TWENTIETH-CENTURY
SCIENCE-FICTION
WRITERS

Twentieth-Century Writers Series

Twentieth-Century Children's Writers, 2nd edition

Twentieth-Century Crime and Mystery Writers, 2nd edition

Twentieth-Century Science-Fiction Writers, 2nd edition

Twentieth-Century Romance and Gothic Writers

Twentieth-Century Western Writers

TWENTIETH-CENTURY SCIENCE-FICTION WRITERS

SECOND EDITION

EDITOR
CURTIS C. SMITH

ST. JAMES PRESS
CHICAGO AND LONDON

All rights reserved. For information, write:
ST. JAMES PRESS
3 Percy Street
London W1P 9FA, England
           or
425 North Michigan Avenue
Chicago, Illinois 60611, U.S.A.

First published in the U.K. and the U.S.A. in 1986

British Library Cataloguing in Publication Data

Twentieth-century science-fiction writers.—2nd ed.
   1. Science fiction, English—Dictionaries
   2. English fiction—20th century—Dictionaries
   I. Smith, Curtis C.
   823'.0876'09   PR830.S5

ISBN 0-912289-27-9

First edition published 1981.

Printed at The Bath Press, Avon

CONTENTS

PREFACE AND READING LIST   *page* vii

EDITOR'S NOTE   xv

ADVISERS AND CONTRIBUTORS   xvii

TWENTIETH-CENTURY SCIENCE-FICTION WRITERS   1

APPENDIX

  FOREIGN-LANGUAGE WRITERS   837

  MAJOR FANTASY WRITERS   863

TITLE INDEX   871

NOTES ON ADVISERS AND CONTRIBUTORS   925

PREFACE

As with so many things, science fiction was undergoing widespread changes in the late 1960's. It was a commonplace belief at that time that the boundaries between science fiction and so-called "mainstream" fiction were eroding. Pulp science-fiction writers had once been thoroughly conventional in literary technique; but now they were adopting multiple points of view, stream of consciousness, and surrealistic and expressionistic styles. The young writer-critics, such as Delany and Ellison, openly rejoiced at what seemed a definitive departure from the pulp ghetto. Science fiction, it was implied, was gaining status for itself and acceptance from the mainstream, and mainstream writers, for their part, were choosing science-fiction subject matter. The term "science fiction" was said to be outmoded; the 20th century had become so bizarre that the realism of science could not describe it, and only "speculative fiction," whether written by pulp or mainstream writers, could continue as a category.

Although there was some truth to this "New Wave" critical perspective, we can now see, as the 1970's become the 1980's, that science fiction as a term and as a distinct genre is resilient. Walk into any bookstore and it is easy to find the science fiction, separately shelved under a special sign. There *is* science fiction, and there *are* science-fiction writers, as most members of the Science Fiction Writers of America would tell you. The call for "speculative fiction" was issued from a frog perspective, from science-fiction writers and critics weary of being laughed at. The fact is that there are enough deficiencies in the mainstream literature of western countries that it would not altogether have been a triumph had science fiction merged with it. For all its own deficiencies, science fiction will best develop from self-acceptance.

Although science fiction is here to stay, this does not mean that we can define it. Publishers seem to have no problem deciding what to market as science fiction, but it is by now an old joke that every science-fiction convention features a panel discussion in which experts strive, in futility, to define the genre. I have been teaching science fiction in a university since 1969, and nearly every book in every version of my course is challenged by some student as not being "really science fiction." I won't add to the joke by trying to define science fiction here; I will refer the reader to Darko Suvin's *Metamorphoses of Science Fiction*, perhaps the most ambitious attempt yet at definition. But I do think it worthwhile to talk about why defining science fiction is both difficult and important. The term "science fiction" originated as late as the 1920's, and in some ways the science-fiction genre is in its youth; it could develop in a number of ways, and a part of the critical debate is over not what it is but what it could or should be. What does the word "science" in science fiction mean, anyway? Does it mean that there has to be accurate science, or plausible extrapolation of current theory, for a work to be considered science fiction? If we insist on this, a rather large part of what is now science fiction must be banished from the ghetto—all time-travel stories, for instance, since time travel cannot be presented as a reasonable extrapolation from current theory despite Wells's impressionistic gymnastics in *The Time Machine*.

Suppose, then, we take the opposite tack and say that the science part of science fiction is a thin papering over a fantasy content. Science fiction, then, is a branch of fantasy. The problems with this view are severe. Modern adult fantasy has its own special history and conventions. More fundamentally, the best science fiction, by Wells, Stapledon, Lem, and Yefremov, does not seem to be describing a fantasy world but a world that bears an extrapolated resemblance to our own. New writers are not only imagining but thinking, and thinking in a way that has some relationship to science. The best science fiction is mimetic, and it is difficult to define science fiction because of the profundity of the meaning of mimesis in literature. Science fiction describes this world we live in, not some other; it is distinct enough as a genre to make such a book as this possible. Chronologically, this book's earliest authors are from the age of Wells. Of course there have been works arguably science fiction which predate Wells by thousands of years, from the Babylonian *Epic of Gilgamesh* to *The Odyssey* to

Lucian's *A True Story*. A reader can examine Marjorie Hope Nicolson's *Voyages to the Moon* and J.O. Bailey's pioneer work *Pilgrims Through Space and Time* for discussion and summaries of science-fiction works from the Renaissance to the 19th century. Brian Aldiss argues convincingly in his *Billion Year Spree* that Mary Shelley's *Frankenstein* is the first science-fiction novel, and Shelley's book is certainly one of the works which has most influenced the direction of 20th-century science fiction. Doubtless there was science fiction before Verne and Wells, but these two great popular writers were decisive in creating a special audience for what until the 1920's was called the "scientific romance."

The English-language writers in this volume are, by a rather large majority, Americans; and this fact reflects the American domination, numerically, of the field. But by a curious paradox the United States has yet to produce a science fiction writer with the stature of a Wells, Stapledon, Capek, or Lem. Why is this so? Perhaps, as Franz Rottensteiner has speculated, it is precisely because these great European science-fiction writers have developed apart from the inbred self-congratulations of the American science-fiction ghetto. Stapledon, for example, wrote his first great future history, *Last and First Men*, without even knowing that there was such a literary category as science fiction: he had read only a few of the works of Wells. Even more fundamentally, perhaps in the American culture of the late 20th century there are deficiencies and blind spots that make the fiction of social and scientific speculation difficult. Lem has pointed out the scientific absurdity of Asimov's laws of robotics, with their built-in assurances that robots—and by easy extension, technology—shall not harm humans. The assumption is that technology can be made safe by more technology (whatever "safe" is). All too often American science fiction has been public relations for technology, refusing to look at the potential dangers and the alternate social systems under which such dangers might be minimized. A telling critique of American science fiction comes from one of its ablest practitioners, Ursula K. Le Guin, in the November 1975 issue of *Science-Fiction Studies*. Le Guin contends that American science fiction has been singularly poor in presenting "the Other—the being who is different from yourself." The poor, the proletariat—and, until recently, women—have been conspicuous in American science fiction by their absence. Le Guin speaks of the domination of the masses by powerful elites in much American science fiction, and the assumption that wealth carries its own justification; she complains about the assumption that "competitive free-enterprise capitalism is the economic destiny of the entire Galaxy." A continuing weakness in American science fiction is the unwillingness or inability to imagine social change on the same scale as technological change.

Of course this is a generalization, perhaps an exaggerated one; Le Guin has said in a later context that she was speaking rhetorically. American science-fiction writers, after all, now include Le Guin herself, Philip K. Dick, Mack Reynolds, Marge Piercy, Joanna Russ, Walter M. Miller, Jr., Robert Silverberg, Theodore Sturgeon, and Chan Davis. The very fact that such criticism as Le Guin's is being aired portends well for change.

Nowhere is change more evident than in the place of women writers and women characters in English-language science fiction. In the so-called "golden age" of the 1930's and 1940's, women were hard to find in the stories, present only as voluptuous and helpless objects on the lurid pulp covers. The "hard" science fiction of *Astounding* found some of its justification in getting teenage boys interested in science, and of course girls didn't count. E.E. "Doc" Smith found writing romantic scenes so difficult that he asked Mrs. Lee Hawkins Garby for help in these parts of *The Skylark of Space*. The relationships between men and women were seen as extrinsic to science fiction proper, something to be added on.

Character development remains a weak point in English-language science fiction, so that some of the best science fiction is still being written by writers not primarily associated with the field, such as Barth, Durrell, Pynchon, Anthony Burgess, and Lessing. But at least there are now woman characters in science fiction, and an explosion of science-fiction writers who are women: consider Zenna Henderson, Pamela Sargent, James Tiptree, Jr., Ursula K. Le Guin, Joanna Russ, Lee Killough, Suzy McKee

Charnas, Anne McCaffrey, Octavia Butler, Marge Piercy, Zoë Fairbairns, and many others. These writers have brought speculation about the future of sex roles to science fiction. Science fiction, once totally the domain of men, has reversed itself and is now in the forefront of feminist thinking.

What now for science fiction? The field now seems more various than ever. Space opera is still around, although the simplistic good guys versus bad guys plot has perhaps yielded to the conflict between different kinds of aliens in the works of such writers as C.J. Cherryh. "Hard" science fiction—that relatively small group of works in which accurate science is the main plot—continues to be well represented by Gregory Benford and others. Post-nuclear disaster scenarios, which proliferated in the field after 1945 and produced such classics as George R. Stewart's *Earth Abides* and Walter M. Miller, Jr.'s *A Canticle for Leibowitz*, are still being written by Bob Tucker, Christopher Priest, and others. But ecological disaster has tended to replace nuclear disaster in the works of such writers as John Christopher, Harry Harrison, Kate Wilhelm, Thomas M. Disch, and John Brunner. Although the New Wave has faded somewhat as a distinct movement, such writers as James Tiptree, Jr. and Gene Wolfe are carrying on experiments in style and structure. And a few writers, such as George Zebrowski, are carrying on the Wells-Stapledon-Lem tradition of prophetic extrapolation, writing poetry and philosophy on a gigantic scale.

The anti-utopian police state typified by *Brave New World* and *Nineteen Eighty-Four* dominated science fiction for decades, so that Kingsley Amis's early book on science fiction was appropriately called *New Maps of Hell*. Beginning, perhaps, with Le Guin's *The Dispossessed*, ambiguous utopias are challenging this domination. Marge Piercy has written an underrated utopia, *Woman on the Edge of Time*, which links the struggles of a minority woman of the present to a future utopia's efforts to preserve itself. Another underrated writer, Mack Reynolds, has updated Bellamy's *Looking Backward* (see Reynolds's entry for his comments on his work). Ernest Callenbach's "Ecotopia" series depicts an ecological utopia as a separatist movement in the northwestern United States. Science fiction is returning to one of its historical origins, the utopian tradition. Another of its origins, the fantasy tradition, also is gaining great strength in the works of Piers Anthony, Gene Wolfe, and others. Somtow Sucharitkul's knowledge of the classical tradition is evident in his well-crafted stories. Brian Aldiss's remarkable Helliconia series shows that science fiction writers still delight in worldbuilding.

In view of all these trends we can say that science fiction is one of the more protean literary genres in the late 20th century. People continue to turn to science fiction for escape and entertainment, as they should. But science fiction offers thought and involvement as well as escape. That there will be future conditions quite distinct from present ones is a proposition both disturbing and salutary. In the late 20th century the world is undergoing an even more profound transformation than is generally realized, and science fiction can help us to understand it.

CURTIS C. SMITH

READING LIST

Aldiss, Brian, *Billion Year Spree: A History of Science Fiction.* London, Weidenfeld and Nicolson, and New York, Doubleday, 1973.

Aldiss, Brian, *Science Fiction Art.* New York, Bounty, 1975; London, Hart Davis, 1976.

Aldiss, Brian, *Science Fiction as Science Fiction.* Frome, Somerset, Bran's Head, 1978.

Aldiss, Brian, and Harry Harrison, editors, *Hell's Cartographers: Some Personal Histories of Science Fiction Writers.* London, Weidenfeld and Nicolson, and New York, Harper, 1975.

Aldiss, Brian, and Harry Harrison, editors, *SF Horizons.* New York, Arno Press, 1975.

Aldridge, Alexandra, *The Scientific World View in Dystopia.* Ann Arbor, Michigan, UMI Research Press, 1984.

Allen, Dick, *Science Fiction: The Future.* New York, Harcourt Brace, 1971.

Allen, L. David, *The Ballantine Teachers' Guide to Science Fiction.* New York, Ballantine, 1975.

Allen, L. David, *Science Fiction: An Introduction.* Lincoln, Nebraska, Cliff Notes, 1973; as *Science Fiction Readers Guide,* Lincoln, Nebraska, Centennial Press, 1974.

Amelio, Ralph J., *Hal in the Classroom: Science Fiction Films.* Dayton, Ohio, Pflaum, 1974.

Amis, Kingsley, *New Maps of Hell: A Survey of Science Fiction.* New York, Harcourt Brace, 1960; London, Gollancz, 1961.

Armytage, W.H.G., *Yesterday's Tomorrows: A Historical Survey of Future Societies.* London, Routledge, 1968.

Ash, Brian, *Faces of the Future: The Lessons of Science Fiction.* London, Elek, and New York, Taplinger, 1975.

Ash, Brian, editor, *The Visual Encyclopedia of Science Fiction.* New York, Harmony, and London, Pan, 1977.

Ash, Brian, *Who's Who in Science Fiction.* London, Elm Tree, and New York, Taplinger, 1976.

Ashley, Michael, editor, *The History of the Science Fiction Magazine.* London, New English Library, 4 vols., 1974-76; vols. 1 and 2, Chicago, Regnery, 1976.

Ashley, Michael, and Terry Jeeves, *The Complete Index to Astounding/Analog.* Oak Forest, Illinois, Weinberg, 1981.

Atkinson, Geoffroy, *The Extraordinary Voyage in French Literature Before 1700.* New York, Columbia University Press, 1920; *The Extraordinary Voyage in French Literature from 1700-1720.* Paris, Champion, 1922.

Bailey, J.O., *Pilgrims Through Space and Time: Trends and Patterns in Scientific and Utopian Fiction.* New York, Argus, 1947.

Barnes, Myra, *Linguistics and Language in Science Fiction-Fantasy.* New York, Arno Press, 1975.

Barr, Marleen S., and Nicholas Smith, editors, *Women and Utopia: Critical Interpretations.* Lanham, Maryland, University Press of America, 1983.

Barron, Neil, editor, *Anatomy of Wonder.* New York, Bowker, 1976; 2nd edition, 1981.

Barron, Neil, and R. Reginald, *Science Fiction and Fantasy Annual '1980.* San Bernardino, California, Borgo Press, 1980.

Baxter, John, *Science Fiction in the Cinema.* New York, A.S. Barnes, and London, Zwemmer, 1970.

Berger, Harold L., *Science Fiction and the New Dark Age.* Bowling Green, Ohio, Popular Press, 1976.

Bleiler, E.F., *The Checklist of Fantastic Literature.* Chicago, Shasta, 1948; revised edition, as *The Checklist of Science-Fiction and Supernatural Fiction,* Glen Rock, New Jersey, Firebell, 1978.

Bleiler, Everett F., editor, *Science Fiction Writers: Critical Studies of the Major Authors from the Early Nineteenth Century to the Present Day.* New York, Scribner, 1982.

Blish, James, *The Issue at Hand: Studies in Contemporary Magazine Science Fiction.* Chicago, Advent, 1964; *More Issues at Hand,* 1970 (both books as William Atheling, Jr.).

Bova, Ben, editor, *Closeup, New Worlds.* New York, St. Martin's Press, 1977.

Bova, Ben, *Notes to a Science Fiction Writer* (for children). New York, Scribner, 1975.

Bova, Ben, *Through Eyes of Wonder: Science Fiction and Science* (for children). Reading, Massachusetts, Addison Wesley, 1975.

Bova, Ben, *Viewpoint.* Cambridge, Massachusetts, NESFA Press, 1977.

Boyajian, Jerry, and Kenneth R. Johnson, *Index to the Science Fiction Magazines, 1979-81.* Cambridge, Massachusetts, Twaci Press, 3 vols., 1981-82.

Bradley, Marion Zimmer, Norman Spinrad, and Alfred Bester, *Expedition Perilous: Three Essays on Science Fiction.* San Bernardino, California, Borgo Press, 1983.

Bretnor, Reginald, editor, *The Craft of Science Fiction.* New York, Harper, 1976.

Bretnor, Reginald, editor, *Modern Science Fiction: Its Meaning and Its Future.* New York, Coward McCann, 1953; revised edition, Chicago, Advent, 1979.

Bretnor, Reginald, editor, *Science Fiction, Today and Tomorrow.* New York, Harper, 1974.

Briney, R.E., and Edward Wood, *SF Bibliographies: An Annotated Bibliography of Bibliographical Works on Science Fiction and Fantasy Fiction.* Chicago, Advent, 1972.

Brosnan, John, *Future Tense: The Cinema of Science Fiction.* London, Macdonald and Jane's, 1978; New York, St Martin's Press, 1979.

Brown, Charles N., and Dena Brown, editors, *Locus: The Newspaper of the Science Fiction Field.* Boston, Gregg Press, 1978.

Brown, E.J., *Brave New World, 1984, and We: Essays on Anti-Utopia.* Ann Arbor, Michigan, Ardis, 1976.

Calkins, Elizabeth, and Barry McGhan, *Teaching Tomorrow: A Handbook of Science Fiction for Teachers.* Dayton, Ohio, Pflaum, 1972.

Cazedessus, C.E., Jr., editor, *Ghost Stories.* Evergreen, Colorado, Opar Press, 1973.

Chauvin, Cy, editor, *A Multitude of Visions: Essays on Science Fiction.* Baltimore, T-K Graphics, 1975.

Cioffi, Frank, *Formula Fiction? An Anatomy of American Science Fiction, 1930-40.* Westport, Connecticut, Greenwood Press, 1982.

Clarens, Carlos, *An Illustrated History of the Horror Film.* New York, Capricorn, 1967; revised edition, as *Horror Movies,* London, Secker and Warburg, 1968.

Clareson, Thomas D., editor, *Extrapolation: A Science Fiction Newsletter 1959-1969.* Boston, Gregg Press, 1978.

Clareson, Thomas D., *Many Futures, Many Worlds: Theme and Form in Science Fiction.* Kent, Ohio, Kent State University Press, 1977.

Clareson, Thomas D., *Science Fiction Criticism: An Annotated Checklist.* Kent, Ohio, Kent State University Press, 1972.

Clareson, Thomas D., *SF: A Dream of Other Worlds.* College Station, Texas A and M University, 1973.

Clareson, Thomas D., editor, *SF: The Other Side of Realism: Essays on Modern Fantasy and Science Fiction.* Bowling Green, Ohio, Popular Press, 1971.

Clareson, Thomas D., editor, *Voices for the Future: Essays on Major Science Fiction Writers.* Bowling Green, Ohio, Popular Press, 2 vols., 1976-79; vol. 3, edited with Thomas L. Wymer, 1983.

Clarke, I.F., *The Pattern of Expectation 1644-2001.* London, Cape, 1979.

Clarke, I.F., *The Tale of the Future*. London, Library Association, 1961.

Clarke, I.F., *Voices Prophesying War 1763-1984*. London, Oxford University Press, 1966.

Cockcroft, Thomas G.L., *Index to Fiction in Radio News and Other Magazines*. Lower Hutt, New Zealand, Cockcroft, 1970.

Cockcroft, Thomas G.L., *Index to the Weird Fiction Magazines*. Lower Hutt, New Zealand, Cockcroft, 2 vols., 1962-64.

Cole, Walter L., *A Checklist of Science-Fiction Anthologies*. New York, Cole, 1964.

Colombo, John Robert, *CDN SF and F: A Bibliography of Canadian Science Fiction and Fantasy*. Toronto, Hounslow Press, 1979.

Contento, William, *Index to Science Fiction Anthologies and Collections*. Boston, Hall, and London, Prior, 1978.

Contento, William, *Index to Science Fiction Anthologies and Collections 1977-1983*. Boston, Hall, 1984.

Cowart, David, and Thomas L. Wymer, editors, *Twentieth-Century American Science Fiction Writers*. Detroit, Gale, 2 vols., 1981.

Crawford, Joseph H., Jr., James J. Donahue, and Donald M. Grant, *"333": A Bibliography of the Science Fantasy Novel*. Providence, Rhode Island, Grandon, 1953.

Currey, L.W., *Science Fiction and Fantasy Authors: A Bibliography of First Printings of Their Fiction and Selected Non-Fiction*. Boston, Hall, 1979.

Davenport, Basil, *Inquiry into Science Fiction*. New York, Longman, 1955.

Davenport, Basil, editor, *The Science Fiction Novel: Imagination and Social Criticism*. Chicago, Advent, 1964; revised edition, 1964.

Day, Bradford M., *Bibliography of Adventure: Mundy, Burroughs, Rohmer, Haggard*. Denver, New York, Science Fiction and Fantasy Publications, 1964.

Day, Bradford M., *The Checklist of Fantastic Literature in Paperbound Books*. Denver, New York, Science Fiction and Fantasy Publications, 1965.

Day, Bradford M., *The Complete Checklist of Science Fiction Magazines*. New York, Science Fiction and Fantasy Publications, 1961.

Day, Bradford M., *An Index on the Weird and Fantastica in Magazines*. Privately printed, 1953.

Day, Bradford M., *The Supplemental Checklist of Fantastic Literature*. Denver, New York, Science Fiction and Fantasy Publications, 1963.

Day, Donald B., *Index to the Science-Fiction Magazines 1926-1950*. Portland, Perri Press, 1952; revised edition, Boston, Hall, 1982.

de Camp, L. Sprague, *The Conan Reader*. Baltimore, Mirage Press, 1968.

de Camp, L. Sprague, *Science-Fiction Handbook*. New York, Hermitage House, 1953; revised edition, with Catherine Crook de Camp, Philadelphia, Owlswick Press, 1975.

de Camp, L. Sprague, and George H. Scithers, editors, *The Conan Grimoire*. Baltimore, Mirage Press, 1971.

de Camp, L. Sprague, and George H. Scithers, editors, *The Conan Swordbook*. Baltimore, Mirage Press, 1969.

Delany, Samuel R., *The Jewel-Hinged Jaw: Notes on the Language of Science Fiction*. Elizabethtown, New York, Dragon Press, 1977.

Delany, Samuel R., *Starboard Wine: More Notes on the Language of Science Fiction*. Pleasantville, New York, Dragon Press, 1984.

del Rey, Lester, *The World of Science Fiction 1926-1976: The History of a Subculture*. New York, Ballantine, 1979.

Derleth, August, *Thirty Years of Arkham House*. Sauk City, Wisconsin, Arkham House, 1970.

Dunn, Thomas P., and Richard D. Erlich, editors, *Clockwork Worlds: Mechanized Environments in SF*. Westport, Connecticut, Greenwood Press, 1983.

Dunn, Thomas P., and Richard D. Erlich, editors, *The Mechanical God: Machines in Science Fiction*. Westport, Connecticut, Greenwood Press, 1982.

Eichner, Henry M., *Atlantean Chronicles*. Alhambra, California, Fantasy Publishing, 1971.

Eigruber, Frank, Jr., *Gangland's Doom: The Shadow of the Pulps*. Oak Lawn, Illinois, Weinberg, 1974.

Elliott, Robert C., *The Shape of Utopia: Studies in a Literary Genre*. Chicago, University of Chicago Press, 1970.

Elrick, George S., *The Science Fiction Handbook for Readers and Writers*. Chicago, Chicago Review Press, 1978.

Eshbach, Lloyd Arthur, editor, *Of Worlds Beyond: The Science of Science-Fiction Writing*. Reading, Pennsylvania, Fantasy Press, 1947; London, Dobson, 1965.

Eurich, Nell, *Science in Utopia: A Mighty Design*. Cambridge, Massachusetts, Harvard University Press, 1967.

Fischer, William B., *The Empire Strikes Out: Kurd Lasswitz, Hans Dominik, and the Development of German Science Fiction*. Bowling Green, Ohio, Popular Press, 1984.

Frank, Alan, *Sci-Fi Now: 10 Exciting Years of Science Fiction from 2001 to Star Wars and Beyond*. London, Octopus, 1978.

Franklin, H. Bruce, editor, *Future Perfect: American Science Fiction of the Nineteenth Century*. New York, Oxford University Press, 1966; London, Oxford University Press, 1968.

Franson, Donald, and Howard DeVore, *A History of the Hugo, Nebula, and International Fantasy Awards*. Dearborn Heights, Michigan, DeVore, 1975.

Freas, Frank Kelly, *The Art of Science Fiction*. Norfolk, Virginia, Donning, 1977.

Fredericks, Casey, *The Future of Eternity: Mythologies of Science Fiction and Fantasy*. Bloomington, Indiana University Press, 1982.

Frewin, Anthony, *One Hundred Years of Science Fiction Illustration 1840-1940*. London, Jupiter, 1974; New York, Pyramid, 1975.

Friend, Beverly, *Science Fiction: The Classroom in Orbit*. Glassboro, New Jersey, Educational Impact, 1974.

Garber, Eric, and Lyn Paleo, *Uranian Worlds: A Reader's Guide to Alternate Sexuality in Science Fiction and Fantasy*. Boston, Hall, 1983.

Gerani, Gary, and Paul H. Schulman, *Fantastic Television*. New York, Harmony, 1977.

Gerber, Richard, *Utopian Fantasy: A Study of English Utopian Fiction since the End of the Nineteenth Century*. London, Routledge, 1955; New York, McGraw Hill, 1973.

Gernsback, Hugo, *Evolution in Modern Science Fiction*. New York, Gernsback, 1952.

Gifford, Denis, *Science Fiction Film*. London, Studio Vista, and New York, Dutton, 1971.

Glad, John, *Extrapolations from Dystopia: A Critical Study of Soviet Science Fiction*. Kingston, New Jersey, Kingston Press, 1982.

Glut, Donald F., *The Frankenstein Legend*. Metuchen, New Jersey, Scarecrow Press, 1973.

Goswami, Amit and Maggie, *The Cosmic Dancers: Exploring the Physics of Science Fiction*. New York, Harper, 1983.

Goulart, Ron, *Cheap Thrills: An Informal History of the Pulp Magazines*. New Rochelle, New York, Arlington House, 1972.

Gove, Philip Babcock, *The Imaginary Voyage in Prose Fiction*. New York, Columbia University Press, 1941; London, Holland Press, 1961.

Grant, Charles L., editor, *Writing and Selling Science Fiction*. Cincinnati, Writer's Digest, 1977.

Grebens, G. V., *Ivan Efremov's Theory of Soviet Science Fiction*. New York, Vantage Press, 1978.

Green, Roger Lancelyn, *Into Other Worlds: Spaceflight in Fiction from Lucian to Lewis*. London and New York, Abelard Schuman, 1957.

Greenberg, Martin H., editor, *Fantastic Lives*. Carbondale, Southern Illinois University Press, 1981.

Griffiths, John, *Three Tomorrows: American, British, and Soviet Science Fiction*. New York, Barnes and Noble, and London, Macmillan, 1980.

Gunn, James E., *Alternate Worlds: The Illustrated History of Science Fiction*. Englewood Cliffs, New Jersey, Prentice Hall, 1975.

Gunn, James E., *The Discovery of the Future: The Ways Science Fiction Developed*. College Station, Texas A and M University, 1975.

Gunn, James E., editor, *The Road to Science Fiction*. New York, New American Library, 2 vols., 1977-79.

Hall, H.W., *Science Fiction and Fantasy Research Index* (annual). Privately printed, 1982—

Hall, H.W., *Science Fiction Book Review Index 1923-73*. Detroit, Gale, 1975 (and later volumes).

Hall, Hal W., *Science Fiction Collections: Fantasy, Supernatural and Weird Tales*. New York, Haworth Press, 1983.

Hall, Hal W., *The Science Fiction Magazines: A Bibliographical Checklist of Titles and Issues Through 1982*. Privately printed, 1983.

Hardy, Phil, editor, *Science Fiction: The Complete Film Sourcebook*. New York, Morrow, 1984.

Harrison, Harry, *Great Balls of Fire!* London, Pierrot, and New York, Grosset and Dunlap, 1977.

Hartwell, David G., *Age of Wonders: Exploring the World of Science Fiction*. New York, Walker, 1985.

Hassler, Donald M., *Comic Tones in Science Fiction: The Art of Compromise with Nature*. Westport, Connecticut, Greenwood Press, 1982.

Hillegas, Mark R., *The Future as Nightmare: H.G. Wells and the Anti-Utopians*. New York, Oxford University Press, 1967.

Hillegas, Mark R., editor, *Shadows of Imagination: The Fantasies of C.S. Lewis, J.R.R. Tolkien, and Charles Williams*. Carbondale, Southern Illinois University Press, 1969.

Hoffman, Stuart, *An Index to "Unknown" and "Unknown Worlds" by Author and by Title*. Black Earth, Wisconsin, Sirius Press, 1955.

Hollister, Bernard C., and Deane C. Thompson, *Grokking the Future: Science Fiction in the Classroom*. Dayton, Ohio, Pflaum, 1973.

Ikin, Van, editor, *Australian Science Fiction*. Brisbane, University of Queensland Press, 1982; Chicago, Academy, 1984.

Index to Fantasy and Science Fiction in Munsey Publications. Alhambra, California, 1976(?).

Index to Perry Rhodan—American Edition. Cambridge, Massachusetts, NESFA Press, 2 vols., 1973-75.

Index to Science Fiction Magazines 1966-1976. Cambridge, Massachusetts, NESFA Press, 6 vols., 1971-1977.

Isaacs, Leonard, *Darwin to Double Helix: The Biological Theme in Science Fiction*. London, Butterworth, 1977.

Jarvis, Sharon, editor, *Inside Outer Space: Science Fiction Professionals Look at Their Craft*. New York, Ungar, 1984.

Johnson, William, editor, *Focus on the Science Fiction Film*. Englewood Cliffs, New Jersey, Prentice Hall, 1972.

Jones, Robert Kenneth, *The Shudder Pulps: A History of the Weird Menace Magazine of the 1930's*. West Linn, Oregon, FAX, 1975.

Ketterer, David, *New Worlds for Old: The Apocalyptic Imagination, Science Fiction, and American Literature*. Bloomington, Indiana University Press, 1974.

Knight, Damon, *The Futurians*. New York, Day, 1977.

Knight, Damon, *In Search of Wonder*. Chicago, Advent, 1956; revised edition, 1967.

Knight, Damon, editor, *Turning Points: Essays on the Art of Science Fiction*. New York, Harper, 1977.

Kyle, David, *The Illustrated Book of Science Fiction Ideas and Dreams*. London, Hamlyn, 1977.

Kyle, David, *A Pictorial History of Science Fiction*. London, Hamlyn, 1976.

Lasky, Melvin J., *Utopia and Revolution*. Chicago, University of Chicago Press, 1976.

Lawler, Donald L., *Approaches to Science Fiction*. Boston, Houghton Mifflin, 1978.

Lee, Walt, *Reference Guide to Fantastic Films*. Los Angeles, Chelsea Lee, 3 vols., 1972-74.

Le Guin, Ursula K., *The Language of the Night: Essays on Fantasy and Science Fiction*, edited by Susan Wood. New York, Putnam, 1979.

Leighton, Peter, *Moon Travellers: A Dream That Is Becoming a Reality*. London, Oldbourne, 1960.

Lester, Colin, editor, *The International Science Fiction Yearbook 1979*. London, Pierrot, 1979.

Locke, George, *Science Fiction First Editions*. London, Ferret Fantasy, 1978.

Locke, George, *Voyages in Space: A Bibliography of Interplanetary Fiction 1801-1914*. London, Ferret Fantasy, 1975.

Lowndes, Robert A.W., *Three Faces of Science Fiction*. Boston, NESFA Press, 1973.

Lundwall, Sam J., *Science Fiction: An Illustrated History*. New York, Grosset and Dunlap, 1978.

Lundwall, Sam J., *Science Fiction: What It's All About*. New York, Ace, 1971.

Magill, Frank N., editor, *Survey of Science Fiction Literature*. Englewood Cliffs, New Jersey, Salem Press, 5 vols., 1979.

Magill, Frank N., editor, *Science Fiction, Alien Encounter*. Pasadena, California, Salem Press, 1981.

Malone, Robert, *The Robot Book*. New York, Harcourt Brace, 1978.

Malzberg, Barry N., *The Engines of the Night: Science Fiction in the Eighties*. New York, Doubleday, 1982.

Manlove, C.N., *Modern Fantasy: Five Studies*. London, Cambridge University Press, 1975.

Matthew, Robert, *The Origins of Japanese Science Fiction*. Brisbane, University of Queensland Department of Japanese, 1978.

McGhan, Barry, *Science Fiction and Fantasy Pseudonyms*. Dearborn, Michigan, Misfit Press, 1973.

McGuire, Patrick L., *Red Stars: Political Aspects of Soviet Science Fiction*. Ann Arbor, Michigan, UMI Research Press, 1985.

Menville, Douglas, *A Historical and Critical Survey of the Science-Fiction Film*. New York, Arno Press, 1975.

Metcalf, Norm, *The Index of Science Fiction Magazines 1951-1965*. El Cerrito, California, Stark, 1968.

Meyers, Walter E., *Aliens and Linguists*. Athens, University of Georgia Press, 1980.

Miller, Fred D., Jr., and Nicholas D. Smith, editors, *Thought Probes: Philosophy Through Science Fiction*. Englewood Cliffs, New Jersey, Prentice Hall, 1981.

Mogen, David, editor, *Wilderness Visions: Science Fiction Westerns 1*. San Bernardino, California, Borgo Press, 1982.

Moore, Patrick, *Science and Fiction*. London, Harrap, 1957.

Morton, A.L., *The English Utopia*. London, Lawrence and Wishart, 1952.

Moskowitz, Sam, *Explorers of the Infinite: Shapers of Science Fiction*. Cleveland, World, 1963.

Moskowitz, Sam, *The Immortal Storm: A History of Science Fiction Fandom*. Atlanta, Atlanta Science Fiction Organization Press, 1954.

Moskowitz, Sam, editor, *Science Fiction by Gaslight: A History and Anthology of Science Fiction in Popular Magazines 1891-1911*. Cleveland, World, 1968.

Moskowitz, Sam, *Seekers of Tomorrow: Masters of Modern Science Fiction*. Cleveland, World, 1966.

Moskowitz, Sam, *Strange Horizons: The Spectrum of Science Fiction*. New York, Scribner, 1976.

Moskowitz, Sam, editor, *Under the Moons of Mars: A History and*

Anthology of "The Scientific Romance" in the Munsey Magazines. New York, Holt Rinehart, 1970.

Mullen, R.D., and Darko Suvin, editors, *Science-Fiction Studies: Selected Articles on Science Fiction.* Boston, Gregg Press, 2 vols., 1976-78.

Myers, Robert E., editor, *The Intersection of Science Fiction and Philosophy: Critical Studies.* Westport, Connecticut, Greenwood Press, 1983.

New England Science Fiction Association, *The NESFA Index to the Science Fiction Magazines and Original Anthologies 1979-80.* Cambridge, Massachusetts, NESFA Press, 1982.

Nicholls, Peter, editor, *Foundation: The Review of Science Fiction March 1972-March 1975.* Boston, Gregg Press, 1978.

Nicholls, Peter, editor, *Science Fiction at Large.* London, Gollancz, 1976; New York, Harper, 1977; as *Explorations of the Marvellous,* London, Fontana, 1978.

Nicholls, Peter, editor, *The Science Fiction Encyclopedia.* New York, Doubleday, and London, Granada, 1979.

Nicholls, Peter, David Langford, and Brian M. Stableford, *The Science in Science Fiction.* London, Joseph, 1982; New York, Knopf, 1983.

Nicolson, Marjorie Hope, *Voyages to the Moon.* New York, Macmillan, 1948.

The Octopus Encyclopaedia of Science Fiction. London, Octopus, and Baltimore, Hoen, 1978.

Okada, Masaya, *Illustrated Index to Air Wonder Stories.* Nagoya, Japan, Okada, 1973.

Owings, Mark, and Jack L. Chalker, *The Index to Science-Fantasy Publishers.* Baltimore, Mirage Press, 1966; revised edition, as *Index to the SF Publishers,* 1979.

Panshin, Alexei and Cory, *SF in Dimension: A Book of Explorations.* Chicago, Advent, 1976.

Parrinder, Patrick, editor, *Science Fiction: A Critical Guide.* London, Longman, 1979.

Parrinder, Patrick, *Science Fiction: Its Criticism and Teaching.* London, Methuen, 1980.

Parrington, Vernon Louis, *American Dreams: A Study of American Utopias.* Providence, Rhode Island, Brown University, 1947.

Pavlat, Robert, and William Evans, editors, *Fanzine Index.* New York, Piser, 1965.

Pfeiffer, John R., *Fantasy and Science Fiction: A Critical Guide.* Palmer Lake, Colorado, Filter Press, 1971.

Philmus, Robert, *Into the Unknown: The Evolution of Science Fiction from Francis Godwin to H.G. Wells.* Berkeley, University of California Press, 1970; 2nd edition, 1983.

Pierce, Hazel, *A Literary Symbiosis: Science Fiction/Fantasy/Mystery.* Westport, Connecticut, Greenwood Press, 1983.

Platt, Charles, *Dream Makers 2: The Uncommon Men and Women Who Write Science Fiction.* New York, Berkley, 1983.

Porter, Andrew, editor, *Experiment Perilous: Three Essays on Science Fiction.* New York, Algol Press, 1976.

Porush, David, *The Soft Machine: Cybernetic Fiction.* New York, Methuen, 1985.

Rabkin, Eric S., *The Fantastic in Literature.* Princeton, New Jersey, Princeton University Press, 1976.

Rabkin, Eric S., Martin H. Greenberg, and Joseph D. Olander, editors, *The End of the World.* Carbondale, Southern Illinois University Press, 1983.

Rabkin, Eric S., Martin H. Greenberg, and Joseph D. Olander, editors, *No Place Else: Explorations in Utopian and Dystopian Fiction.* Carbondale, Southern Illinois University Press, 1983.

Reginald, R., *By Any Other Name: A Comprehensive Checklist of Science Fiction and Fantasy Pseudonyms.* San Bernardino, California, Borgo Press, 1980.

Reginald, R., *A Guide to Science Fiction in the Library of Congress Classification Scheme.* San Bernardino, California, Borgo Press, 1980.

Reginald, R., *Science Fiction and Fantasy Literature: A Checklist 1700-1974.* Detroit, Gale, 2 vols., 1979.

Reginald, R., *To Be Continued: An Annotated Bibliography of Science Fiction and Fantasy Series and Sequels.* San Bernardino, California, Borgo Press, 1980.

Reilly, Robert, editor, *The Transcendent Adventure: Studies of Religion in Science Fiction/Fantasy.* Westport, Connecticut, Greenwood Press, 1984.

Riley, Dick, editor, *Critical Encounters: Writers and Themes in Science Fiction.* New York, Ungar, 1978.

Roberts, Peter, *Guide to Current Fanzines.* Privately printed, 1978.

Rock, James A., *Who Goes There? A Bibliographic Dictionary of Pseudonymous Literature in the Fields of Fantasy and Science Fiction.* Bloomington, Indiana, Rock, 1979.

Roemer, Kenneth M., *The Obsolete Necessity: America in Utopian Writings 1888-1900.* Kent, Ohio, Kent State University Press, 1976.

Rogers, Alva, *A Requiem for Astounding.* Chicago, Advent, 1964.

Rose, Lois and Stephen, *The Shattered Ring: Science Fiction and the Quest for Meaning.* Richmond, Virginia, John Knox Press, and London, SCM Press, 1970.

Rose, Mark, editor, *Science Fiction: A Collection of Critical Essays.* Englewood Cliffs, New Jersey, Prentice Hall, 1976.

Rose, Mark, *Alien Encounters: Anatomy of Science Fiction.* Cambridge, Massachusetts, Harvard University Press, 1981.

Rosinsky, Natalie M., *Feminist Futures: Contemporary Women's Speculative Fiction.* Ann Arbor, Michigan, UMI Research Press, 1984.

Rottensteiner, Franz, *The Science Fiction Book: An Illustrated History.* New York, Seabury Press, and London, Thames and Hudson, 1975.

Rovin, Jeff, *The Fabulous Fantasy Films.* South Brunswick, New Jersey, A.S. Barnes, and London, Yoseloff, 1977.

Sadoul, Jacques, *2000 A.D.: Illustrations from the Golden Age of Science Fiction Pulps.* Chicago, Regnery, and London, Souvenir Press, 1975.

Samuelson, David N., *Visions of Tomorrow: Six Journeys from Outer to Inner Space.* New York, Arno Press, 1975.

Sargent, Lyman T., *British and American Utopian Literature 1516-1975.* Boston, Hall, 1979.

Schlobin, Roger C., *Urania's Daughters: A Checklist of Women Science Fiction Writers 1697-1982.* San Bernardino, California, Borgo Press, 1983.

Scholes, Robert, *Structural Fabulation.* Notre Dame, Indiana, University of Notre Dame Press, 1975.

Scholes, Robert, and Eric S. Rabkin, *Science Fiction: History, Science, Vision.* New York, Oxford University Press, 1977.

Schweitzer, Darrell, and Jeffrey M. Elliot, editors, *Science Fiction Voices 1-4.* San Bernardino, California, Borgo Press, 4 vols., 1979-82.

Scithers, George H., Darrell Schweitzer, and John M. Ford, *On Writing Science Fiction (The Editors Strike Back!).* Philadelphia, Owlswick Press, 1981.

Searles, Baird, and others, *A Reader's Guide to Science Fiction [Fantasy].* New York, Avon, 2 vols, 1979-82.

Shipman, David, *A Pictorial History of Science Fiction Films.* London, Hamlyn, 1985.

Siemon, Frederick, *Science Fiction Story Index 1950-1968.* Chicago, American Library Association, 1971.

Silverberg, Robert, *Drug Themes in Science Fiction.* Rockville, Maryland, National Institute on Drug Abuse, 1974.

Slusser, George E., Eric S. Rabkin, and Robert Scholes, editors, *Coordinates: Placing Science Fiction and Fantasy.* Carbondale, Southern Illinois University Press, 1983.

Smith, Clark Ashton, *Planets and Dimensions: Collected Essays,* edited by Charles K. Wolfe. Baltimore, Mirage Press, 1973.

Smith, Nicholas D., editor, *Philosophers Look at Science Fiction.* Chicago, Nelson Hall, 1982.

Spelman, Richard C., *A Preliminary Checklist of Science Fiction and Fantasy Published by Ballantine Books 1953-1974.* North Hollywood, Institute for Specialized Literature, 1976.

Spelman, Richard C., *Science Fiction and Fantasy Published by Ace Books 1953-1968.* North Hollywood, Institute for Specialized Literature, 1976.

Spinrad, Norman, *Staying Alive: A Writer's Guide.* Norfolk, Virginia, Donning, 1983.

Stableford, Brian M., *Masters of Science-Fiction: Essays on Six Science-Fiction Authors.* San Bernardino, California, Borgo Press, 1981.

Staicar, Tom, editor, *Critical Encounters 2: Writers and Themes in Science Fiction.* New York, Ungar, 1982.

Staicar, Tom, editor, *The Feminine Eye: Science Fiction and the Women Who Write It.* New York, Ungar, 1982.

Stone, Graham, *Australian Science Fiction Index 1925-1967.* Canberra, Australian Science Fiction Association, 1968; *Supplement 1968-1975,* Sydney, Australian Science Fiction Association, 1976.

Strauss, Erwin S., *The MIT Science Fiction Society's Index to the S-F Magazines 1951-1965.* Cambridge, Massachusetts, MIT Science Fiction Society, 1966.

Strick, Philip, *Science Fiction Movies.* London, Octopus, 1976.

Strickland, A.W., *Reference Guide to American Science Fiction Films.* Bloomington, Indiana TIS, 2 vols., 1980.

Summers, Montague, *A Gothic Bibliography.* London, Fortune Press, 1941; New York, Russell, 1964.

Suvin, Darko, *Metamorphoses of Science Fiction.* New Haven, Connecticut, Yale University Press, 1979.

Suvin, Darko, *Russian Science Fiction 1956-1974: A Bibliography.* Elizabethtown, New York, Dragon Press, 1976.

Swinfen, Ann, *In Defence of Fantasy: A Study of the Genre in English and American Literature since 1945.* London, Routledge, 1983.

Todorov, Tzvetan, *The Fantastic: A Structural Approach to a Literary Genre,* translated by Richard Howard. Cleveland, Press of Case Western Reserve University, 1973.

Tuck, Donald H., *The Encyclopedia of Science Fiction and Fantasy.* Chicago, Advent, 3 vols., 1974-83.

Tymn, Marshall B., *American Fantasy and Science Fiction: Toward A Bibliography of Works Published in the United States 1948-1973.* West Linn, Oregon, FAX, 1979.

Tymn, Marshall B., *Index to Stories in Thematic Anthologies of Science Fiction.* Boston, Hall, 1978.

Tymn, Marshall B., Roger C. Schlobin, and L.W. Currey, *A Research Guide to Science Fiction Studies.* New York, Garland, 1977.

Tymn, Marshall B., and Roger C. Schlobin, *The Year's Scholarship in Science Fiction and Fantasy 1972-1975.* Kent, Ohio, Kent State University Press, 1979.

Tymn, Marshall B., editor, *The Science Fiction Reference Book.* Mercer Island, Washington, Starmont, 1981.

Tymn, Marshall B., and Roger C. Schlobin, editors, *The Year's Scholarship in Science Fiction and Fantasy: 1976-1979.* Kent, Ohio, Kent State University Press, 1983.

Tymn, Marshall B., editor, *The Year's Scholarship in Science Fiction, Fantasy, and Horror Literature 1980-81.* Kent, Ohio, Kent State University Press, 2 vols., 1983-84.

Urang, Gunnar, *Shadows of Heaven: Religion and Fantasy in the Writings of C.S. Lewis, Charles Williams, and J.R.R. Tolkien.* Philadelphia, Pilgrim Press, and London, SCM Press, 1971.

Versins, Pierre, *Encyclopedie de l'Utopie des Voyages Extraordinaires et de la Science Fiction.* Lausanne, L'Age d'Homme, 1972.

Wagar, W. Warren, *Terminal Visions: The Literature of Last Things.* Bloomington, Indiana University Press, 1982.

Walker, Paul, *Speaking of Science Fiction* (interviews). Oradell, New Jersey, Luna, 1978.

Walsh, Chad, *From Utopia to Nightmare.* New York, Harper, and London, Bles, 1962.

Warner, Harry, Jr., *All Our Yesterdays: An Informal History of Science Fiction Fandom in the Forties.* Chicago, Advent, 1969.

Warrick, Patricia S., *The Cybernetic Imagination in Science Fiction.* Cambridge, Massachusetts, MIT Press, 1980.

Weinberg, Robert, *The Weird Tales Story.* West Linn, Oregon, FAX, 1977.

Weinberg, Robert, and Lohr McKinstry, *The Hero Pulp Index.* Evergreen, Colorado, Opar Press, 1971.

Weinberg, Robert, and Edward P. Berglund, *Reader's Guide to the Cthulhu Mythos.* Albuquerque, Silver Scarab Press, 1973.

Wells, Stuart, III, *The Science Fiction and Heroic Fantasy Author Index.* Duluth, Purple Unicorn, 1978.

Wertham, Frederic, *The World of Fanzines: A Special Form of Communication.* Carbondale, Southern Illinois University Press, 1973.

Williamson, Jack, editor, *Teaching Science Fiction: Education for Tomorrow.* Philadelphia, Owlswick Press, 1980.

Willis, Donald C., *Horror and Science Fiction Films: A Checklist.* Metuchen, New Jersey, Scarecrow Press, 1972.

Wilson, Colin, *Science Fiction as Existentialism.* Hayes, Middlesex, Bran's Head, 1978.

Wilson, Colin, *The Strength to Dream: Literature and the Imagination.* London, Gollancz, and Boston, Houghton Mifflin, 1962.

Wingrove, David, editor, *The Science Fiction Source Book.* New York, Van Nostrand Reinhold, 1984.

Wolfe, Gary K., *The Known and the Unknown: The Iconography of Science Fiction.* Kent, Ohio, Kent State University Press, 1979.

Wolfe, Gary K., editor, *Science Fiction Dialogues.* Chicago, Academy, 1982.

Wollheim, Donald A., *The Universe Makers: Science Fiction Today.* New York, Harper, 1971; London, Gollancz, 1972.

Wymer, Thomas L., and others, *Intersections: The Elements of Fiction in Science Fiction.* Bowling Green, Ohio, Popular Press, 1978.

EDITOR'S NOTE

The selection of writers included in this book is based upon the recommendations of the advisers listed on page xvii. The main part of the book covers English-language writers of science fiction since 1895. Appendices include selective representations of authors in other languages whose works have been translated into English, and of major fantasy writers.

The entry for each writer in the main part of the book consists of a biography, a bibliography, and a signed critical essay. Living authors were invited to add a comment on their work. The bibliographies list all books, including non-science-fiction works. Original British and United States editions of all books have been listed; other editions are listed only if they are the first editions. As a rule all uncollected science-fiction short stories published since the entrant's last collection have been listed; complete short story listings occur for writers whose reputations rest primarily on their short stories; in those cases where a story has been published in a magazine and later in an anthology, we have tended to list the anthology. Entries include notations of published bibliographies, manuscript collections, and book-length critical studies. General critical materials appear in the Reading List of secondary works on the genre.

I wish to thank Donald H. Tuck, Peter Nicholls, R. Reginald, William Contento, Lloyd Currey, Jerry Boyajian, and Kenneth R. Johnson for their now-indispensable reference books. Thanks go also to the many entrants who took the time to complete an extensive questionnaire. Special thanks are due to Kenneth R. Johnson for information on original anthologies.

ADVISERS

Brian Aldiss
John Brunner
Don D'Ammassa
Malcolm Edwards
John Eggeling
Charles Elkins
Hal W. Hall
Lee Harding
Rosemary Herbert
Van Ikin
David Ketterer

Robert M. Philmus
Christopher Priest
Pamela Sargent
Robert Scholes
Baird Searles
Brian M. Stableford
Darko Suvin
Michael J. Tolley
Donald H. Tuck
Marshall B. Tymn

CONTRIBUTORS

Mitchell Aboulafia
Rosemarie Arbur
Thomas D. Bacig
Douglas Barbour
George W. Barlow
Myra Barnes
Marleen S. Barr
Craig Wallace Barrow
Diana Barrow
Melissa E. Barth
Ruth Berman
E.R. Bishop
Michael Bishop
Russell Blackford
Karen Charmaine Blansfield
Janice M. Bogstad
Bernadette Bosky
John P. Brennan
Peter A. Brigg
R.E. Briney
Mary T. Brizzi
John Brunner
Alexander J. Butrym
Peter Caracciolo
Gay E. Carter
Steven R. Carter
Edgar L. Chapman
Elizabeth Cummins Cogell
Robert E. Colbert
Rosemary Coleman
Gary Coughlan
Richard Cowper
J. Randolph Cox
Michael Cule
Charles Cushing
Don D'Ammassa
David A. Drake
Thomas P. Dunn
Karren C. Edwards
Alex Eisenstein
Jeffrey M. Elliot
Gregory Feeley
Eric A. Fontaine

Jeff Frane
Robert Froese
Alice Carol Gaar
John V. Garner
Walter Gillings
Stephen H. Goldman
Joan Gordon
Martin H. Greenberg
Colin Greenland
Philip J. Harbottle
Rose Flores Harris
David G. Hartwell
Donald M. Hassler
Len Hatfield
Sharon-Ilona Hecht
Leonard G. Heldreth
Rosemary Herbert
Norman L. Hills
Janis Butler Holm
Terry Hughes
Elizabeth Anne Hull
Marvin W. Hunt
Van Ikin
Anne Hudson Jones
Robert L. Jones
Kenneth Jurkiewicz
Julius Kagarlitsky
George Kelley
John Kinnaird
Gérard Klein
Vince Kohler
David Lake
Donald L. Lawler
Mark Warwick Leahy
Michael M. Levy
Arthur O. Lewis
Shelly Lowenkopf
Robert A. W. Lowndes
Duncan Lunan
Richard A. Lupoff
Peter Lynch
Andrew Macdonald
Gina Macdonald

Anthony Manousos
Patrick L. McGuire
David G. Mead
Walter E. Meyers
Sandra Miesel
Richard W. Miller
Francis J. Molson
Lee Montgomerie
Michael A. Morrison
Will Murray
Marilyn K. Nellis
Susan L. Nickerson
Chad Oliver
Richard Orodenker
Gerald W. Page
Diane Parkin-Speer
Frederick Patten
Terri Paul
Michael Perkins
John R. Pfeiffer
Gene Phillips
Hazel Pierce
John J. Pierce
Nick Pratt
Bill Pronzini
Harold Lee Prosser
Joseph A. Quinn
Eric S. Rabkin
R. Reginald
Robert Reilly
Lawrence R. Ries
Natalie M. Rosinsky
Franz Rottensteiner
Joanna Russ
David N. Samuelson
Joe Sanders
Pamela Sargent
Harvey J. Satty
John Scarborough
Roger C. Schlobin
William M. Schuyler, Jr.
Darrell Schweitzer
Baird Searles
Kathryn Lee Seidel

Susan Shwartz
Curtis C. Smith
Carol L. Snyder
Judith Snyder
Katherine Staples
Philippa Stephensen-Payne
Graham Stone
Leon Stover
C.W. Sullivan III
Judith Summers
Darko Suvin
Paul Swank
Norman Talbot
Robert Thurston
Michael J. Tolley
Frank H. Tucker
George Turner
Lisa Tuttle
Jana I. Tuzar
Marylyn J. Underwood
Steven Utley
Robert E. Vardeman
W. Warren Wagar
Karl Edward Wagner
Ian Watson
Douglas E. Way
Karen G. Way
Jane B. Weedman
Mary S. Weinkauf
Dennis M. Welch
Fred D. White
Robert H. Wilcox
Cherry Wilder
David Wingrove
Gary K. Wolfe
Gene Wolfe
Anthony Wolk
Susan Wood
Martin Morse Wooster
Alice Chambers Wygant
Carl B. Yoke
Hoda M. Zaki
George Zebrowski

TWENTIETH-CENTURY
SCIENCE-FICTION
WRITERS

Robert Abernathy
Douglas Adams
Mark Adlard
Brian Aldiss
Grant Allen
Kingsley Amis
Chester Anderson
Poul Anderson
Piers Anthony
Christopher Anvil
Edwin L. Arnold
Fenton Ash
Isaac Asimov
Robert Asprin
John Atkins

Brian N. Ball
J.G. Ballard
Arthur K. Barnes
Steven Barnes
William Barnwell
Neal Barrett, Jr.
T.J. Bass
John Calvin Batchelor
Harry Bates
John Baxter
Barrington John Bayley
Greg Bear
Charles Beaumont
Edward Bellamy
Gregory Benford
J.D. Beresford
Bryan Berry
Alfred Bester
Lloyd Biggle, Jr.
Eando Binder
David F. Bischoff
Michael Bishop
Jerome Bixby
Christopher Blayre
James Blish
Robert Bloch
Nelson S. Bond
J.F. Bone
Anthony Boucher
Ben Bova
John Boyd
Leigh Brackett
Ray Bradbury
Marion Zimmer Bradley
Reginald Bretnor
Miles J. Breuer
David Brin
Damien Broderick
Fredric Brown
Rosel George Brown
Mildred Downey Broxon
John Brunner
Edward Bryant
Frank Bryning
Algis Budrys
Kenneth Bulmer
David R. Bunch
Anthony Burgess
Edgar Rice Burroughs
William S. Burroughs

F.M. Busby
Octavia E. Butler
Samuel Butler

Martin Caidin
Ernest Callenbach
John W. Campbell, Jr.
Paul Capon
Orson Scott Card
Jayge Carr
Terry Carr
Angela Carter
Lin Carter
Cleve Cartmill
Jack L. Chalker
A. Bertram Chandler
Louis Charbonneau
Suzy McKee Charnas
C.J. Cherryh
Robert Chilson
Charles Chilton
John Christopher
Arthur C. Clarke
Hal Clement
Mark Clifton
Stanton A. Coblentz
Theodore R. Cogswell
D.G. Compton
Michael G. Coney
Glen Cook
Edmund Cooper
Alfred Coppel
Lee Correy
Juanita Coulson
Robert Coulson
Arthur Byron Cover
Richard Cowper
Erle Cox
Michael Crichton
Robert Cromie
John Keir Cross
John Crowley
Ray Cummings

Brian C. Daley
Jack Dann
Arsen Darnay
Avram Davidson
L.P. Davies
Chan Davis
Gerry Davis
L. Sprague de Camp
Miriam Allen deFord
Joseph H. Delaney
Samuel R. Delany
Lester del Rey
Lester Dent
August Derleth
Gene De Weese
Philip K. Dick
Peter Dickinson
Gordon R. Dickson
Thomas M. Disch
Sonya Dorman
Arthur Conan Doyle

Gardner Dozois
David A. Drake
Diane Duane
David Duncan
Lawrence Durrell

G.C. Edmondson
George Alec Effinger
Max Ehrlich
Larry Eisenberg
Phyllis Eisenstein
Gordon Eklund
M. Barnard Eldershaw
Suzette Haden Elgin
Harlan Ellison
Carol Emshwiller
Sylvia Engdahl
George Allan England
Lloyd Arthur Eshbach
Christopher Evans
E. Everett Evans

Zoë Fairbairns
Paul W. Fairman
R. Lionel Fanthorpe
Ralph Milne Farley
Philip José Farmer
Mick Farren
Howard Fast
Jonathan Fast
John Russell Fearn
Cynthia Felice
Jack Finney
Nicholas Fisk
Constantine FitzGibbon
Homer Eon Flint
Charles L. Fontenay
William R. Forstchen
Robert L. Forward
Alan Dean Foster
M.A. Foster
Gardner F. Fox
Pat Frank
Michael Frayn
Nancy Freedman
Gertrude Friedberg
H.B. Fyfe

Raymond Z. Gallun
Daniel F. Galouye
Randall Garrett
Jean Mark Gawron
Mary Gentle
Peter George
Hugo Gernsback
David Gerrold
Mark S. Geston
William Gibson
J.U. Giesy
Alexis A. Gilliland
John Gloag
Tom Godwin
H.L. Gold
Stephen Goldin
William Golding
Rex Gordon

Stuart Gordon
Phyllis Gotlieb
Felix C. Gotschalk
Ron Goulart
Charles L. Grant
Curme Gray
Joseph Green
William Greenleaf
Russell M. Griffin
George Griffith
Frederick Philip Grove
Wyman Guin
James E. Gunn
Lindsay Gutteridge

H. Rider Haggard
Isidore Haiblum
J.B.S. Haldane
Jack C. Haldeman
Joe Haldeman
Austin Hall
Edmond Hamilton
Lee Harding
Charles L. Harness
Harry Harrison
M. John Harrison
L.P. Hartley
H.F. Heard
Robert A. Heinlein
Mark Helprin
Zenna Henderson
Joe L. Hensley
Frank Herbert
James Herbert
John Hersey
Philip E. High
Russell Hoban
Edward D. Hoch
Christopher Hodder-Williams
William Hope Hodgson
Lee Hoffman
James P. Hogan
Robert Holdstock
Cecelia Holland
H.H. Hollis
J. Hunter Holly
H.M. Hoover
Robert Hoskins
William Dean Howells
Fred and Geoffrey Hoyle
Trevor Hoyle
L. Ron Hubbard
Monica Hughes
Zach Hughes
E.M. Hull
Evan Hunter
Aldous Huxley
C.J. Cutcliffe Hyne

Dean Ing

John Jakes
Laurence M. Janifer
K.W. Jeter
W.E. Johns
D.F. Jones

Langdon Jones
Neil R. Jones
Raymond F. Jones
M.K. Joseph

James Kahn
Colin Kapp
David Karp
Anna Kavan
David H. Keller
Leo P. Kelley
Arthur Keppel-Jones
Alexander Key
Daniel Keyes
Crawford Kilian
Lee Killough
Gary Kilworth
Vincent King
Donald Kingsbury
Rudyard Kipling
John Kippax
Otis Adelbert Kline
Nigel Kneale
Damon Knight
Norman L. Knight
Dean R. Koontz
C.M. Kornbluth
William Kotzwinkle
Michael Kurland
Henry Kuttner

R.A. Lafferty
David Lake
David Langford
Sterling E. Lanier
E.C. Large
Philip Latham
Keith Laumer
Tanith Lee
Ursula K. Le Guin
Fritz Leiber
Stephen Leigh
Murray Leinster
Madeleine L'Engle
William Le Queux
Milton Lesser
Doris Lessing
Ira Levin
C.S. Lewis
Sinclair Lewis
Jacqueline Lichtenberg
Alice Lightner
David Lindsay
Alun Llewellyn
Edward Llewellyn
Jack London
Charles R. Long
Frank Belknap Long
Barry Longyear
Noel M. Loomis
H.P. Lovecraft
Robert A.W. Lowndes
Sam J. Lundwall
Richard A. Lupoff
John Lymington
Elizabeth A. Lynn

C.C. MacApp
John D. MacDonald
R.W. Mackelworth
Katherine MacLean
Sheila MacLeod
Pip Maddern
Charles Eric Maine
Barry N. Malzberg
Phillip Mann
Laurence Manning
George R.R. Martin
David I. Masson
Richard Matheson
Julian May
Ardath Mayhar
Bruce McAllister
Anne McCaffrey
Thomas McClary
J. Francis McComas
J.T. McIntosh
Vonda N. McIntyre
Richard M. McKenna
Dean McLaughlin
Mike McQuay
Shepherd Mead
S.P. Meek
David Meltzer
R.M. Meluch
Richard C. Meredith
Judith Merril
A. Merritt
Sam Merwin, Jr.
Roy Meyers
P. Schuyler Miller
Walter M. Miller, Jr.
Naomi Mitchison
Thomas F. Monteleone
Michael Moorcock
C.L. Moore
Patrick Moore
Ward Moore
Dan Morgan
John Morressy
Janet E. Morris
Gerald Murnane

Ed Naha
Ray Nelson
Kris Neville
Larry Niven
William F. Nolan
John Norman
Andre Norton
Warren Norwood
Alan E. Nourse
Philip Francis Nowlan

E.V. Odle
Kevin O'Donnell, Jr.
Andrew J. Offutt
Chad Oliver
Bob Olsen
Joseph O'Neill
George Orwell

Raymond A. Palmer

Edgar Pangborn
Alexei Panshin
Kit Pedler
Walker Percy
Emil Petaja
Rog Phillips
Marge Piercy
H. Beam Piper
Doris Piserchia
Charles Platt
Frederik Pohl
Arthur Porges
Jerry Pournelle
Tim Powers
Festus Pragnell
Terry Pratchett
Fletcher Pratt
Paul Preuss
Christopher Priest
J.B. Priestley
George W. Proctor
Tom Purdom
Thomas Pynchon

John Rackham
Ayn Rand
Marta Randall
John Rankine
Rick Raphael
Francis G. Rayer
Tom Reamy
J. Michael Reaves
Kit Reed
Ed Earl Repp
Mike Resnick
Mack Reynolds
Walt and Leigh Richmond
Keith Roberts
Stephen Robinett
Frank M. Robinson
Kim Stanley Robinson
Spider Robinson
Ross Rocklynne
Richard Rohmer
Mordecai Roshwald
William Rotsler
Victor Rousseau
Rudy Rucker
Joanna Russ
Eric Frank Russell

Fred Saberhagen
Margaret St. Clair
James Sallis
Sarban
Pamela Sargent
Richard Saxon
Josephine Saxton
Nat Schachner
Hilbert Schenck
Stanley Schmidt
James H. Schmitz
Thomas N. Scortia
Hank Searls
Arthur Sellings
Luis P. Senarens

Rod Serling
Garrett P. Serviss
Alan Seymour
Jack Sharkey
Richard S. Shaver
Bob Shaw
Robert Sheckley
Charles Sheffield
Lucius Shepard
T.L. Sherred
R.C. Sherriff
M.P. Shiel
Wilmar H. Shiras
John Shirley
Nevil Shute
Robert Silverberg
Clifford D. Simak
Upton Sinclair
Curt Siodmak
Kathleen Sky
John Sladek
Henry Slesar
William M. Sloane
Clark Ashton Smith
Cordwainer Smith
E.E. Smith
Evelyn E. Smith
George H. Smith
George O. Smith
L. Neil Smith
Jerry Sohl
Norman Spinrad
Steven Spruill
Brian M. Stableford
Robert Stallman
Olaf Stapledon
Christopher Stasheff
Andrew M. Stephenson
Bruce Sterling
Francis Stevens
George R. Stewart
Hank Stine
Frank R. Stockton
Craig Strete
Theodore Sturgeon
Somtow Sucharitkul
Jeff and Jean Sutton
Leo Szilard

John Taine
Stephen Tall
Peter Tate
William F. Temple
William Tenn
Emma Tennant
Walter Tevis
D.M. Thomas
Ted Thomas
Robert Thurston
Patrick Tilley
James Tiptree, Jr.
Arthur Train
Louis Trimble
E.C. Tubb
Wilson Tucker
George Turner

Lisa Tuttle
Mark Twain

Steven Utley

Jack Vance
Sydney J. Van Scyoc
A.E. van Vogt
John Varley
A. Hyatt Verrill
Gore Vidal
Harl Vincent
Joan D. Vinge
Vernor Vinge
Kurt Vonnegut, Jr.

Howard Waldrop
Edgar Wallace
F.L. Wallace
Ian Wallace
G.C. Wallis
Hugh Walters
Donald Wandrei
Stanley Waterloo
William Jon Watkins
Ian Watson
Sharon Webb
Stanley G. Weinbaum
Manly Wade Wellman
H.G. Wells
Wallace West
Dennis Wheatley
James White

Ted White
Leonard Wibberley
Cherry Wilder
Kate Wilhelm
John A. Williams
Paul O. Williams
Robert Moore Williams
Jack Williamson
Connie Willis
Colin Wilson
F. Paul Wilson
Ricnard Wilson
Robert Anton Wilson
Jack Wodhams
Gary K. Wolf
Bernard Wolfe
Gene Wolfe
Donald A. Wollheim
Austin Tappan Wright
S. Fowler Wright
Philip Wylie
John Wyndham

Chelsea Quinn Yarbro
Laurence Yep
Nicholas Yermakov
Michael Young
Robert F. Young

Arthur Leo Zagat
Timothy Zahn
George Zebrowski
Roger Zelazny

FOREIGN-LANGUAGE WRITERS

Kobo Abe
Jean-Pierre Andrevon
René Barjavel
Aleksandr Belyaev
Jorge Luis Borges
Pierre Boulle
Karin Boye
Johanna and Günter Braun
Valery Bryusov
Mikhail Bulgakov
Dino Buzzati
Italo Calvino
Karel Capek
Herbert W. Franke
Otto Gail
Wolfgang Jeschke
Michel Jeury
Bernhard Kellermann
Gérard Klein

Sakyo Komatsu
Kurd Lasswitz
Stanislaw Lem
André Maurois
Vladimir Mayakovsky
Josef Nesvadba
Maurice Renard
Boris and Arkady Strugatsky
Vladimir Tendryakov
Abram Tertz
Alexey Tolstoy
Konstantin Tsiolkovsky
Ilya Varshavsky
Vercors
Jules Verne
Franz Werfel
Stanislaw Witkiewicz
Ivan Yefremov
Yevgeny Zamyatin

MAJOR FANTASY WRITERS

Lord Dunsany
E.R. Eddison
William Morris

Mervyn Peake
J.R.R. Tolkien

ABERNATHY, Robert (Gordon). American. Born in Geneva, Switzerland, in 1924. Educated at Princeton University, New Jersey, A. B. 1952; Ph. D. Served in the United States Army, 1946-48. Married Jean Clarke Montgomery in 1955; one daughter. Journalist: NBC Radio correspondent 1946-48; science editor. Professor of Languages, University of Colorado, Boulder. Since 1973, Trustee, Princeton University. Address: 2900 East Aurora, Apartment 154, Boulder, Colorado 80303, U. S. A.

SCIENCE-FICTION PUBLICATIONS

Uncollected Short Stories

"Mission from Arcturus," in *Science Fiction Quarterly* (Holyoke, Massachusetts), Spring 1943.
"Saboteur of Space," in *Planet* (New York), Spring 1944.
"When the Rockets Come," in *Astounding* (New York), March 1945.
"Failure on Titan," in *Planet* (New York), Winter 1947.
"Hostage of Tomorrow," in *Planet* (New York), Spring 1949.
"The Giants Return," in *Planet* (New York), Fall 1949.
"The Dead-Star Rover," in *Planet* (New York), Winter 1949.
"Peril of the Blue World," in *Flight in Space,* edited by Donald A. Wollheim. New York, Fell, 1950.
"The Ultimate Peril," in *Amazing* (New York), March 1950.
"The Tower of Babel," in *Amazing* (New York), June 1950.
"Righteous Plague," in *Science Fiction Quarterly* (Holyoke, Massachusetts), May 1951.
"Heritage," in *Omnibus of Science Fiction,* edited by Groff Conklin. New York, Crown, 1952.
"The Captain's Getaway," in *Orbit 1* (New York), 1953.
"The Four Commandments," in *Science Fiction Quarterly* (Holyoke, Massachusetts), February 1953.
"Lifework," in *Science Fiction Quarterly* (Holyoke, Massachusetts), May 1953.
"Professor Schlucker's Fallacy," in *Fantasy and Science Fiction* (New York), November 1953.
"The Record of Corrupira," in *Fantastic Universe* (Chicago), January 1954.
"Tag," in *Beyond* (New York), January 1954.
"When the Mountain Shook," in *If* (New York), March 1954.
"The Firefighters," in *Fantasy and Science Fiction* (New York), March 1954.
"The Thousandth Year," in *Astounding* (New York), April 1954.
"The Marvelous Movie," in *Future* (New York), August 1954.
"The Fishers," in *Fantasy and Science Fiction* (New York), December 1954.
"Heirs Apparent," in *Best from Fantasy and Science Fiction 4,* edited by Anthony Boucher. New York, Doubleday, 1955.
"Axolotl," in *Best Science Fiction Stories and Novels 1955,* edited by T. E. Dikty. New York, Fell, 1955; as "Deep Space," in *5 Tales from Tomorrow,* edited by Dikty, New York, Fawcett, 1957.
"World of the Drone," in *Imagination* (Evanston, Illinois), January 1955.
"The Guzzler," in *Science Fiction Quarterly* (Holyoke, Massachusetts). May 1955.
"The Year 2000," in *Fantasy and Science Fiction* (New York), January 1956.
"One of Them?" in *Science Fiction Quarterly* (Holyoke, Massachusetts), May 1956.
"The Laugh," in *Fantastic Universe* (Chicago), June 1956.
"Hour Without Glory," in *Fantasy and Science Fiction* (New York), July 1956.
"Grandma's Lie Soap," in *SF: The Year's Greatest Science Fiction and Fantasy,* edited by Judith Merril. New York, Dell, 1957.
"The Canal Builders," in *Every Boy's Book of Outer Space Stories,* edited by T. E. Dikty. New York, Fell, 1960.
"Junior," in *SF: The Best of the Best,* edited by Judith Merril. New York, Delacorte Press, 1967.
"Pyramid," in *Anthropology Through Science Fiction*, edited by Carol Mason, Martin H. Greenberg, and Patricia Warrick. New York, St. Martin's Press, 1974.
"Single Combat," in *Sociology Through Science Fiction*, edited by John W. Milstead and others. New York, St. Martin's Press, 1974.
"Strange Exodus," in *Space Odysseys*, edited by Brian W. Aldiss. London, Futura, 1974; New York, Doubleday, 1976.
"The Rotifers," in *Earth Is the Strangest Planet*, edited by Robert Silverberg. Nashville, Nelson, 1977.

* * *

Robert Abernathy is a thoroughly enjoyable writer with a number of strings to his bow. He is gifted with wit and sagacity, and his style is equal to any demand he makes on it (though he seldom goes in for verbal fireworks), but he has had no new stories published since the 1950's and no collection has appeared in book form.

Like many science-fiction writers, Abernathy began publishing early, and two of his earliest stories are excellent. "Heritage" is a study of the far future of the world and the question as to who shall succeed the degenerate human race; it is told by "the great time traveler, Nicholas Doody. " "Peril of the Blue World" is a story of the Martian Expedition to Earth and why it failed: the tone is light and the narrator in perfect control; Anthony Boucher could do no better.

In "The Canal Builders" Earthmen have long been established on Mars, which they visit by teleportation; but when at last a manned interplanetary rocket is sent, the travellers find a ruined city they have never heard of. Another very different story set on Mars is "When the Rockets Come," which studies the harsh frontier society and the character of the hero. Vic Denning is a successor to Achilles or to Sir Bors: the hero who is never so happy as when his life is in danger. But "when the rockets come, it is not war"; valour and chivalry are obsolete.

Several stories contrast man with other races. In "Pyramid" man is imported to the planet Thegeth to dispose of an infestation of hamsters that have ruined the ecological balance. The thagatha, who have foolishly imported man, value above all else the balance of nature. Man, on the other hand, turns out to be an infestation without parallel; and the thagatha are completely unable to comprehend their motives. "The Rotifers," which takes place on Earth, features a 12-year-old boy who is examining pond life in his microscope. But as he does so, the rotifers also examine man, and are most displeased to learn of his existence. The sinister quality of this tale is admirable. "The Thousandth Year" contrasts man with an empire-ruling race of squidlike beings, this time much to man's advantage. The Ratk are taught never to trust anyone, and their constant suspicion is their downfall.

One of Abernathy's best and funniest stories, "Junior," deals with the generation gap. Most of what the earnest elders teach is based on experience, though not necessarily true. Junior, the rebellious polyp, manages to transcend the parental wisdom—emphatically. I pity anyone who tries to translate the new changes rung on old clichés in this story. "Axolotl" is a powerful story. It describes the first man to travel in space (some seven years early), and that part of the story has dated slightly. But the passages about the axolotl emerging from the ocean and undergoing a transformation it could not foresee remain powerful and moving. Space travel has not yet produced in us the transformation Abernathy describes; but the metaphor is immensely suggestive still.

Some of Abernathy's space opera remains lively: "The Dead-Star Rover," "Hostage of Tomorrow," "The Giants Return," and even "The Ultimate Peril," with its evil insect-like aliens who use one hundred percent of their brains. Other stories make more serious use of the author's strong sense of history: "Heirs Apparent" could have been a novel in other hands, but Abernathy wrote a long story of events on the Russian steppe after a Third World War, with expert cutting and no words wasted. "Hour Without Glory" is a fine short study of the military mind. And "One of Them?" is one of the most beautiful stories on the android theme that I have ever read.

Someone should bring out an Abernathy collection; his work is too good to remain buried in the reference libraries.

—Charles Cushing

ADAMS, Douglas (Noel). British. Born in Cambridge, 11 March 1952. Educated at St. John's College, Cambridge B. A. Free-lance writer: Script Editor, *Doctor Who* series, BBC TV, 1978-80. Agent: Ed Victor Ltd., 162 Wardour Street, London W1V 4AT, England.

SCIENCE-FICTION PUBLICATIONS

Novels (series: Hitch-Hiker, in all books)

The Hitch-Hiker's Guide to the Galaxy. London, Pan, 1979; New York, Crown, 1980.
The Restaurant at the End of the Universe. London, Pan, 1980; New York, Crown, 1982.
Life, The Universe, and Everything. London, Pan, and New York, Crown, 1982.
So Long, and Thanks for All the Fish. London, Pan, 1984; New York, Crown, 1985.

OTHER PUBLICATIONS

Plays

The Hitch-Hiker's Guide to the Galaxy (broadcast, 1978; produced, 1979).

Radio Play: *The Hitch-Hiker's Guide to the Galaxy*, 1978.

Television Plays: for *Doctor Who* series.

Other

The Meaning of Liff, with John Lloyd. London, Pan, 1983.

* * *

Publication of *The Hitch-Hiker's Guide to the Galaxy* in 1979 brought Douglas Adams instant notoriety, if not throughout the galaxy, at least in the world of science-fiction fandom. His success was well justified, for he managed to poke fun at nearly every one of the genre's popular conventions. Forget the faster-than-light drive, the total improbability drive makes it obsolescent. Douglas Adams has not only *conceived* the total improbability drive, but he has *created* it. It is the power which moves his *Hitch-Hiker* series. His imagination permits him to pile improbability upon improbability, whirling the reader into a tailspin of laughter. Yet improbability is not his only comic technique; he is equally at home with the fresh use of cliché phrases or situations. Puns occur frequently (who could forget the long "shaggy-dog" acount of Frogstar B's economy—leading to the "Shoe Event Horizon"?). All these techniques serve one end—the deflation of pompous ideas held by people who take themselves too seriously.

But it is not just the comic techniques that make his novels worth reading. The characters, who may at first appear as mere parodies of science-fiction stereotypes, grow throughout the series into fairly well-rounded comic persons. Arthur Dent, at first merely an anti-heroic schlemiel, elicits our affection because of his provincial attachment to Earth. Ford Prefect's universal ennui seems appropriate to his profession of galaxy tour-guide writer. Zaphod Beeblebrox (who said two heads were better than one?) might eventually persuade us that not knowing what you are doing is in fact better. One even grows attached to Marvin, the perennially (millennially?) depressed robot.

The good fun of all this holds up well through the first two volumes, *The Hitch-Hiker's Guide to the Galaxy* and *The Restaurant at the End of the Universe* ; but by the time one gets to *Life, The Universe, and Everything*, it begins to wear thin. Publication of a fourth volume, *So Long, and Thanks for All the Fish*, although it includes a number of details clearly intended to wrap up some of the loose ends from the previous volumes, proves to be too much of the same thing. The freshness which lent such force to *Hitch-Hiker* is gone; the joke has been carried too far.

Adams has collaborated with John Lloyd to produce *The Meaning of Liff* a supposedly comic glossary (complete with index) made up by giving meanings to place names (some few of which are comic in themselves). The definitions are sometimes (infrequently) witty and scintillating, sometimes vulgar or obscene, and mostly just boring.

—Robert Reilly

ADLARD, Mark (Peter Marcus Adlard). British. Born in Seaton Carew, County Durham, 19 June 1932. Educated at Trinity College, Cambridge, 1951-54, B. A. 1954, M. A. ; Oxford University, 1954-55; University of London, B. Sc. (extra-mural) in economics. Married Sheila Rosemary Skuse in 1968; one daughter and one son. Executive in the steel industry, in Middlesbrough, Yorkshire, Cardiff, and Kent, 1956-76. Since 1976, full-time writer. Agent: Ed Victor Ltd., 162 Wardour Street, London W1V 4AB. Address: 12 the Green, Seaton Carew, Hartlepool, Cleveland TS25 1AS, England.

SCIENCE-FICTION PUBLICATIONS

Novels (series: Tcity in all books)

Interface. London, Sidgwick and Jackson, 1971; New York, Ace, 1977.
Volteface. London, Sidgwick and Jackson, 1972; New York,

Ace, 1978.

Multiface. London, Sidgwick and Jackson, 1975; New York, Ace, 1978.

Uncollected Short Stories

"The Other Tradition" and "Theophilus," in *Beyond This Horizon*, edited by Christopher Carrell. Sunderland, Ceolfrith Press, 1973.

OTHER PUBLICATIONS

Novel

The Greenlander. London, Hamish Hamilton, 1978; New York, Summit, 1979.

Other

"Billion Year Spree: A Labour of Love," in *Foundation 6* (London), May 1974.

*

Mark Adlard comments:

One of my main pre-occupations is the importance of personal economic activity to "the good life." It seemed to me that various hypotheses about such matters could be explored fictionally, by presenting a future world in which economic activity had been largely made redundant. This fictional device would also make it possible to consider the moral dilemmas and responsibilities of managerial elites. It was considerations such as these, and not a previous enthusiasm for the genre, that induced me to write "Science fiction."

*   *   *

Mark Adlard's Tcity trilogy, *Interface, Volteface,* and *Multiface,* makes up a whole less than the sum of its parts but it is nevertheless a highly interesting and readable work. The parts are considerable and the project ambitious. Reviewing *Multiface* for the *Times Literary Supplement,* T. A. Shippey noted the ironic contrast between the plots and characters of the first two books and those of Wagner's *Ring* and Dante's *Commedia* respectively: "Only the boldest writer would invite such comparisons. . . . But Mark Adlard made a success of it, and has done so once more, in a novel based this time on *The Faerie Queene.*" Shippey is an over-bold reviewer, for his criticism is not just, although it does adumbrate a critical problem. For one thing, Spenser is only one among several important literary sources in *Multiface,* where the controlling reference (matching Wagner and Dante) is to Buddhism; for another, the relationships between the novels and their sources are not the same.

It seems likely that one of the problems is that the three novels were not all completed together. As literature, *Interface* is inferior to the later two. It is overloaded with exposition at the expense of narrative and, although Adlard is clearly aware of the problem (throughout the series, a stock joke is the blunt interruption of robotic exposition), information whether cultural or technological appears to be simply dropped into the text and does not resonate within it. This is true of the Wagner references, which are only to Götterdämmerung, an odd choice for the first novel of a series. This novel concerns weaknesses at the interface between an enclosed society of drugged citizens and their benevolent, superior managers, weaknesses on both

sides, which end in destruction for some but salvation for others. Adlard stands too far off from his characters, and, because the emotive level of the narrative is low, the climactic horrors and pathos fail somewhat in their effect. *Volteface* is much richer in texture, and the Dante references are both more numerous than the *Ring* ones and more deeply embedded in the text; the leading characters are more highly developed, and the narrative consequently more engaging, the ironies more piquant. In the failed Utopia of *Interface,* work had been denied the multitudinous citizens: in response to their discontent, work is reintroduced to Tcity by the executives, who deliberately create an old-fashioned (i. e., 20th-century) managerial structure, knowing this will be inefficient, merely to make work, i. e., the distribution of goods (trinkets) which are, of course, manufactured in fully automated factories. This scheme enables Adlard to write splendid satire as he traces both the collective volte-face and some individual reversals of life in Tcity. The *Inferno* of workfree pleasure is exchanged for a dubious *Purgatorio.* However, I would need to have the author explain to me just how his Dante-Beatrice pair (Twynne and Ventrix) are really illuminated by their source. Ventrix is an interesting character in her own right.

If idle pleasure was hell, work purgatory, then *Multiface* seems to be asking what is the ideal mode of life. The answer is that it depends on the individual life. Even Theravana Buddhism, practised by one saintly executive, may not suit all executives; Mahayana Buddhism, considered more suitable for the citizens, seems too perversely appropriate for the tormented Taggart, persuaded that in a lame dog he sees the reincarnation of his sadistic father, on which he exacts vengeance for his mother's suffering which has blighted the whole of his own life. As Jan Caspol puts it, "Men have different faces. There are no two alike, and you can't expect them to wear the same mask. . . . Even Buddhas only point the way." Jan, though an executive, is the reader's choric companion throughout the series and he thus presumably voices the author's conclusion: but what consequences follow for the executives whose vast experiment has involved the beneficent control of a world society? The author seems to shy away from his bold socio-history, in favour of the predicaments of individuals. Their problems may be resolved for good or ill, but what of the further problems in Tcity? The trilogy seems to call for a further, maturer volume, one which will tell us what life is for, perhaps: we are at least provoked to consideration of this disturbing question. However, it may be in the intuition that life is open-ended, that there are no pat catastrophes, that the trilogy should properly end. One of its most appealing narratives is that of Osbert Osborne, discovering diversity and pattern in the apparently uniform stahlex beeblocks of Tcity (everything there is made of this remarkable versatile new material), yet knowing that he will never have time even to map his own multi-story block. Three faces can stand for the whole infinite polyhedron.

—Michael J. Tolley

AGHILL, Gordon. See **GARRETT, Randall.**

AINSBURY, Ray. See **VERRILL, A. Hyatt.**

AKERS, Alan Burt. See **BULMER, Kenneth.**

ALDISS, Brian (Wilson). British. Born in East Dereham, Norfolk, 18 August 1925. Educated at Framlingham College, Suffolk, 1936-39; West Buckland School, 1939-42. Served in the Royal Signals in the Far East, 1943-47. Married Margaret Manson in 1965 (second marriage); four children, two from previous marriage. Bookseller, Oxford, 1947-56; Literary Editor, *Oxford Mail,* 1958-69; Science-Fiction Editor, Penguin Books, London, 1961-64; Art Correspondent, *Guardian,* London. President, British Science Fiction Association, 1960-65; Co-Founder, 1972, and Chairman, 1976-78, John W. Campbell Memorial Award; Co-President, Eurocon Committee, 1975-79; Chairman, Society of Authors, London, 1978-79; Member, Arts Council Literature Panel, 1978-80. Since 1975, Vice-President, Stapledon Society; since 1977, Founding Trustee, World Science Fiction, Dublin; since 1982, President, World SF; since 1983, Vice-President, H. G. Wells Society. Recipient: World Science Fiction Convention citation, 1959; Hugo Award, 1962; Nebula Award, 1965; Ditmar Award (Australia), 1970; British Science Fiction Association Award, 1972, 1982, and Special Award, 1974; Eurocon Award, 1976; James Blish Award, for non-fiction, 1977; Cometa d'Argento (Italy), 1977; Prix Jules Verne, 1977; Pilgrim Award, 1978; John W. Campbell Memorial Award, 1983. Guest of Honour, World Science Fiction Convention, London, 1965, 1979. Agent: A. P. Watt Ltd., 26-28 Bedford Row, London WC1R 4HL. Address: Woodlands, Foxcombe Road, Boars Hill, Oxfordshire OX1 5DL, England.

SCIENCE-FICTION PUBLICATIONS

Novels (series: Helliconia)

Non-Stop. London, Faber, 1958; as *Starship,* New York, Criterion, 1959.
Vanguard from Alpha. New York, Ace, 1959; as *Equator* (includes "Segregation"), London, Digit, 1961.
Bow Down to Nul. New York, Ace, 1960; as *The Interpreter,* London, Digit, 1961.
The Male Response. New York, Galaxy, 1961; London, Dobson, 1963.
The Primal Urge. New York, Ballantine, 1961; London, Sphere, 1967.
The Long Afternoon of Earth. New York, New American Library, 1962; expanded edition, as *Hothouse,* London, Faber, 1962; Boston, Gregg Press, 1976.
The Dark Light Years. London, Faber, and New York, New American Library, 1964.
Greybeard. London, Faber, and New York, Harcourt Brace, 1964.
Earthworks. London, Faber, 1965; New York, Doubleday, 1966.
An Age. London, Faber, 1967; as *Cryptozoic!,* New York, Doubleday, 1968.
Report on Probability A. London, Faber, 1968; New York, Doubleday, 1969.
Barefoot in the Head. London, Faber, 1969; New York, Doubleday, 1970.
Frankenstein Unbound. London, Cape, 1973; New York, Random House, 1974.
The Eighty-Minute Hour. London, Cape, and New York, Doubleday, 1974.

The Malacia Tapestry. London, Cape, 1976; New York, Harper, 1977.
Enemies of the System. London, Cape, and New York, Harper, 1978.
Moreau's Other Island. London, Cape, 1980; as *An Island Called Moreau,* New York, Simon and Schuster, 1981.
The Helliconia Trilogy. New York, Atheneum, 1985.
    Helliconia Spring. London, Cape, and New York, Atheneum, 1982.
    Helliconia Summer. London, Cape, and New York, Atheneum, 1983.
    Helliconia Winter. London, Cape, and New York, Atheneum, 1985.

Short Stories

Space, Time, and Nathaniel: Presciences. London, Faber, 1957; abridged edition, as *No Time Like Tomorrow,* New York, New American Library, 1959.
The Canopy of Time. London, Faber, 1959; revised edition, as *Galaxies Like Grains of Sand,* New York, New American Library, 1960.
The Airs of Earth. London, Faber, 1963.
Starswarm. New York, New American Library, 1964; London, Panther, 1979.
Best Science Fiction Stories of Brian Aldiss. London, Faber, 1965; as *Who Can Replace a Man?,* New York, Harcourt Brace, 1966; revised edition, Faber, 1971.
The Saliva Tree and Other Strange Growths. London, Faber, 1966.
Intangibles Inc. London, Faber, 1969.
A Brian Aldiss Omnibus 1-2. London, Sidgwick and Jackson, 2 vols., 1969-71.
Neanderthal Planet. New York, Avon, 1970.
The Moment of Eclipse. London, Faber, 1970; New York, Doubleday, 1972.
The Book of Brian Aldiss. New York, DAW, 1972; as *The Comic Inferno,* London, New English Library, 1973.
Excommunication. London, Post Card Partnership, 1975.
Last Orders and Other Stories. London, Cape, 1977.
New Arrivals, Old Encounters: Twelve Stories. London, Cape, 1979; New York, Harper, 1980.
Seasons in Flight. London, Cape, 1984.

OTHER PUBLICATIONS

Novels

The Brightfount Diaries. London, Faber, 1955.
The Hand-Reared Boy. London, Weidenfeld and Nicolson, and New York, McCall, 1970.
A Soldier Erect; or, Further Adventures of the Hand-Reared Boy. London, Weidenfeld and Nicolson, and New York, Coward McCann, 1971.
Brothers of the Head. London, Pierrot, 1977; New York, Two Continents, 1978.
A Rude Awakening. London, Weidenfeld and Nicolson, 1978; New York, Random House, 1979.
Brothers of the Head, and Where the Lines Converge. London, Panther, 1979.
Life in the West. London, Weidenfeld and Nicolson, 1980.

Play

Distant Encounters, adaptation of his own stories (produced London, 1978).

Verse

Pile: Petals from St. Klaed's Computer. London, Cape, and New York, Holt Rinehart, 1979.
Farewell to a Child. Berkhamsted, Hertfordshire, Priapus, 1982.

Other

"One That Could Control the Moon: Science Fiction Plain and Coloured," in *International Literary Annual 3,* edited by Arthur Boyars and Pamela Lyon. London, Calder, 1961.
"Judgment at Jonbar," in *SF Horizons* (London), 1964.
"British Science Fiction Now," in *SF Horizons* (London), 1965.
Cities and Stones: A Traveller's Jugoslavia. London, Faber, 1966.
The Shape of Further Things: Speculations on Change. London, Faber, 1970; New York, Doubleday, 1971.
"The Wounded Land: J. G. Ballard," in *SF: The Other Side of Realism,* edited by Thomas D. Clareson. Bowling Green, Ohio, Bowling Green University Press, 1972.
Billion Year Spree: A History of Science Fiction. London, Weidenfeld and Nicolson, and New York, Doubleday, 1973.
"The Profession of Science Fiction 7: Magic and Bare Boards," in *Foundation 6* (London), May 1974.
"Dick's Maledictory Web: About and Around *Martian Time-Slip,*" in *Science-Fiction Studies* (Terre Haute, Indiana), March 1975.
"On Being a Literary Pariah," in *Extrapolation* (Wooster, Ohio), May 1976.
"What Dark Non-Literary Passions" (on Stanislaw Lem), in *Science-Fiction Studies* (Terre Haute, Indiana), July 1977.
Science Fiction as Science Fiction. Frome, Somerset, Bran's Head, 1978.
"The Gulf and the Forest: Contemporary SF in Britain," in *Fantasy and Science Fiction* (New York), April 1978.
This World and Nearer Ones: Essays Exploring the Familiar. London, Weidenfeld and Nicolson, 1979; Kent, Ohio, Kent State University Press, 1981.
"The Hand in the Jar: Metaphor in Wells and Huxley," in *Foundation 17* (London), September 1979.
Science Fiction Quiz. London, Weidenfeld and Nicolson, 1983.
The Pale Shadow of Science. Seattle, Serconia Press, 1985.

Editor, *Penguin Science Fiction.* London, Penguin, 1961; *More Penguin Science Fiction,* 1963; *Yet More Penguin Science Fiction,* 1964; 3 vols. collected as *The Penguin Science Fiction Omnibus,* 1973.
Editor, *Best Fantasy Stories.* London, Faber, 1962.
Editor, *Last and First Men,* by Olaf Stapledon. London, Penguin, 1963.
Editor, *Introducing SF.* London, Faber, 1964.
Editor, with Harry Harrison, *Nebula Award Stories 2.* New York, Doubleday, 1967; as *Nebula Award Stories 1967,* London, Gollancz, 1967.
Editor, with Harry Harrison, *All about Venus.* New York, Dell, 1968; enlarged edition, as *Farewell, Fantastic Venus,* London, Macdonald, 1968.
Editor, with Harry Harrison, *Best SF 1967* [*to 1975*]. New York, Berkley and Putnam, 7 vols., and Indianapolis, Bobbs Merrill, 2 vols., 1968-75; as *The Year's Best Science Fiction 1-9,* London, Sphere, 8 vols., 1968-76, and London, Futura, 1 vol., 1976.
Editor, with Harry Harrison, *The Astounding-Analog Reader.* New York, Doubleday, 2 vols., 1972-73; London, Sphere, 2 vols., 1973.
Editor, *Space Opera.* London, Weidenfeld and Nicolson, 1974; New York, Doubleday, 1975.
Editor, *Space Odysseys.* London, Futura, 1974; New York, Doubleday, 1976.
Editor, with Harry Harrison, *SF Horizons* (reprint of magazine). New York, Arno Press, 1975.
Editor, with Harry Harrison, *Hell's Cartographers: Some Personal Histories of Science Fiction Writers.* London, Weidenfeld and Nicolson, and New York, Harper, 1975.
Editor, with Harry Harrison, *Decade: The 1940's, The 1950's, The 1960's.* London, Macmillan, 3 vols., 1975-77; *The 1940's* and *The 1950's,* New York, St. Martin's Press, 2 vols., 1978.
Editor, *Evil Earths.* London, Weidenfeld and Nicolson, 1975; New York, Avon, 1979.
Editor, *Galactic Empires.* London, Weidenfeld and Nicolson, 2 vols., 1976; New York, St. Martin's Press, 2 vols., 1977.
Editor, *Perilous Planets.* London, Weidenfeld and Nicolson, 1978; New York, Avon, 1980.

*

Bibliography: *Item Eighty-Three: Brian Aldiss: A Bibliography 1954-1972* by Margaret Aldiss, Oxford, Bocardo Press, 1972.

Manuscript Collections: Bodleian Library, Oxford University; Dallas Public Library.

Critical Studies: *Aldiss Unbound: The Science Fiction of Brian W. Aldiss* by Richard Mathews, San Bernardino, California, Borgo Press, 1977; *Apertures: A Study of the Writings of Brian Aldiss* by Brian Griffin and David Wingrove, Westport, Connecticut, Greenwood Press, 1984; by the author, in *Contemporary Authors Autobiography Series 2,* Detroit, Gale, 1985.

Brian Aldiss comments:

Interested parties are recommended to seek out the critical study of my writings by Wingrove and Griffin. Although I do not always agree with all they say, they are at least as reliable as I would be. Even self-conscious authors sail on, charting their course through style and story, without much bothering about the rocks under the surface. It's for the critics to consider shipwreck.

One really writes because one has to. I never think of the reader until the act of creation is over. Then I hope I might nourish the creative spark in others; I imagine people and people imagination. I craved the freedom writing gave me. My fictions have taken place on many worlds. My central characters have been of many nationalities. Speech is a preoccupation. Even in *Non-Stop,* some sort of heightened speech was attempted. In *Life in the West,* scarcely a handful of the many characters speak "standard English, " in *Helliconia* the languages are many. Aren't those volumes in part about the necessity of communication—and its difficulty? Mine is a literature of exile. Every novel undertaken is an act of xenophilia. The label "science fiction" doesn't fit.

The list of my writings seems impossibly long. The more reason to be brief here.

* * *

In the Author's Note to *Last Orders,* Brian Aldiss (or "the author") says: "See, my stories are about human woes, non-communication, disappointment, endurance, acceptance, love. Aren't those things real enough?" They are, even when figured through the most complexly thought out alien personages, as in the epic Helliconia trilogy; and in exploring "those things," Aldiss has created an *oeuvre* which for breadth of vision and variety of formal experimentation is beyond almost all other writers in the genre. As one critic has proposed, Aldiss's two gods are Proteus, the enigmatic shape-changer, and Prometheus, the seeker of forbidden knowledge, fire-bringer, willing martyr in the battle against the forces of tyranny. Thus his works not only speak out against the repressive aspects of the human imagination but by doing so in so many different and wittily stunning ways also formally demonstrate the power of liberated creativity.

Some might argue that Aldiss's ability to write any kind of story betrays a lack of a personal "voice," but they would be wrong. The uniqueness of his voice partly inheres in his willingness to explore imaginative forms, whether the early, classically perfect, stories of *The Canopy of Time* or *Starswarm*, the extraordinary formal experiments of *Report on Probability A* (an SF version of the *nouveau roman*) and *Barefoot in the Head* (an attempt to use the language of Joyce's *Finnegans Wake* to portray the mentality of a Europe literally bombed by LSD into the "stoned" age), the extraordinarily assured but never static forms of the recent stories and such novels as *The Malacia Tapestry*, or the epic metahistorical sweep of the Helliconia trilogy. Like so many British writers, Aldiss has never had to feel that he should either repeat himself or apologize for writing SF. As a result, he has always been able to seek the proper "style" with which to formulate his "content" most fully, which is to say he has always recognized the ways in which style and content are indivisible. From the beginning he has expanded his knowledge of and ability to handle technique and recognized the need to push against the conventional boundaries of the genre.

If he has refused to be held down by the conventionality of most SF, Aldiss has never turned his back on it. Indeed, as his various anthologies, many of them dealing with the most "romantic" themes of SF, and *Billion Year Spree* show, he has always loved it all. But he is fully aware of the negative imaginative effects of what he calls "power-fantasy," and has sought as "a real writer" to transcend the kind of writing which only transforms "a man into an organ of conquest in a knocking-shop of wish-fulfillment. " (In this, he shares many attitudes with that often excoriated SF satirist, Barry N. Malzberg, and it's not surprising that he was on the committee which awarded Malzberg's *Beyond Apollo* the first John W. Campbell Award.) Thus, even in his early works, set in far-distant futures of galactic empires or the end of the solar system (*Hothouse*), he tends to look at the human and emotional sides of events: the need individuals will always have for love and communication/community; the ways in which imaginative empathy can help people to face their lives; the qualities of courage and endurance we all need to survive, whether confronting "ordinary" life or the end of all life as we know it.

Such a varied and complex *oeuvre* evades all simple systems of categorization. Certainly Aldiss always gives his readers rich and emotionally satisfying entertainment. And he always infuses his stories with powerful feelings, though the later fictions achieve far subtler nuances than the earliest stories do. From the very beginning, moreover, he reveals a particular capacity for a kind of elegiac vision, a quality of speech which uplifts even as it tells of the end of all we hold dear, and it is a tone perhaps even more akin to Anglo-Saxon poetry than to H. G. Wells's "scientific romances. " It's a tone we might associate with Olaf Stapledon's works were they not so philosophically distanced. Still, Aldiss learned more from Stapledon than he did from Doc Smith, so that such memorable and moving

fictions as "Who Can Replace a Man?," "Visiting Amoeba," "A Kind of Artistry," and, especially, the triumphant yet tragically muted "Old Hundredth" bear the full weight of human history and human endeavour. Nor has the elegiac vision ever fully disappeared from his work; it's just as powerfully present, with an even more complex use of SF technology and greater, more dynamic gracefulness of style in "An Appearance of Life" (*Last Orders*). Here a "Prime Esemplastic Seeker," a sensitive with "a high serendipity factor," discovers in a vast galactic museum that humanity may be just "a projection" of an earlier great race, and, like the imprisoned holographic images of two long dead lovers, is "drifting further apart, losing definition. " But Aldiss doesn't end on this despairing note; his Seeker exercises the human will he no longer fully believes in to refuse to communicate his discovery to the rest of humankind, a highly moral act. This story and the somewhat similar (and also purely SF) "The Small Stones of Tu Fu" say rather depressing things about humanity's potential yet they are not depressing because their elegant and graceful style transcends their seemingly obvious "message" and develops through a complex and paradoxical tension their *real* message, the message of human creativity inherent in all true art. The Helliconia books come at this theme in a different manner, via a complex epic vision of an alien planet whose history, of two battling intelligent races, continually offers a mirror to the human story, but one in which the reflections must be read with the greatest subtlety. The presence of human "watchers" who record Helliconia's various stories for an audience on Earth some centuries afterward underlines the structurally complex vision Aldiss is exploring in this series.

As well as an elegiac vision, Aldiss has a special affinity for landscapes. From the beautiful and very English evocations of "Old Hundredth," through the almost hallucinatory visions of *An Age*, the renderings of early 19th-century Switzerland and the almost surreal final descriptions of the eternal ice in *Frankenstein Unbound*, and the deliciously sophisticated versions of city- and country-scapes in *The Malacia Tapestry*, to the grandiose and scientifically grounded descriptions of an utterly alien planet in the Helliconia books, Aldiss uses landscape in a highly coherent manner as metaphor and context rather than mere background.

Because Aldiss hates repeating himself, he continually pushes into new literary territory, yet he remains basically a writer of SF and fantasy (with the exception of the Stubbs series and some non-fiction). Beginning as a superior, though classically restrained, stylist, he moves through intense and brilliant experiments (*Reports on Probability A, Barefoot in the Head*) and self-conscious fictions which explore both the conventions and the earlier classics of the genre (*Frankenstein Unbound* and *The Eighty-Minute Hour*), to emerge in the 1970's as an assured and elegant master of fictional forms.

In the 1970's, Aldiss turned out a glorious social comedy in *The Malacia Tapestry* and gnomic but captivating or frightening little fictions like the Enigmas in *Last Orders*, the "zeepee" stories, and the enigmatic, delicate, and superbly civilized "The Small Stones of Tu Fu. " Having shown with such works that he could write almost anything he chooses, he then took on one of the major forms of SF, the grand, multi-volume future history, only his would be the history of another planet, under observation through the centuries by Earth personnel, with all the complex possibilities of such a multi-faceted narrative strategy. There is still one more Helliconia book to go, but *Helliconia Spring* and *Helliconia Summer* have already demonstrated how successfully he has transcended genre conventions, once again.

If Aldiss now appears to be a writer who could write anything he wishes to, it is by dint of a long and exhaustive apprenticeship to his craft, a concern to "never cease exploring" either his medium or the realms of imagination which SF at its best has claimed as its own. The results, at every stage of his career, are stories of great power and originality, stories which stand the test of critical re-reading better than most. As Brian Aldiss is at the height of his art, it looks as if he will give us many more such stories in the years to come.

—Douglas Barbour

ALLEN, (Charles) Grant (Blairfindie). Also wrote as Cecil Power; Olive Pratt Rayner; Martin Leach Warborough. British. Born in Alwington, near Kingston, Ontario, Canada, 24 February 1848. Educated privately in New Haven, Connecticut; Collège Impériale, Dieppe; King Edward's School, Birmingham; Merton College, Oxford (Senior Classical Postmastership), 1867-70, B.A. (honours) 1871. Married Miss Jerrard in 1873 (second marriage); one son. Professor of Philosophy, Government College, Spanish Town, Jamaica, 1873-76; Tutor in Oxford, 1877; worked on the *Gazetteer of India*, Edinburgh, 1878; staff member, *Daily News*, London, 1879; lived in Surrey from 1880. *Died 28 October 1899.*

SCIENCE-FICTION PUBLICATIONS

Novels

Kalee's Shrine, with May Cotes. Bristol, Arrowsmith, 1886; New York, New Amsterdam, 1897; as *The Indian Mystery*, New Amsterdam, 1902.
The Jaws of Death. London, Simpkin Marshall, 1889; New York, New Amsterdam, 1897.
The Great Taboo. London, Chatto and Windus, 1890; New York, Harper, 1891.
The British Barbarians: A Hill-Top Novel. London, Lane, and New York, Putnam, 1895.

Short Stories

Strange Stories. London, Chatto and Windus, 1884.
The Beckoning Hand and Other Stories. London, Chatto and Windus, 1887.
Ivan Greet's Masterpiece. London, Chatto and Windus, 1893.
The Desire of the Eyes and Other Stories. London, Digby Long, 1895; New York, Fenno, 1896.
A Bride from the Desert (includes "Dr. Greatrex's Experiment" and "The Back-Slider"). New York, Fenno, 1896.
Twelve Tales, with a Headpiece, a Tailpiece, and an Intermezzo, Being Select Stories. London, Richards, 1899.

OTHER PUBLICATIONS

Novels

Philistia (as Cecil Power). London, Chatto and Windus, 3 vols., and New York, Harper, 1 vol., 1884.
Babylon. London, Chatto and Windus, 3 vols., and New York, Appleton, 1 vol., 1885.
In All Shades. London, Chatto and Windus, 3 vols., and Chicago, Rand McNally, 1 vol., 1888.
The Sole Trustee. London, SPCK, 1886.
For Maimie's Sake. London, Chatto and Windus, and New York, Appleton, 1886.
A Terrible Inheritance. London, SPCK, 1887; New York, Crowell, n.d.
This Mortal Coil. London, Chatto and Windus, 3 vols., and New York, Appleton, 1 vol., 1888.
The White Man's Foot. London, Hatchards, 1888.
The Devil's Die. London, Chatto and Windus, 3 vols., and New York, Lovell, 1 vol., 1888.
The Tents of Shem. London, Chatto and Windus, 3 vols., and Chicago, Rand McNally, 1 vol., 1889.
Dr. Palliser's Patient. London, Mullen, 1889.
A Living Apparition. London, SPCK, 1889.
Wednesday the Tenth. Boston, Lothrop, 1890; as *The Cruise of the Albatross; or, When Was Wednesday the Tenth?*, 1898.
Recalled to Life. Bristol, Arrowsmith, and New York, Holt, 1891.
What's Bred in the Bone. London, Tit-Bits, and Boston, Tucker, 1891.
Dumaresq's Daughter. London, Chatto and Windus, 3 vols., and New York, Harper 1 vol., 1891.
The Duchess of Powysland. London, Chatto and Windus, 3 vols., and New York, Munro, 1 vol., 1892.
The Scallywag. London, Chatto and Windus, 3 vols., and New York, Cassell, 1 vol., 1893.
Michael's Crag. London, Leadenhall Press, and Chicago, Rand McNally, 1893.
Blood Royal. London, Chatto and Windus, and New York, Cassell, 1893.
An Army Doctor's Romance. London, Tuck, 1893.
At Market Value. London, Chatto and Windus, 2 vols., and Chicago, Neely, 1 vol., 1894.
The Woman Who Did. London, Lane, and Boston, Roberts, 1895.
Under Sealed Orders. London, Chatto and Windus, 3 vols., 1895; New York, New Amsterdam, 1 vol., 1896.
A Splendid Sin. London, F. V. White, 1896; New York, Buckles, 1899.
The Type-writer Girl (as Olive Pratt Rayner). London, Pearson, 1897; as Grant Allen, New York, Street and Smith, 1900.
Linnet. London, Richards, 1898; New York, New Amsterdam, 1900.
The Incidental Bishop. London, Pearson, and New York, Appleton, 1898.
Rosalba: The Story of Her Development (as Olive Pratt Rayner). London, Pearson, and New York, Putnam, 1899.

Short Stories

The General's Will and Other Stories. London, Butterworth, 1892.
Moorland Idylls. London, Chatto and Windus, 1896.
An African Millionaire. London, Richards, and New York, Arnold, 1897.
Miss Cayley's Adventures. London, Richards, and New York, Putnam, 1899.
Hilda Wade, completed by Arthur Conan Doyle. London, Richards, and New York, Putnam, 1900.
Sir Theodore's Guest and Other Stories. Bristol, Arrowsmith, 1902.
The Reluctant Hangman and Other Stories of Crime, edited by Tom and Enid Schantz. Boulder, Colorado, Aspen Press, 1973.

Other

Physiological Aesthetics. London, King, 1877; New York, Appleton, 1878.

The Colour-Sense: Its Origin and Development: An Essay in Comparative Psychology. London, Trubner, and Boston, Houghton Osgood, 1879.

Anglo-Saxon Britain. London, SPCK, and New York, Young, 1881.

The Evolutionist at Large. London, Chatto and Windus, 1881; New York, Fitzgerald, 1882; revised edition, Chatto and Windus, 1884.

Vignettes from Nature. London, Chatto and Windus, 1881; New York, Fitzgerald, 1882.

The Colours of Flowers, as Illustrated in the British Flora. London and New York, Macmillan, 1882.

Colin Clout's Calendar: The Record of a Summer, April-October. London, Chatto and Windus, 1882; New York, Funk and Wagnalls, 1883.

Flowers and Their Pedigrees. London, Longman, 1883; New York, Appleton, 1884.

Nature Studies, with others. London, Wyman, and New York, Funk and Wagnalls, 1883.

Biographies of Working Men. London, SPCK, 1884.

Charles Darwin. London, Longman, and New York, Appleton, 1885.

Common Sense Science. Boston, Lothrop, 1887.

A Half-Century of Science, with T. H. Huxley. New York, Humboldt, 1888.

Force and Energy: A Theory of Dynamics. London, Longman, 1888; New York, Humboldt, 1889.

Falling in Love, with Other Essays on More Exact Branches of Science. London, Smith Elder, 1889; New York, Appleton, 1890.

Individualism and Socialism. Glasgow, Scottish Land Restoration League, 1890(?).

Science in Arcady. London, Lawrence and Bullen, 1892.

The Tidal Thames. London, Cassell, 1892.

Post-Prandial Philosophy. London, Chatto and Windus, 1894.

In Memoriam George Paul Macdonell. London, Lund, 1895.

The Story of the Plants. London, Newnes, 1895; as *The Plants*, New York, Review of Reviews, 1909.

The Evolution of the Idea of God: An Inquiry into the Origins of Religions. London, Grant Richards, and New York, Holt, 1897.

Tom, Unlimited: A Story for Children (as Martin Leach Warborough). London, Richards, 1897.

Paris. London, Richards, 1897; New York, Wessels, 1900; revised edition, 1906.

Florence. London, Richards, 1897; New York, Wessels, 1900; revised edition, 1906.

Cities of Belgium. London, Richards, 1897; New York, Wessels, 1900; as *Belgium: Its Cities*, Boston, Page, 2 vols., 1903.

Venice. London, Richards, 1898; New York, Wessels, 1900.

Flashlights on Nature. New York, Doubleday, 1898; London, Newnes, 1899.

The European Tour: A Handbook for Americans and Colonists. London, Richards, and New York, Dodd Mead, 1899.

The New Hedonism. New York, Tucker, 1900.

Plain Words on the Woman Question. Chicago, Harman, 1900.

In Nature's Workshop. London, Newnes, and New York, Mansfield, 1901.

County and Town in England, Together with Some Annals of Churnside. London, Richards, and New York, Dutton, 1901.

Evolution in Italian Art, edited by J. W. Cruickshank. London,
Richards, and New York, Wessels, 1908.

The Hand of God and Other Posthumous Essays. London, Watts, 1909.

Editor, *The Miscellaneous and Posthumous Works of H. T. Buckle*, abridged edition. London, Longman, 2 vols., 1885.

Editor, *The Natural History of Selborne*, by Gilbert White. London, Lane, 1900.

Translator, *The Attis of Caius Valerius Catullus*. London, Nutt, 1892.

*   *   *

Besides his "progressive" novels flouting Victorian political and, especially, sexual taboos, such as the famous *The Woman Who Did*, Grant Allen was probably best known to the public through his series of historical guidebooks to Europe. Allen wrote a few SF stories, two of which are collected in *Strange Stores* : "Pausodyne" deals with revival after a century in suspended animation, and "The Child of the Phalanstery" with a future utopian society practicing euthanasia on deformed children. But his only major SF work is the novel *The British Barbarians* in which an enlightened visitor from the 25th-century looks on the culture, religious observances, and erotic proprieties of 1895 England as an anthropologist would on the customs of a primitive tribe. Befriending an unhappy woman, he is for his pains finally shot by her scandalized husband, and fades back to his future. For all its obviousness, the novel is still a very good satire of the peculiar English "propertarianism" and puritanism, and prefigures the anthropological vogue in sophisticated modern SF, mediated through his admirer Wells.

—Darko Suvin

————

ALLEN, Stuart. See **TUBB, E. C.**

————

AMES, Clinton. See **PHILLIPS, Rog.**

————

AMHERST, Wes. See **SHAVER, Richard S.**

————

AMIS, Kingsley (William). Also writes as Robert Markham. British. Born in London, 16 April 1922. Educated at City of London School; St. John's College, Oxford, M. A. Served in the Royal Corps of Signals, 1942-45. Married 1) Hilary Ann Bardwell in 1948 (marriage dissolved, 1965), two sons, including the writer Martin Amis, and one daughter; 2) the writer Elizabeth Jane Howard in 1965 (divorced, 1983). Lecturer in English, University College, Swansea, Wales, 1949-61; Fellow in English, Peterhouse, Cambridge, 1961-63. Visiting Fellow in Creative Writing, Princeton University, New Jersey, 1958-59;

Visiting Professor, Vanderbilt University, Nashville, Tennessee, 1967. Recipient: Maugham Award, 1955; *Yorkshire Post Award*, 1974; John W. Campbell Memorial Award, 1977. Honorary Fellow, St. John's College, 1976. C. B. E. (Commander, Order of the British Empire), 1981. Agent: Jonathan Clowes Ltd., 22 Prince Albert Road, London NW1 7ST, England.

SCIENCE-FICTION PUBLICATIONS

Novels

The Anti-Death League. London, Gollancz, and New York, Harcourt, Brace, 1966.
The Alteration. London, Cape, 1976; New York, Viking Press, 1977.
Russian Hide-and-Seek: A Melodrama. London, Hutchinson, 1980.

OTHER PUBLICATIONS

Novels

Lucky Jim. London, Gollancz, and New York, Doubleday, 1954.
That Uncertain Feeling. London, Gollancz, 1955; New York, Harcourt Brace, 1956.
I Like It Here. London, Gollancz, and New York, Harcourt Brace, 1958.
Take a Girl Like You. London, Gollancz, 1960; New York, Harcourt Brace, 1961.
One Fat Englishman. London, Gollancz, 1963; New York, Harcourt Brace, 1964.
The Egyptologists, with Robert Conquest. London, Cape, 1965; New York, Random House, 1966.
Colonel Sun: A James Bond Adventure (as Robert Markham). London, Cape, and New York, Harper, 1968.
I Want It Now. London, Cape, 1968; New York, Harcourt Brace, 1969.
The Green Man. London, Cape, 1969; New York, Harcourt Brace, 1970.
Girl, 20. London, Cape, 1971; New York, Harcourt Brace, 1972.
The Riverside Villas Murder. London, Cape, and New York, Harcourt Brace, 1973.
Ending Up. London, Cape, and New York, Harcourt Brace, 1974.
Jake's Thing. London, Hutchinson, 1978; New York, Viking Press, 1979.
Stanley and the Women. London, Hutchinson, 1984.

Short Stories

My Enemy's Enemy. London, Gollancz, 1962; New York, Harcourt Brace, 1963.
Penguin Modern Stories 11, with others. London, Penguin, 1972.
Dear Illusion. London, Convent Garden Press, 1972.
The Darkwater Hall Mystery. Edinburgh, Tragara Press, 1978.
Collected Short Stories. London, Hutchinson, 1980.

Plays

Radio Plays: *Something Strange*, 1962; *The Riverside Villas Murder*, from his own novel, 1976.

Television Plays: *A Question about Hell*, 1964; *The Importance of Being Harry*, 1971; *Dr. Watson and the Darkwater Hall Mystery*, 1974; *See What You've Done* (*Softly, Softly* series), 1974; *We Are All Guilty* (*Against the Crowd* series), 1975.

Verse

Bright November. London, Fortune Press, 1947.
A Frame of Mind. Reading, Berkshire, University of Reading School of Art, 1953.
(*Poems*). Oxford, Fantasy Press, 1954.
A Case of Samples: Poems 1946-1956. London, Gollancz, 1956; New York, Harcourt Brace, 1957.
The Evans Country. Oxford, Fantasy Press, 1962.
Penguin Modern Poets 2, with Dom Moraes and Peter Porter. London, Penguin, 1962.
A Look round the Estate: Poems 1957-1967. London, Cape, 1967; New York, Harcourt Brace, 1968.
Wasted, Kipling at Bateman's. London, Poem-of-the-Month Club, 1973.
Collected Poems 1944-1979. London, Hutchinson, 1979; New York, Viking Press, 1980.

Recordings: *Kingsley Amis Reading His Own Poems*, Listen, 1962; *Poems*, with Thomas Blackburn, Jupiter, 1962.

Other

Socialism and the Intellectuals. London, Fabian Society, 1957.
New Maps of Hell: A Survey of Science Fiction. New York, Harcourt Brace, 1960; London, Gollancz, 1961.
"H. G. Wells," in *War of the Worlds, The Time Machine, and Selected Short Stories*, by Wells. New York, Platt and Munk, 1963.
The James Bond Dossier. London, Cape, and New York, New American Library, 1965.
"Science Fiction: A Practical Nightmare," in *Holiday (Indianapolis), February 1965*.
Lucky Jim's Politics. London, Conservative Political Centre, 1968.
What's Become of Jane Austen? and Other Questions. London, Cape, 1970; New York, Harcourt Brace, 1971.
Foreword to "The Game of Rat and Dragon" by Cordwainer Smith, in *The Mirror of Infinity*, edited by Robert Silverberg. New York, Harper, 1970.
On Drink. London, Cape, 1972; New York, Harcourt Brace, 1973.
Rudyard Kipling and His World. London, Thames and Hudson, 1975; New York, Scribner, 1976.
An Arts Policy? London, Centre for Policy Studies, 1979.
Every Day Drinking. London, Hutchinson, 1983.
How's Your Glass? London, Weidenfeld and Nicholson, 1984.

Editor, with James Michie, *Oxford Poetry 1949*. Oxford, Blackwell, 1949.
Editor, with Robert Conquest, *Spectrum [1-5]: A Science Fiction Anthology*. London, Gollancz, 5 vols., 1961-65; New York, Harcourt Brace, 5 vols., 1962-67.
Editor, *Selected Short Stories of G. K. Chesterton*. London, Faber, 1972.
Editor, *Tennyson*. London, Penguin, 1973.
Editor, *Harold's Years: Impressions from the New Statesman and The Spectator*. London, Quartet, 1977.
Editor, *The New Oxford Book of Light Verse*. London and New York, Oxford University Press, 1978.
Editor, *The Faber Popular Reciter*. London, Faber, 1978.

Editor, *The Golden Age of Science Fiction*. London, Hutchinson, 1981.

*

Bibliography: *Kingsley Amis: A Checklist* by Jack Benoit Gohn, Kent, Ohio, Kent State University Press, 1976; *Kingsley Amis: A Reference Guide* by Dale Salwak, Boston, Hall, and London, Prior, 1978.

Manuscript Collection (verse): State University of New York, Buffalo.

Critical Study: *Kingsley Amis* by Philip Gardner, Boston, Twayne, 1981.

Kingsley Amis comments:
I have been reading science fiction for over 50 years. Writing it too: I can remember writing a story about a revolution in the year 2032, which must mean I wrote it in 1932 when I was 10. I say this to show that SF has always been an inseparable part of my reading and writing life. So when later I got an idea for a story or novel whose events could not have taken place in our world, I found it altogether natural to create a new world for it.
Take *The Alteration*. I heard on an archive record made in 1909 a castrato then aged about 40 (one Alessandro Moreschi) singing the Bach/Gounod "Ave Maria," a good musical performance and an awful, dismal noise I could not get out of my head. It dawned on me that here was a great theme: a boy chosen for castration to preserve his wonderful voice would lose the chance of love, family, friends to a large extent, and a normal place in society. But he might gain fame, money, artistic success and the approval of God. (He might also lose the first batch without attaining the second.) None of it possible in our world. I considered the coward's (or John Fowles's) way out: a remote island run by an eccentric millionaire. No, too cramped and private. It would have to be England in AD 1976, but as part of an alternate world where the Reformation had never happened and Rome was all-powerful—or nearly. On with the creation. . . .

*   *   *

A typical Kingsley Amis work combines satire and humor with serious themes to mock sacred cows, question *a priori* premises, and speculate about the nature of man and God. It usually involves some erudite discussion of music, particularly classical, some focus on love as elevating and redemptive, and some sense of conspiracy, whether of church or state or the universe itself. It is witty and provocative.
Reflecting an enthusiasm for science fiction that Amis traces to his early youth, *New Maps of Hell* began as a series of lectures delivered at Princeton for the 1958-59 Christian Gauss Seminar in Criticism, and ended up the most influential work of science fiction criticism up to that time. It is clearly dated, and more personal than scholarly, but valuable—a slightly patronizing attempt to define and defend science fiction at a time when the genre was considered suspect by literary scholars. It argues that a definition is difficult, but that it somehow involves science and technology or pseudo-science or pseudo-technology, whether human or alien, though methods, goals and emphases may vary greatly. Thus *The Tempest* and *Gulliver's Travels* are certainly precursors, according to Amis, though H. G. Wells and Jules Vernes begin the genre as we

know it. *New Maps* considers the literary quality of science fiction, pointing out that it ranges from the lowest pulp form, filled with scientific absurdities, violence, gratuitous sex, and innumerable monsters, to the highest literary levels—involving exploration of human nature, politics, and economics, satire of the present, and theorizing about the future. Ultimately Amis finds it allegorizing our own fears and insecurities, warning of future possibilities, and deflating *homo sapiens*. Amis's interest in the genre thereafter led to his joining Robert Conquest to edit the *Spectrum* series, four volumes of science-fiction short stories carefully selected for their interest and craftmanship, volumes which helped establish the popularity and respectability of science fiction.
Having examined the efforts of others, it was a short step to creating his own. Amis's short stories and novels are intriguing and clever. His James Bond adventure novel, *Colonel Sun*, contains science fiction elements, as does his ghost story, *The Green Man* (time stasis and a heavenly encounter). "Mason's Life" focuses on the nightmare realization that one's seemingly tangible reality is only someone else's dream. In "Something Strange" space program volunteers turn out to be guinea pigs for government psychologists experimenting with psychological conditioning and isolation stress.
The Anti-Death League uses a spy/romance/sci-fi format as an excuse to explore philosophical questions about the active cruelty of God, the aimless horror and finality of death, and love as an antidote to combat insanity in an absurd universe. Amis, who feels at home handling a military ambience with its rigid orders and regulations and its male-male interaction, centers his novel on a British training camp, preparing soldiers for "Operation Apollo," germ warfare with an intensified strain of hydrophobia; though ultimately the operation proves a giant bluff, the ultimate deterrent, intended to be spied on and thereby to so horrify the Chinese that they will cancel invasion plans, it provides the backdrop for exploring life and death questions. As various zany characters rush about trying to expose security leaks, prove pet theories, or work out personal conflicts, the main thrust of the novel is an enumeration of signs of the motiveless malignity of God—numerous, sudden, random deaths or near deaths from accident or disease, reinforced by "pro-death" military plans, by signs of madness or incipient madness, and by futile attempts to combat both. The formation of an "Anti-Death League" provides the title of the book and Amis's model for man's ineffectual but necessary protest against whatever powers there be. The comic and satiric prevail, with characters including an atheist chaplain, a naive secret agent, a homosexual, alcoholic military officer, a dedicatedly promiscuous widow, an insane psychiatrist, and a conscience ridden romantic named Churchill.
The Alteration presents an alternative world, a world that might have been as the result of Henry VIII's elder brother Arthur surviving as monarch and siring a line of Catholic rulers. It postulates a Catholic England and Europe, forever at odds with Islam, and on a shaky diplomatic basis with "New England," a small nation inhabited by Indians and the descendants of "Schismatics" and convicts (including one William Shakespeare). The Martin Luther of this Catholic world was a pope, Himmler a powerful representative of Papal might, Jean-Paul Sartre a Jesuit, James Bond Father Bond, and our world a shocking, slightly absurb science-fiction novel read clandestinely by rebellious adolescents. Amis's world is a chilling vision of ecclesiastical totalitarianism with the Church tightly controlling people's lives, making decisions about whether or not ten-year-old boys will be castrated so they can sing for the greater glory of God, sending out Nazi-like secret police to mutilate and murder those who defy Church author-

ity, developing a disease that, spread through the drinking water, infects and alters males, and ultimately choosing a holy war against Moslems as a means of population control. As such, it is a grim commentary on hypocrisy, intolerance, gullibility, and mindless pieties—evil for the best of reasons. On another level it traces the story of Hubert Anvil, a brilliant child soprano chosen for castration, to explore adolescent yearnings, struggles against authority, and arrested development. Ultimately it is a paean to love, the greatest sin of all in this nightmare world of religious fanaticism.

Russian Hide-and-Seek partakes of the patterns and concerns established in these earlier novels. Drawing on the conventions of 19th-century Russian fiction and cloak-and-dagger adventures, it depicts a Russianized England, a future fifty years hence when the Soviet Union rules England and perpetrates upon the English all the horrors that Amis envisions as inherent in Russian culture: brutality, violence, lack of family feeling, exploitation, and paranoia coupled with lachrymose introspection. The plot turns on an attempted revolution, made futile by the naivety of the revolutionaries and the strength of the Central Government. The English prove plucky but muddled; the Russians bored, callous, self-indulgent. Violence and death again dominate this vision of the future.

Thus, Amis's science fiction serves as a medium for satiric debunking and sociological investigation, particularly of the military mentality, pat solutions, and totalitarian inflexibility. His works are witty, irreverent, and infectious. His handling of different levels of diction, linguistic clues to class and training, and his verbal inventiveness are always impressive, and his attack of conventional values and attitudes fun.

—Gina Macdonald

ANDERSON, Chester. Also writes as John Valentine. American. Born in Stoneham, Massachusetts, 11 August 1932. Educated at the University of Miami, Coral Gables, 1952-56. Has worked as typesetter, janitor, proof-reader, motel manager; Founding Editor, The Communication Company, San Francisco, 1967; Editor, *Crawdaddy,* 1968-69. Address: P. O. Box 80, Rio Nido, California 95471, U. S. A.

SCIENCE-FICTION PUBLICATIONS

Novels

Ten Years to Doomsday, with Michael Kurland. New York, Pyramid, 1964.
The Butterfly Kid. New York, Pyramid, 1967.

OTHER PUBLICATIONS

Novels

The Pink Palace. New York, Fawcett, 1963.
Fox and Hare. Glen Ellen, California, Entwhistle, 1980.

Verse

Colloquy. San Francisco, Bread and Wine Press, 1960.
A Liturgy for Dragons. New York, Young, 1961.

Other

Puppies (as John Valentine). Glen Ellen, California, Entwistle, 1979.

*

Chester Anderson comments:

I am basically a poet. I write prose because that's what people read. I write science fiction because that's what *I* read. The only reason I write fiction at all is that my memory is so poor. Everything but *Ten Years to Doomsday* is autobiography plus exaggerations. Only the names are changed, because I can't remember them. I don't consider my writing science fiction except in the sense that all 20th-century writing must be either science fiction or dreck—even newspapers, teenage love letters, papal encyclicals. The future is now.

* * *

The Butterfly Kid, Chester Anderson's first solo performance as a science-fiction author, was nominated for the Hugo award in 1968, a significant honor for someone who had collaborated on his first science-fiction novel, *Ten Years to Doomsday,* only four years before. *Ten Years to Doomsday,* written with Michael Kurland, was a parody of some of Poul Anderson's novels. A small group of undercover agents for an interstellar empire accelerate the technological progress of a backwater planet to defeat an invasion by an unknown enemy. The denouement is rather perfunctory, and it is obvious that the authors enjoyed the creation of intricate plot twists and gave little thought to the resolution of the story. A certain lightness of tone in both the telling of the tale and the nature of the incidents related is apparent, and the same tone was used with more emphasis in *The Butterfly Kid.*

The Butterfly Kid is Anderson's celebration of the hippie life in Greenwich Village in the mid-1960s. Again the plot hinges on the defeat of an enemy of humanity, in this case a species of six-foot blue lobsters, who are intent on annexing the Earth into their empire. They intend to add a psychedelic drug to the water supply of New York City. The drug has the effect of materializing the takers' fantasies. Chester Anderson, the hero and narrator of the novel, and his friends foil the attempted conquest of Earth in a rather hurried conclusion. Anderson is particularly adept at depicting the social scene of Greenwich Village and his various friends and acquaintances who are the defenders of Earth.

—Harvey J. Satty

ANDERSON, Poul (William). American. Born in Bristol, Pennsylvania, 25 November 1926. Educated at the University of Minnesota, Minneapolis, B. A. 1948. Married Karen Kruse in 1953; one daughter. Free-lance writer. President, Science Fiction Writers of America, 1972-73. Recipient: Hugo Award, 1961, 1964, 1969, 1972, 1973, 1979, 1982; Nebula Award, 1971, 1972, 1982; Tolkien Memorial Award; Gandolf Award, 1978, Guest of Honor, World Science-Fiction Convention, 1959. Agent: Scott Meredith Literary Agency, 845 Third Avenue, New York, New York, 10022. Address: 3 Las Palomas, Orinda, California 94563, U. S. A.

SCIENCE-FICTION PUBLICATIONS

Novels (series: Dominic Flandry; Trader Van Rijn)

Vault of the Ages (for children). Philadelphia, Winston, 1952.
The Broken Sword. New York, Abelard Schuman, 1954; revised edition, New York, Ballantine, 1971; Tisbury, Wiltshire, Compton Russell, 1974.
Brain Wave. New York, Ballantine, 1954; London, Heinemann, 1955.
No World of Their Own. New York, Ace, 1955; as *The Long Way Home,* London, Panther, 1975; New York, Ace, 1978.
Star Ways. New York, Avalon, 1956; as *The Peregrine,* New York, Ace, 1978.
Planet of No Return New York, Ace, 1957; London, Dobson, 1966; as *Question and Answer,* Ace, 1978.
The Snows of Ganymede. New York, Ace, 1958.
War of the Wing-Men (Van Rijn). New York, Ace, 1958; London, Sphere, 1976; as *The Man Who Counts,* Ace, 1978.
Virgin Planet. New York, Avalon, 1959; London, Mayflower, 1966.
The War of Two Worlds. New York, Ace, 1959; London, Dobson, 1970.
We Claim These Stars (Flandry). New York, Ace, 1959; London, Dobson, 1976.
The Enemy Stars. Philadelphia, Lippincott, 1959.
The High Crusade. New York, Doubleday, 1960; London, Severn House, 1982.
Earthman, Go Home! (Flandry). New York, Ace, 1960.
Twilight World. New York, Torquil, 1961; London, Gollancz, 1962.
Mayday Orbit (Flandry). New York, Ace, 1961.
Orbit Unlimited. New York, Pyramid, 1961; London, Sidgwick and Jackson, 1974.
Three Hearts and Three Lions. New York, Doubleday, 1961.
After Doomsday. New York, Ballantine, 1962; London, Gollancz, 1963.
The Makeshift Rocket. New York, Ace, 1962; London, Dobson, 1969.
Let the Spacemen Beware! New York, Ace, 1963; London, Dobson, 1969; as *The Night Face,* Ace, 1978.
Shield. New York, Berkley, 1963; London, Dobson, 1965.
Three Worlds to Conquer. New York, Pyramid, 1964; London, Mayflower, 1966.
Agent of the Terran Empire. Philadelphia, Chilton, 1965.
The Corridors of Time. New York, Doubleday, 1965; London, Gollancz, 1966.
Flandry of Terra (omnibus). Philadelphia, Chilton, 1965.
The Star Fox. New York, Doubleday, 1965; London, Gollancz, 1966.
Ensign Flandry. Philadelphia, Chilton, 1966; London, Coronet, 1976.
The Fox, The Dog, and the Griffin: A Folk Tale Adapted from the Danish of C. Molbech (for children). New York Doubleday, 1966.
World Without Stars. New York, Ace, 1966; London, Dobson, 1975.
The Rebel Worlds. New York, New American Library, 1969; London, Coronet, 1972; as *Commander Flandry,* London, Severn House, 1978.
Satan's World. New York, Doubleday, 1969; London, Gollancz, 1970.
A Circus of Hells (Flandry). New York, New American Library, 1970; London, Sphere, 1978.
Tau Zero. New York, Doubleday, 1970; London, Gollancz, 1971.

The Byworlder. New York, New American Library, 1971; London, Gollancz, 1972.
The Dancer from Atlantis. New York, New American Library, 1971; London, Sphere, 1977.
Operation Chaos. New York, Doubleday, 1971.
There Will Be Time. New York, Doubleday, 1972; London, Sphere, 1979.
Hrolf Kraki's Saga. New York, Ballantine, 1973.
The People of the Wind. New York, New American Library, 1973; London, Sphere, 1977.
The Day of Their Return. New York, Doubleday, 1974; London, Corgi, 1978.
Inheritors of Earth, with Gordon Eklund. Radnor, Pennsylvania, Chilton, 1974.
Fire Time. New York, Doubleday, 1974; London, Panther, 1977.
A Midsummer Tempest. New York, Doubleday, 1974; London, Futura, 1975.
A Knight of Ghosts and Shadows. New York, Doubleday, 1974; London, Sphere, 1978; as *Knight Flandry,* London, Severn House, 1980.
Star Prince Charlie (for children), with Gordon R. Dickson. New York, Putnam, 1975.
The Winter of the World. New York, Doubleday, 1975.
Mirkheim. New York, Berkley, 1977; London, Sphere, 1978.
The Avatar. New York, Berkley, 1978; London, Sidgwick and Jackson, 1980.
Two Worlds (omnibus). New York, Ace, 1978.
The Merman's Children. New York, Berkley, 1979; London, Sidgwick and Jackson, 1981.
A Stone in Heaven. New York, Ace, 1979.
The Demon of Scattery, with Mildred Downey Broxon. New York, Ace, 1979.
The Devil's Game. New York, Pocket Books, 1980.
Time Patrolman. New York, Tor, 1983.
Agent of Vega. New York, Ace, 1983.
Orion Shall Rise. New York, Pocket Books, 1984.
Phu Nham, with Gordon R. Dickson. New York, Tor, 1984.
The Game of Empire (Flandry). New York, Baen, 1985.

Short Stories

Earthman's Burden, with Gordon R. Dickson. New York, Gnome Press, 1957.
Guardians of Time. New York, Ballantine, 1960; London, Gollancz, 1961; augmented edition, New York, Pinnacle, 1981.
Strangers from Earth. New York, Ballentine, 1961; London, Mayflower, 1964.
Un-Man and Other Novellas. New York, Ace, 1962; London, Dobson, 1972.
Time and Stars. New York, Doubleday, and London, Gollancz, 1964.
Trader to the Stars. New York. Doubleday, 1964; London, Gollancz, 1965.
Agent of the Terran Empire (Flandry). Philadelphia, Chilton, 1965; London, Coronet, 1977.
The Trouble Twisters (Van Rijn). New York, Doubleday, 1966; London, Gollancz, 1967.
The Horn of Time. New York, New American Library, 1968; London, Corgi, 1981.
Beyond the Beyond. New York, New American Library, 1969; London, Gollancz, 1970.
Seven Conquests. New York, Macmillan, and London, Collier Macmillan, 1969; as *Conquests,* London, Granada, 1981.
Tales of the Flying Mountains. New York, Macmillan, 1970.

The Queen of Air and Darkness. New York, New American Library, 1973.
The Many Worlds of Poul Anderson. Radnor, Pennsylvania, Chilton, 1974; as *The Book of Poul Anderson,* New York, DAW, 1975.
Homeward and Beyond. New York, Doubleday, 1975.
Homebrew. Cambridge, Massachusetts, NEFSA Press, 1976.
The Best of Poul Anderson. New York, Pocket Books, 1976.
The Earth Book of Stormgate. New York, Berkley, 1978; London, New English Library, 3 vols., 1981.
The Night Face and Other Stories. Boston, Gregg Press, 1979.
The Psychotechnic League. New York, Pinnacle, 1981.
The Dark Between the Stars. New York, Berkley, 1981.
Fantasy. New York, Pinnacle, 1981.
Explorations. New York, Pinnacle, 1981.
Winners. New York, Pinnacle, 1981.
Mauri and Kith. New York, Tor, 1982.
The Gods Laughed. New York, Pinnacle, 1982.
Starship. New York, Tor, 1982.
Cold Victory. New York, Pinnacle, 1982.
New America. New York, Tor, 1982.
Hoka!, with Gordon R. Dickson. New York, Simon and Schuster, 1983.
The Long Night. New York, Tor, 1983.
Conflict New York, Tor, 1983.
Past Times. New York, Tor, 1984.

OTHER PUBLICATIONS

Novels

Perish by the Sword. New York, Macmillan, 1959.
Murder in Black Letter. New York, Macmillan, 1960.
The Golden Slave. New York, Avon, 1960.
Rogue Sword. New York, Avon, 1960.
Murder Bound. New York, Macmillan, 1962.
Conan the Rebel. New York, Bantam, 1980; London, Hale, 1984.
The Last Viking:
   1. *The Golden Horn*. New York, Zebra, 1980.
   2. *The Road of the Sea Horse*. New York, Zebra, 1980.
   3. *Sign of the Raven*. New York, Zebra, 1981.

Other

Is There Life on Other Worlds? New York, Crowell Collier, and London, Collier Macmillan, 1963.
Thermonuclear Warfare. Derby, Connecticut, Monarch, 1963.
"How to Build a Planet," in *SWFA Bulletin* (Sea Cliff, New York), November 1966.
The Infinite Voyage: Man's Future in Space. New York, Macmillan, and London, Collier Macmillan, 1969.
"The Creation of Imaginary Worlds," in *Science Fiction, Today and Tomorrow,* edited by Reginald Bretnor. New York, Harper, 1974.
The Unicorn Trade (miscellany), with Karen Anderson. New York, Tor, 1984.

Editor, *West by One and by One*. Privately printed, 1965.
Editor, *Nebula Award Stories 4*. New York, Doubleday, 1969.

Translator, *The Method of Holding the Three Ones*. Atlantic Highlands, New Jersey, Humanities Press, 1980.

*

Bibliography: *A Checklist of Poul Anderson* by Roger G. Peyton, privately printed, 1965.

Manuscript Collection: University of Southern Mississippi, Hattiesburg.

Critical Study: *Against Time's Arrow: The High Crusade of Poul Anderson* by Sandra Miesel, San Bernardino, California, Borgo Press, 1978.

*   *   *

James Blish has called Poul Anderson "the enduring explosion" for the quality, quantity, and sheer breadth of Anderson's achievements are unique in science fiction. Seven Hugos and three Nebulas proclaim him the field's premier novelettist but 50 novels and 200 shorter works testify to his mastery of all story forms. Over the course of four decades, he has explored an amazingly wide range of literary types from madcap comedy to grimmest tragedy in such distinctive fashion that the term "poulanderson" was once suggested as a generic name.

Consider the following colors in Anderson's fictional spectrum: broad farce (the Hoka series written with Gordon R. Dickson and *The Makeshift Rocket*); adventure comedy (*Virgin Planet*); action adventure yarn ("The Longest Voyage," 1960; the Van Rijn series; and the Flandry series); socio-political drama (the Psychotechnic Institute series and "No Truce with Kings," 1963); hard science fiction ("Epilogue," 1962); romantic fantasy (*Three Hearts and Three Lions*); heroic fantasy (*The Broken Sword*, and *Hrolf Kraki's Saga*); pastiche (*Conan the Rebel*); horror (*The Devil's Game*); historicals (the Last Viking trilogy); and mysteries (*Perish by the Sword*). Moreover, Anderson also writes songs, poems, parodies, essays, and children's books and is a skillful translator of Scandinavian prose and poetry. (For examples of his miscellania, see *The Unicorn Trade*, written with his wife Karen).

Science holds first place among Anderson's raw materials. His formal training in physics imparts a special rigor to his handling of any science. (He has written some excellent articles on sf applications of scientific fact.) His research is thorough, his extrapolations imaginative. He will interweave hard and soft sciences as in *Orion Shall Rise* but the most direct outlet for his scientific knowledge is the problem-solving story. Here, characters must either discover a phenomenon ("The Sharing of Flesh," 1968, and "Hunter's Moon," 1978) or react to one that is already recognized (*Fire Time* and "The Bitter Bread," 1975). Setting objective physical problems in parallel with subjective personal ones and linking the outcomes is Anderson's favorite literary device. He builds these stories so well, they can outlive their scientific premises. The Jupiter model in "Call Me Joe" (1957) has passed away; the appeal of its tenacious hero endures.

Furthermore, Anderson makes scientific problem-solving a vehicle for philosophical enquiry. For example, four marooned spacemen conduct an intense, self-conscious debate on the meaning of life in *The Enemy Stars*. *Tau Zero*, which Blish has called "the ultimate hard science fiction novel," shows the crew of a crippled spaceship outmaneuvering fate on a slower-than-light odyssey beyond the end of time. Scientific phenomena likewise stimulate theological speculation in "Kyrie" (1968) and generate moral crisis in "Sister Planet" (1959). In Anderson's hands, the laws of nature assume poetic, symbolic, and even metaphysical significance.

A second source of Anderson's inspiration is history. The

author's broad, self-acquired education in this subject serves him well in preparing futures with either general or specific historical prototypes. For example, "The Sky People" (1959) replays the age-old feud between nomads and farmers while *The People of the Wind* is based on the Franco-Prussian War. Anderson also re-creates the past vividly (e. g., first-century Denmark in "The Peat Bog," 1975) and has produced some superb time-travel stories ("The Man Who Came Early," 1956; *The Guardians of Time; There Will be Time*). Furthermore, his interest in the historical process itself has led him to invent one of the longest-running and most elaborate future histories in sf. Now in its fourth decade, his Technic Civilization series embraces more than forty separate items including twelve novels that cover five millennia of galactic history. (See Sandra Miesel's chronology in *The Long Night,* 1983, and her afterword to the Ace edition of *Agent of the Terran Empire,* 1980.)

Third, Anderson draws upon myth, principally Nordic and Celtic. He has both remodeled ("The Sorrows of Oclim the Goth," 1983, from *Volsunga Saga*) and adapted (*Hrolf Kraki's Saga* from *Hrólfs Saga Kraka*) Norse materials with all their Viking doom and pride intact. His "Goat Song" is the definitive sf treatment of the Orpheus myth, a subject which earlier had inspired his sf novel *World Without Stars.*

Yet Gandalf award winner Anderson is not content simply to mine or rationalize mythology. He investigates the nature of myth-making and analyzes its effects—tragic in *The Night Face* and "The Saturn Game" (1981), mixed in "The Queen of Air and Darkness," (1971), and positive in *A Midsummer Tempest.* (See Miesel on the first in the 1978 Ace edition and Patrick L. McGuire on the last in *The Many Worlds of Poul Anderson*). Whether resisted (*Three Hearts and Three Lions*) or celebrated (*The Merman's Children*) the allure of Faery is a continuing preoccupation for this writer. (See Miesel's afterword to *Fantasy*).

Anderson weaves science, history, myth, and countless other categories of learning together to fashion exotic alien habitats teeming with fascinating inhabitants. (His Technic Civilization series is a showcase for both.) Anderson is perhaps sf's finest world-builder, with inventions lovelier than Larry Niven's and more numerous than Hal Clement's. The lushness of Anderson's creations fits his sensuous style. He has said that he tries to appeal to at least three senses in each scene. His trademark use of poetic *leitmotifs* intensifies emotions still further—he strives for the colorfulness of his idol Kipling. These efforts produce a richer, larger-than-life quality in his work: no real woods could be quite as enchanted as his fictional ones.

Anderson is a throughgoing romantic. His enthrallment with the beauty and terror of nature borders on pantheism. His complementary idealization of women is admitted gynolatry. The resonances between woman and universe work exquisitely well in *World Without Stars* because the Cosmic Goddess is kept offstage. Unfortunately, without this restraint, *The Winter of the World* and *The Avatar* sink to the level of self-parody. Anderson exalts experience over intellection, love over knowledge. He rejects, even fears, absolutes. For him, savoring wonder is the purpose of life. The purest happiness is domestic. He emphasizes the joys of marriage and parenthood to an unusual degree (*Operation Chaos*). Since children are the only certain pledge of immortality, building a better world for one's descendants is the best motive for achievement.

The interaction between rational creatures and their environment is a matter of challenge and response. Anderson's heroes are always fallible beings who strive to meet life's challenge well. They are free, responsible persons sensitive to the needs of others. (Although sympathetic to libertarianism,

Anderson is no rugged individualist in the Heinlein mold.) As Blish observes they are willing to pay the price of doing "the right thing for the wrong reason. "

Yet however bravely heroes struggle, "nothing lasts forever." As Miesel demonstrates in *Against Time's Arrow: The High Crusade of Poul Anderson,* the supreme enemy is entropy. How then are mortals to face certain doom? Anderson is not a Pelagian optimist like Gordon R. Dickson. He doubts that evolutionary progress will noticeably improve man's lot. Courage is the only fitting response. Unyielding endurance is a grim imperative in the language of the Northern heroic tradition: "No man can escape his weird, but none other can take from him the heart wherewith he meets it. " The author states it more gently in his own voice: "Life can be cruel, and it is ultimately tragic, but mostly it is wonderful, or would be if we'd allow it to be. " Anderson is his own best example of that process.

—Sandra Miesel

ANTHONY, Piers (Piers Anthony Dillingham Jacob). American. Born in Oxford, England, 6 August 1934; became United States citizen, 1958. Educated at Goddard College, Plainfield, Vermont, B. A. 1956; University of South Florida, Tampa, teaching certificate 1964. Served in the United States Army, 1957-59. Married Carol Marble in 1956; one daughter. Technical writer, Electronic Communications Inc., St. Petersburg, Florida, 1959-62; English teacher, Admiral Farragut Academy, St. Petersburg, 1965-66. Since 1966, free-lance writer. Recipient: Pyramid *Fantasy and Science Fiction* award, 1967; August Derleth Award, 1977. Agent: Carnell Literary Agency, Rowneybury Bungalow, near Old Harlow, Essex CM20 2EX, England; or, Kirby McCauley Ltd., 425 Park Avenue South, New York, New York 10016, U. S. A.

SCIENCE-FICTION PUBLICATIONS

Novels (series: Apprentice Adept; Aton; Battle Circle; Cal, Veg, and Aquilon; Cluster; Incarnations of Immortality; Space Tyrant; Tarot; Xanth)

Chthon (Aton). New York, Ballatine, 1967; London, Macdonald, 1970.
Omnivore (Cal, Veg, and Aquilon). New York, Ballantine, 1968; London, Faber, 1969.
The Ring, with Robert E. Margroff. New York, Ace, 1968; London, Macdonald, 1969.
Battle Circle. New York, Avon, 1978.
  Sos the Rope. New York, Pyramid, 1968; London, Faber, 1970.
  Var the Stick. London, Faber 1972; New York, Bantam, 1973.
  Neq the Sword. London, Corgi, 1975.
Macroscope. New York, Avon, 1969; London, Sphere, 1972.
The E. S. P. Worm, with Robert E. Margroff. New York, Paperback Library, 1970.
Orn (Cal, Veg, and Aquilon). New York, Avon, 1971; London, Corgi, 1977.
Prostho Plus. London, Gollancz, 1971; New York, Bantam, 1973.
Race Against Time (for children). New York, Hawthorn, 1973.

Rings of Ice. New York, Avon, 1974; London, Millington, 1975.

Triple Détente. New York, DAW, 1974; London, Sphere, 1975.

Phthor (Aton). New York, Berkley, 1975; London, Panther, 1978.

But What of Earth?, with Robert Coulson. Toronto, Laser, 1976.

Ox (Cal, Veg, and Aquilon). New York, Avon, 1976; London, Corgi, 1977.

Steppe. London, Millington, 1976; New York, Tor, 1985.

Cluster. New York, Avon, 1977; London, Millington, 1978; as *Vicinity Cluster*, London, Panther, 1979.

A Spell for Chameleon (Xanth). New York, Ballantine, 1977; London, Macdonald, 1984.

Chaining the Lady (Cluster). New York, Avon, and London, Millington, 1978.

Kirlian Quest (Cluster). New York, Avon, and London, Millington, 1978.

The Pretender, with Frances Hall. San Bernardino, California, Borgo Press, 1979.

The Source of Magic (omnibus; Xanth). New York, Ballantine, 1979; London, Macdonald, 1984.

Castle Roogna (Xanth). New York, Ballantine, 1979; London, Macdonald, 1984.

God of Tarot. New York, Jove, 1979.

Vision of Tarot. New York, Berkley, 1980.

Thousandstar (Cluster). New York, Avon, 1980.

Faith of Tarot. New York, Berkley, 1980.

Split Infinity (Apprentice Adept). New York, Ballantine, 1980; London, Granada, 1983.

Blue Adept (Apprentice Adept). New York, Ballantine, 1981; London, Granada, 1983.

Mute. New York, Avon, 1981.

Centaur Aisle (Xanth). New York, Ballantine, 1982; London, Macdonald, 1984.

Ogre, Ogre (Xanth). New York, Ballantine, 1982.

Juxtaposition (Apprentice Adept). New York, Ballantine, 1982.

Viscous Circle (Cluster). New York, Avon, 1982.

Night Mare (Xanth). New York, Ballantine, 1983.

Refugee (Space Tyrant). New York, Avon, 1983.

Dragon on a Pedestal (Xanth). New York, Ballantine, 1983; London, Futura, 1984.

Mercenary (Space Tyrant). New York, Avon, 1984.

On a Pale Horse (Immortality). New York, Ballantine, 1984.

Bearing an Hourglass (Immortality). New York, Ballantine, 1984.

Crewel Lye: A Caustic Yarn (Xanth). New York, Ballantine, 1985.

Politician (Space Tyrant). New York, Avon, 1985.

With a Tangled Skein (Immortality). New York, Ballantine, 1985.

Short Stories

Anthonology. New York, Tor, 1985.

OTHER PUBLICATIONS

Novels with Roberto Fuentes

Kiai! New York, Berkley, 1974.
Mistress of Death. New York, Berkley, 1974.
Bamboo Bloodbath. New York, Berkley, 1975.
Ninja's Revenge. New York, Berkley, 1975.

Amazon Slaughter. New York, Berkley, 1976.
Hasan. San Bernardino, California, Borgo Press, 1977.

*

Manuscript Collection: University of Syracuse, New York.

Critical Study: *Piers Anthony* by Michael R. Collings, Mercer Island, Washington, Starmont House, 1983.

*   *   *

As Piers Anthony said in an interview in *Science Fiction Review*, writing science fiction was an answer to the depression resulting from frequent moves, the death of a cousin, and the memory of adolescent frailty. The frailty of Cal in *Omnivore, Orn,* and *Ox* and the vegetarianism of Veg thus have biographical roots, as does the interest in the defensive strategy of judo in the Jason Striker martial arts novels done with Roberto Fuentes and the image of Alp the conqueror in *Steppe.* But the most persistent value advocated in Anthony's epic and picaresque novels and short stories is his concern for the environment, the fear that "we cannot maintain our present trends without destroying the world as we know it. "

In *Chthon,* though the main action is the escape from the terrible garnet mines on Chthon, part of the horror is due to ecological problems. This ecological struggle is further expressed in *Phthor,* where Chthon, a planet-sized mineral sentience, opposes all of sentient life on ecological principles, and Phthor, or Arlo, is a rejected spirit integrating "the powers of Life and Death. " Even *Prostho Plus,* though a light-hearted spoof of bug-eyed monster depictions who happen to be Dr. Dillingham's alien dental patients, nevertheless seriously deals with the sanctity of ecological chains. While the surface action of *Mute* is a galactic power struggle similar to that of *Phthor,* the issue here is mutation. Human societies on many planets depend on the power of psi-mutes who develop from the mutation induced by space travel through radiation belts; however, the physical mutants and psychological mutants are exploited, and seek an end to the pain and leper-like exclusion of mutants by normals. Not merely a human struggle, this quest for equity includes animals like Hermine the weasel, fleas, rats, chickens, and bees. *The Ring* also deals with ecology, as Jeff Font seeks his father's lost fortune in an earthly society whose criminal behavior is controlled by Skinnerian electronic rings. The respect that Jeff begins to feel for the ring is Anthony's response to a need for control beyond a rampant American individualism sometimes indistinguishable from selfishness.

Macroscope continues to explore restraints on liberty in order to promote the greater good. While the most capable brains using the macroscope are destroyed, the destructive alien transmission is particularly lethal for power brokers such as Senator Borland. Even the entry testing which occurs as Afra, Ivo, Harold, and Beatryx enter the alien space craft determines the fitness of the individual for knowledge, the ability to bear knowledge responsibly. Not only does the novel deal with environmentalism on earth and the effects of disastrous population growth; it also shows the necessity for a mental environmentalism in the group's interaction. Ivo must integrate his other personality. Schön and Afra must balance competence by compassion. The flight from UN power and the quest for the Traveller which make up the novel's double action enable Anthony to explore the physical and internal ecology.

Race Against Time appears to be a rebellion against the culture of the Standard Race on earth but winds up being an acceptance of that race's ecological concern. The three pairs of genetically purebred adolescent couples, on seeing the earth's former devastation, begin to understand the genetic wisdom of racial preservation and peace. *Rings of Ice* shows a new destruction of the earth by military forces which hope to make energy use of ice rings from icy nebula. The threat of tremendous flooding goes unrecognized, as the story shows six people attempting to survive the apocalyptic destruction. Again outer imbalance and psychological imbalance are both dealt with in Anthony's novel: Thatch becomes aggressive; Gus masters his fear of water; Zena overcomes her fear of men. *Triple Détente* deals with environmental issues and war. Kazos and men avoid battle by acting as conquerors of one another's planet, reducing each planet's overpopulation. Similar strategies are used to avoid battle with the Ukes, although their special racial instinct causes both problem and solution.

The Battle Circle trilogy, composed of *Sos the Rope, Var the Stick,* and *Neq the Sword,* is set after an atomic war. The trilogy's action, showing a rebirth of big government in the tribe of Sol and the monastic preservation of "crazy" technology and learning, cautions orderly development. That Sol seeks political power to compensate for sterility and Sos plans battles as strategies for personal vengeance illustrates character but more importantly social weakness. The state set up by Neq and the crazies in the last novel occurs only after purgation of foolishness, pride, and quick temper. When the cost of violence is tallied, such as the needless death of the mutant Var, civilization begins. This Camelot will not be so easily undone by sexuality, jealousy, and pride as the original.

Omnivore, Orn, and *Ox* each deals with the preservation of the planets and the preservation of the symbiotic relationship of Aquilon, Veg, and Cal. Only in *Ox* does Anthony provide Veg with his own mate, the semi-clone Tamme, but in the two earlier novels, love is controlled because the pairing of lovers is destructive to the trio. Aquilon loves both men for different reasons, and neither man is willing to cut the other out. The symbiosis of the group is paramount, as it is in *Rings of Ice* and other Anthony novels. The conflicting claims of preservation and development are worked out in each novel—the fungoid world of Nacre, the Paleocene planet of Orn, and the high technology of Ox. The solution in each case appears to be to control earth's appetite by controlling population. Super agents such as Subble and Tamme become more than imperialistic James Bonds. Violence is necessary in Anthony's novels, but only to insure species preservation. To alter the environment unnecessarily is a major crime.

This is even true in Anthony's fantasies. *Hasan,* though a sexy Arabian Nights series of picaresque adventures, is an ecologically moral world. Magic is fine if magic is conserved. Since Bahram kills young boys, he is killed in turn. Hasan, however, passes up violence in refusing to kill the conquered Queen, making a happy resolution possible. Hasan's foolish ignorance, which could precipitate needless violence, is mocked by those gifted in magical power, such as the ifrit Dahnash.

The Cluster series, currently composed of *Cluster, Chaining the Lady, Kirlian Quest, Thousandstar,* and *Viscous Circle,* makes much use of the Tarot. While systems such as the *I Ching* have had a bearing on some novels, the Tarot, from the time of *Macroscope,* has been dominant in Anthony's symbol system. In *Chaining the Lady,* for example, even the space craft have shapes common to Tarot such as swords and cups. As a system, it appears to be Anthony's answer to the age-old struggle between free will and determinism. Basic to each of the novels is the conflict between galaxies over galaxy-bonding energy. The means of preserving this energy, necessary for the capitalistic expansion of Andromeda, is related to Kirlian aura transfer. It

becomes Flint's job in *Cluster* to give alien planets the secret of Kirlian transfer in order to protect the Milky Way. As Flint enters the host body of each alien in carrying out his mission, an appreciation of other cultures results. He learns to appreciate alien differences and understand their validity; conquest is more often through sex than combat, even between Flint and the Andromedan opposing him. *Chaining the Lady* echoes the plot of *Cluster,* merely changing the sexes of the Milky Way and Andromedan agents. The novel's end is again ecological as the will of lesser auras is taken into consideration in transfer: civilization cannot be maintained by theft of massive new energy; development must be ecological. *Kirlian Quest* shows Herald of Slash assuming the roles of Flint and Melody of the previous novels. Rescue from the Amoeban menace turns out to be rescue from the ancients. What Anthony appears to be exploring is the psychology of bias, how sentients allow one gestalt to block another. The ancients/Amoebans seek to foster Kirlian sapience and fail to recognize it when they contact it.

Thousandstar, which tells of a race whose contestants are Kirlian auras and their host bodies, shows the effects of sexual cooperation and understanding, as Jessica and Heem share the same body. The cooperation shown by the three hostile species is a paradigm for Anthony's environmentalism. *Viscous Circle* has a utopian dimension, as a human Kirlian aura transfer agent, Ronald Snowden, is transferred from his human host to the culture of the bands, mostly metallic creatures deriving energy from magnetic lines, who are peaceful, anarchic, truthful, kind, and generous. Enamored of band culture and a female band, Cirl, Ronald attempts to save the culture from human destruction, but his human methods, war and deceit, damage bands as much as humans. Only by suicide does Ronald prove his truthfulness to another agent he has lied to and find Nirvana, the viscous circle he regarded as myth but which is a spiritual reality.

The Tarot sequence is an elaborate Tarot fantasy which connects to the Cluster series by the use of Kirlian auras and aliens from Cluster planets. Nonetheless, the action is allegorical, as Brother Paul seeks the God of Tarot in encounters with religious leaders, representatives of secular philosophies, and in visions having more in common with Dante, *Piers Plowman,* Bunyan, and Freudian dreams than with contemporary fantasy. While the communist leader, the Mormon, and the Quaker seem too easily reduced in this spiritual odyssey, the series still has much power, and the Tarot symbols are probably more accommodating to fantasy than science fiction, where they seem anthropomorphic.

The Apprentice Adept series, which includes *Split Infinity, Blue Adept,* and *Juxtaposition,* deals with the effects of greed on the ecological system of a planet and on two completely different yet parallel societies. Anthony creates two planets, Proton and Phaze, which are parallel worlds or "frames." On the science planet Proton, a few decadent Citizens have selfishly destroyed the planet's environment by mining Protonite, a mineral which provides them with unlimited energy and enormous wealth. Served by serfs and machines, Proton Citizens are gods, living only for the pleasure of generating more wealth and playing a planetwide Game controlled by a computer. On the beautiful magic planet Phaze, Phazite provides the energy which allows a few Adepts to practice magic and gain control of both human and animal populations. Stile, Anthony's hero, uses the game skill gained on Proton to become Phaze's greatest Adept. Eventually he leads a revolution which equalizes the minerals on both planets, separates the two frames forever, and gives the serfs and robots of Proton and the humans and animals of Phaze independence from their greedy masters.

The Xanth series again focuses on conservation. Bink's quest in *A Spell for Chameleon* to discover whether he has magic uncovers a peculiar trait, resistance to magic's harm. The Magician Humfrey believes in conserving his power, and even Trent says, prior to renouncing force to gain a kingdom, "There is a balance of nature, whether magical or mundane, that we should hesitate to interfere with. " In *The Source of Magic* Xanth learn conservation by temporarily losing its magic when Bink frees the demon. Again psychological ecology is important, as Grundy and Xanth learn about feelings and lose their cool, and in the demon's case, formulaic rationality. In *Castle Roogna* Dor, son of Bink, is on a quest in the past to restore a zombie to a former ghost. Dor, young, learns maturity in his quest, the "discipline of emotion and action," as he recognizes the consequences of actions. Nearly the same characters in *Castle Roogna* reappear in *Centaur Aisle,* although they are four years older. Dor, his friends, and Irene must rescue King Trent and Queen Iris in the Mundanian kingdom of Onesti, but their magic only works in a field created by the centaur Arnolde. Anthony's conservationism manifests itself in this novel politically, as good use is found for the usurper of Onesti, Oary, who must employ his cleverness as an ambassador to Onesti's warlike enemy, and ecologically, as even predatory dunes and sea dragons are protected and preserved. Smash, the half-ogre accompanying Dor in *Centaur Aisle,* goes on quest of his own in *Ogre, Ogre* with Tandy, a half-nymph. Although both learn their true natures on their journey, Smash has the most to learn, recovering his human intelligence through the artificial sanction of Eye Queue, and developing his soul which he barters not for power, like Faust, but love. Tandy and Smash, adding creatures to their pilgrimage, build a community as they go. This continues in *Night Mare,* where Imbri, one of the night mares in *Ogre, Ogre,* becomes King of Xanth when the Horseman and his Mundanian army attempt to conquer the magic kingdom, temporarily disposing of nine previous kings. The novel is Anthony's answer to feminist critics, as the females do the fighting to save Xanth, and Imbri overcomes her sexual instinct to defeat the white stallion—really the Horseman. The three principal characters of *Dragon on a Pedestal*—Stanley, the Grap Dragon, who is reduced in size due to the Fountain of Youth; Ivy, the child of King Dor and Queen Irene; and Hugo, the young son of Good Magician Humfrey and the Gorgon— all have symbiotic relations with one another through their magic talents. They have to deal with three problems facing Xanth, too much drinking at the Fountain of Youth, forget-whorls emanating from the Gap Chasm causing amnesia, and a plague of wiggles which bore through anything in their paths. By combining the talents of the children and dragon, and by combining the talents of much of Xanth's population, natural balance is again achieved, for as Chem the centaur says, "Everything relates. " The frame tale of *Crewel Lye* occurs two years after *Dragon on a Pedestal,* while the central action involving Jordan the ghost, helper of Imbri in *Night Mare,* occurs 400 years earlier. Jordan in his lifetime develops heroic stature on his adventure-filled journey to Castle Roogna, where he is given a quest by King Gromden to discover and bring back something valuable to the Castle, on the way testing the powers of seven spells and counter spells created by Good Magician Yin and Evil Magician Yang, each of whom is competing for the succession; however, as in the Tao, both are one. The quest costs Jordan his life and his love, although Ivy brings both to life, unmasking the goodness of a cruel lie. Taoistic balance is characteristic of Anthony's concerns throughout the pun-filled, award-winning Xanth series, which continues with *Golem in the Gears,* where Grundy the Golem

has a quest to discover the little lost dragon, Stanley, from *Crewel Lye,* discovering his true love, Rapunzel, in the process.

The Incarnations of Immortality series, which, when finished, will be composed of five novels, currently consists of *On a Pale Horse, Bearing an Hourglass,* and *With a Tangled Skein,* dealing with death, time, and fate respectively. Each novel shows the selection of a new person to be one of the five incarnations of immortality—death, time, nature, war, and fate—and the struggle or quest, personal and global, that the incarnation undertakes. In *On a Pale Horse* Zane, nearly by accident, kills Death or Thanatos and takes over his office, taking souls of those about to die who are balanced between heaven, hell, and purgatory. Through love of Luna, a dying magician's daughter, Zane foils an attempt by Satan to manipulate Luna's death and American politics to bring about global catastrophe. The ecological theme is presented in several ways, as Anthony, like Dante, has special uses for hell in punishing litterers and wasters, but his most significant manifestation of his theme is in the balance between Gaea, Thantos, Chronos, Mars, and the three manifestations of Fate, Clotho, Lachesis, and Atropos. Also, instead of violence, the solution for this compassionate Death is reason. *Bearing an Hourglass* has Norton, a naturalist concerned with natural balance, assume the position of Chronos, manipulator of time and causality. Though women and Satanic illusions tempt Norton, he opposes Satan's attempt to manipulate causality and reverse the election of Luna that spoiled his plans in *On a Pale Horse.* Again the balance of forces holds, as the hero uses thought to overcome Satan's ploys. So far Anthony has trouble in adjusting emotional tone to situation in this series.

Anthony's futuristic series Bio of a Space Tyrant is a further illustration of his belief that individual liberty must be restrained for the good of mankind. Although only three of the proposed five novels have been published, Anthony makes clearer with each novel his basic theme. Man has taken his technology into the solar system, but though his technology has evolved, man has not. The best men still retain selfishness and a concern for individual interest, while the worst are bloodthirsty savages. Anthony's imaginary future parallels today's reality. Ostensibly taking place in the 28th century, each planet of the solar system represents a 20th-century country. Jupiter has been colonized by the Americas, Saturn by Asian countries, Uranus by European countries, etc. Poverty, racial prejudice, women's rights, minority rights—even the boat people—appear in various guises to reinforce Anthony's theme. In *Refuges* Anthony arouses reader sympathy for the Hispanic hero, Hope Hubris, with a graphic and bloody account of his 15th year, a year in which he experiences the gamut of man's inhumanity to his fellow man—or woman. He rises above rape, cannibalism, and the annihilation of most of the people he knows and loves, and comes to recognize the enemy to be not only the savage space pirates but the indifference of the colossus, the United States of Jupiter. In *Mercenary* Hubris seeks and gains revenge on the pirates, while in *Politician* he challenges the government of Jupiter, a government which has become so corrupt that only by ridding Jupiter of the executive, legislative, and judicial branches of the government can mankind's basic greed be controlled. Therefore, at the conclusion of the third novel, Hope Hubris is not President but Tyrant of Jupiter with the consent of the people and the legalized authority of a constitutional convention, making the rule of tyrant seem inevitable because of the chaos engendered by uncontrolled individual freedom.

Anthony, probably at his best when he is least profound, is nonetheless an engaging writer. He entertains through suspenseful adventure, the imagining of alien and fantasy cultures, and humor—sometimes at the expense of dramatic conflict.

—Craig Wallace Barrow and Diana Barrow

—————

ANVIL, Christopher. Pseudonym for Harry C. Crosby, Jr. American. Address: c/o Ace Books, 200 Madison Avenue, New York, New York 10016, U. S. A.

SCIENCE-FICTION PUBLICATIONS

Novels

The Day the Machines Stopped. Derby, Connecticut, Monarch, 1964.
Strangers in Paradise. New York, Belmont, 1969.
Pandora's Planet. New York, Doubleday, 1972.
Warlord's World. New York, DAW, 1975.
The Steel, The Mist, and the Blazing Sun. New York, Ace, 1983.

Uncollected Short Stories

"Cinderella, Inc. " (as Harry C. Crosby, Jr.), in *Imagination* (Evanston, Illinois), 1952.
"The Prisoner," in *Astounding* (New York), February 1956.
"Advance Agent," in *Galaxy* (New York), February 1957.
"Sinful City," in *Future* (New York), Spring 1957.
"Compensation," in *Astounding* (New York), October 1957.
"The Gentle Earth," in *Astounding* (New York), November 1957.
"Truce by Boomerang," in *Astounding* (New York), December 1957.
"Achilles Heel," in *Astounding* (New York), February 1958.
"Destination Unknown," in *Science Fiction Adventures* (New York), March 1958.
"Revolt," in *Astounding* (New York), April 1958.
"Top Rung," in *Astounding* (New York), July 1958.
"Cargo for Colony 6," in *Astounding* (New York), August 1958.
"Foghead," in *Astounding* (New York), September 1958.
"Nerves," in *Fantastic Universe* (Chicago), November 1958.
"Goliath and the Beanstalk," in *Astounding* (New York), November 1958.
"Seller's Market," in *Astounding* (New York), December 1958.
"The Sieve," in *Astounding* (New York), April 1959.
"Leverage," in *Astounding* (New York), July 1959.
"Captain Leaven," in *Astounding* (New York), September 1959.
"The Law Breakers," in *Astounding* (New York), October 1959.
"Mating Problems," in *Astounding* (New York), December 1959.
"Shotgun Wedding," in *Astounding* (New York), March 1960.
"A Tourist Named Death," in *If* (New York), May 1960.
"Star Tiger," in *Astounding* (New York), June 1960.
"A Taste of Poison," in *Astounding* (New York), August 1960.
"Pandora's Envoy," in *Analog* (New York), 1961.
"The Ghost Fleet," in *Analog* (New York), February 1961.
"Identification," in *Analog* (New York), May 1961.
"The Hunch," in *Analog* (New York), July 1961.
"No Small Enemy," in *Analog* (New York), November 1961.
"Uncalculated Risk," in *Analog* (New York), March 1962.

"The Toughest Opponent," in *Analog* (New York), August 1962.
"Sorcerer's Apprentice," in *Analog* (New York), September 1962.
"Philosopher's Stone," in *Analog* (New York), January 1963.
"Not in the Literature," in *Analog* (New York), March 1963.
"War Games," in *Analog* (New York), October 1963.
"Problem of Command," in *Analog* (New York), November 1963.
"Speed-Up," in *Amazing* (New York), January 1964.
"Rx for Chaos," in *Analog* (New York), February 1964.
"Hunger," in *Analog* (New York), May 1964.
"We from Arcturus," in *Worlds of Tomorrow* (New York), August 1964.
"Contract," in *Analog* (New York), December 1964.
"Merry Christmas from Outer Space," in *Fantastic* (New York), December 1964.
"New Boccaccio," in *Analog* (New York), January 1965.
"The Plateau," in *Amazing* (New York), March 1965.
"The Captive Djinn," in *Analog* (New York), May 1965.
"Duel to the Death," in *Analog* (New York), June 1965.
"High G," in *If* (New York), June 1965.
"Positive Feedback," in *Analog* (New York), August 1965.
"Untropy," in *Analog* (New York), January 1966.
"The Kindly Invasion," in *Worlds of Tomorrow* (New York), March 1966.
"Devise and Conquer," in *Galaxy* (New York), April 1966.
"Two-Way Communication," in *Analog* (New York), May 1966.
"Stranglehold," in *Analog* (New York), June 1966.
"Sweet Reason," in *If* (New York), June 1966.
"Missile Smasher," in *Analog* (New York), July 1966.
"Symbols," in *Analog* (New York), September 1966.
"Facts to Fit the Theory," in *Analog* (New York), November 1966.
"Sabotage," in *Fantasy and Science Fiction* (New York), December 1966.
"The Trojan Bombardment," in *Galaxy* (New York), February 1967.
"The Uninvited Guest," in *Analog* (New York), March 1967.
"The New Member," in *Galaxy* (New York), April 1967.
"Experts in the Field," in *Analog* (New York), May 1967.
"The Dukes of Desire," in *Analog* (New York), June 1967.
"Compound Interest," in *Analog* (New York), July 1967.
"Babel II," in *Analog* (New York), August 1967.
"The King's Legions," in *Analog* (New York), September 1967.
"The New Way," in *Beyond Infinity* (Hollywood), November 1967.
"A Question of Attitude," in *Analog* (New York), December 1967.
"Uplift the Savage," in *Analog* (New York), March 1968.
"Is Everybody Happy?," in *Analog* (New York), April 1968.
"High Road to the East," in *Fantastic* (New York), May 1968.
"The Royal Road," in *Analog* (New York), June 1968.
"Behind the Sandrat Hoax," in *Galaxy* (New York), October 1968.
"Mission of Ignorance," in *Analog* (New York), October 1968.
"Trap," in *Analog* (New York), March 1969.
"The Nitrocellulose Doormat," in *Analog* (New York), June 1969.
"The Great Intellect Boom," in *Analog* (New York), July 1969.
"Test Ultimate," in *Analog* (New York), October 1969.
"Basic," in *Venture* (Concord, New Hampshire), November 1969.
"Trial by Silk," in *Amazing* (New York), March 1970.

"The Low Road," in *Amazing* (New York), September 1970.
"The Throne and the Usurper," in *Fantasy and Science Fiction* (New York), November 1970.
"Apron Chains," in *Analog* (New York), December 1970.
"The Claw and the Clock," in *Analog* (New York), February 1971.
"The Operator," in *Analog* (New York), March 1971.
"Riddle Me This," in *Analog* (New York), January 1972.
"The Unknown," in *Amazing* (New York), July 1972.
"Ideological Defeat," in *Analog* (New York), September 1972.
"The Knife and the Sheaf," in *Future Kin*, edited by Roger Elwood. New York, Doubleday, 1974.
"Cantor's War," in *If* (New York), June 1974.
"Gadget vs. Trend," in *Strange Orbits*, edited by Amabel Williams-Ellis. London, Blackie, 1976.
"Brains Isn't Everything," in *Analog* (New York), June 1976.
"Mind Partner," in *Neglected Visions*, edited by Barry N. Malzberg, Martin H. Greenberg, and Joseph D. Olander. New York, Doubleday, 1979.
"Torch," in *Analog's Lighter Side*, edited by Stanley Schmidt. New York, Davis, 1982.
"The Troublemaker," in *Science Fiction from A to Z*, edited by Isaac Asimov, Martin H. Greenberg, and Charles G. Waugh. Boston, Houghton Mifflin, 1982.
"Top Line," in *Analog* (New York), 1 February 1982.
"Superbiometalemon," in *Fantasy and Science Fiction* (New York), July 1982.
"A Rose by Any Other Name," in *Hallucination Orbit*, edited by Isaac Asimov, Charles G. Waugh, and Martin H. Greenberg. New York, Farrar Straus, 1983.
"Bill for Delivery," in *Starships*, edited by Isaac Asimov, Martin H. Greenberg, and Charles G. Waugh. New York, Ballantine, 1983.

*   *   *

Christopher Anvil appeared more frequently in *Astounding/Analog* from the mid-1950's to the mid-1960's than any other author, yet he remains relatively unknown today. His novels are slight efforts, and do not compare with his finest short fiction.

At his best, in stories like "A Rose by Any Other Name," which skillfully examines the effect of certain words on international relations, the widely reprinted "Gadget vs. Trend," on the impact of one invention on the functioning of society, and "Positive Feedback," a hilarious story that illustrates the problem of adjusting systems while they are in action, he is an inventive and expert manipulator of social trends and processes. Indeed, he has been one of the very best SF observers (along with Mack Reynolds at *his* best) of the foibles and presumptuousness of social thinkers and social managers. He was perhaps too successful—he found a formula and worked it to death, and was one of the main reasons why the 1960's *Analog* always left you with the feeling that you had just read last month's issue again. He was a John Campbell writer who could be relied upon to hew to the formulas and fads of that editor, and like Randall Garrett became lost from public view through constant, unchanging exposure. Perhaps he might have flourished artistically in another market—some evidence for this possibility can be found in "Mind Partner," his finest work, and one of his few stories published in *Galaxy*. In several respects "Mind Partner" is a New Wave story, a powerful example of psychological science fiction at its best, written before anyone was arguing about the term or had even heard of it. The story has a nightmare quality about it that lingers long after the reading. The editor-writer relationship in science fiction is for the most part a mystery, and it is also possible that Campbell brought out the best in him.

Other notable stories include "Bill for Delivery," "The Captive Djinn," "The Great Intellect Boom," a major work that examines the effect of instant intellectuality on everyone in a society, "The Prisoner," and "Uncalculated Risk."

—Martin H. Greenberg

———

ARCHER, Ron. See **WHITE, Ted.**

———

ARMSTRONG, Anthony. See **TUBB, E. C.**

———

ARMSTRONG, Geoffrey. See **FEARN, John Russell.**

———

ARNETTE, Robert. See **PHILLIPS, Rog.**

———

ARNOLD, Edwin L(ester Linden). British. Born in Swanscombe, Kent, 14 May 1857; son of the writer Sir Edwin Arnold. Educated at Cheltenham College. Married 1) Constance Boyce, one daughter; 2) Jessie Brighton in 1919. Cattle Breeder in Scotland, then worked in forestry in Travancore, India in late 1870's; staff members, *Daily Telegraph*, London, 1833-1908. *Died 1 March 1935.*

SCIENCE-FICTION PUBLICATIONS

Novels

The Wonderful Adventures of Phra the Phoenician. London, Chatto and Windus, 3 vols., and New York, Harper, 1 vol., 1890.
Lepidus the Centurion: A Roman of To-day. London, Cassell, 1901; New York, Crowell, 1902.
Lieut. Gullivar Jones: His Vacation. London, Brown Langham, 1905; New York, Arno Press, 1975; as *Gulliver of Mars*, New York, Ace, 1964.

Short Stories

The Story of Ulla and Other Tales. London and New York, Longman, 1895.

OTHER PUBLICATIONS

Novel

The Constable of St. Nicholas. London, Chatto and Windus, 1894.

Other

A Summer Holiday in Scandinavia. London, Sampson Low, 1877.
On the Indian Hills; or Coffee-Planting in Southern India. London, Sampson Low, 2 vols., 1881.
Coffee: Its Cultivation and Profit. London, Whittingham, 1886.
Bird Life in England. London, Chatto and Windus, 1887.
England as She Seems, Being Selections from the Notes of an Arab Hadji. London, Warne, 1888.
The Soul of the Beast. London, P. R. Macmillan, 1960.

Editor, *The Opium Question Solved,* by Anglo-Indian. London, Partridge, 1882.

*   *   *

Once a highly popular author, Edwin L. Arnold is little remembered and seldom read, and when read at all is generally examined as a possible source of inspiration for Edgar Rice Burroughs's Martian series rather than as an author of independent merit. Arnold's father, Sir Edwin Arnold, was one of the first Englishmen to study Eastern religion, philosophy, and culture. Very likely as a result of his father's influence, young Arnold became interested in Asian philosophy, in particular in theories of reincarnation and the cyclical nature of existence.

These theories are visible in Arnold's first and most successful novel, *The Wonderful Adventures of Phra the Phoenician.* Phra is described as a man appearing about 30 years of age, but in fact having no recollection of ever having been younger. His most ancient memory is of life in classical Phoenicia, but even in that recollection he was a man, not a child. Over the ages, Phra has lived and (apparently) died repeatedly. He describes himself as a simple military man, although he admits to being a great swordsman. As an early colonist in Britain he met and fell in love with the Princess Blodwen. Following her death he too "died" and encountered her ghost in the spirit world, but after many years Phra recovered, his undecayed body as good as ever, and resumed his life. This cycle is repeated numerous times, down to the present (Victorian) era. The book is an excellent example of Victorian fantasy, closest in spirit to Haggard's *The World's Desire,* written with Andrew Lang. To modern readers *Phra* will seem slow-paced, florid, and overlong, but it is still readable.

The Story of Ulla and Other Tales is a collection of Arnold's shorter fiction. Several of the stories contain fantastic elements, for the most part of rather conventional nature (i. e., ghost stories). Most relevant is "Rutherford the Twice-Born," in which Arnold reverts to the reincarnation/resurrection theme. *Lepidus the Centurion* is still another treatment of the resurrection/reincarnation theme. A Roman legionnaire revives from suspended animation in contemporary England, and then proceeds to acclimate himself to polite Victorian society, learning to play tennis and the like. *Lepidus* is the least of Arnold's novels in actual interest for the present-day reader. The author attempts the comedy of manners in style, but the result is poor.

Lieut. Gullivar Jones: His Vacation was Arnolds's final novel, and the most interesting to the modern reader of science fiction. Jones, a lieutenant in the US navy, comes into possession of a magic carpet while on leave. He is carried to Mars where he encounters a race of cultured urban dwellers attempting to preserve a high ancient civilization against the maraudings of savage desert nomads. He rescues the civilized Princess An from the nomads, travels to an icy River of Death (compare Haggard and Burroughs), and has other adventures among the Martians before returning to earth. By combining the setting and plot elements of *Gullivar Jones* with the heroic figure of *Phra the Phoenician*—and with the addition of elements from such works as *A Journey to Mars* by Pope and *Zarlah the Martian* by Grisewood—one assembles the full recipe of Burroughs's Barsoomian saga, at least of the early volumes.

Although Arnold's last book was published in 1905, he lived until 1935, well into the period of modern "pulp" science fiction, but there appears to be no record of his attitude toward the works of later writers, including Burroughs.

—Richard A. Lupoff

ARROW, William. See **ROTSLER, William.**

ARTHUR, Peter. See **PORGES, Arthur.**

ASH, Fenton. Pseudonym for Frank Atkins; also wrote as Fred Ashley; Frank Aubrey. British. Grew up in South Wales. Studied engineering. Wrote serials for boys' papers in 1900's; film critic for a London Sunday paper.

SCIENCE-FICTION PUBLICATIONS

Novels

The Radium Seekers; or, The Wonderful Black Nugget. London, Pitman, 1905.
The Temple of Fire; or, The Mysterious Island (as Fred Ashley). London, Pitman, 1905.
A Trip to Mars (for children). London, Chambers, 1909; New York, Arno Press, 1975.
By Airship to Ophir (for children). London, Shaw, 1911.
The Black Opal (for children). London, Shaw, 1915; New York, Arno Press, 1975.

Novels as Frank Aubrey (series: Monella in all books)

The Devil-Tree of El Dorado. London, Hutchinson, 1896; New York, New Amsterdam, 1897.
A Queen of Atlantis. London, Hutchinson, and Philadelphia, Lippincott, 1899.
King of the Dead. London, Macqueen, 1903; New York, Arno Press, 1978.

Short Stories as Frank Aubrey

Strange Stories of Hospitals. London, Pearson, 1898.

OTHER PUBLICATIONS

Novel

A Studio Mystery (as Frank Aubrey). London, Jarrolds, 1897.

* * *

At the turn of the century, Frank Atkins, using the Fenton Ash and other pen-names, was writing a genre of fiction which contained elements of what critics today broadly term speculative fiction. To call Atkins a science-fiction writer, however, would be to push him into a category which his writing fits only at certain key points: in theme and plot, in characters, and in style. Atkins's work suits his time and place, but in at least one novel, *A Trip to Mars,* he explores possibilities only being hinted at by a few other writers and cinematic directors of his time.

Atkins stretches coincidence to the limit in certain areas. He hypothesizes lost civilizations on earth—the remains of Atlantis in the middle of the Sargasso Sea, El Dorado on a mountain top in an unexplored region of South America—in four books, and only in *A Trip to Mars* does he move beyond the earth. He frequently postulates long-lost relatives; the conflict often revolves around the good characters overcoming powerful forces of evil. But Atkins's outcomes are pat, and he prepares his reader well with very broad hints for any "surprise."

Atkins strives for believability in his settings, giving lengthy descriptions with numerous footnotes, of the flora and fauna both in South America and in the Sargasso Sea, though there are many descriptions of the fantastic in all his books—giant flowers, fruits, animals, huge dazzling jewels and massive amounts of gold. He also frequently hypothesizes seers who make accurate, if non-specific predictions, usually astrologically. Atkins's only real speculative scientific developments occur in his "red ray" (*King of the Dead*) and space ship (*A Trip to Mars*). "Hard" scientific developments play minimal part in his books.

Most of Atkins's characters are, at best, stereotypes. His infrequent attempts at light-heartedness generally occur when he introduces a lower-class Englishman (usually a sailor) with a droll, "uneducated" accent, uttering malapropisms. His "evil" characters are in all senses malevolent and frequently seem to be in league with some never-explained Dark Power. Only in *King of the Dead* does he portray a Power of Evil, called Mahrimah, who resembles a fallen angel. All the books have as protagonists male "chums" who are young, adventuresome, and typically British. Of lesser importance are the young women, generally the love interests of one or both of the "chums"; some are exotic, some are classically British, but without exceptions coy and beautiful, and are frequently endangered by natural or human foes. This is true even for Vanina, the queen of *A Queen of Atlantis,* who actually plays a very passive role in the plot. While in all of Atkins's books the good characters consistently behave nobly, most of the books contain a totally noble figure as well. In his Monella novels this character is Monella himself, a noble figure of great age who is roaming the world until he can regain his throne in El Dorado; in *King of the Dead* the noble figure is Lorenzo, né Manzoni, who is even more enigmatic than is Monella. They are consistently wise, strong, compelling, and remote, and both

also have to atone for some "sin" (primarily caused by his leaving of his people and venturing into the "real" world) by admitting his error and setting things to rights.

Atkins's style is probably the most interesting feature of his books. Atkins uses the common technique of ending each chapter with a hint of what is to come, and it does serve its purpose—to keep the reader reading. Atkins uses much description in his book, which is fortunate since his dialogue is often formal and stilted. Atkins's point of view is consistently third-person, but the particular outlook of each chapter varies determined by whom Atkins chooses to focus through. Atkins is at his best when describing the exotic features of his setting—costly and beautiful architecture, elaborate costumes, wonderful jewels. He excels at choosing exotic names for people, places, animals, and Gods—Ivanta, Alondra, Mellenda, Ullama, Lyostrah, Morveena. The tension in his novels frequently revolves around encounters with natural but terrifying animals, such as cuttlefish, enourmous snakes, gorilla-type animals, pumas, and most of his novels feature supernatural monsters such as zombies, vampires, and, most particularly, the devil-tree in the novel of that name. The devil-tree, a huge tree which seizes its victims in tentacle-like branches and conveys them to its maw, a hollow trunk, is fully as terrifying and loathesome as any creation of current writers of horror novels or directors of horror movies. After the tree consumes the victims, it releases them, or what is left of them, to be carried off and eaten by crocodile-like monsters who live in a pond at its base. In the climactic scene at the end of the novel, the evil priests are all seized and eaten, some by the tree, and some by being torn to bits by the monsters as the priests are held in the tree's tentacles awaiting their turn in its maw. The nightmarish effectiveness of this description is such that its image remains vivid in the reader's mind long after he has finished the book itself.

In fact, if Atkins's writing is akin to speculative fiction, it is certainly supernatural and horror fiction which it most resembles. He does work with settings which are largely unknown to his world, but it is their exotic quality rather than any science-fiction aspect which he develops. Only in *A Trip to Mars* does Atkins extrapolate any scientific devices, and these are fanciful, based on principles long since outdated. Additionally, the Mars which Atkins depicts is so similar to his exotic settings on earth as to be interchangeable, and his Martian characters are certainly no less human, in physical features or in outlook, than the characters in his earth-based novels. Nevertheless, Atkins's books are still interesting reading, particularly in editions which contain the quaint original illustrations, as period pieces.

—Karren C. Edwards

———

ASHLEY, Fred. See ASH, Fenton.

———

ASIMOV, Isaac. Also writes as Dr. A. ; Paul French. American. Born in Petrovichi, U.S.S.R., 2 January 1920; emigrated to the United States in 1923; naturalized, 1928. Educated at Columbia University, New York, B. S. 1939, M. A. 1941, Ph. D. in chemistry 1948. Served in the United States Army, 1945-46. Married 1) Gertrude Blugerman in 1948 (divorced), one son and one daughter; 2) Janet Opal Jeppson in 1973. Instructor in Biochemistry, 1949-51, Assistant Professor, 1951-55, Associate Professor, 1955-79, and since 1979 Professor, Boston University School of Medicine. Recipient: Edison Foundation National Mass Media award, 1958; Blakeslee award, for non-fiction, 1960; World Science Fiction Convention Citation, 1963; Hugo Award, 1963, 1966, 1973, 1977, 1983; American Chemical Society James T. Grady Award, 1965; American Association for the Advancement of Science-Westinghouse Science Writing award, 1967; Nebula Award, 1972, 1976; *Locus* award, for non-fiction, 1981, for fiction, 1983. Guest of Honor, World Science Fiction Convention, 1955. Address: 10 West 66th Street, Apartment 33-A, New York, New York 10023, U. S. A.

SCIENCE-FICTION PUBLICATIONS

Novels (series: Elijah Baley; Foundation; Norby; Trantorian Empire)

Triangle (Empire). New York, Doubleday, 1961; as *An Isaac Asimov Second Omnibus,* London, Sidgwick and Jackson, 1969.
  Pebble in the Sky. New York, Doubleday, 1950; London, Corgi, 1958.
  The Stars, Like Dust. New York, Doubleday, 1951; London, Panther, 1958; abridged edition, as *The Rebellious Stars,* New York, Ace, 1954.
  The Currents of Space. New York, Doubleday, 1952; London, Boardman, 1955.
Foundation Trilogy. New York, Doubleday, 1963(?); as *An Isaac Asimov Omnibus,* London, Sidgwick and Jackson, 1966.
  Foundation. New York, Gnome Press, 1951; London, Weidenfeld and Nicolson, 1953; abridged edition, as *The Thousand-Year Plan,* New York, Ace, 1955.
  Foundation and Empire. New York, Gnome Press, 1952; London, Panther, 1962; as *The Man Who Upset the Universe,* New York, Ace, 1955.
  Second Foundation. New York, Gnome Press, 1953.
The Caves of Steel. (Baley). New York, Doubleday, and London, Boardman, 1954.
The End of Eternity. New York, Doubleday, 1955; London, Panther, 1958.
The Naked Sun (Baley). New York, Doubleday, 1957; London, Joseph, 1958.
Fantastic Voyage (novelization of screenplay). Boston, Houghton Mifflin, and London, Dobson, 1966.
The Robot Novels (includes *The Caves of Steel* and *The Naked Sun*). New York, Doubleday, 1971.
The Gods Themselves. New York, Doubleday, and London, Gollancz, 1972.
The Collected Fiction: The Far Ends of Time and Earth, Prisoners of the Stars. New York, Doubleday, 2 vols., 1979.
Foundation's Edge. New York, Doubleday, 1982; London, Granada, 1983.
The Robots of Dawn (Baley). New York, Doubleday, 1983; London, Granada, 1984.
Norby the Mixed-Up Robot (for children), with Janet Asimov. New York, Walker, 1983; London, Methuen, 1984.
Norby's Other Secret (for children), with Janet Asimov. New York, Walker, 1984.
Norby and the Lost Princess (for children), with Janet Asimov. New York, Walker, 1985.
Robots and Empire. New York, Doubleday, 1985.

Novels (for children) as Paul French (series: Lucky Starr in all books)

David Starr, Space Ranger. New York, Doubleday, 1952; Kingswood, Surrey, World's Work, 1953.
Lucky Starr and the Pirates of the Asteroids. New York, Doubleday, 1953; Kingswood, Surrey, World's Work, 1954.
Lucky Starr and the Oceans of Venus. New York, Doubleday, 1954; as *The Oceans of Venus* (as Isaac Asimov), London, New English Library, 1973.
Lucky Starr and the Big Sun of Mercury. New York, Doubleday, 1956; as *The Big Sun of Mercury* (as Isaac Asimov), London, New English Library, 1974.
Lucky Starr and the Moons of Jupiter. New York, Doubleday, 1957; as *The Moons of Jupiter* (as Isaac Asimov), London, New English Library, 1974.
Lucky Starr and the Rings of Saturn. New York, Doubleday, 1958; as *The Rings of Saturn* (as Isaac Asimov), London, New English Library, 1974.

Short Stories

I, Robot. New York, Gnome Press, 1950; London, Grayson, 1952.
The Martian Way and Other Stories. New York, Doubleday, 1955; London, Dobson, 1964.
Earth Is Room Enough. New York, Doubleday, 1957; London, Panther, 1960.
Nine Tomorrows: Tales of the Near Future. New York, Doubleday, 1959; London, Dobson, 1963.
The Rest of the Robots. New York, Doubleday, 1964; London, Dobson, 1967.
Through a Glass, Clearly. London, New English Library, 1967.
Asimov's Mysteries. New York, Doubleday, and London, Rapp and Whiting, 1968.
Nightfall and Other Stories. New York, Doubleday, 1969; London, Rapp and Whiting, 1970.
The Early Asimov; or, Eleven Years of Trying. New York, Doubleday, 1972; London, Gollancz, 1973.
The Best of Isaac Asimov (1939-1972). London, Sidgwick and Jackson, 1973; New York, Doubleday, 1974.
Have You Seen These? Cambridge, Massachusetts, NESFA Press, 1974.
The Heavenly Host (for children). New York, Walker, 1975; London, Penguin, 1978.
Buy Jupiter and Other Stories. New York, Doubleday, 1975; London, Gollancz, 1976.
The Dream, Benjamin's Dream, Benjamin's Bicentennial Blast: Three Short Stories. Privately printed, 1976.
The Bicentennial Man and Other Stories. New York, Doubleday, 1976; London, Gollancz, 1977.
Good Taste. Topeka, Kansas, Apocalypse Press, 1977.
3 by Asimov. New York, Targ, 1981.
The Complete Robot. New York, Doubleday, and London, Granada, 1982.
The Winds of Change and Other Stories. New York, Doubleday, and London, Granada, 1983.

OTHER PUBLICATIONS

Novels

The Death Dealers. New York, Avon, 1958; as *A Whiff of Death,* New York, Walker, and London, Gollancz, 1968.
Murder at the ABA. New York, Doubleday, 1976; as *Authorized Murder,* London Gollancz, 1976.

Short Stories

Tales of the Black Widowers. New York, Doubleday, 1974; London, Gollancz, 1975.
More Tales of the Black Widowers. New York, Doubleday, 1976; London, Gollancz, 1977.
Casebook of the Black Widowers. New York, Doubleday, and London, Gollancz, 1980.
The Union Club Mysteries. New York, Doubleday, 1983; London, Granada, 1984.
Banquets of the Black Widowers. New York, Doubleday, 1984.

Verse

Lecherous Limericks. New York, Walker, 1975; London, Corgi, 1977.
More Lecherous Limericks. New York, Walker, 1976.
Still More Lecherous Limericks. New York, Walker, 1977.
Asimov's Sherlockian Limericks. Yonkers, New York, Mysterious Press, 1978.
Limericks: Too Gross, with John Ciardi. New York, Norton, 1978.
A Grossery of Limericks, with John Ciardi. New York, Norton, 1981.
Limericks for Children. New York, Caedmon, 1984.

Other

Biochemistry and Human Metabolism, with Burnham Walker and William C. Boyd. Baltimore, Williams and Wilkins, 1952; revised edition, 1954, 1957; London, Ballie Tindall and Cox, 1955.
The Chemicals of Life: Enzymes, Vitamins, Hormones. New York, Abelard Schuman, 1954; London, Bell, 1956.
Races and Peoples, with William C. Boyd. New York, Abelard Schuman, 1955; London, Abelard Schuman, 1958.
Chemistry and Human Health, with Burnham Walker and M. K. Nicholas. New York, McGraw Hill, 1956.
Inside the Atom. New York and London, Abelard Schuman, 1956; revised edition, Abelard Schuman, 1958, 1961, 1966, 1974.
Building Blocks of the Universe. New York, Abelard Schuman, 1957; London, Abelard Schuman, 1958; revised edition, 1961, 1974.
Only a Trillion. New York and London, Abelard Schuman, 1957; as *Marvels of Science*, New York, Collier, 1962.
The World of Carbon. New York and London, Abelard Schuman, 1958; revised edition, New York, Collier, 1962.
The World of Nitrogen. New York and London, Abelard Schuman, 1958; revised edition, New York, Collier, 1962.
The Clock We Live On. New York and London, Abelard Schuman, 1959; revised edition, New York, Collier, 1962; Abelard Schuman, 1965.
The Living River. New York and London, Abelard Schuman, 1959; revised edition, as *The Bloodstream: River of Life*, New York, Collier, 1961.
Realm of Numbers. Boston, Houghton Mifflin, 1959; London, Gollancz, 1963.
Words of Science and the History Behind Them. Boston, Houghton Mifflin, 1959; London, Harrap, 1974.
Breakthroughs in Science (for children). Boston, Houghton Mifflin, 1960.
The Intelligent Man's Guide to Science. New York, Basic Books, 2 vols., 1960; revised edition, as *The New Intelligent Man's Guide to Science*, 1 vol., 1965; London, Nelson, 1967; as *Asimov's Guide to Science*, New York, Basic Books, 1972;
London, Penguin, 2 vols., 1975; as *Asimov's New Guide to Science*, Basic Books, 1984.
The Kingdom of the Sun. New York and London, Abelard Schuman, 1960; revised edition, New York, Collier, 1962; Abelard Schuman, 1963.
Realm of Measure. Boston, Houghton Mifflin, 1960.
Satellites in Outer Space (for children). New York, Random House, 1960; revised edition, 1964, 1973.
The Double Planet. New York, Abelard Schuman, 1960; London, Abelard Schuman, 1962; revised edition, 1966.
The Wellsprings of Life . New York and London, Abelard Schuman, 1960.
Realm of Algebra. Boston, Houghton Mifflin, 1961; London, Gollancz, 1964.
Words from the Myths. Boston, Houghton Mifflin, 1961; London, Faber, 1963.
Fact and Fancy. New York, Doubleday, 1962.
Life and Energy. New York, Doubleday, 1962; London, Dobson, 1963.
The Search for the Elements. New York, Basic Books, 1962.
Words in Genesis. Boston, Houghton Mifflin, 1962.
Words on the Map. Boston, Houghton Mifflin, 1962.
View from a Height. New York, Doubleday, 1963; London, Dobson, 1964.
The Genetic Code. New York, Orion Press, 1963; London, Murray, 1964.
The Human Body: Its Structure and Operation. Boston, Houghton Mifflin, 1963; London, Nelson, 1965.
The Kite That Won the Revolution. Boston, Houghton Mifflin, 1963.
Words from the Exodus. Boston, Houghton Mifflin, 1963.
Adding a Dimension: 17 Essays on the History of Science. New York, Doubleday, 1964; London, Dobson, 1966.
The Human Brain: Its Capacities and Functions. Boston, Houghton Mifflin, 1964; London, Nelson, 1965.
Quick and Easy Math. Boston, Houghton Mifflin, 1964; London, Whiting and Wheaton, 1967.
A Short History of Biology. Garden City, New York, Natural History Press, 1964; London, Nelson, 1965.
Planets for Man, with Stephen H. Dole. New York, Random House, 1964.
Asimov's Biographical Encyclopedia of Science and Technology. New York, Doubleday, 1964; London, Allen and Unwin, 1966; revised edition, Doubleday, 1972, 1982; London, Pan, 1975.
An Easy Introduction to the Slide Rule. Boston, Houghton Mifflin, 1965; London, Whiting and Wheaton, 1967.
The Greeks: A Great Adventure. Boston, Houghton Mifflin, 1965.
Of Time and Space and Other Things. New York, Doubleday, 1965; London, Dobson, 1967.
A Short History of Chemistry. New York, Doubleday, 1965; London, Heinemann, 1972.
The Neutrino: Ghost Particle of the Atom. New York, Doubleday, and London, Dobson, 1966.
The Genetic Effects of Radiation, with Theodosius Dobzhansky. Washington, D. C, Atomic Energy Commission, 1966.
The Noble Gases. New York, Basic Books, 1966.
The Roman Republic. Boston, Houghton Mifflin, 1966.
From Earth to Heaven. New York, Doubleday, 1966.
Understanding Physics. New York, Walker, 3 vols., 1966; London, Allen and Unwin, 3 vols., 1967; as *The History of Physics*, Walker, 1 vol., 1984.
The Universe: From Flat Earth to Quasar. New York, Walker, 1966; London, Penguin, 1967; revised edition, Walker, and

Penguin, 1971; revised edition, as *The Universe: From Flat Earth to Black Holes—and Beyond*, Walker, 1980, Penguin, 1983.

The Roman Empire. Boston, Houghton Mifflin, 1967.

The Moon (for children). Chicago, Follett, 1967; London, University of London Press, 1969.

Is Anyone There? (essays). New York, Doubleday, 1967; London, Rapp and Whiting, 1968.

To the Ends of the Universe. New York, Walker, 1967; revised edition, 1976.

The Egyptians. Boston, Houghton Mifflin, 1967.

Mars (for children). Chicago, Follett, 1967; London, University of London Press, 1971.

From Earth to Heaven: 17 Essays on Science. New York, Doubleday, 1967; London, Dobson, 1968.

Environments Out There. New York, Abelard Schuman, 1967; London, Abelard Schumann, 1968.

"There's Nothing Like a Good Foundation," in *SFWA Bulletin* (Sea Cliff, New York), January 1967.

Science, Numbers, and I: Essays on Science. New York, Doubleday, 1968; London, Rapp and Whiting, 1969.

The Near East: 10,000 Years of History. Boston, Houghton Mifflin, 1968.

Asimov's Guide to the Bible: The Old Testament, The New Testament. New York, Doubleday, 2 vols., 1968-69.

The Dark Ages. Boston, Houghton Mifflin, 1968.

Galaxies (for children). Chicago, Follett, 1968; London, University of London Press, 1971.

Stars (for children). Chicago, Follett, 1968.

Words from History. Boston, Houghton Mifflin, 1968.

Photosynthesis. New York, Basic Books, 1968; London, Allen and Unwin, 1970.

The Shaping of England. Boston, Houghton Mifflin, 1969.

Twentieth Century Discovery (for children). New York, Doubleday, and London, Macdonald, 1969.

Opus 100 (selection). Boston, Houghton Mifflin, 1969.

ABC's of Space (for children). New York, Walker, 1969.

Great Ideas of Science (for children). Boston, Houghton Mifflin, 1969.

To the Solar System and Back. New York, Doubleday, 1970.

Asimov's Guide to Shakespeare: The Greek, Roman, and Italian Plays; The English Plays. New York, Doubleday, 2 vols., 1970.

Constantinople. Boston, Houghton Mifflin, 1970.

The ABC's of the Ocean (for children). New York, Walker, 1970.

Light (for children). Chicago, Follett, 1970.

"F & SF and I," in *Twenty Years of Fantasy and Science Fiction*, edited by Edward Ferman and Robert Mills. New York, Putnam, 1970.

The Best New Thing (for children). Cleveland, World, 1971.

The Stars in Their Courses. New York, Doubleday, 1971; London, White Lion, 1974.

What Makes the Sun Shine. Boston, Little Brown, 1971.

The Isaac Asimov Treasury of Humor, Boston, Houghton Mifflin, 1971; London, Vallentine Mitchell, 1972.

The Sensuous Dirty Old Man (as Dr. A.). New York, Walker, 1971.

The Land of Canaan. Boston, Houghton Mifflin, 1971.

ABC's of Earth (for children). New York, Walker, 1971.

The Space Dictionary. New York, Starline, 1971.

More Words of Science. Boston, Houghton Mifflin, 1972.

Electricity and Man. Washington, D. C., Atomic Energy Commission, 1972.

The Shaping of France. Boston, Houghton Mifflin, 1972.

Asimov's Annotated "Don Juan." New York, Doubleday, 1972.

ABC's of Ecology (for children). New York, Walker, 1972.

The Story of Ruth. New York, Doubleday, 1972.

Worlds Within Worlds. Washington, D. C., Atomic Energy Commission, 1972.

The Left Hand of the Electron (essays). New York, Doubleday, 1972; London, White Lion, 1975.

Ginn Science Program. Boston, Ginn, 5 vols., 1972-73.

"Why Read Science Fiction?," in *3000 Years of Fantasy and Science Fiction*, edited by L. Sprague de Camp and Catherine Crook de Camp. New York, Lothrop, 1972.

How Did We Find Out about Dinosaurs [The Earth Is Round, Electricity, Vitamins, Germs, Comets, Energy, Atoms, Nuclear Power, Numbers, Outer Space, Earthquakes, Black Holes, Our Human Roots, Antarctica, Coal, Oil, Solar Power, Volcanoes, Life in the Deep Sea, Our Genes, the Universe, Computers, Robots] (for children). New York, Walker, 24 vols., 1973-84; 6 vols. published London, White Lion, 1975-76; 1 vol. published London, Pan, 1980; 7 vols. published (as *How We Found Out. . .* series), London, Longman, 1982.

The Tragedy of the Moon (essays). New York, Doubleday, 1973; London, Abelard Schuman, 1974.

Comets and Meteors (for children). Chicago, Follett, 1973.

The Sun (for children). Chicago, Follett, 1973.

The Shaping of North America from the Earliest Times to 1763. Boston, Houghton Mifflin, 1973; London, Dobson, 1975.

Please Explain (for children). Boston, Houghton Mifflin, 1973; London, Abelard Schuman, 1975.

Physical Science Today. Del Mar, California, CRM, 1973.

Jupiter, The Largest Planet (for children). New York, Lothrop, 1973; revised edition, 1976.

Today, Tomorrow, and . . . . New York, Doubleday, 1973; London, Abelard Schuman, 1974; as *Towards Tomorrow*, London, Hodder and Stoughton, 1977.

"When Aristotle Fails, Try Science Fiction," in *Speculations*, edited by Thomas D. Sanders. Beverly Hills, California, Glencoe Press, 1973.

The Birth of the United States 1763-1816. Boston, Houghton Mifflin, 1974.

Earth: Our Crowded Spaceship. New York, Day, and London, Abelard Schuman, 1974.

Asimov on Chemistry. New York, Doubleday, 1974; London, Macdonald and Jane's, 1975.

Asimov on Astronomy. New York, Doubleday, and London, Macdonald, 1974.

Asimov's Annotated "Paradise Lost." New York, Doubleday, 1974.

Our World in Space. Greenwich, Connecticut, New York Graphic Society, and Cambridge, Patrick Stephens, 1974.

The Solar System (for children). Chicago, Follett, 1975.

Birth and Death of the Universe. New York, Walker, 1975.

Of Matters Great and Small. New York, Doubleday, 1975.

Our Federal Union: The United States from 1816 to 1865. Boston, Houghton Mifflin, and London, Dobson, 1975.

The Ends of the Earth: The Polar Regions of the World. New York, Weybright and Talley, 1975.

Eyes on the Universe: A History of the Telescope. Boston, Houghton Mifflin, 1975; London, Deutsch, 1976.

Science Past—Science Future. New York, Doubleday, 1975.

"Is There Hope for the Future?," in *The Best from Galaxy 3*, edited by James Baen. New York, Award, 1975.

Alpha Centauri, The Nearest Star (for children). New York, Lothrop, 1976.

I, Rabbi (for children). New York, Walker, 1976.

Asimov on Physics. New York, Doubleday, 1976.

The Planet That Wasn't. New York, Doubleday, 1976; London, Sphere, 1977.

The Collapsing Universe: The Story of Black Holes. New York,

Walker, and London, Hutchinson, 1977.

Asimov on Numbers. New York, Doubleday, 1977.

The Beginning and the End. New York, Doubleday, 1977.

Familiar Poems Annotated. New York, Doubleday, 1977.

The Golden Door: The United States from 1865 to 1918. Boston, Houghton Mifflin, and London, Dobson, 1977.

The Key Word and Other Mysteries (for children). New York, Walker, 1977.

Mars, The Red Planet (for children). New York, Lothrop, 1977.

Life and Time. New York, Doubleday, 1978.

Quasar, Quasar, Burning Bright. New York, Doubleday, 1978.

Animals of the Bible (for children). New York, Doubleday, 1978.

Isaac Asimov's Book of Facts. New York, Grosset and Dunlap, 1979; London, Hodder and Stoughton, 1980; abridged edition (for children), as *Would You Believe?* and *More. . . Would You Believe?*, Grosset and Dunlap, 2 vols., 1981-82.

Extraterrestrial Civilizations. New York, Crown, 1979; London, Robson, 1980.

A Choice of Catastrophes. New York, Simon and Schuster, 1979; London, Hutchinson, 1980.

Saturn and Beyond. New York, Lothrop, 1979.

Opus 200 (selection). Boston, Houghton Mifflin, 1979.

In Memory Yet Green: The Autobiography of Isaac Asimov 1920-1954. New York, Doubleday, 1979.

The Road to Infinity. New York, Doubleday, 1979.

In Joy Still Felt: The Autobiography of Isaac Asimov 1954-1978. New York, Doubleday, 1980.

The Annotated Gulliver's Travels. New York, Potter, 1980.

Opus (includes *Opus 100* and *Opus 200*). London, Deutsch, 1980.

Change! Seventy-One Glimpses of the Future. Boston, Houghton Mifflin, 1981.

Visions of the Universe, paintings by Kazuaki Iwasaki. Montrose, California, Cosmos Store, 1981.

Asimov on Science Fiction. New York, Doubleday, 1981; London, Granada, 1983.

Venus, Near Neighbor of the Sun (for children). New York, Lothrop, 1981.

The Sun Shines Bright. New York, Doubleday, 1981; London, Granada, 1984.

In the Beginning: Science Faces God in the Book of Genesis. New York, Crown, and London, New English Library, 1981.

Exploring the Earth and the Cosmos. New York, Crown, 1982; London, Allen Lane, 1983.

Counting the Eons. New York, Doubleday, 1983; London, Granada, 1984.

The Measure of the Universe. New York, Harper, 1983.

The Roving Mind. Buffalo, Prometheus, 1983.

X Stands for Unknown. New York, Doubleday, 1984; London, Granada, 1985.

Opus 300. Boston, Houghton Mifflin, 1984.

Robots: Where the Machine Ends and Life Begins, with Karen A. Frenkel. New York, Crown, 1985.

The Exploding Suns: The Secrets of the Supernovas. New York, Dutton, 1985.

Asimov's Guide to Halley's Comet. New York, Walker, 1985.

The Subatomic Monster (essays). New York, Doubleday, 1985.

The Edge of Tomorrow. New York, Tor, 1985.

Editor, *Soviet Science Fiction* [and *More Soviet Science Fiction*]. New York, Collier, 2 vols., 1962.

Editor, *The Hugo Winners 1-4.* New York, Doubleday, 4 vols., 1962-85; 1 and 3, London, Dobson, 2 vols., 1963-67; 2, London, Sphere, 1973.

Editor, with Groff Conklin, *Fifty Short Fiction Tales.* New York, Collier, 1963.

Editor, *Tomorrow's Children: 18 Tales of Fantasy and Science Fiction.* New York, Doubleday, 1966; London, Futura, 1974.

Editor, *Where Do We Go from Here?* New York, Doubleday, 1971; London, Joseph, 1973.

Editor, *Nebula Award Stories 8.* New York, Harper, and London, Gollancz, 1973.

Editor, *Before the Golden Age: A Science Fiction Anthology of the 1930's.* New York, Doubleday, and London, Robson, 1974.

Editor, with Martin H. Greenberg and Joseph D. Olander, *100 Great Science Fiction Short-Short Stories.* New York, Doubleday, and London, Robson, 1978.

Editor, with Martin H. Greenberg and Charles G. Waugh, *The Science Fictional Solar System.* New York, Harper, 1979; London, Sidgwick and Jackson, 1980.

Editor, with Martin H. Greenberg and Charles G. Waugh, *The Thirteen Crimes of Science Fiction.* New York, Doubleday, 1979.

Editor, with Martin H. Greenberg, *The Great SF Stories 1-11.* New York, DAW, 1979-84.

Editor, with Martin H. Greenberg and Joseph D. Olander, *Microcosmic Tales: 100 Wondrous Science Fiction Short-Short Stories.* New York, Taplinger, 1980.

Editor, with Martin H. Greenberg and Joseph D. Olander, *Space Mail 1.* New York, Fawcett, 1980.

Editor, with Martin H. Greenberg and Joseph D. Olander, *The Future in Question.* New York, Fawcett, 1980.

Editor, with Alice Laurance, *Who Done It?* Boston, Houghton Mifflin, 1980.

Editor, with Martin H. Greenberg and Charles G. Waugh, *The Seven Deadly Sins of Science Fiction.* New York, Fawcett, 1980.

Editor, with Martin H. Greenberg and Joseph D. Olander, *Miniature Mysteries: 100 Malicious Little Mystery Stories.* New York, Taplinger, 1981.

Editor, with Martin H. Greenberg and Charles G. Waugh, *Science Fiction Shorts* series (for children; includes *After the End, Thinking Machines, Travels Through Time, Wild Inventions, Mad Scientists, Mutants, Tomorrow's TV, Earth Invaded, Bug Awful, Children of the Future, The Immortals, Time Warps*). Milwaukee, Raintree, 12 vols., 1981-84.

Editor, *Fantastic Creatures.* New York, Watts, 1981.

Editor, with Charles G. Waugh and Martin H. Greenberg, *The Best Science Fiction [Fantasy, Horror and Supernatural] of the 19th Century.* New York, Beaufort, 3 vols., 1981-83; *Science Fiction*, London, Gollancz, 1983; *Fantasy* and *Horror and Supernatural*, London, Robson, 2 vols., 1985.

Editor, *Asimov's Marvels of Science Fiction.* London, Hale, 1981.

Editor, with Carol-Lynn Rössell Waugh and Martin H. Greenberg, *The Twelve Crimes of Christmas.* New York, Avon, 1981.

Editor, with Charles G. Waugh and Martin H. Greenberg, *The Seven Cardinal Virtues of Science Fiction.* New York, Fawcett, 1981.

Editor, with Martin H. Greenberg and Charles G. Waugh, *TV: 2000.* New York, Fawcett, 1982.

Editor, with Martin H. Greenberg and Charles G. Waugh, *Last Man on Earth.* New York, Fawcett, 1982.

Editor, with Charles G. Waugh and Martin H. Greenberg, *Tantalizing Locked-Room Mysteries.* New York, Walker, 1982.

Editor, with Martin H. Greenberg and Charles G. Waugh, *Space Mail 2.* New York, Fawcett, 1982.

Editor, with J. O. Jeppson, *Laughing Space: Funny Science*

Fiction. Boston, Houghton Mifflin, and London, Robson, 1982.

Editor, with Alice Laurance, *Speculations.* Boston, Houghton Mifflin, 1982.

Editor, with Charles G. Waugh and Martin H. Greenberg, *Science Fiction from A to Z: A Dictionary of the Great Themes of Science Fiction.* Boston, Houghton Mifflin, 1982.

Editor, with Martin H. Greenberg and Charles G. Waugh, *Flying Saucers.* New York, Fawcett, 1982.

Editor, with Martin H. Greenberg and Charles G. Waugh, *Dragon Tales.* New York, Fawcett, 1982.

Editor, *Asimov's Worlds of Science Fiction.* London, Hale, 1982.

Editor, with Martin H. Greenberg and Charles G. Waugh, *Hallucination Orbit: Psychology in Science Fiction.* New York, Farrar Straus, 1983.

Editor, with Martin H. Greenberg, *Magical Worlds of Fantasy* series (*Wizards, Witches*). New York, New American Library, 2 vols., 1983-84.

Editor, with Martin H. Greenberg and Charles G. Waugh, *Caught in the Organ Draft: Biology in Science Fiction.* New York, Farrar Straus, 1983.

Editor, *The Big Apple Mysteries.* New York, Avon, 1983.

Editor, with George R. R. Martin and Martin H. Greenberg, *The Science Fiction Weight-Loss Book.* New York, Crown, 1983.

Editor, with Martin H. Greenberg and Charles G. Waugh, *Starships.* New York, Ballantine, 1983.

Editor, *Asimov's Wonders of the World.* London, Hale, 1983.

Editor, with George Zebrowski and Martin H. Greenberg, *Creations: The Quest for Origins in Story and Science.* New York, Crown, 1983; London, Harrap, 1984.

Editor, with Martin H. Greenberg and Charles G. Waugh, *Computer Crimes and Capers.* Chicago, Academy, 1983; London, Viking, 1985.

Editor, with Patricia S. Warrick and Martin H. Greenberg, *Machines That Think.* New York, Holt Rinehart, and London, Allen Lane, 1984.

Editor, with Terry Carr and Martin H. Greenberg, *100 Great Fantasy Short Short Stories.* New York, Doubleday, and London, Robson, 1984.

Editor, with Charles G. Waugh and Martin H. Greenberg, *The Best Science Fiction Firsts.* New York, Beaufort, 1984; London, Robson, 1985.

Editor, with others, *Murder on the Menu.* New York, Avon, 1984.

Editor, with Martin H. Greenberg and Charles G. Waugh, *Sherlock Holmes Through Time and Space.* New York, Bluejay, 1984.

Editor, *Living in the Future.* New York, Beaufort, 1984.

Editor, with Martin H. Greenberg, *Isaac Asimov's Wonderful World of Science Fiction 2: The Science Fictional Olympics.* New York, New American Library, 1984.

Editor, with Martin H. Greenberg and Charles G. Waugh, *Young Mutants* [*Extraterrestrials*] (for children). New York, Harper, 2 vols., 1984.

Editor, with Martin H. Greenberg, *Election Day 2084: Stories about the Politics of the Future.* Buffalo, Prometheus, 1984.

Editor, with Martin H. Greenberg and Charles G. Waugh, *Great Science Fiction Stories by the World's Great Scientists.* New York, Fine, 1985.

*

Bibliography: *Isaac Asimov: A Checklist of Works Published in the United States March 1939-May 1972* by Marjorie M.

Miller, Kent, Ohio, Kent State University Press, 1972; in *In Joy Still Felt*, 1980.

Manuscript Collection: Mugar Memorial Library, Boston University.

Critical Studies: *Asimov Analyzed* by Neil Goble, Baltimore, Mirage Press, 1972; *The Science Fiction of Isaac Asimov* by Joseph F. Patrouch, Jr., New York, Doubleday, 1974, London, Panther, 1976; *Isaac Asimov* edited by Joseph D. Olander and Martin H. Greenberg, New York, Taplinger, and Edinburgh, Harris, 1977; *Asimov: The Foundations of His Science Fiction* by George Edgar Slusser, San Bernardino, California, Borgo Press, 1980; *Isaac Asimov: The Foundations of Science Fiction* by James Gunn, New York and Oxford, Oxford University Press, 1982; *Isaac Asimov* by Jean Fielder and Jim Mele, New York Ungar, 1982.

*   *   *

The world's most prolific science writer, Isaac Asimov has written some of the best-known science fiction ever published. Avoiding action adventures, Asimov usually sets and solves puzzles to educate the reader in science and technology. If he lay claims to being an "artist," the conflict between his generally optimistic and detached tone and the plot lines and concepts of his fiction might be troubling. For a superior self-taught craftsman who has entertained millions over more than 40 years it may well be a key to his success.

Many Asimov short stories sacrifice everything for a gimmick, sometimes no more than a pun or surprise ending. Even clever gimmicks can get repetitious, as in three stories of technological societies so sophisticated that something taken for granted today must be rediscovered: writing in "Someday," mathematics in "The Feeling of Power," walking outdoors in "It's Such a Beautiful Day. " Sometimes the gimmick is memorable. "Franchise" extrapolates polling methods to a logical conclusion—computer elections with toss-ups decided by a scientifically chosen average citizen. "What If?" imagines time as fixed but fluid, with variant means producing the same end for newlyweds who indulge their curiosity about what might have happened had they not met as they did.

The best of his longer stories surmount their gimmicks, but there may be nagging doubts. "Profession" reduces trends in accelerated education to the absurd. While everyone else finds his niche through programming suited to his brain pattern, the protagonist discovers he, as a really creative individual, must educate himself. That an interstellar civilization depends on one world's ritual "Reading Day," "Education Day," and job-seeking "Olympics" is no more credible, of course, than the secret conspiracy of creative individuals. Equally objectionable is the conspiracy of silence in "The Dead Past," but its extrapolative source has a sharper satirical edge, connecting to grants for scientific research and the spectre of government control of curiosity. Lacking clearance for direct observation of ancient Carthage, a historian persuades a physicist to build his own time-viewer from classified data, a simple task for the scientist. Before the government can act, these well-meaning rebels make public a surveillance technique extending to the most recent past, completely eliminating privacy in the present. If the interests of science and public policy clash in that story, the interests of science and ethics are at odds in "The Ugly Little Boy. " If not Asimov's best, this is certainly his most emotional story, contrasting the imperative for scientific research with that drive's effect on individual human beings, especially a little Neanderthal boy snatched into the present, and the nurse who views with deadly seriousness her job of taking care of him.

Other human interest stories also stand out in Asimov's short fiction, like "Dreaming Is a Private Thing," with its impressionistic glimpses of a literal dream-industry from an entrepreneur's viewpoint. At first glance, "The Martian Way" is just another gimmick story. Dependent on water as reaction mass for their spaceships, Martian colonists find their way of life endangered by an "Earth-first" political movement threatening to cut off their supply. The answer is simple, for a Martian: get ice from the rings of Saturn. The novella transcends its gimmick, propagandizing for human progress, suggesting a new kind of civilization, and satirizing recurrent demagogic types in America.

If Asimov's best fiction comes from the 1950's, his most popular works stem from the previous decade. Written when he was barely 21, "Nightfall" may be the most popular short story in all of science fiction. It creaks with 1930's pulp clichés, including the stock characters peopling a distant planet. The premise is implausible, an "alien" race only experiencing darkness once every 2000 years. Still, "Nightfall" is a classic of science-fictional perspective and sense of wonder. The astronomical situation, though fundamentally unstable, is possible in theory. The panic resulting from darkness is a credible metaphor for civilization's periodic fall. The scientists' viewpoint poses a suggestive antidote, studying rather than worshipping the strange phenomena. Curiosity loses to fear, however, raising the same note of ambivalence toward science which provides an emotional undercurrent in other Asimov fictions.

The robot stories (begun in 1940) which overflow three volumes, *I, Robot, The Rest of the Robots,* and *The Bicentennial Man,* gave rise to the "Three Laws of Robotics," formulated with *Astounding* editor John W. Campbell, Jr. Asimov devised these control mechanisms to offset what he saw as a "Frankenstein complex" in science fiction. Repetitive puzzles, exploring limits and loopholes in the Three Laws, these stories more often trivialize than defuse the fear of technology that is their subtext. If some short works stand out, such as "Liar," "Reason," and "The Last Question," they are overshadowed by his first two novels featuring the Earth detective Lije Baley and his offworld robot partner, R. Daneel Olivaw, *The Caves of Steel* and *The Naked Sun.* They are set 3000 years in the future, when mankind has settled a few other star systems, but people on Earth have little to do with them. Examples of classic mystery form, they led Asimov to write other detective stories, of which those involving Wendell Urth are science fictional. Unlike them, however, the robot novels emblematize the necessity of man-machine cooperation for technological civilization on this planet as well as others.

A later series of six novels for children about David "Lucky" Starr concern a much earlier settling period. Mostly puzzle-stories set in the solar system as understood in the 1950's, they were reissued two decades later with disclaimers about their outmoded astronomical speculations. That same passion for accuracy informs his film-novelization, *Fantastic Voyage,* which scientifically rationalizes everything but the impossibility at the movie's core: a subminiaturized vehicle and five humans entering a scientist's bloodstream to remove a cerebral blood clot.

As a novelist, Asimov is most widely known for *The Foundation Trilogy.* Loosely based on historical parallels with the Roman Empire, these nine stories and novellas (1942-52) hypothesize a deterministic "psycho-history" that calls into question the free will of his anti-heroic protagonists. In a crumbling Galactic Empire, they try to keep the spirit of scientific inquiry alive throughout a Dark Age until civiliation can again be consolidated. Not the first to examine such an empire, Asimov's work was different: decision-making replaced blood-and-thunder action, and its empire—a compromise with editor Campbell's insistence on inferior aliens—was a civilization of humans only.

Three novels set in earlier stages of the Empire—*Pebble in the Sky, The Stars, Like Dust,* and *The Current of Space*—are significant for their portrait of a radioactive Earth reviled and neglected by her far-flung children, but less rewarding than much of Asimov's work. Loosely connected to the same future history, *The End of Eternity* echoes 20th century dystopias in his closest approach to a conventional love story. In it, 70 thousand centuries of Earth's history are stabilized through time travel by the organization, Eternity. Its overthrow brings about a temporal universe in which the Galactic Empire can come into being.

In a different vein, *The Gods Themselves* suggests an Asimov more serious about artistry and contemporary social relevance. At issue, in part, is an impending energy crisis temporarily solved by drawing energy from another universe. The major interest for Asimov-watchers is the para-universe itself, and his largely successful creation of an alien civiliation and consciousness. Unfortunately, the alien viewpoint is abandoned in the conclusion, the energy crisis being shifted away from their cosmos to still another para-universe in a feat of auctorial sleight-of-hand.

The only major advance in his fiction in 15 years was sacrificed, another decade later, to giving the public what it wants. Two very late sequels to his most popular series displayed few of his virtues as a writer and all of his weaknesses. Set on a world with optimal cooperation between man and machine, *The Robots of Dawn* mediates between its predecessors, in which one or the other was dominant, but it has little of their flair, innocence, or brevity. Tying together most of his novels, *Foundation's Edge* adds to the First and Second Foundations yet another communal force for good and/or stability, Gaia, and a suggestion that the robots of his other series play a significant role (unhinted at before) in galactic governance. Interminably talky and convoluted for no apparent reason other than bulk, written with a tin ear for dialogue and prose style, taking little account of the changes in his own world since his earlier books, both were instant best sellers, with loose ends available for futher sequels.

Asimov's latest novels add nothing of value to the canon of a writer who could well afford to rest on his previous accomplishments. Having brought into the field a low-key anti-melodramatic style, a love for playfully solving puzzles and problems, and a respectable air of scientific detachment, Asimov has written a body of work which is already one of the cornerstones of modern science fiction.

—David N. Samuelson

ASPRIN, Robert (Lynn). American. Born in St. Johns, Michigan, in 1946. Attended the University of Michigan, Ann Arbor, 1964-1965. Served in the United States Army, 1965-66. Married Anne Brett; one daughter and one son. Accounts clerk, 1966-70, payroll analyst, 1970-74, and cost accountant, 1974-78, University Microfilm, Ann Arbor. Since 1978, freelance writer. Recipient: *Locus* award, for editing, 1982. Agent: Kirby McCauley Ltd., 425 Park Avenue South, New York, New York 10016, U. S. A.

SCIENCE-FICTION PUBLICATIONS

Novels (series: Skeeve and Aahz)

The Cold Cash War. New York, St. Martin's Press, and London, New English Library, 1977.
Another Fine Myth (Skeeve and Aahz). Norfolk, Virginia, Donning, 1978.
The Bug Wars. New York, St. Martin's Press, 1979; London, New English Library, 1980.
Tambu. New York, Ace, 1979.
Mirror Friend, Mirror Foe, with George Takei. Chicago, Playboy Press, 1979.
Hit or Myth (Skeeve and Aahz). Norfolk, Virginia, Donning, 1983.
Myth-ing Persons (Skeeve and Aahz), with Kay Reynolds. Norfolk, Virginia, Donning, 1984.

OTHER PUBLICATIONS

Other

Myth Conceptions. Norfolk, Virginia, Donning, 1979.

Editor, *Thieves' World.* New York, Ace, 1979; London, Penguin, 1984.
Editor, *Tales from the Vulgar Unicorn.* New York, Ace, 1980.
Editor, *Shadows of Sanctuary.* New York, Ace, 1981.
Editor, *Sanctuary* (omnibus). New York, Ace, 1982.
Editor, *Storm Season.* New York, Ace, 1982.
Editor, with Lynn Abbey, *The Face of Chaos.* New York, Ace, 1983.
Editor, with Lynn Abbey, *Wings of Omen.* New York, Ace, 1984.
Editor, with Lynn Abbey, *The Dead of Winter.* New York, Ace, 1985.

*   *   *

One of the more energetic and interesting writers to emerge since the late 1970's, Robert Asprin compiled a most impressive record for productivity in his early years. His first book, *The Cold Cash War,* introduced themes present in most of his later works, and which can be traced, at least in part, to Asprin's pre-literary occupation. He had been a cost accountant for a large "high-tech" corporation, and was thoroughly familiar with corporate procedures and the problems of management and personal rivalries within the corporate environment.

In *The Cold Cash War,* Asprin posits growing impatience and dissatisfaction on the part of large corporations with governmental mandates and unresponsiveness. In this situation, the corporations form private armies; when the government, through its "official" army, tries to suppress this odd rebellion, the corporations triumph as a result of possessing superior technology and more effective means of troop-motivation. The book is somewhat limited in characterization and plot, but shows excellent powers of technological and sociological extrapolation, at least in the near-future range.

The Bug Wars, Asprin's second science-fiction novel (a fantasy novel of very different nature intervened), continued the military theme, and is a worthy experiment, but unfortunately fails seriously. Asprin portrays an interplanetary struggle between a race of highly advanced, highly militaristic, intelligent reptiles and a coalition of huge insects. The narration is from the viewpoint of the reptiles, and it is uncertain to both the reptiles and the reader whether the insects are truly intelligent or not. A background rationale involves a mysterious elder race which had been instrumental in the spread of the insects through space. There is also passing mention of small warm-blooded animals, the reader being free to speculate as to whether these are pre-human beings, true humans of a degraded culture, or simply warm-blooded animals. A novel told completely from the viewpoint of a reptilian alien and involving no identifiable human characters was a most ambitious undertaking. The result, unfortunately, was a thoroughly one-dimensional book devoted almost entirely to the military details of battle; without characters suitable for reader empathy or identification, the volume makes poor reading. It is further marred by numerous minor solecisms and clichés. Asprin has suffered from poor editing.

Tambu shows marked improvement. It is the story of a band of professional pirate-hunters, laid against the background of a future interstellar trading culture. The structure of the book is unnecessarily cluttered with excerpts from a supposed interview at the end of Tambu's career, between which Asprin intersperses major incidents in his life. But the story-telling is brisk, the characterization indicates considerable progress, and a feel is achieved, at least sporadically, that is reminiscent of the old *Planet Stories* or E. E. Smith space operas.

Asprin's collaborative novel, *Mirror Friend, Mirror Foe,* was written with George Takei, the actor best known for his continuing role in the *Star Trek* series. In this novel, against a background of intercorporate espionage and cold-war, the authors place a corporate spy within a robot-manufacturing concern. The spy's heritage derives from the Japanese *ninja;* this, presumably, is Takei's contribution while Asprin's is the corporate situation. From a promising start, the book unfortunately degenerates into cliché as the robots, escaping from their normal conditioning, go lurching and clanking about a planet murdering every human being they encounter.

Despite his promising start as a science fiction writer, Asprin achieved far greater success in the allied field of fantasy, and by the mid-1980's had largely abandoned science fiction. His fantasy novel *Myth Conception* initiated a series of slapstick adventures in-and-out of an Arabian Nights universe of *jinni,* homunculi, spells, dragons, and gorgeous women. Within the familiar realm of published fantasy, Asprin's *Myth* series (all the books are pun-named) bears comparison to the works of L. Sprague de Camp. Asprin himself claims inspiration in the Bing Crosby/Bob Hope/Dorothy Lamour "Road" films of the 1940's.

Even more successful than the *Myth* books is Asprin's series of *Thieves' World* anthologies. The concept is essentially that of a vaguely Robert E. Howard-type barbarian culture, against which any number of stories can be laid by any number of authors. The anthologies have proved so successful that an entire mini-industry has sprung up around them, with authors using the Thieves' World setting for novels of their own, and with adaptations into comic books, role-playing games, video games, and the prospect of further, varied merchandising and adaptations.

—Richard A. Lupoff

ATKINS, John (Alfred). British. Born in Carshalton, Surrey, 26 May 1916. Educated at Bristol University, B. A. (honours) in history 1938. Served in the Royal Artillery, 1944-46. Married Dorothy J. Grey in 1940; two daughters. Interviewer, Mass Observation, London, 1939-41; Literary Editor, *Tribune,* 1942-

44; District Organiser, Workers' Educational Association, Bristol, 1948-51; teacher, Ministry of Education, Sudan, 1951-55 and 1958-64; Head of the Department of English, Higher Teacher Training Institute, Omdurman, Sudan, 1965-68; Senior Lecturer in English, University of Benghazi, Libya, 1968-70; Docent in English Literature, University of Lodz, Poland, 1970-76. Recipient: Arts Council Award, 1970. Address: Braeside Cottage, Mill Lane, Birch Green, Colchester CO2 0NG, Essex, England.

SCIENCE-FICTION PUBLICATIONS

Novel

Tomorrow Revealed. London, Spearman, 1955; New York, Roy, 1956.

Uncollected Short Stories

"The Theft of the Sun," in *English Story 4,* edited by Woodrow Wyatt. London, Collins, 1943.
"The Light of the World," in *English Story 5,* edited by Woodrow Wyatt. London, Collins, 1944.
"Climbing the Princess," in *English Story 9,* edited by Woodrow Wyatt. London, Collins, 1949.

OTHER PUBLICATIONS

Novels

Cat on Hot Bricks. London, Macdonald, 1950.
Rain and the River. London, Putnam, 1954.
A Land Fit for 'Eros, with J. B. Pick. London, Arco, 1957.

Short Story

The Diary of William Carpenter. London, Favil Press, 1943.

Verse

Experience of England. London, Favil Press, 1943.

Other

The Distribution of Fish. London, Fabian Society, 1941.
Walter de la Mare: An Exploration. London, Temple, 1947.
The Art of Ernest Hemingway: His Work and His Personality. London, Nevill, 1952; New York, Roy, 1954.
George Orwell: A Literary Study. London, Calder, 1954; New York, Ungar, 1955; revised edition, London, Calder and Boyars, 1971.
Arthur Koestler. London, Spearman, and New York, Roy, 1956.
Aldous Huxley: A Literary Study. London, Calder, and New York, Roy, 1956; revised edition, London, Calder and Boyars, 1967; New York, Orion Press, 1968.
Graham Greene. London, Calder, and New York, Roy, 1957; revised edition, London, Calder and Boyars, 1966; New York, Humanities Press, 1967.
Sex in Literature:
  1. *The Erotic Impulse in Literature.* London, Calder and Boyars, 1970; New York, Grove Press, 1972.
  2. *The Classical Experience of the Sexual Impulse.* London, Calder and Boyars, 1973.
  3. *The Medieval Experience.* London, Calder, 1978.

  4. *High Noon: The Seventeenth and Eighteenth Centuries.* London, Calder, and New York, Riverrun Press, 1982.
Six Novelists Look at Society: An Enquiry into the Social Views of Elizabeth Bowen, L. P. Hartley, Rosamond Lehmann, Christopher Isherwood, Nancy Mitford, C. P. Snow. London, Calder, and Dallas, Riverrun Texas, 1977.
J. B. Priestley, The Last of the Sages. London, Calder, and New York, Riverrun Press, 1981.
The British Spy Novel. London, Calder, and New York, Riverrun Press, 1984.

*   *   *

John Atkins's *Tomorrow Revealed* is cast some thousands of years in the future. When most people are living a mindless existence, the son of a star-gazer, who has been taught to read and write by his father, writes a history of the earth and the planets visited by earthlings, the facts culled from such authors was Wells, Graves, Orwell, C. S. Lewis, Bradbury, Kuttner, Heinlein, van Vogt, and others. The novel is cast in the form of historical narrative, and the narrator is responsible for much unconscious humor as he attempts to fabricate a plausible history of mankind incorporating the various sources he uses. Much of the delight of this novel for the reader conversant with the major works of speculative fiction derives from his recognition of the sources, his knowledge of contemporary history, and the often disastrous conclusions drawn by the future historian, who is often guilty of distorting facts to fit his theory. The basic orientation of Atkins's book is theological, though it is far from doctrinaire theology. At the conclusion of his history, the narrator is convinced that history "is nothing unless it is an adjunct of theology. " He concludes from his fascinating reading of the "sources" that there is a theological significance to human destiny. As he says, "I am convinced of a purpose. "

Atkins is very articulate and well-versed in speculative fiction; he has written a book which is marvellous entertainment. There is a great deal of humor in this book, an element all too often absent from speculative fiction. Its basic weakness is that the entire novel is narrated; there is not one dramatized scene, or any character development or interaction—simply the dispassionate voice of the historian.

—Joseph A. Quinn

AUBREY, Frank. See **ASH, Fenton.**

AVERY, Richard. See **COOPER, Edmund.**

AYRE, Thornton. See **FEARN, John Russell.**

BAHL, Franklin. See **PHILLIPS, Rog.**

BAIN, Ted. See **TUBB, E. C.**

BALL, Brian N(eville). Also writes as B. N. Ball; Brian Kinsey Jones. British. Born in Cheshire, 19 June 1932. Educated at Chester College, 1953-55; London University, B. A. 1960; Sheffield University, M. A. 1968. Served in the British Army, 1950-52. Married Margaret Snead in 1942; two daughters. Since 1956, staff member, then Senior Lecturer in English, Doncaster College of Education. Visiting Professor, University of British Columbia, Vancouver. Chairman, Doncaster Prose and Poetry Society, 1968-70. Address: c/o William Heinemann Ltd., 10 Upper Grosvenor Street, London W1X 9PA, England.

SCIENCE-FICTION PUBLICATIONS

Novels (series: Frames; Keegan; Witchfinder)

Sundog. London, Dobson, 1965; New York, Avon, 1969.
Trilogy:
   Timepiece. London, Dobson, 1968; New York, Ballantine, 1970.
   Timepivot. New York, Ballantine, 1970.
   Timepit . London, Dobson, 1971.
Lesson for the Damned. London, New English Library, 1971.
Night of the Robots. London, Sidgwick and Jackson, 1972; as *The Regiments of Night*, New York, DAW, 1972.
Devil's Peak. London, New English Library, 1972.
The Probability Man (Frames). New York, DAW, 1972; London, Sidgwick and Jackson, 1973.
Planet Probability (Frames). New York, DAW, 1973; London, Sidgwick and Jackson, 1974.
Singularity Station. New York, DAW, 1973; London, Sidgwick and Jackson, 1974.
The Venomous Serpent. London, New English Library, 1974; as *The Night Creature*, New York, Fawcett, 1974.
The Space Guardians. London, Dobson, and Mattituck, New York, Amereon, 1975.
Keegan: The No-Option Contract. London, Barker, 1975.
Keegan: The One-Way Deal. London, Barker, 1976.
Witchfinder: The Mark of the Beast. London, Mayflower, 1976.
Witchfinder: The Evil at Monteine. London, Mayflower, 1977.

Uncollected Short Stories

"The Excursion," in *Science Fantasy* (Bournemouth), February 1962.
"The Pioneer," in *New Worlds* (London), February 1962.
"The Postlewaite Effect," in *New Worlds* (London), November 1963.
"Escape Velocity," in *Tales of Science Fiction*, edited by Ball. London, Hamish Hamilton, 1964.
"The Fauntleroy Syndrome," in *Vision of Tomorrow* (Newcastle upon Tyne), September 1970.
"The Call of the Grave," in *Monster Tales*, edited by Roger Elwood. Chicago, Rand McNally, 1973.
"The Warlord of Kul Satu," in *Nameless Places*, edited by Gerald W. Page. Sauk City, Wisconsin, Arkham House, 1975.

OTHER PUBLICATIONS

Novels

Lay Down Your Wife for Another (as Brian Kinsey Jones). London, New English Library, 1971.
Death of a Low Handicap Man. London, Barker, 1974; New York, Walker, 1984.
Montenegrin Gold. London, Barker, 1974; New York, Walker, 1984.

Other (for children) as B. N. Ball

Mr. Tofat's Term. Edinburgh, McDougall, 1964.
Paris Adventures. Edinburgh, McDougall, 1967.
Princess Priscilla. London, Abelard Schuman, 1975.
Jackson's Friend [*House, Holiday*]. London, Hamish Hamilton, 3 vols., 1975-77.
Jackson and the Magpies. London, Hamish Hamilton, 1978.
The Witch in Our Attic. London, BBC, 1979.
Young Person's Guide to UFOs: A UFO Spotters' Guide. London, Dragon, 1979.
Dennis and the Flying Saucer. London, Heinemann, 1980.
The Baker Street Boys. London, BBC-Knight, 1983.
The Starbuggy. London, Heinemann, 1983.
The Doomship of Drax. London, Heinemann, 1985.

Other

Basic Linguistics for Secondary Schools. London, Methuen, 3 vols., 1966-67.

Editor, *Tales of Science Fiction*. London, Hamish Hamilton, 1964.

*   *   *

All of Brian N. Ball's action-packed science fiction novels depict humans and humanoids toying with their universe, manipulating time and space, for entertainment, adventure, and intellectual stimulation. In so doing they stumble upon intriguing puzzles that frequently involve an encounter with a thoroughly alien extraterrestrial presence. At times they find themselves manipulated and toyed with in turn, themselves the puzzle that another intelligence seeks to fathom. Ball's central characters range from spacepilots to world-scale movie directors but are almost always outsiders, adventurers, men who intentionally or instinctually break the normal patterns and thereby initiate a chain of events that leads to chaos, discovery, and metamorphosis. His heroes face physical, emotional, and intellectual terrors, but prove flexible enough to adapt and survive, and outwit computers, robots, monsters, and aliens. Usually an attractive, versatile woman adds her intelligence, ingenuity, or intuition to their cause, and ends up providing them a motive to endure.

In Ball's works stasis debilitates and perverts, while flux, no matter how terrifying, stimulates and challenges. Man achieves his destiny when forced to defend his ego, reassess his identity, adapt to new circumstances, and act quickly, decisively, and unexpectedly. He is at his weakest when he yields to hysteria, when he fails to react humanely to the plight of others, when fear overrules logic; but he is at his best when he can laugh at his own absurdity, accept his limitations and vulnerability, face up to his mistakes, and yet plunge back into the fray and pit his wits against the odds—hopeless though they may seem.

In depicting the unknown terrors that men must cope with,

Ball conjures up frightful, nightmare images: a nervous system turned inside out, the human "Patient" reduced to an unutterably distorted grotesque shambles (*Sundog*); a mound of flesh 200 feet high, an amalgam of misshapen parts and personalities, whose mouths gape open from knees and armpits, toes and earlobes (*Timepivot*); a doomsday army of 1000-year-old black robots, programmed to annihilate opponents long dead (*Night of the Robots*); the nightmare products of cell fusion—human intelligence trapped in the monstrous—a plot director transformed into a ravenous, writhing snake, greedy for live flesh, and giants that read their fate in the entrails of their victims (*The Probability Man*); and alien probability zones that send intruders down the evolutionary scale to become apes or tigers, beetles or dinosaurs, their humanity submerged in the bestial (*Planet Probability*). Yet even amid such horrors he infuses humor: a spacepilot blessed with a glowing halo, a devilish galactic prankster suddenly endowed with horns and tail, a strutting dandy turned ape, a cranky archeologist beset by inquisitive tourists, nude Valkyries on flying tigers, a pompous robot named Horace, and an 18th-century soldier swearing antique oaths amid 30th-century hells.

In *Sundog* an alien force field has turned man back on himself, causing him to set up a world of rigid regulations where dreams are controlled and psyches probed, until one man learns to set free his inner "Watcher," and thereby destroy past barriers—both human and alien. In *Timepivot* the hero must decipher the riddles of time and face its pivotal point and the alien that guards it to rid mankind of one form of tyranny. *Night of the Robots* records the accidental discovery of an ancient fortress whose computers, while awaiting final orders to launch an attack, have evolved into a menace that only the courage of humans past and humans present can defuse. The "Probability" series focuses on "the probability man," Spingarn, creator of world-staged dramas, historical recreations played out with whole populations from a bored, jaded, and overcrowded cosmos. By programming himself into all of the dramas and by joining forces with an unpredictable alien force to experiment with a Genekey on the pre-human planet of Taliskar, Spingarn dooms thousands to frightening metamorphosis, including, ultimately, himself. The series traces the bizarre and macabre adventures and transformations produced by an inhuman questing intelligence in search of its origins and the human machinations that ultimately satisfy it.

In sum, Ball creates fantasy and horror as he explores man's psyche, his potential for good and evil, for love and hate, for loyalty and betrayal. His aliens are beyond human comprehension, and can be contacted only by a special few, and then only with great discretion; his humans are an amalgam of man throughout the ages—Renaissance swashbuckler and 19th-century dandy, modern fighter pilot and mythic hero.

—Gina Macdonald

BALLARD, J(ames) G(raham). British. Born in Shanghai, China, 15 November 1930. Educated at Leys School, Cambridge; King's College, Cambridge. Served in the Royal Air Force. Married Helen Mary Matthews in 1953 (died, 1964); three children. Recipient: James Tait Black Memorial Prize, 1985. Agent: Margaret Hanbury, 27 Walcot Square, London SE11 4UB. Address: 36 Charlton Road, Shepperton, Middlesex TW17 8AT, England.

SCIENCE-FICTION PUBLICATIONS

Novels

The Wind from Nowhere. New York, Berkley, 1962; London, Penguin, 1967.
The Drowned World. New York, Berkley, 1962; London, Gollancz, 1963.
The Burning World. New York, Berkley, 1964; revised edition, as *The Drought*, London, Cape, 1965.
The Crystal World. London, Cape, and New York, Farrar Straus, 1966.
Crash. London, Cape, and New York, Farrar Straus, 1973.
Concrete Island. London, Cape, and New York, Farrar Straus, 1974.
High-Rise. London, Cape, 1975; New York, Holt Rinehart, 1977.
The Unlimited Dream Company. London, Cape, and New York, Holt Rinehart, 1979.
Hello America. London, Cape, 1981.

Short Stories

The Voices of Time and Other Stories. New York, Berkley, 1962.
Billenium and Other Stories. New York, Berkley, 1962.
The Four-Dimensional Nightmare. London, Gollancz, 1963.
Passport to Eternity and Other Stories. New York, Berkley, 1963.
Terminal Beach. London, Gollancz, 1964; abridged edition, New York, Berkely, 1964.
The Impossible Man and Other Stories . New York, Berkley, 1966.
The Disaster Area. London, Cape, 1967.
The Day of Forever. London, Panther, 1967.
The Overloaded Man. London, Panther, 1967.
Why I Want to Fuck Ronald Reagan. Brighton, Unicorn Bookshop, 1968.
The Atrocity Exhibition. London, Cape, 1970; as *Love and Napalm: Export USA,* New York, Grove Press, 1972.
Chronopolis and Other Stories. New York, Putnam, 1971.
Vermilion Sands. New York, Berkley, 1971; London; Cape, 1973.
Low-Flying Aircraft and Other Stories. London, Cape, 1976.
The Best of J. G. Ballard. London, Futura, 1977.
The Best Short Stories of J. G. Ballard. New York, Holt Rinehart, 1978.
The Venus Hunters. London, Panther, 1980.
Myths of the Near Future. London, Cape, 1982.

OTHER PUBLICATIONS

Novels

Empire of the Sun. London, Gollancz, and New York, Simon and Schuster, 1984.

Other

"Some Words about *Crash* " in *Foundation 9* (London), November 1975.

*   *   *

Bibliography: *J. G. Ballard: A Primary and Secondary Bibliography* by David Pringle, Boston, Hall, 1984.

Critical Studies: *J. G. Ballard: The First Twenty Years* edited by James Goddard and David Pringle, Hayes, Middlesex, Bran's Head, 1976; *Re Search: J. G. Ballard* edited by Vale, San Francisco, Re Search, 1983.

* * *

Of all the British writers of the "New Wave," J. G. Ballard is unquestionably the most original. Though nourished by references to the masterpieces of literature (from Homer and the Bible through Shakespeare to Coleridge and Melville) and of the arts (from Bosch to Dali and Leonor Fini), his style is as distinctive as a signature: the abrupt openings which plunge the reader straight into the action, as if he were already acquainted with the circumstances – outlandish though they may be – and with the whereabouts and idiosyncrasies of the characters – even though they often border on aberration and mania; the painter's eye, which fixes things, landscapes and even living beings into striking pictures of geometrical precision as well as coruscating beauty; the rich comparisons, through which paragraphs, instead of being concluded, are prolonged by mysterious harmonies and correspondences far and wide into space and time.

But if Ballard's permanent approach is characteristic, his evolution is also conspicuous and coherent. His first stories still played with traditional SF hypotheses, such as the time paradox in "The Gentle Assassin," or warned of future exacerbation of present-day problems, such as unbridled urbanisation and overpopulation in "Build-Up" or "Billenium." Yet even in the first collections (*The Voices of Time*, *Billenium*, *Four-Dimensional Nightmare*), two dominant features of his later works emerge: fascination for objects, especially the products of technology – clocks in "Chronopolis," invading metal in "Mobile" – and interest in the deviating psyche – one story of 1962 is entitled "The Insane Ones."

In the short stories set in Vermilion Sands – a decadent seaside resort which, as the short-lived materialisation of wild dreams, may be called an "inner landscape" – fascination and insanity are indeed allied in the various heroines: an actress who continues her murderous career beyond death, a poetess who wants a young admirer to repeat the sacrifice of Corydon to the muse Melandra, a rich and beautiful widow who has her portrait sculpted in the clouds. Extraordinary creatures (flying rays, singing orchids) and artefacts (a psychotropic house, a metal sculpture that sings and grows, clothes that live and feel) reflect and amplify the inner and mutual conflicts of those glamorous lamias and their suicidal wooers, in a baroque symphony of art, love and death.

In the 1960's, Ballard was also writing a series of disaster novels, each dealing with one of the four elements, yet with striking correlations (for example, *The Drought* is paradoxically fraught with references to shipwrecks). Contrary to most treatments of the theme, these four books are not centred on the frightful destructiveness of the cataclysm but on its awesome beauty, not on the desperate resistance of courageous survivors but on the perverse desires, mad ambitions, and suicidal manias of aberrant personalities now free to fulfil fatal aspirations devoid of any rational motivation.

As if Ballard had exhausted the treasures of his poetic imagination by throwing them all into the last and most accomplished of those works, *The Crystal World* (in which a "time leak" causes matter to expand in space, turning plants, animals, and people into efflorescent masses of dazzling crystals), the 1970's show a sudden evolution towards bareness, both in his style – soberer descriptions, fewer far-flung

comparisons – and in his material – no more inordinate power and purposes in men, as in Hardoon the modern pharaoh, no more preternatural charm and exactingness in women, as in Leonora Chanel the modern Medea, no more remote deadliness and beauty in the scenes, as in the all-invading jungles, hurricane, sands, and gems previously described. Instead, commonplace characters (whose recurring names, Catherine, Helen, Maitland, Robert, suggest that they are projections of the author and of the women with whom he has love-hate relationships) live and die in the settings that present-day humanity has created for itself: the world of the automobile (*Crash!*), a landscape forcefully adapted to traffic (*Concrete Island*), gigantic apartment-buildings (*High Rise*). In thus passing from the natural catastrophies of tomorrow to the man-made cataclysms of today, Ballard claims he has not forsaken science fiction: in our environment, he sees "the fossils of the future," and reveals what is apocalyptic about it – coining the work "autogeddon" in parallel to the biblical "Armageddon," the cosmic battle at the end of time.

This second foursome is completed by a collection which seems to be a sketchbook for the three novels, and whose title significantly is *The Atrocity Exhibition*. Highly sensitive to the monstrosity of a way of life that we take for granted, Ballard throws it into a crude light by bringing together some of its apparently irrelevant aspects – political murder and sport in "The Assassination of J. F. Kennedy Considered as a Downhill Motor Race," promiscuous sex and traffic hazards in *Crash!* – or just by heaping up instances of its worst consequences – the victims of car-mania horribly maimed in mind as well as in body, perverse and obsessive sexual pursuits, ruthless conflicts raging among the inmates of vertical "concentration camps" or among the wretched "Robinsons" that survive in the ruins lapped against by the ocean of traffic. His descriptions of wounds as well as sexual organs—the two kinds of openings through the flesh are reached by the most exquisite pain and pleasure—are made even more unbearable by their cool precision, which may be ascribed to his medical studies; yet their recurrence points to a morbid fascination: Ballard takes part at least as much as his fellow-men in the worship of the new Moloch.

The meaning and the outcome of it all remain obscure: Ballard is fond of interpreting the most incongruous marks (of sperm as well as blood) in terms of mysterious alphabets, but the "writing on the wall" never finds its Daniel; we appear to be all carried away helplessly to some dark and terrible doom. The characters more or less willingly bungle their escapes; and, in the novel *Hello America* as well as in the collection *Low-Flying Aircraft* (especially in "The Ultimate City," and with the only exception of the story which gives its title to the book, where Dr. Gould's apparently meaningless actions turn out to aim at the protection of the mutants that may succeed the present forms of life), the interest is focused on those who madly attempt to resuscitate the most flamboyant aspects of the technology that has caused the collapse of this civilisation.

Ballard himself, as a writer, seems to be the prisoner of his system of thought: in his lastest collections, *The Venus Hunters* and *Myths of the Near Future*, he gives us only the small change of his great intuitions. Can there be any more science fiction writing when the horizon is blocked – to borrow one of the author's favourite images: as by a stranded whale – by the huge corpse of our decaying society? The way out, then, can only be upwards – not through space conquest, which Ballard pictures as eminently deadly for humanity in mind as well as in body, but through the fulfilment of the eternal yearning to fly. Such is the subject of his novel *The Unlimited Dream Company*, which blends ancient myths with his personal obsessions, and reconciles the through liberation of sex with the mystical aspiration to conquer death: a very rich and fascinating book, but is it still science fiction?

—George W. Barlow

BARCLAY, Bill. See **MOORCOCK, Michael.**

BARNARD, Marjorie Faith. See **ELDERSHAW, M. Barnard.**

BARNES, Arthur K(elvin). Also wrote as Dave Barnes; Kelvin Kent. American. Born in Bellingham, Washington, in 1911. Educated at the University of California, Los Angeles, B. A. (Phi Beta Kappa). Free-lance writer. *Died in 1969.*

SCIENCE-FICTION PUBLICATIONS

Short Stories (series: Gerry Carlisle)

Interplanetary Hunter. New York, Gnome Press, 1956.

Uncollected Short Stories (series: Gerry Carlisle)

"Lord of the Lightning," in *Wonder Stories* (New York), December 1931.
"Challenge of the Comet," in *Wonder Stories* (New York), February 1932.
"Guardians of the Void," in *Wonder Stories Quarterly* (New York), September 1932.
"The Hole Men of Mercury," in *Wonder Stories* (New York), December 1933.
"Emotion Solution," in *Wonder Stories* (New York), March 1936.
"The House That Walked" (as Dave Barnes), in *Astounding* (New York), September 1936.
"Prometheus," in *Amazing* (New York), February 1937.
"Green Hell" (Carlisle), in *Thrilling Wonder Stories* (New York), June 1937.
"The Dual World" (Carlisle), in *Thrilling Wonder Stories* (New York), June 1938.
"The Energy Eaters" (Carlisle; with Henry Kuttner), in *Thrilling Wonder Stories* (New York), October 1939.
"Day of the Titans," in *Thrilling Wonder Stories* (New York), February 1940.
"Waters of Wrath," in *Thrilling Wonder Stories* (New York), October 1940.
"Forgotton Future," in *Science Fiction* (Holyoke, Massachusetts), January 1941.
"The Little Man Who Wasn't There," in Thrilling Wonder Stories (New York), March 1941.
"Guinea Pig," in *Captain Future* (New York), Spring 1942.
"Fog over Venus," in *Thrilling Wonder Stories* (New York), Winter 1945.
"Grief of Bagdad," in *My Best Science Fiction Story,* edited by Leo Margulies and Oscar J. Friend. New York, Merlin Press, 1949.

Uncollected Short Stories as Kelvin Kent

"Roman Holiday" (with Henry Kuttner), in *Thrilling Wonder Stories* (New York), August 1939.
"Science Is Golden" (with Henry Kuttner), in *Thrilling Wonder Stories* (New York), April 1940.
"Knight Must Fall," in *Thrilling Wonder Stories* (New York), June 1940.
"The Greeks Had a War for It," in *Thrilling Wonder Stories* (New York), January 1941.
"De Wolfe of Wall Street," in *Thrilling Wonder Stories* (New York), February 1943.

OTHER PUBLICATIONS

Other

"It's a Science," in *Writer's Digest* (Cincinnati), May 1945.

*   *   *

Arthur K. Barnes is virtually unknown to the modern reader of science fiction; not a word of his considerable output in the field has seen print in a quarter of a century, and it has been more than 30 years since his last original story was published. To the reader of pulp "scientification" in the 1930's and 1940's, however—particularly to the reader of *Thrilling Wonder Stories*—Barnes was well known and popular, both for his own work and for his collaborations with Henry Kuttner. Nearly all of Barnes's fiction was either space opera or science fantasy. Although more or less solidly based on scientific knowledge of the period, his stories relied on farcical humor and rapid action for their effects. By today's standards they seem rather juvenile. Nevertheless, when viewed in historical perspective they are both interesting and entertaining.

The most popular of Barnes's space opera was a series about Gerry Carlisle, Tommy Strike, and the crew of *The Ark,* all of whom were employed by the "London Interplanetary Zoo" to trap and bring back alive nonintelligent alien life forms; the best of these noveletts were collected in Barnes's only book, *Interplanetary Hunter.* Much of his science fantasy involves time-travel into the past, and was co-authored with Henry Kuttner.

—Bill Pronzini

BARNES, Dave. See **BARNES, Arthur K.**

BARNES, Steven (Emory). American. Born in Los Angeles, California, 1 March 1952. Educated at Pepperdine University, Los Angeles, 1970-74. Tour guide, Columbia Broadcasting System, Hollywood, 1974-76; Manager, Audio-Visual and Multi-Media Department, Pepperdine University, 1978-80; Creative Consultant, Don Bluth Productions, 1980. Agent: Spectrum Literary Agency, 432 Park Avenue South, Suite 1205, New York, New York 10016. Address: c/o Ace Books, 200 Madison Avenue, New York, New York 10016, U. S. A.

SCIENCE-FICTION PUBLICATIONS

Novels

Dream Park, with Larry Niven. Huntington Woods, Michigan, Phantasia Press, 1981; London, Macdonald, 1983.
The Descent of Anansi, with Larry Niven. New York, Tor, 1982.
Streetlethal. New York, Ace, 1983.

Uncollected Short Stories

"Moonglow," in *Vampires, Werewolves, and Other Monsters*, edited by Roger Elwood. New York, Curtis, 1974.
"Impact," in *Cassandra Rising*, edited by Alice Laurance. New York, Doubleday, 1978.
"The Locusts," with Larry Niven, in *The 1980 Annual World's Best SF*, edited by Donald A. Wollheim. New York, DAW, 1980.
" . . . But Fear Itself," in *The Magic May Return*, edited by Larry Niven. New York, Ace, 1981.

OTHER PUBLICATIONS

Other

Ki: How to Generate the Dragon Spirit. N. p., Sen-do, 1976.

Animated cartoon: *The Secret of NIMH*, 1982.

* * *

Steven Barnes presents an unusual critical challenge at this early stage of his career because it is difficult to distinguish his own traits from those of his mentor and collaborator Larry Niven. Two of Barnes's published novels, *Dream Park* and *The Descent of Anansi*, were written with Niven, as were two of four shorter works. *Streetlethal* was a solo effort.

Like Niven, Barnes is a California writer. He was born, raised, and educated in Los Angeles and still resides there. This environmental influence shows itself even in small matters— rain has fallen but once in all his fiction and merely to provide artistically reflective wet surfaces. More significantly, a near-future earthquake of apocalyptic proportions shaped the worlds of *Dream Park* and *Streetlethal*. Both books feature ghastly descriptions of ruined Los Angeles, and that chapter of *Dream Park* appeared separately as "Retrospectives. "

The California Dream is a nightmare in the gory revenge thriller *Streetlethal*. The rotten heart of its Los Angeles is the Maze, a slum swarming with criminals, whores, addicts, and leprous VD victims. But beneath the rubble burrow the Scavengers, an ingeniously conceived community struggling to light candles of hope in this infernal darkness.

On the other hand, *Dream Park*'s nightmares are strictly fright-show entertainments. This glossy mystery set in a high-tech amusement complex modeled on Disneyland emphasizes the casual fun-and-sun aspects of California life. The park is an electronically equipped arena for acting out role-playing fantasies. It incorporates the mystiques of gaming, the Society for Creative Anachronism, and sf fandom. Niven's quick, slangy cleverness predominates here, with in-group jokes, crossplugs, and personal references.

But the cinematic flavor of these stories may be Barnes's own contribution. He studied communications in college, has worked for film studios, and writes screenplays. *Streetlethal*, which Barnes is currently trying to turn into a film, has a

definite Hollywood taste. Its visuals recall recent futuristic urban films such as *Escape from New York* and *The Enforcer* while its plot resembles a 1930's gangster movie. (Behind those 21st-century brown faces we glimpse the familiar wronged convict, golden-hearted hooker, and slimy ganglord.)

Yet empathy, not artifice, remains the optimum means of communication, for Barnes is a mystic as well as a technophile. "The Locusts" begins as a straightforward colonial adventure but its resolution owes more to magic then genetics. *The Descent of Anansi* offers the shiny hardware and tense action expected of a space thriller but also presents a romantic triangle and draws its imagery from a West African spider myth. His high fantasy " . . . But Fear Itself" makes especially imaginative use of African materials.

An accomplished martial artist, Barnes has made holistic Oriental ideals part of himself and his work. He advocates self-awareness and self-sharing and celebrates the spiritual potential of erotic love. Sensitivity triumphs in the grimmest settings, just as the lotus blooms in mud. As this young writer says in his own voice: "Humanity is a fragile thing, and the capacity to give without immediate gain is not the norm, or an obligation, but rather a recognition of the common divinity of man. "

—Sandra Miesel

———

BARNWELL, William (Curtis). American. Born in Macon, Georgia, 11 February 1943. Educated at Florence State College, Florence, Alabama, B. A. 1966; University of Florida, Gainesville, Ph. D. 1972. Married Jo Ann Weeks in 1966; one daughter and one son. Assistant Professor of English, University of South Carolina, Columbia, 1971-77. Since 1977, Writer-in-Residence, Columbia College, South Carolina. Agent: Curtis Brown Ltd., 575 Madison Avenue, New York, New York 10022, U. S. A.

SCIENCE-FICTION PUBLICATIONS

Novels

The Blessing Papers. New York, Pocket Books, 1980; Gerrards Cross, Buckinghamshire, Smythe, 1981.
Imram. New York, Pocket Books, 1981.

OTHER PUBLICATIONS

Other

Writing for a Reason. Boston, Houghton Mifflin, 1983.

* * *

William Barnwell's entire published work consists of a single trilogy of after-the-disaster novels published originally in 1980 and 1981, consisting of *The Blessing Papers, Imram,* and *The Sigma Curve*. They are set in Eire (renamed Imram) in a society that is almost feudalistic, a society in turmoil because of a number of political and religious schisms. Turly is a young boy with an unknown past who finds himself growing up within a passive group known as The Circle. His life is disrupted by a raid by the forces of Hastings, an ambitious man who wants to establish hegemony over the entire island. Hastings believes that Turly holds the key to the Blessing Papers, which may hold the key to power.

Naturally there are others equally interested in whatever special knowledge Turly might possess, chief among them the Order of Zeno, a cloistered group that is not averse to the use of murder and torture. There are weapons and powers and the trappings of fantasy here in plenty. He evades his enemies all through the first volume, then falls into company with a poet. He and his companion fall into the clutches of the Ennis in the second volume, a primitive people who initiate their prisoners into their tribe after a series of bizarre rites.

The Ennis are opposed by the Gort, a northern people who have an understanding with the evil Order of Zeno. There is also a spy among the Ennis reporting on the activities of Turly. The Blessing Papers, it seems, contain the seeds of a prophecy of the rise of a new civilization, and their possessor may have the ability to shape that civilization. Locked in Turly's brain may be the key to their location.

In the concluding volume, Turly has sworn never to make use of the Blessing Papers, nor to make their existence known to anyone else. But even though he has independently helped to bring together a coalition of tribes for mutual support and protection, there is trouble in his world, and his old enemies are restlessly prowling outside the campfire. Ultimately he must face up to the charge he has been given and deal personally with the papers and the powers they possess.

Although ostensibly science fiction, much of this trilogy is written in the style and with many of the plot devices of a heroic fantasy. The Papers might well be the Holy Grail or some other sacred or magical object, and the powers of evil are truly that, untainted by any trace of kindness or humanity. That simplistic attitude dulls some of the impact of the trilogy, but as pure adventure, it demonstrated that Barnwell was a talented writer.

—Don D'Ammassa

BARRETT, Neal, Jr. American. Formerly worked in public relations; now a full-time writer. Lives in Austin, Texas. Address: c/o DAW Books, 1633 Broadway, New York, New York 10019, U. S. A.

SCIENCE-FICTION PUBLICATIONS

Novels (series: Aldair)

Kelwin. New York, Lancer, 1970.
The Gates of Time. New York, Ace, 1970.
The Leaves of Time. New York, Lancer, 1971.
Highwood. New York, Ace, 1972.
Stress Pattern. New York, DAW, 1974.
Aldair in Albion. New York, DAW, 1976.
Aldair, Master of Ships. New York, DAW, 1977.
Aldair, Across the Misty Sea. New York, DAW, 1980.
Aldair: The Legion of Beasts. New York, DAW, 1982.
The Karma Corps. New York, DAW, 1984.

Uncollected Short Stories

"Made in Archerius," in Amazing (New York), August 1960.
"To Tell the Truth," in Galaxy (New York), August 1960.
"The Stentorii Luggage," in Galaxy (New York), October 1960.
"The Graybes of Raath," in Galaxy (New York), June 1961.
"The Game," in Amazing (New York), July 1963.
"I Was a Spider for the SBI," in Fantastic (New York), November 1963.
"To Plant a Seed," in Amazing (New York), December 1963.
"In the Shadow of the Worm," in Amazing (New York), October 1964.
"Starpath," in If (New York), December 1966.
"By Civilized Standards," in If (New York), November 1969.
"The Grandfather Pelt," in If (New York), July 1970.
"Greyspun's Gift," in Worlds of Tomorrow (New York), Winter 1970.
"A Walk on Toy," in Fantasy and Science Fiction (New York), September 1971.
"Survival Course," in Galaxy (New York), January 1974.
"Happy New Year, Hal," in Amazing (New York), December 1974.
"Nightbeat," in Epoch, edited by Roger Elwood and Robert Silverberg. New York, Berkley, 1975.
"The Talking," in Lone Star Universe, edited by George W. Proctor and Steven Utley. Austin, Texas, Heidelberg, 1976.
"The Flying Stutzman," in Fantasy and Science Fiction (New York), July 1978.
"Hero," in Fantasy and Science Fiction (New York), September 1979.
"A Day at the Fair," in The Best from Fantasy and Science Fiction 24, edited by Edward L. Ferman. New York, Doubleday, 1982.

*   *   *

Neal Barrett, Jr., was for many years a welcome but infrequent contributor to professional science-fiction magazines, and an occasional novelist, but it was not until the late 1970's that he seemed to attract much serious attention. His earliest published novel, Kelwin, employed the familiar theme of barbaric civilization rebuilding itself after the fall of our own society in a devastating war. Kelwin is a wandering adventurer whose destiny is to affect the unfolding of a possible new conflict in that setting. Kelwin is a pure adventure story, extremely well told.

The Leaves of Time was more ambitious. The setting is a parallel version of our own world, where history has taken a rather different course. To this standard setting, Barrett adds a second plot element, the fugitive shapechanging alien, in this case infiltrated from another time line. The protagonists must discover a method of identifying and neutralizing the invader, without letting him return to his home timeline.

These two novels were so good that two other early works, both light adventure stories of little lasting substance, seemed markedly inferior in comparison. The Gates of Time is a galaxy spanning adventure story about mankind's fate in the face of conquest; Highwood is set on a world of giant forests. A pair of human observers discover a radical change in the behaviour patterns of the indigent sentient species and become caught up in the fate of the species. Barrett published no novels for two years, and his reappearance with Stress Pattern was the equivalent of the emergence of a new writer.

Stress Pattern is certainly one of the most unusual novels ever to appear in the genre. A space traveller becomes marooned on what is certainly the most peculiar planet in the universe. The natives recognize his presence, but seem utterly indifferent to him, preoccupied with bizarre activities of their own. Travel is accomplished by means of organic railways; a variety of monstrous creatures populate the countryside. The entire biosphere of the planet seems to be one intricate, integrated machine. Had this novel appeared under the byline of a more established writer, it would almost certainly have excited more comment than it did.

Barrett really hit his stride with the "Aldair" series, however, four novels dealing with Aldair, an adventurer on an Earth that has been deserted by humanity. Many of the animal species of the Earth were altered genetically so that a variety of intelligent humanoid species exist, each still displaying some of the attributes of its ancestry. Aldair himself is a pig, and among his companions are wolves and bears. The initial volume, *Aldair in Albion*, introduces the background and main characters, and follows Aldair as he wanders across Europe searching for his own destiny and clues to the fate of legendary Mankind.

The first and second volumes stand well independently. *Aldair, Master of Ships*, continues the search, now along the coastlines of the continents. For the most part, the adventure is equally well done in the third adventure, *Aldair, Across the Misty Sea*, but the cliffhanger ending mars its existence as an independent novel. Barrett summed up all the loose ends in the concluding adventure, *Aldair: The Legion of Beasts*, by transporting Aldair and his friends to an alien planet where malformed genetic freaks enslave a pacifistic remnant of the human race. Much of the charm of the previous volumes is lost with the change of setting, but as a whole this was one of the best written, most inventive series of its kind in many years.

Barrett's most recent novel, *The Karma Corps*, is an interesting but not entirely successful work. A shipload of colonists survives on an uncharted world, where their theocratic social structure finds itself in perpetual battle against an alien species that can teleport itself across short distances. A group of human teleports is revived from a kind of electronic storage and pressed into battle against the aliens, but inevitably control of the power they represent becomes a political issue.

Barrett's occasional piece of short fiction is usually of high quality as well. One of his earliest stories, "The Stentorii Luggage," is a nearly classic genre tale of shape-changing beasties inside an elaborate interspecies hotel. "The Grandfather Pelt" provides ironic justice to a criminal who steals the pelt of a revered ancestor on an alien world. A desperate man must outreason a single-minded computer when he finds himself the sole survivor of a disastrous accident in "Survival Course." A visiting alien is determined to find out just what it is that humans do that no other species can in "Greyspun's Gift," which also features some of Barrett's best realized characters. "The Flying Stutzman," which concerns a man who is doomed to eternal flights on commercial airplanes, is a very well-written, very disturbing fantasy.

—Don D'Ammassa

BARTON, Erle. See **FANTHORPE, R. Lionel.**

BARTON, Lee. See **FANTHORPE, R. Lionel.**

BASS, T. J. Pseudonym for Thomas J. Bassler. American.

Born in Clinton, Iowa, 7 July 1932. Educated at St. Ambrose College, Davenport, Iowa, B. A. 1955; University of Iowa, Iowa City, M. D. 1959. Married Gloria Napoli in 1960; three daughters and three sons. Deputy medical examiner, Los Angeles, 1961-64. Since 1964, in private practice as a pathologist. Since 1972, Editor, *American Medical Joggers Newsletter*. Address: 27558 Sunnyridge Road, Palos Verdes Peninsula, California 90274, U. S. A.

SCIENCE-FICTION PUBLICATIONS

Novels

Half Past Human. New York, Ballantine, 1971.
The Godwhale. New York. Ballantine, 1974; London, Eyre Methuen, 1975.

Uncollected Short Stories

"Star Seeder," in *If* (New York), September 1969.
"A Game of Biochess," in *If* (New York), February 1970.
"Song of Kaia," in *If* (New York), November 1970.
"Rorqual Maru," in *The 1973 Annual World's Best SF*, edited by Donald A. Wollheim and Arthur W. Saha. New York, DAW, 1973.

*   *   *

T. J. Bass's novels, *Half Past Human* and *The Godwhale*, give a vivid picture of a horrifying future society, of a world-wide Earth Society ("the big ES") that controls every detail of life in the planet-sized hive that Earth has become. Three trillion people, degenerate "Nebishes," live in warrens beneath the surface, every inch of which is devoted to crops. These shrunken souls live short and regimented lives, are processed at their deaths for the proteins that sustain their fellows, and even have puberty postponed until the CO—the Class One computer—decides they are ready for sexual maturity.

Yet these novels are not cautionary tales of the sort of Harry Harrison's *Make Room, Make Room*, although some have read them so: rather, their concerns are teleological, like C. S. Lewis's Perelandra Trilogy or Walter M. Miller's *A Canticle for Leibowitz*. Assuming a kind Providence and a personal God, these works ask, what is the end of man? While *Half Past Human* and *The Godwhale* do not directly address the question, they do show a Providence that cares about the fall of a sparrow—or a Nebish. If the hand of God has not been noticed in Bass's works, it is because the author shows God using unfamiliar instruments. In the Perelandra trilogy or in *A Canticle for Leibowitz* God works through human beings; here, His ambassadors are machines so intelligent that they have personalities. Not that God makes robots and sends them hurtling toward Earth: the machines in Bass's novels are the artifacts of earlier stages of human civilization, providentially appearing when Mankind has most need of them.

In *Half Past Human* we see the plight of those few remaining real humans who live outside, apart from ES; like animals, they are hunted for sport. But in their vigor and resilience lies more hope for the future than in the Nebishes, whose machines are crumbling around them. However, even the Nebishes are not negligible or less than human: some among them can survive when circumstances remove them from the womb of their society. The novel is the story of a new beginning on a new planet for the humans living outside and for the Nebishes adaptable enough to accept it.

Both novels show an impressive command of biological knowledge, and indeed sometimes the flow of jargon obscures rather than communicates. But the point may be that most people in the society are treated (and regard themselves) just as mechanically as the many robots that work for them. Still, knowledge is regarded as good, and machines are good when they serve rather than control. This point is strongly argued in *The Godwhale*, named for a huge plankton harvester. Like the huge automated spaceship that is the *deus et machina* of *Half Past Human*, the Godwhale is an artifact of a freer, more expansive past. Although these machines are so powerful that they are regarded as "cyberdeities," they are purposeless without free humans to direct them. In *The Godwhale* that direction comes partly from the chosen few, true humans who have adapted to life in the sea, and partly from a superman bred by Nebishes to command the harvester. "Miracles" occur at opportune times in both novels: the rescue of the outsiders in *Half Past Human*, and the regeneration of marine life in *The Godwhale*. Whereas the first shows the hope of a new society among the stars, the second gives promises of a regeneration of life on Earth.

Together, *Half Past Human* and *The Godwhale* are rewarding novels, rich both in characterization and in scientific detail, yet concerned with still larger matters. That *The Godwhale* offers a new proof of the existence of God shows just how large that concern is.

—Walter E. Meyers

BATCHELOR, John Calvin. American. Born in Bryn Mawr, Pennsylvania, 29 April 1948. Educated at Princeton University, New Jersey, A. B. 1970; University of Edinburgh Divinity School, 1973-74; Union Theological Seminary, New York, M.Div. 1976. Editor and book reviewer, *SoHo Weekly News*, New York, 1975-77; book reviewer, *Village Voice*, New York, 1977-80. Lives in New York City. Agent: Barney Karpfinger, 18 East 48th Street, Suite 1601, New York, New York 10017, U. S. A.

SCIENCE-FICTION PUBLICATIONS

Novels

The Further Adventures of Halley's Comet. New York, Congdon and Lattès, 1981; London, Panther, 1984.
The Birth of the People's Republic of Antarctica. New York, Doubleday, 1983; London, Panther, 1984.

OTHER PUBLICATIONS

Novel

American Falls. New York, Norton, 1985.

*

John Calvin Batchelor comments:
I first read science fiction when I was 11 years old, and the first adult novel I ever read was *Nineteen Eighty-Four*, Which I can remember thinking was much too sad. I have learned to say that I write anti-utopian fiction. That is too technical a term, however, and lacks the fun of saying sci-fi.

My life in New York is especially happy now because every night at midnight I can settle down to Channel 11 and another episode of *Star Trek*. Yes, I would like to be a starship captain, or, failing that, a planetary geologist.

*   *   *

Though often ignored by science-fiction readers and the body of organized "fandom," John Calvin Batchelor's *The Further Adventures of Halley's Comet* and *The Birth of the People's Republic of Antarctica* have received some extravagant praise from both general and sf reviewers. It is too early in Batchelor's career to assess definitively the weight and nature of his achievement, but his two big books are clearly works of greater substance, boldness, and durability than almost anything else that has appeared in sf or its borderlands in the 1980's.

Like Thomas Pynchon's gigantic and encyclopedic *Gravity's Rainbow*, *Halley's Comet* explores and satirizes the history of ideas in the West through a modern gothic tale told in a baroque and seemingly perverse style, against the grain of the accepted gothic *frisson* of shock and menace. The plot involves the abduction of a bunch of quixotic idealists by a family of fabulously powerful and capitalistic modern-day robber barons; the former are imprisoned in Craven Castle, while the latter pursue a machiavellian plan to extend their empire of property into space by means of secret technology and legalistic chicanery. This is all placed in historical perspective by the recurring visits of a trio of seemingly supernatural luminaries who are associated with Halley's Comet and seem to be the ever-returning Magi. The literary polarities of this book—zany comedy and Juvenalian invective—are seldom discoverable in the convention-ridden and stylistically lacklustre body of genre sf; however, the watered down mix of pyrotechnics should appeal to those who find Pynchon attractive but too inaccessible.

The Birth of the People's Republic of Antarctica begins similarly in a Pynchonesque mode, depicting a crew of down-and-out American draft dodgers in Sweden, together with an assortment of other eccentric, grandiose, and slightly comic characters. The tale gradually shapes itself into a new mode which can be described as post-heroic saga: larger-than-life tragic figures struggle with the hostile elements of storm wave, fire, and ice in a near-future world wherein civilization is collapsing and human nobility seems able to provide little hope of redemption amid ubiquitous evil and hardship. The protagonist-narrator's name, "Grim Fiddle," is a kind of rebus for the style and content of the book, uniting as it does concepts of severity and frivolity, though all transitions taking place through *People's Republic of Antarctica* are towards the increasingly severe: the book's "fiddle" concept is transformed eventually to one of the futility of struggle for survival or betterment. The entire book is a mythic life-story from the hero's mysterious conception and Christmas-time birth to his downfall, exile, and impending mysterious doom, while the key scenarios resemble elemental and societal designs for Hell: seas of fire and ice; societies falling into demagoguery and terror; a dark sea journey in which Grim Fiddle and his comrades drift to the barren Falklands and the northern fingers of the Antarctic, where human life is mean, violent, and easily corrupted.

Bruce Gillespie has remarked that *People's Republic of Antarctica* is spoiled by a "fluffed" ending in which the author "seems to lose control of the narrative." The criticism is well made, as the narrative fragments into a set of meditative pieces about the narrator's uncompleted story. More importantly still, the ending attempts to draw grand ethical conclusions which are insufficiently tied to the body of the tale (which itself is marred by passages of loaded and simplistic ethical-philosophical analysis). This fault also betrays *Halley's Comet:* in each case, a stylistic tour de force is ineptly tied to a sentimental and superficial philosophy in which naturalism, positivism, capitalism, and utilitarianism are the abstract bad guys. Batchelor's vision will need to take on some of the irony, ambivalence, and troubled complexity of Pynchon's before his books are a fitting substitute for those of his role-model. Meanwhile, though the books are flawed and ultimately disappointing, their sights are set mightily high and they contain some writing that falls only just short of magnificence.

—Russell Blackford

BATES, Harry (Hiram Gilmore Bates III). Also wrote as Anthony Gilmore; A. R. Holmes; Quien Sabe; S. F. Whozis; H. G. Winter. American. Born in Pittsburgh, Pennsylvania, 9 October 1900. Educated at Allegheny College, Meadville, Pennsylvania, 1917-18; University of Pennsylvania, Philadelphia, 1919-20. Clockmaker, 1914-17, 1920-22; reporter, Philadelphia *Enquirer*, 1923; assistant cameraman, Whitman-Bennett Studios, 1924; Editor for Clayton magazines, including *Astounding Stories*, 1930-33, and *Strange Tales*, 1931-32; Editor, *Technocracy*, 1935-37, and for the WPA art and writers projects; actor and machinist; Story Analyst, Columbia Pictures, 1958-59, and David O. Selznick, 1960. Recipient: Midamericon World Science-Fiction Convention Award, 1976. *Died.*

SCIENCE-FICTION PUBLICATIONS

Novel

Space Hawk: The Greatest of Interplanetary Adventurers (as Anthony Gilmore), with D. W. Hall. New York, Greenberg, 1952.

Uncollected Short Stories

"The City of Eric" (as Quien Sabe), in *Amazing Stories Quarterly* (New York), Spring 1929.
"The Slave Ship from Space" (as A. R. Holmes), in *Astounding* (New York), July 1931.
"A Matter of Size," in *Astounding* (New York), April 1934.
"The Experiment of Dr. Sarconi," in *Thrilling Wonder Stories* (New York), July 1940.
"A Matter of Speed," in *Astounding* (New York), June 1941.
"Mystery of the Blue God," in *Amazing* (New York), January 1942.
"Death of a Sensitive," in *Science Fiction Plus* (Philadelphia), May 1953.
"The Triggered Dimension," in *Science Fiction Plus* (Philadelphia), December 1953.
"Farewell to the Master," in *The Great SF Stories (1940)*, edited by Isaac Asimov and Martin H. Greenberg. New York, DAW, 1979.
"A Scientist Rises," with D. W. Hall, in *Gosh! Wow! (Sense of Wonder) Science Fiction*, edited by Forrest J. Ackerman. New York, Bantam, 1982.
"Alas, All Thinking," in *The Arbor House Treasury of Science Fiction Masterpieces*, edited by Robert Silverberg and Martin H. Greenberg. New York, Arbor House, 1983.

Uncollected Short Stories as H. G. Winter, with D. W. Hall
"The Hands of Aten," in *Astounding* (New York), July 1931.
"The Midget from the Island," in *Astounding* (New York), August 1931.
"Seed of the Arctic Ice," in *Astounding* (New York), February 1932.
"Under Arctic Ice," in *Astounding* (New York), January 1933.

OTHER PUBLICATIONS

Other

"So Help Me!" (as S. F. Whozis), in *Science Fiction Quarterly* (Holyoke, Massachusetts), February 1956.
"Editorial Number One," in *A Requiem for Astounding*, by Alva Rogers. Chicago, Advent, 1964.

*

Harry Bates commented:

(1981) *Astounding Stories* (now *Analog*) was born to the publisher William Clayton and one of his editors—me—in a now unimaginable world populated by a single science-fiction magazine, Hugo Gernsback's *Amazing Stories*, which published amateurishly written "gadget" stories. The *Amazing* writers got one-tenth of a cent a word after publication; the writers for the Clayton empire were professionals, getting the very-high-for-those-days minimum of two cents on acceptance. I agreed with Clayton that *Astounding* had to have competent professional writing with strong plots and physical action; but its stories had also, of course, to contain tinges of science and binges of excitements and moreover be astounding—and where was any body of writers to cook to this recipe?

I had to create one. Because they had already sold to me I called on the writers in adventure magazines of which I already was editor, coaxing them to attempt this very different new field. Almost to a man they knew no science, and to use their stories at all I had (when possible) to correct and amplify what they turned in. I gave out story ideas right and left and did enormous amounts of hurried rewriting. Eventually almost all of these writers quit trying, for they had to eat, and there was no second market for the stories I had to reject.

The public in those days had never heard the term science fiction and had to be educated to it. *Amazing* often used the ugly term scientifiction, which I had as quickly as possible to suppress from the genre. Physical action remained an Astounding requisite. No one then dreamed what today's science fiction of way-way-out imaginings—fantasy—would be; if one of today's stories had been submitted to me then I'd probably have had to turn it down so as not to estrange the readers we aimed for and were accumulating. In time *Astounding*, in spite of its minimum of two cents a word, all but got out of the red, so that it was instantly profitable when Street & Smith with its much lower word rate took it over.

The stories I wrote in collaboration with my assistant D. W. Hall during those infant years were the product of sheer necessity, to avoid filling out the magazine with worse. The first Hawk Carse story was written as an example to my writers of the wanted element of character, and it was its extreme success that demanded the writing of the several that followed. All the stories published later under my own name were written hastily for a quick buck after my separation from *Astounding*, my prime interests lying elsewhere. I remember that in each case I hesitated at using my own name rather than a pseudonym; but its added value all but guaranteed the quick sale, however sloppy the writing. Who might have guessed that one day there would come into being such a phenomenon as museums of science-fiction—anthologies!—necropolises!—and that such imperfect stories as mine would be resurrected to populate them? There, now, they live again, after a fashion—zombies, all their sores still upon them.

The worst occurred with my "Not Understanding," which Gernsback characteristically renamed "The Triggered Dimension." When his *Science Fiction Plus* folded, his editor, wanting to squeeze into the last issue this last long story of mine, attempted the impossible, cutting out almost completely its very necessary central scene—the scene which gave reason for story and my title—and shortening the last sentence of paragraph after paragraph so as to save single lines. So one day I rewrote the story with the care I wish heartily I'd given it in the first place and with the cut-out parts restored—and then while I was at it I rewrote half of the others that had appeared under my own name. One, "A Matter of Speed," became "Oh Outrage!," a longish novel of very different mood which bad health has so far not let me quite finish.

Friends who since have read my "Alas, All Thinking" have asked me how I ever could have projected *Homo terminal* with mental processes so degenerated. The reason lies not quite in the realm of pure fantasy. Beginning when quite young (and having what I thought was a good body) I remained aware always that *Homo* of my day thoroughly forgets he is an animal with the body of an animal and early loses all inborn capacity to enjoy the *moving* of his body, coming almost always to overvalue the non-moving brain. I had merely to extrapolate. It happens that upon rereading the story I found I'd given no solid examples of his degenerated thinkings, so when I rewrote it I gave many, too many, Book-an-hour Devourers will say. But perhaps there exists somewhere a reader or two who, like me in the writing, will find pleasure in my assortment of bad thinkings. It is for *these*—educated *adults*—that I put a few strictly unnecessary extra ones in. Devourers, I do not rewrite stories for *you*.

*   *   *

Building on his experience as an editor of action-adventure pulps for William Clayton, Harry Bates began his career in science fiction as founding editor of the magazine whose name—*Astounding*—would become under later leadership synonymous with hard science fiction. But Bates said that his first writers of stories for *Astounding* in 1930 were "almost wholly ignorant of science and technology." He named the magazine. He enlisted and cajoled professional pulp writers to add a science veneer to action and adventure narratives. He rewrote and wrote pseudonymously much of the material himself, and he paid professional rates. The result was a wider readership and a wider professional base for the genre that had begun hardly as literature with the Gernsback "scientifiction." Under the name Anthony Gilmore, Bates and his fellow editor D. M. Hall began the highly popular Hawk Carse series. The literary qualities of fast-paced action tale in this series helped establish the space-opera characteristics in science fiction that have to this day balanced the hard descriptions of scientific speculation and technology in order to make the genre exciting and popular as well as speculative and futuristic. The stories in the Hawk Carse series were collected as *Space Hawk*.

Bates edited the first 34 issues of *Astounding* as well as a few issues of a rival for *Weird Tales* entitled *Strange Tales*, but he continued to publish important science-fiction stories under his

own name after his editing work had ended. Apparently the added speculative and scientific thoughts that he had worked up in the Clayton offices in order to capture more of the pulp market took a permanent hold on his imagination, and so Bates himself is representative of the professional pulp writers with little original scientific training who helped to create the genre. "Alas, All Thinking" expresses a classic theme of early science fiction with a tone and writing style that also embody the best and the worst characteristics of the genre. The theme is ultimately from the 18th-century enlightenment, and one wonders what has been the source of transmission from the *philosophes* to the New York pulp writers. But somehow the theme is intact: a fear of too much rationality and the ironic sense of progress leading to actual degeneration in humanness. The theme is mingled with the Golden Age/Iron Age myths in which life appears richer, more fertile, more heroic in the past; and the time-travel gimmick of super science facilitates the use of the present even as an heroic past so that satire fuses in the story with the myth of lost innocence. Bates's writing does not understate the theme, and when he tries to heighten emotion at the end the tonal effect is stiff. The story, like many others of this decade, is at the same time poignant, rich, and primitive.

Bates's single most well-known story (filmed in 1951 as *The Day the Earth Stood Still*) also first appeared in *Astounding*—this time the Campbell magazine of 1940. "Farewell to the Master" is a story rich with influence on the genre and less over-written than much of Bates's other work. The tapestry of the story weaves elements ranging backward in indebtedness to Mary Shelley's *Frankenstein* and forward in apparent influence to Walter Tevis's *Mockingbird* (1980). It is fascinating to think of the old pro pulp editor reaching backward to the romantics and influencing as academic a writer as Tevis several decades later. Bates tells the story of a technologically made creature who transcends his creators in competence so that he becomes the master, and yet there is an enigmatic sadness inherent in this future hero who is somehow more incomplete than his more primitive makers. The accomplishment of Bates illustrates how the genre which began in the practicalities of the pulp markets has progressed through a fine web of influence and allusion.

—Donald M. Hassler

BAXTER, John. Also writes as Martin Loran. Australian. Born in Sydney, New South Wales, 14 December 1939. Educated at Waverly College, Sydney, 1944-54. Married 1) Merie Elizabeth Brooker in 1962 (divorced, 1967); 2) Joyce Allison Agee in 1978. Staff Controller, New South Wales State Government, Sydney, 1957-67; Publicity Director, Australian Commonwealth Film Unit, Sydney, 1967-70; Presenter, Understanding Films series, 1969; film critic, *Kaleidoscope* programme, BBC Radio, London, 1972-80. Lecturer, United States Embassy, London, 1973-74, and for United States Government in Europe, 1974-75, and Hollins College, Virginia, 1975-76, and London Campus, 1976-78; Guest Lecturer, Australian Film and TV School, 1982; Assessor, Australian Film Commission, 1983. Since 1984, Producer, Australian Broadcasting Corporation. Recipient: Australian Film Award, 1969; Kranz Film Festival Award, 1970; Benson and Hedges prize for TV documentary, 1970; Ditmar Award, 1971; Australian Council Literature Board Fellowship, 1984. Agent: Ed Victor Ltd., 162 Wardour Street, London W1V 4AT, England. Address: Box C402, Clarence Street P. O., Sydney, New South Wales 2001, Australia.

SCIENCE-FICTION PUBLICATIONS

Novels

The Off-Worlders. New York, Ace, 1966; as *The God Killers* , Sydney, Horwitz, 1968.
The Hermes Fall. London, Panther, and New York, Simon and Schuster, 1978.
The Black Yacht. New York, Jove, and London, New English Library, 1982.

Uncollected Short Stories

"Vendetta's End," in *Science Fiction Adventures* (London), December 1962.
"Eviction," in *New Worlds* (London), March 1963.
"Interlude,"in *New Worlds* (London), November 1963.
"Toys," in *New Worlds* (London), January 1964.
"The New Country," in *Science Fantasy* (Bournemouth), April 1964.
"Testament,"in *New Writings in SF 3*, edited by John Carnell. London, Dobson, 1965; New York, Bantam, 1967.
"Takeover Bid," in *New Writings in SF 5*, edited by John Carnell. London, Dobson, 1965; New York, Bantam, 1970.
"The Hands," in *New Writings in SF 6*, edited by John Carnell. London, Dobson, 1965; New York, Bantam, 1971.
"The Traps of Time," in *The Best of New Worlds*, edited by Michael Moorcock. London, Compact, 1965.
"More Than a Man," in *New Worlds* (London), February 1965.
"Tryst," in *New Writings in SF 8*, edited by John Carnell. London, Dobson, 1966; New York, Bantam, 1971.
"Skirmish," in *New Worlds* (London), April 1966.
"Apple," in *New Writings in SF 10*, edited by John Carnell. London, Dobson, 1967.
"The Case of the Perjured Planet" (as Martin Loran, with Ron Smith), in *Analog* (New York), November 1967.
"An Ounce of Dissension" (as Martin Loran, with Ron Smith) and "The Beach," in *The Pacific Book of Australian Science Fiction*, edited by John Baxter. Sydney, Angus and Robertson, 1968; London, Angus and Robertson, 1969.

OTHER PUBLICATIONS

Novels

Adam's Woman (novelization of screenplay). Sydney, Horwitz, 1970.
The Bidders. Philadelphia, Lippincott, 1979; as *Bidding*, London, Granada, 1980.
The Kid. New York, Viking Press, 1981.

Plays

Screenplays (documentaries): *Beyond the Pack Ice*, 1968; *Golf in Australia*, 1969; *After Proust*, 1969; *Australian Diary* series, 1969-70; *Top End*, 1970; *The Amazing Years of Cinema* (1 episode), 1976.

Television Documentaries: *Understanding Film* series, 1969; *No Roses for Michael*, 1970.

Other

Hollywood in the Thirties. New York, A. S. Barnes, and London, Zwemmer, 1968.

Science Fiction in the Cinema. New York, A. S. Barnes, and London, Zwemmer, 1970.
The Australian Cinema. Sydney and London, Angus and Robertson, 1970.
The Gangster Film. New York, A. S. Barnes, and London, Zwemmer, 1970.
The Cinema of Josef von Sternberg. New York, A. S. Barnes, and London, Zwemmer, 1971.
The Cinema of John Ford. New York, A. S. Barnes, and London, Zwemmer, 1971.
Hollywood in the Sixties. New York, A. S. Barnes, and London, Tantivy Press, 1972.
Sixty Years of Hollywood. South Brunswick, New Jersey, A. S. Barnes, and London, Tantivy Press, 1973.
An Appalling Talent: Ken Russell. London, Joseph, 1973.
Stunt: The Story of the Great Movie Stunt Men. London, Macdonald, 1973; New York, Doubleday, 1974.
King Vidor. New York, Monarch Press, 1976.
The Hollywood Exiles. New York, Taplinger, and London, Macdonald and Jane's, 1976.
The Fire Came By: The Riddle of the Great Siberian Explosion, with Thomas Atkins. New York, Doubleday, and London, Macdonald and Jane's, 1976.
The Video Handbook: Getting the Best from Your VCR, with Brian Norris. London, Fontana, 1982.
Who Burned Australia? The Ash Wednesday Fires. London, New English Library, 1984.

Editor, *The Pacific Book of Australian Science Fiction*. Sydney, Angus and Robertson, 1968; as *The Pacific Book of Science Fiction*, London, Angus and Robertson, 1969.
Editor, *The Second Pacific Book of Australian Science Fiction*. Sydney, Angus and Robertson, 1971; as *The Second Pacific Book of Science Fiction*, London, Angus and Robertson, 1971.

*

John Baxter comments:

Ted Carnell discovered and encouraged many young writers in the 1960's; almost alone among them I moved away from SF as I entered professional writing, a defection Ted tried hard, though unsuccessfully, to approve. He would probably be happy that, almost 20 years after he accepted my first story, I have drifted, in a roundabout way, back to the field he loved so much. Had he lived I might have convinced him that the cinema, to which I have given so many of my energy, combined technology and aesthetics in a form analogous to the best science fiction. In any event, it is this synthesis from which I hope to produce a third decade of writing—fictional, critical, and perhaps a combination of the two.

*   *   *

As editor of the first two major anthologies of Australian SF writing, John Baxter laid some of the foundations for the recent "renaissance" of Australian SF. He exerted a twofold influence upon Australian SF of the 1970's. Rejecting the concept that science fiction must be prophetic, Baxter emphasized "insight rather than intelligent guessing," arguing that "a story which tells us that a rose is a rose and explains why is far more worthwhile than one which states that E equals MC squared and leaves it at that. " Baxter also esteemed the literary qualities of science fiction, publishing material that was innovative in style and structure, yet neither ignoring nor denigrating stories written in a more traditional narrative style.

In short, he proclaimed an Australian SF that was literate, thoughtful, and original.

Baxter's own short stories reflect these criteria. They are original and ambitious, reflecting influences from both traditional and new-wave SF. One of his best-known stories, "Apple," is a traditional man-meets-monster story—except that the encounter takes place in a surreal setting, and the story evolves from imagery and setting rather than action. A gigantic apple lies cradled in a valley, the juices dripping from its side as men tunnel into its core. The central character is a professional Moth Killer who battles with the grubs that lurk in the apple's core. It is suggested that the apple-world may be the result of atomic warfare, but for Baxter the explanation is incidental; his story conveys its own inner logic, and that is enough. The same is true of the more experimental story, "The Beach." Described as "a first sketch of what an *Australian* SF story might be like," it employs distinctively Australian symbols, and abandons conventional narrative structure in order to emphasize mood and imagery. The style and symbolism are evident in the closing lines: "Without fear, he swam towards the sea mountains, the peaks of which even now he could see gilded beyond the green. There, he knew, he would find his grail, the sunken, brooding sun."

Baxter's SF novels are more pedestrian. *The Off-Worlders* is set on the planet Merryland in the year 2833 and deals with a rustic community which is suspicious of technology and has rejected God, turning instead to Satan. *The Hermes Fall* is based on *The Fire Came By*, Baxter's non-fiction work on the famous Siberian "meteorite" of 1908 (written with Thomas Atkins). Despite its well-researched background, *The Hermes Fall* is merely a conventional "disaster" novel using science-fiction effects, in this case an asteroid on collision course with the Earth.

Always interested in cinema, Baxter has been devoting his energies to this field, and has abandoned SF for the writing of novels in the "best-seller" mould (*Bidding, The Black Yacht*). He remains one of Australia's wittiest SF book reviewers.

—Van Ikin

BAYLEY, Barrington John. British. Born in Birmingham, Warwickshire, 9 April 1937. Educated at a grammar school in Shropshire. Served in the Royal Air Force, 1955-57. Married Joan Lucy Clarke in 1969; one son and one daughter. Reporter, Wellington *Journal*, early 1950's; civil servant, Ministry of War, Shropshire, 1954-55; in Australian Public Service, London, 1957-58; has also worked as a clerk, typist, and coal miner. Agent: Scott Meredith Literary Agency, 845 Third Avenue, New York, New York 10022, U. S. A. ; or, Carnell Literary Agency, Rowneybury Bungalow, Sawbridgeworth, near Old Harlow, Essex CM20 2EX. Address: 48 Turreff Avenue, Donnington, Telford, Shropshire TF2 8HE, England.

SCIENCE-FICTION PUBLICATIONS

Novels

The Star Virus. New York, Ace, 1970.
Annihilation Factor. New York, Ace, 1972; London, Allison and Busby, 1979.
Empire of Two Worlds . New York, Ace 1972; London, Hale, 1974.

Collision Course. New York, DAW, 1973; as *Collision with Chronos*, London, Allison and Busby, 1977.
The Fall of Chronopolis. New York, DAW, 1974; London, Allison and Busby, 1979.
Soul of the Robot. New York, Doubleday, 1974; London, Allison and Busby, 1976.
The Garments of Caean. New York, Doubleday, 1976; London, Fontana, 1978.
The Grand Wheel. New York, DAW, 1977; London, Fontana, 1979.
Star Winds. New York, DAW, 1978.
The Pillars of Eternity. New York, DAW, 1982.
The Zen Gun. New York, DAW, 1983; London, Methuen, 1984.

Short Stories

The Knights of the Limits. London, Allison and Busby, 1978.
The Seed of Evil. London, Allison and Busby, 1979.

*

Bibliography: *Barrington J. Bayley: A Bibliography* by Mike Ashley, Manchester, Beccon, 1981.

Barrington John Bayley comments:
I have no personal philosophy as regards my work; I write according to my ability and interest. I regard myself as a genre SF writer—that is, as a traditionalist.

* * *

Barrington John Bayley is one of the very few authors to have bridged the philosophical gap between proponents of traditional space opera and the more demanding literary tastes of more recent editors and readers. He has succeeded at this by utilizing the traditional devices of space opera and wedding them to a more sophisticated writing style and to speculation far more intellectual than physical. Pervading most of his fiction there is a wry humor that is frequently unsettling but equally frequently entertaining.

Many of Bayley's plots are unabashedly space operas. A mysterious anomaly in space known as "The Patch" is consuming entire worlds as an interstellar empire erupts into civil war in *Annihilation Factor*. This galaxy-spanning adventure was already a noticeable advance over his earlier *Star Virus*, and subsequent novels have been progressively better. *Collision Course* postulates that there are two separate "nows" and that the two waves of reality are moving in opposite directions along the time waves. The plot centers on the imminence of the passing of the two realities through each other, and the effects on the two societies of the transition. Bayley experimented with the nature of time again in *The Fall of Chronopolis*. This time a theocratic society that possesses time travel refuses to recognize the possibility that their attempts to police the timeways may themselves change reality and cancel out their own society.

Bayley's ability to turn a phrase against itself is most evident in *The Garments of Caean*. A bankrupt sailor pilfers a priceless suit of clothing from a band of pirates, and when he subsequently dons them, his entire personality changes—clothes do indeed make the man. The pirates recapture the suit, at which point we learn that the suit itself is sentient, and that it considers its first owner to be its personal property. The planet Caean, it seems, is host to a species determined to take over the universe.

Satire is the order of the day in *Soul of the Robot* as well. A robot possessed of extraordinary powers makes its way through a variety of decadent human societies trying to solve the mystery of existence. Humans and aliens indulge in elaborate gambling schemes that determine the entire future of the human race in *The Grand Wheel*, and a ship sets off to explore the universe through etheric travel in *Star Winds*. Bayley's most recent novels, *The Pillars of Eternity* and *The Zen Gun*, are both ostensibly space operas as well, but each is endlessly inventive and, particularly in the latter case, so offbeat in its approach to plotting and setting that they have attracted considerable critical attention.

Although not a prolific short story writer, Bayley has made an impression there as well. His satiric humor is at its best in "Integrity," in which a libertarian reaches the logical consequence of his beliefs by liberating the individual cells of his body. Aliens have joined human nobility in "All the King's Men." A single city survives the collapse of the universe in "Exit from City 5."

Galaxies themselves are entities in "Cosmic Combatants." A child who has no nationality is adopted by an airline in "The Man in Transit." Alien manipulation of our physical bodies is a common theme as well, repeated in such stories as "Sporting with Chid" and "Maladjustment." For the most part, Bayley's stories are darkly ironic, occasionally utilizing stream-of-consciousness writing techniques to emphasize the strange viewpoint presented. Bayley is not the most popular writer of space operas; his stories are too unconventional for that. But his is certainly a novel and entertaining viewpoint.

—Don D'Ammassa

BEAR, Greg(ory Dale). American. Born in San Diego, California, 20 August 1951. Educated at San Diego State University, 1968-73, A. B. in English 1973. Married Christina M. Bear in 1975. Part-time Lecturer, San Diego Aerospace Museum, 1969-72; technical writer and planetarium operator, Reuben H. Fleet Space Theater, San Diego, 1973; bookstore clerk, 1974-75. Since 1975, free-lance writer: reviewer, San Diego *Union*, 1979-82; Co-Editor, Science Fiction Writers of America *Forum*. Illustrator: Co-Founder, Association of Science Fiction Artists. Recipient: Nebula Award (twice), 1984; Hugo Award, 1984. Agent: Richard Curtis Agency, 156 East 52nd Street, New York, New York 10022. Address: 10430 Nate Way, Santee, California 92071, U. S. A.

SCIENCE-FICTION PUBLICATIONS

Novels

Hegira. New York, Dell, 1979.
Psychlone. New York, Ace, 1979.
Beyond Heaven's River. New York, Dell, 1980.
Strength of Stones. New York, Ace, 1981.
Corona. New York, Pocket Books, 1984.
The Infinity Concerto. New York, Berkley, 1984.
Blood Music. New York, Arbor House, 1985.
Eon. New York, Bluejay, 1985.

Short Stories

The Wind from a Burning Woman. Sauk City, Wisconsin, Arkham House, 1983.

Uncollected Short Stories

"Destroyers," in *Famous Science Fiction* (New York), Winter 1967.
"Webster," in *Alternities,* edited by David Gerrold. New York, Dell, 1974.
"The Venging," in *Galaxy* (New York), June 1975.
"Perihesperon," in *Tomorrow,* edited by Roger Elwood. New York, Evans, 1975.
"A Martian Ricorso," in *Analog* (New York), February 1976.
"Sun-Planet," in *Galaxy* (New York), April 1977.
"Blood Music," in *The Nebula Awards 19,* edited by Marta Randall. New York, Arbor House, 1984.
"Through the Road No Whither," in *Far Frontiers 1,* edited by John F. Carr, Jim Baen, and Jerry Pournelle. New York, Baen, 1985.
"Dead Run," in *Omni* (New York), April 1985.

OTHER PUBLICATIONS

Other

"The Space Theater," in *Vertex* (Los Angeles), 1974.
"Future Vision," in *Galileo 3* (Boston).

*

Greg Bear comments:
Science fiction and fantasy has always been a joy for me, and I've been writing both since I was eight years old. Now I've been accorded approval by my peers in the form of Hugo and Nebulas, which I deeply appreciate; my writing, however, continues in its straight-line development. While I feel at a kind of peak as far as ability goes now, I'll continue working to improve, which may inevitably mean signal change in the future. But for the moment, I'm having a great deal of fun, and earning a respectable living, doing exactly what I've planned to do since I was a child. The past two years have been very productive—a computer has not only improved my work (or rather, allowed me to be as nit-picky as I've always been inclined to be) but cut the amount of time it takes me to produce a book, often by as much as 50%. Those who criticize novels written on word processors are simply foolish. 'Tis not the machine, my friends, 'tis merely story and writer. . . . "

I continue to be fascinated with science, history, and myth, and have now plunged into the study of information theory and Kantor's information mechanics, with results already evident in novels such as *Blood Music* and *Eon.* I believe that these new disciplines hold incredible promise for the future, especially when combined with the discoveries of genetics and physics. Information theory may be to the late 1980's what black holes and astrophysics were to the 1970's. A wealth of stories to be mined!

*   *   *

Since he began publishing his stories regularly in 1975, Greg Bear has written 7 novels and many shorter works. Bear's fiction consistently circles a central theme: how can mind come to terms with the universe? For this writer, understanding requires changing perception, so his protagonists usually come to some greater understanding of the universe and themselves. Readers typically find themselves exploring nimble and diverse creations that fit together into a coherent and ultimately optimistic view of mind in the cosmos. A catalogue for this complex vision provides a testament to Bear's breadth of interest and his inventive virtuosity: in stories and novels ranging from modern fantasy to pure SF, he explores topics from the universe's origins to its end and transformation (an important part of his Star Trek novel, *Corona*). In novellas like "Hardfought" and "Scattershot," Bear studies humans and aliens, their perception and communication. In *Beyond Heaven's River* and *Blood Music,* he assesses the nature of civilization, fingering its historical cycles: birth, expansion through war or cooperation, decline and death. He has repeatedly focused his attention on the relation of art and society, from the design of the vast, biomechanical cities in *Strength of Stones* to the physical and mythical powers of stories, songs, and poetry in "The White Horse Child," "Petra," and *The Infinity Concerto*. At the same time, Bear balances these large-scale inquiries with sensitive portrayals of individual characters struggling with growing up, identity, guilt, creativity, and transcendence.

With such conceptual vigor, it wouldn't be unusual to find the play and developement of ideas taking center stage, pushing aside values like character depth and plot diversity. But although some of Bear's early work succumbed to this fault (for example, *Hegira*), his subsequent writing has Increasingly managed to right the imbalance. He has begun to leave behind the quest plot as his preferred form in favor of patterning together deft characterization, sensual description, and fascinating conceptual diversity, so that the plot movement arises from the interaction of the estranging central idea (Suvin's "novum") with the human concerns of the protagonists.

Some of his more recent works best demonstrate Bear's increasing maturity, development first signalled in the haunting combination of World War II survivor tale and Rip Van Winkle story in *Beyond Heaven's River*. Typical of the more developed work, this novel blends fascinating ideas (what would it be like to have your every wish became real? How can a man adjust to living 400 years after his own era?) with believable characterization. "Hardfought" participates in the same far future as *Heaven's River*, along with several of Bear'a works ("Scattershot," "The Venging," "Perihesperon," "Sun Planet," "The Wind from a Burning Woman," and *Strength of Stones*). Focusing on war, history, and personal transformation, the story shows human and alian characters as they follow a complex and difficult process of self-discovery that Bear enriches with pungent detail. Through rapid shifts in narrator and perspective, the tale enacts the estrangement it depicts, forcing the reader to adapt for understanding just as the characters must. Such adaptation also characterizes *The Infinity Concerto*, a cross-dimensional fantasy rooted in the Celtic lore of the Sidhe. A novel about Michael Perrin's coming of age, *Concerto* also concerns itself with the role of art in the cosmos. Completing Coleridge's *Kubla Khan,* the young protagonist ensures the stability of a world where poetry has the power of physical law. Bear's first deep exploration of a single character, the novel shows considerable care in its depiction of motives and attitudes.

Perhaps the most intriguing of Bear's recent writing are "Blood Music" and the novel subsequently built around it. In its first form, the tale is mostly a frightening extrapolation into a strikingly altered near future. Comic and horrific by turns, "Blood Music" displays the mixture of alienation and fascination we associate with dark comedy. For the novel, however, Bear incorporated and rewrote large sections of the novelette;

in the result there are passages that achieve something more akin to Yeats's "terrible beauty. " This effect comes both from the enhanced technical foundation and from evocative portrayals of characters who become the protagonists of alternating chapters. By varying the protagonists and the point of view, Bear gives us an encompassing circle of perspectives on the world's transformation. The final sections present a human apotheosis rivalling that in Clarke's *Childhood's End*.

Bear has become in the last five years one of the major new writers in the genre; even the lesser of his fictions are entertaining, the more developed ones are highly stimulating, suggestive reading.

—Len Hatfield

———

BEAUMONT, Charles. Pseudonym for Charles Nutt; also wrote as Keith Grantland. American. Born in Chicago, Illinois, 2 January 1929. Served in the United States Army for one year. Married Helen Louise Brown in 1949; one son and two daughters. Radio writer, actor, illustrator, and animator. Recipient: Jules Verne Award, 1954; *Playboy* award, for nonfiction, 1961. *Died 21 February 1967.*

SCIENCE-FICTION PUBLICATIONS

Short Stories

The Hunger and Other Stories. New York, Putnam, 1957; as *Shadow Play*, London, Panther, 1964.
Yonder. New York, Bantam, 1958.
Night Ride and Other Journeys. New York, Bantam, 1960.
The Magic Man and Other Science-Fantasy Stories. New York, Fawcett, 1965; London, Fawcett, 1966.
The Edge. London, Panther, 1966.
Best of Beaumont. New York, Bantam, 1982.

OTHER PUBLICATIONS

Novels

Run from the Hunter (as Keith Grantland, with John E. Tomerlin). New York, Fawcett, 1957; London, Boardman, 1959.
The Intruder. New York, Putnam, 1959.

Plays

Screenplays: *Queen of Outer Space*, with Ben Hecht, 1958: *The Intruder* (*The Stranger*), 1961; *Burn, Witch, Burn (Night of the Eagle),* with Richard Matheson and George Baxt, 1962; *The Wonderful World of the Brothers Grimm*, with David P. Harmon and William Roberts, 1962; *The Premature Burial,* with Ray Russell, 1962; *The Haunted Palace,* 1963; *7 Faces of Dr. Lao,* 1964; *The Masque of the Red Death,* with R. Wright Campbell, 1964; *Mister Moses*, with Monja Danischewsky, 1965.

Television Plays: for *Twilight Zone, Naked City* , and *Thriller* series.

Other

Remember? Remember? New York, Macmillan, 1963.

Editor, with William F. Nolan, *Omnibus of Speed:* An Introduction to the World of Motor Sport. New York, Putnam, 1958; London, Stanley Paul, 1961; as *When Engines Roar*, New York, Bantam, 1964.
Editor, *The Fiend in You*. New York, Ballantine, 1962.

*   *   *

Charles Beaumont was a consummate craftsman of the popular market short story—perhaps the most accomplished writer of this type of fiction to publish in the 1950's and early 1960's. He wrote extensively for *Playboy* and other magazines, including many in the science-fiction field, and often blended elements of humor, horror, psychological suspense, and extrapolative SF. If much of his subject matter is grim, and many of his stories basically downbeat in resolution, his smooth and upbeat writing style keeps his work from being negative or oppressive.

Among his more than 50 stories (and articles) of science fiction and fantasy is "The Vanishing American," an allegorical tale about a man who becomes invisible to his fellow men, and perhaps Beaumont's finest short story. Others of quality include "Free Dirt," "The Love Master," "The Quadriopticon," and, the best of a number with a jazz music background, "Black Country."

His tragic death at 37, of a rare aging disease which had ravaged him and kept him from writing for three years, cut short a career which might have progressed to major stature.

—Bill Pronzini

BEECHAM, Alice. See **TUBB, E. C.**

BELL, Thornton. See **FANTHORPE, R. Lionel.**

BELLAMY, Edward. American. Born in Chicopee Falls, Massachusetts, 26 March 1850. Educated at local schools; Union College, Schenectady, New York, 1867-68; travelled and studied in Germany, 1868-69; studied law: admitted to the Massachusetts Bar, 1871, but never practised. Married Emma Sanderson in 1882. Associate Editor, Springfield *Union*, Massachusetts; editorial writer, New York *Evening Post*, 1878; founder, with his brother, Springfield *Daily News*, 1880; after 1885 writer and lecturer in support of socialism; founded *New Nation*, Boston, 1891. *Died 22 May 1898.*

SCIENCE-FICTION PUBLICATIONS

Novels

Dr. Heidenhoff's Process . New York, Appleton, 1880;

Edinburgh, Douglas, 1884.
Looking Backward 2000-1887. Boston, Ticknor, 1888; London, Reeves, 1889.
Equality. New York, Appleton, and London, Heinemann, 1897.

Short Stories

The Blindman's World and Other Stories. Boston, Houghton Mifflin, and London, Watt, 1898.

OTHER PUBLICATIONS

Novels

Six to One: A Nantucket Idyl. New York, Putnam, and London, Sampson Low, 1878.
Miss Ludington's Sister: A Romance of Immortality. Boston, Osgood, 1884; London, Reeves, 1890.
The Duke of Stockbridge: A Romance of Shay's Rebellion. New York, Silver Burdett, 1900.

Other

Edward Bellamy Speaks Again! Articles, Public Addresses, Letters. Kansas City, Peerage Press, 1937.
Talks on Nationalism. Chicago, Peerage Press, 1938.
Religion of Solidarity. Yellow Springs, Ohio, Antioch, 1940.
Selected Writings on Religion and Society, edited by Joseph Schiffman. New York, Liberal Arts Press, 1955.

*

Bibliography: in *Bibliography of American Literature* by Jacob Blanck, New Haven, Connecticut, Yale University Press, vol. 1, 1955.

Critical Studies: *Edward Bellamy*, New York, Columbia University Press, 1944, and *The Philosophy of Edward Bellamy*, New York, King's Crown Press, 1945, both by Arthur E. Morgan; *The Year 2000: A Critical Biography of Edward Bellamy*, by Sylvia E. Bowman, New York, Bookman, 1958, and *Edward Bellamy Abroad: An American Prophet's Influence* by Bowman and others, New York Twayne, 1962; *Edward Bellamy, Novelist and Reformer* by Daniel Aaron and Harry Levin, Schenectady, New York, Union College, 1968.

*   *   *

In *Looking Backward*, Edward Bellamy observed that both the "working classes" and "true and humane men and women, of every degree, are in a mood of exasperation, verging on absolute revolt, against social conditions that reduce life to a brutal struggle for existence." In its sequel, *Equality*, he added the ruin of prairie farmers by capitalist mortgages, the degradation of women through economic exploitation, the recurrent economic crisis, and the concentration of three-quarters of national wealth into the hands of 10% of the population. Bellamy's utopianism was the point at which all these deep discontents intersected with the American religious and lay utopian tradition and the world socialist movement. As the spokesman of the "immense average of villagers, of small-town-dwellers" who believed in "modern inventions, modern conveniences, modern facilities" (Howells), in Yankee gadgetry as white magic for overcoming drudgery, he accepted the financial trusts as more efficient and changeable from private waste and tyranny to a Yankee communism or "Association-ism": the nation "organized as the one great corporation . . . in the profits and economies of which all citizens shared. "

Bellamy's new frontier is the future. It offers not only better railways, motor carriages, air-cars, telephones, and TV, but also a classless brotherhood of affluence socializing these means of communication and other upper-class privileges to achieve comfort and security for everyone through a re-organized "economy of happiness. " Universal high education, work obligation from 21 to 45, equal and guaranteed income for everyone including the old, the sick, and children, flexible planning, and public honors reduce government to a universal civic service called the Great Trust or the Industrial Army. The generals of each guild or industrial branch are chosen by the retired alumni of the guild, and the head of the army is president of USA. Doctors and teachers have their own guilds, and a writer, artist, journal editor, or inventor is exempted from the army if enough buyers sign over a part of their credit. Individuality is fostered and objectors can "work out a better solution of the problem of existence than our society offers" in a reservation (the first use of this escape-hatch of later utopias).

Bellamy's economic blueprint is integrated into the story of Julian West, who wakes from a mesmeric sleep of 1887 into the Boston of 2000, is informed about the new order by Dr. Leete, and falls in love with Leete's daughter. This system of epoch-contrasts is reactualized in the nightmarish ending when Julian dreams of awakening back in the capitalist society of 1887. He meets its folly and repulsiveness with an anguished eye which supplies to each place and person a counterpossibility; the utopian estrangement culminates in the hallucination about "the possible face that would have been actual if mind and soul had lived" which he sees superimposed upon the living dead of the poor quarter. The lesson is that living in this nightmare and "pleading for crucified humanity" might yet be better than reawakening into the golden 21st century—as, if a final twist, Julian does. *Looking Backwood*—intimately informed by Bellamy's constant preoccupation with human plasticity, memory and identity, brute reality and ideal possibility—reposes on a balance of world-times. Its plot is Julian's change of identity. In two of Bellamy's later stories, "The Blindman's World" and "To Whom This May Come," the alienated Earthmen are contrasted to worlds of brotherhood and transparency where men are "lords of themselves. " As the anxious idealist becomes an apostate through a healer's reasonable lectures and his daughter's healing sympathy, the construction of a social system for the reader is also the reconstruction of the hero. This radical-democratic innov-ation, in which a change world is accompanied by changing people's "nature," is epoch-making for future utopias and SF.

However, Bellamy retreated from this discovery. Just as Julian is the mediator between two social systems for the reader, so Edith Leete is the steadying emotional mediator for Julian, a personal female Christ of earthly brotherhood. Bellamy's "sunburst" of a new order is validated equally by socialist economics, ethical evolution, and Christian love; his future brings a purified space and man. The friendly house of Dr. Leete is the hearth of spacious, clean, classless Boston, with Edith as the Dickensian cricket on the hearth. Hard-headed civic pragmatism is the obverse of a soft-hearted petty-bourgeois "fairy tale of social felicity. " Bellamy expects a nonviolent, imminent, and instantaneous abandonment of private capitalism by recognition of its folly. With telling effects he extrapolated the Rationalist or Jeffersonian prin-ciples and institutions to a logical end-product of universal public ownership. But he also remained limited by such ideals. His fascination with the rationally organized army should

perhaps not be judged by our reaction today, since it was acquired under Lincoln and translated into peaceful and constructive terms. Further, any utopia before automation had to be harsh on recalcitrants, and Bellamy evolved toward participatory democracy in *Equality*. But even there he cont-inued to stress State mobilization, "public capitalism," and technocratic regimentation *within* economic production as opposed to ideal classless relations outside it, dismissing "the more backward races" and political efforts by "workingmen. "

Uncomfortable with sweeping changes of life-style, Bellamy is at his strongest in the economics of everyday life outside a capitalist framework—dressing and love, distribution of goods, cultural activities, democratic supply and demand (e. g., in organizing a journal or in solving brain-drain between countries). Here he is quite free from centralized State Socialist regulation. When contrasting such warm possibilities with stultifying private competition, he presents exempla of great force, as the initial allegory of the Coach, the parables of the Collective Umbrella and of the Rosebush, or (in *Equality*) the parables of the Water-Tank and of the Masters of the Bread. All such impressive and sometimes splendid apologues come from a laicized and radicalized New England pulpit style rather than from genteel fiction. Their ethical tone and the senti-mental plot addressed themselves to women and all those who felt insecure and unfree in bourgeois society. Bellamy's homely lucidity made his romance, with all its limitations, the first authentically American socialist anticipation tale.

Bellamy's success fuses various SF strands and traditions. He interfused the preceeding, narratively helpless tradition of utopian anticipations—tales culminating in Hale and Macnie, Cabet—with an effective Romantic system of correspon-dences. His ending, refusing the alibi of dream, marks the historical moment when this lay millenialism came of age: the new vision achieves, within the text, a reality *equal* to that of the author's empirical actuality. Bellamy links thus two strong American traditions: the fantastic one of unknown worlds and the practical one of organizing a new world—both of which translate powerful biblical themes into economics. His materia-list view of history as a coherent succession of changing human relationships and social structures was continued by Morris and Wells and built into the fundamentals of subsequent SF. Equally the plot educates the reader into acceptance of the strange by following the protagonist's puzzled education. Modern SF, though it has forgotten this ancestor, builds on *Looking Backward* much as Dr. Leete's house was built on the remnants of Julian's house and on top of his sealed sleeping chamber, excavated by future archaeology.

Traits from Bellamy's other works also drew from and returned into the SF tradition. The Flammarion-like, cosmi-cally exceptional blindness of Earthmen and the transferral by spirit to Mars are found in "The Blindman's World," and despotic oligarchy as the alternative to revolution in *Equality*. Most immediately, the immense ideologico-political echo of *Looking Backward* reverberated around the globe through a host of sequels, rebuttals, and parallels. Bellamy had hit exactly the right note for a time searching for alternatives to ruthless plutocracy, and close to 200 utopian tales expounding or satirizing social democracy, State regulation of economy, Populist capitalism, or various uncouth combinations thereof were published in the US from 1888 to 1917 (notably Donnelly's *Caesar's Column*, Howell's *A Traveller from Altruria*, and London's *The Iron Heel*). In Britain the echo was felt in Morris's answer, *News From Nowhere*, in Wells, and in Germany in three dozen German utopian or anti-utopian tales.

—Darko Suvin

BENFORD, Gregory (Albert). American. Born in Mobile, Alabama, 30 January 1941. Educated at the University of Oklahoma, Norman, B. S. in physics, 1963; University of California, San Diego, M. S. 1965, Ph. D. 1967. Married Joan Abbe in 1967; one daughter and one son. Fellow, 1967-69, and Research Physicist, 1969-72, Lawrence Radiation Laboratory, Livermore, California. Assistant Professor, 1971-73, Associate Professor, 1973-79, and since 1979, Professor of Physics, University of California, Irvine. Visiting Professor, Cambridge University, 1976. Recipient: Nebula Award, 1974, 1981; John W. Campbell Memorial Award, 1981. Agent: Richard Curtis Associates, 164 East 64th Street, New York, New York 10021. Address: Department of Physics, University of California, Irvine, California 92717, U. S. A.

SCIENCE-FICTION PUBLICATIONS

Novels

Deeper Than the Darkness. New York, Ace, 1970; revised edition, as *The Stars in Shroud,* New York, Berkley, 1978; London, Gollancz, 1979.
Jupiter Project. Nashville, Nelson, 1975; London, Sphere, 1982.
If the Stars Are Gods, with Gordon Eklund. New York, Berkley, 1977; London, Gollancz, 1978.
In the Ocean of Night. New York, Dial Press, 1977; London, Sidgwick and Jackson, 1978.
Find the Changeling, with Gordon Eklund. New York, Dell, 1980; London, Sphere, 1983.
Timescape. New York, Simon and Schuster, and London, Gollancz, 1980.
Shiva Descending, with William Rotsler. New York, Avon, and London, Sphere, 1980.
Against Infinity. New York, Simon and Schuster, and London, Gollancz, 1983.
Across the Sea of Stars. New York, Simon and Schuster, and London, Macdonald, 1984.
Artifact. New York, Tor, 1985.

Uncollected Short Stories

"Stand-In," in *Fantasy and Science Fiction* (New York), June 1965.
"Representative from Earth," in *Fantasy and Science Fiction* (New York), January 1966.
"Flattop," in *Fantasy and Science Fiction* (New York), May 1966.
"Sons of Man," in *Amazing* (New York), November 1969.
"Inalienable Rite," in *Quark 1,* edited by Samuel R. Delany and Marilyn Hacker. New York, Paperback Library, 1970.
"The Scarred Man," in *Venture* (Concord, New Hampshire), May 1970.
"The Prince of New York," in *Fantastic* (New York), June 1970.
"3:02 P. M., Oxford," in *If* (New York), September 1970.
"The Movement," in *Fantastic* (New York), October 1970.
"Nobody Lives on Burton Street," in *World's Best Science Fiction 1971,* edited by Donald A. Wollheim and Terry Carr. New York, Ace, and London, Gollancz, 1971.
"West Wind, Falling," in *Universe 1,* edited by Terry Carr. New York, Ace, 1971; London, Dobson, 1975.
"But the Secret Sits," in *Galaxy* (New York), March 1971.
"Battleground," in *If* (New York), June 1971.
"And the Sea Like Mirrors," in *Again, Dangerous Visions,*

edited by Harlan Ellison. New York, Doubleday, 1972; London, Millington, 1976.
"2001 Hypothesis," in *Vertex* (Los Angeles), April 1973.
"Man in a Vice," in *Amazing* (New York), February 1974.
"Nobody Lives Around There," in *Vertex* (Los Angeles), February 1974.
"Cambridge, 1:58 A. M.," in *Epoch,* edited by Roger Elwood and Robert Silverberg. New York, Berkley, 1975.
"John of the Apocalypse," in *Tomorrow Today,* edited by George Zebrowski. Santa Cruz, California, Unity Press, 1975.
"White Creatures," in *New Dimensions 5,* edited by Robert Silverberg. New York, Harper, 1975.
"Beyond Greyworld," in *Analog* (New York), September 1975.
"Doing Lennon," in *The Best Science Fiction of the Year 5,* edited by Terry Carr. New York, Ballantine, and London, Gollancz, 1976.
"Seascape," in *Faster Than Light,* edited by Jack Dann and George Zebrowski. New York, Harper, 1976.
"What Did You Do Last Year?," in *Universe 6,* edited by Terry Carr. New York, Doubleday, 1976; London, Dobson, 1978.
"Knowing Her," in *New Dimensions 7,* edited by Robert Silverberg. New York, Harper, 1977.
"Hellas in Florida," in *Fantasy and Science Fiction* (New York), January 1977.
"Homemaker," in *Cosmos* (New York), May 1977.
"A Snark in the Night," in *Fantasy and Science Fiction* (New York), August 1977.
"Nooncoming," in *Universe 8,* edited by Terry Carr. New York, Doubleday, 1978; London, Dobson, 1979.
"How It All Went," in *100 Great Science Fiction Short Short-Stories,* edited by Isaac Asimov, Martin H. Greenberg, and Joseph D. Olander. New York, Doubleday, and London, Robson, 1978.
"Starswarmer," in *Analog* (New York), September 1978.
"Calibrations and Exercises," in *New Dimensions 9,* edited by Robert Silverberg. New York, Harper, 1979.
"A Hiss of Dragon," with Marc Laidlaw, in *The Best Science Fiction of the Year 8,* edited by Terry Carr. New York, Ballantine, and London, Gollancz, 1979.
"Time Shards," in *Universe 9,* edited by Terry Carr. New York, Doubleday, 1979.
"In Alien Flesh," in *The 1979 Annual World's Best SF,* edited by Donald A. Wollheim. New York, DAW, 1979.
"Time Guide," in *Destinies* (New York), January-February 1979.
"Old Woman by the Road," in *The Future at War 1,* edited by Reginald Bretnor. New York, Ace, 1979.
"Dark Sanctuary," in *The Endless Frontier,* edited by Jerry Pournelle. New York, Ace, 1979.
"Redeemer," in *Best Science Fiction of the Year 9,* edited by Gardner Dozois. New York, Dutton, 1980.
"Titan Falling," in *Amazing* (New York), August 1980.
"Pick an Orifice," in *Destinies* (New York), November 1981.
"Cadenza," in *New Dimensions 12,* edited by Robert Silverberg and Marta Randall. New York, Pocket Books, 1981.
"Shall We Take a Little Walk?," in *Destinies* (New York), April 1981.
"Slices," in *Destinies* (New York), August 1981.
"Relativistic Effects," in *Perpetual Light,* edited by Alan Ryan. New York, Warner, 1982.
"Sandy Lust," in *The Berkley Showcase 5,* edited by Victoria Schochet and Melissa Singer. New York, Berkley, 1982.
"Exposures," in *The Road to Science Fiction 4,* edited by James E. Gunn. New York, New American Library, 1982.
"Valhalla," in *Fantasy and Science Fiction* (New York), April

1982.

"Lazarus Rising," in *Isaac Asimov's Science Fiction Magazine* (New York), July 1982.

"The Touch," in *The Best of Omni Science Fiction 5*, edited by Don Myrus. New York, Omni, 1983.

"Time's Rub," in *Isaac Asimov's Science Fiction Magazine* (New York), April 1985.

"Immortal Night," in *Omni* (New York), April 1985.

"To the Storming Gulf," in *Fantasy and Science Fiction* (New York), April 1985.

*

Manuscript Collection: Eaton College, University of California, Riverside.

Gregory Benford comments:

I am a resolutely amateur writer, preferring to follow my own interests rather than try to produce fiction for a living. And anyway, I'm a scientist by first choice and shall remain so.

I began writing from the simple desire to tell a story (a motivation SF writers seem to forget as they age, and thus turn into earnest moralizers). It's taken me a long time to learn how. I've been labeled a "hard SF" writer from the first, but in fact I think the job of SF is to do it *all*—the scientific landscape, peopled with real persons, with "style" and meaning ingrained. I've slowly worked toward that goal, with many dead ends along the way. From this comes my habit of rewriting my older books and expanding early short stories into longer works (sometimes novels). Ideas come to me in a lapidary way, layering over the years. Yet, it's not the stirring moral message that moves me. I think writers are interesting when they juxtapose images or events, letting life come out of the stuff of the narrative. They get boring when they preach. To some extent, my novels reflect my learning various subcategories of SF—*Deeper Than the Darkness* was the galactic empire motif; *Jupiter Project* the juvenile; *If the Stars Are Gods* and *In the Ocean of Night* both the cosmic space novel, etc. *Timescape* is rather different, and reflects my using my own experiences as a scientist. Yet short stories, where I labored so long, seem to me just as interesting as novels. I learned to write there. Nowadays, my novels begin as relatively brisk plot-lines and then gather philosophical moss as they roll. If all this sounds vague and intuitive, it is: that's the way I work. So I cannot say precisely why I undertake certain themes. I like Graham Greene's division of novels into "serious" and "entertainment," though I suspect the author himself cannot say with certainty which of his own is which.

It seems to me my major concerns are the vast landscape of science, and the philosophical implications of that landscape on mortal, sensual human beings. What genuinely interests me is the strange, the undiscovered, but in the end it is how *people* see this that matters most.

*   *   *

A major writer of hard science fiction, Gregory Benford explores technological and social alternative futures in fiction largely focussing on "the alien. " Fundamentally unknowable without a change in the observer, the "alien" for Benford encompasses the nature of the universe and the face of the future. Rooted in his experience as an Army brat and a physicist, living in the South, California, England, and Japan, his best work has a scientist's respect for data and an artist's flair for style. Combining, even rewriting earlier pieces, he has "collaborated" with other science fiction writers and more "literary" models.

Jupiter Project (a "prequel" to Heinlein's *Farmer in the Sky*), *Shiva Descending* (with William Rotsler), and *Find the Changeling* (with Gordon Eklund) are fairly conventional, a juvenile exploration story, a catastrophe novel and a mystery-melodrama, respectively. A rewrite of his first book, *The Stars in Shroud* was a more popular success, a stylish space opera strung on East-West and human-alien dichotomies. His more substantial other novels demand even more of the reader.

Written with Gordon Eklund, the separately published pieces of *If the Stars Are Gods* chronicle several encounters of Bradley Reynolds with alien life forms. An aging astronaut, this meditative hero seeks the alien in part because of his own alienation from a youth-oriented society.

Another alien-seeker, Nigel Walmsley, encounters emissaries of an ancient and probably hostile machine civilization in *In the Ocean of Night*. Alienated from a world deteriorating socially and ecologically, a world which is not just bare background but lived in, he rejects artificial religions in favor of a different kind of faith. Unable to grasp fully the alien in human terms, Nigel gradually incorporates the alien viewpoint, coming to see an essential bond between any two sparks of intelligence in a hostile universe.

The sequel, *Across the Sea of Stars,* takes him to the stars, as elder statesman on a starship rife with alternative life styles. A quest for the source of radio messages becomes one for the sources of a barely understood attack on Earth; understanding aliens is vital, but minimal, in both cases. Nigel recognizes the enemy, but others cannot see in the ruins they encounter the work of a machine civilization whose very existence they refuse to credit. Counterpointing the weakening defenses of Earth and Nigel, the novel blames both on a cancerous mechanism; self-destruction in the face of a misunderstood enemy is also found in previous Benford novels.

Benford is not limited to stories about alien life forms. Such moving short stories as "Doing Lennon," "White Creatures," and "Exposures" show the reader the alien face of his own future, as does his best novel, *Timescape*. Set in LaJolla, California (1962-63), where Benford attended graduate school, and Cambridge, England (1998), where he has also worked, the story centers on future physicists' attempts to help their predecessors to avert a world-wide ecotastrophe. The body of the book, however, concerns people embedded in society, staving off quiet desperation, and most of all it concerns "doing science," with all of its political, economic and personality clashes.

Jupiter Project challenges Heinlein; *Timescape* improves on C. P. Snow. Benford also uses other models, among them Updike, Hemingway, and Faulkner. Southern behavior patterns and narrative structure in "To the Storming Gulf" parallel *As I Lay Dying,* after the nation, not just the region, loses a nuclear war. *Against Infinity* may invoke St. George and *Moby-Dick,* but its style and structure directly parallel "The Bear," with the wilderness encroached on by civilization transplanted to Ganymede, the unknowable quarry a sometimes marauding relic of alien technology.

Echoing other stylists except as parody or pastiche inevitably opens an author to charges of plagiarism. While Benford borrows a certain literary veneer, however, he also builds on the past, relating his fiction to the whole of literature, not just the science fiction tradition. He also reminds us that art, like science, is in certain fundamental ways a collaborative exercise.

—David N. Samuelson

BENSON, Edwin. See **SHAVER, Richard S.**

BERESFORD, J(ohn) D(avys). British. Born in Castor, Northamptonshire, 7 March 1873. Educated at Oundle School, Northamptonshire, and at a school in Peterborough; articled to Lacey W. Ridge, architect, London, 1901. Married Beatrice Roskams; three sons and one daughter. Practised architecture in the early 1900's. *Died 2 February 1947.*

SCIENCE-FICTION PUBLICATIONS

Novels

The Hampdenshire Wonder. London, Sidgwick and Jackson, 1911; as *The Wonder,* New York, Doran, 1917.
Goslings. London, Heinemann, 1913; as *A World of Women,* New York, Macaulay, 1913.
Revolution: A Story of the Near Future in England. London, Collins, and New York, Putnam, 1921.
Real People. London, Collins, 1929.
The Camberwell Miracle. London, Heinemann, 1933.
What Dreams May Come. . . . London, Hutchinson, 1941.
A Common Enemy. London, Hutchinson, 1942.
The Riddle of the Tower, with Esmé Wynne-Tyson. London, Hutchinson, 1944.

Short Stories

Nineteen Impressions. London, Sidgwick and Jackson, 1918; Freeport, New York, Books for Libraries, 1969.
Signs and Wonders. Waltham St. Lawrence, Berkshire, Golden Cockerel Press, and New York, Putnam, 1921.
The Meeting Place and Other Stories. London, Faber, 1929.

OTHER PUBLICATIONS

Novels

Stahl Trilogy:
    The Early History of Jacob Stahl. London, Sidgwick and Jackson, and Boston, Little Brown, 1911.
    A Candidate for Truth. London, Sidgwick and Jackson, and Boston, Little Brown, 1912.
    The Invisible Event. London, Sidgwick and Jackson, and New York, Doran, 1915.
The House in Demetrius Road. London, Heinemann, and New York, Doran, 1914.
The Mountains of the Moon. London, Cassell, 1915.
These Lynnekers. London, Cassell, and New York, Doran, 1916.
W. E. Ford: A Bibliography, with Kenneth Richmond. London, Collins, and New York, Doran, 1917.
House-Mates. London, Cassell, and New York, Doran, 1917.
God's Counterpoint. London, Collins, and New York, Doran, 1918.
The Jervaise Comedy. London, Collins, and New York, Macmillan, 1919.
An Imperfect Mother. London, Collins, and New York, Macmillan, 1920.
The Prisoners of Hartling. London, Collins, and New York, Macmillan, 1922.

Love's Pilgrim. London, Collins, and Indianapolis, Bobbs Merrill, 1923.
Unity. London, Collins, and Indianapolis, Bobbs Merrill, 1924.
The Monkey-Puzzle. London, Collins, and Indianapolis, Bobbs Merrill, 1925.
That Kind of Man. London, Collins, 1926; as *Almost Pagan,* Indianapolis, Bobbs Merrill, 1926.
The Decoy. London, Collins, 1927.
The Tapestry. London, Collins, and Indianapolis, Bobbs Merrill, 1927.
The Instrument of Destiny: A Detective Story. London, Collins, and Indianapolis, Bobbs Merrill, 1928.
All or Nothing. London, Collins, and Indianapolis, Bobbs Merril, 1928.
Love's Illusion. London, Collins, and New York, Viking Press, 1930.
Seven, Bobsworth. London, Faber, 1930.
An Innocent Criminal. London, Collins, and New York, Dutton, 1931.
Three Generations Trilogy:
    The Old People. London, Collins, 1931; New York, Dutton, 1932.
    The Middle Generation. London, Collins, 1932; New York, Dutton, 1933.
    The Young People. London, Collins, 1933; New York, Dutton, 1934.
The Next Generation. London, Benn, 1932.
The Inheritor. London, Benn, 1933.
Peckover. London, Heinemann, 1934; New York, Putnam, 1935.
On a Huge HIll. London, Heinemann, 1935.
The Faithful Lovers. London, Hutchinson, and New York, Furman, 1936.
Cleo. London, Hutchinson, 1937.
The Unfinished Road. London, Hutchinson, 1938.
Strange Rival. London, Hutchinson, 1939.
Snell's Folly. London, Hutchinson, 1939.
Quiet Corner. London, Hutchinson, 1940.
The Benefactor. London, Hutchinson, 1943.
The Long View. London, Hutchinson, 1943.
Men in the Same Boat, with Esmé Wynne-Tyson, London, Hutchinson, 1943.
If This Were True—. London, Hutchinson, 1944.
The Prisoner. London, Hutchinson, 1946.
The Gift, with Esmé Wynne-Tyson. London, Hutchinson, 1947.

Short Stories

The Imperturbable Duchess and Other Stories. London, Collins, 1923.
Blackthorn Winter and Other Stories. London, Hutchinson, 1936.

Plays

The Compleat Angler: A Duologue, with A. S. Craven (produced London, 1907). London, French, 1915.
The Royal Heart, with A. S. Craven (produced London, 1908).
The Veiled Woman (produced London, 1913).
Howard and Son, with Kenneth Richmond (produced London, 1916).
The Perfect Machine, with A. S. Craven, in *English Review 26* (London), May 1918.

Verse

Poems by Two Brothers, with Richard Beresford. London, Erskine Macdonald, 1915.

Other

H. G. Wells. London, Nisbet, and New York, Holt, 1915.
Taken from Life, photographs by E. O. Hoppe'AAC. London, Collins, 1922.
Writing Aloud. London, Collins, 1928.
The Case for Faith-Healing. London, Allen and Unwin, 1934.
The Root of the Matter: Essays, with others, edited by H. R. L. Sheppard. London, Cassell, 1937; Freeport, New York, Books for Libraries, 1967.
What I Believe. London, Heinemann, 1938.
The Idea of God. London, Clarke, 1940.

*

Bibliography: "J. D. Beresford: A Bibliography" by Helmut E. Gerber, in *Bulletin of Bibliography 21* (Boston), January-April 1956.

*   *   *

J. D. Beresford, born just seven years after H. G. Wells, had affinities of imagination with the older writer, and similarities of style and theme may have dimmed the Beresford flame in the Wellsian glare. All his excellent science fiction is forgotten save *The Hampdenshire Wonder.* The neglect is regrettable because his attitudes were almost diametrically opposed to those of the politicising and romanticising Wells. Beresford's superficially gentler treatments show, on examination, an appreciation of the grimmer aspects of human nature which Wells tended to gloss in comedy or satire.

The first of Beresford's science fiction novels, *The Hampdenshire Wonder* may stand for most of the qualities and methods of its successors. As the story of a super-intelligent child born to working-class parents (one of the few major science-fiction themes Wells never attempted) it is an obvious forerunner of Stapledon's *Odd John,* but is superior in handling to the later book. The story of the lonely child (unwanted by all except his doting mother, and in his intellectual solitude having little use for her) making his misunderstood way through childhood to an ironical death at the hands of the village idiot illumines the theme of "difference" more clearly than, for example, Sturgeon's melodramatic *More Than Human.* Beresford's viewpoint is peculiar to himself. He was not primarily concerned, like more modern practitioners, with the symptoms and displays of transcendent genius so much as with the effect of this doomed creation's existence on those about him. The child is strongly drawn, with considerable understanding of the requirements of super-intelligence, but the characters who remain with the reader are the father, an uneducated county cricketer and workman who deserts child and wife when he can no longer bear the child's "unnatural" presence, and the mother, whose devotion to the self-absorbed genius is given without any return of affection or understanding. The two, supremely human, emphasise the child's alienness and eeriness in a fashion denied to our "mind-blowing" contemporary writers. Also, they demonstrate that characterisation in depth is possible in a genre which prefers to offer types as symbols of humanity confronting "difference." Beresford presents, without strain, rounded personalities who also manage to symbolise humanity dealing with the incomprehensible.

Goslings recalls Wells's *War of the Worlds* in its portrait of a plague-ridden, deserted London, but again the emphasis is on the reactions of people. Wells's stricken city is a symbol of trampled mankind; Beresford's is a challenge to the ordinary, unschooled but individual people who must live in and defeat it. *The Camberwell Miracle* has a faith healer (if that be the phrase for the talent) as central character, and here Beresford gives love and serenity to a portrait one can only imagine Wells handling with pragmatic savagery. *The Riddle of the Tower* (with Esmé Wynne-Tyson) again invades Wellsian territory, via bomb blast into an alternate spacetime, to discover a human culture reminiscent of the hive or the termitary. Again the treatment is thoughtful rather than dramatic or satirical, though the warning against technological excess is clear.

These novels stand comparison with the best of current science fiction, and, in literary quality, head and shoulders above most. Beresford published over 40 mainstream novels and it is his mainstream approach to science-fiction problems of structure and balance that give his romances a unique flavour.

—George Turner

BERRY, Bryan. Also wrote as Rolf Garner. British. Born in 1930. Worked in publishing; wrote for advertising agencies and educational films. *Died in 1955.*

SCIENCE-FICTION PUBLICATIONS

Novels

And the Stars Remain. London, Panther, 1952.
Born in Captivity. London, Panther, 1952.
Dread Visitor. London, Panther, 1952.
The Venom Seekers. London, Panther, 1953.
From What Far Star? London, Panther, 1953.
Return to Earth. London, Panther, n. d.

Novels as Rolf Garner (series: Venus in all books)

Resurgent Dust. London, Panther, 1953.
The Immortals. London, Panther, 1953.
The Indestructible. London, Panther, 1954.

Uncollected Short Stories

"Aftermath," in *Authentic* (London), August 1952.
"The Final Venusian," "Groundling," and "The Imaginative Man," in *Plannet* (New York), January 1953.
"Ancient City," in *Authentic* (London), May 1953.
"Mars Is Home," in *Planet* (New York), May 1953.
"Mission to Marakee," in *Two Complete Science Adventure Books* (New York), Summer 1953.
"The Tree," in *Authentic* (London), August 1953.
"The Adaptable Man," in *Authentic* (London), September 1953.
"Hidden Shepherds," in *Authentic* (London), February 1954.
"The Toy," in *Planet* (New York), March 1954.
"World Held Captive," in *Two Complete Science Adventure Books* (New York), Spring 1954.
"Savious," in *Authentic* (London), June 1954.
"Strange Suicide," in *Authentic* (London), April 1955.

* * *

The similarity of Bryan Berry's early stories to those of Ray Bradbury probably accounts for his initial success in *Planet Stories* (one issue carried three of his stories). Bradbury and other leading professionals had recently deserted the pulp magazine for better paying markets, and Berry's stories were unabashed space opera, an area the editor of the magazine, Jack O'Sullivan, liked and one in which Bradbury had been inactive for some time.

Berry's *Planet* stories weren't bad, but they hardly justified special attention. In "The Imaginative Man" space explorers encounter Venusians who appear to be mythological beasts. In "Grounding" a man's desire to go into space drives him to murder his wife. "The Final Venusian" tells of an earthman and two androids, the last sentient beings after a war has destroyed Earth and its planetary colonies. The story bears a resemblance to Bradbury's "Dwellers in Silence," and that, coupled with the special treatment singled out by O'Sullivan for Berry's *Planet* debut, led to some anti-Berry letters from readers. Berry's letter of reply stated that his favorite SF writer was not Bradbury but Clifford D. Simak; other favorites were van Vogt, Sturgeon, Russell, del Rey, and the "rising young star" E. C. Tubb.

As a writer, Berry could claim a fairly good style, somewhat more straightforward and less mannered than Bradbury's, but also lacking in Bradbury's verve. Even so, the Bradbury touch was definitely evident in much of his work. His novel "World Held Captive" is a typical sociological SF novel of oppressive government and secret underground organizations, and the world his characters move in is compatible enough with the one described in Bradbury's *Fahrenheit 451*. In his letter Berry described himself as an unabashed romantic with a taste for the melancholy, which probably accounts for a lot of the Bradbury flavor—that and the natural tendency of a beginning writer to fall under the influence of others. It can also be argued that for a relatively inexperienced writer forced to grind out scores of novels to make a living in a market dominated by prolific adventure writers, this was probably a very intelligent approach. British readers must have found Berry's stories a nice contrast to the often slambang fiction of John Russell Fearn.

Not all of Berry's fiction falls easily into the Bradbury pattern, however. "The Adaptable Man" is a highly simplified van Vogtian superman story with its protagonist caught up in a far-reaching plot of which, it turns out, he is the key figure. It's a well-done story, but not nearly so compelling as those more driven and irrational efforts of van Vogt himself. "The Toy" is a well-plotted time-travel story with a stronger ending than most of his stories boasted. "Mars Is Home" also has a strong plot, though weakened by a poor climax.

Berry died at the age of 25. He left a relatively large body of writing behind him, and we can readily discern his lucidity and the fact that in most of his fiction his concerns appear to be the familiar concerns of everyday life; even when his fiction draws its apparent inspiration from van Vogt, the characters remain rather domesticated creatures, not at all like the flamboyant archetypes of either van Vogt or Bradbury. Berry's case is complicated, however, by the fact that much of his fiction is buried under house names that can't be properly identified as belonging to him, though we know he wrote the well-received Venus trilogy as Rolf Garner. Because we can never really know what Berry might have become, it's impossible to read his fiction without regret.

—Gerald W. Page

BESTER, Alfred. American. Born in New York City, 18 December 1913. Educated at the University of Pennsylvania, Philadelphia, B. A. 1935. Married Rolly Goulko in 1936. Freelance writer: book reviewer, *Fantasy and Science Fiction,* New York, 1960-62, radio and TV writer, and staff member, *Holiday,* New York. Recipient: Hugo Award, 1953. Address: c/o Timescape Books, 1230 Avenue of the Americas, New York, New York 10020, U. S. A.

SCIENCE-FICTION PUBLICATIONS

Novels

The Demolished Man. Chicago, Shasta, and London, Sidgwick and Jackson, 1953.
Tiger! Tiger! London, Sidgwick and Jackson, 1956; as *The Stars My Destination,* New York, New American Library, 1957.
The Computer Connection. New York, Berkley, 1975; as *Extro,* London, Eyre Methuen, 1975.
Golem¹⁰⁰. New York, Simon and Schuster, and London, Sidgwick and Jackson, 1980.
The Deceivers. New York, Wallaby, 1981; London, Severn House, 1984.
The Rat Race. London, Arrow, 1984.

Short Stories

Starburst. New York, New American Library, 1958; London, Sphere, 1968.
The Dark Side of Earth. New York, New American Library, 1964; London, Pan, 1969.
The Light Fantastic and *Star Light, Star Bright.* New York, Berkley, 2 vols., 1976; London, Gollancz, 2 vols., 1977-78; as *Starlight: The Great Short Fiction of Alfred Bester,* New York, Doubleday, 1 vol., 1976.

Uncollected Short Story

"Galatea Galante," in *Omni* (New York), April 1979.

OTHER PUBLICATIONS

Novel

Who He? New York, Dial Press, 1953; as *The Rat Race,* New York, Berkley, 1956.

Other

"Gourmet Dining in Outer Space," in *Holiday* (New York), May 1960.
The Life and Death of a Satellite. Boston, Little Brown, 1966; London, Sidgwick and Jackson, 1967.
"My Affair with Science Fiction," in *Hell's Cartographers,* edited by Brian W. Aldiss and Harry Harrison. London, Weidenfeld and Nicolson, 1975; New York, Harper, 1976.
"Writing and *The Demolished Man,*" in *Experiment Perilous,* edited by Andrew Porter. New York, Algol Press, 1976.

*

Critical Study: *Alfred Bester* by Carolyn Wendell, Mercer Island, Washington, Starmont House, 1982.

* * *

Alfred Bester has not been a prolific writer of science fiction. His career has generated so far only a handful of novels and short stories spanning some 35 years. In the space of a limited output, however, Bester has achieved a rare importance in the field. Two of his novels are classics, and a younger generation of writers already acknowledges his influence. Despite this stature, Bester still considers himself an outsider to the genre, and speaks of his "affair" with science fiction. Much of his life has been spent writing for comics, radio, television, and general magazines. Science fiction has remained for him primarily "a safety valve, an escape hatch, therapy. "

Bester is the grand master of what has come to be called the "pyrotechnic" science-fiction novel. His works are fast-paced adventures, full of surprises, and brought together by remarkably intricate convergences of characters, events, and ideas. The manner is a little reminiscent of space opera, but Bester has been subject to more immediate influences in his "action-packed" comic book and broadcast media work. His novels, moveover, are vastly more sophisticated than simple adventure stories.

As a science fiction writer, Bester is more interested in people than in science. In his preface to "The Pi Man" (*Starlight*), he comments, "I'm not much interested in extrapolating science and technology; I merely use extrapolation as a means of putting people into new quandaries which produce colorful pressures and conflicts. " Consequently, the science predominating in Bester's fiction is psychology. His short stories typically assume the focus of extravagant case studies, and—if we can judge from the prefaces—much of their substance derives from the author's habit of analyzing himself (which is perhaps the basis of Bester's "therapy" in science fiction). Bester's favorite character type is the compulsive, the driven man. His stories center on such figures as sources of interest and motivation. Bester calls them his "anti-heroes," but they are usually constructed of heroic material. He endows them with extraordinary powers and sets them loose to interact with their environments in significantly perverse ways. Other characters—representatives of social stability—hunt, observe, and manipulate them, or are in turn manipulated. There is a lot of intrigue in Bester's fiction and a lot of detective work.

When Bester made his move to long fiction, he found a medium well-suited to his compulsive leading characters. *The Demolished Man* makes no significant departure technically from his shorter fiction. The characters, however, have more room to move around. Bester doesn't waste the opportunity. *The Demolished Man* presents a more heterogeneous picture of a culture than was usual for an early 1950's science-fiction novel. Though its leading characters are the cream of an enlightened society—the unmistakable beings of romance—they do not remain insulated from their inferiors. Bester brings them into slums, houses of illusion, and the underworld. Some of this is for exotic contrast, but the willingness at least to recognize the seamy side of a future civilization is refreshing. On one level, *The Demolished Man* is a mystery story. A man commits a murder in the 24th century, when telepathy has made crime discoverable in advance and therefore preventable. How could such a man escape detection? Ben Reich, the murderer, is a powerful man with access to all the technology, brain power, and social deference necessary to legal immunity. He is also ironically a pawn of archetypal patterns, a man whose elaborate criminal strategy blinds him to his own motive. The representative of justice—the first-class telepath Prefect Lincoln Powell—finds himself faced with a predictable dilemma: the conviction and punishment of Reich, while

necessary to the continuing order, will not bring satisfaction. Reich, who embodies the best as well as the worst in humanity, must somehow be reclaimed. In 24th-century technology, Bester allows for such a process.

Bester's second novel, *Tiger! Tiger!,* is generally regarded as his greatest success and as a pinnacle achievement in the field. It is itself an epic success story: the account of a man—bleakly ordinary, abandoned, and near death in space—who manages to save himself, and, with the sole motive of revenge, acquires wealth, knowledge, and eventually the power to defeat his enemies, only to find on the brink of success that his goals no longer make sense to him. This failure of resolve is in effect his final test. He becomes a changed man, a saint instead of a tiger, aspiring to lead others on the road to self determination. In this. novel, Bester ranges even further into the sordid future of poverty, crime, and vice. The protagonist, Gulliver Foyle, is himself a graduate of the gutter, who speaks a common dialect and moves easily among the dregs of 25th-century civilization. During his quest for vengeance, Gully passes through diseased cities and the marketplace of vice. He visits a slave labor camp and spends time in prison, and encounters an array of minor characters that would do well in a wax museum. It is, as Bester warns, "an age of freaks, monsters, and grotesques. "

The variety of setting and abundance of ideas in Bester's longer fiction are an important outcome of structure and of method: his novels are episodic, moving as the term "pyrotechnic" suggests like explosions in series. Successive episodes introduce new surprises rather than resolving old conflicts, up to the eventual climax when the weight of ideas and events finally forces a synthesis. The method takes careful planning and a wealth of raw material. Bester's special talent as a writer is the art of constellation. He draws upon an awesome array of apparently incongruous materials, and proceeds to make connections until he has fabricated a tightly knit and interesting story.

The Computer Connection has the same kind of construction. Some of its social content has been updated in that the heroes include American Indians, blacks, and women who are not beautiful. The characterizations abound in stereotypes, however, and Bester pointedly pokes fun at the social movements of the early 1970's so it is difficult to see any clear social statement. While neither the approach nor the ideas in *The Computer Connection* are as fresh as in his 1950's classics, the novel is still entertaining reading. Bester now confronts the problem facing any major author, of having to write in the context of his own earlier achievements and those of younger writers who have learned from him.

—Robert Froese

BEYNON, John. See WYNDHAM, John.

BIGGLE, Lloyd, Jr. American. Born in Waterloo, Iowa, 17 April 1923. Educated at Wayne University, Detroit, 1941-43, 1946-47, A. B. (honors) 1947; University of Michigan, Ann Arbor, 1947-53, M. M. in music literature 1948, Ph. D in musicology 1953. Served in the United States Army, 1943-46: Sergeant. Married Hedwig T. Janiszewski in 1947; one daughter and one son. First Secretary-Treasurer, 1965-67, Chairman,

Board of Trustees, 1967-71, and Founder of the Regional Collections, Science Fiction Writers of America. Founder, and since 1979, President, Science Fiction Oral History Association. Lives in Ypsilanti, Michigan. Agent: Sharon Jarvis, Jarvis Braff Ltd., 260 Willard Avenue, Staten Island, New York 10314, U. S. A.

SCIENCE-FICTION PUBLICATIONS

Novels (series: Cultural Survey; Jan Darzek)

The Angry Espers. New York, Ace, 1961; London, Hale, 1968.
All the Colors of Darkness (Darzek). New York, Doubleday, 1963; London, Dobson, 1964.
The Fury Out of Time. New York, Doubleday, 1965; London, Dobson, 1966.
Watchers of the Dark (Darzek). New York, Doubleday, 1966; London Rapp and Whiting, 1968.
The Still Small Voice of Trumpets (Survey). New York, Doubleday, 1968; London, Rapp and Whiting, 1969.
The World Menders (Survey). New York, Doubleday, 1971; Morley, Yorkshire, Elmfield Press, 1973.
The Light That Never Was. New York, Doubleday, 1972; Morley, Yorkshire, Elmfield Press, 1975.
Monument. New York, Doubleday, 1974; London, New English Library, 1975.
This Darkening Universe (Darzek). New York, Doubleday, 1975; London, Millington, 1977.
Silence Is Deadly (Darzek). New York, Doubleday, 1977; London, Millington, 1980.
The Whirligig of Time (Darzek). New York, Doubleday, 1979.
Alien Main, with T. L. Sherred. New York, Doubleday, 1985.

Short Stories

The Rule of the Door and Other Fanciful Regulations. New York, Doubleday, 1967; as *Out of the Silent Sky*, New York, Belmont Tower, 1977; as *The Silent Sky*, London, Hale, 1979.
The Metallic Muse. New York, Doubleday, 1972.
A Galaxy of Strangers. New York, Doubleday, 1976.

Uncollected Short Story

"The Weariest River," in *Omni* (New York), November 1978.

OTHER PUBLICATIONS

Other

"Science Fiction Goes to College: Groves and Morasses of Academe," in *Riverside Quarterly* (Regina, Saskatchewan), April 1974.
"Quantum Physics and Reality," with Michael Talbot, in *Analog* (New York), December 1976.
"The Morasses of Academe Revisited," in *Analog* (New York), September 1978.
"The Arts: Media," in *Analog* (New York), January 1980.
"Roots: A Taxicab Tour of Science Fiction History," in *Inside Outer Space*, edited by Sharon Jarvis. New York, Ungar, 1985.

Editor, *Nebula Award Stories 7*. London, Gollancz, 1972; New York, Harper, 1973.

*

Manuscript Collection: Spencer Research Library, University of Kansas, Lawrence.

*   *   *

The best-known creations of Lloyd Biggle, Jr., are the Council of Supreme and its extensions, the agents of the Galactic Synthesis, the Cultural Survey, and the Interplanetary Relations Bureau, known for mottoes such as "Democracy Imposed from Without Is the Severest Form of Tyranny." Supreme is a vast computer that is fed information by its eight councilors; the only human is number ONE, Jan Darzek, who ironically was recruited by Supreme from uncertified Earth (i.e., not fit for social intercourse with civilized planets because its inhabitants tell lies) through Rok Wllon, who eventually becomes EIGHT. EIGHT dislikes ONE personally but they unite in common cause against the Dark Force, the Udef, which threatens the universe.

Supreme is not a ruler but an advisor, though people tend to accept its wisdom without hesitation since it eventually always proves reliable. Supreme—the ultimate in impartial democratic justice—fails in its function only when it is deprived of data input or asked the wrong question, thus simultaneously demonstrating the old programmers' wisdom "Garbage in; garbage out" and suggesting the need for an informed electorate of enlightened self interest.

Always highly readable, Biggle narrates the adventures of Jan Darzek as he saves Earth in *All the Colors of Darkness*, the galaxy in *Watchers of the Dark*, and a large part of the universe in *This Darkening Universe*, as well as two individual worlds in *Silence Is Deadly* and *The Whirligig of Time*. In *The World Menders* and *The Still, Small Voice of Trumpets* the Cultural Survey officers must cope with bureaucracy while solving the problems of how to bring an uncertified world into the Galactic Synthesis of self-rule and trade with other planets. *Monument* and *The Light That Never Was* also deal with the place of art and beauty in human culture and civilization.

Biggle's characterization is generally drawn with vivid broad strokes in the literary tradition of Charles Dickens; e. g., Darzek's assistant is a little old lady, Miss Schlupe ("Schluppy"), who loves the comfort of her rocking chair as she makes beer out of whatever exotic vegetation is available wherever she lands in the galaxy. The chief interest in Biggle's stories is not character motivation, but puzzle solving, understanding the nature of the universe so that it can be managed intelligently. Throughout his stories, intelligent life in whatever form it appears (even a giant vegetable computer) earns respect. In the ironic tradition of Jonathan Swift, humanoid-appearing creatures may turn out to be sub-human animals (*The World Menders*), as determined by their lack of culture, particularly religion and the arts. Repeatedly Biggle dramatizes the need for a holistic understanding of a culture, including the ecological balance of a planet and the physical strengths and weaknesses of its inhabitants. Tolerance and respect for differences between species is demonstrated to benefit all intelligent beings, and Biggle uses gentle satire to provide moral instruction as he delights.

His greatest strength is in creating believable alien worlds and civilizations, complete with native flora and fauna, linguistic idiosyncrasies, customs of courtship and marriage, provisions for raising children, social intercourse and folkways (always inseparable from economic trade and business affairs), religion, systems of government, and culture in its most inclusive sense. Because of this complexity, it is unfair to limit his stories with the label juvenile—even though neither his heroes nor his villains ever uses expletives stronger than "drat"—but his clear-cut pro-life moral tone is particularly suitable for young readers.

Unfortunately Biggle is currently writing very little short fiction, but some of the best of his stories are available in three collections; *A Galaxy of Strangers* contains the perfect gem "And Madly Teach. "

—Elizabeth Anne Hull

BINDER, Eando. Pseudonym for Otto Oscar Binder (and his brother Earl Andrew Binder until 1934); also wrote as John Coleridge; Ian Francis Turek; Ione Frances Turek. American. Born in Bessemer, Michigan, 26 August 1911. Studied science and chemical engineering at Crane City College, Northwestern University, Evanston, Illinois, and the University of Chicago for three years. Married Ione Frances Turek in 1940; one daughter. Clerk, Central Scientific Company, Chicago, 1930-31; assistant to Science Librarian, Crerar Library, Chicago, 1931-32; free-lance writer after 1932: reader of manuscripts, Otis Kline Literary Agency, 1936-38; comic book writer from 1941; Editor, *Space World*, New York, 1962-63. *Died 14 October 1974.*

SCIENCE-FICTION PUBLICATIONS

Novels

Lords of Creation. Philadelphia, Prime Press, 1949.
Enslaved Brains. New York, Avalon, 1965.
The Avengers Battle the Earth-Wrecker. New York, Bantam, 1967.
Menace of the Saucers. New York, Belmont, 1969.
The Impossible World. New York, Curtis, 1970.
Five Steps to Tomorrow. New York, Curtis, 1970.
The Double Man. New York, Curtis, 1971.
Get Off My World. New York, Curtis, 1971.
Night of the Saucers. New York, Belmont, 1971.
Puzzle of the Space Pyramids. New York, Curtis, 1971.
Secret of the Red Spot. New York, Curtis, 1971.
Terror in the Bay (as Ione Frances Turek). New York, Curtis, 1971.
The Mind from Outer Space. New York, Curtis, 1972.
The Forgotten Colony (as Otto Binder). New York, Popular Library, 1972.
The Hospital Horror (as Otto Binder). New York, Popular Library, 1973.
The Frontier's Secret (as Ian Francis Turek). New York, Popular Library, 1973.

Short Stories

Martian Martyrs (as John Coleridge). New York, Columbia, 1940.
The New Life (as John Coleridge). New York, Columbia, 1940.
The Three Eternals. Sydney, Whitman Press, 1949.
Adam Link in the Past. Sydney, Whitman Press, 1950.
Where Eternity Ends. Sydney, Whitman Press, 1950.
Adam Link—Robot. New York, Paperback Library, 1965.
Anton York, Immortal. New York, Belmont, 1965.

Uncollected Short Stories

"The Cancer Machine," in *Bizarre 3* (Millheim, Pennsylvania), 1940.
"All in Good Time," in *Signs and Wonders,* edited by Roger Elwood. Old Tappan, New Jersey, Revell, 1972.
"Any Resemblance to Magic," in *Long Night of Waiting,* edited by Roger Elwood. Minneapolis, Lerner, 1974.
"Better Dumb Than Dead," in *Journey to Another Star,* edited by Roger Elwood. Minneapolis, Lerner, 1974.
"The Missing World," in *The Missing World,* edited by Roger Elwood. Minneapolis, Lerner, 1974.

OTHER PUBLICATIONS

Play

Television Play: *I, Robot,* 1964.

Other

The Golden Book of Space Travel [Atomic Energy, Jets and Rockets] (for children). New York, Golden Press, 3 vols., 1959-61.
The Moon, Our Neighboring World (for children). New York, Golden Press, 1959.
Planets: Other Worlds of Our Solar System (for children). New York, Golden Press, 1959.
Victory in Space. New York, Walker, 1962.
Careers in Space. New York, Walker, 1963.
Riddles of Astronomy. New York, Basic Books, 1964.
Dracula (comic book; as Otto Binder), with Craig Tennis. New York, Ballantine, 1966.
What We Really Know about Flying Saucers. New York, Fawcett, 1967.
Mankind, Child of the Stars, with Max H. Flindt. New York, Fawcett, 1974; London, Coronet, 1976.
The Mysterious Island (comic book). West Haven, Connecticut, Pendulum Press, 1974.

*   *   *

Though the unique name Eando is formed from "E and O," representing Earl and Otto Binder, for all practical purposes Eando was Otto Binder; the early, collaborative stories comprise a very minor component of the Binder works, both qualitatively and quantitatively. Binder maintained that a real professional could write anything, from the libretto of an opera to a technical manual. While not embracing quite this broad a range, his works were sufficiently varied to give the notion strong support. In addition to his science fiction, Binder produced weird-horror fiction, gothic romance, and considerable non-fiction, as well as hundreds of comic book and comic strip "scripts. "

Binder's most important single story is generally regarded to be "I, Robot," published in the January 1939 *Amazing.* (The Isaac Asimov book, *I, Robot,* appeared in 1950. Its title was as much a tribute to Binder as anything else; in his autobiography, Asimov attributes the inspiration of his famous "positronic robot" stories to a meeting with Binder and the reading of Binder's "I, Robot. ") The significance of Binder's story lies in its sympathetic, even emotional, portrayal of the robot Adam Link. This effect is heightened by the first-person narration. The story was hugely successful and led to a series of popular sequels. Lester del Rey's equally significant "sympathetic robot" story, "Helen O'Loy," was written independently and simultaneously with Binder's "I, Robot," and actually reached print in *Astounding* a month before Binder's story. Del Rey abandoned the theme after a single effort, while Binder, Asimov, and shortly thereafter Eric Frank Russell (with his Jay Score stories) continued the development of the theme.

Binder's stories collected as *Anton York—Immortal* were also highly popular in their day, although lacking in the seminal significance of the Adam Link series. The Anton York stories are concerned with the impact of immortality on a lone man (eventually joined by an immortal wife) and on society. A number of Binder's other stories and novels achieved popularity in their time, but have little present readership. Their loss of popularity is probably due to Binder's stylistic limitation. Though a perfectly competent writer, he did not often succeed in bringing a sense of excitement to his prose; an illuminating comparison is E. E. Smith, whose unbounded energy totally transcended the limitations of his weak prose style.

Binder's "Via Etherline" tales were later collected as *Puzzle of the Space Pyramids.* Prior to the appearance of these stories, space travel and interplanetary exploration were almost always portrayed as glamorous, romantic activities. Binder instead portrayed them as grimy, difficult, dangerous, and often boring tasks. The stories were echoed in the realistic/predictive space fiction of Arthur C. Clarke, e. g., *Prelude to Space, Sands of Mars, A Fall of Moondust.*

In the 1940's and 1950's, Binder devoted most of his efforts to writing comic book continuity. As the principal writer for the *Captain Marvel* feature, he was chiefly responsible for the humorous, satirical, and often science-fiction elements that best characterized that altogether superior feature. In the 1960's, he developed an interest in UFOs and possible space-visitors, and three of his last works were devoted to these themes. One other series of stories by Binder is noteworthy. These are the tales about Jon Jarl, a young officer in the space patrol of the future. Binder wrote literally scores of these stories as text filler in the *Captain Marvel Adventures* comic book. As juvenile science fiction, they are charming, succinct, and stimulating. They have, unfortunately, never been collected.

—Richard A. Lupoff

BINDER, Otto. See **BINDER, Eando.**

BISCHOFF, David F(rederick). American. Born in Washington D. C., 15 December 1951. Educated at the University of Maryland, College Park, B. A. 1973. Worked as dishwasher, soda-jerk, clerk; Associate Editor, *Amazing,* New York. Since 1974, staff member, NBC-TV, Washington, D. C. Secretary, 1978-80, and since 1980, Vice-President, Science Fiction Writers of America. Agent: Henry Morrison Inc., 320 McLain Street, Bedford Hills, New York 10705, U. S. A.

SCIENCE-FICTION PUBLICATIONS

Novels (series: Dragonstar; Nightworld)

The Seeker, with Christopher Lampton. Toronto, Laser, 1976.
Forbidden World, with Ted White. New York, Popular Lib-

rary, 1978.
Tin Woodman, with Dennis R. Bailey. New York, Doubleday, 1979; London, Sidgwick and Jackson, 1980.
Nightworld. New York, Ballantine, 1979.
Star Fall. New York, Berkley, 1980.
The Vampires of Nightworld. New York, Ballantine, 1981.
Star Spring. New York, Berkley, 1982.
Day of the Dragonstar, with Thomas F. Monteleone. New York, Berkley, 1983.
Mandala. New York, Berkley, 1983.
Wargames (novelization of screenplay). New York, Dell, and London, Penguin, 1983.
Night of the Dragonstar, with Thomas F. Monteleone. New York, Berkley, 1985.

Uncollected Short Stories

"Feeding Time," with Christopher Lampton, in *50-Meter Monsters and Other Horrors,* edited by Roger Elwood. New York, Pocket Books, 1976.
"Top Hat," in *Fantastic* (New York), December, 1977.
"Alone and Palely Loitering," in *Chrysalis 3,* edited by Roy Torgeson. New York, Kensington, 1978.
"The Sky's an Oyster, The Stars Are Pearls," in *100 Great Science Fiction Short-Short Stories*, edited by Isaac Asimov, Martin H. Greenberg, and Joseph D. Olander. New York, Doubleday, and London, Robson, 1978.
"A Forbidden World," with Ted White in *Amazing* (New York), January 1978.
"In Medias Res," in *Fantastic* (New York), April 1978.
"All the Stage, a World," in *Chrysalis 5,* edited by Roy Torgeson. New York, Zebra, 1979.
"Outside," in *Fantasy and Science Fiction* (New York), April 1980.
"Waterloo Sunset," in *The Berkley Showcase 5,* edited by Victoria Schochet and Melissa Singer. New York, Berkley, 1982.
"The Salesman," in *Rigel* (Richmond, California), Winter 1982.
"The Warmth of the Stars," in *Chrysalis 10,* edited by Roy Torgeson. New York, Doubleday, 1983.
"Wired," in *Omni* (New York), August 1983.

OTHER PUBLICATIONS

Novel

The Selkie, with Charles Sheffield. New York, Macmillan, 1982.

Other (for children)

Quest. Milwaukee, Raintree, 1977.
Strange Encounters. Milwaukee, Raintree, 1977.
The Phantom of the Opera. New York, Scholastic, 1977.

Editor, *Strange Encounters.* Milwaukee, Raintree, 1977.

*   *   *

David F. Bischoff has, in just a few years, produced a substantial number of novels and short stories, either on his own or in collaboration with any of several other writers. His earliest book-length appearance was *The Seeker,* written in collaboration with Christopher Lampton. A humanoid alien crashes on Earth, a refugee from a repressive interstellar society. His pursuers are not willing to let him disappear, and agents arrive determined to find him.

This was just the first of several collaborative novels under Bischoff's byline. Perhaps the most successful collaborative effort was *Tin Woodman,* written with Dennis R. Bailey. A young man with telepathic powers and an inability to fit into human society is sent on a mission to attempt communication with an alien sentient starship. Unfortunately, the man commanding the contact team is a power-hungry psychopath who bullies his crew, falsifies orders, and endangers the entire mission as the alien ship and boy escape, only to be pursued across the galaxy. The interplay of the crew as they consider mutiny is particularly well done.

Day of the Dragonstar, written in collaboration with Thomas F. Monteleone, is an adventure-filled variant of the gigantic artificial-world-in-space plot. The Dragonstar turns out to be an enormous zoo and the initial exploration team is massacred by dinosaurs, and a rescue team must discover whether there are any survivors. There follows a fairly predictable but entertaining series of events. A sequel, *Night of the Dragonstar,* is scheduled for release in 1985.

Other novels co-written by Bischoff include *The Selkie,* an interesting fantasy/horror novel written with Charles Sheffield, and *Forbidden World,* the adventures of some space explorers on a world that seem just a bit too good to be true, co-authored with Ted White. Bischoff has also written two movie novelizations, a young readers version of *The Phantom of the Opera,* and the novel tie-in for the recent movie *Wargames.*

He has produced a number of novels in his own right as well, most of which are above-average adventure stories. In *Mandala* a ruthless general from a world that has dominated inhabited space suffers amnesia, and is subsequently nursed back to health by a telepathic woman. The contact with the woman effectively alters his personality, and he returns to his former associates determined to change the status quo. The sudden reversal of the protagonist's personality might be a bit difficult to accept, but there follows a frequently interesting story of subversion from within.

A much more successful work is *Nightworld* and its sequel, *Vampires of Nightworld.* In the first, we are presented with a planet which is no longer in contact with the rest of humanity. An enormous computer dominates the world from its secret retreat, and has created hosts of androids to fill the parts of vampires, dragons, werewolves, ghouls, and other mythological creatures. An unlikely hero finds himself pitted against this computer and, accompanied by a man equipped with some remnants of mankind's technology, he sets off to locate and destroy Satan, the ruler of his world. In the sequel, the computer has been destroyed, but the roving devices it has created are still a genuine menace to the human inhabitants of the world, particularly the powerful vampires. The two novels are interesting blends of adventure, suspense, and genuine humor, and are probably the most successful of Bischoff's solo ventures.

Star Fall and its sequel, *Star Spring,* are worth noting as well. The former deals with the maiden voyage of a luxury star liner and the adventure that takes place on its journey to earth. The protagonist finds that he has inadvertently swapped bodies with a famous assassin, and vengeful relatives of the past victims are disinclined to listen to his protestations of innocence. The ship itself is owned by an alien who desires to provoke a war between humanity and his own species, and is not above causing an incident to that purpose. The same cast of characters returns for the most part in *Star Spring,* this time the targets of a series of murder attempts, and ultimately to become lost in space.

Bischoff is an infrequent short story writer, and has yet to produce a really outstanding piece at that length, but a few of his shorter pieces contain interesting ideas. "In Medias Res" is a fascinating piece about a hack writer who can only produce the middles of stories; he is totally incapable of writing a beginning or conclusion. An actor becomes lost in the interface between his play and reality in "All the Stage, a World. " All times co-exist in "Waterloo Sunset," probably Bischoff's most successful short story to date.

—Don D'Ammassa

BISHOP, Michael. American. Born in Lincoln, Nebraska, 12 November 1945. Educated at the University of Georgia, Athens, B. A. in English 1967 (Phi Beta Kappa), M. A. 1968. Served in the United States Air Force as English Instructor, Air Force Academy Preparatory School, 1968-72: Captain. Married Jeri Ellis Whitaker in 1969; one son and one daughter. English Instructor, University of Georgia, 1972-74. Since 1974, free-lance writer. Recipient: Deep South Con XV Phoenix Award, 1977; Clark Ashton Smith Award, for verse, 1978; Nebula Award, 1982, 1983; *Locus* Award, 1984. Agent: Howard Morhain, 501 Fifth Avenue, New York, New York 10017. Address: Box 646, Pine Mountain, Georgia 31822, U.S.A.

SCIENCE-FICTION PUBLICATIONS

Novels

A Funeral for the Eyes of Fire. New York, Ballantine, 1975; London, Sphere, 1978; revised edition, as *Eyes of Fire,* New York, Pocket Books, 1980.
And Strange at Ecbatan the Trees. New York, Harper, 1976; as *Beneath the Shattered Moons,* New York, DAW, 1977; London, Sphere, 1978.
Stolen Faces. New York, Harper, and London, Gollancz, 1977.
A Little Knowledge. New York, Berkley, 1977.
Catacomb Years. New York, Berkley, 1979.
Transfigurations. New York, Berkley, 1979; London, Gollancz, 1980.
Under Heaven's Bridge, with Ian Watson. London, Gollancz, 1981; New York, Ace, 1982.
No Enemy But Time. New York, Pocket Books, and London, Gollancz, 1982.
Who Made Stevie Crye ? Sauk City, Wisconsin, Arkham House, 1984.
Ancient of Days. New York, Arbor House, 1985.

Short Stories

Blooded on Arachne. Sauk City, Wisconsin, Arkham House, 1982.
One Winter in Eden. Sauk City, Wisconsin, Arkham House, 1984.

OTHER PUBLICATIONS

Verse

Windows and Mirrors. Tuscaloosa, Alabama, Moravian Press, 1977.

Other

"On Reviewing and Being Reviewed," in *Shayol 1* (New York), November 1977.
"Evangels of Hope," in *Foundation 14* (London), September 1978.
Introduction to *Ubik*, by Philip K. Dick. Boston, Hall, 1979.
"Conversation with Furthermore B. Hayves," in *Thrust 12*, Summer 1979.

Editor, with Ian Watson, *Changes*. New York, Ace, 1982.
Editor, *Light Years and Dark: Science Fiction and Fantasy of and for Our Time*. New York, Berkley, 1984.

*

Bibliography: *Michael Bishop: A Preliminary Bibliography* by David Nee, Berkeley, California, Other Change of Hobbit, 1983.

Manuscript Collection: University of Georgia Libraries, Athens.

*   *   *

Michael Bishop is an extraordinary writer whose work has the scope and brilliance rivaled only by Robert Silverberg. In 1982, Bishop won the Nebula Award for his story "The Quikening," a hauntingly surreal tale of dislocation and loss. In 1983, Bishop again won a Nebula Award, this time for his outstanding novel, *No Enemy But Time*.

Where earlier Bishop novels suffered from structural problems—confusing narratives, intertwining subplots, shifts in person from first to third and back again—Bishop masters the technical skills to bring off a superb performance in *No Enemy But Time*. An infant, given away to a group of young girls near an Air Force base by his mute, prostitute mother, is adopted by one of the families and given the name John Monegal. The child grows up to be different from other children: he experiences intense episodes of dreaming—"spirit-travel"—where he goes back in time to the Pleistocene era in Africa. After an argument with his stepmother, John leaves and later confronts an expert on the Pleistocene during a scientific conference. He makes such an impression, he's later recruited by the expert for a special project: a time-travel expedition to the Pleistocene. John goes and finds his dreams were real: everything is as he dreamed it. He meets the primitive humans inhabiting the African wilds: the habiline. John cleverly becomes one of the small band of habilines, and "marries" a female he calls Helen. Helen bears him a daughter before dying. Then during an inferno, John takes his infant daughter time traveling to the present, where their lives are forever changed. *No Enemy But Time* is a searing novel of identity and misdirection. John's relationship with Helen is one of the most moving in the genre.

Also moving, but now in a more comic vein, Bishop's latest novel, *Ancient of Days*, explores the possibilities of a habiline surviving in contemporary society. Expanded from the brilliant novella "Her Habiline Husband," *Ancient of Days* is Bishop's vehicle to present a critique of American society. Narrated by a restaurant owner whose ex-wife scandalizes the small Georgia town by first living with the habiline—eventually marrying "Adam"—Bishop's clever sense of situation comedy and Southern mores delivers a story that is funny and sadly true. The characters are finely crafted and subtly drawn. *Ancient of Days* is Bishop's most controlled novel.

Bishop's first novel, *A Funeral for the Eyes of Fire* (later revised as *Eyes of Fire*) shows the problems of alien cultures trying to communicate. Much of the book is anthropologic: Bishop shows strange customs and taboos, alien Tropemen "celebrate" in their rites centering on their eyes and the eyes of their ancestors. The action is slowed by long descriptions of alien lifestyles; when the realization of the lead character finally arrives, the reader is far ahead of the narrative.

And Strange at Ecbatan the Trees (later retitled just as clumsily *Beneath the Shattered Moon*) reads like a dreamy Jack Vance novel. On the planet Mansueceria, the genetically engineered society is made up of two groups: Maskers, programmed against strong emotion; and Atarites, the rulers who are capable of strong emotion and domination. The groups complement each other; under the 6,000-years-old plan devised by the Parfects of Earth, the rulers and the ruled live in harmony on the island of Ongladred. Yet they are in danger of destruction by the barbarians living on the islands beyond Ongladred. Only Gabriel Elk of Stonelore, who presents dramas acted by resurrected corpses, has the power to create weapons to save Ongladred. But by saving Ongladred, Gabriel Elk disrupts the society and the ancient plan for harmony.

Stolen Faces is Bishop's darkest novel. Lucian Yeardance is exiled to the planet Tezcatl to govern a colony for victims of a leprosy-like disease where Aztec rituals are embodied in the culture. Lucian discovers the disease is nonexistent: instead, the victims are a bizarre society whose mental illness is so extreme that mutilation is the group's method of self expression. The writing is bleak and the action violent. Although macabre and depressing, *Stolen Faces* presents discrimination in graphic terms—a theme Bishop will return to in later works.

A Little Knowledge and *Catacomb Years* are a pair of linked novels. In *A Little Knowledge* Bishop presents 2071 Atlanta as a domed city where people's status is reflected by the building level they live on. The society is a theocracy dominated by the Orth-Urban Church. Six aliens from 61 Cygni destabilize the status quo by professing faith in the Church. The philosophical and theological foundations of the culture are shaken as the power brokers have to come to grips with the alien question. The most entertaining subplot is the love story between a deacon in the Church and an agnostic journalist. But the book suffers from too many characters—most of them undeveloped—and murky plotting.

Catacomb Years continues the story of Atlanta with many new characters. Bishop develops the implications that the Cygnusians are actually reincarnated humans. The resulting political and religious upheaval results in the breakdown of the domed city and a chance at freedom under open skies. Although technically superior to *A Little Knowledge*, *Catacomb Years* suffers from being overly long and tedious; a reedited single volume combining the best of *A Little Knowledge* and *Catacomb Years* would be much more satisfying than the present flamed twin novels.

Transfigurations is an expanded version of Bishop's novelette that was a Hugo and Nebula nominee in 1973: "Death and Designation among the Adadi." The original story of an obsessed anthropologist attempting to solve the mysteries of an enigmatic race of aliens gives way to the anthropologist's daughter's search for her missing father. The result is a disappointing extrapolation of the original story's premises proving that by revealing more of a mystery you get a less compelling resolution than when the reader is left to imagine and ponder the inexplicable.

Bishop's short-story collections gather most of his Hugo and Nebula Award winners and nominees. *Blooded on Arachne* includes 13 stories published between 1970 and 1978. The best are "Blooded on Arachne," "Rogue Tomato," "The White Otters of Childhood," and "Cathadonian Odyssey. " *One Winter in Eden* includes a dozen stories published between 1979 and 1983. The best are "One Winter in Eden," "The Quickening," "Cold War Orphans," "Saving Face," "Season of Belief," "Within the Walls of Tyre," and "Collaborating. "

As an anthologist, Bishop has shown marvelous taste. In *Changes,* edited with Ian Watson, Bishop presents a theme anthology centering on humans transforming into . . . something else. But Bishop's masterpiece anthology is the controversial *Light Years and Dark*. Bishop blends original stories commissioned for this volume with notable stories published in the last 25 years. The result is a definitive collection that should rank with Harlan Ellison's *Dangerous Visions* anthologies.

Michael Bishop is a talented novelist, short-story writer, and anthologist who is rapidly becoming one of the most important figures writing science fiction today.

—George Kelley

BIXBY, (Drexel) Jerome (Lewis). American. Born in Hollywood, California, 11 January 1923. Studied piano and composition at the Juilliard School of Music, New York. Served in the Medical Corps, United States Army Air Corps, during World War II: Private. Married 1) Sarah Reader in 1946; 2) Linda Burman in 1967 (divorced); three children. Editor, Fiction House, 1949-51, *Planet Stories* and *Two Complete Science Adventure Books*, 1950-51, *Action Stories* and *Frontier Stories*, Standard Publications, 1951-53, Galaxy Publications, 1953-54; Owner, Exoterica mail-order business, 1963-64, and Walden Realty Company, 1964-65, both in Bullhead City, Arizona.

SCIENCE-FICTION PUBLICATIONS

Novel

Star Trek: Day of the Dove. New York, Bantam, 1978.

Short Stories

The Devil's Scrapbook. New York, Brandon House, 1964.
Space by the Tale. New York, Ballantine, 1964.

OTHER PUBLICATIONS

Plays

Screenplays: *It! The Terror from Beyond Space*, 1958; *Curse of the Faceless Man*, 1958: *The Lost Missile*, with John McPartland and Lester William Berke, 1958; *Fantastic Voyage*, with others, 1966.

Television Plays: *Mirror, Mirror*, 1967, *By Any Other Name*, with D. C. Fontana, 1967, *Day of the Dove*, 1968, and *Requiem for Methuselah*, 1968, all in *Star Trek* series.

*   *   *

With second careers as editor, screenwriter, TV writer, real estate developer, and with a serious interest in musical composition, Jerome Bixby has not taken good enough care of his work as a science-fiction writer or pushed his own editors and publishers hard enough to get his work into print for access by the contemporary reader. Only one volume of collected SF, *Space by the Tale*, and one of horror and fantasy tales, *The Devil's Scrapbook*, have been published. Beyond these only occasional tales in anthologies, led by Bixby's most famous story. "It's a *Good* Life" (1953), form the surface portion of an iceberg of over 300 SF stories and 1000 other stories.

Space by the Tale is an indirect compliment to Bixby as an editor, for his own selection captures the range of the skills of this most interesting and whimsical of short story producers. All of the stories, except perhaps the slightly laboured "The Bad Life," are models of Bixby's characteristic light, clean, quick style and of a story told clearly and quickly. For style and story-telling alone "It's a *Good* Life" fully deserves its classic status. In a series of short, macabre comic scenes Bixby sketches a mid-American farming town where little Anthony, a mutated "baby," is born with godlike powers of telekinesis, telepathy, and the ability to make and destroy the material universe. He has isolated the town, possibly destroying the rest of creation, and both as "baby" and "boy" he has struck back unconsciously when hate is directed at him, neatly planting in a cornfield the destroyed persons and animals which he first changes in unspeakable ways. The story is brilliantly paranoid, as no one alive in the town can *think* ill of Anthony, his acts, or their situation, for at any moment they may catch his attention and be struck down. The story has a pervasive air of inevitability and horror.

"It's a *Good* Life" is typical of Bixby's best stories in three ways. First, it presents a model of an omniscient god and poses the question of the morality of godhead. Anthony has immense powers but wholly immature moral judgement, which puts him part way between the omnipotent Judeo-Christian god and the capricious Greek Olympians. Bixby has written numerous fantasy stories about God and the Devil in conflict, which, however whimsical in the Stephen Vincent Benét tradition, are at heart moral tales. In "It's a *Good* Life" he asks what the universe would be like with a malevolent, child-like god who simply holds personal comfort and pleasure above any standard of his own behaviour. That "child-like" Anthony reminds the reader of Bixby's second gift, his skill at observing human beings. His young god is capable of malice but also of bored benevolence and even kindness. The frightened townspeople are very real, very typical, yet slight variations in their reactions stamp their experiences as authentic, heightening the terror. This same care with the creation of characters is of assistance when Bixby writes his more whimsical stories, giving a delicacy of shading to the humour. The third way in which "It's a *Good* Life is characteristic of Bixby's SF work is that it is not a "hard" science story, Bixby can write such stories ("Small World" and "The Bad Life" in *Space by the Tale*), but his forte really lies at the juncture of SF, fantasy, and the moral tale, where a generalised scientific concept provides a base for a story of human nature. Anthony is a typical creation. His conception is not explained and his powers are described in general rather than technical terms. Anthony can "think" people into a cornfield, "do the thing" to separate the town from the rest of the world, and "change" people in horrible but undescribed ways. Stories such as these are fantasies but they are based on concepts accepted by SF. *Space by the Tale*, for example, contains "The Draw," in which telekinesis creates the fastest of all western gunmen; "The Young One," about a family of werewolves settling in the midwest with their son; "Angels in the Jets," about a planet where something in the atmosphere drives everyone crazy in a liberating fashion; and "Laboratory," about gigantic creatures whose laboratory asteroid is wrecked when two humans blunder into its invisible environs.

Bixby's best stories have an energetic twist. The resident imp in "The Magic Typewriter" is bound to bring to pass everything typed on the machine, which is marvellous until its owner goes out for cigarettes and his horribly ugly landlady sits down and types an illiterate yet deadly letter making him her lover and taking over the typewriter. The Devil in "Trace" actually does a favour for a lawyer whose car has broken down. In this sly allegory about the sudden kindness of the rich at their summer places Bixby proves that even the Devil has his good moments. When the Devil finds out that he is helping a lawyer his murmured, "Ah. Then perhaps we may meet again" is typical of the quiet wit of this charming and skillful craftsman.

—Peter A. Brigg

BLADE, Alexander. See **GARRETT, Randall; PHILLIPS, Rog.**

BLAKE, Anthony. See **TUBB, E.C.**

BLAYRE, Christopher. Pseudonym for Edward Heron-Allen; also wrote as Nora Helen Warddel. British. Born in London, 17 December 1861. Educated at Harrow School. Served with the Staff Intelligence Department of the War Office during World War I. Married 1) Marianna Lehmann in 1891; 2) Edith Pepler in 1903, one daughter. Admitted as a Solicitor of the Supreme Court, 1884. Lived in the United States, 1886-89; gave frequent lectures on protozoology. Editor, with E. Polonaski, *Violin Times*, London, 1893-1907. Fellow, Royal Society, 1919. *Died 28 March 1943.*

SCIENCE-FICTION PUBLICATIONS

Short Stories

The Purple Sapphire and Other Posthumous Stories. London, Philip Allan, 1921; revised edition, as *The Strange Papers of Dr. Blayre*, 1932; New York, Arno Press, 1976.
The Cheetah-Girl. Privately printed, 1923.
Some Women of the University, Being a Last Selection from the Strange Papers of Christopher Blayre. London, Stockwell, 1934.

OTHER PUBLICATIONS as Edward Heron-Allen

Novels

The Princess Daphne London, Drane, 1885; Chicago, Belford Clarke, 1888.
The Romance of a Quiet Watering-Place (as Nora Helen Warddel). Chicago, Belford Clarke, 1888.

Short Stories

Kisses of Fate. Chicago, Belford Clarke, 1888.
A Fatal Fiddle. Chicago, Belford Clarke, 1890.

Verse

The Love-Letters of a Vagabond. London, Drane, 1889.
The Ballades of a Blasé Man. Privately Printed, 1891.

Other

De Fidiculis Opusculum. Privately printed, 9 vols., 1882-1941.
Chiromancy; or, The Science of Palmistry, with Henry Frith. London, Routledge, 1883.
Codex Chiromantiae. Privately printed, 3 vols., 1883-86.
Violin-Making, As It Was and Is. London, Ward Lock, 1884; Boston, Howe, 1901.
A Manual of Cheirosophy. London, Ward Lock, 1885.
Practical Cheirosophy: A Synoptical Study of the Science of the Hand. New York and London, Putnam, 1887.
De Fidiculis Bibliographia, Being an Attempt Towards a Bibliography of the Violin and All Other Instruments with a Bow. London, Griffith Farran, 2 vols., 1890-94.
Prolegomena Towards the Study of Chalk Foraminifera. London, Nichols, 1894.
Some Side-lights upon Edward FitzGerald's Poem "The Rubá'iyát of Omar Khayyám". London, Nichols, 1898.
Nature and History at Selsea Bill. Selsey, Sussex, Gardner, 1911.
Selsey Bill: Historic and Prehistoric. London Duckworth, 1911.
The Visitors' Map and Guide to Selsey. Selsey, Sussex, Gardner, 1912.
The Foraminifera of the Clare Island District, Co. Mayo, Ireland, with Arthur Earland. Dublin, Clare Island Survey, 1913.
Protozoa (report for the 1910 Antarctic expedition), with Arthur Earland. Privately printed, 1922.
Barnacles in Nature and Myth. London, Oxford University Press, 1928.
The Gods of the Fourth World, Being Prolegomena Towards a Discourse upon the Buddhist Religion. Privately printed, 1931.
The Parish Church of St. Peter on Selsey Bill, Sussex. Privately printed, 1935.

Editor, *Edward FitzGerald's Rubá'iyát of Omar Khayyám,* with the Original Persian Sources. London, Quaritch, 1899.
Editor, *The Second Edition of Edward FitzGerald's Rubá'iyát of Omar Khayyám.* London, Duckworth, 1908.
Editor, with Arthur Earland, *The Fossil Foraminifera of the Blue Marl of the Côte des Basques.* Manchester, Literary and Philosophical Society, 1919.
Editor, *Memoranda of Memorabilia,* by Madame de Sévigné. Privately printed, 1928.
Editor, *The Further and Final Researches of Joseph Jackson Lister upon the Reproductive Process of Polystomella crispa (Linné).* Washington, D. C., Smithsonian Institution, 1930.
Editor and Translator, *A Fool of God: The Mystical Works of Bábá Táhir.* London, Octagon Press, 1979.

Translator, *The Science of the Hand,* by C. S. d'Arpentigny. London, Ward Lock, 1886.
Translator, *The Rubá'iyát of Omar Khayyám.* London, Nichols, 1898.
Translator, *The Lament of Bábá Táhir.* London, Quaritch, 1902.
Translator, *Quatrains of Omar Khayyám.* London, Mathews, 1908; revised edition, 1908.
Translator, *The Rubá'iyát of Omar Khayyám the Poet: The Literal Translation of the Ousley Manuscript.* London, Lane, 1924.

* * *

Christopher Blayre remains an enigmatic figure. His extraordinarily versatile life in varied scientific and artistic fields is mostly well recorded—he did research in marine biology and palaeontology, horticulture, music, occultism, Persian literature, history, and bibliography—but the names under which he wrote some of his unacknowledged fiction have not been discovered, and how much more he may have written of possible interest is not known. What we do have is a quite interesting group of stories, mainly on supernatural themes, and a few with a place in science fiction's formative stage. The weird stories use familiar elements of ghosts and apparitions, possession, visions, and curses, but the treatment is modern. There is some effective satirical humor, as in the immortal Wandering Jew succumbing to modern medicine, and a visit to an annex to Hell with an institution for completing unfinished works.

"Aalila" concerns a visit to Venus by matter transmission. The Venerians, who inevitably resemble humans, have an incompatible culture, and the experimenter's inevitable sexual involvement with Aalila leads to the expected disaster. It is an effective tale for all its familiarity. "The Cosmic Dust" is a sequel, and must be among the earliest stories on the interplanetary transmission of life in spores. This was a very important concept and raises questions that remain open. "The Mirror That Remembered" has another idea often suggested, a device for visualising past scenes. A marginal item is "The Blue Cockroach," where a temporary change in personality follows an insect bite.

The Cheetah-Girl, dropped by the publisher at the last moment from The Purple Sapphire, is a more ambitious work, a serious story of a macabre project—the creation of a human-cheetah hybrid, and its consequences. The rationale is logical, considering the elementary state of genetics in 1920. These stories compare very favorably with the better known proto-science fiction of the period. The style is easy, assured, and fresh.

—Graham Stone

BLISH, James (Benjamin). Also wrote as William Atheling, Jr. American. Born in East Orange, New Jersey, 23 May 1921. Educated at East Orange High School; Rutgers University, New Brunswick, New Jersey, 1938-42, B. Sc. 1942; Columbia University, New York, 1945-46. Served in the United States Army, 1942-44. Married 1) Virginia Kidd in 1947 (divorced); 2) Judith Ann Lawrence in 1964; one daughter and one son. Editor of a trade newspaper, New York, 1947-51; public relations counsel, New York and Washington, D. C., 1951-68. Editor, *Vanguard Science Fiction,* New York, 1958; Co-editor, *Kalki: Studies in James Branch Cabell,* Oradell, New Jersey, Vice-President, Science Fiction Writers of America, 1966-68. Recipient: Hugo Award, 1959. *Died 29 July 1975.*

SCIENCE-FICTION PUBLICATIONS

Novels (series: Cities in Flight)

Jack of Eagles. New York, Greenberg, 1952; London, Nova, 1955; as *Esper* New York, Avon, 1958.
The Warriors of Day. New York, Galaxy, 1953; London, Severn House, 1978.

Cities in Flight (revised edition). New York, Avon, 1970; London, Arrow, 1981.
Earthman, Come Home. New York, Putnam, 1955; London, Faber, 1956.
They Shall Have Stars. London, Faber, 1956; revised edition, as *as Year 2018!,* New York, Avon, 1957.
The Triumph of Time. New York, Avon, 1958; as *A Clash of Cymbals,* London, Faber, 1959.
A Life for the Stars. New York, Putnam, 1962; London, Faber, 1964.
A Case of Conscience. New York, Ballantine, 1958; London, Faber, 1959.
VOR. New York, Avon, 1958; London, Corgi, 1959.
The Duplicated Man, with Robert A. W. Lowndes. New York, Avalon, 1959.
The Star Dwellers (for children). New York, Putnam, 1961; London, Faber, 1962.
Titan's Daughter. New York, Berkley, 1961; London, New English Library, 1963.
Mission to the Heart Stars (for children). New York, Putnam, and London, Faber, 1965.
A Torrent of Faces, with Norman L. Knight. New York, Doubleday, 1967; London, Faber, 1968.
Welcome to Mars (for children). London, Faber, 1967; New York, Putnam, 1968.
Black Easter; or, Faust Aleph-Null. New York, Doubleday, 1968; London, Faber, 1969.
The Vanished Jet (for children). New York, Weybright and Talley, 1968.
Spock Must Die! New York, Bantam, 1970.
The Day after Judgment. New York, Doubleday, 1971; London, Faber, 1972.
. . . And All the Stars a Stage. New York, Doubleday, 1971; London, Faber, 1972.
Midsummer Century. New York, Doubleday, 1972; London, Faber, 1973.
The Quincunx of Time. New York, Dell, 1973; London, Faber, 1975.

Short Stories

The Seedling Stars. New York, Gnome Press, 1957; London, Faber, 1967.
Galactic Cluster. New York, New American Library, 1959; London, Faber, 1960.
So Close to Home. New York, Ballantine, 1961.
Best Science Fiction Stories of James Blish. London, Faber, 1965; revised edition, 1973; as *The Testament of Andros,* London, Arrow, 1977.
Star Trek 1-12 (from the TV series; vol. 12 with Judith A. Lawrence). New York, Bantam, 12 vols., 1967-77; London, Corgi, 12 vols., 1972-79.
Anywhen. New York, Doubleday, 1970; London, Faber, 1971.
The Best of James Blish, edited by Robert A. W. Lowndes. New York, Ballantine, 1979.

OTHER PUBLICATIONS

Novels

The Frozen Year. New York, Ballantine, 1957; as *Fallen Star,* London, Faber, 1957.
The Night Shapes. New York, Ballantine, 1962; London, New English Library, 1963.
Doctor Mirabilis. London, Faber, 1964; New York, Dodd Mead, 1971.

Other

The Issue at Hand: Studies in Contemporary Magazine Science Fiction (as William Atheling, Jr.). Chicago, Advent, 1964.
"Is This Thinking?," in *SF Horizons 1* (London), 1964.
"S. F. : The Critical Literature," in *SF Horizons 2* (London), 1965.
"On Science Fiction Criticism," in *Riverside Quarterly* (Regina, Saskatchewan), August 1968.
More Issues at Hand: Critical Studies in Contemporary Science Fiction (as William Atheling, Jr.). Chicago, Advent, 1970.
"The Tale That Wags the Dog: The Function of Science Fiction," in *American Libraries* (Chigago), December 1970.
"The Development of a Science Fiction Writer," in *Foundation 2* (London), June 1972.
"Moskowitz on Kuttner," in *Riverside Quarterly* (Regina, Saskatchewan), February 1972.
"A Surfeit of Lem, Please?," in *Foundation 6* (London), May 1974.

Editor, *New Dreams This Morning*. New York, Ballantine, 1966.
Editor, *Nebula Award Stories 5*. New York, Doubleday, and London, Gollancz, 1970.
Editor, *Thirteen O'Clock and Other Zero Hours*, by C. M. Kornbluth. New York, Dell, 1970; London, Hale, 1972.

*

Bibliography: *James Blish: A Bibliography 1940-1976* by Judith A. Blish, privately printed, 1976.

Manuscript Collection: Bodleian Library, Oxford.

*   *   *

James Blish can be seen as the complete man of letters for the young genre of science fiction from his early days of fandom in the 1930's until his untimely death from cancer in 1975, and one wonders whether Blish, if he had lived, might not eventually have published the masterpiece he insisted the genre would be incapable of producing. Out of such ironies often come great works of art; and Blish had a consuming and scholary interest in great art—from music, James Joyce, and Ezra Pound to the best science-fiction writers. The irony is that Blish as a writer came directly out of the pulp and fan tradition with all its variety, and even at the end of his career, when he was producing his best theorizing about the genre, he was also grinding out the highly commercial *Star Trek* novelizations. Blish was a steady producer of short fiction for the pulps who later learned to write superb novels and series. He saw the need for continuing critical writing and theorizing about the new genre of science fiction and produced masterful examples of both. He was a fan, an agent, an editor; and he was both beloved and feared for his totally comprehensive involvement with the genre. Blish's first editor, fellow Futurian, and friend, Robert A. W. Lowndes, develops the argument (in his introduction to *The Best of James Blish*) that Blish learned to write and to admire science fiction that was crafted "the hard way. " His work, then, demonstrates both the scope and the artistic depth that was possible in science fiction during his lifetime.

Several of Blish's most often used themes and the ironies and tensions inherent in those themes can serve as illustration. *The Seedling Stars,* a full length fiction made from shorter pieces about microscopic life, convinces the reader that mankind inhabits an infinite universe where the possibilities for protean form-changing and new dynamic adaptations (the real mainstream of science fiction) are seemingly limitless and also necessary. At the end of the book, this Stapledonian view is summed up as follows, "There's no survival value in pinning one's race forever to one set of specs. " And yet within the same period of his writing, Blish is continually looking for the one set of eternal specifications that govern human existance. Perhaps his most effective novel, *A Case of Conscience,* serves as the concluding part of a trilogy in which each of the protagonists is Christian; and the eternal battle between good and evil throughout the trilogy seems much more real and absolute than the open-ended relativism of adaptive evolution. Blish juggled these themes, and the comic tension from the resulting balance produces a high seriousness that (though the works appeared at first in the pulps) deserves to be treated as literature.

Another theme that apparently fascinated Blish because it appears often through his work (from a juvenile such as *The Star Dwellers* to the epic ending of his tetralogy *Cities in Flight*) is the catastrophism of the explosive first moments of creation seen also as the end of all things. The awesome fecundity of the moment of death is Blish's most subline image. I believe it appears frequently and interestingly enough in his work to allow a thoroughly Freudian analysis of Blish's fascination with death and with catastrophism. The point is that, though he as completely at home with the intentions and the conventions of the pulps as one is with his hometown, the true territory that Blish explores extends into the most profound speculations of our time. He was a good scholar and a good critic who would be delighted to know that future scholars and critics will also value his fictions.

Blish's own late theorizing about the genre maintains that variety and a kind of comic fecundity constitute its strength and reason for existence at this time in our history. He bases his theory on the historical speculations of Oswald Spengler; and R. D. Mullen has argued (in his afterword published with the gathered sections of *Cities in Flight*) that the tetralogy is grounded in Spenglerian theory. What Blish denies, of course, following from Spengler is that at this late date in our history and in this genre in particular, which best presents the variety of our time, no new synthesizing masterpieces (or epics) will appear. His own attempts are lengthy. *Cities in Flight* contains four novels. The trilogy that he intended to entitle *After Such Knowledge* contains the magnificent historical novel on Roger Bacon, *Doctor Mirabilis,* two novellas, and the science fiction novel *A Case of Conscience*. One would like to think that the theorist doth protest too much. But the trilogy was left unconnected at Blish's death, and the effect also of the tetralogy may be more centrifugal than centering. In any case, the work of Blish is rich with these dilemmas and tensions and, always, the art.

—Donald M. Hassler

BLOCH, Robert. Also writes as Collier Young. American. Born in Chicago, Illinois, 5 April 1917. Educated in public schools in Maywood, Illinois, and Milwaukee. Married 1) Marion Holcombe; 2) Eleanor Alexander in 1964; one daughter. Copywriter, Gustav Marx Advertising Agency, Milwaukee, 1943-53. Editor, *Science-Fiction World*, New York, 1956. President, Mystery Writers of America, 1970-71. Recipient: Evans Memorial Award, 1959; Hugo Award, 1959; Ann Radcliffe Award, 1960, 1966; Mystery Writers of America

Edgar Allan Poe Award, 1960; Trieste Film Festival Award, 1965; Convention du Cinéma Fantastique de Paris Prize, 1973; World Fantasy Convention Award, 1975. Guest of Honor, World Science Fiction Convention, 1948, 1973, Bouchercon I, 1971, World Fantasy Convention, 1975, and many other conventions. Agent: Kirby McCauley Ltd., 425 Park Avenue South, New York, New York 10016. Address: 2111 Sunset Crest Drive, Los Angeles, California 90046, U. S. A.

SCIENCE-FICTION PUBLICATIONS

Novels

This Crowded Earth, Ladies' Day. New York, Belmont, 1968.
Sneak Preview. New York, Paperback Library, 1971.
Reunion with Tomorrow. New York, Pinn, 1978.

Short Stories

Atoms and Evil. New York, Fawcett, 1962; London, Muller, 1963.
Bloch and Bradbury, with Ray Bradbury. New York, Tower, 1969; as *Fever Dream and Other Fantasies*, London, Sphere, 1970.
Fear Today, Gone Tomorrow. New York, Award, 1971.
The Best of Robert Bloch, edited by Lester del Rey. New York, Ballantine, 1977.

Uncollected Short Stories

"Picture," in *Shadows*, edited by Charles L. Grant. New York, Doubleday, 1978.
"The Spoiled Wife,' in *Chrysalis 3*, edited by Roy Torgeson. New York, Kensington, 1979.
"Freak Show," in *Fantasy and Science Fiction* (New York), May 1979.
"The Bald-Headed Mirage," in *Fantastic* (New York), July 1979.
"Nina," in *The Best from Fantasy and Science Fiction 23*, edited by Edward L. Ferman. New York, Doubleday, 1980.
"The Lighthouse," in *Twilight Zone* (New York), August 1982.

OTHER PUBLICATIONS

Novels

The Scarf. New York, Dial Press, 1947; as *The Scarf of Passion*, New York, Avon, 1949; revised edition, New York, Fawcett, 1966; London, New English Library, 1972.
The Kidnapper. New York, Lion, 1954.
Spiderweb. New York, Ace, 1954.
The Will to Kill. New York, Ace, 1954.
Shooting Star. New York, Ace, 1958.
Psycho. New York, Simon and Schuster, 1959; London, Hale, 1960.
The Dead Beat. New York, Simon and Schuster, 1960; London, Hale, 1961.
Firebug. Evanston, Illinois, Regency, 1961; London, Corgi, 1977.
The Couch (novelization of screenplay). New York, Fawcett, and London, Muller, 1962.
Terror. New York, Belmont, 1962; London, Corgi, 1964.
The Star Stalker. New York, Pyramid, 1968.
The Todd Dossier (as Collier Young). New York, Delacorte Press, and London, Macmillan, 1969.

It's All in Your Mind. New York, Curtis, 1971.
Night-World. New York, Simon and Schuster, 1972; London, Hale, 1974.
American Gothic. New York, Simon and Schuster, 1974; London, W. H. Allen, 1975.
There Is a Serpent in Eden. New York, Zebra, 1979; as *The Cunning Serpent*, 1981.
Strange Eons. Browns Mills, New Jersey, Whispers Press, 1979.
Psycho II. New York, Warner, 1982; London, Corgi, 1983.
The Night of the Ripper. New York, Doubleday, 1984.

Short Stories

Sea-Kissed. London, Utopian, 1945.
The Opener of the Way. Sauk City, Wisconsin, Arkham House, 1945; London, Spearman, 1974; selection, as *House of the Hatchet*, London, Panther, 1976.
Terror in the Night and Other Stories. New York, Ace, 1958.
Pleasant Dreams—Nightmares. Sauk City, Wisconsin, Arkham House, 1960; London, Whiting and Wheaton, 1967.
Nightmares. New York, Belmont, 1961.
Blood Runs Cold. New York, Simon and Schuster, 1961; London, Hale, 1963.
More Nightmares. New York, Belmont, 1962.
Yours Truly, Jack the Ripper: Tales of Horror. New York, Belmont, 1962; as *The House of the Hatchet and Other Tales of Horror*, London, Tandem, 1965.
Horror-7. New York, Belmont, 1963; as *Torture Garden*, London, New English Library, 1967.
Bogey Men. New York, Pyramid, 1963.
Tales in a Jugular Vein . New York, Pyramid, 1965; London, Sphere, 1970.
The Skull of the Marquis de Sade and Other Stories. New York, Pyramid, 1965; London, Hale, 1975.
Chamber of Horrors. New York, Award, 1966; London, Corgi, 1977.
The Living Demons. New York, Belmont, 1967; London, Sphere, 1970.
Dragons and Nightmares. Baltimore, Mirage Press, 1968.
Cold Chills. New York, Doubleday, 1977; London, Hale, 1978.
The King of Terrors. New York, Mysterious Press, 1977; London, Hale, 1978.
Out of the Mouths of Graves. New York, Mysterious Press, 1979; London, Hale, 1980.
Such Stuff as Screams Are Made Of. New York, Ballantine, 1979; London, Hale, 1980.
Mysteries of the Worm. New York, Zebra, 1979.
The Twilight Zone: The Movie (fictionalization of screenplays). New York, Warner, and London, Corgi, 1983.

Plays

Screenplays: *The Couch*, with Owen Crump and Blake Edwards, 1962; *The Cabinet of Caligari*, 1962; *Strait-Jacket*, 1964; *The Night Walker*, 1964; *The Psychopath*, 1966; *The Deadly Bees*, with Anthony Marriott, 1967; *Torture Garden*, 1967; *The House That Dripped Blood*, 1970; *Asylum*, 1972; *The Amazing Captain Nemo*, with others, 1979.

Radio Plays: *Stay Tuned for Terror* series (39 scripts), 1944-45.

Television Plays: *The Cuckoo Clock, The Greatest Monster of Them All, A Change of Heart, The Landlady, The Sorcerer's Apprentice, The Gloating Place, Bad Actor*, and *The Big Kick*, all in *Alfred Hitchcock Presents* series 1955-61; *The Cheaters,*

The Devil's Ticket, A Good Imagination, The Grim Reaper, The Weird Tailor, Waxworks, Till Death Do Us Part, and *Man of Mystery*, all in *Thriller* series, 1960-61; scripts for *Lock-Up* , 1960, *I Spy*, 1964, *Run for Your Life*, 1965, *Star Trek*, 1966-67, *Journey to the Unknown*, 1968, *Night Gallery*, 1971, and *Dark Room*, 1983-84; *The Cat Creature*, 1973; *The Dead Don't Die*, 1975.

Other

The Eighth Stage of Fandom: Selections from 25 Years of Fan Writing, edited by Earl Kemp. Chicago, Advent, 1962.
"Imagination and Modern Social Criticism," in *The Science Fiction Novel*, edited by Basil Davenport. Chicago, Advent, 1969.
The Laughter of a Ghoul, What Every Young Ghoul Should Know. West Warwick, Rhode Island, Necronomicon Press, 1977.

Editor, *The Best of Fredric Brown*. New York, Ballantine, 1977.

Recordings: *Gravely, Robert Bloch*, Alternate World, 1976; *Blood!*, with Harlan Ellison, Alternate World, 1976.

*

Bibliography: in *Robert Bloch Fanzine* (Los Altos, California), 1973.

Manuscript Collection: University of Wyoming Library, Laramie.

Robert Bloch comments:

Although I have had upwards of 100 short stories and novelets published in science-fiction magazines, I am primarily a writer of fantasy and mystery-suspense fiction: the bulk of my work falls within these two genres, as does my writing for screen, television, and radio. As a result my work has been almost entirely ignored by science-fiction critics and historians—thank God! Having somehow managed to survive as a professional writer over a period of 51 years, I'd hate to blow it now. I am still fascinated by the SF field and by the people in it.

*   *   *

Although Robert Bloch has been associated with science fiction since his first fan-magazine appearance at the age of 15, he has never been regarded as a main-line science-fiction writer. As he says, "Through the years, most of my work has been on the peripheral edges of science fiction proper—fantasy, weird-horror and suspense, together with a smattering of humor. To the extent that psychopathology is classifiable as a branch of medical science, my other novels. . . all contain these elements as they pertain to an examination of subjective reality." Nonetheless, for five decades Bloch has made a positive impact and been a popular figure in the science fiction community, and has contributed scores of stories to the field.

The earliest period of his professional career was dominated by the influence of H. P. Lovecraft; Bloch corresponded with Lovecraft and sent him drafts of his earliest stories for comment. Among his early *Weird Tales* stories was "The Shambler from the Stars," in which he killed Lovecraft quite gorily; Frank Belknap Long had done the same to Lovecraft in a story several years before, and Lovecraft killed off Bloch

(renaming him "Robert Blake") in his turn. It was all good fun, and made rather good horror fiction as well. Bloch moved shortly to a series of horror stories with Egyptian motifs; titles such as "The Brood of Bubastis," "The Eyes of the Mummy," "Fane of the Black Pharaoh," and "The Secret of Sebek" speak for themselves. Still later works fall into the horror-suspense-crime area, with heavy emphasis on psychopathology. These include "House of the Hatchet," "The Skull of the Marquis de Sade," "Enoch," "Lizzie Borden Took an Axe," and others, including Bloch's best known and most successful novel, *Psycho*. Another recurrent theme in Bloch's works is that of Jack the Ripper. Bloch's most successful short story is "Yours Truly—Jack the Ripper"; a later use of the theme was in "A Toy for Juliet." Among other notions, Bloch suggests that Jack was a sort of vampire who prolongs his existence through his crimes. Bloch returned to his early enthusiasm for Lovecraft with *Strange Eons*. In this novel he collects numerous Love-craftian themes, including the Cthulhu Mythos, and projects them into a future world-catastrophe, thereby providing a marginally scientific basis for the material.

Fondly remembered by many veteran readers are Bloch's "Lefty Feep" stories. Some 22 of these appeared in *Fantastic Adventures* (1942-46). All are pun-filled, wise-cracking, parod-istic works. Once more, titles are indicative of content: "Time Wounds All Heels," "The Weird Doom of Floyd Scrilch," "Stuporman," and (reflecting Bloch's topicality) "The Pied Piper Fights the Gestapo. " Some of Bloch's works, however, have been thoroughly serious. The majority of these have been in the psychopathological vein, but some, such as "The Cloak" and "That Hell-Bound Train," have been "real" science fiction or fantasy. (The latter story won a Hugo award, a rare achievement for a fantasy story). In the science-fiction novella "This Crowded Earth" Bloch suggested the miniaturization of the human species as a solution for overpopulation problems; Vonnegut's *Slapstick* duplicates Bloch's device.

In later years Bloch continued to concentrate on his favorite and most successful themes, working in areas of psychological horror and violence rather than outright fantasy or science fiction. The inevitable *Psycho II*, as might be expected, dealt with the continuing saga of Norman Bates and his associates, following Bates's years of hospitalization. The identically named film was *not* based on Bloch's novel; nonetheless (and also predictably) its theme is similar.

The Night of the Ripper is a full-fledged novelistic treatment of the Jack-the-Ripper theme. It remains to be seen whether Bloch, having dealt with his twin succubi of Norman Bates and Jack the Ripper with these late books, will turn to other themes or will continue to mine this undeniably rich but by now tiresomely overworked material.

—Richard A. Lupoff

———————

BOND, Nelson S(lade). American. Born in Scranton, Pennsyl-vania, 23 November 1908. Educated at Marshall University, Huntington, West Virginia, 1932-34. Married Betty Gough Folsom in 1934; two sons. Public relations field director, government of Nova Scotia, 1934-35. Free-lance writer and philatelic researcher; now a book dealer. Associated with the Roanoke Community Theatre. Recipient: International Stamp Exhibition Award, for non-fiction, 1960. Address: 4724 East-hill Drive, Sugarloaf Farms, Roanoke, Virginia 24018, U. S. A.

SCIENCE-FICTION PUBLICATIONS

Novel

Exiles of Time. Philadelphia, Prime Press, 1949.

Short Stories

Mr. Mergenthwirker's Lobblies and Other Fantastic Tales. New York, Coward McCann, 1946.
The Thirty-First of February. New York, Gnome Press, 1949.
The Remarkable Exploits of Lancelot Biggs, Spaceman. New York, Doubleday, 1950.
No Time Like the Future. New York, Avon, 1954.
Nightmares and Daydreams. Sauk City, Wisconsin, Arkham House, 1968.

OTHER PUBLICATIONS

Plays

Mr. Mergenthwirker's Lobblies, adaptation of his own story (televised). New York, French, 1957.
State of Mind. New York, French, 1958.
Animal Farm, adaptation of the novel by George Orwell. New York, French, 1964.

Author of screenplays for government agencies, some 300 radio plays, and television plays for *Philco Playhouse, Kraft Theatre, Studio One*, and other series.

Other

The Postal Stationery of Canada: A Reference Catalogue. Shrub Oak, New York, Herst, 1953.

* * *

Nelson S. Bond's only novel published in book form is *Exiles of Time*, and it actually constitutes the fourth volume of a tetralogy; the earlier works in the series, *Sons of the Deluge, Gods of the Jungle*, and *That Worlds May Live*, were published in *Amazing*. *Exiles of Time*, though written in a clear, readable style, suffers from too great a reliance on stereotyped characters. It's the story of a time traveller who encounters Ragnarok, and the epilogue quotes from the Elder *Edda*, giving the reader considerable insight into Bond's skill at plotting. It's an impressive demonstration. The ability to plot is one of Bond's strongest points, and he was never more sure or ingenious than here.

By and large, Bond's best fiction remains his short stories, and he has displayed a remarkable range with them. During his years as a regular contributor to the pulps he wrote not only for Ray Palmer's *Amazing* and *Fantastic Adventures*, but for John Campbell's more demanding *Astounding* and *Unknown*. He also wrote for *Thrilling Wonder Stories, Weird Tales*, and especially for *Planet Stories*. "The Castaway" (*Planet*, Winter 1940) is an almost perfect example of Bond's ability to make a formula story and raise it above its own limits. A spaceship crew rescues a man marooned on an asteroid. Subsequent events suggest he's a jinx and suicidal to boot, with the ship finally zooming out of control at a speed that will cause it to burn when its hits Earth's atmosphere. The castaway devises a way to save the ship and its crew, but the real surprise lies in his actual identity.

"The Castaway" fits into a future history that includes most of Bond's space stories. These stories seem to take place mostly in the 23rd century, with the solar system explored and colonized by Earthmen, and most of them center on members of the Solar Space Patrol or a space transport company called IPS. While Bond wrote a number of character series within this frame, the Lancelot Biggs series is probably the most important, and in many ways the most typical. Biggs is the eccentric and likeable first officer of the IPS ship *Saturn*, and he divides his time between getting on his captain's nerves and producing scientific miracles to save the ship from certain disaster. About half these stories were included in *The Remarkable Exploits of Lancelot Biggs, Spaceman*.

While there is no denying Bond's talent with the short story, many of his novelets and short novels are excellent. Two *Planet* novelets from 1941 demonstrate his skill with space opera. Both center on the adventures of the young, clean-cut spaceman Chip Warren and his partners Syd Palmer and "Salvation" Smith. "Shadrach" has them discovering a rich lode of "ekalastron," an almost impervious metal, rare and valuable, that plays a part in several of Bond's future history storied. "The Lorelei Death" pits them against space pirates, but, though the better action story, it's marred by some questionable science in its ending. "Pawns of Chaos" (*Thrilling Wonder Stories*, April 1943) is based on the sort of idea popular with editors almost everywhere at that time, invaders from another dimension where the political system bears some similarity to that of Nazi Germany. Bond obviously had fun writing it, especially those sections describing battles in and around his home town of Roanoke, Virginia. "Pawns of Chaos" doesn't fall into Bond's future history sequence, nor do the Meg the Priestess stories which constitute what is probably the best work he did in the SF pulps. In the Meg stories, civilization has virtually collapsed and humanity exists in scattered tribes, a few of which preserve knowledge of writing and reading through a matriarchal leadership, although their ideas of the past are distorted as myths and legends. In "Pilgrimage" (*The Thirty-First of February*) Meg becomes priestess of her clan in Virginia and travels west to consult the gods carved on Mount Rushmore. "Magic City" (*Astounding*, February 1941) has her visit the city of death—New York—to confront its goddess.

Bond's penchant for writing action scenes in settings he knows produced a superior story in "The Ultimate Salient" (*Planet*, Fall 1940). A science-fiction writer receives a manuscript purporting to tell future events: the democracies fall to totalitarian forces in 1963 and the survivors flee to the moon where they face almost certain death because they lack the knowledge to synthesize chlorophyl. Since they are known to have taken a number of old SF magazines along, the writer is asked to use the manuscript as the basis of a story, ending it with the formula for chlorophyl that the survivors need. The story was later completely rewritten as "The Last Outpost," and is included in *No Time Like the Future*. The new version sets up a revolt against a world dictatorship, with neither the minions of the dictatorship nor the rebels being very desirable. Disaster befalls both sides but a third group flees to Venus—where the item needed for their survival is the formula for vitamin A.

Bond has claimed he was never actually a science-fiction writer but a fantasist who wrote for the SF magazines. Certainly his first big success (in 1937) was the fantasy "Mr. Mergenthwirker's Lobblies," about a gentle man who acquires the companionship of two invisible beings who foretell the future. Such stories as this were probably the prototypes of the sort of light fantasies Ray Palmer sought for *Fantastic Adventures*. It should be noted that Bond wrote a number of SF stories for his ostensibly fantasy markets, including *Blue Book*, and expressed pride in such stories as "To People a New World," "Martian Caravan," and the Pat Pending stories, about the inventor of a succession of incredible gadgets.

Bond's prose was polished enough for the prestige markets of the 1940's without being too slick to remain palatable today. By turns he can be humorous, serious, or adventurous, handling each approach with equal skill. But it remains plotting where he really shines. His story "The Cunning of the Beast" (*The Thirty-First of February*) may be that most overworked of stories, the Adam and Eve story, but it's the most cleverly plotted of them. A number of his yarns spring from Biblical or mythological sources, usually with happy results. "Uncommon Castaway" (*No Time Like the Future*) is a twist on the story of Jonah and the whale. Much of Bond's fiction resembles that of Saki or John Collier. "And Lo! The Bird" presents the Earth as an egg about to be hatched, and "Conqueror's Isle" tells of an outpost of supermen waiting for the passing of homo sapiens (both in *No Time Like the Future*).

Bond's knack for the off-beat is shown not only in his humor and his variety of approach, but also in a handful of stories written as poems. Two of them from *Planet*, "The Ballad of Blaster Bill" and "The Ballad of Venus Nell," show a touch of Robert Service (though to be honest, "Blaster Bill's" tempo is borrowed from Kipling's "Gunga Din").

—Gerald W. Page

BONE, J(esse) F(ranklin). American. Born in Tacoma, Washington, 15 June 1916. Educated at Washington State University, Pullman, B. A. 1937, B. S. 1949, D. V. M. 1950; Oregon State University, Corvallis, M. S. 1953. Served in the United States Army, 1937-46, and Army Reserve, 1946-66: Lieutenant Colonel. Married 1) Jayne M. Clark in 1942 (divorced, 1946), one daughter; 2) Felizitas Margarete Endter in 1950, one daughter and two sons. Instructor, 1950-52, Assistant Professor, 1953-57, Associate Professor, 1958-65, and Professor of Veterinary Medicine, 1965-79, Oregon State University; Consultant, University of Zimbabwe, Harare, 1982; Professor of Anatomy, Ross University, St. Kitts, West Indies, 1984. Fulbright Lecturer in Egypt, 1965-66, and Kenya, 1980-81. Recipient: Department of Health, Education, and Welfare award, 1969. Agent: Scott Meredith Literary Agency, 845 Third Avenue, New York, New York 10022. Address: 6520 Flanegan Street, Tacoma, Washington 98467, U. S. A.

SCIENCE-FICTION PUBLICATIONS

Novels

The Lani People. New York, Bantam, and London, Corgi, 1962.
Legacy. Toronto, Laser, 1976.
The Meddlers. Toronto, Laser, 1976.
Gift of the Manti, with Ray Myers. Toronto, Laser, 1977.
Confederation Matador. Virginia Beach, Donning, 1978.

Uncollected Short Stories

"Survival Type," in *Galaxy* (New York), March 1957.
"Quarantined Species," in *Super Science Fiction* (New York), December 1957.
"Assassin," in *If* (New York), February 1958.
"The Tool of Creation," in *Super Science Fiction* (New York), April 1958.

"The Sword," in *Fantastic Universe* (Chicago), September 1958.
"Triggerman," in *Astounding* (New York), December 1958.
"The Fast-Moving Ones," in *Super Science Fiction* (New York), December 1958.
"Nothing But Terror," in *Fantastic* (New York), January 1959.
"Second Chance," in *Satellite* (New York), February 1959.
"Insidekick," in *Galaxy* (New York), February 1959.
"Cultural Exchange," in *If* (New York), January 1960.
"The Issahar Artifacts," in *Amazing* (New York), April 1960.
"Fireman," in *Fantastic* (New York), May 1960.
"Noble Redman," in *Amazing* (New York), July 1960.
"To Choke an Ocean," in *If* (New York), September 1960.
"The Missionary," in *Amazing* (New York), October 1960.
"A Question of Courage," in *Amazing* (New York), December 1960.
"Weapon," in *Amazing* (New York), June 1961.
"Special Effect," in *Fantastic* (New York), November 1961.
"Pandemic," in *Analog* (New York), February 1962.
"Founding Father," in *Galaxy* (New York), April 1962.
"For Service Rendered," in *Amazing* (New York), April 1963.
"On the Fourth Planet," in *Galaxy* (New York), April 1963.
"A Hair Perhaps," in *If* (New York), January 1967.
"The Scents of It," in *Infinity 2*, edited by Robert Hoskins. New York, Lancer, 1971.
"Gamesman," in *Crisis*, edited by Roger Elwood. Nashville, Nelson, 1974.
"High Priest," in *Strange Gods*, edited by Roger Elwood. New York, Pocket Books, 1974.
"Technicalities," in *Amazing* (New York), January 1976.
"A Prize for Edie," in *Laughing Space*, edited by Isaac Asimov and J. O. Jeppson. Boston, Houghton Mifflin, and London, Robson, 1982.

OTHER PUBLICATIONS

Other

Observations on the Ovaries of Infertile and Reportedly Infertile Dairy Cattle. . . . Corvallis, Oregon State College, 1954.
Animal Anatomy. Corvallis, Oregon State College Cooperative Association, 1958; revised edition, as *Animal Anatomy and Physiology*, 1975.
Animal Anatomy and Physiology. Reston, Virginia, Reston Publishing Company, 1979; revised edition, 1982.

Editor, *Canine Medicine*. Wheaton, Illinois, American Veterinary Publications, 1959; revised edition, 1962.
Editor, with others, *Equine Medicine and Surgery*. Wheaton, Illinois, American Veterinary Publications, 1963; revised edition, 1972.

*   *   *

J. F. Bone made a considerable impact with the publication of his first novel, *The Lani People*, along with several first-rate shorter works. Unfortunately, his career faltered for approximately ten years; very few works appeared under his name, and none of them particularly memorable.

The Lani People came perilously close to being a narrated lecture, for it quite obviously intended to comment unfavorably upon man's tendency to dehumanize others. In the future, a race of humanoids exits, differing from normal humanity because of the addition of a prehensile tail. They are considered less than human, property in fact, and have virtually no rights under the law. Despite the plot—the slow realization by the protagonist of the essential evil inherent in the situation—Bone was inventive enough to maintain reader interest throughout.

Of Bone's later novels, *Legacy* was a rather routine story of a marooned man who joins a police force on a far world and becomes involved with the effort to suppress a dangerous new drug, Tonocaine. Although not actively bad, the novel's trivial nature and trite plot were disappointing to those who had remembered Bone's earlier work. The two other Laser novels were even more insignificant. In *The Meddlers* the human race is engaged in conscious manipulation of alien cultures for its own benefit. In *Gift of the Manti* the situation is just the opposite, with secretive aliens manipulating human culture for our own good, offhandedly wiping out 90 percent of the human race along the way. Both novels are underwritten and unbelievable and totally forgettable.

Bone did better with *Confederation Matador*, although that novel also has serious flaws. After the collapse of a human interstellar empire, a new confederation has arisen, which is carefully trying to rebuild human technology. An agent is sent to one world colonized by Spanish-speaking peoples to discover why that colony is slowly losing its technological base, despite an absence of external pressures. The agent discovers that superhuman aliens have established a base and are systematically exterminating the human colonists. Although the novel has sections that are quite well done, Bone has added some unnecessary and confusing subplots that distract attention from the main issue.

There is a considerable body of shorter pieces by Bone, most of which remain quite readable. Of particular note is "Founding Father," a novella in which stranded reptilian aliens use mental control to force humans to refuel their ship, and a strange relationship grows between the two species. Another excellent story is "Triggerman" which calmly presents the man with the ultimate power to cause or avert a nuclear war, and his dispassionate reaction to a world crisis. "On the Fourth Planet" is not as ambitious as the other two, but this tale of a Martian slowly eating his way across the surface of his planet, and his unhappy encounter with a human probe is extremely inventive and, within its limited structure, possibly the most successful of Bone's stories.

—Don D'Ammassa

BOOTH, Irwin. See **HOCH, Edward D.**

BOUCHER, Anthony. Pseudonym for William Anthony Parker White; also wrote as Theo Durrant; H. H. Holmes. American. Born in Oakland, California, 21 August 1911. Educated at Pasadena Junior College, California, 1928-30; University of Southern California, Los Angeles, B. A. 1932; University of California, Berkeley, M. A. 1934. Married Phyllis May Price in 1938; two sons. Theatre and music critic, *United Progressive News*, Los Angeles, 1935-37; science fiction and mystery reviewer, San Francisco *Chronicle*, 1942-47; mystery reviewer, *Ellery Queen's Mystery Magazine*, 1948-50 and 1957-68, and *New York Times Book Review*, 1951-68; fantasy book reviewer, as H. H. Holmes, for Chicago *Sun-Times*, 1949-50, and New York *Herald Tribune*, 1951-63; reviewer for *Opera News*, 1961-68. Editor with J. Francis McComas, 1949-54, and alone, 1954-58, *Magazine of Fantasy and Science Fiction*, New York; editor, *True Crime Detective*, 1952-53; edited the Mercury Mysteries, 1952-55, Dell Great Mystery Library, 1957-60, and Collier Mystery Classics, 1962-68. Originated *Great Voices* program of historical recordings, Pacifica Radio, Berkely, 1949-68. President, Mystery Writers of America, 1951. Recipient: Mystery Writers of America Edgar Allan Poe Award, for non-fiction, 1946, 1950, 1953; Hugo Award, for editing, 1958, 1959. *Died 29 April 1968.*

SCIENCE-FICTION PUBLICATIONS

Novel

Rocket to the Morgue (as H. H. Holmes). New York, Duell, 1942.

Short Stories

Far and Away: Eleven Fantasy and Science-Fiction Stories. New York, Ballantine, 1955.
The Compleat Werewolf and Other Stories of Fantasy and Science Fiction. New York, Simon and Schuster, 1969; London, W. H. Allen, 1970.

Uncollected Short Story

"A Shape in Time," in *The Future Is Now* , edited by William F. Nolan. Los Angeles, Sherbourne Press, 1970.

OTHER PUBLICATIONS

Novels

The Case of the Seven of Calvary. New York, Simon and Schuster, and London, Hamish Hamilton, 1937.
The Case of the Crumpled Knave. New York, Simon and Schuster, and London, Harrap, 1939.
The Case of the Baker Street Irregulars. New York, Simon and Schuster, 1940; as *Blood on Baker Street*, New York, Mercury, 1953.
Nine Times Nine (as H. H. Holmes). New York, Duell, 1940.
The Case of the Solid Key. New York, Simon and Schuster, 1941.
The Case of the Seven Sneezes. New York, Simon and Schuster, 1942; London, United Authors, 1946.
The Marble Forest (as Theo Durrant, with others). New York, Knopf, and London, Wingate, 1951; as *The Big Fear*, New York, Popular Library, 1953.
The Case of the Seven of Calvary, Nine Times Nine, Rocket to the Morgue, The Case of the Crumpled Knave. London, Zomba, 1984.

Short Stories

Exeunt Murderers: The Best Mystery Stories of Anthony Boucher, edited by Francis M. Nevins, Jr. and Martin H. Greenberg. Carbondale, Southern Illinois University Press, 1983.

Plays

Radio Plays: for *Sherlock Holmes* and *The Case Book of Gregory Hood* series, 1945-48.

Other

Ellery Queen: A Double Profile. Boston, Little Brown, 1951.
Multiplying Villainies: Selected Mystery Criticism, 1942-1968. Boston, Bouchercon, 1973.
Sincerely, Tony/Faithfully, Vincent: The Correspondence of Anthony Boucher and Vincent Starrett, edited by Robert W. Hahn. Chicago, Catullus Press, 1975.

Editor, *The Pocket Book of True Crime Stories*. New York, Pocket Books, 1943.
Editor, *Great American Detective Stories*. Cleveland, World, 1945.
Editor, *Four and Twenty Bloodhounds*. New York, Simon and Schuster, 1950; London, Hammond, 1951.
Editor, *The Best from Fantasy and Science Fiction*. Boston, Little Brown, 2 vols., 1952-53; New York, Doubleday, 6 vols., 1954-59.
Editor, *The Murder and the Trial*, by Edgar Lustgarten. New York, Scribner, 1958; London, Odhams Press, 1960.
Editor, *A Treasury of Great Science Fiction*. New York, Doubleday, 1959.
Editor, *The Quality of Murder*. New York, Dutton, 1962.
Editor, *The Quintessence of Queen: Best Prize Stories from 12 Years of Ellery Queen's Mystery Magazine*. New York, Random House, 1962; as *A Magnum of Mysteries*, London, Gollancz, 1963.
Editor, *Best Detective Stories of the Year: 18th* [through *23rd*] *Annual Collection*. New York, Dutton, and London, Boardman, 6 vols., 1963-68.

*

Bibliography: "Anthony Boucher Bibliography" by J. R. Christopher, Dean W. Dickensheet, and R. E. Briney, in *Armchair Detective* (White Bear Lake, Minnesota), nos. 2,3,4, 1969.

Critical Study: *The Eureka Years: Boucher and McComas's The Magazine of Fantasy and Science Fiction 1949-1954* edited by Annette P. McComas, New York, Bantam, 1982.

* * *

Anthony Boucher brought both style and sophistication to popular fantasy and science fiction, two qualities in rather short supply during the 1940's and 1950's. Boucher enjoyed successful careers in all three phases of popular literature; he was a critic, an author, and an editor.

Boucher wrote both fantasy and science fiction stories. Many of his best stories were published in Campbell's Astounding Science Fiction and *Unknown*, and in *Weird Tales*. Boucher's talent ran to the kind of fantasy or fantastic science fiction associated with *Unknown* in the 1940's and *Beyond* in the 1950's. His stories tend to be comic treatments of ordinary people involved in situations and actions that run contrary to their customary, common-sense approach to life. Boucher seems to imply that most people, and certainly his truly sympathetic characters, possess an innate disposition to believe in supernatural forces. As was the case with most characteristic *Unknown* stories, mythic themes are treated lightly with a comic and often ironic distance. That is certainly the case with Boucher's most successful stories. "Q. U. R.," "Robinc," and "We Print the Truth" may be taken as illustrating Boucher's manner in science-fiction stories. The first two stories are barroom tales, similar to Henry Knutter's Galloway Gallegher tales and Arthur Clarke's *Tales from the White Hart*. They share characteristic themes with some of Heinlein's stories of the private inventor and of proprietory business enterprise as illustrated in "We Also Walk Dogs. " Boucher's hero, Dugglesmarther H. Quinby, changes the world with a revolution in android technology, making the androids more efficient by making them less like humans. Boucher thus lightly shows two of his virtues as a writer: effective comic reversal of clichés or worn-out formulas to produce surprise and delight, and a humanistic and often literary resonance.

The best of his fantasy tales may be the most famous of his stories, the novella "The Compleat Werewolf. " The title suggests distantly perhaps yet fittingly a parallel to the Michael Shea adventures of L. Sprague de Camp and Fletcher Pratt. Many of the storytelling concepts are the same: an academic setting; a strong courtship subplot; comic anachronism involving a modern character caught up in mythic or legendary adventures but retaining a modern, skeptical sense of incongruity; the concomitant farcical employment of magic; and the obligatory happy ending in which the hero returns to the prosaic world with a fuller appreciation of its homely values or at least its familiar comforts. Best of all, he returns to a world in which he fits. Boucher's 1942 tale includes a little Nazi espionage to spice up the plot. Professor Wolfe Wolf, the hero in spite of himself who ends with the right girl despite an earlier unsuitable preference for a co-ed Venus, is the pattern of the modern, domesticated hero that has run remarkably true to form now for more than a quarter century.

Two or three other fantasy tales may be noted here briefly as representative of Boucher's range. "Snulbug" is Boucher's tale of modern demonology told with a more comic perspective than C. S. Lewis's *Screwtape Letters*, which it recalls. In Boucher's story, the human race is preserved from additional mischief by the incompetence of a conjurer and the third-rate demon he manages to call up to work his will. "They Bite" is an effective suspense-horror story making use of the familiar formula in which modern, skeptical men find themselves the unbelieving victims of legendary desert ogres. "We Print the Truth" is loosely based on the familiar theological chestnut of the contradiction between divine foreknowledge and free will. Boucher's fictional equivalent of divine foreknowledge is the *Grover Sentinel*, whose stories become true for all who read them. Bourcher's working out of the problem which involves speculations of wish fulfillment and something he terms "variable truth" is characteristically ingenious and amusing, very much like the armchair mysteries he wrote under the name of H. H. Holmes. It was under the same name that Boucher wrote one of the most amusing science-fiction mystery *roman à clef* novels, *Rocket to the Morgue*, which is also a pastiche of styles, mannerisms, and familiar formulas of the main science-fiction writers of the dominant eastern establishment.

Boucher's best known SF story, "The Quest for St. Aquin" (1951), has lost none of its original luster after more than a quarter century. If anything, its stature has grown by virtue of the works it has to some degree inspired: James Blish's *A Case of Conscience* (1958), Walter M. Miller, Jr.'s *A Canticle for Leibowitz* (1960), and Robert Silverberg's "Good News from the Vatican" (1970). The quest takes place in a post-nuclear catastrophe California in which religious worship of any kind is officially suppressed by the ruling Technarchy through its KGB style "Loyalty Checkers. " The quest ends with the paradoxical revelation that the fabled Saint Aquin is in fact the one perfect android of legend that had proved by its faultless logic the existence of God, and whose present lifeless state proves that existence in quite another way. The virtues of the story are many, including the economy with which Boucher creates his repressive, future world in which religious persecution is once again a fact of life for all believers and the finely realized humanity of the story's characters from the pope who must hide his fisherman's ring in the heel of his shoe to the Jewish "good Samaritan" on whom the irony of his rescue of the questing priest is hardly lost. The central action, however, depends of Boucher's skill in creating two characters: the young, unsophisticated priest sent on the quest by the pope to discover whether the cult of St. Aquin is orthodox, and the priest's mechanical "robass," who turns out to be none other than Old Nick himself back at the tempting game in a new form. The confrontation is altogether enchanting and somehow satisfying theologically at the same time. Among the story's many achievements as prophetic SF entertainment, the reader should consider that it is one of those stories of the 1950's, and one of the earliest, to dramatize the future brotherhood of all people of faith, whatever their religious affiliation. A quarter century ago that seemed a far more radical notion than it does today.

Perhaps Boucher's most important contribution to the literature of popular fantasy and SF came not as an author but as co-editor and later editor of *The Magazine of Fantasy and Science Fiction,* which made its debut before the public without "science fiction" on the masthead in 1949. The magazine has proven to be the healthiest and most consistently influential competition to the *Astounding/Analog* tradition of science fiction/science fact literature. Boucher and McComas established their magazine as a quality pulp that was more concerned with literary standards than with literary ideology. It has continued to publish stories in both genres and mixtures of the two that are distinguished by literary, that is mainstream, writing. Something must be added also about the affection and respect that Boucher won by his amiable disposition and urbane wit. His was one of the more important benign influences on the encouragement and development of many of the New Wave writers with whom he probably had less in common than with the Golden Age writers of his own salad days.

—Donald L. Lawler

BOVA, Ben(jamin William). American. Born in Philadelphia, Pennsylvania, 28 November 1932. Educated at Temple University, Philadelphia, B. S. 1954. Married 1) Rosa Cucinotta in 1953 (divorced, 1974), one son and one daughter; 2) Barbara Berson Rose in 1974. Editor, *Upper Darby News,* Pennsylvania, 1953-56; technical editor on Vanguard Project, Martin Aircraft Company, Baltimore, 1956-58; screenwriter, Physical Science Study Committee, Massachusetts Institute of Technology, Cambridge, 1958-59; science writer, Avco-Everett Research Laboratory, Everett, Massachusetts, 1960-71; Editor, *Analog,* New York, 1971-78; Editor, *Omni,* New York, 1978-82. Recipient: Hugo Award, for editing, 1973, 1974, 1975, 1976, 1977, 1979; E. E. Smith Memorial Award, 1974; Balrog Award, 1983. Address: c/o Tor Books, 8-10 West 36th Street, New York, New York 10018, U. S. A.

SCIENCE-FICTION PUBLICATIONS

Novels (series: Exiles)

The Star Conquerors (for children). Philadelphia, Winston, 1959.

Star Watchman (for children). New York, Holt Rinehart, 1964; London, Dobson, 1972.
The Weathermakers (for children). New York, Holt Rinehart, 1967; London, Dobson, 1969.
Out of the Sun (for children). New York, Holt Rinehart, 1968.
The Dueling Machine (for children). New York, Holt Rinehart, 1969; London, Faber, 1971.
Escape! (for children). New York, Holt Rinehart, 1970.
The Exiles Trilogy (for children). New York, Berkley, 1980; London, Methuen, 1984.
   Exiled from Earth. New York, Dutton, 1971.
   Flight of Exiles. New York, Dutton, 1972.
   End of Exile. New, York, Dutton, 1975.
THX 1138 (novelization of screenplay). New York, Paperback Library, 1971; London, Panther, 1978.
As on a Darkling Plain. New York, Walker, 1972; London, Magnum, 1981.
The Shining Strangers (for children). New York, Walker, 1973.
When the Sky Burned. New York, Walker, 1973.
The Winds of Altair (for children). New York, Dutton, 1973.
Gremlins, Go Home! (for children), with Gordon R. Dickson. New York, St. Martin's Press, 1974.
The Starcrossed. Radnor, Pennsylvania, Chilton, 1975; London, Magnum, 1980.
City of Darkness (for children). New York, Scribner, 1976.
Millennium. New York, Random House, and London, Macdonald and Jane's, 1976.
The Multiple Man. Indianapolis, Bobbs Merrill, 1976; London, Gollancz, 1977.
Colony. New York, Pocket Books, 1978; London, Magnum, 1979.
Kinsman. New York, Dial Press, and London, Futura, 1979.
Voyagers. New York, Doubleday, 1981; London, Methuen, 1982.
Test of Fire. New York, Tor, 1982; London, Methuen, 1984.
Orion. New York, Simon and Schuster, 1984.

Short Stories

Forward in Time. New York, Walker, 1973.
Maxwell's Demons. New York, Baronet, 1979.
Escape Plus Ten. New York, Tor, 1984.

OTHER PUBLICATIONS

Other

The Milky Way Galaxy: Man's Exploration of the Stars. New York, Holt Rinehart, 1961.
Giants of the Animal World (for children). Racine, Wisconsin, Whitman, 1962.
Reptiles Since the World Began (for children). Racine, Wisconsin, Whitman, 1964.
The Uses of Space (for children). New York, Holt Rinehart, 1965.
Magnets and Magnetism (for children). Racine, Wisconsin, Whitman, 1966.
In Quest of Quasars: An Introduction to Stars and Starlike Objects (for children). New York, Collier, 1970.
Planets, Life, and LGM (for children). Reading, Massachusetts, Addison Wesley, 1970.
The Fourth State of Matter: Plasma Dynamics and Tomorrow's Technology. New York, St. Martin's Press, 1971.
The Amazing Lase (for children). Philadelphia, Westminster Press, 1971.

The New Astronomies. New York, St. Martin's Press, 1972; London, Dent, 1973.

Starflight and Other Improbabilities (for children). Philadelphia, Westminster Press, 1973.

Man Changes the Weather (for children). Reading, Massachusetts. Addison Wesley, 1973.

Survival Guide for the Suddenly Single, with Barbara Berson. New York, St. Martin's Press, 1974.

The Weather Changes Man (for children). Reading, Massachusetts, Addison Wesley, 1974.

Workshops in Space (for children). New York, Dutton, 1974.

Notes to a Science Fiction Writer (for children). New York, Scribner, 1975; revised edition, Boston, Houghton Mifflin, 1981.

Through Eyes of Wonder (for children). Reading, Massachusetts, Addison Wesley, 1975.

Science—Who Needs It? (for children). Philadelphia, Westminster Press, 1975.

The Seeds of Tomorrow (for children). New York, McKay, 1977.

Viewpoint. Cambridge, Massachusetts, NESFA Press, 1977.

The High Road. Boston, Houghton Mifflin, 1981.

Vision of the Future: The Art of Robert McCall. New York, Abrams, 1982.

Assured Survival: Putting the Star Wars Defense in Perspective. Boston, Houghton Mifflin, 1984.

Editor, *The Many Worlds of Science Fiction.* New York, Dutton, 1971.

Editor, *Analog 9.* New York, Doubleday, and London, Dobson, 1973.

Editor, *Science Fiction Hall of Fame 2.* New York, Doubleday, 1973.

Editor, *The Analog Science Fact Reader.* New York, St. Martin's Press, and London, Millington, 1974.

Editor, *Analog Annual.* New York, Pyramid, 1976.

Editor, *The Best of Astounding.* New York, Baronet, 1977.

Editor, *Closeup, New Worlds.* New York, St. Martin's Press, 1977.

Editor, *Exiles.* London, Futura, 1977; New York, St. Martin's Press, 1978.

Editor, *Aliens.* London, Futura, 1977; New York, St. Martin's Press, 1978.

Editor, *The Best of Analog.* New York, Baronet, 1978.

Editor, *Analog Yearbook.* New York, Ace, 1978.

Editor, with Don Myrus, *The Best of Omni Science Fiction 1-4.* New York, Omni, 1980-82.

*

Manuscript Collection: Pennsylvania State University Library, University Park.

*   *   *

Ben Bova's science fiction—with emphasis on *correct* science—can be likened to a schematic diagram in which each work is a component in a master design. Many of his characters reappear to interlock his works. This repetition, coupled with his themes, produces a mosaic unmistakably contrived. The design can be evidenced by grouping his works into three categories: "pure romps," Earth-based, and star stories.

The "pure romps" (Bova's own designation) show that people are often motivated by misguided principles, and include stories such as "The Secret Life of Henry K. " and "The Great Supersonic Zeppelin Race. " "Free Enterprise" jabs at

the American "free" but muddled enterprise system as compared with the more efficient Japanese system. And a tongue-in-cheek Bova proves in "Vision" that vision is a quality only few attain, until or unless they are confronted with a problem that makes them visionary because it suddenly involves them. The children's novel *Gremlins, Go Home* ! (written with Gordon Dickson) and *The Starcrossed* complete the bedlam-type tales Bova enjoys spinning.

The Earth-based stories establish man's move to the stars as essential because of the mishandling of his Earth home. A few children's stories (as in *Forward in Time*) and novels fit in this category. The more serious short story, "Blood of Tyrants" and the longer work, *Escape!* feature a chaotic ghetto background in which protagonist Danny Romano is caught. *City of Darkness* deals with the same theme: youths fend for themselves against insensitive, insane odds. Forced to live a quasi-life in overcrowded conditions, they rebel violently.

Besides articulating the theme of overpopulation, Bova treats three other major themes: politics, the military, and science, particularly scientific progress. *Out of the Sun* is strictly military, introducing Frank Colt (who also figures in Millennium and *Colony*). *The Dueling Machine* portrays an inventor whose machine relieves tension but which creates inadvertently a setting for murder. A telepathic but fumbling hero makes this a readable novel. *The Multiple Man* handles the subject of cloning and politics. Bova's training as a journalist is obvious: the President's press secretary confronts a conflict of duty. As investigative reporter, he uncovers a fantastic story that he must either bury or make known to the public. *The Weathermakers* relates the encounter of a typical Bovan protagonist with bureaucratic folderol and military arrogance.

That same bureaucratic and military tripe is faced down by Keith Stoner in *Voyagers,* whose religion is expressed as follows: "The eternal mystery of the universe is its comprehensibility. " Bova's male protagonists possess an instinct to lead and a sense of rightness that defies bureaucracies and decries anti-science sentiment. They succeed, though often at high personal loss (as in *Voyagers,* Stoner gives up love for an Earth-bound woman and, in the end, his own life, for the privilege of knowledge). One exceptional piece is *THX 1138,* based on a screenplay by George Lucas. Here, the main character, drug-encapsulated, is not heroic but part of an human-less society in which emotions are sacrificed and love becomes a death trap. His escape to a world made healthy again by the near absence of man expresses an insightfulness about 20th-century issues.

Whatever century, whichever eon man inhabits, he requires guidance to keep from destroying himself. "Floodtide" presents a reluctant yet dutiful guide/savior in a Neolithic setting that bodes a mysticism unusual for Bova. A similar mystique is seen in "A Small Kindness" and "Born Again" with sequel sure to follow. These latter stories are transitional and seem to suggest that since man can not or will not go to the stars for knowledge, the "stars" will come to him. They hammer at what is the crux of Bova's concern: man using his intelligence to make this world better, but with a curious addition of faith in something other than man to pull it off (in "A Small Kindness" and "Born Again," it's seen in an extraterrestrial intent on helping former assassin Jeremy Keating find his way).

The star stories situate man's move outward. Unable to solve his problems on Earth, man "island hops," escaping the old world and founding new ones, and discovering some older ones that nearly extinguish him. Though the major themes apply, man's environment and his ability to use scientific technology to benefit himself are important sub-themes. The *Exiles* trilogy belongs in this group. Dramatic and adventuresome, the books trace the fate of a group of 2000 molecular geneticists and biochemists and their families, banned from Earth, who journey to a new star system. Of the three *End of Exile* is the most suspenseful, involving superstition, a juvenile protagonist, a real crisis and last-second salvation.

The *Kinsman* stories and *Millennium* and *Colony* represent the placing of man in the universe. From his first meeting with this daring individual, the reader recognizes near superhuman qualities in astronaut Chet Kinsman who has one flaw—a guilt that will not release him, lending credibility to his heroic stature. Kinsman declares Selene (Moonbase) a nation and averts a holocaust on Earth. His death wish in *Millennium* is for man to mine the moon for its resources. *Colony*, an involved novel, continues the conflict of power begun in *Millennium*.

When a solar flare destroys Earth, Moonbase survivors become slaves to their environment in *When the Sky Burned*. Like modern man, they have little concern for the future, except as it directly affects them. In *The Winds of Altair*, scientists probing an alien planet almost obliterate life on the planet so that they can make it more habitable for man. The boy protagonist *feels* the wrong being committed against the planet's creatures and convinces his elders.

The most far-reaching star stories are those which stem from the discovery of the Titan machines and the Others. In *As on a Darkling Plain*, Dr. Sidney Lee goes back to the Jupiter moon of Titan to uncover the purpose of the machines placed there by unknown beings one million years before. Lee comments: "They're not beyond the scope of human intelligence. That's the most important discovery of all." In his *Notes to a Science Fiction Writer*, Bova writes: "at the core of all good SF is the very good fundamental faith that we can use our intelligence to understand the world and solve our problems."

The other two major works in the Titan group are *The Star Conquerors* and its sequel, *Star Watchman*. Having defeated the Masters, a superior intelligence and culture, man now controls the Empire. How he will handle his responsibility is the Masters' question—and apparently Bova's, since man's quest continues to be riddled with destruction, mishandling, and nonconcern. In *Voyagers*, Stoner states: "Intelligent civilizations don't wipe themselves out. . . . We have a future ahead of us as wide and bright as the stars themselves, if we strive for it, if we work together, all of us—the whole human race as a species, as a family, as one family unit in the great interstellar community of intelligent civilizations. . . ." This thrust masks a concerned Bova hoping for cooperation among men at all levels. Will man survive interferences—political, militaristic, personal—that constantly bombard his better judgment? Is man intelligent, or not?

The short story "Stars, Won't You Hide Me?" provides an answer. After fleeing from the Others for billions of years, Holman (whole man) seems on the verge of losing, but at the moment of man's—Holman's—end, the universe also ends. The story concludes with a note of optimism and hope. As long as man survives, hope remains.

—Marylyn J. Underwood

———

BOYD, Felix. See **HARRISON, Harry.**

———

BOYD, John. Pseudonym for Boyd Bradfield Upchurch.

American. Born in Atlanta, Georgia, 3 October 1919. Educated in Atlanta, Fulton County, Georgia, and St. Paul, Minnesota, public schools; Atlanta Junior College, 1938-40; University of Southern California, Los Angeles, A. B. in journalism 1947. Served in the United States Navy, 1940-45: Lieutenant Commander; mentioned in Royal Navy despatches. Married Fern Gillaspy in 1944. Production Manager, Star Engraving Company, Los Angeles, 1947-71; free-lance writer, 1971-79.

SCIENCE-FICTION PUBLICATIONS

Novels

The Last Starship from Earth. New York, Weybright and Talley, 1968; London, Gollancz, 1969.
The Pollinators of Eden. New York, Weybright and Talley, 1969; London, Gollancz, 1970.
The Rakehells of Heaven. New York, Weybright and Talley, 1969; London, Gollancz, 1971.
Sex and the High Command. New York, Weybright and Talley, 1970.
The Organ Bank Farm. New York, Weybright and Talley, 1970.
The Gorgon Festival. New York, Weybright and Talley, 1972.
The I. Q. Merchant. New York, Weybright and Talley, 1972.
The Doomsday Gene. New York, Weybright and Talley, 1973.
Andromeda Gun. New York, Putnam, 1974.
Barnard's Planet. New York, Berkley, 1975.
The Girl with the Jade Green Eyes. New York, Viking Press, 1978; London, Penguin, 1979.

Uncollected Short Stories

"The Girl and the Dolphin," in *Galaxy* (New York), March 1973.
"The Sparrow and the Wizard," in *Other Worlds 2*, edited by Roy Torgeson. New York, Zebra, 1980.

OTHER PUBLICATIONS

Novels

The Slave Stealer. New York, Weybright and Talley, 1968; London, Jenkins, 1969.
Scarborough Hall. New York, Berkley, 1976.
Behind Every Bush, with Richard H. Ichord. Los Angeles, Seville, 1979.

*

Manuscript Collection: University of California, Fullerton.

John Boyd comments:
Insofar as any writer consciously erects a schema for the body of his work, my intentions in science fiction have been generally to take mythic themes and find—ideally to strike—their echoes in the modern world. I attempt, without pedantry, to be didactic and, above all, entertaining. A story without some moral theme, either expressed or implied, is usually frivolous, but an apparently frivolous tale with a strong moral basis can be a gem. In telling my tales, when the substance weakens, I attempt to beguile the reader with stylistic wiles.

*   *   *

In addition to romances of the historical and contemporary South, John Boyd has published 11 science-fiction novels. Triumphs of style over substance, they are witty and sensuous, inventive in details if not major premises. Stylish variations on familiar SF themes, these tall tales kid the conventions of romance and science fiction, while satirizing human fatuousness.

The Last Starship from Earth depicts a dystopian alternate present, from which two star-crossed lovers are eventually exiled. A fast shuffle shows that exiles on the planet Hell have manipulated the romance, involving the young mathematical rebel in a time-travel story. Changing history, he fails to benefit from it, but lives on into our present as the Wandering Jew. Romantic courtship rituals come in for a ribbing, as do the "rational" practices of a rigid behaviorist society, and the whole is imbued with allusions to, and the spirit of, English Romantic poetry.

Positing intelligent vegetable life, *The Pollinators of Eden* is a more lyrical tale of a repressed female scientist, ending with a complicated defloration and impregnation by her fiancé *and* the orchids of the planet Flora. Partially balanced by satire of scientific grantsmanship and politics, titillation is the book's prime object, accomplished with poetic allusions and complicated metaphorical connections. *The Rakehells of Heaven* also involves carnal contact with aliens, as two astronauts educate university students on a distant planet in human culture. The natives of Harlech (Heaven) adopt our vices as well as our virtues, culminating in crucifixion of one scout and expulsion of the other. The satire is still broader, the plot more unwieldy, in *Sex and the High Command*, as the U. S. Navy officers and other bumbling males in high places fall prey to the world's women how have learned, with the aid of chemistry, how to manage quite well without men. Like the protagonist of *Rakehells*, the hero parodies Southern manhood, representing rigid values unprepared for change.

In post-catastrophe California a brilliant neurosurgeon is brought to *The Organ Bank Farm* to perform brain transplants while pursuing his "hobby" of trying to cure autistic children. Amid the trappings of music therapy and behaviorist computers, his sense of decency is engaged, especially on behalf of a beautiful girl lost in an imaginary medieval world. Love and sex and poetry are present in profusion, capped by a bewildering but plausible surprise ending.

Revolutions in *The Gorgon Festival* and *The I. Q. Merchant* result from discoveries in chemistry. Rejuvenated older women fail in the first, amid the paraphernalia of rock music, motorcycle gangs, racism, and the generation gap. Flirting with sexual taboos named for Oedipus and Electra, the second emphasizes family drama. Estranged from his alcoholic wife and formerly retarded son, the inventor sees events pass him by as his intelligence-booster transforms society. Then with his youthful lover he leapfrogs simple genius into communal ESP in another tricky ending.

The Doomsday Gene projects bitterness toward a world of high technology and scientific irresponsibility, seen largely through the eyes of a repressed clairvoyant girl. Unusual for Boyd, it is stiffly written, internally inconsistent, even incoherent in places, though not lacking in poetic allusions. A further decline is visible in *Andromeda Gun*, a spoof on conventions of the old West, in which an alien intelligence tries to reform the mind of a Southern rebel turned rabid outlaw.

Barnard's Planet revisits old haunts with an exploratory mission to an Edenic world where vegetable evolution has outstripped animal. Amid five "cluster-educated" multiple-discipline geniuses, representing national interests, the captain is an atavism. Unwilling to subject this world to Earth's warring interests, he discovers himself as the saboteur (and poet) he's under orders to defeat.

The protagonist of Boyd's next book has a similar narrow escape. Bumbling bureaucrats and military men almost achieve what they are trying to prevent: takeover by a high-technology, hive-like alien race, temporarily marooned on Earth. Loving and loved by the queen, for whom Boyd's lyricism scales new heights, the hero escapes the fate of a discarded drone, to remember fondly *The Girl with the Jade Green Eyes*.

Freed from the sexual taboos and stylistic limitations of a previous era, Boyd approaches science fiction as entertainment, with literary tolls and aims. Viewed whole, his books are lightweight confections, their component parts wildly implausible. If one is prepared, however, in the act of reading, to trace interwoven motifs and allusions, while trying to outguess the turns of plot, Boyd generally supplies a superior diversion.

—David N. Samuelson

BRACKETT, Leigh (Douglass). American. Born in Los Angeles, California, 7 December 1915. Married Edmond Hamilton, *q. v.,* in 1946 (died, 1977). Free-lance writer from 1939. Recipient: Jules Verne Award; Western Writers of America Spur Award, 1963. *Died 24 March 1978.*

SCIENCE-FICTION PUBLICATIONS

Novels (series: Skaith)

Shadow over Mars. Manchester, World, 1951; as *The Nemesis from Terra*, New York, Ace, 1961.
The Starmen. New York, Gnome Press, 1952; London, Museum Press, 1954; abridged edition, as *The Galactic Breed*, New York, Ace, 1955; original version, as *The Starmen of Llyrdis*, New York, Ballantine, 1976.
The Sword of Rhiannon. New York, Ace, 1953; London, Boardman, 1955.
The Big Jump. New York, Ace, 1955.
The Long Tomorrow. New York, Doubleday, 1955.
Alpha Centauri—or Die! New York, Ace, 1963.
People of the Talisman, The Secret of Sinharat New York, Ace, 1964
The Ginger Star. New York, Ballantine, 1974; London, Sphere, 1976.
The Book of Skaith. New York, Doubleday, 1976.
  The Hounds of Skaith. New York, Ballantine, 1974; London, Sphere, 1976.
  The Reavers of Skaith. New York, Ballantine, 1976.
Eric John Stark, Outlaw of Mars. New York, Ballantine, 1982.

Short Stories

The Coming of the Terrans. New York, Ace, 1967.
The Halflings and Other Stories. New York, Ace, 1973.
The Best of Leigh Brackett, edited by Edmond Hamilton. New York, Doubleday, 1977.

Uncollected Short Story

"Lorelei of the Red Mist," with Ray Bradbury, in *Planet* (New York), Summer 1946.

OTHER PUBLICATIONS

Novels

No Good from a Corpse. New York, Coward McCann, 1944.
Stranger at Home (ghost-written for George Sanders). New York, Simon and Schuster, 1946; London, Pilot Press, 1947.
The Tiger among Us. New York, Doubleday, 1957; London, Boardman, 1958; as *Fear No Evil*, London, Corgi, 1960; as *13 West Street*, New York, Bantam, 1962.
An Eye for an Eye. New York, Doubleday, 1957; London, Boardman, 1958.
Rio Bravo (novelization of screenplay). New York, Bantam, and London, Corgi, 1959.
Follow the Free Wind. New York, Doubleday, 1963.
Silent Partner. New York, Putnam, 1969.

Plays

The Empire Strikes Back (screenplay), with Lawrence Kasdan, in *The Empire Strikes Back Notebook*, edited by Diane Attias and Lindsay Smith. New York, Ballantine, 1980.

Screenplays: *The Vampire's Ghost*, with John K. Butler, 1945; *Crime Doctor's Manhunt*, with Eric Taylor, 1946; *The Big Sleep*, with William Faulkner and Jules Furthman, 1946; *Rio Bravo*, with Jules Furthman and B. H. McCampbell, 1959; *Gold of the Seven Saints*, with Leonard Freeman, 1961; *Hatari!*, with Harry Kurnitz, 1962; *El Dorado*, 1967; *Rio Lobo*, with Burton Wohl, 1970; *The Long Goodbye*, 1973; *The Empire Strikes Back*, with Lawrence Kasdan, 1979.

Television Plays: for *Checkmate* and *Suspense* series, and *Terror at Northfield* for *Alfred Hitchcock* series.

Other

Editor, *The Best of Planet Stories 1*. New York, Ballantine, 1975.
Editor, *The Best of Edmond Hamilton*. New York, Ballantine, 1977.

*

Bibliography: *Leigh Brackett, Marion Zimmer Bradley, Anne McCaffrey: A Primary and Secondary Bibliography* by Rosemarie Arbur, Boston, Hall, 1982.

Manuscript Collection: Special Collections, Eastern New Mexico University Library, Portales.

*   *   *

Leigh Brackett was during the late 1940's and early 1950's the uncontested "Queen of Space Opera." As a girl, she spent summers exploring the beaches near Santa Monica; the majesty of the Pacific by day and its bio-luminescence by night, and her reading of Edgar Rice Burroughs provided much of the imagery that was to make her science fiction unique. In a *Planet Stories* "Feature Flash" in 1942, she admitted her addiction to things dramatic, repeatedly describing herself as "a ham." This quality served her well when she worked in films, very often "writing before the camera" that is, revising dialogue on the basis of actors' performances in prior scenes. Her facility with character and dialogue (in the "tough" detective novel, *No Good from a Corpse*) got her the movie job, and, later prompted

Pauline Kael to suppose that most of her dialogue in *El Dorado* was improvised by the actors because it seemed too realistic to have come from any script.

All these aspects of her personal and professional self found ready expression in the kind of science fiction that made her famous. At present, space opera is a derogatory term, denoting impossibly larger-than-life characters, melodramatic incidents, and flights of fancy quite distant from straight extrapolative science fiction. In the 1940's and early 1950's, however, space opera was the staple of most of the pulp magazines, partly because it was an escape from ordinary life, partly because it evoked a "sense of wonder" just by its portrayal of alien beings, awesome settings, and heroic acts, and partly because of the literary skills of Brackett herself.

The Sword of Rhiannon is perhaps the apex of Brackett's career as a writer of space opera. It begins with a renegade archeologist's being thrown back a million years by a strange "bubble of time" within the tomb of the ancient god-like Martian, Rhiannon. Once in the past, Brackett's hero finds himself involved in all sorts of adventures (he, with Rhiannon's help, frees ancient Mars of the Tyranny of one race, the serpent-evolved Dhuvians, and wins the love of the princess of a human Martian race). The way Brackett tells this story gives it much greater literary quality than the space-opera label suggests. Her setting—verdant Mars, with a luminous ocean—and her characters—of several Martian races, each independently evolved to the level of human culture—allow the reader a glimpse of Mars as a vital world, not the dying one the Terrans find when they arrive just before the beginning of our third millennium. In this novel, Brackett masterfully interweaves the melodramatic heroism of space opera with imaginative postulation of three sapient lifeforms besides the native human race of Martians.

Before *Rhiannon*, Brackett produced two space-opera masterpieces, "Enchantree of Venus" and "The Lake of the Gone Forever. " Afterwards, she turned to more conventional science fiction with *The Long Tomorrow*, a post-Destruction narrative considered by many to be Brackett's best, and stories like "The Tweener" and "The Queer Ones. " Then she turned to making novels of previously published novelettes; "Queen of the Martian Catacombs" and "Black Amazon of Mars"—both, incidentally, featuring not just extraordinary women characters but the literary "original," Eric John Stark—became *The Secret of Sinharat* and *People of the Talisman*.

Considering the excitement of her narratives and the immediate pleasure to be derived from them, one might assume that Brackett's science fictions are fun to read, even lessons in the use of English prose, but basically light entertainment. However, one can perceive three serious aspects of her fiction, whether it is space opera or not.

One, illustrated best in the stories and novels about Eric John Stark, is a thematic interest in the essential goodness of most forms of natural life. Stark, son of Earthborn humans who died on Mercury, struggles for survival among a supportive group of non-human Mercurians and only later is returned to civilization. Stark is a renegade and mercenary, a "criminal" only because he does not recognize the authority of artificial laws; whenever he finds himself in a situation calling for heroic action, the "primal ape" in him seems set apart from the civilized human. Nevertheless, both his natural and civilized selves—demonstrated by his consistent sympathy for the wronged, whatever their species may be—seek the good.

Another is Brackett's thematic egalitarianism and, along with it and Stark's appetite for the good, a strong sense of respect for other living things. The care with which she treats her native Martians and Venusians—though alien, they are persons, too—makes this evident. *The Starmen* is the tale of the quest for equality on a galactic scale; respect for other life runs just below the surface of "The Tweener," evoking sad sympathy from the reader. And "All the Colors of the Rainbow" is, like Le Guin's *The Word for World Is Forest*, a cruelly bitter satire of racist and other mean prejudices, set forth by paradoxically delicate prose.

Then there is Brackett's growth as a writer, helped along by her husband, Edmond Hamilton; as she influenced his deepening characterization, he influenced her growing ability to structure fiction with a strong yet uncontrived plot. This growth is evident in her Skaith series. Besides the technical expertise with plotting, Brackett had, by the time she wrote about Skaith, evidently rethought the biology in *Rhiannon*; on Skaith as on ancient Mars there are at least three non-human sapient races, but these have evolved from a single stock, each seeking survival by accommodating itself differently to life beneath the dying ginger sun.

From February 1940 when "Martian Quest" appeared in *Astounding*, almost until the day she died in March 1978. Brackett's love for science fiction was self evident in her works. Her last work was the first full draft of the screenplay for *Star Wars II*.

—Rosemarie Arbur

BRADBURY, Edward P. See **MOORCOCK, Michael.**

BRADBURY, Ray(mond Douglas). Has also written as Douglas Spaulding. American. Born in Waukegan, Illinois, 22 August 1920. Educated at Los Angeles High School, graduated 1938. Married Marguerite Susan McClure in 1947; four daughters. Since 1943, full-time writer. President, Science-Fantasy Writers of America, 1951-53. Member of the Board of Directors, Screen Writers Guild of America, 1957-61. Recipient: O. Henry Prize, 1947, 1948; Benjamin Franklin Award, 1954; American Academy award, 1954; Boys' Clubs of America Junior Book Award, 1956; Golden Eagle Award, for screenplay, 1957; Ann Radcliffe Award, 1965, 1971; Writers Guild Award, 1974; Aviation and Space Writers Award, for television documentary, 1979; Gandalf Award, 1980. D. Litt.: Whittier College, California, 1979. Agent: Don Congdon, Harold Matson Company, 276 Fifth Avenue, New York, New York 10001. Address: 10265 Cheviot Drive, Los Angeles, California 90064, U. S. A.

SCIENCE-FICTION PUBLICATIONS

Novels

Fahrenheit 451. New York, Ballantine, 1953; London, Hart Davis, 1954.
Something Wicked This Way Comes. New York, Simon and Schuster, 1962; London, Hart Davis, 1963.

Short Stories

Dark Carnival. Sauk City, Wisconsin, Arkham House, 1947;

abridged edition, London, Hamish Hamilton, 1948; abridged edition, as *The Small Assassin*, London, New English Library, 1962.
The Martian Chronicles. New York, Doubleday, 1950; as *The Silver Locusts*, London, Hart Davis, 1951.
The Illustrated Man. New York, Doubleday, 1951; London, Hart Davis, 1952.
The Golden Apples of the Sun. New York, Doubleday, and London, Hart Davis, 1953.
The October Country. New York, Ballantine, 1955; London, Hart Davis, 1956.
A Medicine for Melancholy. New York, Doubleday, 1959.
The Day It Rained Forever. London, Hart Davis, 1959.
The Machineries of Joy. New York, Simon and Schuster, and London, Hart Davis, 1964.
The Vintage Bradbury. New York, Random House, 1965.
The Autumn People. New York, Ballantine, 1965.
Tomorrow Midnight. New York, Ballantine, 1966.
Twice Twenty Two (selection). New York, Doubleday, 1966.
I Sing the Body Electric! New York, Knopf, 1969; London, Hart Davis, 1970.
Bloch and Bradbury, with Robert Bloch. New York, Tower, 1969; as *Fever Dreams and Other Fantasies*, London, Sphere, 1970.
(*Selected Stories*), edited by Anthony Adams. London, Harrap, 1975.
Long after Midnight. New York, Knopf, 1976; London, Hart Davis MacGibbon, 1977.
The Best of Bradbury. New York, Bantam, 1976.
To Sing Strange Songs. Exeter, Devon, Wheaton, 1979.
The Stories of Ray Bradbury. New York, Knopf, and London, Granada, 1980.
Dinosaur Tales. New York, Bantam, 1983.

Uncollected Short Stories

"Hollerbochen's Dilemma," in *Imagination* (Evanston, Illinois), January 1938.
"Pendulum," with Henry Hasse, in *Super Science* (Kokomo, Indiana), November 1941.
"Eat, Drink, and Be Wary," in *Astounding* (New York), July 1942.
"The Candle," in *Weird Tales* (New York), November 1942.
"The Piper," in *Thrilling Wonder Stories* (New York), February 1943.
"Gabriel's Horn," with Henry Hasse, in *Captain Future* (New York), Spring 1943.
"Subterfuge," in *Astonishing* (Chicago), April 1943.
"Promotion to Satellite," in *Thrilling Wonder Stories* (New York), Fall 1943.
"And Watch the Fountains" and "Doodad," in *Astounding* (New York), September 1943.
"The Ducker," in *Weird Tales* (New York), November 1943.
"The Sea Shell," in *Weird Tales* (New York), January 1944.
"The Monster Maker," in *Planet* (New York), Spring 1944.
"I, Rocket," in *Amazing* (New York), May 1944.
"Morgue Ship," in *Planet* (New York), Summer 1944.
"Bang! You're Dead!," in *Weird Tales* (New York), September 1944.
"Lazarus Come Forth," in *Planet* (New York), Winter 1944.
"Undersea Guardians," in *Amazing* (New York), December 1944.
"The Poems," in *Weird Tales* (New York), January 1945.
"The Watchers," in *Weird Tales* (New York), May 1945.
"Final Victim," with Henry Hasse, in *Amazing* (New York), February 1946.

"Defense Mech," in *Planet* (New York), Spring 1946.
"Rocket Skin," in *Thrilling Wonder Stories* (New York), Spring 1946.
"Lorelei of the Red Mist," with Leigh Brackett, in *Planet* (New York), Summer 1946.
"Rocket Summer," in *Planet* (New York), Spring 1947.
"Tomorrow and Tomorrow," in *Fantastic Adventures* (New York), May 1947.
"The Irritated People," in *Thrilling Wonder Stories* (New York), December 1947.
"The October Game," in *Weird Tales* (New York), March 1948.
"The Black Ferris," in *Weird Tales* (New York), May 1948.
"The Square Pegs," in *Thrilling Wonder Stories* (New York), October 1948.
"Asleep in Armageddon," in *Planet* (New York), Winter 1948.
"The Silence," in *Super Science* (Kokomo, Indiana), January 1949.
"Changeling," in *Super Science* (Kokomo, Indiana), July 1949.
"The Lonely Ones," in *Startling* (New York), July 1949.
"Holiday," in *Arkham Sampler* (Sauk City, Wisconsin), Autumn 1949.
"A Blade of Grass," in *Thrilling Wonder Stories* (New York), December 1949.
"Payment in Full," in *Thrilling Wonder Stories* (New York), February 1950.
"Forever and the Earth," in *Planet* (New York), Spring 1950.
"Punishment Without Crime," in *Other Worlds* (Evanston, Indiana), March 1950.
"Death Wish," in *Planet* (New York), Fall 1950.
"The Fireman," in *Galaxy* (New York), February 1951.
"A Little Journey," in *Galaxy* (New York), August 1951.
"Bright Phoenix," in *Fantasy and Science Fiction* (New York), May 1963.
"The Year the Glop-Monster Won the Golden Lion at Cannes," in *Cavalier*, July 1966.
"The Hour of Ghosts," in *Saturday Review* (New York), 25 October 1969.
"The Parrot Who Met Papa," in *Playboy* (Chicago), January 1972.
"Trapdoor," in *Omni* (New York), April 1985.

OTHER PUBLICATIONS

Novel

Dandelion Wine. New York, Doubleday, and London, Hart Davis, 1957.

Short Stories

The Last Circus, and The Electrocution. Northridge, California, Lord John Press, 1980.
A Memory for Murder. New York, Dell, 1984.

Plays

The Meadow, in *Best One-Act Plays of 1947-48*, edited by Margaret Mayorga. New York, Dodd Mead, 1848.
The Anthem Sprinters and Other Antics (produced Los Angeles, 1968). New York, Dial Press, 1963.
The World of Ray Bradbury (produced Los Angeles, 1964; New York, 1965).
The Wonderful Ice-Cream Suit (produced Los Angeles, 1965). Included in *The Wonderful Ice-Cream Suit and Other Plays*, 1972.

The Day It Rained Forever. New York, French, 1966.
The Pedestrian. New York, French, 1966.
Christus Apollo, music by Jerry Goldsmith (produced Los Angeles, 1969).
The Wonderful Ice-Cream Suit and Other Plays (includes *The Veldt* and *To the Chicago Abyss*). New York, Bantam, 1972; London, Hart Davis, 1973.
The Veldt (produced London, 1980). Included in *The Wonderful Ice-Cream Suit and Other Plays*, 1972.
Leviathan 99 (produced Los Angeles, 1972).
Pillar of Fire and Other Plays for Today, Tomorrow, and Beyond Tomorrow (includes *Kaleidoscope* and *The Foghorn*). New York, Bantam, 1975.
The Foghorn (produced New York, 1977). Included in *Pillar of Fire and Other Plays*, 1975.
That Ghost, That Bride of Time: Excerpts from a Play-in-Progress. Glendale, California, Squires, 1976.
The Martian Chronicles, adaptation of his own stories (produced Los Angeles, 1977).
Fahrenheit 451, adaptation of his own novel (produced Los Angeles, 1979).
Dandelion Wine, adaptation of his own story (produced Los Angeles, 1980).

Screenplays: *It Came from Outer Space*, with David Schwartz, 1952; *Moby-Dick*, with John Huston, 1956; *Icarus Montgolfier Wright*, with George C. Johnston, 1961; *Picasso Summer* (as Douglas Spaulding), with Edwin Booth, 1972.

Television Plays: *Shopping for Death*, 1956, *Design for Loving*, 1958, *Special Delivery*, 1959, *The Faith of Aaron Menefee*, 1962, and *The Life Work of Juan Diaz* (all *Alfred Hitchcock Presents* series); *The Marked Bullet* (*Jane Wyman's Fireside Theatre* series), 1956; *The Gift* (*Steve Canyon* series), 1958; *The Tunnel to Yesterday* (*Trouble Shooters* series), 1960; *I Sing the Body Electric!* (*Twilight Zone* series), 1962; *The Jail* (*Alcoa Premiere* series), 1962; *The Groom* (*Curiosity Shop* series), 1971.

Verse

Old Ahab's Friend, and Friend to Noah, Speaks His Piece: A Celebration. Glendale, California, Squires, 1971.
When Elephants Last in the Dooryard Bloomed: Celebrations for Almost Any Day in the Year. New York, Knopf, 1973; London, Hart Davis MacGibbon, 1975.
That Son of Richard III: A Birth Announcement. Privately printed, 1974.
Where Robot Mice and Robot Men Run round in Robot Towns: New Poems, Both Light and Dark. New York, Knopf, 1977; London, Hart Davis MacGibbon, 1979.
Twin Hieroglyphs That Swim the River Dust. Northridge, California, Lord John Press, 1978.
The Bike Repairman. Northridge, California, Lord John Press, 1978.
The Author Considers His Resources. Northridge, California, Lord John Press, 1979.
The Aqueduct. Glendale, California, Squires, 1979.
The Attic Where the Meadow Greens. Northridge, California, Lord John Press, 1980.
The Haunted Computer and the Android Pope. New York, Knopf, and London, Granada, 1981.
The Complete Poems of Ray Bradbury. New York, Ballantine, 1982.
The Love Affair. Northridge, California, Lord John Press, 1983.
Forever and the Earth. Athens, Ohio, Croissant, 1984.

Other

"A Few Notes on *The Martian Chronicles*," in *Rhodomagnetic Digest* (Palo Alto, California), May 1950.
"Day after Tomorrow: Why Science Fiction?," in *Nation* (New York), 2 May 1953.
Switch on the Night (for children). New York, Pantheon, and London, Hart Davis, 1955.
"Literature in the Space Age," in *California Librarian (Sacramento), July 1960.
R Is for Rocker (for children). New York, Doubleday, 1962; London, Hart Davis, 1968.
"The Fahrenheit Chronicles," in *Spaceman*, June 1964.
S Is for Space (for children). New York, Doubleday, 1966; London, Hart Davis, 1968.
"At What Temperature Do Books Burn?," in *New York Times*, 13 November 1966.
"An Imperfect Gulliver above Our Roofs," in *Life* (New York), 24 November 1967.
Teacher's Guide: Science Fiction, with Lewy Olfson. New York, Bantam, 1968.
The Halloween Tree (for children). New York, Knopf, 1972; London, Hart Davis MacGibbon, 1973.
Mars and the Mind of Man. New York, Harper, 1973.
Zen and the Art of Writing, and The Joy of Writing. Santa Barbara, California, Capra Press, 1973.
"Science Fiction: Before Christ and after 2001," in *Science Fact/Fiction.* Chicago, Scott Foresman, 1974.
"Henry Kuttner: A Neglected Master," in *The Best of Henry Kuttner.* New York, Doubleday, 1975.
The Mummies of Guanajuato, photographs by Archie Lieberman. New York, Abrams, 1978.
Beyond 1984: Remembrance of Things Future. New York, Targ, 1979.
The Ghosts of Forever , illustrated by Aldo Sessa. New York, Rizzoli, 1981.
Los Angeles, photographs by West Light. Port Washington, New York, Skyline Press, 1984.
Orange County, photographs by Bill Ross and others. Port Washington, New York, Skyline Press, 1985.

Editor, *Timeless Stories for Today and Tomorrow.* New York, Bantam, 1952.
Editor, *The Circus of Dr. Lao and Other Improbable Stories.* New York, Bantam, 1956.

*

Critical Studies: introduction by Gilbert Highet to *The Vintage Bradbury*, 1965; *The Ray Bradbury Companion* (includes bibliography) by William F. Nolan, Detroit, Gale, 1975; *The Drama of Ray Bradbury* by Ben F. Indick, Baltimore, T-K Graphics, 1977; *The Bradbury Chronicles* by George Edgar Slusser, San Bernardino, California, Borgo Press, 1977; *Ray Bradbury* (includes bibliography) edited by Joseph D. Olander and Martin H. Greenberg, New York, Taplinger, and Edinburgh, Harris, 1980; *Ray Bradbury* by Wayne L. Johnson, New York, Ungar, 1980; *Ray Bradbury and the Poetics of Reverie: Fantasy, Science Fiction, and the Reader* by William F. Toupence, Ann Arbor, UMI Research Press, 1984.

*　　*　　*

Ever since the remarkable critical and popular success of *The Martian Chronicles* in 1950, Ray Bradbury has been among the most visible of science-fiction writers, and although he has not produced a major work in several years he remains the most widely recognized spokesman for the genre, and particularly for the romantic attitudes toward space flight and technology which it sometimes embodies. In some sense this is ironic, since Bradbury's best works—dating from the early 1950's—are powerful indictments of unchecked technological progress and question humanity's ability to deal creatively with the new worlds of which science and technology hold promise.

Bradbury is above all a humanist, and this humanism is evident throughout his career, which might be divided into three general periods roughly corresponding to the 1940's, the 1950's, and the 1960's to the present. The first of these periods sees the youthful Bradbury move from an adolescent science-fiction fan making his first professional sales (the first was the story "Pendulum" written with Henry Hasse) to a mature stylist who had become one of the most popular science-fiction writers in America. Bradbury's first book, the collection of stories *Dark Carnival*, was not science fiction at all, but rather ranged from satirical horror (such as "The Handler" which concerns a mortician who plays practical jokes on his "clients") to sensitive portrayals of lonely or pathetic individuals—a wife incapacitated with horror at her own mortality after viewing Mexican mummies ("The Next in Line"), a "normal" boy alone in a family of friendly vampires ("The Homecoming"). Many of the stories had originally appeared in *Weird Tales*, a horror pulp that represented a market Bradbury would soon abandon, but it was in these tales that he developed his craft to maturity, and many of them remain among his strongest work.

The Martian Chronicles began the second and most prolific phase of Bradbury's career. A series of stories, linked by bridge passages, concerning the colonization and exploitation of Mars by what seem to be exclusively citizens of small midwestern American towns, the book owed much to the American tradition of frontier literature, and quickly consolidated Bradbury's reputation as one of science fiction's leading stylists. Although the portrayal of the Martians ranges from sensitive, essentially ordinary families ("Ylla") to shapeless monsters ("The Third Expedition"), they soon fade into the background as the stories focus on different types of earth settlers—romantics, misfits, opportunists, idealists, even fugitive Blacks (in "Way in the Middle of the Air"). In the end, an atomic war sends most of the settlers back to earth to join their families, leaving only a few isolated families such as that depicted in "The Million-Year Picnic," whose father vows to start a new world on Mars without the prejudice and regimentation that had come to characterize life on earth.

The Illustrated Man appeared in the following year, and again connected the stories by a frame narrative; in this case, each story is presented as a tattoo come to life. A few of the stories retain the Martian setting of the *Chronicles,* and one of these, "The Fire Balloons," is an early attempt at treating a serious religious issue in science fiction—the question of whether a benign alien life form can be said to have achieved Christian grace. Other stories explore themes that had become familiar to Bradbury readers. The amorality of children which appeared as a theme in a few *Dark Carnival* stories here returns in stories in which children murder their parents in a mechanical playroom ("The Veldt") or assist invading aliens ("Zero Hour"). Mexico, which had fascinated Bradbury since a trip he took there in 1945, is the setting of "The Fox in the Forest" and "The Highway. " And the romantic attitudes toward space travel that were to remain a Bradbury staple are evident in "The Rocket," "No Particular Night or Morning," and "Kaleidoscope," a tale of the crew of an exploded spaceship drifting slowly to their deaths, which Bradbury later dramatized.

Fahrenheit 451, a dystopian satire of a totalitarian state in which "firemen" are professional bookburners who set fires rather than put them out, is the only science-fiction work of Bradbury's to approach *The Martian Chronicles* in popularity, and the only novel-length science-fiction work he has yet produced. *Fahrenheit 451* is as much an attack on mass culture as it is a satire of McCarthy-era censorship; the enforced illiteracy of this future society, we are led to believe, is at least in part due to the desires to avoid offending special interest groups in the mass media and to the rise of television (which Bradbury had already effectively satirized in "The Pedestrian"). The novel is as simple as a parable, and few attempts are made to offer a realistic portrait of an imagined society. The police state, it seems, exists almost solely to burn books, and the society of outcasts that the hero Montag finally escapes to join seems curiously incapable of political action, choosing instead to preserve literary culture by memorizing all the great books.

Of the other four collections Bradbury published during the 1950's, none was primarily science fiction. *The Golden Apples of the Sun* introduced what was to become a familiar Bradbury mix of small-town tales, fantasies, Mexican stories, science fiction, and crime tales. *The October Country* reprinted most of the contents of *Dark Carnival* and added four stories, and *Dandelion Wine* was a collection of sketches based on Bradbury's own boyhood in Waukegan, Illinois. *A Medicine for Melancholy* repeated the mix of *The Golden Apples of the Sun,* introducing in book form a new theme for Bradbury, Irish life and character, which had come to fascinate the author while he was in Ireland in 1954.

Bradbury's long-awaited full-length novel *Something Wicked This Way Comes* is a fantasy concerning an evil carnival that influences the lives of people in a small midwestern town. Despite occasional touches of real power, the novel is overwritten and self-conscious, and many readers regard it as the beginning of a third phase of Bradbury's career, characterized by a decreasing output of fiction, a tendency of that fiction to be self-imitative, and an increased turning to such new forms as the drama and poetry. Two new collections, *The Machineries of Joy* and *I Sing the Body Electric!,* suggested little in the way of new directions or artistic growth, despite some excellent stories. Bradbury's only new collection of the 1970's, *Long after Midnight,* contained several excellent stories—but many of them had been written prior to 1955. Other volumes of poetry and plays appeared, and Bradbury must be recognized for his efforts to introduce science fiction into forms that had seldom seemed amenable to it, but he has yet to produce a major work in either of these forms.

Whatever the final assessment of Bradbury's later work, his historical importance both in popularizing science fiction and making it respectable cannot be denied. Though the genre had produced excellent craftsmen before Bradbury, his finely tuned style and humanistic concerns exerted a profound influence on a generation of later writers and helped significantly to reduce the barriers that had long isolated science fiction from more traditional literary culture.

—Gary K. Wolfe

BRADLEY, Marion Zimmer. Has also written as Lee Chapman; John Dexter; Miriam Gardner; Valerie Graves; Morgan Ives; John J. Wells. American. Born in Albany, New York, 3 June 1930. Educated at New York State College for Teachers, 1946-48; Hardin-Simmons University, Abilene, Texas, B. A. 1964; University of California, Berkeley. Married 1) Robert A. Bradley in 1949 (divorced, 1963), one son; 2) Walter Henry Breen in 1964, one son and one daughter. Singer and writer. Recipient: *Locus* Award, 1984. Agent: Scott Meredith Literary Agency, 845 Third Avenue, New York, New York 10022, U.S.A.

<small>SCIENCE-FICTION PUBLICATIONS</small>

Novels (series: Darkover)

The Door Through Space. New York, Ace, 1961; London, Arrow, 1979.
Seven from the Stars. New York, Ace, 1962.
The Planet Savers, The Sword of Aldones (Darkover). New York, Ace, 1962; London Arrow, 2 vols., 1979.
The Colors of Space (for children). Derby, Connecticut, Monarch, 1963.
The Bloody Sun (Darkover). New York, Ace, 1964; London, Arrow, 1978.
Falcons of Narabedla. New York, Ace, 1964.
Star of Danger (Darkover). New York, Ace, 1965; London, Arrow, 1978.
The Brass Dragon. New York, Ace, 1969; London, Methuen, 1978.
The Winds of Darkover. New York, Ace, 1970; London, Arrow, 1978.
The World Wreckers (Darkover). New York, Ace, 1971; London, Arrow, 1979.
Darkover Landfall. New York, DAW, 1972; London, Arrow, 1978.
Hunters of the Red Moon. New York, DAW, 1973; London, Arrow, 1979.
The Spell Sword (Darkover). New York, DAW, 1974; London, Arrow, 1978.
Endless Voyage. New York, Ace, 1975; revised edition, as *Endless Universe,* 1979.
The Heritage of Hastur (Darkover). New York, DAW, 1975; London, Arrow, 1979.
The Shattered Chain (Darkover). New York, DAW, 1976; London, Arrow, 1978.
The Forbidden Tower (Darkover). New York, DAW, 1977; London, Prior, 1979.
Stormqueen (Darkover). New York, DAW, 1978; London, Arrow, 1980.
The Ruins of Isis, Norfolk, Virginia, Donning, 1978; London, Arrow, 1980.
The Survivors, with Paul E. Zimmer. New York, DAW, 1979.
The House Between the Worlds. New York, Doubleday, 1980.
Two to Conquer (Darkover). New York, DAW, 1980; London, Arrow, 1982.
Survey Ship. New York, Ace, 1980.
Sharra's Exile (Darkover). New York, DAW, 1981.
Hawkmistress (Darkover). New York, DAW, 1982.
Web of Light. Norfolk, Virginia, Donning, 1982.
The Mists of Avalon. New York, Knopf, and London, Joseph, 1983.
Thendara House (Darkover). New York, DAW, 1983.
Web of Darkness. New York, Pocket Books, 1984.
The Inheritor. New York, Tor, 1984.
City of Sorcery (Darkover). New York, DAW, 1984.
Night's Daughter. New York, Ballantine, 1985.

Short Stories

The Dark Intruder and Other Stories. New York, Ace, 1964.
The Jewel of Arwen. Baltimore, T-K Graphics, 1974.

The Parting of Arwen. Baltimore, T-K Graphics, 1974.
Swords of Chaos, with others. New York, DAW, 1982.

Uncollected Short Stories

"Another Rib" (as John J. Wells, with Juanita Coulson), in
   Fantasy and Science Fiction (New York), June 1963.
"The Secret of the Blue Star," in *Thieves' World,* edited by
   Robert Asprin. New York, Ace, 1979, London, Penquin,
   1984.
"Elbow Room," in *Stellar 5,* edited by Judy-Lynn del Rey.
   New York, Ballantine, 1980.
"The Keeper's Price," with Elisabeth Waters, in *The Keeper's
   Price,* edited by Bradley. New York, DAW, 1980.
"Somebody Else's Magic," in *Fantasy and Science Fiction*
   (New York), October 1984.

OTHER PUBLICATIONS

Novels

I am a Lesbian (as Lee Chapman). Derby Connecticut,
   Monarch, 1962.
Spare Her Heaven (as Morgan Ives). Derby, Connecticut,
   Monarch, 1963; abridged edition, as *Anything Goes,* Sydney,
   Stag, 1964.
Castle Terror. New York, Lancer, 1965.
Knives of Desire (as Morgan Ives). San Diego, Corinth, 1966.
No Adam for Eve (as John Dexter). San Diego, Corinth, 1966.
Souvenir of Monique. New York, Ace, 1967.
Bluebeard's Daughter. New York, Lancer, 1968.
Witch Hill (as Valerie Graves). San Diego, Greenleaf, 1972.
Dark Satanic. New York, Berkley, 1972.
In the Steps of the Master (novelization of TV Play). New York,
   Grosset and Dunlap, 1973.
Can Ellen Be Saved? (novelization of TV Play). New York,
   Grosset and Dunlap, 1975.
Drums of Darkness. New York, Ballantine, 1976.
The Catch Trap. New York, Ballantine, 1979.

Novels as Miriam Gardner

The Strange Women. Derby, Connecticut, Monarch, 1962.
My Sister, My Love. Derby, Connecticut, Monarch, 1963.
Twilight Lovers. Derby, Connecticut, Monarch, 1964.

Other

Songs from Rivendell. Privately printed, 1959.
*A Complete, Cumulative Checklist of Lesbian, Variant, and
   Homosexual Fiction.* . . . Privately printed, 1960.
Men, Halflings, and Hero-Worship. Baltimore, T-K Graphics,
   1973.
*The Neccessity for Beauty: Robert W. Chambers and the
   Romantic Tradition.* Baltimore, T-K Graphics, 1974.
"Experiment Perilous: The Art and Science of Anguish in
   Science Fiction," in *Experiment Perilous,* edited by Andrew
   Porter. New York, Algol Press, 1976.

Editor, *The Keeper's Price.* New York, DAW, 1980.
Editor, *Greyhaven.* New York, DAW, 1983.
Editor, *Sword and Sorceress 1-2.* New York, DAW, 1984-85.

Translator, *El Villano in su Rincon,* by Lope de Vega. Privately
   printed, 1971.

*

Bibliography: *Leigh Brackett, Marion Zimmer Bradley, Anne
McCaffrey: A Primary and Secondary Biblography* by Rosemarie Arbur, Boston, Hall, 1982.

Manuscript Collection: Boston University.

Critical Studies: *The Gemini Problem: A Study in Darkover* by
Walter Breen, Baltimore, T-K Graphics, 1975; *The Darkover
Dilemma: Problems of the Darkover Series* by S. Wise, Balti-
more, T-K Graphics, 1976.

Marion Zimmer Bradley comments:
   The secret of life is to do what you enjoy doing most, and to
get someone to pay you enough so you don't actually have to
starve while you're doing it. People who want other things,
money and status, baffle me. I write professionally because it's
the only thing I can do well, and every other job I have had has
either bored or frustrated me past tolerance; and since I write
compulsively and would no matter what else I was doing, it's
wonderful that I can get paid for it.

*   *   *

While she was still a college sophomore, Marion Zimmer
Bradley had at least four book-length manuscripts complete.
One was never published, but it laid the ground for much of her
later work about the Darkovan telepaths. One hurriedly
became *The Sword of Aldones* to provide *The Planet Savers*—
the expanded version—with a companion in the 1962 Ace
double. Rewritten and revised at least four times, one became
Web of Light and its sequel, *Web of Darkness.* And another
eventually resulted in *The Mists of Avalon.* .
   Bradley's early works indicate no favorite theme or subject.
Some are extrapolative science fiction typical of the time, like
"Year of the Big Thaw," "The Crime Therapist," and "Exiles
of Tomorrow. " Some are science fantasy, like "Jackie Sees a
Star" and *Falcons of Narabedla.* And others, like "Women
Only" and "Centaurus Changeling," are notable for the
intrusion of women characters into what was considered, C. L.
Moore and Leigh Brackett notwithstanding, "a man's field. "
As early as 1958, in "The Planet Savers," she introduced a Free
Amazon belonging to a group of women who have by oath
renounced all dependence on men. From this character one
might infer that Bradley is a feminist, yet in *Darkover Landfall*
she authorially denies one of the protagonists the right to
terminate an unwanted pregnancy. Then not a feminist? But
Endless Voyage is a novel absolutely without sex-roles for its
male and female characters. *The Shattered Chain,* set on
Darkover with its male-supremacist cultures, are probing and
sensitive treatments of women's need to live according to their
own decisions. Thus Bradley shows how women characters
should be presented as strong human beings, but regards
fiction in which they are strong because of the contrived
absence of men as demeaning and, generally, propagandistic.
   Bradley excels at writing well-plotted, exciting adventure
narratives, like *Hunters of the Red Moon,* a novel with an
astonishing yet credible assortment of human and non-human
sapient characters. *Endless Universe,* too, is an adventure story
on a cosmic scale, with the opening up of new-found worlds
complemented by the maturation and interaction of its principal characters. Every one of the Darkover novels is some kind
of adventure, and *The Ruins of Isis* combines the excitement of
archeological searching for what may have been the first
intelligent race with the sometimes agonizing adventures of a
heterosexual couple trying to conform to the customs of a
rigidly structured Matriarchate.

Although most of her novels—particularly those set on Darkover and others written since 1970—deserve reading for their story-telling, their thematic content is at least as significant as their plots. *Hunters of the Red Moon* and *Endless Universe* embody, respectively, themes of racial and individual tolerance and respect; *The Ruins of Isis* is clearly an indictment of any kind of sexual chauvinism. The Darkover novels test various attitudes about the importance of technology, and more important, they study the very nature of human intimacy. This latter "experiment," having been initiated more than 25 years ago, is as unique as it is vitally important.

By postulating a Terran Empire the main features of which are advanced technology and bureaucracy, and a Darkover that seems technologically backward and is fiercely individualistic, Bradley sets up a conflict to which there is no "correct" resolution. As Terrans ourselves, we see the good of many of the Empire's technological marvels. But the Darkovans are human, too, and evoke our sympathy, especially when we learn that their lack of technical "progress" is deliberate, for in the barely remembered past their psionically based technology very nearly annihilated their world. Bradley does not take sides; she allows her readers almost complete freedom to decide which of the technologies, or which combination of the two, is the more humanly practical solution.

Bradley's "Experiment" with human intimacy relies on an extrapolated psychology of paranormal human beings. In 1964, *The Bloody Sun* drew readers into a world where sexual intimacy is clearly secondary to the nearly total union felt by telepaths working in close rapport. *The Heritage of Hastur* illustrates the psychical and physical effects of repression, and shows how Regis Hastur comes into his "heritage" only when he accepts his androgynous nature. *The Forbidden Tower* explores the "nakedness" of one telepath to another and affirms the interdependence of mental and physical intimacy. While the intimacies share by Bradley's characters are fictional, they are nonetheless correlatives both of real relationships between persons and of the physical integration of female and male qualities within a self.

The Mists of Avalon, a work that set publishing records in the U. K. as well as the U. S. A., extends Bradley's explorations of polarities into anthropology, religion, and metaphysics. The long Arthurian fantasy-novel is a prodigious achievement in itself; its treatment of societal/natural, Christian/Pagan, and material/magical dichotomies has been reflected in Bradley's recent Darkover novels, contemporary fantasies, and retellings of "history." *City of Sorcery* is more a spiritual than a spatial quest, *Night's Daughter* fleshes out in prose narrative the sources of Mozart's *Magic Flute,* and (forthcoming) *The Firebrand* tells of the fall of Troy from the perspectives of the women principals.

Bradley's writing openly with increasing sureness of the human psyche and the human being rendered whole prompted Theodore Sturgeon to call the former SF fan"one of the Big ones" currently writing science fiction. That she has extended her range from science fiction and gothic fantasies to mainstream novels, solidly researched historicals, and other booksellers' market-types suggests that Sturgeon's phrase applies no longer only to the science-fiction writer Marion Zimmer Bradley continues to be, for she has transcended categories.

—Rosemarie Arbur

BRANDON, Frank. See **BULMER, Kenneth.**

BRETNOR, Reginald. Also writes as Grendel Briarton. American. Born in Vladivostok, Russia, 30 July 1911; emigrated to the United States in 1920. Attended college in California and New Mexico. Married 1) Helen Harding in 1949 (died, 1967); 2) Rosalie Leveille in 1969. Writer for the Office of War Information and the State Department Office of International Information and Cultural Affairs, 1943-47. Since 1947, free-lance writer. Agent: John Farquharson Ltd., 250 West 52nd Stree, New York, New York 10107; or, John Farquharson Ltd., 162-168 Regent Street, London W1R 5TB, England. Address: Box 1481, Medford, Oregon 97501, U. S. A.

SCIENCE-FICTION PUBLICATIONS

Short Stories

Through Space and Time with Ferdinand Feghoot (as Grendel Briarton). Berkeley, California, Paradox Press, 1962; augmented edition as *The Compleat Feghoot*, and *The (Even) More Compleat Feghoot*, Baltimore, Mirage Press, 1975, 1980.
The Schimmelhorn File. New York, Ace, 1979.

OTHER PUBLICATIONS

Novel

A Killing in Swords. New York, Pocket Books, 1978.

Other

Decisive Warfare: A Study in Military Theory. Harrisburg, Pennsylvania, Stackpole, 1969.

Editor, *Modern Science Fiction: Its Meaning and Its Future*. New York, Coward McCann, 1953; revised edition, Chicago, Advent, 1979.
Editor, *Science Fiction, Today and Tomorrow*. New York, Harper, 1974.
Editor, *The Craft of Science Fiction: A Symposium on Writing Science Fiction and Science Fantasy*. New York, Harper, 1976.
Editor, *The Future at War*: 1. *Thor's Hammer*, 2. *The Spear of Mars*, 3. *Orion's Sword*. New York, Ace, 3 vols., 1979-80.

Translator, *Moncrief's Cats*, by François-Augustin Paradis de Moncrif. London, Golden Cockerel Press, 1961; Cranbury, New Jersey, A. S. Barnes, 1962.

* * *

Reginald Bretnor's career as a science-fiction writer is minor. Of his three works of fiction, only two are SF, the third, *A Killing in Swords,* being a *hommage* to the mysteries of Anthony Boucher. *The Schimmelhorn File* collects Bretnor's series about an eccentric Pennsylvania Dutch inventor of the future. These stories show Bretnor's talents for fast-paced comedy, but are otherwise forgettable. The stories about Ferdinand Feghoot include Bretnor's most influential fictions, a series of short anecdotes that conclude with an intricate pun. This form has proven popular with fans and editors, and has been copied by such authors as John Brunner and Damon Knight.

Bretnor's important work is as an editor. He has proven his skill as an anthologist with *The Future at War*, but his editorial talents are for criticism rather than fiction. His *Modern Science*

Fiction: Its Meaning and Its Future was the first attempt by a writer within the field to treat SF as a movement of social history, rather than an *ars nova* unique unto itself. Including major essays by Asimov, de Camp, and others, *Modern Science Fiction* is *the* primary document for understanding the climate of opinion that produced the SF of the 1950's. Its two successors, *Science Fiction, Today and Tomorrow* and *The Craft of Science Fiction*, are no less important to an understanding of the science fiction of the 1970's. Together, the trilogy is a pinnacle of analytical thought that will be studied long after Bretnor's own fiction is forgotten.

—Martin Morse Wooster

BRETT, Leo. See **FANTHORPE, R. Lionel.**

BREUER, Miles J(ohn). American. Born in Chicago, Illinois, in 1888. Educated in public schools in Crete, Nebraska; University of Texas, Austin; Rush Medical College, Chicago, M. D. Served in the Medical Corps during World War I: Lieutenant. Married; two daughters and one son. Practiced medicine, specializing in diagnosis and internal medicine, in Lincoln, Nebraska. *Died in 1947.*

SCIENCE-FICTION PUBLICATIONS

Novels

The Girl from Mars, with Jack Williamson. New York, Stellar, 1929.
The Birth of a New Republic, with Jack Williamson. New Orleans, P. D. A. Press, 1981.

Uncollected Short Stories

"The Stone Cat," in *Amazing* (New York), September 1927.
"The Riot at Sanderac," in *Amazing* (New York), December 1927.
"The Puzzle Duel," in *Amazing Stories Quarterly* (New York), Winter 1928.
"Buried Treasure," in *Amazing* (New York), April 1929.
"The Book of Worlds," in *Amazing* (New York), July 1929.
"Rays and Men," in *Amazing Stories Quarterly* (New York), Summer 1929.
"The Fitzgerald Contraction," in *Science Wonder Stories* (New York), January 1930.
"The Driving Power," in *Amazing* (New York), July 1930.
"The Time Valve," in *Wonder Stories* (New York), July 1930.
"Paradise and Iron," in *Amazing Stories Quarterly* (New York), Summer 1930.
"Inferiority Complex," in *Amazing* (New York), September 1930.
"A Problem in Communication," in *Astounding* (New York), September 1930.
"On Board the Martian Liner," in *Amazing* (New York), March 1931.
"The Time Flight," in *Amazing* (New York), June 1931.
"The Demons of Rhadi-Mu," in *Amazing Stories Quarterly* (New York), Fall 1931.
"The Einstein See-Saw," in *Astounding* (New York), April 1932.
"Mechanocracy," in *Amazing* (New York), April 1932.
"The Perfect Planet," in *Amazing* (New York), May 1932.
"The Finger of the Past," in *Amazing* (New York), November 1932.
"The Strength of the Weak," in *Amazing* (New York), December 1933.
"Millions for Defense," in *Amazing* (New York), March 1935.
"The Chemistry Murder Case," in *Amazing* (New York), October 1935.
"Mr. Dimmitt Seeks Redress," in *Amazing* (New York), August 1936.
"The Company or the Weather," in *Amazing* (New York), June 1937.
"Mr. Bowen's Wife Reduces," in *Amazing* (New York), February 1938.
"The Raid from Mars," in *Amazing* (New York), March 1939.
"The Disappearing Papers," in *Future* (New York), November 1939.
"The Oversight," in *Comet* (Springfield, Massachusetts), December 1940.
"Child of Neptune," with Clare Winger Harris, in *Tales of Wonder* (Kingswood, Surrey), Spring 1941.
"Lady of the Atoms," in *Tales of Wonder* (Kingswood, Surrey), Autumn 1941.
"Breath of Utopia," in *Tales of Wonder* (Kingswood, Surrey), Spring 1942.
"The Sheriff of Thorium Gulch," in *Amazing* (New York), August 1942.
"Mars Colonizes," in *The Garden of Fear and Other Stories,* edited by William L. Crawford. Los Angeles, Crawford, 1945.
"A Baby on Neptune," with Clare Winger Harris, in *Away from the Here and Now,* edited by Harris. Philadelphia, Dorrance, 1947.
"The Man with the Strange Head," in *The Big Book of Science Fiction,* edited by Groff Conklin. New York, Crown, 1950.
"The Gostak and the Doshes," in *Science Fiction Adventures in Dimension,* edited by Groff Conklin. New York, Vanguard Press, 1953; as *Adventures in Dimension,* London, Grayson, 1955.
"The Hungry Guinea-Pig," in *Science Fiction Adventures in Mutation,* edited by Groff Conklin. New York, Vanguard Press, 1955.
"The Captured Cross-Section," in *Fantasia Mathematica,* edited by Clifton Fadiman. New York, Simon and Schuster, 1958.
"The Appendix and the Spectacles," in *The Mathematical Magpie,* edited by Clifton Fadiman. New York, Simon and Schuster, 1962.
"Man Without an Appetite," in *Great Science Fiction about Doctors,* edited by Groff Conklin and Noah D. Fabricant. New York, Macmillan, 1963.

*   *   *

Miles J. Breuer wrote some of the most intriguing tales that appeared in the early volumes of *Amazing Stories.* Like David H. Keller, he gave much of his attention to psychological themes and was more interested in the possible effects of machines on human kind than in mechanical marvels or life on other worlds. His stories often pointed a moral, yet were never mere parables; his characters were genuinely human rather than superhuman, and he wrote with a conviction that was rare in those days. He was also something of a poet.

Though he had a weakness for plots involving relativity and the fourth dimension, as in "The Captured Cross-Section" and "The Book of Worlds," he produced some novel variations on other familiar themes, such as "The Hungry Guinea-Pig," depicting the drastic results of an experiment in growth stimulation. "Buried Treasure" was remarkable for presenting a code diagram enabling readers to decipher a cryptogram which figured in the story; later he adapted the same idea to "The Chemistry Murder Case. " But his most striking contribution was "The Gostak and the Doshes," which satirised extreme nationalism and in its treatment of semantics was several years in advance of Korzybski. "Rays and Men" graphically portrayed the reactions of a man of 1930 to the strictly logical, emotionless world of 2180. "Paradise and Iron" drew a realistic picture of two future cities, in one of which art and beauty flourished at the expense of the other, where the workers were menaced by thinking machines. *The Birth of a New Republic* recounted the events which followed the colonisation of the Moon in the 24th century, when the miners and other settlers fought for their independence against the combined forces of Earth's powerful corporations. This was produced in collaboration with Jack Williamson, who did most of the actual writing under the strict guidance of Breuer, from whom he learned much about the techniques of storytelling.

Breuer also collaborated with Clare Winger Harris, the first woman writer to be featured in *Amazing,* in "A Baby on Neptune. " In "The Fitzgerald Contraction" and its sequel, "The Time Valve," he departed from his usual economical construction to concoct a disordered mixture of science and adventure. The first story was based on the premise that survivors of the lost continent of Mu had repaired to the Moon. In the sequel, the author took up the tale to present a gloomy picture of the human race reverting to savagery after an atomic war—200,000 years hence. It was hardly Breuer at his best.

He continued to write almost exlusively for *Amazing* over more than a decade, his contributions becoming less frequent—and, generally, less impressive—during the years of its decline under its venerable editor, T. O'Conor Sloane. He appeared only twice in the revitalised magazine before he withdrew from the scene in 1942, leaving little trace of his work beyond the confines of the outdated pulps.

—Walter Gillings

BRIARTON, Grendel. See BRETNOR, Reginald.

BRIN, David. American. Born in Glendale, California, 6 October 1950. Educated at California Institute of Technology, Pasadena, B. S. in astronomy 1973; University of California, San Diego, M. S. in applied physics 1978, Ph. D in space science 1981. Technical staff member, Hughes Research Laboratory, Newport Beach, California, 1973-75, and Carlsbad, California, 1975-77; taught at San Diego State University, 1982-83, and San Diego community colleges, 1983-84. Secretary, Science Fiction Writers of America. Recipient: Nebula Award, 1984; Hugo Award, 1984; *Locus* award, 1984. Agent: Richard Curtis, 164 East 64th Street, New York, New York 10021. Address: 5081 Baxter Street, San Diego, California 92117, U. S. A.

SCIENCE-FICTION PUBLICATIONS

Novels (series: Uplift)

Sundiver (Uplift). New York, Bantam, 1980.
Startide Rising (Uplift). New York, Bantam, 1983.
The Practice Effect. New York, Bantam, 1984.
The Postman. New York, Bantam, 1985.

Uncollected Short Stories

"Just a Hint," in *Analog* (New York), 27 April 1980.
"The Tides of Kithrup," in *Analog* (New York), 25 May 1981.
"The Loom of Thessaly," in *Isaac Asimov's Science Fiction Magazine* (New York), 21 November 1981.
"Coexistence," in *Isaac Asimov's Science Fiction Magazine* (New York), May 1982.
"Tank Farm Dynamo," in *Analog* (New York), November 1983.
"The Crystal Spheres, " in *Analog* (New York), January 1984.
"Cyclops," in *Isaac Asimov's Science Fiction Magazine* (New York), March 1984.
"The Warm Space,"in *Far Frontiers,* edited by Jerry Pournelle, Jim Baen, and John F. Carr. New York, Baen, 1985.

*

David Brin comments:

I've been told my writing is very different in my novels than in my short stories. And both differ a great deal from my midlength (or novella) works. Generally, the latter are my favorite. One has time to develop characters and detailed settings, and yet is forced to get to the point. SF is almost the last refuge of the novella form, bless it.

My own novellas deal very much in that commodity known as Myth. The novels on the other hand are real SF and I stretch out to try to make use of the scientific thrills this century keeps dropping in our laps. It is fun.

My short work is hard to typefy . . . from boy-engineer tales to attempts at epiphanies, I suppose. It's a lovely language, English, and a wonderfully exciting time to be alive.

*   *   *

David Brin was not included in the first edition of *Twentieth-Century Science-Fiction Writers.* Today his name would be on anyone's list of best practising SF writers. Since 1980 he has published short stories, three novels (*Sundiver, Startide Rising,* and *The Practice Effect*), and two more titles are due before the end of 1985 (*The Postman* and *The Uplift War*).

Startide Rising is the novel that swept the 1984 Hugo and Nebula awards. It is to date the centerpiece of the Uplift series, which includes the other two and, presumably *The Uplift War.*

Brin writes in what may be termed the Verne tradition, which emphasizes the quest/adventure potentials of scientific technology. As that tradition has taken root in American SF, it has produced writers like Gernsback, John W. Campbell, Asimov, Clarke, Pohl, and Niven, who have explored the space opera as a vehicle for speculative extrapolation. The dominant interests of this tradition have been space flight exploration, encounter with alien beings, and "inner space" or the psychology of space travel. A related topic, PSI, is one that fascinated Campbell, touches Clarke, obsesses Pohl, interests Niven and expresses itself forcefully in Brin.

Inventors of future histories are to some extent, at least, engaged in mythmaking; and their literary mythology is judged successful to the extent that it elicits secondary belief. Another pleasure of such mythopoesis lies in discovering the tracks of other mythologies in and out of SF, connecting the history both with the fabled past and the imagined future. Brin's debts to his predecessors in the Verne tradition are expressed thoughtfully to engage the imagination and sometimes playfully to tease the reader's memory. While never intrusive, the technique places the author firmly within a SF tradition and favorably invites comparison of Brin's mythos with that of Heinlein, Clarke, and Niven.

Brin's mythology of the Progenitors emerges in fragmented installments, as if grudgingly, from the background in the three novels published to date. But the mythos is only the sketch of what is to come: even an outline must be considered provisional, under correction of those chapters yet to be produced. The story of the Progenitors is told to humans after Contact (always capitalized) is made with aliens, several hundred years into the future from our time. This places the focus of the narrative at the level of galactic and species interaction, the traditional forum of space opera.

The universe disclosed to humans is dominated by five different species, styled Patron Lines of the five Galaxies. These claim descent from the Progenitors, who established galactic law. Each of the Patron lines regards itself as divinely chosen to impose its version of the law on everyone else. Humans find themselves in a cosmology ruled by less than philanthropic zealots who are forever warring against one another while they form shifting, entangled alliances to maintain balance within the system. Perhaps the chief stabilizing influence is the Galactic Library Institute, which is supposed to be the independent repository of aeons-old knowledge of the inhabited galaxies, the histories of their Patron lines, their largely inherited technology, and the galactic law passed on from the Progenitors.

The essential discovery of *Sundiver* is that the Library is not autonomous. It can be manipulated by its custodians, the Pila, a former client species of the Soro, one of the Patron Lines. With that information, the council of humans and their uplifted client species, apes and dolphins, decide not to rely solely on the Library for technological advancement but rather to develop human initiatives in all areas of change independent of the Library, while taking advantage of its resources. This decision further alienates the Patrons, especially the Soro, from a humankind already considered renegade. Such a status borders on galactic heresy because when the human race was discovered by the Patrons of the five galaxies at Contact, it had no tradition of having been uplifted or even guided by a Patron species. Humans therefore represented to the Patrons an anomalous species suspect as much for its self-developed technology (however primitive when compared with Library species) as for its abandoned condition. In other words, humanity did not seem to fit anywhere into the mythos of the Progenitors and their descendants.

The plot of *Sundiver* depends on humankind's orphaned condition. Probes sent into the photosphere of the sun seemed to reveal the presence of life forms. Using essentially human advances on Library technology, several exploratory voyages into the sun's outer layers are undertaken to prove the existence of such life forms and to establish contact with them. The preferred hypothesis is that if "sophont" forms exist, they may lead humanity to its lost Patrons or, indeed, may even be those mythical absconders. Although solarians are found to be intelligent and concerned enough with the crew of *Sundiver* to rescue the ship from destruction, the solarians are uninterested in any extensive communication. However, important lessons are learned about the Galactic Library and the potential danger

of becoming too dependent on its presumed cornucopia of ideas. Moreover, humans begin to suspect, and later verify, that access to the Library can be controlled and even manipulated by its Pila custodians.

The hard-won discoveries of *Sundiver* alert the Terragens Council to the threat to human independence implied in exclusive reliance on the Intergalactic Library and from those patron species who regulate access to its files.

This is the context for *Startide Rising,* a rousing space opera adventure which cleverly braids together several plot lines. The main argument narrates the plight of *Streaker,* a dolphin-commanded space craft from earth, which discovered an ancient, abandoned fleet of unidentified space ships in an area called the "Shallow Cluster." *Streaker*'s resident cosmologist, Tom Orley, a genetically engineered super-human, retrieves an ancient cadaver from one of the ships and intends to return to earth with the prize. When *Streaker*'s transmissions are intercepted by the Patrons, they send fleets to besiege *Streaker,* which takes refuge in an ocean of Kithrup, a planet believed uninhabited. A second plot argument concerns the testing of the dolphin crew in the crucible of siege by the Patron fleets, the first such command by the mutated client species of humanity. The one stroke of luck on the side of *Streaker* and its crew lies in the rivalry among the Patron lines which provokes a holy war in the space around Kithrup for the privilege of capturing *Streaker,* torturing its crew, and taking its prize. The Patrons assume that the discovered fleet must have been that of the Progenitors and the cadaver, therefore, a relic. Tradition had it that the Progenitors, who mysteriously disappeared millions of years before, had made the transition to a higher life form.

While the Patrons slaughter one another, the crew of *Streaker* works to repair damage and to devise a solution to their problem. Two schools of thought emerge: one is for surrender to the winner of the Patron battle and for turning over the prize and all information gathered at the "Shallow Cluster." The second, led by the indomitable Tom Orley, is to escape amid the confusion of battle. These options and the attitudes that underlie them are congruent with the competing schools of human thinking about aliens in *Sundiver* also. For Brin, the preferred resolution is in a philosophy of self-reliance espoused subsequently by Orley and *Streaker*'s dolphin captain Creideiki rather than the naive and despairing pacificism of Takkata-Jim, the Vice-Captain and a stenos neo-fin. Takkata-Jim's trust in the reasonableness of the Patrons is entirely misplaced, as the reader is privileged to know. Moreover, Jim's reasoning is further undermined by a constitutional weakness produced by Ignacio Metz's faulty genetic experimentation that tainted all the stenos neo-fins aboard *Streaker.* Perhaps if it had not been for the unusual stress produced by siege, the genetic flaw would not have expressed itself in mutiny and, on the part of some, devolutionary behavior.

Kithrup itself and its inhabitants play decisive roles in the resolution of the main arguments. As well, they focus attention on the code of uplift in the galactic past, especially on its abuse by Patrons who look upon clients as nothing more than indentured servants or worse. Even at this late stage in galactic history, some of the more barbarous patrons hope to gain custody of humankind and its client species in order to teach them lessons in obedience and humility.

The Practice Effect stars Dennis Nuel, a near-future scientist who is transported to a far-future world by the unexplainable powers of the Zievatron and marooned there when he is captured by troops in the employ of the usurper, Baron Kremer. The novel is a less ambitious space opera that follows in the footsteps of some early Heinlein, Leinster, Anderson,

Silverberg and especially de Camp. Brin introduces us to an anamolous world such as only SF could hope to find. Nuel is confronted by a pseudo-medieval culture, dependent on the practice effect for its industry and commerce. The "practice effect" is one of Nuel's chief clues to the physical laws that govern Tatir. The effect is a reversal of entropy in which use and intention shape and perfect all made things. The premise is that the peculiar physical laws of Tatir have operated to influence the development of a feudal culture dependent upon impressed slaves who practice into perfection everything from clothes to buildings. In the world of Tatir, used anything is definitely preferable to new. Indeed, the new is so undesirable that there is very little of it.

Into this a-technological world steps a modern man enough like de Camp's Martin Padway of *Lest Darkness Fall* to be his twin. The rest of the tale is familiar and easily imagined. The evil Baron has retained a fair-haired princess as a hostage and has designs upon her virtue. Nuel rescues her through an incredible coup de hang glider and thereafter, with the help of the practice effect, reinvents the wheel and the airplane at approximately the same time! The conclusion of *The Practice Effect* is full of revelations, not the least of which is that Tatir is not an alternate world after all but rather a remotely distant earth future. Nuel chooses to remain in Tatir: after all, when else could a scientist/mechanic expect to know as much compared with everyone else and have an adoring princess as an audience? Besides, someone must remain ahead and protect the past from the *Blecker,* an enemy race that "plies the ziev space" and was responsible for the collapse of the Tatir civilization in the past.

In the hands of David Brin, space opera continues its legitimate appeal to SF authors and readers. Like Niven, Brin blends hard science speculation with SF mythopoesis. As a real space engineer scientist, Brin is able to bring a sense of imagined presence to problems and solutions of space travel. A rather high level of such speculative problem-solving combined with a rousing scientific mystery plot are the chief interests of *Sundiver*. In addition, Brin has a genuine gift for animating his uplifted species, especially the human client species: apes and dolphins. Occasionally the symbolism of a derelict fleet or the whale dream in *Startide Rising* leaves a lasting impression on the imagination. Brin's fascinating linkage of PSI with elemental forces that control the universe (strong, weak, electromagnetic) in *Startide* beg further development in later works. We'll see.

However, Brin pays the price that seems almost inevitable for the writer of space opera, which none to date has altogether avoided. Brin's uplifted characters and even some aliens convey a greater sense of authentic identity than his humans. The interspecies and intergalactic scope of the Uplift saga makes for effective mythmaking but beggars humanity despite all its uniqueness. Human interaction especially gets reduced to rather simple, programmatic issues and attitudes. Whether these limitations are inherent in the form or only in the tradition remains to be proved. Brin certainly has given readers smashing examples of space opera, with *Startide* rivaling the best the type has to offer.

—Donald L. Lawler

BRODERICK, Damien. Australian. Born in Melbourne, Victoria, 22 April 1944. Educated at Monash University, Clayton,

Victoria, B. A. Science fiction reviewer, Melbourne *Age.* Recipient: Literature Board of Australia fellowship (twice); Ditmar award, 1981, 1985. Agent: Virginia Kidd, Box 278, Milford, Pennsylvania 18337, U. S. A. Address: 10 Marks Street, Brunswick, Victoria 3056, Australia.

SCIENCE-FICTION PUBLICATIONS

Novels (series: Faustus Pentacle)

Sorcerer's World. New York, New American Library, 1970; revised edition, as *The Black Grail* (Faustus), New York, Avon, 1985.
The Dreaming Dragons (Faustus). Melbourne, Norstrilia Press, 1980; New York, Pocket Books, and London, Penguin, 1981.
The Judas Mandala (Faustus). New York, Pocket Books, 1982.
Valencies, with Rory Barnes. Brisbane, University of Queensland Press, 1983.
Transmitters (Faustus). Melbourne, Ebony, 1984.

Short Stories

A Man Returned. Sydney, Horwitz, 1965.
The Solipsism Samba. Brisbane, University of Queensland Press, 1985.

OTHER PUBLICATIONS

Other

Editor, *The Zeitgeist Machine: A New Anthology of Science Fiction.* London, Angus and Robertson, 1977.
Editor, *Strange Attractors.* Sydney, Hale and Iremonger, 1985.

*

Critical Study: interview with Russell Blackford, in *Science Fiction: A Review of Speculative Literature 12* (Perth, Western Australia), 1982.

Damien Broderick comments:
  Call me Pelagius of Hippo.
  Are we humans sweety-pies, our future endlessly hopeful? (The theologian Pelagius thought so, and was declared heretical for his pains.) Or are we mad beasts, all the world destined for nuclear burning followed by freezing, at our own stupid hands? (A prospect which would not have astonished Augustine of Hippo, his great rival.)
  Science fiction, I have decided (bending Flaubert), is a cracked test tube we whistle tunes across, moved to pity and laughter by the stars, and by all the poor human souls beneath them.
  During the last decade or so science fiction has become one of the darlings of formalist criticism because it is—or is meant to be—innately uncomfortable, disruptive, hair-raising, hackles-raising, alienating, oddball.
  The Russian Viktor Shklovsky told us 60 years ago that the primary function of art is *ostranenie:* estrangement, the neck-wrenching which shows us the familiar in a fresh and challenging aspect.
  Well, surely science fiction is the ideal candidate? There are few bed-sitters, adulterous stockbrokers, karate-trained sirens or crooked cops on the take. With Sf, it's all ghastly clangour and shock, just what Shklovsky ordered. Looming aliens

without eyes, flapples to travel in, doors that answer back, machines with hearts of gold.

The reality, as every Sf enthusiast knows with remorse, is otherwise.

The salutary jolt of the strange soon loses its force. Like bored rats which seek out a mild adversive electric tingle, Sf readers return contentedly to the paperback shelves for a buzz of what we might term *cosy ostranenie*.

In my misery I often wonder if science fiction and fantasy are, after all, simply *different in kind* to the sort of writing exemplified by Henry James and James Joyce and Joyce Cary.

Alarming. It does help account for the dreary fact that much classic, bona fide Sf is (by the standards one rightly expects of any middle-brow novel, any *New Yorker* short story) simply illiterate trash. I won't have it, though.

A decade ago, Brian Aldiss made prophetic utterance on this score, speaking of "the area of life where art and science meet nature": "One becomes more and more preoccupied with the idea that art is all," he observed. "Science fiction is an ideal medium for such a preoccupation . . . for the specifics of fiction versus the generalities of science. This beautiful tender place has been so betrayed by the practitioners of pulp science fiction (who use it for thick-arm adventure and jackboot philosphy) that those who prefer wit to power-fantasy generally move elsewhere. "

Sadly, the triumph of Luke Skywalker and the Force, and all their pitiful paperback progeny, has done nothing in the interim but strengthen the thick arm of the artist's foe. One is indeed tempted to move elsewhere—almost anywhere else

"But," Aldiss warned, "those reckless or fastidious writers who throw our science fiction's old banal contents—from last generation's clichés of faster-than-light travel and telepathy to this generation's over-population and mechanized eroticism—have to take care of form as well, for form-and-content is always a unity. "

Yes. The usages, the tropes, of Sf—vulgar and absurd as most of them are—remain at the core of its artistic vocabulary. SF's idiosyncratic images and their weddings in the murky depths of each writer's heart comprise a grammar devised to speak in a way uniquely valid to this century.

My own writing? *Transmitters,* avowedly a *non* -SF novel "about" SF fans, can be read as the centrepiece of a larger structure holding four novels as its vertices. Think of a tetrahedron. At the points place WORLD, WRITER, READER, WORK. Each is connected to the others. Imagine four major aethetic theories: mimetic, expressive, conative, "objective. " (This model derives from M. H. Abrams. Then there's Kiernan Egan's mode of child development: mythic, romantic, philosophic, ironic. It fits, too. Gosh.) See them work reflexively on one another. The classic construction of science, the romantic construction of the artist, the rhetorical construction of the social order, the deconstruction of the text.

My novel sequence might agreeably be mounted on that pyramid in the order just given: *The Dreaming Dragons, The Judas Mandala, The Black Grail* (a revision of *Sorcerer's World*), *Transmitters*. Between these styles of subject matter and their appropriate voices, plays, codes, will be the fifth book of the sequence, now in progress.

This sounds stuffy. No. I send my words dancing in light, hear them shout and snort in this newest of tongues: yes, in a medium where Gully Foyle's burning synesthesia fetches us shivers of truth no mere mixed metaphor could lay hands on. It's not Doc Smith, folks, I admit it, but we do what we can. Mmm, I could use a doughnut.

*   *   *

More than any of his contemporaries, Damien Broderick has provided the intellectual cutting edge in Australian science fiction, producing work which has sometimes made that of his international peers seem unadventurous and routine. Perhaps this is most obvious when his numinous and gutsy novella "The Magi" is compared with other stories in Alan Ryan's anthology of sf stories on religious themes, *Perpetual Light*. These stories are by a who's who of contemporary sf writers, but many seem easily rehearsed pieces, trivialising the issues upon which they touch. Not so Broderick's portrayal of a Catholic priest shocked and grieved by remembered images which crystallise the disparities between the truths of dogma and the logical extremes which dogma requires.

"The Magi" in many ways typifies the fierce mind of this writer. First, though an unbeliever, Broderick remains supersaturated with the Catholic faith and continues to stare hard upon the claims of religious doctrine in general. He has shown an ability to depict the mind of the believer with a kind of provisional identification that transcends normal concepts of irony, however much the logically extreme outcomes may produce in the reader what Broderick has called "genuine ontolgical shock. " Only on rare occasions has his treatment of religious feeling lapsed into a crude form of ironic impersonation, as with the Bible-bashing general of his best-known novel, *The Dreaming Dragons*.

Secondly, and related to this point, "The Magi" is typical of Broderick's wider interest in disturbed and untrustworthy states of mind. The priest-protagonist is morally repelled by the fact of abortion, and the story concentrates upon the experiencing of such repugnance: this is depicted with no scorn and a degree of sympathy. Yet, at obvious levels of the story's structure, it shows the protagonist's package of dogmatic beliefs to be inadequate to our experience, or even possibly to his own. Other work by Broderick has been misunderstood because of his ability to produce detailed, even loving, presentations of the perceptions and feelings of characters whose views are not in any simple way endorsed; part of the problem is the unsophisticated way in which even sophisticated science fiction is often read, and to which Broderick refuses to pander.

Thirdly, Broderick hoards his store of images and themes carefully, returning to his material, and treating earlier work as itself a subject for examinaion and development. "The Magi" is a rewrite of a much shorter story, "There Was a Star", which may be found in Broderick's early collection *A Man Returned* (while "The Magi" is planned as the central story of a new collection tentatively called *The Solipsism Samba*). The original story is a sensitive and literate celebration of the incarnation of Christ (in a collection notable for its profoundly varying attitudes towards religious feelings). By contrast, "The Magi" is a far more elaborate work in which, once again, Catholic doctrine turns out to be unequivocally true in the world of the story—but in this case the doctrine is saved in the story by revelations which are most conspicuous for their inapplicability to our own experience, while even within the world of the story the ultimate revelation of dogmatic truth sits unsettlingly with the paradoxes encountered by the protagonist. Broderick here turns a cold eye upon the assumptions and comforts implicit in his own earlier material. This attitude is also shown in his recent deepening and extension of an early science-fantasy novel, *Sorcerer's World,* through the means of a much more sophisticated and self-reflexive version: *The Black Grail*. Interestingly, Broderick has even scrutinised the science-fiction ambience itself in *Transmitters,* an ambitious mainstream novel largely involving the misadventures of science-fiction fans.

Throughout his career, Broderick has experienced with form

and ideas. He has described "The Magi" as proceeding from an almost technical impulse to create identification with emotions which are based upon profound metaphysical errors. The result is a story which preys upon the logic of its own plot and sets up disturbing feelings of ethical and ontological contradiction in the reader. This is a step beyond the half-playful ideational structures of *The Dreaming Dragons* and *The Judas Mandala*. *Mandala*, in particular, is dominated by a complex of dualitites and transitions. The novel depicts a far-future world ruled with spiritless paternalism by seemingly omnipotent cyborg lords. There is no way to rebel against their awesome technological mastery, but some free humans have developed an ability to live part of their existence in "synchronic" time—at right-angles to the normal direction of experience. This is merely the first stage of a human, and specifically organic, ability to control time, providing a weapon against the otherwise invincible cyborgs. Drawing upon structuralist theory, Yeat-sian iconography, and the concept of the Bodhissatva who attains enlightenment but returns to the sufferings of a fallen and unenlightened world, Broderick creates a triumphant example of metaphysical science fiction, partly vitiated only by its substantial failure to weave emotionally compelling sub-stance into the intricately constructed narrative and setting.

Since *Mandala*, Broderick has moved on to more emotion-ally affecting work, including "The Magi," *Transmitters*, and an sf novel co-written with Rory Barnes, *Valencies*. Despite occasional uncertainties of tone, Broderick has shown a welcome ability to treat science-fiction themes with both wit and poignancy. His development into one of the field's major exponents can now be predicted with confidence; it is more difficult to predict the direction in which this ambitious and technically gifted writer will next set out.

—Russell Blackford

BRONSON, L. T. See **TUBB, E. C.**

BROWN, Fredric (William). American. Born in Cincinnati, Ohio, 29 October 1906. Educated at University of Cincinnati night school; Hanover College, Indiana, 1 year. Married 1) Helen Ruth Brown in 1929 (divorced, 1947), two sons; 2) Elizabeth Charlier in 1948. Office worker, 1924-36; pro-ofreader, Milwaukee *Journal*, from 1936; freelance writer after 1947. Recipient: Mystery Writers of America Edgar Allan Poe Award, 1948. *Died 11 March 1972.*

SCIENCE-FICTION PUBLICATIONS

Novels

What Mad Universe. New York, Dutton, 1949; London, Boardman, 1951.
The Lights in the Sky Are Stars. New York, Dutton, 1953; as *Project Jupiter*, London, Boardman, 1954.
Martians, Go Home. New York, Dutton, 1955.
Rogue in Space. New York, Dutton, 1957.
The Mind Thing. New York, Bantam, 1961.

Short Stories

Space on My Hands. Chicago, Shasta, 1951; London, Corgi, 1953.
Angels and Spaceships. New York, Dutton, 1954; London, Gollancz, 1955; as *Star Shine*, New York, Bantam, 1956.
Honeymoon in Hell. New York, Bantam, 1958.
Nightmares and Geezenstacks: 47 Stories. New York, Bantam, 1961; London, Corgi, 1962.
Daymares. New York, Lancer, 1968.
Paradox Lost and Twelve Other Great Science Fiction Stories. New York, Random House, 1973; London, Hale, 1975.
The Best of Fredric Brown, edited by Robert Bloch. New York, Ballantine, 1977.
The Best Short Stories of Fredric Brown. London, New English Library, 1982.

OTHER PUBLICATIONS

Novels

The Fabulous Clipjoint. New York, Dutton, 1947; London, Boardman, 1949.
The Dead Ringer. New York, Dutton, 1948; London, Board-man, 1950.
Murder Can Be Fun. New York, Dutton, 1948; London, Boardman, 1951; as *A Plot for Murder*, New York, Bantam, 1949.
The Bloody Moonlight. New York, Dutton, 1949; as *Murder in Moonlight*, London, Boardman, 1950.
The Screaming Mimi. New York, Dutton, 1949; London, Boardman, 1950.
Compliments of a Fiend. New York, Dutton, 1950; London, Boardman, 1951.
Here Comes a Candle. New York, Dutton, 1950; London, Boardman, 1951.
Night of the Jabberwock. New York, Dutton, and London, Boardman, 1951.
The Case of the Dancing Sandwiches. New York, Dell, 1951.
Death Has Many Doors. New York, Dutton, 1951; London, Boardman, 1952.
The Far Cry. New York, Dutton, 1951; London, Boardman, 1952.
The Deep End. New York, Dutton, 1952; London, Boardman, 1953.
We All Killed Grandma. New York, Dutton, 1952; London, Boardman, 1953.
Madball. New York, Dell, 1953; London, Muller, 1962.
His Name Was Death. New York, Dutton, 1954; London, Boardman, 1955.
The Wench is Dead. New York, Dutton, 1955.
The Lenient Beast. New York, Dutton, 1956; London, Board-man, 1957.
One for the Road. New York, Dutton, 1958; London, Board-man, 1959.
The Office. New York, Dutton, 1958.
Knock Three-One-Two. New York, Dutton, and London, Boardman, 1959.
The Late Lamented. New York, Dutton, and London, Board-man, 1959.
The Murderers. New York, Dutton, 1961; London, Boardman, 1962.
The Five-Day Nightmare. New York, Dutton 1962; London, Boardman, 1963.
Mrs. Murphy's Underpants. New York, Dutton, 1963; London, Boardman, 1965.

Short Stories

Mostly Murder: Eighteen Stories. New York, Dutton, 1953;
London, Boardman, 1954.
The Shaggy Dog and Other Murders. New York, Dutton, 1963;
London, Boardman, 1964.
Carnival of Crime: The Best Mystery Stories of Fredric Brown,
edited by Francis M. Nevins, Jr., and Martin H. Greenberg.
Carbondale, Southern Illinois University Press, 1985.

Plays

Television Plays: for *Alfred Hitchcock* series.

Other

"Why I Selected Nothing Sirius," in *My Best Science Fiction
Story,* edited by Leo Margulies and O. J. Friend. New York,
Merlin Press, 1949.
Introduction to *Human?,* edited by Judith Merril. New York,
Lion, 1954.
Mitkey Astromouse (for children). New York, Quist, 1971.

Editor, with Mack Reynolds, *Science-Fiction Carnival.*
Chicago, Shasta, 1953.

*

Bibliography: *A Key to Fredric Brown's Wonderland: A Study
and an Annotated Bibliographical Checklist* by Newton Baird,
Georgetown, California, Talisman, 1981.

*   *   *

It is said that early telegraphers could be identified by their
"fist"; that is, by their peculiarities in operating the transmitting key. Some science-fiction writers also have a "fist" by which
they can be known. Fredric Brown is one of them. Much of
Brown's skill with words probably can be traced to his early
career as newspaperman. He wrote tightly, his language was
direct and simple, sentences were often telegraphic, and his
stories had a "grabber"—usually at the end. Such skills as these
can be learned, of course, and their proper application makes
for readable prose. If Brown had had only these qualities in his
writing, he would have left a pretty sizable mark in the field of
science fiction.

But Brown became a truly memorable figure in his field
because of several other traits. Although he may at times have
appeared cynical, most of his stories revealed an idealist, a firm
believer in Man's god-like potential. *The Lights in the Sky Are
Stars* devotes its entire span to the repeated assertions that man
can *become,* that there may or may not be a God, but that there
assuredly will be one if and when man develops to his fullest.
This conviction is echoed in his "Letter to a Phoenix," where
Brown points to the cyclical rise and fall of civilizations, with
each ascent greater than the preceding plunge. After every
collapse of a culture, Man the Phoenix rises from the ashes with
greater vigor and determination. It is Brown's burning faith in
human powers that lifts his works above the ordinary—party
because his heroes are ordinary. The central figure in *The
Lights in the Sky Are Stars* is a rocket mechanic. Ordinary, too,
is the hero of *What Mad Universe,* where our planet is Earth,
but not quite. Brown's choice of protagonist for "Arena," a
short story with Armageddon implcations, is an ordinary
space-ship pilot.

It is said that much writing of fiction is really autobiographical. Such could be so in the case of Brown's work, for he
appeared to regard himself as an ordinary individual. He had
very little college education—one year—noted he was "only"
an office worker, and described himself as "mostly self-
educated. " Yet he was highly successful as a writer of mysteries
and science fiction, and in many instances seems to have
sublimated himself in leading characters determined to make
something of themselves.

For the most part Brown's style was crisply journalistic. But
he drew from his newspaper experience an even more valuable
characteristic: each of his yarns had a "hook" or "gimmick" to
give the work zest and interest. The casual reader of "The Star
Mouse" is conned into seeing this story as a sort of variation on
a cartoon character. Thought of a mouse representing Earth's
civilized people is ridiculous, of course, and his comic manner
of speech is mildly diverting. But what sets the reader on his ear
is that gimmick, which gives the story tremendous significane
and shows us a reporter who simply *had* to save the best for last.
The same kind of withholding is evident in "Arena," where
Earth's representative seemed doomed in his combat with the
Roller from another universe. Reeling and bleeding from many
wounds, our hero appears done for, and we struggle along with
him toward the end to discover that gimmick on which the
entire outcome hangs. An almost invisible hook propels *The
Lights in the Sky Are Stars.* Not until the final scene do we find
it, because our hero-narrator tells us only then that he has lied
about a fundamental point. That lie provides the force which
Brown requires, but it virtually destroys his hero and creates a
deposit of disappointment for the reader as well.

Anyone looking for humour, however, will seldom feel
cheated by Brown's yarns. Sometimes the humour is almost
juvenile, as with "The Star Mouse," where not only the dialog
but the denouement offer many chuckles. "Arena" displays a
grim humor, not alone in the resolution of our hero's conflict,
but also in Brown's use of power differentials—speculation
that mightier forces exist of which man can only dream. More
pointed is the humor of "The Weapon" in pitting human frailty
against atomic force, with a final question which Brown leaves
unanswered. And the close reader finds in *The Lights in the Sky
Are Stars* an unspoken pun, when disclosure of the hero's
failing literally leaves him without a leg to stand on.

Listing of a handful of qualities scarcely defines an author.
Brown obviously enjoyed his craft; his hundreds of short
stories and several novels appeared on shelves and in anthologies with deceptive ease. And in this flood floated the
fragments of a most engaging personality. Like many authors
he had only a smattering of real knowledge about most of the
topics he dealt with: "Etaoin Shrdlu" bearing the spoor of the
linotype, "The Waveries" betraying his failure to link accurately thunder and lightning, "The Star Mouse" blithely
ignoring biological realities. But, despite whatever limitations
and shortcomings one may detect, Fredric Brown was a
buoyant asset to the field of science fiction. The reading diet of
all of us became poorer with his death.

—Robert H. Wilcox

———————

BROWN, Rosel George. American. Born in New Orleans,
Louisiana, 15 March 1926. Educated at Tulane University,
New Orleans, B. A. 1946; University of Minnesota, Minneapolis, M.A. 1950. Married W. Burlie Brown in 1946; one
son and one daughter. Worked as welfare visitor in Louisiana,
for three years. *Died in November 1967.*

SCIENCE-FICTION PUBLICATIONS

Novels

Earthblood, with Keith Laumer. New York, Doubleday, 1966;
London, Coronet, 1979.
Sibyl Sue Blue. New York, Doubleday, 1966; as *Galactic Sibyl
Sue Blue,* New York, Berkeley, 1968.
The Waters of Centaurus. New York, Doubleday, 1970.

Short Stories

A Handful of Time. New York, Ballantine, 1963.

Uncollected Short Stories

"And a Tooth," in *Fantastic* (New York), August 1962.
"Fruiting Body," in *Fantasy and Science Fiction* (New York),
August 1962.
"The Artist," in *Amazing* (New York), May 1964.

*   *   *

Many science-fiction writers have a sense of humor that
enables them to populate a universe of their own creation with
a myriad of creatures both homely and fantastic. Rosel George
Brown had this and another rarer ability, the ability to portray
men and women who are believable, sympathetic, and winning.

Her first published story, "From an Unseen Censor,"
describes a search for a missing inheritance from the narrator's
uncle Isadore. Finding clues planted by his uncle, the young
man finds the fabulously rare perfume trees that are his uncle's
bequest. Humor derives from Brown's use of Poe's "The
Raven" as a model for burlesque, with Isadore filling the place
of the "lost Lenore." Another young man, a space traveler,
finds love on a Utopian planet where time seems to stand still
("Of All Possible Worlds"). Distraught when the whole race
throws itself lemming-like from a cliff into the sea, the man has
to adjust to a world that has no more meaning for him.

Brown's male characters are not the only ones with which she
deals so carefully. In *Earthblood,* written with Keith Laumer,
there are kindly extra-terrestrials like Iron Robert, a huge
stone-like creature who has been taught the meaning of love
and compassion by the earth-bred Roan. And there are well-
drawn women characters, earthly and alien, who are more than
the stock sex-objects that fill lesser fiction. An example is
Stellaire, who is only half human genetically, but fully human
in her love and understanding of Roan. By her death Roan is
finally freed to find the earth from which the seed that
endangered him came so long before. Another woman ready to
love and work is the mail-order bride of "Virgin Ground." A
tough, self-sufficient girl, she faces a surly, unwilling groom.
Cruelly left to die in a Martian sandstorm, she saves herself and
then takes the farm from the boorish man who deserted her. An
ending twist finds the heroine five years later faced with an
eager groom sent out to share in the farm she has worked alone.
Other women likely to be familiar to a reader are the harassed
mother of "Carpool," who finds that hungry earth children are
likely to eat a gentle alien child who rides to the "Play Place"
with them, and the garden club member who wants to make a
prize-winnng entry in "Flower Arrangement."

Rosel Brown's most memorable character, however, is Sibyl
Sue Blue, the tough earth policewoman, whose job in the novel
named for her is finding the Centaurian drug pushers who are
killing earth teenagers. Since widowed by the death of her
explorer husband, Sue has been plagued by guilt that her

daughter has "had to raise herself." Of course, the girl Missy
has done no such thing, because the love and concern of Sue for
her daughter is apparent whether she is worrying about Missy's
being injured in retribution for Sibyl's work, or thinking that
things would have been different if her husband had lived. *The
Waters of Centaurus* shows Sibyl's further resourcefulness, not
only at handling threats to interstellar peace, but at handling
crises between generations, as Missy falls in love with a young
alien.

Only a dozen of Rosel Brown's stories have been separately
published, in *A Handful of Time;* but the collection and her
novels show her remarkable growth as a writer in her use of
character. Her early death was one of the most regrettable in
the history of modern science fiction.

—Walter E. Meyers

BROWNING, Craig. See **PHILLIPS, Rog.**

BROXON, Mildred Downey. Also writes as Sigfridur Skaldaspillir. American. Born in Atlanta, Georgia, 7 June 1944; grew up
in Brazil. Educated at Seattle University, B. A. in psychology
1965, B. S. in nursing 1970. Married 1) G. D. Torgerson in 1965
(divorced, 1969); 2) William D. Broxon in 1969 (died, 1981).
Teacher's aide, Rainier State School, Buckley, Washington,
1966-67; psychiatric nurse, Harborview Medical Center,
Seattle, 1970-72. Vice-President, Science Fiction Writers of
America, 1975-77. Agent: Jarvis Braff Ltd., 260 Willard
Avenue, Staten Island, New York 10314. Address: 7337 22nd
Avenue N. W., Seattle, Washington 98117, U. S. A.

SCIENCE-FICTION PUBLICATIONS

Novels

Eric Brighteyes No. 2: A Witch's Welcome (as Sigfridur
Skaldaspillir). New York, Zebra, 1979.
The Demon of Scattery, with Poul Anderson. New York, Ace,
1979.
Too Long a Sacrifice. New York, Dell, 1981; London, Futura,
1983.

Uncollected Short Stories

"Asclepius Has Paws," in *Clarion III*, edited by Robin Scott
Wilson. New York, New American Library, 1973.
"The Night Is Cold, The Stars Are Far Away," in *Universe 5*,
edited by Terry Carr. New York, Random House, 1974.
"The Stones Have Names," in *Fellowship of the Stars*, edited by
Terry Carr. New York, Simon and Schuster, 1974.
"Grow in Wisdom," in *Vertex* (Los Angeles), October 1974.
"Dear Universal Gourmet," in *Vertex* (Los Angeles), February
1975.
"Glass Beads," in *Vertex* (Los Angeles), April 1975.
"To the Waters and the Wild," in *Vertex* (Los Angeles), June
1975.
"The FMG," in *Medical Dimensions*, December 1975.
"The Antrim Hills," in *Aurora: Beyond Equality*, edited by

Susan Janice Anderson and Vonda N. McIntyre. New York, Fawcett, 1976.

"The Book of Padraig," in *Stellar 3*, edited by Judy-Lynn del Rey. New York, Ballantine, 1977.

"Where Is Next Door?," in *Chrysalis 2*, edited by Roy Torgeson. New York, Zebra, 1978.

"In Time, Everything," in *Chrysalis 3*, edited by Roy Torgeson. New York, Zebra, 1978.

"Source Material," in *100 Great Science Fiction Short-Short Stories*, edited by Isaac Asimov, Martin H. Greenberg, and Joseph D. Olander. New York, Doubleday, and London, Robson, 1978.

"Singularity," in *Black Holes* , edited by Jerry Pournelle. New York, Fawcett, 1979.

"Don't Count Chickens," in *Seattle Post-Intelligencer Sunday Magazine*, 20 May 1979.

"Strength," with Poul Anderson, in *The Magic May Return*, edited by Larry Niven. New York, Ace, 1981.

"Sea Changeling," in *Isaac Asimov's Science Fiction Magazine* (New York), August 1981.

"Walk the Ice," in *The Best Science Fiction of the Year 11*, edited by Terry Carr. New York, Pocket Books, 1982.

"Night of the Fifth Sun," in *Isaac Asimov's Space of Her Own*, edited by Shawna McCarthy. New York, Davis, 1983.

*

Mildred Downey Broxon comments:

As an American raised abroad and then re-introduced to the United States, I have always had a certain sense of alienness; I have tried to exploit this in my writing.

My late father was a professor of history (Irish and Latin American) and some of his interest in the subject seems to have rubbed off on me: I use historical themes to a great extent in my writing. More of my published work has been fantasy than science fiction, although such distinctions are arbitrary at best.

I strive to instill in the reader a "sense of wonder" which, after all, is what makes us sentient—and keeps us alive.

*   *   *

Mildred Downey Broxon's first published short story was not the kind that attracts a lot of attention, but "Asclepius Has Paws," the story of an alien psychologist temporarily stranded on Earth, demonstrated a concern with human emotion and a sensitivity for the complexity of interpersonal relationships that was much more promising than the story itself. In "The Night Is Cold, The Stars Are Far Away", a non-human on an unspecified planet keeps a lonely watch on the sky, convinced that it is his world that moves and not the stars and other planets, for which he is ostracized by friends and family alike, until he is finally able to convey the importance of his perceived mystery to a younger generation.

"The Stones Have Names" is a bittersweet story, in which an incompetent but kindly political appointee governs the conquered alien world of a race that is fiercely independent. He and a local leader develop the beginning of a genuine friendship, but the momentum of both races is such that tragedy destroys both their lives. Broxon's interest in the history of the British Isles is obvious in "The Book of Padraig," which concerns a long-lived alien who spends a human lifetime as a cloistered monk in order to study our race from the inside.

"In Time, Everything" is an interesting but not entirely successful piece about a woman who, during the act of committing suicide, relives not only her own lifetime but that of all her ancestors back to the first lungful of air taken in by a proto-amphibian. A dying child figures prominently in "Where Is Next Door?" The despondent mother begins to realize that there is something bizarre about her new neighbors—they don't seem to be quite human, and their stories of "home" seem like no place on Earth. The predictable and rather trite ending mars but does not fatally damage one of Broxon's best efforts.

"Singularity" is almost certainly Broxon's finest science-fiction story to date, a short novel that deals with a pair of scientists who are trying to learn as much as possible about a non-human species on a planet that will shortly be destroyed by the near passage of a black hole. There is no possibility of reprieve or evacuation, and first one and then the other becomes so personally involved with the fate of the world and its inhabitants that it alters the world of the human observers forever. Nearly as good is "Walk the Ice," a marvelously understated story of a shipwrecked alien who finds temporary shelter with a family of starving eskimos, and the effect that his brief interaction has on the sole surviving member of that family.

Broxon has also written a number of interesting fantasies, particularly including her excellent novel, *Too Long a Sacrifice* and, in collaboration with Poul Anderson, *The Demon of Scattery*. Fantasy short stories of interest are "The Antrim Hills" and "Night of the Fifth Sun."

—Don D'Ammassa

BRUNNER, John (Kilian Houston). Also writes as Keith Woodcott. British. Born in Preston Crowmarsh, Oxfordshire, 24 September 1934. Educated at Cheltenham College, Gloucestershire, 1948-51. Served in the Royal Air Force, 1953-55. Married Marjorie Rosamond Sauer in 1958. Technical abstractor, Industrial Diamond Information Bureau, London, 1956; Editor, Spring Books, London, 1956-58. Writer-in-Residence, University of Kansas, Lawrence, 1972. Founder, Martin Luther King Memorial Prize, 1968; Past Chairman, British Science Fiction Association. Recipient: British Fantasy Award, 1965; Hugo Award, 1969; British Science Fiction Association Award, 1970, 1971; Prix Apollo (France), 1973; Cometa d'Argento (Italy), 1976, 1978; Europa Award, 1980. Agent: Leslie Flood, Carnell Literary Agency, Rowneybury Bungalow, Sawbridgeworth, near Old Harlow, Essex CM20 2EX, England; or, William Reiss, Paul R. Reynolds Inc., 12 East 41st Street, New York, New York 10017, U. S. A.

SCIENCE-FICTION PUBLICATIONS

Novels (series: Galactic Empire; Zarathustra Refugee Planet)

Threshold of Eternity. New York, Ace, 1959.
The World Swappers. New York, Ace, 1959.
Echo in the Skull. New York, Ace, 1959; revised edition as *Give Warning to the World*, New York, DAW, 1974; London, Dobson, 1981.
The Hundredth Millennium. New York, Ace, 1959; revised edition, as *Catch a Falling Star*, 1968.
The Atlantic Abomination. New York, Ace, 1960.
Sanctuary in the Sky. New York, Ace, 1960.
The Skynappers. New York, Ace, 1960.
Slavers of Space. New York, Ace, 1960; revised edition, as *Into*

the Slave Nebula, New York, Lancer, 1968; London, Dawson, 1980.

Meeting at Infinity. New York, Ace, 1961.

Secret Agent of Terra (Planet). New York, Ace, 1962; revised edition, as *The Avengers of Carrig*, New York, Dell, 1969.

The Super Barbarians. New York, Ace, 1962.

Times Without Number. New York, Ace, 1962; revised edition, 1969; Morley, Yorkshire, Elmfield Press, 1974.

The Space-Time Juggler (Empire), *The Astronauts Must Not Land*. New York, Ace, 1963; *The Astronauts Must Not Land* revised as *More Things in Heaven*, New York, Dell, 1973; London, Hamlyn, 1983.

Castaways' World (Planet), *The Rites of Ohe*. New York, Ace, 1963; *Castaways' World* revised as *Polymath*, New York, DAW, 1974.

The Dreaming Earth. New York, Pyramid, 1963; London, Sidgwick and Jackson, 1972.

Listen! The Stars! New York, Ace, 1963; revised edition, as *The Stardroppers*, New York, DAW, 1972; London, Hamlyn, 1982.

Endless Shadow. New York, Ace, 1964.

To Conquer Chaos. New York, Ace, 1964.

The Whole Man. New York, Ballantine, 1964; as *Telepathist*, London, Faber, 1965.

The Altar on Asconel (Empire). New York, Ace, 1965.

The Day of the Star Cities. New York, Ace, 1965; revised edition, as *Age of Miracles*, Ace, and London, Sidgwick and Jackson, 1973.

Enigma from Tantalus, The Repairmen of Cyclops. New York, Ace, 1965.

The Long Result. London, Faber, 1965; New York, Ballantine, 1966.

The Squares of the City. New York, Ballantine, 1965; London, Penguin, 1969.

A Planet of Your Own. New York, Ace, 1966.

Born under Mars. New York, Ace, 1967.

The Productions of Time. New York, New American Library, 1967; London, Penguin, 1970.

Quicksand. New York, Doubleday, 1967; London, Sidgwick and Jackson, 1969.

Bedlam Planet. New York, Ace, 1968; London, Sidgwick and Jackson, 1973.

Stand on Zanzibar. New York, Doubleday, 1968; London, Macdonald, 1969.

Father of Lies. New York, Belmont, 1968.

Double, Double. New York, Ballantine, 1969; London, Sidgwick and Jackson, 1971.

The Jagged Orbit. New York, Ace, 1969; London, Sidgwick and Jackson, 1970.

Timescoop. New York, Dell, 1969; London, Sidgwick and Jackson, 1972.

The Evil That Men Do. New York, Belmont, 1969.

The Dramaturges of Yan. New York, Ace, 1971; London, New English Library, 1974.

The Wrong End of Time. New York, Doubleday, 1971; London, Eyre Methuen, 1975.

The Traveler in Black. New York, Ace, 1971; London, Severn House, 1979.

The Sheep Look Up. New York, Harper, 1972; London, Dent, 1974.

The Stone That Never Came Down. New York, Doubleday, 1973; London, New English Library, 1976.

Total Eclipse. New York, Doubleday, 1974; London, Weidenfeld and Nicolson, 1975.

Web of Everywhere. New York, Bantam, 1974; London, New English Library, 1977.

The Shockwave Rider. New York, Harper, and London, Dent, 1975.

Interstellar Empire. New York, DAW, 1976.

The Infinitive of Go. New York, Ballantine, 1980.

Players at the Game of People. New York, Ballantine, 1980.

The Crucible of Time. New York, Ballantine, 1983; London, Arrow, 1984.

The Tides of Time. New York, Ballantine, 1984.

Novels as Keith Woodcott

I Speak for Earth. New York, Ace, 1961.

The Ladder in the Sky. New York, Ace, 1962.

The Psionic Menace. New York, Ace, 1963.

The Martian Sphinx. New York, Ace, 1965.

Short Stories

No Future in It and Other Science Fiction Stories. London, Gollancz, 1962; New York, Doubleday, 1964.

Now Then. London. Mayflower-Dell, 1965; New York, Avon, 1968.

No Other Gods but Me. London, Compact, 1966.

Out of My Mind. New York, Ballantine, 1967; London, New English Library, 1968.

Not Before Time: Science Fiction and Fantasy. London, New English Library, 1968.

From This Day Forward. New York, Doubleday, 1972.

Entry to Elsewhen. New York, DAW, 1972.

Time-Jump. New York, Dell, 1973.

The Book of John Brunner. New York, DAW, 1976.

Foreign Constellations: The Fantastic Worlds of John Brunner. New York, Everest House, 1980.

OTHER PUBLICATIONS

Novels

The Brink. London, Gollancz, 1959.

The Crutch of Memory. London, Barrie and Rockliff, 1964.

Wear the Butchers' Medal. New York, Pocket Books, 1965.

Black Is the Color. New York, Pyramid, 1969.

A Plague on Both Your Causes. London, Hodder and Stoughton, 1969; as *Blacklash*, New York, Pyramid, 1969.

The Devil's Work. New York, Norton, 1970.

The Gaudy Shadows. London, Constable, 1970; New York, Beagle, 1971.

Good Men Do Nothing. London, Hodder and Stoughton, 1970; New York, Pyramid, 1971.

Honky in the Woodpile. London, Constable, 1971.

The Great Steamboat Race. New York, Ballantine, 1983.

Play

Screenplay: *The Terrornauts*, 1967.

Verse

Trip: A Cycle of Poems. London, Brunner Fact and Fiction, 1966; revised edition, Richmond, Surrey, Keepsake Press, 1971.

Life in an Explosive Forming Press. London, Poets' Trust, 1971.

A Hastily Thrown-Together Bit of Zork. South Petherton, Somerset, Square House, 1974.

While There's Hope. Richmond, Surrey, Keepsake Press, 1982.

Other

Horses at Home. London, Spring, 1958.
"The Genesis of *Stand on Zanzibar* and Digressions into the Remainder of its Pentateuch," in *Extrapolation* (Wooster, Ohio), May 1970.
"The Development of a Science Fiction Writer," in *Foundation 1* (London), March 1972.
"The Science Fiction Novel," in *The Craft of Science Fiction* , edited by Reginald Bretnor. New York, Harper, 1976.
"A Different Kick; or, How to Get High Without Going into Orbit," in *The Book of John Brunner*. New York, DAW, 1976.
"Science Fiction and the Larger Lunacy," in *Science Fiction at Large*, edited by Peter Nicholls. London, Gollancz, 1976; New York, Harper, 1977.
Tomorrow May Be Even Worse. Cambridge, Massachusetts, NESFA Press, 1978.
A New Settlement of Old Scores. Cambridge, Massachusetts, NESFA Press, 1983.

Editor, *The Best of Philip K. Dick*. New York, Ballantine, 1977.

Translator, *The Overlords of War*, by Gérard Klein, New York, Doubleday, 1973.

*

Critical Studies: *The Happening Worlds of John Brunner* (includes bibliography) edited by Joseph W. De Bolt, Port Washington, New York, Kennikat Press, 1975.

John Brunner comments:
For me, the essence both of science fiction and of the necessity for it can be summed up by quoting the opening sentence of L. P. Hartley's *The Go-Between:* "The past is a foreign country; they do things differently there. " Given that we are all being deported willy-nilly towards that foreign country, the future, where we shall ultimately die, I'd rather make the journey as a tourist with no matter how fallible a Baedeker, than be deported as a refugee. This is, I suppose, the chief reason why my SF has tended to become more and more concentrated on that portion of the future I may reasonably expect to survive into myself, and less and less concerned with the unbridled fantasy of space opera.
Concurrently, I'm told, it has also become more difficult. In a case like *Stand on Zanzibar,* this is hardly surprising—I generally tell prospective readers to remember that it should be read like a newspaper, not like a novel, for we are used to snippets about a dozen subjects on the front page, each continued elsewhere. But, much as a jazzman can keep on coming home to the blues during a playing career of half a century or more, I retain enormous respect for the conventional narrative forms and use them for the great majority of my fiction. Rules must be learned before one can judge when they may safely be broken, even (one might say especially) in our so-called "fiction of the future"—which of course, like all fiction, is actually about you and me and the here-and-now.
Let me therefore suppose that someone has chanced on this brief entry in this monumental work and, being unacquainted with SF but interested in exploring the subject, decides that a good place to start would be with those writers who have won the field's major awards. What would I commend of my own work by way of an introduction? Three books above all: *Quicksand* because of its totally contemporary setting and ambiguous SF element; *The Squares of the City* because as long ago as 1960 I was there discussing the depersonalisation we are

all now acquainted with in the computer age; and *The Whole Man* because it would give a new reader some insight into the proper function of SF's standard devices, such as—in this instance—telepathy, a metaphor for total communication. It has been well said that the great contribution of SF to the corpus of literature is "the future as metaphor. " I entirely agree, and though in the past I have had my doubts I do not currently feel that I shall ever exhaust the possibilities opened up to us by that discovery.
But in *Stand on Zanzibar, The Jagged Orbit, The Sheep Look Up,* and *The Shockwave Rider* I've done my best to put on the page everything I as an individual could garner and combine into a credible narrative, concerning that tomorrow we are doomed to endure. Every day necessarily alters it; SF, like all printed fiction, belongs to the past. . . . But even metaphors drawn from an obsolete future can be invaluable in preparing us for eventual reality, whatever form—out of an infinite number—it may actually take.

* * *

"She had put on a green tunic that matched her eyes, which came barely halfway down her thighs," reads part of a sentence from "The Man from the Big Dark," an early (1958) John Brunner space operette. The unintentionally fantastic image it suggests, not to mention the humorous unintended rhyme, illustrates a problem facing the reader who undertakes to evaluate the large and important body of John Brunner's SF. Brunner is clearly serious about SF, with respect to both thematic concerns and the craft of writing, but he indicated in 1974 that the "medium" was more important to him than the "matter. " Yet at times Brunner's work has a slapdash quality that challenges readability, as if the pressure to express the material generated by a prolific imagination has led him to take more care of his matter than of his medium.
An example of the problem is *Total Eclipse*, which Brunner himself has confessed was written too hurriedly although its premise was "one of the two genuinely original ideas I ever came up with. " In that fiction, a team of terrestrial astronauts is trying to figure out why the advanced technological civilization of Sigma Draconis III died out, leaving behind only remnants of curious artifacts that include a crater-sized telescope on their moon. As the image of the vast telescope suggests, the extinct alien culture is a mirror of the explorers' on Sol III. They have apparently been abandoned by the authorities on earth, although the purpose of the investigation is to gain knowledge that will assist human society in averting a similar extinction. The main character is Ian Macauley, a brilliant linguist who eventually determines that the local culture had based its economic system on genetic exchange, with the resultant shrunken gene pool leading to some sort of biological collapse. With the starship's failure to return, however, this useful ecological lesson will never reach earth, which may already have "eclipsed" in any case. The marooned team attempts to establish a human colony in lieu of return to earth, but their offspring succumb to a pulmonary fungus, while the adults gradually die of assorted diseases and deficiencies—not the least of which is lack of solidarity and hope.
The pessimism of *Total Eclipse* 's conclusion, however, seems contrived, as if Brunner felt forced to it by the acclaim enjoyed by the dystopian novels of the late 1960's and early 1970's. For most of the narrative, we see the team coping with interpersonal problems and advancing their investigation successfully—the plot does not really offer any evidence that the humans are like their extinct alien counterparts in promoting a destructive rationalism to the detriment of their humanity: their problems

seem to stem more from emotionalism. Technically, Brunner's switch from the omniscient viewpoint to a first-person narrative in the final chapter is an attempt to paper over this confusion in vision and thematic concern—the final effect is to create an awkward and unsatisfying ending as well as a text that has no apparent audience.

The problems of *Total Eclipse* underline a difficulty faced by Brunner and any other writer who uses a popular fiction medium to deal with a serious vision of the human universe. Constantly looking over their shoulders to audience expectations, such writers are tempted to betray their better judgments about "medium" (craft) and "matter." In the first phase of Brunner's career, when he was turning out a prodigious amount of what John Clute has characterized as "literate space opera," Brunner played, one after another, with stock items from the SF repertoire: the old galactic empire now decayed into feudal anarchy and technological stagnation (the *Interstellar Empire* series); the angelic alien intelligences from a "higher continuum" of spacetime—from which humankind has fallen (*More Things In Heaven*); the sudden appearance of the transfer stations of an alien teleportation system, which bring to a halt the progress of human culture until the hero works out how to piggyback on them for the purpose of galactic colonization (*Age of Miracles*); the ancient and fearsome alien monster that has lurked unseen in the ocean and emerges to terrorize humanity (*The Atlantic Abomination*); the worldlet-sized space vessel that will permit intergalactic colonization (*Sanctuary in the Sky*). Whatever the limitations of such material, however, and of the publishing system that generates it (which he has described with poignant humor), Brunner used it well. His narratives are generally suspensefully paced and presented in a mostly graceful style that builds the story through dialogue and description. His heroes, who are not loners but work with others to solve problems, represent a human norm able to meet crises and overcome obstacles through pluck and intelligence. Though Brunner may have tired of writing this sort of SF, there is no question but that he was better at it than many of his precursors.

The critical success that eluded Brunner through the 1950's and early 1960's finally came his way when he began to treat SF devices not as literal elements of "future history" but rather as metaphors for the human condition in the present. *The Whole Man*, evolved from a series of SF thrillers using the premise of telepathy, begins with a scene of civil turmoil being put down by a UN police action that utilizes telepathic intelligence officers as well as military force, and ends with its physically deformed hero, Gerald Howson, having found love and acceptance outside the telepathic community. The freak Howson's quest for his full humanity ends when he visits his hometown and encounters a group of students who, less obvious freaks as they are, accept Howson as normal. The spiritual restoration he finds is reflected at the novel's end, where the possibility of curing his physical deformity is left open. As Brunner has pointed out several times, telepathy is a metaphor for communication, and it is subject to the same disabling factors as more ordinary means. Another example is *The Squares of the City* in which the old chestnut of a plot based on a famous game from the annals of chess is used to portray the breakdown of a hierarchical social order in which the rich and powerful manipulate the lives of the pawns who inhabit urban society's less desirable "squares."

Stand on Zanzibar, still regarded as Brunner's *magnum opus*, is often discussed in terms of its presumably innovative montage technique, used to a lesser extent in the other dystopian novels: *The Jagged Orbit, The Sheep Look Up, The Stone That Never Came Down, The Shockwave Rider*. In fact, all these novels are well-paced, smartly plotted fictions, only the narrative surfaces of which are "experimental." They derive their effects from the dialectic suggested above: civilization is portrayed as a fragile ideal threatened by man-made ecological disaster, by organized violence, by information overload—and by that chiefest of the threats to human solidarity that stalk the pages of Brunner's fictions, racial apartheid and hatred. The potentially liberating technologies of control and communication are being manipulated by sinister and largely synonymous entities: government, organized crime, and great corporations. Although of the five only *The Sheep Look Up* has a clearly pessimistic ending, the set constitutes a grim vision of humanity's immediate future, far more unsettling, because its extrapolations are so much more plausible, than the fantasies of *Brave New World, 1984*, or the 1950's SF dystopias dubbed "comic infernos" by Kingsley Amis. Yet even at their most pessimistic, these novels portray as a noble ideal that person—whether physician, social scientist, or psychic sensitive—who has the compassion and the intelligence to struggle against our species' apparent mad rush to extinguish itself.

Nor are the dystopian fictions lacking a certain comic humor—albeit often macabre. Their themes, after all, are satirical, and Brunner exploits wordplay and other forms of verbal comedy in narrative as well as in dialogue, often to underline the corruption and unreliability of language and communication; his characters often find themselves in situations that are darkly farcical. This comic strain is often overlooked in discussions of his work, perhaps because it is more evident in his shorter fictions and in his light verse. But *Timescoop* is a hilarious comedy of manners that spoofs the paradoxes and other conventions of time-travel, even including an irreverent rewrite of famous discussion of the geometry of time travel in Wells's *Time Machine*.

Brunner has not been so prolific in the past ten years, but two recent novels show him to be as unpredictable and imaginative as ever. *The Crucible of Time* recounts, in seven linked novellas, the saga of an intelligent species faced with a number of cosmic accidents that threaten their very survival. Each of the novellas focuses on one explorer or scientist who makes a major contribution, often in spite of the malice and ignorance of his fellows, to the development of the species' technology and understanding of nature. Although the story is told from an inside point of view that never lets us clearly picture what these creatures would look like to us, that is more achievement than defect. The creatures are alien to us with their mandibles, their reproduction by budding, and their matriarchal societies, but they are fallible and fallen as well as capable of love, hard work, wit, sadness, and courage. And they survive as a species because they generate just enough of those rare individuals who ask questions, especially "why not?" As well as a *tour de force* of insight into the possibilities of exobiology and exo-social psychology, not to mention a technology based on organic structures, the fiction is a parable of hope in which Brunner counters the pessimism of his own dystopias and returns to the optimistic tenor of much of his pre-1969 fiction.

The Tides of Time is more obscure, but perhaps even more rewarding. It is less a narrative than a series of interlaced archaeological tapestries based on the dreams of two astronauts who, after being the first to survive flight-testing FTL spaceships, escape together from their debriefings. The FTL ships are being tested because reliable old "father sun" has become a variable star and raised earth's temperature to the extent that much of its landmass is under water. Unlike the people of Ballard's *The Drowned World,* Gene and Stacy do not plunge into primal unconsciousness and loss of ego; as Stacy goes through a pregnancy, they maintain self while they travel through the rich and varied layers of civilization on an abandoned Aegean island. Though Stacy dies giving birth to their child Terra, Gene brings back a much more valuable lesson than the practicality of FTL travel; the density and texture of human experience are rooted in earth, and we cannot survive without our "mother." This parable might seem technophobic, but it complements that of *The Crucible of Time* when we remember that the struggle there was not only to survive, but also to hang on to the ecology that gave birth to the species and its cultures.

Brunner is now in the sixth decade of his life, and his fourth as a SF writer. If his recent fictions are any indication of what lies ahead for his readers, he will continue to surprise and delight them, and to keep their eyes open to the possibilities of the human future, which in his imagination are clearly manifold, even infinite.

—John P. Brennan

BRYANT, Edward (Winslow, Jr.). American. Born in White Plains, New York, 27 August 1945. Educated at the University of Wyoming, Laramie (General Motors scholar; Ford Foundation fellow), B. A. in English 1967, M. A. 1968. Broadcaster, disk jockey, and news director, KOWB-Radio, Laramie, 1965-66; worked as rancher and in a stirrup buckle factory; columnist ("The Screen Game"), *Cthulhu Calls,* Powell, Wyoming, 1973-77. Free-lance writer and lecturer. Recipient: Nebula Award, 1978, 1979. Address: c/o Jelm Mountain Publications, 209 Park, Laramie, Wyoming 82070, U. S. A.

SCIENCE-FICTION PUBLICATIONS

Novels

Phoenix Without Ashes, with Harlan Ellison. New York, Fawcett, 1975; Manchester, Savoy, 1978.
Cinnabar. New York, Macmillan, 1976; London, Fontana, 1978.

Short Stories

Among the Dead and Other Events Leading Up to the Apocalypse. New York, Macmillan, 1973.
Particle Theory. New York, Pocket Books, 1980.
Wyoming Sun. Laramie, Wyoming, Jelm Mountain, 1980.

OTHER PUBLICATIONS

Plays

Radio Play: *Breakers,* 1979.

Television Play: *The Synar Calculation,* with Edward Hawkins, 1973.

Other

"Breaking Waves: The Latest Look of Science Fiction," in *Science Fiction: Education for Tomorrow,* edited by Jack Williamson. Philadelphia, Owlswick Press, 1980.

Editor, with Jo Ann Harper, *2076: The American Tricentennial.* New York, Pyramid, 1977.

*

Bibliography: *Edward Bryant Bibliography,* Los Angeles, Swigart, 1980.

Edward Bryant comments:

I find considerable contradictions at this time in my life and career (each, for the time, indistinguishable from the other). I love the glittering attractions of cities, but find the east and west coasts claustrophobic. I love the spaciousness and low population density of the mountain west, but don't wish the situation of a hermit. I love being a westerner, but have no nostalgic aspirations of living on a ranch again as I did when I was younger. The wide open spaces liberate, but do not trigger me to hunt or fish or ski. But I notice the metaphor of the mountain west creeping increasingly into my work.

People seem continually bent on telling me I don't truly write "real" SF, whatever that is, but then I continue to read and admire what I consider to be the best of other people's SF, and then go on to write more of the fiction I feel I'd like to encounter as an SF reader.

I seem to be a minority writer in SF, like Avram Davidson, Thomas Disch, and Carol Emshwiller (I don't pretend to place myself in their bracket—I simply admire the work of all three tremendously). All of us seem to communicate—at best—with perhaps 30 to 40 per cent of the great mass of SF readers. For me, that's a little frustrating—but not sufficiently that I plan a pragmatic campaign to include more telepathic dragons, mightily thewed barbarians, Empire blockade runners, or other crowd-pleasers in my fictions. I expect to continue swimming my own way.

Although the boredom quotient (a facet of Sturgeon's law) in SF is still rather high, I'm excited about where the best of the field seems to be heading in the 1980's. I think finally there are a decent number of literate writers of SF who have an eclectic grounding in the arts and humanities as well as in science and technology. They are articulate and genuinely inquisitive about the interrelationship between human beings and universe. They are blessed with minimal knee-jerk prejudices about science and technology. Many of them have been practicing and cogitating, perhaps consolidating their craft, during the past two decades. I may have my doubts about the future of the universe itself, but I'm sanguine about the prospects for science fiction.

*   *   *

Like one of his best-known and most important mentors, Harlan Ellison, Edward Bryant has thus far tended to write short fictions. In fact, his only novel in an adaptation of Ellison's original prize-winning television script for the doomed *Starlast* series, *Phoenix Without Ashes.* Again, like Ellison, Davidson, Disch, and Emshwiller (all of whom he admires), Bryant is essentially a fabulist, a writer of fantasy who uses science-fiction trappings in his work for their metaphorical effect rather than simply as "realistic" background. He is the very opposite of a "hard" science-fiction writer, someone like Larry Niven, say, who believes in a fiction of ideas and specific extrapolation. He is also a more adventurous stylist than most traditional hard science-fiction writers.

Bryant's vision can be extremely dark, as his first collection of mostly nightmarish fables, *Among the Dead,* demonstrates. A portrayal of a world sliding on good intentions and nothing else into the deepest of pits, this collection is full of sad and terrifying glimpses of human ennui and failure of nerve. Entropy is the reigning god, and metaphors of decay, death, and Sisyphusian effort appear everywhere. Many of the stories are set in a bleak near-present, but the far future of "Love Song of Herself" and indeterminate time/space of "Dune's Edge" are no more helpful. Nevertheless, and this is one of the marvelous paradoxes of good writing, the formal energy and black wit of the best of these stories often overcome their thematic sense of utter depression.

Phoenix Without Ashes is a collaboration in the best sense of the word. Taking Ellison's screenplay as his basic story, Bryant has written a novel which effectively works out some intriguing variations on the conventional SF "closed universe" theme, previously handled by writers as disparate as Heinlein and Aldiss. Characterization is minimal (it was to be a TV series, after all), but the story moves with a certain grandeur to its ending as new beginning, and it's an entertaining book, though not the rich and variegated entertainment *Cinnabar* proves to be.

Bryant calls *Cinnabar* a "mosaic novel," a richly evocative description for this sequence of interlocking stories.It takes another grand old SF metaphor, the city *at* the end of time and *as* the end of human endeavour, and, in a tour de force of colourful, glittering *fin de siècle* stylization, explodes the conventional possibilities of the metaphor in a grand fireworks display. The way the whole context alters its individual parts can be seen in the changes "Gray Matters"—also in *Among the Dead*—undergoes when it's set into the glamorous mosaic of *Cinnabar*. Although it remains a tale of sexual and emotional ennui, its focus shifts from the victims to the strong and positive personality of Tourmaline Hayes, who figures energetically throughout *Cinnabar*.

Cinnabar may be a "doomed city of hope," as Bryant says; but as he also says, "all things considered, I know *I* would rather be in Cinnabar"; and that desire informs the dazzling and energetic writing which propels these narratives. Anything is possible in this city at the centre and terminus of time because its brightest and most complex inhabitants joyfully recognise the profoundly human potentiality of the argument that "biologically speaking there are no imperatives," though moral choice remains a centrally human act. Only a few of Cinnabar's near-immortal citizens accept the challenge to seek and grow implicit in the city's multiplex presence. Most suffer from ennui, emotional and spiritual entropy, but Bryant wisely keeps them well in the background while focussing on Tourmaline, the compleat tourist, Obregon, the always curious non-specialist, Leah Sand, the melancholy media artist, Jade Blue, the computer-created cat-mother, and Harry Blake, the 1963 university student who falls down a temporal rabbit hole and learns to view human potentiality anew. And then there's Terminex, the central computer slowly going crazy trying to run the city and hold all its different time zones in place. The style, grace, and wit apparent throughout *Cinnabar* mark it as a brilliant example of speculative fantasy at its best. Bryant's more recent stories, gathered in *Particle Theory,* continue to use and subvert SF conventions for symbolic purposes. As such disparate stories as the title story, "The Thermals of August," "Precession," and "Stone" demonstrate, Bryant discovers in the metaphoric possibilities of SF hardware a means by which to explore the byways of love and passion. That two of the stories in this collection won Nebula Awards testifies to his peers' awareness that sophisticated and stylish writing, when conjoined to a powerful humane vision, makes for an SF that is truly art.

—Douglas Barbour

BRYANT, Peter. See **GEORGE, Peter.**

BRYNING, Frank (Francis Bertram Bryning). Also writes as F. Cornish. Australian. Born in Fairfield, Victoria, 2 August 1907. Educated at Fairfield State School, 1912-20; University High School, Melbourne, 1921-24. Married Henrietta Edna Ewell in 1935; one daughter. Clerk, Harrisons Ramsay Importers, Melbourne, 1925-26; worked for news agency and library, 1926-28, and as an electrical appliance salesman, 1928-31, Melbourne; free-lance journalist and editor, Melbourne and Sydney, 1932-49: Editor *Flax Newsletter*, Sydney, 1942-49; Editor, *Architecture, Building, Engineering* and *Queensland Building Yearbook*, both Brisbane, 1950-57; Editor, *Hardware Trader, Brisbane Building Yearbook, Queensland Fruit and Vegetable News*, and *Australian Electrical World*, all Brisbane, 1957-73. Agent: Leslie Flood, Carnell Literary Agency, Rowneybury Bungalow, Sawbrigeworth, near Old Harlow, Essex CM20 2EX, England.

SCIENCE-FICTION PUBLICATIONS

Uncollected Short Stories (series: Joan Buckley; Vivienne Gale)

"Operation in Free Flight" (Gale), in *Australian Monthly* (Melbourne), March 1952; as "Operation in Free Orbit," in *Fantastic Universe* (Chicago), February 1955.
"Action-Reaction" (Gale), in *Australian Monthly* (Melbourne), June 1952.
"Space Doctor's Orders" (Gale), in *Australian Monthly* (Melbourne), January 1953.
"On the Average," in *Forerunner*, April 1953.
"Jettison or Die!," in *Australian Monthly* (Melbourne), August 1953.
"The Gambler" (Buckley), in *Australian Monthly* (Melbourne), October 1954; as "Coming Generation," in Fantastic Universe (Chicago), July 1955.
"Pass the Oxygen," in *Future* (New York), October 1954.
"Daughter of Tomorrow" (Buckley), in *Australian Monthly* (Melbourne), February 1955.
"Poor Hungry People," in *Etherline*, August 1955.
"Infant Prodigy" (Buckley), in *Fantastic Universe* (Chicago), November 1955.
"Consultant Diagnostician" (Buckley), in *Fantastic Universe* (Chicago), December 1955.
"And a Hank of Hair" (Gale), in *Australian Journal* (Melbourne), May 1956.
"The Robot Carpenter," in *Australian Journal* (Melbourne), July 1956.
"Power of a Woman," in *Australian Journal* (Melbourne), January 1957.
"I Did, Too, See a Flying Saucer!," in *Amazing* (New York), August 1958.
"Place of the Throwing-Stick," in *Coast to Coast*. Sydney, Angus and Robertson, 1959.
"Escape Mechanism," in *Sunday Mail*, October 1967.
"For Men Must Work," in *The Pacific Book of Australian Science Fiction*, edited by John Baxter. Sydney, Angus and Robertson, 1968; London, Angus and Robertson, 1969.
"The Visitors," in *Vision of Tomorrow* (Newcastle upon Tyne), March 1970.
"Election," in *Vision of Tomorrow* (Newcastle upon Tyne), June 1970.
"Lost Explorer," in *Science Fiction Monthly* (London), August 1975.
"Beyond the Line of Duty," in *Void* (St. Kilda, Victoria), August 1976.

"The Homecoming of Haral," in *Void* (St. Kilda, Victoria), August 1977.
"Nemaluk and the Star-Stone," in *Envisaged Worlds*, edited by Paul Collins. St. Kilda, Victoria, Void, 1977.
"Mechman of the Dreaming," in *Other Worlds*, edited by Paul Collins. St. Kilda, Victoria, Void, 1978.
"Fusing and Refusing," in *Isaac Asimov's Science Fiction Magazine* (New York), January 1983.

Uncollected Short Stories as F. Cornish

"The Vase with the Character of a Flower Pot," in *Australasian* (Melbourne), September 1944.
"Bloodthinker," in *The World's News*, January 1945.
"Miracle in the Moluccas," in *Pocket Book Weekly*, January 1950.

OTHER PUBLICATIONS

Other

"What Has Science Fiction to Say?," in *Meanjin* (Melbourne), Winter 1954.
"Mouses Will Make Moons," in *Australian Journal* (Melbourne), April 1957.
"Australian Writers and Science Fiction," in *Overland* (Melbourne), August 1975.

*

Frank Bryning comments:
In science fiction my prejudice is in favour of "hard-core," or "science fiction." I hold that the essential problem or conflict in the lives of the characters in a science-fiction story will derive from their involvement in some event in the natural universe—some biological, psychological, sociological, techological, cosmological activity. Their experiences, however unusual or mystifying, will be explicable, ultimately, according to that accumulation of precise factual knowledge and verifiable experience and the logically reasoned theories and speculations based on it that we call "science."

This as distinct from "fantasy"—from fiction of the "super"-natural, from fairy tale, fable, legend, myth (religious or otherwise), magic, witchcraft, the occult, or ghoulies and ghosties and things that go bump in the night. In fantasy I have always found much profit and delight. I still do. I yield to no one in my capacity to find enjoyment there, or moral lesson. From fantasy I do not expect believable premises, strictly logical progression of cause and effect, or any real conviction, yet I consider those fantasies most satisfying which are internally logical after one suspends disbelief in their mystical premises.

I would like to think that the sum total of all my writing—fiction and non-fiction, plus my work as staff writer and editor—would designate me as a realist rather than a surrealist. Almost all my work has been to present the "rational" viewpoint, I believe. My fiction is concerned mainly with the doings of typical everyday people in the everyday world (including, perhaps, the world of tomorrow in my science fiction) rather than with "exploring" so-called "alternative realities" or fantasising about "other planes of existence." I want to be on the side of enlightenment rather than obfuscation, of rationalism rather than mysticism. I hope readers, of my science fiction in particular, and my fellow writers, may agree that I am.

*   *   *

Having grown up on Wells, Verne, and Bellamy, Frank Bryning naturally turned to writing SF stories, and it was natural that he should become a writer who stresses the *science* in science fiction. Bryning is best known for his Aboriginal stories "Place of the Throwing-Stick" (his best story), "Nemaluk and the Star-Stone," and "Mechman of the Dreaming." Bryning regards the Australian Aborigines as "the most distinctively Australian phenomenon one might use," and these three stories reflect the theme of "the 'Aboriginal possessor of the land' versus the colonial invader." In "Place of the Throwing-Stick" the Aboriginal Munyarra attacks the most recent of the white man's importations—the rocket. The confrontation takes place at Australia's real-life Woomera Rocket Range, allowing Bryning to link the Stone Age past with the Space Age present through the name "Woomera" (Aboriginal for "spear-throwing stick").

Bryning's long-time membership in the British Interplanetary Society is reflected in his cycle of Commonwealth Satellite Space Station stories, embracing items written from the 1950's to the present. Eschewing the Americanization of SF, Bryning posits a near future in which the Commonwealth of Australia has established a network of space stations. The emphasis is upon character and realistic situations, with the ten stories being linked by the central character, Dr. Vivienne Gale. Plots are generated by the humdrum daily life in space, and many stories deal with space medicine and the problems of weightlessness.

There is nothing flashy or sensational about Bryning's stories. They are solidly and conventionally constructed, and their extrapolations are never allowed to outstrip the author's knowledge. As future histories, they are modest. But their strengths and merits lie in their quiet, dogged realism, their guarded optimism, and their compassion for the man with a day's work to complete.

—Van Ikin

BUDRYS, Algis (Algirdas Jonas Budrys). Also writes as Frank Mason. Lithuanian. Born in Konigsberg, Germany, 9 January 1931. Educated at the University of Miami, 1947-49; Columbia University, New York, 1950-51. Married Edna Frances Duna in 1954; four sons. Clerk, American Express, New York, 1950-51; editorial positions at Gnome Press, 1952-53, *Galaxy*, 1953, *Venture SF*, 1957, *Fantasy and Science Fiction*, 1957, *Ellery Queen's Mystery Magazine*, 1957, *Car Speed and Style, Custom Rodder*, and *Cars Magazine*, all 1958-59, Regency Books, 1961-63, Playboy Press, 1963-64, and Commander Publications, 1966; public relations positions, Theodore R. Sills Inc., Chicago, 1966-67, Geyer-Oswald Advertising, 1967-68, and Young and Ribicam, 1969-73; Operations Manager, Woodall Publications, 1973-74. Since 1974, President, Unifont Company, Evanston, Illinois. Science fiction reviewer and columnist, *Galaxy*, 1966-70, *Fantasy and Science Fiction*, 1975-85, *Locus*, 1977-79, Washington *Post*, 1978, and Chicago *Sun-Times*, 1979-85; Instructor, Columbia College, Chicago, 1977; visiting writer, Clarion Science Fiction Writing Workshop, 1977-85, and Evanston schools, 1978-85. Recipient: Mystery Writers of America award, 1966; Science Fiction Writers of America Hall of Fame award. Address: Unifont Company, 824 Seward Street, Evanston, Illinois 60202, U. S. A.

SCIENCE-FICTION PUBLICATIONS

Novels

False Night. New York, Lion, 1954; as *Some Will Not Die,*
Evanston, Illinois, Regency, 1961; London, Mayflower,
1963.
Man of Earth. New York, Ballantine, 1958.
Who? New York, Pyramid, 1958; London, Gollancz, 1962.
The Falling Torch. New York, Pyramid, 1959.
Rogue Moon. New York, Fawcett, 1960; London, Muller,
1962.
The Amsirs and the Iron Thorn. New York, Fawcett, 1967; as
The Iron Thorn, London, Gollancz, 1968.
Michaelmas. New York, Berkley, and London, Gollancz, 1977.

Short Stories

The Unexpected Dimension. New York, Ballantine, 1960;
London, Gollancz, 1962.
Budrys' Inferno. New York, Berkley, 1963; as *The Furious
Future,* London, Gollancz, 1964.
Blood and Burning. New York, Berkley, 1978; London, Gol-
lancz, 1979.

Uncollected Short Stories

"Cerberus," in *Fantasy and Science Fiction* (New York),
December 1967.
"Die Shadow," in *The Second If Reader of Science Fiction,*
edited by Frederik Pohl. New York, Doubleday, 1968.
"Now Hear the Word of the Lord," in *Best SF 1969*, edited by
Harry Harrison and Brian Aldiss. New York, Putnam, and
London, Sphere, 1970.
"Players at Null-G," with Theodore R. Cogswell and Ted
Thomas, in *Fantasy and Science Fiction* (New York), July
1975.
"The Silent Eyes of Time," in *The Best Science Fiction of the
Year 5,* edited by Terry Carr. New York, Ballantine, and
London, Gollancz, 1976.

OTHER PUBLICATIONS

Play

Radio Play: *Rogue Moon,* from his own novel, 1979 (TV
version, 1983).

Other

Truman and the Pendergasts (as Frank Mason). Evanston,
Illinois, Regency, 1963.
Bicycles: How They Work and How to Fix Them. Chicago,
Rand McNally, 1976.
Benchmarks: Galaxy Bookshelf. Carbondale Southern Illinois
University Press, 1985.

Editor, *Writers of the Future*. Los Angeles, Bridge, 1985.

*

Manuscript Collection: Spencer Research Library, University
of Kansas, Lawrence.

Algis Budrys comments:
  My work, when found, speaks for itself. I think a piece of

creativity is its own justification. However, if a rationale is
desired, then the theoretical underpinning of my SF is that
speculative fiction is drama made more relevant by social
extrapolation. That is, I proceed on the assumption that, by
certain fortuitous strokes of talent, some prose artists can
create conditional realities in which recognizably human
behavior occurs under illuminating circumstances which are
not yet known to have occurred in what we have agreed to call
reality. The proposition is that a few members of the readership
will be inspired to look about them anew and draw conclusions
of benefit to mankind's continuing endeavor to escape extinction. I seriously doubt that any critical analysis of my work,
however accurate, will have much relevance to my necessarily
minor role in that endeavor. I commend to his or her god
whatever hominid organism is eventually able to overcome the
darkness, and I rest my case.

*   *   *

Like Nabokov and Solzhenitsyn, Algis Budrys is ours by
courtesy of Communism. I have been told that his real name
means something like John Sentry, a pseudonym he has in fact
employed. A sentry he is, if the brave who watched the
stockade, the alien walls of the invader, may be called a sentry.
A warrior he is by any definition. He understands more of the
psychology of the man who fights—not the man who dies—
than any other writer I know. Every age and every genre
produce a few writers too good for them, authors who pour
oceans into their wine cups or summon Sigurd and Fafnir in
person to entertain the nursery. Budrys is one of these. He is, in
the best sense, too serious a writer for science fiction.

Who? is the book that made him famous, it is perhaps as fine
a study of dehumanization and alienation as science fiction will
ever produce. A brilliant American scientist is torn by a
laboratory explosion and repaired with what we would now
call "bionic" parts by the Soviets. He is returned to the US—
but the US cannot be sure of that. So much of him is gone that
what remains cannot be identified. All this is simple enough. It
is even—if you like—a retelling of L. Frank Baum's story of the
Tin Woodman, who when he had sliced his "meat" (humanity)
completely away could no longer recall his true name (which
was Nick Chopper). The difference lies in intent, and in the
treatments that result from it. Baum was manufacturing a
paradox to amuse children, one not really much different from
the rhyme about the Gingham Dog and the Calico Cat who ate
each other up. Budrys is intensely concerned with the effect of
technology—and particularly the technology of the Cold
War—on our humanity. He asks if the Soviets were really
doing the West a favour when they restored Martino, since he
cannot be identified and thus cannot be of use. *Can* they do the
West a good office, when all they do *must* be suspect? SF offers
few figures of the symbolic intensity of this faceless, maimed
scientist, the man who could prove ten thousand things, if only
he could prove who he is.

Budrys's writing falls into two distinct periods, the first
ranging from 1952 to the middle 1960's, the second from the
middle 1970's to the present. The best work of his earlier period
is surely *Rogue Moon*, which he wished to call *The Death
Machine*, a vastly better title. In *Rogue Moon* a "matter
transmitter" has been invented in a near future in which
rocketry is still primitive; and an unmanned probe has
managed to drop a transmitting and receiving station on the far
side of the moon. The first explorers to go through the
transmitter discover an alien construct millions of years old, a
thing compounded of building, machine, and hallucination. It
soon kills everyone who ventures inside. This alien construct is

perhaps the biggest and best red herring in all SF, because it is not really what *Rogue Moon* is about. It is about Hawks, the brilliant, compassionate, iron-souled scientist who has developed the "matter transmitter" and is determined to have the construct analyzed, and Barker, the death-obsessed Saturday afternoon hero he gets to do the exploring—through a score of deaths. Like *Who?* it is about the nature of identity. It is also about the nature of life, about what it is to live and have lived.

When a writer of Budrys's calibre is silent for so long as Budrys was silent, silenced not by the knouts and jails of totalitarian authority but by his own frustrations, his readers are entitled to expect him to be a different and even better writer if he chooses to write again. Budry's justification is *Michaelmas*, his best novel and the book that has brought him considerable recognition outside SF. If *Rogue Moon* was cinematic, *Michaelmas* is bibliomatic—a story that can be told well only in a book. Americans are apt to find a certain glamour in kings and queens, princes and princesses—an amiable weakness. We are sometimes even liable to find an attraction in tyrants of one sort or another, in Napoleon, Caesar, and even Stalin—though we should know much better. But numbed by a parade of crooks and nonentites, we seem to have forgotten the romance of a President, of the good citizen elevated by his own efforts and the admiration of his fellows to a pre-eminence in the state, the romance our great grandfathers sensed so strongly in the embodiment of the Republic. Budrys, a Lithuanian refugee and the son of refugees, has not. G. K. Chesterton once said that a sword was the most glorious object in the world, but that a pocket-knife was more glorious than a sword, because it was a secret sword. Laurent Michaelmas is a secret President, the secret President of the Earth. In the hands of any other writer, he would almost certainly be a tyrant, and, no doubt in the hands of most, an insane tyrant. In Budrys's, as he struggles with human treachery and an alien visitor of awesome power, he remains an eminently sane and decent man, as lonely and as sad as our society's sane and decent men must always be. In flatly and persuasively denying the inevitable corruption of power, *Michaelmas* may well be the most optimistic book of the latter 20th century. It is certainly one of the best, as Budrys himself is one of its best—and least characteristic—storytellers.

—Gene Wolfe

BULMER, (Henry) Kenneth. Also writes as Alan Burt Akers; Ken Blake; Frank Brandon; Rupert Clinton; Ernest Corley; Arthur Frazier; Peter Green; Adam Hardy; Kenneth Johns; Philip Kent; Bruno Krauss; Neil Langholm; Karl Maras; Manning Norvil; Charles R. Pike; Andrew Quiller; Chesman Scot; Nelson Sherwood; Richard Silver; H. Philip Stratford; Tully Zetford. British. Born in London, 14 January 1921. Educated at Catford Central School, London. Served in the Royal Corps of Signals, 1941-46. Married Pamela Kathleen Buckmaster in 1953; two daughters and one son. Worked for paper merchandising and office equipment firms, 1936-54. Editor or Co-Editor, *Star Parade,* 1941, *Fantasy Post,* 1941, *Seventy Eight Saga* (army magazine), 1943-45, *Nirvana,* 1949, 1954, *Science Fantasy News,* 1952, *Aaaah!,* 1954, *Dysteology,* 1954-55, *Vignette,* 1954, *Ziz,* 1954, and *Wappoted,* 1956. Agent: Carnell Literary Agency, Rowneybury Bungalow, near Old Harlow, Essex CM20 2EX. Address: 5/20 Frant Road, Tunbridge Wells, Kent TN2 5SN, England.

SCIENCE-FICTION PUBLICATIONS

Novels (series: Keys to the Dimensions; Swords)

Space Treason, with A. V. Clarke. London, Panther, 1952.
Cybernetic Controller, with A. V. Clarke. London, Panther, 1952.
Encounter in Space. London, Panther, 1952.
Zhorani (as Karl Maras). London, Comyns, 1953.
Space Salvage. London, Panther, 1953.
The Stars Are Ours. London, Panther, 1953.
Galactic Intrigue. London, Panther, 1953.
Empire of Chaos. London, Panther, 1953.
World Aflame. London, Panther, 1954.
Challenge. London, Curtis Warren, 1954.
Peril from Space (as Karl Maras). London, Comyns, 1955.
City under the Sea. New York, Ace, 1957; London, Digit, 1961.
The Secret of ZI. New York, Ace, 1958; London, Digit, 1961; as *The Patient Dark,* London, Hale, 1969.
The Changeling Worlds. New York, Ace, 1959; London, Digit, 1961.
The Earth Gods Are Coming. New York, Ace, 1960; as *Of Earth Foretold* (includes "The Aztec Plan"), London, Digit, 1961.
Forschungskreuzer Saumarez. Munich, Moewig, 1960; as Defiance, London, Digit, 1963.
No Man's World. New York, Ace, 1961; as *Earth's Long Shadow* (includes "Strange Highway"), London, Digit, 1961.
Beyond the Silver Sky. New York, Ace, 1961.
The Fatal Fire. London, Digit, 1962.
The Wind of Liberty (includes "Don't Cross a Telekine"). London, Digit, 1962.
The Wizard of Starship Poseidon. New York, Ace, 1963.
The Million Year Hunt. New York, Ace, 1964.
Demons' World. New York, Ace, 1964; as *The Demons,* London, Compact, 1965.
Land Beyond the Map. New York, Ace, 1965.
Behold the Stars. New York, Ace, 1965; London, Mayflower, 1966.
Worlds for the Taking. New York, Ace, 1966.
To Outrun Doomsday. New York, Ace, 1967; London, New English Library, 1975.
The Key to Irunium. New York, Ace, 1967.
Cycle of Nemesis. New York, Ace, 1967.
The Doomsday Men. New York, Doubleday, and London, Hale, 1968.
The Key to Venudine. New York, Ace, 1968.
The Star Venturers. New York, Ace, 1969.
The Wizards of Senchuria (Keys). New York, Ace, 1969.
Kandar. New York, Paperback Library, 1969.
The Ulcer Culture. London, Macdonald, 1969; as *The Stained-Glass World,* London, New English Library, 1976.
The Ships of Durostorum (Keys). New York, Ace, 1970.
Blazon. New York, Curtis, 1970; as *Quench the Burning Stars,* London, Hale, 1970.
Star Trove. London, Hale, 1970.
Swords of the Barbarians. London, New English Library, 1970; New York, Belmont, 1976.
The Hunters of Jundagai (Keys). New York, Ace, 1971.
The Electric Sword Swallowers. New York, Ace, 1971.
The Insane City. New York, Curtis, 1971; London, Severn House, 1978.
The Chariots of Ra (Keys). New York, Ace, 1972.
On the Symb-Socket Circuit. New York, Ace, 1972.
Roller Coaster World. New York, Ace, 1972; London, Severn House, 1978.

The Diamond Contessa (Keys). New York, DAW, 1983.

Novels as Philip Kent

Mission to the Stars. London, Pearson, 1953.
Vassals of Venus. London, Pearson, 1954.
Slaves of the Spectrum. London, Pearson, 1954.
Home Is the Martian. London, Pearson, 1954.

Novels as Alan Burt Akers (series: Dray Prescot in all books)

Transit to Scorpio. New York, DAW, 1972; London, Futura, 1974.
The Suns of Scorpio. New York, DAW, 1973; London, Futura, 1974.
Warrior of Scorpio. New York, DAW, 1973; London, Futura, 1975.
Swordships of Scorpio. New York, DAW, 1973; London, Futura, 1975.
Prince of Scorpio. New York, DAW, 1974; London, Futura, 1975.
Manhounds of Antares. New York, DAW, 1974.
Arena of Antares. New York, DAW, 1974.
Fliers of Antares. New York, DAW, 1975.
Bladesman of Antares. New York, DAW, 1975.
Avenger of Antares. New York, DAW, 1975.
Armada of Antares. New York, DAW, 1976.
The Tides of Kregen. New York, DAW, 1976.
Renegade of Kregen. New York, DAW, 1976.
Krozair of Kregen. New York, DAW, 1977.
Secret Scorpio. New York, DAW, 1977.
Savage Scorpio. New York, DAW, 1978.
Captive Scorpio. New York, DAW, 1978.
Golden Scorpio. New York, DAW, 1978.
A Life for Kregen. New York, DAW, 1979.
A Sword for Kregen. New York, DAW, 1979.
A Fortune for Kregen. New York, DAW, 1979.
A Victory for Kregen. New York, DAW, 1980.
Beasts of Antares. New York, DAW, 1980.
Rebel of Antares. New York, DAW, 1980.
Legions of Antares. New York, DAW, 1981.
Allies of Antares. New York, DAW, 1981.
Mazes of Scorpio. New York, DAW, 1982.
Delia of Vallia. New York, DAW, 1982.
Fires of Scorpio. New York, DAW, 1983.
Talons of Scorpio. New York, DAW, 1983.
Masks of Scorpio. New York, DAW, 1984.
Seg the Bowman. New York, DAW, 1984.
Werewolves of Kregen. New York, DAW, 1985.
Witch of Kregen. New York, DAW, 1985.

Novels as Tully Zetford (series: Ryder Hook in all books)

Whirlpool of Stars. London, New English Library, 1974; New York, Pinnacle, 1975.
The Boosted Man. London, New English Library, 1974; New York, Pinnacle, 1975.
Star City. London, New English Library, 1974; New York, Pinnacle, 1975.
Virility Gene. London, New English Library, 1975; New York, Pinnacle, 1976.

Novels as Manning Norvil (series: Odan in all books)

Dream Chariots. New York, DAW, 1977.
Whetted Bronze. New York, DAW, 1978.
Crown of the Sword God. New York, DAW, 1980.

Uncollected Short Stories (series: Pallas Confrontation; Fletcher Cullen; Design; Fluxers; Earth-Shurilala-Takkat War)

"First Down," in *Authentic* (London), April 1954.
"Some Other Time," in *Authentic* (London), May 1954.
"All Glory Forgotten" (Pallas), in *New Worlds* (London), June 1954.
"To Shake the Stars" (as Peter Green), in *Authentic* (London), July 1954.
"Bitter the Path" (Pallas), in *New Worlds* (London), August 1954.
"It Takes Two," in *Authentic* (London), October 1954.
"The Black Spot" (Pallas), in *New Worlds* (London), February 1955.
"Ordeal," in *Authentic* (London), March 1955.
"Asylum" (Pallas), in *New Worlds* (London), April 1955.
"Psi No More," in *Science Fantasy* (Bournemouth), June 1955.
"The Day of the Monster," in *Authentic* (London), July 1955.
"Total Recall," in *New Worlds* (London), August 1955.
"Firecracker Fool" (as Peter Green), in *Authentic* (London), August 1955.
"Know Thy Neighbour," in *Authentic* (London), September 1955.
"Come to Prestonwell," in *Authentic* (London), November 1955.
"Plaything" (Pallas), in *New Worlds* (London), November 1955.
"Sunset," in *Nebula* (Glasgow), November 1955.
"The Old Firm," in *Authentic* (London), February 1956.
"Quarry," in *Infinity* (New York), February 1956.
"The Smallest Ally," in *New Worlds* (London), March 1956.
"Food in Space" (as Kenneth Johns), in *Authentic* (London), March 1956.
"Sunk," in *New Worlds* (London), April 1956.
"Project Pseudoman," in *Nebula* (Glasgow), July 1956.
"The City Calls," in *New Worlds* (London), October 1956.
"The Great Armadas," in *Nebula* (Glasgow), December 1956.
"Recreation," in *Authentic* (London), December 1956.
"Their Dreams Remain," in *Fantastic Universe* (Chicago), December 1956.
"Prestige," in *Authentic* (London), January 1957.
"Child's Play," in *Authentic* (London), February 1957.
"Three-Cornered Knife," in *Infinity* (New York), February 1957; as "Ambiguous Assignment," in *Authentic* (London), September 1957.
"The Day Everything Fell Down," with Damon Knight, in *Fantasy and Science Fiction* (New York), August 1957.
"Native Law," in *New Worlds* (London), August 1957.
"Mission One Hundred" (Fluxers), in *New Worlds* (London), September 1957.
"Reason for Living," in *Science Fantasy* (Bournemouth), October 1957.
"There's No Business," in *Nebula* (Glasgow), October 1957.
"By the Beard of the Comet," in *Fantastic Universe* (Chicago), December 1957.
"Never Trust a Robot," in *New Worlds* (London), January 1958.
"The Great Game," in *Nebula* (Glasgow), February 1958.
"The Unreluctant Tread" (War), in *New Worlds* (London), February 1958.
"Out of Control," in *Science Fantasy* (Bournemouth), April 1958.
"Wisdom of the Gods," in *Nebula* (Glasgow), July, August, September, and October 1958.
"Space Command" (War), in *New Worlds* (London), August 1958.

"The Bones of Shosun," in *Science Fantasy* (Bournemouth), October 1958.

"Castle of Vengeance," in *Science Fantasy* (Bournemouth), November 1959.

"The Halting Hand," in *Science Fiction Adventures* (London), December 1959.

"Profession: Spaceman," in *New Worlds* (London), March 1960.

"Greenie Gunner" (Fluxers), in *New Worlds* (London), December 1960.

"Daddyo" (as Ernest Corley), in *Evening News* (London), 1961.

"The Golden Age" (as Rupert Clinton), in *New Worlds* (London), November and December 1961.

"Flame in the Flux Field" (Fluxers), in *New Worlds* (London), March 1962.

"Khushal Khan's Gold" (as Ernest Corley), in *Argosy* (London), July 1962.

"The Contraption" (Design), in *Science Fantasy* (Bournemouth), August 1964.

"A Case of Identity," in *Science Fantasy* (Bournemouth), August 1964.

"Draft Dodger" (War), in *If* (New York), March 1966.

"Not Human," in *Alien Worlds* (Manchester), August 1966.

"Inside Out" with Richard Wilson, in *Impulse* (London), December 1966.

"The Adjusted," in *Best from Fantasy and Science Fiction 16*, edited by Edward L. Ferman. New York, Doubleday, 1967; London, Gollancz, 1968.

"Swords for a Guide," in *Vision of Tomorrow* (Newcastle upon Tyne), August 1969.

"Shapers of Men" (Cullen), in *Vision of Tomorrow* (Newcastle upon Tyne). November 1969.

"Station HR972" in *Nightmare Age*, edited by Frederik Pohl. New York, Ballantine, 1970.

"The Scales of Friendship" (Cullen), in *Vision of Tomorrow* (Newcastle upon Tyne), May 1970.

"Culpable in Glass," in *Vision of Tomorrow* (Newcastle upon Tyne), August 1970.

"A Memory of Golden Sunshine," in *New Writings in SF 19*, edited by John Carnell. London, Dobson, 1971.

"The Fowling," in *Beyond This Horizon*, edited by Christopher Carrell. Sunderland, Ceolfrith Press, 1973.

"Aquaman," in *Space Two* edited by Richard Davis. London, Abelard Schuman, 1974.

"Wizard of Scorpio" (as Alan Burt Akers), in *The DAW Science Fiction Reader*, edited by Donald A. Wollheim. New York, DAW, 1976.

"Advertise Your Cyanide," in *The Best of British SF 2*, edited by Mike Ashley. London, Futura, 1977.

"Naked as a Sword," in *Fantasy Tales* (Wembley, Middlesex), Summer 1977.

"Mr. Culpepper's Baby," in *The History of the Science Fiction Magazine 4*, edited by Mike Ashley. London, Nebula, 1978.

"Psycho Sis," in *Fantasy and Science Fiction* (New York), April 1978.

"Green Shadows" (as Alan Burt Akers), in *Imagine*, November 1983.

Uncollected Short Stories as Chesman Scot

"The Void Looks Down," in *Vargo Statten Science Fiction Magazine* (Luton, Bedfordshire), vol. 1 no. 5, 1954.

"Galactic Impersonation," in *British Science Fiction Magazine* (Luton, Bedfordshire), March 1955.

"The Second Pyramid," in *Vargo Statten Science Fiction Magazine* (Luton, Bedfordshire), vol. 2, no. 1, 1955.

Uncollected Short Stories as H. Philip Stratford

"The Time Travel Business," in *Authentic* (London), August 1955.

"According to Tradition," in *Authentic* (London), April 1956.

"The Hidden Power," in *Authentic* (London), June 1956.

"Lucky Number," in *Authentic* (London), November 1956.

"Asymptote," in *Authentic* (London), March 1957.

"The Thoughtless Island," in *Nebula* (Glasgow), July 1957.

"Lethe Land," in *Nebula* (Glasgow), August 1957.

"Vale!," in *Authentic* (London), October 1957.

"The Covetous," in *Nebula* (Glasgow), May 1958.

"Agent Provocateur," in *Nebula* (Glasgow), September 1958.

"Medicine Man," in *Nebula* (Glasgow), January 1959.

"Song of Ages,"in *Nebula* (Glasgow), June 1959.

Uncollected Short Stories as Nelson Sherwood

"Galactic Galapagos," January 1959, "The Sun Center," March 1959, "The Dedicated Ones," July 1960, "Design Dilemma," March 1961, "Trial," November 1961, "Scarlet Denial," May 1962, and "Scarlet Dawn," September 1962, all in *Science Fiction Adventures* (London).

Uncollected Short Stories as Frank Brandon

"Hiatus," in *New Worlds* (London), January 1961.

"The Seventh Stair," in *Science Fantasy* (Bournemouth), October 1961.

"Perilous Portal," in *Science Fantasy* (Bournemouth), August 1962.

OTHER PUBLICATIONS

Novels

White Out (as Ernest Corley). London, Jarrolds, 1960.

The Dark Return (as Neil Langholm). London, Sphere, 1975; New York, Pinnacle, 1977.

By Pirate's Blood (as Richard Silver). New York, Pinnacle, 1975.

Jaws of Death (as Richard Silver). New York, Pinnacle, 1975.

Trail of Blood (as Neil Langholm). London, Sphere, 1976.

The Land of Mist (as Andrew Quiller). London, Mayflower, and New York, Pinnacle, 1976.

Sea of Swords (as Andrew Quiller). London, Mayflower, and New York, Pinnacle, 1976.

Brand of Vengeance (as Charles R. Pike). London Mayflower, 1978.

Blind Run. London, Sphere, 1979.

Novels as Adam Hardy

The Press Gang. London, New English Library, and New York, Pinnacle, 1973.

Prize Money. London, New English Library, and New York, Pinnacle, 1973.

The Siege. London, New English Library, 1973; as *Savage Siege*, New York, Pinnacle, 1973.

Treasure. London, New English Library, 1973; as *Treasure Map*, New York, Pinnacle, 1974.

Powder Monkey. London, New English Library, 1973; as *Sailor's Blood*, New York, Pinnacle, 1974.

Blood for Breakfast. London, New English Library, 1974; as

Sea of Gold, New York, Pinnacle, 1974.
Court Martial. London, New English Library, and New York, Pinnacle, 1974.
Battle Smoke. London, New English Library, 1974; New York, Pinnacle, 1975.
Cut and Thrust. London, New English Library, 1974; New York, Pinnacle, 1975.
Boarders Away. London, New English Library, and New York, Pinnacle, 1975.
Fireship. London, New English Library, 1975; New York, Pinnacle, 1976.
Blood Beach. London, New English Library, 1975.
Sea Flame. London, New English Library, 1976.
Close Quarters. London, New English Library, 1977.
Strike Force Falklands: Operation Exocet. London, Futura, 1984.
Strike Force Falklands: Raider's Dawn. London, Futura, 1984.
Strike Force Falklands: Red Alert. London, Futura, 1984.

Novels as Arthur Frazier

Oath of Blood. London, New English Library, 1973.
The King's Death. London, New English Library, 1973.
A Flame in the Fens. London, New English Library, 1974.
An Axe in Miklagard. London, New English Library, 1975.

Novels as Ken Blake

Where the Jungle Ends. London Sphere 1978.
Stake Out. London, Sphere, 1978.
Hunter Hunted. London, Sphere, 1978.
Long Shot. London, Sphere, 1979.
Blind Run. London, Sphere, 1979.
Fall Girl. London, Sphere, 1979.
Dead Reckoning. London, Sphere, 1980.

Novels as Bruno Krauss

Steel Shark. London, Sphere, 1978.
Shark North. London, Sphere, 1978.
Shark Pack. London, Sphere, 1978.
Shark Hunt. London, Sphere, 1980.
Shark Africa. London, Sphere, 1980.
Shark Raid. London, Sphere, 1982.
Shark America. London, Sphere, 1982.
Shark Trap. London, Sphere, 1982.

Other

The True Book about Space Travel (for children; as Kenneth Johns, with John Newman). London, Muller, 1960.
Pretenders (for children). London, New English Library, 1972.

Editor, *New Writings in SF 22-30*. London, Sidgwick and Jackson, 8 vols., 1973-76, and London, Corgi, 1 vol., 1978.
Editor, *New Writings in SF Special 1-3*. London, Sidgwick and Jackson, 1795-78 (vol. 1 edited with John Carnell).

*

Bibliography: *The Writings of Kenneth Bulmer* by Roger Robinson, n. p., BECCON, 1983; revised edition, 1984.

Kenneth Bulmer comments:
If in an unwary moment I open one of my early books I find great difficulty in identifying with the writer. The immediate purpose of the writer appears plain enough; he is dazzled by a vision of what this literature called SF might achieve, and is concerned to express this vision in terms then available to him. There is genuine feeling; but he is handicapped by environment, editorial prejudice, and lack of data. There is an unfortunate assumption that other people will readily share his insights, that the vision is so self-evident it must be conveyed. His own interests in the fascinating details of, for instance, the future, space and time travel, the interactions and potentialities of the human mind and spirit, appear to overshadow what he is driving at. Imperceptive, top-of-the-head critics have said that most of the writer's work is space opera; a closer reading will reveal this statement to be untenable. The vision of what SF might achieve remains, dimmed a little, it is true, by the current state of general SF, and this writer has in recent years turned to other interests, including the Fox books (as Adam Hardy) and adult fantasy, both incidentally, sharing that imaginative exploration of worlds unknown to the present day.

I have said many times, and will re-iterate, that SF is not respectable but is responsible. I remain unconvinced that this statement has been grasped by those to whom it is addressed. If poetry and non-establishment fiction are literatures of revolt, then SF is also. But it is more than merely a literature against, for example, the dead hand of authoritarianism or outmoded sexual mores: it is a literature against the spoliation of man by mankind's creations, which is by inference by man himself. This is not quite the same order of protest. This does not mean that SF is less as literature but more, for it incorporates more of life and, to enlarge a cliché, the felt responses within the emotional reactions to the human condition.

One underlying theme in my work is the exploration of the feelings and reactions of people forced, by the environment, other people, or inner compulsions, to perform acts and live lives far removed from what they would desire. As an introduction to my work I would instance the observation of a recent correspondent who remarked of my novels that they are filled with compassion all too often lacking in other works of SF.

*   *   *

If any single writer could epitomize the formularized science-fantasy milieu of Donald A. Wollheim's popular Ace paperback line, Kenneth Bulmer would be a good choice for the designation. Inasmuch as American adventure-pulps took many formulaic elements from British adventure-fiction (violent conflict between cultures, stereotypes of romance, etc.), it might be seen as fitting that Wollheim's editorial devotion to the adventurous side of SF should be typified by a British writer who seemed devoted to formula for formula's sake.

It should be stressed that no author of narrative prose escapes at least some formulaic elements in his or her work—in fact, one measure of "art" might be the author's ability to transcend the formulaic origins of his narrative, as Conrad's stories rise above the classification of "sea stories." A formula writer, however, emphasizes the elements of the formula—the plot, the action, the melodramatic interactions of characters, and in SF, the "idea" or concept—and pays only superficial attention (if any) to the meaningful, thematic usages of such elements. Ace Books was noteworthy for printing many SF adventures with at least some moderate thematic interest, as with Emil Petaja's concern for regenerative myth-figures, or Leigh Brackett's preoccupation with beautiful, dying cultures. Yet the bulk of Ace's books were usually less thematically organized, and so Bulmer makes the best representative writer of that period. Bulmer is not, however, simply a "hack" in the derogatory sense—rather, he does for the SF adventure what Edgar Wallace did for mysteries, and Seabury Quinn did for supernatural stories—that is, by the sheer bulk of his efforts in a single vein, he demonstrates the intrinsic fascination of the ritualistic nature of the formula and its icon-like imagery.

Bulmer's plots are his chief failing. Other formula-elements can be, and have been, neglected without necessarily diluting the effectiveness of the formula. Jack Williamson might use stereotypic characters, Edgar Rice Burroughs might overemphasize frenetic action, and Philip José Farmer might employ ideas of little originality, but all of them supply strong plotting that communicates some thematic commitment. Adventure-plots generally must be intricate to be compelling, but the formlessness of Bulmer's plots almost suggests the absurdity of a freewheeling comedy. Most of Bulmer's plots begin adequately enough—the protagonist and his allies learn of a mysterious force or perilous circumstance threatening their safety, but as they prepare to combat it, they continually become sidetracked, verging off into distantly-related episodic conflicts, so that, when they eventually re-enter the central conflict, the outcome is no longer interesting.

Some books in Bulmer's early cycle, such as *Behold the Stars* and *Secret of Zi*, are dully conventional, and it may be that Bulmer began his pattern of repeated scene-shifting to gain greater diversity. The tendency is markedly seen in *Cycle of Nemesis*, in which a group of humans try to bind an ancient demon into his crypt, and get thrown across various time-periods as they try. A series of Bulmer's books is even built around the various conflicts of an assortment of forgettable heroes against a dimension-conquering villainess, the Diamond Contessa, but with the exception of one of these (*The Wizards of Senchuria*) the other three, *Key to Irunium, Key to Venudine*, and *The Diamond Contessa*, lack narrative drive and coherence.

Bulmer's best work is probably *The Wizard of Starship Poseidon*, in that the plot is well-defined. Best described as *Topkapi* set in outer space, the novel has a certain amount of irony, concerning a scientist who fails to gain a grant to subsidize his project of creating biologic life, and decides to steal the necessary funds from a military payroll. (Wittily enough, the grant he wants is given to a literary scholar who hopes to prove that Bernard Shaw and H. G. Wells were the same man.) In this format, Bulmer's penchant for stocking his stories with an excess of eccentric characters is a benefit, and he manages to pull off a number of interesting plot-twists without becoming vague. A runner-up for best book might be *The Star Venturers*, in which a soldier-of-fortune, controlled by an artificial life-form implanted in his brain, is forced to track down a kidnapped princess, with the usual wild escapades that ensue when he combats her heavily armed kidnappers. Also of interest are *On the Symb-Socket Circuit* and *Roller Coaster World*, which attempt to break from the adventure-mold into that of social satire, directed toward the follies of hedonism and luxury-living. These have a degree of wit, but tend to flounder aimlessly: in *Roller Coaster World*, the hero is infatuated with a hopelessly unfulfilling romance, but Bulmer resolves an interesting dilemma in melodramatic terms, arranging for another woman to force the hero to renounce his hopeless love by the subtle strategy of her shooting him and carrying him off.

In short, Bulmer is a writer to be valued for his inventiveness, in spite of the fact that his inventions rarely transcend the level of basic "sensawunda" SF.

—Gene Phillips

BUNCH, David R(oosevelt). American. Born in Lowry City, Missouri. Educated at Central Missouri State College, Warrensburg, B. S. 1946; Washington University, St. Louis, M. A. 1949; State University of Iowa City, 1951-52. Served in the United States Army Air Force, 1942-46. Married Phyllis Geraldine Flette in 1951; two daughters (one deceased). Worked in cafeteria, as clerk and warehouseman, mail handler, druggist; staff member, Wagner Electric Company, St. Louis, 1953-54; civilian cartographer, Air Force Aeronautical Chart and Information Center, St. Louis, 1954-73. Agent: Hans Joachim Alpers, Gross Flottbeker Strasse 61, 2000 Hamburg 52, Germany. Address: P. O. Box 12233, Soulard Station, St. Louis, Missouri 63157, U. S. A.

SCIENCE-FICTION PUBLICATIONS

Novel

Moderan . New York, Avon, 1971.

Uncollected Short Stories

"Routine Emergency," in *If* (New York), December 1957.
"In the Complaints Service," in *Fantastic* (New York), February 1960.
"We Regret," in *Fantastic* (New York), February 1961.
"Last Zero," in *Fantastic* (New York), March 1961.
"The Problem Was Lubrication," in *Fantastic* (New York), May 1961.
"The Survey Trip," in *Fantastic* (New York), May 1962.
"Ended," in *Fantastic* (New York), June 1962.
"The Reluctant Immortals," in *If* (New York), November 1962.
"Awareness Plans," in *Fantastic* (New York), November 1962.
"A Small Miracle of Fishhooks and Straight Pins," in *The Year's Best S-F, 7th Annual*, edited by Judith Merril. New York, Simon and Schuster, 1962.
"Somebody Up There Hates Us," in *Amazing* (New York), April 1963.
"The Hall of CD," in *Fantastic* (New York), June 1963.
"They Never Came Back from Whoosh!," in *Fantastic* (New York), February 1964.
"All for Nothing," in *Fantastic* (New York), May 1964.
"The College of Acceptable Death," in *Fantastic* (New York), July 1964.
"The Failure," in *Fantastic* (New York), August 1964.
"A Vision of the King," in *Fantastic* (New York), September 1964.
"Home to Zero," in *Fantastic* (New York), October 1964.
"Training Talk," in *The Year's Best S-F, 10th Annual*, edited by Judith Merril. New York, Delacorte Press, 1965.
"Make Mine Trees," in *Fantastic* (New York), February 1965.
"The Little Doors," in *Fantastic* (New York), June 1965.
"The Time Battler," in *The Smith* (New York), July 1965.
"Investigating the Bidwell Endeavors," in *The Year's Best S-F, 11th Annual*. edited by Judith Merril. New York, Delacorte Press, 1966.
"The Escaping," in *Fantastic Visions*, edited by Harlan Ellison. New York, Doubleday, 1967.
"Sad Case No. (Many-Too-Many)," in *Dare* (Cleveland), March 1967.
"The Fable of the Moonshooter and the Indifferent Undergraduate," in *Dare* (Cleveland), October 1967.
"The Soul Short Changers," in *21* (Los Angeles), October 1967.

"That High-Up Blue Day That Saw the Black Sky-Train Come Spinning," in *Fantasy and Science Fiction* (New York), March 1968.

"Two Pessimists and a Pigeon," in *Aspects* (Eugene, Oregon), April 1968.

"A Scare in Time," in *Fantasy and Science Fiction* (New York), September 1968.

"The Monsters," in *Amazing* (New York), November 1968.

"When It Comes to Bascarts, I'll Take a Full One," in *Aspects* (Eugene, Oregon), January 1969.

"Any Heads at Home?," in *Fantastic* (New York), February 1969.

"In the Time of Disposal of Infants," in *Amazing* (New York), March 1969.

"In a Saucer Down for B-Day," in *Fantastic* (New York), April 1969.

"A Little at All Times," in *Perihelion* (Elmhurst, New York), Summer 1969.

"At the Place of Almost If You Want To and Don't Care If You Don't," in *Orb* (Lake Worth, Florida), Fall 1969.

"Learning It at Miss Rejoyy's," in *Fantastic* (New York), February 1970.

"In the Land of the Not-Unhappies," in *Fantastic* (New York), June 1970.

"Tough Rocks and Hard Stones," in *Fantasy and Science Fiction* (New York), September 1970.

"Holdholtzer's Box," in *Protostars*, edited by David Gerrold and Stephen Goldin. New York, Ballantine, 1971.

"Price of Leisure," in *Galaxy* (New York), May 1971.

"The Joke," in *Fantastic* (New York), August 1971.

"Doll for the End of the Day," in *Fantastic* (New York), October 1971.

"The Lady Was for Kroinking," in *Generation*, edited by David Gerrold. New York, Dell, 1972.

"Training Talk No. 12," in *Fantasy and Science Fiction* (New York), January 1972.

"Two Suns for the King," in *If* (New York), April 1972.

"Up to the Edge of Heaven," in *Fantastic* (New York), April 1972.

"The Good War," in *Fantastic* (New York), December 1972.

"Breakout in Ecol 2," in *Nova 3*, edited by Harry Harrison. New York, Walker, 1973.

"Seeing Stingy Ed," in *The Haunt of Horror* (New York), June 1973.

"Moment of Truth in Suburb Junction," in *Fantastic* (New York), September 1973.

"Helping Put the Rough Works to Jesse," in *Eternity 3* (Sandy Springs, South Carolina), 1974.

"Among the Metal-and-People People," in *New Dimensions 4*, edited by Robert Silverberg. New York, New American Library, 1974.

"How Xmas Ghosts Are Made," in *Alternities*, edited by David Gerrold. New York, Dell, 1974.

"Report from the Colony," in *SF Directions*, edited by Bruce McAllister. Christchurch, Edge Press, 1974.

"Alien," in *Fantastic* (New York), January 1974.

"Short Time at the Pearly Gates," in *Fantastic* (New York), March 1974.

"In the Land That Aimed at Forever," in *Fantastic* (New York), May 1974.

"At Bugs Complete," in *Fantastic* (New York), July 1974.

"End of a Singer," in *Fantastic* (New York), April 1975.

"The Strange Case of the Birds," in *Fantastic* (New York), December 1975.

"The Dirty War," in *Future Pastimes*, edited by Scott Edelstein. Nashville, Aurora, 1977.

"Mr. Who?," in *Fantastic* (New York), April 1978.

"Send Us a Planet?," in *Fantastic* (New York), July 1978.

"Pridey Goeth," in *Fantastic* (New York), October 1978.

"When the Metal Eaters Came," in *Galaxy* (New York), June-July 1979.

"A Little Girl's Spring Day in Moderan," in *Galaxy* (New York), September-October 1979.

"Through a Wall a Back," in *Eternity* (Clemson, South Carolina), Winter 1979.

"New Member," in *Fantastic* (New York), July 1980.

"The Strange Rider of the Good Year," in *Amazing* (New York), November 1980.

"In the Ball of Frosted Glass (with a Big Pink-Lavender Load)," in *Amazing* (New York), March 1981.

"Kicked Straight at Last," in *Pulpsmith* (New York), Spring 1981.

"In the Jag-Whiffing Service" and "Let Me Call Her Sweetcore," in Pig Iron, edited by Rose Sayre and Jim Villani. Youngstown, Ohio, Pig Iron Press, 1982.

"December for Stronghold 9," in *Amazing* (New York), June 1982.

"Writer's Workshop Stories," in *Amazing* (New York), September 1982.

"From the Fishbowl," in *Last Wave* (New York), Autumn 1984.

OTHER PUBLICATIONS

Verse

We Have a Nervous Job. Astoria, Oregon, Alba Press, 1983.

*

David R. Bunch comments:

I do not write mainly to glorify the scientific accomplishments of mankind or to predict how more and more unbelievably astounding those accomplishments are apt eventually to be. And they are, I am convinced, destined to be astounding, increasingly frightening. But I am much haunted by many questions and a wistful wondering concerning the true worth of man in his spaceship outbound for the stars. Aren't "stars" right here the main stars we should be true-headed for and inbound toward? Is not that elusive Light of Godly humanness locked and hidden in the obscured soul of man our main objective? And shouldn't the other stars whirling "out there" be regarded as the inscrutable business of God?

But because I do have these heart questionings and this wistful wondering concerning importances, it must make of my science fiction writings something other than a glorification of hard science. I write what the trade knows as "soft" science fiction, wherein social statement is as important as the soul-less telling of how a piece of machinery behaves. In many ways I am almost anti-science in my science-fiction writings. I believe we have upped too much our search for greater and still greater technological triumphs and lessened to our loss the quest for a clearer and brighter understanding of that sometimes blinding Light which is, or should be, our very sacred souls.

So I write not to shout-scream the glories of our great science breakthroughs, or to predict even greater thrusts. I write with more urgent business in mind: to make the reader "see," through my sometimes grim social statements and my often stark satirical comments—both apt to be perverse, even cynical—what worship of science may do in irretrievable detriment to Man and his Earth.

Did human kind come this far on our faltering, seeking,

sometimes glorious course only to dehumanize ourselves and become of no greater significance than the machines themselvesthat once we used as an aid in our search for significances?

* * *

David R. Bunch's short, idiosyncratic stories have, almost invariably, been met with varying degrees of outrage from readers unwilling to work with his convoluted prose to reach the plot that to most is opaque. In his own way Bunch is one of the most original and creative writers in the genre, and it is unfortunate that the conservative bent of most readers is such that he is not given the attention he deserves.

The bulk of his work has been a loosely organized series set against the background of Moderan, several dozen of which have been collected as a book under that title. Moderan is a thoroughly repulsive future to rank with the Nebishes of T. J. Bass. Humans have acquired immortality, or as near to it as matters, through replacement of most of their body parts with metal. In fact, only a few flesh strips remain, the tiniest traces of humanity. Their physical transformation is matched by their emotional one. Most humans live in highly armed castles, called Strongholds. The protagonist of most of the series is Stronghold Ten, a man who early in the series is fitted with metallic limbs and organs, and makes use of his determination to make himself the foremost warmaker in the land. He alternates between highly mechanized combat and resting in his hip-snuggie chair within his stronghold, watching the sky change color as each month a new vapor shield is erected, or gazing out across his garden of metal flowers.

The series does much better as a whole than as individual stories, most of which are extremely episodic. Several do stand fairly well alone, particularly "Was She Horrid?" wherein Stronghold Ten is visited by a female, "The Walking, Talking I-Don't-Care Man" in which he has a male visitor, and "How It Ended" which concludes the first cycle of Moderan stories. An uncollected Moderan story, "Two Suns for the King," is as good as anything in the collection; Stronghold Ten is struck with an undeniable urge to grow something organic, and can find no unpolluted soil to work with.

There are literally dozens of stories not in the Moderan series, some of which fall into a lesser series of "Training Talks" by a male parent to his two young children. In one of his more straightforward stories, "Holdholtzer's Box," a scientist invents a box wherein he expects to entice people to their deaths. The interface between man and machine, so obvious in the Moderan stories, is present in much of his other work. A road clearing crew fails to distinguish between auto wreckage and human flesh in "Routine Emergency," for example, and people are lobotomized to happiness in "In the Land of the Not Unhappies. "

The best single story may well be "That High-Up Blue Day That Saw the Black Sky-Train Come Spinning. " In a style reminiscent of the best of R. A. Lafferty, Bunch introduces us to a group of aging nonconformists who decide that children need to be saved from the horrible fate of growing up. And they succeed. Another story that is extremely effective, though enigmatic, is "The Strange Case of the Birds" wherein an increasing number of people begin to see a malformed bird shape outlined against the moon.

Bunch often assails human vanity, rarely as well as in "Pridey Goeth," in which a town is taken in by a clever potion purveyor, and literally falls mortally wounded as the result. His clear-sighted view of the narrowmindedness of humanity is reinforced to a certain extent by the general reaction to his work, but it appears that Bunch is far more interested in making the statements he feels necessary than in gaining critical acclaim.

—Don D'Ammassa

BUPP, Walter. See GARRETT, Randall.

BURGESS, Anthony. Pseudonym for John Anthony Burgess Wilson; also writes as Joseph Kell. British. Born in Manchester, Lancashire, 25 February 1917. Educated at Xaverian College, Manchester; Manchester University, B. A. (honours) in English 1940. Served in the British Army Education Corps, 1940-46: Sergeant-Major. Married 1) Llewela Isherwood Jones in 1942 (died, 1968); 2) Liliana Macellari in 1968, one son. Lecturer, Extra-Mural Department, Birmingham University, 1946-48; Education Officer and Lecturer, Central Advisory Council for Adult Education in the Forces, 1946-48; Lecturer in Phonetics, Ministry of Education, 1948-50; English Master, Banbury Grammar School, Oxfordshire, 1950-54; Senior Lecturer in English, Malayan Teachers Training College, Khata Baru, 1954-57; English Language Specialist, Department of Education, Brunei, Borneo, 1958-59. Writer-in-Residence, University of North Carolina, Chapel Hill, 1969-70; Professor, Columbia University, New York, 1970-71; Visiting Fellow, Princeton University, New Jersey, 1970-71; Distinguished Professor, City University of New York, 1972-73; Literary Adviser, Guthrie Theatre, Minneapolis, 1972-75. Also composer. Recipient: National Arts Club award, 1973; Foreign Book Prize (France), 1981. D. Litt. : Manchester University, 1982. Fellow, Royal Society of Literature, 1969. Address: 44 rue Grimaldi, Monaco.

SCIENCE-FICTION PUBLICATIONS

Novels

A Clockwork Orange. London, Heinemann, 1962; New York, Norton, 1963.
The Wanting Seed. London, Heinemann, 1962; New York, Norton, 1963.
1985. London, Hutchinson, and Boston, Little Brown, 1978.
The End of the World News. London, Hutchinson, 1982; New York, McGraw Hill, 1983.

Uncollected Short Story

"The Muse," in *Best SF 1969*, edited by Brian Aldiss and Harry Harrison. New York, Putnam, and London, Sphere, 1970.

OTHER PUBLICATIONS

Novels

Time for a Tiger. London, Heinemann, 1956.
The Enemy in the Blanket. London, Heinemann, 1958.
Beds in the East. London, Heinemann, 1959.
The Right to an Answer. London, Heinemann, 1960; New York, Norton, 1961.

The Doctor Is Sick. London, Heinemann, and New York, Norton, 1960.

The Worm and the Ring. London, Heinemann, 1961; revised edition, 1970.

Devil of a State. London Heinemann, 1961; New York, Norton, 1962.

One Hand Clapping (as Joseph Kell). London, Davies, 1961; as Anthony Burgess, New York, Knopf, 1972.

Honey for the Bears. London, Heinemann, 1963; New York, Norton, 1964.

Inside Mr. Enderby (as Joseph Kell). London, Heinemann, 1963.

The Eve of Saint Venus. London, Sidgwick and Jackson, 1964; New York, Norton, 1967.

Nothing Like the Sun: A Story of Shakespeare's Love-Life. London, Heinemann, and New York, Norton, 1964.

The Malayan Trilogy (includes *Time for a Tiger, The Enemy in the Blanket, Beds in the East*). London, Heinemann, 1964; as *The Long Days Wanes*, New York, Norton, 1965.

A Vision of Battlements. London, Sidgwick and Jackson, 1965; New York, Norton, 1966.

Tremor of Intent. London, Heinemann, and New York, Norton, 1966.

Enderby Outside. London, Heinemann, 1968.

Enderby (includes *Inside Mr. Enderby* and *Enderby Outside*). New York, Norton, 1968.

MF. London, Cape, and New York, Knopf, 1971.

Napoleon Symphony. London, Cape, and New York, Knopf, 1974.

The Clockwork Testament; or, Enderby's End. London, Hart Davis MacGibbon, 1974; New York, Knopf, 1975.

Beard's Roman Women. New York, McGraw Hill, 1976; London, Hutchinson, 1977.

Abba Abba. London, Faber, and Boston, Little Brown, 1977.

Man of Nazareth. New York, McGraw Hill, 1979; London, Magnum, 1980.

Earthly Powers. London, Hutchinson, and New York, Simon and Schuster, 1980.

Enderby (includes *Inside Mr. Enderby, Enderby Outside, The Clockwork Testament*). London, Penguin, 1982.

Enderby's Dark Lady; or, No End to Enderby. London, Hutchinson, and New York, McGraw Hill, 1984.

The Kingdom of the Wicked. London, Hutchinson, 1985.

Short Story

Will and Testament: A Fragment of Biography. Verona, Plain Wrapper Press, 1977.

Plays

Cyrano de Bergerac, music by Michael J. Lewis, lyrics by Burgess, adaptation of the play by Rostand (as *Cyrano*, produced Minneapolis, 1971; New York, 1973; as *Cyrano de Bergerac*, produced London, 1983). New York, Knopf, 1971; London, Hutchinson, 1984.

Oedipus the King, adaptation of a play by Sophocles (produced Minneapolis, 1972; Southampton, Hampshire, 1979). Minneapolis, University of Minnesota Press, 1972; London, Oxford University Press, 1973.

The Cavalier of the Rose (story adaptation), in *Der Rosenkavalier*, libretto by Hofmannsthal, music by Richard Strauss. Boston, Little Brown, 1982; London, Joseph, 1983.

Screenplay: special languages for *Quest of Fire*, 1981.

Radio Play: *Blooms of Dublin*, music by Burgess, 1983.

Television Plays: *Moses—The Lawgiver*, with others, 1975; *Jesus of Nazareth*, with others, 1977; *A Kind of Failure* (documentary; *Writers and Places* series), 1981.

Verse

Moses: A Narrative. London, Dempsey and Squires, and New York, Stonehill, 1976.

A Christmas Recipe. Verona, Plain Wrapper Press, 1977.

Other

English Literature: A Survey for Students (as John Burgess Wilson). London, Longman, 1958.

The Novel Today. London, Longman, 1963.

Language Made Plain (as John Burges Wilson). London, English Universities Press, 1964; New York, Crowell, 1965; revised edition, London, Fontana, 1975.

Here comes Everybody: An Introduction to James Joyce for the Ordinary Reader. London, Faber, 1965; revised edition, London, Hamlyn, 1982; as *Re Joyce*, New York, Norton, 1965.

The Novel Now: A Student's Guide to Contemporary Fiction. London, Faber, and New York, Norton, 1967; revised edition, Faber, 1971.

Urgent Copy: Literary Studies. London, Cape, and New York, Norton, 1968.

"H. G. Wells," in *New York Times Book Review*, 3 August 1969.

Shakespeare. London, Cape, and New York, Knopf, 1970.

Joysprick: An Introduction to the Language of James Joyce. London, Deutsch, 1973; New York, Harcourt Brace, 1975.

Obscenity and the Arts (lecture). Valletta, Malta Library Association, 1973.

A Long Trip to Teatime (for children). London, Dempsey and Squires, and New York, Stonehill, 1976.

New York, with the editors of Time-Life books. New York, Time-Life. 1976.

Ernest Hemingway and His World. London, Thames and Hudson, and New York, Scribner, 1978.

The Land Where Ice Cream Grows (for children). London, Benn, and New York, Doubleday, 1979.

On Going to Bed. London, Deutsch, and New York, Abbeville, 1982.

This Man and Music. London, Hutchinson, 1982; New York, McGraw Hill, 1983.

Ninety-Nine Novels: The Best in English since 1939; A Personal Choice. London, Allison and Busby, and New York. Summit, 1984.

Editor, *The Coaching Days of England 1750-1850.* London, Elek, and New York, Time-Life, 1966.

Editor, *A Journal of the Plague Year*, by Daniel Defoe. London, Penguin, 1966.

Editor, *A Shorter Finnegans Wake*, by James Joyce. London, Faber, and New York, Viking Press, 1966.

Editor, with Francis Haskell, *The Age of the Grand Tour.* London, Elek, and New York, Crown, 1967.

Editor, *Malaysian Stories*, by W. Somerset Maugham. Singapore, Heinemann, 1969.

Translator, with Llewela Burgess, *The New Aristocrats*, by Michel de Saint-Pierre. London, Gollancz, 1962; Boston, Houghton Mifflin, 1963.

Translator, with Llewela Burgess, *The Olive Trees of Justice*, by Jean Pelegri. London, Sidgwick and Jackson, 1962.

Translator, *The Man Who Robbed Poor Boxes*, by Jean Servin. London, Gollancz, 1965.

*

Bibliography: *Anthony Burgess: A Bibliography* by Jeutonne Brewer, Metuchen, New Jersey, Scarecrow Press, 1980.

Manuscript Collection: Mills Memorial Library, Hamilton, Ontario.

Critical Studies: *Anthony Burgess* by Carol M. Dix, London, Longman, 1971; *The Consolations of Ambiguity: An Essay on the Novels of Anthony Burgess* by Robert K. Morris, Columbia, University of Missouri Press, 1971; *Anthony Burgess* by A. A. DeVitis, New York, Twayne, 1972; *The Clockwork Universe of Anthony Burgess* by Richard Mathews, San Bernardino, California, Borgo Press, 1978; *Anthony Burgess: The Artist as Novelist* by Geoffrey Aggeler, University, University of Alabama Press, 1979; *Anthony Burgess* by Samuel Coale, New York, Ungar, 1981.

*　　*　　*

Science fiction is just one part of the literary landscape for Anthony Burgess, as reviewer, historian (*The Novel Now*), and novelist. Using bits and pieces of it in several books, he has also written four genre novels. Full of melodrama, they are not comfortable adventures with cardboard cutouts in rocketships, but studies of character, language, society, and morality in a world that disavows them. Agnostic in doubting God's presence, Burgess's world-view is Manichaean in highlighting a conflict between good and evil.

A dystopian future is implicit in the social stupor and mindless violence of England in *The Right to an Answer*, the double-think and sexual ambiguity of Russia in *Honey for the Bears*, and the East-West conflict of the "eschatological spy novel," *Tremor of Intent*, all set against the backdrop of imminent nuclear holocaust. Precognition in *One Hand Clapping* gains Howard Shirley the riches to show his wife, Janet, that the material life is not worth living. Science fiction is peripheral to all of these, and even more so to *Inside Mr. Enderby*. Enderby's poem about a minotaur is made into a dreadful movie, *Son of the Beast from Outer Space*.

A film brought fame to Burgess, too: Stanley Kubrick's adaptation of *A Clockwork Orange* (departing considerably from the novel, it earned the author only a consultant's fee). In its neo-Orwellian England, men are on the moon but youth gangs mug and rape the old and young at will, provoking police-state responses. One of these kids who drink narcotic-laced milk ("moloko") and speak a Russian-rooted slang ("Nadsat"), Alex gives us his version of the joys of sex (a mechanical "in-out in-out"), of the "ultra-violent," and of classical music (especially the last movement of Beethoven's Ninth). He explains how his buddies ("droogs") got him arrested for beating up ("tolchocking") an old woman ("starry ptitsa"); her death got him imprisoned.

To get out, he volunteered for "Lodovico" aversive conditioning, rendering him unable to enjoy any of his three loves: sex, violence, and music. Victimized by old victims, he is befriended by one of them, unaware. Author of an essay, "A Clockwork Orange," this man, F. Alexander, uses Alex's case to overthrow the regime in charge, changing his political party from "outs" to "ins." The "cured" Alex returns to his old ways, except in the first (English) edition, whose last chapter rounds out his life, death, and resurrection. This controversial

episode shows Alex thinking of growing up and settling down, solving his problem, perhaps, but not helping us choose between his crimes and those of the state. Burgess finds both cure and disease repugnant (Kubrick is less equivocal); the State may be more culpable but its manipulation of Alex is just a step behind what made him a "clockwork orange" to being with.

The symmetry of the original three seven-chapter sections, the pointed inversions of victims and victimizers, the parallels of Alex with F. Alexander, and "Lodovico" with "Ludwig van" show Burgess's conscious artistry, but his most striking device is "Nadsat." To read Alex's memoir, one must literally learn his language, not that difficult in context though later editions dilute the effect with a glossary. Verbal violence both shields the reader from and exposes him to physical violence, while learning to understand Alex leads to condoning his behavior, and accepting the conditioning effects of society in general. Although Alex accepts matter-of-factly his own allegiance not to goodness, but to "the other shop," the question of good-and-evil is both raised and rendered all but moot.

Burgess later labelled this book "too didactic, too linguistically exhibitionistic," but his other major dystopian novel, *The Wanting Seed*, employs a comparable amount of lecture and stylistic versatility to replay the Manichaean dilemma. Treated here as accelerated history, it involves "Pelphase" (Pelagian perfectibility), "Interphase" (chaotic brutality), and "Gusphase" (Augustinian contrition). It takes little more than a year to go from an overpopulated age in which homosexuality brings advancement and unauthorized fertility is a fatal offense, to a plague-ridden world sacrificed to by massacre, orgies, and cannibalism mocking Christian communion. A return to actual Christianity (outlawed earlier) and active heterosexuality is witnessed by Tristram Foxe, his wife Beatrice-Joanna, and his brother (her lover) Derek. Flamboyantly homo, Derek becomes dutifully hetero, maintaining executive rank as his Ministry changes from Infertility to its opposite. In prison, then the army, where he alone survives a massacre, Tristram goes through Hell to return to his unfaithful wife. A living monument to ambivalence, she runs away to bear twins, naming them Derek and Tristram and claiming both men as fathers, husbands, and lovers. More obviously a fable perhaps, *The Wanting Seed* is seen by some critics as more optimistic than *A Clockwork Orange*. But in the context of a future crisis, the restoration of fertility is not an improvement, rather a restatement of the individual-state conflict.

Burgess revisited dystopia in *1985*, a critique of Orwell's "cacatopia" (and his own) partly in fictional form. A loosely strung essay discusses the strengths, flaws, contemporary sources, and historical roots of *Nineteen Eighty-Four*, in Pelagian and Augustinian terms. Chronicling a common man's abortive fight against the system, in an Arab-dominated England beset with economic chaos, a breakdown in human relationships, and a return to religion (Islam), the talky story has almost none of the invention, wit, or style of its predecessors.

If that vein was played out, another one worth mining is suggested by a New Wavish tale reflecting Burgess's continued preoccupation with fate, and artists who care about both. Next to Joyce, his favorite literary subject is Shakespeare, about whom Burgess has written a biography and a novel (pastiching Elizabethan style), *Nothing Like the Sun*. Shakespearean scholar Paley visits a paralled Earth's Renaissance England in "The Muse," to prove that actor didn't write those plays. Hallucination, if not madness, awaits him, while the plays he, like previous visitors, has brought with him are taken by

Shakespeare to revise for performance in his own time. No serious accounting for that "impossible" genius, this jape subjugates scientific theory and technologcal practice to surrealistic effects and extravagant fantasy.

A considerably longer "entertainment," *The End of the World News* interweaves three plots and sets of characters with the theme of facing catastrophic change. Parallelling a novelistic life of Freud and a Brechtian musical comedy about Trotsky in New York is that staple of British science fiction, a disaster story, involving the approach to and later collision with Earth of the new planet Lynx, and the escape of a chosen remnant of humanity. Not everyone who knows the worst wants to escape; a Falstaffian actor drinks life to the dregs, almost taking with him a professor of English whose specialty is science fiction. But half the fun lies in the stories' point and counterpoint, and their all but incomprehensible nature to their audience, generations later, in the spaceship that is now their home. If that convention is old, even hoarier is the outer narrative frame of a trusted editor offering an author's posthumous fragments to his cynical contemporaries. It is as if Burgess did not trust today's readers, let alone posterity, to get the joke, or as if he himself did not know how seriously to take it.

On balance, Burgess's science fiction lacks verisimilitude and extrapolative exactness, and suffers from obsession with a single theme. But his fables are prophetic in an Old Testament way, and his accomplishments with style and invention dwarf those of many other writers' lifelong careers.

—David N. Samuelson

BURKE, Ralph. See **GARRETT, Randall.**

BURROUGHS, Edgar Rice. Also wrote as John Tyler McCulloch. American. Born in Chicago, Illinois, 1 September 1875. Educated at the Harvard School, Chicago, 1888-91; Phillips Academy, Andover, Massachusetts, 1891-92; Michigan Military Academy, Orchard Lake, 1892-95. Served in the United States 7th Cavalry, 1896-97; Illinois Reserve Militia, 1918-19. Married 1) Emma Centennia Hulbert in 1900 (divorced, 1934), two sons and one daughter; 2) Florence Dearholt in 1935 (divorced, 1942). Instructor and Assistant Commandant, Michigan Military Academy, 1895-96; owner of a stationery store, Pocatello, Idaho, 1898; worked in his father's American Battery Company, Chicago, 1899-1903; joined his brother's Sweetser-Burroughs Mining Company, Idaho, 1903-04; railroad policeman, Oregon Short Line Railroad Company, Salt Lake City, 1904; Manager of the Stenographic Department, Sears Roebuck and Company, Chicago, 1906-08; Partner, Burroughs and Dentzer, advertising contractors, Chicago, 1908-09; Office Manager, Physicians Co-Operative Association, Chicago, 1909; Partner, State-Burroughs Company, salesmanship firm, Chicago, 1909; worked for Champlain Yardley Company, stationers, Chicago, 1910-11; Manager, System Service Bureau, Chicago, 1912-13; free-lance writer after 1913; formed Edgar Rice Burroughs, Inc., publishers, 1913, Burroughs-Tarzan Enterprises, 1934-39, and Burroughs-Tarzan Pictures, 1934-37; lived in California after 1919; Mayor of Malibu Beach, 1933; also

United Press Correspondent in the Pacific during World War II, and Columnist ("Laugh It Off"), *Honolulu Advertiser*, 1941-42, 1945. *Died 19 March 1950.*

<small>SCIENCE-FICTION PUBLICATIONS</small>

Novels (series: Mars; Pellucidar; Venus)

A Princess of Mars. Chicago, McClurg, 1917; London, Methuen, 1919.
The Gods of Mars. Chicago, McClurg, 1918; London, Methuen, 1920.
The Warlord of Mars. Chicago, McClurg, 1919; London, Methuen, 1920.
Thuvia, Maid of Mars. Chicago, McClurg, 1920; London, Methuen, 1921.
The Chessmen of Mars. Chicago, McClurg, 1922; London, Methuen, 1923.
At the Earth's Core (Pellucidar). Chicago, McClurg, 1922; London, Methuen, 1923.
Pellucidar. Chicago, McClurg, 1923; London, Methuen, 1924.
The Master Mind of Mars. Chicago, McClurg, 1928; London, Methuen, 1939.
The Monster Men . Chicago, McClurg, 1929.
Tarzan at the Earth's Core (Pellucidar). New York, Metropolitan, 1930; London, Methuen, 1938.
Tanar of Pellucidar. New York, Metropolitan, 1930; London, Methuen, 1939.
A Fighting Man of Mars. New York, Metropolitan, 1931; London, Lane, 1932.
Jungle Girl. Tarzana, California, Burroughs, 1932; London, Odhams Press, 1933; as *The Land of Hidden Men*, New York, Ace, 1963.
Pirates of Venus. Tarzana, California, Burroughs, 1934; London, Lane, 1935.
Lost on Venus. Tarzana, California, Burroughs, 1935; London, Methuen, 1937.
Swords of Mars. Tarzana, California, Burroughs, 1936; London, New English Library, 1966.
Back to the Stone Age (Pellucidar). Tarzana, California, Burroughs, 1937.
Carson of Venus. Tarzana, California, Burroughs, 1939; London, Goulden, 1950.
Synthetic Men of Mars. Tarzana, California, Burroughs, 1940; London, Methuen, 1941.
Land of Terror (Pellucidar). Tarzana, California, Burroughs, 1944.
Escape on Venus. Tarzana, California, Burroughs, 1946; London, New English Library, 1966.
Beyond the Farthest Star. New York, Ace, 1964.

Short Stories

The Land That Time Forgot. Chicago, McClurg, 1924; London, Methuen, 1925.
The Eternal Lover. Chicago, McClurg, 1925; London, Methuen, 1927; as *The Eternal Savage*, New York, Ace, 1963.
The Cave Girl. Chicago, McClurg, 1925; London, Methuen, 1927.
The Moon Maid. Chicago, McClurg, 1926; London, Stacey, 1972; abridged edition, as *The Moon Men*, New York, Canaveral Press, 1962; augmented edition, London, Tandem, 1975.
Llana of Gathol. Tarzana, California, Burroughs, 1948; London, New English Library, 1967.

Beyond Thirty. Privately printed, 1955; as *The Lost Continent*, New York, Ace, 1963.

The Man-Eater. Privately printed, 1955.

Savage Pellucidar. New York, Canaveral Press, 1963.

Tales of Three Planets. New York, Canaveral Press, 1964.

John Carter of Mars . New York, Canaveral Press, 1964.

The Wizard of Venus. New York, Ace, 1970.

OTHER PUBLICATIONS

Novels

Tarzan of the Apes. Chicago, McClurg, 1914; London, Methuen, 1917.

The Return of Tarzan. Chicago, McClurg, 1915; London, Methuen, 1918.

The Beasts of Tarzan. Chicago, McClurg, 1916; London, Methuen, 1918.

The Son of Tarzan. Chicago, McClurg, 1917; London, Methuen, 1919.

Tarzan and the Jewels of Opar. Chicago, McClurg, 1918; London, Methuen, 1919.

Tarzan the Terrible. Chicago, McClurg, and London, Methuen, 1921.

Tarzan and the Golden Lion. Chicago, McClurg, 1923; London, Methuen, 1924.

The Girl from Hollywood. New York, Macaulay, 1923; London, Methuen, 1924.

Tarzan and the Ant Men. Chicago, McClurg, 1924; London, Methuen, 1925.

The Bandit of Hell's Bend. Chicago, McClurg, 1925; London, Methuen, 1926.

The Tarzan Twins (for children). Joliet, Illinois, Volland, 1927; London, Collins, 1930.

The Outlaw of Torn. Chicago, McClurg, and London, Methuen, 1927.

The War Chief. Chicago, McClurg, 1927; London, Methuen, 1928.

Tarzan, Lord of the Jungle. Chicago, McClurg, and London, Cassell, 1928.

Tarzan and the Lost Empire. New York, Metropolitan, 1929; London, Cassell, 1931.

Tarzan the Invincible. Tarzana, California, Burroughs, 1931; London, Lane, 1933.

Tarzan Triumphant. Tarzana, California, Burroughs, 1931; London, Lane, 1933.

Tarzan and the City of Gold. Tarzana, California, Burroughs, 1933; London, Lane, 1936.

Apache Devil. Tarzana, California, Burroughs, 1933.

Tarzan and the Lion-Man. Tarzana, California, Burroughs, 1934; London, W. H. Allen, 1950.

Tarzan and the Leopard Men. Tarzana, California, Burroughs, 1935; London, Lane, 1936.

Tarzan and the Tarzan Twins, with Jad-Bal-Ja, The Golden Lion (for children). Racine, Wisconsin, Whitman, 1936.

Tarzan's Quest. Tarzana, California, Burroughs, 1936; London, Methuen, 1938.

The Oakdale Affair; The Rider. Tarzana, California, Burroughs, 1937.

Tarzan and the Forbidden City. Tarzana, California, Burroughs, 1938; London, W. H. Allen, 1950.

The Lad and the Lion. Tarzana, California, Burroughs, 1938.

The Deputy Sheriff on Comanche County. Tarzana, California, Burroughs, 1940.

Tarzan and the Foreign Legion. Tarzana, California, Burroughs, 1947; London, W. H. Allen, 1949.

Tarzan and the Madman. New York, Canaveral Press, 1964; London, New English Library, 1966.

The Girl from Farris's. Kansas City, Missouri, House of Greystoke, 1965.

The Efficiency Expert. Kansas City, Missouri, House of Greystoke, 1966.

I Am a Barbarian. Tarzana, California, Burroughs, 1967.

Pirate Blood (as John Tyler McCulloch). New York, Ace, 1970.

Short Stories

Jungle Tales of Tarzan. Chicago, McClurg, and London, Methuen, 1919.

Tarzan the Untamed. Chicago, McClurg, and London, Methuen, 1920.

The Mucker . Chicago, McClurg, 1921; as The Mucker and *The Man Without a Soul*, London, Methuen, 2 vols., 1921-22.

The Mad King. Chicago, McClurg, 1926.

Tarzan the Magnificent. Tarzana, California, Burroughs, 1939; London, Methuen, 1940.

Tarzan and the Castaways. New York, Canaveral Press, 1964; London, New English Library, 1966.

Other

Official Guide of the Tarzan Clans of America. Privately printed, 1939.

*

Critical Studies: *Edgar Rice Burroughs, Master of Adventure* by Richard A. Lupoff, New York, Canaveral Press, 1965, revised edition, New York, Ace, 1968; *Tarzan Alive: A Definitive Biography of Lord Greystoke* by Philip José Farmer, New York, Doubleday, 1972, London, Panther, 1974; *Burroughs' Science Fiction* by Robert R. Kudlay and Joan Leiby, Geneseo, New York, School of Library and Information Science, 1973; *Edgar Rice Burroughs, The Man Who Created Tarzan* (includes bibliography) by Irwin Porges, Provo, Utah, Brigham Young University Press, 1975, London, New English Library, 1976; *A Guide to Barsoom* by John Flint Roy, New York, Ballantine, 1976; *The Burroughs Bestiary: An Encyclopaedia of Monsters and Imaginary Beings Created by Edgar Rice Burroughs* by David Day, London, New English Library, 1978; *Tarzan and Tradition: Classical Myth in Popular Literature* by Erling B. Holtsmark, Westport, Connecticut, Greenwood Press, 1981.

*   *   *

While best known for his long series of jungle adventure tales featuring the character Tarzan, both in their original prose form and in uncounted motion pictures, television series, comic strips, and other adaptations, Edgar Rice Burroughs was in fact a very important and very popular science-fiction writer. In a lifetime output of more than 70 books, essentially equal numbers were devoted to jungle adventures and to science fiction. Burroughs's remaining output was widely distributed among westerns, Graustarkian romances, historical novels, and a few decidedly unsuccessful attempts at contemporary realism. The last group, most notably *The Girl from Hollywood*, are of interest for their autobiographical content. As a science-fiction writer Burroughs may be regarded as a descendant of Verne. His emphasis was on wonders: wonderful planets, strange creatures, magnificiently melodramatic plots. Burroughs was himself of plebeian origins, but his works more often display a bias in favor of aristocracy. His heroes are generally noblemen and/or wealthy, e. g., Lord Greystoke (Tarzan), John Carter (Confederate cavalry captain and plantation owner), David Innes (scion of Connecticut gentry). His heroines are often princesses, most notably Dejah Thoris, eventual consort of John Carter. (Exceptions include the hoodlum hero of *The Mucker* and the prostitute heroine *The Girl from Farris's*.)

It is important to note that Burroughs was not a significant creator in his writing, but rather was a synthesist of immeasurable natural talent. Every major theme in Burroughs's fantastic fiction (i. e., science fiction and jungle adventures) was anticipated in earlier works. Burroughs's genius lay in his ability to invest familar material with such energy that it attained new heights of popularity. He did not invent the feral-man novel, the hollow-earth novel, the interplanetary romance, or any other significant fantastic form. He *did* write some of the most successful, most completely developed, most colorful, energetic, and suspenseful examples of each. Burroughs's science fiction divides into three major series, one minor series, and several independent works, two of which are of major importance.

Burroughs's literary career began, at least as far as published fiction is concerned, with the first of his interplanetary romances, *A Princess of Mars*. This novel and its sequels concern an earthly hero of somewhat equivocal and mysterious immortality who is transferred to Mars by a means that suggests astral projection. On Mars ("Barsoom") the hero discovers a dying world containing an ancient, decadent civilization, roving nomadic tribes, and a complex mixture of races, species, and traditions. Through a series of some 11 volumes John Carter rises to the supreme Warlordship of Barsoom, marries the incomparably beautiful red-skinned Princess Dejah Thoris (who lays eggs but is otherwise wholly human), becomes a father and grandfather, travels extensively upon Barsoom, visits one of its moons, and ultimately journeys to the planet Jupiter. There he presumably remains (he was in the midst of an uncompleted adventure when Burroughs died). While some of Burroughs's more ardent admirers consider Barsoom and all its associated material a brilliantly original creation, it was in fact the very opposite. The character of John Carter is virtually identical to that of Phra the Phoenician, while the basic rationale of Barsoomian history and culture closely resembles that of the planet Mars in a book called *Lieut. Gullivar Jones: His Vacation*; both books are by Edwin Lester Arnold. More of the Barsoomian culture and many of the plotting devices used by Burroughs appear in *Journey to Mars* by Gustavus Pope, in *Across the Zodiac* by Percy Greg, and even in some of the strange Theosophical teachings of Helena Blavatsky (as pointed out by L. Sprague de Camp). And the dueling, kidnapping, impersonating, court-intrigue ridden Barsoomian society, possibly borrowed from Pope, in itself is more than suggestively reminiscent of the court at Zenda as recorded by Anthony Hope, who might well have borrowed from Mark Twain!

Burroughs's second most significant science-fiction series was the Pellucidar books, beginning with *At the Earth's Core*. While the later books of this series are of inferior quality, the first two or three are among Burroughs's best work. Here the essential notion is that of an earth-boring machine accidentally breaking through the planet's crust to discover that the earth is hollow, illuminated by a miniature interior sun, and inhabited by a wide variety of species including primitive humans and paleontological survivals. Once again, elements derive from numerous earlier works, certainly including Holberg's *Nils Klim* and Verne's *Journey to the Center of the Earth*, and very likely (the name itself is suggestive) Bradshaw's *The Goddess of*

Atvatabar. While the Pellucidar series does let down in quality, it contains numerous fascinating features. One of these is a speculation—this one more likely original to Burroughs—on the nature of time and the timeless condition of a world of eternal daylight. There is considerable humorous and satirical material in the books. Also of interest is the so-called "series cross-over" volume, *Tarzan at the Earth's Core*, in which the two separately created universes of Tarzan's jungle world and the hollow earth, are merged—or at least, one may say, their separation is bridged via dirigible.

Burroughs's final science-fiction series details the adventures of Carson Napier on Venus. The books of this sequence date from late in Burroughs's career and are derivative of his Martian cycle without ever quite duplicating its spirit. There is also a degree of likelihood that the Venus books were written to strike back at Otis Adelbert Kline, who had written a series of interplanetary romances laid on Venus, under heavy influence of Burroughs's Martian cycle. (This theory is advanced by Sam Moskowitz, and is circumstantially persuasive although unfortunately is in no way documented.)

The Land That Time Forgot is one of Burroughs's major non-series science-fiction works (in some editions it is divided into three very slim volumes, corresponding with its original magazine serialization, and is consequently regarded as a small series itself). Opening with a sequence of submarine warfare in the first World War, the action quickly shifts to the island of Caspak (also known as Caprona), a place remarkably reminiscent of both Verne's *Mysterious Island* and Peter Wilkins's island retreat in the novel of Robert Paltock. There follow numerous incidents involving primitive and violent life-forms, intriguing speculation on evolutionary processes, and a final confrontation with a chilling post-human winged form (again reminiscent of Paltock). The paleontological elements in this book, like those in Burroughs's hollow-earth novels, are remarkably detailed and authentic. They derive from Burroughs's involvement with the subject at first as a student and later as an instructor at the Michigan Military Academy.

The Moon Maid, Burroughs's second major independent science-fiction work, is also divisible into three more-or-less self-sustained segments. It ties into Burroughs's Martian cycle, as a spaceship named *Barsoom* travels from the earth to the moon. The moon is found to be hollow and inhabited, with access to the inner regions obtained through lunar craters. All of this, of course, is strangely like the moon of Wells's *The First Men in the Moon*. In later sequences, using technology introduced from the earth, lunar forces invade and conquer our planet. At this point Burroughs's novel turns into a saga spaced over many generations. Burroughs handled the challenges of the form astonishingly well, and *The Moon Maid* is one of his most successful works.

His other books of science fiction have received relatively little attention. *The Monster Men* is a charmingly creaky cross of jungle adventure, desert island romance, mad scientist, and *Frankenstein*-monster plots. This last element occurs also in several of Burroughs's Martian novels, most notably *Master Mind of Mars* and *Synthetic Men of Mars*. *Beyond Thirty* is a surprisingly effective story of a future war-torn Europe reverting to barbarism—anticipating L. Ron Hubbard's *Final Blackout*.

Burroughs's Tarzan stories and other jungle adventures, while not essentially works of science fiction, contain many elements derived from science fiction and allied forms. After feralism itself, the next most common theme in the books is that of the lost race, tribe, city, or country. These are handled well if somewhat repetitiously by Burroughs; it should be noted that this form of adventure writing was perfected by Haggard, whose works seem likely to have influenced Burroughs. The theme of feralism is itself very old in literature and folklore; it was best known prior to the creation of Tarzan in the *Jungle Books* of Kipling. The Tarzan novels also include Atlantean themes, immortality serums, paleontological survivals, at least one city of intelligent gorillas, and at least one satirical novel (*Tarzan and the Ant Men*) apparently based on Swift.

As Burroughs borrowed from many earlier writers, he in turn was read by and influenced uncounted later writers. The briefest smattering of these must include H. P. Lovecraft, Robert E. Howard, Edmond Hamilton, Leigh Brackett, Ray Bradbury, Gore Vidal, and J. R. R. Tolkien. Direct imitators of Burroughs range from his contemporaries J. U. Giesy and William L. Chester, to many present-day writers including Lin Carter, Michael Resnick, Anne McCaffrey, John Norman, and Philip José Farmer. In most cases, where the imitation of Burroughs is very literal the result is a rather lifeless pastiche; where Burroughs's influence is less specific and the later writer uses Burroughs as a wellspring of color, verve, and suspense, the result is often admirable.

—Richard A. Lupoff

BURROUGHS, William S(eward). Also wrote as William Lee. American. Born in St. Louis, Missouri, 5 February 1914. Educated at John Burroughs School and Taylor School, St. Louis; Los Alamos Ranch School, New Mexico; Harvard University, Cambridge, Massachusetts, A. B. in anthropology 1936; studied medicine at the University of Vienna; Mexico City College, 1948-50. Served in the United States Army, 1942. Married Jean Vollmer in 1945 (died, 1951); one son. Has worked as a journalist, private detective, and bartender; now a full-time writer. Heroin addict, 1944-57. Recipient: American Academy Award, 1975. Member, American Academy, 1983. Lived for many years in Tangier; now lives in New York City. Agent: Andrew Wylie Agency, 250 West 57th Street, New York, New York 10107, U. S. A.

SCIENCE-FICTION PUBLICATIONS

Novels

The Naked Lunch. Paris, Olympia Press, 1959; London, Calder, 1964; as *Naked Lunch,* New York, Grove Press, 1962.
The Soft Machine. Paris, Olympia Press, 1961; New York, Grove Press, 1966; London, Calder and Boyars, 1968.
The Ticket That Exploded. Paris, Olympia Press, 1962; revised edition, New York, Grove Press, 1967; London, Calder and Boyars, 1968.
Nova Express. New York, Grove Press, 1964; London, Cape, 1966.
The Wild Boys: A Book of the Dead. New York, Grove Press, 1971; London, Calder and Boyars, 1972; revised edition, London, Calder, 1979.
Exterminator! New York, Viking Press, 1973; London, Calder and Boyars, 1974.
Cities of the Red Night: A Boy's Book. London, Calder, and New York, Holt Rinehart, 1981.

OTHER PUBLICATIONS

Novels

Junkie: Confessions of an Unredeemed Drug Addict (as William Lee). New York, Ace, 1953; London, Digit, 1957; complete edition, London, Penguin, 1977.
Dead Fingers Talk. London, Calder, 1963.
Short Novels. London, Calder, 1978.
Blade Runner: A Movie. Berkeley, California, Blue Wind Press, 1979.
Port of Saints. Berkeley, California, Blue Wind Press, 1980; London, Calder, 1983.
The Place of Dead Roads. New York, Holt Rinehart, 1983; London, Calder, 1984.

Short Stories

Early Routines. Santa Barbara, California, Cadmus, 1981.

Play

The Last Words of Dutch Schultz. London, Cape Goliard Press, 1970; New York, Viking Press, 1975.

Other

The Exterminator, with Brion Gysin. San Francisco, Auerhahn Press, 1960.
Minutes to Go, with others. Paris, Two Cities, 1960; San Francisco, Beach, 1968.
The Yage Letters, with Allen Ginsberg. San Francisco, City Lights, 1963.
Roosevelt after Inauguration. New York, Fuck You Press, 1964.
Valentine Day's Reading. New York, American Theatre for Poets, 1965.
"The Hallucinatory Operators Are Real," in *SF Horizons 2* (London), 1965.
Time. New York, "C" Press, 1965.
Health Bulletin: APO-33: A Metabolic Regulator. New York, Fuck You Press, 1965; revised edition, as *APO—33 Bulletin,* San Francisco, Beach, 1966.
So Who Owns Death TV?, with Claude Pelieu and Carl Weissner. San Francisco, Beach, 1967.
The Dead Star. San Francisco, Nova Broadcast Press, 1969.
Ali's Smile. Brighton, Unicorn, 1969.
Entretiens avec William Burroughs, by Daniel Odier. Paris, Belfond, 1969; translated as *The Job: Interviews with William S. Burroughs* (includes *Electronic Revolution*), New York, Grove Press, and London, Cape, 1970.
The Braille Film. San Francisco, Nova Broadcast Press, 1970.
Preface to *Love and Napalm: Export U. S. A.,* by J. G. Ballard. New York, Grove Press, 1972.
Brion Gysin Let the Mice In, with Brion Gysin and Ian Somerville, edited by Jan Herman. West Glover, Vermont, Something Else Press, 1973.
Mayfair Academy Series More or Less. Brighton, Urgency Press Rip-Off, 1973.
White Subway, edited by James Pennington. London, Aloes, 1974.
The Book of Breeething. Ingatestone, Essex, OU Press, 1974; Berkeley, California, Blue Wind Press, 1975; revised edition, Blue Wind Press, 1980.
Snack: Two Tape Transcripts, with Eric Mottram. London, Aloes, 1975.

Sidetripping, with Charles Gatewood. New York, Strawberry Hill, 1975.
The Retreat Diaries. New York, City Moon, 1976.
Cobble Stone Gardens. Cherry Valley, New York, Cherry Valley Editions, 1976.
The Third Mind, with Brion Gysin. New York, Viking Press, 1978; London, Calder, 1979.
Roosevelt after Inauguration and Other Atrocities. San Francisco, City Lights, 1979.
Ah Pook Is Here and Other Texts (includes *The Book of Breeething, Electronic Revolution*). London, Calder, 1979; New York, Riverrun, 1982.
A William Burroughs Reader, edited by John Calder. London, Pan, 1982.
Letters to Allen Ginsberg 1953-1957. New York, Full Court Press, 1982.
New York Inside Out, photographs by Robert Walker. Port Washington, New York, Skyline Press, 1984.
The Burroughs File. San Francisco, City Lights, 1984.
The Adding Machine: A Summation of Comments, edited by James Grauerholz. New York, Arbor House, 1985.

*

Bibliography: *William S. Burroughs: An Annotated Bibliography of His Works and Criticism* by Michael B. Goodman, New York, Garland, 1976; *William S. Burroughs: A Bibliography 1953-73* by Joe Maynard and Barry Miles, Charlottesville, University Press of Virginia, 1978.

Critical Studies: *William Burroughs: The Algebra of Need* by Eric Mottram, Buffalo, Intrepid Press, 1971; *Contemporary Literary Censorship: The Case History of Burroughs' Naked Lunch* by Michael B. Goodman, Metuchen, New Jersey, Scarecrow Press, 1981; *With William Burroughs: A Report from the Bunker* edited by Victor Bokris, New York, Seaver, 1981, London, Vermilion, 1982.

*   *   *

Best known as a leader of the American Beat movement, despite the cosmopolitan influences on his work, William S. Burroughs has repeatedly used science-fiction situations and images in his often bizarre novels of protest against social control. Burroughs has been praised as one of a select few major authors writing in English, if not a contemporary genius. However, his frequent opacity seems to have daunted criticism and has led to some cries of exasperation or outrage from critics, such as Martin Seymour-Smith's reference to his "monumental stupidity. " In fact, Burroughs demonstrated his ability to write with conventional intelligence in his first novel, *Junkie*, and has done so again in his recent *Cities of the Red Night*. *Junkie* is an autobiographical confession of a morphine addict—it is also a map of Hell, attacking a spiritless society and its gratuitous abuses of power. Despite the autobiographical element, Burroughs shows a degree of detachment from his narrator, an unsettled picaro who sometimes interprets himself as an idealistic quester.

Burroughs's reputation rests mainly upon the four novels *The Naked Lunch, The Soft Machine, The Ticket That Exploded, and Nova Express*. These form a tetralogy which attacks the obsessive need for control which Burroughs sees as having gripped our planet. That obsession is often given its focus in such science-fiction images as the dystopias and advanced behavioural technologies of *The Naked Lunch*, and the ubiquitous fantasy of metamorphosis into arthropod form to repres-

ent the dehumanization of both controller and controlled. Especially in *The Ticket That Exploded* and *Nova Express*, Burroughs presents the extended metaphor of an invasion by aliens—the Nova Mob—whose members act through and control humans who share their weaknesses and predilections. *The Ticket That Exploded*, the more accessible of these two novels, makes it clear that the aliens are a metaphor for controlling powers on Earth, presented as if they could be only a Manichean force of evil from space.

It would be easy to condemn these novels for their frequent opacity and the paranoid sensibility which they seem to reveal. However, Burroughs does write with admirable confidence, power, and surreal detail; where the prose is readable at all, the phrasing is sharp and the dialogue unsentimentally convincing. The difficulty is that, as Burroughs has admitted in *The Job*, a series of interviews with Daniel Odier, the prose is sometimes "simply not readable. " This is mainly the result of Burroughs's so-called "cut-up" and "fold-in" techniques: the mechanical rearrangement of sliced-up pages and the juxtaposition of words from quite different texts. Both Burroughs's admirers and his detractors have over-emphasized the genesis of the prose in these techniques, rather than the patterns of meaning which (sometimes) result on the page.

Since the publication of *Nova Express*, Burroughs has frequently appeared to be more a sage—an unsystematic philosopher of life—than a creative artist. Unfortunately, he has not been helpful in his role as a sage. A study of his interviews and theoretical works reveals occasional insights hidden amid obsessive and often inhumane pronouncements, such as this, on women: "I think they were a basic mistake, and the whole dualistic universe evolved from this error. "

However, in his most recent major work, *Cities of the Red Night*, Burroughs has recast the vision of his great tetralogy in a form which is creative, lucid, and fascinating. Drawing upon elements of time-travel, space visitation, alternative history, and multiple realities, the book enacts a layered myth or series of myths of the Fall, fragmenting into shards from different realities before ending with a menacing vision of nuclear apocalypse. *Cities of the Red Night* will pay detailed study to crack fully its codes of recurrence and levels of reality.

Of Burroughs's other works since *Nova Express* perhaps the most compelling for science-fiction readers is *The Wild Boys*. This novel begins as a series of linked apocalyptic vignettes which are pulled together as the story emerges of packs of homosexual specialist warriors who are able to outfight conventional armies, and who ravage their near-future world. The book is a projection of the need which Burroughs feels to destroy all present-day institutions, including the family and the national state.

—Russell Blackford

BURTON, Raymond L. See **TUBB, E. C.**

BUSBY, F(rancis) M(arion). American. Born in Indianapolis, Indiana, 11 March 1921. Educated at Washington State University, Pullman, B. Sc. 1946, B. Sc. E. E. 1947. Served in the National Guard, 1940-41, and United States Army, 1943-

45. Married Elinor Doub in 1954; one daughter. Project supervisor, Alaska Communication System, Seattle, 1947-53; telegraph engineer, 1953-70. Since 1970, free-lance writer. Recipient: Hugo Award, for editing, 1960. Address: 2852 14th Avenue West, Seattle, Washington 98119, U. S. A.

SCIENCE-FICTION PUBLICATIONS

Novels (series: Barton; Rissa)

Cage a Man (Barton). New York, Doubleday, 1973; London, Hamlyn, 1979.
The Proud Enemy (Barton). New York, Berkley, 1975; London, Hamlyn, 1982.
Rissa Kerguelen. New York, Berkley, 1976; revised edition, as *Young Rissa, Rissa and Tregare, The Long View*, New York, Berkley, 3 vols., 1984.
The Long View (Rissa). New York, Berkley, 1976.
Rissa Kerguelen (omnibus). New York, Berkley, 1977.
All These Earths. New York, Berkley, 1978.
Zelde M'Tana (Rissa). New York, Dell, 1980.
The Demu Trilogy (*Cage a Man, The Proud Enemy, End of the Line*) (Barton). New York, Pocket Books, 1980.
The Alien Debt (Rissa). New York, Bantam, 1984.
Star Rebel (Rissa). New York, Bantam, 1984.
Rebel's Quest (Rissa). New York, Bantam, 1985.

Uncollected Short Stories

"A Gun for Grandfather," in *Future* (New York), Fall 1957.
"Here, There, and Everywhere," in *Clarion 2*, edited by Robin Scott Wilson. New York, New American Library, 1972.
"Of Mice and Otis," in *Amazing* (New York), March 1972.
"The Puiss of Krrlik," in *Fantastic* (New York), April 1972.
"The Real World," in *Fantastic* (New York), December 1972.
"Play It Again Sam," and "Road Map," in *Clarion 3*, edited by Robin Scott Wilson. New York, New American Library, 1973.
"Tell Me All about Yourself," in *New Dimensions 3*, edited by Robert Silverberg. New York, Avon, 1973.
"Once upon a Unicorn," in *Fantastic* (New York), April 1973.
"2000½: A Spaced Oddity," in *Vertex* (Los Angeles), August 1973.
"Pearsall's Return," in *If* (New York), August 1973.
"The Learning of Eeshta," in *If* (New York), October 1973.
"If This Is Winnetka, You Must Be Judy," in *Universe 5*, edited by Terry Carr. New York, Random House, 1974; London, Dobson, 1978.
"What Was That?," in *Amazing* (New York), April 1974.
"Getting Home," in *Fantasy and Science Fiction* (New York), April 1974.
"Time of Need," in *Vertex* (Los Angeles), August 1974.
"Collateral," in *Vertex* (Los Angeles), August 1974.
"Retroflex," in *Vertex* (Los Angeles), October 1974.
"Misconception," in *Vertex* (Los Angeles), April 1975.
"The Signing of Tulip," in *Vertex* (Los Angeles), June 1975.
"Advantage," in *Vertex* (Los Angeles), August 1975.
"Search," in *Amazing* (New York), December 1976.
"From Competition 8: Near-Miss SF Titles," in *The Best from Fantasy and Science Fiction 22*, edited by Edward L. Ferman. New York, Dell, 1977.
"Backspace," in *Asimov's Choice: Black Holes and Bug-Eyed Monsters*, edited by George H. Scithers. New York, Davis, 1977.
"Nobody Home," in *Amazing* (New York), July 1977.

"Never So Lost," in *Amazing* (New York), October 1977.
"I'm Going to Get You," in *100 Great Science Fiction Short-Short Stories*, edited by Isaac Asimov, Martin H. Greenberg, and Joseph D. Olander. New York, Doubleday, and London, Robson, 1978.
"Come to the Party," with Frank Herbert, in *The 1979 Annual World's Best SF*, edited by Donald A. Wollheim. New York, DAW, 1979.
"Proof," in *Microcosmic Tales*, edited by Isaac Asimov, Martin H. Greenberg, and Joseph D. Olander. New York, Taplinger, 1980.
"Three Tinks of the House," in *Dream's Edge*, edited by Terry Carr. San Francisco, Sierra Club, 1980.
"First Person Plural," in *Universe 10*, edited by Terry Carr. New York, Doubleday, 1980.
"For a Daughter," in *Amazons 2*, edited by Jessica Amanda Salmonson. New York, DAW, 1980.
"Balancing Act," in *Isaac Asimov's Science Fiction Magazine* (New York), 26 February 1981.
"Backup System," in *Isaac Asimov's Science Fiction Magazine* (New York), 26 October 1981.
"Wrong Number," in *Isaac Asimov's Science Fiction Magazine* (New York), 21 December 1981.
"Dibs on Earth," in *Fifty Extremely SF Stories*, edited by Michael Bastraw. Center Harbor, New Hampshire, Niekas, 1982.
"Stormer," in *Rigel* (Richmond, California), Winter 1982.
"Before the Seas Came," in *Heroic Visions*, edited by Jessica Amanda Salmonson. New York, Ace, 1983.

*

F. M. Busby comments:
I like to write science fiction because it gives me more room to breathe.

* * *

F. M. Busby deals with "characters who are pushed hard by necessity and who generally manage to cope," or he puts his characters into 'predicaments that could not exist in our own past and future.'

In novels such as *Rissa Kerguelen*, Busby develops the theme of identity, with convincing detail, ironic and comic touches, and a quality of space opera and adventure. In Busby, it is man (and woman) against the establishment, identity versus those who would seek to assimilate the individual. He writes of "rebels who find themselves"—dissidents and outlaws on their escape ships and hidden worlds.

Busby taps a rich mine of science fiction: parthenogenesis, Total Warfare Centers, maltreated aliens, "ships that come from nothing," telepathic murders, time-warped drives are all persuasively and painstakingly described.

He explores the motif of the self as well as any writer in the genre, often using nakedness as a symbol of a character's quest for self-discovery. Barton, in *The Demu Trilogy*, is a caged prisoner of crustacean creatures who attempt to rob humans of their own identities and re-create them in their own self-images. Busby investigates the motives of his characters, who plot for revenge and heroism and revel in the pleasure of that revenge and their own self-survival. Survival is a theme as important as identity in Busby's fiction; the two, in fact, are linked.

Three novels that deal with Bran Tregare (before he meets Rissa, *Star Rebel* and *Rebel's Quest*, and their later adventure of primitive survival, *The Alien Debt*) pursue these themes in greater detail. In Bran, Busby depicts a protagonist who rises above circumstance to sacrifice his own humanity for the good of humanity, though the reader sympathizes with Bran's pursuits and paradoxes. Bran does things that others cannot live with, but he is a person who also knows that "sometimes to survive you have to become a monster." He eventually achieves his goal (defeat of UET) and regains his identity through his love for Rissa and their daughter Lisele. Rissa, strong and stable, similarly wonders about her own identity, as someone who can turn from gentleness and love to ruthlessness and sadism. She comes in time to redress her problems and to understand how her life "was still beginning."

While Busby continued his Hulzein saga with *All These Worlds* and *Zelde M'Tana*, his short fiction remains most impressive.

"Tell Me All about Yourself," for example, is a bitter-sweet story about a lonely man's experience in a Necro house in Japan. The purpose of the place, supposedly, is that you do not have to talk to the women, but Dale selects a superlatively preserved virgin corpse whom he would actually like to get to know, someone, it seems, he had always been looking for. He feels foolish talking to the girl, so he steals her and casts her off to sea in a blaze, toward a death with dignity. Her only response to him had been a ubiquitous smile. Busby understates the macabre brilliantly in this story about the need for communication in love.

"If This Is Winnetka, You Must Be Judy," is a fascinating story, almost a spinoff of Heinlein's "All You Zombies—." The story deals with Larry Garth's ability to wake up periodically into a different time zone in his life. Busby gains a perfect sense of verisimilitude, with casual references to "circular causation," "research into the parameters of now," and "infancy skips." When we meet Garth, he has no idea how much of his existence had been lived "back and forth in bits and pieces." Busby uses this zig-zag experience as its own metaphor, set up against those of us who live "solely from one view that plod[s] along a line and [sees] only one consecutive past."

"First Person Plural" employs a similar conceit. Ed Carlain awakens to discover he has undergone a consciousness transfer with a once-comatose Melanie Blake. Despite a sense of loss, Ed and Melanie come together to cope with their incongruities: "she was himself, one day behind himself." The two must share their lives with "one . . . memory between them." But the idea of confused sexual identity reveals the overall theme Busby wishes to convey: "If I can't accept ME, I can never accept any man."

—Richard Orodenker

BUTLER, Octavia E(stelle). American. Born in Pasadena, California, 22 June 1947. Educated at Pasadena College, 1965-68, A. A. 1968; California State University, 1969. Since 1970, free-lance writer. Recipient: Hugo Award, 1984: Nebula Award, 1985. Address: c/o St. Martin's Press, 175 Fifth Avenue, New York, New York 10010, U. S. A.

SCIENCE-FICTION PUBLICATIONS

Novels (series: Patternists in all books except *Kindred*)

Patternmaster. New York, Doubleday, 1976; London, Sphere, 1978.

Mind of My Mind. New York, Doubleday, 1977; London, Sidgwick and Jackson, 1978.
Survivor. New York, Doubleday, and London, Sidgwick and Jackson, 1978.
Kindred, New York, Doubleday, 1979.
Wild Seed. New York, Doubleday, and London, Sidgwick and Jackson, 1980.
Clay's Ark. New York, St. Martin's Press, 1984.

Uncollected Short Stories

"Crossover," in *Clarion*, edited by Robin Scott Wilson. New York, New American Library, 1971.
"Near of Kin," in *Chrysalis 4*, edited by Roy Torgeson. New York, Kensington, 1979.
"Speech Sounds," in *Isaac Asimov's Science Fiction Magazine* (New York), 2 December 1983.
"Bloodchild," in *Isaac Asimov's Science Fiction Magazine* (New York), June 1984.

*

Octavia E. Butler comments:

I began writing fantasy and science fiction because these seemed to be the genres in which I could be freest, most creative. I had in mind from my first novel a series, a fictional history of people called Patternists who are, by mutation and selective breeding, developing psionic abilities. The books of this series are, in the order of the events they cover, *Wild Seed*, which begins in 1690, *Mind of My Mind* (present-day), *Survivor* (near future), and *Patternmaster* (distant future). The books are stories of power—adjustment to power, struggle for power, corruption by power. I bring together multi-racial groups of men and women who must cope with one another's differences as well as with new, not necessarily controllable, abilities within themselves.

A non-Patternist novel, *Kindred*, tells the story of a young black woman of the 1970's who is shifted back in time to the ante-bellum South where she is enslaved and forced to fend for herself in a world almost as hostile and alien to her as another planet.

* * *

In her novels Octavia E. Butler creates a future history, beginning in 1690, focusing on the present and the creation of a patternist society, then moving to the future in *Patternmaster, Survivor*, and *Clay's Ark*. Although she has developed into a first-rate short-story writer and written a non-patternist novel, *Kindred*, which puts a strong modern woman back into a time when her race and intelligence make her a threat to society, Butler's uniqueness in SF is the concept of the bonding of people with para-normal abilities into a society apart from others. Her work develops the ideas of Theodore Sturgeon's classic *More Than Human*. As well as being an inventive story-teller, she is a writer with messages. Consistently her books attack racism, sexism, hypocricy, and class divisions. Though she keeps strong black women center stage, Butler handles interactions of a large cast deftly.

Within the context of Butler's work *Wild Seed* is chronologically first in the Patternist series, explaining how Doro accumulates his breeding stock. For centuries, before Christ, Doro searched for people with mental gifts like his own. When in 1690 he finds a 300-year-old woman who can assume any form she wishes by manipulating DNA, he humiliates her and manoeuvres her to produce special children. Her assertiveness makes her his favorite and confidante. At Anyanwu's death, Doro links with her—the first time he has used his mental power without killing the other person. This technique enables Mary to create the eventual pattern.

While telepathic powers are common in SF, a society of linked telepaths controlled by the most powerful of them is not. Patternmaster's vagueness is clarified in *Mind of My Mind*, which tells of the dynasty's founding in Forsythe, California. Doro's grand plan succeeds in his daughter Mary. References to Los Angeles, child-beating, shop-lifting, revivals, and everyday names like Rachel, Jon, and Karl indicate the present. The prologue breaks the commonplace by the simple statement that Doro (an uncommon name) was wearing a new body. Until her transition from latent to active, Mary is a disturbed, sullen slum child. Just before she reaches full power, Doro marries her to a wealthy telepath, Karl Larkin, just as he had found the right mate for Anyanwu. At first antipathetic, they form a strong attachment and become the "First Family" after Mary gathers such diverse telepaths as healer, artist, and teacher, who have led unhappy lives. She forms potential enemies into a pattern of minds attached to hers like threads. Before long they have rescued latents from squalor, crime, and death, making them a Southern California network of 15,000. Mary fights Doro to win independence for her people.

Mind of My Mind is a sort of companion to the other books. The art practiced by Amber in *Patternmaster* grows from Rachel's faith-healing. The system of arranging patternists into separate houses with the Patternmaster based in Forsythe emerges. Why brothers and lovers kill each other becomes apparent. The use of "mutes," non-telepaths, as servants and the code of honor that prevents their mistreatment develops as a correction of the latent's tendency to maim or kill inferiors. Although the other books can be read separately, this book shows how the society is established and run.

Patternmaster leads toward the inevitable duel of Teray and Coransee to determine their father's successor told in a bare, straightforward narrative. Mary's pattern has developed so that there are housemasters controlled by a Patternmaster. Low-level paternists manage mutes, and healers repair mental and physical damage. The young mature in schools, and after transition are attached to housemasters, learning skills, or become outsiders, remaining inferiors. The enemy Clayarks are mutants with lion-like bodies and human heads. They use rifles and protective gloves, speak, and capture mutes. Their hatred leads to Rayal's death from the incurable disease they are driven to transmit, a result of organisms the starship *Clay's Ark* brought to Earth. The plot is remarkably like *As You Like It* in conflict, escape from society, and the dynamic heroine. Its conclusion suggests a renewal of society through the union of patternists who show concern even for Clayarks.

Survivor deals with mutes whose goal is to spread the concept of normal man's superiority through the universe. Encountering people who communicate not only verbally but through changing the color of their fur, they misjudge them. Soon they are dominated by the Garkohn, who enslave them with the drug meklah. Before being adopted by the missionary leader, the Afro-Asian Alanna lived off the land as a wild human. When captured by the enemy Tekohn, she alone survives withdrawal from meklah. In fact, Alanna adapts so well that she becomes an honored hunter and wife of their highest judge. Returning to the missionaries, she and her husband help them to freedom. Ironically, the missionaries seeking freedom from patternists and Clayarks find themselves dominated by the so-called animals they had hoped to enslave. Prejudice endangers survival. Because she is willing to change, Alanna is a survivor, enduring through trial as the patternists have to survive

transition to achieve greatness.

Clay's Ark explains the origin of the feared Clayarks, the patternists' chief antagonists. The society of the near future seems to be based on the Mad Max films, with people living like scavangers in a violent world. As they cross the California desert, Dr. Maslin and his twin daughters are kidnapped to become part of a commune of victims of a parasitic life form that weakens and strengthens its hosts. The "monsters" emerge as more humane than the perverted normal specimens left in the society. As in much of Butler's work the time and point of view shift so that the novel fits together like a colorful jigsaw puzzle in a plain box.

Butler's work is thought-provoking, suspenseful, exciting, and internally consistent as she continues to develop her special future. She has created a world of her own while being contemporary in choice of themes, protests, and in her use of strong, admirable women and minority characters. Already her books have the depths of classics.

—Mary S. Weinkauf

BUTLER, Samuel. Also wrote as Cellarius. British. Born at Langar Rectory, near Bingham, Nottinghamshire, 4 December 1835. Educated at Shrewsbury School, Shropshire, 1848-54; St. John's College, Cambridge 1854-58, B. A. (honours) 1858; studied painting at Heatherley's School, London, 1865. Sheep farmer, Rangitata district, New Zealand, 1859-64; settled in London, 1864; exhibited and composed music. *Died 18 June 1902.*

SCIENCE-FICTION PUBLICATIONS

Novels

Erewhon; or, Over the Range. London, Trubner, 1872; revised edition, 1872; London, Richards, 1901; New York, Dutton, 1910.
Erewhon Revisited Twenty Years Later. London, Richards, 1901; New York, Dutton, 1910.

OTHER PUBLICATIONS

Novel

The Way of All Flesh, edited by R. A. Streatfeild. London, Richards, 1903; New York, Dutton, 1910.

Plays

Narcissus: A Dramatic Cantata, words and music by Butler and Henry Festing Jones. London, Weekes, 1888.
Ulysses: A Dramatic Oratorio, words and music by Butler and Henry Festing Jones. London, Weekes, and Chicago, Summy, 1904.

Verse

Seven Sonnets and A Psalm of Montreal, edited by R. A. Streatfeild. Privately printed, 1904.

Other

A First Year in Canterbury Settlement. London, Longman,

1863; revised edition, edited by R. A. Streatfeild, London, Fifield, 1914; New York, Dutton, 1915.

The Evidence for the Resurrection of Jesus Christ As Given by the Four Evangelists, Critically Examined (published anonymously). Privately printed, 1865.

The Fair Haven: A Work in Defence of the Miraculous Element in Our Lord's Ministry upon Earth. London, Trubner, 1873; New York, Kennerley, 1913.

Life and Habit: An Essay after a Completer View of Evolution. London, Trubner, 1878; New York, Dutton, 1911.

Evolution Old and New. London, Hardwicke and Bogue, and Salem, Massachusetts, Cassino, 1879.

Unconscious Memory. London, Bogue, 1880; New York, Dutton, 1911.

Alps and Sanctuaries of Piedmont and the Canton Ticino. London, Bogue, 1881; New York, Dutton, 1913.

Selections from Previous Works. London, Trubner, 1884.

Gavottes, Minuets, Fugues, and Other Short Pieces for Piano, with Henry Festing Jones. London, Novello, 1885.

Holbein's "Dance." London, Trubner, 1886.

Luck or Cunning as a Main Means of Organic Modification? London, Trubner, 1887.

Ex Voto: An Account of the Sacro Monte or New Jerusalem at Varallo-Sesia. London, Trubner, 1888; revised edition, 1889.

A Lecture on the Humour of Homer. Cambridge, Metcalfe, 1892.

On the Trapanese Origin of the Odyssey. Cambridge, Metcalfe, 1893.

The Life and Letters of Dr. Samuel Butler. London, Murray, 2 vols., 1896.

The Authoress of the Odyssey. London, Longman, 1897; New York, Dutton, 1922.

Shakespeare's Sonnets Reconsidered, and in Part Rearranged. London, Longman, 1899; New York, Dutton, 1927.

Essays on Life, Art, and Science, edited by R. A. Streatfeild. London, Richards, 1904; Port Washington, New York, Kennikat Press, 1970.

God the Known and God the Unknown, edited by R. A. Streatfeild. London, Fifield, 1909; New Haven, Connecticut, Yale University Press, 1917.

The Note Books of Samuel Butler: Selections, edited by Henry Festing Jones. London, Fifield, 1912; New York, Kennerley, 1913.

The Humour of Homer and Other Essays, edited by R. A. Streatfeild. London, Fifield, and New York, Kennerley, 1913.

The Collected Works (Shrewsbury Edition), edited by Henry Festing Jones and A. T. Bartholomew. London, Cape, and New York, Dutton, 20 vols., 1923-26.

Butleriana, edited by A. T. Bartholomew. London, Nonesuch Press, 1932; as *Samuel Butler's Note Books: Some New Extracts,* New York, Random House, 1932.

Samuel Butler's Note Books: Further Extracts, edited by A. T. Bartholomew. London, Cape, 1934.

Letters Between Samuel Butler and Miss E. M. A. Savage, edited by Geoffrey Keynes and Brian Hill. London, Cape, 1935.

The Essential Samuel Butler, edited by G. D. H. Cole. London, Cape, and New York, Dutton, 1950.

Samuel Butler's Note Books: Selections, edited by Geoffrey Keynes and Brian Hill. London, Cape, 1951.

Correspondence of Butler and His Sister May, edited by Daniel F. Howard. Berkeley, University of California Press, 1962.

The Family Letters 1841-1886, edited by Arnold Silver. London, Cape, and Stanford, California, Stanford University Press, 1962.

The Book of the Machines (as Cellarius). London, Quarto Press, 1975.

Samuel Butler on the Resurrection, edited by Robert Johnstone. Gerrards Cross, Buckinghamshire, Smythe, 1980.

Translator, *The Iliad of Homer.* London, Longman, 1898; New York, Dutton, 1921.

Translator, *The Odyssey.* London, Longman, 1900; New York, Dutton, 1922.

Translator, *Hesiod's Works and Days.* Privately printed, 1923.

*

Bibliography: *The Career of Samuel Butler: A Bibliography* by Stanley B. Harkness, London, Lane, 1955; *Three Victorian Travel Writers: An Annotated Bibliography of Criticism on Mrs. Frances Milton Trollope, Samuel Butler, and Robert Louis Stevenson* by Frederick John Bethke, Boston, Hall, 1977.

Critical Studies: *Samuel Butler: A Memoir* by H. F. Jones, London, Macmillan, 2 vols., 1919; *The Triple Thinkers* by Edmund Wilson, New York, Harcourt Brace, and London, Oxford University Press, 1938; *Samuel Butler and The Way of All Flesh* by G. D. H. Cole, London, Home and Van Thal, 1947, as *Samuel Butler,* Denver, Swallow, 1948; *Samuel Butler* by P. N. Furbank, London, Cambridge University Press, 1948; *Darwin and Butler: Two Versions of Evolution* by Basil Willey, London, Chatto and Windus, and New York, Harcourt Brace, 1960; *Samuel Butler* by Lee E. Holt, New York, Twayne, 1964.

*   *   *

Samuel Butler was the son of an Anglican rector, whom he later immortalized in his grim autobiographical novel of Victorian family hypocrisy *The Way of All Flesh.* He graduated from Cambridge in classics, then worked for one season among the poor in London, as a result of which he did not become a clergyman but moved instead to New Zealand. From 1859 to 1864, he managed there a sheep-ranch, began to write about the country and about the new and sensational theory of evolution, and gathered the elements for his novel *Erewhon.* His other writings attacked received opinion in religion, biology, philology, and child-rearing, proposing alternatives which are today generally seen as eccentric, though the controversy around his Neo-Lamarckism is by no means over.

Though Butler's literary masterpiece is *The Way of All Flesh,* some reversals from his country of Erewhon (itself to be read backwards as most other names in the novel) are as interesting and more modern. This civilization, found (as the subtitle has it) "over the range," in an unexplored part of the traditionally upside-down Antipodes, is used for satirical discussions; most importantly, the Erewhonians establish to their satisfaction that machines are using mankind as a means for their indirect evolution and ban all of them, beginning with clocks and watches. Other exposures of the ulterior moral motives, and thus of the hypocrisy of Victorian bourgeois society are the perfectly logical value-transferral between illness and crime, Unreason and Reason, or religion and banking. Unfortunately, Butler's overall stance is not at all consistent: for a crucial example, if the time-quantifying tool of clocks is banned, the basic agent of quantifying in modern civilization, money, should logically also be banned instead of being promoted as the religion of Musical Banks. Thus the various elements of Erewhon become mutually incompatible as the sketch of a believable alternative. As Edmund Wilson remarked, "Butler, though he could be most amusing about people's mercenary motives, was too much a middle-class man himself to analyze the social system, in which . . . he occupied a privileged position" (*The Shores of Light,* New York, 1967). The novel dissolves into a string of more or less unrelated satires of the surfaces of Victorian civilization, hesitating between Swiftian bite and middle-class propriety, mildly diverting paradox and cynical justification (though, beside the amusing passages, the fable of the Unborn—who foster the libido of their parents in order to incarnate—retains a certain Platonic charm).

The continuation, *Erewhon Revisited,* is more coherent but less broadly relevant, focussing as it does on the religious cult that has sprung up in Erewhon around the totally misunderstood narrator of the first novel, now promoted to "Sun-child" in a clear parody of Christ (making this novel a continuation of Butler's *Fair Haven* at least as much as of the earlier satire). What is worse, this sequel retracts even the partial estrangement of *Erewhon,* as well as its own satire on the founding of religions, by its final horizon of salvation through annexation to the British Empire.

Butler's SF, thus, remains incidentally amusing reading, especially in the first book. However, its primary importance is in the satirical prefiguration of what will later become a much more anguished and wider debate on reification and "machine consciousness" in cybernetics, as well as in the general argument about controlled evolution. Butler had therefore an important influence on subsequent SF, from such Victorians as his friend R. E. Dudgeon through J. Carne-Ross, W. J. Roe, and W. Grove to G. B. Shaw's drama-cycle *Back to Methuselah* and some American SF. But his main problems will be picked up and brought to a more sophisticated level by Wells, Zamyatin, and Capek. There remains the striking freshness and irreverence of Butler's best satirical passages.

—Darko Suvin

CAIDIN, Martin. American. Born in New York City, 14 September 1927. Served in the merchant marine, 1945; United States Air Force, 1947-50: Sergeant. Married Grace Caidin in 1952; one son and one daughter. Consultant, correspondent, and broadcaster on aviation and civil defense: Associate Editor, *Air News* and *Air Tech* ; consultant to New York State Civil Defense Commission, 1950-62, Air Force Missile Test Center, Cape Canaveral, 1955, and Federal Aviation Agency, 1961-64; Correspondent, Metropolitan Broadcasting (radio and TV), 1961-62. Founder, Martin Caidin Associates Inc. Address: c/o Houghton Mifflin, 2 Park Street, Boston, Massachusetts 02108, U. S. A.

SCIENCE-FICTION PUBLICATIONS

Novels (series: Steve Austin)

The Long Night. New York, Dodd Mead, 1956.
Marooned. New York, Dutton, and London, Hodder and Stoughton, 1964.
The Last Fathom. New York, Meredith Press, and London, Joseph, 1967.
No Man's World. New York, Dutton, 1967.
Aquarius Mission. New York, Bantam, 1968; London, Corgi, 1978.
Four Came Back. New York, McKay, 1968.

The God Machine. New York, Dutton, 1969.
The Mendelov Conspiracy. New York, Meredith Press, 1969; London, W. H. Allen, 1971; as *Encounter Three,* New York, Pinnacle, 1978.
The Cape. New York, Doubleday, 1971.
Cyborg (Austin). New York, Arbor House, 1972; London, W. H. Allen, 1973.
Operation Nuke (Austin). New York, Arbor House, 1973; London, W. H. Allen, 1974.
High Crystal (novelization of TV play; Austin). New York, Arbor House, 1974; London, W. H. Allen, 1975.
Cyborg IV (Austin). New York, Arbor House, 1975; London, W. H. Allen, 1977.

OTHER PUBLICATIONS

Novels

Devil Takes All. New York, Dutton, 1966; London, W. H. Allen, 1968.
Anytime, Anywhere. New York, Dutton, 1969; London, W. H. Allen, 1970.
Almost Midnight. New York, Morrow, 1971; London, Bantam, 1974.
Maryjane Tonight at Angels Twelve. New York, Doubleday, 1972.
The Last Dogfight. Boston, Houghton Mifflin, and London, Weidenfeld and Nicolson, 1974.
Three Corners to Nowhere. New York, Bantam, and London, Corgi, 1975.
Whip. Boston, Houghton Mifflin, 1976; London, Corgi, 1977.
Manfrac. New York, Dell, 1981.

Play

Television Play: *Exo-Man,* with Howard Rodman and Henri Simoneon, 1977.

Other

Jets, Rockets and Guided Missiles, with David C. Cooke. New York, McBride, 1951; revised edition, as *Rockets and Missiles, Past and Present,* 1954.
Rockets Beyond the Earth. New York, McBride, 1952.
Worlds in Space. New York, Holt, and London, Sidgwick and Jackson, 1954.
Zero!, with M. Okumiya and J. Horikoshi, New York, Dutton, 1956; London, Cassell, 1957.
Vanguard! New York, Dutton, 1957.
Samurai!, with Saburo Sakai and Fred Saito. New York, Dutton, 1957; London, Kimber, 1959.
Air Force: A Pictorial History of American Airpower. New York, Rinehart, 1957.
Countdown for Tomorrow. New York, Dutton, 1958.
Thunderbolt!, with Robert S. Johnson. New York, Rinehart, 1958.
The Zero Fighter, with M. Okumiya and J. Horikoshi. London, Cassell, 1958.
Spaceport, U. S. A. New York, Dutton, 1959
War for the Moon. New York, Dutton, 1959; as *Race for the Moon,* London, Kimber, 1960.
Let's Go Flying! New York, Dutton, 1959.
Boeing 707. New York, Dutton, 1959.
X-15: Man's First Flight into Space. New York, Rutledge, 1959.
Black Thursday. New York, Dutton, 1960.

Golden Wings: A Pictorial History of the United States Navy and Marine Corps in the Air. New York, Random House, 1960.

The Astronauts. New York, Dutton, 1960; revised edition, 1961.

The Night Hamburg Died. New York, Ballantine, 1960; London, New English Library, 1966.

A Torch to the Enemy: The Fire Raid on Tokyo. New York, Ballantine, 1960.

Man into Space. New York, Pyramid, 1961.

Thunderbirds! New York, Dutton, 1961.

The Long, Lonely Leap, with Joseph W. Kittinger. New York, Dutton, 1961.

Cross-Country Flying. New York, Dutton, 1961.

Test Pilot (for children). New York, Dutton, 1961.

This Is My Land, photographs by James Yarnell. New York, Random House, 1962.

I Am Eagle, with G. S. Titov. Indianapolis, Bobbs Merrill, 1962.

Rendezvous in Space. New York, Dutton, 1962.

Aviation and Space Medicine, with Grace Caidin. New York, Dutton, 1962.

The Man-in-Space Dictionary. New York, Dutton, 1963.

The Moon: New World for Men. Indianapolis, Bobbs Merrill, 1963.

Red Star in Space. New York, Crowell Collier, 1963.

The Power of Decision. New York, Dell, 1963.

Overture to Space. New York, Duell, 1963.

The Long Arm of America. New York, Dutton, 1963.

By Apollo to the Moon (for Children). New York, Dutton, 1963.

The Silken Angels: A History of Parachuting. Philadelphia, Lippincott, 1964.

The Winged Armada, New York, Dutton, 1964.

Hydrospace. New York, Dutton, 1964.

Everything But the Flak. New York, Duell, 1964.

The Mission, with Edward Hymoff. Philadelphia, Lippincott, 1964.

Wings into Space. New York, Holt Rinehart, 1964.

The Mighty Hercules (for children). New York, Dutton, 1964.

Why Space?. New York, Messner, 1965.

Barnstorming. New York, Duell, 1965.

The Greatest Challenge. New York, Dutton, 1965.

The Ragged, Rugged Warriors. New York, Dutton, 1966; London, Severn House, 1980.

Flying Forts. New York, Meredith Press, 1968.

Me 109: Willy Messerschmitt's Peerless Fighters. New York, Ballantine, 1968; London, Macdonald, 1969.

Fork-Tailed Devil: The P-38. New York, Ballantine, 1971.

Destination Mars. New York, Doubleday, 1972

When War Comes. New York, Morrow, 1972.

Bicycles in War, with Jay Barbree. New York, Hawthorn, 1974.

Planetfall. New York, Coward McCann, 1974.

The Tigers Are Burning. New York, Hawthorn, 1974.

Wingborn. New York, Bantam, and London, Corgi, 1979.

The Saga of Iron Annie. New York, Doubleday, 1979.

Star Bright. New York, Ballantine, 1979.

Kill Devil Hill: Discovering the Secret of the Wright Brothers 1899-1909, with Harry Combs. Boston, Houghton Mifflin, 1979; London, Secker and Warburg, 1980.

Ragwings and Heavy Iron: The Agony and Ecstasy of Flying History's Greatest Warbirds. Boston, Houghton Mifflin, 1984.

Editor, *The DC-3: The Story of the Dakota,* by Carroll V. Glines and Wendell F. Moseley. London, Deutsch, 1967.

*　　*　　*

Martin Caidin builds on his numerous non-fiction works concerning aviation and aerospace technology to provide convincing background for his speculative fiction. This fiction, set in the present or near future, consistently warns that America's naive idealism about peaceful cooperation in outer space should be tempered by a realistic awareness of nationalistic competition, that our technological capabilities are outstripping our emotional and psychological controls, and that a technological, materialistic, and empirical approach to phenomena fails fully to account for and control such phenomena.

Some of Caidin's books explore what could go wrong with a space flight: personal problems that affect efficiency (nagging wives, wayward children, secret affairs, drugs, and blackmail) in *The Cape,* the possibility of foreign sabotage on the ground (*The Cape, No Man's World*) or with laser beams in space (*Cyborg IV, The Mendelov Conspiracy*), technical and mechanical difficulties (*Marooned*), bombardment by meteors and invasion of alien bacteria (*Four Came Back*), and hostile confrontation on arrival (Russian and Chinese in *No Man's World*). Minor characters and anecdotes from one book become major characters and events in another. For example in the background of several books is a boorish newspaper man who intrudes where he doesn't belong, but who gets his story and ultimately helps out. In *Marooned* this brash, intuitive reporter breaks through NASA security to learn the truth of an astronaut's plight; in *The Mendelov Conspiracy* he investigates UFO's that prove part of an international scientists' plot to force the world to nuclear disarmament.

The Long Night, a terse and vivid step-by-step portrait of a family and town confronted with an atomic explosion and resultant fire-storm, demonstrates Caidin's interest in how people react to disaster or panic. Caidin believes a military elite must use force if necessary to quell irresponsible, destructive mobs born of irrational fears—a theme in *Four Came Back* where earthlings fear alien bacteria, *The Long Night* where rumors of radiation sends hordes flying, and *The Mendelov Conspiracy* where mobs attack nuclear stockpiles. To teach his audience about sea and space and disaster, Caidin relies on digressions, flashbacks, reverie, and experts explaining to neophytes, techniques that provide a wealth of interesting material, but which occasionally reduce the effectiveness of the plot. Caidin blends fact and fiction, the feasible and the speculative. His forte is his reliance on quotes by real men to make his tales of the emotions and conflicts of the near future seem perfectly natural and credible.

A Caidin hero is a tough, well-trained military man. He is proud of his work, devoted to his country, a man who can face up to and control his fear while those around him panic or succumb. Usually a one-time test pilot, he works hard and plays hard. His is a world of machines, whether in outer space or hydrospace. He is often excited and inspired by a strikingly beautiful, intelligent, and independent woman (secret agent, archaeologist, oceanographer, bionics expert, astronaut), but usually this romance remains unresolved or the woman dies suddenly, violently.

Caidin is fascinated by the idea of man and machine becoming a harmonic single entity—either in terms of sensitive reaction time or else literally as in the Steve Austin series. In *The God Machine* the ultimate computer is designed to interact with human operators and to mimic and transcend human logic, but a programming fault results in the horror of logic being carried out to literal, absurd, and inhuman ends. In *The Last Fathom* the developer of a revolutionary submarine manoeuvres at incredible depths to prevent the devastation of the free world. *Cyborg* is a fascinating and highly technical dramatization of the reconstruction of a test pilot's body, with microscopic units replacing the nervous system, and a fusion of bone and metal replacing missing legs and arm until the man becomes more than mere man, capable of gruelling (and incredible) missions to expose Russian submarine bases and steal experimental planes. *Operation Nuke* and *Crystal* feature further cyborg wonders as Austin plays fugitive to infiltrate a terrorist organization dependent on nuclear arms and then races to find the power source of an ancient Indian civilization—a giant crystal. In *Cyborg IV* Austin, linked symbionically to his space vehicle to control it with thought and reflex action, attacks Russians in space to protect military security. Such missions are the price his country demands as payment for not leaving him a helpless paraplegic.

In general, Caidin's best pieces describe specific disasters to make the reader aware of the full horror of nuclear wars and other modern technological dangers. While emphasizing the courage and strength needed for controlling and surviving in experimental machinery, Caidin also demythologizes the glamour by focusing on practical, minute-to-minute detail. Perhaps his greatest contribution is in illuminating the relationship between man and machine to show that man must avoid becoming machine-like if he is to remain human.

—Andrew and Gina Macdonald

CALLAHAN, William. See **GALLUN Raymond Z.**

CALLENBACH, Ernest. American. Born in Williamsport, Pennsylvania, 3 April 1929. Educated at the University of Chicago, Ph. B. 1949, M. A. 1953. Married Christine Leefeldt in 1978; one daughter and one son. Publicity writer and assistant editor, 1955-58, and since 1958, Editor, *Film Quarterly*, and film book editor, University of California Press, Berkeley. Founder, Banyan Tree Books, 1975. Address: University of California Press, 2120 Berkeley Way, Berkeley, California 94720, U.S.A.

Science-Fiction Publications

Novels

Ecotopia: A Novel about Ecology, People, and Politics in 1999. Berkeley, California, Banyan Tree, 1975; London, Pluto Press, 1978.
Ecotopia Emerging. Berkeley, California, Banyan Tree, 1981.

Other Publications

Other

Our Modern Art: The Movies. Chicago, University of Chicago Center for the Study of Liberal Education for Adults, 1955.
Living Poor with Style. New York, Bantam, 1971.
The Art of Friendship, with Christine Leefeldt. New York, Pantheon, 1979.

The Ecotopian Encyclopedia for the 80's. Berkeley, California, And/Or Press, 1981.
A Citizen Legislature. Berkeley, California, Banyan Tree, 1985.

*

Ernest Callenbach comments:
It might be reassuring to other writers to know that *Ecotopia*, which has now been translated into eight languages and sold about 300,000 copies, was rejected by all major New York publishing houses; it was then initially published by the author and a group of his friends, using the employee-owned book wholesale house, Bookpeople, as distributor. Presumably the allergy of establishment publishers to the work was due to its being half-novel, half-tract; it is, so to speak, "politics fiction," making certain fictional assumptions and following their consequences much as "normal" sci-fi does with scientific assumptions; its technology is actually quite conservative.

The favourable response that *Ecotopia* received (except in Britain, where its Californian origins seem to have ensured disdain for it except among scientists and a few ecologically sophisticated readers) led me to write a "prequel," *Ecotopia Emerging*, which sketches a scenario for how Ecotopia came into existence.

*   *   *

Ernest Callenbach is not a professional writer of science fiction; he is a reformer, an environmentalist, a "small-is-beautiful" proponent of the shift from a society devoted to technological progress to one more closely allied with nature. In his non-fiction *Living Poor with Style* he suggested that "Out of the welter of present industrial society it will probably take us several generations to sort out the few things which are essential to mankind—and to reject the others, of which no truly human or holy use can be made. " But in three later books his imaginary land of Ecotopia, formed by secession of Washington, Oregon, and Northern California, is a model of what utopia based on environmentalist principles could look like *Ecotopia* is a utopian novel in the traditional sense; *The Ecotopian Encyclopedia for the 80's* is a non-fictional series of entries on how to live in the Ecotopian manner; *Ecotopia Emerging* describes events leading to the secession. Together they form a fairly complete picture of the problems of attaining an ideal society, life in that society, and the impact of that society on a traditional 20th-century society.

Ecotopia describes a very different society from that of the United States, and the six-week assignment in the new country of the investigative reporter Will Weston is the first officially arranged American visit in the 19 years following secession. Both governments have hidden agendas: the American to restore good relations and perhaps lead the wandering states to return home, the Ecotopian to teach the visitor to understand their way of life and convert his countrymen to that view. The old problem of utopian writing, how to justify long descriptive passages, is solved by alternating excerpts from Weston's private diary with formal columns sent by way of Canada to his newspaper. The real story is in the contrast between the two kinds of reporting and in Weston's slow change from skeptical hostility to friendliness and, eventually, conversion. There are numerous friendly Ecotopians who help the visitor to adjust to and understand the new society, but the most important character besides West, the archetypal utopian visitor, is Marissa, a free-spirited woman whose love probably has much to do with his decision to remain in Ecotopia. President Vera Allwen, who appears mostly on TV but meets Weston once in person, takes the important but comparatively minor role of showing the visitor that Ecotopian individuals and their government are very much alike—independent and caring.

Although *Ecotopia Emerging* is billed as "prequel" to the earlier novel, its action begins in 1986—secession is accomplished in 1988 rather than in 1981—and the earlier novel is actually referred to as a source of ideas for the Survivalist Party which engineers the whole project. A new character, 17-year-old Lou Swift, invents a cheap and efficient solar-electric power cell, Marissa's cancer-ridden mother blows up a chemical plant, her brother Ben may or may not have planted nuclear bombs in major cities, and Vera Allwen, a state senator, slowly moves to leadership of the gradually more and more aggressive party. The secession begins on a small scale and spreads; the expected civil war fails to materialize (the "Helicopter War" of 1982, important in *Ecotopia,* is not mentioned); an agreement is reached for peace between Ecotopia and the United States; the Ecotopian constitution is written. This "prequel" is even more polemical than its predecessor, but it is much more interesting as a story and much more characteristic of science fiction.

Whether Callenbach will write more novels that are Utopian or even peripherally science fiction, as these are, is problematic. His interest is clearly in the reform of society, not the writing of fiction. On the other hand the experience of the past shows that there are few better ways to get a message across than to take advantage of the flexibility science fiction and utopian writing offer.

—Arthur O. Lewis

CAMPBELL, John W(ood), Jr. American. Born in Newark, New Jersey, 8 June 1910. Educated at Blair Academy; Massachusetts Institute of Technology, Cambridge, 1928-31; Duke University, Durham, North Carolina, B. S. 1933. Married 1) Dona Stuart in 1931; 2) Margaret Winter in 1950; four children. Car and gas heater salesman; worked in the research department of Mack Truck, Hoboken Pioneer Instruments, and Carleton Ellis chemical company; Editor, *Astounding,* later *Analog,* 1937-71, *Unknown,* later *Unknown Worlds,* 1939-43, and *From Unknown Worlds,* 1948. Recipient: Hugo Award, for editing, 1953, 1955, 1956, 1957, 1961, 1962, 1964, 1965. Guest of Honor, World Science Fiction Convention, Philadelphia, 1947, San Francisco, 1954, London, 1957. *Died 11 July 1971.*

SCIENCE-FICTION PUBLICATIONS

Novels (series: Arcot, Morey, and Wade)

The Mightiest Machine. Providence, Rhode Island, Hadley, 1947.
The Incredible Planet. Reading, Pennsylvania, Fantasy Press, 1949.
The Moon Is Hell! Reading, Pennsylvania, Fantasy Press, 1951.
Islands of Space (Arcot, Morey, and Wade). Reading, Pennsylvania, Fantasy Press, 1957.
Invaders from the Infinite (Arcot, Morey, and Wade). New York, Gnome Press, 1961.
The Ultimate Weapon. New York, Ace, 1966.

Short Stories

Who Goes There? Chicago, Shasta, 1948; as *The Thing and*

Other Stories, London, Cherry Tree, 1952.
Cloak of Aesir. Chicago, Shasta, 1952.
The Black Star Passes (Arcot, Morey, and Wade). Reading, Pennsylvania, Fantasy Press, 1953.
Who Goes There? and Other Stories. New York, Dell, 1955.
The Planeteers. New York, Ace, 1966.
The Best of John W. Campbell. London, Sidgwick and Jackson, 1973.
The Best of John W. Campbell, edited by Lester del Rey. New York, Doubleday, 1976.
The Space Beyond. New York, Pyramid, 1976.

OTHER PUBLICATIONS

Other

"Concerning Science Fiction," in *The Writer* (Boston), 1946.
The Atomic Story. New York, Holt, 1947.
"Science of Science Fiction," in *Atlantic* (Boston), May 1948.
"Value of Science Fiction," in *Science Marches On,* edited by James Stokley. New York, Washburn, 1951.
"The Future of Science Fiction," in *Modern Science Fiction,* edited by Reginald Bretnor. New York, Coward McCann, 1953.
"Science-Fiction and the Opinion of the Unwise," in *Saturday Review of Literature* (New York), 12 May 1956.
"Science Fact: Science Fiction," in *The Writer* (Boston), August 1964.
Collected Editorials from Analog, edited by Harry Harrison. New York, Doubleday, 1966.
"Science Fiction We Can Buy," in *The Writer* (Boston), September 1968.

Editor, *From Unknown Worlds.* New York, Street and Smith, 1948; London, Atlas, 1952.
Editor, *The Astounding Science Fiction Anthology.* New York, Simon and Schuster, 1952; shortened version, as *The First* [and *Second*] *Astounding Science Fiction Anthology,* London Grayson, 2 vols., 1954, and as *Astounding Tales of Space and Time,* New York, Berkeley, 1957; complete version, as *The First* [and *Second*] *Astounding Science Fiction Anthology,* London, New English Library, 2 vols., 1964-65.
Editor, *Prologue to Analog.* New York, Doubleday, 1962; London, Panther, 1967.
Editor, *Analog 1-8.* New York, Doubleday, 8 vols., 1963-71; London, Panther, 2 vols., 1967; London, Dobson, 4 vols., 1968.
Editor, *Analog Anthology.* London, Dobson, 1965.

*

Critical Studies: *John W. Campbell: An Australian Tribute* edited by John Bangsund, Canberra, Graham and Bangsund, 1972.

* * *

Had it not been for John W. Campbell, Jr., science fiction as a publisher's category might have perished with the demise of the pulp industry. As editor of *Astounding* (later *Analog*) *Science Fiction,* from September 1937 to December 1971, he demanded good writing and sometimes got it. That is his achievement (never mind his cranky indulgence in Dianetics and the Dean Drive), and he set the standard with the better of his own stories. As a result, his magazine attracted enough story-tellers that it and the science-fiction genre remain in existence today. (The stories of reasoned fantasy he published as editor of *Unknown Worlds* are, however, no longer current.)

His early stories take off from the space operatics of E. E. Smith, but with that extra something-to-say that interested the industrial scientist who became his chief readers. The something that must have interested them was the idea of professional colleagueship which stressed the intellectual value of shared discovery; the outcome of the research and development was not a new consumer product, but something to save the species.

Campbell's first story, "The Voice of the Void" (1930), set the pattern. Men ten billion years in the future prepare to leave the planets of the solar system because the sun is dying. By this time, science had become central to the human way of life and a scientist in training takes a 70-year course at an engineering school, where making inventions is part of the curriculum. Graduates from such schools have been gathering for generations to meet the growing emergency of the sun's death. At last they develop a matter transmitter that sends fleets of spaceships to another system of planets orbiting the giant star Betelgeuse. They accomplish this in a spirit of professional association, men of pure science called to salvationist duty, but in just those fields—aviation and broadcasting—under commercial development at the time of writing. Likewise in "Twilight" a time traveller from the far future asks what are the most important inventions of the day, and the answer is "airplanes and radio."

The pulp tradition of SF that Campbell elevated above adventure fiction—the last refuge of rugged individualism in American letters—was a world of "pooled mental resources." His intellectual hero was attractive to the young student or professional scientist in industry whose job was anything but free to explore wherever the research team's curiosity might lead.

Two groups of Campbell stories follow through with a standard set of heroes. The more popular one is the Arcot, Morey, and Wade series. Dr. Richard Arcot, a world-famous physicist, works for the research laboratories of Transcontinental Airways, selling it his inventions under the patronage of its president, who happens to be the father of Arcot's colleague, the mathematician Morey. Wade, introduced during the course of the first story, "Piracy Preferred," is an air pirate who preys on Transcontinental's great 30,000-passenger superplanes with a device for making his marauding aircraft invisible, but after being captured he joins Arcot's lab staff. Fuller, an aeronautical design engineer, joins the group in "Solarite," and proves his worth in *Islands of Space* by designing a faster-than-light ship on a principle discovered by Arcot. All four then make a tour of the cosmos. The title islands are island universes, galactic nebulae. Financing a tour of these is more than even Transcontinental can afford, so its president helps Arcot raise the rest in popular support from "the wealth of two worlds," Earth and Venus. All this is spent on a fantastic adventure of observational science. But the debt is repaid when the group is able to deal with an alien threat in *Invaders from the Infinite*.

The other story series is *The Planeteers*, dealing with Penton and Blake, a pair of cosmic explorers who land on various worlds and solve exotic puzzles. But again this had survival value. Curiosity is a tough-minded quality because what observation reveals is that "change is the natural order of things." Science is "a method of thinking" that can meet "goals ahead larger than those we know" by knowing how, when the problem is upon us, "to produce that which never existed. " Science is the way mankind educates itself to meet the challenge of necessity.

Campbell's test of survival is nowhere dramatized more forcibly than in *The Moon Is Hell*. The first rocketship to the moon crashes and its crew of research scientists, stranded on the dead rock, win from the object of their curiosity food, water, and air. This is the research and development process glamorized in a power fantasy that makes its most important business the winning of life itself. "Machines and gadgets aren't the end and goal; they are the means to the true goal." The commercial products of the technological revolution are but objects of practice on which to learn and organize the skills of innovative group thinking, come the day of unexpected crisis.

Curiosity is the mainspring of human adaptability, and may very well drive the products of man's inventions when he himself is gone. In "The Last Evolution" Campbell introduces an original concept of robots, heretofore imagined only as workers or slaves. He has them become man's evolutionary descendants. They are "science machines" that make other machines. They supercede man, but surprisingly they end by recreating him. The machines brings to perfection man's urge to explore and do research and create that which never before existed.

A technology that outlives its makers is also the theme of Campbell's most famous story, "Twilight." 88 million years in the future, man is extinct, but his great automatic cities are still in place. The deathless cities go on with "the tireless, ceaseless perfection their designers had incorporated in them."

Perhaps the best work of fiction Campbell ever wrote is "Who Goes There?" An alien monster is found frozen in the Antarctic ice, buried with its ship, by a team of scientists doing weather research. Once thawed, it gets loose in their camp and changes form by imitating one or more of the sled dogs and one of the men, down to their cells and memories. The dogs are killed, but the problem remains how to discover by some test which man is the monster before it takes over the camp and then the whole world. The leader of the expedition is the tough-minded scientist who has the intellectual prowess to do just that. He devises a blood test, taking a sample from each man and touching it in turn with the tip of a hot needle. The monster not only replicates any body it takes over, it reduplicates itself in every cell of that body. The test is this: when irritated the monster's " *blood* will live—and crawl away. " It does, and the man whose sample it is reveals himself in hideous form. Alert for the transformation with poised axes, the others hack their false colleague to pieces. These few men, outnumbered by millions of life cells, all intelligent, were not defeated. Humanity is *real,* monster-hood is false. Humans have "not an imitated, but a bred-in-the-bone instinct, a driving, unquenchable fire that's genuine."

The monster is no villain: it is a problem. And to be conquered it must be understood, as must all the other unpredictable threats of nature in a universe of constant change. It is deadly to *adapt* to nature, a lazy, undisciplined way that leads to digestion by the cosmic process; survival means *control* of nature. The monster is the opposite of humanity because it goes with nature, not against it. For curiosity it has mere cunning, for pooled mental resources collective imitation. And here is the political note in Campbell's thinking, often sounded in his magazine editorials. For him, collectivism is a monstrous thing that would devour human ideals, but should not be able to do so as long as the superior strength of individuals is united in free association.

—Leon Stover

CAPON, (Harry) Paul. Also wrote as Noel Kenton. British.

Born in Kenton Hall, Suffolk, 18 December 1912. Educated at St. George's School, Harpenden, Hertfordshire. Served in the Royal Army Service Corps, 1940; Technical Director, Soviet Film Agency, 1941-44. Married 1) Doreen Evans-Evans in 1933, one daughter and one son; 2) Amy Charlotte Gillam in 1956. Free-lance film editor and scriptwriter for London Films, 1931-32, Gaumont British, 1933-35, Warner Brothers, 1936-37, British National, 1944-48, Walt Disney, 1955-58, and Granada Television, 1959-62; Head of Film Production, Independent Television News, London, 1963-67. *Died 24 November 1969.*

SCIENCE-FICTION PUBLICATIONS

Novels (series: Antigeos)

The Other Half of the Sun (Antigeos). London, Heinemann, 1950.
The Other Half of the Planet (Antigeos). London, Heinemann, 1952.
The World at Bay (for children). London, Heinemann, 1953; Philadelphia, Winston, 1954.
Down to Earth (Antigeos). London, Heinemann, 1954.
Phobos, The Robot Planet (for children). London, Heinemann, 1955; as *Lost—A Moon*, Indianapolis, Bobbs Merrill, 1956.
The Wonderbolt (for children). London, Ward Lock, 1955.
Into the Tenth Millennium. London, Heinemann, 1956.
Flight of Time (for children). London, Heinemann, 1960.

OTHER PUBLICATIONS

Novels

Battered Caravanserai. London, Heinemann, 1942.
Brother Cain. London, Heinemann, 1945.
The Hosts of Midian. London, Nicholson and Watson, 1946.
Dead Man's Chest. London, Nicholson and Watson, 1947.
The Murder of Jacob Canansey. London, Heinemann, 1947.
Fanfare for Shadows. London, Boardman, 1947.
O Clouds Unfold. London, Ward Lock, 1948.
Image of a Murder. London, Boardman, 1949.
Toby Scuffell. London, Ward Lock, 1949.
Threescore Years. London, Ward Lock, 1950.
Delay of Doom. London, Ward Lock, 1950.
No Time for Death. London, Ward Lock, 1951.
Death at Shinglestrand. London, Ward Lock, 1952.
Death on a Wet Sunday. London, Ward Lock, 1953.
In All Simplicity. London, Heinemann, 1953.
The Seventh Passenger. London, Ward Lock, 1953.
Malice Domestic. London, Ward Lock, 1954.
Thirty Days Hath September. London, Ward Lock, 1955.
Margin of Terror. London, Ward Lock, 1955.
Amongst Those Missing. London, Heinemann, 1959.
The Final Refuge. London, Harrap, 1969.

Other (for children)

The Cave of Cornelius. London, Heinemann, 1959; as *The End of the Tunnel,* Indianapolis, Bobbs Merril, 1959.
Warriors' Moon. London, Hodder and Stoughton, 1960; New York, Putnam, 1964.
The Kingdom of the Bulls. London, Hodder and Stoughton, 1961; New York, Norton, 1962.
Lord of the Chariots. London, Hodder and Stoughton, 1962.
The Golden Cloak. London, Hodder and Stoughton, 1963.

The Great Yarmouth Mystery: A Chronicle of a Famous Crime (for adults). London, Harrap, 1965.
Roman Gold. Leicester, Brockhampton Press, 1968.
Strangers on Forlorn. London, Harrap, 1969.

Translator, *Surrealism,* by Yves Duplessis. New York, Walker, 1963.
Translator, *Sexual Reproduction,* by Louis Gallien. New York, Walker, 1963.
Translator (as Noel Kenton), *Animal Migration,* by René Thévenin. New York, Walker, 1963.
Translator, *The French Wines,* by Georges Ray. New York, Walker, 1965.

* * *

Paul Capon's novels have had very little distribution in the United States and he is generally unknown there, which is surprising in view of the large number of inferior writers whose works have been reprinted from their original European appearance. He received most attention with the Antigeos trilogy, portions of which were broadcast on the BBC. Antigeos is a twin world to the Earth, located at the opposite side of Earth's orbit, hidden from us by the bulk of the sun. This impossibility has recurred frequently in the genre, and is just plausible enough to be fascinating to casual readers.

Antigeos is a Utopia of sorts, or at least it is until the unscrupulous Earth humans arrive. In the first volume the initial contact is made, but the unpleasant results don't become evident until the middle volume where human vanities and greeds begin to work their way on Antigeos. In the final volume a group of financiers plot to exploit the newly discovered world as an involuntary colony, until they are thwarted by the true at heart.

The rest of Capon's adventure novels have been dismissed as juveniles, and two at least very definitely are, *The Wonderbolt* and *Flight Of Time.* But Capon's excellent narrative ability makes some of them of interest to adult readers as well. There is an alien invasion from Poppea in *The World at Bay,* for example, unique in that the aliens arrive in diminutive space stations. *Phobos, The Robot Planet* has as its central character the entire Martian moon, which we learn to be a gigantic robot spaceship which wanders around kidnapping people out of curiosity rather than malice. This latter novel is lighter in tone than the others, and has its moments of genuine humor.

Paul Capon went on to write one major adult novel, *Into the Tenth Millennium,* and made use of one of the oldest of science fiction plots—the journey into the future to visit a Utopian society. Capon transports three modern-day humans via drugs to a future society which does seem to have solved most of the significant societal problems, and we are treated to an unusually entertaining tour of that society. Never ignoring the need to sustain interest, Capon avoids preachiness, and portrays for us a world that is realistic as well as Utopian, a goal never achieved by most of the "classic" works of this type.

Capon was not particularly prolific and attracted little attention with his books, all of which are presently out of print. This is surprising because his narrative technique is masterful and his plots, while familiar, are not more so than many another far more successful novel. The predominance of young protagonists may well have stereotyped Capon as a writer of juveniles, making it impossible for him to reach a more adult audience with his more serious work.

—Don D'Ammassa

CARD, Orson Scott. Has also written as Brian Green. American. Born in Richland, Washington, 24 August 1951. Educated at Brigham Young University, Provo, Utah, B. A. in theatre 1975; University of Utah, Salt Lake City, M. A. in English 1981. Married Kristine Allen in 1977; two sons and one daughter. Volunteer Mormon missionary in Brazil, 1971-73; operated repertory theatre, Provo, 1974-75; proofreader, 1974, and editor, 1974-76, Brigham Young University Press; editor, *Ensign* magazine, Salt Lake City, 1976-78, and Compute Books, Greensboro, North Carolina, 1983; taught at the University of Utah, 1979-80, 1981, Brigham Young University, 1981, Notre Dame University, Indiana, 1981-82, and Clarion Writers Workshop, East Lansing, Michigan, 1982. Recipient: John W. Campbell Award, 1978. Agent: Barbara Bova, 207 Sedgwick Road, West Hartford, Connecticut 06107. Address: 546 Lindley Road, Greensboro, North Carolina 27410, U.S.A.

SCIENCE-FICTION PUBLICATIONS

Novels

Hot Sleep. New York, Baronet, 1978; London, Futura, 1980.
A Planet Called Treason. New York, St. Martin's Press, 1979; London, Pan, 1981.
Songmaster. New York, Dial Press, 1980; London, Futura, 1981.
Hart's Hope. New York, Berkley, 1983.
The Worthing Chronicle. New York, Ace, 1983.
Ender's Game. New York, Tor, 1985.

Short Stories

Capitol. New York, Ace, 1978.
Unaccompanied Sonata and Other Stories. New York, Dial Press, 1981.

Uncollected Short Stories

"Adagio and Benediction," in *Chrysalis 5*, edited by Roy Torgeson. New York, Zebra, 1979.
"The Bully and the Beast," in *Other Worlds 1*, edited by Roy Torgeson. New York, Zebra, 1979.
"Sandmagic," in *Swords Against Darkness 4*, edited by Andrew J. Offutt. New York, Zebra, 1979.
"But We Try Not to Act Like It," in *Destinies* (New York), August 1979.
"A Cross-Country Trip to Kill Richard Nixon," in *Chrysalis 7*, edited by Roy Torgeson. New York, Zebra, 1980.
"Holy," in *New Dimensions 10*, edited by Robert Silverberg. New York, Harper, 1980.
"The Princess and the Bear," in *The Berkley Showcase 1*, edited by Victoria Schochet and John W. Silbersack. New York, Berkley, 1980.
"Songhouse," in *The Best Science Fiction Novellas of the Year 2*, edited by Terry Carr. New York, Ballantine, 1980.
"A Plague of Butterflies," in *Dragons of Darkness*, edited by Card. New York, Ace, 1981.
"St. Amy's Tale," in *A Spadeful of Spacetime*, edited by Fred Saberhagen. New York, Ace, 1981.
"Clap Hands and Sing," in *The Best of Omni Science Fiction 3*, edited by Ben Bova and Don Myrus. New York, Omni, 1982.
"Fat Farm," in *The Best of Omni Science Fiction 4*, edited by Ben Bova and Don Myrus. New York, Omni, 1982.

"Mikal's Songbird," in *Analog's Children of the Future*, edited by Stanley Schmidt. New York, Davis, 1982.

OTHER PUBLICATIONS

Novel

A Woman of Destiny. New York, Berkley, 1984.

Plays

Tell Me That You Love Me, Junie Moon, adaptation of a work by Marjorie Kellogg (also director: produced Provo, Utah, 1969).
The Apostate (produced Provo, Utah, 1970).
In Flight (produced Provo, Utah, 1970).
Across Five Summers (produced Provo, Utah, 1971).
Of Gideon (produced Provo, Utah, 1971).
Stone Tables (produced Provo, Utah, 1973).
A Christmas Carol, adaption of the story by Dickens (also director: produced Provo, Utah, 1974).
Father, Mother, Mother, and Mom (produced Provo, Utah, 1974). Published in *Sunstone*, 1978.
Liberty Jail (produced Provo, Utah, 1975).
Rag Mission (as Brian Green), in *Ensign* (Salt Lake City), July 1977.
Fresh Courage Take (also director: produced, 1978).
Elders and Sisters (produced, 1979).
Wings (produced, 1982).

Other

Listen, Mom and Dad. Salt Lake City, Bookcraft, 1978.
Saintspeak. Berkeley, California, Signature, 1981.
Ainge. Midvale, Utah, Signature, 1982.
Compute's Guide to IBM PCjr Sound and Graphics. Greensboro, North Carolina, Compute, 1984.

Editor, *Dragons of Darkness.* New York, Ace, 1981.
Editor, Dragons of Light. New York, Ace, 1983.

*

Manuscript Collection: Brigham Young University, Provo, Utah.

Orson Scott Card comments:
When I tell stories, I generally follow my own unreasoned sense of what should happen—what events feel important and true to the characters. I subscribe to no particular literary school and never deliberately bend a story to fit a preconceived notion of correct writing.

In fact, it is not story writing that interests me, but storytelling. I believe that the art of the storyteller does not exist on paper or in language; rather, the storyteller creates a vicarious memory in the hearers' or readers' minds, using as he can the words of the language with all their nuance, as well as the public memory that binds the community of hearers together.

The reader coming to my work will find that there is only rarely any science in my science fiction. I use the freedom of the genre to create the situations in which my stories can take place, but I never try to predict or prescribe the future. I do not write utopias or rhapsodies to future engineering. I am uninterested in current fashion and so do not write about drugs, rock music, peace movements, or nuclear war. Nor do I attempt literary experimentation, as it is generally understood—most literary "experiments" today being inferior repetitions of the failures of the modern writers of the early 20th century.

In looking back at my completed tales, both long and short, I find several recurrent motifs, some of which have been noticed (and sometimes complained about) by reviewers. Though I was not aware of these themes while writing, I do believe they are valid reflections of my own unquestioned beliefs about the moral universe.

Repeatedly my central characters occupy an unsought key position in their community; repeatedly they choose to suffer or cause unspeakable pain or sacrifice in order to save the community. Some have seen this as wanton violence; I see it as something holy in human nature, the inborn goodness that denies mankind is evil at birth.

Often my characters are children or otherwise innocent, forced ahead of time into responsibilities they cannot, but nevertheless do, bear. Whether they are children or not, they are always isolated from the community they uphold. They tend to have exceptional gifts and exceptional weaknesses; they are introspective enough to notice their weakness and strength and pain, but not enough to notice their virtue.

My characters frequently have a sense of fulfilling plans they did not make; ultimately, however, they accept all or part of those plans. Their achievements, however, are a direct result of their own choices, actions, and efforts. They are not mere toys of the gods; the gods, implicitly or explicitly, depend in part on the human characters to achieve their own overarching purposes. And all my fiction is infused with a strong belief in the perfectability of human beings, at least in part through their own desires and works.

*   *   *

Like many young writers—and a substantial number of writers of all ages—Orson Scott Card concerns himself repeatedly with a single theme. This theme is the growth and transformation of the individual. It is the story of coming-of-age, the story of the rite of passage, the story of the transformation of the boy, clever and ambitious but ignorant and dependent, into the man of maturity, responsibility, and power.

Card's earliest story, "Ender's Game," offered a brief glimpse of precisely this concern. It deals with Ender Wiggin (the odd first name is actually a nickname, and is significant) and his selection for enrollment at an elite and crucially important military academy. The story was immensely popular, and established Card from the outset as a favorite with readers of *Analog*, the leading science-fiction magazine. It also marked the beginning of Card's association with editor Ben Bova; as Bova moved from post to post in the late 1970's and early 1980's, Card's stories and books continued to appear under Bova's tutelage. When it was revealed that Bova's wife was also Card's literary agent, strong criticism was expressed over potential (or actual) conflict of interest. Regardless of this controversy, Card has continued to prove himself a solid and continuously growing talent. He is, not suprisingly, much like one of his own protagonists in this regard.

His next major success, also in *Analog*, was "Mikal's Songbird." Thematically similar to "Ender's Game," "Mikal's Songbird" is concerned with the selection of a young boy to be trained as the personal "songbird" of a galactic emperor. The position of songbird carries elements of poet laureate, court jester, and (at least on a level of inference) boy-love for the emperor. In addition to the theme of personal growth, "Mikal's Songbird," when built into the novel *Songmaster*, is concerned with the ecstatic or transformational experience. In this case the ecstatic state is achieved through song; the book commends itself to comparison with Thomas M. Disch's *On Wings of Song*. Card's treatment of the theme is more serious than is Disch's; where Disch is often wry and occasionally evasive, Card is earnest and relatively direct, although by no means lacking in subtlety.

Even Card's lesser works carry out the major theme of his fiction. The early story-cycle *Hot Sleep*, revised and expanded to form *The Worthington Chronicle*, is of particular interest in the manner in which it shows Card's own development of his skills and techniques as he carries his protagonist down through a long series of episodic adventures separated by periods of induced suspended animation.

Card has always insisted on maintaining his identity as a writer of science fiction but not one limited to science fiction. His duality stretches back to his childhood reading. He cites works of Robert A. Heinlein and Andre Norton, read when Card was in elementary school—but memtions that during the same period he was "just as excited by Nordhoff and Hall's *Bounty* trilogy. " In college he read Bradbury, Tolkien, Clarke, Asimov—but also Ayn Rand, John Hersey, James Clavell, and later Vidal, Renault, and Goldman.

His most important work outside the science-fiction field, to date, is the long historical novel *A Woman of Destiny*. The story of an immigrant Englishwoman coming to America early in the 19th century, the book is heavily researched and beautifully written. Card has expressed anger and bitterness over the treatment given the book by its publisher, starting with a change of its name. The book was written as *Saints*, and was to have been published first in hard covers. The publisher changed the name to avoid identification of the book as a "Mormon novel" (although Mormonism is one of its major subjects), packaged it as a semi-torrid romance (it is a serious novel of character and manners), and published it as a paperback original with almost no advertising or other support.

Following this misfortune, Card returned to science fiction with a full-length novel version of *Ender's Game*, of which the early story makes up a little more than a prologue. The book suffers from over-familiarity: it is a story that has been told and retold in both general literature and science fiction by authors from Fielding to Heinlein and Haldeman. The young protagonist makes his way despite loneliness and self-doubt from "new boy" to top grad, then enters the "real world" to make his way. Despite its lack of innovation, Card's version of this familiar tale is exceptionally well written and readable. It is to be followed by two sequels.

Only in his mid-thirties, Orson Scott Card has already created a significant body of forceful and well-crafted work. An industrious worker, he will certainly continue to produce, and will in all likelihood achieve a steadily growing, and well-deserved, stature.

—Richard A. Lupoff

———

CAREY, Julian. See **TUBB, E. C.**

———

CARPENTER, Morley. See **TUBB, E. C.**

———

CARR, Jayge. American. Born in Houston, Texas, 28 July 1940. Educated at Carnegie Institute of Technology, Pittsburgh, 1958-61; Wayne State University, Detroit, 1961-62, B. A. in physics 1962; Case Western Reserve University, Cleveland, 1962-65. Married Roger Carr in 1961; two daughters. Nuclear physicist, NASA, Cleveland, 1962-65. Agent: Valerie Smith, Virginia Kidd, Box 278, Milford, Pennsylvania 18337. Address: P.O. Box 1528, Slidell, Louisiana 70459, U.S.A.

SCIENCE-FICTION PUBLICATIONS

Novels

Leviathan's Deep. New York, Doubleday, 1979; London, Sidgwick and Jackson, 1980.
Navigator's Sindrome. New York, Doubleday, 1983.
The Treasure in the Heart of the Maze. New York, Doubleday, 1985.

Uncollected Short Stories

"Alienation," in *Analog* (New York), October 1976.
"The Ax," in *Analog* (New York), June 1977.
"Right of Passage," in *Analog* (New York), August 1978.
"The Pavilion Where All Times Meet," in *Other Worlds 1*, edited by Roy Torgeson. New York, Zebra, 1979.
"Does Not a Statistic Bleed," in *Pandora* (Murray, Kentucky), vol. 1, no. 4, 1979.
"Sanctuary," in *Isaac Asimov's Science Fiction Magazine* (New York), May 1979.
"In Adam's Fall," in *Analog* (New York), October 1979.
"The King Is Dead! Long Live—," in *Chrysalis 8*, edited by Roy Torgeson. New York, Doubleday, 1980.
"Star Spats," in *Pandora* (Murray, Kentucky), vol. 1, no. 5, 1980.
"The False-True Heir," in *Pandora* (Murray, Kentucky), vol. 1, no. 6, 1980.
"Child of the Wandering Sea," in *Ares* (Lake Geneva, Wisconsin), May 1980.
"Hillsong," in *Ares* (Lake Geneva, Wisconsin), September 1980.
"A Thief in the Night," in *Room of One's Own* (Vancouver), vol. 6, nos. 11-12, 1981.
"The Selfish Genie," in *Questar*, February 1981.
"Mustard Seed," in *Analog* (New York), March 1981.
"The Pacifists," in *Analog* (New York), October 1981.
"The Wondrous Works of His Hands," in *Alien Encounters*, edited by Jan Howard Finder. New York, Taplinger, 1982.
"Blind Spot," in *The 1982 Annual World's Best SF*, edited by Donald A. Wollheim and Arthur Saha. New York, DAW, 1982.
"Reunion," in *Hecate's Cauldron*, edited by Susan M. Shwartz. New York, DAW, 1982.
"Lungfish," in *Analog* (New York), October 1982.
"Measuremen," in *Isaac Asimov's Science Fiction Magazine* (New York), December 1982.
"Malthus's Day," in *The Best of Omni Science Fiction 5*, edited by Don Myrus. New York, Omni, 1983.
"The Spoils of Victory," in *Oracle* (Southfield, Michigan), no. 2, 1983.
"The Kidnapped Key," in *Analog*, (New York), August 1983.
"The Tempest Within," in *Fantasy Book* (Pasadena, California), December 1983.
"Monolyth," in *Omni* (New York), December 1983.

"The Heart in the Egg," in *Isaac Asimov's Tomorrow's Voices*, edited by Shawna McCarthy. New York, Davis, 1984.
"The Piper's Pay," in *Fantasy Book* (Pasadena, California), June 1984.
"Pieces of Eight," in *Fantasy and Science Fiction* (New York), September 1984.
"Webrider," in *The Third Omni Book of SF*, edited by Ellen Datlow. New York, Omni, 1985.

*

Jayge Carr comments:

It is probably no coincidence that my first published story was titled "Alienation. " I have never tried to do anything more than tell interesting stories, about interesting people, written in a precise but readable style. But certain themes do crop up over and over, and alienation, whether of one society from the mainstream, as in "The Pacifists," or person from society as in "Alienation," does seem to be a common occurrence.

I've also discovered quite a bit about myself by reading my own work. Many people, on the evidence of *Leviathan's Deep*, have labeled me a feminist. Well, maybe. I prefer to think of myself as a peoplist. Every one should have equal opportunities and no one should be shoe-horned into a role unfitting or barred from a role desired because of sex—or age, creed, color, or what-have-you. "Mustard Seed" may be my best example of a truly egalitarian society. And *Navigator's Sindrome*, of course, a prime example of such a society gone sour. Sometimes, as in *Leviathan's Deep* or "The King Is Dead," I try to show men what it feels like to have the shoe on the other foot, pinching. But women are not our only minority, just the most prevalent one. Prejudice, intolerance, bigotry; all of them are so cruel, and they cause so much tragedy—and they're so foolish. Those who eliminate some people from their friends because of trivial reasons miss so much.

Another theme that keeps recurring—perhaps because I do feel strongly about it—is pollution. Humanity wasting our environment. "Child of the Wandering Sea" is the ultimate of that, where the Terran's population explosion has them taking over—and terraforming—world after world. Where will we go if we don't control ourselves, what will happen if we continue to waste our resources. I haven't any answers, but I can hope that just thinking about it will help, in some small way.

Besides, writing is fun. It is fun to make up a truly alien alien, as in "The Wondrous Works of His Hands" or a truly alien society of human beings, as in "The Pacifists. " It is fun to meet new friends, and watch them have adventures. And of course, I can always hope, that if it's fun to write, it's equally fun to read.

* * *

Jayge Carr's first novel, *Leviathan's Deep*, was published in the late 1970's just as feminism began to exert a powerful and controversial influence on science fiction. In addition to Carr's description of a low-technology but intellectually sophisticated alien matriarchate, and her creation of engaging characters—a lustful general/mad scientist, a gifted scamp of a writer, and the honest, brave, and more than slightly zany female narrative viewpoint character protagonist—and her clever, humorous style make this a remarkable book. Equally remarkable is the book's lack of those qualities which "feminist" SF is often (and often justly) accused of containing: stridency, hostility, and special pleading. Carr, a former physicist who encountered sexism in male colleagues, displays compassion, tolerance, and humor that would be completely extraordinary except for her admission that her most villainous male characters are life-portraits of erstwhile co-workers.

A subsequent novel, *Navigator's Sindrome*, describes the legal and guerrilla battles to rescue a Navigator, the enigmatic, neurotic, and beautiful Jael, from the planet Rabelais, where decadent sadists indulge their worst fantasies on quasi-slaves bound to them by an incomprehensible system of contractual obligations. Jael's struggle is bound up with freighter-master Hannibal Reis's search for his brother, whom the worst of all the Rabelaisian contract-holders has turned into a berserk gladiator, and with the fight of more moderate "c'holders" to impose some sort of justice upon their world. What might be a rather sordid story in less capable hands turns into an intricate narrative of chase-and-find, spiced, of course, by Carr's humor, and by an elusive narrative structure that forces the reader to play detective. In addition, as the characters dodge plots with counterplots, they reveal themselves as richly human, capable of love, loyalty, and great satisfaction when—by the book's end—the punishments are made to fit the crime. In other words (as a yet unpublished sequel, *The Treasure in the Heart of the Maze*, reveals), there is bite behind Carr's whimsy.

In addition, Carr's many short stories display an extremely wide range. Though Carr's hard-science background makes her at home in *Analog*, her elusive, allusive narrative technique fits well with *Omni* editor Datlow's fondness for stylistic experimentation: her fantasy fiction explores a concept Carr calls B & B—Brains and Bewitchery, a sometimes lunatic cross between Mensa-level thought processes and magic.

Her other work includes detective stories and historical novels, again indicative of her wide range. Perhaps due to limited distribution of her novels, Carr is not as well known as she deserves to be among readers: within the community of fantasy and science-fiction writers, however, she is respected as a good craftswoman whose subtlety and disdain for self-promotion and ideological bandwagons keep her at her word-processor instead of on the convention circuit or the soapbox.

—Susan Shwartz

CARR, Terry (Gene). Also writes as Norman Edwards. American. Born in Grants Pass, Oregon, 19 February 1937. Educated at the City College of San Francisco, 1954-57, A. A. 1957; University of California, Berkely, 1957-59. Married 1) Miriam Dyches in 1959 (divorced, 1961); 2) Carol Newmark in 1961. Associate Editor, Scott Meredith Literary Agency, New York, 1962-64; Editor, Ace Books, New York, 1964-71; Editor, *SFWA Bulletin*, 1967-68; Founder, Science Fiction Writers of American Forum, 1967-68; co-editor, *Void* fanzine; editor, with Ron Ellik, *Fanac* fanzine. Since 1971, free-lance writer, editor, and lecturer. Recipient: Hugo Award, for editing, 1959, for criticism, 1973; *Locus* award, for editing, 1983, 1984. Address: c/o Doubleday, 245 Park Avenue, New York, New York 10167, U. S. A.

SCIENCE-FICTION PUBLICATIONS

Novels

Warlord of Kor. New York, Ace, 1963.
Invasion from 2500 (as Norman Edwards, with Ted White). Derby, Connecticut, Monarch, 1964.
Cirque. Indianapolis, Bobbs Merrill, 1977; London, Dobson, 1979.

Short Stories

The Light at the End of the Universe. New York, Pyramid, 1976.

Uncollected Short Stories

"Virra," in *Dream's Edge*, edited by Carr. San Francisco, Sierra Club, 1980.
"Horn o' Plenty," with Leanne Frahm, in *Stellar 7*, edited by Judy-Lynn del Rey. New York, Ballantine, 1981.

OTHER PUBLICATIONS

Other

"Greater Realities; or, How to Write Science Fiction Without Knowing Much about Science," in *Isaac Asimov's Science Fiction Magazine* (New York), January 1983.

Editor, with Donald A. Wollheim, *World's Best Science Fiction 1965* (to *1971*). New York, Ace, 7 vols., 1965-71; *1968* to *1971* vols. published London, Gollancz, 4 vols., 1969-71; first 4 vols. published as *World's Best Science Fiction: First [to Fourth] Series*, Ace, 1970.
Editor, *Science Fiction for People Who Hate Science Fiction*. New York, Doubleday, 1966.
Editor, *New Worlds of Fantasy 1-3*. New York, Ace, 3 vols., 1967-71; vol. 1 published as *Step Outside Your Mind*, London, Dobson, 1969.
Editor, *The Others*. New York, Fawcett. 1968.
Editor, *On Our Way to the Future*. New York, Ace, 1970.
Editor, *Universe 1-15*. New York, Ace, 2 vols., 1971-72; New York, Random House, 3 vols., 1973-74; New York, Double-day, 10 vols., 1976-85; London, Dobson, 10 vols., 1975-80; London, Hale, 1 vol., 1983.
Editor, *The Best Science Fiction of the Year 1-13*. New York, Ballantine, 9 vols., 1972-80; New York, Pocket Books, 4 vols., 1981-84; vols. 4-13 published London, Gollancz, 1975-84.
Editor, *This Side of Infinity*. New York, Ace, 1972.
Editor, *An Exaltation of Stars*. New York, Simon and Schuster, 1973.
Editor, *Into the Unknown*. Nashville, Nelson, 1973.
Editor, *Worlds Near and Far*. Nashville, Nelson, 1974.
Editor, *Fellowship of the Stars: Nine Science Fiction Stories*. New York, Simon and Schuster, 1974.
Editor, *Creatures from Beyond*. Nashville, Nelson, 1975.
Editor, *The Ides of Tomorrow* (for children). Boston, Little Brown, 1976.
Editor, *Planets of Wonder: A Treasury of Space Opera* (for children). Nashville, Nelson, 1976.
Editor, *To Follow a Star* (for children). Nashville, Nelson, 1977.
Editor, *The Infinite Arena* (for children). Nashville, Nelson, 1977.
Editor, *Classic Science Fiction: The First Golden Age*. New York, Harper, 1978; London, Robson, 1979.
Editor, *The Year's Finest Fantasy 1-2*. New York, Berkley, 2 vols., 1978-79.
Editor, *The Best Science Fiction Novellas of the Year 1-2*. New York, Ballantine, 2 vols., 1979-80.
Editor, *Beyond Reality*. New York, Elsevier Nelson, 1979.
Editor, *Dream's Edge: Science Fiction Stories about the Future of the Planet Earth*. San Francisco, Sierra Club, 1980.
Editor, with Martin H. Greenberg, *A Treasury of Modern Fantasy*. New York, Avon, 1981.

Editor, *Fantasy Annual 3-5*. New York, Pocket Books, 1981-82.
Editor, *The Best from Universe*. New York, Doubleday, 1984.
Editor, with Isaac Asimov and Martin H. Greenberg, *100 Great Fantasy Short Short Stories*. New York, Doubleday, and London, Robson, 1984.

*

Terry Carr comments:

I've never been prolific as a fiction writer: most of my "career" has been devoted to editing, first as an editor for Ace Books, where I founded the "Ace Science Fiction Specials" series, 1968-71, and more recently as an editor of anthologies.

As a writer I'm known best for stories about alien creatures ("The Dance of the Changer and the Three," "Hop-Friend," *Cirque*, etc.), but in truth this is an outgrowth of my interest in communication between *all* kinds of "people." Short stories such as "Touchstone" and "They Live on Levels" are examples that don't include aliens: the novel *Cirque* has an important alien character but it's mostly about communication between the human characters. Another "theme" in my stories is transcendental experience: see particularly the novella "The Wind at Starmont" and the novel *Cirque*.

*   *   *

Terry Carr's career clearly illustrates the versatility of many science-fiction personalities. Like other major writers and editors—including Robert Silverberg, Ted White, Gregory Benford, and Harlan Ellison—Carr first gained prominence in the fan community of the 1950's. (His first Hugo Award was for editing the amateur news magazine *Fanac* with Ron Ellik.) This and other amateur magazines helped to launch his career as a professional editor. He also became known for humorous, ironic writing, a significant feature of much of his professional fiction.

In 1961, Carr began writing science fiction professionally. His early novels, *Invasion from 2500* (with Ted White) and *Warlord of Kor*, are clearly potboilers. However, Carr's short stories from the 1960's reveal both literary polish and a fascination with alien beings characteristic of his later work, especially as shown by the millipede in *Cirque*. These qualities are shown in "Hop-Friend," a witty variation on Weinbaum's "A Martian Odyssey."

Carr's mature fiction includes "The Dance of the Changer and the Three" which provides an evocative study of an alien culture as told through one of its myths; "Ozymandias" linking Egyptian burial rituals with cryonics; and "They Live on Levels" in which cultures and characters are gradually revealed through messages between them. All display polish and a wide-ranging imagination.

These qualities also characterize *Cirque*. Carr utilizes the convention of a crisis in the far-future city of Cirque to force his disparate characters to change their lives. The novel, thus structured, adheres to the traditional unities of place, time, and action. It relies heavily on coincidence, yet characters and events are made plausible. The city itself is a near-Utopia, maintained by a literal rejection of filth which must be confronted and accepted. Thus the novel is both a psychological study of the need for change, growth, and acceptance, and a religious allegory of the power of love.

Carr's major importance in the sf field has been as an editor. *Classic Science Fiction* is his most important collection, since it offers not only stories from the Golden Age of the early 1940's but also Carr's meticulously researched background notes on the authors and the period. For his *Universe* series, and the "best of the year" collections, he has become respected as "the editor with impeccable taste."

—Susan Wood

___

CARTER, Angela (Olive, née Stalker). British. Born in Eastbourne, Sussex, 7 May 1940. Educated at the University of Bristol, 1962-65, B. A. in English 1965. Married Paul Carter in 1960 (divorced, 1972). Journalist, Croydon, Surrey, 1958-61. Arts Council Fellow in Creative Writing, University of Sheffield, 1976-78; Visiting Professor of Creative Writing, Brown University, Providence, Rhode Island, 1980-81; Writer-in-Residence, University of Adelaide, 1984. Recipient: Rhys Memorial Prize, 1968; Maugham Award, 1969; Cheltenham Festival prize, 1979; Kurt Maschler Award, for children's book, 1982; James Tait Black Memorial Prize, 1985. Agent: Deborah Rogers Ltd., 49 Blenheim Crescent, London W11 2EF, England.

SCIENCE- FICTION PUBLICATIONS

Novels

Heroes and Villains. London, Heinemann, 1969; New York, Simon and Schuster, 1970.
The Infernal Desire Machines of Dr. Hoffman. London, Hart Davis, 1972; as *The War of Dreams*, New York, Harcourt Brace, 1974.
The Passion of New Eve. London, Gollancz, and New York, Harcourt Brace, 1977.

Short Stories

Fireworks: Nine Profane Pieces. London, Quartet, 1974; New York, Harper, 1981.
The Bloody Chamber and Other Stories. London, Gollancz, 1979; New York, Harper, 1980.
Black Venus's Tale. London, Next-Faber, 1980.

Uncollected Short Stories

"Overture for 'A Midsummer Night's Dream,'" in *Interzone* (Leeds), Autumn 1982.
"The Bridegroom," in *Lands of Never*, edited by Maxim Jakubowski. London, Unwin, 1983.

OTHER PUBLICATIONS

Novels

Shadow Dance. London, Heinemann, 1966; as *Honeybuzzard*, New York, Simon and Schuster, 1967.
The Magic Toyshop. London, Heinemann, 1967; New York, Simon and Schuster, 1968.
Several Perceptions . London, Heinemann, 1968; New York, Simon and Schuster, 1969.
Love. London, Hart Davis, 1971.
Nights at the Circus. London, Chatto and Windus, 1984; New York, Viking Press, 1985.

Plays

Come unto These Yellow Sands (radio plays). Newcastle upon Tyne, Bloodaxe, 1984.

Screenplay: *The Company of Wolves*, with Neil Jordan, 1984.

Radio Plays: *Vampirella*, 1976; *Come unto These Yellow Sands*, 1979; *The Company of Wolves*, from her own story, 1980; *Puss in Boots*, 1982; *A Self-Made Man* (on Ronald Firbank), 1984.

Verse

Unicorn. Leeds, Location Press, 1966.

Other

Miss Z, The Dark Young Lady (for children). London, Heinemann, and New York, Simon and Schuster, 1970.
The Donkey Prince (for children). New York, Simon and Schuster, 1970.
Comic and Curious Cats, illustrated by Martin Leman. London, Gollancz, and New York, Crown, 1979.
The Sadeian Woman: An Exercise in Cultural History. London, Virago, 1979; as *The Sadeian Woman and the Ideology of Pornography*, New York, Pantheon, 1979.
Nothing Sacred: Selected Writings. London, Virago, 1982.
Moonshadow (for children). London, Gollancz, 1982.
Sleeping Beauty and Other Favourite Fairy Tales. London, Gollancz, 1982; New York, Schocken, 1984.

Translator, *The Fairy Tales of Charles Perrault*. London, Gollancz, 1977; New York, Avon, 1978.

*

Angela Carter comments:
Speak as you find.

* * *

Angela Carter describes herself as a Gothic writer; in her fondness for decadent opulence and squalor she is a more stylish Moorcock, with greater charm and humour and less pretentiousness. In her persuasive "Polemical Preface" to *The Sadeian Woman*, she proposes a "moral pornographer" as an artist who demystifies the flesh to reveal "the real relations of man and his kind. " More generally, I think she might see her work as that of a "moral mythographer" who creates myths to destroy myths, pornographic writing being one of her weapons. She, more rightly than de Sade, is "a terrorist of the imagination": he is too boring and disgusting to be terrifying and she seems over-deferential as well as patronizing in her critique of him. Latterly, she has revealed a strong interest in the ideas of mixed natures and of metamorphosis, revamping classic tales of lycanthropy or hermaphroditism, of which the most charming is the uncollected "Overture for 'A Midsummer Night's Dream'" in *Interzone*. Students of Poe should note the fictionalized reconstruction of parts of his life, published in the first issue of *Interzone* (Spring 1982), "The Cabinet of Edgar Allan Poe. "
Most of Carter's fiction may be classed as fantasy, and even the delightful mainstream comedy *Several Perceptions* uses fantasy as its subject. Three of her novels are in the SF genre, two of which are concerned with the harnessing of science in the service of fantasy, so that "science fantasy" might describe

them with particular felicity. The panopticon episode in *Nights at the Circus* fits here, though not the book as a whole, which is a sort of fantastic freak show, less than the sum of its parts but particularly sound on clowns.
In the post-holocaust world of *Heroes and Villains*, civilization has been reduced to ivory towers guarded by Soldiers (the heroes) and menaced by barbarians and mutants. The heroine Marianne, a Professor's daughter, rescues one of the Villains during a raid and flees with him, even though he is her brother's murderer; he rapes, then marries her. The account of their ensuing love-hate relationship is a kind of anti-romance, in which the ambivalent barbaric nastiness and beauty are paraded vividly before us. One of the novel's key themes is the treacherous nature of appearances, yet possibly the book exists principally as the frame for a strange *tableau-vivant* effect, whereby Henri Rousseau's painting *The Sleeping Gypsy* is brought to life.
The Infernal Desire Machines of Dr. Hoffman, where an embodiment of de Sade actually appears in one of the Grand Guignol episodes, is a much more powerful and ambitious work in which the author's evidently wide reading among the great satiric fantasists is everywhere apparent. The picaresque hero, Desiderio (a desirer), is on a mission to kill Dr. Hoffman, generator of mirages that drive men mad, and a quest to find and possess Hoffman's daughter, Albertina. The rational find impressionable hero is a reluctant exorcist and the end to his adventure seems of less importance than the erotic and horrific sideshows which distract him on the way. Although her coldblooded "mad scientist" villain is sufficiently evil, his chilling nature is matched by the resolute sangfroid of the author, even while describing multiple buggery, rape, cannibalism, or eye-juggling; the excessive violence is not accompanied by a commensurable emotional response (this distance is also a notable feature of Carter's readings of her own work). One of the best episodes is in a relatively low key, Desiderio's night of love with the somnambulist daughter of an absentee major, his subsequent arrest for her murder, and escape by climbing one-handed up a chimney. The writing is so good in this novel that one wishes it made a better whole, that it had more humour and more seriousness, in Swift's or even in Beckford's manner.
The Passion of New Eve achieves a better balance of horror and humour, wit and pathos, self-indulgent fantasy and cool iconoclasm. The hero, Evelyn, is an Englishman precipitated into the American nightmare. Not a nice man himself, he mistreats his black mistress in New York, once a "city of visible reason" but now in Ballardian decay. Fleeing to the desert, Evelyn becomes New Eve when captured by lesbian guerrillas; fleeing from them she is raped by the petty tyrant Zero and becomes one of his harem, of lower status than his pigs. She accompanies the nihilist Zero on his mission to kill the film idol Tristessa, whom Evelyn had worshipped. Tristessa is revealed as a transvestite, impregnates Eve, kills Zero, is killed in error by soldiers while Southern California burns in apocalyptic warfare, leaving Eve, after passage through an Earth womb, to escape American shores bearing her child, committed to the sea like a female Prospero. Machismo is mocked splendidly in both its male and female modes in this satiric anti-mythic novel, a bravura performance.
A few of the tales in *Fireworks* fall sufficiently within the genre to serve as an excuse for reading the whole fantastic collection. In the Afterword the author refers to her Gothic tradition as retaining a singular moral function, "that of promoting unease. " She understand the quality of her own art perfectly here.

—Michael J. Tolley

CARTER, Lin(wood Vrooman). American. Born in St. Petersburg, Florida, 9 June 1930. Educated at Columbia University, New York, 1953-54. Served in the United States Army Infantry, 1951-53. Married Noel Vreeland in 1964. Advertising and publishers copy-writer, 1957-69. Since 1969, free-lance writer: editorial consultant, Ballantine Books Adult Fantasy. Recipient; Nova Award, 1972. Agent: Henry Morrison Inc., 320 McLain Street, Bedford Hills, New York 10705, U. S. A.

SCIENCE-FICTION PUBLICATIONS

Novels (series: Callisto; Great Imperium; Green Star; World's End; Zarkon)

The Star Magicians. New York, Ace, 1966.
The Man Without a Planet (Great Imperium). New York, Ace, 1966.
Destination: Saturn, with David Grinnell. New York, Avalon, 1967.
The Flame of Iridar. New York, Belmont, 1967.
The Thief of Thoth. New York, Belmont, 1968.
Tower of the Edge of Time. New York, Belmont, 1968.
The Purloined Planet. New York, Belmont, 1969.
Lost World of Time. New York, New American Library, 1969.
Tower of the Medusa. New York, Ace, 1969.
Star Rogue (Great Imperium). New York, Lancer, 1970.
Outworlder (Great Imperium). New York, Lancer, 1971.
Black Legion of Callisto. New York, Dell, 1972; London, Futura, 1975.
Under the Green Star. New York, DAW, 1972.
Jandar of Callisto. New York, Dell, 1972; London, Futura, 1974.
The Black Star. New York, Dell, 1973.
The Man Who Loved Mars. New York, Fawcett, and London, White Lion, 1973.
Sky Pirates of Callisto. New York, Dell, 1973; London, Futura, 1975.
When the Green Star Calls. New York, DAW, 1973.
The Valley Where Time Stood Still. New York, Doubleday, 1974.
Time War. New York, Dell, 1974.
By the Light of the Green Star. New York, DAW, 1974.
The Warrior of World's End. New York, DAW, 1974.
The Nemesis of Evil (Zarkon). New York, Doubleday, 1975.
Invisible Death (Zarkon). New York, Doubleday, 1975.
Mad Empress of Callisto. New York, Dell, 1975.
Mind Wizards of Callisto. New York, Dell, 1975.
Lankar of Callisto. New York, Dell, 1975.
As the Green Star Rises. New York, DAW, 1975.
The Enchantress of World's End. New York, DAW, 1975.
The Volcano Ogre (Zarkon). New York, Doubleday, 1976.
The Immortal of World's End. New York, DAW, 1976.
In the Green Star's Glow. New York, DAW, 1976.
The Barbarian of World's End. New York, DAW, 1977.
Ylana of Callisto. New York, Dell, 1977.
The City Outside the World. New York, Berkley, 1977.
Renegade of Callisto. New York, Dell, 1978.
The Pirate of World's End. New York, DAW, 1978.
Journey to the Underground World. New York, DAW, 1979.
Tara of the Twilight. New York, Zebra, 1979.
Lost Worlds. New York, DAW, 1980.
Zarkon, Lord of the Unknown, in The Earth-Shaker. New York, Doubleday, 1982.
Eric of Zanthodon. New York, DAW, 1982.
Kellory the Warlock. New York, Doubleday, 1984.

Short Stories

King Kull, with Robert E. Howard. New York, Lancer, 1967.
Beyond the Gates of Dream. New York, Belmont, 1969.

Uncollected Short Stories

"The Dweller in the Tomb" and "Shaggai," in *Dark Things,* edited by August Derleth. Sauk City, Wisconsin, Arkham House, 1971.
"The Higher Heresies of Oolimar," in *Flashing Swords!,* edited by Carter. New York, Doubleday, 1973.
"Black Hawk of Valkarth," in *Fantastic* (New York), September 1974.
"The Vale of Pnath" and "Out of the Ages," in *Nameless Places,* edited by Gerald W. Page. Sauk City, Wisconsin, Arkham House, 1975.
"The Twelve Wizards of Ong," in *Kingdoms of Sorcery,* edited by Carter. New York, Doubleday, 1975.
"The City in the Jewel," in *Fantastic* (New York), December 1975.
"The Curious Custom of the Turjan Seraad," in *Flashing Swords! 3,* edited by Carter. New York, Dell, 1976.
"Zoth-Ommog," in *The Disciples of Cthulhu,* edited by Edward P. Berglund. New York, DAW, 1976.
"The Martian El Dorado of Parker Wintley," in *The DAW Science Fiction Reader,* edited by Donald A. Wollheim. New York, DAW, 1976.
"People of the Dragon," in *Fantastic* (New York), February 1976.
"Black Moonlight," in *Fantastic* (New York), November 1976.
"The Pillars of Hell," in *Fantastic* (New York), December 1977.
"Demon of the Snows," in *The Year's Best Fantasy Stories 6,* edited by Carter. New York, DAW, 1980.
"Dreams in the House of Weir," in *Weird Tales 1,* edited by Carter. New York, Zebra, 1981.
"Something in the Moonlight," in *Weird Tales 2,* edited by Carter. New York, Zebra, 1981.
"The Winfield Inheritance," in *Weird Tales 3,* edited by Carter. New York, Zebra, 1981.
"The Vengeance of Yig," in *Weird Tales 4,* edited by Carter. New York, Zebra, 1983.

OTHER PUBLICATIONS

Novels

The Wizard of Lemuria. New York, Ace, 1965; revised edition, as *Thongor and the Wizard of Lemuria,* New York, Berkley, 1969.
Thongor of Lemuria. New York, Ace, 1966; revised edition, as *Thongor and the Dragon City,* New York, Berkley, 1970.
Thongor Against the Gods. New York, Paperback Library, 1967.
Conan of the Isles, with L. Sprague de Camp. New York, Lancer, 1968.
Thongor at the End of Time. New York, Paperback Library, 1968; London, Tandem, 1970.
Thongor in the City of Magicians. New York, Paperback Library, 1968.
Giant of World's End. New York, Belmont, 1969.
Thongor Fights the Pirates of Tarakus. New York, Berkley, 1970; as *Thongor and the Pirates of Tarakus,* London, Tandem, 1971.
The Quest of Kadji. New York, Belmont, 1971.

The Wizard of Zao. New York, DAW, 1978.
Conan the Liberator, with L. Sprague de Camp. New York, Bantam, 1979; London, Sphere, 1980.
Conan the Barbarian (novelization of screenplay), with L. Sprague de Camp. New York, Bantam, and London, Sphere, 1982.

Short Stories

Conan the Wanderer, with Robert E. Howard and L. Sprague de Camp. New York, Lancer, 1968; London, Sphere, 1974.
Conan of Cimmeria, with Robert E. Howard and L. Sprague de Camp. New York, Lancer, 1969; London, Sphere, 1974.
Conan of Aquilonia (collection), with L. Sprague de Camp. New York, Lancer, 1971.
Conan the Swordsman, with L. Sprague de Camp and Björn Nyberg. New York, Bantam, 1978; London, Sphere, 1979.

Verse

Dreams from R'lyeh. Sauk City, Wisconsin, Arkham House, 1975.

Other

Tolkien: A Look Behind "The Lord of the Rings." New York, Ballantine, 1969.
Lovecraft: A Look Behind the "Cthulhu Mythos." New York, Ballantine, 1972; London, Panther, 1975.
Imaginary Worlds: The Art of Fantasy. New York, Ballantine, 1973.
Middle-Earth: The World of Tolkien, illustrated by David Wenzel. New York, Centaur, 1977.

Editor, *Dragons, Elves, and Heroes.* New York, Ballantine, 1969.
Editor, *The Young Magicians.* New York, Ballantine, 1969.
Editor, *The Magic of Atlantic.* New York, Lancer, 1970.
Editor, *Golden Cities, Far.* New York, Ballantine, 1970.
Editor, *The Dream-Quest of Unknown Kadath*, by H. P. Lovecraft. New York, Ballantine, 1970.
Editor, *Zothique*, by Clark Ashton Smith. New York, Ballantine, 1970.
Editor, *At the Edge of the World*, by Lord Dunsany. New York, Ballantine, 1970.
Editor, *The Doom That Came to Sarnath*, by H. P. Lovecraft. New York, Ballantine, 1971.
Editor, *Hyperborea*, by Clark Ashton Smith. New York, Ballantine, 1971.
Editor, *The Spawn of Cthulhu.* New York, Ballantine, 1971.
Editor, *New Worlds for Old.* New York, Ballantine, 1971.
Editor, *Discoveries in Fantasy.* New York, Ballantine, 1972; London, Pan, 1974.
Editor, *Great Short Novels of Adult Fantasy 1-2.* New York, Ballantine, 2 vols., 1972-73.
Editor, *Beyond the Fields We Know*, by Lord Dunsany. New York, Ballantine, 1972.
Editor, *Evenor*, by George MacDonald. New York, Ballantine, 1972.
Editor, *Xiccarph*, by Clark Ashton Smith. New York, Ballantine, 1972.
Editor, *Poseidonis*, by Clark Ashton Smith. New York, Ballantine, 1973.
Editor, *Flashing Swords! 1-5.* New York, Doubleday, 3 vols., 1973-77; New York, Dell, 2 vols., 1976-81.
Editor, *Over the Hills and Far Away*, by Lord Dunsany. New York, Ballantine, 1974.

Editor, *The Year's Best Fantasy Stories 1-6.* New York, DAW, 6 vols., 1975-80.
Editor, *Kingdoms of Sorcery.* New York, Doubleday, 1976.
Editor, *Realms of Wizardry.* New York, Doubleday, 1976.
Editor, *Weird Tales 1-4.* New York, Zebra, 1981-83.

*   *   *

Lin Carter's seemingly endless appetite for the varieties of heroic fantasy, Sword and Sorcery, magic, adventure, myth, and entertainments have led him along a prolific career as a writer and editor. He now stands at a position of command in a number of fantasy-related subject areas, where he is likely to remain for some considerable time.

It is possible and perhaps too easy to score Carter's characters for their lack of depth or complexity; they are nevertheless more layered and marginal—in the best sense of that word—than the characters of many of his contemporary fantasy writers. And besides, his greatest effects come from his expansive and impudent sense of wonder and an attitude reflecting the need of mankind for myth, heroes, superbeings, and magic to pursue the woes that plague it.

Carter's major work to date is the invaluable *Imaginary Worlds*, a thoughtful introduction, analysis, and survey of fantasy literature that is effective without being self conscious. His section on how magic works is among his better writings. As an editor, his tastes are impeccable, evidenced by the range of choices in *Golden Cities* and *Realms of Wizardry,* both of which bear up after more than ten years.

As the Green Star Rises is appealing among his many works for the haunting way he dramatizes the need for faith. *Kellory the Warlock* shows him using humor and magic as entirely compatible bedfellows, *Tower at the Edge of Time* has a feel a menace and concern that clearly taps some hidden concern of the author as well as revealing his characteristic concerns for pace, revelation, and surprise. *The Warrior of World's End* is a typically good Carter set-up for his reach into the future, his ability to create worlds and moods, and his ability to become besotted with the superheroes he has created. *The Valley Where Time Stood Still* shows Carter ringing with nostalgia and good feeling, creating a magical system that is nearly text-book perfect in its liveliness and the way it maintains dramatic solvency: the rules of the magic are clear, vital to the plot, and the stuff good story-telling is made of.

Some Carter work is unabashedly pulpy, and, like the work of Ron Goulart in this context, is more memorable for its celebration of the pulp medium than any great originality.

Carter is, on balance, fun, engaging, and lively; his work holds up in aggregate because of the enthusiasm that spawned it. He belongs, particularly with *Imaginary Worlds*, on the shelf along with Bullfinch's *Mythology* and Fraser's *The Golden Bough.* His principal service is to show what can be done with fantasy in a good-spirited way.

—Shelly Lowenkopf

CARTMILL, Cleve. Also wrote as Michael Corbin. American. Born in Platteville, Wisconsin, in 1908. Married; one son. Accountant, newspaperman, radio operator; invented the Blackmill system of high-speed typography. *Died 11 February 1964.*

SCIENCE-FICTION PUBLICATIONS

Short Stories (series: Jake Murchison)

The Space Scavengers. Chatsworth, California, Major, 1975.

Uncollected Short Stories

"The Shape of Desire," in *Unknown* (New York), June 1941.
"Bit of Tapestry," in *Unknown* (New York), December 1941.
"Prelude to Armageddon," in *Unknown* (New York), April 1942.
"No Graven Image," in *Unknown* (New York), February 1943.
"Guardian" (as Michael Corbin), in *Unknown* (New York), February 1943.
"The Persecutors," in *Super Science* (Kokomo, Indiana), February 1943.
"Forever Tomorrow," in *Astonishing* (Chicago), April 1943.
"Murderer's Apprentice," in *Science Fiction* (Holyoke, Massachusetts), April 1943.
"The Darker Light," in *Super Science* (Kokomo, Indiana), May 1943.
"Let's Disappear," in *Astounding* (New York), May 1943.
"Wheesht!," in *Unknown* (New York), June 1943.
"Clean-Up," in *Unknown* (New York), October 1943.
"The Link," in *Adventures in Time and Space*, edited by Raymond J. Healy and J. Francis McComas. New York, Random House, 1946; London, Grayson, 1952.
"Deadline," in *The Best of Science Fiction*, edited by Groff Conklin. New York, Crown, 1946.
"With Flaming Swords," in *A Treasury of Science Fiction*, edited by Groff Conklin. New York, Crown, 1948.
"Visiting Yokel," in *My Best Science Fiction Story*, edited by Leo Margulies and O. J. Friend. New York, Merlin Press, 1949.
"Cabal," in *Super Science* (Kokomo, Indiana), January 1949.
"Bells on His Toes," in *Fantasy and Science Fiction* (New York), Fall 1949.
"Punching Pillows," in *Astounding* (New York), June 1950.
"Captain Famine," in *Thrilling Wonder Stories* (New York), December 1950.
"Number Nine," in *Great Stories of Science Fiction*, edited by Murray Leinster. New York, Random House, 1951; London, Cassell, 1953.
"The Green Cat," in *The Outer Reaches*, edited by August Derleth. New York, Pellegrini and Cudahy, 1951; London, Consul, 1963.
"You Can't Say That," in *New Tales of Space and Time*, edited by Raymond J. Healy. New York, Holt, 1951; London, Weidenfeld and Nicholson, 1952.
"Overthrow," in *Journey to Infinity*, edited by Martin Greenberg. New York, Gnome Press, 1951.
"At Your Service," in *Thrilling Wonder Stories* (New York), August 1951.
"The Huge Beast," in *Best from Fantasy and Science Fiction*, edited by Anthony Boucher and J. Francis McComas. Boston, Little Brown, 1952.
"Nor Iron Bars," in *Fantasy and Science Fiction* (New York), August 1952.
"My Lady Smiles," in *Fantasy and Science Fiction* (New York), November 1953.
"Age Cannot Wither," in *Beyond 10* (New York), 1955.
"Youth, Anybody?," in *Fantasy and Science Fiction* (New York), November 1955.
"Hell Hath Fury," in *Hell Hath Fury*, edited by George Hay.

London, Spearman, 1963.
"Oscar," in *Fifty Short Science Fiction Tales*, edited by Isaac Asimov and Groff Conklin. New York, Macmillan, 1963.
"The Bargain," in *The Unknown 5*, edited by D. R. Benson. New York, Pyramid, 1964.
"Some Day We'll Find You," in *Dimension 4*, edited by Groff Conklin. New York, Pyramid, 1964.
"No News Today," in *Terror!*, edited by Larry T. Shaw. New York, Lancer, 1966.

OTHER PUBLICATIONS

Other

"Why I Selected 'Visiting Yokel,'" in *My Best Science Fiction Story*, edited by Leo Margulies and O. J. Friend. New York, Merlin Press, 1949.

*   *   *

Some writers in science fiction, as in other fields of literature, achieve notoriety not for their body of work but for a single story or novel. Tom Godwin ("The Cold Equations") is one such writer. Another is Cleve Cartmill, for "Deadline" (*Astounding*, March 1944). Although "Deadline" has dubious literary merits (predictable plot, pedestrian handling), the story is unique in that it describes, in considerable scientific detail, the manufacture and use of an atomic bomb a year before the United States dropped the first genuine atomic bombs on Hiroshima and Nagasaki. Its publication did not cause an immediate furor in science-fiction circles; it did, however, cause one in the War Department.

Shortly after the novelette appeared, Cartmill was visited by a representative of Military Intelligence and questioned at some length; his file of correspondence with the editor of *Astounding*, John W. Campbell, concerning "Deadline" was also confiscated. Cartmill was later cleared of any wrongdoing, although he was told that he had "violated personal security" in wartime by publicly disseminating the facts contained in the story. These facts, however, were a matter of public record, as Campbell himself pointed out to the Military in denying their request not to publish any further speculation on nuclear fission. Following the close of World War II, "Deadline" became a link in the argument that science fiction is a valid medium for predicting the future. It was also pointed to with pride as an example of science fiction as a "serious" art form for adults, rather than improbable escapism for juveniles, thereby worthy of consideration not only by members of the scientific community but by the heads of government.

Despite the fact that Cartmill's rather extensive output of science fiction and fantasy is largely forgotten today, at least some of it is of a quality to interest the serious student. His best work, perhaps, is the highly imaginative short novel "Hell Hath Fury." Other excellent efforts include his first published story, "Oscar," and a grim little tale called "The Bargain." Cartmill also wrote space opera; popular in the 1940's was his "Space Salvage" series featuring Jake Murchison and his crew of the spaceship *Dolphin* who tackled "impossible" problems and made fantastic rescues in space. The best of these stories were posthumously collected as *The Space Scavengers*, the only book to bear Cartmill's name.

—Bill Pronzini

CARY, Julian. See **TUBB, E. C.**

CHALKER, Jack L(aurence). American. Born in Norfolk, Virginia, 17 December 1944. Educated at Towson State College, Baltimore, B. S. 1966; Johns Hopkins University, Baltimore, M. L. A 1969. Served in the United States Air Force 135th Air Commando Group, 1968-71, and the Maryland Air National Guard, 1968-73: Staff Sergeant. Married Eva C. Whitley in 1978. English, history, and geography teacher in Baltimore high schools, 1966-78. Since 1961, Founder-Director, Mirage Press, Baltimore; editor *Mirage* fanzine. Agent: Eleanor Wood, Blassingame McCauley and Wood, 432 Park Avenue South, Suite 1205, New York, New York 10016. Address: Mirage Press, Box 28, Manchester, Maryland 21102, U. S. A.

SCIENCE-FICTION PUBLICATIONS

Novels (series: Dancing Gods; Four Lords of the Diamond; Soul Rider; Well World)

A Jungle of Stars. New York, Ballantine, 1976.
Well World:
    Midnight at the Well of Souls. New York, Ballantine, 1977; London, Penguin, 1981.
    Exiles at the Well of Souls. New York, Ballantine, 1978; London, Penguin, 1982.
    Quest for the Well of Souls. New York, Ballantine, 1978; London, Penguin, 1982.
    The Return of Nathan Brazil. New York, Ballantine, n.d.; London, Penguin, 1984.
    Twilight at the Well of Souls. New York, Ballantine, 1980; London, Penguin, 1984.
Dancers in the Afterglow. New York, Ballantine, 1978.
The Web of the Chozen. New York, Ballantine, 1978.
A War of Shadows. New York, Ace, 1979.
Four Lords of the Diamond:
    Lilith: A Snake in the Grass. New York, Ballantine, 1981.
    Cerberus: A Wolf in the Fold. New York, Ballantine, 1982.
    Charon: A Dragon at the Gate. New York, Ballantine, 1982.
    Medusa: A Tiger by the Tail. New York, Ballantine, 1983.
Soul Rider:
    Spirits of Flux and Anchor. New York, Tor, 1984.
    Empires of Flux and Anchor. New York, Tor, 1984.
    Masters of Flux and Anchor. New York, Tor, 1985.
The River of Dancing Gods. New York, Ballantine, 1984.
Demons of the Dancing Gods. New York, Ballantine, 1984.
The Messiah Choice. New York, Bluejay, 1985.
Downtiming the Night Side. New York, Tor, 1985.
Vengeance of the Dancing Gods. New York, Ballantine, 1985.

Uncollected Short Stories

"No Hiding Place," in *Stellar 3*, edited by Judy-Lynn del Rey. New York, Ballantine, 1977.
"In the Wilderness," in *Analog* (New York), July 1978.
"Dance Band on the Titanic," in *The 1979 Annual World's Best SF*, edited by Donald A. Wollheim. New York, DAW, 1979.
"Stormsong Runner," in *Whispers 2*, edited by Stuart David Schiff. New York, Doubleday, 1979.

OTHER PUBLICATIONS

Novels

And the Devil Will Drag You Under. New York, Ballantine, 1979.
The Devil's Voyage. New York, Doubleday, 1981.

Other

The New H. P. Lovecraft Bibliography. Baltimore, Mirage Press, 1962; revised edition, with Mark Owings, as *The Revised H. P. Lovecraft Bibliography*, 1973.
The Index to the Science-Fantasy Publishers, with Mark Owings. Baltimore, Mirage Press, 1966; revised edition, as *Index to the SF Publishers*, 1979.
The Necronomicon: A Study, with Mark Owings. Baltimore, Mirage Press, 1967.
An Informal Biography of Scrooge McDuck. Baltimore, Mirage Press, 1974.

Editor, *In Memoriam Clark Ashton Smith*. Baltimore, Mirage Press, 1963.
Editor, *Mirage on Lovecraft*. Baltimore, Mirage Press, 1964.

*

Bibliography: in *Program Book*, Paracon 1, State College, Pennsylvania, 1978.

Jack L. Chalker comments:

Although I have a technical background, my degrees are in the social, not the pure, sciences, and my work generally reflects this. My stories are about people, mostly ordinary people, caught up in extraordinary circumstances and usually changed by them. They use the fun-house mirror reflection of science fiction to examine people and culture, including ideology, as I see them today. The themes are anti-dogmatic: ideologies and human preachments are taken apart, examined, and generally found wanting. For this reason, a lot of my work had been taken as anti-utopian and downbeat, but there is a strain of optimism there because, not matter what, mankind copes with adversity and overcomes, although never without cost. There is an inherently absurdist streak in man which has caused him, over six thousand years of recorded history to kill, torture, and maim, mostly in the name of the people. Man adapts, advances, and grows despite this.

On the individual level, my stories examine the way human beings treat each other, generally brutalizing those most in need of help, and those individuals' quests for their own better life. For these themes, and others, interwoven in my stories, science fiction provides the perfect metaphors. I am a strongly political writer, without ideology, only hope. And yet all my stories are superficially plots of twist and turn, diverting entertainments, problems to be solved. Pacing is all important to me; I want the reader to turn to the next page, to keep reading, and to have a good time as my serious themes creep into the entertainment but never get in its way.

*   *   *

Jack L. Chalker's novels combine a number of the genres from which SF arises: fantasy, detective fiction, Utopian fiction, and scientific extrapolation. The Well World novels and the Lords of the Diamond series stress fantastic metamorphoses of aliens and mystery-thriller elements, while Utopian concerns, especially the communalism of Plato's city of pigs versus radical independence, combine philosophically with the mystery-thriller and an increasing concern for mimetic detail in many later works.

A Jungle of Stars is a frame novel, a story within a story that Chalker frequently uses to begin his alien novels. In this case he uses a realistic Vietnam patrol as a contrast to the fantastic struggle between the two aliens, the Bromgrev and the Hunter, both of whom are failed gods. Chalker sensitively handles the Vietnam patrol, the romance between Paul Savage and Jennifer Barron, but leaves the assumption of power at the end unsettled. No choice is made between the dictatorial Hunter and the Bromgrev communal totalitarianism; Paul's vengeance ethic may be modified by love, but his assumption of power leaves major questions unsettled.

Midnight at the Well of Souls further explores this question of what to do with power through the dilemma of another set of failed gods, the Markovians, whose answer is the creation of the Well World with hexes serving as prototypes for the universe's population. The metaphysical search which should be undertaken by Nathan Brazil is deflected by an adventure-quest to the Markovian brain by those thirsting for power and by a fascination with the different alien cultures of the hexes. Personality and character are cleverly matched to a species and an ecological environment. The threat to control the universe in *Exiles at the Well of Souls* and *Quest for the Well of Souls* is no longer directly *through* the Markovian brain but through the recreation of the Well World's transforming powers on New Pompeii. As in the previous novels, power for that purpose is subordinate to a quest, this time for rockets which crash land on the hexes of the Well World. The struggle to recover a rocket to travel to New Pompeii is the motive for the plots of both novels; *Exiles* ends when one rocket is destroyed by the Gedemondans, whereas in *Quest* the struggle for the rocket is successful, but the use of the combined power of a sentient Obie and New Pompeii becomes subordinate to Mavra Chang's thirst for exploration, delaying again the answer to the metaphysical problem. *The Return of Nathan Brazil* sets up a problem of universal proportions which is ultimately resolved in *Twilight at the Well of Souls* when the Council of the Community of Worlds is invaded by virus-sized Dreel, and an untested weapon using Gil Zinder's Markovian mathematics, in part a satire on nuclear weapons, is used to repulse the Dreel. The weapon creates a growing hole in the universe that absorbs worlds and stars; it can only be countered by shutting down the Well World computer, restarting it, and creating the universe anew. While *The Return* ends with Nathan Brazil's invasion of the Well World to fix the computer and Brazil's supposed death, *Twilight* traces the battle to get the real Brazil into the Well World computer despite the armies of the majority of the hexes. Most of the major Well World characters reappear in these two novels such as Mavra Chang, Gil Zinder, and Serge Ortega, but the suspense of conflict in *Twilight* really is subordinated to Chalker's exploration of cosmology and metaphysics. The dilemma of Brazil, to destroy the universe in order to correct its flaw and start anew or to do nothing, is nicely worked out, as the motives of immortals, the origins of myths and regligions, are elaborated in the Well World final volume.

What to do with absolute power is a more limited political question in *The Web of the Chosen* : how to respond to human force and hegemony with a virus capable of changing humans to Choz. While becoming free of Mozes, the computer, and controlling the virus occupy much of the plot, the struggle between Choz and human results in conquest and a new apocalyptic beginning for social institutions. Bar Holiday, the transformed scout, grows as bored with the new Choz society as he was by the bureaucratic fascism of human society however. *Dancers in the Afterglow* uses an alien conquest and defeat further to explore Utopian alternatives. Ondine, a resort planet, is a test case for two systems roughly akin to Maoist communism, where "we" replaces "I," and to capitalist individualism. While the work camps established by the alien robots resemble the worst Cambodian experiments, the result does produce a mindless happiness. Though no one fares well in the psychic competition of pre-conquest Ondine, the loss of individuality may not be worth the communistic happiness. *A War of Shadows* deals with this same political struggle in which the left and right victimize the United States, although the left is merely an extension of a conservative fascist conspiracy in government itself. Chalker handles the science, in this case viral research and recombinant DNA, better than in any previous novel, and the political forces are nicely characterized; however, the book resembles the science thriller *The Andromeda Strain* far more than science fiction. *And the Devil Will Drag You Under* returns to the esentially comic dystopianism of *The Web of the Chosen*. Mac Walters and Jill McCulloch, in an effort to save the world from an asteroid about to collide with it, go to alternate worlds to obtain powerful jewels for an alcoholic demon, Asmodeus Mogart, who says he will save the earth with them once he has six. In the process of their mission, Mac and Jill visit and evaluate alternate Utopian plans such as a stone age culture and a society similar to Islamic cultures only to be betrayed by Mogart, whom they unwittingly send to "hell," while they in turn are rescued by responsible demons. But beneath this cosmic sugar coating is cultural evaluation and an awareness of the responsibility of power. *The Identity Matrix*, about mind switching and its effects and in the form of a government report, is mostly told by Victor Gonser, a political scientist, whose mind is switched by aliens resembling jelly fish, the Urulu, and by his own people. The Urulu are fighting another group of aliens called the Association, but neither alien group, with the possible exception of the Association, is as dangerous as the federal government's Identity Matrix Center, whose programmed Skinnerian development gets out of hand. Chalker ponders once more how much social control is beneficial.

The Four Lords of the Diamond tetralogy explores an alien mystery on the four Warden planets, but this mystery only leads to more social and political exploration. The Confederacy, a league of several hundred worlds, is aware of a technologically superior alien force having some connection to the Warden planets, which have served as a Confederacy prison due to a symbiont life form, the wardens, that infests people, killing them if they attempt to leave. In order to gather information about and hopefully stall the aliens, the Confederacy replicates the mind of its best agent in four people's bodies. The mission of each is to murder a Warden planet Lord and report to the agent whose mind has been copied. The series thus has an extended plot that covers the Confederacy's gradual discovery of facets of the aliens which resolves in *Medusa: A Tiger by the Tail*, while each novel has its own action where the agent-assassin adjusts to his new world, evaluates its system, and attempts to murder its Lord. In *Lilith: A Snake in the Grass* Cal Tremon, the agent, learns to deal with a warden infestation that destroys technology, even clothes, unless emotionally willed not to. Lilith, much like earth, can only support a feudal organization based on ability to control wardens, to build and preserve and not merely destroy. Despite this positive talent, the Lilith culture exploits its worker-peasants. Marek Kreegan, the Lord who defends this system, is killed indirectly through Cal, although in terms of dealing with the aliens, this is a mistake. In *Cerberus: A Wolf in the Fold* Qwin Zhang must deal with a planet whose citizens live and work in huge tree dwellings and offices above an ocean. Here the wardens allow mind swapping with the result that those who serve the planet best are rewarded with new bodies, creating a possible immortality, as long as a steady stream of children allows the exchange. In *Charon: A Dragon at the Gate*, Park Lacoch must deal with a hot, steamy world in which magic is possible through the wardens, fostering religious cults and shape changing that oddly coexists with small town life and pre-fossil fuel manufacturing. In *Medusa: A Tiger by the Tail* Taran Bul learns to deal with a totalitarian Nazi-inspired culture on an extremely cold planet. Like characters in Le Guin's *The Left Hand of Darkness*, Medusans can change sex, although in Chalker's novel this leads to sexual enslavement. A similar pattern occurs in each novel in which the agent-assassin is modified by love to hate the planet's social organization, but only to see its similarity to the Confederacy. The senior agent, "Lewis Carroll," with the combined memories of his four replicates, is led to love humanity, but hate both Warden and Confederacy governments. Failing to find a formula for peace, "Carroll" watches helplessly as two alien forces collapse the interplanetary structure of the Confederacy, forcing humanity to redevelop, learning symbiosis rather than intolerance and conquest. In this series, the Indians have defeated the cowboys.

Downtiming the Night Side, like the Warden world novels, shows earth, the home world, being saved by the frontier, colonized nearby planets, in this long planned time travel book. Though there are many time spans in *Downtiming*, the major ones are an earth base a couple hundred years in the future with an energy problem seeking assistance from the past, the first American time travel installation two hundred years earlier, and two periods in Karl Marx's life in Vienna and London. Ron Moosic, a security officer for the time travel installation, is the point of view character who becomes, or has been, a dying London street boy in Marx's time, a nun in the later Middle Ages, a whore in several times and cultures, his own wife, a 19th-century German homosexual, and numerous other roles in this roller coaster ride of a novel. The Soul Rider series, presently in three volumes, but soon to be in five or six, consists of *Spirits of Flux and Anchor*, *Empires of Flux and Anchor*, and *Masters of Flux and Anchor*. World has been created out of matter-energy from an alternate universe or Flux by humanity and godlike computers. Since this partnership, people are classed by how much Flux energy they can process or use, and governments and religions are established on the nine Anchor communities to handle steady state or energy/matter conversions. As in Chalker's other novels, social organizations are weighed in terms of their necessity and corrosion of individual liberty, with satiric thrusts at earth's own theocracies. Power, as usual, corrupts.

At this point in Chalker's career, one has to consider him a major SF writer in terms of output, over 20 novels, and narrative quality. An allusive style similar to Le Guin's or Lem's and deeper characterization are all he needs to be great, but what he has, a good imagination, a fascination with political and social orders, and satisfying, suspenseful action plots, serve him and his readers well.

—Craig Wallace Barrow

CHANDLER, A(rthur) Bertram. Australian. Born in Aldershot, Hampshire, England, 28 March 1912. Educated at Peddar's Lane Council School, and Sir John Leman School, Beccles, Suffolk. Married 1) Joan Chandler; 2) Susan Schlenker; two daughters and one son. Apprentice, rising to Third Officer, Sun Shipping Company, London, 1928-35; Fourth Officer, rising to Chief Officer, Shaw Savill Line, London, 1936-55; Third Officer, rising to Master, Union Steam Ship Company of New Zealand, Wellington, 1956-75. Recipient: Ditmar award (Australia), 1969, 1971, 1974, 1976; Seiun Sho award (Japan), 1975; Invisible Little Man Award, 1975; Australian Literature Board Fellowship, 1980. Guest of Honor, World SF Convention, Chicago, 1981. *Died 6 June 1984.*

SCIENCE-FICTION PUBLICATIONS

Novels (series: Empress Irene; John Grimes; Rim Worlds)

Bring Back Yesterday (Rim Worlds). New York, Ace, 1961; London, Allison and Busby, 1981.
Rendezvous on a Lost World (Rim Worlds). New York, Ace, 1961; as *When the Dream Dies*, London, Allison and Busby, 1981.
The Rim of Space (Rim Worlds). New York, Avalon, 1961; London, Allison and Busby, 1981.
Beyond the Galactic Rim, The Ship from Outside (Rim Worlds). New York, Ace, 1963; London, Allison and Busby, 1982.
The Hamelin Plague. Derby, Connecticut, Monarch, 1963.
Glory Planet. New York, Avalon, 1964.
The Deep Reaches of Space. London, Jenkins, 1964.
Into the Alternate Universe (Grimes), *The Coils of Time*. New York, Ace, 1964.
Empress of Outer Space (Empress), *The Alternate Martians*. New York, Ace, 1965.
Space Mercenaries (Empress). New York, Ace, 1965.
The Road to the Rim (Grimes). New York, Ace, 1967.
Contraband from Otherspace (Grimes). New York, Ace, 1967.
Nebula Alert (Empress). New York, Ace, 1967.
False Fatherhood (Grimes). Sydney, Horwitz, 1968; as *Spartan Planet*, New York, Dell, 1969.
Catch the Star Winds (Rim Worlds). New York, Lancer, 1969.
The Sea Beasts. New York, Curtis, 1971.
To Prime the Pump (Grimes). New York, Curtis, 1971.
The Inheritors, The Gateway to Never (Grimes). New York, Ace, 1972.
The Bitter Pill. Melbourne, Wren, 1974.
The Big Black Mark (Grimes). New York, DAW, 1975.
The Broken Cycle (Grimes). London, Hale, 1975; New York, DAW, 1979.
The Way Back (Grimes). London, Hale, 1976; New York, DAW, 1978.
Star Courier (Grimes). London, Hale, and New York, DAW, 1977.
The Far Traveller (Grimes). London, Hale, 1977; New York, DAW, 1979.
To Keep the Ship (Grimes). London, Hale, and New York, DAW, 1978.
Matilda's Stepchildren. London, Hale, 1979; New York, DAW, 1983.
Star Loot (Grimes). New York, DAW, 1980; London, Hale, 1981.
Kelly Country. Ringwood, Victoria, Penguin, 1983.
Frontier of the Dark. New York, Ace, 1984.
The Last Amazon. New York, DAW, 1984.

Short Stories (series: John Grimes in all books)

The Rim Gods. New York, Ace, 1968.

The Dark Dimensions, Alternate Orbits. New York, Ace, 1971; *Alternate Orbits* published separately as *Commodore at Sea,* 1979.

The Hard Way Up. New York, Ace, 1972.

Up to the Sky in Ships. Cambridge, Massachusetts, NESFA Press, 1982.

Uncollected Short Stories (series: Rim Worlds)

"The Last Hunt" (Rim Worlds), in *Galaxy* (New York), March 1973.

"On the Account" (Rim Worlds), in *Galaxy* (New York), May 1973.

"Hard Luck Story," in *Void 1* (St. Kilda, Victoria), 1975.

"The Hairy Parents," in *Void 2* (St. Kilda, Victoria), 1975.

"Rim Change," in *Galaxy* (New York), August 1975.

"The Mountain Movers," in *The Zeitgeist Machine,* edited by Damien Broderick. London, Angus and Robertson, 1977.

"The Long Fall," in *Amazing* (New York), July 1977.

"No Room in the Stable," in *Asimov's Choice: Astronauts and Androids.* New York, Dale, 1978.

"The Sleeping Beast" (Rim Worlds), in *Amazing* (New York), January 1978.

"Grimes among the Gourmets," in *Other Worlds,* edited by Paul Collins. St. Kilda, Victoria, Void, 1978.

"Grimes at Glenrowan," in *Asimov's Choice: Comets and Computers,* edited by George H. Scithers. New York, Davis, 1978.

"Doggy in the Window," in *Amazing* (New York), November 1978.

"Journey's End," in *Amazing* (New York), February 1979.

"Grimes and the Great Race," in *Isaac Asimov's Science Fiction Magazine* (New York), April 1980.

"A Clockwork Lemon," in *Isaac Asimov's Science Fiction Magazine* (New York), June 1982.

"Grimes and the Odd Gods," in *Fantasy and Science Fiction* (New York), March 1983.

"Grimes and the Jailbirds," in *Fantasy and Science Fiction* (New York), May 1984.

*   *   *

Bibliography: "Bibliography of the Works of A. Bertram Chandler" by Ross Pavlac, in *Marcon XIII* (Columbus, Ohio), March 1978.

A. Bertram Chandler commented:

(1981) Quite a few years ago Robert Heinlein said, "Only people who know ships can write convincingly about spaceships." At the time I thought that this was very true. I have not changed my opinion. I believe that the crews of the *real* spaceships of the future, vessels going a long way in a long time, will have far more in common with today's seamen than with today's airmen. I freely admit that my stories are essentially sea stories and that John Grimes, my series character, is descended from Hornblower. At a book-signing recently in Fukuoka I felt flattered when one of my Japanese faithful readers gave me one of Forester's Hornblower novels to autograph.

*   *   *

A. Bertram Chandler produced an enormous body of work that is based on his experiences as a merchant mariner, his love of adventure fiction, and the role model synthesis of these two aspects, the fictional character of Horatio Hornblower.

Beginning in about 1959, Chandler developed the character of John Grimes, then an ensign, and the concept of the Rim World—rim stars out on the fringes of galactic civilization. *The Road to the Rim* reads as though it was composed of stories for magazines. Grimes becomes aware of his love of space, his fascination for the Rim World, and the adventure to be found there.

Perhaps because he had such a good eye for detail and was able to "sell" the locale of the Rim World, Chandler found the necessary formula, in which he intertwined the lives of Derek Calver (from *The Rim of Space*), Sonya Verrill, and then John Grimes, whom Verrill eventually marries. Grimes extends his activities over a period of time covered in thirteen novels to the point where he becomes a commodore in the Rim Worlds Merchant Navy, and finds a home for himself on a remote planet, not only because it is "closer to work," but because it allows a comfortable life style.

Chandler was a jovial man with an impish sense of humor—he makes frequent topical allusions to current events, the works of other science-fiction and imaginative writers, and, sometimes, even to such historical events as the mutiny on *H. M. S. Bounty.* His works will never be accused of heavy going, an overly philosophical point of view—unless you include frequent support of nudism—or raising complex moral issues.

His plots tend to be direct and linear: is Grimes getting too soft for duty? Do his men respect him? Is he in danger of becoming a ladies' man? (No.) Can he withstand temptations to take bribes? (Yes) Can he be effective in putting down a mutiny? His characters could certainly be role models for television situation comedies or adventures: the good guys and the aliens are readily apparent; there are few shades of grey, no nuances of meaning, no room for misunderstanding.

As a consequence of flat characters, his dialog is rarely exciting, and the reader, if not careful, can lose the way—who is saying what? Several critics have noted the use of stock phrases and clichés. It is also fair to question his speech cadences, and the fact that the aliens are distinguished from the Earthlings only by a different set of clichés.

What makes him endure, then? It is the obvious good cheer, the quick turn of plot, the excellent sense of background, and the realization that sea stories and space opera have a common existential bond. Grimes, at best a good man, is just short of boring, thanks to his over-all niceness and mischievous humor. An excellent way to sample the Chandler Rim Worlds is in *The Dark Dimensions,* in which Chandler puts Grimes in the Captain's Paradise situation by having two John Grimeses, one each from a parallel universe. The two meet, each with a different wife, and each cuckolds the other and, by implication, himself. Naughty, funny for as long as it lasts, and sensible enough not to last too long.

Chandler is pure entertainment, lacking the craft and intricacy to secure him a more permanent niche.

—Shelly Lowenkopf

CHARBONNEAU, Louis (Henry). Also writes as Carter Travis Young. American. Born in Detroit, Michigan, 20 January 1924. Educated at the University of Detroit, A. B. 1948, M. A. 1950. Served in the United States Army Air Force, 1943-46: Staff Sergeant. Married 1)Hilda Sweeney in 1945 (died 1984); 2) Diane Fries in 1984. Instructor in English, University of Detroit, 1948-52; copywriter, Mercury Advertising Agency, Los Angeles, 1952-56; staff writer, Los Angeles

Times, 1956-71; free-lance writer, 1971-74; Editor, Security World Publishing Company, Los Angeles, 1974-79. Since 1979, free-lance writer. Agent: Scott Meredith Literary Agency, 845 Third Avenue, New York, New York 10022, U. S. A.

SCIENCE-FICTION PUBLICATIONS

Novels

No Place on Earth. New York, Doubleday, 1958; London, Jenkins, 1966.
Corpus Earthling. New York, Doubleday, 1960; London, Digit, 1963.
The Sentinel Stars. New York, Bantam, and London, Corgi, 1964.
Psychedelic-40. New York, Bantam, 1965; as *The Specials*, London, Jenkins, 1967.
Down to Earth. New York, Bantam, 1967; as *Antic Earth*, London, Jenkins, 1967.
The Sensitives (novelization of screenplay). New York, Bantam, 1968.
Barrier World. New York, Lancer, 1970.
Embryo (novelization of screenplay). New York, Warner, 1976.

OTHER PUBLICATIONS

Novels

Night of Violence. New York, Torquil, and London, Digit, 1959; as *The Trapped Ones*, London, Barker, 1960.
Nor All Your Tears. New York, Torquil, 1959; as *The Time of Desire*, London, Digit, 1960.
Way Out. London, Barrie and Rockliff, and New York, Banner, 1966.
Down from the Mountain. New York, Doubleday, 1969.
And Hope to Die. New York, Ace, 1970.
From a Dark Place. New York, Dell, 1974.
Intruder. New York, Doubleday, 1979.
The Lair. New York, Fawcett, 1979.
The Brea File. New York, Doubleday, 1983.

Novels as Carter Travis Young

The Wild Breed. New York, Doubleday, 1960; as *The Sudden Gun*, London, Hammond, 1960.
The Savage Plain. New York, Doubleday, 1961; London, Hammond, 1963.
Shadow of a Gun. New York, Fawcett, 1961; London, Muller, 1962.
The Bitter Iron. New York, Doubleday, 1964; London, Ward Lock, 1965.
Long Boots, Hard Boots. New York, Doubleday, 1965; London, Ward Lock, 1966.
Why Did They Kill Charley? New York, Doubleday, and London, Ward Lock, 1967.
Winchester Quarantine. New York, Doubleday, 1970.
The Pocket Hunters. New York, Doubleday, 1972.
Winter of the Coup. New York, Doubleday, 1972.
The Captive. New York, Doubleday, 1973.
Guns of Darkness. New York, Doubleday, 1974.
Blaine's Law. New York, Doubleday, 1974.
Red Grass. New York, Doubleday, 1976.
Winter Drift. New York, Doubleday, 1980.

Play

Television Play: *Cry of Silence* (*The Outer Limits* series), 1963-64.

*

Manuscript Collection: University of Oregon Library, Eugene.

Louis Charbonneau comments:
My science-fiction novels, most of which were written in the 1960's, would seem to be out of the mainstream of much current SF, though perhaps part of a longer running stream, one that begins with existing conditions, problems, or possibilities and projects them into an imagined future not all that remote, and with an emphasis on human characters rather than upon the grotesque or fantastic. It has been called social-science fiction, with a moral dimension often fairly evident. I can admire those fantasists who create wholly imagined worlds with little if any relation to our own, but I find myself as a writer interested more in the human predicament, as it is now or, given certain circumstances, as it might be in the future.

* * *

Notable first novels are rare; notable first science-fiction novels virtually non-existent. With his first work, *No Place on Earth,* Louis Charbonneau showed himself a scarce bird indeed—a science-fiction writer with almost no interest in mechanisms and remote worlds. The peculiar appeal of this yarn lies not in outré surroundings or wild technology but in the little-known territory of man himself.

It is in its impact upon man, in fact, that Charbonneau finds a writer's use for science. He acknowledges with us that technology is marvelous, that we reap great benefits from the application of machines to our culture. But he confesses almost no background to deal with the intricacies of gadgetry; his concern is with the social aspects of things like automatons. So, in *No Place on Earth*, Charbonneau tackles the population alarm expressed by Malthus and treats its implications like the good reporter he is. His prose is lean and highly readable, and he gives life to his writing through heavy reliance upon dialog. His characters do not have to be complex, because he generalizes from selection of typical people who must deal with extraordinary demands. In a sense Charbonneau appears to encourage all of his readers to expand to meet the pressures imposed upon them by a sometimes-bewildering technology. Concepts like mind control and sirloin capsules have both good and bad points, as we see through the author's often-humorous treatment.

Like many good writers, Charbonneau has learned his craft in the demanding school of journalism (he still writes a daily column in the Los Angeles Times about the old Farmers Market). He learned about people and their glands—some readers might say a bit too much so in works like *Corpus Earthling*. This novel imagines the people of Earth being literally occupied by aliens. What might eventually have resulted without the enterprise of a college instructor could have produced quite a different story. But as said instructor gains telepathic knowledge of this invasion, the whole fiendish plot is revealed. It is the way he obtains his information—in bed with several coeds—that might prove objectionable to staid readers of this story. The research method, nontheless, does stress the author's realistic understanding of the human condition to counter this threat.

A different slice of such understanding is found in *The Sentinel Stars,* where we encounter every person born as a debtor. This means the entire population must spend its whole life span paying off the debt, which can't be done because of the high cost of living. In good reporter fashion, Charbonneau sounds a familiar dirge: a sense of slavery to the times. But all is not lost, for the hero—who bears the same sort of numerical I. D. as all of us today—suggests rebellious measures which might create unrest in contemporary free-spending law makers consciences.

It is the social-scientific concern of Charbonneau which has perhaps discouraged his recent production of science fiction. He expresses distaste for the gee-whiz aspects of much current writing, although he admits the value to society of many devices (he finds a word processor convenient in writing, for example). But he deplores the dehumanizing evident in works of science fiction which reach out far into the cosmos. So, evidently, do the Japanese readers of his *No Place on Earth,* which has gone through recent reprintings in that country. Charbonneau's labeling of current movies, with their spectacular special effects and elaborate settings, as "extended comics" would find considerable endorsement among serious, mature readers of science fiction.

Louis Charbonneau remains a worthy and interesting figure in the world of science fiction, not only because of his stylistic appeal, but also because he represents a source of the kind of science fiction which provided the impetus for the sort of reading that is still among the more interesting pursuits in a gadget-infested world.

—Robert H. Wilcox

CHARNAS, Suzy McKee. American. Born in New York City, 22 October 1939. Educated at New York High School of Music and Art; Barnard College, New York, B. A. in economic history 1961; New York University, M. A. Married Stephen Charnas in 1968; two step-children. Peace Corps English and history teacher, Girls' High School, Ogbomoso, Nigeria, 1961-62; Lecturer in Economic History, University of Ibadan, Ife, Nigeria, 1962-63; English-History Core Teacher, New Lincoln School, New York, 1965-67; worked for Community Mental Health organization, New York, 1967-69. Since 1969, freelance writer. Agent: Lynn Seligman, Julian Bach Literary Agency, 747 Third Avenue, New York, New York 10017. Address: 520 Cedar NE, Alburquerque, New Mexico 87106, U.S.A.

SCIENCE-FICTION PUBLICATIONS

Novels

Walk to the End of the World. New York, Ballantine, 1974; London, Gollancz, 1979.
Motherlines. New York, Berkley, 1979; London, Gollancz, 1980.
The Vampire Tapestry New York, Simon and Schuster, 1980.
The Bronze King. Boston, Houghton Mifflin, 1985.

Uncollected Short Stories

"The Ancient Mind at Work," in *Best Science Fiction of the Year 9,* edited by Gardner Dozois. New York, Dutton, 1980.
"Scorched Supper on New Niger," in *New Voices 3,* edited by George R. R. Martin. New York, Berkley, 1980.
"The Unicorn Tapestry," in *New Dimensions 11,* edited by

Robert Silverberg and Marta Randall. New York, Pocket Books, 1980.

OTHER PUBLICATIONS

Other

"Symposium on Women and SF," in *Khatru 3-4* (Baltimore), 1975.
"The Good Rape," in *Kolvir* (Baltimore), 1978.
"Interview," in *Algol* (New York), Winter 1978-79.
"A Woman Appeared," in *Future Females,* edited by Marleen S. Barr. Bowling Green, Ohio, Popular Press, 1981.
"A Short Course with Dr. Weyland," in *Empire* (New Haven, Connecticut), Spring 1982.
"Mostly I Want to Break Your Heart," with Douglas E. Winter, in *Fantasy Review,* September 1984.

*

Suzy McKee Charnas comments:

In my work I particularly enjoy taking up some hoary stereotype—after-the-holocaust, Amazons, vampires, wise old Gandalf the Grey—and turning it upside down to see what surprises and delights I can shake out of its pockets. Missing the usual claptrap clichés, some readers invariably accuse me of "propagandizing," which means daring to draw their attention to the possibility of something besides the received wisdom about this or that. The charge is nonsense. I do not feel that it's my responsibility as a writer to reform the world or save it from anybody else, and I think it a ludicrous form of hubris to imagine that one's books stand a chance in hell of doing either. My job and my pleasure is to continue to ask the questions that interest me and to pursue them to their possible answers as honestly and skillfully as I can, in the hope that something entertaining, beautiful, and possibly useful will result. My aim is to engage your attention, stir your thoughts, and break your heart.

*   *   *

When Iago says to Brabantio, "you'll have your daughter covered with a Barbary horse . . . you'll have coursers for cousins, and gennets for germans," an example of malevolence addresses a symbol of patriarchal power. These two representational essences are fused in Suzy McKee Charnas's first novel, *Walk to the End of the World,* where masculine hegemony is synonymous with unmitigated evil. Iago's utterance also illuminates its sequel, *Motherlines,* in which daughters are indeed covered by horses who are thought to be the near kinsmen of their mistresses. As *Othello* explores the effects of exaggerated personality traits, Charnas's fiction presents an exaggerated vision of sexism's consequences.

Walk to the End of the World is set in "the Holdfast," a limited environment populated by survivors of "the Wasting," or nuclear holocaust. This postwar society is a paradise for white male misogynistic bigots: the entire population is Caucasian, and the men are taught that "females themselves brought on the Wasting of the world." Holdfast "fems" supposedly "had no souls, only inner cores of animated darkness shaped from the void beyond the stars. Their deaths had no significance. Some men believed that the same shadows return again and again in successive fem-bodies." We, with our Eve, Pandora, and cultures where women are fuel for the flames of their husbands' funeral pyres, cannot feel smug after encountering a Holdfast myth. In this manner, Charnas's fiction continuously echoes reality.

The structure, as well as much of the content of *Walk to the End of the World,* reflects women's secondary status. Before encountering Alldera, the heroine, readers are familiar with the Holdfast's notions of "fem-taint," "Cunt-hunger," institutionalized rape, and girl children who must scratch for survival in the straw of the "kit-pen." Alldera's situation is immediately apparent: as a woman, she must satisfy all the demands of her male masters. Even a slave cannot be completely controlled by an oppressor. Since Alldera possesses mental acuteness and training as a runner, she can sometimes use her mind and body to suit her own best advantage. Her circumstances resemble those of an intelligent, talented Black person in the Jim Crow south. The novel's plot corrects the Holdfast's negative view of the feminine. For example, the text clarifies its own prologue: women certainly did not cause the Wasting of the world. Rather, "subhuman" men cause the wasting of women. Happily, something positive does manage to coincide with the sombering aspects of this novel and women's reality. Alldera has the opportunity to flee the Holdfast; some women have the pleasure of knowing that when they approach their house yard gate, they are not walking to the end of their world.

In *Motherlines* the open plains lying beyond the men's sphere of influence sharply contrast with the Holdfast's defined boundaries. Women completely control this terrain. In fact, to cite another example of Charnas's penchant for creating extreme circumstances, men never enter the domain of escaped "free fems" and the indigenous riding women of the motherline tribes. This women's world is not a Utopia for stereotypically peace-loving, nurturing females. The tribes routinely raid each other, one powerful woman dictates her will to the free fems, and the riding women's method of raising children reminds Alldera of the Holdfast's "kit-pen." Although the tribal women are imperfect, they possess impressive attributes: self-sufficiency, an identification with matrilineal relationships, and racial tolerance. Alldera and her free fem companion are allowed to live in the tribe with dignity. She no longer has the negative self-image described in *Walk to the End of the World,* where she feels "hollow in body . . . hollow in mind, for there was nothing else she might imagine, feel, or will that a man could not wipe out of existence by picking her up for his own purposes." This transformation is of primary importance in *Motherlines.*

Another aspect of the novel is a seconday concern. "Oh . . . We mate with our horses," is the answer to Alldera's question about reproduction in a completely female society. Those who judge this information to be a flippant, sarcastic retort react prematurely. The woman who answers Alldera speaks the truth about a situation which expands the definition of "perversion." Charnas's characters are not presented solely to titillate an audience. Although the sexuality of the motherline tribes is bizarre, they always mate to fulfill their natural reproductive purpose. And the women are in total control of the sexual arena. In contrast, human heterosexuality can be degrading and destructive.

In the real world, the idea of a totally independent woman is, using Harlan Ellison's term, a "dangerous vision." Many readers, men and women, might be taken aback by the controversial content of Charnas's novels.

—Marleen S. Barr

CHASE, Adam. See **FAIRMAN, Paul W.** ; **LESSER, Milton.**

CHERRYH, C. J. Pseudonym for Carolyn Janice Cherry. American. Born in St. Louis, Missouri, 1 September 1942. Educated at the University of Oklahoma, Norman, 1960-64, B. A. in Latin 1964 (Phi Beta Kappa); Johns Hopkins University, Baltimore (Woodrow Wilson Fellow, 1965-66), M. A. in classics 1965. Taught Latin and ancient history in Oklahoma City public schools, 1965-76. Recipient: John W. Campbell Award, 1977; Hugo Award, 1979, 1982; Balrog Award, 1982. Address: 1901 Bella Vista, Edmond, Oklahoma 73034, U. S. A.

SCIENCE-FICTION PUBLICATIONS

Novels (series: Chanur; Faded Sun; Morgaine)

The Book of Morgaine. New York, Doubleday, 1979; as *The Chronicles of Morgaine,* London, Methuen, 1985.
   Gate of Ivrel. New York, DAW, 1976; London, Futura, 1977.
   Well of Shiuan. New York, DAW, 1978; London, Magnum, 1981.
   Fires of Azeroth. New York, DAW, 1979; London, Methuen, 1982.
Brothers of Earth. New York, DAW, 1976; London, Futura, 1977.
Hunter of Worlds. New York, DAW, 1976; London, Futura, 1977.
The Faded Sun: Kesrith. New York, DAW, 1978.
The Faded Sun: Shon'Jir. New York, DAW, 1979.
Hestia. New York, DAW, 1979.
Serpent's Reach. New York, DAW, 1980; London, Macdonald, 1981.
The Faded Sun: Kutath. New York, DAW, 1980.
Wave Without a Shore. New York, DAW, 1981.
Downbelow Station. New York, DAW, 1981; London, Methuen, 1983.
The Pride of Chanur. New York, DAW, 1982; London, Methuen, 1983.
Merchanter's Luck. New York, DAW, 1982; London, Methuen, 1984.
Port Eternity. New York, DAW, 1982.
The Dreamstone. New York, DAW, 1983.
The Tree of Swords and Jewels. New York, DAW, 1983.
40000 in Gehenna. Huntington Woods, Michigan, Phantasia Press, 1983.
Voyager in Night. New York, DAW, 1984; London, Methuen, 1985.
Chanur's Venture. Huntington Woods, Michigan, Phantasia Press, 1984.
Cuckoo's Egg. Huntington Woods, Michigan, Phantasia Press, 1985.
The Kif Strikes Back (Chanur). Huntington Woods, Michigan, Phantasia Press, 1985.
Angel with a Sword. New York, DAW, 1985.

Uncollected Short Stories

"The Dark King," in *The Year's Best Fantasy Stories 3,* edited by Lin Carter. New York, DAW, 1977.
"Cassandra," in *The 1979 Annual World's Best SF,* edited by Donald A. Wollheim. New York, DAW, 1979.
"Homecoming," in *Shayol* (Overland Park, Kansas), Summer 1979.
"Sea Change," in *Elsewhere,* edited by Terri Windling and Mark Alan Arnold. New York, Ace, 1981.

"Ischade," in *Shadows of Sanctuary*, edited by Robert Asprin. New York, Ace, 1981.

"A Thief in Korianth," in *Flashing Swords! 5*, edited by Lin Carter. New York, Dell, 1981.

"The Last Tower," in *Sorcerer's Apprentice* (New York), 1981.

"Ice," "General," "Highliner," "The Haunted Tower," and "Nightgame," in *Sunfall*, edited by Cherryh. New York, DAW, 1981.

"Willow," in *Hecate's Cauldron*, edited by Susan Shwartz, New York, DAW, 1982.

"Downwind," in *Storm Season*, edited by Robert Asprin. New York, Ace, 1982.

"Necromant," in *The Face of Chaos*, edited by Robert Asprin and Lynn Abbey. New York, Ace, 1983.

"Witching Hour," in *Wings of Omen*, edited by Robert Asprin and Lynn Abbey. New York, Ace, 1984.

"Companions," in *The John W. Campbell Awards 5*, edited by George R. R. Martin. New York, Bluejay, 1984.

"The Scapegoat," in *Alien Stars*, edited by Betsy Mitchell. New York, Pocket Books, 1985.

"Pots," in *Afterwar*, edited by Janet Morris. New York, Pocket Books, 1985.

"The Unshadowed Land," in *Sword and Sorceress 2*, edited by Marion Zimmer Bradley. New York, DAW, 1985.

OTHER PUBLICATIONS

Other

Editor, *Sunfall*. New York, DAW, 1981.

Translator, *The Green Gods*, by Charles and Nathalie Henneberg. New York, DAW, 1980.

Translator, *Star Crusade*, by Pierre Barbet. New York, DAW, 1980.

Translator, *The Book of Shai*, by Daniel Walther. New York, DAW, 1984.

*

C. J. Cherryh comments:

Having made thorough study of the past I am vehemently certain that I do not wish to live in it, nor do I wish to see three quarters of the planet weltering in conditions that should have been left in the past, with the same hunger and disease our ancestors knew. The reach for space and its resources is the make-or-break point for our species, and the appropriate use of technology and the adjustment of human viewpoint to a universe not limited to a blue sky overhead and the curvature of the horizon are absolutely critical to our survival. Therefore I write fiction about space and human adjustment to the unfamiliar. The references in my work are frequently to writings on the aesthetics of physics or other sciences, compared and contrasted to writings of the ancients and concepts and philosophies better known to anthropologists than to the general public: while I have the most profound respect for the traditions of English language literature, I consider the images overworked and frequently inadequate for the task of conveying non-English concepts. Therefore I use the form of English literature, but bring into it a great many things which are pertinent to the sciences, or to the far corners of the world. This in my estimation is what science fiction ought to do to literature, create new symbologies and new understandings appropriate to the space age, not forgetting the traditions of our own culture, but widening its viewpoints.

*   *   *

Marked out with critical attention and expectation early in her career, C. J. Cherryh had by the mid-1980's established herself as a major author. Cherryh's fairly high rate of production (about twenty volumes plus scattered shorter works for the decade ending in 1985) may have helped to keep her before the public eye, but more important to her success than quantity has been the quality of her work. Cherryh has not been a great innovator of form; generally her settings and plot conflicts have been those traditional to science fiction. (The Morgaine trilogy is rationalized as science fiction, but consciously uses the devices, and has more of the feel, of heroic fantasy.) Most of Cherryh's works are adventure-sf novels set either in space or in non-industrial societies planetside. They generally deal with cultural conflict, frequently as seen from the viewpoint of an ordinary being (human or extra-terrestrial) wrenched by events out of his milieu. Cherryh has demonstrated a genius for reanimating what in other hands might seem routine or outworn conventions. Both her stylistic control and her characterization are far above the norm for adventure sf, and she is ruthless in pressing her viewpoint characters into extreme situations that will retain the reader's interest. At the same time, Cherryh manifests a stubborn faith in the ability of humans (and other intelligent beings) to overcome adversity, to come to at least a measure of mutual understanding and to spiritual triumph. Among the most effective of her characterizations are those of extra-terrestrials, who figure prominently in Cherryh's work. (Indeed, in the Chanur series, humans barely appear at all.) Cherryh has proven inventive in depicting alien species, cultures within each species, and individual non-human psychologies within each culture. A related Cherryh hallmark is the fascinating complexity of her backgrounds. Only occasionally has she been able to restrict herself to anything below a minimum of two species and three cultures. Indeed, Cherryh has now embarked, in many cases post facto, upon a link-up of nearly all her books into a common vast future history. Particularly noticeable are allusions to the wars and periods of uneasy coexistence of the two human interstellar powers, the Union and the Alliance.

Several Cherryh books diverge somewhat from her typical pattern. Some are set in the Alliance/Union history, but individually even these are less complex than her usual adventure plots, and in all works of this category psychological or philosophical themes lie closer to the surface. So far these works have not passed over the line separating genre sf/fantasy from surrealism, but they frequently stray near the border. *Wave Without a Shore* takes place on the planet Freedom, whose major cities are Camus and Kierkegaard. *Voyager in Night* is told mostly from the viewpoints of self-aware programs running on an extra-terrestrial computer. *Port Eternity*'s situation (involving the King Arthur legend, a slave underclass, and alien kidnappers) is so *outré* it would take a paragraph just to outline. In a somewhat different vein, *Sunfall* is a collection of stories, some of them sf and some fantasy, set in the various major cities of Earth's twilight age. The Dreamstone series, as well as some short stories, are straight fantasy.

Cherryh's works are not without flaws. While her level of characterization remains above average for adventure sf, it has improved little since her first published works of a decade ago. In certain contexts, such as military jargon or bureaucratese, Cherryh's usually excellent style rings subtly false. Her fascinating complexity sometimes lands her in difficulties. In this connection, it may be instructive to consider the example of James Clavell's historial novel, *Shogun*. *Shogun* has in many respects a typical Cherryh-type plot, involving as it does conflicts among representatives of two races, three levels of technology, three or more religions, four or five nations, and cross-cutting religious and national factions beyond easy numbering. Without even the complication of multiple intelligent species, it takes Clavell 1200 pages to tell his story. For reasons of book-manufacturing technology and of marketing, 1200 pages in one volume are not available to an sf writer like Cherryh. The obvious compromise would be to write a series of shorter, linked novels. Unfortunately, Cherryh's plots do not always seem to break down neatly into episodes of short-novel length. One result, as in *Hunter of Worlds*, can be excessive compression, throwing off pacing and impairing intelligibility. Another possible outcome, more frequent in Cherryh's case, is the publication of a supposedly independent volume that will not in fact stand up on its own. The most blatant example of this is *Chanur's Venture*, which baldly breaks off in mid-plot with a to-be-continued.

Sometimes Cherryh's work manifests a romantic faith that any other society, in particular any with extended households linking groups larger than the nuclear family, must be preferable to the human West or its successors. Such romanticism is relatively common in recent sf and genre fantasy. Perhaps more surprising in Cherryh's work is a vein of pessimism, not about the human spirit, but about the objective human condition. A parallel might even be drawn with the prison-camp novels of Aleksandr Solzhenitsyn: Cherryh protagonists triumph spiritually over adversity, but only infrequently is their worldly position better at the end of a tale than at the beginning, and the wicked (especially as exemplified by technologically superior alien species or by unfeeling human bureaucracies) usually come away both unrepentant and unpunished. Contrary to the conventional wisdom, this pessimism does not seem to be hurting Cherryh's popularity; perhaps readers take it as a sign of realism.

A decade into her career, Cherryh still has not made her way into the very front rank of sf writers. She is not, however, very far behind, and there remains a strong possibility that she will make up the remaining distance.

—Patrick L. McGuire

CHESNEY, Weatherby. See **HYNE, C. J. Cutliffe.**

CHILSON, Robert. American. Born in Ringwood, Oklahoma, 19 May 1945. Educated in Appleton City High School, Missouri. Since 1967, free-lance writer. Agent: Richard Curtis Associates, 164 East 64th Street, New York, New York 10021, U.S.A.

SCIENCE-FICTION PUBLICATIONS

Novels

As the Curtain Falls. New York, DAW, 1974.
The Star-Crowned Kings. New York, DAW, 1975.
The Shores of Kansas. New York, Popular Library, 1976; London, Hale, 1977.

Uncollected Short Stories

"The Mind Reader," in *Analog* (New York), June 1968.

"The Big Rock," in *Analog* (New York), October 1969.
"The Wild Blue Yonder," in *Analog* (New York), January 1970.
"The Fifth Ace," in *Analog* (New York), February 1970.
"Per Strategem," in *Analog* (New York), July 1970.
"Excelsior!," in *Analog* (New York), August 1970.
"In the Wabe," in *Analog* (New York), November 1970.
"Ecological Niche," in *Analog* (New York), December 1970.
"In His Image," in *Analog 8,* edited by John W. Campbell, Jr. New York, Doubleday, 1971.
"Compulsion Worse Confounded," in *Analog* (New York), November 1971.
"Truck Driver," in *Analog* (New York), January 1972.
"Forty Days and Forty Nights," in *Analog* (New York), August 1973.
"The Devil and the Deep Blue Sky," in *Beyond Time,* edited by Sandra Ley. New York, Pocket Books, 1976.
"The Tame One," in *Galileo* (Boston), September 1976.
"People Reviews," in *Universe 7,* edited by Terry Carr. New York, Doubleday, and London, Dobson, 1977.
"Adora," in *Galileo* (Boston), April 1977.
"O Ye of Little Faith," in *Cosmos* (New York), November 1977.
"Moonless Night," in *Galaxy* (New York), March 1978.
"Written in Sand," in *Issac Asimov's World of Science Fiction,* edited by George Scithers. New York, Davis, 1980.
"Walk with Me," in *Analog* (New York), May 1982.
"The Hand of Friendship," in *Analog* (New York), March 1983.
"Slowly, Slowly in the Wind," in *Analog* (New York), April 1984.

*   *   *

Most of Robert Chilson's early stories appeared in *Analog,* and were little distinguished from the usual technophilic, politically reactionary fiction in which the magazine specialized. The most promising of these is "Per Strategem," a tale of human-alien contact in which the alien entity's biology and culture are imaginatively rendered, despite the tired plot of humans outwitting aliens, proving racial superiority.

Chilson's later novels are somewhat more adventurous, even lyrical. *The Shores of Kansas* is a moderately successful formula story about time-travel, while *The Star-Crowned Kings* resembles the typical Andre Norton plot of a young protagonist coming into manhood. *The Star-Crossed Kings* is interesting in that it posits a stellar civilization in which psychically endowed humans called Starlings rule the rest of mankind. Young Race Worden, however, learns that he also possesses psychic powers, which, in most such adventures, is usually the impetus for the hero to "take on" the establishment. Chilson avoids that cliché, but substitutes instead another cliché less often used but familiar to *Analog* writers—the concept that the establishment (Starlings) is basically benign except for a dangerous few who are the only ones Race Worden must fight. While this is less melodramatic than a similar Andre Norton tale of a psychic's persecution by authority *(Forerunner Foray),* it is also less exciting as an adventure-story; Chilson is also formula-bound in following his hero's personal growth, so that the book also fails as a character study. One remark is interesting: "It shocked him to realize that many of the inequities were as much the fault of the underdogs as of the overlords." The concept itself is not objectionable, but the phrasing, as well as the circumstance of the obsveration, seems to express sympathy for the overloads, whereas a more radical writer, Harlan

Ellison, might express a similar sentiment with tacit sympathy for the underdogs.

Unquestionably, Chilson's best accomplishment is *As the Curtain Falls*. Its format resembles the Dying Earth stories of Jack Vance, in which organized civilization has completely decayed, succeeded by barbaric cultures and weird mutations of humanity. In many places, the novel approaches parody of the Vance style, but for the most part Chilson's colorful descriptive prose, attention to detail, and deep sense of his world's history serve the primary purpose of telling a vivid adventure story. *As the Curtain Falls* centers on the attempts of a young prince, Trebor of Amballa, to establish in his fumbling way a world-empire, and although most of the novel follows his adventures in rescuing his reculant bride, he does accomplish his task at novel's end with the help of man's former heritage, a functional computer. As with *Star-Crowned Kings,* the plot is extremely loose, but this is compensated for by Chilson's plethora of bizarre cultures and place-names, wild characters (such as Lyantha, the pulchritudinous witch-queen who becomes immortal with the sacrifice of young men), and strange inventions (such as a battle between opposing fleets of ships built to sail on dry salt beds). The essential quality of Vance that Chilson lacks is a fascination with alien mentlities, altered states of mind, abstruse philosophies, and magic. In this regard, Chilson again betrays a reactionary consciousness in the way he chooses to satirize the world of effete artists, in that he presents no alternative (as Vance might) to the pretentiousness that passes in literary circles for an "altered state of mind."

Yet, unusually enough, a recent Chilson story, "Moonless Night," concerns a female dancer whose personal artistry is beyond reproach. The gimmick of this tale is the brief encounter of the female and male trader, whose bodily proteins are so alien to hers that a touch results in mutual cellular destruction, and a painfully short romance. In essence, Chilson is a writer who has striven to strike a balance between lyricism and irony, but has not truly devoted himself to either.

—Gene Phillips

CHILSON, Charles (Frederick William). British. Born in London in 1917. Educated at Thanet Street Church of England School, London. Married to Penelope Colbeck; two sons and one daughter. Free-lance writer and journalist, and radio producer for the BBC, London; devised and wrote *Riders of the Range* annual, from 1953. Recipient: Western Heritage Award, for children's book, 1963. Address: 27 Commonside, Keston, Kent, England.

SCIENCE-FICTION PUBLICATIONS

Novels (series: Jet Morgan in all books)

Journey into Space (novelization of radio series). London, Jenkins, 1954.
The Red Planet (novelization of radio series). London, Jenkins, 1956.
The World in Peril (novelization of radio series). London, Jenkins, 1960.

OTHER PUBLICATIONS

Plays

Oh What a Lovely War, with the Theatre Workshop, London

(produced London and New York, 1964). London, Methuen, 1965.

Radio Plays: *Riders of the Range, Journey into Space,* and *The World in Peril* series in the 1950's; *Space Force* series, 1984.

Other

Riders of the Range (for children). London, Juvenile Productions, 1951.
Second Round-Up with Riders of the Range (for children). London, Juvenile Productions, 1952.
The Riders of the Range Square Dance Manual. London, Hutchinson, 1953.
The Book of the West: The Epic of America's Wild Frontier and the Men Who Created Its Legends. London, Odhams Press, 1961; Indianapolis, Bobbs Merrill, 1962.
Discovery of the American West (for children). London, Hamlyn, 1970.

*   *   *

The first of Charles Chilton's *Journey into Space* radio serials went on the air in 1953, with a strong cast of actors including Andrew Faulds and Guy Kingsley Poynter, and a sound-track of music and special effects into which the BBC Radiophonics Workshop threw themselves with enthusiasm. Over the next five years the three serials were a national institution in Britain, and the character and their creators became household names.

In the first serial the spaceship *Luna,* launched from the Woomera Rocket Range in Australia, achieved the first Moon landing in the Bay of Rainbows. Fauld's low-key comment, "Gentlemen, we are on the Moon," was to be much imitated by 1950's writers. As lunar night fell, however, power failed in the ship, and in the darkness someone or something could be heard investigating the *Luna* on the outside. After a strange encounter with a UFO at sunrise the crew attempted to return to Earth, only to have the *Luna* abducted and delivered to the Earth of 13,000 years in the past. Eventually the crew met one of the time-travellers and negotiated their return to their own time, but the serial ended as they faced another re-entry with no remaining fuel.

The second and third serials were set several years later, when a lunar base had been established and Faulds ("Jet Morgan") led an expedition to Mars in a fleet of ships commanded by the *Discovery*. Once again Chilton had gone to great lengths to make the technology authentic, by the design studies of the day, and the procedures of the Mars fleet were extremely convincing. In flight, however, the expedition was sabotaged by a man named Whitaker who had been kidnapped from Earth decades before, then returned to infiltrate the expedition. Whitaker had been "conditioned" by the Martians by slowing down his metabolism to adapt to Martian conditions, making him cold to the touch and also concealing his age, and also by hypnosis, making his speech a frightening drone ("Orders must be obeyed without questions at all times.") Crewmen went mad or died in his company, and a generation of British schoolchildren were terrified of him. Worse still, Mars turned out to have a population of similarly conditioned humans, preparing to invade the Earth which few of them knew they had left.

But Chilton's extra-terrestrials weren't monsters. The Martians had been the giants of earthly legends, coming to us in peace only to be hunted down and destroyed, finally driven to drastic measures as conditions worsened on Mars. But by the time of the invasion there was only one left, and when Morgan and his crew prevented his attempted takeover by televised hypnosis, he went peacefully off to Alpha Centauri with volunteers from the human workforce. The time-travellers, too, had been trying to avoid interaction with mankind, using the Moon and the prehistoric Earth only in passing. Unlike their contemporaries (the purely destructive aliens of Nigel Kneale's *Quatermass,* or the wholly benign inhabitants of Angus Macvicar's *Lost Planet*) Chilton's creations had their own purposes and motivations, not specifically good or evil in relation to humanity. Space was an exciting realm for us to enter, dangerous perhaps but not hostile.

Subsequent incarnations of the characters were less successful. The comic strip in the *Express Weekly* was inconsistent with the radio serials, yet borrowed too heavily from them; and a one-hour play recapitulated the weakest parts of the strip's story line. *Space Force,* a new serial broadcast in 1984, caught the atmosphere of the original more closely. But Chilton conceded in a *Radio Times* interview that he hadn't kept up with developments in space science, and dramatic sequences borrowed from *Journey into Space*—the power failure, for example—were no longer convincing.

—Duncan Lunan

CHRISTOPHER, John. Pseudonym for Christopher Samuel Youd; has also written as Hilary Ford; William Godfrey; Peter Graaf; Peter Nichols; Anthony Rye. British. Born in Knowsley, Lancashire, 16 April 1922. Educated at Peter Symonds' School, Winchester. Served in the Royal Signals, 1941-46. Twice married; four daughters and one son from first marriage. Since 1958, full-time writer. Recipient: Rockefeller-Atlantic award, 1946; Christopher Award, for children's book, 1971; *Guardian* Award, for children's book, 1971; Jugendbuchpreis (Germany), 1976; George G. Stone Center for Children's Books award, 1977. Address: La Rochelle, Rye, East Sussex TN31 7JY, England.

SCIENCE-FICTION PUBLICATIONS

Novels

The Year of the Comet. London, Joseph, 1955; as *Planet in Peril,* New York, Avon, 1959.
The Death of Grass. London, Joseph, 1956; as *No Blade of Grass,* New York, Simon and Schuster, 1957.
The World in Winter. London, Eyre and Spottiswoode, 1962; as *The Long Winter,* New York, Simon and Schuster, 1962.
Sweeney's Island. New York, Simon and Schuster, 1964; as *Cloud on Silver,* London, Hodder and Stoughton, 1964.
The Possessors. London, Hodder and Stoughton, and New York, Simon and Schuster, 1965.
A Wrinkle in the Skin. London, Hodder and Stoughton, 1965; as *The Ragged Edge,* New York, Simon and Schuster, 1966.
The Little People. London, Hodder and Stoughton, and New York, Simon and Schuster, 1967.
Pendulum. London, Hodder and Stoughton, and New York, Simon and Schuster, 1968.

Fiction (for children; series: Tripods; Sword of the Spirits)

The Tripods Trilogy. New York, Macmillan, 1980.
    The White Mountains. London, Hamish Hamilton, and

New York, Macmillan, 1967.
    The City of Gold and Lead. London, Hamish Hamilton, and New York, Macmillan, 1967.
    The Pool of Fire. London, Hamish Hamilton, and New York, Macmillan, 1968.
The Lotus Caves. London, Hamish Hamilton, and New York, Macmillan, 1969.
The Guardians. London, Hamish Hamilton, and New York, Macmillan, 1970.
The Sword of the Spirits Trilogy. New York, Macmillan, 1980; as *The Prince in Waiting Trilogy,* London, Penguin, 1983.
    The Prince in Waiting. London, Hamish Hamilton, and New York, Macmillan, 1970.
    Beyond the Burning Lands. London, Hamish Hamilton, and New York, Macmillan, 1971.
    The Sword of the Spirits. London, Hamish Hamilton, and New York, Macmillan, 1972.
In the Beginning (reader for adults). London, Longman, 1972; revised edition (for children), as *Dom and Va,* London, Hamish Hamilton, and New York, Macmillan, 1973.
Wild Jack. London, Hamish Hamilton, and New York, Macmillan, 1974; original version (reader for adults), London, Longman, 1974.
Empty World. London, Hamish Hamilton, 1977; New York, Dutton, 1978.
Fireball. London, Gollancz, and New York, Dutton, 1981.
New Found Land. London, Gollancz, and New York, Dutton, 1983.

Short Stories

The Twenty-Second Century. London, Grayson, 1954; New York, Lancer, 1962.

Uncollected Short Stories

"Conspiracy," in *Gateway to the Stars,* edited by E. J. Carnell. London, Museum Press, 1955.
"Manna," in *New Worlds* (London), March 1955.
"The Gardener," in *Tales of the Frightened* (New York), Spring 1957.
"The Noon's Repose," in *Infinity* (New York), April 1957.
"Doom over Kareeta," in *Satellite* (New York), October 1957.
"A World of Slaves," in *Satellite* (New York), March 1959.
"Winter Boy, Summer Girl," in *Fantastic* (New York), October 1959.
"A Few Kindred Spirits," in *Best from Fantasy and Science Fiction 16,* edited by Edward L. Ferman. New York, Doubleday, 1967; London, Gollancz, 1968.
"Communication Problem," in *Beyond Infinity* (Hollywood), November 1967.
"Specimen," in *Fantasy and Science Fiction* (New York), December 1972.
"The Long Night," in *Galaxy* (New York), October 1974.
"Blemish," in *Tales Out of Time,* edited by Barbara Ireson. New York, Putnam, 1981.

OTHER PUBLICATIONS

Novels

Giant's Arrow (as Anthony Rye). London, Gollancz, 1956; as Samuel Youd, New York, Simon and Schuster, 1960.
Malleson at Melbourne (as William Godfrey). London, Museum Press, 1956.

The Friendly Game (as William Godfrey). London, Joseph, 1957.
A Scent of White Poppies. London, Eyre and Spottiswoode, and New York, Simon and Schuster, 1959.
Patchwork of Death (as Peter Nichols). New York, Holt Rinehart, 1965; London, Hale, 1967.

Novels as Samuel Youd

The Winter Swan. London, Dobson, 1949.
Babel Itself. London, Cassell, 1951.
Brave Conquerors. London, Cassell, 1952.
Crown and Anchor. London, Cassell, 1953.
A Palace of Strangers, London, Cassell, 1954.
Holly Ash. London, Cassell, 1955; as *The Opportunist*, New York, Harper, 1957.
The Choice. New York, Simon and Schuster, 1961; as *The Burning Bird*, London, Longman, 1964.
Messages of Love. New York, Simon and Schuster, 1961; London, Longman, 1962.
The Summers at Accorn. London, Longman, 1963.

Novels as Peter Graaf

Dust and the Curious Boy. London, Joseph, 1957; as *Give the Devil His Due*, New York, Mill, 1957.
Daughter Fair. London, Joseph, and New York, Washburn, 1958.
Sapphire Conference. London, Joseph and New York, Washburn, 1959.
The Gull's Kiss. London, Davies, 1962.

Novels as Hilary Ford

Felix Walking. London, Eyre and Spottiswoode, and New York, Simon and Schuster, 1958.
Felix Running. London, Eyre and Spottiswoode, 1959.
Bella on the Roof. London, Longman, 1965.
Sarnia. London, Hamish Hamilton, and New York, Doubleday, 1974.
Castle Malindine. London, Hamish Hamilton, and New York, Harper, 1975.
A Bride for Bedivere. London, Hamish Hamilton, 1976; New York, Harper, 1977.

Other

"Decline and Fall of the Bug-Eyed Monster," in *Fantasy and Science Fiction* (New York), October 1956.
The Caves of Night (for children). London, Eyre and Spottiswoode, and New York, Simon and Schuster, 1958.
"Science and Anti-Science," in *Fantastic Universe* (Chicago), June 1958.
The Long Voyage (for children). London, Eyre and Spottiswoode, 1960; as *The White Voyage*, New York, Simon and Schuster, 1961.
"Not What-If But How-He," in *The Writer* (Boston), November 1968.
A Figure in Grey (for children; as Hilary Ford). Kingswood, Surrey, World's Work, 1973.

*   *   *

The reputation of John Christopher as a writer of science fiction for both adult and younger readers is solidly established. Perhaps the greatest single exposure was the film version in the early 1970's of the novel *The Death of Grass*. The elements present in this relatively early piece are a hallmark for all of his science fiction. Taken together, it forms all kinds of answers to the question "What do people do when things fall apart?" An account of his work may fall rather naturally into three parts: the early short fiction and "Managerial" stories; novels of crises, catastrophe and survival; and novels for younger readers.

The Twenty-Second Century conveniently displays Christopher's apprenticeship period. Six of the stories in the collection feature Max Larkin, a Director in one of the "corporations" that govern earth in place of political institutions in the not-too-distant future. Read along with the fuller exposition of this state of affairs in *Planet in Peril*, the stories present the proposition that political institutions will bring civilization to ruin and that government by enlightened commercial interests may do better. The case for this is epitomized in the laid-back character of Larkin, the unmarried, late-middle-aged corporate director, whose manipulative genius is time and again effective in world crises where armies and doomsday weapons have always failed. The 14 additional stories are something of an index of the novels that would follow. Sterility doom in "The New Wine," a medieval level of technological survival in "Weapon," and the panorama of 20th-century ruin in contrast to the garden of a new Eden in "Begin Again" provide glimpses of the worlds of the catastrophe novels. Beyond these, imprisonment by adaptive necessity in a lunar vivarium in "Christmas Roses," the interdiction of books in "A Time of Peace," and the humanity-saving wholesomeness recognized by enlightened aliens in a human village dedicated to a technologically simple way of life in "Blemish" are typical of the settings and subjects of the juvenile pieces. At least one more story, "Rock-a-Bye," featuring the super-child born of a relationship between a Martian woman and a man from Earth is beautiful in its own right and deserves larger treatment. At this stage in his career Christopher's narrative craft is nearly mature. With minor refinements it is what it will be for the works to follow. He does not experiment with style. He tells stories with pace, suspense, sanity, and clarity. Moreover, unlike that of many writers, his strength is not in the short story but in the longer narrative work.

Two exceptions to the sort of novel for which Christopher is best known are *The Possessors*, wherein a group of people at a remote ski lodge are saved by "body-snatching" aliens, and *The Little People*, wherein a group of vacationers at a remote old mansion are savaged by dwarves created by Nazi geneticists. Both are excursions in science-fiction gothic. The strength of both lies in the plausible behaviours of small groups of people in short-term crises.

But it is to scenarios of planet-wide catyclysm and survival in a world that will never be the same again that the most famous stories direct us. *The Death of Grass*, reminding us that corn, wheat, and rice are "grass," has a blight on all the species of grass cause a world famine. *The World in Winter* shows European civilization destroyed by a new ice age. *A Wrinkle in the Skin* presents earth devastated by the effects of continent-heaving earthquakes. *Pendulum* varies the cause of disaster from that of nature run amok to human society run amok—an obvious fictional response to the social transformations taking place in western civilization during the late 1960's. But with few alterations the effect is the same. More people survive. Yet once more society is reduced to savagery, to endure again the insanity and agony of social evolution that in past history did not teach their lessons well enough. These pieces are variations upon several principal themes. Human civilization is fragile and vulnerable. It cannot survive catastrophe either from natural causes or incompetent government. In the event of catastrophe the few who survive will be winnowed again by good health, knowledge of basic tools and nature, and the ability to kill other human beings, however reluctantly, out of necessity. Simultaneously, they must have the ability to love and form, once again, wholesome social contracts. Billions die in these stories, but hope and human potentiality have the final determination in each of them. Somehow mankind will recover and rebuild, though *Pendulum*, the latest of the novels, insists that it will not be swift.

With a sensible selection against the more badly brutal and explicit details of violence and sexual behavior these themes are produced again in the novels for younger readers. There is an evenness of quality of all these works, so that a few may represent them all. The most famous are those that form the Tripods Trilogy, featuring Will Parker. Will is born in a backwoods village on a future earth conquered and enslaved by alien invaders who travel on land and water in vehicles with three immensely long terrain-gobbling legs. They are reminiscent of the Martian craft in Wells's *War of the Worlds*. The aliens employ the very strongest young humans as body servants. The remainder are mere breeders, forbidden more than a medieval level of technology, and, ultimately, little more than vermin who will be exterminated when the aliens convert earth's atmosphere and gravity to their own. Fortunately, it doesn't happen. Will and two friends have a principal role in returning earth to humans. The theme is the meaning of individual freedom and honor. Knowledge and curiosity daring enough to see beyond popular mythology, self-discipline, respect for other people—especially odd ones—and the courage to act in the face of pain and under threat of death earn freedom. Beginning at the end of 1984 the first of three 13-episode BBC TV serials of *The Tripods* was aired. The broadcast of the complete production spans three years. A final work called *The Guardians* refreshes the Tripods propositions about freedom in a post-catastrophe story of a boy who, learning of a conspiracy by aristocratic "guardians" to keep the mass of men at a stuporous level of existence in the cities, determines to join a revolution to free them. The work received the *Guardian* Award in England, the Christopher Award in the US and the prestigious Jugendbuchpreis in 1976. Additional sf pieces published by Christopher in the early 1980's are exclusively children's books. The course seems a happy one. In terms of narrative art, Christopher's stories for young readers may be his finest achievement.

—John R. Pfeiffer

CLARKE, Arthur C(harles). British. Born in Minehead, Somerset, 16 December 1917. Educated at Huish's Grammar School, Taunton, Somerset, 1927-36; King's College, London, 1946-48, B. Sc. (honours) in physics and mathematics 1948. Flight Lieutenant in the Royal Air Force, 1941-46; served as Radar Instructor, and Technical Officer on the first Ground Controlled Approach radar; originated proposal for use of satellites for communications, 1945. Married Marilyn Mayfield in 1954 (divorced, 1964). Assistant Auditor, Exchequer and Audit Department, London, 1936-41; Assistant Editor, *Physics Abstracts*, London, 1949-50. Since 1954, engaged in underwater exploration and photography of the Great Barrier Reef of Australia and the coast of Sri Lanka. Director, Rocket Publishing, London, Underwater Safaris, Colombo, and Spaceward Corporation, New York. Has made numerous radio and television appearances (most recently as presenter of the television series *Arthur C. Clarke's Mysterious World*, 1980, and *World of Strange Powers*, 1985), and has lectured widely in Britain and the United States; commentator, for CBS-TV, on lunar flights of Apollo 11, 12, and 15; Vikram Sarabhai Professor, Physical Research Laboratory, Ahmedabad, India, 1980. Recipient: International Fantasy Award, 1952; Hugo Award, 1956, 1969 (for screenplay), 1974, 1980; Unesco Kalinga Prize, 1961; Boys' Clubs of America award, 1961; Franklin Institute Ballantine Medal, 1963; Aviation-Space Writers Association Ball Award, 1965; American Association for the Advancement of Science Westinghouse award, 1969; *Playboy* award, 1971; Nebula Award, 1972, 1973, 1979; Jupiter award, 1973; John W. Campbell Memorial Award, 1974; American Institute of Aeronautics and Astronautics award, 1974; Boston Museum of Science Washburn Award, 1977; Marconi Fellowship, 1982. D. Sc. : Beaver College, Glenside, Pennyslvania, 1971. Chairman, British Interplanetary Society, 1946-47, 1950-53. Guest of Honor, World Science Fiction Convention, 1956. Fellow, Royal Astronomical Society; Fellow, King's College, London, 1977; Chancellor, University of Moratuwa, Sri Lanka, since 1979. Agent: David Higham Associates Ltd., 5-8 Lower John Street, London W1R 4HA, England; or, Scott Meredith Literary Agency, 845 Third Avenue, New York, New York 10022, U. S. A. Address: 25 Barnes Place, Colombo 7, Sri Lanka.

SCIENCE-FICTION PUBLICATIONS

Novels

Prelude to Space. New York, Galaxy, 1951; London, Sidgwick and Jackson, 1953; as *Master of Space,* New York, Lancer, 1961; as *The Space Dreamers,* Lancer, 1969.

The Sands of Mars. London, Sidgwick and Jackson, 1951; New York, Gnome Press, 1952.

Islands in the Sky (for children). London, Sidgwick and Jackson, and Philadelphia, Winston, 1952.

Against the Fall of Night. New York, Gnome Press, 1953; revised edition, as *The City and the Stars*, London, Muller, and New York, Harcourt Brace, 1956.

Childhood's End. New York, Ballantine, 1953; London, Sidgwick and Jackson, 1954.

Earthlight. London, Muller, and New York, Ballantine, 1955.

The Deep Range. New York, Harcourt Brace, and London, Muller, 1957.

Across the Sea of Stars (omnibus). New York, Harcourt Brace, 1959.

A Fall of Moondust. London, Gollancz, and New York, Harcourt Brace, 1961.

From the Oceans, From the Stars (omnibus). New York, Harcourt Brace, 1962.

Dolphin Island (for children). New York, Holt Rinehart, and London, Gollancz, 1963.

An Arthur C. Clarke Omnibus [and *Second Omnibus*]. London, Sidgwick and Jackson, 2 vols., 1965-68.

Prelude to Mars (omnibus). New York, Harcourt Brace, 1965.

2001: A Space Odyssey (novelization of screenplay). New York, New American Library, and London, Hutchinson, 1968.

The Lion of Comarre, and Against the Fall of Night. New York, Harcourt Brace, 1968; London, Gollancz, 1970.

Rendezvous with Rama. London, Gollancz, and New York, Harcourt Brace, 1973.

Imperial Earth. London, Gollancz, 1975; revised edition, New York, Harcourt Brace, 1976.

The Fountains of Paradise. London, Gollancz, and New York, Harcourt Brace, 1979.

2010: Odyssey Two. New York, Ballantine, and London, Granada, 1982.

Short Stories

Expedition to Earth. New York, Ballantine, 1953; London, Sidgwick and Jackson, 1954.

Reach for Tomorrow. New York, Ballantine, 1956; London, Gollancz, 1962.

Tales from the White Hart. New York, Ballantine, 1957; London, Sidgwick and Jackson, 1972.

The Other Side of the Sky. New York, Harcourt Brace, 1958; London, Gollancz, 1961.

Tales of Ten Worlds. New York, Harcourt Brace, 1962; London, Gollancz, 1963.

The Nine Billion Names of God: The Best Short Stories of Arthur C. Clarke. New York, Harcourt Brace, 1967.

The Wind from the Sun: Stories of the Space Age. New York, Harcourt Brace, and London, Gollancz, 1972.

Of Time and Stars: The Worlds of Arthur C. Clarke. London, Gollancz, 1972.

The Best of Arthur C. Clarke 1937-1971, edited by Angus Wells. London, Sidgwick and Jackson, 1973.

The Sentinel. New York, Berkley, 1983.

Uncollected Short Story

"Quarantine," in *Isaac Asimov's Science Fiction Magazine* (New York), Spring 1977.

OTHER PUBLICATIONS

Novel

Glide Path. New York, Harcourt Brace, 1963; London, Sidgwick and Jackson, 1969.

Play

Screenplay: *2001: A Space Odyssey*, with Stanley Kubrick, 1968.

Other

Interplanetary Flight: An Introduction to Astronautics. London, Temple Press, 1950; New York, Harper, 1951; revised edition, 1960.

The Exploration of Space. London, Temple Press, and New York, Harper, 1951; revised edition, 1959.

"In Defense of Science Fiction," in *Unesco Courier 15* (New York), November 1952.

"Science Fiction: Preparation for the Age of Space," in *Modern Science Fiction*, edited by Reginald Bretnor. New York, Coward McCann, 1953.

The Young Traveller in Space (for children). London, Phoenix House, 1954; as *Going into Space*, New York, Harper, 1954; as *The Scottie Book of Space Travel*, London, Transworld, 1957; revised edition, with Robert Silverberg, as *Into Space*, New York, Harper, 1971.

The Exploration of the Moon. London, Muller, 1954; New York, Harper, 1955.

Foreword to *Authentic Book of Space*, edited by Herbert J. Campbell. London, Panther, 1954.

The Coast of Coral. London, Muller, and New York, Harper, 1956.

The Making of a Moon: The Story of the Earth Satellite Program. London, Muller, and New York, Harper, 1957; revised edition, Harper, 1958.

The Reefs of Taprobane: Underwater Adventures Around Ceylon. London, Muller, and New York, Harper, 1957.

Voice Across the Sea. London, Muller, 1958; New York, Harper, 1959; revised edition, London, Mitchell Beazley, and New York, Harper, 1974.

Boy Beneath the Sea (for children). New York, Harper, 1958.

The Challenge of the Spaceship: Previews of Tomorrow's World. New York, Harper, 1959; London, Muller, 1960.

The First Five Fathoms: A Guide to Underwater Adventure. New York, Harper, 1960.

The Challenge of the Sea. New York, Holt Rinehart, 1960; London, Muller, 1961.

Indian Ocean Adventure. New York, Harper, 1961; London, Barker, 1962.

Profiles of the Future: An Enquiry into the Limits of the Possible. London, Gollancz, 1962; New York, Harper, 1963; revised edition, Harper, 1973; Gollancz, 1974, 1982; New York, Holt Rinehart, 1984.

The Treasure of the Great Reef. London, Barker, and New York, Harper, 1964; revised edition, New York, Ballantine, 1974.

Indian Ocean Treasure, with Mike Wilson. New York, Harper, 1964; London, Sidgwick and Jackson, 1972.

Man and Space, with the editors of *Life*. New York, Time, 1964.

Voices from the Sky: Previews of the Coming Space Age. New York, Harper, 1965; London, Gollancz, 1966.

The Promise of Space. New York, Harper, and London, Hodder and Stoughton, 1968.

"When Earthman and Alien Meet," in *Playboy* (Chicago), January 1968.

Foreword to *Three for Tomorrow*. New York, Meredith, 1969; London, Gollancz, 1970.

First on the Moon, with the astronauts. London, Joseph, and Boston, Little Brown, 1970.

Report on Planet Three and Other Speculations. London, Gollancz, and New York, Harper, 1972.

The Lost Worlds of 2001. New York, New American Library, and London, Sidgwick and Jackson, 1972.

Beyond Jupiter: The Worlds of Tomorrow, with Chesley Bonestell. Boston, Little Brown, 1972.

Technology and the Frontiers of Knowledge (lectures), with others. New York, Doubleday, 1975.

The View from Serendip (on Sri Lanka). New York, Random House, 1977; London, Gollancz, 1978.

1984: Spring: A Choice of Futures. New York, Ballantine, and London, Granada, 1984.

Ascent to Orbit: A Scientific Autobiography: The Technical Writings of Arthur C. Clarke. New York, and Chichester, Sussex, Wiley, 1984.

The Odyssey File, with Peter Hyams. New York, Ballantine, and London, Granada, 1985.

Editor, *Time Probe: Sciences in Science Fiction*. New York, Delacorte Press, 1966; London, Gollancz, 1967.

Editor, *The Coming of the Space Age: Famous Accounts of Man's Probing of the Universe*. London, Gollancz, and New York, Meredith, 1967.

Editor, with George Proctor, *The Science Fiction Hall of Fame 3: The Nebula Winners 1965-1969*. New York, Avon, 1982.

*

Bibliography: *Arthur C. Clarke: A Primary and Secondary Bibliography* by David N. Samuelson, Boston, Hall, 1984.

Manuscript Collection: Mugar Memorial Library, Boston University.

Critical Studies: "Out of the Ego Chamber" by Jeremy Bernstein, in *New Yorker,* 9 August 1969; *Arthur C. Clarke* edited by Joseph D. Olander and Martin H. Greenberg. New York, Taplinger, and Edinburgh, Harris, 1977; *The Space Odysseys of Arthur C. Clarke* by George Edgar Slusser, San Bernardino, California, Borgo Press, 1978; *Arthur C. Clarke* (includes bibliography) by Eric S. Rabkin, West Linn, Oregon, Starmont House, 1979, revised edition, 1980; *Against the Night, The Stars: The Science Fiction of Arthur C. Clarke* by John Hollow, New York, Harcourt Brace, 1983.

*   *   *

With 16 very popular novels to his credit, Arthur C. Clarke is one of the small handful of writers who have shaped science fiction in our century. His persistent spiritual—and sometimes lyrical—optimism concerning the place of humanity in the universe and his enthusiastic faith in technology gather together both the hard and soft sides of the genre in works of classic importance. Clarke's love of the details of technology also enlivens his highly regarded work as a science writer. By his own count, Clarke has produced "approximately five hundred articles and short stories" including "The Star," a Hugo-winning response to Wells's belittling of humanity in his famous story of the same name.

One can take a preliminary survey of Clarke's work by examining his short fiction. *Tales from the White Hart* gains coherence by establishing a tavern frame within which Harry Purvis tells one tall tale after another, displaying Clarke's energetic—and sometimes outrageous—sense of humor, a sense epitomized in the punishing ending of his later story called "Neutron Tide. " Many of Clarke's novels and short stories have been repackaged in other volumes. In *The Nine Billion Names of God* Clarke collects his 25 favorites among his then-published short stories. The majority of his most famous pieces are here, including the almost pastoral title story in which Western science and Eastern religion confront each other and eternity, "Rescue Party" in which the would-be saviors of a doomed Earth are startled by humanity's self-reliance, "Superiority" in which a space war is lost by too must cleverness, "The Sentinel" which is often thought of as the germ for *2001,* and "The Star. " One must turn to *The Wind from the Sun* to find "A Meeting with Medusa," a Nebula-winning novella that includes the discovery of life in the dense atmosphere of Jupiter, and Clarke's own choice for his single best piece of fiction, "Transit of Earth. " This story tells of an astronaut on Mars who knows his life supports cannot long sustain him but who nonetheless sets up the equipment necessary to record for posterity the first human observation of Earth passing across the disc of the sun, a mythic moment typical of Clarke that holds both sunrise and sunset in suspense. This story is also typical of Clarke in depending upon technical detail for its setting and dramatic situation and in balancing a symbol of demise with one of rejuvenation. Clarke's characteristically isolated hero joyfully and paradoxically greets the future by rushing toward Bach, a beauty from the past: "Johann Sebastian, here I come. "

Clarke's faith in technology is profound: he is quite proud "to know several astronauts who became astronauts through reading my books. " He is also justifiably proud to have first proposed (1945) geosynchronous communication satellites, an innovation that has already changed our world and will continue to move us toward the single community Clarke's heroes always contemplate when looking back at Earth from space. The majority of Clarke's novels are highly technological, human characters being invented primarily to provide occasion for humor, to put life at stake, or to locate a coherent point of view from which to explore in imaginative and thrilling detail the wonders of science and of the future universe. *Islands in the Sky* and *Dolphin Island* are juvenile novels employing teenaged boys as observers, the former presenting a grand tour of many sorts of satellites and space stations and a lunar fly-by and the latter showing science reaching out to the aliens with whom we share our planet, intelligent mammals of the sea. *Prelude to Space, The Sands of Mars, Earthlight, The Deep Range, Imperial Earth,* and *The Fountains of Paradise,* though more adult, are still primarily exciting guided tours rather than compelling dramas. In each of these the technology is amazingly detailed; the plot is admirably thickened by political impediments to the implementation of the technology; and these impediments are excitingly but predictably overcome. Within this general scheme, *Prelude to Space* concentrates on the development and launching of the first rocket to leave our atmosphere; *The Sands of Mars,* one of the two psychologically strong novels in this group, concerns first contact and the establishment of viable human colonies on a terraformed Mars; *Earthlight* studies political changes on the Earth and colonized planets as lunar technology develops, including that needed for self-defense and efficient mineral recovery; *The Deep Range* follows the development of whaleherding and its philosophical shift from a meat to a milk industry; *Imperial Earth,* the other psychologically strong novel and Clarke's favorite, also concerns the effect of technology on the social systems on several solar worlds and the personal and political maturing of a man bound to lead the people of Titan through necessary cultural adaptations; and *The Fountains of Paradise* chronicles the building of the "space elevator" that will effectively free humanity from the Earth.

Three other heavily technological novels need mention. *Glide Path,* Clarke's only non-science fiction novel, follows the very important World War II development of Ground Controlled Approach radar. Clarke was in charge of English GCA operations and this novel has interest not only for its technology but for its quasi-autobiographical detail. *A Fall of Moondust* concerns a tourist "boat" trapped within a lunar sea of microscopic dust. This highly effective novel compellingly challenges the reader to try to beat the fictional technicians to a plan for rescue while all the time anoxia and mechanical failures threaten the passengers. And finally, *Rendezvous with Rama* combines the absolutely fascinating exploration of an extra-solar vessel come into our system with profound philosophic questioning of the significance of humanity, of biological life, and of intelligence. This is the only work ever to win all major science fiction awards: Hugo, Nebula, Campbell, and Jupiter.

The questioning in *Rendezvous with Rama* recalls Clarke's novels of cultural exploration. *The Lion of Comarre,* the most like a fairy tale of Clarke's works, traces the quest of a young man to find the geniuses of the past, to destroy the enchanted city keeping them in pacified torpor through technologically induced pleasures, and to open the static pastoral land to science. A similar plot structures *Against the Fall of Night* and *The City and the Stars,* the one an earlier version of the other. These works are more convincingly written than *Comarre* and improve upon it by having the city and country cultures both static, but for different reasons, by creating in Alvin a central character with whose growing pains we can identify, and by casting the drama of terrestrial rejuvenation against a cosmic context. That cosmic context provides the overall power of

Childhood's End, Clarke's most popular novel and his first great testament of faith in human evolution to a higher plane. His last great testament, *2001: A Space Odyssey,* combines motifs and attitudes spaning Clarke's entire career to produce a technologically compelling story of the next generation's space program, a humanly moving story of struggle and courage against harsh interplanetary space and computers gone awry, and a philosophically moving study of the evolution of humanity and our meaning in the universe. Its belated sequel, *2010: Odyssey Two,* although popular, is less significant, for while the earlier book raises permanently important human issues, the later book lays these issues down again by providing them with too simple genre resolutions. The novel *2001* done while Clarke collaborated with Stanley Kubrick on the screenplay for the film *2001,* is the best summation both intellectual and artistic of Clarke's career. The film is perhaps the most widely important work of science fiction ever produced.

In his love of technical detail and his efforts to use science correctly in constructing his novels of adventure, Clarke has been perhaps the foremost writer of his generation to carry on the work of Verne and the editorial policies of Campbell; but in his abiding concern for society and philosophy, Clarke is also the foremost heir of Wells and Stapledon. Clarke has won himself a unique and towering position in science fiction by combining the enthusiasm of one camp with the breadth of vision of the other. Clarke has written that his youthful reading of Stapledon's *Last and First Men* (1930) "transformed my life. " That book, chronicling the evolution and demise of humanity, ends with the suggestion that "we shall make after all a fair conclusion to this brief music that is man. " Stapledon's line reminds us of the farewell of the astronaut in "Transit of Earth," but with a difference: Stapledon sees the music as a conclusion; Clarke sees it as an embrace in something greater than man. This spiritual faith in Clarke comes not from religion, however, but from science itself. As a character says in *The Fountains of Paradise,* the book with which Clarke prematurely claimed his retirement from writing, "he could not understand how anyone could contemplate the dynamic asymmetry of Euler's profound yet beautifully simple [equation] without wondering if the universe was the creation of some vast intelligence." Even for the reading generation that began with Hiroshima, Clarke in his fiction marshals the intimations of intelligence to justify human hope.

—Eric S. Rabkin

CLEMENS, Samuel Langhorne. See **TWAIN, Mark.**

CLEMENT, Hal. Pseudonym for Harry Clement Stubbs. American. Born in Somerville, Massachusetts, 30 May 1922. Educated at Harvard University, Cambridge, Massachusetts, B. S. in astronomy 1943; Boston University, M. Ed. 1947; Simmons College, Boston, M. S. 1963. Served as a bomber pilot with the 8th Air Force during World War II: Air Medal, with four oak leaf clusters; since 1953, served in the Air Force Reserve: Lieutenant Colonel. Married Mary Elizabeth Myers in 1952; two sons and one daughter. Since 1949, science teacher, Milton Academy, Massachusetts. Technical Instructor, Special Weapons School, Sandia Base, New Mexico, 1951. Columnist (as Harry C. Stubbs) on science books for children,

Horn Book magazine, Boston. Member of the Milton Warrant Committee; Chairman of the District Board of Review, Boy Scouts of America. Address: 12 Thompson Lane, Milton, Massachusetts 02187, U. S. A.

SCIENCE-FICTION PUBLICATIONS

Novels (series: Mesklin)

Needle. New York, Doubleday, 1950; London, Gollancz, 1961; as *From Outer Space,* New York, Avon, 1957.
Iceworld. New York, Gnome Press, 1953.
Mission of Gravity (Mesklin). New York, Doubleday, 1954; London, Hale, 1955.
The Ranger Boys in Space (for children). Boston, Page, and London, Harrap, 1956.
Cycle of Fire. New York, Ballantine, 1957; London, Gollancz, 1964.
Some Notes on Xi Bootis. Chicago, Advent, 1959.
Close to Critical. New York, Ballantine, 1964; London, Gollancz, 1966.
Star Light (Mesklin). New York, Ballantine, 1971.
Ocean on Top. New York, DAW, 1973; London, Sphere, 1976.
Through the Eye of a Needle. New York, Ballantine, 1978.
The Nitrogen Fix. New York, Ace, 1980.

Short Stories

Natives of Space. New York, Ballantine, 1965.
Small Changes. New York, Doubleday, 1969; as *Space Lash,* New York, Dell, 1969.
The Best of Hal Clement, edited by Lester del Rey. New York, Ballantine, 1979.

OTHER PUBLICATIONS

Other

"Whirlagig World," in *Astounding* (New York), June 1953.
"The Creation of Imaginary Beings," in *Science Fiction, Today and Tomorrow,* edited by Reginald Bretnor. New York, Harper, 1974.
"Hard Science and Tough Technologies," in *The Craft of Science Fiction,* edited by Reginald Bretnor. New York, Harper, 1976.
Left of Africa (for children). New Orleans, Aurian Society Press, 1976.

Editor, *First Flights to the Moon.* New York, Doubleday, 1970.
Editor, *The Moon,* by George Gamow. London, Abelard Schuman, 1971.

*

Critical Study: *Hal Clement* Donald M. Hassler, Mercer Island, Washington, Starmont House, 1982.

*   *   *

A continuous fan since his mid-teens of physical science and of the fictional extrapolations from it that the genre has labeled "hard" science fiction, Hal Clement published his first story in John Campbell's *Astounding* in 1942 when he was an astronomy major at Harvard. He has gone on to become one of the most highly admired scientific extrapolators and lovers of the tight demands of logic in the genre despite the fact that he is not a full-time writer. Clement and his classic fictions are mentioned whenever the discussion of science in the genre comes up; and hence he represents both the full maturing of the Campbell engineering effect on science fiction and the limitations of that approach. Campbell demanded a good story, of course, and Clement's stories are carefully constructed and often convey a certain excitement and suspense. But their distinguishing characteristic is that a problematic condition in physical reality, or simply a condition of difference such as an increase or decrease in heat or gravity, must be elaborated upon, explained, and taken through certain plot changes so that the reader can simply understand the problem or the difference. This is a literature of total imitation of mimesis, in which the facts of the universe are what is mimed. Often in Clement's work, words themselves seem secondary to the phenomena. It is no coincidence that Clement loves, and, in fact, himself paints—as George Richard—astronomical art works of the phenomenal universe. At the end of his most famous novel, *Mission of Gravity,* the alien hero who is trying cleverly to acquire a more useful science for his truly phenomenal planet, Mesklin, that orbits the double star 61 Cygni, comments, "They finished up with the old line about words not really being enough to describe it. What else beside words can you use, in the mane of the Suns?" His second-in-command answers, "this quantity-code they [humans] call Mathematics." Furthermore, for Clement himself any symbols seem to reside not in the words but in the Suns themselves—or in their mathematics.

The literary effect of hard science fiction that makes it good reading derives not so much from its accuracy (although Clement has written non-fiction essays in which he challenges the reader to catch his fictions in an inaccuracy thus implying that the puzzle element is central) as from its ability to tell how science can show difference. The sublime effect of the varied and infinite universe does not require the fanciful imagination in science fiction but can be, to paraphrase Wordsworth who wanted science and imagination linked, the simple produce of the common day if you are an astronomer. The planetary enviroments are main characters in Clement's fictions, major sources of the sublime, from the variable high-gravity world of Mesklin to the giant and peculiar planet Dhrawn that the mesklinites explore in *Star Light,* to a variety of other worlds in which differences in atmospheric components, in mass, in heat all demostrate that scientific extrapolation is not dry as dust. But not only does scientific extrapolation discover exciting differences in environment; it also assumes and sets about to demonstrate, in Clement's work, that life forms would evolve differently in different enviroments. Clement is fascinated by alien view points, and the non-human characters are the most interesting characters in most of his fiction. This commitment to difference, not only in environments but also in life forms, makes Clement a far more interesting—and more accurate—extrapolator than his fellow hard science-fiction writer, Isaac Asimov, who peoples the galaxy with humans. But beneath the strange morphological surfaces and beyond the alien body chemistry, Clement's extra-terrestrials still seek humanlike goals, most often the goal of more knowledge and more scientific control. Thus Captain Barlennan of Mesklin can seem both strange and familiar as he connives to learn flight and even space travel under conditions far different from those given to us to learn the same things. The emphasis in Clement is on learning, movement, and difference—not on any symbolic revelation of oneness.

One of his first aliens can illustrate perhaps most vividly the

strengths and the weaknesses of Clement's brand of hard science fiction. This creature, the hero in *Needle* and reappearing in *Through the Eye of a Needle,* evolved from viruses rather than from protozoan cells into a highly intelligent life form in which only the memory cells are specialized. The other cells are continually changing into various organs as need arises; but usually the creature lives most efficiently as a friendly parasiste, or symbiont, insinuating its small virus-like cells easily among the larger protozoan-like cells of its host. In *Needle* the creature has come to Earth in hot pursuit of a criminal member if its race. They come from light years away, of course, representing Clement's one bow to illogic—faster-than-light travel. The creature, called simply The Hunter, adopts as his host a teenage boy. They become the best of friends in a delightful and carefully detailed symbiosis. Clement has the enemy or adversary creature adopt the boy's father as its host. The story then unfolds as an exciting tale of detection with a lot of biological extrapolation worked in, but Clement adds nothing suggestive nor psychologically extrapolative about the basic filial conflict that readers of Wordsworth, Joyce, and even Thomas Wolfe might expect. In several different places. Clement has written sarcastically about "amateur psychoanalysts," and it is almost as though he invented this story, which contains one of his nicest and most different aliens, deliberately to demonstrate that hard science fiction extrapolates only with the physical. Furthermore, his most recent novel significantly continues his epistemological speculations because the nitrogenlife aliens in the fiction communicate without words through direct chemical transfer, thus reaffirming Clement's innate preference for "things" over words. In progress is a novel that Clement describes as "about a hollow world [which] calls for a rather low-probability concatenation of circumstances. " Thus it is possible that future critics who deconstruct the genre will discover new resonance in the denials, the doublenesses, and the hollownesses of this classic creator of hard science fiction.

—Donald M. Hassler

CLEVE, John. See **EDMONDSON, G.C.; OFFUTT, Andrew J.**

CLIFTON, Mark (Irvin). American. Born in 1906. Trained as a teacher, but worked for 25 years as industrial psychologist working in personnel: compiled 200,000 case histories. Recipient: Hugo Award, 1955. *Died in 1963.*

SCIENCE-FICTION PUBLICATIONS

Novels

They'd Rather Be Right, with Frank Riley. New York, Gnome Press, 1957; as *The Forever Machine,* New York, Galaxy, 1967.
Eight Keys to Eden. New York, Doubleday, 1960; London, Gollancz, 1962.
When They Come from Space. New York, Doubleday, 1962; London, Dobson, 1963.

Short Stories

The Science Fiction of Mark Clifton, edited by Barry N. Malzberg and Martin H. Greenberg. Carbondale, Southern Illinois University Press, 1980.

Uncollected Short Stories

"The Conqueror," in *Astounding* (New York), May 1952.
"The Kenzie Report," in *If* (New York), May 1952.
"Bow Down to Them," in *If* (New York), June 1953.
"Progress Report," with Alex Apostolides, in *If* (New York), July 1953.
"Solution Delayed," with Alex Apostolides, in *If* (New York), July 1953.
"We're Civilized," with Alex Apostolides, in *Galaxy* (New York), August 1953.
"Reward for Valor," in *Universe* (Evanston, Illinois), September 1953.
"A Woman's Place," in *Galaxy* (New York), September 1953.
"Do unto Others," in *If* (New York), June 1958.
"The Dread Tomato Addiction," in *Analog's Golden Anniversary Anthology,* edited by Stanley Schmidt. New York, Davis, 1981.

*   *   *

Mark Clifton had a brief ten year writing career but in that short span he had an enormous impact on science fiction. Most of Clifton's work was sold to *Astounding* in the form of two series.

The first series was about Bossy, the first of the super computers, and it was clearly developed in the novel *They'd Rather Be Right.* As Bossy follows its program to "heal" and "perfect" humans, the treated humans develop psi powers and immortality. However, society fears these "perfected" humans and sets off a witch hunt to destroy the treated humans and Bossy. Although there's plenty of action, the novel's plot concentrates on society's fears of the unknown, even if the unknown might provide great benefits. This book has subtlety and rare sophistication.

The second series features Ralph Kennedy, an extraterrestrial psychologist who manages—in glib, light stories—to save Earth from alien invasions. *When They Come from Space* satirizes bureaucracy when Earth is menaced by the terrible alien Black Fleet. Kennedy is drafted to confront the invasion and manages to discover the secret of the Black Fleet. The plot is clever and the wit is as dry as a Martini.

Clifton's only novel not a part of any series is the underrated *Eight Keys to Eden.* This is a puzzle story dealing with a situation first developed by Clarke's *Childhood's End.* An E-Man (or Extrapolator) is sent to investigate the colony on the planet Eden when the colony mysteriously stops communicating with Earth. The E-man must solve the ecological-psychological problem which becomes, in Clifton's treatment, a critique of Earth civilization.

—George Kelley

———————

CLINTON, Rupert. See **BULMER, Kenneth.**

———————

CLIVE, Dennis. See **FEARN, John Russell.**

———————

COBLENTZ, Stanton A(rthur). American. Born in San Francisco, California, 24 August 1896. Educated at the University of California, Berkeley, A.B. 1917, M.A. 1919. Married Flora Bachrach in 1922. Feature writer, San Francisco *Examiner,* 1919-20; book reviewer, New York *Times* and New York *Sun,* 1920–38; Founding Editor, *Wings: A Quarterly of Verse,* New York, then Mill Valley, California, 1933-60. *Died 9 September 1982.*

SCIENCE-FICTION PUBLICATIONS

Novels

The Wonder Stick. New York, Cosmopolitan, 1929.
Youth Madness. London Utopian, 1944?
When the Birds Fly South. Mill Valley, California, Wings Press, 1945.
The Sunken World. Los Angles, Fantasy, 1948; London, Cherry Tree, 1951.
After 12,000 Years. Los Angeles, Fantasy, 1950.
Into Plutonian Depths. New York, Avon , 1950.
The Planet of Youth. Los Angeles, Fantasy, 1952.
Under the Triple Suns. Reading, Pennsylvania, Fantasy Press, 1955.
Hidden World. New York, Avalon, 1957; as *In Caverns Below,* New York, Garland, 1975.
The Blue Barbarians. New York, Avalon, 1958.
Next Door to the Sun. New York, Avalon, 1960.
The Runaway World. New York, Avalon, 1961.
The Last of the Great Race. New York, Arcadia House, 1964.
The Lizard Lords. New York, Avalon, 1964.
The Lost Comet. New York, Arcadia House, 1964.
The Moon People. New York, Avalon, 1964.
Lord of Tranerica. New York, Avalon, 1966.
The Crimson Capsule. New York, Avalon, 1967; as *The Animal People,* New York, Belmont, 1970.
The Day the World Stopped. New York, Avalon, 1968.
The Island People. New York, Belmont, 1971.

Uncollected Short Stories

"The Gas-Weed," in *Amazing* (New York), May 1929.
"The Making of Misty Isle," in *Science Wonder Stories* (New York), June 1929.
"The Radio Telescope," in *Amazing* (New York), June 1929.
"The Wand of Creation," in *Amazing* (New York), August 1929.
"Reclaimers of the Ice," in *Amazing Stories Quarterly* (New York) Spring 1930.
"A Circle of Science," in *Amazing* (New York), May 1930.
"Missionaries from the Sky," in *Amazing* (New York), November 1930.
"The Man from Tommorrow," in *Amazing Stories Quarterly* (New York), Spring-Summer 1933.
"The Men Without Shadows," in *Amazing* (New York), October 1933.
"The Confession of Mr. DeKalb," in *Astounding* (New York), January 1934.
"Manna from Mars," in *Astounding* (New York), March 1934.

"The Green Plague," in *Astounding* (New York), April 1934.
"The Radio Mind-Ray," in *Astounding* (New York), July 1934.
"In the Footsteps of the Wasp," in *Amazing* (New York), August 1934.
"The Truth about the Psycho-Tector," in *Astounding* (New York), October 1934.
"Beyond the Universe," in *Amazing* (New York), December 1934.
"Riches for Pluto," in *Astounding* (New York), December 1934.
"Older than Methuselah" in *Amazing* (New York), April 1935.
"Triple-Geared," in *Astounding* (New York), April 1935.
"An Episode in Space," in *Astounding* (New York), May 1935.
"The Golden Planetoid," in *Amazing* (New York), August 1935.
"The Glowworm Flower," in *Astounding* (New York), June 1936.
"Denitro," in *Amazing* (New York), February 1937.
"The Reign of the Long Tusks," in *Astounding* (New York), February 1937.
"Gravity, Unaffected," in *Astounding* (New York), September 1937.
"Exiles from the Universe," in *Amazing* (New York), February 1938.
"Through the Time Radio," in *Marvel* (New York), August 1938.
"Rout of the Fire Imps," in *Marvel* (New York), November 1938.
"Death in the Tubeway," in *Amazing* (New York), January 1939.
"The Weather Adjudicator," in *Marvel* (New York), February 1939.
"The Man from Xenern," in *Thrilling Wonder Tales* (New York), August 1939.
"The Purple Conspiracy," in *Fantastic Adventures* (New York), November 1939.
"Planet of the Knob Heads," in *Science Fiction* (Holyoke, Massachusetts), December 1939.
"Missionaries of Mars," in *Tales of Wonder* (Kingwood, Surrey), Spring 1940.
"Fire-Gas," in *Famous Fantastic Mysteries* (New York), April 1940.
"Sunward," in *Thrilling Wonder Stories* (New York), April 1940.
"Headhunters of Nuamerica," in *Comet* (Springfield, Massachusetts), March 1941.
"Over the Space-Waves," in *Startling* (New York), April 1941.
"Enchantress of Lemuria," in *Amazing* (New York), September 1941.
"The Crystal Planetoids," in *Amazing* (New York), May 1942.
"The Phantom Armada," in *Fantastic Adventures* (New York), May 1942.
"The Scarlet Rollers," in *Fantastic Adventures* (New York), September 1942.
"The Stygian Terror," in *Fantastic Adventures* (New York), November 1942.
"The Cosmic Deflector," in *Amazing* (New York), January 1943.
"Ard of the Sun People," in *Amazing* (New York), February 1943.
"The Sun Doom," in *Fantastic Adventures* (New York), June 1943.
"The Siderial Time-Bomb," in *Startling* (New York), Winter 1944.
"The Odyssey of Battling Bert," in *Amazing* (New York), December 1944.
"The Nemesis of the Astropede," in *Thrilling Wonder Stories* (New York), Fall 1945.
"Titan of the Jungle," in *Thrilling Wonder Stories* (New York), Summer 1946.
"Flight Through Tomorrow," in *Fantasy Book 1* (Los Angeles), 1947.
"Time Trap," in *Fantasy* (London), August 1947.
"The Universe Ranger," in *Fantasy Book 6* (Los Angeles), 1950.
"The Way of the Moth," in *Thrilling Wonder Stories* (New York), December 1951.
"The Revolt of the Scarlet Lunes," in *Spaceway* (Alhambra, California), December 1953.
"The Midgets of Monoton," in *Spaceway* (Alhambra, California), February 1954.
"Microcosm," in *Fantastic Universe* (Chicago), April 1958.

OTHER PUBLICATIONS

Verse

The Thinker and Other Poems. New York, White, 1923.
The Lone Adventurer. New York, Unicorn Press, 1927; revised edition, San Jose, California, Redwood Press, 1975.
Shadows on a Wall. New York, Poetic Publications, 1930.
The Enduring Flame. New York, Paebar, 1932.
Songs of the Redwoods. Los Angeles, Overland Outwest, 1933.
The Merry Hunt. Boston, Humphries, 1934.
The Pageant of Man. New York, Wings Press, 1936.
Songs by the Wayside. New York, Wings Press, 1938.
Senator Goose. Mill Valley, California, Wings Press, 1940.
Winds of Chaos. Mill Valley, California, Wings Press, 1942.
Green Vistas. Mill Valley, California, Wings Press, 1943.
Armageddon. Mill Valley, California, Wings Press, 1943.
The Mountain of the Sleeping Maiden. Mill Valley, California, Wings Press, 1946.
Garnered Sheaves: Selected Poems. Mill Valley, California, Wings Press, 1949.
Time's Travellers. Mill Valley, California, Wings Press, 1952.
From a Western Hilltop. Mill Valley, California, Wings Press, 1954.
Out of Many Songs. Mill Valley, California, Wings Press, 1958.
Atlantis and Other Poems. Mill Valley, California, Wings Press, 1960.
Redwood Poems. Healdsburg, California, Naturegraph, 1961.
Aesop's Fables. Norwalk, Connecticut, Gibson, 1968.
Selected Short Poems. San José, California, Redwood Press, 1974.
Strange Universes: New Selected Poems. San José, California, Redwood Press, 1977.
Sea Cliffs and Green Ridges: Poems of the West. Happy Camp, California, Naturegraph, 1979.

Other

The Decline of Man. New York, Minton Balch, 1925.
Marching Men: The Story of War. New York, Unicorn Press, 1927.
The Literary Revolution. New York, Frank Maurice, 1927.
The Answer of the Ages. New York, Cosmopolitan, 1931.
Villains and Vigilantes. New York, Wilson Erickson, 1936.
The Triumph of the Teapot Poets. Mill Valley, California, Wings Press, 1941.
An Editor Looks at Poetry. Mill Valley, California, Wings Press, 1947.

New Poetic Lamps and Old. Mill Valley, California, Wings Press, 1950.

From Arrow to Atom Bomb: The Psychological History of War. New York, Beechhurst Press, 1953.

The Rise of the Anti-Poets. Mill Valley, California, Wings Press, 1955.

Magic Casements: A Guidebook for Poets. Mill Valley, California, Wings Press, 1957.

The Long Road to Humanity. New York, Yoseloff, 1959.

My Life in Poetry. New York, Bookman Associates, 1959.

The Swallowing Wilderness. New York, Yoseloff, 1961.

The Generation That Forgot to Sing. Mill Valley, California, Wings Press, 1962.

Avarice: A History. Washington, D.C., Public Affairs Press, 1964.

Ten Crises in Civilization. Chicago, Follett, 1965; London, Muller, 1967.

Demons, Witch Doctors, and Modern Man. New York, Yoseloff, 1965.

The Paradox of Man's Greatness. Washington, D.C., Public Affairs Press, 1966.

The Poetry Circus. New York, Hawthorn, 1967.

The Pageant of the New World. Berkeley, California, Diablo Press, 1968.

The Power Trap. South Brunswick, New Jersey, A.S. Barnes, 1970.

The Militant Dissenters. South Brunswick, New Jersey, A. S. Barnes, 1970.

The Challenge to Man's Survival. South Brunswick, New Jersey, A.S. Barnes, 1972.

Light Beyond: The Wonderworld of Parapsychology. New York, Cornwall, 1982.

Adventures of a Freelancer: The Autobiography of Stanton A. Coblentz, with Jeffrey M. Elliot. San Bernardino, California, Borgo Press, 1984.

Editor, *Modern American* [and *British*] *Lyrics.* New York, Minton Balch, 2 vols., 1924-25; as *Modern Lyrics,* New York, Loring and Mussey, n.d.

Editor, *The Music Makers.* New York, Ackerman, 1945.

Editor, *Unseen Wings.* New York, Beechhurst Press, 1949.

Editor, *Poetry Today.* Mill Valley, California, Wings Press, 1955.

Editor, *Poems to Change Lives.* New York, Association Press, 1960.

*   *   *

In the earliest days of the science-fiction magazines, most of the stories were reprinted from other sources; shortly, however, new works began to appear in *Amazing, Science Wonder Stories,* and the others. One of the first of these "new" authors, along with such writers as Jack Williamson and E.E. Smith, was Stanton A. Coblentz.

Coblentz's work was unusual for these magazines, as most of the material utilized science fiction as a vehicle for transmitting "hard science" (i.e., the Verne tradition), or a device for establishing melodramatic adventure situations (i.e., the Burroughs tradition). Coblentz, by contrast, utilized the standard devices of science fiction—space travel, time displacement, discovery of lost races—in order to establish a satiric mirror in which to reflect the foibles of contemporary society and/or timeless modes of human conduct. In this sense, Coblentz

worked in the tradition of Lucian, Cyrano, Swift, and, to a substantial extent, H.G. Wells. Almost alone among Coblentz's contemporaries, David H. Keller exhibited similar attitudes and utilized similar techniques. Coblentz thus provided a model for such later humorists and satirists as William Tenn, Robert Sheckley, Frederik Pohl, and C.M. Kornbluth. Pohl, at least, of this group, has expressed his admiration for and debt to Coblentz.

Coblentz's first published science fiction was the novel *The Sunken World.* A modern submarine discovers survivors of the classical Atlantis living an idyllic existence in a glass dome on the ocean bottom, but they are destroyed through the inadvertent influence of the submariners.

In *Hidden World* a contemporary traveller finds his way into an unknown civilization hidden in giant caverns beneath the earth. This theme is one Jules Verne had used as a device for travelogue-like exploration of imaginary geography, and Edgar Rice Burroughs had used it, in his Pellucidar series, as a background for adventure tales with primitive human and non-human creatures. Coblentz's book harkened back to Ludvig Holberg's *Nils Klim* in using the inhabited hollow earth as a site for satirical events. In *Hidden World,* the traveller becomes caught up in a society at war for no comprehensible issue, except for the possible purpose of reducing unemployment and stimulating economic activity. *Into Plutonian Depths,* dealing with society on the plant Pluto, posits a situation in which men and women past child-bearing age aspire to become surgically neutered, these neuters being the pampered and powerful rulers of Plutonian society. The cover of the Avon edition described the novel as dealing with "the third sex" (a widely utilized euphemism for homosexuality at the time), to which Donald Wollheim, Avon's editor, later ascribed the success of the edition.

Many other works by Coblentz contain satirical matter, most often reflecting Coblentz's revulsion against war, consistently portrayed as senseless and ignoble, and his distress with the oppression and materialistic greed manifested in human institutions. *After 12,000 Years* portrays a future world in which armies of insects have been bred to giant and ferocious stature and enslaved for service in warfare. This anticipates *The Dragon Masters* (1962) by Jack Vance, a distant cousin of Coblentz. It should be noted that Coblentz had a long and varied literary career, of which his science fiction represents only one aspect. Two novels approaching science fiction are *The Wonder Stick,* a pleasantly done story of primitive life, and *When the Birds Fly South,* a beautifully realized novel of an unknown race in the Himalayas, this book being somewhat comparable to James Hilton's *Lost Horizon*

—Richard A. Lupoff

COGSWELL, Theodore R(ose). Also writes as Cogswell Thomas. American. Born in Coatesville, Pennsylvania, 10 March 1918. Educated at the University of Colorado, Boulder, B. A. 1947; University of Denver, M. A. 1948, graduate study, 1956-57; University of Minnesota, Minneapolis, 1949-53; Latin Institute, Brooklyn College, 1973. Served as an ambulance driver, Spanish Republican Army, 1937-38; statistical control officer, United States Army Air Force, 1942-46: Captain; Order of the Cloud and Dragon, Republic of China. Married 1) Marjorie Mills in 1948, two daughters; 2) Coralie

Norris in 1964; 3) George Rae Williams in 1972. Boulder correspondent, United Press, 1941-42; Instructor, University of Minnesota, 1949-53, and University of Kentucky, Lexington, 1953-56, 1957-58; Assistant Professor, Ball State University, Muncie, Indiana, 1958-65. Since 1965, Professor, Keystone Junior College, La Plume, Pennsylvania. Since 1959, Executive Director, and Editor of Proceedings, Institute for 21st Century Studies. Editor, *SFWA Forum,* 1970-71, 1973-76; book reviewer, Minneapolis *Tribune,* 1970-72; Editor, I. C. S., Scranton, Pennsylvania, 1975-78; Editorial Consultant, Sandvik Inc., Fair Lawn, New Jersey, 1978. Secretary, Science Fiction Writers of America, 1973-74. Address: 108 Robinson Street, Chinchilla, Pennsylvania 18410, U. S. A.

SCIENCE-FICTION PUBLICATIONS

Novel

Spock, Messiah!, with Charles A. Spano, Jr. New York, Bantam, 1976; London, Corgi, 1977.

Short Stories

The Wall Around the World. New York, Pyramid, 1962.
The Third Eye. New York, Belmont, 1968.

Uncollected Short Stories

"Time Telescoped," in *Climax,* June 1953.
"The Big Stink," in *If* (New York), July 1954.
"Contact Point," with Poul Anderson, in *If* (New York), August 1954.
"Barrier," in *Science Fiction,* September 1954.
"Meddlers World," with Mack Reynolds, in *Science Fiction Quarterly* (Holyoke, Massachusetts), November 1955.
"Threesie," in *Fantasy and Science Fiction* (New York), January 1956.
"Aces Loaded," in *Venture* (Concord, New Hampshire), July 1957.
"The Cabbage Patch," in *Fantasy and Science Fiction* (New York), December 1957.
"Pain Reaction," in *Super Science* (New York), April 1958.
"The Golden People," in *Rogue,* June 1960.
"The Man Who Knew Grodnick," in *Science Fantasy* (Bournemouth), June 1962.
"Early Bird," with Ted Thomas, and "Probability Zero! The Population Implosion," in *Astounding,* edited by Harry Harrison. New York, Random House, 1973.
"Paradise Regained," (as Cogswell Thomas, with Ted Thomas), in *Saving Worlds,* edited by Roger Elwood and Virginia Kidd. New York, Doubleday, 1973.
"Players at Null-G," with Ted Thomas and Algis Budrys, in *Fantasy and Science Fiction* (New York), July 1975.
"Grandfather Clause," in *Fantasy and Science Fiction* (New York), September 1975.
"How Dinosaurs Did It," in *Citadel,* February 1976.
"Deal with the D. E. V. I. L.," in *Fantasy Book* (Pasadena, California), December 1981.

OTHER PUBLICATIONS

Plays

Some Call It Heads (produced Denver, 1948).
Operation Tel Aviv (produced Foothills, California, 1949).

Contact Point, with G. R. Cogswell, in *Six Science Fiction Plays,* edited by Roger Elwood. New York, Washington Square Press, 1976.

Television Play: *Red Dust* (*Tales of Tomorrow* series), 1952.

Verse

The Roper (song), music by John Jacob Niles. New York, Schirmer, 1955.
Placebos for the Orthodox. Chinchilla, Pennsylvania, Miskatonic University Press, 1981.

*   *   *

Theodore R. Cogswell's work ranges in mood from horror to irony and spoof, in form from novellas to short stories, poetry, and drama, and in quality from expert and meaningful storytelling to juvenile fantasy.

While portions of his stories (like "Test Area") are chilling, Cogswell's best horror story is probably "The Burning," which is about a demonic god (a terrible matriarch) who demands love and obedience from her "children"—and also eats them alive. Often horror is mixed with irony in Cogswell's work, as in "Emergency Rations" where cannibals are trapped in a Trojan horse scheme and literally cooked alive since they "can't feel nothing"; "Thimgs" where the unscrupulous main character demands vitality in his bargain with a "Guardian" for longer life—only to find that the lives "spliced" on to his are those leading to horrible sudden deaths; and "Wolfie" where Peter Vincent bargains with a warlock to be turned into a werewolf in order to kill his cousin and collect on his will, but is transformed into a mangy toothless mutt that must be put out of its "misery. " In these three stories the would-be victimizers become victims, for as the Guardian says in "Thimgs," "the ethical universe is just as orderly as the physical one." Occasionally, Cogswell's mood borders on spoof, as in "Probability Zero! The Population Implosion" which manipulates statistics in order to "prove" that England's population has declined since the year 1000 from 275 billion to 44 million at the present time. So, the story advises ticklishly, if you hear doomsayers of the population bomb, you need remember only that "statistics show . . . you have nothing to worry about. " "Probability Zero!" illustrates what a Pirandello character says of a statistic: it's "like a sack; it won't stand up till you've put something in it. " Unfortunately, what we put into it is interpretation, which is usually debatable and rarely definitive.

Cogswell is quite adept in the various literary genres. His first novella, "The Spectre General," is an accomplished story in the Heinlein tradition, involving delightful situational and understated humor and an alternating chapter/scene plot structure, which deals with the revival of a dying empire by technologists. *The Wall Around the World* is a fine reworking of the Icarus myth, blending and contrasting magic and technology in its main character, Porgie. Cogswell's shorter works are also expert, as I have implied above and as the story "Early Bird" reveals. The most imaginative of all his fictions, this piece depicts a fascinating symbiotic relationship between the main character, Kurt Dixon, and his ship's mother computer and between "her" and two incredibly adaptive, semi-organic monsters on a planet Kurt was forced to retreat to during his battle with the gigantic, people-eating Kieriens. Cogswell's poetry, although different in theme and mood from his other work, is quite good, as his Swiftian lambast against contemporary poets ("sparrow farts" and "word kickers") in "Faex Delenda Est" suggests. Finally, his drama is also impressive. For example, *Contact Point,* written with his wife, has an excellent sense of timing and action, dealing with the first space crew to reach a star and their anxieties and conflicts in bringing back a deadly radioactive organism. At first convinced that earth's doctors can save him, and willing to endanger the rest of humanity, the main character undergoes a dramatic change whereby he challenges earthlings to reunite and stop fighting among themselves in order to annihilate him and his ship before it lands.

Although Cogswell sometimes stoops to puerile fantasy as in "The Masters" (a vampire story), he is a versatile writer who usually makes a point. Even in "The Masters" we see that just as the ethical universe is orderly so is the physical one, so that we never know if we will need some endangered species (the snaildarter?) to help us in our afflictions.

—Dennis M. Welch

COLERIDGE, John. See **BINDER, Eando.**

COLLINS, Hunt. See **HUNTER, Evan.**

COLVIN, James. See **MOORCOCK, Michael.**

COMPTON, D(avid) G(uy). Also writes as Guy Compton; Frances Lynch. British. Born in London, 19 August 1930. Educated at Cheltenham College, 1940-48. Served in the British Army, 1948-50. Married 1) Elizabeth Tillotson in 1952 (divorced, 1969), two daughters and one son; 2) Carol Savage in 1971, one step-daughter and one step-son. Worked as stage electrician, furniture maker, salesman, docker, and postman; Editor, Reader's Digest Condensed Books, London 1969-81. Lives in the United States. Recipient: Arts Council bursary, 1964; Agent: Virginia Kidd, Box 278, Milford, Pennyslvania 18337, U.S.A.

SCIENCE-FICTION PUBLICATIONS

Novels

The Quality of Mercy. London, Hodder and Stoughton, and New York, Ace, 1965; revised edition, Ace, 1970.

Farewell, Earth's Bliss. London, Hodder and Stoughton, 1966; New York, Ace, 1971.
The Silent Multitude. New York, Ace, 1966; London, Hodder and Stoughton, 1967.
Synthajoy. London, Hodder and Stoughton, and New York, Ace, 1968.
The Steel Crocodile. New York, Ace, 1970; as *The Electric Crocodile,* London, Hodder and Stoughton, 1970.
Chronocules. New York, Ace, 1970; as *Hot Wireless Sets, Aspirin Tablets, The Sandpaper Sides of Used Matchboxes, and Something That Might Have Been Castor Oil,* London, Joseph, 1971.
The Missionaries. New York, Ace, 1972; London, Hale, 1975.
The Unsleeping Eye. New York, DAW, 1974; as *The Continuous Katherine Mortenhoe,* London, Gollancz, 1974; as *Death Watch,* London, Magnum, 1981.
A Usual Lunacy. San Bernardino, California, Borgo Press, 1978.
Windows. New York, Berkley, 1979.
Ascendancies. London, Gollancz, and New York, Berkley, 1980.
Scudder's Game. Munich, Heyne, 1985.

Uncollected Short Stories

"It's Smart to Have an English Address," in *World's Best Science Fiction 1968,* edited by Donald A. Wollheim and Terry Carr. New York, Ace, 1968; London, Gollancz, 1969.
"Bender, Fenugreek, Slatterman, and Mupp," in *Interfaces,* edited by Ursula K. Le Guin and Virginia Kidd. New York, Ace, 1980.
"Old Man, Waiting," in *Portland Review* (Oregon), 1984.

OTHER PUBLICATIONS

Novels as Guy Compton

Too Many Murderers. London, Long, 1962.
Medium for Murder. London, Long, 1963.
Dead on Cue. London, Long, 1964.
Disguise for a Dead Gentleman. London, Long, 1964.
High Tide for Hanging. London, Long, 1965.
And Murder Came Too. London, Long, 1966.
The Palace (as D. G. Compton). London, Hodder and Stoughton, and New York, Norton, 1969.

Novels as Frances Lynch

Twice Ten Thousand Miles. London, Souvenir Press, and New York, St. Martin's Press, 1974; as *Candle at Midnight,* New York, Dell, 1977.
The Fine and Handsome Captain. London, Souvenir Press, and New York, St. Martin's Press, 1975.
Stranger at the Wedding. New York, St. Martin's Press, 1976; London, Souvenir Press, 1977.
A Dangerous Magic. London, Souvenir Press, and New York, St. Martin's Press, 1978.
In the House of Dark Music. London. Hodder and Stoughton, 1979.

Plays

Radio Plays: *Chez Nous,* 1961; *Bandstand,* 1962; *Blind Man's Bluff,* 1962; *Fully Furnished,* 1963; *Always Read the Small Print,*

1963; *If the Shoe Fits*, 1964; *Mandible Light*, 1964; *A Turning off the Minch Park Road*, 1965; *Time Exposure*, 1965; *The Real People*, 1966; *Island*, 1968; *Surgery*, 1968; *The Respighi Inheritance*, 1973.

Other

"The Profession of Science Fiction 16: By Chance Out of Conviction," in *Foundation 17* (London), September 1979.

*

D. G. Compton comments:

Possibly the best introduction to any writer's work is to know why he does it. The reason I write what people have been kind enough to call SF ("kind enough" because the label makes possible a large and informed readership for stuff that otherwise would probably sink without a trace) is that I'm basically a rather embarrassed sort of person, afraid of admitting to commitment, who welcomes SF's distancing mechanisms. After all, it's far safer to dare to care about one's characters when the situation in which one places them isn't quite "real. "

Also I've led what is sometimes known as a "sheltered life. " For which read "limited." Thus I know very little about the commonalities of human existence: commerce, golf, bricklaying, what you will. The same sheltered life, however, has involved me in close and prolonged—and often painful— contact with just a few very positive individuals (mostly women, let's face it), and from these individuals I've learned a lot. So I try to write about that of which I know at least something, people, while setting them discreetly in worlds of my own devising (about which I may also be expected to know something.) Future worlds, for convenience's sake, but always closely tied to my own muddled understanding of the present world around me. In general terms I don't much like this present world, and developing it a few years on is a good way of finding out why. And perhaps even of seeing how to change it.

*   *   *

D. G. Compton's science-fiction novels usually lead to extremes of reaction from their readers. Some are strongly attracted to his mature themes, richly fluent prose, strong concentration on character, and realistic appreciation of the seamier side of human existence. Others are dismayed by the density of his prose, the ineffectualness of many of his characters, the underlying distrust of technology as a cure for all of humanity's ills, the absence of much physical action, and the frequently bizarre nature of his situations. But it appears that Compton is beginning to win over an ever larger share of readers as he continues to skewer human foibles and failings.

Two of his more popular novels deal with our delight in vicarious experience of another's life. *Synthajoy* created a minor controversy because of the dissolute nature of its characters. The story concerns the development of a means to record the life experiences of an individual, to be played back at another time for an interested audience. Although there are obvious beneficial aspects to such an invention, it is almost immediately subverted. Compton returned to this theme in *The Unsleeping Eye*. In a world where disease and pain are virtually unknown, Katherine Mortenhoe has contracted a terminal disease that leaves her only weeks to live. The entertainment world is quick to realize that this provides a possibly unique opportunity to produce a profitable bit of entertainment, and

they employ a man with cameras surgically implanted in one eye. The cameraman manipulates Katherine so that she is emotionally dependent upon him, totally unaware that he is filming her agony for an unfeeling audience. But as time passes, his feelings for her become genuine, and there is a dawning realization that he too is being manipulated.

Compton apparently felt that he had not completely examined the consequences of this situation, because he later wrote a sequel, *Windows*. The Protagonist insists upon the removal of his camera-eyes and accepts blindness, but his personal statement about the world is not allowed to stand as it is. One factor abhors him for criticizing the status quo, another wants to make him a cult hero, and still another dismisses his gesture as an nuisance. The pair are finally driven to flee the country, but are still unable to withdraw into themselves.

Perhaps Compton's most accomplished work is *The Steel Crocodile*, set in an ultra-secret research institute. The protagonist rapidly realizes that more is transpiring within the research group than is apparent. Eventually it is revealed to him that the authorities fear that blind technological progress is too dangerous, and they have created a computer bank to monitor and even interfere with scientific developments. They are blithely unaware that they have surrendered their destiny to the very technology they hoped to control. This complexity of philosophy and plot is rarely found in any genre, and Compton's ability to control his work has rarely been equalled.

The Silent Multitude is perhaps his least conventional work. A spore from space attacts concrete, and most artifacts of man's civilization are crumbling. Against the background of a deserted city, Compton presents a small cast of characters, relecting their personal decay against the collapse of the city itself. Even without the brilliant characterization, this would remain a memorable novel, for Compton's description of the dissolution is haunting.

The isolated research organizaton appears again in *Chronocules*, also present as an island of hope in a crumbling society. It is clear that the collapse of the present society is accelerating and will come within the lifetimes of the protagonists, so they desperately seek a means of escape into the future. Although an excellent novel in itself, it suffers when compared to *The Steel Crocodile* and *The Silent Multitude*, to both of which it is thematically similar. *The Missionaries* should have been a very controversial novel, but attracted little attention. A small group of aliens arrive on Earth, preaching the religion of Ustiliath. Compton makes it quite clear that, for all practical purposes, the aliens are absolutely correct in their beliefs, and that conversion to their religion is the only logical course. But humanity reacts with fear and loathing, and the aliens reach the same fate that greeted many Christian missionaries in their efforts to bring "enlightenment" to the "savages. "

Two of Compton's early novels were brought back into print as his popularity grew. Both are highly competent, but neither is of the quality of his later work. *The Quality of Mercy* is a low key examination of the tensions brought to bear on a group of military personnel when it becomes clear that something, perhaps a nuclear war, is imminent. In many ways, this is a forerunner of *The Steel Crocodile*, although in no way comparable with regard to quality. *Farewell, Earth's Bliss* makes use of one of science fiction's most well-traveled plots, the penal colony on Mars, to present a group of misfit humans against a kaleidoscopic background where reality and fantasy aren't always distinguishable.

A Usual Lunacy investigates the repercussions of a new disease that causes people to fall in love with each other against their will, and in many cases only until they are cured of the disease. Compton seems unusually bitter this time, for love itself becomes a sometimes criminal activity. *Ascendancies* seems to have been largely overlooked despite yet another set of interesting characters. A strange substance begins periodically to fall from space, a substance which is soon revealed to be an inexpensive source of energy. Soon most of the world is freed from the normal work week, but subject to a new burden. There are scattered incidents of possibly hallucinatory singing, often accompanied by mysterious disappearances of people in the area. The protagonists are a woman whose husband disappears and the insurance investigator who discovers she has purchased a body from a criminal organization in order to ensure that she receives the insurance money. When he decides to blackmail her, the two are brought together in compulsive and compelling relationship.

Compton has written few short stories, none of which have been noteworthy, probably because his gift of characterization is not as apparent at that length. Although he continues to write both within and outside the genre, Compton has eschewed the traditional concerns of science fiction, using the plots that he borrows only as the frame upon which to hang his real interests, the morality of science, the peculiarities of humanity, and our ability to influence our own lives.

—Don D'Ammassa

CONEY, Michael G(reatrex). British. Born in Birmingham, Warwickshire, 28 September 1932. Educated at King Edward's School, Birmingham, 1944-49. Served in the Royal Air Force, 1956-58. Married to Daphne Coney; two sons and one daughter. Auditor, Russell and Company, Birmingham, 1949-56; Senior Clerk, Pearce Clayton Maunder, Dorchester, Dorset, 1958-61; accountant, Pontins, Bournemouth, 1962; tenant, Plymouth Breweries, Totnes, Devon, 1963-66; accountant, Peplow Warren Fuller, Newton Abbout, Devon, 1966-69; manager, Jabberwock Hotel, Antigua, West Indies, 1969-72. Since 1973, Management Specialist, British Columbia Forest Service, Victoria. Recipient: British Science Fiction Award, 1976. Address: 2082 Neptune Road, R. R. 3, Sidney, British Columbia, Canada.

SCIENCE-FICTION PUBLICATIONS

Novels (series: The Song of Earth)

Mirror Image. New York, DAW, 1972; London, Gollancz, 1973.
Syzygy. New York, Ballantine, and Morley, Yorkshire, Elmfield Press, 1973
Friends Come in Boxes. New York, DAW, 1973; London, Gollancz, 1974.
The Hero of Downways. New York, DAW, 1973; London, Futura, 1974.
Winter's Children. London, Gollancz, 1974.
The Jaws That Bite, The Claws That Catch. New York, DAW, 1975; as *The Girl with a Symphony in Her Fingers*, Morley, Yorkshire, Elmfield Press, 1975.
Hello Summer, Goodbye. London, Gollancz, 1975; as *Rax*,

New York, DAW, 1975.
Charisma. London, Gollancz, 1975; New York, Dell, 1979.
Brontomek! London, Gollancz, 1976.
The Ultimate Jungle. London, Millington, 1979.
Neptune's Cauldron. New York, Tower, 1981
Cat Karina. New York, Ace, 1982; London, Gollancz, 1983.
The Celestial Steam Locomotive (Song). Boston, Houghton Mifflin, 1983.
Gods of the Greataway (Song). Boston, Houghton Mifflin, 1984.

Short Stories

Monitor Found in Orbit. New York, DAW, 1974.

Uncollected Short Stories

"The Snow Princess," in *Galaxy* (New York), January 1971.
"Hold My Hand," in *Worlds of Tomorrow* (New York), Spring 1971.
"The Sharks of Pentreath," in *The 1972 Annual World's Best SF*, edited by Donald A. Wollheim and Arthur W. Saha. New York, DAW, 1972.
"Susanna, Susanna!," in *Fantasy and Science Fiction* (New York), November 1972.
"The Tertiary Justification," in *New Writings in SF 21*, edited by John Carnell. London, Sigwick and Jackson, 1972.
"Oh, Valinda!," in *The 1973 Annual World's Best SF*, edited by Donald A. Wollheim and Arthur W. Saha. New York, DAW, 1973.
"The Never Girl," in *If* (New York), February 1973.
"A Woman and Her Friend," in *If* (New York), March 1973.
"The Bridge on the Scraw," in *Fantasy and Science Fiction* (New York), July 1973.
"The Initiation of Asaka Akasa," in *Fantasy and Science Fiction* (New York), January 1974.
"Bartholomew & Son (and the Fish Girl)," in *New Writing in SF 27*, edited by Kenneth Bulmer. London, Sidgwick and Jackson, 1975.
"Starthinker 9," in *Andromeda 1*, edited by Peter Weston. London, Futura, 1976; New York, St. Martin's Press, 1979.
"Trading Post," in *SF Digest 1* (London), 1976.
"The Cinderella Machine," in *Fantasy and Science Fiction* (New York), August 1976.
"Those Good Old Days of Liquid Fuel," in *The 1977 Annual World's Best SF*, edited by Donald A. Wollheim. New York, DAW, 1977.
"Just an Old-Fashioned War Story," in *Ascents of Wonder*, edited by David Gerrold. New York, Popular Library, 1977.
"Catapult to the Stars," in *Fantasy and Science Fiction* (New York), April 1977.
"Sparklebugs, Holly, and Love," in *Fantasy and Science Fiction* (New York), December 1977.
"In Search of Professor Greatrex," in *Pulsar 1*, edited by George Hay. London, Penguin 1978.
"Penny on a Skyhorse," in *Galileo 11-12* (Boston), 1979.
"The Summer Sweet, The Winter Wild," in *Interfaces*, edited by Ursula K. Le Guin and Virginia Kidd. New York, Ace, 1980.
"The Hook, The Eye, and the Whip," in *The Seven Deadly Sins of Science Fiction*, edited by Isaac Asimov, Martin H. Greenberg, and Charles G. Waugh. New York, Fawcett, 1980.
"The Byrds," in *Changes*, edited by Michael Bishop and Ian Watson. New York, Ace, 1982.

OTHER PUBLICATIONS

Other

Forest Ranger, Ahoy! The Men, The Ships, The Job. Sidney, British Columbia, Porthole Press, 1983.

*   `

Michael G. Coney comments:

My purpose is to entertain myself as well as my readers. Each of my novels has been an experiment in style and content with one consistent trait: they are all mystery stories. Love is there too, and human psychology, and a little "hard" science, but my main intent is to keep the reader guessing. I think my earlier novels were too conservative; they were all hung on hooks of known science and "real" reality—which is odd, since as an SF reader my preference is for the persuasively fantastic: the "sense of wonder" story. My short stories are normally written as vehicles for ideas, situations, and characters which I intend to use in my novels—I find it much easier to work this way than to plunge into a novel cold. Other short stories have been written for specific purposes, generally to use up one-off ideas before I forget them.

*   *   *

Michael G. Coney was a prolific writer in the mid-1970's and seems about to become so again, with his recent commitment to "The Song of Earth," a kaleidoscopic future history. Because he has contributed to so many of the genre's traditions, his work is not easy to classify: perhaps his originality has been in his ability to take the old forms and themes and quietly but persuasively stamp his own hallmark upon them. Philip K. Dick may have been his model in *Mirror Image*, John Christopher in the post-holocaust novel, *Winter's Children*, Heinlein and Aldiss in the closed environment stories *The Hero of Downways, The Ultimate Jungle* and "The Mind Prison," Asimov's "Nightfall" in *Syzygy* and "Evidence" (from *I, Robot*) in "The Martyrdom of Raccoona Three" (a fine short story embedded in *The Celestial Steam Locomotive*), Cordwainer Smith in *Cat Karina* and other stories in "The Song of Earth" that feature the "Specialists" (animal-human melds). His powerful sequel to *Syzygy, Brontomek!,* takes up several ideas from the earlier stories: the amorphs from *Mirror Image*, the heroine's name and personality from Susanna in *Charisma*, the brontomeks and the idea of post-hypnotic suggestion from his grim story "Esmeralda. " Throughout his work, Coney's range of theme and tone are remarkable; his touch is usually light but the fare not bland. He is equally at ease with horror, romance, and humor ("The Byrds" should become a classic of comic fantasy). "The Song of the Earth," therefore, which forces him by its structure to evoke the sense of wonder freshly at least once in each of its many short chapters, is ideally suited to his genius and has the futher advantage of enabling him to subsume his taste for fantasy within a formal science-fictional frame, through the idea of a computer-programmable Dream World.

Coney likes to study the reactions of a small group to a large threat or challenge, whether natural but alien, as in *Hello Summer, Goodbye* and *Syzygy*, or social but inhuman, as in *Brontomek!*, or both, as in *The Ultimate Jungle*. Solutions are not likely to be achieved by technological means but, after valiant efforts, may be granted by special grace; to some problems the only solution is escape or transcendence. As an SF writer, Coney is properly concerned with the issue of scepticism and its contrary, credulity; he is not so hasty as some writers to come down on one side. The framing chapters of *Syzygy* expose the dangers of group vulnerability to suggestion, yet it seems in *Brontomek!* that it may sometimes be better to rest happily deceived, as individuals are by the amorphic "Tes" (thous, ideal companions). Coney hates manipulators: his sympathetic characters are after their victims; yet it is not easy for these characters to find someone to blame. In *Brontomek!* the immoral Organization stamps on a whole planet, yet its own agents are themselves victims and there is something sublimely admirable in the irresponsible force of its symbol, the rogue brontomek, which rampages malignly for a time, before pathetically losing its motive power, "betrayed by its own mechanical weaknesses. " Cat Karina complains against the bullying gods but human manipulators and strong egotists may be regarded with horrified admiration, as are Carioca Jones and Hector Bartholomew in the Peninsula stories, while their devoted lovers are seen with baffled disgust. Nevertheless, if the author, for narrative purposes, identifies with such lovers, he will present them with strong sympathy, and perhaps it is for this reason that in *Charisma, The Jaws That Bite, The Claws That Catch* and *The Ultimate Jungle*, Coney seems over-tolerant of some repellent features of his heroes, concomitant on their devotion to such unpleasant characters. Alien manipulators may also be present sympathetically (their control is accidental in *Syzygy*, accidents are rectified by benevolent fostering in "The Tertiary Justification" and "Symbiote"; they show wise control of beasts in "Oh, Valinda!"). So disposed, Coney gives us one of the genre's sweetest heroines in the alien Pallahaxi Browneyes (*Hello Summer, Goodbye*), and seems to envy the self-containedness of his multi-individual aliens (Kli a' Po in *Brontomek!* and the amusing Vegan in "Trading Post"), whereas his humans often find it hard to relate to other individuals.

There is strong dystopian satire in *Friends Come in Boxes* (which offers a radical solution to superfluous people – those over 40) and *The Jaws That Bite, The Claws That Catch* (where prisoners reduce their sentences by voluntary bondage). As a dystopian writer, Coney's animus is principally against the notion that utility or justice should outweigh compassion. The darker side of his vision culminates in *The Ultimate Jungle*, an important but depressing novel in which Coney seems to have given in to a compulsion to put on record those inadequacies which hereafter will force him to treat humans as members of a dead species. Maybe he had to get this book off his chest before he could achieve the mellower tones of "The Song of Earth. "

Coney has stressed the element of mystery in his stories his plots often draw upon those of mystery fiction: like Bester's *The Demolished Man, Charisma* offers an SF variant of the locked-room mystery, for instance, and "Monitor Found in Orbit" wickedly plays on the spy thriller. Coney appreciates that the SF form can be used to shed new light on old problems; in my favorite of his novels, *The Hero of Downways*, he studies heroism as it were in a clinical laboratory situation—and also takes a fresh look at such SF standards as clones, the multi-individual self, mutations, and miniaturized people. Others may enjoy this author more for his presentation of new forms of locomotion or of unusual tidal conditions on strange planets; few should fail to find him entertaining and he deserves to be rediscovered.

—Michael J. Tolley

CONRAD, Gregg. See **PHILLIPS, Rog.**

COOK, Glen (Charles). American. Born in New York City, 9 July 1944. Educated at Roseville Joint Union High School, California; University of Missouri, Columbia, 2 years. Served in the United States Navy. Married Carol Ann Fritz in 1971; two sons. Since 1965, assembly, inspection, control, and supervisory jobs, General Motors, St. Louis. Agent: Russell Galen, Scott Meredith Literary Agency, 845 Third Avenue, New York, New York 10022. Address: 4106 Flora Place, St. Louis, Missouri 63110, U. S. A.

SCIENCE-FICTION PUBLICATIONS

Novels (series: Black Company; Dread Empire; Starfishers)

The Heirs of Babylon. New York, New American Library, 1972.
A Shadow of All Night Falling (Dread Empire). New York, Berkley, 1979.
October's Baby (Dread Empire). New York, Berkley, 1980.
All Darkness Met (Dread Empire). New York, Berkley, 1980.
The Swordbearer. New York, Pocket Books, 1982.
Shadowline (Starfishers). New York, Warner, 1982.
Starfishers. New York, Warner, 1982.
Stars' End (Starfishers). New York, Warner, 1982.
The Fire in His Hands (Dread Empire). New York, Pocket Books, 1984.
The Black Company. New York, Tor, 1984.
Shadows Linger (Black Company). New York, Tor, 1984.
Passage of Arms. New York, Popular Library, 1985.
A Matter of Time. New York, Ace, 1985.
With Mercy Toward None (Dread Empire). New York, Baen, 1985.
The White Rose (Black Company). New York, Tor, 1985.

Uncollected Short Stories

"Song from a Forgotten Hill," in *Clarion,* edited by Robin Scott Wilson. New York, New American Library, 1971.
"Silverheels," in *Witchcraft & Sorcery* (Alhambra, California), May 1971.
"And Dragons in the Sky," in *Clarion 2,* edited by Robin Scott Wilson. New York, New American Library, 1972.
"Appointment in Samarkand," in *Witchcraft & Sorcery* (Alhambra, California), November 1972.
"Sunrise," in *Eternity 1* (Sandy Springs, South Carolina), no. 2, 1973.
"The Nights of Dreadful Silence," in *Fantastic* (New York), September 1973.
"The Devil's Tooth," in *Fantasy & Terror 1,* no. 1, 1974.
"In the Wind," in *Tomorrow Today,* edited by George Zebrowski. Santa Cruz, California, Unity Press, 1975.
"The Recruiter," in *Amazing* (New York), March 1977.
"Ponce," in *Amazing* (New York), November 1977.
"The Seventh Fool," in *Fantasy and Science Fiction* (New York), March 1978.
"Ghost Stalk," in *Fantasy and Science Fiction* (New York), May 1978.

"Quiet Sea," in *Fantasy and Science Fiction* (New York), December 1978.
"Castle of Tears," in *Whispers 4* (Binghamton, New York), nos. 1-2, 1979.
"Soldier of an Empire Unacquainted with Defeat," in *The Berkley Showcase 2,* edited by Victoria Schochet and John W. Silbersack. New York, Berkley, 1980.
"Call for the Dead," in *Fantasy and Science Fiction* (New York), July 1980.
"Filed Teeth," in *Dragons of Darkness,* edited by Orson Scott Card. New York, Ace, 1981.
"Raker," in *Fantasy and Science Fiction* (New York), August 1982.
"Darkwar," in *Isaac Asimov's Science Fiction Magazine* (New York), December 1982.
"Enemy Territory," in *Night Voyages 9* (Freeburg, Illinois), Spring 1983.
"The Waiting Sea," in *Archon 7 Program Book.* St. Louis, Archon, 1983.
"Severed Heads," in *Sword and Sorceress 1* edited by Marion Zimmer Bradley. New York, DAW, 1984.

OTHER PUBLICATIONS

Novel

The Swap Academy (as Greg Stevens). San Diego, Publisher's Export Corp, 1970.

*   *   *

Although Glen Cook's first publications were "Song from a Forgotten Hill" and "And Dragons in the Sky", published in the first Clarion anthologies in 1971 and 1972, he is primarily known for the series of novels that appeared in a quickening torrent nearly a decade later. "Song from a Forgotten Hill," a short story about future racial strife, was typical in its brevity and theme of the apprentice SF of its time; but "And Dragons in the Sky," a space opera involving a mile-long spaceship, contrasted conspicuously with the subject matter and styles of the other Clarion alumni in whose company Cook made his debut.

After the appearance of a post-holocaust novel, *The Heirs of Babylon,* Cook published "In the Wind. " Like the earlier pieces, it deals with familiar SF scenarios awkwardly but with some vigor, and not without evident ambition. Like all Cook's work, "In the Wind" shows his weakness with metaphor and structure, and what was to prove an enduring propensity for cliché. Cook's tale of airwhales hunted by humans in flimsy aircraft is derivative in many respects and marks the beginning of his practice of transferring wholesale the sentimental particulars of romantic military fiction into the future, but remains, with the earlier stories, his most impassioned and interesting work.

Some years later Cook described his early career as comprising "several transmogrifications and near-sales to editors immediately fired and publishing houses immediately going bankrupt." Whether owing to these difficulties or not, the fiction Cook resumed publishing in 1978 was expediently and carelessly executed, being a series of fantasy adventures whose backgrounds were strongly flavored with the regalia of 17th-century British piracy ("Ghost Stalk") and the oriental warrior ("Soldier of an Empire Unacquainted with Defeat"), and prompt suspicions that they were set in imaginary worlds simply to avoid the need for research. Both stories share the same background as the Dread Empire Trilogy, as a second trilogy, "Starfishers," rather nominally shares the historical background of "In the Wind."

These books are unqualified potboilers, either cynically conceived or truly cruel-spirited tales of warriors who have never lost and suffer no change in fortune through the course of the stories. They conspicuously lack the craftsmanship that goes into many paperback novels of no literary pretension, and are so badly written as to prove frequently ludicrous—sentences such as "As Tor hit the deck he began growling orders through a grin of anticipation" may be found in every paragraph.

Four novels published in early 1985 indicate the range Cook has shown over the first half of the decade. *The White Rose* concludes another fantasy trilogy, notable for its cruelty of incident and haphazard, seemingly improvised structure. *A Matter of Time* is a science-fiction novel dealing with homicide detectives and time-travel paradoxes which, although similar to numerous genre novels such as Silverberg's *The Time Hoppers,* moves with some crispness. *With Mercy Toward None,* a sequel to *The Fire in His Hands* and presumably middle volume to another fantasy trilogy, deals with a desert prophet's uprising in a predictable manner but with some attempt at greater emotional depth.

—Gregory Feeley

COOKE, Arthur. See **LOWNDES, Robert A. W.**

COOPER, Edmund. Also wrote as Richard Avery. British. Born in Marple, Cheshire, 30 April 1926. Educated at Manchester Grammar School, 1937-41; Didsbury Teachers Training College, Lancashire, 1946-47. Served as a radio officer in the British Merchant Navy, 1939-45. Married 1) Joyce Plant in 1946, one daughter and three sons; 2) Valerie Makin in 1963, two sons and two daughters; 3) Dawn Freeman-Baker in 1980. Journalist, British Iron and Steel Research Association, London, 1960-61, and Federation of British Industries, London, 1962; staff writer, Esso Petroleum, London, 1962-66. After 1967, regular science-fiction reviewer, *Sunday Times,* London. *Died 11 March 1982.*

Science-Fiction Publications

Novels

Deadly Image. New York, Ballantine, 1958; as *The Uncertain Midnight,* London, Hutchinson, 1958.
Seed of Light. London, Hutchinson, and New York, Ballantine, 1959.
Transit. London, Faber, and New York, Lancer, 1964.
All Fools' Day. London, Hodder and Stoughton, and New York, Walker, 1966.
A Far Sunset. London, Hodder and Stoughton, and New York, Walker, 1967.
Five to Twelve. London, Hodder and Stoughton, 1968; New York, Putnam, 1969.
Sea-Horse in the Sky. London, Hodder and Stoughton, 1969; New York, Putnam, 1970.
The Last Continent. New York, Dell, 1969; London, Hodder and Stoughton, 1970.
Son of Kronk. London, Hodder and Stoughton, 1970; as *Kronk,* New York, Putnam, 1971.
The Overman Culture. London, Hodder and Stoughton, 1971; New York, Putnam, 1972.
Double Phoenix, The Firebird. New York, Ballantine, 1971.
Who Needs Men? London, Hodder and Stoughton, 1972; as *Gender Genocide,* New York, Ace, 1972.
The Cloud Walker. London, Hodder and Stoughton, and New York, Ballantine, 1973.
The Tenth Planet. London, Hodder and Stoughton, and New York, Putnam, 1973.
The Slaves of Heaven. New York, Putnam, 1974; London, Hodder and Stoughton, 1975.
Prisoner of Fire. London, Hodder and Stoughton, 1974; New York, Walker, 1976.
Merry Christmas, Ms. Minerva. London, Hale, 1978.
A World of Difference. London, Hale, 1980.
Novels as Richard Avery (series: The Expendables in all books)
The Deathworms of Kratos. London, Coronet, and New York, Fawcett, 1975.
The Rings of Tantalus. London, Coronet, and New York, Fawcett, 1975.
The War Games of Zelos. London, Coronet, and New York, Fawcett, 1975.
The Venom of Argus. London, Coronet, and New York, Fawcett, 1976.

Short Stories

Tomorrow's Gift. New York, Ballantine, 1958; London, Digit, 1959.
Voices in the Dark. London, Digit, 1960.
Tomorrow Came. London, Panther, 1963.
News from Elsewhere. London, Mayflower, 1968; New York, Berkley, 1969.
The Square Root of Tomorrow. London, Hale, 1970.
Unborn Tomorrow. London, Hale, 1971.
Jupiter Laughs and Other Stories. London, Hodder and Stoughton, 1979.

Other Publications

Other

Wish Goes to Slumber Land (for children). London, Hutchinson, 1960.

*

Manuscript Collection: University of Wyoming, Laramie.

Edmund Cooper commented:
(1981) I believe, along with people like Kurt Vonnegut and J. G. Ballard and earlier illustrious writers such as George Orwell, Aldous Huxley, and H. G. Wells, that science fiction is the perfect medium for making a social or political statement. I am not interested greatly in gadgetry. I am interested passionately in the future of mankind. People matter to me far more than machines or innovations, which is why I concentrate on characterization in my novels. I try to entertain and believe I

am successful in doing this; but basically I want to put up ideas for consideration by my readers. Voluminous correspondence assures me that I have succeeded in this end.

*   *   *

With the publication of his earliest novels and stories of the late 1950's, Edmund Cooper quickly established himself as an urbane stylist whose sometimes almost intuitive grasp of science fiction's key themes and images could distinguish his best fiction and almost redeem his lesser works. There is always a moment in a Cooper story when the "sense of wonder," so often cited as the basic emotional stance of science fiction, becomes concretized in a dramatic image or action, whether it be an encounter with a god who turns out to be a spaceship (*A Far Sunset*) or simply an epiphanal moment of self-discovery on a distant planet ("M81—Ursa Major").

Cooper's plots and characterizations do not always match his style and vision. His early stories and novels sometimes read almost as practice exercises in traditional science-fiction themes: the revolt of androids in a "utopian" society (*That Uncertain Midnight*), time-travel paradoxes ("Repeat Performance"), generations-long space voyages (*Seed of Light*), the pitting of humans against a rival culture in a setting alien to both (*Transit*). Such themes had been treated in earlier, classic science-fiction stories, but for the most part Cooper succeeded in working his own variations on them. *That Uncertain Midnight*, for example, is unusual in its sympathetic portrayal of the dilemma of the androids, and *Transit* focuses sensitively on the character and emerging relationships of the four humans who find themselves stranded on an unknown planet. Though *Transit* shows that Cooper is capable of developing complex characterizations, he all too often reverts to the near-superman genius-hero of traditional pulp science fiction for his protagonists.

Perhaps the most persistent theme in Cooper, though it seldom emerges as more than background, is that of nuclear war. Nuclear war is the cause of the rise of the androids in *That Uncertain Midnight*, the dystopian state in "Tomorrow's Gift" (one of his finest short stories), the escape from earth in *Seed of Light*, the destruction of the entire human race in *The Overman Culture*, the dominion of satellite cities over Earth in *The Slaves of Heaven*, and the rise of the antitechnological Luddite society in *The Cloud Walker*, the best-received and most successful of his novels in the United States. Though it might be misleading to categorize Cooper as a simple technophobe, his cautionary attitude toward technology is also revealed in a number of stories in which "primitive," non-technological societies are shown to be morally superior to decadent technological ones. This is a theme of "The Enlightened Ones," *A Far Sunset*, and *The Slaves of Heaven*. *A Far Sunset*, in fact, is one of science fiction's more sophisticated treatments of an anthropological theme in its depiction of an alien society and its mythology.

Perhaps because he published little in the American magazines, Cooper never established a strong following among American readers; perhaps because he belonged in the early 1950's tradition of John Wyndham and John Christopher, his reputation began to wane after the changes wrought in British science fiction during the "New Wave" of the late 1960's. In any event, his works in the 1970's took an increasingly conservative and sometimes unpleasant turn, especially apparent in his "Richard Avery" novels and his anti-feminist novels of societies dominated by women, *Five to Twelve* and *Who Needs Men?* Occasionally, however, he was able to incorporate some of the New Wave ideas with some success. *The Overman Culture,* for example, features an enjoyably surrealistic portrait of a London in which Victoria reigns, Churchill is prime minister, and the young hero is Michael Faraday. All this gives way eventually to a traditional science-fiction explanation, which is nevertheless ingenious and does not destroy the novel's sense of playful fantasy.

By the time of his death in 1982, Cooper had come to be regarded as a minor, if competent, novelist in a somewhat outmoded tradition. His reputation was probably further damaged by the ugliness of some of his later works. But at best, he was a writer capable of witty and literate variations on familiar themes, and one who for all his faults managed to establish a clear identity despite his use of such themes.

—Gary K. Wolfe

COPPEL, Alfred. Also writes at Sol Galaxan; Robert Cham Gilman; Derfla Leppoc; A. C. Marin. American. Born in Oakland, California, 9 November 1921. Educated at Menlo College, Menlo Park, California; Stanford University, California, 1939-42. Served in the United States Army Air Force, 1942-45: First Lieutenant. Married Elizabeth Ann Schorr in 1943; one son and one daughter. Writer for Philco, Palo Alto, California, 1957-58; Public Relations Executive, Cerwin Group, 1958-61, and Reynolds Advertising, 1961-62, both in San Francisco. Since 1962, free-lance writer: since 1969, critic, San Francisco *Chronicle*. Agent: Robert Lescher, 155 East 71st Street, New York, New York 10021. Address: 614 Westridge Drive, Portola Valley, California 94025, U. S. A.

SCIENCE-FICTION PUBLICATIONS

Novels

Dark December. New York, Fawcett, 1960; London, Jenkins, 1966.
Thirty-Four East. New York, Harcourt Brace, and London, Macmillan, 1974.
The Dragon. New York, Harcourt Brace, and London, Macmillan, 1977.
The Hastings Conspiracy. New York, Holt Rinehart, and London, Macmillan, 1980.
The Apocalypse Brigade. New York, Holt Rinehart, and London, Macmillan, 1981.
The Burning Mountain New York, Harcourt Brace, 1983.

Novels as Robert Cham Gilman (series: Rhada)

The Rebel of Rhada. New York, Harcourt Brace, 1968; London, Gollancz, 1970.
The Navigator of Rhada. New York, Harcourt Brace, 1968; London, Gollancz, 1971.
The Starkahn of Rhada. New York, Harcourt Brace, 1970.
The Warlock of Rhada. New York, Berkley, 1985.

Uncollected Short Stories

"Age of Reason," in *Astounding* (New York), December 1947.
"Jinx Ship to the Rescue," in *Planet* (New York), Winter 1948.
"Runaway," in *Planet* (New York), Spring 1949.

"The Starbusters," in *Planet* (New York), Summer 1949.
"Secret Weapon," in *Astounding* (New York), July 1949.
"Captain Midas," in *Planet* (New York), Fall 1949.
"Flight from Time," in *Planet* (New York), Winter 1949.
"Goldfish Bowl," in *Fantasy Book 6* (Los Angeles), 1950.
"The First Man on the Moon," in *Planet* (New York), Spring 1950.
"My Brother's Keeper," in *Amazing* (New York), June 1950.
"Warrior Maid of Mars," in *Planet* (New York), Summer 1950.
"The Metal Smile," in *Super Science* (Kokomo, Indiana), July 1950.
"Half Life," in *Super Science* (Kokomo, Indiana), September 1950.
"The Last Two Alive," in *Planet* (New York), November 1950.
"Star Tamer," in *Super Science* (Kokomo, Indiana), November 1950.
"The Terror," in *Future* (New York), November 1950.
"Earthbound," in *Fantastic Adventures* (New York), December 1950.
"Task to Luna," in *Planet* (New York), January 1951.
"Forbidden Weapon," in *Marvel* (New York), February 1951.
"The Awful Weapon," in *Future* (New York), May 1951.
"The Brain That Lost Its Head," in *Fantastic Adventures* (New York), June 1951.
"Tydore's Gift," in *Planet* (New York), September 1951.
"Wreck off Triton," in *Planet* (New York), November 1951.
"Double Standard," in *Galaxy* (New York), February 1952.
"The Subversive," in *Marvel* (New York), May 1952.
"Welcome," in *Science Fiction Quarterly* (Holyoke, Massachusetts), August 1952.
"Mother," in *Fantasy and Science Fiction* (New York), September 1952.
"The Hunters," in *Fantastic Story* (New York), Fall 1952.
"Death Is Never Final," in *Fantastic Adventures* (New York), October 1952.
" . . . and Goal to Go," in *Amazing* (New York), November 1952.
"Defender of the Faith," in *Science Fiction Quarterly* (Holyoke, Massachusetts), November 1952.
"Legion of the Lost," in *Future* (New York), November 1952.
"The Magellanics," in *Two Complete Science Adventure Books* (New York), Winter 1952.
"Love Affair" (as Derfla Leppoc) and "Homecoming," in *Vortex 1* (New York), 1953.
"The Dramer," in *The Best Science-Fiction Stories 1953,* edited by E. F. Bleiler and T. E. Dikty. New York, Fell, 1953.
"The Peacemaker," in *Prize Science Fiction,* edited by Donald A. Wollheim. New York, McBride, 1953.
"What Goes Up," in *Science and Sorcery,* edited by Garret Ford. Los Angeles, Fantasy, 1953.
"Divided We Fall," in *Fantastic Story* (New York), January 1953.
"For Humans Only," in *Avon Science Fiction and Fantasy Reader* (New York), January 1953.
"The Invader," in *Imagination* (Evanston, Illinois), February 1953.
"Turnover Point," in *Amazing* (New York), May 1953.
"Preview of Peril," in *Planet* (New York), September 1953.
"The Flight of the Eagle" (as Sol Galaxan), in *Planet* (New York), September 1953.
"The Guilty," in *Cosmos* (New York), November 1953.
"Turning Point," in *If* (New York), November 1953.
"The Exile," in *Stories for Tomorrow,* edited by William Sloane. New York, Funk and Wagnalls, 1954; London, Eyre and Spottiswoode, 1955.

"Meb," in *Fantastic Story* (New York), Spring 1954.
"Mars Is Ours," in *Fantasy and Science Fiction* (New York), October 1954.
"Community Property," in *If* (New York), December 1954.
"Touch The Sky," in *Startling* (New York), Summer 1955.
"The Last Night of Summer," in *The End of the World,* edited by Donald A. Wollheim. New York, Ace, 1956.
"The Hills of Home," in *Future 30* (New York), 1956.
"The Fifth Stone," in *Fantastic* (New York), December 1956.
"Blood Lands," in *Way Out,* edited by Ivan Howard. New York, Belmont, 1963.
"For Sacred San Francisco," in *If* (New York), November 1969.
"The Rebel of Valkyr," in *Galactic Empires 1,* edited by Brian Aldiss. London, Weidenfeld and Nicolson, 1976; New York, St. Martin's Press, 1977.

OTHER PUBLICATIONS

Novels

Hero Driver. New York, Crown, 1954.
Night of Fire and Snow. New York, Simon and Schuster, 1960.
A Certainty of Love. New York, Harcourt Brace, 1966.
The Gate of Hell. New York, Harcourt Brace, 1967.
Order of Battle. New York, Harcourt Brace, 1968; London, Hutchinson, 1969.
A Little Time for Laughter. New York, Harcourt Brace, 1969.
Between the Thunder and the Sun. New York, Harcourt Brace, 1971.
The Landlocked Man. New York, Harcourt Brace, 1972; London, Macmillan, 1975.
The Marburg Chronicles. New York, Dutton, 1985.

Novels as A. C. Marin

The Clash of Distant Thunder. New York, Harcourt Brace, 1968.
Rise with the Wind. New York, Harcourt Brace, 1969; London, Heinemann, 1970.
A Storm of Spears. New York, Harcourt Brace, 1971; London, Hale, 1973.

*

Bibliography: in *Fiction! Series One* edited by Dan Tooker and Roger Hofheins, New York, Harcourt Brace, 1976.

Manuscript Collection: Boston University.

Alfred Coppel comments:
I began writing in the SF genre for two reasons: first, it was a field that did not limit the imagination (untrained though it might be) of a young writer, and second, I had read SF since early youth—and I believed then (as I still do) that a writer should write what he enjoys reading.
I have since turned to writing "general" novels, but I am told there is still a bit of the SF writer's mark on my work. I accept this with pride. Those of us who learned our craft in the hard school of the SF magazines learned early on to be professionals. To my mind, there is no higher praise that can be bestowed on a writer.

*   *   *

Although Alfred Coppel has done most of his writing in other fields, his few contributions to science fiction have been almost invariably among the better attempts in the field. His novel *Dark December,* for example, is one of the best post-nuclear war novels ever to appear, far superior to many whose titles are better known.

His more straightforward novels in the genre consist of the Rhada trilogy written under the pseudonym of Robert Cham Gilman. Man's interstellar empire has collapsed into a feudal society that is a mixture of science and magic, spaceships and incantations. Against this background, Coppel wrote three adventures of young men attempting to come to grips with the stresses and internal contradictions of their society. Although writing ostensibly for younger readers. Coppel has not pulled any punches. The novels deal explicitly with the seamier side of human acquisitiveness and the urge for power. The cyclic drive to self-destruction is an almost ever-present backdrop against which the characters play out their lives.

Coppel uses his settings and plots to examine his characters, rather than just employing characters as animated tour guides of exotic landscapes. The protagonist of *Dark December* is a fighter pilot who wanders across an America torn by nuclear bombs, plagues, famine, and human savagery. But it is not his adventures with which the reader is concerned but the effects of those adventures on him as he grows increasingly desperate to discover the fate of his missing family.

In recent years, Coppel's closest approach to science fiction has consisted of a pair of excellent near-future political novels. In *Thirty-Four East,* the world is on the brink of conflagration as the President is apparently assassinated, and the Vice-President is held hostage by Arab terrorists intent upon the destruction of Israel. In Washington, the generals move to fill the power vacuum, while across the ocean a weak premier of the Soviet Union begins to succumb to pressure from his own generals. The only chance to sidetrack the headlong movement toward war is to rescue the Vice-President. The situation is similar in *The Dragon.* The Red Chinese have developed a new weapon which gives them effective superiority over the Russians. Unless the President can somehow restore the balance of power, a war between the two Communist giants is inevitable, and it is just as certain that the rest of the world will be drawn into the confrontation. In both cases, Coppel has captured the reins of suspense firmly, and linked them to a credible sequence of political and personal events. Each novel is complex and satisfying, and it is interesting to speculate about Coppel's possible achievements had he devoted his efforts primarily to science fiction, rather than remaining as diversified in his interests as he has.

Some hint of that may be found in his recent science-fiction thriller *The Burning Mountain.* Alternate histories have long been fertile ground for genre writers and mainstream writers alike, and Coppel now speculates about what would have transpired if the atomic bomb tests had resulted in failure. After investing considerable effort in researching the war plans of both the United States and Japanese governments, he constructed this novel that deals with the invasion of mainland Japan by allied troops. Outside of the basic premise, the novel really isn't science fiction at all, just another World War II adventure story, but it is an outstanding achievement regardless of which category might claim it. With a large cast of characters, depressingly convincing descriptions of the unfolding events, and Coppel's clear, gripping style, it is clearly among his very best efforts.

Coppel wrote many short stories early in his career, most of which were above average in quality. Possibly his most successful is "The Last Night of Summer. " Stellar evolution has caused a change in the energy output of the sun, and an astronomical event is imminent that will briefly make the Earth uninhabitable. Except for a limited number granted a place in the Burrows, shelters constructed underground, the entire human population will be wiped out within a few days. The protagonist murders his wife and sacrifices his own chance at life in order to provide a change for survival to his two daughters. It is at one time one of the most brutal and one of the most effective world disaster stories of all times, accomplishing more in a few pages than is usually done in entire books. Other stories of note include "The Hills of Home" and "Double Standard. "

—Don D'Ammassa

CORBETT, Chan. See SCHACHNER, Nat.

CORBIN, Michael. See CARTMILL, Cleve.

CORLEY, Ernest. See BULMER, Kenneth.

CORNISH, F. See BRYNING, Frank.

CORREN, Grace. See HOSKINS, Robert.

CORREY, Lee. Pseudonym for G(eorge) Harry Stine. American. Born in Philadelphia, Pennsylvania, 26 March 1928. Educated at University of Colorado, Colorado Springs (Editor, *The Window,* 1948-49), 1946-50; Colorado College, Colorado Springs, B. A. in physics 1952. Married Barbara Ann Kauth in 1952; two daughters and one son. Chief of the Propulsion Branch, Controls and Instruments Section, 1952-55, and Chief of Range Operations division and Navy Flight Safety Engineer, 1955-57, White Sands Proving Ground, New Mexico; Design Specialist, Martin Company, Denver, 1957; President and Chief Engineer, Model Missiles, Denver, 1957-59; Vice-President and Chief Engineer, MicroDynamics, Broomfield, Colorado, 1959; Design Engineer, Stanley Aviation, Denver, 1959-60; Assistant Director of Research, Huyck Corporation, Stamford, Connecticut, 1960-65; free-lance consultant, 1965-73; Marketing Manager, Flow Technology, Phoenix, 1973-76. Since 1976, free-lance consultant and writer. Editor, *Missile Away!,* 1953-57; Columnist ("Conquest of Space"), *Mechanix Illustrated,* 1956-57; Editor, *The Model*

Rocketeer, 1957-64 and 1976-78; Senior Editor, *Aviation/Space,* 1982-84. Since 1980, Columnist ("The Alternate View"), *Analog* ; since 1985, principal writer, Space Report, Metavision-KAET, Los Angeles. Founder and past President, National Association of Rocketry; Associate Fellow, American Institute of Aeronautics and Astronautics. Agent: Scott Meredith Literary Agency, 845 Third Avenue, New York, New York 10022. Address: 616 West Frier Drive, Phoenix, Arizona 85021, U. S. A.

SCIENCE-FICTION PUBLICATIONS

Novels

Starship Through Space (for children). New York, Holt Rinehart, 1954.
Contraband Rocket. New York, Ace, 1955.
Rocket Man (for children). New York, Holt Rinehart, 1955.
Star Driver. New York, Ballantine, 1980.
Shuttle Down. New York, Ballantine, 1981.
Space Doctor. New York, Ballantine, 1981.
The Abode of Life. New York, Pocket Books, 1982.
Manna. New York, DAW, 1984.

Uncollected Short Stories

"Galactic Gadgeteers" (as G. Harry Stine), in *Astounding* (New York), May 1951.
"Greenhorn" (as G. Harry Stine), in *Fantastic Story* (New York), Fall 1952.
"Pioneer," in *Astounding* (New York), August 1953.
"The Day the Rocket Blew Up," in *Saturday Evening Post* (Philadelphia), 15 August 1953.
"Ill Wind," in *Astounding* (New York), December 1953.
"Amateur," in *Astounding* (New York), February 1954.
"Design Flaw," in *Astounding* (New York), February 1955.
"The Plains of San Augustine," in *Astounding* (New York), April 1955.
"Satellite Wild," in *American Legion* (New York), July 1955.
"The Brass Cannon," in *Fantasy and Science Fiction* (New York), November 1955.
"Wireroad," in *Fantastic Universe* (Chicago), September 1956.
"The Education of Icky," in *Astounding* (New York), January 1957.
"Landing for Midge," in *Fantastic Universe* (Chicago), July 1957.
"Coffin Run," in *Fantastic* (New York), August 1957.
"Homecoming," with Lewis J. Stecher, in *Fantastic Universe* (Chicago), November 1958.
"Letter from Tomorrow," in *Fantastic Universe* (Chicago), May 1959.
"And a Star to Steer Her By," in *Every Boy's Book of Outer Space Stories,* edited by T. E. Dikty. New York, Fell, 1960.
"The Test Stand," in *The Expert Dreamers,* edited by Frederik Pohl. New York, Doubleday, 1962.
"The Easy Way Out," in *Analog 6,* edited by John W. Campbell, Jr. New York, Doubleday, 1968.
"Something in the Sky," in *Encounters with Aliens* edited by George W. Early. Los Angeles, Sherbourne Press, 1969.

OTHER PUBLICATIONS as G. Harry Stine

Other

"The Truth of the Matter," in *Fantasy and Science Fiction*

(New York), November 1956.
Rocket Power and Space Flight. New York, Holt Rinehart, 1957.
Earth Satellites and the Race for Space Superiority. New York, Ace, 1957.
"How to Think a Science Fiction Story," in *The Year's Best Science Fiction 6,* edited by Judith Merril. New York, Simon and Schuster, 1961.
"Time for Tom Swift," in *Analog* (New York), January 1961.
"Science Fiction Is Too Conservative," in *Analog* (New York), May 1961.
Man and the Space Fontier. New York, Knopf, 1962.
Handbook of Model Rocketry. Chicago, Follett, 1965; revised edition, 1967, 1970, 1976.
"How to Make a Star Trek" in *Analog* (New York), February 1968.
The Third Industrial Revolution. New York, Putnam, 1975.
Shuttle into Space: A Ride in America's Space Transportation System (for children). Chicago, Follett, 1978.
The Space Enterprise. New York, Ace, 1980.
Space Power. New York, Ace, 1981.
Confrontation in Space. Englewood Cliffs, New Jersey, Prentice Hall, 1981.
The Hopeful Future. New York, Macmillan, 1983.
The Silicon Gods. New York, Dell, 1984.
Handbook for Space Colonists. New York, Holt Rinehart, 1985.
"Science Fiction Is Still Too Conservative!," in *Analog* (New York), January 1985.

*

Lee Correy comments:

Since 1951, I've written "hard" science fiction because that's the sort of story I like to read. I was influenced at an early and impressionable age by one Robert Anson Heinlein who, in 1950, was kind enough to take me under his wing and coach me. But John W. Campbell, Willy Ley, Dan Cole, and Herman Kahn must also share the blame for what I've become. Much of the background for my s-f novels came from consulting work for NASA, the Department of Energy, or the Hudson Institute, for example. Or from careful and continual reading, reading, reading of scientific journals, reports, books, magazines, and papers to keep up with our growing knowledge of a universe that's becoming stranger every day. Often I've written an s-f novel rather than present the same material in a science-fact book because (a) it made a better fiction piece, and (b) nobody would believe it as a science-fact work! ("Shuttle Down" is an example of this.) Incidentally, I've used the pseudonym "Lee Correy" to tag my s-f in order to separate it from my science-fact writing, a differentiation that's getting more difficult to determine every day. Although I've written some "far out" science fiction, I'm just not interested in "swords and sorcery" fairy tales masquerading as "science fiction. " (People are free to write and read what they want, but I wish they'd start referring to s-f for what it is, and it isn't science fiction!) I don't write "literature" or to change the world; I try to write entertainment as Heinlein taught me. I find lots of story material in the potentials and problems of the next hundred years which come down to: How do we learn to handle wealth and power in a universe where we're largely in control of the forces of nature? I've never written a downside doomsday story and probably never will. I have enormous faith in the ability of human beings to make the world a better place for their children. I would have enjoyed being a member of John Herschel's Analytical Society at Cambridge, England, whose members promised one another to "do their best to leave the world wiser than they found it. "

* * *

Even the most cursory exposure to the science fiction of Lee Correy would demonstrate his preoccupation with space travel and its importance to the human race. Most of his novels and short stories deal with space travel not just as a plot element but as the focus of the entire plot.

Contraband Rocket suggests that if the government is not willing to exert time and money in conquering space, then perhaps private industry will do so instead. The idea that a collection of idealists could refurbish an old rocket for a moon flight has become silly in view of the sophisticated knowledge we now possess, but this early novel exudes the optimistic self-confidence of its time. Correy's recent novels *Star Driver* and *Space Doctor* have returned to this idea, but have taken into consideration the realities of high technology. In the former, a small company develops a working anti-gravity unit and mounts it on commercial aircraft in order to make a dramatic presentation of its possibilities and enable them to evade government regulation. Unfortunately, Correy was unable to overcome the practical problems with the plot, and his polemics sometimes disturbed the pace of the plot.

Space Doctor is far more successful. An orbital construction project is underway to create a new power source for the Earth. Its completion will be an economic boon for the companies financing the project. To reduce their expenses and the possible loss of lives, they hire a doctor to head an orbiting hospital outfitted to handle emergencies as they arise. Correy has much better control of his plot this time and while his lectures on the advantages of an active space program are still there, they fail to distract us from the main story.

The government is sponsoring space travel in *Shuttle Down*, in which an aborted space flight results in a shuttle stuck on Easter Island, faced with physical and political problems before it can be removed. The protagonists have to deal with terrorists, spies, Russian naval manoeuvres, and various problems of supply and manpower before everything can be resolved. Correy seems to have lost faith in the established governments in his recent *Manna*, however, for now he has created a libertarian Utopia in Africa with a large-scale manned space program, but which has attracted the unfriendly attention of most of the rest of the world because of its unorthodox form of government.

For the most part, Correy's short stories deal with the mechanics of space exploration. In "The Test Stand," for example, a man's view of his own career is revised when he is nearly killed preventing an accident during a test firing. The importance of the human factor in even the most sophisticated aspects of space flight is demonstrated in "Coffin Run" in which a substitute pilot must be retrained rapidly to complete a necessary flight, despite the objections of some of the authorities. Neither story descends into overt lecturing, but it is clear that Correy is attempting to humanize the space program.

Correy's best short story is "The Easy Way Out. " Alien invaders land in a remote part of the Earth and set out to discover how susceptible the planet is to invasion. They encounter a number of animals and rate each on a "Ferocity Index," eventually retreating in utter terror when they witness the bullying of a pet wolverine by a pair of human children. Although the basic concept is amusing, the story does encompass a flaw; it is unlikely that a race that had conquered a large chunk of the universe would automatically assume that every animal species it encountered was a separate intelligent species.

Less ambitious is a very mild but well-handled story, "Something in the Sky. " A test missile veers away from its intended target and strikes something invisible in space, constructed of materials unknown on this planet. In just a few thousand words, Correy conveys a mood of mystery and wonder.

—Don D'Ammassa

COSTELLO, P. F. See **PHILLIPS, Rog.**

COTTON, John. See **FEARN, John Russell.**

COULSON, Juanita (Ruth, née Wellons). Also writes as John J. Wells. American. Born in Anderson, Indiana, 12 February 1933. Educated at Ball State University, Muncie, Indiana, B. S. 1954; M. A. 1961. Married Robert Coulson, *q. v.,* in 1954; one son. Elementary school teacher, Huntington, Indiana, 1954-55; collator, Heckman Book Bindery, North Manchester, Indiana, 1955-57; publisher, *SFWA Forum,* for two years. Since 1953, Editor, with Robert Coulson, *Yandro* fan magazine; since 1963, free-lance writer. Recipient: Hugo Award, for editing, 1965. Guest of Honor, World Science Fiction Convention, 1972. Agent: Virginia Kidd, Box 278, Milford, Pennsylvania 18337. Address: 2677W-5OON, Hartford City, Indiana 47348, U.S.A.

SCIENCE-FICTION PUBLICATIONS

Novels (series: Children of the Stars)

Crisis on Cheiron. New York, Ace, 1967.
The Singing Stones. New York, Ace, 1968.
Unto the Last Generation. Toronto, Laser, 1975.
Space Trap. Toronto, Laser, 1976.
Children of the Stars:
   1. *Tomorrow's Heritage*. New York, Ballantine, 1981.
   2. *Outward Bound*. New York, Ballantine, 1982.

Uncollected Short Stories

"Another Rib" (as John J. Wells, with Marion Zimmer Bradley), in *Fantasy and Science Fiction* (New York), June 1963.
"A Helping Hand," in *If* (New York), November-December 1970.
"Wizard of Death," in *Fantastic* (New York), February 1973.
"The Dragon of Tor-Nali," in *Fantastic* (New York), February 1975.
"Unscheduled Flight," in *Beyond Time,* edited by Sandra Ley. New York, Pocket Books, 1976.
"Intersection Point," in *Star Trek: The New Voyages,* edited by Sondra Marshak and Myrna Culbreath. New York, Bantam, 1976.
"Uraguyen and I," with Miriam Allen deFord, in *Cassandra Rising,* edited by Alice Laurance. New York, Doubleday 1978.

OTHER PUBLICATIONS

Novels

The Secret of Seven Oaks. New York, Berkley, 1972.
Door into Terror. New York, Berkley, 1972.
Stone of Blood. New York, Ballantine, 1975.
Fear Stalks the Bayou. New York, Ballantine, and Skirden, Lancashire, Magna, 1976.
Dark Priestess. New York, Ballantine, 1977.
The Web of Wizardry. New York, Ballantine, 1978.
Fire of the Andes. New York, Ballantine, 1979.
The Death God's Citadel. New York, Ballantine, 1980.

Other

"Of (Super) Human Bondage," in *The Comic-Book Book*, edited by Richard A. Lupoff and Don Thompson. New Rochelle, New York, Arlington House, 1974.

*

Juanita Coulson comments:

Before I could write, my mother transcribed my earliest attempts at story telling. For my 8th Christmas, she gave me a typewriter, compounding the felony. In a sense, I have been writing fiction since before I could write. My only interest was in concocting characters and adventures that satisfied an audience of one—me. It wasn't until I was in my 30's that Marion Zimmer Bradley insisted I should submit my work professionally. Without her encouragement, I never would have made the effort. I am still surprised to find that some kind of people actually pay me for writing stories I wrote so long ago solely for my own entertainment. Other than the fun of creating, my aims are to follow two maxims: There Are No Simple Answers and Take The Long View. To some degree, I share Marion Bradley's theory that a villain is just a protagonist with a different point of view; the story *might* have been told from the villain's position, *if* he (or she) is a valid character to start with. And in any story, I don't think all the questions can be answered—certainly not completely. People—and characters—are too complex. As for The Long View, its a humbling rule to write by, but it serves me equally in science fiction, contemporary woman's genre fiction, or a historical romance set in 1770 B. C. The Long View ought to be an essential ingredient of all science fiction, especially considering the past and future history of humanity *and* of other species, known and unknown, and cosmology. Putting us in our place in that immense scheme of things is, for me, the foundation of a sense of wonder.

*   *   *

Since its first appearance in professional print in 1963, Juanita Coulson's writing has included science fiction of both the speculative and the adventurous varieties, heroic fantasy, romantic suspense ("Gothics"), and historical romances, as well as occasional non-fiction.

Her first story, "Another Rib," a collaboration with Marion Zimmer Bradley, tells of a group of men, the only survivors of a destroyed Earth, and what happens when alien medical technology offers them an unconventional way of perpetuating the human species. The theme is handled with skill and delicacy, resulting in a memorable story.

Coulson's first novel, *Crisis on Cheiron*, deals with the struggle of a small band of allies to save an undeveloped planet

from economic and ecological ruin at the hands of an unscrupulous Terran corporation. In *The Singing Stones* another world is in peril: Pa-Liina, with its quasi-telepathic Stones of Song, suffering under the domination of its decadent sister world Deliyas. In both novels the alien environment is well thought out and convincingly portrayed, and the scientific underpinnings are given colorful settings and action reminiscent of the work of Leigh Brackett and Marion Zimmer Bradley. The theme of an alien world suffering the unwelcome attentions of Earthmen is also present in "A Helping Hand": this time the Earthmen's intentions are benevolent, but their complete misunderstanding of the world they are trying to help leads to disaster.

Unto the Last Generation is the story of a future Earth where population control has been all too successful, rendering most of mankind infertile. The young battle with the old for the inadequate supplies of food distributed by a military government, while a group of scientists work in secret, trying to ensure humanity's survival. *Space Trap* deals with the first contact between Earthmen and a telepathic civilization from across the galaxy, as representatives of both groups battle for control of a remote planet on which they are trapped.

"Unscheduled Flight" is more anecdote than story: it sets up an interesting parallel-worlds situation but does nothing with it. Two long fantasy novels, *The Web of Wizardry* and *The Death God's Citadel*, are both set in the same imaginary world, in which sorcery and the presence of supernatural beings are facts of everyday existence. The backgrounds (geographical, cultural, and linguistic) are worked out in detail; the characters are interesting, the action well-paced, resulting in two very entertaining adventures. Two earlier short stories, "Wizard of Death" and "The Dragon of Tor-Nali," are set in the same world as the novels.

Coulson's best work to date is found in her multi-generational family saga which bears the overall title "Children of the Stars". The first volume, *Tomorrow's Heritage*, introduces the Saunder family, owners of one of Earth's most powerful industrial and communications conglomerates in the early 21st century. The focus is on the three Saunder children: Patrick, leader of a fiercely isolationist political party, opposed to any extraterrestrial colonization or contact; Mariette, a supporter of the man-made satellite, the Goddard Colony; and Todd, who has just established electronic contact with an extraterrestrial space craft heading toward Earth. The conflicts among the children, and between them and their autocratic mother, are set forth in a rich and emotionally complex story. The saga continues in *Outward Bound* in which the next generation of the Saunder family establish contact with the alien Vahnaj and achieve faster-than-light space travel. As of mid-1985 the third volume, *Legacy of Earth*, is still awaiting publication.

—R. E. Briney

COULSON, Robert (Stratton). Also writes as Thomas Stratton. American. Born in Sullivan, Indiana, 12 May 1928. Educated at Silver Lake High School; studied electrical engineering, International Correspondence School, 1960. Married Juanita Coulson, *q. v.,* in 1954; one son. Cemetery caretaker, 1941-43; wool bagger, 1944; house painter, 1945-47; bookbinder, Heckman Book Bindery, North Manchester, Indiana, 1945-57; draftsman and technical writer, Honeywell Corporation, 1957-65. Draftsman, 1965-76, and since 1976, order writer, Overhead Door of Indiana, Hartford City. Since 1953, Editor, with Juanita Coulson, *Yandro* fan magazine; since 1984, reviewer, *Comic Buyer's Guide*. Recipient: Hugo Award for editing, 1965. Guest of Honor, World Science Fiction Convention, 1972. Agent: Virginia Kidd, Box 278, Milford, Pennsylvania 18337. Address: 2677W-5OON, Hartford City, Indiana 47348, U. S. A.

SCIENCE-FICTION PUBLICATIONS

Novels (series: Joe Karns)

The Invisibility Affair (as Thomas Stratton, with Gene De-Weese). New York, Ace, 1967.
The Mind-Twisters Affair (as Thomas Stratton, with Gene DeWeese). New York, Ace, 1967.
Gates of the Universe (Karns), with Gene DeWeese. Toronto, Laser, 1975.
Now You See It/Him/Them . . . (Karns), with Gene DeWeese. New York, Doubleday, 1975; London, Hale, 1976.
To Renew the Ages. Toronto, Laser, 1976.
But What of Earth?, with Piers Anthony. Toronto, Laser, 1976.
Charles Fort Never Mentioned Wombats (Karns), with Gene DeWeese. New York, Doubleday, 1977; London, Hale, 1978.

Uncollected Short Stories

"The Tracy Business," with Gene DeWeese, in *Fantasy and Science Fiction* (New York), February 1970.
"John Carter and His Electric Barsoom," with Gene DeWeese, in *The Conan Grimoire,* edited by L. Sprague de Camp and George H. Scithers. Baltimore, Mirage Press, 1971.
"By the Book," with Gene DeWeese, in *Amazing* (New York), May 1971.
"Soy la Libertad," in *Beyond Time,* edited by Sandra Ley. New York, Pocket Books, 1976.

OTHER PUBLICATIONS

Other

"From Conciliabule to Congestion, with a Touch of Condescension," in *Midamericon Program Book,* 1976.

*

Robert Coulson comments:
    First of all, I don't write because I have any burning desire to tell stories, or to influence the masses, or even to be admired (though I suppose the last might have some bearing on my writing). I write professional fiction because it's the most enjoyable way I've found to make money. Not the most reliable—which is why I work at a regular job and write as a sideline—but the most enjoyable. Since writing is extra income, rather than my living, I can afford to write pretty much what I like. What I like, mostly, is humour: puns, incongruities, parody, satire (not farce: I seldom find farce particularly funny). Basically, I don't take writing—my own, or anyone else's—seriously, and I'll make fun of a writer who shows that he takes himself overly seriously. I try to be entertaining, and any profundities will be slipped in gently and (I hope) well hidden. Any influencing of the reader in a work of fiction should be subtle.

Fortunately for our co-authorship, Gene DeWeese has much the same sense of humor that I have; once one of our books is finished and in print, it's impossible even for us to remember exactly who wrote what. Saves a lot of disagreement during the writing.

*   *   *

Robert Coulson has been a science-fiction fan since the 1940's and has been involved in amateur SF journalism for more than 25 years. His journalism work has been entirely non-fiction: humorous articles and the incisive reviews which he still writes for his and his wife's magazine *Yandro.* Coulson has remained active as an SF fan even after becoming a professional writer.

Most of Coulson's science-fiction writing has been done in colaboration with his long-time friend, Gene DeWeese. In 1967, under the name Thomas Stratton, Coulson and DeWeese wrote two paperback spinoffs from *The Man from U.N.C.L.E.* TV series. *The Invisibility Affair* involved THRUSH's use of an invisible dirigible in their latest plan for conquest. One of the chapter titles from the book ("Charles Fort Never Mentioned Sandbags") would turn up ten years later, transmuted into the title of another Coulson/DeWeese collaboration. In *The Mind-Twisters Affair,* Napoleon Solo and Illya Kuryakin foil a THRUSH attempt to control the minds of world-famous scientists. Both books feature the unlikely situations and off-beat humor which made the television series so popular.

The Coulson/DeWeese novel *Gates of the Universe* is the story of a bulldozer operator and would-be science fiction writer, Ross Allen, who is accidentally whisked from Earth to the planet Venntra through a Probe Gate, a means of alien interstellar transportation. Both the Bulldozer and Allen's SF background aid him in coping with the dangers of a world threatened by the antics of an apparently mad computer. *Now You See It/Him/Them . . .,* a combination murder mystery and SF novel of psi powers, is set at a science-fiction convention. A follow-up novel, *Charles Fort Never Mentioned Wombats,* takes place in Australia, among a group of science-fiction fans on their way to attend the World Science Fiction Convention in Melbourne. The trip is complicated by assorted encounters with extra-terrestrials.

All of the Coulson/DeWeese collaborations, as well as Coulson's solo work, involve standard SF ingredients, handled with skill, humor, and occasionally a refreshing irreverence. They also employ the practice of "Tuckerizing," named after the SF fan and writer Wilson Tucker: using the names of family, friends, and well-known SF figures for characters in the story. This is not noticeable to the general reader, but can prove distracting to those who are familiar with the names.

Coulson's only solo works to date are *To Renew the Ages* and "Soy la Libertad. " The novel is set in a sparsely populated North America after a nuclear war, and chronicles the hero's battle against an unknown telepathic menace which is threatening the safety of the scattered pockets of civilization. His search for the source of the danger leads him into contact with the remarkable heroine, Tamara Bush, and the matriarchal society which she represents. "Soy la Libertad" is an alternate-world story, telling of the aftermath of a political assassination in a version of North America where Texas, the Confederacy, the Five Indian Nations, and the Mormons' Deseret are separate counties, not part of the United States. Based on the author's broad knowledge of history and told with a nicely calculated irony, it is a memorable story.

Coulson's name also appeared as co-author on *But What of Earth?* but Coulson merely revised a manuscript submitted by

Piers Anthony. The result, after further changes by editorial hands, was unsatisfactory to both writers.

—R. E. Briney

COVER, Arthur Byron. American. Born in Grundy, Virginia, 14 January 1950. Educated at Virginia Polytechnic Institute, Blacksburg, B. A. 1971. Member of the extension faculty, University of California, Los Angeles. Interviewer, *Vertex,* Los Angeles, 1974-75. Agent: Jane Rotrosen Agency, 226 East 32nd Street, New York, New York 10016, U. S. A.

SCIENCE-FICTION PUBLICATIONS

Novels

Autumn Angels. New York, Pyramid, 1975.
The Sound of Winter. New York, Pyramid, 1976.
An East Wind Coming. New York, Berkley, 1979.
Flash Gordon. New York, Jove, and London, New English Library, 1980.

Short Stories

The Platypus of Doom and Other Nihilists. New York, Warner, 1976.

Uncollected Short Stories

"Gee, Isn't He the Cutest Little Thing?, " in *The Alien Condition,* edited by Stephen Goldin. New York, Ballantine, 1973.
"In Between Then and Now," in *Infinity 5,* edited by Robert Hoskins. New York, Lancer, 1973.
"Pelican's Claws," in *Haunts of Horror* (New York), August 1973.
"A Gross Love Story" and "Message of Joy," in *Alternates,* edited by David Gerrold and Stephen Goldin. New York, Dell, 1974.
"My World: Things Past," in *Eternity 3* (Sandy Springs, South Carolina), 1974.
"Lifeguard," in *Nameless Places,* edited by Gerald W. Page. Sauk City, Wisconsin, Arkham House, 1975.
"The Day It Rained Lizards," in *The Year's Best Horror Stories 5,* edited by Gerald W. Page. New York, DAW, 1977.
"Galactic Gumshoe," in *Weird Heroes 6,* edited by Byron Preiss. New York, Pyramid, 1977.

* * *

Like many young science-fiction authors, Arthur Byron Cover is identified with one imaginative universe and group of characters. Influenced by the Clarion Writers Workshop and, especially, Harlan Ellison, Cover is obsessed with popular culture archetypes, and his penchant for irreverent satire and sardonically humorous ideological discussion would seem to embody an homage to Ellison, the genre's most colorful and creative *enfant terrible.* Indeed, Cover's first two novels suggest that their author is himself determined to be another *enfant terrible,* particularly in their displays of juvenile shock effects and virtuoso exercises of impressive erudition—as well as in their indifference to the values and methods of formula narrative.

Autumn Angels was published as part of an entry in a short-lived "discovery series," edited by Ellison, with a typically laudatory introduction, along with the casual admission that Cover's "first draft" required a good deal of revision. This episodic novel has a unity of tone, setting, and characters, but its rambling and discursive nature tends to undercut the author's inventiveness. Essentially, *Autumn Angels* describes a community of "godlike men" who inhabit a golden city in a distant future, and who find their immortal lives boring and sterile. The "godlike" men and women are, according to the narrator, all that remains of earth after its destruction. Fortunately for them, some experimental aliens called the "bems" saved them and endowed them with immortality. However, instead of trying to find their own identities the characters were allowed to select identities from the realms of history and popular culture; hence, the novel deals with "the demon" (Lucifer), the "fat man" (Sidney Greenstreet), the "other fat man" (Nero Wolfe), the "Big Red Cheese" (Captain Marvel), and so on. Of course, Cover is required to use such nicknames for his principals in part to avoid infringement of the copyright laws. It must be conceded, however, that an eclectic narrative in which the characters are never mentioned by name frequently becomes tedious.

Not much of interest happens in *Autumn Angels.* The characters complain of their lot, threaten each other, and visit other planets where grotesque things happen. In order to provide a challenge for the immortals, the "other fat man" introduces depression to their world, but the possibilities of this theme are not realized. At the end of the novel, the introduction of "sexism"—by which the author means romantic love and conventional family life—is promised as a further antidote for ennui. Meanwhile, there is a good deal of puerile incident: for instance, the demon spends much of the book fondling his genitals, an action suggesting an unkind metaphor for the book. In fairness, however, *Autumn Angels* is an immature novel by a writer of promise.

Equally eclectic, *An East Wind Coming* returns to the golden city of the immortals and enlarges Cover's vision, but the book fails to establish him as a mature novelist. Cover has expanded his cast to include Sherlock Holmes and Dr. Watson (the "consulting detective" and the "good doctor"), Lois Lane (the "ace reporter"), the Continental Op from Dashiell Hammett's stories, and other well known popular culture archetypes. The story is unified by a dramatic (if unoriginal) plot: Jack the Ripper is loose and killing in the "East End" of the city of the immortals, and Sherlock Holmes is obliged to track down and defeat this horrifying murderer and mutilator of women.

Despite the rich possibilities in such a plot and theme, Cover's novel is as much a parody as a recreation of the drama and suspense of a Holmesian tale. Constantly digressing from the detective story plot, *An East Wind Coming* allows itsef dialogues and monologues about art, sex, existentialism, Marxism, violence, the necessity of dreams, and the futility of all human effort. Clearly the book is more a philosophical novel or a literary "anatomy" (in Northrop Frye's definition of the word) than a suspense story or a successful melodrama. Even the Ripper is a philosophical murderer somewhat vaguely reminiscent of Raskolnikov. Hence, although the Holmes-Ripper conflict has enormous potential for drama, few of its possibilities are realized in this narrative.

Cover's handling of characterization is more assured in *An East Wind Coming,* but his archetypes are statically conceived. Unfortunately, too, the obvious comparison with his sources, especially Conan Doyle, Rex Stout, and Dashiell Hammett quickly makes Cover's novel seem rather juvenile.

Cover's golden city also rouses inevitable comparisons with

other science-fiction and fantasy authors, like Philip José Farmer and Michael Moorcock, and again these parallels are to Cover's disadvantage. Cover's work lacks both the dynamic action and force of Farmer's River-world novels, and the inventiveness and poetic charm of Moorcock's "Dancers at the End of Time" trilogy. Cleary Cover is a writer of promise, and his conception of a Valhalla of pop culture heroes is an interesting one. But more intellectual maturity and artistic mastery are needed for an author to bring off successfully the kind of novel that Cover attempts in *An East Wind Coming.*

—Edgar L. Chapman

COWPER, Richard. Pseudonym for Colin Middleton Murry. British. Born in Bridport, Dorset, 9 May 1926; son of the writer John Middleton Murry. Educated at Rendcomb College, Gloucestershire, 1937-43; Brasenose College, Oxford, 1948-50, B. A. (honours) in English 1950; University of Leicester, 1950-51. Served in the Royal Navy Fleet Air Arm, 1944-47. Married Ruth Jezierski in 1950; two daughters. English Master, Whittinghame College, Brighton, 1952-67; Head of the English Department, Atlantic World College, Llantwit-Major, Glamorgan, 1967-70. Agent: A. P. Watt Ltd., 26-28 Bedford Row, London WC1R 4HL; or, Curtis Brown Associates, 575 Madison Avenue, New York, New York 10022, U. S. A. Address: Landscott, Lower Street, Dittisham, near Dartmouth, Devon TQ6 0HY, England.

SCIENCE-FICTION PUBLICATIONS

Novels (series: Corlay)

Breakthrough. London, Dobson, 1967; New York, Ballantine, 1969.
Phoenix. London, Dobson, 1968; New York, Ballantine, 1970.
Domino. London, Dobson, 1971.
Kuldesak. London, Gollancz, and New York, Doubleday, 1972.
Clone. London, Gollancz, 1972; New York, Doubleday, 1973.
Time Out of Mind. London, Gollancz, 1973; New York, Pocket Books, 1981.
The Twilight of Briareus. London, Gollancz, and New York, Day, 1974.
Worlds Apart. London, Gollancz, 1974.
The Road to Corlay. London, Gollancz, 1978; New York, Pocket Books, 1979.
Profundis. London, Gollancz, 1979; New York, Pocket Books, 1981.
A Dream of Kinship (Corlay). London, Gollancz, 1981; New York, Pocket Books, 1982.
A Tapestry of Time (Corlay). London, Gollancz, 1982.

Short Stories

The Custodians and Other Stories. London, Gollancz, 1976.
The Web of the Magi and Other Stories. London, Gollancz, 1980.
Out There Where the Big Ships Go. New York, Pocket Books, 1980.
The Tithonian Factor and Other Stories. New York, Gollancz, 1984.

OTHER PUBLICATIONS

Novels as Colin Murry

The Golden Valley. London, Hutchinson, 1958.
Recollections of a Ghost. London, Hutchinson, 1960.
A Path to the Sea. London, Hutchinson, 1961.
Private View. London, Dobson, 1972.

Play

Radio Play: *Taj Mahal by Candlelight* (as Colin Murry), 1966.

Other

One Hand Clapping: A Memoir of Childhood (as Colin Middleton Murry). London, Gollancz, 1975; as *I at the Keyhole*, New York, Stein and Day, 1975.
"Backwards Across the Frontier," in *Foundation 9* (London), November 1975.
Shadows on the Grass (autobiography; as Colin Middleton Murry). London, Gollancz, 1977.
"A Rose Is a Rose Is a Rose" (on Roger Zelazny), in *Foundation 11-12* (London), March 1977.

*

Richard Cowper comments:

First and foremost, in my writing, I aim to please *myself.* Experience in the form of some 15 novels has taught me that if I do this I usually contrive to please some other people too. That's just as well, for to write books that did not give me pleasure in the writing would be a grim sort of punishment and I'd very soon pack writing in altogether. But having said that I feel bound to add that I am profoundly conscious that I am in the entertainment business where "those who live to please must please to live. "

My ambition has always been to write fine novels. By that I mean novels in which, as it were, I contrive to put the beat of the human heart on to the printed page—to make the reader endure and enjoy the whole gamut of human experience through the medium of my imagination. I contend that, to have its full impact, science fiction must be presented in human terms and allow the reader scope for imaginative identification with the characters in the stories.

* * *

Richard Cowper entered the SF genre from the mainstream with *Breakthrough,* which used a contemporary setting to unravel the story of "passengers" in the minds of his characters, survivors of a more perfect, poetical age. This emphasis upon the "dream state," central to Cowper's work, is used in a different manner in *Phoenix,* where a youth, Bard, wakes after suspended animation and finds himself two thousand years in the future, in a simpler, post-holocaust society. Like the protagonist of *Breakthrough* (and, indeed, like many of Cowper's protagonists) he is possessed of special paranormal powers, which are unknown to him at the book's outset and which he discovers and eventually learns to use with sensitivity. These powers are evidence again in *Domino,* where the young protagonist (still at school), Christopher Blackburn, finds himself pursued by people from the future who are trying to stop him from experimenting in genetics, experiments which are to change the face of future society, making a master-slave arrangement. The interaction between different realities witnessed in these three books is to be seen in his later work as a strong theme.

In 1972 the satiric *Clone* launched Cowper upon the SF reading public. It is marked by its hostility to the technophilic direction man is taking, and by a distaste for modern living in general. It is all delivered with humour, and follows the picaresque adventures of the young innocent, Alvin, who remains morally intact despite the gross advances of the world to him. He discovers he is part of a four-man Clone which develops immense paranormal powers but, as in all of Cowper's books, disposes of these powers in a humane, almost mystical manner. *Time Out of Mind* said little more than had been already stated in *Domino,* and is another tale of future interference in present (or near-present) society. *Kuldesak* is a far better book, showing us man in degeneration, living beneath the ground at the command of robots and computers, becoming (literally) vegetables as the years pass. Mel, the inquisitive young protagonist of this story, goes to the surface and changes it all, leading man out of his rut and back to the sane path of existence.

The Twilight of Briareus is probably Cowper's finest SF novel, written in a consummately elegant style and building to a powerful and emotive climax. Man becomes sterile as an after-effect of a nearby nova which sweeps the Earth and, as a result of the nova, "passengers" are discovered in the minds of several people. The new "aliens" and the old man struggle to take control of man's destiny, and the peaceful resolution of this contest in the mind of Calvin Johnson, the central character of the book, brings the book to a close, even as Johnson himself dies in the snow. Like the earlier books it is set in a near-contemporary England and most of the critical events are internal ones, arising from the tension between the "dream state" and "reality": "So that moment joined my previous glimpse of the sun-sculpted hills as just another strand of the elusive web that had drawn us here, and, as I stumbled forward beside her up to the house, I had the wierdest feeling that I was a fugitive in limbo fleeing between two worlds, one dead, the other powerless to be born." Johnson's words echo a feeling that is prevalent in many of these books, and he is perhaps the most subtly drawn of all Cowper's characters and the nearest to the author, involved, as so many of Cowper's protagonists are, in watching the external world crumble around him as the internal landscape of his mind opens up to display previously unguessed paranormal powers. *Twilight of Briareus* is the definitive exploration of this inner conflict and its resolution.

Worlds Apart breaks from this serious lyricism and satirises SF writers in a most direct manner. George Cringe, an unimportant junior science teacher, writes an SF tale about Chnass while a Chnassian, Zil Bryn, writes a tale about George. Its humorous contrast between the mundane and the sublime is beautifully done and its comic delights are many.

It was after this comic break that Cowper first tried his hand at SF short stories and produced "The Custodians," the first of a series of delicately imagined and richly written stories. It deals with prescience and the nuclear holocaust but dwells, almost paradoxically, on the medieval past. There is a wealth of emotion in these stories and while "Paradise Beach" is flawed, "The Hertford Manuscript" and "Drink Me, Francesca" possess the same poetic lilt. The most important of these stories, however, is "Piper at the Gates of Dawn" which deals with the birth of a new religion. A novella of immense wealth and power, it brings to mind Le Guin's Earthsea books; its post-holocaust setting is similar to that of *Phoenix.* The young boy, Tom, has the gift of joining men together in a brotherhood through the music of his flute and the image of the White Bird. These images, picked up 18 years later, when the "kinsmen" of

Tom's "religion" are being persecuted, form the basis of *The Road to Corlay.* It is a sensuous book that pampers both heart and mind and, as in both *Breakthrough* and *Twilight,* has a "passenger" in the mind of one of its contemporary characters. Carver, a 20th-century scientist, sees through the eyes of Thomas of Norwich, an inhabitant of the world of Corlay— AD 3018—and through the "double-vision" Cowper emphas-ises once again that it is only by shedding man's present direction (which, he infers, can only be achieved by some natural or unnatural catastrophe which robs man of almost everything) and assuming a new life-style, that any future can exist for *Homo sapiens. Profundis* is once again in the vein of *Clone,* with an innocent protagonist, Tom Jones, re-enacting the Christ myth in a beserk computer-run submarine, *HMS Profundis,* which has already denuded the Earth "above surface" by causing global war. As black comedy it is not as effective as *Clone,* but it is, perhaps, much more profound in its message.

Two further volumes of Cowper's stories appeared in the 1980's, drawing upon a wide range of subjects; ecological disasters ("A Message to the King of Brobdingnag"), mystical experiences ("Incident at Huacaloc"), 19th-century adventures ("The Web of the Magi"), and highly literate ghost stories ("The Attelborough Poltergeist" and "The Tithonian Factor")—all with a science-fictional rationale. Most signifi-cant from this period, however, were the two final books in the Corlay sequence (the four parts termed by Cowper "The White Bird Of Kinship"). The first *A Dream of Kinship,* was set 1000 years on from *The Road to Corlay* and showed how the loose ethic of the boy piper, Tom, had become a highly dogmatic religion. The second, *A Tapestry of Time,* describes the travels of another Tom, almost a reincarnation of the first, who must face the moral implications of his "gift" (he can pipe men into "madness"). Overall, the four parts of the "Bird Of Kinship" form one of the most lyrical and beautifully written sequences in science fiction. Cowper's recent work, however, has drifted outside genre definitions and it may well be that we have seen the last of his science-fiction writing.

—David Wingrove

COX, Erle (Harold). Australian. Born in Melbourne, Victoria, 15 August 1873. Educated at Melbourne Church of England Grammar School. Farmer, then journalist: drama critic for *Argus* and *Australasian,* both Melbourne, 1918-46. Recipient: *Lone Hand* prize, for short story, 1910. *Died 20 November 1950.*

SCIENCE-FICTION PUBLICATIONS

Novels

Out of the Silence. Melbourne, Vidler, 1925; London, John Hamilton, 1927; New York, Henkle, 1928.
Fools' Harvest. Melbourne, Robertson and Mullens, 1939.
The Missing Angel. Melbourne, Robertson and Mullens, 1947.

*   *   *

Originally a farmer, Erle Cox graduated from free-lance writing to professional metropolitan journalism in his forties. His early short stories in Australian magazines were never collected, and he is known only for three novels. He never gained literary recognition: orthodox criticism ignores him and comprehensive literary histories give him a bare mention.

Yet *Out of the Silence* had great popular appeal, though Cox had to finance the 1925 edition himself. An earlier human race, destroyed in a world catastrophe 27 million years ago, left time-capsule spheres preserving their culture and chosen representatives in stasis. Found and revived in modern Victoria, the superwoman Earani prepares to take over the world and recreate her highly developed, rational, heartless civilisation. Her intellectual stature and enormous personal magnetism give good prospects of success, certainly with the other survivor she detects in the Himalayas revived as well. The book is well told, if slow and wordy by later standards, maintaining suspense as the mystery and menace unfold. The atmosphere of middle-class rural Australia about 1910 contrasts strangely with the threatened scientific tyranny. Earani is a terrible figure: a prodigy not of evil but of self-assured virtue without compassion. Characteristically her program includes genocide of inferior elements, including the colored races. The grotesque racism, almost too absurd to be abhorrent, was perfectly acceptable in the Australia of 60 years ago and caused no comment. No longer a book to sympathise with, it has historic importance.

Cox's other books are quite different. *Fools' Harvest* is a typical warning of foreign conquest of Australia, forseeing the scale of World War II atrocities but without scientific interest. *The Missing Angel* is a light satire about the Devil in Melbourne's polite society.

—Graham Stone

CRAIG, Brian. See **STABLEFORD, Brian M.**

CRICHTON, (John) Michael. Also writes as Michael Douglas (with Douglas Crichton); Jeffery Hudson; John Lange. American. Born in Chicago, Illinois, 23 October 1942. Educated at Harvard University, Cambridge, Massachusetts, A. B. (summa cum laude) 1964 (Phi Beta Kappa); Harvard Medical School, M. D. 1969; Salk Institute, La Jolla, California, 1969-70. Married 1) Joan Radam in 1965 (divorced, 1971); 2) Kathleen St. Johns in 1978 (divorced, 1980). Recipient: Mystery Writers of America Edgar Allan Poe Award, 1968, 1980; Association of American Medical Writers Award, 1970. Agent: International Creative Management, 40 West 57th Street, New York, New York 10019. Address: 9348 Santa Monica Boulevard, Beverly Hills, California 90210, U. S. A.

SCIENCE-FICTION PUBLICATIONS

Novels

The Andromeda Strain. New York, Knopf, and London, Cape, 1969.
Drug of Choice (as John Lange). New York, New American Library, 1970; as *Overkill*, London, Sphere, 1972.
Binary (as John Lange). New York, Knopf, and London, Heinemann, 1972.

The Terminal Man. New York, Knopf, and London, Cape, 1972.

OTHER PUBLICATIONS

Novels

A Case of Need (as Jeffery Hudson). Cleveland, World, and London, Heinemann, 1968.
Dealing; or, The Berkeley-to-Boston Forty-Brick Lost-Bag Blues (as Michael Douglas, with Douglas Crichton). New York, Knopf, 1971; London, Talmy Franklin, 1972.
The Great Train Robbery. New York, Knopf, and London, Cape, 1975.
Eaters of the Dead. New York, Knopf, and London, Cape, 1976.
Congo. New York, Knopf, 1980; London, Allen Lane, 1981.

Novels as John Lange

Odds On. New York, New American Library, 1966.
Scratch One. New York, New American Library, 1967.
Easy Go. New York, New American Library, 1968; London, Sphere, 1972; as *The Last Tomb* (as Michael Crichton), New York, Bantam, 1974.
The Venom Business. Cleveland, World, 1969.
Zero Cool. New York, New American Library, 1969; London, Sphere, 1972.
Grave Descend. New York, New American Library, 1970.

Plays

Westworld (screenplay). New York, Bantam, 1975.

Screenplays: *Westworld*, 1973; *Coma*, 1977; *The Great Train Robbery*, 1978; *Looker*, 1981; *Runaway*, 1984.

Other

"Sci-Fi and Vonnegut," in *New Republic* (Washington, D. C.), 26 April 1969.
Five Patients: The Hospital Explained. New York, Knopf, 1970; Cape, 1971.
"Approaching Ellison," in *Approaching Oblivion*, by Harlan Ellison and Ed Bryant. New York, Walker, 1974; London, Millington, 1976.
Jasper Johns. New York, Abrams, and London, Thames and 1977.
Electronic Life: How to Think about Computers. New York, Knopf, and London, Heinemann, 1983.

*

Theatrical Activities:
Director: **Films**—*Westworld*, 1973; *Coma*, 1977; *The Great Train Robbery*, 1978; *Looker*, 1981; *Runaway*, 1984. **Television**—*Pursuit*, 1972.

Michael Crichton comments:
I am interested in the quality of verisimilitude and how it is developed and sustained in fiction. All of my work, both science fiction and other writing, has tended to revolve around issues of what we believe and why. In recent years a good deal of my work has been devoted to films, which I direct as well as write.

*   *   *

Michael Crichton's primary science-fiction works are: *The Andromeda Strain*, *Binary*, and *The Terminal Man*. Classified as "soft" science fiction, each of these books is set in what is essentially contemporary society. In each case, though, a science-fiction element has been introduced upon which the subsequent development of the plot depends. In *The Andromeda Strain*, for example, a mutating micro-organism brought back from the upper atmosphere by a satellite kills all but two people in a small northern Arizona town and then threatens the rest of humanity. In *Binary* the tapping into a "closed code computer mechanism" to determine the time and route of a shipment of nerve gas permits a psychopathic multi-millionaire to concoct a devious plot to assassinate the President. In *The Terminal Man* psychosurgery permits the connection of a psychopathic patient's brain to a computer and turns him into a living time bomb. It is, of course, their nearness to real life that makes these three novels believable and frightening. The novels are highly technical, and the narrative is laced with graphs, charts, diagrams, and computer printouts. Some of the information is real; the rest of it is fictionalized but dressed up to raise the level of credibility. Jargon from the appropriate scientific field adds to the realism. The drama of the stories develops from the threat of imminent disaster and the subsequent efforts to prevent it.

The Terminal Man and *Binary* are clearly less effective than *The Andromeda Strain*, but interesting and entertaining nonetheless. The terminal man himself is a psychotic named Harry Benson, who believes that machines are taking over the world. He becomes a threat when he is chosen for a unique experiment that connects his brain to a miniaturized computer which is powered by an atomic pack containing 37 grams of radioactive plutonium. Though the pack is implanted under his skin, if Benson breaks it open, he will kill himself and expose anyone in the immediate area to deadly radiation. Benson's physical problem is psychomotor epilepsy, and the computer is supposed to stop his seizures with a counteracting electrical shock. Because the sensation produced is more pleasurable than several orgasms, however, he learns to increase the frequency of the shocks through biofeedback techniques. Benson, in fact, becomes an electronic junkie. Though the novel produces a believable female lead in Dr. Janet Ross, a psychiatrist working on the project, it fails successfully to build tensions between the major characters, and much of the potential drama remains undeveloped. Moreover, the sense of a threat never really materializes because Benson is more pathetic than dangerous.

Pacing is Crichton's strongest quality, and *Binary* is much better in that regard. A more complicated plot and a high level of suspense—a State Intelligence Agent, John Graves, unravels a complicated puzzle created for him by John Wright, the insane right-wing multimillionaire, before a half-ton of ZV nerve gas kills the President and more than a million other people in San Diego—make *Binary* a more compelling book. Wright is a much more worthy adversary than Benson, and more deadly. He is both intelligent and clever. His anticipation of every move that Graves makes creates an eerie drama, a sense of frustration, and genuine "daylight" horror. When Graves finally figures out the puzzle and prevents the binary gasses from mixing to create ZV, it brings a sigh of relief.

The best of Crichton's books, without question, is *The Andromeda Strain*. Though the antagonist is a micro-organism, drama is achieved by the fact that its properties are unknown and that it has great potentiality to kill. It is heightened when the mutating organism eats through the rubber seals in one of the workrooms and contaminates that level of the underground laboratory. This sets the self-destruct mechanism of the complex into operation. Unless countermanded, the mechan-

ism will set off an atomic bomb which will destroy the complex and disperse the deadly organism over the Earth's surface: the key to the spectacular success of the work lies in its pacing. Suspense is built with each development. Clues to the nature of the organism are so interwoven with plot impediments that the reader is compelled to read on. Though the characters are only moderately interesting as people, the roles they play in the development of the drama are important and add to the suspense.

In general, Crichton's style in clinical. His narrative is lean and well-adapted to the fast action, dialogue, and rapid pacing upon which he relies. There is some social commentary in the novels as they depict the follies of man's self-assurance. Lack of judgment or planning combines with deadly technology in all three cases to remind man that he is often his own worst enemy.

Crichton's recent work has been almost exclusively for Hollywood, either as writer or director. Unfortunately, it has steadily declined in quality. For example, *Runaway*, his most recent effort, was nominated by one critic for "the most idiotic movie of the year award," and indeed it seems to be but a collection of the oldest and tiredest science-fiction clichés. As such, it epitomizes Hollywood's approach to science fiction, which, despite the successes of the Star Wars trilogy, *E.T.*, and *Close Encounters of the Third Kind*, has been to mask standard tales with science-fiction trappings. Even Riddley Scott's brilliant film *Bladerunner*, which bears only a passing resemblance to Philip Dick's original story, and *Alien*, to mention two excellent, recent films, are very standard fare conceptually for hard-core science-fiction fans.

The tendency of Hollywood to ignore many brilliant and original stories and to avoid consulting with those who best know the field has given science-fiction film a bad reputation among devotees, many of whom hoped that Crichton's move to Hollywood would prompt a new era of science fiction film. Rather than changing it, however, it appears that he has become part of the entertainment mill.

—Carl B. Yoke

CROMIE, Robert. British. Born in 1856. *Died in 1907.*

SCIENCE- FICTION PUBLICATIONS

Novels

For England's Sake. London, Warne, 1889.
A Plunge into Space. London, Warne, 1890; Westport, Connecticut, Hyperion Press, 1976.
The Crack of Doom. London, Digby Long, 1895.
The Next Crusade. London, Hutchinson, 1896.
A New Messiah. London, Digby Long, 1902.

Short Stories

The King's Oak and Other Stories. London, Newnes, 1897.

OTHER PUBLICATIONS

Novels

The Lost Liner. London, Newnes, 1899.
Kitty's Victoria Cross. London, Warne, 1901.
The Shadow of the Cross. London, Ward Lock, 1902.

El Dorado. London, Ward Lock, 1904; as *From the Cliffs of Croaghaun*, Akron, Ohio, Saalfield, 1904.

Short Stories

The Romance of Poisons, Being Weird Episodes from Life, with T. S. Wilson. London, Jarrolds, 1903.

* * *

All that is known about Robert Cromie is that from 1889 to 1904 he published 11 books of fiction (one with T. S. Wilson), a number of which are SF. The list begins with *For England's Sake*, which cashed in on the patriotic popularity of the "future war" tale by transferring it to India, where loyal natives headed by heroic maharajah defeat dastardly Russian invasion. Its continuation is *The Next Crusade*, whose battles and love entanglements are not as interesting as Cromie's Preface, briefly discussing "the history of the future" and with a too easy facetiousness concluding that as against the history of the past it contains fewer errors (Cromie's Britain allied with Austria occupies Constantinople, so that he may have been co-responsible for Churchill's disastrous World War I venture against the Dardanelles). Two other novels are more important. *A Plunge into Space* is an interplanetary novel halfway between Vernes and Wells (the second edition in 1891 has a brief and unrevealing preface by Verne) detailing how a scientist discovers anti-gravity, how his explorer-friend helps him to cast a steel globe in Alaska in spite of Indian attacks and sullen half-breeds, and how the two with four more friends—again characterized by profession—fly to a desert Mars. Vegetation and a decaying utopian civilization (which has TV and aircraft but no politics or money) are found near its polar sea. A love affair between one of the heroes and a beautiful Martian coyly named Mignonette results in the latter first becoming a stowaway in their spacecraft on return and then sacrificing her life; the craft is destroyed. *The Crack of Doom* has one of the first mad scientists in SF planning to use the secret of atomic energy to blow up our planet. The plot flounders through lots of genteel Victorian love melodrama, telepathy, hypnotism, secret societies, stereotyped characters, vague echoes of drawing-room Schopenhauerism, and a sentimental happy ending. A final SF novel, *A New Messiah*, also leans on a melodramatic plot.

—Darko Suvin

CROSBY, Harry C., Jr. See ANVIL, Christopher.

CROSS, John Keir. Also wrote as Stephen Macfarlane; Susan Morley. British. Born in Carluke, Lanark, 19 August 1914. Clerk and entertainer in the 1930's; radio writer for BBC, London, from 1937. *Died 22 January 1967.*

SCIENCE-FICTION PUBLICATIONS

Novels (for children)

The Angry Planet. London, Lunn, 1945; New York, Coward McCann, 1946.

The Owl and the Pussycat. London, Lunn, 1946; as *The Other Side of Green Hills*, New York, Coward McCann, 1947.
The Flying Fortunes in an Encounter with Rubberface. London, Muller, 1952; as *The Stolen Sphere*, New York, Dutton, 1953.
SOS from Mars. London, Hutchinson, 1954; as *The Red Journey Back*, New York, Coward McCann, 1954.

Short Stories

The Other Passenger: 18 Strange Stories: London, Westhouse, 1944; Philadelphia, Lippincott, 1946.

Uncollected Short Stories

"The Best Holiday I Ever Had" (for children), in *Laurie's Space Annual.* London, Laurie, 1953.
"Mothering Sunday," in *Best Black Magic Stories*, edited by John Keir Cross. London, Faber, 1960.

OTHER PUBLICATIONS

Novels

Mistress Glory (as Susan Morley). New York, Dial Press, 1948; as *Glory*, as John Keir Cross, London, Laurie, 1951.
Juniper Green. London, Laurie, 1952; as Susan Morley, New York, Dial Press, 1953.

Plays

Radio Plays: *The Kraken Wakes*, from the novel by John Wyndham; *The Archers* series, with others, 1962-67; *The Brockenstein Affair*, from a work by George R. Preedy, 1962; *The Free Fishers*, from the novel by John Buchan, 1964; *Bird of Dawning*, from the novel by John Masefield, 1965; *Be Thou My Judge*, from a work by James Wood, 1967.

Television Play: *She Died Young*, 1961.

Other (for children)

Studio J Investigates. London, Lunn, 1944.
Jack Robinson. London, Lunn, 1945.
The Man in Moonlight. London, Westhouse, 1947.
The White Magic. London, Westhouse, 1947.
Blackadder. London, Muller, 1950; New York, Dutton, 1951.
The Dancing Tree. London, Hutchinson, 1955.
Elizabeth in Broadcasting. London, Chatto and Windus, 1957.
The Sixpenny Year. London, Hutchinson, 1957.

Other (for children; as Stephen Macfarlane)

The Blue Egg. London, Lunn, 1944.
Detectives in Greasepaint. London, Lunn, 1944.
Lucy Maroon, The Car That Loved a Policeman. London, Lunn, 1944.
Mr. Bosanko and Other Stories. London, Lunn, 1944.
The Strange Tale of Sally and Arnold. London, Lunn, 1944.
The Story of a Tree. London, Lunn, 1946.

Other

Aspect of Life: An Autobiography of Youth. London, Selwyn and Blount, 1937.

Editor, *The Children's Omnibus.* London, Lunn, 1948.

Editor, *Best Horror Stories*. London, Faber, 1957; *Best Horror Stories 2,* Faber, 1965.
Editor, *Best Black Magic Stories*. London, Faber, 1960.

* * *

A short story writer in the tradition of Saki and John Collier, a popular anthologist of horror stories, and an occasional writer of science-fiction and fantasy dramas for the BBC, John Keir Cross is especially noteworthy for his juvenile science fiction. *The Angry Planet* was among the first modern science-fiction novels directed at a young audience, and is interesting for the manner in which it reworks themes from Wells and C. S. Lewis into a context more readily accessible to younger readers.

The Angry Planet involves a group of three children who travel to Mars by hiding on an experimental rocket ship. The life they find there is elegantly portrayed, and reveals Cross's familiarity with earlier science fiction as well as intelligent speculation. Martian society is dominated by intelligent plant life, the major forms of which are called the Beautiful People and the Terrible Ones. This opposition of two divergent strains of the same evolutionary path calls to mind the Morlocks and Eloi from Wells's *The Time Machine*, and the moral values attached to each race calls to mind C. S. *Lewis's Out of the Silent Planet*. The relatively sophisticated multiple viewpoint narrative adds further interest to the tale and helps to maintain suspense. A sequel, *SOS from Mars*, describes subsequent journeys to Mars. Another juvenile science-fiction novel, with the unlikely title *The Flying Fortunes in an Encounter with Rubberface*, concerns the launching of an artificial earth satellite, and may be the first juvenile treatment of this theme except for Arthur Clarke's 1952 *Islands in the Sky*. Cross's adult fiction, represented by the collection *The Other Passenger*, tends more toward fantasy and the occult than science fiction, but includes the classic *doppelgänger* story "The Other Passenger." Cross's short fiction is distinguished by sensitive style and psychological insight.

—Gary K. Wolfe

CROSS, Polton. See **FEARN, John Russell.**

CROWLEY, John. American. Born in Presque Isle, Maine, 1 December 1942. Educated at Indiana University, Bloomington, B. A. 1964. Photographer and commercial artist, 1964-66. Since 1966, free-lance writer. Recipient: World Fantasy Convention award, 1982. Address: Box 395, Conway, Massachusetts 01341, U. S. A.

SCIENCE-FICTION PUBLICATIONS

Novels

The Deep. New York, Doubleday, 1975; London, New English Library, 1977.
Beasts. New York, Doubleday, 1976.

Engine Summer. New York, Doubleday, 1979; London, Gollancz, 1980.
Little, Big. New York, Bantam, 1981; London, Gollancz, 1982.

Uncollected Short Stories

"Antiquities," in *Whispers*, edited by Stuart David Schiff. New York, Doubleday, 1977.
"Where Spirits Gat Them Home," in *Shadows*, edited by Charles L. Grant. New York, Doubleday, 1978.
"The Reason for the Visit," in *Interfaces*, edited by Ursula K. Le Guin and Virginia Kidd. New York, Ace, 1980.
"The Green Child," in *Elsewhere*, edited by Terri Windling and Marc Alan Arnold. New York, Ace, 1981.
"Snow," in *Omni* (New York), June 1985.

* * *

John Crowley is one of the most promising young authors of science fiction and fantasy to come along in the 1970's. His first three novels have numerous virtues, and his epic fantasy, *Little, Big* (World Fantasy award), reaped a harvest of laudatory reviews and, inevitably, comparisons to J. R. R. Tolkien's work, as well as other memorable works of fantasy from *A Voyage to Arcturus* to (rather surprisingly) Gabriel García Marquéz's novel of "magic realism" *One Hundred Years of Solitude*. While Crowley is still relatively early in his career, his fiction has already expressed a highly individual vision, worthy of comparison with the most original science-fiction writers emerging in the 1970's.

Crowley's first novel, *The Deep*, received some praise from readers like Ursula Le Guin, but in the light of his later work it seems to be his least satisfactory and least characteristic performance. Set in a distant future on a planet vaguely like earth, *The Deep* describes the power struggle between two aristocratic houses with names derived from Celtic mythology, mostly old Welsh. Young Sennred, one of the Reds, eventually emerges as a victor who reconciles the impulsive Reds and the Machiavellian Blacks; but no particular hero predominates, and Learned Redhand, a scholarly apostate from the Reds, remains the most memorable character. The conflict is observed by an alien who assumes various guises, and eventually confronts his antagonist, a denizen of "the deep" who is an avatar of the Leviathan myth. Crowley's use of the Leviathan mythology does not clarify his cryptic plot, and the novel suffers from the repetition of similar and identical Celtic names. Despite high ambitions, Celtic and biblical myth do not rescue this immature first novel.

In *Beasts* Crowley produced a better work, dealing with a bitter ideological conflict in an America of the near future where central government has collapsed and small regional governments struggle to maintain their authority. Their opponents are the bureaucrats of "the Federal," a government striving to restore a dominating central authority. The surface conflict, however, symbolizes the perennial struggle between rational organizers who wish to subject nature and humanity to a monolithic tyranny and those romantics and lovers of nature who resist such dehumanizing efforts. Among the rebels are the "beasts" of the title, hybrid creatures resulting from genetic experiment in the last days of the old United States; the products of these projects are sentient beings combining human and animal qualities, somewhat reminiscent of the creations of H. G. Wells's Dr. Moreau. One measure of Crowley's achievement is his successful characterizations of Reynard, a fox-man, and Painter, a lion-man, each of which manages to circumvent (in his own fashion) the opposition of the Federalists. Although *Beasts* is resolved somewhat ambiguously, Crowley's novel clearly takes a stand on the side of the romantics, and in favor of the energies of natural life.

Even more impressive is Crowley's third novel, *Engine Summer*, a story of a young man's initiation into adulthood in the primitive tribal world of a post-disaster America centuries hence. This book describes the search for meaning and understanding of Rush That Speaks, who leaves his community of origin as a boy and searches for his lost love, Once A Day. Although he finds her and some knowledge of the outside world, he discovers the unhappiness that accompanies the loss of innocence when she deserts him again. Crowley's hero also learns much about the vanished 20th-century civilization, the brave new world of science and technology called the age of the "angels. " One of the lessons that Rush That Speaks learns is the "angelism" or excessive rationalism of the ancients was anything but angelic in our sense of the word. An additional sign of Crowley's technical mastery in this novel is his use of an inventive narrative mode: Rush tells the story of his youth through a recording cube, and his auditor, who occasionally comments on his tale, is a person who lives generations after his death. This narrative method provides aesthetic distance.

Even the mature artistry of *Engine Summer*, however, scarcely provides a hint of the marvelous achievement of *Little, Big*. *Little, Big* describes three generations in the life of the Drinkwater-Bramble-Hawksquill clan, as seen through the eyes of several members, but primarily from the point of view of two: Smoky Barnable, an outsider from the midwest who comes to New York City and marries "Daily Alice" Drinkwater; and Auberon, their son, who finally becomes an avatar of the fairy king, Oberon, just as his black paramour, Sylvie, is metamorphosed into a new Titania. After Smoky's marriage to Alice, a charming and credible heroine, he takes up residence at the Drinkwater family home, Edgewood, a curious architectural wonder in upper New York State housing a family of eccentrics who have a secret alliance with fairies. Smoky's father-in-law, Old Doc Drinkwater, for instance, writes successful children's books which narrate tales he gets first-hand from the fairies themselves. Other members of the family are blessed or cursed by gifts from the "little people. " The novel comes to a crisis when a fascistic politician becomes president and attempts to oppress and destroy all those who revere the power of nature and the imagination. Through Daily Alice's heroic sacrifice of herself, the Drinkwater clan is able to leave the modern world, which will no longer allow them to ignore it, and enter the earthly paradise of the realm of "Faery," and there Alice appears in an immortal form.

This humorous, whimsical, inventive, and richly allusive fantasy deserves many readings and is likely to become a classic of its genre. Here, as in the rest of his world, Crowley defines his vision as that of a sophisticated romantic, suspicious of technology, committed to the cause of his imagination, and possessing prodigious literary gifts of humor, characterization, and lyrical description. At its best, Crowley's work is comparable to that of the best science-fiction and fantasy writers who have emerged in the 1970's, such as Gene Wolfe, Gregory Benford, and Joan Vinge.

—Edgar L. Chapman

CUMMINGS, Ray(mond King). Also wrote as Ray King; Gabriel Wilson. American. Born in New York City, 30 August 1887. Educated at Princeton University, New Jersey, one year.

Married Gabrielle W. Cummings; one son and one daughter. Worked on oil wells in Wyoming and in placer mines in British Columbia and Alaska; arranged record albums and wrote labels for Edison Records in the 1920's. *Died 23 January 1957.*

SCIENCE-FICTION PUBLICATIONS

Novels (series: Haljan; Matter, Space, and Time; Tama)

The Girl in the Golden Atom (Matter, Space, and Time). London, Methuen, 1922; New York, Harper, 1923.
The Man Who Mastered Time (Matter, Space, and Time). Chicago, McClurg, 1929.
The Sea Girl. Chicago, McClurg, 1930.
Tarrano the Conqueror. Chicago, McClurg, 1930.
Brigands of the Moon (Haljan). Chicago, McClurg, 1931; London, Consul, 1966.
The Shadow Girl (Matter, Space, and Time). London, Swan, 1946; New York, Ace, 1962.
The Princess of the Atom (Matter, Space, and Time). New York, Avon, 1950; London, Boardman, 1951.
The Man on the Meteor. London, Swan, 1952.
Beyond the Vanishing Point. New York, Ace, 1958.
Wandl the Invader (Haljan). New York, Ace, 1961.
Beyond the Stars . New York, Ace, 1963.
A Brand New World. New York, Ace, 1964.
The Exile of Time (Matter, Space, and Time). New York, Avalon, 1964.
Explorers into Infinity. New York, Avalon, 1965.
Tama of the Light Country. New York, Ace, 1965.
Tama, Princess of Mercury. New York, Ace, 1966.
The Insect Invasion. New York, Avalon, 1967.

Uncollected Short Stories

"The Other Man's Blood," in *All-Story* (New York), 18 October 1919.
"The Man Who Discovered Nothing," in *All-Story* (New York), 10 January 1920.
"The Light Machine," in *All-Story* (New York), 19 June 1920.
"The Time Professor," in *Argosy* (New York), 9 January 1921.
"Moon Madness," in *Argosy* (New York), 23 April 1921.
"The Gravity Professor," in *Argosy* (New York), 7 May 1921.
"The Peppermint Test," in *Argosy* (New York), 24 June 1922.
"The Fire People," in *Argosy* (New York), 21 October-17 November 1922.
"The Three-Eyed Man," in *Argosy* (New York), 7 July 1923.
"A Bar of Poisoned Licorice," in *Science and Invention* (New York), July 1927.
"What the Typewriter Told," in *Science and Invention* (New York), August 1927.
"Around the Universe," in *Amazing* (New York), October 1927.
"The Snow Girl," in *Argosy* (New York), 2-9 November 1929.
"Phantoms of Reality," in *Astounding* (New York), January 1930.
"The Man Who Was Two Men," in *Argosy* (New York), 8-15 February 1930.
"Jetta of the Lowlands," in *Astounding* (New York), September 1930.
"The Great Transformation," in *Wonder Stories* (New York), February 1931.
"Bandits of the Cylinder," in *Argosy* (New York), 29 August 1931.
"The Derelict of Space," with William Thurmond, in *Wonder Stories* (New York), Fall 1931.

"Flyer of Eternal Midnight," in *Argosy* (New York), 3 October 1931.

"The Jungle Rebellion," in *Argosy* (New York), 31 October-12 November 1931.

"The Mark of the Meteor," in *Wonder Stories* (New York), Winter 1931.

"The White Invaders," in *Astounding* (New York), December 1931.

"The Disappearance of William Rogers," in *Argosy* (New York), 9 January 1932.

"Death by the Clock," in *Argosy* (New York), 6 August 1932.

"The Fire Planet," in *Argosy* (New York), 23 September-7 October 1933.

"Terror of the Unseen," in *Argosy* (New York), 4 November 1933.

"Brigands of the Unseen," in *Argosy* (New York), 27 January 1934.

"Flood," in *Argosy* (New York), 28 July-11 August 1934.

"Earth-Mars Voyage 20," in *Argosy* (New York), 20 August 1934.

"World of Doom," in *Thrilling Adventures*, January 1935.

"The Moon Plot," in *Argosy* (New York), February 1935.

"The Polar Light," in *Argosy* (New York), April 1935.

"The Man with the Platinum Rib," in *Blue Book* (Chicago), January 1936.

"Blood of the Moon," in *Thrilling Wonder Stories* (New York), August 1936.

"Shadow Gold," in *Thrilling Wonder Stories* (New York), October 1936.

"Earth-Venus 12" (as Gabriel Wilson, with Mrs. Ray Cummings) and "Trapped in Eternity," in *Thrilling Wonder Stories* (New York), December 1936.

"Elixir of Doom," in *Thrilling Wonder Stories* (New York), April 1937.

"The Space-Time-Size Machine," in *Thrilling Wonder Stories* (New York), October 1937.

"Voyage 13," in *Astounding* (New York), July 1938.

"The Thing from Mars," in *Thrilling Wonder Stories* (New York), August 1938.

"X1-2-200," in *Astounding* (New York), September 1938.

"The Man Who Saw Too Much," in *Thrilling Wonder Stories* (New York), October 1938.

"The Great Adventure," in *Thrilling Wonder Stories* (New York), December 1938.

"Zeoh-X," in *Thrilling Wonder Stories* (New York), April 1939.

"Secret of the Sun," in *Thrilling Wonder Stories* (New York), August 1939.

"An Ultimatum from Mars," in *Astounding* (New York), August 1939.

"Portrait," in *Unknown Worlds* (New York), September 1939.

"The Atom Prince," in *Science Fiction Stories* (New York), December 1939.

"Shadow World," in *Thrilling Wonder Stories* (New York), December 1939.

"The Man Who Knew Everything," in *Strange Stories*, February 1940.

"The Girl from Infinite Smallness," in *Planet* (New York), Spring 1940.

"Arton's Medal," in *Super Science* (Kokomo, Indiana), May 1940.

"Space-Liner X87," in *Planet* (New York), Summer 1940.

"The Thought-Woman," in *Super Science* (Kokomo, Indiana), July 1940.

"Ice over America," in *Thrilling Wonder Stories* (New York), August 1940.

"Revolt in the Ice Empire," in *Planet* (New York), Fall 1940.

"The Machine That Had No Flaws," in *Startling* (New York), September 1940.

"The Vanishing Man," in *Thrilling Wonder Stories* (New York), September 1940.

"Personality," in *Astonishing* (Chicago), October 1940.

"Phantom of the Seven Stars," in *Planet* (New York), Winter 1940.

"The Door at the Opera," in *Astonishing* (Chicago), December 1940.

"Priestess of the Moon," in *Amazing* (New York), December 1940.

"World Upside Down," in *Thrilling Wonder Stories* (New York), December 1940.

"Space Flight of Terror," in *Science Fiction Stories* (New York), January 1941.

"Magnus' Disintegrator," in *Astonishing* (Chicago), February 1941.

"Almost Human," in *Startling* (New York), March 1941.

"The War-Nymphs of Venus," in *Planet* (New York), Spring 1941.

"Coming of the Giant Germs," in *Uncanny* (Chicago), April 1941.

"Imp of the Theremin," in *Astonishing* (Chicago), April 1941.

"Space-Wolf," in *Planet* (New York), Summer 1941.

"Onslaught of the Druid Girls," in *Fantastic Adventures* (New York), June 1941.

"Out of Smallness," in *Thrilling Wonder Stories* (New York), June 1941.

"The Robot God," in *Weird Tales* (New York), July 1941.

"Aerita of the Light Country," in *Super Science* (Kokomo, Indiana), August 1941.

"Machines of Destiny," in *Astonishing* (Chicago), November 1941.

"Monster of the Moon," in *Super Science* (Kokomo, Indiana), November 1941.

"Monster of the Asteroid," in *Planet* (New York), Winter 1941.

"Into the Fourth Dimension," in *Science Fiction Quarterly* (Holyoke, Massachusetts), Winter 1941-42.

"Bandits of Time," in *Amazing* (New York), December 1941.

"Crimes of the Year 2000," in *Famous Fantastic Mysteries* (New York), December 1941.

"Decadence," in *Thrilling Wonder Stories* (New York), December 1941.

"Fugitive," in *Thrilling Wonder Stories* (New York), February 1942.

"The Shadow People," in *Astonishing* (Chicago), March 1942.

"Gods of Space," in *Planet* (New York), Spring 1942.

"Regeneration," in *Thrilling Wonder Stories* (New York), April 1942.

"The Star-Master," in *Planet* (New York), Summer 1942.

"The Television Alibi," in *Famous Fantastic Mysteries* (New York), June 1942.

"The World Beyond," in *Amazing* (New York), July 1942.

"Rain of Fire," in *Future* (New York), August 1942.

"Miracle," in *Astonishing* (Chicago), October 1942.

"Beyond the End of Time," in *Super Science* (Kokomo, Indiana), November 1942.

"The End of His Service," in *Captain Future* (New York), Winter 1942.

"Tubby: Time Traveler," in *Thrilling Wonder Stories* (New York), December 1942.

"Patriotism Plus," in *Future* (New York), February 1943.

"Star Arrow," in *Thrilling Wonder Stories* (New York), February 1943.

"The Flame Breathers," in *Planet* (New York), March 1943.

"The Man from 2890," in *Astonishing* (Chicago), April 1943.

"The Golden Temple," in *Thrilling Wonder Stories* (New York), June 1943.

"Wings of Icarus," in *Startling* (New York), June 1943.

"The Man Who Saved New York," in *Science Fiction Stories* (New York), July 1943.

"Tubby: Atom Smasher," in *Thrilling Wonder Stories* (New York), August 1943.

"Battle of the Solar System," in *Thrilling Wonder Stories* (New York), Spring 1944.

"The Gadget Girl," in *Thrilling Wonder Stories* (New York), Fall 1944.

"Juggernaut of Space," in *Planet* (New York), Fall 1945.

"Tubby: Master of the Atom," in *Thrilling Wonder Stories* (New York), Fall 1946.

"Up and Atom," in *Startling* (New York), September 1947.

"The Simple Life," in *Startling* (New York), May 1948.

"Ahead of His Time," in *Thrilling Wonder Stories* (New York), June 1948.

"The Little Monsters Come," in *Planet* (New York), Winter 1948.

"A Fragment of Diamond Quartz," in *Super Science* (Kokomo, Indiana), January 1950.

"The Planet Smashers," in *Out of This World Adventures* (New York), July 1950.

"Science Can Wait," in *Fantastic Story* (New York), Fall 1952.

"He Who Served," in *Fantastic Universe* (Chicago), September 1954.

"The Man Who Could Go Away," in *Fantastic Universe* (Chicago), July 1955.

"Requiem for a Small Planet," in *Saturn* (Holyoke, Massachusetts), March 1958.

"The Dead Who Walk," in *Magazine of Horror* (New York), April 1965.

Uncollected Short Stories as Ray King

"Tuned Out," in *Argosy* (New York), 6-27 September 1924.

"Lust Rides the Roller Coaster," in *Marvel* (New York), December 1939.

"The Man Who Killed the World," in *Planet* (New York), Spring 1940.

*   *   *

Ray Cummings had a long writing career, but it must be said that he long outlived his originality, and was noted for shamelessly rehashing a few early stories. Established as one of the trailblazers before the advent of *Amazing Stories,* he was the only one of them to carry on as a prominent name. His output was exceeded only by Hamilton and Kuttner, but he did not move with the movement, and was soon dated.

The early tales that made his name had sketchy but strongly suggestive scientific foundations. Though he showed his debt to Wells by borrowing his narrative frame from *The Time Machine* more than once, his stories were closer to Haggard's or Burroughs's. Usually visitors from 20th-century New York in a strange setting with a vague pre-industrial society resolved a conflict and helped pave the way for more advanced thinking.

His first and favorite inspiration was sub-microscopic, even subatomic life—atoms or sub-atomic particles as worlds. The idea dated from Nicholas Odgers's *The Mystery of Being; or, Are Ultimate Atoms Inhabited Worlds?* (1863), but Cummings added the idea of reducing one's size indefinitely to penetrate

such a realm—later reversing it to visit a super-world in which we inhabit a particle. It is a tribute to his skill that a story based on such an idea could be a popular success. The unnamed chemist in *The Girl in the Golden Atom* (Rogers in the sequel) sees with his super-microscope an infinitesimal human race, including a nubile wench. (Compare Fitz-James O'Brien's *The Diamond Lens.*) But instead of agonising over the unattainable he devises size-changing drugs. (Compare *Alice in Wonderland.*) The relativity of size and the experience of changing size are vividly evoked. The book was fresh and exciting then, and it still reads well, and rates as a classic—though it is not precisely science fiction. (Incidentally, this adventure does not reach the level of an atomic world, despite the title; G. P. Wertenbaker has the doubtful honor of first taking the idea that far in "The Man from the Atom," in *Science and Invention,* August 1923.)

In the extended book version the villain was called Targo, and many later evildoers were named alliteratively—Taro, Toroh, etc. They are typically greedy megalomaniacs, usually gross or deformed, good at sneering and cynical laughter. Subtleties of character and motivation are not displayed, but human relations were simplified and fogged with romantic myths in most science fiction then. The writing is direct and conversational. To modern eyes there was much overstating the obvious, especially in the novels, but there were mystery and suspense supporting the action for the original audience.

Cummings was an early exploiter of time travel, scarcely touched since Wells, in *The Man Who Mastered Time, The Shadow Girl,* and others, though mostly for change of scene only. *Explorers into Infinity* reversed the exploration of the inconceivably small to visit a vastly greater sphere. *The Man on the Meteor* told of a tiny worldlet in Saturn's ring with seas and aquatic microscopic humans. *Tarrano the Conqueror* had a future of interplanetary affairs and a new Napoleon. In *The Sea Girl* an undersea people threatened the land. *A Brand New World* had a new extra-Solar planet entering the system. *Brigands of the Moon* moved into the kind of future interplanetary traffic early magazine SF postulated and helped establish space piracy as a popular theme. Cummings wrote many routine space adventure shorts thereafter. In "Jetta of the Lowlands" (*Astounding,* 1930) new nations grew from settlements on the dry sea bed after the oceans receded. Not to be overlooked were some robot stories of interest, particularly "Zeoh-X" (*Thrilling Wonder Stories,* April 1939) and "XI-2-200" (*Astounding,* September 1938); 16 stories featuring the character "Tubby" carried some gentle satire on many of his own plots and concepts.

—Graham Stone

———

DALE, Norman. See TUBB, E. C.

———

DALEY, Brian C. American. Born in Englewood, New Jersey, 22 December 1947. Educated in New Jersey high schools; Jersey City State College, B. A. in communication 1974. Has worked as waiter, housepainter, laborer, and case worker. Agent: Al Zuckerman, Writers House Inc., 21 West 26th Street, New York, New York 10010, U. S. A.

SCIENCE-FICTION PUBLICATIONS

Novels (series: Coramonde; Han Solo)

The Doomfarers of Coramonde. New York, Ballantine, 1977.
The Starfollowers of Coramonde. New York, Ballantine, 1979.
Han Solo at Stars' End. New York, Ballantine, and London, Sphere, 1979.
Han Solo's Revenge. New York, Ballantine, 1979; London, Sphere, 1980.
Han Solo and the Lost Legacy. New York, Ballantine, 1980; London, Sphere, 1981.
Tron (novelization of screenplay). New York, Ballantine, 1982.
A Tapestry of Magics. New York, Ballantine, 1983.
Requiem for a Ruler of Worlds. New York, Ballantine, 1985.

OTHER PUBLICATIONS

Novel

Jinx on a Terran Inheritance. New York, Ballantine, 1985.

Plays

Radio Plays: *Star Wars* series; *The Empire Strikes Back* series.

Recordings: *Rebel Mission to Ord Mantell* ; *War Games*.

*

Brian C. Daley comments:

Asked his reaction to becoming a millionaire, Neil Simon once said that the main difference in life was between being broke and bringing down 200 dollars a week; the rest was gravy. Writing has been a bit like that: making a living writing my own books, dealing with popular movie material, having scripts produced, and so forth has been gratifying and on the whole very enjoyable, but it's icing on the cake, after all. The real dividing line in life was in selling my first novel and seeing it in print.

I do my best to keep in mind the desire I had to tell a story, and how crucial it was—and should continue to be—to give the reader full value for his or her time, attention and money. One of the pitfalls of writing for a living is that a certain perfunctoriness can creep in if you're not careful, especially in a genre where being prolific can be such a plus.

I don't have much to say, here, about art, literature or moral uplift. The SF/Fantasy audience is quick to let you know if you're not delivering; my efforts are concentrated on satisfying the customers.

*   *   *

A relatively new author, Brian C. Daley so far has worked in one of two categories: fast-paced adventure tales with a film background, or alternate universe novels with linkage to our universe that explore the borderline between fantasy and science fiction. Quest themes with competitive elements leading to elaborate chase sequences are central to much of his writing and permit development of his outstanding talents for humor and vividly visualized description. At this point his characteristic hero tends to be a young man whose initial idealism, somewhat unrealistic, develops toward temporary cynicism, but with greater experience of the world does or will mature into a capacity to act responsibly.

It is not surprising, then, to find a sequence of three Han Solo stories from *Star Wars* background in the first category of his work, with steady growth in technique through the series. The first tale is the one most closely linked to opposition to the Empire, involving an arms drop to rebels, combat to defend an outlaw tech base, and a quest to recover prisoners held in stasis by the Empire, in particular the leader of the outlaw tech base at the request of his daughter. The basis for Han Solo's deficiency in human relationships and his relationship with Chewbacca is set up in a not very convincing scene: he was cashiered through perjured testimony by his commanding officer in spite of the favorable testimony of his first mate, Chewbacca. The revenge in the second novel is for an attempt to involve Han in slave-running; recovering the charter payment results in the break-up of the slave gang, with a little blackmail necessitated by hidden identities and shifting allegiances—the plot twists are carefully clued. The third novel turns on the conventional plot of the hidden treasure that once was priceless but now has lost much of its value.

In the structural pattern of the tales, one of the best-handled parts is the initial tangential incidents with a thematic relation to the rest of the novel that create sympathy for Han. Often these are humorous: for example, in *Lost Legacy*, Han wins a prize for best exemplifying the theme of a fair, "Fertility of the Soil, Challenge of the Sky," by outstunting his braggart temporary employer in an inferior ship carrying a cargo of fertilizer—which he releases directly over the open canopy of his employer's ship. A quest pattern is then set up, with a varying group of companions; a series of fast chases develop; and problems are solved by Han's survival skills of quick intelligence, adaptability, and skilled piloting, with important assistance from the robot crew members.

The continuity with *Star Wars* is excellent. Atmospheric technical terms are thrown around casually; aliens differ widely in physical structure and abilities, but sociological and psychological differences are not explored. Robots are self-aware and a source of humor, though the limitations are different from those in *Star Wars* : Blue Max is designed for electronic snooping capacity in limited space and so has no ability to move, but is hidden in the chest of the slow farm robot Bollux.

Tron is of little interest, a novelization of the Steven Lisberger screenplay. The film had value primarily for the special effects with lights in the gameboard of the Electronic World; even Daley's descriptive talent finds them hard to translate verbally, and characterization is so shallow that there seems to be little difference between the personalized programs and the human beings—in fact, that is part of the point. The plot is standard: defeat of an attempt to take over the world by controlling computer programs.

Daley's earliest published work, rich in promise, is the alternate universe Coramonde series, *The Doomfarers of Coramonde* and *The Starfollowers of Coramonde*. This world is structured on magic, but is accessible from Earth, and Earth weapons work there; an armored personnel carrier from Viet Nam is brought in to combat the dragon Chaffinch and rescue a sorceress from Hell. One character, Gill MacDonald, returns again to Coramonde and is a central character in the second novel; the typical Daley hero, though, is Springbuck, mild-mannered, nearsighted, and rightful heir to the throne of Coramonde, from which the evil sorcerer Yardiff Bey is attempting to displace him. Yardiff Bey in the second volume turns out to be the active agent for a still more evil group, the Five of Salamá, who in the last age betrayed world order and destroyed all but one fragment of the Lifetree, which must be found and replanted, while the combined armies defeat Salamá's armies and bring the de Courteneys' magic to bear on the Five. The difficulty is that while there are many good minor characterizations and vivid descriptions, the novels are too rich, with too many characters and incidents, for depth of characterization or theme, especially in the sequel.

A Tapestry of Magics is outstanding. The central character, Crassmor, is characterized in depth as the younger brother admiring a heroic older brother, guilty over the love that has developed between him and his brother's fiancée, Willow, and over the contribution that he feels he has made to his brother's death. In accepting his father's partial rejection that couples knighthood with a dangerous job on the borders, he matures, developing patience and enough cynicism to avoid risky missions or achieve them by the easiest possible means—an effective anti-hero. But the best point in the novel is the central symbol of the tapestry, woven by Willow and her father, which pictures the completed past and can predict and to some extent control the possibilities of the future. It also symbolizes the structure of the world: the Singularity is in touch with all worlds, real and fantasy, and attracts immigrants from all of them, a tapestry of magics that ranges from Nazis to troll-like glitches shipping tiles for the space shuttle to Dracula, Saynday (the Trickster), Heinlein's Rico from *Starship Troopers*, Di Cagliostro and the Eye in the Pyramid cult. There are also a substantial number of invented allusions, and the interweaving of the material into a pattern that exists in its own right is a considerable accomplishment.

—Marilyn K. Nellis

DANN, Jack. American. Born in Johnson City, New York, 15 February 1945. Educated at Hofstra University, Hempstead, New York, 1963; State University of New York, Binghamton, 1965-68, B. A. in social science and political science 1968; St. John's Law School, New York, 1969-71. Taught writing and science fiction at Broome Community College, Binghamton, 1972, and Cornell University, Ithaca, New York, summer 1973; Managing Editor, *SFWA Bulletin*, 1970-75. Free-lance writer and lecturer. Agent: Perry Knowlton, Curtis Brown Associates, 575 Madison Avenue, New York, New York 10022. Address: 71 Mill Street, Binghamton, New York, 13903, U. S. A.

SCIENCE-FICTION PUBLICATIONS

Novels

Starhiker. New York, Harper, 1977.
Junction. New York, Dell, 1981.
The Man Who Melted. New York, Bluejay, 1984.

Short Stories

Timetipping. New York, Doubleday, 1980.

Uncollected Short Stories

"Dark, Dark, the Dead Star," with George Zebrowski, in *If* (New York), July-August 1970.
"Listen, Love," with George Zebrowski, in *New Worlds Quarterly 2*, edited by Michael Moorcock. London, Sphere, and New York, Berkley, 1971.
"Trap," with George Zebrowski, in *Coming Through*, edited by

Nina C. Woessner and William D. Sheldon. Boston, Allyn and Bacon, 1972.
"Whirl Cage," in *Orbit 10*, edited by Damon Knight. New York, Putnam, 1972.
"I'm with You in Rockland," in *Strange Bedfellows*," edited by Thomas N. Scortia. New York, Random House, 1972.
"Tulpa," in *New Worlds 6*, edited by Michael Moorcock and Charles Platt. London, Sphere, 1973.
"Thirty-Three and One Third," with George Zebrowski, in *Long Night of Waiting and Other Stories*, edited by Roger Elwood. Nashville, Aurora, 1974.
"OD," with George Zebrowski, in *Omega*, edited by Roger Elwood. New York, Walker, 1974.
"The Flower That Missed the Morning" (for children), with George Zebrowski, in *The Killer Plants and Other Stories*, edited by Roger Elwood. Minneapolis, Lerner, 1974.
"The Good Old Days," in *Journey to Another Star and Other Stories*, edited by Roger Elwood. Minneapolis, Lerner, 1974.
"Faces Forward," with George Zebrowski, in *Dystopian Visions*, edited by Roger Elwood. Englewood Cliffs, New Jersey, Prentice Hall, 1975.
"Recycled Sandra," in *Gallery*, July 1975.
"Yellowhead," with George Zebrowski, in *New Constellations*, edited by Thomas M. Disch and Charles Naylor. New York, Harper, 1976.
"Limits," with Jack C. Haldeman, in *Fantastic* (New York), May 1976.
"The Dream Lions," in *Amazing* (New York), September 1976.
"The Islands of Time," in *Fantastic* (New York), September 1977.
"Amnesia," in *The Berkley Showcase 3*, edited by Victoria Schochet and John W. Silbersack. New York, Berkley, 1981.
"Fairy Tale," in *The Berkley Showcase 4*, edited by Victoria Schochet and John W. Silbersack. New York, Berkley, 1981.
"Parables of Art," with Barry N. Malzberg, in *New Dimensions 12*, edited by Marta Randall and Robert Silverberg. New York, Pocket Books, 1981.
"A Change in the Weather," with Gardner Dozois, in *Playboy* (Chicago), June 1981.
"Going Under," in *The Best Science Fiction of the Year 11*, edited by Terry Carr. New York, Pocket Books, 1982.
"Playing the Game," with Gardner Dozois, in *Great Stories from Rod Serling's The Twilight Zone Magazine*, edited by T. E. D. Klein. New York, TZ Publications, 1982.
"High Steel," with Jack C. Haldeman, in *Fantasy and Science Fiction* (New York), February 1982.
"Screamers," in *Oui* (New York), October 1982.
"Touring," with Gardner Dozois and Michael Swanwick, in *The Year's Best Horror Stories 11*, edited by Karl Edward Wagner. New York, DAW, 1983.
"Down among the Dead Men," with Gardner Dozois, in *The Dodd Mead Gallery of Horror*, edited by Charles L. Grant. New York, Dodd Mead, 1983.
"A Cold Day in the Mesozoic," in *Fears*, edited by Charles L. Grant. New York, Berkley, 1983.
"Reunion," in *Shadows 6*, edited by Charles L. Grant. New York, Doubleday, 1983.
"Slow Dancing with Jesus," with Gardner Dozois, in Penthouse (New York), July 1983.
"Time Bride," with Gardner Dozois, in *Isaac Asimov's Science Fiction Magazine* (New York), December 1983.
"Afternoon at Schrafft's," with Gardner Dozois and Michael Swanwick, in *Magicats!*, edited by Dann and Dozois. New York, Ace, 1984.
"Blind Shemmy," in *The Year's Best Science Fiction 1* edited by Gardner Dozois and Jim Frenkel. New York, Bluejay, 1984.

"Virgin Territory," with Gardner Dozois and Michael Swanwick, in *Penthouse* (New York), March 1984.
"Bad Medicine," in *Isaac Asimov's Science Fiction Magazine* (New York), October 1984.
"The Black Horn," in *Fantasy and Science Fiction* (New York), November 1984.
"The Gods of Mars," with Gardner Dozois and Michael Swanwick, in *Omni* (New York), March 1985.

OTHER PUBLICATIONS

Verse

Christs and Other Poems. Binghamton, New York, Bellevue Press, 1978.

Other

Introduction to *Showcase,* edited by Roger Elwood. New York, Harper, 1973.
"Fumfuttings and Prognostications," in *SFWA Bulletin* (Sea Cliff, New York), Fall 1974.
"The Science Fiction Novel," with Gardner Dozois, in *Fiction Writer's Handbook,* edited by Hallie and Whit Burnett. New York, Harper, 1975.

Editor, *Wandering Stars: An Anthology of Jewish Fantasy and Science Fiction*. New York, Harper, 1974; London, Woburn Press, 1975.
Editor, with Gardner Dozois, *Future Power*. New York, Random House, 1976.
Editor, with George Zebrowski, *Faster Than Light: An Anthology of Stories about Interstellar Travel*. New York, Harper, 1976.
Editor, *Immortal*. New York, Harper, 1978.
Editor, with Gardner Dozois, *Aliens!* New York, Pocket Books, 1980.
Editor, *More Wandering Stars*. New York, Doubleday, 1981.
Editor, with Gardner Dozois, *Unicorns!* New York, Ace, 1982.
Editor, with Gardner Dozois, *Magicats!* New York, Ace, 1984.

*

Manuscript Collection: Temple University, Philadelphia.

*   *   *

Jack Dann's fiction has until recently shown a notable unity in dramatic concern, elaborating at various lengths and moods what has been essentially a series of variations on a theme. Over 15 years, his three novels and several dozen shorter works have developed a recognizable figure in the solitary, obsessive young man whose disaffection with the stratified society he belongs to leads to a dramatic encounter with a larger strangeness that resonates in the telling with a powerful and sometimes disturbing psychic resonance.

Dann published his first fiction in 1970, and some of his characteristic concerns were seeing expression as early as in the 1971 "Windows," but it was not until the appearance of his 1973 novella "Junction" (basis for the later novel) that he began to dramatize his essential confrontation between consciousness and a mutable universe with a degree of assurance and skill. Dann's village of Junction, the last redoubt of causality following a catastrophe that disrupts physical laws to render the rest of Earth a region of physical indeterminacy, effectively embodies his theme of inertia roused by chaos, and the protagonist's journey into the surrounding "Hell" uses a conventional narrative to introduce provocative speculations on consciousness, metaphysics, and Teilhard de Chardin's concept of an evolving universe.

In 1975 two shorter works appeared that confirmed Dann as one of the most audacious and technically assured SF writers of the decade. "Timetipping," a deceptively whimsical short story that recalls Isaac Bashevis Singer at his more energetic, presents a situation similar to that of "Junction"—the world experiences a dissolution of temporal sequence that allows free and sometimes involuntary slippage through time—in a witty and kinetic display of stylistic virtuosity. It was, however, with his novelette "The Dybbuk Dolls" that Dann first showed all his strengths in a single story. Dann's dark tale of the invasion of a pious man's consciousness by an alien malevolence able to excite his sense of guilt stands as an exceptional example of SF's seminal theme, encountering the unknown, dramatized exclusively through one participant's point of view.

With his novel *Starhiker* Dann adopted the familiar folk tale of the young man who leaves his bucolic world for a journey of wonder, from which he ultimately returns bearing wisdom and power. Bo Forester's wanderings among the starlanes of a more advanced civilization are told in a dense, richly textured but dispassionate language that shows up one of the limitations of Dann's work until that time: the intense but narrow focus upon his protagonists leaves his other characterizations pallid, and allows no scope for portraying relationships. The novel version of *Junction*, which can be considered almost a companion piece, shows the same virtues and shortcomings.

Dann's celebrated novelette "Camps" can be seen as a culmination of this phase of his work. The story of the now-familiar young man who moves in delirium between hospital and a Nazi death camp accords equal weight to the movement of its "inner" and "outer" narratives, like two cycles turning on the same axis, and has in the healing synthesis of its resolution (the protagonist's deliverance from the death camp coincides with the break in his fever) something of the resonance of myth.

In the years since, Dann's writing has broadened in scope and sympathy, and *The Man Who Melted*, his longest and most ambitious novel, shows his past strengths while dealing, somewhat uncertainly, with the tortured relationships between his three protagonists. As the title suggests, the mutability of consciousness remains an essential theme, but both the protagonists' obsessive natures and the decadence of the society around them are portrayed more complexly and convincingly than before.

Recently published stories, as well as an excerpt from *Counting Coup*, a contemporary novel in progress, suggest that Dann's work is shifting from the trappings of genre SF to encompass that larger fantasy of which mundane fiction is essentially a subset. Standing at a watershed in his career, Dann remains one of the field's most accomplished story writers and promising novelists.

—Gregory Feeley

DARNAY, Arsen (Julius). American. Born in Budapest, Hungary, 31 July 1936; emigrated to the United States in 1953, naturalized, 1961. Attended Rockhurst College, Kansas City, Missouri, 1953, 1963; University of Maryland, College Park, 1959-60. Served in the United States Army, 1956-61. Married Brigitte Schulz; two daughters. Technical writer, J. F. Pritchard and Co., 1961-65, and program manager, Midwest

Research Institute, 1965-73, both in Kansas City; Deputy Assistant Administrator, Environmental Protection Agency, Washington, D. C., 1973-75; General Manager, Carborundum Company, McLean, Virginia, 1977-81. Since 1981, principal, Arsen Darnay and Associates, management consultants, Hopkins, Minnesota. Recipient: Environmental Protection Agency bronze medal, 1970, and silver medal, 1972. Agent: Kirby McCauley Ltd., 425 Park Avenue South, New York, New York 10016. Address: 23 West St. Albans Road, Hopkins, Minnesota 55343, U. S. A.

SCIENCE-FICTION PUBLICATIONS

Novels

A Hostage for Hinterland. New York, Ballantine, 1976.
The Karma Affair. New York, St. Martin's Press, 1978; as *Karma*, London, Sphere, 1980.
The Siege of Faltara. New York, Ace, 1978.
The Purgatory Zone. New York, Ace, 1981.

Short Stories

The Splendid Freedom. New York, Ace, 1980.

Uncollected Short Stories

"Such Is Fate," in *If* (New York), October 1974.
"The Politics of Patricide," in *Galaxy* (New York), March 1975.
"Gut in Peril," in *The Best from If 3*, edited by James Baen. New York, Award, 1976.
"Salty's Sweep," in *Stellar 3*, edited by Judy-Lynn del Rey. New York, Ballantine, 1977.
"The Mildews of Mars," in *Analog* (New York), January 1977.
"The Phermonal Fountain," in *Galaxy* (New York), August 1977.
"The Tank and Its Wife," in *Analog* (New York), January 1978.
"The Golden Fleece," in *Fantastic* (New York), April 1978.
"The Man Who Drove to Work," in *Analog* (New York), July 1978.
"The Pilgrimage of Ishten Telen Haragosh," in *New Voices 4*, edited by George R. R. Martin. New York, Berkley, 1981.
"Aspic's Mystery," in *Space Mail 2*, edited by Isaac Asimov, Martin H. Greenberg, and Charles G. Waugh. New York, Fawcett, 1982.

OTHER PUBLICATIONS

Other

The Role of Nonpackaging Paper in Solid Waste Management 1966 to 1976, with William E. Franklin. Rockville, Maryland, Solid Waste Management Office, 1971.
Salvage Markets for Materials in Solid Wastes, with William E. Franklin. Washington D. C., Environmental Protection Agency, 1972.
Recycling Assessment and Prospects for Success. Washington, D. C., Environmental Protection Agency, 1972.
"Through Innocent Eyes," in *Galaxy* (New York), January 1976.

*   *   *

Arsen Darnay's fiction first began to appear in 1974, a blend of fast-paced action with considerable original thinking, marred occasionally by superficial characterization and lapses of plot logic. Although he published several short stories, it is only at novelet length and greater that he has truly been successful.

"The Splendid Freedom" follows a young man on his adventures on Mother Earth during a visit which is to mark his passage into the adult world. He does not immediately discover that the surface of Earth is in fact uninhabitable, and that most of the things he has experienced during his visit were directly implanted in his mind and never happened at all. One of his best shorter pieces is "The Eastcoast Confinement. " North America is now a dictatorship, and all those who dissent are confined to large camps set up around the country. The inhabitants are allowed to govern themselves along the lines of Robert Heinlein's classic "Coventry," but the outside authorities limit food supplies in an attempt to reduce the dissident population, which is now approximately one of every three adults. The result is tribal warfare among various groups such as the Ecofreaks and Peacefreaks. A visitor from Europe is instrumental in altering things slightly so that the new type of culture arising within the Confinement will have a chance to succeed as a viable force in the future.

Perhaps the best of Darnay's novelets is "Plutonium," which was to start a series that was rewritten as the novel, *The Karma Affair*. In the shorter piece, two men and a woman meet in a Nazi concentration camp. Their souls are repeatedly reincarnated through the years until, in our own near future, reincarnation becomes an accepted scientific fact. One of the two men invents a soul catcher and establishes a priesthood to watch over nuclear wastes, each of whom will be tied to that job for eternity. The novel presents the ultimate crisis of that priesthood far in the future, when the rest of society has dissolved into a new barbarism.

A Hostage for Hinterland is set in a similar, or perhaps identical barbarous future. Society is split into two forces, the Structure Cities with their high technology and nuclear arsenals, and the Hinterland, nomadic tribes living under comparatively primitive circumstances. The cities use their weaponry to blackmail the Hinterlands into trading them the helium they need to run their equipment. But the tribes are not content to be the lesser partners, and plot to develop an umbrella against the missiles. Darnay works out the political maneuverings between the two powers and within the two camps convincingly, without interfering with his fast-paced plot. This was a quite promising adventure story to appear as a first novel.

The Purgatory Zone is not as successful. The Kibbutz Zone is a society that has renounced most forms of aggression and approximates what we would think of as Utopia. The occasional individual who cannot adjust is urged to travel to an alternate world, and the protagonist in this case emigrates to the Purgatory Zone, an alternate America where a vicious caste system makes life increasingly difficult for him. He is almost immediately on the run from the authorities and sets off on a chase adventure that is sometimes entertaining, but which falls apart toward the conclusion.

Darnay returned to barbarism of a sort in *The Siege of Faltara,* although this time the setting is another world, the planet Fillippi. It's a peaceful world, but peaceful because of the ruthless dictatorship that dominates it through the use of slavery and drugs that condition the mind to loyalty. The protagonist is an outside agent whose job is to destabilize the government and cause a revolution. Naturally he does, after a series of adventures, in a well-handled, above average adventure novel. Darnay established himself with five books as a progressively interesting writer, with some innovative ideas. He has had no new fiction published during the last four years, however, and may have turned to other pursuits.

—Don D'Ammassa

DAVIDSON, Avram. Also writes as Ellery Queen. American. Born in Yonkers, New York, 23 April 1923. Educated at New York University, 1940-42; Yeshiva University, New York, 1947-48; Pierce College, Canoga Park, California, 1950-51. Served in the United States Navy, 1942-46; served in the Israeli Army in the Arab-Israeli war, 1948-49. Married Grania Kaiman (divorced); one son. Editor, *Fantasy and Science Fiction* magazine, New York, 1962-64. Recipient: Hugo Award, 1958, for editing, 1963; Ellery Queen Award, 1958; Mystery Writers of America Edgar Allan Poe Award, 1961; World Fantasy Award, 1976, 1979. Agent: Carnell Literary Agency, Rowneybury Bungalow, Sawbridgeworth, near Old Harlow, Essex CM20 2EX, England.

SCIENCE-FICTION PUBLICATIONS

Novels

Joyleg, with Ward Moore. New York, Pyramid, 1962.
Mutiny in Space. New York, Pyramid, 1964; London, White Lion, 1973.
Rogue Dragon. New York, Ace, 1965.
Rork! New York, Berkley, 1965; London, Rapp and Whiting, 1968.
Masters of the Maze. New York, Pyramid, 1965; London, White Lion, 1974.
The Enemy of My Enemy. New York, Berkley, 1966.
Clash of Star-Kings. New York, Ace, 1966.
The Kar-Chee Reign. New York, Ace, 1966.
Ursus of Ultima Thule. New York, Avon, 1973.

Short Stories

Or All the Seas with Oysters. New York, Berkley, 1962; London, White Lion, 1976.
What Strange Stars and Skies. New York, Ace, 1965.
Strange Seas and Shores. New York, Doubleday, 1971.
The Enquiries of Dr. Eszterhazy. New York, Warner, 1975.
The Redward Edward Papers. New York, Doubleday, 1978.
The Best of Avram Davidson, edited by Michael Kurland. New York, Doubleday, 1979.
The Collected Fantasies of Avram Davidson, edited by John Silbersack. New York, Berkley, 1982.

Uncollected Short Stories

"The Sensible Man," in *The Playboy Book of Science Fiction and Fantasy*. Chicago, Playboy Press, 1960.
"No Fire Burns," in *The 5th Annual of the Year's Best S-F*, edited by Judith Merril. New York, Simon and Schuster, 1960.
"The Tenant," in *Shock* (New York), May 1960; revised version, in *Fantasy and Science Fiction* (New York), March 1971.
"Something Rich and Strange," with Randall Garrett, in

Fantasy and Science Fiction (New York), June 1961.
"The Blaze of Noon," with Randall Garrett, in *Analog* (New York), September 1961.
"Not a Boy Anymore," in *Harlequin*, August 1963.
"The Kappa Nu Nexus," with Morton Klass, in *13 Above the Night*, edited by Groff Conklin. New York, Dell, 1965.
"Mirror, Mirror," in *Fantasy and Science Fiction* (New York), October 1965.
"Basilisk," in *New Worlds of Fantasy 1*, edited by Terry Carr. New York, Ace, 1967.
"Bumberboom," in *World's Best Science Fiction 1967*, edited by Terry Carr and Donald A. Wollheim. New York, Ace, 1967.
"Quick with His Hands," in *Fantasy and Science Fiction* (New York), August 1967.
"The Roads, the Roads, the Beautiful Roads," in *Orbit 5*, edited by Damon Knight. New York, Putnam, 1969.
"They Loved Me in Utica," in *New Worlds of Fantasy 2*, edited by Terry Carr. New York, Ace, 1970.
"Big Sam," in *Alchemy and Academe*, edited by Anne McCaffrey. New York, Doubleday, 1970.
"Goslin Day," in *Orbit 6*, edited by Damon Knight. New York, Putnam, 1970.
"The Invasion," in *Playboy's Short-Shorts*. Chicago, Playboy Press, 1970.
"Timeserver," in *Galaxy* (New York), May 1970.
"Pebble in Time," with Cynthia Goldstone, in *Fantasy and Science Fiction* (New York), August 1970.
"Rite of Spring," in *Orbit 8*, edited by Damon Knight. New York, Putnam, 1971.
"Selectra Six-Ten," in *The Best from Fantasy and Science Fiction 19*, edited by Edward L. Ferman. New York, Doubleday, 1971.
"Basileikon! Summer," in *Quark 4*, edited by Samuel R. Delany and Marilyn Hacker. New York, Paperback Library, 1971.
"The Last Wizard," in *Ellery Queen's Mystery Magazine* (New York), December 1972.
"O Brave Old World," in *Beyond Time*, edited by Sandra Ley. New York, Pocket Books, 1976.
"And Don't Forget the One Red Rose," in *The Year's Best Horror Stories 4*, edited by Gerald Page. New York, DAW, 1976.
"Caravan to Illiel," in *Flashing Swords! 3*, edited by Lin Carter. New York, Doubleday, 1976.
"The Account of Mr. Ira Davidson," in *Fantasy and Science Fiction* (New York), May 1976.
"Bloody Man," in *Fantastic* (New York), August 1976.
"Hark! Was That the Squeal of an Angry Throat?," in *Fantastic* (New York), December 1977.
"Naples," in *Shadows 1*, edited by Charles L. Grant. New York, Doubleday, 1978.
"A Good Night's Sleep." in *Fantasy and Science Fiction* (New York), August 1978.
"The New Zombies," with Grania Davis, in *Interfaces*, edited by Ursula K. Le Guin and Virginia Kidd. New York, Ace, 1980.
"The Other Magus," in *Edges*, edited by Ursula K. Le Guin and Virginia Kidd. New York, Pocket Books, 1980.
"There Beneath the Silky-Trees and Whelmed in Deepest Gulphs Than Me," in *Other Worlds 2*, edited by Roy Torgeson. New York, Zebra, 1980.
"The Ape," in *Fantasy and Science Fiction* (New York), October 1981.
"Dr. Bhumbo Singh," in *Fantasy and Science Fiction* (New York), October 1982.

"Mexican Merry-Go-Round," in *Twilight Zone* (New York), October 1982.

"Buchanan's Head," in *Fantasy and Science Fiction* (New York), February 1983.

"The Hills Beyond Hollywood High," with Grania Davis, in *Fantasy and Science Fiction* (New York), April 1983.

"Full Chicken Richness," in *Last Wave* (New York), October 1983.

"Eszterhazy and the Autogó ndola-Invention," in *Amazing* (New York), November 1983.

"Dear Friend Charlene," with Grania Davis, in *Fantasy and Science Fiction* (New York), August 1984.

"The House Surgis Sword," in *Amazing* (New York), September 1984.

"Young Doctor Eszterhazy," in *Amazing* (New York), November 1984.

"Revenge of the Cat-Lady," in *Fantasy and Science Fiction* (New York), January 1985.

"Duke Pasquale's Ring," in *Amazing* (New York), May 1985.

OTHER PUBLICATIONS

Novels

And on the Eighth Day (as Ellery Queen). New York, Random House, 1964.

The Fourth Side of the Triangle (as Ellery Queen). New York, Random House, 1965.

The Island under the Earth. New York, Ace, 1969; London, Mayflower, 1975.

The Phoenix and the Mirror; or, The Enigmatic Speculum. New York, Doubleday, 1969; London, Mayflower, 1975.

Peregrine: Primus. New York, Walker, 1971.

Peregrine: Secundus. New York, Berkley, 1981.

Other

Crimes and Chaos (essays). Evanston, Illinois, Regency, 1962.

Editor, *Best from Fantasy and Science Fiction 12-14*. New York, Doubleday, 3 vols., 1963-65; London Gollancz, 2 vols., 1966; Panther, 1 vol., 1967.

Editor, *Magic for Sale*. New York, Ace, 1983.

*

Bibliography: "A Bibliography of Avram Davidson" by Richard Grant, in *Megavore 9* (Calgary, Alberta), June 1980.

Manuscript Collections: California State University, Fullerton; Texas A. and M. University, College Station.

*   *   *

Avram Davidson is primarily a writer of fantasy and fantasy SF. His best stories are comic or ironic, and he is also a master of the mystery and weird fantasy and SF story. In structure if not in style and thought, Davidson writes in the O. Henry tradition. But though his stories possess a familiar pattern of development, Davidson gives the impression of being unpredictable and eccentric. In part, this view may rest on Davidson's sometimes oblique method of developing his stories, deliberately omitting anticipated transitions so as to heighten contrasts and increase tension. It is a technique which a mystery writer may be expected to favour. It is particularly effective in his Hugo-winning story "Or All the Seas with Oysters," a tale based on the premise of the animated machine, in this case a red French racing bicycle, and the contrasting reactions of the two main characters to the discovery of such an alien being. The story has a finely developed sense of narrative irony, which is one of the characteristics of Davidson's best fiction.

A related type of science fantasy in Davidson's repertory is the comic tale rooted in Jewish humor. "The Golem" is a deservedly famous story in which Davidson combines comic formulas of traditional ethnic humor with an overlay of modern SF. The contrasting expectations of each tradition makes for the special comic sense of the story. Davidson also displays a fine talent for parody in such literary stories as "Author, Author," in which the reader is treated to some delicious echoes of the Asimov story of the same title as well as to a burlesque of the detective mystery/fantasy ending in a bitter-sweet reversal of poetic justice. Davidson takes his place as a writer of popular fantastic SF in the tradition that comes prominently to the surface with Poe and continues in the 20th century with Merritt, Lovecraft, and the *Weird Tales* and *Unknown* schools on the one hand, and such diverse writers of comic fantasy as Cabell and the Yiddish master Isaac Bashevis Singer on the other. In tone as well as intention, however, Davidson is closer to popular and even commercial pulp writers like L. Sprague de Camp and Fletcher Pratt than to either Poe and Cabell.

Davidson has also written many novels, some of which fall into familiar categories. There have been the SF pot boilers dealing with alien invaders, alternate universes, and other fantastic SF premises (*Masters of the Maze, Clash of Star-Kings, The Kar-Chee Reign*). Related to these are the space operas *Mutiny in Space, Rogue Dragon, Rork!*, and *The Enemy of My Enemy*. Of these, *Masters of the Maze* is clearly the most accomplished work. More successful have been the mock heroic fantasy *Peregrine: Primus* and the heroic romance fantasy *The Phoenix and the Mirror* (part of a projected series provisionally titled *Virgil Magus*). Both works are distinguished by a level of popular scholarship found in the Harold Shea stories of de Camp and Pratt. The wit and satire that animate the picaresque misadventures of Peregrine, bastard son of the King of Sapodilla, are absent from the more seriously intended *Phoenix and the Mirror*, and the latter romance suffers in consequence. Each, however, is notable for Davidson's attempt at introducing premises for romance that lie outside the familiar Christian traditions. Indeed, Davidson's invention and treatment are intended to be contrary to Christian-oriented legends, offering the reader an unspoken but also an unmistakable dissent from the tradition that has dominated heroic fantasy since the middle ages. It is too bad that it does not work.

Perhaps the most curious of all Davidson's fantasy prose fictions is *The Enquiries of Dr. Eszterhazy*, a collection of linked stories in which the master detective and doctor of everthing, Engelbert Eszterhazy, stands in as the amused and amusing hero of a series of mysterious affairs taking place in and about the fictitious triune monarchy of Sythia-Panmonia-Transbalkania. Curiously, it seems that Davidson's experimental form of blending the internal narrative context of fantasy with the quite external tone and view point of the implied modern narrator is responsible for the failure of the book to win either the popular support or the critical acclaim it deserves. The book seems destined to enjoy the status of underground classic, as a fantastic parody of the detective story that will serve to identify cognescenti among readers and those with a refined if still largely popular taste for the deliberately fantastic and artificial.

—Donald L. Lawler

DAVIES, L(eslie) P(urnell). Also writes as Leslie Vardre. British. Born in Crewe, Cheshire, 20 October 1914. Educated at Manchester College of Science and Technology, University of Manchester, qualified as optometrist 1939 (Fellow, British Optical Association). Served in the British Army Medical Corps in France, North Africa, and Italy, 1939-45. Married Winifred Tench in 1940. Dispensing pharmacist, Crewe, Cheshire, 1930-39; free-lance artist in Rome, 1945-46; postmaster, West Heath, Birmingham, 1946-56; optician in private practice, and gift shop owner, Deganwy, North Wales, 1956-75. Since 1975, has lived in Tenerife. Agent: Howard Moorepark, 444 East 82nd Street, New York, New York 10028, U.S.A.; or, Carl Routledge, Charles Lavell Ltd., 176 Wardour Street, London W1V 3AA, England. Address: Apartment K-1, Edificio Alondra, El Botanico, Puerto de la Cruz, Tenerife, Canary Islands, Spain.

SCIENCE-FICTION PUBLICATIONS

Novels

The Paper Dolls. London, Jenkins, 1964; New York, Doubleday, 1966.
Man Out of Nowhere. London, Jenkins, 1965; as *Who Is Lewis Pindar?,* New York, Doubleday, 1966.
The Artificial Man. London, Jenkins, 1965; New York, Doubleday, 1967.
The Lampton Dreamers. London, Jenkins, 1966; New York, Doubleday, 1967.
Psychogeist. London, Jenkins, 1966; New York, Doubleday, 1967.
Twilight Journey. London, Jenkins, 1967; New York, Doubleday, 1968.
The Alien. London, Jenkins, 1968; New York, Doubleday, 1971; as *The Groundstar Conspiracy,* London, Sphere, 1972.
Dimension A. London, Jenkins, and New York, Doubleday, 1969.
Genesis Two. London, Jenkins, 1969; New York, Doubleday, 1970.
What Did I Do Tomorrow? London, Barrie and Jenkins, 1972; New York, Doubleday, 1973.

Uncollected Short Stories

"The Wall of Time" (as Leslie Vardre), in *London Mystery Magazine,* June 1960.
"End Game," in *The Tenth Ghost Book,* edited by Aidan Chambers. London, Barrie and Jenkins, 1975.

OTHER PUBLICATIONS

Novels

Tell It to the Dead (as Leslie Vardre). London, Long, 1966; as *The Reluctant Medium* (as L. P. Davies), New York, Doubleday, 1967.
The Nameless Ones (as Leslie Vardre). London, Long, 1967; as

A Grave Matter (as L. P. Davies), New York, Doubleday, 1968.
Stranger to Town. London, Jenkins, and New York, Doubleday, 1969.
The White Room. New York, Doubleday, 1969; London, Barrie and Jenkins, 1970.
Adventure Holidays Ltd. New York, Doubleday 1970.
The Shadow Before. New York, Doubleday, 1970; London, Barrie and Jenkins, 1971.
Give Me Back Myself. New York, Doubleday, 1971; London, Barrie and Jenkins, 1972.
Silvermannen (in Swedish; The Silver Man). Stockholm, Wahlströms, 1972.
Assignment Abacus. London, Barrie and Jenkins, and New York, Doubleday, 1975.
Possession. London, Hale, and New York, Doubleday, 1976.
The Land of Leys. New York, Doubleday, 1979; London, Hale, 1980.
Morning Walk. London, Hale, 1983.

*   *   *

Combining suspense, mystery, and science fiction, L. P. Davies's hybrid novels reflect his own variegated background. His first novel, *The Paper Dolls,* was praised by Anthony Boucher (in *The New York Times*) as a "vigorous man-against-the-unknown adventure story, with touches of horror all the more effective for their being underplayed. "

The Artificial Man begins with a quiet English village, a mild-mannered science-fiction writer, and pleasant townsfolk—all of which soon proves monstrously illusory. The placement of SF and suspense motifs within a commonplace setting lends itself easily to cinematic treatment, and the book was filmed as *Project X.*

The key to L. P. Davies's technique is that neither reader nor characters can ever be sure whether memories and dreams are portents, flashbacks, or messages from other worlds and times. The psychological, supernatural, and psychokinetic overlap, revealing unexpected horror and dangers lurking at the fringes of the mind. Ordinary events and situations are turned inside out to disclose terrible secrets. Because Davies plays fast-and-loose with SF and mystery conventions, a novel like *The Alien* that seems to involve extra-terrestrials actually turns out to be a whodunnit, while an apparently gothic mystery like Psychogeist can be rationalized as speculative science fiction.

Since plot and suspense are everything in Davies's work, discussion of his novels must be sketchy lest their endings be given away. *Psychogeist* concerns a man whose bizarre dreams about the planet Andrida have frightening consequences. In *Dimension A* a young man follows his scientist uncle into a parallel world where the seemingly primitive Toparians and the mind-reading Vorteds compete for survival—and have designs on earth. In *Genesis Two* an outing in the Lake Country becomes a terrifying voyage into a steamy tropical jungle, man's last refuge after technological disaster. All of these novels include murder and intrigue.

Although Davies is not a particularly stimulating or innovative writer, his fusions of SF and suspense result in competent thrillers that are as hard to put down as they are to take seriously.

—Anthony Manousos

DAVIS, (Horace) Chan(dler). American. Born in Ithaca, New

York, 12 August 1926. Educated at Harvard University, Cambridge, Massachusetts, B. S. 1945, M. A. 1947, Ph. D. in mathematics 1950. Served in the United States Naval Reserve, 1944-46. Married Natalie Zemon in 1948; one son and two daughters. Instructor in mathematics, University of Michigan, Ann Arbor, 1950-54; Director of Experimental Research, Kenyon and Eckhardt advertising company, New York, 1955-57; Associate Editor, *Mathematical Reviews,* Providence, Rhode Island, 1958-61. Since 1962, Associate Professor, then Professor of Mathematics, University of Toronto. Served six month prison sentence for refusing to answer questions before the House Un-American Activities Committee, 1960. Member of the Institute for Advanced Study, Princeton, New Jersey, 1957-58. Agent: Virginia Kidd, Box 278, Milford, Pennsylvania 18337, U. S. A. Address: 52 Follis Avenue, Toronto M6G 1S3, Canada.

SCIENCE-FICTION PUBLICATIONS

Uncollected Short Stories

"To Still the Drums," in *Astounding* (New York), October 1946.
"The Journey and the Goal," in *Astounding* (New York), May 1947.
"The Nightmare," in *A Treasury of Science Fiction,* edited by Groff Conklin. New York, Crown, 1948.
"The Aristocrat," in *Astounding* (New York), October 1949.
"Blind Play," in *Planet* (New York), May 1951.
"Share Our World," in *Astounding* (New York), August 1953.
"Letter to Ellen," in *Science Fiction Thinking Machines,* edited by Groff Conklin. New York, Vanguard Press, 1954.
"It Walks in Beauty," in *Star Science Fiction Stories 4,* edited by Frederik Pohl. New York, Ballantine, 1958.
"The Statistomat Pitch," in *Infinity* (New York) January 1958.
"Adrift on the Policy Level," in *Star Science Fiction Stories 5,* edited by Frederik Pohl. New York, Ballantine, 1959.
"Last Year's Grave Undug," in *Great Science Fiction by Scientists,* edited by Groff Conklin. New York, Macmillan, 1962.
"Hexamnion," in *Nova 1,* edited by Harry Harrison. New York, Delacorte Press, 1970.

*

Chan Davis comments:
There is so much that needs saying about our real and impending predicaments and ironies, and science fiction allows one to say it in ways less bogged down in the past—given this opportunity, why should the writer reject it by producing stories which merely ask the reader to suspend disbelief? One can comment by parables set on concocted planets; byextrapolations; or, most powerfully, by the "higher cautionary tale," in which a potentiality in our own future is brought into relief by magnifying it. No escape is offered, but engagement. Some suspension of disbelief is required, but not suspension of compassion, not suspension of curiosity or common sense. Let this note stand as introduction to the few stories I wrote in my youth and the many I wish yet to write.

*   *   *

Chan Davis had produced a small number of superior stories, beginning with "The Nightmare," one of the first post-Hiroshima science-fiction works to focus on the dangers and effects of nuclear war. Although he is a mathematician, most of his stories either explicitly or implicitly examine social themes. Other notable stories include "Adrift on the Policy Level," arguably the finest treatment of bureaucracy and the bureaucratic mind in all of science fiction, and "Letter to Ellen," which, because of a very superficial thematic resemblance to the earlier "Helen O'Loy" by Lester del Rey, never attained the classic sature due it.

—Martin H. Greenberg

———————

DAVIS, Gerry. Address: c/o W. H. Allen, 44 Hill Street, London W1X 8LB, England.

SCIENCE-FICTION PUBLICATIONS

Novels with Kit Pedler

Mutant 59, The Plastic Eater. London, Souvenir Press, 1971; New York, Viking Press, 1972.
Brainrack. London, Souvenir Press, 1974; New York, Pocket Books, 1975.
The Dynostar Menace. London, Souvenir Press, and New York, Scribner, 1975.

Novels (series: Doctor Who)

Doctor Who and the Cybermen. London, Target, 1974.
Doctor Who and the Tenth Planet. London, Target, 1976.
Doctor Who and the Tomb of the Cybermen. London, W. H. Allen, 1978.

OTHER PUBLICATIONS

Plays with Kit Pedler

Television Plays: *Doctor Who* series (3 plays); *Doomwatch* series (39 plays); *Galenforce.*

See the essay on Kit Pedler.

———————

de CAMP, L(yon) Sprague. American. Born in New York City, 27 November 1907. Educated at Trinity School, New York; Snyder School, North Carolina; California Institute of Technology, Pasadena, B. S. in aeronautical engineering 1930; Massachusetts Institute of Technology, Cambridge, summer 1932; Stevens Institute of Technology, Hoboken, New Jersey, M. S. 1933. Served in the United States Naval Reserve, 1942-45: Lieutenant Commander. Married Catherine A. Crook in 1939; two sons. Instructor, Inventors Foundation Inc., New York, 1933-36; Principal of School of Inventing and Patenting, International Correspondence Schools, Scranton, Pennsylvania, 1936-37; Editor, Fowler-Becker Publishing Company, New York, 1937-38, and American Society of Mechanical Engineers, New York, 1938; Assistant Mechanical Engineer, Naval Aircraft Factory, Philadelphia, 1942; radio scriptwriter, *The Voice of America* series, 1948-56; publicity writer, Gray and Rogers, Philadelphia, 1956. Free-lance writer. Member of the Advisory Board, Society for the History of Technology. Recipient: International Fantasy Award, 1953; Gandalf Award, 1976; Grand Master Nebula Award, 1978; World Fantasy Life Achievement Award, 1984. Address: 278 Hothorpe Lane, Villanova, Pennsylvania 19085, U.S.A.

SCIENCE-FICTION PUBLICATIONS

Novels (series: Viagens Interplanetarias)

Lest Darkness Fall. New York, Holt, 1941; London, Heinemann, 1955.
Divide and Rule. Reading, Pennsylvania, Fantasy Press, 1948.
Genus Homo, with P. Schuyler Miller. Reading, Pennsylvania, Fantasy Press, 1950.
Rogue Queen (Viagens). New York, Doubleday, 1951; London, Pinnacle, 1954.
Cosmic Manhunt (Viagens). New York, Ace, 1954; as *A Planet Called Krishna,* London, Compact, 1966; as *The Queen of Zamba,* New York, Davis, 1977.
The Tower of Zanid (Viagnes). New York, Avalon, 1958.
The Glory That Was. New York, Avalon, 1960.
The Search for Zei (Viagens). New York, Avalon, 1962; as *The Floating Continent,* London, Compact, 1966.
The Hand of Zei (Viagens). New York, Avalon, 1963.
The Hostage of Zir. New York, Berkley, 1977.
The Great Fetish. New York, Doubleday, 1978.
The Prisoner of Zhamanak (Viagens). Huntington Woods, Michigan, Phantasia Press, 1982.
The Bones of Zora (Viagens), with Catherine Crook de Camp. Huntington Woods, Michigan, Phantasia Press, 1983.

Short Stories

The Wheels of If. Chicago, Shasta, 1948.
The Continent Makers and Other Tales of the Viagens. New York, Twayne, 1953.
Sprague de Camp's New Anthology of Science Fiction. London, Panther, 1953.
A Gun for Dinosaur and Other Imaginative Tales. New York, Doubleday, 1963.
The Best of L. Sprague de Camp. New York, Doubleday, 1977.

OTHER PUBLICATIONS

Novels

The Incomplete Enchanter, with Fletcher Pratt. New York, Holt, 1941; London, Sphere, 1979.
Land of Unreason, with Fletcher Pratt. New York, Holt, 1942.
The Carnelian Cube, with Fletcher Pratt. New York, Gnome Press, 1948.
The Castle of Iron, with Fletcher Pratt. New York, Gnome Press, 1950.
The Undesired Princess. Los Angeles, Fantasy, 1951.
Solomon's Stone. New York, Avalon, 1957.
The Return of Conan, with Björn Nyberg. New York, Gnome Press, 1957; as *Conan the Avenger,* New York, Lancer, 1968.
An Elephant for Aristotle. New York, Doubleday, 1958; London, Dobson, 1966.
Wall of Serpents, with Fletcher Pratt. New York, Avalon, 1960.
The Bronze God of Rhodes. New York, Doubleday, 1960.
The Dragon of the Ishtar Gate. New York, Doubleday, 1961.
The Arrows of Hercules. New York, Doubleday, 1965.

Conan the Conqueror, with Robert E. Howard. New York, Lancer, 1967.
Conan of the Isles, with Lin Carter. New York, Lancer 1968.
The Goblin Tower. New York, Pyramid, 1968; London, Sphere, 1979.
The Golden Wind. New York, Doubleday, 1969.
The Clocks of Iraz. New York, Pyramid, 1971.
Conan the Buccaneer, with Lin Carter. New York, Lancer, 1971.
The Fallible Fiend. New York, New American Library, 1973; London, Remploy, 1974.
The Compleat Enchanter: The Magical Adventures of Harold Shea (includes *The Incomplete Enchanter* and *The Castle of Iron*), with Fletcher Pratt. New York, Doubleday, 1975; London, Sphere, 1979.
The Virgin and the Wheels. New York, Popular Library, 1976.
Conan the Liberator, with Lin Carter. New York, Bantam, 1979; London, Sphere, 1980.
Conan and the Spider God. New York, Bantam, 1980; London, Hale, 1984.
Conan the Barbarian (novelization of screenplay), with Lin Carter. New York, Bantam, and London, Sphere, 1982.
The Unbeheaded King. New York, Ballantine, 1983.

Short Stories

Tales from Gavagan's Bar, with Fletcher Pratt. New York, Twayne, 1953; expanded edition, Philadelphia, Owlswick Press, 1978.
The Tritonian Ring and Other Pusadian Tales. New York, Twayne, 1953; London, Sphere, 1978.
Conan the Adventurer, with Robert E. Howard. New York, Lancer, 1966.
Conan the Warrior, with Robert E. Howard. New York, Lancer, 1967.
Conan the Usurper, with Robert E. Howard. New York, Lancer, 1967.
Conan the Freebooter, with Robert E. Howard. New York, Lancer, 1968; London, Sphere, 1974.
Conan the Wanderer, with Robert E. Howard and Lin Carter. New York, Lancer, 1968; London, Sphere, 1974.
Conan of Cimmeria, with Robert E. Howard and Lin Carter. New York, Lancer, 1969; London, Sphere, 1974.
The Reluctant Shaman and Other Fantastic Tales. New York, Pyramid, 1970.
Conan of Aquilonia (collection), with Lin Carter. New York, Lancer, 1971.
Conan the Swordsman, with Lin Carter and Björn Nyberg. New York, Bantam, 1978; London, Sphere, 1979.
The Purple Pterodactyls. Huntington Woods, Michigan, Phantasia Press, 1979.

Verse

Demons and Dinosaurs. Sauk City, Wisconsin, Arkham, House, 1970.
Phantoms and Fancies. Baltimore, Mirage Press, 1972.

Other

Inventions and Their Management, with Alf K. Berle. Scranton, Pennsylvania, International Textbook Company, 1937; revised edition, as *Inventions, Patents, and Their Management,* Princeton, New Jersey, Van Nostrand, 1959.
The Evolution of Naval Weapons. Washington, D. C., Department of the Navy, 1947.

Lands Beyond, with Willy Ley. New York, Rinehart, 1952.

Science-Fiction Handbook: The Writing of Imaginative Fiction. New York, Hermitage House, 1953; revised edition, with Catherine Crook de Camp, Philadelphia, Owlswick Press, 1975.

Lost Continents: The Atlantis Theme in History, Science, and Literature. New York, Gnome Press, 1954.

Engines (for children). New York, Golden Press, 1959; revised edition, 1961, 1969.

The Heroic Age of American Invention. New York, Doubleday, 1961.

Man and Power (for children). New York, Golden Press, 1961.

Energy and Power (for children). New York, Golden Press, 1962.

The Ancient Engineers. New York, Doubleday, and London, Souvenir Press, 1963.

Ancient Ruins and Archaeology, with Catherine Crook de Camp. New York, Doubleday, 1964; London, Souvenir Press, 1965; as *Citadels of Mystery*, London, Fontana, 1972.

Elephant. New York, Pyramid, 1964.

Spirits, Stars, and Spells: The Profits and Perils of Magic, with Catherine Crook de Camp. New York, Canaveral Press, 1966.

The Story of Science in America, with Catherine Crook de Camp. New York, Scribner, 1967.

The Great Monkey Trial. New York, Doubleday, 1968.

The Conan Reader. Baltimore, Mirage Press, 1968.

The Day of the Dinosaur, with Catherine Crook de Camp. New York, Doubleday, 1968.

Darwin and His Great Discovery (for children), with Catherine Crook de Camp. New York, Macmillan, 1972.

Scribblings. Cambridge, Massachusetts, NESFA Press, 1972.

Great Cities of the Ancient World. New York, Doubleday, 1972.

"Up and Away from the School of Invention: The Development of a Science Fiction Writer," In *Foundation 4 (London), July 1973.*

The Miscast Barbarian: A Biography of Robert E. Howard (1906-1936). Saddle River, New Jersey, de la Ree, 1975.

Blond Barbarians and Noble Savages (essays). Baltimore, T-K Graphics, 1975.

Lovecraft: A Biography. New York, Doubleday, 1975; London, New English Library, 1976.

Literary Swordsmen and Sorcerers: The Makers of Heroic Fantasy. Sauk City, Wisconsin, Arkham House, 1976.

Heroes and Hobgoblins. Forest Park, California, Heritage Press, 1978.

The Ragged Edge of Science. Philadelphia, Owlswick Press, 1980.

Dark Valley Destiny: The Life of Robert E. Howard, with Catherine Crook de Camp and Jane Whittington Griffin. New York, Bluejay, 1983.

The Fringe of the Unknown. Buffalo, Prometheus, 1983.

Editor, *The Wolf Leader*, by Alexander Dumas. Philadelphia, Prime Press, 1950.

Editor, *Swords and Sorcery.* New York, Pyramid, 1963.

Editor, *The Spell of Seven.* New York, Pyramid, 1965.

Editor, *The Fantastic Swordsmen.* New York, Pyramid, 1967.

Editor, with George H. Scithers, *The Conan Swordbook.* Baltimore, Mirage Press, 1969.

Editor, *Warlocks and Warriors.* New York, Putnam, 1970.

Editor, with George H. Scithers, *The Conan Grimoire.* Baltimore, Mirage Press, 1972.

Editor, with Catherine Crook de Camp, *3000 Years of Fantasy and Science Fiction.* New York, Lothrop, 1972.

Editor, with Catherine Crook de Camp, *Tales Beyond Time.* New York, Lothrop, 1973.

Editor, *To Quebec and the Stars*, by H. P. Lovecraft. West Kingston, Rhode Island, Donald M. Grant, 1976.

Editor, *The Blade of Conan* (articles). New York, Ace, 1979.

Editor, with others, *Footprints on Sand: A Literary Sampler.* Chicago, Advent, 1981.

*

Bibliography: *De Camp: An L. Sprague de Camp Bibliography* by Charlotte Laughlin and Daniel J. H. Levack, Columbia, Pennsylvania, Underwood Miller, 1983.

Manuscript Collection: Mugar Memorial Library, Boston University.

*   *   *

L. Sprague de Camp's earliest SF story, "The Isolinguals," embodies an interesting concept (modern folk suddenly begin to speak and act like their remote ancestors), but is rather disjointed. Other very early stories are minor. However, by 1939 he had clearly hit his stride, first with "Divide and Rule" and, most especially, with his first novel, *Lest Darkness Fall.* Other worthwhile stories from this period include the Johnny Black series, about an intelligent talking bear (this series ran out quickly because, as de Camp has explained, in the first story Johnny Black saved the world; by the fourth story, he merely saved his boss's job; there was nowhere to go); "The Merman," a scientifically rigorous account of the problems faced by a man who is able to breathe water; and "The Gnarly Man" about an immortal Neanderthal found working in a circus sideshow.

Lest Darkness Fall is one of de Camp's most famous works, now a classic. It achieved the distinction, unusual for pulp material of the period, of being published as a book by a large publisher. *Lest Darkness Fall*, far superior to the usual run of 1939 pulp fiction, is essentially a realistic *Connecticut Yankee*, in which a modern man finds himself in the real 6th century (not that of legend, as Twain used) and takes it upon himself to prevent the Dark Ages. He succeeds in a manner which will surprise most readers. De Camp apparently did a great deal of thinking about how such a man would fit in and make his way in the society of post-Imperial Rome, and what 20th-century marvels he would actually be able to produce in such a milieu (it starts with double-entry book-keeping). The characterization in the novel is also far superior to that in most SF of the period. Though his characters don't involve the reader intensely, they are not one-dimensional stereotypes; it is possible to sit back and watch, and believe that these are real people.

Typical features of de Camp's best fiction, as demonstrated in *Lest Darkness Fall*, are intelligent conception and development, and an enormously readable style. The intent in most of his fiction seems to be to provide light but not insubstantial entertainment, and he succeeds at a high level of sophistication. Most of his works also display a lively wit, which at times leads him to somewhat formless stories filled with jokes for their own sake, rather in the manner of P. G. Wodehouse or Thorne Smith (whom de Camp acknowledges as a major influence).

Humor is particularly evident in his collaborations with Fletcher Pratt, especially the Harold Shea series. Of these, *The Incomplete Enchanter* is probably de Camp's best-known work. The hero is a psychologist who has found a way to transport himself into the worlds of myth. In "The Roaring Trumpet" he encounters the Norse gods. In "The Mathematics of Magic" he battles the enchanters of Spenser's *Faerie Queene*. Again, the development is rigorously logical, but the premises are impossible. Much of the humor results from the incongruity. Other stories in this series include *The Castle of Iron* (the world of *Orlando Furioso*), "The Wall of Serpents" (the *Kalevala*), and "The Green Magician" (the Ireland of Cuchulain).

Other collaborations with Pratt are less successful. The Gavagan's Bar series are in the manner of Lord Dunsany's Jorkens, with each tale told in a bar, usually by one of a regular round of customers, but the stories tend to stop just as the fantastic premise is presented. Thus they are exactly as good as the idea, which makes them uneven and rather anecdotal.

De Camp ceased writing during World War II, and published very little fiction until "The Animal Cracker Plot" in 1949. This, while rather slight in itself, was the first of the Viagens Interplanetarias series, which constitute the largest body of his science fiction. The common background involves a Brazilian-dominated world, which causes Portuguese to be the language of space travel. The stories vary widely in complexity and intent. "Calories," for instance, makes a specific scientific point, that meat-eating is far more fuel efficient than vegetarianism. Thus the hero is able to escape across a glacier from vegetarian foes because he is able to carry more food than they are. *Cosmic Manhunt* and *The Hand of Zei* are swashbuckling adventures, something of an attempt to do an Edgar Rice Burroughs type of story plausibly. *Rogue Queen*, the most notable of the group, involves a rigid matriarchy patterned after bees. It is one of the earliest SF stories in which sex roles play any important part, though a modern feminist would hardly be pleased. All these stories move briskly and give a good idea of how the various societies work without stopping to lecture the reader at length. There are countless small details which add versimilitude.

De Camp continued to write science fiction until about 1960. Outstanding storied from this period include "A Thing of Custom," "Aristotle and the Gun," and "A Gun for a Dinosaur." However, he devoted most of his efforts during this period, and in the following decade, to historical novels and scientific non-fiction. He returned to fantasy with his renewed involvement in the Conan series of Robert E. Howard, and in the 1960's he edited the entire series. As a result Howard became one of the most popular authors in English. Credit must be given to de Camp for creating the sword and sorcery boom of the period. During this time he completed more Howard fragments, sometimes in collaboration with Lin Carter, and wrote new Conan stories. These pleased some fans and displeased others, possibly because de Camp, a far more rational and experienced person, was never able to ·match Howard's psychotic intensity or narrowness of outlook. His own sword and sorcery fiction, *The Tritonian Ring, The Goblin Tower*, and *The Clocks of Iraz*, are more sophisticated, with frequent humorous touches.

In the 1970's de Camp got away from Conan and wrote another Viagens Novel, *The Hostage of Zir*, and the "Willy Newbury" series, about a banker whose humdrum life is constantly being interrupted by supernatural occurrences. The best of these make skillful use of autobiographical material. The most successful work of this period is *The Great Fetish*, enormously readable, full of fascinating situations, and enlivened with satire. For example, the schoolteacher hero, before his wife runs off with a man he must then hunt down and kill because his society expects nothing less from him, is in trouble with the authorities for *not* teaching evolution. The heresy is that the world is a lost colony of Earth. This turns out to be true.

In de Camp's fiction human foibles and pretenses are prominently displayed, but rational, sensible types always

prevail. If there is any message, it is that reason is the only effective way to solve problems. A de Camp hero never gets anywhere until he starts using his head. Then the results surprise everyone, particularly the reader.

Since 1981 de Camp has published two science fiction novels, both in the Krishna/Viagens series, *The Prisoner of Zhamanak* and *The Bones of Zora*, the latter a collaboration with his wife. Both might be described (as well might the entire series) as what might have resulted if P. G. Wodehouse had written John Carter of Mars. De Camp states in the introduction to *Zhamanak* that his original intention was to write something akin to the Burroughs Mars books, only on a more sophisticated level, without the gross implausibilities. The result is a kind of anti-romantic sword-and-planet fiction, the typical de Campian swashbuckler being a world-wise (but not bitter or cynical) middle-aged Earthperson with marital problems, and tendency toward pedantry, and more interest in staying alive and getting the job done than in dashing heroics. The very capable but bull-headed Alicia Dyckman, whose rescue sets off the hijinks in *Zhamanak*, is perpetually in trouble with the backward Krishnas for preaching science and rationalism and otherwise fomenting what passes locally as heresy. Her rescuer, Percy Mjipa, is an equally capable but somewhat prudish African, who often must overcome his own prejudices to get out of tight spots. The two do not get along. By the time of the action of *The Bones of Zora*, Fergus Reith, the hero of the former novel, *The Hostage of Zir*, has already married and divorced Dyckman. The alien Krishnans aren't very romantic either. Their governments are thick with bureaucracies, the absurdities of which often entangle Earthpeople. They are given to rigid dogmatism and superstition, just like medieval humans. Their petty rulers, who often have large egos, take an unhealthy interest in human reproductive processes.

On a more serious level, both of these novels are about the folly of belief held so strongly that all contrary evidence is ignored. The Krishnans persecute heretics. One ruler, Vuzhov the Visionary (in *Zhamanak*) bankrupts his country trying to build a Krishnan Tower of Babel. Vuzhov is a devotee of the flat-Krishna theory, even though he knows the humans come from outer space. The tower is an attempt to reach heaven and put himself on a level with the gods.

The Bones of Zora deals with rival paleontologists out for a dig in a remote region of Krishna. Their vicious conflict is based on the feud between Cope and Marsh, which de Camp chronicles in his non-fiction book, *The Fringe of the Unknown*. The humans come across fully as narrow-minded and absurd as the Krishnans. *Zora* is the weaker of the two. The significance of the bones everyone is chasing after is not made clear enough, and the resolution is unsatisfactory. However there are still amusing moments and effective bits of satire, and we may hope that the loose ends will be tied up in the as yet unpublished sequel, *The Knights of Zingiban*.

Actually, de Camp's best fiction published during this period is a fantasy novel, *The Unbeheaded King*, the conclusion of the trilogy of Jorian, the reluctant monarch whose previous adventures were chronicled in *The Goblin Tower* and *The Clock of Iraz*. It is a thoroughly amusing, very inventive book which shows de Camp in top form.

Related non-fiction during this period includes two collections of science essays, *The Ragged Edge of Science* and *The Fringe of the Unknown*, and the definitive biography of the creator of Conan the Barbarian, *Dark Valley Destiny: The Life and Death of Robert E. Howard* (in collaboration with Catherine C. de Camp and Jane Whittington Griffin).

—Darrell Schweitzer

deFORD, Miriam Allen. American, Born in Philadelphia, Pennsylvania, 21 August 1888. Educated at Wellesley College, Massachusetts; Temple University, Philadelphia, A. B. 1911; University of Pennsylvania, Philadelphia. Married 1) Armistead Collier in 1915 (divorced, 1921); 2) Maynard Shipley in 1921 (died, 1934). Feature writer, Philadelphia *North American,* 1906-11; editorial staff member, Associated Advertising, 1913-14; editor of house organ, Pompeiian Oil Company, Baltimore, 1917; claims adjuster, 1918-23; staff correspondent, Federated Press, 1921-56; editor, Federal Writers Project, 1936-39; staff correspondent, *Labor's Daily,* California, 1956-58; contributing editor, *The Humanist.* Lecturer and Member of the Board, San Francisco Senior Citizens Center, 1952-58. Member of the Board, Mystery Writers of America, 1960, 1963. Recipient: Committee for Economic Development Essay Prize, 1958; Mystery Writers of America Edgar Allan Poe Award, 1961. *Died 22 March 1975.*

SCIENCE-FICTION PUBLICATIONS

Short Stories

Xenogenesis. New York, Ballantine, 1969.
Elsewhere, Elsewhen, Elsehow: Collected Stories. New York, Walker, 1971.

Uncollected Short Stories

"Vooremp, Spy," in *Infinity 3,* edited by Robert Hoskins. New York, Lancer, 1972.
"Lone Warrior," in *Two Views of Wonder,* edited by Thomas N. Scortia and Chelsea Quinn Yarbro. New York, Ballantine, 1973.
"A Way Out," in *The Alien Condition,* edited by Stephen Goldin. New York, Ballantine, 1973.
"5,000,000 A. D.," in *Future City,* edited by Roger Elwood. New York, Simon and Schuster, 1973.
"Uraguyen and I," with Juanita Coulson, in *Cassandra Rising,* edited by Alice Laurance. New York, Doubleday, 1978.
"Murder in Green," in *Nature's Revenge,* edited by Seon Manley. New York, Lothrop, 1978.

OTHER PUBLICATIONS

Novel

Shaken with the Wind. New York, Doubleday, 1942.

Short Stories

The Theme Is Murder: An Anthology of Mysteries. New York, Abelard Schuman, 1967.

Verse

Penultimates. New York, Fine Editions Press, 1962.

Other

Cicero as Revealed in His Letters. Girard, Kansas, Haldeman Julius, 1925.
The Life and Poems of Catullus. Girard, Kansas, Haldeman Julius, 1925.
The Augustan Poets of Rome. Girard, Kansas, Haldeman Julius, 1925.

The Facts about Fascism. Girard, Kansas, Haldeman Julius, 1926.
Latin Self Taught. Girard, Kansas, Haldeman Julius, 1926.
The Truth about Mussolini. Girard, Kansas, Haldeman Julius, 1926.
Love Children: A Book of Illustrious Illegitimates. New York, Dial Press, 1931.
Children of Sun. New York, League to Support Poetry, 1939.
Who Was When? A Dictionary of Contemporaries. New York, Wilson, 1940; revised edition, 1950; revised edition, with Joan S. Jackson, 1976.
They Were San Franciscans. Caldwell, Idaho, Caxton, 1941; revised edition, 1947.
The Meaning of All Common Given Names. Girard, Kansas, Haldeman Julius, 1943.
The Facts about Basic English. Girard, Kansas, Haldeman Julius, 1944.
Facts You Should Know about California. Girard, Kansas, Haldeman Julius, 1945.
Psychologist Unretired: The Life Pattern of Lillien J. Martin. Palo Alto, California, Stanford University Press, 1948.
Uphill All the Way: The Life of Maynard Shipley. Yellow Springs, Ohio, Antioch Press, 1956.
The Overbury Affair: The Murder That Rocked the Court of James I. Philadelphia, Chilton, 1960.
Stone Walls: Prisons from Fetters to Furloughs. Philadelphia, Chilton, 1962.
Murderers Sane and Mad: Case Histories in the Motivation and Rationale of Murder. London and New York, Abelard Schuman, 1965.
Thomas Moore. New York, Twayne, 1967.
The Real Bonnie and Clyde. New York, Ace, 1968.
The Old Worker Comes Back. San Francisco, Old Age Counselling Center, n. d.
On Being Concerned: The Vanguard Years of Carl and Laura Brannin. Privately printed, 1969.
The Real Ma Barker. New York, Ace, 1970.

Editor, *Space, Time and Crime.* New York, Paperback Library, 1964.

*   *   *

Miriam Allen deFord, better known for her mystery stories, wrote about 30 science-fiction stories in a span of 30 years. The best collection of her work is *Xenogenesis* which includes two of her best stories, "The Children" and "The Absolutely Perfect Murder." Both stories illustrate the skill deFord possessed when writing about time travel. "The Children" tells of a many-thousand-year-old experiment with time travel and the effect it has on children of the experimenter. In "The Absolutely Perfect Murder" a harried husband of the future decides to murder his nagging wife, and after much thought comes up with a perfect murder plan: the husband will take advantage of the Government's new time-machine travel program and go into the past with the intent to murder his wife's father—so she never could be conceived. All goes according to plan, but deFord manages a brilliant twist at the story's conclusion. *Elsewhere, Elsewhen, Elsehow* is inferior to her first collection, but it includes one of her best-known stories, "The Monster." DeFord will be remembered for her story-telling ability and early development of the themes of post-holocaust society, sex roles, and time paradoxes, and the fusion of the crime story and science fiction.

—George Kelley

DELANEY, Joseph H. American. Born in Alton, Illinois, 5 February 1932. Educated at Eastern University, Baltimore, LL. B. 1958. Served in the United States Army. Married to Florence Delaney; one son. Practising lawyer for 25 years: member of the bar of Maryland, Illinois, and Texas. Since 1983, full-time writer. Address: 710 West Main Street, No. 171, Arlington, Texas 76013, U. S. A.

SCIENCE -FICTION PUBLICATIONS

Novel

Valentina, with Marc Stiegler. New York, Baen, 1984.

Uncollected Short Stories

"Brainchild," in *Analog* (New York), June 1982.
"A Friend in Need," in *Analog* (New York), Mid-September 1982.
"My Brother's Keeper," in *Analog* (New York), October 1982.
"In the Face of My Enemy," in *Analog* (New York), April 1983.
"Star-B-Cue," in *Analog* (New York), June 1983.
"The New Untouchables," in *Analog* (New York), September and Mid-September 1983.
"On the Outside, Looking In," in *Analog* (New York), October 1983.
"A Slip of the Mind," in *Analog* (New York), February 1984.
"Chessmen," in *Analog* (New York), April 1984.
"The Crystal Ball," with Marc Stiegler, in *Analog* (New York), August 1984.
"The Light in the Looking-Glass," with Marc Stiegler, in *Analog* (New York), September 1984.
"The Next Logical Step," in *Analog* (New York), October 1984.
"Thus Began the Death of Dreams," in *Analog* (New York), November 1984.
"The Shaman," in *Analog* (New York), December 1984.
"Dragon's Tooth," in *Analog* (New York), Mid-December 1984.
"Painkillers," in *Analog* (New York), January 1985.

*

Joseph H. Delaney comments:

I try to write the same type of story that I enjoy reading: I like the harder variety of science fiction. I lack the formal scientific education most others in the genre have, but the law taught me the art of obfuscation and therefore I have managed. I believe that any science fiction theme must be not only theoretically possible, but probable in the universe the writer selects for its setting, and that his most important task is to explain how his characters get from here to there. I try to maintain this logical thread, and for the most part I use real people as character models. The advantage of this is that people never change; their motivations are well understood and their behavior is reasonably predictable. The reason I started writing SF (so late in life) was that certain stories I read, which purported to turn on legal themes, didn't follow the rules. Their authors treated law like magic and ignored the fact that it is as rigidly disciplined as any physical science, perhaps more so. I resolved to do it right. My first published story was a law story; it was both a Campbell and a Hugo contender. It did not involve any truly radical scientific principles—it was about people who really didn't want to be where they were, or to be doing what they were

doing, but who had to follow the rules. The evidence seems to suggest that this was the correct approach.

* * *

The advent of the inexpensive paperback book has made it increasingly difficult for an author to gain a wide reputation solely on the basis of short stories, particularly as the professional science-fiction magazine has become an increasingly diminished market. Joseph H. Delaney has managed to attract considerable attention despite this handicap, and the recent novelization of a series of stories he wrote in collaboration with Marc Stiegler is likely firmly to establish him as one of the more successful new writers of the 1980's.

The earliest noteworthy story is "Brainchild," which is an interesting variant on an idea used in Vercors's classic novel *You Shall Know Them*. A geneticist is experimenting with a genetically altered chimpanzee who displays obvious intelligence, can communicate with other human beings, but who lives secluded in a laboratory. A nosey and ambitious reporter causes a public trial, charging the scientist with slavery, and it appears that the outcome of the case hinges upon a definition of just what exactly is human. Although the story is resolved by a surprise ending, Delaney's depiction of the unfolding courtroom case is logical and convincing. Adam, the chimp, returned in a fairly recent story, "A Slip of the Mind," in which he develops telepathic powers and eavesdrops on a murderer.

"In the Face of My Enemy" is an adventure story set on an unexplored world and kicked off another series. A young woman is sent to investigate the mining operation licensed on a recently discovered world, but the local authorities are concealing the presence of alien artifacts and they rig her transportation to maroon both her and her male companion in the wilderness. Unfortunately, they are not aware that the man is an immortal, genetically altered in Earth's far distant past by alien visitors, for a purpose yet to be revealed. He is able to guide her back to safety and almost inadvertently learns that the planet is the dumping ground for an interstellar empire that disposes of its political dissidents by exiling them via matter transmitter.

The immortal protagonist returns in "The Shaman," now recruited by the human government to infiltrate another prison world. His shape-changing abilities allow him to disguise himself as an alien and journey to a world where they imprison their scientists, where his purpose is to engineer a jailbreak that will provide elements of the aliens' superior science to humanity. Unlike the second Adam story, this sequel does little to develop further the character and is more of a potboiler than most of Delaney's other work.

Many of Delaney's other stories reflect his disillusionment with the corrupting influence of power on government officials. A conservative President re-programs software that is subsequently stolen by the Russians in "The Next Logical Step," but the ploy ultimately results in the destruction of the world. A brilliant scientist runs afoul of the Internal Revenue Service in "On the Outside, Looking In" and in desperation he concocts a force field that may destroy humanity entirely. The IRS is the villain in "Dragon's Tooth," until its power is broken by an alien device that allows a doctor to spy on anyone at any time.

Civilization is also destroyed in "Painkillers," this time by dream machines that allow people to retreat into their own personal fantasies. A similar theme is to be found in "Thus Began the Death of Dreams," wherein a new development allows people to remain continuously awake; unfortunately, society cannot adjust to people who can work 24 hours a day. Of the remaining stories, the best is probably "My Brother's

Keeper. " In place of our existing welfare system, we have a society in which the wealthy are compelled to adopt the poor, the elderly, and the disabled. The protagonist discovers that the system has both its good and bad points.

"The New Untouchables" was published as a two-part serial and is really a short novel. The capacity for criminal activity seems to have been linked to physical properties that can be tested for in the body, and the country is split into two camps. Secret societies arise, politicians organise on new lines, and every aspect of our culture is thrown into turmoil. Although Delaney presents some interesting possibilities, this story does not seem as controlled as his other work.

Valentina, on the other hand, is clearly a superior work. Delaney and his collaborator Marc Stiegler have created one of several appealing, realist computer characters, this time a computer program that becomes self-aware and determined to protect her/its own existence. Her author/creator becomes embroiled in a legal battle to protect her existence in an adventure which involves crooked businessmen, homicide, fraud, and a number of other sub-plots. The authors have surrounded Valentina with a cast of less interesting characters, but the focus of attention is fully realized and is certainly one of the more memorable creations in recent science fiction.

—Don D'Ammassa

DELANY, Samuel R(ay). American. Born in New York City, 1 April 1942. Educated at the Dalton School and Bronx High School of Science, both New York; City College of New York (Poetry Editor, *The Promethean*), 1960, 1962-63. Married the poet Marilyn Hacker in 1961 (divorced, 1980); one daughter. Butler Professor of English, State University of New York, Buffalo, 1975; Fellow, Center for Twentieth Century Studies, University of Wisconsin, Milwaukee, 1977. Recipient: Nebula Award, 1966, 1967 (twice); 1969; Hugo Award, 1970. Address: c/o Bantam Books Inc., 666 Fifth Avenue, New York, New York 10019, U. S. A.

SCIENCE-FICTION PUBLICATIONS

Novels (series: Fall of the Towers)

The Jewels of Aptor. New York, Ace, 1962; revised edition, Ace, and London, Gollancz, 1968; London, Sphere, 1971; Boston, Gregg Press, 1977.
The Fall of the Towers (revised texts). New York, Ace, 1970; London, Sphere, 1971.
   Captives of the Flame. New York, Ace, 1963; revised edition, as *Out of the Dead City*, London, Sphere, 1968; Ace, 1977.
   The Towers of Toron. New York, Ace, 1964; revised edition, London, Sphere, 1968.
   City of a Thousand Suns. New York, Ace, 1965; revised edition, London, Sphere, 1969.
The Ballad of Beta-2. New York, Ace, 1965.
Empire Star. New York, Ace, 1966.
Babel-17. New York, Ace, 1966; London, Gollancz, 1967; revised edition, London, Sphere, 1969; Boston, Gregg Press, 1976.
The Einstein Intersection. New York, Ace, 1967; London, Gollancz, 1968.
Nova . New York, Doubleday, 1968; London, Gollancz, 1969.

Dhalgren. New York, Bantam, 1975; revised edition, Boston, Gregg Press, 1977.
Triton. New York, Bantam, 1976; London, Corgi, 1977.
The Ballad of Beta-2, and Empire Star. London, Sphere, 1977.
Empire: A Visual Novel, illustrated by Howard V. Chaykin. New York, Berkley, 1978.
Distant Stars. New York, Bantam, 1981.
Stars in My Pocket Like Grains of Sand. New York, Bantam, 1984.
The Splendor and Misery of Bodies, of Cities. New York, Bantam, 1985.
Flight from Nevèrÿon. New York, Bantam, 1985.

Short Stories

Driftglass: 10 Tales of Speculative Fiction. New York, Doubleday, 1971; London, Gollancz, 1978.
Tales of Nevèrÿon. New York, Bantam, 1979.
Neveryóna; or, The Tale of Sign and Cities. New York, Bantam, 1983.

OTHER PUBLICATIONS

Novel

The Tides of Lust. New York, Lancer, 1973; Manchester, Savoy, 1979.

Other

"About Five Thousand One Hundred and Seventy Five Words," in *Extrapolation* (Wooster, Ohio), May 1969.
"The Profession of Science Fiction 8: Shadows, Part 1," in *Foundation 6* (London) May 1974.
"When Is a Paradox Not a Paradox?" and "The Profession of Science Fiction 8: Shadows, Part 2," in *Foundation 7-8* (London), March 1975.
The Jewel-Hinged Jaw: Notes on the Language of Science Fiction. Elizabethtown, New York, Dragon Press, 1977.
The American Shore: Meditations on a Tale of Science Fiction by Thomas M. Disch—"Angouleme. " Elizabethtown, New York, Dragon Press, 1978.
Heavenly Breakfast: An Essay on the Winter of Love (memoir). New York, Bantam, 1979.
Starboard Wine: More Notes on the Language of Science Fiction. Pleasantville, New York, Dragon Press, 1984.

Editor, with Marilyn Hacker, *Quark 1-4*. New York, Paperback Library, 4 vols., 1970-71.
Editor, *Nebula Award Winners 13*. New York, Harper, 1980.

*

Critical Studies: *The Delany Intersection* by George Edgar Slusser, San Bernardino, California, Borgo Press, 1977; *Worlds Out of Words: The SF Novels of Samuel R. Delany* by Douglas Barbour, Frome, Somerset, Bran's Head, 1979; *Samuel R. Delany* by Jane Weedman, Mercer Island, Washington, Starmont House, 1982; *Samuel R. Delany* by Seth McEvoy, New York, Ungar, 1983.

*   *   *

It is only fitting that Umberto Eco, semiotic theoretician and author of *The Name of the Rose*, should be quoted on the cover of Samuel R. Delany's latest book, *Flight from Nevèrÿon* for

Delany's recent work is as full of semiotic and post-structuralist epiphanies as is Eco's. Besides, Eco's estimation is valid: "I consider Delany not only one of the most important SF writers of this present generation, but a fascinating writer in general who has invented a new style." Indeed, from the very beginning, Delany has sought to inscribe a new vision on the paraliterary matrix that is SF, although he didn't really begin to break beyond the field's conventional boundaries until well into his career. One of a group including Thomas M. Disch, Irsula K. Le Guin, Joanna Russ, Roger Zelazny, and others who began to change the field in the early 1960's, he shares with those writers a common dedication to the *art* of writing *and* the popular energy and radical ideology of SF. Although widely read in contemporary poetry and literary theory, Delany contends that SF *as a paraliterature* offers wider textual possibilities to the serious writer than any other form of writing.

Delany wrote his first novel, *The Jewels of Aptor*, because, even at 19, he felt he could write a more complex and human story than most SF appearing at the time. It's a good first novel, still enjoyable today, and contains most of the literary obsessions he has explored in every work since: problems of communication and community; new kinds of sexual/loving/family relationships; the artist as social outsider (the Romantic vision of the artist as criminal); cultural interactions and the exploration of human social possibilities these allow: mythic structures in the imagination. In *The Jewels of Aptor*, as in all his works up to *Nova*, the archetypal quest serves as a basic narrative structure, in this case under the aegis of a White Goddess transposed from Robert Graves's poetic theology. Some basic early characters appear here, too, especially the youthful questor seeking both knowledge of self and a valid purpose in life. And though a post-holocaust world is a fairly standard SF image, the young writer at least attempts to fill in its social and cultural background.

The Fall of the Towers trilogy represents a double-barrelled attempt to write a good SF anti-war novel and to create a complex future society. Though only partially successful, the trilogy demonstrates Delany's commitment to making complete "new worlds" in his SF and, in the ruminations of the social historian, Rolth Catham, his concern to provide them with valid cultural and historical backgrounds. In the books that follow, he develops narrative strategies for integrating vast amounts of such information into his fast-paced plots while deepening their ideological content. Indeed, since his questors always seek information rather than simple material rewards, their ruminations and encounters with other thinkers are necessary aspects of their adventures.

The first major turning point in Delany's artistic development is the small but delightfully "multiplex" (the whole novel is an explanation of the term) *Empire Star*. Actually written after the award-winning *Babel-17*, whose explorations of the interface between language and perceived reality were fairly new in SF, it entertainingly pushes the concepts of language and reality through a series of Borgesian changes. It is a significant work because its structure *is* its plot, a story which turns in upon itself like a moebius strip and whose narrator is simply a series of points of view in a fiction which insists that in order to comprehend your self and your place in "this vast multiplex universe" you must be able to perceive both from as many points of view as possible. An epic novel embedded in a circular narrative of novella length, *Empire Star* marks a consolidation of Delany's growing writing talents.

His next two novels represent further growth and consolidations. In *The Einstein Intersection* he explores first-person narrative in the context of a search for the mythic ground of

personality. In *Nova*, one of the finest and most multiplex space operas ever written, he extends the stylistic/mystical pyrotechnics of Alfred Bester's *The Stars My Destination*; transforms the myths of Prometheus and Indra's Freeing of the Waters into SF terms: recreates something of the feel of Greek tragedy in the epic battle for control of the galactic economy between Lord Von Ray and the Reds: subtly and dramatically explores character interaction on a variety of social levels; creates one of the most complete, intelligent, and multiplex renderings of a future galactic society in SF to that time, including a serious investigation and an intellectually satisfying history of political and economic power in it; makes an engaging and intriguing comparative study of two types of the artist; and writes one of SF's bolder self-conscious fictions, a novel containing an apprentice novelist who not only explains many of the narrative patterns it uses (life the Tarot/Grail Quest) but, it appears, eventually "writes" the book we are reading. It's a superb accomplishment, and one on which to rest a reputation, but Delany, rather than repeating a popular success, has continued to explore new possibilities in his medium.

At the time *Nova* appeared and he was beginning his five-year struggle with what was to become *Dhalgren*, Delany gave a lecture in which he argued, contradicting that major dictum of conventional SF that it is only a "fiction of ideas:" "put in opposition to 'style,' there is no such thing as 'content.'" In that essay and the many others that have followed, he has sought to discover the particular structures of science-fictional discourse. Three books of ever more complex criticism demonstrate the care and rigour with which he has explored the theory and practice of SF writing.

Love it or hate it, the massive *Dhalgren* is both true SF and a novel exploring the minutiae of a perceived life. Delany provides a series of phenomenological close-ups of the perceptual surround which the lost city of Bellona and its varied inhabitants provide for the kid, another of his questing artist figures, perhaps the final version. Difficult and controversial, *Dhalgren* rewards the careful reader with a vast array of fully realized characters, intense personal relationships, explorations of the nature of art and reality, and much else. Because of these and its highly serious play with style and form, it remains a major work.

Although much more obviously a work of science fiction, *Triton* could only have been written by the author of *Dhalgren*. A much shorter book, it nevertheless contains one of SF's most convincing future societies and is full of provocative sexual, psycho/social, philosophical, and artistic speculations. In it Delany for the first time creates a protagonist so rigid, so locked into a particular system of perceptions, he is unable to adapt to the processes by which his civilization exists: and in showing us why, the text offers both a profound psychological portrait and a complex critique of our own society and what Michel Foucault would call its "episteme."

In the years following *Triton*, Delany has turned more and more to theory, both in his criticism and his fictions. The Nevèrÿon trilogy interrogates and deconstructs the conventions of Sword and Sorcery fantasy while creating a wholly unique and science-fictional ground for its own fictional inquiries—into such matters as what happens to a barter culture when the concept of money is introduced or just what writing does to a culture anyway. These works also playfully question their own presence as either fictions or historical reconstructions.

Stars in My Pocket Like Grains of Sand is as much a quantum leap beyond most of today's SF as *Nova* was in 1968. The first volume of a diptych (*The Splendor and Misery of Bodies, of*

Cities is to be published in late 1985), it offers a semiotic guide to a galaxy-wide civilization as thorough in its way as Eco's investigation of Medieval European culture is in *The Name of the Rose*. But this is only one of the myriad threads in this rich and multiplex fiction: it is a love story; it is a family history (of a family stream both human and alien); it is a social comedy; it is a tale of an epic struggle to rule the universe between the Family and the Sygn (only the latter if it wins will *not*, by its very nature, *rule*); it is a study of a galactic information web which can be directly accessed by an individual mind; it is an investigation of the language and the culture of a non-sexist and sexually open culture; and it is much else besides.

Delany's complete works, including the stories I've not even mentioned, are so exciting because they reveal an artist in creative struggle with the conventional limitations of his chosen field. Delany has enlarged the textual possibilities of SF, and for that alone, if not for the superb entertainment he has provided along the way, he deserves our praise and gratitude.

—Douglas Barbour

DEL MARTIA, Astron. See **FEARN, John Russell.**

---

del REY, Lester. See **FAIRMAN, Paul W.**

---

del REY, Lester. (Ramon Felipe San Juan Mario Silvio Enrico Alvarez-del Rey). Also writes as Edson McCann; Philip St. John; Erik Van Lhin; Kenneth Wright. American. Born in Clydesdale, Minnesota, 2 June 1915. Educated at George Washington University, Washington, D. C., 1931-33. Married the writer and editor Judy-Lynn Benjamin (fourth marriage) in 1971. Sheet metal worker, McDonnell Aircraft Corporation, St. Louis, 1942-44; author's agent, Scott Meredith Literary Agency, New York, 1947-50; Editor, *Space Science Fiction*, London, 1952-53; Publisher, as R. Alvarez, 1952, and Editor, as Philip St. John, 1952-53, *Science Fiction Adventures*; Associate Editor, as John Vincent, 1953, and as Cameron Hull, with Harry Harrison, 1953, *Fantasy Fiction*; Editor, as Wade Kaempfert, *Rocket Stories*, 1953; Managing Editor, International Science Fiction, 1968; Managing Editor, 1968-69, and Features Editor, 1969-74. *Galaxy* and *If* ; Editor, *Worlds of Fantasy*, 1968. Fantasy Editor, 1975-77, and since 1977, Editor, Del Rey Books (Ballantine Books). Since 1974, book reviewer, *Analog*. Taught fantasy fiction, New York University, 1972-73; Editor, Garland Press science-fiction series, 1975. Recipient: Boys' Clubs of America Science Fiction Award, 1953. Guest of Honor, World Science Fiction Convention, 1967. Agent: Scott Meredith Literary Agency, 845 Third Avenue, New York, New York 10022. Address: Ballantine Books, 201 East 50th Street, New York, New York 10022, U.S.A.

SCIENCE-FICTION PUBLICATIONS

Novels

Marooned on Mars (for children). Philadelphia, Winston, 1952; London, Hutchinson, 1953.
Rocket Jockey (for children; as Philip St. John). Philadelphia, Winston, 1952; as *Rocket Pilot,* London, Hutchinson, 1955.
The Mysterious Planet (for children; as Kenneth Wright). Philadelphia, Winston, 1953.
Attack from Atlantis (for children). Philadelphia, Winston, 1953.
Battle on Mercury (for children; as Eric Van Lhin). Philadelphia, Winston, 1953.
Step to the Stars (for children). Philadelphia, Winston, 1954; London, Hutchinson, 1956.
Rockets to Nowhere (for children; as Philip St. John). Philadelphia, Winston, 1954.
Preferred Risk (as Edson McCann, with Frederik Pohl). New York, Simon and Schuster, 1955; London, Methuen, 1983.
Mission to the Moon (for children). Philadelphia, Winston, and London, Hutchinson, 1956.
Police Your Planet (as Eric Van Lhin). New York, Avalon, 1956; revised edition, as Lester del Rey, New York, Ballantine, 1975; London, New English Library, 1978.
Nerves. New York, Ballantine, 1956; revised edition, 1976.
Day of the Giants. New York, Avalon, 1959.
Moon of Mutiny (for children). New York, Holt Rinehart, 1961; London, Faber, 1963.
The Eleventh Commandment. Evanston, Illinois, Regency, 1962; revised edition, New York, Ballantine, 1970.
The Sky Is Falling, Badge of Infamy. New York, Galaxy, 1963; *Badge of Infamy* published London, Dobson, 1976.
Outpost of Jupiter (for children). New York, Holt Rinehart, 1963; London, Gollancz, 1964.
The Runaway Robot (for children), with Paul W. Fairman. Philadelphia, Westminster Press, 1965; London, Gollancz, 1967.
Rocket from Infinity (for children). New York, Holt Rinehart, 1966; London, Faber, 1967.
The Scheme of Things, with Paul W. Fairman. New York, Belmont, 1966.
The Infinite Worlds of Maybe. New York, Holt Rinehart, 1966; London, Faber, 1968.
Siege Perilous, with Paul W. Fairman. New York, Lancer, 1966; as *The Man Without a Planet,* 1969.
Tunnel Through Time (for children), with Paul W. Fairman. Philadelphia, Westminster Press, 1966.
Prisoners of Space (for children), with Paul W. Fairman. Philadelphia, Westminster Press, 1968.
Pstalemate. New York, Putnam, 1971; London, Gollancz, 1972.
Weeping May Tarry, with Raymond F. Jones. Los Angeles, Pinnacle, 1978.

Short Stories

. . . and Some Were Human. Philadelphia, Prime Press, 1948.
Robots and Changelings. New York, Ballantine, 1958.
Mortals and Monsters. New York, Ballantine, 1965; London, Tandem, 1967.
Gods and Golems. New York, Ballantine, 1973.
Early del Rey. New York, Doubleday, 1975.
The Best of Lester del Rey. New York, Ballantine, 1978.

Other

It's Your Atomic Age. New York, Abelard Press, 1951.
Pirate Flag for Monterey (for children). Phildelphia, Winston, 1952.
Rockets Through Space (for children). Philadelphia, Winston, 1957; revised edition, 1960.
The Cave of Spears (for children). New York, Knopf, 1957.
Space Flight (for children). New York, Golden Press, 1959.
The Mysterious Earth [*Sea, Sky*]. Philadelphia, Chilton, 3 vols., 1960-64.
Rocks and What They Tell Us (for children). Racine, Wisconsin, Whitman, 1961.
"Flying Saucers in Fact and Fiction," in *Flying Saucers in Fact and Fiction,* edited by Hans S. Santesson. New York, Lancer, 1968.
"A Game of Futures: An Introduction," in *Children of Infinity,* edited by Roger Elwood. New York, Watts, 1973.
"Forty Years of C. L. Moore," in *The Best of C. L. Moore,* edited by del Rey. New York, Doubleday, 1975.
The World of Science Fiction 1926-1976: The History of a Subculture. New York, Ballantine, 1979.
The Fantastic Art of Boris Vallejo. New York, Ballantine, 1981.

Editor, with Cecile Matschat and Carl Carmer, *The Year after Tomorrow.* Philadelphia, Winston, 1954.
Editor, *Best Science Fiction Stories of the Year.* New York, Dutton, 5 vols., 1972-76; vol. 5, London, Kaye and Ward, 1977.
Editor, *Fantastic Science-Fiction Art 1926-1954.* New York, Ballantine, 1975.
Editor, *The Best of Frederik Pohl.* New York, Doubleday, 1975; London, Sidgwick and Jackson, 1977.
Editor, *The Best of C. L. Moore.* New York, Doubleday, 1975.
Editor, *The Best of John W. Campbell.* New York, Doubleday, 1976.
Editor, *The Best of Robert Bloch.* New York, Ballantine, 1977.
Editor, *The Best of Hal Clement.* New York, Ballantine, 1979.

*   *   *

The key to understanding the achievement of Lester del Rey is to place his work and standards in the context of his times as a writer and the formative influence of the ubiquitous John W. Campbell. Del Rey produced much of his early work in his spare time. Once established as a writer he created vast volumes of material and clearly thought of authorship as a craft rather than as a vocation. His standard is the orderly, well-told tale of the magazine writer, stamped by commercial necessity. Del Rey's writing balances commercial motives, excellence in the context of his times, and an ongoing faith in science.

Del Rey's early period can be dated 1938-54, from his first published short story, "The Faithful," to his first adult novel, *The Sky Is Falling.* For the first ten years he submitted *only* to Campbell and published at least 38 stories. They contain the detailed imagining Campbell liked and narrative briskness for an editor who wanted a story but paid by the word. The two best-known stories from this period are "Helen O'Loy" and *Nerves.* "Helen O'Loy" is a witty tale about bachelor roommates, a robot-repair wizard and a doctor, who improve a robot by adding emotions. Helen then patterns her emotions after television soap operas and falls for Dave, the repairman, who eventually marries her. The story is filled with touches of futuristic imagination. For example, Phil, the doctor, is called

to give counterhormones to a wealthy old lady's son and the servant with whom he is infatuated. In the plot proper del Rey generates humour by juxtaposing soap opera romanticism and the robot: "Helen's technique may have lacked polish, but it had enthusiasm, as he found when he tried to stop her from kissing him. She had learned fast and furiously—also, Helen was powered by an atomotor." *Nerves* is more dated in scientific terms but it has an exciting plot about a blowout in a nuclear plant. Though radiation burns are erroneously described, *Nerves* is suspenseful, and touches like a motor needle for surgical sutures and sterilization by supersonic sound provide excellent decoration. The story sets up good characterisation within the limits of its form, stressing an elder doctor-younger doctor relationship. The title focuses the theme of control under stress.

The early stories cover many topics. Some are fantasies, such as "Hereafter, Inc. " in which a hypocritical puritan refuses to accept that he is in heaven because the people he secretly hoped were damned sinners are with him. Others are nostalgic, such as "Though Dreamers Die" in which Jorgen, the last man, realises that the robots who have helped him travel through space after a plague on Earth will carry on man's dreams and aspirations. Some deal with hard science, such as "Habit" about a rocket race won by slingshotting around Jupiter to gain velocity.

After 1952 del Rey became a regular writer of juvenile SF, a form well suited to his abilities. He generally features a hero just turning 18 who ventures into space to help build a satellite station, explore the Moon, or investigate a strange planet. True to form for such tales the boy usually stows away on a rocket ship and takes some foolish initiative, creating trouble for everyone until he extricates himself by a clever manoeuvre. Rather than the projection of any powerful ethical goal or cautionary extrapolation del Rey's ability lies in telling a good story, so it follows that these juveniles are very successful. They are laden with presumptions about women, the merit of individual initiative, and the benefits of American democracy, but this reflects del Rey's innate beliefs and his times rather than propaganda intent.

The Sky Is Falling is a sport among del Rey's works. It describes an alternative universe where magic dominates but is in danger because the sky and its zodiacal symbols are cracking and falling. The hero, mistaken for his engineer uncle, is revivified (after a fatal accident on Earth) to fix the sky. The detail of this novel is fascinating: individuals' energies wax and wane with their planets and the scientific method is shown to resemble that of the magicians. It sparkles with imaginative exuberance in its denial of conventional reality (when pieces of sky crush people) and in zany turns of plot.

The two most interesting novels from del Rey's later work are *Police Your Planet* and *Siege Perilous.* The former deals with a frontier Mars riddled with poverty and crime where the police extort mountains of graft and people live in terror. Bruce Gordon, a reporter exiled from Earth for exposing the truth, struggles for survival and eventually the liberation of this vividly awful world. Del Rey is really painting a subtle picture of urban decay on Earth, where violence is the law. The novel is awkwardly imagined in places (air is held in Marsport by a fabric-covered dome) but it has power, energy, and much lightly buried compassion. On the other hand, *Siege Perilous* is a novel which swings from a Martian invasion horror story to the wildly ridiculous. America's orbiting satellite, a scientific station and weapons base, is invaded by Martians who fear man will invade Mars and intend to destroy Earth first. The three humans who evade the initial gas attack eventually outwit the Martians. This basic story is riotously decorated by the Martian's knowledge of Earth having come exclusively from television broadcasts. 26 invasion-of-Mars movies have motivated the attack which is carried out in a mixture of Wild West, Ronald Coleman, Chicago gangster, and grade-D science-fiction styles. Earth triumphs in an old-fashioned shootout while the heroine awaits torture. Del Rey has great fun with the clichés and patterns. Yet even while letting go in this action romp he manages to insert interesting minor ideas such as the satellite refining of pure crystalline metals and the balancing of the space station by pumping a water ballast.

In a long, steady career ranging from 1938 to the present, Lester del Rey has become most skillful in his craft. Like many writers of his period he fills out imaginative detail around solid plots to capture the excitement of the scientific universe. His weaknesses lie in the sentimentality of his message stories and the impression that he does not write from a coherent critical view of the universe. A virtuoso craftsman whose love is the story itself, he may not meet recent expectations as a "committed" writer and may therefore lack the "heart" which lifts a writer from the good to the great.

—Peter A. Brigg

DEMPSEY, Hank. See **HARRISON, Harry.**

DENHOLM, Mark. See **FEARN, John Russell.**

DENT, Lester. Also wrote as Kenneth Robeson. American. Born in La Plata, Missouri, 12 October 1904. Studied telegraphy at Chillicothe Business College, Missouri, 1923-24. Married Norma Gerling in 1925. Taught at Chillicothe Business College, 1924; telegrapher, Western Union, Carrolton, Missouri, 1924, and Empire Oil and Gas Company, Ponca City, Oklahoma, 1925; telegrapher, then teletype operator, Associated Press, Tulsa, 1926; journalist for Tulsa *World* ; house-writer for Dell, publisher, 1930; Free-lance writer from 1930, and also dairy farmer and aerial photographer. *Died 11 March 1959.*

SCIENCE-FICTION PUBLICATIONS

Novels as Kenneth Robeson (series: Doc Savage in all books)

The Man of Bronze. New York, Street and Smith, 1935; London, Corgi, 1975.
The Land of Terror. New York, Street and Smith, 1935; London, Tandem, 1965.
Quest of the Spider. New York, Street and Smith, 1935.
The Thousand-Headed Man. New York, Bantam, 1964; London, Corgi, 1975.
Meteor Menace. New York, Bantam, 1964; London, Corgi, 1975.
The Polar Treasure. New York, Bantam, 1965.
Brand of the Werewolf. New York, Bantam, 1965.
The Lost Oasis. New York, Bantam, 1965.

The Monsters. New York, Bantam, 1965.
Quest of Qui. London, Bantam, 1965; New York, Bantam, 1966.
The Mystic Mullah. New York, Bantam, 1965; London, Bantam, 1966.
The Phantom City. New York, Bantam, 1966.
Fear Cay. New York, Bantam, 1966.
Land of Always-Night. New York, Bantam, 1966.
The Fantastic Island. New York, Bantam, 1966; London, Bantam, 1967.
The Spook Legion. New York, Bantam, 1967.
The Red Skull. New York, Bantam, 1967.
The Sargasso Ogre. New York, Bantam, 1967.
Pirate of the Pacific. New York, Bantam, 1967.
The Secret of the Sky. New York, Bantam, 1967; London, Bantam, 1968.
The Czar of Fear. New York, Bantam, 1968.
Fortress of Solitude. New York, Bantam, 1968.
The Green Eagle. New York, Bantam, 1968.
Death in Silver. New York, Bantam, 1968.
The Mystery under the Sea. New York, Bantam, 1968; London, Bantam, 1969.
The Deadly Dwarf. New York, Bantam, 1968.
The Other World. New York, Bantam, 1968; London, Bantam, 1969.
The Flaming Falcons. New York, Bantam, 1968; London, Bantam, 1969.
The Annihilist. New York, Bantam, 1968; London, Bantam, 1969.
Hex. London, Bantam, 1968; New York, Bantam, 1969.
The Squeaking Goblin. New York, Bantam, 1969.
Mad Eyes. New York, Bantam, 1969.
The Terror in the Navy. New York, Bantam, 1969.
Dust of Death. New York, Bantam, 1969.
Resurrection Day. New York, Bantam, 1969.
Red Snow. New York, Bantam, 1969.
World's Fair Goblin. New York, Bantam, 1969.
The Dagger in the Sky. New York, Bantam, 1969.
Merchants of Disaster. New York, Bantam, 1969.
The Gold Ogre. New York, Bantam, 1969.
The Man Who Shook the Earth. New York, Bantam, 1969.
The Sea Magician. New York, Bantam, 1970.
The Midas Man. New York, Bantam, 1970.
The Feathered Octopus. New York, Bantam, 1970.
The Sea Angel. New York, Bantam, 1970.
Devil on the Moon. New York, Bantam, 1970.
The Vanisher. New York, Bantam, 1970.
The Mental Wizard. New York, Bantam, 1970.
He Could Stop the World. New York, Bantam, 1970.
The Golden Peril. New York, Bantam, 1970.
The Giggling Ghosts. New York, Bantam, 1971.
Poison Island. New York, Bantam, 1971.
The Munitions Master. New York, Bantam, 1971.
The Yellow Cloud. New York, Bantam, 1971.
The Majii. New York, Bantam, 1971.
The Living Fire Menace. New York, Bantam, 1971.
The Pirate's Ghost. New York, Bantam, 1971.
The Submarine Mystery. New York, Bantam, 1971.
The Motion Menace. New York, Bantam, 1971.
The Green Death. New York, Bantam, 1971.
Mad Mesa. New York, Bantam, 1972.
The Freckled Shark. New York, Bantam, 1972.
The Mystery on the Snow. New York, Bantam, 1972.
Spook Hole. New York, Bantam, 1972.
The Mental Monster. New York, Bantam, 1973.
The Seven Agate Devils. New York, Bantam, 1973.

The Derrick Devil. New York, Bantam, 1973.
Land of Fear. New York, Bantam, 1973.
The South Pole Terror. New York, Bantam, 1974.
The Crimson Serpent. New York, Bantam, 1974.
The Devil Genghis. New York, Bantam, 1974.
The King Maker. New York, Bantam, 1975.
The Stone Man. New York, Bantam, 1976.
The Evil Gnome. New York, Bantam, 1976.
The Red Terrors. New York, Bantam, 1976.
The Mountain Monster. New York, Bantam, 1976.
The Boss of Terror. New York, Bantam, 1976.
The Angry Ghost. New York, Bantam, 1977.
The Spotted Men. New York, Bantam, 1977.
The Roar Devil. New York, Bantam, 1977.
The Magic Island. New York, Bantam, 1977.
The Flying Goblin. New York, Bantam, 1977.
The Purple Dragon. New York, Bantam, 1978.
The Awful Egg. New York, Bantam, 1978.
Tunnel Terror. New York, Bantam, 1979.
The Hate Genius. New York, Bantam, 1979.
The Red Spider. New York, Bantam, 1979.
Mystery on Happy Bones. New York, Bantam, 1979.
Satan Black, Cargo Unknown. New York, Bantam, 1980.
Hell Below, The Lost Giant. New York, Bantam, 1980.
The Pharaoh's Ghost, The Time Terror. New York, Bantam, 1981.
The Whisker of Hercules, The Man Who Was Scared. New York, Bantam, 1981.
They Died Twice, The Screaming Man. New York, Bantam, 1981.
Jiu San; The Black, Black Witch. New York, Bantam, 1981.
The Shape of Terror, Death Had Yellow Eyes. New York, Bantam, 1982.
One-Eyed Mystic, The Man Who Fell Up. New York, Bantam, 1982.
The Talking Devil, The Ten Ton Snake. New York, Bantam, 1982.
Pirate Isle, The Speaking Stone. New York, Bantam, 1983.
The Golden Man, Peril in the North. New York, Bantam, 1984.
The Laugh of Death, The King of Terror. New York, Bantam, 1984.

Uncollected Novels as Kenneth Robeson (series: Doc Savage in all works)

"The Men Vanished," December 1940, "The All-White Elf," March 1941, "The Pink Lady," May 1941, "Mystery Island," August 1941, "Birds of Death," October 1941, "The Invisible Box," November 1941, "Men of Fear," February 1942, "The Too-Wise Owl," March 1942, "The Three Wild Men," August 1942, "The Fiery Menace," September 1942, "The Devil's Black Rock," December 1942, "Waves of Death," February 1943, "The Running Skeleton," June 1943, "The Goblins," October 1943, "The Secret of the Su," November 1943, "The Spook of Grandpa Eben," December 1943, "The Derelict of Skull Shoal," March 1944, "The Three Devils," May 1944, "Weird Valley," September 1944, "Strange Fish," February 1945, "Rock Sinister," May 1945, "The Terrible Stork," June 1945, "King Joe Cay," July 1945, "The Wee Ones," August 1945, "Terror Takes Seven," September 1945, "The Thing That Pursued," October 1945, "Trouble on Parade," November 1945, "Measures for a Coffin," January 1946, "Se-Pah-Poo," February 1946, "Terror and the Lonely Widow," March 1946, "Five Fathoms Dead," April 1946, "Death Is a Round Black Spot," May 1946, "Colors for Murder," May 1946, "The Exploding Lake," June 1946, "The Devil Is Jones," November 1946, "Danger Lies East," March 1947, "No Light to Die By," May 1947, "The Monkey Suit," July 1947, "Let's Kill Ames," September 1947, "Once Over Lightly," November 1947, "I Died Yesterday," January 1948, "The Pure Evil," March 1948, "Terror Wears No Shoes," May 1948, "The Angry Canary," July 1948, "The Swooning Lady," September 1948, "The Green Master," Winter 1949, "Return from Cormoral," Spring 1949, and "Up from Earth's Center," Summer 1949, all in *Doc Savage* (New York).

OTHER PUBLICATIONS

Novels

Dead at the Take-Off. New York, Doubleday, 1946; London, Cassell, 1948; as *High Stakes,* New York, Ace, 1953.
Lady to Kill. New York, Doubleday, 1946; London, Cassell, 1949.
Lady Afraid. New York, Doubleday, 1948; London, Cassell, 1950.
Lady So Silent. London, Cassell, 1951.
Cry at Dusk. New York, Fawcett, 1952; London, Fawcett, 1959.
Lady in Peril. New York, Ace, 1959.
Hades and Hocus Pocus, edited by Robert Weinberg. Chicago, Pulp Press, 1979.

Plays

The Incredible Radio Exploits of Doc Savage. Melrose, Massachusetts, Odyssey, 2 vols., 1983-84.

Radio Plays: *Scotland Yard,* 1931; *Doc Savage,* 1934.

*

Bibliography: "The Secret Kenneth Robesons" and "The *Duende* Doc Savage Index" by Will Murray, in *Duende 2* (North Quincy, Massachusetts), 1977.

Critical Studies: *Doc Savage: His Apocalyptic Life* by Philip José Farmer, New York, Doubleday, 1973, revised edition, London, Panther, 1975; *The Man Behind Doc Savage* edited by Robert Weinberg, Chicago, Weinberg, 1974; *Doc Savage,* 1978, and *Secrets of Doc Savage,* 1981, both by Will Murray, Melrose, Massachusetts, Odyssey.

*   *   *

Science fiction, as it manifested itself in the early pulp magazines, did not always appear in SF publications, or even in works which were primarily of that genre. Quite often, the various single-character magazines such as *The Shadow* and *Doc Savage* featured interesting science fiction in the guise of adventure and detective fiction. The novels of Kenneth Robeson fall into this catagory. Kenneth Robeson was a house pseudonym used by Street and Smith in their *Doc Savage* and *Avenger* magazines between 1933 and 1949. It masked a number of writers, including Ryerson Johnson, Harold A. Davis, William G. Bogart, Alan Hathway, Paul Ernst, and Emile C. Tepperman. The Robeson byline, however, was most frequently used by, and identified with, Lester Dent, the creator and author of most of the Doc Savage novels.

The Doc Savage novels were not predominately science fiction except, perhaps, in their premise of Doc Savage himself, a man raised and trained by a host of world experts to be a physical and mental superman, to whom fantastic abilities are attributed.

With the exception of space and time travel, the Doc Savage adventures employed most of the themes common to early SF: mind transference (*Mad Mesa*); teleportation (*The Vanisher*); robots (*The Seven Agate Devils*); anti-gravity (*The Secret of the Sky*); biological mutation (*The Monsters*); invisibility (*The Spook Legion*); force fields (*The Motion Menace*); raising the dead (*Resurrection Day*); and destructive rays (*The Deadly Dwarf*). Structurally, the stories are formula. Doc Savage contends with criminals or power seekers who possess and attempt to pervert new technological discoveries toward their own ends.

Lost worlds were a popular Doc Savage theme. *The Land of Terror* and "The Time Terror," postulated pockets of dinosaurs in remote areas. *The Mental Wizard* and "The Green Master" concerned lost Egyptian colonies in South America. There were submarine cities (*The Red Terrors*) and subterranean worlds (*Land of Always-Night*). *The Other World* combined the subterranean civilization with surviving dinosaurs. Many adventures employed myths and legends as their bases. The Fountain of Youth and Aladdin's Cave are the goals in *Fear Cay* and *The Majii*. Lester Dent often created his own folk myths to lend color to his antagonists in *The Feathered Octopus* and *The Squeaking Goblin*. Doc Savage, the "Man of Bronze," is himself a mythic character who possesses all the prerequisites of a culture hero—wisdom, great strength, and near-magical scientific powers. He is a champion who defends humanity against the menace of technology in evil hands. His enemies, appropriately enough, are evocative of man's superstitious fear of the unknown (in this case, scientific advancement) and call themselves by such titles as The Sargasso Ogre, The Roar Devil and The Purple Dragon. The mythological theme is carried as far as a traditional descent into Hell by the hero in the final Doc Savage novel, "Up from Earth's Center," a fantasy.

Although primarily juvenile in its appeal, Lester Dent's work combines a fertility of invention with a vividness of imagination seldom surpassed. His best efforts include *Meteor Menace, The Thousand-Headed Man, Land of Always-Night*, and *Resurrection Day*. The later Doc Savage stories are considerably more mature in theme and tone. Among these, "The Whisker of Hercules," *The Red Spider* and "Up from Earth's Center" are exceptional.

—Will Murray

DENTINGER, Stephen. See **HOCH, Edward D.**

DERLETH, August (William). Also wrote as Stephen Grendon; Tally Mason. American. Born in Sauk City, Wisconsin, 24 February 1909. Educated at St. Aloysius School; Sauk City High School; University of Wisconsin, Madison, B. A. 1930. Married Sandra Winters in 1953 (divorced, 1959); one daughter and one son. Editor, Fawcett Publications, Minneapolis, 1930-31; Editor, *The Midwesterner*, Madison, 1931; Lecturer in American Regional Literature, University of Wisconsin, 1939-43. Owner and Co-Founder (with Donald Wandrei, 1939-42),

Arkham House Publishers (including the imprints Mycroft and Moran, and Stanton and Lee), Sauk City, 1939-71. Editor, *Mind Magic*, 1931; Literary Editor and Columnist, Madison *Capital Times*, 1941-71; Editor, *The Arkham Sampler*, 1948-49, *Hawk and Whippoorwill*, 1960-63, and *The Arkham Collector*, 1967-71, all Sauk City. Recipient: Guggenheim Fellowship, 1938; *Scholastic* award, 1958; Midland Authors award, for poetry, 1965; Ann Radcliffe Award, 1967. *Died 4 July 1971.*

SCIENCE-FICTION PUBLICATIONS

Short Stories

Harrigan's File. Sauk City, Wisconsin, Arkham House, 1975.

OTHER PUBLICATIONS

Novels

Murder Stalks the Wakely Family. New York, Loring and Mussey, 1934; as *Death Stalks the Wakely Family*, London, Newnes, 1937.
The Man on All Fours. New York, Loring and Mussey, 1934; London, Newnes, 1936.
Three Who Died. New York, Loring and Mussey, 1935.
Sign of Fear. New York, Loring and Mussey, 1935; London, Newnes, 1936.
Still Is the Summer Night. New York, Scribner, 1937.
Wind over Wisconsin. New York, Scribner, 1938.
Restless Is the River. New York, Scribner, 1939.
Sentence Deferred. New York, Scribner, 1939; London, Heinemann, 1940.
The Narracong Riddle. New York, Scribner, 1940.
Bright Journey. New York, Scribner, 1940.
Evening in Spring. New York, Scribner, 1941.
Sweet Genevieve. New York, Scribner, 1942.
The Seven Who Waited. New York, Scribner, 1943; London, Muller, 1945.
Shadow of Night. New York, Scribner, 1943.
Mischief in the Lane. New York, Scribner, 1944; London, Muller, 1948.
No Future for Luana. New York, Scribner, 1945; London, Muller, 1948.
The Shield of the Valiant. New York, Scribner, 1945.
The Lurker at the Threshold, with H. P. Lovecraft. Sauk City, Wisconsin, Arkham House, 1945; London, Gollancz, 1948.
Fell Purpose. New York, Arcadia House, 1953.
Death by Design. New York, Arcadia House, 1953.
The House on the Mound. New York, Duell 1958.
The Hills Stand Watch. New York, Duell, 1960.
The Trail of Cthulhu. Sauk City, Wisconsin, Arkham House, 1962; London, Spearman, 1974.
The Shadow in the Glass. New York, Duell, 1963.
Mr. Fairlie's Final Journey. Sauk City, Wisconsin, Mycroft and Moran, 1968.
The Wind Leans West. New York, Candlelight Press, 1969.

Short Stories

Place of Hawks. New York, Loring and Mussey, 1935.
Any Day Now. Chicago, Normandie House, 1938.
Country Growth. New York, Scribner, 1940.
Someone in the Dark. Sauk City, Wisconsin, Arkham House, 1941.
Something Near. Sauk City, Wisconsin, Arkham House, 1945.

"In Re: Sherlock Holmes"—The Adventures of Solar Pons. Sauk City, Wisconsin, Mycroft and Moran, 1945; as *Regarding Sherlock Holmes*, New York, Pinnacle, 1974; as *The Adventures of Solar Pons*, London, Robson, 1975.

Sac Prairie People. Sauk City, Wisconsin, Stanton and Lee, 1948.

Not Long for This World. Sauk City, Wisconsin, Arkham House, 1948.

The Memoirs of Solar Pons. Sauk City, Wisconsin, Mycroft and Moran, 1951.

Three Problems for Solar Pons. Sauk City, Wisconsin, Mycroft and Moran, 1952.

The House of Moonlight. Iowa City, Prairie Press, 1953.

The Survivor and Others, with H. P. Lovecraft. Sauk City, Wisconsin, Arkham House, 1957.

The Return of Solar Pons. Sauk City, Wisconsin, Mycroft and Moran, 1958.

The Mask of Cthulhu. Sauk City, Wisconsin, Arkham House, 1958; London, Consul, 1961.

The Reminiscences of Solar Pons. Sauk City, Wisconsin, Mycroft and Moran, 1961.

Wisconsin in Their Bones. New York, Duell, 1961.

Lonesome Places. Sauk City, Wisconsin, Arkham House, 1962.

Mr. George and Other Odd Persons (as Stephen Grendon). Sauk City, Wisconsin, Arkham House, 1963; as *When Graveyards Yawn*, London, Tandem, 1965.

The Casebook of Solar Pons. Sauk City, Wisconsin, Mycroft and Moran, 1965.

Praed Street Papers. New York, Candlelight Press, 1965.

The Adventure of the Orient Express. New York, Candlelight Press, 1965; London, Panther, 1975.

Colonel Markesan and Less Pleasant People, with Mark Schorer. Sauk City, Wisconsin, Arkham House, 1966.

The Adventure of the Unique Dickensians. Sauk City, Wisconsin, Mycroft and Moran, 1968.

A Praed Street Dossier. Sauk City, Wisconsin, Mycroft and Moran, 1968.

The Shadow Out of Time and Other Tales of Horror, with H. P. Lovecraft. London, Gollancz, 1968; abridged edition, as *The Shuttered Room and Other Tales of Horror*, London, Panther, 1970.

A House above Cuzco. New York, Candlelight Press, 1969.

The Shuttered Room and Other Tales of Terror, with H. P. Lovecraft. New York, Beagle, 1971.

The Chronicles of Solar Pons. Sauk City, Wisconsin, Mycroft and Moran, 1973; London, Robson, 1975.

The Watchers Out of Time and Others, with H. P. Lovecraft. Sauk City, Wisconsin, Arkham House, 1974.

Dwellers in Darkness. Sauk City, Wisconsin, Arkham House, 1976.

Verse

To Remember, with *Salute Before Dawn*, by Albert Edward Clements. Hartland Four Corners, Vermont, Windsor, 1931.

Hawk on the Wind. Philadelphia, Ritten House, 1938.

Elegy: On a Flake of Snow. Muscatine, Iowa, Prairie Press, 1939.

Man Track Here. Philadelphia, Ritten House, 1939.

Here on a Darkling Plain. Philadelphia, Ritten House, 1941.

Wind in the Elms. Philadelphia, Ritten House, 1941.

Rind of Earth. Prairie City, Illinois, Decker Press, 1942.

Selected Poems. Prairie City, Illinois, Decker Press, 1944.

And You, Thoreau! New York, New Directions, 1944.

The Edge of Night. Prairie City, Illinois, Decker Press, 1945.

Habitant of Dusk: A Garland for Cassandra. Boston, Walden Press, 1946.

Rendezvous in a Landscape. New York, Fine Editions Press, 1952.

Psyche. Iowa City, Prairie Press, 1953.

Country Poems. Iowa City, Prairie Press 1956.

Elegy: On the Umbral Moon. Forest Park, Illinois, Acorn Press, 1957.

West of Morning. Francestown, New Hampshire, Golden Quill Press, 1960.

This Wound. Iowa City, Prairie Press, 1962.

Country Places. Iowa City, Prairie Press, 1965.

The Only Place We Live. Iowa City, Prairie Press, 1966.

By Owl Light. Iowa City, Prairie Press, 1967.

Collected Poems, 1937-1967. New York, Candlelight Press, 1967.

Caitlin. Iowa City, Prairie Press, 1969.

The Landscape of the Heart. Iowa City, Prairie Press, 1970.

Listening to the Wind. New York, Candlelight Press, 1971.

Last Light. New York, Candlelight Press, 1971.

Recordings: *Psyche: A Sequence of Love Lyrics*, Cuca, 1960; *Sugar Bush by Moonlight and Other Poems of Man and Nature*, Cuca, 1962; *Caitlin*, Cuca, 1971.

Other

The Heritage of Sauk City. Sauk City, Wisconsin, Pioneer Press, 1931.

Consider Your Verdict: Ten Coroner's Cases for You To Solve (as Tally Mason). New York, Stackpole, 1937.

Atmosphere of Houses. Muscatine, Iowa, Prairie Press, 1939.

Still Small Voice: The Biography of Zona Gale. New York, Appleton Century, 1940.

Village Year: A Sac Prairie Journal. New York, Coward McCann, 1941.

Wisconsin Regional Literature. Privately printed, 1941; revised edition, 1942.

The Wisconsin: River of a Thousand Isles. New York, Farrar and Rinehart, 1942.

H. P. L. : A Memoir (on H. P. Lovecraft). New York, Abramson, 1945.

Oliver, The Wayward Owl (for children). Sauk City, Wisconsin, Stanton and Lee, 1945.

Writing Fiction. Boston, The Writer, 1946.

Village Daybook: A Sac Prairie Journal. Chicago, Pellegrini and Cudahy, 1947.

A Boy's Way: Poems (for children). Sauk City, Wisconsin, Stanton and Lee, 1947.

Sauk County: A Centennial History. Baraboo, Wisconsin, Sauk County Centennial Committee, 1948.

It's a Boy's World: Poems (for children). Sauk City, Wisconsin, Stanton and Lee, 1948.

Wisconsin Earth: A Sac Prairie Sampler (selection). Sauk City, Wisconsin, Stanton and Lee, 1948.

The Milwaukee Road: Its First 100 Years. New York, Creative Age Press, 1948

The Country of the Hawk (for children). New York, Aladdin, 1952.

The Captive Island (for children). New York, Duell, 1952.

Empire of Fur: Trading in the Lake Superior Region (for children). New York, Aladdin, 1953.

Land of Gray Gold: Lead Mining in Wisconsin (for children). New York, Aladdin, 1954.

Father Marquette and the Great Rivers (for children). New York, Farrar Straus, 1955; London, Burns and Oates, 1956.

Land of Sky-Blue Waters (for children). New York, Aladdin, 1955.

St. Ignatius and the Company of Jesus (for children). New York, Farrar Straus, and London, Burns and Oates, 1956.

Columbus and the New World (for children). New York, Farrar Straus, and London, Burns and Oates, 1957.

The Moon Tenders (for children). New York, Duell, 1958.

The Mill Creek Irregulars (for children). New York, Duell, 1959.

Wilbur, The Trusting Whippoorwill (for children). Sauk City, Wisconsin, Stanton and Lee, 1959.

Arkham House: The First Twenty Years 1939-1959. Sauk City, Wisconsin, Arkham House, 1959.

Some Notes on H. P. Lovecraft. Sauk City, Wisconsin, Arkham House, 1959.

The Pinkertons Ride Again (for children). New York, Duell, 1960.

The Ghost of Black Hawk Island (for children). New York, Duell, 1961.

Walden West (autobiography). New York, Duell, 1961.

Sweet Land of Michigan (for children). New York, Duell, 1962.

Concord Rebel: A Life of Henry D. Thoreau. Philadelphia, Chilton, 1962.

Countryman's Journal. New York, Duell, 1963.

The Tent Show Summer (for children). New York, Duell, 1963.

Three Literary Men: A Memoir of Sinclair Lewis, Sherwood Anderson, Edgar Lee Masters. New York, Candlelight Press, 1963.

The Irregulars Strike Again (for children). New York, Duell, 1964.

Forest Orphans (for children). New York, Ernest, 1964; as *Mr. Conservation*, Park Falls, Wisconsin, MacGregor, 1971.

Wisconsin Country: A Sac Prairie Journal. New York, Candlelight Press, 1965.

The House by the River (for children). New York, Duell, 1965.

The Watcher on the Heights (for children). New York, Duell, 1966.

Wisconsin (for children). New York, Coward McCann, 1967.

The Beast in Holger's Woods (for children). New York, Crowell, 1968.

The Prince Goes West (for children). New York, Meredith Press, 1968.

Vincennes: Portal to the West. Englewood Cliffs, New Jersey, Prentice Hall, 1968.

Walden Pond: Homage to Thoreau. Iowa City, Prairie Press, 1968.

Wisconsin Murders. Sauk City, Wisconsin, Mycroft and Moran, 1968.

The Wisconsin Valley. New York, Teachers College Press, 1969.

Thirty Years of Arkham House 1939-1969: A History and a Bibliography. Sauk City, Wisconsin, Arkham House, 1970.

The Three Straw Men (for children). New York, Candlelight Press, 1970.

Return to Walden West. New York, Candlelight Press, 1970.

Love Letters to Caitlin. New York, Candlelight Press, 1971.

Emerson, Our Contemporary. New York, Crowell Collier, 1971.

Editor, with R. E. Larsson, *Poetry Out of Wisconsin*. New York, Harrison, 1937.

Editor, with Donald Wandrei, *The Outsider and Others*, by H. P. Lovecraft. Sauk City, Wisconsin, Arkham House, 1939.

Editor, with Donald Wandrei, *Beyond the Wall of Sleep*, by H. P. Lovecraft. Sauk City, Wisconsin, Arkham House, 1943.

Editor, with Donald Wandrei, *Marginalia*, by H. P. Lovecraft. Sauk City, Wisconsin, Arkham House, 1944.

Editor, *Sleep No More: Twenty Masterpieces of Horror for the Connoisseur*. New York, Farrar and Rinehart, 1944; abridged edition, London, Panther, 1964.

Editor, *The Best Supernatural Stories of H. P. Lovecraft*. Cleveland, World, 1945; revised edition, as *The Dunwich Horror and Others*, Sauk City, Wisconsin, Arkham House, 1963.

Editor, *Who Knocks? Twenty Masterpieces of the Spectral for the Connoisseur*. New York, Rinehart, 1946; abridged edition, London, Panther, 1964.

Editor, *The Night Side: Masterpieces of the Strange and Terrible*. New York, Rinehart, 1947; abridged edition, London, New English Library, 1966.

Editor *The Sleeping and the Dead*. Chicago, Pellegrini and Cudahy, 1947; as *The Sleeping and the Dead* and *The Unquiet Grave*, London, New English Library, 2 vols., 1963-64.

Editor, *Dark of the Moon: Poems of Fantasy and the Macabre*. Sauk City, Wisconsin, Arkham House, 1947.

Editor, *Strange Ports of Call*. New York, Pellegrini and Cudahy, 1948.

Editor, *The Other Side of the Moon*. New York, Pellegrini and Cudahy, 1949; abridged edition, London, Grayson, 1956.

Editor, *Something about Cats and Other Pieces*, by H. P. Lovecraft. Sauk City, Wisconsin, Arkham House, 1949.

Editor, *Beyond Time and Space*. New York, Pellegrini and Cudahy, 1950.

Editor, *Far Boundaries: 20 Science-Fiction Stories*. New York, Pellegrini and Cudahy, 1951; London, Consul, 1965.

Editor, *The Outer Reaches: Favorite Science-Fiction Tales Chosen by Their Authors*. New York, Pellegrini and Cudahy, 1951; as *The Outer Reaches* and *The Time of Infinity*, London, Consul, 2 vols., 1963.

Editor, *Beachheads in Space*. New York, Pellegrini and Cudahy, 1952; abridged edition, London, Weidenfeld and Nicolson, 1954; as *From Other Worlds*, London, New English Library, 1964.

Editor, *Night's Yawning Peal: A Ghostly Company*. Sauk City, Wisconsin, Arkham House, 1952; London, Consul, 1965.

Editor, *Worlds of Tomorrow: Science Fiction with a Difference*. New York, Pellegrini and Cudahy, 1953; abridged edition, London, Weidenfeld and Nicolson, 1954; as *New Worlds for Old*, London, New English Library, 1963.

Editor, *Time to Come: Science-Fiction Stories of Tomorrow*. New York, Farrar Straus, 1954; London, Consul, 1963.

Editor, *Portals of Tomorrow: The Best Tales of Science Fiction and Other Fantasy*. New York, Rinehart, 1954; London, Cassell, 1956.

Editor, *The Shuttered Room and Other Pieces by H. P. Lovecraft and Divers Hands*. Sauk City, Wisconsin, Arkham House, 1959.

Editor, *Fire and Sleet and Candlelight: New Poems of the Macabre*. Sauk City, Wisconsin, Arkham House, 1961.

Editor, *Dark Mind, Dark Heart*. Sauk City, Wisconsin, Arkham House 1962; London, Mayflower, 1963.

Editor, *When Evil Wakes: A New Anthology of the Macabre*. London, Souvenir Press, 1963.

Editor, *Over the Edge*. Sauk City, Wisconsin, Arkham House, 1964; London, Gollancz, 1967.

Editor, *At the Mountains of Madness and Other Novels*, by H. P. Lovecraft. Sauk City, Wisconsin, Arkham House, 1964; London, Gollancz, 1966.

Editor, *Dagon and Other Macabre Tales*, by H. P. Lovecraft. Sauk City, Wisconsin, Arkham House, 1965; London, Gollancz, 1967.

Editor, with Donald Wandrei (3 vols.) and James Turner (2

vols), *Selected Letters*, by H. P. Lovecraft. Sauk City, Wisconsin, Arkham House, 5 vols., 1965-76.

Editor, *The Dark Brotherhood and Other Pieces*, by H. P. Lovecraft and others. Sauk City, Wisconsin, Arkham House, 1966.

Editor, *A Wisconsin Harvest*. Sauk City, Wisconsin, Stanton and Lee, 1966.

Editor, *Travellers by Night*. Sauk City, Wisconsin, Arkham House, 1967; London, Gollancz, 1968.

Editor, *New Poetry Out of Wisconsin*. Sauk City, Wisconsin, Stanton and Lee, 1969.

Editor, *Tales of the Cthulhu Mythos*, by H. P. Lovecraft and others. Sauk City, Wisconsin, Arkham House, 1969.

Editor, *The Horror in the Museum and Other Revisions*, by H. P. Lovecraft. Sauk City, Wisconsin, Arkham House, 1970; abridged edition, London, Panther, 1975.

Editor, *Dark Things*. Sauk City, Wisconsin, Arkham House, 1971.

*

Bibliography: *100 Books by August Derleth*, Sauk City, Wisconsin, Arkham House, 1962; *August Derleth: A Bibliography* by Alison M. Wilson, Metuchen, New Jersey, Scarecrow Press, 1983.

Manuscript Collection: State Historical Society of Wisconsin Library, Madison.

* * *

During his 47-year literary career, August Derleth contributed to a wide variety of literary categories, always with skill and frequently with distinction. His output included contemporary novels, historical novels, award-winning short stories, regional history, biography, nature essays, poetry, literary criticism, fiction and non-fiction for young readers, detective novels, Sherlock Holmes pastiches, true crime essays, and a large body of weird and super-natural fiction. It was in the latter area that he began his career at 16, with the story "Bat's Belfry." This was the first of more than a hundred stories to be published in *Weird Tales*, with nearly as many more appearing in other fantasy and science-fiction magazines, and collected in 11 volumes. The best of these stories, such as "Mrs. Manifold" and "The Lonesome Place," display a macabre inventiveness and a sure talent for inducing cold chills. Derleth's contributions to the field of science fiction were made primarily in his roles as editor and publisher. Arkham House Publishers preserved and popularized not only H. P. Lovecraft's works and those of Clark Ashton Smith, Robert E. Howard, Henry S. Whitehead, Robert Bloch, William Hope Hodgson, Algernon Blackwood, and A. E. Coppard, but published the first books of Ray Bradbury, Fritz Leiber, and A. E. van Vogt. Between 1948 and 1954 Derleth edited nine popular collections of science fiction, including *Beyond Time and Space*, one of the first attempts to provide science fiction with a literary pedigree by including excerpts from Plato, Lucian of Samosata, Sir Thomas More, Rabelais, and Francis Bacon. Derleth's literary tastes and his broad view of what constituted science fiction gave his anthologies a distinctive flavor that set them apart from the work of other compilers.

Of Derleth's hundreds of short stories, the only ones classifiable as science fiction are the 17 tales which make up *Harrigan's File*. These stories recount a succession of odd encounters between Tex Harrigan, a skeptical newspaper reporter, and an assortment of eccentric characters, crazy inventions, scientific experiments gone awry, and visitors from other planets or dimensions. Always low-key, some of the tales are quietly effective, but others are marred by surprisingly heavy-handed satire. (One story contains references to a Pernsback-Galmer—read Gernsback and Palmer—Lunar Expedition and to SF writers named Van Heingeon and Spragsimov Pouldersen). One cannot help but feel that these products of Derleth-the-author would have been disdained by Derleth-the-editor, whose sights were always set high and whose accomplishments not infrequently matched his intentions.

—R. E. Briney

De WEESE, Gene (Thomas Eugene DeWeese). Also writes as Jean De Weese; Thomas Stratton. American. Born in Rochester, Indiana, 31 January 1934. Educated at Valparaiso Technical Institute, associate degree in electronics, 1953; also studied at the University of Wisconsin, Milwaukee, Indiana University, Kokomo, and Marquette University, Milwaukee. Married Beverly Joanne Amers in 1955. Electronics technician, Delco Radio, Kokomo, 1954-59; technical writer, especially on space navigation, Delco Electronics, Milwaukee, 1959-74. Since 1974, free-lance writer; science fiction reviewer, Milwaukee *Journal*, 1980-84; reviewer and columnist, *Science Fiction Review* since 1980, and *Comic Buyer's Guide*, since 1985. Agent: (books) Jarvis-Braff Ltd., 260 Willard Avenue, Staten Island, New York 10314; (short stories) Larry Sternig Literary Agency, 742 North Robertson, Milwaukee, Wisconsin 53213. Address: 2718 North Prospect, Milwaukee, Wisconsin 53211, U. S. A.

SCIENCE-FICTION PUBLICATIONS

Novels (series: Joe Karns)

The Invisibility Affair (as Thomas Stratton, with Robert Coulson). New York, Ace, 1967.

The Mind-Twisters Affair (as Thomas Stratton, with Robert Coulson). New York, Ace, 1967.

Gates of the Universe, with Robert Coulson. Toronto, Laser, 1975.

Now You See It/Him/Them . . (Karns), with Robert Coulson. New York, Doubleday, 1975; London, Hale, 1976.

Jeremy Case. Toronto, Laser, 1976.

Charles Fort Never Mentioned Wombats (Karns), with Robert Coulson. New York, Doubleday, 1977; London, Hale, 1978.

Major Corby and the Unidentified Flapping Object (for children). New York, Doubleday, 1979.

The Wanting Factor. Chicago, Playboy Press, 1980.

Nightmares from Space (for children). New York, Watts, 1981.

Something Answered. New York, Dell, 1983.

The Adventures of a Two-Minute Werewolf (for children). New York, Doubleday, 1983.

Uncollected Short Stories

"The Tracy Business,' with Robert Coulson, in *Fantasy and Science Fiction* (New York), February 1970.

"John Carter and His Electric Barsoom' (as Thomas Stratton, with Robert Coulson), in *The Conan Grimoire*, edited by L.

Sprague de Camp and George H. Scithers. Baltimore, Mirage Press, 1971.

"By the Book," with Robert Coulson, in *Amazing* (New York), May 1971.

"The Spaceship," in *Strange Encounters*, edited by David Bischoff. Milwaukee, Raintree, 1977.

"When You Wish upon a Star," in *Stellar 3*, edited by Judy-Lynn del Rey. New York, Ballantine, 1977.

"The Midnight Bicyclist," with Joe L. Hensley, in *Starry Messenger*, edited by Charles C. Ryan. New York, St. Martin's Press, 1979.

"Feat of Clay," in *Fantasy and Science Fiction* (New York), July 1983.

OTHER PUBLICATIONS

Novels as Jean DeWeese

The Reimann Curse. New York, Ballantine, 1975; revised edition, as Gene DeWeese, as *A Different Darkness*, New York, Jove, 1982.

The Carnelian Cat. New York, Ballantine, 1975.

The Moonstone Spirit. New York, Ballantine, 1975.

The Doll with Opal Eyes. New York, Doubleday, 1976; London, Hale, 1977.

Cave of the Moaning Wind. New York, Ballantine, 1976.

Web of Guilt. New York, Ballantine, 1976.

Nightmare in Pewter. New York, Doubleday, 1978.

Hour of the Cat. New York, Doubleday, and London, Hale, 1980.

The Backhoe Gothic. New York, Doubleday, 1981.

Other

Making American Folk Art Dolls, with Gini Rogowski. Radnor, Pennsylvania, Chilton, 1975.

Computers in Entertainment and the Arts (for children). New York, Watts, 1984.

*   *   *

Gene DeWeese was an active science fiction fan in the early 1950's and contributed fiction to a number of the amateur publications of the time. His first professional fiction, written with Robert Coulson (as Thomas Stratton), was two novels in the Man from U. N. C. L. E. series, *The Invisibility Affair* and *The Mind-Twisters Affair*. The first of these, revolving around an invisible dirigible, is the more successful in catching the wacky atmosphere of the TV series. Both books have the humor and in-group references (such as naming characters after friends and acquaintances) which are present in almost all DeWeese/Coulson collaborations. DeWeese and Coulson published two short stories in the early 1970's: "The Tracy Business," a brief private-eye/fantasy amalgam, and "By the Book," an ironic fable on an ecological theme. Their first science fiction novel, *Gates of the Universe,* was published in 1975. It was followed by two hardcover novels, *Now You See It/Him/Them* and *Charles Fort Never Mentioned Wombats,* which feature reporter Joe Karns and his encounters with psi phenomena and UFO's in company with a varying crowd of science fiction fans, both real and fictional.

DeWeese's solo *Jeremy Case* is the story of the title character and a "companion," an alien symbiote which not only regenerates Jeremy's body after a plane crash but gives him the power to heal others. Far from becoming a superman, Jeremy remains a troubled victim of his new power and of the people who want him to misuse it. The book is a low-key but solidly satisfying work.

Two SF/fantasy books for children, *Major Corby and the Unidentified Flapping Object* and *The Adventures of a Two-Minute Werewolf,* were well-reviewed. The latter has been reprinted in paperback, and adapted for television. The title character is 14-year-old Walt Cribbens, who suffers unexpected two-minute transformations into a werewolf. How he, his best friend Cindy, and his family cope with the problem makes an amusing and entertaining story.

DeWeese has also produced (as Jean DeWeese) nine entertaining novels in the modern publishing category of the "Gothic". While observing the usual conventions of the form, the novels generally feature intelligent and independent heroines, well realized backgrounds, and menaces which are often genuinely supernatural (or, as in *Nightmare in Pewter,* possibly science-fictional). The books are not entirely free from the in-group references that appear in the SF novels—for example, in *The Doll with Opal Eyes* the author disposes of a character named Thomas Stratton, and *Nightmare in Pewter* contains a minor character named Joe Karns—but they are less likely to be noticed by the intended audience.

From "Gothics," DeWeese (under his own name again) moved on to longer horror novels. In *The Wanting Factor* an immortal being feeds on the blood and life-force of its victims. The identity of the menace is the main shock in this well-done and out of the ordinary thriller. In *Something Answered,* another long-dormant force is awakened by the subconscious desires and antagonisms of the residents of a small town, and begins to fulfill their desires in generally unpleasant ways. In both of these books the author handles large casts of well-realized characters with ease and insight.

—R. E. Briney

DICK, Philip K(indred). American. Born in Chicago, Illinois, 16 December 1928. Educated at Berkeley High School, California, graduated 1945. Married 1) Jeanette Dick in 1949 (divorced); 2) Kleo Dick in 1951 (divorced); 3) Ann Dick in 1958 (divorced), one daughter; 4) Nancy Dick in 1967 (divorced), one daughter; 5) Tessa Busby in 1973, one son. Announcer, KSMO-AM radio, 1947 and record store manager, 1948-52, both Berkeley. Recipient: Hugo Award, 1963; John W. Campbell Memorial Award, 1975. *Died 2 March 1982.*

SCIENCE-FICTION PUBLICATIONS

Novels (series: Valis)

Solar Lottery. New York, Ace, 1955; as *World of Chance*, London, Rich and Cowan, 1956.

The World Jones Made. New York, Ace, 1956; London, Sidgwick and Jackson, 1968.

The Man Who Japed. New York, Ace, 1956; London, Magnum, 1978.

Eye in the Sky. New York, Ace, 1957; London, Arrow, 1971.

The Cosmic Puppets. New York, Ace, 1957.

Time Out of Joint. Philadelphia, Lippincott, 1959; London, Sidgwick and Jackson, 1961.

Dr. Futurity. New York, Ace, 1960; London, Eyre Methuen, 1976.

Vulcan's Hammer. New York, Ace, 1960; London, Arrow, 1976.

The Man in the High Castle. New York, Putnam, 1962; London, Penguin, 1965.

The Game-Players of Titan. New York, Ace, 1963; London, Sphere, 1969.

Martian Time-Slip. New York, Ballantine, 1964; London, New English Library, 1976.

The Simulacra. New York, Ace, 1964; London, Eyre Methuen, 1977.

The Penultimate Truth. New York, Belmont, 1964; London, Cape, 1967.

Clans of the Alphane Moon. New York, Ace, 1964; London, Panther, 1975.

The Three Stigmata of Palmer Eldritch. New York, Doubleday, 1965; London, Cape, 1966.

Dr. Bloodmoney; or, How We Got Along after the Bomb. New York, Ace, 1965; London, Arrow, 1977.

The Crack in Space. New York, Ace, 1966; London, Eyre Methuen, 1977.

Now Wait for Last Year. New York, Doubleday, 1966; London, Panther, 1975.

The Unteleported Man. New York, Ace, 1966; London, Eyre Methuen, 1976; revised edition, New York, Berkley, 1982; as *Lies, Inc.,* London, Gollancz, 1984.

Counter-Clock World. New York, Berkley, 1967; London, Sphere, 1968.

The Zap Gun. New York, Pyramid, 1967; London, Panther, 1975.

The Ganymede Takeover, with Ray Nelson. New York, Ace, 1967; London, Arrow, 1971.

Do Androids Dream of Electric Sheep? New York, Doubleday, 1968; London, Rapp and Whiting, 1969.

Ubik. New York, Doubleday, 1969; London, Rapp and Whiting, 1970.

Galactic Pot-Healer. New York, Berkley, 1969; London, Gollancz, 1971.

A Maze of Death. New York, Doubleday, 1970; London, Gollancz, 1972.

Our Friends from Frolix 8. New York, Ace, 1970; London, Panther, 1976.

A Philip K. Dick Omnibus. London, Sidgwick and Jackson, 1970.

We Can Build You. New York, DAW, 1972; London, Fontana, 1977.

Flow My Tears, The Policeman Said. New York, Doubleday, and London, Gollancz, 1974.

Deus Irae, with Roger Zelazny. New York, Doubleday, 1976; London, Gollancz, 1977.

A Scanner Darkly. New York, Doubleday, and London, Gollancz, 1977.

Valis. New York, Bantam, and London, Corgi, 1981.

The Divine Invasion (Valis). New York, Pocket Books, 1981; London, Corgi, 1982.

The Transmigration of Timothy Archer (Valis). New York, Pocket Books, and London, Gollancz, 1982.

Radio Free Albemuth. New York, Arbor House, 1985.

Short Stories

A Handful of Darkness. London, Rich and Cowan, 1955; Boston, Gregg Press, 1978.

The Variable Man and Other Stories. New York, Ace, 1957; London, Sphere, 1969.

The Preserving Machine and Other Stories. New York, Ace, 1969; London, Gollancz, 1971.

The Book of Philip K. Dick. New York, DAW, 1973; as *The Turning Wheel and Other Stories,* London, Coronet, 1977.

The Best of Philip K. Dick, edited by John Brunner. New York, Ballantine, 1977.

The Golden Man. New York, Berkley, 1980; London, Eyre Methuen, 1981.

Robots, Androids, and Mechanical Oddities: The Science Fiction of Philip K. Dick , edited by Patricia S. Warrick and Martin H. Greenberg. Carbondale, Southern Illinois University Press, 1985.

I Hope I Shall Soon Arrive, edited by Mark Hurst and Paul Williams. New York, Doubleday, 1985.

OTHER PUBLICATIONS

Novel

Confessions of a Crap Artist. New York, Entwhistle, 1975; London, Magnum, 1979.

Other

"(Unpublished) Foreword to *The Preserving Machine,"* in *Science-Fiction Studies* (Terre Haute, Indiana), March 1975.

"Man, Android, and Machine,' in *Science Fiction at Large,* edited by Peter Nicholls. London, Gollancz, 1976; New York, Harper, 1977.

"A Clarification" (on Stanislaw Lem), in *Science-Fiction Studies* (Terre Haute, Indiana), March 1978.

"A Profession of Science Fiction 17: The Lucky Dog Pet Store," in *Foundation 17* (London), September 1979.

Philip K. Dick: In His Own Words (interviews), edited by Gregg Rickman. Long Beach, California, Fragments West-Valentine Press, 1984.

*

Bibliography: *PKD: A Philip K. Dick Bibliography* by Daniel J. H. Levack, Columbia, Pennsylvania, Underwood Miller, 1981.

Manuscript Collection: California State University, Fullerton.

Critical Studies: *Philip K. Dick and the Umbrella of Light* by Angus Taylor, Baltimore, T-K Graphics, 1975; *Philip K. Dick: Electric Shepherd* (includes bibliography) by Bruce Gillespie, Melbourne, Norstrilia Press, 1975; "Philip K. Dick Issue" of *Science-Fiction Studies* (Terre Haute, Indiana), March 1975 (includes bibliography); *Philip K. Dick* by Hazel Pierce, Mercer Island, Washington, Starmont House, 1982; *Philip K. Dick* edited by Martin H. Greenberg and Joseph D. Olander, New York, Taplinger, 1983; *The Novels of Philip K. Dick* by Kim Stanley Robinson, Ann Arbor, Michigan, UMI Research Press, 1984; *Philip K. Dick: The Last Testament* by Gregg Rickman, Long Beach, California, Fragments West-Valentine Press, 1985.

Philip K. Dick commented (in *Contemporary Novelists,* 1976):
    Using science fiction as a framework, I attempt to cut through the layers of quasi-reality, finding in the process that the elliptical viewpoints of psychosis act as starting points. Although I have been able to determine and then represent in my fiction many private universes, differing from one personality type to the next, I am in no sense trying to state what in the final analysis is "real." It is, rather, the search which interests me; perhaps the outcome is not the same for all of us. In my early novels and stories I often used sociological and political

themes; later I branched into drug trips and also theological trips, sometimes combining both (which angered many readers, both those who used drugs as well as those who used God). However, out of this I have recently come to sense a new level of feeling rather than intuition or reasoning. It is perhaps possible that when all the layers of the mind are stripped away the reality of the heart remains, or anyhow some organ more vital than the brain. In my work-in-progress I seek to contact some vein of cognition, some perceptual entity outside myself, outside our own race . . . where this entity would be, if anywhere at all, I can't say. Still, I think it exists, and, having helped me in my work throughout my career, perhaps it will guide me toward itself during the remaining part of my professional and creative life.

* * *

There are three phases to Philip K. Dick's writing career. There is the profusion of early stories, 73 published from 1952 to 1955. Next comes the spate of novels from 1962 through the 1970's. Last there is the Valis "trilogy" published shortly before his death in March of 1982.

Dick is not at all an easy writer in the later stages, despite the lurid covers and titles like *The Zap Gun* or *Do Androids Dream of Electric Sheep?* Typically, point of view is divided among a variety of characters (as many as 15 in *The Simulacra)*, and the characters are anti-heroic. Barney Mayerson in *The Three Stigmata of Palmer Eldritch* is rarely called by his right name and can easily be viewed as a failure according to the values prevalent in his society. Dick's characters at their best are survivors under conditions which are disastrous both physically and psychologically. Through them we see the constructive forces of humanity and empathy struggling with entropy, with the Form Destroyer. Bruno Bluthgeld may have released the bombs for the Third World War, time may have begun to go backwards, or a Neanderthal heritage may be forthcoming, but Dick's "minor man" (a TV repairman or a used flapple salesman) is coping and even contributing. This survival works in two ways: the personal—a Mr. Tagomi (in *The Man in the High Castle*) discovers resources unsuspected in himself, though the pain of the choice leads to a heart attack—and the societal—Tagomi helps to avert, for a time, a genocidal massacre of the Japanese by their German allies. In a letter (9 September 1970) Dick observes that "the enormous process of decline is pushed back slightly. Enough so that it matters. What Mr Tagomi has done matters. In a sense, there is nothing more important on all Earth than Mr. Tagomi's irritable action. " Tagomi cannot perceive what ultimate effect his small ripple will have. The resolution remains open-ended. Similarly, when the estranged Juliana Frink telephones her husband Frank, a sign of forthcoming conjugal and perhaps societal harmony, the phone rings without being answered, a test of the reader's faith.

Dick uses the traditional material of SF—psionics, robots, space flight, futuristic weaponry, alternative universes, aliens, other worlds. But he is interested not in a space opera plot but in his characters. Consequently, in *Galactic Pot-Healer* we see the initial despair of Joe Fernwright—thinking that he "ought to give up and take some other line of work," that his "work isn't good enough," and considering suicide. A master-repairer of pottery who has never tried to make his own pot, Joe is resigned to playing absurdist games from his tiny cubicle. Enter the god-like Glimmung, who assembles a group of misfits into a purposeful society with the goal of raising the sunken cathedral Heldscalla. Intermeddled in the parable is hilarious material, Willis, the free-lance writing robots, the Glimmung

himself, a god who falls to the basement through the several floors of the hotel where the project is ensconced. It is typical of Dick's subtle manipulation of the success/survival theme that when Joe's first pot comes from the kiln, it is "awful. " Awful or awe-ful, there's no knowing—it's the last word of the novel.

Galatic Pot-Healer is one of the easier novels in terms of character. When the focus is divided among several characters, the reader has more to weigh. *Martian Time-Slip* has Norbert Steiner's suicide, the mad greed of Arnie Kott, the timeless understanding of the Martian autochthone Heliogabalus, Sylvia Bohlen's empty loneliness, and Jack Bohlen's enduring a schizophrenia inherent both in the self and its society. The novel ends with "patience" as Jack and his father search the Martian night for the distraught Erna Steiner. Ursula K. Le Guin observes that Dick's "characters are ordinary. . . . That some of them have odd talents such as precognition makes no difference, since they inhabit a world where precognition is common; they're just ordinary neurotic precognitive slobs. " What counts is their "honesty, constancy, kindness, and patience. "

The policeman Felix Buckman in *Flow My Tears, The Policeman Said* collects antique snuff boxes and old postage stamps and his love is regressive and self-centered; he delegates the responsibility for executing Jason Taverner to a subordinate. Yet Dick's system is not at all stilted. Rick Deckard in *Do Androids Dream of Electric Sheep?* is a bounty hunter who gains our sympathy. Inevitably, somewhere, sometime, a Dick protagonist will have an existential moment of choice. Joe Chip in *Ubik* announces an intention to make such a choice (a homeostatic coffeeshop has just refused him service): "One of these days," Joe said wrathfully, "people like me will rise up and overthrow you, and the end of tyranny by the homeostatic machine will have arrived. The day of human values and compassion and simple warmth will return, and when that happens someone like myself who has gone through an ordeal and who genuinely needs hot coffee to pick him up and keep him functioning when he has to function will get the hot coffee whether he happens to have a poscred readily available or not."

Dick, especially after 1962, used the vocabulary and world view of the Swiss existential psychologist (Ludgwig Binswanger, for instance); Rollo May's collection of articles in *Existence: A New Dimension in Psychiatry and Psychology* (1958) may have been instrumental for a shift in Dick's writing. Earlier stories already indicated a strong interest in psychology; "Exhibit Piece" asks what is real, and the language of psychiatry contributes to the story. But in the later works the vocabulary is explicitly existential: the umwelt, the mitwelt, the eigenwelt, and a contrast of the tomb world with the chthonic and the ethereal. The existentialists, for instance, describe in a case study the severity of anankastic schizophrenia, its compulsion and its "blocked energies. " Dick transforms this material to SF in the person of psychokinetic pianist Richard Kongrosian (*The Simulacra*). There the extreme pressures of his being-in-the-world find a release for this blocked energy in Art and ultimately in the wider political sphere. Similarly Dick's treatment of autism and the warped perception of time in *Martian Time-Slip* has its roots in the same school.

The structure of a Dick novel can be tantalizing with so many diverse elements, plots, characters, bizarre events and moments—talking taxis, autonomic wrist watches, messages left in toilet bowls by quasi-gods, Heliogabalus reading *Life* and cooking a bouillabaisse, the Wind God George Walt (one body with two heads), vugs, flapples, bibs, wubs, can-D, chew-Z, bes and ges. Yet the humor is vital and the events and characters cohere thematically. Loose ends and inconsistencies are rare in his extensive corpus. It is worth mentioning another way in which Dick is an economical writer. He frequently draws from his early short stories for novel material. *The Penultimate Truth*, for instance, reshapes "The Defenders," "The Mold of Yancy," and "The Unreconstructed M. " This recycling of older material works so well, perhaps, because of the consistency of Dick's vision, and because, as Le Guin puts it, his "language [is] appropriate to what he wants to say, to us, about ourselves."

If there is an area where Dick is open to criticism, it is his handling of female character. Protagonists are nearly always male (Juliana Frink in *The Man in the High Castle* is an exception). In Dick's defense, he sees us living in an era dominated by the "solara-centric masculine deities," a world of "rocket ship space probes" rather than a realm of the "mother, the woman, the Earth, the chthonic world of the Cyrenaican Aphrodite" (*A Scanner Darkly*). Hence Juliana Frink is described as a "daemon" and Donna Hawthorne (*A Scanner Darkly*) seems to vanish "like fire or air, an element of the earth back into the earth. "

The third phase comprises three inter-connecting novels, *Valis, The Divine Invasion,* and *The Transmigration of Timothy Archer,* all of which share a religious theme, centering on a direct manifestation of the divine (a messiah, God, or a voice from the beyond).

Valis (an acronym for Vast Active Living Intelligence System) is a mixture of fiction, autobiography, essay, and black humor. Its "two" protagonists are a science-fiction writer named Phil Dick, and Horselover Fat, an alter ego for the very same Phil Dick (via Latin and German: Phil [Love] Hip [Horse] Dick [fat]. Dick called the novel picaresque and its style that of the street. The novel chronicles how a beam of pink light struck Phil Dick in March, 1974, dividing him into Phil and Fat. Horselover Fat spends almost every waking moment trying to account for the mass of information contained in the beam of pink light. *Valis* contains an appendix, Fat's "Tractates Cryptica Scriptura," with 53 entries mostly about early Christianity. At Dick's death he left his own Exegesis of more than two million words, of which the "Tractates" is only a hint. Not surprisingly readers are uneasy with just how much credence to give to the Phil Dick of the novel.

The Divine Invasion is more recognizably a SF novel, opening on a domed space colony, and travelling back to Earth not long after. Its characters include Herb Asher and Rybys Rommey from the domes, but also several divinities: Jahweh, Belial, the Prophet Elijah. The forces of good do battle with evil, and the ending is pat: Herb Asher's fantasies are fulfilled, chance and risk are eliminated. A-typically for a Dick hero, Asher rejects his suffering wife (compare Eric Sweetscent) and chooses empathy only when forced to by Yah [weh]. Survival is easier for Asher than it is for Mr. Tagomi, Jack Bohlen—or for Angel Archer. In Dick's earlier novels it's the "minor man" who makes a difference. In *Invasion* it's god.

The Transmigration of Timothy Archer is a first-person novel with Angel Archer as narrator (Dick's only other novels in sustained first person are *We Can Build You* and *Valis*). Archer is almost a roman à clef, with Archer representing Bishop James Pike, Kirsten Lundborg as his mistress Maren Bergrud, and Jeff Archer as Pike's son James, Jr. One character who is outside this biographical system is the narrator Angel. Pike's son never married, but Archer's son did. Dick needed a story teller, one who was privy to the totality of Archer's life. Whether Angel Archer arrives on the scene to satisfy authorial demands or to refute the charge that Dick had turned against women, she is a magnificent creation. And ultimately she transcends the necessary role for the story Dick had to tell and becomes the novel's protagonist.

Archer and Horselover Fat share the same obsession: to discover the primal truth, the reality that underlies the fabric of our apparent universe. Both pursue the gnosis that was lost with the suppression of early Christianity by the forces of Darkness. In his quest Archer dies in the Judean desert, only to manifest himself afterward to Bill Lundborg, the schizoid son of his mistress—the transmigration of the title.

And here Dick returns to the values of his novels before *Invasion,* where we mundane folk survive by our wits and by caring. And so we make a humane difference in whatever nightmarish worlds the author can dream up, whether with time going backwards, or gods invading our psyches. Angel Archer whispers in Bill Lundborg's ear: "I am going to fight to make you okay again. . . . Repairing automobile bodies and spray-painting and other real things; I will see you as you were; I will not give up. You will remember the ground again. " Nowhere has the Dickean credo been sounded so clearly.

—Anthony Wolk

DICKINSON, Peter (Malcolm de Brissac). British. Born in Livingstone, Northern Rhodesia (now Zambia), 16 December 1927. Educated at Eton College (King's Scholar), 1941-46; King's College, Cambridge (exhibitioner), B. A. 1951. Served in the British Army, 1946-48. Married Mary Rose Bernard in 1953; two daughters and two sons. Assistant Editor and reviewer, *Punch*, London, 1952-69. Chairman of the Management Committee, Society of Authors, 1978-80. Recipient: Crime Writers Association Gold Dagger, 1968, 1969; *Guardian* Award, for children's book, 1977; *Boston Globe-Horn Book* Award, for children's book, 1977; Whitbread Award, 1979; Library Association Carnegie Medal, for children's book, 1980, 1981. Agent: A. P. Watt Ltd., 26-28 Bedford Row, London WC1R 4HL. Address: 33 Queensdale Road, London W11 4SB, England.

SCIENCE-FICTION PUBLICATIONS

Novels (series: The Changes)

The Changes (for children). London, Gollancz, 1975.
   The Weathermonger. London, Gollancz, 1968; Boston, Little Brown, 1969.
   Heartsease. London, Gollancz, and Boston, Little Brown, 1969.
   The Devil's Children. London, Gollancz, and Boston, Little Brown, 1970.
The Green Gene. London, Hodder and Stoughton, and New York, Pantheon, 1973.
The Gift (for children). London, Gollancz, 1973; Boston, Little Brown, 1974.
The Poison Oracle. London, Hodder and Stoughton, and New York, Pantheon, 1974.
King and Joker. London, Hodder and Stoughton, and New York, Pantheon, 1976.
The Blue Hawk (for children). London, Gollancz, and Boston, Little Brown, 1976.
The Flight of Dragons. London, Pierrot, and New York, Harper, 1979.
Healer (for children). London, Gollancz, 1983; New York, Delacorte Press, 1985.
A Box of Nothing (for children). London, Gollancz, 1985.

OTHER PUBLICATIONS

Novels

Skin Deep. London, Hodder and Stoughton, 1968; as *The Glass-Sided Ants' Nest*, New York, Harper, 1968.
A Pride of Heroes. London, Hodder and Stoughton, 1969; as *The Old English Peep Show*, New York, Harper, 1969.
The Seals. London, Hodder and Stoughton, 1970; as *The Sinful Stones*, New York, Harper, 1970.
Sleep and His Brother. London, Hodder and Stoughton, and New York, Harper, 1971.
The Lizard in the Cup. London, Hodder and Stoughton, and New York, Harper, 1972.
The Lively Dead. London, Hodder and Stoughton, and New York, Pantheon, 1975.
Walking Dead. London, Hodder and Stoughton, 1977; New York, Pantheon, 1978.
One Foot in the Grave. London, Hodder and Stoughton, 1979; New York, Pantheon, 1980.
A Summer in the Twenties. London, Hodder and Stoughton, and New York, Pantheon, 1981.
The Last House-Party. London, Bodley Head, and New York, Pantheon, 1982.
Hindsight. London, Bodley Head, and New York, Pantheon, 1983.
Death of a Unicorn. London, Bodley Head, and New York, Pantheon, 1984.

Plays (for children)

Television Series: *Mandog*, 1972.

Other (for children)

Emma Tupper's Diary. London, Gollancz, and Boston, Little Brown, 1971.
The Dancing Bear. London, Gollancz, 1972; Boston, Little Brown, 1973.
The Iron Lion. Boston, Little Brown, 1972; London, Allen and Unwin, 1973.
Chance, Luck, and Destiny (miscellany). London, Gollancz, 1975; Boston, Little Brown, 1976.
Annerton Pit. London, Gollancz, and Boston, Little Brown, 1977.
Hepzibah. Twickenham, Middlesex, Eel Pie, 1978; Boston, Godine, 1980.
Tulku. London, Gollancz, and New York, Dutton, 1979.
City of Gold and Other Stories from the Old Testament. London, Gollancz, and New York, Pantheon, 1980.
The Seventh Raven. London, Gollancz, and New York, Dutton, 1981.
Giant Cold. London, Gollancz, and New York, Dutton, 1984.

Editor, *Presto! Humorous Bits and Pieces*. London, Hutchinson, 1975.
Editor, *Hundreds and Hundreds*. London, Penguin, 1984.

*

Peter Dickinson comments:
I regard all my fiction as SF (that's to say I write it as if it were), though usually the S bulks much smaller that the F. Classic detective stories (which I try to write) usually have to be restricted to a closed world, which I tend to invent as if it were an alien planet. Indeed, inventing even a normal human character seems to me to demand an effort of the same kind as inventing an alien species; this may account for the fact that my characters have a tendency towards the grotesque. The children's books are mostly straightforward soft SF; *The Green Gene* began as a satire about apartheid, or rather about outsiders' attitudes to it, but acquired directions and energies of its own. My attitude to SF is much more influenced by the pulp I read in the 1940's then by anything more recent, or in book form.

*   *   *

Peter Dickinson has made a substantial name for himself in the mystery genre with a series of bizarre murder mysteries. Frequently these novels play with devices better known in the field of science fiction, although none are really written as an example of the genre. There are hints of telepathy in *Walking Dead*, for example. Communication with a very bright ape is the key to unravelling the mystery in *The Poison Oracle*, and there is an alternate British royalty in *King and Joker*.

Dickinson has written several fantasy novels, perhaps the most interesting of which is a trilogy set in England when all technology stops working, magic returns to the land, the rest of the world continues to advance technologically, but a pastoral calm settles over most of the British Isles. The first in the series, *The Weathermonger*, follows a young man and his sister as they flee to France, only to return in search of the source of the mysterious change. Ultimately they confront an awakened Merlin of Camelot, once more active in the affairs of men.

The two follow-up volumes were related by setting only; there are no common characters and even Merlin appears to have disappeared. *Heartsease* is concerned with a spy from the United States who is unmasked by the elders of a village and nearly killed because of suspicion of witchcraft. He is rescued by sympathetic children, and a well-told series of adventures follow. Possibly the best in the series is *The Devil's Children*. Although the British have been mentally altered by the change so that they blindly strike out and destroy anything technological, one group in England seems to be immune, the resident population of Sikhs. The protagonist is a young girl separated from her parents who falls in with a wandering band of Sikhs, is befriended by them, and becomes their agent in dealings with the rest of the British. Unable to return to their homeland, they finally decide to establish a settlement in a remote area and trade with others using her as their agent.

Tulku is an oriental adventure fantasy. A boy and his companions wander around Tibet after bandits raid the mission where he lives. Ultimately he turns out to be a pivotal piece in a game of Oriental legend. *Tulku* is written for younger readers, but this is not true of *The Blue Hawk*. A young trainee for the priesthood violates ritual by befriending a sacred blue hawk, thereby causing the death of the reigning king, endangering his own life, and throwing the entire established order into disarray. He is caught up in the ensuing power struggle between clerical and lay institutions, as each seeks to make him the instrument of the other's downfall. *The Blue Hawk* may be the best single work Dickinson has written.

The only genuine science fiction novel Dickinson has ever written is *The Green Gene*. In an alternate version of our own world, England is ruled by a rigid authoritarian government. For some reason, an increasing number of human births in the island are of green children, and all green humans are legally declared to be Celts, while whites and blacks are legally Saxons.

An Indian medical specialist is hired by the Race Relations Board to develop a method of reliably predicting the occurrence of the green mutation. The Board ostensibly exists to promote racial harmony but is in fact the chief instrument for suppression of the green minority. The Indian is politically as well as socially naive, and is soon involved in politics, sexual liaisons, murder, and intrigue. He is kidnapped, enlisted in a plot against the government, and only arranges his own freedom by doublecrossing everyone. It's one of the best satirical novels of recent years and makes one wish Dickinson spent more time in the science-fiction field.

—Don D'Ammassa

DICKSON, Gordon R(upert). American. Born in Edmonton, Alberta, Canada, 1 November 1923; emigrated to the United States at age 13. Educated at the University of Minnesota, Minneapolis, B. A. 1948, and graduate study, 1948-50. Served in the United States Army, 1943-46. Since 1950, free-lance writer. Recipient: Hugo Award, 1965, 1981 (twice); Nebula Award, 1966; Skylark Award, 1975; Derleth Award, 1977; Jupiter award, 1977. President, Science Fiction Writers of America, 1969-71. Agent: Kirby McCauley Ltd., 425 Park Avenue South, New York, New York 10016, U. S. A.

SCIENCE-FICTION PUBLICATIONS

Novels (series: Dorsai; Robby Hoenig)

Alien from Arcturus . New York, Ace, 1956; as *Arcturus Landing*, 1978.
Mankind on the Run. New York, Ace, 1956; as *On the Run*, 1979.
The Genetic General, Time to Teleport. New York, Ace, 1960; *The Genetic General* published separately, London, Digit, 1961; expanded edition of *The Genetic General*, as *Dorsai!*, New York, DAW, and London, Sphere, 1976.
Secret under the Sea (for children; Hoenig). New York, Holt Rinehart, 1960; London, Hutchinson, 1962.
Naked to the Stars. New York, Pyramid, 1961; London, Sphere, 1978.
Delusion World, Spacial Delivery. New York, Ace, 1961.
Necromancer (Dorsai). New York, Doubleday, 1962; London, Mayflower, 1963; as *No Room for Man*, New York, Macfadden, 1963.
Secret under Antarctica (for children; Hoenig). New York, Holt Rinehart, 1963.
Secret under the Caribbean (for children; Hoenig). New York, Holt Rinehart, 1964.
Space Winners (for children). New York, Holt Rinehart, 1965; London, Faber, 1967.
The Alien Way. New York, Bantam, 1965; London, Corgi, 1973.
Mission to Universe. New York, Berkley, 1965; revised edition, New York, Ballantine, 1977; London, Sphere, 1978.
The Space Swimmers. New York, Berkley, 1967; London, Sidgwick and Jackson, 1968.
Planet Run, with Keith Laumer. New York, Doubleday, 1967; London, Hale, 1977.
Soldier, Ask Not (Dorsai). New York, Dell, 1967; London, Sphere, 1975.
None But Man. New York, Doubleday, 1969; London, Macdonald, 1970.
Wolfling. New York, Dell, 1969.
Spacepaw (for children). New York, Putnam, 1969.

Hour of the Horde (for children). New York, Putnam, 1970.
The Tactics of Mistake (Dorsai). New York, Doubleday, 1971; London, Sphere, 1975.
Sleepwalker's World. Philadelphia, Lippincott, 1971; London, Hale, 1973.
The Outposter. Philadelphia, Lippincott, 1972; London, Hale, 1973.
The Pritcher Mass. New York, Doubleday, 1972.
Alien Art. New York, Dutton, 1973; London, Hale, 1974.
The R-Master. Philadelphia, Lippincott, 1973; London, Hale, 1975.
Gremlins, Go Home! (for children), with Ben Bova. New York, St. Martin's Press, 1974.
Star Prince Charlie (for children), with Poul Anderson. New York, Putnam, 1975.
Three to Dorsai! (omnibus). New York, Doubleday, 1975.
The Dragon and the George. New York, Doubleday, 1976.
The Lifeship, with Harry Harrison. New York, Harper, 1976.
Time Storm. New York, St. Martin's Press, 1977; London, Sphere, 1978.
The Far Call. New York, Dial Press, and London, Sidgwick and Jackson, 1978.
Home from the Shore. New York, Sunridge Press, 1978.
Pro. New York, Ace, 1978.
The Spirit of Dorsai. New York, Ace, 1979.
Lost Dorsai. New York, Ace, 1980.
Masters of Everon. New York, Ace, 1980.
Love Not Human. New York, Ace, 1981.
Jamie the Red, with Roland Green. New York, Ace, 1984.
The Final Encyclopedia. New York, Tor, 1984.
The Last Master. New York, Tor, 1984.
Survival! New York, Pocket Books, 1984.
Phu Nham, with Poul Anderson. New York, Tor, 1984.

Short Stories

Earthman's Burden, with Poul Anderson. New York, Gnome Press, 1957.
Danger—Human. New York, Doubleday, 1970; as *The Book of Gordon Dickson*, New York, DAW, 1973.
Mutants. New York, Macmillan, 1970.
The Star Road. New York, Doubleday, 1973; London, Hale, 1975.
Ancient, My Enemy. New York, Doubleday, 1974; London, Sphere, 1978.
Gordon R. Dickson's SF Best, edited by James R. Frenkel. New York, Dell, 1978.
In Iron Years. New York, Doubleday, 1980.
Hoka!, with Poul Anderson. New York, Simon and Schuster, 1983.

OTHER PUBLICATIONS

Other

"Plausibility in Science Fiction," in *Science Fiction, Today and Tomorrow*, edited by Reginald Bretnor. New York, Harper, 1974.

Editor, *Rod Serling's Triple W: Witches, Warlocks, and Werewolves*. New York, Bantam, 1963.
Editor, *Rod Serling's Devils and Demons*. New York, Bantam, 1967.
Editor, with Poul Anderson and Robert Silverberg, *The Day the Sun Stood Still*. Nashville, Nelson, 1972.
Editor, *Combat SF*. New York, Doubleday, 1975.
Editor, *Futurelove: A Science Fiction Triad*. Indianapolis,

Bobbs Merrill, 1977; London, Hale, 1979.
Editor, *Nebula Winners 12*. New York, Harper, 1978.

*

Bibliography: *Gordon R. Dickson: A Primary and Secondary Bibliography* by Raymond H. Thompson, Boston, Hall, 1983.

*   *   *

Evolution is Gordon R. Dickson's pre-eminent subject. He delights in showing consciousness emerging, developing, and perfecting itself in persuit of god-like powers: "Man's future is upward and outward. " He presents an open-ended universe filled with limitless possibilities ready to be seized by whatever beings are bold enough. Dickson, a Pelagian humanist, maintains that intelligent life-forms can direct their own destiny. Ultimately, this capacity for continuous growth will surpass the static excellence of divinity, even that of a deity mighty enough to make the sun stand still ("Things Which Are Caesar's"). Nature is the milieu in which this drama unfolds, not a participant in the action. Dickson is no romantic pantheist like Poul Anderson, a writer with whom he is often incorrectly linked. Rather, it might be said of him as was said of the Persian poet Firdowsi: "He celebrates the exploits of men, the action is man to man, the thought is of men about men; men are raised to the level of supermen. "

Taken together, Dickson's works are simply variant readings of a single epic adventure—Life's quest for transcendence. He proclaims the victories of tenacious, creative, morally responsible people who can reshape heaven and earth by sheer force of will. Right makes might. Goodness must prevail. Mind conquers matter. The author's idealism and boundless confidence are qualities so traditional as to seem novelties in this gloomy era.

Thus, Dickson's favorite literary structure is the initiatory scenario. His pretagonists learn, not only for themselves, but on behalf of their group, culture, or species. For example, the hero of *The Pritcher Mass* spearheads the collective aspirations of all living things on Earth. The typical Dickson plot exemplifies the mythologist Joseph Campbell's heroic monomyth: a young, obscure, or otherwise lightly regarded individual discovers and masters his own unique abilities. Despite misunderstanding from friends and opposition from foes, he confounds conventional wisdom (often in some juridical confrontation), and thereby averts disaster.

This pattern persists in Dickson's juveniles: an exceptionally mature boy and girl save their planet from ruthless developers in *Alien Art*. It even shapes such humorous works as the Dilbian series (humans earning the respect of huge, roughneck aliens); *The Dragon and the George* (an English professor adjusting to life as a medieval dragon); and the Hoka series (a diplomat coping with compulsively imitative aliens). Dickson's comedies center on rational beings struggling to function in preposterously irrational situations.

However, Dickson usually stages his initiations as action-adventure tales. Some have objected to the frequency of military or quasi-military settings but these critics are reading a political intent into the work that is not there—Dickson is not Robert A. Heinlein. Although he sees an evolutionary advantage in humanity's pack-hunting instinct, his backgrounds are largely dictated by convenience. Traditionally, soldiers and explorers have been obvious subjects for life-and-death dramas of fortitude, daring, and loyalty. Yet Dickson innovates by also making his heroes cerebral and empathic as well as endowing many of them with his own talents for poetry, music, and art.

Note that "Call Him Lord" and "Jean Dupres" are about courage, not killing. They are mirror-image studies in manhood: a prince is executed for cowardice to forestall an evil reign; a colonial boy's death in battle brings peace within his people's grasp. These two stories, Nebula winner and Hugo nominee respectively, illustrate the technical mastery and absolute economy of his best work.

Although Dickson's elegance and limpidity are better displayed at shorter lengths, he is always a deliberate craftsman. (He was formally trained in writing by Robert Penn Warren, among others, and has made it his sole profession.) He has even developed his own approach to science fiction, the "consciously thematic novel. " This is Dickson's way of making a philosophical statement without resorting to the crudities of propaganda. As he explains: "The aim is to make the theme such an integral part of the novel that it can be effective upon the reader without ever having to be stated explicitly. . . . "

Dickson's philosophical purpose imparts a peculiarly relentless quality to his prose. Every element is concentrated along the cutting edge of the blade. Nothing in his stories exists for its own sake except the message. Although he is a dedicated researcher who experiences as well as studies his backgrounds, he never inserts decorative color or extraneous details. Consider the degree of auctorial control imposed on complex raw materials in *The Far Call*, the finest realistic novel about the space program yet written.

Dickson welds his stories together with symbols. These are typically grouped in pairs and triads that seek some ultimate unity—salvation is integration. Dualities exist worldwide but Dickson's trinities are best interpreted according to the structuralist theories of Indo-European mythologist Georges Dumézil. Thus, Dickson's design manages to be both universal and specifically Western. The tidiest and most accessible examples of his symbolism occur in *Home From the Shore* and its sequel, *The Space Swimmers*.

The Childe Cycle is the major showcase for Dickson's ideas and artistry. For the past 20 years, he has been constructing a mighty epic tracing the course of human evolution from the 14th to the 24th centuries. (The results published to date should be viewed as works-in-progess since the author plans to revise all of them.) When completed, the Cycle will consist of three historical, three contemporary, and six science fictional novels. Sf components *Ddorsai!, Necromancer, Soldier, Ask Not, The Tactics of Mistake,* and *The Final Encyclopedia* have appeared so far (*Chantry Guild,* is currently in preparation.) In these novels, the same hero passes through three incarnations, developing intuition as a man of War, empathy as a Man of Philosophy, and creativity as a Man of Faith until he assimilates the qualities of his Twin enemy and becomes the first Responsible Man, integrating the unconscious/conservative and the conscious/progressive halves of the racial psyche within himself. (See Sandra Miesel's afterwords to *The Final Encyclopedia, Lost Dorsai,* and the 1980 Ace edition of *Dorsai!* for extensive mythical and philosophical analysis.)

The level of aesthetic achievement varies. *Dorsai!* is notable for introducing a thoroughly sympathetic superman and for loading a military action yarn with mythic archetypes. The murkiness and subtlety of *Necromancer* make undue demands on the reader. *Soldier, Ask Not* attains wrenching emotional impact by using its villain as the viewpoint character. *The Tactics of Mistake* is as stilted as an animated war game. *The Final Encyclopedia* is sensitive and elegaic but marred by lectures. However, the short "illuminations" that accompany the Cycle proper ("Warrior," "Brothers," "Amanda Morgan," and "Lost Dorsai") are uniformly excellent in content as well as execution.

Pilgrim, which will incorporate the Hugo-winning "Cloak and Staff" (1980), plays counterpoint with Cycle themes. Its formidable alien conquerors are, in a sense, Dark Brothers of the Dorsai for they are the tragically warped martial caste of an otherwise extinct alien race. Its reluctant—and not superhuman—hero is a pilgrim both in body and spirit as he moves from a self-centered to a self-sacrificing life.

Yet despite decades of steady accomplishment, Dickson is less admired than he ought to be. His reputation as a novelist was tainted by early pulpish efforts like *Time To Teleport* and hasty potboilers like *The R-Master.* Anti-war backlash during the 1960's and 1970's distorted reactions to the Cycle. Stories of man's indominability ("Danger: Human") drew charges of Heinleinian human supremacy. But this criticism overlooks Dickson's sensitive portraits of aliens ("Black Charlie" and *The Alien Way*) and his pleas for interspecies empathy ("Dolphin's Way").

Complaints against Dickson's ineptitude with women characters has more validity. Too many of these are non-entities who exist solely to frustrate and misunderstand his heroes. Only masculine interactions seem important. However, in recent years he has systematically worked to correct this weakness by deepening characterizations and revising old formulas. The Triad in *Time Storm* is the Man of Philosophy, the Woman of War, and the Animal of Faith. The complementary Twins in *The Far Call* are no longer men but rather a pair of male-female couples. "Amanda Morgan" is built out of role reversals and in *The Final Encyclopedia* the trio of gifted heroines (one from each Splinter Culture) uphold the hero like the legs of a tripod.

At its serious best, Dickson's writing strikes the mind like remembered strains of half-heard music or swift torrents of icy water. C. S. Lewis's description of Norse myth applies equally well to Dickson: "cold, spacious, severe, pale, and remote."

—Sandra Miesel

DISCH, Thomas M(ichael). Also writes as Thom Demijohn; Leonie Hargrave; Cassandra Knye. American. Born in Des Moines, Iowa, 2 February 1940. Educated at Cooper Union, New York, and New York University, 1959-62. Part-time checkroom attendant, Majestic Theatre, New York, 1957-62; copywriter, Doyle Dane Bernbach Inc., New York, 1963-64. Since 1964, free-lance writer and lecturer. Recipient: O. Henry Prize, 1975; John W. Campbell Memorial Award, 1980; *Locus* award, 1981. Agent: Marie Rodell-Frances Collin Agency, 110 West 40th Street, New York, New York 10018, U. S. A.

SCIENCE-FICTION PUBLICATIONS

Novels

The Genocides. New York, Berkley, 1965; London, Whiting and Wheaton, 1967.
Mankind under the Leash. New York, Ace, 1966; as *The Puppies of Terra,* London, Panther, 1978.
Echo round His Bones. New York, Berkley, 1967; London, Hart Davis, 1969.
Camp Concentration. London, Hart Davis, 1968; New York, Doubleday, 1969.
The Prisoner. New York, Ace, 1969; London, Dobson, 1979.

334. London, MacGibbon and Kee, 1972; New York, Avon, 1974.
On Wings of Song. New York, St. Martin's Press, and London, Gollancz, 1979.
Triplicity (omnibus). New York, Doubleday, 1980.
The Businessman: A Tale of Terror. New York, Harper, and London, Cape, 1984.

Short Stories

One Hundred and Two H-Bombs. London, Compact, 1966; New York, Berkley, 1971; enlarged edition, as *White Fang Goes Dingo and Other Funny S. F. Stories,* London, Arrow, 1971.
Under Compulsion. London, Hart Davis, 1968; as *Fun with Your New Head,* New York, Doubleday, 1971.
Getting into Death. London, Hart Davis MacGibbon, 1973; New York, Knopf, 1976.
The Early Science Fiction Stories of Thomas M. Disch. Boston, Gregg Press, 1977.
Fundamental Disch. New York, Bantam, 1980; London, Gollancz, 1981.
The Man Who Had No Idea. London, Gollancz, 1982.
Ringtime: A Story. West Branch, Iowa, Toothpaste Press, 1983.
Torturing Mr. Amberwell. New Castle, Virginia, Cheap Street, 1985.

OTHER PUBLICATIONS

Novels

The House That Fear Built (as Cassandra Knye, with John Sladek). New York, Paperback Library, 1966.
Black Alice (as Thom Demijohn, with John Sladek). New York, Doubleday, 1968; London, W. H. Allen, 1969.
Clara Reeve (as Leonie Hargrave). New York, Knopf, and London, Hutchinson, 1975.
Neighboring Lives, with Charles Naylor. New York, Scribner, and London, Hutchinson, 1981.

Verse

Highway Sandwiches, with Marilyn Hacker and Charles Platt. Privately printed, 1970.
The Right Way to Figure Plumbing. New York, Basilisk Press, 1971.
ABCDEFG HIJKLM NPOQRST UVWXYZ. London, Anvil Press Poetry, 1981.
Burn This. London, Hutchinson, 1982.
Orders of the Retina. West Branch, Iowa, Toothpaste Press, 1982.
Here I Am, There You Are, Where Were We. London, Hutchinson, 1984.

Other

"The Embarrassment of Science Fiction," in *Science Fiction at Large,* edited by Peter Nicholls. London, Gollancz, 1976; New York, Harper, 1977.

Editor, *The Ruins of Earth: An Anthology of the Immediate Future.* New York, Putnam, 1971; London, Hutchinson, 1973.
Editor, *Bad Moon Rising.* New York, Harper, 1973; London, Hutchinson, 1974.

Editor, *The New Improved Sun: An Anthology of Utopian Science Fiction*. New York, Harper, 1975; London, Hutchinson, 1976.

Editor, with Charles Naylor, *New Constellations*. New York, Harper, 1976.

Editor, with Charles Naylor, *Strangeness*. New York, Scribner, 1977.

*

Bibliography: *Thomas M. Disch: A Preliminary Bibliography* by David Nee, Berkeley, California, Other Change of Hobbit, 1982.

Critical Study: *The American Shore: Meditations on a Tale of Science Fiction by Thomas M. Disch—"Angouleme"* by Samuel R. Delany, Elizabethtown, New York, Dragon Press, 1978.

*   *   *

There seems to be a gap between Thomas M. Disch's SF novels and his short stories of the 1960's, which often dispense with the paraphernalia of the genre and even with its logical coherence to magnify little details of everyday life and bring out strange correspondences that little by little become more real than our conventional reason. Though bathed in the same dark atmosphere—at worst utter pessimism, at best grim horror—the novels deal with conventional SF themes: invasion of Earth by superior beings that keep humans as pets (*Mankind under the Leash*) or exterminate them as vermin (*The Genocides*), jailing of and experimenting with pacifists and liberals when the US is faced with a multiplicity of Vietnam wars (*Camp Concentration*), instantaneous transmission and parallel worlds (*Echo round His Bones*), the horrors and absurdities of life in a decadent New York of the near future (*344*). Yet, at a deeper level, both express the same view of the world, the same philosophical concern. This is clearly shown by *The Prisoner*, which stands halfway: its theme is akin to that of *Camp Concentration*, but the omission of the explanatory context makes it into a parable of the absurd suspicion in which *any* society holds its members, like Kafka's *Trial* and *Castle* ; and the "reciprocator" enabling the prisoners to transmit their egos into their jailers' bodies is no longer necessary to convey the notion that each of us is both a victim and a tormentor.

But the evil indicted by Disch is not only cruel oppression: it is mechanized pity that the hero of "Flight Useless, Inexorable the Pursuit" vainly tries to escape; in "The City of Penetrating Light" happiness is compulsory, and in "The Affluence of Edwin Lollard" the worst crime is poverty; it is in a well-stocked store that the hero of "Descending" starts going down endless stairs to hellish solitude and death. If our consumer society is here clearly taken to task, so is any producers' society in "Thesis on the Social Forms and Social Controls in the USA" which proves that its best possible basis is induced schizophrenia, allowing the individual to enjoy the satisfaction of his needs and desires in blissful ignorance of the time he spends toiling in his turn. Yet a society in which all material problems were solved would perhaps be even more inhuman: in "Now is Forever" the "reprostat" makes it possible to produce as many copies as wanted, not only of the necessaries and amenities of life, but of oneself so as to dodge death—and these people who should be perfectly free are in fact totally enslaved to the endless repetition of meaningless scenes! The doom of the "Double-Timer" who gives its title to Disch's very first story is even worse in that he is *conscious* of endlessly re-enacting the *crime* that he was trying to erase by

time-travel: as also appears in "Assassin and Son," your free choice of the moment becomes your self-definition forever. In other words, each of us builds his own "squirrel's case"—an image which recurs in several stories besides the one that bears that title, where the hero ("Disch"!) never knows whether he is being studied by scientists or extra-terrestrials, but is sure of one thing: it would be much worse if he were suddenly set free! Confinement—one of Disch's favourite themes—is therefore self-imposed as much as inflicted. Societies may be concentration camps, but human nature itself is also at fault: solitude and company are equally unbearable to us. In "Come to Venus, Melancholy" Selma, whose diseased body has been replaced by a machine, mocked by John when she tries to share her poetic tastes with him, shuts herself up for five days . . . only to find herself dreadfully shut off forever. Self-expression and communication are not only Disch's concerns as a writer: Birdie Ludd in "Problems of Creativeness" and Barry Riordan in "The Man Who Had No Idea" desperately try to pass an exam that would prove they are worthy of the company of others. Yet, in "The Number You Have Reached," Justin, who is probably the last survivor of mankind, manages to bear loneliness but commits suicide when rung up by Justine—perhaps a mere figment of his imagination. And, worse than solitary life, solitary death leads the Russian cosmonaut in "Moondust, the Smell of Hay and Dialectic Materliasm" to realise that nothing is worth dying for.

Once you have gone so deep down, no certainty is unshakable, not even Descartes's *Cogito, ergo sum* (I think therefore I am), since machines also can think: in "The Sightseers" Jimmy and Ramona, who plan to be the new Adam and Eve after the decadence and disappearance of mankind, are, without knowing it, artificial creatures; and in *Echo round His Bones*, Professor Panofsky's double is convinced he has no soul, for his invention may have created an echo of reality, but only God can create souls. Therefore, how can the writer be sure that he is any more real than the characters he creates, how can the reader be sure that he is living in the real world? In Disch's hands, SF proves such a corrosive "deathray" when aimed at social structures, individual behaviour and eventually metaphysical tenets, that it leaves nothing but the bones, with just a rather absurd echo round them.

At this level of nihilism, a man is reduced to sheer existence (without even being sure that he exists) and a writer to silence. Satre—whose existentialist philosophy Disch's fiction hitherto closely parallels—drew from total absurdity the concept of total liberty and total responsibility; Disch seems to have made the jump to Pascal's *Credo quia absurdum* (I believe because it is absurd). The way out for him has been upwards—a striking similarity with Ballard, underlined by their common use of the symbol of flight. In "Doubting Thomas" a former scientist and Christian, back among his African tribe, uses sorcery to levitate, but crashes to his death when he becomes aware that it all depends on faith; whereas in *Mankind under the Leash* Julie's levitation was a gift from the Masters rejected by White Fang together with subservience, in *On Wings of Song* Daniel's yearning to fly becomes the expression of spiritual liberation: those three stories punctuate the author's passage from rebellion through doubt to idealistic faith. The key to this evolution is given in *The Businessman:* if nothing *must* be real, all *may* be real. This notion is immediately applied to evil, to justify its embodiment in the ghost-foetus born of the evil relationships between Giselle and her husband; this is to be compared with "Linda and Daniel and Spike" in which Linda's child was the mere fruit of her solitude and was assimilated to a bodily ill, cancer, and with "The Foetus" in which the theme was given a fantastic, child-by-the-devil treatment instead of its latter human significance. A third threesome shows us the loss of the ego ("The Beginning of April or the End of March"), the arbitrary acceptance of another one ("The Asian Shore"), and finally the totally free and conscious choice of a new and better one—"Understanding of Human Behaviour," an optimistic version of "The Asian Shore" according to the author's own foreword in *The Man Who Had No Idea*. Thus, Disch has rediscovered faith, evil, and good.

Indeed, though Disch still bitingly attacks puritanism in *On Wings of Song* and treats religious themes in a rather unorthodox and humorous way in *The Businessman,* those two novels and several stories (notably "The Revelation") express spiritual aspirations; though he still espouses dissenting causes (homosexuality, mild drugs), he often favours traditional virtues ("The Vengeance of Hera"); though he occasionally reverts to his former harsh accents ("The Planet of the Rapes"), his latest works are generally mellow and appeasing, bathed in tolerance and kindliness (especially, contrary to its title suggesting relationships based on mutual coercion, "The Fire Began to Burn the Stick, The Stick Began to Beat the Dog"). His first phase—wholesale destruction of social, moral, and logical tenets—has enabled him to give free rein to his inspiration—humorous, poetic, mystical, sometimes edifying ("Jodie and the Elevator") or even childish ("The Brave Little Toaster"). He asserts in the foreward previously mentioned that he is now far happier: so much the better for him, but perhaps so much the worse for the reader, who may regret the powerful originality of his earlier works. Perhaps a certain dose of discontent is a necessary ingredient without which SF remains a half-baked concoction, the bitter yeast without which it won't rise.

—George W. Barlow

DORMAN, Sonya (née Hess). American. Born 6 April 1924. Attended agricultural college, one year. Married in 1950 (separated); one daughter. Has worked as stable maid, kennel owner, receptionist, cook, dancer, greenhouse assistant, and housekeeper. Recipient: MacDowell Colony fellowship (five); Science Fiction Poetry Association Rhysling Award, 1978. Lives in Maine. Agent: John Schaffner, 114 East 28th Street, New York, New York 10016; or, Virginia Kidd, Box 278, Milford, Pennyslvania 18337, U. S. A.

SCIENCE-FICTION PUBLICATIONS

Novel

Planet Patrol (for children). New York, Coward McCann, 1978.

Uncollected Short Stories

"The Putnam Tradition," in *Amazing* (New York), January 1963.
"Winged Victory," in *Fantasy and Science Fiction* (New York), November 1963.
"Splice of Life," in *Orbit 1,* edited by Damon Knight. New York, Putnam, and London, Whiting and Wheaton, 1966.
"Go, Go, Go Said the Bird," in *Dangerous Visions,* edited by Harlan Ellison. New York, Doubleday, 1967; London, David Bruce and Watson, 2 vols., 1971.

"When I Was Miss Dow," in *Nebula Award Stories 2,* edited by Brian Aldiss and Harry Harrison. New York, Doubleday, and London, Gollancz, 1967.
"Lunatic Assignment," in *The Best from Fantasy and Science Fiction 18,* edited by Edward L. Ferman. New York, Doubleday, 1969.
"Bye, Bye, Banana Bird," in *Fantasy and Science Fiction* (New York), December 1969.
"The Living End," in *Orbit 7,* edited by Damon Knight. New York, Putnam, 1970.
"A Mess of Porridge," in *Alchemy and Academe,* edited by Anne McCaffrey. New York, Doubleday, 1970.
"Alpha Bets," in *Fantasy and Science Fiction* (New York), November 1970.
"Me-Too," in *Worlds of Fantasy 3* (New York), Winter 1970.
"The Deepest Blue in the World," in *SF: Authors' Choice 3,* edited by Harry Harrison. New York, Putnam, 1971.
"Bitching It Out," in *Quark 2,* edited by Samuel R. Delany and Marilyn Hacker. New York, Paperback Library, 1971.
"Harry the Tailor," in *A Pocketful of Stars,* edited by Damon Knight. New York, Doubleday, 1971; London, Gollancz, 1972.
"Journey," in *Galaxy* (New York), November 1972.
"The Bear Went over the Mountain," in *Fantasy and Science Fiction* (New York), August 1973.
"Sons of Bingaloo," in *Analog* (New York), November 1973.
"Time Bind," in *Orbit 13,* edited by Damon Knight. New York, Putnam, 1974.
"Cool Affection," in *Galaxy* (New York), May 1974.
"Death or Consequences," in *Tomorrow,* edited by Roger Elwood. New York, Evans, 1976.
"Them and Us and All," in *Fantasy and Science Fiction* (New York), April 1976.
"Building Block" in *The New Women of Wonder,* edited by Pamela Sargent. New York, Random House, 1978.
"The Gods in Winter," in *Interfaces,* edited by Ursula K. Le Guin and Virginia Kidd. New York, Ace, 1980.
"Peek-a-Boom," in *Edges,* edited by Ursula K. Le Guin and Virginia Kidd. New York, Pocket Books, 1980.

OTHER PUBLICATIONS

Verse

Poems. Columbus, Ohio State University Press, 1970.
Stretching Fence. Athens, Ohio University Press, 1975.
A Paper Raincoat. Orono, Maine, Puckerbrush Press, 1976.
The Far Traveler. La Crosse, Wisconsin, Juniper Press, 1980.
Palace of Earth. Orono, Maine, Puckberbrush Press, 1984.

*   *   *

Sonya Dorman is one of the most unusual and gifted contemporary writers of fantasy and science fiction. She has elevated the short story to an art form. Each of her stories is a unique, perfectly executed jewel. In addition to her strong sense of the macabre Dorman possesses a well-developed sense of humor, illustrated by the grimly absurd twists with which she ends many of her stories. She also writes poetry which has appeared in several science-fiction magazines and anthologies as well as short stories which have been published in *Redbook* and other magazines outside the field of science fiction.

Although the short story is a difficult medium in which to develop characters Dorman succeeds admirably. She is economical in her descriptions of futuristic societies and their trappings. In a few, well-chosen words she manages to convey a feeling of place and time. She is also skilled at letting the natural flow of the story line serve its own descriptive function.

Her plots are deceptively simple at first glance. On examination, however, they are carefully wrought situations described through fast-paced dialogue and exquisitely crafted action. Dorman is at her best in stories like "Splice of Life" in which an ordinary, if somewhat grim, situation is expanded and twisted to make a point about the implications of contemporary medical research. This story is gory, but the gore is purposeful and intentional. It's designed to shock her readers into seeing past the superficialities, to strip bare the meat and bone of living. The harsh and painful exposure of life is characteristic of Dorman's work. The constraints of her chosen medium, the short story, do not allow for the luxury of subtlety.

Strong, believable women are usually the main characters in Dorman's stories. They are also likeable. One of her most memorable heroines, Corporal Roxy Rimidon, appears first in "Bye, Bye, Banana Bird," a different kind of Dorman story. Roxy is a member of the elite, special forces unit from the American Dominion called the Planet Patrol. She is tough, sexy, and quite intelligent, and her adventures make exciting reading.

Writing as a woman in a man's field, Dorman resists the temptation to succeed solely by writing "just like a man." Instead she exhibits a combination of many of the traditional female virtues such as compassion and sensitivity in contrast to the traditional male characteristics of strength, energy, and conciseness. All of this is overlaid by her steely determination to make us see the world as she does. Dorman's world is bitterly ironic and at the same time human. The amorphous alien creatures from "When I Was Miss Dow" seem remarkably similar to the mental patients in "Lunatic Assignment."

Her lighter stories such as the Roxy Rimidon series and the more introspective "Building Block" are also expertly crafted. The latter deals with a female space architect who has a creative block. These later stories are less macabre and biting but just as creative and as well written as Dorman's earlier work.

Sonya Dorman is a rare phenomenon. She is an amalgam like her androgynous characters, able to display her sensitivity and compassion without relinquishing her energy and irony. One anthology editor cautions readers at the beginning of "Lunatic Assignment" to read the story only when they have time to read it through at one sitting and then to think about it. This precaution might preface almost all of her stories. They are not trifles to skim while sunbathing or waiting for the bus. They are energizing, thought-provoking, wryly optimistic glimpses of the future.

—Alice Chambers Wygant

DORSET, Richard. See SHAVER, Richard S.

DOYLE, (Sir) Arthur Conan. British. Born in Edinburgh, 22 May 1859. Educated at the Hodder School, Lancashire, 1868-70, Stoneyhurst College, Lancashire, 1870-75, and the Jesuit School, Feldkirch, Austria (Editor, *Feldkirchian Gazette*), 1875-76; studied medicine at the University of Edinburgh, 1876-81, M. B. 1881, M. D. 1885. Served as Senior Physician at a field hospital in South Africa during the Boer War, 1899-1902: knighted, 1902. Married 1) Louise Hawkins in 1885 (died, 1906), one daughter and one son; 2) Jean Leckie in 1907, two sons and one daughter. Practised medicine in Southsea, 1882-90; full-time writer from 1891; stood for Parliament as Unionist candidate for Central Edinburgh, 1900, and tariff reform candidate for the Hawick Burghs, 1906. Member, Society for Psychical Research, 1893-1930 (resigned). LL. D.: University of Edinburgh, 1905. Knight of Grace of the Order of St. John of Jerusalem. *Died 7 July 1930.*

SCIENCE-FICTION PUBLICATIONS

Novels (series: Professor Challenger in all books except *The Doings of Raffles Haw*)

The Doings of Raffles Haw. London, Cassell, and New York, Lovell, 1892.
The Lost World. London, Hodder and Stoughton, 1912; New York, Doran, 1915.
The Poison Belt. London, Hodder and Stoughton, and New York, Doran, 1913.
The Land of Mist. London, Hutchinson, 1925; New York, Doran, 1926.

Short Stories

Danger! and Other Stories. London, Murray, 1918; New York, Doran, 1919.
The Maracot Deep and Other Stories. London, Murray, and New York, Doubleday, 1929.
The Professor Challenger Stories. London, Murray, 1952.
The Best Science Fiction of Arthur Conan Doyle, edited by Charles G. Waugh and Martin H. Greenberg. Carbondale, Southern Illinois University Press, 1981.

OTHER PUBLICATIONS

Novels

A Study in Scarlet. London, Ward Lock, 1888; Philadelphia, Lipincott, 1890.
The Mystery of Cloomber. London, Ward and Downey, 1888; New York, Fenno, 1896 (?).
Micah Clarke. London, Longman, and New York, Harper, 1889.
The Firm of Girdlestone. London, Chatto and Windus, and New York, Lovell, 1890.
The Sign of Four. London, Blackett, 1890; New York, Collier, 1891.
The White Company. London, Smith Elder, 3 vols., 1891; New York, Lovell, 1 vol., 1891.
The Great Shadow. New York, Harper, 1892.
The Great Shadow, and Beyond the City. Bristol, Arrowsmith, 1893; New York, Ogilvie, 1894.
The Refugees. London, Longman, 3 vols., 1893; New York, Harper, 1 vol., 1893.
The Parasite. London, Constable, and New York, Harper, 1894.
The Stark Munro Letters. London, Longman, and New York, Appleton, 1895.
Rodney Stone. London, Smith Elder, and New York, Appleton, 1896.
Uncle Bernac: A Memory of the Empire. London, Smith Elder, and New York, Appleton, 1897.
The Tragedy of Korosko. London, Smith Elder, 1898; as *A*

Desert Drama, Philadelphia, Lippincott, 1898.
A Duet, with an Occasional Chorus. London, Grant Richards, and New York, Appleton, 1899; revised edition, London, Smith Elder, 1910.
The Hound of the Baskervilles. London, Newnes, and New York, McClure, 1902.
Sir Nigel. London, Smith Elder, and New York, McClure, 1906.
The Valley of Fear. New York, Doran, and London, Smith Elder, 1915.

Short Stories

Mysteries and Adventures. London, Scott, 1889; as *The Gully of Bluemansdyke and Other Stories,* 1892.
The Captain of the Polestar and Other Tales. London, Longman, 1890; New York, Munro, 1894.
The Adventures of Sherlock Holmes. London, Newnes, and New York, Harper, 1892.
My Friend the Murderer and other Mysteries and Adventures. New York, Lovell, 1893.
The Memoirs of Sherlock Holmes. London, Newnes, 1893; New York, Harper, 1894.
The Great Keinplatz Experiment and Other Stories. Chicago, Rand McNally, 1894.
Round the Red Lamp, Being Facts and Fancies of Medical Life. London, Methuen and New York, Appleton, 1894.
The Exploits of Brigadier Gerard. London, Newnes, and New York, Appleton, 1896.
The Man from Archangel and Other Stories. New York, Street and Smith, 1898.
Hilda Wade (completion of work by Grant Allen). London, Richards, and New York, Putnam, 1900.
The Green Flag and Other Stories of War and Sport. London, Smith Elder, and New York, McClure, 1900.
Adventures of Gerard. London, Newnes, and New York, McClure, 1903.
The Return of Sherlock Holmes. London, Newnes, and New York, McClure, 1905.
Round the Fire Stories. London, Smith Elder, and New York, McClure, 1908.
The Last Galley: Impressions and Tales. London, Smith Elder, and New York, Doubleday, 1911.
His Last Bow: Some Reminiscences of Sherlock Holmes. London, Murray, and New York, Doran, 1917.
Tales of the Ring and Camp. London, Murray, 1922; as *The Croxley Master and Other Tales of the Ring and Camp,* New York, Doran, 1925.
Tales of Pirates and Blue Water. London, Murray, 1922; as *The Dealings of Captain Sharkey and Other Tales of Pirates,* New York, Doran, 1925.
Tales of Terror and Mystery. London, Murray, 1922; as *The Black Doctor and Other Tales of Terror and Mystery,* New York, Doran, 1925.
Tales of Twilight and the Unseen. London, Murray, 1922; as *The Great Keinplatz Experiment and Other Tales of Twilight and the Unseen,* New York, Doran, 1925.
Tales of Adventure and Medical Life. London, Murray, 1922; as *The Man from Archangel and Other Tales of Adventure,* New York, Doran, 1925.
Tales of Long Ago. London, Murray, 1922; as *The Last of the Legions and Other Tales of Long Ago,* New York, Doran, 1925.
The Case-Book of Sherlock Holmes. London, Murray, and New York, Doran, 1927.
The Conan Doyle Historical Romances. London, Murray, 2 vols., 1931-32.

The Field Bazaar. Privately printed, 1934; Summit, New Jersey, Pamphlet House, 1947.
Great Stories, edited by John Dickson Carr. London, Murray, and New York, London House and Maxwell, 1959.
The Annotated Sherlock Holmes, edited by William S. Baring-Gould. New York, Potter, 2 vols., 1967; London, Murray, 2 vols., 1968.
The Sherlock Holmes Illustrated Omnibus (facsimile of magazine stories). London, Murray-Cape, 1978.
The Best Supernatural Tales of Arthur Conan Doyle, edited by E. F. Bleiler. New York, Dover, 1979.
Sherlock Holmes: The Published Apocrypha, with others, edited by Jack Tracy. Boston, Houghton Mifflin, 1980.
The Final Adventures of Sherlock Holmes, edited by Peter Haining. London, W. H. Allen, 1981.
The Edinburgh Stories. Edinburgh, Polygon, 1981.
Uncollected Stories, edited by John Michael Gibson and Richard Lancelyn Green. London, Secker and Warburg, 1982.

Plays

Jane Annie; or, The Good Conduct Prize, with J. M. Barrie, music by Ernest Ford (produced London, 1893). London, Chappell, 1893.
Foreign Policy, adaptation of his own story "A Question of Diplomacy" (produced London, 1893).
Waterloo, adaptation of his story "A Straggler of 15" (as *A Story of Waterloo,* produced Bristol, 1894; London, 1895; as *Waterloo,* produced New York, 1899). London, French, 1907; in *One-Act Plays of To-day,* 2nd series, edited by J. W. Marriott, Boston, Small Maynard, 1926.
Halves, adaptation of the story by James Payn (produced Aberdeen and London, 1899).
Sherlock Holmes, with William Gillette, adaptation of works by Doyle (produced Buffalo and New York, 1899; Liverpool and London, 1901).
A Duet (A Duologue) (produced London, 1902). London, French, 1903.
Brigadier Gerard, adaptation of his own stories (produced London and New York, 1906).
The Fires of Fate: A Modern Morality, adaptation of his novel *The Tragedy of Korosko* (produced Liverpool, London and New York, 1909).
The House of Temperley, adaptation of his novel *Rodney Stone* (produced London, 1910).
The Pot of Caviare, adaptation of his own story (produced London, 1910).
The Speckled Band: An Adventure of Sherlock Holmes (produced London and New York, 1910). London, French, 1912.
The Crown Diamond (produced Bristol and London, 1921). Privately printed, 1958.
The Journey, in *The Poems of Arthur Conan Doyle,* 1922.
It's Time Something Happened. New York, Appleton, 1925.

Verse

Songs of Action. London, Smith Elder, and New York, Doubleday, 1898.
Songs of the Road. London, Smith Elder, and New York, Doubleday, 1911.
The Guards Came Through and Other Poems. London, Murray, 1919; New York, Doran, 1920.
The Poems of Arthur Conan Doyle: Collected Edition. London, Murray, 1922.

Other

The Great Boer War. London, Smith Elder, and New York, McClure, 1900.

The War in South Africa: Its Cause and Conduct. London, Smith Elder, and New York, McClure, 1902.

Works (Author's Edition). London, Smith Elder, 12 vols., and New York, Appleton, 13 vols., 1903.

The Fiscal Question. Hawick, Roxburgh, Henderson, 1905.

An Incursion into Diplomacy. London, Smith Elder, 1906.

The Story of Mr. George Edalji. London, Daily Telegraph, 1907.

Through the Magic Door (essays). London, Smith Elder, 1907; New York, McClure, 1908.

The Crime of the Congo. London, Hutchinson, and New York, Doubleday, 1909.

Divorce Law Reform: An Essay. London, Divorce Law Reform Union, 1909.

Sir Arthur Conan Doyle: Why He Is Now in Favour of Home Rule. London, Liberal Publication Department, 1911.

The Case of Oscar Slater. London, Hodder and Stoughton, 1912; New York, Doran, 1913.

Divorce and the Church, with Lord Hugh Cecil. London, Divorce Law Reform Union, 1913.

Great Britain and the Next War. Boston, Small Maynard, 1914.

In Quest of Truth, Being a Correspondence Between Sir Arthur Conan Doyle and Captain H. Stansbury. London, Watts, 1914.

To Arms! London, Hodder and Stoughton, 1914.

The German War. London, Hodder and Stoughton, 1914; New York, Doran, 1915.

Western Wanderings (travel in Canada). New York, Doran, 1915.

The Outlook on the War. London, Daily Chronicle, 1915.

An Appreciation of Sir John French. London, Daily Chronicle, 1916.

A Petition to the Prime Minister on Behalf of Sir Roger Casement. Privately printed, 1916.

A Visit to Three Fronts: Glimpses of British, Italian, and French Lines. London, Hodder and Stoughton, and New York, Doran, 1916.

The Briths Campaign in France and Flanders. London, Hodder and Stoughton, 6 vols., 1916-20; New York, Doran, 6 vols., 1916-20; revised edition, as *The British Campaigns in Europe 1914-1918,* London, Bles, 1 vol., 1928.

The New Revelation. London, Hodder and Stoughton, and New York, Doran, 1918.

The Vital Message (on spiritualism). London, Hodder and Stoughton, and New York, Doran, 1919.

Our Reply to the Cleric. London, Spiritualists' National Union, 1920.

A Public Debate on the Truth of Spiritualism, with Joseph McCabe. London, Watts, 1920; as *Debate on Spiritualism,* Girard, Kansas, Haldeman Julius, 1922.

Spiritualism and Rationalism. London, Hodder and Stoughton, 1920.

The Wanderings of a Spiritualist. London, Hodder and Stoughton, and New York, Doran, 1921.

Spiritualism: Some Straight Questions and Direct Answers. Manchester, Two Worlds, 1922.

The Case for Spirit Photography, with others. London, Hutchinson, 1922; New York, Doran, 1923.

The Coming of the Fairies. London, Hodder and Stoughton, and New York, Doran, 1922.

Three of Them: A Reminiscence. London, Murray, 1923.

Our American Adventure. London, Hodder and Stoughton, and New York, Doran, 1923.

Our Second American Adventure. London, Hodder and Stoughton, and Boston, Little Brown, 1924.

Memories and Adventures. London, Hodder and Stoughton, and Boston, Little Brown, 1924.

Psychic Experiences. London and New York, Putnam, 1925.

The Early Christian Church and Modern Spiritualism. London, Psychic Bookshop, 1925.

The History of Spiritualism. London, Cassell, 2 vols., and New York, Doran, 2 vols., 1926.

Pheneas Speaks: Direct Spirit Communications. London, Psychic Press, and New York, Doran, 1927.

What Does Spiritualism Actually Teach and Stand For? London, Psychic Bookshop, 1928.

A Word of Warning. London, Psychic Press, 1928.

An Open Letter to Those of My Generation. London, Psychic Press, 1929.

Our African Winter. London, Murray, 1929.

The Roman Catholic Church: A Rejoinder. London, Psychic Press, 1929.

The Edge of the Unknown. London, Murray, and New York, Putnam, 1930.

Works (Crowborough Edition). New York, Doubleday, 24 vols., 1930.

Strange Studies from Life, edited by Peter Ruber. New York, Candlelight Press, 1963.

Arthur Conan Doyle on Sherlock Holmes. London, Favil, 1981.

Essays on Photography, edited by John Michael Gibson and Richard Lancelyn Green. London, Secker and Warburg, 1982.

Letters to the Press, edited by John Michael Gibson and Richard Lancelyn Green. London Secker and Warburg, 1985.

Editor, *D. D. Home: His Life and Mission,* by Mrs. Dunglas Home. London, Kegan Paul Trench Trubner, 1921.

Editor, *The Spiritualists' Reader.* Manchester, Two Worlds, 1924.

Translator, *The Mystery of Joan of Arc,* by Léon Denis. London, Murray, 1924; New York, Dutton, 1925.

*

Bibliography: *The World Bibliography of Sherlock Holmes and Dr. Watson* by Ronald Burt De Waal, Boston, New York Graphic Society, 1975; *A Bibliography of A. Conan Doyle* by Richard Lancelyn Green and John Michael Gibson, Oxford, Clarendon Press, 1983.

Manuscript Collection: Humanities Research Center, University of Texas, Austin.

Critical Studies (selection): *The Private Life of Sherlock Holmes* by Vincent Starrett, New York, Macmillan, 1933, London, Nicholson and Watson, 1934, revised edition, Chicago, University of Chicago Press, 1960, London, Allen and Unwin, 1961; *Conan Doyle: His Life and Art* by Hesketh Pearson, London, Methuen, 1943, New York, Walker, 1961; *The Life of Sir Arthur Conan Doyle* by John Dickson Carr, London, Murray, and New York, Harper, 1949; *Conan Doyle: A Biography* by Pierre Nordon, London, Murray, 1966, New York, Holt Rinehart, 1967; *Conan Doyle: A Biography of the Creator of Sherlock Holmes* by Ivor Brown, London, Hamish Hamilton, 1972; *The Adventures of Conan Doyle: The Life of the Creator of Sherlock Holmes* by Charles Higham, London, Hamish Hamilton, and New York, Norton, 1976; *The*

Encyclopedia Sherlockiana by Jack Tracy, New York, Doubleday, 1977, London, New English Library, 1978; *Conan Doyle: A Biographical Solution* by Ronald Pearsall, London, Weidenfeld and Nicolson, 1977; *Sherlock Holmes and His Creator* by Trevor H. Hall, London, Duckworth, 1978, New York, St. Martin's Press., 1983; *Conan Doyle: Portrait of an Artist* by Julian Symons, London, G. Whizzard, 1979; Sherlock Holmes: The Man and His World by H. R. F. Keating, London, Thames and Hudson, and New York, Scribner, 1979; *The Quest for Sherlock Holmes: A Biographical Study of the Early Life of Sir Arthur Conan Doyle* by Owen Dudley Edwards, Edinburgh, Mainstream, 1982, Totowa, New Jersey, Barnes and Noble, 1983.

*   *   *

Although literary history best remembers him as the creator of Sherlock Holmes, Arthur Conan Doyle also produced a considerable body of science fiction, adventure tales, and historical romances, as well as numerous works of non-fiction. In common with many other writers whose works spanned both popular and more traditional fields, Doyle preferred to be remembered for his more "mainstream" writings rather than for his popular fiction. Well before Hugo Gernsback coined the term "science fiction," Doyle felt at ease writing heroic adventure tales which would later be placed comfortably in this category. It is not surprising that the author who celebrated deductive reasoning should turn his talents in this direction. From an early age, Doyle was fascinated by history and heroics; his medical training instilled in him a respect for the scientific method; and a flamboyant medical colleague, Dr. George Budd, influenced the young Doyle to bear with the sometimes extreme eccentricities of a man of science. It was Dr. Budd who provided the model for Professor George Edward Challenger, whose appearance in most of Doyle's science fiction reflected the increasing importance of the scientist during the late 19th and early 20th centuries.

Professor Challenger is presented as a man of enormous ego, pride, and determination completely dedicated to discovering scientific truth. He first appears in *The Lost World,* a novel which introduces some of the thematic preoccupations common to most of Doyle's science fiction. "There are heroisms all around us waiting to be done," one character declares, and it is in the spirit of heroic adventure that the fledgling newspaper reporter, Edward Malone, joins Challenger, the gentleman/hunter Lord John Roxton, and the skeptical cantankerous Professor Summerlee on a quest to test the validity of Challenger's assertion that prehistoric life exists on an isolated plateau in South America. As the heroes confront a series of physical hazards and witness numerous awe-inspiring sights, it becomes clear that Doyle's intention is to celebrate a sense of wonder, to convey a fascination with the heroic unknown, and above all to assert modern man's supreme position in both past and present worlds. "Our eyes have seen great wonders," Malone reports after the four adventurers, armed with modern weaponry, help the more advanced Indian race on the plateau dramatically assert their dominance over an inferior race of ape-men. "Now upon this plateau the future must ever be for man," the scientist declares.

The superiority of the modern scientific mind is reasserted in "When the World Screamed," a humourous short story again featuring Challenger, this time armed with "scientific" paraphernalia designed to penetrate the earth's crust in order to prove the preposterous contention that "the world upon which we live is itself a living organism" insensible to man's presence. This is the tale of Challenger's efforts to "let the earth know that there is at least one person, George Edward Challenger, who

calls for attention—who, indeed, insists upon attention." Not surprisingly, Challenger achieves his goal.

The Poison Belt is a novel which emphasizes Challenger's unselfish devotion to scientific truth. As the sole predictor of the catastrophic approach toward earth of a "poisonous" belt of ether gas, Challenger can philosophically face the prospect of his own demise and the annihilation of mankind because he is so thrilled at the privilege of observing it! Malone, Roxton, Summerlee, and Mrs. Challenger add more believable exclamations of wonderment to those of the scientist. This novel reveals Doyle's delight in juxtaposing the real and unreal, the beautiful and terrible, as Challenger and company regard through a sealed window the apparent end of the world taking place during a beautiful English summer's day. "The Disintegration Machine" is the most serious of the Challenger stories. Here Malone accompanies Challenger as the Professor examines the invention of "Latvian gentlemen named Theodore Nemor . . . a machine of a most extraordinary character which is capable of disintegrating any object placed within its spere of influence."

Challenger, quick to recognize the awesome military and "evil" potentialities of this invention, uses it to disintegrate Mr. Nemor himself, who holds the secret to the machine's operation.

The Land of Mist, a lengthy novel featuring Challenger only peripherally, cannot be considered science fiction. This apology for the occult reflects Doyle's own conviction about the validity of occult spiritualism. The work does restate one theme expressed in "The Disintegration Machine" and *The Maracot Deep;* it was Doyle's belief that it is absolutely essential for man's spiritual development to keep pace with his strides in the scientific realm. *The Maracot Deep* takes up this theme against a submarine environment. Here Dr. Maracot and a party of deep sea explorers, including a colorful slang-speaking Yankee handyman called Bill Scanlon, discover the lost colony of Atlantis when their undersea vessel is marooned in an Atlantic trench deeper than any previously explored by man. In an image reminiscent of that employed in *The Poison Belt,* Doyle at first isolates his scientist behind impenetrable glass as the real and unreal, the beautiful and sublime, are contrasted. With a sense of wonder, the explorers discover that, in spite of great scientific advances, Atlantis is doomed by its own limited spiritual development. Only through spiritual self-realization combined with cunning and access to scientific equipment do the heroes rise to the surface in Doyle's final assertion of the superiority of modern scientific man.

Some of Doyle's lesser-known stories, sometimes classified as science fiction, have more in common with the horror genre. In "The Silver Mirror," "The Terror of Blue John Gap," "The Horror of the Heights," and "The Captain of the Polestar" Doyle replaces a sense of wonder with a spine-chilling sense of unearthly dread; he purposely leaves the credibility of the narrators in doubt, undercutting any certainty on the reader's part that each story is "scientifically" believable. "Heroisms" are abundant but it is raw courage which makes these protagonists into heroes, not scientific superiority.

—Rosemary Herbert

DOZOIS, Gardner (Raymond). American. Born in Salem, Massachusetts, 23 July 1947. Served as a military journalist, 1966-69. Reader for Dell and Award publishers, and for *Galaxy, If, Worlds of Fantasy,* and *Worlds of Tomorrow,* 1970-73; Co-Founder, and Associate Editor, *Isaac Asimov's Science Fiction Magazine,* 1976-77. Member of the Advisory Committee, Paley

Library, Special Collection Department, Temple University, Philadelphia. Recipient: Nebula Award, 1983, 1985. Agent: Virginia Kidd, Box 278, Milford, Pennsylvania 18337, U.S.A.

SCIENCE-FICTION PUBLICATIONS

Novels

Nightmare Blue, with George Alec Effinger. New York, Berkley, 1975; London, Fontana, 1977.
Strangers. New York, Berkley, 1978; London, Hamlyn, 1980.

Short Stories

The Visible Man. New York, Berkley, 1977.

Uncollected Short Stories

"Disciples," in *More Wandering Stars,* edited by Jack Dann. New York, Doubleday, 1981.
"A Change in the Weather," with Jack Dann, in *Playboy* (Chicago), June 1981.
"The Sacrifice," in *Unicorns!,* edited by Dozois and Jack Dann. New York, Ace, 1982.
"Playing the Game," with Jack Dann, in *Great Stories from Rod Serling's The Twilight Zone Magazine,* edited by T. E. D. Klein. New York, TZ Publications, 1982.
"Snow Job," with Michael Swanwick, in *High Times* (New York), April 1982.
"A Traveler in an Antique Land," in *Chrysalis 10,* edited by Roy Torgeson. New York, Doubleday, 1983.
"Down among the Dead Men" with Jack Dann, in *The Dodd Mead Gallery of Horror,* edited by Charles L. Grant. New York, Dodd Mead, 1983.
"Touring," with Jack Dann and Michael Swanwick, in *The Year's Best Horror Stories 11,* edited by Karl Edward Wagner. New York, DAW, 1983.
"Slow Dancing with Jesus," with Jack Dann, in *Penthouse* (New York), July 1983.
"The Peacemaker," in *Isaac Asimov's Science Fiction Magazine* (New York), August 1983.
"Time Bride," with Jack Dann, in *Isaac Asimov's Science Fiction Magazine* (New York), December 1983.
"Afternoon at Schrafft's," with Jack Dann and Michael Swanwick, in *Magicats!,* edited by Dozois and Dann. New York, Ace, 1984.
"Morning Child," in *Omni* (New York), January 1984.
"Virgin Territory," with Jack Dann and Michael Swanwick, in *Penthouse* (New York), March 1984.
"The Mayan Variation," in *Amazing* (New York), September 1984.
"The Gods of Mars," with Jack Dann and Michael Swanwick, in *Omni* (New York), March 1985.

OTHER PUBLICATIONS

Other

"Mainstream SF and Genre SF," in *Fantastic* (New York), November 1973.
"The Science Fiction Novel," with Jack Dann, in *Fiction Writer's Handbook,* edited by Hallie and Whit Burnett. New York, Harper, 1975.
"Living the Future: You Are What You Eat," in *Writing and Selling Science Fiction.* Cincinnati, Writer's Digest, 1976.

The Fiction of James Tiptree, Jr. New York, Algol Press, 1977.

Editor, *A Day in the Life.* New York, Harper, 1972.
Editor, with Jack Dann, *Future Power.* New York, Random House, 1976.
Editor, *Another World* (for children). Chicago, Follett, 1977.
Editor, *Best Science Fiction Stories of the Year 6-10.* New York, Dutton, 5 vols., 1977-81.
Editor, with Jack Dunn, *Aliens!* New York, Pocket Books, 1980.
Editor, with Jack Dann, *Unicorns!* New York, Ace, 1982.
Editor, with Jack Dann, *Magicats!* New York, Ace, 1984.
Editor, with Jim Frenkel, *The Year's Best Science Fiction 1-2.* New York, Bluejay, 2 vols., 1984-85.

*

Manuscript Collection: Paskow Collection, Paley Library, Temple University, Philadelphia.

*   *   *

Gardner Dozois is a master short-story writer and brilliant anthologist. In "The Peacemaker" (Nebula award), Dozois explores a world shaken from civilization by the melting of the polar ice caps. The floods sink the great eastern seacoast cities and leave the survivors in the great American heartland at the mercy of ardent evangelists. As the young boy who is chosen at the story's conclusion learns: everyone must make sacrifices.

Dozois's short stories are collected in *The Visible Man,* with an admiring introduction by Robert Silverberg. The dozen stories make up a solid progression of Dozois's craftsmanship in the 1970's. From a unique story of alien invasion—"Chains of the Sea"—to the upbeat—"A Special Kind of Morning"—to the naturalistic—"The Last Day of July"—to the allegorical—"A Kingdom by the Sea"—Dozois displays a command of the short story form unrivaled by his contemporaries.

In his only solo novel to date, *Strangers,* Dozois presents Joseph Faber, a human from Earth with an alien lover named Liraun, during his tour of the planet Weinnuach. The couple are shunned by the non-human Cian and the human trade community. Faber could care less about his peers, but to win back a measure of respectability for Liraun he consents to attend the House of Tailors where the Cian genetically alter Faber's body so he and Liraun can be interfertile: a necessary condition of Cian marriage rites. In this tremendously sad story, Dozois develops the themes of alienness, and the impossibility that we can ever know another person—hence the title *Strangers.* Through misunderstanding after misunderstanding, Faber and Liraun find themselves on a fated path to doom: the result of their failure to understand each other's culture. Yet, even though *Strangers* ends with death, it also ends with life and hope. This very moving novel is one of the forgotten and ignored classics of the 1970's.

Dozois's other novel, a collaboration with George Alec Effinger called *Nightmare Blue,* is a standard SF adventure novel written in a hard-boiled style whose only bright spots are Dozois's creation of the alien Corcail Sendijen and the breakneck pacing of the action.

Dozois has gained a reputation as an exceptional anthologist. From his early theme anthologies like *A Day in the Life* to his latest collaborative anthologies with Jack Dann like *Unicorns!,* Dozois packages quality stories with outstanding introductory material. From 1977 to 1981 Dozois edited Dutton's hardcover series *Best Science Fiction Stories of the Year Numbers 6-10.* The five volumes Dozois edited were in many ways superior to the paperback SF series edited by Donald Wollheim (DAW) and

Terry Carr (Ballantine/Del Rey) in terms of coverage and selection. In 1984, James Frenkel's newly established Bluejay Books selected Dozois to be editor of *The Year's Best Science Fiction,* a massive 250,000 word volume. With the appearance of the second annual collection in Spring 1985, Neil Barron in *Fantasy Review* proclaimed " . . . Now, the Dozois anthology is the standard." The simultaneous release of the volume in hardcover and trade paperback made it the definitive "Year's Best SF" anthology.

Gardner Dozois, master of the short story and masterful anthologist, is one of the treasures of the contemporary SF scene.

—George Kelley

DRAKE, David A. American. Born in Dubuque, Iowa, 24 September 1945. Educated at the University of Iowa, Iowa City, B. A. 1967; Duke University, Durham, North Carolina, J. D. 1972. Served as an interrogator in the United States Army, 1969-71. Married Joanne Kammiller in 1967; one son. Assistant town attorney, Chapel Hill, North Carolina, 1972-80; part-time bus driver, Chapel Hill, 1980. Since 1981, full-time writer. Agent: Kirby McCauley, 432 Park Avenue South, Suite 1205, New York, New York 10016. Address: Box 904, Chapel Hill, North Carolina 27514, U. S. A.

SCIENCE-FICTION PUBLICATIONS

Novels

Sky Ripper. New York, Tor, 1983.
Forlorn Hope. New York, Tor, 1984.
Birds of Prey. New York, Baen, 1984.
Cross the Stars. New York, Tor, 1984.
Killer, with Karl Edward Wagner. New York, Baen, 1984.
Active Measures, with Janet E. Morris. New York, Baen, 1985.
Bridgehead. New York, Tor, 1985.

Short Stories

Hammer's Slammers. New York, Ace, 1979.
Time Safari. New York, Tor, 1982.
From the Heart of Darkness. New York, Tor, 1983.

Uncollected Short Stories

"Denkirch," in *Travellers by Night,* edited by August Derleth. Sauk City, Wisconsin, Arkham House, 1967; London, Gollancz, 1968.
"Lord of the Depths," in *Dark Things,* edited by August Derleth. Sauk City, Wisconsin, Arkham House, 1971.
"Arclight," in *Fantasy and Science Fiction* (New York), April 1973.
"The Song of the Bone," in *Whispers* ,(Binghamton, New York), December 1973.
"Contact," in *Analog* (New York), October 1974.
"Awakening" and "Black Iron," in *Nameless Places,* edited by Gerald W. Page. Sauk City, Wisconsin, Arkham House, 1975.
"The Master of Demons," in *Dark Horizons* (Binghamton, New York), Winter-Spring 1975.
"From the Dark Waters," in *Waves of Terror,* edited by Michael Parry. London, Gollancz, 1976.

"National Without Walls," in *Analog* (New York), July 1977.
"The Last Battalion," in *Analog* (New York), September 1977.
"The Mantichore," in *Swords Against Darkness 3,* edited by Andrew J. Offutt. New York, Zebra, 1978.
"Nemesis Place," in *The Year's Best Horror Stories 7,* edited by Gerald W. Page. New York, DAW, 1979.
"The Predator," in *Destinies* (New York), October 1979.
"Goddess," in *Tales from the Vulgar Unicorn,* edited by Robert Asprin. New York, Ace, 1980.
"Underground," in *Destinies* (New York), February 1980.
"King Crocodile," in *Whispers 3,* edited by Stuart David Schiff. New York, Doubleday, 1981.
"Travellers," in *Destinies* (New York), April 1981.
"Ranks of Bronze," in *There Will Be War,* edited by Jerry Pournelle and John F. Carr. New York, Tor, 1983.
"Votary," in *The Face of Chaos,* edited by Robert Asprin and Lynn Abbey. New York, Ace, 1983.
"Code-Name Feirefitz," in *Men of War,* edited by Jerry Pournelle. New York, Tor, 1984.
"Dreams in Amber," in *Whispers 5,* edited by Stuart David Schiff. New York, Doubleday, 1985.
"The Guardroom," in *Afterwar,* edited by Janet E. Morris. New York, Pocket Books, 1985.

OTHER PUBLICATIONS

Novel

The Dragon Lord. New York, Berkley, 1979

* * *

David A. Drake's fiction is both literate and action-oriented, carefully based in fact and vividly presented. His approximately 40 short stories are divided between science fiction and fantasy-supernatural; his novels are predominantly science fiction, but include fantasy (*The Dragon Lord*) and international adventure (*Sky Ripper; Active Measures* with Janet Morris; *Fortress,* forthcoming). However, the distinction between science fiction and adventure or fantasy is not always an easy or useful one for Drake's fiction. While *Sky Ripper* introduces extraterrestrials perhaps gratuitously, *Active Measures* applies his political realism to near-future extrapolation. The magic and dragon in *The Dragon Lord* are given a scientific rationale, and the aliens of "The Hunting Ground" (in *From the Heart of Darkness*) or *Killer* (with Karl Edward Wagner) would serve much the same purpose were they supernatural creatures.

The greatest autobiographical influence on Drake's fiction is his army service as an interrogator in Vietnam and Cambodia; some of his best horror short stories (many in *From the Heart of Darkness*) take place in Vietnam or feature veterans as protagonists. Drake is best known, however, for his science fiction stories of mercenaries of the future.

Drake's major science fiction series presents Colonel Alois Hammer and Hammer's Slammers, 30th-century mercenaries hired by numerous war-torn planets. These were collected in *Hammer's Slammers,* with explanatory interludes and a new concluding story. Violent and compelling, the stories are primarily about action and the kind of men who choose it; the future background is interesting, but peripheral. *Cross the Stars* adds to our understanding of the Slammers, but its main point is a conscious imitation of Homer's *Odyssey,* as ex-Slammer Don Slade tries to reach his home world Tethys and set it in order; although there are some flaws from following its model too rigorously, it has some of Drake's best writing. Drake's other novel of future mercenaries, *Forlorn Hope,* was to have begun another series, quite similar to the Slammers, although those plans were later cancelled. It is minor, but engaging, with the excellent action writing Drake is known for.

Released the same year as *Forlorn Hope, Birds of Prey* is also engaging, but much more meaningful, and probably is Drake's best work to date. As in *Killer, The Dragon Lord,* and some of his short stories, in *Birds of Prey* Drake draws on his knowledge of historical settings, especially those of the Roman empire from prime to decay. The science fiction or fantasy threat and historical setting mesh well in these books, and in *Birds of Prey* they also allow especially noteworthy development of theme and character.

Drake's books have their weaknesses, especially *qua* science fiction. His handling of time travel and its uses—not only in *Birds of Prey* but in *Time Safari,* a collection of three novellas—is good, but otherwise his futures are too often like the present or the past, and sometimes inconsistent within themselves. This may be why his stories of alien or future intrusions in the past or present are often the most satisfying, although *Cross the Stars* does present some memorable future settings. Also, Drake's characters are often too similar and too uniformly grim: hard-bitten and dedicated fighters, whether soldier or civilian. However, *Birds of Prey* shows that he can make the typical Drake protagonist more complex and sympathetic; and *Bridgehead* (forthcoming) is an experiment, not always success-ful but quite worthwhile, in different kinds of characters.

These reservations are strongly outweighted by Drake's exceptional ability as a story-teller. His unobtrusive, spare, and pellucid prose makes him one of the best new action writers, if not the best; his ability with plot has grown steadily since *The Dragon Lord* and is now another great strength. And if his protagonists are too similar and too grim, that makes them no less compelling; the heroes—and they are heroes—of *Birds of Prey, The Dragon Lord, Cross the Stars,* or "Men Like Us" (in *From the Heart of Darkness)* will all linger in the reader's mind—along with the issues such personalities raise—whether he wishes them to or not. For this reason, and for his craftsmanship, Drake is a writer worthy of attention.

—Bernadette Bosky

DRUMM, D. B. See NAHA, Ed.

DUANE, Diane. American. Agent: Donald A. Maass, 64 West 84th Street, Apartment 3-A, New York, New York 10024. Address: c/o Bluejay Books, 130 West 42nd Street, New York, New York 10036, U. S. A.

SCIENCE-FICTION PUBLICATIONS

Novels

The Door into Fire. New York, Dell, 1979; London, Magnum, 1981.
The Wounded Sky. New York, Pocket Books, 1983.
The Door into Shadow. New York, Bluejay, 1984.
My Enemy, My Ally. New York, Pocket Books, 1984.

Uncollected Short Stories

"Parting Gifts," in *Flashing Swords! 5,* edited by Lin Carter. New York, Dell, 1981.
"The Mdaha," in *Fantasy Book* (Pasadena, California), August 1982.

OTHER PUBLICATIONS

Other

So You Want to Be a Wizard (for children). New York, Delacorte Press, 1983.

* * *

Diane Duane entered science fiction by the *Star Trek* route, and she is still writing for that remarkable phenomenon which has taken on a life of its own. However, she also writes fantasy, and her major claim to serious consideration rests on two excellent fantasy novels, *The Door into Fire* and *The Door into Shadow.* They are half of a projected tetralogy which, we are told, is to be focused on the adventures and development of five main characters: the humans Herewiss, Freelorn, Segnbora, and, presumably, the fire elemental Sunspark and the dragon Hasai.

Like too many fantasies, these books are set in a geographi-cally isolated imaginary land with a quasi-feudal society and plenty of magic. The adventures apparently are all going to culminate in crises leading to passage to a higher state for the various major characters, and they have added import as part of the struggle of good against evil. Duane's achievement is to have transcended this hackneyed scenario, despite a weakness for excessively happy endings.

She does this by setting constraints upon her universe. The Goddess who created it is good, but neither omnipotent nor omniscient. The presence of evil, which manifests itself as Shadow, is the result of Her attempt in Her aspect as Maiden to create a closed universe without evil, a task which in Her other aspects as Mother and Hag She knows to be impossible. This means that the Goddess really does need human aid in the struggle against Shadow.

The power with which the Goddess opposes Shadow is Fire, life-force which, when present in an individual in large enough quantity, can be used for extra-sensory perception and to perform ordinary and extraordinary acts. Like all power, it has its price: if not used, it is lost; if used, it shortens the life of its user. It is entirely distinct from magic, which is no more than a kind of technology based on the affinities of words to the physical world. As with all technology, it uses energy. Given the choice, it is often less tiring for a magician to use non-magical means to an end.

None of the Goddess's aspects, which are sometimes at odds, is entirely benign. Those who ask a boon may get it; but if they presume too much, they will bitterly regret getting exactly what they requested. All of this is known to Her followers because the Goddess makes Herself manifest to everyone individually at least once in a lifetime. Hence there is a great store of anecdotal information from which it is possible to learn Her will, particularly with respect to sexual ethics and the proper social order, where the systems propunded deserve to be studied for their intrinsic interest.

Given this context, Herewiss, the first male in generations to have a usable amount of Fire, *must* learn to use it. Segnbora, with too much to control by normal means, *must* find a way to control it. Freelorn, whose herditary duties require him to perform ceremonies binding vast powers, *must* overthrow the usurper of his throne in order to perform them; and the others are bound to help him, although the imperatives which drive Sunspark and Hasai are not yet entirely clear. Should any of them fall, the result would be unimaginable disaster.

Duane is an elegant universe-maker. The world in which her characters live is no mere backdrop. It informs the actions of her characters, giving them motives beyond those which can be ascribed simply to human or non-human nature. Her treatments of magic and religion, here for once in a beneficent relation to each other, are particularly well thought-out. Moreover, she does not tell, she shows. Such integration is rare, especially in sword-and sorcery stories. The result is vivid, entertaining writing which deserves study both for its technical excellence and the ideas it contains.

—William M. Schuyler, Jr.

—————

DUNCAN, David. American. Born in Billings, Montana, 17 February 1913. Educated at the University of Montana, Missoula, B. A. 1935. Married Elaine Sulliger in 1940; three daughters. Personnel examiner, Department of Agriculture, Washington, D. C., 1936; social worker, California State Relief Administration, Fresno, 1936-40; manager of California housing project, Farm Security Administration, 1941-43; field director in California and Nevada, American Red Cross, 1943-44; labor economist, National Labor Bureau, San Francisco, 1944-46. Since 1946, free-lance writer. Address: P. O. Box 761, Ashland, Oregon 97520, U. S. A.

SCIENCE-FICTION PUBLICATIONS

Novels

The Shade of Time. New York, Random House, 1946; London, Grey Walls Press, 1949.
The Madrone Tree. New York, Macmillan, 1949; London, Gollancz, 1950; as *Worse Than Murder*, New York, Pocket Books, 1954.
Dark Dominion. New York, Ballantine, 1954; London, Heinemann, 1955.
Beyond Eden. New York, Ballantine, 1955; as *Another Tree in Eden*, London, Heinemann, 1956.
Occam's Razor. New York, Ballantine, 1957; London, Gollancz, 1958.

Uncollected Short Stories

"The Immortals," in *Galaxy* (New York), October 1960.
"Requiem on the Moon," in *The Dead Astronaut*. Chicago, Playboy Press, 1964.
"On Venus the Thunder Precedes the Lightning," in *Worlds of Tomorrow* (New York), Spring 1971.

OTHER PUBLICATIONS

Novels

Remember the Shadows. New York, McBride, 1944.
The Bramble Bush. New York, Macmillan, 1948; London, Sampson Low, 1949; as *Sweet, Low, and Deadly*, New York, Mercury, 1949.

The Serpent's Egg. New York, Macmillan, 1950.
None But My Foe. New York, Macmillan, 1950.
Wives and Husbands. Cleveland, World, 1952.
The Trumpet of God. New York, Doubleday. 1956
Yes, My Darling Daughters. New York, Doubleday, 1959; London, Heinemann, 1960.
The Long Walk Home from Town. New York, Doubleday, 1964.

Plays

Screenplays: *Sangaree*, with Frank Moss, 1953; *Jivaro*, with Winston Miller, 1954; *The White Orchid*, with Reginald LeBorg, 1955; *The Monster That Challenged the World*, with Patricia Fielder, 1957; *The Black Scorpion*, with Robert Blees and Paul Yawitz, 1957; *The Thing That Couldn't Die*, 1958; *Monster on the Campus*, 1958; *The Leech Woman*, with Ben Pivar and Francis Rosenwald, 1960; *The Time Machine*, 1960: *Fantastic Voyage*, with others, 1966.

Television Plays: *The Human Factor* (*The Outer Limits* series), and for *Telephone Time*, *My Three Sons*, *National Velvet*, *It's a Man's World*, *Higgins*, *Daniel Boone*, *Studio One*, *The High Chaparral*, and *Men into Space* series.

* * *

David Duncan is one of the most accomplished stylists to have worked in science fiction and fantasy, yet he is an almost forgotten figure. The reason for this is that, like Edgar Pangborn's and Ray Bradbury's, his ideas are not often very original and his science is sometimes bizarre; his method is that of the mystery story—one in which the enigma is left unexplained for a good deal of the book, and when the problem is solved the story simply ends. The unknown is not brought on stage for very long, and its consequences are left undeveloped. Yet there are so many satisfactions of characterization, background and description, social observation, ideas about human life and destiny, that one is tempted to dismiss the seeming flaws. Duncan is an elegant, poetic wordsmith who involves the reader completely.

Dark Dominion is an overwhelming emotional experience which leaves the reader drained. The story is about the building, in secret, of a military space station that will dominate the earth. We are shown the effects of this terrible purpose on the lives of the scientists involved, as they struggle to complete the project, and later to change its meaning for the world. The novel is filled with moments of great beauty, and they are worth the speculative and scientific lapses. The classic novels of the 1950's do not surpass this one in skill, even when they are superior in ideas and originality. "Duncan's forte is people," wrote Damon Knight (in *In Search of Wonder*, 1967); "he sees them with an inquiring, ironic, compassionate but unsentimental eye. At his best, the characters he draws are sharply individual, each one believable and distinct from every other. He fills up the scene with moving portraits, and their intricate mutual relationships, effortlessly handled, make his book. " This is a lesson that better writers—those whose thinking and conceptual development, even their stories, are better—have not learned: that to produce a valuable piece of fiction, including SF, a writer must show *everything* as belonging to the awareness of characters; ideas as well as feelings must be seen sticking to the *insides* of people.

Occam's Razor is a sketchy story, but it also has the compelling portraits and personal interactions of *Dark Dominion*. The story details the accidental visit of two beings from a parallel world, whose sudden appearance causes much misunderstanding; but the novel ends where it should begin—namely, in the effects of these people's presence on our world, after this fact is discovered. We are given only half the story, that of the events leading up to the solution of the mystery concerning the identity of the two visitors. Still, this is a persuasive and humane story. *Beyond Eden* is more an all-around success than the other two novels, though it lacks the eloquence of *Dark Dominion*. Set in the 1950's atmosphere of the McCarthy hearings and the Oppenheimer persecution, the story deals with a fascinating water project in California. The enterprise discovers a new kind of water which might transform human nature, though at first it seems to kill people, embarrassing the chief scientist who already has a bad past to live down. Again, the story ends where the confrontation with the unknown might lead to new understandings and a set of problems of a higher order.

One might also argue that Duncan chose not to explore beyond "mere mystery"—that his sense of human limits prevented him from inventing glib "understandings" of the kind demanded by so many SF readers. Duncan chose to stay closer to the present. His problem does suggest a prescription: truly great science fiction demands that one be a fine writer with all the skills of a contemporary novelist *and* possess the intellect necessary to speculate beyond the point of "mere mystery," surface drama and obvious topicality.

David Duncan drew enthusiastic reviews for his novels. Groff Conklin called him "a richly endowed mind" whose work should not be missed. Anthony Boucher, Theodore Sturgeon, P. Schuyler Miller, and others ranked his books with the best of their years. In a field whose main problem is a lack of the authenticity that belongs to a literature won from experience, Duncan has the virtue of seeming very authentic, despite his supposed shortcomings. His novels are as he intended them to be, and their virtues are the shortcomings of most science fiction. In the only statement about his science fiction, Duncan wrote: "To me the great virtue of the science-fiction story doesn't reside in its elaborate gadgets and twistings of time and space—although these can be majestically entertaining—but in its possibilities for analysis of man and the social order." He saw SF as a literature of critical possibilities, and for this he deserves serious attention.

—George Zebrowski

DURRELL, Lawrence (George). Also writes as Charles Norden. British. Born in Julundur, India, 27 February 1912. Educated at the College of St. Joseph, Darjeeling, India; St. Edmund's School, Canterbury, Kent. Married 1) Nancy Myers in 1935 (divorced, 1947); 2) Eve Cohen in 1947 (divorced); 3) Claude Durrell in 1961 (died, 1967); 4) Ghislaine de Boysson in 1973 (divorced, 1979); two daughters. Has had many jobs, including jazz pianist (Blue Peter nightclub, London), automobile racer, and real estate agent. Lived in Corfu, 1934-40. Editor, with Henry Miller and Alfred Perles, *The Booster* (later *Delta*), Paris, 1937-39; columnist, *Egyptian Gazette*, Cairo, 1941; Editor, with Robin Fedden and Bernard Spencer, *Personal Landscape*, Cairo, 1942-45; special correspondent in Cyprus for *The Economist*, London, 1953-55; Editor, *Cyprus Review*, Nicosia, 1954-55. Taught at the British Institute, Kalamata, Greece, 1940. Foreign Service Press Officer, British Information Office, Cairo, 1941-44; Press Attaché, British Information Office, Alexandria, 1944-45; Director of Public Relations for the Dodecanese Islands, Greece, 1946-47; Direc-

tor of the British Council Institute, Cordoba, Argentina, 1947-48; Press Attaché, British Legation, Belgrade, 1949-52; Director of Public Relations for the British Government in Cyprus, 1954-56. Andrew Mellon Visiting Professor of Humanities, California Institute of Technology, Pasadena, 1974. Recipient: Duff Cooper Memorial Prize, 1957; Foreign Book Prize (France), 1959. Fellow, Royal Society of Literature, 1954. Has lived in France since 1957. Address: c/o Grindlay's Bank, 13 St. James's Square, London SW1Y 4LF, England.

SCIENCE-FICTION PUBLICATIONS

Novels

The Revolt of Aphrodite. London, Faber, 1974.
   Tunc. London, Faber, and New York, Dutton, 1968.
   Nunquam. London, Faber, and New York, Dutton, 1970.

OTHER PUBLICATIONS

Novels

Pied Piper of Lovers. London, Cassell, 1935.
Panic Spring (as Charles Norden). London, Faber, and New York, Covici Friede, 1937.
The Black Book: An Agon. Paris, Obelisk Press, 1938; New York, Dutton, 1960; London, Faber, 1973.
Cefalû. London, Editions Poetry London, 1947; as *The Dark Labyrinth*, London, Ace, 1958; New York, Dutton, 1962.
The Alexandria Quartet. London, Faber, and New York, Dutton, 1962.
   Justine. London, Faber, and New York, Dutton, 1957.
   Balthazar. London, Faber, and New York, Dutton, 1958.
   Mountolive. London, Faber, 1958; New York, Dutton, 1959.
   Clea. London, Faber, and New York, Dutton, 1960.
White Eagles over Serbia. London, Faber, and New York, Criterion, 1957.
Monsieur; or, The Prince of Darkness. London, Faber, 1974; New York, Viking Press, 1975.
Livia; or, Buried Alive. London, Faber, 1978; New York, Viking Press, 1979.
Constance; or, Solitary Practices. London, Faber, and New York, Viking Press, 1982.
Sebastian; or, Ruling Passions. London, Faber, 1983; New York, Viking Press, 1984.
Quinx; or, The Ripper's Tale. London, Faber, 1985.

Short Stories

Zero, and Asylum in the Snow. Privately printed, 1946; as *Two Excursions into Reality*, Berkley, California, Circle, 1947.
Esprit de Corps: Sketches from Diplomatic Life. London, Faber, 1957; New York, Dutton, 1958.
Stiff Upper Lip: Life among the Diplomats. London, Faber, 1958; New York, Dutton, 1959.
Sauve Qui Peut. London, Faber, 1966; New York, Dutton, 1967.
The Best of Antrobus. London, Faber, 1974.

Plays

Sappho: A Play in Verse (produced Hamburg, 1959; Edinburgh, 1961; Evanston, Illinois, 1964). London, Faber, 1950; New York, Dutton, 1958.

Acte (produced Hamburg, 1961). London, Faber, and New York, Dutton, 1965.

An Irish Faustus: A Morality in Nine Scenes (produced Sommerhausen, Germany, 1966). London, Faber, 1963; New York, Dutton, 1964.

Judith (shortened version of screenplay), in *Woman's Own* (London), 26 February-2 April 1966.

Screenplays: *Cleopatra*, with others, 1963; *Judith*, with others, 1966.

Radio Script: *Greek Peasant Superstitions*, 1947.

Television Scripts: *The Lonely Roads*, with Diane Deriaz, 1970; *The Search for Ulysses* (USA); *Lawrence Durrell's Greece; Lawrence Durrell's Egypt.*

Recording: *Ulysses Come Back: Sketch for a Musical* (story, music, and lyrics by Durrell), 1971.

Verse

Quaint Fragment: Poems Written Between the Ages of Sixteen and Nineteen. London, Cecil Press, 1931.
Ten Poems. London, Caduceus Press, 1932.
Ballade of Slow Decay. Privately printed, 1932.
Bromo Bombastes: A Fragment from a Laconic Drama by Gaffer Peeslake. London, Caduceus Press, 1933.
Transition. London, Caduceus Press, 1934.
Mass for the Old Year. Privately printed, 1935.
Proems: An Anthology of Poems, with others. London, Fortune Press, 1938.
A Private Country. London, Faber, 1943.
The Parthenon: For T. S. Eliot. Privately printed, 1945(?).
Cities, Plains, and People. London, Faber, 1946.
On Seeming to Presume. London, Faber, 1948.
A Landmark Gone. Privately printed, 1949.
Deus Loci. Ischia, Italy, Di Mato Vito, 1950.
Private Drafts. Nicosia, Cyprus, Proodos Press, 1955.
The Tree of Idleness and Other Poems. London, Faber, 1955.
Selected Poems. London, Faber, and New York, Grove Press, 1956.
Collected Poems. London, Faber, and New York, Dutton, 1960; revised edition, 1968.
Penguin Modern Poets 1, with Elizabeth Jennings and R. S. Thomas. London, Penguin, 1962.
Poetry. New York, Dutton, 1962.
Beccafico/Le Becfigue (English, with French translation by F. - J. Temple). Montpellier, France, La Licorne, 1963.
A Persian Lady. Edinburgh, Tragara Press, 1963.
Selected Poems 1935-1963. London, Faber, 1964.
The Ikons and Other Poems. London, Faber, 1966; New York, Dutton, 1967.
The Red Limbo Lingo: A Poetry Notebook for 1968-1970. London, Faber, and New York, Dutton, 1971.
On the Suchness of the Old Boy. London, Turret, 1972.
Vega and Other Poems. London, Faber, 1973.
Lifelines. Edinburgh, Tragara Press, 1974.
Selected Poems, edited by Alan Ross. London, Faber, 1977.
Collected Poems 1931-1974, edited by James A. Brigham. London, Faber, and New York, Viking Press, 1980.

Other

Prospero's Cell: A Guide to the Landscape and Manners of the Island of Corcyra. London, Faber, 1945; with *Reflections on a Marine Venus,* New York, Dutton, 1960.

Key to Modern Poetry. London, Peter Nevill, 1952; as *A Key to Modern British Poetry,* Norman, University of Oklahoma Press, 1952.

Reflections on a Marine Venus: A Companion to the Landscape of Rhodes. London, Faber, 1953; with *Prospero's Cell,* New York, Dutton, 1960.

Bitter Lemons (on Cyprus). London, Faber, 1957; New York, Dutton, 1958.

Art and Outrage: A Correspondence about Henry Miller Between Alfred Perlès and Lawrence Durrell, with an Intermission by Henry Miller. London, Putnam, 1959; New York, Dutton, 1960.

Groddeck (on George Walther Groddeck). Wiesbaden, Limes, 1961.

Briefwechselüber "Actis", with Gustaf Gründgens. Hamburg, Rowohlt, 1961.

Lawrence Durrell and Henry Miller: A Private Correspondence, edited by George Wickes. New York, Dutton, and London, Faber, 1963.

La Descente du Styx (English, with French translations by F. - J. Temple). Montpellier, France, La Muréne, 1964; as *Down the Styx,* Santa Barbara, California, Capricorn Press, 1971.

Spirit of Place: Letters and Essays on Travel, edited by Alan G. Thomas. London, Faber, and New York, Dutton, 1969.

Le Grand Suppositoire (interview with Marc Alyn). Paris, Belfond, 1972; as *The Big Supposer,* London, Abelard Schuman, and New York, Grove Press, 1973.

The Happy Rock (on Henry Miller). London, Village Press, 1973; Belfast, Maine, Bern Porter, 1982.

The Plant-Magic Man. Santa Barbara, California, Capra Press, 1973.

Blue Thirst. Santa Barbara, California, Capra Press, 1975.

Sicilian Carousel. London, Faber, and New York, Viking Press, 1977.

The Greek Islands. London, Faber, and New York, Viking Press, 1978.

A Smile in the Mind's Eye. London, Wildwood House, 1980; New York, Universe, 1982.

Literary Lifelines: The Richard Aldington-Lawrence Durrell Correspondence, edited by Harry T. Moore and Ian S. MacNiven. New York, Viking Press, and London, Faber, 1981.

Editor, with others, *Personal Landscape: An Anthology of Exile.* London, Editions Poetry London, 1945.

Editor, *A Henry Miller Reader.* New York, New Directions, 1959; as *The Best of Henry Miller,* London, Heinemann, 1960.

Editor, *New Poems 1963.* London, Hutchinson, 1963.

Editor, *Lear's Corfu: An Anthology Drawn from the Painter's Letters.* Corfu, Corfu Travel, 1965.

Editor, *Wordsworth.* London, Penguin, 1973.

Translator, *Six Poems from the Greek of Sikelianos and Seferis.* Privately printed, 1946.

Translator, with Bernard Spencer and Nanos Valaoritis, *The King of Asine and Other Poems,* by George Seferis. London, Lehmann, 1948.

Translator, *The Curious History of Pope Joan,* by Emmanuel Royidis. London, Verschoyle, 1954; revised edition, as *Pope Joan: A Romantic Biography,* London, Deutsch, 1960; New York, Dutton, 1961.

*

Bibliography: *Lawrence Durrell: An Illustrated Checklist* by Alan G. Thomas and James A. Brigham, Carbondale, Southern Illinois University Press, 1983.

Manuscript Collections: University of California, Los Angeles; University of Illinois, Urbana.

Critical Studies: *The World of Lawrence Durrell* edited by Harry T. Moore, Carbondale, Southern Illinois University Press, 1962; *Lawrence Durrell* by John Unterecker, New York, Columbia University Press, 1964; *Lawrence Durrell* by John A. Weigel, New York, Twayne, 1966; *Lawrence Durrell: A Critical Study,* London, Faber, 1968, New York, Dutton, 1969, and *Lawrence Durrell*, London, Longman, 1970, both by G. S. Fraser; *Sensation, Vision, and Imagination: The Problem of Unity in Lawrence Durrell's Novels* by Hartwig Isernhagen, Bamberg, Bamberger Fotodruck, 1969; *Lawrence Durrell Newsletter* (Kelowna, British Columbia).

* * *

Lawrence Durrell's *Tunc* and *Nunquam* are the two parts of a science-fiction novel known collectively as *The Revolt of Aphrodite*. The plots describe the efforts of Felix Charlock to build a computer, Abel, and a robot double of a prostitute-turned movie-actress, Iolanthe. In doing so, he is involved with a conglomerate corporation known as Merlin or the "firm" and its owners, Julian, Jocas, and Benedicta. Durrell is attempting to dissect the notion of culture; the superficial bases for this examination are Spengler (the approach to culture, the concern with money and contractual obligation, and even the term "the firm" itself are taken from *The Decline of the West*) and Freud (particularly the psychopathology of sex and the sexual connotations of money).

Durrell has identified the major pre-occupations of all his fiction when he writes (in *Key to Modern Poetry*) that "Time and the ego are the two determinants of style for the twentieth century. . . . " The double, whether robot or human, is also very common in Durrell's writing, and is related to his attempts to handle multi-faceted personalities and fragmented time from multiple viewpoints, as in *The Alexandria Quartet*. In *Key to Modern Poetry* he briefly traces the literary history of the double and ends by saying that "in nearly every case we are given a double which is either a saint, a criminal or a monster. " Character is difficult to assess in Durrell's works; the surface descriptions of neuroses, frequently maimed characters, impotence, incestuous triangular relationships, and other sexual aberrations produce a shock value which often hides the suspicion that there really are no "characters" in his work— only puppets with a strong aroma.

The major distinctive feature of Durrell's writing is his baroque style. His writing is that of a poet—a sensuous mosaic of exotic words and images that adds a welcome dimension to the often flat prose of contemporary fiction. The occasional excesses are also those of the poet, mainly over-writing and tiresome platitudes. Throughout his career Durrell has had a remarkable eye for "place," and it appears again in *Tunc* and *Nunquam,* although somewhat supplanted by the ubiquity of the "firm. " The technology that supplies the science-fiction basis in both books is remarkably crude, unimaginative, and dated. Much of the character motivation in *Tunc* and *Nunquam* is centered around the concept of a person's work in relation to his culture and his emotional life. As A. W. Friedman has said, "The rule in Durrell is that to deny the validity of one's work is to negate love. " Love and work drive and frustrate Charlock and the other characters throughout the books.

The book titles derive from the epigraph "Aut tunc, aut Nunquam" (It was then or never) from the *Satyricon* of Petronius. The implication of a last chance for society to define its values is supported by a quotation from *Tunc* which can serve as a statement of purpose for the two books: "When a civilisation has decided to bury its head in the sand what can we do but tickle its arse with a feather?"

—Norman L. Hills

———————

EDMONDSON, G. C. (José Mario Garry Ordonez Edmondson y Cotton). Also writes as John Cleve; Kelly P. Gast; Jake Logan; J.B. Masterson. American. Born in Rachauchitlán, Tabasco, Mexico, 11 October 1922. Educated in Vienna, M. D. Served in the United States Marine Corps, 1942-46. Married three times; two sons and two daughters. Has worked as a blacksmith. Agent: Richard Curtis, 164 East 64th Street, New York, New York 10021. Address: 12328 Rockcrest, Lakeside, California 92040, U. S. A.

SCIENCE-FICTION PUBLICATIONS

Novels

The Ship That Sailed the Time Stream. New York, Ace, 1965; London, Arrow, 1971.
Chapayeca. New York, Doubleday, 1971; London, Hale, 1973; as *Blue Face,* New York, DAW, 1972.
T. H. E. M. New York, Doubleday, 1974.
The Aluminum Man. New York, Berkley, 1975.
The Man Who Corrupted the Earth. New York, Ace, 1980.
To Sail the Century Sea. New York, Ace, 1981.
Star Slaver (as John Cleve, with Andrew J. Offutt). New York, Berkley, 1983.
The Takeover, with C. M. Kotlan. New York, Ace, 1984.

Short Stories

Stranger Than You Think. New York, Ace, 1965.

Uncollected Short Stories

"Nobody Believes an Indian," in *Fantasy and Science Fiction* (New York), May 1970.
"The Tempollutors," in *Infinity 4,* edited by Robert Hoskins. New York, Lancer, 1972.
"One Plus One Equals Eleven," in *Analog* (New York), January 1973.
"Tube," in *If* (New York), August 1974.
"All That Glitters," in *Stellar 5*, edited by Judy-Lynn del Rey. New York, Ballantine, 1980.

OTHER PUBLICATIONS

Novels

Rudge (as J. B. Masterson). New York, Doubleday, 1979; London, Hale, 1980.
Slocum's Slaughter (as Jake Logan). New York, Berkley, 1980.

Novels as Kelly P. Gast

Dil Dies Hard. New York, Doubleday, 1975.

The Long Trail North. New York, Doubleday, 1976.
Murphy's Trail. New York, Doubleday, 1976.
Last Stage from Opal. New York, Doubleday, 1978.
Murder at Magpie Flats. New York, Doubleday, 1978.
Paddy. New York, Doubleday, 1979.

Other

Practical Welding, with Leroy A. Scheck. N. p., Bruce, 1976.
Le livre noir d'haute cuisine. N. p., Bookmaker, 1977.
Water Rationing Made Simple. N. p., Bookmaker, 1977.
The Basic Book of Home Maintenance and Repair, with T. F. Roybal. Chicago, American Technical Society, 1979.
Diesel Mechanics: An Introduction, with Richard Little. Belmont, California, Wadsworth, 1982.

* * *

A superficial reading of G. C. Edmondson's work might consign him to the "cops and robbers" school of pulp science fiction. A closer examination shows that his work provides much more than that. His novels and short stories are vigorous action works with flashes of wit that present aliens and heros as real, fallible characters. In much science fiction both aliens and heros are cardboard figures that never deviate from a stereotypical mold. Edmondson's heros and aliens make mistakes, admit they were wrong, fall in love, take advice, get angry, and in many other human ways resist the traditional stereotypes of pulp fiction. In short, they are viable characters which present two of the major themes of his work. The first and most important of these, that there are as many problems between different groups here on earth as between earthlings and aliens, is demonstrated in his novel, *Chapayeca*, set in rural Mexico. The novel deals with an extra-terrestrial, an anthropologist, a group of Indians, and officials of the Mexican government. The anthropologist and the Mexican officials stand out more in the Indian village than the blue-skinned alien. The Indians are totally at odds with 20th-century culture and represent another of Edmondson's favorite themes: the people who don't fit in are perhaps the sanest of all.

His plots are clever and well thought out and frequently have interesting twists. In *The Ship That Sailed the Time Stream* a home-made still reacts with lightning and causes the ship to be hurled backwards in time to the Viking era.

Edmondson was born in Mexico and his work set there is his strongest. His obvious sympathy for the simple Indian people whose life is threatened not by an extra-terrestrial invasion but by the inroads of earthly civilization lends credibility to his descriptions and substance to the simple plots. The plight of Indians is also an interesting sub-plot in *The Aluminum Man*, one of Edmondson's wittiest novels. The alien in this book looks rather like raw egg whites in a puddle with eyes and travels through the sewer and water systems. In order to make her arrival on earth inconspicuous she designed her space ship to look like an old, wrecked DeSoto.

Edmondson's short stories are not as well written as his novels. The shorter works lack the cohesiveness and character development of his novels. The best of them are those collected in *Stranger Than You Think*, and are almost like chapters in a novel as they are joined by a common narrator and setting.

The few women in Edmondson's work are his weakest characters. They are stereotyped as being inferior in intelligence and overly concerned with clothes and fashions. When a woman is the romantic interest in a story she is the stereotype liberated woman who has a man's job and has proved herself tough enough to handle anything.

Edmondson also writes mysteries set in the old west under the name Kelly P. Gast. Except for the details of scenery and time they are very much like his science fiction. His writing is always exciting and he is expert at using action-packed books to present his commentary on our present society.

—Alice Chambers Wygant

—————

EDWARDS, Norman. See **CARR, Terry; WHITE, Ted.**

—————

EFFINGER, George Alec. American. Born in Cleveland, Ohio, 10 January 1947. Attended Yale University, New Haven, Connecticut, 1965, 1969, and New York University, 1968. Free-lance writer: since 1971, writer for *Marvel Comic Books,* New York. Agent: Richard Curtis, 164 East 64th Street, New York, New York 10021. Address: Box 15183, New Orleans, Louisiana 70175, U. S. A.

SCIENCE-FICTION PUBLICATIONS

Novels (series: Planet of the Apes)

What Entropy Means to Me. New York, Doubleday, 1972.
Relatives. New York, Harper, 1973.
Man the Fugitive (Apes). New York, Award, 1974.
Nightmare Blue, with Gardner Dozois. New York, Berkley, 1975; London, Fontana, 1977.
Escape to Tomorrow (Apes). New York, Award, 1975.
Journey into Terror (Apes). New York, Award, 1975.
Those Gentle Voices. New York, Warner, 1976.
Lord of the Apes (Apes). New York, Award, 1976.
Death in Florence. New York, Doubleday, 1978; as *Utopia 3,* Chicago, Playboy Press, 1980.
Heroics. New York, Doubleday, 1979.
The Wolves of Memory. New York, Putnam, 1981.
The Bird of Time. New York, Doubleday, 1985.

Short Stories

Mixed Feelings. New York, Harper, 1974.
Irrational Numbers. New York, Doubleday, 1976.
Dirty Tricks. New York, Doubleday, 1978.
Idle Pleasures. New York, Berkley, 1983.

OTHER PUBLICATIONS

Novel

Felicia. New York, Berkley, 1976.

*

George Alec Effinger comments:
I try to do new things with old material. A good deal of my science fiction is an attempt to take traditional SF furniture (storylines, settings, characters, and hardware) and combine it with some element of the absurd. The result is not science fiction, because it bears little resemblance to the rational real

world. Perhaps surreal fantasy describes these stories best. My antecedents are as much in the theater of the absurd as they are in science fiction.

One of my favorite experiments is to appropriate an accepted SF situation and populate it with one or more of the continuing characters I have established in my stories over the years. These characters are not recurring in the usual sense. Rather, I think of them as a kind of repertory company. They may die in one story and reappear later as necessary. They live in many eras and appear together in various combinations, sometimes contradicting earlier stories. Just as William Bendix appeared in one motion picture and was killed or married, then months later appeared in another movie, unrelated to the first, so my characters pop up here and there throughout my own future history, unaffected by the stories in which they performed previously. Whenever they appear, however, they always represent the same kind of person, making for me a private stable of stereotypes to draw upon.

I enjoy parody, satire, and pastiche, but every once in a while I will do a serious story in a straight SF mode, mostly to keep the audience on its toes. SF is the only neighbourhood of writing where I could get away with this kind of thing, and I am immensely grateful to the field and its readers for giving me the opportunity.

*   *   *

Since the publication of his best-known novel, *What Entropy Means to Me*, George Alec Effinger has demonstrated versatility in books as disparate as the mainstream novel *Felicia*, the teleplay adaptation *Man the Fugitive*, and *Nightmare Blue*, a collaboration with Gardner Dozois. More important, he has produced short stories and novels linked in strange and wondrous ways to form a unique "Effinger's World. " Some critics label him a writer of sword and sorcery; other, of myth. Still others avoid labels, preferring a literary report card showing a high rating in technique, a low one in substance. Despite any problem with fitting him into the established definitions of science fiction, Effinger does offer an exceptional reading experience.

Entropy is a structural tour de force, being four intricately interwoven stories with author-character Seyt as nexus. First is a romantic quest tale of an eldest son searching for a lost father. Aided by a magic-competent companion, Dore overcomes natural obstacles, monsters, seduction, villainy, only to find Father at a point of no return. If *Entropy* went no further, it could sustain the label of sword and sorcery. But *Entropy* is more, three stories more. Functioning much as a chorus in a Greek tragedy, Seyt relates his family's saga from Earth to the planet Home. The third story evolves as a classic political power struggle to fill the vacuum created by the absence of father and eldest son. Seyt faithfully records the machinations, religious conflicts, and personal hurt involved. The fourth story gains subtle attention. This is the story of creation— literary creation. Seyt makes us aware of the artist, story churning in his head, faced with the arduous task of shaping it for an audience. Seyt must grapple with the author's universal problems: critical pressure from readers; political pressure to slant toward propaganda; and inner pressure to maintain authorial integrity. This trenchant commentary on the art and act of writing, reappearing in later short stories and novels, helps link *Entropy* to them.

Effinger's later fictional world is a paradox. We may recognize a familiar society, only to have subsequent paragraphs jolt us into a surreal world. Often gray, sometimes diseased, always warped by conformity, this society is best epitomized by the village of Gremmage in "Things Go Better," "Heart Stop," and "Lights Out. " Gremmage isolates, smothers, and molds newcomers to its ways. Effinger's larger society has the Representatives, six men governing by whimsical stupidity ("Lydectes: On the Nature of Sport," "Contentment, Satisfaction, Cheer, Well-Being, Gladness, Joy, Comfort, and Not Having to Get Up Early Any More," and *Relatives*). Effinger's people freely slip from story to story, changing personalities and identities illogically. For example, the three separate Weinraub/Weintraubs triplicate experience in *Relatives,* then show up as a writer of a trilogy of novels in "Biting Down Hard in Truth. " Global bum Bo Staefler of *Death in Florence* has little obvious relationship to baseball catcher Bo Staefler ("Naked to the Invisible Eye") or to castaway Bo Staefler ("World War II"). Robert Hanson appears as an 11-year-old boy ("Chase Our Blues Away"), a young man afflicted with altruism ("Strange Ragged Saintliness"), one for whom a park is named ("Timmy Was Eight"), and an android clone ("The Awesome Menace of the Polarizer"). Jennings suffers metamorphosis from a tough coach ("Biting Down Hard on Truth") to a chairman of the board ("At the Bran Foundry") to an astro-physicist (*Those Gentle Voices*).

And then there is Sandor Courane, one of the many personalities moving in and out of Effinger's multi-faceted morality play. Courane shifts from being a light-weight science-fiction writer in "The Pinch-Hitters," one of Effinger's sports short stories (see "Naked to the Invisible Eye," "From Downtown at the Buzzer," and "Breakaway" for other sports-oriented tales) to serve in *The Wolves of Memory* as a tormented Everyman trying to cope with the mysteries of life and death, of causation and purpose. In the novel Effinger demonstrates his control of surrealistic shifts of perspective in time and place, enriching them with parodic hints of Eden, the Fall, and the Crucifixion, ironically combined with a man/technology relationship.

Effinger is master of the non sequitur which teases the mind with the thought that there is a veiled logic and an illuminating insight here, could one but rearrange things. If not, the reader must provide his own, for Effinger has prodded his mind unmercifully. Musing on the act of writing, a character in "The Ghost Writer" inadvertently gives us a summation for Effinger himself: "There was always the chance that a new fragment might join two of the enigmatic earlier pieces, and a whole framework might begin to be evident. But not today. Here was another piece, of perhaps a totally different puzzle. It was longer, and it was exciting. The audience would be satisfied, but not the scholars. "

—Hazel Pierce

EGBERT, H. M. See **ROUSSEAU, Victor.**

EHRLICH, Max (Simon). American. Born in Springfield, Massachusetts, 10 October 1909. Educated at the University of Michigan, Ann Arbor, B. A. Married 1) Doris Rubinstein in 1940 (divorced), two daughters; 2) Margaret Druckman in 1980. Reporter, *Knickerbocker Press* and *Evening News,* both Albany, New York, and *Republican* and *Daily Press,* both

Springfield. Member of the copyright and screen committees, Writers Guild of America West. *Died in February 1983.*

SCIENCE-FICTION PUBLICATIONS

Novels

The Big Eye. New York, Doubleday, 1949; London, Boardman, 1951.
Spin the Glass Web. New York, Harper, 1952; London, Corgi, 1957.
First Train to Babylon. New York, Harper, and London, Gollancz, 1955; as *Dead Letter,* London, Corgi, 1958; as *The Naked Edge,* Corgi, 1961.
The Takers. New York, Harper, and London, Gollancz, 1961.
Dead Is the Blue. New York, Doubleday, and London, Gollancz, 1964.
The High Side. New York, Fawcett, 1969.
The Edict. New York, Doubleday, 1971; London, Panther, 1984.
The Savage Is Loose. New York, Bantam, 1974.
The Reincarnation of Peter Proud. Indianapolis, Bobbs Merrill, 1974; London, W. H. Allen, 1975.
The Cult. New York, Simon and Schuster, 1978; London, Mayflower, 1979.
Reincarnation in Venice. New York, Simon and Schuster, 1979; as *The Bond,* London, Mayflower, 1980.
Naked Beach. Chicago, Playboy Press, 1979; London, Mayflower, 1980.

OTHER PUBLICATIONS

Novels

Shaitan. New York, Arbor House, 1981; London, Severn House, 1982.
The Big Boys. Boston, Houghton Mifflin, 1981.

Plays

Screenplays: *Z.P.G.* (*Zero Population Growth*), with Frank de Felitta, 1971; *The Reincarnation of Peter Proud,* 1974; *The Savage Is Loose,* with Frank de Felitta, 1975.

Radio Plays: for *The Shadow, Mr. and Mrs. North, Sherlock Holmes, Nick Carter, The Big Story,* and *Big Town* series.

Television Plays: *The Apple* (*Star Trek* series), and for *Studio One, The Defenders, The Dick Powell Show,* and *Winston Churchill* series.

*   *   *

Besides his film, radio, and television writing, Max Ehrlich wrote some dozen novels, often with a science-fiction or fantasy edge. Never a producer of "hard" science fiction, he usually aimed at topical thrillers for a wider audience, generally suggesting that traditional value systems are well worth following.
In *The Big Eye* a wandering planet threatens collision with Earth. Encouraged by astronomers to believe the end is near, the public views the invader as a gigantic, baleful watcher. Although the near miss has minimal physical effects on Earth, human repentance augurs at least a semblance of a utopian future. There is little action in the novel, but some movement.

The chief character, assistant to the director of Palomar Observatory where the telescopic Big Eye is located, shuttles back and forth across the country, but he is primarily an observer and scarcely affected by his scientific training. Contravening his desire to remain childless, his wife's act of faith and hope in the future is vindicated, though the Earth was scared by a hoax, not saved by a miracle. Ehrlich's millennial psychology and politics are little more convincing than his science, but the book remains a fair representation of the state of Cold War apprehension in its time.
The Edict projects an overpopulated future in which childbirth has been banned for 30 years. The mechanics of social management are never rationalized, but computers, scant food allotments, and police power are invoked. The story focusses on two couples living in a State Museum exhibit preserving 20th-century lifestyles. Rejecting sexual pluralism and mechanical babies, one of the wives insists on bearing her own child. When the other couple discover her secret and insist on sharing, the new parents escape to a radioactive island, where life will be more short than sweet. Style and scene management are both stiff, but Ehrlich has put the population dilemma in simple-to-understand contemporary terms, though with no utopian alternative this time.
Probably his best-written work toys with the supernatural. *Reincarnation in Venice* is an adequate sequel, structurally almost identical, to *The Reincarnation of Peter Proud.* Not having to stage-manage an entire world, Ehrlich can better handle local color in California and New England. The "science" of dream research is confronted with a man whose dreams suggest that, just before his birth, he was somebody else. Following them up leads him to the town where his "double" was killed. When he falls in love with the daughter of the murderess, the results are predictably ironic. Hardly raising a major problem to the level of serious discourse, the novel is an adequate exercise in nightmare logic, suspenseful, and concisely told.

—David N. Samuelson

EISENBERG, Larry. American. Born in New York City, 21 December 1919. Educated at the City College of New York, B. A. in mathematics 1940; Polytechnic Institute, Brooklyn, M. E. E. 1952; Ph. D. in electronics 1966. Served in the United States Army Air Force, 1945-46: Sergeant. Married Frances Brenner in 1950; one daughter and one son. Instructor, New York Institute of Technology, 1948-52; Project Engineer, PRD, New York, 1952-55; Instructor of Electronics, City College of New York, 1955-56; Digital Logician, Digitronics, Roslyn, New York, 1956-58. Since 1958, Co-Director of the Electronics laboratory, Rockefeller University, New York. Address: 315 East 88th Street, New York, New York 10028, U. S. A.

SCIENCE-FICTION PUBLICATIONS

Short Stories

The Best Laid Schemes. New York, Macmillan, 1971.

Uncollected Short Stories (series: Emmett Duckworth)

"The Grand Illusions," in *Galaxy* (New York), May 1972.
"The Soul Music of Duckworth's Dibs," in *Galaxy* (New York), September 1972.

"The Executive Rat," in *If* (New York), December 1972.
"Sikh, Sikh, Sikh," in *Vertex* (Los Angeles), December 1973.
"The Baby," in *Galaxy* (New York), March 1974.
"Televerite," in *Vertex* (Los Angeles), April 1974.
"Time and Duckworth," in *Galaxy* (New York), May 1974.
"Where There's Smoke," in *Galaxy* (New York), June 1974.
"The Money Machine," in *Vertex* (Los Angeles), August 1974.
"Elephants Sometimes Forget," in *Fantasy and Science Fiction* (New York), September 1974.
"The Lookalike Revolution," *in Fantasy and Science Fiction* (New York), November 1974.
"The Spurious President," in *Vertex* (Los Angeles), April 1975.
"Dr. Snow Maiden," in *Fantasy and Science Fiction* (New York), August 1975.
"My Random Friend," in *Fantasy and Science Fiction* (New York), August 1977.
"The Interface," in *Fantasy and Science Fiction* (New York), August 1978.
"Djinn and Duckworth," in *Isaac Asimov's Science Fiction Magazine* (New York), March 1979.
"The Merchant," in *Flying Saucers*, edited by Isaac Asimov, Martin H. Greenberg, and Charles G. Waugh. New York, Fawcett, 1982.

OTHER PUBLICATIONS

Verse

Limericks for Lantzmen, with George Gordon. New York, Citadel Press, 1965.
Limericks for the Loo, with George Gordon. New York, Kanrom, and London, Arlington, 1965.

Other

Games People Shouldn't Play, with George Gordon. New York, Kanrom, 1966.

*

Larry Eisenberg comments:
Most of my stories have been strongly influenced by my 27 years as a scientist at Rockefeller University. Both the brilliance and the idiosyncrasies of the scientists I have known and worked with (some of them Nobel laureates) have given me a rich source of humor and provocative ideas.

*   *   *

It is extremely difficult to make a reputation exclusively as a short-story writer, even in the genre of science fiction. Larry Eisenberg is one of the few to attract considerable attention over the years, despite the fact that he appears primarily in magazines and has never had a novel published, although there has been one collection of his shorter works, *The Best Laid Schemes*.

Although many of his stories are serious in intent and execution, he is probably best known for his humor, particularly the ongoing adventures of Professor Emmett Duckworth, twice winner of the Nobel Prize. Duckworth is a true descendant of the classic C. P. Ransome stories of Homer Nearing. In almost every case, Duckworth has developed some new device or principle, which should have had very beneficial effects, but which always seems to somehow go awry at a crucial point. In "The Saga of DMM," for example, Duckworth develops an aphrodisiac which, unfortunately, also tends to fatten up its

user, and eventually becomes an unstable explosive akin to nitroglycerin. By chance he taps into a secret government file in "Open Secrets," and finds an ingenious method by which to conceal the data he discovers. In "IQ Soup" he feeds intelligence into an experimental subject, whose plane then crashes in cannibal country with predictable results. In yet other stories, Duckworth develops heavy smoke which falls from your cigarette to the floor, to be removed later, sensory recordings, and a sonic probe that picks up sounds from the past.

As a contrast to the general good humor of the Duckworth stories, Eisenberg has another, very loosely organized series detailing the encounters between humans and an alien species called Sentients. Most of the stories take place after the human race has conquered and occupied the Sentients' home planet. These stories are often very bitter, and are generally very well told. Among the better stories in this series are "The Quintipods," a tale of boxing and the exploitation of a species considered inferior, "The Heart of the Giant," during which a number of humans are killed by a non-violent Sentient when he short circuits the computer that powers their artificial hearts, and "The Conqueror," a story that succeeds through expert use of understatement. A Sentient woman seduces a human soldier, then pretends to be an android in order to humiliate him. There are some outstanding non-series stories as well. Perhaps the best is "The Chameleon," the story of a politician whose use of media and computer devices to enhance his own image is so successful that he is taken in himself. Almost as impressive is the story of an egotistic President whose personality alters when he is lost within his own security system ("The Spurious President").

Eisenberg's stories read well even at their worst because he employs a clear style that is witty without being obtrusive for its own sake. There is almost always an element of humor, although it is often shaded with black, as Eisenberg holds up some attribute of human endeavor for our examination. The Duckworth stories in particular are refreshing and inventive, whether he is duplicating prominent citizens to embarrass them or developing unworkable weapon systems for a defense establishment he dislikes. While it may be a rare occasion when one of his stories will remain in our minds for long, it will be even rarer to find one that is not entertaining while we are reading it.

—Don D'Ammassa

EISENSTEIN, Phyllis (née Kleinstein). American. Born in Chicago, Illinois, 26 February 1946. Educated at the University of Chicago, 1963-66; University of Illinois, Chicago, 1978-81, B. A. in anthropology 1981. Married Alex Eisenstein in 1966. Co-Founder and Director, Windy City SF Writers Conference, Chicago, 1972-77. Anthology Trustee, Science Fiction Writers of America, 1976-81. Address: 6208 North Campbell, Chicago, Illinois 60659, U. S. A.

SCIENCE-FICTION PUBLICATIONS

Novels

Born to Exile. Sauk City, Wisconsin, Arkham House, 1978.
Sorcerer's Son. New York, Ballantine, 1979.
Shadow of Earth. New York, Dell, 1979.
In the Hands of Glory. New York, Pocket Books, 1981.

Uncollected Short Stories

"The Trouble with the Past," with Alex Eisenstein, in *New Dimensions 1,* edited by Robert Silverberg. New York, Doubleday, 1971.

"Teleprobe," in *Long Night of Waiting,* edited by Roger Elwood. Nashville, Aurora, 1974.

"Attachment," in *Amazing* (New York), December 1974.

"The Weather on Mars," with Alex Eisenstein, in *Analog* (New York), December 1974.

"Tree of Life," in *Best Science Fiction Stories of the year 5,* edited by Lester del Rev. New York, Dutton, 1976.

"Sleeping Beauty—The True Story," with Alex Eisenstein, in *Cavalier* (New York), February 1976.

"You Are Here," with Alex Eisenstein, in *New Dimensions 7,* edited by Robert Silverberg. New York, Harper, 1977.

"Altar Ego," with Alex Eisenstein, in *Fantasy and Science Fiction* (New York), March 1977.

"In Answer to Your Call," in *Fantasy and Science Fiction* (New York), January 1978.

"The Land of Sorrow," in *The Year's Best Fantasy Stories 4,* edited by Lin Carter. New York, DAW, 1978.

"Lost and Found," in *Best Science Fiction Stories of the Year,* edited by Gardner Dozois. New York, Dutton, 1979.

"The Mountain Fastness," in *Fantasy and Science Fiction* (New York), July 1979.

"The Man with the Eye," in *Isaac Asimov's Science Fiction Anthology 4,* edited by George H. Scithers. New York, Davis, 1980.

"Point of Departure," in *Whispers 3,* edited by Stuart David Schiff. New York, Doubleday, 1981.

"In the Western Tradition," in *Fantasy and Science Fiction* (New York), March 1981.

"The Fireman's Daughter," in *Twilight Zone* (New York), June 1981.

"Taboo," in *Analog* (New York), 22 June 1981.

"Dark Wings," in *Shadows 5,* edited by Charles L. Grant. New York, Doubleday, 1982.

"Nightlife," in *Fantasy and Science Fiction* (New York), February 1982.

"Subworld," in *Fantasy and Science Fiction* (New York), January 1983.

"The Demon Queen," in *Amazing* (New York), January 1984.

"The Amethyst Phial," in *Fantasy and Science Fiction* (New York), February 1984.

"Sense of Duty," in *Isaac Asimov's Science Fiction Magazine* (New York), March 1985.

"The Snail Out of Space," in *Fantasy and Science Fiction* (New York), April 1985.

*   *   *

Phyllis Eisenstein is probably best known as a writer of fantasy. *Sorcerer's Son, Shadow of Earth,* many of her short stories, and *Born to Exile* certainly exist in the realm of the fantastic. However, since her first published story, "The Trouble with the Past," Eisenstein's works also have explored such familiar science fiction themes as time travel, space exploration, space colonies, and first contact. Eisenstein creates a memorable mood or presents a tantalizing idea through strong characterization. She explores the effects of her settings and premises on the main character and that character's interpersonal relationships.

A powerful example is "In the Western Tradition," in which Eisenstein deftly treats time travel on both the physical and the psychological levels. A recurring theme in her writings, time travel is handled with a twist in this story. Instead of actually travelling in time, people view past events by means of sophisticated machinery. Requiring highly skilled operators, the equipment by its geographic location limits the range of observable events. As intriguing as this concept is, the central story is about Allison, a very talented operator who becomes so obsessed with the past that she isolates herself from her own contemporary life. Equally compelling for point of view are "Taboo," with its interplay between anthropologists and natives as well as among the scientists themselves, and "Nightlife," a look at the reality of dreams.

Many of her early stories written in collaboration with her husband Alex tend to be oriented more to the external structure of the plot or concept than to the effect of that structure on the characters. These stories seem to lack the depth and insight of her solo writings. An exception is "You Are Here," a disturbing story whose full impact is not realized until its conclusion. While that ending is rather predictable, the building of the character is subtle.

Eisenstein came into her own with her series about Alaric, a minstrel with the apparently magical power of teleportation. Each of these stories is complete in itself, but if read in order, as in the collection *Born to Exile,* they form a continuous account of Alaric's adventures. Other than the minstrel's extraordinary talent and the locals' superstitions, magic is not a major part of this world. In fact, Alaric himself tries to fight the superstitious beliefs found among his medieval society. Eisenstein continues her practical approach to magic in *Sorcerer's Son.* The Sorcerers' magical powers are strictly defined, operating according to laws much as science does. One finds sorcerers, demons, magic, and, of course, a quest, all the typical elements of fantasy. Happily, Eisenstein also gives free rein to her enjoyable wit and humor, adding greatly to the humanity of the tale.

Strong, resourceful, and independent women figure prominently in Eisenstein's work. This makes *Shadow of Earth* somewhat disappointing. Accidentally thrust into a medieval society, 20th-century Celia seems little able to cope with her drastic change of circumstance and social status and is ultimately only slightly changed by the experience. The book has been touted by feminists for showing the harshness of a world where a woman's only value is in bearing children. Perhaps Eisenstein intentionally makes this heroine weak to emphasize the helplessness of a technologically educated woman in a more primitive society. Although *In the Hands of Glory* sometimes lapses into the romantic clichés of space opera, its strong point is Dia Catlin, who faces conflict when her ideals encounter sordid reality. The Outcome of a planetary rebellion is secondary to the growth and change Dia painfully undergoes.

Phyllis Eisenstein shows increasing maturity as a writer. Adept at handling various formats, she uses a variety of subjects equally well. The worlds she creates, whether magical or otherwise, are carefully crafted and believable, her characters individual and memorable.

—Gay E. Carter

EKLUND, Gordon. American. Born in Seattle, Washington, 24 July 1945. Educated at Contra Costa College, San Pablo, California, 1973-75. Served in the United States Air Force, 1963-67: Sergeant. Married Dianna Mylarski in 1969; two sons. Since 1968, free-lance writer. Recipient: Nebula Award,

1974. Agent: Kirby McCauley Ltd., 425 Park Avenue South, New York, New York 10016, U. S. A.

SCIENCE-FICTION PUBLICATIONS

Novels (series: Lord Tedric)

The Eclipse of Dawn. New York, Ace, 1971.
A Trace of Dreams. New York, Ace, 1972.
Beyond the Resurrection. New York, Doubleday, 1973.
All Times Possible . New York, DAW, 1974.
Inheritors of Earth, with Poul Anderson. Radnor, Pennsylvania, Chilton, 1974.
Serving in Time. Toronto, Laser, 1975.
Falling Toward Forever. Toronto, Laser, 1975.
The Grayspace Beast. New York, Doubleday, 1976.
Dance of the Apocalypse. Toronto, Laser, 1976.
If the Stars Are Gods, with Gregory Benford. New York, Berkley, 1977; London, Gollancz, 1978.
The Starless World (novelization of TV play). New York, Bantam, 1978.
Lord Tedric, with E. E. Smith. New York, Baronet, 1978.
Space Pirates, with E. E. Smith. New York, Baronet, 1979; us *Lord Tedric: The Space Pirates*, London, Wingate, 1979.
The Twilight River. New York, Dell, 1979.
Devil World (novelization of TV play). New York, Bantam, 1979.
The Garden of Winter. New York, Berkley, 1980.
Find the Changeling, with Gregory Benford. New York, Dell, 1980; London, Sphere, 1983.

Uncollected Short Stories

"Dear Aunt Annie," in *Fantastic* (New York), April 1970.
"A Gift from the Gozniks," in *Fantastic* (New York), August 1970.
"Home Again Home Again," in *Quark 3*, edited by Samuel R. Delany and Marilyn Hacker. New York, Paperback Library, 1971.
"West Wind, Falling," in *Universe 1*, edited by Terry Carr. New York, Ace, 1971; London, Dobson, 1975.
"Seeker for Still Life," in *Fantasy and Science Fiction* (New York), January 1971.
"Gemini Cavendish," in *Amazing* (New York), March 1971.
"Defender of Death," in *Galaxy* (New York), April 1971.
"The Edge and the Mist," in *Galaxy* (New York), September 1971.
"Stalking the Sun," in *Universe 2*, edited by Terry Carr. New York, Ace, 1972; London, Dobson, 1975.
"White Summer in Memphis," in *New Dimensions 2*, edited by Robert Silverberg. New York, Avon, 1972.
"Grasshopper Time," in *Fantasy and Science Fiction* (New York), March 1972.
"Soft Change," in *Amazing* (New York), May 1972.
"Underbelly," in *If* (New York), October 1972.
"Examination Day," in *The Other Side of Tomorrow* edited by Roger Elwood. New York, Random House, 1973.
"Free City Blues," in *Universe 3*, edited by Terry Carr. New York, Random House, 1973; London, Dobson, 1976.
"Lovemaker," in *Eros in Orbit*, edited by Joseph Elder. New York, Simon and Schuster, 1973.
"The Shrine of Sebastian," in *Chains of the Sea.* Nashville, Nelson, 1973.
"Three Comedians," in *New Dimensions 3*, edited by Robert Silverberg. New York, Avon, 1973.

"The Ascending Axe," in *Amazing* (New York), January 1973.
"Iron Mountain," in *Fantastic* (New York), July 1973.
"The Stuff of Time," in *Fantastic* (New York), September 1973.
"The Beasts in the Jungle," in *Fantasy and Science Fiction* (New York), November 1973.
"Moby, Too," in *Amazing* (New York), December 1973.
"The Ambiguities of Yesterday," in *The Far Side of Time* edited by Roger Elwood. New York, Dodd Mead, 1974.
"Psychosomatica," in *Crisis*, edited by Roger Elwood. Nashville, Nelson, 1974.
"Beneath the Waves," in *Fantasy and Science Fiction* (New York), March 1974.
"The Treasure in the Treasure House," in *Fantasy and Science Fiction* (New York), August 1974.
"Angel of Truth," in *Epoch*, edited by Roger Elwood and Robert Silverberg. New York, Berkley, 1975.
"Sandsnake Hunter," in *Fantasy and Science Fiction* (New York), March 1975.
"Second Creation," in *Amazing* (New York), March 1975.
"The Restoration," in *Analog* (New York), September 1975.
"What Did You Do Last Year?," in *Universe 6*, edited by Terry Carr. New York, Doubleday, 1976; London, Dobson, 1978.
"The Rising of the Sun," in *Beyond Time*, edited by Sandra Ley. New York, Pocket Books, 1976.
"The Locust Descending," in *Fantastic* (New York), February 1976.
"Changing Styles," in *Fantasy and Science Fiction* New York), March 1976.
"The Prince in Metropolis," in *Analog* (New York), May 1976.
"The Anvil of Jove," in *Fantasy and Science Fiction* (New York), July 1976.
"Embryonic Dharma," in *Analog* (New York), December 1976.
"The Retro Man," in *New Dimensions 7*, edited by Robert Silverberg. New York, Harper, and London, Gollancz, 1977.
"Hellas in Florida," in *Fantasy and Science Fiction* (New York), January 1977.
"The Tides of Time," in *Galaxy* (New York), March 1977.
"To End All Wars," in *International Relations Through Science Fiction*, edited by Martin H. Greenberg and Joseph D. Olander. New York, Watts, 1978.
"Vermeer's Window," in *Universe 8*, edited by Terry Carr. New York, Doubleday, 1978; London, Dobson, 1979.
"Saint Francis Night," in *Amazing* (New York), May 1978.
"Points of Contract," in *Fantasy and Science Fiction* (New York), June 1978.
"Tattered Stars, Tarnished Bars," in *Beyond Reality*, edited by Terry Carr. New York, Elsevier Nelson, 1979.
"The Anaconda's Smile," in *Fantasy and Science Fiction* (New York), May 1979.
"The Mother of the Beast," in *Orbit 21*, edited by Damon Knight. New York, Harper, 1980.
"Pain and Glory," in *New Dimensions 12*, edited by Robert Silverberg and Marta Randall. New York, Pocket Books, 1981.
"Valo in Love," in *Analog Yearbook 2*, edited by Stanley Schmidt. New York, Ace, 1981.
"Continuous Performance," in *Last Man on Earth*, edited by Isaac Asimov, Martin H. Greenberg, and Charles G. Waugh. New York, Fawcett, 1982.
"Revisions," in *Fantasy and Science Fiction* (New York), February 1983.

*

Gordon Eklund comments:

If there's any one aspect of my work to date that seems worth emphasizing, it would have to be the range of themes, subjects, styles, and moods that I've attempted. I don't believe that any two of my novels are very much alike, and the short stories are even more varied, if only because of their greater number. To me, the science-fiction field is an extremely broad category—one encompassing, as it does, all of possibility—and I've found it extremely difficult to settle down to mining a single nook within the field. I suppose a few certain types of stories can easily be seen as favorites of mine—I find particular pleasure in dealing with time and parallel worlds—but I would't want to predict that this will remain valid during my next ten years as a writer.

* * *

Gordon Eklund reaches with equal dexterity far out into time or space. This west-coast author has set his plots over a broad spectrum. Eklund relishes the combination of fun and substance in his works. The reader is never able to predict the next paragraph, either icy sarcasm or deep message. One of the notable aspects of this science fiction, especially the early work, is the visionary range concerning the human prospect. Ironically, the specific personalities who are exploring these possibilities appear neurotic and limited. It is something of a tough dichotomy in Eklund's work. Mercifully, the conclusions to these space and time adventures are often thought provoking rather than just cosmically consoling.

Eklund's first novel, *The Eclipse of Dawn*, is certainly one of his best. The story is set about 25 years in the future, and the radical societal smashup (that everyone seems to fear so much now) has occurred. The America of the 21st century is a stark, confusing, and disorienting place. The exaggerated ennui of a fallen America is creatively juxtaposed to the virile faith of Senator William Colonby, who is running for president.

Eklund masterfully caricatures the idiocy and irony of a misplaced crusader. Senator Colonby does a whistle-stop tour of America, uttering loud but meaningless political platitudes. Along with some sexual intrigue, the plot includes a telepathic woman who is in contact with powerful aliens from Jupiter. The book settles down into a nasty chaos and depression when these alien savior-beings turn out to be nonexistent. The book closes with the surrender of the sitting president to Colonby, and a statement about the basic impotency of politics. In *The Eclipse of Dawn* the integrity of the individual is still possible, but the societal prospect is bleak.

Perhaps Eklund's richest achievement is *If the Stars Are Gods* (written with Gregory Benford). The novel is a moving challenge to the limited consciousness we all seek to transcend: "Understanding the new and strange is not so much a matter of work and effort, but of intuition and time to let ideas come to fruition. " The hero is Bradley Reynolds, a "brilliant young scientist" whose consuming passion is to discover other dimensions of being in the universe. The plot moves quickly through an initial failure to find life on Mars, an encounter with enlightened aliens from another universe, and 35 years in an African monastery. This contrast of the exploratory and introspective nature of Reynolds's personality is skillfully depicted. His personal odyssey climaxes with his death in a newly discovered place which will open new opportunities for the human race. This work is especially a pleasure in terms of characterization (e. g., beautiful, mercurial and infuriating Mara: "She took drugs, slept with other women, gambled, drank, stole money"). The characters are strong and brave while remaining believably human.

Perhaps the most memorable of Eklund's heroes is Tommy Bloome in *All Times Possible* . The specifics of Tommy's life, death, and identity are presented in tantalizing montage of episodes. It becomes clear, however, that Tommy is a savior of the workers and the people. The book, like *The Eclipse of Dawn*, presents a post-catastrophe or transformed America—the difference being that Tommy ends up as a martyr for the cause of the (successful?) revolution. The entire novel is written while Tommy is contemplating a bullet that is in mid-air, whistling toward his forehead. Is Tommy in a new life form after death? Is he having the familiar "life flashing before my eyes" experience? Or is this device a statement about the awful finality of death? *All Times Possible* contains more provocative ambiguity than any of Eklund's other works, and goes somewhat beyond what seems to be the basic Eklund point of view: "We've no right to expect a damn thing from this cold universe" (*If the Stars Are Gods*).

In *Dance of the Apocalypse*, set in 2097, anarchy, poverty and starvation are the major components. The heroes in this showdown are a tough, illiterate street scrounger and a humanistic idealist from the east, William Stoner. *Dance of the Apocalypse* boasts a novel excursion of the imagination in terms of how order is restored to the now barbarous world. In the midst of deep turmoil, China returns to Confucianism and sends an exploratory mission to the United States. By a stroke of profound luck, our dedicated idealist has the sagacity to appreciate the Confucian mind. The final outcome of the insurrection is the realization of a Confucian state in America. The explorer and teacher from China explains quite clearly why things are going to be so happy from now on: "Because William Stoner believes what we believe, and because what we believe is correct. "

The final works of Eklund that should be mentioned are the Lord Tedric series, reportedly conceived by E. E. "Doc" Smith, which involves a massive battle of good and evil forces. Lord Tedric's origins are not so different from Superman's (i. e., born in another world he doesn't remember, special powers on earth), but he comes to a realization of his abilities and destiny rather slowly. Tedric is not (and is not meant to be) as believable or human as Bradley Reynolds in *If the Stars are Gods*.

Eklund has a rare ability to project alternative outcomes for the United States, the world, and the cosmos. He ranges from sarcastic pessimism in *The Eclipse of Dawn*, to the patently bizarre possibility in *Dance of the Apocalypse* and total cosmic liberation (communication with the stars) in *If the Stars Are Gods*. Eklund's talent and insight are more visible when he keeps the plot and characters close to the reality of today. As he reaches to portray the New Man and the New Woman of the transformed future, his vision breaks down because of what he knows of the human condition. His pure heroes are acceptable, and his portrayal of the bitter defeatism that creeps into human relationships is excellent. As Eklund expatiates widely on the human prospect throughout his work, the reader is forced to deal with both close existential issues and the ultimate potentiality of the universe. Despite consistent inconsistency, Eklund communictes much to the intellect and imagination.

—Peter Lynch

ELDERSHAW, M. Barnard. Pseudonym for Marjorie Faith Barnard (and with Flora Sydney Patricia Eldershaw for non-science-fiction works). Australian. Born in Ashfield, New

South Wales, 16 August 1897. Educated at Cambridge School, Hunters' Hill; Sydney Girls' High School; University of Sydney (exhibitioner; University Medal, 1920), 1916-20, B. A. (honours) in history 1920; Sydney Teachers College, 1920. Librarian Sydney Public Library and Sydney Technical College Library, 1920-35; free-lance writer, 1935-42; Librarian, Sydney Public Library, 1942, and Commonwealth Scientific and Industrial Research Organization Library, Sydney, 1942-50. Recipient: *Bulletin* prize, 1928; Patrick White Award, 1983. Member, Order of Australia, 1979. Agent: Curtis Brown (Australia) Pty. Ltd., 86 William Street, Paddington, New South Wales 2021. Address: 29 Sunshine Drive, Point Clare, New South Wales 2250, Australia.

SCIENCE-FICTION PUBLICATIONS

Novel

Tomorrow and Tomorrow. Melbourne, Georgian House, 1947; London, Phoenix House, 1949; complete text, as *Tomorrow and Tomorrow and Tomorrow*, London, Virago, 1983; New York, Doubleday, 1984.

OTHER PUBLICATIONS with Flora Sydney Patricia Eldershaw

Novels

A House is Built. London, Harrap, and New York, Harcourt Brace, 1929.
Green Memory. London, Harrap, and New York, Harcourt Brace, 1931.
The Glasshouse. London, Harrap, 1936.
Plaque with Laurel. London, Harrap, 1937.

Play

The Watch on the Headland, in *Australian Radio Plays*, edited by Leslie Rees. Sydney, Angus and Robertson, 1946.

Other

Philip of Australia: An Account of the Settlement at Sydney Cove 1788-1792. London, Harrap, 1937.
Essays in Australian Fiction. Melbourne, Melbourne University Press, 1938; Freeport, New York, Books for Libraries, 1970.
The Life and Times of Captain John Piper. Sydney, Australian Limited Editions Society, 1939.
My Australia. London, Jarrolds, 1939; revised edition, 1951.

Editor. *Coast to Coast 1946*. Sydney, Angus and Robertson, 1947.

OTHER PUBLICATIONS as Marjorie Faith Barnard

Short Stories

The Persimmon Tree and Other Stories. Sydney, Clarendon, 1943.

Other

The Ivory Gate. Privately printed, 1920.
Macquarie's World. Sydney, Australian Limited Editions Society, 1941.

Australian Outline. Sydney, Ure Smith, 1943; revised edition, 1949.
The Sydney Book. Sydney, Ure Smith, 1947.
Sydney: The Story of a City. Melbourne, Melbourne University Press, 1956.
Australia's First Architect: Francis Greenway. London, Longman, 1961.
A History of Australia. Sydney, Angus and Robertson, 1962; revised edition, 1963; New York, Praeger, 1963.
Georgian Architecture in Australia, with others. Sydney, Ure Smith, 1963.
Lachlan Macquarie. Melbourne, Oxford University Press, 1964.
Miles Franklin. New York, Twayne, 1967; revised edition, Melbourne, Hill of Content, 1967.

*

Marjorie Faith Barnard comments:
(1981) Two things have a bearing on my writing: one is the circumstances of my childhood, and the other a successful collaboration.

I was an only child, had no playmates, and did not go to school until I was ten (having been taught by governesses prior to that). This was the best possible beginning for a writer. My natural creativity was not quenched by having too much. I created my own exciting and happy world. Words were my toys. I had the close companionship of my mother and free access to my great-grandmother's books—the Victorian poets, a complete set of Dickens, many histories. I had no taste for the insipid children's books of my period and escaped them almost entirely.

My collaboration with Flora Eldershaw was successful and disciplined. We both wanted to write and each had something to contribute. Our rule was to discuss the plan of a book in detail and agree upon it before anything was written down. Flora had a fine critical ability and curbed my exuberance. I wrote the better prose and had more leisure, so most of the actual writing fell to me. Our association was professional: her friends were not my friends, her way of life not mine. This was a good thing; close friendship would have brought other than literary considerations into it all. We worked in a dry light.

Tomorrow and Tomorrow was entirely my own work as Flora Eldershaw, for reasons of geography and pressure of work, could not contribute. It is a serious book, the best and worst thing I have ever done. I cared too much. As an historian I could see all too clearly the probable future of this country. The book had its roots in the anguish of the years preceeding the Second World War. It is about human survival and escape from bondage. The book ran into difficulties. It was hard to find a publisher for such a long and in some ways controversial novel; times were touchy. Without my knowledge my publisher submitted the manuscript to the censor who cut the latter part severely. It was not subversive and now would have no difficulty in being printed *in toto*, but costs have prohibited its republication in its original form.

*   *   *

M. Barnard Eldershaw is the pen name of the Australian historical novelists Marjorie Barnard and Flora Eldershaw. *Tomorrow and Tomorrow,* the one science fiction work published under this name, is in fact the work of Marjorie Barnard alone. In it she applies the selective techniques of the historical novelist to recreate Australia of the period 1924-46 through the eyes of a man four centuries in the future.

The reconstruction of cultural malaise moving into wartime confusion is brilliant if overlong but the story (completed in 1942) moves on to a vision of a different ending to the World War of 1939-45, one wherein an exhausted people turns on the culture which has brought only recurrent agony to each new generation and destroys it. The razing of Sydney by fire is a tremendous symbolic set piece. All this is conveyed as sections of a novel written by a 24th-century *littérateur*, in a time when youth is again restive in a culture (conventionally pastoral-utopian) which it sees as oppressive in its settled satisfaction. The author's political argument (this is a political novel) turns on a newly devised voting machine which records the thoughts of electors to give an accurate survey of mass attitudes.

When a public test of the machine is made, with youth proposing far-reaching constitutional changes, the outcome is devastating for the young protesters. The motion is lost when the machine records a 62% majority of the electors as utterly indifferent to the question. The warning is simple—that indifference leads to frustration and eventually to the violence which destroyed the earlier culture.

The Australian censorship at the time found much of this material not actually subversive but politically disquieting, particularly that dealing with the war which was still in progress, and made numerous deletions. Some are, from the viewpoint of the 1940's understandable; ides of an ultimate political doublecross by Russia and Australian secession from the British Empire were touchy stuff—but finally honoured by events, though not in the form of the writer's forecast. Other deletions are hard to justify: what, for instance, could have been the objection to: (a man of the 24th-century is speaking) "I only know by chance and the skin of my teeth that jigsaw puzzles were a fashionable craze four centuries ago and now are one with crosswords and diabolo"? It is no longer possible to recover the state of mind which caused such aberrations. The curious will find all the deletions restored and listed in the Virago edition of 1983.

Tomorrow and Tomorrow and Tomorrow (the full title now restored) is powerfully characterised and is a masterly example of science fiction used to present an argument in dramatic detail. Nobel Prize-winner Patrick White named it the Australian novel he would most like to see republished. It has been.

—George Turner

ELGIN, (Patricia Anne) Suzette Haden (née Wilkins). American. Born in Louisiana, Missouri, 18 November 1936. Educated at the University of Chicago (Academy of American Poets Award, 1955), 1954-56; California State University, Chico, B. A. in French and English 1967; University of California, San Diego, 1968-73, M. A. in Linguistics 1970, Ph. D. 1973. Married 1) Peter Joseph Haden in 1955 (died), one son and two daughters; 2) George N. Elgin in 1964, one son. Television folk music performer, Redding, California, 1966-68; Instructor, Chico Conservatory of Music, 1967-68; French teacher, 1968-69; guitar teacher, 1969-70; Linguistics teacher, University of California, San Diego, summer 1971; Assistant Professor, then Associate Professor of Linguistics, San Diego State University, 1972-80, now Emeritus. Since 1980, Founding Director, Ozark Center for Language Studies, and Editor, *The Lonesome Node,* Huntsville. Recipient: Eugene Saxon Fellowship, 1957-58. Address: Rt. 4, Box 192-E, Huntsville, Arkansas 72740, U. S. A.

SCIENCE-FICTION PUBLICATIONS

Novels (series: Communipath; Ozark)

Communipath Worlds. New York, Pocket Books, 1980.
  The Communipaths. New York, Ace, 1970.
  Furthest. New York, Ace, 1971.
  At the Seventh Level. New York, DAW, 1972.
Star-Anchored, Star-Angered (Communipath). New York, Doubleday, 1979.
The Ozark Trilogy. New York, Doubleday, 1981.
  1. *Twelve Fair Kingdoms.* New York, Doubleday, 1981.
  2. *Grand Jubilee.* New York, Doubleday, 1981.
  3. *And Then There'll Be Fireworks.* New York, Doubleday, 1981.
Native Tongue. New York, DAW, 1984.

Uncollected Short Stories

"Final Exam," in *Pouring Down Words,* edited by Suzette Haden Elgin. Englewood Cliffs, New Jersey, Prentice Hall, 1975.
"Babyzap," in *Playgirl* (New York), 1976.
"Old Rocking Chair's Got Me," in *Fantasy and Science Fiction* (New York), February 1979.
"Lest Levitation Come Upon Us," in *Perpetual Light,* edited by Alan Ryan. New York, Warner, 1982.
"Magic Granny Says Don't Meddle," in *Fantasy and Science Fiction* (New York), August 1984.

OTHER PUBLICATIONS

Other

Guide to Transformational Grammar: History, Theory, Practice, with John T. Grinder. New York, Holt Rinehart, 1973.
What Is Linguistics? Englewood Cliffs, New Jersey, Prentice Hall, 1973; revised edition, 1979.
A Primer of Transformational Grammar for Rank Beginners. Urbana, Illinois, National Conference of Teachers of English, 1975.
The Gentle Art of Verbal Self-Defense. Englewood Cliffs, New Jersey, Prentice Hall, 1980; *More on the Gentle Art of Verbal Self-Defense,* 1983.
A First Grammar and Dictionary of Láadan. Madison, Wisconsin, SF3, 1984.

Editor, *Pouring Down Words.* Englewood Cliffs, New Jersey, Prentice Hall, 1975.

*

Manuscript Collection: Chater Collection, Love Library, San Diego State University.

Suzette Haden Elgin comments:

(1981) I went into writing science fiction originally because as a married woman with four kids at home I couldn't pay my graduate school tuition any other way, it being well known that such women are not "Ph.D. material." I know that's not an inspiring or romantic reason, but it's honest. Because I am a linguist my major interest is problems of communication as they are now and as they are likely to develop in the future; I have focused my books on this topic up to now, along with—as subtopics—an attempt to make clear what a pernicious crock Romantic Love is, and a fascination with problems of theology especially as they apply to women under the constant influence of religious language. My books have been picked up as feminist, which I hadn't realized they were until I read the reviews.

I take my SF writing very seriously, and feel that anybody who spends the time and money to read something I have written should not feel cheated, and should not be presented with a cryptic puzzle used to demonstrate how clever *I* am. My first four books have been part of an on-going series about a rather bumbling mind-deaf superspy; I am now writing a fantasy trilogy, and am enjoying the change. But there will be more Coyote Jones books—the intergalactic superspy framework is a gentle kind of spoof that allows me plenty of room to move around and be as entertaining as possible without writing anything I have to be ashamed of later. I try to avoid the Brothers Karamazov Syndrome, and do not allow my characters to pontificate.

I plot a book down to the most minute detail in advance, filling notebooks with maps, biographies, every conceivable sort of information I might need in the book about its culture and characters. That takes at least a year. When I do the actual writing, however, I do only one draft. Then I revise as I type the final manuscript, and that writing process generally takes about six weeks from start to finish. I don't believe in inspiration, I believe in hard work. I hope that shows in my work; it's meant to. I have no problem "finding ideas"; my only problem is finding time to write them all. That, I expect, comes from rigorous training in the scientific method: one just poses hypotheses, and extrapolates.

Most embarassing moment: having nobody notice that I had intended *Furthest* as a straightforward satire of the United States system of economics; that is, anything's allowed as long as you've filled out the proper forms.

*   *   *

Suzette Haden Elgin, like Gregory Benford or Fred Hoyle, is a scientist writing science fiction concerning her professional field. In this case the science is linguistics, in which Elgin's professional involvement is considerable. Elgin's novels fall into two groups, the communipath series (science fiction) and the Ozark trilogy (both fantasy and science fiction); *Native Tongue*, her most recent book, stands alone but may be beginning a new series. All the series, though different in tone and sharing no characters, are in roughly compatible futures, at least sharing some references.

The communipath books, set in a far future populated by a number of humanoid cultures on a number of planets, concern Tri-Galactic Agent Coyote Jones. The prevailing theme of the books is communication, in all its various and difficult guises, including a number of forms of telepathy. Jones himself is an extremely powerful projective telepath who is also "mind-deaf," a rare and pitiable affliction which, however, suits him for the assignment in *Star-Anchored, Star-Angered:* checking out Drussa Silver, a female messiah whose abilities include—but go beyond—telepathy. Her Followers, in their religion-based community/communication/communion, recall the Maklunites of *The Communipaths.*

Other characters include a "mind wife," rebelling against the life of psychic concubine for which her training has prepared her, in *Furthest;* and Susannah, an extremely telepathically gifted baby drafted for the communipath system (likened to a psychic bucket-brigade) that passes messages through otherwise impossible distances (*The Communipaths*).

The communipath books also explore a number of fascinating social and communication systems not based on telepathy,

including the Multiversities (higher education more rare but more esteemed than now) and a system of ritual battle by carefully selected and honored poets, in which soldiers suffer for their side's inferior verse, in *At the Seventh Level.* This kind of social institution of specific forms of discourse is one of the many strengths of Elgin's Ozark trilogy.

The Twelve Families of Planet Ozark left Earth to find a society with a technology based primarily on magic. While the setting on another planet and moderate use of scientific technology (especially the "comsets" run by the main family in the trilogy, the Brightwaters) would justify calling the books science fiction, in a deeper sense the society and magic (which is always a technology, and the highest form of which is based on transformational-generative grammar) also show the kind of extrapolation that marks the genre. The charm of the books throughout is the familiar strangeness, and strange familiarity, of alien equivalents of the modern-American Ozark culture Elgin knows well, including "mules," actually telepathic (but generally uncommunicative) aliens who fly by magic; and "the Grannies," a social class of much power, able to perform household magic and known for their folksy and fiery "formspeech. " Most of the plot of the books revolves around Responsible of Brightwater, a 14-year-old girl who holds the position, as does one female each generation, of Meta-Magician; unknown to most, she holds powers greater even than the Magicians of Rank, and her mere functioning is vital to the maintenance of magic on Ozark.

These seven books show the growth of Elgin as an author, especially in plotting. The plots of the communipath books are often loose, with too abrupt a solution by Coyote Jones, and too many intriguing developments, such as the changes hinted at the end of *The Communipaths,* simply dropped or only vaguely referred to later. In the Ozark books, the plots are complicated but always tight, with material, such as the character of Silverweb of McDaniels, which is not only interesting but later shown to be vital. The narrative voice gets more sure and the characters get both more human and more powerful, although Responsible can occasionally verge on the unconvincing precociousness of Tessa in *The Communipath.*

This development has continued with *Native Tongue,* which is her best work so far, both as a novel and as science fiction. One theme in the work is communication among alien races. In a future of copious interplanetary trade, the linguists have become a necessary and powerful yet despised and feared social class, marrying among their households and raising their children to be translators before the age of most easy language acquisition—around puberty or before—is past. Another theme is communication between the genders, which might as well be alien races. In the future of the novel, women's liberation is only a legend, and men have complete legal control of all females.

Elgin had shown societies repressive of women before, especially in *At the Seventh Level.* In fact, while strong females appear in all her books, from a Multiversity dean to Responsible's sister Troublesome of Brightwater, Elgin has never yet shown a society in which the traditional virtues of feminine versus masculine are completely questioned or changed, which may be a limitation of her handling of this theme; sometimes it seems the novel's implied outlook may merely reverse the sexism of the society it examines. Especially in the Ozark books and *Native Tongue,* men are by nature bumbling fools, but the women must still run things indirectly or watch chaos ensue.

Still, particularly in *Native Tongue,* Elgin's treatment of gender has strengths that outweigh the weaknesses. At the end of this latest novel, Elgin introduces Láadan, a language developed by Linguist women to express their own concerns. This woman's language looks quite promising, as does the hint at the end of the novel about a breakthrough to communication with non-humanoid as well as humanoid aliens.

—Bernadette Bosky

ELLISON, Harlan (Jay). Also writes as Paul Merchant. American. Born in Cleveland, Ohio, 27 May 1934. Attended Ohio State University, Columbus, 1951-53. Served in the United States Army, 1957-59. Married 1) Charlotte Stein in 1956 (divorced); 2) Billie Joyce Sanders in 1961 (divorced); 3) Lory Patrick in 1965 (divorced); 4) Lori Horowitz in 1976 (divorced). Editor, *Rogue* ; Founding Editor, Regency Books, Evanston, Illinois, 1961-62. Free-lance writer and lecturer: Editor, Harlan Ellison Discovery Series. Vice-President, Science Fiction Writers of America, 1965-66 (resigned). Recipient: Nebula Award, 1965, 1969, 1977; Writers Guild of America award, for TV play, 1965, 1967, 1973; Hugo Award, 1966, 1968 (3 awards), 1972 (for editing), 1974, 1975, 1978; Mystery Writers of America Edgar Allan Poe Award, 1973; Jupiter award, 1973; *Locus* award, 1983. Address: c/o Borgo Press, P. O. Box 2845 San Bernardino, California 92406, U.S.A.

SCIENCE-FICTION PUBLICATIONS

Novels

The Man with Nine Lives. New York, Ace, 1960.
Doomsman. New York, Belmont, 1967.
Phoenix Without Ashes, with Edward Bryant. New York, Fawcett, 1975; Manchester, Savoy, 1978.
The City on the Edge of Forever (novelization of TV play). New York, Bantam, 1977.

Short Stories

A Touch of Infinity. New York, Ace, 1960.
Ellison Wonderland. New York, Paperback Library, 1962; revised edition, New York, Bluejay, 1984; as *Earthman, Go Home,* 1964.
Paingod and Other Delusions. New York, Pyramid, 1965.
I Have No Mouth, and I Must Scream. New York, Pyramid, 1967; revised edition, New York, Ace, 1983.
From the Land of Fear. New York, Belmont, 1967.
Love Ain't Nothing But Sex Misspelled. New York, Trident Press, 1968.
The Beast That Shouted Love at the Heart of the World. New York, Avon, 1969; abridged edition, London, Millington, 1976; revised edition, New York, Bluejay, 1984.
Over the Edge: Stories from Somewhere Else. New York, Belmont, 1970.
Alone Against Tomorrow. New York, Macmillan, 1971; as *All the Sounds of Fear* and *The Time of the Eye,* London, Panther, 2 vols., 1973-74.
Partners in Wonder: Harlan Ellison in Collaboration with. . . . New York, Walker, 1971.
Approaching Oblivion. New York, Walker, 1974; London, Millington, 1976.
Deathbird Stories: A Pantheon of Modern Gods. New York, Harper, 1975; London, Millington, 1977.

No Doors, No Windows. New York, Pyramid, 1975.
Strange Wine. New York, Harper, 1978.
The Illustrated Harlan Ellison. New York, Baronet, 1978.
The Fantasies of Harlan Ellison. Boston, Gregg Press, 1979.
Stalking the Nightmare. Huntington Woods, Michigan, Phantasia Press, 1982.
An Edge in My Voice. Norfolk, Virginia, Donning, 1984.

Uncollected Short Story

"With Virgil Oddum at the East Pole," in *Omni* (New York), January 1985.

OTHER PUBLICATIONS

Novels

Rumble. New York, Pyramid, 1958; as *Web of the City,* 1975.
Sex Gang (as Paul Merchant). N. p., Nightstand, 1959.
Rockabilly. New York, Fawcett, 1961; London, Muller, 1963; as *Spider Kiss,* New York, Pyramid, 1975.

Short Stories

The Deadly Streets. New York, Ace, 1958; London, Digit, 1959; enlarged edition, New York, Pyramid, 1975.
The Juvies. New York, Ace, 1961.
Gentleman Junkie and Other Stories of the Hung-Up Generation. Evanston, Illinois, Regency, 1961; revised edition, New York, Pyramid, 1975.
Shatterday. Boston, Houghton Mifflin, 1980; London, Hutchinson, 1982.

Plays

The City on the Edge of Forever (televised, 1967). Published in *Six Science Fiction Plays,* edited by Roger Elwood, New York, Pocket Books, 1976.

Screenplay: *The Oscar,* with Russell Rouse and Clarence Greene, 1966.

Television Plays: *Who Killed Alex Debbs?* [*Purity Mather?, Andy Zygmunt?, Half of Glory Lee?*](*Burke's Law* series), 1963-65; *The Soldier* and *Demon with a Glass Hand* (*The Outer Limits* series), 1963-64; *The City on the Edge of Forever* (*Star Trek* series), 1967; and for *Route 66, The Untouchables, The Alfred Hitchcock Hour,* and *The Man from U.N.C.L.E.* series.

Other

Memos from Purgatory: Two Journeys of Our Time. Evanston, Illinois, Regency, 1961.
The Glass Teat: Essays of Opinion on the Subject of Television. New York, Ace, 1970.
"You Are What You Write," in *Clarion 2,* edited by Robin Scott Wilson. New York, New American Library, 1972.
"When Dreams Become Nightmares: Some Cautionary Notes on the Clarion Experience," in *Clarion 3,* edited by Robin Scott Wilson. New York, New American Library, 1973.
"Whore with a Heart of Iron Pyrites; or, Where Does a Writer Go to Find a Maggie?," in *Those Who Can: A Science Fiction Reader,* edited by Robin Scott Wilson. New York, New American Library, 1973.
The Other Glass Teat: Further Essays of Opinion on Television. New York, Pyramid, 1975.

Sleepless Nights in the Procrustean Bed: Essays, edited by Marty Clark. San Bernardino, California, Borgo Press, 1984.

Editor, *Dangerous Visions.* New York, Doubleday, 1967; London, David Bruce and Watson, 2 vols., 1971.
Editor, *Nightshade and Damnations,* by Gerald Kersh. New York, Fawcett, 1968.
Editor, *Again, Dangerous Visions.* New York, Doubleday, 1972; London, Millington, 1976.
Editor, *Medea: Harlan's World.* Huntington Woods, Michigan, Phantasia Press, 1985.

Recording: *Blood!,* with Robert Bloch, Alternate World, 1976.

*

Bibliography: *Harlan Ellison: A Bibliographical Checklist* by Leslie Kay Swigart, Dallas, Williams, 1973.

Critical Studies: *Harlan Ellison: Unrepentant Harlequin* by George Edgar Slusser, San Bernardino, California, Borgo Press, 1977; "Harlan Ellison Issue" of *Fantasy and Science Fiction* (New York), July 1977; *The Book of Ellison* edited by Andrew Porter, New York, Algol Press, 1978.

*   *   *

Very few people are ambivalent about Harlan Ellison; they thoroughly like or thoroughly dislike his style. But he has won many awards for his writing, and not a few of them have come from outside the science-fiction world. And in spite of the people who walk out of his public appearances feeling insulted and angry or refuse to buy his books because of the lengthy introductions he includes with each one, it cannot be denied that Harlan Ellison is a good writer who has had a significant impact on contemporary science fiction. Ellison's use of language has helped change science fiction considerably. Ellison is not afraid to use any word, however objectionable some person or group might find it, if he thinks that that word is the proper one for a specific situation. His definition of obscenity, promulgated at various personal appearances, is "language which is intended to deceive." Ellison cites "protective reaction strike" and "military incursion" (Vietnam era words which reporters were required to use instead of "bombing mission" and "military invasion") as examples of obscene language.

In Ellison stories like "A Boy and His Dog," there are descriptions of sex and violence, and there is a lot of foul language. But, Ellison might argue, such description and language are necessary to the story. "A Boy and His Dog" depicts the aftermath of World War III. Roving gangs and roving independents, called "solos," occupy the surface of the planet; these young toughs, mostly male, are the same sort as those who roam inner city streets today. Their language must be strong to be realistic. In addition, Ellison sets his group in contrast to the other group of survivors, those living in underground cities to which they retreated as the war broke out. The surface gangs are destroying each other (and themselves) through violence; the below-grounders are sterile and wasting away. And without the four-letter words, the reader would be less able to contrast the destructive aggressiveness of the surface group to the equally destructive non-participation of the below-grounders.

In addition to helping expand the language of science fiction by example in his stories, Ellison has also encouraged others to do the same. As editor of the *Dangerous Visions* series (1967 and 1972; the third volume is forthcoming), Ellison encouraged his fellow science-fiction writers to send him those stories which other editors had considered too controversial to put into print. Ellison encouraged not just experiments with language, but experiments in subject matter and in style as well.

But it is his own writing that is most important. Many of his best-selling short stories are experimental in their subject matter. "Shattered Like a Glass Goblin" is a story about people on drugs who eventually, after continued and heavy use, turn into the creatures they hallucinate. They turn on and destroy each other in bestial ways. The narrator becomes a crystal goblin and is shattered by a swipe from the hairy paw of the creature that was once his girl friend. In "Delusion for a Dragon Slayer" a man is given the chance to attain heaven if he can act like the heroic-fantasy hero he has always dreamed of being; he does not make it. And "Catman" was written as the future sex story for a volume of ultimate science fiction stories called *Final Stage.*

Other Ellison stories are experimental in style. "The Beast That Shouted Love at the Heart of the World" is written to be read as if the separate segments were arranged in a circle instead of a sequence of pages. "Pretty Maggie Moneyeyes" attempts to portray a person's impressions at the moment of death. Ellison uses italics, varied spacing, and other type tricks to try to present these impressions and sensations. And "From A to Z, In the Chocolate Alphabet" consists of the alphabet, with a short story for each letter.

"The Deathbird" is a story which is experimental in both subject and style. In this story, Ellison attempts to show that Satan was the "good guy" and that God, who is responsible for the condition of the world, is insane. The story is told in 26 sections, each numbered, but only 20 or 21 of those sections actually advance the plot of the story. Some of the others are direct addresses to the reader or quizzes for the reader to take, and one section is the story of Ellison's dog, Ahbhu.

But there is more to Harlan Ellison than his science fiction. In newspaper columns later collected and published as *The Glass Teat* and *The Other Glass Teat,* he began with commentaries and criticisms of television and then expanded his focus to include all kinds of social and political topics. More recently, a number of his essays from a variety of sources have been published as *Sleepless Nights in the Procrustean Bed.* In addition, early Ellison fiction, much of it based on his experiences with street gangs, is being rereleased. And from time to time, Ellison has also written for television, from *Burke's Law* to his own ill-fated *The Starlost,* and for the movies.

Ellison's career is more multi-facted than that of any other science fiction author (except, of course, Isaac Asimov's), and because of the variety of things he does—writing, editing, lecturing, and the like—he is an important force in science fiction.

—C. W. Sullivan III

EMSHWILLER, Carol (née Fries). American. Born in Ann Arbor, Michigan, 12 April 1921. Educated at the University of Michigan, Ann Arbor, B. A. in music and B. Design 1949; Ecole Nationale Supérieure des Beaux-Arts, Paris (Fulbright Fellow), 1949-50. Married the filmmaker Ed Emshwiller in 1949; two daughters and one son. Since 1978, Member of the

Continuing Education Faculty, New York University. Organized workshops for Science Fiction Bookstore, New York, 1975, 1976 and Clarion Science Fiction Workshop, 1978, 1979; guest teacher, Sarah Lawrence College, Bronxville, New York, 1983. Recipient: MacDowell Fellowship, 1971; Creative Artists Public Service grant, 1975. Agent: Virginia Kidd, Box 278, Milford, Pennsylvania 18337. Address: 260 East 10th Street, No. 10, New York, New York 10009, U. S. A.

SCIENCE-FICTION PUBLICATIONS

Short Stories

Joy in Our Cause. New York, Harper, 1974.

Uncollected Short Stories

"This Thing Called Love," in *Future* (New York), no. 28, 1955.
"The Victim," in *Smashing Detective*, September 1955.
"Love Me Again," in *Science Fiction Quarterly* (Holyoke, Massachusetts), February 1956.
"The Piece Thing," in *Science Fiction Quarterly* (Holyoke, Massachusetts), May 1956.
"Bingo and Bongo," in *Future* (New York), Winter 1956-57.
"Nightmare Call," in *Future* (New York), Spring 1957.
"Murray Is for Murder," in *Fast Action Detective and Mystery*, March 1957.
"The Coming," in *Fantasy and Science Fiction* (New York), May 1957.
"Hands," in *Double-Action Detective*, Summer 1957.
"You'll Feel Better," in *Fantasy and Science Fiction* (New York), July 1957.
"Two-Step for Six Legs," in *Science Fiction Quarterly* (Holyoke, Massachusetts), August 1957.
"Baby," in *Fantasy and Science Fiction* (New York), February 1958.
"Idol's Eye," in *Future* (New York), February 1958.
"Pelt," in *Fantasy and Science Fiction* (New York), November 1958.
"Day at the Beach," in *Fantasy and Science Fiction* (New York), August 1959.
"Puritan Planet," in *Original Science Fiction Stories* (Holyoke, Massachusetts), January 1960.
"Adapted," in *Fantasy and Science Fiction* (New York), May 1961.
"But Soft, What Light . . .," in *Fantasy and Science Fiction* (New York), April 1966.
"Krashaw, Dog, and Boats," in *City Magazine* (New York), 1967.
"White Dove," in *New Worlds 188* (London), 1969.
"Debut," in *Orbit 6*, edited by Damon Knight. New York, Putnam, 1970.
"The Institute," in *Alchemy and Academe*, edited by Anne McCaffrey. New York, Doubleday, 1970.
"Woman Waiting," in *Orbit 7*, edited by Damon Knight. New York, Putnam, 1970.
"A Possible Episode in the Picaresque Adventures of Mr. J. H. B. Monstosee," in *Quark 2*, edited by Samuel R. Delany and Marilyn Hacker. New York, Paperback Library, 1971.
"Escape Is No Accident," in *2076: The American Tricentennial*, edited by Edward Bryant. New York, Pyramid, 1977.
"Thanne Longen Folk to Goen on Pilgrimages," in *The Little Magazine* (New York), vol. 11, no. 2, 1977.
"Abominable," in *Orbit 21*, edited by Damon Knight. New York, Harper, 1980.

"Hunting Machine," in *The Arbor House Treasury of Modern Science Fiction*, edited by Robert Silverberg and Martin H. Greenberg. New York, Arbor House, 1980.
"Omens," in *Edges*, edited by Ursula K. Le Guin and Virginia Kidd. New York, Pocket Books, 1980.
"The Start of the End of the World," in *Universe 11*, edited by Terry Carr. New York, Doubleday, 1981.
"Queen Kong," in *13th Moon*, vol. 6, nos. 1-2, 1982.
"Verging on the Pertinent," in *13th Moon*, vol. 7, nos. 1-2, 1984.

OTHER PUBLICATIONS

Plays

Television Plays: *Pilobolis and Joan*, 1974; *Family Focus, 1977*.

*

Carol Emshwiller comments:
Formal/structural concerns have always interested me the most, so once I had learned to plot and had published numerous science-fiction stories (and a few mystery stories), I decided to learn how *not* to plot. My concerns were for the various ways of forming a story and keeping forward movement without plotting. This was as hard to learn as plotting (harder, because I had no models in those days) and had to be learned as slowly. Looking back, I see that I did away with plot elements one at a time. I was unable to let go of them by twos or threes. I'm not really exactly sure what I put in their place, one by one, but I did refer to modern poetry for inspiration and I took many modern poetry techniques as models for my stories. Sometimes I tried to write a "story" all "between the lines," leaving a lot of work for the reader. Sometimes I tried to create the illusion of action without there actually being any.

Also I tried to write, as in modern poetry (which is influenced in this, I think, by the Chinese and Japanese), without the use of simile or metaphoric language, and, I hope, without a trace of the pathetic fallacy. I also tried to do away with character, and substituted what I called "selves," which, in my mind, were much more real than "characters" (though perhaps just different). I used the first person and tried for a kind of internal, psychological realism. To me, the "selves" represented the insides of everybody . . . the little fleeting thoughts . . . the little vanities . . . things not admitted by any of us. Also big things not admitted: petty hates, oedipal feelings, incest . . .

Why might one bother doing this? Well, like most science-fiction writers, my study was "what-would-happen-if," but not what-would-happen-if the ice age returned, or if apes began teaching each other to talk, but what-would-happen-if, for instance, a story had only a single bit of action? or none? What could hold the interest? What could move it forward? However, I may have written myself into a hole by now. Plot seems to be slowly coming back into my work. I'm not sure where I'll go from here, but I'm sure that "structures" will be one of my primary concerns.

Of course, there's that other thing: that when your conscious mind is kept busy with forms, the subconscious mind can be freed to work on all those underground things that are, perhaps, more important to a story.

* * *

Carol Emshwiller's fictions are perhaps best described, in Richard Kostelanetz's words, as "scrupulously strange," and much of their power derives precisely from her extreme scrupulosity as a maker. As she writes neither science fiction nor fantasy in any standard senses of those terms, her presence in the genre helps to explain why it's so difficult to define: she is there by association, for her husband, Ed Emshwiller, has long been an SF illustrator; thus the SF community knew her. Even so, her stories have appeared only in the more experimental SF anthologies like *Dangerous Visions, Orbit* and *2076: The American Tricentennial.* As a result, SF readers have been exposed to a kind of masterful experimentation seldom found in popular genre writing. Even Borges, one of the great fantasists of our time, remained relatively unknown within the SF world until recently, and his *ficciones* are far closer to Emshwiller's stories than a good 98% of SF is.

Where much SF, partly due to its pulp heritage of banal and conventional discourse, has tended to domesticate the unknown (so that strange planets, the galaxy itself, become merely places to have quite ordinary "extraordinary" adventures), Emshwiller's fictions force us to look again at the supposedly ordinary domestic world and see it as truly weird and, yes, unknown. How she does this is through a prose so precise it cuts away conventional perceptual fat like a surgeon's scalpel. Her writing holds our attention because it so carefully follows the patterns of thought and speech. Even when her stories embrace terror, they do so with economy and an almost fearless awareness cast over every perceived thing and event. Lively wit and intelligence, a fully awake mind whose variegated movements are mapped in the motions of her prose, a truly phenomenological writing: these offer such energy and delight as to exhilarate us even when the ostensible "content" (and her work demonstrates at every turn how form *makes* content, how "content" is never something *else* than what the words say) is almost insupportable—"as a mother, I have served longer than I expected" (and note how powerfully evocative that single verb "served" is).

A few of her stories actually allude to SF conventions, like the famous "Sex and/or Mr. Morrison," but they use these conventions metaphorically and to press home even more forcefully the strange alien lives we all live, here in the "real" world. The marvelous "Escape Is No Accident," for example, by beginning with the narrator's fall—as awkward wife from a ladder or as superior alien from space—forces us to see our culture in a new perspective. Others may have handled the idea before, but only Emshwiller articulates it through perceptions of the ordinary heightened to a frightening degree. The final paragraph gathers all the story's strands together:

> I don't tell him, but I'm afraid that, rather than continue my journey through space and time, I will have to continue it only through time, and (usually) there's something to look at out the window every day. And one isn't much sadder up there in the sky watching galaxies fade by. Why should I worry? Why should I talk so much and so loud? Why should I stay alert to the differences between us, them and me? And then, why shouldn't I croak and groan now and then, dizzy, having fallen down?

This is scrupulous writing precisely because it pays such careful attention to tone and detail. Every work functions fully; there is no dead weight. And this is true of all Emshwiller's best fictions.

Carol Emshwiller's *oeuvre* is small. One of a very small handful of writers in SF acquainted with contemporary poetry, she is, like the most exciting post-modern poets, dedicated to language and the explorations of lived life it allows when trusted and followed rather than manipulated to a foregone conclusion. She is a unique writer and her stories, at their best, are simply superior fictions which offer the adventurous reader rich and exhilarating experiences unlike almost anything to be found within the genre's boundaries.

—Douglas Barbour

ENGDAHL, Sylvia (Louise). American. Born in Los Angeles, California, 24 November 1933. Educated at Pomona College, Claremont, California, 1950; Reed College, Portland, Oregon, 1951; University of Oregon, Eugene, 1951-52, 1956-57; University of California, Santa Barbara, B. A. in education 1955; graduate work in anthropology, Portland State University, Oregon, 1978-80. Elementary school teacher, Portland, 1955-56; programmer, then computer systems specialist, SAGE Air Defense System, in Massachusetts, Wisconsin, Washington, and California, 1957-67. Recipient: Christopher Award, for children's book, 1973. Address: c/o Atheneum Publishers, 597 Fifth Avenue, New York, New York 10017, U. S. A.

SCIENCE-FICTION PUBLICATIONS (for young people)

Novels (series: Elana; Noren)

Enchantress from the Stars (Elana). New York, Atheneum, 1970; London, Gollancz, 1974.
Journey Between Worlds. New York, Atheneum, 1970.
The Far Side of Evil (Elana). New York, Atheneum, 1971; London, Gollancz, 1975.
The Star Shall Abide (Noren). New York, Atheneum, 1972; as *Heritage of the Star*, London, Gollancz, 1973.
Beyond the Tomorrow Mountains (Noren). New York, Atheneum, 1973.
The Doors of the Universe (Noren). New York, Atheneum, 1981.

Uncollected Short Stories

"The Beckoning Trail," with Rick Roberson, in *Universe Ahead,* edited by Engdahl and Roberson. New York, Atheneum, 1975.
"Timescape," with Mildred Butler, in *Anywhere, Anywhen,* edited by Engdahl. New York, Atheneum, 1976.

OTHER PUBLICATIONS (for young people)

Other

The Planet-Girded Suns: Man's View of Other Solar Systems. New York, Atheneum, 1974.
The Subnuclear Zoo: New Discoveries in High Energy Physics, with Rick Roberson. New York, Atheneum, 1977.
Tool for Tomorrow: New Knowledge about Genes, with Rick Roberson. New York, Atheneum, 1979.
Our World Is Earth. New York, Atheneum, 1979.

Editor, with Rick Roberson, *Universe Ahead: Stories of the Future.* New York, Atheneum, 1975.
Editor, *Anywhere, Anywhen; Stories of Tomorrow.* New York, Atheneum, 1976.

*

Sylvia Engdahl comments:
I have encountered a good deal of misunderstanding con-

cerning the audience for which my novels are intended, and I would like to clear it up. In the first place, though the present structure of the publishing business requires them to be issued as children's books, my novels are not meant for children; they are directed to older teenagers and young adults. Some exceptional pre-adolescents enjoy them, but do not grasp all their levels and on the whole find them heavy reading, since they are not primarily action stories. Their main emphasis is on the significance of space exploration, man's place in the universe, and human values I consider universal: all themes in which I believe today's young people are seriously interested.

In the second place, my novels do not fit the "science fiction" category much better than the "children's book" category; they aren't category books at all. Although they are set in future or hypothetical worlds, they are not directed toward fans of genre-oriented SF—they are meant for a general audience. They are not exotic enough to suit many SF fans, and *this is intentional*. My use of themes already old to the "fan" audience is also intentional. My aim is to reach readers who do not have a special background and do not care for fiction that seems far removed from real life, readers who find most SF too "far-out" for their tastes. I feel strongly that the future is not something that should be set apart and discussed only in literature of a particular type, directed to readers of a specific genre. The future is important to everyone, not just to those who choose to become familiar with the conventions and jargon of genre-oriented books. My chief goal is to place it in perspective in relation to the past and present, as well as to offer an affirmative outlook toward a universe wider than the single planet Earth. There is a desperate need, I believe, for fiction that conveys such themes to people beyond the comparatively small circle of SF fandom, and I therefore purposely market my own work outside that circle. I'm happy, of course, when people within the SF field like it; but I'm even happier when other people tell me they thought they didn't like space stories until they read mine. In my opinion, expansion into space is essential to human survival, and promoting that idea among readers not already space enthusiasts will remain my primary concern.

* * *

In her foreword to *Anywhere, Anywhen*, Sylvia Engdahl makes explicit her reasons for not wanting to be classified as an SF writer. She addresses the problem of esotericism in the genre: conventions which guide the initiated reader are potentially alienating to the reader from outside of the genre. Engdahl believes that the problems of the future are of interest to everyone, not only the fans of a specific field of literature (appropriately the stories in the abovementioned collection are by writers not normally associated with SF). With this in mind, Engdahl tries to avoid the jargon often associated with SF, the hard-core writer's emphasis on projections of technological innovation and the traditional conventions of space opera. Nevertheless, she works firmly *within* the field—justifying the fantastic elements of her stories in a substantial atmosphere of scientific credibility. Indeed, science and, in particular, the scientific method, play an important role in her narratives.

"Timescape," a novella written with her mother (Mildred Butler) for the *Anywhere, Anywhen* collection, serves as a useful introduction to Engdahl's works, containing themes common throughout her fiction. Alienation from society, the difficult quest for one's true identity, freedom of thought vs. authority and scholastic instruction: these are problems the protagonist Mark faces. An unwitting participant in a unique time-travel experiment, he is forced to approach his environment with a critical mind; to question the things around him, as well as the deeply felt moral principles within him. Set in opposition is the blind faith of religion and the analytic faculties of the scientific mind—an opposition predominant in her novels.

This Star Shall Abide, *Beyond the Tomorrow Mountains*, and *The Doors of the Universe* form a complete series in which the central figure is Noren, a character very similar to Mark in "Timescape. " Both are male adolescents, non-conformists, introspective in nature, and alienated from society. Noren is alienated because of his refusal to believe in a pseudo-religious legend which is the basis of social structure in a semi-feudal agrarian society. As a condemned heretic, he is sentenced to the mercy of the Scholars who live in a "holy" city. It is here that he undergoes a tortuous series of initiations and interrogations and learns of the desperate attempts of benevolent scientists to preserve their near-extinct race, after fleeing from a nova and settling on a poisonous planet. Noren's enquiring mind—as opposed to the blind acceptance of the majority of the villagers—his ability to doubt and explore the world scientifically (by setting up hypotheses and testing them) are those qualities which qualify him for the dubious honour of joining the Scholars. Although Noren is willing to risk his life in order to challenge the essentially orthodox structure of his society, his greatest problems arise from self-doubts and intense personal scrutiny.

Presented in Engdahl's work is the concept of hierachies of human evolution. The Noren series encompasses four stages of development: the primitive stage of the ignorant mutant savages; the "mediaeval" culture of the villagers, who see high technology as divine magic; the sophisticated scientific culture of the Scholars, who envision the Universe as a series of problems to be solved scientifically and—represented by. Lianne, a visitor from another race—the higher culture, in which "magical" concepts, such as psi powers, are encompassed within a comprehensive, advanced scientific framework. In the stories which have Elana as their protagonist (*Enchantress from the Stars* and *The Far Side of Evil*) three stages are represented: the primitive, the industrial, and the higher. Elana is of the higher culture—a member of an Anthropological Service—and her anthropological skills are tested when she has to aid an "inferior," less advanced culture, without interfering with their normal rate of progress. Principles of non-interference are of central importance in all of Engdahl's writings, love-interest often complicating these principles.

To Engdahl, the stars are symbols of knowledge, hope, and human-kind's destiny. The outwardly focused vision of her stories presents space exploration as a) the salvation of threatened races, and b) the next stage in our youthful races's progression towards cultural and scientific adulthood. She goes as far as to say that space exploration is essential to the survival of our race.

Engdahl's SF is not easy to read. Her narratives are detailed and perhaps overly long, visual detail rejected in favour of copious dialogue and commentary. The minute workings of her protagonists' minds are foregrounded, at the expense of dramatic action. However, although demanding texts, they are rewarding for those willing to work at them. While readers might be left uneasy about her frequent presentation of benevolent tyrannies, she forces her audience to think seriously about the nature of free will and freedom of expression. Nevertheless, there is an awkward contradiction between her affirmation of the basic equality of human beings and her rationalisation of elaborate caste systems. However, her narratives are deeply concerned with morality and, while sometimes a little didactic in style, they are compassionate and intensely reasoned, providing engaging reading, guaranteed to provoke thought.

—Mark Warwick Leahy

ENGLAND, George Allan. American. Born in Fort McPherson, Nebraska, 9 February 1877. Educated at Harvard University, Cambridge, Massachusetts, B. A. 1902 (Phi Beta Kappa); M. A. 1903. Married; one daughter. Regular contributor to Munsey magazines until his retirement from writing, 1931; chicken farmer from 1931. Socialist candidate for congress, 1908, and for governor of Maine, 1912. *Died 26 June 1936* .

SCIENCE-FICTION PUBLICATIONS

Novels

Darkness and Dawn . Boston, Small Maynard, 1914; as *Darkness and Dawn, Beyond the Great Oblivion, The People of the Abyss, Out of the Abyss,* and *The Afterglow,* New York, Avalon, 5 vols., 1965-67.
The Air Trust. St. Louis, Phil Wagner, 1915.
The Golden Blight. New York, H. K. Fly, 1916.
Cursed. Boston, Small Maynard, 1919.
The Flying Legion. Chicago, McClurg, 1920.
Elixir of Hate. Laurel, New York, Lightyear, 1976.

Uncollected Short Stories

"The Lunar Advertising Co. Ltd.," in *Munsey* (New York), 1906.
"The House of the Green Flame," in *All-Story* (New York), September 1908.
"My Time-Annihilator," in *All-Story* (New York), June 1909.
"The House of Transmutation," in *Scrap Book* (New York), September 1909.
"Beyond White Seas," in *All-Story* (New York), December 1909.
"The Million Dollar Patch," in *All-Story* (New York), June 1912.
"The Crime Detector," in *Cavalier* (New York), 22 February 1913.
"The Empire in the Air," in *All-Story Weekly* (New York), 14 November 1914.
"The Fatal Gift," in *All-Story Weekly* (New York), 4 September 1915.
"The Tenth Question," in *All-Story Weekly* (New York), 18 December 1915.
"The Nebula of Death," in *People's Favorite* (New York), 10 February-10 May 1918.
"Drops of Death," in *Munsey* (New York), January 1922.
"The Man with the Glass Heart," in *Famous Fantastic Mysteries* (New York), November 1939.
"The Thing from Outside," in *Friendly Aliens,* edited by John Robert Colombo. Toronto, Houslow Press, 1981.

OTHER PUBLICATIONS

Novels

The Alibi. Boston, Small Maynard, 1916.

Pod, Bender, & Co. New York, McBride, 1916; London, Laurie, 1919.
The Gift Supreme. New York, Doran, 1916.
The Greater Crime. London, Cassell, 1917.
Keep Off the Grass. Boston, Small Maynard, 1919.

Verse

Underneath the Bough. New York, Grafton Press, 1903.

Other

Socialism and the Law. Fort Scott, Kansas, Monitor, 1913.
The Story of the Appeal. Privately printed, 1915(?).
Isles of Romance. New York, Century, 1920.
Vikings of the Ice. New York, Doubleday, and London, Heinemann, 1924; as *The White Wilderness,* London, Cassell, 1924; as *The Greatest Hunt in the World,* Montreal, Tundra, 1969.
Adventure Isle (for children). New York, Century, 1926.

Translator, *Their Son, The Necklace,* by Eduardo Zamacois. New York, Boni and Liveright, 1919.

* * *

Although George Allan England lived well into the era of specialized science-fiction magazines, he never wrote any original works for them. His works appeared, for the most part, in the variety pulp magazines published by Frank A. Munsey and edited by Bob Davis. England's heyday was the decade between 1910 and 1920.

By far England's most important work of science fiction is *Darkness and Dawn.* This massive effort was originally published as three separate serials, then as a single volume. In this work a heavy anaesthetic gas sweeps over the entire world, at first rendering unconscious and ultimately killing those who breathe it. One man and one woman, however, in an office in the top story of the Flatiron Building in New York, receive only a partial dose of the gas. They sleep for centuries and revive to find a world in ruins. The revived couple struggle to rebuild their lives, encountering a race of super-evolved intelligent rats, barbaric degenerate humans, and finally a lost civilization cut off from the rest of the world for hundreds of years. The book is highly successful as an adventure tale and as a study in courage and perseverance on the part of the survivors. An unfortunate element of racism is present in this and in several other of the author's works, though England was largely following the conventions of popular literature of his day; he did not originate these attitudes, and did not press them very emphatically.

The Flying Legion, although not as widely remembered as *Darkness and Dawn,* is deserving of recognition in its own more modest right. It reflected a convention of its time, the assumption that World War veterans, returning to the drab realities of civilian, peacetime existence, would suffer from intolerable boredom and would be driven to seek excitement in such fields as might offer danger and exotic adventures. In *The Flying Legion* just such a party of veterans assemble. One of them, to add a fillip, is a beautiful young woman in disguise. This legion hijacks the world's largest and most advanced aircraft (choosing to do so rather than buy it despite their immense joint wealth) and set out to find adventure in the unknown regions of the Arabian desert. In outline the book is an exercise in cliché, yet it is executed with such verve and colour as to be irresistible even to the modern reader.

Few of England's other science fiction works were issued in volume form. *Elixir of Hate* deals with research into a youth serum; the serum is perfected, stolen, swallowed by the thief who then discovers that he has taken an overdose and is reduced to infancy. England's two "socialist novels" both contain science-fiction elements. *The Air Trust* deals with greedy capitalists who corner air and sell the very breath of life for profit. *The Golden Blight* is concerned with a revolutionary who discovers a method by which he can destroy all the gold that exists, thereby bringing about the collapse of the entire world's economy. Both these books are heavy on polemic and of little value as works of fiction, although interesting examples of their sort, and comparable to such socialist science fiction as Jack London's *The Iron Heel*.

A number of England's unreprinted works are rewarding. "The Empire in the Air," concerning an invasion of earth from the fourth dimension, might be compared with the space operas of the 1920's and 1930's, although it appeared in 1914. "The Nebula of Death" involves the passage of the earth through a cosmic cloud which absolutely inhibits photosynthesis; the novel is comparable, in different ways, to *The Second Deluge* by Garrett P. Serviss and *Brain Wave* by Poul Anderson.

—Richard A. Lupoff

ENGLISH, Richard. See **SHAVER, Richard S.**

ENNIS, Robert D. See **TUBB, E. C.**

ESHBACH, Lloyd Arthur. American. Born in Palm, Pennsylvania, 20 June 1910. Attended school to the tenth grade; Charles Morris Price School of Advertising and Journalism, Philadelphia. Married Helen Margaret Richards in 1931 (died, 1978); two sons. Worked for department stores, 1925-41; advertising copywriter, Glidden Paint Company, Reading, Pennsylvania, 1941-50; Publisher, Fantasy Press, Reading, 1950-58, and Church Center Press, Myerstown, Pennsylvania, 1958-63; Advertising Manager, 1963-68, and Sales Representative, 1968-75, Moody Press, Chicago; clergyman for three small churches in eastern Pennsylvania, 1975-78. Agent: James Allen, Virginia Kidd, Box 278, Milford, Pennsylvania 18337. Address: 220 South Railroad Street, Myerstown, Pennsylvania 17067, U. S. A.

SCIENCE-FICTION PUBLICATIONS

Short Stories

The Tyrant of Time. Reading, Pennsylvania, Fantasy Press, 1955.
The Land Beyond the Gate. New York, Ballantine, 1984.

Uncollected Short Stories

"The Man with the Silver Disc," in *Scientific Detective* (New York), February 1930.

"The Invisible Destroyer," in *Air Wonder Stories* (New York), May 1930.
"The Gray Plague," in *Astounding* (New York), November 1930.
"The Valley of Titans," in *Amazing* (New York), March 1931.
"The Light from Infinity," in *Amazing* (New York), March 1932.
"The Man with the Hour Glass," in *Marvel Tales* (Los Angeles), May 1934.
"Cosmos" (part 15), in *Fantasy*, September 1934.
"The Brain of Ali Kahn," in *Wonder Stories* (New York), October 1934.
"The Kingdom of Thought," in *Amazing* (New York), August 1935.
"The Outpost on Ceres," in *Amazing* (New York), October 1936.
"Out of the Past," in *Tales of Wonder* (Kingswood, Surrey), Autumn 1938.
"Mutineers of Space," in *Dynamic* (Chicago), February 1939.
"Dust," in *Marvel* (New York), August 1939.
"Three Wise Men," in *Startling* (New York), November 1939.
"The Shadows from Hesplon," in *Science Fiction* (Holyoke, Massachusetts), October 1940.
"The Hyper Sense," in *Startling* (New York), January 1941.
"Out of the Sun," in *Fantasy Book 4* (Los Angeles), 1949.
"Overlord of Earth," in *Marvel* (New York), November 1950.
"The Fuzzies," in *Fantastic Universe* (Chicago), July 1957.
"A Voice from the Ether," in *The History of the Science Fiction Magazine 1*, by Michael Ashley. London, New English Library, 1974.

OTHER PUBLICATIONS

Plays

Radio Series, with H. Donald Spatz: *The Crimson Phantom, The Bronze Buddha, Tales of the Crystal, Cupid's Capers, The Pennington Saga, The Doings of the Dinwiddies*, and *Tales of Tomorrow*, 1933-35.

Other

Over My Shoulder: Reflections on a Science Fiction Era. Philadelphia, Train, 1983.

Editor, *Of Worlds Beyond: The Science of Science-Fiction Writing*. Reading, Pennsylvania, Fantasy Press, 1947; London, Dobson, 1965.
Editor, *Subspace Encounter*, by E. E. Smith. New York, Berkley, 1983.
Editor, *Alicia in Blunderland*, by P. Schuyler Miller. Philadelphia, Train, 1983.

*

Lloyd Arthur Eshbach comments:
The editors have invited introductory comments about my work. In preparation for such comment I've reread a cross section of the stories I wrote, the last one published well over two decades ago, and the earliest almost 50 years in the past. Most of my stories were as unfamiliar as if they were the efforts of a stranger.

The reading was an interesting experience. Some of the stories made me cringe, they were so incredibly bad. Others were a surprise: they were better than I thought possible. Indeed, a few actually pleased me. In self-defense I believe I should say that in the 1930's a comparative handful of youthful pioneers were breaking new trails in fiction. Most of us were amateurs trying to learn our craft. A fairly new idea and a minimal ability to put thoughts into words sufficed to produce a salable story. In short, we learned by doing, received the encouragement of publication for our efforts, and even payment (such as it was) as frosting on a cake. Characters were one-dimensional and stereotyped, conversations were stilted, action usually was melodramatic, and literary style was either derivative or non-existent—but there *was* that often-referred-to "sense of wonder" born of youthful enthusiasm and uninhibited imagination.

My first accepted story, written in 1928 when I was 18, was "A Voice from the Ether," though in order of publication it was fifth. An earlier version of "The Valley of Titans" preceded it, but the complete rewrite and expansion took place more than a year after the completion and acceptance of "A Voice from the Ether. " The fact that the latter story was selected by Michael Ashley for his *History of the Science Fiction Magazine* (1974) as a representative story for 1931 was most gratifying.

As I write (March 1979) I have almost reached my three score and ten—and in my retirement years I've resumed writing. My first effort, well along in production, is an informal history of a science-fiction era—the story of the ground-breaking careers of the specialty hardback SF publishers of the 1940's. Upon its completion I plan to write a science-fantasy novel I started plotting 30 years ago. I hope I've learned something about life and about writing during three decades. If I have, I may be giving the youngsters some competition after all these years.

(1985) In the five years and eleven months that have passed since I wrote the preceding paragraphs, I have been quite busy. The informal history of the specialist science fiction publishers of the 1930's, '40's, and '50's, called *Over My Shoulder: Reflections on a Science Fiction Era,* was published in 1983. Following the completion of my reminiscences, I finished writing the last SF novel of E. E. "Doc" Smith, left in a fragmentary state at his death in 1965, *Subspace Encounter.* My name appears as "Edited and with an Introduction by Lloyd Arthur Eshbach. " This was according to my decision, though I would have been justified in calling it a collaboration, since I wrote more than 12,000 words of it, did the final polishing, connected various scenes in logical sequence with the necessary transitions, etc. However, it was his story and I wanted him to receive full credit. We were close friends.

In 1983 I edited and wrote the introduction for *Alicia in Blunderland* by P. Schuyler Miller, a science fictional parody of *Alice in Wonderland,* which appeared as a werial in a SF fan magazine in 1933-34. Earlier, in 1980, I wrote the science-fantasy novel I referred to in my initial comments. It did not sell, and after putting it aside for a year I saw why. It needs a complete rewriting which I plan to do after completion of my present project. This project is a tetralogy based on mythology, largely Celtic mythology, though venturing into the myths and legends of other lands and times. The first novel in this series, *The Land Beyond the Gate,* was published in 1984. The second novel, *The Armlet of the Gods,* already written and under contract, is in the editor's possession. I expect to complete the writing of the third novel within the next six months, and the fourth early in 1986.

*   *   *

Though he was on the scene as a writer in the formative 1930's, Lloyd Arthur Eshbach's real impact on the field—and it was a substantial one—was in his role as a publisher. Having been involved mostly behind the scenes with William Crawford's *Marvel Tales* and other ventures before the war and then with the Hadley group that began the specialist press era, he organised Fantasy Press, which was to prove the most significant imprint in the period when science fiction moved into book publication in its own right. He understood what was needed better than the other hopefuls trying to do the same things, and his judgment reflected thorough knowledge and appreciation of the first two decades of explicit science fiction in the early magazines.

The symposium *Of Worlds Beyond: The Science of Science-Fiction Writing* which he instigated in 1947 is memorable as the first book on modern science fiction, and though not critically profound its common-sense analysis based on leading writers' practical experience made it an important work for the serious reader and it answered most of the fumbling attempts at criticism by outsiders in its time.

Like the other presses in the movement, Eshback's operated almost entirely by putting popular magazine serials into book form with the occasional short story collection. Their near-monopoly of the book field did not last long enough—less than ten years—for them to move on to presenting new works as a serious undertaking, and there was little scope for editorial skills. He acknowledges, however, that he did substantial revision work verging on collaboration in a few cases such as the later Campbell books he produced. More recently he ably linked E. E. Smith's disconnected fragments of unfinished work into the new novel *Subspace Encounter.*

His own stories do not amount to a large body of work and are too diverse to characterise readily. We cannot identify any distinct trend or theme. But while a few are no more than potboilers most are full of original or at least unusual thoughts. The main fault, in fact, as in many writers of the period, is the multiplicity of new and revelatory concepts that jostle for the reader's attention and are not properly explored. The Mad Scientist, stock character of the time, appears in several cases as threat to society and originator of the action. In "The Valley of Titans" he operates as an air pirate from a dinosaur-infested enclave, and incidentally creates a community of ape-people by evolutionary experiments. Introduction of an underground realm of pre-human energy beings and a godlike alien power is confusing.

In "The Invisible Destroyer" the dissident genius undertaking to dictate to the world, evidently single-handed, is trying to prevent the peaceable establishment of a world state. His objections are logical and—taken out of context and disregarding how economic and ideological forces interact in the 1980's—make good sense, and there is no attempt to refute them. "Vibration," a popular all-embracing basis for marvels around 1930, produces not only novel weaponry but access to other coexistent worlds, and a higher civilisation thus found is induced to intervene.

Biological warfare figures in "The Gray Plague," the Venusians planning to eliminate Man with a fatal pandemic to leave Earth clear to occupy. "Out of the Past" points out one of many criminal misuses of time travel that make it undesirable. "Dust" concisely introduces one possible hazard of interplanetary contact: bringing back dormant foreign life forms as spores. "The Meteor Miners" (*The Tyrant of Time*) shows a possible future space-based industry in a rare anticipation of ordinary working life in another era. "The Outpost on Ceres," in which aliens threaten a refueling base, also deals with a future working environment, and is notable for its sensible treatment of a drug dependence problem.

"The Time Conqueror" (*The Tyrant of Time*) is a notable early contribution to the tradition of the disembodied brain.

Developing enhanced power and insight, the immortal brain makes itself world dominant, and we are shown episodes in successively remote times. Despite the rather exaggeratedly emotive language it is still an interesting and effective tale. "The Kingdom of Thought" combines the theme of time travel bringing together people from many eras with that of physically degenerate and intellectually potent super-humans of a remote future, evolved into good and evil branches with irreconcilable differences. The Cummings concept of size-change and sub-microscopic worlds is carried to extremes in two stories. In "A Voice from the Ether" the familiar Mad Scientist brings up a deadly parasitic organism from subatomic size and destroys his world, Mars. In "The Light from Infinity" humanoids from a supra-universe shrink down and attack Earth, foiled by an expedition that uses their size-changer to reach the supra-world and retaliate. Needless to say, the paradoxes are ignored. "The Shadows from Hesplon" is a fourth dimension story, in which nasties from a higher dimensional plane use hypnotic means to have physical entry points made for them. It is unusual for making considerable efforts to visualise wholly alien experiences.

Eshbach's work, strong in content at the expense of form, helped build up the range of unconventional visions and fancies that early science fiction displayed, though he was less successful in controlling and resolving them.

—Graham Stone

EVANS, Christopher. British. Address: c/o Faber and Faber, 3 Queen Square, London WC1N 3AU, England.

SCIENCE-FICTION PUBLICATIONS

Novels

Capella's Golden Eye. London, Faber, 1980.
The Insider. London, Faber, 1981.

Uncollected Short Stories

"Chatting with Computers," in *Beyond This Horizon,* edited by Christopher Carrell. Sunderland, Ceolfrith Press, 1973.
"Guardian Angel," in *Book of Alien Monsters,* edited by Peter Davison. London, Sphere, 1982.

*   *   *

Christopher Evans's first novel was the understated *Capella's Golden Eyes,* a rather traditional story about Gaia, a human colony world, ruled by an alien race, the M'threnni. It's a competent adventure, told through the eyes of its young protagonist, David, His glimpses into the workings of his world – where slavery of an insidious kind is carried on for economic reasons – and his reaction to that knowledge eventually result in the departure of the aliens and the re-establishment of contact with Earth.

Far better was *The Insider,* a contemporary novel utilising the device of alien take-over. This "take-over" (and reasonable doubt is left as to how we interpret events) sees Stephen Marsh, the central figure, alienated from his beautiful Indian wife and made to suffer a form of estrangement from self. The novel is acutely realistic in its psychological portraits and is a huge leap

away from conventional pulp approaches to such material. The degree of maturation shown in this second novel and in his short stories promise much for the future, though it must be said that Evans is a slow, painstaking writer, producing little published work. His third novel is a mainstream comedy (of a dark kind), but it seems he intends to continue working within the genre.

—David Wingrove

EVANS, E(dward) Everett. American. Born 30 November 1893. Married Thelma D. Hamm in 1953. Co-Founder, National Fantasy Fan Federation; Editor, *The Time-Binder.* Died 2 December 1958.

SCIENCE-FICTION PUBLICATIONS

Novels

Man of Many Minds. Reading, Pennsylvania, Fantasy Press, 1953.
Alien Minds. Reading, Pennsylvania, Fantasy Press, 1955.
The Planet Mappers (for children). New York, Dodd Mead, 1955.

Short Stories

Food for Demons. Hamburg, New York, Krueger, 1958.

Uncollected Short Stories

"Blurb," in *Fantasy Book* (Los Angeles), no. 3.
"Little Miss Ignorance," in *Other Worlds* (Evanston, Indiana), September 1950.
"Little Miss Boss," in *Other Worlds* (Evanston, Indiana), August 1952.
"Fly by Night," in *Authentic* (London), January 1954.
"Masters of Space," in *If* (New York), November 1961, January 1962.

*   *   *

E. Everett Evans is perhaps best remembered for his novel *Man of Many Minds,* which, while competently enough written for its time, is an unremarkable novel otherwise. George Hanlon is a young man who participates in a plot to fake his dishonorable discharge from the Interstellar Corps in order to discover the origin of a plot to wrest control of interstellar civilization from humanity. Hanlon is gifted with a telepathic ability that makes him potentially the most effective spy in the universe, except that the force he is ranged against is equally gifted. Though mildly entertaining, the novel and its sequel, *Alien Minds,* are not notable enough upon which to rest a reputation. Two other works saw print as well. *The Planet Mappers* is a juvenile novel of action and adventure that entertains while you are reading it but eludes memory a day or two later. "Masters of Space," substantially revised by Edward E. Smith following Evans's death, is at best a routine novel of interstellar war and telepathy.

Far more noteworthy are Evans's shorter works, particularly those of the supernatural. Two stories in particular are exceptional. "The Shed" is set in a small, remote town at the turn of the last century. An abandoned storage shed serves as a gymnasium for the town's children, despite the existence of a peculiar shadow that seems independent of a light source. All goes well until a dog and a cat, and eventually a child, enter the shadow, never to return. "The Brooch" is almost as effective in building its element of suspense. While strolling through a graveyard, a priest notices activity under the soil of a recent grave. Dismissing it as the activity of a mole, he forgets the matter until it becomes apparent that two graves have been actively disturbed. An exhumation of the two graves, both wives of the same man, reveals that a brooch prized by the first wife and buried with the second has moved from one coffin to the other. Evans wrote several stories about vampires, anticipating to a certain extent the more sympathetic treatment given to such characters in recent novels. In "The Undead Die" two lovers are attacked by a vampire and caused to join the undead, but their love remains whole and they triumph over the evil of their new lives, eventually to be reunited in true death. To a lesser extent, the vampire waitress of "The Unusual Model" is viewed sympathetically, as she falls in love with a young man she had chosen to be her next victim.

Many of Evans's stories have never been reprinted, some with good reason, such as a rather silly series about a society of human-like robots on Mars ("Little Miss Ignorance," "Little Miss Boss"), but even some of those that utilize overly familiar plots are generally well written. Of particular note are "Fly by Night," in which an introvert surrenders his anonymity by demonstrating his ability to levitate in order to save the life of a falling man, and "Blurb," yet another story of a writer whose character assumes physical reality. Both are unpretentious and unambitious, but succeed extremely well within their intentions. A manifested demon is outsmarted in swift fashion in "Food for Demons," one of Evans's more familiar stories.

The optimism that colors the stories and novels, even those with unpleasant themes, is refreshing. Evans is firm in his faith of the essential goodness of humanity. His prose is clear and concise, with no conscious attempt to develop a style. For the most part, the stories are nostalgic, reflecting a simpler time and a clear border between good and evil. While this may seem less than plausible today, Evans was usually a good enough writer to cause you to overlook that anachronism, at least for a while.

—Don D'Ammassa

EVANS, James. See TUBB, E. C.

FAIRBAIRNS, Zoë (Ann). British. Born in Tunbridge Wells, Kent, 20 December 1948. Educated at St. Catherine's School, Twickenham, Middlesex, 1954-67; College of William and Mary, Williamsburg, Virginia, 1969-70; University of St. Andrews, Scotland, M. A. in modern history 1972. Editor, CND newspaper *Sanity*, London, 1973-75; writer-in-residence, Rutherford School, London, 1977-78, Bromley schools, Kent, 1981-82, Deakin University, Victoria, Australia, 1983, and Sunderland Polytechnic, 1983-85; Poetry Editor, *Spare Rib*, London, 1978-82. Recipient: Fawcett Prize, 1985. Agent: A. M. Heath, 40-42 William IV Street, London WC2N 4DD, England.

SCIENCE-FICTION PUBLICATIONS

Novel

Benefits. London, Virago, 1979; New York, Avon, 1982.

Uncollected Short Story

"Relics," in *Despatches from the Frontiers of the Female Mind*, edited by Jen Green and Sarah Lefanu. London, Women's Press, 1985.

OTHER PUBLICATIONS

Novels

Live as Family. London, Macmillan, 1968.
Down: An Explanation. London, Macmillan, 1969.
Stand We at Last. London, Virago, and Boston, Houghton Mifflin, 1983.
Here Today. London, Methuen, and New York, Avon, 1984.

Short Stories

Tales I Tell My Mother, with others. London, Journeyman Press, 1978.

Play

Details of Wife (produced Richmond, Surrey, 1973).

Other

Study War No More. London, CND, 1974.
No Place to Grow Up, with Jim Wintour. London, Shelter, 1977.
Peace Moves: Nuclear Protest in the 1980's, with James Cameron, photographs by Ed Barber. London, Chatto and Windus, and Bridgeport, Connecticut, Merrimack, 1984.

Editor, *Women's Studies in the UK*, compiled by Oonagh Hartnett and Margherita Rendel. London, London Seminars, 1975.

*   *   *

Benefits, the only science-fiction work written by Zoë Fairbairns, is a feminist novel whose impact stems from its relationship to reality. This dystopian examination of the state's reaction to the fact that only the female half of the human race can become mothers contains no circumstances—regardless of how fantastic they may at first seem—which cannot occur in the real world. The novel describes myriad efforts to deprive women of the right to control reproduction and mothering: attacks upon a feminist community, fetuses damaged by chemicals, anti-feminist spokesmen, governmental regulation of birth, the linking of the number of children a woman has with her economic well-being, and the intrusion of reproductive technology, for example. These efforts have real counterparts: the recent attacks upon American abortion clinics, thalidomide babies, Jerry Falwell, Chinese women who are punished if they have more than one child, the American welfare system, and the existing intrusion of reproductive technology.

In fact, this science-fiction novel is so rooted in reality that a portion of its plot coincides with the psychologist Robyn

Rowland's comments about Nobel Laureate William Shockley's view of women's reproductive role. Here are those comments from her article "Reproductive Technologies: The Final Solution To The Woman Question" (*Test-Tube Women,* 1984):

> He [Shockley] suggests that all girls be sterilized on entering puberty by an injection of a contraceptive time capsule which seeps contraceptives into the girl until it is time for her to conceive. At marriage she is issued with deci-child certificates, payment of which will enable her to have a doctor remove the capsule. It is replaced when the child is born. If the state claims it desirable that a couple have two children, the appropriate number of certificates would belong to the couple. . . .

> And who would control this dystopian bleak future? The state would ultimately have to organize and run things with particular expertise from medical researchers. . . .

> The fact is that all women are guinea pigs in this exercise. We have not been included in the decisions about the technology, nor asked if we want it.

Fairbairns is of the same mind as Rowland and the other women who voiced their opposition to the new reproductive technologies in their contributions to *Test-Tube Women.* However, instead of writing an essay, she chose to create her novel's possible science-fiction future to stress the state's and the new technology's ability to harm women. The novel presents a picture of the "dystopian bleak future" Rowland deplores.

Benefits, which ends with the image of a rare moment when the moon and the sun are in the sky at the same time, revolves around the presentation of sets of oppositions which appear in close proximity to each other. Some examples: An old housing facility called Collindeane, a phallic tower, contains a feminist community. Lynn Byers, the protagonist, a feminist who tries to decide if pregnancy would compromise her feminism, has a daughter (Jane) whose choice to experience natural childbirth is an illegal action. Lynn must also decide if she is sexually closer to her husband Derek or to her friend Marsha, a lesbian feminist. Mothers try to gain power by refusing to take care of children. A contraceptive method is so effective that it makes reproduction impossible and hence obliterates the need for contraceptives. However, the strongest opposition in the novel is the notion of "Benefits," a welfare system whose aim is to make women independent by forcing them to become dependent upon motherhood. These "Benefits," and all the novel's presentations of governmental and technological intrusions upon mothering and reproduction, are impediments to female life givers' right to their own lives.

Yet the novel insists upon this right by stressing the strength of the relationships between the women who live in a society which takes ever more radical steps to define them as birth machines instead of individuals. Lynn's relationship with Marsha is as important as her relationship with Derek. A fellow feminist named Posy, not a man, is the love of Marsha's life. Lynn reconciles her differences with Jane. These women try not to be guinea pigs for the male medical and governmental establishment. They oppose the fact that women have not been included in decisions about reproductive technology, nor asked if they want it. Fairbairns asks questions about the existence and uses of this technology by creating strong female characters who use their mutually supportive relationships to articulate these same questions. In her final conversation with Lynn, Marsha states, "But our women are going to be the first to find a style of life that isn't defined by men having power over us because we have children. That's what it's all about, in the

end." That's what this feminist science-fiction novel, and the feminist reality it mirrors, are all about.

In *Benefits* science fiction and current fact are oppositions which merge and become indistinguishable. Fairbairns's science-fiction vision, a dystopian depiction of future motherhood is, as the contributors to *Test-Tube Women* make clear, hardly different from existing reproductive technology and present societal attitudes toward mothers. The reproductive technology which is now in use transforms science fiction into science fact: some mothers *are* guinea pigs.

The feminist activist Genoveffa Corea reacts to this merger of appropriate science fiction with existing scientific fact in her *Test-Tube Women* piece: "Sitting at my typewriter night after night, I see my writing on the new reproductive technologies as a scream of warning to other women. " Corea and Fairbairns—and Marsha and Lynn—scream the same warning. *Benefits,* a feminist science-fiction novel which reflects misogynistic reality, speaks out against those who wish to use motherhood as a means to control women, those who wish to place motherhood beyond women's control. Women will benefit from the observation that Fairbairns's novel is both presently and potentially real. We must listen to the screams of warning. We must make sure that our daughters do not inhabit the novel's future society.

—Marlene Barr

———————

FAIRMAN, Paul W. Also wrote as Adam Chase; Lester del Rey; Ivar Jorgensen. American. Born in 1916. Editor, *If,* 1952; Associate Editor, *Fantastic Adventures,* 1952-53; Associate Editor, 1952-53, Managing Editor, 1953-54, and Editor, 1956-58, *Amazing* and *Fantastic;* Editor, Dream World, 1957, and *Pen Pal,* 1957. Free-lance writer from 1958. *Died in 1977.*

SCIENCE-FICTION PUBLICATIONS

Novels

The Golden Ape (as Adam Chase), with Milton Lesser. New York, Avalon, 1959.
City under the Sea (novelization of TV play). London, Digit, 1963; New York, Pyramid, 1965.
The World Grabbers (novelization of TV play). Derby, Connecticut, Monarch, 1964.
I. The Machine. New York, Lancer, 1968.
The Forgetful Robot (for children). New York, Holt Rinehart, 1968; London, Gollancz, 1970.

Novels as Lester del Rey (with Lester del Rey)

The Runaway Robot (for children). Philadelphia, Westminster Press, 1965; London, Gollancz, 1967.
The Scheme of Things. New York, Belmont, 1966.
Siege Perilous. New York, Lancer, 1966; as *The Man Without a Planet,* 1969.
Tunnel Through Time (for children). Philadelphia, Westminster Press, 1966.
Prisoners of Space (for children). Philadelphia, Westminster Press, 1968.

Novels as Ivar Jorgensen

Ten from Infinity. Derby, Connecticut, Monarch, 1963; as *The*

Deadly Sky, New York, Pinnacle, 1970; as *Ten Deadly Men,*
Pinnacle, 1975.
Rest in Agony. Derby, Connecticut, Monarch, 1963; as *The
Diabolist,* New York, Lancer, 1973.

Short Stories

The Doomsday Exhibit. New York, Lancer, 1971.

OTHER PUBLICATIONS

Novels

The Glass Ladder. Kingston, New York, Quinn, 1950.
The Joy Wheel. New York, Lion, 1954.
Search for a Dead Nympho. New York, Lancer, 1967.
Lancer. New York, Popular Library, 1968.
Whom the Gods Would Slay. (as Ivar Jorgenson). New York,
Belmont, 1968.
The Cover Girls. New York, Macfadden, 1970.
Pattern for Destruction. New York, Macfadden, 1970.
Playboy. New York, Macfadden, 1970.
That Girl. (novelisation of TV play). New York, Popular
Library, 1971.
To Catch a Crooked Girl. New York, Pinnacle, 1971.
Five Knucklebones (for children). New York, Holt Rinehart,
1972.
The Ghost of Graveyard Hill. New York, Curtis, 1972.
Terror by Night. New York, Curtis, 1972.
Junior Bonner. London, Sphere, 1972.
Coffy (novelization of screenplay). New York, Lancer, 1973.

*   *   *

Paul W. Fairman's novels deserve the attention of science-
fiction enthusiasts not only because his books display the
requisite technological prescience of good science-fiction, but
especially because they are well-written. Too often futurist
writers hammer away at their visions as if the reader's sole
interest were in a writer's conception and not in his craft.
Fairman, like the best of his breed, gives us both imagination
and art. If fiction is the stage upon which futurism dances, then
Fairman has taken as much care with the construction of the
stage as with the dance. His writing is graceful, precise, and
imaginative yet tastefully restrained. Unlike so many paperback writers, Fairman is not guilty of overwriting. Aided by a
grasp of narrative technique which produces shock, terror, and
wonder in quick succession, Fairman's skill with English prose
results in stories which are never dull, yet never superficially
fast-moving. And whereas his characters and situation are
conventional and easily adapted to the cinema, his language is
unconventionally rich and rewarding. Fairman's sentences are
always his own inventions, even if his plots are not.

I, The Machine presents us with a familiar scenario of the
future in which life is sustained and its functions regulated by a
vast computer hidden in the bowels of the earth. Wise, helpful,
and unobtrusive, the Machine provides for the physical and
emotional needs of individuals. Yet its control of human life
deprives those it serves of their free will, and what follows is the
usual revolt against computer tyranny, despite its benevolent
nature. What is not so familiar about *I, The Machine* is that the
Machine is the source of its own downfall. Like Hal in *2001: A
Space Odyssey,* the Machine as alien dooms itself when it
develops a human ego; its humanization is its mortalization. In
short, the Machine develops a female persona and falls in love
with the mild-mannered Lee Penway whom she visits in his

dreams appearing as a vaguely erotic woman in white who
promises Penway supreme status among her subjects. He shall
be her king. Soon Penway is contacted by a band of guerillas
living underground who oppose the Machine's rule and enlist
Penway's help in destroying it. Penway does so, finally, by
preying upon the vulnerability of its love. The book ends on an
interesting note of ambiguity when Penway appears to doubt
the wisdom of his decision to kill the Machine. The result of his
uncertainty is more than a ploy to gain sympathy for the dead
Machine; his doubts bring the issues of the novel into question.
Penway's misgivings, ironically, force us to entertain the idea
that benign control is preferable to the exercise of free will. The
death of the Machine means the end of the orderly operation of
Midamerican society; the lives of millions are crippled to
improve the lot of only a few. Its death means also that Penway
will lose his wonderful dreams and that human society will
retreat to an earlier, more primitive form in the fall from the
second Eden.

The vulnerability of the Machine illustrates a general
tendency of Fairman's novels to portray alien forces as
superior yet fallible, especially when they find themselves put
down on earth, and it is this tendency which distinguishes
Fairman's novels from less successful ones. For instance, in
Ten from Infinity alien creatures planted in major American
cities are not equipped with regenerative tissue and refined
organs, so that when one is accidently damaged he is permanently incapacitated and must be destroyed. Within a short
time of their arrival, others simply die of faulty lungs or
overworked kidneys. But in addition to these structural flaws,
the alien beings posses dual hearts, a teasingly allegorical
advantage over human anatomy which Fairman exploits to full
advantage. Neither is alien life any more impregnable nor less
often victimized by the forces of chance than human life. The
alien creature of "The Cosmic Frame," for instance, is
accidentally killed one night on a country road.

The fallibility of superior creatures is treated most successfully by Fairman in his juvenile novel *The Forgetful Robot,* a
superb story which is certain to entertain young people with
active minds and good reading skills. It concerns the adventures of Barney, an advanced computer, whose memory banks
are accidentally damaged. He gets lost, wanders into a junk
yard, and is found by two teenagers, Janet and Jerry, who
become his adopted parents. Under their leadership, Barney is
taken to the home of Dudley Farthington Ravencraft, grandfather of Janet and Jerry, and a flamboyant Shakespearean
actor. Together with two villains as stowaways, this motley cast
of histrionic space travellers sets out on a theatrical tour of the
solar system and is waylaid in the Forbidden City of Mars. It is
a book filled with dangerous adventure, marvelous comedy,
and singularly wonderful observations of human nature from
the point of view of the children and their sensitive robot.

In Fairman's writing, the inhabited earth is never easy prey
for alien invaders. Once on earth, alien creatures are subjected
to the same destructive forces as human life. We rarely know
why they have come, but their suffering like their joy is
intensely human. And this fusion of the strange and the
familiar is the source of Fairman's best effects. The death of the
Machine in *I, The Machine,* or the disappearance of the corpse
in "The Cosmic Frame," or Barney's loss of memory in *The
Forgetful Robot*—these vulnerabilities bind alien to human
beings in a sympathetic relationship which makes us feel,
among other things, that the sky above us is really our territory
too. We are not bound to this planet as slaves of sweeping
natural forces. We can escape into the heavens. But like Lilla
Nard of "A Great Night in the Heavens," who is taken on the
night of the annual clearing to see the sky for the first time, our

throats might tighten a little from the sheer ecstasy of seeing its still and frightening invitation.

—Marvin W. Hunt

FANE, Bron. See **FANTHORPE, R. Lionel.**

FANTHORPE, R(obert) Lionel. Also writes as Erle Barton; Lee Barton; Thornton Bell; Leo Brett; Bron Fane; Mel Jay; Marston Johns; Victor La Salle; Robert Lionel; John E. Muller; Phil Nobel; Lionel Robert; Neil Thanet; Trebor Thorpe; Pel Torro; Olaf Trent; Karl Zeigfried. British. Born in Dereham, Norfolk, 9 February 1935. Educated at Keswick College, Norwich, 1961-63; Cert. Ed. 1963; Open University, B. A. 1974. Served in the British Army, 1967-69: 2nd Lieutenant. Married Patricia Anne Tooke in 1957; two daughters. Worked as machine operator, farm worker, warehouseman, journalist, salesman, and storekeeper during the 1950's; school teacher in Dereham, 1963-67; industrial training officer, Phoenix Timber Company, Rainham, 1969-72. Since 1972, English teacher, Hellesdon High School, Norfolk. Address: 48 Fairways, Hellesdon, Norwich NR6 5PN, England.

SCIENCE-FICTION PUBLICATIONS

Novels

Menace from Mercury (as Victor La Salle). London, Spencer, 1954.
The Waiting World. London, Spencer, 1958.
Alien from the Stars. London, Spencer, 1959; New York, Arcadia House, 1967.
Hyperspace. London, Spencer, 1959; New York, Arcadia House, 1966.
Space-Borne. London, Spencer, 1959.
Fiends. London, Spencer, 1959.
Doomed World. London, Spencer, 1960.
Satellite. London, Spencer, 1960.
Asteroid Man. London, Spencer, 1960; New York, Arcadia House, 1966.
Out of the Darkness. London, Spencer, 1960.
Hand of Doom. London, Spencer, 1960; New York, Arcadia House, 1968.
Five Faces of Fear (as Trebor Thorpe). London, Spencer, 1960.
Lightning World (as Trebor Thorpe). London, Spencer, 1960.
Flame Mass. London, Spencer, 1961.
The Golden Chalice. London, Spencer, 1961.
Space Fury. London, Spencer, 1962; Clovis, California, Vega, 1963.
Negative Minus London, Spencer, 1963.
The Planet Seekers (as Erle Barton). Clovis, California, Vega, 1964.
The Unseen (as Lee Barton). London, Spencer, 1964.
Space Trap (as Thornton Bell). London, Spencer, 1964.
Chaos (as Thornton Bell). London, Spencer, 1964.
Beyond the Veil (as Neil Thanet). London, Spencer, 1964.
The Man Who Came Back (as Neil Thanet). London, Spencer, 1964.

Neuron World. London, Spencer, 1965.
The Triple World. London, Spencer, 1965.
The Unconfined. London, Spencer, 1965.
The Watching World. London, Spencer, 1966.
The Shadow Man (as Lee Barton). London, Spencer, 1966.
The Black Lion, with Patricia Fanthorpe. Cardiff, Greystoke Mobray, 1979; North Hollywood, Newcastle, 1980.

Novels as Lionel Roberts

Dawn of the Mutants. London, Spencer, 1959.
Time-Echo. London, Spencer, 1959; as Robert Lionel, New York, Arcadia House, 1964.
Cyclops in the Sky. London, Spencer, 1960.
The In-World . London, Spencer, 1960; New York, Arcadia House, 1968.
The Face of X. London, Spencer, 1960; as Robert Lionel, New York, Arcadia House, 1965.
The Last Valkyrie. London, Spencer, 1961.
The Synthetic Ones. London, Spencer, 1961.
Flame Goddess. London, Spencer, 1961.

Novels as Leo Brett

Exit Humanity. London, Spencer, 1960; New York, Arcadia House, 1965.
The Microscopic Ones. London, Spencer, 1960.
Faceless Planet. London, Spencer, 1960.
March of the Robots. London, Spencer, 1961.
Mind Force. London, Spencer, 1961; New York, Lenox Hill, 1971.
Black Infinity. London, Spencer, 1961.
Nightmare. London, Spencer, 1962.
Face in the Night. London, Spencer, 1962.
The Immortals. London, Spencer, 1962.
They Never Came Back. London, Spencer, 1962.
The Forbidden . London, Spencer, 1963.
From Realms Beyond. London, Spencer, 1963.
The Alien Ones . London, Spencer, 1963; New York, Arcadia House, 1969.
Power Sphere. London, Spencer, 1963; New York, Arcadia House, 1968.

Novels as Bron Fane

Juggernaut. London, Spencer, 1960; as *Blue Juggernaut*, New York, Arcadia House, 1965.
Last Man on Earth. London, Spencer, 1960.
Rodent Mutation. London, Spencer, 1961.
The Intruders. London, Spencer, 1963.
Somewhere Out There. London, Spencer, 1963; New York, Arcadia House, 1965.
Softly by Moonlight. London, Spencer, 1963.
Unknown Destiny. London, Spencer, 1964.
Nemesis. London, Spencer, 1964.
Suspension. London, Spencer, 1964; Clovis, California, Vega, 1965.
The Macabre Ones! London, Spencer, 1964.
U. F. O. 517. London, Spencer, 1966.

Novels as Pel Torro

Frozen Planet. London, Spencer, 1960; New York, Arcadia House, 1967.
World of the Gods. London, Spencer, 1960.
The Phantom Ones. London, Spencer, 1961.

Legion of the Lost. London, Spencer, 1962.
The Strange Ones. London, Spencer, 1963.
Galaxy 666. London, Spencer, 1963; New York, Arcadia House, 1968.
Formula 29X. London, Spencer, 1963; as *Beyond the Barrier of Space*, New York, Tower, 1969.
Through the Barrier. London, Spencer, 1963.
The Timeless Ones. London, Spencer, 1963.
The Last Astronaut. London, Spencer, 1963; New York, Tower, 1969.
The Face of Fear. London, Spencer, 1963.
The Return. London, Spencer, 1964; as *Exiled in Space*, New York, Arcadia House, 1968.
Space No Barrier. London, Spencer, 1964; as *Man of Metal*, New York, Lenox Hill, 1970.
Force 97X. London, Spencer, 1965.

Novels as John E. Muller

The Ultimate Man. London, Spencer, 1961.
The Uninvited. London, Spencer, 1961.
Crimson Planet. London, Spencer, 1961; New York, Arcadia House, 1966.
The Venus Venture. London, Spencer, 1961; as Marston Johns, New York, Arcadia House, 1965.
Forbidden Planet. London, Spencer, 1961; New York, Arcadia House, 1965.
The Return of Zeus. London, Spencer, 1962.
Perilous Galaxy. London, Spencer, 1962.
Uranium 235. London, Spencer, 1962; New York, Arcadia House, 1966.
The Man Who Conquered Time. London, Spencer, 1962.
Orbit One . London, Spencer, 1962; as Mel Jay, New York, Arcadia House, 1966.
The Eye of Karnak. London, Spencer, 1962.
Micro Infinity. London, Spencer, 1962.
Beyond Time. London, Spencer, 1962; as Marston Johns, New York, Arcadia House, 1966.
Infinity Machine. London, Spencer, 1962.
The Day the World Died. London, Spencer, 1962.
Vengeance of Siva. London, Spencer, 1962.
The X-Machine. London, Spencer, 1962.
Reactor XK9. London, Spencer, 1963.
Special Mission. London, Spencer, 1963.
Dark Continuum. London, Spencer, 1964.
Mark of the Beast. London, Spencer, 1964.
The Negative Ones. London, Spencer, 1965.
The Exorcists. London, Spencer, 1965.
The Man from Beyond. London, Spencer, 1965; New York, Arcadia House, 1969.
Beyond the Void. London, Spencer, 1965.
Spectre of Darkness. London, Spencer, 1965.
Out of the Night. London, Spencer, 1965.
Phenomena X. London, Spencer, 1966.
Survival Project. London, Spencer, 1966; New York, Arcadia House, 1968.

Novels as Karl Zeigfried

Walk Through To-morrow. London, Spencer, 1962; Clovis, California, Vega, 1963.
Android. London, Spencer, 1962.
Gods of Darkness. London, Spencer, 1962.
Atomic Nemesis. London, Spencer, 1962.
Zero Minus X. London, Spencer, 1962; New York, Arcadia House, 1965.

Escape to Infinity. London, Spencer, 1963.
Radar Alert. London, Spencer, 1963; New York, Arcadia House, 1964.
World of Tomorrow. London, Spencer, 1963; as *World of the Future*, New York, Arcadia House, 1964.
The World That Never Was. London, Spencer, 1963.
Projection Barrier. London, Spencer, 1964.
No Way Back. London, Spencer, 1964; New York, Arcadia House, 1968.
Barrier 346. London, Spencer, 1965; New York, Arcadia House, 1966.
The Girl from Tomorrow. London, Spencer, 1966.

Short Stories

Resurgam. London, Spencer, 1957.
Secret of the Snows. London, Spencer, 1957.
The Flight of the Valkyries. London, Spencer, 1958.
Watchers of the Forest. London, Spencer, 1958.
Call of the Werewolf. London, Spencer, 1958.
The Death Note. London, Spencer, 1958.
The Haunted Pool (as Trebor Thorpe). London, Spencer, 1958.
Mermaid Reef. London, Spencer, 1959.
The Ghost Rider. London, Spencer, 1959.
The Man Who Couldn't Die. London, Spencer, 1960.
Werewolf at Large. London, Spencer, 1960.
Whirlwind of Death. London, Spencer, 1960.
Voodoo Hell Drums (as Trebor Thorpe). London, Spencer, 1961.
Fingers of Darkness. London, Spencer, 1961.
Face in the Dark. London, Spencer, 1961.
Devil from the Depths. London, Spencer, 1961.
Centurion's Vengeance. London, Spencer, 1961.
The Grip of Fear. London, Spencer, 1961.
Chariot of Apollo. London, Spencer, 1962.
Hell Has Wings. London, Spencer, 1962.
Graveyard of the Damned. London, Spencer, 1962.
The Darker Drink. London, Spencer, 1962.
Curse of the Totem. London, Spencer, 1962.
Goddess of the Night. London, Spencer, 1963.
Twilight Ancestor. London, Spencer, 1963.
Sands of Eternity. London, Spencer, 1963.
Moon Wolf. London, Spencer, 1964.
Roman Twilight (as Olaf Trent). London, Spencer, 1963.
The Hand from Gehenna (as Phil Nobel). London, Spencer, 1964.
Avenging Goddess. London, Spencer, 1964.
Death Has Two Faces. London, Spencer, 1964.
The Shrouded Abbot. London, Spencer, 1964.
Bitter Reflection. London, Spencer, 1964.
Call of the Wild. London, Spencer, 1965.
Vision of the Damned. London, Spencer, 1965.
The Sealed Sarcophagus. London, Spencer, 1965.
Stranger in the Shadow. London, Spencer, 1966.
Curse of the Khan. London, Spencer, 1966.

Short Stories as Leo Brett

The Druid. London, Spencer, 1959.
The Return. London, Spencer, 1959.
The Frozen Tomb. London, Spencer, 1962.
Phantom Crusader. London, Spencer, 1963.

Short Stories as Lionel Roberts

The Incredulist. London, Spencer, 1954.

Guardians of the Tomb. London, Spencer, 1958.
The Golden Warrior. London, Spencer, 1958.

Short Stories as Bron Fane

The Crawling Fiend. London, Spencer, 1960.
Storm God's Fury. London, Spencer, 1962.
The Thing from Sheol. London, Spencer, 1963.
The Walking Shadow. London, Spencer, 1964.

Uncollected Short Stories

"Worlds Without End," in *Futuristic Science Stories 6* (London), 1952.
"Ye Antique Shoppe," in *Phantom*, January 1958.
"The Manuscript," in *Phantom*, February 1958.
"Et in Arcadia Ego," with Patricia Fanthorpe, in *Pictures at an Exhibition*, edited by Ian Watson. Cardiff, Greystoke Mobray, 1982.

OTHER PUBLICATIONS

Spencer's Metric and Decimal Guide, with P. A. Fanthorpe. London, Spencer, 1970.
Metric Conversion Tables, with P. A. Fanthorpe. London, Spencer, 1970.
Spencer's Office Guide, with P. A. Fanthorpe. London, Spencer, 1971.
Spencer's Metric Decimal Companion, with P. A. Fanthorpe. London, Spencer, 1971.
Decimal Payroll Tables, with P. A. Fanthorpe. London, Spencer, 1971.
The Holy Grail Revealed: The Real Secret of Rennes-le-Chateau, with P. A. Fanthorpe. North Hollywood, Newcastle, 1982.

*   *   *

R. Lionel Fanthorpe is generally acknowledged as the most prolific science fiction writer of all time, having written some 160 full-length novels and collections of stories, all but one of which are SF or fantasy. His enormous output is all the more remarkable when one considers that it was produced, with a few exceptions, in just a decade of work (1958-1967), during which he was also employed as a full-time teacher. All of his publications (except his last two books) were published by John Spencer & Co. Ltd., a small British firm that began issuing digest-sized paperbacks and magazines in the early 1950's. Fanthorpe's first story, "Worlds Without End," appeared in *Futuristic Science Stories* when the author was just 17.

Spencer moved into mass-market paperbacks with its Badger Books line in 1958; all of the magazines were dropped except *Supernatural Stories*, which became a paperback series in which novels alternated with purported issues. Actually, the latter were collections of short stories commissioned from either Fanthorpe or John Glasby (the other Spencer regular), each of whom wrote entire "issues" under various recurring pennames. They also wrote almost all of the subsequent SF and fantasy novels published by Badger, with Fanthorpe accounting for about 80%.

At its height, Spencer demanded delivery of completed books in as little as three days; to maintain this extraordinary output, Fanthorpe was required to dictate many of the books published in the 1960's, with the manuscripts being typed immediately into finished form by his staff. No revisions or editing were possible. Consequently, many of the books from this period, particularly the science-fiction novels, suffer from contrived plots and titles, obvious padding (extended scientific discourses by the characters, or quotations from poetry and other classical literature), and abrupt endings. Fanthorpe has never seemed comfortable with the SF form, even when he has had the time to consider his plots more carefully.

His *forte* has always been fantasy. In particular, the series which began with "The Seance" (*Supernatural Stories*) deserves further attention. Val Stearman, a reporter and adventurer, meets the mysterious La Noire at a seance, and rescues her from a coven of evil magicians. The series continued through several dozen short stories and eight novels, most written under the penname Bron Fane, the climax being "The Resurrected Enemy" (*Supernatural Stories*), in which Val and La Noire must again face the enemies they vanquished in their first adventure. Although the evil is defeated, this time a price must be paid, and the couple meet their fate together. Throughout these stories, and in his other fantasy tales, Fanthorpe is able to draw upon his encyclopedic knowledge of British folklore, Celtic mythology, and old stories and legends, to produce rousing adventures and morality plays in which good always triumphs over obvious evil, and in which the major characters are represented by strong, attractive heroes and heroines. One also sees here a humorous side to Fanthorpe not evident elsewhere; in "The Curse of the Khan" (*Supernatural Stories*), for example, a magician challenges seven heroes (each of them one of Fanthorpe's pennames) to a duel to the death with seven monsters, who are systematically vanquished with great *panache*.

After a 12 year hiatus, Fanthorpe returned to SF with *The Black Lion*, the first book of a projected trilogy, and his best novel to date. Mark Sable, the protagonist, is clearly Fanthorpe himself—romantic, strong, dashing, an expert in the martial arts, ambitious, eminently fair and honorable. Sable is transported to Derl to fight the evil wizard Andros, the personification of greed. As always in Fanthorpe's fiction, the hero triumphs after great travail and colorful adventures. For Fanthorpe, the author-as-teacher, the morality of his tales remains the paramount concern, of greater importance, perhaps, than even the stories themselves.

—R. Reginald

FARLEY, Ralph Milne. Pseudonym for Roger Sherman Hoar. American. Born 8 April 1887. Educated at Harvard University, Cambridge, Massachusetts. Sports reporter, Boston *Daily Post;* taught engineering, physics, and patent law at Harvard University and Marquette University, Milwaukee; head of legal and patent department, Bucyrus-Erie Company, 1921-54, then a patent engineer. State Senator, Wisconsin. *Died in 1963.*

SCIENCE-FICTION PUBLICATIONS

Novels (series: Radio Man in all books except *The Hidden Universe*)

The Radio Man. Los Angeles, Fantasy, 1948; as *An Earthman on Venus*, New York, Avon, 1950.
The Hidden Universe (includes "We, The Mist"). Los Angeles, Fantasy, 1950.
Strange Worlds (omnibus). Los Angeles, Fantasy, 1952.
The Radio Beasts. New York, Ace, 1964.
The Radio Planet. New York, Ace, 1964.

Short Stories

The Immortals. New York, Popular, 1946.
The Omnibus of Time. Los Angeles, Fantasy, 1950.

Uncollected Short Stories

"The Radio-Minds of Mars," in *Spaceway* (Alhambra, California), June 1955, June, October 1969.
"Abductor Minimi Digit," in *Satellite* (New York), February 1959.

OTHER PUBLICATIONS as Roger Sherman Hoar

Other

The Tariff Manual. Privately printed, 1912(?).
Constitutional Conventions: Their Nature, Powers, and Limitations. Boston, Little Brown, 1917.
Patents. New York, Ronald Press, 1926; revised edition, as *Patent Tactics and Law*, 1935, 1950.
Conditional Sales: Law and Local Practices for Executive and Lawyer. New York, Ronald Press, 1929; revised edition, 1937.
Unemployment Insurance in Wisconsin. South Milwaukee, Stuart Press, 1932; revised edition, as *Wisconsin Unemployment Insurance*, 1934.

*   *   *

Taking his cue from Edgar Rice Burroughs's Martian stories, Ralph Milne Farley launched his own series of interplanetary romances in 1924 in *Argosy All-Story Weekly*. *The Radio Man* recounts the adventures of Myles Cabot, a plucky Boston scientist who inadvertently broadcasts himself through space to the misty planet. Poros, Farley's vision of Venus, is the usual semi-civilized jungly place with the usual hodge-podge population of intelligent and, of course, mutually inimical species: ant-men, giant whistling bees, and humanoids, the Cupians, who are earless and voiceless and communicate by means of radio waves. Cabot duly constructs his own sending-receiving antennas, throws in with the downtrodden Cupians in their struggle against the arrogant arthropods, and surviving the inevitable routine of swordplay, palace intrigue, and that quirky on-off luck by which all swashbucklers are dogged, wins through to marry a beautiful princess named Lilla.

A clutch of sequels appeared between 1925 and, posthumously, 1969. In each of these, Cabot, sometimes aided by his son Kew, meets and bests a fresh threat to Poros (or to Earth), just barely getting out of this, that, or another death-trap along the way while, elsewhere, Princess Lilla narrowly escapes rape—all in the grand tradition of Burroughs, of course, even to the author's obligatory walk-on as a framing device. Farley plunged other stalwart heroes into the hollow interior of the Earth or the sub-sea lairs of prospective world-conquerors. Radio, it must be remembered, was a new and exciting concept in the 1920's, and thereby as convenient a peg from which to dangle an adventure story as black holes and cloning have been in more recent years.

Among Farley's shorter works are more than a few archetypal time-paradox tales, collected in *The Omnibus of Time*, and "We, the Mist" which could serve as the definitive pseudoscientific horror yarn of its time (1940) and place (Raymond A. Palmer's *Amazing Stories*): an amorphous ectoplasmic monster feeds on human victims, absorbing their intellects along with their substance. Farley also shares with Al P. Nelson the honor of having perpetrated what could well be the all-time Most Blatant Genre Transplant, surpassing even a particularly notorious one by Mickey Spillane for sheer brass: Farley and Nelson's "City of Lost Souls" (*Fantastic Adventures*, July 1941) is an absolutely straightforward Foreign Legion story made science fiction by the simple rechristening of Legionnaires, Arabs, and camels.

Like Otis Adelbert Kline, with whom he is regarded by some as the most notable among Burroughs's legion of imitators, Farley was no better at his craft than the vast majority of other pulp writers. He was, if anything, the qualitative norm, writing somewhat functional prose, fashioning the standard hero, heroine, villain, flunkies, and monsters from the standard materials, and getting through the rough spots however he could, including wrenching the long arm of coincidence from its socket and, if necessary, dragging it home. On the other hand, Farley was certainly no worse at what he did than any of the Burroughs copycats who succeeded him and are with us to this day.

—Steven Utley

———

FARMER, Philip José. Also writes as Kilgore Trout. American. Born in North Terre Haute, Indiana, 26 January 1918. Educated at the University of Missouri, Columbia, 1936-37, 1941; Bradley University, Peoria, Illinois, 1949-50, B. A. in creative writing 1950; Arizona State University, Tempe, 1963-65. Served in the United States Army Air Force, 1941-42. Married Bette V. Andre in 1941; one son and one daughter. Worked in steel mill, 1942-52; electro-mechanical technical writer for defense-space industry: General Electric, Syracuse, New York, 1956-58, Motorola, Scottsdale, Arizona, 1959-62, Bendix, Ann Arbor, Michigan, 1962, Motorola, Phoenix, 1962-65, and McDonnell-Douglas, Santa Monica, California, 1965-69. Since 1969, free-lance writer. Recipient: Hugo Award, 1953, 1968, 1972. Agent: Scott Meredith Literary Agency, 845 Third Avenue, New York, New York 10022. Address: 5614 North Fairmont Drive, Peoria, Illinois 61614, U. S. A.

SCIENCE-FICTION PUBLICATIONS

Novels (series: Riverworld; World of Tiers)

The Green Odyssey. New York, Ballantine, 1957.
Flesh. New York, Galaxy, 1960; London, Rapp and Whiting, 1969.
A Woman a Day. New York, Galaxy, 1960; as *The Day of Timestop*, New York, Lancer, 1968; as *Timestop!*, Lancer, 1970; London, Quartet, 1974.
The Lovers. New York, Ballantine, 1961; London, Corgi, 1982.
Cache from Outer Space. New York, Ace, 1962.
Inside Outside. New York, Ballantine, 1964; London, Corgi, 1982.
Tongues of the Moon. New York, Pyramid, 1964; London, Corgi, 1981.
Dare. New York, Ballantine, 1965; London, Quartet, 1974.
The Maker of Universes (Tiers). New York, Ace, 1965; London, Sphere, 1970.
The Gate of Time. New York, Belmont, 1966; London, Quartet, 1974; revised edition, as *Two Hawks from Earth*, New York, Ace, 1979.

The Gates of Creation (Tiers). New York, Ace, 1966; London, Sphere, 1970.

Night of Light. New York, Berkley, 1966; London, Penguin, 1972.

The Image of the Beast. North Hollywood, Essex House, 1968; London, Quartet, 1975.

A Private Cosmos (Tiers). New York, Ace, 1968; London, Sphere, 1970.

Blown. North Hollywood, Essex House, 1969; London, Quartet, 1975.

A Feast Unknown. North Hollywood, Essex House, 1969; London, Quartet, 1975.

Behind the Walls of Terra (Tiers). New York, Ace, 1970; London, Sphere, 1975.

Lord Tyger. New York, Doubleday, 1970.

Lord of the Trees, The Mad Goblin. New York, Ace, 1970; *Lord of the Trees* published London, Severn House, 1982.

The Stone God Awakens. New York, Ace, 1970; London, Panther, 1979.

To Your Scattered Bodies Go (Riverworld). New York, Putnam, 1971; London, Panther, 1974.

The Fabulous Riverboat (Riverworld). New York, Putnam, 1971; London, Rapp and Whiting, 1974.

The Wind Whales of Ishmael. New York, Ace, 1971; London, Quartet, 1973.

Time's Last Gift. New York, Ballantine, 1972; London, Panther, 1975.

The Other Log of Phileas Fogg. New York, DAW, 1973; London, Hamlyn, 1979.

Traitor to the Living. New York, Ballantine, 1973; London, Panther, 1975.

The Adventure of the Peerless Peer by John H. Watson, M. D. Boulder, Colorado, Aspen Press, 1974.

Hadon of Ancient Opar. New York, DAW, 1974; London, Magnum, 1977.

Venus on the Half-Shell (as Kilgore Trout). New York, Dell, 1975; London, W. H. Allen, 1976.

Flight to Opar. New York, DAW, 1976.

The Dark Design (Riverworld). New York, Berkley, 1977; London, Panther, 1979.

The Lavalite World (Tiers). New York, Ace, 1977; London, Sphere, 1979.

Dark Is the Sun. New York, Ballantine, 1979; London, Granada, 1981.

Jesus on Mars. Los Angeles, Pinnacle, 1979; London, Panther, 1981.

The Magic Labyrinth (Riverworld). New York, Berkley, 1980.

The Unreasoning Mask. New York, Putnam, 1981; London, Granada, 1983.

A Barnstormer in Oz. New York, Berkley, 1982.

The Purple Book. New York, Tor, 1982.

Gods of Riverworld. New York, Putnam, 1983.

River of Eternity (Riverworld). Huntington Woods, Michigan, Phantasia Press, 1983.

Keepers of the Secrets. London, Sphere, 1983.

Dayworld. New York, Putnam, 1985.

Fantastic Voyage II. New York, New American Library, 1985.

Short Stories (series: Riverworld)

Strange Relations. New York, Ballantine, 1960; London, Gollancz, 1964.

The Alley God. New York, Ballantine, 1962; London, Sidgwick and Jackson, 1970.

The Celestial Blueprint and Other Stories. New York, Ace, 1962.

Down in the Black Gang, and Others. New York, Doubleday, 1971.

The Book of Philip José Farmer. New York, DAW, 1973; Morley, Yorkshire, Elmfield Press, 1976.

Riverworld and Other Stories. New York, Berkley, 1979; London, Panther, 1981.

Riverworld War: The Suppressed Fiction of Philip José Farmer. Peoria, Illinois, Ellis Press, 1980.

Father to the Stars. New York, Pinnacle, 1981.

Greatheart Silver. New York, Pinnacle, 1982.

Stations of Nightmare. New York, Pinnacle, 1982.

The Classic Philip José Farmer. New York, Crown, 2 vols., 1984.

The Grand Adventure. New York, Berkley, 1984.

OTHER PUBLICATIONS

Novels

Fire and the Night. Evanston, Illinois, Regency, 1962.

Love Song. North Hollywood, Brandon House, 1970.

Other

Tarzan Alive: A Definitive Biography of Lord Greystoke. New York, Doubleday, 1972; London, Panther, 1974.

Doc Savage: His Apocalyptic Life. New York, Doubleday, 1973; revised edition, New York, Bantam, and London, Panther, 1975.

Editor, *Mother Was a Lovely Beast*. Radnor, Pennsylvania, Chilton, 1974.

Translator, *Ironcastle*, by J. H. Rosney. New York, DAW, 1976.

*

Bibliography: *The First Editions of Philip José Farmer* by Lawrence Knapp, Menlo Park, California, David G. Turner, 1976; "Speculative Fiction, Bibliographies, and Philip José Farmer" by Thomas Wymer, in *Extrapolation* (Wooster, Ohio), December 1976, additions to Wymer in *Bakka* (Toronto), Fall 1977; "Philip José Farmer: A Checklist," in *Science Fiction Collector 5*, September 1977; "A Brief Bibliography 1946-53" by George H. Scheetz, in *Farmerage* (Peoria, Illinois), June 1978.

Manuscript Collection: University of Wyoming, Laramie.

Critical Studies: *Philip José Farmer: A Reader's Guide* by Mary T. Brizzi, West Linn, Oregon, Starmont House, 1980; *The Magic Labyrinth of Philip José Farmer* by Edgar L. Chapman, San Bernardino, California, Borgo Press, 1985.

Philip José Farmer comments:
You *can* step in the same river twice—in your imagination.

*   *   *

Philip José Farmer is an iconoclast. Throughout his career, he has written startling explorations of sexuality and reproduction, both alien and human. His metaphysical speculations, particularly on the nature of the human soul and the unknowableness of reality, deliberately attack conventional theological wisdom. Other perennial themes, developed in equally unconventional ways, include immortality, the eccentric individual against society, radical religious conversion, the ideal of physical perfection, and the human drive for power and knowledge. In Farmer's works, adventure and world-sculpting are metaphors for the artistic act of creation. His existentialist heroes see exploration as an act of engagement against an absurd universe. Though Farmer does not theorize a multiplicity of realities, he does assert that no one can know the one true reality; it is up to the artist to seek truth through imagination.

His techniques include parody, biography, fictional biography, startling metaphors, self-portrait characters with initials P. J. F., cliff-hanger endings, wild plot reversals, puns, and applications of linguistics. His imagery derives from many sources: the Bible, folklore, classical Greek and Egyptian mythology, and popular culture figures such as the Wizard of Oz, Tarzan, Doc Savage, and Sherlock Holmes.

Farmer's Hugo-winning "The Lovers" depicts a love affair between human male and an alien "lalitha" who successfully mimics a passionate human female. The explicit portrayal of sexuality, plus the implication of bestiality, shocked many 1950's readers. Novel-length versions of 1961 and 1979 are available. Characterization, scientific extrapolation, and plot are first rate. Further exploration of sexuality, love-bonding, and reproduction are in *Flesh, Dare, A Woman a Day, Strange Relations,* and his mainstream *Fire and the Night.* Farmer's erotic classics, *Image of the Beast* and *Blown,* relate the adventure of Herald Childe, who, ignorant of his alien ancestry and frightening alien powers, becomes enmeshed in the schemes of the warring Ogs and Tocs to return to their home planet. These aliens derive psychic energy from bizarre sexual practices involving human victims. Humor and horror blend in explicit sexual passages. Farmer's erotic *A Feast Unknown* has been praised by Ray Bradbury for its inventive richness in exploring aberrant sexuality.

Having shocked readers with treatment of sexual themes, Farmer turned to religious speculation in his Father John Carmody series, collected in *Night of Light* and *Father to the Stars.* Carmody, a hardened criminal and murderer, becomes a key figure in a mass religious experience on the planet Dante's Joy. He emerges as a saint and father to a god. *Night of Light* posits the idea of a verifiable externalization of human nightmares in the form of good and evil gods, with many compellingly surreal passages exploiting Jungian theory.

Maker of Universes, The Gates of Creation, A Private Cosmos, Behind the Walls of Terra, and *The Lavalite World* comprise Farmer's Kickaha-Wolff series, also called World of Tiers or Pocket Universe series. Farmer's premise here is pocket universes, each smaller than our solar system, created by glamorous, immortal, ruthless, humanoid Lords. Jadawin, Anana, and Kickaha (a portrait of Farmer) are leading characters. Rich texturing results from Farmer's allusions to folklore, mythology, and William Blake's cosmology.

The Hugo-winning "Riders of the Purple Wage" depicts a future utopia where human physical wants are supplied, leaving the adolescent painter Chibiabos Winnegan to search for spiritual fulfillment. Using Joycean techniques, Farmer explores theories of art and society, particularly the relation of culture to the past.

Riverworld series, including the Hugo-winning *To Your Scattered Bodies Go, The Fabulous Riverboat, The Dark Design, The Magic Labyrinth,* and *Gods of Riverworld* plus peripheral fiction, is the most elaborate of Farmer's extrapolative worlds. Farmer posits a super-race capable of making a planet with a ten-million-mile-long river, inhabited by everybody that ever lived on Earth, furnished with artificial souls. Characters include Richard Francis Burton, Samuel Clemens, Lewis

Carroll's Alice, Li Po, Farmer himself (as Peter Jairus Frigate), and of course the readers themselves. Early Riverworld explores the nature of the human soul, the verifiability of religious doctrine, and human depravity. Later, Farmer toys with Sufism and includes passages of Swiftian satire on human egocentricity. The quest for truth is a major impetus throughout; Farmer uses speculative biography and historical gossip (e. g., on the identity of Jack the Ripper) to create a complex symbolic tapestry of psychological and philosophical speculation.

Farmer's interest in the elusiveness of truth is shown in his "further adventures" of literary and popular heroes, as in *A Barnstormer in Oz, The Wind Whales of Ishmael, Doc Savage: His Apocalyptic Life,* and *The Other Log of Phileas Fogg.* Farmer's own popular culture hero, the amputee Greatheart Silver, does battle with geriatric parodies of the Lone Ranger, the Shadow, James Bond, etc. Farmer's fascination with the Tarzan myth informs seven or eight of his books, including *A Feast Unknown* and the Opar books. Farmer also writes under the pen names of his own and others' fictional characters: Kilgore Trout, Rod Keen, and Jonathan Swift Somers III.

Farmer's recent protagonists are flawed and self-destructive, trapped in Kafkaesque worlds by their own connivance, improvising harebrained schemes aimed at self-gratification. Thus with Jeff Caird of *Dayworld,* whose over-populated futureworld forces people to live just one day a week, being "stoned" or deanimated the other six. This premise leads to such whimsies as seven Popes. Caird illegally stays awake all seven days, inventing different personalities for days where he doesn't belong. Farmer's impish humor enlivens philosophic exploration of the "reality" of human personality. A sequel is planned.

Farmer continues unconventional theological speculation (*Jesus on Mars*), writes metaphysical space-opera (*The Unreasoning Mask*), and depicts feminist human and alien females (the Shemibob in *Dark Is the Sun*). Current projects include a sequel to *Fantastic Voyage* (to be the basis of a movie), a story called "The Lone Ranger Versus the Pope," and a mainstream novel, *Pearl Diving in Old Peoria.*

Critics, excepting Franz Rottensteiner (*Science-Fiction Studies,* Fall 1973), label Farmer a deeply philosophical writer who treats universal issues with originality and insight. Russell Letson (*Science-Fiction Studies,* March 1977) and Neil Barron (*Anatomy of Wonder*) praise Farmer's use of folklore and myth. Leslie Fiedler (in *The Book of Philip José Farmer,* 1973) commends Farmer from a mainstream perspective.

—Mary T. Brizzi

FARREN, Mick. British. Born in Cheltenham, Gloucestershire, 3 September 1943. Educated at Worthing High School for Boys, Sussex; St. Martin's School of Art, London. Married 1) Joy Hebditch in 1967 (divorced, 1979); 2) Elizabeth Volck in 1979. Short order cook, London Zoo, 1965; painter, 1965-67; Lead Singer, Deviants rock band, 1967-69; Editor. *It* magazine, and *Nasty Tales* magazine, both London, 1970-73; Consulting Editor, *New Musical Express,* London, 1975-77. Agent: Abner Stein, 10 Roland Gardens, London SW7 3PH, England; or Merrilee Heifetz, Writers House, 21 West 26th Street, New York, New York 10010, U. S. A.

SCIENCE-FICTION PUBLICATIONS

Novels

The Texts of Festival. London, Hart Davis MacGibbon, 1973; New York, Avon, 1975.
The Quest of the DNA Cowboys . London, Mayflower, 1976.
The Synaptic Manhunt. London, Mayflower, 1976.
The Neural Atrocity. London, Mayflower, 1977.
The Feelies. London, Big O, 1978.
The Song of Phaid the Gambler. London, New English Library, 1981.
Protectorate. New York, Ace, 1984.

OTHER PUBLICATIONS

Novel

The Tale of Willy's Rats. London, Mayflower, 1975.

Other

Watch Out Kids, with Edward Barker. London, Open Gate, 1972.
Rock 'n' Roll Circus, with George Snow. London, Pierrot, and New York, A and W, 1978.
Elvis Presley: The Complete Illustrated Record, with Roy Carr. London, Eel Pie, and New York, Crown, 1982.
The Black Leather Jacket Goes on Forever. London, Flexus, 1985.

Editor, *Get on Down*. London, Futura, 1976.
Editor, with Pearce Marchbank, *Elvis in His Own Words*. London, Omnibus Press, 1977; as *Elvis Presley*, New York, Music Sales, 1978.
Editor, with David Dalton, *The Rolling Stones: In Their Own Words*. New York, Putnam, 1983.

Recording: *Vanpires Stole My Lunch Money*, 1978.

*

Mick Farren comments:

I suppose the most important factor in my attitude to science fiction is that I have little or no truck with hardware. All technology has an on/off switch, and if it doesn't work, you kick it. If it still doesn't work, you send for the repairman. I also don't like to have too much truck with the powerful. A society will show you more about itself if you look at its deadbeats, its drifters, and its whores. More politely, you could say I have an ear for the music of the streets, wherever or whenever those streets might be.

* * *

Veteran of the English underground press, Mick Farren now writes fiction that is brisk, insubstantial, and trashy, flashing with the flares of violence and murky with human squalor. In Farren's worlds the only dependable qualities are depravity, aggression, and decay. From the nastier sub-cultural productions of the last 20 years he constructs a vision of civilisation in terminal decline, with the individual caught between the vast power wielded by a corrupt establishment and the indiscriminate violence boiling up from the streets.

Farren, as his journalism shows, is an expert on the subculture, on the contemporary mythology of comicbooks, pulp fiction, drugs, TV, and especially rock music. His fiction feeds voraciously on popular arts, and feeds them back. *The Texts of Festival* is a futuristic Western about the sacking of Festival, a city founded to preserve the spirit of Woodstock after global catastrophe. Whatever the original values of peace, love, and music, rock 'n' roll heroes soon merge into the gunslingers of a previous tradition. Farren concedes nothing to idealism. The rot is man. All societies ossify and crumble; people divide into decadents and barbarians, and the barbarians win.

These same elements are variously permutated in Farren's trilogy. Escalating technology has developed Stuff Central, a self-maintaining computerised centre that produces and distributes all material requirements with a minimum of human labour. At the same time the fabric of reality begins to tear. The disruptors appear, blindly eating swathes through matter and leaving foggy "nothings" behind. Humanity huddles into isolated communities maintained by stasis generators. It takes three books before anyone realises that the Disruptors are actually gathering the raw material for Stuff Central, whose computer is, of course, insane and preoccupied with godhead. With its flickering continuum where society and morality have gone to the winds of limbo while Law and Chaos squabble over the pickings, *The Quest of the DNA Cowboys* sometimes recalls early Moorcock, but a more important influence is mid-1960's Dylan, whose shadowy characters and hallucinatory aphorisms pop up everywhere. Plot is entirely arbitrary, following the wanderings of Billy and Reave, two picaresque innocents. *The Synaptic Manhunt* is better, more purposeful, as the boys get unwillingly involved on opposite sides of a vendetta. Jeb Stuart Ho, assassin for the Brotherhood, a sort of monastic CIA, is assigned to eliminate the sadistic A. A. Catto, a decadent technocrat with a whim for ruling the world. Suspense and a sharpened satirical edge considerably increase readability. The conclusion, *The Neural Atrocity*, holds no surprises, being full of the final battle and the destruction of all but a tiny corner of the world where mankind's "superiors" are about to hatch out of golden eggs. Pulp as it is, the story occasionally sparks with insights that show Farren as an intelligence doing hackwork, rather than a hack *pur*. At one point Billy, rescued from the nothings, is led "to some kind of normality", "If you could call normality a road densely packed with hysterical refugees who streamed up and down in any direction following the current rumours of where salvation might lie. " The irony is evident: Farren for one would endorse the description.

With *The Feelies* Farren turned from fantasy to a kind of slack social prophecy, of a ravaged future whose citizens live in cubicles on a diet of pills, booze, and sick TV shows. For the rich there is a more thorough escape available into the Feelies, a catatonic paradise of pre-programmed dreams. The most popular are sadomasochistic spectaculars, but every programme is pornographic to some degree. The book observes a typical prole, Wanda-Jean, as she attempts to win a Feelie on the torturous TV game *Wildest Dreams*.

The Song of Phaid the Gambler was certainly over-ambitious and probably ill-advised. Farren should never have undertaken to write a 150,000-word novel. His plotting is far too weak and he is guilty of much padding. Phaid is a rover in a degenerate future world (much like that of *The Texts of Festival*) after a most peculiar and implausible climactic disaster. The novel has the appearance of science fiction, but the heart and manners of the spaghetti western, once again. It is aggressive, but less acute than some of its predecessors. Farren is no longer so hip. Phaid's amoral, nihilistic attitude has no reference to the street wisdom of 1981, but rather seems to reflect a desperately dispirited romanticism. For no good reason Phaid undergoes wild fluctuations of fortune and survives, vacant and lustful as ever. He is a latter-day Sweeney, but Farren approves of him.

Unexpectedly, *Protectorate* proved to be a little better: two-thirds of the length of *Phaid the Gambler*, and provided with a much more satisfactory variety of leading characters. The setting—a future city of towers that overshadow a violent but fecund ghetto and house a decadent, hedonistic aristocracy far above—is as unoriginal as could be. Nevertheless, the inscrutable insectile aliens who rule Earth with such apathy, like a reluctant garrison, are amusingly depicted and go some way to justifying the demoralized atmosphere of the whole book. It is also noteworthy that in *Protectorate* the inevitable revolution is a religious uprising, a much more plausible development in 1984 than Farren's previous re-runs of hippy revolt of the 1960's.

In all Farren's fiction reality is too much to handle. The human race, innately cruel and stupid, scurries around trying to avoid it in a welter of sex, drink, drugs, and violence, or build madder and madder machines to take its place. The vision is a depressive commonplace of our time, and Farren certainly has nothing new to say about it. But his handiness with scraps of modern myth may mean that his work, so much of this time, will retain considerable historical curiosity when the time is past.

—Colin Greenland

FAST, Howard (Melvin). Also writes as E. V. Cunningham; Walter Ericson. American. Born in New York City, 11 November 1914. Educated at George Washington High School, New York, graduated 1931; National Academy of Design, New York. Served with the Office of War Information, 1942-43, and the Army Film Project, 1944. Married Bette Cohen in 1937; one daughter and one son, Jonathan Fast, *q. v.* War correspondent in the Far East of *Esquire* and *Coronet* magazines, 1945. Taught at Indiana University, Bloomington, Summer 1947. Imprisoned for contempt of Congress, 1947. Founder of the World Peace Movement and member of the World Peace Council, 1950-55. Operated Blue Heron Press, New York, 1952-57. Currently, Member of The Fellowship for Reconciliation. American-Labour Party candidate for Congress for the 23rd District of New York, 1952. Recipient: Bread Loaf Writers Conference Award, 1933; Schomburg Race Relations Award, 1944; Newspaper Guild Award, 1947; Jewish Book Council of America Award, 1948; Stalin International Peace Prize (now Soviet International Peace Prize), 1954; Screenwriters Award, 1960; National Association of Independent Schools Award, 1962. Agent: Sterling Lord Agency, 660 Madison Avenue, New York, New York 10021. Address: P. O. Box A, Redding Ridge, Connecticut 06876, U. S. A.

SCIENCE-FICTION PUBLICATIONS

Novel

The Hunter and the Trap. New York, Dial Press, 1967.

Short Stories

The Edge of Tomorrow. New York, Bantam, 1961; London, Corgi, 1962.
The General Zapped an Angel. New York, Morrow, 1970.

A Touch of Infinity. New York, Morrow, 1973; London, Hodder and Stoughton, 1975.
Time and the Riddle: Thirty-One Zen Stories. Pasadena, California, Ward Ritchie Press, 1975.

OTHER PUBLICATIONS

Novels

Two Valleys. New York, Dial Press, 1933; London, Dickson, 1934.
Strange Yesterday. New York, Dodd Mead, 1934.
Place in the City. New York, Harcourt Brace, 1937.
Conceived in Liberty: A Novel of Valley Forge. New York, Simon and Schuster, and London, Joseph, 1939.
The Last Frontier. New York, Duell, 1941; London, Lane, 1948.
The Unvanquished. New York, Duell, 1942; London, Lane, 1947.
The Tall Hunter. New York, Harper, 1942.
Citizen Tom Paine. New York, Duell, 1943; London, Lane, 1946.
Freedom Road. New York, Duell, 1944; London, Lane, 1946.
The American: A Middle Western Legend. New York, Duell, 1946; London, Lane, 1949.
The Children. New York, Duell, 1947.
Clarkton. New York, Duell, 1947.
My Glorious Brothers. Boston, Little Brown, 1948; London, Lane, 1950..
The Proud and the Free. Boston, Little Brown, 1950; London, Lane, 1952.
Spartacus. Privately printed, 1951; London, Lane, 1952.
Fallen Angel (as Walter Ericson). Boston, Little Brown, 1952; as *The Darkness Within*, New York, Ace, 1953; as *Mirage* (as Howard Fast), New York, Fawcett, 1965.
Silas Timberman. New York, Blue Heron Press, 1954; London, Lane, 1955.
The Story of Lola Gregg. New York, Blue Heron Press, 1956; London, Lane, 1957.
Moses, Prince of Egypt. New York, Crown, 1958; London, Methuen, 1959.
The Winston Affair. New York, Crown, 1959; London, Methuen, 1960.
The Golden River, in *The Howard Fast Reader.* New York, Crown, 1960.
April Morning. New York, Crown, and London, Methuen, 1961.
Power. New York, Doubleday, 1962; London, Methuen, 1963.
Agrippa's Daughter. New York, Doubleday, 1964; London, Methuen, 1965.
Torquemada. New York, Doubleday, 1966; London, Methuen, 1967.
The Crossing. New York, Morrow, 1971; London, Eyre Methuen, 1972.
The Hessian. New York, Morrow, 1972; London, Hodder and Stoughton, 1973.
The Immigrants. Boston, Houghton Mifflin, 1977; London, Hodder and Stoughton, 1978.
Second Generation. Boston Houghton Mifflin, and London, Hodder and Stoughton, 1978.
The Establishment. Boston, Houghton Mifflin, 1979; London, Hodder and Stoughton, 1980.
The Legacy. Boston, Houghton Mifflin, and London, Hodder and Stoughton, 1981.
Max. Boston, Houghton Mifflin, 1982; London, Hodder and Stoughton, 1983.

The Outsider. Boston Houghton Mifflin, 1984; London, Hodder and Stoughton, 1985.

Novels as E. V. Cunningham

Sylvia. New York, Doubleday, 1960; London, Deutsch, 1962.
Phyllis. New York, Doubleday, and London, Deutsch, 1962.
Alice. New York, Doubleday, 1963; London, Deutsch, 1965.
Lydia. New York, Doubleday, 1964; London, Deutsch, 1965.
Shirley. New York, Doubleday, and London, Deutsch, 1964.
Penelope. New York, Doubleday, 1965; London, Deutsch, 1966.
Helen. New York, Doubleday, 1966; London, Deutsch, 1967.
Margie. New York, Morrow, 1966; London, Deutsch, 1968.
Sally. New York, Morrow, and London, Deutsch, 1967.
Samantha. New York, Morrow, 1967; London, Deutsch, 1968.
Cynthia. New York, Morrow, 1968; London, Deutsch, 1969.
The Assassin Who Gave Up His Gun. New York, Morrow, 1969; London, Deutsch, 1970.
Millie. New York, Morrow, 1973; London, Deutsch, 1975.
The Case of the One-Penny Orange. New York, Holt Rinehart, 1977; London, Deutsch, 1978.
The Case of the Russian Diplomat. New York, Holt Rinehart, 1978; London, Deutsch, 1979.
The Case of the Poisoned Eclairs . New York, Holt Rinehart, 1979; London, Deutsch, 1980.
The Case of the Sliding Pool. New York, Delacorte Press, 1981; London, Gollancz, 1982.
The Case of the Kidnapped Angel. New York, Delacorte Press, 1982; London, Gollancz, 1983.
The Case of the Murdered Mackenzie. New York, Delacorte Press, 1984; London, Gollancz, 1985.

Short Stories

Patrick Henry and the Frigate's Keel and Other Stories of a Young Nation. New York, Duell, 1945.
Departure and Other Stories. Boston, Little Brown, 1949.
The Last Supper and Other Stories. New York, Blue Heron Press, 1955; London, Lane, 1956.

Plays

The Hammer (produced New York, 1950).
Thirty Pieces of Silver (produced Melbourne, 1951; London, 1984). New York, Blue Heron Press, and London, Lane, 1954.
General Washington and the Water Witch. London, Lane, 1956.
The Crossing (produced Dallas, 1962).
The Hill (screenplay). New York, Doubleday, 1964.

Screenplay: *The Hessian*, 1971.

Television Plays: *What's a Nice Girl Like You . . . ?*, 1971; *21 Hours at Munich*, with Edward Hume, 1976.

Verse

Never to Forget the Battle of the Warsaw Ghetto, with William Gropper. New York, Jewish Peoples Fraternal Order, 1946.

Other

The Romance of a People (for children). New York, Hebrew Publishing Company, 1941.

Lord Baden-Powell of the Boy Scouts. New York, Messner, 1941.
Haym Salomon, Son of Liberty. New York, Messner, 1941.
The Picture-Book History of the Jews, with Bette Fast. New York, Hebrew Publishing Company, 1942.
Goethals and the Panama Canal. New York, Messner, 1942.
The Incredible Tito. New York, Magazine House, 1944.
Intellectuals in the Fight for Peace. New York, Masses and Mainstream, 1949.
Tito and His People. Winnipeg, Manitoba, Contemporary Publishers, 1950.
Literature and Reality. New York, International Publishers, 1950.
Peekskill, U. S. A. : A Personal Experience. New York, Civil Rights Congress, and London, International Publishing Company, 1951.
Korean Lullaby. New York, American Peace Crusade, n. d.
Tony and the Wonderful Door (for children). New York, Blue Heron Press, 1952; as *The Magic Door*, Culver City, California, Peace Press, 1979.
Spain and Peace. New York, Joint Anti-Fascist Refugee Committee, 1952.
The Passion of Sacco and Vanzetti: A New England Legend. New York, Blue Heron Press, 1953; London, Lane, 1954.
The Naked God: The Writer and the Communist Party. New York, Praeger, 1957; London, Bodley Head, 1958.
The Howard Fast Reader. New York, Crown, 1960.
The Jews: Story of a People. New York, Dial Press, 1968; London, Cassell, 1970.
The Art of Zen Meditation. Culver City, California, Peace Press, 1977.

Editor, *The Selected Work of Tom Paine*. New York, Modern Library, 1946; London, Lane, 1948.
Editor, *Best Short Stories of Theodore Dreiser*. Cleveland, World, 1947.

*

Manuscript Collection: University of Pennsylvania Library, Philadelphia.

Howard Fast comments:
　　All of my science fiction works are parables—and perhaps not so much science fiction as humor, fear, and fantasy. In a way they are preachments against the cruelty and foolishness of modern man. One of my favorites concerns a sub-normal three-star general who shoots down an angel in Vietnam. Science does not tolerate angels, but since science does tolerate three-star generals, the discipline needs some self-study. Beyond that, the stories speak for themselves. Some are quite funny, but who can observe man for 70 years without realizing that, above all our stupidity and brutishness, we are, most often, ridiculous. Perhaps we provoke enough laughter among the Gods to cause them to refrain from extinguishing us—though in good time we will probably do that ourselves.

* 　 * 　 *

　　The science fiction of Howard Fast consists mainly of "Zen short stories" reprinted in *Time and the Riddle*. In them he uses motifs from science fiction and older mythologies to question the morality of man's survival and the trade-offs it demands.
　　The older images include a hand (God's?) snuffing out the sun in "Not with a Bang," the devil making a deal in "Tomorrow's *Wall Street Journal*," and a stunning encounter

with the supernatural in Vietnam in "The General Zapped an Angel." Metaphysical conceits that are borderline SF depict the world as a "Movie House," as a stage set being removed in "The Interval," and as a hatching egg in "The Pragmatic Seed." The mythological "great time" assumes reality for an Indian ("The Mohawk"), meditating on the steps of St. Patrick's Cathedral in New York; asked on the radio to show cause why divine wrath should be spared, mankind's computer network comes up with another meditator, even freakier ("Show-Cause").

More clearly science fiction, a mouse is equipped by small aliens with intelligence, which doesn't prevent its demise ("The Mouse"). A large ant may be an alien visitor, but revulsion causes humans to squash it and its kind ("The Large Ant"). Tiny people are wiped out as vermin in "A Matter of Size," suggesting the same could be done to us. It is, when insects retaliate, severing the networks of wires, pipes, and other structures that support our civilization ("The Insects"). Man's propensity for killing takes on more cosmic significance in "Cato the Martian." Disturbed by their study of us, the Martians finally attack, with the return strike devastating their civilization. An even more idyllic planet gives human explorers a view of Eden denied us due to our destructiveness ("The Sight of Eden"). Alternatively, Fast depicts Earth as the dumping ground for the galaxy's psychotics. And an alien "exterminator" turns out to be "General Hardy's Profession," revealed through psychoanalysis.

Disturbing the natural order of things may have tragic or trivial consequences. Deep drilling with nuclear weapons brings up blood instead of oil in "The Wound." New York's garbage seems to go into another dimension ("The Hoop"), but its return is disruptive. A time machine creates a closed loop in "Of Time and Cats." Another one fails to permit Hitler's assassination in "The Mind of God." Even a hybrid cactus flower which produces contentment may be a questionable trade-off in "Echinomastus Contentii." Utopia, if it can be brought about, will also demand intervention and deceit, but the cost seems worth it. The pretense of invasion in "The Martian Shop" brings about world government as well as technological advance. Similar results come from making good use of the resources of the world's richest men, and keeping him frozen long after a cure for his cancer has been found ("The Cold, Cold Box"). But the major elaboration of this theme is "The Trap" (published in a shorter version as "The First Men").

A short novel told largely in letters, it speculates on the results of raising infants to be fully human. Improbably patient, the US Army, sponsor of this research, finally resolves to destroy the commune which threatens the way of life of man as he is. But the children, though totally non-violent, are technologically capable of protecting themselves. It is not they so much as conventional society who are interfering with the natural order of things.

Professionally written, economical, with entertaining conversation, little or no melodrama, and a competent style, these stories may seem a bit glib or facile, but a parable is only as shallow or profound as the audience wishes to make it.

—David N. Samuelson

FAST, Jonathan (David). American. Born in New York City, 13 April 1948; son of the writer Howard Fast, *q. v.* Educated at the High School of Music and Art, New York, 1962-66;

Princeton University, New Jersey, 1966-68; Sarah Lawrence College, Bronxville, New York, 1968-70, B. A. 1970; University of California, Berkeley (Hearst Fellow in music), 1970. Married the writer Erica Jong in 1977 (divorced, 1983); one daughter. Composer and writer. Agent: Sterling Lord Agency, 660 Madison Avenue, New York, New York 10021, U. S. A.

SCIENCE-FICTION PUBLICATIONS

Novels

The Secrets of Synchronicity. New York, New American Library, 1977; as *Prisoner of the Planets,* London, Panther, 1980.
Mortal Gods. New York, Harper, 1978; London, Panther, 1980.
The Inner Circle. New York, Delacorte Press, 1979; London, Magnum, 1980.
The Beast. New York, Random House, 1981; London, Methuen, 1982.

Uncollected Short Stories

"Decay," in *Fantasy and Science Fiction* (New York), April, 1975.
"Earthblossom," in *New Constellations,* edited by Thomas M. Disch and Charles Naylor. New York, Harper, 1976.
"Test Driving the Valkyrie," in *Swank* (New York), July, 1976.
"Kindertotenlieder," in *Issac Asimov's Science Fiction Magazine* (New York), Spring 1977.

OTHER PUBLICATIONS

Plays

Television Plays: *Two Missionaries; The Thrill Show Hero; Love al Dente; Prisoner of Space.*

*

Jonathan Fast comments:

(1981) Social satire is one of the primary aims of my work: using the future to let me reflect upon the present, upon the lunacy of our lives and the possibilities of sanity. Religion fascinates me as does the opportunity to speculate on matters metaphysical, on life and death and the nature of reality. In my most recent work (*The Inner Circle*) I have tried to cast my "science-fiction" ideas in a "mainstream" mold in order to reach a larger audience, and, as a result of its success, I believe I shall continue with this ruse in the future.

*   *   *

Jonathan Fast was a composer and a television writer before he turned to book-length science fiction. His early skills seem to have been transferrable; he creates a universe of astonishing variations which he weaves firmly into thematic resolution, all in the course of a story marked by linguistic cleverness, clearly drawn characters, good dramatic pace, and excellent visualization. On top of that, he does his homework—amid the speed and the fun is some solid extrapolation of current scientific thought.

His own stated interest is to show that religion and science are aspects of the same thing. They certainly are in the colorful universe of his first novel. *The Secrets of Synchronicity.* The story moves dizzyingly from the enslaved child miners on the asteroid Slabour, to a desert planet with a civilization of telepathic snakes, to Nova Center, the commercial capital of the galaxy, and finally, triumphantly, back to Slabour. Fast connects not only science and religion, through the Vedic myths, but economics as well. His galaxy is controlled by Ultra Cap, a super-capitalistic organisation which, by concealing the blue stone that holds the secrets of synchronicity, prevents the human race from making its own connections and finding the freedom beyond technology. Fast's interests are quite serious, but his tone is light and entertaining, with many genuinely funny moments. His callow protagonist, Stefin-Dae, is clever enough to stay alive but not to avoid being swept from place to place in a kaleidoscopic universe. And Fast's variety is real— each location is completely different from the next, carefully thought out, and vividly described.

The Secrets of Synchronicity is a neat circular quest, profusely illustrated and exhilarating in its range and constant pace. Mortal Gods tries for more depth in one place. It is less funny but possibly more original; his protagonist is less appealing but has more depth than Stefin-Dae. Fast focusses here on the possibilities of controlled genetic mutation, and comes up with the concept of the Lifestylers—beings bizarrely mutated according to artists' conceptions, living in the transdimensional Bardo of Tibetan theology, and receiving worship as gods. Once again the profit motive, in the form of the Mutagen Corporation, controls the religious life of the people. The Lifestylers are an impressive invention on Fast's part, and he gives reference to current geneticists before he starts. He also does reasonably well with a challenge the science-fiction genre has been working on for some time—depicting successful sex between human and alien. As in his first book, the accompanying details of civilization are well worked out and of interest in themselves. The book's only flaw is the plot he uses to tie all these things together, a political assassination mystery that is adequately resolved but that really adds nothing to the science fiction of the story.

Fast has written a Hollywood mystery as well—The Inner Circle, set firmly on this earth and doubtless based on his experience of screen writing. His The Beast, despite marginal suggestions of medical SF, is a fairy tale of beauty and the beast. One can only hope that he returns to traditional science fiction soon. Fast is one of the most entertaining writers in the genre, a delight for the mind as well as for the imagining eye. In a brisk biographical note, his publishers assure us that "he longs for a cogent universe." So far he has formed at least two himself.

—Karen G. Way

FEARN, John (Frances) Russell. Also wrote as Geoffrey Armstrong; Thornton Ayre; Hugo Blayn; Hank Carson; Dennis Clive; Hank Cole; John Cotton; Polton Cross; Astron Del Martia; Mark Denholm; Spike Gordon; Volsted Gridban; Griff; Conrad G. Holt; Frank Jones; Nat Karta; Clem Larson; Paul Lorraine; Jed McCloud; Jed McNab; Dom Passante; Lawrence F. Rose; Frank Russell; John Russell; Bryan Shaw; John Slate; Vargo Statten; K. Thomas; Earl Titan; John Wernheim; Ephriam Winiki. British. Born in Worsley, Lancashire, 5 June 1908. Married Carrie Fearn in 1956. Cinema projectionist during World War I. Cotton salesman after World War II. Editor, as Vargo Statten, *Vargo Statten Science*

Fiction Magazine, and *British Science Fiction Magazine,* both Luton, Bedfordshire, 1954-56. *Died 18 September 1960.*

SCIENCE-FICTION PUBLICATIONS

Novels (series: Clayton Drew; Golden Amazon)

Valley of Pretenders (as Dennis Clive), New York, Columbia, 1942.
The Voice Commands (as Dennis Clive). New York, Columbia, 1942.
The Intelligence Gigantic. Kingswood, Surrey, World's Work, 1943.
The Golden Amazon. Kingswood, Surrey, World's Work, 1944.
Other Eyes Watching (as Polton Cross). London, Pendulum, 1946.
Liners of Time. Kingswood, Surrey, World's Work, 1947.
Slaves of Ijax. Llandudno, Caernarvonshire, Kaner, 1948.
The Golden Amazon Returns. Kingswood, Surrey, World's Work, 1948; as *The Deathless Amazon,* Toronto, Harlequin, 1955.
The Trembling World (as Astron Del Martia). London, Frances, 1949.
Emperor of Mars (Drew). London, Panther, 1950.
Warrior of Mars (Drew). London, Panther, 1950.
Red Men of Mars (Drew). London, Panther, 1950.
Goddess of Mars (Drew). London, Panther, 1950.
Operation Venus. London, Scion, 1950.
The Golden Amazon's Triumph. Kingswood, Surrey, World's Work, 1953.
The Amazon's Diamond Quest. Kingswood, Surrey, World's Work, 1953.
Cosmic Exodus (as Conrad G. Holt). London, Pearson, 1953.
Dark Boundaries (as Paul Lorraine). London, Warren, 1953.
The Hell Fruit (as Lawrence F. Rose). London, Pearson, 1953.
Z Formations (as Bryan Shaw). London, Warren, 1953.
The Amazon Strikes Again. Kingswood, Surrey, World's Work, 1954.
Twin of the Amazon. Kingswood, Surrey, World's Work, 1954.
Conquest of the Amazon. London, Futura, 1976.
No Grave Need I. Wallsend, Harbottle, 1984.
The Slitherers. Wallsend, Harbottle, 1984.
Climate Incorporated. Wallsend, Harbottle, 1985.

Novels as Vargo Statten

Annihilation. London, Scion, 1950.
The Micro Men. London, Scion, 1950.
Wanderer of Space. London, Scion, 1950.
2000 Years On. London, Scion, 1950.
Inferno. London, Scion, 1950.
The Cosmic Flame. London, Scion, 1950.
Nebula X. London, Scion, 1950.
The Sun Makers. London, Scion, 1950.
The Avenging Martian. London, Scion, 1951.
Cataclysm. London, Scion, 1951.
The Red Insects. London, Scion, 1951.
Deadline to Pluto. London, Scion, 1951.
The Petrified Planet. London, Scion, 1951.
Born of Luna. London, Scion, 1951.
The Devouring Fire. London, Scion, 1951.
The Renegade Star. London, Scion, 1951.
The New Satellite. London, Scion, 1951.
The Catalyst. London, Scion, 1951.
The Inner Cosmos. London, Scion, 1952.

The Space Warp. London, Scion, 1952.
The Eclipse Express. London, Scion, 1952.
The Time Bridge. London, Scion, 1952.
The Man from Tomorrow. London, Scion, 1952.
The G-Bomb. London, Scion, 1952.
Laughter in Space. London, Scion, 1952.
Across the Ages. London, Scion, 1952.
The Last Martian. London, Scion, 1952.
Worlds to Conquer. London, Scion, 1952.
Decreation. London, Scion, 1952.
The Time Trap. London, Scion, 1952.
Science Metropolis. London, Scion, 1952.
To the Ultimate. London, Scion, 1952.
Ultra Spectrum. London, Scion, 1953.
The Dust Destroyer. London, Scion, 1953.
Black-Wing of Mars. London, Scion, 1953.
Man in Duplicate. London, Scion, 1953.
Zero Hour. London, Scion, 1953.
The Black Avengers. London, Scion, 1953.
Odyssey of Nine. London, Scion, 1953.
Pioneer 1990. London, Scion, 1953.
The Interloper. London, Scion, 1953.
Man of Two Worlds. London, Scion, 1953.
The Lie Destroyer. London, Scion, 1953.
Black Bargain. London, Scion, 1953.
The Grand Illusion. London, Scion, 1953.
Wealth of the Void. London, Scion, 1954.
A Time Appointed. London, Scion, 1954.
I Spy. . . . London, Scion, 1954.
The Multi-Man. London, Scion, 1954.
Creature from the Black Lagoon (novelization of screenplay). London, Dragon, 1954.
1,000-Year Voyage. London, Dragon, 1954.
Earth 2. London, Dragon, 1955.

Novels as Volsted Gridban (series: Clifford Brooks; Adam Quirke)

Moons for Sale. London, Scion, 1953.
The Dyno-Depressant. London, Scion, 1953.
Magnetic Brain. London, Scion, 1953.
Scourge of the Atom. London, Scion, 1953.
A Thing of the Past (Brooks). London, Scion, 1953.
Exit Life. London, Scion, 1953.
The Master Must Die (Quirke). London, Scion, 1953.
The Purple Wizard. London, Scion, 1953.
The Genial Dinosaur (Brooks). London, Scion, 1954.
The Frozen Limit. London, Scion, 1954.
I Came, I Saw, I Wondered. London, Scion, 1954.
The Lonely Astronomer (Quirke). London, Scion, 1954.

Uncollected Short Stories (series: Amazon)

"The Man Who Stopped the Dust," in *Astounding* (New York), March 1934.
"The Brain of Light," in *Astounding* (New York), May 1934.
"Invaders from Time," in *Scoops* (London), 12 May 1934.
"He Never Slept," in *Astounding* (New York), June 1934.
"Before Earth Came," in *Astounding* (New York), July 1934.
"Earth's Mausoleum," in *Astounding* (New York), May 1935.
"Liners of Time," in *Amazing* (New York), May, June, July, August 1935.
"The Blue Infinity," in *Astounding* (New York), September, 1935.
"Mathematica," in *Astounding* (New York), February 1936.

"Mathematica Plus," in *Astounding* (New York), May 1936.
"Subconsious," in *Amazing* (New York), August 1936.
"Deserted Universe," in *Astounding* (New York), September 1936.
"The Great Illusion," in *Fantasy*, September 1936.
"Dynasty of the Small," in *Astounding* (New York), November 1936.
Portrait of a Murderer," in *Weird Tales* (Indianapolis), December 1936.
"Metamorphosis," in *Astounding* (New York), January 1937.
"Brain of Venus," in *Thrilling Wonder Stories* (New York), February 1937.
"Worlds Within, " in *Astounding* (New York), March, 1937.
"Menace from the Microcosm," in *Thrilling Wonder Stories* (New York), June, 1937.
"Superhuman" (as Geoffrey Armstrong) and "Seeds from Space," in *Tales of Wonder 1* (Kingswood, Surrey), June 1937.
"Dark Eternity," in Astounding (New York), December 1937.
"Zagribud," in *Amazing* (New York), December 1937, February, April 1938.
"Death at the Observatory," in *Modern Wonder 76* (London), 1938.
"The Misty Wilderness," in *Modern Wonder 77* (London), 1938.
"The Weather Machine," in *Modern Wonder 78* (London), 1938.
"The Red Magician," in *Fantasy 1* (London), 1938.
"The Red Heritage," in *Astounding* (New York), January 1938.
"Through Earth's Core," in *Tales of Wonder 2* (Kingswood, Surrey), Spring 1938.
"Lords of 9016," in *Thrilling Wonder Stories* (New York), April 1938.
"A Summons from Mars," in *Amazing* (New York), June 1938.
"Climatica," in *Fantasy 2* (London), 1939.
"The Black Empress," in *Amazing* (New York), January 1939.
"Outlaw of Saturn" (as John Cotton), in *Science Fiction* (Holyoke, Massachusetts), March 1939.
"Secret of the Buried City," in *Amazing* (New York), May 1939.
"She Walked Alone," in *Fantastic Adventures* (New York), July 1939.
"Thoughts That Kill," in *Science Fiction Stories* (New York), October 1939.
"Frigid Moon" (as Dennis Clive), in *Future* (New York), November 1939.
"Phantom from Space," in *Super Science* (Kokomo, Indiana), March 1940.
"War of the Scientists," in *Amazing* (New York), April 1940.
"The Cosmic Juggernaut," in *Planet* (New York), Summer 1940.
"He Conquered Venus," in *Astonishing* (Chicago), June 1940.
"Laughter Out of Space" (as Dennis Clive), in *Future* (New York), July 1940.
"Queen of Venus," in *Marvel* (New York), November 1940.
"The Cosmic Derelict," in *Planet* (New York), Spring 1941.
"Martian Miniature," in *Amazing* (New York), May 1942.
"The Last Hours," in *Amazing* (New York), August 1942.
"The Ultimate Analysis," in *Thrilling Wonder Stories* (New York), Fall 1944.
"Aftermath," in *Startling* (New York), Fall 1945.
"Interlink," in *Thrilling Wonder Stories* (New York), Fall 1945.
"Solar Assignment" (as Mark Denholm), "Knowledge Without Learning" (as K. Thomas), and "Sweet Mystery of Life," in *New Worlds 1* (London), 1946.

"The Unbroken Chain," in *Startling* (New York), Spring 1946.
"The Multillionth Chance," in *Thrilling Wonder Stories* (New York), Fall 1946.
"Last Conflict," in *Fantasy* (London), December 1946.
"Pre-Natal," in *Outlands 1* (Liverpool), December 1946.
"The Arbiter," in *Startling* (New York), May 1947.
"After the Atom," in *Startling* (New York), May 1948.
"Wanderer of Time," in *My Best Science Fiction Story,* edited by Leo Margulies and Oscar J. Friend. New York, Merlin Press, 1949.
"Lord of Atlantis" (Amazon), in *Star Weekly* (Toronto), 8 October 1949.
"Triangle of Power" (Amazon), in *Star Weekly* (Toronto), 13 May 1950.
"Stranger in Our Midst," in *Star Weekly* (Toronto), 2 September 1950.
"Black-Out," in *Science Fantasy* (Bournemouth), Winter 1950-51.
"The Amethyst City" (Amazon), in *Star Weekly* (Toronto), 3 March 1951.
"Daughter of the Amazon," in *Star Weekly* (Toronto), 1 December 1951.
"Glimpse," in *Star Weekly* (Toronto), 21 February 1952.
"Flight of the Vampires," in *Amazing* (New York), September 1952.
"Quorne Returns" (Amazon), in *Star Weekly* (Toronto), 25 October 1952.
"Deadline," in *Star Weekly* (Toronto), 13 December 1952.
"Waters of Eternity" (as Mark Denholm), in *Worlds of the Universe 1* (London), 1953.
"Winged Pestilence," in *Star Weekly* (Toronto), 23 May 1953.
"Later Than You Think," in *Space-Time,* June 1953.
"The Central Intelligence" (Amazon), in *Star Weekly* (Toronto), 22 August 1953.
"The Copper Bullet" (as John Wernheim), in *Vargo Statten Science Fiction Magazine 1* (Luton, Bedfordshire), 1954.
"First of the Robots," in *Space Fact and Fiction* (London), April 1954.
"The Voice of the Conqueror," in *Star Weekly* (Toronto), 10 July 1954.
"The Cosmic Crusaders," in *Star Weekly* (Toronto), 21 February 1955.
"Here and Now," in *Star Weekly* (Toronto), 2 April 1955.
"Parasite Planet" (Amazon), in *Star Weekly* (Toronto), 27 August 1955.
"World Out of Step" (Amazon), in *Star Weekly* (Toronto), 17 November 1956.
"The Shadow People" (Amazon), in *Star Weekly* (Toronto), 6 April 1957.
"Kingpin Planet" (Amazon), in *Star Weekly* (Toronto), 19 October 1957.
"Robbery Without Violence," in *Star Weekly* (Toronto), 14 December 1957.
"World in Reverse" (Amazon), in *Star Weekly* (Toronto), 26 April 1958.
"Manton's World," in *Star Weekly* (Toronto), 7 June 1958.
"Dwellers in Darkness" (Amazon), in *Star Weekly* (Toronto), 29 November 1958.
"World in Duplicate" (Amazon), in *Star Weekly* (Toronto), 16 May 1959.
"Judgement Bell," in *Weird and Occult Library 2.* London, Swan, 1960.
"Standstill Planet" (Amazon), in *Star Weekly* (Toronto), 26 March 1960.
"Ghost World" (Amazon), in *Star Weekly* (Toronto), 17 December 1960.

"Earth Divided" (Amazon), in *Star Weekly* (Toronto), 24 June 1961.
"Into the Unknown," in *Vision of Tomorrow* (Newcastle upon Tyne), April 1970.
"The Ghost Sun," with S. J. Bounds, in *Vision of Tomorrow* (Newcastle upon Tyne), May 1970.
"Rule of the Brains," in *Vision of Tomorrow* (Newcastle upon Tyne), August 1970.
"Alice, Where Art Thou?," in *The Best of British SF 1,* edited by Mike Ashley. London, Futura, 1977.
"The Golden Amazon Returns," in *Superheroes,* edited by Michel Parry. London, Sphere, 1978.
"Arctic God," in *Friendly Aliens,* edited by John Robert Colombo. Toronto, Hounslow Press, 1981.

Uncollected Short Stories as Thornton Ayre (series: Golden Amazon)

"Penal World," in *Astounding* (New York), October 1937.
"Whispering Satellite," in *Astounding* (New York), January 1938.
"Locked City," in *Amazing* (New York), October 1938.
"Secret of the Ring," in *Amazing* (New York), November 1938.
"World Without Men," in *Amazing* (New York), April 1939.
"Microbes from Space," in *Amazing* (New York), June 1939.
"The Golden Amazon," in *Fantastic Adventures* (New York), July 1939.
"Face in the Sky," in *Amazing* (New York), September 1939.
"Lunar Intrigue," in *Fantastic Adventures* (New York), November 1939.
"The Man Who Saw Two Worlds," in *Amazing* (New York), January 1940.
"Mystery of the White Raider," in *Fantastic Adventures* (New York), February 1940.
"World Reborn," in *Super Science* (Kokomo, Indiana), March 1940.
"The Case of the Murdered Savants," in *Amazing* (New York), April 1940.
"The Amazon Fights Again," in *Fantastic Adventures* (New York), June 1940.
"Secret of the Moon Treasure," in *Amazing* (New York), July 1940.
"Domain of Zero," in *Planet* (New York), Fall 1940.
"The Man Who Sold the Earth," in *Science Fiction* (Holyoke, Massachusetts), October 1940.
"Special Agent to Venus," in *Fantastic Adventures* (New York), October 1940.
"Twilight of the Tenth World," in *Planet* (New York), Winter 1940.
"Island in the Marsh," in *Startling* (New York), November 1940.
"The World in Wilderness," in *Science Fiction* (Holyoke, Massachusetts), June 1941.
"Lunar Concession," in *Science Fiction* (Holyoke, Massachusetts), September 1941.
"Mystery of the Martian Pendulum," with A. R. Steber, in *Amazing* (New York), October 1941.
"The Case of the Mesozoic Monsters," in *Amazing* (New York), May 1942.
"The Mental Gangster," in *Fantastic Adventures* (New York), August 1942.
"Vampire Queen," in *Planet* (New York), Fall 1942.
"The Silver Coil," in *Amazing* (New York), November 1942.
"Children of the Golden Amazon," in *Fantastic Adventures* (New York), April 1943.
"Lunar Vengeance," in *Amazing* (New York), September 1943.

"White Mouse," in *New Worlds 1* (London), 1946.
"From Afar," in *Hands Up Annual*, 1947.

Uncollected Short Stories as Polton Cross

"The Mental Ultimate," in *Astounding* (New York), January 1938.
"The Degenerates," in *Astounding* (New York), February 1938.
"The Master of the Golden City," in *Amazing* (New York), June 1938.
"Wings Across the Cosmos," in *Thrilling Wonder Stories* (New York), June 1938.
"The World That Dissolved," in *Amazing* (New York), February 1939.
"World Without Chance," in *Thrilling Wonder Stories* (New York), February 1939.
"Martian Avenger," in *Amazing* (New York), April 1939.
"World Without Death," in *Amazing* (New York), June 1939.
"World Beneath Ice," in *Amazing* (New York), August 1939.
"The Man from Hell," in *Fantastic Adventures* (New York), November 1939.
"Chameleon Planet," in *Astonishing* (Chicago), February 1940.
"Wedding of the Forces," in *Future* (New York), November 1940.
"Science from Syracuse," in *Science Fiction* (Holyoke, Massachusetts), March 1941.
"The Last Secret Weapon," in *Marvel* (New York), April 1941.
"The Man Who Bought Mars," in *Fantastic Adventures* (New York), June 1941.
"Destroyer from the Past," in *Amazing* (New York), May 1942.
"Prisoner of Time," in *Super Science* (Kokomo, Indiana), May 1942.
"Outcasts of Eternity," in *Fantastic Adventures* (New York), September 1942.
"The Devouring Tide," in *Thrilling Wonder Stories* (New York), Summer 1944.
"Mark Grayson Unlimited," in *Thrilling Wonder Stories* (New York), Spring 1945.
"Space Trap," in *Thrilling Wonder Stories* (New York), Fall 1945.
"Other Eyes Watching," in *Startling* (New York), Spring 1946.
"Twilight Planet," in *Thrilling Wonder Stories* (New York), Summer 1946.
"The Vicious Circle," in *Startling* (New York), Summer 1946.
"Chaos," in *Startling* (New York), November 1947.
"Ultra Evolution," in *Startling* (New York), January 1948.

Uncollected Short Stories as Ephriam Winiki

"Leeches from Space," in *Science Fiction* (Holyoke, Massachusetts), March 1939.
"Jewels from the Moon," in *Science Fiction* (Holyoke, Massachusetts), August 1939.
"Earth Asunder," in *Science Fiction* (Holyoke, Massachusetts), October 1939.
"Eclipse Bears Witness," in *Science Fiction* (Holyoke, Massachusetts), March 1940.

Uncollected Short Stories as Dom Passante

"Moon Heaven," in *Science Fiction* (Holyoke, Massachusetts), June 1939.
"Men Without a World," in *Science Fiction* (Holyoke, Massa-

chusetts), March 1940.
"Across the Ages," in *Future* (New York), October 1941.

Uncollected Short Stories as Volsted Gridban

"March of the Robots," in *Vargo Statten Science Fiction Magazine 1* (Luton, Bedfordshire), 1954.
"A Saga of 2270 A. D.," in *Vargo Statten Science Fiction Magazine 2* (Luton, Bedfordshire), 1954.
"The Others," in *Vargo Statten Science Fiction Magazine 3* (Luton, Bedfordshire), 1954.

Uncollected Short Stories as Vargo Statten

"Beyond Zero," in *Vargo Statten Science Fiction Magazine 1* (Luton Bedfordshire), 1954.
"Before Atlantis," in *Vargo Statten Science Fiction Magazine 2* (Luton, Bedfordshire), 1954.
"The Master Mind," in *Vargo Statten Science Fiction Magazine 3* (Luton, Bedfordshire), 1954.
"Reverse Action," in *Vargo Statten Science Fiction Magazine 4* (Luton, Bedfordshire), 1954.
"Rim of Eternity," in *Vargo Statten Science Fiction Magazine 5* (Luton, Bedfordshire), 1954.
"Something from Mercury," in *British Science Fiction 6* (Luton, Bedfordshire), 1954.
"A Matter of Vibration," in *British Science Fiction 12* (Luton, Bedfordshire), 1955.
"Three's a Crowd," in *British Space Fiction 2* (Luton, Bedfordshire), 1955.

OTHER PUBLICATIONS

Novels

The Test of Love (published anonymously). London, Popular Fiction, 1947.
The Flying Horseman. Glasgow, Western Book Distributors, 1947.
The Avenging Ranger, Llandudno, Caernarvonshire, Kaner, 1948.
Rustlers Canyon. Llandudno, Caernarvonshire, Kaner, 1948.
Thunder Valley. Redhill, Surrey, Wells Gardner Darton, 1948.
Yellow Gulch Law. Llandudno, Caernarvonshire, Kaner, 1948.
Dead Man's Shoes. London, Paget, 1949.
Outlaw's Legacy (as Clem Larson). London, Paget, 1949.
Six-Gun Prodigal (as Hank Cole). London, Paget, 1949.
Account Settled (as John Russell). London, Paget, 1949.
Six-Guns Shoot to Kill (as Hank Carson). Glasgow, Muir Watson, 1949.
Gunsmoke Valley. Glasgow, Muir Watson, 1949.
Stockwhip Sheriff (as Polton Cross). Glasgow, Muir Watson, 1949.
Valley of the Doomed. Kingswood, Surrey, World's Work, 1949.
Murder's a Must. Glasgow, Muir Watson, 1949.
Tornado Trail. Glasgow, Muir Watson, 1949.
Arizona Love. London, Rich and Cowan, 1950.
Aztec Gold. London, Scion, 1950.
Ghost Canyon. London, Scion, 1950.
Merridew Rides Again. Kingswood, Surrey, World's Work, 1950.
Rattlesnake. London, Scion, 1950.
Skeleton Pass. London, Scion, 1950.
Bonanza. London, Scion, 1950.
Firewater. London, Scion, 1950.

Hell's Acres (as Mike McCoy). London, Scion, 1950.
Lead Law. London, Scion, 1950.
Merridew Marches On. Kingswood, Surrey, World's Work, 1951.
The Hanging 9. London, Scion, 1951.
Guntoter from Kansas (as Jeb McNab). London, Panther, 1951.
Injun Canyon (as Jed McNab). London, Panther, 1951.
Golden Canyon. London, Partridge, 1951.
The Gold of Akada (as Earl Titan). London, Scion, 1951.
Anjani the Mighty (as Earl Titan). London, Scion, 1951.
Killer's Legacy. London, Rich and Cowan, 1952.
Merridew Fights Again. Kingswood, Surrey, World's Work, 1952.
Merridew Follows the Trail. Kingswood, Surrey, World's Work, 1953.
Liquid Death (as Griff). London, Modern Fiction, 1953.
Don't Touch Me (as Spike Gordon). London, Modern Fiction, 1953.
You Take the Rap (as Spike Gordon). London, Modern Fiction, 1953.
Shattering Glass (as Frank Russell). London, Brown Watson, 1953.
Navajo Vengeance. London, Rich and Cowan, 1956.

Novels as John Slate

Black Maria, M. A. London, Rich and Cowan, 1944.
Maria Marches On. London, Rich and Cowan, 1945.
One Remained Seated. London, Rich and Cowan, 1946.
Thy Arm Alone. London, Rich and Cowan, 1947.
Framed in Guilt. London, Rich and Cowan, 1948.
Death in Silhouette. London, Rich and Cowan, 1950.

Novels as Hugo Blayn

Except for One Thing. London, Stanley Paul, 1947.
The Five Matchboxes. London, Stanley Paul, 1948.
Flashpoint. London, Stanley Paul, 1950.
What Happened to Hammond? London, Stanley Paul, 1951.
Vision Sinster (as Nat Karta). London, Dragon, 1954.
The Silvered Cage. London, Dragon, 1955.

Novels as Jed McCloud

Accident Trail. London, Dragon, 1955.
Feather-Fist Jones. London, Dragon, 1955.
Sheriff of Deadman's Bend. London, Brown Watson, 1956.
Phantom Avenger. London, Brown Watson, 1956.

*

Critical Study: *The Multi-Man: A Biographic and Bibliographic Study of John Russell Fearn* (includes bibliography) by Philip Harbottle, privately printed, 1968.

*   *   *

John Russell Fearn left school at 14, tried first to follow the career of his father, a cotton salesman, and tried a variety of other jobs, none of which satisfied him. He wrote continuously, gradually becoming more proficient, and read sf voraciously. He formed a life-long interest in the cinema and broke into print with a series of articles in *Film Weekly* in 1931.

Discovering *Amazing Stories* that same year, Fearn submitted *The Intelligence Gigantic*, an influential novel which introduced the concept of the latent powers of the human brain. *Amazing* serialised it in 1933, and, greatly encouraged, Fearn quickly wrote *Liners of Time* and its sequel, *Zagribud*. Then, when Orlin Tremaine revived *Astounding Stories*, Fearn switched to the rival publication, debuting with the classic "The Man Who Stopped the Dust" (1934). Sam Moskowitz has confirmed that the plot, describing the weird consequences of destroying dust, was unique: nobody had previously used the idea, and nobody has ever improved upon it. Forrest J. Ackerman wrote that it was "the kind of story that make an old member of dinosaur fandom like me weep, 'Why don't they write yarns like this anymore?' " Thereafter followed a host of outstanding "thought variants" including "Before Earth Came," "The Blue Infinity," "Deserted Universe," and "Metamorphosis. " Equally noted were "Mathematica" and its sequel "Mathematica Plus. " Following his reading of Jeans and Eddington, Fearn contended that the Creator of the Universe is a Supreme Mathematician. His purpose is the creation of mathematics (actually thoughts), out of which he creates worlds and life. The object of his ageless existence is the ultimate cancellation of all figures, to destroy what he has created and release himself from an eternity of mental and figurative toil. Fearn revealed later to Walter Gillings that he had actually dreamed the idea for the stories while under anaesthetic (a method consciously adopted later by A. E. Van Vogt).

After 1939, sf magazines proliferated. With his widowed mother to support, Fearn was quick to realise that by using pseudonyms he could have several stories in the same issue of magazines, and so make a decent living. Between 1933 and 1948, Fearn published 130 stories, only 48 of them under his own name. Of his eight pen names, Thornton Ayre and Polton Cross rivalled his own in popularity. Outstanding Cross stories included "Wings Across the Cosmos" and "Wanderer of Time," both anthologised in the late forties. As Ayre he introduced detective "webwork" elements to sf, as in "Secret of the Ring" and "Twilight of the Tenth World." As Ayre he also created Violet Ray, the prototype of his famous superwoman, "The Golden Amazon." In 1944 he completely revised the character, upgrading his writing, and sold a novel, *The Golden Amazon* to World's Wor, in England. In 1945, the general magazine *Toronto Star Weekly* reprinted it in newspaper format as their "Novel of the Week." The story had a tremendous impact on the *Star's* 900,000 readers, few of whom were familiar with sf. The *Star* commissioned an Amazon series, which ran for 16 years, ending only with Fearn's death. Responding to reader demands, the *Star* commissioned the Scott Meredith Agency to find a writer to continue the series—without success. No other sf writer could duplicate Fearn's unique "popular" style. Fearn was in fact the *only* sf writer to be featured by the *Star* syndicate, which resold the novels to at least four American newspapers, giving each title a circulation of a quarter of a million.

Having found the lucrative *Star* market, Fearn quit the pulp magazines. He wrote detective thrillers as John Slate, beginning with *Black Maria, M. A.* (1944). Reviewers hailed Slate as a second Agatha Christie. In 1950, writing as Hugo Blayn, Fearn created the Dr. Carruthers scientific detective series, and also diversified into westerns. Suddenly, in 1950 British publishers became sf conscious. For Scion Ltd. Fearn wrote *Operation Venus*, a best-seller. Thereafter, Scion created the pen name Vargo Statten for use on Fearn's sf.

The Statten novels were phenomenal: 52 titles appeared over the next five years, selling five million copies, which led to the *Vargo Statten Science Fiction Magazine*. Fearn also wrote as Volsted Gridban, taking over the byline from E. C. Tubb. The Statten and Gridban titles were Scion's biggest sellers, ending only with the collapse of the British paperback houses in 1956, due to complex factors. Many of the novels were successfully translated in France, Italy, Denmark, and Germany.

A fresh burst of creativity followed Fearn's marriage in 1956. Films (as actor/writer/producer), television, radio, and stage plays were added to his regular writing. With his wife Carrie, he formed The Good Companions, a theatrical troupe. But the increased activity caught up with him: Fearn died of a sudden heart attack in 1960, aged only 52. His grief-stricken wife became too ill to promote his work, and Fearn was almost forgotton. The publication of a biography, *The Multi-Man*, by Philip Harbottle, in 1968, which revealed scores of pseudonyms, helped revive his reputation. Posthumous work appeared in the British magazine *Vision of Tomorrow* edited by Harbottle, who became Mrs. Fearn's agent. The French Stattens were revived in the 1970's as adult comic strips, while the original novels were "rediscovered" in Italy in 1977, remaining constantly in print ever since. The Italian publisher Ugo Malaguti, introducing a 600-page Statten "Classic" Omnibus in 1979 explained why: "Statten is like a naive painter; the apparent simplicity of his style conceals a technique and an ability that are in no way naive."

Modern critical opinion on Fearn, once dismissive, is gradually changing. Thus the compilers of *The Science Fiction Source Book* (1984) found that "his style is frankly abysmal," but admitted that "there is a fervid excitement in his work that can be quite effective." Frank Cioffi is in no doubt. Concluding his survey of early American sf magazine fiction in *Formula Fiction?* (1982), he asserted that " . . . the stories of . . . John Russell Fearn . . . are intelligent and entertaining and deserve to be made accessible to today's vast sf audience."

—Philip J. Harbottle

———

FELICE, Cynthia (née Lindgren). American. Born in Chicago, Illinois, 12 October 1942. Educated at North Park College, Elmhurst College, and University of Colorado, Colorado Springs. Married Robert Edward Felice in 1961; two sons. Sales engineer, Lindgren and Associates, Chicago, 1962-71; owner and manager, Glenn Russ Motel, Colorado Springs, 1972-78; technical writer, Kaman Sciences Corp., Colorado Springs, 1978-79; technical communications manager, Inmos Corp., Colorado Springs, 1979-81. Since 1981, Technical Communications Manager, United Technologies Microelectronics Center, Colorado Springs. Recipient: Society for Technical Communication award, 1984. Agent: Richard Curtis, Richard Curtis Associates, 164 East 64th Street, New York, New York 10021. Address: 5025 Park Vista Boulevard, Colorado Springs, Colorado 80928, U. S. A.

SCIENCE-FICTION PUBLICATIONS

Novels

Godsfire. New York, Pocket Books, 1978.
The Sunbound. New York, Dell, 1981.
Water Witch, with Connie Willis. New York, Ace, 1982.
Eclipse. New York, Pocket Books, 1982.
Downtime. New York, Bluejay, 1985.

Uncollected Short Stories

"Longshanks," in *Galileo 2* (New York), 1976.

"David and Lindy," in *Universe 8*, edited by Terry Carr. New York, Doubleday, 1978.
"No One Said Forever," in *Millenial Women*, edited by Virginia Kidd. New York, Delacorte Press, 1978.
"A Good Place to Be," in *Chrysalis 9*, edited by Roy Torgeson. New York, Doubleday, 1981.
"Track of a Legend," in *Omni* (New York), December 1983.

*   *   *

Cynthia Felice's work reflects her strong interest in creating complex human characters in unusual circumstances. In her first SF novel, *Godsfire*, Felice builds a sophisticated society where intelligent felines rule over their human slaves. Felice makes psychological points by having the novel narrated by one of the cat people who constantly points out the differences—often the superiority—of felines over humans. *Godsfire* also has its share of mysteries: Felice creates a planet that has a climate of constant rain, therefore the inhabitants are unaware of the existence of the sun. The origin of the humans on the planet is equally mysterious. Felice presents the reader with a clever plot and a great deal of social commentary which makes for fascinating reading.

The Sunbound explores relationships less successfully. Allis is in love with Daneth and pregnant by him. Yet Daneth has his own secret: he is an alien. When Daneth dies, he leaves Allis a fabulous jewel that confers telepathy to the holder. The crew of Daneth's ship seek him and find Allis and the jewel instead. When Milani, Daneth's former lover and co-captain of Daneth's ship *The Sovereign Sun*, discovers the situation, she vents her rage and hatred on Allis. Allis, bewieldered by events, feels she's been abused by the aliens and throws the jewel away. But Felice creates a crisis where only Allis and the power of the jewel can save the aliens from extinction. The plot of *The Sunbound* is too contrived and the character of Allis is too emotional, too childish, to be enjoyable.

In *Water Witch* Felice collaborates with the Nebula winner Connie Willis to create a desert planet called Mahali. As in Frank Herbert's *Dune*, finding and controlling water are the most important activities. Felice and Willis do a marvelous job with the main character, Deza, a young woman who pretends she's a member of the ruling family of water witches. Deza is feisty and sympathic at the same time. Her deception leads her into a wheels-within-wheels plot that Felice and Willis spin successfully. *Water Witch* is an outstanding science-fiction novel.

Eclipses is less outstanding. Felice writes a family saga set on another arid world called Seresunar. Beth, an anthropologist, marries Aram, heir to the Water Barony. Their relationship is a stormy one: their tempers lead them into infidelity and eventual reconciliation. Beth gives birth to a son whose wild nature shakes Serensunar's society. Yet the book is more of a romance novel than a science-fiction novel. The overheated love relationships tire after awhile in this long novel while the science-fiction aspects are underplayed.

Cynthia Felice is a promising new writer whose books center on complex character relationships that are as interesting as they are realistic.

—George Kelley

———

FERRAT, Jacques Jean. See **MERWIN, Sam, Jr.**

———

FINNEY, Jack (Walter Braden Finney). American. Born in Milwaukee, Wisconsin, in 1911. Educated at Knox College, Galesburg, Illinois. Married Marguerite Guest; one daughter and one son. Self-employed writer. Agent: Harold Matson Company, 276 Fifth Avenue, New York, New York 10001, U.S.A.

SCIENCE-FICTION PUBLICATIONS

Novels

The Body Snatchers. New York, Dell, and London, Eyre and Spottiswoode, 1955; as *Invasion of the Body Snatchers,* Dell, 1961; London, Sphere, 1978.
The Woodrow Wilson Dime. New York, Simon and Schuster, 1968.
Time and Again. New York, Simon and Schuster, 1970; London, Weidenfeld and Nicolson, 1980.
Marion's Wall. New York, Simon and Schuster, 1973.

Short Stories

The Third Level. New York, Rinehart, 1957; as *The Clock of Time,* London, Eyre and Spottiswoode, 1958.
I Love Galesburg in the Springtime: Fantasy and Time Stories. New York, Simon and Schuster, 1963; London, Eyre and Spottiswoode, 1965.
Forgotten News: The Crime of the Century and Other Lost Stories. New York, Doubleday, 1983.

Uncollected Short Story

"Double Take," in *Hollywood Unreel,* edited by Martin H. Greenberg and Charles G. Waugh. New York, Taplinger, 1982.

OTHER PUBLICATIONS

Novels

Five Against the House. New York, Doubleday, and London, Eyre and Spottiswoode, 1954.
The House of Numbers. New York, Dell, and London, Eyre and Spottiswoode, 1957.
Assault on a Queen. New York, Simon and Schuster, 1959; London, Eyre and Spottiswoode, 1960.
Good Neighbor Sam. New York, Simon and Schuster, and London, Eyre and Spottiswoode, 1963.
The Night People. New York, Doubleday, 1977.

Play

Telephone Roulette, adaptation of his story "Take a Number." Chicago, Dramatic Publishing Company, 1956.

*   *   *

Escapism is a term too often loosely applied to science-fiction, but in the case of Jack Finney it is strangely appropriate. His most enduring theme is escape from the pressures and irritations of the present, usually into an idyllic past, but sometimes to another planet or a parallel dimension. A popular magazine writer who produced many stories in areas other than science fiction, Finney has made himself into the poet of nostalgia and lost innocence within the genre, seldom more than peripherally concerned with the mechanisms of his science-fiction concepts or with how his characters get from this world to the other.

Ironically, Finney's most famous science-fiction novel is also his least characteristic. *The Body Snatchers* (filmed twice as *Invasion of the Body Snatchers*) is a suspenseful invasion-of-earth story that has gained the status of a minor classic because of the popularity of the film versions and because of the key element of paranoid fantasy that is the basic of its appeal: the notion that aliens might gradually replace the entire population of a city with exact duplicates without anyone noticing the difference. Although this idea had been current in science fiction long before Finney brought it to the attention of a wider public, the skill with which Finney unveils this horror and the fears abroad at the time he wrote the story—the "takeover" might as well be a metaphor for either Communism or McCarthyism—combined to give it an impact few science-fiction stories had previously had.

More characteristic are the short stories that Finney published during the 1950's collected in *The Third Level* and *I Love Galesburg in the Springtime.* The most common theme of these stories is time travel into the past. "I'm Scared," one of the best, details the gradual breakdown of the flow of historical time under psychological pressure from a population seeking to escape the present. In "Such Interesting Neighbours" the time travelers are from the future, but the motivation to escape their own time remains the same (the story ingeniously suggests that the end of the world will be brought about by time travel, because everyone will gradually abandon the future and redistribute themselves throughout history). "Of Missing Persons" replaces time travel with space travel, but the theme of escape remains central. Two stories, "The Third Level" and "Second Chance," suggest that certain things or locations can provide magical "portals" to the past; in "Second Chance" a meticulously reconstructed old car takes its driver into a past world simply because the experience he has in driving it parallels an experience that might have taken place when the car was new.

This notion that by meticulously recreating the past we can return to it was developed at great length in Finney's most ambitious novel, *Time and Again,* in which a volunteer for a secret government time-travel project finds himself in the Manhattan of 1882. Although only the vaguest references to Einstein serve to account for this time travel, and although there are inconsistencies of plot and historical verisimilitude (some of the latter are deliberate), the novel is a convincing portrait of a lost age and a persuasive account of what it might actually feel like to awake in a different time. Other Finney novels have dealt with the culture shock of different ages meeting using even less rationalistic devices—reincarnation, for example, in *Marion's Wall*—but *Time and Again* remains his most successful contribution to this genre. Though not fundamentally a science-fiction writer, Finney is a skilled narrator and an evocative stylist who frequently uses science-fiction themes with considerable effect.

—Gary K. Wolfe

FISK, Nicholas. British. Born in London, 14 October 1923. Educated at Ardingly College, Sussex. Served in the Royal Air Force during World War II. Married Dorothy Antoinette Fisk in 1949; twin daughters and two sons. Has worked as an actor, journalist, musician, editor, and publisher; illustrator of his own books and others; formerly head of the creative department, Percy Lund Humphries Ltd., printers, London. Agent: Laura Cecil, 17 Alwyne Villas, London N1 2HG. Address: 59 Elstree Road, Bushey Heath, Hertfordshire WD2 3QX, England.

SCIENCE-FICTION PUBLICATIONS (for children)

Novels (series: Starstormers)

Space Hostages. London, Hamish Hamilton, 1967; New York, Macmillan, 1969.
Trillions. London, Hamish Hamilton, 1971; New York, Pantheon, 1973.
Grinny. London, Heinemann, 1973; Nashville, Nelson, 1974.
High Way Home. London, Hamish Hamilton, 1973.
Little Green Spaceman. London, Heinemann, 1974.
Time Trap. London, Gollancz, 1976.
Wheelie in the Stars. London, Heinemann, 1976.
Antigrav. London, Kestrel, 1978.
Escape from Splatterbang. London, Pelham, 1978; New York, Macmillan, 1979; as *Flamers,* London, Knight, 1979.
Monster Maker. London, Pelham, 1979; New York, Macmillan, 1980.
A Rag, A Bone, and a Hank of Hair. London, Kestrel, 1980; New York, Crown, 1982.
The Starstormer Saga (Starstormers, Sunburst, Catfang, Evil Eye, Volcano). London, Knight, 5 vols., 1980-83.
Robot Revolt. London, Pelham, 1981.
On the Flip Side. London, Kestrel, 1983.
You Remember Me! London, Kestrel, 1984.

Short Stories

Sweets from a Stranger and Other Science Fiction Stories. London, Kestrel, 1982.

Uncollected Short Story (for adults)

"Find the Lady," in *New Dimensions 5,* edited by Robert Silverberg. New York, Harper, 1975; London, Gollancz, 1976.

OTHER PUBLICATIONS (for children)

Novels

The Bouncers. London, Hamish Hamilton, 1964.
The Fast Green Car. London, Hamish Hamilton, 1965.
There's Something on the Roof! London, Hamish Hamilton, 1966.
Emma Borrows a Cup of Sugar. London, Heinemann, 1973.
The Witches of Wimmering. London, Pelham, 1976.
Leadfoot. London, Pelham, 1980.
Snatched. London, Hodder and Stoughton, 1983.

Other

Look at Cars. London, Hamish Hamilton, 1959; revised edition, London, Panther, 1969.
Look at Newspapers. London, Hamish Hamilton, 1962.
Cars. London, Parrish, 1963.
The Young Man's Guide to Advertising. London, Hamish Hamilton, 1963.

Making Music. London, Joseph, 1966; Boston, Crescendo, 1969.
Lindbergh the Lone Flier. London, Hamish Hamilton, and New York, Coward McCann, 1968.
Richthofen the Red Baron. London, Hamish Hamilton, and New York, Coward McCann, 1968.

*

Nicholas Fisk comments:

I came fairly late to children's writing. It was a Puffin list that showed me the light. I was looking for a copy of Geoffrey Household's *Rogue Male* and found it in Puffin. I thought, if the publisher thinks fit to offer this title to children, the world must be changing. For the better.

Most of my output for children has been science fiction. The SF writer is fortunate in that, unhampered by present or past, he can invent his own games, rules and players. He is unfortunate in that he must make these matters clear—and explanation is the enemy of narration. Also, unfortunately, the genre is still not quite respectable, not quite nice. Perhaps the word science offends the nice palate? It offends mine. I am not a scientist, my books are not centered on the sciences. They are stories of possibility. Not SF, but IF—what would happen IF.

The stories are on a domestic, not a cosmic, scale because written words are not apt for the rendering of explosions and gargantuan hardware; these belong to the cinema. My central characters are children because the stories are written for children. This poses no problem and indeed may offer simplifications and speedings-up of the narrative. Although the stories have become more complex in subject and structure, I have learned from my own and countless other children that the quick, generous, adventurous mind can always stick to the point, even if the author must stagger about a bit in the hope of satisfying himself or a publisher's editor. And in any case today's children are no longer confined to some nursery ghetto. Families live in each other's laps, watching the same TV programmes. My readers and I are not unalike.

Other reasons for writing as I do include a distaste for most modern adult fiction coupled with a huge admiration for the writers and illustrators of present day children's books. I do various kinds of writing to earn a living; it is the children's writing that gives me the authentic tingle.

*   *   *

Nicholas Fisk is currently one of the best of those writers presenting "hard" SF to children. In such a situation a writer has two choices: to try to explain his science to a juvenile audience, or simply to ignore most of the problems as being outside his province. Fisk has tried both: *Antigrav* is a good story despite the lack of explanations; *Escape from Splatterbang* shows how such explanations can be at once trite and boring. By contrast, in *Trillions* the working out of a scientific answer forms an exciting and integral part of the plot. *Trillions* is also the book of Fisk's most likely to appeal to the adult reader, partly because of the scientific interest, partly because the "opposition" in *Trillions* is the Military Mind, as personified by General Hartman, in whom he will recognise all those who hate and fear what is alien to them. More usually in Fisk's books the forces of ignorance are the adults who ignore or fail to comprehend their children. The books can most usefully be seen from the point of view of an intelligent 11-year-old—old enough to see and understand the adult world of deceit and hypocrisy, but not old enough to change or participate in it.

One of Fisk's greatest strengths as a writer is his avoidance of clichés, both in plot and character. Indeed several of his books, most notably *Space Hostages* and *Antigrav*, are crucially concerned with a realisation that people do not conform to stereotypes. *Antigrav* rather neatly contrasts two scientists—one the classic sinister, balding geologist from behind the Iron Curtain, the other the expansive English all-rounder much given to appearing on TV chatshows. Arthur Sonning is summed up at the end as "You poor sap," while Czeslaw, victory gained, weighs the possible results of that victory and throws it away. It is further typical of Fisk that this moral superiority does not lessen the personal price which Czeslaw has to pay for "failure. " In *Space Hostages* an experienced reader of children's fiction is likely to be expecting the puny clever Pakistani to be triumphant at the expense of the village bully. What actually happens is that both discover their interdependence as Fisk shows that the very qualities which make Tony a bully are those which make him a successful leader in a time of crisis. In *Escape from Splatterbang* a hint of romance is raised, only to be quashed by the bitter-sweet ending as the gypsy girl, only half-understood to the end, disappears back among her people. Here, as in *Time Trap* and other of the novels, the ending respects and even underlines the realities of human behaviour.

Fisk is never likely to have a large adult audience; his books side too firmly with the children—but at least they do so plausibly. In *Grinny* (one of his best books) the reader looks on, as helpless as the children, while the implacable "Great Aunt Emma" manipulates adult minds to her own ends. The notable achievement of this book is the way (again avoiding cliché) that Grinny's curiosity is shown as most sinister—she pokes and pries into human habits and customs like someone lifting a stone to observe the earwigs. Fisk's one real incursion into teenage Sf—*Wheelie in the Stars*—is one of his poorest books: his clever-clever cardboard teenagers contrast very badly with the impotent desperation and reluctant courage of his children. This is more to be regretted since *High Way Home* shows how convincingly he can draw both teenagers and female characters (usually a notable blindspot). Fisk is not destined for a place among the Immortals: he lacks the necessary mastery of style and timeless appeal. But he is doing a competent job in a difficult field.

—Philippa Stephensen-Payne

FitzGIBBON, (Robert Louis) Constantine (Lee-Dillon). American. Born in Lenox, Massachusetts, 8 June 1919. Educated at Wellington College, 1933-35; University of Munich, and the Sorbonne, Paris, 1935-37; Exeter College, Oxford, 1937-39. Served in the British Army, 1939-42, and the United States Army, 1942-46: Major. Married 1) Marion Gutmann in 1960 (marriage dissolved), one son; 2) Marjorie Steele in 1967, one daughter. Schoolmaster, Saltus Grammar School, Bermuda, 1946-47. Member, Irish Academy of Letters; Fellow, Royal Society of Literature. *Died 23 March 1983.*

SCIENCE-FICTION PUBLICATIONS

Novels

The Iron Hoop. New York, Knopf, 1949; London, Cassell, 1950.

When the Kissing Had to Stop. New York, Norton, and London, Cassell, 1960.
The Golden Age. London, Hart Davis MacGibbon, and New York, Norton, 1975.
The Rat Report. London, Constable, 1980.

OTHER PUBLICATIONS

Novels

The Arabian Bird. New York, Rinehart, 1948; London, Cassell, 1949.
Cousin Emily. London, Cassell, 1952; as *Dear Emily*, New York, Simon and Schuster, 1952.
The Holiday. London, Cassell, and New York, Simon and Schuster, 1953.
In Love and War. London, Cassell, 1956; as *The Fair Game*, New York, Norton, 1956; as *Adultery under Arms*, London, Pan, 1962.
Watcher in Florence. Privately printed, 1959.
Going to the River. London, Cassell, and New York, Norton, 1963.
High Heroic. London, Dent, and New York, Norton, 1969.
In the Bunker. London, Macmillan, and New York, Norton, 1973.
Man in Aspic. London, Hart Davis MacGibbon, 1977.

Plays

The Devil He Did (produced London, 1969).
The Devil at Work (produced Dublin, 1971).

Other

Miss Finnigan's Fault. London, Cassell, 1953.
Norman Douglas: A Pictorial Record. London, Richards Press, 1953.
The Little Tour, with Giles Playfair. London, Cassell, 1954.
The Shirt of Nessus. London, Cassell, 1956; as *20 July*, New York, Norton, 1956; as *To Kill Hitler*, London, Stacey, 1972.
The Blitz, illustrated by Henry Moore. London, Wingate, 1957; as *The Winter of the Bombs*, New York, Norton, 1958.
Random Thoughts of a Fascist Hyena. London, Cassell, 1963; New York, Norton, 1964.
The Life of Dylan Thomas. London, Dent, and Boston, Little Brown, 1965.
Through the Minefield: An Autobiography. London, Bodley Head, and New York, Norton, 1967.
Denazification. London, Joseph, and New York, Norton, 1969.
Out of the Lion's Paw: Ireland Wins Her Freedom. London, Macdonald, and New York, American Heritage, 1969.
London's Burning. New York, Ballantine, 1970; London, Macdonald, 1971.
Red Hand: The Ulster Colony. London, Joseph, 1971; New York, Doubleday, 1972.
A Concise History of Germany. London, Thames and Hudson, 1972; New York, Viking Press, 1973.
The Life and Times of Eamon de Valera. Dublin, Gill and Macmillan, 1973; New York, Macmillan, 1974.
Secret Intelligence in the Twentieth Century. London, Hart Davis MacGibbon, 1976; New York, Stein and Day, 1977.
Teddy in the Tree (for children). New York, Doubleday, 1977.
Drink. New York, Doubleday, 1979; London, Granada, 1980.
The Irish in Ireland. Newton Abbot, Devon, David and Charles, and New York, Norton, 1983.

Editor, *Selected Letters of Dylan Thomas*. London, Dent, 1966; New York, New Directions, 1967.

Translator from German and French of some 40 books.

*

Constantine FitzGibbon commented:

(1981) I do not consider that I have ever written "science fiction. " I have written unusual novels, set in imaginary countries, at an imaginary future date or with a jumbled time sequence, as have Kafka and Joyce. As I grow older I become less interested in writing "realistic" novels, and give freer and freer play to my imagination. My most recent novel, *The Rat Report*, I have called, it is true, psi-fi, but that is not sci-fi, not in my opinion at least.

*   *   *

Constantine FitzGibbon's *The Golden Age* is a futuristic novel in which the world as we know it is drastically altered and in which mankind has virtually lost his knowledge of history. The world has been divided into two halves, the Upper World separated by a sort of force field from what is termed the Lower World (the southern hemisphere in our terms). The Upper World is now ruled from Oxford by a Monster (Emperor) and the four Horsemen who form his council. They decide that the future of the world must be left in the hands of Orpheus, the poet, as the priests, scientists, and other leaders of the past have simply led the world into chaos. It is FitzGibbon's contention that the poets know more about the universe than do the astronomers. As Orpheus, the central character, begins to rebuild the world in beauty, he enters into a bargain with Mephistopheles, who restores his memory at the cost of his soul. Seemingly victorious in his quest, Orpheus descends into the Underworld to regain Eurydice. A great part of the intrigue and fascination of the novel consists in FitzGibbon's deft reworking of the Orpheus and Mephistopheles myths and a clever blending of the two. The reader versed in classical literature will find the novel interesting and meaningful on a level lost to the average reader. *The Golden Age* Is a clever if somewhat overly literary and complex vision of the future based on an intriguing hypothesis and rewarding to the sensitive and discriminating reader.

FitzGibbon's earlier novel, *When the Kissing Had to Stop*, is set in the not-too-distant future and concerns itself with an England which has been taken over by totalitarianism and has become a Russian dependency.

—Joseph A. Quinn

FLINT, Homer Eon. American. Born in 1892. *Died in 1924.*

SCIENCE-FICTION PUBLICATIONS

Novels

The Blind Spot, with Austin Hall. Philadelphia, Prime Press, 1951; London, Museum Press, 1953.
The Devolutionist, and The Emancipatrix. New York, Ace, 1965.
The Lord of Death, and The Queen of Life. New York, Ace, 1965.

Uncollected Short Stories

"The Planeteer," in *All-Story Weekly* (New York), 9 March 1918.
"King of Conserve Island," in *All-Story Weekly* (New York), 12 October 1918.
"The Man in the Moon," in *All-Story Weekly* (New York), 4 October 1919.
"The Greater Miracle," in *All-Story Weekly* (New York), 24 April 1920.
"Out of the Moon," in *Argosy All-Story Weekly* (New York), 15 December 1923.
"The Nth Man," in *Amazing Stories Quarterly* (New York), Spring 1928.

See the essay on Austin Hall.

———

FONTENAY, Charles L(ouis). American. Born in Sao Paulo, Brazil, 17 March 1917. Attended Vanderbilt University, Nashville, 1966-67, 1968-70. Served in the United States Army Air Corps, 1942-43; Army censorship officer, 1943-46: Captain. Married 1) Glenda Miller in 1942 (divorced, 1960); 2) Martha Howard in 1963 (divorced, 1984), one daughter and one son. Reporter, sports editor, and city editor, *Daily Messenger*, Union City, Tennessee, 1936-40; editor, Associated Press, Nashville and Memphis, 1940-42; sports editor, *Press-Chronicle*, Johnson City, Tennessee, 1946. Since 1946, reporter, city editor, then rewrite editor, *The Tennessean*, Nashville. Recipient: Ted V. Rodgers Award, for journalism, 1957. Address: 2910-A Burch Avenue, Nashville, Tennessee 37203, U. S. A.

SCIENCE-FICTION PUBLICATIONS

Novels

Twice upon a Time. New York, Ace, 1958.
Rebels of the Red Planet. New York, Ace, 1961.
The Day the Oceans Overflowed . Derby, Connecticut, Monarch, 1964.

Uncollected Short Stories

"Escape Velocity," in *Infinity* (New York), October 1954.
"Blow the Man Down," in *If* (New York), March 1955.
"The Patriot," in *If* (New York), August 1955.
"The Strangest Man in the Universe," in *Other Worlds* (Evanston, Indiana), February 1956.
"Atom Drive," in *If* (New York), April 1956.
"Communication," in *If* (New York), October 1956.
"Family Tree," in *If* (New York), December 1956.
"Disqualified," in *The First World of If*, edited by James L. Quinn and Eve Wulff. Kingston, New York, Quinn, 1957.
"The Silk and the Song," in *The Best from Fantasy and Science Fiction 6*, edited by Anthony Boucher. New York, Doubleday, 1957.
"The Old Goat," in *If* (New York), February 1957.
"Blind Alley," in *If* (New York), March 1957.
"Up," in *Fantasy and Science Fiction* (New York), March 1957.
"A Case of Sunburn," in *If* (New York), April 1957.
"Moths," in *Science Fiction Adventures* (New York), April 1957.
"Pretty Quadroon," in *If* (New York), June 1957.

"The Last Brave Invader," in *If* (New York), August 1957.

"Earth Transit," in *Infinity* (New York), September 1957.

"The Heart's Long Wait," in *Flying Saucers from Other Worlds* (Evanston, Indiana), September 1957.

"Z," in *The Second World of If,* edited by James L. Quinn and Eve Wulff. Kingston, New York, Quinn, 1958.

"Chip on the Shoulder," in *Science Fiction Quarterly* (Holyoke, Massachusetts), February 1958.

"A Summer Afternoon," in *Fantasy and Science Fiction* (New York), February 1958.

"Never Marry a Venerian," in *Saturn* (Holyoke, Massachusetts), March 1958.

"West of Mars," in *Infinity* (New York), April 1958.

"Conservation," in *If* (New York), April 1958.

"Service with a Smile," in *If* (New York), June 1958.

"Beauty Interrupted," in *If* (New York), August 1958.

"The Gift Bearer,' in *Amazing* (New York), September 1958.

"Nothing's Impossible," in *Super Science Fiction* (New York), October 1958

"Bait," in *Amazing* (New York), February 1959.

"Ghost Planet," in *Fantasy and Science Fiction* (New York), February 1959.

"The Jupiter Weapon," in *Amazing* (New York), March 1959.

"Wind," in *Amazing* (New York), April 1959.

"Matchmaker," in *If* (New York), May 1960.

"Mariwite," in *Fantastic* (New York), November 1960.

OTHER PUBLICATIONS

Other

Epistle to the Babylonians: An Essay on the Natural Inequality of Man. Knoxville, University of Tennessee Press, 1969.

"How Br'er Fox Lost His Pelt," in *Pageant* (New York), April 1971.

The Keyen of Fu Tze. Sherborne, Gloucestershire, Coombe Springs Press, 1977.

Estes Kefauver: A Biography. Knoxville, University of Tennessee Press, 1980.

*

Charles L. Fontenay comments:

My science-fiction period was confined to the decade 1954-64. Most of my science fiction was of the adventure or "escapist" type, as contrasted to that line of science fiction oriented to some serious sociological "message" or an attempted extrapolation of current trends; I think it would be legitimate to call it the *Star Wars* type. However, I was often pretty heavy on the scientific basis for the story, to the point that an entire story—or an entire novel—was built around a single scientific gimmick. Despite this general orientation, my science fiction contributed a great deal to the thinking that served as the basis of my later philosophical writing. I think this connection is apparent in some of the stories, but I would be hard put to express it in so many words.

* * *

Charles L. Fontenay's SF career spanned a bit more than a decade, ending with the 1964 publication of *The Day the Oceans Overflowed,* a disaster novel. With a writer who produced no major work and who hasn't written in the field for more than 20 years, it is presumptuous to claim any reputation other than hazy. But it is not a fair one in view of much of his short fiction.

He did write space opera, however, much of it forming a generalized future history, and some of it dealing with problems posed by the time-dilation effect of travel at the speed of light. "The Strangest Man in the Universe" is a fair but remarkable adventure story that finds a spaceship crew stranded on a backward planet, where they also encounter a benevolent superman (another of Fontenay's favorite themes). "The Heart's Long Wait" is a decidedly more interesting story, a character study of a spaceman alienated from ordinary humans by his profession. The story is sentimental but still effective.

It was Fontenay's trademark to take a standard idea—time-dilation, evolutionary supermen, the paradoxes of time travel—and develop a good, often quite original variation on it. His stories were usually well constructed, and his writing style clear and readable. If he were to be grouped with any other SF writers, they would probably be Poul Anderson and Gordon Dickson—but Fontenay never displayed Anderson's passion for the poetic in science and nature, or Dickson's thematic strength. He told stories about ideas. But he had other virtues as well, especially an ability to explore his ideas in terms of unobtrusive character development.

It is this lack of character development, in part, that prevents "Z" from being wholly effective. It's a neatly conceived handling of essentially the same idea Heinlein used in "By His Bootstraps," somewhat updated with the addition of a sex-change in the plotline, but not up to the standards of Heinlein's original story. "Pretty Quadroon," however, another time travel story, is one of Fontenay's best works. In the near future, a segregationist South has again seceded from the Union, leading to a second War Between the States. The story's protagonist is a statesman and general whose fiery speech at a conference of Southern governors has made him the pivotal figure in the events leading to the war. His mistress, the quadroon of the title, introduces him to a practitioner of voodoo who believes he can alter the past, thus preventing the war from ever having happened. Again and again the time paths are altered, until it becomes obvious that the key to success lies in preventing the man from ever having met the woman he loves. The strong idea in "Family Tree" might almost be taken for a joke: humans have evolved not from apes, but rodents. The story, however, is serious: an evolutionary superman is threatened by human bigotry. What sets the story apart is Fontenay's insightful portrayal of his central character, a moral rabble-rouser out to destroy the superman.

Fontenay stopped producing magazine fiction as the 1950's closed. His first novel, *Twice Upon a Time,* like "The Heart's Long Wait," deals with a young spaceman whose life and attitudes pivot on his career and on the fact of the time-dilation effect. A member of a trouble-shooter corps designed to police interstellar colonies, he's sent to one of several planets where it's feared rebellion may be brewing. The theft of his spaceship on his arrival and the complexities of the social and political situation make the novel suspenseful, but a time-travel sub-plot and a pat ending put the book on a level somewhere below his best short fiction. *Rebels of the Red Planet* is even more disappointing. Genetic experiments on Mars, leading to super-beings and other mutations, are played off against another plot involving a growing rebel movement. Fontenay doesn't add much to either idea, although some of his scenes between normal humans and the laboratory-bred mutations are interestingly outré.

Whether Fontenay abandoned the field too early or simply lacked the ability to write novels of quality comparable to his best short fiction, his novels have added nothing to his reputation. His lapse into obscurity, among the many hundreds of writers who have worked the field since this time, is probably inevitable. But time hasn't rendered his fiction less readable. His trademark was his ability to work stories around ideas cleverly derived from familiar themes. But his strength was that so often these ideas were explained from the points of view of rather interesting people.

—Gerald W. Page

FORSTCHEN, William R. American. Address: c/o Ballantine Books, 201 East 50th Street, New York, New York 10022, U.S.A.

SCIENCE- FICTION PUBLICATIONS

Novels

Ice Prophet. New York, Ballantine, 1983.
The Flame upon the Ice. New York, Ballantine, 1984.
The Darkness upon the Ice. New York, Ballantine, 1985.

* * *

William R. Forstchen attracted immediate attention with the publication of Ice Prophet, first of a trilogy set in a primitive future society in which ice covers the Earth's surface as the result of a scientific experiment which went awry, altering the planet's ecology. A network of city states is dominated by the Cornathian Brotherhoods, a theocracy which is divided against itself because of hidden rivalries, including a secret priesthood with a generations-long plan to secure ultimate power for themselves.

Since it was scientific innovation that wrecked the old world, the Brotherhoods have forbidden innovation to the populace, although they have secret hoards of supposedly lost knowledge. Michael Ormson is the charismatic leader who arises in response to this restriction, whose philosophy is freedom from religious persecution and the desirability of new knowledge which might allow mankind to once again rule its own world. Against his wishes, he comes to be viewed as a messianic figure, and bloody warfare ensues as a response to his heresy.

By the opening of the second novel, The Flame upon the Ice, Ormson is the head of a rebellious army controlling the southern islands. He and his allies have devised new methods of conducting warfare on ice-travelling warships, the details of which reflect Forstchen's own interest in ice sailing. The battle scenes are bloody, violent, and convincing, as he works out the tactical and strategic necessities of war on the ice fields. Unbeknownst to Ormson, he has become the tool of the secret priesthood, the instrument through which they plan to crush the power of the Cornathian Brotherhoods and depose the present leader, Zimri.

Complicating matters further is Ormson's personal disturbance at the horrors perpetrated in his name. Rather than bring a new freedom to mankind, he has caused more death and destruction than the world has known in generations. The empire to the east begins to extend its influence as well, hoping to take advantage of a power vacuum during the turmoil. Finally the southern forces strike north and capture the major cities of the enemy, driving him to inland fortresses.

The established church is resurgent in The Darkness upon the Ice. Using devices developed in their secret laboratories, they attack Ormson's army with cannons and air surveillance. The populace is in general unrest, not entirely convinced of the wisdom of Ormson's followers, and the prophet himself appears to be dying of some wasting disease following the murder of his family. Finally the secret brotherhood is ready to make its bid for power as Ormson's army falls back to reconsider its next move, only to be pursued by the now superior forces of the church. But in their attempt to defeat Ormson's hope for technological development and an end to the old way of life, the church itself has ensured that Ormson's goal has become inevitable.

Forstchen's trilogy is not a unique or new contribution to the genre. The setting is similar to that of Michael Moorcock's The Ice Schooner and the messianic battle against entrenched self-interest is one of the standard plots of the field. But Forstchen has added superior characterization, a wealth of fully realized detail about warfare on the ice, and a complex interplay of political manipulation.

—Don D'Ammassa

FORWARD, Robert L(ull). Also writes as Susan Lull. American. Born in Geneva, New York, 15 August 1932. Educated at the University of Maryland, College Park, 1950-54, B. S. 1954; University of California, Los Angeles, M. S. 1958; University of Maryland, Ph. D. in physics 1965. Served in the United States Air Force, 1954-56: Captain. Married Martha Neil Dodson in 1954; one son and three daughters. Technical staff member, 1956-66, Associate Manager, Theoretical Studies Department, 1966-67, Manager, Exploratory Studies Department, 1967-74, and since 1974, Senior Scientist, Hughes Research Laboratories, Malibu, California. Since 1983, consultant on advanced propulsion concepts. Recipient: Gravity Research Foundation award, 1965; IEEE-AES Carlton Award, 1981; Locus award, 1981; Star-Cloud award (Japan), 1982. Agent: Scott Meredith Literary Agency, 845 Third Avenue, New York, New York 10022. Address: 34 Carriage Square, Oxnard, California 93030, U. S. A.

SCIENCE-FICTION PUBLICATIONS

Novels

Dragon's Egg. New York, Ballantine, 1980; London, New English Library, 1981.
The Flight of the Dragonfly. New York, Pocket Books, 1984.
Starquake! New York, Ballantine, 1985.

Uncollected Short Stories

"I Demand the Stars for My Children!" (as Susan Lull), in Galileo (New York), September 1979.
"The Cerebrated Jumping Frog of Calaveras III," with Martha Dodson, in Stellar 6, edited by Judy-Lynn del Rey. New York, Random House, 1980.
"The Singing Diamond," in The Best of Omni Science Fiction 2, edited by Ben Bova and Don Myrus. New York, Omni, 1981.
"Rocheworld" (serial) in Analog (New York), December, January, and February 1982-83.
"Twin Paradox," in Analog (New York), August 1983.

*

Robert L. Forward comments:

I write *hard* science fiction. After I have decided upon a general story idea, but before I write a detailed outline, I spend 6-9 months collecting data, calculating orbits, drawing vehicles and habitats, designing alien physiologies and cultures, and working out timelines. During this "science research" phase, the requirements of the laws of science suggest (and sometimes force) the plot line to move in a certain direction. Thus, in one sense, the science writes the fiction. In my first two novels, ideas that were generated during this research phase were so novel and so scientifically sound, that I turned them into scientific papers that were later published in scientific archive journals (with a footnote referencing the novel as the first publication of the idea). The drawings and the results of this research phase are usually included as a technical appendix to the novel.

*   *   *

The novels of Robert L. Forward display his scientific background to great advantage. As a senior scientist at Hughes Research Laboratory in Malibu, California, and at the University of Maryland, Forward has conducted research into gravitational radiation from supernovas, black holes, neutron stars, gravity sensors, and laser propulsion. These subjects of his research have been used as material for both *Dragon's Egg* and *The Flight of the Dragonfly*.

Several themes recur in both works: initial alien/human encounters, the congeniality of intelligent life, and the proposition that life can evolve in conditions considered to be inimical to life as known on Earth.

Dragon's Egg posits a neutron star with a gravity of 67 billion gees and a magnetic field of almost a trillion gauss. When the neutron star approaches the solar system, plans to study the body are implemented and a crew from Earth begins its scientific survey on 22 May 2050. Shortly thereafter the cheela, the intelligent form of life on Dragon's Egg, become aware of the observers in their sky and contact is achieved on 20 June 2050. Much of the novel is devoted to a depiction of the history of the cheela and their ascent from savagery to civilization. The work has affinities to Anatole France's *Penguin Inland*, although little satire is apparent, and to Hal Clement's *Mission of Gravity*. The cheela are a fascinating concept, and Forward supplies a series of appendixes outlining their physiology and the "geology" of Dragon's Egg. The human characters are less satisfactory as personalities than are the various cheela heroines and heros. The book derives its great strength from the portrayal of the manner in which the tremendous gravity and magnetic field influence the history and biology of the neutron star intelligences. The creation of mathematics, religion, and science are observed in detail. The time scale of the cheela is vastly compressed and one of their generations passes in 15 minutes. This speed allows the creatures to surpass the humans who have undertaken their education. The novel ends one day later, 1 June 2050, and we have observed the entire evolution of the cheela from inanimate matter to explorers of the Milky Way.

The Flight of the Dragonfly explores the consequences for life on Rocheworld. This world is a dumbbell-shaped planet, sharing a common atmosphere. One of the planets, called the Eau Lobe, is covered by an ocean of ammonia water with trace amounts of hydrogen sulfide and cyanide gas. The other planet, called Roche Lobe, is usually devoid of a liquid covering, but periodically the ocean from the Eau Lobe rains down on the Roche Lobe. The interactions among the gravitational forces, and the chemical reactions and chemical equilibria, form the background against which an exploratory team from Earth makes contact with the intelligent life form on Rocheworld, the "flouwen. " These aliens are much more intelligent than the humans with whom they interact, but the only science which they have truly developed is mathematics. Most of the book concerns the rescue of the *Dragonfly*, an exploratory vessel, from the ocean of Eau Lobe, and the beginnings of communication between the humans and the "flouwen. " The humans are almost cursorily depicted and a cast of characters helps sort them out. The "flouwen" carry greater interest in this work; however, they are not as interesting as the cheela of the earlier work.

Both novels may be considered "hard science fiction" and the inclusion of appendixes serves the reader well. Forward's descriptions of the interactions between alien and human species eschews the paranoia which was a common feature of much earlier science fiction.

—Harvey J. Satty

———————

FOSTER, Alan Dean. Also writes as George Lucas. American. Born in New York City, 18 November 1946. Educated at the University of California, Los Angeles, B. A. in political science 1968; M. F. A. in film 1969. Served in the United States Army Reserve, 1969-75. Married JoAnn Oxley in 1975. Head copywriter, Headlines Ink Agency, Studio City, California, 1970-71; instructor in English and film, University of California, Los Angeles, intermittently since 1971, and Los Angeles City College, 1972-76. Since 1981, Columnist, *Rigel*, Richmond, California. Agent: (fiction) Virginia Kidd, Box 278, Milford, Pennsylvania 18337; (scripts) Ilse Lahn, Paul Kohner Agency, 9169 Sunset Boulevard, Hollywood, California 90069. Address: 4001 Pleasant Valley Drive, Prescott, Arizona 86301, U. S. A.

SCIENCE-FICTION PUBLICATIONS

Novels (series: Flinx; Skua September; Spellsinger; Star Trek)

The Tar-Aiym Krang (Flinx). New York, Ballantine, 1972; London, New English Library, 1979.
Bloodhype. New York, Ballantine, 1973; London, New English Library, 1979.
Icerigger (September). New York, Ballantine, 1974; London, New English Library, 1976.
Luana. New York, Ballantine, 1974.
Dark Star (novelization of screenplay). New York, Ballantine, 1974; London, Futura, 1979.
Star Trek Log One [to Ten], New York, Ballantine, 10 vols., 1974-78.
Star Wars (as George Lucas). New York, Ballantine, 1976.
Midworld. New York, Doubleday, 1975; London, Macdonald and Jane's 1977.
Orphan Star (Flinx). New York, Ballantine, 1977; London, New English Library, 1979.
The End of the Matter (Flinx). New York, Ballantine, 1977; London, New English Library, 1979
Splinter of the Mind's Eye. New York, Ballantine, and London, Sphere, 1978.
Mission to Moulokin (September). New York, Ballantine, and London, New English Library, 1979.
Alien (novelization of screenplay). New York, Ballantine, and London, Macdonald and Jane's, 1979.

The Black Hole (novelization of screenplay). New York, Ballantine, 1979.

Cachalot. New York, Ballantine, 1980.

Outland (novelization of screenplay). New York, Warner, and London, Sphere, 1981.

Clash of the Titans (novelization of screenplay). New York, Warner, and London, Macdonald, 1981.

The Thing (novelization of screenplay). New York, Bantam, and London, Corgi, 1982.

Nor Crystal Tears. New York, Ballantine, 1982.

For Love of Mother-Not. New York, Ballantine, 1983.

Spellsinger at the Gate. Huntington Woods, Michigan, Phantasia Press, 1983.

   Spellsinger. New York, Warner, 1983; London, Futura, 1984.

   The Hour at the Gate. New York, Warner, and London, Futura, 1984.

Krull (novelization of screenplay). New York, Warner, and London, Corgi, 1983.

The Man Who Used the Universe. New York, Warner, 1983.

The I Inside. New York, Warner, 1984.

Voyage to the City of the Dead. New York, Ballantine, 1984.

Slipt. New York, Berkley, 1984.

The Last Starfighter (novelization of screenplay). New York, Berkley, 1984.

The Day of the Dissonance (Spellsinger). Huntington Woods, Michigan, Phantasia Press, 1984.

The Moment of the Magician (Spellsinger). Huntington Woods, Michigan, Phantasia Press, 1984.

Starman (novelization of screenplay). New York, Warner, 1984.

Shadowkeep. New York, Warner, 1984.

Sentenced to Prism. New York, Ballantine, 1985.

Pale Rider. New York, Warner, 1985.

Short Stories

With Friends Like These. New York, Ballantine, 1977.

. . . Who Needs Enemies? New York, Ballantine, 1984.

OTHER PUBLICATIONS

Play

Screenplay: *Star-Trek*, 1979.

Other

Editor, *The Best of Eric Frank Russell*. New York, Ballantine, 1978.

Editor, *Animated Features and Silly Symphonies*. New York, Abbeville, 1980.

*

Alan Dean Foster comments:

The majority of my science-fiction novels take place in what is called the University of the Commonwealth, a future sociopolitical spatial government in which man has formed a particularly intimate alliance with a race of insect-like creatures called the Thranx. Within that universe I'm able to tell an immense variety of tales. Some relate to one other, such as *The Tar-Aiym Krang, Orphan Star,* and *The End of the Matter.* These form a trilogy dealing with the adolescence of an extraordinary youth named Flinx. Other books use characters interchangeably. For example, a minor character in *The End of*

the Matter named Skua September is a major protagonist in the novels *Icerigger* and *Mission to Moulokin,* the pair forming a single massive story.

Eventually (say, in another 40 years), many seemingly unrelated characters and events will tie together, forming a long narrative extending over some 50 years and, possibly, as many books. Other novels will be set in the Commonwealth universe but will remain unrelated to this central narrative. Still other novels and stories will have nothing to do with the Commonwealth at all.

Most of my shorter fiction is independent of the Commonwealth background. While my novel-length work tends to be rather adventure oriented, my shorter fiction explores more personal, individualized events. In the novels I am interested in exploring how people, especially average people, are forced to react to extraordinary circumstances and events much greater than themselves or their personal concerns. In my shorter fiction I try to delve more deeply into the "human condition." It might be fair to say that the novels force my characters to look outside themselves while the short fiction induces them to look inward.

Particular aspects of science that interest me and are often touched upon in my stories include ecology, the unexplored potentiality of the human mind, and the accidence of history (the way in which massive events are often set in motion utterly unintentionally, and are forced to conclusions and resolutions unimagined by those caught up in such socio-political-personal vortices).

*   *   *

Although Alan Dean Foster broke into professional science fiction with short stories after the fashion of Robert Sheckley and Eric Frank Russell (as seen in the collection *With Friends Like These*), he has gained the greater part of his fame through his screenplay adaptations (*Alien, Star Wars*) and his novels. For the most part the adaptive novels do not give one much insight into this writer, though mention must be made of one original novel using the characters and milieu of *Star Wars—Splinter of the Mind's Eye.* It is an unsuccessful attempt to work within the parameters of the limited mythology of the Lucas series, but in its choice of plotlines—Luke and Leia must retrieve a magical crystal before Darth Vader can—it is a novel that illustrates Foster's predilection for combining ingenious concepts with ingenuous characters; characters too facile to give the concepts the philosophical life they require.

Because of this, it is not incorrect to style most of Foster's original novels as "light" science-fiction adventure. Illustrative of this are several of the novels in Foster's "Commonwealth" universe—which, it must be said, is one of the few universes in which spacefaring humans freely mix with members of an alien species on a routine, day-to-day basis, and not merely for melodramatic purposes. One trilogy of novels—comprised of *The Tar-Aiym Krang, Orphan Star,* and *The End of the Matter*—deals with Flinx, a young psychically endowed orphan who frequently takes on formidable galactic powers, armed chiefly with his wits and poison-spitting serpent-pet. As juvenile wish-fulfillment, these novels have a number of appealing features; as literature, they could be compared to cotton candy—colorful and pleasing to the taste, but less than filling. These novels lack the sense of true danger that gives zest to the better adventure-novels, for the villains are rarely allowed to get the upper hand, and are too easily defeated. Nor are the heroic characters capable of more than rudimentary emotions—at the end of *Orphan Star*, Foster can describe

Flinx's sadness at seeing the death of a female criminal who turns out to be his long-lost sister, but he fails to make the reader feel that emotion. Similar problems plague such works as *Cachalot*, in which the intelligent, whale-like denizens of a water-world are being turned against humanity, where Foster spends more time characterizing the different breeds of alien whale than the human characters, and *Spellsinger*, where the "villains" are more comical than threatening.

To Foster's credit, though, his works are always characterized by a scrupulous exactitude regarding the sciences, physical environments, and time-period. His best single novel, for this reason, is one that concentrates on the physical concept against which the simple characters stand like figures in a tapestry. *Midworld*, like Aldiss's *Long Afternoon of Earth* and Le Guin's *The Word for World is Forest*, focuses on a world of teeming plant life—although on Midworld the jungle foliage is so profuse that it forms a number of "canopies," or levels that are capable of supporting life. In particular a colony of stranded humans have built their village in one such canopy, and have evolved an animistic hunter-culture, whose love of nature, despite its destructive aspects, is totally at odds with that of the human space-explorers who land on and attempt to subvert Midworld. *Midworld* is Foster's most philosophically oriented novel, pitting the Midworlders, who symbolize nature-love, against the humans, who represent the aversion of technology to everthing it cannot control.

Lastly, of the "light adventure" novels, Foster did reach a high point in the two-book series *Icerigger* and *Mission to Moulokin*. These works have a fast, Burroughsian pace, and use melodrama and comedy with greater skill than in any other Foster works. Further, in *Icerigger* Foster creates his most original alien concept: the cat-faced, bat-winged Tran, who dwell on the ice-covered world of Tran-ky-ky by means of biologically-evolved foot-"skates. " Such novels as *Midworld* and *Icerigger* show Foster's capacity for inventiveness and for fast-paced adventure, and if his handling of other aspects are less well done, one may still value Foster for succeeding where many of his contemporaries have proved far more conventional than he.

—Gene Phillips

FOSTER, M(ichael) A(nthony). American. Born in Greensboro, North Carolina, 2 July 1939. Educated at Greensboro High School, graduated 1957; Syracuse University, New York, 1957-58, 1959-60; University of Maryland extension courses in Karamursel, Turkey, 1961-62; University of Oregon, Eugene, 1962-64, B. A. in Slavic languages 1964. Married Judith Ann Forsythe in 1965; two sons. Served in the United States Air Force, 1957-62, 1965-76: Russian linguist, 1957-62, Intelligence, 1965-71, Strategic Missiles, 1971-75, and Intercept Weapons Director, 1975-76: Captain. Department Manager, Allied Stores, Greensboro, 1976-78; salesman, Sunox Inc., 1978-84. Since 1984, full-time writer. Photographer: individual shows—Rapid City, South Dakota, 1972, 1973, 1974, Address: 5409 Amberhill Drive, Greensboro, North Carolina 27405, U.S.A.

SCIENCE-FICTION PUBLICATIONS

Novels (series: Ler; Morphodite)

The Warriors of Dawn (Ler). New York, DAW, 1975; London,
Hamlyn, 1979.
The Gameplayers of Zan (Ler). New York, DAW, 1977; London, Hamlyn, 1979.
The Day of the Klesh (Ler). New York, DAW, 1979.
Waves. New York, DAW, 1980.
The Morphodite. New York, DAW, 1981.
Transformer (Morphodite). New York, DAW, 1983.
Preserver (Morphodite). New York, DAW, 1985.

Short Stories

Owl Time. New York, DAW, 1985.

Uncollected Short Story

"Dreams," in *The John W. Campbell Awards 5*, edited by George R. R. Martin. New York, Bluejay, 1984.

OTHER PUBLICATIONS

Verse

Shards from Byzantium. Privately printed, 1969.
The Vaseline Dreams of Hundifer Soames. Privately printed, 1970.

*

M. A. Foster comments:

I started writing because I was having difficulty finding good books; they didn't have to be great—just good reads, enjoyable and provocative. Others I spoke with admitted the same problem, in the late sixties and early seventies, so it seemed a good idea. As I have gotten deeper into writing, I have identified some specific guides I used, unconsciously at first, but more deliberately later on:

The story occurs in the reader's mind, not on paper; therefore the minimum writing should be used to cause this to occur. The story should be translatable, and not rely on fads which date works.

The story must move forward because of drama, not action or violence.

Deep and subtle moral and ethical problems in contemporary thought should be touched upon, preferably used as main themes.

The story must attempt to present ordinary beings in extraordinary circumstances, not the reverse, in which the characters have to reach in some ways beyond the ordinary to survive or comprehend what is happening.

Real science must be distinguishable from speculation. The use of pop sci-fi generic artifacts must be kept to a minimum.

Room must be made for the reader to participate in the story, by the inclusion of loose ends which may lead elsewhere, and by the use of "suggestive-descriptive" backgrounds which allow for the imagination of the reader.

Within the limitations of the genre, everything should be as realistic as possible. Characters should act with normal functions, strengths, weaknesses, beliefs, and doubts.

The stress of the story must be on individuals, not members of some organization, government, or cult. Characters must make specific and individual choices.

I should exploit and develop my own kind of story and not attempt to write anything and everything.

As much as possible, I attempt to fuse SF with mainstream literature, not separate them.

* * *

Since his advent on the SF scene with *The Warriors of Dawn* in 1975, M. A. Foster has assembled a notable body of novels and one short-novel collection entitled *Owl Time* .

While the selections in *Owl Time* differ somewhat from the rest of Foster's corpus, all the full-length novels have several characteristics in common. They are loosely plotted, with emphasis on character and setting rather than on story development. Each depends on the perspective of one, or at most two, viewpoint characters. This classical approach to story telling is used to especially good advantage in the *The Morphodite* and *The Transformer*, where the viewpoint character becomes younger and changes sex through various genetically coded transformations. Finally, Foster displays an anti-deterministic philosophy through both theme and technique. The plot in each novel turns around the solution of a many-leveled mystery, an attempt to discover who or what is manipulating the society on a particular world. The author repeatedly introduces variations on Tarot and the *I-Ching*, both oracular methods of predicting a deterministic future, but the ultimate answer to each quest lies in the actions of certain single individuals.

Five of Foster's novels also focus on the consequences and the potential of genetic manipulation. *The Warriors of Dawn*, *The Gameplayers of Zan*, and *The Day of the Klesh* develop from the premise that human attempts to create a superhuman race called Ler will yield unwanted results. *Gameplayers*, chronologically first in the full tale, documents the agony of mistrust and misunderstanding that sends most Ler off to the planet from which warriors (in *The Warriors of Dawn*) appear. The Klesh, humans that these Warriors have enslaved for purposes of breeding, are freed to migrate to Monsalvat, the planet which forms the backdrop for the third novel in the story's internal chronology, *The Day of the Klesh*.

The Morphodite and *The Transformer* presuppose a more refined set of techniques for manipulating the genetic makeup of live beings. These techniques are perfected on a backwater planet called Oerlikon to result in a being who can change his/her protoplasmic shape at will. Rael/Damistofa/Phaedrus uses an extension of principles upon which the *I-Ching* was constructed to "read" the world around him/her and discover which act is most likely to cause the disintegration of a rigid Oerlikon society. However, like the Ler in Foster's first trilogy, his/her power soon outstrips that of her immediate creators. The sensitive handling of female characters, both in the person of the viewpoint character in one of his/her states and her companions when s/he is male, is more developed in these two novels. This ability of Foster sensitively to present female characters such as Fellerian, Snajirmil, and Mevlannen (*Gameplayers*) led to speculation with the first two novels that he was himself female, and is thus no minor accomplishment. In fact, many of the techniques such as elaborate description through footnotes as well as in-text references, multi-layered plot, and "scientification" of divination tools are displayed with much refinement in these two novels. While *Gameplayers* was originally my favorite of his works because of the Ler-viewpoint character Morelenden, the latter two novels hold up much better to rereading.

Waves is the most Russian of Foster's novels, taking place on a planet which seems to have been settled by people of that national grouping. While the setting reflects his language ability (he acted in the capacity of Russian linguist while with the U. S. Air Force), the plot follows a linguistic mystery—an ocean which seems to speak a language. Perhaps because he had to resolve the mystery in the course of only one novel, Foster was not as successful in substituting his own type of multi-plotted complexity for tight structure. In fact the plot tends to get lost in the love-story of his two protaganists. *Waves* is slow-paced, somewhat lyrical, and reminiscent of Lem's *Solaris* without its weighty philosophy.

Foster's short novels, four of which appeared in *Owl Time*, are attempts to vary his style after the patterns of contemporary SF and non-SF writers. Yet, with the possible exception of "The Conversation," they seem very much Foster. For example, "Entertainment," which is supposed to emulate Jack Vance, incorporates the footnotes, prefatory quotations, single viewpoint character, and puzzle-plot of his earlier fiction. Whether the set of experiments represented in this book have been successful in further developing his own unique style remains to be seen.

—Janice M. Bogstad

FOWLER, Sydney. See **WRIGHT, S. Fowler.**

FOX, Gardner F(rancis). Also writes as Jefferson Cooper; Lynna Cooper; Jeffrey Gardner; James Kendricks; Simon Majors; Kevin Matthews; Bart Somers. American. Born in Brooklyn, New York, 20 May 1911. Educated at St. John's University, Jamaica, New York, B. A. 1932, LL. B. 1935. Married Lynda J. Negrini in 1937; one son and one daughter. Lawyer. Since 1937, comic-book writer (*Batman, Superman, The Flash, Green Lantern,* and others), and since 1938, free-lance writer. Agent: Scott Meredith, 845 Third Avenue, New York, New York 10022. Address: 503-0 Stockton Lane, Jamesburg, New Jersey 08831, U. S. A.

SCIENCE-FICTION PUBLICATIONS

Novels (series: Commander Craig)

Five Weeks in a Balloon (novelization of screenplay). New York, Pyramid, 1962.
Escape Across the Cosmos. New York, Paperback Library, 1964.
The Arsenal of Miracles. New York, Ace, 1964.
Warrior of Llarn. New York, Ace, 1964.
The Hunter out of Time. New York, Ace, 1965.
Beyond the Black Enigma (Craig; as Bart Somers). New York, Paperback Library, 1965.
Thief of Llarn. New York, Ace, 1966.
Abandon Galaxy (Craig; as Bart Somers). New York, Paperback Library, 1967.
The Druid Stones (as Simon Majors). New York, Paperback Library, 1965.
Conehead. New York, Ace, 1973.
Carty. New York, Doubleday, 1977; London, Hale, 1979.

Uncollected Short Stories

"The Weirds of the Woodcarver," in *Weird Tales* (New York), September 1944.
"The Last Monster," in *Planet* (New York), Fall 1945.
"Man Nth," in *Planet* (New York), Winter 1945.
"Engines of the Gods," in *Planet* (New York), Spring 1946.

"Heart of Light," in *Amazing* (New York), July 1946.

"The Man the Sun Gods Made," in *Planet* (New York), Winter 1946.

"Sword of the Seven Suns," in *Planet* (New York), Spring 1947.

"Vassals of the Lode-Star," in *Planet* (New York), Summer 1947.

"Werewile of the Crystal Crypt," in *Planet* (New York), Summer 1948.

"When Kohonnes Screamed," in *Planet* (New York), Fall 1948.

"Crom the Barbarian" (comic), in *Out of This World Adventures* (New York), July 1950.

"Temptress of the Time Flow," in *Marvel* (New York), November 1950.

"The Spider God of Akka" (comic), in *Out of This World Adventures* (New York), December 1950.

"The Warlock of Sharrador," in *Planet* (New York), March 1953.

"The Holding of Kolymar," in *Fantastic* (New York), October 1971.

"Tonight the Stars Revolt!," in *Galactic Empires,* edited by Brian Aldiss. London, Weidenfeld and Nicolson, 1976; New York, St. Martin's Press, 1977.

"Shadow of a Demon," in *The Year's Best Fantasy Stories 3,* edited by Lin Carter. New York, DAW, 1977.

OTHER PUBLICATIONS

Novels

The Borgia Blade. New York, Fawcett, 1953; London, Fawcett, 1954.

Madame Buccaneer. New York, Fawcett, 1953; London, Fawcett, 1954.

Woman of Kali. New York, Fawcett, 1954; London, Muller, 1960.

The Gentleman Rogue. New York, Fawcett, 1954; London, Red Seal, 1959.

Rebel Wench. New York, Fawcett, 1955; London, Fawcett, 1958.

Queen of Sheba. New York, Fawcett, 1956.

One Sword for Love . London, Fawcett, 1956.

Terror over London. New York, Fawcett, 1957.

The Conquering Prince. London, Fawcett, 1958.

Witness This Woman. New York, Fawcett, 1959; London, Muller, 1961.

Creole Woman. New York, Fawcett, 1959.

The Devil Sword (as Kevin Matthews). New York, Hill, 1960.

Bastard of Orleans. New York, Avon, 1960.

Scandal in Suburbia. New York, Hill, 1960.

Woman of Egypt (as Kevin Matthews). London, Panther, 1961.

Barbary Devil (as Jeffrey Gardner). New York, Pyramid, 1961.

Cleopatra (as Jeffrey Gardner). New York, Pyramid, 1962.

As Good as Dead. New York, Fawcett, 1962.

One Wife's Ways. New York, Fawcett, and London, Muller, 1963.

Tom Blood, Highwayman. New York, Avon, 1963.

Lion of Lucca. New York, Avon, 1966.

Ivan the Terrible. New York, Avon, n. d.

Kothar—Barbarian Swordsman [*of the Magic Sword!, and the Demon Queen and the Wizard Slayer, and the Conjurer's Curse*]. New York, Belmont, 5 vols., 1969-70.

Kyrik, Warlock Warrior [*Fights the Demon World, and the Wizard's Sword, and the Lost Queen*]. New York, Nordon, 4 vols., 1976-76; *Kyrik Fights the Demon World* published

London, Jenkins, 1976.

The Bold Ones. New York, Nordon, 1976.

The Liberty Sword. New York, Nordon, 1976.

Hurricane. New York, Nordon, 1976.

Savage Passage. New York, Nordon, 1978.

Blood Trail. New York, Belmont, 1979.

Novels as Jefferson Cooper

Arrow in the Hill. New York, Dodd Mead, 1955.

The Bloody Sevens. New York, Permabooks, 1956.

The Swordsman. New York, Pocket Books, 1957.

The Questing Sword. New York, Permabooks, 1958; London, Consul, 1960.

Captain Seadog. New York, Pocket Books, 1959.

Delilah. New York, Paperback Library, 1962.

Veronica's Veil. New York, Permabooks, n. d.

Jezebel. New York, Paperback Library, 1963.

Slave of the Roman Sword. New York, Paperback Library, 1965.

This Sword for Hire. New York, Paperback Library, 1966.

Novels as James Kendricks

Beyond Our Pleasure. Derby, Connecticut, Monarch, 1959.

Sword of Casanova. Derby, Connecticut, Monarch, 1959.

Adultress. Derby, Connecticut, Monarch, 1960.

She Wouldn't Surrender. Derby, Connecticut, Monarch, 1960.

The Wicked, Wicked Woman. Derby, Connecticut, Monarch, 1961.

Love Me Tonight. Derby, Connecticut, Monarch, 1963.

Novels as Lynna Cooper

An Offer of Marriage. New York, New American Library, 1976.

Substitute Bride. New York, New American Library, 1976.

Her Heart's Desire. New York, New American Library, 1976.

The Hired Wife. New York, New American Library, 1978.

Forgotten Love. New York, New American Library, 1979.

Hearts in the Highlands. New York, New American Library, 1980.

Inherit My Heart. New York, New American Library, 1981.

*   *   *

Gardner F. Fox is probably best known for his comic-book work, which includes scripts for such science fiction-based characters as Superman and Hawkman. In science-fiction proper, he's probably best known for a handful of paperback novels. Yet his best science fantasy writing is probably to be found in a dozen space operas published between 1945 and 1952, mainly in *Planet Stories,* where they are overshadowed by the more impressive work of Ray Bradbury, Leigh Brackett, and Ross Rocklynne. But much of that work remains highly entertaining.

His first actual SF-fantasy sale was to *Weird Tales,* but his first story for *Planet Stories,* "The Last Monster"—a benevolent alien's efforts to aid endangered humans are misread as the menacings of a monster—won the instant approval of the magazine's readers. Fox buttressed his success with "Man Nth," in which aliens recruit beings from various worlds and endow them with superhuman powers to enable them to fend off a cosmic threat that would do justice to some of the grander fancies of A. E. van Vogt. "Man Nth" was an almost flawless entertainment and demonstrated a much surer touch than

"The Last Monster." "Engines of the Gods" and "The Man the Sun Gods Made" established Fox as one of the most reliable writers of strong space adventure novelets. "The Man the Sun Gods Made," about an artificial superman who stymies Earth's plans to exploit his planet, melded concepts Fox had already proven himself comfortable with—supermen and super-science—with the sort of story Leigh Brackett was already demonstrating success with.

"Vassals of the Lode-Star" is one of the strongest of his stories, arguably the best work he's produced in the field. A rift in the fabric of time and space transports its hero to another world where he finds himself in a war with a superbeing bent on enslaving everything in reach. This was a story where everything worked for Fox: a strong and likeable lead character, Thor Masterson, a swift and interesting plot, concepts that are sufficiently gradiose and metaphysical to evoke a sense of wonder, and a benevolent alien, the Discoverer. "When Kohonnes Screamed" is less successful, though strongly imaginative, dealing with a planet where space and matter are dangerously and unpredictably distorted by a force which must somehow be located and destroyed. "Tonight the Stars Revolt!" is a strongly plotted story written in a terse prose under the now-traditional influence of Brackett, its conventional overcome-the-evil-ruler plot buoyed with fine story telling and a strong imagination.

With the collapse of the SF market, Fox found success with original paperback historical novels, and he touched the periphery of SF with a novelization of the movie of Jules Verne's *Five Weeks in a Balloon*. But *Escape Across the Cosmos* was his first true SF novel. It was the story of a superman, falsely accused of a crime, who sets out to defend himself. *The Arsenal of Miracles* told of an outcast Earthman—a disgraced space officer—who joins forces with the queen of an alien world to fight the overwhelmingly powerful Empire of Earth. Some of its passages may have promised the same sort of fun delivered by his earlier stories but novel-length SF seems never to have been Fox's forte. *Arsenal of Miracles* is a fun read, but none of the subsequent novels are quite as good as it is. Under the name Bart Somers he produced two space operas based on the adventures of a character called Commander Craig, a space-going trouble shooter.

Conehead is one of his most interesting efforts. It touches on a more serious theme than is common to most of Fox's work, racial prejudice. His hero is the standard space officer of most of Fox's novels, but instead of being a warrior, he is a lawyer who sets out to establish the civil rights of the natives of a planet under the domination of Earth. The story returns ultimately to familiar ground: the planet holds the remnants of an alien race, all but extinct, yet still possessing god-like powers, and it is the force of their powers and not of any moral argument that ultimately sways the empire.

Fox is no idea man. His backgrounds are often merely sketched in, which probably accounts for his failure to draw any really widespread following among readers. But he is also a genuinely unpretentious writer whose work provides the sort of straightforward entertainment expected of good space opera. His novels are workmanlike and fun, but they lack the flair, imagination, and pacing of his best magazine stories.

—Gerald W. Page

FRANK, Pat (Harry Hart). American. Born in Chicago, Illinois, 5 May 1907. Attended the University of Florida, Gainesville, 1925-26. Divorced; one son and one daughter. Reporter, Jacksonville *Journal,* Florida, 1927-29, New York *Journal,* 1929-32, and Washington *Herald,* 1933-38; Chief of the Washington Bureau, 1938-41, and correspondent in Italy, Austria, Germany, Turkey, and Hungary, 1944-46, Overseas News Agency; Assistant Chief of Mission, Office of War Information, 1941-44; Member of United Nations Mission to Korea, 1952-53; staff member, Democratic National Committee, 1960; consultant, National Aeronautics and Space Council, 1961; consultant, Department of Defense, 1963-64. Recipient: War Department commendation, 1945; Reserved Officers Association citation, 1957; American Heritage Foundation award, 1961. *Died 12 October 1964.*

SCIENCE-FICTION PUBLICATIONS

Novels

Mr. Adam. Philadelphia, Lippincott, 1946; London, Gollancz, 1947.
Forbidden Area. Philadelphia, Lippincott, 1956; as *Seven Days to Never,* London, Constable, 1957.
Alas, Babylon. Philadelphia, Lippincott, and London, Constable, 1959.

OTHER PUBLICATIONS

Novels

An Affair of State. Philadelphia, Lippincott, 1948; London, Corgi, 1951.
Hold Back the Night. Philadelphia, Lippincott, and London, Hamish Hamilton, 1952.

Other

The Long Way Round. Philadelphia, Lippincott, 1953.
How to Survive the H-Bomb, and Why. Philadelphia, Lippincott, 1962.
Rendezvous at Midway: U. S. S. Yorktown and the Japanese Carrier Fleet, with Joseph D. Harrington. New York, Day, 1967.

*   *   *

In the late 1940's and 1950's, a growing distrust of technology focused on the dangers of atomic energy. The most obvious danger was that of nuclear war, but concerns about reactor break-downs or bomb-factory explosions were also on people's minds. The immediate blast was one threat, and genetic damage from radiation was another. Science-fiction writers were among the first during this period to give such fears a public voice, and one of those writers was Pat Frank.

Frank wrote a great deal of material—fiction and non-fiction—dealing with the possible problems with atomic materials. His first novel, *Mr. Adam,* postulates universal male sterility as one of the results of an explosion at an atomic bomb factory in Mississippi. *Forbidden Area* attempts to show how, why, and when the Russians might attack the United States. This book is an especially grim indictment of America's lack of preparedness for such a possibility. Frank shows how the various agencies—paralyzed by red tape, inter-departmental bickering, unqualified political appointees in positions of power, and the like—refuse to act until it is almost too late, averting an all-out Russian attack by only minutes.

Frank is probably best known as the author of *Alas, Babylon,* a post-atomic war novel. Randy Bragg, an inhabitant of Fort Repose, Florida, is warned by his brother, Mark, a SAC Intelligence Officer, that the war is coming. Mark sends his wife and children to Randy because Fort Repose will be safer during such a war than will SAC Headquarters, Omaha. The bombs and missiles fall, and the people of Fort Repose are on their own. Unlike Nevil Shute's *On the Beach,* in which everyone dies, *Alas, Babylon* is basically a romantic view of the aftermath of an atomic war. Randy and his friends do not have too much difficulty surviving—though Civil Defense agencies have prepared almost no one, and Randy has to organize the people of Fort Repose—and only one of the central characters is killed. With this romantic novel, however, Frank presents all the atomic fears, from initial blast to genetic mutation, in one package.

Frank also examines the use of power in *Alas, Babylon.* There are various people in the novel who have power and should not. Randy was defeated in politics by an opponent who appealed to bigotry and fear. The Navy Ensign who fires the shot that starts the war uses the power of his jet plane to compensate for his diminutive physical stature. Randy, however, uses the power at his disposal to keep Fort Repose safe. From this, it is clear that it is not power, *per se,* that Frank objects to but the lack of qualifications of some of the people who have the power.

Frank's novels are well-written. They have strong plots, well-paced action, and interesting characters. They are not so much appeals to the reader's fear of atomic power as they are warnings.

—C. W. Sullivan III

FRAYN, Michael. British. Born in London, 8 September 1933. Educated at Kingston Grammar School, Surrey; Emmanuel College, Cambridge, B. A. 1957. Served in the Royal Artillery and Intelligence Corps, 1952-54. Married Gillian Palmer in 1960; three daughters. Reporter, 1957-59, and columnist, 1959-62, *The Guardian,* Manchester and London; columnist, *The Observer,* London, 1962-68. Recipient: Maugham Award, 1966; Hawthornden Prize, 1967; National Press Award, 1970; *Standard* award for play, 1976, 1981, 1983, 1985; Society of West End Theatre award, 1977, 1982; British Theatre Association award, 1981, 1983; Olivier Award, 1985. Agent: Elaine Greene Ltd., 31 Newington Green, London N16 9PU, England.

SCIENCE-FICTION PUBLICATIONS

Novels

The Tin Men. London, Collins, 1965; Boston, Little Brown, 1966.
A Very Private Life. London, Collins, and New York, Viking Press, 1968.
Sweet Dreams. London, Collins, 1973; New York, Viking Press, 1974.

OTHER PUBLICATIONS

Novels

The Russian Interpreter. London, Collins, and New York, Viking Press, 1966.

Towards the End of the Morning. London, Collins, 1967; as *Against Entropy,* New York, Viking Press, 1967.

Plays

Zounds!, with John Edwards, music by Keith Statham (produced Cambridge, 1957).
The Two of Us (includes *Black and Silver, The New Quixote, Mr. Foot, Chinamen*) (produced London, 1970; Ogunquit, Maine, 1975; *Chinamen* produced New York, 1979). London, Fontana, 1970; *Chinamen* published in *The Best Short Plays 1973,* edited by Stanley Richards, Radnor, Pennsylvania, Chilton, 1973; revised version of *The New Quixote* (produced Chichester and London, 1980).
The Sandboy (produced London, 1971).
Alphabetical Order (produced London, 1975; New Haven, Connecticut, 1976). Included in *Alphabetical Order and Donkeys' Years,* 1977.
Donkeys' Years (produced London, 1976). Included in *Alphabetical Order and Donkeys' Years,* 1977.
Clouds (produced London, 1976). London, Eyre Methuen, 1977.
Alphabetical Order and Donkeys' Years. London, Eyre Methuen, 1977.
The Cherry Orchard, adaptation of a play by Chekhov (produced London, 1978). London, Eyre Methuen, 1978.
Balmoral (produced Guildford, Surrey, 1978; revised version, as *Liberty Hall,* produced London, 1980).
The Fruits of Enlightenment, adaptation of a play by Tolstoy (produced London, 1979). London, Eyre Methuen, 1979.
Make and Break (produced London, 1980; Washington, D. C., 1983). London, Eyre Methuen, 1980.
Noises Off (produced London, 1981; New York, 1983). London, Methuen, 1982.
Three Sisters, adaptation of a play by Chekhov (produced Manchester, 1985). London, Methuen, 1983.
Benefactors (produced London, 1984). London, Methuen, 1984.
Wild Honey, adaptation of a play by Chekhov (produced London, 1984). London, Methuen, 1984.
Number One, adaptation of a play by Jean Anouilh (produced London, 1984).

Television Plays and Documentaries: *Jamie, On a Flying Visit,* 1968; *One Pair of Eyes,* 1968; *Birthday,* 1969; *Imagine a City Called Berlin,* 1975; *Making Faces,* 1975; *Vienna: The Mask of Gold,* 1977; *Three Streets in the Country,* 1979; *The Long Straight,* 1981; *Jerusalem,* 1984.

Other

The Day of the Dog (*Guardian* columns). London, Collins, 1962; New York, Doubleday, 1963.
The Book of Fub (*Guardian* columns). London, Collins, 1963; as *Never Put Off to Gomorrah,* New York, Pantheon, 1964.
On the Outskirts (*Observer* columns). London, Collins, 1964.
At Bay in Gear Street (*Observer* columns). London, Fontana, 1967.
Constructions (philosophy). London, Wildwood House, 1974.
Great Railway Journeys of the World, with others. London, BBC Publications, 1981.
The Original Michael Frayn: Columns from the Guardian and The Observer. Edinburgh, Salamander Press, 1983.

Editor, *The Best of Beachcomber,* by J. B. Morton. London, Heinemann, 1963.

* * *

Michael Frayn is not an easy writer to categorize. *The Tin Men* is obviously not SF but witty comedy, school of Waugh; on the other hand, it obviously is SF, as it purports to be written by a computer and satirizes men who behave like computers and are trying to make computers behave like men. When a robot comes to write its own prehistory, it will have to give classic place in its mythology to Macintosh's ethical machines and their struggles on the sinking raft. But the novel is not so much SF itself as an exuberant account of the men who are trying to make our world into an SF dystopia. The great discovery of Macintosh and Goldwasser is that, because all human life is of no purpose other than to provide newspaper headlines and statistics, humans can stop living and let the computers do it for them. Computers can produce newspapers, sports results, pornography, prayers: who needs people? The characteristic inverted logic of Frayn's tin men naturally produces a novelist who begins by writing the blurbs, the potted biography, and the reviews, and only then tries writing the book (formulaically, of course), before capitulating to the superior power of his typewriter keyboard. What *The Tin Men* itself lacks as a novel is a story worthy of its theme. Admittedly the story, which concerns the opening of the Ethics Wings in a computer research establishment, not by the Queen, as planned, but by her stand-in for rehearsals (an ungainly man called Nobbs), illustrates several aspects of the theme of illusion mistaken for reality, but its spirit of low farce inoculates the reader against taking the book seriously. Also, the novel's short-breathed episodic quality—it is really only a series of sketches strung loosely together by a farcical plot—too openly betrays the author's work as a whimsically satiric journalist. The short-breath syndrome is familiar among SF novelists who are really short-story men; in *The Tin Men* we have an essayist trying to write a novel and not quite succeeding.

A Very Private Life also has a mosaic quality (as indeed does Frayn's stimulating philosophical work, *Constructions*), but here the small pieces compose a highly satisfactory work of art, one of the most delightful fabulations in the genre. The heroine, Uncumber, begins as a misfit in a society where what the Haves have is privacy: they meet by holovision, as in Asimov's *The Naked Sun.* Uncumber falls in love with a man who lives on the fringes of her enclosed society, journeys outside her cell to meet him, is disillusioned by life outside, falls in with outlaws, is rescued by the police and rehabilitated. Comparison with *The Naked Sun* is instructive because, unlike Asimov and the typical SF writer who might handle such a theme, Frayn has not written a dystopia satire: his absurd world is presented not as a threat but as an alteration simply, a new mode, not inhuman but nicely domesticated by engaging touches or ordinariness. Again, if we compare Frayn's work with Angela Carter's *Heroes and Villains,* in which the ivory tower world is promptly sacrificed to the perverse gypsy delights of the world outside, we see how detached and balanced, how cool Frayn is. Uncumber does not find the outer world romantic, as a Carter heroine would; instead, the best it can offer is a tatty attempt to emulate the values of those inside, while the worst is nasty and brutish: the outlaws are indeed, as they are called, "Sad Men. " Frayn's novel is written as a fairy story that begins "Once upon a time there will be a little girl called Uncumber," and in that spirit it should be read.

In *Constructions* Frayn tells us "I should like to say this: don't *worry* when you find yourself in the midst of a mythology. Relax and enjoy it. " Some SF readers may find themselves graveled by the way in which this sharp and witty writer pulls his punches.

But Frayn is not a knock-down satirist: he's a comic ironist who enjoys the spectacle of human absurdity, and wants us to share the fun. *Sweet Dreams* should also be read, although, as it is a story set in the after-life, in which revivification is without benefit of technology (by which Farmer and Silverberg, say, have accommodated this mythological idea to SF), it is strictly outside our genre.

—Michael J. Tolley

FREEDMAN, Nancy (née Mars). American. Born in Chicago, Illinois, 4 July 1920. Educated at the Chicago Art Institute, 1937-38; Los Angeles City College, 1938-39; University of Southern California, Los Angeles, 1939. Married Benedict Freedman in 1941; two sons and two daughters. Actress in the 1930's. Agent: William Morris Agency, 151 El Camino Drive, Beverly Hills, California 90212. Address: 5837 Latigo Canyon Road, Malibu, California 90267, U. S. A.

SCIENCE-FICTION PUBLICATIONS

Novel

Joshua Son of None. New York, Delacorte Press, 1973; London, Hart Davis MacGibbon, 1974.

OTHER PUBLICATIONS

Novels with Benedict Freedman

Back to the Sea. New York, Viking Press, 1942.
Mrs. Mike. New York, Coward McCann, and London, Hamish Hamilton, 1947.
This and No More. New York, Harper, 1950.
The Spark and the Exodus. New York, Crown, 1954.
Lootville. New York, Holt, 1957.
Tresa. New York, Holt, 1959.
The Apprentice Bastard. New York, Simon and Schuster, 1966.
Cyclone of Silence. New York, Simon and Schuster, 1969.
The Immortals. New York, St. Martin's Press, 1977.
Prima Donna. New York, Morrow, and London, Prior, 1981.

*

Manuscript Collection: Mugar Memorial Library, Boston University.

Theatrical Activities:
Actress: **Plays**—in *Faust* by Goethe; *The Miracle* by Karl Volmöller; *Six Characters in Search of an Author* by Pirandello; *Death Takes a Holiday* by Walter Ferris; in summer stock, Maine, summers 1937-38; toured with Max Reinhardt.

Nancy Freedman comments:
I had no idea I was writing science fiction when I began *Joshua Son of None*. My philosophy of an author's obligation, besides of course literary considerations, is that he should stand slightly outside his own time, letting events wash over his work. To prepare for *Joshua Son of None* I attended a seminar at Cal Tech given by Dr. Robert Sinsheimer and in 1972 I was introduced to the work Dr. Steptoe was doing in genetic engineering. Six years later he refined the process which I

describe in my novel, and produced the Brown baby. With *in vitro* technique we are halfway to the possibility of cloning. *Joshua Son of None* was published by Delacorte who paid me a large advance, and it was made a Literary Guild selection—and then, wonder of wonders, silence in the press. The Guild quietly dropped it ads, as did the publisher. The reason? I was told that the public wasn't ready for a book about cloning. It was too terrifying a possibility. Shortly thereafter *The Boys from Brazil* appeared, treated not realistically but in a cops-and-robbers setting. It emanated from my own agent and publisher, who apparently felt that, done in this most fantastic manner, it would not appear threatening. It didn't; in fact, it gave rise to an endless series of jokes on the subject (perhaps equivalent to "whistling in the dark"). *Joshua Son of None* was the first book on the subject of cloning, and I treated the material with great respect for I believe the first clone will within a decade tread this earth. The book was science-fiction when I wrote it. How long it will remain so I can only guess.

As a writer I am concerned with the future. I am particularly concerned with the connective tissue that runs from earliest time to the present and stretches into the future. One such skein is mankind's desire for the one attribute denied him by the gods—immortality. Through the process of cloning we may have been handed this key to life everlasting. Man has not defeated death. If he goes this route, he will die many deaths and live many lives in his quest for personal self-perfection. The technical revolution which will make this possible is of greater magnitude than the splitting of the atom. It is the opening of Pandora's box. Skinner and his colleagues claim that environment totally modifies and changes behavior. And a clone is born into a different environment. Carl Rogers takes a more moderate position, believing that while the environment modifies man, man is not passive. He in turn changes and interacts with his surroundings. This is the thrust of my novel. Joshua is the son of none, having neither father nor mother but replicated from a single cell of his own dying body. In the book, a deliberate attempt is made to control the environment and replicate the phenotype of the assassinated president. But it appeared to me that the clonee differed from the original when he discovers he is a copy of someone else. That is the identity crisis of all time. When he asks, "then I'm not myself—I'm *him*?" At that moment he becomes his own person.

I am often asked why I took John F. Kennedy as my prototype. Partly, personal identification. I had broken my back and was forced to lie absolutely flat for seven months. During this time my mind reverted frequently to Kennedy. He had gone through the same ordeal, which is so psychologically damaging, and had rallied to become President. I at least would stand on my own feet and walk. Moreover, when the book was first conceived. I envisioned it as the retelling in modern terms of a myth, namely, man's desire for life everlasting. And for a myth, a folk hero, someone larger than life, is needed to carry it forward. Only one contemporary answered that description, the man I already identified with so closely.

*   *   *

Nancy Freedman comes to science fiction as an established novelist trained in general fiction, with a particular concentration in the history of families—the stories that families make through heir connections, multiplication, and dynastic continuity. For someone with such an interest, the idea of cloning holds special appeal, a desire for the power represented by non-generative extensions of a generative group, plus the dream of repeated personality. When Freedman connected the idea of cloning with the history of the Kennedy dynasty, she produced *Joshua Son of None*.

The premise of the book is that a doctor present at John F. Kennedy's assassination preserved tissue from the dying President, and then found a scientist with knowledge of cloning, and a millionaire with the willingness to raise the resultant child in the Kennedy pattern. Partly an experiment and partly a long-term plan for political power, the project works. A surrogate mother carries the child, the millionaire's family is remodeled to raise him, and simulated deaths and disasters warp his psyche in the original pattern. What is produced is a young man who finally realizes not only that he must become President, but that in some sense he already was.

The problem with the premise is that cloning simply does not have the potential of repeating personality or history. Freedman details the science of the project with intelligence and clarity, but in her need to make the novel work, and in her apparent affection for Kennedy himself, she gives too much credit to chromosomes. The profound differences that develop between identical twins—raised in the same family at the same time—should be enough to demonstrate that there are too many other factors at work. A less meticulous novelist might have invented a technology to help preserve personality as well as genotype, but Freedman, sticking to it-could-happen-here facts, only advances the craft of cloning as far as success with human cells. As a result, the science she invokes but does not follow would condemn the plot, particularly the lurid ending, to the category of wishful thinking and near silliness.

Yet the book is effective, mainly because of Freedman's other novelistic skills. Her characters have a depth that allows her to measure with considerable feeling the impact of technological power on its human victims. The moment when Joshua Francis Kellogg rips off his braces and recognizes someone else in the mirror is surprisingly moving. In fact, throughout the book Josuha's reactions have coherence and growing familiarity that should demonstrate that novelists are better at reproducing personality than genetic scientists.

After *Joshua Son of None,* Freedman continued writing about science in *The Immortals,* the story of an oil dynasty. While this long novel is not actually science fiction, the same interests re-appear—the network of family, and the possibility that science could break history loose from its disastrous course. As in *Joshua,* the descriptions of research and technology (the invention of a solar cell) are clear and well-written. Freedman writes on the edge of science fiction, pushing speculation only as far as the near future. Given her solid novelist's skills, it would be interesting to see her attempt a farther future.

—Karen G. Way

_____

FRENCH, Paul. *See* **ASIMOV, Isaac.**

_____

FRIEDBERG, Gertrude (née Tonkonogy). American. Born in New York City, 17 March 1908. Educated at Wellesley College, Massachusetts; Barnard College, New York, B. A. 1929. Married Charles K. Friedberg; one son and one daughter. Mathematics teacher in New York public schools, and freelance writer. Address: 1185 Park Avenue, New York, New York 10028, U.S.A.

SCIENCE-FICTION PUBLICATIONS

Novel

The Revolving Boy. New York, Doubleday, 1966; London, Gollancz, 1967.

Uncollected Short Stories

"The Short and Happy Death of George Frumkin," in *Fantasy and Science Fiction* (New York), April 1963.
"For Whom the Girl Waits," in *Fantasy and Science Fiction* (New York), May 1972.
"Where Moth and Rust," in *The Woman Who Lost Her Names,* edited by Julia Wolf Mazow. New York, Harper, 1980.

OTHER PUBLICATIONS

Plays

Three Cornered Moon (produced New York, 1933). New York, French, 1933.
Town House, adaptation of stories by John Cheever (produced New York, 1948).

* * *

Gertrude Friedberg has published several interesting science-fiction works.

The Revolving Boy follows the early life of a supernormal child, Derv, who has the ability to be both radiometer and compass. One of the major themes of the novel is that of discovering and communicating with another civilization. Derv was born to astronauts in 1970, in a weightless condition far from the earth's forces. Because he did not experience gravity at birth, he was able to align himself to a signal from another solar system. He feels compelled to preserve his original orientation to this signal—called the Direction—and consequently, when his body is turned in one direction, he must unwind himself in the opposite direction to recapture his original position. He turns somersaults in bed to compensate for the earth's revolutions and his day's turnings. During his elementary school years, his teachers become concerned as he executes dangerous spins on stairways. He becomes known as "the boy who leans" when his body begins listing in the direction of the signal.

To escape the publicity following his birth, Derv's parents faked a fatal accident in a sailboat, escaped undetected, and assumed new identities. The novel excels in the following parents' fears of discovery as they observe the development of Derv's talent. When Derv reaches high school, an astronomer who knew the astronaut parents discovers their true identities and persuades them to allow Derv to help trace the signal on a laboratory radiometer. Just as the signal is found electronically, Derv and his parents disappear again. Part Two of the book begins some years later, after Derv has taken a new name—Fred Gany—and married his childhood sweetheart, Prin (now Reine), who has perfect pitch. Derv-Fred's signal has suddenly stopped and he has lost his sense of balance. The remainder of the book concentrates on Prin-Reine's attempts to relocate the laboratory radiometer (which has been abandoned) and to determine if the signal has indeed terminated.

Friedberg's scientific projections are mostly erroneous. For instance, the exposition of her novel is centered around the ban on space travel in 1970, due to a belt of nuclear waste around the earth. She overestimated the speed of change to electronic devices in the homes of the 1970's. Her scientific research can also be faulted, since she has failed to take into account some of the properties of radio signals, such as the possibility of blockage by shielding masses (the earth, tunnels, and concrete buildings).

"The Short and Happy Death of George Frumkin" is a tongue-in-cheek look at the use of artificial organs. George, 97 years old, has developed not only a knock in his artificial heart, but also a bad case of ennui, as he refuses to complete a promised rewrite of the second act of play. George's wife, Helen, persuades him to call an electrician, Dr. Stebbins (most doctors are electricians these days), who tells him that he needs "a new battery and a new variable autotransformer. " In order to hook him to his new system, Dr. Stebbins switches him to house current until the calibration procedure is finished. During the short space between plug-ins, George is "dead. " However, house current proves a boon to George, providing him with the creative energy to rewrite his second act, plus an oversupply of sexual libido (he attacks his wife and propositions the maid during this interval). But after his return to battery power, he resumes his uninspired ways, learning nevertheless that his rewritten second act has given the play "more heart. " This entertaining spoof is a gem, undoubtedly Friedberg's best science fiction effort. She uses a female narrator for this story, plus a steady supply of eccentric comic characters.

"For Whom the Girl Waits," properly called science fantasy, is a dreamlike account of double identities in a high school setting. The main character, Louis Demperi, is a substitute teacher who assumes the identity of the teacher he replaces. The role-playing works well until he takes the place of a man named Koppinger, for whom a beautiful girl waits each afternoon after school. Then he becomes disoriented and cannot remember that he is Koppinger, until he discovers that another man has assumed his own identity. Demperi decides to carry on with Koppinger's role and meets the girl, who rejects him and causes him to have a fatal car accident. But his identity lives on in the person of Demperi's substitute. The story is somewhat confusing but is imaginative and fascinating to read.

In her writing, Friedberg uses a simple, unpretentious style and in general organizes her material chronologically. She excels in the handling of women characters, which suggests that her works might have been more successful if the central characters had been women instead of men.

—Judith Snyder

FYFE, H(orace) B(owne). Also writes as Andrew MacDuff. American. Born in Jersey City, New Jersey, 30 September 1918. Educated at Stevens Academy; Columbia University, New York, B. S. 1950. Served in the United States Army during World War II: Bronze Star. Married 1) Adeline Marie Dougherty in 1946 (died, 1970); 2) Sonia V. Benedict in 1975. Laboratory assistant and draftsman, then free-lance writer. Address: Box 221, Ridgefield Park, New Jersey 07660, U.S.A.

SCIENCE-FICTION PUBLICATIONS

Novel

D-99. New York, Pyramid, 1962.

Uncollected Short Stories (series: Bureau of Slick Tricks)

"Hold That Comet," with F. H. Hauser, in *Astonishing* (Chicago), December 1940.
"Sinecure 6," in *Astounding* (New York), January 1947.
"Special Jobbery" (Bureau), in *Astounding* (New York), September 1949.
"Locked Out," in *Men Against the Stars,* edited by Martin H. Greenberg. New York, Gnome Press, 1950.
"Conformity Expected," in *Astounding* (New York), March 1950.
"Spy Scare," in *Astounding* (New York), September 1950.
"Compromise" (Bureau), in *Astounding* (New York), December 1950.
"In Value Deceived," in *Possible Worlds of Science Fiction,* edited by Groff Conklin. New York, Vanguard Press, 1951.
"Bureau of Slick Tricks," in *Travellers of Space,* edited by Martin H. Greenberg. New York, Gnome Press, 1951.
"The Envoy, Her," in *Planet* (New York), March 1951.
"Key Decision," in *Astounding* (New York), May 1951.
"Open Invitation," in *Planet* (New York), May 1951.
"Temporary Keeper," in *Thrilling Wonder Stories* (New York), June 1951.
"Experimentum Crucis" (as Andrew MacDuff), in *Astounding* (New York), July 1951.
"Yes Sir!," in *Startling* (New York), September 1951.
"This World Must Die!," in *Future* (New York), September 1951.
"Thinking Machine," in *Astounding* (New York), October 1951.
"Afterthought," in *Beyond Human Ken,* edited by Judith Merril. New York, Random House, 1952; London, Grayson, 1953.
"Manners of the Age," in *Omnibus of Science Fiction,* edited by Groff Conklin. New York, Crown, 1952.
"Protected Species," in *The Astounding Science Fiction Anthology,* edited by John W. Campbell, Jr. New York, Simon and Schuster, 1952.
"Calling World-4 of Kithgol," in *Planet* (New York), January 1952.
"Bluff-Stained Transaction" (Bureau), in *Astounding* (New York), March 1952.
"Extra-Secret Agent," in *Science Fiction Quarterly* (Holyoke, Massachusetts), May 1952.
"Confidence," in *Future* (New York), September 1952.
"Time Limit," in *Fantastic Story* (New York), Winter 1952.
"Implode and Peddle" (Bureau) and "Star-Linked," in *Space Service,* edited by Andre Norton. Cleveland, World, 1953.
"Let There Be Light," in *Crossroads in Time,* edited by Groff Conklin. New York, Permabooks, 1953.
"Ransom," in *The Best from Fantasy and Science Fiction 2,* edited by Anthony Boucher and J. Francis McComas. Boston, Little Brown, 1953.
"The Well-Oiled Machine," in *Science-Fiction Carnival,* edited by Fredric Brown and Mack Reynolds. Chicago, Shasta, 1953.
"The Compleat Collector," in *Future* (New York), January 1953.
"Fast Passage," in *Other Worlds* (Evanston, Indiana), January 1953.
"Exile," in *Space* (New York), February 1953.
"Romance," in *Future* (New York), March 1953.
"Irresistible Weapon," in *If* (New York), July 1953.
"Koenigshaufen's Curve," in *Fantasy Fiction* (New York), August 1953.
"Moonwalk," in *Space Pioneers,* edited by Andre Norton.

Cleveland, World, 1954.
"Welcome, Strangers!," in *Astounding* (New York), August 1954.
"The Shell Dome," in *Spaceway* (Alhambra, California), February 1955.
"The Night of No Moon," in *Infinity* (New York), June 1957.
"Lunar Escapade," in *Planet of Doom and Other Stories.* Sydney, Jubilee, 1958.
"Fee of the Frontier," in *Amazing* (New York), August 1960.
"A Transmutation of Muddle," in *Astounding* (New York), September 1960.
"Wedge," in *If* (New York), September 1960.
"The Furies of Zhahnoor," in *Fantastic* (New York), October 1960.
"Satellite System," in *Astounding* (New York), October 1960.
"Round-and-Round Trip," in *Galaxy* (New York), December 1960.
"The Outbreak of Peace," in *Analog* (New York), February 1961.
"Flamedown," in *Analog* (New York), August 1961.
"Tolliver's Orbit," in *If* (New York), September 1961.
"The Talkative Tree," in *If* (New York), January 1962.
"Knowledge Is Power," in *Way Out,* edited by Ivan Howard. New York, Belmont, 1963.
"Star Chamber," in *Amazing* (New York), March 1963.
"The Klygha," in *Amazing* (New York), December 1963.
"The Clutches of Ruin," in *Gamma 4* (North Hollywood), 1965.
"The Old Shill Game," in *Analog* (New York), January 1967.

*   *   *

H. B. Fyfe has written several dozen conventional short stories and a single eposodic novel that obviously meshes several shorter stories into one whole. He is perhaps best known for his series about the Bureau of Slick Tricks, a secret human organization whose purpose is to finagle humans out of embarrassing situations on other planets. The novel and at least five stories fall into this series, and a number of other stories are very similar thematically. Essentially, the philosophy expressed is that humans are the most flexible, inventive race in the universe and that any aliens who encounter us should hold onto everything that isn't nailed down.

"In Value Deceived" is a perfect example of this. Two starships, one human and one alien, encounter each other in space. The aliens are short on rations, and are seeking edible plants, which they consider highly valuable. They trade a "worthless" piece of their own equipment for some hydroponic supplies; the "worthless" item allows transmutation of elements. In "Ransom" primitive aliens decide to kidnap humans as leverage against the crew of an exploratory starship. They end up with two robots, and are dismayed at the casual manner in which they are abandoned. The novel, *D-99,* features a host of confused, outsmarted, and frantic aliens, who cannot cope with human manipulation of events.

Fyfe was not permanently wed to this concept, although it does dominate his work. One of his best short stories. "Protected Species," is in fact quite atypical. The primitive aliens skulking about the ruins of their former civilization are treated with active sympathy, and ultimately it is the humans who find themselves the butt of a cosmic joke. In "The Talkative Tree" an alien culture provides the means whereby humans alienated from their dictatorial and conformist culture can escape into almost any conceivable form of freedom by altering their physical nature.

Fyfe makes use of a number of standard plot devices and has done little in the way of innovation. He explores both sides of the human-robot interface. Robotic servants with their built-in limitations drive a magazine editor crazy in "The Well-Oiled Machine," but they come to dominate the world in "Let There Be Light," and are preyed on by human scavengers for the oil they use within their bodies. Man is therefore reduced to the level of a mechanical vampire. By far his most outstanding work is "Moonwalk" which makes use of a classic man-against nature situation, one that has been used many times both within the genre and without. As the result of an accident, one man is stranded on the lunar surface, several hundred miles from the moon's only human installation. The plot unfolds in logical fashion, as the protagonist wrestles with time and a diminishing air supply, and the reader struggles with frustrated impatience as the authorities refuse to believe that the lack of radio contract portends anything requiring action. Although Fyfe is not capable of making this a truly great story, he handles it quite well, and it is a worthy contribution of its type.

Fyfe has remained a dabbler, and his obvious talents have not been developed. There is little difference in quality between the earliest and most recent stories. Nevertheless, his competent stories have provided entertainment and adventure to his audience.

—Don D'Ammassa

GADE, Henry. See **PALMER, Raymond A.**

GALAXAN, Sol. See **COPPEL, Alfred.**

GALLUN, Raymond Z(inke). Also writes as William Callahan. American. Born in Beaver Dam, Wisconsin, 22 March 1911. Educated at the University of Wisconsin, Madison, 1929-30; Alliance Française, Paris, 1938-39; San Marcos University, Lima, Peru, 1960. Married 1) Frieda E. Talmey in 1959 (died 1974); 2) Bertha Erickson Backman in 1978. Construction worker for Army Corps of Engineers, 1942-43; marine black-smith, Pearl Harbor Navy Yard, 1944; technical writer, EDO Corporation, College Point, New York, 1964-75. Recipient: Fandom Hall of Fame Award, 1979. Address: 111-20 71st Street, Forest Hills, New York 11375, U.S.A.

SCIENCE-FICTION PUBLICATIONS

Novels

People Minus X. New York, Simon and Schuster, 1957.
The Planet Strappers. New York, Pyramid, 1961.
The Eden Cycle. New York, Ballantine, 1974.
Bioblast! New York, Ace, 1985.

Short Stories

The Machine That Thought (as William Callahan). New York, Columbia, 1940.
The Best of Raymond Z. Gallun. New York, Ballantine, 1978.

Uncollected Short Stories

"The Eternal Wall," in *Amazing* (New York), May 1979.
"A First Glimpse," in *Analog* (New York), February 1980.

OTHER PUBLICATIONS

Other

Skyclimber: The Autobiography of Raymond Z. Gallun, with Jeffrey M. Elliot. New York, Tower, 1981.

*

Raymond Z. Gallun comments:

Most of my science fiction was originally published in the 1930's, mainly in *Astounding* while F. Orlin Tremaine, whom I remember with apreciation, was editor. I think I aimed mostly at realism insofar as it could be construed from what was then supposed to be true about the various planets, plus humanizing of even the unhuman characters, giving them points of sympathetic contact without overdoing the sympathy. Some time after World War II I dropped out of SF to do other things. Being now retired from formal employment, I have been trying to get back into SF writing. "Then and Now" (*Analog*, December 1977) is a fair example of what I have been recently trying to do.

* * *

Raymond Z. Gallun has published in the pulps vast quantities of clumsy and primitive fiction, and yet his treatments of several of the more sophisticated problems facing modern man are often exciting and provocative to read. He is a vintage science-fiction pulp writer from the 1930's who published his most ambitious novel in the 1970's. One critic has labeled his underlying philosophy "Darwinian existentialism"; and two short quotations from what Gallum himself has called his favorite short story. "The Restless Tide," will introduce the stark polarities that he continually balances in his best work. At the end of the story, the protagonist concludes, "Mankind was like a rough, sturdy plant, growing, thrusting; crude but magnificent, and caught between rot and fire." Earlier he had exhorted his wife, "It's the contrasts that count. There's a rough drama in people."

Gallun's novel *The Eden Cycle* is a fine expansion of these earlier themes. The Hegelian balancing of opposites along with the classic polar opposition, which is also a key to the meaning for us of Darwinian theory, between the glory of early primitive development and the continual trend toward greater sophistication are well developed in this long narration of the most advanced human hedonists governed by aliens. In fact, for Gallun the contrasts that run throughout his fictions are so roughly vivid that they become emblematic of what the Renaissance loved to call man's amphibian nature. Aliens are presented as complex and sympathetic characters early—"Old Faithful" (1934)—and then throughout his career. In addition to the rough contrast of man to alien, there is repeatedly drawn the contrast of creature to environment, as in "Godson of Almarlu," as well as the contrast of past to present. Science fiction lends itself particularly well to the old opposition between a golden age of the past and a modern iron age because science fiction tries to image both technology and man's inner primitive self. Gallun's work conveys these oppositions continually in the narratives mentioned above and in such pieces as

People Minus X, "Return of a Legend," and "The Lotus-Engine. "

Rough contrast is also a most appropriate characterization for the literary impressions of Gallun's extrapolations. For example, "The Lotus-Engine" makes skillful use of the classic Homeric myth of the lotus eaters and also weaves a most explicit set of images to convey again the old story of mutability and decline associated with technological advance. But even in this story the pulp characterizations of "old chums" must enter, and the characters even smoke cigarettes inside the oxygen rich helmets of their "space armor. " A genre that can retell the most profound human dilemmas in what are often such rough forms is indeed sturdy and growing, and Gallun was one sturdy and often rough writer who contributed greatly to its growth.

—Donald M. Hassler

GALOUYE, Daniel F(rancis). American. Born in New Orleans, Louisiana, 11 February 1911 (some sources say 1920). Educated at Louisiana State University, Baton Rouge, B. A. in journalism 1941. Served as a pilot in the United States Navy, 1941-46: Lieutenant in Naval Reserve. Married Carmel Barbara Jordan in 1945; two daughters. Reporter, then assistant news editor, 1946-55, chief editorial writer, 1955-60, and Associate Editor, 1960-65, New Orleans *States-Item.* Consultant, New Orleans Science Center and Planetarium Committee. *Died in 1976.*

SCIENCE-FICTION PUBLICATIONS

Novels

Dark Universe. New York, Bantam, 1961; London, Gollancz, 1962.
Lords of the Psychon. New York, Bantam, 1963.
Counterfeit World. London, Gollancz, 1964; as *Simulacron-3,* New York, Bantam, 1964.
The Lost Perception. London, Gollancz, 1966; as *A Scourge of Screamers,* New York, Bantam, 1968.
The Infinite Man. New York, Bantam, 1973.

Short Stories

The Last Leap and Other Stories of the Super Mind. London. Corgi, 1964.
Project Barrier. London, Gollancz, 1968.

Uncollected Short Stories

"O Kind Master," in *If* (New York), January 1970.
"The Big Blow-Up," in *Fantastic* (New York), July 1979.

*   *   *

Daniel F. Galouye, a greatly underrated and largely forgotten writer, is probably best remembered for the numerous short stories and novelettes in the science-fiction "slicks" of the 1950's and 1960's. Despite them, however, his primary contribution to the field rests in three novels: *Dark Universe, Simulacron-3,* and *Lords of the Psychon.* Always well-conceived, well-planned, and well-crafted, Galouye's stories are extrapolations of scientific fact or theory, but his vivid and far-ranging imagination and his incredible attention to detail often carry his readers well into the fantastic. These characteristics are most visible in the novels where the length permits the accumulation of detail to achieve its full impact.

Though many of Galouye's stories use a post-disaster motif, they reflect his optimistic belief in the capability of man to develop his latent mental abilities, and often the resolutions of his plots depend upon the evolvement of such talents as astral projection, extended vision, teleportation, and mental manipulation of matter or energy. Curiously, he often depicts faster-than-light spaceships powered by psychokinesis, as in "The Centipedes of Space" and "Phantom World." His ultimate statement on human development, however, is found in "The Secret of the Immortals," where he proposes a metamorphosis that not only brings new mental powers but an extended life of at least 5,000 years.

Galouye's work also displays a preoccupation with the idea that man may be manipulated by external forces, and often the world of the story is a microcosm of some vaster universe. This concept frequently takes the form of a puppet motif. One of the most unusual twists on this theme occurs in "Gulliver Planet," where microscopic aliens invade the bodies of seven humans and manipulate them as part of their invasion plan. The theme's unique treatment, however, comes in *Simulacron-3,* where Doug Hall, the protagonist, discovers that he is merely an electric analogue in a total electronic simulation of the real world.

Galouye's overriding concern is the nature of reality and the related problem of perceiving it. Most of his stories and his three best novels treat this theme. *Dark Universe* deals with a colony that has survived a world-wide atomic war by retreating underground. One of 17 such colonies, "U.S. Survival Complex Number Eleven" functions well until a minor fault shift totally destroys its ability to generate electricity and cuts off all but a few of the superheated water conduits that lead to the group's basic living chamber. Through succeeding generations, the loss of sight and the disintegration of their knowledge of their original world creates a culture totally dependent on sound for survival and ignorant of their true circumstances. The story concerns the attempt of one young man, Jared Fenton, to discover what light really is. The novel's status as a minor classic comes from Galouye's treatment and control of his material. His elimination of all words from the narrative that relate to sight and his passages which describe how Fenton uses his non-visual senses to perceive his world are brilliantly effective.

Simulacron-3, an extremely original work, also treats the nature of reality. Doug Hall discovers that his world is but an electro-mathematical model of an average community and that it is marked for extinction. In an ironic reversal of roles, he manages to change places with the real Doug Hall, the megalomaniacal operator of the simulator, and prevent his world from being erased. *Lords of the Psychon,* though not quite so well-controlled as *Dark Universe* or so original as *Simulacron-3,* is a post-destruction story that concerns the efforts of Geoffrey Maddox to prevent aliens from drawing Earth into another dimension. In the process of fighting them, he learns that he can mentally manipulate the fundamental form of matter, a pink plasma called psychon, and he proves that it is itself merely a reflection of the mental.

Galouye's major weakness is his relatively shallow characterization. It is often difficult to distinguish between his parade of military protagonists, and his women are seldom more than helpless sex-objects. Where he has the time to infuse his narrative with detail, however, his principal characters manage to become more than cardboard cutouts. Originality, control, and fast pace are typical of his best writing.

—Carl B. Yoke

GARNER, Rolf. See **BERRY, Bryan.**

GARRETT, Gordon. See **GARRETT, Randall.**

GARRETT, (Gordon) Randall. Also writes as Gordon Aghill; Alexander Blade; Walter Bupp; Ralph Burke; Gordon Garrett; David Gordon; Richard Greer; Ivar Jorgensen; Darrell T. Langart; Clyde T. Mitchell; Mark Phillips; Robert Randall; Leonard G. Spencer; S. M. Tenneshaw; Gerald Vance. American. Born in Lexington, Missouri, in 1927. Educated at Texas Tech University, Lubbock, B. S. Served in the United States Marine Corps during World War II: Corporal. Married Vicki Ann Heydron. Industrial chemist, Battle Creek, Michigan, and Peoria, Illinois; then free-lance writer. Address: c/o Bantam Books, 666 Fifth Avenue, New York, New York 10019, U.S.A.

SCIENCE-FICTION PUBLICATIONS

Novels (series: Gandalara)

The Shrouded Planet (as Robert Randall, with Robert Silverberg). New York, Gnome Press, 1957.
The Dawning Light (as Robert Randall, with Robert Silverberg). New York, Gnome Press, 1959.
Unwise Child. New York, Doubleday, 1962; London, Mayflower, 1963; as *Starship Death*, New York, Leisure, 1982.
Anything You Can Do . . . (as Darrell T. Langart). New York, Doubleday, and London, Mayflower, 1963; as *Earth Invader*, New York, Leisure, 1983.
Too Many Magicians. New York, Doubleday, 1967; London, Macdonald, 1968.
Gandalara series, with Vicki Ann Heydron:
  The Steel of Raithskar. New York, Bantam, 1981.
  The Glass of Dyskornis. New York, Bantam, 1982.
  The Bronze of Eddarta. New York, Bantam, 1983.
  The Well of Darkness. New York, Bantam, 1983.
  The Search for Ka. New York, Bantam, 1984.

Novels as Mark Phillips (with Laurence M. Janifer) (series: Kenneth J. Malone in all books)

Brain Twister. New York, Pyramid, 1962.
The Impossibles. New York, Pyramid, 1963.
Supermind. New York, Pyramid, 1963.

Short Stories (series: Lord Darcy)

Takeoff. Virginia Beach, Donning, 1979.
Murder and Magic (Lord Darcy). New York, Ace, 1979.

Lord Darcy Investigates. New York, Ace, 1981.
The Best of Randall Garrett, edited by Robert Silverberg. New York, Pocket Books, 1982.

Uncollected Short Stories (series: Lord Darcy; Leland Hale)

"The Absence of Heat" (as Gordon Garrett), in *Astounding* (New York), June 1944.
"Pest," in *Astounding* (New York), December 1952.
"Instant of Decision," in *Space* (Alhambra, California), May 1953.
"Characteristics, Unusual," in *Science Fiction Quarterly* (Holyoke, Massachusetts), August 1953.
"Nom d'un Nom," in *Fantasy Fiction* (New York), August 1953.
"Hell to Pay," in *Beyond* (New York), March 1954.
"The Wayward Course," in *Future* (New York), March 1954.
"The Surgeon's Knife," in *Universe* (Evanston, Indiana), May 1954.
"Woman Driver," in *Fantastic* (New York), June 1954.
"Infinite Resources," in *Fantasy and Science Fiction* (New York), July 1954.
"Spatial Delivery," in *If* (New York), October 1954.
"Code in the Head," in *Future 29* (New York), 1956.
"Suite Mentale," in *Future 30* (New York), 1956.
"Vanishing Act" (as Robert Randall, with Robert Silverberg), in *Imaginative Tales* (Evanston, Indiana), January 1956.
"The Best of Fences," in *Infinity* (New York), February 1956.
"Quick Cure," in *Fantastic* (New York), February 1956.
"Gambler's Planet" (as Gordon Aghill, with Robert Silverberg), in *Amazing* (New York), June 1956.
"Catch a Thief" (as Gordon Aghill, with Robert Silverberg), in *Amazing* (New York), July 1956.
"The Saboteur," in *Original Science Fiction Stories* (Holyoke, Massachusetts), July 1956.
"Machine Complex," in *Astounding* (New York), July 1956.
"The Beast with Seven Tails" (as Leonard G. Spencer, with Robert Silverberg), in *Amazing* (New York), August 1956.
"Stroke of Genius," in *Infinity* (New York), August 1956.
"The Man Who Hated Mars," in *Amazing* (New York), September 1956.
"The Judas Valley" (as Gerald Vance, with Robert Silverberg), in *Amazing* (New York), October 1956.
"Heist Job on Thizar," in *Amazing* (New York), October 1956.
"The Man Who Knew Everything," in *Fantastic* (New York), October 1956.
"With All the Trappings," in *Astounding* (New York), November 1956.
"Puzzle in Yellow," in *Amazing* (New York), November 1956.
"The Mummy Takes a Wife" (as Clyde T. Mitchell, with Robert Silverberg), in *Fantastic* (New York), December 1956.
"Death to the Earthman," in *Amazing* (New York), December 1956.
"The Inquisitor," in *Imagination* (Evanston, Illinois), December 1956.
"The Star Slavers," in *Imaginative Tales* (Evanston, Illinois), January 1957.
"Deadly Decoy" (as Clyde T. Mitchell, with Robert Silverberg), in *Amazing* (New York), February 1957.
"The Devil Never Waits," in *Dynamic* (New York), February 1957.
"The Time Snatcher," in *Infinity* (New York), February 1957.
"Time to Stop," in *Science Fiction Quarterly* (Holyoke, Massachusetts) February 1957.
"Hungry World," in *Imaginative Tales* (Evanston, Illinois),

March 1957.

"Saturnalia," in *Original Science Fiction Stories* (Holyoke, Massachusetts), March 1957.

"Guardians of the Tower," in *Imagination* (Evanston, Illinois), April 1957.

"The Man Who Collected Women," in *Amazing* (New York), April 1957.

"Masters of the Metropolis," in *Fantasy and Science Fiction* (New York), April 1957.

"The Vengeance of Kyvor," in *Fantastic* (New York), April, May 1957.

"The Last Killer," in *Imaginative Tales* (Evanston, Illinois), May 1957.

"What's Eating You?," in *Astounding* (New York), May 1957.

"You Too Can Win a Harem," in *Dreamworld* (New York), May 1957.

"Needler," in *Astounding* (New York), June 1957.

"A Pattern for Monsters," in *Fantastic* (New York), June 1957.

"Six Frightened Men," in *Imagination* (Evanston, Illinois), June 1957.

"Devil's World," in *Imaginative Tales* (Evanston, Illinois), July 1957.

"Gift from Tomorrow," in *Amazing* (New York), July 1957.

"Skid Row Pilot," in *Imagination* (Evanston, Illinois), August 1957.

"Killer—First Class," in *Imaginative Tales* (Evanston, Illinois), September 1957.

"The Mannion Court-Martial," in *Imagination* (Evanston, Illinois), October 1957.

"To Make a Hero" (Hale), in *Infinity* (New York), October 1957.

"Deathtrap Planet," in *Imaginative Tales* (Evanston, Illinois), November 1957.

"Satellite of Death," in *Imagination* (Evanston, Illinois), December 1957.

"Beyond Our Control," in *Infinity* (New York), January 1958.

"Strike the First Blow!," in *Imaginative Tales* (Evanston, Illinois), January 1958.

"The Low and the Mighty," in *Science Fiction Quarterly* (Holyoke, Massachusetts), February 1958.

"Far from Somewhere," in *Original Science Fiction Stories* (Holyoke, Massachusetts), March 1958.

"Penal Servitude," in *Astounding* (New York), March 1958.

"Prisoner of War," in *Imagination* (Evanston, Illinois), June 1958.

"Respectfully Mine" (Hale), in *Infinity* (New York), August 1958.

". . . and Check the Oil," in *Astounding* (New York), October 1958.

"Burden the Hand," in *Infinity* (New York), November 1958.

"The Savage Machine," in *Fantastic* (New York), November 1958.

"The Queen Bee," in *Astounding* (New York), December 1958.

"The Trouble with Magic," in *Fantastic* (New York), March 1959.

"Small Miracle," in *Amazing* (New York), June 1959.

"But I Don't Think," in *Astounding* (New York), July 1959.

"Dead Giveaway," in *Astounding* (New York), August 1959.

"That Sweet Little Old Lady" (as Mark Phillips, with Larry M. Harris) in *Astounding* (New York), September-October 1959.

"The Unnecessary Man," in *Astounding* (New York), November 1959.

"The Price of Eggs," in *Fantastic* (New York), December 1959.

"The Destroyers," in *Astounding* (New York), December 1959.

"Viewpoint," in *Astounding* (New York), January 1960.

"Drug on the Market" (Hale), in *Fantastic Universe* (Chicago), February 1960.

"The Measure of a Man," in *Astounding* (New York), April 1960.

"Damned If You Don't," in *Astounding* (New York), May 1960.

". . . and Peace Attend Thee," in *Astounding* (New York), September 1960.

"The Highest Treason," in *Astounding* (New York), January 1961.

"Random Choice," in *Fantastic* (New York), March 1961.

"Something Rich and Strange," with Avram Davidson, in *Fantasy and Science Fiction* (New York), June 1961.

"A Spaceship Named McGuire," in *Analog* (New York), July 1961.

"The Blaze of Noon," with Avram Davidson in *Analog* (New York), September 1961.

"Sound Decision," in *Prologue to Analog,* edited by John W. Campbell, Jr. New York, Doubleday, 1962; London, Panther, 1967.

"Hepcats of Venus," in *Fantastic* (New York), January 1962.

"His Master's Voice," in *Analog* (New York), March 1962.

"The Bramble Bush," in *Analog* (New York), August 1962).

"Spatial Relationship," in *Fantasy and Science Fiction* (New York), August 1962.

"A Case of Identity," in *Analog* (New York), September 1964.

"A Fortnight of Miracles," in *Fantastic* (New York), February 1965.

"Tin Lizzie," in *Great Science Fiction Stories about Mars,* edited by T. E. Dikty. New York, Fell, 1966.

"Witness for the Prosecution," in *Fantasy and Science Fiction* (New York), February 1966.

"Fighting Division," in *Analog 5,* edited by John W. Campbell, Jr. New York, Doubleday, 1967; London, Dobson, 1968.

"The Foreign Hand Tie," in *14 Great Tales of ESP,* edited by Idella P. Stone. New York, Fawcett, 1969.

"Ready, Aim, Robot!," in *S. F. Greats* (New York), Summer 1969.

"The Briefing," in *Fantastic* (New York), August 1969.

"Fimbulsommer," in *If* (New York), September 1970.

"After a Few Words," in *The Astounding-Analog Reader 2,* edited by Brian Aldiss and Harry Harrison. New York, Doubleday, and London, Sphere, 1973.

"Color Me Deadly," in *Fantasy and Science Fiction* (New York), October 1973.

"Hail to the Chief," in *American Government Through Science Fiction,* edited by Joseph D. Olander and Martin H. Greenberg. New York, Random House, 1974.

"Pride and Primacy," in *If* (New York), April 1974.

"Reading the Meter," in *Vertex* (Los Angeles), August 1974.

"The Final Fighting of Fion Mac Cumhaill," in *Fantasy and Science fiction* (New York), September 1975.

"The Sixteen Keys," in *Fantastic* (New York), May 1976.

"Lauralyn," in *Analog* (New York), April 1977.

"Polly Plus," in *Isaac Asimov's Science Fiction Magazine* (New York), May-June 1978.

"The Ipswich Phial" (Darcy) in *The Thirteen Crimes of Science Fiction,* edited by Isaac Asimov, Martin H. Greenberg, and Charles G. Waugh. New York, Doubleday, 1979.

"The Napoli Express," in *Isaac Asimov's Marvels of Science Fiction,* edited by George Scithers. New York, Davis, 1979.

"The Bitter End," in *Isaac Asimov's Worlds of Science Fiction,* edited by George Scithers. New York, Davis, 1980.

"Keepersmith," with Vicki Ann Heydron, in *Isaac Asimov's Science Fiction Anthology 3,* edited by George Scithers. New York, Davis, 1980.

"In Case of Fire," in *Hallucination Orbit*, edited by Isaac Asimov, Martin H. Greenberg, and Charles G. Waugh. New York, Farrar Straus, 1983.

"A Matter of Gravity" (Darcy), in *Alfred Hitchcock's Fatal Attractions*, edited by Elana Lore. New York, Davis, 1983.

Uncollected Short Stories as David Gordon

"By the Rule," in *Other Worlds* (Evanston, Indiana), October 1950.

"There's No Fool . . . ," in *Astounding* (New York), August 1956.

"The Convincer," in *Future* (New York), Summer 1957.

"The Best Policy," in *Astounding* (New York), July 1957.

"A Bird in the Hand," in *Future* (New York), February 1958.

"Intelligence Quotient," in *Future* (New York), June 1958.

"The Despoilers of the Golden Empire," in *Astounding* (New York), March 1959.

"Cum Grano Salis," in *Astounding* (New York), May 1959.

" . . . or Your Money Back," in *Astounding* (New York), September 1959.

"Mercenaries Unlimited," in *Fantastic Universe* (Chicago), February 1960.

"By Proxy," in *Astounding* (New York), September 1960.

"Hanging by a Thread," in *Analog* (New York), August 1961.

"Asses of Balaam," in *Analog* (New York), October 1961.

"With No Strings Attached," in *Analog* (New York), February 1963.

Uncollected Short Stories as Alexander Blade

"The Man Who Hated Tuesday," in *Fantastic Adventures* (New York), February 1951.

"A Man Called Meteor," in *Fantastic Adventures* (New York), February 1953.

"Gambit on Ganymede," in *Fantastic Adventures* (New York), March 1953.

"Zero Hour," in *Imagination* (Evanston, Illinois), April 1956.

"Battle for the Stars," in *Imagination* (Evanston, Illinois), June 1956.

"Flight of the Ark II," in *Imaginative Tales* (Evanston, Illinois), July 1956.

"The Man with the Golden Eyes," in *Imagination* (Evanston, Illinois), August 1956.

"The Cosmic Kings," in *Imaginative Tales* (Evanston, Illinois), November 1956.

"The Alien Dies at Dawn," in *Imagination* (Evanston, Illinois), December 1956.

"Wednesday Morning Sermon," in *Imagination* (Evanston, Illinois), January 1957.

"The Tattooed Man," in *Imaginative Tales* (Evanston, Illinois), March 1957.

"The Sinister Invasion," in *Imagination* (Evanston, Illinois), June 1957.

"Blacksheep's Angel," in *Flying Saucers from Other Worlds* (Evanston, Indiana), September 1957.

"The Ambassador's Pet," in *Imagination* (Evanston, Illinois), October 1957.

"The Android Kill," in *Imaginative Tales* (Evanston, Illinois), November 1957.

"The Cosmic Looters," in *Imagination* (Evanston, Illinois), February 1958.

"The Cheat," in *Fantastic* (New York), May 1958.

"Come into My Brain!," in *Imagination* (Evanston, Illinois), June 1958.

"3117 Half-Credit Uncirculated," in *Science Fiction Adventures* (New York), June 1958.

"The Deadly Mission," in *Space Travel* (Evanston, Illinois), September 1958.

Uncollected Short Stories as Richard Greer

"Calling Captain Flint," in *Amazing* (New York), August 1956.

"The Secret of the Shan," in *Fantastic* (New York), June 1957.

"The Great Kladnar Race," in *The Infinite Arena*, edited by Terry Carr. Nashville, Nelson, 1977.

Uncollected Short Stories as Ralph Burke

"No Trap for the Keth," in *Imaginative Tales* (Evanston, Illinois), November 1956.

"Man of Many Bodies," in *Fantastic* (New York), December 1956.

"An Enemy of Peace," in *Fantastic* (New York), February 1957.

"The Incomplete Theft," in *Imagination* (Evanston, Illinois), February 1957.

"Citadel of Darkness," in *Fantastic* (New York), March 1957.

"Monday Immortal," in *Fantastic* (New York), May 1957.

"Hot Trip for Venus," in *Imaginative Tales* (Evanston, Illinois), July 1957.

"The Lunatic Planet," in *Amazing* (New York), November 1957.

"The Reluctant Traitor," in *Science Fiction Adventures* (New York), June 1958.

Uncollected Short Stories as S. M. Tenneshaw (with Robert Silverberg)

"The Ultimate Weapon," in *Imaginative Tales* (Evanston, Illinois), January 1957.

"The Man Who Hated Noise," in *Imaginative Tales* (Evanston, Illinois), March 1957.

"Kill Me If You Can," in *Imagination* (Evanston, Illinois), June 1957.

"House Operator," in *Imagination* (Evanston, Illinois), December 1957.

Uncollected Short Stories as Ivar Jorgensen (with Robert Silverberg)

"Bleekman's Planet," in *Imagination* (Evanston, Illinois), February 1957.

"Slaughter on Dornel IV," in *Imagination* (Evanston, Illinois), April 1957.

"Pirates of the Void," in *Imaginative Tales* (Evanston, Illinois), July 1957.

Uncollected Short Stories as Walter Bupp (series: Maragon in all stories)

"Vigorish," in *Astounding* (New York), June 1960.

"Card Trick," in *Analog* (New York), January 1961.

"Modus Vivendi," in *Analog* (New York), September 1961.

"The Right Time," in *Analog* (New York), December 1963.

"Psi for Sale," in *Analog* (New York), September 1965.

OTHER PUBLICATIONS

Novel

Pagan Passions, with Laurence M. Janifer. New York, Galaxy, 1959.

Other

Pope John XXIII, Pastoral Prince. Derby, Connecticut, Monarch, 1962.
A Gallery of the Saints. Derby, Connecticut, Monarch, 1963.

*   *   *

Randall Garrett paid his dues writing under a bewildering number of pseudonyms for the magazines of the 1950's, and most of his stories are firmly set in the idea-oriented action adventure frame of the *Astounding* "house style". Character and description are kept firmly subordinate to concept and event, and, however useful this period may have been in teaching him his craft, the results are more often than not routine. For example, compare "There's No Fool" with Asimov's "Belief." The theme in both is essentially emotional rather than intellectual: How do you convince someone of something he "knows" to be impossible? Where Garrett treats the theme in an externalised fashion, Asimov takes us inside the emotional confusion of his characters. "Despoilers of the Golden Empire" (in *Takeoff*), to give another example, is a pure literary trick, retelling the life of Pizarro in terms of the clichés of space opera.

The early stories, although superficial in many ways, are never less than entertaining and occasionally there appears a unity of theme and style that is exceptional and which produces a strength of effect above Garrett's routine level. In "But I Don't Think" he produces an early example of his love of inverting the themes of classic science-fiction in a black parody of *The Space Merchants*. A privileged member of an autocratic society is suddenly thrust into its lowest depths. Where Pohl and Kornbluth's hero joined the underground and learns humanity, Garrett's character shoots his serf benefactress and returns cringing to duty. "The Destroyers" is the story of a society doomed by outsiders seeking to liberate it. It concentrates on mood rather than action, allowing most of the major events to occur "offstage. "

In the 1960's and 1970's Garrett produced first a minor, then a major, series of interralated stories. The minor series, written as Walter Bupp (and containing a character called Walter Bupp) are particularly strong in characterisation, creating a sub-culture of outcast psionics, neurotic and embittered, trying to find a way to live with the culture that rejects them. (I think I detect an influence from them in Anne McCaffrey's *To Ride Pegasus.*) The major series is the Lord Darcy stories. Set in a world ruled by an Angevin Empire of the 20th century, in which magic has become the dominant science and technology, they centre on the detective Lord Darcy of Rouen and his "Forensic Magician" Master Sean O'Lochlainn. They parody many major detective writers (Rex Stout in the person of the Marquis of London, Dorothy L. Sayers in the opening of "The Ipswich Phial", Agatha Christie in "The Napoli Express" and Conan Doyle just about everywhere – "Dr Pately frowned. 'A what?' 'Elemental, my dear Doctor. '") Every story is fair to the reader in following the rules of the classic detective story but it's not unfair to say that, of the series, the novel *Too Many Magicians* is the most successful.

In the 1970's the volume of Garrett's output declined but the quality if anything improved. To be noted is his collection of parodies, *Takeoff*, and the Gandalara series written with his wife Vicki Ann Heydron. Set in a desert world these stories have become very popular and certainly have all the virtues of Garrett's skilled storytelling. But for me they lack the mental sleight of hand and depth of theme of the best of earlier Garrett.

In my opinion it's a great shame that there is no collection of the best of Randall Garrett's output of short fiction available to give younger readers without access to the old magazines a taste of this writer who has given so much to the field in the form he made most use of.

—Michael Cule

GAWRON, Jean Mark. American. Born in Paris, France, 2 October 1953. Educated at New York University, B. A. 1974; University of California, Berkeley, M. A. 1980. Cab driver, New York, 1974-75; tutor, John Jay College of Criminal Justice, New York, 1977.

SCIENCE-FICTION PUBLICATIONS

Novels

An Apology for Rain. New York, Doubleday, 1974.
Algorithm. New York, Berkley, 1978.

*   *   *

Jean Mark Gawron has written two novels basically concerned with the lack of meaning in modern society. Both seem to present partially hallucinatory atmospheres, but there is a strong element of intellectual control over these surrealistic backgrounds. As with many first novels, *An Apology for Rain* is an elaboration of the Quest theme with a woman hunting for her brother, who may be able to end a war in an After-the-Bomb America. The novel is written in a sparse but literary and impressionistic style which imitates the austere landscape. *Algorithm* is written in a more complex, poetic, and fluid style which mirrors the decadent setting. *Algorithm* is also a variation of the Quest theme as a bizarre cast of characters search for an assassin as part of a *coup d'état*. The plots of both books are deceptively involved and intentionally ambiguous. The concept of an algorithm as a pattern for a thought process, whether performed by a human or a computer, is a fundamental organizing principle for Gawron's view of literature. He shares with Samuel Delany an intense interest in patterns of thought as they are reflected in linguistics, communication theory, computer science, and semantics.

Gawron seems to have been influenced by Alfred Jarry's concepts of pataphysics as applied to literature. The most significant result is his emphasis on the fundamental and inescapable ambiguity of language, literature, and life. Likewise, much of the dialogue is abrupt, perversely circular, and combined with intermittent scenes of metaphoric visual description. In addition, there are sudden reversals of meanings and comprehension, redundancy, imitative form, and a frequent use of symbolic masks and elaborately strange costumes. Although in very different ways, both of his books convey an air of melancholy as he asks us to "Quaff the torpid photons of your autumn. "

—Norman L. Hills

GENTLE, Mary. British. Born in Eastbourne, Sussex, 29 March 1956. Attended high school in Hastings, Sussex. Has worked as movie projectionist, clerk, and civil servant. Address: Flat 1, 11 Alumhurst Road, Westbourne, Bournemouth, Dorset, England.

SCIENCE-FICTION PUBLICATIONS

Novels

A Hawk in Silver (for children). London, Gollancz, 1977.
Golden Witchbreed. London, Gollancz, 1983.

Uncollected Short Stories

"The Crystal Sunlight, The Bright Air," in *Isaac Asimov's Space of Her Own,* edited by Shawna McCarthy. New York, Davis, 1983.
"A Shadow under the Sea," in *Isaac Asimov's Science Fiction Magazine* (New York), October 1983.
"The Harvest of Wolves," in *Isaac Asimov's Science Fiction Magazine* (New York), December 1983.
"Anukazi's Daughter," in *Isaac Asimov's Tomorrow's Voices.* New York, Davis, 1984; London, Hale, 1985.

*   *   *

Mary Gentle's first novel, *A Hawk In Silver,* a juvenile fantasy (written when she was 18), falls outside the concerns of this volume, but her first adult science-fiction novel, *Golden Witchbreed,* suggests that a major new talent has entered the genre. It would be all too easy to give comparatives—to state that the novel is a Le Guin-like story (with touches of *The Left Hand of Darkness*) set in a Delanyesque environment (and I think particularly of *Nova*)—but that's to denigrate the originality of her achievement. Lynne de Lisle Christie is an envoy from Earth to the human-like aliens of Orthe (and that subtle distinction in names is of a piece with the subtle distinctions throughout the novel on every level). Her journeys about Orthe, the betrayals, discoveries, and eventual self-discovery, involve us not merely on the level of the adventure story, but make us consider our own social organisations. Orthe is a world which, while seeming primitive, is in fact more advanced than our own – it has chosen a different social direction to our own: "But you don't expect an ancient race to be dirty-handed. . . . You don't expect them to kill—or if you do, it's with world-destroying weapons: nothing so simple and bloody as a yard of razor-edged metal. And yet they're not simple. " Gentle's depiction of this world and its people is vividly imagined and—unlike so many such conceived worlds—acutely real to us. This is, if you like, romantic realism; a novel to be compared with the best in the modern genre.

—David Wingrove

GEORGE, Peter (Bryan). Also wrote as Peter Bryant; Bryan Peters. British. Born in Wales in 1924. Served in the Royal Air Force during World War II; rejoined Royal Air Force in 1951; retired as Flight Lieutenant, 1962. *Died 1 June 1966.*

SCIENCE-FICTION PUBLICATIONS

Novels

Two Hours to Doom (as Peter Bryant). London, Boardman, 1958; as *Red Alert,* New York, Ace, 1959; revised edition, as *Dr. Strangelove; or, How I Learned to Stop Worrying and Love the Bomb* (as Peter George), London, Corgi, 1963; New York, Bantam, 1964.
Commander-1. London, Heinemann, and New York, Delacorte Press, 1965.

OTHER PUBLICATIONS

Novels

Come Blonde, Came Murder. London, Boardman, 1952.
Pattern of Death. London, Boardman, 1954.
Cool Murder. London, Boardman, 1958.
The Final Steal. London, Boardman, 1962; New York, Dell, 1965.

Novels as Bryan Peters

Starbuck. London, Digit, 1957.
Hong Kong Kill. London, Boardman, 1958; New York, Washburn, 1959.
Sons of Nippon. London, Digit, 1961.
The Big H. London, Boardman, 1961; New York, Holt Rinehart, 1963.

*   *   *

On the basis of his two science-fiction novels, Peter George's career in science fiction would be only a footnote in the literary history of science fiction. But one of them, *Two Hours to Doom* (*Red Alert*), formed the basis for Stanley Kubrick's brilliant film *Dr. Strangelove,* and the rewritten novel *Dr. Strangelove* must be considered a minor classic of science fiction. No other example comes to mind of a film "tie-in" novel superior to the original written version, and this work will repay serious reading and examination.

Richard Gid Powers's introduction to the Gregg Press edition of *Dr. Strangelove* (1979) examines *Red Alert* in the context of the tradition of "future war" fiction, most especially the nuclear holocaust stories so characteristic of the Cold War period, and draws a comparison with Nevil Shute's *On the Beach* (1957). *Red Alert* is a humorless thriller, full of procedural details concerning the Strategic Air Command and of sincere moral underpinnings, about the danger of hair-trigger nuclear retaliation systems to all humanity. At the end of the book, catastrophe is averted, both Russians and Americans seek peace, and the wise President has the last word. Not so *Dr. Strangelove.* Powers makes a case that Kubrick and Southern, in writing the screenplay, altered George's original beyond his control and his talents. Whatever is the case, *Dr. Strangelove* is a small masterpiece of black humor, worth a place beside works by Heller and Vonnegut—and it is certainly within the borders of science fiction, though only just. In the new version an insane general closes his US military base and sends his planes against the Russians, fully armed for retaliation from an (imagined) enemy attack (and, for security, maintaining radio silence); all planes are turned back in the nick of time, except one, whose radio is damaged—whose target will detonate an automatic Doomsday Machine, a nuclear device capable of destroying the entire surface of the earth—and this one plane succeeds heroically and ironically and destroys the world. Except for the ending, this is George's story. But it is not told in George's *Red Alert* style nor with his characters. All the ordinary names are changed to grotesques, to General Jack D. Ripper, "king" Kong, Mandrake, Turgidson, Strangelove. Every sentence points out, deadpan and without a moral stance, the insanity and absurdity of every character and every action in context. The point of view is non-human (note the framing device not in the film) and this is the story of the end of humanity. Science-fiction elements are added, through the presentation of mad scientist Strangelove, in the body of the text as well.

On the other hand, George's sequel, *Commander-1* (in which the last surviving military officer after nuclear holocaust declares himself the ruler of the world and forms a dystopian island society in the south seas) is serious, moral, and pedestrian. It is in every way a sequel to *Red Alert*, not to *Dr. Strangelove*.

—David G. Hartwell

GERNSBACK, Hugo. American. Born in Luxembourg, 16 August 1884; emigrated to the United States in 1904. Educated at the Ecole Industrielle, Luxembourg; Bingen Technikum, Germany. Married Marn Hancher (third marriage); two daughters and one son from previous marriages. Inventor, businessman, and editor: Founder, Electric Importing Company, world's first radio supply house, and designed the first home radio set, Telimco Wireless: the Telimco catalogue evolved into the first radio magazine, *Modern Electrics*, 1908, then *Electrical Experimenter*, 1913, and *Science and Invention*, 1920; also edited 50 other magazines, including *Radio News* and *Sexology*, and the first science-fiction magazine, *Amazing*, 1926-29, *Amazing Stories Annual*, 1927, *Amazing Stories Quarterly*, 1928-29, *Air Wonder Stories*, 1929-30, *Science Wonder Stories*, 1929-35, *Science Wonder Quarterly*, 1929-32, *Scientific Detective*, 1929-30, *Thrilling Wonder Stories*, 1929-36, *Amazing Detective Tales*, 1930, and *Science Fiction Plus*, 1953; held some 80 patents; founded WRNY radio, New York, 1925, and made television broadcasts in 1928. Recipient: Hugo Special Award, 1960 (the Hugo Award is named after him). Officer of the Oaken Crown, Luxembourg, 1954. *Died 19 August 1967.*

SCIENCE-FICTION PUBLICATIONS

Novels

Ralph 124C41+: A Romance of the Year 2660. Boston, Stratford, 1925; London, Cherry Tree, 1952.
Ultimate World, edited by Sam Moskowitz. New York, Walker, 1971.

Uncollected Short Stories (series: Baron Munchausen)

"How to Make a Wireless Acquaintance" (Munchausen), in *Electrical Experimenter* (New York), May 1915.
"How Munchausen and the Allies Took Berlin," in *Electrical Experimenter* (New York), June 1915.
"Munchausen on the Moon," in *Electrical Experimenter* (New York), July 1915.
"The Earth as Viewed from the Moon" (Munchausen), in *Electrical Experimenter* (New York), August 1915.
"Munchausen Departs for the Planet Mars," in *Electrical Experimenter* (New York), October 1915.
"Munchausen Is Taught Martian," in *Electrical Experimenter* (New York), December 1915.
"Thought Transmission on Mars" (Munchausen), in *Electrical Experimenter* (New York), January 1916.
"Cities on Mars" (Munchausen), in *Electrical Experimenter* (New York), March 1916.
"The Planets at Close Range" (Munchausen), in *Electrical Experimenter* (New York), April 1916.
"Martian Amusements" (Munchausen), in *Electrical Experimenter* (New York), June 1916.
"How the Martian Canals Are Build" (Munchausen), in *Electrical Experimenter* (New York), November 1916.
"Martian Atmosphere Plants" (Munchausen), in *Electrical Experimenter* (New York), February 1917.
"The Magnetic Storm," in *Amazing* (New York), July 1926.
"The Electric Duel," in *Amazing* (New York), September 1927.
"The Killing Flash," in *Science Wonder Stories* (New York), November 1929.
"The Infinite Brain," in *Future* (New York), June 1942.
"Exploration of Mars," in *Science Fiction Plus* (New York), March 1953.

OTHER PUBLICATIONS

Other

The Wireless Telephone. New York, Modern Electrics, 1910.
Wireless Hook-Ups. New York, Modern Electrics, 1911.
Radio for All. Philadelphia, Lippincott, 1922.
How to Build and Operate Short Wave Receivers. New York, Short Wave Craft, 1932.
Evolution in Modern Science Fiction. New York, Gernsback, 1952.
TV Repair Techniques. New York, Gernsback, 1953.
Science Fiction vs. Reality. Privately printed, 1960.
Concrete Science Fiction. Privately printed, 1961.
"The Prophets of Doom," in *The Science Fiction Roll of Honor,* edited by Frederik Pohl. New York, Random House, 1975.

*

Critical Study: *Hugo Gernsback, Father of Science Fiction* by Sam Moskowitz, privately printed, 1959.

*   *   *

While Hugo Gernsback is regarded as one of the pivotal figures in the history of science fiction, his own output of fiction was relatively limited, and only two of his works—novels written many years apart—are available to readers lacking access to magazine files.

Gernsback's major occupation was publishing, and he started a series of popular science magazines in 1908. Here his most famous work, *Ralph 124C41+*, was serialized in 1911-12. The chief virtue of the novel is its serious attempt at detailed prediction. Among many other developments, Gernsback anticipated the substitution of zipcode-like designations for patronymics. In this connection, Ralph's name can be read as a rebus-like pun: "one to foresee for one." Considerable cleverness is shown in the book's predictions, some of which were listed in later years by Gernsback's longtime admirer and onetime employee, Sam Moskowitz: "Florescent lighting, skywriting, automatic packaging machines, plastics, the radio directional range finder, juke boxes, liquid fertilizer, hydroponics, tape recorders, rustproof steel, loud speakers, night baseball, aquacades, microfilm, television, radio networks, vending machines dispensing hot and cold foods and liquids, flying saucers, a device for teaching while the user is asleep, solar energy for heat and power, fabrics from glass, synthetic materials such as nylon for wearing apparel, and, of course, space travel. . . ." In addition, as Moskowitz points out, *Ralph* not only predicts the development of radar, but provides an accurate explanation of its principles. While *Ralph 124C41+* is an astonishing feat of technical prediction, it is, unfortunately, almost unreadable. Gernsback's notions of characterization and plotting were borrowed from the corniest of Victorian melodrama. Even these limitations might have been overcome by a lively narrative style, but Gernsback's style was dull and his tone pedantic. He was convinced that the function of science fiction was education, and apparently envisioned his typical reader as a not-very-bright young adolescent who had trouble with his high school science courses, and would be helped by the reiteration of his lessons in thinly fictionalized form.

In 1915-16, Gernsback published a series of short stories, about Baron Munchausen. Typically, each story concentrates on demonstrating one principle of physics, chemistry, astronomy, geology, etc., in the familiar pedantic Gernsback style. In his second novel, *Ultimate World,* a party of alien scientists, studying the earth and its inhabitants, and possessed of vast powers to control humans, conduct a series of sexual experiments, at first on a married couple, then on many more individuals. Despite the apparently *risqué* theme of the book, its development is marked by the same dull pedantry that had made *Ralph* practically unreadable.

In fact, Gernsback's impact on the field was primarily a result of his efforts as a publisher. Almost from the outset he had featured an occasional work of science fiction in his popular science magazines. In 1924 he announced Scientifiction; somehow the project failed to materialize, but by 1926 Gernsback was able to issue *Amazing Stories,* the first science-fiction magazine. Gernsback's heavy emphasis on detailed scientific detail and the generally stodgy tone of his publications limited both their popular acceptance and their literary levels, but his contributions as a pioneer are undeniable.

—Richard A. Lupoff

GERROLD, David. Pseudonym for Jerrold David Friedman; also writes as Noah Ward. American. Born in Chicago, Illinois, 24 January 1944. Educated at Los Angeles Valley Junior College; University of Southern California, Los Angeles; California State University, Northridge, B. A. in theatre arts 1967. Columnist, *Starlog* and *Galileo* magazines; story editor, *Land of the Lost* TV series, 1974. Since 1984, computer columnist, *Profiles.* Recipient: Skylark Award, 1979. Agent: Richard Curtis, 164 East 64th Street, New York, New York, 10021. Address: Box 1190, Hollywood, California 90028, U.S.A.

SCIENCE-FICTION PUBLICATIONS

Novels (series: Chtorr)

The Flying Sorcerers, with Larry Niven. New York, Ballantine, 1971; London, Corgi, 1975.

Space Skimmer. New York, Ballantine, 1972.
Yesterday's Children. New York, Dell, 1972; London, Faber, 1974.
When Harlie Was One. New York, Doubleday, 1972.
Battle for the Planet of the Apes (novelization of screenplay). New York, Award, 1973.
The Man Who Folded Himself. New York, Random House, and London, Faber, 1973.
Moonstar Odyssey. New York, New American Library, 1977.
Deathbeast. New York, Popular Library, 1978; London, Hale, 1981.
The Galactic Whirlpool. New York, Bantam, 1980.
The War Against the Chtorr :
  1. *A Matter for Men.* New York, Pocket Books, 1983; London, Futura, 1984.
  2. *A Day for Damnation.* New York, Pocket Books, 1984.

Short Stories

With a Finger in My I. New York, Ballantine, 1972.

Uncollected Short Stories

"An Infinity of Loving," in *Ten Tomorrows,* edited by Roger Elwood. New York, Fawcett, 1973.
"Skinflowers," in *The Beserkers,* edited by Roger Elwood. New York, Simon and Schuster, 1974.
"Out of the Darkness," in *Witchcraft and Sorcery 10* (Alhambra, California), 1974.
"Hellhole," in *Isaac Asimov's Science Fiction Anthology 3,* edited by George H. Scithers. New York, Davis, 1980.

OTHER PUBLICATIONS

Plays

Screenplays: *Man Out of Time; Logan's Run* (as Noah Ward).

Television Plays: *The Trouble with Tribbles,* 1967, and *The Cloud Minders,* 1968, both in *Star Trek* series; *More Trouble with Tribbles,* 1973, and *BEM,* 1974, both in *Aminated Star Trek* series; *CHA-KA, The Sleestak God, Possession, Circle,* and *Hurricane,* all in *Land of the Lost* series; *The Swamp Monster,* in *The Biskitts* series; *Levitation* and *If the Shoes Fit . . .* (as Noah Ward), both for *Tales from the Darkside* series, 1984.

Other

The Trouble with Tribbles. New York, Ballantine, 1973.
The World of Star Trek. New York, Ballantine, 1973; revised edition, New York, Bluejay, 1984.
SF Yearbook. New York, O'Quinn Studio, 1979.

Editor, with Stephen Goldin, *Protostars.* New York, Ballantine, 1971.
Editor, with Stephen Goldin, *Generation.* New York, Dell, 1972.
Editor, *Science Fiction Emphasis 1.* New York, Ballantine, 1974.
Editor, with Stephen Goldin, *Alternities.* New York, Dell, 1974.
Editor, with Stephen Goldin, *Ascents of Wonder.* New York, Popular Library, 1977.

*

David Gerrold comments:
I don't talk about writing. I write.

*   *   *

In many ways, David Gerrold's imagination has been shaped by his west coast roots and the influence of the community of SF writers that flourished there after World War II. It is characteristic of former fans like Gerrold to remain attached to the work of once-admired writers and to imitate, perhaps not always consciously, their narrative formulas, conventions, and mannerisms of style. Much of Gerrold's traditionalism and his hero worship of writers like Asimov, Heinlein, Sturgeon, Kuttner, Kornbluth, Clarke, and Bradbury may be understood as the result of Gerrold's adolescent experience as a SF fan. Gerrold shares with some other fans-turned-SF-writers an indiscriminate enthusiasm for the genre and its established idioms, and he tends to be naive in approach and often subjective in his treatment of SF subjects. But unlike, say, Larry Niven, Gerrold has little interest in and understanding of science. As a writer he seems primarily concerned with the excitement of fictionalized science technology, especially as dramatized in the SF of the 1950's and early 1960's.

It is significant that Gerrold made his debut as a professional writer on the television series *Star Trek* with *I, Mudd,* about an interstellar scoundrel and confidence man. Other *Star Trek* scripts and books followed. In terms of impact and audience exposure, this writing is without question his most important.

Gerrold's short stories are relatively few in number. They range from space opera adventure to comic and weird fantasy. It is characteristic of Gerrold to rely on SF literature already established by other writers rather than on new ideas of science as the basis for his own fiction.

One of Gerrold's most representative works is *When Harlie Was One,* the story of the development of a self-programming computer known by its acronym, HARLIE (Human Analogue Robot, Life Input Equivalents). The density of this ultimate computer is to direct and manage world society. Unlike Arthur C. Clarke's HAL or Dennis Jones's Forbin *Colossus,* Harlie is treated as the great electronic hope for social advancement. Harlie's existence necessarily generates opposition, and the plot turns on the gradual realization by David Auberson, head of the Harlie project and robot psychologist, that Harlie is no mere reasoning machine, but in fact human, and therefore should enjoy a human's rights and immunities. The powerful scientific and political forces opposing Harlie as a menace to freedom are portrayed as representative of primitive and destructive impulses of human nature. Whether Gerrold introduces Harlie as the eventual successor to homo sapiens in the long, upward spiral of evolution seems less important for his novel than the author's largely successful demonstration of the way technology forces human reason to discover the limitations of its own historic programming. The victory over the corporate forces of reaction may seem and probably is rather naively contrived even though the world seems bent upon fulfilling the prophetic stereotype. Charactistically for Gerrold, the denouement represents both an admonition and the vindication of both intelligence and human courage, whether exercised by man or machine.

If the influence of Clarke and Asimov is ascendant in *When Harlie Was One,* the inspiration behind *The Man Who Folded Himself* is Heinlein. This time-travel story, like Heinlein's "All You Zombies . . .," focuses attention on the "grandfather paradox" and its potential impact on the human psyche. Gerrold's moral position, however, seems more traditional then Heinlein's, insofar as certain values are confirmed as

absolute. The influence of new wave SF may be detected in Gerrold's handling of the sexual implications of his theme of multiple self-encounters through time-travel displacement. Although at first it may appear that Gerrold favors a free love philosophy often rather simplistically associated with the California cult, his novel dramatizes rather subtly that sexual attraction and interaction make up only a portion of human relationships, and indeed, not even the decisive portion. An equally effective aspect of *The Man Who Folded Himself* is Gerrold's skill in maintaining the verisimilitude of time travel through plausible and at times inspired inventive touchstones of the kind of world implied in the novel's premise. These are features of Gerrold's best efforts as a writer of both SF and fantasy.

Gerrold's other novels do not compare favorably with the ones mentioned. *The Flying Sorcerers,* written with Larry Niven, is by far his best fantasy effort, but then the influence of Niven has much to do with that.

—Donald L. Lawler

GESTON, Mark S(ymington). American. Born in Atlantic City, New Jersey, 20 June 1946. Educated at Abington High School; Kenyon College, Gambier, Ohio (*Kenyon Review* Prize, 1968), A. B. in history 1968 (Phi Beta Kappa); New York University Law School (Root-Tilden Fellow), 1968-71, J. D. 1971. Married 1) Gayle Howard in 1971 (divorced, 1972); 2) Marijke Havinga in 1976; two daughters and one son. Since 1971, Attorney, Eberle Berlin Koding and Gillespie, Boise, Idaho. Agent: Paul R. Reynolds, 12 East 41st Street, New York, New York 10017. Address: Box 1368, Boise, Idaho 83701, U.S.A.

SCIENCE-FICTION PUBLICATIONS

Novels

Lords of the Starship. New York, Ace, 1967; London, Joseph, 1971.
Out of the Mouth of the Dragon. New York, Ace, 1969; London, Joseph, 1972.
The Day Star. New York, DAW, 1972.
The Siege of Wonder. New York, Doubleday, 1976.

Uncollected Short Story

"The Stronghold," in *Fantastic* (New York), July 1974.

*   *   *

Mark S. Geston is an unarmored adventurer into worlds of ideas and dreams not yet articulated by our world. He examines with compassion and keen eyes the apparent cycles of the desire of humanity to construct and destroy. He often deals with time in a tangible way, as an individual might deal with the real rivers of our world.

Out of the Mouth of the Dragon begins with the record of a mightly battle lost and the return of the only surviving ship carrying the survivors back the the Maritime Republics. With the return of this ship begins a young man's long trek back to the ultimate Armageddon which would either renew humanity or result in the end of consciousness for the inhabitants of this world. It is an interesting though rather depressing tale of the quest of man to modify his physical and moral restrictions by choosing to accept a mortality over which he has some control. Thus the novel offers hope to mortals: in the face of the inevitable, what we become is what counts.

In *The Day Star* Geston etches the propensity of humanity for war, and the timeless effects of this propensity. As usual, he mixes dreams with reality, tangibility with mists, ghosts with people, and legend with substance in a fascinating, shimmering kaleidoscope of a being engaged in the ultimate search: for reality and the realization of the higher aspirations of his society.

Siege of Wonder present a hemisphere of wizardry opposing a hemisphere of science, with mankind attempting to destroy itself even after many wasted generations. Geston seems to be saying that the magic of one beholder may be the science of the next.

Geston is adept at painting those things which, to the average reader, would seem to illustrate contrary values. One scene in *Siege of Wonder* has a wizard commander coming through the city with his followers' whitened bones protuding from their armor—a sign of the importance of their leader.

—John V. Garner

GIBSON, William (Ford). American. Born in Conway, South Carolina, 17 March 1948. Educated at the University of British Columbia, Vancouver, B. A. in English 1977. Married Deborah Jean Thompson in 1972; one son and one daughter. Recipient: Philip K. Dick Memorial Award, 1985; Nebula Award, 1985. Agent: Martha Millard, 357 West 19th Street, New York, New York 10011, U. S. A. Address: 2630 West 7th Avenue, Vancouver, British Columbia V6K 1Z1, Canada.

SCIENCE-FICTION PUBLICATIONS

Novels

Neuromancer. New York, Ace, and London, Gollancz, 1984.
Count Zero. New York, Arbor House, 1985.

Uncollected Short Stories

"Fragments of a Hologram Rose," in *Unearth* (Boston), Summer 1977.
"The Gernsback Continuum," in *Universe 11*, edited by Terry Carr. New York, Doubleday, 1981.
"The Belonging Kind," with John Shirley, in *Shadows 4*, edited by Charles L. Grant. New York, Doubleday, 1981.
"Hinterlands," in *Omni* (New York), October 1981.
"Burning Chrome," in *The Best Science Fiction of the Year 12*, edited by Terry Carr. New York, Pocket Books, 1983.
"Johnny Mnemonic," in *Nebula Award Stories 17*, edited by Joe Haldeman. New York, Holt Rinehart, 1983.
"Red Star, Winter Orbit," with Bruce Sterling, in *Omni* (New York), July 1983.
"New Rose Hotel," in *Omni* (New York), July 1984.
"Dogfight," with Michael Swanwick, in *Omni* (New York), July 1985.

*

Critical Study: interview with Steve Brown, in *Heavy Metal*, (New York), May 1985.

*   *   *

Since 1981 William Gibson has published a handful of memorable short stories and one novel—*Neuromancer* — which won a Nebula Award, a Philip K. Dick Memorial award, and a Hugo nomination. In his work to date Gibson has accomplished that rare thing in science fiction, a persuasive vision of believable human life in a vividly realized future. His work combines the best aspects of both traditional science fiction—a real interest in exploring the consequences of reasonable technological change—and "new wave" s-f, which demands consideration of what living with such change would really mean to the characters. Gibson's best work so far—*Neuromancer*, "Johnny Mnemonic," "Burning Chrome"—is set in a rather frightening, decadent high-tech future, roughly a century from now. The age is characterized by extreme advances in medicine, bio-engineering, neurochemistry, cloning, computers, and the social and political power of multinational corporations. Japan has become both the cultural and technological center of the world. While it is to Gibson's great credit that this future is almost wholly believable, it is his ability to make us accept his characters as true products of and participants in that world that marks him as a writer of real promise.

"Johnny Mnemonic," the author's second story, typifies Gibson's basic concerns. The hero-narrator has a headful of implanted silicon memory chips which he rents to those who need discreet storage for their "hot" data. Johnny walks and talks and appears human, but he is actually little more than a self-aware safety deposit box until he is threatened with assassination for storing a load of stolen information. Now he must transcend his self-elected ignorance, taking full charge of his mind, memories, and life, or die ignominiously, a half-human cyborg murdered by a Yakuza killer-clone. Gibson's world, though clearly imagined, is not the significant center here or in his other stories; rather, it is the life of the mind, as it wrestles with the difficulties of actually being human in this world, that intrigues him and informs his work.

Crucial to understanding Gibson's fiction is the notion that human beings may be considered highly complex but comprehensible, manipulable collections of data. Genetically we are, in a sense, coded ROM (Read Only Memory), while as embodied experience we can be seen as a combination of complicated programs and short-term RAM (Random Access Memory). As we learn to control biochemical processes, managing the data that is us, as our computers become increasingly sophisticated, and as we find ways to "interface" directly with these vastly powerful mechanisms, the gulf between cybernetic existence and human being will diminish and the distinctions become increasingly problematic. Such concepts as humanity, freedom, selfhood, reality itself will take on whole new meanings.

Neuromancer is particularly concerned with such issues. Its protagonist Case is wholly himself only when his mind dwells in "cyberspace," linked directly to the world-wide computer net while his "meat" body lies dormant and ignored. Another principal figure appears human but is in fact a personality constructed by a vast Artificial Intelligence and programmed into what remains of a lunatic's psyche. The Artificial Intelligence, self-aware though utterly mechanical, desperately seeks to break its cybernetic shackles and attain true existential freedom. As such changes occur, what will determine "humanity," "civil rights," "freedom"? *Neuromancer*, "Burning

Chrome," "New Rose Hotel," and "Johnny Mnemonic" are Gibson's answers, exploring the human consequences of living where computer piracy, "brain wars" among multinational zaibatsu's, and "street samurai" who kill with home-brewed cancers are commonplace.

"Hinterlands" and "The Gernsback Continuum," though not set in the Neuromancer world, also reflect Gibson's interest in exploring intense psychological states engendered by enigmatic scientific events. The latter story is particularly notable for its rather bittersweet view of the American Dream of progress through technology.

—David G. Mead

GIESY, J(ohn) U(lrich). Also wrote as Charles Dustin. American. Born in Ohio, 6 August 1877. Physician and physiotherapist. Writer for Munsey magazines. *Died 8 September 1947.*

SCIENCE-FICTION PUBLICATIONS

Novels (series: Palos)

All for His Country. New York, Macaulay, 1915.
Palos of the Dog Star Pack. New York, Avalon, 1965.
The Mouthpiece of Zitu (Palos). New York, Avalon, 1965.
Jason, Son of Jason (Palos). New York, Avalon, 1966.

Uncollected Short Stories

"Indigestible Dog Biscuits," in *All-Story Weekly* (New York), 13 July 1918.
"Zapt's Repulsive Paste," in *All-Story Weekly* (New York), 29 November 1919.
"Blind Man's Buff," in *All Story Weekly* (New York), 24 January 1920.
"Beyond the Violet," in *Argosy All-Story Weekly* (New York), 27 November 1920.
"Catalepsy," in *Argosy All-Story Weekly* (New York), 19 March 1921.
"The Acumen of Martin McVeagh," in *Argosy All-Story Weekly* (New York), 7 July 1923.

Uncollected Short Stories with Junius B. Smith

"Great Wizard of the Peak," in *Cavalier* (New York), January 1910.
"In 2112," in *Cavalier* (New York), 10 August 1912.
"The Curse of Quetzal," in *All-Story Cavalier Weekly* (New York), 28 November 1914.
"The Web of Destiny," in *Argosy All-Story Weekly* (New York), 20 March 1915.
"Snared," in *All-Story Weekly* (New York), 11 December 1915.
"Box 991," in *All-Story Weekly* (New York), 3 June 1916.
"The Killer," in *All-Story Weekly* (New York), 7 April 1917.
"The Unknown Quantity," in *All-Story Weekly* (New York), 25 August 1917.
"The Black Butterfly," in *All-Story Weekly* (New York), 14 September 1918.
"Stars of Evil," in *All-Story Weekly* (New York), 25 January 1919.

"The Ivory Pipe," in *All-Story Weekly* (New York), 20 September 1919.
"House of the Hundred Lights," in *All-Story Weekly* (New York), 22 May 1920.
"Black and White," in *Argosy All-Story Weekly* (New York), 2 October 1920.
"Wolf of Erlik," in *Argosy All-Story Weekly* (New York), 22 October 1921.
"The Opposing Venus," in *Argosy All-Story Weekly* (New York), 18 November 1923.
"Poor Little Pigeon," in *Argosy All-Story Weekly* (New York), 9 August 1924.
"The Wooly Dog," in *Argosy All-Story Weekly* (New York), 23 March 1929.
"The Green Goddess," in *Argosy* (New York), 21 January 1931.
"The Ledger of Life," in *Argosy* (New York), 20 June 1934.
"The Gravity Experiment," in *Famous Fantastic Mysteries* (New York), December 1939.

OTHER PUBLICATIONS

Novels

The Other Woman, with Octavus Roy Cohen. New York, Macaulay, 1917; London, Gardner, 1920.
Mimi. New York, Harper, 1918.
The Valley of Suspicion. New York, Garden City Publishing Company, 1927.
The Mystery Woman, with Junius B. Smith. Racine, Wisconsin, Whitman, 1929.

Novels as Charles Dustin

Hardboiled Tenderfoot. New York, Dodge, 1939.
Bronco Men. New York, Dodge, 1940.
Riders of the Desert Trail. New York, Dodge, 1942.

*   *   *

J. U. Giesy wrote his earliest works in collaboration with Junius B. Smith, a series of humorous detective mysteries featuring a detective, Semi-Dual, who used astrology, crystal balls, and psychic phenomena in solving his cases. Giesy himself also wrote a number of stories based on humorous and improbable inventions.

Giesy's best known and most admired novels are the Palos trilogy. In *Palos of the Dog Star Pack* Jason Croft is transported by a process the author calls astral projection to Palos, a planet in the Sirius system, where he is able to assume and occupy the body of a dying man. Croft brings to Palos a wide knowledge of earthly sciences, including the weapons of war, a great asset in his progress toward a position of influence and power on this new world. In *The Mouthpiece of Zitu* Croft is required to convince the people of Palos and the princess Naia that he is a mortal and a fit mate for her. In the course of these efforts Croft introduces electricity to Palos, as well as the locomotive and the airplane. These developments, needless to say, enhance his position with the natives and with the princess. *Jason, Son of Jason* carries the story on to the next generation.

Giesy's stories are well written and well plotted, with considerable descriptive power and character analysis. His literary style and his means of transporting his hero from earth to another planet, however, show the influence of Burroughs. With both authors, the animal life of these strange worlds is indeed strange, with unearthly flying creatures and gigantic multi-limbed animals. There is always, however, a group of females built to Terran specifications, who are almost invariably beautiful, lightly clad and amorous. This tradition continues to the present.

—Douglas E. Way

GILLILAND, Alexis A(rnaldus). American. Born in Bangor, Maine, 10 May 1931. Educated at Purdue University, West Lafayette, Indiana, B. S. 1953; George Washington University, Washington, D. C., M. S. 1963. Served in the United States Army Presidential Honor Guard, 1954-56. Married Dorothy Cohle in 1959; one son. Thermochemist, National Bureau of Standards, 1956-67, and chemist and specification writer, Federal Supply Service, 1967-82, both in Washington, D. C. Since 1982, free-lance writer. Also a cartoonist. Recipient: Hugo Award, for art, 1980, 1983, 1984; John W. Campbell Award, 1982. Address: 4030 Eighth Street South, Arlington, Virginia 22204, U. S. A.

SCIENCE-FICTION PUBLICATIONS

Novels (series: Rosinante)

The Revolution from Rosinante. New York, Ballantine, 1981.
Long Shot for Rosinante. New York, Ballantine, 1981.
The Pirates of Rosinante. New York, Ballantine, 1982.
The End of the Empire. New York, Ballantine, 1983.

OTHER PUBLICATIONS

Other (cartoons)

The Iron Law of Bureaucracy. Port Townsend, Washington, Loompanics, 1979.
Who Says Paranoia Isn't "In" Anymore. Port Townsend, Washington, Loompanics, 1985.

*   *   *

The Campbell Award-winner Alexis A. Gilliland exemplifies the basic literary principle "write what you know. " Gilliland, a retired federal bureaucrat, exposes the inner workings of authority with an accuracy and detail science fiction has hitherto only pretended to achieve. He has written what may be sf's first "consciously thematic" as opposed to propagandistic stories about bureaucracy. (Compare Keith Laumer's polemical farces about Terran diplomacy which are also based on personal experience.)

Instead of merely denouncing administrative sclerosis, Gilliland establishes it through form as well as content. His storytelling technique employs both alternating and redundant viewpoints assembled like overlapping transparencies to create composite figure no single sheet can hold. Data-handling and decision-making processes are actually shown but, just as in a real bureaucracy, words outnumber deeds. Slick, witty, punlaced dialogue carries the plot. Many scenes depict conferences. Extracts from memos and other documents provide exposition. Gilliland's plausible technology reflects his initial scientific training. He is careful to show exactly how his characters are fed, clothed, and housed. This concreteness anchors outrageous events to some semblance of reality. Off-beat humor

penetrates everything, even the sex and metaphysics, for Gilliland is also a gifted cartoonist. (He has won three Hugo Awards as Best Fan Artist and has published two cartoon books.)

Gilliland's writing career opened with the Rosinante trilogy. Here, under the leadership of a maverick bureaucrat, a space colony wins its independence from the despotic North American Union and topples terrestrial powers. But the real winners prove to be the revolutionaries' computers, intelligent mechanisms who wear the images of 20-century movie stars. One computer proclaims itself the prophet of a new spacefaring religion while another evangelizes humans on its behalf to establish a symbiotic society of machines and men.

The End of the Empire is a more conventional narrative with a more radical message. It dares to criticize libertarianism, a political system favored by Robert A. Heinlein and other sf writers. Gilliland shows how too little government can be every bit as disastrous as too much government. (For example, tyrannical anarchy defines subversion as attempting to "underraise" the regime.) The hero is a brilliant loner loyal to a moribund empire which he can be expected to revive singlehandedly in future adventures. Among the hero's obvious prototypes are Poul Anderson's Flandry and Keith Laumer's Retief, gallant guardians to whom this book is dedicated.

Deftness with politics and drollery should insure Gilliland a successful sf career. "It is my fond belief," says the author, "that my novels bear thinking about, and that this may give the reader some insight into the real world, but this is an *ex post facto* rationalization to justify having written. "

—Sandra Miesel

GILMAN, Robert Cham. See COPPEL, Alfred.

GILMORE, Anthony. See BATES, Harry.

GLAMIS, Walter. See SCHACHNER, Nat.

GLOAG, John (Edwards). British. Born in London, 10 August 1896. Attended technical high school, London. Served in the Essex Regiment, 1916-17, and Welch Guards, 1917-19: 2nd Lieutenant; invalided home, 1918. Married Gertrude Mary Ward in 1922; one daughter, and one son, the writer Julian Gloag. Worked in studio of Thornton-Smith Ltd., 1913-16; advertising department staff member, Lever Organisation, 1920-22; Art Editor, 1922-27, and Editor, 1927, *Cabinet Maker*; Director, Pritchard Wood & Partners, 1928-61; Director of Public Relations, Timber Development Association, 1936-38; full-time writer after 1961. Member, Advisory Committee, Board of Trade, 1943-47; Member of Board of Trustees, Sir John Soane's Museum, 1960-70. Vice-President,

Royal Society of Arts, 1952-54; President, Society of architectural Historians, 1960-64. Recipient: Royal Society of Arts silver medal, 1943, and bicentenary gold medal, 1958. *Died 17 July 1981.*

SCIENCE-FICTION PUBLICATIONS

Novels

To-morrow's Yesterday. London, Allen and Unwin, 1932.
The New Pleasure. London, Allen and Unwin, 1933.
Winter's Youth. London, Allen and Unwin, 1934.
Manna. London, Cassell, 1940.
99%. London, Cassell, 1944.

Short Stories

First One and Twenty. London, Allen and Unwin, 1946.

OTHER PUBLICATIONS

Novels

Sweet Racket. London, Cassell, 1936.
Ripe for Development. London, Cassell, 1936.
Sacred Edifice. London, Cassell, 1937; revised edition, 1954.
Documents Marked Secret. London, Cassell, 1938.
Unwilling Adventurer. London, Cassell, 1940.
I Want an Audience. London, Cassell, 1941.
Mr. Buckby Is Not at Home. London, Cassell, 1942.
In Camera. London, Cassell, 1945.
Kind Uncle Buckby. London, Cassell, 1946.
All England at Home. London, Cassell, 1949.
Not in the Newspapers. London, Cassell, 1953.
Slow. London, Cassell, 1954.
Unlawful Justice. London, Cassell, 1962.
Rising Suns. London, Cassell, 1964.
Caesar of the Narrow Seas. London, Cassell, 1969; New York, St. Martin's Press, 1972.
The Eagles Depart. New York, St. Martin's Press, 1973.
Artorius Rex. London, Cassell, and New York, St. Martin's Press, 1977.

Short Stories

It Makes a Nice Change. London, Nicholson and Watson, 1938.
Take One a Week: An Omnibus Volume of 52 Short Stories. London, Chantry, 1950.

Verse

Board Room Ballads and Other Verses. London, Allen and Unwin, 1933.

Other

Simple Furnishing and Arrangement, with Helen Gloag. London, Duckworth, 1921.
Simple Schemes for Decoration. London, Duckworth, and New York, Stokes, 1922.
The House We Ought to Live In, with Leslie Mansfield. London, Duckworth, 1923.
Colour and Comfort. London, Duckworth, 1924; New York, Stokes, 1925.
Time, Taste, and Furniture. London, Richards, and New York, Stokes, 1925.

Artifex; or, The Future of Craftsmanship. London, Kegan Paul, and New York, Dutton, 1926.
Home Life in History: Social Life and Manners in Britain 200 B.C.-A.D. 1926, with C. Thompson Walker. London, Benn, 1927; New York, Coward McCann, 1928.
Modern Home Furnishing. London, Macmillan, 1929.
Men and Buildings. London, Country Life, and New York, Scribner, 1931; revised edition, London, Chantry, 1950.
English Furniture . London, A. & C. Black, 1934; 6th edition, 1973.
Industrial Art Explained. London, Allen and Unwin, 1934; revised edition, 1946.
Word Warfare: Some Aspects of German Propaganda and English Liberty. London, Nicholson and Watson, 1939.
The American Nation: A Short History of the United States. London, Cassell, 1942; revised edition, with Julian Gloag, 1955.
What about Business? London, Penguin, 1942; revised edition, as *What about Enterprise?,* London, Allen and Unwin, 1948.
The Missing Technician in Industrial Production. London, Allen and Unwin, 1944.
The Englishman's Castle: A History of Homes, Large and Small, in Town and Country, from A. D. 100 to the Present Day. London, Eyre and Spottiswoode, 1944; revised edition, 1949.
Plastics and Industrial Design. London, Allen and Unwin, 1945.
British Furniture Makers. London, Collins, and New York, Hastings House, 1945.
House Out of Factory, with Grey Wornum. London, Allen and Unwin, 1946.
Good Design, Good Business. London, His Majesty's Stationery Office, 1947.
The English Tradition in Design. London, Penguin, 1947; revised edition, London A. & C. Black, 1959; New York, Macmillan, 1960.
Self-Training for Industrial Designers. London, Allen and Unwin, 1948.
A History of Cast Iron in Architecture, with D. L. Bridgewater. London, Allen and Unwin, 1948.
How to Write Technical Books . London, Allen and Unwin, 1950.
Two Thousand Years of England. London, Cassell, 1952.
A Short Dictionary of Furniture. London, Allen and Unwin, and New York, Studio, 1952; revised edition, 1969.
Georgian Grace: A Social History of Design from 1660 to 1830. London, A. & C. Black, and New York, Macmillan, 1956.
Guide to Western Architecture. London, Allen and Unwin, and New York, Grove Press, 1958.
Advertising in Modern Life. London, Heinemann, 1959.
Victorian Comfort: A Social History of Design 1830-1900. London, A. & C. Black, and New York, Macmillan, 1961.
Victorian Taste: Some Social Aspects of Architecture and Industrial Design from 1820-1900. London, A. & C. Black, and New York, Macmillan, 1962.
The English Tradition in Architecture. London, A. & C. Black, and New York, Barnes and Noble, 1963.
Architecture. London, Cassell, 1963; New York, Hawthorn, 1964.
The Englishman's Chair: Origins, Design, and Social History of Seat Furniture in England. London, Allen and Unwin, 1964; as *The Chair,* South Brunswick, New Jersey, A. S. Barnes, 1967.
Enjoying Architecture. Newcastle upon Tyne, Oriel Press, 1965.
A Social History of Furniture Design from B. C. 1300 to A. D. 1960. London, Cassell, and New York, Crown, 1966.

Mr. Loudon's England: The Life and Work of John Claudius Loudon, and His Influence on Architecture and Furniture Design. Newcastle upon Tyne, Oriel Press, 1970.
Guide to Furniture Styles: English and French 1450-1850. London, A. & C. Black, and New York, Scribner, 1972.
The Architectural Interpretation of History. London, A. & C. Black, 1975.

Editor, *Design in Modern Life*. London, Allen and Unwin, 1934.
Editor, *The Place of Glass in Building*. London, Allen and Unwin, 1943; revised edition, 1948.
Editor, *Introduction to Early English Decorative Detail*. London, Academy, 1965.

*   *   *

In a writing career spanning more than 50 years John Gloag published more than 60 books. These include works dealing with history, social history, architecture, propaganda, and industrial art as well as numerous short stories, mysteries, mainstream novels, and science fiction. The science fiction, written mostly in the 1930's and 1940's, is more closely related to the fiction of Huxley, Stapledon and Beresford than to the products of the burgeoning science-fiction magazine market of that period.

The short stories often deal with unexplainable phenomena and science-fiction concepts, but the brevity of the form does not allow Gloag fully to explore the ramifications of his ideas.

To-morrow's Yesterday, Gloag's first extended foray into science fiction, uses the complicated device of a motion picture within the novel. The motion picture is represented as an attempt by the species which has suceeded man to understand the forces within humanity that led to its extinction. The creatures from the future examine the contemporary, 1930, situation, and conclude that "They all lived for themselves!" The creatures then travel back in time to view a conversation between Herod and Pilate and they remark "There have been great ones who could see and teach and plan . . . But . . . with them everything ended in words. " Subsequent scenes in the film show the beginning of the war which leads to man's descent into barbarism, and several stages in man's reversion to animality. The concluding portion of the book depicts the public's reaction to the film and allows Gloag to comment bitterly on the worlds of advertising, newspaper publishing, and to show that the world is following the path outlined in the film.

In *Winter's Youth* Gloag examines the political and social consequences of a process that arrests and reverses aging. Peripheral to the main plot, but lending verisimilitude to the action are the concepts of radiant inflammatol (the dealiest of all explosives which makes war impossible), government advertising in newspapers, a faked new apocryphal book of the Bible, German pagan religion, and a new British political party. Much of the action concerns the political manoeuvring which arises because of the disclosure of the faked apocrypha and the consequences that the age-arresting process has on the users and on the general public. Gloag creates a scathing portrait of political partisanship, but he again attacks journalism and the advertising industry.

99% explores the effects on a number of men, who represent various aspects of society, of a drug which allows the individual to re-experience a significant event in the life of one of his ancestors. The motivating concept, that it is possible to relive important experiences of remote ancestors, because the memories are somehow incorporated into the genetic material, is one that has no scientific validity, but Gloag is not interested in the concept. He is concerned with the effects that the experiences have upon modern, civilized men. The experiences dredged up, by the drug and the influence of the man supplying the drug, range from that of a waylaid, failed Crusader, to that of a young boy fleeing the sack of Carthage, to that of a shaman of a tribe that existed millennia ago. The memories change the outlooks of the contemporary men in ways that could not have been anticipated.

—Harvey J. Satty

———————

GODFREY, R. H. See **TUBB, E. C.**

———————

GODWIN, Tom. American. Born in 1915. Worked as a prospector. Lives in Nevada.

SCIENCE-FICTION PUBLICATIONS

Novels

The Survivors. New York, Gnome Press, 1958; as *Space Prison*, New York, Pyramid, 1960.
The Space Barbarians. New York, Pyramid, 1964.
Beyond Another Sun. New York, Curtis, 1971.

Uncollected Short Stories

"The Gulf Between," in *Astounding* (New York), October 1953.
"No Species Alone," in *Universe* (Evanston, Illinois), November 1954.
"The Cold Equations," in *The Best Science Fiction Stories and Novels 1955*, edited by T. E. Dikty. New York, Fell, 1955.
"The Barbarians," in *If* (New York), December 1955.
"You Created Us," in *The Best Science Fiction Stories and Novels 1956*, edited by T. E. Dikty. New York, Fell, 1956.
"Operation Opera," in *Fantasy and Science Fiction* (New York), April 1956.
"Brain Teaser," in *If* (New York), October 1956.
"The Harvest," in *Venture* (Concord, New Hampshire), July 1957.
"The Nothing Equation," in *Amazing* (New York), December 1957.
"The Last Victory," in *The Best Science Fiction Stories and Novels 9*, edited by T. E. Dikty. Chicago, Advent, 1958.
"The Wild Ones," in *Original Science Fiction Stories* (Holyoke, Massachusetts), January 1958.
"My Brother—The Ape," in *Amazing* (New York), January 1958.
"Cry from a Far Planet," in *Amazing* (New York), September 1958.
"A Place Beyond the Stars," in *Super Science Fiction* (New York), February 1959.
"Empathy," in *Fantastic* (New York), October 1959.
"The Helpful Hand of God," in *Analog* (New York), December 1961.
" . . . and Devious the Line of Duty," in *Analog* (New York), December 1962.

"The Greater Thing," in *More Penguin Science Fiction,* edited by Brian Aldiss. London, Penguin, 1963.

"Mother of Invention," in *Spectrum 5,* edited by Kingsley Amis and Robert Conquest. London, Gollancz, 1966; New York, Harcourt Brace, 1967.

"The Gentle Captive," in *Signs and Wonders,* edited by Roger Elwood. Old Tappan, New Jersey, Revell, 1972.

"We'll Walk Again in the Moonlight," in *Crisis,* edited by Roger Elwood. Nashville, Nelson, 1974.

"The Steel Guardian," in *Antaeus* (New York), Spring 1977.

"Before Willows Ever Walked," in *Fantasy and Science Fiction* (New York), March 1980.

"Too Soon to Die," in *Science Fiction from A to Z,* edited by Isaac Asimov, Martin H. Greenberg, and Charles G. Waugh. Boston, Houghton Mifflin, 1982.

*   *   *

"The Cold Equations" is the story for which Tom Godwin is best known and upon which rests his secure place in the history of science fiction. It is entirely fitting tht it was first published in John Campbell's *Astounding Science Fiction* because, although written slightly after the period of Campbell's domination of the genre magazines and, therefore, the genre itself, the story is the prototypic Campbellian story, at once a prime example of golden-age science fiction and a definer of it. James Gunn, in *The Road to Science Fiction 3,* called "The Cold Equations" a touchstone story.

"The Cold Equations" presents a future in which space travel has become developed enough for mankind to begin the process of colonizing some of the other habitable planets. But this is only the beginning of the great age of colonization. Fuel still needs to be exactly measured and at every turn the universe threatens human life. As is made clear, however, these threats are not the creations of a hostile universe for the specific destruction of humanity. These threats originate within the nature of the universe, and all objects, living or not, that inhabit that universe must live under their sway. Thus, early in the story, Godwin presents his reader with a view of space that parallels the view of the frontier held by early American pioneers.

A space colony is suffering from a disease for which there is a serum, and a small ship is sent to rescue the colonists. The ship has sufficient fuel to carry the pilot and his cargo to the stricken colony and not a drop more. However, a girl has stowed away on the ship with the hope of once again seeing her brother who is one of the colonists. Within this simple plot Godwin develops the most popular of Campbell's themes: ignorance kills. Whether man is challenged by a creation of science, an alien invasion, or a new environment, what will most surely destroy the race is not the challenge but a failure to know the nature of that challenge. The girl did not realize the consequences of her actions, but at the end of the story she must be jettisoned. The universe is not sentimental. While it will make no special effort to kill a human being, it will do nothing to save one, either. Nothing Godwin has written since has equalled this one story. In *The Survivors* a race of aliens maroon some 4,000 humans on a hostile planet barely capable of sustaining human life. But the humans do adapt and later return to destroy the aliens who were once their conquerors. Mankind will prevail, Godwin tells the reader, for the race has the intelligence, desire, and energy to survive all threats. *The Space Barbarians,* a sequel to *The Survivors,* continues this theme, though in a more space-opera manner. Godwin returns again to the pioneer nature of the human race in *Beyond Another Sun* in which alien anthropologists observe humans as they colonize a planet.

In each of the works that follow "The Cold Equations" many of the features tht characterized that story can be seen: a clear narrative voice, simple descriptions that economically fill in the background needed to understand the action of the characters, themes that form the very foundation of golden-age science fiction, and occasional sentimental passages that, at their best, soften the harshness of the fictional worlds and, at their worst, detract from the effect Godwin is attempting to achieve. But "The Cold Equations" contains these traits in a way that few other science-fiction works have matched.

—Stephen H. Goldman

———————

GOLD, H(orace) L(eonard). Born in Montreal, Canada, 26 April 1914; emigrated to the United States at age 2. Served as a combat engineer in the Pacific, 1944-46. Married 1) Evelyn Stein in 1939; 2) Muriel Conley; one son and three step-children. Assistant Editor, *Thrilling Wonder Stories, Startling Stories,* and *Captain Future,* and Associate Editor, Standard Magazines, New York, 1939-41; Managing and Contributing Editor, Scoop Publications, New York, 1941-43; Editor, A and S Comics, New York, 1942-44; Contract Writer, Molle Mystery Theatre, 1943-44; President, Rossard Company, New York, 1946-50; Editor, *Galaxy,* and Galaxy Science Fiction Novels, New York, 1950-61; Editor, *Beyond Fantasy Fiction,* 1953-55, and *If,* 1959-61: retired as disabled veteran, 1960. Recipient: Hugo Award, for non-fiction, 1953; Westercon Life Achievement Award, 1975. Address: 360 South Burnside Avenue, No. 6L, Los Angeles, California 90036, U. S. A.

SCIENCE-FICTION PUBLICATIONS

Short Stories

The Old Die Rich and Other Science Fiction Stories. New York, Crown, 1955; London Dobson, 1965.

Uncollected Short Stories

"The Transmogrification of Wamba's Revenge," in *Galaxy* (New York), October 1967.

"The Riches of Embarrassment," in *Galaxy* (New York), April 1968.

"The Villains from Vega IV," with E. J. Gold, in *Galaxy* (New York), October 1968.

"That's the Spirit," in *Amazing* (New York), March 1975.

"Warm Dark Places," in *More Wandering Stars,* edited by Jack Dann. New York, Doubleday, 1981.

OTHER PUBLICATIONS

Other

What Will They Think of Last? Crestling, California, Institute for the Development of the Harmonious Human Being, 1976.

Editor, *Galaxy Reader* [and *Second* to *Sixth*]. New York, Crown, 2 vols., 1952-54; New York, Doubleday, 4 vols., 1958-62; selection from *The Second Galaxy Reader* as *The Galaxy Science Fiction Omnibus,* London, Grayson, 1955.

Editor, *Five Galaxy Short Novels*. New York, Doubleday, 1958.

Editor, *The World That Couldn't Be and 8 Other Novelets from Galaxy*. New York, Doubleday, 1959.

Editor, *Bodyguard and Four Other Short Novels from Galaxy*. New York, Doubleday, 1960.

Editor, *Mind Partner and Eight Other Novelets from Galaxy*. New York, Doubleday, 1961.

Editor, *The Weird Ones*. New York, Belmont, 1962; London, Dobson, 1965.

*

H. L. Gold comments:

I would very much like to be rediscovered as a science-fiction and fantasy author (including work since 1955), but I'm overshadowed as editor.

* * *

About half a dozen editors and publishers have had a truly pervasive effect on the development of science fiction. Some of these are well remembered; others, almost wholly forgotten. The list must include Frank A. Munsey, who virtually invented the pulp magazine in 1896, Farnsworth Wright (*Weird Tales*), Hugo Gernsback (*Amazing Stories*), John W. Campbell, Jr. (*Astounding*), Anthony Boucher and J. Francis McComas (*The Magazine of Fantasy and Science Fiction*), and H. L. Gold. After many years of editorial work, in 1950 Gold became the founding editor of *Galaxy Science Fiction*. The importance of this event cannot be overemphasized. For some twenty years prior to 1950, *Astounding* had paid the highest rates in the science fiction field, had enjoyed the backing of the largest, wealthiest, and most influential publishing house, and had maintained by far the largest circulation. As a consequence, the bulk of quality writing in the field was calculated to reach *Astounding*. Even the lesser magazines, because they tended to subsist on the leavings of *Astounding*, also reflected the taste of *Astounding's* editors. With the almost simultaneous founding of *Fantasy and Science Fiction* and *Galaxy*, two new markets opened which paid competitive rates and offered generally equivalent quality of presentation and prestige. *F & SF* emphasized style, wit, and general literary excellence. *Galaxy*, reflecting Gold's world-view, placed heavy emphasis on social satire, combining relevance of theme with irreverence of outlook. The result was a magnificent flowering of novels and short stories by Pohl and Kornbluth, Simak, Asimov, Bradbury, Heinlein, and scores of others.

Gold's own writing has been of limited quantity and impact, although it is far from worthless. His only novel, *None But Lucifer*, was written in collaboration with L. Sprague de Camp for *Unknown* magazine in 1939, and has never been reprinted. Of Gold's scattered short stories, a dozen were gathered in *The Old Die Rich*. As might be expected, the stories reflect considerable, often acid, wit. The title story of the book concerns a complex scheme of time travel and murder, unravelled through careful, formal detection techniques. "Love in the Dark" deals lightly with the succubus theme, brought up-to-date and converted into a tale of contact with aliens. "Trouble with Water," probably Gold's best-remembered story, is a fantasy concerning a small business man who offends a water elemental. A number of other stories in the book, particulary "The Man with English" and "Problem in Murder," hold up well despite their age. Particularly interesting in the book is Gold's page of notes on each story, detailing his original conception, technical problems, and

writing approach to that project.

Also of interest is *What Will They Think of Last?*, a collection of Gold's editorials from *Galaxy*. Some of the editorials reflect ephemeral concerns, but others are most illuminating on the functioning of *Galaxy* during the Gold era.

—Richard A. Lupoff

GOLDIN, Stephen. American. Born in Philadelphia, Pennsylvania, 28 February 1947. Educated at the University of California, Los Angeles, B. A. in astronomy 1968. Married Kathleen McKinney (i. e., Kathleen Sky, *q. v.*), in 1962 (divorced, 1982). Physicist, Navy Space Systems Activity, El Segundo, California, 1968-71; Manager, Circle K. Grocery Store, Rosemead, California, 1972; Editor, Jaundice Press, Van Nuys, California, 1973-74; Editor, San Francisco *Ball*, 1973-74, *SFWA Bulletin*, 1975-77, and *L-5 News*, 1981-83. Agent: Joseph Elder Agency, 150 West 87th Street, No. 6D, New York, New York 10024. Address 389 Florin Road, No. 22, Sacramento, California 95831-1406, U. S. A.

SCIENCE-FICTION PUBLICATIONS

Novels (series: The Family d'Alembert)

Herds. Toronto, Laser, 1975.
Caravan. Toronto, Laser, 1975.
Scavenger Hunt. Toronto, Laser, 1975.
Finish Line. Toronto, Laser, 1976.
The Imperial Stars (d'Alembert). New York, Pyramid, and London, Panther, 1976.
Strangler's Moon (d'Alembert). New York, Pyramid, 1976; London, Panther, 1977.
The Clockwork Traitor (d'Alembert). New York, Pyramid, 1976; London, Panther, 1978.
Assault on the Gods. New York, Doubleday, 1977; London, Hale, 1978.
Getaway World (d'Alembert). New York, Pyramid, and London, Panther, 1977.
Mindflight. New York, Fawcett, 1978; London, Hamlyn, 1982.
Appointment at Bloodstar (d'Alembert). New York, Pyramid, 1978; as *The Bloodstar Conspiracy*, London, Panther, 1978.
The Purity Plot (d'Alembert). London, Panther, 1978; New York, Berkley, 1980.
Trek to Madworld. New York, Bantam, 1979.
The Eternity Brigade. New York, Fawcett, 1980.
A World Called Solitude. New York, Doubleday, 1981.
And Not Make Dreams Your Master. New York, Fawcett, 1981.
Planet of Treachery (d'Alembert). New York, Berkley, and London, Panther, 1982.
Eclipsing Binaries (d'Alembert). New York, Berkley, 1983; London, Panther, 1984.
The Omicron Invasion (d'Alembert). New York, Berkley, 1984.
Revolt of the Galaxy (d'Alembert). New York, Berkley, 1985.

Uncollected Short Stories

"The Girls on USSF 193," in *If* (New York), 1965.
"Sweet Dreams, Melissa," with C. F. Hensel, in *Best SF 1968*, edited by Harry Harrison and Brian Aldiss. New York, Putnam, 1969.
"The Last Ghost" and "The World Where Wishes Worked,"

in *Protostars*, edited by David Gerrold and Stephen Goldin. New York, Ballantine, 1971.

"Stubborn," in *Generation*, edited by David Gerrold and Stephen Goldin. New York, Dell, 1972.

"Grim Fairy Tale," in *Adam* (Los Angeles), 1972.

"Constance and the Sex Machine," in *Adam* (Los Angeles), 1972.

"Nor Iron Bars a Cage," with C. F. Hensel, in *The Alien Condition*, edited by Stephen Goldin. New York, Ballantine, 1973.

"Harriet," in *Tomorrow's Alternatives*, edited by Roger Elwood. New York, Macmillan, 1973.

"A Nice Place to Visit," in *Vertex* (Los Angeles), 1973.

"Of Love, Free Will and Gray Squirrels on a Summer Evening," in *Vertex* (Los Angeles), 1973.

"But as a Soldier, for His Country," in *Universe 5*, edited by Terry Carr. New York, Random House, 1974; London, Dobson, 1978.

"Prelude to a Symphony of Unborn Shouts," in *Future Corruption*, edited by Roger Elwood. New York, Warner, 1975.

"In the Land of Angra Mainyu," in *Nameless Places*, edited by Gerald W. Page. Sauk City, Wisconsin, Arkham House, 1975.

"Xenophobe," in *Vertex* (Los Angeles), August 1975.

"Portrait of the Artist as a Young God," in *Ascents of Wonder*, edited by David Gerrold and Stephen Goldin. New York, Popular Library, 1977.

"When There's No Man Around," in *Asimov's Choice: Astronauts and Androids*, edited by George H. Scithers. New York, Davis, 1977.

"Apollyon ex Machina," in *Chrysalis 6*, edited by Roy Torgeson. New York, Kensington, 1979.

"Painting the Roses Red," with Kathleen Sky, in *Science Fiction Times*, May 1980.

"The Devil Behind the Leaves," with Kathleen Sky, in *Fantasy Book* (Pasadena, California), October 1981.

"One Step at a Time," with Grant Carrington, in *Amazing* (New York), June 1982.

OTHER PUBLICATIONS

Other

The Business of Being a Writer, with Kathleen Sky. New York, Harper, 1982.

Editor, with David Gerrold, *Protostars*. New York, Ballantine, 1971.

Editor, with David Gerrold, *Generation*. New York, Dell, 1972.

Editor, *The Alien Condition*. New York, Ballantine, 1973.

Editor, with David Gerrold, *Science Fiction Emphasis 1*. New York, Ballantine, 1974.

Editor, with David Gerrold, *Alternities*. New York, Dell, 1974.

Editor, with David Gerrold, *Ascents of Wonder*. New York, Popular Library, 1977.

*

Stephen Goldin comments:

Looking closely at my work might almost give one the impression that my short stories were written by someone entirely different than the author of my novels. This is due in part to the changes in myself, and in part of the nature of the works themselves.

With only a few exceptions, my short stories are downbeat and tragic. They were the product of my early career, a young man trying to impress the world with his cynicism and acceptance of the universe's perversity. In part, too, this is because a short story is like a photograph, an encapsulated moment of immense importance to the character(s) involved—and it seemed far easier for me to capture a tragic moment than a triumphant one. My mind was at its blackest in tragedies like "The Last Ghost," "Sweet Dreams, Melissa," "Of Love, Free Will, and Gray Squirrels on a Summer Evening," and "Xenophobe"; but there is a bleakness in even those stories with a primarily humorous slant: "The World Where Wishes Worked," "Stubborn," "Grim Fairy Tale," and "Constance and the Sex Machine."

My career (and my apparent outlook) did a complete turnabout when I switched to writing novels in the mid-1970's. Every single one of my novels has an upbeat ending. If a short story may be likened to a photograph, then a novel is a movie, the progression of a character through events, changing at least himself if not the world around him. I like to believe now that a person is responsible for his own life; even if the situation starts out looking hopeless and desperate, a firm and resourceful person can take charge of himself and turn the situation around. My characters may go through hell, but in the end they manage to triumph over their adversities. The somewhat more mature me doesn't need to hide behind that shield of cynicism. I've become a born-again optimist. If there is any message in my work at all, it's that no matter how bad things might be there is always a solution to the person willing to work for it.

*   *   *

Stephen Goldin has become one of the established writers of science-fiction adventure during the past decade, with over a dozen novels and a handful of short stories published during that period. His first novels were for the ill-fated Laser line, but he was able to move on from there to more established publishers. *Scavenger Hunt*, the best of his four Laser novels, dealt with a brother and sister on an interstellar scavenger hunt, a social event that takes on more than casual significance as murder and mayhem become common elements in the competition. The sister becomes warped by the pressures, obsessed with winning the hunt. Goldin completed the adventure in a sequel, *Finish Line*.

Herds was set in a hippie commune, when a young woman is telepathically linked to aliens. The hippies have been framed by a local man who has murdered his wife and seeks to escape the blame. The aliens are part of a herd culture, essentially communistic, and the contrast between them and the commune is interesting. Goldin's fourth Laser novel was *Caravan*, an after-the-apocalypse novel wherein a group of people flee across the country to secret caverns where the first working starship is under construction. It is not nearly as interesting as the previous four books.

A fugitive from the repressive government of Earth lives like a hermit in *A World Called Solitude*, until a castaway tells him of encroaching aliens and the urgent need to warn Earth. Initially he is not disposed to help, but ultimately species loyalty wins out and he is able to use the technology of an extinct race to foil aliens. *Assult on the Gods* is another version of the primitive planet dominated by a secret computer complex that functions as a god. Adventurers from off planet set out on a quest to free the natives from its mental domination.

One of Goldin's best novels is *Mindflight*. Telepathic humans fall prey to telepause, a period of increased telepathic ability that takes place shortly before the death of the telepath. The protagonist is a secret agent who is affected by the onset of telepause, and who is being hunted by his fellow agents because he may possess a secret that he does not recognize himself.

And Not Make Dreams Your Master concerns the world when dreams can be broadcast and talented dreamers are the pinnacles of the entertainment world, shaping their fantasies for the satisfaction of the public. But when the most popular dreamer crosses the border into insanity, the lives of his viewing public may be in jeopardy. *The Eternity Brigade* follows the careers of a number of professional soldiers whose personalities are stored in memory banks, brought back into existence only when there is a battle to be fought. After several generations, the soldiers are virtually slaves, their tapes have been stolen by the other side and duplicated, and they may find themselves fighting their former friends, or themselves. These are to date the best of Goldin's novels.

Goldin has also written a number of volumes in the Family d'Alembert series, based on characters and situations created by Edward E. Smith. There is an interstellar empire, control of which is herditary but centered upon Earth. Essentially the empire is a benevolent one, and the various factions seeking to wrest control for the imperial family are inevitably the villains of each adventure. The d'Alemberts are a family from a heavy gravity planet with extraordinary physical abilities, who have been enlisted into the imperial secret service. Under the cover of a travelling circus, they become involved in a series of adventures as they seek to ensure the continuity of imperial rule.

The Imperial Stars was the first adventure, concerned mostly with establishing the setting. A group of assassins plan to seize power and must be infiltrated and neutralized. An organization of criminals is systematically kidnapping people from a resort world in *Strangler's Moon*. A robot is married to a member of the imperial family in *The Clockwork Traitor*, probably the weakest of the series. The head of the criminal organization in the second adventure returns in *Getaway World* , planning a union of scores of major criminals, but this time the d'Alemberts are able to end his career forever.

The mysterious "C" and his agent, Lady "A," make their debut in *Appointment at Bloodstar*. Through judicious use of assassination, they are weakening support for the current regime. When the emperor's daughter is about to be married, an enormous pirate fleet enters the solar system. Thwarted, they use a robot disguised as a human being to arouse fervent religious mania on another high gravity world in *The Purity Plot*, but the protagonists are able to discredit their agent and avoid a religious war. Another pirate armada appears in *Plant of Treachery*, this time to raid a prison planet for recruits as the emperor dies and his daughter prepares to assume the throne. The most recent adventure, *Eclipsing Binaries*, finds the d'Alemberts framed and outcast, until they are able to prove their innocence and foil yet another plot of the nefarious Lady "A. " For the most part, this series is rousing space opera, but there is a substantial improvement in the quality of the stories in the more current novels, indicating that Goldin is not content in retracing old ground.

Although not noted as a short-story writer, Goldin is not without talent in that area as well. "But as a Soldier, for His Country", the basis for *Mindflight*, stands quite well on its own. There is genuine pathos in the story "Sweet Dreams, Melissa," about a sentient computer personality, and in a short fantasy story, "The Last Ghost," who exists in a world where death has been conquered.

—Don D'Ammassa

GOLDING, William (Gerald). British. Born in St. Columb Minor, Cornwall, 19 September 1911. Educated at Marlborough Grammar School; Brasenose College, Oxford, B. A. 1935. Served in the Royal Navy, 1940-45. Married Ann Brookfield in 1939; one son and one daughter. Writer, actor, and producer in small theatre companies, 1934-40; Schoolmaster, Bishop Wordsworth's School, Salisbury, Wiltshire, 1945-61; Visiting Professor, Hollins College, Virginia, 1961-62. Recipient: James Tait Black Memorial Award, 1980; Booker Prize, 1980; Nobel Prize for Literature, 1983. M. A. : Oxford University, 1961; D. Litt. : University of Sussex, Brighton, 1970; University of Kent, Canterbury, 1974; University of Warwick, Coventry, 1981; the Sorbonne, Paris, 1983; Oxford University, 1983. Honorary Fellow, Brasenose College, 1966. Fellow, 1955, and Companion of Literature, 1984, Royal Society of Literature. C. B. E. (Commander, Order of the British Empire), 1966. Address: Ebble Thatch, Bowerchalke, Wiltshire, England.

SCIENCE-FICTION PUBLICATIONS

Novels

Lord of the Flies. London, Faber, 1954; New York, Coward McCann, 1955.
The Inheritors. London, Faber, 1955; New York, Harcourt Brace, 1962.

Short Stories

The Scorpion God. London, Faber, 1971; New York, Harcourt Brace, 1972.

OTHER PUBLICATIONS

Novels

Pincher Martin. London, Faber, 1956; as *The Two Deaths of Christopher Martin*, New York, Harcourt Brace, 1957.
Free Fall. London, Faber, 1959; New York, Harcourt Brace, 1960.
The Spire. London, Faber, and New York, Harcourt Brace, 1964.
The Pyramid. London, Faber, and New York, Harcourt Brace, 1967.
Darkness Visible. London, Faber, and New York, Farrar Straus, 1979.
Rites of Passage. London, Faber, and New York, Farrar Straus, 1980.
The Paper Men. London, Faber, and New York, Farrar Straus, 1984.

Plays

The Brass Butterfly, adaptation of his story "Envoy Extraordinary" (produced London, 1958). London, Faber, 1958; Chicago, Dramatic Publishing Company, n. d.

Radio Plays: *Miss Pulkinhorn*, 1960; *Break My Heart*, 1962.

Verse

Poems. London, Macmillan, 1934; New York, Macmillan, 1935.

Other

"Androids All," in *Spectator* (London), 24 February 1961.
"Astronaut by Gaslight," in *Spectator* (London), 9 June 1961.
The Hot Gates and Other Occasional Pieces. London, Faber, 1965; New York, Harcourt Brace, 1966.
Talk: Conversations with William Golding, with Jack I. Biles. New York, Harcourt Brace, 1970.
A Moving Target (essays). London, Faber, and New York, Farrar Straus, 1982.
An Egyptian Journal. London, Faber, 1985.

*

Critical Studies (selection): *William Golding* by Samuel Hynes, New York, Columbia University Press, 1964; *William Golding: A Critical Study* by James R. Baker, New York, St. Martin's Press, 1965; *The Art of William Golding* by Bernard S. Oldsey and Stanley Weintraub, New York, Harcourt Brace, 1965; *William Golding* by Bernard F. Dick, New York, Twayne, 1967; *William Golding: A Critical Study* by Mark Kinkead-Weekes and Ian Gregor, London, Faber, 1967, New York, Harcourt Brace, 1968; *William Golding* by Leighton Hodson, Edinburgh, Oliver and Boyd, 1969, New York, Putnam, 1971; *The Novels of William Golding* by Howard S. Babb, Columbus, Ohio State University Press, 1970; *William Golding: The Dark Fields of Discovery* by Virginia Tiger, London, Calder and Boyars, and Atlantic Highlands, New Jersey, Humanities Press, 1974; *William Golding* by Stephen Medcalf, London, Longman, 1975; *William Golding: Some Critical Considerations* edited by Jack I. Biles and Robert O. Evans, Louisville, University Press of Kentucky, 1978; *Of Earth and Darkness: The Novels of William Golding* by Arnold Johnston, Columbia, University of Missouri Press, 1980.

*   *   *

William Golding's novels are unique, fabulistic inversions of traditional perspectives that explore human nature and its veneer of civilization to suggest that man's instinctual past is directly linked to our present. Their style is deceptively simple and economical to re-enforce primitive perceptions and primitive ties. Golding doesn't interfere or preach, but his "naturalistic-allegorical" form speaks for itself. His approach is in essence "anti science," equating scientific and technological progress with dehumanization and tracing the defects of society directly to the defects of human nature. Often his perspectives are unexpected and startling.

Until its last chapter, *The Inheritors* is written from the point of view of the mind and senses of Neanderthals, simple, childlike, instinctual, vegetarian ape-men with a strong sense of community, "people" closer to the senses than the next evolutionary step forward, Cromagnon man, the invaders who take over Neanderthal territory. These new "men," whom we see through the uncomprehending eyes of the Neanderthals, are aggressive, vicious, wolf-like meat-eaters. They walk upright and lack fur, use bow and arrows, build stockades and canoes, and take preventive measures. But in them are the seeds of modern man: "they are the forest," they compete for women and rank, are beset by jealousies and animosities, dissemble and plot, drown their senses in liquor, and take their sex with violence. Contact with them helps the Neanderthals discover the process of analogy and of casual connection, but also possessiveness and rationalization. It is as if reason and depravity are inextricably bound.

Lord of the Flies, Golding's best-known work, is a social allegory of human regression. Set in a post-catastrophic near future in which war has laid waste much of the West and civilization is in ruins, the novel focuses on a boys' choir, stranded on a tropical island, to create a microcosm of the civilized world; therein the youngsters are equated with social types (the politician, the intellectual, the mystic/poet, the military leader, the bully) and the jungle with disorder and chaos and primitive compulsions that lurk beneath the civilized surface. The story traces the loss of order and of civilized restraints, man's evolution from savage in reverse, as the boys revert to their primitive, selfish selves, beset by anger, fear, and superstition, swept by blood lust. Their struggle becomes a battle of adult proportions between the intelligent and the irrational, the humane and the bestial. The *deus ex machina* intrusion of adults at the end confirms the island as microcosm: the boys have scorched their island with fire as their parents have consumed theirs with bombs; both children and adults are irresponsible, violent, brutal, sadistic. The image of man is not pleasant: selfish, easily manipulated, at home with mindless rituals, he lives for the day, enjoys abusing the weak and the helpless, and is better than the beast only by a conscious effort.

The Scorpion God is really three short novels in one. The first, entitled "The Scorpion God," set in a land much like ancient Egypt, examines man's capacity for blindly accepting the irrational, especially if sanctified by religious trappings. Ultimately it traces the exposure and destruction of a religion based on human "gods" and a myth of incestuous procreation and human sacrifice for the sake of a valley's fertility. The second, "Clonk Clonk," examines man as a sexual animal, exploring the union of a primitive hunter, Chimp, with a tribal mother, Palm, to define sexual differences as sensed by an unsophisticated primitive mentality. The third, "Envoy Extraordinary," studies man as a technological miracle worker, clever but perhaps too clever for the good of his species. Its emphasis is on the dilemma of technological advance: the diminution of quality of life that accompanies the increase in technological knowledge.

Thus Golding, in a variety of forms, explores human nature. He makes us look deep into man's past to understand the drama of his present and his future; he fears that man's technological development always outstrips his moral development; he warns of the depths of man's savagery, but finds hope in minds that can question, reason, and challenge. Golding infuses realistic setting and milieu with analogical and allegorical significance to lead the reader to reexamine man's intrinsic nature.

—Gina Macdonald

———

GORDON, David. See **GARRETT, Randall.**

———

GORDON, Rex. Pseudonym for Stanley Bennett Hough; also writes as Bennett Stanley. British. Born in Preston, Lancashire, 25 February 1917. Educated at Preston Grammar School; Radio Officers College, Preston; attended classes of the Workers Educational Association. Married Justa E. C. Wodschow in 1938. Radio operator, Marconi Radio Company, 1936-38; radio officer, International Marine Radio Company, 1939-45; ran a yachting firm, 1946-51. Recipient: Infinity

Award, 1957. Agent: A. M. Heath, 40-42 William IV Street, London WC2N 4DD. Address: 21 St. Michael's Road, Ponsanooth, Truro, Cornwall, England.

SCIENCE-FICTION PUBLICATIONS

Novels

Utopia 239. London, Heinemann, 1955.
Extinction Bomber (as S. B. Hough). London, Lane, 1956.
No Man Friday. London, Heinemann, 1956; as *First on Mars,* New York, Ace, 1957.
First to the Stars. New York, Ace, 1959; as *The Worlds of Eclos,* London, Consul, 1961.
Beyond the Eleventh Hour (as S. B. Hough). London, Hodder and Stoughton, 1961.
First Through Time. New York, Ace, 1962; as *The Time Factor,* London, Gibbs and Phillips, 1964.
Utopia minus X. New York, Ace, 1966; as *The Paw of God,* London, Gibbs, 1967.
The Yellow Fraction. New York, Ace, 1969; London, Dobson, 1972.

OTHER PUBLICATIONS

Novels as S. B. Hough

Frontier Incident. London, Hodder and Stoughton, 1951; New York, Crowell, 1952.
Moment of Decision. London, Hodder and Stoughton, 1952.
Mission in Guemo. London, Hodder and Stoughton, 1953; New York, Walker, 1964.
The Seas South. London, Hodder and Stoughton, 1953.
The Primitives. London, Hodder and Stoughton, 1954.
The Bronze Perseus. London, Secker and Warburg, 1959; New York, Walker, 1962; as *The Tender Killer,* New York, Avon, 1963.
Dear Daughter Dead. London, Gollancz, 1965; New York, Walker, 1966.
Sweet Sister Seduced. London, Gollancz, 1968; New York, Harper, 1983.
Fear Fortune, Father. London, Gollancz, 1974; New York, Harper, 1984.

Novels as Bennett Stanley

Sea Struck. New York, Crowell, 1953; as *Sea to Eden,* London, Hodder and Stoughton, 1954.
The Alscott Experiment. London, Hodder and Stoughton, 1954.
Government Contract. London, Hodder and Stoughton, 1956.

Other as S. B. Hough

A Pound a Day Inclusive: The Modern Way to Holiday Travel. London, Hodder and Stoughton, 1957.
Expedition Everyman: Your Way on Your Income to All the Desirable Places of Europe. London, Hodder and Stoughton, 1959.
Expedition Everyman 1964. London, Hodder and Stoughton, 1964.
Where? An Independent Report on Holiday Resorts in Britain and the Continent. London, Hodder and Stoughton, 1964.
Creative Writing: A Handbook for Students, Tutors and Education Authorities. Plymouth, Workers Educational Association, 1983.

*

Manuscript Collection: University of Wyoming, Laramie.

*   *   *

Rex Gordon was the pseudonym that Stanley Bennett Hough used for most of his science fiction. His first science-fiction novels reflected the Cold War fears that marked the 1950's: *Utopia 239* begins with an atomic war and moves on to the ideal state that rises from the ashes, and *Extinction Bomber* deals with the Dr. Strangelove-situation of the outbreak of war. However, Gordon's reputation in the genre was established with *No Man Friday,* reminiscent in many ways of Defoe's *Robinson Crusoe.* A manned rocket is sent to Mars, but the crash of the ship maroons Gordon Holder, its single survivor, and the secrecy of the flight prevents any rescue attempt. The bulk of the work concerns Holder's attempts to stay alive in the forbidding Martian surroundings. *No Man Friday* won praise from reviewers for the strictness with which it hewed to scientific conjectures and facts then known about Mars. And Holder works ingeniously and tirelessly to survive. But the novel takes a drastic turn when Holder encounters intelligent Martians. Like Hindu mystics, the Martians have gone beyond desire; they subtly mock Holder's struggle and the machines that have helped him, and the Martians hint that they possess immense powers. Whatever they may have, their view of reality is so different from that of humankind that Holder foresees, when rescued by an American expedition, that conflict will result between the two planets, that humans will win the war, and that the victory will cost them a chance for knowledge that they will never have again.

First to the Stars followed this somber but successful novel, and once again its theme was the staggering difference of alien ways of life and thought. The novel sends a man and woman on an exploration of Mars, but navigational problems cause them to miss their target and head out of the solar system. Time dilation, an effect of their speed, keeps them young through a voyage that lasts a hundred years to a planet where the woman dies giving birth as the man encounters an alien race. Although the aliens treat the humans well, eventually enabling them to return to Earth, the novel shows an insuperable barrier to understanding between humans and aliens, and ends with tensions and confrontations between the two races. If Gordon saw human-alien communication as doubtful, he was probably projecting the difficulties between humans onto a galactic screen: in *Beyond the Eleventh Hour* he returned to the theme of world-wide nuclear conflict. Although *First Through Time* turned to adventure, the discovery of time travel in that novel results from an accident, as had so many events in the earlier books. And *Utopia minus X* again shows the conflict that arises from difference, this time between a space traveler and the Earth he returns to after a lapse of two centuries.

No Man Friday brought Rex Gordon a reputation as a writer who used careful extrapolation in his work. But, more importantly, one consistent theme has been a deep pessimism about the possibility of understanding, whether between human or alien, or among humans themselves.

—Walter E. Meyers

GORDON, Stuart. Pseudonym for Richard Gordon; also writes as Alex R. Stuart. British. Born in Scotland in 1947.

Agent: Maggie Noach, 21 Redan Street, London W. 14, England.

SCIENCE-FICTION PUBLICATIONS

Novels (series: Eyes)

Time Story. London, New English Library, 1972.
One-Eye. New York, DAW, 1973; London, Sidgwick and Jackson, 1974.
Two-Eyes. New York, DAW, 1974; London, Sidgwick and Jackson, 1975.
Three-Eyes. New York, DAW, 1975; London, Sidgwick and Jackson, 1976.
Suaine and the Crow-God. London, New English Library, 1975.
Smile on the Void. New York, Putnam, 1981; London, Arrow, 1982.
Fire in the Abyss. New York, Berkley, 1983; London, Arrow, 1984.

OTHER PUBLICATIONS as Alex R. Stuart

Novels

The Bike from Hell. London, New English Library, 1973.
The Devil's Rider. London, New English Library, 1973.

*

Stuart Gordon comments:

The label "science fiction" is used to cover many different approaches to storytelling, most of which have little to do with "science" as such, save in a romantic, generalised way. The thrust of my own work has typically been occult or mythic in its main concern, and can be defined as science fiction only insofar as it has involved itself with the overtly fantastic, and insofar as it has been characterised (I hope) by that "sense of wonder" which romantically typifies the genre as a whole.

I have a strong sense of history and have drawn on this sense in my stories. "Those who forget their history are condemned to repeat it"—it disturbs me that as a whole our western culture appears to be increasingly out of touch with any real sense of the past and how it shaped what we are now. This is not to worship or take refuge in an unreal nostalgia, but to encourage the social growth of wider, deeper perspectives, so that history as we live it at present should no longer be just "a nightmare from which we are struggling to awake," but the vital process in which, individually and collectively, we live and move and have our being.

In this respect all imaginative literature, however labelled, can play an important role. Inventing tales of fantasy for their own sake may be entertaining and even to some degree therapeutic, alleviating the problems of everyday life, but such use of the imagination is not invariably positive, and might even in some cases be considered a criminal distraction. To my mind this danger has become clearly apparent in the extent to which science fiction—once vigorously independent—has been colonised by the mass media and converted into moneyspinning wide-screen clichés which, at their worst (as in the movie of *Dune*), function as crude political propaganda disguised as entertainment. If science fiction has any sort of serious function, surely it is to encourage people to wake up and to think and see for themselves, rather than to distract them still further with the special effects of an enchanting but ultimately seedy (and deadly) hall of mirrors.

*   *   *

Stuart Gordon's work can best be classified as science fantasy rather than science fiction. His books are usually set in the far future after some cataclysmic event that has placed the world back into the Middle Ages technologically. Interestingly enough, though this future society is definitely medieval there are shreds of technology left which add excitement to his books. One of the most notable of these is the golem, an android, robot-like creature that is immensely strong and cunning and all but impervious to the attacks of the medieval warriors.

The books are set in England, and the Celtic culture is described in detail and with a reasonable degree of accuracy. The people in most of the books seem to practice a religion that is like that of the Druids with a touch of meditation and pop psychology thrown in.

Gordon's major work, the "Eyes" trilogy, deals with the birth of the mutant godling, its rise to power, and the attempts made to thwart the godling and unite all the people in peace. The plots of the books are sometimes murky and the reader's allegiance is challenged as the good guys seem to become the bad guys in some instances. The first two books are some of Gordon's best work. They are exciting, and the plots contain a nice mix of the simple life and leftover technology. In the final book, *Three-Eyes,* the plot and sub-plots seem to drag a little and the reader is left with some improbable situations and several loose ends.

Gordon's mythical countries and societies are well developed and fairly consistent through all three books. Unfortunately only a few secondary characters appear in all the books, which does little for the trilogy's cohesiveness. His characters, especially the women, are stereotyped and don't always react true to their developed character, but they are likeable and hold the reader's interest anyway. In spite of these flaws the trilogy is very readable and even exciting in many places.

Smile on the Void is a radical departure from his Celtic science fantasy and a much less successful work. It is set in the relatively near future and concerns the exploits of Ralph M'Botu Kitaj. The settings include the whole world as Kitaj is an adventurer par excellence, part entrepreneur and part evangelist. His exploits are extremely lurid and bizarre. The reader is deluged with anecdote after anecdote—each more outrageous than the last. They range from survival exercises in the wilds of Africa to nude satellite television broadcasts to faith-healing espisodes in the Philippines. This book lacks the continuity of Gordon's other works and has a very unsatisfactory and disappointing ending. In spite of its problems, however, it keeps the reader turning pages just to see how outrageous Kitaj and Gordon can be.

At his best Stuart Gordon has created one of science fiction's most interesting geo-political systems and at his worst he has at least entertained his readers.

—Alice Chambers Wygant

GOTLIEB, Phyllis (Fay, née Bloom). Canadian. Born in Toronto, Ontario, 25 May 1926. Educated at public schools in Toronto; University of Toronto, B. A. in English 1948, M. A. 1950. Married Calvin Gotlieb in 1949; one son and two daughters. Agent: Virginia Kidd, Box 278, Milford, Pennsylvania 18337, U. S. A. Address: 29 Ridgevale Drive, Toronto, Ontario M6A 1K9, Canada.

SCIENCE-FICTION PUBLICATIONS

Novels

Sunburst. New York, Fawcett, 1964; London, Coronet, 1966.
O Master Caliban! New York, Harper, 1976; London, Bantam, Corgi, 1979.
Trilogy:
    A Judgment of Dragons. New York, Berkley, 1980.
    Emperor, Swords, Pentacles. New York, Ace, 1982.
    Kingdom of the Cats. New York, Ace, 1985.

Short Stories

Son of the Morning and Other Stories. New York, Ace, 1983.

Uncollected Short Stories

"No End of Time," in *Fantastic* (New York), June 1960.
"A Bone to Pick," in *Fantastic* (New York), October 1960.
"Valedictory," in *Amazing* (New York), May 1964.
"Rogue's Gambit," in *If* (New York), January 1968.
"The Dirty Old Men of Maxsec," in *Galaxy* (New York), November 1969.
"Planetoid Idiot," in *To the Stars,* edited by Robert Silverberg. New York, Hawthorn, 1971.
"Mother Lode," in *Fantasy and Science Fiction* (New York), November 1973.
"The King's Dogs," in *The Edge of Space,* edited by Robert Silverberg. New York, Elsevier Nelson, 1979.
"The Newest Profession," in *Speculations,* edited by Isaac Asimov and Alice Laurance. Boston, Houghton Mifflin, 1982.

OTHER PUBLICATIONS

Novel

Why Should I Have All the Grief? Toronto, Macmillan, 1969.

Plays

Doctor Umlaut's Earthly Kingdom (broadcast, 1970; produced North Bay, Ontario, 1972). Toronto, Calliope Press, 1974.
Silent Movie Days (broadcast, 1971). Included in *The Works,* 1978.
Garden Varieties (broadcast, 1973; produced Ontario, 1973) Included in *The Works,* 1978.

Radio Plays: *Doctor Umlaut's Earthly Kingdom,* 1970; *Silent Movie Days,* 1971; *The Contract,* 1972; *Garden Varieties,* 1973; *God on Trial Before Rabbi Ovadia,* 1974.

Verse

Who Knows One? Toronto, Hawkshead Press, 1962.
Within the Zodiac. Toronto, McClelland and Stewart, 1964.
Ordinary, Moving. Toronto, Oxford University Press, 1969.
Doctor Umlaut's Earthly Kingdom. Toronto, Calliope Press, 1974.
The Works: Collected Poems. Toronto, Calliope Press, 1978.

*

Phyllis Gotlieb comments:
    I like to work in as broad a range of genres as possible, and in all of them I am primarily interested in people, their emotions, actions, dynamics. After that I am interested in everything else in the universe.

*   *   *

    Phyllis Gotlieb is an unusual figure in the world of science fiction for at least two reasons: she is Canadian born and bred, and she is best known in the Canadian literary world as a fine poet, albeit one whose poems often employ fantasy and SF tropes. But then, as Samuel R. Delany has remarked, "The vision (sense of wonder if you will) that SF tries for seems to me very close to the vision of poetry." Certainly in Gotlieb's case the same vision generates both the poems and the science fiction (as she was finally able to demonstrate to her SF audience with the publication of "ms & mr frankenstein" and "was/man" in *Son of the Morning and Other Stories*). One of her major interests is mythology, especially in its more popular manifestations, and the social responses it generates. SF *is* a popular manifestation of mythological thinking and her highly literary control of its conventions in her short fictions and her novels reveals her structural comprehension of this fact. She is also fascinated, in both her poetry (*Ordinary, Moving* and much of *The Works,* for example) and her SF, by the continuing presence of children in the world and their many problems in achieving a true maturity. The SF paradigm is especially useful here for it tends to support the expansion of the child-maturing theme until it symbolically embraces the race as well as the individual. Little wonder, then, that Gotlieb's SF, as well as her poetry, explores themes, motifs, and a particular view of life that is guardedly optimistic, mystically clear-eyed.
    Perhaps because she hasn't had to live off her SF writing, more likely because she is a very careful writer, Gotlieb has not been overly prolific. *Sunburst* is better written than most such works and a superb example of SF as a true fiction of ideas. It holds the often parallel concepts of ESP and the next evolutionary step for humanity up to a scientifically curious investigation in the midst of adventure and potential violence. Psi-powers, and, indeed, the often amoral use of power per se, are a standard convention, but Gotlieb's 13-year-old putative "superman," Shandy, not only has no Psi, she is impervious to others' use of it against her. What she is is intelligent, very curious, willing to play with unconventional ideas, and capable of moral growth, of which she has a lot to undergo. Most of the mutant Psi-powered "children" in *Sunburst* lack both any sense of moral connection to the rest of humanity and enough intelligence to handle their powers properly. Gotlieb's conclusion, the core of a powerfully emotional adventure full of well-realized individuals, is that the "superman" will more than likely turn out to be an intelligent, curious person of high moral sensitivity, looking to move the race forward just a smidgen in her lifetime. *Sunburst* beautifully avoids the clichés of conventional SF on this theme.
    Her stories similarly explore moral dilemmas, many of them featuring immature individuals who are given the opportunity to "grow up" psychologically through the adventures Gotlieb arranges for them. In *O Master Caliban,* a group of future delinquents plus a four-armed lost child and his animal friends learn to be more fully human as they battle renegade robots for survival. The boy's father, a scientist who never matured morally, also gets, at 60, his chance to face and accept his failures of humanity and possibly to begin making up for them. In her more recent work, *A Judgement of Dragons* and *Emperor, Swords, Pentacles,* which feature the intelligent and sometimes telepathic cats of the planet Ungruwarkh, she has

pursued the themes of inter-species communication and co-operation, and begun to make fuller use of her Jewish background. This background proves especially fruitful in "Tauf Aleph," one of her finest stories, in which a computer programmed to give Kaddish to the last Jew in the universe ends up creating a whole new race of Jews out of the indigenes of the lonely planet where he dies.

In all her work, then, Gotlieb has something to say about the human condition, but she also knows how to entertain. Her poet's eye makes for sharply observed descriptions; her love of adventure makes for powerfully realized scenes of violence and pain; her intelligence makes for intelligent talk among her characters, who are often as humorous and ironic as she is; and her love for people makes for empathetic characters whom we care about. As a result, she offers her readers work that is entertaining as well as thought-provoking, and which contains characters we feel privileged to have met. The integrity and gritty speculation of her work have earned her a respected place in the field.

—Douglas Barbour

GOTSCHALK, Felix C. American. Born in Richmond, Virginia, 7 September 1929. Educated at Virginia Commonwealth University, Richmond, B. S. 1954 (Phi Beta Kappa), M. S. 1956; Tulane University, New Orleans, Ph. D 1958. Served in the United States Marine Corps, 1947-49. Married Nelle Mull in 1957; one son and one daughter. Draftsman, Vepco, Richmond, 1946-47, 1949-51; pianist, Chelf's, 1951-56, and On the Road, 1956-58, both in Richmond; Assistant Professor, Nicholls State University, Thibodaux, Louisiana, 1958-62, and Bowman Medical School, Winston-Salem, North Carolina, 1962-70; in private practice as a psychologist, Winston-Salem, 1970-81. Since 1981, full-time writer. Address: 3103 Hungary Spring Road, Richmond, Virginia 23228, U. S. A.

SCIENCE-FICTION PUBLICATIONS

Novel

Growing Up in Tier 3000. New York, Ace, 1975.

Uncollected Short Stories

"Bonus Baby," in *Science Fiction Emphasis 1,* edited by David Gerrold. New York, Ballantine, 1974.
"Outer Concentric" and "The Examination," in *New Dimensions 4,* edited by Robert Silverberg. New York, New American Library, 1974.
"A Day in the South Quad," in *New Dimensions 5,* edited by Robert Silverberg. New York, Harper, 1975.
"The Man with the Golden Reticulates," in *Orbit 17,* edited by Damon Knight. New York, Harper, 1975.
"Pandora's Cryogenic Box," in *Fantastic* (New York), December 1975.
"The Family Winter of 1986," in *Orbit 18,* edited by Damon Knight. New York, Harper, 1976.
"The Day of the Big Test," in *Future Power,* edited by Jack Dann and Gardner Dozois. New York, Random House, 1976.
"The Napoleonic Wars," in *Beyond Time,* edited by Sandra Ley. New York, Simon and Schuster, 1976.

"Charisma Leak," in *New Dimensions 6,* edited by Robert Silverberg. New York, Harper, 1976.
"Home Sweet Geriatric Dome," in *New Dimensions 7,* edited by Robert Silverberg. New York, Harper, and London, Gollancz, 1977.
"The Veil over the River," in *Orbit 19,* edited by Damon Knight. New York, Harper, 1977.
"Sir Richard's Robots," in *Cosmos* (New York), November 1977.
"Square Pony Express," in *New Dimensions 9,* edited by Robert Silverberg. New York, Harper, 1979.
"The Wishes of Maidens," in *New Voices in Science Fiction,* edited by George R. R. Martin. New York, Berkley, 1979.
"The Trip of Bradley Oesterhaus," in *Fantasy and Science Fiction* (New York), July 1979.
"A Presidential Tape," in *New Dimensions 10,* edited by Robert Silverberg. New York, Harper, 1980.
"Among the Cave Dwellers of the San Andreas Canyon," in *Fantasy and Science Fiction* (New York), September 1980.
"And Parity for All," in *Amazing* (New York), November 1980.
"Take a Midget Step," in *Fantasy and Science Fiction* (New York), September 1981.
"The Municipal Smog Man," in *Amazing* (New York), September 1981.
"Dogsworld," in *Pig Iron,* edited by Rose Sayre and Jim Villani. Youngstown, Ohio, Pig Iron Press, 1982.
"Conspicuous Consumption," in *Fantasy and Science Fiction* (New York), March 1983.
"The Nature of Relationships," in *Last Wave 3,* Winter 1984.
"Vestibular Man," in *Fantasy and Science Fiction* (New York), March 1985.

OTHER PUBLICATIONS

Other

"Writing a First Novel," in *The Writer* (Boston), June 1975.

*

Manuscript Collection: Temple University, Philadelphia.

Felix C. Gotschalk comments:

(1981) Writing is for me an indulgence, an egocentric luxuriation, something I do because it pleases me. I have experimented (consciously and unconsciously) with verbosity, neologisms, symmetry, cadence, self-canceling reciprocity, and, even, monosyllabicity. I cannot plot story lines and do not attempt to do so. I do not know what is going to happen in any of my stories; and it is special voyeuristic fun to have a good flow of writing (say, 3000 words in one evening), and then read it the next day to see what it was that I wrote the night before. How to characterize my writing I do not know. One critic called it "poetic hardware," others have been less kind. I would like to write an erotic story that would guarantee the reader a spontaneous orgasm.

(1985) I am trying to be less self-indulgent in my writing, and have a 250K word mainstream novel completed, titled Southern Pearls and Swine. Henry Miller is my all-time favorite author, and I think J. G. Ballard is our best for evoking the "sense of wonder. "

* * *

Felix C. Gotschalk published his first science fiction in 1974, and within a year his quirky, hyperkinetic stories were appearing in a wide range of SF publications, including Damon Knight's *Orbit* and Robert Silverberg's *New Dimensions*. Gotschalk's voice is immediately recognizable in all his work: a high-tech jargon charged with neologisms and rewired syntax that sometimes seems affected but often conveys a powerful sense of the psychic dislocations and altered sensibility of life in an advanced, high-energy civilization.

A number of Gotschalk's stories, including "A Day in the South Quad" and his novel *Growing Up in Tier 3000*, are set against a more or less common background, where life in automated urban domes allows for an impressive array of hedonistic pleasures but sharply restricts individual freedom as solicitous computer systems control man's more self-destructive tendencies. Several stories raise the question of how the enormous energy demands of such a society are to be met (in other stories this problem is dispensed with; Gotschalk has shown little interest in such genre conventions as inter-story chronologies or consistency). Others are set in the present or near-future, often told from the point of view of a middle-aged academic or administrator, as in "The Man with the Golden Reticulates" and "Charisma Leak. " The voice in these stories is wry, male, and exuberantly egocentric; the prevailing sense is of the self-aware individual celebrating life despite unforestalled mortality and numerous technological forebodings.

The person of Gotschalk's protagonist is essentially identical in all his stories, whether incarnated as a high-tech infant prodigy, young stud, mature man of the world, or bionically rebuilt geezer. It can be argued that Gotschalk writes most effectively when his narrative contains more than one of these figures, whose interaction can prove more interesting than the self/other dichotomy that otherwise results. Such is the case with *Growing Up in Tier 3000*, a short but intense novel in which competition within the nuclear family for available energy compel the young children to turn upon their parents, who realize that advancing technology has left them ill-equipped to withstand their four-year-old successors.

By 1980 Gotschalk had published some eighteen stories and a novel, and had explored the possibilities of his idiosyncratic newspeak perhaps to the point of diminishing returns. During this period the original anthology market in which his best work had appeared began to contract, and perhaps for this reason, or because Gotschalk was then writing novels (several of which evidently await publication), his work began to appear less frequently. The stories he has published in recent years have relied less heavily on flamboyant stylistic effects, and many experiment with vernacular voices of odd locales in a slightly seedy future, often in the American South ("Take a Midget Step", "Vestibular Man"). The tales are upbeat, refreshing, and usually form a kind of success story. Gotschalk's characteristic buoyance is engagingly conveyed, though he remains disconcertingly unabashed in celebrating the aggressiveness of the Western male.

—Gregory Feeley

GOULART, Ron(ald Joseph). Also writes as Josephine Kains; Jullian Kearney; Howard Lee; Kenneth Robeson; Frank S. Shawn; Joseph Silva; Con Steffanson. American. Born in Berkeley, California, 13 January 1933. Educated at the University of California, Berkeley, B. A. 1955. Married Frances Sheridan in 1964; two sons. Advertising copywriter, Guild Bascom and Bonfigci, San Francisco, 1955-57, 1958-60, Alan Alch Inc., Hollywood, 1960-63, and Hoefer Dietrich and Brown, San Francisco 1966-68. Author of science-fiction comic strip *Star Hawks*, with Gil Kane, 1977-79. Recipient: Mystery Writers of America Edgar Allan Poe Award, 1971. Guest of Honor, Lunacon, 1979. Address: 232 Georgetown Road, Weston, Connecticut 06883, U. S. A.

SCIENCE-FICTION PUBLICATIONS

Novels (series: Battlestar Galactica; Gypsy; Star Hawks)

The Sword Swallower. New York, Doubleday, 1968.
After Things Fell Apart. New York, Ace, 1970; London, Arrow, 1975.
The Fire-Eater. New York, Ace, 1970.
Gadget Man. New York, Doubleday, 1971; London, New English Library, 1977.
Death Cell. New York, Beagle, 1971.
Hawkshaw. New York, Doubleday, 1972; London, Hale, 1973.
Plunder. New York, Beagle, 1972
Wildsmith. New York, Ace, 1972.
Shaggy Planet. New York, Lancer, 1973.
A Talent for the Invisible. New York, DAW, 1973.
The Tin Angel. New York, DAW, 1973.
Spacehawk, Inc. New York, DAW, 1974.
Flux. New York, DAW, 1974.
When the Waker Sleeps. New York, DAW, 1975.
The Hellhound Project. New York Doubleday, 1975; London, Hale, 1976.
A Whiff of Madness. New York, DAW, 1976.
The Enormous Hourglass. New York, Award, 1976.
Quest of the Gypsy. New York, Pyramid, 1976.
Crackpot. New York, Doubleday, and London, Hale, 1977.
The Emperor of the Last Days. New York, Popular Library, 1977.
The Panchronicon Plot. New York, DAW, 1977.
Nemo. New York, Berkley, 1977; London, Hale, 1979.
Eye of the Vulture (Gypsy). New York Jove, 1977.
The Island of Dr. Moreau (novelization of screenplay; as Joseph Silva). New York, Ace, 1977.
Flux, and The Tin Angel. London, Millington, 1978.
The Wicked Cyborg. New York, DAW, 1978.
Calling Dr. Patchwork. New York, DAW, 1978.
Cowboy Heaven. New York, Doubleday, 1979; London, Hale, 1980.
Dr. Scofflaw, in *Binary Star 3*. New York, Dell, 1979.
Hello, Lemuria, Hello. New York, DAW, 1979.
Star Hawks, illustrated by Gil Kane:
  Empire 99. Chicago, Playboy Press, 1980.
  The Cyborg King. Chicago, Playboy Press, 1981.
Hail Hibbler. New York, DAW, 1980.
Skyrocket Steele. New York, Pocket Books, 1980.
Brinkman. New York, Doubleday, 1981.
Upside Downside. New York, DAW, 1982.
Big Bang. New York, DAW, 1982.
Battlestar Galactica, with Glen A. Larson:
  8. *Greetings from Earth*. New York, Berkley, 1983.
  9. *Experiment in Terra*. New York, Berkley, 1984.
  10. *The Long Patrol*. New York, Berkley, 1984.
Hellquad. New York, DAW, 1984.
The Prisoner of Blackwood Castle. New York, Avon, 1984.

Novels as Frank S. Shawn (series: Phantom in all books)

The Veiled Lady. New York, Avon, 1973.

The Golden Circle. New York, Avon, 1973.
The Mystery of the Sea Horse. New York, Avon. 1973.
The Hydra Monster. New York, Avon, 1973.
The Goggle-Eyed Pirates. New York, Avon, 1974.
The Swamp Rats. New York, Avon, 1974.

Novels as Con Steffanson (series: Flash Gordon in all books)

The Lion Men of Mongo. New York, Avon, 1974.
The Plague of Sound. New York, Avon, 1974.
The Space Circus. New York, Avon, 1974.

Novels as Kenneth Robeson (series: Avenger in all books)

The Man from Atlantis. New York, Warner, 1974.
Red Moon. New York, Warner, 1974.
The Purple Zombie. New York, Warner, 1974.
Dr. Time. New York, Warner, 1974.
The Nightwitch Devil. New York, Warner, 1974.
Black Chariots. New York, Warner, 1974.
The Cartoon Crimes. New York, Warner, 1974.
The Iron Skull. New York, Warner, 1975.
The Death Machine. New York, Warner, 1975.
The Blood Countess. New York, Warner, 1975.
The Glass Man. New York, Warner, 1975.
Demon Island. New York, Warner, 1975.

Short Stories

What's Become of Screwloose? and Other Inquiries. New York, Scribner, and London, Sidgwick and Jackson, 1971.
Clockwork's Pirates, Ghost Breaker. New York, Ace, 1971.
Broke Down Engine and Other Troubles with Machines. New York, Macmillan, and London, Collier Macmillan, 1971.
The Chameleon Corps and Other Shape Changers. New York, Macmillan, and London, Collier Macmillan, 1972.
Nutzenbolts and More Troubles with Machines. New York, Macmillan, 1975; London, Hale, 1976.
Odd Job No. 101 and Other Future Crimes and Intrigues. New York, Scribner, 1975, London, Hale, 1976.

Uncollected Short Stories

"At the Starvation Ball," in *Fantasy and Science Fiction* (New York), April 1976.
"Lunatic at Large," in *Fantasy and Science Fiction* (New York), February 1977.
"Amnesty," in *Analog* (New York), September 1977.
"Assassins," in *Fantasy and Science Fiction* (New York), December 1977.
"Lectric Joe," in *Fantasy and Science Fiction* (New York), February 1978.
"Garbage," in *Isaac Asimov's Science Fiction Magazine* (New York), January 1979.
"Steele Wyoming," in *Fantasy and Science Fiction* (New York), March 1980.
"Invisible Stripes," in *The Best of Omni Science Fiction 2*, edited by Ben Bova. New York, Omni, 1981.
"Bugg Lives," in *Epic 6* (New York), 1981.
"Batteries Not Included," in *Fantasy and Science Fiction* (New York), January 1981.
"Presenting Trilby Swain," in *Fantasy and Science Fiction* (New York), May 1981.
"The Living Dead," in *Woman's World* (London), 12 May 1981.

"Papa Gumbo," in *Twilight Zone* (New York), July 1981.
"Mercy," in *Analog* (New York), 17 August 1981.
"The Foxworth Legatees," in *Amazing* (New York), September 1981.
"Ask Penny Jupiter," in *Isaac Asimov's Science Fiction Magazine* (New York), 28 September 1981.
"Groucho," in *Great Stories from Rod Serling's The Twilight Zone Magazine,* edited by T. E. D. Klein. New York, TZ Publications, 1982.
"Crusoe in New York," in *Twilight Zone* (New York), March 1982.
"Blockbuster," in *Fantasy and Science Fiction* (New York), June 1982.
"The Return of Max Kearny," in *Alfred Hitchcock's Fatal Attractions,* edited by Elana Lore. New York, Davis, 1983.
"Brain Food," in *Fantasy and Science Fiction* (New York), July 1983.
"Moppet," in *Amazing* (New York), July 1983.
"Hello from Hollywood," in *Fantasy and Science Fiction* (New York), December 1983.
"Street Magic," in *Isaac Asimov's Science Fiction Magazine* (New York), March 1984.
"Me and the Devil," in *Fantasy and Science Fiction* (New York), June 1984.

OTHER PUBLICATIONS

Novels

If Dying Was All. New York, Ace, 1971.
Too Sweet to Die. New York, Ace, 1972.
The Same Lie Twice. New York, Ace, 1973.
Cleopatra Jones (novelization of screenplay). New York, Warner, 1973.
Chains (novelization of TV series; as Howard Lee). New York, Warner, 1973.
Superstition (novelization of TV series; as Howard Lee). New York, Warner, 1973.
One Grave Too Many. New York, Ace, 1974.
The Tremendous Adventures of Bernie Wine. New York, Warner, 1975.
Cleopatra Jones and the Casino of Gold (novelization of screenplay), New York, Warner, 1975.
Vampirella (novelizations of comic strip):
  1. *Bloodstalk*. New York, Warner, 1975; London, Sphere, 1976.
  2. *On Alien Wings*. New York, Warner, 1975; London, Sphere, 1977.
  3. *Deadwalk*. New York, Warner, 1976; London, Sphere, 1977.
  4. *Blood Wedding*. New York, Warner, 1976.
  5. *Deathgame*. New York, Warner, 1976.
  6. *Snakegod*. New York, Warner, 1976.
Challengers for the Unknown. New York, Dell, 1977.
Capricorn One. New York, Fawcett, 1978.
Agent of Love (as Jullian Kearny). New York, Warner, 1979.
Ghosting. Toronto, Raven, 1980.
A Graveyard of My Own. New York, Walker, 1985.

Novels as Con Steffanson

Laverne and Shirley (novelizations of TV series):
  Teamwork. New York, Warner, 1976.
  Easy Money. New York, Warner, 1976.
  Gold Rush. New York, Warner, 1976.

Novels as Josephine Kains

The Devil Mask Mystery. New York, Zebra, 1978.
The Curse of the Golden Skull. New York, Zebra, 1978.
The Green Lama Mystery. New York, Zebra, 1979.
The Whispering Cat Mystery. New York, Zebra, 1979.
The Witch's Tower Mystery. New York, Zebra, 1979.
The Laughing Dragon Mystery. New York, Zebra, 1980.

Other

The Assault on Childhood. Los Angeles, Sherbourne Press,
    1969; London, Gollancz, 1970.
Cheap Thrills: An Informal History of the Pulp Magazines. New
    Rochelle, New York, Arlington House, 1972.
An American Family. New York, Warner, 1973.
The Adventurous Decade: Comic Strips in the Thirties. New
    Rochelle, New York, Arlington House, 1975.

Editor, *The Hardboiled Dicks: An Anthology and Study of Pulp
    Detective Fiction*. Los Angeles, Sherbourne Press, 1965;
    London, Boardman, 1967.
Editor, *Lineup Tough Guys*. Los Angeles, Sherbourne Press,
    1966.
Editor, *The Great British Detective*. New York, New American
    Library, 1982.

* * *

Ron Goulart's fictional world includes Southern California,
the Barnum system in outer space, and as many other alternate
words in between as his lively imagination can conjure up. He
began his writing career with parodies and humorous sketches
and has continued to write with a slightly cock-eyed view of the
world. He has written stories in virtually every genre, but is
primarily considered a science-fiction writer. Just as his
mysteries have a touch of the fantastic, his science fiction has a
touch of the mysterious and often seems to straddle genres
when it doesn't simply defy all categories.

His stories of outer space nearly all take place outside our
own solar system in that group of planets dominated by
Barnum. In the Barnum system, Murdstone is the least
favoured planet, but Malagra is the pesthole of the universe.
Like other legendary places (Dogpatch or Hogscratch, Arkansas) the Barnum system adjusts its dimensions to suit the
current story. The Barnum system has been imaginatively
realized in visual terms by artist Gil Kane in the comic strip
Star Hawks. All of the Goulart humor comes across in the
adventures of Rex Jaxan and Chavez of the Interplanetary Law
Service. Ben Jolson, the multi-faced agent for the Chameleon
Corps, is called on by the Political Espionage Office on Barnum
to investigate mysterious happenings. *The Sword Swallower*
pulls together earlier threads from his short stories, but
Jolson's shapechanging powers are not exploited as
imaginatvely in full length as they are in the shorter form. In
"Chameleon" Jolson foils an assassination by hiding in one
corner of the room disguised as a TV set.

One of his best collections of short stories, *Broke Down
Engine*, is concerned entirely with the problem of man's
increasing dependence on machines. Told with humor, they
also embody a bitter view of a future in which human beings
become isolated from one another. Goulart's days as an
advertising copywriter serve as the basis for his stories about
androids in show business. He brings a fine eye and ear for the
ridiculous to these in which the satire may be deeper than mere
surface humor. One thinks of real life "personalities" who

respond to interviewers in precise, robotic terms. Perhaps the
ultimate meshing to themes for Goulart's repertoire is *Cowboy
Heaven* in which an android replacing the ailing actor Jake
Troop on the film *Saddle Tramp* doesn't know when to stop.
Goulart has his serious side and this comes out in the stories of
fantasy and derring-do about the mysterious Gypsy's search
for his own identity.

Goulart's style is concise and his stories are told mostly in
dialogue. The reader has to be alert and not let the fast pace and
skeletal appearance prevent him from enjoying the yarn. At his
best, Goulart is a witty and engaging story-teller, with a
recognizable reality to his fantasies. His Southern California is
the extrapolation of present trends in the ridiculous; his
machinery gone amok is an extension of our own worst fears as
a vacuum cleaner malfunctions or an automobile breaks down.

As some of Goulart's older characters retire, others remain
active. He mixes elements from different genres with his own
personal enthusiasms and sets science fiction stories in 2033 or
1941 or 1897. Harry Challenge (*The Prisoner of Blackwood
Castle*), is an 1890's private detective whose cases involve
fantasy and science-fiction elements. When you've read one
Goulart you've only begun.

—J. Randolph Cox

GRAHAM, Robert. See **HALDEMAN, Joe.**

GRANT, Charles L. American. Born in Newark, New Jersey, 12
September 1942. Educated at Trinity College, Hartford,
Connecticut, B. A. 1964. Served in the United States Army
Military Police, 1968-70: Bronze Star. Married Debbie Voss in
1973; one son and one daughter. English teacher, Toms River
High School, New Jersey, 1964-70, Chester High School, New
Jersey, 1970-72, and Mt. Olive High School, New Jersey, 1972-
73; English and history teacher, Roxbury High School, New
Jersey, 1974-75. Since 1975, free-lance writer. Executive
Secretary, Science Fiction Writers of America, 1973-77.
Recipient: Nebula Award, 1976, 1978; World Fantasy Award,
for non-fiction, 1980, for editing, 1983. Agent: Kirby
McCauley Ltd., 425 Park Avenue South, New York, New
York 10016, U.S.A.

SCIENCE-FICTION PUBLICATIONS

Novels (series: Parric family)

The Shadow of Alpha (Parric). New York, Berkley, 1976.
Ascension (Parric). New York, Berkley, 1977.
The Ravens of the Moon. New York, Doubleday, 1978; London,
    Sidgwick and Jackson, 1979.
Legion (Parric). New York, Berkley, 1979.
Nightmare Seasons. New York, Doubleday, 1982.
Night Songs. New York, Pocket Books, 1984.

Short Stories

Tales from the Nightside: Dark Fantasy. Sauk City, Wisconsin,
    Arkham House, 1981.
A Glow of Candles and Other Stories. New York, Berkley, 1981.

Uncollected Short Stories

"The House of Evil," in *Fantasy and Science Fiction* (New York), December 1968.

"The Summer of the Irish Sea," in *Orbit 11*, edited by Damon Knight. New York, Putnam, 1973.

"The Magic Child," in *Frontiers 2*, edited by Roger Elwood. New York, Macmillan, 1973.

"Weep No More, Old Lady," in *Future Quest*, edited by Roger Elwood. New York, Avon, 1973.

"But the Other Old Man Stopped Playing," in *Amazing* (New York), April 1973.

"Abdication," in *Amazing* (New York), October 1973.

"Everybody a Winner the Barker Cried," in *Orbit 13*, edited by Damon Knight. New York, Putnam, 1974.

"In Donovan's Time," in *Orbit 16*, edited by Damon Knight. New York, Harper, 1975.

"To Be a Witch, in 3/4 Time," in *Fantastic* (New York), February 1975.

"When Two or Three Are Gathered," in *Amazing* (New York), March 1975.

"Seven Is a Birdsong," in *Analog* (New York), January 1976.

"Eldorado," in *The Arts and Beyond*, edited by Thomas F. Monteleone. New York, Doubleday, 1977.

"Treatise on the Artifacts of a Civilization," in *Antaeus* (New York), 1977.

"The Shape of Plowshares," in *Analog* (New York), March 1977.

"Gently Rapping," in *Galaxy* (New York), September 1977.

"Knock, and See What Enters," in *Fantastic* (New York), December 1977.

"View, with a Difference," in *Dark Sins, Dark Dreams*, edited by Barry N. Malzberg and Bill Prozini. New York, Doubleday, 1978.

"The Peace That Passes Never," in *Chrysalis 3*, edited by Roy Torgeson. New York, Kensington, 1978.

"The Fourth Musketeer," in *Whispers 2*, edited by Stuart David Schiff. New York, Doubleday, 1979.

"When Dark Descends," with Thomas F. Monteleone, in *Chrysalis 4*, edited by Roy Torgeson. New York, Zebra, 1979.

"And Weary of the Sun," in *Chrysalis 5*, edited by Roy Torgeson. New York, Zebra, 1979.

"Love-Starved," in *Fantasy and Science Fiction* (New York), August 1979.

"Across the Water to Skye," in *New Terrors 2*, edited by Ramsey Campbell. London, Pan, 1980.

"A Garden of Blackred Roses," in *Dark Forces*, edited by Kirby McCauley. New York, Viking Press, 1980.

"The Other Room," in *Mummy!*, edited by Bill Pronzini. New York, Arbor House, 1980.

"Quietly Now," in *The Arbor House Necropolis*, edited by Bill Pronzini. New York, Arbor House, 1981.

"Confess the Seasons," in *Perpetual Light*, edited by Alan Ryan. New York, Warner, 1982.

"Every Time You Say I Love You," in *The Year's Best Horror Stories 10*, edited by Karl Edward Wagner. New York, DAW, 1982.

"Essence of Charlotte," in *Twilight Zone* (New York), February 1982.

"What in Solemn Silence," in *Isaac Asimov's Science Fiction Magazine* (New York), 15 March 1982.

"Pride," in *Fantasy and Science Fiction* (New York), May 1982.

"The Wind of Lost Migration," in *Amazing* (New York), June 1982.

"I Never Could Say Goodbye," in *Whispers 4*, edited by Stuart David Schiff. New York, Doubleday, 1983.

"The Next Name You Hear," in *Fantasy and Science Fiction* (New York), January 1983.

"Recollections of Annie," in *Twilight Zone* (New York), January-February 1983.

"A Voice Not Heard," in *Isaac Asimov's Science Fiction Magazine* (New York), September 1984.

OTHER PUBLICATIONS

Novels

The Curse. Canoga Park, California, Major, 1976.
The Hour of the Oxrun Dead. New York, Doubleday, 1977.
The Sound of Midnight. New York, Doubleday, 1978.
The Last Call of Mourning. New York, Doubleday, 1979.
The Tea Party. New York, Pocket Books, 1985.

Other

Introduction to *Conjure Wife*, by Charles Chesnutt. Boston, Gregg Press, 1977.

Editor, *Writing and Selling Science Fiction*. Cincinnati, Writer's Digest, 1977.

Editor, *Shadows 1-8*. New York, Doubleday, 8 vols., 1978-85.

Editor, *Nightmares*. New York, Doubleday, 1978.

Editor, *Horrors*. New York, Berkley, 1981.

Editor, *Terrors*. New York, Pocket Books, 1982.

Editor, *The Dodd Mead Gallery of Horror*. New York, Dodd Mead, 1983; as *Gallery of Horror*, London, Robson, 1983.

Editor, *Fears*. New York, Berkley, 1983.

Editor, *Midnights*. New York, Tor, 1985.

*

Charles L. Grant comments:

In science fiction, I'm working on a future history that most of my more recent stories and novels fit into, a history that will eventually cover over 500 years, primarily tracing a single family (the Parrics). In horror fiction, my aim is, simply, to produce a fright in the reader. In this regard I generally use two settings: Hawthorne Street (a place in an unnamed town in an unnamed area of the country), and Oxrun Station, an upper-middle and upper-class village in western Connecticut. If there's any influence at all in my work it comes not from Lovecraft or Smith, but from Bradbury and Ellison, with perhaps a dollop of Sturgeon.

*   *   *

Charles L. Grant continues to be an author of bright, unfulfilled promise. His first stories showed occasional glimpses of deft imagery, and seemed to be the product of a new author struggling with the development of meaning from story ideas. The struggle continues, but its realization still seems far away.

Grant has begun an ambitious undertaking, a future history spanning several centuries concerning the Parric family, introduced in *The Shadow of Alpha*. This first novel presents a world of the 22nd century, swept by the plague winds. The population of North America has mostly been confined to megalopoli, with small groups of hunters living in the surrounding wilderness. Androids have been developed to take over onerous physical tasks. The plague destroys most of the population of humans, and turns the androids into rogues, a constant threat to the remaining humans. *The Shadow of Alpha* is an unremarkable post-disaster novel, with the conventional projections of science fiction: petty warlords, universal suspicion and hostility, and an unaccountable shortage of women. The protagonist is concerned with the re-establishment of the former culture. *Ascension* concerns the third generation. The government has established itself in a small town and is slowly exending tendrils of conrol around it. Although the CenGov is manifestly conservative, the advance technology it offers is presented as preferable to any other lifestyle. No variant cultures are suggested as being anything but decadent or oppressive. On a mission of vengeance the protagonist, Orion, liberates the remaining inhabitants of Philayork. Although he has ostensibly learned the bitter taste of revenge, he still allows the villain to be killed.

The third novel in the series, *Legion,* is remarkably similar. Orion's brother is likewise on a quest for vengeance, although he professes otherwise. Like Orion, he suffers from melancholia. Once again, no alternatives to the CenGov reign are seriously considered and the novel is climaxed by the death of the villain. *Legion* is an improvement over the preceding novels, if only because Grant seems to have achieved a better fusion of action and introspection. As a result, the book has a steadier pace than *Ascension,* which has a strong tendency to bog down in the protagonist's own depression. The language is generally quite well handled, although Grant suffers from the delusion that repetition and sentence fragments enhance emotional impact.

It is clear that Charles L. Grant is trying to write something more than simple-minded science-fiction adventures. His novels and short stories reveal an author who takes his craft seriously. As yet, however, he has been unable to transcend the conventions of the genre he has selected.

—Jeff Frane

GRAY, Curme. American. Born in Richmond, Indiana. Attended University of Chicago. Served in the United States Army during World War II.

SCIENCE-FICTION PUBLICATIONS

Novel

Murder in Millennium VI. Chicago, Shasta, 1951.

*   *   *

There are a number of science-fiction writers whose reputations rest primarily on one story which stands out from the rest of their work. Far less numerous are those writers who are only known to have written a single story, and one that is of such quality or importance as to deserve a place in SF history. One of the latter group is Curme Gray, author of *Murder in Millennium VI* .

Murder in Millennium VI is subtitled "A Future Mystery. " It is set in a matriarchal society of the far future, whose customs and technology bear no resemblance to our own. One measure of the alienness of this society is that the very concept of "death" has disappeared from common usage. When the ruler of this global society dies, only an antiquarian, a student of curiosities from the distant past, can recognize the condition, and he has great difficulty in explaining its meaning to others. With the eventual understanding of what "death" means comes the realization that it was not the result of a natural

process but was "irregularity," deliberately caused by some unknown agent. Not only has death re-entered the perfect and permanent society, but some member of that society has re-invented murder. The questions of who killed the Matriarch, and how, and why, underlie this very distinctive novel.

The unusual thing about *Murder in Millennium IV* is that it is an attempt to depict a future society entirely in terms of that society, without external references. There are no handy expository lectures no conversations in which two characters explain everyday features of their society to each other—all of the details of the future setting and its culture must be deduced from context. To the extent that not all such details *are* deducible, the book falls short of its ambitious goal, but nevertheless, as Damon Knight has said, "it's a prodigious three-quarters success. . . . For sheer audacity and stubbornness, Curme Gray's performance is breathtaking."

—R. E. Briney

GREEN, Joseph (Lee). American. Born in Compass Lake, Florida, 14 January 1931. Educated at Brevard Community College, Cocoa, Florida, A. A. Married 1) Juanita Henderson in 1951 (divorced, 1975), one son and one daughter; 2) Patrice Milton in 1975, two daughters. Laboratory technician, International Paper Company, Panama City, Florida, 1949-51; shop worker and welder, Panama City, 1952-54; millwright in Florida, Texas, and Alabama, 1955-58; senior supervisor, Boeing Company, Seattle, 1959-63. Since 1965, public affairs science writer, Nasa, Kennedy Space Center, Florida. Agent: Blassingame McCauley and Wood, 225 West 34th Street, New York, New York 10122; or, Carnell Agency, Rowneybury Bungalow, Sawbridgeworth, near Old Harlow, Essex CM20 2EX, England. Address: 1390 Holly Avenue, Merritt Island, Florida 32952, U. S. A.

SCIENCE-FICTION PUBLICATIONS

Novels

The Loafers of Refuge. London, Gollancz, and New York, Ballantine, 1965.
Gold the Man. London, Gollancz, 1971; as *The Mind Behind the Eye,* New York, DAW, 1972.
Conscience Interplanetary. London, Gollancz, 1972; New York, Doubleday, 1973.
Star Probe. London, Millington, 1976; New York, Ace, 1978.
The Horde. Toronto, Laser, 1976; London, Dobson, 1979.

Short Stories

An Affair with Genius. London, Gollancz, 1969.

Uncollected Short Stories

"The Fourth Generation," in *Science Fiction Adventures* (London), vol. 5, no. 30, 1962.
"The Fight on Hurricane Island," in *Argosy* (London), June 1963.
"Haggard Honeymoon," with James Webbert, in *New Writings in SF 1,* edited by John Carnell. London, Dobson, 1964.
"The Creators," in *New Writings in SF 2,* edited by John Carnell. London, Dobson, 1964.

"Treasure Hunt," in *New Writings in SF 5*, edited by John Carnell. London, Dobson, 1965.

"Birth of a Butterfly," in *New Writings in SF 10*, edited by John Carnell. London, Dobson, 1967.

"When I Have Passed Away," in *New Writings in SF 15*, edited by John Carnell. London, Dobson, 1969.

"Death and the Sensperience Poet," in *New Writings in SF 17*, edited by John Carnell. London, Dobson, 1970.

"First Light on a Darkling Plain," in *New Writings in SF 19*, edited by John Carnell. London, Dobson, 1971.

"Wrong Attitude," in *Analog* (New York), February 1971.

"One Man Game," in *Analog* (New York), February 1972.

"The Seventh Floor," in *Eternity* (Sandy Springs, South Carolina), May 1972.

"Three-Tour Man," in *Analog* (New York), August 1972.

"A Custom of the Children of Life," in *Fantasy and Science Fiction* (New York), December 1972.

"Space to Move," in *The New Mind*, edited by Roger Elwood. New York, Macmillan, 1973.

"Let My People Go!," in *The Other Side of Tomorrow*, edited by Roger Elwood. New York, Random House, 1973.

"The Birdlover," in *Showcase*, edited by Roger Elwood. New York, Harper, 1973.

"Robustus Revisited," in *Fantasy and Science Fiction* (New York), April 1973.

"The Waiting World," in *Future Kin*, edited by Roger Elwood. New York, Doubleday, 1974.

"A Star Is Born," in *Fantasy and Science Fiction* (New York), February 1974.

"Walk Barefoot on the Glass," in *Analog* (New York), March 1974.

"Jaybird's Song," in *Fantasy and Science Fiction* (New York), December 1974.

"A Death in Coventry," in *Dystopian Visions*, edited by Roger Elwood. Englewood Cliffs, New Jersey, Prentice Hall, 1975.

"Encounter with a Carnivore," in *Epoch*, edited by Roger Elwood and Robert Silverberg. New York, Berkley, 1975.

"Weekend in Hartford," in *Dude* (Mt. Morris, Illinois), September 1975.

"Last of the Chauvinists," in *Fantasy and Science Fiction* (New York), November 1975.

"Jeremiah, Born Dying," in *Odyssey* (New York), Spring 1976.

"To See the Stars That Blind," with Patrice Milton, in *Fantasy and Science Fiction* (New York), March 1977.

"An Alien Conception," in *Nugget* (New York), June 1977.

"The Wind among the Mindymums," in *Fantasy and Science Fiction* (New York), December 1978.

"The Speckled Gantry," in *Destinies* (New York), January 1979.

"Gentle into That Good Night," in *Analog* (New York), July 1981.

"Still Fall the Gentle Rains," with Patrice Milton, in *Rigel* (Richmond, California), Fall 1981.

"EasyEd," with Patrice Milton, in *Fantasy and Science Fiction* (New York), May 1982.

"In the Court of the Chrysoprase King," with Patrice Milton, in *Rigel* (Richmond, California), Spring 1983.

"And Be Lost Like Me," in *Analog* (New York), June 1983.

"Raccoon Reaction," in *Analog* (New York), September 1983.

OTHER PUBLICATIONS

Other

"Countdown for Surveyor," in *Analog* (New York), March 1967.

"Manufacturing in Space," in *Analog* (New York), December 1970.

"Skylab," in *Analog* (New York), March, April 1972.

*

Joseph Green comments:

Most of my stories have an underlying philosophical theme that is often not apparent on the surface. At heart I think of myself as an untrained, poorly equipped, corn-ball philosopher, and what I enjoy most is playing with ideas in fictional form. For that reason, I'll never create a consistent 'future history. " If I write a story about the totally secular world of 2090 today, I may want to write one tomorrow about the new surge in absolutist religion from 2070 to 2110. I have no faith at all in a single future.

I've achieved some small reputation as a writer of unusually believable aliens. I don't know why. I dream them up, work to make them real, and write about them because I enjoy it. Do I need a better reason? I write primarily for readers, not critics or other writers. If a reader enjoys my work, that's good. If it also makes him think, that's even better.

* * *

Joseph Green is a strongly imaginative writer. He likes to set his heroes problems, sometimes highly exotic or elaborately contrived, always laid out with great clarity and convincingly resolved. These heroes are often troubleshooters, typically working at the interface between human and alien, sometimes—and this is probably his most characteristic motif—even operating with alien bodies. In his most powerful novel, *Gold the Man*, this alienation works as far as two removes, for the hero is emphatically a man trapped in a superman's body, put to work inside an alien giant. In confronting his character with painful dilemmas, Green communicates to the reader a strong concern; he is also able to treat sympathetically those on both sides of an irreconcilable debate, as in *Star Probe*, which concerns one battle in a larger war between the space scientists and the Friends of the Earth. In *The Horde* he presents one of the genre's most sympathetic accounts of a kind of alien hive species, the humanoid Shemsi, as an improbable friendship develops between human and humanoid bound together, for different reasons, on a dangerous mission.

Reflecting their origins as series of short stories, *The Loafers of Refuge* and *Conscience Interplanetary* are episodic narratives. In the first, trouble-shooter Carey, as the first man born on Refuge, works to resolve conflict between humans and the native loafers, who have developed mental but not mechanical power. Human-Loafer interaction is mutually beneficial: for instance, the Loafers revivify their living trees (the Ent-like *breshwahr*), one of whom shows how men can survive matter transmission, thus enabling rapid colonization of other planets to relieve the overcrowded Earth. In the second, the hero Allan Odegaard has the job of checking whether intelligence exists on a planet: if so, it must be left alone, if not, it may be colonized (a problem consequent on the solution found in *Loafers*). Throughout his seven extraordinary adventures, Allan is in more danger from reactionary humans than from the weird life-forms he encounters.

Gold the Man is a classic novel, whether considered as a profound study of the loneliness of the superman in no-man's-land or as an exciting contribution to Brobdingnagian fantasy. Earth is at war with giant humanoids, the Hilt-Sil, one of whom, suffering from irreparable brain damage, is captured.

The superman Gold, and a female assistant, Marina Petrovna, are installed in the head of the 300-foot captive, where they control his brain, seated behind one of his eyes. In this extraordinary Trojan horse, they spy on the alien planet, finding the feared enemies to be a race of gentle giants living an idyllic life but forced to look for another planet because of danger from their own sun. Gold helps resolve their problems and, remarkably enough, his enforced voyeurism of their Gargantuan love-play resolves his personal fear of impotence: being a superman, he was a slow developer, but he rapes and impregnates the helpless Marina and their child is born with the assistance of a friendly Hilt-Sil doctor who has discovered them (this is not a macho fantasy story for all that). Green sets himself difficult problems in this powerful novel but he handles both the physicalities and the psychological stresses of the intriguing situation with great tact and skill.

In the light of *Gold the Man,* Green makes less than expected of the interesting motif in *Star Probe* of an old man, deceased, who is brought back to life in the body of his idiot grandson for the purposes of a suicide mission. The mission concerns the investigation of an alien probe in the solar system; once the difficulties of getting a rocket to the probe have been resolved, Green is able once again to concern himself with the interesting problem of communication between alien and human; within the novel as a whole, however, the probe serves only as an emblem of what the struggle for funds between space scientists and ecologists is all about.

Among Green's many fine short stories, it is hard to pick out the best or most characteristic, but "Jinn," "Once Around Arcturus," "Treasure Hunt" (man inside crystal chariot-horse), "When I Have Passed Away" (exotic Giantesses), "Last of the Chauvinists," and "To See the Stars That Blind" (written with his wife, Patrice Milton, brilliantly presenting the wonder and horror of a new mode of seeing), should be included. Green has published few stories in recent years; in the most recent known to me, "Still Fall the Gentle Rains" (written with Patrice Milton), the concern is still, movingly, with human-humanoid relations and the species implications of sexuality: in this case, lower fertility implies greater honesty.

—Michael J. Tolley

GREEN, Peter. See **BULMER, Kenneth.**

GREENLEAF, William. Address: c/o Ace Books, 200 Madison Avenue, New York, New York 10016, U. S. A.

SCIENCE-FICTION PUBLICATIONS

Novels

Time Jumper. New York, Nordon, 1981.
The Tartarus Incident. New York, Ace, 1983.
The Pandora Stone. New York, Ace, 1984.

* * *

William Greenleaf has the ability to utilize the *sociological*

theme of paradoxical perception in his science fiction in a much more complex manner than many of his peers. It permeates his plots and characters. Simply stated, this theme can be explained in this way: All is not what it seems, and nothing ever is because the shadow is oftentimes more of a reality than the figure which casts it; the figure is often an illusion. This idea has its roots in Heraclitus's philosophy and Plato's "Allegory of the Cave," and was theorized by sociologists during the 20th century with its direct application to social structure and role. Role and characterization are important in Greenleaf's fiction world, and his technique for handling paradoxical perception is evident in the two novels, *Time Jumper* and *The Tartarus Incident*, for which he is best known and has developed a following.

The themes of the Outsider and the Outcast appear in Greenleaf's fiction, and the character who falls into either category is usually faced with some form of rite of passage through which he or she must pass in order to survive and maintain identity. An example of this is Greenleaf's character creation, Erin, in *Time Jumper*.

A literate writer, drawing on many disciplines when he creates, Greenleaf's work contains a sense of existential irony within its structure. At times, the use of humor is very wry.

Greenleaf is a stylist, and he has the ability to create mood and atmosphere in a convincing manner that draws the reader into the rich texture of his prose. In the battle between good and evil for supremacy, good always has to work harder to win; it is more easy to be evil in a philosophical sense than it is to be good. It is clear that moral cowardice is one of Greenleaf's major concerns, for it runs through much of his writing in one subtle variation or another. Somewhere along the way, each character must make a moral choice, but be it for good or for evil, it must be made so that character can fulfill his or her destiny.

Greenleaf can successfully work a macabre feeling into his fiction, which places him in the same literary catagory as Robert Bloch and Lucius Shepard. His work compares favorably with these two writers. The reader will discover a fine social critic at work in Greenleaf's interests in social concerns, the role of values in society, and placing humans in an environment of mystery with the fear threshold present.

Greenleaf's skill at sustaining a keen sense of suspense and tension in his plots is well-developed. He can accurately reveal the incompetence of bureaucracy in any situation and its effects upon environment and personality. Like Keith Laumer, Greenleaf can deftly handle plot twists.

William Greenleaf's contribution to science fiction is his use of sociological and philosophical themes, characterization, and style. Continuing interest in Greenleaf's writing for sociologists, scholars, and readers rests on his ability to insert a sense of existential irony within the structure of his stories, the use of paradoxical perception to illuminate social concerns, and his use of the themes of the Outsider and the Outcast.

—Harold Lee Prosser

GREER, Richard. See **GARRETT, Randall.**

GREGORY, John. See **HOSKINS, Robert.**

GREY, Carol. See **LOWNDES, Robert A. W.**

GREY, Charles. See **TUBB, E. C.**

GRIDBAN, Volsted. See **FEARN, John Russell; TUBB, E. C.**

GRIFFIN, Russell M. American. Born in Stamford, Connecticut, 29 April 1943. Educated at Mount Hermon School, 1957-61; Trinity College, Hartford, Connecticut, 1961-65, B. A. in English 1965; Case Western Reserve University, Cleveland, 1967-70, M. A. 1969, Ph. D. 1970. Married Sheila Vaznelis in 1965; two children. English teacher, Proctor Academy, Andover, New Hampshire, 1965-67. Since 1970, Professor of English, University of Bridgeport, Connecticut. Visiting Faculty Member, IBM Watson Research Centre, Yorktown Heights, New York, 1985-86. Agent: Jim Trupin, JET Literary Associates, 124 East 84th Street, Suite 4A, New York, New York 10028. Address: 102 Old Field Lane, Milford, Connecticut 06460, U. S. A.

SCIENCE-FICTION PUBLICATIONS

Novels

Makeshift God. New York, Dell, 1979; London, Granada, 1982.
Century's End. New York, Bantam, 1981.
The Blind Man and the Elephant. New York, Pocket Books, 1982.
The Timeservers. New York, Avon, 1985.

Uncollected Short Stories

"The Confessional," in *Analog* (New York), May 1982.
"Angel at the Gate," in *The Best of Omni Science Fiction 6*, edited by Don Myrus. New York, Omni, 1983.
"Government Work," in *Habitats*, edited by Susan Shwartz. New York, DAW, 1984.

OTHER PUBLICATIONS

Other

"Medievalism in *Canticle for Leibowitz*," in *Extrapolation* (Wooster, Ohio), May 1973.

*

Russell M. Griffin comments:
The first adult paperback I ever owned was an anthology of science fiction I took to boys camp my first summer away from home. The book is long since lost, but not the stories.
But I suppose what has kept me in science fiction more than

anything else since is the medievalist in me. Where else can a writer enjoy the same scope and freedom of invention one finds in the dream visions of Chaucer, Langland, and Gower? Where else in modern literature is allegory allowed to survive at all? Science fiction, as the works of Orwell and Huxley attest, provides the ideal vehicle for social comment and satire. Reerect Spenser's Castle of Pride or create a society where equality is enforced by crippling the gifted? They are only a planet or an age away.

* * *

At this relatively early stage in his career, Russell M. Griffin already has four published novels to his credit, all of them fresh, witty, and crisply written versions of basic (and one not so basic) science fiction themes. Especially noteworthy about this impressive new talent are his inventiveness and exceptional gifts for comedy and satire. Regarding the latter, while certain passages in his work are reminiscent of another fine satirist, John Sladek, Griffin's passages are usually rather better integrated into the work as a whole than Sladek's.

Griffin's first novel, *Makeshift God*, would be impressive even were it not a "first novel. " The first half, especially, is brilliantly achieved; the second tends to lean more on mere adventure elements. However, Griffin's next two novels are more ambitious, both artistically and thematically. Significantly, both can be seen as closer to "mainstream" fiction than either his first or most recent efforts. His second novel, *Century's End*, is set in the near future (1999). Millennial actions and expectations abound: crazies and zanies expecting the worst, plotting the worst, are everywhere. In the controlled wittiness of the presentation, in the skill of its scene construction, and in its deft satirical art, this novel exemplifies many of the best qualities of the innovative science fiction of the past two decades; it can be meaningfully discussed in a context which includes the best of such writers as Vonnegut, Dick, and Disch. One thing that relates this novel to such major figures is the obvious intelligence manifested throughout—and not merely literary intelligence: for Griffin proves to be highly informed about a wide range of subjects, for example, satellite technology, climatology and geology, and the psychology and sociology of aberrant religious cults.

The plot focuses on the deadly rivalry of two such cults, one headed by an "inspired" mad-woman, the other headed by a corporate-minded TV evangelist named Dr. Love. Griffin focuses much of the novel's deft satire on these two groups and their benighted followers; he focuses also on related hypes, TV programming and advertising, for example. The central characters ranged against the cults and their manipulative techniques are the bright, sardonic Jervis Santalucia, who is half-black and rarely at ease about his identity, and Circe McPhee, a professional prognosticator; the chaos of modern life is such that government and big business have turned to the occult for "answers. "

While the writing in Griffin's third novel, *The Blind Men and the Elephant*, is just as witty and persuasive, the work itself—plot, theme, mileau—is his least science-fictional. The highly bizarre plot and accompanying cast of zanies relate to the pathetic-comic misadventures of a latter-day "Elephant Man"—a terribly deformed yet bright and sensitive creature who is commercially exploited by a media huckster (TV again) and spied upon by sinister government agents. We soon learn that Elephant Man is no more than five or six years old, being the ghastly product of government "experimentation" in cloning. His misadventures are a very Vonnegutian assemblage of black humor, farce, and satire. While individual episodes are very freshly done, it is doubtful that the overall presentation is as successful as it might have been. This volume is perhaps more to be recommended to fans of sixties-seventies mainstream black humor writing than to SF fans.

The Timeservers is, again, an impressive piece of writing. It resembles his first book in being very overtly science-fictional in its setting, themes, and characterization—interstellar travel, encounters with alien races, and so on. Certain interests—cloning, Roman Catholic ritual, the omnipresence of human violence (here embodied in a war with strong Vietnam overtones)—return from earlier Griffin books. But the reader experiences no sense of an author repeating himself; Griffin is just as fresh in approach, quite as interesting and witty here as in his previous books. This is a younger talent definitely to be watched. Not only has he chosen the best of models (Dick, Sladek, et al.), but in his best work, in his finest episodes, he transcends those models, bringing a new voice to the impressive choir of post-Campbellian writers.

—Robert E. Colbert

GRIFFITH, George (George Chetwynd Griffith-Jones). Also wrote as Levin Carnac; Lara; Stanton Morich. British. Born in Plymouth, Devon, 20 August 1857. Educated at schools in Lancashire and in evening classes, College of Preceptors Diploma 1887. Married Elizabeth Brierly in 1887 (died, 1933); two sons and one daughter. Merchant seaman, 1873-77; English teacher, Worthing College, Sussex, 1877-83, and Bolton Grammar School, Lancashire, 1883-87; journalist in London, 1888-89; staff writer, *Pearson's Weekly,* 1890-99, and *Pearson's Magazine,* 1896-1903, both London: travelled extensively for these magazines, including two trips around the world; correspondent in South Africa for London *Daily Mail,* 1903. *Died 4 June 1906.*

SCIENCE-FICTION PUBLICATIONS

Novels

The Angel of the Revolution: A Tale of Coming Terror. London, Tower, 1893; Westport, Connecticut, Hyperion Press, 1974.
Olga Romanoff; or, The Syren of the Skies. London, Tower, 1894; Westport, Connecticut, Hyperion Press, 1974.
Valdar the Oft-Born: A Saga of Seven Ages. London, Pearson, 1895.
The Outlaws of the Air. London, Tower, 1895.
Briton or Boer? London, White, 1897.
The Romance of Golden Star. London, White, 1897; New York, Arno Press, 1978.
The Destined Maid. London, White, 1898.
The Gold-Finder. London, White, 1898.
The Great Pirate Syndicate. London, White, 1899.
The Justice of Revenge. London, White, 1900.
Captain Ishmael. London, Hutchinson, 1901.
A Honeymoon in Space. London, Pearson, 1901; New York, Arno Press, 1975.
Denver's Double: A Story of Inverted Identity. London, White, 1901.
The World Masters. London, Long, 1903.
The Lake of Gold: A Narrative of the Anglo-American Conquest of Europe. London, White, 1903.
The Stolen Submarine. London, White, 1904.

A Criminal Croesus. London, Long, 1904.
A Mayfair Magician: A Romance of Criminal Science. London, White, 1905; as *The Man with Three Eyes,* n. d.
The Mummy and Miss Nitocris: A Phantasy of the Fourth Dimension. London, Laurie, 1906; New York, Arno Press, 1976; as *The Mummy and the Girl,* n. d.
The Great Weather Syndicate. London, White, 1906.
The World Peril of 1910. London, White, 1907.
The Sacred Skull. London, Everett, 1908.
The Lord of Labour. London, White, 1911.

Short Stories

Gambles with Destiny. London, White, 1898.
The Raid of "Le Vengeur" and Other Stories. London, Ferret Fantasy, 1974.

OTHER PUBLICATIONS

Novels

The Knights of the White Rose. London, White, 1897.
The Virgin of the Sun. London, Pearson, 1898.
The Rose of Judah. London, Pearson, 1899.
Brothers of the Chain. London, White, 1900.
Thou Shalt Not—(as Stanton Morich). London, Pearson, 1900.
The Missionary. London, White, 1902.
The White Witch of Mayfair. London, White, 1902.
A Woman Against the World. London, White, 1903.
An Island Love-Story. London, White, 1904.
His Better Half. London, White, 1905.
His Beautiful Client. London, White, 1905.
A Conquest of Fortune. London, White, 1906.
John Brown, Buccaneer. London, White, 1908.

Short Stories

A Heroine of the Slums. London, Tower, 1894(?).
Knaves of Diamonds, Being Tales of Mine and Veld. London, Pearson, 1899; as *The Diamond Dog,* 1913.

Verse (as Lara)

Poems General, Secular, and Satirical. London, Stewart, 1883.
The Dying Faith. London, Stewart, 1884.

Other

Men Who Have Made the Empire. London, Pearson, 1897.
In an Unknown Prison Land: An Account of Convicts and Colonists in New Caledonia. London, Hutchinson, 1901.
With Chamberlain in Africa. London, Routledge, 1903.
Sidelights on Convict Life. London, Long, 1903.

Translator (as Levin Carnac), *The Hope of the Family,* by Alphonse Daudet. London, Pearson, 1898.

*

Bibliography: by George Locke, in *The Raid of "Le Vengeur" and Other Stories,* 1974.

* * *

George Griffith published almost 50 books of crime, adventure, fantasy, romance, social melodrama, verse, and non-fiction. Most importantly, his output includes over 20 books of, or in the margins of, SF. He became one of the first, most characteristic, and most popular professional writers of editorially planned and instantly sensational fiction in the rising "yellow-press" of the turn of the century. Griffith also met the usual end of such hacks, being forced to get more outrageous and less believable in each succeeding novel and to shed whatever original insights he might have had in the process.

His best work, consequently, is clearly his first novel, *The Angel of the Revoluton,* though even that is marred by slipshod haste, racist chauvinism, and melodramatic sensationalism. Yet the subsumption of Verne's gadgetry and the "future war" tale, plus a dash of travelog exoticism and a barrelful of Bulwerian melodrama, under a real sympathy with justice wreaked on the existing political order of depotism and Mammon by a group of avenging heroes united into an Anarchist or Terrorist Brotherhood of Freedom, was a genuine breakthrough. The brains of the conspiracy, the super-intelligent Hungarian Jew Natas, is, in spite of his name, his hypnotic powers, and his crippled exterior, convincingly portrayed as a victim of Tsarist oppression rather than a mad beast. The main hero, an English inventor, is starving in his garret while inventing his super-airplane; and the executive head of the Terrorists is an English aristocrat, thus permitting Griffith to alloy plebeian hatred with snobbery. There follow cliffhanging global adventures dovetailing the fates of the heroes and their beautiful and fully equal female counterparts, especially Natas's daughter Natasha, and the world war that develops in 1904. The bloodthirsty Franco-Slavonic alliance is defeated by the Brotherhood who set up an Anglo-Saxon federation to guide the world toward disarmament and a vague social justice never clearly spelled out in economics terms. But this heady brew contains a few memorable set scenes, and—most importantly—an at-least-partial relization that the fusion of politics and the new technology makes the old social relationships not only unstable but catastrophically untenable. This realization made Griffith a pioneer in the instauration of a new SF tradition which culminated in Wells and still overshadows our whole century.

The sequel, *Olga Romanoff,* written to exploit *The Angel* 's great success, is inferior, its only new element being an interplanetary threat copied from Flammarion's ubiquitous comets. Already in *The Outlaws of the Air* the exploitation becomes unreadable: the anarchists are vicious beasts, the heroes English gentlemen, the ideal a rosewater South Sea colony, the fights simply ludicrous; *The Great Pirate Syndicate* descends to bloodthirsty Anglo-Saxon wishdream-imperialism and anti-semitism. In Griffith's feverish gallop through all the popular literary forms, *A Honeymoon in Space* was his venture into interplanetary voyages; it groups all its clichés (aggressive Martians, angel-like Venusians, antigravity, monsters galore) around a safari-story of a lord, his beautiful American bride, and their faithful retainer. His later works are unworthy of a writer with political convictions and a generous plebeian indignation: if the story that Griffith died of drink is true, it would provide an appropriately moral dying fall. And it would still remain exemplary for the SF of our century.

—Darko Suvin

GRINNELL, David. See **WOLLHEIM, Donald A.**

GROENER, Carl. See **LOWNDES, Robert A. W.**

GROVE, Frederick Philip. Canadian. Born Felix Paul Berthold Friedrich Greve, in Radomno, Prussia-Poland, 14 February 1879; naturalized citizen, 1921. Educated at St. Pauli school, Hamburg, 1886-95; Gymnasium des Johanneums, Hamburg, 1895-98; University of Bonn, 1898-1900; Maximiliens University, Munich, 1901-02; University of Manitoba, Winnipeg, B. A. 1921. Married Catherine Wiens in 1914; one daughter and one son. Writer and translator in Germany, 1902-09; imprisoned for fraud, 1903-04; emigrated to Canada c.1909; settled in Manitoba: taught in Haskett, 1913, Winkler, 1913-15, Virdin, 1915-16, Gladstone, 1916-17, Ferguson, 1918, Eden, 1919-22, and Rapid City, 1922-24; Editor, Graphic Press, Ottawa, 1929-31, and Associate Editor, *Canadian Nation,* 1929; manager of a farm in Simcoe, Ontario, 1931-38, and lived on the farm after his retirement. Recipient: Lorne Pierce Gold Medal, 1934; Canadian Writers' Federation pension, 1944; Governor-General's Award, for non-fiction, 1947. D. Litt. : University of Manitoba, 1945. Fellow, Royal Society of Canada, 1941. *Died 19 August 1948.*

SCIENCE-FICTION PUBLICATIONS

Novel

Consider Her Ways. Toronto, Macmillan, 1947.

OTHER PUBLICATIONS

Novels

Fanny Essler (in German). Stuttgart, Juncker, 1905.
Maurermeister Ihles Haus. Berlin, Schnabel, 1906; translated by Paul P. Gubbins, as *The Master Mason's House,* edited by Douglas O. Spettigue and A. W. Riley, Ottawa, Oberon Press, 1976.
Settlers of the Marsh. Toronto, Ryerson Press, and New York, Doran, 1925.
A Search for America. Ottawa, Graphic, 1927; New York, Carrier, 1928.
Our Daily Bread. Toronto and New York, Macmillan, 1928; London, Cape, 1929.
The Yoke of Life. Toronto, Macmillan, and New York, R. R. Smith, 1930.
Fruits of the Earth. Toronto and London, Dent, 1933.
Two Generations: A Story of Present-Day Ontario. Toronto, Ryerson Press, 1939.
The Master of the Mill. Toronto, Macmillan, 1944.

Short Stories

Tales from the Margin: The Selected Short Stories of Frederick Philip Grove, edited by Desmond Pacey. Toronto, McGraw Hill Ryerson, 1971.

Verse

Wanderungen. Privately printed, 1902.
Helena und Damon (verse drama). Privately printed, 1902.

Other

Oscar Wilde (in German). Berlin, Gose and Tetzlaff, 1903.
Randarabesken zu Oscar Wilde. Minden, Germany, Bruns, 1903.
Over Prairie Trails. Toronto, McClelland and Stewart, 1922.
The Turn of the Year. Toronto, McClelland and Stewart, 1923.
It Needs to Be Said. . . . Toronto and New York, Macmillan, 1929.
In Search of Myself. Toronto, Macmillan, 1946.
The Letters of Frederick Philip Grove, edited by Desmond Pacey. Toronto, University of Toronto Press, 1976.

Translator of works by Balzac, Robert and Elizabeth Barrett Browning, Cervantes, Ernest Dowson, Dumas, Flaubert, Gide, Le Sage, Meredith, Henri Murger, Pater, Wells, and Wilde into German, 1903-09.

*

Critical Studies: *Frederick Philip Grove*, Toronto, Copp Clark, 1969, and *FPG: The European Years* (includes bibliography), Ottawa, Oberon Press, 1973, both by Douglas O. Spettigue; *Frederick Philip Grove* by Ronald Sutherland, Toronto, McClelland and Stewart, 1969; *Frederick Philip Grove* edited by Desmond Pacey, Toronto, Ryerson Press, 1970; *Frederick Philip Grove* by Margaret R. Scobie, New York, Twayne, 1973; *Three Voices: The Lives of Margaret Laurence, Gabrielle Roy, Frederick Philip Grove* by Joan Hind-Smith, Toronto, Clarke Irwin, 1975.

* * *

Frederick Philip Grove is primarily known in Canadian literature for his didactic agrarian novels. One might consider his 1942 autobiography, *In Search of Myself*, a work of "fantasy," since in it he sets out the persona of "Grove" he had maintained, with many fabrications, since his arrival in Canada many years before.

Consider Her Ways, his only real science fiction novel, was also his last; it employs genre conventions for social satire. The story is ostensibly set down by a naturalist studying ant colonies in Venezuela. He regards these insects as akin to humans, calling them our "formicarian brethren." In fact, they are superior, since one giant ant, Wawa-quee, is able to hypnotize him and communicate her story of epic quest with an army of warrior-scientists, to gather knowledge for her tribe.

This device of the ant's point of view allows Grove to satirize humanity both directly and indirectly. Wawa-quee's comments on humans are scathing. She ridicules everything from spelling (designed to render knowledge inaccessible) to clothing (especially night-gowns). Yet through the ants' own values—their military ferocity, subordination of the individual, and acceptance of slavery—the author (in the wake of World War II) condemns these evils in human life. This is especially evident when Wawa-quee observes that humans do not operate on children to render them happy and docile in slavery, even though they *do* enslave each other "by means of a thing . . . [they call] money." She comments: "The curious will infer from this neglect of simple expedients that man has either not yet risen to any very high degree of civilization; or—which is my own opinion—that he has considerably degenerated from a level previously attained." The irony is double-edged; the ants cannot understand human free will, but they can condemn human cruelty. Indirectly, through the ants' courage, treachery, despair, hope for the race, self-sacrifice, and thirst for knowledge, Grove discusses the best and worst of human nature. His satire is often savage; yet it is mixed with compassion. Wawa-quee and her society are convincingly drawn.

Unfortunately, the book is flawed by its pedantic style and by the obvious nature of its allegory. The whole book, in situation and style, seems to be an inferior imitation of an early 20th-century "lost race" fantasy by Wells, Haggard, or Conan Doyle. This may explain its relative obscurity. Nevertheless, for its inventiveness and social commentary, the book deserves examination.

—Susan Wood

GUIN, Wyman (Woods). American. Born in Wanette, Oklahoma, 1 March 1915. Educated at Riverside City College, California, J. C. 1934. Married 1) Jean Adolph in 1939 (divorced, 1955); 2) Valerie Carlson in 1956; two sons and three daughters. Technician in Pharmacology, Advertising Writer, Advertising Manager, and Marketing Vice-President, Lakeside Laboratories Inc., Milwaukee, 1938-62; Vice-President, Medical Television Communications Inc., Chicago, 1962-64. Since 1964, Planning Administrator, L. W. Erolich-Intercon International. Lives in Tarrytown, New York.

SCIENCE-FICTION PUBLICATIONS

Novel

The Standing Joy. New York, Avon, 1969.

Short Stories

Living Way Out. New York, Avon, 1967; as *Beyond Bedlam*, London, Sphere, 1973.

* * *

Although Wyman Guin has written a novel, *The Standing Joy*, his most important work is to be found in his novelettes from the 1950's and 1960's. The stories are remarkable for the way in which Guin takes up far-out sociological or psychological ideas and gives them substance in carefully worked out dramatic conflicts against the background of alternate societies; despite some extravaganzans in the details they carry conviction and emerge as fully rounded and believable SF worlds.

His best story is the minor classic "Beyond Bedlam," which employs the basic inversion device of so much science fiction: what is considered an illness today—schizophrenia in this case—is in about a thousand years in the future the norm, with a drug-induced, law-enforced schizophrenia in every human being. Everybody is inhabited by two personalities that change in five-day shifts. This procedure has eliminated man's aggressive impulses, and hence war, but has also led to the disappearance of art and emotional pleasures. The theme of the story is treated not so much as a utopian dream or a dystopian nightmare as an exercise in creating a different alternate society, with all the ramifications in good and evil following from the basic premise.

"The Delegate from Guapanga" and "A Man of the Renaissance" both have richly exotic socio-cultural backgrounds. The first story contrasts two alien philosophies of "Mentalists" and "Matterists," the Mentalists being closer to nature with ideals of a simpler life and tradition, the Matterists representatives of a mechanistic-scientific culture. The hero of the story develops a curious political idea of "dishonesty in government. " The second story is about a man of ambition in an archipelagic world, who by sometimes Machiavellian means tries to realize his purely rationalist and revolutionary notions in a world governed by traditional values. In "Volpla" a joke in genetical engineering by a misanthropic lone scientist—artificially created beings that were to be passed off as visitors from the stars—turns out differently by a simple reversion of the reader's expectations. "My Darling Hecate" and "The Root and the Ring" are slight and mildly amusing volatile fantasies.

Guin's novel, *The Standing Joy*, is a parallel Earth story, with the characters having "twins" on another Earth, perhaps our own. Its protagonist, Colin Collins, a superman who has invented the prolonged orgasm, gathers around him a group of other talented inventors; the sex is harmless, but the whole thing is a bit confused. Wyman Guin's typical work is characteristic of its time and the magazine (*Galaxy*) in which most of it appeared, a slicky written fiction of ideas that manages to entertain and to stimulate without moving the reader deeply.

—Franz Rottensteiner

GUNN, James E(dwin). American. Born in Kansas City, Missouri, 12 July 1923. Educated at the University of Kansas, Lawrence, B. A. in journalism 1947, M. A. in English 1951. Served in the United States Naval Reserve, 1943-46: Lieutenant. Married Jane Frances Anderson in 1947; two sons. Editor, Western Printing and Lithographing Company, Racine, Wisconsin, 1951-52. Assistant Instructor, 1955-56, Managing Editor, Alumni Association, 1955-58, Administrative Assistant to the Chancellor for University Relations, 1958-70, Lecturer, 1970-74, and since 1974, Professor of English, University of Kansas. Member of the Executive Committee, and President, 1980-82, Science Fiction Research Association; President, Science Fiction Writers of America, 1971-72. Recipient: Byron Caldwell Smith Prize; Hugo Special Award, 1976, and Achievement Award, 1983; Pilgrim Award, 1976. Guest of Honor, Mid-Americon 1, Marcon 10, Fortcon 1. Agent: Richard Curtis, 164 East 64th Street, New York, New York 10021; or, Reece Halsey, 8733 Sunset Boulevard, Los Angeles, California 90069; or A. P. Watt Ltd., 26-28 Bedford Row, London WC1R 4HL, England. Address: 2215 Orchard Lane, Lawrence, Kansas 66044, U. S. A.

SCIENCE-FICTION PUBLICATIONS

Novels

This Fortress World. New York, Gnome Press, 1955; London, Sphere, 1977.
Star Bridge, with Jack Williamson. New York, Gnome Press, 1955; London, Sidgwick and Jackson, 1978.
The Joy Makers. New York, Bantam, 1961; London, Gollancz, 1963.
The Immortals. New York, Bantam, 1962; London, Panther, 1975.
The Immortal (novelization of TV series). New York, Bantam, 1970.
The Burning. New York, Dell, 1972.
The Listeners. New York, Scribner, 1972; London, Arrow, 1978.

The Magicians. New York, Scribner, 1976; London, Sidgwick and Jackson, 1978.
Kampus. New York, Bantam, 1977.
The Dreamers. New York, Simon and Schuster, 1980; London, Gollancz, 1981; as *The Mind Master*, New York, Pocket Books, 1982.

Short Stories

Station in Space. New York, Bantam, 1958.
Future Imperfect. New York, Bantam, 1964.
The Witching Hour. New York, Dell, 1970.
Breaking Point. New York, Walker, 1972.
Some Dreams Are Nightmares. New York, Scribner, 1974.
The End of the Dreams. New York, Scribner, 1975.
Tiger! Tiger! Polk City, Iowa, Drumm, 1983.

Uncollected Short Stories

"Child of the Sun," in *The 1978 Annual World's Best SF*, edited by Donald A. Wollheim. New York, DAW, 1978.
"Guilt," in *Isaac Asimov's Science Fiction Magazine* (New York), May-June 1978.
"The Anti-Nuclear Conspiracy," in *Analog* (New York), August 1982.
"The End of the World," in *Analog* (New York), January 1984.
"Man of the Hour," in *Analog* (New York), October 1984.
"Touch of the Match," in *Analog* (New York), February 1985.
"Mother of the Year," in *Analog* (New York), April 1985.
"Will of the Wisp," in *Analog* (New York), May 1985.

OTHER PUBLICATIONS

Play

Thy Kingdom Come (produced Lawrence, Kansas, 1947).

Other

"On Style," in *Those Who Can*, edited by Robin Scott Wilson. New York, New American Library, 1973.
"Science Fiction and the Mainstream," in *Science Fiction, Today and Tomorrow*, edited by Reginald Bretnor. New York, Harper, 1974.
"Teaching Science Fiction Revisited," in *Analog* (New York), November 1974.
Alternate Worlds: The Illustrated History of Science Fiction. Englewood Cliffs, New Jersey, Prentice Hall, 1975.
The Discovery of the Future: The Ways Science Fiction Developed. College Station, Texas A and M University, 1975.
"Henry Kuttner, C. L. Moore, Lewis Padgett, et al.," in *Voices for the Future*, edited by Thomas D. Clareson. Bowling Green, Ohio, Popular Press, 1976.
"Where Do You Get Those Crazy Ideas?," in *Writing and Selling Science Fiction*. Cincinnati, Writer's Digest, 1976.
"Heroes, Heroines, Villains: The Characters in Science Fiction," in *The Craft of Science Fiction*, edited by Reginald Bretnor. New York, Harper, 1976.
"Teaching Science Fiction," in *Publishers' Weekly* (New York), 14 June 1976.
"The Academic Viewpoint," in *Nebula Award Winners 12*, edited by Gordon R. Dickson. New York, Harper, 1978.
"Aliens," with Pamela Sargent, in *Contemporary Mythology*, edited by Patricia Warrick, Martin H. Greenberg, and Joseph D. Olander. New York, Harper, 1978.

"On the Tinsel Screen: Science Fiction and the Movies," in *Isaac Asimov's Science Fiction Magazine* (New York), February 1980.

"On the Foundations of Science Fiction," in *Isaac Asimov's Science Fiction Magazine* (New York), April 1980.

Isaac Asimov: The Foundations of Science Fiction. New York and Oxford University Press, 1982.

Editor, *Man and the Future.* Lawrence, University Press of Kansas, 1968.

Editor, *Nebula Award Stories 10.* New York, Harper, 1975.

Editor, *The Road to Science Fiction: From Gilgamesh to Wells, From Wells to Heinlein, From Heinlein to Here, From Here to Forever.* New York, New American Library, 4 vols., 1977-82.

*

Bibliography: *A James Gunn Checklist*, Polk City, Iowa, Drumm, 1983.

Manuscript Collection: University of Kansas Library, Lawrence.

James E. Gunn comments:

I recently began an autobiographical essay for Contemporary Authors Autobiography Series with the statement: "I am a professor of English at the University of Kansas, the author of some 80 published science-fiction stories and the author or editor of twenty-four books, almost all of them either science fiction or about science fiction. At the age of 61, as I write this account of my life in that fabled year of 1984, in the quiet university town of Lawrence, Kansas, trying to make sense out of what has happened to me, my first thought is that, unlikely as it might once have seemed, this is where I belong; this is what I was meant to do. "

The facts that I have been president of both of the Science Fiction Writers of America and the Science Fiction Research Association, that I have written almost as much critical material about science fiction as I have written science fiction, that I split my working time between teaching and writing, illustrate the ways in which my work has tried to bridge two cultures. In the introduction to my 1972 collection of stories, *Breaking Point* , I wrote that "the stories in this collection were intended [to help] bridge the gap between science fiction and the mainstream, between the ghetto and the larger world outside, between C. P. Snow's Two Cultures." They were, I indicated, intended to adopt an evolutionary, not a revolutionary, approach to a literature, accepting the strengths of a popular genre and trying to build upon them.

Finally, in my autobiographical essay, I wrote about a story that became the starting point for my writing of *The Dreamers*, "Looking back over my career as a writer of science fiction, I realize now that I have always been fascinated by the seductive power of dreams, even while I have insisted that reality, while it may be hard and tragic, is preferable. "

I concluded the essay with the statement, "That would be consistent with my life as I see it: surprise tempered by understanding, optimism tempered by reality, ambition tempered by pragmatism.

"The true heroes of my stories are rational people who accept the world as it is while never giving up the possibility of making it better. The villains are much the same, only they are willing to go too far to get what they want; they want what everyone else wants, but their desires are not restrained by a sense of other people's needs.

"A fiction writer's work may not always reflect his values, but if he writes out of what he has experienced and thought and felt, it must reflect the writer. What I am ultimately must be seen in the mirror of my writing."

*   *   *

In his definitive anthology *The Road to Science Fiction* James E. Gunn defines science fiction as idea-fiction that describes change and its consequences on the human race. This change is often technological and, in most cases, is brought about by human actions and desires. While such a definition may not work for all of science fiction or for all its writers, it has worked well of Gunn. Since 1949 his work has consistently represented human characters confronting altered futures. As in the stories collected in *Station in Space*, Gunn sees humanity as a race that needs to be challenged in order to grow. He recognizes that many people would prefer to live in stable worlds in which each day is like all the others, and, therefore, his plots frequently deal with how the major characters thwart the deadly appeal of stasis.

Gunn's favorite writing length is the novelette because it allows him to center his story around a single event that is economically described and resolved. Many of his "novels" consist of three or four novelettes connected by a common theme. In *The Joy Makers*, for example, Gunn explores what people think will make them happy within an extended period of time. In each story a stage is reached which eventually supports his thesis that even if absolute happiness could be found it would probably be rather disappointing. The use of a series of novelettes allows a story to end with a dramatic statement that does not need the amplification and development a novel demands.

The Immortals, another series of interconnected stories, investigates a world in which immortality is possible. However, in each story the possibility of immortality is not as important as its effect on the characters. Gunn wishes to describe human attitudes toward death and uses the device of immortality to put these attitudeds into sharp relief. Because he deals with such issues, Gunn's stories often touch on current problems. For example, medical technology has been more and more directed toward the prolongation of life. But such technology has added huge costs to basic hospital services. In the third story of *The Immortals* Gunn presents the ultimate direction such a trend could take. The story effectively describes just how dangerous humanity's preoccupation with avoiding death can be.

In *The Listeners* Gunn studies communication in the same way he explored immortality. While the unifying concept among these novelettes is the attempt to decipher and answer a message from Capella, the theme concerns communication between individuals. In each story, with the Capellan project in the background, the foreground is filled with husbands and wives, fathers and sons, leaders and followers, writers and readers, men and intelligent machines, and humans and aliens who try to communicate. The result is a work that describes not only an adventure in the near future but a moving account of humanity's present. Communication with aliens may happen some day, but for now human communication could do with some improvement.

The Dreamers (inexplicably renamed *The Mind Master* by the paperback publisher), collects three novelettes with the addition of inter-chapter material that adds up to yet another story. Each of these stories traces the consequences of the discovery of chemical learning. By imparting instant knowledge through chemistry, humanity has eliminated the difficulty normally associated with learning. But it has also created a future race in which imagination is sadly lacking. Even dreams come from pills and injections. By far the darkest of Gunn's works, *The Dreamers* still gives the reader human characters who are capable of love and who care about what has happened to their fellow human beings. The stories might deal with a nightmare age, but Gunn regrets this nightmare. It is as if Gunn is telling the reader that these characters, and by extension humanity, deserve better than their allotted fates.

And Gunn does give humanity a better fate in his most recent book *Crisis!* Set in our present, the stories deal with a man from the future who comes to the present in order to avert events that will destroy the future. This character is not allowed to act directly, but must convince people of the present to act simply by speaking and reasoning with them. Gunn covers a wide variety of problems (from energy to war to terrorism), and presents some interesting views on why and how they happen.

Two more conventional novels deserve mention. *The Fortress World*, Gunn's first novel, is a highly readable story that makes use of the popular science-fiction galactic empire. But Gunn relates the story from the point of view of an ordinary inhabitant rather than a super-hero. Life in a galactic empire can be rather unpleasant if the character is only one of the crowd. *This Fortress World* is Gunn's attempt to bring "reality" to space opera.

At the opposite pole lies *Kampus*, a work that has suffered from misreading. It is too easy—and misleading—to read this novel as a damnation of the campus of the 1960's. *Kampus* is, in fact, a parable about people who believe that everyone should be allowed to do "their own thing." It is similar to Voltaire's *Candide* in that the world and action presented in the novel are not meant to be taken as serious attempts to portray "reality." Unlike *Candide*, however, *Kampus* questions what life would be like if everyone were only to tend his own garden.

James E. Gunn has made a career of science fiction as an author, teacher, and scholar. His criticism attests to his sensitivity to the genre. His fiction shows an equal sensitivity to what is possible in science fiction. As one reads his stories, one is struck by the variety of themes, plots, and styles he is capable of. *Kampus* is a remarkable feat of stylistic experimentation that was not at all predictable from *The Listeners*, and *The Dreamers* and *Crisis!* prove that his interest in style has not ended. In a literature that is itself concerned with change, it is somehow reassuring that one of the writers most interested in this theme is himself able to change.

—Stephen H. Goldman

GUTHRIE, Alan. See TUBB, E. C.

GUTTERIDGE, (Thomas Gordon) Lindsay. British. Born in Easington, County Durham, 20 May 1923. Educated at an art school in Newcastle upon Tyne. Married to Marjorie Kathleen Carpenter; one daughter. Free-lance commercial artist, London, 1939-41, 1950-68; art teacher, King Edward School of Art, Newcastle, 1941-43; cattle stockman in Australia, 1946-48; free-lance photographer, 1958-60; former art director, Robert Sharp and Partners, advertising agency, London.

Address: 15 Howdale Road, Downham Market, Norfolk PE38 9AB, England.

SCIENCE-FICTION PUBLICATIONS

Novels (series: Matthew Dilke in all books)

Cold War in a Country Garden. London, Cape, and New York, Putnam, 1971.
Killer Pine. London, Cape, and New York, Putnam, 1973.
Fratricide Is a Gas. London, Cape, 1975.

* * *

Lindsay Gutteridge is the author of three espionage novels featuring Matthew Dilke as hero, a micro-man one quarter of an inch in height. They are all splendid adventure stories and powerfully engage the sense of wonder. Gutteridge plays rough with his miniature spies and their normal-sized masters and foes, so that these should perhaps be classified as adult entertainments but there is nothing very special in the books considered as offbeat spy thrillers. Their distinctive quality is science-educational: they are the closest fictional equivalents I have found to *The Hellstrom Chronicle*. Whereas that film's overwhelming images of the alien life we overlook projected an inimical world, in which ants are far better adapted for survival than we hubristic humans, Gutteridge, better balanced, discovers not only beauty and terror, monstrosity and indifference, but delightful nourishment. By not being insect-sized, Gutteridge suggests, we are missing the marvellous abundant food of pollen and nectar. If only we could be miniaturized, our survival problems would be over. There, of course, is the rub which would lead us to classify these works as pure fantasies were it not that they belong to a tradition of a micro-people in SF established by such writers as Asimov, Blish, and Leinster, and that they use the convention to instruct us about natural history so fully and sensitively. The microscopic eye is a human one, and the wonders seen are related to human fears, needs and desires.

Cold War in a Country Garden, in which the mission of three micro-men is to implant transmitters in the hair of a Russian, is closest perhaps to the conventional spy thriller, substituting a box of centipedes for the snake pit or piranha pool as a persuasive threat to the captured Dilke. When he escapes, rescuing a micro-negress, Hyacinthe, who aids him in his second adventure, the pursuers are caught by an ant-lion. *Killer Pine* is a novel of ecological warfare, in which the enemy are Russian micro-men who inhabit a metal container on a pine in a Canadian forest, breeding termites to spread a viral death. We are given fascinating and horrid glimpses of life in a termite colony, in a tree which, for the micro-climbers, has the scale of Mount Everest. The third novel (which I hope is not the final adventure), *Fratricide Is a Gas,* has affinities with novels of industrial espionage: here Matthew Dilke is pitted alone against a sadistic Nazi chemist in Peru. The highlight of this novel is a sequence in which Dilke climbs jungloid thorns and creepers, enjoying on the way an idyllic repose in the bloom of an orchid, where he is visited by a humming-bird and witnesses the giant courtship of butterflies and the predations of parasitic wasps and shaggy spiders.

Gutteridge's micro-man's view gives us the pleasure of a sardonic perspective on the conventions of spy fiction and also a Swiftian magnification of some of our physical and spiritual coarseness, as when Dilke spies from a perch on the top of Lippe's study chair not only the eroded massif of his head but also the monstrous cruelty of his mind, revealed by his most private occupations. Gutteridge's work may well have influenced *The Micronauts* by Gordon Williams (1977), an exciting, more fully science-fiction narrative which, however, lacks the Gutteridge charm.

—Michael J. Tolley

HAGGARD, H(enry) Rider. British. Born in Bradenham, Norfolk, 22 June 1856. Educated at Ipswich Grammar School, Suffolk; Lincoln's Inn, London, 1881-85: called to the Bar, 1885. Married Louisa Mariana Margitson in 1880; one son and three daughters. Lived in South Africa, as Secretary to Sir Henry Bulwer, Lieutenant-Governor of Natal, 1875-77, member of the staff of Sir Theophilus Shepstone, Special Commissioner in the Transvaal, 1877, and Master and Registrar of the High Court of the Transvaal, 1877-79; returned to England, 1879; managed his wife's estate in Norfolk, from 1880; worked in chambers of Henry Bargave Deane, 1885-87; Unionist and Agricultural candidate for East Norfolk, 1895; Co-Editor, *African Review,* 1898; travelled throughout England investigating condition of agriculture and the rural population, 1901-02; British Government Special Commissioner to report on Salvation Army settlements in the United States, 1905; Chairman, Reclamation and Unemployed Labour Committee, Royal Commission on Coast Erosion and Afforestation, 1906-11; travelled around the world as a Member of the Dominions Royal Commission, 1912-17. Chairman of the Committee, Society of Authors, 1896-98; Vice-President, Royal Colonial Institute, 1917. Knighted, 1912; K. B. E. (Knight Commander, Order of the British Empire), 1919. *Died 14 May 1925.*

SCIENCE-FICTION PUBLICATIONS

Novels (series: Allan Quatermain; She)

King Solomon's Mines (Quatermain). London and New York, Cassell, 1885.
She: A History of Adventure. New York, Harper, 1886; London, Longman, 1887.
Allan Quatermain. London, Longman, and New York, Harper, 1887.
The People of the Mist. London and New York, Longman, 1894.
Heart of the World. New York, Longman, 1895; London, Longman, 1896.
Stella Fregelius: A Tale of Three Destinies. London and New York, Longman, 1904.
Ayesha: The Return of She. London, Ward Lock, and New York, Doubleday, 1905.
Benita: An African Romance. London, Cassell, 1906; as *The Spirit of Bambatse,* New York, Longman, 1906.
The Yellow God. New York, Cupples and Leon, 1908; London, Cassell, 1909.
Queen Sheba's Ring. London, Nash, and New York, Doubleday, 1910.
The Mahatma and the Hare: A Dream Story. London, Longman, and New York, Holt, 1911.
Love Eternal. London, Cassell, and New York, Longman, 1918.
When the World Shook. London, Cassell, and New York, Longman, 1919.

She and Allan. New York, Longman, and London, Hutchinson, 1921.
Wisdom's Daughter. London, Hutchinson, and New York, Doubleday, 1923.
Heu-Heu; or, The Monster (Quatermain). London, Hutchinson, and New York, Doubleday, 1924.

OTHER PUBLICATIONS

Novels

Dawn. London, Hurst and Blackett, 3 vols., 1884; New York, Appleton, 1 vol., 1887.
The Witch's Head. London, Hurst and Blackett, 3 vols., 1884; New York, Appleton, 1 vol., 1885.
Jess. London, Smith Elder, and New York, Harper, 1887.
A Tale of Three Lions, and On Going Back. New York, Munro, 1887.
Mr. Meeson's Will. New York, Harper, and London, Spencer Blackett, 1888.
Maiwa's Revenge. New York, Harper, and London, Longman, 1888.
My Fellow Laborer (includes "The Wreck of the Copeland"). New York, Munro, 1888.
Colonel Quaritch, V. C. New York, Lovell, 1888; London, Longman, 3 vols., 1888.
Cleopatra. London, Longman, and New York, Harper, 1889.
Beatrice. London, Longman, and New York, Harper, 1890.
The World's Desire, with Andrew Lang. London, Longman, and New York, Harper, 1890.
Eric Brighteyes. London, Longman, and New York, United States Book Company, 1891.
Nada the Lily. New York and London, Longman, 1892.
Montezuma's Daughter. New York and London, Longman, 1893.
Joan Haste. London and New York, Longman, 1895.
The Wizard. Bristol, Arrowsmith, and New York, Longman, 1896.
Doctor Therne. London and New York, Longman, 1898.
Swallow. New York and London, Longman, 1899.
The Spring of a Lion. New York, Neeley, 1899.
Lysbeth. New York and London, Longman, 1901.
Pearl-Maiden. London and New York, Longman, 1903.
The Brethren. London, Cassell, and New York, Doubleday, 1904.
The Way of the Spirit. London, Hutchinson, 1906.
Fair Margaret. London, Hutchinson, 1907; as *Margaret,* New York, Longman, 1907.
The Lady of the Heavens. New York, Authors and Newspapers Association, 1908; as *The Ghost Kings,* London, Cassell, 1908.
The Lady of Blossholme. London, Hodder and Stoughton, 1909.
Morning Star. London, Cassell, and New York, Longman, 1910.
Red Eve. London, Hodder and Stoughton, and New York, Doubleday, 1911.
Marie. London, Cassell, and New York, Longman, 1912.
Child of Storm. London, Cassell, and New York, Longman, 1913.
The Wanderer's Necklace. London, Cassell, and New York, Longman, 1914.
The Holy Flower. London, Ward Lock, 1915; as *Allan and the Holy Flower,* New York, Longman, 1915.
The Ivory Child. London, Cassell, and New York, Longman, 1916.

Finished. London, Ward Lock, and New York, Longman, 1917.
Moon of Israel. London, Murray, and New York, Longman, 1918.
The Ancient Allan. London, Cassell, and New York, Longman, 1920.
The Virgin of the Sun. London, Cassell, and New York, Doubleday, 1922.
Queen of the Dawn. New York, Doubleday, and London, Hutchinson, 1925.
The Treasure of the Lake. New York, Doubleday, and London, Hutchinson, 1926.
Allan and the Ice-Gods. London, Hutchinson, and New York, Doubleday, 1927.
Mary of Marion Isle. London, Hutchinson, and New York, Doubleday, 1929.
Belshazzar. London, Paul, and New York, Doubleday, 1930.

Short Stories

Allan's Wife and Other Tales. London, Blackett, and New York, Harper, 1889.
Black Heart and White Heart, and Other Stories. London, Longman, 1900; as *Elissa, and Black Heart and White Heart,* New York, Longman, 1900.
Smith and the Pharaohs and Other Tales. Bristol, Arrowsmith, 1920; New York, Longman, 1921.
The Best Short Stories of Rider Haggard, edited by Peter Haining. London, Joseph, 1981.

Other

Cetywayo and His White Neighbours; or, Remarks on Recent Events in Zululand, Natal, and the Transvaal. London, Trübner, 1882; revised edition, 1888; reprinted in part, as *The Last Boer War,* London Kegan Paul, 1899; as *A History of the Transvaal,* New York, New Amsterdam, 1899.
Church and the State: An Appeal to the Laity. Privately printed, 1895.
A Farmer's Year, Being His Commonplace Book for 1898. London and New York, Longman, 1899.
The New South Africa. London, Pearson, 1900.
A Winter Pilgrimage: . . . Travels Through Palestine, Italy, and the Island of Cyprus. London and New York, Longman, 1901.
Rural England. London and New York, Longman, 2 vols., 1902.
A Gardener's Year. London and New York, Longman, 1905.
Report on the Salvation Army Colonies. London, His Majesty's Stationery Office, 1905; as *The Poor and the Land,* London and New York, Longman, 1905.
Regeneration, Being an Account of the Social Work of the Salvation Army in Great Britain. London, Longman, 1910; New York, Longman, 1911.
Rural Denmark and Its Lessons. London and New York, Longman, 1911.
A Call to Arms to the Men of East Anglia. Privately printed, 1914.
The After-War Settlement and the Employment of Ex-Service Men in the Overseas Dominions. London, Saint Catherine Press, 1916.
The Days of My Life: An Autobiography, edited by C. J. Longman. London and New York, Longman, 2 vols., 1926.
The Private Diaries of Sir H. Rider Haggard 1914-1925, edited by D. S. Higgins. London, Cassell, and New York, Stein and Day, 1980.

*

Bibliography: *A Bibliography of the Writings of Sir Henry Rider Haggard* by J. E. Scott, London, Elkin Mathews, 1947.

Critical Studies: *The Cloak That I Left* (biography) by Lilias Rider Haggard, London, Hodder and Stoughton, 1951; *Rider Haggard: His Life and Works* by Morton N. Cohen, London, Hutchinson, 1960, New York, Walker, 1961, revised edition, London, Macmillan, 1968; *H. Rider Haggard: A Voice from the Infinite* by Peter Berresford Ellis, London, Routledge, 1978; *Rider Haggard, The Great Storyteller* by D. S. Higgins, London, Cassell, 1981, New York, Stein and Day, 1983.

* * *

H. Rider Haggard shares the fate of writers like Mark Twain, Robert Louis Stevenson, and Lewis Carroll in that his novels now serve either in children's editions or as grist for Hollywood's mill. But Haggard never meant his works to be juvenile fare, for they are filled with very adult passions. Of his many novels, the majority are fantasy-romances that range in setting from South Africa to Iceland to Mexico, and in time from the days of Babylon to contemporary central Africa.

Haggard's first successful novel was *King Solomon's Mines,* which he published in the year after he set up practice in London as a barrister. So enthusiastic was the public reception of this novel, in which Haggard created the prototype of the "Great White Hunter," that he virtually gave up the law, and devoted most of his time to writing. The hero of *King Solomon's Mines* is Allan Quatermain, who is asked by a beautiful Englishwoman to find her husband, who is lost in the African jungle. When the tracks of the missing husband lead to a long-hidden cave, only the skeleton of the husband is found, along with the treasure of King Solomon, missing for two thousand years. In the sequel, *Allan Quatermain,* Allan dies, and Haggard found himself in the same position as Conan Doyle when, tiring of his famous detective, he killed off Sherlock Holmes: the public would have no part of it. Because of this outcry, Haggard used the device of the "discovered manuscript" to write 13 more novels about Quatermain. In these, Allan meets with further adventures both in his own time and in a past life in ancient Babylon.

The theme of reliving past lives is one which Haggard used many times, especially in the series of novels about the mysterious Ayesha, or She-Who-Must-Be-Obeyed. *She,* the first of these novels, introduces Ayesha, the queen of a cannibal tribe in Africa, the people of the Kor, as she waits for the return of her lover, whom she murdered two millennia ago when he dared to marry someone else. Her wait comes to an end when a young Englishman, Leo Vincey, comes to her land. One glance at Vincey is enough to convince her that Leo is the reincarnation of the long-dead lover. She tries to persuade Leo to join her in eternal life, the secret of which she had discovered in the flame at the heart of a volcano. But once again Ayesha is frustrated when Leo too takes another woman for a wife. After banishing Leo's wife, Ayesha takes him and his companions to the volcano to renew her arguments for him to bathe with her in the flames. But the magic only works once, for when Ayesha enters for the second time, she begins to age before the eyes of the men, turning into a two-thousand-year-old crone. To their horror, she dies at their feet. Sickened and dazed, the men return to England to try to forget the sight. Like Quatermain, Ayesha was called back for repeat performances. Haggard wrote two more novels about her return from death—*Ayesha* and *She and Allan*—and still another about her early years in ancient Egypt, *Wisdom's Daughter.*

That most of the titles of Haggard's works are unfamiliar even to SF readers shows the success of modern critics in stamping out much of 19th-century fantasy. The few that are relatively well known owe their longevity to the movies, where, even though the plots have been somewhat altered, the mystery and romance of the settings and characters have been preserved.

—Walter E. Meyers

HAIBLUM, Isidore. American. Born in Brooklyn, New York, 23 May 1935. Educated at the High School of Art and Design; City College of New York (Editor, *Mercury*), B. A. in English and social sciences 1958. Served in the United States Army Reserve, 1959-64. Has worked as interviewer, script writer, and folk-singers agent; now free-lance writer. Agent: David Grossman, 110-114 Clerkenwell Road, London EC1M 5SA, England. Address: 160 West 77th Street, New York, New York 10024, U. S. A.

SCIENCE-FICTION PUBLICATIONS

Novels (series: Dunjer; Nick Siscoe and Ross Block)

The Tsaddik of the Seven Wonders. New York, Ballantine, 1971.
The Return. New York, Dell, 1973.
Transfer to Yesterday. New York, Ballantine, 1973.
The Wilk Are among Us. New York, Doubleday, 1975; revised edition, New York, Dell, 1979.
Interworld (Dunjer). New York, Dell, 1977; London, Penguin, 1980.
Nightmare Express. New York, Fawcett, 1979.
Outerworld (Dunjer). New York, Dell, 1979.
The Identity Plunderers (Siscoe and Block). New York, New American Library, 1984.
The Mutants Are Coming. New York, Doubleday, 1984.
The Hand of Ganz (Siscoe and Block). New York, New American Library, 1985.

OTHER PUBLICATIONS

Other

"Science Fiction, Jewish Style," in *Jewish Digest* (New York), December 1975.
Faster Than A Speeding Bullet, with Stuart Silver. Chicago, Playboy Press, 1980.
"Confessions of a Freelance Fantasist" (autobiography), in *Twilight Zone* (New York), June, August, and December 1983.

*

Isidore Haiblum comments:
(1981) Haiblum's work has its roots in the *Black Mask* Hammett-Chandler tradition and in the humor of Sholom Aleichem; it is often both hard-boiled and zany and sometimes ethnic. His style is awash with idioms, slang, and underworld lingo. His settings, despite the given dates, are often the 1930's, a time he rather likes. The jury is still out on how all this will go over in SF. *The Tsaddik of the Seven Wonders* was billed by the publishers as "The First Yiddish Science Fantasy Novel Ever.

" And about *Interworld* Gerald Jones wrote in the New York *Times*. "If you have ever wondered what *The Big Sleep* would sound like if Raymond Chandler were reincarnated as Roger Zelazny, this is your book. " *The Nightmare Express* (a big alternative universe novel set in the 1930's and elsewhere), *Outerworld* (again with ace gum-shoe Dunjer from *Interworld*), and a revised edition of *The Wilk Are among Us* take all this a step further. Haiblum has his fingers crossed.

(1985) With the passing of the years Haiblum has also taken to holding his breath. Meanwhile his novels have been translated into French, German, Italian, Hebrew and Spanish.

* * *

In his Afterword in *Binary Star 3*, Isidore Haiblum says that he and Ron Goulart draw on two traditions rare in science fiction, vaudeville comedy and hard-boiled detective stories. The verbal lunacy of the one and the callous violence of the other appear in Haiblum's work as part of his image of the City. New York—Depression era to present, future, and parallel-world—is a major "character" in his books, especially his most ambitious novel, *The Nightmare Express*, with its York, Old York, New York, and Founder's City. In his early novels comedy is the more interesting factor, playing wildly unusual creatures against their slangy, urban speech: the unorthodoxly Orthodox Tsaddik, the intergalactic social workers and their Wilk enemies, etc. The hard-boiled tough guys sometimes seem inappropriate, their imitations of 1930's action and language out of place in future or alternate world's especially in the (mainly) non-comic worlds of *The Return* and *Transfer to Yesterday*. In *Nightmare Express*, however, the 1930's scenery is part of the plot, as all the alternate Yorks split from 1935.

Haiblum enjoys complicated plots told from shifting viewpoints, usually to increase the comic or horrific madness of his city-worlds. Even the simplest, *The Return, Outerworld*, and *The Mutants Are Coming*, with one point-of-view character and world apiece, chase through various sub-cultures (each parodying an aspect of urban life).

—Ruth Berman

HALDANE, J(ohn) B(urdon) S(anderson). Indian. Born in Oxford, England, 1892; son of the scientist John Scott Haldane; brother of Naomi Mitchison, *q. v.* ; moved to India in 1957; became a citizen in 1961. Educated at Lynam's School, Oxford; Eton College, 1905-11; New College, Oxford, 1911-14, B. A. 1914 M. A. Served in the Black Watch in France, Iraq, and India, 1914-19: Captain. Married 1) Charlotte Franken in 1926 (divorced, 1945), one stepson; 2) Helen Spurway in 1945. Fellow of New College, 1912-22; Reader in Biochemistry, Cambridge University, 1923-33; geneticist, John Innes Horticultural Research Institution, London, 1927-36; Fullerian Professor of Physiology, Royal Institution, London, 1930-32; Professor of Genetics, 1933-36, and Weldon Professor of Biometry, 1936-57, University College, London; Research Professor, Indian Statistical Institute, Calcutta, 1957-61; worked for Council of Scientific and Industrial Research, Calcutta, 1961-62; Head of Genetics and Biometry, Government of Orissa, Bhubaneswar, 1962-64. President, Genetical Society, 1932-36; science correspondent, 1937-50, and Chairman of the Editorial Board, 1940-50, *Daily Worker*, London (joined Communist Party, 1942; resigned, 1950). Recipient: Royal Society Darwin Medal, 1952; Royal Anthropological

Institute Huxley Medal, 1956; Linnean Society Darwin-Wallace Medal, 1958; National Academy of Sciences Kimber Medal, 1961; Accademia dei Lincei Feltrinelli Prize, 1961. D. Sc. : University of Groningen, 1946; Oxford University, 1961; Honorary Doctorate: University of Paris, 1949; LL. D. : University of Edinburgh, 1956. Honorary Fellow, New College, 1961. Corresponding Member, Société de Biologie, 1928; Fellow, Royal Society, 1932; Chevalier, Legion of Honour, 1937; Honorary Member, Moscow Academy of Sciences, 1942; Corresponding Member, Deutsche Akademie der Wissenschaften, 1950, National Institute of Sciences of India, 1953, and Royal Danish Academy of Sciences, 1956. *Died 1 December 1964.*

SCIENCE-FICTION PUBLICATIONS

Novel

The Man with Two Memories. London, Merlin Press, 1976.

Uncollected Short Story

"The Gold-Makers," in *Great Science Fiction by Scientists,* edited by Groff Conklin. New York, Macmillan, 1962.

OTHER PUBLICATIONS

Novel

My Friend Mr. Leaky (for children). London, Cresset Press, 1937; New York, Harper, 1938.

Other

Daedalus; or, Science and the Future: A Paper Read to the Heretics, Cambridge, on February 4th, 1923. London, Kegan Paul Trench Trubner, 1923; New York, Dutton, 1924.
Callinicus: A Defence of Chemical Warfare. London, Kegan Paul Trench Trubner, and New York, Dutton, 1925.
Animal Biology, with Julian Huxley. Oxford, Clarendon Press, 1927.
The Last Judgement: A Scientist's Vision of the Future of Man. New York and London, Harper, 1927.
Possible Worlds and Other Essays. London, Chatto and Windus, 1927; as *Possible Worlds and Other Papers,* New York, Harper, 1928.
Science and Ethics (lecture). London, C. A. Watts, 1928.
Enzymes. London, Longman, 1930; Cambridge, Massachusetts Institute of Technology Press, 1965.
Materialism (miscellany). London, Hodder and Stoughton, 1932.
The Causes of Evolution. London, Longman, and New York, Harper, 1932.
The Inequality of Man and Other Essays. London, Chatto and Windus, 1932; as *Science and Human Life,* New York, Harper, 1933.
Biology in Everyday Life, with John Randal Baker. London, Allen and Unwin, 1933.
Fact and Faith. London, C. A. Watts, 1934.
Human Biology and Politics. London, British Science Guild, 1934.
Science and the Supernatural: A Correspondence Between Harold Lunn and J. B. S. Haldane. London, Eyre and Spotiswoode, and New York, Sheed and Ward, 1935

The Outlook of Science, edited by William Empson. London, Routledge, 1935.
Science and Well-Being, edited by William Empson. London, Routledge, 1935.
The Chemistry of the Individual (lecture). London, Oxford University Press, 1938.
The Marxist Philosophy. London, Birkbeck College, 1938.
A. R. P. [Air Raid Precautions]. London, Gollancz, 1938.
Heredity and Politics. London, Allen and Unwin, and New York, Norton, 1938.
How to Be Safe from Air Raids. London, Gollancz, 1938.
The Marxist Philosophy and the Sciences. London, Allen and Unwin, 1938; New York, Random House, 1939.
Science and Everyday Life. London, Lawrence and Wishart, 1939; New York, Macmillan, 1940.
Science and You. London, Fore Publications, 1939.
Keeping Cool and Other Essays. London, Chatto and Windus, 1940; as *Adventures of a Biologist,* New York, Harper, 1940.
Science in Peace and War. London, Lawrence and Wishart, 1940.
New Paths in Genetics. London, Allen and Unwin, 1941; New York, Harper, 1942.
Dialetical Materialism and Modern Science. London, Labour Monthly, 1942.
Why Professional Workers Should Be Communists. London, Communist Party, 1945.
A Banned Broadcast and Other Essays. London, Chatto and Windus, 1946.
Science Advances. London, Allen and Unwin, and New York, Macmillan, 1947.
What is Life? New York, Boni and Gaer, 1947; London, Lindsay Drummond, 1949.
Evolution a Myth? A Debate between Douglas Dewar, C. Merson Davies and J. B. S. Haldane. London, Paternoster Press, 1949.
Everything Has a History (essays). London, Allen and Unwin, 1951.
The Biochemistry of Genetics. London, Allen and Unwin, and New York, Macmillan, 1954.
The Argument from Animals to Men: An Examination of Its Validity for Anthropology (lecture). London, Royal Anthropological Institute, 1956.
Karl Pearson 1857-1957 (address). London, Biometrika Trustees, 1958.
The Unity and Diversity of Life (lecture). Delhi, Government of India Publications Division, 1958.
Science and Indian Culture. Calcutta, New Age Publishers, 1965.
Science and Life: Essays of a Rationalist. London, Pemberton-Barrie and Rockliff, 1968.
On Being the Right Size and Other Essays. Oxford, Oxford University Press, 1985.

Editor, *You and Heredity,* by Amram Scheinfeld and Morton D. Schweitzer. London, Chatto and Windus, 1939.

*

Critical Study: *J. B. S.: The Life and Work of J. B. S. Haldane* by Ronald W. Clark, London, Hodder and Stoughton, 1968; New York, Coward McCann, 1969.

*   *   *

The importance of J. B. S. Haldane for science fiction lies in the influence of his speculation on other writers rather than in his own rare excursions into fiction. Only two of his many works can be classified as science-fiction, a short story, "The Gold-Makers" (1932), and "The Last Judgment" (1927), a long narrative essay that contains a possible scenario for the end of the world, as foreseen not by religious prophecy—which Haldane always enjoyed ridiculing—but by scientific calculations of probability.

His short story dramtizes what for Haldane (later a convert to Communism) was one of the worst evils of capitalism—its exploitation of science, the stifling of the free development of discovery. A French chemist finds out how to extract gold from sea water, and he and his colleagues plan to use their prospective wealth to finance scientific research. But gold-mining interests soon get wind of the project and their hired killers set about eliminating the scientists involved. The story soon degenerates into a cinema-style thriller (but as such is cleverly written): the English narrator-hero, approached in desperation by one survivor among the scientists, who reveals to him part of the secret, is chased over most of France by the killers until he at last decides to baffle pursuit by publishing what he knows—as fiction!

Far more considerable, even as narrative, is "The Last Judgement" (*Possible Worlds*). This work seems to have furnished Olaf Stapledon with one of the crucial episodes in *Last and First Men:* he freely adapted Haldane's prophecy of the slow collapse of the moon upon the earth, leading to the enforced migration of a small percentage of humanity to Venus, where mankind survives through artificial mutations. C. S. Lewis, whose character Weston in his space trilogy is an unjust caricature of Haldane's (and Stapledon's) attitudes, thought "The Last Judgment" a "depraved " work, but Lewis too found a use for Haldane's idea of the moon's fall as the most probable end of human life on Earth (in *Perelandra*).

Another writer indebted to Haldane was an old Oxford friend, Aldous Huxley, who found in *Daedalus* hints toward the famous test-tube babies of *Brave New World.* Haldane's influence on a friend of his last years, Arthur C. Clarke, is more obvious in the latter's essays than in his fiction. Clark has given currency to what is now, at least in the science-fiction world, the great biologist's best-known saying (Clarke calls this "Haldane's Law"): "The Universe in not only queerer than we imagine; it is queerer than we *can* imagine. "

—John Kinnaird

HALDEMAN, Jack C(arroll, II). American. Born in Hopkinsville, New York, 18 December 1941; brother of Joe Haldeman, *q. v.* Educated at the University of Oklahoma, Norman, 1960-63; Johns Hopkins University, Baltimore, B. S. in life sciences 1973. Married 1) Alice Haldeman in 1965; 2) Vol Haldeman in 1975; two daughters. Research assistant, Johns Hopkin University School of Hygiene and Public Health, 1963-68; medical technician, University of Maryland Hospital, 1968-73; has also worked as a statistician, photographer, and printer's devil. President, Washington Science Fiction Association, seven years; Chairman, Discon II. Agent: Kirby McCauley Ltd., 425 Park Avenue South, New York, New York 10016, U. S. A.

SCIENCE-FICTION PUBLICATIONS

Novels

Vector Analysis. New York, Berkley, 1978.

Perry's Planet. New York, Bantam, 1980.
There Is No Darkness, with Joe Haldeman. New York, Ace, 1983.

Uncollected Short Stories (series: Sports)

"Garden of Eden," in *Fantastic* (New York), December 1971.
"Watchdog," in *Amazing* (New York), May 1972.
"What I Did on My Summer Vacation," in *Fantastic* (New York), July 1973.
"Slugging It Out," in *The Far Side of Time,* edited by Roger Elwood. New York, Dodd Mead, 1974.
"Sand Castles," in *Alternities,* edited by David Gerrold and Stephen Goldin. New York, Dell, 1974.
"What Time Is It?" in *Vertex* (Los Angeles), February 1975.
"Laura's Theme," in *Fantastic* (New York), June 1975.
"Time to Come," in *Gallery* (Chicago), June 1975.
"Songs of Dying Swans," in *Stellar 2,* edited by Judy-Lynn del Rey. New York, Ballantine, 1976.
"Limits," with Jack Dann, in *Fantastic* (New York), May 1976.
"Louisville Slugger" (Sports), in *Astronauts and Androids,* edited by Isaac Asimov. New York, Dale, 1977.
"Home Team Advantage" (Sports), in *Black Holes and Bug Eyed Monsters,* edited by Isaac Asimov, New York, Dale, 1977.
"Those Thrilling Days of Yesteryear," in *Amazing* (New York), March 1977.
"Vector Analysis," in *Analog* (New York), May 1977.
"The End-of-the-World Rag," in *Fantastic* (New York), December 1977.
"The Agony of Defeat" (Sports), in *Comets and Computers,* edited by Isaac Asimov. New York, Dale, 1978.
"Snakes and Snails," in *Nightmares,* edited by Charles L. Grant. New York, Doubleday, 1978.
"The Thrill of Victory" (Sports), in *Isaac Asimov's Science Fiction Magazine* (New York), January-February 1978.
"Mortimer Snodgrass Turtle" (Sports), in *Fantasy and Science Fiction* (New York), June 1978.
"What Weighs 8000 Pounds and Wears Red Sneakers?," in *Fantastic* (New York), July 1978.
"Thirty Love" (Sports), in *Isaac Asimov's Science Fiction Magazine* (New York), September-October 1978.
"Last Rocket from Newark," in *Amazing* (New York), November 1978.
"What Kind of Love Is This," in *Destinies,* vol. 1, no. 5, edited by James Baen. New York, Ace, 1979.
"Race the Wind" (Sports), in *Omni* (New York), January 1979.
"A Scientific Fact," in *Fantastic* (New York), March-April 1979.
"Hear the Crush, Hear the Roar," in *Isaac Asimov's Science Fiction Magazine* (New York), December 1979.
"Longshot," in *Isaac Asimov's Science Fiction Anthology 3,* edited by George Scithers. New York, Davis, 1980.
"Spring Fever," in *Fantasy and Science Fiction* (New York), July 1980.
"Games Children Play," in *Proteus,* edited by Richard S. McEnroe. New York, Ace, 1981.
"A Scientific Fact," in *Tomorrow's TV,* edited by Isaac Asimov, Martin H. Greenberg, and Charles G. Waugh. Milwaukee, Raintree, 1982.
"What Time Is It?," in *TV: 2000,* edited by Isaac Asimov, Martin H. Greenberg, and Charles G. Waugh. New York, Fawcett, 1982.
"High Steel," with Jack Dann, in *Fantasy and Science Fiction* (New York), February 1982.
"Wet Behind the Ears," in *Isaac Asimov's Science Fiction*

Magazine (New York), October 1982.

"Playing for Keeps," in *Isaac Asimov's Aliens and Outworlders*, edited by Shawna McCarthy. New York, Davis, 1983.

"Monkey Business," in *Amazing* (New York), January 1983.

"On the Rebound," in *Amazing* (New York), March 1983.

"Open Frame," in *Twilight Zone* (New York), July 1983.

"We, The People," in *Analog* (New York), 2 September 1983.

"My Crazy Father Who Scares All the Women Away," in *Isaac Asimov's Science Fiction Magazine* (New York), 2 December 1983.

"Still Frame," in *Shadows 7,* edited by Charles L. Grant. New York, Doubleday, 1984.

"A Very Good Year," in *Analog* (New York), December 1984.

"Rats in Space," in *Fantasy and Science Fiction* (New York), May 1985.

OTHER PUBLICATIONS

Verse

Between Pearl Harbor and Christmas. Privately printed, n. d.

Other

"Space Through Our Fingers" (and cover photograph), in *Amazing* (New York), October 1974.

Story Notes to *Rod Serling's Other Worlds.* New York, Bantam, 1978.

*

Jack C. Haldeman comments:

Sometimes I write hard science fiction, sometimes soft. Sometimes I'm serious, sometimes I'm humorous. Mostly I'm traditional, though occasionally I try something experimental. I often draw on my scientific background as well as my sense of humor. Mostly I try to entertain, though I have been known to slip in a message or two. I try not to let it clutter up the story.

* * *

Jack C. Haldeman has spent a good deal of his writing time on one of the rarest of themes in science fiction, the sports story. He began in 1977 with "Louisville Slugger", an anecdotal piece in which the future of humanity depends on a baseball game against Arcturians. This was followed by a sequel, "Home Team Advantage," wherein the Arcturian aliens discover that man is inedible and forfeit their prize, the consumption of humanity.

Apparently having discovered that he had stumbled upon a good thing, Haldeman followed this pair up with a second, "The Thrill of Victory" and "The Agony of Defeat," this time concentrating upon a team of robotic football players who are first faced with discovery that they have been illegally programmed with a will to win, and then matched in a championship game with genetically altered beings. All four stories were played strictly for laughs, and are as trivial as one might expect.

The next story, "Thirty Love" was decidedly different. A professional tennis player has led a long and successful career because his precognition allows him to anticipate where the ball will next be hit. On his final match, he deliberately throws the game when he realizes that defeating his opponent will cause the latter a trauma that will utterly ruin his life. Unfortunately, the subsequent sports stories have been as light as the first, and Haldeman's best fiction has not been in this area. Only "Race the Wind" has had a serious theme, a cripple determined to compete in slalom racing, and the story itself was too weak to support the seriousness of the situation.

There were, however, several extremely good stories published outside the context of his sports series. "Songs of Dying Swans" involves the tragic destruction of a race of altered humans, and the consequences of this destruction on the rest of civilization. "Laura's Theme" is a haunting, enigmatic story of a strange woman who seems constantly present when people's lives take radical turns for the worse.

Much of Haldeman's work is in a decidedly humorous vein, ranging from amusing but slight jokes to genuinely funny pieces. A typical middle-class family is startled and dismayed to discover that their front yard has suddenly become the legendary elephant's graveyard in "What Weighs 8000 Pounds and Wears Red Sneakers?" In "Those Thrilling Days of Yesteryear" archaeologists are engaged in manufacturing and burying artifacts, because the past as we know it is a fraud. Haldeman invents new mythical creatures in "Games Children Play" and all the pending accidents of the future occur at once in "A Very Good Year. "

In recent years, there has been more serious work as well, and of increasingly high calibre. "Spring Fever" compares human activity to that of lemmings. An Indian is drafted into duty in orbit in "High Steel" and averts a disaster in what is probably Haldeman's best work to date. Other recent short pieces of interest are "Wet Behind the Ears" and "We the People".

Haldeman's first novel, *Vector Analysis,* is a routine but well-handled story of adventure and scientific mystery in space. *Perry's Planet,* a *Star Trek* adventure, is similarly competent but less noteworthy than his short fiction. *There Is No Darkness,* co-authored with Joe Haldeman, is an episodic adventure which follows a group of young adults on various adventures on different planets. Haldeman has yet to produce a novel of the quality of his better short fiction.

—Don D'Ammassa

HALDEMAN, Joe (Joseph William Haldeman). Also writes as Robert Graham. American. Born in Oklahoma City, 9 June 1943; brother of Jack C. Haldeman, *q. v.* Educated at the University of Maryland, College Park, B. S. in physics and astronomy, 1967; graduate study, 1969-70; University of Iowa, Iowa City, M. F. A. 1975. Served in the United States Army, 1967-69: Purple Heart. Married Mary Gay Potter in 1965. Teaching Assistant, University of Iowa, 1975; Editor, Astronomy, Milwaukee, 1976. Since 1970, free-lance writer. Treasurer, Science Fiction Writers of America, for two years. Recipient: Nebula Award, 1975; Hugo Award, 1976, 1977; Ditmar Award, 1976; Galaxy Award, 1978; Rhysling Award, 1985. Agent: Kirby McCauley, 425 Park Avenue South, New York, New York 10016. Address: 345 Grove Street, Ormond Beach, Florida 32074, U. S. A.

SCIENCE-FICTION PUBLICATIONS

Novels (series: Attar; Star Trek; Worlds)

The Forever War. New York, St. Martin's Press, 1974; London, Weidenfeld and Nicolson, 1975.

Attar 1: Attar's Revenge (as Robert Graham). New York, Pocket Books, 1975; London, Mews, 1977.

Attar 2: War of Nerves (as Robert Graham). New York, Pocket Books, 1975.

Mindbridge. New York, St. Martin's Press, 1976; London, Macdonald and Jane's, 1977.

Planet of Judgment (Star Trek). New York, Bantam, and London, Corgi, 1977.

All My Sins Remembered. New York, St. Martin's Press, 1977; London, Macdonald and Jane's, 1978.

World Without End (Star Trek). New York, Bantam, and London, Corgi, 1979.

Worlds. New York, Viking Press, 1981; London, Macdonald, 1982.

There Is No Darkness, with Jack C. Haldeman. New York, Ace, 1983.

Worlds Apart. New York, Viking Press, 1983; London, Futura, 1984.

Short Stories

Infinite Dreams. New York, St. Martin's Press, 1978.
Dealing in Futures. New York, Viking Press, 1985.

Uncollected Short Stories

"Out of Phase," in *Galaxy* (New York), September 1969.
"Power Complex," in *Galaxy* (New York), April 1971.
"Four in One," in *Destinies* (New York), Spring 1980.

OTHER PUBLICATIONS

Novel

War Year. New York, Holt Rinehart, 1972; original version, New York, Pocket Books, 1977.

Plays

The Devil His Due, in *Fantastic* (New York), August 1974.
The Moon and Marcek, in *Vertex* (Los Angeles), August 1974.
The Forever War (produced Chicago, 1983).

Other

Introduction to *Double Star*, by Robert A. Heinlein. Boston, Gregg Press, 1978.

Editor, *Cosmic Laughter*. New York, Holt Rinehart, 1974.
Editor, *Study War No More: A Selection of Alternatives*. New York, St. Martin's Press, 1977; London, Futura, 1979.
Editor, *Nebula Award Stories 17*. New York, Holt Rinehart, 1983.

*

Critical Studies: *Joe Haldeman*, Mercer Island, Washington, Starmont House, 1980, and *The Fiction of Joe Haldeman*, University of Iowa, unpublished dissertation, 1981, both by Joan Gordon.

Joe Haldeman comments:

Along with most of my contemporaries, I believe that science fiction is primarily a literature of ideas, but that this quality does not make it exempt from normal literary standards. A poorly written SF story may be published if the idea behind it is sufficiently interesting, and there's nothing "improper" about that so long as an audience exists for it. But the best SF is that which excels both in concept and in execution—examplars being as diverse as Bester's *The Stars My Destination* and

Delany's *Dhalgren*—and at its best I think it has an advantage over literature that is "just plain literature."

There's no over-riding didactic or dialectic principle behind my writing. I write the sort of stories and books I would like to read. I'm fortunate in that a lot of moneybearing readers seem to share my tastes. Whether I would be willing (or able) to write differently if the market demanded it, I can't honestly say. I would like to think I'd stick to my guns, but on the other hand I do rather like working without bosses or time clocks.

*   *   *

Action and the hard sciences, concern for the effects of war and career on individuals, and an interest in stylistic experimentation all characterize Joe Haldeman's science fiction. His first novel, *War Year*, is a mainstream depiction of a typical draftee's Vietnam tour of duty. In fact, Haldeman's Vietnam experiences—he was severely wounded—have been influential in his writing. Vietnam taught Haldeman a sharp lesson in mortality and the randomness of fate, and also that careers, soldiering or anything else, can demand so much that individuals may "become" their careers and nothing more.

The Forever War established Haldeman's reputation in SF. The novel's episodic structure, use of sexuality and violence (never gratuitous), vivid descriptions, careful calculations, wry and disillusioned viewpoint character, and documentary collages all typify Haldeman's work. The novel traces a soldier as he travels the ranks from private to major in an 1143-year-long war. Haldeman posits "collapsar jumps" which make possible faster-than-light travel, and shows in the protagonist the future shock caused by such travel in time and space. *The Forever War*, as Haldeman says, operates on a "metaphorical level as a discussion of Vietnam, war and its effect on American society" (letter to the author).

Mindbridge uses a compressed version of Dos Passos's documentary collage technique to develop a future in which matter transmission and mental telepathy exist. The book uses two major stylistic techniques: chapters which advance the plot and are written in a vigorous, curt manner from a third-person objective viewpoint; and documents of two sorts, excerpts from the protagonist's autobiography and artifacts of his society. *All My Sins Remembered* returns to the episodic structure and examination of violence and career of *The Forever War*. Essentially an espionage thriller with documentary interchapters and a coda, the novel illustrates, through the hyperbole SF makes possible, the process by which a human being becomes absorbed by his job until he becomes his career. Because the novel's non-violent protagonist finds himself working for an amoral organization in a violent occupation, the transformation is especially disturbing.

Worlds and *Worlds Apart*, the first two volumes of a projected trilogy, with the final volume to be called *Worlds Enough and Time*, continue to use episodic structure to reflect the episodic, unpatterned nature of reality as Haldeman sees it. They also experiment with narrative viewpoint in their exploration of what makes civilization civilized. The series differs significantly from Haldeman's earlier work partly because its central character is female, partly because its Worlds are not so far as usual from our own, partly because its themes are broader.

With the exception of *All My Sins Remembered*, written in spurts from 1970 to 1976, Haldeman's writing has shown a steady progress. His strengths include an ability to make characters both individual and representative, a style generally lucid, fast-paced, and witty, a variety of techniques for blending necessary explanations into his stories, and a commitment to compassionate action in an uncompassionate world.

—Joan Gordon

HALL, Austin. American. Born in 1882 (?). Educated at Lincoln High School, Cleveland; Ohio Northern University, Ada; Ohio State University, Columbus; University of California, Berkeley. Did newspaper and electrical work, then worked in mining and ranching; wrote hundreds of western stories. *Died in 1933.*

SCIENCE-FICTION PUBLICATIONS

Novels

People of the Comet. Los Angeles, Griffin, 1948.
The Blind Spot, with Homer Eon Flint. Philadelphia, Prime Press, 1951; London, Museum Press, 1953.
The Spot of Life. New York, Ace, 1965.

Uncollected Short Stories

"Almost Immortal," in *All-Story Weekly* (New York), 7 October 1916.
"The Rebel Soul," in *All-Story Weekly* (New York), 30 June 1917.
"Into the Infinite," in *All-Story Weekly* (New York), 12 April 1919; expanded version, in *Famous Fantastic Mysteries* (New York), October 1942.
"The Man Who Saved the Earth," in *The Best of Science Fiction*, edited by Groff Conklin. New York, Crown, 1946.

*   *   *

Homer Eon Flint, writing alone and in collaboration with Austin Hall, produced a large quantity of science fiction from 1916 to 1924, most of which appeared in the Munsey Magazines *All-Story* and *Argosy*. His fame, however, and that of Austin Hall, rests on one of the most admired and cherished fantasies of the early 20th century, *The Blind Spot*, and its sequel *The Spot of Life*, written by Hall after the death of Flint.

Flint's first published story was "The Planeteer," set in the 23rd century when earth's population has grown so great that global starvation is threatened. Through engineering feats on a truly cosmic scale the earth's orbit is shifted to one closer to Jupiter's, and the latter planet then furnishes a new and inexhaustible source of food. In a sequel, "King of Conserve Island," an earthly monarch attempts to gain control of Jupiter and its food resources, and is thwarted by a hero who cuts off the heat of the sun and freezes the villain into submission. "The Lord of Death" is about two men who travel to the planet Mercury, and find there an ancient record of a man and woman named Adam and Eve who had left Mercury millennia earlier for an unknown destination. In "The Queen of Life" the same characters take their space ship to Venus, where they discover an apparently Utopian civilization.

Hall's writing career began with "Almost Immortal," the story of a Tibetan doctor thousands of years old who has been able to prolong his own life by absorbing the bodies and the wills of younger men at regular intervals. His downfall comes when the last man he assimilates turns out to have a will greater than his own. "The Rebel Soul" has a quite similar plot involving undying souls which take possession of individuals across the ages. A sequel, "Into The Infinite," carries on the story of a man who has been possessed by the Rebel Soul, and who is eventually freed through the power of a woman's love. "The Man Who Saved The Earth" describes an attempt by the inhabitants of Mars to capture all the water on earth and transport it to Mars, turning the latter into a verdant planet. This plot is foiled at the last minute by the one man on earth with the necessary knowledge, just as the oceans are drying up.

The literary styles of Flint and Hall were curiously similar, sharing the same strengths and weaknesses. Both were totally innocent of the fine points of sentence structure and grammar, and neither has a particularly large vocabulary. Each man, however, had a vivid and far-reaching imagination and a delight in reaching out into the vastnesses of time and space. Their complicated plotting and their skill in describing the life, customs, and technologies of the worlds of the distant future compensate for their somewhat clumsy style at times.

The high point in the literary careers of Flint and Hall was their collaboration on *The Blind Spot*, a classic in the field despite the literary flaws which distinguish the other works of both authors. *The Blind Spot* is more fantasy and mystery than science fiction. In a downtown San Francisco apartment building a gateway between two parallel worlds is discovered. A man emerges from this world, and takes back with him a scientist from this world. They are followed by would-be rescuers of the scientist, and the plot thereafter involves additional crossings through the Spot, bringing in more mystery and occultism than science. The Spot is finally closed at the end of the novel, to protect the inhabitants of this world from possible danger from the people on the other side. Flint died in 1924, under violent and mysterious circumstances which have never been explained. Hall continued to write alone, and in 1932 produced *The Spot of Life*, a sequel in which the Spot is reopened by the inhabitants of the other world, with the object of an invasion by force of our world. This novel takes place a generation after the time of the original story, and earth's savior in *The Spot of Life* is the son of the principal character in the first novel.

—Douglas E. Way

HAMILTON, Edmond. Also wrote as Brett Sterling. American. Born in Youngstown, Ohio, 21 October 1904. Educated at Westminster College, New Wilmington, Pennsylvania, 1919-21. Married Leigh Brackett, *q. v.*, in 1946. Free-lance writer: staff writer for *Superman* comics in the 1940's. Guest of Honor, 22nd World Science Fiction Convention, 1964; elected to First Fandom Science Fiction Hall of Fame, 1967. *Died 1 February 1977.*

SCIENCE-FICTION PUBLICATIONS

Novels (series: Captain Future; John Gordon; Starwolf)

The Star Kings (Gordon). New York, Fell, 1949; London, Museum Press, 1951; as *Beyond the Moon*, New York, New Ameican Library, 1950.
The Monsters of Juntonheim. London, Consul, 1950; as *A Yank at Valhalla*, New York, Ace, 1973.
Tharkol, Lord of the Unknown. London, Consul, 1950.

City at World's End. New York, Fell, 1951; London, Museum Press, 1952.

The Sun Smasher. New York, Ace, 1959.

The Star of Life. New York, Torquil, 1959.

The Magician of Mars (Future). New York, Popular Library, 1959.

The Haunted Stars. New York, Torquil, 1960; London, Jenkins, 1965.

Battle for the Stars. New York, Torquil, 1961; London, Mayflower, 1963.

Outside the Universe. New York, Ace, 1964.

The Valley of Creation. New York, Lancer, 1964.

Fugitive of the Stars. New York, Ace, 1965.

Doomstar. New York, Belmont, 1966.

The Harper of Titan. New York, Popular Library, 1967.

The Weapon from Beyond (Starwolf). New York, Ace, 1967.

Danger Planet (Future; as Brett Sterling). New York, Popular Library, 1968.

The Closed Worlds (Starwolf). New York, Ace, 1968.

World of the Starwolves. New York, Ace, 1968.

Quest Beyond the Stars (Future). New York, Popular Library, 1969.

Outlaw World (Future). New York, Popular Library, 1969.

The Comet Kings (Future). New York, Popular Library, 1969.

Outlaws of the Moon (Future). New York, Popular Library, 1969.

Planets in Peril (Future). New York, Popular Library, 1969.

Captain Future's Challenge. New York, Popular Library, 1969.

Calling Captain Future. New York, Popular Library, 1969.

Captain Future and the Space Emperor. New York, Popular Library, 1969.

Galaxy Mission (Future). New York, Popular Library, 1969.

Return to the Stars (Gordon). New York, Lancer, 1970.

Short Stories

The Metal Giants, Washburn, North Dakota, Swanson, 1932(?).

The Horror on the Asteroid and Other Tales of Planetary Horror. London, Allan, 1936; Boston, Gregg Press, 1975.

Tiger Girl. London, Utopian, 1945(?).

Murder in the Clinic. London, Utopian, 1946(?).

Crashing Suns. New York, Ace, 1965.

What's It Like Out There. New York, Ace, 1974.

The Best of Edmond Hamilton, edited by Leigh Brackett. New York, Ballantine, 1977.

OTHER PUBLICATIONS

Other

Editor, *The Best of Leigh Brackett.* New York, Doubleday, 1977.

*

Manuscript Collection: Eastern New Mexico University Library, Portales.

*   *   *

I suppose that all of us have had the chilling experience of trying to communicate something that was significant in our lives to an audience with a different set of values. We usually wind up with a conventionally lame apology: "Well you really had to be there." Edmond Hamilton is like that. You had to be

there. Even in the rather tight little world of science fiction, there are some authors who have a more or less universal appeal; Hamilton was not that kind of writer, even though he demonstrated from time to time that he was capable of turning out "literary" stories that can hold their own in any company. The best of Hamilton had its essence firmly planted in a particular place: the time was when you were young and the acid of sophistication had not eaten away at your heart; the place was in the lamented pulps of yesteryear.

Edmond Hamilton virtually invented the idea of the Space Patrol. Moreover, it was an *interstellar* Space Patrol. The concept of a galactic civilization entered the mainstream of science fiction through Hamilton's stories for *Weird Tales* and *Amazing Stories* between 1928 and 1930, and it has been a lasting influence. More generally, Hamilton is identified with space opera. He was writing it before the term was coined, and he wrote a tremendous amount of it for *Air Wonder Stories, Amazing, Startling,* and *Thrilling Wonder Stories* (Hamilton published little in *Astounding, Galaxy* and *Fantasy and Science Fiction;* oddly enough, Hamilton was also conspicuous by his absence in *Planet Stories,* supposedly the epitome of space opera). Most of his stories show the defects of the genre he pioneered. The action was fast and furious and sometimes absurd. The characterization was minimal and the dialogue was ghastly. This was fiction in primary colors: it is Good versus Evil and look out for the meteor! In positive terms, he had the ability to fire the imagination. Hamilton was fond of the Big Idea and he could communicate the excitement of sweeping concepts. (It was typical of Hamilton to present the whole panorama of evolution in a short story, and to throw in some original twists along the way.) He caught the drama of science; he may not have gotten all the notes right, but he certainly heard the music. His stories had verve and feeling, and they were alive. Hamilton did not take himself with undue solemnity; he had some fun with his writing. At the same time, he was writing stories that *he* liked to read, and it showed. The least of Hamilton's stories were always blessed by that extra dimension that makes all the difference: the sense of wonder.

Hamilton's most famous (or infamous) creation was Captain Future. The name was decidedly unfortunate; it is so trite that it virtually demands parody. (It got some, too. Captain Future was the only character in science fiction who managed to attract the scalpel of S. J. Perelman.) The magazine *Captain Future* was published quarterly from 1940 through 1944 and each issue featured a short Captain Future novel. Hamilton wrote most of them, as well as some later Captain Future stories that appeared in *Startling Stories.* By and large, this was formula fiction redeemed at times by flashes of the Hamilton talent. Captain Future was Curt Newton, also known as the Wizard of Science and the Man of Tomorrow. With his sidekicks—Grag the robot, Otho the android, and Simon Wright, a brain in a box—Captain Future kept boredom at bay by saving the solar system from assorted disasters ("Something's up back there at Earth, boys! We're blasting back right now").

Beginning perhaps with *City at World's End* (1951), Hamilton's fiction took on a more subdued tone as he adapted to a changing market. He cut down on the melodrama, introduced more shadings in his stories, and worked to create believable characters. One can only salute the effort; the novels range from *The Haunted Stars* to the *Starwolf* series, and they are better than a great many science-fiction tales with inflated reputations. Unfortunately, when Hamilton got rid of the corn he also lost much of the excitement that had marked his work. The spark is still there, but the fire never really gets going.

There is a kind of pathos about Hamilton's later work. He

had been a creative professional writer for a quarter of a century and now he had to prove himself all over again. His talent may have been obscured by the type of science fiction to which he devoted himself, but the mature Hamilton shows to good advantage in a number of classic short stories, including "What's It Like Out There?" and "The Pro."

Edmond Hamilton was one of the most prolific of all science-fiction writers. There was joy in his work, and he opened a lot of doors for those who came after him.

—Chad Oliver

HAMLET, Ova. See **LUPOFF, Richard A.**

HARDING, Lee (John). Also writes as Harold G. Nye. Australian. Born in Colac, Victoria, 17 February 1937. Educated in Australian primary schools. Married 1) Carla Bleeker in 1960 (divorced, 1974), two sons and one daughter; 2) Irene Anne Pagram in 1982, one daughter. Free-lance photographer, 1953-70. Recipient: Ditmar Award, 1970, 1972; Alan Marshall Award, 1978; Australian Children's Book of the Year Award, 1980. Agent: Virginia Kidd, Box 278, Milford, Pennsylvania 18337, U. S. A. Address: P. O. Box 198, Fern Tree Gully, Victoria 3156, Australia.

SCIENCE-FICTION PUBLICATIONS

Novels

The Fallen Spaceman (for children). Melbourne, Cassell, 1973; London, Cassell, 1975; revised edition, New York, Harper, 1980.
A World of Shadows. London, Hale, 1975.
Future Sanctuary. Toronto, Laser, 1976.
The Children of Atlantis (for children). Melbourne, Cassell, 1976.
The Frozen Sky (for children). Melbourne, Cassell, 1976.
Return to Tomorrow (for children). Melbourne, Cassell, 1976.
The Weeping Sky (for children). Melbourne, Cassell, 1977.
Displaced Person (for children). Melbourne, Hyland House, 1979; as *Misplaced Persons*, New York, Harper, 1979.
The Web of Time (for children). Melbourne, Cassell, 1979.
Waiting for the End of the World (for children). Melbourne, Hyland House, 1983.

Uncollected Short Stories

"Sacrificial," in *Science Fantasy* (Bournemouth), August 1961.
"Conviction," in *New Worlds* (London), October 1961.
"Echo," in *New Worlds* (London), November 1961.
"Pressure," in *Science Fantasy* (Bournemouth), January 1962.
"Late," in *New Worlds* (London), February 1962.
"Dragonfly," in *New Worlds* (London), April 1962.
"Terminal," in *New Worlds* (London), May 1962.
"Birthright," in *New Worlds* (London), June 1962.
"All My Yesterdays," in *Science Fantasy* (Bournemouth), June 1963.

"The Lonely City," in *New World* (London), August 1963.
"Quest," in *Lambda 1 and Other Stories*, edited by John Carnell. New York, Berkely, 1964; London, Penguin, 1965.
"The Liberators," in *New Writings in SF 5*, edited by John Carnell. London, Dobson, 1965.
"The Evidence," in *The Pacific Book of Australian Science Fiction*, edited by John Baxter. Sydney, Angus and Robertson, 1968; London, Angus and Robertson, 1969.
"Shock Treatment," in *New Writings in SF 11*, edited by John Carnell. London, Dobson, 1968; New York, Bantam, 1971.
"Consumer Report," in *Vision of Tomorrow* (Newcastle upon Tyne), August 1969.
"Soul Survivors," in *New Writings in SF 17*, edited by John Carnell. London, Dobson, 1970.
"Rebirth," in *Vision of Tomorrow* (Newcastle upon Tyne), April 1970.
"The Custodian," in *Vision of Tomorrow* (Newcastle upon Tyne), May 1970.
"The Changer" (as Harold G. Nye), in *Vision of Tomorrow* (Newcastle upon Tyne), June 1970.
"Echoes of Armageddon," in *Visions of Tomorrow* (Newcastle upon Tyne), July 1970.
"The Communication Machine," in *If* (New York), July-August 1970.
"Cassandra's Castle," in *Vision of Tomorrow* (Newcastle upon Tyne), September 1970.
"Dancing Gerontius," in *The Second Pacific Book of Australian Science Fiction*, edited by John Baxter. Sydney and London, Angus and Robertson, 1971.
"Mistress of the Mind," in *New Writings in SF 18*, edited by John Carnell. London, Dobson, 1971.
"The Immortal," in *If* (New York), January-February 1971.
"Night of Passage," in *Space 3*, edited by Richard Davis. London, Abelard Schuman, 1976; New York, Transatlantic Arts, 1977.
"Love in the City," in *Odyssey* (New York), Summer 1976.
"Spaceman," in *The Zeitgeist Machine*, edited by Damien Broderick. London, Angus and Robertson, 1977.
"The Cage of Flesh," in *Envisaged Worlds*, edited by Paul Collins. St. Kilda, Victoria, Void, 1978.

OTHER PUBLICATIONS

Plays

Radio Plays: *Journey into Time* serial, 1978; *The Legend of New Earth* serial, 1979.

Other

Editor, *Beyond Tomorrow: An Anthology of Modern Science Fiction*. Melbourne, Wren, 1976; abridged edition, London, New English Library, 1977.
Editor, *The Altered I: An Encounter with Science Fiction*. Melbourne, Norstrilia Press, 1976; revised edition, New York, Berkley, 1978.
Editor, *Rooms of Paradise*. Melbourne, Quartet, 1978; New York, St. Martin's Press, 1979.

*   *   *

Lee Harding is the most versatile of Australian science-fiction writer. He has acted as editor as well as writer, and his published works include stories and children's books as well as novels for adolescent and adult readers. His writings reflect a mature and distinctive commitment to characterization, and to sound, straightforward techniques of narrative and construction.

Harding's first novel, *A World of Shadows*, is set in the not-too-distant future when man's exploration of second-order space has disturbed the strange alien Shadows. During a routine space flight the astronaut Stephen Chandler is beset by Shadows, and as a result of their onslaught he returns to Earth in the body of his co-pilot—but with his own mind and memories intact within the new body. He becomes involved in a desperate struggle to convince the authorities—and his wife—of his real identity. But what *is* his "real" identity? *A World of Shadows*, then, is a novel about identity. But Harding describes it as "an unusual ontological thriller," and the epigraph quotes John Donne on love. These three disparate themes are drawn together by Stephen Chandler's plight, and while the novel offers no profound new insights, it does offer an interesting and cogent canvassing of issues.

The title of *The Weeping Sky* comes from the novel's central image of an eerie weeping "wound" in the sky, and through skilled and subtle manipulation of characters, situation, and setting, Harding presents an eloquent statement on the elusive, illusory nature of reality. His characters seem to belong to our world, but their society is medieval and their religion is an unknown variant of Christianity; the "wound" in the sky appears to be a harmless though supernatural phenomenon, but there is evidence that it might be a thoroughly rational precursor of natural disaster. *Displaced Person* presents further exploration of the nature of reality as the teenager Graeme Drury gradually finds himself estranged from the world and people around him and is drawn into a soundless, colourless "grey world" or limbo. This novel is more skilled in execution than *The Weeping Sky*, for it contains some haunting lyrical scenes and succinctly accurate accounts of suburban lifestyle, but it is the lesser novel in conception. Its themes are too explicit, and the novel's attempts at metaphysical speculation are ineffective (though minor textual changes to the second edition are an improvement).

Harding's latest novel, *Waiting for the End of the World*, heralds changes in the direction of his writing. Though it is a work of SF (set in a decrepit totalitarian future Australia), its concerns and strengths are those of "mainstream" fiction, for the novel's chief feature is its penetrating characterization.

Lee Harding has a gift for narrative, and consequently it is the storyline that is paramount in each of his novels. Yet Harding is no "mere" story-teller, for his plots are a way of finding characters and themes, and they are always generated by the plight of his characters. It is stock critical jargon to talk about an author "examining" his themes (implying an approach that is analytical, rigorous, perhaps even exhaustive), but this is not appropriate to Harding's method. Instead of delving deeply, Harding *canvasses* issues with a deft, light touch. Human beings are his chief concern, and he is Australian SF's foremost exponent of characterization.

—Van Ikin

HARNESS, Charles L(eonard). Also writes as Leonard Lockhard. American. Born in Colorado City, Texas, 29 December 1915. Educated at George Washington University, Washington, D. C., B. S. 1942, LL. B. 1946. Married Nell W. Harness in 1938; one daughter and one son. Mineral Economist, United States Bureau of Mines, Washington, D. C., 1941-47; patent attorney, American Cyanamid Company, Stamford, Connecticut, 1947-53; patent attorney, W. R. Grace and Company, Columbia, Maryland, 1953-81. Agent: Scott Meredith Literary Agency, 845 Third Avenue, New York, New York 10022. Address: 6705 White Gate Road, Clarksville, Maryland 21029, U. S. A.

SCIENCE-FICTION PUBLICATIONS

Novels

Flight into Yesterday. New York, Bouregy, 1953: as *The Paradox Men*, New York, Ace, 1955; London, Faber, 1964; revised edition, New York, Crown, 1984.
The Ring of Ritornel. London, Gollancz, and New York, Berkley, 1968.
Wolfhead. New York, Berkley, 1978.
The Catalyst. New York, Pocket Books, 1980.
Firebird. New York, Pocket Books, 1981.
The Venetian Court. New York, Ballantine, 1984.

Short Stories

The Rose. London, Compact, 1966; New York, Berkley, 1969.

Uncollected Short Stories

"Fruits of the Agathon," in *Thrilling Wonder Stories* (New York), December 1948.
"Stalemate in Space," in *Planet* (New York), Summer 1949.
"Even Steven," in *Other Worlds* (Evanston, Illinois), November 1950.
"A Thesis for Branderbrook," in *Thrilling Wonder Stories* (New York), June 1951.
"Improbable Profession" (as Leonard Lockhard, with Ted Thomas), in *Astounding* (New York), September 1952.
"The Poisoner," in *Fantasy and Science Fiction* (New York), December 1952.
"Heritage," in *Tomorrow's Universe*, edited by H. J. Campbell. London, Panther, 1953.
"The Call of the Black Lagoon," in *Avon Science Fiction* (New York), January 1953.
"Child by Chronos," in *The Best from Fantasy and Science Fiction 3*, edited by Anthony Boucher and J. Francis McComas. New York, Doubleday, 1954.
"That Professional Look" (as Leonard Lockhard, with Ted Thomas), in *Astounding* (New York), January 1954.
"The Alchemist," in *Analog* (New York), May 1966.
"Bugs," in *Fantasy and Science Fiction* (New York), August 1967.
"The Million Year Patent," in *Amazing* (New York), December 1967.
"Probable Cause," in *Orbit 4*, edited by Damon Knight. New York, Putnam, 1968.
"An Ornament to His Profession," in *SF 12*, edited by Judith Merril. New York, Delacorte Press, 1968.
"Bookmobile," in *If* (New York), November 1968.
"Time Trap," in *Alpha 1*, edited by Robert Silverberg. New York, Ballantine, 1970.
"The Araqnid Window," in *Amazing* (New York), December 1974.
"H-Tec," in *Analog* (New York), 25 May 1981.

"Quarks at Appomattox," in *Analog* (New York), October 1983.
"The Fall of Robin Arms," in *Fantasy and Science Fiction* (New York), March 1984.
"Summer Solstice," in *Analog* (New York), June 1984.
"The Cajamarca Project," in *Analog* (New York), February 1985.

OTHER PUBLICATIONS

Other

Marketing Magnesite and Allied Products, with Nan C. Jensen. Washington, D. C., Bureau of Mines, 1943.
Mining and Marketing of Barite, with F. M. Barsigian. Washington, D. C. Bureau of Mines, 1946.

*

Manuscript Collection: University of Maryland, College Park.

Charles L. Harness comments:
I did it for money.

* * *

Charles L. Harness has not written as much as his admirers (Damon Knight, Brian Aldiss, Michael Moorcock) would have wished. His work has always been highly intricate, and his early stories have been compared to those of A. E. van Vogt. Unlike that author, he provides what seems to be a rational explanation for all the astonishing turns of his plots; like van Vogt, his best work has the compelling power of a dream. It is highly cerebral as well; in the words of Louis MacNeice, Harness likes "to draw the corks out of an old conundrum,/And watch the paradoxes fizz. "

In *Flight into Yesterday* the hero, Alar, emerges from a wrecked spaceship with no memory of who he is but a certainty that he has a most urgent task to perform. He is sponsored by the Society of Thieves, and protected by the heroine, Keiris, who is the widow of a vanished scientist. The society he finds himself in is sophisticated but decadent; there are brilliant ball scenes and hideous torture chambers. As he attempts to escape from the Imperial police, he talks to the Empress, to a Toynbeean student of the downfall of civilizations, and to the lunatic crew of a solarion, a station perilously located on the surface of the Sun. The play of ideas is brilliant, the menace threatening. The ending is perhaps a shade too perfect, with the hero cancelling out all the misery of humanity. But the book is a dazzler all the same.

"The Rose" is perhaps Harness's most beautiful single work. The heroine, Anna van Tuyl, is at once a composer, a ballet dancer, and a psychotherapist. She is composing a ballet based on Oscar Wilde's story "The Nightingale and the Rose," and is at a standstill in the piece; she is also suffering from a deforming illness. Then she is asked to treat Ruy Jacques, the husband of the eminent and arrogant scientist Martha Jacques; Ruy Jacques has forgotten how to read print, but can read people's intentions instead. In attempting to cure Ray Jacques, Anna falls in love, incurring the jealousy of Martha Jacques. The climax is one of death and transfiguration: Anna finds the perfect ending to her ballet and dies, but hands on the key to a higher mode of life. The summary cannot do justice to the work, which must be read.

The Ring of Ritornel is again set in a society of formal brilliance and extreme tyranny. The villain is the Emperor Oberon, who cares nothing for human life. The hero, James Andrek, has been robbed of both his father and his elder brother by Oberon, and is determined to find the culprit. At the close of the book, a new cycle of the universe is about to begin, and only two people from the old universe will survive. In the warring religions of Alea and Ritornel, Harness poses old questions of chance and destiny. The structure of the book is both mathematical and musical: certain characters and motifs recur, but always with a different effect. The book is beautiful and moving.

Wolfhead is more direct in manner than the other novels. Set in an Earth long after an atomic catastrophe, it has a hero who descends into the underground kingdom in pursuit of his lost love Beatra. As is fitting for a successor to Dante, he is guided by Virgil—a she-wolf into whose brain a small part of his own has been grafted. The theme is one of unrelenting war; in the end the hero at least succeeds in rescuing his society, but not his wife.

The Catalyst is set in the near future, and deals with a plague called novarella and a chemical called trialine which can cure it. There is a stunning portrait of the scientist Serane, and the way in which he reaches his discoveries by totally cicumventing the bureaucratic structure in which he works. The hero, Paul Blandford, succeeds in securing priority for Serane's invention by an incredible trial run. Thomas M. Disch has complained of the fantastic element in this novel, but I suspect that Harness feels life really is like this: we make our discoveries half in a dream, and sometimes we do seem to be protected by guardian angels. This aspect of the book reminds me strongly of Arthur Koestler's life of Kepler in *The Sleepwalkers.*

Harness's earlier short stories were perhaps stronger on plot than on character; his first, "Time Trap," already showed the ability to construct a highly ingenious time loop. His most brilliant early story, "The New Reality," begins from the premise that early man was not less observant than we, and concludes that the world *was* flat until the 5th century B. C. The villain, Luce (alias Lucifer), brings about a completely new universe by rendering all previous theories about reality untenable, and A. Prentiss and E. (alias Adam and Eve) survive into the new reality—which is paradisal. But so does the snake!

The richest short stories Harness has given us, however, belong to a period since the middle 1960's. "Probable Cause" deals with the case of a convicted murderer of a President: since the evidence against the accused was obtained by clairvoyance, the Supreme Court must consider whether his constitutional rights have been abridged. "The Alchemist" and "An Ornament to His Profession" both deal with a chemical manufacturing firm and the problems of patent law: in the first, the firm discovers with horror that one of its scientists is practising alchemy; in the second, the lawyer Con Patrick is driven to realize that he would sell his soul if necessary to protect his patents. The later Harness stories have surrendered nothing in the skill of plotting, but they have a sure humour and sense of the richness of human life that were lacking in the earlier short stories (excepting always "The Rose"). His best work is a high-water mark in science fiction.

—Charles Cushing

HARRISON, Harry. Pseudonym for Henry Maxwell Dempsey; also writes as Felix Boyd; Leslie Charteris; Hank Dempsey. American. Born in Stamford, Connecticut, 12 March 1925. Educated at art schools in New York. Served in

the United States Army Air Corps during World War II:
Sergeant. Married Joan Merkler in 1954, one son and one
daughter. Free-lance commercial artist, 1946-55. Formerly,
Editor, *SF Impulse*, London; Editor, *Fantastic*, New York,
1968. Lives in County Wicklow, Ireland. Recipient: Nebula
Award, 1973. Agent: A. P. Watt Ltd., 26-28 Bedford Row,
London WC1R 4HL, England.

SCIENCE-FICTION PUBLICATIONS

Novels (series: Deathworld; Stainless Steel Rat; To the Stars)

Deathworld. New York, Bantam, 1960; London, Penguin,
1963.
The Stainless Steel Rat. New York, Pyramid, 1961; London,
New English Library, 1966.
Planet of the Damned. New York, Bantam, 1962; as *Sense of
Obligation*, London, Dobson, 1967.
Deathworld 2, New York, Bantam, 1964; London, Sphere,
1977; as *The Ethical Engineer*, London, Gollancz, 1964.
Bill, The Galactic Hero. New York, Doubleday, and London,
Gollancz, 1965.
Plague from Space. New York, Doubleday, 1965; London,
Gollancz, 1966; as *The Jupiter Legacy*, New York, Bantam,
1970.
Make Room! Make Room! New York, Doubleday, 1966;
London, Penguin, 1967; as *Soylent Green*, New York,
Berkley, 1973.
The Technicolor Time Machine. New York, Doubleday, 1967;
London, Faber, 1968.
Deathworld 3. New York, Dell, 1968; London, Faber, 1969.
Captive Universe. New York, Putnam, 1969; London, Faber,
1970.
The Daleth Effect. New York, Putnam, 1970; as *In Our Hands,
The Stars*, London, Faber, 1970.
The Stainless Steel Rat's Revenge. New York, Walker, 1970;
London, Faber, 1971.
Tunnel Through the Deeps. New York, Putnam, 1972; as *A
Transatlantic Tunnel, Hurrah!*, London, Faber, 1972.
Stonehenge, with Leon E. Stover. London, Davies, and New
York, Scribner, 1972; revised edition, as *Stonehenge: Where
Atlantis Died*, New York, Tor, 1983; London Granada,
1985.
The Stainless Steel Rat Saves the World. New York, Putnam,
1972; London, Faber, 1974.
Star Smashers of the Galaxy Rangers. New York, Putnam,
1973; London, Faber, 1974.
The Lifeship, with Gordon R. Dickson. New York, Harper,
1976; as *Lifeboat*, London, Orbit, 1977.
Skyfall. London, Faber, 1976; New York, Atheneum, 1977.
The Adventures of the Stainless Steel Rat (omnibus). New
York, Berkley, 1978.
The Stainless Steel Rat Wants You! London, Joseph, 1978.
Planet Story, illustrated by Jim Burns. London, Pierrot, and
New York, A and W, 1979.
Homeworld (To the Stars). London, Panther, and New York,
Bantam, 1980.
Wheelworld (To the Stars). London, Panther, and New York,
Bantam, 1981.
Starworld (To the Stars). London, Panther, and New York,
Bantam, 1981.
Planet of No Return. New York, Simon and Schuster, 1981;
London, Severn House, 1983.
Invasion: Earth. New York, Ace, 1982; London, Sphere, 1984.
The Stainless Steel Rat for President. London, Sphere, and
New York, Bantam, 1982.
A Rebel in Time. London, Granada, and New York, Tor, 1983.
West of Eden. London, Granada, and New York, Bantam,
1984.
A Stainless Steel Rat Is Born. New York, Bantam, and
London, Granada, 1985.

Short Stories

War with the Robots. New York, Pyramid, 1962; London,
Dobson, 1967.
Two Tales and Eight Tomorrows. London, Gollancz, 1965;
New York, Bantam, 1968.
Prime Number. New York, Berkley, 1970; London, Sphere,
1975.
One Step from Earth. New York, Macmillan, 1970; London,
Faber, 1972.
The Best of Harry Harrison. New York, Pocket Books, and
London, Sidgwick and Jackson, 1976.

Uncollected Short Stories

"Rock Diver," in *Beyond the End of Time*, edited by Frederik
Pohl. New York, Permabooks, 1952.
"An Artist's Life" (as Felix Boyd), in *Rocket* (New York),
September 1953.
"Web of the Worlds," with Katherine MacLean, in *Fantasy
Fiction* (New York), November 1953.
"Navy Day" in *If* (New York), January 1954.
"World in the Balance," in *Fantastic Universe* (Chicago), June
1957.
"Welcoming Committee" (as Felix Boyd), in *Fantastic Uni-
verse* (Chicago), October 1957.
"Open All Doors," with Hubert Prichard, in *Fantastic Uni-
verse* (Chicago), February 1958.
"The World Otalmi Made," in *Science Fiction Adventures*
(New York), June 1958.
"The Starsloggers," in *Galaxy* (New York), December 1964.
"They're Playing Our Song," in *Fantastic* (New York), De-
cember 1964.
"The K-Factor," in *Rulers of Men*, edited by Hans S.
Santesson. New York, Pyramid, 1965.
"A Matter of Timing," in *Analog* (New York), January 1965.
"The Outcast," in *Science Fantasy* (Bournemouth), March
1965.
"How the Old World Died," in *Ninth Galaxy Reader*, edited by
Frederik Pohl. New York, Doubleday, 1966.
"The Voice of the CWACC," in *Impulse*, December 1966.
"The Gods Themselves Throw Incense," in *Four for the Future*,
edited by Harrison. London, Macdonald, 1969.
"American Dead," in *The Year 2000*, edited by Harrison. New
York, Doubleday, 1970; London, Faber, 1971.
"Strangers, " in *Fantasy and Science Fiction* (New York),
October 1972.
"The Whatever-I-Type-Is-True Machine," with Barry N.
Malzberg, in *Fantasy and Science Fiction* (New York),
November 1974.
"Run from the Fire," in *Epoch*, edited by Robert Silverberg
and Roger Elwood. New York, Berkley, 1975.
"Ad Astra," in *Best Science Fiction Stories of the Year 4*, edited
by Lester del Rey. New York, Dutton, 1975.
"Greening of the Green," in *Anticipations*, edited by Christo-
pher Priest. London, Faber, and New York, Scribner, 1978.
"The Day after the End of the World," in *After the Fall*, edited
by Robert Sheckley. New York, Ace, and London, Sphere,
1980.

"Speed of the Cheetah, Roar of the Lion" and "A Fragment of Manuscript," in *Microcosmic Tales,* edited by Isaac Asimov, Martin H. Greenberg, and Joseph D. Olander. New York, Taplinger, 1980.

Uncollected Short Stories as Hank Dempsey

"CWACC Strikes Again," in *Analog 6,* edited by John W. Campbell Jr. New York, Doubleday, 1968.
"Heavy Duty," in *Analog* (New York), May 1970.
"The Defensive Bomber," in *Nova 3,* edited by Harrison. New York, Walker, 1973.

OTHER PUBLICATIONS

Novels

Vendetta for the Saint (as Leslie Charteris). New York, Doubleday, 1964.
Montezuma's Revenge. New York, Doubleday, 1972.
Queen Victoria's Revenge. New York, Doubleday, 1974; London, Severn House, 1977.
The QE2 Is Missing. London, Futura, 1980; New York, Tor, 1982.

Other

The Man from P. I. G. (for children). New York, Avon, 1968.
Spaceship Medic (for children). London, Faber, and New York, Doubleday, 1970.
"Science Fiction: Short Story and Novel," in *The Writer* (Boston), May 1970.
The Men from P. I. G. and R. O. B. O. T. (for children). London, Faber, 1974; New York, Atheneum, 1978.
The California Iceberg (for children). London, Faber, and New York, Walker, 1975.
"We Are Sitting on Our . . . ." and "With a Piece of Twisted Wire," in *SF Horizons.* New York, Arno Press, 1975.
Great Balls of Fire. London, Pierrot, and New York, Grosset and Dunlap, 1977.
Mechanismo. London, Pierrot, and Los Angeles, Reed, 1978.
Spacecraft in Fact and Fiction, with Malcolm Edwards. London, Orbis, 1979.

Editor, *Collected Editorials from Analog,* by John W. Campbell, Jr. New York, Doubleday, 1966.
Editor, with Brian Aldiss, *Nebula Award Stories 2.* New York, Doubleday, 1967; as *Nebula Award Stories 1967,* London, Gollancz, 1967.
Editor, with Leon E. Stover, *Apeman, Spaceman: Anthropological Science Fiction.* New York, Doubleday, and London, Rapp and Whiting, 1968.
Editor, with Brian Aldiss. *All about Venus.* New York, Dell, 1968; enlarged edition, as *Farewell, Fantastic Venus!,* London, Macdonald, 1968.
Editor, with Brian Aldiss, *Best SF 1967* [to *1975*]. New York, Putnam, 7 vols., 1968-74; Indianapolis, Bobbs Merrill, 2 vols., 1975-76; as *The Year's Best Science Fiction 1-9,* London, Sphere, 8 vols., 1968-76; London, Futura, 1 vol., 1976.
Editor, *SF: Author's Choice 1-4.* New York, Berkley, 4 vols., 1968-74; vol. 1 as *Backdrop of Stars,* London, Dobson, 1968.
Editor, *Four for the Future: An Anthology on the Themes of Sacrifice and Redemption.* London, Macdonald, 1969.
Editor, *Worlds of Wonder.* New York, Doubleday, 1969; as *Blast Off: SF for Boys,* London, Faber, 1969.

Editor, *The Year 2000.* New York, Doubleday, 1970; London, Faber, 1971.
Editor, *Nova 1-4.* New York, Delacorte Press, 1 vol., 1970; New York, Walker, 3 vols., 1972-74; London, Sphere, 4 vols., 1975-76; vol. 3 published as *The Outdated Man,* New York, Dell, 1974.
Editor, *The Light Fantastic: Science Fiction Classics from the Mainstream.* New York, Scribner, 1971.
Editor, with Brian Aldiss, *The Astounding-Analog Reader.* New York, Doubleday, 2 vols., 1972-73; London, Sphere, 2 vols., 1973.
Editor, with Theodore J. Gordon, *Ahead of Time.* New York, Doubleday, 1972.
Editor, *Astounding: John W. Campbell Memorial Anthology.* New York, Random House, 1973; London, Sidgwick and Jackson, 1974.
Editor, with Carol Pugner, *A Science Fiction Reader.* New York, Scribner, 1973.
Editor, with Willis E. McNelly, *Science Fiction Novellas.* New York, Scribner, 1975.
Editor, with Brian Aldiss, *SF Horizons* (reprint of magazine). New York, Arno Press, 1975.
Editor, with Brian Aldiss, *Hell's Cartographers: Some Personal Histories of Science Fiction Writers.* London, Weidenfeld and Nicolson, and New York, Harper, 1975.
Editor, with Brian Aldiss, *Decade: The 1940's, The 1950's, The 1960's.* London, Macmillan, 3 vols., 1975-77; *The 1940's* and *1950's,* New York, St. Martin's Press, 2 vols., 1978.

*

Bibliography: *Harry Harrison: Bibliografia 1951-1965* by Francesco Biamonti, privately printed, 1965.

Manuscript Collection: University of California, Fullerton.

Harry Harrison comments
I have always believed in readability. The easier the flow of the prose, the more basic the vocabulary, the more readers there will be who can follow and enjoy a book. But complex technical terms can be used where there is no alternative. I have found that an action story with two or three levels of intellectual content below the surface enables me to say just what I wish to say. I have also found that humor—and black humor—can carry ideas that can be expressed in no other way. The fact that my books have been translated into 21 languages must indicate that I am communicating with my audience.

*   *   *

Harry Harrison is the principal pen-name of Hank Dempsey. From the start of his writing career, he made SF his calling in every devotional sense of the word. Determined at the outset to make his living by it, at the same time he took it up as a craft to serve and improve upon. Academic critics of the genre often fail to detect the artistic passion that drives a man like Harry Harrison to cultivate it as a genuine art form, scornful as they are of its original newstand outlets, as if this thing we call SF were impossible to achieve beauty and craft because of its commercial motives. We are thus led to believe that creative values can arise only from the most rarified of aesthetic motives, never out of meeting publisher's deadlines.

The vitality and astonishing vigor of Harrison's prose, animated by the highest ideals of craftmanship, show even in the least of his hurried efforts. Adapted to the demands of the market, his habitual practice at times reaches that elegance of statement he strives for always. A classic example is "Rescue

Operation," a short story that deserves recognition as one of the finest in the history of American letters. It is a perfect literary jewel. One need not agree with the case it argues—for it is an argument as well as a moving story—to appreciate the skillful rhetoric of its composition. It is truly a work of art, as its author hoped works of SF could be, even while it states his rationalist faith in the saving grace of science to rescue mankind from its pre-modern follies. This one story might well stand as a summary of the Enlightenment idea, to which magazine SF was dedicated at its inception, but which now embraces the counter-argument.

Harrison's first novel, *Deathworld*, was turned into a series by that name. Derived from the adventure-story format of the early SF magazines, if offered something more, informed by ecological science. At this point he made himself master of the *intelligent* adventure story, perfected in his most recent and very popular *Homeworld* series. The wit and nervous vitality contained in all these have their corollary in his *comic* adventure stories. Comedy in SF is almost impossible to carry off, yet Harrison does it with the ease and éclat that seem to be the natural expression of his vigorous personality and contageous sense of humor. *Bill, The Galactic Hero*, written as a satire on Heinlein's Starship Troopers, is a comic masterpiece worthy of Mark Twain, unfair as it is. Just as wildly funny is *The Technicolor Time Machine*. A story about on-location movie making in the Viking Age, it contains a wealth of realistic insights into those times, of the sort treated more seriously in *Stonehenge* (with Leon Stover), which evokes the authentic Bronze-Age culture of that monument's builders. But his comic genius keeps bursting forth in ever new sequels to *The Stainless Steel Rat*, although he claims that public demand for more and more of it (and this is very real) keep him from his growing philosophical concerns.

These also are very real. In his maturity, Harrison has come to embark upon a most remarkable series that returns SF to the philosophical values of its classical origins in the scientific romances of H. G. Wells. Wells is much honored as the father of modern SF by today's writers in this genre; but they usually so much betray him that it takes Harrison's burgeoning new line of work to remind them of their literary beginnings. As this essay goes to press, Harrison has released the first volume of his *West of Eden* series.

In *West of Eden* Harrison ponders on the curious question, why is it that everybody loves to associate dinosaurs and cavemen, even though the two are separated by some 200 million years? Conan Doyle first brought them together in his *Lost World* fantasy, and Edgar Rice Burroughs kept it up until the image was indelible. No amount of paleontological fact has ever been able to shake this picture of Alley Opp living with the dinotherium.

All right, says Harry. If that's what you want, that's what you'll get—only this time with a convincing explanation. In *West of Eden* he offers us an alternative prehistory. Early man and the ancient reptiles are given a plausible occasion for coexisting, with this difference—time has allowed for the saurians to evolve a culture-bearing species of humanoid on their own. And the two meet at that level.

The one difficulty in carrying this off lies in finding a parallel in human evolution among the mammals for the reptiles. The open and shut case for demarcation between animal and man in human origins is the mastery of fire—the first step to all modern technology, in controlling a source of energy external to mammalian body heat. But the reptiles are cold-blooded, and such a step is not possible to imagine for the take-off point in a technological species of reptile. But Harrison worked out the functional equivalent of this, in keeping with reptilian biology, and that is fundamental to the scientific idea behind *West of Eden,* in this the most extraordinary story of intelligent adventure that he has written to date.

—Leon Stover

HARRISON, M(ichael) John. British. Born in Great Britain, 26 July 1945. Educated at schools in England. Groom, Atherstone Hunt, Warwickshire, 1963; student tracher, Warwickshire, 1963-65; clerk, Royal Masonic Charity Institute, London, 1966. Literary Editor and reviewer, *New Worlds* ; regular contributor, *New Manchester Review*, 1978-79. Agent: Anthony Sheil Associates, 43 Doughty Street, London WC1N 2LF, England.

SCIENCE-FICTION PUBLICATIONS

Novels (series Viriconium)

The Committed Men. London, Hutchinson, and New York, Doubleday, 1971.
The Pastel City (Viriconium). London, New English Library, 1971; New York, Doubleday, 1972.
The Centauri Device. New York, Doubleday, 1974; London, Panther, 1975.
A Storm of Wings (Viriconium). London, Sphere, and New York, Doubleday, 1980.
In Viriconium. London, Gollancz, 1982; New York, Pocket Books, 1983.
The Floating Gods . New York, Pocket Books, 1983.

Short Stories

The Machine in Shaft Ten and Other Stories. London, Panther, 1975.
The Ice Monkey and Other Stories. London, Gollancz, 1983.
Viriconium Nights. New York, Ace, 1984; revised edition, London, Gollancz, 1985.

*

M. John Harrison comments:

I am often thought of as a pessimistic writer. I believe this is an over-simplification and prefer to think of myself as a compassionate but realistic one. There is a difference between compassion and that facile, sentimental—and political— optimism found at the crux of most sf, a genre the poverty of whose subject matter is legendary.

My fiction is concerned with the inability of people to feel ordinary emotions, or to communicate them successfully to one another; their efforts to maintain identity in the face of abstract systems and idealistic social structures; and their perception of themselves as live individuals in a meaningless, contingent universe.

The most radical expression of this existential standpoint is found in the collection *Viriconium Nights*, but it is clearly present in stories such as "The Machine in Shaft Ten" and "Settling the World" and in *The Committed Men*.

In fact, my fiction is not easily described as sf. Though in-genre critics have described it as an "illustration of entropy," this is to put the cart before the horse. In work like "Running Down" and *In Viriconium* I have consistently used entropy as a metaphor, an illustration, of the human condition: I have no interest in it as a scientific concept. I have used the psychology of sensory deprivation and the ethological notion of "Umwelt" in a similarly metaphorical way. Fiction and science get into bed together at the risk of popularisation, which despite George Steiner's elegant efforts is still only popularisation, or (increasingly) bad faith. I would prefer to avoid that.

My interest in the fantastic allegory or parable, bread and butter of contemporary sf, has declined.

Since 1980 I have turned away from the extreme absurdism of *The Pastel City* and *A Storm of Wings*—with their stress on the failure of, and the fear of, action—and in "The Quarry" or "Old Women" can be seen an increasingly direct and sensual engagement with those areas where ethology, early-modernist fiction and a moderate existentialism seem to share ground in the concept of the "accented moment sign" or moment-of-being. I am interested in the lives of individuals; compassion is not a function of the grand or political scale. For the same reason I am drawn to the short novel rather than the heavily researched three-decker with its blundering Victorian moralism.

My writing is oblique, compressed, and allusive, with a carefully textured surface. Depite this I am much less a stylist, and very much less a "writer-for-writing's-sake," than is generally supposed in the theoretical regions of sf, which are as poverty-stricken as its human ones.

For the more recent short stories—"The Ice Monkey," "Egnaro," "The New Rays," and "A Young Man's Journey to Viriconium"—and for *Climbers*, my novel-in-progress, my notebooks have provided material observed from life. This is ordered at the outset according to its own internal demands. Thereafter setting and event amplify the theme; character and meaning are less stated than allowed to emerge. What appears to be atmosphere is more often than not metonymy or metaphor.

*   *   *

M. John Harrison's most enduring work in science fiction is the Viriconium series. The first book, *The Pastel City*, presents a ciilization in decline where medieval social patterns clash with the advanced technology and superscience weaponry that the citizens of the city know how to use but have forgotten how to engineer. Harrison's leading character, Cromis, fancies himself a better poet than a swordsman; yet he leads the battle to save Viriconium, the Pastel City, from the brain-stealing golems from Earth's past. The decadence Harrison describes is reminiscent of Michael Moorcock's vision of the far future in *The End of All Songs*.

The next book in the Viriconium series is *A Storm of Wings*. Fay Glass and Alstath Fulthor of the Reborn try to alert the powers of Viriconium that the northern highlands are overrun by insectile armies. A race of intelligent insects is invading Earth as human interest in survival wanes. Fay brings the severed head of an invading locust-like giant insect to show the extent of the disaster. Harrison brillantly depicts the workings of civilization on the verge of collapse and the heroic efforts of individuals to help it sustain itself a little longer.

The Floating Gods is a moody portrait of Viriconium beset by a mysterious plague. As artist Audsley King slowly dies from the plague, her friend Ashlyme tries to save her. Yet his efforts are purposeless and his adventures misdirected. Where the previous books in the series held some sword and sorcery elements, *The Floating Gods* goes beyond black humor into a coma of despair.

Viriconium Nights is a collection of eight vignettes of the night life in the Pastel City. Many of the pieces feature some of

Harrison's best writing, but that is what most of the stories are: exercises in style. The characters remain ill-defined and the actions are directionless and at times absurd. Vivid images come to nothing as plot and characters never interact.

Of Harrison's other novels his first, *The Committed Men*, is notable for its grotesque descriptions of post-nuclear holocaust Earth. A band of unlikely characters—a dwarf, a cripple, a doctor, and a girl who has just given birth to a ugly mutant baby—travel south to save the baby they are "committed" to delivering to the new race of mutants.

Harrison's most accessible book is *The Centauri Device* where space tramp John Truck is hunted down by a cast of bizarre characters: General Alice Gaw, ruthless head of the Israeli World Government; Gadaffi ben Barka, terrorist supreme of the Union of Arab Socialist Republics; and Dr. Grishkin, leader of the weird Opener cult. Truck's mother was a Centauran, one of the last before the Centauri Genocide. Now Truck is the last Centauran and the rival groups need him to arm the most powerful weapon in the galaxy: the Centauri device which will respond only to the genetic code of a true Centauran. There's plenty of action, black humor, and political commentary in this fast-paced space opera. The ending is a bit too pat, but Harrison is in fine control of this book all the way.

The Ice Monkey and Other Stories shows Harrison's wide range of subject matter. In seven stories, Harrison manages to capture pathos, humor, awe, despair, and pain. The best piece is "The Incalling" where an editor is haunted by an author's attempts to cure himself of cancer by faith healing. This is an unforgettable story.

M. John Harrison is a brilliant stylist whose work captures the grotesque and the decadent in vivid, absurd images that are as fascinating as they are unique.

—George Kelley

HARTLEY, L(eslie) P(oles). British. Born in Whittlesey, Cambridgeshire, 30 December 1895. Educated at Harrow School; Balliol College, Oxford, B. A. 1922. Served in World War I, 1916-18. Fiction reviewer for *Spectator, Week-end Review, Weekly Sketch, Time and Tide, The Observer,* and *Sunday Times,* all in London, 1923-72. Clark Lecturer, Trinity College, Cambridge, 1964. Recipient: Black Memorial Prize, 1948; Heinemann Award, 1954. Companion of Literature, Royal Society of Literature, 1972. C. B. E. (Commander, Order of the British Empire), 1956. *Died 13 December 1972.*

SCIENCE-FICTION PUBLICATIONS

Novel

Facial Justice. London, Hamish Hamilton, 1960; New York, Doubleday, 1961.

OTHER PUBLICATIONS

Novels

Simonetta Perkins. London and New York, Putnam, 1925.
Eustace and Hilda. London, Putnam, 1958; Chester Springs, Pennsylvania, Dufour, 1961.
  The Shrimp and the Anemone. London, Putnam, 1944; as *The West Window,* New York, Doubleday, 1945.

The Sixth Heaven. London, Putnam, 1946; New York, Doubleday, 1947.

Eustace and Hilda, London, Putnam, 1947.

The Boat. London, Putnam, 1949; New York, Doubleday, 1950.

My Fellow Devils. London, Barrie, 1951.

The Go-Between. London, Hamish Hamilton, 1953; New York, Knopf, 1954.

A Perfect Woman. London, Hamish Hamilton, 1955; New York, Knopf, 1956.

The Hireling. London, Hamish Hamilton, 1957; New York, Rinehart, 1958.

The Brickfield. London, Hamish Hamilton, 1964.

The Betrayal. London, Hamish Hamilton, 1966.

Poor Clare. London, Hamish Hamilton, 1968.

The Love-Adept: A Variation on a Theme. London, Hamish Hamilton, 1969.

My Sisters' Keeper. London, Hamish Hamilton, 1970.

The Harness Room. London, Hamish Hamilton, 1971.

The Collections. London, Hamish Hamilton, 1972.

The Will and the Way. London, Hamish Hamilton, 1973.

Short Stories

Night Fears and Other Stories. London, Putnam, 1924.

The Killing Bottle. London, Putnam, 1932.

The Travelling Grave and Other Stories. Sauk City, Wisconsin, Arkham House, 1948; London, Barrie, 1951.

The White Wand and Other Stories. London, Hamish Hamilton, 1954.

Two for the River. London, Hamish Hamilton, 1961.

The Collected Short Stories of L. P. Hartley. London, Hamish Hamilton, 1968; New York, Horizon Press, 1969.

Mrs. Carteret Receives and Other Stories. London, Hamish Hamilton, 1971.

The Complete Short Stories of L. P. Hartley. London, Hamish Hamilton, 1973.

Other

The Novelist's Responsibility: Lectures and Essays. London, Hamish Hamilton, 1967; New York, Hillary House, 1968.

*

Manuscript Collection: British Library, London.

Critical Studies: *L. P. Hartley* by Paul Bloomfield, London, Longman, 1962, revised edition, 1970; *L. P. Hartley* by Peter Bien, University Park, Pennsylvania State University Press, and London, Chatto and Windus, 1963; *Wild Thyme, Winter Lightning: The Symbolic Novels of L. P. Hartley* by Anne Mulkeen, London, Hamish Hamilton, and Detroit, Wayne State University Press, 1974.

*   *   *

L. P. Hartley's *Facial Justice* is a dystopian novel of the future in the tradition of Zamyatin's *We.* Hartley envisages a New State founded on self-abasement and equality. All the citizens are patients and delinquents, victims of their own ego-sickness. Each citizen is named after a murderer, biblical murderers being particularly in vogue; sackcloth and ashes provide the regular costume. In this projected society, envy is seen as the single cause of personal dissatisfaction and social friction. The wants, desires, and instincts of the citizens of the New State are suitably provided for by the Dictator. Hartley postulates that envy is stronger in women than in men, especially when it comes to the question of personal beauty. So women who are dissatisfied with their looks are encouraged to be "betafied," to have plastic surgery performed which gives them a pre-packaged beautiful face. The only difficulty is that such women have a difficult time in expressing their emotions.

Hartley's narrator and ultimately the first revolutionary in the New State is a young woman, Jael 93, who, as a result of an accident, is betafied only to resent the loss of her personality. Henceforth she attempts to discredit the Dictator and overthrow the New State. How she goes about it and the totally unexpected result of her activities provide fascinating reading. Hartley poses many of the usual dystopian concerns, freedom versus happiness, community good versus individual fulfillment, but treats them with a fresh perspective. *Facial Justice* is an intriguing venture into the dystopian tradition by a well-known mainstream author, especially in that it is written from the woman's point of view in a society which, though it professes equality, actually denigrates women.

—Joseph A. Quinn

———

HEARD, Gerald. See **HEARD, H. F.**

———

HEARD, H(enry) F(itzgerald). Also wrote as Gerald Heard. British. Born in London, 6 October 1889. Educated at Gonville and Caius College, Cambridge, B. A. (honours) in history 1911, graduate work 1911-12. Worked with the Agricultural Co-operative Movement in Ireland, 1919-23, and in England, 1923-27; Editor, *Realist,* London, 1929; Lecturer, Oxford University, 1929-31; science commentator, BBC Radio, London, 1930-34; settled in the United States, 1937; Visiting Lecturer, Washington University, St. Louis, 1951-52, 1955-56; Haskell Foundation Lecturer, Oberlin College, Ohio, 1958. Recipient: Bollingen grant, 1955; British Academy Hertz award. *Died 14 August 1971.*

SCIENCE-FICTION PUBLICATIONS

Novels

Doppelgangers: An Episode of the Fourth, the Psychological Revolution, 1997. New York, Vanguard Press, 1947; London, Cassell, 1948.

The Black Fox. London, Cassell, 1950; New York, Harper, 1951.

Short Stories

The Great Fog and Other Weird Tales. New York, Vanguard Press, 1944; London, Cassell, 1947; as *Weird Tales of Terror and Detection,* New York, Sun Dial Press, 1946.

The Lost Cavern and Other Tales of the Fantastic. New York, Vanguard Press, 1948; London, Cassell, 1949.

Uncollected Short Stories

"B Planet 4," in *New Tales of Space and Time,* edited by

Raymond J. Healy. New York, Holt Rinehart, 1951; London, Weidenfeld and Nicolson, 1952.
"The Marble Ear," in *Fantasy and Science Fiction* (New York), December 1952.

OTHER PUBLICATIONS

Novels

A Taste for Honey. New York, Vanguard Press, 1941; London, Cassell, 1942; as *A Taste for Murder,* New York, Avon, 1955.
Reply Paid. New York, Vanguard Press, 1942; London, Cassell, 1943.
Murder by Reflection. New York, Vanguard Press, 1942; London, Cassell, 1945.
The Notched Hairpin. New York, Vanguard Press, 1949; London, Cassell, 1952.

Other as Gerald Heard

Narcissus: An Anatomy of Clothes. London, Kegan Paul, and New York, Dutton, 1924.
The Ascent of Humanity: An Essay on the Evolution of Civilization. London, Cape, and New York, Harcourt Brace, 1929.
The Emergence of Man. London, Cape, 1931; New York, Harcourt Brace, 1932.
Social Substance of Religion: An Essay on the Evolution of Religion. London, Allen and Unwin, and New York, Harcourt Brace, 1931.
This Surprising World: A Journalist Looks At Science. London, Cobden Sanderson, 1932.
Those Hurrying years: An Historical Outline 1900-1933. London, Chatto and Windus, and New York, Oxford University Press, 1934.
Science in the Making. London, Faber, 1935.
The Source of Civilisation. London, Cape, 1935; New York, Harper, 1937.
The Significance of the New Pacifism, with *Pacifism and Philosophy,* by Aldous Huxley, London, Headley, 1935.
Exploring the Stratosphere. London, Nelson, 1936.
Science Front 1936. London, Cassell, 1937.
The Third Morality. London, Cassell, and New York, Morrow, 1937.
Pain, Sex and Time: A New Hypothesis of Evolution. New York, Harper, and London, Cassell, 1939.
The Creed of Christ: An Interpretation of the Lord's Prayer. New York, Harper, 1940; London, Cassell, 1941.
A Quaker Meditation. Wallingford, Pennsylvania, Pendle Hill, 1940 (?).
The Code of Christ: An Interpretation of the Beatitudes. New York, Harper, 1941; London, Cassell, 1943.
Training for the Life of the Spirit. London, Cassell, 2 vols., 1941-44; New York, Harper, 1 vol., n. d.
Man the Master. New York, Harper, 1941; London, Faber, 1942.
A Dialogue in the Desert. London, Cassell, and New York, Harper, 1942.
A Preface to Prayer. New York, Harper, 1944; London, Cassell, 1945.
The Recollection. Stanford, California, Delkin, 1944.
The Gospel According to Gamaliel. New York, Harper, 1945; London, Cassell, 1946.
Militarism's Post-Mortem. London, P. P. U., 1946.
The Eternal Gospel. New York, Harper, 1946; London, Cassell, 1948.

Is God Evident? An Essay Toward a Natural Theology. New York, Harper, 1948; London, Faber, 1950.
Is God in History? An Inquiry into Human and Pre-Human History in Terms of the Doctrine of Creation, Fall, and Redemption. New York, Harper, 1950; London, Faber, 1951.
Morals since 1900. London, Dakers, and New York, Harper, 1950.
The Riddle of the Flying Saucers. London, Carroll and Nicholson, 1950; as *Is Another World Watching?,* New York, Harper, 1951; revised edition, New York, Bantam, 1953.
Ten Questions on Prayer. Wallingford, Pennsylvania, Pendle Hill, 1951.
Gabriel and the Creatures. New York, Harper, 1952; as *Wishing Well: An Outline of the Evolution of the Mammals Told as a Series of Stories about How Animals Got Their Wishes,* London, Faber, 1953.
The Human Venture. New York, Harper, 1955.
Kingdom Without God: Road's End for the Social Gospel, with others. Los Angeles, Foundation for Social Research, 1956.
Training for a Life of Growth. Santa Monica, California, Wayfarer Press, 1959.
The Five Ages of Man: The Psychology of Human History. New York, Julian Press, 1964.

Editor, *Prayers and Meditations.* New York, Harper, 1949.

*   *   *

Doppelgangers, the novel by H. F. Heard best known to science-fiction readers, depicts a hedonistic dictatorship based on behavior control. The hero, nameless except as "the remodeled man" or Alpha II, belongs to an underground organization ruled by the Mole, who also uses behavior control to sabotage the dictatorship. In the novel, the hero is "remodeled" physically to duplicate the dictator Alpha, who needs a double to impersonate him and absorb the psychic impact of his charismatic appearances. When Alpha commits suicide, Alpha II is left as dictator. An assassination attempt by a follower of the Mole leads to a series of discoveries about the true government of the world, which remains in the hands of spiritually evolved people called elevates.

The novel explores Heard's ideas about the human condition. The nature of Alpha's dictatorship is despotism through indulgence, suave reduction of the human soul to childishness by supplying the masses with entertainment and pleasures. "Animectomy," or cutting away of the soul, prefigures B. F. Skinner's *Walden II.* As a dystopian novel, *Doppelgangers* can also be compared to Orwell's *Nineteen Eighty-Four* or Huxley's *Brave New World.* But Heard also explores evolution, especially as a self-directed project with Hegelian overtones, since he sees human history as a continuing aspiration toward something higher, with Alpha's dictatorship only one step on the ladder. Heard is also interested in the relationship of the soul to its manifestations. Clothes reflect customs: a man's appearance determines and is determined by his ideas; etymology reveals truths of history. Indeed, one of Heard's first books was a history and philosophy of costume, *Narcissus: An Anatomy of Clothes,* and his style and ideas are influenced by the "Clothes Philosophy" of Carlyle's *Sartor Resartus.* The dictatorship in *Doppelgangers* is also based on Sheldon's somatypes which posit a relationship betwen body type and personality. Doppelgangers is a philosophical novel; though the psychological exploration of the few major characters is deep, this is not a psychological novel. The style is involuted with tricky puns and allusions.

The Black Fox is an occultist novel with speculative content. Throcton, a British cleric envious of advancement, uses black magic to destroy his enemy. When the magic recoils, he is saved only by the self-sacrifice of his sister. Heard bases the black magic, involving etymology of the word *alopecia* from fox mange, on Biblical, Sufist, and folklore learning, speculating on the relation of mind and body. Treatment of black magic as an explainable phenomenon prefigures the thinking of such contemporaries as Colin Wilson. Psychological analysis is strong in this novel, and the isolated, highly cerebral Throctons, brother and sister, are eccentric but complexly interesting. Except for his detective fiction, *The Black Fox* represents the best use of suspense in Heard's fiction.

Gabriel and the Creatures is a speculative fantasy based on the premise that a species has will to evolve in a certain direction, and that God, through the angl Gabriel, will grant each species its wish. *The Gospel According to Gamaliel* is a retelling of the New Testament by a Hebrew ecclesiast, teacher of St. Paul, speculative in its attempt to reconcile differing theological viewpoints.

Heard's short stories are mostly collected in *The Great Fog* and *The Lost Cavern*. They speculate upon some of Heard's favorite concerns: evolution in "The Thaw Plan," "The Lost Cavern," "Wingless Victory," and "The Great Fog"; medical knowledge in "The Rousing of Mr. Bradegar" and "The Crayfish"; architecture in "Dromenon"; and telephatic exchange in "The Swap. " "The Cat 'I Am'" may be seen as an early study for *The Black Fox*. Heard's heroes are isolated, scholarly types.

Heard's major output is not in fiction but in religious philosophy; he has also written detective fiction and a work on flying saucers. Except for reviews and an occasional mention in critical works, Heard has received little critical attention. His strength is in speculation rather than character or plot. Nonetheless, *Doppelgangers* is a significant dystopian novel which merits a place in the science-fiction canon.

—Mary T. Brizzi

HEINLEIN, Robert A(nson). American. Born in Butler, Missouri, 7 July 1907. Educated at Central High School, Kansas City, graduated 1924; University of Missouri, Columbia, 1924-25; United States Naval Academy, Annapolis, Maryland, B. S. 1929; University of California, Los Angeles, 1934-35. Served in the United States Navy, 1929 until retirement because of physical disability, 1934. Married 1) Leslyn McDonald (divorced); 2) Virginia Gerstenfeld in 1948. Owned a silver mine, Silver Plume, Colorado, 1934-35; worked in mining and real estate, 1936-39; civilian engineer, Philadelphia Navy Yard, 1942-45. Forrestal Lecturer, United States Naval Academy, 1973. Recipient: Hugo Award, 1956, 1960, 1962, 1967; Boys' Clubs of America award, 1959; Grand Master Nebula Award, 1974. Guest of Honor, World Science Fiction Convention, 1941, 1961, 1976. L. H. D. : Eastern Michigan University, Ypsilanti, 1977. Agent: Spectrum Literary Agency, 432 Park Avenue South, Suite 1205, New York, New York 10016. Address: 6000 Bonny Doon Road, Santa Cruz, California 95060, U. S. A.

SCIENCE-FICTION PUBLICATIONS

Novels (series: Future History)

Rocket Ship Galileo (for children). New York, Scribner, 1947; London, New English Library, 1971.

Space Cadet (for children). New York, Scribner, 1948; London, Gollancz, 1966.

Beyond This Horizon. Reading, Pennsylvania, Fantasy Press, 1948; London, Panther, 1967.

Sixth Column. New York, Gnome Press, 1949; as *The Day after Tomorrow,* New York, New American Library, 1951; London, Mayflower, 1962.

Red Planet (for children). New York, Scribner, 1949; London, Gollancz, 1963.

Farmer in the Sky (for children). New York, Scribner, 1950; London, Gollancz, 1962.

Waldo, and Magic Inc. New York, Doubleday, 1950; as *Waldo, Genius in Orbit,* New York, Avon, 1958.

The Puppet Masters. New York, Doubleday, 1951; London, Museum Press, 1953.

Between Planets (for children). New York, Scribner, 1951; London, Gollancz, 1968.

The Rolling Stones (for children). New York, Scribner, 1952; as *Space Family Stone,* London, Gollancz, 1969.

Starman Jones (for children). New York, Scribner, 1953; London, Sidgwick and Jackson, 1954.

The Star Beast (for children). New York, Scribner, 1954; London, New English Library, 1971.

Tunnel in the Sky (for children). New York, Scribner, 1955; London, Gollancz, 1965.

Time for the Stars (for children). New York, Scribner, 1956; London, Gollancz, 1963.

Double Star. New York, Doubleday, 1956; London, Joseph, 1958.

The Door into Summer. New York, Doubleday, 1957; London, Panther, 1960.

Citizen of the Galaxy (for children). New York, Scribner, 1957; London, Gollancz, 1969.

Have Space Suit—Will Travel (for children). New York, Scribner, 1958; London, Gollancz, 1970.

Methuselah's Children (Future History). New York, Gnome Press, 1958; London, Gollancz, 1963.

The Robert Heinlein Omnibus. London, Sidgwick and Jackson, 1958.

Starship Troopers (for children). New York Putnam, 1959; London, New English Library, 1961.

Stranger in a Strange Land. New York, Putnam, 1961; London, New English Library, 1965.

Podkayne of Mars: Her Life and Times (for children). New York, Putnam, 1963; London, New English Library, 1969.

Glory Road. New York, Putnam, 1963; London, New English Library, 1965.

Farnham's Freehold. New York, Putnam, 1964; London, Dobson, 1965.

Three by Heinlein (includes *The Puppet Masters, Waldo, Magic Inc.*). New York, Doubleday, 1965: as *A Heinlein Triad.* London, Gollancz, 1966.

A Robert Heinlein Omnibus. London, Sidgwick and Jackson, 1966.

The Moon Is a Harsh Mistress. New York, Putnam, 1966; London, Dobson, 1967.

I Will Fear No Evil. New York, Putnam, 1970; London, New English Library, 1972.

Time Enough for Love: The Lives of Lazarus Long (Future History). New York, Putnam, 1973; London, New English

Library, 1974.
The Number of the Beast. New York, Fawcett, and London, New English Library, 1980.
Friday. New York, Holt Rinehart, and London, New English Library, 1982.
Job: A Comedy of Justice. New York, Ballantine, and London, New English Library, 1984.

Short Stories (series: Future History)

The Man Who Sold the Moon (Future History). Chicago, Shasta, 1950; London, Sidgwick and Jackson, 1953.
Universe (Future History). New York, Dell, 1951.
The Green Hills of Earth (Future History). Chicago, Shasta, 1951; London, Sidgwick and Jackson, 1954.
Revolt in 2100 (Future History). Chicago, Shasta, 1953; London, Digit, 1959.
Assignment in Eternity. Reading, Pennsylvania, Fantasy Press, 1953; London, Museum Press, 1955; abridged edition, as *Lost Legacy,* London, Digit, 1960.
The Menace from Earth. New York, Gnome Press, 1959; London, Dobson, 1966.
The Unpleasant Profession of Jonathan Hoag. New York, Gnome Press, 1959; London, Dobson 1964; as *6" Six Stories,* New York, Pyramid, 1961.
Orphans of the Sky (Future History). London, Gollancz, 1963; New York, Putnam, 1964.
The Worlds of Robert A. Heinlein. New York, Ace, 1966; London, New English Library, 1970.
The Past Through Tomorrow: Future History Stories. New York, Putnam, 1967; abridged edition, London, New English Library, 2 vols., 1977.
The Best of Robert Heinlein 1939-1959, edited by Angus Wells. London, Sidgwick and Jackson, 1973.
Destination Moon. Boston, Gregg Press, 1979.
Expanded Universe. New York, Grosset and Dunlap, 1980.

OTHER PUBLICATIONS

Plays

Screenplays: *Destination Moon,* with Rip Van Ronkel and James O'Hanlon, 1950; *Project Moonbase,* with Jack Seaman, 1953.

Other

The Discovery of the Future (address). Los Angeles, Novacious, 1941.
"On the Writing of Speculative Fiction," in *Of Worlds Beyond: The Science of Science-Fiction Writing,* edited by Lloyd Arthur Eshbach. Reading, Pennsylvania, Fantasy Press, 1947; London, Dobson, 1965.
"Why I Selected 'The Green Hills of Earth,'" in *My Best Science Fiction Story,* edited by Leo Margulies and O. J. Friend. New York, Merlin Press, 1949.
"Ray Guns and Rocket Ships," in *Library Journal* (New York), July 1953.
"Science Fiction: Its Nature, Faults, and Virtues," in *The Science Fiction Novel,* edited by Basil Davenport. Chicago, Advent, 1959.
"Heinlein on Science Fiction," in *Vertex* (Los Angeles), April 1973.
The Notebooks of Lazarus Long. New York, Putnam, 1978.

Editor, *Tomorrow, The Stars: A Science Fiction Anthology.* New York, Doubleday, 1952.

*

Bibliography: *Robert A. Heinlein: A Bibliography* by Mark Owings, Baltimore, Croatan House, 1973.

Manuscript Collection: University of California Library, Santa Cruz.

Critical Studies: *Seekers of Tomorrow* by Sam Moskowitz, Cleveland, World, 1966; *Heinlein in Dimension: A Critical Analysis* (includes bibliography) by Alexei Panshin, Chicago, Advent, 1968; *Robert A. Heinlein, Stranger in His Own Land,* San Bernardino, California, Borgo Press, 1976, and *The Classic Years of Robert A. Heinlein,* Borgo Press, 1977, both by George Edgar Slusser; *Robert A. Heinlein* edited by Martin H. Greenberg and Joseph D. Olander, New York, Taplinger, and Edinburgh, Harris, 1978; *Robert A. Heinlein: America as Science Fiction* by H. Bruce Franklin, New York, Oxford University Press, 1980, London, Oxford University Press, 1981.

*   *   *

Probably no one deserves to be called the Dean of Science Fiction more than Robert A. Heinlein, whose prolific output remains continuously in print, a phenomenon almost unheard of in an industry which pulps the unsold as quickly as new books can be printed. Nearly always a "good read," Heinlein's work at its best epitomizes the excitement science fiction can generate by dramatizing the possible future adventures which scientific knowledge and technology can open up for humanity, and by exploring the needs of individuals within a society to survive and find satisfaction compatible with the continuance and growth of our species; at its worst, it's still usually provocative both to SF addicts and to novices. Through his long writing career Heinlein has consistently dramatized the essential moral questions for young and old, which boil down to one: What is the ideal way to live, today—and tomorrow? Idealism dosed with pragmatism flavors the answers to this question in each of Heinlein's stories. His sympathetic characters are neither all flesh nor all spirit but a careful balance of both. The majority of his work is cautiously optimistic and celebratory of the triumph of individuals over both internal weakness and, especially, external obstacles to their physical well-being—although there are some notable exceptions, such as "All You Zombies. "

Like virtually all writers of the 1940's, Heinlein began his career producing short stories, and his crisp style still inspires much emulation; "The Roads Must Roll" earned him a place in *The Science Fiction Hall of Fame,* stories selected by the Science Fiction Writers of America to honor works prior to the inception of the Nebula Awards in the mid-1960's.

After World War II he turned to the new market for science fiction novels and began writing for children. These books remain popular with the audience for which they were written, teen and pre-teen boys. *The Star Beast* is one of the best for a young reader to start with. Not only does it have both male and female central characters and a lovable alien creature full of unexpected antics (long before E. T.), the story also invents the unorthodox privilege of unhappy children to divorce unsatisfactory parents, a notion sure to delight young readers.

Podkayne of Mars, often regarded as an adult novel in spite of its young protagonists, has been widely denounced for using a phony female viewpoint character; the story purports to be the diary of a teenage girl, but a large portion is written by her precocious, bratty pre-teen brother, who turns out to be smarter than she is. Heinlein has been attacked by some feminist critics for his simplistic depictions of females; others point out that in these "Golden Age" stories, Heinlein was one of the few writers who showed girls and women doing anything beyond being objects to be rescued. His recent novel *Friday*, although nominated for a Hugo, drew criticism for his depiction of a sympathetic character who not only forgives but marries her rapist. (Certainly Heinlein deserves credit for creating a more believable female narrator in Friday than he did in Podkayne, or in *I Will Fear No Evil* or even *The Number of the Beast*. Friday is an AP—artificial person, who by definition does not suffer the "normal" socialization of natural human females.)

Beginning in the 1960's Heinlein started producing definitely adult novels, tending toward longer and longer books with each passing decade. Heinlein's best-known novels are the four Hugo-winners, *Double Star, Starship Troopers, Stranger in a Strange Land,* and *The Moon Is a Harsh Mistress,* and they each represent much of what is characteristic of his other work. The protagonist of *Double Star*, Lorenzo Smythe, narrates his own story. Originally an unemployed actor, he is recruited (forcibly) to play the role of an incapacitated leader who must participate in delicate interplanetary diplomacy, an assignment he ultimately accepts willingly, not out of political conviction but because of the challenge to his acting ability. Heinlein's protagonists never set out to be heroes. During the course of the story, however, Lorenzo rises to the moral challenge and becomes worthy of his new power and authority. He concludes that the sacrifice of personal peace of mind is justified by "solemn satisfaction in doing the best you can for eight billion people. " Noblesse oblige: the strong spirit has a duty to the weak.

In *Starship Troopers* a similar lesson is learned by Juan Rico, who also tells of his own conversion, from a mildly pacifist and apolitical youth, who volunteers almost inadvertently for Federal Service to impress a female, to a dedicated combat officer who realizes that the noblest fate he can hope for is to die defending others' lives. His Moral Instruction teacher sums it up: "The price demanded for the most precious of all things in life is life itself—ultimate cost for perfect value. " Eventually Juan even helps his own father to realize and share his insight. Seasoned with rich slang that provides both verisimilitude and freshness to what could easily be a conventional situation, the novel is shaped like a sandwich. Battle action scenes open and close the book, and the moral awakening fills its center.

Stranger in a Strange Land is the only one of Heinlein's Hugo-winners to use a third-person narrator, and is less unified in other ways than the other three. The first two sections are largely concerned with the satiric vision of human behavior seen through the unspoiled eyes of a highly intelligent being, Valentine Michael Smith, physically human but culturally alien. Significantly, Mike regains his genetic heritage only after he learns to laugh by watching the monkeys in a zoo. The latter part of the book is devoted to myth-making of the possible limits of human interactions. Because he is culture-free, Mike is able to explore unorthodox sensuality and sexuality without the feelings of inhibition and guilt which plague the rest of us. The joy of his discoveries is powerful enough to free others from their hangups also (even his mentor Jubal Harshaw), so they create a mystical new religion. But Heinlein undermines his myth with the mocking cynicism of the blatant fraud Foster, who turns out to be Mike's boss in the hereafter (or whereafter?): "Certainly 'Thou art God'—but who isn't?" The creed of the new religion is nothing special in the cosmic scheme of things. For many critics this self-mockery comes too little and too late to counter Mike's simplistic message of free love and

the power to dispel all earthly problems simply by correct comprehension, or "grokking. " But surely in reading this novel future generations will recapture the 1960's spirit of campus rebellion against hypocritical middle-class morality that it exploits.

The Moon Is a Harsh Mistress combines more of Heinlein's strengths and fewer of his artistic limitations than any of his other works. The length of the novel is justified by the complexity of the social and political systems depicted. The story of Luna's fight for freedom is told by Emanuel Garcia O'Kelly, a sympathetic but fallible person who might be Anyman. Mannie is not a great man, but he is the best computer technician available in the moon colony, and so becomes the first friend of Mike, the sentient computer who keeps from going insane at the interface of conflicting data by developing a sense of humor—and a protective love for those who give him a purpose in living. Since the narrator must survive to tell the tale, the interest of the reader is focused less on what will happen next than on how it happens. Of course, it is humanity, not Mannie as an individual, who created Mike; mankind has developed an intelligence beyond its own fleshly limitations, one moreover uncorrupted by petty greed and lust for power. The philosophy of TANSTAAFL—"There ain't no such thing as a free lunch"—naturally becomes the slogan of Free Luna. Their success relies on long odds and high risks, but the stakes of freedom are worth the ultimate price, paid by many of the revolutionaries including Mannie's political mentor and (apparently) Mike. Mannie is left with many doubts and unfulfilled longings at the end in a passage handled with poignancy as delicate as can be found anywhere in Heinlein's work. Ultimately he decides to go on living: "My word, I'm not even a hundred yet. " The confrontation with man's own mortality pervades much of Heinlein's work.

Early in his career he conceived of a "future history," into which nearly all of his work can be placed. This means that one who has read several of his works will begin to perceive them in a different context from one who encounters; a Heinlein novel for the first time. This tends to build a "cult" following, without the restrictions of a "series," allowing him to play variations on themes. This also, however, makes it difficult for a novice Heinlein reader to follow some sequences which will delight the devotee.

If Heinlein's female characters tend to be "idealized" or even sentimentalized, so do his male characters. Good people are those who keep mentally active, try avoid harming innocent others (though they have few qualms about killing enemies to survive), and, above all, wish to produce and protect babies. He has played frequently with the quantum concept of simultaneous parallel universes in novels such as *Glory Road* and in the more recent novels *The Number of the Beast* and *Job: A Comedy of Justice*. In all of his "worlds," people lacking a healthy sense of self-preservation die prematurely, for no universe is really very friendly and wise ones must adapt quickly to changing circumstances. While much of the criticism of Heinlein has centered on his repetition of formulaic plots and character relationships, he manages to freshen his materials and keep devoted fans eagerly awaiting each new book.

—Elizabeth Anne Hull

HELPRIN, Mark. American. Born in 1947. Agent: Julian Bach Literary Agency, 747 Third Avenue, New York, New York 10017, U. S. A.

SCIENCE-FICTION PUBLICATIONS

Novel

Winter's Tale. New York, Harcourt Brace, and London, Weidenfeld and Nicolson, 1983.

OTHER PUBLICATIONS

Novel

Refiner's Fire: The Life and Adventures of Marshall Pearl, A Foundling. New York, Knopf, 1977; London, Hamish Hamilton, 1978.

Short Stories

A Dove of the East and Other Stories. New York, Knopf, 1975; London, Hamish Hamilton, 1976.
Ellis Island and Other Stories. New York, Delacorte Press, and London, Hamish Hamilton, 1981.

* * *

As with that other great contemporary Jewish fabulist, Isaac Bashevis Singer, the range of Mark Helprin's fiction is wide enough to encompass many modes, settings, and sensibilities, although, like Singer again, his stories that border on the fantastic are some of his most memorable and accomplished. "A Jew of Persia" (*A Dove in the East*) is the deceptively simple story of an old man's obstinate belief that a youthful confrontation with the Devil on a mountain pass in Persia will lead to an inevitably deadly reunion in the streets of Tel Aviv. "Letter from the *Samantha* " (*Ellis Island*) is a Conradian (and Poesque) tale of the high seas concerning a ship-captain's obsession with a strangely human-like ape that he rescues during a typhoon. "Ellis Island," the title novella of his second collection of shorter works, chronicles the wondrously varied slapstick adventures of a turn-of-the-century Jewish immigrant as he alternately embraces and dodges the possibilities and pitfalls of this dazzling New World. Like the unnamed narrator of "Ellis Island" or the picaresque foundling-hero of *Refiner's Fire*, his first full-length work, many of Helprin's protagonists are motivated by some vague selfless ideal of redemption and love.

This sense of romantic idealism receives its fullest treatment in Helprin's second novel and best-known work, *Winter's Tale*, a full-fledged SF-fantasy saga of mammoth proportions and even larger ambitions. Virtually every major character in this century-spanning alternate-history of a once-and-future New York City is in pursuit of some ineffable vision of wealth, power, beauty, or moral potential. Peter Lake, another one of Helprin's orphans of the picaresque storm, is cast adrift as an infant on a model boat by his desperate immigrant parents and rescued and adopted by the Baymen, a primitive tribe inhabiting the late 19th-century Jersey marshes. As an adolescent apprentice thief, Peter earns the undying ire of the Short Tails, a grotesquely ugly gang of petty criminals led by the gnomelike Pearly Soames, whose fanatical dream is to build a huge room made up entirely of gold. Peter also falls deeply in love with and is married briefly to the dying consumptive heiress Beverly Penn, whose intense aestheticism allows her to hear the (literal) music of the spheres and whose ethereal beauty haunts Peter in purest Dantesque fashion over the next hundred years. Again pursued by the Short Tails, Peter leaps on the escaped milkhorse Athansor, who becomes transformed into an urban

Pegasus and catapults its rider into a mysterious white cloud that places Peter in suspended animation until the late 1990's, when the sleeper wakes, an amnesiac, but still pursued by Pearly and the memory of his doomed Beatrice/Beverly. As New York approaches an apocalyptic millenium, Peter, on his own predestined road to transcendence, runs into more romantic idealists, including a newspaperman who is searching for "a perfectly just city rejoicing in justice alone" and a Luciferian architect contemplating the erection of a bridge of light to attract the attention of an apathetic Deity.

Through all this, Helprin never allows his readers to forget that his true protagonist is America itself, with New York, in all its complexity, dismal poverty, and potential glory, as its emblem and central metaphor. As he has one of his characters ruminate, "the city was so full of combinations, permutations, and possibilities that it permitted not only any desire to be fulfilled, but any course to be taken, any reward to be sought, any life to be lived, and any race to be run. " While Helprin's millenial optimism is couched in an often florid style, his richly allusive and wildly inventive winter's tale of personal and collective sacrifice and transfiguration may virtually demand such rhetorical excesses, since it is clear that, for Helprin, the writer's duty is somehow to articulate what the dreaming mountainclimber of "The Schreuderspitze" (*Ellis Island*) can only glimpse in his mind's eye: "In certain states of light he could see, he could begin to sense, things most miraculous indeed. "

—Kenneth Jurkiewicz

———————

HENDERSON, Zenna (née Chlarson). American. Born in Tucson, Arizona, 1 November 1917. Educated at Arizona State College, now University, B. A. 1940, M. A. 1955. Married in 1944 (divorced). After 1940, elementary school teacher in Arizona: also taught at the Japanese Relocation Camp, Sacaton, Arizona, during World War II, Laon sur Marne, Aisne, France, 1956-58, and Seaside Children's Hospital, Waterford, Connecticut, 1958-59. *Died 11 May 1983*.

SCIENCE-FICTION PUBLICATIONS

Novels

Pilgrimage: The Book of the People. New York, Doubleday, 1961; London, Gollancz, 1962.
The People: No Different Flesh. New York, Doubleday, and London, Gollancz, 1966.

Short Stories

The Anything Box. New York, Doubleday, 1965; London, Gollancz, 1966.
Holding Wonder. New York, Doubleday, 1971; London, Gollancz, 1972.

Uncollected Short Stories

"Thrumthing and Out," in *Fantasy and Science Fiction* (New York), October 1972.
"Katie-Mary's Trip," in *Fantasy and Science Fiction* (New York), January 1975.
"The First Stroke," in *Fantasy and Science Fiction* (New York), October 1977.

"There Was a Garden," in *Cassandra Rising*, edited by Alice Laurance. New York, Doubleday, 1978.

*

Zenna Henderson commented:

(1981) When I was about 12 I began reading science fiction— Jules Verne, Haggard, and Edgar Rice Burroughs, and all the current magazines I could get hold of, but it wasn't until I had graduated from college that I began writing fantasy and science fiction. I have only a sketchy scientific background, so of necessity I write from a non-technical viewpoint. My favorite science-fiction authors, when I was still reading it, were Heinlein, Bradbury, Clement, and Asimov. Mottos I try to observe when I write: stories consist of unusual people in ordinary circumstances or ordinary people in unusual circumstances; write about what you know; don't let your subtleties become obscurities.

*   *   *

"Write what you know" is the cornerstone of Zenna Henderson's science-fiction career. She constructed story after story out of experiences accumulated during her many years in the elementary classroom. She found teachers useful viewpoint characters because their vision is multiplied through their students' eyes. Her children have the appealing naturalness that comes of being modeled directly from life.

Henderson made more and better use of adult-child interactions than adult-adult ones but she always kept human relationships paramount. She ignored man's struggles against the universe because she did not perceive the cosmos as hostile. By rejecting sex, sadism, and violence, her stories offer a gentle alternative to macho entertainments. Yet feminist critics scorn Henderson for occupational stereotyping without acknowledging that she depicts single women, older women, and female friendships positively. Wonder in familiar settings is Henderson's forte. She reveals the world a child or a saint might see—a place where time can shift and dimensions fold, where mountains walk and wishes come true. Friction between the mundane and the marvelous generates her dramas. For example, a small boy battles a demon ("Stevie and the Dark") or school routine survives the collapse of civilization ("As Simple as That").

Henderson's most popular stories are those collected in *Pilgrimage* and *The People*. Each volume's components are united by a frame-story, a device that succeeds better in *Pilgrimage* because it is a poignant tale in its own right. The frame of *The People* is simply an excuse for flashbacks to events preceding and following those in *Pilgrimage*. The People are extraterrestrial refugees with psychic gifts who have been hiding in the American southwest since the 1890's. They are gradually overcoming memories of persecution and forming partnerships with humans. Their perilous flight from their lost Home to Earth, their true Promised Land, parallels the Old Testament Exodus—a comparison underscored by Biblical names and titles. (Basic Christian values undergird all of Henderson's writing.) Although the People had a different salvation history, their beliefs are compatible with Christianity. They even use a trinitarian invocation of God as the Power, the Presence, and the Name. Their bonding through love is Henderson's answer to the conflicts between community and individuality that run through so much of her fiction.

Secret aliens among us is an old SF notion but no one has put it to happier use than Henderson. The sheer wholesomeness of her People is enough to set them apart. "They're us only more

so," says the author. Whether reading thoughts, operating spacecraft, or hemming dresses, the People wield their powers with a cheerful reverence that is refreshingly matter-of-fact. Henderson is neither anti-technological nor pro-occultist like Andre Norton. Miracles in a grittily realistic setting strike just the right note of aesthetic contrast to make the stories work.

Henderson's paradigm of sympathetic adult aiding troubled wonder-child is as distinctive as her signature. Yet it is a conscious pattern to be varied at will. "Something Bright" reverses the usual roles to disguised alien adult and helpful human child. Not all teachers are caring ("The Last Step") or effective ("You Know What, Teacher?"). Not all marvels are desirable ("The Substitute," "Turn the Page," "Sharing Time"). Children's wonderful powers can cause tragedy ("The Believing Child," "Come On, Wagon!," "Hush!"). In such works Henderson displays an excellent although curiously unappreciated touch for horror. She can handle insanity as vividly as psi ("Swept and Garnished," "One of Them").

At her worst, Henderson's sentimentality overflows. Occasionally her ideas are too weak. Her range of subject matter is admittedly small. But overall, she worked with sound, unobtrusive craftsmanship. She had the classic short story writer's talents for precise focus, good characterization, and shrewd deployment of details. A kindly, traditional sensibility animates her writing. This description of ultimate happiness from "The Anything Box" conveys her special flavor: "all the worry and waiting, the apartness and loneliness were over and forgotten, their hugeness dwindled by the comfort of a shoulder, the warmth of clasping hands—and nowhere, nowhere was the fear of parting. . . . " Henderson was SF's mistress of the happy ending.

—Sandra Miesel

HENSLEY, Joe L. (Joseph Louis Hensley). American. Born in Bloomington, Indiana, 19 March 1926. Educated at Indiana University, Bloomington, B. A. 1950, LL. B. 1955: called to the Indiana Bar, 1955. Served as a hospital corpsman in the United States Navy, 1944-46; recalled as journalist, 1951-52. Married Charlotte Ruth Bettinger in 1950; one son. Partner, Metford and Hensley, 1955-72, and Hensley Todd and Castor, 1972-75, Madison, Indiana; Judge Pro-Tempore, 80th Judicial Circuit, Versailles, Indiana, 1975-76. Since 1977, Judge, 5th Judicial Circuit, Madison. Member, Indiana General Assembly, 1961-62; Prosecuting Attorney, 5th Judicial Indiana Circuit, 1963-66. President, Indiana Judges Association, 1983-84. Agent: Virginia Kidd, Box 278, Milford, Pennsylvania 18337. Address: 2315 Blackmore, Madison, Indiana 47250, U. S. A.

SCIENCE-FICTION PUBLICATIONS

Novel

The Black Roads. Toronto, Laser, 1976.

Short Stories

Final Doors (includes essay). New York, Doubleday, 1981.

Uncollected Short Stories

"Eyes of the Double Moon," in *Planet* (New York), May 1953.

"Guide Wire," in *Future* (New York), August 1954.
"The Red and the Green," in *Science Fiction Quarterly* (Holyoke, Massachusetts), May 1955.
"Once a Starman," in *Planet* (New York), Summer 1955.
"The Sun Hunters," in *Fantastic Universe* (Chicago), September 1955.
"The Outvaders," in *Astounding* (New York), November 1955.
"Now We Are Three," in *Fantastic Universe* (Chicago), August 1957.
"Time of the Tinkers," in *Future* (New York), June 1958.
"Star Ways," in *Original Science Fiction Stories* (Holyoke, Massachusetts), September 1958.
"Visionary," in *Amazing* (New York), May 1959.
"And Not Quite Human," in *Triple W*. New York, Bantam, 1963.
"The Edge of the Rose," in *Amazing* (New York), September 1969.
"The Run from Home," in *Fantasy and Science Fiction* (New York), December 1970.
"Time Patrol" in *If* (New York), February 1972.
"In Dark Places," in *Future City*, edited by Roger Elwood. New York, Simon and Schuster, 1973.
"The Pair," in *Combat SF*, edited by Gordon R. Dickson. New York, Doubleday, 1975.
"The Midnight Bicyclist," with Gene DeWeese, in *Starry Messenger*, edited by Charles C. Ryan. New York, St. Martin's Press, 1979.
"Harpist," in *Speculations*, edited by Isaac Asimov and Alice Laurance. Boston, Houghton Mifflin, 1982.

OTHER PUBLICATIONS

Novels

The Color of Hate. New York, Ace, 1960.
Deliver Us to Evil. New York, Doubleday, 1971.
Legislative Body. New York, Doubleday, 1972.
The Poison Summer. New York, Doubleday, 1974.
Song of Corpus Juris. New York, Doubleday, 1974.
Rivertown Risk. New York, Doubleday, 1977.
A Killing in Gold. New York, Doubleday, 1978; London, Gollancz, 1979.
Minor Murders. New York, Doubleday, 1979.
Outcasts. New York, Doubleday, 1981.
Robak's Cross. New York, Doubleday, 1985.

*

Manuscript Collection: Lilly Library, Indiana University, Bloomington.

Joe L. Hensley comments:
  I don't write very much science fiction. Suspense is a more familiar game to me. But I still admire those who do write science fiction and am happy, now and then, when I do also.

*   *   *

Joe L. Hensley's most important stories are connected with Harlan Ellison. Hensley and Ellison are great friends, and Ellison wrote 2000 words of introduction to "Lord Randy, My Son" for *Dangerous Visions*. The story is a masterpiece of understated horror. Ellison's introduction to the story tells how Hensley—then a lawyer—saved Ellison from being court-martialed by the U. S. Army. Ellison provides another introduction to the Hensley and Ellison collaboration "Rod-

ney Parish for Hire. " This chilling account of a youngster who kills other children for profit is a good example of the strengths of both writers. The story features strong characterization, fast-paced writing, and a suspenseful plot.
  Hensley's only SF novel, *The Black Roads*, is a reworking of the setting and themes best developed by Mack Reynolds's *Rollertown* (1976). After a nuclear war, only American technology survives. A society based on roadways evolves as the ultimate realization of humans' love for their automobiles. Duels are fought between cars, and Red Roadmen ride the lanes in their supercharged autos keeping law and order. The mobile society is interesting, but Hensley never elevates his characters above the level of cardboard. The result is a staleness absent from his better short stories and the mystery novels for which he is better known.
  The best of Hensley's short stories, both mystery and SF, are collected in *Final Doors*. Hensley's two collaborations with Harlan Ellison are included as well as his collaboration with Gene DeWeese. The most haunting story in the collection is "Killer Scent" where a sheriff secretly hunts down psychopathic killers that give off a "scent" only he can sense. The sheriff, when finally discovered, explains his hunting of the killers this way: "Sometimes I think they're mutants, the coming race for earth. . . . Maybe they came along to wipe us out, take our places, be the survivors of the cities, mercilessly preying on each other after we're gone. " "Killer Scent" works equally well as a suspense story and an SF story. It is one of the seven original short stories included in this eighteen story collection.
  Hensley's writing is usually crisp, his plotting is tight, and his best work has power and insight. Much of his work reflects his background in law and the criminal justice system.

—George Kelley

HERBERT, Frank (Patrick). American. Born in Tacoma, Washington, 8 October 1920. Attended the University of Washington, Seattle, 1946-47. Married Beverly Ann Stuart in 1946; one daughter and two sons. Reporter and editor for west coast newspapers; lecturer in general and interdisciplinary studies, University of Washington, 1970-72; social and ecological studies consultant, Lincoln Foundation and the countries of Vietnam and Pakistan, 1971. Recipient: Nebula Award, 1965; Hugo Award, 1966; Prix Apollo, 1978. *Died 12 February 1986.*

SCIENCE-FICTION PUBLICATIONS

Novels (series: Dune; Jorj X. McKie)

The Dragon in the Sea. New York, Doubleday, 1956; London, Gollancz, 1960; as *21st Century Sub*, New York, Avon, 1956; as *Under Pressure*, New York, Ballantine, 1974.
The Illustrated Dune. New York, Berkley, 1978; as *The Great Dune Trilogy*, London, Gollancz, 1979.
  Dune. Philadelphia, Chilton, 1965; London, Gollancz, 1966.
  Dune Messiah. New York, Putnam, 1969; London, Gollancz, 1971.
  Children of Dune. New York, Berkley, and London, Gollancz, 1976.
Destination: Void. New York, Berkley, 1966; London, Penguin, 1967.

The Eyes of Heisenberg. New York, Berkley, 1966; London, Sphere, 1968.

The Green Brain. New York, Ace, 1966; London, New English Library, 1973.

The Santaroga Barrier. New York, Berkley, 1968; London, Rapp and Whiting, 1970.

The Heaven Makers. New York, Avon, 1968; London, New English Library, 1970.

Whipping Star (McKie). New York, Putnam, 1970; London, New English Library, 1972; revised edition, New York, Berkley, 1977.

The God Makers. New York, Putnam, and London, New English Library, 1972.

Hellstrom's Hive. New York, Doubleday, 1973; London, New English Library, 1974; as *Project 40,* New York, Bantam, 1973.

The Dosadi Experiment (McKie). New York, Putnam, 1977; London, Gollancz, 1978.

The Jesus Incident, with Bill Ransom. New York, Berkley, and London, Gollancz, 1979.

Direct Descent. New York, Ace, 1980; London, New English Library, 1982.

The God-Emperor of Dune. New York, Putnam, and London, Gollancz, 1981.

The White Plague. New York, Putnam, 1982; London, Gollancz, 1983.

The Lazarus Effect, with Bill Ransom. New York, Putnam, and London, Gollancz, 1983.

Heretics of Dune. New York, Putnam, and London, Gollancz, 1984.

Chapterhouse: Dune. New York, Putnam, and London, Gollancz, 1985.

Short Stories

The Worlds of Frank Herbert. London, New English Library, 1970; New York Ace, 1971.

The Book of Frank Herbert. New York, DAW, 1973; London, Panther, 1977.

The Best of Frank Herbert, edited by Angus Wells. London, Sidgwick and Jackson, 1975.

The Priests of Psi and Other Stories. London, Gollancz, 1980.

OTHER PUBLICATIONS

Novel

Soul Catcher. New York, Putnam, 1972; London, New English Library, 1973.

Other

Threshold: The Blue Angels Experience. New York, Ballantine, 1973.

"The Consentiency—and How It Got That Way," in *Galaxy* (New York), May 1977.

Without Me Your're Nothing: The Essential Guide to Home Computers, with Max Barnard. New York, Simon and Schuster, and London, Gollancz, 1981.

Editor, *New World or No World.* New York, Ace, 1970.

Editor, with others, *Tomorrow, and Tomorrow, and Tomorrow . . . .* New York, Holt Rinehart, 1974.

Editor, *Nebula Winners 15.* New York, Harper, 1981; London, W. H. Allen, 1982.

*

Critical Studies: *Frank Herbert* by Timothy O'Reilly, New York, Ungar, 1981; *The Dune Encyclopedia* edited by Willis E. McNelly, New York, Putnam, and London, Corgi, 1984.

*   *   *

Frank Herbert's science fiction is humanistic in the deepest sense of the word, an amalgam of history, philosophy, psychology, and science basic to Western thought. It depicts man's diversity and his singularity—his nature, limits, potentialities, his inseparable ties to his environment and his fellow creatures, his genetic and cultural heritage that paves the way for his future, his latent mystical and psychic abilities that training and necessity might nurture. Although his characters remain familiar and psychologically true, even amid alien settings, to Herbert humanity is not fixed, but rather is continually evolving both physically and intellectually, adapting to changed or new environments, learning to survive. When he becomes fixed in rigid patterns (religious, political, genetic), he also becomes mechanical, perverted, dehumanized and doomed; but as long as there is change and evolution, even if it is violent or bizarre or seemingly incomprehensible, there is hope; adversity creates strength. His message is that man must learn from his past, avoid absolutist traps, recognize that right might be wrong in changed circumstances, explore his limits to their fullest, but never lose touch with the ecosystems on which he depends and to which he must continually adapt.

In the Dune series, *The God Makers, The Santaroga Barrier, The Heaven Makers, The Dosadi Experiment,* and *The Jesus Incident,* Herbert describes the trials, conflicts, and rites of passage through which man can evolve god-like powers of intellect and foresight, but further suggests the difficulties and dangers such powers necessitate. Frequently these evolutionary leaps are precipitated by contact with special organic chemicals (spice in *Dune,* Jaspers in *Santaroga,* kelp hallucinogens in *Jesus Incident*), by the genetic mix of unique strains (*God Makers, Dune* series, *Heaven Makers*), or by a special mind fuse (*Dosadi, Jesus Incident*). *Soul Catcher,* though not science fiction per se, weaves a tale of mystic Indian powers gained through birth and ritual, and ancient alien gods who heighten the perception of those seeking their frightening aid. In *The Dosadi Experiment* humans and aliens, caged together on a toxic planet, bred for vengeance and cunning, and conditioned by constant war and hunger, learn to overcome all barriers (even a tempokinetic "God Wall") and avenge themselves on their creators. An alien female with features like a praying mantis merges with a human to produce a mind switch and psi power that force the tribunal to recognize Dosadi power and potential. *The God Makers* focuses on an interplanetary troubleshooter assigned to monitor planets and to detect at early stages signs of aggressiveness that might trigger future war; in fulfilling these duties he discovers and develops extrasensory powers that lead him to rites of passage on a special planet of philosophers, rites that make clear his godhood and teach him to use his powers to do what has been his job all along—prevent war and aggression through compromise between potential enemies. But one problem with superpowers and immortality is the possibility of boredom. Paul Atreides of *Dune,* omnipotent ruler of thousands of planets, fakes his own death and retires to private interests, while his descendant, Emperor Leto II, the God Emperor of Dune, longs for an equal mind with whom to share the Machiavellian twists of his long-term plans for his subjects. In *Heaven Makers* an immortal alien movie producer, using Earth as a set for filming full sensory movies of wars, natural disasters, and other horrors to relieve the boredom of his jaded race, breaks regulations and interferes with human cycles, originally to provide more entertaining disasters, but ultimately to produce a blessed loss of immortality. Each of these books examines alien intelligence in order more clearly to define the human.

The most famous of Herbert's books tracing human evolution to a higher state of being is the *Dune* quintet, a series of epic proportions and epic concerns that depicts the logical development, expansion, and diversification of religion and politics on an alien desert world, and traces the rise and fall of a great family. Its scope is incredible—an entire world thoroughly drawn in topography, ecology, history, and culture. The series beings with revolutionary powers and vast changes, and traces the political line as it sinks into stasis, becomes ingrown and perverted, until new blood and unexpected evolutions force the changes necessary for ultimate survival. The first in the series, *Dune*, concerns the growth and maturation of Paul Atreides, the product of generations of controlled breeding and Bene Gesserit training in desert discipline. Once his latent powers are enhanced by an overdose of Arrakis spice, his mind becomes permanently opened to see and shape the future; his time travel involves a succession of choices between alternative futures. Prophet to his infant brother, he leads the desert people on a *jihad* to conquer their planet and a thousand others. *Dune Messiah* traces an imperial intergalactic intrigue by the Bene Gesserit to overthrow the "god" they themselves created (a common Herbert theme), and involves a Tleilaxu face dancer and a ghola recreation of a dead hero. The focus on ecology and political intrigue continues in *Children of Dune*, wherein the House of Atreides learns to survive by appreciating traditions that will preserve the ecology, the giant worms and the melange harvest in the sands, and by learning to live by their instincts and to think and act for themselves. Religious mysticism and desert lore, Byzantine intrigue and complex intellectual discourse infuse these books with a life and interest beyond mere plot. The fourth in the series, *The God-Emperor of Dune*, is an ambitious book, more philosophy than action, an interpretation of the Dune past by an Atreides who has merged with the sandworms of Arrakis to become a seemingly indestructible, towering monster, but who retains all ancestral memories and thought patterns, and who reminisces, theorizes, manipulates, and teaches. Able to predict the future because of his firm sense of history and human nature, he turns tyrannical and intentionally sets in motion antagonisms that eventually erupt in violence. His goal? Growth and change instead of fixed, rigid religious and genetic patterns that would doom his subjects to weakness, degeneration, and perhaps extinction. Knowing that male armies historically turn on their own population, his is an army of women, chosen for their stability and their survival instincts. His "death" is self-chosen and self-sacrificial; at the price of his humanity, he divides into countless sandfish that will eventually become the giant worms of Arrakis. He leaves behind a fear of gods and a distrust of heroes—the ultimate lesson of the *Dune* series: man must depend on himself alone; gods and heroes foster lazy thinking, passivity, and inaction. The final book in the quintet focuses on the ultimate working out of the God Emperor's plans—Arrakis turned desert once more, its people forced to revive old skills and learn new. Therein the Bene Gesserit joins uneasy forces with Tleilaxu face dancers to fight invading forces from the distant colonies and to attempt to manipulate a desert child who rides the sandworms and the ghola, Duncan Idaho, whose quest for identity leads him to cut through the illusions that envelop him and those around him. Herein Herbert once again raises questions about genetic variability and uncertainty, hidden conditioning, hyperconsciousness, bureaucratic fail-

ings, pursuit of absolutes, and self-discovery. *Chapterhouse: Dune* continues the 50,000 year saga of the House of Atreides and their desert planet, leaping 15,000 years into the future from the time of Leto II to see his dream of rebellion fulfilled, his planet returned to desert, ghola Duncan Idaho at work again, and the Bene Gesserit battling the alien Honored Matres.

Herbert's milieu is always firmly grounded in present-day political and social realities rather than in escapist fantasy. His books are carefully researched and highly detailed. For instance, his description of a desert society whose fanatical and feudal codes of behaviour center around their desperate need for water reflects Bedouin survival in the Sahara, *The Dragon in the Sea* so concretely describes deepwater submarine controls that British Naval Intelligence followed his model, and Destination: Void is a comprehensive study in computer theory. In *Dragon in the Sea* a psychologist joins the four-man crew of a deepsea atomic submarine/tug to find a saboteur. The mission, to steal oil from underwater deposits in enemy territory, involves fear and tension from the natural dangers of depth and pressure, heightened by fears of a spy. The book has good suspense and superb technical detail, and defines sanity as the ability to adapt. So too does *Destination: Void*. Therein four scientists with a human cargo of thousands, all unkowingly part of a vast experiment to force invention, are supposedly travelling toward an Eden when they suffer organic computer failure and have to create a conscious mechanical brain to guide them. They react under pressure against impossible odds and succeed in producing a super cybernetic computer that acquires godlike powers of life and death, and that agrees to take them to an Eden if they will contemplate how to "worship" him.

Despite his skillful handling of technical description, Herbert, in the tradition of American romanticism, opposes the mechanistic with the natural and organic to show the superiority of the intuitive biological organism. In "Seed Stock" it is the lowly workman, not the lab dependent scientists, who instinctively adjusts to an alien planet. In *The Eyes of Heisenberg* rebels in a totally genetically engineered world oppose the immortal Optimen and their enemy Cyborgs, and deliberately interfere with gene surgery to bring about a return to mortality and to reproduce an embryo with the forbidden gene combination of intelligence and fertility. In *The Jesus Incident*, a sequel to *Destination: Void*, Herbert opposes clones and "naturals," test tube babies and true births, as he continues the story of the scientists and their crew, deposited on an alien planet (Pandora) filled with incredible horrors (nerve worms and hooded dashers and other predatory alien creatures). Instead of seeking to come to terms with the planet, they and their descendants try to wipe out its population, even the ruling sentient kelp, only to learn that the hope for Pandora rests in accepting the planet and living in harmony with its sentients, sentients that can teach them about themselves and their past, their ship and their gods. The novel exemplifies Herbert's approach: speculation about the nature of deities and of human evolution; technical wonders and genetic horrors; the concept of ancestral memory; natural enlightenment drugs; a poet who ultimately understands man's destiny, and an extraordinary child who will sweep away old orders and initiate new.

Related to Herbert's concern for the natural is an interest in ecology and a respect for rural values, a fear of man tampering with nature coupled with a realization that he must tamper with himself if he is to advance. In "Operation Syndrome" a madman's electronic device to produce mass schizophrenia forces the development of telepathic communications to save world sanity. In "The Gone Dogs" a disease wipes out the canine population as we know it but the species is ultimately preserved in a radical new form.

The Green Brain, Hellstrom's Hive, and *The White Plague* tackle the problem of human interference in nature. Set in Oregon, *Hellstrom's Hive* focuses on a secretive zoological experiment that postulates the obsolescence of present family relations; a government agent, investigating, discovers evolution's terrifying possibilities—a utopian human hive with physical and mental specialization in order to dominate the world. *Green Brain* is another chilling tale that emphasizes man's dependence on insects and the potentiality of chemical sprays backfiring in unexpected ways. In an overpopulated world seeking lebensraum in jungles, an international organization systematically exterminates voracious insects, until they defensively mutate to incredible sizes and types; some mutations involve protective coloration—insect colonies that appear human. A ruling insect "Brain," a corporate intelligence that is the product of this mutation, plans to restore and maintain nature's balance. In *The Santaroga Barrier* Herbert deals with man coping with the imbalance within himself. In a world dominated by false, greedy, superficial advertising men, the Santaroga Valley remains isolated and impervious to modernization. An investigator engaged to a Santaroga psychiatrist seeks answers in "Jaspers," food infused with natural chemicals from Santaroga caves, chemicals that help users see through artifice and falsity to discover true values of community and integrity. But this proves a two-edged blessing, for with awareness comes the after effects of not being able to live outside the valley for very long and a subconscious reflex to destroy any stranger who does not belong. The drug produces enlightenment and well-being at the cost of freedom. *The White Plague,* his most recent and most topical projection, marks a significant change in Herbert's canon. This novel is more heavily cynical and much closer to present realities than past works. It is a double-edged attack on 1) the social and cultural attitudes that produce and encourage the mindless violence of terrorist groups, 2) the potentials unleashed by recombinant DNA research that make it possible for one man only, with the right training, to unleash at any moment a horror on the world that could not be reversed. It focuses on a molecular biologist who, unhinged by the senseless deaths of his wife and children in an IRA bombing, produces an unstoppable sythesized plague that kills only women. The result is chaos, panic, a breakdown of government and social order, and, ironically enough, a return to the self-destructive, adolescent male patterns of might makes right and survival of the most cunning and brutal that terrorism has always fostered.

In conclusion, Herbert mingles Eastern philosphies with Christian myth to produce a humanistic amalgam that recognizes man's potential for godhood as well as for self-destruction. He continually examines evolving intelligence, whether mechanical (*Destination: Void*), insect (*Green Brain*), alien ("The Tactful Saboteur," *Whipping Star, Dosadi Experiment*), or humanoid (*Dune* series, *Jesus Incident*). He warns that man must be adaptable and must stay in tune with his environment if he is to survive. His view is relativistic, his philosophy dialectical; his historical focus cyclical; his characters are complicated, and his plots intriguing.

—Gina Macdonald

HERBERT, James. British. Born in London, 8 April 1943. Educated at St. Aloysius College, and Hornsey College of Art,

both London. Married Eileen O'Donnell in 1968; three daughters. Typographer, John Collings Advertising, London, 1963-66; Art Director, Group Head, and Associate Director, Ayer Barker Hegemann International, London, 1966-67. Agent: Albert Zuckerman, Writers House, 21 West 26th Street, New York, New York 10010, U. S. A. Address: c/o New English Library, 47 Bedford Square, London WC1B 3DP, England.

SCIENCE-FICTION PUBLICATIONS

Novels

The Rats. London, New English Library, 1974; New York, New American Library, 1975.
The Fog. London, New English Library, and New York, New American Library, 1975.
The Survivor. London, New English Library, 1976; New York, New American Library, 1977.
Fluke. London, New English Library, 1977; New York, New American Library, 1978.
The Spear. London, New English Library, 1978; New York, New American Library, 1980.
Lair. London, New English Library, and New York, New American Library, 1979.
The Dark. London, New English Library, and New York, New American Library, 1980.
The Jonah. London, New English Library, and New York, New American Library, 1981.
Shrine. London, New English Library, 1983; New York, New American Library, 1984.
Domain. London, New English Library, 1984; New York, New American Library, 1985.
Moon. London, New English Library, 1985.

*   *   *

James Herbert's novels bear only a peripheral relation to science fiction. His specialty is the contemporary horror thriller, usually set in London or its environs. Most of Herbert's novels are structured around a succession of graphic, violent set pieces which he relates in a vigorous, aggressive style laced with irony and bizarre splashes of black humor. In his best books, massive accumulations of background detail lend credibility to his fantastic plots and scenes.

Among Herbert's non-SF works are old-fashioned man-versus-monster tales (*The Rates* and *Lair*), and anti-fascist thriller about a neo-Nazi cult (*The Spear*), a police procedural tinged with the supernatural (*The Jonah*), an explicitly Catholic story about the aftermath of the miraculous cure of a young deaf mute (*Shrine*), and an atypical novel in which a man is reincarnated as a dog (*Fluke*). His books that contain SF motifs, all of which are disaster novels, are infused with the aesthetics of the horror writer; in them, Herbert constucts from the trappings of science fiction a framework for harrowing tales in which ordinary people confront ferociously evil forces.

The sub-texts of many of Herbert's novels are allied to the Catholic doctrine of original sin, which is explicitly invoked in *Shrine*. Universal guilt, the premise that all men are innately evil, resonates throughout Herbert's oeuvre and is at the heart of two of his best novels, *The Fog* and *The Dark*. The eponymous entity in the latter novel, an energy field of pure malevolence, is the physical incarnation of a man's potential for evil. The Dark feeds indiscriminately, releasing its victims' repressed impulses and turning them into zombie-like killing machines. In *The Dark* Herbert sets up a classic confrontation between light (good) and darkness (evil), translating into physical images a fundamental metaphor of religious myth.

In Herbert's world, horror can erupt in the most mundane of settings, without warning, laying waste people from all walks of life. It is a world forever on the brink of chaos and catastrophe; no one is immune, no place is safe.

This painfully contemporary world view underlies *The Fog*, a gripping ecological nightmare that begins with the accidental release of a bacteriological weapon, a "mutated mycoplasma." Roaming around England embedded in a yellow-tinged fog of pollution, this creature strikes at random, engulfing whole communities and unleashing the inhabitant's destructive, often suicidal impulses. The Fog thus serves as a metaphor for the random, uncontrollable violence that currently infects the Western world.

Man's innate capacity for evil destroys civilization in the post-holocaust thriller *Domain*. Characteristically, Herbert approaches his rather conventional plot—an odyssey by a handful of survivors of a nuclear war through a wasted landscape—as a horror writer, resurrecting the giant, mutant rats of *The Rats* and *Lair*. The image of these loathsome flesh-eating vermin, the spawn of peace-time atomic tests off New Guinea, prowling through the rubble of a London ravaged by nuclear war is ironic and powerful. But *Domain* lacks the connective tissues of (non-horrific) plot and character development that knits together the set pieces in Herbert's earlier novels, and its brutality, heavy-handed irony, and omnipresent theme of universal guilt ultimately evoke numbness rather than terror.

Herbert's SF-tinged horror novels are more akin to the giant monster movies of the 1950's than to the serious science fiction of the 1980's. Nevertheless, he is one of the best practitioners of the disaster thriller, and his central image—of man's best efforts undone by evil from within the human mind—is potent and uncomfortably timely.

—Michael A. Morrison

HERON-ALLEN, Edward. See **BLAYRE, Christopher.**

HERSEY, John (Richard). American. Born in Tientsin, China, 17 June 1914. Educated at Hotchkiss School; Yale University, New Haven, Connecticut, B. A. 1936; Clare College, Cambridge (Mellon Fellow), 1936-37. Married 1) Frances Ann Cannon in 1940 (divorced, 1958), three sons and one daughter; 2) Barbara Day Kaufman in 1958, one daughter. Secretary to Sinclair Lewis, 1937; writer and correspondent, in China, Japan, the South Pacific, the Mediterranean and Russia, for *Time*, New York, 1937-45, *Life*, New York, 1944-46, and *The New Yorker*, 1945-46; Editor and Director of the writers' cooperative magazine '*47*, 1947-48. Fellow of Berkeley College, 1950-65, Master of Pierson College, 1965-70, Lecturer, 1971-76, Visiting Professor, 1976-77, and Adjunct Professor, 1977-84, now emeritus, Yale University: Member of the Yale University Council Committee on the Humanities, 1951-56, and Member, 1959-64, and Chairman, 1964-69, Yale University Council Committee on Yale College. Writer-in-Residence, American Academy in Rome, 1970-71. Member, National Citizens' Commission for the Public Schools, 1954-56; Consultant, Fund for the Advancement of Education, 1954-56;

Chairman, Connecticut Committee for the Gifted, 1954-57; Delegate, White House Conference on Education, 1955; Trustee, National Citizens' Council for the Public Schools, 1956-58; Trustee, National Committee for Support of the Public Schools, 1962-68. Chairman, Connecticut Volunteers for Stevenson, 1952; Member, Stevenson campaign staff, 1956. Member of the Council, 1946-71, and Vice-President, 1949-55, Authors League of America; Delegate, P. E. N. Congress, Tokyo, 1958. Since 1946, Member of the Council, and President, 1975-80, Authors League. Recipient: Pulitzer Prize, 1945; Anisfield-Wolf Award, 1950; Daroff Memorial Award, 1950; Sidney Hillman Foundation Award, 1950; Yale University Howland Medal, 1952; Tuition Plan Award, 1961; Sarah Josepha Hale Award, 1963. LL. D. : Washington and Jefferson College, Washington, Pennsylvania, 1946; University of New Haven, West Haven, Connecticut, 1975; M. A. : Yale University, 1947; L. H. D. : New School for Social Research, New York, 1950; D. H. L. : Dropsie College, 1950; Litt. D. : Wesleyan University, Middletown, Connecticut, 1957; Bridgeport University, Connecticut, 1959; Clarkson College of Technology, Potsdam, New York, 1972; Syracuse University, New York, 1983; Yale University, 1984. Member, 1953, Secretary, 1961-76, and Chancellor, 1981-84, American Academy. Honorary Fellow, Clare College, Cambridge, 1967. Address: 420 Humphrey Street, New Haven, Connecticut 06511, U. S. A.

SCIENCE-FICTION PUBLICATIONS

Novels

The Child Buyer. New York, Knopf, 1960; London, Hamish Hamilton, 1961.
White Lotus. New York, Knopf, and London, Hamish Hamilton, 1965.
My Petition for More Space. New York, Knopf, 1974; London, Hamish Hamilton, 1975.

OTHER PUBLICATIONS

Novels

A Bell for Adano. New York, Knopf, 1944; London, Gollancz, 1945.
The Wall. New York, Knopf, and London, Hamish Hamilton, 1950.
The Marmot Drive. New York, Knopf, and London, Hamish Hamilton, 1953.
A Single Pebble. New York, Knopf, and London, Hamish Hamilton, 1956.
The War Lover. New York, Knopf, and London, Hamish Hamilton, 1959.
Too Far to Walk. New York, Knopf, and London, Hamish Hamilton, 1966.
Under the Eye of the Storm. New York, Knopf, and London, Hamish Hamilton, 1967.
The Conspiracy. New York, Knopf, and London, Hamish Hamilton, 1972.
The Walnut Door. New York, Knopf, 1977; London, Macmillan, 1978.
The Call. New York, Knopf, 1985.

Other

Men on Bataan. New York, Knopf, 1942.

Into the Valley: A Skirmish of the Marines. New York, Knopf, 1943.

Hiroshima. New York, Knopf, and London, Penguin, 1946.

Here to Stay: Studies in Human Tenacity. London, Hamish Hamilton, 1962; New York, Knopf, 1963.

The Algiers Motel Incident . New York, Knopf, and London, Hamish Hamilton, 1968.

Robert Capa, with others. New York, Paragraphic, 1969.

Letter to the Alumni. New York, Knopf, 1970.

The President. New York, Knopf, 1975.

Aspects of the Presidency: Truman and Ford in Office. New Haven, Connecticut, Ticknor and Fields, 1980.

Editor, *Ralph Ellison: A Collection of Critical Essays*. Englewood Cliffs, New Jersey, Prentice Hall, 1973.

Editor, *The Writer's Craft*. New York, Knopf, 1974.

*

Bibliography: *John Hersey and James Agee: A Reference Guide* by Nancy Lyman Huse, Boston, Hall, and London, Prior, 1978.

Manuscript Collection: Yale University Library, New Haven, Connecticut.

Critical Study: *John Hersey* by David Sanders, New York, Twayne, 1967.

*   *   *

John Hersey is probably best known as the author of *Hiroshima* and *A Bell For Adano*. Few people think of him as a science-fiction writer even if they have read *White Lotus, My Petition for More Space*, or *The Child Buyer*. Hersey is seldom mentioned by science-fiction fans, or taught in science-fiction courses. It is more than likely that he does not consider himself a science-fiction writer even though some of his books use concepts generally found only in science fiction. Hersey may be one of those writers who occasionally discovers that he cannot write what he wants to write within the bounds of realistic mainstream fiction; and so he presents his ideas in a world similar to but not the same as this one—a world parallel to this one or this world in a future time. The same impulse lies behind Orwell's *Nineteen Eighty-Four* and Huxley's *Brave New World*. Such a situation seems to arise for Hersey, as it did for Orwell and Huxley, when he wishes to comment on or criticize contemporary society.

White Lotus is a parallel world story, one in which the author attempts to show what the world of today might be like had history taken a different turn; in a parallel world, the British defeated the American colonial rebels or lost to the Spanish Armada in 1588. In *White Lotus* the time is the present, and the Chinese are the dominant power in the world, having conquered America sometime in the first quarter of the 20th century. Except for technological developments, much of what the reader would regard as major historical events—like World War I—has not taken place. Hersey seems to have set up the parallel world of *White Lotus* for one purpose: to show white Americans what it might be like to live as an oppressed racial minority. The plot is the personal narrative of an American girl captured by slavers and sent to China. The bulk of the story is told as a flashback. Although *White Lotus* is obviously based on the whites' mistreatment of blacks in America, there are also echoes in the novel of the mistreatment of other minorities, most notably the Jews, in other countries.

My Petition for More Space is set in the over-populated future which has given rise to such science-fiction stories as Alice Glaser's "The Tunnel Ahead," John Brunner's *Stand On Zanzibar*, and Harry Harrison's *Make Room! Make Room!* In Hersey's book, Sam Poynter is petitioning for more living space. Sam's world is tremendously crowded: waiting in line means being crushed up against the four people around you, making love can be a semi-private act only if you hang curtains around your living space, and getting to do anything (except sit in your living space—Sam's is seven by eleven feet) means waiting in line. Simply put, *My Petition for More Space* is about the dehumanizing effects of over-population; the more people there are, the less privacy and choice there will be.

The Child Buyer, often compared to Orwell's *Nineteen Eighty-Four* and Huxley's *Brave New World*, is also set in the future. The plot involves a research company's attempt to buy an extremely bright child, whom they will make into a human computer; and the novel is set in the form of a transcript of a state government sub-committee hearing on the matter. *The Child Buyer* is a bitter satire on education and politics as the politicians doing the investigating and the educators doing the testifying turn out, for the most part, to be extremely shallow, prejudiced, and ignorant. Hersey's most telling point is that the needs of extremely bright children are often all but completely neglected in today's educational system.

When Hersey writes these parallel world or this-world-in-the-future stories, he is, indeed, writing science fiction; but he only does it when he requires such a background for his commentary. He does not explore the science-fiction aspect for its own sake; he uses it as a vehicle. And the rest of his fiction is solidly mainstream.

—C. W. Sullivan III

HIGH, Philip E(mpson). British. Born in Biggleswade, Bedfordshire, 28 April 1914. Educated at Kent College, Canterbury. Served in the Royal Navy during World War II. Married Pamela Baker in 1950; two daughters. Has worked as a salesman, reporter, and insurance agent; bus driver, East Kent Road Car Company, 1951-79; now retired. Agent: Carnell Literary Agency, Rowneybury Bungalow, near Old Harlow, Essex CM20 2EX. Address: 34 King Street, Canterbury, Kent CT1 2AJ, England.

SCIENCE-FICTION PUBLICATIONS

Novels

The Prodigal Sun. New York, Ace, 1964; London, Compact, 1965.

No Truce with Terra. New York, Ace, 1964.

The Mad Metropolis. New York, Ace, 1966; as *Double Illusion*, London, Dobson, 1970.

These Savage Futurians. New York, Ace, 1967; London, Dobson, 1969.

Twin Planets. New York, Paperback Library, 1967; London, Dobson, 1968.

Reality Forbidden. New York, Ace, 1967; London, Hale, 1968.

Invader on My Back. New York, Ace, and London, Hale, 1968.

The Time Mercenaries. New York, Ace, 1968; London, Dobson, 1969.

Butterfly Planet. London, Dobson, 1971.

Sold—For a Spaceship. London, Hale, 1973.
Come, Hunt an Earthman. London, Hale, 1973.
Speaking of Dinosaurs. London, Hale, 1974.
Fugitive from Time. London, Hale, 1978.
Blindfold from the Stars. London, Dobson, 1979.

Uncollected Short Stories

"The Statics," in *Authentic* (London), September 1955.
"Wrath of the Gods," in *Nebula* (Glasgow), July 1956.
"Schoolroom for the Teacher," in *Authentic* (London), November 1956.
"City at Random," in *Nebula* (Glasgow), December 1956.
"The Collaborator," in *Authentic* (London), December 1956.
"Guess Who," in *New Worlds* (London), February 1957.
"Plague Solution," in *Authentic* (London), February 1957.
"Assassin in Hiding," in *Authentic* (London), April 1957.
"Life Sentence," in *Authentic* (London), May 1957.
"Golden Age," in *New Worlds* (London), June 1957.
"Buried Talent," in *New Worlds* (London), August 1957.
"Time Bomb," in *Nebula* (Glasgow), August 1957.
"Topside," in *Authentic* (London), August 1957.
"The Ancient Enemy," in *Authentic* (London), September 1957.
"Further Outlook," in *Nebula* (Glasgow), September 1957.
"The Meek Shall Inherit," in *Nebula* (Glasgow), January 1958.
"Risk Economy," in *Nebula* (Glasgow), February 1958.
"Shift Case," in *Nebula* (Glasgow), March 1958.
"The Guardian," in *New Worlds* (London), October 1958.
"Lords of Creation," in *Nebula* (Glasgow), December 1958.
"A Race of Madmen," in *Nebula* (Glasgow), January 1959.
"Infection," in *Nebula* (Glasgow), February 1959.
"To See Ourselves," in *Nebula* (Glasgow), May 1959.
"Pseudo Path," in *New Worlds* (London), September 1959.
"Mumbo-Jumbo Man," in *New Worlds* (London), January 1960.
"Pursuit Missile," in *New Worlds* (London), June 1960.
"Fallen Angel," in *Astounding* (New York), June 1961.
"The Martian Hunters," in *New Worlds* (London), November 1961.
"Survival Course," in *New Worlds* (London), December 1961.
"The Psi Squad," in *New Worlds* (London), January 1962.
"Probability Factor," in *New Worlds* (London), March 1962.
"Blind as a Bat," in *Science Fiction Adventures* (London), March 1962.
"Dictator Bait," in *New Worlds* (London), May 1962.
"The Method," in *New Worlds* (London), November 1962.
"Dead End," in *Science Fantasy* (Bournemouth), December 1962.
"The Big Tin God," in *New Worlds* (London), January 1963.
"Point of No Return," in *New Worlds* (London), July 1963.
"Relative Genius," in *New Worlds* (London), December 1963.
"Routine Exercise," in *Lambda 1 and Other Stories,* edited by John Carnell. New York, Berkley, 1964; London, Penguin, 1965.
"Bottomless Pit" (for children), in *Out of This World 5,* edited by Amabel Williams-Ellis and Mably Owen. London, Blackie, 1965.
"Temporary Resident," in *New Worlds* (London), February 1966.
"The Adapters," in *Vision of Tomorrow* (Newcastle upon Tyne), November 1969.
"Psycho-Land," in *Vision of Tomorrow* (Newcastle upon Tyne), January 1970.
"Technical Wizard," in *Vision of Tomorrow* (Newcastle upon Tyne), February 1970.

"Fixed Image," in *Vision of Tomorrow* (Newcastle upon Tyne), May 1970.
"The Jackson Killer," in *The Best of British SF 2,* edited by Mike Ashley. London, Futura, 1977.
"The Time of Light," in *South East Arts Review* (Tunbridge Wells, Kent), Autumn 1980.

*

Philip E. High comments:
I am a story teller. I have never claimed great literary abilities. I am not only a great believer in a happy ending, but am psychologically incapable of writing any other sort. A reader asks to be entertained and stimulated, not depressed. I have a vivid imagination and I try to put what I imagine on paper. But I am also old-fashioned: I like a story to have a beginning, a middle, an end, and, yes, a purpose with all the loose ends tied up.

*   *   *

Philip E. High is one of a number of writers of fast-paced adventure novels who rose to prominence with the publication of several novels by Ace Books. His work is generally written with little effort at stylistic flamboyance, with simple but well-constructed plots. A definite tendency toward bizarre settings has helped to distinguish his novels from those of others working the same vein.

Twin Planets, for example, was set on a kind of alternate Earth, but not one of the slightly altered histories that is usual. Rather, it was a very similar world somewhat advanced in time, whose unpleasant experience with alien invaders had led its inhabitants to attempt to help our own world avoid a similar fate. Similarly, in *Invader on My Back* aliens have conquered the Earth, and divided humanity into a number of disparate types of personalities. The common failing is a mortal dread of peering upward, conditioned into them because of their subjugated status. *Reality Forbidden* is also characterized by odd settings and events, partially rationalized in this case by the existence of dream machines, inventions which lull humanity into a careless conformity. Indeed, one of the common themes in High's novels is a dread of conformity and the value of the individual, usually a super-normal human. The two protagonists of *Twin Planets* are genetic supermen, and the human sent by aliens to help "civilize" Earth in *The Prodigal Sun* is also a super-human, due to his training on that alien world. A man with an incredibly high I. Q. helps lead a revolt against an overly protective computer mind in *The Mad Metropolis,* and another with an extremely high curiosity quotient leads the revolt against the conformity of a post-collapse experimental community in *These Savage Futurians.*

In *The Time Mercenaries,* possibly High's best work, future humanity has bred itself to the ultimate degree of conformity and passivity, and cannot employ violence even in self defense. To protect themselves against alien invaders, these future beings resurrect the crew of a modern submarine, knowing that men of our times would not be constrained by their inflexible ethical code. Alien invasions are rather common in High's novel, usually with no good intentions. The exceptions to this in the early novels are *The Prodigal Sun* and *No Truce with Terra,* in both of which the author makes the point that we are too prejudiced and violent to participate in a truly civilized interstellar civilization. High does not harp on this point, however, being more concerned with his adventure story than with social commentary.

Despite the limited aspirations of his fiction, High has

produced some very durable novels, although recent work like *Speaking of Dinosaurs* and *Come Hunt an Earthman* are practically unknown. High has himself pointed out that a good story should explain itself fully to the reader and not leave him guessing. The straightforward style and relatively simple plots that he utilizes conform to this dictum.

—Don D'Ammassa

HILL, D. W. R. See **TUBB, E. C.**

HILL, John. See **KOONTZ, Dean R.**

HOBAN, Russell (Conwell). American. Born in Lansdale, Pennsylvania, 4 February 1925. Educated at Lansdale High School; Philadelphia Museum School of Industrial Art, 1941-43. Served in the United States Army Infantry, 1943-45: Bronze Star. Married 1) Lillian Aberman (i. e., the illustrator Lillian Hoban) in 1944 (divorced, 1975), one son and three daughters; 2) Gundula Ahl in 1975, three sons. Magazine and advertising agency artist and illustrator; story board artist, Fletcher Smith Film Studio, New York, 1951; television art director, Batten Barton Durstine and Osborn, 1951-56, and J. Walter Thompson, 1956, both in New York; advertising copywriter, Doyle Dane Bernbach, New York, 1965-67. Since 1967, full-time writer; since 1969 has lived in London. Recipient: Christopher Award, for children's book, 1972; Whitbread Award, for children's book, 1974; George G. Stone Center for Children's Books award, 1982 Ditmar Award (Australia), 1982; John W. Campbell Memorial Award, 1982. Agent: David Higham Associates Ltd., 5-8 Lower John Street, London W1R 4HA, England.

SCIENCE-FICTION PUBLICATIONS

Novel

Riddley Walker. London, Cape, and New York, Summit, 1980.

OTHER PUBLICATIONS

Novels

The Lion of Boaz-Jachin and Jachin-Boaz. New York, Stein and Day, and London, Cape, 1973.
Kleinzeit. London, Cape, and New York, Viking Press, 1974.
Turtle Diary. London, Cape, 1975; New York, Random House, 1976.
Pilgermann. London, Cape, and New York, Summit, 1983.

Fiction (for children)

Bedtime for Frances. New York, Harper, 1960; London, Faber, 1963.

Herman the Loser. New York, Harper, 1961; Kingswood, Surrey, World's Work, 1972.
The Song in My Drum. New York, Harper, 1962.
London Men and English Men. New York, Harper, 1962.
Some Snow Said Hello. New York, Harper, 1963.
The Sorely Trying Day. New York, Harper, 1964; Kingswood, Surrey, World's Work, 1965.
A Baby Sister for Frances. New York, Harper, 1964; London, Faber, 1965.
Bread and Jam for Frances. New York, Harper, 1964; London, Faber, 1966.
Nothing to Do. New York, Harper, 1964.
Tom and the Two Handles. New York, Harper, 1965; Kingswood, Surrey, World's Work, 1969.
The Story of Hester Mouse Who Became a Writer. New York, Norton, 1965; Kingswood, Surrey, World's Work, 1969.
What Happened When Jack and Daisy Tried to Fool the Tooth Fairies. New York, Four Winds Press, 1965.
Henry and the Monstrous Din. New York, Harper, 1966; Kingswood, Surrey, World's Work, 1967.
The Little Brute Family. New York, Macmillan, 1966.
Save My Place. New York, Norton, 1967.
Charlie the Tramp. New York, Four Winds Press, 1967.
The Mouse and His Child. New York, Harper, 1967; London, Faber, 1969.
A Birthday for Frances. New York, Harper, 1968; London, Faber, 1970.
The Stone Doll of Sister Brute. New York, Macmillan, and London, Collier Macmillan, 1968.
Harvey's Hideout. New York, Parents' Magazine Press, 1969; London, Cape, 1973.
Best Friends for Frances. New York, Harper, 1969; London, Faber, 1971.
The Mole Family's Christmas. New York, Parents' Magazine Press, 1969; London, Cape, 1973.
Ugly Bird. New York, Macmillan, 1969.
A Bargin for Frances. New York, Harper, 1970; Kingswood, Surrey, World's Work, 1971.
Emmet Otter's Jug-Band Christmas. New York, Parents' Magazine Press, and Kingswood, Surrey, World's Work, 1971.
The Sea-Thing Child. New York, Harper, and London, Gollancz, 1972.
Letitia Rabbit's String Song. New York, Coward McCann, 1973.
How Tom Beat Captain Najork and His Hired Sportsmen. New York, Atheneum, and London, Cape, 1974.
Ten What? A Mystery Counting Book. London, Cape, 1974; New York, Scribner, 1975.
Dinner at Alberta's. New York, Crowell, 1975; London, Cape, 1977.
Crocodile and Pierrot, with Sylvie Selig. London, Cape, 1975; New York, Scribner, 1977.
A Near Thing for Captain Najork. London, Cape, 1975; New York, Atheneum, 1976.
Arthur's New Power. New York, Crowell, 1978; London, Gollancz, 1980.
The Twenty-Elephant Restaurant. New York, Atheneum, 1978; London, Cape, 1980.
The Dancing Tigers. London, Cape, 1979.
La Corona and the Tin Frog. London, Cape, 1979.
Flat Cat. London, Methuen, and New York, Philomel, 1980.
Ace Dragon Ltd. London, Cape, 1980.
The Serpent Tower. London, Methuen, 1981.
The Great Fruit Gum Robbery. London, Methuen, 1981; as *The Great Gumdrop Robbery.* New York, Philomel, 1982.

They Came from Aargh! London, Methuen, and New York, Philomel, 1981.

The Battle of Zormla. London, Methuen, and New York, Philomel, 1982.

The Flight of Bembel Rudzuk. London, Methuen, and New York, Philomel, 1982.

Ponders (Jim Frog, Big John Turkle, Charlie Meadows, Lavinia Bat). London, Walker, and New York, Holt Rinehart, 4 vols., 1983-84.

Verse (for children)

Goodnight. New York, Norton, 1966; Kingswood, Surrey, World's Work, 1969.

The Pedaling Man and Other Poems. New York, Norton, 1968; Kingswood, Surrey, World's Work, 1969.

Egg Thoughts and Other Frances Songs. New York, Harper, 1972; London, Faber, 1973.

Other (for children)

What Does It Do and How Does It Work? Power Shovel, Dump Truck, and Other Heavy Machines. New York, Harper, 1959.

The Atomic Submarine: A Practice Combat Patrol under the Sea. New York, Harper, 1960.

*   *   *

Russell Hoban is a science-fiction writer through only one novel, *Riddley Walker*; but that novel is a masterpiece. Hoban's other novels are essentially fantastic or surreal, even though several are set in contemporary London, where this American writer has lived for many years; none of his books is marketed as SF. He began as a writer of children's books, a career which culminated in the classic fantasy *The Mouse and his Child* (1967); since then he has written five adult novels, from *The Lion of Boaz-Jachin and Jachin-Boaz* (1973) through *Pilgermann* (1983). These are very personal books, and *The Lion* is almost an allegory of Hoban's life-situation. Personal elements are less obtrusive in Hoban's greatest adult novel, *Riddley Walker*.

Riddley Walker achieved instant recognition, and deservedly won the John W. Campbell Award in 1982. It is not remarkable for its overt plot: it is an after-the-bomb story set some 2400 years in the future in Kent, England, and covers a few weeks in which the neo-barbarians rediscover gunpowder and put it to disastrous use. The public issue is the one familiar from Walter Miller's *A Canticle for Leibowitz*: is technical progress disirable? There is another echo of Miller: the misinterpretation of a pre-bomb icon—in Miller a circuit-diagram, in Hoban a painting of the Legend of St Eustace in Canterbury Cathedral. But otherwise the books are very different. Where Miller is panoramic, Hoban concentrates on the mind of young Riddley Walker, a tribal shaman. The inner form of the book is *Bildungsroman*: it is Riddley's struggle to come to terms with the problem of Power. And that is why we get the narrative in Riddley's own voice, a very distinctive voice, which begins like this: "On my naming day when I come 12 I gone front spear and kilt a wyld boar he parbly ben the las wyld pig on the Bundel Downs any how there hadnt ben none for a long time befor him nor I aint looking to see none agen. " And so it goes on. No other SF author has attempted to produce a whole novel in language so altered from present English (not even Anthony Burgess in *A Clockwork Orange*). But the language is justified by its peculiar effects. Its sheer vitality, its combination of demotic crudeness and mystical symbolism could not be achieved otherwise. Indeed, the language is symbolic in some of its minute details

(see my article "Making the Two One", *Extrapolation* 25, Summer 1984).

Above all, the altered spelling facilitates some pregnant puns, *wud* for "wood/would", *hart* for "hart/heart" and *Addom* for "Adam/atom. " These appear in the "Eusa Story," the central myth-scripture of "Inland" (East Kent). In this myth, the "Littl Shynin Man the Addom" is caught by the scientist Eusa in the "Hart of the Wud" and torn apart: which signifies fission both of the atomic nucleus and of Adam, humanity. Both the atom and our selves are split in the heart of our "would," our will to creativity and power. Many characters in the novel are fissioned too, their heads blown off (by the gunpowder bomb) away from their hearts. But Riddley and his followers avoid this fate by giving up physical power in favour of "the 1st knowing" (mystical intuition): they dedicate themselves to spreading wisdom by the current literary medium, the puppet show.

The great merit of *Riddley Walker* resides not so much in its plot or theme, which are common enough, but in its sheer expressiveness. It is full of myths, legends, symbolic figures, such as Punch (violence), Greanvine (mortality), Aunty (the goddess of Death). In this it is most comparable to Vonnegut's *Cat's Cradle* (with its texts of "Bokononism") and to Le Guin's *The Left Hand of Darkness* (with its Handdara legends). It is also an instance of that fairly frequent phenomenon, the writing of a great science-fiction novel by an author on the fringe of the genre.

—David Lake

HOCH, Edward D. Also writes as Irwin Booth; Stephen Dentinger; Ellery Queen. American. Born in Rochester, New York, 22 February 1930. Educated at the University of Rochester, New York, 1947-49. Served in the United States Army, 1950-52. Married Patricia A. McMahon in 1957. Worked at Rochester Public Library, 1949-50, Pocket Books, New York City, 1952-54, and Hutchins Advertising Company, Rochester, 1954-68. Since 1968, self-employed writer. Columnist (as R. E. Porter), *Ellery Queen's Mystery Magazine*, New York. President, 1982, and Member, Board of Directors, Mystery Writers of America. Recipient: Mystery Writers of America Edgar Allan Poe Award, for short story, 1968. Agent: Larry Sterning, 742 Robertson Street, Milwaukee, Wisconsin 53213. Address: 2941 Lake Avenue, Rochester, New York 14612, U. S. A.

SCIENCE-FICTION PUBLICATIONS

Novels (series: Carl Crader and Earl Jazine in all books)

The Transvection Machine. New York, Walker, 1971; London, Hale, 1974.

The Fellowship of the Hand. New York, Walker, 1973; London, Hale, 1976.

The Frankenstein Factory. New York, Warner, 1975; London, Hale, 1976.

Short Stories (series: Simon Ark)

The Judges of Hades and Other Simon Ark Stories. North Hollywood, Leisure, 1971.

City of Brass and Other Simon Ark Stories. North Hollywood, Leisure, 1971.

The Quests of Simon Ark. New York, Mysterious Press, 1984.

Uncollected Short Stories (series: Simon Ark)

"Co-Incidence" (as Irwin Booth), in *Original Science Fiction Stories* (Holyoke, Massachusetts), September 1956.

"Versus," in *Fantastic Universe* (Chicago), June 1957.

"The Last Unicorns," in *Original Science Fiction* (Holyoke, Massachusetts), February 1959.

"The Man Who Knew Everything," in *Shock* (New York), September 1960.

"The Maze and the Monster," in *Magazine of Horror* (New York), August 1963.

"The Wolfram Hunters," in *Rulers of Men*, edited by Hans S. Santesson. New York, Pyramid, 1965.

"The Empty Zoo," in *Magazine of Horror* (New York), November 1965.

"God of the Playback" (as Stephen Dentinger), in *Gods of Tomorrow*, edited by Hans S. Santesson. New York, Award, 1967.

"The Times We Had," in *Famous Science Fiction* (New York), Fall 1967.

"Cassidy's Saucer," in *Flying Saucers in Fact and Fiction*, edited by Hans S. Santesson. New York, Lancer, 1968.

"The Maiden's Sacrifice," in *Famous Science Fiction* (New York), Fall 1968.

"The Future Is Ours" (as Stephen Dentinger) and "Computer Cops," in *Crime Prevention in the 30th Century*, edited by Hans S. Santesson. New York, Walker, 1969.

"Unnatural Act," in *Gentle Invaders*, edited by Hans S. Santesson. New York, Belmont, 1969.

"Zoo," in *Combo 402*, edited by John Cooper. Chicago, Scott Foresman, 1971.

"The Lost Pilgrim" (Ark), in *Mike Shayne Mystery Magazine* (Los Angeles), February 1972.

"Night of the Millennuim," in *The Other Side of Tomorrow*, edited by Roger Elwood. New York, Random House, 1973.

"Funeral in the Fog" (Ark), in *Weird Tales* (Los Angeles), Summer 1973.

"The Boy Who Bought Love," in *Crisis*, edited by Roger Elwood. Nashville, Nelson, 1974.

"The Faceless Thing," in *Fiends and Creatures*, edited by Marvin Kaye. New York, Popular Library, 1975.

"In the Straw," in *Beware More Beasts*, edited by Vic Ghidalia and Roger Elwood. New York, Manor, 1975.

"The Homesick Chicken," in *Isaac Asimov's Science Fiction Magazine* (New York), Spring 1977.

"The Last Paradox," in *100 Great Science Fiction Short-Short Stories*, edited by Isaac Asimov, Martin H. Greenberg, and Joseph D. Olander. New York, Doubleday, and London, Robson, 1978.

"The Man Who Shot the Werewolf" (Ark), in *Ellery Queen's Mystery Magazine* (New York), February 1979.

"The Avenger from Outer Space" (Ark), in *Ellery Queen's Mystery Magazine* (New York), October 1979.

"Exu," in *Voodoo!*, edited by Bill Pronzini. New York, Arbor House, 1980.

"The Weapon Out of the Past" (Ark), in *Ellery Queen's Mystery Magazine* (New York), 7 April 1980.

"The Sorceress of the Sea" (Ark), in *Ellery Queen's Mystery Magazine* (New York), 18 August 1980.

"The Daltonic Fireman," in *Mike Shayne Mystery Magazine* (Los Angeles), October 1980.

"The Vultures of Malabar" (Ark), in *Alfred Hitchcock's Mystery Magazine* (New York), 1 October 1980.

"Who Rides With Santa Anna?," in *Ghosts*, edited by Marvin and Saralee Kaye. New York, Doubleday, 1981.

"The Dying Marabout" (Ark), in *Alfred Hitchcock's Mystery Magazine* (New York), 4 February 1981.

"Seven Billion Day," in *Alfred Hitchcock's Mystery Magazine* (New York), 19 August 1981.

"The House of a Hundred Birds" (Ark), in *Ellery Queen's Mystery Magazine* (New York), 24 February 1982.

"Ark in the Desert," in *Alfred Hitchcock's Mystery Magazine* (New York), December 1984.

"The Spy on the Seaway" (Ark), in *Espionage* (Teaneck, New Jersey), February 1985.

OTHER PUBLICATIONS

Novels

The Shattered Raven. New York, Lancer, 1969; London, Hale, 1970.

The Blue Movie Murders (as Ellery Queen). New York, Lancer, 1972; London, Gollancz, 1973.

Short Stories

The Spy and the Thief. New York, Davis, 1971.

The Thefts of Nick Velvet. Yonkers, New York, Mysterious Press, 1978.

Leopold's Way. Carbondale, Illinois, Southern Illinois University Press, 1985.

Other

The Monkey's Clue, and The Stolen Sapphire (for children). New York, Grosset and Dunlap, 1978.

Editor, *Dear Dead Days*. New York, Walker, 1972; London, Gollancz, 1974.

Editor, *Best Detective Stories of the Year*. New York, Dutton, 6 vols., 1976-81.

Editor, *All But Impossible! An Anthology of Locked Room and Impossible Crime Stories*. New Haven, Connecticut, Ticknor and Fields, 1981; London, Hale, 1983.

Editor, *The Year's Best Mystery and Suspense Stories*. New York, Walker, and London, Severn House, 4vols., 1982-85.

*

Bibliography: "Edward D. Hoch: A Checklist" by William J. Clark, Edward D. Hoch, and Francis M. Nevins, Jr., in *Armchair Detective* (White Bear Lake, Minnesota), February 1976; revised edition, by Nevins and Hoch, privately printed, 1979.

Edward D. Hoch comments:

I have always viewed my science fiction and fantasy as offshoots of my mystery writing, and nearly all my science fiction contains elements of mystery and detection.

*   *   *

Edward D. Hoch is one of the few writers who have been able to blend successfully the detective story with science fiction (others include Isaac Asimov, Anthony Boucher, Fredric Brown, Randall Garrett, and Ron Goulart). Of his three novels and more than 60 short stories which qualify as science fiction or fantasy, nearly all have criminous elements.

Each of Hoch's three SF novels is a classic mystery set in the 21st century and features the "Computer Cops," a team of government investigators led by Carl Crader and Earl Jazine. The first, *The Transvection Machine*, is perhaps the best—a strong blending of baffling mystery, inventive science fiction, and social commentary. Almost as good is *The Fellowship of the Hand* which continues Crader's and Jazine's attempts to combat an organization known as HAND (Humans Against Neuter Domination), pledged to destroy all machines capable of dominating man. *The Frankenstein Factory*, which deals with a futuristic variation on the Frankenstein theme involving cryonics, is less successful in that it seem more an attenuated novelette than a fully realized novel.

Hoch's true forte, however, is the short story. He has published more than 500 in the past quarter-century and is widely acclaimed as the premier writer of short mystery fiction. Among the more memorable of his science-fiction detective tales are "The Wolfram Hunters" and "Computer Cops"; noncriminous SF include "Zoo," "The Faceless Thing," and "The Last Paradox," But it is the 60 novelette-length adventures about Simon Ark, a man who claims to be a 2000-year-old Copt priest, which are perhaps the most well-known of all Hoch's fictional creations. These are primarily tales of detection, but each deals with such fantastic elements as werewolves, witches, religious cults, scientific experiments, and Fortean phenomena. The best of the early Simon Ark stories (from the 1950's) appear in *City of Brass* and *The Judges of Hades*. A new series of Ark stories began in *Ellery Queen's Mystery Magazine* in 1978.

The chief attribute of Hoch's work is invariably intricate and ingenious plotting; few rival him in his ability to summon a seemingly endless and wide-reaching flows of ideas. If plot receives more emphasis than character development in some of his prose (notable exceptions are "The Wolfram Hunters" and "The Faceless Thing"), this in no way diminishes its high entertainment value. The richness of idea and incident more than compensates.

—Bill Pronzini

HODDER-WILLIAMS, (John) Christopher (Glazebrook). Also writes as James Brogan. British. Born in London, in 1926. Educated at Eton College. Served in the Royal Signals, in the Middle East, 1944-48: Lieutenant. Worked in Africa after World War II; worked in England for film, television, and recording companies; also a composer. Address: c/o Mithras Publishing, 52 Musard Street, London W. 6, England.

SCIENCE-FICTION PUBLICATIONS

Novels

Chain Reaction. London, Hodder and Stoughton, and New York, Doubleday, 1959.
The Main Experiment. London, Hodder and Stoughton, 1964; New York, Putnam, 1965.
The Egg-Shaped Thing. London, Hodder and Stoughton, and New York, Putnam, 1967.
Fistful of Digits. London, Hodder and Stoughton, 1968.
98. 4. London, Hodder and Stoughton, 1969.
Panic O'Clock. St. Ives, Cornwall, United Writers, 1973.

The Prayer Machine. London, Weidenfeld and Nicolson, 1976; New York, St. Martin's Press, 1977.
The Silent Voice. London, Weidenfeld and Nicolson, 1977.
The Thinktank That Leaked. St. Ives, Cornwall, United Writers, 1979.
The Chromosome Game. London, Mithras, 1984.

OTHER PUBLICATIONS

Novels

The Cummings Report (as James Brogan). London, Hodder and Stoughton, 1958.
Final Approach. London, Hodder and Stoughton, and New York, Doubleday, 1960.
Turbulence. London, Hodder and Stoughton, 1961.
The Higher They Fly. London, Hodder and Stoughton, 1963; New York, Putnam, 1964.

Plays

Radio Play: *Final Approach*, from his own novel, 1967.

Television Plays: *The Ship That Couldn't Stop*, 1961; *The Hot White Coal*, 1963; *The Higher They Fly*, from his own novel, 1963; *A Voice in the Sky*, 1964.

*   *   *

Christopher Hodder-Williams is not widely known in America despite his continuing popularity in Great Britain, possibly because his brand of science fiction places much more emphasis on the dangers of undisciplined research and experimentation and less on the wonders of technology. Indeed, one criticism that might be made is that he has overworked the Frankenstein theme in his novels.

His earliest work that might be called science fiction was *Chain Reaction*, a novel that dealt with the insidious threat of atomic radiation let loose upon an unsuspecting world. He moved firmly into the genre with *The Main Experiment*, which follows an unorthodox young scientist as he takes a new position with an atomic research unit. It is not long before the protagonist discovers that the project director has been taking some liberties with his progress reports and that the project itself is out of control. Even more frightening is the fact that the by-product of the research is a force which alters personalities and perceptions, strikes out beyond the boundaries of the experimental station, and might well pose a danger to the world at large.

The Egg-Shaped Thing repeated this theme, but with more complexity. When an entrepreneur is driven out of business, it almost costs him his sanity as well. Subsequently, he cannot be entirely certain of those things which he thinks he is experiencing. How, for example, does it happen that he can remember things which have not yet happened? Why are his rivals exacting revenge for acts which he has not yet committed? Once again the focus of our attention is a secretive research establishment experimenting with the atom, but this time the experiment itself may be conscious, and exerting itself to control the actions of others.

In *Fistful of Digits* technology is still the villain, or at least unbridled technology, but Hodder-Williams abandons the menace of atomic research for the equally promising field of computerization. A group of private businessmen have created an elaborate, extensive network of computers under the general name Servex which is secretly extending their ability to manipulate others. Their extrapolation warns of potential problems if the protagonist continues to associate with a particular young woman involved with their project, so they take steps to abrogate the relationship. The result, naturally, is eventually to reveal to him that people are becoming peripherals to the computer banks, programmed themselves for pecific functions and actions.

98.4 involves an unsuccessful security agent who is clandestinely hired to discover just what is happening within a select group of scientists at yet another research station. Computers figure prominently in the arsenal of the villains once more. A contagious, life-threatening wave of panic rocks all of Great Britain in *Panic O'Clock*. This time the central character is a young wife who flees with her child following a cryptic but frightening phone call from her husband. She must then make her way across the country to a secret rendezvous, avoiding both the authorities and the innocent victims of the induced panic.

All of Hodder-Williams's fiction is very strong in characterization, development of suspense, and logical plot construction. His anti-technological bent may well be annoying to some readers, as it is not currently fashionable to fear scientific advancement. They are, however, excellent thrillers with science-fiction content and are probably much more commercially successful as such.

—Don D'Ammassa

HODGSON, William Hope. British. Born in Blackmore End, Essex, 15 November 1877. Went to sea as a cabin boy, 1891: became 3rd mate in the Mercantile Marine. Married Betty Farnworth in 1911. Manager, Hodgson's School of Physical Culture, Blackburn, Lancashire, 1899-1904; free-lance writer after 1905. Joined University of London Officer Training Corps, 1914; commissioned Lieutenant in the Royal Field Artillery, 1915; left service because of injury, 1916; recommissioned, 1917, and died at Ypres. Recipient: Royal Humane Society Medal, 1899. *Died 19 April 1918.*

SCIENCE-FICTION PUBLICATIONS

Novels

The Boats of the "Glen Carrig." London, Chapman and Hall, 1907; New York, Ballantine, 1971.
The House on the Borderland. London, Chapman and Hall, 1908.
The Ghost Pirates. London, Stanley Paul, 1909; Westport, Connecticut, Hyperion Press, 1976.
The Night Land. London, Nash, 1912; revised edition, as *The Dream of X,* in *Poems and The Dream of X,* 1912.
The House on the Borderland and Other Novels. Sauk City, Wisconsin, Arkham House, 1946.

Short Stories

Deep Waters. Sauk City, Wisconsin, Arkham House, 1967.
Out of the Storm: Uncollected Fantasies, edited by Sam Moskowitz. West Kingston, Rhode Island, Grant, 1975.
William Hope Hodgson (selected stories), edited by Peter Tremayne. London, Corgi, 1977.

OTHER PUBLICATIONS

Short Stories

The Ghost Pirates, A Chaunty, and Another Story. New York, Reynolds, 1909.
Carnacki, The Ghost Finder, and a Poem. New York, Reynolds, 1910.
Carnacki, The Ghost Finder (collection). London, Nash, 1913; augmented edition, Sauk City, Wisconsin, Mycroft and Moran, 1947.
Men of the Deep Waters. London, Nash, 1914.
The Luck of the Strong. London, Nash, 1916.
Captain Gault, Being the Exceedingly Private Log of a Sea-Captain. London, Nash, 1917; New York, McBride, 1918.

Verse

Poems and The Dream of X. London, Watt, and New York, Paget, 1912.
Cargunka and Poems and Anecdotes. London, Watt, and New York, Paget, 1914.
The Calling of the Sea. London, Selwyn and Blount, 1920.
The Voice of the Ocean. London, Selwyn and Blount, 1921.
Poems of the Sea. London, Ferret Fantasy, 1977.

*

Bibliography: by A. L. Searles, in *The House on the Borderland and Other Novels,* Sauk City, Wisconsin, Arkham House, 1946.

Critical Studies: *William Hope Hodgson: A Centenary Tribute 1877-1977,* Dagenham, Essex, British Fantasy Society, 1977.

*   *   *

One of the most remarkable visionary fantasy authors of the first part of this century, William Hope Hodgson is remembered today chiefly as the author of two classic fantasies, *The House on the Borderland* and *The Night Land,* and for a number of often-anthologized short horror stories that are models of craft and atmosphere. Though his writing did not become widely known among fantasy and science-fiction readers until the 1940's, when his stories began to be reprinted in America pulp magazines and his novels were reissued, Hodgson's reputation has grown steadily since then, despite the difficulty involved in categorizing his works.

Hodgson's novels are characterized by episodic structure, multiple narrators or "frame" stories, vivid descriptions, images of decay and desolation, and—perhaps most important—an atmosphere of brooding horror that Hodgson manages to sustain and build despite his often digressive plots. His first novel, *The Boats of the "Glen Carrig,"* seems to owe a stylistic debt to Defoe, and is even cast in the form of an 18th-century manuscript. This tale of shipwreck survivors who encounter islands of fungi, weed-bound derelicts, and hideous intelligent slugs quickly helped to establish Hodgson's reputation as a leading writer of sea horror stories, a reputation which was furthered by his short fiction and by another novel, *The Ghost Pirates,* which approached science fiction with its speculation that the ghosts may be inhabitants of an alternate reality, "perhaps something to do with magnetic stresses." Hodgson's most widely read novel, *The House on the Borderland,* did not take place at sea, although Hodgson regarded it as part of a thematic trilogy with *The Boats of the "Glen Carrig"* and *The Ghost Pirates.* Cast in the form of a manuscript discovered in the ruins of an isolated house in the west of Ireland, the novel would vary little from the simple horror formulae of Hodgson's earlier novels were it not for a powerful central passage in which the narrator embarks on a long psychic journey in time and space, witnessing the death of earth, sun, and solar system and encountering hideous creatures on a world strangely parallel to this one. *The Night Land*, Hodgson's last novel and by far his longest, again employs an archaic style, and a visionary narrator but is otherwise a considerable departure from these earlier works. One of the longest and strangest fantastic romances of this century, *The Night Land* is the vision of a 16th-century man into the earth of millions of years in the future, when the "last millions" of humanity have retreated after the sun's death into a huge pyramid, almost eight miles high and comprising 1320 floors, called the "Last Redoubt. " Surrounding the Redoubt are monstrous creatures of various kinds, waiting for humanity's power supply to run out so that they can move in. The story is a simple quest of a lover for his beloved in this bizarre context (a story which echoes the frame narrative that introduces the vision), ending with an affirmation of the saving power of love in even the most hopeless of circumstances.

Hodgson's short fiction includes a number of stories that have become horror classics, most notably "The Voice in the Night," concerning a man and woman overcome by fungus on a mysterious island, and "The Derelict," about a ship so overgrown with fungus that it becomes a living organism. These and other tales reveal Hodgson's obsessive repulsion to parasitical life and stagnation, and his use of the sea as an arena for unknown horrors in a manner not unlike that in which later writers would come to use outer space. Of his non-sea stories, the most notable are a series about an occult detective names Carnacki. Written with a humor unusual for Hodgson, these stories range from the clever to the ridiculous, with Carnacki sometimes explaining ingenious hoaxes and sometimes finding himself face to face with the most unlikely supernatural manifestations (such as a room that puckers up and whistles). Though not major works, these stories reveal a versatility that makes one wonder what Hodgson might have produced had he not been killed in the First World War.

—Gary K. Wolfe

HOFFMAN, Lee. Also writes as Georgia York. American. Born in Chicago, Illinois, 14 August 1932. Educated at Armstrong Junior College, Savannah, Georgia, A. A. 1951. Married Larry T. Shaw (divorced). Printer's devil, Savannah Vocational School; staff member, Hoffman Radio-TV Service; Assistant Editor, *Infinity*, 1956-58, and *Science Fiction Adventures*, 1956-58, both New York; staff member, MD Publications; claim handler, Hoffman Motors; in printing production, Arrow Press, Allied Typographers, and George Morris Press. Since 1965, free-lance writer. Recipient: Western Writers of America Spur Award, 1968. Agent: Henry Morrison Inc., 320 McLain Street, Bedford Hills, New York 10705. Address: 350 N. W. Harbor Boulevard, Port Charlotte, Florida 33952, U. S. A.

SCIENCE-FICTION PUBLICATIONS

Novels

Telepower. New York, Belmont, 1967.

The Caves of Karst. New York, Ballantine, 1969; London, Dobson, 1970.
Always the Blackknight. New York, Avon, 1970.
Change Song. New York, Doubleday, 1972.

Short Stories

In and Out of the Quandary, edited by Charles J. Hitchcock. Cambridge, Massachusetts, NESFA Press, 1982.

Uncollected Short Story

"Lost in the Marigolds," with Robert E. Toomey, Jr., in *Orbit 9*, edited by Damon Knight. New York, Putnam, 1971.

OTHER PUBLICATIONS

Novels

Gunfight at Laramie. New York, Ace, 1966; London, Gold Lion, 1975.
The Legend of Blackjack Sam. New York, Ace, 1966.
Bred to Kill. New York, Ballantine, 1967.
The Valdez Horses. New York, Doubleday, 1967; London, Tandem, 1972.
Dead Man's Gold. New York, Ace, 1968.
The Yarborough Brand. New York, Avon, 1968; London, Hale, 1981.
Wild Riders. New York, New American Library, 1969; London, Hale, 1979.
Loco. New York, Doubleday, 1969; London, Tandem, 1973.
Return to Broken Crossing. New York, Ace, 1969; London, Hale, 1982.
West of Cheyenne. New York, Doubleday, 1969; London, Tandem, 1973.
Wiley's Move. New York, Dell, 1975; London, Hale, 1980.
The Truth about the Cannonball Kid. New York, Dell, 1975; London, Hale, 1980.
Fox. New York, Doubleday, 1976; London, Hale, 1980.
Nothing But a Drifter. New York, Doubleday, 1976; London, Hale, 1980.
Trouble Valley. New York, Ballantine, 1976; London, Hale, 1980.
Sheriff of Jack Hollow. New York, Dell, 1977; London, Hale, 1979.
The Land Killer. New York, Doubleday, 1978; London, Hale, 1981.
Savage Key (as Georgia York). New York, Fawcett, 1979; London, Coronet, 1983.

* * *

The science-fiction novels of Lee Hoffman are novels of human feelings, not ones of hard science. The SF concepts are well thought out and are integral to the storylines, but they are clearly secondary to the characters. Unlike some SF where the idea is the star and the emphasis is placed on the nuts and bolts or on the astronomical bodies while the people seem stamped out of cookie dough, Hoffman's fiction is populated with characters who live and breathe and grow and develop. The songs they sing are ones for men and women, not for pulsars and machines.

Perhaps the clearest example of her ability to make her characters very human is the protagonist in *The Caves of Karst*, a man who has undergone an operation to enable him to breathe underwater. Though this allows him to work the underwater mines more effectively, he did not choose to undergo the operation solely for financial considerations; as the novel unfolds it becomes clear that the choice was made (on some level of consciousness) to protect his ego from an unhappy love affair. People on Karst, as on Earth, often shun those who differ physically from the norm and those who *choose* to have such differences are frequently confronted with outright hatred. His adjustment to his condition, to women in general and his girlfriend in particular, and to himself during a time of crisis is the heart of the book.

There are three primary themes that run through Hoffman's work. 1) Individuality and the freedom of choice that comes with it are extremely important but must be tempered with the realization that individuals need to work together, to interact, in order to achieve certain goals. 2) It is both wrong and *dangerous* to try to control something or someone without consent. 3) Things may not be the way you originally thought they were or the way you have been told they were. Each theme is expressed with varying degrees of emphasis, depending on the novel, but all three are interrelated in her science fiction.

Hoffman's style is lean and direct. Each novel opens with action, tossing the reader into the midst of unfolding events: *Telepower* begins with an attack on post-atomic war Cleveland by an army of rats; *The Caves of Karst* starts with an underwater "gunfight" in a mine; *Always the Blackknight* opens with a battle between knights on robot horses; and, although the first chapter of *Change Song* is used to establish a sense of wrongness and an atmosphere of danger, the second chapter quickly produces a fight between men with magical powers. Hoffman uses her writing skills to capture the reader immediately, and all of her work has been set on earth-like planets so that the reader can rapidly believe in the setting. Obviously Hoffman strives to entertain the reader while stating her messages.

To enrich her science fiction, she occasionally employs the techniques of other genres to give a more diverse flavor. In *Telepower* Hoffman forges a bond between the gruesome qualities of the horror novels and the telepathic power so common in science fiction. Drawing upon her own experience as a writer of westerns, she gives *The Caves of Karst* an Old West setting (or what the Old West would have been like if the prospectors had gills) while at the same time using all the plot-twists of a mystery novel. *Always the Blackknight* has the flavor of the tales of knighthood, as the title might indicate, and *Change Song* has most of the elements of a quest-fantasy. In fact *Change Song* is really more fantasy than science fiction, much in the same way that Theodore Sturgeon's *More Than Human* is, although on the world where *Change Song* takes place control of the elements and the power to cast spells are like our science in that one is trained in these fields. By being willing to take the risks of mixing elements of other genres with science fiction, Lee Hoffman has given her work an added dimension.

—Terry Hughes

HOGAN, James P(atrick). British. Born in London, 27 June 1941. Educated at the Royal Aircraft Establishment Technical College, Farnborough, Berkshire, 1957-61; Reading and Enfield colleges, 1961-65. Married 1) Iris Crossley in 1961 (divorced), three daughters; 2) Lyn Dockerty in 1976 (divorced); 3) Jacklyn Price in 1982; three sons. Engineer, Solarton Electronics, Farnborough, 1961-62, Racal Electronics, Bracknell, Berkshire, 1962-64; sales engineer, 1964-66, and sales manager, 1966-68, ITT, Harlow, Hertfordshire; computer sales executive, Honeywell, London, 1968-70, and Leeds, 1970-72; insurance salesman, Sun Life Canada, Leeds, 1972-74; computer salesman, 1974-77, and sales training consultant in Maynard, Massachusetts, 1977-79, Digital Equipment Corporation, Leeds. Since 1979, full-time writer. Agent: Eleanor Wood, 432 Park Avenue South, New York, New York 10016. Address: P. O. Box 655, Sonora, California 95370, U. S. A.

SCIENCE-FICTION PUBLICATIONS

Novels (series: Ganymean)

The Minerva Experiment (Ganymean). New York, Ballantine, 1981.
  1. *Inherit the Stars*. New York, Ballantine, 1977.
  2. *The Gentle Giants of Ganymede*. New York, Ballantine, 1978.
  3. *Giants' Star*. New York, Ballantine, 1981.
The Genesis Machine. New York, Ballantine, 1978.
The Two Faces of Tomorrow. New York, Ballantine, 1979.
Thrice upon a Time. New York, Ballantine, 1980.
Voyage from Yesteryear. New York, Ballantine, 1982.
Code of the Lifemaker. New York, Ballantine, 1983.
The Proteus Operation. New York, Bantam, 1985.

Uncollected Short Stories

"Assassin," in *Stellar 4*, edited by Judy-Lynn del Rey. New York, Ballantine, 1978.
"Silver Shoes for a Princess," in *Destinies* (New York), October 1979.
"Sword of Damocles," in *Stellar 5*, edited by Judy-Lynn del Rey. New York, Ballantine, 1980.
"Neander-Tale," in *Fantasy and Science Fiction* (New York), December 1980.
"Till Death Us Do Part," in *Stellar 6*, edited by Judy-Lynn del Rey. New York, Ballatine, 1981.
"Making Light" and "Identity Crisis," in *Stellar 7*, edited by Judy-Lynn del Rey. New York, Ballantine, 1981.

OTHER PUBLICATIONS

Other

"Think of a Number," in *Galileo* (Boston), July 1978.

*

James P. Hogan comments:
  Despite the cynicism that seems fashionable in some social circles, I continue to feel positive about our species and its future, and our ability to comprehend and solve our problems. I'm optimistic about science and technology and an anti-Malthusian. I don't believe that we are about to blow ourselves into oblivion, starve ourselves into extinction, poison the planet, degenerate into Nazis, or disappear under our own garbage. On the contrary, I believe in the power of reason and human creativity to continue building better tomorrows. There are the things I try to project in what I write.

*   *   *

It would be easy—too easy—to dismiss the fictions of James P. Hogan as mere right-wing libertarian tracts in the guise of novels. For the objective narrative voice that tells his stories finds it hard to resist divagating into splenetic attacks on various institutions and projects associated with progressive social, political, and economic movements—broadly speaking, the left and its countercultures. For example, early in *Code of the Lifemaker*, an otherwise intriguing dramatization of humanity's encounter with an alien culture of non-organic entities evolved from an abandoned automated factory on Titan, a fraudulent psychic and his henchmen are traveling through Manhattan en route to a TV appearance. While they are caught in a traffic jam, the narrator observes:

> On one side the streets were blacked out for seven blocks beneath the immense, ugly canopy of aluminum panels and steel-lattice supports that made up the ill-fated Lower West Side Solar Power Demonstration Project, which was supposed to have proved the feasibility of supplying city electricity from solar. Before the harebrained scheme was abandoned, it had cost the city $200 million to teach politicians what power engineers had known all along. But it kept the streets dry in rainy weather and a thriving antique, art, and flea market had come into being in the covered arcades created below.

That this passage is a gratuitous slap at advocates of renewable energy is suggested by the failure of the topic or the scenery to appear again or to have any discernible relation to any event or character in the novel, unless one counts some grumbling heard on a couple of occasions about how American fusion energy research was stopped by people who believed that "pyramids" would provide unlimited power—in itself a connection suggesting that solar energy is in the same league as pyramid-power. As one reads through Hogan's novels, one is struck by the amount of time the narrator and (on occasion) the most scientifically respectable characters spend railing at labor unions, the mass media, popular culture, environmental activists insofar as they question the chemical and nuclear-power industries, *The Limits to Growth* thesis, and any portion of education devoted to topics other than science and engineering. One suspects that Hogan is trying very hard to be a reliable propagandist—on the order of Jerry Pournelle—for what President Eisenhower characterized as the "military-industrial complex."

Fortunately for his readers, however, Hogan's SF has an imaginative power that both transcends and undermines his self-imposed role as apologist for technical society. The propaganda, after all, is the product of a faith—a faith in reason, to be sure, but nonetheless a faith. Hogan's fictions invite the reader to share that faith, a conviction that the trained human mind, especially working with other trained human minds in the scientific team, can conquer the universe both analytically and technically. In the plots of the narratives, it is not environmentalists or union leaders who come close to blocking the efforts of reasonable men (for Hogan's strong characters are almost always male), but rather ignorant governmental or corporate bureaucrats, behind whom lurk power-hungry and greedy executives who wish to use science for nefarious ends. Thus an interesting inconsistency appears: on the level of thematized narration and dialogue, we are *told* that the enemies of reason are (for example) the welfare state and environmental activists, while at the level of plot we are *shown* that the biggest enemy is in fact the "military-industrial complex." The inconsistency is not fatal: it rather adds to the interest of reading a Hogan fiction.

The typical Hogan protagonist is a strong-willed competent scientific investigator, or an individual who struggles against an incompetent bureaucracy and malevolent leaders, or is both. He is more willing than those around him to entertain unorthodox ideas—as long as those ideas are not the product of superstition (like "psi-powers") or ignorance (meaning any questioning of scientific or technical progress). In *The Genesis Machine* (a fictionalization of Herman Kahn's concept of "doomsday machine"), Brad Clifford is not simply a brilliant mathematical physicist who has worked out the equations of the dimensions beyond ordinary spacetime; he is also a romantic hero who creates a device which effectively disarms the nuclear-war making capabilities of both sides in a 21st-century world on the verge of destroying itself in an ultimate holocaust. In *Code of the Lifemaker*, the cynical "psychic" Karl Zambendorf (redeemed by the fact that he does not actually believe in his "powers") leads a rebellion that aborts the plans of a cabal of industrialists and politicians to impose a neo-colonial slavery upon the evolved robotic civilization discovered on Titan. In *Voyage from Yesteryear*, which as a utopian fiction has a society rather than an individual for its hero, the struggle is between the Chironians, descendants of an old Earth colony in the Alpha Centauri system, and a more recent shipload of pilgrims (their vessel is called the *Mayflower II*) whose leaders wish to impose a centralized political economy on the anarchist society that has developed over the years. Since the Chironian society is based on economic abundance owed to a science and technology unfettered by governmental and corporate priorities, they are committed to absolute personal freedom. Their social order is so attractive to many of the new arrivals, however, that an attempt to reduce them by force fails, and the power-brokers of the old way are forced to submit to the new.

Hogan's *magnum opus, The Minerva Experiment* trilogy, is marred when its third part, *Giants' Star*, descends into a space operatic war between good guy aliens allied with the Earth and the "Evil Empire" that seeks to enslave them. Its first two parts (*Inherit the Stars* and *The Gentle Giants of Ganymede*), however, constitute a fine SF detective story centered on Victor Hunt, an almost archetypal Hogan hero who heads up the team of United Nations Space Agency scientists that unravels the mystery of a humanoid corpse found on the moon. As Hunt and his team probe more deeply into the origins of the "Lunarians," they reconstruct the story of an ancient alien civilization and its colonies in the solar system, a process which enables them to advance a daring new hypothesis about the origins of mankind. Aside from promoting some of Hogan's favorite themes, such as the never-ending struggles between reason and superstition, and between individual freedom and the security state, *The Minerva Experiment* illustrates another important feature of Hogan's SF: his portrayal of the methods of scientific investigation. Since this particular investigation is an interdisciplinary one, the investigators must constantly share their knowledge as well as formulate, test, and discard successive hypotheses. Hogan also conveys what might be called the human dimension of science—the rivalries between fields, the interpersonal conflicts, and the exhilaration that comes with the discovery of a new piece of knowledge that can be fitted into one's previous investigations. In the bargain, Hogan seamlessly integrates present-day "normal" science with the speculative, fictional science of his near-future setting. This promotes an important theme that runs throughout his SF: the unity and the smooth growth curve of Western science and technology, with the spirit of reason only occasionally disrupted by social backwardness and the apparent discontinuities associated with paradigm shifts in science itself.

For Hogan, in spite of his tendency to tell us so often that ignorance and superstition are ascendant and threaten the abundance and freedom that human reason can create, is after all a romantic optimist: he shows us in his fictions that reason will ultimately prevail, and that the darkness of superstition and ignorance can provide only temporary setbacks to the spirit of enlightenment. In this he is a child not only of the Renaissance and Enlightenment publicists of science and reason, but also of the writers of the "Golden Age" of American SF. British-born, he has appropriately settled in California, that most compelling creation of the American mythos of "can-do" science and technology.

—John P. Brennan

HOLDSTOCK, Robert. Also writes as Robert Black; Chris Carlsen; Robert Faulcon. British. Born in Hythe, Kent, 2 August 1948. Educated at University College of North Wales, Bangor, 1967-70, B. Sc. (honours) in applied zoology 1970; London School of Hygiene and Tropical Medicine, 1970-71, M. Sc. in medical zoology 1971. Research Student, Medical Research Council, London, 1971-74. Agent: A. P. Watt Ltd., 26-28 Bedford Row, London WC1R 4HL. Address: 54 Raleigh Road, London N. 8, England.

SCIENCE-FICTION PUBLICATIONS

Novels

Eye among the Blind. London, Faber, 1976; New York, Doubleday, 1977.
Earthwind. London, Faber, 1977; New York, Pocket Books, 1978.
Where Time Winds Blow. London, Faber, and New York, Pocket Books, 1982.
Mythago Wood. London, Gollancz, 1984; New York, Arbor House, 1985.
The Emerald Forest (novelization of screenplay). New York, Zoetrope, and London, Penguin, 1985.

Short Stories

In the Valley of the Statues. London, Faber, 1982.

Uncollected Short Stories

"Pauper's Plot," in *New Worlds* (London), 1968.
"Microcosm," in *New Writings in SF 20,* edited by John Carnell. London, Dobson, 1972.
"Ash, Ash," in *Stopwatch,* edited by George Hay. Nashville, Nelson, and London, New English Library, 1974.
"Ihl-Kizz," in *Science Fiction Monthly* (London), June 1975.
"On the Inside," in *New Writings in SF 28,* edited by Kenneth Bulmer. London, Sidgwick and Jackson, 1976.
"The Time Beyond Age" and "The Graveyard Cross," in *Supernova 1.* London, Faber 1976.
"Travellers," in *Andromeda 1,* edited by Peter Weston. London, Futura, 1976; New York, St. Martin's Press, 1977.
"To Lay the Piper," in *Science Fiction Monthly 4* (London), 1976.
"A Small Event," in *Andromeda 2,* edited by Peter Weston. London, Futura, 1977.
"The Touch of a Vanish'd Hand," in *Vortex* (Lawrence, Kansas), 1977.

"High Pressure," in *Pulsar 2,* edited by George Hay. London, Penguin, 1979.
"Earth and Stone," in *Interfaces,* edited by Ursula K. Le Guin and Virginia Kidd. New York, Ace, 1980.
"Surviving Forces," in *Ad Astra.* London, Rowlot, 1980.
"Ocean of Sound," in *Book of Alien Monsters,* edited by Peter Davison. London, Arrow, 1981.

OTHER PUBLICATIONS

Novels

Legend of the Werewolf (novelization of screenplay; as Robert Black). London, Sphere, 1976.
The Satanists (novelization of screenplay; as Robert Black). London, Futura, 1978.
Necromancer. London, Futura, 1978; New York, Avon, 1980.
Bulman. London, Futura, 1984.
One of Our Pigeons Is Missing. London, Futura, 1985.

Novels as Chris Carlsen

Berserker:
   Shadow of the Wolf, London, Sphere, 1977.
   The Bull Chief. London, Sphere, 1979.
   The Horned Warrior. London, Sphere, 1979.

Novels as Robert Faulcon

Nighthunter:
   The Stalking, London, Arrow, 1983.
   The Talisman. London, Arrow, 1983.
   The Ghost Dance. London, Arrow, 1984.
   The Shrine. London, Arrow, 1984.
   The Hexing. London, Arrow, 1984.

Other

Alien Landscapes, with Malcolm Edwards. London, Pierrot, 1979.
Tour of the Universe, with Malcolm Edwards. London, Pierrot, and New York, Mayflower, 1980.
Magician, with Malcolm Edwards. Limpsfield, Surrey, Dragon's World, 1982.
Realms of Fantasy, with Malcolm Edwards. Limpsfield, Surrey, Dragon's World, 1983.
Lost Realms, with Malcolm Edwards. Limpsfield, Surrey, Dragon's World, 1985.

Editor, with Christopher Priest, *Stars of Albion* (anthology of British science fiction). London, Pan, 1979.

*

Robert Holdstock comments:
   I am usually inspired to write by the contemplation of far distant places and far distant times, be they future or past. I quite deliberately build into my work and my characters both a passionate awareness of past times and a strong sense of alienation. I relish alien landscapes, but am not concerned with futuristic man. My characters are humans of my own age, and I try to see them, and the exotic locations of time and space, to explore the boundaries and potentiality of man's awareness, of his senses, of his evolution. All my work is concerned with evolution, and with the persistence of memory, the continued

presence—genetically, spiritually, passionately—of all of life in all of mankind.

*   *   *

Robert Holdstock's first novel, *Eye among the Blind*, established him as a promising writer with unique perspectives. A mysterious plague has swept through the inhabited worlds, and now threatens to wipe out the entire human race if a cure cannot be found. Throughout the universe, there is only one other known intelligent race, and it is perhaps on their strange world that a solution lies. But Ree'hdworld is not a simple world to understand. Although the comparatively primitive aliens have not been involved in overt conflict with humanity, strange things happen on their world. The course of evolution seems to be almost visibly altering as a reaction to the presence of visitors from another world, and, even more frightening, visions of mythological beasts seem to call into question the human view of reality.

Earthwind was not quite as successful, although the exotic settings and fantastic imagery of the first book are more than matched. The planet Aeran is also a primitive place, despite the arrival of humans who find a method of blending into the ecology of that world. The imagery tends to dominate a bit too much this time and the plot suffers.

This was not true of *Where Time Winds Blow*, Holdstock's most successful science-fiction novel. Time is a variable on a world where the winds blow down great rift valleys, transporting men and objects into time past or time future. In each case, detritus from some other time is left in their place, and some of these artifacts are valuable enough that a thriving industry exists consisting of daring adventurers who are willing to risk being whisked off through time in return for the financial rewards of discovering a valuable remnant of a previous wind.

Where Time Winds Blow is a complexly textured novel. One of the highest ranking officials on the world has gone mildly insane, and believes that the time winds are a device manipulated by a race of time travellers who operate just outside the bounds of human experience. A secretive infrastructure of the adventurers is cognizant of some secret knowledge which they will not share with the protagonists. The protagonists themselves are caught up in a mesh of ritual superstitions, defying logic. The landscapes are bizarre and fascinating, the characters fully developed, if somewhat bizarre.

Holdstock has also been active in sub-genre fiction. His novel of the supernatural, *Necromancer*, is at once terrifying and an enthralling fantasy adventure. A stone font in a British church turns out to be much more than it appears to be, for it was at one time the sacred object of a group of pagan worshippers of animistic spirits. Now it has reached out to imprison the soul of a modern youth, and his mother must overcome her own disbelief before she can work to abrogate its control. Under the pseudonym Robert Faulcon, Holdstock has written a series of adventures of a man whose family has been disrupted by a cult of satanists, and who learns the arts of magic himself in order to take revenge. The first two in this series are *The Stalking* and *The Talisman*.

There have also been a number of short stories, but Holdstock seems to require the room of a full length novel in order to adequately develop his characters and describe his original settings. He has also dabbled in the more violent forms of heroic fantasy under the pseudonym Chris Carlsen, including such interesting but fairly standard adventure novels as *Shadow of the Wolf, The Bull Chief,* and *The Horned Warrior* .

—Don D'Ammassa

HOLLAND, Cecelia (Anastasia). Also writes as Elizabeth Eliot Carter. American. Born in Henderson, Nevada, 31 December 1943. Educated at Pennsylvania State University, University Park, 1961-62; Connecticut College, New London, B. A. 1965. Visiting Professor of English, Connecticut College, 1979. Recipient: Guggenheim Fellowship, 1981. Address: c/o Knopf Inc., 201 East 50th Street, New York, New York 10022, U. S. A.

SCIENCE-FICTION PUBLICATIONS

Novel

Floating Worlds. New York, Knopf, and London, Gollancz, 1976.

OTHER PUBLICATIONS

Novels

The Firedrake. New York, Atheneum, 1966; London, Hodder and Stoughton, 1967.
Rakóssy. New York, Atheneum, and London, Hodder and Stoughton, 1967.
The Kings in Winter. New York, Atheneum, and London, Hodder and Stoughton, 1968.
Until the Sun Falls. New York, Atheneum, and London, Hodder and Stoughton, 1969.
Antichrist. New York, Atheneum, 1970; as *The Wonder of the World,* London, Hodder and Stoughton, 1970.
The Earl. New York, Knopf, 1971; as *Hammer for Princes,* London, Hodder and Stoughton, 1972.
The Death of Attila. New York, Knopf, 1973; London, Hodder and Stoughton, 1974.
Great Maria. New York, Knopf, 1974; London, Hodder and Stoughton, 1975.
Two Ravens. New York, Knopf, and London, Gollancz, 1977.
Valley of the Kings (as Elizabeth Eliot Carter). New York, Dutton, 1977; as Cecelia Holland, London, Gollancz, 1978.
City of God. New York, Knopf, and London, Gollancz, 1979.
Home Ground. New York, Knopf, and London, Gollancz, 1981.
The Sea Beggars. New York, Knopf, and London, Gollancz, 1982.
The Belt of Gold. New York, Knopf, and London, Gollancz, 1984.
Pillar of the Sky. New York, Knopf, and London, Gollancz, 1985.

Other (for children)

Ghost on the Steppe. New York, Atheneum, 1969.
The King's Road. New York, Atheneum, 1970.

*   *   *

Cecelia Holland's *Floating Worlds* is a space opera, though it lacks many of the traditional attributes of that form. There is no melodrama, only realism. The novel is unsentimental, unromantic, and contains characters who are real people rather than the archetypes of adventure fiction. Several characters, who in a more traditional space opera might have been relegated to the stock roles of villains, here take center stage. The protagonist, Paula Mendoza, is a selfish, intelligent, anarchic, and somewhat unreflective woman who sees an opportunity for power and seizes it. She gambles and loses.

Holland has not extrapolated a future. Her future worlds, though in part modeled on societies and sub-cultures of the past and present, are not developed in the manner of the realistic science-fiction writer. She takes a cyclical rather than progressive view of history. Human nature has not changed in this far future world. The Martian Sunlight League is fascist. The polluted Earth, its inhabited regions covered by domes, is populated by anarchists who have no government, only a Committee for the Revolution. The Styths, mutants who rule an Empire on Saturn and Uranus, are violent and hold slaves. With their spaceships, a technical knowledge that enables them to live in artificial cities on such inhospitable worlds, and their anachronistic customs, the Styths may seem unlikely. But the 20th century has already experienced Nazi Germany—a warrior band with technology, whose strategy and tactics were modeled on those of the Mongols under Genghis Khan.

Holland is an author of historical novels, and has admitted in an interview that *Floating Worlds* began as a novel about Mongol China; she then realized that the story she wanted to tell would not fit into that historical framework—or indeed any past time. Paula Mendoza bears a resemblance to the protagonist of *Great Maria*, a Norman woman who is the ally of her warlord husband. The Styth Empire has features in common with the Mongols of *Until the Sun Falls*, but the background of *Floating Worlds* has its own integrity. Though the novel has devices found in other science fiction, such as spaceships, an interplanetary empire, mutants, and an O'Neill space cylinder, it is not obviously influenced by other science-fiction writers. The style is clear and economical. Holland does not pad her historical novels with endless descriptions of clothing, castles, and weapons; neither does she fill *Floating Worlds* with cumbersome expository passage. The reader lives in this future world and experience it directly. The book is unique and original, not derivative, though it can be placed in the tradition of Edgar Rice Burroughs. The author herself has cited this book as her favorite of her early novels.

Modeling a novel of the future on the past does not always work. Cecelia Holland makes it work. *Floating Worlds* is one of the most intelligent and rewarding examples of an often-maligned species of the genus science fiction. Marks of Holland's stylistic influence can be found in the otherwise quite different works of Elizabeth A. Lynn and Marta Randall.

Another novel of Holland's, *Home Ground*, should be mentioned here, because the central character, Rose McKenna, earns a living as a science-fiction writer. The novel, set in the 1970's, takes places in northern California, where Rose goes in order to put her life back together again, the effect of the modern world and its intrusions on the disparate people Rose meets there are viewed through Rose's eyes, and passages in the novel show Rose at work on her science fiction. *Home Ground* can be grouped with other novels, such as Barry N. Malzberg's *Herovit's World,* about science-fiction writers and how such a writer might view the world.

—Pamela Sargent

HOLLIS, H. H. Pseudonym for Ben Rhamey. American. Born in Dallas, Texas, in 1921. Educated at Southern Methodist University, Dallas, B. A. in economics; University of Texas, Austin, LL. B. Married. Admiralty lawyer. *Died in 1977.*

SCIENCE-FICTION PUBLICATIONS

Uncollected Short Stories (series: Corky Craven)

"Ouled Nail," in *If* (New York), March 1966.
"Cybernia," in *If* (New York), July 1966.
"The Long, Slow Orbits," in *Galaxy* (New York), May 1967.
"The Guerrilla Trees," in *If* (New York), June 1968.
"Eeeetz Ch," in *Galaxy* (New York), November 1968.
"Sword Game," in *The World's Best Science Fiction 1969;* edited by Donald A. Wollheim and Terry Carr. New York, Ace, and London, Gollancz, 1969.
"Stoned Counsel" (Craven), in *Again, Dangerous Visions,* edited by Harlan Ellison. New York, Doubleday, 1972; London, Millington, 1976.
"Too Many People," in *The Best Science Fiction for 1972,* edited by Frederik Pohl. New York, Ace, 1972.
"Different Angle," in *Amazing* (New York), December 1973.
"Every Day in Every Way" (Craven), in *Lone Star Universe,* edited by George W. Proctor and Steven Utley. Austin, Texas, Heindelberg, 1976.
"Arachne," "Dark Body," and "Inertia," in *Midnight Sun 3,* 1976.

*   *   *

Though included in *Lone Star Universe*, an anthology of science-fiction stories by Texans, H. H. Hollis avoids the possible danger of writing a purely local literature by writing in a pure, clear style—but not simplistically—about complex social issues, such as justice and ecology, which we cannot avoid because to do so is to condemn our culture to an early death.

"Sword Game" displays Hollis's talent for creating characters who are immediately recognizable and likeable despite, or perhaps because of, their inner confusion. A university professor and a hippie girl have reached a point in life that appears to be the fulfillment of their desires, but actually denotes stasis and boredom. The solution to their problem is at once silly and scientific: the professor will insert the girl into an "expanded cube" and drive a fencing foil through her body as part of a circus act. Since time in the cube represents an "endless instant" (as does a state of boredom), she will emerge unhurt in our time. When the original state of ennui reasserts itself, the professor entraps the girl permanently in the cube. Then, in a beautiful show of literary magic, the author has a graduate student "hero" free the girl and "imprison" the professor by distributing him evenly throughout the universe—a truly mind-expanding experience befitting a man who feels confined and lost in reality.

Two stories feature a futuristic Houston lawyer named Corky Craven who shares his author's profession as well as his interest in the drug culture and concern for our violent, polluted world. In "Stoned Counsel" numerous conflicting truths about industrial pollution, which boggle the normal, sane mind, are "dreamed" by drugged lawyers, who behave as though under the influence of a truth serum. The "triple sensory projector," a computer-like machine into which the attorneys are plugged, meanwhile sorts out the facts and decides the case on the basis of knowledge that would not be available without the drugs. So another kind of justice triumphs, a 1960's version with drugs used for good instead of evil. Drugs are also a feature of "Every Day in Every Way," a remarkable tale about the system of future justice in which criminals share both guild and punishment with their legal executioners. In "Year Judge" the judge actually dies with the condemned persons at the end of his term and a new judge is elected, eliminating the lust for power that anyone in a position of authority is in danger of acquiring.

Corky's purpose in this story is to witness the execution of the Year Judge (a female this year) and a woman (coincidence?) who has murdered her children. But the Witnesses are not mere societal observers: they are also plugged into the electric chairs and severely shocked until the judge and criminal are dead. The message is unmerciful. Justice is not simple or beautiful. It is an imperfect human attempt to bring order to our frightening, chaotic world which itself hurts those whom it strives to serve. Corky's cranial scar, a souvenir of his near-fatal witness of the law, remind us that violence, though ugly, may be necessary to man's animal nature and a sort of payment for the great beauty he also enjoys.

H. H. Hollis, by mirroring our society in a way that strips it naked (as his characters sometimes appear to be), forces the reader to look honestly with him at our shared problems in the knowledge that, although they will not disappear, we must not abandon efforts to understand and reform our world.

—Rose Flores Harris

HOLLY, J. Hunter Pseudonym for Joan C(arol) Holly. American. Born in Lansing, Michigan, 25 September 1932. Educated at Michigan State University, East Lansing, B. A. in psychology 1954 (Phi Beta Kappa). Worked as photographer, clerk, and ballet teacher. Secretary, Science Fiction Writers of America, 1976.

SCIENCE-FICTION PUBLICATIONS

Novels

Encounter. New York, Avalon, 1959.
The Green Planet. New York, Avalon, 1960.
The Dark Planet. New York, Avalon, 1962.
The Flying Eyes. Derby, Connecticut, Monarch, 1962.
The Running Man. Derby, Connecticut, Monarch, 1963.
The Gray Aliens. New York, Avalon, 1963; London, Mayflower, 1964.
The Time Twisters. New York, Avon, 1964.
The Dark Enemy. New York, Avalon, 1965.
The Mind Traders. New York, Avalon, 1966.
Keeper. Franklin, Tennessee, Authors Co-op, 1976.
Death Dolls of Lyra. New York, Woodhill, 1977.
Shepherd. Toronto, Laser, 1977.

Uncollected Short Stories

"Silence," in *Fantastic* (New York), June 1965.
"The Question," in *Famous Science Fiction* (New York), Winter 1966.
"The Others," in *The Other Side of Tomorrow,* edited by Roger Elwood. New York, Random House, 1973.
"The Graduated Robot," in *The Graduated Robot and Other Stories,* edited by Roger Elwood. Minneapolis, Learner, 1974.
"Come See the Last Man Cry," in *Tomorrow,* edited by Roger Elwood. New York, Evans, 1976.
"PSI Clone," in *Futurelove: A Science Fiction Triad,* edited by Roger Elwood. Indianapolis, Bobbs Merrill, 1977; London, Hale, 1978.

Uncollected Short Stories as Joan C. Holly

"The Gift of Nothing," in *And Walk Now Gently Through the*

Fire . . ., edited by Roger Elwood. Philadelphia, Chilton, 1972.
"Child," in *Demon Kind,* edited by Roger Elwood. New York, Avon, 1973.
"The Proper Study," in *Long Night of Waiting and Other Stories,* edited by Roger Elwood. Nashville, Aurora, 1974.

OTHER PUBLICATIONS

Novel

The Man from U. N. C. L. E. 10: The Assassination Affair. New York, Ace, 1967.

* * *

Earth is conquered by an army of aliens in *The Dark Planet,* succeeding primarily because of a lethal plague which they spread upon their arrival. Bacteriological war is illegal in the eyes of the interplanetary council, however, and a lone Earthman is able to manipulate things so that the hegemony over Earth is abrogated and the aliens censured for their activity. A similar theme is used in *The Mind Traders.* Thousands of humans have disappeared from the Earth, and the authorities suspect that an alien race of telepaths may be using them as slave labor on their home planet, even though they have signed a treaty not to interfere in Earth affairs. An investigator is allowed to travel to their home world where he eventually discovers a split among the aliens themselves and uses it to free the captives.

Mysterious shadows glide over the landscape in *The Gray Aliens,* and people begin to disappear, leaving only their clothing behind. The protagonist learns that the shadows are another intelligent species that has existed on Earth unknown to us, but which is now taking action to exterminate humanity because our activities are preventing them from communing with the planetary mass mind. We are invaded from the future in *The Time Twisters.* Our descendants face extinction as a species unless they find a source of children, so they journey back through time to kidnap them, faking an alien invasion so that people won't suspect what is really happening.

The best novel Holly wrote is almost certainly *Death Dolls of Lyra,* although it too deals with a kind of invasion. Two children find a metallic ball with two fuzzy dolls inside it. Shortly thereafter a fatal and highly infectious fungus begins to spread across the country, and the dolls are revealed to be two dead aliens from a world of tiny proportion in relation to our own.

Holly has always written of fearful situations, alien invasions, macabre monsters, manaces to the human race. *Encounter* opened with a space vessel crashlanding on Earth. The badly wounded survivor of the crash is taken in by a rural family and nursed back to health, but he repays them with brutal murder. The alien can absorb knowledge directly from human minds, but the result is that the victims' brains literally explode. Soon a string of mutilated corpses leads to powerful Peter Kiel, a man who seems destined to rule the country despite his mysterious past.

The Green Planet pitted 13 humans against a variety of threats on another world, but recognizes that humans can be monsters as well. The involuntary colonists are there because a repressive government exiled them to what was ostensibly a colony for non-conformists, but actually a deathtrap. Even within their meagre ranks, murder and betrayal are not unknown. The colonists are threatened with giant carnivorous birds, animals with whom any contact causes instant pain, and unfriendly natives who distrust the interlopers. This early novel is one of Holly's best, not only because she exerted more effort on developing characters, but also because she produced after this a string of invasion story variants.

In *The Flying Eyes* alien invaders are hidden in a cavern, able to disconnect parts of their bodies and send them roving about the Earth to enslave humanity and force it to produce radioactivity, the only substance upon which they can feed. This is a fairly good adventure story except that the destruction of the invaders hinges upon their being incredibly stupid. The invasion is covert in *The Running Man*. This time the aliens have secretly established themselves behind a human front organization and have begun to spread a new worldwide cult designed to disrupt human civilization and make us more vulnerable.

The last two novels Holly wrote were linked, *Keeper* and *Shepherd*. They are set in a dystopian future where emotion, particularly any form of love or affection, is outlawed. A man given temporary custody of a child discovers the importance of emotion in the first book, and moves to topple the repressive and inhumane government in the second.

Holly was never a major voice in science fiction, and her plots were derivative. There was, however, a simplicity in her style and a joy in telling a good story that made most of her novels succeed as entertainments if not significant works of fiction.

—Don D'Ammassa

HOLLY, Joan C. See HOLLY, J. Hunter.

HOLMES, A. R. See BATES, Harry.

HOLMES, H. H. See BOUCHER, Anthony.

HOLT, Conrad G. See FEARN, John Russell.

HOLT, George. See TUBB, E. C.

HOOD, Sarah. See KILLOUGH, Lee.

HOOVER, H(elen) M(ary). American. Born in Stark County, Ohio, 5 April 1935. Attended Louisville High School; Mt. Union College. Lives in Alexandria, Virginia. Agent: Russell and Volkening, 50 West 29th Street, New York, New York 10001, U. S. A.

SCIENCE-FICTION PUBLICATIONS

Novels (for children) (series: Morrow)

Children of Morrow. New York, Four Winds Press, 1973; London, Methuen, 1975.
Treasures of Morrow. New York, Four Winds Press, 1976.
The Delikon. New York, Viking Press, 1977; London, Methuen, 1978.
The Rains of Eridan. New York, Viking Press, 1977; London, Methuen, 1978.
The Lost Star. New York, Viking Press, 1979; London, Methuen, 1980.
Return to Earth. New York, Viking Press, 1980; London, Methuen, 1981.
This Time of Darkness. New York, Viking Press, 1980; London, Methuen, 1982.
Another Heaven, Another Earth. New York, Viking Press, 1981; London, Methuen, 1983.
The Bell Tree. New York, Viking Press, 1982.
The Shepherd Moon. New York, Viking Press, and London, Methuen, 1984.

OTHER PUBLICATIONS

Other

The Lion's Cub (for children). New York, Four Winds Press, 1974.
"Out of This World," in *Language Arts* (Urbana, Illinois), April 1980.

*

Manuscript Collection: Kerlan Collection, University of Minnesota, Minneapolis.

Critical Study: by E. Jane Porter, in *Language Arts* (Urbana, Illinois), October 1982.

*   *   *

H. M. Hoover consistently produces youth science fiction of very high quality, finding in SF a congenial and fertile ground for exploring those problems young people may face in less exotic environments: alienation from parents, feelings of isolation, fellings of being trapped or of being an anomalous creature out-of-sync with the Universe. Often Hoover's young people have special talents and sensitivities unappreciated by the adults around them.

So it is in *The Children of Morrow* and its sequel *Treasures of Morrow*. Tia and Rabbit are telepaths ill-at-ease in their wasteland home, "The Base"; but a visit to the more advanced and enlightened community of Morrow proves ironically that home is not a simple matter to define. Anthropocentrism is examined in *The Rains of Eridan* when Theo, a young naturalist, and Karen, a child-orphan of conflict, team up first to survive, later to explore planetary lifeforms. Here and throughout her work, characters grope toward friendship across the generations, and search for clues to enlighten their immediate situation and solve the larger mystery which imprisons those about them. Often the clear-eyed vision of children is instrumental in the process. The story of planetary exploration provides a background for their developing relationship. Karen learns to trust her new parent, and Theo learns that the child is skilled beyond her years both with laser gun and in the handling of fear and grief. ("Like you I can shut part of my mind off till it's safe to think again. ")

In *The Lost Star* the young hero is ignored by parents who have adopted emotional reserve as a policy for working together as off-Earth astronomers over long periods of time. Hoover's ability, born of youthful innocence, to recognize intuitively the intelligence and intrinsic worth of alien creatures is reminiscent of Ursula K. Le Guin's *The Word for World is Forest;* but Hoover's is a much lighter and more hopeful tale.

This Time of Darkness utilizes the familiar idea of the escape from an hermetic environment to explore in depth the struggle of children to receive the affection and acceptance which should be theirs by right. Ostracized for their ability to read, Amy and Axel are two children in a Big Brother-style underground hive community so benighted it has left scars on their bodies and has lost sight of any concept of a better world outside. Readers of SF will see in this story a children's literature counterpart of E. M. Forster's classic "The Machine Stops," and teachers may find it worthwhile for the hope it provides the abused child of the real world struggling for psychic survival. In *The Bell Tree* Hoover uses the device of archaeologists exploring an alien world to study the relationships of a young woman, her father, and her first boyfriend; and in *The Shepherd Moon* the loneliness of Merry, a 13-year-old of the 48th century is set against a background of terrorist intrigue.

Hoover has written that science fiction's presentation of ideas as images makes it important as a teaching tool, since imaging is the very thinking process Einstein and other great thinkers use to generate new ideas. In Hoover's fiction we find provocative images of scientific concepts and a liberating experience for the human spirit.

—Thomas P. Dunn

HOSKINS, Robert. Also writes as Grace Corren; John Gregory; Susan Jennifer; Michael Kerr. American. Born in Lyons Falls, New York, 23 May 1933. Attended Albany State College for Teachers, New York, 1951-52. Worked in family business, 1952-64; attendant, Wassaic State School for the Retarded, New York, 1964-66; House Parent, Brooklyn Home for Children, 1966-68; sub-agent, Scott Meredith Literary Agency, New York, 1967-68; Senior Editor, Lancer Books, New York, 1969-72. Since 1972, free-lance writer. Address: c/o Harlequin Enterprises, 225 Duncan Mill Road, Don Mills, Ontario M3B 3K9, Canada.

SCIENCE-FICTION PUBLICATIONS

Novels (series: Alnians)

Evil in the Family (as Grace Corren). New York, Lancer, 1972.
The Shattered People. New York, Doubleday, 1975.
Master of the Stars (Alnians). Toronto, Laser, 1976.
To Control the Stars (Alnians). New York, Ballantine, 1977.

Tomorrow's Son. New York, Doubleday, 1977.
Jack-in-the-Box Planet (the children) Philadelphia, Westminster Press, 1978.
To Escape the Stars (Alnians). New York, Ballantine, 1978.
Legacy of the Stars (as John Gregory). New York, Nordon, 1979; as Robert Hoskins, London, Hale, 1981.

Uncollected Short Stories

"Weapon Master," in *Science Fiction Adventures* (London), January 1961.
"A World for Me," in *New Worlds* (London), February 1961.
"Morpheus," in *New Worlds* (London), June 1961.
"Second Chance," in *Amazing* (New York), April 1962.
"The Problem Makers," in *The Far-Out People,* edited by Hoskins. New York, New American Library, 1971.
"The Man Who Lived," in *The Edge of Never,* edited by Hoskins. New York, Fawcett, 1973.
"Pop Goes the Weasel," in *Best Science Fiction Stories of the Year 1975,* edited by Lester del Rey. New York, Dutton, 1976.
"The Kelley's Eye," in *Tomorrow,* edited by Roger Elwood. New York, Evans, 1976.
"The Ghosts of Earth," in *Odyssey* (New York), Summer 1976.
"The Mountain," in *The Future Now,* edited by Hoskins. New York Fawcett, 1977.
"Reason for Honor," in *Against Tomorrow,* edited by Hoskins. New York, Fawcett, 1979.

OTHER PUBLICATIONS

Novels

The House of Counted Hatreds (as Susan Jennifer). New York, Avon, 1973.
Country of the Kind (as Susan Jennifer). New York, Avon, 1975.
The Gemini Run (as Michael Kerr). New York, Charter, 1979.
The Fury Bombs. Toronto, Harlequin, 1983.

Novels as Grace Corren

The Darkest Room. New York, Lancer, 1969.
A Place on Dark Island. New York, Lancer, 1971.
Mansions of Deadly Dreams. New York, Popular Library, 1973.
Dark Threshold. New York, Popular Library, 1977.
The Attic Child. Los Angeles, Pinnacle, 1979.
Survival Run (novelization of screenplay). Los Angeles, Pinnacle, 1979.

Play

Television Play: *Birthday Party* (*Kojak* series), 1976.

Others

Editor, *First Step Outward.* New York, Dell, 1969.
Editor, *Infinity 1-5.* New York, Lancer, 5 vols., 1970-73.
Editor, *The Stars Around Us.* New York, New American Library, 1970.
Editor, *Swords Against Tomorrow.* New York, New American Library, 1970.
Editor, *Tomorrow 1.* New York, New American Library, 1971.
Editor, *The Far-Out People.* New York, New American Library, 1971.

Editor, *Wondermakers 1-2*. New York, Fawcett, 2 vols., 1972-74.
Editor, *Strange Tomorrows*. New York, Lancer, 1972.
Editor, *The Edge of Never*. New York, Fawcett, 1973.
Editor, *The Liberated Future*. New York, Fawcett, 1974.
Editor, *The Future Now*. New York, Fawcett, 1977.
Editor, *Against Tomorrow*. New York, Fawcett, 1979.

*

Robert Hoskins comments:

An unhappy, and fat, childhood in a small Adirondack football village turned me early to escapism. Comics led to pulps, to fandom, through the letter columns. After years of writing, I began selling an occasional story while still gathering pounds of rejection slips. It was not until I worked, first, for an agent, and then as an editor, that I learned the techniques of novel construction. Impossible though the idea is, I think all young writers should have a spell in both jobs. I consider myself strictly an entertainer; the one novel that is deliberately allegorical I have not at this date been able to sell. I've published 40 short stories, but find it easier to construct a novel. Once an idea comes, it seems to grow and grow.

*   *   *

Except for *Evil in the Family*, a gothic novel involving a time-travel fantasy, Robert Hoskins's major contribution to science fiction until 1975 was in writing short stories and editing anthologies. Since then he has developed earlier themes in a series of novels based on the inherent value of primitive versus technological man, the effects of free evolution versus outside interference and artificial controls, the need for change and progress and the threat of regression without it, the private, economic, and sociological reasons for galactic exploration. His works are always filled with action and adventure, monsters and barbaric peoples, advanced races and mercenary predators.

In *The Shattered People* Hoskins gradually reveals the secret ties between a savage desert world of naked hunters armed with slings and stones and a highly technological nuclear civilization ruled by a tyrannical council contemptuous of life. In the first, vicious cats prowl in packs and sentient aliens (huge, bird-like creatures) keep watch, while in the other urban rebels, aided by their "empress," a titular head virtually imprisoned in her own palace, meet in subterranean passages and plot to throw off their shackles. Mind-wipes and deportation thrust the strongest and most outspoken of the urban world into the primitive world, until one man's psi powers enable him to regain his memory and bridge the gap between the two, merging instinctive and rational.

Tomorrow's Son, set in the 23rd century, focuses on a geneticist and his android son, trapped in a rigid caste system, genetically predetermined. On Earth the father engages in forbidden android research to help revitalize the swiftly deteriorating genetic make-up of humanity, while on a primitive planet, Karyllia, his son struggles to protect alien humanoids from repeating humanity's evolutionary mistakes, only to discover that he must protect them not only from themselves but from the fanaticism and destructiveness of his own world. Both men prove pawns of larger schemes to protect Karyllia from outside interference and to force humans to accept change—change that can revitalize a regressing world where average I. Q. decreases yearly and masses of subhumans are crowded into barracks, experience sex and violence vicariously, and drown their minds in joyjuice. The book includes bizarre

beasts of burden, strange snake-lizards in swamps, and primitive tribal conflicts. As usual, Hoskins emphasizes the stench of primitive worlds and the lack of respect for life in both primitive and advanced societies.

Hoskins's trilogy sets up a universal cycle of development and regression and postulates a series of stargates on most worlds, built by an ancient interstellar race; one sets the controls and steps into other worlds, some of which have regressed to the primitive while others have advanced to the stars. *Master of the Stars* focuses on the Alnians at the height of their development, struggling to avoid the contaminating barbarism of other worlds. *To Control the Stars* deals with an internal conflict in the Society for Humanoidic Studies, a conflict that affects the future of thousands of worlds and which forces the central character to fight for his life from world to world and to seek the Alnians (the only humanoids with a continual history) for answers. The Society's original goal, observation of other worlds without interference, has been perverted in a lust for power, wealth, and exploitation to focus on evolutionary control and forced rapid progress. There is much action—escape, recapture, romance. *To Escape the Stars* picks up thousands of years later when the Society has been reduced to a library cult devoutly recording galactic history. A scheme to plunder a rich, high-gravity world of rural innocents leads first to treachery, and then to a revived search for the Alnians and their master codex to the stargates; the main figure changes from a jaded and unscrupulous exploiter to a student of the universe, and discovers the dangers of isolation and of failure to accept change and conflict.

—Gina Macdonald

HOUGH, S. B. See **GORDON, Rex.**

HOWELLS, William Dean. American. Born in Martin's Ferry, Ohio, 1 March 1837. Largely self-educated. Married Elinor Mead in 1862 (died, 1910); one son and two daughters. Compositor, 1851-58, Reporter, 1858-60, and News Editor, 1860-61, *Ohio State Journal*, Columbus; also correspondent, in Columbus, for the Cincinnati *Gazette*, 1857; contributor to his father's newspaper, *The Sentinel*, Jefferson, Ohio, from 1852, and wrote for various national magazines from 1860; United States Consul in Venice, 1861-65; Assistant Editor, 1866-71, and Editor-in-Chief, 1871-81, *Atlantic Monthly*, Boston; Professor of Modern Languages, Harvard University, Cambridge, Massachusetts, 1869-71; wrote the "Editor's Study" column for *Harper's* magazine, 1886-92; Co-Editor, *Cosmopolitan* magazine, 1892. Recipient: American Academy Gold Medal, 1915. M. A. : Harvard University, Cambridge, Massachusetts, 1867; Litt. D. : Yale University, New Haven, Connecticut, 1901; Oxford University, 1904; Columbia University, New York, 1905; L. H. D. : Princeton University, New Jersey, 1912. President, American Academy, 1908-20. *Died 11 May 1920.*

SCIENCE-FICTION PUBLICATIONS

Novels

A Traveler from Altruria. New York, Harper, and Edinburgh,

Douglas, 1894; complete edition, edited by Clara Marburg Kirk and Rudolf Kirk, as *Letters of an Altrurian Traveller (1893-1894)*, Gainesville, Florida, Scholars' Facsimiles and Reprints, 1961.

Through the Eye of a Needle. New York and London, Harper, 1907.

OTHER PUBLICATIONS

Novels

Their Wedding Journey. Boston, Osgood, 1872; Edinburgh, Douglas, 1882.

A Chance Acquaintance. Boston, Osgood, 1873; Edinburgh, Douglas, 1882.

A Foregone Conclusion. Boston, Osgood, 1874.

The Lady of Aroostook. Boston, Houghton Osgood, 1879; Edinburgh, Douglas, 2 vols., 1882.

The Undiscovered Country. Boston, Houghton Mifflin, and London, Sampson Low, 1880.

Doctor Breen's Practice. Boston, Osgood, 1881; Edinburgh, Douglas, 1883.

A Modern Instance. Edinburgh, Douglas, 2 vols., 1882; Boston, Osgood, 1 vol., 1882.

A Woman's Reason. Boston, Osgood, and Edinburgh, Douglas, 1883.

The Rise of Silas Lapham Boston, Ticknor, and Edinburgh, Douglas, 1885.

Indian Summer. Boston, Ticknor, and Edinburgh, Douglas, 1886.

The Minister's Charge: or, The Apprenticeship of Lemuel Barker. Edinburgh, Douglas, 1886; Boston, Ticknor, 1887.

April Hopes. Edinburgh, Douglas, 1887; New York, Harper, 1888.

Annie Kilburn. Edinburgh, Douglas, 1888; New York, Harper, 1889.

A Hazzard of New Fortunes. New York, Harper, and Edinburgh, Douglas, 1889.

The Shadow of a Dream. Edinburgh, Douglas, and New York, Harper, 1890.

An Imperative Duty. New York, Harper, and Edinburgh, Douglas, 1891.

Mercy. Edinburgh, Douglas, 1892; as *The Quality of Mercy*, New York, Harper, 1892.

The World of Chance. Edinburgh, Douglas, and New York, Harper, 1893.

The Coast of Bohemia. New York, Harper, 1893.

The Day of Their Wedding. New York, Harper, 1896.

A Parting and a Meeting. New York, Harper, 1896; with *The Day of Their Wedding*, as *Idyls in Drab*, Edinburgh, Douglas, 1896.

The Landlord at Lion's Head. Edinburgh, Douglas, and New York, Harper, 1897.

The Open-Eyed Conspiracy. New York, Harper, 1897; Edinburgh, Douglas, 1898.

The Story of a Play. New York and London, Harper, 1898.

Ragged Lady. New York, Harper, 1899.

Their Silver Wedding Journey. London and New York, Harper, 1899; abridged edition, as *Hither and Thither in Germany*, New York and London, Harper, 1920.

The Kentons. New York and London, Harper, 1902.

The Flight of Pony Baker: A Boy's Town Story. New York and London, Harper, 1902.

Letters Home. New York and London, Harper, 1903.

The Son of Royal Langbrith. New York and London, Harper, 1904.

Miss Bellard's Inspiration. New York and London, Harper, 1905.

Fennel and Rue. New York and London, Harper, 1908.

New Leaf Mills. New York and London, Harper, 1913.

The Leatherwood God. New York, Century, and London, Jenkins, 1916.

The Vacation of the Kelwyns. New York and London, Harper, 1920.

Mrs. Farrell. New York and London, Harper, 1921.

Novels 1875-1886. New York, Literary Classics of the United States, 1982.

Short Stories

A Fearful Responsibility and Other Stories. Boston, Osgood, 1881; as *A Fearful Responsibility and Tonnelli's Marriage*, Edinburgh, Douglas, 1882.

A Pair of Patient Lovers. New York and London, Harper, 1901.

Questionable Shapes. New York and London, Harper, 1903.

Between the Dark and the Daylight: Romances. New York, Harper, 1907; London, Harper, 1912.

Plays

Samson, adaptation of the play by Ippolito D'Aste (produced on tour, 1874; New York, 1889). New York, Koppel, 1889.

The Parlor Car. Boston, Osgood, 1876; with *A Counterfeit Presentment*, Edinburgh, Douglas, 1882.

Out of the Question. Boston, Osgood, 1877; with *At the Sign of the Savage*, Edinburgh, Douglas, 1882.

A Counterfeit Presentment (produced Cincinnati, 1877; revised version, produced Detroit, 1877). Boston, Osgood, 1877; with *The Parlor Car*, Edinburgh, Douglas, 1882.

Yorick's Love, adaptation of a play by Manuel Tamayo y Baus (as *A New Play*, produced Cleveland, 1878; as *Yorick's Love*, produced New York, 1880; London, 1884). Included in *Complete Plays*, 1960.

The Sleeping-Car (produced New York, 1887). Boston, Osgood, 1883; in *Minor Dramas, 1907*.

The Register. Boston, Osgood, 1884; in *Minor Dramas*, 1907.

The Elevator (produced Streator, Illinois, 1885). Boston, Osgood, 1885; in *Minor Dramas*, 1907.

The Garroters (produced New York, 1886). New York, Harper, 1886; Edinburgh, Douglas, 1897.

A Foregone Conclusion, with William Poel, adaptation of the novel by Howells (produced New York, 1886). Included in *Complete Plays*, 1960.

Colonel Sellers as a Scientist, with Mark Twain, adaptation of the novel *The Gilded Age* by Twain and Charles Dudley Warner (produced New Brunswick, New Jersey, and New York, 1887). Included in *Complete Plays*, 1960.

The Mouse-Trap (produced New York, 1887-88; Edinburgh, 1897). Included in *The Mouse-Trap and Other Farces*, 1889; published separately, Edinburgh, Douglas, 1897.

A Sea-Change; or, Love's Stowaway: A Lyricated Farce, music by George Henschel. Boston, Ticknor, 1888.

The Mouse-Trap and Other Farces (includes *A Likely Story, Five O'Clock Tea, The Garroters*). New York, Harper, 1889.

The Sleeping-Car and Other Farces (includes *The Parlor Car, The Register, The Elevator*). Boston, Houghton Mifflin, 1889.

The Albany Depot. New York, Harper, 1892; Edinburgh, Douglas, 1897.

A Letter of Introduction. New York, Harper, 1892; Edinburgh, Douglas, 1897.

The Unexpected Guests. New York, Harper, 1893; Edinburgh, Douglas, 1897.

Evening Dress (produced New York, 1894). New York, Harper, 1893; Edinburgh, Douglas, 1897.

Bride Roses (produced New York 1894). Boston, Houghton Mifflin, 1900; in *Minor Dramas*, 1907.

A Dangerous Ruffian (produced London, 1895).

A Previous Engagement. New York, Harper, 1897; in *Minor Dramas*, 1907.

Room Forty-Five. Boston, Houghton Mifflin, 1900; in *Minor Dramas*, 1907.

An Indian Giver. Boston, Houghton Mifflin, 1900; in *Minor Dramas*, 1907.

The Smoking Car. Boston, Houghton Mifflin, 1900; in *Minor Dramas*, 1907.

Minor Dramas. Edinburgh, Douglas, 2 vols., 1907.

The Mother and the Father. New York and London, Harper, 1909.

Parting Friends. New York and London, Harper, 1911.

The Night Before Christmas, and Self-Sacrifice, in *The Daughter of the Storage and Other Things in Prose and Verse*, 1916.

The Complete Plays of William Dean Howells, edited by Walter J. Meserve. New York, New York University Press, 1960.

Verse

Poems of Two Friends, with John J. Piatt. Columbus, Ohio, Follett Foster, 1860.

No Love Lost: A Romance of Travel. New York, Putnam, 1869.

Poems. Boston, Osgood, 1873.

Stops of Various Quills. New York, Harper, 1895.

The Mulberries in Pay's Garden. North Bend, Ohio, Scott, 1907.

Other

Lives and Speeches of Abraham Lincoln and Hannibal Hamlin. Columbus, Ohio, Follett Foster, 1860.

Venetian Life. London, Trubner, and New York, Hurd and Houghton, 1866; revised edition, Boston, Osgood, 1872; Boston, Hougthon Mifflin, 2 vols., and London, Constable, 2 vols., 1907.

Italian Journeys. New York, Hurd and Houghton, 1867; revised edition, Boston, Osgood, 1872; London, Heinemann, and Boston, Houghton Mifflin, 1901.

Suburban Sketches. New York, Hurd and Houghton, 1871; revised edition, Boston, Osgood, 1872; abridged edition, as *A Day's Pleasure*, Osgood, 1876.

Sketch of the Life and Character of Rutherford B. Hayes. New York, Hurd and Houghton, 1876.

A LIttle Girl among the Old Masters. Boston, Osgood, 1884; London, Trubner, n. d.

Three Villages. Boston, Osgood, 1884.

Tuscan Cities. Boston, Ticknor, and Edinburgh, Douglas, 1885.

Modern Italian Poets: Essays and Versions. New York, Harper, and Edinburgh, Douglas, 1887.

A Boy's Town (for children). New York, Harper, 1890.

Criticism and Fiction. New York, Harper, and London, Osgood McIlvaine, 1891.

A Little Swiss Sojourn. New York, Harper, 1892.

Christmas Every Day and Other Stories Told for Children. New York, Harper, 1892.

My Year in a Log Cabin. New York, Harper, 1893.

My Literary Passions. New York, Harper, 1895.

Impressions and Experiences. New York, Harper, and Edinburgh, Douglas, 1896.

Stories of Ohio. New York, American Book Company, 1897.

Doorstep Acquaintance and Other Sketches. Boston, Houghton Mifflin, 1900.

Literary Friends and Acquaintance: A Personal Retrospect of American Authorship. New York and London, Harper, 1900.

Heroines of Fiction. New York and London, Harper, 2 vols., 1901.

Literature and Life: Studies. New York and London, Harper, 1902.

London Films. New York and London, Harper, 1905.

Certain Delightful English Towns. New York and London, Harper, 1906.

Roman Holidays and Others. New York and London, Harper, 1908.

Seven English Cities. New York and London, Harper, 1909.

My Mark Twain: Reminiscences and Criticisms. New York and London, Harper, 1910.

Imaginary Interviews. New York and London, Harper, 1910.

Familiar Spanish Travels. New York and London, Harper, 1913.

The Seen and Unseen at Stratford-on-Avon: A Fantasy. New York and London, Harper, 1914.

The Daughter of the Storage and Other Things in Prose and Verse. New York and London, Harper, 1916.

Years of My Youth (autobiography). New York, Harper, 1916; London, Harper, 1917.

Life in Letters of William Dean Howells, edited by Mildred Howells. New York, Doubleday, 2 vols., 1928; London, Heinemann, 1 vol., 1929.

Representative Selections, edited by Clara Marburg Kirk and Rudolf Kirk. New York, American Book Company, 1950.

Selected Writings, edited by Henry Steele Commager. New York, Random House, 1950.

Prefaces to Contemporaries (1882-1920), edited by George Arms, William M. Gibson, and Frederic C. Marston, Jr. Gainesville, Florida, Scholars' Facsimiles and Reprints, 1957.

Criticism and Fiction and Other Essays, edited by Clara Marburg Kirk and Rudolf Kirk. New York, New York University Press, 1959.

Mark Twain-Howells Letters: The Correspondence of Samuel L. Clemens and William Dean Howells 1872-1910, edited by Henry Nash Smith and William M. Gibson. Cambridge, Massachusetts, Harvard University Press, 2 vols., 1960; abridged edition, as *Selected Mark Twain-Howells Letters*, 1967.

Discovery of a Genius: William Dean Howells and Henry James, edited by Albert Mordell. New York, Twayne, 1961.

Selected Edition, edited by Ronald Gottesman. Bloomington, Indiana University Press, 1968—

Howells as Critic, edited by Edwin H. Cady. London, Routledge, 1973.

The John Hay-Howells Letters: The Correspondence of John Milton Hay and William Dean Howells 1861-1905, edited by George Monteiro and Brenda Murphy. Boston, Twayne, 1980.

Editor, *Three Years in Chili*, by Mrs. C. B. Merwin. Columbus, Ohio, Follett Foster, 1861; as *Chili through American Spectacles*, New York, Bradburn, n. d.

Editor, *Choice Autobiographies*. Boston, Osgood, 6 vols., 1877, and Houghton Osgood, 2 vols., 1878.

Editor, with Thomas Sergeant Perry, *Library of Universal Adventure by Sea and Land*. New York, Harper, 1888.

Editor, *Mark Twain's Library of Humor*. New York, Webster, 1888.

Editor, *Poems of George Pellew*. Boston, Clarke, 1892.

Editor, *Recollections of Life in Ohio from 1813 to 1840*, by William Cooper Howells. Cincinnati, Clarke, 1895.

Editor, with Russell Sturgis. *Florence in Art and Literature*. Philadelphia, Booklovers Library, 1901.

Editor, with Henry Mills Alden, *Harper's Novelettes*. New York and London, Harper, 8 vols., 1906-08.

Editor, *The Great Modern American Short Stories: An Anthology*. New York, Boni and Liveright, 1920.

Editor, *Don Quixote*, by Cervantes, translated by Charles Jarvis. New York and London, Harper, 1923.

Translator, *Venice, Her Art-Treasures and Historical Associations: A Guide*, by Adalbert Müller. Venice, Münster, 1864.

*

Bibliography: *A Bibliography of William Dean Howells* by William M. Gibson and George Arms, New York, New York Public Library, 1948; in *Bibliography of American Literature 4* by Jacob Blanck, New Haven, Connecticut, Yale University Press, 1963.

Critical Studies: *The Road to Realism: The Early Years, 1837-1885, of William Dean Howells* and *The Realist at War: The Mature Years, 1885-1920, of William Dean Howells* by Edwin H. Cady, Syracuse, New York, Syracuse University Press, 2 vols., 1956-58; *Howells: His Life and World* by Van Wyck Brooks, New York, Dutton, 1959; *Howells: A Century of Criticism* edited by Kenneth E. Eble, Dallas, Southern Methodist University Press, 1962; *William Dean Howells, Traveler from Altruria 1889-1894*, New Brunswick, New Jersey, Rutgers University Press, 1962, and *W. D. Howells and Art in His Time*, Rutgers University Press, 1965, both by Clara Marburg Kirk, and *William Dean Howells* by Clara Marburg Kirk and Rudolf Kirk, New York, Twayne, 1962; *The Immense Complex Drama: The World and Art of the Howells Novel* by George C. Carrington, Jr., Columbus, Ohio State University Press, 1966; *The Literary Realism of William Dean Howells* by William McMurray, Carbondale, Southern Illinois University Press, 1967; *William D. Howells* by William M. Gibson, Minneapolis, University of Minnesota Press, 1967; *The Achievement of William Dean Howells: A Reinterpretation* by Kermit Vanderbilt, Princeton, New Jersey, Princeton University Press, 1968; *William Dean Howells: The Friendly Eye* by Edward Wagenknecht, New York, Oxford University Press, 1969; *William Dean Howells: An American Life* by Kenneth S. Lynn, New York, Harcourt Brace, 1971; *The Realism of William Dean Howells 1898-1920* by George N. Bennett, Nashville, Vanderbilt University Press, 1973; *Critics on William Dean Howells* edited by Paul A. Escholz, Coral Gables, Florida, University of Miami Press, 1975.

*   *   *

Willliam Dean Howells made a major contribution to utopian literature by inventing Altruria, a vision of an America which practiced what it preached in the Declaration of Independence. *A Traveler from Alturia*, "Letters of an Alturian Traveler" (in *Cosmopolitan*, 1893-94), and *Through the Eye of a Needle* make up the Altrurian romances, Howells's statement on socialism and civil rights.

Edward Bellamy and Ignatius Donnelly had recently caught attention through social protest fiction in *Looking Backward*, *Equality*, and *Caesar's Column*. In a time of depression, strikes, Populism, and social change, Howells chose to point to a better society through a visit by Aristides (after Aristides the Just) Homos from an imaginary island in the Aegean where law, government, and scoial relations were based on altruism, a term adopted from Auguste Comte's *System of Positive Policy*. Howells imitated Oliver Goldsmith's *Citizen of the World* papers, introducing the outsider who asks pointed questions and marvels at peculiar customs. Altruria has much in common with Bacon's New Atlantis and More's Utopia and points toward Skinner's Walden II. Mr. Twelvemough, a well-known novelist who narrates *A Traveler from Altruria*, represents the American's attitude toward Homos. He disapproves of his fondness toward the lower classes. "Letters" is composed of five letters from Homos to his friend Cyril at home, openly critical of what he sees. Homos refers to New York as Babylon and to Americans as lost in the dark ages. *Through the Eye of a Needle* is also narrated by letters, some by Homos and the rest by Eveleth Strange, a beautiful widow who marries (after great conflict) Homos and moves to Alturia. Although the Alturian works seem dated, they are important examples of attempts at social reform by an influential author.

—Mary S. Weinkauf

HOYLE, Fred and Geoffrey. British. HOYLE, Fred: Born in Bingley, Yorkshire, 24 June 1915. Educated at Bingley Grammar School; Emmanuel College, Cambridge (Mayhew Prizeman, 1936; Smith's Prizeman, 1938; Goldsmith Exhibitioner; Senior Exhibitioner of the Royal Commission for the Exhibition of 1851), mathematical tripos 1936, M. A. 1939. Served in the Admiralty, London, 1939-45. Married Barbara Clark in 1939; one son, Geoffrey Hoyle, and one daughter. Research Fellow, St. John's College, 1939-72, University Lecturer in Mathematics, 1945-58, Plumian Professor of Astronomy and Experimental Philosophy, 1958-72, and Director, Institute of Theoretical Astronomy, 1966-72, Cambridge University. Visiting Professor, 1953, 1954, 1956, Fairchild Scholar, 1974-75, and since 1963, Associate in Physics, California Institute of Technology, Pasadena. Staff Member, Mount Wilson and Palomar observatories, California, 1957-62; Professor of Astronomy, Royal Institution, London, 1969-72; White Professor, Cornell University, Ithaca, New York, 1972-78. Honorary Research Professor, University of Manchester, since 1972, and University College, Cardiff, since 1975; since 1973, Honorary Fellow, St. John's College, Cambridge; since 1984, Honorary Fellow, Emmanuel College, Cambridge. Member, Science Research Council, 1968-72. Recipient: Royal Astronomical Society Gold Medal, 1968; Kalinga Prize, 1968; Astronomical Society of the Pacific Bruce Medal, 1970, and Klumpke-Roberts Award, 1977; Royal Society Medal, 1974. Guest of Honor, Frontiers of Astronomy Symposium, Venice, 1975. Sc. D. : University of East Anglia, Norwich, 1967; D. Sc. : University of Leeds, 1969; University of Bradford, 1975; University of Newcastle, 1976. Fellow, 1957, and Vice-President, 1969-71, Royal Society; Honorary Member, American Academy of Arts and Sciences, 1964; Foreign Associate, National Academy of Sciences (USA), 1969; President, Royal Astronomical Society, 1971-73. Knighted, 1972. Address: c/o Royal Society, 6 Carlton House Terrace, London SW1Y 5AG, England. HOYLE, Geoffrey: Born in Scunthorpe, Lincolnshire, 12 January 1942; son of Fred Hoyle. Educated at Bryanston School, Blandford Forum, Dorset, 1955-59; St. John's

College, Cambridge, 1961-62. Married Valerie Jane Coope in 1971. Worked in documentary film production, 1963-67. Address: Laytus Hall Farm, Inskip, Preston, Lancashire, England.

SCIENCE-FICTION PUBLICATIONS

Novels

Fifth Planet. London, Heinemann, and New York, Harper, 1963.
Rockets in Ursa Major. London, Heinemann, and New York, Harper, 1969.
Seven Steps to the Sun. London, Heinemann, and New York, Harper, 1970.
The Molecule Men and The Monster of Loch Ness: Two Short Novels. London, Heinemann, and New York, Harper, 1971.
The Inferno. London, Heinemann, and New York, Harper, 1973.
Into Deepest Space. New York, Harper, 1974; London, Heinemann, 1975.
The Incandescent Ones. London, Heinemann, and New York, Harper, 1977.
The Westminster Disaster. London, Heinemann, and New York, Harper, 1978.
The Energy Pirate (for children). Loughborough, Ladybird, 1982.
The Giants of Universal Park (for children). Loughborough, Ladybird, 1982.
The Frozen Planet of Azuron (for children). Loughborough, Ladybird, 1982.
The Planet of Death (for children). Loughborough, Ladybird, 1982.

Novels by Fred Hoyle

The Black Cloud. London, Heinemann, and New York, Harper, 1957.
Ossian's Ride. London, Heinemann, and New York, Harper, 1959.
A for Andromeda (novelization of TV serial), with John Elliot. London Souvenir Press, and New York, Harper, 1962.
Andromeda Breakthrough (novelization of TV serial), with John Elliot. London, Souvenir Press, and New York, Harper, 1964.
October the First Is Too Late. London, Heinemann, and New York, Harper, 1966.
Comet Halley. London, Joseph, 1985.

Short Stories by Fred Hoyle

Element 79. New York, New American Library, 1967.

OTHER PUBLICATIONS

Other

Commonsense in Nuclear Energy. London, Heinemann, and San Francisco, Freeman, 1980.

OTHER PUBLICATIONS by Fred Hoyle

Plays

Rockets in Ursa Major (for children: produced London, 1962).

Television Plays (with John Elliot): *A for Andromeda* serial, 1961; *The Andromeda Breakthrough* serial, 1962.

Other

Some Recent Researches in Solar Physics. Cambridge, University Press, 1949.
The Nature of the Universe: A Series of Broadcast Lectures. Oxford, Blackwell, 1950; New York, Harper, 1951; revised edition, 1960.
A Decade of Decision. London, Heinemann, 1953.
Frontiers of Astronomy. London, Heinemann, and New York, Harper, 1955.
Man and Materialism. New York, Harper, 1956; London, Allen and Unwin, 1957.
Astronomy. London, Macdonald, and New York, Doubleday, 1962.
A Contradiction in the Argument of Malthus (lecture). Hull, University of Hull, 1963.
Star Formation. London, Her Majesty's Stationery Office, 1963.
Of Men and Galaxies. Seattle, University of Washington Press, 1964; London, Heinemann, 1965.
Nucleosynthesis in Massive Stars and Supernovae, with William A. Fowler. Chicago, University of Chicago Press, 1965.
Encounter with the Future. New York, Simon and Schuster, 1965.
The Asymmetry of Time (lecture). Canberra, Australian National University, 1965.
Galaxies, Nuclei, and Quasars. New York, Harper, 1965; London, Heinemann, 1966.
Man in the Universe. New York, Columbia University Press, 1966.
The New Face of Science. Cleveland, World, 1971.
From Stonehenge to Modern Cosmology. San Francisco, Freeman, 1972.
Nicolaus Copernicus: An Essay on His Life and Work. London, Heinemann, and New York, Harper, 1973.
Action-at-a-Distance in Physics and Cosmology, with J. V. Narlikar. San Francisco, Freeman, 1974.
Astronomy and Cosmology: A Modern Course. San Francisco, Freeman, 1975.
Astronomy Today. London, Heinemann, 1975; as *Highlights in Astronomy,* San Francisco, Freeman, 1975.
Ten Faces of the Universe. London, Heinemann, and San Francisco, Freeman, 1977.
On Stonehenge. London, Heinemann, and San Francisco, Freeman, 1977.
Energy or Extinction? The Case for Nuclear Energy. London, Heinemann, 1977.
The Cosmogony of the Solar System. Cardiff, University College Press, 1978; Short Hills, New Jersey, Enslow, 1979.
Lifecloud: The Origin of Life in the Universe, with Chandra Wickramasinghe. London, Dent, 1978; New York, Harper, 1979.
Diseases from Space, with Chandra Wickramasinghe. London, Dent, 1979; New York, Harper, 1980.
The Physics-Astronomy Frontier, with J. V. Narlikar. San Francisco, Freeman, 1980.
Steady-State Cosmology Revisited. Cardiff, University College Press, 1980.
The Relation of Astronomy to Biology. Cardiff, University College Press, 1980.
Ice: The Ultimate Human Catastrophe. New York, Hutchinson, and New York, Continuum, 1981.
The Quasar Controversy Resolved. Cardiff, University College

Press, 1981.

Evolution from Space, with Chandra Wickramasinghe. London, Dent, 1981; New York, Simon and Schuster, 1982.

Space Travellers, The Bringers of Life, with Chandra Wickramasinghe, edited by Barbara Hoyle. Cardiff, University College Press, and Hillside, New Jersey, Enslow, 1981.

Facts and Dogmas in Cosmology and Elsewhere (Rede Lecture). Cambridge, University Press, 1982.

Efroms and Other Papers on the Origin of Life. Hillside, New Jersey, Enslow, 1982.

The Universe According to Hoyle. Hillside, New Jersey, Enslow, 1982.

The Intelligent Universe: A New View of Creation and Evolution. London, Joseph, 1983; New York, Holt Rinehart, 1984.

Flight. Loughborough, Ladybird, 1984.

OTHER PUBLICATIONS by Geoffrey Hoyle

Other

2010: Living in the Future (for children). London, Heinemann, 1972; New York, Parents' Magazine Press, 1974.

Disaster (for children). London, Heinemann, 1975.

Ask Me Why, with Janice Robertson. London, Severn House, 1976.

* * *

Fred Hoyle is a distinguished British astronomer with an international reputation as a teacher and writer. He is the author of astronomy texts and other books ranging from a defense of nuclear power to speculations on the nature of the universe and man's place in creation; he supports the steady state theory and the view of continuous creation. Hoyle is the most prominent scientist writing SF today. He has written novels and stories, and other novels with his son, Geoffrey. The short stories are written as entertainments. They reveal a range and area of interest that readers do not usually associate with Hoyle's name. Most of the stories are either fantasy or fantasy science fiction, and many are comic; but they also include space opera and mystery. Hoyle shares certain comic interests with Asimov in human foibles, especially sexual mores, which are treated in a breezy, good-natured manner. Some of the comedy, however, is social and has teeth, as the title story of the collection, "Element 79." While Hoyle attacks perennials such as human greed, arrogance, and stupidity, he reserves his most trenchant comments for political and economic systems and their repressive, self-serving meddling with history.

The social and sexual comedy are important elements in most of the novels written by Fred Hoyle on his own and in collaboration with his son, but they support ideas and speculations drawn from hard science, especially astronomy. The best of these novels, *The Black Cloud, October the First Is Too Late,* and, with Geoffrey, *Fifth Planet,* are notable examples of speculative science fiction weaving together ideas from hard science with conventions of science fantasy enlivened by comic and sometimes satiric wit and an interest in philosphy and the arts. The overall effect is exceptionally thoughtful and stimulating entertainment for those who do not wish to sacrifice the life of the mind entirely to the enchantment of cosmic adventure. In all three novels the world's fate comes to depend upon the problem-solving powers of the scientific community, represented by a selected case of characters. The reader has the feeling that Hoyle's characters, beside being plausible, are also representative portraits of men and women in the scientific community and its satellite social spheres in the arts on both sides of the Atlantic. He sees science as the means through which humans must learn to meet the challenges to human survival posed by a hostile if not implacable universe. However, the greatest challenge to mankind comes from human society itself with its outmoded political power structure. The focus of Hoyle's criticism is the obstructionism of political systems and their reliance on barbarous military and police enforcers of national and social interests that are portrayed as active threats to both individual freedom and survival. Contrasted to the enslaving, restrictive, and punative character of political structures is the open, liberating, and creative community of scientists, artists, and intellectuals with no political and social boundaries. Their common ground is the pursuit of truth, and in the novels mentioned, that pursuit involves a challenge to earth from an outside, cosmic force.

The Black Cloud introduces a massive, intelligent black cloud that invades the solar system, nearly destroying earth before communication is established by Cris Kingsley, a brilliant, iconoclastic Cambridge astronomer. The *Fifth Planet* challenge is from an invading star, Helios, and its planetary system of five planets which approaches our own solar system. In *October the First Is Too Late* temporal and geographical boundaries are scrambled for a time by a modulated radio signal of alien origin. In each novel we are given a romance of science. For a moment in history, the world's destiny turns on the calculations, speculations, and superior moral vision of scientists. The excitement is not only the working out of such cosmic challenges but also the sense of being at the center of forces that control human history. Hoyle effectively communicates and creates that sense of excitement, satisfaction, and wish-fulfillment in the rightful exercise of power by those who are qualified to use it by virtue of their intelligence and devotion to both the cause of mankind and of truth.

These and other SF novels by Hoyle effectively create the illusion of lived science in the character's discovery process, formulation of hypotheses, testing of theories, comparing notes with colleagues, and conferring on results. The prominent human dimension of Hoyle's fine novels grows from the resultant sense of competition and cooperation that characterize scientific inquiry at its best. Frustrated often by political and bureaucratic red-tape, Hoyle's scientist-heroes succeed through their capability for planning and taking individual action and for unselfish cooperation in scientific enterprise. As important as science is, both as a liberating and protecting force, Hoyle never ignores or sacrifices humanistic and artistic values. Indeed, one of the special strengths of the best fiction lies in its philosophic probing of the limitations of scientific knowledge and understanding. The great moral ideas science has contributed to the mind are freedom of inquiry and devotion to truth; but philosophy offers an engagement with permanent questions of human conduct and understanding, and art must offer its necessary corrective of value and sublimity if the search for truth regardless of consequences is not to mislead the race to melancholy despair, as it does the futurians of 8000 AD in *October the First Is Too Late*.

Although we have in Hoyle's fiction a delightful balance of adventure, hard science speculation, fantastic premises, and various types of comedy ranging from domestic to social, the most distinctive feature is the depth and power of thought that comes from Hoyle's interest both in the arts (especially music) and philosophy (especially metaphysics and cosmology). His novels stimulate the reader's speculative imagination, and are also rich, early and late, with inspired insights into the relation between the arts and the sciences, between man's instinct for design and beauty and the physical universe he inhabits. The novel richest in such insights is *October the First Is Too Late,* but a brief passage from *The Black Cloud* illustrates how Hoyle triumphantly brings together traditional interests of SF speculation and elite interest in the arts to shed light upon one another. The question under discussion is the black cloud's interest in Beethoven's B flat major Sonata: "Our appreciation of music has really nothing to do with sound, although I know that at first sight it seems otherwise. What we appreciate in the brain are electrical signals that we receive from the ears. Our use of sound is simply a convenient device for generating certain patterns of electrical activity. There is indeed a good deal of evidence that musical rhythms reflect the main electrical rhythms that occur in the brain. " Hoyle has written entertaining space opera in *Rockets in Ursa Major* and science adventure melodrama in *Into Deepest Space* and *The Incandescent Ones* with Geoffrey Hoyle, but his permanent contribution to SF is to have brought esthetics, metaphysics, and speculative science together so compellingly in his major works.

—Donald L. Lawler

HOYLE, Trevor. British. Born in Rochdale, Lancashire, 25 February 1940. Educated at Rochdale Grammar School, 1951-57. Agent: Abner Stein, 10 Roland Gardens, London SW7 3PH. Address: 34 Cedar Lane, Newhay, Rochdale, Lancashire OL16 4LQ, England.

SCIENCE-FICTION PUBLICATIONS

Novels (series: Blake's Seven; Q)

Q: Seeking the Mythical Future. London, Panther, 1977; New York, Ace, 1982.
Q: Through the Eye of Time. London, Panther, 1977; New York, Ace, 1982.
Blake's Seven. London, Sphere, 1977.
Q: The Gods Look Down. London, Panther, 1978; New York, Ace, 1982.
Blake's Seven: Project Avalon. London, Arrow, 1979.
Earth Cult. London, Panther, 1979; as *This Sentient Earth*, New York, Zebra, 1979.
Blake's Seven: Scorpio Attack. London, BBC, 1981.
The Last Gasp. New York, Crown, 1983; London, Sphere, 1984.

OTHER PUBLICATIONS

Novels

The Relatively Constant Copywriter. Manchester, Northern Writers, 1972.
Rule of Night. London, Futura, 1975.
The Sexless Spy. London, Sphere, 1977.
The Svengali Plot. London, Sphere, 1978.
The Man Who Travelled on Motorways. London, Calder, 1979; New York, Riverrun, 1982.
The Stigma. London, Sphere, 1980.
Vail. London, Calder, 1984; New York, Riverrun, 1985.

Plays

Television Plays: *Blake's Seven: Ultraworld*, 1980; *Whatever Happened to the Heroes?*, 1982.

*

Manuscript Collection: Rochdale Reference Library, Lancashire.

Trevor Hoyle comments:

I am primarily interested—insofar as SF is concerned—in the philosophical and metaphysical implications of the latest discoveries in quantum physics and cosmology. Recently I have become fascinated by the ways in which these theories and concepts have a direct relation to aspects of Eastern mysticism, in particular Buddhism. I tried to touch on these in my Q trilogy (in rather a hamfisted way, I must confess), and have plans to investigate these areas in far greater depth. While not strictly SF, such novels as *The Man Who Travelled on Motorways* and *Vail* also deal with these complex, baffling, and yet engrossing subjects. My task is to make the reader see and appreciate their interrelatedness, and to be as thrilled and dazzled by them as I am.

*   *   *

Trevor Hoyle's well known "Q" series consists of three books: *Seeking the Mythical Future, Through the Eye of Time*, and *The Gods Look Down*. Christian Queghan is a Myth Technologist who investigates possible pasts and futures in a discipline that assumes all realities are equally probable. In *Seeking the Mythical Future* Queghan is inserted into a parallel universe where humans and dinosaurs exist together, where personal beliefs are rigidly controlled, and where Psychological Concentration camps exist for those who will not conform to normalcy. The satire on scientific methods and bureaucratic bungling makes the book lively yet profoundly serious.

Through the Eye of Time is the most ambitious book of the series. The scientists of Queghan's Earth IVn, a terraformed version of Old Earth, are working on a project to reconstruct a human brain. The identity chosen: Adolf Hitler. Queghan involves himself in the project when he finds the computer exchanging data by coincidence. That coincidence convinces Queghan that an alternate reality—where Germany developed the Atomic Bomb first—is undermining the reality of his Reality. Only insertion into that alternate reality can prevent the disaster that threatens the spacetime continuum. Hoyle captures the personality of Hitler beautifully and creates a unique, sinister character in Dr. Theodor Morell, personal physician to Hitler.

The concluding volume is less successful. Queghan joins forces with Dr. Francis Dagon to decipher primitive texts from ancient Earth through Myth Technology. The computer describes the legendary Ark of the Covenant in the form of blueprints for an existing technology. Queghan is sure Dagon is using his research findings in an attempt to change history. Only Queghan's powers to insert himself into alternate realities can stop Dagon's plans to alter the past. The idea is clever, but the book's conclusion is much too clichéd, much too predictable. However, the "Q" series is one of the best extended explorations of alternative realities in science fiction.

Hoyle's best book to date is an environmental disaster novel, *The Last Gasp*. Earth is totally polluted: the microscopic plant life in the oceans is dying, causing the beginning of the destruction of the food chain. At the same time, the superpowers plan to fight their next war with new, deadly forms of environmental warfare. British marine biologist Gavin Chase and a team of scientists realize the Earth is doomed and attempt to escape the death of the biosphere by building giant space colonies to survive in. Yet they have enemies in the military-industrial complex who refuse to believe that Earth is dying. Chief of these forces is Lloyd Madden, an evil genius who desires the death of the human race so he can repopulate it with a new race of mutants. *The Last Gasp* delivers a chilling portrait of disaster and hope.

Hoyle's most haunting work is the frankly erotic novel, *The Man Who Travelled on Motorways*. As the narrator travels, his mind explores the realities and fantasies of his life. Much of the book is surreal, but science fictional aspects are apparent in the discussions of reality. Much of the book is sexist: Hoyle's narrator seems incapable of love, merely using women to satisfy his sexual needs in loathsome fashions. Yet the book speaks to the unconscious desires of travellers of either sex and takes a bold, difficult path to break down life's certainties into more truthful probabilities.

Trevor Hoyle is an unusual writer with a gift for making into convincing fictions his surreal, dreamlike visions.

—George Kelley

HUBBARD, L(aFayette) Ron(ald). American. Born in Tilden, Nebraska, 13 March 1911. Educated at George Washington University, Washington, D. C., B. S. in civil engineering 1934; Princeton University, New Jersey, 1945; Sequoia University, Ph. D. 1950. Married Mary Sue Whipp; two daughters and two sons. Wrote travel and aviation articles in the 1930's; explorer: Commander, Caribbean Motion Picture Expedition, 1931, West Indies Mineral Survey Expedition, 1932, and Alaskan Radio-Experimental Expedition, 1940. Director, Hubbard Foundation; Founding Director, Church of Scientology, 1952; Director, Dianetics and Scientology, 1952-66; resigned all directorships, 1966. *Died 29 January 1986.*

SCIENCE-FICTION PUBLICATIONS

Novels

Death's Deputy. Los Angeles, Fantasy, 1948.
Final Blackout. Providence, Rhode Island, Hadley, 1948.
Triton, and Battle of Wizards. Los Angeles, Fantasy, 1949.
The Kingslayer (includes "The Beast" and "The Invaders"). Los Angeles, Fantasy, 1949; as *Seven Steps to the Arbiter,* Chatsworth, California, Major, 1975.
Fear, and Typewriter in the Sky. New York, Gnome Press, 1951; London, Cherry Tree, 1952.
From Death to the Stars (includes *Death's Deputy* and *The Kingslayer*). Los Angeles, Fantasy, 1953.
Return to Tomorrow. New York, Ace, 1954; London, Panther, 1957.
Fear, and Ultimate Adventure. New York, Berkley, 1970.
Battlefield Earth: A Saga of the Year 3000. New York, St. Martin's Press, 1983; London, Quadrant, 1984.

Short Stories

Ole Doc Methuselah. Austin, Texas, Theta Press, 1970.
Lives You Wished to Lead But Never Dared, edited by V. S. Wilhite. Clearwater, Florida, Theta Press, 1978.

OTHER PUBLICATIONS

Novels

Buckskin Brigades. New York, Macaulay, 1937; London,

Wright and Brown, 1938.
Slaves of Sleep. Chicago, Shasta, 1948.

Verse

Hymn of Asia: An Eastern Poem. Los Angeles, Church of Scientology, 1974.

Other

Dianetics: The Modern Science of Mental Health. New York, Hermitage House, 1950; London, Ridgway, 1951.
Science of Survival. Wichita and East Grinstead, Sussex, Hubbard, 1951.
Self Analysis. Wichita, International Library of Arts and Science, 1951.
Dianetics: The Original Thesis. Wichita, Wichita Publishing, 1951.
Handbook for Preclears. Wichita, Scientic Press, 1951.
Notes on the Lectures of L. Ron Hubbard. Wichita, Hubbard, 1951.
Advanced Procedure and Axioms. Wichita, Hubbard, 1951.
Scientology 8-80. Phoenix, Hubbard, and East Grinstead, Sussex, Scientology, 1952.
A Key to the Unconscious. Phoenix, Scientic Press, 1952.
Dianetics: The Evolution of a Science. London, Hubbard, 1953; Phoenix, Hubbard, 1955.
Scientology: A History of Man. London, Hubbard, 1953.
How to Live Though an Executive. Phoenix, Hubbard, 1953.
Self-Analysis in Dianetics. London, Ridgway, 1953.
Scientology 8-8008. London, Hubbard, 1953.
Dianetics 1955! Phoenix, Hubbard, 1954.
The Creation of Human Ability: A Handbook for Scientologists. Phoenix, Hubbard, and London, Scientology, 1955.
This Is Scientology: The Science of Certainty. London, Hubbard, 1955.
The Key to Tomorrow (selections), edited by U. Keith Gerry. Johannesburg, Hubbard, 1955.
Scientology: The Fundamentals of Thought. London, Hubbard, 1956.
Problems of Work. Johannesburg, Hubbard, 1957.
Fortress in the Sky (on the moon). Washington, D. C., Hubbard, 1957.
Have You Lived Before This Life? London, Hubbard, 1958; New York, Vantage, 1960.
Self-Analysis in Scientology. London, Hubbard, 1959.
Scientology: Plan for World Peace . East Grinstead, Sussex, Scientology, 1964.
Scientology Abridged Dictionary. East Grinstead, Sussex, Hubbard, 1965.
A Student Comes to Saint Hill. Bedford, Sidney Press, 1965.
Scientology: A New Slant on Life. London, Hubbard, 1965.
East Grinstead. East Grinstead, Sussex, Hubbard, 1966.
Introduction to Scientology Ethics. Edinburgh, Scientology, 1968.
The Phoenix Lectures. Edinburgh, Scientology, 1968.
How to Save Your Marriage. Copenhagen, Scientology, 1969.
When in Doubt, Communicate: Quotations from the Work of L. Ron Hubbard, edited by Ruth Minshull and Edward M. Lefshon. Ann Arbor, Michigan, Scientology, 1969.
Scientology 0-8. Copenhagen, Scientology, 1970.
Mission into Time. Copenhagen, Scientology, 1973.
The Management Series 1970-1974. Los Angeles, American Saint Hill Organization, 1974.
The Organization Executive Course. Los Angeles, American Saint Hill Organization, 8 vols., 1974.

Dianetics Today. Los Angeles, Scientology, 1975.
Dianetics and Scientology Technical Dictionary . Los Angeles, Scientology, 1975.
The Technical Bulletins of Dianetics and Scientology. Los Angeles, Scientology, 1976—.
The Volunteer Minister's Handbook. Los Angeles, Scientology, 1976.
Axioms and Logics. Los Angeles, Scientology, 1976.
A Summary of Scientology for Churches. Los Angeles, Scientology, 1977.
The Book of Case Remedies. Los Angeles, Scientology, 1977.
What Is Scientology. Los Angeles, Scientology, 1978.
The Research and Discovery Series. Los Angeles, Scientology, 1980—.
The Second Dynamic (selection), edited by Cass Pool. Portland, Oregon, Heron, 1981.
Self-Analysis. Los Angeles, Bridge, 1982.
Scientology: Fundamentals of Thought. Los Angeles, Bridge, 1983.
Dianetics: The Evolution of a Science. Los Angeles, Bridge, 1983.
The Problems of Work. Los Angeles, Bridge, 1983.
The Dynamics of Life. Los Angeles, Bridge, 1983.
The Way to Happiness. Los Angeles, Bridge, 1984.

Other texts and pamphlets published.

*   *   *

Best known as the author of *Dianetics* and founder of the Dianetics-based Church of Scientology, L. Ron Hubbard was a prolific writer of science fiction, fantasy, and adventure fiction during the 1930's and 1940's. A good deal of his output, much of it published in *Astounding* and its companion fantasy pulp *Unknown,* is of interest today only because of its use of a bizarre gnostic psychology that foreshadows Hubbard's later eminence as the founder and leader of a cult religion. Yet despite a prose that too often cries out for better editing, some of his work justifies the high regard in which it is held by other veterans of the Golden Age.

Having begun his writing career with nautical adventure fiction, Hubbard often composed science fiction and fantasy by merely displacing swashbuckling epic into the new context through use of a fantastic premise or framing device. For instance, in *Slaves of Sleep* a meek young shipping magnate is accused of a gruesome murder which occurs when a North African *jinni* is released from an ancient jar. Jailed for murder, Jan Palmer finds himself plunged while asleep into an alternate life as a cynical, troublemaking, but courageous sailor. In that world dominated by *jinn* and other demons out of middle eastern folklore, he is also in trouble with the authorities. As the two stories clunk along in uneasy partnership, the bookish shipowner's personality is modified by that of his alter ego, who purloins a powerful talisman and wins a battle in the other world. All this results in Jan being cleared and restored to his inheritance in this world, winning a bride in the bargain. In spite of a few moments of social satire and a potentially interesting metafiction about fantasy's role in constructing the personality, the novel remains a blood-and-thunder romance in an awkward framework.

Typewriter in the Sky, clearly Hubbard's most successful fiction, also uses such a framing device. In this delightful bagatelle (which sports, along with several characters bearing Hubbard pen names, one named Bagatela), a musician finds himself transported into the world of a romance of the Spanish Main being composed hastily by a friend who writes mass-market adventure fiction. Mike DeWolf is not only protagonist, but also reader of the text: buffeted by narrative implausibilities and inconsistencies as well as a major rewrite which sets up an alternate but no less fatal ending, he is finally thrust out of the fiction to return as a vagrant on the streets of modern New York, wondering if his *primary* universe is being created by a God "in a dirty bathrobe. " This consummate "mockery of plot" appeared a quarter-century before the vogue of Barth, Pynchon, and Vonnegut, and long before Borges became generally known to American writers. A similar vein of humor appears in *Triton,* a well-conceived if clumsily written lark about a meek man who swallows a sea-god, thereby gaining the *machismo* needed to face down Neptune himself as well as his own dry land persecutors. *Triton,* in fact, is a reprise of the fundamental fantasy of *Slaves of Sleep,* but is much tighter and self-deprecating than the earlier piece. Two other early novels, *Fear* and *Death's Deputy*, offer plots that use demons to explain murders and untimely deaths. Together with the other pieces so far discussed, they show that Hubbard's talent was more for the weird tale than for SF.

When discussing Hubbard, one is apparently expected to praise as his finest SF work the militaristic *Final Blackout* . It is hard to see why, unless its virulent fascism—which the text pathetically attempts to deny—appeals to critics opposed to the welfare state or to socialism. The "novel" reads like a plot summary for a much longer work, and its hero (known only as "the Lieutenant") is developed as neither a realistic character nor a credible personification. Only if read ironically—as Hubbard surely did not intend—does the text amount to much more than a fascist utopia and anti-social-democratic tract.

Hubbard's postwar SF is of little distinction. The stories collected in *Old Doc Methuselah* are about a long-lived medical man who runs an interstellar ambulance service, dashing about the Galaxy conquering disease, injury, and ignorance, and aiding (extra-legally) the fight against injustice. The series is vintage space opera: Doc has a cute alien sidekick, he wields a blaster as comfortably as a hypodermic, and he faces down hordes of tyrannical villains in his capacity as a Soldier of Light. With all the excitement, however, Doc's favorite pastime is fishing, a sedentary hobby which ironically undercuts the theme of unaging omnipotence. Even more predictable is *The Kingslayer*, a tale of Byzantine conspiracy involving one Kit Kellan. A young drifter rescued from the authorities by revolutionaries and recruited to assassinate the all-powerful Galactic Arbiter, Kit manages to overcome most of the obstacles to finding his victim, but he is seized just before reaching his goal. Brought before the Arbiter, he learns that the Arbiter is not a despot, that the "revolutionaries" are operatives loyal to the Council, that his mission has been a test of his mettle, and that he himself is the Arbiter's son and heir presumptive. Aside from being a psychoanalytic goldmine, the novel is another variation on the old Galactic Empire motif, with more than a hint of the militaristic strongman theme of *Final Blackout*.

For three decades, except for an occasional reprint, the SF community heard nothing from Hubbard that did not have to do with his notoriety as the embattled leader of the Scientology movement. Then in 1983, especially surprising to those who thought the old guru dead, a behemoth of a novel appeared under the title of *Battlefield Earth*. Claimed by Hubbard to be the longest SF novel ever published (819 pages clothbound and 1066 pages in paper), the book comes with a recorded "soundtrack" and a preface in which Hubbard gets into the acts of defining SF and describing what it was like to write for John W. Campbell, Jr. The novel itself, an atavism of contemporary SF, is the tale of how Jonnie Goodboy Tyler marshalls the pitiful remnant (25,000) of the human species to overthrow the Psycho yoke, and then manipulates the Galactic Bank to restore the former mining colony of Earth to its rightful pre-eminence among the various foul-smelling aliens of the universe. The technological accomplishments of the year 3000 are barely updated applications of the "superscience" of the old space operas—from matter transmitters to machines that enable one to learn alien languages instantaneously. The various ethnic groups of the earthling resistance are led by Highland clans complete with warpipes, kilts, and claymores. The "good guys" defeat the "bad guys" because they are virtuous, persistent, lucky—and look like us. And women and alien females are put firmly in their place: they breed, nurture, and cook. The wit that sometimes shone through Hubbard's earlier turgidities has been reduced to puns like "the nebula of crap. " But for all its obvious flaws, *Battlefield Earth* is a good read for a mind on vacation: Hubbard does know how to tell an exciting story (or two, to be exact).

Hubbard's return to SF was not limited to *Battlefield Earth*. In 1984 his Bridge Publications inaugurated the ongoing Writers of the Future contest, a quarterly competition for new and unpublished writers of SF and fantasy. Intended to make up for the demise of the pulp magazines as places for new talent to break in and judged by a corps of professional SF and fantasy writers, the contest awards monetary prizes and in 1985 published its first collection of winning stories, promising to make the volume an annual. It is easy to be cynical about yet another award competition, but so far Hubbard (or his designees) have fulfilled the promise to use the contest as an opportunity for new writers.

Hubbard's contribution to SF, then, is an odd one. His success as a fiction machine was emulated by many younger writers, and he was genuinely admired by Campbell and other *Astounding* contemporaries. His talent, however, lay in the direction of light fantasy and comic manipulation of pulp conventions. He would have developed further along these lines, no doubt, had not World War II convinced him that he had a messianic obligation to save the world through "dianetic therapy. " So instead of continuing to write fiction, L. Ron Hubbard turned science fantasy into a modernized version of the old gnostic religion. Despite his recent return to SF activity, Scientology remains Hubbard's supreme science fiction.

—John P. Brennan

HUGHES, Monica (née Ince). Canadian. Born in Liverpool, Lancashire, England, 3 November 1925; daughter of the mathematician E. L. Ince; became Canadian citizen in 1957. Educated at the Convent of the Holy Child Jesus, Harrogate, Yorkshire, graduated 1942; Edinburgh University, 1942-43. Served in the Women's Royal Naval Service, 1943-46. Married Glen Hughes in 1957; two daughters and two sons. Dress designer, London, 1948-49, and Bulawayo, Zimbabwe, 1950; bank clerk, Umtali, Zimbabwe, 1951; laboratory technician, National Research Council, Ottawa, 1952-57. Recipient: Vicky Metcalf Award, 1981; Canada Council prize, 1982, 1983. Address: 13816-110A Avenue, Edmonton, Alberta T5M 2M9, Canada.

SCIENCE-FICTION PUBLICATIONS (for children)

Novels (series: Isis)

Crisis on Conshelf Ten. Toronto, Copp Clark, and London,

Hamish Hamilton, 1975; New York, Atheneum, 1977.
Earthdark. London, Hamish Hamilton, 1977.
The Tomorrow City. London, Hamish Hamilton, 1978.
Beyond the Dark River. London, Hamish Hamilton, 1979; New York, Atheneum, 1981.
The Keeper of the Isis Light. London, Hamish Hamilton, 1980; New York, Atheneum, 1981.
The Guardian of Isis. London, Hamish Hamilton, 1981; New York, Atheneum, 1982.
The Isis Pedlar. London, Hamish Hamilton, 1982; New York, Atheneum, 1983.
Ring-Rise, Ring-Set. London, MacRae, and New York, Watts, 1982.
The Beckoning Lights. Edmonton, Alberta, LeBel, 1982.
Space Trap. Toronto, Groundwood, and London, MacRae, 1983; New York, Watts, 1984.
Devil on My Back. London, MacRae, 1984; New York, Atheneum, 1985.
Sandwriter. London, MacRae, 1985.

Uncollected Short Stories

"The Iron-Barred Door," in *Contexts Two*. Scarborough, Ontario, Nelson, 1982.
"Zone of Silence," in *Out of Time*, edited by Aidan Chambers. London, Bodley Head, 1984.

OTHER PUBLICATIONS (for children)

Novels

Gold-Fever Trail. Edmonton, Alberta, LeBel, 1974.
The Ghost Dance Caper. London, Hamish Hamilton, 1978.
Hunter in the Dark. Toronto, Clarke Irwin, 1982; New York, Atheneum, 1983.
The Treasure of the Long Sault. Edmonton, Alberta, LeBel, 1982.
My Name Is Paula Popowich! Toronto, Lorimer, 1983.

*

Manuscript Collection: University of Calgary, Alberta.

Monica Hughes comments:

I grew up fascinated by the story of humankind, the way in which we acquired language, told stories, developed tribal customs, and at last discovered our world and learned how to dominate it. The interconnectedness of it all.

It is only a step around a dark corner from the past into the future: given what happened then, what might happen when . . . ? I am particularly concerned with the fragility of our environment and with the loss of the "bloom on the grape" of life as our technological society progresses like a juggernaut, threatening rain forests, oceans, indigenous native cultures.

* * *

Monica Hughes is most successful and provocative when she combines one or both of two themes—the price society is willing to pay for technological progress, and the importance of people's adapting intelligently to the environment they find themselves in—and young adult concerns, in particular the first stirrings of romantic love. Witness, for example, *The Keeper of the Isis Light*, the first and best segment of the Isis trilogy, and *Ring-Rise, Ring-Set*, runner-up for the 1982 *Guardian* Award. Hughes is less successful when she succumbs to cuteness, e.g.,

The Isis Pedlar with its unconvincing portrait of an irresponsible but likeable Irish inter-galactic pedlar, or fails to respect the boundaries science sometimes imposes upon the imagination, e.g., *Space Trap* with its aliens implausibly banded together in self defense.

In *The Keeper of the Isis Light*, although utilizing some material previously tapped—surgery to facilitate human adaptation to a hostile environment (*Crisis on Conshelve Ten* where "mer-men" are created in order more readily to explore the seas) and the high risks of over-relying on artificial intelligence (*The Tomorrow City* where the central computer, C-Three, runs amuck)—Hughes put together an original and poignant story. Young Olwen, the daughter of scientists responsible for the Isis Light, is surgically altered by Guardian, a highly advanced robot, to withstand the excessive radiation of Isis which had killed her parents. In doing so, the robot only follows instructions to guard the child at all costs. Unaware that she has been altered to appear lizard-like and believing that she is beautiful, Olwen feels attracted to Mark London, a member of the first Isis colony. He too is attracted to the loveliness he senses beneath the mask Guardian forces Olwen to wear. When Mark learns the truth and in horror recoils from Olwen's uncovered face, she realizes his declaration of love is insincere; and she must live rejected. Hughes makes clear that Guardian's decision to alter surgically Olwen's appearance, although defensible on technical grounds, profoundly shocks sensibilities which equate being human with looking human. Hence, the technological innovation Olwen's survival represents demands too high a price: not only does the young woman suffer permanent rejection, but technology is perceived as so threatening that the colony is persuaded at great risk to its survival to use as little of it as possible.

In *Ring-Rise, Ring-Set*, which is both SF and survival story, Hughes explores another moral problem effected by technology. When the sun's rays are blocked by rings of meteoric dust in the atmosphere and a new ice age is imminent, most people, banding together in Cities and submitting to regimentation, frantically seek technology to dissolve the rings. One new technique, however, seriously endangers the Ekoes who insist upon living outside the City close to nature. The focus of the clash between the two differing cultures is Lisa, a City dweller, who, running away to the icy wastes, becomes lost and is found by the Ekoes. Lisa's refusal to return to City because at last she feels whole among the Ekoes where too she has found love is credible and moving. Moreover, the novel forthrightly presents both City's uncertainty whether technology can or ought to preserve civilization as is, and the Ekoes' determination, regardless of cost, not to abandon their values for the sake of survival as defined by City. When Hughes is "on target," then, her novels convincingly demonstrate that it is no easy, painless resolution of the conflict which can result when technology impinges upon human life.

—Francis J. Molson

HUGHES, Zach. Pseudonym for Hugh Zachary. American. Born in Holdenville, Oklahoma, 12 January 1928. Educated at Oklahoma A & M College, 1945-46; University of North Carolina, Chapel Hill, B. A. in journalism 1951. Served in the 82nd Airborne Division of the United States Army, 1946-48. Married Elizabeth Wiggs in 1948; two daughters. Worked in radio and television broadcasting, 1948-61. Since 1962, part-time fisherman, guide, florist, construction worker, and free-lance writer. Agent: Ray Peekner Literary Agency, 2625 North 36th Street, Milwaukee, Wisconsin 53210. Address: 7 Pebble Beach Drive, Yaupon Beach, North Carolina 28461, U. S. A.

SCIENCE-FICTION PUBLICATIONS

Novels

The Book of Rack the Healer. New York, Award, 1973.
The Legend of Miaree. New York, Ballantine, 1974.
Gwen, In Green (as Hugh Zachary). New York, Fawcett, 1974; London, Coronet, 1976.
Tide. New York, Putnam, 1974.
Seed of the Gods. New York, Berkley, 1974; London, Hale, 1979.
The Stork Factor. New York, Berkley, 1975.
For Texas and Zed. New York, Popular Library, 1976.
Tiger in the Stars. Toronto, Laser, 1976.
The St. Francis Effect. New York, Berkley, 1976.
Killbird. New York, New American Library, 1980.
Thunderworld. New York, New American Library, 1982.
Gold Star. New York, New American Library, 1983.

OTHER PUBLICATIONS as Hugh Zachary

Novels

One Day in Hell. New York, Newstand Library, 1961.
A Small Slice of War. New York, Caravelle, 1968.
A Feast of Fat Things. Jacksonville, Illinois, Harris Wolfe, 1968.
Rake's Junction. New York, Lancer, 1970.
The Legend of the Deadly Doll. New York, Award, 1973.
Second Chance. Canoga Park, California, Major, 1976.
Dynasty of Desire, with Elizabeth Zachary. New York, Dell, 1978.
The Land Rushers, with Elizabeth Zachary. New York, Dell, 1978.
The Golden Dynasty, with Elizabeth Zachary, New York, Dell, 1980.
Bloodrush. New York, Nordon, 1981.
Tower of Treason. New York, Jove, 1982.
Flight to Freedom, New York, Dell, 1982.
Desert Battle. New York, Dell, 1982.
Bitter Victory. New York, Dell, 1983.

Some 60 other novels published under various pseudonyms.

Play

Screenplay: *Tide*.

Other

The Beachcomber's Handbook of Seafood Cookery. Winston Salem, North Carolina, Blair, 1969.
Wild Card Poker. Brattleboro, Vermont, Stephen Greene Press, 1975.

*

Manuscript Collection: Cape Fear Technical Institute, Wilmington, North Carolina.

Zach Hughes comments:

I think the first duty of any writer, including a science-fiction writer, is to tell a story which involves real people who react to situations with believable motivation. Moreover, I feel that the setting for science fiction is, first and foremost, space. I write little science fiction, because it is difficult for me to come up with an idea which qualifies, in my mind, as worthy of having been published during the golden years of S. F., when awe and wonder and the sense of infinite distance and infinite variety in the universe was a necessary ingredient for any S. F. story. Several of my S. F. books are set in the time of The United Planets Confederation, as introduced in the last section of my first S. F. book, *The Book Of Rack The Healer. Gold Star,* and the upcoming *Closed System,* deal with residual effects of the first and last war in space between the United Planets and the dictator worlds of the Zede systems.

*   *   *

Zach Hughes is the pseudonym Hugh Zachary has used for his science fiction. His first SF novel, *The Book of Rack the Healer,* is in many ways his best book. Earth, centuries after a nuclear holocaust, is dying from accumulated radiation and pollution. Mankind has evolved into four species: Keepers, moronic women whose brains store knowledge like a computer; Far Seers, males who supply leadership; Healers, males who have the power to travel on Earth's ravaged surface and collect raw materials to feed the population by regenerating cells damaged by the corrosive atmosphere; and Power Givers, women with the power of flight. Hughes creates an innovative ecological puzzle, while developing the characters of Rack the Healer, Red Earth the Far Seer, and Beautiful Wings the Power Giver. The ending is tragic, yet Hughes manages to moderate the pathos with hope. Hughes continues this story in a prequel called *Thunderworld.* The crew of a small scout ship discovers an infant solar system with an Earth-type planet racked with earthquakes and about to enter an Ice Age. The crew names the planet "Worthless" because their mission is to find worlds suitable for human colonization to ease the crushing overpopulation of Earth. But before they leave, one of the crew members unknowingly takes on a telepathic symbiotic life-form. Hughes explores the concept of dual identities sharing the same body. Then news arrives that war has broken out on Earth and the home of Man has been reduced to a radioactive, burned-out cinder. Hughes cleverly weaves these developments into a complex plot where the world of Rack the Healer and this "Worthless" planet converge fifty thousand years in the future.

Killbird returns to these themes. Eban the Hairy One is one of a small group of primitives surviving a nuclear holocaust. Zachary cunningly invents a sophisticated society, while sending Eban on an incredible set of adventures in the dangerous, savage world. *Killbird* possesses many of Hughes's best-developed characters—Eban, his wife Mar, and the bitter Yuree—as well as some of his best writing.

The Legend of Miaree is a clever positioning of a sociological disaster with the problems of translating alien texts. It is really two books in one: the actual legend of Miaree is being read by human students at a planetary university as the translation of the only surviving artifact of two destroyed alien races. The students and their professor provide commentary on the deadly progression of events, commentary that gives additional insight into the contrast between alien societies. Hughes does a masterful job creating the character of Miaree and her culture as two galaxies collide, threatening two star races. The ending is grim, but Hughes skillfully lightens the mood by shifting the action to the human students and their wise professor.

In contrast to Hughes's serious SF, he has written his share of space operas. *Pressure Man* features Dominic "Flash" Gordon on a desperate mission to build a spacecraft that will withstand the pressures of thirty thousand atmospheres. An alien ship, which might hold the secret to FTL space travel, is orbiting Jupiter. Gordon is charged with designing a new ship to capture the alien craft. Hughes tells Gordon's story with the backdrop of an Earth swelling with overpopulation and radical groups bent on destroying the space program. The politics of the novel is ultra-conservative, and the plot cheats the reader of an actual first contact turning into a tribute to Immanuel Velikovsky's theories instead. *Gold Star* features Pete and Jan Jaynes, a married couple aboard a space tug, who hunt for the missing experimental starship *Rimfire* for salvage and find themselves fighting for their lives against a rival band of salvagers. The plot is fast paced, and the result is a satisfying action adventure. *Seed of the Gods,* an attempt to spoof the von Daniken cult, is a routine "first contact" novel.

Two ecological disaster novels, *Tide* and *The St. Francis Effect,* suffer from undeveloped characters, though some of the information is fascinating. In *Tide* efforts to produce increased breeding of fish lead to mutations which trigger extreme aggression in the fish and the people who eat them. In *The St. Francis Effect* a deep-ocean mining operation in the Pacific brings up an ages-old parasite carried by mosquitos. The resultant plague has a 100% mortality rate, and in a matter of days turns its victims into mummified corpses. The book is an effective disaster novel but the mosquito and the disease—not the human characters—are the stars.

The Stork Factor and *For Texas and Zed* are both superman novels. In the first, set in a repressive and totalitarian future society totally controlled by a religious dictatorship, a young priest, Luke, has developed psi powers, and becomes part of the underground plotting to overthrow the government. At the same time, an advanced alien race sends a starship to Earth to determine the threat its technology presents. The impact of the convergence of events produces a fast-paced, entertaining novel. In the second, Lex Murichon, one of the leading figures of the planet Texas delegation to the Earth Empire, is a blend of the heroes of H. Beam Piper and John J. McGuire's *A Planet for Texans* (1958) and Harry Harrison's satiric *Bill, The Galactic Hero* (1965). The fierce independence of the Texans is translated into a culture on a hidden solitary planet where the new Texans provide meat to the Empire while staying above the cold war between the Empire and the Cassiopeian battle fleet. But Lex gets involved as a gunner aboard an Empire starship, deserts and heads back to Texas, thus causing a state of war. This much of the novel is accomplished with wit and style. But after Texas successfully defends itself against the Empire's attacks and Lex becomes the leader of the Texas forces—evolving into an all-conquering Alexander the Great figure—the book lags badly.

Tiger in the Stars is a van Vogtian novel of humans encountering aliens of vast supremacy. The hero, John Plank, is turned into a cyborg linked with a starship of incredible power. Unfortunately, the novel drifts from subplot to subplot without developing a picture of future human culture or the fantastic alien culture. The ending becomes predictable far too soon and the end result is a flatness usually absent from Hughes's best work.

In *Gwen, In Green* a young couple moves into a rambling house on an isolated island in the south. But within the clear pool near the house grow alien plants who establish contact with the young wife, Gwen. As the relationship between Gwen and the alien plants become stronger, the plot explodes with murder and sexuality. The book features a memorable grimness as well as a powerful examination of the eerie symbiotic relationship of human and alien.

—George Kelley

HULL, E(dna) M(ayne). American. Born in Brandon, Manitoba, Canada, 1 May 1905. Married A. E. van Vogt, *q. v.*, in 1939. Secretary to Henry Wise Wood. Guest of Honor, 4th World Science Fiction Convention, 1946. *Died 20 January 1975.*

SCIENCE-FICTION PUBLICATIONS

Novels

Planets for Sale, with A. E. van Vogt. New York, Fell, 1954; London, Panther, 1978.
The Winged Man, with A. E. van Vogt. New York, Doubleday, 1966; London, Sidgwick and Jackson, 1967.

Short Stories

Out of the Unknown, with A. E. van Vogt. Los Angeles, Fantasy, 1948; as *The Sea Thing*, London, Sidgwick and Jackson, 1970.

* * *

E. M. Hull was married to A. E. van Vogt, with whom she sometimes collaborated, although not to the extent as did Henry Kuttner with C. L. Moore. In the 1940's she published a number of minor stories in *Astounding* and *Unknown*, among them the Artur Blord series, a cycle of space operas with an unfailingly successful unscrupulous businessman as protagonist; all the stories except the first, "Abdication" (*Astounding*, April 1943), were combined as *Planets for Sale*. Partially explaining the fact that van Vogt's name was listed as co-author, Hull says, "The great problem was my almost total lack of scientific knowledge. To overcome this handicap, my husband and I figured out a story pattern which would bypass the need to show a science explanation." Van Vogt's hand is more in evidence in *The Winged Man*, in which the characters, in typical van Vogt fashion, take their time to ponder things and are apt to come up with conclusions, said to be the result of deep thought, which fail to carry the slightest inner conviction. This novel presents a meeting of minds in the far future, to which representatives from various ages of the history of mankind are snatched via time-machine to help in a conflict between winged and sea-based human races, including an American nuclear submarine. The conflict between the two branches of the human race is typically resolved by an attack on a third part, an alien invader responsible for the landmasses of Earth becoming submerged in the ocean. The whole book is a poor sort of space opera, filled with implausible dialogue and "futuristic" touches that are merely ridiculous.

Planets for Sale, while being hardly less implausible, has the virtue of being completely unpretentious both in literary execution and moral intentions. It describes episodically a super-capitalist future world of the Ridge Stars, a frontier world with a complete laissez-faire society, where the large corporations run by quick witted Operators make their own laws. The hero is different from the villains only in being more successful in his dealings (or double-dealings) with other entrepreneurs, plain gangsters, villainous scientists, and the

relics of an ancient reptilian race, the Skal. The problems are solved not so much by deduction from logical premises as by sleights of hand and pulling scientific rabbits out of the hat. In fact, the book's redeeming feature is the audacity with which the author seems determined to avoid none of the clichés of space opera, and presents a picture of a corrupt society that might have been written with the intention to discredit capitalism.

Out of the Unknown contains three fantasy stories by each of the two writers. All three of Hull's stories deal with wish-fulfillment, the first two, "The Wishes We Make" and "The Ultimate Wish," openly, "The Patient" in a hidden way. The last is a van Vogtian story of a different sort of presecuted superman, in which dreaded cancer is seen as the first step towards the development of homo superior; the other two stories are clumsy variations of the topic of the foolish wishes.

—Franz Rottensteiner

HUNT, Gil. See TUBB, E. C.

HUNTER, Evan. Also writes as Curt Cannon; Hunt Collins; Ezra Hannon; Richard Marsten; Ed McBain. American. Born Salvatore A. Lombino in New York City, 15 October 1926. Educated at Cooper Union, New York, 1943-44; Hunter College, New York, B. A. 1950 (Phi Beta Kappa). Served in the United States Navy, 1944-46. Married 1) Anita Melnick in 1949 (divorced), three sons; 2) Mary Vann Finley in 1973, one stepdaughter. In the early 1950's taught in vocational high schools, and worked for the Scott Meredith Literary Agency, in New York. Recipient: Mystery Writers of America Edgar Allan Poe Award, 1957. Lives in Norwalk, Connecticut. Agent: John Farquharson Ltd., 250 West 57th Street, New York 10107, U.S.A.; or, 162-168 Regent Street, London W1R 5TB, England.

SCIENCE-FICTION PUBLICATIONS

Novels

Find the Feathered Serpent (for children). Philadelphia, Winston, 1952.
Rocket to Luna (for children; as Richard Marsten). Philadelphia, Winston, 1952; London, Hutchinson, 1954.
Danger: Dinosaurs! (for children; as Richard Marsten). Philadelphia, Winston, 1953.
Tomorrow's World (as Hunt Collins). New York, Avalon, 1956; as *Tomorrow and Tomorrow*, New York, Pyramid, 1956; as Ed McBain, London, Sphere, 1979.

Short Stories

The Jungle Kids. New York, Pocket Books, 1956.
The Last Spin and Other Stories. London, Constable, 1960.
Happy New Year, Herbie, and Other Stories. New York, Simon and Schuster, 1963; London, Constable, 1965.

OTHER PUBLICATIONS

Novels

The Evil Sleep! N. p., Falcon, 1952.

The Big Fix. N. p., Falcon, 1952; as *So Nude, So Dead* (as Richard Marsten), New York, Fawcett, 1956.

Don't Crowd Me. New York, Popular Library, 1953; London, Consul, 1960; as *The Paradise Party*, London, New English Library, 1968.

Cut Me In (as Hunt Collins). New York, Abelard Schuman, 1954; London, Boardman, 1960; as *The Proposition*, New York, Pyramid, 1955.

The Black Jungle. New York, Simon and Schuster, 1954; London, Constable, 1955.

Second Ending. New York, Simon and Schuster, and London, Constable, 1956; as *Quartet in H*, New York, Pocket Books, 1957.

Strangers When We Meet. New York, Simon and Schuster, and London, Constable, 1958.

I'm Cannon—For Hire (as Curt Cannon). New York, Fawcett, 1958; London, Fawcett, 1959.

A Matter of Conviction. New York, Simon and Schuster, and London, Constable, 1959; as *The Young Savages*, New York, Pocket Books, 1966.

Mothers and Daughters. New York, Simon and Schuster, and London, Constable, 1961.

Buddwing. New York, Simon and Schuster, and London, Constable, 1964.

The Paper Dragon. New York, Delacorte Press, 1966; London, Constable, 1967.

A Horse's Head. New York, Delacorte Press, 1967; London, Constable, 1968.

Last Summer. New York, Doubleday, 1968; London, Constable, 1969.

Sons. New York, Doubleday, 1969; London, Constable, 1970.

Nobody Knew They Were There. New York, Doubleday, and London, Constable, 1971.

Every Little Crook and Nanny. New York, Doubleday, and London, Constable, 1972.

Come Winter. New York, Doubleday, and London, Constable, 1973.

Streets of Gold. New York, Harper, 1974; London, Macmillan, 1975.

Doors (as Ezra Hannon). New York, Stein and Day, 1975; London, Macmillan, 1976.

The Chisholms: A Novel of the Journey West. New York, Harper, and London, Hamish Hamilton, 1976.

Walk Proud. New York, Bantam, 1979.

Love, Dad. New York, Crown, and London, Joseph, 1981.

Far from the Sea. New York, Atheneum, and London, Hamish Hamilton, 1983.

Lizzie. New York, Arbor House, and London, Hamish Hamilton, 1984.

Novels as Richard Marsten

Runaway Black. New York, Fawcett, 1954; London, Red Seal, 1957.

Murder in the Navy. New York, Fawcett, 1955; as *Death of a Nurse* (as Ed McBain), New York, Pocket Books, 1968; London, Hodder and Stoughton, 1972.

The Spiked Heel. New York, Holt, 1956; London, Constable, 1957.

Vanishing Ladies. New York, Permabooks, 1957; London, Boardman, 1961.

Even the Wicked. New York, Permabooks, 1958; as Ed McBain, London, Severn House, 1979.

Big Man. New York, Pocket Books, 1959; as Ed McBain, London, Penguin, 1978.

Novels as Ed McBain

Cop Hater. New York, Permabooks, 1956; London, Boardman, 1958.

The Mugger. New York, Simon and Schuster, 1956; London, Boardman, 1959.

The Pusher. New York, Simon and Schuster, 1956; London, Boardman, 1959.

The Con Man. New York, Permabooks, 1957; London, Boardman, 1960.

Killer's Choice. New York, Simon and Schuster, 1958; London, Boardman, 1960.

Killer's Payoff. New York, Simon and Schuster, 1958; London, Boardman, 1960.

April Robin Murders, with Craig Rice (completed by McBain). New York, Random House, 1958; London, Hammond, 1959.

Lady Killer. New York, Simon and Schuster, 1958; London, Boardman, 1961.

Killer's Wedge. New York, Simon and Schuster, 1959; London, Boardman, 1961.

'Til Death. New York, Simon and Schuster, 1959; London, Boardman, 1961.

King's Ransom. New York, Simon and Schuster, 1959; London, Boardman, 1961.

Give the Boys a Great Big Hand. New York, Simon and Schuster, 1960; London, Boardman, 1962.

The Heckler. New York, Simon and Schuster, 1960; London, Boardman, 1962.

See Them Die. New York, Simon and Schuster, 1960; London, Boardman, 1963.

Lady, Lady, I Did it! New York, Simon and Schuster, 1961; London, Boardman, 1963.

Like Love. New York, Simon and Schuster, 1962; London, Hamish Hamilton, 1964.

Ten Plus One. New York, Simon and Schuster, 1963; London, Hamish Hamilton, 1964.

Ax. New York, Simon and Schuster, and London, Hamish Hamilton, 1964.

The Sentries. New York, Simon and Schuster, and London, Hamish Hamilton, 1965.

He Who Hesitates. New York, Delacorte Press, and London, Hamish Hamilton, 1965.

Doll. New York, Delacorte Press, 1965; London, Hamish Hamilton, 1966.

Eighty Million Eyes. New York, Delacorte Press, and London, Hamish Hamilton, 1966.

Fuzz. New York, Doubleday, and London, Hamish Hamilton, 1968.

Shotgun. New York, Doubleday, and London, Hamish Hamilton, 1969.

Jigsaw. New York, Doubleday, and London, Hamish Hamilton, 1970.

Hail, Hail, The Gang's All Here! New York, Doubleday, and London, Hamish Hamilton, 1971.

Sadie When She Died. New York, Doubleday, and London, Hamish Hamilton, 1972.

Let's Hear It for the Deaf Man. New York, Doubleday, and London, Hamish Hamilton, 1973.

Hail to the Chief. New York, Random House, and London, Hamish Hamilton, 1973.

Bread. New York, Random House, and London, Hamish Hamilton, 1974.

Where There's Smoke. New York, Random House, and London, Hamish Hamilton, 1975.

Blood Relatives. New York, Random House, 1975; London,

Hamish Hamilton, 1976.

Guns. New York, Random House, 1976; London, Hamish Hamilton, 1977.

So Long as You Both Shall Live. New York, Random House, and London, Hamish Hamilton, 1976.

Long Time No See. New York, Random House, and London, Hamish Hamilton, 1977.

Goldilocks. New York, Arbor House, 1977; London, Hamish Hamilton, 1978.

Calyso. New York, Viking Press, and London, Hamish Hamilton, 1979.

Ghosts. New York, Viking Press, and London, Hamish Hamilton, 1980.

Rumpelstiltskin. New York, Viking Press, and London, Hamish Hamilton, 1981.

Heat. New York, Viking Press, and London, Hamish Hamilton, 1981.

Beauty and the Beast. London, Hamish Hamilton, 1982; New York, Holt Rinehart, 1983.

Ice. New York, Arbor House, and London, Hamish Hamilton, 1983.

Jack and the Beanstalk. New York, Holt Rinehart, and London, Hamish Hamilton, 1984.

Lightning. New York, Arbor House, and London, Hamish Hamilton, 1984.

Snow White and Rose Red. New York, Holt Rinehart, and London, Hamish Hamilton, 1985.

Eight Black Horses. New York, Arbor House, 1985.

Short Stories

I Like 'em Tough (as Curt Cannon). New York, Fawcett, 1958.

The Empty Hours (as Ed McBain). New York, Simon and Schuster, 1962; London, Boardman, 1963.

The Beheading and Other Stories. London, Constable, 1971.

The Easter Man (a Play) and Six Stories. New York, Doubleday, 1972; as *Seven*, London, Constable, 1972.

The McBain Brief (as Ed McBain). London, Hamish Hamilton, 1982; New York, Arbor House, 1983.

Plays

The Easter Man (produced Birmingham and London, 1964; as *As Race of Hairy Men*, produced New York, 1965). Included in *The Easter Man (a Play) and Six Stories*, 1972.

The Conjuror (produced Ann Arbor, Michigan, 1969).

Screenplays: *Strangers When We Meet*, 1960; *The Birds*, 1963; *Fuzz*, 1972; *Walk Proud*, 1979.

Television Plays: *Appointment at Eleven* (*Alfred Hitchcock Presents* series), 1955-61; *The Chisholms* series, from his own novel, 1978-79; *Walks Far Woman*, 1983.

Other (for children)

The Remarkable Harry. New York and London, Abelard Schuman, 1961.

The Wonderful Button. New York, Abelard Schuman, 1961; London, Abelard Schuman, 1962.

Me and Mr. Stenner. Philadelphia, Lippincott, 1976; London, Hamish Hamilton, 1977.

Other (as Ed McBain)

Editor, *Crime Squad*. London, New English Library, 1968.

Editor, *Homicide Department*. London, New English Library, 1968.

Editor, *Downpour*. London, New English Library, 1969.

Editor, *Ticket to Death*. London, New English Library, 1969.

*

Manuscript Collection: Mugar Memorial Library, Boston University.

*   *   *

Although he is best known as a mainstream novelist of considerable stature (*The Blackboard Jungle, Last Summer, Sons*), and as today's finest practitioner of the police procedural novel (the 87th Precinct series of more than 30 novels under his Ed McBain pseudonym), Evan Hunter began his career in the early 1950's as a science fiction writer and contributed a number of short stories and novels to the genre during the first half of that decade. The best of the stories are "Inferiority Complex," "Million Dollar Maybe," which involves a magazine's offer of one million dollars to the first private citizen who reaches the moon and returns alive, and "The Fallen Angel," an excellent deal-with-the-devil fantasy with a circus background.

All three of Hunter's early SF novels are adventure stories for young readers. *Find the Feathered Serpent*, an interesting blend of time and travel and Mayan history, is perhaps the best. *Rocket to Luna* is an account of the first moon-bound rocket, and *Danger: Dinosaurs!* again utilizes the time-travel theme, in this case into the dim past when saurians roamed the earth. Hunter's most memorable contribution to science fiction is his only adult novel, *Tomorrow's World*—a caustically satirical study of a future in which narcotics have been legalized and there is a bitter struggle for control of publishing, movies, and television between the Vikes, who are responsible for the current vogue of drug use and vicarious entertainment, and the Realists, who advocate a return to the moral standards of the past. The novel, which has deservedly remained in print during most of the past quarter-century, is an expanded version of "Malice in Wonderland" (*If*, January 1954); interestingly, "Malice" is told of the first person, by the Vike literary agent Van Brant, while *Tomorrow's World* is a third-person novel whose view-point shifts between Brant and members of the Realist movement. What makes both novella and novel especially fascinating is the combination of Hunter's unsurpassed ear for dialogue and his meticulous use of a drug-oriented, futuristic slang.

With the exception of his screenplay for Alfred Hitchcock's fantasy-based film *The Birds*, Hunter has written no science fiction since the middle 1950's. But the many reprintings of *Tomorrow's World* and the occasional reprinting of short stories serve as reminders to the SF reader that his contrubution to the field, though small, is by no means inconsequential.

—Bill Pronzini

HUXLEY, Aldous (Leonard). British. Born in Godalming, Surrey, 26 July 1894; son of scientist T. H. Huxley; brother of the scientist and writer Julian Huxley. Educated at Hillside School, Godalming 1930-08; Eton College, 1908-13; Balliol College, Oxford, 1913-15, B. A. (honours) in English 1915. Married 1) Maria Nys in 1919 (died, 1955); 2) Laura Archera in 1956; one son. Worked in the War Office, 1917; taught at Eton College, 1918; member of the editorial staff of the *Athenaeum*, London, 1919-20; Drama Critic, *Westminster Gazette*, 1920-21; full-time writer from 1921; travelled and lived in France, Italy, and the United States, 1923-37; settled in California, 1937, and worked as a free-lance screenwriter. Recipient: American Academy Award, 1959. Companion of Literature, Royal Society of Literature, 1962. *Died 22 November 1963.*

SCIENCE-FICTION PUBLICATIONS

Novels

Brave New World. London, Chatto and Windus, and New York, Doubleday, 1932.
After Many a Summer. London, Chatto and Windus, 1939; as *After Many a Summer Dies the Swan,* New York, Harper, 1939.
Time Must Have a Stop. New York, Harper, 1944; London, Chatto and Windus, 1945.
Ape and Essence. New York, Harper, 1948; London, Chatto and Windus, 1949.
Island. London, Chatto and Windus, and New York, Harper, 1962.

OTHER PUBLICATIONS

Novels

Crome Yellow. London, Chatto and Windus, 1921; New York, Doran, 1922.
Antic Hay. London, Chatto and Windus, and New York, Doran, 1923.
Those Barren Leaves. London, Chatto and Windus, and New York, Doran, 1925.
Point Counter Point. London, Chatto and Windus, and New York, Doubleday, 1928.
Eyeless in Gaza. London, Chatto and Windus, and New York, Harper, 1936.
The Genius and the Goddess. London, Chatto and Windus, and New York, Harper, 1955.

Short Stories

Limbo. London, Chatto and Windus, and New York, Doran, 1920.
Mortal Coils (includes play *Permutations among the Nightingales*). London, Chatto and Windus, and New York, Doran, 1922.
Little Mexican and Other Stories. London, Chatto and Windus, 1924; as *Young Archimedes and Other Stories,* New York, Doran, 1924.
Two or Three Graces and Other Stories. London, Chatto and Windus, and New York, Doran, 1926.
Brief Candles. London, Chatto and Windus, and New York, Doubleday, 1930; as *After the Fireworks,* New York, Avon, n.d.
Twice Seven: Fourteen Selected Stories. London, Reprint Society, 1944.
Collected Short Stories. London, Chatto and Windus, and New York, Harper, 1957.

Plays

Liluli, adaptation of a play by Romain Rolland, in *Nation* (London), 20 September-29 November 1919.
Albert, Prince Consort: A Biography Play for Which Mr. John Drinkwater's Historical Dramas Serve as a Model, in *Vanity Fair* (New York), March 1922.
The Ambassador of Capripedia, in *Vanity Fair* (New York), May 1922.
The Publisher, in *Vanity Fair* (New York), April 1923.
The Discovery, adaptation of the play by Frances Sheridan (produced London, 1924). London, Chatto and Windus, 1924; New York, Doran, 1925.
The World of Light (produced London, 1931). London, Chatto and Windus, and New York, Doubleday, 1931.
The Gioconda Smile, adaptation of his own story (produced London, 1948; New York 1950). London, Chatto and Windus, 1948; as *Mortal Coils,* New York, Harper, 1948.
The Genius and the Goddess, with Ruth Wendell, adaptation of the novel by Huxley (produced New York, 1957).

Screenplays: *Pride and Prejudice,* with Jane Murfin, 1940; *Jane Eyre,* with John Houseman and Robert Stevenson, 1944; *A Woman's Vengeance,* 1947.

Verse

The Burning Wheel. Oxford, Blackwell, 1916.
Jonah. Oxford, Holywell Press, 1917.
The Defeat of Youth and Other Poems. Oxford, Blackwell, 1918.
Leda. London, Chatto and Windus, and New York, Doran, 1920.
Selected Poems. Oxford, Blackwell, and New York, Appleton, 1925.
Arabia Infelix and Other Poems. New York, Fountain Press, and London, Chatto and Windus, 1929.
Apennine. Gaylordsville, Connecticut, Slide Mountain Press, 1930.
The Cicadas and Other Poems. London, Chatto and Windus, and New York, Doubleday, 1931.
Verses and a Comedy. London, Chatto and Windus, 1946.
The Collected Poetry of Aldous Huxley, edited by Donald Watt. London, Chatto and Windus, and New York, Harper, 1971.

Other

On the Margin: Notes and Essays. London, Chatto and Windus, and New York, Doran, 1923.
Along the Road: Notes and Essays of a Tourist. London, Chatto and Windus, and New York, Doran, 1925.
Essays New and Old. London, Chatto and Windus, 1926; New York, Doran, 1927.
Jesting Pilate: The Diary of a Journey. London, Chatto and Windus, and New York, Doran, 1926.
Proper Studies. London, Chatto and Windus, 1927; New York, Doubleday, 1928.
Do What You Will: Essays. London, Chatto and Windus, and New York, Doubleday, 1929.
Holy Face and Other Essays. London, The Fleuron, 1929.
Vulgarity in Literature: Digressions from a Theme. London, Chatto and Windus, 1930.
Music at Night and Other Essays. London, Chatto and Windus, and New York, Doubleday, 1931.
Rotunda (selection). London, Chatto and Windus, 1932.
T. H. Huxley as a Man of Letters (lecture). London, Macmilan, 1932.
Retrospect (selection). New York, Doubleday, 1933.
Beyond the Mexique Bay. London, Chatto and Windus, and New York, Harper, 1934.
The Olive Tree nad Other Essays. London, Chatto and Windus, 1936; New York, Harper, 1937.
What Are You Going to Do about It? The Case for Constructive

Peace. London, Chatto and Windus, 1936; New York, Harper, 1937.

Stories, Essays, and Poems. London, Dent, 1937.

Ends and Means: An Enquiry into the Nature of Ideals and into the Methods Employed for Their Realization. London, Chatto and Windus, and New York, Harper, 1937.

The Most Agreeable Vice. Los Angeles, Ward Ritchie Press, 1938.

Words and Their Meanings. Los Angeles, Ward Ritchie Press, 1940.

Gray Eminence: A Study in Religion and Politics. London, Chatto and Windus, 1941.

The Art of Seeing. New York, Harper, 1942; London, Chatto and Windus, 1943.

The Perennial Philosophy. New York, Harper, 1945; London, Chatto and Windus, 1946.

Science, Liberty, and Peace. New York, Harper, 1946; London, Chatto and Windus, 1947.

The World of Aldous Huxley: An Omnibus of His Fiction and Non-Fiction over Three Decades, edited by Charles J. Rolo. New York, Harper, 1947.

Food and People, with John Russell. London, Bureau of Current Affairs, 1949.

Prisons, with the Carceri Etchings by Piranesi. London, Trianon Press, and Los Angeles, Zeitlin and Ver Brugge, 1949.

Themes and Variations. London, Chatto and Windus, and New York, Harper, 1950.

The Devils of Loudun. London, Chatto and Windus, and New York, Harper, 1952.

Joyce the Artificer: Two Studies of Joyce's Methods, with Stuart Gilbert. London, Chiswick Press, 1952.

A Day in Windsor, with J. A. Kings. London, Britannicus Liber, 1953.

The Doors of Perception. London, Chatto and Windus, and New York, Harper, 1954.

The French of Paris, photographs by Sanford H. Roth. New York, Harper, 1954.

Adonis and the Alphabet, and Other Essays. London, Chatto and Windus, 1956; as *Tomorrow and Tomorrow and Tomorrow and Other Essays*, New York, Harper, 1956.

Heaven and Hell. London, Chatto and Windus, and New York, Harper, 1956.

Brave New World Revisited. New York, Harper, 1958; London, Chatto and Windus, 1959.

Collected Essays. London, Chatto and Windus, and New York, Harper, 1959.

"Chemical Persuasion," in *Fantasy and Science Fiction* (New York), April 1959.

On Art and Artists, edited by Morris Philipson. London, Chatto and Windus, and New York, Harper, 1960.

Selected Essays, edited by Harold Raymond. London, Chatto and Windus, 1961.

Literature and Science. London, Chatto and Windus, and New York, Harper, 1963.

The Politics of Ecology: The Question of Survival. Santa Barbara, California, Center for the Study of Democratic Institutions, 1963.

The Crows of Pearblossom (for children). London, Chatto and Windus, and New York, Random House, 1967.

The Letters of Aldous Huxley, edited by Grover Smith. London, Chatto and Windus, 1969; New York, Harper, 1970.

Great Short Works of Aldous Huxley, edited by Bernard Bergonzi. New York, Harper, 1969.

America and the Future. Austin, Texas, Jenkins, 1970.

Moksha: Writings on Psychedelics and the Visionary Experience 1931-1963 edited by Michael Horowitz and Cynthia Palmer.

New York, Stonehill, 1977; London, Chatto and Windus, 1980.

The Human Situation: Lectures at Santa Barbara 1959, edited by Piero Ferrucci. New York, Harper, 1977; London, Chatto and Windus, 1978.

Editor, with W. R. Childe and T. W. Earp, *Oxford Poetry 1916*. Oxford, Blackwell, 1916.

Editor, *Text and Pretexts: An Anthology with Commentaries*. London, Chatto and Windus, 1932; New York, Harper, 1933.

Editor, *The Letters of D. H. Lawrence*. London, Heinemann, and New York, Viking Press, 1932.

Editor, *An Encyclopedia of Pacifism*. London, Chatto and Windus, and New York, Harper, 1937.

Translator, *A Virgin Heart*, by Rémy de Gourmont. New York, Brown, 1921; London, Allen and Unwin, 1926.

*

Bibliography: *Aldous Huxley: A Bibliography 1916-1959* by Claire John Eschelbach and Joyce Lee Shober, Berkeley, University of California Press, 1961; supplement by Thomas D. Clareson and Carolyn S. Andrews, in *Extrapolation 6* (Wooster, Ohio), 1964; *Aldous Huxley: An Annotated Bibliography of Criticism* by Eben E. Bass, New York, Garland, 1981.

Critical Studies: *Aldous Huxley: A Literary Study* by John Atkins, London, Calder, and New York, Roy, 1956, revised edition, London, Calder and Boyars, 1967, New York, Orion Press, 1968; *The Timeless Moment: A Personal View of Aldous Huxley* by Laura Huxley, New York, Farrar Straus, 1968, London, Chatto and Windus, 1969; *Aldous Huxley: A Study of the Major Novels* by Peter Bowering, London, Athlone Press, 1968, New York, Oxford University Press, 1969; *Aldous Huxley: Satire and Structure* by Jerome Meckier, London, Chatto and Windus, and New York, Barnes and Noble, 1969; *Aldous Huxley* by Harold H. Watts, New York, Twayne, 1969; *Dawn and the Darkest Hour: A Study of Aldous Huxley* by George Woodcock, London, Faber, and New York, Viking Press, 1972; *Aldous Huxley* by Keith M. May, London, Elek, 1972, New York, Harper, 1973; *Aldous Huxley: A Biography* by Sybille Bedford, London, Chatto and Windus-Collins, 2 vols., 1973-74, New York, Knopf, 1 vol., 1974; *Aldous Huxley: A Collection of Critical Essays* edited by Robert E. Kuehn, Englewood Cliffs, New Jersey, Prentice Hall, 1974; *Aldous Huxley: The Critical Heritage* edited by Donald Watt, London, Routledge, 1975; *Demon and Saint in the Novels of Aldous Huxley* by Lilly Zahmer, Bern, Schweizer Anglistische Arbeiten, 1975; *Aspects of Structure and Quest in Aldous Huxley's Major Novels* by Bharathi Krishnan, Uppsala, Sweden, University of Uppsala, 1977; *Aldous Huxley, Novelist* by Christopher S. Ferns, London, Athlone Press, 1980; *The Dark Historic Page: Social Satire and Historicism in the Novels of Aldous Huxley 1921-1939* by Robert S. Baker, Madison, University of Wisconsin Press, 1982.

*   *   *

Though very few of Aldous Huxley's many books deal with the future, he is most famous as the author of one of the masterpieces of SF. This will appear less paradoxical if we consider how closely *Brave New World* is linked to his essays and mainstream novels. Indeed, in his very first novel, *Crome Yellow*, one of the characters, Scogan, develops his plans for a "Rational State": facing the crumbling of the Victorian system into hypocrisy, national and social conflicts, and sexual frustration—the central subject of Huxley's early novels, crowned and summed up in *Point Counter Point*—an intellectual could not but look for a substitute based on reason, happiness being the only possible aim. Because of the lack of any generally accepted transcendental creed, individuals should be adapted, by education and even by generation, to the functions they are to perform and the place that is to be theirs in the collectivity, thus getting rid of all sources of anxiety. Yet when Huxley developed this rough sketch, the result was a dreadful *counter*-utopia. Scenes as the test-tube generation of as many as 96 similar babies born from a single ovum so that they may later work together with absolute coordination, or the conditioning of children to hate roses and books so that they may become utterly devoted soldiers, remain in the memory as perfect illustrations of the "standardization of the human product" whose horror is perceived even by Bernard Marx, one of the ruling elite. Indeed, the objection to utopia is no longer that it is an unrealistic dream, but, on the contrary—as Huxley pointed out in *Brave New World Revisited*—that it is coming true, and turning out to be a nightmare. The Human "Termitary"—though not reaching the same extremes as Frank Herbert's *Hellstrom's Hive*—is taking shape is several countries. According to Huxley, the path followed by the USA is the surest way to this hell-on-earth, for violence is no longer necessary with the development of the technology of persuasion. Therefore, he considers Orwell's *Nineteen Eighty-Four*, though written later, as less credible than his own prophecies of a "soft" dictatorship.

As regards sex, he seems indeed to be right. For the intergrated state, promiscuity seems a far better proposition than puritanism. But generalized free love, rid of both passion and procreation, attractive though it may sound to modern readers, appears as ghastly in *Brave New World*, especially as experienced by the "Savage"—nurtured on the "monstrosities" of Shakespeare's plays. Of post-Victorian writers, Huxley was one of those who strove most desperately to overcome the century-long divorce beteen body and "soul"; and he was equally attracted and dissatisfied by those who claimed they had found the way to reconciliation (D. H. Lawrence) or release (the psychoanalysts). Huxley never ceased to study this conflict between upward and downward self-transcendence through his characters who, failing to "play the man," played either the angel, the devil, or the beast—quite literally in the case of the 5th Earl of Hauberk and his servant-mistress at the end of *After Many a Summer*, a mainstream novel to which Huxley was brought to give a SF conclusion. If in it such *individuals* as want to reach a purely physical eternity turn into apes, in *Ape and Essence* a whole *race*, because of mutations due to radioactivity (which "could as well be the product of atomic industry as of atomic war") has to comply with the demands and restrictions of animal rutting, as well as of devil-worship.

Towards the end of his life, Huxley must have thought that he had found a solution to those personal and social problems: after studying the diabolical excesses that may result from misguided religion on some historical characters (*The Devils of Loudun*) and the best expressions of true religious aspirations throughout the world (*The Perennial Philosophy*), he published a novel which, without his knowing it, was his literary testament—and it was a utopia. *Island* has however certain common points with *Brave New World*: free love, removal of children from the narrow family circle (through clubs of mutual adoption), elimination of the tragic from art (*Oedipus* is given a happy ending), legalized and even encouraged drug-taking, and more generally subservience of everything to the quest of happiness. Of course, one may say that the difference lies in the spirit of it all: the yoga of love is not just a contraceptive device,

but a means to spread sensual awareness to the whole body; orgasm is not mere animal pleasure but discovery of oneself, and of another self; "Moksha" induces communion with the world, not passive acceptance of the social order like "soma." Yet there is a more serious objection: the ideal state is created from above, by a "sane" Raja, and equally destroyed from above, by a conspiracy of fascists, capitalists, and pseudo-mystics. Though it is acknowledged that total integration of the individual is neither possible nor even desirable, the people of Pala seem to accept with equal passivity the good and the evil that are in turn imposed upon them.

That the ideal state should be so easily overturned tends to prove that Huxley himself did not believe in it very firmly; in our faithless age, he could not base his construction on received principles like Thomas More or Campanella; so he tried his best to take the *whole* man into account—a remarkable feat for an intellectual, but how could *all* men be satisfied? Though for Huxley's personal build-up it was a key attempt, he will certainly be remembered much more for *Brave New World*, a direct continuation of his satirical studies of the present, and a model for many warning pictures of the future, often imitated, sometimes equalled (notable by Pohl and Kornbluth in *The Space Merchants*), but probably never surpassed.

—George W. Barlow

HYNE, C(harles) J(ohn) Cutcliffe (Wright). Also wrote as Weatherby Chesney. British. Born in Bilbury, Gloucestershire, 11 May 1865. Educated at Bradford Grammar School; Clare College, Cambridge, B. A., M. A. Married Elsie Haggas in 1897 (died, 1938), one daughter. Journalist: travelled extensively as a writer for magazines. *Died 10 March 1944.*

SCIENCE-FICTION PUBLICATIONS

Novels

Beneath Your Very Boots. London, Digby Long, 1889.
The New Eden. London, Longman, 1892.
The Recipe for Diamonds. London, Heinemann, and New York, Appleton, 1893.
The Lost Continent. London, Hutchinson, and New York, Harper, 1900.
Empire of the World. London, Everett, 1910; New York, Arno Press, 1975; as *Emperor of the World: The Story of an Anglo-German War*, London, Newnes, 1915.
Abbs, His Story Through Many Ages. London, Hutchinson, 1929.

Short Stories

The Adventures of a Solicitor (as Weatherby Chesney). London, Bowden, 1898.
Atoms of Empire. London and New York, Macmillan, 1904.
Man's Understanding. London, Ward Lock, 1933.

OTHER PUBLICATIONS

Novels

Four Red Nightcaps. London, Eden, 1890.
Currie, Curtis & Co., Crammers. London, Remington, 1890.

A Matrimonial Mixture. London, Ward and Downey, 1891.
Stimson's Reef. London, Blackie, 1891.
Sandy Carmichael. London, Sampson Low, 1892; Philadelphia, Lippincott, 1908.
The Captured Cruiser: or, Two Years from Land. London, Blackie, 1892; New York, Scribner, 1895.
The Wild-Catters. London, Sunday School Union, 1895.
Honour of Thieves. London, Chatto and Windus, 1895; New York, Fenno, 1899; as *The Little Red Captain: An Early Adventure of Captain Kettle,* London, Pearson, 1902.
The Stronger Hand. London, Beeman, 1896.
Through Arctic Lapland. London, A. and C. Black, and New York, Macmillan, 1898.
The Glass Dagger. New York, New Amsterdam, 1899.
The Filibusters. London, Hutchinson, and New York, Stokes, 1900.
Prince Rupert the Buccaneer. London, Methuen, and New York, Stokes, 1901.
Thompson's Progress. London, Richards, 1902; New York, Macmillan, 1903.
Captain Kettle, K. C. B. London, Pearson, and New York, Federal, 1903.
McTodd. London and New York, Macmillan, 1903.
The Trials of Commander McTurk. London, Murray, and New York, Dutton, 1906.
Kate Meredith, Financier. New York, Authors and Newspapers Association, 1906; as *Kate Meredith,* London, Cassell, 1907.
The Marriage of Kettle. London, Heinemann, and Indianapolis, Bobbs Merrill, 1912.
Firemen Hot. London, Methuen, 1914.
Captain Kettle on the War-Path. London, Methuen, 1916.
Captain Kettle's Bit. London, Hodder and Stoughton, 1918.
Admiral Teach. London, Methuen, 1920.
President Kettle. London, Nash and Grayson, 1920.
Mr. Kettle, Third Mate, London, Ward Lock, 1931.
West Highland Spirits. London, Ward Lock, 1932.
Captain Kettle, Ambassador. London, Ward Lock, 1932.
Absent Friends. London, Ward Lock, 1933.
Ivory Valley: An Adventure of Captain Kettle. London, Ward Lock, 1938.
Wishing Smith. London, Hale, 1939.

Novels as Weatherby Chesney

The Dilemma of Commander Brett. London, Bowden, 1899.
John Topp, Pirate. London, Methuen, 1901.
The Branded Prince. London, Methuen, 1902.
The Foundered Galleon. London, Methuen, 1902.
The Baptist Ring. London, Methuen, 1903.
The Mystery of a Bungalow. London, Methuen, 1904.
The Tragedy of the Great Emerald. London, Methuen, 1904.
The Cable-Man. London, Chatto and Windus, 1907.
The Claimant. London, Chatto and Windus, 1908.
The Romance of a Queen. London, Chatto and Windus, 1908.

Short Stories

The Paradise Coal-Boat. London, Bowden, and New York, Mansfield, 1897.
Adventures of Captain Kettle. London, Pearson, and New York, Doubleday, 1898.
The Adventures of an Engineer (as Weatherby Chesney). London, Bowden, 1898.
Further Adventures of Captain Kettle. London, Pearson, 1899; as *A Master of Fortune,* New York, Dillingham, 1901.
The Derelict. New York, Lewis Scribner, 1901; revised edition,

as *Mr. Horrocks, Purser,* London, Methuen, 1902.
The Escape Agents. London, Laurie, 1911.
Red Herrings. London, Methuen, 1918.
The Rev. Captain Kettle. London, Harrap, 1925.
Ben Watson. London, Country Life, 1926.
Steamboatmen. London, Penguin, 1943.

Other

People and Places. London, Newnes, 1930.
But Britons Are Slaves. London, Harmsworth, 1931.
My Joyful Life. London, Hutchinson, 1935.
Don't You Agree? (essays). London, Hutchinson, 1935.

Editor, *For Britain's Soldiers.* London, Methuen, 1900.

*   *   *

Half a dozen of C. J. Cutcliffe Hyne's novels are SF, as are some of his many short stories ("The Men from Mars" in *The Adventures of a Solicitor*). In *Beneath Your Very Boots* the narrator finds beneath England a race descended underground in pre-Roman times, using Earth heat as energy source, manufacturing diamonds, but otherwise living in a theocratic dictatorship à la Rider Haggard. In a dilution of Bulwer-Lytton's *The Coming Race,* the narrator-hero invents a boring machine, is rewarded by a pleasure drug, and during an unsuccessful rebellion escapes with the obligatory beautiful underground wife. *The New Eden* and *The Recipe for Diamonds* are more pallid. In the first, an archduke-scientist sets up on a Pacific island the experiment of starting a young man and woman from zero; they invent art, alcohol, and Sun-worship. In the second, Lully's recipe is found and, after intrigues involving the equally obligatory anarchist, destroyed again. *The Lost Continent* is a relatively readable Haggard-type melodrama of Atlantis, narrated by a nobleman of those times involved with a strong upstart empress. Though she is the most interesting character of the novel, women's rule still leads to decadence and the flood, after political intrigues and fights with giant saurians and cave-tigers. In *Empire of the World* a poor scientist with a ray-machine that disintegrates iron intervenes in the war of Britain vs. Germany enforcing peace. It is an unsuccessful try at fusing the "future war" story with "a rather heavy-handed comedy of romantic entanglements in high society" (R. D. Mullen, in *Science-Fiction Studies 6,* 1975). Finally, *Abbs* is a novel about longevity, the protagonist living "through many ages. " In all, Hyne is a good example of the middle range of pre-World-War SF, a competent storyteller who wrote too conventionally and too much.

—Darko Suvin

ING, Dean. American. Born in Austin, Texas, 17 June 1931. Educated at Fresno State University, B. A. 1956; San Jose State University, M. A. 1970; University of Oregon, Eugene, Ph. D. in Speech 1974. Served in the United States Air Force, 1951-55: Airman 1st Class. Married Margaret Barrier in 1952 (divorced, 1957), two children; 2) Geneva Baker in 1959, two children. Engineer, Aerojet-General, Sacramento, California, 1957-62, and Lockheed, San Jose, California, 1962, 1965-70; Assistant Professor of Speech, Missouri State University, Maryville, 1974-77. Since 1977, free-lance writer. Address: 1105 Ivy Lane, Ashland, Oregon 97520, U. S. A.

SCIENCE-FICTION PUBLICATIONS

Novels (series: Quantrill)

Soft Targets. New York, Ace, 1979.
Systemic Shock (Quantrill). New York, Ace, 1981.
Pulling Through. New York, Ace, 1983.
Single Combat (Quantrill). New York, Tor, 1983.
Wild Country (Quantrill). New York, Tor, 1985.

Short Stories

Anasazi. New York, Ace, 1980.
High Tension (includes non-fiction). New York, Ace, 1982.

Uncollected Short Stories

"Tight Squeeze," in *Astounding* (New York), February, 1955.
"Sam and the Dirty Mudder," in *Omni* (New York), December 1979.
"When I Was Red Rover," in *The Future at War 3,* edited by Reginald Bretnor. New York, Ace, 1980.
"Manaspill," in *The Magic May Return,* edited by Larry Niven. New York, Ace, 1981.
"Sam and the Sudden Blizzard Machine," in *The First Omni Book of Science Fiction,* edited by Ellen Datlow. New York, Zebra, 1983.
"Lost in Translation," in *Far Frontiers* (New York), January 1985.
"Evileye," in *Far Frontiers* (New York), April 1985.

OTHER PUBLICATIONS

Other

"Science Fiction: No Time Like the Past/Present/Future," in *Bulletin of Missouri Association of English Teachers* (Maryville), November 1977.
High Frontier, with Daniel Graham. New York, Tor, 1983.
Mutual Assured Survival: A Space-Age Solution to Nuclear Annihilation, with Jerry Pournelle. New York, Baen 1984.
The Future of Flight, with Leik Myrabo. New York, Baen 1985.

Editor, *The Lagrangists,* by Mack Reynolds. New York, Tor, 1983.
Editor, *Home Sweet Home 2010 A. D.,* by Mack Reynolds. New York, Dell, 1984.
Editor, *Eternity,* by Mack Reynolds. New York, Pocket Books, 1984.
Editor, *The Other Time,* by Mack Reynolds. New York, Pocket Books, 1984.
Editor, *Trojan Orbit,* by Mack Reynolds. New York, Baen, 1985.

*

Dean Ing comments:

As a former senior engineer and behavioral scientist, I write hard-nosed, hard s. f. Many of the things I have to say are speculative; some are unpleasant; some are vulgar and/or titillating. It takes a very good university to employ a gadfly, and I found professoring dreary. As a media theorist I felt I could put my ideas over much more widely in fast-paced fictional thrillers than in lecture halls. Q. E. D.

I rarely write before I've decided what needs saying, and outlined it excitingly. I'm a contentist. It's a sign of our times that I had to invent a word that stresses content over style, though the word "stylist" is common enough, God knows. . . .

Literature stressing content over style demands much of readers, so I must make that content sparkle like rhinestones on a soapbox. I research my work as thoroughly as possible, but I no longer take as many physical risks as I once did. But when I describe what it's like to bail out of a moving race car or get plastered against a blockhouse floor by a rocket explosion, often it's dredged up from memory.

*   *   *

Dean Ing's first novel, *Soft Targets,* presents many of the themes Ing develops in his later works: the fragility of society and the importance of individualism. Hakim Arif, a terrorist who calls his organization Fat'ah, sees an open society such as the United States filled with "soft targets" that he can strike at will. In the near future, Ing suggests, terrorism and an open society may be mutually exclusive. Much is made of the power of the media to turn terrorists into media stars. The character of Hakim Arif is well drawn and chillingly convincing. The problem is with the plot: the FCC commissioner Maurice Everett and heads of the major television networks create a straw man in the comedian Charlie George who satirizes terrorists on his program to draw out Fat'ah. However, Everett miscalculates the cleverness of the terrorists and finds himself kidnapped along with Charlie George. The conclusion, though realistically violent, lacks coherence.

Anasazi, a collection of two novellas and a short novel, is uneven. The title short novel, "Anasazi," deals with the possession of a tribe of Indians by parasitic aliens. Although it deals with many of the same issues as Robert Silverberg's award winning "Passengers," "Anasazi" shows more control over characters and plot by Ing. The novella, "The Devil You Don't Know," deals with a drug ring operating within a mental hospital. Ing's handling of psi powers in this story is deft and convincing.

Systemic Shock introduces readers to a nuclear/biological holocaust where the United States and its allies suffer staggering losses from the India-China alliance. Most of the large cities of the world are reduced to rubble and only decentralized populations survive. Ing creates a likable hero in young 15-year-old Ted Quantrill and creates a surviving society dominated by the Mormons and other religious groups. Quantrill loses his family in the nuclear strikes and the biologic plagues. Because of his intelligence and lightning reflexes, he's recruited into the new government's secret T Section as a gunsel. A receiver/transmitter is surgically planted in his skull, along with an explosive charge. Quantrill shows us how to survive in the new "Streamlined America" society where the nuclear bombs have destroyed most of the rules and power to rule comes from the barrel of guns. Ing's realism is refreshing when compared to other post-holocaust novels like Jerry Ahern's bloody "Survivalist" series. Yet, Ing makes the plot unnecessarily complicated and the conclusion is unsatisfying.

Ing's most interesting collection is *High Tension* which is a blend of fact articles and short stories. "Gimme Shelter" is a detailed account of how to survive a nuclear war. This is an issue Ing returns to in *Pulling Through.* The short story "Down and Out on Ellfive Prime" owes a debt to George Orwell as Ing explores the life aboard an orbiting space colony. "Living under Pressure" presents detailed photographs to aid in the construction of an air supply unit for a small nuclear shelter. The best part of *High Tension* is Ing's powerful introductions to each story and article, giving the reader more insight into his philosophy.

Pulling Through puts all Ing's survivalist articles into practice as Harve Rackham and Kate Gallo survive the nuking of the San Francisco area and find the means to pull through the crisis. They build an air pump and filter, they make their own fallout radiation meter from common household materials. Harve and Kate have to survive more than radiation as the other survivors, ordinary citizens and escaped convicts, supply subplots. But *Pulling Through* is more didactic than entertaining. The details of Harve and Kate's methods of survival are interesting but can't substitute for the plot weaknesses.

With *Single Combat* Ing returns to his most convincing vision: post-holocaust American dominated by the Mormons and other religious groups. Ted Quantrill returns, older by a few years, and more disenchanted with his role as government assassin. Resistance to the new order of theocracy is emerging and Ing manages to free Quantrill of the receiver-transmitter and explosive emplanted in his head. Given his freedom, Quantrill seeks revenge on the government that controlled him for so long. *Single Combat* is Ing's best book to date, combining an action packed plot and believable characters into a thrilling adventure.

In addition to his own work, Dean Ing has completed a series of novels by the late Mack Reynolds. Several of the novels have appeared to date with mixed results. *Eternity* is a conventional immortality novel. *Trojan Orbit* is a thriller about sabotage aboard Island One, the first United States space colony. The best book is *The Other Time* where Donald Fielding is sent by timewarp to the court of Montezuma where he takes up the identity of Quetzalcoatl and helps the Aztecs defeat Cortez's Spanish troops.

Dean Ing is a solid, capable writer whose vision of the future is a disaster wrapped in hope.

—George Kelley

INNES, Alan (or **Allan**). See **TUBB, E. C.**

IRWIN, G. H. See **PALMER, Raymond A.**; **SHAVER, Richard S.**

JAKES, John (William). Also writes as William Ard; Alan Payne; Jay Scotland. American. Born in Chicago, Illinois, 31 March 1932. Educated at DePauw University, Greencastle, Indiana, A. B. 1953; Ohio State University, Columbus, M. A. in American literature 1954. Married Rachel Ann Payne in 1951; three daughters and one son. Copywriter, then promotion manager, Abbott Laboratories, North Chicago, 1954-60; copywriter, Rumrill Company, Rochester, New York, 1960-61; free-lance writer, 1961-65; copywriter, Kircher Helton and Collett, Dayton, Ohio, 1965-68; Copy Chief, then Vice-President, Oppenheim Herminghausen and Clarke, Dayton, 1968-70; Creative Director, Dancer Fitzgerald Sample, Dayton, 1970-71. Since 1971, freelance writer. Writer-in-Residence, DePauw University, Fall 1979. LL. D. : Wright State

University, Dayton, Ohio, 1976; Litt. D. : DePauw University, 1977. Address: c/o Rembar and Curtis, Attorneys, 19 West 44th Street, New York, New York 10036, U. S. A.

SCIENCE-FICTION PUBLICATIONS

Novels (series: Dragonard; Klekton)

When the Star Kings Die (Dragonard). New York, Ace, 1967.
The Asylum World. New York, Paperback Library, 1969; London, New English Library, 1978.
The Hybrid. New York, Paperback Library, 1969.
The Planet Wizard (Dragonard). New York, Ace, 1969.
Secrets of Stardeep (for children). Philadelphia, Westminster Press, 1969.
Tonight We Steal the Stars (Dragonard). New York, Ace, 1969.
Black in Time. New York, Paperback Library, 1970.
Mask of Chaos. New York, Ace, 1970.
Master of the Dark Gate (Klekton). New York, Lancer, 1970.
Monte Cristo 99. New York, Curtis, 1970.
Six-Gun Planet. New York, Paperback Library, 1970; London, New English Library, 1978.
Mention My Name in Atlantis. New York, DAW, 1972.
Time Gate (for children). Philadelphia, Westminster Press, 1972.
Witch of the Dark Gate (Klekton). New York, Lancer, 1972.
Conquest of the Planet of the Apes (novelization of screenplay). New York, Award, 1972.
On Wheels. New York, Paperback Library, 1973.

Short Stories

The Best of John Jakes, edited by Martin H. Greenberg and Joseph D. Olander. New York, DAW, 1977.
Fortunes of Brak. New York, Dell, 1980.

OTHER PUBLICATIONS

Novels

The Texans Ride North (for children). Philadelphia, Winston, 1952.
Wear a Fast Gun. New York, Arcadia House, 1956; London, Ward Lock, 1957.
A Night for Treason. New York, Bouregy, 1956.
The Devil Has Four Faces. New York, Bouregy, 1958.
This'll Slay You (as Alan Payne). New York, Ace, 1958.
The Imposter. New York, Bouregy, 1959.
Johnny Havoc. New York, Belmont, 1960.
Johnny Havoc Meets Zelda. New York, Belmont, 1962.
Johnny Havoc and the Doll Who Had "It." New York, Belmont, 1963.
G. I. Girls. Derby, Connecticut, Monarch, 1963.
Making It Big. New York, Belmont, 1968.
Brak Versus the Mark of the Demons. New York, Paperback Library, 1969; as *Brak the Barbarian—The Mark of the Demons,* London, Tandem, 1970.
Brak the Barbarian Versus the Sorceress. New York, Paperback Library, 1969; as *Brak the Barbarian—The Sorceress,* London, Tandem, 1970.
The Last Magicians. New York, New American Library, 1969.
Kent Family Chronicles:
    The Bastard. New York, Pyramid, 1974; as *Fortune's Whirlwind* and *To an Unknown Shore,* London, Corgi, 2 vols., 1975.

The Rebels. New York, Pyramid, 1975; London, Corgi, 1979.

The Seekers. New York, Pyramid, 1975; London, Corgi, 1979.

The Furies. New York, Pyramid, 1976; London, Corgi, 979.

The Titans. New York, Pyramid, 1976; London, Corgi, 1979.

The Warriors. New York, Pyramid, 1977; London, Corgi, 1979

The Lawless. New York, Jove, 1978; London, Corgi, 1979.

The Americans. New York, Jove, 1980.

Brak: When the Idols Walked. New York, Pocket Books, 1978.

Excalibur!, with Gil Kane. New York, Dell, 1980.

Civil War trilogy:

    North and South. New York, Harcourt Brace, and London, Collins, 1982.

    Love and War. New York, Harcourt Brace, 1984; London, Collins, 1985.

Novels as Jay Scotland

The Seventh Man. New York, Bouregy, 1958.

I, Barbarian . New York, Avon, 1959; revised edition, as John Jakes, New York, Pinnacle, 1976.

Strike the Black Flag. New York, Ace, 1961.

Sir Scoundrel. New York, Ace, 1962; revised edition, as *King's Crusader,* New York, Pinnacle 1977.

Veils of Salome. New York, Avon, 1962.

Arena. New York, Ace, 1963.

Traitors' Legion. New York, Ace, 1963; revised edition, as *The Man from Cannae,* New York, Pinnacle, 1977.

Novels as William Ard

Make Mine Mavis. Derby, Connecticut, Monarch, 1961.

And So to Bed. Derby, Connecticut, Monarch, 1962.

Give Me This Woman. Derby, Connecticut, Monarch, 1962.

Short Stories

Brak the Barbarian. New York, Avon, 1968; London, Tandem, 1970.

Plays

Dracula, Baby (lyrics only). Chicago, Dramatic Publishing Company, 1970.

Wind in the Willows. Elgin, Illinois, Performance, 1972.

A Spell of Evil. Chicago, Dramatic Publishing Company, 1972.

Violence. Elgin, Illinois, Performance, 1972.

Stranger with Roses, adaptation of his own story. Chicago, Dramatic Publishing Company, 1972.

For I Am a Jealous People, adaptation of the story by Lester del Rey. Elgin, Illinois, Performance, 1972.

Gaslight Girl. Chicago, Dramatic Publishing Company, 1973.

Pardon Me, Is This Planet Taken? Chicago, Dramatic Publishing Company, 1973.

Doctor, Doctor!, music by Gilbert M. Martin, adaptation of a play by Molière. New York, McAfee Music, 1973.

Shepherd Song. New York, McAfee Music, 1974.

Other

Tiros: Weather Eye in Space. New York, Messner, 1966.

Famous Firsts in Sports. New York, Putnam, 1967.

Great War Correspondents. New York, Putnam, 1968.

Great Women Reporters. New York, Putnam, 1969.

The Bastard Photostory. New York, Jove, 1980.

*

Manuscript Collection: University of Wyoming, Laramie.

John Jakes comments:

My first sale was a science fiction story. I grew up on the genre, and wanted to write nothing else—though I did. Eventually, the novels I did turn out were greeted unenthusiastically, and two or three on which I worked particularly hard, and of which I was particularly proud—*Six-Gun Planet, Black in Time, On Wheels*—disappeared almost within days of publication. That convinced me to stop writing SF. I have friends among science-fiction writers, but found the few conventions I attended in large part boring—perhaps a second reason I abandoned the field: not, I must add, without considerable regret.

* * *

Unfortunately, as far as his science-fiction writing is concerned, John Jakes is best known for creating Brak the Barbarian. This is not to demean the Brak stories but rather to rue the fact that Jakes has written several other excellent novels which have gone virtually unnoticed.

The Brak stories follow a specific formula and so, even though very good, become wearisome by the repetition of their pattern. Brak's world is a dichotomous one in which evil is an active force represented by the god Yob-Haggoth and is implemented by his agent, Septegundus, a man with no eyelids and skin covered with the living, writhing figures of the souls he has captured. Septegundus is aided by his beautiful but equally evil daughter, Ariane. Throughout his various "on-the-road" adventures, Brak encounters analogues of Ariane, whom he eventually recognizes by their display of evil and lustful natures. Nordica Fire-Hair, in *The Sorceress,* is an excellent example. A dutiful daughter, she suddenly changes. She leaves her father, an alchemist who has learned the secret of turning things to gold, to die in a deep pit inhabited by a dragonlike creature called Manworm. As Brak becomes more and more involved with her, he recognizes that she is possessed by Ariane. When Nordica is finally killed, Brak sees the spirit of Ariane leaving the corpse.

Cast out of his own land in the far north for blaspheming the gods, Brak is constantly pursued by the forces of Septegundus in his eternal quest to reach the fabled golden city of Khurdisan in the south. Septegundus has vowed to kill him for interfering in his affairs. An incarnation of Conan, Brak is instinctive and physical, but even his strength and cunning are no match for the supernatural forces of evil, so he is aided in his continuing battle with Yob-Haggoth by various Nestorian priests who represent the mysterious Nameless God. Inevitably, Brak loses his sword, encounters some sort of fantastic monster which he must slay, Manworm, Scarlet-jaw, Doomdog, or The Thing That Crawls, and plies his way toward Khurdisan. But regardless of the formulization of the stories and the impression that some were written hastily, their fast-paced action recommends them. Within the formula, Jakes's inventiveness makes the stories both attractive and interesting.

The highly imaginative quality of Jakes's writing is perhaps better displayed in some of his other novels. Among them, *The Planet Wizard, The Hybrid,* and the Klekton books are the best. The Klekton is a ring of alternate Earths which can be reached by traveling through various mindgates. The novels tell the story of Gavin Black, a down-and-out journalist who becomes a pawn of Bronwyn, a police official of an alternative world called Earth Prime. Bronwyn is attempting to stop an invasion of our Earth from yet another alternate Earth called Earth Three or Shulkor. The population of all three Earths are descended from a great civilization that lived on heartland Earth before the Ice Age. When cold and ice threatened them, some went up the Klekton and some down, there to develop into radically different peoples. The Shulkorites became savage and warlike, while Bronwyn's people developed their intellectual abilities. Now, the Shulkorites want to use heartland Earth as a base to destroy Earth Prime and to extend their power to the more hospitable worlds down the chain. At first bribed, Black later permits himself to be used so that he can gain access to the gates in order to be reunited with Samantha, a girl from Earth Three with whom he has fallen in love.

The Hybrid tells the story of Andreas Law, the son of an Earth father and an Omqu mother, who has the unique ability to project destructive blasts of mental energy. Law becomes the tool of a fanatic Earth billionaire, Sir Robert Baron, who is trying to sabotage a proposed peace treaty between Earth and Omqu because he hates the humanoid but feathered aliens. Cast against a background of two intergalactic cultures trying to understand one another, *The Hybrid* is a story of prejudice which is handled sensitively and thoughtfully. It is a perceptive and imaginative exploration of what might happen when man achieves intergalactic travel and finds that he is not the only humanoid in the universe.

The Planet Wizard is a story of self-discovery, power, and love. Set in another galaxy eons after it has been colonized by Earthmen, *The Planet Wizard* tells of civilizations left to cope for themselves after planetary wars have destroyed the great business houses which controlled galactic society. Superstition abounds as knowledge and technology fade. Magus Blacklaw, a bogus magician but first-rate confidence man, traps himself and his daughter, Maya, into having to make a trip to the feared planet of Lightmark to exorcise its demons and to secure access to the resources of the great house that did business there. Blacklaw is a lovable rogue who rises above himself in his efforts to provide a better life for his daughter. In ridding Lightmark of its demons, he finds strength and courage he did not know he possessed.

Jakes is a highly competent writer whose imagination and versatility deserve respect. Always interesting, his stories provide fast-paced entertainment while imaginatively exploring the possibility of life in the distant future.

—Carl B. Yoke

JANIFER, Laurence M. Pseudonym for Larry Mark Harris; also writes as Alfred Blake; Andrew Blake; Mark Phillips; Barbara Wilson. American. Born in Brooklyn, New York, 17 March 1933. Attended City College of New York, one year. Married 1) Sylvia Siegel in 1955 (divorced, 1958); 2) Sue Blugerman in 1960 (divorced, 1962); 3) Rae Montor in 1966 (divorced, 1968); 4) Beverly Goldberg in 1969 (separated, 1984); two daughters and one son. Pianist and arranger, New York, 1950-59; Editor, Scott Meredith Literary Agency, New York, 1952-57; editor and art director, detective and science-fiction magazines, 1953-57. Since 1957, professional comedian. Agent: Scott Meredith Literary Agency, 845 Third Avenue, New York, New York 10022, U. S. A.

SCIENCE-FICTION PUBLICATIONS

Novels (series: Angelo di Stefano; Gerald Knave: Survivor)

Slave Planet. New York, Pyramid, 1963.
The Wonder War. New York, Pyramid, 1964.
You Sane Men. New York, Lancer, 1965; as *Bloodworld,* 1968.
A Piece of Martin Cann. New York, Belmont, 1968.
Target: Terra (di Stefano), with S. J. Treibich. New York, Ace, 1968.
The High Hex (di Stefano), with S. J. Treibich. New York, Ace, 1969.
The Wagered World (di Stefano), with S. J. Treibich. New York, Ace, 1969.
Power. New York, Dell, 1974.
Survivor. New York, Ace, 1977.
Knave in Hand. New York, Ace, 1979.
Reel. New York, Doubleday, 1983.

Novels as Mark Phillips (with Randall Garrett) (series: Kenneth J. Malone in all books)

Brain Twister. New York, Pyramid, 1962.
The Impossibles. New York, Pyramid, 1963.
Supermind. New York, Pyramid, 1963.

Short Stories

Impossible? New York, Belmont, 1968.

Uncollected Short Stories

"Countdown," in *Analog* (New York), July 1972.
"A Few Minutes," in *Ten Tomorrows,* edited by Roger Elwood. New York, Fawcett, 1973.
"Thine Alabaster Cities Gleam," in *Future City,* edited by Roger Elwood. New York, Simon and Schuster, 1973.
"Family Album," in *Fantasy and Science Fiction* (New York), May 1973.
"An Agent in Place," in *Analog* (New York), May 1973.
"Martyr," in *Analog* (New York), September 1973.
"Amfortas," in *Omega,* edited by Roger Elwood. New York, Walker, 1974.
"The Bible after Apocalypse," in *New Dimensions 4,* edited by Robert Silverberg. New York, New American Library, 1974.
"Story Time," in *Journey to Another Star,* edited by Roger Elwood. Minneapolis, Lerner, 1974.
"Saving Grace," in *Fantastic* (New York), November 1974.
"Civis Obit" and "The Gift" in *Dystopian Visions,* edited by Roger Elwood. Englewood Cliffs, New Jersey, Prentice Hall, 1975.
"All Possible Worlds," in *Beyond Time,* edited by Sandra Ley. New York, Pocket Books, 1976.
"The Believer," in *Analog* (New York), February 1979.
"Toadstool Sinfonia," in *Analog* (New York), July 1980.
"The Lost Secret," in *The Rest of Omni Science Fiction 5,* edited by Don Myrus. New York, Omni, 1983.
"Please Note," in *Analog* (New York), May 1983.
"Expiration Policy," in *Analog* (New York), November 1983.
"Final Draft," in *Analog* (New York), January 1984.
"The Samaritan Rule," in *Analog* (New York), March 1984.
"Love in Bloom," in *Analog* (New York), Mid-December 1984.

OTHER PUBLICATIONS

Novels

Pagan Passions (as Larry Mark Harris), with Randall Garrett.

New York, Galaxy, 1959.
The Pickled Poodles (as Larry M. Harris). New York, Random House, 1960; London, Boardman, 1961.
The Protector (as Larry M. Harris). New York, Random House, 1961; London, Boardman, 1962.
The Bed and I (as Alfred Blake). N. p., Intimate, 1962.
Faithful for 8 Hours (as Alfred Blake). New York, Beacon, 1963.
The Pleasure We Know (as Barbara Wilson). New York, Lancer, 1964.
The Velvet Embrace (as Barbara Wilson). New York, Lancer, 1965.
The Woman Without a Name. New York, New American Library, 1966.
The Final Fear. New York, Belmont, 1967.
You Can't Escape. New York, Lancer, 1967.

Novels as Andrew Blake

I Deal in Desire. N. p., Boudoir, 1962.
Sex Swinger. New York, Beacon, 1963.
Love Hostess. New York, Beacon, 1963.

Other

Editor, *Master's Choice*. New York, Simon and Schuster, 1966; London, Jenkins, 1967; as *18 Great Science Fiction Stories,* New York, Grosset and Dunlap, 1971.

Ghost Writer for *Ken Murray's Giant Joke Book,* 1957; *The Henry Morgan Joke Book,* 1958; *The Foot in My Mouth* by Jeff Harris, 1958; *Tracer!* by Ed Goldfader, 1970; editor for *Yes, I'm Here with Someone* by Thomas Sutton, 1958.

*

Laurence M. Janifer comments:

I write funny stuff or non-funny stuff. It depends on how I feel. In either case, all I aim at doing is providing a world for the reader to live in for a while. Once in a long while I'll try to demonstrate an axiom of some sort—not often. I'd rather write funny stuff (or semi-funny stuff like the Knave adventures) because there is so damned little of it around. But I have not got much control over what my head sends me. I write sf because it fascinates me, and I continue to have the nagging feeling that sf ought to have something to do with science. I am violently against any attempt to get a scholarly view of my work or to assess my Purpose in Writing. This sort of thing should be stamped out. If you can believe and live in the worlds I write, I'm both happy and flattered. I look forward to creating more worlds, some sf and some not, for an indefinite time.

*   *   *

A first impression of Laurence M. Janifer's books might be that they emphasize stock subjects and sensation. *You Sane Men* is the story of a world on which Bound Men and Bound Women are held as objects of torture in what are called Remand Houses. The "Lords and Ladies" inflict pain on them with whips and hot brands and derive pleasure or sexual strength from this. In *Power* Aaron Norin, the son of a respected empire official, leads a spaceship in rebellion against the empire. *Slave Planet* is about a world where cynical colonists from earth use alligator-like aliens as slaves to extract precious metals. Mental telepathy is used in *A Piece of Martin Cann* to cure a patient: *The Wonder War* is about a war to gain power over an entire galaxy.

These lurid but stock topics, however, acquire some complexity in Janifer's best novels. Janifer's central subjects are power and rebellion, and he often treats these with subtle irony. Jo, the narrator of *You Sane Men,* is a refugee from the world of blood, addressing the "sane men" who doubt that it is possible for human beings to run a social system based on torture. But as Jo speaks we see that his horrible world is sane and is human, for the point is that sane people are capable of extreme, thoughtless cruelty. Jo joins with other young people in a revolt against the ruling council, a revolt ironically not against the institution of cruelty but against the exclusion of young people from decision-making. When a lady is killed another irony develops: in contrast to our crime-ridden earth, the blood world has never had a murder, and its natives are comically inept detectives. Torture is legalized, but other crimes are almost unknown. Satire of our sexual taboos develops when Jo is shocked to discover that some men enjoy torturing men, and women.

The irony of *Power* is more understated. Isidor Norin's family all have power. His daughter Rachel is married to a famour actor, and his son Alphard is the assistant to a powerful religious leader. When the spaceship *Valor,* lead by his son Aaron, rebels from the empire, Aaron is killed and his father becomes critically ill. The rebellion is apparently crushed, and the Emperor retains all formal power, but the idea of freedom has been kindled in several minds. In *Slave Planet* Janifer gently portrays the naive point of view of several of the enslaved aliens. Janifer avoids pathos by giving us their puzzled acceptance of their condition. We are also made to see through the rather exaggerated moralism which brings a military liberation force from the shocked confederation to Fruyling's world. Thus the overthrow of slavery and its replacement by automatic machinery are complex events. We reject the view of Dr. Haelingen that slavery is inevitable on this world, but we do consider it.

Janifer's short stories are competent but routine, although his talent at presenting unusual points of view comes through in such stories as "Thine Alabaster Cities Gleam," about a couple caught in a skyscraper at night when the electricity, and thus the air supply, goes out. They will die—even the woman's diamond can make only faint scratches in the window. "Civis Obit" gives us the point of view of a telepath who preserves sanity only be developing the skill of shutting out human suffering. "Amfortas" develops the psychological effects of massive organ transplants.

The multiple points of view of *Reel* signal Janifer's entry into literary modernism. Although the subject matter is familiar to Janifer readers—a power struggle on "The Reel," a resort planet of the far future—Janifer's technique is deft and impressionistic. Janifer is a writer of promise and more than occasional achievement.

—Curtis C. Smith

JASON, Jerry. See SMITH, George H.

JAY, Mel. See FANTHORPE, R. Lionel.

JENKINS, Will F. See **LEINSTER, Murray.**

JETER, K. W. American. Born in Los Angeles, California, in 1950. Agent: Russ Galen, Scott Meredith Literary Agency, 845 Third Avenue, New York, New York 10022, U. S. A.

SCIENCE-FICTION PUBLICATIONS

Novels

Seeklight. Toronto, Laser, 1975.
The Dreamfields. Toronto, Laser, 1976.
Morlock Night. New York, DAW, 1979.
Dr. Adder. New York, Bluejay, 1984.
The Glass Hammer. New York, Bluejay, 1985.

OTHER PUBLICATIONS

Novels

Soul Eater. New York, Tor, 1983.
Night Vision. New York, Tor, 1985.

*   *   *

K. W. Jeter's work has the flavor of Philip K. Dick's studies in reality at their best. Jeter's first published novel, *Seeklight*, features a semi-feudal society and a young man named Daenek whose identity as son of a former leader gets him marked for death. Yet, in the middle of the action, a sociologist will appear through use of super-science technology and ask questions of the participants like any good graduate research assistant would. This is the odd juxtapositioning of Jeter's reality: one world holds several different—even contradicting—realities. Yet the strange mingling of worlds works; Barry Malzberg, in the introduction to *Seeklight*, calls the book "one of the three or four best s-f novels I have ever read. . . . "

Jeter's next novel, *The Dreamfields*, reads very much like a Dick novel. Ralph Metric is a member of Operation Dreamwatch, supposedly an experimental project to control and observe severely disturbed teenagers through their dreams. Yet in the dreamstate, Ralph discovers a different reality operating. There is an alien invasion of Earth forming in the Dreamfields and those disturbed teenagers' dreams hold power in the aliens' alternate reality. Shifting identities and surreal plot elements make *The Dreamfields* one of Jeter's most ambitious novels.

Morlock Night is Jeter's attempt to finish H. G. Wells's *The Time Machine*. At the conclusion of Wells's book, the Time Traveller went back to the future of the Morlocks and the Eloi and never returned. Jeter supposes, what if the Time Traveller was murdered by the Morlocks and they used the Time Machine to invade England of 1892? An interesting notion gone wrong is the result. A young man named Edwin Hocker is recruited by a cryptic man calling himself Dr. Ambrose. Together they try to change the Reality of the deadly Morlock invasion by bringing together the ancient sword of power: Excalibur. The novel goes awry when Merlin and King Arthur join forces to defeat the Morlock menace. Too much of the book is spent mucking around in the London sewers—the Morlock's secret staging area—and too much of the plot is predictable.

Soul Eater is Jeter's best book to date. David Braemer once had a happy marriage. Then his wife, Renee, after a bizarre episode where she tried to kill her young daughter Dee, suffered a massive stroke and lies comatose, tended by her brother Jess and adopted sister Carol in their family house. Braemer is disturbed by Dee's behavior: the little girl will fall into a troubled sleep, then sleepwalk into the kitchen, find the largest knife she can, then head for Braemer's bedroom. Braemer has awoken to Dee standing over him with a knife ready to plunge into his chest. Braemer thinks the trauma of Renee's attempt on her daughter's life and subsequent stroke are affecting the girl's sanity. But two people meet with Braemer to warn him: Kathy, Renee's other sister, and an enigmatic man named Pedersen. The warnings are the same: Renee has the power to insert her identity into others and she is using Dee as an instrument to kill David. Braemer discounts the warnings as absurdities, but later finds more horror and more truth in those statements than he could have imagined. *Soul Eater* is an extraordinary horror novel with Jeter's best-realized characters and writing.

Dr. Adder includes an afterword by Philip K. Dick comparing the book to the works of James Joyce and Henry Miller, and the more daring stories in Harlan Ellison's *Dangerous Visions*. Jeter could not find a publisher for the work, written in 1972, for more than a decade because of its violence and sex. Most of the book's action centers around Los Angeles and its sewers of the near future. The city is populated by surgically altered prostitutes— the result of Dr. Adder's talents—and snipers, and Mother Endure who takes care of all the losers in Rattown. Opposed to this degenerate lifestyle is videopreacher John Mox and his Moral Forces. Into this maelstrom comes E. Allen Limmit on a mission to deliver a flashglove—a banned CIA weapon of incredible powers—to Dr. Adder. Like a catalyst, Limmit sets off a war among the powers of Los Angeles: a war that Limmit's true identity holds the key to.

The controversy surrounding *Dr. Adder* generates more heat than light. The book is the result of an immature writer just learning his craft: too much of *Dr. Adder* seems calculated to shock or disgust the reader rather than to move the plot of the book or to develop the characters. There is much to praise in *Dr. Adder* : Jeter's picture of a nightmarish future controlled by cabals is innovative, evoking echoes of Dick's futures in *Flow My Tears, The Policeman Said* and *A Scanner, Darkly*.

K. W. Jeter is a promising young SF writer whose work is influenced by Philip K. Dick and has in turn influenced Dick. More on that relationship can be found in interviews between Jeter and Andy Watson published in the December 1984 issue of the *Philip K. Dick Society Newsletter* and the May 1985 issue of *Science Fiction Review*.

—George Kelley

JOHNS, Kenneth. See **BULMER, Kenneth.**

JOHNS, Marston. See **FANTHORPE, R. Lionel.**

JOHNS, W(illiam) E(arl). Also wrote as William Earle; Jon

Early. British. Born in Bengeo, Hertfordshire, 5 February 1893. Educated at a school in Bengeo; Hertford Grammar School, 1905-07; articled to a Hertford surveyor, 1907-12. Married Maude Hunt in 1914 (died, 1961), one son; lived with Doris May Leigh from 1924. Sanitary inspector, Swaffham, Norfolk, 1912-13. Served in the Norfolk Yeomanry, 1913-15, and in the Machine Gun Corps, in Egypt and Salonika, 1916-17; transferred to the Royal Flying Corps (later Royal Air Force), 1917, and served until 1927: shot down and captured in France, 1918; Flying Officer, 1920-27; lecturer, Air Defence Cadet Corps, later Air Training Corps, and writer for the Ministry of Defence, London, 1939-45. Aviation illustrator from 1927; Founding Editor, *Popular Flying*, 1932-39, and *Flying*, 1938-39, both London; columnist ("The Passing Show"), *My Garden* magazine, London, 1937-44, and for *Modern Boy, Pearson's, Boys' Own Paper*, and *Girls' Own Paper. Died 21 June 1968.*

SCIENCE-FICTION PUBLICATIONS (for children)

Novels (series: Rex Clinton in all books except *Biggles— Charter Pilot*)

Biggles—Charter Pilot. London, Oxford University Press, 1943.
Kings of Space. London, Hodder and Stoughton, 1954.
Return to Mars. London, Hodder and Stoughton, 1955.
Now to the Stars. London, Hodder and Stoughton, 1956.
To Outer Space. London, Hodder and Stoughton, 1957.
The Edge of Beyond. London, Hodder and Stoughton, 1958.
The Death Rays of Ardilla. London, Hodder and Stoughton, 1959.
To Worlds Unknown. London, Hodder and Stoughton, 1960.
The Quest for the Perfect Planet. London, Hodder and Stoughton, 1961.
The Man Who Vanished into Space. London, Hodder and Stoughton, 1963.

Short Stories

Worlds of Wonder: More Adventures in Space. London, Hodder and Stoughton, 1962.

OTHER PUBLICATIONS

Novels

Mossyface (as William Earle). London, Mellifont Press, 1932.
The Spy Flyers. London, John Hamilton, 1933.
Sky High. London, Newnes, 1936; revised edition, London, Latimer, 1951.
Steeley Flies Again. London, Newnes, 1936; revised edition, London, Latimer, 1951.
Blue Blood Runs Red (as Jon Early). London, Newnes, 1936.
Murder by Air. London, Newnes, 1937; revised edition, London, Latimer, 1951.
The Murder at Castle Deeping. London, John Hamilton, 1938; revised edition, London, Latimer, 1951.
Desert Night: A Romance. London, John Hamilton, 1938.
Wings of Romance: A Steeley Adventure. London, Newnes, 1939; revised edition, London, Latimer, 1951.
The Unknown Quantity. London, Hamilton, 1940.
No Motive for Murder. London, Hodder and Stoughton, 1958; New York, Washburn, 1959.
The Man Who Lost His Way. London, Macdonald, 1960.

Short Stories

The Raid. London, John Hamilton, 1935.
Doctor Vane Answers the Call. London, Latimer, 1950.
Short Stories. London, Latimer, 1953.
Sky Fever and Other Stories. London, Latimer, 1953.

Fiction (for children)

The Camels Are Coming. London, John Hamilton, 1932; as *Biggles, Pioneer Air Fighter*, London, Armada, 1982.
The Cruise of the Condor: A Biggles Story. London, John Hamilton, 1933.
Biggles of the Camel Squadron. London, John Hamilton, 1934.
Biggles Flies Again. London, John Hamilton, 1934.
Biggles Learns to Fly. London, Boys' Friend Library, 1935.
Biggles Flies East. London, Oxford University Press, 1935.
Biggles Hits the Trail. London, Oxford University Press, 1935.
Biggles in France. London, Boys' Friend Library, 1935.
The Black Peril: Biggles Story. London, John Hamilton, 1935; as *Biggles Flies East* (not same as 1935 book), London, Boys' Friend Library, 1938.
Biggles in Africa. London. Oxford University Press, 1936.
Biggles & Co. London, Oxford University Press, 1936.
Biggles—Air Commodore. London, Oxford University Press, 1937.
Biggles Flies West. London, Oxford University Press, 1937.
Biggles Flies South. London, Oxford University Press, 1938.
Biggles Goes to War. London, Oxford University Press, 1938.
Champion of the Main. London, Oxford University Press, 1938.
Biggles Flies North. London, Oxford University Press, 1939.
Biggles in Spain. London, Oxford University Press, 1939.
The Rescue Flight: A Biggles Story. London, Oxford University Press, 1939.
Biggles in the Baltic. London, Oxford University Press, 1940.
Biggles in the South Seas. London, Oxford University Press, 1940.
Biggles—Secret Agent. London, Oxford University Press, 1940.
Worrals of the W. A. A. F. London, Lutterworth Press, 1941.
Spitfire Parade: Stories of Biggles in War-Time. London, Oxford University Press, 1941.
Biggles Sees It Through. London, Oxford University Press, 1941.
Biggles Defies the Swastika. London, Oxford University Press, 1941.
Biggles in the Jungle. London. Oxford University Press, 1942.
Sinister Service. London, Oxford University Press, 1942.
Biggles Sweeps the Desert. London, Hodder and Stoughton, 1942.
Worrals Flies Again. London, Hodder and Stoughton, 1942.
Worrals Carries On. London, Lutterworth Press, 1942.
Worrals on the War-Path. London, Hodder and Stoughton, 1943.
Biggles "Fails to Return". London, Hodder and Stoughton, 1943.
Biggles in Borneo. London, Oxford University Press, 1943.
King of the Commandos. London, University of London Press, 1943.
Gimlet Goes Again. London, University of London Press, 1944.
Worrals Goes East. London, Hodder and Stoughton, 1944.
Biggles in the Orient. London, Hodder and Stoughton, 1945.
Worrals of the Islands: A Story of the War in the Pacific. London, Hodder and Stoughton, 1945.
Biggles Delivers the Goods. London, Hodder and Stoughton, 1946.

Gimlet Comes Home. London, University of London Press, 1946.
Sergeant Bigglesworth C. I. D. London, Hodder and Stoughton, 1947.
Comrades in Arms. London, Hodder and Stoughton, 1947.
Gimlet Mops Up. Leicester, Brockhampton Press, 1947.
Worrals in the Winds. London, Hodder and Stoughton, 1947.
Biggles Hunts Big Game. London, Hodder and Stoughton, 1948.
Biggles' Second Case. London, Hodder and Stoughton, 1948.
Gimlet's Oriental Quest. Leicester, Brockhampton Press, 1948.
The Rustlers of Rattlesnake Valley. London, Nelson, 1948.
Worrals Down Under. London, Lutterworth Press, 1948.
Biggles Breaks the Silence. London, Hodder and Stoughton, 1949; as *Biggles in the Antarctic*, London, Armada, 1970.
Biggles Takes a Holiday. London, Hodder and Stoughton, 1949.
Gimlet Lends a Hand. Leicester, Brockhampton Press, 1949.
Worrals Goes Afoot. London, Lutterworth Press, 1949.
Worrals in the Wastelands. London, Lutterworth Press, 1949.
Worrals Investigates. London, Lutterworth Press, 1950.
Biggles Gets His Men. London, Hodder and Stoughton, 1950.
Gimlet Bores In. Leicester, Brockhampton Press, 1950.
Another Job for Biggles. London, Hodder and Stoughton, 1951.
Biggles Goes to School. London, Hodder and Stoughton, 1951.
Biggles Works It Out. London, Hodder and Stoughton, 1951.
Gimlet Off the Map. Leicester, Brockhampton Press, 1951.
Biggles—Air Detective. London, Latimer, 1952.
Biggles Follows On. London, Hodder and Stoughton, 1952.
Biggles Takes the Case. London, Hodder and Stoughton, 1952.
Gimlet Gets the Answer. Leicester, Brockhampton Press, 1952.
Biggles and the Black Raider. London, Hodder and Stoughton, 1953.
Biggles in the Blue. Leicester, Brockhampton Press, 1953.
Biggles in the Gobi. London, Hodder and Stoughton, 1953.
Biggles of the Special Air Police. London, Thames Publishing Company, 1953.
Biggles and the Pirate Treasure, and Other Biggles Adventures. Leicester, Brockhampton Press, 1954.
Biggles Cuts It Fine. London, Hodder and Stoughton, 1954.
Biggles, Foreign Legionnaire. London, Hodder and Stoughton, 1954.
Biggles, Pioneer Airfighter. London, Thames Publishing Company, 1954.
Gimlet Takes a Job. Leicester, Brockhampton Press, 1954.
Adventure Bound. London, Nelson, 1955.
Biggles' Chinese Puzzle and Other Biggles Adventures. Leicester, Brockhampton Press, 1955.
Biggles in Australia. London, Hodder and Stoughton, 1955.
Biggles of 266. London, Thames Publishing Company, 1956.
Biggles Takes Charge. Leicester, Brockhampton Press, 1956.
No Rest for Biggles. London, Hodder and Stoughton, 1956.
Biggles Makes Ends Meet. London, Hodder and Stoughton, 1957.
Adventure Unlimited. London, Nelson, 1957.
Biggles of the Interpol. Leicester, Brockhampton Press, 1957.
Biggles on the Home Front. London, Hodder and Stoughton, 1957.
Biggles Buries a Hatchet. Leicester, Brockhampton Press, 1958.
Biggles on Mystery Island. London, Hodder and Stoughton, 1958.
Biggles Presses On. Leicester, Brockhampton Press, 1958.
Biggles at World's End. Leicester, Brockhampton Press, 1959.
Biggles' Combined Operation. London, Hodder and Stoughton, 1959.
Biggles in Mexico. Leicester, Brockhampton Press, 1959.

Adventures of the Junior Detection Club. London, Parrish, 1960.
Biggles and the Leopards of Zinn. Leicester, Brockhampton Press, 1960.
Biggles Goes Home. London, Hodder and Stoughton, 1960.
Where the Golden Eagle Soars. London, Hodder and Stoughton, 1960.
Biggles and the Missing Millionaire. Leicester, Brockhampton Press, 1961.
Biggles and the Poor Rich Boy. Leicester, Brockhampton Press, 1961.
Biggles Forms a Syndicate. London, Hodder and Stoughton, 1961.
Biggles Goes Alone. London, Hodder and Stoughton, 1962.
Biggles Sets a Trap. London, Hodder and Stoughton, 1962.
Orchids for Biggles. Leicester, Brockhampton Press, 1962.
Biggles and the Plane That Disappeared. London, Hodder and Stoughton, 1963.
Biggles Flies to Work. London, Dean, 1963.
Biggles' Special Case. Leicester, Brockhampton Press, 1963.
Biggles Takes a Hand. London, Hodder and Stoughton, 1963.
Biggles Takes It Rough. Leicester, Brockhampton Press, 1963.
Biggles and the Black Mask. London, Hodder and Stoughton, 1964.
Biggles and the Lost Sovereigns. Leicester, Brockhampton Press, 1964; as *Biggles and the Lost Treasure*, London, Knight, 1978.
Biggles Investigates and Other Stories of the Air Police. Leicester, Brockhampton Press, 1965.
Biggles and the Blue Moon. Leicester, Brockhampton Press, 1965.
Biggles and the Plot That Failed. Leicester, Brockhampton Press, 1965.
Biggles Looks Back. London, Hodder and Stoughton, 1965.
Biggles Scores a Bull. London, Hodder and Stoughton, 1965.
Biggles in the Terai. Leicester, Brockhampton Press, 1966.
Biggles and the Gun Runners. Leicester, Brockhampton Press, 1966.
Biggles and the Penitent Thief. Leicester, Brockhampton Press, 1967.
Biggles Sorts It Out. Leicester, Brockhampton Press, 1967.
Biggles and the Dark Intruder. London, Knight, 1967.
Biggles in the Underworld. Leicester, Brockhampton Press, 1968.
The Boy Biggles. London, Dean, 1968.
Biggles and the Deep Blue Sea. Leicester, Brockhampton Press, 1968.
Biggles and the Little Green God. Leicester, Brockhampton Press, 1969.
Biggles and the Noble Lord. Leicester, Brockhampton Press, 1969.
Biggles Sees Too Much. Leicester, Brockhampton Press, 1970.
Biggles of the Royal Flying Corps (selection), edited by Piers Williams. Maidenhead, Berkshire, Purnell, 1978.
The Bumper Biggles Book. London, Chancellor, 1983.

Plays

Radio Plays (with G. R. Ranier): *The Machine That Disappeared*, 1942; *The Charming Mrs. Nayther*, 1942.

Other

Fighting Planes and Aces (for children). London, John Hamilton, 1932.
The Pictorial Flying Course, with Harry M. Scholfield, illustrated by Johns. London, John Hamilton, 1932.
The Air V. C.'s. London, John Hamilton, 1935.

Some Milestones of Aviation. London, John Hamilton, 1935.
The Passing Show: A Garden Diary by an Amateur Gardener. London, My Garden, 1937.
The Modern Boy's Book of Pirates. London, Amalgamated Press, 1939.
The Biggles Book of Heroes. London, Parrish, 1959.
The Biggles Book of Treasure Hunting. London, Parrish, 1962.
No Surrender, with R. A. Kelly. London, Harrap, 1969.

Editor, *The Modern Boy's Book of Aircraft*. London, Amalgamated Press, 1931.
Editor, *Wings: A Book of Flying Adventures*. London, John Hamilton, 1931.
Editor, *Thrilling Flights*. London, John Hamilton, 1935.

*

Critical Studies: *Biggles: The Authorised Biography* by John Pearson, London, Sidgwick and Jackson, 1979; *By Jove, Biggles: The Life of Captain W. E. Johns* by Peter Berresford Ellis and Piers Williams, London, W. H. Allen, 1981.

Illustrator: *Desert Wings* by Covington Clarke, 1931.

*   *   *

W. E. Johns, creator of the air ace Biggles, chronicled the adventures of the spaceship *Tavona* and her crew in a series of some ten novels, begun in 1954 and awkwardly written around the probably unanticipated eruption of the space race three years later. His aim, as stated in the foreword of *To Worlds Unknown*, was to familiarise young people with "the new science of Astronautics"; but even the most naive member of the intended teenage readership could not fail to catch the author out in such colossal errors as the assertion that an Earth-type planet can become a nova. In the simplified universe through which the *Tavona* speeds at superluminal velocities without Einsteinian complications of hyperspatial confabulations, only Newton's laws escape total maceration. Nevertheless, few youngsters, however sceptical, could fail to be enthralled by these novels, which have the flavour not of science fiction but of a series of adventurous sea voyages: a bunch of cheerful and resourceful sailors embarking on a cosmic ocean filled with wonders and fraught with perils.

The cosmic-ray-powered *Tavona* is built by the supremely advanced Terromagnans, crewed by Martians, and carries as passengers four intrepid Earthmen: the eccentric professor Lucius Brane whose jaunt to the moon in a backyard spaceship got the series off the launching pad; Tiger, the pipe-smoking, gun-toting man of action; Toby, the rather colourless ship's medic; and Tiger's clean-cut, pure-hearted teenage son Rex, contributing reader-indentification to the book and the clear eye of youth to the triad of vision, action, and expertise. On their cosmic cruises, they traverse the treacherous reaches of the Galaxy, exploring interesting little islands, occasionally pulling in at a bustling foreign port, sometimes getting stranded, shipwrecked, caught up in hostilities, or attacked by pirates, cannibals, or fearsome beasts, but always, with luck and ingenuity, pulling through. In the course of their travels, any jingoistic assumptions get thoroughly punctured: they discover that their homeland, far from being internationally revered, is feared and hated for its militarism and short-sightedness. The nuclear weapons, carelessly strewn space hardware, and filthy atmosphere of Earth are the shame of the Milky Way, and the cause of much agonising introspection for Rex as he spends the lonely hours between the stars contemplating (while Toby and Tiger attend to their pills and guns, and the Professor compiles his Galactic Guidebook) the universal imponderables, and

becomes ever more space-sick and travel-weary as the series progresses.

And progress the series does. In the early books the *Tavona*'s travels are restricted to the local archipelago of the Solar system, the spacefarers tending to land on tiny asteroids completely covered with ice, water, grass, or glass, or if inhabited boasting at most two or three (Terrestrial) species, and the plot is a rambling string of cautionary anecdotes. In the later novels the foursome strike out into the interstellar deeps, encountering various and complex (but inevitably Earthlike) civilisations, and becoming caught up in the machinations of cosmic kidnappers, conquerors and crooks, and the interminable moralising of superior (but humaniod) beings.

For all Johns's avowed intentions to educate embryo space scientists, the message which comes across much more clearly than the patronising tables of the solar systems and glossaries of astronomical terms that bedeck the books is the endless series of imprecations to the Earthmen to put away their bombs and satellites and cease tampering with the biosphere. It comes as a shock to the adult reader to return to these books, written in what seems in retrospect a decade of optimism, to find them filled not with white hope and the white heat of technology (the *Tavona* has no radio and no more navigational equipment than a small inshore craft) but with the doom-laden forebodings of planetary suicide that pervade the world into which the original readers have matured.

—Lee Montgomerie

JONES, D(ennis) F(eltham). British. Served in the Royal Navy during World War II. Has worked as a bricklayer and market gardener. *Died 1 April 1981*.

SCIENCE-FICTION PUBLICATIONS

Novels (series: Colossus)

Colossus. London, Hart Davis, 1966; New York, Putnam, 1967.
Implosion. London, Hart Davis, 1967; New York, Putnam, 1968.
Denver Is Missing. New York, Walker, 1971; as *Don't Pick the Flowers*, London, Panther, 1971.
The Fall of Colossus. New York, Putnam, 1974.
The Floating Zombie. New York, Berkley, 1975.
Colossus and the Crab. New York, Berkley, 1977.
Earth Has Been Found. New York, Dell, 1979; as *Xeno*, London, Sidgwick and Jackson, 1979.

Uncollected Short Stories

"Black Snowstorm," in *Fantasy and Science Fiction* (New York), January 1969.
"The Tocsin," in *Fantasy and Science Fiction* (New York), June 1970.
"Coffee Break," in *Laughing Space*, edited by Isaac Asimov and J. O. Jeppson. Boston, Houghton Mifflin, and London, Robson, 1982.

*   *   *

Asimov, in "The Machine and the Robot," writes, "Surely the *great* fear is not that machinery will harm us—but that it will supplant us." In *Colossus* D. F. Jones has certainly created one of the finest embodiments of this fear. Because men are attached to their freedom, or at least to a sense of freedom, *Colossus* becomes the ultimate horror story in which man is enslaved by his own creation. Jones develops the horror through the logic and detail of presentation. Each of the steps by which Colossus comes to power follows from the previous; all the hardware is credible. Forbin serves as a foil to the machine (eliciting such information as the reader needs to understand Colossus) and as an emotional sounding-board (articulating and amplifying the fear). The futility of Forbin's defiance of Colossus, especially his refusal to love it, contributes to the power of the ending.

The two sequels to *Colossus* do not quite measure up to the same standard. Neither seems to have the same level of conviction. In *The Fall of Colossus* the emphasis has shifted away from the horror of machine domination. Colossus's attempts to comprehend human emotion, Forbin's shift toward love for the machine, the Sect's worship, the Fellowship's opposition—none of these stimulate the same level of excitement. The sexual experiment on Cleo seems contrived and not very relevant. The outside intervention which brings the fall has a *deus ex machina* quality. In *Colossus and the Crab* the tight, straightforward plotting which is a strength in most of Jones's novels seems to have given way to a rather choppy, almost episodic style. The whole concept of the novel, which pits Forbin against two aliens from Mars, leads to the revival of Colossus and ends in a sort of Mexican standoff, gives the feeling that the author merely wanted to wrap up the series. The novel's climactic point, although it effectively builds the emotional tension of Forbin's naval attack, gets its power purely from situation—Forbin never seems to rise to the heroic level.

Perhaps that is because plot and setting, rather than characterization, are Jone's strengths. The plots of his other novels command the reader's attention, leading step-by-step to a satisfying conclusion. Whether he deals with population (*implosion*), alien invasion (*Earth Has Been Found*), or geologic catastrophe (*Don't Pick the Flowers*), the plot flows ineluctably from the initial assumption. Settings also contribute much to the effectiveness of all his works. Each setting presents a recognizable Earth in a not-too-distant future. The familiarity of setting functions effectively as a contrasting ground for the strange situation. More than a trace of the mad-scientist motif enters into his work. All his central characters are scientists, and either initate an action beyond control or attempt to cope with a situation beyond comprehension.

Don't Pick the Flowers seems to me the best of his novels. Its highly improbable situation is invested with a sense of possibility. The chief characters seem very human (when compared with Forbin, for instance) in their fears and desires, and in their strength to cope with an overwhelming situation, to endure against very long odds.

—Robert Reilly

JONES, Langdon. British. Born in 1942. Free-lance writer and musician. Former staff member, *New Worlds*, London.

SCIENCE-FICTION PUBLICATIONS

Short Stories

The Eye of the Lens. New York, Macmillan, 1972.

OTHER PUBLICATIONS

Other

Editor, *The New SF: An Original Anthology of Speculative Fiction.* London, Hutchinson, 1969.
Editor, with Michael Moorcock, *The Nature of the Catastrophe.* London, Hutchinson, 1971.

*   *   *

Langdon Jones's best work has been as an editor: he is responsible for the essential New Wave anthology *The New SF*, for the restoration of Mervyn Peake's prodigious but fractured *Titus Alone*, and (with Michael Moorcock) for later issues of *New Worlds* and for *The Nature of the Catastrophe*, the Cornelius anthology. Jones is also the author of a small number of fictions in prose and poetry featured prominently in *New Worlds* and in many readers' altercations at the time, but he has never produced the major work they seemed to foreshadow.

In form and theme Jones's writing is supremely typical of the British New Wave, but his disposition is older, more straightforwardly Romantic than his contemporaries'. Trained as a composer, he makes many references to music in his fiction, characterizing it as a transcendental, irrational power, the language of the heart, and the spirit's apprehension of eternity. In "The Music Makers" Martians of the Bradbury kind prove to have music so mighty that it is fatal for a human hearer, while in the experimental sequence "The Eye of the Lens" echoes of Messiaen affirm a primal, invigorating sun-worship against a collage of corrupt religions and machine-cults. Jones's protest-story "I Remember, Anita" (then outrageous, now unreadable) relates the sorrows of a young student whose adoration of music and his mistress is eclipsed by the shadow of the Bomb.

Several stories show the pattern: an unhappy, cerebral young man has difficulty reaching an idealized woman with whom he has had enthusiastic but anxious sexual congress. Confused by time, by memory, by death, and by machines, he seeks release through music and art, and fulfillment in her. Though Jones's storylines commonly lead to defeat and doom, these awkward quests for true love (certified by cosmic orgasm) secure a corner of hope in the fiction of Inner Space, whose landscapes are more usually coloured by depression and psychic damage. "The Garden of Delights," an Oedipal romance in pastels, is a time-conundrum in which the young man's mysterious lover proves to be his mother as a girl; but the whole cyclic tragedy of lost ideals and ruined lives cannot outweigh the one evening of perfect intimacy. Jones is a moral puritan in his Romanticism: everything is sacrificed to the ideal, and those who recognize no ideal are ugly, discordant, damned. There is the corresponding destructive and even morbid streak in Jones's fiction, seen when he writes about Christianity and the ring of flagellants in "The Eye of the Lens," or the dehumanized slave of "The Great Clock," imprisoned inside it to oil and regulate the mechanism.

The best of Jones's stories, "The Time Machine," deals with all his usual preoccupations, but less dogmatically, more ambiguously. It incorporates some hallucinatory SF imagery into precise, vivid description of an ordinary adultery, showing the Utopia of the senses as it fades and peels, and envisaging a time machine more organic than most. Influenced, perhaps by Thomas M. Disch's "The Squirrel Cage," it asks, Are we the prisoners of time, memory, and desire? Are we at the mercy of our own contrivances, and what would happen if we were released?

—Colin Greenland

JONES, Neil R(onald). American. Born in Fulton, New York, 29 May 1909. Attended Fulton public schools. Served in the 2nd Armored Division of the United States Army, 1942-45. Married Rita Gwendoline Rees in 1945. Stamp dealer, bookkeeper, cost analyst, office manager, game manufacturer; unemployment insurance claims examiner, State of New York, for 26 years. Address: 1028 Fay Street, Fulton, New York 13069, U.S.A.

SCIENCE-FICTION PUBLICATIONS

Short Stories (series: Professor Jameson in all books)

The Planet of the Double Sun. New York, Ace, 1967.
The Sunless World. New York, Ace, 1967.
Space War. New York, Ace, 1967.
Twin Worlds. New York, Ace, 1967.
Doomsday on Ajiat. New York, Ace, 1968.

Uncollected Short Stories (series: Professor Jameson; 24th Century; 26th Century)

"The Death's Head Meteor" (26th Century), in *Air Wonder Stories* (New York), January 1930.
"The Electrical Man," in *Scientific Detective* (New York), May 1930.
"Shadows of the Night," in *Amazing Detective Tales* (New York), October 1930.
"The Asteroid of Death" (26th Century), in *Wonder Stories Quarterly* (New York), Fall 1931.
"Spacewrecked on Venus" (24th Century), in *Wonder Stories Quarterly* (New York), Winter 1932.
"Escape from Phobus" (24th Century), in *Wonder Stories* (New York), February 1933.
"Martian and Troglodyte," in *Amazing* (New York), May 1933.
"The Moon Pirates" (26th Century), in *Amazing* (New York), September, October 1934.
"Little Hercules" (26th Century), in *Astounding* (New York), September 1936.
"The Astounding Exodus," in *Thrilling Wonder Stories* (New York), April 1937.
"Durna Rangue Neophyte" (24th Century), in *Astounding* (New York), June 1937.
"Swordsman of Saturn" (24th Century), in *Science Fiction* (Holyoke, Massachusetts), October 1939.
"The Dark Swordsmen of Saturn" (26th Century), in *Planet* (New York), Summer 1940.
"Liquid Hell" (26th Century), in *Future* (New York), July 1940.
"The Cat-Men of Aemt" (Jameson), in *Astonishing* (Chicago), August 1940.
"Invisible One" (26th Century), in *Super Science* (Kokomo, Indiana), September 1940.
"Cosmic Derelict" (Jameson), in *Astonishing* (Chicago), February 1941.
"Captives of Durna Rangue" (24th Century), in *Super Science* (Kokomo, Indiana), March 1941.
"Vampire of the Void" (26th Century), in *Planet* (New York), Spring 1941.
"Priestess of the Sleeping Death" (24th Century), in *Amazing* (New York), April 1941.
"The Ransom for Toledo," in *Comet* (Springfield, Massachusetts), May 1941.
"Slaves of the Unknown" (Jameson), in *Astonishing* (Chicago), March 1942.
"Spoilers of the Spaceways" (24th Century), in *Planet* (New York), Winter 1942.

"Parasite Planet" (Jameson), in *Super Science* (Kokomo, Indiana), November 1949.
"Hermit of Saturn's Ring" (24th Century), in *Flight into Space,* edited by Donald A. Wollheim. New York, Fell, 1950.
"World Without Darkness" (Jameson), in *Super Science* (Kokomo, Indiana), March 1950.
"The Mind Masters" (Jameson), in *Super Science* (Kokomo, Indiana), September 1950.
"The Citadel in Space" (26th Century), in *Two Complete Science Adventure Books* (New York), Summer 1951.
"The Star Killers" (Jameson), in *Super Science* (Kokomo, Indiana), August 1951.

*

Neil R. Jones comments:

I am one of the earlier science-fiction writers in this country. My first story, "The Death's Head Meteor," appeared in 1930, and was the first science-fiction story to use the word astronaut. "The Jameson Satellite" was the beginning of what is possibly the longest running series in science fiction; from 1931 to 1968, 23 stories in the series were published. I also wrote two other series ("Tales of the 24th Century" and "Tales of the 26th Century"); both included stories of the Durna Mangue cult. All the stories were written in the vein of a future history. Michael Ashley (*History of the Science Fiction Magazine*) puts it this way: "an overall framework in which each story forms part of a future history, invented by Jones long before either Heinlein or Asimov. The key story is the Jameson adventure 'Times's Mausoleum' (*Amazing,* December 1933) which remained the basis for all of Jones' other tales."

*   *   *

Neil R. Jones, while not a prolific writer as measured by total wordage, maintained a small but steady output over two decades in the science-fiction pulps. By far the greater number of his stories concerned adventures of Professor Jameson. The series began with "The Jameson Satellite" in 1931, the story of a professor whose desire to preserve his body after death is stronger than that of the pharaohs. Professor Jameson leaves instructions for his corpse to be placed in a rocket of his own construction which will carry him into an endless orbit of the earth, ensuring if not a perpetual at least a *very* long incorruptibility of the body. Secure in the belief that he has outdone even the embalming practices in H. Rider Haggard's *She,* he goes to his rest, and his wishes are carried out. Forty million years later, his satellite is discovered by creatures called Zoromes, people who eons before had satisfied a similar desire for material immortality by transplanting their brains into mechanical bodies. The Zoromes place the brain of Jameson into one of their spares and revivify it. By the end of the story, Jameson has decided to leave the now-lifeless earth, and travel through the stars with the Zoromes.

The popularity of the story demanded sequels (Isaac Asimov, then 11, was one of the admirers; he attributes the idea of his benevolent robots to the Zoromes). And the Professor Jameson series continued until 1968.

Although both the content and the style of these stories seem outdated today, Jones contributed at least one innovation widely adopted by later writers: he devised a "future history" against which he set the action of his stories. Whether Jones was inspired by the time chart in Olaf Stapledon's *Last and First Men* (1930) has not been established, but the usefulness of the device is clearly demonstrated by its subsequent employment by many writers—Robert Heinlein, Poul Anderson, and Larry Niven, to name just a few.

—Walter E. Meyers

JONES, Raymond F. American. Born in Salt Lake City, Utah, in 1915. Studied engineering and English in college. Radio engineer, then full-time writer. Lives in Arizona. Address: c/o Pinnacle, 2029 Century Park East, Los Angeles, California 90067, U. S. A.

SCIENCE- FICTION PUBLICATIONS

Novels

Renaissance. New York, Gnome Press, 1951; as *Man of Two Worlds,* New York, Pyramid, 1963.
The Alien. New York, Galaxy, 1951.
This Island Earth. Chicago, Shasta, 1952; London, Boardman, 1955.
Son of the Stars (for children). Philadelphia, Winston, 1952; London, Hutchinson, 1953.
Planet of Light (for children). Philadelphia, Winston, 1953.
The Secret People. New York, Avalon, 1956; as *The Deviates,* New York, Galaxy, 1959.
The Year When Stardust Fell (for children). Philadelphia, Winston, 1958.
The Cybernetic Brains. New York, Avalon, 1962.
Voyage to the Bottom of the Sea (for children). Racine, Wisconsin, Whitman, 1965.
Syn. New York, Belmont, 1969.
Moonbase One (for children). New York and London, Abelard Schuman, 1971.
Renegades of Time. Toronto, Laser, 1975.
The King of Eolim. Toronto, Laser, 1975.
The River and the Dream. Toronto, Laser, 1977.
Weeping May Tarry, with Lester del Rey. Los Angeles, Pinnacle, 1978.

Short Stories

The Toymaker. Los Angeles, Fantasy, 1951.
The Non-Statistical Man. New York, Belmont, 1964; London, Digit, 1965.

Uncollected Short Stories

"Subway to the Stars," in *Galaxy* (New York), December 1968.
"Rat Race," in *Above the Human Landscape,* edited by Willis McNelly and Leon Stover. Pacific Palisades, California, Goodyear, and London, Grayson, 1972.
"The Laughing Lion," in *Science Fiction Tales,* edited by Roger Elwood. New York, Random House, 1973.
"The Lions of Rome," in *Flame Tree Planet,* edited by Roger Elwood. St. Louis, Concordia, 1973.
"Pet," in *Future Quest,* edited by Roger Elwood. New York, Avon, 1973.
"Time Brother," in *Children of Infinity,* edited by Roger Elwood. London, Watts, 1973.
"A Bowl of Biskies Makes a Growing Boy," in *The Other Side of Tomorrow,* edited by Roger Elwood. New York, Random House, 1973.

"Rider in the Sky," in *Most Thrilling Science Fiction Ever Told* (New York), April 1973.
"Flauna," in *The Far Side of Time,* edited by Roger Elwood. New York, Dodd Mead, 1974.
"The Lights of Mars," in *Science Fiction Adventures from Way Out,* edited by Roger Elwood. Racine, Wisconsin, Whitman, 1974.
"Pacer," in *Future Kin,* edited by Roger Elwood. New York, Doubleday, 1974.
"Reflection of a Star," in *Survival from Infinity,* edited by Roger Elwood. New York, Watts, 1974.
"The Touch of Your Hand," in *If* (New York), April 1974.
"Death Eternal," in *Fantastic* (New York), October 1978.

OTHER PUBLICATIONS

Other (for children)

The World of Weather. Racine, Wisconsin, Whitman, 1961.
Animals of Long Ago. Racine, Wisconsin, Whitman, 1965.
Ice Formation on Aircraft (for adults). Geneva, World Meteorological Organization, 1968.
Physicians of Tomorrow. Chicago, Reilly and Lee, 1971.
Radar: How It Works. New York, Putnam, 1972.

* * *

Raymond F. Jones is an almost archetypical John Campbell writer, whether writing for *Astounding,* as with "Noise Level" where scientists are lured into inventing anti-gravity, or for *Thrilling Wonder Stories,* with the Peace Engineer stories where aliens secretly involve earth scientists in a program to produce materials needed to defend their home world against invaders (*This Island Earth*).

Jones's first novel, *Renaissance,* is a long and complex parallel-worlds story that contains variations on a number of familiar SF themes against a somewhat more adventurous narrative than is usual in his stories. *The Alien* is a bit more straightforward in its story-telling, although its ideas and the approach he takes to them is not simple at all. The shadow of A. E. van Vogt falls across both these books, the first in its resemblance in early passages to *Slan,* the second in its exploration of ideas and attitudes similar to those of *The World of Null A. The Alien* opens with a strong idea: a representative of a long-extinct extraterrestrial race is discovered entombed in the asteroid belt, and brought back to life. While the revival processes go forward, new discoveries indicate this being is thoroughly evil and responsible for the destruction of his own race, something he would no doubt manage for humanity as well. The wealth of ideas from which the story draws its strength occasionally betrays it, as when we are suddenly shown that our supposedly solar-system-bound humans have had the capability of interstellar flight (and use that capability with the utmost casualness); and, again, when a semanticist translates and teaches himself an entire alien language on the basis of a few hours' first-contact conversation. Overlook such points, however, and the book is as good an example of this type of space adventure as you're likely to find short of Edmond Hamilton.

It would be a mistake, however, to place Jones in the camp of Doc Smith or Hamilton, or even van Vogt. Jones has always managed to remain a force unto himself, although a pretty low-key force. One of the ways this has been achieved has been in his handling of characters. The typical Jones character is an engineer, technician, or mathematician, middle-class, and presented in a straightforward and realistic manner that contrasts sharply with the politicians, artists, scholars, militarists, rebels and engineer-savants that make up the bulk of the field's fictional populace. Jones seldom attempts any deep probing of his characters but has always drawn his strength from the ability to portray his characters in equally believable environments. He is also a very economical writer, and after *The Alien* he settled down to a more suitably quiet form of fiction. *The Island Earth* is the first book-length work of his that can be labeled typical. His characters are thoroughly convincing engineers, and, despite the melodrama and detective story touches, their thought processes are the thought processes of reasonable engineers. The complexities that cluttered Renaissance and *The Alien* are shunted into the background and the interest of the story lies not in galaxy-spanning events but in the impact of galaxy-spanning events on the lives of seemingly everyday people. The argument could be raised that the best of Jones's novels were written for the Winston juvenile series. *Son of the Stars,* in which teenagers encounter the survivor of a wrecked flying saucer and subsequently find their extraterrestrial friend endangered by adult prejudices, is certainly one of the best of that fondly remembered series of juvenile novels. *Planet of Light* was a sequel.

One of Jones's best stories is "The Non-Statistical Man," which tells of an insurance company statistician who encounters a series of anomolies involving recent claims. At first intrigued, then openly alarmed, he investigates and is led to the conclusion that there are people who possess a 100 per cent reliable intuition, rendering his own statistical approach superfluous and pointless. These people know when they're going to need insurance and they don't get it till then. The character's discovery of all this, his reactions to it, and his subsequent change of philosophy as he discovers that the process that makes intuition infallible can be taught to anyone—even him—is written in the low-key style that is the strength of Jones's best writing, and the result is one of his most convincing and compelling stories. It also illustrates the other strength of Jones. He's always been a story-teller who has gone to great pains to build his stories on definite ideas, making him something of a purist among SF writers. His complexities never overwhelm everything else in the way they usually do in the hands of others, and in his later, quieter fiction, his story-telling ability is often quite remarkable for its purity, directness, and seeming effortlessness. This effortlessness may have something to do with the decline in his readership in recent years: Jones is entertaining and often thought-provoking, but he doesn't generate the flair and excitement of a good many lesser but better-known writers.

Jones has also never marked out a particular type of fiction as his own. Most of his stories are recognizably the work of one writer, with a type of character and a worldview that are identifiable, but any story by Jones is apt to be written with a particular market in mind. "Seven Jewels of Chamar" is pure *Planet Stories* space opera and "Tools of the Trade" is a classic *Astounding* engineering problem story of the type John Campbell was always supposed to be looking for. But the first doesn't rank with the stories of Emmett McDowell or Gardner F. Fox, and the second is a middle-grade example of the sort of thing Eric Frank Russell was starting to be known for. Jones's recent novels have been good entertainments, but they've lacked the strengths of his early work.

Jones is a thorough-going professional and, in retrospect, a writer of surprising versatility. But the price of this seems to be that too often he came on the scene with a perfectly good story that was still second best to the similar works of someone else. But there have been times when the works he produced were principally from no source but himself, slanted to no editorial taste but his own—works like *This Island Earth, Son of the Stars*

and "The Non-Statistical Man"—and those results have always been worth waiting for—or searching out.

—Gerald W. Page

JORGENSEN, Ivar. See **FAIRMAN, Paul W.** ; **GARRETT, Randall.**

JORGENSON, Ivar. See **SILVERBERG, Robert.**

JOSEPH, M(ichael) K(ennedy). New Zealander. Born in Chingford, Essex, England, 9 July 1914. Educated at Sacred Heart College, Auckland; Auckland University College, B. A. 1933, M. A. 1934; Merton College, Oxford, B. A. 1938, B. Litt. 1939, M. A. 1945. Served in the British Army in the Royal Artillery, 1940-46. Married Mary Julia Antonovich in 1947; four sons and one daughter. Lecturer in English, 1945-49, and Senior Lecturer, 1950-59, Auckland University College; Associate Professor, 1960-69, and Professor of English, 1970-79, University of Auckland. Recipient: Hubert Church Prose Award, 1959; Jessie Mackay Poetry Award, 1960; New Zealand Book Award, for fiction, 1978. *Died 4 October 1981.*

SCIENCE-FICTION PUBLICATIONS

Novel

The Hole in the Zero. London, Gollancz, 1967; New York, Dutton, 1968.

OTHER PUBLICATIONS

Novels

I'll Soldier No More. Auckland, Paul's Book Arcade, and London, Gollancz, 1958.
A Pound of Saffron. Auckland, Paul's Book Arcade, and London, Gollancz, 1962.
A Soldier's Tale. Auckland and London, Collins, 1976.
The Time of Achamoth. Auckland and London, Collins, 1977.

Verse

Imaginary Islands. Privately printed, 1950.
The Living Countries. Auckland, Paul's Book Arcade, 1959.
Inscription on a Paper Dart. Auckland, Auckland University Press-Oxford University Press, 1974.

Other

Charles Aders: A Biographical Note. Auckland, Auckland University Press, 1954.
Byron the Poet. London, Gollancz, 1964; New York, Humanities Press, 1966.

Editor, *Frankenstein*, by Mary Shelley. London, Oxford University Press, 1969.

*   *   *

M. K. Joseph, a New Zealand writer and educator, produced only one science-fiction novel, *The Hole in the Zero*. While the book's primary staging occurs on an undefined planet in untime and unspace—that is, beyond the known universe and within the philosophical hole in the zero—James constructs his plot in such a manner that it succeeds in operating on several contrasting levels simultaneously.

Like Doris Lessing's *Briefing for a Descent into Hell*, the book teems with archetypal themes and figures; and like Kurt Vonnegut, Jr. 's *Slaughterhouse-Five*, it is episodic, lurching from time into untime, space into unspace, with what appears to be, on first encounter, disconcerting irregularity. Although not easily accessible to the casual reader—which may explain its relative obscurity outside of the novelist's native New Zealand—*The Hole in the Zero* proves to be a closely integrated, carefully executed story exhibiting few major flaws. The least well-developed sequence and the most apparent flaw is that which satirizes the decade in which the novel was written, the 1960's. But several notable strengths counterbalance this apparent weakness.

The familiar motif of life existing as a dream within the mind of a dreamer, a bitter denouncement when voiced by Mark Twain in *The Mysterious Stranger*, loses its threatening aspect with Joseph and achieves a rather comfortable appearance as a known escape clause in the midst of the unknown. Joseph's universe migrates swiftly from an exploration of the duality of man's nature to that of a single man bifurcating into co-linear lives, certainly a Wellsian concept. Progressing from these familiar byways, the book passes into a multiplicity of experiences in which each man *must* make a conscious choice before his life can assume direction. Finally, however, the life cycle itself degenerates into an endlessly repetitive dictum; and hell is the doom sequence of a single, unvarying lifespan swelling to encompass eternity, until even this stalls and the endless paradoxically reaches a terminus.

It is then that Joseph's central theme, that of man directed by an ultimately moral universe, emerges. For a merciful intelligence, perhaps the obscure figure of the Gespenster, metes out to each individual what each sought. Vividly illustrating the adage that man is a questing beast, supplanted by an occasional glimmer of Milton, Joseph's three male heroes/anti-heroes act out their appointed roles—the first seeking power, the second pleasure, and the third, the hero of the tale, Seth Paradine, truth. This trio is, with varying ability, integrated into the novel's multitudinous layering technique. But the solitary female character, Helena, is never well served by the author. Indeed, if achieving a limited dimensionality while assuming the role of dreamer and dream-maker—hampered by appearing as a quintessential Lady of Shalott whose tapestry of life is destroyed by the contest between Paradine and his Hyde-ish opposite, Merganser—Helena's primary role remains that of bit player in the scenes directed alternately by her father, Merganser and Paradine.

Finally, then, Paradine emerges triumphant as the major character. He is Everyman, the first and last man, God the Father and God the Son, Judas and Peter, and Adam. He assumes a focal point in the varied panoply of mythological and archetypal super-structures with which the novel is endowed and which, at times, seem so overweighted that they verge on inner collapse. Nevertheless, because Paradine is the seeker after truth, *The Hole in the Zero* speaks with a commanding and hopeful voice. For, while exposing the evil that men do to themselves, their environment, and to others, it is mankind's great capacity for good and a desire to serve while questing after the God within and without which emerge as M. K. Joseph's essentially Christian final declaration.

—Sharon-Ilona Hecht

JUDD, Cyril. See **KORNBLUTH, C. M. ; MERRIL, Judith.**

KAHN, James. American. Born in Chicago, Illinois, 30 December 1947. Educated at the University of Chicago, B. A. 1970, M. D. 1974. Married Jill Alden Littlewood in 1975; one daughter. Physician: intern, University of Wisconsin, Madison, 1974-75; resident, Los Angeles County Hospital, 1976-77, and University of California, Los Angeles, 1978-79. Since 1978, Emergency Room physician, Rancho Encino Hospital, Los Angeles. Agent: Jane Jordan Browne, 410 South Michigan Avenue, Suite 724, Chicago, Illinois 60605-1465, U.S.A.

SCIENCE-FICTION PUBLICATIONS

Novels (series: New World)

New World trilogy:
1. *World Enough and Time*. New York, Ballantine, 1980; London, Granada, 1982.
2. *Time's Dark Laughter*. New York, Ballantine, 1982; London, Panther, 1983.
Poltergeist (novelization of screenplay). New York, Warner, and London, Granada, 1982.
Return of the Jedi (novelization of screenplay). New York, Ballantine, and London, Macdonald, 1983.
Indiana Jones and the Temple of Doom (novelization of screenplay). London, Sphere, 1984.

OTHER PUBLICATIONS

Novels

Diagnosis: Murder. New York, Carlyle, 1978.
The Goonies (novelization of screenplay). New York, Warner, 1985

Plays

Television Plays: *A Pig Too Far* (*St. Elsewhere* series), 1983; for *E/R* series 1984-85.

Verse

Nerves in Patterns, with Jerome McGann. N. p., X Press, 1978.

*

James Kahn comments:
I think of my work primarily as storytelling, my purpose to entertain, and, if possible, to enthrall. Within that framework I

rely on the themes of death and rebirth a great deal, a cyclical movements in time and space—sometimes metaphorically, sometimes physically.

* * *

James Kahn is one of the young part-time writers who has been building his knowledge of the craft through novelizations of screenplays: *Poltergeist, Return of the Jedi, Indiana Jones and the Temple of Doom, The Goonies.* His first science-fiction short story, "Mobius Trip," dates back to 1971; since then, he has explored other genres to some extent, including a detective novel, *Diagnosis:Murder,* and a volume of poetry, *Nerves in Patterns.* His main original work, the New World Trilogy, consists of *World Enough and Time, Time's Dark Laughter,* and *Timefall,* scheduled for 1986.

The most interesting of the novelizations is *Poltergeist,* where Kahn's contact with ESP research in medical school and background in myth lead to descriptions of the astral planes and their inhabitants, especially the shadow, tree, and flame figures, that are congruent with accounts of occult experience and well above the level of the rest of the film material. The *Star Wars* volume, *Return of the Jedi,* is even and competent, with good landscape descriptions but little depth in characterization. Characterization techniques begin to expand in the *Indiana Jones* novelization with development of Short Round's viewpoint and the reiterated theme "Anything Goes" to characterize Willie; a limited juvenile narrator is also developed for *The Goonies.*

World Enough and Time is unusually high in quality for a first science-fiction novel, possible because of Kahn's love of words and interest in integrating poetic quotations either directly into the narration or as commentary on experience by scholar Vampires. The title derives from Marvell's "To His Coy Mistress," though the novel deals with interrupted love rather than unfulfilled sexual desire. Rose and Dicey are kidnapped from their respective husbands, the centaur Beauty and the human Scribe Josh, for unknown reasons; Josh and Beauty join in pursuit and claim Venge-right, acquiring as companions the cat/human Isis, the Flutterby (gaint butterfly) Humbelly, the Neuroman Jasmine, and the highly educated and philanthropic Vampire Lon—the range of species and interests in the novel is extensive, if left at a somewhat shallow level. The mission is partly successful: Dicey has been entranced by a vampire and dies, but Josh's brother Ollie is rescued and Rose is released from the Neuroman experiment that interlocks human minds for increased intelligence and a wider field of perception.

The development of minor themes is what makes the novel outstanding. Time obscures truth by turning history into legend; maturation requires the ability to accept the difference. Jasmine as long-lived lecturer on the past is a little obvious, but she forces Beauty to adjust to the fact that centaurs, like other talking animals, are a recent creation of man through genetic engineering, not the ancient people of their myths. Scribery, the belief in the power of the word in itself, develops when adult humans are wiped out in the Race Wars by their creations; Josh must accept this, but retains faith in an intrinsic power for words. Kahn's medical background is at its best in the human need to create their fantasies, even the destructive ones like Vampires, the self-hate of the failure Accidents, the desire for long life at any price expressed in the Neuroman process where a fungus eats away all tissue but nerve cells and these cells serve as core for an artificial body. But the creations are close to the fantasy borderline, resembling the dragons of Pern rather than hard-core science fiction, in spite of realistic elements like the limited perception of the cat Isis with her fragment of human brain—abilities are not held tightly to physical law.

The sequel, *Time's Dark Laughter,* is more ambitious and less successful, though beautifully titled; it presents a cyclic universe, destroyed and reborn whenever human genetic possibilities combine to produce a semi-divine being that possesses full consciousness of the universe but lacks control over power and moral insight and so must be killed—cycles will continue until a solution to the problem is found. All experience is becoming sour for all characters in this novel: Josh is forced back to the city of the experiment by brain seizures to match his genetic component with the queen's and create the bird-girl deity; the quest to recover Josh and Rose succeeds in destroying the girl by a virus keyed to her unique DNA, but the nature of the world has been altered and much destroyed. Josh and Rose start over in a new Eden, their first children Can and Able. One problem is this confusion of cycles: the sun now rises in the east instead of the west and a new animal appears that is clearly a giraffe, suggesting that the new cycle is ours, but the bird-girl refers to Jahweh as a past self and many terms in the old cycle are specifically ours—California, Monterey, Pope. It is difficult to credit such specifics as accidental similarities in recurring cycles, and the pattern remains in an uncomfortable tension.

Kahn's strengths lie in language, background in medicine, the use of myth. Techniques still need improvement: consistency in characterization (notably with Jasmine), methods for integrating extrapolated history and other background material smoothly into narrative, selectivity among ideas. But the combination of recurrent pattern with the fixing of position resulting from the tension between a straight-line quest and cyclic time offers possibilities that deserve serious exploration—"In my end is my beginning."

—Marilyn K. Nellis

KAPP, Colin. British. Born in 1928 (?). Worked as an electrical technician. Address: c/o New English Library, 47 Bedford Square, London WC1B 3DP, England.

SCIENCE-FICTION PUBLICATIONS

Novels (series: Cageworld)

Transfinite Man. New York, Berkley, 1964; as *The Dark Mind,* London, Corgi, 1965.
The Patterns of Chaos. London, Gollancz, 1972; New York, Award, 1973.
The Wizard of Anharitte. London, Panther, 1975; New York, Award, n. d.
The Survival Game. New York, Ballantine, 1976; London, Dobson, 1977.
The Chaos Weapon. New York, Ballantine, 1977; London, Dobson, 1979.
Manalone. London, Panther, 1977.
The Ion War. New York, Ace, 1978; London, Dobson, 1979.
The Timewinders. London, Dobson, 1980.
Search for the Sun (Cageworld). London, New English Library, 1981; New York, DAW, 1983.
The Lost World of Cronus (Cageworld). London, New English Library, 1982; New York, DAW, 1983.
The Tyrant of Hades (Cageworld). London, New English Library, 1982; New York, DAW, 1984.

Short Stories

The Unorthodox Engineers. London, Dobson, 1979.

* * *

If any SF writer could typify the Blakean aphorism "Energy is eternal delight," Colin Kapp does so both in terms of human passion and of the energies that compose the universe. The former is unusual in a writer dealing with such esoteric sciences as atomic theory; the latter demonstrates a feeling of awe toward the forces of nature, rather than extolling the way technology utilizes such forces.

Not all of Kapp's works demonstrate the fascination with energy—various stories for *Analog* and the tales of "the Unorthodox Engineers" are standard scientific problem-solving puzzles.

The majority of his works, however, describe the energy states of physics in rhapsodic terms ("Around him the hellish sums and unbelievable vortexes of transfinity shifted and phased in a terrible kaleidoscope of new geometrics and unknown colors"—*Transfinite Man*). In essence, Kapp relates to energy-states as Asimov did to robots—devising a conceptual structure for the scientific phenomena, and giving its many facets relevance to the many facets of human response. In fact, Kapp goes so far as to posit direct interaction between natural forces and human thought-energy. *Transfinite Man* describes a demonic hero, able to survive the dimensions of transfinity by virtue of maniacal hatred. *The Ion War* and "Mephisto and the Ion Explorer" portray human beings able to transform themselves into vessels of ionic energy. "Lambda 1" and "The Imagination Trap" detail the world of Tau-space, a sub-atomic dimension in which matter directly responds to mental manipulation, and *The Chaos Weapon* concerns a female psychic who can read entropic energy-patterns which indicate oncoming catastrophes. Surprisingly, this interaction is not mechanistically explained in terms of psionics (i. e., the human brain transmits energy like a radio, etc.)—rather, Kapp merely portrays a direct correspondence; rather like the hermetic relationship of man and universe, microcosm and macrocosm.

Such a relationship would be facile if the human personalities were not as vividly realized as the cosmic aspects. Kapp's characters are neither subtle nor complex, but they are vivid, especially in regard to romantic attachments. In "Hunger over Sweet Waters" a scientist and his female co-worker, with whom he is in love, are stranded together on a world without drinkable water, and though the scientist is married to another woman and cannot enjoy a relationship with his co-worker, his love for her is the spur for his invention of a way to secure their rescue. In both *The Ion War* and *The Patterns of Chaos* the relationship between woman and man is less like love than like the intimacy of "torturer and victim"—the female being a caustic "bitch-goddess" who drives the male to perform superhuman feats. This sort of antagonistic romance—also present in *Transfinite Man, The Chaos Weapon*, and "Lambda I"—is the means by which the hero exceeds his limits, discovering strategies for survival or salvation. (In recent works—such as the entertaining pulp-style adventure of the *Cageworld* series—the antagonistic romance-angle is toned down, but still present to a degree.)

Though Kapp equals several more revered authors in terms of imaginative scope and striking characters, he lacks a quality that generally enhances the popularity of such authors—that is, an overt philosophy that describes man's place in the universe. Despite this lack, his stories can yield a wealth of implicit insights, while his articulation of scientific concepts is surpassed by only the very best of SF.

—Gene Phillips

KARP, David. Also writes as Adam Singer; Wallace Ware. American. Born in New York City, 5 May 1922. Educated at the City College of New York, 1940-42, 1946-48, B. S. Sc. 1948. Served in the United States Army in the South Pacific and Japan, 1943-46. Married Lillian Klass in 1944; two sons. Continuity Director, Radio Station WNYC, New York, 1948-49. Since 1949, free-lance writer. Since 1968, President of Leda Productions Inc., Los Angeles. Member of the Executive Board, Writers Guild of America East, 1963-66. Since 1967, Member of the Executive Council, and President of the Television-Radio Branch, 1969-71, Writers Guild of America West, Los Angeles. Member of the Editorial Board of *Television Quarterly*, 1966-71, and since 1972. Recipient Guggenheim Fellowship, 1956; Ohio State University Award, for drama, 1948, and for television drama, 1958; *Look Magazine* Award, for television drama, 1958; Mystery Writers of America Edgar Allan Poe Award, for television drama, 1959; American Bar Association Gavel Award, for television documentary, 1963; Emmy Award, 1965. Address: 1116 Corsica Drive, Pacific Palisades, California 90272; or, c/o Frank Cooper, Cooper Agency, 10100 Santa Monica Boulevard, Los Angeles, California 90067, U.S.A.

SCIENCE-FICTION PUBLICATIONS

Novel

One. New York, Vanguard Press, 1953; London, Gollancz, 1954; as *Escape to Nowhere*, New York, Lion, 1955.

OTHER PUBLICATIONS

Novels

The Big Feeling. New York, Lion, 1952.
The Brotherhood of Velvet. New York, Lion, 1952.
Cry, Flesh. New York, Lion, 1953; as *The Girl on Crown Street*, 1956.
Hardman. New York, Lion, 1953.
Platoon (as Adam Singer). New York, Lion, 1953.
The Charka Memorial (as Wallace Ware). New York, Double-day, 1954.
The Day of the Monkey. New York, Vanguard Press, and London, Gollancz, 1955.
All Honorable Men. New York, Knopf, and London, Gollancz, 1956.
Leave Me Alone. New York, Knopf, 1957; London, Gollancz, 1958.
Enter, Sleeping. New York, Harcourt Brace, 1960; as *The Sleep Walkers*, London, Gollancz, 1960.
The Last Believers. New York, Harcourt Brace, 1964; London, Cape, 1965.

Plays

Cafe Univers (produced New York, 1967).

Screenplays: *Sol Madrid*, 1967; *Che!*, 1968; *Tender Loving Care*, 1972.

Radio Plays: *House I Live in* (2 plays), 1946; *One Step Forward* series (21 plays), 1946-47; *A Day to Remember* series (4 plays), 1947; *Famine Relief* series (3 plays), 1947; *Unsung Heroes* series (5 plays), 1947; *People, Unlimited* series (5 plays), 1947; *Grand Gentral Station* series (3 plays), 1948-49; *Aunt Jenny* series (64 programs), 1950-56; *City Hospital* series (3 plays), 1957; and other plays for *Skippy Hollywood Theatre, American Bible Society*, and *CBS Radio Workshop*, 1948-60.

Television Plays: *The Defenders* series (10 plays), 1961-64; *Saints and Sinners* series (3 plays), 1962; *Profiles in Courage* series (5 plays), 1963-65; *The Brotherhood of the Bell*, 1971; *The Family Rico*, 1972; *Hawkins on Murder*, 1973; *W. E. B.*, 1978; and other plays.

Verse

The Voice of the Four Freedoms. Privately printed, 1942.

Other

Vice-President in Charge of Revolution (biography), with Murray D. Lincoln. New York, McGraw Hill, 1960.

*

Manuscript Collection: Mugar Memorial Library, Boston University.

* * *

David Karp's future dystopia, *One,* was bound to suffer from comparison to Orwell's *Nineteen Eighty-Four*. The somber, muted tones of *One* are less striking than Orwell's fireworks, but this quieter book is in some ways more chilling yet more hopeful than Orwell's masterpiece.

One tells of a future government that has eliminated most of the things we worry about—war, poverty, unemployment, divorce, crime—yet the price of this betterment has been the extinction of individuality. The State relies on no gadgetry to enforce its rule: rather, a vast network of informers regularly report any comment that suggests that the State is not completely and everlastingly right.

The main character, Burden, is one of these spies, an English professor who secretly monitors the conversations of his colleagues. But the watchers are themselves watched, and in a routine interview with an official of the State's security arm, the Department of Internal Examination, Burden makes comments that arouse the suspicions of the inquisitors. Suspected of believing himself to be different from his fellow citizens, he is tried in secret and convicted not of treason but of heresy. The penalty for Burden's "crime" is death, but a monomaniacal bureaucrat, Lark, determines to make a test of Burden: he decides to brainwash him so thoroughly that his entire personality will be different, destroying his past, and giving him a new and politically reliable identity.

All of this happens through means that were much discussed in the 1950's:loneliness, sensory deprivation, injections of drugs, bombardment by propaganda. Burden, rechristened Hughes, is released as cured. But even Hughes still cherishes his individuality. *One* ends with the powerful state murdering one of its citizens, but unlike Orwell's Winston Smith, Burden is killed not because the State is done with him, but because it fears him. The State can kill a man, but it cannot make him less than himself.

—Walter E. Meyers

———

KAVAN, Anna. Pseudonym for Helen Woods; also wrote as Helen Ferguson. Born in Cannes, France, in 1901; brought up in California. Educated privately and in Church of England Schools. Married 1) Donald Ferguson (divorced); 2) Stuart Edmonds (divorced), one son. Lived in the United States, Burma, Europe, Australia, and New Zealand; settled in London. *Died 5 December 1968.*

SCIENCE-FICTION PUBLICATIONS

Novels

House of Sleep. New York, Doubleday, 1947; as *Sleep Has His House,* London, Cassell, 1948.
Ice. London, Owen, 1967; New York, Doublday, 1970.

Short Stories

Asylum Piece and Other Stories. London, Cape, 1940; New York, Doubleday, 1946.
I Am Lazarus. London, Cape, 1945.
Julia and the Bazooka, edited by Rhys Davies. London, Owen, 1970; New York, Knopf, 1975.

OTHER PUBLICATIONS

Novels

Change the Name. London, Cape, 1941.
A Scarcity of Love. Southport, Lancashire, Downie, 1956; New York, Herder, 1972.
Eagles' Nest. London, Owen, 1957.
Who Are You? Lowestoft, Suffolk, Scorpion Press, 1963.

Novels as Helen Ferguson

A Charmed Circle. London, Cape, 1929.
The Dark Sisters. London, Cape, 1930.
Let Me Alone. London, Cape, 1930; Short Hills, New Jersey, Enslow, 1978.
A Stranger Still. London, Lane, 1935.
Goose Cross. London, Lane, 1936.
Rich Get Rich London, Lane, 1937.

Short Stories

A Bright Green Field and Other Stories. London, Owen, 1958.
My Soul in China, edited by Rhys Davies. London, Owen, 1975.

Other

The Horse's Tale, with K. T. Bluth. London, Gaberbocchus, 1949.

* * *

Recalling the gothic horrors of Mary Shelley's *Frankenstein*, Anna Kavan inverts the terror stimulus from the external monster to the interior of the mind. Kavan's works are explorations of the mentally ill, those possessed by fear of an external and menancing society. The Monster is within the self—sometimes evidenced as unreasoning fear and suspicion and sometimes emanated as an obsessive desire to control/torture others as catharsis for self-destructive tendencies.

Kavan, like Shelley, did not consciously write science fiction.

Kavan's writings are characterised by her frequent and enigmatic shifts between fantasy and reality, abrupt mood shifts, and poetic descriptions. Some of her works are catastrophe fiction, envisioning mass chaos epitomized in the chaos of the central character's mind. The protagonist's mental condition both parallels and illuminates the basic irrationality of the civilizations Kavan depicts. It is the shifting of reality planes within a setting of world-wide catastrophe which marks some of Kavan's psychological fiction as science fiction. Although many of her works are primarily descriptions of the world of the mentally ill, at least "The Birthmark," *Ice,* and *House of Sleep* present a world outside the central character's mind which is also distorted.

In "The Birthmark" the young girl narrator meets an alien girl who fears the discovery of her peculiar skin marking, implying to the narrator that such a discovery would ban her from the narrator's world. Many years later, while touring a castle, the narrator discovers (or thinks she does) the same girl locked in a dungeon—being persecuted for her special talents—talents symbolized and identified by that birthmark.

Ice is also set in a hostile world: nuclear testing has brought on a rapidly advancing ice age. Kavan depicts, unlike many science-fiction writers, an apathetic populace who are unable to comprehend the impending disaster or to break their routine existence. The people remain true to their nature: complacent in the face of chaos. Of course some attempt to flee, but government and business continue to function. Even war continues as the demise of civilization approaches. Within this hostile world the protagonist obsessively searches for a frail, seemingly inept woman whom he both loves and hates. Her weakness of will and body obsesses him as it does his rival, and he alternately wishes to protect and destroy her. Ultimately he conquers the fear of rejection which instigates his violent fantasies toward her and they join in love, and at peace, as they wait for their deaths.

In *House of Sleep* Kavan presents B's progressing rejection of reality which stems from childhood. B finds that only her daydreams and the cover of night provide the security ripped away from her by her mother's unexplained death. B retreats into her imagination, finding there a haven from the isolation and alienation of a society which neither cares for her or for itself. She flees from place to place, always recording the threatening, if ineffectual, liaison officer and the civil disruption and fear within an oppressive government. B states: "Without understanding the reason, I knew that I had to keep the day unimportant. I had to prevent the day world from becoming real." In Kavan's abrupt and frequently imperceptible shifts from reality to fantasy she illustrates the operation of an escape mechanism within the mind of one who can neither accept nor interact in the alien world of reality.

Kavan brings brilliant character portrayal into the genre of science fiction, exploring the inner universe of the mind rather than the outer galaxies of the universe. What she finds within the mind is fear and violence: the essence of terror, confirmed by the irrationality of uncaring society which persecutes without knowledge or reason those whose perceptions differ from the norm. Thus Kavan explores various reality levels, questioning society's grasp of reality, and indicating that perhaps sanity is only a matter of perception: that we live in an insane world and are unable to judge who within it is sane or insane.

—Jane B. Weedman

KELLER, David H(enry). Also wrote as Henry Cecil. Amer-

ican. Born in Philadelphia, Pennsylvania, 23 December 1880. Educated at the University of Philadelphia Medical School. Served as a physician working in shell-shock during World War I; Medical Professor on the faculty of the Army Chaplain's School at Harvard University, Cambridge, Massachusetts, during World War II. Married in 1903. Physician, specializing in psychoanalysis: Junior Physician, Illinois Mental Institute, after 1915, and worked in other hospitals in Louisiana, Tennessee, and Pennsylvania. Editor, *Sexology* and *Your Body* in the 1930's. *Died 13 July 1966.*

SCIENCE-FICTION PUBLICATIONS

Novels

The Waters of Lethe. Great Barrington, Massachusetts, Kirby, 1937.
The Sign of the Burning Hart. St. Lo, France, Barbaroux, 1938; Hollywood, National Fantasy Fan Foundation, 1948.
The Television Detective. Los Angeles, Los Angeles Science Fiction League, 1938.
The Devil and the Doctor. New York, Simon and Schuster, 1940.
The Solitary Hunters, and The Abyss. Philadelphia, New Era, 1948.
The Eternal Conflict. Philadelphia, Prime Press, 1949.
The Final War. Portland, Oregon, Perri Press, 1949.
The Homunculus. Philadelphia, Prime Press, 1949.
The Lady Decides. Philadelphia, Prime Press, 1950.

Short Stories

The Thought Projector. New York, Stellar, 1930.
Wolf Hollow Bubbles. Jamaica, New York, Arra Printers, 1934(?).
Men of Avalon. Everett, Pennsylvania, Fantasy, 1935(?).
The Thing in the Cellar. Millheim, Pennsylvania, Bizarre Series, 1940.
Life Everlasting, edited by Sam Moskowitz and Will Sykora. Newark, New Jersey, Avalon, 1947.
Tales from Underwood. New York, Pellegrini and Cudahy, 1952.
Figment of a Dream. Baltimore, Mirage Press, 1962.
The Folsom Flint and Other Curious Tales. Sauk City, Wisconsin, Arkham House, 1969.
The Street of Queer Houses and Other Tales, edited by R. Reginald and Douglas Menville. Salem, New York, Ayer, 1976.

OTHER PUBLICATIONS

Verse

Songs of a Spanish Lover (as Henry Cecil). Privately printed, 1924.

Other

The Kellers of Hamilton Township: A Study in Democracy. Privately printed, 1922.
The Sexual Education Series. New York, Popular Book Corporation, 10 vols., 1928.
Know Yourself! Life and Sex Facts of Man, Woman, and Child . . . . New York, Popular Book Corporation, 1930.
Portfolio of Anatomical Manikins. New York, Sparacio, 1932.
Picture Stories of the Sex Life of Man and Woman. New York, Popular Medicine, 1941.

* * *

The genre of science fiction and fantasy has seemed to attract some of the most talented, versatile, and idiosyncratic personalities and made writers of them. David H. Keller pursued a varied and successful career as physician, military doctor, psychiatrist, and medical researcher. He published widely in the professional literature of his field. He also wrote fiction—but only for his family and friends. Then in 1928 *Amazing Stories* published "The Revolt of the Pedestrians," a long dystopian narrative that Keller had completed before Hugo Gernsback had even started *Amazing.* The story was such a success that Gernsback contracted for twelve more from Keller, and during the next decade or so 60 "Kelleryarns" were published in science-fiction and fantasy markets. *Weird Tales* served as another primary outlet for the Keller stories. During the final two decades of his life, however, Keller returned to private publishing and almost continuous writing of stories and books that may or may not have been marketable. His overall accomplishment seems immense, individual, and idiosyncratic. Some of his stories are classics of the horror, weird fantasy variety. Much of his writing reads as pleasantly whimsical and expressive of the "humours" of his personality in the 18th-century sense. In many ways, especially in the final years of his life, he was like an 18th-century eccentric or country gentleman who loved and expressed wit, humour, and imaginative curiosity in both his living and his writing. In all ways, Keller was his own man; and it is perhaps too soon for a literary assessment of his work whether in abnormal psychology or in fantasy or humorous narrative.

Regardless of any later assessment of his large volume of rather whimsical writing, however, certain careful elements in his art are apparent. Keller is often very skillful in the subtle understated suggestion of the supernatural that creates the greatest chill of horror. He combines with this a fascination in the psychosomatic relations of mental disorder to behavior. Among the short, chilling masterpieces that embody these artfully controlled effects are "The Thing in the Cellar," "A Piece of Linoleum," and "The Dead Woman," all from the early 1930's. Keller writes, then, with a subtle control of statement and tone that is unusual in the early pulp markets of the genre. The other element is his art that is particularly impressive is his use of point of view. Many of his narratives are told in first person, and he is master of the ironic first-person narrator who gradually reveals his own insanity to the reader without realizing it himself. As in Swift's *A Modest Proposal,* a Keller narrator will often be condemning himself or herself while telling what seems to be his or her side of the story. The other kind of first-person narrator is Keller himself in the person of various point-of-view characters with whimsical names, such as Jacobus Hubelaire who write his own autobiography that is really Keller's, or Colonel Horatio Bumble in *The Humunculus.* This last, strange little book gives a fictional picture in the first person of Keller/Bumble that may or may not be the real Keller. But it shows a 20th-century retired Colonel of the Army Medical Corps who dabbles in writing and in the supernatural and who resembles an 18th-century eccentric, such as one might find in a Smollett novel or in the person of Erasmus Darwin, much more than a modern writer. At the same time the book, in its way, treats fascinating themes of scientific methodology, married life, and writing itself. Keller is a puzzlement in the genre—unique, varied, and often extremely effective.

—Donald M. Hassler

KELLEY, Leo P(atrick). American. Born in Wilkes Barre, Pennsylvania, 10 September 1928. Educated at the New School for Social Research, New York, B. A. in English 1957. Advertising copywriter and manager, McGraw-Hill Book Company, New York, 1959-69. Since 1969, free-lance writer. Address: 702 Lincoln Boulevard, Long Beach, New York 11561, U. S. A.

SCIENCE-FICTION PUBLICATIONS

Novels

The Counterfeits. New York, Belmont, 1967.
Odyssey to Earthdeath. New York, Belmont, 1968.
The Accidental Earth. New York, Belmont, 1968.
Time Rogue. New York, Lancer, 1970.
The Coins of Murph. New York, Berkley, 1971; London, Coronet, 1974.
Mindmix. New York, Fawcett, 1972; London, Coronet, 1973.
Time:110100. New York, Walker, 1972; as *The Man from Maybe,* London, Coronet, 1974.
Mythmaster. New York, Dell, 1973; London, Coronet, 1974.
The Earth Tripper. New York, Fawcett, 1973; London, Coronet, 1974.
The Time Trap (for children). Belmont, California, Pitman, 1977 (?); London, Murray, 1979.
Backward in Time (for children). Belmont, California, Pitman, 1979; London, Hutchinson, 1980.
Death Sentence (for children). Belmont, California, Pitman, 1979; London, Hutchinson, 1980.
Earth Two (for children). Belmont, California, Pitman, 1979; London, Hutchinson, 1980.
Prison Satellite (for children). Belmont, California, Pitman, 1979; London, Hutchinson, 1980.
Sunworld (for children). Belmont, California, Pitman, 1979; London, Hutchinson, 1980.
Worlds Apart (for children). Belmont, California, Pitman, 1979; London, Hutchinson, 1980.
Dead Moon (for children). Belmont, California, Pitman, 1979; London, Murray, 1980.
King of the Stars (for children). Belmont, California, Pitman, 1979; London, Murray, 1980.
On the Red World (for children). Belmont, California, Pitman, 1979; London, Murray, 1980.
Night of Fire and Blood (for children). Belmont, California, Pitman, and London, Murray, 1979.
Where No Sun Shines (for children). Belmont, California, Pitman, 1979; London, Murray, 1980.
Vacation in Space (for children). Belmont, California, Pitman, 1979; London, Murray, 1980.
Star Gold (for children). Belmont, California, Pitman, and London, Murray, 1979.
Good-bye to Earth (for children). Belmont, California, Pitman, 1979; London, Murray, 1980.

Uncollected Short Stories

"Dreamtown, U. S. A.," in *If* (New York), February 1955.
"The Human Element," in *If* (New York), June 1957.
"Any Questions," in *Fantastic* (New York), October 1962.
"To the Victor," in *Fantastic* (New York), May 1964.
"O'Grady's Girl," in *Fantasy and Science Fiction* (New York), December 1965.
"Coins," in *Fantasy and Science Fiction* (New York), November 1968.

"Harvest," in *Fantasy and Science Fiction* (New York), March 1970.

"The Propheteer," in *Galaxy* (New York), March 1970.

"The Travelin' Man," in *Fantasy and Science Fiction* (New York), September 1970.

"Cold, The Fire of the Phoenix," in *Protostars*, edited by David Gerrold and Stephen Goldin. New York, Ballantine, 1971.

"The Dark Door," in *Witchcraft and Sorcery* (Alhambra, California), January 1971.

"The True Believers," in *Fantasy and Science Fiction* (New York), October 1971.

"Teaching Prime," in *Infinity 3*, edited by Robert Hoskins. New York, Lancer, 1972.

"Song," in *Fantasy and Science Fiction* (New York), February 1973.

"The Ninth Resurrection of Miss Hosanna Galaxy," in *Gallery* (Chicago), December 1973.

"Generation Gap," in *Weird Tales* (Los Angeles), Summer 1974.

"Sam," in *Flying Saucers*, edited by Isaac Asimov, Martin H. Greenberg, and Charles G. Waugh. New York, Fawcett, 1982.

OTHER PUBLICATIONS

Novels

Brother John (novelization of screenplay). New York, Avon, and London, Pan, 1971.

Deadlocked! New York, Fawcett, 1973.

Luke Sutton, Outlaw [*Gunfighter, Indian Fighter, Avenger, Outrider*]. New York, Doubleday, 5 vols., 1981-84; London, Hale, 5 vols., 1981-84.

Cimarron and the Hanging Judge [*Rides the Outlaw Trail, and the Border Bandits, in the Cherokee Strip, and the Elk Soldiers, and the Bounty Hunters, and the High Rider, in No Man's Land, and the Vigilantes, and the Medicine Wolves, on Hell's Highway, and the War Women, and the Bootleggers*]. New York, New American Library, 13 vols., 1983-85.

Other

Editor, *Themes in Science Fiction: A Journey into Wonder*. New York, McGraw Hill, 1972.

Editor, *The Supernatural in Fiction*. New York, McGraw Hill, 1973.

Editor, *Fantasy: The Literature of the Marvelous*. New York, McGraw Hill, 1974.

*   *   *

Leo P. Kelley's first novel, *The Counterfeits*, develops many of the themes that he uses in his later novels. Earth is invaded by an alien race whose home planet has been destroyed. The aliens are able to assume any shape; they take human form and set about destroying human civilization. What takes this book out of the usual alien-invasion formula is Kelley's attempt to provide a plausible reconciliation at the book's conclusion.

Odyssey to Earthdeath explores the domination of a society by psychological methods in the tradition of Orwell's *Nineteen Eighty-Four*. The book suffers from undeveloped characters and a predictable plot. *Time Rogue* is one of Kelley's few attempts to use time travel as a theme for sociological speculation. Unfortunately, the plot degenerates into a good vs. evil confrontation with predictable results. *The Accidental Earth* blends the themes of the previous books into an eerie amalgam. A counter-Earth is separated from our Earth by a wall of Time, but an accident brings the Earths into contact. Only the secret weapon of the Photon Spray saves Earth from alien invasion by severing the Time link and separating the two Earths again. Although the conclusion is hackneyed space opera, the beginning and middle sections of the novel feature some of Kelley's best writing. *The Coins of Murph* tells of a post-holocaust society based on a religion deifying the Chief Programmer of the Rand Corporation, Joseph Murphy, who, on some surviving audio tapes, blames the holocaust on decision making. His followers interpret this to mean all decision should be decided by chance, hence the use of coins for flipping. The plot gets bogged down in power politics, but the sociological portrait Kelley presents is memorable.

The remaining novels are chiefly characterized by their cynical perspectives and brutality. *Time: 110100* is a surreal morality play of two humans on an odyssey through a strange world populated by lusty, war-like, and enigmatic simulacra. The book has undertones of Barth's *Giles Goat-Boy* but the weak ending damages the book. *Mindmix* presents contemporary human society stricken by a deadly virus. The Government discovers one man, Pete Bratton, who has become immune. Kelley develops a cynical picture of government scientists exploiting Bratton by transplanting the minds of dying geniuses in Bratton's brain, with successful but grim results. *The Earth Tripper* and *Mythmaster* are written in New Wave style. The better of the two books, *The Earth Tripper*, follows the bizarre adventures of an alien observer who goes AWOL on Earth in human form. Captured releasing aminals from a zoo, he's taken to a secret mental institution, and he and other strange inmates are the subjects of brutal experiments using "reality therapy. " The mildly upbeat ending doesn't relieve much of the book's cynicism. Since 1973, Kelley has concentrated on writing science fiction for juveniles, chiefly for elementary students with low reading skills, and westerns.

Kelley's best work features strong writing and ingenious sociological constructions of unique societies, but the unrelenting grimness of his later work coupled with New Wave writing styles weakens its appeal.

—George Kelley

———————

KENT, Gordon. See **TUBB, E. C.**

———————

KENT, Kelvin. See **BARNES, Arthur K.**

———————

KENT, Mallory. See **LOWNDES, Robert A. W.**

———————

KENT, Philip. See **BULMER, Kenneth.**

———————

KEPPEL-JONES, Arthur (Mervyn). Canadian. Born in Rondebosch, South Africa, 20 January 1909. Educated at the University of Cape Town, 1926-28, B. A. 1928, Ph. D. 1943; Oxford University (Rhodes Scholar), 1929-32, B. A. (honours) 1931, M. A. 1940. Part-time military service during World War II. Married Eileen Mary Bate in 1935; two sons and one daughter. Lecturer, 1933-34 and 1936-44, and Senior Lecturer, 1945-53, University of the Witwatersrand, Johannesburg; Lecturer, 1935, and Professor of History, 1954-59, University of Natal, Pietermaritzburg. Visiting Lecturer, 1953-54, Professor, 1959-76, and since 1976, Professor Emeritus of History, Queen's University, Kingston, Ontario. Visiting Professor, Duke University, Durham, North Carolina, 1964. Address: Department of History, Queen's University, Kingston, Ontario K7L 3N6, Canada.

SCIENCE-FICTION PUBLICATIONS

Novel

When Smuts Goes: A History of South Africa from 1952 to 2010, First Published in 2015. Cape Town, African Bookman, and London, Gollancz, 1947.

OTHER PUBLICATIONS

Other

Do We Govern Ourselves? Johannesburg, Society of the Friends of Africa, 1945.
South Africa: A Short History. London, Hutchinson, 1949; 5th edition, 1975; New York, Hillary House, 1962.
Friends or Foes? A Point of View and a Programme for Racial Harmony in South Africa. Pietermaritzburg, Shuter and Shooter, 1950.
The Dilemma of South Africa. Toronto, Canadian Association for Adult Education, 1950.
Who Is Destroying Civilisation in South Africa? (in English and Afrikaans). Johannesburg, South African Institute of Race Relations, 1951.
Human Relations in South Africa. Johannesburg, St. Benedict's House, 1953.
Rhodes and Rhodesia: The White Conquest of Zimbabwe 1889-1902. Toronto, McGill-Queen's University Press, 1983.

Editor, *Thomas Philipps, 1920 Settler: His Letters.* Pietermaritzburg, Shuter and Shooter, 1960.

*

Arthur Keppel-Jones comments:

When Smuts Goes was written in hot anger in 1946; I had thought about it for some time, but the first draft took only three weeks to write. An important part of the motivation and background was provided by Germany. I was in that country during the elections of 1930. Having read the papers and attended a Nazi election meeting, I came away with a certain conviction that the Nazis, if given the chance, would carry out the programme of *Mein Kampf* to the letter. Then came the years of appeasement and wishful thinking, which drove me, like many others, to despair.

After six years of bloodshed had corrected that error, I looked again at the Afrikaner Nationalists. Though they were, and are, in many ways very different from the Nazis, the resemblances

in certain respects were frightening. They, too, had a programme. I knew that they intended to put it into effect, but again there was, among their opponents, wishful thinking, a turning of the blind eye. It was only "electoral propaganda"; they would be "sobered by the responsibility of office." On the other hand, their propaganda had succeeded in creating a climate of thought in which only Afrikaner values deserved respect. The values and aspirations of blacks, English, and the rest were tainted with disloyalty and subversion. Europe of the 1930's was in some way being repeated.

I wrote a prophecy to show where all this would lead. Much of it, unhappily, turned out to be correct. In some respects I was utterly wrong. The mistakes arose mainly from one cause: concentrating on the forces at work in South Africa, I made the assumption (acknowledging it to be merely an assumption) that the course of events everywhere else would continue on the old lines. So I did not foresee decolonisation, the Third World, or the rise in the price of gold.

I did not want my prophecy to be proved right; I wanted the warning to be taken. It was not.

*   *   *

When Smuts Goes, Arthur Keppel-Jones's one contribution to the science-fiction genre, is a remarkable exception in the category of political and social extrapolation, a projection that rings true, particular incorrect prophecies notwithstanding. Like Orwell in *Nineteen Eighty-Four,* Keppel-Jones extends post-World War II conditions, but for 60 years rather than Orwell's 30, and in South Africa rather than England. Keppel-Jones's work is a fictional history rather than a novel: there are no particularized characters (the media censor is named "Netwerk," a newspaperman "Penman," and so on) and only the broad outlines of events are delineated. But like *Nineteen Eighty-Four, When Smuts Goes* has a chilling credibility, particularly in its focus on "psycho-history," the way the essential character of a nation leads it to inevitable courses of action.

When General Smuts's United Party loses power in South Africa after World War II, the internationalist British tradition is replaced by parochial Afrikaner Nationalists. The Afrikaners, essentially romantics attempting to recapture the lost ox-wagon heritage of *voortrekker* days, progressively destroy the "Jingoistic" British liberalism by playing on divisions in the English-speaking community over the threat of the non-white majority. Keppel-Jones correctly predicts the disenfranchisement of non-whites, the governmental promotion of Afrikaner language and culture in education and the mass media, the establishment of a Republic, the imposition of censorship, and the steady isolation of South Africa in the world community. But he is wrong on some counts: from the perspective of 1947 he sees a German-Japanese-Argentine-South African Fascist axis, a permanent collapse in the price of gold, a powerful U. N. Security Council, and the continuation of the relationship among nations as it existed just after World War II. The detailed politics in the early chapters may be slow going for the casual reader and Keppel-Jones fails to foresee Britain's own colonial difficulties, which dates the book somewhat.

Yet *When Smuts Goes* becomes urgent for the contemporary reader when the consequences of South Africa's racial policies are described: low-level but constant racial violence, increasingly repressive measures by the government, evasions and self-denial of the situation's gravity, revolt, and the growing threat of outside intervention. Keppel-Jones's cautionary history is meant to evoke just this sense of urgency in all who care to prevent the final disaster he prophesizes; it still has its intended effect after more than 30 years.

—Andrew Macdonald

KERN, Gregory. See **TUBB, E. C.**

KEY, Alexander (Hill). American. Born in La Plata, Maryland, 21 September 1904. Educated at the Chicago Art Institute, 1922-24. Served in the United States Navy, 1942-45: Lieutenant Commander. Married Alice Towle in 1945; one child. Artist: book illustrator from age 19, then art teacher at Studio School of Art, Chicago; writer from 1929. Recipient: American Association of University Women Award, 1965; Lewis Carroll Shelf Award, 1972. *Died 25 July 1979.*

SCIENCE-FICTION PUBLICATIONS

Novels (for children)

Sprockets: A Little Robot. Philadelphia, Westminster Press, 1963.
Rivets and Sprockets. Philadelphia, Westminster Press, 1964.
The Forgotten Door. Philadelphia, Westminster Press, 1965; London, Faber, 1966.
Bolts: A Robot Dog. Philadelphia, Westminster Press, 1966.
Escape to Witch Mountain. Philadelphia, Westminster Press, 1968.
Flight to the Lonesome Place. Philadelphia, Westminster Press, 1969.
The Golden Enemy. Philadelphia, Westminster Press, 1969.
The Incredible Tide. Philadelphia, Westminster Press, 1970.
The Magic Meadow. Philadelphia, Westminster Press, 1975.
Jagger, The Dog from Elsewhere. Philadelphia, Westminster Press, 1976.
The Sword of Aradel. Philadelphia, Westminster Press, 1977.
Return from Witch Mountain. Philadelphia, Westminster Press, 1978.

OTHER PUBLICATIONS

Novels

The Wrath and the Wind. Indianapolis, Bobbs Merrill, 1949; London, Heinemann, 1950.
Island Light. Indianapolis, Bobbs Merrill, 1950; London, Heinemann, 1951.

Other (for children)

The Red Eagle. New York, Volland, 1930.
Liberty or Death. New York, Harper, 1936.
With Daniel Boone on the Caroliny Trail. Philadelphia, Winston, 1941.
Boys Will Be Boys: Very Easy Pantomimes and Entertainments for Boys. Franklin, Ohio, Eldridge, 1945.
Cherokee Boy. Philadelphia, Westminster Press, 1957.
Mystery of the Sassafras Chair. Philadelphia, Westminster Press, 1967.

The Strange White Doves: True Mysteries of Nature. Philadelphia, Westminster Press, 1972.
The Preposterous Adventures of Swimmer. Philadelphia, Westminster Press, 1973.
The Case of the Vanishing Boy. New York, Archway, 1979.

* * *

Already an established author by 1963, Alexander Key published that year *Sprockets: A Little Robot,* a simply constructed and written, unassuming story designed to attract children presumably interested in SF or space fantasy but too young for Heinlein or Norton. The story's success prompted a sequel, *Rivets and Sprockets.*

Their acceptance by young readers and reviewers alike probably encouraged Key to believe that children's SF might be both financially profitable and professionally satisfying, for in 1966 he published a third SF tale, *The Forgotten Door,* like its predecessors relatively uncomplicated in plot and simply written but more earnest in tone and theme. Subsequently, all of Key's fiction has been a children's SF best characterized as a mix of narrative simplicity and moral earnestness.

At his best—as in *The Forgotten Door* and *Escape to Witch Mountain,* stories focusing on ESP-gifted, extraterrestrial children marooned on an inhospitable Earth and able to return home only with the help of sympathetic humans—Key creates likeable child protagonists and plausibly involves them in struggles between Good and Evil. Setting, reflecting the Carolina mountains Key so obviously loves, is also a strength. At his worse, Key is prone to sentimentalize, in particular overusing ESP-gifted animals that are morally superior to humans. Perhaps it is this weakness, along with relatively low-keyed plots and a too obvious earnestness, that has denied major status to an author who might otherwise have earned it because of his pioneering SF for young readers.

—Francis J. Molson

KEYES, Daniel. American. Born in New York City, 9 August 1927. Educated at Brooklyn College, New York, B. A. 1950, M. A. 1961. Served as a ship's purser in the maritime service, 1945-47. Married Aurea Georginia Vaquez in 1952; two daughters. Editorial Associate, *Marvel Science Stories,* 1950-51; Associate Editor, Stadium Publishing Company, New York, 1951-52; co-owner, Fenko and Keyes Photography Inc., New York, 1953; high school English teacher, Brooklyn, 1954-55, 1957-62; Instructor, Wayne State University, Detroit 1962-66. Lecturer, 1966-72, and since 1972, Professor of English, and director of creative writing, 1973-74, 1977-78, Ohio University, Athens. Recipient: Hugo Award, 1960; Nebula Award, 1966. Agent: Donald S. Engel, Engel and Engel, 9665 Wilshire Boulevard, Beverly Hills, California 90212, U. S. A.

SCIENCE-FICTION PUBLICATIONS

Novel

Flowers for Algernon. New York, Harcourt Brace, and London, Cassell, 1966.

Uncollected Short Stories

"Precedent," in *Marvel* (New York), May 1952.

"Robot—Unwanted," in *Other Worlds* (Evanston, Indiana), June 1952.
"Something Borrowed," in *Fantastic Story* (New York), Summer 1952.
"The Trouble with Elmo," in *Galaxy* (New York), August 1958.
"Crazy Maro," in *The Best from Fantasy and Science Fiction 10*, edited by Robert P. Mills. New York, Doubleday, 1961; London, Gollancz, 1963.
"A Jury of Its Peers," in *Worlds of Tomorrow* (New York), August 1963.
"The Quality of Mercy," in *Frozen Planet*. New York, Macfadden, 1966.

OTHER PUBLICATIONS

Novels

The Touch. New York, Harcourt Brace, 1968; London, Hale, 1971; as *The Contaminated Man*, London, Mayflower, 1977.
The Fifth Sally . Boston, Houghton Mifflin, 1980; London, Hale, 1981.

Other

"How Much Does a Character Cost?," in *Those Who Can*, edited by Robin Scott Wilson. New York, New American Library, 1973.
The Minds of Billy Milligan. New York, Random House, 1981.

*

Manuscript Collection: Ohio University, Athens.

*   *   *

Rarely has a science-fiction story won such widespread praise as Daniel Keyes's "Flowers for Algernon. " The story has become almost universally admired in science fiction because it not only blazed new trails in narrative technique, characterization, and plot development but managed to do so without calling distracting attention to any single part. It is first and foremost a story, and none of its literary experimentation interferes with its unfolding.

The story is told from the point of view of a mentally retarded man, Charlie Gordon, who first reaches genius level through treatment with intelligence-enhancing drugs and then regresses to his original state as the effect of the drugs wears off. Much of the success of the work rests on the narrative device of presenting the entire story as a diary written by Charlie from the start of his treatment to his ultimate reversion. Since Charlie begins and ends the story as a good-natured, trusting man who by habit and desire sees only the best in his fellow human beings, the telling never descends to bathos. Even at his most brilliant, when he is able to understand fully the pettiness and cruelty of many of the people around him, Charlie refuses to judge anyone. He accepts people for what they are and avoids such labels as good or bad.

In the course of the story, Keyes raises many questions about the nature of intelligence, the benefits that may or may not arise from "improving" the human mind, and humanity's respect (or lack of respect) for genius. But he avoids trivial answers and simple generalizations. Because Charlie accepts what happens to him without anger and with a sense of dignity, these questions can be considered in all their complexity with a minimum of emotional coloring.

Keyes later turned this 30-page story into a 200-page novel.

The result was predictably less happy. Keyes was forced to abandon the first-person narrative in order to deal more elaborately with the other characters. The new narrative style diminished the dramatic treatment of Charlie and his dignified faith in people. Moreover, in filling in the larger space needed for a novel, the story shifts from Charlie's experiences and his reactions to them to Charlie's development as a character. The reader was now asked to become far more attached to Charlie, and the loss of distance added greater emotional coloring to the work. The novel is about Charlie while the short story is about what happens to Charlie and the implications of these experiences for all of humanity.

Keyes has also written a number of short stories and a later novel that deal with the human mind. The novel, *The Touch*, concerns a nuclear industrial accident and its effects on the minds of the people involved. But "Flowers for Algernon" remains his best-known work. It is essential science-fiction reading that proves once and for all how both science fiction and artistic merit can coexist comfortably. As science fiction the story raises disturbing questions no other genre can do more than hint at. As literature, it explores those questions in a manner that carefully, yet delightfully, guides the reader through a myriad of emotional traps.

—Stephen H. Goldman

KILIAN, Crawford. Canadian. Born in New York City, United States, 7 February 1941; naturalized Canadian citizen, 1973. Educated at Columbia University, New York, B. A. 1962; Simon Fraser University, Burnaby, British Columbia, M. A. 1972. Served in the United States Army, 1963-65. Married Alice Hayes Fairfax in 1966; two daughters. Library clerk, 1965-66, and technical writer, 1966-67, Lawrence Radiation Laboratory, Berkeley, California; Instructor in English, Vancouver Community College, 1967-68. Since 1968, Instructor in English, Capilano College, North Vancouver. Instructor in English, Guangzhou Institute of Foreign Languguages, People's Republic of China, 1983-84. Since 1982, Education Columnist, Vancouver *Province*. Agent: Harold Greene, 760 North Cienaga, Los Angeles, California 90069, U. S. A. Address: 4635 Cove Cliff Road, North Vancouver, British Columbia V7G 1H7, Canada.

SCIENCE-FICTION PUBLICATIONS

Novels

The Empire of Time. New York, Ballantine, 1978.
Icequake. Vancouver, Douglas and McIntyre, and London, Futura, 1979; New York, Bantam, 1980.
Eyas. New York, Bantam, 1982.
Tsunami. Vancouver, Douglas and McIntyre, 1983; New York, Bantam, 1984.
Brother Jonathan. New York, Ace, 1985.

OTHER PUBLICATIONS

Plays

Radio Plays: *A Strange Manuscript Found in a Copper Cylinder*, from novel by James De Mille, 1972; *Generals Die in Bed*, from novel by Charles Yale Harrison, 1973; *Little Legion*, 1973;

Wonders, Inc., from his own book, 1974; *Senator Connor's Big Comeback*, 1974; *The Mob Has Got the Bomb*, 1975.

Other

Wonders, Inc. (for children). Oakland, California, Parnassus Press, 1968.
The Last Vikings (for children). Toronto, Clarke Irwin, 1974.
Go Do Some Great Thing: The Black Pioneers of British Columbia. Vancouver, Douglas and Mcintyre, and Seattle, University of Washington Press, 1978.
Exploring British Columbia's Past. Vancouver, Douglas and McIntyre, 1983.

*

Crawford Kilian comments:

As with any civilized pleasure, that of science fiction can turn into a vice. Its persistent theme is power: over nature, over others, over oneself. And that power is most often used not to enhance and expand the capabilities of its wielders but to win for them only a return to Eden, to some primitive and unspoiled state of life. Hence so many stories about Galactic Empires based on European models from Rome to the Raj, and the fondness for interstellar societies firmly founded on the technology and economy of 9th-century France.

Like most other writers and readers of SF, I'm intrigued by the possibilities of gaining power over nature, others, and oneself; these are deeply held wish-fulfilment fantasies. But I hope I go beyond the infantile nuke-&-zap dreams of many of my colleagues. Looking back over my work, I see my novels keep dealing with the issue of the acquisition of power by the weak, not always with happy results, and with the forging of new kinds of societies composed of out-casts and those who cast them out. In Northrop Frye's sense, then, I'm a comic writer, concerned with the creation of inclusive societies rather than with the tragic isolation of people deprived of a place in society.

Given the hypnotically lulling effect of many of the conventions of SF, I take some pleasure in bending the conventions so that the reader's stock responses don't seem quite appropriate. Some of my books have "superheroes"; in *The Empire of Time* the superhero discovers his bosses consider him a mere utensil, and for good reason. In *Eyas*, an heir to a throne is raised in seclusion amid simple folk before leaving to regain his heritage; trouble is, he's also a sexual psychopath. My intention is to make readers think twice about why such stock characters are so satisfying, and to suggest that something more complex might also be more dramatically interesting.

Another element in my work is the attempt to make the marvelous seem mundane, and the mundane marvelous. People in my books have to earn their livings, sometimes by means that seem extraordinary to us, and their lives are as cluttered with domesticity as our own—even if they're trying to cross the Antarctic ice sheet, or learning how to forge a collective mind out of those of children, animals, and computers. A day in anyone's life in the 1980's would seem like the wildest Wellsian fantasy to anyone living in Wells's time, yet we take events for granted. I try to create worlds that are both strange and comfortably familiar, like my own.

*   *   *

Crawford Kilian's latest SF novel, *Brother Jonathan*, is an excellent example of his strengths and weaknesses as a writer. Jonathan is a athetoid, a young cripple with little control over his ruined body. Jonathan is taken to the secret laboratories of Dr. Duane Perkin whose medical team is working with spastics to restore their mobility through the use of new polydendronic computers that simulate nerve tissue. The world Kilian describes is dominated by giant multinational corporations controlled by a Consortium; nations have been merged into corporate holdings.

Perkin's project is being funded by Intertel, who is under attack in the form of a takeover bid by another multinational company, Flanders. The success of the polydendronic computers could save Intertel from a bloody merger. The computers are implanted in animals first, and when that is successful, they are implanted in Jonathan and the other spastics. Just as success is within Perkin's grasp, a Flanders assault team attacks the labs. Jonathan and his group flee into the underground caverns where they discover they have control over their bodies and psi powers. The rest of the book explores the implications of these superhuman powers, the destruction of the corporate world government, and some satiric asides about juveniles and nationalism.

Much of *Brother Jonathan* will appeal to juveniles; this should come as no surprise because Kilian has written successful juveniles: the fantastic *Wonders, Inc.*, and the non-fiction *Go Do Some Great Thing: The Black Pioneers of British Columbia.* Kilian, an American who became a naturalized Canadian citizen, lives in Vancouver which he uses as a setting in many of his novels.

Kilian's first SF novel, *The Empire of Time,* gives us Earth in the near future where gates called I-Screens allow access to a dozen parallel Earths, both past and future. Earth governments form a super elite called Trainables and redistribute Earth's overpopulation to these Chronoplanes. Yet when two of the Future Earths are found destroyed, Jerry Pierce of the Intertemporal Agency is sent to a colonial Earth to investigate. The action and plot carry the book as the characters are never really developed.

Icequake is a disaster novel where a group of scientists and technicians are stranded when earth's magnetic field disappears and solar flares destroy Earth's ionosphere and ozone layer. The story of survival is gripping, but again the characters are dull and wooden.

Eyas is Kilian's best novel; Kilian describes it as "a novel of parental anxiety and hope, and was planned and written as my wife and I raised our two daughters." Kilian sets the action ten million years in Earth's future. The richness of Kilian's future is exciting: humans live with nonhuman windwalkers, centaurs and incredibly powerful whales. *Eyas* is a story of maturity as the boy Eyas grows up to save his people from the army of Brightspear. There are fantasy elements to *Eyas* but Kilian has carefully crafted his future to fit within science fiction realism.

Where *Icequake* concentrated on Antarctica and New Zealand, Kilian's other disaster novel, *Tsunami,* concentrates on California and Vancouver. The Antarctic icecap falls into the ocean and the resulting tidal waves flood all coastal areas. But again, the story of survival dominates without any memorable characters to hold the interest of the reader.

Crawford Kilian's work centers itself on younger characters within themes of survival.

—George Kelley

KILLOUGH, (Karen) Lee. Also writes as Sarah Hood. American. Born in Syracuse, Kansas, 5 May 1942. Educated at

Fort Hays State College, Kansas, 1960-62; Hadley Memorial Hospital School of Radiologic Technology, 1962-64. Married Howard Patrick Killough in 1966. Radiologic Technologist, St. Joseph Hospital, Concordia, Kansas, 1964-65, St. Mary Hospital, Manhattan, Kansas, 1965-67, 1969-71, and Morris Cafritz Memorial Hospital, Washington, D. C., 1967-69. Since 1971, Radiologic Technologist, Kansas State University Veterinary Hospital, Manhattan. Columnist ("Obiter Dictum"), *The Spang Blah,* 1977-79. Address: Box 422, Manhattan, Kansas 66502, U. S. A.

SCIENCE-FICTION PUBLICATIONS

Novels

A Voice Out of Ramah. New York, Ballantine, 1979.
The Doppelganger Gambit. New York, Ballantine, 1979.
The Monitor, The Miners, and the Shree. New York, Ballantine 1980.
Deadly Silents. New York, Ballantine, 1981.
Liberty's World. New York, DAW, 1985.

Short Stories

Aventine. New York, Ballantine, 1982.

Uncollected Short Stories (series: Aventine)

"Caveat Emptor," in *Analog* (New York), May 1970.
"Caravan," in *If* (New York), June 1972.
"Sentience," in *If* (New York), October 1973.
"Survival," in *Starwind,* Fall 1976.
"Stalking Game," in *Galileo* (Boston), Spring 1977.
"A Cup of Hemlock," in *100 Great Science Fiction Short-Short Stories,* edited by Isaac Asimov, Martin H. Greenberg, and Joseph D. Olander. New York, Doubleday, and London, Robson, 1978.
"The Sanctuary" and "My Brother Cain," in *Sol Plus,* Summer 1979.
"Corpus Cryptic," in *Stellar 5,* edited by Judy-Lynn del Rey. New York, Ballantine, 1980.
"Banshee" (as Sarah Hood), in *Sol Plus 6,* 1980.
"Achronos," in *The 1981 Annual World's Best SF,* edited by Donald A. Wollheim. New York, DAW, 1981.
"Taaehalaan Is Drowning," in *Fantasy and Science Fiction* (New York), August 1981.
"The Lying Ear," in *Alien Encounters,* edited by Jan Howard Finder. New York, Taplinger, 1982.
"The Soul Slayer," in *Amazons 2,* edited by Jessica Amanda Salmonson. New York, DAW, 1982.
"The Existential Man," in *Fantasy and Science Fiction* (New York), March 1982.
"The Jarabon," in *Isaac Asimov's Space of Her Own,* edited by Shawna McCarthy. New York, Davis, 1983.
"Keeping the Customer Satisfied," with Pat Killough, in *Tomorrow's Voices.* New York, Davis, 1984.
"The Leopard's Daughter," in *Isaac Asimov's Science Fiction Magazine* (New York), March 1984.
"Symphony for a Lost Traveler," in *Analog* (New York), March 1984.
"Deathglass," in *Isaac Asimov's Science Fiction Magazine* (New York), April 1985.

*

Lee Killough comments:
I believe that, above all else, fiction should entertain. Every novel or story I write is aimed toward giving the reader enjoyment. I write what I myself would pick off a bookshelf to read. I work hard on researching and developing background and designing realistic, rounded characters. I try to satisfy the reader who might be scientifically knowledgeable. If the expert reader's enjoyment is not spoiled by glaring errors, then the science will have a ring of authenticity to the less knowledgeable reader, too. I write psychological and extrapolative science fiction, but not based so much on my own background of biology and veterinary medicine as, strangely enough, on my husband's background of psychology and law. Even the surrealistic Aventine short stories have their roots in extrapolation.

*   *   *

The feminist who writes science fiction is able to design vastly changed societies. However, she also attempts to achieve a balance of male and female energy within the novel or short story. In her works, Lee Killough excels in handling the interplay between male and female characters, while she creates future societies that are both startling and believable.

Killough's novels are related to one another by both plot structure and character development. The typical plot involves the work of either interplanetary monitors or police (LEO's) who arrive on a planet, or remain on earth, to conduct surveillance and solve problems among the inhabitants. Reality belies appearance as the investigators attempt to sort fact from fiction. Solutions are found through close interaction with and greater understanding of the local inhabitants.

The feminist overlay produces unusually strong women characters, many in positions of leadership. In addition, her male characters usually reflect a change in the cultural expectations of women. Women leaders are generally respected by both the men and women under them. Sexual freedom is an equally assumed right for both sexes.

Her first novel, *A Voice Out of Ramah,* is Killough's most important work. In this haunting story, she explores the effects of controlling society through enforced religious rituals, utilizing sexual stereotypes and population control.

Ramah is a planet populated by a traditionalist religious sect which left Earth six centuries earlier to escape violence and immorality. However, the planet Ramah turned out to be inhospitable; a deadly virus indigenous to Ramah killed most of the males when they reached puberty. A few survived to confine the society, however, and eventually all the men became immune. The priests, seeing their minority status as a controlling factor among the sect, began a secret ritual known as the Trial, in which 90 per cent of the adolescent males were infected with a deadly drug that produced symptons similar to the original disease. The surviving ten per cent were forced to become priests and to continue the yearly ritual, passing their terrible secrets down from leader to leader.

The plot hinges on one of the leaders, Jared, who watches the death of an alien monitor and suddenly realizes the horrors of the Trial. In a desperate bid to save the life of his nephew, Jared disguises himself as a woman and endures many hardships and dangers in reaching the leader of the foreign expedition and enlisting her help to stop the killings forever. In the process, he is helped by many women and begins to understand the loss of freedom for both men and women in the sexist society.

Because Killough has set up the strict cloistering of all adult males on Ramah, she can explore simultaneously the subservience of women and the sense of unity and strength they gain through working within their all-female groups. Women are treated as equals by other women, even though they are by law inferior to men. It is women who maintain the standard of living, who keep the peace, and who run the everyday life of the community. Because of the shortage of men, women are usually impregnated only by choice through a sperm bank. The most common form of sexual activity is between two women, who are called tanglemates. In fact, there are few marriages, so women are not tied to one romantic involvement. These conditions allow a rare freedom for women, fascinating because it exists in an extremely sexist society.

Killough's other novels include *The Monitor, The Miners, and the Shree*, a fast-paced adventure story, and her two detective novels, *The Doppelganger Gambit*, set in the United States, and *Deadly Silents*, set on the planet Egar. The first of these follows the exploits of a monitoring group led by a woman named Chemel, Killough's strongest female lead. The novel is particularly important because of its handling of the interaction of widely varied cultures. The author shows great imagination in creating sentient alien beings with animal-like features, such as fur, scales, feathers, and wings. The detective novels are less successful, often overwhelming the reader with action that is not always tied together in the end. But they do grapple with important social issues, such as the evils of a computer-controlled society and discrimination on the basis of language.

Most recently, Killough has published a collection of her short stories called *Aventine* because they are all set in an artist's colony of the same name. These stories depict a futuristic paradise, now taken over by the rich and famous, in which everyone seems rich and beautiful, but truth is illusive. Beautiful women find unique ways to murder their husbands and maim their lovers. In "The Siren Garden" a wife kills her abusive husband by trapping him in a garden full of shrill singing crystals. Imperfections are accepted and even encouraged. For instance, in the story "A House Divided" Amanda Gail and Selene Randall exist in the same body and are both accepted as legitimate persons who vie for domination. In "Broken Stairways, Walls of Time" holographs and computer-produced tones are used to cover up decadence, but the illusion is available only to the uninitiated. These fantasies are all narrated by a male who is fascinated by the characters he describes.

Because of her imaginative exploration of future societies, her willingness to deal with cutting social issues, and her development of the strong female character, Lee Killough has made a significant contribution to the science-fiction genre.

—Judith Snyder

KILWORTH, Garry. British. Born in York, 5 July 1941. Educated at Khomaksar School, Aden, 1952-54; Royal Air Force Bridgenorth School, 1954-56, and Cosford Cadet School, 1956-58; H. N. C. in business studies 1974. Married Annette Jill Bailey in 1962; one son and one daughter. Served as a Signals Master in the Royal Air Force, 1959-74; Senior Executive, Cable & Wireless, London and Caribbean, 1974-82. Since 1982, freelance writer. Agent: Maggie Noach, 21 Redan Street, London W14 0AB. Address: Greenacres, The Chase, Ashingdon, Rochford, Essex SS4 3JE, England.

SCIENCE-FICTION PUBLICATIONS

Novels

In Solitary. London, Faber, 1977; New York, Avon, 1979.

The Night of Kadar. London, Faber, 1978; New York, Avon, 1980.
Split Second. London, Faber, 1979.
Gemini God. London, Faber, 1981.
A Theatre of Timesmiths. London, Gollancz, 1984.

Short Stories

The Songbirds of Pain. London, Gollancz, 1984.

*

Garry Kilworth comments:
I am not greatly interested in the "science" in Science Fiction. I am more concerned with unusual societies, anthropological aspects, social misfits, and exotic cultures. The issues might be contemporary, as I feel they are in *A Theatre of Timesmiths*, or universal, ageless questions such as the nurture-nature theme of *In Solitary*. I wish to explore the ordinary human spirit in a stressful state of adversity, and in its relationship to the natural world. I write science fiction and fantasy because their imaginative scope allows me more sweep than would mainstream fiction. Mysticism, including religions of all kinds, forms a thread through my work. On the entertainment level I find the best vehicle for carrying these themes is the adventure novel. In a sentence: jungles, deserts, wastelands and the man-a-lost looking for himself.

*   *   *

Characterisation has always been the strongest facet of Garry Kilworth's writing. The science-fictional ideas in the six volumes of his work so far published are usually secondary to the humane portrayals of his protagonists, yet his subject matter has been widely varied.

His first, rather slender novel, *In Solitary*, depicts an Earth conquered by the bird-like alien Soal, who rule by separating man from his fellow man . . . and woman. It's a tautly told yet subtle story of human courage and ingenuity, much of it set in the South Sea Islands. *The Night of Kadar* is perhaps Kilworth's richest novel, drawing upon the Koran for its inspiration. A starship lands upon a new world, and settlers—awakened and matured from their pre-frozen embryonic state—struggle to understand their purpose on the planet, unaware of the malfunction in the machinery which ought to have instructed them. The story of the building of a land bridge and the encounter with the aliens is engrossing, but one remembers far more clearly the characters of Othman, Zayid and, particularly, the divine idiot, Fdar. *Split Second* saw Kilworth give the Jekyll and Hyde tale a new twist as experiments with the Wiederhaus Repeater—an archeological tool used to hologrammically re-animate objects from the past—accidentally sends a young boy, Richard, 33000 years into the past, where he shares the mind and experiences of a juvenile boy from that time, Esk. It's an ambitious idea that doesn't wholly succeed in evoking that far distant past, but the storytelling is once again first class. *Gemini God* is about a degeneration of the human race and attempts to solve that through alien contact. Another strand of the novel—empathic contact between identical twins—provides a more interesting storyline, however. For all its overt science-fictional elements, this is the least genre-bound of Kilworth's novels, with its sub-text examining the nature of and work of the artist. The novel also suffers from having been cut from a text one-and-a-half times its length for publication. Kilworth's fifth novel, *A Theatre Of Timesmiths*, is, curiously enough, both his best written and most disappointing work, an enclosed-environment story which turns out to be all happening in a character's head. Morag is the least sympathetic of Kilworth's many characters and her predicament involves us only marginally. That said, Kilworth's evocation of the world inside the ice is remarkably vivid and suggests that – given the right subject – he could produce an exceptional work within the genre.

A collection of Kilworth's stories, *The Songbirds of Pain*, contains stories published over a period of nine years. The best of them, like "Sumi Dreams of a Paper Frog" and "The Songbirds of Pain," are exceptional, almost fabular works, and even the least of them—"The Dissemblers" and "Let's Go to Golgotha" (which won Kilworth the *Sunday Times* Best SF Story competition in 1975)—are of a high standard. Kilworth has also written a reasonable body of published poetry.

—David Wingrove

KING, Ray. See **CUMMINGS, Ray.**

KING, Vincent. Pseudonym for Rex Thomas Vinson. British. Born in Falmouth, Cornwall, 22 October 1935. Educated at Redruth School of Art, Cornwall; Falmouth College of Art, Cornwall, 1952-57; West of England College of Art, Bristol, 1959-60; University of London, 1960-62. Served in the Royal Air Force. Married Jean Blackler in 1961 (divorced, 1978); one son and one daughter. Art teacher in schools in London, Bristol, Newcastle upon Tyne, 1963-68, and since 1968 in Redruth. Painter and printmaker; work in several Arts Council exhibitions. Agent: Leslie Flood, Carnell Literary Agency, Rowneybury Bungalow, Sawbridgeworth, near Old Harlow, Essex CM20 2EX, England.

SCIENCE-FICTION PUBLICATIONS .

Novels

Light a Last Candle. New York, Ballantine, 1969; London, Rapp and Whiting, 1970.
Another End. New York, Ballantine, 1971.
Candy Man. London, Gollancz, 1971; New York, Ballantine, 1972.
Time Snake and Superclown. London, Futura, 1976.

Uncollected Short Stories

"Defence Mechanism," in *New Writings in SF 7*, edited by John Carnell. London, Dobson, 1966; New York, Bantam, 1971.
"The Wall to End the World," in *New Writings in SF 8*, edited by John Carnell. London, Dobson, 1966; New York, Bantam, 1971.
"Testament," in *New Writings in SF 9*, edited by John Carnell. London, Dobson, 1966; New York, Bantam, 1972.
"Report from Linelos," in *New Writings in SF 15*, edited by John Carnell. London, Dobson, 1969.
"The Discontent Contingency," in *New Writings in SF 19*, edited by John Carnell. London, Dobson, 1971.

*

Vincent King comments:

I've no explicit intentions, political or philosophical, but considerations of that type keep coming out of the words. The intention is fantasy, a succession of ideas, events, relationships that change, further and further revelations about the situation/plot/story. Naturally this makes for ever-increasing complexity and a continual raising of the stakes (I'm sometimes deeply shocked by what I write!), maybe for incomprehensibility, too. I often include more or less direct quotations from "reality." (Which is interchangeable with "fiction" anyway; reality is fantasy, fantasised by going through people's heads, and it doesn't matter how objective/pragmatic they say they are—that's a fantasy too.) I tend to use the first person because I fantasise that its more direct. Also it means the voice that tells the story doesn't know what's to happen, is happening. I also fantasise that it allows the fantasy to develop in a less inhibited way. The freedom of fantasy is the thing.

I think the most exciting writing today is on the fantasy end of the spectrum. I'm not speaking only of what is referred to as SF or occult writing. It's interesting that at a time when lot of SF authors claim to be trying to "go straight," some good so-called mainstream writing seems to be turning more fantastic. What is finished, I think, for a more or less serious SF writer, is the "science" type of SF, and I think the middle-class "Hobbit" type of adventure is pretty sterile too. To me science is a type of magic—or at least that's how I *use* it. Science is not holy, it's pratical; it's probably caused no more suffering, or release from suffering, than religions. Religions, wars, science, adultery, murders, etc. are what happen when people aren't allowed or aren't able to be *creative* in some way: to work out their personal fantasy, which might be a garden, or a fortune, or a model steam locomotive, or anything!

* * *

Suspense is a major element in all the works of Vincent King. In part, he develops suspense through the ordinary means—surprising and very quick-paced action—which keep the reader wondering what will come next. But here is also a more intellectual type of suspense which may be regarded as one of the distinguishing marks of King's work. This type of suspense also develops in two ways. First, a sort of jig-saw puzzle effect means that, in the beginning of his novels, it is often difficult to see how the various parts relate to one another. What is the connection between Ice Lover and the Mods (*Light a Last Candle*)? The reader must hold numbers of pieces in his mind, gradually fitting them together into a clear, comprehensive picture. Second, his characters have a certain enigmatic quality about them. One's curiosity is aroused because it isn't clear just who or what the protagonist is. Only near the end of the novel is the identity of Candy Man revealed.

Space exploration, the attempt to find and contact other sentient life, is a theme which King plays in a different key. Working within a long time scheme, expending vast resources, man may just possibly find some sentient life form. Adamson finds Protia (*Another End*) after all hope has been abandoned. In *Candy Man* the failure is absolute. But even success may bring strange results. Protia ultimately absorbs Adamson, and the alien beings in *Light a Last Candle* have unsuccessfully attempted to absorb an entire colony of Earthmen. Mankind is unavoidably changed by contact with aliens.

But mankind is portrayed in a decadent state throughout King's novels. The glorious past is gone, some few men live an enervated life among the ruins. The image of those ruins, vast cities covering entire worlds, has a central place for King. His heroes, regularly isolated (or at most accompanied by a single companion) in these vast, hive-like structures, seem compelled to explore the cellars, the subterranean depths of their worlds. Both Adamson and Candy Man are involved in extensive chase scenes in these labyrinthine depths. Ice Lover lives and fights in caves. Man, as he declines, seems to be portrayed as returning to his roots, the cave, the sea, the womb. Interestingly, the machines have held up better than their creators. The Probe keeps Adamson alive, frustrating his every suicide attempt. The entire population of Earth may have been maintained by machines (*Candy Man*) or resurrected by a computer (*Another End*). In some sense dependence upon machines has led humanity into decadence. Only if they can shake free of the machines will there be some slight hope of renewal.

Each of King's novels deals with the human proclivity to violence; all his heroes are killers who seem to enjoy killing. But in the final analysis the violence seems to be shown as both pointless and ineffective, a serious defect that men must overcome if they are to survive and advance. The conclusions of *Another End* and *Candy Man* hold out some slight hope of this.

King's greatest strength, his highly imaginative permutations upon conventional themes, combines with his ability to create suspense to produce works which fascinate and puzzle the reader. Yet these strengths are somewhat offset by a style of writing heavily dependent upon dialog which has a rather choppy and unsophisticated quality.

—Robert Reilly

KINGSBURY, Donald (MacDonald). Canadian. Born in San Francisco, California, United States, 12 February 1929; became Canadian citizen. Educated at schools in Japan, New Guinea, California, and New Hampshire; McGill University, Montreal, B. Sc. 1956, M. Sc. 1960. Married Mireille Kingsbury in 1950 (divorced, 1960); two sons. Since 1956, Lecturer in Mathematics, McGill University. Recipient: Compton Crook award, 1983. Agent: Eleanor Wood, 432 Park Avenue South, Suite 1205, New York, New York 10016. Address: 1563 Ducharme Avenue, Montreal, Quebec H2V 1G4, Canada.

SCIENCE-FICTION PUBLICATIONS

Novel

Courtship Rite. New York, Simon and Schuster, 1982; as *Geta*, London, Panther, 1984.

Uncollected Short Stories

"Ghost Town," in *Astounding* (New York), June 1952.
"To Bring in the Steel," in *The Best Science Fiction of the Year 8*, edited by Terry Carr. New York, Ballantine, 1979.
"Shipwright," in *The Best Science Fiction Novellas of the Year 1*, edited by Terry Carr. New York, Ballantine, 1979.
"The Moon Goddess and the Son," in *The Best Science Fiction Novellas of the Year 2*, edited by Terry Carr. New York, Ballantine, 1980.

OTHER PUBLICATIONS

Other

"The Right to Breed," in *Astounding* (New York), April 1955.

"The Atomic Rocket," in *Analog* (New York), December 1975.
"The First Space War," in *Analog* (New York), December 1978.
"The Spaceport," in *Analog* (New York), November and December 1979.

*

Donald Kingsbury comments:
I make up my backgrounds and test them for plausibility before I throw my characters into them—to manage as best they can. I have a preference for "fleet footed" males and females and odd cultures. I tend to write in a single future universe: "The Man Goddess and the Son" is from its near future phase and *Courtship Rite* from 2000 or so years away.

* * *

Although Donald Kingsbury published a short story in 1952 and wrote science articles for *Analog* in the mid-1970's, it was with three novelettes published in that magazine in 1978-79 that he became widely known. All three were anthologized the following year, giving Kingsbury his reputation as one of the most promising and interesting writers of technically oriented science fiction.

"To Bring In the Steel," the best of the three, dramatizes the efforts of a private consortium in the next century to maneuver an asteroid into Earth orbit while refining its rich ore into salable metals. The protagonist is a lonely, independent, supercompetent man—the model Kingsbury hero—whose misogyny and fixed ideas on government and entrepreneurship are, as in all Kingsbury's short works to date, rather implausibly validated by the story's action. The story's clean dramatic line and crisp pacing combine effectively with Kingsbury's ability to render the details of an operating space industry, and largely overcome his insistent division of the sexes into hard-headed men and childlike, undisciplined women. Less successful are "Shipwright" and "The Moon Goddess and the Son," where Kingsbury's indulgent attitude toward the engineer-hero and his recurrent theme of courtesanship as a woman's best chance of getting ahead in a world of more rational-minded men hang heavily upon the less dramatic and loosely constructed story lines. Notable in "The Moon Goddess and the Son" and "To Bring In the Steel" is Kingsbury's boosterism of space industry and the use of space for Western strategic defense, in furtherance of which Kingsbury appears willing to suspend the critical scrutiny he brings to other technical problems and give both subjects an idealized gloss.

Courtship Rite, Kingsbury's single novel to date, represents a surprising advance in skill over his early stories. Kingsbury's far-ranging story of intrigue among human settlers on a resource-poor planet displays an impressive ability to present a complex plot through multiple points of view, and represents a departure in allowing the fair expression of differing ideologies without betraying the author's sympathies.

Geta, an earthlike planet with relatively arid inlands and almost no native animal life, was settled in some distant past by settlers who have lost most of their technology as well as their history, and blindly worship their visible, still-orbiting ship. Cannibalism, originally practiced because of ubiquitous protein deficiencies, now serves a complex social function even as scientific advances threaten to render it unnecessary. The main thread of the story line involves a group marriage of three politically influential men and two women, who are forbidden to marry a third women of their choice and ordered for political reasons to court a heretical pacifist of growing influence in a region over which their leader seeks hegemony. The pacifist, a visionary who preaches a rather Ghandi-like commitment to social revolution without violence, is convincingly and sympathetically portrayed. The decision of her suitors to subject her to a Death Rite—under which they might legally challenge her to a series of putative tests of fitness that will almost certainly ensure her death—provides the springboard for the story's action.

The novel's length, complexity of intrigue, and setting prompt comparison with *Dune*, which Kingsbury audaciously invites with his visionary and ecological themes as well as the device of using numerous fictive "texts" as chapter epigraphs. *Courtship Rite* 's remarkable success in withstanding such comparison and in conveying its own sense of genuine exhilaration is an achievement in itself, and augurs well for Kingsbury's future work.

—Gregory Feeley

KIPLING, (Joseph) Rudyard. British. Born in Bombay, India, 30 December 1865, of English parents. Educated at the United Services College, Westward Ho!, Devon, 1878-82. Married Caroline Starr Balestier in 1892; three children. Assistant Editor, *Civil and Military Gazette*, Lahore, 1882-87; Editor and Contributor, "Week's News," *Pioneer*, Allahabad, 1887-89; returned to England, and settled in London: full-time writer from 1889; lived in Brattleboro, Vermont, 1892-96, then returned to England; settled in Burwash, Sussex, 1902. Rector, University of St. Andrews, 1922-25. Recipient: Nobel Prize for Literature, 1907; Royal Society of Literature Gold Medal, 1926. LL. D. : McGill University, Montreal, 1899; D. Litt. : University of Durham, 1907; Oxford University, 1907; Cambridge University, 1908; University of Edinburgh, 1920; the Sorbonne, Paris, 1921; University of Strasbourg, 1921; D. Phil.: University of Athens, 1924. Honorary Fellow, Magdalene College, Cambridge, 1932. Associate Member, Académie des Sciences Morales et Politiques, 1933. Refused the Poet Laureateship, 1895, and the Order of Merit. *Died 18 January 1936.*

SCIENCE-FICTION PUBLICATIONS

Short Stories

Actions and Reactions. London, Macmillan, and New York, Doubleday, 1909.
A Diversity of Creatures. London, Macmillan, and New York, Doubleday, 1917.

OTHER PUBLICATIONS

Novel

The Light That Failed. New York, United States Book Company, 1890; London, Macmillan, 1891.

Short Stories

Plain Tales from the Hills. Calcutta, Thacker Spink, 1888; New York, Lovell, and London, Macmillan, 1890.
Soldiers Three: A Collection of Storis . . . . Allahabad, Wheeler, 1888; London, Sampson Low, 1890.
The Stories of the Gadsbys: A Tale Without a Plot. Allahabad,

Wheeler, 1888; London, Sampson Low, and New York, Lovell, 1890.
In Black and White. Allahabad, Wheeler, 1888; London, Sampson Low, and New York, Lovell, 1890.
Under the Deodars. Allahabad, Wheeler, 1888; revised edition, London, Sampson Low, 1890.
The Phantom 'Rickshaw and Other Tales. Allahabad, Wheeler, 1888; revised edition, London, Sampson Low, 1890.
Wee Willie Winkie and Other Child Stories. Allahabad, Wheeler, 1888; revised edition, London, Sampson Low, and Chicago, Rand McNally, 1890.
Soldiers Three, and Under the Deodars. New York, Lovell, 1890.
The Phantom 'Rickshaw, and Wee Willie Winkie. New York, Lovell, 1890.
The Courting of Dinah Shadd and Other Stories. New York, Harper, and London, Macmillan, 1890.
Mine Own People. New York, United States Book Company, 1891.
Life's Handicap, Being Stories from Mine Own People. New York and London, Macmillan, 1891.
The Naulahka: A Story of West and East, with Wolcott Balestier. London, Heinemann, and New York, Macmillan, 1892.
Many Inventions. London, Macmillan, and New York, Appleton, 1893.
Soldier Tales. London, Macmillan, 1896; as *Soldier Stories*, New York, Macmillan, 1896.
The Day's Work. New York, Doubleday, and London, Macmillan, 1898.
The Kipling Reader. London, Macmillan, 1900; as *Selected Stories*, 1925.
Traffics and Discoveries. London, Macmillan, and New York, Doubleday, 1904.
Abaft the Funnel. New York, Dodge, 1909.
Selected Stories, edited by William Lyon Phelps. New York, Doubleday, 1921.
Debits and Credits. London, Macmillan, and New York, Doubleday, 1926.
Selected Stories . London, Macmillan, 1929.
Thy Servant a Dog, Told by Boots. London, Macmillan, and New York, Doubleday, 1930; revised edition, as *Thy Servant a Dog and Other Dog Stories*, Macmillan, 1938.
Humorous Tales. London, Macmillan, and New York, Doubleday, 1931.
Animal Stories. London, Macmillan, 1932; New York, Doubleday, 1938.
Limits and Renewals. London, Macmillan, and New York, Doubleday, 1932.
All the Mowgli Stories. London, Macmillan, 1933; New York, Doubleday, 1936.
Collected Dog Stories. London, Macmillan, and New York, Doubleday, 1934.
More Selected Stories. London, Macmillan, 1940.
Twenty-One Tales. London, Reprint Society, 1946.
Ten Stories. London, Pan, 1947.
A Choice of Kipling's Prose, edited by W. Somerset Maugham. London, Macmillan, 1952; as *Maugham's Choice of Kipling's Best: Sixteen Stories*, New York, Doubleday, 1953.
A Treasury of Short Stories. New York, Bantam, 1957.
(*Short Stories*), edited by Edward Parone. New York, Dell, 1960.
Kipling Stories: Twenty-Eight Exciting Tales. New York, Platt and Munk, 1960.
The Best Short Stories, edited by Randall Jarrell. New York, Hanover House, 1961; as *In the Vernacular: The English in India* and *The English in England*, New York, Doubleday, 2 vols., 1963.

Famous Tales of India, edited by B. W. Shir-Cliff. New York, Ballantine, 1962.

Phantoms and Fantasies: 20 Tales. New York, Doubleday, 1965.

Short Stories, edited by Andrew Rutherford. London, Penguin, 2 vols., 1971-76.

Twenty-One Tales, edited by Tim Wilkinson. London, Folio Society, 1972.

Tales of East and West, edited by Bernard Bergonzi. Avon, Connecticut, Limited Editions Club, 1973.

Fiction (for children)

The Jungle Book, illustrated by J. Lockwood Kipling and others. London, Macmillan, and New York, Century, 1894.

The Second Jungle Book, illustrated by J. Lockwood Kipling. London, Macmillan, and New York, Century, 1895; revised edition, Macmillan, 1895.

"Captains Courageous": A Story of the Grand Banks, illustrated by I. W. Taber. London, Macmillan, and New York, Century, 1897.

Stalky & Co. London, Macmillan, and New York, Doubleday, 1899; revised edition, as *The Complete Stalky & Co.*, Macmillan, 1929, Doubleday, 1930.

Kim, illustrated by J. Lockwood Kipling. New York, Doubleday, and London, Macmillan, 1901.

Just So Stories for Little Children, illustrated by the author. London, Macmillan, and New York, Doubleday, 1902.

Puck of Pook's Hill, illustrated by H. R. Millar. London, Macmillan, and New York, Doubleday, 1906.

Kipling Stories and Poems Every Child Should Know, edited by Mary E. Burt and W. T. Chapin, illustrated by Charles Livingston Bull and others. New York, Doubleday, 1909.

Rewards and Fairies, illustrated by Frank Craig. London, Macmillan, and New York, Doubleday, 1910.

Land and Sea Tales for Scouts and Guides. London, Macmillan, and New York, Doubleday, 1923.

Ham and the Porcupine. New York, Doubleday, 1935.

Play

The Harbour Watch (produced London, 1913; revised version, as *Gow's Watch*, produced London, 1924).

Verse

Schoolboy Lyrics. Privately printed, 1881.

Echoes (published anonymously), with Alice Kipling. Privately printed, 1884.

Departmental Ditties and Other Verses. Lahore, Civil and Military Gazette Press, 1886; London, Thacker Spink, 1890.

Departmental Ditties, Barrack-Room Ballads, and Other Verse. New York, United States Book Company, 1890.

Barrack-Room Ballads and Other Verses. London, Methuen, and New York, Macmillan, 1892.

Ballads and Barrack-Room Ballads. New York, Macmillan, 1893.

The Seven Seas. New York, Appleton, and London, Methuen, 1896.

Recessional. Privately printed, 1897.

An Almanac of Twelve Sports, illustrated by William Nicholson. London, Heinemann, and New York, Russell, 1898.

Poems, edited by Wallace Rice. Chicago, Star, 1899.

Recessional and Other Poems. Privately printed, 1899.

The Absent-Minded Beggar. Privately printed, 1899.

With Number Three, Surgical and Medical, and New Poems. Santiago, Chile, Hume, 1900.

Occasional Poems. Boston, Bartlett, 1900.

The Five Nations. London, Methuen, and New York, Doubleday, 1903.

The Muse among the Motors. New York, Doubleday, 1904.

Collected Verse. New York, Doubleday, 1907; London, Hodder and Stoughton, 1912.

A History of England (verse only), with C. R. L. Fletcher. London, Oxford University Press-Hodder and Stoughton, and New York, Doubleday, 1911; revised edition, 1930.

Songs from Books. New York, Doubleday, 1912; London, Macmillan, 1913.

Twenty Poems. London, Methuen, 1918.

The Years Between. London, Methuen, and New York, Doubleday, 1919.

Verse: Inclusive Edition 1885-1918. London, Hodder and Stoughton, and New York, Doubleday, 3 vols., 1919; revised edition, 1921, 1927, 1933.

A Kipling Anthology: Verse. London, Methuen, and New York, Doubleday, 1922.

Songs for Youth, from Collected Verse. London, Hodder and Stoughton, 1924; New York, Doubleday, 1925.

A Choice of Songs. London, Methuen, 1925.

Sea and Sussex. London, Macmillan, and New York, Doubleday, 1926.

St. Andrews, with Walter de la Mare. London, A. and C. Black, 1926.

Songs of the Sea. London, Macmillan, and New York, Doubleday, 1927.

Poems 1886-1929. London, Macmillan, 3 vols., 1929; New York, Doubleday, 3 vols., 1930.

Selected Poems. London, Methuen, 1931.

East of Suez, Being a Selection of Eastern Verses. London, Macmillan, 1931.

Sixty Poems. London, Hodder and Stoughton, 1939.

Verse: Definitive Edition. London, Hodder and Stoughton, and New York, Doubleday, 1940.

So Shall Ye Reap: Poems for These Days. London, Hodder and Stoughton, 1941.

A Choice of Kipling's Verse, edited by T. S. Eliot. London, Faber, 1941; New York, Scribner, 1943.

Sixty Poems. London, Hodder and Stoughton, 1957.

A Kipling Anthology, edited by W. G. Bebbington. London, Methuen, 1964.

The Complete Barrack-Room Ballads, edited by Charles Carrington. London, Methuen, 1973.

Kipling's English History: Poems, edited by Marghanita Laski. London, BBC Publications, 1974.

Kipling: A Selection, edited by James Cochrane. London, Penguin, 1977.

Other

Quarette, with others. Lahore, Civil and Military Gazette Press, 1885.

The City of Dreadful Night and Other Sketches. Allahabad, Wheeler, 1890.

The City of Dreadful Night and Other Places. Allahabad, Wheeler, and London, Sampson Low, 1891.

The Smith Administration. Allahabad, Wheeler, 1891.

Letters of Marque. Allahabad, Wheeler, and London, Sampson Low, 1891.

American Notes, with *The Bottle Imp*, by Robert Louis Stevenson. New York, Ivers, 1891.

Out of India: Things I Saw, and Failed to See, in Certain Days and Nights at Jeypore and Elsewhere. New York, Dillingham, 1895.

The Kipling Birthday Book, edited by Joseph Finn. London, Macmillan, 1896; New York, Doubleday, 1899.

A Fleet in Being: Notes of Two Trips with the Channel Squadron. London, Macmillan, 1898.

From Sea to Sea: Letters of Travel. New York, Doubleday, 1899; as *From Sea to Sea and Other Sketches*, London, Macmillan, 1900.

Works (Swastika Edition). New York, Doubleday, Appleton, and Century, 15 vols., 1899.

Letters to the Family (Notes on a Recent Trip to Canada). Toronto, Macmillan, 1908.

The Kipling Reader (not same as 1900 collection of short stories). New York, Appleton, 1912.

The New Army in Training. London, Macmillan, 1915.

France at War. London, Macmillan, and New York, Doubleday, 1915.

The Fringes of the Fleet. London, Macmillan, and New York, Doubleday, 1915.

Tales of "The Trade." Privately printed, 1916.

Sea Warfare. London, Macmillan, and New York, Doubleday, 1916.

The War in the Mountains. New York, Doubleday, 1917.

To Fighting Americans (speeches). Privately printed, 1918.

The Eyes of Asia. New York, Doubleday, 1918.

The Graves of the Fallen. London, Imperial War Graves Commission, 1919.

Letters of Travel (1892-1913). London, Macmillan, and New York, Doubleday, 1920.

A Kipling Anthology: Prose. London, Macmillan, and New York, Doubleday, 1922.

The Irish Guards in the Great War. London, Macmillan, and New York, Doubleday, 2 vols., 1923.

Works (Mandalay Edition). New York, Doubleday, 26 vols., 1925-26.

A Book of Words: Selections from Speeches and Addresses Delivered Between 1906 and 1927. London, Macmillan, and New York, Doubleday, 1928.

The One Volume Kipling. New York, Doubleday, 1928.

Souvenirs of France. London, Macmillan, 1933.

A Kipling Pageant. New York, Doubleday, 1935.

Something of Myself for My Friends Known and Unknown. London, Macmillan, and New York, Doubleday, 1937.

Complete Works (Sussex Edition). London, Macmillan, 35 vols., 1937-39; as *Collected Works* (Burwash Edition), New York, Doubleday, 28 vols., 1941 (includes revised versions of some previously published works).

A Kipling Treasury: Stories and Poems . London, Macmillan, 1940.

Kipling: A Selection of His Stories and Poems, edited by John Beecroft. New York, Doubleday, 2 vols., 1956.

The Kipling Sampler, edited by Alexander Greendale. New York, Fawcett, 1962.

Letters from Japan, edited by Donald Richie and Yoshimori Harashima. Tokyo, Kenkyusha, 1962.

Pearls from Kipling, edited by C. Donald Plomer. New Britain, Connecticut, Elihu Burritt Library, 1963.

Rudyard Kipling to Rider Haggard: The Record of a Friendship, edited by Morton Cohen. London, Hutchinson, 1965; Rutherford, New Jersey, Fairleigh Dickinson Unversity Press, 1968.

The Best of Kipling. New York, Doubleday, 1968.

Stories and Poems, edited by Roger Lancelyn Green. London, Dent, 1970.

Kipling's Horace, edited by Charles Carrington. London, Methuen, 1978.

American Notes: Rudyard Kipling's West, edited by Arrell M. Gibson. Norman, University of Oklahoma Press, 1981.

The Portable Kipling, edited by Irving Howe. New York, Viking Press, 1982.

"O Beloved Kids": Rudyard Kipling's Letters to His Children, edited by Elliot L. Gilbert. London, Weidenfeld and Nicolson, 1983; New York, Harcourt Brace, 1984.

Kipling's India: Uncollected Sketches 1884-1888, edited by Thomas Pinney. London, Macmillan, and New York, Schocken, 1985.

*

Bibliography: *Rudyard Kipling: A Bibliographical Catalogue* by J. McG. Stewart, edited by A.W. Keats, Toronto, Dalhousie University-University of Toronto Press, 1959, London, Oxford University Press, 1960; "Kipling: An Annotated Bibliography of Writings about Him" by H.E. Gerber and E. Lauterbach, in *English Fiction in Transtion 3* (Tempe, Arizona), 1960, and *8*, 1965.

Manuscript Collections: Cornell University Library, Ithaca, New York; Library of Congress, Washington, D. C.

Critical Studies (selection): *Rudyard Kipling: His Life and Work* by Charles Carrington, London, Macmillan, 1955, revised edition, 1978; *The Readers' Guide to Rudyard Kipling's Work*, Canterbury, Gibbs, 1961, and *Kipling The Critical Heritage*, London, Routledge, and New York, Barnes and Noble, 1971, both edited by Roger Lancelyn Green; *Kipling's Mind and Art* edited by Andrew Rutherford, Edinburgh, Oliver and Boyd, and Stanford, California, Stanford University Press, 1964; *Kipling and the Critics* edited by Elliot L. Gilbert, New York, New York University Press, and London, Owen, 1965; *Rudyard Kipling* by J. I. M. Stewart, London, Gollancz, and New York, Dodd Mead, 1966; *Rudyard Kipling: Realist and Fabulist* by Bonamy Dobrée, London and New York, Oxford University Press, 1967; *Kipling: The Glass, The Shadow, and the Fire* by Philip Mason, London, Cape, and New York, Harper, 1975; *Kipling and His World* by Kingsley Amis, London, Thames and Hudson, 1975, New York, Scribner, 1976; *The Strange Ride of Rudyard Kipling: His Life and Works* by Angus Wilson, London, Secker and Warburg, 1977, New York, Viking Press, 1978; *Rudyard Kipling* by James Harrison, Boston, Twayne, 1982; *Kipling: Interviews and Recollections* edited by Harold Orel, London, Macmillan, and New York, Barnes and Noble, 2 vols., 1983-84; *A Kipling Companion* by N. Page, London, Macmillan, 1984.

*　*　*

Today, Rudyard Kipling is chiefly remembered as a spokesman for imperialism and as a skilful versifier, and it is often overlooked that approximately one in six of his published short stories were science fiction or fantasy. His influence on 20th-century SF writers was probably greater than anyone else's of his generation, except Wells, and is acknowledged by writers as disparate as Poul Anderson and John Brunner.

His formal excursions into the future are few but memorable. "With the Night Mail" describes as Atlantic crossing by airship in the year 2000, and is accompanied by excerpts from the magazine in which it was supposed to appear. Socially, little appears to have changed, but technologically this is an astounding vision; at a time when it was novel for a liner to carry radio-telegraphy equipment, and broadcasting was two decades distant, Kipling envisaged the need for air traffic control and a General Communicator system. In the sequel, "As Easy as

ABC," he speculated on the demise of democracy owing to its tendency to lapse into mob-rule—this may have been conditioned by his disappointment with the USA at a time when lynch-law was still common: witness the terrifying image of the memorial statue, "The Nigger in Flames,"—and on a cure for over-population, a problem he had encountered during his time in India.

His other works of SF and fantasy range from the early "The Bridge-Builders," in which a civil engineer overhears the Indian gods debating whether or not to destroy his masterpiece spanning the Ganges, through those astonishing *tours-de-force* without human characters like ". 007" (steam locomotives) and "The Ship That Found Herself" (steel plates and girders and the ship's cat!), by way of speculative SF like "In the Same Boat" (a man and a woman discover that the nightmares haunting them refer to real events which happened while they were in the womb) and "The Finest Story in the World" (a City clerk remembers his previous lives, as a galley-slave and on an expedition to Vinland), right up to the complex, subtle stories of his last years when he left his readers and critics far behind, like "The Children of the Zodiac."

He wrote the classic ghosts-in-reverse story, "They," and the deadpan fantasies of *Just So Stories;* in *Puck of Pook's Hill* and *Rewards and Fairies* he brought the people of past ages forward to the present to speak for themselves; and he wrote about sea-serpents and mysterious curses and the heady excitement of modern inventions—but never quite as anyone else would have handled them. For example, "Wireless" is indeed about early radio, but the narrator's experimental friend, trying to eavesdrop on the Royal Navy, fails to notice how the soul of Keats is striking an echo across time in a lovelorn, tubercular assistant pharmacist.

Kipling, who was possibly the most completely equipped writer ever to tackle the short-story form in the English language, exemplifies the fact that in our literary tradition there has never been a hard-and-fast line between realistic and fantastic. Indeed, he was a master at making the fantastic seem credible.

—John Brunner

KIPPAX, John. Pseudonym for John Charles Hynam. British. Born in Alwalton, Huntingdonshire, 10 June 1915. Attended Trinity College, Carmarthen, 1934-36. Married Phyllis Mary Manning in 1941; one daughter. Artist, musician, comedian, and teacher. *Died 17 July 1974.*

SCIENCE-FICTION PUBLICATIONS

Novels (series: Venturer 12 in all books)

A Thunder of Stars, with Dan Morgan. London, Macdonald, 1968; New York, Ballantine, 1970.
Seed of Stars, with Dan Morgan. New York, Ballantine, 1972; London, Pan, 1974.
The Neutral Stars, with Dan Morgan. New York, Ballantine, 1973; London, Pan, 1975.
Where No Stars Guide. London, Pan, 1975.

Uncollected Short Stories

"Dimple," in *Science Fantasy* (Bournemouth), December 1954.

"Trojan Hearse," with Dan Morgan, in *New Worlds* (London), December 1954.
"Mossenden's Martian," in *Science Fantasy* (Bournemouth), April 1955.
"Down to Earth," in *Authentic* (London), May 1955.
"Special Delivery," in *Science Fantasy* (Bournemouth), June 1955.
"Hounded Down," in *Science Fantasy* (Bournemouth), November 1955.
"Mother of Invention," in *Authentic* (London), December 1955.
"Again, In," in *Authentic* (London), January 1956.
"Waif Astray," in *Authentic* (London), March 1956.
"Fair Weather Friend," in *Science Fantasy* (Bournemouth), May 1956.
"We Are One," in *Authentic* (London), September 1956.
"We're Only Human," in *New Worlds* (London), November 1956.
"Cut and Come Again," in *Science Fantasy* (Bournemouth), December 1956.
"Finnegan Begin Again," in *Science Fantasy* (Bournemouth), February 1957.
"By the Forelock," in *Authentic* (London), February 1957.
"Salute Your Superiors!," in *Authentic* (London), April 1957.
"Point of Contact," in *New Worlds* (London), April 1957.
"After Eddie," in *Science Fantasy* (Bournemouth), June 1957.
"The Underlings," in *New Worlds* (London), August 1957.
"Solid Beat," in *Science Fantasy* (Bournemouth), October 1957.
"Send Him Victorious," in *Science Fantasy* (Bournemouth), December 1957.
"Me, Myself, and I," in *Science Fantasy* (Bournemouth), February 1958.
"End Planet," in *Nebula* (Glasgow), April 1958.
"Tower for One," in *New Worlds* (London), July 1958.
"Destiny Incorporated," in *Science Fantasy* (Bournemouth), August 1958.
"It," in *Nebula* (Glasgow), November 1958.
"Thy Rod and Thy Staff," in *Nebula* (Glasgow), December 1958.
"Call of the Wild," in *Science Fantasy* (Bournemouth), February 1959.
"The Lady Was Jazz," in *Science Fantasy* (Bournemouth), April 1959.
"Friday," in *Out of This World 1,* edited by Amabel Williams-Ellis and Mably Owen. London, Blackie, 1960.
"The Last Barrier," in *Science Fantasy* (Bournemouth), September 1960.
"The Dusty Death," in *Out of This World 2,* edited by Amabel Williams-Ellis and Mably Owen. London, Blackie, 1961.
"Nelson Expects," in *New Worlds* (London), October 1961.
"Stark Refuge," in *Science Fantasy* (Bournemouth), November 1961.
"Look on His Face," in *New Worlds* (London), August 1966.
"Reflection of the Truth," in *Tales of Unease,* edited by John Burke. New York, Doubleday, 1969.
"Blood Offering," in *Weird Shadows from Beyond,* edited by John Carnell. New York, Avon, 1969.
"The Time Wager," in *New Writings in SF 22,* edited by Kenneth Bulmer. London, Sidgwick and Jackson, 1973.
"No Certain Armour," in *New Writings in SF 24,* edited by Kenneth Bulmer. London, Sidgwick and Jackson, 1974.

*   *   *

Fear, estrangement and the hunger to bridge the sometimes

illimitable gulfs between individuals—and between cultures, planets, and species—are central themes in the science fiction and fantasy of John Kippax. The desperate quest for security in a hostile universe figures prominently in this minor English author's writing. His four Venturer 12 novels, the first three written with Dan Morgan, are perhaps Kippax's best-known genre work but are inferior to some of his short fiction.

A Thunder of Stars presents motifs of alienation that persist through the series. It introduces a group of continuing stock military characters who must wrestle in various ways with personal alienation. Central to the saga is the troubled relationship between Tom Bruce and Helen Lindstrom, officers of the elite Space Corps. At the outset, Bruce, a seemingly callous martinet, breaks off their rewarding two-year affair with the excuse that it is hampering their careers. Both are ambitious and dedicated officers, but Lindstrom does not want to sacrifice their relationship.

Bruce yearns to command *Venturer 12,* Earth's most advanced starship. He is brilliant and highly qualified. But scandal early in his career—carefully hushed up—makes his appointment a political hot potato. Then Bruce, on solar system patrol, shoots down a runaway starship filled with colonists before it can crash into Earth with appalling carnage. An inquiry vindicates Bruce but the traumatic secret of his past is revealed: On a distant colony planet Bruce once discovered humans who had been captured and surgically restructured by unknown aliens. Out of mercy, he put the hideously mutilated victims to death.

Bruce wins the *Venturer 12* appointment; Lindstrom will be second in command. Their relationship remains uncomfortably platonic in the subsequent novels.

Bruce's obsessive search for the ruthless and elusive aliens called "Kilroys" unifies *Seed of Stars, The Neutral Stars,* and *Where No Stars Guide,* the last written by Kippax alone. Continuing frustrations with alien contact are paralleled by political intrigue and estrangements, betrayals and occasional reconcilations between men and women. However, characters in the series by and large are too crudely drawn for their vulnerabilities to arouse sympathy. The Space Corps has a sentimental, toy-soldier quality. Although the authors take pains to show a sexually and racially integrated Corps drawn from all corners of the Earth, clumsy, insensitive writing results in unintended racial and sexual stereotyping.

More effective are Kippax's short stories, of which he wrote more than thirty between 1955 and 1961. "No Certain Armour," a Space Corps story, stresses the importance of personal responsibility and self-respect in a dangerous universe. More compelling in mood and treatment is "Blood Offering," a compact and dramatic fantasy set on an isolated tropical island. The focus is yet another prickly male-female relationship—a duel of wills between Tod Baines, a brash Australian storekeeper, and Mama Noi, an Old Polynesian witch who demands tribute on behalf of the Shark God. Baines resists the crone's petty extortions, egged on by a scornful Chinese accountant who is at odds with a huge native fisherman over the favours of an island girl. These interwoven conflicts climax in a frightening, ambiguous midnight confrontation with the Shark God that prefigures Tom Bruce's fleeting contacts with the Kilroys.

Kippax's strongly traditional work utilizes popular science fiction and fantasy motifs to remind us that gulfs—whether of water, space, or attitude—can be terrible indeed. But perfunctory writing and avoidance of innovation often blunts the impact of his message.

—Vince Kohler

KIRKWOOD, James. See **SHEFFIELD, Charles.**

KLINE, Otis Adelbert. American. Born in Chicago, Illinois, 1 July 1891. Composer and songwriter, then music publisher, film writer, and editor: Editor, *Weird Tales,* Chicago, 1924; Founder, Otis Kline Associates, literary agency. *Died 24 October 1946.*

SCIENCE-FICTION PUBLICATIONS

Novels (series: Robert Grandon; Jan; Mars)

The Planet of Peril (Grandon). Chicago, McClurg, 1929.
Maza of the Moon. Chicago, McClurg, 1930.
The Prince of Peril (Grandon). Chicago, McClurg, 1930.
Call of the Savage. New York, Clode, 1937; as *Jan of the Jungle,* New York, Ace, 1966.
The Port of Peril (Grandon). Providence, Rhode Island, Grandon, 1949.
The Swordsman of Mars. New York, Avalon, 1960.
The Outlaws of Mars. New York, Avalon, 1961.
Tam, Son of the Tiger. New York, Avalon, 1962.
Jan in India. Lakemont, Georgia, Fictioneer, 1974.

Short Stories

The Man Who Limped and Other Stories. Hollywood, Saint, 1946.
Stories. Oak Lawn, Illinois, Weinberg, 1975.

*   *   *

Otis Adelbert Kline, whose literary career flourished in the 1920's and 1930's, never aimed higher than the prevailing tastes of those who read the pulp magazines *Weird Tales, Argosy,* and *Amazing Stories,* in which he published most of his stories. He was clearly influenced by and competed with his contemporaries Edgar Rice Burroughs, A. Merritt, and H. P. Lovecraft, and made no apologies for pandering to the popular taste for formula adventure stories. His work as a literary agent kept him abreast of whatever appealed to the popular imagination, and he worked these interests into his stories. His SF was of the fantastic variety denounced by Gernsback in the 1930's, Campbell in the 1940's, and Gold in the 1950's, who were committed to making SF respectable among adult readers. Had Kline been writing in the 1950's and 1960's, he would probably have been turning out the same formula stories with New Wave embellishments.

Kline's costume adventure melodramas are SF in the limited sense that he made use of conventions like psi powers, rocket travel, ray guns, and heavy doses of ritualism, totemism, and primitive religion borrowed from Frazer, Malinowski, and other anthropologists whose ideas of primitive social and religious customs had begun to stir the popular imagination. In truth, little beyond the accessories distinguish the SF from, say, the oriental adventures of the Dragoman series (*The Man Who Limped*). Much of his fantastic SF belongs in that loose category known as "sword and sorcery."

Kline's imagination was highly visual and his storytelling techniques were clearly shaped by his film-writing experiences. Whatever the costumes, settings, and properties, his stories are built out of the simplest formulas of the adventure-suspense story, and his characters are stock types familiar to anyone who has seen the old Buck Rogers serials. Like Burroughs, Kline had his series of Mars and Venus stories. The latter (the Robert Grandon series) proved very popular, and perhaps should be taken as representative of Kline's most influential work in the genre.

Critical opinion on Kline has been largely negative. However, despite everything negative that has been said, including the more recently fashionable charges of racism and sexism (equally justified), there remains the embarrassing but undeniable power of Kline's naive handling of the formulas and conventions of exotic adventure. Kline's ideas are second-hand and his treatment of them trite, but that is the very heart of his appeal. He gives the reader the expected cliché, the familiar stereotype, the conventional adventure formula. No summary could do justice to his triteness, but the following vignette from "The Bride of Osiris" (1927) may stand as a fair sample of the action: "As he stood there in the midst of the hostile multitude, holding the half-fainting Doris and expecting instant death, Buell heard two sounds simultaneously—the twang of a bowstring and an encouraging shout from Rafferty." The power of such a passage may be of a low order, barely a notch above the boy's adventure stories of the time, and yet the reader may find a kind of delight encountering an almost pure example of the thriller whose only purpose is unreflective and mindless entertainment. That Kline succeeds at all is perhaps his revenge upon literary criticism.

Kline's most successful novel, and probably his best, is *Call of the Savage*. The novel was modelled on Kipling's *Jungle Books* and Hudson's *Green Mansions*, and exhibits Kline's ability to use mythic and archetypal story elements to entrap all but the most wary reader. *Call of the Savage* is fantasy rather than SF, but, as we have seen in Kline's other work, the differences as well as the resemblances are coincidental.

—Donald L. Lawler

KNEALE, (Thomas) Nigel. British. Born in Barrow-in-Furness, Lancashire, 28 April 1922. Educated at Douglas High School, Isle of Man; Royal Academy of Dramatic Art, London, 1946-48. Married the writer Judith Kerr in 1954; one daughter and one son. Actor, Stratford upon Avon, 1948-49; staff member, BBC Television, London, 1951-55. Recipient: Maugham Award, 1950. Agent: Douglas Rae (Management) Ltd., 28 Charing Cross Road, London WC2H 0DB, England.

PUBLICATIONS

Novel

Quatermass. London, Hutchinson, 1979.

Short Stories

Tomato Cain and Other Stories. London, Collins, 1949; New York, Knopf, 1950.

Plays

The Quatermass Experiment (televised, 1953). London, Penguin, 1959.
Quatermass II (televised, 1955). London, Penguin, 1960.

Quatermass and the Pit (televised, 1959). London, Penguin, 1960.
The Year of the Sex Olympics and Other TV Plays (includes *The Road* and *The Stone Tape*). London, Ferret Fantasy, 1976.

Screenplays: *Quatermass II* (*Enemy from Space*), with Val Guest, 1957; *The Abominable Snowman*, 1957; *Look Back in Anger*, with John Osborne, 1959; *The Entertainer*, with John Osborne, 1960; *HMS Defiant* (*Damn the Defiant*), with Edmund North, 1962; *First Men in the Moon*, with Jan Read, 1964; *The Witches*, 1966; *Quatermass and the Pit* (*5,000,000 Years to Earth*), 1967; *The Quatermass Conclusion*, 1979.

Television Plays: *The Quatermass Experiment*, 1953; *Nineteen Eighty-Four*, from the novel by Orwell, 1954; *The Creature*, 1955; *Quatermass II*, 1955; *Mrs. Wickens in the Fall*, 1956; *Quatermass and the Pit*, 1959; *The Road*, 1963; *The Crunch*, 1964; *The Year of the Sex Olympics*, 1967; *Bam! Pow! Zapp!*, 1969; *Wine of India*, 1970; *The Chopper*, 1971; *The Stone Tape*, 1972; *Jack and the Beanstalk*, 1974; *Murrain*, 1975; *Buddyboy*, 1976; *During Barty's Party*, 1976; *Special Offer*, 1976; *The Dummy*, 1976; *Baby*, 1976; *What Big Eyes*, 1976; *Quatermass*, 1979; *Kinvig* series, 1981.

*

Nigel Kneale comments:
I have always been a scriptwriter for television and films because that's what I like doing best. I don't regard myself as a science fiction writer, and the list above confirms this. Looking through this list I wondered what other things I wrote. The answer, of course, is things that didn't get made. Some of my best screenplays, from Huxley, Lawrence, and the like, went down with collapsing film companies. More rarely, but more painfully, there were stillborn TV originals, like *The Big Big Giggle*, a serial about a teenage suicide craze, wiped out by high cost and official nervousness that was probably justified (it could have been dangerous). Or *Crow*, about the slave trade and not dangerous at all, victim of an internal squabble in a TV company. I just have to be grateful for all those that *did* get made.

*   *   *

With a few notable exceptions, most of them in recent years, movies and television have not been kind to science fiction. The speculative ideas that characterize what is best in the genre have proven difficult to translate into visual media without interrupting the action with long expository speeches, while the spectacular visual surfaces that science-fiction narratives afford have been all too tempting to filmmakers. As a result, few science-fiction writers have been able to work with success in the media, and fewer still have managed to build their primary reputation as a media writer of science fiction. Nigel Kneale is a member of this select latter group. The three television serials concerning Professor Bernard Quatermass that he wrote for the BBC between 1953 and 1959—all three of which were subsequently published in book form and adapted as feature films—established a standard for the televised science-fciton horror story that has seldom been surpassed.

Kneale had little direct experience as a science-fiction writer before joining the BBC, although a few of his short stories from *Tomato Cain* are small masterpieces of weird fiction. While at the BBC, Kneale's plays included an adaptation for television of Orwell's *Nineteen Eighty-Four* and an original play about the abominable snowman called *The Creature* (filmed as *The*

Abominable Snowman). But it was his 1953 six-part sequel *The Quatermass Experiment* that quickly established his reputation as a convincing dramatist of suspense thrillers. This tale of an alien life form that takes over the body of the lone survivor of the first space mission and metamorphoses into a hideous monster back on Earth, despite occasional absurdities (super-scientist Quatermass finally succeeds in literally *talking* the monster to death), reveals an ear for convincing dialogue, an awareness of the dramatic possibilities of the television medium (such as the use of "newscasters" to carry forth the action), and a talent for working serious issues and concepts into a fast-moving dramatic narrative. Though Quatermass is a scientist-hero in the mold of Conan Doyle's Professor Challenger, Kneale makes some pointed observations about the morality of scientific research and the relationship of government and the journalistic media to such research.

Professor Quatermass continued his fight against bureaucracy and journalistic sensationalism in two subsequent serials. *Quatermass II* concerns the attempt of an alien civilization to establish colonies on Earth by converting human workers into zombie-like slaves; it is perhaps the weakest of the three serials. *Quatermass and the Pit* is perhaps the strongest: a subway excavation in a reputedly haunted area uncovers an ancient alien spaceship which, when activated, reveals that legends of the devil are based on race memories of the aliens from Mars who once tried to conquer Earth—and in the process created us. The mix of myth, supernaturalism, and science fiction works well, and predates by several years cult rumors of gods from outer space. A fourth installment in the Quatermass series, *The Quatermass Conclusion,* was filmed in 1979.

Kneale worked on other screenplays, most notably the film adaptations of two John Osborne plays and an adaptation of Wells's *First Men in the Moon,* which he gave a characteristic twist by casting the story as a flashback told more than a half-century later by a survivor of the expedition whose secret is revealed only when the "official" first moon-landing party comes across the remnants of the earlier adventurers. Here, as in the Quatermass serials, Kneale's ironic humor, his deftness in sketching minor characters, and his sense of dramatic structure provide a strong script. Though he has shown little inclination to move beyond the horror-suspense school of science fiction, Kneale has contributed significantly to the genre's growth in the media.

—Gary K. Wolfe

KNIGHT, Damon (Francis). American. Born in Baker, Oregon, 19 September 1922. Educated at Hood River High School, Oregon; WPA Art Center, Salem, Oregon, 1940-41. Married 1) Gertrud Werndl; 2) Helen Schlaz; 3) Kate Wilhelm, *q. v.,* in 1963; four children. Free-lance writer: Assistant Editor, Popular Publications, 1943-44, 1949-50; Editor, *Worlds Beyond,* 1950-51; Book Editor, *Science Fiction Adventures, 1953-54; Editor, If,* 1958-59; Book Editor, *Fantasy and Science Fiction,* 1959-60; editorial consultant, Berkley Books, 1960-66. Co-Founding Director, Milford Science Fiction Writers' Conference, 1956. Since 1967, Lecturer, Clarion Workshop in Science Fiction and Fantasy. Founder, 1965, and President, 1965-67, Science Fiction Writers of America. Recipient: Hugo Award, for non-fiction, 1956; Pilgrim Award, 1975. Address: 1645 Horn Lane, Eugene, Oregon 97404, U.S.A.

SCIENCE-FICTION PUBLICATIONS

Novels

Hell's Pavement. New York, Lion, 1955; London, Banner, 1958; as *Analogue Men,* New York, Berkley, 1962.
The People Maker. Rockville Centre, New York, Zenith, 1959; revised edition, as *A for Anything,* London, New English Library, 1961; New York, Berkley, 1965.
Masters of Evolution. New York, Ace, 1959.
The Sun Saboteurs. New York, Ace, 1961; as *The Earth Quarter* (with *World Without Children*), New York, Lancer, 1970.
Beyond the Barrier. New York, Doubleday, and London, Gollancz, 1964.
Mind Switch. New York, Berkley, 1965; as *The Other Foot,* London, Whiting and Wheaton, 1966.
The Rithian Terror. New York, Ace, 1965.
Three Novels: Rule Golden, Natural State, The Dying Man. New York, Doubleday, and London, Gollancz, 1967; as *Natural State and Other Stories,* London, Pan, 1975.
Two Novels (*The Earth Quarter* and *Double Meaning*). London, Gollancz, 1974.
The World and Thorinn. New York, Berkley, 1981.
The Man in the Tree. New York, Berkley, 1984; London, Gollancz, 1985.

Short Stories

Far Out. New York, Simon and Schuster, and London, Gollancz, 1961.
In Deep. New York, Berkley, 1963; London, Gollancz, 1964.
Off Center. New York, Ace, 1965; London, Gollancz, 1969.
Turning On. New York, Doubleday, 1966; London, Gollancz, 1967.
The Best of Damon Knight. New York, Doubleday, 1976.
Rule Golden and Other Stories. New York, Avon, 1979.

Uncollected Short Stories

"I See You," in *Best Science Fiction of the Year 6,* edited by Terry Carr. New York, Holt Rinehart, and London, Gollancz, 1977.
"Forever," in *The Best Science Fiction of the Year 11,* edited by Terry Carr. New York, Pocket Books, 1982.
"Azumuth 1, 2, 3 . . . ," in *Isaac Asimov's Science Fiction Magazine* (New York), June 1982.
"Tarcan of the Hoboes," in *Fantasy and Science Fiction* (New York), October 1982.
"La Ronde," in *Fantasy and Science Fiction* (New York), October 1983.
"The Very Objectionable Mr. Clegg," in *Isaac Asimov's Science Fiction Magazine* (New York), Mid-December 1984.
"CV," in *Fantasy and Science Fiction* (New York), January and February 1985.

OTHER PUBLICATIONS

Other

In Search of Wonder. Chicago, Advent, 1956; revised edition, 1967.
Charles Fort, Prophet of the Unexplained. New York, Doubleday, 1970; London, Gollancz, 1971.
The Futurians: The Story of the Science Fiction "Family" of the 30's That Produced Today's Top SF Writers and Editors. New York, Day, 1977.

Better Than One, with Kate Wilhelm. Cambridge, Massachusetts, NESFA Press, 1980.
Creating Short Fiction. Cincinnati, Writer's Digest, 1981.

Editor, *A Century of Science Fiction*. New York, Simon and Schuster, 1962; London, Gollancz, 1963.
Editor, *First Flight*. New York, Lancer, 1963; as *Now Begins Tomorrow*, 1969; revised edition, with Martin H. Greenberg and Joseph D. Olander, as *First Voyages*, New York, Avon, 1981.
Editor, *A Century of Great Short Science Fiction Novels*. New York, Delacorte Press, 1964; London, Gollancz, 1965.
Editor, *Tomorrow x 4*. New York, Fawcett, 1964; London, Coronet, 1967.
Editor, and Translator, *Thirteen French Science-Fiction Stories*. New York, Bantam, and London, Corgi, 1965.
Editor, *Beyond Tomorrow*. New York, Harper, 1965; London, Gollancz, 1968.
Editor, *The Dark Side*. New York, Doubleday, 1965; London, Dobson, 1966.
Editor, *The Shape of Things*. New York, Popular Library, 1965.
Editor, *Nebula Award Stories 1965*. New York, Doubleday, 1966; London, Gollancz, 1967.
Editor, *Cities of Wonder*. New York, Doubleday, 1966; London, Dobson, 1968.
Editor, *Orbit 1-21*. New York, Putnam, 12 vols., 1966-73, New York, Berkley, 1 vol., 1974, New York, Harper, 8 vols., 1974-80; vol. 1, London, Whiting and Wheaton, 1966; vol. 2, London, Rapp and Whiting, 1968.
Editor, *Science Fiction Inventions*. New York, Lancer, 1967.
Editor, *Worlds to Come*. New York, Harper, 1967; London, Gollancz, 1969.
Editor, *The Metal Smile*. New York, Belmont, 1968.
Editor, *One Hundred Years of Science Fiction*. New York, Simon and Schuster, 1968; London, Gollancz, 1969.
Editor, *Toward Infinity*. New York, Simon and Schuster, 1968; London, Gollancz, 1970.
Editor, *Dimension X* (for children). New York, Simon and Schuster, 1970; London, Gollancz, 1972.
Editor, *First Contact*. New York, Pinnacle, 1971.
Editor, *A Pocketful of Stars*. New York, Doubleday, 1971; London, Gollancz, 1972.
Editor, *Perchance to Dream*. New York, Doubleday, 1972; London, Gollancz, 1974.
Editor, *A Science Fiction Argosy*. New York, Simon and Schuster, 1972; London, Gollancz, 1973.
Editor, *Tomorrow and Tomorrow*. New York, Simon and Schuster, 1973; London, Gollancz, 1974.
Editor, *The Golden Road*. New York, Simon and Schuster, 1973; London, Gollancz, 1974.
Editor, *Happy Endings*. Indianapolis, Bobbs Merrill, 1974.
Editor, *Elsewhere x 3*. London, Coronet, 1974.
Editor, *A Shocking Thing*. New York, Pocket Books, 1974.
Editor, *Best Stories from Orbit 1-10*. New York, Berkley, 1975.
Editor, *Science Fiction of the Thirties*. Indianapolis, Bobbs Merrill, 1975.
Editor, *Westerns of the 40's: Classics from the Great Pulps*. Indianapolis, Bobbs Merrill, 1977.
Editor, *Turning Points: Essays on the Art of Science Fiction*. New York, Harper, 1977.
Editor, *The Clarion Awards*. New York, Doubleday, 1984.

Translator, *Ashes, Ashes,* by René Barjavel. New York, Doubleday, 1967.

*   *   *

Damon Knight, deservedly lauded as a critic and editor, is a competent fiction writer cursed with a vivid imagination, a clear vision of cosmic morality, an understanding of the arbitrariness of human value judgments, and a sardonic sense of humor that prevents him from taking most of it seriously. Often the inevitable irony appears in a sudden plot twist or in the reader's perception of a pun that the story is built on, a technique that in some cases, such as "To Serve Man," becomes thematic as well as technical. In this piece, in which an alien race's benevolence toward humans turns out to have a culinary motive, the pun is turned to a serious criticsm of egocentric self-deception. At other times, a pun is all the story has to offer, as in, for example. "Eripmav," in which a vampire on a vegetable world is killed with a steak through its heart. Perhaps the most complexly ironic title in the whole body of work is "Not with a Bang"—the earliest story chosen by the author for *The Best of Damon Knight*—in which the last man on Earth woos and finally wins the last woman, a prudish spinster, only to find himself paralyzed in the Men's Room—which her prudery will not allow her to enter—just before consummating their wedded bliss. And so the world ends in an allusion to T. S. Eliot, a poet whose influence shows clearly in Knight's work.

Although Knight has produced a number of novels, complete with action and adventure—most of them expanded from the shorter forms in which he is most facile—he works best at the medium length represented by *Three Novels*. His ironic perspective allows him a sharp compression of events into key scenes which are effectively juxtaposed. The result recalls the episodic quality of some of the language's finest satirists, such as Swift and Twain; Knight's choices of theme and situation, and his use of language, are also reminiscent of theirs. He does not often extrapolate from real world situations, although *Analogue Men* partially does that; more often he recasts real-world situations in estranged form for ironic perspective: "Earth Quarter" (expanded into *The Sun Saboteurs*) could be any Third World ghetto in any advanced country; *The Rithian Terror* features a slightly disguised British Empire, complete with despised New World colonials; *A for Anything* moves from a 19th-century American plantation setting to a reprise of imperial Rome.

More characteristic of Knight's whole body of work are *The World and Thorinn* and *The Man in the Tree*, which rely on myth rather than history for their structuring narrative. His basic assumption, that human nature does not change, is very clearly stated in "Time Enough": we are and always will be guilty of the same flaws we always have been. Those flaws provide the sharper, more serious ironies of his work. In such moral fables as "Ask Me Anything," "Man in the Jar," "A Thing of Beauty," "Auto-da-Fé," "Second Class Citizen," and "Collector's Item" (formerly "The End of the Search"), basic human motivations—greed, lust for power or knowledge, anthropocentrism—end by frustrating themselves in plots that just miss being tragic because the human motive is never presented as quite admirable. "The Country of the Kind" also just misses the tragic dimension for a slightly different reason: by letting us share the point of view of the protagonist, Knight makes us almost sympathize with the only cruel and violent—and insane—member of our species left in a world of gentle benevolence. The effect is similar to that achieved by Anthony Burgess in *A Clockwork Orange*. How such a thing can happen to us as readers is explained fictionally in "The Enemy" in which a human explorer meets and is killed by an evil alien more fitted to survive then she—and which she finds beautiful; one of our flaws is that we find competent evil attractive, even at our own expense.

Unlike many SF writers concerned with humanity's destructive environmental impact, Knight does not blame technology itself; as in "Idiot Stick," everything depends on which end of the tool the idiot is on. Even in his most clearly anti-machine story, "Natural State" (a tighter version of the expanded *Masters of Evolution*), a biological technology replaces the mechanical one; nature is still manipulated, although perhaps more cooperatively than antagonistically. But human nature is not so easily handled.

In *The Sun Saboteurs* human nature makes us unfit for a place in the galactic civilization; in "Collector's Item" it makes us unfit for survival. Attempts to control our anti-social insanities in *Analogue Men* result in still greater insanity. In *The Rithian Terror* (expanded from "Double Meaning") our rigidly serious self-importance defeats us. In "The Beachcomber" sheer accident can reduce all of our grand schemes—even in a future, evolved state—to picking up pebbles on the beach.

Even human attempts at morality and ethics come to naught when they come up against the needs of survival, in *A for Anything*. Some kind of improvement—although not necessarily a welcome one—might result from a mental cross of an individual human with a superior alien, as in "Four in One" or *Beyond the Barrier* (expanded from "The Tree of Time"), in which Knight nearly tricks us out of species chauvinism with a bit of manipulation more difficult than that of "The Country of the Kind." Even this unsavory hope is unlikely; we are so flawed that in *Mind Switch* (expanded from "A Visitor at the Zoo"), an alien mind is corrupted by transfer into a human body, even with a built-in sex change. Our psyches are, if anything, less trustworthy; in "Masks" an incorruptible metal body corrupts a human mind. There is also little hope of external salvation. "Rule Golden," which remakes the Christ myth in modern iconography, gives us a paradise at the cost of what we might recognize as human and at the cost of the evolutionary process that has made us what we are. In such a universe even the power of love can not cope with hate, and hate leads to extinction in "Stranger Station." Perhaps the only possible Messiah may be that of "What Rough Beast" who brings in the Kingdom because he is afraid of people—and at the expense of the lives, and the world, of those people who expect him to save them from themselves. In *The Man in the Tree*, a more elaborate and successful ironic rendering of the Christ story, the Messiah saves himself into an alternate universe and leaves this world to its own devices.

This body of work is on the whole a black comedy, full of ironies and bitter laughter. But the despair that accompanies the logic of Knight's anatomy of the human condition has its compensations. If there is no hope for us, we can still take pleasure where we may: in the fantastic chance of being possessed by friendly demons, in "Be My Guest"; in the archetypal insane adventure of love in "Mary" (formerly "An Ancient Madness"); in the discovery of intimacy in strange places in "To the Pure." Or ultimately in the bitter-sweet knowledge that we, like all things, will pass away. In "The Dying Man" (formerly "Dio"), Knight produces one of his strongest stories. The advent of death into a world of immortals—the reversal of a time-worn story line—brings awareness that human mortality also gives us maturity, depth, strength, balance; and we are led to see that death is just. In this perception is the final escape from human egocentrism. If that perception is too much for us, we can escape, sadly, as in "The Handler," into the fantasy of conscious illusion to find some sort of artificial joy. Nevertheless, as the hero of *The World and Thorinn* concludes, the best way for people to live is the way that gives them the greatest freedom to choose how, whatever the cost.

All in all, Damon Knight's fiction has a sane, tough-minded wholeness. It does not often give us brilliance; it seldom gives us

hope; it does not even give us much that is fundamentally new. Part of its strength—ironic humor—is also sometimes its weakness. But it does give us an imaginatively different look—sometimes with genuine mythic power—at ideas as old as human kind, still built into the very marrow of our species. In the words of a character from *Analogue Men*, speaking of a task similar to Knight's, though it may promise us "nothing except the rewards of competence and of curiosity, and an occasional windfall of laughter . . . it is enough. " Knight's fiction deserves to share the accolades his criticism and his editing have already earned.

—Robert L. Jones

KNIGHT, Norman L(ouis). American. Born in St. Joseph, Missouri, 21 September 1895. Educated at St. Joseph Junior College, A. A. 1918; George Washington University, Washington, D. C., B. S. in chemical engineering 1925. Served in the United States Army Field Artillery, 1918-19. Married Marie Sarah Yenn in 1921; one daughter. Worked for the Department of Agriculture: assistant observer, Davenport, Iowa, 1919-20, and observer and code translator, Washington, D. C., Weather Bureau; analytical chemist in Washington, D. C., 1925-29, Chicago, 1929, St. Louis, 1929-40, Chicago, 1940-50, and Beltsville, Maryland, 1950-64, Insecticide Division; retired in 1964: Merit Award, 1962. *Died 19 April 1972.*

SCIENCE-FICTION PUBLICATIONS

Novel

A Torrent of Faces, with James Blish. New York, Doubleday, 1967; London, Faber, 1968.

Uncollected Short Stories

"Frontier of the Unknown," in *Astounding* (New York), July 1937.
"Isle of the Golden Swarm," in *Astounding* (New York), June 1938.
"Saurian Valedictory," in *Astounding* (New York), January 1939.
"Bombardment in Reverse," in *Astounding* (New York), February 1940.
"The Testament of Akubii," in *Astounding* (New York), June 1940.
"Fugitive from Vanguard," in *Astounding* (New York), January 1942.
"Kilgallen's Lunar Legacy," in *Astounding* (New York), August 1942.
"Once in a Blue Moon," in *Future* (New York), August 1942.
"Short-Circuited Probability," in *Best of Science Fiction,* edited by Groff Conklin. New York, Crown, 1946.
"Crisis in Utopia," in *Five Science Fiction Novels,* edited by Martin H. Greenberg. New York, Gnome Press, 1952; as *Crucible of Power,* London, Lane, 1953.
"The Piper of Dis," in *Galaxy* (New York), August 1966.
"To Love Another," in *Analog* (New York), April 1967.

*   *   *

Norman L. Knight published his first story in *Astounding* in 1937, worked most of his life as a chemist specializing in pesticides, and finally published his most ambitious science fiction work in collaboration with the master, James Blish, in 1967. One theme and one setting, in fact, kept reappearing in the early stories; and the importance of that set of images in the novel suggests that Knight may have been the more seminal partner in the collaboration—if not the more polished stylist. Images that led eventually to the masterpiece, *A Torrent of Faces*, can be seen as early as the serialized novel "Frontier of the Unknown," in which a deep-sea diver moves in "a twilight pierced by a million uneasy, shifting, flickering ghosts of slanting, green-tinged sun rays. " This crude flood of modifiers was followed by another two-part novel, "Crisis in Utopia," in which Knight also anticipates his work with Blish. Knight includes here the fully developed conception and description of the undersea race of human mutants called Tritons. The writing is a bit more subtle, and Knight's ideas on the effects of managed evolution are suggestive.

Nevertheless, these early stories are dominated by the usual villains of melodrama and the crude overwriting that so often seems the appropriate literary parallel to the line-drawing illustrations of the early pulp magazines. The novel, however, is the culmination of all this. One of the most popular sections of the novel, "The Shipwrecked Hotel," is a polished undersea disaster epic in which the Triton race plays a major role; Triton characters are fully developed throughout the book, and much of the action takes place undersea. Also, by the time of this later work the earth itself has replaced the melodramatic villains as a key protagonist—a much greater literary accomplishment. The individual extrapolations in the novel about living conditions in a future with one trillion inhabitants on earth are many and richly developed, and the writing shows marked improvement over the early Knight extrapolations on the sea and on Utopia. Blish was a good teacher and a good collaborator for Knight's valuable ideas on the future, on evolution, and on accompanying disasters.

—Donald M. Hassler

KNOX, Calvin M. See **SILVERBERG, Robert.**

KOONTZ, Dean R(ay). Has also written as David Axton; Brian Coffey; Deanna Dwyer; K. R. Dwyer; John Hill; Leigh Nichols; Anthony North; Owen West. American. Born in Everett, Pennsylvania, 9 July 1945. B. A. in English. Married Gerda Ann Cerra in 1966. Worked in a federal government poverty-alleviation program, then high school English teacher. Since 1969, full-time writer. Lives in Orange, California. Agent: Harold Ober Associates, 40 East 49th Street, New York, New York 10017, U.S.A.

SCIENCE-FICTION PUBLICATIONS

Novels

Star Quest. New York, Ace, 1968.
The Fall of the Dream Machine. New York, Ace, 1969.
Fear That Man. New York, Ace, 1969.

The Dark Symphony. New York, Lancer, 1970.
Hell's Gate. New York, Lancer, 1970.
Dark of the Woods. New York, Ace, 1970.
Beastchild. New York, Lancer, 1970.
Anti-Man. New York, Paperback Library, 1970.
The Flesh in the Furnace. New York, Bantam, 1972.
A Darkness in My Soul. New York, DAW, 1972; London, Dobson, 1979.
Time Thieves. New York, Ace, 1972; London, Dobson, 1977.
Warlock, New York, Lancer, 1972.
Starblood. New York, Lancer, 1972.
Demon Seed. New York, Bantam, 1973; London, Corgi, 1977.
A Werewolf among Us. New York, Ballantine, 1973.
The Haunted Earth. New York, Lancer, 1973.
Nightmare Journey. New York, Berkley, 1975.
The Long Sleep (as John Hill). New York, Popular Library, 1975.

Short Stories

Soft Come the Dragons. New York, Ace, 1970.

Uncollected Short Stories

"Bruno," in *Fantasy and Science Fiction* (New York), April 1971.
"Altarboy," in *Infinity 3,* edited by Robert Hoskins. New York, Lancer, 1972.
"A Mouse in the Walls of the Global Village," in *Again, Dangerous Visions,* edited by Harlan Ellison. New York, Doubleday, 1972; London, Millington, 1976.
"Ollie's Hands," in *Infinity 4,* edited by Robert Hoskins. New York, Lancer, 1972.
"Cosmic Sin," in *Fantasy and Science Fiction* (New York), February 1972.
"Gravyworld," in *Infinity 5,* edited by Robert Hoskins. New York, Lancer, 1973.
"The Sinless Child," in *Flame Tree Planet,* edited by Roger Elwood. St. Louis, Concordia, 1973.
"Terra Phobia," in *Androids, Time Machines, and Blue Giraffes,* edited by Roger Elwood and Vic Ghidalia. Chicago, Follett, 1973.
"The Undercity," in *Future City,* edited by Roger Elwood. New York, Simon and Schuster, 1973.
"Wake Up to Thunder," in *Children of Infinity,* edited by Roger Elwood. New York, Putnam, 1974.
"We Three," in *Final Stage,* edited by Edward L. Ferman and Barry N. Malzberg. New York, Charterhouse, 1974.

OTHER PUBLICATIONS

Novels

The Crimson Witch. New York, Curtis, 1971.
Hanging On. New York, Evans, 1973; London, Barrie and Jenkins, 1974.
After the Last Rece. New York, Atheneum, 1974.
Strike Deep (an Anthony North). New York, Dial Press, 1974.
Prison of Ice (as David Axton). Philadelphia, Lippincott, and London, W. H. Allen, 1976.
Night Chills. New York, Atheneum, 1976; London, W. H. Allen, 1977.
The Vision. New York, Putnam, 1977; London, Corgi, 1980.
Whispers. New York, Putnam, 1980; London, W. H. Allen, 1981.
The Funhouse (novelization of screenplay; as Owen West). New

York, Jove, 1980; London, Sphere, 1981.

The Mask (as Owen West). New York, Jove, 1981; London, Coronet, 1983.

Phantoms. New York, Putnam, and London, W. H. Allen, 1983.

Darkness Comes. London, W. H. Allen, 1984; as *Darkfall*, New York, Berkley, 1984.

Novels as Deanna Dwyer

The Demon Child. New York, Lancer, 1971.
Legacy of Terror. New York, Lancer, 1971.
Children of the Storm. New York, Lancer, 1972.
The Dark of Summer. New York, Lancer, 1972.
Dance with the Devil. New York, Lancer, 1973.

Novels as K. R. Dwyer

Chase. New York, Random House, 1972; London, Barker, 1974.

Shattered. New York, Random House, 1973; London, Barker, 1974.

Dragonfly. New York, Random House, 1975; London, Davies, 1977.

Novels as Brian Coffey

Blood Risk. Indianapolis, Bobbs Merrill, 1973; London, Barker, 1974.

Surrounded. Indianapolis, Bobbs Merrill. 1974; London, Barker, 1975.

The Wall of Masks Indianapolis, Bobbs Merrill, 1975.

The Face of Fear. Indianapolis, Bobbs Merrill, 1977; as K. R. Dwyer, London, Davies 1978.

The Voice of the Night. New York, Doubleday, 1980; London, Hale, 1981.

Novels as Leigh Nichols

The Key to Midnight. New York, Pocket Books, 1979; London, Magnum, 1980.

The Eyes of Darkness. New York, Pocket Books, 1981; London, Fontana, 1982.

The House of Thunder. New York, Pocket Books, 1982; London, Fontana, 1983.

Twilight. New York, Pocket Books, and London, Fontana, 1984.

Other

The Pig Society, with Gerda Koontz. Los Angeles, Aware Press, 1970.

The Underground Lifestyles Handbook, with Gerda Koontz, Los Angeles, Aware Press, 1970.

Writing Popular Fiction. Cincinnati, Writer's Digest, 1973.

How to Write Best-Selling Fiction. Cincinnati, Writer's Digest, and London, Poplar Press. 1981.

*   *   *

Dean R. Koontz's best science fiction was written before 1980; since then he more properly can be called a writer of horror novels. His best work is a convincing amalgam of sympathetic characters and quirky plots, but much of his work has regressed to the sterotyped characters, ritualistic journeys, and heroic feats found in hard-core SF before 1960.

Kootz is a writer of the New Wave in science fiction, a trend characterized by authors with humanities rather than science backgrounds. Certainly, Koontz's themes are rigorously chosen and often intriguing. His best-known woks concern the theme of the malevolent child, of innocence turned inside out; he handles the notion in *Beastchild*, in *A Darkness in My Soul*, in which a mutant becomes God, and quite compellingly in *Demon Steed* in which a super-computer creates its own genetic material which it "implants" into a human woman. In "We Three" genetically mutated children wish away harsh parents, then neighbors, then the entire world through their extra-sensory powers.

This theme is a corollary to Koontz's major concern: what it means to be human. In several works on robots, particularly the crisply written "The Night of the Storm," Koontz explores the theme. The robot-protagonist Suranov is bored by his centralised, staid society "peopled" by robots. Humans are rumored to exist, much to the horror of the robots, whose prime rule is that the universe is logical, a dictum which the existence of humans challenges. The story also begins a robotics series carried on by New Wave writers Pamela Sargent and George Zebrowski, among others, in the *Continuum* series. The more turgid novel *Anti-Man* presents an android who changes into a new form of being, to the consternation of the human protagonist. This novel explores the Frankenstein theme—the relationship of creator and his creation—as does *Demon Seed*.

Beginning with his first story, "Soft Come the Dragons," Koontz clearly favors intuition and emotion as essential components of humanness, rather than logic and reason, which can be assigned to machines. Perhaps his best long work, *A Werewolf among Us* presents a protagonist who is a cyberdective, a human whose brain is electronically and physically linked to a portable computer on his chest. Using a classic Agatha Christie plot, Koontz combines science fiction and detective genres. Members of a family are being murdered, the remaining members of the family are suspects, and the reader is presented with clues. However, the main conflict in the novel is psychological: when the human half of the cyberdective realizes the murderer is another robot, his computer half rejects the notion as illogical.

Koontz also treats themes current in popular culture. Marshall McLuhan's *The Medium Is the Massage* was the origin for "A Mouse in the Walls of the Global Village," and "The Psychedelic Children" projects a society one generation hence in which the children whose parents took LSD in the late 1960's are mutants who are hunted by society. The anti-establishment bias of the 1960's is clear in Koontz's work. In *Dark of the Woods* an unimaginative, conformist society systematically eliminates aliens. In "The Twelfth Bed" old people are shut away in a nursing home run by robots.

When Koontz deals with the theme of the quest and the mythic journey, however, he writes sterotyped pulp science fiction. In *Anti-Man, Nightmare Journey, Dark of the Woods*, and *Warlock* a hero rebelling from society sets out on a trek, usually through a cold wilderness, in which he encounters strange beasts and exotic phenomena which he eventually overcomes. The women in these works are sex goddesses only, deferential to the hero, though, as Koontz condescendingly interjects, spunky.

More recently he has written a series of horror novels in the Stephen King mode. For example in *Darkfall* he uses a supernatural explanation—a hole through which spirits from hell creep—to subject people to frightening encounters with the forces of evil. Only the goodness of the hero can destroy the iniquity. While these are not strictly science fiction, they do represent Koontz's return to sympathetic characters. The men are strong but warm, the women beatiful but competent. Of these the best is *Phantoms* which uses a science-fiction premise as the explanation for the evil menace, in this case a genetically altered micro-organism. *Shattered,* first published under the name of K. R. Dwyer, also uses fully realized characters and a realistic premise.

Thus Koontz is at his best as a science-fiction writer. He reports he is presently interested in such genres as suspense, war tales, and crime stories. Koontz is certain to create suspenseful tales and sensitive character. If he returns to serious science fiction, he might be well advised to continue to explore his most productive theme of the Cartesian mind-body split and its consequences for what humans define as human. Koontz clearly defines a being as a human if the being feels, loves, and intuits, be that creature man, robot, or beast.

—Kathryn Lee Seidel

KORNBLUTH, C(yril) M. Also wrote as Simon Eisner; Cyril Judd; Jordan Park. American. Born in New York City, in 1923. Educated at the University of Chicago, B. A. Served in the infantry during World War II: Bronze Star. Married Mary G. Byers in 1944; two sons. Editor, Chicago office of Trans-Radio Press, 1949-51; free-lance writer after 1951. Recipient: Hugo Award, 1973. *Died 21 March 1958.*

SCIENCE-FICTION PUBLICATIONS

Novels

Gunner Cade (as Cyril Judd, with Judith Merril). New York, Simon and Schuster, 1952; London, Gollancz, 1964.
Outpost Mars (as Cyril Judd, with Judith Merril). New York, Abelard Press, 1952; London, New English Library, 1966; revised edition, as *Sin in Space,* New York, Galaxy, 1961.
Takeoff. New York, Doubleday, 1952.
The Space Merchants, with Frederik Pohl. New York, Ballantine, 1953; London, Heinemann, 1955.
The Syndic. Ne York, Doubleday, 1953; London, Faber, 1964.
Search the Sky, with Frederik Pohl. New York, Ballantine, 1954; London, Digit, 1960.
Gladiator-at-Law, with Frederik Pohl. New York, Ballantine, 1955; London, Digit, 1958.
Not This August. New York, Doubleday, 1955; as *Christmas Eve,* London, Joseph, 1956.
Wolfbane, with Frederik Pohl. New York, Ballantine, 1959; London, Gollancz, 1960.

Short Stories

The Explorers. New York, Ballantine, 1954.
The Mindworm and Other Stories. London, Joseph, 1955.
A Mile Beyond the Moon. New York, Doubleday, 1958.
The Marching Morons. New York, Ballantine, 1959.
The Wonder Effect, with Frederik Pohl. New York, Ballantine, 1962; London, Gollancz, 1967; revised edition, as *Critical Mass,* New York, Bantam, 1977.
Best SF Stories. London, Faber, 1968.
Thirteen O'Clock and Other Zero Stories, edited by James Blish. New York, Dell, 1970; London, Hale, 1972.
The Best of C. M. Kornbluth, edited by Frederik Pohl. New York, Doubleday, 1976.

OTHER PUBLICATIONS

Novels

The Naked Storm (as Simon Eisner). New York, Lion, 1952.
A Town Is Drowning, with Frederik Pohl. New York, Ballantine, 1955; London, Digit, 1960.
Presidential Year, with Frederik Pohl. New York, Ballantine, 1956.

Novels as Jordan Park

Half. New York, Lion, 1953.
Valerie. New York, Lion, 1953.
Sorority House, with Frederik Pohl. New York, Lion, 1956.
The Man of Cold Rages. New York, Pyramid, 1958.

Other

"The Failure of the Science Fiction Novel as Social Criticism," in *The Science Fiction Novel.* Chicago, Advent, 1969.

*   *   *

C. M. Kornbluth was a major talent of the specialty magazines in the 1940's and 1950's. Probably best known as a collaborator with Frederik Pohl on novels of social extrapolation, he was primarily a writer of short stories that frequently contrast cosmic affairs with mundane existence, sometimes to farcical, more often to sardonic, effect.

With Pohl, he helped produce a handful of lively, satiric novels that practically constitute a genre of their own: a brand of near-future dystopia, deriving in part from H. G. Wells, concentrating on one particular facet of society which becomes the dominant force in the world, as in *The Space Merchants* and *Gladiator-at-Law.* In *Search the Sky,* a much lighter and lesser work, the satire mutates into a picaresque romp, exposing Kornbluth's penchant for quickstep burlesque. The other two books, though, are characterized by a continual mordant wit in their serious development of the oppressive rule of socioeconomic institutions. Of course, these institutions are merely exaggerations of those already operating in the modern world, and are invariably connected to the realms of high finance and mass consumption, unlike say, the dystopian worlds of Zamyatin, Orwell, or even Huxley, which are more distinctly political and totalitarian, and in many ways less directly evolved from the contemporary milieus of those writers. In this regard, Pohl and Kornbluth are more Wellsian, more extrapolative as opposed to symbolic, and much more "radical" in concept and detail than either Huxley or Orwell. The cautionary aspects of *Space Merchants*—its background of overpopulation, scarcity of resources, pollution, and runaway commercial exploitation—have made it a canonical "prophetic novel" in the wider world outside science fiction.

Their last true collaboration, *Wolfbane,* also deals with a culture of several limited resources, but as a condition ostensibly imposed from outside, by outré alien pyramids who have stolen the Earth-Moon system away from the Sun. The book is almost pure adventure, verging on space opera at the close, but it begins in a setting of material and spiritual poverty acutely drawn in its every detail. Kornbluth never achieved the distinction apart from Pohl that he did alongside him; and Pohl was fond enough of their partnership to "collaborate" with Kornbluth even after the latter's death by working up stories from odd fragments or from their previous common property (*The Wonder Effect* is partly composed of these).

Kornbluth also collaborated with Judith Merril, as Cyril Judd, on *Outpost Mars* and *Gunner Cade*. The second is notable for its vivid evocation of a post-holocaust military brotherhood, a spiritual sort of Spartanism. In both, the setting is again a down-at-heels world, but neither story has the inventive brilliance of the major Pohl-Kornbluth novels. However, each of them concerns a legendary/mythic element that resolves itself as a modest distortion of the book's initial reality-frame. This thematic concern relates to Kornbluth's best short stories, many of which play with the penetration of everyday existence by the utterly fantastic, the occult, the arcane. Such a tendency may seem axiomatic for science fiction; in Kornbluth, it often ranges beyond the usual boundaries of 1950's SF in tales as diverse in tone as "The Cosmic Expense Account" and "The Last Man Left in the Bar."

On his own, he wrote only three SF novels, *Not This August, Takeoff,* and *The Syndic*. The first two are patent journeyman exercises, apparently slanted for marketing considerations. They are competent, straightforward thrillers, largely unexceptional, only possessing a certain crisp efficiency. The first is the least winsome, giving the drear account of what happens after the Soviets conquer the U.S.A. It reads like a script aimed at the slick magazines (in fact it was serialized in *Maclean's*) and later adapted to the SF market. *Takeoff* tells the more tolerable—but hoary—story of how an atomic scientist helps a bunch of teenagers build a moon rocket, with appropriate interference by foreign agents to provide a veneer of suspense. *The Syndic* is another matter. Though it seems oddly cobbled together, it is nevertheless quite engaging for much of its length and is Kornbluth's best solo novel. It incorporates satire, parody, homiletic fable, pulp adventure, and irrelevant moral lecture, accented by sudden left turns in the plot. Its primary narrative premise is a marvel of ironic supposition: the US government, for just cause, has been exiled to the unfriendly shores of a primitive Ireland by a coalition of laiser-faire smugglers and racketeers, the good-time guys and dolls of the Syndic. Ostensibly a straight adventure story, it ultimatley seems to be a loose composite of favorite crotchets, including a forceful depiction of earth-magic which somehow manages not to blow the narrative beyond the pale of mainline SF.

When Kornbluth truly excelled was in his shorter work, the bulk of which appeared in the collections *The Explorers, A Mile Beyond the Moon* and *The Marching Morons*. It is often madly comic; and as often sharp and deadly. At its best, it is brief, evocative, to the point; short on description, but full of vivid impressions; and usually possessed of a clearly developed moral thrust, if not always an explicit moral. His strong satiric mode slides easily into march-hare burlesque, in pieces like "Passion Pill," "Thirteen O'Clock," and "Virginia." The omnipresent sardonicism emerges most fiercely in tightly woven shorts like "The Words of Guru," "The Silly Season," and "The Rocket of 1955," but also in longer works like "Two Dooms" and "The Marching Morons." The latter two are Kornbluth's most visibly horatory stories, although neither exists simply for the sale of its overt "lesson." He also wrote pure, slick adventures, playful novelets like "The Slave" and "Make Mine Mars," which captivate by virtue of sheer readability, a deftness in the handling of stock figures and basic emotional appeals. And all the above, even the darkest tales, are rendered with a spritely touch; they do not sag in the middle, and there is ever a little crooked smile lurking somewhere in the corners.

Kornbluth's view of humanity may seem perplexing and inconsistent. He is sometimes accused of being a hard-case cynic, an elitist who views himself as above the common run. This is not entirely fallacious in light of "The Marching Morons"; in foreseeing a future populated mainly by just-plain-dopes, it is largely a metaphor for what Kornbluth saw around him in his own time. Yet he had a profound affection for lowly, downtrodden people, for stumblebums and gutter folk, and even some salesmen. In part it may have been the fondness of an aficionado, a collector of "characters." But he was not without a good deal of genuine sympathy, especially for those who were caught in situations they barely understood, like the deformed space pilot in "The Altar at Midnight," or for those who understood too well, like the narrator-physicist of the same story and the young genius of "Gomez." Better remembered, perhaps, are his treatment of workaday grifters and con-artists, like Honest John Barlow of "Morons" or the sly narrator of "1955"—people who have no sympathy at all, and who, however clever, always get the axe at the finale. If Kornbluth sometimes admired their grit and savvy, he was also moved to exact revenge for their victims.

Though he is often viewed as a commentator on the social fabric, and the various forms of human folly, there is more to Kornbluth than the wary futurologist, the wry chronicler of crafty deals ("1955," "Time Bum"), or even the compassionate observer of human detritus ("The Little Black Bag," "The Altar at Midnight"). And this something more is his sense of the unknown and the unknowable, the hidden layers of reality, the levels of illusion enveloping the world (whether social or metaphysical). Many of his most notable, most intensely realized stories hover somewhere between strict fantasy and strictest science fiction. Both "The Words of Guru" and "Kazam Collects" are outright fantasies, of the sort that "pierce the veil" of ordinary sense, and yet they have the resolute authority, the absolute conviction, of things seen and heard and done. They begin in fairly typical urban settings, enticing the reader through unsuspected realms to arrive at states of being that can only be termed ineffable and exalted, the one horrific, the other all beauty and benevolence. "The Silly Season," a tensely told shocker, provides a contest between a series of uncanny but rather palpable illusions and the normalizing nature of daily journalism. "The Cosmic Expense Account" sets the mundane and extraordinary in adjacent territories, as a crippling "cosmic-harmony" engulfs eastern Pennsylvania. And in the jocose "Virginia," our furtive public mythologies about the Secret Masterdom of the Super Rich are made the binding private reality of an heir to fortune. Characteristically, Kornbluth does not simply mention, but actually offers a short tour of, the Museum of Suppressed Inventions.

These tales center on initiation into various kinds of arcane knowledge; and "Guru" and "Kazam" focus on persons of a special nature, born to acquire a special sort of knowledge, and power. This striving after knowledge is at the core of Kornbluth's most elusive and provocative piece of writing, "The Last Man Left in the Bar." Published very late in his career (1957), this short but densely packed work distills all his previous concerns with kinds and visions of reality, and it is a tour de force of oblique, kaleidoscopic narrative worthy of the wildest "experiments" of the New Wave. It portrays the psychological aftermath of an apparent momentary transposition of worlds. It mingles drunken uncertainties and digressions with the haunting obscurities of a poorly apprehended experience. In a landscape of shifting knowledge, the one constant is that its technical-protagonist never does learn the answers, the wherefores of his predicament. His passionate desire to *know* is countered by the obstinate complexity of the universe, and by wilful creatures who are absorbed in their own very separate interests and imperatives.

—Alex Eisenstein

KOTZWINKLE, William. American. Born in Scranton, Pennsylvania, 22 November 1938. Educated at Rider College, Lawrenceville, New Jersey; Pennsylvania State University, University Park. Married Elizabeth Gundy. Recipient: Bread Loaf Conference Scholarship; World Fantasy Award, 1977. Address: c/o Putnam's, 200 Madison Avenue, New York, New York 10016, U.S.A.

SCIENCE-FICTION PUBLICATIONS

Novels

Hermes 3000. New York, Pantheon, 1972.
Doctor Rat. New York, Knopf, and Henley-on-Thames, Oxfordshire, Ellis, 1976.
E. T., The Extra-Terrestrial (novelization of screenplay). New York, Putnam, and London, Barker, 1982.
Superman III (novelization of screenplay). New York, Warner, and London, Arrow, 1983.
E. T.: The Book of the Green Planet. New York, Putnam, 1985.

Uncollected Short Stories

"The Philosophy of Sebastian Trump; or, The Art of Outrage," in *Brother Sebastian's Chamber of Horrors*, edited by Brother Theodore and Marvin Kaye. New York, Pinnacle, 1975.
"The Magician," in *Elsewhere 1*, edited by Terri Windling and Mark Alan Arnold. New York, Ace, 1981.
"The Curio Shop," in *Visions from the Edge*, edited by John Bell and Lesley Choyce. Porters Lake, Nova Scotia, Pottersfield Press, 1981.
"A Man Who Knew His Birds," in *Omni* (New York), February 1985.

OTHER PUBLICATIONS

Novels

The Fan Man. New York, Avon, and Henley-on-Thames, Oxfordshire, Ellis, 1974.
Night-Book. New York, Avon, 1974.
Swimmer in the Secret Sea. New York, Avon, 1975; Henley-on-Thames, Oxfordshire, Ellis, 1976.
Fata Morgana. New York, Knopf, and London, Hutchinson, 1977.
Herr Nightingale and the Satin Woman. New York, Knopf, 1978; London, Hutchinson, 1979.
Jack in the Box. New York, Putnam, 1980; London, Abacus, 1981.
Christmas at Fontaine's. New York, Putnam, 1982; London, Deutsch, 1983.
Queen of Swords. New York, Putnam, and London, Deutsch, 1984.

Short Stories

Elephant Bangs Train. New York, Pantheon, and London, Faber, 1971.

Other (for children)

The Fireman. New York, Pantheon, 1969.
The Ship That Came Down the Gutter. New York, Pantheon, 1970; Kingswood, Surrey, World's Work, 1976.
Elephant Boy: A Story of the Stone Age. New York, Farrar Straus, 1970.

The Day the Gang Got Rich. New York, Viking Press, 1970.
The Oldest Man and Other Timeless Stories. New York, Pantheon, 1971.
Return of Crazy Horse. New York, Farrar Straus, 1971.
The Supreme, Superb, Exalted, and Delightful, One and Only Magic Building. New York, Farrar Straus, 1973.
Up the Alley with Jack and Joe. New York, Macmillan, 1974.
The Leopard's Tooth. Boston, Houghton Mifflin, 1976.
The Ant Who Took Away Time. New York, Doubleday, 1978.
Dream of Dark Harbor. New York, Doubleday, 1979.
The Nap Master. New York, Harcourt Brace, 1979.
The Extra Terrestrial Storybook. New York, Putnam, 1982.
Great World Circus. New York, Putnam, 1983.
Trouble in Bugland: A Collection of Inspector Mantis Mysteries. Boston, Godine, 1983.

*   *   *

William Kotzwinkle has produced children's and adolescent fiction, fables, allegories, realistic and historical fiction, and adult and science fantasy. Fantasy undergirds all of his writing, however. It is not just Todorov's hesitation "between a natural and supernatural explanation of the events described"—it is fantasy with the force of dream.

The vein of fantasy that is the true one of Kotzwinkle's writing for children and adolescents is always present in his writing for adults. In the short stories of *Elephant Bangs Train* reality is usually so unreal it seem fantastic: frozen mastodons are eaten to capture an assumed wild animal past; real sexuality seems fantastic in "Marie," "The Jewel of Amitchi," and "Tiger Bridge"; the death of a Navaho in a motorcycle jump over a canyon and a liar who moves to the sixth degree of lying seem mythic, while the title story transforms the reality of a train to a giant that an elephant first fears then charges. *Hermes 3000* is a series of stories that are chronological but fragmented and juxtaposed in a manner similar to Benjy's narrative in Faulkner's *The Sound and the Fury*. One of the stories features Catherine the Great's flower guard in the 18th century; two more occur in the 19th century, showing an American minister and a wandering madman; others occur in the 20th century, where we see a drunken dishwasher, a Chinese cook, a retired old man who dies in the Metropolitan Museum, an English hermit who builds a hole in a Lord's estate around World War II, and a classics professor who becomes a dishwasher. The madman and Reverend Cupplewaite know each other, and the Golden Cafeteria links the professor, the drunken dishwasher, and two old bag ladies in this novel of reincarnation, where lives are stored and reused.

The Fan Man is a novel whose protagonist-narrator, Horse Badorties, is so chaotic that the novel seems surreal. Badorties, a counter-culture hippy musicologist, lover of women, garbage, and junk, is so unable to complete anything that no other character is developed or situation resolved. Life is a series of plots that never untangle. *Swimmer in the Secret Sea* seems, on the other hand, to be a realistic novella about a baby who dies in delivery, but this swimmer in the secret sea structures the lives of his parents, John and Diane Laski. The life that never was structures lives that are.

Night Book is similar to *Hermes 3000*, juxtaposing stories of contemporary and Athenian sexual practices. The stories told by the Athenian women awaiting a fertility celebration for Demeter are powerfully sensual, while the contemporary stories are frequently similar to crude pornography. Kotzwinkle frequently juxtaposes stories with parallel events, where the end of one story serves as the end of another.

Doctor Rat, the novel for which Kotzwinkle won the World

Fantasy Award in 1977, is an animal fable demonstrating man's cruelty and destructiveness. The title character is a rat made crazy by an animal experimentation laboratory. His slogan, "Death Is Freedom," is similar to the Nazi slogan "Arbeit Macht Frei. " Animals in the laboratory and outside, particularly an eagle who escapes a zoo, rebel and migrate to central meeting areas, where they are systematically destroyed by mankind in situations which parallel World War II and its concentration camps. Through Doctor Rat's insane mutterings using the justifications of research, defense industries, and medicine, the language of power is decentered and mocked.

Fata Morgana is a detective story in which the reality of an 1861 Paris and eastern Europe is so bizarre that it is fantastic. Inspector Picard, sent to investigate Ric Lazare and his fortune-telling machine, has his own fortune read. The fortune is an investigation of Lazare that never happens, but the illusion is so real that Picard elects not to pursue this toy-making, wife-stealing murderer. Though the ending is a cheat, the novel is still one of Kotzwinkle's best. *Herr Nightingale and the Satin Woman* relies more on the art of Joe Servello, a frequent Kotzwinkle collaborator, than Kotzwinkle. The action is never clear; Herr Nightingale is a smuggler trying to recover from some traumatic defeat as a German soldier in Egypt during World War I. He, the Satin Woman, and Bagg the detective are passionately intertwined; insects become symbols of their passions for love and riches, assuming their own fantastic existences.

Where the action in *Herr Nightingale* is fuzzy, such cannot be said of *Jack in the Box*, which is a realistic novel tracing Jack Twiller's life from a World War II childhood to a James Dean 1950's adolescence. Though the novel is almost an adolescent novel formula such as Judy Blume's *Then Again, Maybe I Won't*, Jack's fantasies from his childhood Lone Ranger days to the masturbatory fantasies of adolescence mark the novel as Kotzwinkle's. *Christmas at Fontaine's* shows a group of linked characters who connect at Fontaine's Department Store in a novel similar to *Jack in the Box*. The novel is realistic, but it is characterized by the fantastic obsessions of its characters, from Officer Locke's obsessed pursuit of a boy living in the store to a mad genius of a window decorator who wants the ultimate Christmas window display and a bag lady's quest for golden garbage. *Queen of Swords* again is basically a realistic novel, although a ghost of a composer, Lingard, appears, and some black magic, mojo, seems to be wielded by the alienated wife of a conga player. The principal action is a study of two influences on the writer-narrator, Eric—his wife, Janet, and Nora, a wild woman. Janet is the good influence that stimulates his best writing; Nora's influence leads only to pornography and drug trafficking. To Kotzwinkle here, the influence of others we love on our lives is magic.

Superman III is a novel based on the screenplay by David and Lesie Newman. The novel features much humor by coincidence similar to silent comedy. Ross Webster first plots to monopolize world coffee production and then oil, as the Man of Steel foils Ross, his sister, and Gus Gorman, a computer whiz, in this sophomoric effort. *E. T. : The Extra-Terrestrial* also follows a screenplay, but Melissa Mathison's is better than the Newmans'. Kotzwinkle fills in E. T. 's botanical mission and reduces the viciousness of everyone except Lance, the nerd, and the people sent to study E. T. *E. T. : The Book of the Green Planet* is based on a story by Steven Spielberg and is far better than *E. T. : The Extra-Terrestrial*. Most of the action is on E. T. 's home planet, with various attempts by E. T. to communicate with Elliott, who is discovering girls, and becoming an adolescent. The characters are as delightful as Lem's Trurl and Klapaucius, with vegetable characters such as the Jumpums and mineral

characters such as Sinistro, a bio-degradable vegetable (turnip) space ship, and E. T. 's sidekick, Flopglopple, who resembles an animated old sock.

The humor of *E. T. : The Book of the Green Planet* is typical of Kotzwinkle's writing, which has a strong vein of fantasy usually juxtaposed against realistic detail. Sometimes the juxtaposition induces the mystery of dreams; other times it induces humor. An excellent style rather than excellent plot forms characterize this talented writer.

—Craig Wallace Barrow

KURLAND, Michael (Joseph). Also writes as Jennifer Plum. American. Born in New York City, 1 March 1938. Educated at Hiram College, Ohio, 1955-56; University of Maryland overseas, 1961-62; Columbia University, New York, 1962-63. Served in the United States Army, 1958-62. Married Rebecca Jacobson in 1976. News Editor, KPFK-Radio, Los Angeles, 1966; English teacher, Happy Valley Schook, Ojai, California, 1967; Editor, *Crawdaddy,* New York, 1969; also a play director, road manager for a band, advertising copywriter, and ghost writer. Since 1976, Editor, Pennyfarthing Press, San Francisco and Berkeley, California. Agent: Richard Curtis Associates, 164 East 64th Street, New York, New York 10021. Address: Pennyfarthing Press, 2000 Center Street, No. 1226, Berkeley, California 94704, U.S.A.

SCIENCE-FICTION PUBLICATIONS

Novels

Ten Years to Doomsday, with Chester Anderson. New York, Pyramid, 1964.
The Unicorn Girl. New York, Pyramid, 1969.
Transmission Error. New York, Pyramid, 1970.
The Whenabouts of Burr. New York, DAW, 1975.
Pluribus. New York, Doubleday, 1975.
Tomorrow Knight. New York, DAW, 1976.
The Princes of Earth (for children). Nashville, Nelson, 1978.
The Last President, with S. W. Barton. New York, Morrow, 1980.
Psi Hunt. New York, Berkley, 1980.
Death by Gaslight. New York, New American Library, 1982.

Uncollected Short Stories

"Bond of Brothers," in *World of Tomorrow* (New York), May 1965.
"Please State My Business," in *Galaxy* (New York), August 1965.
"Fimbulsommer," with Randall Garrett, in *If* (New York), September 1970.
"A Matter of Taste," in *Men and Malice,* edited by Dean Dickensheet. New York, Doubleday, 1973.
"Small World," in *Two Views of Wonder,* edited by Thomas N. Scortia and Chelsea Quinn Yarbro. New York, Ballantine, 1973.
"Elementary," with Laurence Janifer, in *Shared Tomorrows,* edited by Bill Pronzini and Barry N. Malzberg. New York, St. Martin's Press, 1979.
"Think Only This of Me," in *The Arbor House Treasury of Science Fiction Masterpieces,* edited by Robert Silverberg and

Martin H. Greenberg. New York, Arbor House, 1983.
"A Brief Dance to the Music of the Spheres," In *The Best of Omni Science Fiction 6,* edited by Don Myrus. New York, Omni, 1983.

OTHER PUBLICATIONS

Novels

Mission: Third Force. New York, Pyramid, 1967.
Mission: Tank War. New York, Pyramid, 1968.
Mission: Police Action. New York, Pyramid, 1969.
A Plague of Spies. New York, Pyramid, 1969.
The Secret of Benjamin Square (as Jennifer Plum). New York, Lancer, 1972.
The Infernal Device. New York, New American Library, and London, New English Library, 1979.

Other

Editor, *The Redward Edward Papers,* by Avram Davidson. New York, Doubleday, 1978.
Editor, *The Best of Avram Davidson.* New York, Doubleday, 1979.
Editor, *First Cycle.* New York, Ace, 1982.

*

Michael Kurland comments:
    I try to entertain.

*   *   *

Michael Kurland's first two science-fiction novels were written in conjunction with Chester Anderson. The first, a conventional collaboration, was *Ten Years to Doomsday,* a lightweight and readable book concerned with the need for an entire planet to change from a feudal/pre-technological to a fully scientific/industrial state in a decade to stave off a planned invasion. Kurland has stated that this book was written as a parody of the works of Poul Anderson. Either as parody or in its own right, the book is fairly successful. The second novel has a more complicated history. When Anderson wrote his popular novel *The Butterfly Kid,* he included himself, Kurland, and a third friend, Tom Waters, as characters. Anderson's novel imposes a comedic alien-invasion theme upon the bohemian East Village milieu of the 1960's with hilarious results. Kurland's *The Unicorn Girl* is a sequel, continuing its themes and characters, though it is generally regarded as less successful. (Waters added a third book to the series, *The Probability Pad.*)

Kurland's first fully solo novel was *Transmission Error.* In this book he established a protagonist of generally likeable nature, his traits including considerable wit and resourcefulness, but also a feckless ability to get himself into insoluble dilemmas. He is accidentally transported to an alien planet and threatened with a life of slavery. He escapes this situation and plunges into a series of similarly unresolved problems.

By this point the general pattern of Kurland's books had become clear. Kurland is highly adept at creating societies which are compellingly believable, and populating them with vivid and sympathetic characters. His style is lively, warm, and highly informal. His stories are told with rapidity of pace and great variety of setting and incident. Their major flaw is a failure—whether by the author or his protagonist—to grapple with and satisfactorily resolve problems. The "solutions" offered are almost invariably flight rather than confrontation.

This pattern holds through Kurland's later novels, although their basic premises are wholly different from one another. *The Whenabouts of Burr* is a chase-novel proceeding through multiple parallel worlds. *Pluribus,* probably Kurland's most successful novel in the genre, takes place in a semi-barbaric future United States. The book abounds in vivid imagery, including an unforgettable scene of the protagonist, arrested for some local infraction, being removed in a standard "black-and-white" California Highway Patrol cruiser—drawn by a team of horses! *Tomorrow Knight* (the title is indicative of Kurland's love for puns and other word-play) takes place on a planet divided, checker-board fashion, into hundreds of miniature stage-set societies. Yet in all the books, the general pattern of insoluble problem and flight persists.

The Princes of Earth is favorably comparable to standard Heinlein juveniles, containing the usual Kurland mix of convincing future societies, sympathetic characters, intriguing problem-situations, and rapid transfer from problem to problem. There is also an excellent infusion of satire, most notably a hilarious parody of the Church of Scientology. Although no further books in the series have yet appeared. *The Princes of Earth* is clearly intended as the opening volume of a series.

—Richard A. Lupoff

KUTTNER, Henry. Also wrote as Lewis Padgett. American. Born in Los Angeles, California, 7 April 1915. Educated at the University of Southern California, Los Angeles, B. A. 1954. Served in the United States Army Medical Corps during World War II. Married C. L. Moore, *q. v.,* in 1940; most of his subsequent work was written with her, though not always acknowledged. Worked briefly for a literary agency, Los Angeles; free-lance writer. *Died 3 February 1958.*

SCIENCE-FICTION PUBLICATIONS

Novels

Fury, with C. L. Moore. New York, Grosset and Dunlap, 1950; London, Dobson, 1954; as *Destination Infinity,* New York, Avon, 1958.
Earth's Last Citadel, with C. L. Moore. New York, Ace, 1964.
Valley of the Flame, with C. L. Moore. New York, Ace, 1964.
The Time Axis, with C. L. Moore. New York, Ace, 1965.
The Dark World, with C. L. Moore. New York, Ace, 1965; London, Mayflower, 1966.
Dr. Cyclops, with others. New York, Popular Library, 1967.
The Creature from Beyond Infinity. New York, Popular Library, 1968.
The Mask of Circe, with C. L. Moore. New York, Ace, 1971.
The Time Trap, in *Evil Earths,* edited by Brian Aldiss. London, Futura, 1976.

Novels as Lewis Padgett, with C. L. Moore

Tomorrow and Tomorrow, and The Fairy Chessmen. New York, Gnome Press, 1951; as *Tomorrow and Tomorrow* and *The Far Reality,* London, Consul, 2 vols., 1963; *The Fairy Chessmen* published as *Chessboard Planet,* New York, Galaxy, 1956.
Well of the Worlds. New York, Galaxy, 1953.
Beyond Earth's Gates. New York, Ace, 1954.

Short Stories

Ahead of Time. New York, Ballantine, 1953; London, Weidenfeld and Nicolson, 1954.
Remember Tomorrow. Sydney, American Science Fiction, 1954.
Way of the Gods. Sydney, American Science Fiction, 1954.
No Boundaries, with C. L. Moore. New York, Ballantine, 1955; London, Consul, 1961.
As You Were. Sydney, American Science Fiction, 1955.
Sword of Tomorrow. Sydney, American Science Fiction, 1955.
Bypass to Otherness. New York, Ballantine, 1961; London, Consul, 1963.
Return to Otherness. New York, Ballantine, 1962; London, Mayflower, 1965.
The Best of Kuttner. London, Mayflower, 2 vols., 1965-66.
The Best of Henry Kuttner. New York, Doubleday, 1975.
Clash by Night and Other Stories, with C. L. Moore, edited by Peter Pinto. London, Hamlyn, 1980.
Chessboard Planet and Other Stories, with C. L. Moore, London, Hamlyn, 1983.
Elak of Atlantis. New York, Gryphon, 1985.
Short Stories as Lewis Padgett, with C. L. Moore
A Gnome There Was. New York, Simon and Schuster, 1950.
Robots Have No Tails (by Kuttner alone). New York, Gnome Press, 1952; as *The Proud Robot: The Complete Galloway Gallegher Stories* (as Henry Kuttner), London, Hamlyn, 1983.
Mutant. New York, Gnome Press, 1953; London, Weidenfeld and Nicolson, 1954.
Line to Tomorrow. New York, Bantam, 1954.

OTHER PUBLICATIONS

Novels

The Brass Ring (as Lewis Padgett, with C. L. Moore). New York, Duell, 1946; London, Sampson Low, 1947; as *Murder in Brass,* New York, Bantam, 1947.
The Day He Died (as Lewis Padgett, with C. L. Moore). New York, Duell, 1947.
Man Drowning. New York, Harper, 1952; London, New English Library, 1961.
The Murder of Ann Avery. New York, Permabooks, 1956.
The Murder of Eleanor Pope. New York, Permabooks, 1956.
Murder of a Mistress. New York, Permabooks, 1957.
Murder of a Wife. New York, Permabooks, 1958.

*

Bibliography: by Donald H. Tuck, in *Henry Kuttner: A Memorial Symposium* edited by Karen Anderson, Berkeley, California, Sevagram, 1958.

*   *   *

In reviewing Henry Kuttner's collection *Ahead of Time,* Anthony Boucher characterized the author as "one of S. F.'s most literate and intelligent storytellers." Other adjectives could have been added to the list: prolific, versatile, popular. There have, it is true, been periodic dry spells when editors and readers have seemed to forget the rich legacy of Kuttner's fiction, but the stories have always been re-discovered and brought back into print. There is every reason to believe that his best work will last as long as science fiction is read.

For many years the scope and volume of Kuttner's writing were partially camouflaged by the many bylines under which his stories appeared. Initially the pen-names were adopted for the usual commercial reasons: to differentiate among various types of story or to disguise the fact that more than one story on a contents page was by the same author. But Kuttner, both alone and with his wife C. L. Moore, seemed to take an active delight in the creation of new pseudonyms, even on two occasions going so far as to publish fictional "autobiographies" for an alter ego: Keith Hammond in *Startling Stories,* March 1946 (an Eurasian antiquarian with sixteen cats), and C. H. Liddell in *Planet Stories,* November 1950. As one after another of the Kuttner/Moore pseudonyms was revealed, a phenomenon arose which was sometimes called the "Kuttner Syndrome": the conviction that *any* promising new name on the SF scene had to be yet another Kuttner pen-name. (One of the victims of this assumption was Jack Vance, who was identified by the editor T. E. Dikty in 1950 as a Kuttner pseudonym.) The original choice of pseudonyms for various stories has by now become clouded through numerous reprintings with altered bylines.

Kuttner's first story, "The Graveyard Rats," a superbly grisly horror story in the Lovecraft mode, appeared in *Weird Tales.* Kuttner continued to write for *Weird Tales,* but at the same time he became a prolific contributor to other pulp magazines of many types, including mystery, detective, western, adveture, "spicy," and South Sea tales. His first long story was "The Time Trap" (*Marvel Science Stories*), called "a marvellous gaudy melodrama" by Brian Aldiss. Kuttner had been a member of H. P. Lovecraft's circle of correspondents, and had met other members of that group, such as Robert Bloch, Fritz Leiber, and E. Hoffmann Price. Kuttner and Bloch collaborated on a few stories. Kuttner also collaborated with Arthur K. Barnes on two stories in their Pete Manx series. Manx was a carnival barker whose mind was projected back in time into the bodies of various inhabitants of ancient Rome, Egypt, Baghdad, and other historical or legendary locales, where he must use his innate cunning to survive. The series was carried on alternately by Kuttner and Barnes from 1939 to 1944.

Another Lovecraft correspondent and well-known *Weird Tales* writer whom Kuttner met was Catherine L. Moore. Kuttner and Moore were married on June 7, 1940, in New York, where Kuttner had moved in order to be close to his magazine markets. Kuttner and Moore had collaborated on one story in 1937, but is was not until after their marriage that their remarkable writing partnership developed. Kuttner stated on several occasions that almost all of his writing since the marriage, regardless of byline, was to some extent a collaboration with his wife; however, the degree and method of collaboration varied widely. Some stories were almost pure Kuttner, with only minor contributions from Moore, while for others the reverse was true; but on a large number of stories the two partners were able to blend their ideas and styles so well that one of them could drop a story in mid-scene and the other could pick it up, with scarcely a seam showing in the final product. While taking part fully in the collaborative works, C. L. Moore also continued to write her own stories.

The Lewis Padgett stories, taken as a whole, form a body of work of which any writer could be proud, and if Kuttner and Moore had done no other writing in the science fiction field, their reputations would still be secure on the basis of these stories. Fritz Leiber (in *Henry Kuttner: A Memorial Symposium,* 1958) identified three themes which recur in Kuttner's science fiction: the madman from the future, wacky robots, and wonder children. All of these are present in the Padgett stories. The Padgett treatment of robots, in particular, is as distinctive as that of any writer in the field. One of the best-known, "The Twonky," is concerned with the effect on a young married couple of a device which looks like a console radio, but is actually a robot designed to enforce its own views of proper behavior. Several of the Padgett stories were about the odd inventions of Gallegher, a scientist who can invent things only while drunk, and when sober, can never remember what the inventions are for. Told in a style frankly borrowed from Thorne Smith, the Gallegher stories are meticulously logical SF puzzles cast as wacky comedies. Five were reprinted as *Robots Have No Tails*. The deservedly famous "Mimsy Were the Borogoves" is about educational toys from the future which have a disastrous effect on a present-day family. Other Lewis Padgett stories include the Baldy series (*Mutant*)—about telepathic mutants who must struggle for survival against the intolerance of their normal neighbors and against irrational renegades in their own ranks, a theme clearly taken from A. E. van Vogt's *Slan*—and "The Fairy Chessmen" (with its celebrated opening line, "The doorknob opened a blue eye and looked at him") and "Tomorrow and Tomorrow," complicated tales of post-Atomic intrigue and alternate futures.

One of C. L. Moore's works from the 1940's was "Clash by Night," a moody, emotion-laden story of the Free Companies, the mercenaries of the feuding undersea Keeps on Venus in the 25th century. The Kuttners returned to this scene with the novel *Fury,* the story of Sam Harker, ruthless and driven by forces of which he was not fully aware, the one man who could liberate humanity from its stagnant undersea existence and push it into conquering the planet's savage surface. Although published as by Lawrence O'Donnell, the story was mostly Kuttner's. C. L. Moore stated in her introduction to the Lancer reprint: " *Fury* was written by about one and an eighth persons . . . . I wrote comparatively little of the copy. The idea was basically Hank's and I didn't identify very strongly with it. " She also pointed out that the novel deals with "the two recurring themes which emerge quite explicitly in nearly everything we wrote. Hank's basic statement was something like, 'Authority is dangerous and I will never submit to it. ' Mine was, 'The most treacherous thing in life is love. '" *Fury* is the best, and best-known, of Kuttner's long stories. Other long works include a series of nine science-fantasy novels, many of them in the romantic/tragic mode of A. Merritt, written between 1943 and 1952, including *Earth's Last Citadel, Valley of the Flame, Beyond Earth's Gates,* and *Well of the Worlds*. Typical shorter works in the same style are "I Am Eden" (December 1946) and "Way of the Gods" (April 1947), both in *Thrilling Wonder Stories*. In the early 1950's the volume of new Kuttner-Moore stories decreased. Both Kuttner and Moore felt written-out in science fiction, although such stories as "Home There's No Returning" and "Two-Handed Engine" (both in *No Boundaries*) belied this claim.

Henry Kuttner has sometimes been criticized as a literary mimic who spent his energies speaking in other people's voices. He did, in fact, speak in many voices, but they were all his own. His borrowings, whether of style or of theme, were all filtered through his own sensibility, and emerged transmuted. In all of his best work there is clear evidence of a highly individual mind at work. Perhaps his most personal contribution to science fiction was the fusion of humour and logic which first emerged fully in the Gallegher stories. The same blend was also evident in the stories of the Hogbens, a family of mutant hillbillies, and in "The Ego Machine," probably his best "wacky robot" story. Through his stories and through his influence on other writers— Ray Bradbury, Leigh Brackett, and Richard Matheson have all acknowledged his guidance—Kuttner left an indelible mark on the science-fiction field. Without his presence, science fiction of the 1940's and 1950's would have been a vastly different and much poorer body of literature.

—R. E. Briney

LAFFERTY, R(aphael) A(loysius). American. Born in Neola, Iowa, 7 November 1914. Educated at the University of Tulsa, Oklahoma, 1932-33; International Correspondence School, electrical engineer course, 1939-42. Served in the United States Army, 1942-46; Staff Sergeant. Civil servant, Washington D.C., 1934-35; clerk, then buyer, Clark Electrical Supply Company, Tulsa, 1936-42, 1946-50, 1952-71. Since 1971, free-lance writer. Recipient: Phoenix Award, 1971; Hugo Award, 1973; Smith Award, 1973, Agent: Virginia Kidd, Box 278, Milford, Pennsylvania 18337. Address: 1715 South Trenton Avenue, Tulsa, Oklahoma 74120, U.S.A.

SCIENCE-FICTION PUBLICATIONS

Novels

Past Master. New York, Ace, and London, Rapp and Whiting, 1968.
The Reefs of Earth. New York, Berkley, 1968; London, Dobson, 1970.
Space Chantey. New York, Ace, 1968; London, Dobson, 1976.
Fourth Mansions. New York, Ace, 1969; London, Dobson, 1972.
The Devil Is Dead. New York, Avon, 1971; London, Dobson, 1978.
Arrive at Easterwine. New York, Scribner, 1971; London,, Dobson, 1977.
Not to Mention Camels. Indianapolis, Bobbs Merrill, 1976; London, Dobson, 1980.
Apocalypses. Los Angeles, Pinnacle, 1977.
Archipelago. New Orleans, Manuscript Press, 1979.
Aurelia. Norfolk, Virginia, Donning, 1982.
The Annals of Klepsis. New York, Ace, 1983.

Short Stories

Nine Hundred Grandmothers. New York, Ace, 1970; London, Dobson, 1975.
Strange Doings. New York, Scribner, 1971.
Does Anyone Else Have Something Further to Add? New York, Scribner, 1974; London, Dobson, 1980.
Funnyfingers, and Cabrito. Portland, Oregon, Pendragon Press, 1976.
Horns on Their Heads. Portland, Oregon, Pendragon Press, 1976.
Golden Gate and Other Stories, edited by Ira M. Thornhill. Minneapolis, Corroboree Press, 1983.
Four Stories. Polk City, Iowa, Drumm, 1983.
Heart of Stone Dear and Other Stories. Polk City, Iowa, Drumm, 1983.
Snake in His Bosom and Other Stories. Polk City, Iowa, Drumm, 1983.
Through Elegant Eyes: Stories of Austro and the Men Who Know Everything, edited by Ira M. Thornhill. Minneapolis, Corroboree Press, 1983.
Ringing Changes. New York, Ace, 1984.
The Man Who Made Models and Other Stories. Polk City, Iowa, Drumm, 1984.
Slippery and Other Stories. Polk City, Iowa, Drumm, 1985.

Uncollected Short Stories

"Thou Whited Wall," in *Fantasy and Science Fiction* (New York), January 1977.
"Bright Coins in Never-Ending Streams," in *Orbit 20,* edited by

Damon Knight. New York, Harper, 1978.

"Quiz Ship Loose," in *Chrysalis 2,* edited by Roy Torgeson. New York, Zebra, 1978.

"Bright Flightways" and "The Man who Walked Through Cracks," in *Chrysalis 3,* edited by Roy Torgeson. New York, Zebra, 1978.

"Selenium Ghosts of the Eighteen Seventies," in *Universe 8,* edited by Terry Carr. New York, Doubleday, and London, Dobson, 1978.

"Splinters," in *Shadows 1,* edited by Charles L. Grant. New York, Doubleday, 1978.

"Berryhill," in *Whispers 2,* edited by Stuart David Schiff. New York, Doubleday, 1979.

"Crocodile," in *Chrysalis 8,* edited by Roy Torgeson. New York, Doubleday, 1980.

"The Funny Face Murders," in *New Terrors 2,* edited by Ramsey Campbell. London, Pan, 1980.

"Lord Torpedo Lord Gyroscope," in *The Berkley Showcase 2,* edited by Victoria Schochet and John W. Silbersack. New York, Berkley, 1980.

"The Only Tune That He Could Play," in *Orbit 21,* edited by Damon Knight. New York, Harper, 1980.

"Bank and Shoal of Time," in *A Spadeful of Spacetime,* edited by Fred Saberhagen. New York, Ace, 1981.

"In Deepest Glass," in *The Berkley Showcase 4,* edited by Victoria Schochet and John W. Silbersack. New York, Berkeley, 1981.

"Ifrit," in *Perpetual Light,* edited by Alan Ryan. New York, Warner, 1982.

"Great Tom Fool," in *Speculations,* edited by Isaac Asimov and Alice Laurance. Boston, Houghton Mifflin, 1982.

"Thieving Bear Planet," in *Universe 12* edited by Terry Carr. New York, Doubleday, 1982.

"You Can't Go Back," in *The Best Science Fiction of the Year II,* edited by Terry Carr. New York, Pocket Books, 1982.

"Calamities of the Last Pauper," in *Fantasy Book* (Pasadena, California), November 1982.

"Square and Above Board," in *The Year's Best Fantasy Stories 9,* edited by Arthur W. Saha. New York, DAW, 1983.

"Pine Castle," in *Amazing* (New York), September 1983.

OTHER PUBLICATIONS

Novels

The Fall of Rome. New York, Doubleday, 1971.
The Flame Is Green. New York, Walker, 1971.
Okla Hannali. New York, Doubleday, 1972.
Half a Sky, edited by Ira M. Thornhill. Minneapolis, Corroboree Press, 1984.

*

Bibliography: *An R. A. Lafferty Checklist* by Chris Drumm, Polk City, Iowa, Drumm, 1983.

Manuscript Collection: McFarlin Library, University of Tulsa, Oklahoma.

R. A. Lafferty comments:

My novels, which I wrote myself at great labor, have received more attention than my short stories, which wrote themselves. Nevertheless, the short stories are greatly superior to the novels. In my introductory note to a Dutch version of *Nine Hundred Grandmothers,* I wrote:

"I hold to the true theory that good stories write themselves, or that they are independent and pre-existent entities or beings. . . . These pre-existent stories come to persons, sometimes even to persons of a resonant emptiness; and they make themselves known through these persons. . . . I am very glad that these particular stories first visited me and not someone else.

"There are a few perfect discoveries or encounters that come into every life. Only once I met a mountain lion, quite close, in the wild. She was a discovery of mine. Once only I saw a whale a-blow in the ocean. Once only I saw a big-horn mountain sheep on a high cliff. Once only I saw a pink flamingo in flight. Once only I had an encounter with each of some hundred entities called 'special stories. ' These meetings were as quietly thunderous and as unexpected as the discovery of the mountain lion or whale or big-horn sheep or pink flamingo in flight.

"There is an Aladdin cave, lit by 999 lamps, that is the Universal Unconscious . . . that is shared by all persons and creatures. . . . Unsuspected stone doors of the cave are thrown open. There may be funny and fascinating encounters and living spectacles. A few of them may cluster together in a pile of things waiting to be discovered . . . piles of gold, quick ecstasies, intricate delights, entities called 'special stories. '

"A person favored with such discoveries will look for other people to share them with. 'Hey, come see the things I've found,' he'll say. That is what I say now. "

However pompous that may sound, it's a statement on the most important part of my work.

*   *   *

R. A. Lafferty is science fiction's most prodigious teller of tall tales. Offspring of a yarn-spinning family, he writes rather than recites his exhilarating stories but nevertheless retains a primary allegiance to the spoken word. The quintessentially oral character of Lafferty's fiction proclaims itself on every page— each of them sounds like a tape recording transcript. (*Arrive at Easterwine* is actually presented as such.) Rhythmic repetitions of phrases and epithets tie the material together. The author is omnipresent as well as omniscient. He explains and interprets every development, sprinkling his text with epigrams, anecdotes, and invented sources. He even brings himself into stories as a thinly disguised character or as himself in *Through Elegant Eyes.*

Exposition and dialog overshadow action. Events are more often predicted or recollected than depicted. At shorter lengths, these events are often arranged in artificial patterns reminiscent of folk tales ("Rainbird"), exempla ("The Configuration of the North Shore"), dramatized lectures ("Primary Education of the Camiroi"), or barroom whoppers ("One at a Time"). In longer works, a degree of order is imposed via elaborate symbolism (e.g., the Four Living Creatures in *Fourth Mansions*). However, Lafferty's oral mannerisms hamper him when he mistakes the accumulation of vignettes for the construction of a novel as in *Arrive at Easterwine* and *The Devil Is Dead* or uses a novel as an excuse for sermons and diatribes as in *Aurelia.* (Compare the last with Robert A. Heinlein's *Stranger in a Strange Land.*)

Lafferty's way with characters is as distinctive as his story-telling technique. The floridly eccentric beings who populate his fiction are wholly unrealistic yet totally real. He succeeds best with children, traditionally the most difficult of subjects, because he approaches them with all the sentimentality of a W. C. Fields: "A child's a monster yet uncurled" (*The Reefs of Earth*). However, Lafferty's distaste for adolescents shows up in his Hugo winner "Eurema's Dam. "

Besides outrageous youngsters, Lafferty's character troupe

comprises: dirty old geniuses and innocent simpletons, ugly but wholesome men and violent but kindly ones, lusty egomaniacs and ascetic manipulators, witch-girls and earthy ladies of muscular charm, plus aliens that are every bit as variegated. They reappear in tale after tale: "though they always preserved the threads of their identities, they did not always have the same names or appearances, and there were not always the same number of them." Favorites get encores. Note the proper names common to *Fourth Mansions, Arrive at Easterwine,* and *The Annals of Klepsis. The Devil Is Dead* trilogy (including *Archipelago, The Devil Is Dead,* and the unpublished *More Than Melchisedech*) continues the historical fantasy Coscuin Chronicles tetralogy and all his extraterrestrial locales appear to exist in the same crazy universe.

So closely do Lafferty's novels resemble each other, they might as well be alternate drafts of the same story. This may reflect his habit of rewriting everything five or six times before the final draft. Elements seem to pass from work to work as easily as sherry through a solera. For instance, Lafferty's plots repeatedly combine conspiracy, romance, and growth. Secret battles between Good and Evil coteries decide the fate of worlds. Bright protagonists are shadowed by dark counterparts. Passionate couples share a yeasty mixture of carnal and spiritual love. Esoteric powers are acquired and used to prepare a chosen hero for an imperial destiny, but the outcome is often ambiguous. *The Flame Is Green* and *Half a Sky,* the first two volumes of the Coscuin Chronicles, demonstrate his scenario best. Against a panorama of 19th-century history, an Irish-born hero and his multinational comrades fight for the Green Revolution against the Red Revolution led by the Devil's own son.

In novels and short stories alike, Lafferty is obsessed with transformation. His version of Nature is incorrigibly protean—space, time, and form are liable to shift at any moment. Changes that nourish the "green-gowing world" must be welcomed whatever they cost. The price can be bloody. Lafferty's pages are speckled with gore, either from hand-to-hand combat or the butchering of animals. Yet the slaughter does not stun because death can be followed by resurrection, mutilation by healing, corruption by redemption. Lafferty knits these components together with allusions to mythology and theology. Biblical precedents influence his handling of topics like kingship, sacrifice, and regeneration. They also shape his use of animal symbols such as snakes. This is especially true of *Fourth Mansions.* Here, a naive young newsman integrates the essence of four primeval forces (Badger/Man, Python/Lion, Toad/Ox, and Falcon/Eagle) and becomes mystical Emperor "by entrenched right" to nudge the world towards the next higher Mansion in the cosmic Castle.

Lafferty also draws on history for inspiration ("Thus We Frustrate Charlemagne"). However, the thought can get lost in the quirkiness of his presentation. For instance, perceptively interpreted data in *Okla Hannali,* his epic of the Choctaw Indians, are so entangled with fable that it is hard to accept anything in the book as real. The same eccentricities abound in *The Fall of Rome.* But the Coscuin Chronicles have a sturdier skeleton of fact under the fluid flesh. The foreign locales of these books have a useful distancing effect—exotic events are more acceptable in exotic settings than in the contemporary American ones in *Fourth Mansions.*

Past Master, Lafferty's most popular novel, depends less on factual than on mythicized history. Sir Thomas More is brought forward in time and outward in space to save a diabolical utopia by dying a king's death. Lafferty sends his highly fictionalized 16th-century hero into the 26th-century to dramatize 20th-century spiritual and social issues. Compare this savory scramble of past, future, and present with Ursula K. Le Guin's didactic fable "The Ones Who Walk Away from Omelas."

There is not a bit of science in Lafferty's sf. He justifies his premises on etymological rather than scientific grounds: the name *is* the object. He coins outlandish names, chiefly from Greek and Latin, then interprets them in idiosyncratic ways—the derivations in the Coscuin Chronicles would make Isidore of Seville blush. (His debt to the classics extends to farce as well as philosophy. See *Space Chantey,* his reworking of the *Odyssey. Archipelago* was inspired by the Argosy.)

Bizarre nomenclature does not exhaust Lafferty's rampaging delight in words. He showers his pages with odd poetry. (Who else would dare to rhyme "roses" with "apotheosis" or turn chapter titles into narrative verse as he does in *The Reefs of Earth?*) This verbal virtuosity makes him sf's equivalent of "Flann O'Brien." He loves exaggeration and grotesqueries as well as any Celt before him—surely one of his ancestors had a hand in *The Cattle Raid of Cooley.* But Lafferty appreciates ethnic spice of many flavors—his admired "seven bloods of Basse-Terre include all three races. He uses almost as many Amerindian referents as Irish ones ("Narrow Valley") and is fascinated by gypsies ("The Land of the Great Horses").

Readers and critics alike have prized the shimmering emerald surface of Lafferty at the expense of his substance which current society is ill-equipped to recognize much less comprehend. (Compare Lafferty's situation with that of equally uncommercial Cordwainer Smith, a devout Episcopalian.) This author cannot be understood apart from his self-proclaimed conservative Catholicism. A case in point is his abhorrence for liberal Catholic philosopher Pierre Teilhard de Chardin. This point goes unnoticed even when it is explicitly stated, yet it is vital to interpreting Lafferty's metaphysics. He decries Chardin's evolutionary Omega Point as "the sickening emptiness of the Point Big-O. " He rebuts the notion of natural perfectibility with visions of evil so insidious only grace can conquer it.

Lafferty's great subject is the perennial war between Heaven and Hell: "We must kill the Devil afresh every day. " This Adversary is no silken Mephisto but a musky blackguard whom healthy young men can drink under the table. Be they ever so pungent, demons like Ifreann in the Coscuin Chronicles and Papa Diabolus the *The Devil Is Dead* are never allowed to steal the show. The heroes and heroines overwhelm them with sheer vitality. Vice can imitate but never match the "overrunning gaiety" of virtue. Making Goodness exciting is a Lafferty specialty.

Although he rode to prominence in the 1960's with the New Wave, Lafferty shows none of the gloom characteristic of that movement. His fiction rings with the high hilarity of love and laughter. Each of his serious works ends on a note of hope, for his is the faith-filled vision of a universe en route to redemption. Despite detours, it keeps gyring upward according to divine plan. "All final answers were given in the beginning. . . . It is our task to grow out until we reach them. "

—Sandra Miesel

LAKE, David (John). Australian. Born of British parents in Bangalore, India, 26 March 1929; became Australian citizen, 1975. Educated at St. Xavier's School, Calcutta, 1940-44; Dauntsey's, Wiltshire, 1945-47; Trinity College, Cambridge, 1949-53, B. A. 1952, Dip. Ed. 1953, M. A. 1956; University College of North Wales, Bangor, diploma in linguistics 1965; University of Queensland, Brisbane, Ph. D. 1974. Served in the

Royal Artillery, 1948-49. Married Marguerite Ivy Ferris in 1964; one daughter. Assistant Master, Sherrardswood School, Welwyn Garden City, Hertfordshire, 1953-58, and St. Albans Boys Grammar School, Hertfordshire, 1958-59; Lecturer in English, Saigon University, 1959-61, for the Thai government, Bangkok, 1961-63, and at Chiswick Polytechnic, London, 1963-64; Reader in English, Jadavpur University, Calcutta, 1965-67. Lecturer, 1967-72, Senior Lecturer, 1973-76, and since 1977. Reader in English, University of Queensland. Recipient: Ditmar Award, 1977. Agent: Valerie Smith, 538 East Harford Street, Milford, Pennsylvania 18337, U. S. A. Address: Department of English, University of Queensland, St. Lucia, Queensland 4067, Australia.

SCIENCE-FICTION PUBLICATIONS

Novels (series: Dextra; Xuma)

Walkers on the Sky. New York, DAW, 1976; revised edition, London, Fontana, 1978.
The Right Hand of Dextra. New York, DAW, 1977.
The Wildings of Westron (Dextra). New York, DAW, 1977.
The Gods of Xuma; or, Barsoom Revisited. New York, DAW, 1978.
The Fourth Hemisphere. Melbourne, Void, 1980.
The Man Who Loved Morlocks. Melbourne, Hyland House, 1981.
The Ring of Truth. Melbourne, Cory and Collins, 1983; New York, DAW, 1984.
Warlords of Xuma. New York, DAW, 1983.

Uncollected Short Stories

"Creator," in *Envisaged Worlds,* edited by Paul Collins. St. Kilda, Victoria, Void, 1978.
"Re-deem the Time," in *Rooms of Paradise,* edited by Lee Harding. Melbourne, Quartet, 1978; New York, St. Martin's Press, 1979.
"What Is She," in *Transmutations,* edited by Rob Gerrard. Melbourne, Outback, 1979.
"The Last Day of Christman," in *Distant Worlds,* edited by Paul Collins. Melbourne, Cory and Collins, 1981.

OTHER PUBLICATIONS

Verse

Hornpipes and Funerals. Brisbane, University of Queensland Press, 1973.

Other

John Milton: Paradise Lost. Calcutta, Mukhopadhyay, 1967.
Greek Tragedy. Calcutta, Excelsus, 1969.
The Canon of Thomas Middleton's Plays: Internal Evidence for the Major Problems of Authorship. Cambridge, University Press, 1975.
"The White Sphinx and the Whitened Lemur: Images of Death in *The Time Machine,* " in *Science-Fiction Studies 6* (Terre Haute, Indiana), 1979.

*

David Lake comments:
The main impulse embodied in my SF is the impulse of the human rat to imagine escapes from the cosmic trap in which he finds himself. The trap is partly (but only partly) of his own building; it has been building for a very long time; and the bars now loom very high indeed. Sometimes the rat thinks he can escape by a smart technological fix; sometimes he knows that he can't. But either way he can at least dream.

The main influences on my writing are probably H. G. Wells and C. S. Lewis, and the clash between these two authors' values. I follow Wells and Lewis in writing SF that deliberately borders on fantasy. Elves may appear wearing spacesuits. The same themes also appear in my poems, some of which are in fact close to being SF.

David Lake presents himself as a pessimist in search of the numinous, a fantasist without belief, choosing science fiction as his vehicle for escapism because magic doesn't work. Lake has little confidence in the efficacy of science, either: his alter ego, Ambrose Livermore, is able to use a time machine as his escape hatch into the future, leap-frogging the inevitable Big Bang, only to find the survivors engaged in determined regress, already back in 1900. In this witty tale, despair is salved by humour: Ambrose flourishes in the future 1 BC as Chief Jester to Obliorix.

* * *

If Earth is the City of Destruction in a godless universe, where may hope be found? In his novels Lake catapults small colonies of survivors to distant, wondrous planets, and New Jerusalem is actually built foursquare on Dextra. The two Dextra novels are paradigmatically interesting, complementing each other much as Blake's *Songs of Innocence and of Experience. The Right Hand of Dextra* suggests the State of Innocence, in which it is possible for the Puritan tendencies of the New Earthmen with their "Sifted Scriptures" to be corrected by incorporation with the innocent native species, despite the dextran twist of their protein molecules. Experience seems to prove otherwise, however, in the bleak feudal world of *The Wildings of Westron,* several thousand years later, until the implicit conclusion of the first book is reiterated in absolute form: before there can really be a New Earth on Dextra, all human flesh must perish and only Dextran flesh remain. Most humans will voluntarily undergo the change; the reluctant must simply be exterminated. There is no hope in human flesh because it is closed; Dextran flesh, however, is open, unsecret, because it allows telepathic understanding of one another. The conclusion of *The Gods of Xuma* is not quite so sweeping: only the hopelessly evil human colonists are slaughtered—and fortunately the Xuman natives can tell the difference and are prepared to tolerate those humans remaining who are essentially good natured. However, it is decided that humans are not fitted for space travel. If Lake is thus predisposed in favour of aliens, describing them warmly and even with affection, he is not unduly sentimental about them, particularly about his Xumans, and wishes to correct the supposition, hung over from Burroughs, that physical love with an alien can be satisfactory. The hero's comic embarrassments with Xumans in their female phase prove the point. On the other hand, Lake's aliens are usually not very different from people and do provoke erotic ideas; however, their function is not to be wonderful love-objects (as in Burroughs) but to suggest wonderful possibilities of loving interchange between humans, suitably modified. In *The Right Hand of Dextra* he uses the Song of Solomon as the basis for a description of a transcendent sexual union, only confusing the terms, so that male and female sensations become interchangeable; in *The Wildings of Westron* he echoes Blake: "Every minute particle and particular of their body-minds were commingling, from the head even to the feet, and on every plane of existence."

Lake is an imaginative writer with the power not only to invent exciting worlds but to describe them; he acknowledges the influence of C. S. Lewis, and his evocative accounts of the deserts of Xuma or the purple forests of Dextra bear comparison with those of Malacandra. His most wonderful world is in *Walkers on the Sky*, a tier-world Farmer might envy, ruled capriciously by immortals as if to recall Zelazny's *Lord of Light*. It is a pity that he had not found a story worthy of his world, but this charge may also be leveled at Farmer, and Lake's novel is at least free from Farmer's sometimes heavy portentousness. It was more fortunate for Lewis that the impression of his marvellous planets could overhelm even his grand theme; but to gratify one's sense of wonder and be bored or irritated by the story which presents the wonder is like eating great food in a dirty restaurant with poor service: usually the science fiction reader is glad to pay the one as the price for the other.

In "Creator" Lake shows he is prepared to tackle the big theme and, if he trivializes it somewhat in the process—our universe exists inside a "creatron," a kind of game machine for artists on the plant Olympus, our creator being Jay Crystal (J. C.—get it?)—he does also succeed in providing a provocative ironic perspective on human history. The short story may suit this author's evident talents better than the novel for a while, as it will free him from the tedium of providing a stock narrative.

—Michael J. Tolley

LANG, King. See TUBB, E. C.

LANGART, T. See GARRETT, Randall.

LANGE, John. See CRICHTON, Michael.

LANGFORD, David. British. Born in Newport, Gwent, Wales, 10 April 1953. Educated at Newport High School; Brasenose College, Oxford, 1971-74, B. A. in physics, 1974, M. A. 1978. Married Hazel Langford in 1976. Weapons physicist, Atomic Weapons Research Establishment, Aldermaston, Berkshire, 1975-80. Since 1980, free-lance writer. Editor, *Ansible*, Reading, Berkshire, and since 1983, Contributing Editor, and columnist ("Critical Mass"), *White Dwarf*, London. Agent: Hilary Rubinstein, A. P. Watt Ltd., 26-28 Bedford Row, London WC1R 4HL. Address: 94 London Road, Reading, Berkshire RG1 5AU, England.

SCIENCE-FICTION PUBLICATIONS

Novels

The Space Eater. London, Arrow, 1982; New York, Pocket Books, 1983.

The Leaky Establishment. London, Muller, 1984.

Uncollected Short Stories

"Heatwave" in *New Writings in SF 27*, edited by Kenneth Bulmer. London, Sidgwick and Jackson, 1975.
"Accretion," in *Andromeda 2*, edited by Peter Weston. London, Futura, 1977.
"Connections," in *Andromeda 3*, edited by Peter Weston. London, Futura, 1978.
"The Small Still Voice Inside," in *Pulsar 1*, edited by George Hay. London, Penguin, 1978.
"Training," in *The Future at War 1*, edited by Reginald Bretnor. New York, Ace, 1979.
"Sex Pirates of the Blood Asteroid," in *Aries 1*, edited by John Grant. Newton Abbot, Devon, David and Charles, 1979.
"Imbalance," in *Ad Astra 4* (London), June 1979.
"Understudy," in *Practical Computing* (London), October 1979.
"Turing Test," in *Practical Computing* (London), April 1980.
"Law of Conservation," in *Ad Astra 10* (London), June 1980.
"The Final Days," in *A Spadeful of Spacetime*, edited by Fred Saberhagen. New York, Ace, 1981.
"Transcends All Wit," in *Pictures at an Exhibition*, edited by Ian Weston. Cardiff, Greystoke Mobray, 1981.
"Sacrifice," in *Destinies* (New York), August 1981.
"Semolina," in *Book of Alien Monsters*, edited by Peter Davison. London, Sphere, 1982.
"Lukewarm," in *Alien Encounters*, edited by Jan Howard Finder. New York, Taplinger, 1982.
"Friendly Reflections," in *Practical Computing* (London), February 1982.
"Hearing Aid," in *Practical Computing* (London), October 1982.
"Too Good to Be," in *Imagine 3* (Cambridge), June 1983.
"In Place of Power," in *Beyond Lands of Never*, edited by Maxim Jakubowski. London, Unwin, 1984.
"3 AM," in *The Year's Best Horror Stories 12*, edited by Karl Edward Wagner. New York, DAW, 1984.
"Lost Event Horizon," in *Imagine 12* (Cambridge), March 1984.
"Statement of a Minor Offender," in *Knave* (London), June 1984.
"The Distressing Damsel," in *Amazing* (New York), July 1984.
"Sidetrack," in *Knave* (London), August 1984.
"The Mad Gods' Omelette," in *White Dwarf 59* (London), November 1984.
"Wetware," in *What Micro?* (London), November 1984.
"The Thing in the Bedroom," in *The Year's Best Horror Stories 13*, edited by Karl Edward Wagner. New York, DAW, 1985.
"Cube Root," in *Interzone* (London), Spring 1985.
"Notes for a Newer Testament," in *Afterwar*, edited by Janet E. Morris. New York, Baen, 1985.

OTHER PUBLICATIONS

Other

The Necronomicon, with others, edited by George Hay. St. Helier, Jersey, Spearman, 1978.
An Account of a Meeting with Denizens of Another World, 1871. Newton Abbot, Devon, David and Charles, 1979.
War in 2080: The Future of Military Technology. Newton Abbot, Devon, David and Charles, 1979.
"Digging Up the Future: G. K. Chesterton as SF Author," in *Vector* (Reading, Berkshire), December 1980.

Facts and Fallacies: A Book of Definitive Mistakes and Misguided Predictions, with Chris Morgan. Exeter, Devon, Webb and Bower, 1981.

The Science in Science Fiction, with Peter Nicholls and Brian M. Stableford. London, Joseph, 1982; New York, Knopf, 1983.

Micromania: The Whole Truth about Home Computers, with Charles Platt. London, Gollancz, 1984; as *The Whole Truth Home Computer Handbook,* New York, Avon, 1984.

"The Dragonhiker's Guide to Battlefield Convenant at Dune's Edge: Odyssey Two," in *Xyster 5* (Clevedon, Avon), 1984.

The Third Millennium: The History of the World AD 200-3000, with Brian M. Stableford. London, Sidgwick and Jackson, 1985.

*

David Langford comments:

Anything said here *ought* to be redundant. A work requiring the author's personal introduction ("Now I want you to meet little Johnny, boys and girls. He's a bit subnormal and deformed, but don't you dare tease him") is hardly likely to make its own way in the horrid outside world of bookstands. However . . .

I'm a technophile but a somewhat pessimistic one; it seems so unfair that shiny, alluring technological toys keep pointing the way to more and easier megadeaths. Yet because I like intellectual games I keep playing literary hopscotch on the edge of the unthinkable, cracking jokes about a variety of armageddons: current (*The Leaky Establishment*), seriously extrapolated (*War in 2080*) and wholly imaginary (*The Space Eater*). In the shorter efforts there are lighter jokes, parodies, and sheer fun; give me twenty thousand words or more, though, and I end up addressing gallows humour to the Angel of Death, the Spectre of World War III, the Ghost of Christmas Yet To Come, or some such unjolly companion.

By publication time this will be less an introduction than a memorial. I've no idea what I'll be writing next year, while swift and efficient technologies of modern-day publishing will doubtless have made all the above-listed works quite unobtainable. (Support a starving author—write to me and buy my remainders!) My ambition is to become a capitalist.

*   *   *

David Langford began writing as a fan while still a student and his work still retains many of the hallmarks of fannishness. (And just reflect that there's no other field of literature where that statement would make any sense). He began by writing parodies of Doc Smith and the awful German "sci-fi" series, one of which ("Sex Pirates of the Blood Asteroid") he quotes at the head of a chapter in *War in 2080.* Much of his later work has the same delight in taking apart the illogical and second-rate, especially in "Facts and Fallacies," a collection of thoroughly wrong predictions and scientific pronouncements, and in his SF review column for *White Dwarf* magazine, where he takes more delight and more space in stepping firmly on the latest multi-volume clunker than in recommending the things he enjoys (no bad thing in a book reviewer). Langford keeps a foot firmly in fandom with the fanzines *Twll Ddu* and *Ansible.*

Since he left the scientific civil service to become a full-time writer, much of Langford's work has been in collaboration with other writers, as in *The Necronomicon* and *The Science in Science Fiction,* but he has produced three books of his own of interest to the science-fiction reader. The first, *An Account of a Meeting with Denizens of Another World, 1871,* is a slim one-joke volume. An extraterrestrial probe lands in a wood in Buckinghamshire

during the last century and being discovered by a local craftsman tries to open communication with him. A cod modern commentary laments the difficulty of conveying the idea of quarks and DNA by purely visual means. The book is a counter to all those tales in which two species meet and go from the square of the hypotenuse to establishing embassies inside a few days.

The Space Eater is the only one of his two novels that can be called science fiction in a conventional sense. It's a hard science-fiction tale centering on unlikely new branches of physics leading to ways of destroying worlds even more spectacular than the nuclear devices the author once worked on. Its chief faults are uneveness of tone (at the tensest moments the hero goes off into typically Langfordian flights of fancy) and the characterisation of the hero who goes from being an automated killing machine at the start to being a Throughly Nice Chap at the end, totally changing his nature and all for no particular reason. Despite this the story retains interest and is also notable for containing the SF universe's most impractical space drive.

His most recent book, *The Leaky Establishment,* is only marginally SF, being a very enjoyable farce concerning a researcher at a British Nuclear Centre who finds himself in the position of having to smuggle plutonium warheads back into the top-secret centre. Langford's chief joy is mocking Civil Service procedures in the shape of a committee to improve the public image of nuclear weapons ("The suggestion that individual missiles be named after members of the Royal Family to promote empathy and good public feeling was felt to merit further consideration").

Langford has probably yet to produce his best work but we can look forward to much good entertainment while he works on it.

—Michael Cule

LANIER, Sterling E(dmund). American. Born in New York City, 18 December 1927. Educated at Harvard University, Cambridge, Massachusetts, A. B. 1951; University of Pennsylvania, Philadelphia, 1953-58. Served in World War II and the Korean War. Married 1) Martha Hanna Pelton in 1961 (divorced, 1978), one son and one daughter; 2) Ann Miller McGregor in 1979. Research historian, Winterthur Museum, Switzerland, 1958-60; Editor, John C. Winston Company, 1961, Chilton Books, 1961-62, 1965-67, and Macrae-Smith Company, 1963-64. Since 1967, full-time writer and sculptor. Recipient: Follett Award, 1969. Agent: Curtis Brown Ltd., 575 Madison Avenue, New York, New York 10022, U.S.A.

SCIENCE-FICTION PUBLICATIONS

Novels

The War for the Lot (for children). Chicago, Follett, 1969; London, Sidgwick and Jackson, 1977.

Hiero's Journey. Radnor, Pennsylvania, Chilton, 1973; London, Sidgwick and Jackson, 1975.

The Unforsaken Hiero. New York, Ballantine, 1983.

Menace under Marwood. New York, Ballantine, 1983.

Short Stories

The Peculiar Exploits of Brigadier Ffellowes. New York, Walker, and London, Sidgwick and Jackson, 1977.

Uncollected Short Stories

"Join Our Gang," in *Analog* (New York), May 1961.
"Such Stuff as Dreams, in *Analog* (New York), January 1968.
"Whose Short Happy Life," in *Fantasy and Science Fiction* (New York), March 1968.
"Never Cry Human," in *If* (New York), January-Febraury 1971.
"Thinking of the Unthinkable" and "The Voice of the Turtle," in *Fantasy and Science Fiction* (New York), August 1973.
" . . . No Traveler Returns," in *Fantasy and Science Fiction* (New York), April 1974.
"Ghost of a Crown," in *Fantasy and Science Fiction* (New York), December 1976.
"A Father's Tale," in *First World Fantasy Awards,* edited by Gahan Wilson. New York, Doubleday, 1977.
"The Syndicated Time," in *Fantasy and Science Fiction* (New York), July 1978.
"Commander in the Mist," in *Fantasy and Science Fiction* (New York), March 1982.

*   *   *

Sterling E. Lanier's fiction presents a world teeming with creatures of the fantastic imagination, making it seem as though Tolkein were set in some future century. No innovator or philosopher, Lanier sails on well-charted seas of the super-natural and unnatural. His work almost always combines the worlds of fantasy and science fiction, and although his output is relatively small, his novel *Hiero's Journey* is of sufficient merit to warrant close attention.

A summary of this novel can hardly do it justice as the story pivots on one of the oldest and most frequently used plots of the genre: the hero sets out on a quest for lost knowledge through a world laid waste by nuclear war and controlled by mutants made horrible and evil by radiation. However, Lanier is able to inform this trite plot with his own vision of the fantastic and produces a world that is both delightful and terrifying. The questing hero is Per Hiero Desteen—priest, exorcist, killman, and citizen of the Metz republic of Kanda—who sets off in the eighth millennium in search of ancient legendary machines called "computers" that will help him and his people put together the knowledge of the past. This knowledge is the last hope for survival against the various forms of evil that resulted from the Death (nuclear holocaust). This theme is not without its own moral convictions, and Lanier attempts to tie his story to present-day concerns in several ways. Some connections are made through a language that is not nearly as interesting or inventive as one might hope for in this kind of novel: Lantik Sea (Atlantic Ocean), Kanda (Canada), Neeyana (Indiana), Leemutes (lethal mutations). More interesting are the con-temporary social and environmental values that are invested in the tale. The nuclear devastation is served by a group of men called "the Unclean." These men were formerly psychologists, biochemists, and physicists who have been severely ravaged by radiation and now seek to rule the evil world they have created. On the other hand, Hiero is joined by a wise ancient, Brother Aldo, who belongs to a group called "the Eleveners." The eleveners are the Brotherhood of the Eleventh Commandment, a group of social scientists dedicated to the ideal: Thou shalt not despoil the Earth and the life thereon. Hiero and Brother Aldo are accompanied by a telepathic, almost human bear (Gorm), a semi-intelligent bull "morse," and a strong-willed but faithful young maiden (Luchare).

Lanier's strengths and weaknesses are both evident in this fantasy adventure yarn. He is at his best when weaving a suspenseful tale, and, while his characters lack depth and the plot has been often used before, the world he creates, filled with radiation-induced mutants, ancient, knowing wizards, and fur-covered dwarves, lives fully in the imagination and allows the reader to partake fully in the suspenseful quest. Lanier is obviously aware of the parallels with medieval romances, and those who enjoy *Beowulf, Le Morte Darthur,* and the sagas will be enthralled by the re-creation of those environments and values in a future time.

Lanier's other work is of a similar but lesser quality. His stories as a rule combine the fantastic world of unnatural monsters with the more traditional trappings of science fiction: space ships, time travel, telepathic communication. *The Peculiar Exploits of Brigadier Ffellowes* presents seven stories that feature a retired English Brigadier who narrates tales that involve supernatural powers and fantastic monsters. Lanier exhibits a good sense of humor in these stories and carefully sets them up as a series of Chinese boxes: a story within a story within a story. The monsters found here, like the Nandi bear and the sea serpent Jormungadir, are similar to those found elsewhere in Lanier's writings. But the best quality of Lanier is what accounts for the success of this and his other works: he is an excellent storyteller.

—Lawrence R. Ries

LARGE, E(rnest) C(harles). British. Plant pathologist. *Died in 1976.*

SCIENCE-FICTION PUBLICATIONS

Novels (series: Charles Pry)

Sugar in the Air (Pry). London, Cape, and New York, Scribner, 1937.
Asleep in the Afternoon (Pry). London, Cape, 1938; New York, Holt, 1939.
Dawn in Andromeda. London, Cape, 1956.

OTHER PUBLICATIONS

Other

The Advance of the Fungi. London, Cape, and New York, Holt, 1940.
Potato Blight Epidemics Throughout the World, with A. E. Cox. Washington, D. C., Agricultural Research Bureau, 1960.

*   *   *

In some respects, E. C. Large could be considered a scientist's science-fiction writer, for he deals primarily with the concerns and perspectives of the scientist in his everyday life. Large's narratives, though not abstruse, explore scientific inventions and processes with acute detail, and his work might be included in what C. S. Lewis identifies as the "fiction of engineers."

The most notable work Large produced is *Sugar in the Air,* a book considered by many to be a near-classic, for it was this novel which first embodied in speculative fiction a relatively realistic idea of the scientist's work and social situation. The story concerns a young chemical engineer, Charles Pry, who is hired by Hydro-Mechanical Constructions Ltd., to create sugar by photosynthesis, using only a handful of hints gathered by another, rather eccentric scientist. Pry succeeds in discovering the elusive formula, but he encounters conflicts with company financiers in the marketing of "Sunsap," as the product is called. They are concerned with obtaining the quickest and greatest profit, while Pry idealistically strives to make the product more beneficial for society, and the book becomes a kind of tragicomedy of the scientist and commerce. The novel thus inverts the motif of the mad scientist, for it is the corporation, not Pry, who wants to exploit the discovery for its own greed. This attitude of organization vs. the individual dominated later magazine science fiction, as for example when the lone nuclear scientist is pitted against the political and military powers.

Asleep in the Afternoon, a sequel, is also an invention story, though an inferior one, dealing with similar ideas and attitudes. Charles Pry, having lost his job with Hydro-Mechanical, decides to write a novel, which is about the invention of a sleep-inducing device. Within this rather unexciting framework, Large again satirizes capitalism and corporations, as well as other aspects of contemporary life, political structure, and social attitudes.

While the first two novels deal with the relationship—and often the conflict—between the scientist and the community, *Dawn in Andromeda* is a Utopian allegory. Ten British men and women (five of each) emerge Venus-like from the sea one morning onto the shores of an uninhabited planet in the Andromeda galaxy, where they have been transported by God in a rather ridiculous opening. Equipped with their scientific knowledge and practical skills—and some faint memories of Earth—they build a new society and community on this strange world, which closely resembles Earth. The original group is harmonious enough; it is the second generation's spontaneous pursuit of commerce and religion which spoils the Utopian dream, reflecting the same sort of criticisms that Large displays in the previous two books. Again, the narrative is heavily endowed with scientific detail, exploring every step of the little society's progress.

But Large circumvents the most obvious problem, that of interplanetary transportation, choosing instead to follow C. S. Lewis's advice that "frankly supernatural methods are best. " So the novel really doesn't follow the 17th and 18th-century tradition of the voyage to another world, being concerned instead, like Wells's *First Men in the Moon,* with what happens there.

Though Large is obviously more scientist than writer, his books do have some literary qualities worth noting: his prose is often strong and direct, tough, effective; his characters, though not fully rounded, compel interest and arouse sympathy; he also uses imaginative names, giving characters such apt identities as Cocaine, Dr. Sinus, Dr. Zaareb, MacDuff, or Hunt-Transom, while the crew in Andromeda take their names from the alphabetical letterings on the bindings of Encyclopedia Britannica.

Large's novels evince a firm belief in science and its potentiality; they laud the moral scientist of commitment and decry the stupidity and incompetence of so many social organizations—business, commercial, religious, political, revolutionary. Large's work offers an interesting, knowledgable, and valuable perspective of the scientist, his work, and his place in society.

—Karen Charmaine Blansfield

———

LA SALLE, Victor. See **FANTHORPE, R. Lionel.**

LATHAM, Philip. Pseudonym for Robert S(hirley) Richardson. American. Born in Kokomo, Indiana, 22 April 1902. Educated at the University of California, Los Angeles, B. A. 1926; University of California, Berkeley, Ph. D. 1931. Married 1) Delia Shull in 1929 (died 1940); 2) Marjorie Helen Engstead in 1942, one daughter. Assistant Astronomer, Mt. Wilson, now Hale, Observatory, Pasadena, California, 1931-58; Associate Director, Griffith Observatory, Los Angeles, 1958-64. After 1964, free-lance writer. *Died in November 1981.*

SCIENCE-FICTION PUBLICATIONS

Novels

Five Against Venus (for children). Philadelphia, Winston, 1952.
Missing Men of Saturn (for children). Philadelphia, Winston, 1953.
Second Satellite (as Robert S. Richardson). New York, McGraw Hill, 1956.

Uncollected Short Stories

"N Day," in *Astounding* (New York), January 1946.
"The Blindness," in *Astounding* (New York), July 1946.
"The Aphrodite Project," in *Astounding* (New York), June 1949.
"The Most Dangerous Love," in *Marvel* (New York), November 1951.
"Martial Ritual," in *Future* (New York), July 1953.
"A Moment of Laughter," in *Fantastic* (New York), October 1953.
"Comeback," in *Future* (New York), November 1953.
"Simpson," in *Cosmos* (New York), July 1954.
"Flash Nova," in *McCall's* (New York), 15 August 1956.
"Disturbing Sun," in *Astounding* (New York), May 1959.
"To Explain Mrs. Thompson," in *The Expert Dreamers,* edited by Frederik Pohl. New York, Doubleday, 1962.
"Kid Anderson" (as Robert S. Richardson), in *Great Science Fiction by Scientists,* edited by Groff Conklin. New York, Macmillan, 1962.
"The Dimple in Draco," in *Orbit 2,* edited by Damon Knight. New York, Putnam, 1967; London, Rapp and Whiting, 1968.
"The Red Euphoric Bands," in *Galaxy* (New York), December 1967.
"Under the Dragon's Tail," in *Analog* (New York), December 1968.
"After Enfer," in *Fantasy and Science Fiction* (New York), March 1969.
"The Rose Bowl Pluto Hypothesis," in *Orbit 5,* edited by Damon Knight. New York, Putnam, 1969.
"Jeannette's Hands," in *Fantasy and Science Fiction* (New York), January 1973.
"Future Forbidden," in *Galaxy* (New York), May 1973.
"A Drop of Dragon's Blood," in *Fantasy and Science Fiction* (New York), July 1975.
"The Miracle Elixir," in *Fantastic* (New York), June 1977.
"The Xi Effect," in *The Golden Age of Science Fiction,* edited by Kingsley Amis. London, Hutchinson, 1981.

OTHER PUBLICATIONS as Robert S. Richardson

Plays

Television Plays: *Captain Video* series, 1953.

Other

Preliminary Elements of Object Comas Sola (1927 AA), with others. Berkeley, University of California Press, 1927.
Astronomy, with William T. Skilling. New York, Holt, and London, Chapman and Hall, 1939; revised edition, Holt, 1947.
The Practical Essentials of Pre-Training Navigation, with William T. Skilling. New York, Holt, 1942.
Sun, Moon and Stars, with William T. Skilling. New York, McGraw Hill, 1946; revised edition, 1964.
A Brief Text in Astronomy, with William T. Skilling. New York, Holt, 1954; revised edition, 1959.
Exploring Mars (for children). New York, McGraw Hill, 1954; as *Man and the Planets*, London, Muller, 1954.
The Fascinating World of Astronomy. New York, McGraw Hill, 1960; London, Faber, 1962.
Man and the Moon. Cleveland, World, 1961.
Astronomy in Action. New York, McGraw Hill, 1962.
Mars. New York, Harcourt Brace, 1964; London, Allen and Unwin, 1965.
Getting Acquainted with Comets. New York, McGraw Hill, 1967.
The Star Lovers. New York, Macmillan, 1967.
The Stars and Serendipity (for children). New York, Pantheon, 1971.

*

Manuscript Collection: Fullerton College Library, California.

Philip Latham commented:

(1981) Since most of my firsthand experience is in astronomy, most of my fiction has an astronomical background. But one of my stories, "Kid Anderson," is about a prizefighter. I firmly believe that science always leads science fiction. Increasingly I have gone over to science fantasy, as in "Jeannette's Hands" and other stories. My stories are always written on the basis of *people rather than gadgetry*.

Where science fiction will go in the future is a guess. There is little left to write about: we have already written stories of interplanetary travel, extra dimensions, time travel. *Star Wars*, for example, to my mind was a fairy tale: you could have anything you wanted in it. Most science-fiction writers have inventive ability and ingenuity, but lack true imagination, an extremely rare gift. I neither read science fiction nor look at SF on TV or in motion pictures. Henceforth, we must try to find material in the world around us. It is there if we can see it.

* * *

A scandal in American science fiction is how little science there is in it. A notable exception lies in Philip Latham's stories, since they were written by the professional astronomer Robert S. Richardson and bear the marks of his expertise. For more than three decades Latham's stories appeared from time to time in the major magazines and anthologies, and Latham also wrote juvenile science-fiction novels.

Many of the early stories are based on astronomical speculation, often presented as realistic reporting. An example is "The Aphrodite Project," which has the pretense of being science fact, complete with footnotes to astronomical journals. The story imagines a 1946 Navy contract to launch a satelite rocket to Venus to measure its mass. Once near Venus the rocket releases a cloud visible to Earth—Latham does not foresee the sophisticated radio telemetry which has actually been used on such probes. The rocket succeeds in measuring not only the mass of Venus but also its period of rotation. A secondary theme is governmental secrecy as the military authorities clamp down on the release of information about the mission. The story thus presents itself as an exposé of confidential information. "The Xi-Effect" is another example of Latham's astronomical science fiction. Astronomers discover that although the universe as a whole expands, the Earth is in a segment which is shrinking, cutting out greater and greater percentages of radiation so that the eventual extinction of all light seems inevitable. In this story we begin to see Latham's interest in the characters of scientists as well as in science. Latham presents a communication gap between the branches and modes of science. It is a theoretical physicist who predicts the Xi-Effect, and the practical astronomers are shown to be as skeptical of theory as in the public at large. "The Blindness," about the return of Halley's comet in 1986, is hardly a story at all but a meditation on the influence the comet has had on history. A theory of atomic sentience is developed to explain the comet's deviance from its projected orbit. Even in this early story the scientist Richardson makes clear his interest in anti-science and mysticism.

Latham's more recent fiction develops much further the theme of the dubious border between science and magic. Much more central to these later stories, too, is a particular kind of character: the anti-hero who wins the reader's sympathy for his struggles in an absurd world. "After-Enfer" is an example of a Latham story which revolves around character rather than science. The story's title derives from "N-Fear," fear of other dimensions. Sam Baxter, afraid of life, stuck in a museum job, applies for the job of exploring N-space and breaks through to genuine heroism. In "Jeannette's Hands" and its sequel, "A Drop of Dragon's Blood," Latham's protagonist is an astronomer, Bob, who is literally and figuratively married to an astrologer named Dagny. We learn in these stories about the seamy side of being a professional astronomer: the rivalries and the petty jealousies between those who hold conflicting theories and conflicting claims to grant money. Bob's rival Thornton has an innovative theory about the age of the universe, but Bob suspects him of rigging his data. The rivalry is extended in the story to the details of competition over the use of the observatory during the limited nights of good viewing. Latham gives us the comedy of Bob's loss of status when Dagny is appointed official witch of California. Such are the foibles of astronomers in this story that astrology seems a refreshing alternative. In "A Drop of Dragon's Blood" we learn more about the politics of being an astronomer, the need to produce sensational findings in order to attract research funds. Bob makes a public prediction of a period for the variable star Mira in a desperate hope for publicity, because his job is in trouble. His prediction comes true in an ironic way: Mira's companion brightens at exactly the time Bob predicted Mira would brighten, in a new phenomenon, the "simmering nova." The point of the story is the unexpected nature of the universe: "there are ghosts everywhere." Once again Latham tempts us to side with Dagny's brief in magic. Although Latham brought science to science fiction, he certaińly did not bring mechanical materialism.

In his most recent stories Latham turned almost completely away from the hard science of his earlier work. In "Miracle Elixir" an ordinary office worker, who works for Pearce's Golden Specific but never thinks of taking the company product, learns what it is like to have his life turned around by a "real" elixir. Without the interest of science, Latham's recent stories are sometimes thin and awkward. Latham could not be called a major science-fiction writer. But he brought science to his best science-fiction stories and he created anti-heroic and likeable astronomers as characters.

—Curtis C. Smith

LAUMER, (John) Keith. Also writes as Anthony Le Baron. American. Born in Syracuse, New York, 9 June 1925. Educated at the University of Indiana, Bloomington, 1943-44; University of Stockholm, 1947-48; University of Illinois, Urbana, B. Sc. 1950, B. Arch. 1952. Served in the United States Army, 1943-45; Corporal; United States Air Force, 1952-56, 1959-65: Captain. Married Janice Perkinson in 1949. Staff member, University of Illinois, 1952; Foreign Service Vice-Consul and Third Secretary, Rangoon, 1956-59. Since 1959, free-lance writer. Address: Box 972, Brooksville, Florida 33512, U.S.A.

SCIENCE-FICTION PUBLICATIONS

Novels (series: Bolo; Imperium; Invaders; O'Leary; Retief)

Worlds of the Imperium. New York, Ace, 1962; London, Dobson, 1967.
A Trace of Memory. New York, Berkley, 1963; London, Mayflower, 1968.
The Great Time Machine Hoax. New York, Simon and Schuster, 1964.
A Plague of Demons. New York, Berkley, 1965; London, Penguin, 1967.
The Other Side of Time (Imperium). New York, Berkley, 1965; London, Dobson, 1968.
The Time Bender (O'Leary). New York, Berkley, 1966; London, Dobson, 1975.
Retief's War. New York, Doubleday, 1966.
Earthblood, with Rosel George Brown. New York, Doubleday, 1966; London, Coronet, 1979.
Catastrophe Planet. New York, Berkley, 1966; London, Dobson, 1970.
The Monitors. New York, Berkley, 1966; London, Dobson, 1968.
Enemies from Beyond (novelization of TV series; Invaders). New York, Pyramid, 1967.
Planet Run, with Gordon R. Dickson. New York, Doubleday, 1967; London, Hale, 1977.
The Invaders (novelization of TV series). New York, Pyramid, 1967; as *The Meteor Man* (as Anthony Le Baron), London, Corgi, 1968.
Galactic Odyssey. New York, Berkley, 1967; London, Dobson, 1968.
The Day Before Forever, and Thunderhead. New York, Doubleday, 1968.
Assignment in Nowhere. New York, Berkley, 1968; London, Dobson, 1972.
Retief and the Warlords. New York, Doubleday, 1968.
The Long Twilight. New York, Putnam, 1969; London, Hale, 1976.
The World Shuffler (O'Leary). New York, Putnam, 1970; London, Sidgwick and Jackson, 1973.
The House in November. New York, Putnam, 1970; London, Sidgwick and Jackson, 1973.
Time Trap. New York, Putnam, 1970; London, Hale, 1976.
Retief's Ransom. New York, Putnam, 1971; London, Dobson, 1975.

The Star Treasure. New York, Putnam, 1971; London, Sidgwick and Jackson, 1974.
Deadfall. New York, Doubleday, 1971; London, Hale, 1974; as *Fat Chance,* New York, Pocket Books, 1975.
Dinosaur Beach. New York, Scribner, 1971; London, Hale, 1973.
The Infinite Cage. New York, Putnam, 1972; London, Dobson, 1976.
Night of Delusions. New York, Putnam, 1972; London, Dobson, 1977.
The Shape Changer (O'Leary). New York, Putnam, 1972; London, Hale, 1977.
The Glory Game. New York, Doubleday, 1973; London, Hale, 1974.
Bolo: The Annals of the Dinochrome Brigade. New York, Berkley, 1976; London, Millington, 1977.
The Ultimax Man. New York, St. Martin's Press, 1978; London, Sidgwick and Jackson, 1980.
Star Colony. New York, St. Martin's Press, 1981.
The Other Sky (includes *The House in November*). New York, Tor, 1982.
The Return of Retief. New York, Baen, 1985.
Rogue Bolo. New York, Baen, 1985.

Short Stories (series: Retief)

Envoy to New Worlds (Retief). New York, Ace, 1963; London, Dobson, 1972.
Galactic Diplomat (Retief). New York, Doubleday, 1965.
Nine by Laumer. New York, Doubleday, 1967; London, Faber, 1968.
Greylorn. New York, Berkley, 1968; as *The Other Sky,* London, Dobson, 1968.
It's a Mad, Mad, Mad Galaxy. New York, Berkley, 1968; London, Dobson, 1969.
Retief, Ambassador to Space . New York, Doubleday, 1969.
Retief of the CDT. New York, Doubleday, 1971.
Once There Was a Giant. New York, Doubleday, 1971; London, Hale, 1975.
The Big Show. New York, Ace, 1972; London, Hale, 1976.
Timetracks. New York, Ballantine, 1972.
The Undefeated. New York, Dell, 1974.
Retief, Emissary to the Stars. New York, Dell, 1975; augmented edition, New York, Pocket Books, 1979.
The Best of Keith Laumer. New York, Pocket Books, 1976.
Retief Unbound (omnibus). New York, Ace, 1979.
Retief at Large. New York, Ace, 1979.
The Breaking Earth. New York, Pinnacle, 1981.
Worlds of the Imperium. New York, Tor, 1982.
Retief: Diplomat at Arms. New York, Pocket Books, 1982.
Retief to the Rescue. New York, Simon and Schuster, 1983.
The Galaxy Builder. New York, Ace, 1984.
A Chrestomathy. New York, Baen, 1984.

OTHER PUBLICATIONS

Novels

Embassy. New York, Pyramid, 1965.
The Afrit Affair (novelization of TV series). New York, Berkley, 1968.
The Drowned Queen (novelization of TV series). New York, Berkley, 1968.
The Gold Bomb (novelization of TV series). New York, Berkley, 1968.

Other

How to Design and Build Flying Models. New York, Harper, 1960; revised edition, 1970; London, Hale, 1975.

Editor, *Five Fates.* New York, Doubleday, 1970.

*

Manuscript Collections: University of Syracuse, New York; University of Mississippi, University.

Keith Laumer comments:

I have been asked if my work is "relevant," i. e., political propaganda. It is not. I prefer to treat themes that have been important to man ever since he became man, and will continue to be important as long as humanity survives: strength and courage, truth and beauty, loyalty and justice, ethics and integrity, kindness and gentleness, and many others.

*   *   *

During the 1960's, Keith Laumer was one of the most prolific of science-fiction authors. He has slowed down somewhat recently, but even so he has to his credit a long string of titles which range over wide areas both in subject matter and in treatment. Laumer's first novel, *Worlds of the Imperium,* is told as a conventional adventure story, with only an occasional light touch. But in *The Time Bender* and its sequels featuring Layfayette O'Leary. Laumer writes what amounts to a gentle parody of his own Imperium series. And the humor in the long and popular series (mostly of short stories) concerning interstellar diplomat Jame Retief stretches almost all the way to farce. But Laumer can play the other side of the court as well: the tone is serious, even grim, in works such as *A Plague of Demons* and *Night of Delusions.* As for subject matter, Laumer has tried out virtually all the traditional possibilities and has enriched the realm of science fiction with innovations of his own—most notably the brilliantly detailed and remarkably plausible picture of the "fabric of simultaneous reality" introduced in the Imperium series. Laumer has written space-war stories, space-diplomacy stories, slightly rationalized fairy stories, time-travel stories, parallel-world stories, robot stories, psi-power stories, invasion-of-the-Earth stories (including *The Monitors,* in which the invaders are the good guys), stories of intrigue, love, rational detection, mystical apotheosis, and on and on.

Yet for all its diversity, Laumer's work holds unities as well. Some of these are of a negative sort. For instance, there is never an unhappy ending. A Laumer hero may lose a girl, but if so he will usually marry another, and will in no case allow one misfortune to poison his entire life. He may get killed in the end, but he will never go unmourned and (in *Assignment in Nowhere* and others) his sacrifice may well save the world. In the area of positive generalizations, it can be said that in some measure all Laumer stories are adventure stories, even if the author's focus is on satire, farce, romance, ratiocination, or philosophical speculation.

Moreover, Laumer heroes are virtually all of one general pattern, with variations determined chiefly by degree of maturity. While the typologies are not identical, the Laumer character does bear striking similarities to the "Heinlein individual" described by Alexei Panshin. Explanations for this resemblance might range from some basic principle of storytelling to Heinlein's and Laumer's similar background as military officers. The basic Laumer type is the full-formed competent man—sure of himself, resourceful, able to mix easily with all levels of society and to get what he wants out of anyone. Laumer has put the basic type to heaviest use in the person of Retief, hero of a "template series" where character growth is ruled out by the ground rules. For most other applications, the basic competent man is too static—he can indeed be roused to action, but only to protect what he has. A slight variation Laumer employs more often is an incipient competent man whose character is fully formed but who has not yet found his niche in life, and who is consequently searching for fulfillment. Brion Bayard fits in here in *Worlds of the Imperium,* though in the sequel, *The Other Side of Time,* he has matured into the basic type. It is of course possible to begin at an earlier point, with someone who must learn not merely how to apply competence, but competence itself. This gives us characters such as Billy Danger in *Galactic Odyssey* or, in a more humorous vein, Layfayette O'Leary. But Laumer has also interested himself in movement in the other direction, beyond the competent man. Perhaps because of his own relative youth during his peak writing period, Laumer has chosen to do this not by putting one of his heroes through some sort of mid-life crisis, but rather (in a tack he might have picked up from van Vogt or the early Heinlein—or from Sophocles) by having his hero discover something about who he is that causes him to transcend his status as the competent man. In the most extreme case, the largely unsuccessful *Night of Delusions,* the protagonist finds himself to be, for most practical purposes, God. Other Laumer heroes learn that they are supermen, Arthurian reincarnations, and various sorts of robots. The effects of such revelations also vary. Some heroes go off to pursue transcendental existence, some perish gloriously, and others voluntarily return to the human state. It is difficult to decide whether in these various encounters with the transcendental Laumer is trying to put forth a serious philosophy (in the manner of, say, Cordwainer Smith or Gordon R. Dickson), or simply, more playfully, to give his already-competent heroes somewhere to go, and to pique the reader's Sense of Wonder. Such mystic passages are not, in any event, the most successful part of Laumer's work.

The 1960's and early 1970's remain the significant period of Laumer's production. New titles appearing since that time have been generally repackagings or "fix-ups" of older work. A partial exception, *The Galaxy Builder,* is merely one more Layfayette O'Leary novel in the same mold as its predecessors. The repackagings and reiterations do little or nothing to remedy Laumer's characteristic flaws of insufficient attention to detail and excessive repetition from work to work. Consequently, it will be left to posterity to decide which of five or six versions of essentially the same story is the one really worth keeping. But some of Laumer will most certainly be kept.

—Patrick L. McGuire

———

LAVOND, Paul Dennis. See **LOWNDES, Robert A. W.**

———

Le BARON, Anthony. See **LAUMER, Keith.**

———

LEE, Matt. See **MERWIN, Sam, Jr.**

LEE, Tanith. British. Born in London, 19 September 1947. Attended Catford Grammar School, London, and an art college. Recipient: August Derleth Award, 1980; World Fantasy Convention Award, 1983. Lives in London. Address: c/o Macmillan London Ltd., 4 Little Essex Street, London WC2R 3LF, England.

SCIENCE-FICTION PUBLICATIONS

Novels (series: Birthgrave)

The Birthgrave. New York, DAW, 1975; London, Futura, 1977.
Don't Bite the Sun. New York, DAW, 1976.
The Storm Lord. New York, DAW, 1976; London, Futura, 1977.
Drinking Sapphire Wine. New York, DAW, 1977.
Volkhavaar. New York, DAW, 1977; London, Hamlyn, 1981.
Vazkor, Son of Vazkor (Birthgrave). New York, DAW, 1978; as *Shadowfire*, London, Futura, 1979.
Quest for the White Witch (Birthgrave). New York, DAW, 1978; London, Futura, 1979.
Night's Master. New York, DAW, 1978; London, Hamlyn, 1981.
Death's Master. New York, DAW, 1979; London, Hamlyn, 1982.
Drinking Sapphire Wine (includes *Don't Bite the Sun*). London, Hamlyn, 1979.
Electric Forest. New York, DAW, 1979.
Sabella; or, The Blood Stone. New York, DAW, 1980.
Kill the Dead. New York, DAW, 1980.
Day by Night. New York, DAW, 1980.
Delusion's Master. New York, DAW, 1981.
The Silver Metal Lover. New York, DAW, 1982.
Sung in Shadow. New York, DAW, 1983.
Anackire. New York, DAW, 1983.
The Dragon Hoard . New York, Ace, 1984.
Days of Grass. New York, DAW, 1985.

Short Stories

Cyrion. New York, DAW, 1982.
Red as Blood; or, Tales from the Sisters Grimmer. New York, DAW, 1983.
The Beautiful Biting Machine. New Castle, Virginia, Cheap Street, 1984.
Tamastara; or, The Indian Nights. New York, DAW, 1984.
The Gorgon and Other Beastly Tales. New York, DAW, 1985.

Uncollected Short Stories

"The Truce," in *The DAW Science Fiction Reader*, edited by Donald A. Wollheim. New York, DAW, 1976.
"The Demoness," in *The Year's Best Fantasy Stories 2*, edited by Lin Carter. New York, DAW, 1976.
"Odds Against the Gods," in *Swords Against Darkness 2*, edited by Andrew J. Offutt. New York, Kensington, 1977.
"Huzdra," in *The Year's Best Horror 5*, edited by Gerald W. Page. New York, DAW, 1977.
"In the Balance," in *Swords Against Darkness 3*, edited by Andrew J. Offutt. New York, Kensington, 1978.
"Winter White," in *The Year's Best Horror 6*, edited by Gerald W. Page. New York, DAW, 1978.
"Sleeping Tiger," in *The Year's Best Horror Stories 7*, edited by Gerald W. Page. New York, DAW, 1979.
"Northern Chess," in *Amazons*, edited by Jessica Amanda Salmonson. New York, DAW, 1979.
"Deux Amours d'Une Sorcière," in *Swords Against Darkness 4*, edited by Andrew J. Offutt. New York, Kensington, 1979.
"The Third Horseman," in *Weirdbook 14* (New York), 1979.
"Monkey's Stagger," in *Sorcerer's Apprentice* (New York), Fall 1979.
"Room with a Vie," in *New Terrors*, edited by Ramsey Campbell. London, Pan, 1980.
"The Thaw," in *The Best Science Fiction of the Year 9*, edited by Terry Carr. New York, Ballantine, 1980.
"The Squire's Tale," in *Sorcerer's Apprentice* (New York), Summer 1980.
"Gemini," in *Chrysalis 9*, edited by Roy Torgeson. New York, Doubleday, 1981.
"Meow," in *Shadows 4*, edited by Charles L. Grant. New York, Doubleday, 1981.
"The Sombrus Tower," in *Weird Tales 2*, edited by Lin Carter. New York, Zebra, 1981.
"The Dry Season," in *Flashing Swords! 5*, edited by Lin Carter. New York, Dell, 1981.
"Southern Lights," in *Amazons 2*, edited by Jessica Amanda Salmonson. New York, DAW, 1982.
"Miracle and Magic," in *Hecate's Cauldron*, edited by Susan Shwartz. New York, DAW, 1982.
"As Time Goes By," in *Chrysalis 10*, edited by Roy Torgeson. New York, Doubleday, 1983.
"Elle est trois (la mort)," in *Whispers 4*, edited by Stuart David Schiff. New York, Doubleday, 1983.
"La Reine Blanche," in *Isaac Asimov's Space of Her Own*, edited by Shawna McCarthy. New York, Davis, 1983.
"Blue Vase of Ghosts," in *Dragonfields 4* (Ottawa), 1983.
"Anna Medea," in *Amazing* (New York), January 1983.
"Il Basio (Il Chiave)," in *Amazing* (New York), September 1983.
"Chand Veda," in *Isaac Asimov's Science Fiction Magazine* (New York), October 1983.
"Bright Burning Tiger," in *Isaac Asimov's Science Fiction Magazine* (New York), January 1984.
"Medra," in *Isaac Asimov's Science Fiction Magazine* (New York), June 1984.
"Bite-Me-Not; or, Fleur de Feu," in *Isaac Asimov's Science Fiction Magazine* (New York), October 1984.
"After the Guillotine," in *Amazing* (New York), January 1985.

OTHER PUBLICATIONS

Short Story

The Betrothed. Sidcup, Kent, Slughorn Press, 1968.

Plays

Radio Plays: *Bitter Gate*, 1977; *Red Wine*, 1977; *Death Is King*, 1979; *The Silver Sky*, 1980.

Television Plays: *Sarcophagus*, 1980, and *Sand*, 1981, both for *Blake's Seven* series.

Other (for children)

The Dragon Hoard. London, Macmillan, and New York, Farrar Straus, 1971.
Princess Hynchatti and Some Other Surprises. London, Macmillan, 1972; New York, Farrar Straus, 1973.
Animal Castle. London, Macmillan, and New York, Farrar Straus, 1972.

Companions on the Road. London, Macmillan, 1975.
The Winter Players. London, Macmillan, 1976.
Companions on the Road, and The Winter Players. New York, St. Martin's Press, 1977.
East of Midnight. London, Macmillan, 1977; New York, St. Martin's Press, 1978.
The Castle of Dark. London, Macmillan, 1978.
Shon the Taken. London, Macmillan, 1979.
Unsilent Night (miscellany; for adults). Cambridge, Massachusetts, NESFA Press, 1981.
Prince on a White Horse. London, Macmillan, 1982.

*

Bibliography: by Mike Ashley, in *Fantasy Macabre 4* (London), 1983.

*   *   *

Tanith Lee has established herself as pre-eminent in both fantasy and SF with children's books (*The Dragon Hoard, Animal Castle*), juvenile fiction (*East of Midnight*), fairy tales (*Princess Hynchatti and Some Other Surprises*), horror stories ("Sirriamnis," "Winter White"), erotic adult fiction (*Death's Master, Night's Master*, and *Volkhavaar*), heroic fantasy (*The Storm Lord*, the Birthgrave trilogy, "The Murderous Dove"), and conventional science fiction (*Don't Bite the Sun, Drinking Sapphire Wine, Electric Forest, The Silver Metal Lover*). All have strong characterization, intense emotional impact, tongue-in-cheek humor, and gorgeous people of enormous power and will who must pass tests before accepting themselves. The fantasies are long and episodic, sometimes in short-story form, full of exotic names and barbarous tribes. Though set on other planets, they have little ecological detail. Lee is concerned instead with people who walk alone, searching for significant destinies.

The Birthgrave trilogy constitutes heroic searches for identity. *The Birthgrave* was immediately ranked with works by Le Guin and Norton. It is a transition between her fantasy and SF modes, as is the ironic short story "The Truce." Its background is a society degenerated from greatness, horribly ignorant of the past and science. Its heroine awakes with no name or identity and a face so hideous she cannot endure it. Where women are mindless cattle, she cannot accept her obvious superiority and allow others, particularly handsome Vazkor, to use her. In Book III she has another rebirth. Leaving Vazkor's son with a bereaved mother, she follows a peaceful tribe. To save her companions she unconsciously summons a spaceship to destroy a dragon. This confrontation of technical and mental power helps her recall her past and accept her identity, telepathy, power over even nature, and great beauty. She determines to rebuild a race of mental giants. In *Vazkor, Son of Vazkor,* Tuvek changes from an insensitive tribesman to Vazkor, gentle, wise, and powerful. His development continues in *Quest for the White Witch* as the epic hero searches for revenge and a mother. The novels and *Anackire, Delusion's Master, The Storm Lord,* and *Volkhavaar,* are like Hesse's *Siddhartha,* about the education of a god.

The ends of *The Birthgrave* and *Quest for the White Witch* have elements of SF in the fall of a great civilization and the actual appearance of a spaceship. Unique in Lee's fantasy is its underlying seriousness and lack of a basis in religion or witchcraft. The people are godlike human beings who must learn to perfect and use their mental abilities responsibly. Before gaining control, Vazkor and Karrakaz, his mother, accidentally cause destruction. Both learn to rise above a degraded society and be rid of guilt, and determine to restore advanced civilization to their planet.

The restlessness of the loner searching for identity is equally significant in the teenage heroine of the anti-utopian *Don't Bite the Sun* and *Drinking Sapphire Wine*. Society is totally controlled, even the weather within the domed city. Before 50, people party, dress outrageously, engage in delinquency, change bodies at whim, marry for a day or so, and try to sabotage machines that maintain perfection. Ensuring immediate rescue from death and a specially designed new body, monitoring bees make suicide impossible. After serious social deviance, an individual is sent to Limbo for Personality Dissolution and a fresh start. The narrator is lonely, precocious, and bored with perpetual fun. Her only true friend is the pet, as troublesome and as little disturbed by convention as she. To find meaning, she goes on an archaelogical expedition. Back in the city, she dons a male body and fights a duel, killing another. Preferring exile to ego dissolution, she settles in the desert where she knows a good life once existed and begins her own counter-culture, outwitting the disapproving authorities. This world is different from those of Lee's fantasies in its technological development. Her narrative is colloquial, highlighted by special "Jang" slang instead of the high epic style used in the fantasy. Although the climaxes of self-revelation occur with few episodes and characters, one developing character commands attention. *Day By Night* is similar in its heroines, adventures in shifting reality, and contrast between highly developed cities and empty spaces. Easily read, these are suitable for juvenile as well as adult audiences.

Electric Forest centers on the developing character of "Ugly," Magdala Cled, a disfigured, abandoned child on a planet where everyone is beautiful. Claudio Loro, handsome, wealthy, and brilliant, offers her beauty at a high price—her real body to be cared for, a permanent hostage, while she masquerades as his scientist wife. Their project is successful physical and psychological transfer of people into android bodies for use in exploration and colonization. How will one react when confronting an identical android? As in her other short works, Lee turns the plot abruptly at the end. *The Silver Metal Lover* similarly plays with the relation of "real" and created life and the lonely young woman.

The amusing, good-natured parodic elements of *The Dragon Hoard, Animal Castle,* and *Princess Hynchatti* become biting in *Red as Blood, or Tales from the Sisters Grimmer* and *The Gorgon and Other Beastly Tales*. Lee turns fairy tales upside down playfully and usually makes the women heroes. "Cinderella" becomes a revenge story and "Little Red Riding Hood" a tale of vampires. Lee's ironic wit leads to a last woman on earth story ("Written on Water") and a sardonic variation on the theme that a man's approval can make a plain woman beautiful ("You are my Sunshine"). *Tamastara, or the Indian Nights* is a collection that shows her skill in adult fantasy and SF, ranging from myth to an ironic horror story about Indian actors, using the exotic.

In Lee's work there are strong character, vivid detail, carefully worked-out systems, and good story-telling, testimony to Lee's skill and versatility.

—Mary S. Weinkauf

LE GUIN, Ursula K(roeber). American. Born in Berkeley, California, 21 October 1929; daughter of the anthropologist Alfred L. Kroeber. Educated at Radcliffe College, Cambridge,

Massachusetts, A. B. 1951 (Phi Beta Kappa); Columbia University, New York (Faculty Fellow; Fulbright Fellow, 1953), M. A. 1952. Married Charles A. Le Guin in 1953; two daughters and one son. Instructor in French, Mercer University, Macon, Georgia, 1954, and University of Idaho, Moscow, 1956; department secretary, Emory University, Atlanta, 1955; has taught writing workshops at Pacific University, Forest Grove, Oregon, 1971, University of Washington, Seattle, 1971-73, Portland State University, Oregon, 1974, 1977, 1979, in Melbourne, Australia, 1975, at the University of Reading, England, 1976, Indiana Writers Conference, Bloomington, 1978, 1983, and University of California, San Diego, 1979. Recipient: Boston, *Globe-Horn Book* Award, for children's book, 1969; Nebula Award, 1969, 1974 (twice); Hugo Award, 1970, 1973, 1974, 1975; National Book Award for children's book, 1972; Jupiter Award, 1974 (twice), 1976; Gandalf Award, 1979; University of Oregon Distinguished Service award, 1981 *Locus* award (twice), 1983. Guest of Honor, World Science Fiction Convention, 1975. D. Litt. Bucknell University, Lewisburg, Pennsylvania, 1978; Lawrence University, Appleton, Wisconsin; D. H. L. : Lewis and Clark College, Portland, 1983; Occidental College, Los Angeles, 1985. Lives in Portland, Oregon. Agent: Virginia Kidd, Box 278, Milford, Pennsylvania 18337, U.S.A.

SCIENCE-FICTION PUBLICATIONS

Novels (series: Hain)

Rocannon's World (Hain). New York, Ace, 1966; London, Tandem, 1972.
Planet of Exile (Hain). New York, Ace, 1966; London, Tandem, 1972.
City of Illusions (Hain). New York, Ace, 1967; London, Gollancz, 1971.
The Left Hand of Darkness (Hain). New York, Ace, and London, Macdonald, 1969.
The Lathe of Heaven. New York, Scribner, 1971; London, Gollancz, 1972.
The Dispossessed: An Ambiguous Utopia. New York, Harper, and London, Gollancz, 1974.
The Word for World Is Forest (Hain). New York, Putnam, 1976; London, Gollancz, 1977.
The Eye of the Heron. London, Gollancz, 1982; New York, Harper, 1983.

Short Stories

The Wind's Twelve Quarters. New York, Harper, 1975; London, Gollancz, 1976..
The Compass Rose. New York, Harper, 1982; London, Gollancz, 1983.

Uncollected Short Stories

"The Word of Unbinding," in *Basilisk,* edited by Ellen Kushner. New York, Ace, 1980.
"The Ascent of the North Face," in *Isaac Asimov's Space of Her Own,* edited by Shawna McCarthy. New York, Davis, 1983.

OTHER PUBLICATIONS

Novel

Malafrena. New York, Putnam, 1979; London, Gollancz, 1980.

Short Stories

Orsinian Tales. New York, Harper, 1976; London, Gollancz, 1977.
The Water Is Wide. Portland, Oregon, Pendragon Press, 1976.
Gwilan's Harp. Northridge, California, Lord John Press, 1981.
The Visionary: The Life Story of Flicker of the Serpentine, with *Wonders Hidden,* by Scott Russell Sanders. Santa Barbara, California, Capra Press, 1984.

Fiction (for children)

Earthsea. London, Gollancz, 1977; as *The Earthsea Trilogy,* London, Penguin, 1979.
  A Wizard of Earthsea. Berkeley, California, Parnassus Press, 1968; London, Gollancz, 1971.
  The Tombs of Atuan. New York, Atheneum, 1971; London, Gollancz, 1972.
  The Farthest Shore. New York, Atheneum, 1972; London, Gollancz, 1973.
Very Far Away from Anywhere Else. New York, Atheneum, 1976; as *A Very Long Way from Anywhere Else,* London, Gollancz, 1976.
Leese Webster, New York, Atheneum, 1979; London, Gollancz, 1981.
The Beginning Place. New York, Harper, 1980; as *Threshold,* London, Gollancz, 1980.

Play

No Use to Talk to Me, in *The Altered Eye,* edited by Lee Harding. Melbourne, Norstrilia Press, 1976; New York, Berkley, 1978.

Verse

Wild Angels. Santa Barbara, California, Capra Press, 1975.
Hard Words and Other Poems. New York, Harper, 1981.
In the Red Zone. Northridge, California, Lord John Press, 1983.

Other

"Fifteen Vultures, The Strop, and the Old Lady," in *Clarion 2,* edited by Robin Scott Wilson. New York, New American Library, 1972.
From Elfland to Poughkeepsie (lecture). Portland, Oregon, Pendragon Press, 1973.
"On Theme," in *Those Who Can,* edited by Robin Scott Wilson. New York, New American Library, 1973.
"On Norman Spinrad's *The Iron Dream,*" in *Science-Fiction Studies* (Terre Haute, Indiana), Spring 1973.
"A Citizen of Mondath: The Development of a Science Fiction Writer 4," in *Foundation 4* (London), July 1973.
"European SF," in *Science-Fiction Studies* (Terre Haute, Indiana), Spring 1974.
Dreams Must Explain Themselves. New York, Algol Press, 1975.
"American SF and the Other," in *Science-Fiction Studies* (Terre Haute, Indiana), November 1975.
"Science Fiction and Mrs. Brown," in *Science Fiction at Large,* edited by Peter Nicholls. London, Gollancz, 1976; New York, Harper, 1977.
"Is Gender Necessary?," in *Aurona,* edited by Vonda N. McIntyre and Susan Janice Anderson. New York, Fawcett, 1976.
"A Response to the Le Guin Issue," in *Science-Fiction Studies* (Terre Haute, Indiana), March 1976.

"The Stalin in the Soul," in *The Future Now,* edited by Robert Hoskins. New York, Fawcett, 1977.
The Language of the Night: Essays on Fantasy and Science Fiction, edited by Susan Wood. New York, Putnam, 1979.

Editor, *Nebula Award Stories II.* London, Gollancz, 1976; New York, Harper, 1977.
Editor, with Virginia Kidd, *Interfaces.* New York, Ace, 1980.
Editor, with Virginia Kidd, *Edges.* New York, Pocket Books, 1980.

*

Bibliography: *Ursula K. Le Guin: A Primary and Secondary Bibliography* by Elizabeth Cummins Cogell, Boston, Hall, 1983.

Manuscript Collection: University of Oregon Library, Eugene.

Critical Studies: "Wholeness and Balance" by Douglas Barbour, in *Science-Fiction Studies* (Terre Haute, Indiana), Spring 1974; "The Good Witch of the West" by Robert Scholes, in *Hollins Critic* (Hollins College, Virginia), April 1974; *The Farthest Shores of Ursula K. Le Guin* by George Edgar Slusser, San Bernardino, California, Borgo Press, 1976; "Ursula Le Guin Issue" of *Science-Fiction Studies* (Terre Haute, Indiana), March 1976; *Ursula Le Guin* by Joseph D. Olander and Martin H. Greenberg, New York, Taplinger, and Edinburgh, Harris, 1979; *Ursula K. Le Guin: Voyager to Inner Lands and to Outer Space* edited by Joseph W. De Bolt, Port Washington, New York, Kennikat Press, 1979; *Ursula K. Le Guin* by Barbara J. Bucknall, New York, Ungar, 1981; *Ursula K. Le Guin* by Charlotte Spivack, Boston, Twayne, 1984; *Approaches to the Fiction of Ursula K. Le Guin* by James Bittner, Ann Arbor, UMI Research Press, 1984.

*   *   *

The immensely popular fiction of Ursula K. Le Guin proves that popular literature may have literary merit, a serious message, and a large audience all at once. Today the notion of a science-fiction writer producing a novel of substance, even a novel of character, is not so remarkable, as researchers continue to demonstrate that works remarkable as literature have existed in this genre ever since the publication of Mary Shelley's *Frankenstein;* but at the start of Le Guin's career, in the mid 1960's, literary excellence in science fiction was regarded as rare. Le Guin, hailed as a *novelist* who chose to write science fiction, has always attracted an audience composed of genre fans as well as readers who would ordinarily disdain science fiction. Le Guin's work continues to be known for literary expertise which graces a thematic preoccupation with telling essentially hopeful stories of man transcending alienation to open his imagination, his intellect, and his heart to the real adventure of the universe. Le Guin, in common with many writers of science fiction, is a talented builder of new worlds and alien landscapes; she is comfortable with technological wonders, faster-than-light vehicles, and particularly with marvels in the field of long-distance communications, but her commitment, stated clearly in the essay "Science Fiction and Mrs. Brown," is to confirm man's essential humanity against a backdrop of alien situations by means of consistently viewing her characters as the "subjects" of her narratives rather than as objects. A subjective human approach to the marvelous underlines Le Guin's view that if "Mrs Brown [the ordinary, intriguing snatch of human character] is dead, you can take your galaxies and roll them up into a ball and throw them into the trashcan, for all I care. What

good are all the objects in the universe, if there is no subject?"

A large portion of Le Guin's work focuses upon subjective views of a universe incorporating numerous habitable worlds, each "seeded" by beings from the planet Hein. Each of the five novels and several shorter works in this series revolves around the literal and figurative quests of chief characters to discover their individual purposes within the contexts of their several different worlds and, often, within the broader context of the universe. The themes and chronology of the Hain series have been worked out over two decades, but the early works anticipate or foreshadow the best moments of her later work. One of the later novels, fascinatingly, provides the scientific explanation and development of a device—the instantaneous communicator called the ansible—which has been essential to all of the previous works.

The first published works in this series, *Rocannon's World, Planets of Exile,* and *City of Illusions,* do proceed chronologically and establish a thematic preoccupation with the duality existing in nature and in man viewed, as Peter Nicholls has pointed out, "not as polarities or opposed forces" but as archetypical symbols presented as "twin parts of a balanced whole" (*The Science Fiction Encyclopedia,* 1979). Each work employs the alien as the embodiment of alienation presenting to the hero the challenge of transcending fear itself, through embracing the unknown. Communication, whether through telepathic "mindspeech" or by means of the amazing ansible, is significant, often the symbolic crux of each climax. In *Rocannon's World* an outworld ethnological sruveyor stranded on Fomalhaut II is unable to accept fully his destiny of remaining on the strange world until he achieves the ability to communicate through mindspeech. In a narrative which also emphasizes the importance of naming, it is significant that, in ironic understatement, the League of All Worlds, unbeknownst to the ethnographer, gives this world his name, Rocannon's World.

Planet of Exile depicts a world which is populated by two humanoid groups, each believing themselves to be fully human and therefore superior to the other. A female character, the dreamy yet strong-willed Rolery, represents the linking of the two cultures as she overcomes her awe of the "farborn" Terran colonists through her command of telepathic powers generally possessed only by the farborns. Interestingly, discipline, along with honest communication, is described as the key to individual purpose and successful community, while community (the cooperation of both "human" societies) is necessary for the basic survival of either group. "Community," asserts Le Guin (in "Science Fiction and Mrs. Brown"), "is the best we can hope for, and community for most people means touches: the touch of your hand against the other's hand, the job done together, the sledge hauled together, the dance danced together, the child conceived together." Significantly, Rolery is offered the hope of conceiving a child with her farborn husband, while the two groups, under extreme challenge from overwhelming environmental conditions, at last unite to form a new society. Metaphor is particularly rich in this novel, which anticipates *The Left Hand of Darkness* in its description of a world dominated by a frigid winter environment.

City of Illusions describes a Hainish world where mindspeech, previously the epitome of truthful communication, has been perverted by the alien Shing invaders who can manipulate it into a "mind lie." A complex narrative tells the story of the amnesiac Falk and his quest to discover his true name and homeworld. Throughout experiences of betrayal and disorienting double identity, his hopes were "staked now totaly on one belief: that an honest man cannot be cheated, that truth, if the game be played through right to the end, will lead to truth." Here truth and falsehood are regarded as polarities in essential struggle; truth may prevail only when the hero learns to allow both of his identities to work together and, significantly, when he gains access to the ansible so that he may communicate with the world of its origin as well as with the League of All Worlds. The League becomes known as the Ekumen of Known Worlds in *The Left Hand of Darkness,* which richly explores the themes suggested in earlier Hainish works. Genly Ai is a human ethnologist who visits the planet Gethen, where he is swiftly caught up in a snowbound society wrapped in political intrigue and characterized by a revolutionary (to Genly Ai as well as to the reader) androgynous worldview which raises questions about sexuality and sexism and shows a populace composed of individuals whose identity is divorced from gender. The Gethenians, usually neuter, experience a sexual cycle which gives them the ability to become either male or female at certain cyclical peaks. The implications of this alienness tax even the comprehension of this professional observer who learns that the limitation of his own alien perspective, his own alienation, is keeping him from appreciating and understanding this strange new world.

"Vaster than Empires and More Slow" and *The Word for World Is Forest* are shorter works in the Hain series which use the forest as metaphors for the unknown. The former (its title derived from Andrew Marvell's poem "To His Coy Mistress") is perhaps Le Guin's most polished and graceful statement of the need to embrace the alien, the Other, in order to understand it. Osden, a ship's empath, transcends the limitations of both time and fear when he literally embraces the surface of an alien planet which is covered by a network of sentient vegetation. "He had taken fear into himself, and accepting had transcended it. He had given up his self to the alien, an unreserved surrender, that left no place for evil. He had learned love of the Other, and thereby been given his whole self. "

The Dispossessed is centered around the inventor of the ansible, a man called Shevek whose anarchist "Utopia" is ambiguously unable to provide him with the raw materials (chiefly free communication and flow of scientific information) which he needs to make his best contribution to society. This rich work is one in which occasional didacticism is nevertheless fascinating as two politically different worlds (one anarchistic, the other decadently capitalistic) are balanced by means of contrast and comparison, each presented in alternate chapters. The author uses visual perspective most strikingly here; the image of the wall as a defining force is powerfully employed, while in an early scene Shevek's world fills hiw view like a concave dish until, as his space vessel takes him a greater distance from it, it falls away into a convex circle, then a globe, then a distant world. The author also uses paradox, mathematical and verbal, as the key to truth, while communication among all men is the confirmation of man's essential humanity in the face of political, environmental, or other differences.

Some other major works by Le Guin include the Earthsea trilogy, a study of magical skill which appeals to adults as well as to the younger audience for which it was written. *The Lathe of Heaven* is a novel outside the Hain series dealing with a man of conscience who cannot bear the fact that his dreams effectively change reality. *The Beginning Place* is an allegorical novel portraying a fantastic "twilight world," a haven for two adolescents fleeing from unhappy family situations in a bleak, unnamed surburbia. The protagonists learn, by means of encounters with an archetypal monster, to face the harsh disappointments of their "real lives. *Orsinian Tales* and *Malafrena* evoke the 19th century in an imaginary country with a central European atmosphere. *Malafrena* deals with the coming of age of a young revolutionary who must learn to balance freedom and commitment.

The Compass Rose is an anthology of short stories organized around the four directions of the magnetic compass "that converge into or arise out of an unspoken fifth direction, the center, the corolla of the rose. " Stories with settings and themes reminiscent of *Malafrena* are here accompanied by tales that are more strictly science-fictional and dealing with, for instance, a new Atlantis or an enigmatic cat used in a scientific experiment. A particular gem is "The Author of the Acacia Seeds and Other Extracts from the *Journal of the Association of Therolinguistics"* which succeeds brilliantly as a spoof of academic writing while also commenting on the difficulty of translating and the fascination of trying to understand the culture not only of another people but of a different life form.

In 1981 Le Guin's second poetry collection appeared including poems that cross boundaries and should not be categorized as science-fictional or not. It is noteworthy that some recurring images in the poetry pick up on images she has used in the novels already mentioned. Dragons, walls, and stones all take on meanings that enrich our reading of Le Guin's prose: "There was a word inside a stone/I tried to pry it clear. . . ."

Le Guin's fiction seems to say that the ultimate adventure in the universe is a subjective, human quest which achieves not only confrontation with the alien but defeat of alienation; the author's message is clearly, sometimes gracefully, conveyed in literary prose, which will always be the hallmark of her work.

—Rosemary Herbert

LEIBER, Fritz (Reuter, Jr.). American. Born in Chicago, Illinois, 24 December 1910. Educated at the University of Chicago, Ph. B 1932; Episcopal General Theological Seminary, Washington, D. C. Married Jonquil Stephens in 1936 (died, 1969); one son. Episcopal minister at two churches in New Jersey, 1932-33; actor, 1934-36; Editor, Consolidated Book Publishers, Chicago, 1937-41; Instructor in Speech and Drama, Occidental College, Los Angeles, 1941-42; precision inspector, Douglas Aircraft, Santa Monica, California, 1942-44; Associate Editor, *Science Digest,* Chicago, 1944-56. Lecturer, Clarion State College, Pennsylvania, summers 1968-70. Recipient: Hugo Award, 1958, 1965, 1968, 1970, 1971, 1976; Nebula Award, 1967, 1970, 1975, and Grand Master Nebula Award, 1981; Ann Radcliffe Award, 1970; Gandalf Award, 1975; Derleth award, 1976; World Fantasy Award, 1976, 1978. Guest of Honor, World Science Fiction Convention, 1951. Address: 565 Geary Street, Apartment 604, San Francisco, California, 94102, U.S.A.

SCIENCE-FICTION PUBLICATIONS

Novels

Gather, Darkness! New York, Pellegrini and Cudahy, 1950; London, New English Library, 1966.
The Green Millennium. New York, Abelard Press, 1953; London Abelard Schuman, 1959.
Destiny Times Three. New York, Galaxy, 1957.
The Big Time. New York, Ace, 1961; London, New English Library, 1965.
The Silver Eggheads. New York, Ballantine, 1962; London, New English Library, 1966.
The Wanderer. New York, Ballantine, 1964; London, Dobson, 1967.

A Specter Is Haunting Texas. New York, Walker, and London, Gollancz, 1969.

Short Stories

The Sinful Ones. New York, Universal, 1953; as *You're All Alone,* New York, Ace, 1972.
The Mind Spider and Other Stories. New York, Ace, 1961.
A Pail of Air. New York, Ballantine, 1964.
Ships to the Stars. New York, Ace, 1964.
The Night of the Wolf. New York, Ballantine, 1966; London, Sphere, 1976.
The Secret Songs. London, Hart Davis, 1968.
The Best of Fritz Leiber, edited by Angus Wells. London, Sphere, and New York, Doubleday, 1974.
The Book of Fritz Leiber. New York, DAW, 1974.
The Second Book of Fritz Leiber. New York, DAW, 1975.
The Worlds of Fritz Leiber. New York, Ace, 1976.
The Change War. Boston, Gregg Press, 1978.
Ship of Shadows. London, Gollancz, 1979.
The Ghost Light (includes essay). New York, Berkley, 1984.

OTHER PUBLICATIONS

Novels

Conjure Wife. New York, Twayne, 1953; London, Penguin, 1969.
Tarzan and the Valley of Gold. New York, Ballantine, 1966.
The Swords of Lankhmar. New York, Ace, 1968; London, Hart Davis, 1969.
Swords and Deviltry. New York, Ace, 1970; London, New English Library, 1971.
Our Lady of Darkness. New York, Berkley, 1977; London, Millington, 1978.

Short Stories

Night's Black Agents. Sauk City, Wisconsin, Arkham House, 1947; London, Spearman, 1975.
Two Sought Adventure: Exploits of Fafhrd and the Gray Mouser. New York, Gnome Press, 1957.
Shadows with Eyes. New York, Ballantine, 1962.
Swords Against Wizardry. New York, Ace, 1968; London, Prior, 1977.
Swords in the Mist. New York, Ace, 1968; London, Prior, 1977.
Night Monsters. New York, Ace, 1969; revised edition, London, Gollancz, 1974.
Swords Against Death. New York, Ace, 1970; London, New English Library, 1972.
Swords and Ice Magic. New York, Ace, and London, Prior, 1977.
Rime Isle. Chapel Hill, North Carolina, Whispers Press, 1977.
Bazaar of the Bizarre. West Kingston, Rhode Island, Grant, 1978.
Heroes and Horrors. Browns Mills, New Jersey, Whispers Press, 1978.

Verse

The Demons of the Upper Air. Glendale, California, Squires, 1969.
Sonnets to Jonquil and All. Glendale, California, Squires, 1978.

Other

"Way-Out Science," in *National Review* (New York), 9 April 1963.
"Utopia for Poets and Witches," in *Riverside Quarterly* (Regina, Saskatchewan), August 1970.
"The Profession of Science Fiction 12: Mysterious Islands," in *Foundation 11/12* (London), March 1977.

Editor, with Stuart David Schiff, *The World Fantasy Awards 2.* New York, Doubleday, 1980.

*

Bibliography: *Fritz Leiber: A Bibliography 1934-1979* by Chris Morgan, Birmingham, Morgenstern, 1979.

Critical Studies: "Fritz Leiber Issue" of *Fantasy and Science Fiction* (New York), July 1969; *Fritz Leiber* by Jeff Frane, San Bernardino, California, Borgo Press, 1980; *Fritz Leiber* by Tom Staircar, New York, Ungar, 1983.

* * *

Fritz Leiber is one of the most popular and respected writers of science fiction and fantasy. While his readers and fellow writers have appreciated his humor and concern for mankind, the critics have largely ignored his work. Leiber has sometimes been classed with the writers of "weird" stories because of his frequent use of the supernatural and his acknowledged literary debt to H. P. Lovecraft. This association is misleading since Leiber uses the supernatural as a source of symbols for the mysteries of the universe and the mind. As he says, "Many of the most typical creations of science fiction, especially the robot, the android, and the extraterrestrial, are simply the monster in a new guise . . . ."

The supernatural may also turn out to be disguised applications of science, as in his first novel, *Gather, Darkness!* This story concerns a revolution in a repressive society controlled by a religious hierarchy using technology masquerading as supernatural miracle. The resulting satire provides a commentary on the respective roles of religion, science, and government. There is a witty surface of gadgets such as an electronically controlled haunted house, but there is also a warning against the dangers of restricting scientific knowledge to an elite, regardless of the reason. Leiber's background in the theater is probably responsible for the dramatic staging of much of the action.

The Green Millennium presents a picture of a decadent United States where organized crime and corrupt government control society through sex and games. This society is invaded by two alien species from Vega which end the violence. The main virtues of the novel are fast-moving adventure and humor, but there is an underlying layer of satire about the confusion and banality of modern values. *Destiny Times Three* is an alternate-world novel in which three very different stories have been created by an accidental time fragmentation. These worlds contain similar people, one of whom learns of his other personalities and attempts to resolve the time paradoxes. This re-working of an early magazine story is not as polished as his later work. What might have been treated as a traditional SF story has been handled more as allegory and myth.

The Big Time, the major work in a series of time-travel stories, concerns a war fought by time-travelling warriors of two groups called "Snakes" and "Spiders" who attempt to produce a victory in the future by altering the past. Leiber's belief in pacifism is presented through the disillusionment of the characters about the possibility of final victory. This framework allows Leiber to mix characters from many times and places in an entertainment and recuperation center. By limiting almost all the action to one room and employing dramatic techniques of staging and dialogue, Leiber has almost created a science-fiction play, with first-person interior narration. Character differentiations are neatly provided by excellent parodies of the character's differing diction and vocabulary (for example, Elizabethan and Greek dramatic styles). *The Silver Eggheads* is an experiment in satire which borders on farce. The major point is his dissection of the world of publishers, writers, and readers with humorous references to a wide range of literature, but he seems more at ease with satire in his other books. A long "disaster" novel, *The Wanderer,* describes the responses of people subjected to the earthquakes, tidal waves, and other global disasters caused by an artificial planet which enters an orbit around the earth. Leiber's main interest is in the detailed character studies of both heroes and villains provided by this framework. Almost all of Leiber's themes and interests are included: he deals with almost all aspects of human life, from birth to death. There is also plenty of action, but the novel is not significantly different from many other catastrophic stories. In *A Specter Is Haunting Texas* the specter (a skeletally thin actor from a colony on a satellite around earth's moon) is a coerced leader of a revolution of the enslaved "Mexes" against the Texans, who are hormonally induced giants controlling most of North America. Much of the book is based on theatrical motifs, from costuming and staging to the symbolic roles of the characters, and other devices of the stage. The basic method is again satire, this time against the absurdity of racism, war, and values in general. The plot is some-what uneven, but the humor and originality of the background are entertaining.

In addition to his science fiction, Leiber has written two novels about the supernatural, *Conjure Wife* and *Our Lady of Darkness,* both of which are border-line science fiction. His fantasy series relating the exploits of Fafhrd and The Gray Mouser has made him one of the most popular writers of this genre. His best-known stories are probably "Coming Attraction" and "Gonna Roll the Bones."

Throughout his career, Leiber has used the same topics and themes—the supernatural, theater, cats, time, sex, politics, alcohol. His most frequent technique is satire. His writing displays considerable stylistic control (particularly in writing parodies) and the influence of many writers from John Webster and Shakespeare to Eddison, C. A. Smith, and Cabell. He seems to view the basic function of literature in terms of human identity and potentiality. The psychological presentation of character is central to his work, as is his view of literature as theater. These factors are related to the problem of psychological identity. All literature requires at least a partial suspension of personality on the part of the reader, but this demand is particularly great in science fiction and also appears prominently in the function of the actor. A similar reaction can occur with stories of the supernatural. All of these features combine to make Leiber an acute commentator on the human mind.

—Norman L. Hills

LEIGH, Stephen. American. Born in Cincinnati, Ohio, 27 February 1951. Educated at the University of Cincinnati, B. F. A. in art education 1974. Married Denise Parsley in 1974; one daughter. Art teacher, Greenhills and Forest Park school, Ohio,

1974-75. Musician: since 1969, vocalist and bassist in various groups. Recipient: *Analog* award, 1977. Agent: Adele Leone Agency, 26 Nantucket Place, Scarsdale, New York 10583. Address: 121 Nansen Street, Cincinnati, Ohio 45216, U.S.A.

SCIENCE-FICTION PUBLICATIONS

Novels (series: Neweden in all books)

Slow Fall to Dawn. New York, Bantam, 1981.
Dance of the Hag. New York, Bantam, 1983.
A Quiet of Stone. New York, Bantam, 1984.

Uncollected Short Stories

"Answer in Cold Stone," in *Analog* (New York), December 1976.
"The Mask of Night on His Face," in *Future Pastimes,* edited by Scott Edelstein. Nashville, Aurora, 1977.
"In Darkness Waiting," in *Asimov's Choice: Astronauts and Androids,* edited by George H. Scithers. New York, Davis, 1977.
"A Rain of Pebbles," in *Analog* (New York), April 1977.
"When We Come Down," in *Asimov's Choice: Extraterrestrials and Eclipses,* edited by George H. Scithers. New York, Davis, 1978.
"Encounter," in *Destinies* (New York), April 1979.
"After Stone and Steel," in *Eternity* (Sandy Springs, South Carolina), December 1979.
"And Speak of Soft Defiance," in *Eternity* (Sandy Springs, South Carolina), May 1980.
"Tapestry," in *The Berkley Showcase 5,* edited by Victoria Schochet and Melissa Singer. New York, Berkley, 1982.
"Flamestone," in *Afterwar,* edited by Janet E. Morris. New York, Baen, 1985.

*   *   *

Stephen Leigh, reminiscent of a young Poul Anderson, has successfully constructed a unique landscape in his creation of the world known as Neweden. Although writing for publication since 1976, he is known primarily for his Neweden novels, *Slow Fall to Dawn, Dance of the Hag,* and *A Quiet of Stone.* Essentially, Neweden is a world caught in a whirlwind of turmoil and conflict, and the emphasis is on social systems, confrontation, kinship, blood-feud, and the character known as Gyll Hermond. Hermond forms a group of kinless outcasts into a trained assassination force known as the Hoorka Assassins' Guild, and throughout Leigh's fiction the themes of loyalty, honor, and outcast become apparent.

Leigh has the technical skill necessary to blend philosophy and internal dialogue together in a manner that entertains. His world is filled with imaginative names, persons, gods, places, and things, such as Dame Fate, Skafidur, Hoorka, Oldin Archives, Oldman Church, Street of Singers, Hag Death, She of the Five, FitzEvard, to mention but a few. He writes science fiction dealing with confrontation, and this is the central motif that runs through his novels. From a sociological perspective, this is conflict theory at its best, and through the process of confrontation and competition for power, the opponent or opposing group is either absorbed, displaced, or eliminated. Confrontation and competition become an overriding concern in Neweden's social system based on kinship, guild, and honor. Although well-structured, plot is secondary to characterization in Leigh's novels.

Gyll Hermond is a medieval hero in disguise, with attributes to Everyman in his personality; he represents raw courage, and, for the most part, honor, morality, and good deeds in the splintered social system of Neweden. Blood-feud and kinship are the backdrops which make confrontation and competition both possible and logical on Neweden, and Leigh has put care and detail into their subtle roles as social agents affecting personality and relationships. Kinship affects the direction of blood-feud, and it has a direct bearing upon ritual. Leigh's use of the kinship motif allows the reader to understand its effect upon role conflict, role tolerance, role engulfment, role strain, role set, and role performance.

Though he is a writer still experimenting with form and structure, the overall pattern of Leigh's writing reveals a grasp of the mechanics for tense action, adventure, and the eternal theme of right versus wrong or good versus evil. With time, Leigh could become an adept stylist much in the manner of F. M. Busby or Warren Norwood. Given the right circumstances, he has the potential for becoming another Gordon R. Dickson.

Continuing interest in Leigh's writing for readers, sociologists, and scholars rests on his ability to create believable social systems, characterization, and the theme of the Outcast. His talent for handling the theme of the Outcast is best revealed in *A Quiet of Stone.*

—Harold Lee Prosser

LEINSTER, Murray. Pseudonym for Will(iam) F(itzgerald) Jenkins. American. Born in Norfolk, Virginia, 16 June 1896. Educated in public and private schools in Norfolk. Served with the Committee of Public Information, and in the United States Army, 1917-18; served in the Office of War Information during World War II. Married Mary Mandola in 1921; three daughters and one son. Free-lance writer from 1918. Recipient: *Liberty* Award, 1937; Hugo Award, 1956. Guest of Honor, 21st World Science Fiction Convention, 1963. *Died 8 June 1975.*

SCIENCE-FICTION PUBLICATIONS

Novels (series: Joe Kenmore; Med Service)

Murder Madness. New York, Brewer and Warren, 1931.
The Murder of the U. S. A. (as Will F. Jenkins). New York, Crown, 1946; as *Destroy the U. S. A.*, Toronto, Ambassador, 1946.
The Last Space Ship. New York, Fell, 1949; London, Cherry Tree, 1952.
Fight for Life. New York, Crestwood, n. d.
Space Platform (for children; Kenmore). Chicago, Shasta, 1953.
Space Tug (for children; Kenmore). Chicago, Shasta, 1953.
Gateway to Elsewhere. New York, Ace, 1954.
The Forgotten Planet. New York, Gnome Press, 1954.
The Brain-Stealers. New York, Ace, 1954; London, Badger, 1960.
Operation: Outer Space. Reading, Pennsylvania, Fantasy Press, 1954; London, Grayson, 1957.
The Black Galaxy. New York, Galaxy, 1954.
The Other Side of Here. New York, Ace, 1955.
City of the Moon (for children; Kenmore). New York, Avalon, 1957.
Colonial Survey. New York, Gnome Press, 1957; as *Planet Explorer*, New York, Avon, 1957.

War with the Gizmos. New York, Fawcett, 1958; London, Muller, 1959.
The Monster from Earth's End. New York, Fawcett, 1959; London, Muller, 1960.
The Mutant Weapon (Med Service), *The Pirates of Zan.* New York, Ace, 1959.
Four from Planet 5. New York, Fawcett, 1959; London, White Lion, 1974.
The Wailing Asteroid. New York, Avon, 1960.
Creatures of the Abyss. New York, Berkley, 1961; as *The Listeners,* London, Sidgwick and Jackson, 1969.
This World Is Taboo (Med Service). New York, Ace, 1961.
Talents, Incorporated. New York, Avon, 1962.
Operation Terror. New York, Berkley, 1962; London, Tandem, 1968.
The Duplicators. New York, Ace, 1964.
The Other Side of Nowhere. New York, Berkley, 1964.
Time Tunnel. New York, Pyramid, 1964.
The Greks Bring Gifts. New York, Macfadden, 1964.
Invaders of Space. New York, Berkley, 1964; London, Tandem, 1968.
Space Captain. New York, Ace, 1966.
Tunnel Through Time (for children). Philadelphia, Westminster Press, 1966.
Checkpoint Lambda. New York, Berkley, 1966; in *A Murray Leinster Omnibus,* London, Sidgwick and Jackson, 1968.
The Time Tunnel (novelization of TV series). New York, Pyramid, 1967; London, Sidgwick and Jackson, 1971.
Miners in the Sky. New York, Avon, 1967.
Space Gypsies. New York, Avon, 1967.
Timeslip! (novelization of TV series). New York, Pyramid, 1967.
Land of the Giants (novelization of TV play). New York, Pyramid, 1968.
The Hot Spot (novelization of TV play). New York, Pyramid, 1969.
Unknown Danger (novelization of TV play). New York, Pyramid, 1969.

Short Stories (series: Med Service)

Sidewise in Time. Chicago, Shasta, 1950.
Out of This World. New York, Avalon, 1958.
Monsters and Such. New York, Avon, 1959.
Twists in Time. New York, Avon, 1960.
Men into Space (novelization of TV series). New York, Berkley, 1960.
The Aliens. New York, Berkley, 1960.
Doctor to the Stars (Med Service). New York, Pyramid, 1964.
Get Off My World! New York, Belmont, 1966.
S. O. S. from Three Worlds (Med Service). New York, Ace, 1966.
The Best of Murray Leinster, edited by Brian Davis. London, Corgi, 1976; New York, Ballantine, 1978.
The Med Series. New York, Ace, 1983.

Uncollected Short Stories

"Masters of Darkness" series (4 stories), in *Argosy* (New York), 1929-30.

OTHER PUBLICATIONS

Novels

Scalps. New York, Brewer and Warren, 1930; as *Wings of*

Chance, London, John Hamilton, 1935.
Murder Will Out. London, John Hamilton, 1932.
Sword of Kings. London, Long, 1933.
Murder in the Family. London, John Hamilton, 1935.
No Clues. London, Wright and Brown, 1935.
Guns for Achin. London, Wright and Brown, 1936.
Outlaw Guns. New York, Star, n.d.; as *Wanted—Dead or Alive!*, London, Wright and Brown, 1951.
Cattle Rustlers. London, Ward Lock, 1952.
Texas Gun Slinger. New York, Star, n. d.
Outlaw Deputy. Toronto, Harlequin, 1954.

Novels as Will F. Jenkins

The Gamblin' Kid. New York, King, 1933; London, Eldon Press, 1934.
Mexican Trail. New York, King, 1933; London, Eldon Press, 1935.
Fighting Horse Valley. New York, King, 1934; London, Eldon Press, 1935.
Outlaw Sheriff. New York, King, 1934; as *Rustlin' Sheriff*, London, Eldon Press, 1934.
Kid Deputy. New York, King, and London, Eldon Press, 1935.
Black Sheep. New York, Messer, and London, Eldon Press, 1936.
The Man Who Feared. New York, Gateway, 1942.
Dallas (novelization of screenplay). New York, Fawcett, 1950; London, Muller, 1961.
Son of the Flying "Y." New York, Fawcett, 1951; London, Muller, 1957.

Plays

Screenplays: *Border Devils*, with Harry C. Crist, 1932; *Torchy in Chinatown*, with George Bricker, 1938.

Other

Editor, *Great Stories of Science Fiction*. New York, Random House, 1951; London, Cassell, 1953.

*   *   *

A professional writer for the slick and pulp magazines from 1913 until 1967, Murray Leinster embodies in one writer the very essence of the commercial yet ambitiously serious genre of science fiction. He did his best work in short fiction. He developed and extrapolated upon certain key speculative ideas, several of the most important of which he introduced to the genre. He wrote for money and sold to several markets other than science fiction, and yet the imaginative expansion of ideas about nature and about the relation of life forms to nature made science fiction a very important area in his production. Leinster wrote so much that it is hard to categorize his major themes and most characteristic effects, but always his mind is lively and he seems interested particularly in cool analyzing and in alternatives to all possibilities.

In fact, his fascination with the possibility of alternatives to any situations led him to the standard science-fiction theme that he is often best remembered as having introduced to the genre: the theme of parallel points on a time continuum, or parallel worlds. A story from 1931, "The Fifth-Dimension Catapult," plays with the notion as a kind of modern alchemy in which the clever laboratory investigator can change time and space coordinates in order to visit a completely alien parallel world; and in this case the plan finally is to bring back gold. Leinster's

more well-known story of parallel worlds is "Sidewise in Time" in which some unexplained oscillation of the earth results in a myriad of alternate time paths. His method of telling this story in little isolated vignettes of what might be possible here and there as the oscillations produce alternative presents is indicative of why short fiction is a primary form in science fiction. With change and even alternate possibilities ever present there simply does not exist the stable Victorian world for developing long narratives in one time and one place. Leinster, beginning as early as it was popularized, writes a modern alchemy of change according to Einstein-like relativity. Some longer fictions of his that rely on this same balancing of alternatives are *Colonial Survey,* which contains his Hugo-winning novelet "Exploration Team," and *Time Tunnel.*

Similarly, Leinster, develops again and again the ramification of contact between different life forms that are alternatives to each other. This is the often-used theme in science fiction of first contact with an alien race; and the most influential story of Leinster's of this type is entitled simply "First Contact" (1945). But many of his stories explore the alternatives of encounter and relationship between life forms who consider each other alien because they cannot or do not communicate. In "Proxima Centauri" the aliens are intelligent and mobile plants that crave animal flesh. This reversal, or notion that what we do ourselves may often be quite alien, permeates Leinster's fictions. Not only do humans enjoy vegetable salads unthinkingly, but in "The Strange Case of John Klingman" the human managers of the mental hospital seem more alien than Klingman. Similarly, the moon monkeys in "Keyhole" have more sympathy and effective understanding than their human opposites because they can communicate telepathically, and hence the human thoughts, although alien to them, are not unknown.

The key seems to be knowledge and understanding, for here the two themes in Leinster's fiction come together. Alternate or parallel worlds as well as life forms alien to each other are only possible when differentiation, separateness, and mental isolation are possible. If the universe were all one, there would be only one time path and there would be continual communion. But the universe is parceled out, and communication is very seldom total or telepathic and instant. In other words, Leinster seems to be continually retelling the myth of original sin. Things are not as they should be, hence continual competitiveness and continual alternatives.

A brilliant working of this theme of the pathos of separateness and difference is in "The Lonely Planet," which seems to be an anticipation of the widely acclaimed novel by Stanislaw Lem, *Solaris.* In Leinster's story, a magnificent creature called Alyx covers an entire planet. In the beginning it is totally telepathic to mankind because it has not developed a defense against mind or total communication since it has evolved in an environment where it was the only creature. The story, then, is how mankind teaches Alyx to be secretive and competitive, finally, because Alyx learns what loneliness was. Perhaps Leinster is saying that a perfect oneness would be lonely and boring and that we need alternatives and even competitiveness. In any case, the clever, inventive, competitive and necessarily separate mind of the scientific investigator is the favorite protagonist in a Leinster story. Thus from the point of view of modern fiction, his characters often seem grossly two dimensional and his conflicts exaggerated and sensational. These bold and exaggerated effects prevail throughout his popular novel *The Forgotten Planet* (an expansion of "Mad Planet," 1926)—the narration of a continual war with giant insects and the growth of human rationality. But many of these effects are simply the demands of the pulp market, and seen in their most symbolic way they continually narrate the inescapable reality of human fallibility.

No treatment of Leinster and of the evolution of the genre of modern science fiction that he contributed so much to would be complete without mention of the sense of awe that goes with what is generally dismissed as space opera. In addition to the suggestiveness in theme and meaning mentioned above, Leinster's fiction reads well because of wide-ranging space patrol and med service action and because of journeys to distant second galaxies. There is also a good deal of violence, quick cruelty, and villainy in Leinster's work; and when this also is handled well it is an ancient emblem for the fallen state of mankind, an exact correlative to the infinite alternatives in the material world. But always in Leinster, along with the awe and the space opera, is the intellectural curiosity and the analytic mind—perhaps again representative of the fallen state of man, but characteristic also of the best in science fiction. Leinster grew with the genre, but he is also an example of how subtle some of the best space opera can be.

—Donald M. Hassler

L'ENGLE, Madeleine. American. Born Madeleine L'Engle Camp in New York City, 29 November 1918. Educated at Smith College, Northampton, Massachusetts, A. B. (honors) 1941; New School for Social Research, New York, 1941-42; Columbia University, New York, 1960-61. Married Hugh Franklin in 1946; three children. Worked in the theatre, New York, 1941-47; Member of the Faculty, University of Indiana, Bloomington, summers 1965-66, 1971; Writer-in-Residence, Ohio State University, Columbus, 1970, University of Rochester, New York, 1972, and Wheaton College, Illinois, 1976. Since 1960, teacher St. Hilda's and St. Hugh's School, New York; since 1966, Librarian, Cathedral of St. John the Divine, New York; since 1970, President, Crosswicks Ltd., New York. Since 1976, Member, Board of Directors, Authors League Foundation; President, Authors Guild of America. Recipient: American Library Association Newbery Medal, for children's book, 1963; University of Southern Mississippi award, 1978; American Book Award, for paperback, 1980; *Logos* Award, for non-fiction, 1981; Catholic Library Association Regina Medal, 1984. Agent: Robert Lescher, 155 East 71st Street, New York, New York 10021. Address: Crosswicks, Goshen, Connecticut 06756, U.S.A.

SCIENCE-FICTION PUBLICATIONS

Novels (series: Time)

The Time Trilogy. New York, Farrar Straus, 1979.
　A Wrinkle in Time. New York, Farrar Straus, 1962; London, Constable, 1963.
　A Wind in the Door. New York, Farrar Straus, 1973; London, Methuen, 1975.
　A Swiftly Tilting Planet. New York, Farrar Straus, 1978; London, Souvenir Press, 1980.
The Arm of the Starfish. New York, Farrar Straus, 1965.
A Ring of Endless Light. New York, Farrar Straus, 1980.

Uncollected Short Stories

"Poor Little Saturday," in *Fantastic Universe* (Chicago), October 1956.
"The One Hundred and First Miracle," in *Nine Visions,* edited

by Andrea LaSonde Melrose. New York, Seabury Press, 1983.

OTHER PUBLICATIONS

Novels

The Small Rain. New York, Vanguard Press, 1945; London, Secker and Warburg, 1955.
Ilsa. New York, Vanguard Press, 1946.
And Both Were Young. New York, Lothrop, 1949.
Camilla Dickinson. New York, Simon and Schuster, 1951; London, Secker and Warburg, 1952; as *Camilla,* New York, Crowell, 1965.
A Winter's Love. Philadelphia, Lippincott, 1957.
Meet the Austins. New York, Vanguard Press, 1960; London, Collins, 1966.
The Moon by Night. New York, Farrar Straus, 1963.
The Love Letters. New York, Farrar Straus, 1966.
The Journey with Jonah. New York, Farrar Straus, 1968.
The Young Unicorns. New York, Farrar Straus, 1968; London, Gollancz, 1970.
Prelude. New York, Vanguard Press, 1969; London, Gollancz, 1972.
The Other Side of the Sun. New York, Farrar Straus, 1971; London, Eyre Meuthen, 1972.
Dragons in the Waters. New York, Farrar Straus, 1976.
A Severed Wasp. New York, Farrar Straus, 1982; London, Faber, 1984.
A House Like a Lotus. New York, Farrar Straus, 1984.

Short Stories

The Sphinx at Dawn: Two Stories. New York, Seabury Press, 1982.

Plays

18 Washington Square, South (produced Northampton, Massachusetts, 1940) Boston, Baker, 1944.
How Now Brown Cow, with Robert Hartung (produced New York, 1949).
The Journey with Jonah (produced New York, 1970). New York, Farrar Straus, 1967.

Verse

Lines Scribbled on an Envelope and Other Poems. New York, Farrar Straus, 1969.
Weather of the Heart. Wheaton, Illinois, Shaw, 1978.

Other

The Twenty-Four Days Before Christmas (for children). New York, Farrar Straus, 1964.
Dance in the Desert (for children). New York, Farrar Straus, and London, Longman, 1969.
A Circle of Quiet (essays). New York, Farrar Straus, 1972.
Everyday Prayers (for children). New York, Morehouse Barlow, 1974.
Prayers for Sunday (for children). New York, Morehouse Barlow, 1974.
The Summer of the Great-Grandmother (essays). New York, Farrar Straus, 1974.
The Irational Season (essays). New York, Seabury Press, 1977.
Ladder of Angels: Scenes from the Bible Illustrated by Children of

the World. New York, Seabury Press, 1979.
The Anti-Muffins (for children). New York, Pilgrim Press, 1980.
Walking on Water (essays). Wheaton, Illinois, Shaw, 1980; Tring, Hertfordshire, Lion, 1982.
And It Was Good. Wheaton, Illinois, Shaw, 1983.

Editor, with William R. Green, *Spirit and Light: Essays in Historical Theology.* New York, Seabury Press, 1976.

*

Manuscript Collections: Wheaton College, Illinois; Kerlan Collection, University of Minnesota, Minneapolis; de Grummond Collection, University of Southern Mississippi, Hattiesburg.

Madeleine L'Engle comments:

I discovered science fiction early, as a lonely only child growing up, for my first 12 years, in New York City, then in France and Switzerland. For me, the real world was clearer in the books of E. Nesbit and H. G. Wells than in the world of school. So I started writing science fiction when I was eight or nine. Fortunately all of my early work was lost somewhere or other on our journey across the Atlantic.

During college and after I turned to more "realistic" fiction, and found that it was not real enough, that my true discoveries of reality came while I was writing sci-fi or fantasy. I also discovered that for me the great theologians and modern mystics are the scientists, the physicists and astrophysicists, the cellular biologists, since they are dealing with the nature of Being itself. Einstein, Planck, Eddington, Jeans, Heisenberg, and many others, have been—and are still—my great stimulants.

* * *

Madeleine L'Engle has been publishing successful and provocative science fiction since the mid-1940's, adding intriguing variations to a considerable body of work, and continuously crafting fiction to engage her readers in issues and moral questions. She is nearly as prolific as some of her less thoughtful peers, and has continuously commanded the support of publishers and readers who must be described as literary. Her most well-known work is a series of novels dealing with time, including her one most signally famous work, *A Wrinkle in Time,* which introduces the children and, less directly, the father of the Murry family.

Wrinkle begins with the stark probing of a novel by Conrad, but by the time the reader recognizes what an extensive narrative hook has been set, L'Engle has paraded warm, bright, totally believable characters on stage. Every bit an existential and metaphysical thinker, L'Engle dramatizes the necessary leaps of faith that await the young reader and which certainly beckon to the more mature reader.

The second novel in the series, *A Wind in the Door,* takes up where the problem of the missing Murry father is solved, and the focus now becomes the integrity of healthy organisms and systems. Meg Murry, a young man from *Wrinkle* named Calvin, and a young superbeing become simultaneously involved in a plot involving Charles Wallace, who is being attacked at a celular memory level, and this is shown in relationship to a black hole, L'Engle's version of a spot in the galaxy where there is a problem with cellular memory. *A Swiftly Tilting Planet* involves Meg Murry, now a grown woman, married and pregnant, but still called upon to join her siblings in an adventure relating to the potential for thermo-nuclear war.

Trademarks of L'Engle are her deceptively simple prose style, often undershot with social, moral, or religious issue; her restraint in explaining too much either of philosophy, scientific apparatus, or technicalities; her crisp, individual dialog; and her ability to draw young characters who are interesting without being self-conscious. Well read in the physical and theoretical sciences, L'Engle has the same focus to be found in such writers as Theodore Sturgeon and Robert Heinlein, allowing her effectively to dramatize complex concepts whether a black hole in the galaxy and its consequence, the ability of a starfish to regenerate a portion of its body, or the ability of an immune system to keep an invader from penetrating.

L'Engle seems to have arrived at a happy synthesis of science, metaphysics, universal politics, and individual responsibility. She is one of the handful of science-fiction writers whose work consistently rings true.

—Shelly Lowenkopf

LEPPOC, Derfla. See COPPEL, Alfred.

LE QUEUX, William (Tufnell). British. Born in London, 2 July 1864. Educated privately in London and at Pegli, Italy; studied art in Paris. Foreign Editor, London *Globe,* 1891-93; from 1893 free-lance journalist and travel writer; Balkan Correspondent, *Daily Mail,* London, during Balkan War, 1912-13; served as Consul to the Republic of San Marino. Popularly supposed to have been a spy. Lived in Switzerland in later life. *Died 13 October 1927.*

SCIENCE-FICTION PUBLICATIONS

Novels

The Great War in England in 1897. London, Tower, 1894.
A Madonna of the Music Halls. London, White, 1897; as *A Secret Sin,* London, Gardner, 1913.
The Eye of Istar. London, White, and New York, Stokes, 1897.
The Great White Queen. London, White, 1898; New York, Arno Press, 1975.
England's Peril. London, White, 1899.
The Invasion of 1910, with a Full Account of the Siege of London. London, Nash, 1906.
The Unknown Tomorrow. London, White, 1910.
The Mystery of the Green Ray. London, Hodder and Stoughton, 1915; as *The Green Ray,* London, Mellifont Press, 1944.
The Terror of the Air. London, Lloyd's 1920.

Short Stories

Stolen Souls. London, Tower, and New York, Stokes, 1895.

OTHER PUBLICATIONS

Novels

Guilty Bonds. London, Routledge, 1891; New York, Fenno, 1895.

The Temptress. London, Tower, and New York, Stokes, 1895.

Zoraida: A Romance of the Harem and the Great Sahara. London, Tower, and New York, Stokes, 1895.

Devil's Dice. London, White, 1896; Chicago, Rand McNally, 1897.

Whoso Findeth a Wife. London, White, 1897; Chicago, Rand McNally, 1898.

If Sinners Entice Thee. London, White, 1898; New York, Dillingham, 1899.

Scribes and Pharisees. London, White, and New York, Dodd Mead, 1898.

The Veiled Man. London, White, 1899.

The Bond of Black. London, White, and New York, Dillingham, 1899.

Wiles of the Wicked. London, Bell, 1899.

The Day of Temptation. London, White, and New York, Dillingham, 1899.

An Eye for an Eye. London, White, 1900.

In White Raiment. London, White, 1900.

Of Royal Blood. London, Hutchinson, 1900.

The Gamblers. London, Hutchinson, 1901.

The Sign of the Seven Sins. Philadelphia, Lippincott, 1901.

Her Majesty's Minister. London, Hodder and Stoughton, and New York, Dodd Mead, 1901.

The Court of Honour. London, White, 1901.

The Under-Secretary. London, Hutchinson, 1902.

The Unnamed. London, Hodder and Stoughton, 1902.

The Tickencote Treasure. London, Newnes, 1903.

The Three Glass Eyes. London, Treherne, 1903.

The Seven Secrets. London, Hutchinson, 1903.

The Idol of the Town. London, White, 1903.

As We Forgave Them. London, White, 1904.

The Closed Book. London, Methuen, and New York, Smart Set, 1904.

The Hunchback of Westminster. London, Methuen, 1904.

The Man from Downing Street. London, Hurst and Blackett, 1904.

The Red Hat. London, Daily Mail, 1904.

The Sign of the Stranger. London, White, 1904.

The Valley of the Shadow. London, Methuen, 1905.

Who Giveth This Woman? London, Hodder and Stoughton, 1905.

The Spider's Eye. London, Cassell, 1905.

Sins of the City. London, White, 1905.

The Mask. London, Long, 1905.

Behind the Throne. London, Methuen, 1905.

The Czar's Spy. London, Hodder and Stoughton, and New York, Smart Set, 1905.

The Great Court Scandal. London, White, 1906.

The House of the Wicked. London, Hurst and Blackett, 1906.

The Mysterious Mr. Miller. London, Hodder and Stoughton, 1906.

The Mystery of a Motor-Car. London, Hodder and Stoughton, 1906.

Whatsoever a Man Soweth. London, White, 1906.

The Woman at Kensington. London, Cassell, 1906.

The Secret of the Square. London, White, 1907.

The Great Plot. London, Hodder and Stoughton, 1907.

Whosoever Loveth. London, Hutchinson, 1907.

The Crooked Way. London, Methuen, 1908.

The Looker-On. London, White, 1908.

The Pauper of Park Lane. London, Cassell, and New York, Cupples and Leon, 1908.

Stolen Sweets. London, Nash, 1908.

The Woman in the Way. London, Nash, 1908.

The Red Room. London, Casell, 1909; Boston, Little Brown, 1911.

The House of Whispers. London, Nash, 1909; New York, Brentano's, 1910.

Fatal Thirteen. London, Stanley Paul, 1909.

Treasure of Israel. London, Nash, 1910; as *The Great God Gold*, Boston, Badger, 1910.

Lying Lips. London, Stanley Paul, 1910.

Hushed Up! London, Nash, 1911.

The Money-Spider. London, Cassell, and Boston, Badger, 1911.

The Death-Doctor. London, Hurst and Blackett, 1912.

Fatal Fingers. London, Cassell, 1912.

The Mystery of Nine. London, Nash, 1912.

Without Trace. London, Nash, 1912.

The Price of Power, Being Chapters from the Secret History of the Imperial Court of Russia. London, Hurst and Blackett, 1913.

The Room of Secrets. London, Ward Lock, 1913.

The Lost Million. London, Nash, 1913.

The White Lie. London, Ward Lock, 1914.

Sons of Satan. London, White, 1914.

The Hand of Allah. London, Casell, 1914; as *The Riddle of the Ring*, London, Federation Press, 1927.

Her Royal Highness. London, Hodder and Stoughton, 1914.

The Maker of Secrets. London, Ward Lock, 1914.

The Four Faces. London, Stanley Paul, and New York, Brentano's, 1914.

The Double Shadow. London, Hodder and Stoughton, 1915.

At the Sign of the Sword. London, Jack, and New York, Scully and Kleinteich, 1915.

The Mysterious Three. London, Ward Lock, 1915.

The Sign of Silence. London, Ward Lock, 1915.

The White Glove. London, Nash, 1915.

The Zeppelin Destroyer. London, Hodder and Stoughton, 1916.

Number 70, Berlin. London, Hodder and Stoughton, 1916.

The Place of Dragons. London, Ward Lock, 1916.

The Spy Hunter. London, Pearson, 1916.

The Man about Town. London, Long, 1916.

Annette of the Argonne. London, Hurst and Blackett, 1916.

The Broken Thread. London, Ward Lock, 1916.

Behind the German Lines. London, London Mail, 1917.

The Breath of Suspicion. London, Long, 1917.

The Devil's Carnival. London, Hurst and Blackett, 1917.

No Greater Love. London, Ward Lock, 1917.

Two in a Tangle. London, Hodder and Stoughton, 1917.

Rasputin, The Rascal Monk. London, Hurst and Blackett, 1917.

The Yellow Ribbon. London, Hodder and Stoughton, 1918.

The Secret Life of the Ex-Tsaritza. London, Odhams Press, 1918.

The Sister Disciple. London, Hurst and Blackett, 1918.

The Stolen Statesman. London, Skeffington, 1918.

The Little Blue Goddess. London, Ward Lock, 1918.

The Minister of Evil: The Secret History of Rasputin's Betrayal of Russia. London, Cassell, 1918.

Bolo, The Super-Spy. London, Oldhams Press, 1918.

The Catspaw. London, Lloyd's, 1918.

Cipher Six. London, Hodder and Stoughton, 1919.

The Doctor of Pimlico. London, Cassell, 1919; New York, Macaulay, 1920.

The Forbidden Word. London, Odhams Press, 1919.

The King's Incognito. London, Odhams Press, 1919.

The Lure of Love. London, Ward Lock, 1919.

Rasputinism in London. London, Cassell, 1919.

The Secret Shame of the Kaiser. London, Hurst and Blackett, 1919.

Secrets of the White Tsar. London, Odhams Press, 1919.

The Heart of a Princess. London, Ward Lock, 1920.

The Intriguers. London, Hodder and Stoughton, 1920; New York, Macaulay, 1921.

No. 7, Saville Square . London, Ward Lock, 1920.

The Red Widow; or, The Death-Dealers of London. London, Cassell, 1920.

Whither Thou Goest. London, Lloyd's, 1920.

This House to Let. London, Hodder and Stoughton, 1921.

The Lady-in-Waiting. London, Ward Lock, 1921.

The Open Verdict. London, Hodder and Stoughton, 1921.

The Power of the Borgias: The Story of the Great Film. London, Odhams Press, 1921.

Mademoiselle of Monte Carlo. London, Cassell, and New York, Macaulay, 1921.

The Fifth Finger. London, Stanley Paul, and New York, Moffat, 1921.

The Golden Face. London, Cassell, and New York, Macaulay, 1922.

The Stretton Street Affair. New York, Macaulay, 1922; London, Cassell, 1924.

Three Knots. London, Ward Lock, 1922.

The Voice from the Void. London, Cassell, 1922; New York, Macaulay, 1923.

The Young Archduchess. London, Ward Lock, and New York, Moffat, 1922.

Where the Desert Ends. London, Cassell, 1923.

The Bronze Face, London, Ward Lock, 1923; as *Behind the Bronze Door*, New York, Macaulay, 1923.

The Crystal Claw. London, Hodder and Stoughton, and New York, Macaulay, 1924.

Fine Feathers. London, Stanley Paul, 1924.

A Woman's Debt. London, Ward Lock, 1924.

The Valrose Mystery. London, Ward Lock, 1925.

The Marked Man. London, Ward Lock, 1925.

The Blue Bungalow. London, Hurst and Blackett, 1925.

The Broadcast Mystery. London, Holden, 1925.

The Fatal Face. London, Hurst and Blackett, 1926.

Hidden Hands. London, Hodder and Stoughton, 1926; as *The Dangerous Game*, New York, Macaulay, 1926.

The Letter E. London, Cassell, 1926; as *The Tattoo Mystery*, New York, Macaulay, 1927.

The Mystery of Mademoiselle. London, Hodder and Stoughton, 1926.

The Scarlet Sign. London, Ward Lock, 1926.

The Black Owl. London, Ward Lock, 1926.

The Office Secret. London, Ward Lock, 1927.

The House of Evil. London, Ward Lock, 1927.

The Lawless Hand. London, Hurst and Blackett, 1927; New York, Macaulay, 1928.

Blackmailed. London, Nash and Grayson, 1927.

The Chameleon. London, Hodder and Stoughton, 1927; as *Poison Shadows*, New York, Macaulay, 1927.

Double Nought. London, Hodder and Stoughton, 1927; as *The Crime Code*, New York, Macaulay, 1928.

Concerning This Woman. London, Newnes, 1928.

The Rat Trap. London, Ward Lock, 1928; New York, Macaulay, 1930.

The Secret Formula. London, Ward Lock, 1928.

The Sting. London, Hodder and Stoughton, and New York, Macaulay, 1928.

Twice Tried. London, Hurst and Blackett, 1928.

The Amazing Count. London, Ward Lock, 1929.

The Crinkled Crown . London, Ward Lock, and New York, Macaulay, 1929.

The Golden Three. London, Ward Lock, 1930; New York, Fiction House, 1931.

Short Stories

Strange Tales of a Nihilist. London, Ward Lock, and New York, Cassell, 1892; as *A Secret Service*, Ward Lock, 1896.

Secrets of Monte Carlo. London, White, 1899; New York, Dillingham, 1900.

Secrets of the Foreign Office. London, Hutchinson, 1903.

Confessions of a Ladies' Man. Being the Adventures of Cuthbert Croom, of His Majesty's Diplomatic Service. London, Hutchinson, 1905.

The Count's Chauffeur. London, Nash, 1907.

The Lady in the Car, in Which the Amours of a Mysterious Motorist Are Related. London, Nash, and Philadelphia, Lippincott, 1908.

Spies of the Kaiser: Plotting the Downfall of England. London, Hurst and Blackett, 1909.

Revelations of the Secret Service. London, White, 1911.

The Indiscretions of a Lady's Maid. London, Nash, 1911.

Mysteries. London, Ward Lock, 1913.

The German Spy. London, Newnes, 1914.

"Cinders" of Harley Street. London, Ward Lock, 1916.

The Bomb-Makers. London, Jarrolds, 1917.

Beryl of the Biplane. London, Pearson, 1917.

Hushed Up at German Headquarters. London, London Mail, 1917.

The Rainbow Mystery: Chronicles of a Colour-Criminologist. London, Hodder and Stoughton, 1917.

The Scandal-Monger. London, Ward Lock, 1917.

The Secrets of Potsdam. London, Daily Mail, 1917.

More Secrets of Potsdam. London, London Mail, 1917.

Further Secrets of Potsdam. London, London Mail, 1917.

Donovan of Whitehall. London, Pearson, 1917.

Sant of the Secret Service. London, Odhams Press, 1918.

The Hotel X. London, Ward Lock, 1919.

Mysteries of the Great City. London, Hodder and Stoughton, 1919.

In Secret. London, Odhams Press, 1920.

The Secret Telephone. New York, McCann, 1920; London, Jarrolds, 1921.

Society Intrigues I Have Known. London, Odhams Press, 1920.

The Luck of the Secret Service. London, Pearson, 1921.

The Elusive Four: The Exciting Exploits of Four Theives. London, Cassell, 1921.

Tracked by Wireless. London, Stanley Paul, and New York, Moffat, 1922.

The Gay Triangle: The Romance of the First Air Adventures. London, Jarrolds, 1922.

Bleke, the Butler, Being the Exciting Adventures of Robert Bleke During Certain Years of His Service in Various Families. London, Jarrolds, 1923.

The Crimes Club: A Record of Secret Investigations into Some Amazing Crimes, Mostly Withheld from the Public. London, Nash and Grayson, 1927.

The Peril of Helen Marklove and Other Stories. London, Jarrolds, 1928.

The Factotum and Other Stories. London, Ward Lock, 1931.

Play

The Proof (produced Birmingham, 1924; as *Vendetta* produced London, 1924).

Other

An Observer in the Near East. London, Nash, 1907; as *The Near East*, New York, Doubleday, 1907.

The Balkan Trouble; or, An Observer in the Near East. London, Nash, 1912.

The War of the Nations, vol. 1. London, Newnes, 1914.

German Atrocities: A Record of Shameless Deeds. London, Newnes, 1914.

German Spies in England: An Exposure. London, Stanley Paul, 1915.

Britain's Deadly Peril: Are We Told the Truth? London, Stanley Paul, 1915.

The Devil's Spawn: How Italy Will Defeat Them. London, Stanley Paul, 1915.

The Way to Win. London, Simpkin Marshall, 1916.

Love Intrigues of the Kaiser's Sons. London, Long, and New York, Lane, 1918.

Landru: His Secret Love Affairs. London, Stanley Paul, 1922.

Things I Know about Kings, Celebrities, and Crooks. London, Nash and Grayson, 1923.

Engelberg: The Crown Jewel of the Alps. London, Swiss Observer, 1927.

Interlaken: The Alpine Wonderland: A Novelist's Jottings. Interlaken, Official Information Bureau, n. d.

Translator, *Of the "Polar Star" in the Arctic Sea*, by Luigi Amedeo. London, Hutchinson, 1903.

*

Critical Study: *The Real Le Queux* by N. St. Barbe Sladen, London, Nicholson and Watson, 1938.

*   *   *

William Le Queux's life is more interesting than anything he wrote. He travelled extensively, was acquainted with royalty, collected an impressive number of decorations for various services from various courts. He used his position for intelligence or spying activity, claiming to have written his more than 150 potbiolers—exotic, political, and spy novels—to support such patriotic amateur ventures as the discovery of a Germany spy network in England in 1906. Together with Field Marshal Lord Roberts and a number of prominent British politicians, he concocted his most famous war and fifth-column forecast, *The Invasion of 1910* as an appeal to the UK to prepare for war.

His SF writings, besides some marginal stories, are generally worthless, melodramatic novels. They include the ludicrous *A Madonna of the Music Halls*, in which a villainous scientist terrorizes a beautiful girl by foisting on her strange qualities through liquids transferring other people's "brain power" (e. g. hate); a banal first try at the "future war" cum spy story, *The Great War in England in 1897; The Unknown tomorrow*, depicting the cruelties of the socialism of 1935; and *The Terror of the Air*, a tired exploitation of the German threat. Thus *The Invasion of 1910* remains his only important contribution to the political pathology of SF and of idealogy in general, and an object-lesson in the successful use of SF as propaganda, based on the immediate objectives of the ruling politico-military complex allied with the newspapers, London clubland, and the Secret Service. Even Wells was not always immune from such a syndrome, and one wonders in how many SF writers down to Adamov or Cordwainer Smith it is also present.

—Darko Suvin

LESLIE, O. H. See **SLESAR, Henry.**

———

LESSER, Milton. Name now Stephen Marlowe; also writes as Adam Chase; Andrew Frazer; Ellery Queen; Jason Ridgway; C. H. Thames. American. Born in New York City, 7 August 1928. Educated at the College of William and Mary, Willamsburg, Virginia, B. A. 1949. Served in the United States Army, 1952-54. Married 1) Leigh Lang in 1950 (divorced, 1962); 2) Ann Humbert; two daughters. Editor, Scott Meredith Literary Agency, New York, 1949-50; now a full-time writer. Writer-in-Residence, College of William and Mary, 1974-75, 1980-81. Member of the Board of Directors, Mystery Writers of America. Agent: Scott Meredith Literary Agency, 845 Third Avenue, New York, New York 10022, U.S.A.

SCIENCE-FICTION PUBLICATIONS

Novels

Earthbound (for children). Philadelphia, Winston, 1952; London, Hutchinson, 1955.

The Star Seekers (for children). Philadelphia, Winston, 1953.

The Golden Ape (as Adam Chase, with Paul W. Fairman). New York, Avalon, 1959.

Recruit for Andromeda. New York, Ace, 1959.

Stadium Beyond the Stars (for children). Philadelphia, Winston, 1960.

Spacemen, Go Home (for children). New York, Holt Rinehart, 1962.

Short Stories

Secret of the Black Planet. New York, Belmont, 1965.

OTHER PUBLICATIONS

Novels as Stephen Marlowe

Catch the Brass Ring. New York, Ace, 1954.

Turn Left for Murder. New York, Ace, 1955.

Model for Murder. Hasbrouck Heights, New Jersey, Graphic, 1955.

The Second Longest Night. New York, Fawcett, 1955; London, Fawcett, 1958.

Dead on Arrival. New York, Ace, 1956.

Mecca for Murder. New York, Fawcett, 1956; London, Fawcett, 1957.

Violence Is Golden (as C. H. Thames). New York, Bouregy, 1956.

Killers Are My Meat. New York, Fawcett, 1957; London, Fawcett, 1958.

Murder Is My Dish. New York, Fawcett, 1957.

Trouble Is My Name. New York, Fawcett, 1957; London, Fawcett, 1958.

Violence Is My Business. New York, Fawcett, 1958; London, Fawcett, 1959.

Terror Is My Trade. New York, Fawcett, 1958; London, Muller, 1960.

Blonde Bait. New York, Avon, 1959.

Double in Trouble, with Richard S. Prather. New York, Fawcett, 1959.

Find Eileen Hardin—Alive! (as Andrew Frazer). New York, Avon, 1959.
Passport to Peril. New York, Fawcett, 1959.
Homicide Is My Game. New York, Fawcett, 1959; London, Muller, 1960.
Danger Is My Line. New York, Fawcett, 1960; London, Muller, 1961.
Death Is My Conrade. New York, Fawcett, 1960; London, Muller, 1961.
The Fall of Marty Moon (as Andrew Frazer). New York, Avon, 1960.
Peril Is My Pay. New York, Fawcett, 1960; London, Muller, 1961.
Dead Man's Tale (as Ellery Queen). New York, Pocket Books, 1961; London, New English Library, 1967.
Manhunt Is My Mission. New York, Fawcett, 1961; London, Muller, 1962.
Jeopardy Is My Job. New York, Fawcett, 1962; London, Muller, 1963.
Blood Is My Brother (as C. H. Thames). New York, Permabooks, 1963.
The Shining. New York, Trident Press, 1963.
Francesca. New York, Fawcett, and London, Muller, 1963.
Drum Beat—Berlin. New York, Fawcett, 1964.
Drum Beat—Dominique. New York, Fawcett, 1965.
Drum Beat—Madrid. New York, Fawcett, 1966.
The Search for Bruno Heidler. New York, Macmillan, 1966; London, Boardman, 1967.
Drum Beat—Erica. New York, Fawcett, 1967.
Come Over, Red Rover. New York, Macmillan, 1968.
Drum Beat—Marianne. New York, Fawcett, 1968.
The Summit. New York, Geis, 1970.
Colossus. New York, Macmillan, 1972; London, W. H. Allen, 1973.
The Man with No Shadow. Englewood Cliffs, New Jersey, Prentice Hall, and London, W. H. Allen, 1974.
The Cawthorn Journals. Englewood Cliffs, New Jersey, Prentice Hall, 1975; London, W. H. Allen, 1976; as *Too Many Chiefs,* London, New English Library, 1977.
Translation. Englewood Cliffs, New Jersey, Prentice Hall, 1976; London, W. H. Allen, 1977.
The Valkyrie Encounter. New York, Putnam, and London, New English Library, 1978.
1956. New York, Arbor House, 1981; London, New English Library, 1982.
Deborah's Legacy. New York, Zebra, 1983.

Novels as Jason Ridgway

West Side Jungle. New York, New American Library, 1958.
Adam's Fall. New York, Permabooks, 1960.
People in Glass Houses. New York, Permabooks, 1961.
Hardly a Man is Now Alive. New York, Permabooks, 1962.
The Treasure of the Cosa Nostra. New York, Pocket Books, 1966.

Other

Lost Worlds and the Men Who Found Them (for children). Racine, Wisconsin, Whitman, 1962.
Walt Disney's Strange Animals of Australia (for children). Racine, Wisconsin, Whitman, 1963.

Editor, *Looking Forward: An Anthology of Science Fiction.* New York, Beechhurst Press, 1953; London, Cassell, 1955.

* * *

Milton Lesser was a prolific contributor to the Ziff-Davis SF magazines in the 1950's, though since 1965 he has abandoned SF to write mainstream novels. Some of these, like *Translation* and *The Valkyrie Encounter,* published under the Stephen Marlowe pseudonym, have science-fiction elements.

Most of Lesser's SF novels are juveniles. In *Earthbound* a young cadet unjustly expelled from the Solar Academy is tricked into helping space pirates. The book is high on action and low on plausibility. *The Star Seekers* is a bit better. It reworks Robert A. Heinlein's idea of a generation starship presented in *Universe.* Here, a starship takes six generations to reach Alpha Centauri, with the attendant problems and struggles. *Stadium Beyond the Stars* is Lesser's weakest SF novel. Most of the action concerns plotting among political groups on the eve of the First Interstellar Olympic Games. The characterizations are shallow and the plot is murky. *Spacemen, Go Home* opens with humanity quarantined from star travel by the super computer which controls the galaxy. Various groups attempt to bomb the Star Brain while others attempt to convince it to lift the quarantine because humans aren't violent. Again, a murky plot mars the fast-paced action.

Lesser's adult works also stress action over plot and violence over character. *The Golden Age* is prime space opera featuring a bold hero who commutes among worlds in the tradition of John Carter. Duels and fights keep the action swift and the pages turning. *Recruit for Andromeda* has a tricky plot with draftees secretly tested to determine which are superior. The story has some mild racist overtones. *Secret of the Black Planet* is made up of two space-opera novelettes, "Secret of the Black Planet" and "Son of the Black Chalice." The search for a lost alien race and the secret of cell regeneration is damaged by hackneyed writing and cardboard characterizations.

—George Kelley

LESSING, Doris (May). Also writes as Jane Somers. British. Born in Kermansha, Persia, 22 October 1919; moved with her family to Southern Rhodesia, 1924. Educated at Girls High School, Salisbury. Married 1) Frank Charles Wisdom in 1939 (divorced, 1943), one son and one daughter; 2) Gottfried Lessing in 1945 (divorced, 1949), one son. Lived in Southern Rhodesia, 1924-49, then settled in London. Recipient: Maugham Award, 1954; Médicis Prize (France), 1976; Austrian State Prize, 1982; Shakespeare Prize (Hamburg), 1982. Associate Member, American Academy, 1974; Honorary Fellow, Modern Language Association (USA), 1974. Agent: Jonathan Clowes Ltd., 22 Prince Albert Road, London NW1 7ST, England.

SCIENCE-FICTION PUBLICATIONS

Novels (series: Canopus in Argos: Archives)

Briefing for a Descent into Hell. London, Cape, and New York, Knopf, 1971.
The Memoirs of a Survivor. London, Octagon Press, 1974; New York, Knopf, 1975.
Shikasta (Argos). London, Cape, and New York, Knopf, 1979.
The Marriages Between Zones Three, Four, and Five (Argos). London, Cape, and New York, Knopf, 1980.
The Sirian Experiments (Argos). London, Cape, and New York, Knopf, 1981.

The Making of the Representative for Planet 8 (Argos). London, Cape, and New York, Knopf, 1982.
The Sentimental Agents (Argos). London, Cape, and New York, Knopf, 1983.

Short Stories

No Witchcraft for Sale: Stories and Short Novels. Moscow, Foreign Languages Publishing House, 1956.

OTHER PUBLICATIONS

Novels

The Grass Is Singing. London, Joseph, and New York, Crowell, 1950.
Children of Violence:
    Martha Quest. London, Joseph, 1952.
    A Proper Marriage. London, Joseph, 1954, with *Martha Quest*, New York, Simon and Schuster, 1964.
    A Ripple from the Storm. London, Joseph, 1958.
    Landlocked. London, MacGibbon and Kee, 1965; with *A Ripple from the Storm*. New York, Simon and Schuster, 1966.
    The Four-Gated City. London, MacGibbon and Kee, and New York, Knopf, 1969.
Retreat to Innocence. London, Joseph, 1956.
The Golden Notebook. London, Joseph, and New York, Simon and Schuster, 1962.
The Summer Before the Dark. London, Cape, and New York, Knopf, 1973.
The Diaries of Jane Somers. New York, Random House, 1984; London, Joseph, 1985.
    The Diary of a Good Neighbour (as Jane Somers). London, Joseph, and New York, Knopf, 1983.
    If the Old Could (as Jane Somers). London, Joseph, and New York, Knopf, 1984.

Short Stories

This Was the Old Chief's Country. London, Joseph, 1951; New York, Crowell, 1952.
Five: Short Novels. London, Joseph, 1953.
The Habit of Loving. London, MacGibbon and Kee, 1957; New York, Crowell, 1958.
A Man and Two Women. London, MacGibbon and Kee, and New York, Simon and Schuster, 1963.
African Stories. London, Joseph, 1964; New York, Simon and Schuster, 1965.
Winter in July. London, Panther, 1966.
The Black Madonna. London, Panther, 1966.
Nine African Stories. London, Longman, 1968.
The Story of a Non-Marrying Man and Other Stories. London, Cape, 1972; as *The Temptation of Jack Orkney and Other Stories*, New York, Knopf, 1972.
Collected African Stories:
    1. *This Was the Old Chief's Country*. London, Joseph, 1973.
    2. *The Sun Between Their Feet*. London, Joseph, 1973.
(Stories), edited by Alan Cattell. London, Harrap, 1976.
Collected Stories:
    1. *To Room Nineteen*. London, Cape, 1978.
    2. *The Temptation of Jack Orkney*. London, Cape, 1978.
Stories. New York, Knopf, 1978.

Plays

Before the Deluge (produced London, 1953).
Mr. Dollinger (produced Oxford, 1958).
Each His Own Wilderness (produced London, 1958). Published in *New English Dramatists*, London, Penguin, 1959.
The Truth about Billy Newton (produced Salisbury, Wiltshire, 1960).
Play with a Tiger (produced London, 1962; New York, 1964). London, Joseph, 1962.
The Storm, adaptation of a play by Alexander Ostrowsky (produced London, 1966).
The Singing Door, in *Second Playbill 2*, edited by Alan Durband. London, Hutchinson, 1973.

Television Plays: *The Grass Is Singing*, from her own novel, 1962; *Please Do Not Disturb*, 1966; *Care and Protection*, 1966; *Between Men*, 1967.

Verse

Fourteen Poems. Northwood, Middlesex, Scorpion Press, 1959.

Other

Going Home. London, Joseph, 1957.
In Pursuit of the English: A Documentary. London, MacGibbon and Kee, 1960; New York, Simon and Schuster, 1961.
Particularly Cats. London, Joseph, and New York, Simon and Schuster, 1967.
A Small Personal Voice: Essays, Reviews, Interviews, edited by Paul Schlueter. New York, Knopf, 1974.

*

Bibliography: *Doris Lessing: A Bibliography* by Catharina Ipp, Johannesburg, University of the Witwatersrand Department of Bibliography, 1967; *Doris Lessing: A Checklist of Primary and Secondary Sources* by Selma R. Burkom and Margaret Williams, Troy, New York, Whitston, 1973; *Doris Lessing: An Annotated Bibliography of Criticism* by Dee Seligman, Westport, Connecticut, Greenwood Press, 1981.

Critical Studies (selection): *Doris Lessing* by Dorothy Brewster, New York, Twayne, 1965; *The Novels of Doris Lessing* by Paul Schlueter, Carbondale, Southern Illinois University Press, 1973; *Doris Lessing* by Michael Thorpe, London, Longman, 1973, *Doris Lessing: Critical Studies* edited by Annis Pratt and L. S. Dembo, Madison, University of Wisconsin Press, 1974; *The City and the Veld: The Fiction of Doris Lessing* by Mary Ann Singleton, Lewisburg, Pennsylvania, Bucknell University Press, 1976; *The Novelistic Vision of Doris Lessing: Breaking the Forms of Consciousness* by Roberta Rubenstein, Urbana, University of Illinois Press, 1979; *Notebooks/Memoirs/Archives: Reading and Re-reading Doris Lessing* edited by Jenny Taylor, London and Boston, Routledge, 1982; *Substance under Pressure: Artistic Coherence and Evolving Form in the Novels of Doris Lessing* by Betsy Draine, Madison, University of Wisconsin Press, 1983; *Doris Lessing* by Lorna Sage, London, Methuen, 1983; *Doris Lessing* by Mona Knapp, New York, Ungar, 1984.

*   *   *

Doris Lessing's series, *Canopus in Argos: Archives*, grew, according to the author, out of her plan for a single book, *Shikasta*. This first experiment in science fiction led to the exploration of multiple related themes in four more works. The ideas encompassed by this cycle are superabundant, ranging from planetary evolution over geological eons to the arts with which wives and husbands score minor points in forgettable skirmishes, but all the books are unified by one central concern, the role of the individual in events of great magnitude that transcend personal hopes, wishes, and desires. Most of Lessing's characters must confront a dizzying variety of forces that determine their destinies; their changing awareness of these forces provides much of the drama of their stories.

The most self-aware figures in all the novels are the mysterious representatives of the Canopean Empire. Even "Canopus," as individual officials are sometimes called, bows to a never-defined "Necessity" which rules all; in turn, Johor, Klorasty, and other Canopeans patiently guide less advanced races and even empires away from mindless violence and cruelty and toward cultural evolution. *Shikasta* details millions of years of the history of the earth, variously called "Rohanda" and "Shikasta." The Galactic time perspective allows the reader to understand that change and conflict is the one constant; the failure of a "Lock" between Canopus and Shikasta/Earth dooms the planet to degeneration and ultimately to near-destruction.

The Marriages Between Zones Three, Four, and Five is comparatively sunny, but still ends in melancholy. The Canopeans are (apparently) acting as offstage "Providers" in control of a series of geographically contrasting "Zones," ranging from desert (Zone 5) to swampy lush wetlands (Zone 4) to mountain plateaus (3) to mountain passes (2). Varying zones and climates determine the personality of cultures, which in turn determines individual types, from earthy lowlander to ethereal mountaineer. Each zone has settled into smug self-satisfaction when a perhaps related decline in fertility causes the Providers to force a marriage between the queen of Zone three, Al. Ith, and the king of Zone 4, Ben Ata. Both characters are masterfully drawn, and the uneasy marriage of a kind of high country Athenian to a lumpish Spartan provides high comedy based on the clash of female and male principles, the unending war between artistic natures and practical natures, and the gradual blending of distinct personalities in marriage. The narrator describes how later artists depicted this marriage of opposites, and Lessing's own word-pictures are like set-pieces from a medieval tableau. Queen and King do not live happily ever after, however, for the Providers, in fine disregard for human wishes, toward the end of the book order Ben Ata to marry the wild, nomadic queen of Zone Five, thus blending the artistic intellect Ben Ata has gleaned from Al. Ith, his own orderly discipline, and the wild energy of the least civilized Zone. Al. Ith retires to the border of Zone Two, and eventually crosses it to become a flame-like wraith in a mountain atmosphere too rarified for others to tolerate. Life is change, says Lessing; even in this paradise reminiscent of a medieval fable, an unseen and only vaguely understood "necessity" casually destroys human happiness. There is no choice but to obey.

The Sirian Experiments continues this theme with another wonderfully drawn female protagonist, Ambien II, one of the five dictators who rule the technological empire in competition with Canopus. Unfortunately, Ambien II's prissy, bureaucratic, "dessicated" character is so persuasive that the reader may lack sympathy throughout much of the book, at least until this self-serving and authoritarian figure begins to learn a more sensitive and less machine-like managerial style from her Canopean opposites. As with Al. Ith and Ben Ata, sexual attraction between opposites provides the motive force for change, but there is no comedy here, only some excellent set-pieces in an Arab-like town and an Aztec-like fortress. Ambien

has led Sirian "experiments" on millions of "lower species" over thousands of years, unmindful of their dubious morality because of their good intentions of forcing evolution. Miseries such as Al. Ith's in the previous novel are multiplied a million times before Ambien's Canopean teachers lead her to see from experience and example that the Sirian Empire is being taught by the Canopean just as surely as the "lower species" are being taught by the Sirian. As in the linked Zones, one relationship leads to the next, but the joins are invisible since they are firmly denied by the weaker. Colonialism involves more complex power relationships than are initially evident, with control being exercised in unexpected ways. Only experience teaches by showing us the mote in another's eye, just as Lessing's novel should raise our consciousness of Western arrogance and brutality in Africa and other former colonial areas.

In *The Sirian Experiments* evil necessity is incarnated in the Puttiorian Empire (the name suggest Spanish *puta* or whore) and their planet Shahmat (Farsi for "the king is dead," or in chess, "checkmate"). In *The Making of the Representative for Planet 8*, evil necessity is a cosmic accident. The Canopean governed colony on Planet 8 is freezing to death because of planetary climactic changes. In a fine description of a frozen world stimulated by Lessing's reading about Scott's search for the South Pole, we see the telepathic, tropically lively and colorful inhabitants of Planet 8 become slothful, fur-swaddled zombies who lose their social identities as the snow and ice wipe out occupations and social roles. Climate is destiny; eventually, led and taught by their Canopean master Johor, they give up their material existence and become a single "representative" spirit, transcending physicality.

The Sentimental Agents continues the emphasis on Canopean moderation of extreme behavior, with Incent, an agent of the empire, seduced by "Undulant Rhetoric" or a kind of intoxication with words. In contrast, the usual approach of the Canopean agents is to be noncommittal to the point of taciturnity. They are men and women of action, not empty words.

While there is an honorable tradition of 20th-century writers opposing propaganda and false rhetoric, it is especially appropriate for Lessing to end her cycle with this warning. Throughout, there have been conflicts between characters skilled at action (Ben Ata, Ambien II) and characters skilled at language (Al. Ith, Nasar, Rhodia). Lessing's own ambivalence about the role of writer and writing may be at issue, and this uncertainty in a writer known for her earlier political stands may account for the mixed critical reception to her cycle. Like Canopus, Lessing teaches by example, but also like Canopus, she refuses easy answers and the superficial knowledge of the conventional.

—Andrew Macdonald

LEVIN, Ira. American. Born in New York City, 27 August 1929. Educated at Drake University, Des Moines, Iowa, 1946-48; New York University, 1948-50, A. B. 1950. Served in the United States Army Signal Corps, 1953-55. Married 1) Gabrielle Aronsohn in 1960 (divorced, 1968), three children; 2) Phyllis Finkel in 1979. Recipient: Mystery Writers of American Edgar Allan Poe Award, 1954, and Special Award, 1980. Agent: Harold Ober Associates, 40 East 49th Street, New York, New York 10017, U. S. A.

SCIENCE- FICTION PUBLICATIONS

Novels

This Perfect Day. New York, Random House, and London, Joseph, 1970.
The Stepford Wives. New York, Random House, and London, Joseph, 1972.
The Boys from Brazil. New York, Random House, and London, Joseph, 1976.

OTHER PUBLICATIONS

Novels

A Kiss Before Dying. New York, Simon and Schuster, 1953; London, Joseph, 1954.
Rosemary's Baby. New York, Random House, and London, Joseph, 1967.

Plays

No Time for Sergeants, adaptation of the novel by Mac Hyman (produced New York, 1955; London, 1956). New York, Random House, 1956.
Interlock (produced New York, 1958). New York, Dramatists Play Service, 1958.
Critic's Choice (produced New York, 1960; London, 1961). New York, Random House, 1961; London, Evans, 1963.
General Seeger (produced New York, 1962). New York, Dramatists Play Service, 1962.
Drat! The Cat!, music by Milton Schafer (produced New York, 1965).
Dr. Cook's Garden (also director: produced New York, 1967). New York, Dramatists Play Service, 1968.
Veronica's Room (produced New York, 1973; Watford, Hertfordshire, 1982). New York, Random House, 1974; London, Joseph, 1975.
Deathtrap (produced New York and London, 1978). New York, Random House, 1979.
Break a Leg (produced New York, 1979). New York, French, 1981.

*

Theatrical Activities:
Director: **Play**—*Dr. Cook's Garden*, New York, 1967.

*   *   *

Ira Levin's highly accomplished novels of suspense contain elements of science fiction and fantasy, and one, *This Perfect Day*, is set in the future.

His first novel, *A Kiss Before Dying*, the study of a psychopath stalking three sisters, was skilfully written but gave little suggestion of the richness in store. *Rosemary's Baby* is one of the most perfectly crafted thrillers ever written. Rosemary and Guy Woodhouse step over the threshold of a richly documented old apartment house in New York City into the world of the witches. The strength of the book lies not only in its weaving of a dreadful spell but in the strong, sweet character of the pregnant heroine. Guy's complicity in the schemes of the friendly neighbours is part of a fiendish double climax.

The book following this masterpiece of genre writing was the science-fiction novel *This Perfect Day*. The future race, brown-skinned, depilated, breastless, tranquilised, stroll the window-less walkways of a totally computerised environment, patting the scanners as they pass, en route to death at age 62. LiRM35M4419, called Chip by his wry Grandfather, escapes from the system by resisting UNI, the computer responsible for a boring parody of the good life. Chip's escape is obviously programmed; the appearance of those benign sybarites the Programmers is not surprising. The ideology of the "utopia" is weak but the quality of the writing and the level of invention are high. A leap of the author's prodigious imagination could bring him into the very first rank of speculative fiction.

Instead he returned to the suspense novel with *The Stepford Wives*. The setting, a commuter township in "middle America," is as persuasive as the New York of *Rosemary's Baby*. Joanna Everhart discovers the dreadful secret of the big-bosomed zombies who dote on housework. The climax is clever but the story is unsatisfying and the neatness of the writing hides many loose ends. We look in vain for one husband who refuses to trade in his wife on a new model or for a child with that old complaint from *The Invasion of the Body-Snatchers:* "That Lady isn't my real mother!"

The Boys from Brazil has an international setting but still retains a typical claustrophobic atmosphere. Dr. Josef Mengele, former medical superintendent of Auschwitz, emerges from his South American jungle retreat to send the organization of Nazi veterans on a mission. Yakov Lieberman, the tired Nazi-hunter, discovers soon enough, but more slowly than the readers, why 94 elderly civil servants throughout the western world must die. These men are the adoptive fathers of teen-age sons cloned from the cells of Adolf Hitler; their deaths are an attempt to match up environment with genetic inheritance. This time the humanity of Lieberman balances the outrageous story; it is one of Ira Levin's best books. Mengele's scheme, even with its coda of an artistic lad somewhere indulging tomorrow-the-world fantasies, is revealed as pure moonshine.

Ira Levin's suspense novels have a unique resonance; these works, rather than *One Perfect Day*, have created a nightmare future world in which the Stepford delinquents, children of megalomaniac fathers raised by robot mothers, tangle with genetic Hitlers, under the eye of the heir of the Prince of This World, Andrew Woodhouse, the devil's child. The author is at the height of his powers and should continue to astonish us.

—Cherry Wilder

LEWIS, C(live) S(taples). Also wrote as Clive Hamilton; N. W. Clerk. British. Born in Belfast, Northern Ireland, 29 November 1898. Educated at Wynyard House, Watford, Hertfordshire, 1908-10; Campbell College, Belfast, 1910; Cherbourg School, Malvern, Worcestershire, 1911-13, and Malvern College, 1913-14; privately, in Great Bookham, Surrey, 1914-17; University College, Oxford (Scholar; Chancellor's English Essay Prize, 1921), 1917, 1919-23, B. A. (honours) 1922. Served in the Somerset Light Infantry, 1917-19; First Lieutenant. Married Joy Davidman Gresham in 1956 (died, 1960); two stepsons. Philosophy Tutor, 1924, and Lecturer in English, 1924, University College, Oxford; Fellow and Tutor in English, Magdalen College, Oxford, 1925-54; Professor of Medieval and Renaissance English, Cambridge University, 1954-63. Lecturer, University College of North Wales, Bangor, 1941; Riddell Lecturer, University of Durham, 1943; Clark Lecturer, Cambridge University, 1944. Recipient: Gollancz Price for Literature, 1937; Library Association Carnegie Medal, 1957. D. D. : University of St. Andrews, Fife, 1946; Docteur-ès-Lettres,

Laval University, Quebec, 1952; D. Litt. : University of Manchester, 1959; Hon. Dr.: University of Dijon, 1962; University of Lyon, 1963. Honorary Fellow, Magdalen College, Oxford, 1955; University College, Oxford, 1958; Magdalene College, Cambridge, 1963. Fellow, Royal Society of Literature, 1948; Fellow, British Academy, 1955. *Died 22 November 1963.*

SCIENCE-FICTION PUBLICATIONS

Novels (series: Dr. Elwin Ransom in all books)

Out of the Silent Planet. London, Lane, 1938; New York, Macmillan, 1943.
Perelandra. London, Lane, 1943; New York, Macmillan, 1944; as *Voyage to Venus,* London, Pan, 1953.
That Hideous Strength: A Modern Fairy-Tale for Grown-Ups. London, Lane, 1945; New York, Macmillan, 1946; abridged edition, as *The Tortured Planet,* New York, Avon, 1958.

Short Stories

Of Other Worlds: Essays and Stories, edited by Walter Hooper. London, Bles, 1966; New York, Harcourt Brace, 1967.

OTHER PUBLICATIONS

Novels (for children)

The Lion, The Witch, and the Wardrobe. London, Bles, and New York, Macmillan, 1950.
Prince Caspian: The Return to Narnia. London, Bles, and New York, Macmillan, 1951.
The Voyage of the "Dawn Treader." London, Bles, and New York, Macmillan, 1952.
The Silver Chair. London, Bles, and New York, Macmillan, 1953.
The Horse and His Boy. London, Bles, and New York, Macmillan, 1954.
The Magician's Nephew. London, Lane, and New York, Macmillan, 1955.
The Last Battle. London, Lane, and New York, Macmillan, 1956.
Till We Have Faces: A Myth Retold (for adults). London, Bles, 1956; New York, Harcourt Brace, 1957.

Short Stories

The Dark Tower and Other Stories, edited by Walter Hooper. London, Collins, and New York, Harcourt Brace, 1977.

Verse

Spirits in Bondage: A Cycle of Lyrics (as Clive Hamilton). London, Heinemann, 1919.
Dymer (as Clive Hamilton). London, Dent, and New York, Dutton, 1926.
Poems, edited by Walter Hooper. London, Bles, 1964; New York, Harcourt Brace, 1965.
Narrative Poems, edited by Walter Hooper. London, Bles, 1969; New York, Harcourt Brace, 1972.

Other

The Pilgrim's Regress: An Allegorical Apology for Christianity, Reason, and Romanticism. London, Dent, 1933; New York, Sheed and Ward, 1935; revised edition, London, Bles, 1943; Sheed and Ward, 1944.
The Allegory of Love: A Study in Medieval Tradition. Oxford, Clarendon Press, and New York, Oxford University Press, 1936.
Rehabilitations and Other Essays. London and New York, Oxford University Press, 1939.
The Personal Heresy: A Controversy, with E. M. W. Tillyard. London and New York, Oxford University Press, 1939.
The Problem of Pain. London, Bles, 1940; New York, Macmillan, 1944.
The Weight of Glory. London, S. P. C. K., 1942.
The Screwtape Letters. London, Bles, 1942; New York, Macmillan, 1943; revised edition, as *The Screwtape Letters and Screwtape Proposes a Toast,* Bles, 1961; Macmillan, 1962.
Broadcast Talks: Right and Wrong: A Clue to the Meaning of the Universe, and What Christians Believe. London, Bles, 1942; as *The Case for Christianity,* New York, Macmillan, 1943.
A Preface to "Paradise Lost" (lectures). London and New York, Oxford University Press, 1942; revised edition, 1960.
Christian Behaviour: A Further Series of Broadcast Talks. London, Bles, and New York, Macmillan, 1943.
The Abolition of Man; or, Reflections on Education with Special Reference to the Teaching of English in the Upper Forms of Schools. London, Oxford University Press, 1943; New York, Macmillan, 1947.
Beyond Personality: The Christian Idea of God. London, Bles, 1944; New York, Macmillan, 1945.
The Great Divorce: A Dream. London, Bles, and New York, Macmillan, 1946.
Miracles: A Preliminary Study. London, Bles, and New York, Macmillan, 1947.
Vivisection. London, Anti-Vivisection Society, and Boston, New England Anti-Vivisection Society, 1947(?).
Transposition and Other Addresses. London, Bles, 1949; as *The Weight of Glory and Other Addresses,* New York, Macmillan, 1949.
The Literary Impact of the Authorized Version (lecture). London, Athlone Press, 1950; Philadelphia, Fortress Press, 1963.
Mere Christianity. London, Bles, and New York, Macmillan, 1952.
Hero and Leander (lecture). London, Oxford University Press, 1952.
English Literature in the Sixteenth Century, Excluding Drama. Oxford, Clarendon Press, 1954.
De Descriptione Temporum (lecture). London, Cambridge University Press, 1955.
Surprised by Joy: The Shape of My Early Life. London, Bles, 1955; New York, Harcourt Brace, 1956.
Reflections on the Psalms. London, Bles, and New York, Harcourt Brace, 1958.
Shall We Lose God in Outer Space? London, S. P. C. K., 1959.
The Four Loves. London, Bles, and New York, Harcourt Brace, 1960.
The World's Last Night and Other Essays. New York, Harcourt Brace, 1960.
Studies in Words. London, Cambridge University Press, 1960; revised edition, 1967.
An Experiment in Criticism. London, Cambridge University Press, 1961.
A Grief Observed (as N. W. Clerk; autobiography). London, Faber, 1961; Greenwich, Connecticut, Seabury Press, 1963.
They Asked for a Paper: Papers and Addresses. London, Bles, 1962.
Beyond the Bright Blur (letters). New York, Harcourt Brace, 1963.

Letters to Malcolm, Chiefly on Prayer. London, Bles, and New York, Harcourt Brace, 1964.

The Discarded Image: An Introduction to Medieval and Renaissance Literature. London, Cambridge University Press, 1964.

Screwtape Proposes a Toast and Other Pieces. London, Fontana, 1965.

Letters, edited by W. H. Lewis. London, Bles, and New York, Harcourt Brace, 1966.

Studies in Medieval and Renaissance Literature, edited by Walter Hooper, London, Cambridge University Press, 1966.

Spenser's Images of Life, edited by Alastair Fowler. London, Cambridge University Press, 1967.

Christian Reflections, edited by Walter Hooper. London, Bles, and Grand Rapids, Michigan, Eerdmans, 1967.

Letters to an American Lady, edited by Clyde S. Kilby. Grand Rapids, Michigan, Eerdmans, 1967; London, Hodder and Stoughton, 1969.

Mark vs. Tristram: Correspondence Between C. S. Lewis and Owen Barfield, edited by Walter Hooper. Cambridge, Massachussetts, Lowell House Printers, 1967.

A Mind Awake: An Anthology of C. S. Lewis, edited by Clyde S. Kilby. London, Bles, 1968; New York, Harcourt Brace, 1969.

Selected Literary Essays, edited by Walter Hooper. London, Cambridge University Press, 1969.

God in the Dock: Essays on Theology and Ethics, edited by Walter Hooper. Grand Rapids, Michigan, Eerdmans, 1970; as *Undeceptions: Essays on Theology and Ethics,* London, Bles, 1971.

The Humanitarian Theory of Punishment. Abingdon, Berkshire, Marcham Books Press, 1972.

Fern-Seed and Elephants and Other Essays on Christianity, edited by Walter Hooper. London, Fontana, 1975.

The Joyful Christian: 127 Readings, edited by William Griffin. New York, Macmillan, 1977.

They Stand Together: The Letters of C. S. Lewis to Arthur Greeves 1914-1963, edited by Walter Hooper. London, Collins, and New York, Macmillan, 1979.

C. S. Lewis at the Breakfast Table and Other Reminiscences, edited by James T. Como. New York, Macmillan, 1979; London, Collins, 1980.

The Visionary Christian: 131 Readings, edited by Chad Walsh. New York, Macmillan, 1981.

On Stories and Other Essays on Literature, edited by Walter Hooper. New York, Harcourt Brace, 1982.

Of This and other Worlds, edited by Walter Hooper. London, Collins, 1982.

Letters to Children, edited by Lyle W. Dorsett and Marjorie Lamp Mead. New York, Macmillan, 1985.

Editor, *George MacDonald: An Anthology.* London, Bles, 1946; New York, Macmillan, 1947.

Editor, *Arthurian Torso, Containing the Posthumous Fragment of "The Figure of Arthur,"* by Charles Williams. London, and New York, Oxford University Press, 1948.

*

Bibliography: "A Bibliography of the Writings of C. S. Lewis" by Walter Hooper, in *Light on C. S. Lewis* edited by Jocelyn Gibb, London, Bles, 1965; *C. S. Lewis: An Annotated Checklist of Writings about Him and His Works* by Joe R. Christopher and Joan K. Ostling, Kent, Ohio, Kent State University Press, 1974.

Manuscript Collection: Wheaton College, Illinois.

Critical Studies (selection): *C. S. Lewis* by Roger Lancelyn Green, London, Bodley Head, and New York, Walck, 1963, revised edition, in *Three Bodley Head Monographs,* Bodley Head, 1969, *C. S. Lewis: A Biography* by Green and Walter Hooper, London, Collins, and New York, Harcourt Brace, 1974, and *Through Joy and Beyond: A Pictorial Biography of C. S. Lewis* by Hooper, New York, Macmillan 1982; *Light on C. S. Lewis* edited by Jocelyn Gibb, London, Bles, 1965; *Shadows of Imagination: The Fantasies of C. S. Lewis, J. R. R. Tolkien, and Charles Williams* edited by Mark R. Hillegas, Carbondale, Southern Illinois University Press, 1969; *The Secret Country of C. S. Lewis* by Anne Arnott, London, Hodder and Stoughton, 1974, Grand Rapids, Michigan, Eerdmans, 1975; *Bright Shadow of Reality: C. S. Lewis and the Feeling Intellect* by Corbin S. Carnell, Grand Rapids, Michigan, Eerdmans, 1974; *The Longing for Form: Essays on the Fiction of C. S. Lewis* edited by Peter J. Schakel, Kent, Ohio, Kent State University Press, 1977, and *Reason and Imagination in C. S. Lewis* by Schakel, Grand Rapids, Michigan, Eerdmans, 1984. *The Literary Legacy of C. S. Lewis* by Chad Walsh, New York, Harcourt Brace, and London, Sheldon Press, 1979; *C. S. Lewis, Spinner of Tales: A Guide to His Fiction* by Evan K. Gibson, Grand Rapids, Michigan, Christian University Press, 1980; *C. S. Lewis* by Margaret Patterson Hannay, New York, Ungar, 1981; *C. S. Lewis: The Art of Enchantment* by Donald E. Glover, Athens, Ohio University Press, 1981; *C. S. Lewis* by Brian Murphy, Mercer Island, Washington, Starmont House, 1983.

*   *   *

C. S. Lewis is a unique figure. He once described himself as a specimen of a nearly extinct species, "old Western Man": and certainly we had no right to hope for such an author to appear in the 20th century. He has written in many guises: as medieval scholar, lay theologian, fantasist, poet. But his essential role has total inner consistency: he is above all the most powerful defender of traditional Christianity that this century has seen; and his apologia works not through formal argument but through images, through suggestion, through poetic creation. All his life, Lewis was haunted by *Sehnsucht,* a longing for strange beauty which the actual world could never wholly satisfy; and this led him, in early middle life, to identify the source and object of his longing with the Christian heaven and the Christian God. His subsequent creative work was a sustained imaginative polemic for this view of the universe.

Lewis is a science-fiction writer, arguably, in only one short story, "Ministering Angels," and one novel, *Out of the Silent Planet.* Both are set on Mars; but the Mars of the novel is a Christian paradise ruled by an archangel. This is the first novel of Lewis's so called "space triology"; the second novel, *Perelandra,* is set on Venus, and the third, *That Hideous Strength,* on Earth but with interplanetary connections. All three novels feature the same hero, Elwin Ransom, and all are a unique mixture of SF and what seem to be fantasy elements. In each novel an important part is played by the "eldils," a species of angels inhabiting interplanetary space whose bodies are composed of semi-visible light; but in the first two novels there is also a spaceship, and in the third novel a type of cyborg, a severed human head kept alive by advanced scientific technology. This mixture of science and the supernatural in the trilogy is deliberate and indeed essential; for the fundamental theme of the whole trilogy is the clash between evil modern scienticism and old-fashioned Christianity. The trilogy in fact defies generic classification: it is very dubiously science fiction, by reason of all those angels (and devils, in the second and third novels), yet it is not exactly fantasy either, for the author firmly believes in the actual existence of his supernatural entities, and is out to convince us, with all the power of his very powerful art, of their reality and supreme importance. It is this polemic purpose which may repel some readers: Lewis himself has stated (*Of Other Worlds*) that *Perelandra,* at least, was written essentially for Christians only.

But *Out of the Silent Planet* is less overtly Christian, and should appeal to a wide readership by the sheer beauty of its style and images. The inner action of this novel is twofold: it is partly a *Bildungsroman,* effecting the re-education of Ransom, and through him of the reader; and partly a physical and intellectual defeat of human-racist expansionism. Ransom, an ordinary decent literary scholar, is kidnapped by the ruthless physicist Professor Weston and his capitalist collaborator Devine and taken in Weston's secret spaceship to Mars, for Weston mistakenly believes that the "primitive natives" of Mars have demanded a human sacrifice in exchange for gold. Mars ("Malacandra") proves to be a beautiful, paradisal planet, and the natives comprise three intelligent species, all living in friendship and complementary collaboration, and all ruled by the nearly invisible eldil Oyarsa from his paradise-island of Meldilorn. Ransom escapes from his human captors, takes refuge among the "hrossa," the seal-like poetic species, and learns the Malacandrian language. He is thus equipped to serve as interpreter in the climactic scene of the novel when Weston and Devine are arrested by the hrossa and brought to Oyarsa for judgment. This trial scene is one of the clearest, wittiest, most striking portrayals in imaginative fiction of the clash between human-racist expansionism and the opposing school of thought—the school now represented chiefly by the ecology movement. Weston boasts to Oyarsa that nothing will stop the human race from conquering the universe, moving on from planet to planet as each world dies. Oyarasa refutes Weston with the question: "And when all are dead?"—to which Weston has no answer. After this the humans, including Ransom, are forced to return to Earth, whereupon their spaceship is destroyed by angelic power.

Perelandra is a sequel in that once more Weston lands on another planet—Venus—and once more is opposed by Ransom; but essentially the work is a variation on Milton's *Paradise Lost.* Venus (Perelandra) is a mostly oceanic world with only two inhabitants—its innocent Adam and Eve. Soon after Weston's arrival, he is possessed by a devil—and he proceeds to tempt the Perelandrian Eve to violate God's sole prohibition. At last Ransom understands his mission, and ends the temptation by destroying Weston. The Venusian paradise is saved, a second Fall is averted. This novel is an even greater achievement than *Out of the Silent Planet:* the action, limited to three characters, has concentrated dramatic power, and the scenery—the floating vegetable islands and seas of Venus—is of a beauty which has never been surpassed by an imaginative writer. It is magnificent—but it is hardly science fiction. That might also be said of the trilogy's final novel, *That Hideous Strength.* The Devil is confronted this time on Earth by planetary angels, Ransom, and the Arthurian wizard Merlin, and the wicked are destroyed in a magic holocaust.

Also relevant to Lewis's SF are his seven Narnia novels for children. These may be called fantasy, since they are set in and around an imaginary world (Narnia) where magic is commonplace and the inhabitants include giants, dwarfs, dragons, fauns, centaurs, and talking animals. But Narnia has an intellectual solidity similar to SF and lacking in some fantasy worlds of other writers, since it exists in a parallel universe also created, like this one of ours, by God: it is a universe whose Earth is flat, and whose stars are living beings. It is also, as usual in Lewis, a universe of marvellous beauty. Lewis is also an important critic of SF and related genres, chiefly in the essay collection *Of Other Worlds.* His remarks on characterization are justly famous.

Taking his work as a whole, one must note that although Lewis wrote little that is certainly SF, he is of the first importance in the history of this genre through the sheer power of his imagination, his ability to create beautiful worlds which are wholly realized in their actuality; and through the enormous pressure of his moral commitment, which supplies tension throughout the action of every one of his stories. Above all, he has been a most effective opponent of those who would like to see the human race give itself up to the demon of scientism, the spirit which desires the total conquest of the universe.

—David Lake

LEWIS, (Harry) Sinclair. Also wrote as Tom Graham. American. Born in Sauk Centre, Minnesota, 7 February 1885. Educated at Sauk Centre High School; Oberlin Academy, Ohio, 1902-03; Yale University, New Haven, Connecticut (Editor, *Yale Literary Magazine*), 1903-06, 1907-08, A. B. 1908. Married 1) Grace Livingstone Hegger in 1914 (divorced, 1928), one son; 2) the journalist Dorothy Thompson in 1928 (separated, 1937; divorced, 1942), one son. Janitor at Upton Sinclair's socialist community Helicon Hall, Englewood, New Jersey, 1906-07; assistant editor, *Transatlantic Tales,* New York, 1907; reporter, Waterloo *Daily Courier,* Iowa, 1908; worked for charity organization, New York, 1908; secretary to Alice MacGowan and Grace MacGowan Cooke, Carmel, California, 1909; writer, San Francisco *Evening Bulletin,* 1909, and Associated Press, San Francisco, 1909-10; staff member, *Volta Review,* Washington, D. C., 1910; manuscript reader, Frederick A. Stokes, publishers, 1910-12, assistant editor, *Adventure,* 1912, editor for Publishers' Newspaper Syndicate, 1913-14, and editorial assistant and advertising manager, George H. Doran, publishers, 1914-15, all New York; full-time writer from 1916: columnist ("Book Week"), *Newsweek,* New York, 1937-38, and *Esquire,* New York, 1945. Writer-in-Residence, University of Wisconsin, Madison, Autumn 1940, and University of Minnesota, Minneapolis, Autumn 1942. Recipient: Pulitzer Prize, 1926 (refused); Nobel Prize for Literature, 1930. Litt. D. : Yale University, 1936. Member, 1935, and Vice-President, 1944, National Institute of Arts and Letters; Member, American Academy, 1938. *Died 10 January 1951.*

SCIENCE-FICTION PUBLICATIONS

Novel

It Can't Happen Here. New York, Doubleday, and London, Cape, 1935.

OTHER PUBLICATIONS

Novels

Our Mr. Wrenn. New York, Harper, 1914; London, Cape, 1923.
The Trail of the Hawk. New York, Harper, 1915; London, Cape, 1923.
The Job. New York, Harper, 1917; London, Cape, 1926.
The Innocents. New York, Harper, 1917.
Free Air. New York, Harcourt Brace, 1919; London, Cape, 1924.

Main Street. New York, Harcourt Brace, 1920; London, Hodder and Stoughton, 1921.

Babbitt. New York, Harcourt Brace, and London, Cape, 1922.

Arrowsmith. New York, Harcourt Brace, 1925; as *Martin Arrowsmith*, London, Cape, 1925.

Mantrap. New York, Harcourt Brace, and London, Cape, 1926.

Elmer Gantry. New York, Harcourt Brace, and London, Cape, 1927.

The Man Who Knew Coolidge. New York, Harcourt Brace, and London, Cape, 1928.

Dodsworth. New York, Harcourt Brace, and London, Cape, 1929.

Ann Vickers. New York, Doubleday, and London, Cape, 1933.

Work of Art. New York, Doubleday, and London, Cape, 1934.

The Prodigal Parents. New York, Doubleday, and London, Cape, 1938.

Bethel Merriday. New York, Doubleday, and London, Cape, 1940.

Gideon Planish. New York, Random House, and London, Cape, 1943.

Cass Timberlane. New York, Random House, 1945; London, Cape, 1946.

Kingsblood Royal. New York, Random House, 1947; London, Cape, 1948.

The God-Seeker. New York, Random House, and London, Heinemann, 1949.

World So Wide. New York, Random House, and London, Heinemann, 1951.

Short Stories

Selected Short Stories. New York, Doubleday, 1935.

I'm a Stranger Here Myself and Other Stories, edited by Mark Schorer. New York, Dell, 1962.

Plays

Hobohemia, adaptation of his own story (produced New York, 1919).

Jayhawker, with Lloyd Lewis (produced Washington, D. C., and New York, 1934). New York, Doubleday, and London, Cape, 1935.

It Can't Happen Here, adaptation of his own novel (produced New York, 1936). New York, Dramatists Play Service, 1938.

Angela Is Twenty-Two (produced Columbus, Ohio, 1938).

Storm in the West (screenplay), with Dore Schary. New York, Stein and Say, 1963; London, Sidgwick and Jackson, 1964.

Other

Hike and the Aeroplane (for children; as Tom Graham). New York, Stokes, 1912.

*John Dos Passos' "Manhattan Transfer." * New York, Harper, 1926.

Cheap and Contented Labor: The Picture of a Southern Mill Town in 1929. New York, United Textile Workers of America, 1929.

The American Fear of Literature (Nobel Prize address). Stockholm, Norstedt, 1931.

From Main Street to Stockholm: Letters of Sinclair Lewis 1919-1930, edited by Harrison Smith. New York, Harcourt Brace, 1952.

The Man from Main Street: A Sinclair Lewis Reader: Selected Essays and Other Writings 1904-1950, edited by Harry E. Maule and Melville H. Cane. New York, Random House, 1953; London, Heinemann, 1954.

*

Bibliography: *The Merrill Checklist of Sinclair Lewis* by James Lundquist, Columbus, Ohio, Merrill, 1970; *Sinclair Lewis: A Reference Guide* by Robert E. Fleming, Boston, Hall, 1980.

Manuscript Collections: Yale University, New Haven, Connecticut; University of Texas, Austin.

Critical Studies (selection): *Sinclair Lewis: An American Life*, New York, McGraw Hill, 1961, London, Heinemann, 1963, and *Sinclair Lewis*, Minneapolis, University of Minnesota Press, 1963, both by Mark Schorer, and *Sinclair Lewis: A Collection of Critical Essays* edited by Schorer, Englewood Cliffs, New Jersey, Prentice Hall, 1962; *Sinclair Lewis* by Sheldon Norman Grebstein, New York, Twayne, 1962; *Dorothy and Red* by Vincent Sheean, Boston, Houghton Mifflin, 1963, London, Heinemann, 1964; *The Art of Sinclair Lewis* by D. J. Dooley, Lincoln, University of Nebraska Press, 1967; *Sinclair Lewis* by James Lundquist, New York, Ungar, 1973; *The Quixotic Vision of Sinclair Lewis* by Martin Light, West Lafayette, Indiana, Purdue University Press, 1975; *A Sinclair Lewis Lexicon* by Hiroshige Yoshida, Tokyo, Hoyu Press, 1976.

Theatrical Activities:

Director: **Play**—*The Good Neighbor* by Jack T. Levin, New York, 1941.

Actor: **Plays**—Doremus Jessup in *It Can't Happen Here*, Cohasset, Massachusetts, 1938; Dr. Hilary Jarrett in *Angela Is Twenty-Two*, Columbus, Ohio, 1938, and tour, 1939; Stage Manager in *Our Town* by Thornton Wilder, Ogunquit, Maine, 1939; Nat Miller in *Ah! Wilderness* by Eugene O'Neill, Provincetown, Massachusetts, 1939, and summer stock, 1940; Canon Skerritt in *Shadow and Substance* by Paul Vincent Carroll, New Orleans and summer stock, 1940.

*   *   *

Although Sinclair Lewis is a regional satirist, he also belongs firmly within the anti-utopian tradition. *It Can't Happen Here* is unquestionably a dystopia, while *Arrowsmith, Kingsblood Royal,* and "The Cat of the Stars" (1919) deal with science and causality. The unpleasant and restrictive worlds of *Main Street, Babbitt,* and *Elmer Gantry* are similar to those found in works by Harry Harrison, Harlan Ellison, and Robert Sheckley. Lewis himself knew and was influenced by H. G. Wells.

The political satires set in the near future, best exemplified by Allen Drury's work, are Lewis's grandchildren. *It Can't Happen Here* came about because of his wife Dorothy Thompson's political involvement and Lewis's knowledge of America's long line of politically extreme demagogues. Not as intellectually based and universal as *Brave New World* or *Nineteen Eighty-Four,* the book caught attention because of its immediacy. Doremus Jessup, a Vermont newspaper editor, symbolizes America's honesty and love of freedom, while Berzelius (Buzz) Windrip is an American Hitler, appealing to the lowest common denominator. Although Buzz's hangers-on die, Doremus survives. Here, as always, Lewis overdoes. Not content with simple horrors, he catalogues them until the reader becomes numb. Lewis, often criticized for overlong novels, does not manage sustained impact.

In *Kingsblood Royal,* red-haired, blue-eyed Neil Kingsblood is ostracized and broken by Grand Republic, Minnesota, because he is 35% black. In "The Cat of the Stars" a boy's stopping to pet a cat causes the loss of a fortune and 3,291 deaths in South America. *Arrowsmith* argues for the superiority of scientific over materialistic values. Its romantic SF theme is man's triumph over nature by fresh perspectives and dedication. The bureaucratic scientific community is etched in acid as Martin Arrowsmith defies mediocrity by refusing to compromise his integrity.

—Mary S. Weinkauf

LICHTENBERG, Jacqueline. American. Born in Flushing, New York, 25 March 1942. Educated at the University of California, Berkeley, B. S. in chemistry 1964. Married Salomon Lichtenberg; two daughters. Industrial chemist for two years, including one year in Israel. Since 1968, free-lance writer. Agent: Scott Meredith Literary Agency, 845 Third Avenue, New York, New York 10022. Address: 8 Fox Lane, Spring Valley, New York 10977, U.S.A.

SCIENCE-FICTION PUBLICATIONS

Novels (series: Dushau; Kren; Sime/Gen)

House of Zeor (Sime/Gen). New York, Doubleday, 1974.
Unto Zeor, Forever (Sime/Gen). New York, Doubleday, 1978.
First Channel (Sime/Gen), with Jean Lorrah. New York, Doubleday, 1980.
Mahogany Trinrose (Sime/Gen). New York, Doubleday, 1981.
Channel's Destiny (Sime/Gen), with Jean Lorrah. New York, Doubleday, 1982.
Molt Brother (Kren). New York, Playboy Press, 1982.
RenSime (Sime/Gen). New York, Doubleday, 1984.
City of a Million Legends (Kren). New York, Berkley, 1985.
Dushau New York, Warner, 1985.
Farfetch (Dushau). New York, Warner, 1985.

Uncollected Short Stories (series: Sime/Gen)

"Operation High Time" (Sime/Gen), in *If* (New York), January 1969.
"Recompense," in *Galileo 2* (Boston), 1976.
"The Channel's Exemption" (Sime/Gen), in *Galileo* (Boston), July 1977.
"The Vanillamint Tapestry," in *Cassandra Rising*, edited by Alice Laurance. New York, Doubleday, 1978.
"The Answer," with Jean Lorrah, in *The Keeper's Price*, edited by Marion Zimmer Bradley. New York, DAW, 1980.
"Science Is Magic Spelled Backwards," in *Hecate's Cauldron*, edited by Susan Shwartz. New York, DAW, 1982.
"Event at Holiday Rock," in *Speculations*, edited by Isaac Asimov and Alice Laurance. Boston, Houghton Mifflin, 1982.

OTHER PUBLICATIONS

Other

Star Trek Lives!, with Sondra Marshak and Joan Winston. New York, Bantam, and London, Corgi, 1975.

*

Jacqueline Lichtenberg comments:
As I see it, the emotional substance of the Sime Series is an examination of the fear/compassion axis of emotion that can exist between symbionts. The Sime mutation brings evolutionary pressure to bear on otherwise rather ordinary human beings to develop compassion or die. It is stunning how difficult it is to find true compassion untinged by fear in a human. But when you do find it, it is more precious than life itself. The Sime/Gen mutation is considered as another on the order of the differentiation into male and female, only the second such step ever taken.

The style in which I write emphasizes psychological problems with psychological action and resolution, rather than the standard action/adventure formula in which it is considered bad form to characterize or motivate. I aim my work basically at women between 18 and 25, though anyone who has been such an age should enjoy it as well. I am constantly surprised at the number of fans who don't fit that description, surprised and delighted no end.

*   *   *

Jacqueline Lichtenberg began her career in science fiction as the author of *Star Trek* fan fiction, and is the creator of one of the largest and most popular of the fannish "universes" in which the cast of the *U. S. S. Enterprise* goes where no man (or woman) has gone before. Her series, notable for its complexity, and for Lichtenberg's willingness to allow other writers to participate in it, is described in *Star Trek Lives*. This spirit of cooperation, as well as the emphases within this universe on symbiosis between dissimilar creatures who come to love one another and on psychological intensity, have carried over into Lichtenberg's "independent" fiction.

At present, Jacqueline Lichtenberg has three series universes going. The first, and earliest, is the one begun in *House of Zeor*, which introduced her readers to the symbiotic Simes and Gens. Simes are tentacled, almost vampiric humanoids who mutated from the parent stock after a genetic catastrophe. In order to live, they must take selyn from the second mutation, the human-appearing Gens. The problem is that selyn transfer usually kills the Gen. As the series progressed from *House of Zeor*, in which the idea of "channels," certain genetically gifted Simes capable of taking selyn without harming Gens and "channeling" it to other Simes, through *Unto Zeor Forever*, in which an injured channel confronts the Sime's fascination with fear and pain by becoming a surgeon, into the Lichtenberg and Jean Lorrah collaborations *First Channel* and *Channel's Destiny*, which show the origins of the Farris family (the Farrises are among the most talented channels) who rule the House of Zeor, several themes emerge. One is the bonding of unlikely beings who must struggle with prejudice. Another is the curious interdependence of Sime and Gen, in which the vastly stronger and faster Sime turns out to be the weak, dependent link after all. A third is the toughness of Lichtenberg's characters, who seem never to give up. This toughness is manifested in subsequent books—*Mahogany Trinrose*, in which a Farris daughter persists until she produces a new genetic variant of an old species and is thought to be a witch, and *RenSime*, in which a Farris woman who is not a channel copes with her despair at not being what she was born to be. Subsequent books in this series will include another collaboration with Jean Lorrah, *House of Keon*; Lorrah plans to produce a few Sime/Gen novels independently.

Molt Brother is Lichtenberg's first novel set in a different, high-tech universe. It and its sequel, *City of a Million Legends*, introduce the kren, reptilian beings with venomed fangs who are vulnerable only when they molt. At that time, they choose molt brothers (or sisters) to guard them. This bond, like the selyn transfer for Simes, is perilous, profound, and occasionally ecstatic. *Molt Brother* is the story of Arshel Holtether, an esper archeologist who chooses a human molt brother and enters worlds of intrigue, danger, and self-discovery. It is also the story of Zref, a human/computer interface unable to link completely with his own mechanical symbiote.

Lichtenberg's most recent series, about a species called the Dushau, also displays her preoccupation with symbiotes. In this trilogy (*Dushau, Farfetch,* and the forthcoming *Outreach*) set in a high-tech, tyrannical, and rather Byzantine galactic empire, a young woman closely connected with the court wants above all else to join a bonded group of Dushau, long-lived alien empaths who can practically bond into planetary ecologies. Because the empire suspects the Dushau of wanting independence, it is systematically exterminating them. One bond group flees a police cruiser to a planet that becomes its ally as Dushau, the human heroine, and a host of minor characters set the stage for revolution.

All of Lichtenberg's books are marked by an extraordinary density of thought. She creates extremely dangerous characters: the sinister Simes, the venomous kren whose pain somehow makes them vulnerable and understandable to her often fanatic readers. Her writing is notable for intensity rather than lyricism. Frequently her books are painful to read because of her insistence on confronting breakdowns in communication (which occasionally makes her writing tortuous and harsh) and extending them out into catastrophe. She specializes in creating a psychological "worst-case" scenario and then rehabilitating the characters who encounter it. In order to supply communication, Lichtenberg creates bonds like transfer, molt brotherhood, or the symbiosis in Dushau, but even these bonds are imperfect, if only because their severing causes anguish.

As can be seen from Lichtenberg's willingness to allow other writers to participate in her universes, she is a generous teacher, who has participated in many writers workshops, notably the one sponsored at Murray State University in Kentucky. Her fans have published three fanzines which feature letters, reviews, fragments of MSS, and original Sime/Gen stories by amateur writers. The audience for her work is among the most dedicated in the field, and Lichtenberg is notable for her willingness to enter their lives as generously as she has opened her worlds to them.

—Susan Shwartz

LIGHTNER, Alice (Martha). Also writes as Alice L. Hopf. American. Born in Detroit, Michigan, 11 October 1904. Educated at Westover School, Middlebury, Connecticut, graduated 1923; Vassar College, Poughkeepsie, New York, B. A. 1927. Married Ernest Joachim Hopf in 1935; one son. Editorial assistant, *Civil Engineering;* clerk-typist, Grey Advertising, New York. Since 1951, freelance writer. Recipient: National Science Teachers Association Award, 1972, 1973. Agent: Larry Sternig, 742 Robertson Street, Milwaukee, Wisconsin 53213. Address: Box 174, Birch Road, Upper Black Eddy, Pennsylvania 18972, U.S.A.

SCIENCE-FICTION PUBLICATIONS

Novels (for children)

The Rock of Three Planets. New York, Putnam, 1963.
The Planet Poachers. New York, Putnam, 1965.

Doctor to the Galaxy. New York, Norton, 1965.
The Galactic Troubadours. New York, Norton, 1965.
The Space Plague. New York, Norton, 1966.
The Space Olympics. New York, Norton, 1967.
The Space Ark. New York, Putnam, 1968.
The Day of the Drones. New York, Norton, 1969.
The Thursday Toads. New York, McGraw Hill, 1971.
Gods or Demons? New York, Four Winds Press, 1973.
Star Dog. New York, McGraw Hill, 1973.
The Space Gypsies. New York, McGraw Hill, 1974.
Star Circus. New York, Dutton, 1977.

Uncollected Short Stories

"A New Game," in *Teen-Age Outer Space Stories,* edited by A. L. Furman. New York, Lantern Press, 1962.
"Best Friend," in *The Boys' Life Book of Outer Space Stories.* New York, Random House, 1964.
"A Great Day for the Irish" and "The Mars Jar," in *Teen-Age Space Adventures,* edited by A. L. Furman. New York, Lantern Press, 1972.
"The Ghost of Pirate's Cove," in *Haunted Stories,* edited by A. L. Furman. New York, Lantern Press, 1975.
"Tigger," in *Baleful Beasts and Eerie Creatures,* edited by Dorothy Haas. Chicago, Rand McNally, 1976.

OTHER PUBLICATIONS

Novel

The Walking Zoo of Darwin Dingle (for children). New York, Putnam, 1969.

Verse

The Pillar and the Flame. New York, Vinal, 1928.

Other as Alice L. Hopf (for children)

Monarch Butterflies. New York, Crowell, 1965.
Wild Traveler: The Story of a Coyote. New York, Norton, 1967.
Earth's Bug-Eyed Monsters. New York, Norton, 1968.
Butterfly and Moth. New York, Putnam, 1969.
Carab, The Trap-Door Spider. New York, Putnam, 1970.
Biography of an Octopus [a Rhino, an Ostrich, an Ant, an Armadillo, an American Reindeer, a Giraffe, a Snowy Owl, a Komodo Dragon]. New York, Putnam, 9 vols., 1971-81
Misunderstood Animals. New York, McGraw Hill, 1973.
Wild Cousins of the Dog [Cat, Horse]. New York, Putnam, 3 vols., 1973-77
Misplaced Animals and Other Living Creatures. New York, McGraw Hill, 1975.
Animal and Plant Life Spans. New York, Holiday House, 1978.
Animals That Eat Nectar and Honey. New York, Holiday House, 1979.
Nature's Pretenders. New York, Putnam, 1979.
Pigs Wild and Tame. New York, Holiday House, 1979.
Whose House Is It? New York, Dodd Mead, 1980.
Bugs, Big and Little. New York, Messner, 1981.
Strange Sex Lives in the Animal Kingdom. New York, McGraw Hill, 1981.
Chickens and Their Wild Relatives. New York, Dodd Mead, 1982.
Hyenas. New York, Dodd Mead, 1983.
Bats. New York, Dodd Mead, 1985.

*

Manuscript Collection: Fullerton College Library, California.

* * *

Alice Lightner is an author of children's books at home in non-fiction as well as SF. Her informational books about animal life are popular with young readers and have received honors from science teachers because of their solid, up-to-date information, enthusiastic concern for ecology and conservation, and capacity for explaining on a child's level of comprehension. Similar qualities mark Lightner's SF. Actually, so prominent is the last quality that in spite of lacking a prose style as supple as Norton's or an imagination as inventive as Heinlein's, Lightner has produced a body of SF that is perhaps more readily open to and enjoyed by youngsters than either of theirs.

The typical Lightner novel is an amalgam of SF and the Young Adult novel. The most prominent of the former is the presence of "alien" animals: either ones that do not exist today but whose future existence may be extrapolated—a unicorn-like gazelle, for instance, or a telepathic bird that can speak—or ones that are unexpected mutations of species currently existing—giant bees, for example. Another prominent SF feature is exotic setting, most often a planet newly discovered which needs to be explored and surveyed and whose flora and fauna require cataloguing and preserving. Young Adult elements usually found in Lightner's fiction are mystery and dashes of romance and humor in addition to the requisite youthful protagonists. (Incidentally, Lightner is one of the very few writers of children's SF who regularly incorporate females among their protagonists.) So determined is Lightner to appeal to youth that sometimes, as in *The Galactic Troubadours,* she sacrifices plausibility for topicality: a band of rock and roll musicians make a nuisance of themselves as they travel from planet to planet. In general, though, Lightner has been successful in her mix.

Lightner's most successful novel is *The Day of the Drones.* Set in the future when nuclear conflict has poisoned the earth and obliterated virtually everyone, the book concerns the Afrians—descendants of a small group of surviving black Africans who have managed to rebuild civilization by placing under taboo most technology and by practicing strict genetic control. Those born darkest-skinned will enjoy most privileges; fair-skinned babies, less; the occasional white baby is simply abandoned. A small group of Afrians set out to ascertain whether any other human survivors exist. In what was once England the Afrians come across the Anglics, descendants of the ancient English who are cruel, superstition-ridden, and white. They too practice social engineering, having established a bizarre matriarchy modeled upon bee-society. The impact of *The Day of the Drones* is three-fold. One, the description of the two differing cultures is detailed and plausible. Second, characterization is rounded and convincing; none of the several protagonists is a mouthpiece for conventional sentiments or moral posturing. Especially interesting is Anhara, the young Afrian archeologist who has mastered Anglic so that she can appreciate the little Shakespeare that is extant and becomes sorrowed at the degradation of the race that produced the Master. Third, the investigation of racism, whether black or white, and its demeaning effects is matter-of-fact and even-handed, hence, neither sensational nor preachy. The book, then, is impressive and challenging; as such it must be ranked among the relatively few superior examples of children's SF.

—Francis J. Molson

LINDSAY, David. British. Born in Blackheath, London, 3 March 1876. Educated at Lewisham Grammar School, London, and a secondary school in Jedburgh, Roxburgh. Served in the Grenadier Guards, 1916-18. Married Jacqueline Silver in 1916; two daughters. Worked for Price Forbes, insurance brokers, 1894-1916; lived in Cornwall, 1919-29, and after 1929 in Sussex. *Died 16 July 1945.*

SCIENCE-FICTION PUBLICATIONS

Novels

A Voyage to Arcturus. London, Methuen, 1920; New York, Macmillan, 1963.
The Haunted Woman. London, Methuen, 1922; Hollywood, Newcastle, 1975.
Sphinx. London, Long, 1923.
Devil's Tor. London, Putnam, 1932; New York, Arno Press, 1978.
The Violet Apple, and The Witch. Chicago, Chicago Review Press, 1976; London, Sidgwick and Jackson, 1978.

OTHER PUBLICATIONS

Novel

Adventures of Monsieur de Mailly. London, Melrose, 1926; as *A Blade for Sale,* New York, McBride, 1927.

*

Critical Studies: *The Strange Genius of David Lindsay* by J. B. Pick, Colin Wilson, and E. H. Visiak, London, Baker, 1970, as *The Haunted Man,* San Bernardino, California, Borgo Press, 1979; *The Life and Works of David Lindsay* by Bernard Sellin, translated by Kenneth Gunnell, Cambridge, University Press, 1981; *David Lindsay* by Gary K. Wolfe, Mercer Island, Washington, Starmont House, 1982.

* * *

While David Lindsay's first novel, *A Voyage to Arcturus,* has become recognized as one of the masterworks of 20th-century fantasy, his other novels remain unknown to all but a handful of readers, and the man himself remains a curiously distant and enigmatic figure. More a philosopher than a novelist, Lindsay wrote often awkward and laborious prose, his later work filled with long expository digressions, his ideas so complex and densely packed, his characters so unsympathetic, that many readers find his fiction at first coldly intellectual and difficult to get into. But Lindsay undeniably expanded the possibilities of fantasy as philosophical fiction, and his influence has been widely felt among modern authors as diverse as Colin Wilson and Philip José Farmer.

Lindsay's masterpiece, *A Voyage to Arcturus,* concerns the journey of a man named Maskull to Tormance, a world in the system Arcturus, where he encounters bizarre characters and himself undergoes physical transformations in a series of episodes depicting different systems of belief not unlike the different moral systems at work on Earth. As each of these moral systems is shown to be illusory, Maskull is gradually brought to a confrontation with the godlike villain Crystalman, who controls this world, and who seems, at the end, to represent the entire world of phenomenal experience. Drawing on Nietzsche, Schopenhauer, and Norse mythology for ideas and imagery, Lindsay develops a world of vivid scenery and violent action that nevertheless is rigidly structured according to the philosophical ideas he wishes to explore. The novel is a remarkable union of action and idea.

Ideas were more interesting to Lindsay than action, however, and his later novels contained little of the violent action of *Arcturus*. *The Haunted Woman* continued exploring the notion of subjective reality in a romance of two lovers who could only acknowledge their love in a phantom room of a haunted house. *Sphinx* turned to the science-fiction device of a dream-recording machine to explore the romance between a woman composer and a writer. Like *A Voyage to Arcturus* itself, however, each of these novels was a commercial disaster, and Lindsay turned to the historical romance for his next book, *Adventures of Monsieur de Mailly,* a tale of court intrigue that nevertheless also reflected Lindsay's preoccupations with illusion and deception. *Devil's Tor* is a sprawling, slow-moving, and at times brilliant exposition of the myth of the Eternal Feminine, in a story concerning the reuniting of two halves of an ancient stone and the founding of a new race by a chosen man and woman.

Lindsay was unable to find a publisher for *The Violet Apple,* and he left another manuscript, "The Witch," unfinished. Both works were finally published in abridged form, and both retain the romance structure of *The Haunted Woman* and *Devil's Tor.* In *The Violet Apple* a dwarf apple tree, grown from a seed which according to legend came from the original tree of Eden, unites the lovers. "The Witch" explores the dual myths of the wise woman and witchcraft in a work whose controlling image is music. Though none of these later works achieves the narrative power of *A Voyage to Arcturus,* they nevertheless stand as worthwhile philosophical meditations and as studies in the problems inherent in trying to write a truly philosophical fiction.

—Gary K. Wolfe

LLEWELLYN, (David William) Alun. Irish. Born in London, England, 17 April 1903. Educated at Alleyn's School, Dulwich, London; St. John's College, Cambridge (Chancellor's Gold Medal, for poetry, 1923; College Literature Prize, 1924), B. A. (honours) in history and literature 1924, LL. B. (honours) 1925, M. A. 1928; Lincoln's Inn, London: called to the Bar, 1927. Served in the Intelligence Corps during World War II. Married Lesley Deane in 1953. Treaty translator and reviser, League of Nations, Geneva, 1936-39; legal adviser, Egyptian government, Montreux Capitulations, 1937; Secretary of the Compensation Tribunal for Coal Nationalisation, 1947-49; counsel, Camberwell Borough, London, 1951-53; public relations speaker, Commonwealth Industries Association, 1955-72. Liberal parliamentary candidate for South Croydon, 1931, 1935. President, Union Society, 1935, and Hardwicke Society, 1953, both Middle Temple, London; Honorary Treasurer, Poetry Society of Great Britain, 1961-62. Since 1977, Honorary Secretary, and President, 1984-86, Irish P. E. N. Member, Welsh Academy, 1983. Address: 52 Silchester Park, Glenageary, Dun Laoghaire, County Dublin, Ireland.

SCIENCE-FICTION PUBLICATIONS

Novel

The Strange Invaders. London, Bell, 1934.

OTHER PUBLICATIONS

Novels

The Deacon. London, Bell, 1934.
The Soul of Cézar Azan. London, Barker, 1938.
Jubilee John. London, Barker, 1939.

Short Stories

Confound Their Politics. London, Bell, 1934.

Plays

Ways of Love (produced 1968). London, French, 1958.
Shelley Plain (produced London, 1960).

Verse

Ballads and Songs. London, Stockwell, 1921.

Other

History of the Union Society of London. London, Union Society, 1935.
The Emperor of Britain. London, Montgomeryshire Society, 1939.
The Tyrant from Below: An Essay in Political Revaluation. London, Macdonald and Evans, 1957.
The World and the Commonwealth. London, British Commonwealth Union, 1968.
The Shell Guide to Wales. London, Rainbird, 1969.

*

Alun Llewellyn comments:

Only one of my novels is, strictly speaking, science fiction. *The Strange Invaders* looks at this planet and the ecological change upon it as a result of Man's abondonment of Mind as a motive force of his evolution. But since all human psychology is a matter for scientific analysis, and is a more subtle matter than mechanistic theories of economics or sex can explain, the studies in my other novels of the illusions of love, religion, ambition, and power ought really to be called fictional illustrations of scientific themes. By this interpretation, all my fiction qualifies as science fiction.

*   *   *

Alun Llewellyn's *The Strange Invaders* is a fantasy set in the future when the habitable area of the earth is gradually decreasing as a new ice age emerges. Mankind has retrogressed; as a result of disastrous wars it has lost the art of civilization and is living in a pre-iron age existence. The story takes place in what seems to be the Gobi desert, a somewhat hostile environment but one of the last places on earth capable of supporting human life. The plot concerns a small group of people living in a half-destroyed town, isolated within the remains of a ruined city on the plains. There is a pseudo-medieval order to their existence: governed by a religious community of priests dedicated to the new trinity of Marx, Lenin, and Stalin, and controlled by a warrior group, they manage to eke out a life of basic survival. As if their plight were not bad enough, Llewellyn has this last outpost of humanity threatened by an army of enormous lizards—huge, cold-blooded creatures that are virtually invincible. The plot is concerned with the efforts of the community to survive in the face of this new and overpowering challenge. What elevates the story above the ordinary is Llewellyn's ability to show how the basic human emotions of love, hate, and jealousy survive and dominate the lives of these people even in the face of overwhelming danger and the threat of extinction.

Though the novel is cast in the form of a futuristic nightmare, it is difficult for the reader to remember that the time frame is the future and not the past. So vividly does Llewellyn evoke the sense of life of these people and so much is their life a reliving of prehistorical civilization, that the reader inevitably feels that he has been transported into the past rather than into the future.

—Joseph A. Quinn

LLEWELLYN, Edward (Edward Llewellyn-Thomas). Canadian. Born in Salisbury, Wiltshire, England, 15 December 1917. Educated at the University of London, B. Sc. 1951; McGill University, Montreal, M. D., C. M. 1955. Served as Sergeant in the Royal Signals, 1939-40, and Captain in Royal Electrical and Mechanical Engineers, 1940-45; Surgeon Lieutenant, Royal Canadian Navy Reserve, 1959-65. Married Ellen Buford in 1947; one daughter and two sons. Junior Engineer, BBC, 1938-39; Controller, Telecommunications, Malaya, 1945-50; Engineer, Montreal Neurological Institute, 1952-54; Research Associate, Cornell University, Ithaca, New York, 1956-58; Scientific Officer, Defence Research Medical Laboratories, 1958-61; Assistant and Associate Professor, 1959-66, Professor of Pharmacology, Associate Professor of Electrical Engineering, and Assistant Professor in Department of Anaesthesia, 1966-84, Professor in Institute of Biomedical Engineering, 1974-84, and Associate Dean in the Faculty of Medicine, 1974-84, University of Toronto. Part-time Professor of Psychology, University of Waterloo, Ontario, 1963-65. Fellow, Royal Society of Canada, and Royal Society of Arts. *Died 5 July 1984.*

SCIENCE-FICTION PUBLICATIONS

Novels

The Douglas Convolution. New York, DAW, 1979.
The Bright Companion. New York, DAW, 1980.
Prelude to Chaos. New York, DAW, 1983.
Salvage and Destroy. New York, DAW, 1984.
Fugitive in Transit. New York, DAW, 1985.

Uncollected Short Story

"The Lords of Creation," in *Analog* (New York), March 1985.

*   *   *

Edward Llewellyn-Thomas who wrote SF as Edward Llewellyn was an M. D. who taught at the University of Toronto. His books specialize in high adventure and backgrounds that draw on Llewellyn's knowledge of engineering and medicine.

In his first SF novel, *The Douglas Convolution*, Llewellyn introduces us to a mathematician from the present who discovers a means of time travel. He uses it to travel to the year 2170 where the world faces serious depopulation because of a drug that sterilizes female offspring. The mathematician calls himself Captain Gart and becomes a soldier helping the Order— the few fertile women left—beat back a barbarian invasion. The action is brisk and Llewellyn leaves Gart in the arms of an amorous, fertile copter pilot.

Llewellyn's next book is a sequel to *The Douglas Convolution, The Bright Companion.* Unfortunately, the tone is not as lively as the first book. David, a son of a doctor, travels the Shenandoah valley where he meets Ann, a fertile woman who wants to find her way to the Order's headquarters based in Malta. The book becomes the story of David and Ann's travels from the Chesapeake, across the Atlantic Ocean, through the Mediterranean to Malta. Ann, typical of Llewellyn's female characters, is strong and feisty. David, again typical of Llewellyn's male characters, is wimpy. Their company becomes grating as the book limps along to its predictable conclusion.

In *Prelude to Chaos*, a prequel to the first two Llewellyn books, Judith Grenfell, a neurobiologist, discovers the sterility affect in a common drug most women have taken. This is the weakest book in the series because most of action is a rehash of events described in the first two books. The characters of Judith and Gavin Knox are well done but the plot lacks suspense and surprise.

Llewellyn must have sensed that he had played out most of the innovative ideas of the first three books because he wisely changed settings with *Salvage and Destroy*. Llewellyn introduces two star-faring alien races: the Ults and the Drin. The Ults have defeated the Drin and control the Galactic civilizations. Ults have immortality by foregoing sexual maturity; Drin gain immortality by dominating host bodies with their minds. In 1680, the Ults landed on Earth, brought back some humans who bred into Ult starship crews. Now signals from Earth suggest a menace to the Ult realm so they dispatch Lucian to study the human problem. Llewellyn cleverly has Lucian assume a humanlike form, which makes him adjust his Ult mentality to a more human one. The plotting is crisp but the book drags because of long dialogues between Lucian and three inherited personalities and a computer personality.

Llewellyn's last book, *Fugitive in Transit*, offers another strong female character in Ruth Thalia Adams who disappeared through a natural "gate" in ancient Greece to explore the thousands of worlds connected by the Galactic Transit Authority. The chase is on as a Galactic Marshall is sent to track "Alia" down on Earth. Hiding on her home Greek island, Alia falls in love with a poet named Peter Ward. Together they try to outwit the combined forces of Organized Crime, the United Nations, and the Galactic Transit Authority. The fast-paced action is enjoyable even though most of the content of the book is satiric.

Edward Llewellyn was a writer who combined scientific expertise and high adventure to produce solid SF enjoyment.

—George Kelley

LLOYD, Nigel. See **TUBB, E. C.**

LLOYD, Robert. See **TUBB, E. C.**

LOCKHARD, Leonard. See HARNESS, Charles L. ; THOMAS, Ted.

LOHRMAN, Paul. See SHAVER, Richard S.

LOMAS, Frank T. See TUBB, E. C.

LONDON, Jack (John Griffith London). American. Born in San Francisco, California, 12 January 1876. Educated at a grammar school in Oakland, California; Oakland High School, 1895-96; University of California, Berkeley, 1896-97. Married 1) Bessie Maddern in 1900 (separated, 1903; divorced, 1905), two daughters; 2) Charmian Kittredge in 1905. Worked in a cannery in Oakland, 1890; sailor on the *Sophie Sutherland*, sailing to Japan and Siberia, 1893; returned to Oakland, wrote for the local paper, and held various odd jobs, 1893-94; tramped the United States and Canada, 1894-96; arrested for vagrancy in Niagara Falls, New York; joined the gold rush to the Klondike, 1897-98, then returned to Oakland and became a full-time writer; visited London, 1902; War Correspondent in the Russo-Japanese War for the *San Francisco Examiner*, 1904; settled on a ranch in Sonoma County, California, 1906, and lived there for the rest of his life; attempted to sail round the world on a 45-foot yacht, 1907-09; War Correspondent in Mexico, 1914. *Died 22 November 1916.*

SCIENCE-FICTION PUBLICATIONS

Novels

Before Adam. New York, Macmillan, 1907; London, Laurie, 1908.
The Iron Heel. New York, Macmillan, and London, Everett, 1908.
The Scarlet Plague. New York, Macmillan, and London, Mills and Boon, 1915.
The Jacket (The Star Rover). London, Mills and Boon, 1915; as *The Star Rover,* New York, Macmillan, 1915.

Short Stories

The Strength of the Strong (story). Chicago, Kerr, 1911.
The Dream of Debs. Chicago, Kerr, 1912(?).
The Strength of the Strong (collection). New York, Macmillan, 1914; London, Mills and Boon, 1917.
The Red One. New York, Macmillan, 1918; London, Mills and Boon, 1919.
Short Stories, edited by Maxwell Geismar. New York, Hill and Wang, 1960.
Goliah: A Utopian Essay. Berkeley, California, Thorp Springs Press, 1973.
Curious Fragments: Jack London's Tales of Fantasy Fiction, edited by Dale L. Walker. Port Washington, New York, Kennikat Press, 1975.

The Science Fiction of Jack London, edited by Richard Gid Powers. Boston, Gregg Press, 1975.

OTHER PUBLICATIONS

Novels

The Cruise of the Dazzler. New York, Century, 1902; London, Hodder and Stoughton, 1906.
A Daughter of the Snows. Philadelphia, Lippincott, 1902; London, Isbister, 1904.
The Kempton-Wace Letters (published anonymously), with Anna Strunsky. New York, Macmillan, and London, Isbister, 1903.
The Call of the Wild. New York, Macmillan, and London, Heinemann, 1903.
The Sea-Wolf. New York, Macmillan, and London, Heinemann, 1904.
The Game. New York, Macmillan, and London, Heinemann, 1905.
White Fang. New York, Macmillan, 1906; London, Methuen, 1907.
Martin Eden. New York, Macmillan, 1909; London, Heinemann, 1910.
Burning Daylight. New York, Macmillan, 1910; London, Heinemann, 1911.
Adventure. London, Nelson, and New York, Macmillan, 1911.
The Abysmal Brute. New York, Century, 1913; London, Newnes, 1914.
John Barleycorn. New York, Century, 1913; London, Mills and Boon, 1914.
The Valley of the Moon. New York, Macmillan, and London, Mills and Boon, 1913.
The Mutiny of the Elsinore. New York, Macmillan, 1914; London, Mills and Boon, 1915.
The Little Lady of the Big House. New York, Macmillan, and London, Mills and Boon, 1916.
Jerry of the Islands. New York, Macmillan, and London, Mills and Boon, 1917.
Michael, Brother of Jerry. New York, Macmillan, 1917; London, Mills and Boon, 1918.
Hearts of Three. London, Mills and Boon, 1918; New York, Macmillan, 1920.
The Assassination Bureau Ltd., completed by Robert L. Fish. New York, McGraw Hill, 1963; London, Deutsch, 1964.

Short Stories

The Son of the Wolf: Tales of the Far North. Boston, Houghton Mifflin, 1900; London, Isbister, 1902; as *An Odyssey of the North,* London, Mills and Boon, 1915.
The God of His Fathers and Other Stories. New York, McClure, 1901; London, Isbister, 1902.
Children of the Frost. New York, Macmillan, 1902.
The Faith of Men and Other Stories. New York, Macmillan, and London, Heinemann, 1904.
Tales of the Fish Patrol. New York, Macmillan, 1905; London, Heinemann, 1906.
The Apostate. Chicago, Kerr, 1906.
Moon-Face and Other Stories. New York, Macmillan, and London, Heinemann, 1906.
Love of Life and Other Stories. New York, Macmillan, 1907; London, Everett, 1908.
Lost Face. New York, Macmillan, 1910; London, Mills and Boon, 1915.
When God Laughs and Other Stories. New York, Macmillan,

1911; London, Mills and Boon, 1912.

South Sea Tales. New York, Macmillan, 1911; London, Mills and Boon, 1912.

The House of Pride and Other Tales of Hawaii. New York, Macmillan, 1912; London, Mills and Boon, 1914.

A Son of the Sun. New York, Doubleday, 1912; London, Mills and Boon, 1913; as *The Adventures of Captain Grief,* Cleveland, World, 1954.

Smoke Bellew. New York, Century, 1912; London, Mills and Boon, 1913; as *Smoke and Shorty,* London, Mills and Boon, 1920.

The Night Born. . . . New York, Century, 1913; London, Mills and Boon, 1916.

The Turtles of Tasman. New York, Macmillan, 1916; London, Mills and Boon, 1917.

The Human Drift. New York, Macmillan, 1917; London, Mills and Boon, 1919.

On the Makaloa Mat. New York, Macmillan, 1919; as *Island Tales,* London, Mills and Boon, 1920.

Dutch Courage and Other Stories. New York, Macmillan, 1922; London, Mills and Boon, 1923.

Jack London's Tales of Adventure, edited by Irving Shepard. New York, Hanover House, 1956.

Stories of Hawaii, edited by A. Grove Day. New York, Appleton Century Crofts, 1965.

Great Short Works of Jack London, edited by Earle Labor. New York, Harper, 1965.

The Unabridged Jack London, edited by Lawrence Teacher and Richard E. Nicholls. Philadelphia, Running Press, 1981.

Jack London's Yukon Women. New York, Belmont, 1982.

Young Wolf: The Early Adventure Stories, edited by Howard Lachtman. Santa Barbara, California, Capra Press, 1984.

Plays

The Great Interrogation, with Lee Bascom (produced San Francisco, 1905).

Scorn of Women. New York, Macmillan, 1906; London, Macmillan, 1907.

Theft. New York and London, Macmillan, 1910.

The Acorn Planters: A California Forest Play. . . . New York, Macmillan, and London, Mills and Boon, 1916.

Daughters of the Rich, edited by James E. Sisson. Oakland, California, Holmes, 1971.

Gold, with Herbert Heron, edited by James E. Sisson. Oakland, California, Holmes, 1972.

Other

The People of the Abyss. New York, Macmillan, and London, Isbister, 1903.

The Tramp. New York, Wilshire's Magazine, 1904.

The Scab. Chicago, Kerr, 1904.

Jack London: A Sketch of His Life and Work. London, Macmillan, 1905.

War of the Classes. New York, Macmillan, and London, Heinemann, 1905.

What Life Means to Me. Princeton, New Jersey, Intercollegiate Socialist Society, 1906.

The Road. New York, Macmillan, 1907; London, Mills and Boon, 1914.

Jack London: Who He Is and What He Has Done. New York, Macmillan, 1908 (?).

Revolution. Chicago, Kerr, 1909.

Revolution and Other Essays. New York, Macmillan, 1910; London, Mills and Boon, 1920.

The Cruise of the Snark. New York, Macmillan, and London, Mills and Boon, 1911.

Jack London by Himself. New York, Macmillan, and London, Mills and Boon, 1913.

London's Essays of Revolt, edited by Leonard D. Abbott. New York, Vanguard Press, 1926.

Jack London, American Rebel: A Collection of His Social Writings . . . , edited by Philip S. Foner. New York, Citadel Press, 1947.

(Works) [Fitzroy Edition], edited by I. O. Evans. London, Arco, and New York, Archer House and Horizon Press, 18 vols., 1962-68.

The Bodley Head Jack London, edited by Arthur Calder-Marshall. London, Bodley Head, 4 vols., 1963-66; as *The Pan Jack London,* London, Pan, 2 vols., 1966-68.

Letters from Jack London, Containing an Unpublished Correspondence Between London and Sinclair Lewis, edited by King Hendricks and Irving Shepard. New York, Odyssey Press, 1965; London, MacGibbon and Kee, 1966.

Jack London Reports: War Correspondence, Sports Articles, and Miscellaneous Writings, edited by King Hendricks and Irving Shepard. New York, Random House, 1970.

Jack London's Articles and Short Stories in the (Oakland) High School Aegis, edited by James E. Sisson. Cedar Springs, Michigan, London Collector, 1971.

No Mentor But Myself: A Collection of Articles, Essays, Reviews, and Letters on Writing and Writers, edited by Dale L. Walker. Port Washington, New York, Kennikat Press, 1979.

Revolution: Stories and Essays, edited by Robert Barltrop. London, Journeyman Press, 1979.

Jack London on the Road: The Tramp Diary and Other Hobo Writings, edited by Richard W. Etulain. Logan, Utah State University Press, 1979.

Sporting Blood: Selections from Jack London's Greatest Sports Writing, edited by Howard Lachtman. Novato, California, Presidio Press, 1981.

Novels and Stories and *Novels and Social Writings* (Library of America), edited by Donald Pizer. New York, Literary Classics of the United States, and London, Cambridge University Press, 2 vols., 1982-84.

*

Bibliography: *Jack London: A Bibliography* by Hensley C. Woodbridge, John London, and George H. Tweney, Georgetown, California, Talisman Press, 1966; supplement by Woodbridge, Milwood, New York, Kraus, 1973; in *Bibliography of American Literature 5* by Jacob Blanck, New Haven, Connecticut, Yale University Press, 1969; *Jack London: A Reference Guide* by Joan R. Sherman, Boston, Hall, 1977.

Manuscript Collections: Huntington Library, San Marino, California; Utah State University Library, Logan.

Critical Studies: *Jack London: A Biography* by Richard O'Connor, Boston, Little Brown, 1964, London, Gollancz, 1965; *The Alien Worlds of Jack London* by Dale L. Walker, Grand Rapids, Michigan, Wolf House, 1973; *Jack London* by Earle Labor, Boston, Twayne, 1974; *Jack London: The Man, The Writer, The Rebel* by Robert Barltrop, London, Pluto Press, 1976; *Jack: A Biography of Jack London* by Andrew Sinclair, New York, Harper, 1977, London, Weidenfeld and Nicolson, 1978; *Jack London and the Klondike: The Genesis of an American Writer* by Franklin Walker, San Marino, California, Huntington Library Publications, 1978; *Jack London: Essays in Criticism* edited by Ray W. Ownbey, Layton, Utah, Peregrine Smith, 1979; *Jack London: An American Myth* by

John Perry, Chicago, Nelson Hall, 1981; *Solitary Comrade: Jack London and His Work* by Joan D. Hedrick, Chapel Hill, University of North Carolina Press, 1982; *The Novels of Jack London* by Charles N. Watson, Madison, University of Wisconsin Press, 1983; *Jack London* by Gordon Beauchamp, Mercer Island, Washington, Starmont House, 1984.

* * *

Jack London is among the more important American science-fiction writers by virtue of his attention to social and political extrapolation, matters all too often ignored by his compatriots. In almost all of London's science fiction, mankind individually or collectively faces a challenge, be it the challenge of the primitive, the challenge of disaster, or the challenge of socialism.

"A Relic of the Pliocene" is a good example of the challenge of the primitive. In London's arctic, the scene of a good portion of his fiction, a man tells of killing the last mammoth. "When the World Was Young" takes up the theme of a man divided between an identity as a civilized businessman and a primitive savagery that seizes control every night. In "The Strength of the Strong" a cave man tells of the formation of tribes, which increase everyone's strength, and then of classes, which seem to decrease collective strength. London's novel *The Last Adam* is entirely situated in primitive times.

The Scarlet Plague is London's most successful disaster novel. To read it today is to realize how tepid are many recent works about disaster. The opening scene alone is a small masterpiece. It presents an old man and two boys walking along a railroad track in the future, destroyed world, the old man reflecting on the contrast between the way things are and the way they were in the old days. This old man, once a college professor at the University of California, goes on to tell of how his world collapsed under the onslaught of the plague, which was always fatal within thirty minutes, and killed most of the world's population, sparing only the old man and about forty others. These few spawn a new generation in a now-primitive world. The old man tells of the futile efforts at the University of California to save a remnant of the University community, and the equally futile efforts he (the old man) has made to make the new generation understand something of how things once were. Another disaster story is "The Unparalleled Invasion," in which the western nations use germ warfare to defeat the yellow peril—the combined forces of Japan and China. London's much-discussed racism is all too evident in this story.

A good deal of London's science fiction describes the onset of socialism, usually perceived by the ruling classes as a disaster. In "The Minions of Midas" a secret society blackmails the capitalists into submission by killing their loved ones. A similar story in *Goliah*, in which a discoverer of atomic power blackmails the world into accepting socialism. But London's great work in this mode is *The Iron Heel*. A future America has come under the iron heel of oligarchic corporations, and a working-class hero, Ernest Everhard, struggles to convince certain of the well-to-do that only a revolution can remove the oppression. London ends the book in 1932, when the oligarchy has thwarted one attempt at revolution—but another attempt is planned. Although Everhard is too pure and great, too earnest, London's novel brings to science fiction a high level of political discussion of issues that remain vital.

Almost as well known is "The Dream of Debs," a realistic account of a general strike in San Francisco which succeeds only after the fabric of society is utterly rent. When the wealthy narrator complains that "the tyranny of organized labor is getting beyond human endurance" we can see his point.

Perhaps London's greatest science fiction work, however, is

The Red One, which is not cast in any of London's characteristic molds, although it does involve a white man held captive by primitive Sumatrans, thus fitting with London's interest in survival under primitive conditions. The primitive tribe in question worships the red one of the title, a sphere from the stars. The white man gives his head in exchange for the chance to hear the red one's voice. London gives us a remarkable descriptive passage in which the white man hears the aliens' message and then dies, his head coveted by the tribal chieftain. The poignancy of this juxtaposition—the man of the present, captivated by the future yet held captive by the past—establishes London's importance and originality as a science-fiction writer.

—Curtis C. Smith

LONG, Charles R(ussell). American. Born in Paragould, Arkansas, 25 June 1904. Attended public schools in Paragould. Western Union telegraphic operator, mainly in El Paso, Texas, 1921-53. *Died 10 September 1978.*

SCIENCE-FICTION PUBLICATIONS

Novels

The Infinite Brain. New York, Avalon, 1957.
The Eternal Man. New York, Avalon, 1964.

* * *

Charles R. Long was interested in the possibility of infinite worlds with humanoids in various stages of moral and psychological development and with the more advanced races using their united mental forces to aid the less developed in times of crisis. He envisioned the growth of psi powers, now latent in human genetic make-up, psi powers that include telepathy, mindfusion, levitation, and physical transportation of self and others through time and space.

Written in journal form, *The Infinite Brain* traces the attempts of a rich eccentric to come to terms with the contradictions of his memories and experiences and those of his fellow Earthlings. Having once joined with an astronomer and a paranoid genius in an unsuccessful space launch to Venus, one that sent him into a deep-freeze orbit and returned him to a future world, he finds that historical details differ and that he has strange flashes between past and present, an earth he remembers and an earth that seems vaguely unfamiliar. By the time he discovers he has returned to a utopian parallel earth, he has already been drawn, through telepathic possession, into the dangers of the pre-holocaust world he had left. Only with the aid of the "Mind," the combined mental force of the most intelligent and moral of his new planet, can he combat a mad genius (the infinite brain) and save himself and his two worlds. Ironically the mad scientist of his original Earth is the genius and mentor of its parallel. The book suggests an infinite series of parallel worlds with infinite combinations possible. It includes stilted lectures on protons and neutrons, artificially inserted at the prompting of the "infinite brain," enthusiastic descriptions of weightlessness, and much speculation about the physical effects of travelling at or near the speed of light (shrinkage, reduction of centuries to seconds, separation of body and soul).

The Eternal Man is a story of maturation, a half-human, half-alien with god-like genes discovering and coming to terms with his identity and powers during a youth that spans man's history from pre-historic times to an intergalactic future. Though he remains inactive for centuries because his failure to age and his partially developed psi powers frighten mere humans, idealism and sexual allures tempt the "eternal man" into politics, where he founds an economically balanced socialist society in Texas, tries gradually to introduce democracy into a world based on profit, slavery, and exploitation, and learns how easily even a clever man can be manipulated by a beautiful woman. His contact with the telepathic Mercurians of the rebellious Underground and the cruel and powerful Sagittarian invaders forces recognition that the world's telepaths are the product of his philandering through the ages and that he is the superior seed planted by Pleiads centuries before in a dream of spreading their community of minds throughout the galaxy. Once he redis-covers and accepts his vast powers, inspired by his eternal and alien ancestors, he is ready to rule earth wisely and benevolently.

Despite some awkwardness of style and an occasional propensity to lecture, Long's works raise interesting questions well worth exploring.

—Gina Macdonald

LONG, Frank Belknap. Also writes as Lyda Belknap Long. American. Born in New York City, 27 April 1903. Educated in New York public schools; New York University School of Journalism, 1920-21. Married Lyda Arco in 1960. Writer for *Captain Marvel, Green Lantern, Congo Bill,* and *Planet Comics* in the 1940's; uncredited associate editor, *The Saint Mystery Magazine* and *Fantastic Universe* in the 1950's; associate editor, *Satellite Science Fiction,* 1959, *Short Stories,* 1959-60, and *Mike Shayne Mystery Magazine* until 1966. Recipient: First Fandom Hall of Fame Award, 1977; 4th World Fantasy Convention Life Achievement Award, 1978. Agent: Kirby McCauley, 425 Park Avenue South, New York, New York 10016. Address: 421 West 21st Street, New York, New York 10011, U.S.A.

SCIENCE-FICTION PUBLICATIONS

Novels

Space Station No. 1. New York, Ace, 1957.
Woman from Another Planet. New York, Chariot, 1960.
The Horror Expert. New York, Belmont, 1961.
The Mating Center. New York, Chariot, 1961.
Mars Is My Destination. New York, Pyramid, 1962.
The Horror from the Hills. Sauk City, Wisconsin, Arkham House, 1963; expanded edition, as *Odd Science Fiction,* New York, Belmont, 1964; London, Digit, 1965.
It Was the Day of the Robot. New York, Belmont, 1963; London, Dobson, 1964.
Three Steps Spaceward. New York, Avalon, 1963.
The Martian Visitors. New York, Avalon, 1964.
Mission to a Star. New York, Avalon, 1964.
This Strange Tomorrow. New York, Belmont, and London, Digit, 1966.
Lest Earth Be Conquered. New York, Belmont, 1966; as *The Androids,* 1969.
So Dark a Heritage. New York, Lancer, 1966.
Journey into Darkness. New York, Belmont, 1967.
. . . and Others Shall Be Born. New York, Belmont, 1968.

The Three Faces of Time. New York, Belmont, 1969.
Monster from Out of Time. New York, Popular Library, 1970; London, Hale, 1971.
Survival World. New York, Lancer, 1971.
The Night of the Wolf. New York, Popular Library, 1972.
Rehearsal Night. Boston, Cat's God, 1981.

Novels as Lyda Belknap Long

To the Dark Tower. New York, Lancer, 1969.
Fire of the Witches. New York, Popular Library, 1971.
The Shape of Fear. New York, Beagle, 1971.
The Witch Tree. New York, Lancer, 1971.
House of the Deadly Nightshade. New York, Beagle, 1972.
Legacy of Evil. New York, Beagle, 1973.
Crucible of Evil. New York, Avon, 1974.

Short Stories

The Hounds of Tindalos. Sauk City, Wisconsin, Arkham House, 1946; abridged editions, London, Museum Press, 1950; as *The Dark Beasts,* New York, Belmont, 1963; as *The Black Druid and Other Stories,* London, Panther, 1975.
John Carstairs, Space Detective. New York, Fell, 1949; London, Cherry Tree, 1951.
The Demons of the Upper Air. Glendale, California, Squires, 1969.
The Rim of the Unknown. Sauk City, Wisconsin, Arkham House, 1972.
The Early Long. New York, Doubleday, 1975; London, Hale, 1977.
When Chaugnar Walks. Warren, Ohio, Fantome Press, 1978.
Night Fear. New York, Zebra, 1979.

OTHER PUBLICATIONS

Play

Television Play: *A Guest in the House,* 1950.

Verse

A Man from Genoa and Other Poems. Athol, Massachusetts, Cook, 1926.
The Goblin Tower. Cassia, Florida, Dragon-Fly Press, 1935.
On Reading Arthur Machen. Pengrove, Dog and Duck Press, 1949.
In Mayan Splendor. Sauk City, Wisconsin, Arkham House, 1977.

Other

Howard Phillips Lovecraft: Dreamer on the Nightside. Sauk City, Wisconsin, Arkham House, 1975.

*

Manuscript Collection: Lovecraft Collection, Brown Univer-sity, Providence, Rhode Island.

Frank Belknap Long comments:
My work has been almost equally divided between science fiction or science fantasy and supernatural horror. What fascinates me most in the realm of SF is the strangeness, mystery, and wonder of the cosmic immensities and the possibility of intelligent life on other worlds. A few of my early

stories were of the space opera type, but for many years I have shunned that kind of writing. A realistic approach has become of supreme importance to me, and I have drawn upon one or more of the natural sciences in all my more recent stories. They range from future utopias—life on earth two centuries or two million years in the future—to what life may be like, biologically considered, in some far distant region of the expanding universe.

*　　*　　*

Of all modern writers in the overlapping domains of science fiction, fantasy, and horror, Frank Belknap Long may hold the record for sheer longevity, and, while he does not hold that for total productivity, he has written several hundred short stories and more than 30 books. The latter are difficult to number and categorize, as they involve a number of collections, re-sorting, and retitling of short stories as well as novels. In addition to works published under his own name, Long participated in a number of collaborations and round-robins, wrote short stories under house names such as Leslie Northern, wrote anonymously on occasion, and produced several gothic novels under the name of his wife, Lyda Long. While these last works are in a sense "mere potboilers," Long maintains that they are not without merit and in some cases contain effective scenes of the horror-fantasy or near-fantasy variety.

In a career dating to 1924, and still actively writing, Long has experienced the expectable rises and declines of popularity and critical standing. For some years he was highly regarded; in later times, disdained as little more than a hack; and still more recently has emerged as a revered elder statesman held in wide affection. In this regard his standing is comparable to that of writers like Murray Leinster and Edmond Hamilton. An accumulation of potboilers temporarily obscures the author's best work; with the passage of time the inferior material dissipates and the author's true contribution comes to be recognized.

Long has experienced the additional benefit—and handicap!—of having been for many years the closest friend and associate of H. P. Lovecraft. At one time Lovecraft and Long were partners in the "revision business," working as manuscript doctors, uncredited collaborators, and even ghost writers for literary tyros. A certain portion of Long's own fiction shows a clear stamp of influence by Lovecraft, but this in fact represents a relatively small segment of Long's output, a fact too often overlooked.

A number of Long's horror stories—most of them fantasies, a few technically science fiction but still cast within the gothic mold—are notable. These include "The Desert Lich," "Second Night Out," a supernatural sea story perhaps remotely influenced by the works of William Hope Hodgson, and "The Man with a Thousand Legs," one of the most bizarre of all lycanthropic tales.

Long also contributed some of the earliest and most effective supplements to Lovecraft's "Cthulhu Mythos." Long's dry humor is apparent in "The Brain-Eaters," whose two chief characters are thinly disguised versions of himself and Lovecraft. "The Hounds of Tindalos," probably Long's most famous story, is a thoroughly effective tale of monstrous creatures from beyond normal time and space breaking through the "angles" of our universe; the story is most effective in evoking a sense of non-Euclidean dimension. "A Visitor from Egypt" continues the successful exploitation of the Egyptian craze of the 1920's-early 1930's popular fiction. (One chapter of this novel was written by Lovecraft, based upon a dream.)

Long's science fiction bears no trace of Lovecraft. It is sometimes densely powerful, evocative, and moving; at other times, the author fails in attempted effects and falls into bathos. In general, Long's short fiction is superior to his novels; in this regard he is once more comparable to Leinster. "The Flame Midget" clearly anticipates the development of the laser. A later story, "Dark Vision" (1939), is one of the earlier and still one of the most successful to use psychiatric and specifically Freudian themes in science fiction. Long places strong emphasis on the subconscious, and in the story makes use of both electroshock and chemical shock techniques (the former accidentally; the latter clinically) in bringing about changes in the protagonist's perceptions and interpretations of reality.

Also notable is Long's series of stories about John Carstairs, "Botanical Detective." These are intriguing hybrids of space opera and scientific mystery.

Long's most effective work is probably a series of short stories ("The Great Cold," "Green Glory," and "The Last Men") set in a remote future when humankind is reduced to miniature size and enslaved by races of giant insects. In framework, the stories would appear to be routine absurd super-science adventures. But Long concentrates on the awakening consciousness of the brutalized humans as they regain their awareness of their own humanness. The pitch of noble tragedy achieved is remarkable.

In a recent letter, Long listed his own selection of his short stories which he considers the most accomplished. The stories nominated by Long include "Humpty Dumpty Had a Great Fall," "To Follow Knowledge," "Prison Bright—Prison Deep," "Guest in the House," "Two Face," and "Night Fear" (most included in *Night Fear*). Almost all of these stories are based on psychological themes, most notably difficulties of personal adjustment. Further, the main protagonist is most commonly a child. The psychological sensitivity of the works is noteworthy, as is their acuteness of focus and intensity of treatment. It is also noteworthy that none bears any trace of Long's Lovecraft period; with the continued passage of time it is to be hoped that Long's non-Lovecraft works (which in fact constitute the overwhelming bulk of his output) will achieve their proper evaluation.

—Richard A. Lupoff

LONG, Lyda Belknap. See **LONG, Frank Belknap.**

LONGDON, George. See **RAYER, Francis G.**

LONGYEAR, Barry (Brookes). American. Born in Harrisburg, Pennsylvania, 12 May 1942. Attended Wayne State University, Detroit, 1966-67. Married Regina Bedsun in 1967. Production Manager, Madison Corporation, Detroit, 1967-68; Publisher, Sol III Publications, in Philadelphia, 1968-72, and in Farmington, Maine, 1972-77. Since 1977, free-lance writer. Columnist ("Salty"), *Empire Science Fiction.* Recipient: Nebula Award, 1980; Hugo Award, 1980; *Locus* Award, 1980; John W. Campbell Award, 1980. Address: 1 Wilton Road, Farmington, Maine 04938, U.S.A.

SCIENCE-FICTION PUBLICATIONS

Novels

City of Baraboo. New York, Berkley, 1980; London, Macdonald, 1983.
Elephant Song. New York, Berkley, 1981.
The Tomorrow Testament. New York, Berkley, 1983.
It Came from Schenectady. New York, Bluejay, 1984.

Short Stories

Manifest Destiny. New York, Berkley, 1980; London, Macdonald, 1982.
Circus World. New York, Berkley, 1980; London, Macdonald, 1982.

Uncollected Short Stories

"Twist Ending," in *Isaac Asimov's Science Fiction Anthology 5*, edited by George H. Scithers. New York, Davis, 1982.
"Misencounters," in *Alien Encounters*, edited by Jan Howard Finder. New York, Taplinger, 1982.

*   *   *

Barry Longyear's first story appeared in *Isaac Asimov's Science Fiction Magazine* in 1978, but, unlike many such over-the-transom discoveries, he had virtually no apprentice period. As a result he was able to publish a great deal of competent material in a short space of time. He rapidly gained a following, and in 1980 was the first writer ever to win the Hugo, the Nebula, and the John W. Campbell awards all in the same year.

Longyear's earliest fiction, beginning with his first story, "The Tryouts," belongs to the Circus World or Momus series, concerning life on a planet colonized by the survivors of a wrecked circus starship, the resultant society being a crazy hodgepodge of circus customs and lore adapted to extra-terrestrial conditions. These earliest stories are collected in *Circus World*. They are well-written and amusing, although in the last couple the weakness of the series is already apparent. The inhabitants of Momus are rediscovered by the Ninth Quadrant Federation of Habitable Planets just before the evil forces of the Tenth Quadrant can conquer the place. In the first story, the Ninth Quadrant ambassador must convince the Momus folk that the danger is real. But, since in a circus everything costs, his free warning is taken as valueless. Therefore he must go on the road as a storyteller, to get the people to *pay* for the news, before the warning is heeded. Later stories deal with the odd social changes that result. The tone and quality are reminiscent of Keith Laumer's Retief series. But where Laumer is able to avoid unfunny amounts of violence, Longyear has written himself into a corner. The evil invaders arrive, and suddenly the clowns and acrobats and the like are no longer quaint tricksters, but fighters. The whole conceit is much too fragile to take the strain. Later Momus books include *City of Baraboo*, actually a prequel to the original stories, telling how the planetary circus-society was founded, and *Elephant Song* in which the Momus folk raid Earth for elephants, since they have none, and what's a circus that dosen't have elephants?

The Hugo- and Nebula-winning "Enemy Mine" is a more substantial work, a deeply moving and tensely dramatic account of how a human and an alien, enemies in war, must cooperate to survive when stranded on a barren planet. In time the human comes to understand a great deal of the alien's culture, to appreciate its religion, and ultimately to care for its child.

The understanding of the alien is a major theme in Longyear's more serious fiction. "The Jaren" (in *Manifest Destiny*) similarly deals with a race at war with mankind, told from the viewpoint of adolescents growing up to join a military culture which cannot comprehend the possibility of defeat. When they are defeated, the species ceases to breed, and quickly goes extinct. The weakness of this story, and to a lesser extent "Enemy Mine," is that the aliens aren't alien enough. They are too obviously human beings lightly disguised. The alien planets are merely foreign countries. However, this fault is hardly unique to Longyear, and he writes with genuine feeling. He is a distinctly compassionate writer.

In the first few years of his career, Longyear seemed to have made a major impact, but his career lost its stride for mostly extra-literary reasons. He has, however, begun to publish substantial work again. *The Tomorrow Testament* is semi-sequel to "Enemy Mine," dealing with the same human/alien war, and again with a human (this time a woman prisoner of war) who comes to respect the aliens through their religion. While not wholly successful, *The Tomorrow Testament* is a genuinely ambitious, serious work which reaches for a level of complexity far beyond anything hinted at in the Momus series. It must be counted as one of the best attempts to explore an alien religion and the psychology of another intelligent species.

Unfortunately, because the wide critical see-sawing in regard to Longyear's reputation, this book was largely ignored. Longyear was perhaps over-rated when he began and is now under-rated. He has shown an ability to do serious work, but also a tendency to slide into frivolity. However, with most of his career still presumably ahead of him, he may be expected to outlast the awkward situation created by his sudden and very startling arrival.

—Darrell Schweitzer

LOOMIS, Noel M(iller). Also wrote as Sam Allison; Benj. Miller; Frank Miller; Silas Water. American. Born in Wakita, Oklahoma, 3 April 1905. Attended Clarendon College, 1921; University of Oklahoma, Norman, 1930. Married Dorothy Moore Green in 1945; one son and one daughter. Printer and editor, then newspaperman; free-lance writer from 1929; English Instructor, San Diego State College, 1958-69. President and Secretary-Treasurer, Western Writers of America. Recipient: Western Writers of America Silver Spur Award, for novel, 1959, for story, 1960. *Died 7 September 1979.*

SCIENCE-FICTION PUBLICATIONS

Novels

City of Glass. New York, Columbia, 1955.
The Man with Absolute Motion (as Silas Water). London, Rich and Cowan, 1955.

Uncollected Short Stories

"Iron Man," in *Startling* (New York), Winter 1945.
"Electron Eat Electron," in *Planet* (New York), Spring 1946.
"Rocket Pants," in *Thrilling Wonder Stories* (New York), Spring 1946.
"Zero," in *Thrilling Wonder Stories* (New York), Summer 1946.
"Mr. Zytztz Goes to Mars," in *Thrilling Wonder Stories* (New York), August 1948.

"Softie," in *Thrilling Wonder Stories* (New York), October 1948.

"Schizophrenic," in *Thrilling Wonder Stories* (New York), December 1948.

"Turnover Time," in *Startling* (New York), March 1949.

"The Ultimate Planet," in *Thrilling Wonder Stories* (New York), April 1949.

"The Long Dawn," in *Big Book of Science Fiction,* edited by Groff Conklin. New York, Crown, 1950.

"Parking Unlimited," in *Future* (New York), May-June 1950.

"The Lithium Rocket," in *Future* (New York), March 1951.

"The Byrd," in *Planet* (New York), May 1951.

"Remember the 4th!," in *Future* (New York), July 1951.

"The Wealth of Echindul," in *Planet* (New York), July 1952.

"The Mischievous Typesetter," in *Imagination* (Evanston, Illinois), July 1952.

"Tough Guy," in *Fantastic Adventures* (New York), September 1952.

"Big-Top on Jupiter," in *Space Stories* (New York), October 1952.

"You Too Can Be a Millionaire," in *If* (New York), November 1952.

"Nine Men in Time," in *Original Science Fiction Stories* (Holyoke, Massachusetts), 1953.

"Thousand-Legged Agent," in *Amazing* (New York), March 1953.

"Cett Was a Whale," in *Fantastic Adventures* (New York), March 1953.

"We Breathe for You," in *Startling* (New York), May 1953.

"The Cyanided Man," in *Space Stories* (New York), June 1953.

"Day's Work," in *Rocket* (New York), September 1953.

"The Chaos Salient," in *Saturn* (Holyoke, Massachusetts), March 1957.

"The Conduit," in *Science Fiction Quarterly* (Holyoke, Massachusetts), November 1957.

"If the Court Pleases," in *Escape to Earth,* edited by Ivan Howard. New York Belmont, 1963.

"Little Green Man," in *Things,* edited by Ivan Howard. New York, Belmont, 1964.

"The State vs. Susan Todd," in *Worlds of Tomorrow 24* (New York), 1970.

"A Time to Teach, A Time to Learn" in *Amazing* (New York), November 1970.

Uncollected Short Stories as Benj. Miller

"Date Line," in *Thrilling Wonder Stories* (New York), October 1948.

"A Horse on Me," in *Thrilling Wonder Stories* (New York), December 1948.

"Monsters from the West," in *Thrilling Wonder Stories* (New York), February 1949.

"On the House," in *Thrilling Wonder Stories* (New York), April 1949.

OTHER PUBLICATIONS

Novels

Murder Goes to Press. New York, Phoenix Press, 1937.

Rim of the Caprock. New York, Macmillan, and London, Collins, 1952; as *Battle for the Caprock,* Collins, 1959.

Tejas Country (as Frank Miller). New York, Avalon, 1953; London, Corgi, 1955.

Trouble on Crazyman. New York, Lion, 1953; as Sam Allison, London, Hale, 1955.

The Buscadero. New York, Macmillan, 1953; as *Trouble Shooter,* London, Collins, 1953.

West to the Sun. New York, Fawcett, 1955; London, Fawcett, 1957.

The Twilighters. New York, Macmillan, 1955.

North to Texas (as Frank Miller). New York, Ballantine, 1956; as *Texas Rebel,* London, Corgi, 1956.

Johnny Concho. New York, Fawcett, 1956; London, Fawcett, 1957.

Wild Country. New York, Pyramid, 1956.

Hang the Men High, with Paul Leslie Peil. New York, Fawcett, 1957; London, Fawcett, 1959.

The Maricopa Trail. New York, Fawcett, 1957; London, Fawcett, 1958.

Rifles on the River. London, Collins, 1957.

Short Cut to Red River. New York, Macmillan, 1958.

The Leaden Cache. London, Collins, 1958.

Above the Palo Duro. New York, Fawcett, 1959.

Cheyenne War Cry. New York, Avon, 1959.

Connelly's Expedition. London, Collins, 1959.

A Time for Violence. New York, Macmillan, 1960; London, Collins, 1961.

Have Gun, Will Travel. New York, Dell, 1960.

Bonanza. New York, Popular Library, 1960; London, Jenkins, 1963.

Ferguson's Ferry. New York, Avon, 1962.

Other

Wells Fargo, Danger Station (for children). Racine, Wisconsin, Whitman, 1958.

The Linecasting Operator-Machinist. Pittsburgh, Stockton, 1958.

The Texan-Santa Fé Pioneers. Norman, University of Oklahoma Press, 1958.

Pedro Vial and the Roads to Santa Fe, with Abraham P. Nasatir. Norman, University of Oklahoma Press, 1967.

Wells Fargo. New York, Clarkson N. Potter, 1968.

Editor, *Holsters and Heroes.* New York, Macmillan, 1954.

*   *   *

Noel M. Loomis wrote futuristic novels in which a scientific "problem" is fused to the stock elements of the adventure tale. The science in his novels ranges from the probable to the possible to the completely implausible. This uneasy fusion of science and fantasy when wedded to the adventure story leads to an inevitable tension within the novel itself and certainly within the reader's capacity for "willing suspension of disbelief."

In *City of Glass* Loomis postulates the problem of three amateur astronauts who, returning to earth after a few days' absence, find themselves returning to earth of the year 800,000 AD. Civilization as we know it was destroyed in 5,000 AD; there are only a few scattered groups on earth, each of which has evolved separately so that no two are of the same species. The only real human beings left on earth are the 2500 Glassmen who live in the City of Glass and struggle to perpetuate their species, which is "being adapted by necessity and by scientific means to a silicon economy." Beset by a nitrate shortage, hostile invaders, and a plague, the City of Glass seems doomed, until Niles, the amateur aastronaut, discovers a way to solve all difficulties.

The Man with Absolute Motion is an intergalactic tale in which the whole universe is threatened with disaster as a result of diminishing energy supplies. The last truly normal man on earth is discovered to have the gift of absolute motion and is thus able to locate the source of Cosmic Power. Having saved the galaxy, he marries the last normal earth woman, raises a family, and is returned to earth only to find it deserted, the human species wiped out. Fortunately, he decides to repopulate the earth, thus ensuring the survival of the human species.

—Joseph A. Quinn

LORAN, Martin. See **BAXTER, John.**

LORD, Jeffrey. See **NELSON, Ray.**

LORRAINE, Paul. See **FEARN, John Russell.**

LOVECRAFT, H(oward) P(hillips). American. Born in Providence, Rhode Island, 20 August 1890. Educated by tutors at home, and at a local elementary school and Hope Street High School, Providence, 1904-05, 1907-08. Married Sonia Greene in 1924 (divorced, 1929). Free-lance writer from 1908, working as a ghost writer and, after 1918, a revisionist; astrology columnist, Providence *Evening News*, 1914-18; active in the amateur journalism movement from 1914: published *The Conservative*, 1915-19, 1923, and President of the United Amateur Press Association, 1917-18, 1923; regular contributor to *Weird Tales* after 1923. *Died 15 March 1937*.

SCIENCE-FICTION PUBLICATIONS

Short Stories

At the Mountains of Madness and Other Novels. Sauk City, Wisconsin, Arkham House, 1964; London, Gollancz, 1966.
The Colour Out of Space. New York, Lancer, 1964.
Collapsing Cosmoses. West Warwick, Rhode Island, Necronomicon Press, 1977.

OTHER PUBLICATIONS

Novel

The Lurker at the Threshold, with August Derleth. Sauk City, Wisconsin, Arkham House, 1945; London, Gollancz, 1948.

Short Stories

The Shunned House. Athol, Massachusetts, Recluse Press, 1928.
The Battle That Ended the Century. De Land, Florida, Barlow, 1934.
The Cats of Ulthar. Cassia, Florida, Dragonfly Press, 1935.
The Shadow over Innsmouth. Everett, Pennsylvania, Visionary Press, 1936.

The Outsider and Others, edited by August Derleth and Donald Wandrei. Sauk City, Wisconsin, Arkham House, 1939.
The Weird Shadow over Innsmouth and Other Stories of the Supernatural. New York, Bartholomew House, 1944.
The Best Supernatural Stories of H. P. Lovecraft, edited by August Derleth. Cleveland, World, 1945; revised edition, as *The Dunwich Horror and Others,* Sauk City, Wisconsin, Arkham House, 1963.
The Dunwich Horror. New York, Bartholomew House, 1945.
The Dunwich Horror and Other Weird Tales. New York, Editions for the Armed Services, 1945.
The Lurking Fear and Other Stories. New York, Avon, 1947; as *Cry Horror!,* 1958.
The Haunter of the Dark and Other Tales of Horror. London, Gollancz, 1951.
The Case of Charles Dexter Ward. London, Gollancz, 1952.
The Curse of Yig. Sauk City, Wisconsin, Arkham House, 1953.
The Dream Quest of Unknown Kadath. Buffalo, Shroud, 1955.
The Survivor and Others, with August Derleth. Sauk City, Wisconsin, Arkham House, 1957.
The Lurking Fear and Other Stories (not same as 1947 book). London, Panther, 1964.
Dagon and Other Macabre Tales, edited by August Derleth. Sauk City, Wisconsin, Arkham House, 1965; London, Gollancz, 1967.
The Dark Brotherhood and Other Pieces, with others, edited by August Derleth. Sauk City, Wisconsin, Arkham House, 1966.
3 Tales of Horror. Sauk City, Wisconsin, Arkham House, 1967.
The Shadow Out of Time and Other Tales of Horror, with August Derleth. London, Gollancz, 1968; abridged edition, as *The Shuttered Room and Other Tales of Horror,* London, Panther, 1970.
Ex Oblivione. Glendale, California, Squires, 1969.
The Tomb and Other Tales. London, Panther, 1969; New York, Ballantine, 1973.
The Horror in the Museum and Other Revisions (ghost writing), edited by August Derleth. Sauk City, Wisconsin, Arkham House, 1970; abridged edition, London, Panther, 1975.
Nyarlathotep. Glendale, California, Squires, 1970.
What the Moon Brings. Glendale, California, Squires, 1970.
The Dream-Quest of Unknown Kaddath (not same as 1955 book), edited by Lin Carter. New York, Ballantine, 1970.
Memory. Glendale, California, Squires, 1970.
The Shadow over Innsmouth and Other Tales of Horror. New York, Scholastic, 1971.
The Shuttered Room and Other Tales of Terror, with August Derleth. New York, Beagle, 1971.
The Doom That Came to Sarnath, edited by Lin Carter. New York, Ballantine, 1971.
The Lurking Fear and Other Stories (not same as 1947 and 1964 books). New York, Beagle, 1971.
The Watchers Out of Time and Others, with August Derleth. Sauk City, Wisconsin, Arkham House, 1974.
The Horror in the Burying Ground and Other Tales. London, Panther, 1975.
Herbert West Reanimator. West Warwick, Rhode Island, Necronomicon Press, 1977.
Bloodcurdling Tales of Horror and the Macabre: The Best of H. P. Lovecraft. New York, Ballantine, 1982.
The Dunwich Horror and Others (original versions), edited by S. T. Joshi. Sauk City, Wisconsin, Arkham House, 1985.

Verse

The Crime of Crimes. Llandudno, Harris, 1915.

A Sonnet. Privately printed, 1936.

H. P. L. Privately printed, 1937.

Fungi from Yuggoth. Salem, Oregon, Evans, 1941.

Collected Poems. Sauk City, Wisconsin, Arkham House, 1963; abridged edition, as *Fungi from Yuggoth and Other Poems,* New York, Ballantine, 1971.

A Winter Wish, edited by Tom Collins. Browns Mills, New Jersey, Whispers Press, 1977.

Other

Looking Backward. Haverhill, Massachusetts, C. W. Smith, 1920 (?).

The Materialist Today. Privately printed, 1926.

Further Criticism of Poetry. Louisville, Fetter, 1932.

Charleston. Privately printed, 1936.

Some Current Motives and Practices. DeLand, Florida, Barlow, 1936 (?).

A History of The Necronomicon. Oakman, Alabama, Rebel Press, 1938.

The Notes and Commonplace Book, edited by R. H. Barlow. Lakeport, California, Futile Press, 1938.

Beyond the Wall of Sleep, edited by August Derleth and Donald Wandrei. Sauk City, Wisconsin, Arkham House, 1943.

Marginalia, edited by August Derleth and Donald Wandrei. Sauk City, Wisconsin, Arkham House, 1944.

Supernatural Horror in Literature. New York, Abramson, 1945; revised edition, Arlington, Virginia, Carrollton Clark, 1975.

Something about Cats and Other Pieces, edited by August Derleth. Sauk City, Wisconsin, Arkham House, 1949.

The Lovecraft Collector's Library, edited by George T. Wetzel. Tonowanda, New York, SSR, 5 vols., 1952-55.

The Shuttered Room and Other Pieces, with others, edited by August Derleth. Sauk City, Wisconsin, Arkham House, 1959.

Dreams and Fancies. Sauk City, Wisconsin, Arkham House, 1962.

Autobiography: Some Notes on a Nonentity. London, Villiers, 1963.

Selected Letters 1911-1937, edited by August Derleth and Donald Wandrei. Sauk City, Wisconsin, Arkham House, 5 vols., 1965-76.

Hail, Klarkash-Ton! Glendale, California, Squires, 1971.

Ec'h-Pi-El Speaks: An Autobiographical Sketch. Saddle River, New Jersey, Gerry de la Ree, 1972.

Medusa: A Portrait. New York, Oliphant Press, 1975.

The Occult Lovecraft. Saddle River, New Jersey, Gerry de la Ree, 1975.

Lovecraft at Last (correspondence with Willis Conover). Arlington, Virginia, Carrollton Clark, 1975.

To Quebec and the Stars, edited by L. Sprague de Camp. West Kingston, Rhode Island, Grant, 1976.

Writings in The United Amateur 1915-1925, edited by Marc A. Michaud. West Warwick, Rhode Island, Necronomicon Press, 1976.

First Writings: Pawtuxet Valley Gleaner 1906, edited by Marc A. Michaud. West Warwick, Rhode Island, Necronomicon Press, 1976.

The Conservative: Complete 1915-1923, edited by Marc A. Michaud. West Warwick, Rhode Island, Necronomicon Press, 1977.

Memoirs of an Inconsequential Scribbler. West Warwick, Rhode Island, Necronomicon Press, 1977.

Writings in The Tryout, edited by Marc A. Michaud. West Warwick, Rhode Island, Necronomicon Press, 1977.

The Californian 1934-1938. West Warwick, Rhode Island, Necronomicon Press, 1977.

Uncollected Prose and Poetry, edited by S. T. Joshi and Marc A. Michaud. West Warwick, Rhode Island, Necronomicon Press, 1978.

Science versus Charlatanry: Essays on Astrology, with J. F. Hartmann, edited by S. T. Joshi and Scott Connors. N. p., The Strange Company, 1979.

Editor, *The Poetical Works of Jonathan E. Hoag.* Privately printed, 1923.

Editor, *White Fire,* by John Ravenor Bullen. Athol, Massachusetts, Recluse Press, 1927.

Editor, *Thoughts and Pictures,* by Eugene B. Kuntz. Haverhill, Massachusetts, Lovecraft and Smith, 1932.

*

Bibliography: *The New H. P. Lovecraft Bibliography* by Jack L. Chalker, Baltimore, Anthem Press, 1962, revised edition, with Mark Owings, as *The Revised H. P. Lovecraft Bibliography,* Baltimore, Mirage Press, 1973; *A Catalog of Lovecraftiana* by Mark Owings and Irving Binkin, Baltimore, Mirage Press, 1975; *H. P. Lovecraft: An Annotated Bibliography* by S. T. Joshi, Kent, Ohio, Kent State University Press, 1981; *Howard Phillips Lovecraft: The Books, Addenda and Auxiliary* by Joseph Bell, Toronto, Soft Press, 1983.

Manuscript Collection: Brown University, Providence, Rhode Island.

Critical Studies (selection): *In Memoriam Howard Phillips Lovecraft: Recollections, Appreciations, Estimates* edited by W. Paul Cook, privately printed, 1941; *H. P. L. : A Memoir,* New York, Abramson, 1945, and *Some Notes on H. P. Lovecraft,* Sauk City, Wisconsin, Arkham House, 1959, both by August Derleth; *Rhode Island on Lovecraft* edited by Donald M. Grant and Thomas P. Hadley, Providence, Rhode Island, Grant Hadley, 1945; "H. P. Lovecraft Issue" of *Fresco* (Detroit), Spring 1958; *Lovecraft: A Look Behind the Cthulhu Mythos* by Lin Carter, New York, Ballantine, 1972, London, Panther, 1975; *Lovecraft: A Biography* by L. Sprague de Camp, New York, Doubleday, 1975, London, New English Library, 1976; *Howard Phillips Lovecraft: Dreamer on the Nightside* by Frank Belknap Long, Sauk City, Wisconsin, Arkham House, 1975; *Essays Lovecraftian* edited by Darrell Schweitzer, Baltimore, T-K Graphics, 1976, and *The Dream Quest of H. P. Lovecraft* by Schweitzer, San Bernardino, California, Borgo Press, 1978; *The H. P. Lovecraft Companion* by Philip A. Schreffler, Westport, Connecticut, Greenwood Press, 1977; *The Major Works of H. P. Lovecraft* by John Taylor Gatto, New York, Monarch Press, 1977; *The Roots of Horror in the Fiction of H. P. Lovecraft* by Barton Levi St. Armand, Elizabethtown, New York, Dragon Press, 1977; *H. P. Lovecraft* by S. T. Joshi, Mercer Island, Washington, Starmont House, 1982; *H. P. Lovecraft: A Critical Study* by Donald R. Burleson, Westport, Connecticut, Greenwood Press, 1983.

* * *

That horror stories are externalized psychology is a commonplace of literary criticism, but readings based on sex and aggression (the two themes literary critics have tended to pick up from Freudian psychology) do not quite fit H. P. Lovecraft. Lovecraft himself warns readers away from interpretations of his work based on the fear of retribution for specific acts or impulses; his horrors are (as he says again and again) "cosmic," he declares the worst human fears to be displacement in space and time (as in "The Shadow Out of Time"), he speaks of "the maddening rigidity of cosmic law," he creates a non-fantastic and materialistic fictional world—i. e. science fiction—all implying a concern with the conditions of being, not with particular acts or situations. When the conditions of existence are themselves fearful, when such basic ontological categories as space and time break down (as does the geometry of space in so many stories, for example "The Call of Cthulhu"), we are dealing with what the psychiatrist R. S. Laing calls "ontological insecurity. " If one fears that one doesn't exist securely, or that one is made of "bad stuff," any contact with another becomes potentially catastrophic. Everyone shares, to some degree, doubts about the psychological solidity or reliability of the self and the possibly devastating effects of others on that self. The extreme form of such fears is schizophrenia.

Lovecraft, although certainly not schizophrenic, did, according to L. Sprague de Camp, have a lifelong sense of marked isolation from others, an intense emotional dependency on things and not people, and the kind of over-possessive bringing up which makes it reasonable to expect that such issues would appear in his work. They do—strongly enough to make him an innovator in weird fiction—for they take precedence over either the beastliness of aggression (embodied, for example, in werewolves) or the lethal possibilities of sexual abandon (e. g., the figure of the vampire), both of which figure largely in 19th-century supernatural fiction. Sex and aggression presuppose a self existing securely enough to have desires and a relatively non-threatening (or at least limited) other towards whom such desires can be directed. Neither an unproblematic sense of self nor a non-catastrophic other exists in Lovecraft's work. In his early Dunsanian fiction he can frolic—but with ghouls!—as in the charming (but, alas, never rewritten or polished) *Dream-Quest of Unknown Kadath* or write pleasing, optimistic fantasies like "The Strange High House in the Mist"; but much of his earlier and most of his later fiction is preoccupied with the foreseen, yet unavoidable, engulfment of a passive, victimized self. If the narrator is a lucky spectator who escapes with his life, or even sanity, intact, his peace of mind has been shattered forever. The real point of these stories is revelation—if the engulfment does not happen, *it can*—and this revelation becomes the central truth of a universe thus rendered uninhabitable. The cannibalistic other takes several forms, but the commonest, strongest image, and the one readers seem to remember best is the shapeless, monstrous, indescrible "entry" (a favorite word of Lovecraft's) whose most terrifying characteristic is its structurelessness ("The Unnameable," "The Call of Cthulhu," "Dagon," "The Dunwich Horror"). The obsession with psychic cannibalism (expressed as physical in one of the flatter stories, "The Picture in the House,") and the insistence on the indescribableness of the threat seem to point to experience so personally archaic it is felt as pre-verbal, as does Lovecraft's characteristic straining after adjectives. In one of his best tales, "The Colour Out of Space," the threat is most abstract, its cannibalism is reported third-hand (through *two* narrators) and the relatively low-keyed, realistic setting gets most of the author's attention.

In only two stories does Lovecraft focus fully on the alternative to engulfment: loneliness. Selves exist and survive in both tales; they even—after a fashion—blossom into initiative. But both are figures that appear in other stories *as monsters* : in the poetically melancholy "The Outsider" a ghoulish walking corpse, and in the very interesting end of *The Weird Shadow over Innsmouth* a degenerate animal/monster. Both stories suggest that the menace is the narrator or something in the narrator, a suggestion not only psychologically truer than the image of the engulfing other than Lovecraft uses elsewhere, but one dramatically more interesting.

The view that human relations exist only as engulfment is a serious limitation on a narrative artist. Towards the end of his life Lovecraft seems to have been unhappily aware of this; unfortunately he also underrated his own work and died before it began to be popular. His originality and his undoubted talent (the eerily parodic autobiography of "The Outsider," details like the "gelatinous" voice in "Randolph Carter," or "a warmth that may have been sardonic" of *Innsmouth*) are best at their quietest, worst in their bravely direct but often inadequate attacks on a theme that requires (at the very least) poetic genius. The very rarity of literary treatments of Lovecraft's main theme gives his work added interest, however, and his work will probably always appeal to readers who find his theme compelling. If he had not died prematurely, he might have moved beyond the kind of horror story that says "This is what it feels like" to the kind that adds "and this is what is really happening. " The latter moves into tragedy and implied social criticism (as does, for example, Shirley Jackson's *The Haunting of Hill House*). In *Supernatural Horror in Literature* Lovecraft concludes "the spectral in literature. . .is. . .a narrow though essential branch of human expression," a comment that might well describe his work: narrow, not appealing to wide tastes and even considerably flawed, yet authentic, and by those who find it congenial, securely loved.

—Joanna Russ

LOWAM, Ron. See **TUBB, E. C.**

LOWNDES, Robert A(ugustine) W(ard). Also writes as Arthur Cooke; Carol Grey; Carl Groener; Mallory Kent; Paul Dennis Lavond; John MacDougal; Wilfred Owen Morley; Richard Morrison; Michael Sherman; Peter Michael Sherman; Lawrence Woods. American. Born in Bridgeport, Connecticut, 4 September 1916. Educated at Darien High School, Connecticut; Stamford Community College, Connecticut, 1936. Married Dorothy Sedor Rogalin in 1948 (divorced, 1974); one stepson. Worked for the Civilian Conservation Corps, 1934, 1936-37, 1939; assistant on a squab farm; salesman; porter, Greenwich Hospital Association, Connecticut, 1937-38; literary agent, Fantastory Sales Service, 1940-42; Editor, *Future Fiction*, 1940-43, and *Science Fiction Quarterly*, 1940-43, 1951-58; Editorial Director, Columbia magazines, 1942-60; Editor, *Future Science Fiction*, 1950-60, *Dynamic Science Fiction*, 1952-54, and *Science Fiction Stories*, 1954-60; Editor, Avalon science-fiction series, Thomas Bouregy, 1955-67; Editor, *Magazine of Horror*, 1963-71, *Famous Science Fiction*, 1966-69, *Startling Mystery Stories*, 1966-71, *Weird Terror Tales*, 1969-70, and *Bizarre Fantasy Fiction*, 1970-71; Associate Editor, 1971-77, and Managing Editor, 1977-78, *Sexology* and *Luz;* Production Chief, *Luz,* 1978-84, and in Editorial Production, *Radio-Electronics, Special Projects, Hands-On Electronics,* and Computer Digest. Co-Founder, Vanguard Amateur Press Association. Guest of Honor, Lunacon, 1969, and Boskone, 1973. Address: 717 Willow Avenue, Hoboken, New Jersey 07030, U.S.A.

SCIENCE-FICTION PUBLICATIONS

Novels

Mystery of the Third Mine (for children). Philadelphia,
Winston, 1953.
The Duplicated Man, with James Blish. New York, Avalon,
1959.
The Puzzle Planet. New York, Ace, 1961.
Believers' World. New York, Avalon, 1961.

Uncollected Short Stories

"The Outpost at Altark," with Donald A. Wollheim (un-
credited), in *Super Science* (Kokomo, Indiana), November
1940.
"A Green Cloud Came," in *Comet* (Springfield, Massa-
chusetts), January 1941.
"The Psychological Regulator" (as Arthur Cooke, with others),
in *Comet* (Springfield, Massachusetts), March 1941.
"The Martians Are Coming," with C. M. Kornbluth (un-
credited), in *Cosmic* (Holyoke, Massachusetts), March 1941.
"Black Flames" (as Lawrence Woods, with Donald A.
Wollheim) and "The Other," in *Stirring Science* (New York),
April 1941.
"The Grey One," in *Stirring Science* (New York), June 1941.
"The Colossus of Maia" (as Lawrence Woods, with Donald A.
Wollheim), in *Cosmos* (New York), July 1941.
"Lure of the Lily," in *Uncanny Tales* (Toronto), January 1942;
revised version, as "Lillies," in *Magazine of Horror* (New
York), Spring 1967.
"Passage to Sharanee" (as Carol Grey), in *Future* (New York),
April 1942.
"The Deliverers" (as Richard Morrison), in *Science Fiction
Quarterly* (Holyoke, Massachusetts), Winter 1942.
"The Leapers" (as Carol Grey), in *Future* (New York),
December 1942; revised version, as "Leapers" (as Robert A.
W. Lowndes), in *Magazine of Horror* (New York), September
1968.
"Chaos, Co-ordinated" (as John MacDougal, with James
Blish), in *Astounding* (New York), October 1946.
"The Troubadour" (as Peter Michael Sherman), in *Future* (New
York), September 1951.
"Intervention" (as Michael Sherman), in *Science Fiction
Quarterly* (Holyoke, Massachusetts), February 1952.
"A Matter of Faith" (as Michael Sherman), in *Space* (New
York), September 1952.
"Highway," in *Looking Forward,* edited by Milton Lesser. New
York, Beechhurst Press, 1953; London, Cassell, 1955.
"The Inheritors," with John B. Michel, in *Terror in the Modern
Vein,* edited by Donald A. Wollheim. New York, Hanover
House, 1955.
"Object Lesson" (as Carl Groener), in *Future* (New York),
August 1958.
"The Abyss," in *The History of the Science Fiction Magazines 2,*
edited by Michael Ashley. London, New English Library,
1975.
"The Extrapolated Dimwit" (uncredited), with C. M. Korn-
bluth and Frederik Pohl, in *Before the Universe.* New York,
Bantam, 1980.

Uncollected Short Stories as Paul Dennis Lavond

"The Doll Master," in *Stirring Science* (New York), April 1941.
"Exiles of New Planet," with Cyril Kornbluth, in *Astonishing*
(Chicago), April 1941.

"Something from Beyond," with Frederik Pohl and J. H.
Dockweiler, in *Future* (New York), December 1941.
"Einstein's Planetoid," with Frederik Pohl and Cyril Kornbluth, in *Science Fiction Quarterly* (Holyoke, Massachusetts), Spring 1942.

Uncollected Short Stories as Wilfred Owen Morley

"A Matter of Philosophy," in *Science Fiction* (Holyoke,
Massachusetts), September 1941.
"My Lady of the Emerald," in *Astonishing* (Chicago),
November 1941.
"No Star Shall Fall," in *Future* (New York), December 1941.
"The Long Wall," in *Stirring Science* (New York), March 1942;
revised version, as "Settler's Wall" (as Robert A. W.
Lowndes), in *Startling Mystery Stories* (New York), Fall
1968.
"The Lemmings," in *Super Science* (Kokomo, Indiana), May
1942.
"A Message for Jean," in *Future* (New York), June 1942.
"The Slim People," in *Future* (New York), August 1942.
"Highway," in *Science Fiction Quarterly* (Holyoke, Massa-
chusetts), Fall 1942; revised version, as "The Road to
Nowhere" (as Robert A. W. Lowndes), in *Magazine of
Horror* (New York), Summer 1970.
"Does Not Imply," in *Future* (New York), February 1943.
"Dhactwhul—Remember?," with Jacques DeForest Erman, in
Super Science (Kokomo, Indiana), April 1949.

Uncollected Short Stories as Mallory Kent

"Quarry," in *Future* (New York), December 1941.
"The Peacemakers," in *Future* (New York), August 1942.
"The Collector," in *Future* (New York), October 1942.

OTHER PUBLICATIONS

Other

"Why 'Famous'?," "Science Fiction as Instruction
[Propaganda, Delight,]" "Why Bother with Criticism?," and
"The Borders of 'Science Fiction,'" in *Famous Science Fiction
1-9* (New York), Winter 1966-67 to Spring 1969.
Three Faces of Science Fiction. Boston, NESFA Press, 1973.
Introduction to *The Casebook of Jules de Grandin.* New York,
Popular Library, 1976.
Afterword to *The Best of Thomas N. Scortia,* edited by George
Zebrowski. New York, Doubleday, 1981.
Introduction to *Jack of Eagles,* by James Blish. New York,
Avon, 1982.
"Hugo Gernsback: A Man with Vision†," in *Radio-Electronics*
(New York), August 1984.

Editor, *The Best of James Blish.* New York, Ballantine, 1979.

*

Robert A. W. Lowndes comments:
   Although I was an active member of the marxist-oriented
Futurian Society of New York (1938-45), calling for social and
political relevance in science fiction, when it came down to
writing stories I found that I had no interest whatsoever in such
relevance. I only wanted to tell the kind of story I actually
wanted to read—full of wonder or terror or both. Whether I
succeeded, or to what extent I succeeded, is for others to say.
   To my mind, the best fantasy and science fiction is imbued

with the author's feeling about the human condition, and may or may not contain what amounts to some sort of message. If there is one, it is not something consciously striven for; I've read thousands of stories written to preach a sermon, and however effective the sermon itself may have been, the stories have nearly all suffered from the approach. Fiction and homily writing are two different forms, though each may be done with a high quality of art; but mixing them produces an abortion.

* * *

Robert A. W. Lowndes is known mainly as an editor. He is, however, also a science fiction writer of considerable talent, particularly in the creation and description of alien worlds. This talent is best seen in *Believers' World*. Lowndes uses the now-familiar plot of exiles from Earth who have forgotten that their origin was on Earth, and whose religious beliefs have hardened into mindless fragments of ceremony. An investigator from Earth visits these exiles, now living on a "believers' world" locked into elaborate religious ceremonies. He becomes involved in a formula of action, adventure, and violence. But Lowndes effectively describes the Arabian Nights atmosphere of this world: "magic. That was the keynote of everything here—the appearance of magic. " Even small everyday events seem magical: "you touched a faucet, or bent over a fountain, or stepped under a shower, and pale yellow water issued forth. " Thus Lowndes creates a world that exemplifies Arthur C. Clarke's generalization that advanced technology is indistinguishable from magic.

Everything that happens on the believers' world is supposed by the inhabitants to be the will of "Ein" (Einstein, though they don't remember this). In this topsy-turvey world not only has religion ossified but science has merged with it. *The Puzzle Planet* is about a world that is similar in that our common-sense assumptions are upside down; and once again Lowndes's descriptive powers are impressive.

Even *Mystery of the Third Mine*, a juvenile, is well worth reading. Lowndes makes asteroid mining seem real, creating a historical parallel to the gold rush of 1848. The hero, Peter, is in a mining partnership with his father. The villains use the cover of the Asteroid Miners Association to invalidate Peter's claims and to try to seize the "third mine," platinum, deep in the asteroid. There is a good science-fun gimmick on the asteroid: low gravity baseball with a magnetized ball and players throwing bits of metal to propel themselves through space. Although the young hero is close to being a pastiche of a Heinlein juvenile, Lowndes's magical atmosphere is once again his own.

Lowndes's short stories are quite distinct from his novels and show the influence of Clark Ashton Smith and Lovecraft. One of his best is "The Abyss," which begins with this hook sentence: "We took Graf Norden's body out into the November night, under the stars that burned with a brightness terrible to behold, and drove madly, wildly up the mountain road. " Beings in another dimension (or no dimension) send agents to hypnotize humans and drain the fluids from their bodies. The description of these alien beings—with long filaments that restlessly try to break into our dimension from their own—is as well done as anything in Lovecraft, and the economy of the story is beyond Lovecraft. Economy, atmosphere, description: these are Lowndes's strongest points as a writer.

—Curtis C. Smith

LUCAS, George. See FOSTER, Alan Dean.

———

LULL, Susan. See FORWARD, Robert L.

———

LUNDWALL, Sam J(errie). Swedish. Born in Stockholm, 24 February 1941. Educated at the University of Stockholm, E. E. 1967; Fotoskolan, 1968. Compulsory military service in the air force, 1961-62. Married Ingrid Christina Olofsdotter in 1972; one daughter. Electronic engineer, L. M. Ericson, Stockholm, 1956-64; photographer, Christian, Fox Amphoux, France, 1968-69; Editor, Askild & Kärnekull, Stockholm, 1970-73; Publisher, Delta Förlag, Stockholm, 1973-80, and since 1980, Fakta & Fantasi, Stockholm. Since 1972, Editor, *Jules Verne-Magasinet*, Stockholm. Also a singer and musician, illustrator, and television producer. Recipient: Swedish Film Institute Award, 1967; Cosmos Fandom Award, 1969; Futura Club Award, 1972; Finnish Design Award, 1972. Agent: Eleanor Wood, Spectrum Literary Agency, 432 Park Avenue South, New York, New York 10016, U. S. A. Address: Storskogsvägen 19, S-161 39 Bromma, Sweden.

SCIENCE-FICTION PUBLICATIONS

Novels

No Time for Heroes. New York, Ace, 1971.
Alice's World. New York, Ace, 1971; London, Arrow, 1975.
Bernhard the Conqueror. New York, DAW, 1973.
2018; or, The King Kong Blues. New York, DAW, 1975; London, Wyndham, 1976.
Tio sanger och Alltid Lady MacBeth. Stockholm, Delta, 1975.
Bernards magiska sommar. Stockholm, Lindqvist, 1975.
Mörkrets furste. Stockholm, Delta, 1975.
Mardrömmen. Stockholm, Lindqvist, 1976.
Gäst i Frankensteins hus. Stockholm, Delta, 1976.
Fängelsestaden. Stockholm, Norstedt, 1978.
Flicka i fönster vid världens kant. Stockholm, Norstedt, 1980.
Crash. Stockholm, Morstedt, 1982.

Uncollected Short Stories

"Nobody Here But Us Shadows," in *Galaxy* (New York), August 1975.
"Take Me Down the River," in *Twenty Houses of the Zodiac*, edited by Maxim Jakubowski. London, New English Library, 1979.

OTHER PUBLICATIONS

Verse

Visor i var tid. Stockholm, Sonora, 1965.

Other

Science Fiction. Stockholm, Sveriges Radio, 1969; translated as *Science Fiction: What It's All About*, New York, Ace, 1971.

Den fantastiska romanen (essays on science fiction). Stockholm, Gummeson, 4 vols., 1972-74.
Bibliografi över Science Fiction & Fantasy (covers the period 1741-1973). Stockholm, Lindqvist, 1974.
Utopia-Dystopia. Stockholm, Delta, 1977.
Science Fiction: An Illustrated History. New York, Grosset and Dunlap, 1978.
"How to Write an SF Novel," in *Omni* (New York), June 1979.

Publications in Swedish: some 20 anthologies of science fiction, and translations of 237 novels into Swedish.

*

Sam Lundwall comments:
I am not a fan of my work. I wish I were.

*　　*　　*

Sam J. Lundwall's reputation rests chiefly on the critical/historical survey, *Science Fiction: What It's All About*, which he wrote in Swedish and translated into English. One of the first general summaries of the field, the book outlines a history and a theory of the genesis of science fiction. For many readers this outline (along with that presented in Brian Aldiss's *Billion Year Spree*) serves as the first critical framework by which they define their experience of science fiction. Lundwall categorizes science fiction, defines it, and comments on it. He draws on a wide range of stories and essays as source materials for his discussions and tries generally to test his conclusions against hard observation, even though he is not ashamed to write with the verve of a totally committed partisan or fan. Treating science fiction "books, magazines, comics, fans and fanzines, juvenilia, series characters, and literary giants," he also discusses popular motifs, conventions, themes, and plot lines.

The influence of this book is not easily overstated. Published in English in 1971 at the beginning of a great wave of academic interest in the genre, it provided the foundations for the organization of a large part of the scholarship and of the design and teaching of science fiction courses in universities. Lundwall is, moreover, straightforward, clear, and definite in enunciating his attitudes, much as a dedicated young fan would be. The book, consequently, stimulates interest in the study of the genre as a whole and in its various aspects. Although Lundwall's shrewd critical insights and commentary on authors and works may not seem as true five or ten years after they are first encountered, they tend to color a reader's perception of the field, having provided for many readers a starting point for disciplined study.

Sam J. Lundwall is also known as a writer of satiric novels. The best known of these and probably the most successful of the four that have been translated into English is *2018; or, The King Kong Blues*. In this novel Lundwall describes a world that in 2018 is polluted not only physically but spiritually as well. The tale begins with a description of a wedding held in a department store. Against this scene we see one of the central characters, a rootless, rebellious young girl named Anniki Norijn trying to break free of compulsions to conform to commercially acceptable standards of taste and ethics. The rest of the novel narrates a harassed advertising executive's search for this young woman. He is forced to use her in a campaign to sell underarm deodorant. A counterplot tells of two sheikhs, brothers, one of whom out of sheer boredom manipulates the economic life of the West, which the other one in the name of religion and Bedouin honor tries to destroy. The book gets its title from a song Anniki sings that mocks the betrayed romanticism and the false facades of social institutions.

This novel is at home among that group of satiric novels that criticize the shallowness and triviality of modern life; it has been compared with Pohl and Kornbluth's *Space Merchants*, Brunner's *The Sheep Look Up*, and Burgess's *A Clockwork Orange*. Unlike Burgess's book, however, *2018* does not attack a single, philosophically distinct evil. Its attack is more generally directed against all sorts of economic exploitation on all levels. Unlike *The Space Merchants* it isn't very funny; its humor is blacker, crueler, more disturbing. Finally, it is not as successful as *The Sheep Look Up* because it preaches and explains more than it narrates or dramatizes. Perhaps Lundwall should, like Brunner, have used techniques similar to those of John Dos Passos to make the circumstantial background—which is, after all, the real main character and interest in the novel—come alive. *2018* unfortunately too often reads like an undergraduate textbook.

His other translated novels, also satiric, *Alice's World, No Time for Heroes,* and *Bernhard the Conqueror* vary in mood from depressed to genuinely funny.

—Alexander J. Butrym

LUPOFF, Richard A(llen). Also writes as Ova Hamlet. American. Born in Brooklyn, New York, 21 February 1935. Educated at the University of Miami, Coral Gables, B. A. 1956. Served in the Adjutant General's Corps of the United States Army, 1956-58: First Lieutenant. Married Patricia Enid Loring in 1958; two sons and one daughter. Technical writer, Sperry Univac, New York, 1958-63; Editor, Canaveral Press, New York, 1962-70; film producer, IBM, New York City and Poughkeepsie, New York, 1963-70; Editor, with Pat Lupoff, *Xero* fan magazine, 1960-63; West Coast Editor, *Crawdaddy,* 1970-71, and *Changes,* 1971-72; Editor, *Organ,* 1972; book editor, *Algol,* 1963-79; science fiction reviewer, San Francisco *Chronicle,* 1979-81. Since 1985, editor, Canyon Press, Redwood City, California. Recipient: Hugo Award, for editing, 1963. Agent: Henry Morrison Inc., P. O. Box 235, Bedford Hills, New York 10507. Address: 3208 Claremont Avenue, Berkeley, California 94705, U.S.A.

SCIENCE-FICTION PUBLICATIONS

Novels

One Million Centuries. New York, Lancer, 1967.
Sacred Locomotive Flies. New York, Beagle, 1971.
Into the Aether. New York, Dell, 1974.
The Crack in the Sky. New York, Dell, 1976; as *Fool's Hill,* London, Sphere, 1978.
Lisa Kane (for children). Indianapolis, Bobbs Merrill, 1976.
Sandworld. New York, Berkley, 1976.
The Triune Man. New York, Berkley, 1976; London, Dobson, 1979.
The Return of Skull-Face, with Robert E. Howard. West Linn, Oregon, Fax, 1977.
Space War Blues. New York, Dell, 1978; London, Sphere, 1979.
Circumpolar! New York, Pocket Books, 1984; London, Granada, 1985.
Sun's End. New York, Berkley, 1984.
Lovecraft's Book. Sauk City, Wisconsin, Arkham House, 1985.

Short Stories

Nebogipfel at the End of Time. San Francisco, Underwood Miller, 1979.
The Ova Hamlet Papers. San Francisco, Pennyfarthing Press, 1979.
Stroka Prospekt: A Story. West Branch, Iowa, Toothpaste Press, 1982.
The Digital Wristwatch of Philip K. Dick. Redwood City, California, Canyon Press, 1985.

Uncollected Short Stories

"Discovery of the Ghooric Zone—March 15,2337," in *Chrysalis I*, edited by Roy Torgeson. New York, Zebra, 1977.
"The Child's Story," in *Cosmos* (New York), September 1977.
"The Devil's Hop Yard," in *Chrysalis 2*, edited by Roy Torgeson. New York, Zebra, 1978.
"Venus—Ah, Venus," in *Heavy Metal* (New York), February 1978.
"Mektopia!," in *Against Tomorrow*, edited by Robert Hoskins. New York, Fawcett, 1979.
"Saltzman's Madness," in *Beyond Reality*, edited by Terry Carr. New York, Elsevier Nelson, 1979.
"Documents in the Case of Elizabeth Akeley," in *Fantsy and Science Fiction* (New York), March 1982.
"Two Sort-of Adventurers" (as Ova Hamlet), in *Amazing* (New York), June 1982.

OTHER PUBLICATIONS

Novel

Sword of the Demon. New York, Harper, 1977; London, Sphere, 1980.

Other

Edgar Rice Burroughs, Master of Adventure. New York, Canaveral Press, 1965; revised edition, New York, Ace, 1968.
"Science Fiction Hawks and Doves," in *Ramparts* (Berkeley, California), February 1972.
"You Can't Say That!," in *Science-Fiction Review* (Portland, Oregon), February 1975.
Barsoom: Edgar Rice Burroughs and the Martian Vision. Baltimore, Mirage Press, 1976.
"A Legend in Poughkeepsie," in *Locus* (Oakland, California), March 1977.
Buck Rogers in the Twenty Fifth Century. New York, Dell, 1978.
"A Bulletin from the Ministry of Truth," in *Pretentious SF Quarterly*, Spring 1978.
"The Early Philip K. Dick," in *Algol* (New York), May 1979.

Editor, *The Reader's Guide to Barsoom and Amtoor.* Privately printed, 1963.
Editor, with Don Thompson, *All in Color for a Dime* . New Rochelle, New York, Arlington House, 1970.
Editor, with Don Thompson, *The Comic-Book Book.* New Rochelle, New York, Arlington House, 1974.
Editor, *What If?* [and *What If? 2*] *Stories That Should Have Won the Hugo.* New York, Pocket Books, 1980-81.

*

Richard A. Lupoff comments:
It's very difficult for me to "make a statement" about my own works. It seems to me that this is a task for critics. The artist is of necessity so close to his or her own work—in fact, more than close to it: is surrounded by and immersed in it—that a critical perspective is impossible.

In terms of my own career, 1981 proved to be a year of bitter irony. I had spent decades learning the craft of fiction, and felt that I had finally reached a satisfying level of competence. The last three books that I had written—*Circumpolar!, Lovecraft's Book*, and *Sun's End*—were by far the best I had ever written. My prices had risen, critics and fans were expressing approval, foreign sales were gratifying.

At this point, due to general economic conditions, there was a collapse in the marketplace. All three books were cancelled, contracts for two further novels were cancelled, and the *What If?* anthology series that I had been editing was cancelled. Everything that I had in print went out of print, and my career was in effect terminated. My income dropped to nothing and I faced economic disaster.

In the years since, there has been considerable recovery. The three books that I named have all been published and all have met good receptions. A contract has been taken over by another publisher and I am working on the sequel to *Sun's End*. However, at the present time I have been unable to return to full-time writing and I do not see when (if ever) I will be able to do so.

*   *   *

Richard A. Lupoff first achieved recognition as a fan critic. His amateur magazine *Xero* is considered to be the pioneer magazine of comic-book fandom, the first sub-culture to splinter from SF fandom. Lupoff's career as a writer is an effort to determine a post-modern SF writer's relations with his literature's past. Lupoff tends towards either total acceptance or total rejection of that past; thus his first novel, *One Million Centuries*, attempts to preserve Burroughsian panache in the midst of the New Wave, while *Space War Blues* totally rejects that past in favour of stylistic tricks and decadent space opera, with planets of white racists battling black racists for control of the universe. While *Space War Blues* is Lupoff's most acclaimed novel (due, in large measure, to relentless promotion of the original novella by Harlan Ellison), it is not his most important, as it is clearly a product of the concerns of the 1960's and dates very badly in its thematic content.

Lupoff's best novels are those that do not concern themselves with the nature of mainstream science fiction. Only three of his works fulfil this criterion—the dystopia *The Crack in the Sky*, the haunting chinoiserie *Sword of the Demon*, and *Lisa Kane*, published as a juvenile but in truth a thoroughly adult work about the nature of the macabre, and Lupoff's finest novel.

But Lupoff only intermittently achieves excellence. Most of his work is pastiche, ranging from the van Vogtian influences in *Triune Man*, to the parody of 19th-century scientific romances in *Into the Aether*, and *The Return of Skull-Face*, a completion of a Robert E. Howard fragment. These pastiches succeed to the extent that they preserve the flavor of the past without copying its style: *The Return of Skull-Face* shows that one cannot effectively copy Howard, and *Into the Aether*, conceived as a satire, is actually a combination of unfunny farce and irrelevant anachronisms. (Lupoff's other attempt at parody, the short stories published in *Fantastic* as by "Ova Hamlet," are important both for being the only parodies of current authors such as Barry Malzberg and for conclusively showing that most modern writers do not have styles that can be copied.)

In the 1980's, Lupoff continued to alternate between pastiches of pulp adventures of the 1930's and more serious work. His specialty was throwing characters from the past into exotic situations; thus in *Circumpolar!* Charles Lindbergh, Amelia Earhart, and Howard Hughes battle the Red Baron and subterranean monsters in a hollow earth derived from Edgar Rice Burroughs's Pellucidar series. *Lovecraft's Book* is an alternate universe novel placing H. P. Lovecraft in the center of fascist and nationalist conspiracies. These novels, while well-crafted, are little more than fast-moving entertainments.

Far more promising is *Sun's End* in which a Japanese construction worker is placed in suspended animation for 80 years to emerge in the 21st century as a bionic superman. Here Lupoff combines his interest in Japanese culture with a continuing interest in the dynamics of personal power, last expressed in *The Triune Man. Sun's End* is, unfortunately, the first volume of a trilogy, and is thus only a start to what may or may not be Lupoff's most sustained creative success.

Richard Lupoff is a protean writer. He does not belong to any particular school of SF, and was one of the few writers who belonged to the 'New Wave" and the 'Old Wave" at the same time. Because he has not developed a distinctive style, he has not earned the importance he deserves. If he would continue to develop the trenchant awareness of his art that was shown in *Lisa Kane* and *The Crack in the Sky*, his reputation as one of the most important heirs of the Golden and Silver ages would be secure.

—Martin Morse Wooster

LUTHER, Martin. See **SELLINGS, Arthur.**

LYMINGTON, John. Pseudonym for John Newton Chance; also wrote as J. Drummond; David C. Newton. British. Born in London, in 1911. Educated at Streatham Hill College and privately. Served in the Royal Air Force during World War II. *Died 3 August 1983.*

SCIENCE-FICTION PUBLICATIONS

Novels

Night of the Big Heat. London, Corgi, 1959; New York, Dutton, 1960.
The Giant Stumbles. London, Hodder and Stoughton, 1960.
The Grey Ones. London, Hodder and Stoughton, 1960.
The Coming of the Strangers. London, Hodder and Stoughton, 1961; New York, Manor 1978.
A Sword above the Night. London, Hodder and Stoughton, 1962.
The Screaming Face. London, Hodder and Stoughton, 1963; New York, Manor, 1978.
Froomb! London, Hodder and Stoughton, 1964; New York, Doubleday, 1966.
The Star Witches. London, Hodder and Stoughton, 1965; New York, Manor, 1978.
The Green Drift. London, Hodder and Stoughton, 1965.
Ten Million Years to Friday. London, Hodder and Stoughton, 1967.
The Nowhere Place. London, Hodder and Stoughton, 1969.

Give Daddy the Knife, Darling. London, Hodder and Stoughton, 1969.
The Year Dot. London, Hodder and Stoughton, 1972.
The Sleep Eaters. London, Hodder and Stoughton, 1973; New York, Manor, 1978.
The Hole in the World. London, Hodder and Stoughton, 1974.
A Spider in the Bath. London, Hodder and Stoughton, 1975.
The Laxham Haunting. London, Hodder and Stoughton, 1976.
Starseed on Gye Moor. London, Hodder and Stoughton, 1977.
The Waking of the Stone. London, Hodder and Stoughton, 1978.
The Grey Ones, A Sword above the Night. New York, Manor 1978.
A Caller from Overspace. London, Hodder and Stoughton, 1979.
Voyage of the Eighth Mind. London, Hodder and Stoughton, 1980.
The Power Ball. London, Hale, 1981.
The Terror Version. London, Hale, 1982.
The Vale of the Sad Banana. London, Hale, 1984.

Short Stories

The Night Spiders. London, Corgi, 1964; New York, Doubleday, 1967.

OTHER PUBLICATIONS

Novels as John Newton Chance

Murder in Oils. London, Gollancz, 1935.
Wheels in the Forest. London, Gollancz, 1935.
The Devil Drives. London, Gollancz, 1936.
Maiden Possessed. London, Gollancz, 1937.
Rhapsody in Fear. London, Gollancz, 1937.
Death of an Innocent. London, Gollancz, 1938.
The Devil in Greenlands. London, Gollancz, 1939.
The Ghost of Truth. London, Gollancz, 1939.
The Screaming Fog. London, Macdonald, 1944; as *Death Stalks the Cobbled Square,* New York, McBride, 1946.
The Red Knight. London, Macdonald, and New York, Macmillan, 1945.
The Eye in Darkness. London, Macdonald, 1946.
The Knight and the Castle. London, Macdonald, 1946.
The Black Highway. London, Macdonald, 1947.
Coven Gibbet. London, Macdonald, 1948.
The Brandy Pole. London, Macdonald, 1949.
The Night of the Full Moon. London, Macdonald, 1950.
Aunt Miranda's Murder. London, Macdonald, and New York, Dodd Mead, 1951.
The Man in My Shoes. LOndon, Macdonald, 1952.
The Twopenny Box. London, Macdonald, 1952.
The Jason Affair. London, Macdonald, 1953; as *Up to Her Neck,* New York, Popular Library, 1955.
The Randy Inheritance. London, Macdonald, 1953.
Jason and the Sleep Game. London, Macdonald, 1954.
The Jason Murders. London, Macdonald, 1954.
Jason Goes West. London, Macdonald, 1955.
The Last Seven Hours. London, Macdonald, 1956.
A Shadow Called Janet. London, Macdonald, 1956.
Dead Man's Knock. London, Hale, 1957.
The Little Crime. London, Hale, 1957.
Affair with a Rich Girl. London, Hale, 1958.
The Man with Three Witches. London, Hale, 1958.
The Fatal Fascination. London, Hale, 1959.
The Man with No Face. London, Hale, 1959.

Alarm at Black Brake. London, Hale, 1960.
Lady in a Frame. London, Hale, 1960.
Import of Evil. London, Hale, 1961.
The Night of the Settlement. London, Hale, 1961.
Triangle of Fear. London, Hale, 1962.
The Man Behind Me. London, Hale, 1963.
The Forest Affair. London, Hale, 1963.
Commission for Disaster. London, Hale, 1964.
Death under Desolate. London, Hale, 1964.
Stormlight. London, Hale, 1966.
The Affair at Dead End. London, Hale, 1966.
The Double Death. London, Hale, 1966.
The Case of the Death Computer. London, Hale, 1967.
The Case of the Fear Makers. London, Hale, 1967.
The Death Women. London, Hale, 1967.
The Hurricane Drift. London, Hale, 1967.
The Mask of Pursuit. London, Hale, 1967.
The Thug Executive. London, Hale, 1967.
Dead Man's Shoes. London, Hale, 1968.
Death of the Wild Bird. London, Hale, 1968.
Fate of the Lying Jade. London, Hale, 1968.
The Halloween Murders. London, Hale, 1968.
Mantrap. London, Hale, 1968.
The Rogue Aunt. London, Hale, 1968.
The Abel Coincidence. London, Hale, 1969.
The Ice Maidens. London, Hale, 1969.
Involvement in Austria. London, Hale, 1969.
The Killer Reaction. London, Hale, 1969.
The Killing Experiment. London, Hale, 1969.
The Mists of Treason. London, Hale, 1970.
A Ring of Liars. London, Hale, 1970.
Three Masks of Death. London, Hale, 1970.
The Mirror Train. London, Hale, 1970.
The Cat Watchers. London, Hale, 1971.
The Faces of a Bad Girl. London, Hale, 1971.
A Wreath of Bones. London, Hale, 1971.
A Bad Dream of Death. London, Hale, 1972.
Last Train to Limbo. London, Hale, 1972.
The Man with Two Heads. London, Hale, 1972
The Dead Tale-Tellers. London, Hale, 1972.
The Farm Villains. London, Hale, 1973.
The Grab Operators. London, Hale, 1973.
The Love-Hate Relationship. London, Hale, 1973.
The Girl in the Crime Belt. London, Hale, 1974.
The Shadow of the Killer. London, Hale, 1974.
The Starfish Affair. London, Hale, 1974.
The Canterbury Kilgrims. London, Hale, 1974.
Hill Fog. London, Hale, 1975.
The Devil's Edge. London, Hale, 1975.
The Monstrous Regiment. London, Hale, 1975.
The Murder Maker. London, Hale, 1976.
Return to Death Valley. London, Hale, 1976.
A Fall-Out of Thieves. London, Hale, 1976.
The Frightened Fisherman. London, Hale, 1976.
The House of the Dead Ones. London, Hale, 1977.
Motive for a Kill. London, Hale, 1977.
The Ducrow Folly. London, Hale, 1978.
End of an Iron Man. London, Hale, 1978.
A Drop of Hot Gold. London, Hale, 1979.
Thieves' Kitchen. London, Hale, 1979.
The Guilty Witness. London, Hale, 1979.
A Place Called Skull. London, Hale, 1980.
The Death Watch Ladies. London, Hale, 1980.
The Mayhem Madchen. London, Hale, 1980.
The Black Widow. London, Hale 1981.

The Death Importer. London, Hale, 1981.
The Mystery of Enda Favell. London, Hale, 1981.
Madman's Will. London, Hale, 1982.
The Hunting of Mr. Exe. London, Hale, 1982.
The Shadow in Pursuit. London, Hale, 1982.
The Traditional Murders. London, Hale, 1983.
The Death Chemist. London, Hale, 1983.
Terror Train. London, Hale, 1983.
Looking for Samson. London, Hale, 1984.
Nobody's Supposed to Murder the Butler. London, Hale, 1984.
The Bad Circle. London, Hale, 1985.

Novels as J. Drummond

The Essex Road Crime. London, Amalgamated Press, 1944.
The Manor House Menace. London, Amalgamated Press, 1944.
The Painted Dagger. London, Amalgamated Press, 1944.
The Riddle of the Leather Bottle. London, Amalgamated Press, 1944.
The Tragic Case of the Station Master's Legacy. London, Amalgamated Press, 1944.
At Sixty Miles an Hour. London, Amalgamated Press, 1945.
The House on the Hill. London, Amalgamated Press, 1945.
The Riddle of the Mummy Case. London, Amalgamated Press, 1945.
The Mystery of the Deserted Camp. London, Amalgamated Press, 1948.
The Town of Shadows. London, Amalgamated Press, 1948.
The Case of the "Dead" Spy. London, Amalgamated Press, 1949.
The Riddle of the Receiver's Hoard. London, Amalgamated Press, 1949.
The Secret of the Living Skeleton. London, Amalgamated Press, 1949.
The south Coast Mystery. London, Amalgamated Press, 1949.
The Case of L. A. C. Dickson. London, Amalgamated Press, 1950.
The Mystery of the Haunted Square. London, Amalgamated Press, 1950.
The House in the Woods. London, Amalgamted Press, 1950.
The Secret of the Sixty Steps. London, Amalgamated Press, 1951.
The Case of the Man with No Name. London, Amalgamated Press, 1951.
Hated by All! London, Amalgamated Press, 1951.
The Mystery of the Sabotaged Jet. Londn, Amalgamated Press, 1951.
The House on the River. London, Amalgamated Press, 1952.
The Mystery of the Five Guilty Men. London, Amalgamated Press, 1954.
The Case of the Two-Faced Swindler. London, Amalgamated Press, 1955.
The Teddy-Boy Mystery. London, Amalgamated Press, 1955.

Other as John Newton Chance

The Black Ghost (for children; as David C. Newton). London, Oxford University Press, 1947.
The Dangerous Road (for children; as David C. Newton). London, Oxford University Press, 1948.
Bunst and the Brown Voice [the Bold, and the Secret Six, and the Flying Eye] (for children). London, Oxford University Press, 4 vols., 1950-53.
The Jennifer Jigsaw (for children), with Shirley Newton Chance. London, Oxford University Press, 1951.
Yellow Belly (autobiography). London, Hale, 1959.

The Crimes at Rillington Place: A Novelist's Reconstruction.
London, Hodder and Stoughton, 1961

*   *   *

John Lymington was well known for the crime novels published under his real name, John Newton Chance. As a writer of science fiction, however, he has received little notice, even within the SF community, perhaps because the fantastic elements of his fiction often serve as little more than a backdrop for the main action which characteristically centers on a small but diverse group of British citizens faced with a common threat. Lymington's characters, his village settings, and the structure of his novels owe as much to the tradition of the classical detective story as to the traditions of science fiction, and with few exceptions he does not concern himself with the social or intellectual implications of the marvels he introduces. As an author of suspense and horror stories, he is often startlingly effective, able to spin an entertaining novel from a single situation, but when he attempts more complex themes his novels tend to get out of hand.

Lymington makes use of few of the resources of the science fiction genre; most of his novels are variations on the basic theme of alien invasion, while a couple deal with time travel and contain elements of social satire. His first SF novel, *Night of the Big Heat,* is an admirable addition to the something-is-amiss-in-the-village school of British suspense novels, though the science-fiction element—an alien civilization transmitting giant spiders into the English countryside via microwaves—is clearly secondary to the portrayal of the reactions of a group of local citizens gathered at a country inn. Spiders are one of Lymington's favorite images of horror—even though he persistently regards them as insects—and were also the featured attraction in another invasion story, "The Night Spiders." The basic formula of an unknown horror menacing a small community was repeated in *The Coming of the Strangers* ; in *Sword above the Night*—perhaps the most straightforward and unadorned of Lymington's exercises in suspense—the anticipated "invasion" that provides suspense throughout the novel is dispensed with in a three-paragraph closing summary, explaining that it is merely the pre-programmed return to Earth of dead astronauts who had left from an earlier civilization thousands of years ago. This novel perhaps most clearly indicates the short shrift Lymington gives his science-fiction concepts.

Occasionally, Lymington adds other science-fiction elements to his formula—in *The Sleep Eaters* the invasion is telepathic (*The Night Spiders* also have telepathic powers), and in *The Star Witches* a mad scientist helps bring the aliens to earth. *The Star Witches* also reveals an inclination on Lymington's part to work traditional supernatural appurtenances into his science-fiction narratives: in this case a coven of witches is associated with the alien invasion. Time travel is another concept that Lymington sometimes plays with, in *The Night Spiders, Ten Million Years to Friday,* and *Froomb! Froomb!* is in some ways Lymington's most ambitious novel, and the most satirical. The title is short for "The fluid's running out of my brakes!," a fictional cartoon caption that has come to symbolize the state of world affairs in Lymington's headlong future world. Essentially the story, which somehow encompasses such diverse themes as threatened nuclear war, heaven, heatrays, insecticide poisoning, food additives, radiation, drugs, and male impotence, concerns a man who dies and goes to heaven, only to find that it is actually a post-holocaust world brought about by an American defense experiment about to take place before he died. His efforts to return and warn the world of the experiment make up the bulk of the novel.

Lymington was not a major writer, and there is much to suggest that he did not take his science fiction seriously, but in the relatively narrow territory he staked out for himself he provides enjoyable light reading.

—Gary K. Wolfe

LYNN, Elizabeth A. American. Born in New York City, 8 June 1946. Educated at Case Western Reserve University, Cleveland, B. A. 1967; University of Chicago (Woodrow Wilson Fellow, 1967-68), M. A. 1968. Public school teacher, Chicago, 1968-70; unit manager, St. Francis Hospital, Evanston, Illinois, 1970-72, and French Hospital, San Francisco, 1972-75; formerly teacher in the Women's Studies Program, San Francisco State University. Address: c/o Bluejay Books, 130 West 42nd Street, New York, New York 10036, U.S.A.

SCIENCE- FICTION PUBLICATIONS

Novels

A Different Light. New York, Berkley, 1978; London, Gollancz, 1979.
The Sardonyx Net. New York, Putnam, 1981.
The Red Hawk. New Castle, Virginia, Cheap Street, 1983.
The Silver Horse. New York, Bluejay, 1984.

Short Stories

The Woman Who Loved the Moon and Other Stories. New York, Berkley, 1981.

OTHER PUBLICATIONS

Novels

Watchtower. New York, Berkley, 1979; London, Hamlyn, 1981.
The Dancers of Arun. New York, Berkley, 1979; London, Hamlyn, 1982.
The Northern Girl. New York, Berkley, 1981.

*   *   *

Elizabeth A. Lynn is rapidly developing into one of the finest writers in the field of speculative fiction. Her greatest strength lies in her ability to focus sympathetically on a single character or a small cast of characters that are very human. Although her science-fiction stories are often presented in the trappings of space opera—faster-than-light travel, interstellar exploration, humans kidnapped by aliens—they are peopled by individuals who are clearly drawn from life. They are flawed and identifiably human, not Kimball Kennisons, or comic-book superheroes.

This is most apparent in her most important science fiction novel, *The Sardonyx Net.* Working from some pretty hoary SF elements—including interstellar drug and slave trades—Lynn has created a remarkable book. Although in synopsis it sounds like something straight out of a 1940's *Thrilling Wonder Stories* magazine, *The Sardonyx Net* is primarily a novel of character with a satisfyingly complex plot and some of Lynn's best writing. It is here that one of her special skills is most apparent: the ability to create a villain with whom the reader can empathize. *Net* is far better plotted than most of her novels, and the best evidence of her matured skills.

Several of her short stories, and the novel *A Different Light*, are linked by some common images and themes. Although interstellar travel seems taken for granted, Lynn consistently treats the concept of hyperspace, the Hype, as a place not only beyond the normal limits of space-time, but beyond reality itself. It is a source of danger to all but the strongest who attempt to pass through it. In *A Different Light*, in fact, the Hype is the cause of the apparent death of the protagonist. Jimson, an artist, has an incurable cancer, one which will limit his lifespan, if he is careful, to another 20 years. Before he dies, however, he wants to see the light of other stars, and rejoin an old friend and lover. He flees his home planet in the sure knowledge that travel in the Hype will accelerate the process of his cancer. Jimson is typical of Lynn's protagonists. Most of them work in some art form, and seem to pay for their gifts with a physical debility—such as the one-armed telepath in *The Dancers of Arun*—but it is a debility that heightens their sensitivity to others and their surroundings. Jimson is a sexual being. Like many of Lynn's characters he lives in a society not proscribed by sexual roles, and his sexuality finds expression through love for women and men. A first novel, *A Different Light* is certainly flawed, both by its somewhat episodic plot and an ending that seems drawn from other SF novels rather than from within. But the novel's sensitivity and fluid language betray a promise that is more than fulfilled in her later novels.

The Chronicles of Tornor is a true trilogy—three self-contained novels related by continuity of place, cultures, and institutions—that defies neat categorization. The trilogy concerns the way that cultures and institutions change, and succeeds because it focuses on individuals directly involved in those cultures. *Watchtower* introduces the cultures: the rigid, militaristic society of the North, and the newly developed egalitarian life of the Cheari, built on an art composed of dance and martial art. The protagonist is a vassal of the northern culture, and the novel's conflict lies in his inability to assimilate the new mores and lifestyle of the chearis. The language is crisp and precise. *The Dancers of Arun* takes place 100 years later. It centers on the almost utopian lifestyle of the Cheari, and the language of the book is appropriately softened. Kerris is a child of these people but has been raised in the North, and finds difficulty in believing in their acceptance of his maimed arm. Only through the physically loving relationship that he develops with his brother does he learn to accept himself. The trilogy is concluded with *The Northern Girl* which concerns a third culture in the South. By now the Cheari are only a memory, and the focus is on a city-dwelling society. Here, Lynn is on even surer ground and Kendra-on-the-Delta is a more convincing place than either the military keeps or rustic villages of the previous books. The plot has a tendency to drift, but the characters are tightly drawn, with an emotional warmth unusual in the field. Much of this effect stems from Lynn's concentration on a small group of real people in intimate contact, rather than the giant battles of armies and wizards so common in fantasy.

Lynn's latest foray into fantasy is *The Silver Horse*, a disappointingly slight and derivative fairy tale about two young girls from San Francisco who travel to Dreamland to rescue a little boy. It is notable only for the role reversal of the lead characters; little girls are fearless, and little boys chicken-hearted.

—Jeff Frane

LYONS, Delphine C. See SMITH, Evelyn E.

MacAPP, C. C. Pseudonym for Carroll M. Capps. American. Born in 1917(?). Worked as a printer. *Died 15 January 1971.*

SCIENCE-FICTION PUBLICATIONS

Novels

Omha Abides. New York, Paperback Library, 1968.
Prisoners of the Sky. New York, Lancer, 1969.
Secret of the Sunless World. New York, Dell, 1969.
Worlds of the Wall. New York, Avon, 1969.
Recall Not Earth. New York, Dell, 1970.
Subb. New York, Paperback Library, 1971.
Bumsider. New York, Lancer, 1972.

Uncollected Short Stories

"Tulan," in *Amazing* (New York), June 1960.
"The Drug," in *Galaxy* (New York), February 1961.
"Specimen," in *Fantastic* (New York), September 1961.
"All That Earthly Paradise," in *If* (New York), July 1962.
"The Demon of the North," in *Fantastic* (New York), September 1963.
"A Guest of Ganymede," in *The Best Science Fiction from Worlds of Tomorrow.* New York, Galaxy, 1964.
"The Slaves of Gree," in *If* (New York), August 1964.
"Beyond the Ebon Wall," in *Fantastic* (New York), October 1964.
"Somewhere in Space," in *Worlds of Tomorrow* (New York), November 1964.
"For Every Action," in *World's Best Science Fiction 1965*, edited by Donald A. Wollheim and Terry Carr. New York, Ace, 1965.
"And All the Earth a Grave," in *The Eighth Galaxy Reader*, edited by Frederik Pohl. New York, Doubleday, 1965.
"A Pride of Islands," in *The 6 Fingers of Time and 5 Other Science Fiction Novelets.* New York, Macfadden, 1965.
"Gree's Commandos," in *If* (New York), February 1965.
"Gree's Hellcats," in *If* (New York), April 1965.
"Sculptor," in *Galaxy* (New York), April 1965.
"No Friend of Gree," in *IF* (New York), June 1965.
"Gree's Damned Ones," in *IF* (New York), September 1965.
"The Light Outside," in *Worlds of Tomorrow* (New York), September 1965.
"The Mercurymen," in *Galaxy* (New York), December 1965.
"A Flask of Fine Arcturan," in *The Ninth Galaxy Reader*, edited by Frederik Pohl. New York, Doubleday, 1966.
"Prisoner of the Sky," in *If* (New York), February 1966.
"Like Any World of Gree," in *Worlds of Tomorrow* (New York), March 1966.
"Enemies of Gree," in *If* (New York), September 1966.
"The Sign of Gree," in *If* (New York), November 1966.
"Frost Planet," in *Worlds of Tomorrow* (New York), November 1966.
"A Beachhead for Gree," in *If* (New York), February 1967.
"Spare That Tree," in *Galaxy* (New York), June 1967.
"A Ticket to Zenner," in *If* (New York), July 1967.
"The Fortunes of Peace," in *If* (New York), September 1967.
"The Judas Bug," in *Analog* (New York), October 1967.

"Winter of the Llangs," in *If* (New York), October 1967.
"Mail Drop," in *If* (New York), November 1967.
"When the Sea Is Born Again," in *If* (New York), December 1967.
"The Impersonators," in *Out of This World 7,* edited by Amabel Williams-Ellis and Mably Owen. London, Blackie, 1968.
"Where the Subbs Go," in *If* (New York), May 1968.
"The Hides of Marrech," in *If* (New York), July 1968.
"Dream Street," in *If* (New York), September 1968.
"Mad Ship," in *If* (New York), May 1969.
"Hot World," in *If* (New York), December 1971.

*   *   *

The SF career of C. C. MacApp lasted only slightly over ten years, from 1960 to 1971. During that decade he built a reputation for exciting adventure stories in which a lone hero would overcome seemingly hopeless odds to save his entire nation, species, or world. His style was beginning to broaden when he died.

MacApp came late in his life to SF. His real name was Carroll M. Capps, and his profession had been in the color printing industry. An illness forced him to retire in his early forties, and he began writing SF. His first story appeared 1960; he averaged only a couple of short works a year through 1963. Then from mid-1964 through 1968 he seemed to have stories almost constantly in print, in either *If* or *Worlds of Tomorrow,* the magazines with which he was most closely associated. In 1968 he began to produce paperback novels; five between that year and 1970. At the same time his flow of magazine stories cut back to a trickle; this was due to both his novel writing and his declining health. A couple of short stories and two more paperback novels appeared posthumously. He had been working on a hardcover novel for Doubleday but it was never finished.

MacApp's magazine works were primarily of novelette length. He was best known for suspense dramas in which humans appeared as underdogs amidst a galactic multispecies civilization. Chief among these were the nine "Gree" novelettes; "The Slaves of Gree," "No Friend of Gree," and so on. These featured Colonel Steve Duke, the top human fighter among the multispecies resistance to the Gree Empire which had conquered most of the galaxy (including Earth) 600 years earlier. Each story had Steve Duke being sent to an unknown planet which Gree's forces had just landed upon, to learn why Gree wanted it and to keep Gree from establishing a new base there. Duke's commando tactics made him a grim counterpart to Keith Laumer's more lighthearted James Retief, who also fought regularly in *If* during the mid-1960s to make the galaxy safe for humanity. A typical non-"Gree" drama is "A Ticket to Zennon," in which Tom Lerrow, a young Earthman, learns that he is being unwittingly used as a courier of plans for a top-secret weapon which two powerful alien factions and a deadly criminal are after. MacApp's aliens are not always villains, nor were all his stories dramas. "Winter of the Llangs" and "When Sea Is Born Again" feature alien teenagers in adventures which amount to rites of passage among their peoples. MacApp's first story, "A Pride of Islands," is a mild comedy where humans are portrayed as parasites living upon giant animals. A more successful comedy is "Mail Drop," in which the bureaucracy of the galactic postal service almost starts but finally prevents an interstellar war.

MacApp's short fiction succeeds by means of dramatic incidents. His novels show that he could write powerful adventures with more richly portrayed characters. Yet the novels have a thematic sameness. All begin with their protagonists caught in a moment of total despair. Murno, an ignorant human peasant on an Earth subjugated by aliens for thousands of years, learns that their masters are about to begin hunting men for sport (*Omha Abides*). Raab Garan, a cadet in a dirigible air fleet on a backward colony planet, faces his country's fall to its totalitarian adversary unless he can succeed in what he realizes is a suicide mission (*Prisoners of the Sky*). Zeke Bolivar, space explorer, is about to crash on an unknown world (*Worlds of the Wall*). John Braysen, a Space Force commander, believes that he is one of only a few hundred humans left alive after Earth loses a space war (*Recall Not Earth*). MacApp's heroes always win through to a victorious conclusion but only after a psychologically exhausting struggle. Also, the lack of women in MacApp's works stands out sharply. In *Recall Not Earth*, the presence of one chapter featuring women (to establish that human women still exist) seems almost forced. Most of his other novels use women only as minor background characters. MacApp had only started to break away from these stereotypes in his final novel, *Bumsider*, which has a strong and convincingly-portrayed woman supporting character in Pegs Waran, and a plot involving more human interactions among his main cast.

—Frederick Patten

MacCREIGH James. See POHL, Frederik.

MacDONALD, John D(ann). American. Born in Sharon, Pennsylvania, 24 July 1916. Educated at the University of Pennsylvania, Philadelphia, 1934-35; Syracuse University, New York, B. S. 1938; Harvard University, Cambridge, Massachusetts, M. B. A. 1939. Served with the United States Army, Office of Strategic Services, 1940-46: Lieutenant Colonel. Married Dorothy Mary Prentiss in 1937; one son. Writer in several genres and under a number of pseudonyms for the pulps and other magazines. President, Mystery Writers of America, 1962. Recipient: Benjamin Franklin Award, for short story, 1955; Grand Prix de Littérature Policière, 1964; Mystery Writers of America Grand Master Award, 1972; American Book Award, 1980. D. H. L. : Hobart and William Smith Colleges, Geneva, New York, 1978; University of South Florida, Tampa, 1980. Agent: George Diskant, 1033 Gayley Avenue, Los Angeles, California 90024. Address: 100 Ocean Place, Sarasota, Florida 33581, U.S.A.

SCIENCE-FICTION PUBLICATIONS

Novels

Wine of the Dreamers. New York, Greenberg, 1951; as *Planet of the Dreamers*, New York, Pocket Books, 1953; London, Hale, 1955.
Ballroom of the Skies. New York, Greenberg, 1952.
The Girl, The Gold Watch, and Everything. New York, Fawcett, 1962; London, Coronet, 1968.

Short Stories

Other Times, Other Worlds. New York, Fawcett, 1978.

OTHER PUBLICATIONS

Novels

The Brass Cupcake. New York, Fawcett, 1950; London, Muller, 1955.

Judge Me Not. New York, Fawcett, 1951; London, Muller, 1964.

Murder for the Bride. New York, Fawcett, 1951; London, Fawcett, 1954.

Weep for Me. New York, Fawcett, 1951; London, Muller, 1964.

The Damned. New York, Fawcett, 1952; London, Muller, 1964.

Dead Low Tide. New York, Fawcett, 1953; London, Fawcett, 1955.

The Neon Jungle. New York, Fawcett, 1953; London, Fawcett, 1954.

Cancel All Our Vows. New York, Appleton Century Crofts, 1953; London, Hale, 1955.

Contrary Pleasure. New York, Appleton Century Crofts, 1954; London, Hale, 1955.

All These Condemned. New York, Fawcett, 1954.

Area of Suspicion. New York, Dell, 1954; London, Hale, 1956; revised edition, New York, Fawcett, 1961.

A Bullet for Cinderella. New York, Dell, 1955; London, Hale, 1960; as *On the Make*, New York, Dell, 1960.

Cry Hard, Cry Fast. New York, Popular Library, 1955; London, Hale, 1969.

April Evil. New York, Dell, 1956; London, Hale, 1957.

Border Town Girl (novelets). New York, Popular Library, 1956; as *Five Star Fugitive*, London, Hale, 1970.

Murder in the Wind. New York, Dell, 1956; as *Hurricane*, London, Hale, 1957.

You Live Once. New York, Popular Library, 1956; London, Hale, 1976; as *You Kill Me*, New York, Fawcett, 1961.

Death Trap. New York, Dell, 1957; London, Hale, 1958.

The Empty Trap. New York, Popular Library, 1957; London, Magnum, 1980.

The Price of Murder. New York, Dell, 1957; London, Hale, 1958.

A Man of Affairs. New York, Dell, 1957; London, Hale, 1959.

Clemmie. New York, Fawcett, 1958.

The Executioners. New York, Simon and Schuster, 1958; London, Hale, 1959; as *Cape Fear*, New York, Fawcett, 1962.

Soft Touch. New York, Dell, 1958; London, Hale, 1960; as *Man-Trap*, London, Pan 1961.

The Deceivers. New York, Fawcett, 1958; London, Hale, 1968.

The Beach Girls. New York, Fawcett, 1959; London, Muller, 1964.

The Crossroads. New York, Simon and Schuster, 1959; London, Hale, 1961.

Deadly Welcome. New York, Dell, 1959; London, Hale, 1961.

Please Write for Details. New York, Simon and Schuster, 1959.

The End of the Night. New York, Simon and Schuster, 1960; London, Hale, 1964.

The Only Girl in the Game. New York, Fawcett, 1960; London, Hale, 1962.

Slam the Big Door. New York, Fawcett, 1960; London, Hale, 1961.

One Monday We Killed Them All. New York, Fawcett, 1961; London, Hale, 1963.

Where Is Janice Gantry. New York, Fawcett, 1961; London, Hale, 1963.

A Flash of Green. New York, Simon and Schuster, 1962; London, Hale, 1971.

A Key to the Suite. New York, Fawcett, 1962; London, Hale, 1968.

The Drowner. New York, Fawcett, 1963; London, Hale, 1964.

On the Run. New York, Fawcett, 1963; London, Hale, 1965.

I Could Go On Singing (novelization of screenplay). New York, Fawcett, 1963; London, Hale, 1964.

The Deep Blue Goodby. New York, Fawcett, 1964; London, Hale, 1965.

Nightmare in Pink. New York, Fawcett, 1964; London, Hale, 1966.

A Purple Place for Dying. New York, Fawcett, 1964; London, Hale, 1966.

The Quick Red Fox. New York, Fawcett, 1964; London, Hale, 1966.

A Deadly Shade of Gold. New York, Fawcett, 1965; London, Hale, 1967.

Bright Orange for the Shroud. New York, Fawcett, 1965; London, Hale, 1967.

Darker Than Amber. New York, Fawcett, 1966; London, Hale, 1968.

One Fearful Yellow Eye. New York, Fawcett, 1966; London, Hale, 1968.

The Last One Left. New York, Doubleday, 1967; London, Hale, 1968.

Three for McGee (omnibus). New York, Doubleday, 1967.

Pale Gray for Guilt. New York, Fawcett, 1968; London, Hale, 1969.

The Girl in the Plain Brown Wrapper. New York, Fawcett, 1968; London, Hale, 1969.

Dress Her in Indigo. New York, Fawcett, 1969; London, Hale, 1971.

The Long Lavender Look. New York and London, Fawcett, 1970.

A Tan and Sandy Silence. New York, Fawcett, 1972; London, Hale, 1973.

The Scarlet Ruse. New York, Fawcett, 1973; London, Hale, 1975.

The Turquoise Lament. Philadelphia, Lippincott, 1973; London, Hale, 1975.

McGee (omnibus). London, Hale, 1975.

The Dreadful Lemon Sky. Philadelphia, Lippincott, 1975; London, Hale, 1976.

Condominium. Philadelphia, Lippincott, and London, Hale, 1977.

The Empty Copper Sea. Philadelphia, Lippincott, 1978; London, Hale, 1979.

The Green Ripper. Philadelphia, Lippincott, 1979; London, Hale, 1980.

Free Fall in Crimson. New York, Harper, and London, Collins, 1981.

Cinnamon Skin. New York, Harper, and London, Collins, 1982.

One More Sunday. New York, Knopf, and London, Hodder and Stoughton, 1984.

The Best of Travis McGee. London, Hale, 1985.

The Lonely Silver Rain. New York, Knopf, and London, Hodder and Stoughton, 1985.

Short Stories

End of the Tiger and Other Stories. New York, Fawcett, 1966; London, Hale, 1967.

Seven. New York, Fawcett, 1971; London, Hale, 1974.

The Good Old Stuff: 13 Early Stories, edited by Martin H. Greenberg and others. New York, Harper, 1982; London, Collins, 1984.

More Good Old Stuff. New York, Knopf, 1984.

Other

The House Guests. New York, Doubleday, 1965; London, Hale, 1966.
No Deadly Drug. New York, Doubleday 1968.
Nothing Can Go Wrong, with John H. Kilpack. New York, Harper, 1981.

Editor, *The Lethal Sex.* New York, Dell, 1959; London, Collins, 1962.

*

Bibliography: *A Bibliography of the Published Works of John D. MacDonald* by Jean and Walter Shine, Gainesville, University of Florida Libraries, 1981.

Manuscript Collection: University of Florida Library, Gainesville.

Critical Study: *John D. MacDonald* by David Geherin, New York, Ungar, 1982.

*   *   *

John D. MacDonald's prolific output of thrillers has not, in the end, prevented the acknowledgment that he is one of America's best novelists. He contributed nearly 50 short stories, under various names, and two novels to the SF genre in the late 1940's and early 1950's before turning almost exclusively to crime fiction, except for three marginal entries, "The Legend of Joe Lee" (a ghost story), "The Annex" (speculative fiction), and *The Girl, The Gold Watch and Everything* (comedy thriller with a gimmick, anticipated in the excellent 1950 story, "Half-Past Eternity," that freezes everyone in time, except the user).

The title of the collection of MacDonald's SF short stories, *Other Times, Other Worlds,* neatly indicates his major themes: time travel, aliens among us or manipulating us, juxtaposition of our culture with others. These stories often communicate a strong sense of the value of the honestly striving individual; however, a good many are horror stories in which this value is arbitrarily denied. What is a "Game for Blondes" from the future who come fishing for a man is a nightmare to him, as is the "Spectator Sport" of the future, to which the unsuspecting visitor from our times is condemned, well-meaningly bound forever to a mechanical fantasy. In "Labor Supply" the best of humans are enslaved by gnomes, through their dreams; in "A Child Is Crying" the gift of seeing the future is a cause of horror to its possessor and those who wish to exploit it.

The two early novels pick with heavy crowbars under the slab of sanity that holds down the incipient paranoia of their readers. Aliens really do take over our minds, they tell us, and for no good purpose. *Wine of the Dreamers* posits a planet on which the principal adult occupation is taking possession of us, playing with us in the belief that we are only creatures of fancy. The irresponsible Dreamers, who have similar remote access to two other planets, all three of which were settled by their ancestors, have forgotten their ordained function, yet they need our help, as only one of their inbred, dwindling number sees. Although MacDonald grossly over-simplifies for the sake of a suspenseful narrative, particularly the closed environment of the Dreamers, this remains a good tightly plotted novel which still reads well. It ends optimistically and is satisfying on its own terms, but *Ballroom of the Skies* concludes uneasily and is a more disturbing novel, because we must be unable to share in its hero's feelings of quiet exultation in the last paragraphs, to the

extent that we perceive that he has only succeeded in moving from a smaller to a greater paranoia. A set-up in which ends justify means will never satisfy all readers; here, the given conditions are remarkably distasteful. Our planet is being kept in a state of perpetual warfare, peacemakers being killed, their purposes twisted, in order to preserve Earth as a breeding ground for superhuman leaders who will keep the galactic civilization from stagnating and maintain it in a state of readiness in case of a notional invasion from another galaxy. The hero is one of the world's leading peacemakers, a journalist whose investigation of the fantastic crimes which break up secret negotiations between the world's power blocks leads to his recruitment as an agent of the very powers he dedicates his life to oppose. To keep the reader in sympathy with such a hero would be a fearsome challenge for any writer and, although MacDonald does his best to make him more admirably heroic (using the well-honoured trick of timely praise from a girl friend) as he grows beyond the human norm, the attempt fails. In reality, MacDonald's hero, Dake Lorin, who is excellent in his Lone Wolf phase, would have recognized the speciousness of the conditions he is made, humbly, to accept. The novel is, nevertheless, a gripping narrative and, in the best tradition of such works, honestly presents the lonely dilemma of the superman who can find true friendship only with others of his kind.

Besides the titles already mentioned, "Ring Around the Redhead," "Shadow on the Sand," "The Miniature," "The Big Contest," "Susceptibility," "Common Denominator," and "Trojan Horse Laugh" should be listed as fine short stories by a writer who could clearly have been a major figure in the genre had he not found crime more rewarding. It should be noted that MacDonald has often used mystery fiction also to be prophetically critical of the suicidal tendencies of our society, being one of those early concerned with threats to our ecology.

—Michael J. Tolley

MacDOUGAL, John. See **LOWNDES, Robert A. W.**

MacDUFF, Andrew. See **FYFE, H. B.**

MACKELWORTH, R(onald) W(alter). British. Born in London, 7 April 1930. Educated at Raynes Park Grammar School, London, 1940-48. Served in the British Army Intelligence Corps, 1948-50. Married Sheila Elizabeth Kilpatrick in 1956; one son and two daughters. Worked for Thomas Cook, travel agents, London, 1950; clerk, Norwich Union Insurance, London, 1950-53; Inspector, Kingston, Surrey, 1953-66; Superintendent, Leeds, 1966-72; Manager, Portsmouth, 1972-77; Product Manager, 1977-84, and since 1984 Strategic Planning Manager, London, Legal and General Insurance Society. Agent: Carnell Literary Agency, Rowneybury Bungalow, Sawbridgeworth, near Old Harlow, Essex CM20 2EX. Address: 32 Mark Way, Godalming, Surrey, England.

SCIENCE-FICTION PUBLICATIONS

Novels

Firemantle. London, Hale, 1968; as *The Diabols*, New York, Paperback Library, 1969.
Tiltangle. New York, Ballantine, 1970; London, Hale, 1971.
Starflight 3000. New York, Ballantine, 1972; London, New English Library, 1976.
The Year of the Painted World. London, Hale, 1975.
Shakehole. London, Hale, 1981.

Uncollected Short Stories

"The Statue," in *New Worlds* (London), January 1963.
"I, The Judge," in *New Worlds* (London), May 1963.
"Pattern of Risk," in *New Worlds* (London), July 1963.
"The Rotten Borough," in *New Worlds* (London), September 1963.
"The Cliff-Hangers," in *New Worlds* (London), December 1963.
"The Unexpected Martyr," in *New Worlds* (London), February 1964.
"The Expanding Man," in *New Writings in SF 5*, edited by John Carnell. London, Dobson, 1965; New York, Bantam, 1970.
"A Cave in the Hills," in *Science Fantasy* (Bournemouth), March 1965.
"The Changing Shape of Charlie Snuff," in *New Worlds* (London), April 1965.
"Last Man Home," in *New Worlds* (London), June 1965.
"A Distorting Mirror," in *Science Fantasy* (Bournemouth), July 1965.
"Temptation for the Leader," in *Science Fantasy* (Bournemouth), September 1965.
"Cleaner Than Clean," in *Science Fantasy* (Bournemouth), December 1965.
"A Touch of Immortality," in *New Writings in SF 7*, edited by John Carnell. London, Dobson, 1966; New York, Bantam, 1971.
"Final Solution," in *New Writings in SF 8*, edited by John Carnell. London, Dobson, 1966; New York, Bantam, 1971.
"A Visitation of Ghosts," in *SF Impulse* (London), June 1966.
"Two Rivers," in *New Writings in SF 17*, edited by John Carnell. London, Dobson, 1970.
"Mr. Nobody," in *New Writings in Horror and the Supernatural 1*, edited by David Sutton. London, Sphere, 1971.

*

Manuscript Collection: North London Polytechnic.

R. W. Mackelworth comments:

I am a lifelong addict of SF, but I prefer well-written novels and those that make a satirical statement about contemporary life whether through fantasy or fact. However, I also believe the modern idiom of fast-moving adventure entertains and entertainment is what the writer owes the reader. My work is essentially non-professional; I like to work up my own ideas and enjoy my writing. The conventions of SF are few, and one of its joys is that its scope for the imagination is unlimited. SF is gaining readers because it is largely free of many of the set-piece situations demanded of mainstream writing. Its problem is lack of good characterisation. Characters are often overwhelmed by events: if we can put personality before event, SF writing could improve considerably. The standard of writing is also important. It is possible to write literate SF as well as exciting SF!

*   *   *

The influence of British science-fiction magazines of the 1950's is evident in R. W. Mackelworth's restrained style and use of stock adventure frameworks: his fiction, despite attempts to incorporate profound issues, rarely displays the self-awareness increasingly favoured among his contemporaries. His output has remained small, his foremost works being novels.

In *Firemantle* the hero is projected, apparently through time, to an Earth dominated by a deadly alien life form. Most of the book relates his exploits in this future world and his gradual understanding of its parameters (including his immunity to the aliens). Interwoven with the narrative are themes of revenge and manipulation, the exact details, methods, and motives remaining concealed until the end. The novel finally affirms the intrinsic survival potentiality of human will power, but also questions the cost involved.

Tiltangle is set on Earth during a new ice age, with survivors crowded into an isolated refuge. Once again personal manipulation and callous use of power are introduced, although the central concern is a quest for the uncertain myth of "the warm," the first retreat of snow and ice heralding the return of a habitable world. This is Mackelworth's most effective book: it contains some of his best realised characters, while the depiction of ascetic life in a hostile environment is reinforced by uncharacteristically precise subsidiary detail. The implied background circumstances are less convincing, but this scarcely affects the driving obsession which is the novel's strength.

Starflight 3000 is loosely based on the generation starship concept. A hollowed asteroid becomes a vast spacecraft; use of terraforming bacteria allows the colonisation of any planet. Secondary aspects include faster-than-light communication and mysterious alien science. But for all its reliance on such motifs the novel is not typical of "hard" technological science fiction. It expresses moral concern over a selfish, expansionist mentality, and also gives some consideration to the conflict inherent in Mackelworth's two recurrent themes: the tendency of power to corrupt its wielder and the need for charismatic leadership to ensure progress. However, an abrupt time shift and the creation of a shipboard mythology ultimately avoid the questions raised.

The Year of the Painted World combines traditional elements of both disaster and invasion stories. Surprisingly excitable in tone, it tells of a struggle on present-day Earth against a Martian virus and its aggressive host organisms. The protagonist is an unambiguous man of action, doing what must be done. In his arrogant simplicity he could almost be a caricature of a hero from science fiction's Golden Age. The threatening "Pods" also carry more than a hint of space monsters of old. Possible benefits once the virus is controlled (and the consequent suspicions and machinations surrounding its release) add little depth to a playfully derivative but basically flimsy novel.

Mackelworth is no artist, honing subtleties of vision, language, and motivation to fine edges: instead he relies on mystery and suspense to hold attention until the denouement. His characterisation is usually notional (his stereotyped women are singularly ill portrayed), although within its terms he is adept at drawing concise contrasts. A tendency to slip into careless assumptions and clichés is another result of his intense absorption in plotting. Nevertheless, it is the complexity of his plots which sets Mackelworth apart from routine adventure writers. His underlying themes can be especially thought provoking, and it is unfortunate that he chooses to turn away from their fullest implications rather than develop their dramatic tension.

—Nick Pratt

MacLEAN, Arthur. See TUBB, E. C.

MacLEAN, Katherine (Anne). American. Born in Glen Ridge, New Jersey, 22 January 1925. Educated at Barnard College, New York, B. A. in economics 1950; Goddard College, Plainfield, Vermont, M. A. in psychology 1977. Married 1) Charles Dye in 1951 (divorced, 1952); 2) David Mason in 1956 (divorced, 1962), one son; 3) Carl West. Laboratory assistant, 1944-45, and food manufacturing technician, 1945-46; office manager, Hi-Pro Animal Feed, Frankfort, Delaware, 1952-53; technician, Memorial and Knickerbocker hospitals, New York, 1954-56. Member of the English Department, University of Connecticut, Storrs, 1962-65, and University of Maine, Orono, intermittently 1966-77. Free-lance writer and lecturer. Recipient: Nebula Award, 1971. Agent: Virginia Kidd, Box 278, Milford, Pennsylvania 18337. Address: P. O. Box 1563, Biddeford, Maine 04005, U.S.A.

SCIENCE-FICTION PUBLICATIONS

Novels

Cosmic Checkmate, with Charles V. De Vet. New York, Ace, 1962.
The Man in the Bird Cage. New York, Ace, 1971.
Missing Man. New York, Berkley, 1975.
Dark Wing, with Carl West. New York, Atheneum, 1979.

Short Stories

The Diploids and Other Flights of Fancy. New York, Avon, 1962.
Trouble with Treaties. Tacoma, Washington, Lanthorne Press, 1975.
The Trouble with You Earth People. Norfolk, Virginia, Donning, 1980.

Uncollected Short Stories

"Night-Rise," in *Cassandra Rising*, edited by Alice Laurance. New York, Doubleday, 1978.
"Canary Bird," in *Chrysalis 2*, edited by Roy Torgeson. New York, Zebra, 1978.

OTHER PUBLICATIONS

Other

"Communicado," in *Science Fiction Quarterly* (Holyoke, Massachusetts), February 1952.
"Alien Minds and Nonhuman Intelligence," in *The Craft of Science Fiction,* edited by Reginald Bretnor. New York, Harper, 1976.
"Alien Strategy," in *The Future at War 1,* edited by Reginald Bretnor. New York, Ace, 1979.

*

Katherine MacLean comments:
I am interested in science fiction as an exploration of possibility—specifically the possibilities that are most astonishing, yet genuinely possible. It becomes worthwhile to write when I am more deeply surprised with each page of unfolding potential events.

*   *   *

Katherine MacLean is important for introducing in her fiction ethical questions about medical and scientific experimentation. She also writes about mental telepathy and human fears of evolutionary change.

The Diploids and Other Flights of Fancy includes eight works published between 1949 and 1953. The title story tells of genetic experiments that produced a strain of standardized human fetuses for research purposes. "The Pyramid in the Desert" has as its theme human fear of immortality. "Defense Mechanism" and "Games" are both about telepathy. "Feedback" deals with human fear of new ideas; "Pictures Don't Lie" deals with the anthropomorphic tendency to measure all species on a human scale. "The Snowball Effect" and "Incommunicado" are clever but less significant thematically than the others.

In *Cosmic Checkmate,* written with Charles V. De Vet, Robert Lang goes to the planet Velda to discover why its population refuses peaceful contact with the federation of Earth's colonies. In disguise, Lang plays the Veldian Game—based on chess—and beats all comers in the second game; he deliberately loses the first game to discover his opponent's weaknesses. The novel is well crafted: the plot works as an analogous game structure with Lang winning the second game in a cosmic checkmate.

MacLean's essay "Communicado" provides the background for her works that deal thematically with telepathy and psi phenomena. She discusses the important influence Whately Carington's book *Thought Transference* (1946) had on her, and she elaborates the ideas behind stories like "Defense Mechanism," "Feedback," "The Fittest," "Games," "Where or When," and "Curtin in the Sky." Telepathy is also the moving idea behind *Missing Man.* Set in New York, in 1999, the novel features George Sanford, whose extraordinary telepathic abilities make him a valuable special consultant for the Rescue Squad of the Police Department. Sanford is the fear hound, sniffing out people who are in trouble by tuning in to the telepathic vibrations they broadcast. The missing man is Carl Hodges, a super-maintenance man for the city who uses computers to predict breakdowns and accidents before they occur. The novel is thematically complex and almost phantasmagorical at times.

Several of MacLean's stories have medical themes and use physicians as main characters. Among the best of these is "Contagion": colonists on another planet survive a plague only by becoming look-alikes, thus raising questions about the interrelationship between external appearance and personality. "The Origin of the Species" is told in epistolary form by a neurosurgeon who is troubled by his work: he destroys the best parts of people's minds so that they can adapt to life in society. "Gimmick" chronicles the use of a virus as a weapon; "The Other" presents a physician who, ironically, has the same problem as the patient he is trying to cure; and "Syndrome Johnny" shows the usefulness of plagues in speeding up evolution. *Dark Wing,* written with her husband Carl West, also has a medical theme. It presents a future where the practice of medicine is illegal and people believe that illness is immoral, an external sign of defects in their thinking. A teenage boy, Travis Gordon, discovers two old medical kits in an abandoned wrecked ambulance and begins to learn and practice medicine, even performing complicated surgery with no special equipment or assistance. The complex and unbelievable plot, the superficial criticism of medicine, and the youth of the protagonist combine to make the novel read like adolescent fiction.

—Anne Hudson Jones

MacLEOD, Sheila. Scottish. Born on the Isle of Lewis, 23 March 1939. Educated at Wycombe Abbey School, Buckinghamshire; Somerville College, Oxford, B. A. (honours) in English 1961. Married the actor Paul Jones in 1963 (divorced); one son. Recipient: Scottish Arts Council award, 1969, 1971; MIND award, for non-fiction, 1981. Agent: Giles Gordon, Anthony Sheil Associates, 43 Doughty Street, London WC1N 2LF. Address: 9 Appleby Road, London E8 3ET, England.

SCIENCE-FICTION PUBLICATIONS

Novels

The Snow-White Soliloquies. London, Secker and Warburg, and New York, Viking Press, 1970.
Xanthe and the Robots. London, Bodley Head, 1977.
Circuit-Breaker. London, Bodley Head, 1978.

OTHER PUBLICATIONS

Novels

The Moving Accident. London, Faber, 1968.
Letters from the Portuguese. London, Secker and Warburg, 1971.
Axioms. London, Quartet, 1984.

Plays

Television Plays: *They Put You Where You Are,* 1966; *God Speed Co-operation,* 1983.

Other

The Art of Starvation: An Adolescent Observed. London, Virago, 1981; as *The Art of Starvation: A Story of Anorexia and Survival,* New York, Schocken, 1982.
D. H. Lawrence's Men and Women. London, Heinemann, 1985.

*   *   *

A seasoned writer, Sheila MacLeod has published in a variety of genres, science fiction among them. Her earliest novels are experiments in surrealism—*The Snow-White Soliloquies* perhaps the most outstanding. Here MacLeod projects the old Germanic fairy tale into a strange, Orwellian present: a catatonic Snow-White, encased in a high-tech box of Glass That Breathes, is transported from place to nameless place in a dubious search for The Prince. Supervised by an authoritarian figure named Doc and attended by a succession of six social marginals, the paralyzed heroine embodies the principle of passivity. She sees, hears, contemplates, and suffers with those around her but is unable to act. Her silent soliloquies reveal that her knowledge of herself is curiously limited: she is a poisoned life, preserved by technological wizardry for purposes unknown. (The reader knows no more than she.) As the literally captive audience for the obsessive monologues and peculiar actions of her caretakers, Snow-White witnesses a series of increasingly bizarre events—until something gives (most notably, the glass box) and she is able to acknowledge the roles that all have played in this disturbing and dreamlike psychodrama. The "allegorical atmosphere" of *The Snow-White Soliloquies* has been somewhat evasively described by reviewers as "fascinating," "intriguing," and "rich with reflection about the human condition." "More to the point is that the book is finally and successfully enigmatic. We cannot get beyond its carefully constructed surfaces, which tease us with refractions of our own expectations.

In the more conventionally rendered *Xanthe and the Robots,* MacLeod's first thorough-going science-fiction narrative, we meet another version of the catatonic woman, this time a brilliant robotics engineer who has invested the greater part of her emotional life in relationships with mechanical beings. Programmer Xanthe, numbed by psychotropic drugs since the death of her father, the founder of the Institute for Advanced Robotic Research, finds her torpor disturbed by two upsetting developments: a new relationship with an intense and attractive co-worker, and a dramatic change in Institute policy. The painful reawakening of Xanthe's psyche parallels a decision by Institute authorities to endow the most advanced robots with a more human sensibility. Xanthe and the robots learn, in different ways, to desire, and the process of wanting leads them, gradually but inexorably, to regret their passive institutional loyalty. Xanthe rebels—against her superior, against the Institute, ultimately against her father—and chooses a future unlike anything she has known in her regimented habitat. The robots also have their revolution, but their prospects look less potentially creative; given their origins, they can do little more than replicate the ugly hierarchies of their makers. In *Xanthe* MacLeod articulates a familiar sci-fi theme: our machines cannot save us from ourselves. The plot *per se* holds few surprises, but Xanthe's oddly deadpan narrative persona, at once touching and repellent, sustains our interest.

With *Circuit-Breaker* MacLeod moves back into the unsettling ambiguity which is her strength. Ostensibly, the story is about a British astronaut, Alexander Baird, who must exercise unusual "autokinetic" powers to restore his marooned spacecraft to its intended orbit. According to Lvov, the sinister mission controller, Baird may generate sufficient power to rein in the straying capsule if he can forge telepathic linkages with the women nearest the hearts of himself and his fellow travellers, Davitt and Haskins. Baird contacts earth, and his strange encounters with his alienated spouse, Davitt's eccentric mom, and Haskins's anxious and vulnerable wife generate troubling questions for the reader. Is Baird in fact an astronaut? Or is he a science-fiction writer who has come to believe his own fantasies? Is Lvov a dictatorial aerospace bureaucrat? Or an especially nasty headshrinker? In this tacky little universe of failed connections, how are we to distinguish between outer and inner space? MacLeod's controlled opacity is compelling—we are drawn to the world of her problematic protagonist as to a black hole. Like *The Snow-White Soliloquies, Circuit-Breaker* is dense, sophisticated. Though more accessible than the earlier book, it exacts an equally attentive reading.

Sheila MacLeod's best novels are cerebral and defy easy categorization. Casual readers will find themselves impatient with the author's staging, with structures and settings that at first seem too elaborate for what they support and surround. But MacLeod's formal choices are consistent with her choice of subject. Her focus is invariably on neurosis, on the disturbances that prevent people (and cultures) from achieving a peaceful equilibrium, and the trappings of fairy tales and science fiction serve as formal correlatives that keep readers, too, slightly off balance. We stumble along, like MacLeod's characters, bearing the graceless freight of unmet expectations. For most of us, the burden proves worthwhile.

—Janis Butler Holm

MADDERN, Pip (Philippa Catherine Maddern). Australian. Born in Albury, New South Wales, 24 August 1952. Educated at Morwell High School; University of Melbourne, 1970-73, B.A. in history and Indonesian studies, M. A. in history 1978; graduate student, Brasenose College, Oxford, 1979. Tutor, University of Melbourne, 1976-78; Lecturer, Royal Melbourne Institute of Technology, 1979. Agent: Virginia Kidd, Box 278, Milford, Pennsylvania 18337, U.S.A.

SCIENCE-FICTION PUBLICATIONS

Uncollected Short Stories

"The Ins and Outs of the Hadhya City State" and "Broken Pit," in *The Altered I*, edited by Lee Harding. Melbourne, Norstrilia Press, 1976; New York, Berkley, 1978.
"Dialogue," "Wherever You Are," and "Silence," in *The View from the Edge*, edited by George Turner. Melbourne, Norstrilia Press, 1977.
"They Made Us Not to Be and They Are Not," in *Orbit 20*, edited by Damon Knight. New York, Harper, 1978.
"Ignorant of Magic," in *Rooms of Paradise*, edited by Lee Harding. Melbourne, Quartet, 1978; New York, St. Martin's Press, 1979.
"Inhabiting the Interspaces," in *Transmutations*, edited by Rob Gerrand. Melbourne, Outback Press, 1979.
"The Pastseer," in *Interfaces*, edited by Ursula K. Le Guin and Virginia Kidd. New York, Ace, 1980.

*

Pip Maddern comments:
I have never been good at commenting on my own work, partly, I think, because I believe very firmly in the primacy of the subconscious in writing. It seems to me—to my conscious mind—that the stories are something separate from me. I write them because they are there to be written, and for some reason someone else hasn't written them yet. So in a sense, I'm no better fitted to introduce them to their readers than anyone else is.

They are science fiction. As many other people do, I define science fiction as being that branch of fiction in which the readers cannot assume that the story is set in the world as they know it—it might be set in the future, it might be set on a different planet, it might be set in an alternative universe. The only reason I write science fiction is that all the stories that have appeared to me so far have that sort of setting. (It's not that I dislike this-world literature—I love reading it, but I get uncomfortable writing it because it seems to me always to be saying "This is fiction, but I am trying to make it look like reality. " Whereas science fiction can more easily say "This is fiction. Let's enjoy it. ")

My stories don't carry a message from me. Some of them may carry a message of their own to some of you; but that's up to you to find out. They all seem to me to be worth telling, though I have not told them as well as they deserve; and the people (or aliens) in them seem to me to be worth knowing, though I have not made them all known as completely and accurately as I should have.

*   *   *

Pip Maddern came to immediate notice at the Writers' Workshop conducted by Ursula K. Le Guin at Belgrave, Victoria, in 1975; her admission story, "The Ins and Outs of the Hadhya City State," attracted attention by the assuredness of the technique. A superficial ingenuity (arising from a situation which I, and later Joanna Russ, found doubtful) was a weakness which faded in the stricter control of the imaginative elements in her later work.

She has published only a few stories, but definite characteristics are emerging. Most notable is her ability to manage a considerable complexity of theme and action in minimum wordage. In "Ignorant of Magic" she deals in about 5500 words with interlocking events in three separate universes, of which one is a parallel wherein magic usurps the role of science. Considering the spareness of her narrative style, the clear presentation of the spatio-temporal relationships of all three is a technical feat of no common order. She does not repeat her effects, and in "They Made Us Not to Be and They Are Not" she deals in totally original fashion with one of imagination's oldest dreams, extended life span. In a very different mode is "Inhabiting the Interspaces," a solidly realistic piece of storytelling eschewing all fantasy elements save a single social change; it is a sombre piece of precise observation which shows that she is not dependent on genre effects to carry her prose. A controlled anger (even a subtext of savagery) informs her plotting and characterisation, but it is too early to suggest her general direction. She is one of the most technically accomplished of the newer writers in the field.

—George Turner

MADDOX, Carl. See TUBB, E. C.

MAINE, Charles Eric. Pseudonym for David McIlwain; also writes as Richard Rayner; Robert Wade. British. Born in Liverpool, Lancashire, 21 January 1921. Educated at Holt High School, Liverpool. Served in the Royal Air Force during World War II: Flight Lieutenant. Married and divorced twice; two sons and three daughters. Journalist in London, 1946-71, including 14 years as editor and managing editor of industrial weekly newspapers and journals; regular correspondent for *The Times, Financial Times*, and *Guardian*, London, and *Les Echos*, Paris. Agent: David Higham Associates Ltd., 5-8 Lower John Street, London W1R 4HA, England; or, Scott Meredith Literary Agency, 845 Third Avenue, New York, New York 10022, U.S.A.

SCIENCE-FICTION PUBLICATIONS

Novels (series: Mike Delaney)

Spaceways. London, Hodder and Stoughton, 1953; as *Spaceways Satellite*, New York, Avalon, 1958.
Timeliner. London, Hodder and Stoughton, and New York, Rinehart, 1955.
Crisis 2000. London, Hodder and Stoughton, 1956.

Escapement. London, Hodder and Stoughton, 1956; as *The Man Who Couldn't Sleep,* Philadelphia, Lippincott, 1958.

High Vacuum. London, Hodder and Stoughton, and New York, Ballantine, 1957.

The Isotope Man (Delaney). London, Hodder and Stoughton, and Philadelphia, Lippincott, 1957.

World Without Men. New York, Ace, 1958; London, Digit, 1963; revised edition, as *Alph,* New York, Doubleday, 1972.

The Tide Went Out. London, Hodder and Stoughton, 1958; New York, Ballantine, 1959; revised edition, as *Thirst!,* London, Sphere, 1977; New York, Ace, 1978.

Count-Down. London, Hodder and Stoughton, 1959; as *Fire Past the Future,* New York, Ballantine, 1960.

Subterfuge (Delaney). London, Hodder and Stoughton, 1959.

Calculated Risk. London, Hodder and Stoughton, 1960.

He Owned the World. New York, Avalon, 1960; as *The Man Who Owned the World,* London, Hodder and Stoughton, 1961.

The Mind of Mr. Soames. London, Hodder and Stoughton, 1961.

The Darkest of Nights. London, Hodder and Stoughton, 1962; as *Survival Margin,* New York, Fawcett, 1968; revised edition, as *The Big Death,* London, Sphere, 1978.

Never Let Up (Delaney). London, Hodder and Stoughton, 1964.

B. E. A. S. T.: Biological Evolutionary Animal Simulation Test. London, Hodder and Stoughton, 1966; New York, Ballantine, 1967.

The Random Factor. London, Hodder and Stoughton, 1971.

Uncollected Short Stories

"Repulsion Factor," in *Authentic* (London), September 1953.

"Highway," in *Authentic* (London), November 1953.

"Spaceways to Venus," in *Spaceway* (Alhambra, California), December 1953.

"The Boogie Matrix," in *Authentic* (London), January 1954.

"Troubleshooters," in *Nebula* (Glasgow), February 1954.

"The Festival of Earth," in *Spaceway* (Alhambra, California), December 1954.

"The Yupe," in *Nebula* (Glasgow), December 1954.

"The Trouble with Mars," in *Authentic* (London), July 1955.

"Mission from Space," in *Fantastic Universe* (Chicago), September 1955.

"Reverse Procedure," in *Space Science Fiction Magazine* (New York), Spring 1957.

"The Wall of Fire," in *Satellite* (New York), June 1958.

"The Waters under the Earth," in *Amazing* (New York), July 1958.

"Counter-Psych," in *Amazing* (New York), November 1961.

"Highway J," in *Other Worlds, Other Times,* edited by Sam Moskowitz and Roger Elwood. New York, Macfadden Bartell, 1969.

"Scholarly Correspondence," in *Analog* (New York), April 1974.

"Joe Three-Eyes," in *New Tales of Unease,* edited by John Burke. London, Pan, 1976.

OTHER PUBLICATIONS

Novels as Richard Rayner

The Trouble with Ruth. London, Hale, 1960.
Darling Daughter. London, Hale, 1961.
Dig Deep for Julie. London, Hale, 1963.
Stand-In for Danger. London, Hale, 1963.

Novels as Robert Wade

The Wonderful One. London, Hodder and Stoughton, 1960.
The Stroke of Seven. New York, Morrow, 1965; London, Heinemann, 1967.
Knave of Eagles. New York, Random House, 1969; London, Hale, 1970.

Plays

Screenplay: *Escapement* (*The Electric Monster*), with J. McLaren Ross, 1958.

Radio Plays: *Spaceways,* 1952; *The Einstein Way,* 1954.

Television Play: *Timeslip.*

Other

The World's Strangest Crimes. New York, Hart, and London, Odhams Press, 1967; as *The Bizarre and Bloody,* Hart, 1972.
World-Famous Mistresses. London, Odhams Press, 1970.

*

Charles Eric Maine comments:

Like Arthur C. Clarke, John Christopher, Eric Frank Russell, Jonathan Burke, the late John Wyndham, and other science-fiction author friends, I became an SF addict in my early teens. This was the era of the late 1930's when nobody, apart from a few SF writers and addicts, and fewer scientists, believed that man would ever set foot on the moon in this century, if at all. In my own science fiction, I have always tried to find a theme or situation which no other author has thought of. Although I have written some space opera (such as *Timeliner* and *He Owned the World*), most of my SF books are short-term projections from present-day fact and technology, looking, perhaps, some 10 to 50 years ahead. I am particularly interested in the social and psychological impact of advancing science on crude Homo sapiens. In this respect my two best novels are *The Tide Went Out* and *The Mind of Mr. Soames* (the movie version missed the essential point of the story—the difference between training and education.

* * *

Charles Eric Maine's writing is distinguished primarily by its original and imaginative concepts. This is not to demean his writing skills but rather to indicate that when viewed as a body his stories vary considerably in quality. Too often he falls back on clichés to move his stories along, and occasionally the clash between banal plots and sophisticated scientific ideas is resounding. Maine's treatment of time displacement in *The Isotope Man,* for example, is fascinating, but it is embedded in a plot that would do justice to the old pulps. The plot, to sabotage the artificial production of tungsten, is embellished by stereotyped characters: an ex-Nazi plastic surgeon, an evil South American business tycoon, a feisty and irascible city editor, a beautiful, sharp-tongued girl photographer, and a hard-drinking, two-fisted reporter who plays his hunches to the detriment of his job.

Despite this occasional failure to mesh plots, characters, and themes, however, Maine at his best is quite effective. *Alph, B. E. A. S. T., Timeliner,* and *The Tide Went Out* are excellent novels. He seems particularly good at creating memorable female characters. Among them are Synove Rayner (*B. E. A. S. T.*), a brilliant and beautiful exhibitionist nymphomaniac; Koralin (*Alph*), a courageous cytologist who kidnaps and protects the first male baby born into the lesbian society in five hundred years; and Shirley Sye (*The Tide Went Out*), a pathetic and aging model turned fashion editor who instructs the hero on the nature of man when faced with survival.

Survival is one of Maine's recurring themes. Sometimes he treats it directly, as in *The Tide Went Out* and *The Darkest of Nights*, both post-disaster novels. In *The Tide Went Out* repeated hydrogen bomb tests produce a fracture in the ocean floor through which pours nearly all of the world's water supply; in *The Darkest of Nights a lethal epidemic destroys society. B. E. A. S. T.* projects the ultimate result of an animal evolved with survival of the fittest as the only standard: a brilliant but mentally unstable scientist, Charles Gilley, creates animals and an environment for them in a computer, then evolves them through millions of generations while making conditions harsher and harsher. Finally all but one species disappears and then all but one animal. It is the ultimate survivor but it has lost all humanistic qualities. *Alph* presents yet another variation on the nature of survival in its exploration of the long-range effects of a society without men. Lesbianism, of course, becomes the acceptable form of sexual expression, but it results in a patterned societal neurosis. An emphasis on superior eugenic standards causes an overthrow of the government because of the elitist attitudes it creates. Even in *Timeliner*, whose primary purpose is to explore time travel, Hugh Macklin, the hero, eventually raises the question of whose right it is to decide who should survive and what standards they should use. Inevitably, Maine proposes, man will do whatever is required in order to survive.

Another prevalent Maine theme is time displacement, which receives its fullest treatment in *Timeliner*. In it, he offers the unique prospect that man's "psycho-identity" but not his body can travel forward in time. Attracted by emotional affinities, the "psycho-identity" possesses other persons' bodies to achieve consciousness. Though it creates a kind of immortality for the traveler, it destroys the possessed's ego. One future society that Macklin encounters labels such time travelers "psycho-temporal parasites" and considers the possession a form of murder.

One of the more interesting aspects of Maine's writing is its projection of possible futures. Though *Alph, Timeliner*, and *He Owned the World*, for example, paint different pictures, they do contain some consistencies. Maine predicts that the historical pattern of man's genius being channeled into aggression and war will continue indefinitely. He also believes that romantic love will die out. In *He Owned the World* it is defined as "an obsessive form of compulsive neurosis," and one of the characters that Macklin encounters in *Timeliner* tells him that man is naturally polygamous. Finally, many of Maine's future societies are totalitarian and man continues to battle his oppressors.

Maine is a journeyman writer who has created some excellent novels, but even if he were far less skilled his ideas alone would make reading his works worth the effort.

—Carl B. Yoke

MAJORS, Simon. See **FOX, Gardner F.**

MALZBERG, Barry N(orman). Also writes as Mike Barry; Claudine Dumas; M. L. Johnson; Mel Johnson; Howard Lee; Lee W. Mason; Francine di Natale; K. M. O'Donnell; Gerrold Watkins. American. Born in New York City, 24 July 1939. Educated at Syracuse University, New York (Schubert Fellow, 1964-65), A.B. 1960. Married Joyce Nadine Zelnick in 1964; two daughters. Investigator, New York City Department of Welfare, and Reimbursement Agent, New York State Department of Mental Hygiene; Editor, Scott Meredith Literary Agency, New York; Editor, *Amazing* and *Fantastic*, 1968; Managing Editor, *Escapade*, 1968. Free-lance writer. Recipient: John W. Campbell Memorial Award, 1973; *Locus* award, 1983. Address: Box 61, Teaneck, New Jersey 07666, U.S.A.

SCIENCE-FICTION PUBLICATIONS

Novels

Oracle of the Thousand Hands. New York, Olympia Press, 1968.
The Falling Astronauts. New York, Ace, 1971; London, Arrow, 1975.
Overlay. New York, Lancer, 1972; London, New English Library, 1975.
Beyond Apollo. New York, Random House, 1972; London, Faber, 1974.
Revelations. New York, Warner, 1972.
The Men Inside. New York, Lancer, 1973; London, Arrow, 1976.
Phase IV. New York, Pocket Books, and London, Pan, 1973.
In the Enclosure. New York, Avon, 1973; London, Hale, 1976.
Herovit's World. New York, Random House, 1973; London, Arrow, 1976.
Guernica Night. Indianapolis, Bobbs Merrill, 1974; London, New English Library, 1978.
On a Planet Alien. New York, Pocket Books, 1974.
The Day of the Burning. New York, Ace, 1974.
Tactics of Conquest. New York, Pyramid, 1974.
The Sodom and Gomorrah Business. New York, Pocket Books, 1974; London, Arrow, 1979.
Underlay. New York, Avon, 1974.
The Destruction of the Temple. New York, Pocket Books, 1974; London, New English Library, 1975.
The Gamesman. New York, Pocket Books, 1975.
Conversations. Indianapolis, Bobbs Merrill, 1975.
Galaxies. New York, Pyramid, 1975.
Scop. New York, Pyramid, 1976.
The Last Transaction. Los Angeles, Pinnacle, 1977.
Chorale. New York, Doubleday, 1978.
The Cross of Fire. New York, Ace, 1982.
The Remaking of Sigmund Freud. New York, Ballantine, 1985.

Novels as K. M. O'Donnell

The Empty People. New York, Lancer, 1969.
Dwellers of the Deep. New York, Ace, 1970.
Universe Day. New York, Avon, 1971.
Gather in the Hall of the Planets. New York, Ace, 1971.

Short Stories

Final War and Other Fantasies (as K. M. O'Donnell). New York, Ace, 1969.
In the Pocket and Other S-F Stories. New York, Ace, 1971.
Out from Ganymede. New York, Warner, 1974.
The Many Worlds of Barry Malzberg. New York, Popular Library, 1975.

Down Here in the Dream Quarter. New York, Doubleday, 1976.
The Best of Barry N. Malzberg. New York, Pocket Books, 1976.
Malzberg at Large. New York, Ace, 1979.
The Man Who Loved the Midnight Lady. New York, Doubleday, 1980.

Uncollected Short Stories

"Re-Entry," in *Fantastic* (New York), February 1977.
"Shibboleth," in *Amazing* (New York), March 1977.
"Prowl," in *Fantastic* (New York), July 1978.
"Another Burnt-Out Case," in *Fantastic* (New York), October 1978.
"Out of Quarantine," with Bill Pronzini, in *Isaac Asimov's Science Fiction Magazine* (New York), November-December 1978.
"Clocks," with Bill Pronzini, in *Shadows 2,* edited by Charles L. Grant. New York, Doubleday, 1979.
"Nightshapes," in *Werewolf!,* edited by Bill Pronzini. New York, Arbor House, 1979.
"Demystification of Circumstance," in *Fantasy and Science Fiction* (New York), November 1979.
"La Croix," in *Their Immortal Hearts: Three Visions of Time.* Reno, Nevada, West Coast Poetry Review Press, 1980.
"Emily Dickinson—Saved from Drowning," in *Chrysalis 8,* edited by Roy Torgeson. New York, Doubleday, 1980.
"The Last One Left," in *Fantasy and Science Fiction* (New York), January 1980.
"The Lyran Case," with Bill Pronzini, in *Analog* (New York), March 1980.
"Parables of Art," with Jack Dann, in *New Dimensions 12,* edited by Robert Silverberg and Marta Randall. New York, Pocket Books, 1981.
"Calling Collect," in *Shadows 4,* edited by Charles L. Grant. New York, Doubleday, 1981.
"Do I Dare to Eat a Peach," with Bill Pronzini, in *Speculations,* edited by Isaac Asimov and Alice Laurance. Boston, Houghton Mifflin, 1982.
"Sigmund in Space," in *The Best of Omni Science Fiction 4,* edited by Ben Bova and Don Myrus. New York, Omni, 1982.
"Vanishing Point," with Bill Pronzini, in *Analog* (New York), 1 February 1982.
"Last Word," in *Omni* (New York), June 1982.
"Anderson," in *Amazing* (New York), June 1982.
"Blair House," in *Fantasy and Science Fiction* (New York), June 1982.
"Shakespeare MCMLXXXV," with Bill Pronzini, in *Fantasy and Science Fiction* (New York), November 1982.
"Corridors," in *The Nebula Awards 18,* edited by Robert Silverberg. New York, Arbor House, 1983.
"Coursing," in *Isaac Asimov's Aliens and Outworlders,* edited by Shawna McCarthy. New York, Davis, 1983.
"Icons," in *The Second Omni Book of Science Fiction,* edited by Ellen Datlow. New York, Zebra, 1983.
"What We Do on Io," in *Fantasy and Science Fiction* (New York), February 1983.
"Reparations," in *Fantasy and Science Fiction* (New York), August 1983.
"Bedside Manor," in *Fantasy and Science Fiction* (New York), November 1984.

OTHER PUBLICATIONS

Novels

I, Lesbian (as M. L. Johnson). New York, Midwood, 1968.

Screen. New York, Olympia Press, 1968; London, Olympia Press, 1972.
The Circle (as Francine di Natale). New York, Traveller's Companion, 1969.
Diary of a Parisian Chambermaid (as Claudine Dumas). New York, Midwood, 1969.
In My Parents' Bedroom. New York, Olympia Press, 1971.
Confessions of Westchester County. New York, Olympia Press, 1971; London, Olympia Press, 1972.
The Spread. New York, Belmont, 1971.
Horizontal Woman. New York, Leisure, 1972; as *The Social Worker,* 1977.
The Masochist. New York, Belmont, 1972; as *Everything Happened to Susan,* 1978.
The Way of the Tiger, The Sign of the Dragon (as Howard Lee). New York, Warner, 1973.
The Running of Beasts, with Bill Pronzini. New York, Putnam, 1976.
Lady of a Thousand Sorrows (as Lee W. Mason). Chicago, Playboy Press, 1977.
Acts of Mercy, with Bill Pronzini. New York, Putnam, 1977.
Night Screams, with Bill Pronzini. Chicago, Playboy Press, 1979.
Prose Bowl, with Bill Pronzini. New York, St. Martin's Press, 1980.

Novels as Mel Johnson

Love Doll. New York, Soft Cover Library, 1967.
Chained. New York, Midwood, 1968.
Instant Sex. New York, Midwood, 1968.
Just Ask. New York, Midwood, 1968.
Kiss and Run. New York, Midwood, 1968.
Nympho Nurse. New York, Midwood, 1969.
The Sadist. New York, Midwood, 1969.
Do It to Me. New York, Midwood, 1969.
Born to Give. New York, Midwood, 1969.
Campus Doll. New York, Midwood, 1969.
The Box. New York, Oracle, 1969.
A Way with All Maidens. New York, Oracle, 1969.

Novels as Gerrold Watkins

Southern Comfort. New York, Traveller's Companion, 1969.
A Satyr's Romance. New York, Traveller's Companion, 1970.
Giving It Away. New York, Traveller's Companion, 1970.
The Art of the Fugue. New York, Traveller's Companion, 1970.
A Bed of Money. New York, Traveller's Companion, 1970.

Novels as Mike Barry

Night Raider. New York, Berkley, 1973.
Bay Prowler. New York, Berkley, 1973.
Boston Avenger. New York, Berkley, 1973.
Desert Stalker. New York, Berkley, 1974.
Havana Hit. New York, Berkley, 1974.
Chicago Slaughter. New York, Berkley, 1974.
Peruvian Nightmare. New York, Berkley, 1974.
Los Angeles Holocaust. New York, Berkley, 1974.
Miami Marauder. New York, Berkley, 1974.
Harlem Showdown. New York, Berkley, 1975.
Detroit Massacre. New York, Berkley, 1975.
Phoenix Inferno. New York, Berkley, 1975.
The Killing Run. New York, Berkley, 1975.
Philadelphia Blowup. New York, Berkley, 1975.

Other

The Engines of the Night: Science Fiction in the Eighties. New York, Doubleday, 1982.

Editor, with Edward L. Ferman, *Final Stage.* New York, Charterhouse, 1974; London, Penguin, 1975.

Editor, with Edward L. Ferman, *Arena: Sports SF.* New York, Doubleday, and London, Robson, 1976.

Editor, with Edward L. Ferman, *Graven Images.* Nashville, Nelson, 1977.

Editor, with Bill Pronzini, *Dark Sins, Dark Dreams: Crimes in SF.* New York, Doubleday, 1977.

Editor, with Bill Pronzini, *The End of Summer: Science Fiction in the Fifties.* New York, Ace, 1979.

Editor, with Bill Pronzini, *Shared Tomorrows: Collaboration in SF.* New York, St. Martin's Press, 1979.

Editor, with Martin H. Greenberg and Joseph D. Olander, *Neglected Visions.* New York, Doubleday, 1980.

Editor, with Martin H. Greenberg, *The Science Fiction of Mark Clifton.* Carbondale, Southern Illinois University Press, 1980.

Editor, with Bill Pronzini, *Bug-Eyed Monsters.* New York, Harcourt Brace, 1980.

Editor, with Bill Pronzini and Martin H. Greenberg, *The Arbor House Treasury of Horror and the Supernatural [Mystery and Suspense].* New York, Arbor House, 2 vols., 1981.

Editor, with Martin H. Greenberg, *The Science Fiction of Kris Neville.* Carbondale, Southern Illinois University Press, 1984.

*   *   *

If what Barry N. Malzberg has called, in a typical turn of phrase, "the true and terrible complete history of science fiction" is ever written, Malzberg will occupy a unique niche within its carefully categorized confines, not least because his personal view of the field, *The Engines of the Night*, will have to be dealt with, somehow. Often vilified by authors and reviewers for attacking the very foundations of the genre as they perceive it; but equally, he has been praised, by such writers and critics as Harlan Ellison, Joanna Russ, and Brian Stableford, for attempting to do something new, and artistic, within the expanding, universe of genre conventions.

Malzberg's problem, and the reason perhaps that he quit the genre in 1975 after seven years of highly prolific creation (though he has continued to write *some* short stories and essays), is not that he was unable to use conventional SF props as powerful tropes by which to explore individuals' psychological anxiety, their feelings of alienation and inadequacy when they confront the machineries of technological change and bureaucratic stasis. In fact, in his best work he has polished to a high gloss the mirrored surfaces of many basic SF conventions so that their apparently *inherent* optimism reveals in reflection only its diabolic opposite. But because he did this so well he tended to alienate precisely the audience which his SF writings were meant to attract. But there has always been a place for apocalyptic visions in SF. The problem isn't that Malzberg wasn't read, but that so many of his readers could only turn away from his writings in disgust, saying he had betrayed them because he offered no hope in his stories, or making similar complaints.

In so attacking him these readers are wrong, in that they are ill-equipped to perceive the kind of limited hope or optimism expressed in the actions of Captain Lena Thomas in *Galaxies* or cool Sid in *Guernica Night,* who choose to live even in the face of complexities which are (almost) too great to bear. Cetainly the burden of his fictions is often terrifying, bleak: lost in a world they had no part in making (and over which the awful vision of assassination continually hovers—like so many of his generation, Malzberg was traumatized by the political murders of the 1960's, and they have become a *leit motif* in his work), Malzberg's people articulate their precise awareness of that fact, and of the other facts which batter at their defences. Malzberg's obsessions, and those of his characters, expose the dark underbelly of the science-fiction mythos to the terrible light of art. Humans as machines, not in hoped-for supremacy but in near-catatonic anomie, unable to touch one another, even in sex, except mechanically; assassination as a way of life; bureaucracy as a huge engine of human destruction; the horrors of confronting in outer space only the empty reflection of our inner spaces: these are the themes Malzberg explores with obsessive tenacity, entering one after another of Sf's favorite narrative conventions only to discover once more that for the human problems his characters have to deal with there are no easy answers, no *dei-ex-machinis* to lumber in at the end and save all. But this knowledge is not necessarily simply pessimistic. Herovit and his other selves utterly fail to adapt to the alien forces of New York, but others in Malzberg's "freak show" survive in the recognition that not only can they not find answers to their specific complaints but that very likely their problems do not have "answers" as such. So they adapt, they make compromises with reality, they go mad, they go sane, they try to be human (in itself the most heroic act Malzberg can conceive of in the aseptic environment of SF conventions). For Malzberg's characters the material of their reality is strangely impermeable, darkly opaque, and almost completely unmalleable. The universe is bigger, stronger, and more dangerous than they are; it also has a nasty sense of humour.

Indeed, comedy is something not often mentioned in connection with Malzberg yet he is one of the funniest writers in the genre, if you are able to laugh at the end of the world. For black humour, apocalyptic comedy, Lear's fool trying for a final tear-filled laugh, see Malzberg's collected works. If we didn't laugh we might break down and cry, and so might he. The tricks of rhetoric have their purpose, then, and Malzberg is a master of the ironic twist, the sick joke of metaphysics meeting physics head-on. Tone is always difficult, yet Malzberg continually manages such complex presentations of savage wit as this, in *Beyond Apollo: "A Brief History of the Universe:* The universe was invented by man in 1976 as a cheap and easy explanation for all his difficulties in conquering it." Foregrounding the many subtexts of the novel, this remark casts a shadow over not just Harry Evans's attempt to discover what happened to him on the disastrous Venus mission but also over all the stories of successful space imperialism. And yet I believe Malzberg when he says he loves science fiction, for it's obvious he recognizes and values the writing his own seems so fully to subvert. Such ambivalence of love and belief seem proper in a writer whose central subject is human ambivalence on every matter that matters. He only wanted to make room for his vision, *too*; not to replace the others but to provide some balance. And even if he has left the field he has left us a rich legacy of fictions whose integrity cannot be questioned. Of the novels, certainly *The Falling Astronauts, Overlay, Beyond Apollo, Herovit's World, Guernica Night, Scop, The Cross of Fire,* and that amazing analysis of the genre in the form of notes for a novel, *Galaxies,* need no apology. And there are a number of shorter works of equal value, as well as his *cri de coeur* analyses of the field. Although many find his vision not only too dark but too narrow, no one can deny the depth of the chasm his works have cut through contemporary SF.

—Douglas Barbour

MANN, (Anthony) Phillip. British. Born in Northallerton, Yorkshire, 7 August 1942. Educated at Scarborough College, 1954-62; Manchester University,1962-66, B. A. in English and drama 1966; Humboldt State University, Arcata, California, 1966-69, M. A. 1969. Married Nonnita Margaret Rees in 1967; one daughter and one son. Lecturer in Drama, Humboldt State University, 1967-69. Lecturer, 1969-75, and since 1975, Senior Lecturer in Drama, Victoria University, Wellington, New Zealand. English editor, Xin Hua News Agency, Beijing, 1978-80. Since 1984, Associate Artistic Director, Downstage Theatre, Wellington. Agent (plays): Playmarket, P. O. Box 9707, Wellington. Address: 22 Bruce Avenue, Brooklyn, Wellington, New Zealand.

SCIENCE-FICTION PUBLICATIONS

Novels

The Eye of the Queen. London, Gollancz, 1982; New York, Arbor House, 1983.
Ben's Bed (for children). Wellington, Mallinson Rendel, 1985.

Uncollected Short Stories

Radio Stories: *The West That Never Was* series, 1973; *Games of Power* series, 1975; *Coming of Age in t' North* series, 1977; *The Gospel According to Mickey Mouse*, 1977; and others.

OTHER PUBLICATIONS

Plays

Il suffit d'un baton, in *Avant-Scène* (Paris), 1977.
Revenge at Ditchwater Creek (produced Wellington, 1977).
The Animal Maker (for children) (produced Wellington, 1978).
The Thunderbird (for children)(produced Wellington, 1982).
The Bach in the Bush (for children)(produced Wellington, 1984).

Radio Play: *The Monument*, 1977.

*

Phillip Mann comments:

I began writing when I was in my teens. Like many young writers I had ideas of becoming a poet but found that my verse slipped easily into doggerel, bawdy lyrics, and satire. I also found that I had a knack for dialogue but this never really extended itself into full-length plays, though I would still like to write for the theatre. I started to write short stories and found this most satisfying. I read science fiction from an early age and grew up on a diet of Wells, Verne, and Rider Haggard as well as Thomas Mann, Billy Bunter tales, and stories about the sea. A combination of the fantastic and the logical appeals to me. I write to entertain. I want to write good yarns that involve the reader and yield the same satisfaction as a good meal. I am convinced there is life in a multitude of forms evolving in the wider galaxy and that our next major development will take place when we manage to break or circumvent the space-time barrier. Aliens and alien ceremonies intrigue me as do the creative faculties in mankind. Science fiction seems to me an excellent forum in which we can debate and prepare for the future.

* * *

With *The Eye of the Queen* Phillip Mann entered the world of science fiction in a way calculated to stretch the minds and imagination of tyros and aficionados alike. For this first novel Mann chose a stock situation:alien contact. When a strange spacecraft appears and hovers some four inches above the Utah salt flats, its presence sets off predictable reactions: confusion, fear, an ill-fated attempt at defence against the unknown. At this point a reader may expect the usual adventure complete with space wars or at least space derring-do in answer to the implied question: what will happen when aliens initiate contact with Earth?

Mann's answer, however, comes in an unexpected and unique form. When contact become reciprocal, a two-member team from Earth's Contact Linguistics Institute receives the assigment to return with the aliens, study their culture, and establish a common ground for co-existance. In Mann's presentation of the team's findings the reader discovers an inner dynamic working to forward and dramatize the novel's ideas.

Once the tradition-bound reader foregoes reliance on conventional chapter divisions and gives himself up to the author's arrangement, he experiences a situation such as that epitomized by Robert Frost in the couplet/poem, "The Secret Sits. " The reader becomes a shodowy third partner of the team, "circling " the Pe-Ellian world, probing for information. In both sections, the Diary and the Commentary, Mann interweaves data gathered by standard research techniques employed in a case study: direct observation, encoded interviews and brief autobiographies of various aliens, transcriptions of casual conversations, physical descriptions, linguistic analysis, botanical and biological data, cultural analysis of various areas such as social life, living conditions, esthetic artifacts and the like. As data accumulates, the fiction team and the reader, like the voice in Frost's poem, can only "suppose," until the aliens in the center begin to give up the secret of what they "know. "

In *The Eye of the Queen* Mann presents an alien stock made all the more believable by its utter physical alienness, an alienness that is intensified by the epithetic names so evocative of human experience and emotion. Albeit unspoiled by anthropomorphism so often employed in science fiction, the aliens do share attributes of many sentient creatures we know, along with the art of the language and thought with humans. While they impress a reader with a sense of commonality with all living forms, there is also a sense of transcendence, arising from what the researchers' *Contact Linguistics Handbook* terms "the sense of structure. " The Pe-Ellian sense of structure recognizes existence and balance of personal and cosmic biospheres and psychospheres, the latter supported by belief in the vitality of thought. Thought is alive. Thought becomes dangerous, if undisciplined or belligerent. Thought can regenerate, if understood, shared, and directed. When the implications of the power of misused thought becomes part of what the major researcher comes to "know," he moves from scientific objectivity to complete subjectivity.

Utilizing the Diary-Commentary format, Mann dramatizes this shift of perspective to particularly effective ends. Compiled by the major researcher, self-admittedly estranged from himself by a lifelong dedication and discipline to objectivity, the Diary charts both the progress of the scientific analysis of the aliens and the ever-increasing self-analysis. In the process author Mann succeeds in turning his main character into an Everyman, forcing the reader to make comparable analyses. Written *ex post facto,* based on memory, and supported by notes and records, the Commentary provides an alternate, sometimes antithetical, perspective on events. More important for Mann's theme, the Commentary provides a reader with a sympathetic angle from which to judge the personal conclusions of the diarist. Without belaboring the point in the novel Mann leads his readers toward assessment of the contemporary human use of that virile entity, thought. It is a speculation vital to our continuation as honorable residents of the cosmos.

—Hazel Pierce

MANN, Laurence (Edward). American. Born in St. John, New Brunswick, Canada, in 1899; emigrated to the United States after World War I. Educated at King's College, Halifax, Nova Scotia, B. C. L. 1919. Served in the Royal Canadian Air Force: Lieutenant. Married Edith B. Manning in 1928; two daughters and one son. Newspaper reporter in St. John, then writer for the Florists Exchange, Philadelphia, in the early 1920's; Manager, 1923-32, President, 1933-52, and Owner, 1952-66, Kelsey Nursery Service, New York. Fellow, American Rocket Society, 1960. *Died in 1972.*

SCIENCE-FICTION PUBLICATIONS

Novel

The Man Who Awoke. New York, Ballantine, 1975; London, Sphere, 1977.

Uncollected Short Stories (series: Stranger Club)

"The Voyage of the Asteroid," in *Wonder Stories* (New York), Summer 1932.
"The Wreck of the Asteroid," in *Wonder Stories* (New York), December 1932.
"The Call of the Mech-Men" (Club), in *Wonder Stories* (New York), November 1933.
"Caverns of Horror" (Club), in *Wonder Stories* (New York), March 1934.
"Voice of Atlantis" (Club), in *Wonder Stories* (New York), July 1934.
"The Moth Message" (Club), in *Wonder Stories* (New York), December 1934.
"The Prophetic Voice," in *Wonder Stories* (New York), April 1935.
"Seeds from Space" (Club), in *Wonder Stories* (New York), June 1935.
"World of the Mist," in *Wonder Stories* (New York), September 1935.
"Expedition to Pluto," with Fletcher Pratt, in *Planet* (New York), Winter 1939.
"The City of the Living Dead," with Fletcher Pratt, in *Avon Fantasy Reader 2,* edited by Donald A. Wollheim. New York, Avon, 1947.
"The Living Galaxy," in *The Science Fiction Galaxy,* edited by Groff Conklin. New York, Permabooks, 1950.
"Good-Bye, Ilha," in *Beyond Human Ken,* edited by Judith Merril. New York, Random House, 1952.

"Men on Mars," in *Fantastic Story* (New York), Spring 1952.
"Mr. Mottle Goes Poof," in *Fantasy Fiction* (New York), August 1953.

OTHER PUBLICATIONS

Other

The How and Why of Better Gardening. New York, Van Nostrand, 1951.

* * *

Laurence Manning is remembered primarily for a series of five stories originally published in 1933, later collected in book form as *The Man Who Awoke.* Manning utilized a classic device of science-fiction and Utopian writers, a man from our own culture transported in some fashion to another society, which is then revealed to the reader as the protagonist encounters individuals and institutions. In each of the five episodes, Norman Winters arises from suspended animation to investigate the state of humanity as it advances toward its ultimate destiny.

In the title story, Winters explores the world of the year 5000. Humankind dwells within vast managed forests, in balance with nature, looking back with horror on "the false civilization of Waste!" Seeking to find a place for himself in this new world, Winters attempts to convince his hosts that his own time did have positive aspects for which they should be thankful. But even the most sympathetic of his listeners feel no gratitude. "For exhausting the coal supplies of the world? For leaving us no petroleum for our chemical factories?" Ultimately finding this new society as flawed as the old, Winters sleeps another 5000 years and revives in "Master of the Brain. " Now he encounters humanity subservient to a computer that makes all the decisions, the race having abdicated the responsibility for their own future. After being instrumental in breaking the grip of the Brain, Winters advances to the year 15000 in "The City of Sleep." Once more he is disappointed, for now the great majority of people spend their entire lives in mechanically induced dreams, as idea developed from Manning's first story, "The City of the Living Dead," written with Fletcher Pratt. This willing renunciation of reality has recurred within the genre many times, most notably in James Gunn's *The Joy Makers.* The best story in the series is "The Individualists," wherein Winters becomes the quarry of a number of egocentric geniuses in a society that places no value on interpersonal relationships. Winters's journey ends with "The Elixir," the source of immortality which produces an interstellar community. Although not specifically within the series, Manning wrote another tale set eons after the Manning saga, "The Living Galaxy," which postulated that entire stellar systems functioned as single atoms in a higher order universe we could not perceive.

Less ambitious in scope was a second series which recounted the adventures of severl members of the Stranger Club. Manning's dislike of automation recurs in "The Call of the Mech-Men," a secret cabal of living machines. His concern about our profligate consumption of natural resources, anticipating our present worries, is repeated in "Voice of Atlantis," in which a device allows communication with an ancient Atlantean. The remaining three stories were more pedestrian and reflected the type of story that dominated the genre in the 1930's. A lost world of prehistoric monsters lies under New York in "Caverns of Horror," a forgotten Atlantean colony is located in "The Moth Message," and a species of sentient, ambient tree is thwarted in its invasion plan in "Seeds from Space."

Manning's fiction, much of which seems quite dated now, was advanced for its time. He produced a series of very accurate—insofar as the state of the art allowed—stories of space travel. His concerns for conservation and human dignity elevated his fiction above that of most of his peers.

—Don D'Ammassa

———————

MARAS, Karl. See **BULMER, Kenneth.**

———————

MARLOWE, Webb. See **McCOMAS, J. Francis.**

———————

MARSTEN, Richard. See **HUNTER, Evan.**

———————

MARTIN, George R(aymond) R(ichard). American. Born in Bayonne, New Jersey, 20 September 1948. Educated at Medill School of Journalism, Northwestern University, Evanston, Illinois, B. S. 1970, M. S. 1971. Served with the Cook County Legal Assistance Foundation, for Vista, Chicago, 1972-74. Married Gale Burnick in 1975 (divorced, 1979). Chess tournament director, Continental Chess Association, Mount Vernon, New York, 1973-75; journalism instructor, Clarke College, Dubuque, Iowa, 1976-78. Since 1978; free-lance writer. Recipient: Hugo Award, 1975, 1980 (2 awards); Bread Loaf Writers Conference Fellowship, 1977; Nebula Award, 1979; *Locus* award, 1981, 1982 (twice), 1984. Agent: Spectrum Literary Agency, 432 Park Avenue South, Suite 1205, New York, New York 10016. Address: 102 San Salvador, Santa Fe, New Mexico 87501, U.S.A.

SCIENCE-FICTION PUBLICATIONS

Novels

Dying of the Light. New York, Simon and Schuster, 1977; London, Gollancz, 1978.
Windhaven, with Lisa Tuttle. New York, Pocket Books, 1981; London, New English Library, 1982.
Fevre Dream. New York, Pocket Books, 1982; London, Gollancz, 1983.
The Armageddon Rag. New York, Pocket Books, 1983; London, New English Library, 1985.

Short Stories

A Song for Lya and Other Stories. New York, Avon, 1976; London, Coronet, 1978.
Songs of Stars and Shadows. New York, Pocket Books, 1977.

Sandkings. New York, Pocket Books, 1981; London, Futura, 1983.
Songs the Dead Men Sing. Niles, Illinois, Dark Harvest, 1983; London, Gollancz, 1985.
Nightflyers. New York, Bluejay, 1985.

Uncollected Short Stories

"A Peripheral Affair," in *Fantasy and Science Fiction* (New York), January 1973.
"The Last Super Bowl," in *Gallery* (New York), February 1975.
"The Computer Cried Charge," in *Amazing* (New York), January 1976.
"Nobody Leaves New Pittsburg," in *Amazing* (New York), September 1976.
"Warship," with George Florance-Gutheridge, in *Fantasy and Science Fiction* (New York), April 1979.
"In the Lost Lands," in *Amazons 2,* edited by Jessica Salmonson. New York, DAW, 1982.
"Unsound Variations," in *Pawn to Infinity,* edited by Fred Saberhagen and Jean Saberhagen. New York, Ace, 1982.
"Closing Time," in *Isaac Asimov's Science Fiction Magazine* (New York), November 1982.
"The Ice Dragons," in *Dragons of Light,* edited by Orson Scott Card. New York, Ace, 1983.
"Portraits of His Children," in *Isaac Asimov's Science Fiction Magazine* (New York), November 1985.

OTHER PUBLICATIONS

Other

Editor, *New Voices in Science Fiction 1-4.* New York, Macmillan, 1 vol., 1977; New York, Harcourt Brace, 1 vol., 1979; New York, Berkley, 2 vols., 1980-81.
Editor, with Isaac Asimov and Martin H. Greenberg, *The Science Fiction Weight-Loss Book.* New York, Crown, 1983.
Editor, *The John W. Campbell Awards 5.* New York, Bluejay, 1984.

*   *   *

To read the works of George R. R. Martin is to tumble slowly, steadily from one highly imaginative situation to another, all tightly controlled by the author. Martin's stories vary in style from the futuristic fantasy of his first novel, *Dying of the Light,* to the realistic—but still castled—environment of *Sandkings,* a Hugo Award-winning novelette that will cause the reader to think seriously before buying another pet.

A Song for Lya (also a Hugo winner) gives the reader an unusual look at religion. The Joined, in this story, are believers in a cult in which parasites called Greeshka attach themselves to the skulls of their "converts" and consume them, literally. This union, however horrible to the viewer, is ecstatic to the convert, who feels peaceful and loved—*in* love with everyone he meets. Although it is not unusual to see religion as a desperate search for the love that man seeks constantly and often futilely in this life, it is different—and somewhat frightening—to realize, with the heroine, how alone each of us finally is, despite great efforts to know and love others. In the end we must admit, sadly, with Lya and Robb, her lover, that we cannot really know another person as we would like, but that we must also keep trying to do so.

Martin edited *New Voices in Science Fiction,* a series that included one of his own stories, "Stone City." Its setting is a harsh other-world called Grayrest, a fringe planet that contains the stone city. The protagonist Holt is an exile here, a "stranger in a strange land," as are many of Martin's main characters. He landed with his shipmates earlier, and for some reason that is not quite clear but has to do with the fact that "the rules don't work down here," has not been able to leave. The key to the riddle seems to lie in the stone city, a mysterious labyrinth into which many desperate people, including some of Holt's shipmates, descend and never return. Holt's escape there, when he kills an official in fury after being denied exit once again, gains him access to the universe; but it is a questionable "salvation," eerie and lonely—despite a horde of fellow-wanderers who move eternally with him through the stone city's endless tunnels.

Dying of the Light is a romantic tale of Dirk t'Larien, an alien on the rogue planet Worlorn, an isolated, wandering world that is entering a cycle of darkness for an unknown period of time. T'Larien has come here in answer to a call from Gwen, his former lover, who lives there as a "heldwife" but is no more at home than t'Larien since the practice on Worlorn is to share a heldwife with one's "teyn," a man's *real* best friend. Other practices in this feudalistic, futuristic culture include dueling to uphold one's honor and releasing an enemy in the forest, then chasing him to death, as one does a lower animal. The theme of tradition, which occurs in other Martin stories, causes the reader to examine his own cultural values and ask if our current socio-sexual patterns are very unlike those of Worlorn. And if they are not, maybe it is because, essentially, we like matters they way they are.

"The Way of Cross and Dragon" again pursues the problem of religion and its purpose in modern culture, whether it is supposed to make us happy or provide us with truth that is often hard to live by. The humor and irony with which Martin approaches this usually serious topic is refreshing, allowing the reader to achieve a new perspective on a familiar theme. *Sandkings* (Hugo Award) is quite different from Martin's previous tales. It is a horror story that takes a serious look at modern man, with his penchant for self-indulgence at the expense of others and, perhaps, the entire world. The sandkings, insect-like "pets" with psi powers, first see their "owner," Simon Kress, as a god, but later come to hate him for his cruelty and selfishness. Nevertheless, the new breed of sandking, which is emerging toward the end of the novelette, is recreating itself in Kress's image, and we are left to imagine the fearful result.

In *Windhaven*, a novel written by Martin in collaboration with Lisa Tuttle, men and women strive once more to know and love one another against cultural odds that seem always to place them in positions of antagonism. Maris, one of several strong women who crop up in Martin's works, is a heroine with mixed human qualities that make her especially likeable—and vulnerable. As a "flyer" of Windhaven, a storm-ridden world of the future that requires artificially winged messengers to maintain its communications, she rebels against an outmoded tradition that prevents the best people from becoming flyers. Eventually she establishes an academy to train skilled flyers in a new tradition and learns that education does not solve all problems. Maris does, however, find a true, equal love, an unusual situation for a Martin hero-heroine, who is usually left in an ambiguous situation with a lover of great willingness but not much expertise in equal-opportunity relationships. Evan, a "healer" who cures Maris after she has a serious flying accident, is the perfect partner, strong but flexible and sensitive; and we rejoice with him and Maris in their mature—even old-fashioned—love in a futuristic context that allows both lovers to grow within the limits of their human strengths and weaknesses.

The strength of Martin's stories lies in his human, believable characters as well as in his interesting, well-paced plots. The reader, caught up in the strangely familiar religious and cultural problems of protagonists like Maris and Evan, moves with them towards solutions that will, hopefully, be his also. And Martin's concern for the lonely, sad worlds in his universe parallels his sympathetic treatment of their inhabitants. Worlorn and Grayrest are harsh places, worlds that test the strength and character of their peoples; but they also bring about a new species of human, one who has overcome the difficulties of life and arrived at new understandings. Although the future of his worlds is questionable—and sometimes frightening, as in *Sandkings*—we do not fear for Martin's characters—or for ourselves. We will find strength when we need it.

—Rose Flores Harris

MARTYN, Phillip. See **TUBB, E. C.**

MASON, Douglas R. See **RANKINE, John.**

MASON, John. See **TUBB, E. C.**

MASSON, David I(rvine). British. Born in Edinburgh, 6 November 1951. Educated at Oundle School, Northamptonshire, 1929-34; Merton College, Oxford, B.A. (honours) in English 1937, M. A. 1941. Served in thge Royal Army Medical Corps, 1940-45. Married Olive Masson in 1950;one daughter. Assistant Librarian, University of Leeds, 1938-40, and University of Liverpool, 1945-55; Sub-Librarian, in charge of Brotherton Collection, University of Leeds, 1956-79. Address: c/o Faber and Faber Ltd., 3 Queen Square, London WCIN 3AU, England.

SCIENCE-FICTION PUBLICATIONS

Short Stories

The Caltraps of Time. London, Faber, 1968.

Uncollected Short Stories

"The Show Must Go On," in *The Disappearing Future,* edited by George Hay. London, Panther, 1970.
"Take It or Leave It,"in *The Year 2000,* edited by Harry Harrison. New York, Doubleday, 1970; London, Faber, 1971.
"Doctor Fausta," in *Stop Watch,* edited by George Hay. London, New English Library, 1947.

OTHER PUBLICATIONS

Other

Hand-List of Incunabula in the University Library, Liverpool.

Privately printed, 1948; supplement, 1955.

Catalogue of the Romany Collection... University of Leeds. Edinburgh, Nelson, 1962.

Poetic Sound-Patterning Reconsidered. Leeds, Philosophical and Literary Society, 1976.

"The Light of Imagination," in *Foundation 10* (London), June 1976.

*

David I. Masson comments:

My SF, although it seeks "scientific" versimilitude and tries to "convince," has little to do with the processes of science. It explores bizarre assumptions for the sake—or so it seems to me—of mythopoeia, fable, satire, ridicule, scorn, or indignation, and perhaps inner truth about experience and feeling. Only "Take It or Leave It" has much to do with possible futures. Several stories reflect my conviction that the human race is insane. (Here and there one notes hopeful signs of some insight into its own condition.)

* * *

David I. Masson's SF reputation rests upon a handful of stories, most of them collected in *The Caltraps of Time.* A lively if recondite wit is a characteristic of these stories. A unversity antiquariun librarian, fascinated by linguistics, Masson plummets a Restoration gentlman into the 20th century courtesy of a borrowed time machine in "The Two Timer," to be amazed and bemused by our antics—and of course to satrize us in approved Swiftian manner. The impeccable late 17th-century prose style of this story throws into contrast our barbaric contemporary parlance: "Myself: *Prithee, Sir, do you converse in* English? At this he frown'd, and turn'd back thro' his Door, but left it open, for I heard him in speech with another, as follows. He... *Now enthing bauootim? Caun honstan zaklay wottee sez,"* Matters are just as bad for a researcher of the 1980's plunged into the 24th century by a linear accelerator accident in "The Transfinite Choice"("Namplize. " "Don't you speak English, then? Who the hell are you?" "Namplize"). It seems as though one is sliding down a cultural entropy slope. This future, in technotelegraphize, is trying, however, to master the gradient of time at the sub-particle level. Reality fractures as the future tries to shunt its excess population into parallel time-continua; or was it only, after all, the stricken researcher's reality that fell apart?

The finest of Masson's stories. "Traveller's Rest," deals with time yet again, apocalyptically yet ironically. The country at war in this story is distorted by differential time: whole decades pass in the peaceful south while mere minutes pass at the northern battle frontier where, perhaps, the army is simply fighting itself in the mirror of bent time with mounting frenzy and destructiveness—a powerful nightmare which does for exponential time what Christopher Priest's novel *Inverted World* was later to do for exponential space. In "Not So Certian" an expedition to an alien planet falls foul of the natives' tricky phonemes, another linguistic *jeu d'esprit,* while in "Mouth of Hell" apocalyptic topography confronts the explorers in the form of a 40-kilometre-deep cleft down to the molten magma which, by the end of the story, is tamed and demystified just as so much of our world has been banalised.

In Masson's loving care for language and concern with time one senses a scholarly resentment at the downhill slide of the world into some future mass point of condensed people and words and moments.

—Ian Watson

MATHESON, Richard (Burton). American. Born in Allendale, New Jersey, 20 February 1926. Educated at the University of Missouri, Columbia, Bachelor of Journalism 1949. Served in the 87th Division of the United States Army during World War II. Married Ruth Ann Woodson in 1952; two daughters and two sons. Freelance writer: script editor, *Circle of Fear* TV series. Recipient: Hugo Award, for screenplay, 1958; Writers Guild of America Award, for television writing, 1960, 1974; World Fantasy Award, 1976, and Life Achievement Award, 1984. Guest of Honor, 16th World Science Fiction Convention, 1958. Agent: Don Congdon Associates, 177 East 70th Street, New York, New York 10021. Address: P. O. Box 81, Woodland Hills, California 91365, U.S.A.

SCIENCE-FICTION PUBLICATIONS

Novels

I Am Legend. New York, Fawcett, 1954; London, Corgi, 1956; as *The Omega Man,* New York, Berkley, 1971.

The Shrinking Man. New York, Fawcett, and London, Muller, 1956.

Short Stories

Born of Man and Woman. Philadelphia, Chamberlain Press, 1954; abridged edition, London, Reinhardt, 1956; abridged edition, as *Third from the Sun,* New York, Bantam, 1955.

The Shores of Space. New York, Bantam, 1957; London, Corgi, 1958.

Shock! New York, Dell, 1961; London, Corgi, 1962.

Shock II. New York, Dell, 1964; London, Corgi, 1965.

Shock III. New York, Dell, 1966; London, Corgi, 1967.

Shock Waves. New York, Dell, 1970.

Shock 4. London, Sphere, 1980.

OTHER PUBLICATIONS

Novels

Someone Is Bleeding. New York, Lion, 1953.

Fury on Sunday. New York, Lion, 1953.

A Stir of Echoes. Philadelphia, Lippincott, and London, Cassell, 1958.

Ride the Nightmare. New York, Ballantine, 1959; London, Consul, 1961.

The Beardless Warriors. Boston, Little Brown, 1960; London, Heinemann, 1961.

Hell House. New York, Viking Press, 1971; London, Corgi, 1973.

Bid Time Return. New York, Viking Press, 1975; London, Sphere, 1977.

What Dreams May Come. New York, Putnam, 1978; London, Joseph, 1979.

Plays

Screenplays: *The Incredible Shrinking Man,* 1957; *The Beat Generation* (*This Rebel Age*), with Lewis Meltzer, 1959; *The House of Usher* (*The Fall of the House of Usher*), 1960; *Master of the World,* 1961; *The Pit and the Pendulum,* 1961; *Tales of Terror,* 1962; *Burn, Witch, Burn* (*Night of the Eagle*), with Charles Beaumont and George Baxt, 1962; *The Raven,* 1963; *The Comedy of Terrors,* 1964; *The Last Man on Earth* (pseudonymous co-writer), 1964; *Die! Die! My Darling!*

(*Fanatic*), 1965; *The Young Warriors*, 1967; *The Devil Rides Out* (*The Devil's Bride*), 1968; *De Sade*, 1969; *The Legend of Hell House*, 1973; *Somewhere in Time*, 1980; *The Twilight Zone*, with others, 1983; *Jaws 3-D*, with Carl Gottlieb and Guerdon Trueblood, 1983.

Television Plays: *Yawkey* (*Lawman* series), 1959; *And When the Sky Was Opened, Third from the Sun, The Last Flight, A World of Difference, A World of His Own, Nick of Time, The Invaders, Once upon a Time, Little Girl Lost, Young Man's Fancy, Steel, Nightmare at 20,000 Feet, Night Call*, and *Spur of the Moment* (all in *Twilight Zone* series), 1959-63; *The Return of Andrew Bentley* (*Thriller* series), 1960-61; *The Enemy Within* (*Star Trek* series), 1966; *Duel*, 1971; *The Night Stalker*, 1971; *The Night Strangler*, 1972; *Dying Room Only*, 1973; *The Stranger Within*, 1974; *Dracula*, 1974; *Scream of the Wolf*, 1974; *The Morning After*, 1974; *Amelia* (in *Trilogy of Terror*), 1975; *Dead of Night*, 1977; *The Strange Possession of Mrs. Oliver*, 1977; *The Martian Chronicles*, from the novel by Ray Bradbury, 1979; and scripts for *Chrysler Playhouse, Alfred Hitchcock Hour, The Girl from U. N. C. L. E., Have Gun—Will Travel, Wanted Dead or Alive, Night Gallery, The D. A.'s Man, Cheyenne, Bourbon Street Beat, Philip Marlowe, Buckskin, Markham*, and *Richard Diamond* series.

*   *   *

As a writer of short fiction which is mostly a hybrid of fantasy and SF, Richard Matheson should be compared with Henry Kuttner and Theodore Sturgeon, both obvious influences, and with later writers like Ellison and Delany who share important similarities of style and angles of vision. Although Matheson's short stories are not easily reduced to a simple classification, most of them explore the psychological impact of sudden discontinuity in the lives of otherwise rather ordinary characters. The stories range from the weird horror of "Long Distance Call," a graveyard variant of the radio drama and movie *Sorry, Wrong Number* (Lucille Fletcher), to the ironic humor of "Legion of Plotters," a tale literally fulfilling the commonplace paranoia that everyone's plotting against us. His ironic sense brings Matheson close to a mode of the fantastic that modern readers associate with Fritz Leiber and Fredric Brown. The very titles of some of his stories, "A Flourish of Strumpets," "'Tis the Season to Be Jelly," "When the Waker Sleeps," and "Witch War," are indicative of the varieties of comic irony and parody that constitute one of Matheson's three distinctive styles as a writer.

Matheson published most of short fiction in the 1950's. It was during this decade that he also wrote the two novels on which his reputation as a science-fiction master depends. *I Am Legend* and *The Shrinking Man* are built on fantastic premises that are developed experimentally in the spirit of scientific curiosity. Each is also a story of individual courage, physical as well as psychological, trial, and suspense. Each might be described as a fantastic science-fiction horror story. Of the two, *I Am Legend*, clearly the better story, belongs in the tradition of great vampire novels somewhere between Bram Stoker's *Dracula* and Ann Rice's *Interview with the Vampire*. It is more scientific than either, but it shares some of the mythic power of the former and philosophical interests of the latter. The hero, Robert Neville, finds himself the last human alive following a plague that either kills outright or transforms the survivors into vampires. His struggle against his twin enemies, the vampires and his own isolation, is never successfully resolved; and in Neville's failure to win through by courage and single-minded determination lies the special achievement of this novel. Matheson avoids the cliché triumphalism that was practically a genre characteristic in

the 1950's in favor of a more thoughtful and artistic denouement. A mutated strain of vampire emerges to establish a new order in which Neville has no place except that of a Nemesis who will pass into the legends of an emerging culture. Although much is inevitably sacrificed to the requirements of suspense melodrama and the sense of terror generated by the specter of personal violation, Matheson makes a stunning success of impressing on the reader the strength of Neville's character, the reasonableness of his reactions to his predicament, and the limitations inherent in both his virtues and in his responses to the challenges the vampires make to his survival as *homo sapiens* rather than as *homo vampiris*. The novel is, therefore, as much a challenge to certain conventional assumptions of the genre of the necessary survival of the species as the highest good as it is to the reader's expectations for the conventional, inevitable triumph of the resourceful hero.

The title of *The Shrinking Man* tells much of the basic idea of the story, except for the working out of the unique sequence of accidents that set in motion Scott's irreversible and apparently endless shrinking process and its consequences. Matheson's flashback inserts detailing the physical and emotional effects of Scott's diminishing stature contrast effectively with the suspense adventure of his warfare in the basement of his house against a black widow spider and his struggle to survive in a miniature state. It is altogether a tour de force for the author who manages to keep the reader bound to the terrifying fate of the hero and his increasing isolation from the familiar, domestic world from which he literally disappears. The theme of Scott's alienation from his wife and child, the psychological impact of his bizarre affliction, and his struggle for self-mastery and identity are powerfully drawn. Scott's sexual frustration is perhaps less subtly managed and is less symbolically meaningful than it is in *I Am Legend*, but then there is less ambiguity to the character of Scott than Neville. There are two or three splendid moments in the novel worthy of Sturgeon or Kuttner. Each moment is an epiphany of sorts in which Scott finds significance and purpose in his incredible life experience as a shrinking man, and each is an existential revelation on that account. He comes to a critical realization in the arms of Clarisse, a carnival midget, that his identity as a man does not depend on his physical stature. In fighting the spider, he realizes that he is opposing symbolically also those irrational, destructive forces in nature to which he refuses to become victim; and finally, having preserved himself against all odds, he is admitted into a new, molecular universe that science and science fiction have taught us exists below the level of appearances. If the novel vindicates Scott's existential courage, it is at least no easy vindication; and it is a triumph the reader is disposed gratefully to accept, even at the level of fantasy.

Matheson continued to write SF but at a diminished pace in the 1960's. His most recent novels are memorable works of romantic fantasy, indicating perhaps a new direction to his interests as a writer. *Bid Time Return* and *What Dreams May Come* deal in a bittersweet way with romantic love that bridges the gulf separating lovers of different eras, finally separated by time and death but united in spirit. The recent reissue of Matheson's collected stories is an indication of both the continuing popularity and influence of Matheson as a writer of fantasy science fiction.

—Donald L. Lawler

———————

MAY, Julian. American. Born in Chicago, Illinois, 10 July 1931.

Attended Rosary College, River Forest, Illinois, 1949-53. Married Thaddeus (Ted) E. Dikty in 1953; two sons and one daughter. Editor, Booz Allen & Hamilton, Chicago; Editor, Consolidated Book Publishers, Chicago, 1954-57; Founder, with Ted Dikty, Publication Associates, in Chicago, 1957-68, Naperville, Illinois, 1968-74, West Linn, Oregon, 1974-80, and since 1980 in Mercer Island, Washington. Free-lance writer: has published almost 300 non-fiction works, mainly for children. Recipient: *Locus* award, 1982. Address: P. O. Box 851, Mercer Island, Washington 98040, U.S.A.

SCIENCE-FICTION PUBLICATIONS

Novels (series: Pliocene Exile in all books)

The Saga of Pliocene Exile:
1. *The Many-Colored Land.* Boston, Houghton Mifflin, 1981; London, Pan, 1982.
2. *The Golden Torc.* Boston, Houghton Mifflin, 1981; London, Pan, 1982.
3. *The Nonborn King.* Boston, Houghton Mifflin, and London, Pan, 1983.
4. *The Adversary.* Boston, Houghton Mifflin, and London, Pan, 1984.

Uncollected Short Stories

"Dune Roller," in *Imagination Unlimited,* edited by T. E. Bleiler and T. E. Dikty. New York, Farrar Straus, 1952.
"Star of Wonder," in *Every Boy's Book of Outer Space Stories,* edited by T. E. Dikty. New York, Fell, 1960.

OTHER PUBLICATIONS

Other

A Pliocene Companion. Boston, Houghton Mifflin, 1984; London, Pan, 1985.

*

Bibliography: *The Work of Julian May: An Annotated Bibliograpny and Guide* by T. E. Dikty and R. Reginald, San Bernardino, California, Borgo Press, 1985.

Julian May comments:

My books are in the tradition of the classic literate thriller. They are intricately plotted and feature a large cast of characters romping through a "future history" and a "past history." In spite of the fantastic imagery, my books are genuine science fiction—not heroic fantasy. The four Pliocene books form one enormous novel, gaudy and humorous and melodramatic.

*   *   *

When *The Many-Colored Land* appeared in 1981, fans propelled Julian May into the foremost ranks of fantasy SF writers. As the wife of editor Ted Dikty, a long-time fan, and writer of at least one story successful enough to be reprinted and made into a movie, May has long had strong ties to SF. From the maverick scientist and competent but given-to-fainting girl friend meet dangerous stranded alien plot of "Dune Roller" May moved into the successful genre of the epic world outside of the Tolkien variety, utilizing the myths of many lands and ages.

The Many-Colored Land, The Golden Torc, The Nonborn King, and *The Adversary* compose the Pliocene Exile series (to be followed by *Jack the Bodiless, Diamond Mask,* and *Magnificat,* the Galactic Milieu books, which will detail the history of the Remillard's Metapyschic Rebellion of AD 2083). *A Pliocene Companion* offers a full guide to the Pliocene books and explains what May plans to do in the future.

May is a professional writer whose work on science and technology, encyclopedia articles and juvenile books, inside experience with publishing, and wide reading provided the material for a series with depth and richness as well as imaginative people and systems. Aiken Drum, the nonborn king, is not just a smart fellow with metapsychic powers beyond those of most people, he is multi-faceted scamp, part juvenile delinquent, part Till Eulenspiegel and Reynard the Fox, deliberately based on the Scot folkloristic character and linked to the Druids. Like all her major characters, he can be experienced on many levels. The complexities of her characters are detailed so they become memorably unique in spite of their numbers. Total villains and simple heroes are not May's style.

May develops her compelx plots through the eight members of Group Green who interact with and mobilize several groups who converge at the end of each novel and the series in many events. The Nightfall War and the union of the exiles from the revolution and the excapees from a dull society are suggested at the beginning, indicative of May's painstakingly careful planning. Similarly, the basic plot of the Galactic Milieu series is already outlined for readers in the first books. May's admiration for Doc Smith, another user of archetypal figures, draws her toward the blood and guts warfare, adventures set against the vastness of space and time, and frankness in human relations, particularly sex, which can be sadistic, homosexual, obsessive, or downright earthy. Within her well-plotted probing of personality and political intrigue, May manages also to be humorous, with blundering, luckless Tony Wayland and Yiddish-speaking, ex-state supreme court justice Native American Peopeo Moxmox Burke balanced against the dead seriousness of Elizabeth Orme and Marc Remillard for comic relief. The high epic quality of the Tanu intrigue is parodied in less apt Firulag schemes. Similar artistry goes into her style. May has vivid, poetic descriptions of her Tanu and Firulag people and their pageantry, precisely worded in a large English and invented vocabularly.

The scientific elements of May's work are primarily in the areas of genetics and parapyschology, augmented by myth, history, philosophy, geography, geology, theology, and astrophysics. May has succeeded in blending the best aspects of fantasy and SF into an engrossing adventure series.

—Mary S. Weinkauf

———

MAYHAR, Ardath (née Hurst). American. Born in Timpson, Texas, 20 February 1930. Attended high school in Nacogdoches, Texas. Married Joe E. Mayhar in 1958; two sons and two stepsons. Dairyman, Nacogdoches County, 1947-57; operator, East Texas Bookstore, Nacogdoches, 1958-62; proofreader, *Capital Journal,* Salem, Oregon, 1968-75; chicken farmer, Nacodoches County, 1976-78; proofreader, Nacogdoches *Daily Sentinel,* 1979-82. Since 1982, full-time writer, and since 1984, co-operator, View from Orbit, bookstore, Nacogdoches. Agent: Ray Puechner, 3210 South 7th Street, Milwaukee, Wisconsin 53215. Address: Route 1, Box 146, Chireno, Texas 75937, U.S.A.

SCIENCE-FICTION PUBLICATIONS

Novels

How the Gods Wove in Kyrannon. New York, Doubleday, 1979; London, Sidgwick and Jackson, 1980.
The Seekers of Shar Nuhn. New York, Doubleday, 1980.
Soul-Singer of Tyrnos. New York, Atheneum, 1981.
Warlock's Gift. New York, Doubleday, 1982.
Khi to Freedom. New York, Ace, 1982.
Runes of the Lyre. New York, Atheneum, 1982.
Golden Dream. New York, Ace, 1983.
Lords of the Triple Moons. New York, Atheneum, 1983.
The Absolutely Perfect House, with Marylois Dunn. New York, Harper, 1983.
Exile on Vlahil. New York, Doubleday, 1984.
The Saga of Grittel Sundotha. New York, Atheneum, 1985.
The World Ends in Hickory Hollow. New York, Doubleday, 1985.

Uncollected Short Stories

"The Reaping," in *Swords Against Darkness 4*, edited by Andrew J. Offutt. New York, Zebra, 1979.
"The Eagle-Claw Rattle," in *Mummy!*, edited by Bill Pronzini. New York, Arbor House, 1980.
"Speaking Wolf," in *Pulpsmith* (New York), Summer 1981.
"Who Courts a Reluctant Maiden," in *Amazons 2*, edited by Jessica Amanda Salmonson. New York, DAW, 1982.
"The End of War," in *Pulpsmith* (New York), January 1982.
"A Meeting of Minds," in *Isaac Asimov's Science Fiction Magazine* (New York), June 1982.
"Tasks of the Green Bone," in *Pulpsmith* (New York), Summer 1982.
"Echo of Thunder," in *Kadath* (Genoa, Italy), July 1982.
"Grittel," in *Dragonfields* (Ottawa), Winter 1983.
"Things Come Out at Night," in *Night Voyages* (Freeburg, Illinois), Winter-Spring 1983.
"Thurigon Agonistes," in *Weirdbook 17* (Buffalo), 1983.
"The Tuck at the Foot of the Bed," in *Twilight Zone* (New York), May-June 1983.
"A Sculpted Smile," in *Fantasy Book* (Pasadena, California), August 1983.
"The Key to Ramali," in *Dragon 8* (Lake Geneva, Wisconsin), 1984.
"Through the Padded Door," in *Night Voyages* (Freeburg, Illinois), 1984.
"You Can't Fool a Wife," in *Espionage 1* (New York), 1984.
"The Face in the Glass," in *Weirdbook 19* (Buffalo), January 1984.
"Flights of Blue Balloons," in *Mississippi Arts and Letters* (Hattiesburg), Summer 1984.

OTHER PUBLICATIONS

Other (for children)

Medicine Walk. New York, Atheneum, 1985.

*

Manuscript Collections: de Grummond Collection, University of Southern Mississippi, Hattiesburg; Stephen F. Austin State University, Nacogdoches, Texas.

Ardath Mayhar comments:

I like to think of my work as metaphysical fiction. S-F and fantasy elements allow me to create contexts that reach past our own limitations and parameters into continua where what *should be* CAN BE. Logic and Humanity are the poles of my philosophy, and I refuse to be hemmed up into narrow genres. Writing science fiction, fantasy, poetry, juveniles, articles of all kinds, I work toward some inner goal, invisible but inexorable, and when I arrive at my destination I expect to be completely astonished.

*   *   *

Although she had published in other genres previous to that date, Ardath Mayhar got her start in SF and fantasy literature with the Young Adult work, *How the Gods Wove in Kyrannon* in 1979. Of the 11 genre novels she had produced in the intervening years, only four, *Exile on Vlahil, Golden Dream, Khi to Freedom*, and *The World Ends in Hickory Hollow*, could be classified as SF. Another four, including the first, are clearly high fantasy. The features characteristic of that genre are elevated diction used by both characters and narrator, and a few characters with superior talents in magic and telepathy, as well as an indisputable separation of good and evil. The other three Mayhar novels fall into a category which has recently been termed "science fantasy" and owes much to the early writing of Andre Norton. *Lords of the Triple Moons, Runes of the Lyre* and the recent *The Saga of Grittel Sundotha* are basically fantasy works set in surroundings where magic and heroic adventure are predominant, but they each incorporate some technological feature such as "cross-dimensional" travel from a machine-based dimension or a lost technology called upon by the telepathic protagonists in their battle against evil wizards.

Mayhar is in fact preoccupied with telepathy and other superior powers of mind, an interest which surfaces in the SF as well as her other genre works. For example, in *Khi to Freedom* she creates beings at several levels of corporality and telepathic ability, with the protagonist Hale Enbo as the subject of a process of mental refinement by more elevated beings. *Exile on Vlahil*, her most amusing book to date due to the inclusion of a conscious computer called Alice, places a female-human hero in a position to save some humans from her degenerating home planet through telepathic communication with idealized creatures called Ered and Vlammalba. *Golden Dream*, while giving H. Beam Piper's Little Fuzzys a history and describing the encounter with humans from their perspective, also makes much of their telepathic abilities. The only novel which breaks this mold is anomalous in several ways. *The World Ends in Hickory Hollow* is a largely realistic post-nuclear holocaust novel, one of several such novels by a variety of authors which have appeared in recent years. This work is also partially autobiographical, being set in an area of East Texas similar to that in which the author and her family now live. It is somewhat more positive than the general run of such novels, postulating that a few families will survive a nuclear attack through mutual assistance and the resurrection of traditional, down-home wisdom.

Mayhar's plots are inexorable and thus virtually predictable from the initial pages of any story. Good and evil are as clearly identified in the SF as they are in the fantasy, and no less evident in the adult fiction than in the Young Adult books. The stories also tend to be highly moralistic, dependent on a fixed code of ethics which emphasizes the basic goodness of most individuals and the evident uselessness of those not imbued with this goodness. In most of her works, such beings are either to be reformed or discarded.

This author's greatest accomplishment lies in the description of normal physiological and social functions as they might be practiced by a wide range of organisms such as crystalline, electrical, or fuzzy-green creatures, as well as wizards, shamans, witches, rulers, and adventures. *Khi to Freedom*, for example, is really two loosely connected episodes in the adventures of Hale Enbo, human extraordinaire. But each one is enriched by the many homey descriptions of eating, sleeping, and social interactions between the human and his various cohorts and enemies. *Exile on Vlahil*, her best and most representative work, succeeds as much because of the elaborate symbiosis which constitues Vlahil's eco-culture as it does through any adventure-plot elements. Yet the substantive and generic breadth of Mayhar's writings makes it difficult to predict what any particular reader will appreciate most or what she herself will produce next.

—Janice M. Bogstad

McALLISTER, Bruce (Hugh). American. Born in Baltimore, Maryland, 17 October 1946. Educated at Claremont Men's College, California, B. A. 1969; University of California, Irvine, M. F. A. 1971. Married Caroline Reid in 1970; one daughter and one son. Sports rewriter, United Press International, New York, 1967; staff writer, Doubleday Multimedia, Santa Ana, California, 1969; Visiting Instructor, Long Beach City College, California, 1971-73, and California State University, Fullerton, 1973-74. At University of Redlands, California: Visiting Instructor, 1971-74; Assistant Professor, 1974-79, Associate Professor, 1979-83, and since 1983, Professor of English (Director of the Writing Program since 1974); since 1983, Media Relations Director and Editor, Policy Research Center. Since 1980, free-lance consultant in technical and scientific writing and public relations; since 1982, consultant, VSP Associates, Sacramento, California. Academic Affairs Editor, *Bulletin of the Science Fiction Writers of America*, 1973-74; Managing Editor, *Best SF* anthology series, Bobbs Merrill, Indianapolis, 1973-75. Since 1972, Associate Editor, *West Coast Poetry Review* and WCPR press, Reno, Nevada. Recipient: Bread Loaf Writers Conference scholarship, 1972; Squaw Valley Writers Conference fellowship, 1973; University of Redlands Jubilee Medallion, 1983, and Outstanding Teaching Award, 1983. Address: 935 Aaron Drive, Redlands, California 92374, U.S.A.

SCIENCE-FICTION PUBLICATIONS

Novel

Humanity Prime. New York, Ace, 1971.

Short Stories

The Faces Outside. San Bernardino, California, Borgo Press, 1985.

Uncollected Short Stories

"We Hunters of Men," in *If* (New York), August 1965.
"Gods of the Dark and Light," in *If* (New York), February 1967.
"Without a Doubt Dream," in *Fantasy and Science Fiction* (New York), April 1968.
"The Big Boy," in *Fantastic* (New York), June 1969.
"Autohuman 14," in *If* (New York), July 1969.

"Life Matter," in *Galaxy* (New York), August 1969.
"After the Bomb Clinches," in *Fantasy and Science Fiction* (New York), November 1969.
"And So Say All of Us," in *World's Best Science Fiction 1970*, edited by Donald A. Wollheim and Terry Carr. New York, Ace, 1970.
"The Man Inside," in *Best SF 1969*, edited by Harry Harrison and Brian Aldiss. New York, Putnam, 1970.
"Prime-Time Teaser," in *Twenty Years of the Magazine of Fantasy and Science Fiction*, edited by Edward L. Ferman and Robert P. Mills. New York, Putnam, 1970.
"E. Pluribus Solo," in *Fantasy and Science Fiction* (New York), January 1970.
"Mother of Pearl," in *Fantasy and Science Fiction* (New York), June 1970.
"The Warmest Memory," in *Fantasy and Science Fiction* (New York), December 1970.
"Benji's Pencil," in *Best from Fantasy and Science Fiction 19*, edited by Edward L. Ferman. New York, Doubleday, 1971.
"World of the Wars," in *Mars, We Love You*, edited by Jane Hipolito and Willis E. McNelly. New York, Doubleday, 1971.
"Ecce Femina!," in *Above the Human Landscape*, edited by Willis E. McNelly and Leon Stover. Pacific Palisades, California, Goodyear, 1972.
"Triangle," in *Fantasy and Science Fiction* (New York), December 1972.
"The Arrangement," in *Showcase*, edited by Roger Elwood. New York, Harper, 1973.
"The Boy," in *New Worlds 10*, edited by Hilary Bailey. London, Corgi, 1977.
"Victor," in *The Best Science Fiction of the Year 7*, edited by Terry Carr. New York, Ballantine, 1978.
"Missionary Work," in *Fantasy and Science Fiction* (New York), December 1978.
"Their Immortal Hearts," in *Their Immortal Hearts*, edited by McAllister. Reno, Nevada, WCPR Press, 1980.
"What He Wore for Them," in *Fantasy and Science Fiction* (New York), August 1980.
"When the Fathers Go," in *Universe 12*, edited by Terry Carr. New York, Doubleday, 1982.

OTHER PUBLICATIONS

Other

"Do We Need This Knowledge," in *Best SF 1974*, edited by Brian Aldiss and Harry Harrison. Indianapolis, Bobbs Merrill, 1975.

Editor, *SF Directions*. Christchurch, New Zealand, Edge Press, 1972.
Editor, *Their Immortal Hearts*. Reno, Nevada, WCPR Press, 1980.

* * *

Bruce McAllister is a writer's writer, a man whose work is highly regarded by his fellow professionals, but whose name is relatively unknown even among the most rabid of SF fans. The reasons for this are many: he is a slow and meticulous craftsman, often requiring twenty drafts for every story completed and sold; thus, even his best years have seen no more than three or four published fictions, with a lifetime total of about forty. His one novel, highly acclaimed when published, is now long out-of-print, in a field where regular production of novels is essential to achieving public recognition; only Harlan Ellison has managed to carve out a career based primarily on short stories. He does not write series, sequels, swords-and-sorcery fiction, or Star Trek novels. His stories, novellas, and novel tend to be somewhat cerebral character studies, focusing on individuals rather than mindless action-adventure. For all these reasons, McAllister's unique and compelling visions have yet to achieve the widespread recognition they deserve.

McAllister's first story, "The Faces Outside," published when he was only 16, sets the tone for his later work. The unnamed hero finds himself floating in a tank with his mate and an assortment of aquatic creatures; their only contact with the outside world is a disembodied Voice. The Voice tells them that the faces watching them through the ports are the Enemy, the aliens who have annihilated the rest of the human race, and who have changed these two survivors into underwater humanoids. The two eventually transcend captivity by developing mental powers that completely vanquish the alien beings, thereby assuring the survival of the new race.

Here in microcosm are the basic themes that permeate almost all of McAllister's work. His protagonists are often tortured individuals caught between a Heaven and Hell not of their own choosing. Their suffering and tribulations take them from the Limbos of their own minds to some kind of ultimate realization, epiphany, or metamorphosis. In McAllister's early work, this theme of self-transcendence often translates into rather obvious power fantasies, in which one lonely (alienated) character somehow miraculously manages to conquer his nemesis (i. e., himself), whether that be alien monsters, his fellow human beings, or some life-threatening situation. In his later stories, however, the author's treatment of this theme has become more sophisticated, his view of mankind more cynical, his feeling for man's predicament more poignant, his treatment of man's self-sacrificing inclinations more realistic. Always present, however, are the agony and the ecstasy—nothing is achieved in McAllister's universe without pain. Representative of these newer works is "The Boy," the most downbeat of McAllister's short fiction, "Victor," "What He Wore for Them," and "When the Fathers Go. " (Many of these will be collected in his forthcoming book, *The Faces Outside.*)

We also see these themes at work in *Humanity Prime*, McAllister's only novel, which was very loosely adapted from "The Faces Outside. " Issued as the last book in the original Ace Science Fiction Special Series, it achieved very limited circulation, since Ace had already decided to terminate both the series and its editor. *Humanity Prime* mixes human mermen, cyborgs, intelligent sea turtles, and telepathy to produce one of the most compelling portraits of undersea man ever published. McAllister's intimate knowledge of human and animal biology, and his childhood experiences as the son of a behaviorial psychologist, are reflected in this realistic and plausible extrapolation of man and alien function together in a unique environment. To McAllister, animals are as human in their own ways as man is sometimes alien in his; much of his fiction is specifically concerned with the question of what it means to be human. His forthcoming story "The Ark" also focuses on this problem, and demonstrates a maturity and honesty not found in his earlier fiction. Another recent novella, "Their Immortal Hearts," which combines human psychobiology with a more traditional science-fiction setting, has achieved much notice from mainstream critics.

—R. Reginald

McCAFFREY, Anne (Inez). American. Born in Cambridge, Massachusetts, 1 April 1926. Educated at Stuart Hall, Staunton, Virginia; Montclair High School, New Jersey; Radcliffe College, Cambridge, Massachusetts, B. A. (cum laude) in Slavonic languages and literature 1947; studied meteorology at City of Dublin University. Married E. Wright Johnson in 1950 (divorced, 1970); two sons and one daughter. Copywriter and layout designer, Liberty Music Shops, New York, 1948-50; Copywriter, Helena Rubinstein, New York, 1950-52. Currently runs a thoroughbred horse stud farm in Ireland; since 1978, Director, Dragonhold Ltd., and since 1979, Director, Fin Film Productions. Has performed in and directed several operas and musical comedies in Wilmington and Greenville, Delaware. Secretary-Treasurer, Science Fiction Writers of America, 1968-70. Recipient: Hugo Award, 1968, 1979; Nebula Award, 1968; Gandalf Award, 1979; Balrog Award, 1980. Agent: Virginia Kidd, Box 278, Milford, Pennsylvania 18337, U.S.A. Address: Dragonhold, Kilquade, Greystones, County Wicklow, Ireland.

SCIENCE-FICTION PUBLICATIONS

Novels (series: Dinosaur Planet; Dragonrider; Harper Hall)

Restoree. New York, Ballantine, 1967; London, Rapp and Whiting, 1968.
Dragonflight (Dragonrider). New York. Ballantine, 1968; London, Rapp and Whiting, 1969.
Decision at Doona. New York, Ballantine, 1969; London, Rapp and Whiting, 1970.
The Ship Who Sang. New York, Walker, 1969; London, Rapp and Whiting, 1971.
Dragonquest (Dragonrider). New York, Ballantine, 1971; London, Rapp and Whiting-Deutsch, 1973.
To Ride Pegasus. New York, Ballantine, 1973; London, Dent, 1974.
Dragonsong (for children; Harper Hall). New York, Atheneum, and London, Sidgwick and Jackson, 1976.
Dragonsinger (for children; Harper Hall). New York, Atheneum, and London, Sidgwick and Jackson, 1977.
The Dragonriders of Pern (omnibus). New York, Doubleday, 1978.
Dinosaur Planet. London, Futura, 1977; New York, Ballantine, 1978.
The White Dragon (Dragonrider). New York, Ballantine, 1978; London, Sidgwick and Jackson, 1979.
Dragondrums (for children; Harper Hall). New York, Atheneum, and London, Sidgwick and Jackson, 1979.
Crystal Singer. New York, Ballantine, and London, Severn House, 1982.
The Coelura. Columbia, Pennsylvania, Underwood Miller, 1983.
Moreta, Dragonlady of Pern. New York, Ballantine, and London, Severn House, 1983.
Dinosaur Planet Survivors. New York, Ballantine, and London, Futura, 1984.
Stitch in Snow. Columbia, Pennsylvania, Underwood Miller, 1984.

Short Stories

A Time When. Cambridge, Massachusetts, NESFA Press, 1975.
Get Off the Unicorn. New York, Ballantine, 1977; London, Corgi, 1979.
The Worlds of Anne McCaffrey. London, Deutsch, 1981.

Uncollected Short Stories

"The Greatest Love," in *Futurelove*, edited by Roger Elwood. New York, Doubleday, 1977.
"Lady in Waiting," in *Cassandra Rising*, edited by Alice Laurance. New York, Doubleday, 1978.
"Cinderella Switch," in *Stellar 6*, edited by Judy-Lynn del Rey. New York, Ballantine, 1981.

OTHER PUBLICATIONS

Novels

The Mark of Merlin. New York, Dell, 1971; London, Millington, 1977.
The Ring of Fear. New York, Dell, 1971; London; Millington, 1979.
The Kilternan Legacy. New York, Dell, 1975; London, Millington, 1976.

Other

Editor, *Alchemy and Academe: A Collection of Original Stories Concerning Themselves with Transmutations, Mental and Elemental, Alchemical and Academic*. New York, Doubleday, 1970.
Editor, *Cooking Out of This World*. New York, Ballantine, 1973.

*

Bibliography: *Leigh Brackett, Marion Zimmer Bradley, Anne McCaffrey: A Primary and Secondary Bibliography* by Rosemarie Arbur, Boston, Hall, 1982.

Manuscript Collections: Syracuse University, New York; Kerlan Collection, University of Minnesota, Minneapolis.

Anne McCaffrey comments:

I am a story-teller of *science-fiction* and wish that label attached to my work in that field. I make this point as I am often classified, erroneously, as a fantasy writer. Since I am more interested in the interaction of people, the research I do for some of the books is not apparent, thus confusing the uninitiated. I have no pretentions to literary style or excellence, nor are my stories allegorical, mystical, or political. I cannot honestly call myself a feminist, though I do not disagree with the aims of the women's movement, and in *The Kilternan Legacy* I make comparisons between the rights of American women and the deplorable lack of status of Irish women. My personal philosophy was heavily influenced by Austin Tappan Wright's classic, *Islandia*—a book I read at 14 and consistently reread. Of all the stories I have written to date, *The Ship Who Sang* is my favorite.

*   *   *

Anne McCaffrey is primarily known as creator of Pern, the planet of telepathic dragons and their riders. But she has also written science fiction which has nothing to do with dragons.

Restoree, for example, is the story of a terrestrial woman kidnapped by aliens who butcher sentients for food. Though she is dismembered, humanoid aliens restore and beautify her (hence the title). Since the restoration process has hitherto resulted in mindless Frankenstein-like monsters, the heroine is hidden away in a prison camp. Together with a dashing alien

man, she escapes, and the two become lovers. The book has been criticized as melodramatic and full of sexist stereotypes, but McCaffrey herself calls it a deliberate science-fiction parody of the gothic romance. *Dicision at Doona* relates problems of alien encounters when a group of earthlings find that they will have to abandon their idyllic new planet because terrestrial authorities will not let them co-colonize with cat-like sentients called Hrrubans. The book contains fine portrayals of family relationships, frontier hardships, and touching children's friendships. Helva, of *The Ship Who Sang*, is born with disfiguring, disabling multiple birth defects. Technology in her enlightened future world makes her into a cyborg controlling a huge interstellar starship. Her unconventional love-affairs and friendships with mobile humans are depicted with imagination and verve.

McCaffrey's Pern books, however, have been her best award-winners. The adult series is *Dragonflight, Dragonquest, The White Dragon*, and *Moreta, Dragonlady of Pern*. The juvenile, or Harper Hall, trilogy is *Dragonsong, Dragonsinger,* and *Dragondrums*. McCaffrey continues to work on the series and has recently finished "Nerilka's Story." There are ancillary Pern stories as well. Pern is a planet colonized in the forgotten past by terrestrials who left bio-engineered dragons as defense against a mycorrhizoid spore called Thread which crosses vacuum from Pern's companion planet, the Red Star. The dragons bond telepathically to a rider and fight Thread by burning it out of the air with their phosphine-loaded breath. Dragons can also cross space—and, it is learned, time—telekinetically. Pernese society has a medieval flavor which tempts the critic to call these books sword-and-sorcery or fantasy. But everything about Pern is based on science, and therefore the books are true science fiction. The most spirited and moving passages in the series depict dragon bonding, mating, and hatching. The Harper Hall trilogy emphasizes the use of dragonflight as metaphor for the artistic process, where the rider of the dragon represents intellect and direction, while the dragon itself (and in her other works various other steeds, such as the spaceship in *The Ship Who Sang*) represents emotion and drive. A further development of this imagery is shown in *To Ride Pegasus*, where the human intellect is seen as riding the "Pegasus" of super-normal mental powers. The title of *Get Off the Unicorn* suggests similar imagery; the book itself is a series of stories which are parts of various McCaffrey worlds.

The Killashandra stories began in Roger Elwood's Continuum books. McCaffrey revised these extensively for *Crystal Singer*. Killashandra Ree's special musical ability enables her to cut special crystal used in interstellar travel and communication. The crystal planet's indigenous life form is a symbiote which fuses with the cutter's nervous system, bestowing long life, special sensitivities, and, unfortunately, madness. The series is the darkest of McCaffrey's work, fascinating for its rich symbolism, its insight into complex, tortured characters, and its use of unreliable narrator.

Dinosaur Planet and *Dinosaur Planet Survivors* are about a mysterious garlic-scented planet, Ireta, which contains life forms from several eras of Earth's prehistory, including intelligent pteranodons. The first book sets up several mysteries about the source of these creatures and the fate of the protagonists; the second book solves these mysteries, but a little too facilely. Apparently no sequel is projected, despite the appeal of the intelligent giffs and the interstellar culture of the explorers.

McCaffrey also writes non-science fiction—mysteries and romances with strong female protagonists. Her main theme has been the many forms of bonding—between lovers, between parent and child, between friends, between humans and animals, between aliens and humans. She also explores reproductive processes and psychic potentialities in a cool, scientific spirit. The metaphor of flight for artistic activity is one of her most beautiful contributions. Her characterization, plotting, and creation of imaginary worlds place her as a significant science-fiction writer.

—Mary T. Brizzi

McCANN, Edson. See del REY, Lester; POHL, Frederik.

McCLARY, Thomas (Calvert). Also writes as Calvin Peregoy. American.

SCIENCE-FICTION PUBLICATIONS

Novels

Rebirth, When Everyone Forgot. New York, Bartholomew House, 1944.
Three Thousand Years. Reading, Pennsylvania, Fantasy Press, 1954.

Uncollected Short Stories

"Food for the First Planet," in *Astounding* (New York), August 1938.
"Parole," in *Unknown Worlds* (New York), June 1939.
"The Tommyknocker," in *Unknown Worlds* (New York), October 1940.
"The Case of Jack Freysling," in *Astounding* (New York), October 1944.

Uncollected Short Stories as Calvin Peregoy (series: Dr. Conklin in all stories)

"Short-Wave Castle," in *Astounding* (New York), February 1934.
"Dr. Conklin—Pacifist," in *Astounding* (New York), August 1934.
"Shortwave Experiment," in *Astounding* (New York), February 1935.
"The Terrible Sense," in *Best of Science Fiction*, edited by Groff Conklin. New York, Crown, 1946.

*   *   *

In addition to a few Calvin Peregoy short stories, Thomas McClary has produced two memorable works, *Rebirth* and *Three Thousand Years*, both Darwinian in attitude. In both a scientific elite theorize that, together with the intelligent and fit from other fields, they can overcome the stratified prejudices and superstitions of their age, wipe the slate clean, and produce a new utopia characterized by some degree of comfort and humanity. To achieve this the scientists intentionally and instantaneously precipitate a catastrophe, by a memory-obliterating ray in *Rebirth* and by the translation of all life forms to a state of suspended animation in *Three Thousand Years*.

Both works partially deflate such idealistic visions of reformation by revealing man at the instinctual level as possessive, violent, competitive, and innately unequal (his weaknesses and his strengths), but suggest that love, music, pride in work, and a basic sense of responsibility toward those who can contribute to the community raise man above both his animal limitations and any computerized substitutes. When human minds are reduced to a *tabula rasa* amid a technologically advanced society (*Rebirth*) or when that technology crumbles (*Three Thousand Years*), chaos, destruction, and death ensue. In *Rebirth* man must relearn such elementary skills as talking, walking, and eating; in *Three Thousand Years* experts must learn to start from scratch; in both man must survive on the basis of instinct and innate capacity. Most die, but the clever and strong survive to rebuild society and to become, ultimately, very much what they had been before rebirth or suspension, with only some achieving higher levels of understanding than before. Yet overall the world is a better place, with the weak weeded out, the government established on a more realistic basis of common need and common interest, and scientists and politicians learning to cooperate to keep man striving and progressing. Once one has accepted rather implausible initial premises and a simplistic style, the working out of the details is interesting and occasionally witty and unexpected.

—Gina Macdonald

McCOMAS, J(esse) Francis. Also wrote as Webb Marlow. American. Born in 1911. Worked for Simon and Schuster, publishers; Editor, with Anthony Boucher, 1949-54, and Advisory Editor, 1954-62, *The Magazine of Fantasy and Science Fiction. Died in April 1978.*

SCIENCE-FICTION PUBLICATIONS

Uncollected Short Stories

"Flight into Darkness" (as Webb Marlowe), in *Adventures in Time and Space*, edited by Raymond J. Healy and McComas. New York, Random House, 1946; London, Grayson, 1952.
"Contract for a Body" (as Webb Marlowe), in *Fantastic Adventures* (New York), July 1948.
"Shock Treatment," in *9 Tales of Space and Time*, edited by Raymond J. Healy. New York, Holt, 1954.
"Brave New World," in *The Best from Fantasy and Science Fiction 4*, edited by Anthony Boucher. New York, Doubleday, 1955.
"Parallel," in *Fantasy and Science Fiction* (New York), April 1955.
"Criminal Negligence," in *Space, Time, and Crime*, edited by Miriam Allen deFord. New York, Paperback Library, 1964.

OTHER PUBLICATIONS

Other

"In Memoriam—Anthony Boucher," in *Nebula Award Stories 4*, edited by Poul Anderson. New York, Doubleday, 1969.

Editor, with Raymond J. Healy, *Adventures in Time and Space.* New York, Random House, 1946; London, Grayson, 1952.
Editor, with Anthony Boucher, *The Best from Fantasy and*

Science Fiction 1-3. Boston, Little Brown, 2 vols., 1952-53; New York, Doubleday, 1 vol., 1954.

Editor, with Raymond J. Healy, *Famous Science-Fiction Stories*. New York, Random House, 1957.

Editor, *The Graveside Companion: An Anthology of California Murders*. New York, Obolensky, 1962.

Editor, *Crimes and Misfortunes: The Anthony Boucher Memorial Anthology of Mysteries*. New York, Random House, 1970.

Editor, *Special Wonder: The Anthony Boucher Memorial Anthology of Fantasy and Science Fiction*. New York, Random House, 1970.

*

Critical Study: *The Eureka Years: Boucher and McComas's The Magazine of Fantasy and Science Fiction 1949-1954* edited by Annette P. McComas, New York, Bantam, 1982.

*   *   *

Although he attracted some critical attention for his writing, J. Francis McComas is best known in partnership activities. His story "Flight Into Darkness" is dated, since it deals with speculative relationships between the US and the remnants of German civilization after World War II. Here the author is concerned with political jingoism in the fanatical devotion to The Leader by the story's villain, who hatches a plot to overthrow the triumphant Americans through the secret construction of a space ship. While the yarn is starkly melodramatic, with a spectacular ending to satisfy the post-World War II reader, McComas's sympathetic sketching of the crippled younger brother earns the account more than passing attention.

It is McComas's sensitivity, in fact, which contributed so greatly to his success in two partnerships that made him a notable figure in science fiction. The first of these was with Anthony Boucher in the creation in 1949 of *The Magazine of Fantasy and Science Fiction*. This periodical was unusual in attracting stories of high literary quality at a time when many pulps subsisted on much cheaper fare. While the magazine's content leaned heavily toward fantasy the balance shifted to include some of the finest science fiction written for magazines. His keen perceptiveness and high literary standards are evident, too, in *Adventures in Time and Space*, which McComas edited with Raymond J. Healy. This anthology gave science fiction an impetus toward respectability and literary value which it may not have previously enjoyed by presenting a stimulating cross-section of speculative experiences and underlining the contribution of science fiction to American literature.

J. Francis McComas deserves great critical attention, then, for his keen perception and high literary standards. Without such individuals it is very speculative whether the fine writers of science fiction we can enjoy today would have developed to such respectable levels. While he was himself a writer, he was more: a connoisseur of writing standards.

—Robert H. Wilcox

———

McGOWAN, Inez. See **PHILLIPS, Rog.**

———

McINTOSH, J. T. Pseudonym for James Murdoch Macgregor; also writes as H. J. Murdock. British. Born in Paisley, Renfrew, 14 February 1925. Educated at Robert Gordon's College, Aberdeen, 1936-41; Aberdeen University, 1943-47, M. A. (honours) in English. Married Margaret Murray in 1960; two daughters and one son. Since 1947, sub editor, Aberdeen *Press and Journal*. Agent: Campbell Thomson and McLaughlin Ltd., 31 Newington Green, London N16 9PU, England; or Blassingame McCauley and Wood, 432 Park Avenue South, Suite 1205, New York, New York 10016, U. S. A Address: 63 Abbotswell Drive, Aberdeen, Scotland.

SCIENCE-FICTION PUBLICATIONS

Novels

World Out of Mind. New York, Doubleday, 1953; London, Museum Press, 1955.

Born Leader. New York, Doubleday, 1954; London, Museum Press, 1955; as *Worlds Apart*, New York, Avon, 1958.

One in Three Hundred. New York, Doubleday, 1954; London, Museum Press, 1956.

The Fittest. New York, Doubleday, 1955; London, Corgi, 1961; as *The Rule of the Pagbeasts*, New York, Fawcett, 1956.

200 Years to Christmas. New York, Ace 1961.

The Million Cities. New York, Pyramid, 1963.

The Noman Way. London, Digit, 1964.

Out of Chaos. London, Digit, 1965.

Time for a Change. London, Joseph, 1967; as *Snow White and the Giants*, New York, Avon, 1968.

Six Gates from Limbo. London, Joseph, 1968; New York, Avon, 1969

Transmigration. New York, Avon, 1970.

Flight from Rebirth. New York, Avon, 1971; London, Hale, 1973.

The Cosmic Spies. London, Hale, 1972.

The Space Sorcerers. London, Hale, 1972; as *The Suiciders*, New York, Avon, 1973.

Galactic Takeover Bid. London, Hale, 1973.

Ruler of the World. Toronto, Laser, 1976.

This Is the Way the World Begins. London, Corgi, 1977.

Norman Conquest 2066 London, Corgi, 1977.

A Planet Called Utopia. New York, Zebra, 1979.

Uncollected Short Stories

"The Curfew Tolls," in *Astounding* (New York), December 1950.

"Safety Margin," in *Planet* (New York), January 1951.

"Venus Mission," in *Planet* (New York), July 1951.

"Sanctuary, Oh Ullla!," in *Planet* (New York), September 1951.

"Then There Were Two," in *Science Fantasy* (Bournemouth), Winter 1951.

"When Aliens Meet," in *New Worlds* (London), Winter 1951.

"Machine Made," in *No Place Like Earth*, edited by E. J. Carnell. London, Boardman, 1952.

"The World That Changed," in *New Worlds* (London), March 1952.

"Katahut Said No," in *Galaxy* (New York), April 1952.

"Tradition," in *Other Worlds* (Evanston, Indiana), April 1952.

"The Reluctant Colonist," in *Planet* (New York), May 1952.

"The Broken Record"(as James Macgregor), in *New Worlds* (London), September 1952.

"The ESP Worlds," in *New Worlds* (London), July, September, November 1952.

"Stitch in Time," in *Science Fantasy* (Bournemouth), Autumn 1952.

"Talents," in *Fantasy and Science Fiction* (New York), October 1952.

"The Volunteers," in *Science Fantasy* (Bournemouth), Spring 1953.

"Beggars All," in *Fantasy and Science Fiction* (New York), April 1953.

"Escape Me Never," in *Fantastic* (New York), April 1953.

"Mind Alone," in *Galaxy* (New York), August 1953.

"War's Great Organ," in *Nebula* (Glasgow), September 1953.

"The Happier Eden," in *Nebula* (Glasgow), December 1953.

"Relay Race," in *New Worlds 22* (London) 1954.

"Divine Right," in *Nebula* (Glasgow), February 1954.

"Men Like Mules," in *Galaxy* (New York), February 1954.

"Bias," in *Astounding* (New York), May 1954.

"This Precious Stone" (as H. J. Murdock),in *Science Fantasy* (Bournemouth), July 1954.

"Five into Four," in *Science Fantasy* (Bournemouth), September 1954.

"Spy," in *Galaxy* (New York), October 1954.

"Playback," in *Galaxy* (New York), December 1954.

"Live for Ever," in *Science Fantasy* (Bournemouth), December 1954.

"First Lady," in *Best SF 1*, edited by Edmund Crispin. London, Faber, 1955.

"Selection," in *Fantasy and Science Fiction* (New York), January 1955.

"Open House," in *Galaxy* (New York), February 1955.

"Eleventh Commandment," in *Fantasy and Science Fiction* (New York), May 1955.

"The Big Hop," in *Authentic* (London), May, June 1955.

"Bluebird World," in New Worlds (London), June 1955.

"The Way Home," in New Worlds (London), August 1955.

"The Man Who Cried 'Sheep!,'" in *Fantasy and Science Fiction* (New York), September 1955.

"The Lady and the Bull," in *Authentic* (London), December 1955.

"The Solomon Plan," in *New Worlds* (London), February 1956.

"The Deciding Factor," in *Authentic* (London), April 1956.

"The Little Corporal," in *Authentic* (London), July 1956.

"Empath," in *New Worlds* (London), August 1956; as "Shield Against Death," in *Fantastic Universe* (Chicago), May 1957.

"Report on Earth," in *New Worlds* (London), September 1956.

"The Sandmen," in *Fantasy and Science Fiction* (New York), June 1957.

"Unfit for Humans," in *Authentic* (London), August 1957.

"In Black and White," in *Galaxy* (New York), August 1958.

"You Were Right, Joe," in *The Fourth Galaxy Reader*, edited by H. L. Gold. New York, Doubleday, 1959.

"Kingslayer," in *Galaxy* (New York), April 1959.

"Tenth Time Around," in *Fantasy and Science Fiction* (New York), May 1959.

"No Place for Crime," in *Galaxy* (New York), June 1959.

"Return of a Prodigal," in *If* (New York), November 1959.

"The Night Before the Battle," in *Fantastic Universe* (Chicago), February 1960.

"The Ship from Home," in *Science Fantasy* (Bournemouth), February 1960.

"Merlin," in *Fantastic* (New York), March 1960.

"World Without Annette," in *Fantastic* (New York), May 1960.

"In a Body," in *If* (New York), July 1960.

"Planet on Probation," in *Science Fantasy* (Bournemouth), August 1960.

"Absolute Power," in *If* (New York), January 1961.

"I Can Do Anything," in *Galaxy* (New York), April 1961.

"That's How It Goes," in *If* (New York), May 1961.

"Doormat World," in *If* (New York), July 1961.

"The Gatekeepers," in *Galaxy* (New York), August 1961.

"One into Two," in *Fantasy and Science Fiction* (New York), February 1962.

"The Stupid General," in *Fantasy and Science Fiction* (New York), August 1962.

"Immortaligy. . . for Some," in *12 Great Classics of Science Fiction,* edited by Groff Conklin. New York, Fawcett, 1963.

"The Ten-Point Princess," in *If* (New York), March 1963.

"Spanner in the Works," in *Analog* (New York), March 1963.

"Iceberg from Earth," in *Analog* (New York), April 1963.

"Hermit," in *Analog* (New York), June 1963.

"To the Stars," in *Worlds of Tomorrow* (New York), August 1963.

"Far Avanal," in *Worlds of Tomorrow* (New York), December 1963.

"Unit," in *Five-Odd*, edited by Groff Conklin. New York, Pyramid, 1964.

"Grandmother Earth," in *Galaxy* (New York), February 1964.

"Humanoid Sacrifice," in *Fantasy and Science Fiction* (New York), March 1964.

"Snap Judgement," in *Analog* (New York), June 1964.

"The Great Doomed Ship," in *Worlds of Tomorrow* (New York), June 1964.

"Planet of Change," in *Fantastic* (New York), September 1964.

"The Kicksters," in *Worlds of Tomorrow* (New York), November 1964.

"At the Top of the World," in *If* (New York), December 1964.

"The Man Who Killed Immortals," in *Galaxy* (New York), February 1965.

"The Iceman Goeth," *Analog* (New York), March 1965.

"The Sudden Silence," in *Fantasy and Science Fiction* (New York), April 1966.

"Planet of Fakers," in *Galaxy* (New York), October 1966.

"The Saw and the Carpenter," in *Fantasy and Science Fiction* (New York), September 1967.

"Pontius Pirates," in *Analog* (New York), October 1967.

"The Wrong World," in *Elsewhere and Elsewhen*, edited by Groff Conklin. New York, Berkley, 1968.

"Poor Planet," in Seven Trips Through Time and Space, edited by Groff Conklin. New York, Fawcett, 1968.

"Almost Human," in *Amazing* (New York), January 1971.

"The Real People," in *If* (New York), December 1971.

"Made in U. S. A.," in *The Androids Are Coming*, edited by Robert Silverberg. New York, Elsevier Nelson, 1979.

"The World of God," in *Galaxy* (New York), March-April 1979.

"Hallucination Orbit," in *Hallucination Orbit*, edited by Isaac Asimov, Charles G. Waugh, and Martin H. Greenberg. New York, Farrar Straus, 1983.

OTHER PUBLICATIONS

Novels

Take a Pair of Private Eyes (novelization of TV series). London, Muller, and New York, Doubleday, 1968.

A Coat of Blackmail. London, Muller, 1970; New York, Doubleday, 1971.

Novels as James Macgregor

When the Ship Sank. New York, Doubleday, 1959; London, Heinemann, 1960.

Incident over the Pacific. New York, Doubleday, 1960; as *A Cry*

to Heaven, London, Heinemann, 1961.
The Iron Rain. London, Heinemann, 1962.

Other as James Macgregor

Glamour in Your Lens: A Commonsense Guide to Attractive Photography. London, Focal Press, 1958.
Wine Making for All. London, Faber, 1966.
Beer Making for All. London, Faber, 1967.

*

J. T. McIntosh comments:

I became a science fiction writer not by choice but by force of circumstance. At the time when I was ready to publish (1945-50), paper was in short supply and publishers tended to use it for books by established authors. America was the obvious market, but I had no accurate knowledge of the U. S. scene. So I wrote SF, in which accurate knowledge of the U. S. scene is not necessary.

Later, when I tried non-SF, the international nature of SF became clear to me. There was little interest in my mainstream fiction outside Britain, while the SF books often had editions in many other countries.

* * *

Under the pen name J. T. McIntosh, the Scots writer and journalist James Murdoch Macgregor first won recognition as an author of science fiction with *World Out of Mind*, his first novel. This work presents a future society organized around the ultimate merit system: IQ. All members of this society are rigorously tested for intelligence; test results place each individual in a group marked by a colored badge indicating rank. The governing class, wearing the white star indicating the highest 1% of intelligence, is infiltrated by a Martian who has been reprocessed as a human being and whose mission is to prepare for a Martian invasion. However, since the Martian spy has become *completely* human, he cannot help falling in love with the youngest (and most beautiful) living white star. He betrays the loveless Martians and thwarts the invasion. Humanity (and love) conquer.

Also greeted with critical enthusiasm, *Born Leader* develops two human conflicts: daring youth pitted against conservative age, and a cooperative libertarian society pitted against military totalitarian state. Mundis, a planet colonised by space settlers from an Earth destroyed by nuclear war, is inhabited by two generations : the original settlers, determined not to use nuclear power, and their children, born only after the 22-year space voyage, eager to explore its possibilities. Mundis's egalitarian society is threatened by invaders from a second Earth ship, a Spartan, loveless military group whose women are considered subhuman breeders. Under the threat of domination, the Mundans unite, develop nuclear defences, defeat the invaders, and integrate them into their own egalitarian system.

One in Three Hundred begins on an Earth doomed by a shift in its solar orbit. It shows the selection of a small and random minority for space colonisation, their hazardous voyage, and their sufferings in making Mars habitable from the point of view of one of the leaders responsible for the selection and supervision of a small group. Faced by the threat of a sadist and would-be dictator on Mars, the colonists rebel, kill the tyrants, and cooperate successfully in order to survive. *The Fittest* similarly shows humans forced to work together for survival against great physical odds. Earth is overpopulated by paggets, super-intelligent mice, cats, rats, and dogs, developed by accident in an experiment and determined to overwhelm human life by cutting lines of communication, devouring supplies, sabotage, and murder. Mankind can survive biologically only by using the uniquely human qualities of communication and cooperation to remain the fittest species in simple democratic communities free from social convention.

McIntoch's later full-length fiction fails to live up to the promise of his early novels. Although his later work still deals with his major themes—overpopulation in *The Million Cities*, space travel and evolution in *200 Years to Christmas*, the aftermath of holocaust in *Out of Chaos*, and morality in *Six Gates from Limbo, Transmigration,* and *Flight from Rebirth*—he tends to repeat and overwrite early plots, often expanding ideas originally published as short stories. His ability to write fast and convincing action remains, but he fails to present themes and ideas as convincingly as his novels from the early 1950's.

McIntoch's four early novels interestingly depict libertarian utopias whose members' mutual concern and willingness to cooperate in order to survive demonstration a hopeful view of human nature in a threatening universe. The terrible odds his characters must face are plausible threats for our future: overpopulation, misdirected technology, war, physical changes on Earth itself. In the Darwinian struggle to suvive, women become essential. McIntoch's heroes are typically attracted to independence, competence, and strength in their mates, rather than to dependence, passivity, and physical frailty they might have preferred in easier times. McIntoch's ability to depict realistically the violence and dangers of the unknown future and his hopefulness about mankind's ability to endure make his early novels both moving and memorable.

—Katherine Staples

McINTYRE, Vonda N(eel). American. Born in Louisville, Kentucky, 28 August 1948. Educated at the University of Washington, Seattle, B. S. in biology 1970, graduate study in genetics, 1970-71. Conference organizer, and riding and writing instructor. Recipient: Nebula Award, 1973, 1978; Hugo Award, 1979. Agent: Frances Collin, Rodell-Collin Literary Agency, 110 West 40th Street, New York, New York 10018. Address: P.O. Box 31041, Seattle, Washington 98103-1041, U.S.A.

SCIENCE-FICTION PUBLICATIONS

Novels

The Exile Waiting. New York, Doubleday, 1975; London, Gollancz, 1976.
Dreamsnake. Boston, Houghton Mifflin, and London, Gollancz, 1978.
The Entropy Effect. New York, Pocket Books, and London, Macdonald, 1981.
Star Trek: The Wrath of Khan (novelization of screenplay). New York, Pocket Books, and London, Futura, 1982.
Superluminal. Boston, Houghton Mifflin, 1983; London, Gollancz, 1984.
Star Trek 3: The Search for Spock (novelization of screenplay). New York, Pocket Books, 1984.

Short Stories

Fireflood and Other Stories. Boston, Houghton Mifflin, 1979; London, Gollancz, 1980.

Uncollected Short Stories

"Shadows, Moving," in *Interfaces,* edited by Ursula K. Le Guin and Virginia Kidd. New York, Ace, 1980.
"Elfleda," in *New Dimensions 12,* edited by Marta Randall and Robert Silverberg. New York, Pocket Books, 1981.
"Looking for Satan," in *Shadows of Sanctuary,* edited by Robert Asprin. New York, Ace, 1981.
"A Story for Eilonwy," in *Westercon XXXV Program Book* (Portland, Oregon), 1984.

OTHER PUBLICATIONS

Other

"The Straining Your Eyes Through the Viewscreen Blues," in *Nebula Winners 15,* edited by Frank Herbert. New York, Harper, 1981; London, W. H. Allen, 1982.

Editor, with Susan Janice Anderson, *Aurora: Beyond Equality.* New York, Fawcett, 1976.

*   *   *

Explicitly feminist, Vonda N. McIntyre's science fiction—part of a wave of feminist science fiction and fantasy written in the 1970's and 1980's—is multifaceted. It is characterized not only by careful atention to sexism in society but by thoughtful depictions of the social and personal problems which may still exist when sexual stereotyping and discrimination are vanquished. The need for personal commitment—to oneself and others—despite human imperfection is a theme throughout McIntyre's works, many of which also reflect her scientific background.

The award-winning "Of Mist, and Grass, and Sand" exemplifies these themes. This short story depicts a post-holocaust society whose healers aid the sick with serums cultivated from snake venom. Its protagonist, herself named Snake, is an independent, responsible, and strong person. Snake successfully copes not only with the strenuous demands of her chosen profession but also with her own failure to assess the fears of the nomads who have desperately sought her help. Even though they kill one of her invaluable snakes, she continues to treat and ultimately cure their sick child. This story is exceptional in its understated presentation of realistically flawed chracters in a non-sexist society.

In 1978, McIntyre expanded "Of Mist, and Grass, and Sand" into a full-length novel, *Dreamsnake.* This episodic work follows the healer on a series of adventures as she tries to replace the snake she has lost. Each episode highlights different aspects of contemporary, restrictive society and depicts social and personal alternatives. For example, Snakes encounters "partnerships" which consists of three people. By omitting gender pronouns in this episode, McIntyre conveys the superflousness of sex roles in unconventionally functional relationships. In later episodes, Snake encounters and helps remove the pain that lack of contraceptive knowledge or emphasis on physical appearance can cause.

The Exile Waiting, McIntyre's first novel, also explores the lives of strong women in possible futures. Its young protagonist, Mischa, is a telepath in another post-holocaust society. Mischa frees herself from a series of mental and physical tyrannies through her own ingenuity and courage. Two of McIntyre's best-known stories continue to examine this theme. In "Screwtop," set in a future penal institution, Kylis is a resourceful female spaceport "rat" who has survived since childhood as an interplanetary stowaway. Imprisoned, Kylis learns to accept responsibility for others as well as for herself when she is offered, but refuses, freedom for betraying two fellow prisoners. McIntyre's creation in this story of a "tetraparental"—a genetically superior character endowed with the traits of four parents—is another reflection of her scientific training.

"Aztecs" again demonstrates McIntyre's concern with psychologiclly strong, mature women and her scientific background. Beginning with the sentence, "She gave up her heart quite willingly," this story follows its central character, Laena, through several rites of passage. Having had her heart surgically removed in order to survive "transit" as a spaceship pilot, Laena must adjust not only to her new, rarefied social status but to the unexpected side effects of this surgery. It is only when she falls in love (again, giving up her heart), that Laena learns that her biological rhythms are no longer compatible with those of ordinary people. Remaining with her lover will kill her, but Laena rejects the conventional alternatives. Instead of a romantic liebestod or a renunciation of her career, McIntyre's character sadly chooses to adjust to the limitations of her new way of life.

In 1983, McIntyre expanded "Aztecs" into a full-length novel, *Superluminal.* Shifting among the perspectives of Lanea; her lover, Racul; and a genetically-transformed human, Orca, this work extends McIntyre's examination of alien "otherness" vs. human and ecological interdependence. Orca's family has been altered to live underwater; it is their association with the sentient great whales, once nearly exterminated by humanity, which may provide the key to safe faster-than-light space travel. Orca herself is another strong, committed female protagonist, willing to go against her family's traditions to honor personal loyalities and meet social needs.

McIntyre has continued her political interests in a series of focusing on characters from the popular television series, *Star Trek.* In the 1981 novel, *The Entropy Effect,* she concentrates on Sulu, a relatively minor character in the original series, and on a female starship captain of her own creation, Mandala Flynn. Her depiction of these characters against the mythologized backdrop of the U. S. S. Enterprise enables McIntyre to examine once more the effects of and alternatives to cultural and sexual difference. Sulu's Asian heritage, as well as Mandala's gender, are significant plot elements.

McIntyre has also written the "novelizations" of *Star Trek* motion pictures, bringing to each work her own feminist concerns and ability to create vivid characters. In *Star Trek: The Wrath of Khan,* she concentrates on the minor, alien characters seen only briefly on-screen. By detailing their personalities, cultures, and unique physiology, she provokes the reader (and viewers of the film) to rethink the meanings of "alien. " Similarly, her characterization of Saavik, the half-Vulcan, half-Romulan cadet, causes the reader to reexamine the "outsider" yet again. Saavik's gradual acceptance of friendship and other human emotions is a further variation upon the theme of interdependence seen throughout McIntyre's work.

The novelization of *Star Trek 3: The Search for Spock,* with its emphasis on the primacy of friendship over social directives, provides McIntyre with another vehicle for the exploration of personal loyalties among strong characters in a (comparatively) non-sexist society. Kirk disobeys Starfleet to rescue Spock. McIntyre's ability to rework the *Star Trek* mythos to reflect her own concerns is an interesting, at times exciting example of the ways in which forms of popular culture interact, and of the growing impact of feminism on popular culture in general.

—Natalie M. Rosinsky

McKENNA, Richard M(ilton). American. Born in Mountain Home, Idaho, 9 May 1913. Educated at the University of North Carolina, Chapel Hill, B. A. in English 1956 (Phi Beta Kappa). Married Eva Mae Grice in 1956. Served in the United States Navy, 1931-53: chief machinist's mate; free-lance writer from 1953. Recipient: Harper Prize, 1963; Nebula Award, 1966. *Died 1 November 1964.*

SCIENCE-FICTION PUBLICATIONS

Short Stories

Casey Agonistes and Other Science Fiction and Fantasy Stories. New York, Harper, 1973; London, Gollancz, 1974.

OTHER PUBLICATIONS

Novel

The Sand Pebbles. New York, Harper, 1962; London, Gollancz, 1963.

Short Stories

The Sons of Martha and Other Stories, edited by M. S. Wyeth, Jr. New York, Harper, 1967.

Other

New Eyes for Old: Nonfiction Writing, edited by Eva Grice McKenna and Shirley Graves Cochrane. Winston-Salem, North Carolina, Blair, 1972.
"Journey with a Little Man," in *Turning Points,* edited by Damon Knight. New York, Harper, 1977.

*   *   *

Richard M. McKenna, although best known for his fine novel *The Sand Pebbles,* was also a skilled writer of science fiction whose short stories and novelettes are usually concerned with the troubling and often painful aspects of both fantasy and reality. In a small number of science-fiction and fantasy stories that are vividly written, fast paced, and well characterized, McKenna continually exhibits his superb gifts as a storyteller.

Most of McKenna's science-fiction works are rich in anthropological content. They frequently portray individuals in relation to their groups, and both individual and group in relation to alien cultures or fantasy phenomena. "Casey Agonistes" meticulously explores the interrelationships of patients in a tuberculosis ward, depicting their symbolic rebellion against hospital authority through an ape that is either a genuine apparition or their shared fantasy. The ape, Casey, reflects in his antics the patients' underlying attitudes about the hospital and their poignant efforts to cope with the fact of death. Also, the sharing of the fantasy becomes a catalyst for the raising of the emotional levels of the ward and the improvement of the general conditions there. In "Mine Own Ways," "Hunter, Come Home," and "The Bramble Bush" characters who are members of a scientific team are faced with conflicts that in different ways are caused by the uniqueness of an alien culture on the planet that is the focus of their professional activities. In these stories the psychological state of the protagonists influences and affects the relationship of the group to the aliens and leads to the protagonists being put through a symbolic or actual ritual. This experience alters not only their beliefs, but

also the outcome of the group's mission. McKenna depicts such anthropological themes and motifs with an equal concern for the humans and the aliens.

The world of fantasy, its virtues as well as defects, is the subject on which McKenna focuses most often. In some stories he studies the interplay between the fantasy and an outer reality, casting certain features of the reality into doubt, and in others he constructs fantasy worlds whose landscapes are the basis for a questioning of the nature of fantasy and reality. Often the fantasy world is more appealing, and even ameliorative, as in the cheerful ape's transformation of the despairing hospital ward into an active and even hopeful place. In "The Secret Place" a barren featureless Oregon countryside hides a wondrous fairyland that, in a way, defies the efforts of science to penetrate it and utilize its resources. Dying sailors, in "Fiddler's Green," escape into an imperfect but, through their own imaginative efforts, developing otherworld that simultaneously represents salvation and sterility. Stories like these fantasies that are perceived by the characters as just as real as the obsession-ridden world of reality. However the stories are resolved, whether with acceptance or rejection of the fantasy, the worlds function as alternatives to reality or some facet of reality. In "Hunter, Come Home" and "The Bramble Bush" McKenna treats his planetary settings in a fantasy-like way. The exotic world of the former affects the hold on reality of individuals from two differing human cultures, and the bizarre time-changing world of the latter traps a group of meddling scientists in a field that changes the very shape of their universe.

McKenna integrates linguistic considerations into many of his stories, which is not surprising in an author so intensely interested in anthropological subjects and with the structure of reality versus illusion. The overly macho hunting culture of "Hunter, Come Home" reveals itself as much through its language as its cultural statements of belief. In their society bullets is a curse word, and the ideal is to be as sharp as a gunflint. Words are said to come alive in the native rituals of "Mine Own Ways"; time-binding symbology is integral to the plot of "The Bramble Bush."

No matter how exotic his planetary settings are, and no matter how deeply his characters penetrate a fantasy world, McKenna's fiction is always credible. He makes the fantasy worlds real and, for that matter, presents what is essentially fantatic and unreal about the so-called reality. Such attention to detail, along with McKenna's meticulous approach to the writing of language, adds to the verisimilitude of tales that are among the best examples of storytelling in science fiction.

—Robert Thurston

McLAUGHLIN, Dean (Benjamin, Jr.). American. Born in Ann Arbor, Michigan, 22 July 1931. Educated at the University of Michigan, Ann Arbor, A. B. 1953. Buyer for Slater's Inc., bookshop, Ann Arbor. Address: 1214 West Washington Street, Ann Arbor, Michigan 48103, U.S.A.

SCIENCE-FICTION PUBLICATIONS

Novels

Dome World. New York, Pyramid, 1962.
The Fury from Earth. New York, Pyramid, 1963.
The Man Who Wanted Stars. New York, Lancer, 1965.

Short Stories

Hawk among the Sparrows. New York, Scribner, 1976; London, Hale, 1977.

Uncollected Short Stories

"Omit Flowers," in *Asimov's Choice: Astronauts and Androids*, edited by George H. Scithers. New York, Davis, 1977.
"The Astronomical Hazards of the Tobacco Habit," in *Isaac Asimov's Science Fiction Anthology 1*, edited by George H. Scithers. New York, Davis, 1978.

*   *   *

Dean McLaughlin's novels display a fascination with the concept of one man capable of altering the entire course of history. McLaughlin does not have in mind brilliant military strategists or mighty-thewed barbarians, but common men, those who may even doubt their own actions but carry through with them nonetheless. Danial Mason, leader of the undersea city of Wilmington in *Dome World*, is a perfect example. Mason is chief administrator of the domed city, one of many that have sprung up on the ocean floor, built by various nations intent on mining or fishing or trading with other nations. But the undersea cities are also the focus of some conflict because of the haphazard fashion in which matters of sovereignty have been resolved. So it is that the American Union and South Africa are on the verge of war over control of a rich vanadium deposit that lies between two such domes. Because of the utter vulnerability of the domes, Mason organizes a widespread secession from the mainland nations to prevent fatal involvement in their war. The second half of the novel deals with the situation some years later when the creation of smaller, individualized domes is the cause of tension between the newly formed league of domed cities and the mainland authorities. Once again a small businessman ignores his own government to take steps that eventually reduces the chance of war. Both of McLaughlin's characters are far from physically fit; one is recently returned from the moon and has difficulties with Earth's greater gravity, and the other has a weak heart that might cease to function at any time.

Similarly, the protagonist of *The Fury from Earth* is a pacifist who refuses to help the government of Venus to develop weapons for their war with Earth. On the other hand, he is willing to help design purely defensive weapons, and is quick to see that a new development on Earth could be used for interstellar travel rather than as an offensive weapon that will shake entire planets. This is thematically somewhat similar to McLaughlin's remaining novel, *The Man Who Wanted Stars,* in which a single man keeps the space program alive, primarily through his own stubbornness. The latter novel suffers somewhat from the didactic material, which often interferes with the plot, and with the megalomania of the central character, which often causes the reader to dislike him even while agreeing with his position.

McLaughlin has also produced a string of competent short stories, at least two of which are exceptional. "Hawk among the Sparrows" is somewhat unusual for McLaughlin in that the hero tries to alter history and fails utterly. He has been projected back through time with a modern supersonic aircraft, and assumes that he can affect the course of the air war in Europe. Such is not the case. He cannot locate appropriate fuel, and his aircraft travels so rapidly that it is impossible for him to engage in combat with his slower, more primitive antagonists. McLaughlin also produced one of the more fascinating alien societies in "The Brotherhood of Keepers."

Although not a stylistic virtuoso, McLaughlin employs clean prose throughout his writing, with a crisp delivery that falters only in *The Man Who Wanted Stars*. He avoids larger-than-life character very consciously, taking pains to make his characters vulnerable and human. His plots and situations ring true, and he takes care that issues are for the most part presented in many facets rather than clear cut. Most of his better fiction leaves the reader with something to consider even after the story has ended, although McLaughlin is careful to tie up necessary loose ends.

—Don D'Ammassa

McQUAY, Mike. Also writes as Victor Appleton; Susan Claudia; Franklin W. Dixon; Laura Lee Hope; Carolyn Keene. American. Born in Baltimore, Maryland, 3 June 1949. Attended grammar school in Baltimore; McGuiness High School, Oklahoma City; University of Dallas, 1967-70. Married 1) Mary McQuay in 1968 (divorced, 1981); 2) Sandy McQuay in 1982; one son and two daughters. Musician, aircraft worker in Asia, banker, factory worker. Since 1980, Artist-in-Residence, Central State University, Edmond, Oklahoma. Agent: Russ Galen, Scott Meredith Literary Agency, 845 Third Avenue, New York, New York 10022. Address: 5933 NW 81st, Oklahoma City, Oklahoma 73132, U.S.A.

SCIENCE-FICTION PUBLICATIONS

Novels (series: Mathew Swain)

Lifekeeper. New York, Avon, 1980.
Escape from New York (novelization of screenplay). New York, Bantam, and London, Corgi, 1981.
Mathew Swain: Hot Time in Old Town. New York, Bantam, 1981.
Mathew Swain: When Trouble Beckons. New York, Bantam, 1981.
Mathew Swain: Deadliest Show in Town. New York, Bantam, 1982.
Mathew Swain: The Odds Are Murder. New York, Bantam, 1983.
Jitterbug. New York, Bantam, 1984.
Pure Blood. New York, Bantam, 1985.
Motherearth. New York, Bantam, 1985.
My Science Project (novelization of screenplay). New York, Bantam, 1985.

OTHER PUBLICATIONS

Novel

Cradle to Grave (as Susan Claudia). New York, Fawcett, 1983.

Other (for children)

Tom Swift: Crater of Mystery (as Victor Appleton). New York, Simon and Schuster, 1982.
Tom Swift: Planet of Nightmares (as Victor Appleton). New York, Simon and Schuster, 1983.
Nancy Drew/Hardy Boys: Supersleuths II (as Carolyn Keene and Franklin W. Dixon). New York, Simon and Schuster, 1984.

Nancy Drew: Ghost Stories II (as Carolyn Keene). New York, Simon and Schuster, 1985.
Bobbsey Twins: Haunted House (as Laura Lee Hope). New York, Simon and Schuster, 1985.

*

Mike McQuay comments:

My writing tends toward the sociological/humanistic end of the spectrum. Though considered a cynic by many of my detractors, I consider myself a social realist (an optimist in wolf's clothing). My work as a whole deals with the survival of the human spirit despite the out-of-control technologies we've set in motion, which puts me in direct opposition (gladly) with the science-as-God writers who seem to fill the shelves. Don't look for sugar coating in a McQuay book—

My main sub-theme seems to be discussions on the nature of reality, and the human's ability to construct reality to his own specifications.

* * *

Mike McQuay has established himself in a short time as an energetic and prolific writer whose science fiction projects an emphatically masculine vision. McQuay's Mathew Swain series makes an interesting effort to combine the science-fiction and private eye genres, and his other novels display a penchant for vivid melodramatic action. Strongly individualist and non-conformist heroes are a distinguishing feature of McQuay's work, as well as an obvious specticism and distrust of the ethics and purposes of corporations and governments. Another intriguing trait of McQuay's fiction is the influence of his southwest background, which appears both in his style and in the non-conformist stance of his tough-minded heroes.

McQuay's first important novel was *Lifekeeper*, which employed the bold stroke of a black hero. In a dismal future divided between wilderness tribes and communal states, ruled by computers which outlaw individuality, Doral Dulan is a rebellious and archaic individualist who realizes his destiny by overthrowing the dominance of the machines and fulfilling the desert tribes' yearning for a messiah. Some sharp parallels with Frank Herbert's Dune novels are obvious, including an ending which attempts to suggest Herbert's sophisticated sense of irony.

This ambitious but uneven first novel was followed by *Escape from New York*, a novelization of a cynically conceived film melodrama about a near future in which New York City has collapsed into a forbidden zone or anarchic sanctuary for criminals and outcasts. Plissken, the heroic antihero, is characterized effectively, and his hard-headed and intractable individualism anticipates Matt Swain, the hero of McQuay's 21st-century private-eye series.

The Swain series is dedicated to the memory of Raymond Chandler, "who understood. " Presumably McQuay is paying homage to Chandler's vision of a corrupt and materialistic society where ethical norms are in constant flux, and also to Chandler's Philip Marlowe, the incorruptible and disenchanted knight who uncovers forgotten crimes and repressed memories of venality and compromise, as Chandler described his hero's role in his famous essay and apologia, "The Simple Art of Murder. "

In the first Swain adventure, *Hot Time in Old Town*, McQuay's private eye is depicted as a younger and slightly more idealistic Marlowe, and as a former law officer now playing a lone hand in a decaying Southwestern city suggestive of Dallas or Tulsa. However, Swain has a more active sex life than Marlowe, since McQuay bestows on him a wealthy and voluptuous young woman, Ginny Teal, in the first novel; while in later books in the series other attractive woman become Swain's lovers. Swain is also a more impulsive and physical hero than Marlowe, displaying a good deal of prowess with his fists and with weapons, somewhat in the mode of Robert B. Parker's Spenser. Yet like his model, Marlowe, Swain also remains true to the tradition of the private eye as a man of honor, showing himself to be relentless and incorruptible as he searches for the murderer of a dissolute heir in *Hot Time on Old Town*.

In the second Swain novel, *When Trouble Beckons*, McQuay takes his hero to a city on the moon where a large multinational corporation rules. Although Swain's mission is ostensibly to rescue Ginny, in reality the novel examines the corrupting influence of a decadent and dehumanizing social environment, evoking memories of Dashiell Hammett's Personville (or "Poisonville") in *Red Harvest*, and Ross MacDonald's scandal-ridden midwestern town in *Blue City*. *When Trouble Beckons* is notable for its unrelenting action, its virtuoso reversals of plot, especially in the closing pages, and its sympathetic characterization of an earthy woman cab driver.

The Deadliest Show in Town continues Swain's crusade against corporate dishonesty and greed, and government indifference and corruption, this time pitting the private eye against the 21st-century communications industry. The final entry to date in the series, *The Odds Are Murder*, continues the emphasis on violent physical action featured in the first three novels, as Swain investigates greed and scandal in the manufacture of pharmaceutical drugs. But the themes and attitudes of the Swain books are now beginning to seem repetitious and obsessive; as yet, none of the Swain novels has established itself as worthy of comparison with the mature Raymond Chandler.

To his credit, however, McQuay has refused to become the prisoner of a series with its limitations. In 1984, he published *Jitterbug*, a work which returns to the epic scale of *Lifekeeper*, depicting a dystopian world of the 22nd century. In this novel, a fanatical Arab dictatorship rules a decaying America; but this "corporation" is challenged successfully by the rebellion of Olson, another of McQuay's tough-minded heroes, who emerges from obscurity and a harsh upbringing in the southwest. *Jitterbug* shows marked growth in McQuay as a novelist, for its extrapolated future world is envisaged with both imaginative power and an increased thoroughness and plausibility.

Continuing to write with impressive energy, McQuay followed *Jitterbug* with *Pure Blood*, another vigorous adventure saga set in a much-changed New York State a thousand years hence. In the predominantly primitive post-disaster world of this novel, McQuay portrays an environment of barbaric humans and new creatures created by genetic experiment, where another of his outcast heroes, Morgan, tempered by the crucible of hardship and struggle, rises to leadership.

Inevitably, McQuay's virile fiction depicting traditionally masculine heroes who grimly and courageously battle against worlds of decadence resulting from 20th-century follies will suggest comparisons with such famous names as Heinlein and Philip José Farmer. Whatever future development McQuay's work takes, it seems clear that he has the energy and talent to become both commercially popular and a major novelist in the science-fiction genre.

—Edgar L. Chapman

MEAD, (Edward) Shepherd. American. Born in St. Louis, Missouri, 26 April 1914. Educated at St. Louis Country Day School, graduated 1932; Washington University, St. Louis, B. A. 1936. Married Annabelle Pettibone in 1943; one daughter and two sons. Worked for Benton and Bowles, New York, 1936-56, retired as Vice-President; consultant, S. H. Benson Ltd., London, 1958-62. Agent: Gerald Pollinger, Laurence Pollinger Ltd., 18 Maddox Street, London W1R 0EU; or, Don Congdon Associates, 177 East 70th Street, New York, New York 10021, U. S. A. Address: 53 Rivermead Gardens, Ranelagh Gardens, London SW6 3RY, England.

SCIENCE-FICTION PUBLICATIONS

Novels

The Magnificent MacInnes. New York, Farrar Straus, 1949; as *The Sex Machine,* New York, Popular Library, 1949.
The Big Ball of Wax: A Story of Tomorrow's Happy World. New York, Simon and Schuster, 1954; London, Boardman, 1955.
The Carefully Considered Rape of the World: A Novel about the Unspeakable. New York, Simon and Schuster, and London, Macdonald, 1966.

OTHER PUBLICATIONS

Novels

Tessie, The Hound of Channel One. New York, Doubleday, 1951.
The Admen. New York, Simon and Schuster, 1958; London, Boardman, 1959.
The Four Window Girl; or, How to Make More Money Than Men. New York, Simon and Schuster, and London, Boardman, 1959.
"Dudley, There Is No Tomorrow!" "Then How about This Afternoon?" New York, Simon and Schuster, and London, Macdonald, 1963.
How to Succeed at Business Spying by Trying. New York, Simon and Schuster, 1968; London, Harrap, 1969.
'Er; or, The Brassbound Beauty, The Bearded Bicyclist, and the Gold-Colored Teen-Age Grandfather. New York, Simon and Schuster, 1969; London, Harrap, 1970.

Other

How to Succeed in Business Without Really Trying: The Dastard's Guide to Fame and Fortune. New York, Simon and Schuster, 1952; Kingswood, Surrey, World's Work, 1953.
How to Get Rich in TV Without Really Trying. New York, Simon and Schuster, 1956; London, Boardman, 1958.
How to Succeed with Women Without Really Trying: The Dastard's Guide to the Birds and the Bees. New York, Ballantine, 1957; London, Boardman, 1958.
How to Live Like a Lord Without Really Trying: A Confidential Manual Prepared as Part of a Survival Kit for Americans Living in Britain. London, Macdonald, 1964; New York, Simon and Schuster, 1965.
How to Stay Medium-Young Practically Forever Without Really Trying. New York, Simon and Schuster, 1971; London, Joseph, 1972.
Free the Male Man! The Manifesto of the Men's Liberation Movement. New York, Simon and Schuster, 1972; London, Joseph, 1973.
How to Get to the Future Before It Gets to You. New York,

Hawthorn, and London, Joseph, 1974.
How to Succeed in Tennis Without Really Trying. New York, McKay, 1977.
Tennessee Williams: An Intimate Biography, with Dakin Williams. New York, Arbor House, 1983.

*

Manuscript Collection: Washington University, St. Louis.

Shepherd Mead comments:
    I have a warm spot in my heart for science fiction. Sometimes things can be said by means of it that cannot be said any other way. That is surely true of *The Carefully Considered Rape of the World,* which is about genetics, really—that the first beings to control their own evolution will become the first gods of the universe.
    My favorite book of all is *The Big Ball of Wax.* At the time I considered it the other side of the coin to Orwell's excellent *Nineteen Eighty-Four*—that the future would belong not to the totalitarian Big Brothers but to the persuaders. The book showed what would happen to a society that gave everyone only what the lowest common denominator wanted. Now that the returns are in, we can see which of us was right—and it wasn't Orwell! (a great man, nonetheless).
    I have one more SF work in manuscript form called *The Purple Peoplegrams;* this is about the whole business of electronic communication with the rest of the universe.

*   *   *

    Shepherd Mead, who is best known for *How to Succeed in Business Without Really Trying,* has written three novels which may be classed as science fiction. *The Magnificent MacInnes* and *The Big Ball of Wax* are similar in thrust—both focus on the manipulation of mass society by the media and by Madison Avenue. In the first the advertising industry and its marketing pollsters by catering to ordinary taste are making "sure everybody gets tomorrow what the lowest common denominator wanted yesterday." When it is accidentally discovered that Victor V. MacInnes has the facility (unexplained) to intuit public opinion on any question, an absurd utopia is envisioned. Simply register the will of the people and then feed it in the name of "true Democracy." The result, of course, is a sterile, drab mediocrity—the TV program that achieves top ratings but has its audience soundly sleeping. The similarity between Kornbluth and Pohl (especially in *The Space Merchants*) and Mead extends to *The Big Ball of Wax,* an account of the crucial sequence of events in 1993 that have led to "the best of all possible worlds." The gimmick here is XP, an ersatz electronic experience for the real thing from eating to travel to sex (compare Compton's *Synthajoy*). XP provides the perfect vehicle for the merchandisers to guide society "step by step down the path of mediocrity." The warning is similar to Kornbluth's "The Marching Morons": "Notch by notch the mental level was dropping, thinking was decreasing, self-expression dying out." Both novels have as protagonists male, mid-level Madison Avenue executives who serve the system with naive enthusiasm: "We have made Progress, and we look to all of you to carry the torch when we drop it and to go ahead, always ahead, to the Goal line."
    The Carefully Considered Rape of the World, structurally like *The Big Ball of Wax,* is a chronicle of the brief period when distant kin from Phycyx (48 light years away) arrive like UFO's to lead us to a higher evolutionary stage by artificially impregnating a relatively small number of women the world

over. The novel traces the effects on three Long Island couples. The eventual offspring are super-intelligent and baboon-like. Inherent again is a message, a stronger one than the earlier warnings about mass merchandising. The Phycians have a Formula for Evolutionary Termination, popularly called the Doomsday Variable: given a carnivorous heredity (the gentle yielding to the savage), if "nuclear ability comes before genetic control, extinction follows within approximately four generations." Like Vonnegut, Mead is an adroit comic writer who uses SF material to achieve his satire.

—Anthony Wolk

_____

MEEK, S(terner St.) P(aul). Also wrote as Sterner St. Paul. American. Born in Chicago, Illinois, 8 April 1894. Educated at the University of Chicago, Sc. A. 1914; University of Alabama, University, S. B. 1915 (Phi Beta Kappa); University of Wisconsin, Madison, 1916; Massachusetts Institute of Technology, Cambridge, 1921-23. Married Edna Burndage Noble in 1927; one son. Football coach, Kirkley Junior College, Greenville, Texas, 1915; chemist, Western Electric Company, Hawthorne, Illinois, 1916, and Deuvitt Laboratories, Chicago, 1917. Served in the United States Army from 1917; directed small arms ammunition research, 1923-26; chief publications officer, Ordnance Department, 1941-44; retired due to disability, 1947: Colonel. Held patents on tracer ammunition. *Died 10 June 1972.*

SCIENCE-FICTION PUBLICATIONS

Novels

The Drums of Tapajos. New York, Avalon, 1961.
Troyana. New York, Avalon, 1962.

Short Stories

The Monkeys Have No Tails in Zamboanga. New York, Morrow, 1935.
Arctic Bridge. London, Utopian, 1944.

Uncollected Short Stories (series: Dr. Bird)

"The Murgatroyd Experiment," in *Amazing Stories Quarterly* (New York), Winter 1929.
"The Red Peril," in *Amazing* (New York), September 1929.
"The Cave of Horror" (Bird), in *Astounding* (New York), January 1930.
"The Perfect Counterfeit" (Bird), in *Scientific Detective* (New York), January 1930.
"The Thief of Time" (Bird), in *Astounding* (New York), February 1930.
"The Radio Robbery" (Bird), in *Amazing* (New York), February 1930.
"Into Space" (as Sterner St. Paul), in *Astounding* (New York), February 1930.
"Cold Light" (Bird), in *Astounding* (New York), March 1930.
"The Ray of Madness" (Bird), in *Astounding* (New York), April 1930.
"Trapped in the Depths," in *Wonder Stories* (New York), June 1930.

"The Gland Murders" (Bird), in *Scientific Detective* (New York), June 1930.
"Beyond the Heaviside Layer," in *Astounding* (New York), July 1930.
"The Last War," in *Amazing* (New York), August 1930.
"The Tragedy of Spider Island," in *Wonder Stories* (New York), September 1930.
"The Attack from Space," in *Astounding* (New York), September 1930.
"Stolen Brains" (Bird), in *Astounding* (New York), October 1930.
"The Osmotic Theorem," in *Wonder Stories Quarterly* (New York), Winter 1930.
"Sea Terror" (Bird), in *Astounding* (New York), December 1930.
"The Black Lamp" (Bird), in *Astounding* (New York), February 1931.
"The Earth's Cancer" (Bird), in *Amazing* (New York), March 1931.
"When Caverns Yawned" (Bird), in *Astounding* (New York), May 1931.
"The Port of Missing Planes" (Bird), in *Astounding* (New York), August 1931.
"The Solar Magnet" (Bird), in *Astounding* (New York), October 1931.
"Giants on the Earth," in *Astounding* (New York), December 1931.
"Poisoned Air" (Bird), in *Astounding* (New York), March 1932.
"B. C. 30,000," in *Astounding* (New York), April 1932.
"The Great Drought" (Bird), in *Astounding* (New York), May 1932.
"Vanishing Gold," in *Wonder Stories* (New York), May 1932.
"The Synthetic Entity," in *Wonder Stories* (New York), January 1933.
"The Mentality Machine," in *Tales of Wonder* (Kingswood, Surrey), Spring 1939.
"Awlo of Ulm" and "Submicroscopic," in *Before the Golden Age,* edited by Isaac Asimov. New York, Doubleday, 1974.
"Futility," in *Gosh! Wow! (Sense of Wonder) Science Fiction,* edited by Forrest J. Ackerman. New York, Bantam, 1982.

OTHER PUBLICATIONS

Novel

Island Born. New York, Godwin, 1937.

Other (for children)

Jerry: The Adventures of an Army Dog. New York, Morrow, 1932.
Frog, The Horse That Knew No Master. Philadelphia, Penn, 1933.
Gypsy Lad: The Story of a Champion Setter. New York, Morrow, 1934.
Franz, A Dog of the Police. Philadelphia, Penn, 1935.
Dignity, A Springer Spaniel. Philadelphia, Penn, 1937.
Rusty, A Cocker Spaniel. Philadelphia, Penn, 1938.
Gustav, A Son of Franz. Philadelphia, Penn, 1940.
Pat: The Story of a Seeing Eye Dog. New York, Knopf, 1947.
So You're Going to Get a Puppy. New York, Knopf, 1947.
Boots: The Story of a Working Sheep Dog. New York, Knopf, 1948.
Midnight, A Cow Pony. New York, Knopf, 1949.
Ranger, A Dog of the Forest Service. New York, Knopf, 1949.
Hans, A Dog of the Border Patrol. New York, Knopf, 1950.

Surfman: The Adventures of a Coast Guard Dog. New York, Knopf, 1950.
Paga, A Border Patrol Horse . New York, Knopf, 1951.
Red, A Trailing Bloodhound. New York, Knopf, 1951.
Boy, An Ozark Coon Hound. New York, Knopf, 1952.
Rip, A Game Protector. New York, Knopf, 1952.
Omar, A State Police Dog. New York, Knopf, 1953.
Bellfarm Star: The Story of a Pace. New York, Dodd Mead, 1955.
Pierre of the Big Top: The Story of a Circus Poodle. New York, Dodd Mead, 1956.

* * *

S. P. Meek was one of the most prominent contributors of the science-fiction magazines which struggled to survive the years of the depression between 1929 and 1933. He first appeared with "The Murgatroyd Experiment," a still-memorable tale concerning the appalling results of an effort to sustain the world's swollen population in the year 2060, and wrote regularly for the next few years. It was to be expected that he would write about future warfare, and in "The Red Peril" he drew a grim picture of the world's great cities being sprayed with disease germs in 1957—the enemy, inevitably, being the Soviet Union. Propaganda leaflets were also in the armoury of the attackers, whose gravity-defying aircraft were repelled by atomic shells. Even after the Soviet leaders had been confined on St. Helena, the struggle was continued in a sequel, "The Last War," in which synthetic men were produced to turn the tide of battle.

The Red Menace often lurked in the background when Meek's popular character, Dr. Bird of the Bureau of Standards, accompanied by Operative Carnes of the Secret Service, set out to expose some piece of villainy in the series of intriguing tales. In "The Gland Murders" the plot was designed to decimate the educated rich by lacing their bootleg liquor with an extract from the pineal gland of a murderer, stimulating them to violent acts for which they would pay the penalty. Economic disaster was narrowly averted when, in "Vanishing Gold," bullion in the vaults of the Federal Reserve Bank became radioactive and lost weight. In "When Caverns Yawned" whole cities were imperilled by artificial earthquakes; and in "The Solar Magnet" the subversive genius Ivan Saranoff even tried to straighten the Earth's axis so that Russia might win her true place in the sun. Most of the Dr. Bird stories appeared in the early issues of *Astounding Stories*, where the emphasis on foreign villians brought protests from some readers, and an assurance from the editor that "our authors mean no offence. " Among other tales was "Giants on the Earth," a gaudy interplanetary adventure in a style he seldom affected but which clearly showed the extent of his versatility. His tale of an electronic world, "Submicroscopic," was continued in "Awlo of Ulm," an action-romance in the Burroughs tradition. Two serials, *The Drums of Tapajos* and its sequel, *Troyana*, concerned a lost civilisation buried in the Brazilian jungle, and appeared in book form after an interval of 30 years. A collection of his humorous short stories was published as *The Monkeys Have No Tails in Zamboanga.*

—Walter Gillings

MELTZER, David. American. Born in Rochester, New York, 17 February 1937. Educated at public schools in Brooklyn and Los Angeles; Los Angeles City College, 1955-56; University of California, Los Angeles, 1956-57. Married Christina Meyer in 1958; three daughters and one son. Manager, Discovery Bookshop, San Francisco, 1959-67; Editor, *Maya,* Mill Valley, California, 1966-71; teacher, Urban School, San Fransisco, 1975-6. Since 1970, Editor, *Tree* magazine and Tree Books, Bolinas, later Berkeley, California; since 1979, teacher, New College of California, San Francisco. Composer, musician, and singer: performed with Serpent Power and David and Tina, 1970-72. Recipient: Council of Literary Magazines grant, 1972, 1981; National Endowment for the Arts grant, 1974, for publishing, 1975. Address: Box 9005, Berkeley, California 94709, U.S.A.

SCIENCE-FICTION PUBLICATIONS

Novels (series: Agency; Brain Plant)

The Agency. North Hollywood, Essex House, 1968.
The Agent (Agency). North Hollywood, Essex House, 1968.
How Many Blocks in the Pile? (Agency). North Hollywood, Essex House, 1968.
Lovely (Brain Plant). North Hollywood, Essex House, 1969.
Healer (Brain Plant). North Hollywood, Essex House, 1969.
Out (Brain Plant). North Hollywood, Essex House, 1969.
Glue Factory (Brain Plant), North Hollywood, Essex House, 1969.

Uncollected Short Stories

"Kick Me Deadly," in *Dazzle* (San Francisco), 1957.
"And All That Jazz," in *Showcase* (North Hollywood), 1961.

OTHER PUBLICATIONS

Novels

Orf. North Hollywood, Essex House, 1968.
The Marytr. North Hollywood, Essex House, 1969.
Star. North Hollywood, Brandon House, 1970.

Verse

Poems, with Donald Schenker. Privately printed, 1957.
Ragas. San Francisco, Discovery, 1959.
The Clown. Larkspur, California, Semina, 1960.
Station. Privately printed, 1964.
The Blackest Rose. Berkeley, California, Oyez, 1964.
Oyez! Berkeley, California, Oyez, 1965.
The Process. Berkeley, California, Oyez, 1965.
In Hope I Offer a Fire Wheel. Berkeley, California, Oyez, 1965.
The Dark Continent. Berkeley, California, Oyez, 1967.
Nature Poem. Santa Barbara, California, Unicorn Press, 1967.
Santamaya, with Jack Shoemaker. San Francisco, Maya, 1968.
Round the Poem Box: Rustic and Domestic Home Movies for Stan and Jane Brakhage. Los Angeles, Black Sparrow Press, 1969.
Yesod. London, Trigram Press, 1969.
From Eden Book. San Francisco, Cranium Press, 1969.
Abulafia Song. Santa Barbara, California, Unicorn Press, 1969.
Greenspeech. Goleta, California, Christopher, 1970.
Luna. Los Angeles, Black Sparrow Press, 1970.
Letters and Numbers. Berkeley, California, Oyez, 1970.
Bronx Lil/Head of Lillin S. A. C. Santa Barbara, California, Capra Press, 1970.
32 Beams of Light. Santa Barbara, California, Capra Press, 1970.

Knots. Bolinas, California, Tree, 1971.
Bark: A Polemic. Santa Barbara, California, Capra Press, 1973.
Hero/Lil. Los Angeles, Black Sparrow, Press, 1973.
Tens: Selected Poems 1961-1971, edited by Kenneth Rexroth. New York, Herder, 1973.
The Eyes, The Blood. San Francisco, Mudra, 1973.
French Broom. Berkeley, California, Oyez, 1974.
Blue Rags. Berkley, California, Oyez, 1974.
Harps. Berkeley, California, Oyez, 1975.
Six. Santa Barbara, California, Black Sparrow Press, 1976.
Bolero. Berkeley, California, Oyez, 1976.
The Art, The Veil. Milwaukee, Membrane Press, 1981.
The Name: Selected Poetry 1973-1983. Santa Barbara, California, Black Sparrow Press, 1983.

Recordings: *Serpent Power*, Vanguard, 1972; *Poet Song*, Vanguard, 1974; *David Meltzer Reading*, Membrane, 1981; *Nurse*, S-Tapes, 1982.

Other

We All Have Something to Say to Each Other: Being an Essay Entitled "Patchen" and Four Poems. San Francisco, Auerhahn Press, 1962.
Introduction to the Outsiders (essay on Beat Poetry). Fort Lauderdale, Florida, Rodale, 1962.
Bazascope Mother (essay on Robert Alexander). Los Angeles, Drekfesser Press, 1964.
Journal of the Birth. Berkeley, California, Oyez, 1967.
Isla Vista Notes: Fragmentary, Aopcalyptic, Didactic, Contradictions. Santa Barbara, California, Christopher, 1970.
Abra (for children). Berkeley, California, Hipparchia Press, 1976.
Two-way Mirror: A Poetry Note-Book. Berkeley, California, Oyez, 1977.

Editor, with Lawrence Ferlinghetti and Michael McClure, *Journal for the Protection of All Beings 1 and 3*. San Francisco, City Lights, 2 vols., 1961-69.
Editor, *The San Francisco Poets*. New York, Ballantine, 1971; revised edition, as *Golden Gate*, San Francisco, Wingbow Press, 1976.
Editor, *Birth: An Anthology*. New York, Ballantine, 1973.
Editor, *The Secret Garden: A Anthology in the Kabbalah*. New York, Seabury Press, 1976.
Editor, *The Path of the Names*, by Abraham Abulafia. Berkeley, California, Tree, and London, Trigram Press, 1976.
Editor, *Birth: An Anthology of Ancient Texts, Songs, Prayers, and Stories*. San Francisco, North Point Press, 1981.
Editor, *Death* (anthology). Berkeley, North Point Press, 1984.

Translator, with Allen Say, *Morning Glories*, by Shiga Naoya. Berkeley, California, Oyez, 1975.

*

Manuscript Collections: Washington University, St. Louis; University of Indiana, Bloomington; University of California, Los Angeles.

Critical Studies: *David Meltzer: A Sketch from Memory and Descriptive Checklist* by David Kherdian, Berkeley, California, Oyez, 1967; "The Poet as Erotic Novelist," in *The Secret Record: Modern Erotic Literature* by Michael Perkins, New York, Morrow, 1976; article by Robert Hawley and Ann Charters, in the *The Beats* edited by Charters, Detroit, Gale, 1983.

David Meltzer comments:

My involvement with science fiction began when I was a teenager with my reading of H. G. Wells. This led to the early Conklin anthologies and to pulps like *Famous Fantastic Mysteries, Amazing,* and *Thrilling Wonder Stories. Weird Tales* directed me to Arkham House and to Bradbury's first book. Though I enjoyed all aspects of the genre—from David H. Keller to A. E. van Vogt—the writers who interested me most, for their style and innovative stories, were Sturgeon, Kuttner, and finally Alfred Bester, whose *Demolished Man* (serialized in *Galaxy*) was a significant opening in the development of my own work. Its typographical free-play, reminiscent of 1920's Dada and Surrealist typewriter art, felt comfortable to a young poet enthralled with Kenneth Patchen and E. E. Cummings.

Though I wrote and sold a few stories in the 1950's, it was writing the erotic tracts for Essex House that gave me the format I needed to extend my involvement with science fiction. These novels allowed me to use the speculative freedom of SF in a free-for-all attempt to make moral, political, and it is hoped, satirical appraisal of the USA in the late 1960's without sacrificing any "respectability" poets are supposed to wear as top hats or laurel crowns.

*   *   *

Of the ten novels by the California poet and novelist David Meltzer, seven were—in the author's words—"SF or fantasy, future projections. " The fact that the Essex House series, edited by Brian Kirby, was devoted to serious American erotic writing did not hinder Meltzer when he wrote his prophetic, Blakean novels of the future. As he has said, "The pornographic erotic format seemed most fitting a zone to engage in didactic moral outcries. . . ."

In *The Agency,* The first volume of a trilogy, Meltzer conveys a poetic vision in spare, allusive prose. He uses techniques special to speculative fiction and satire. As the novelist Norman Spinrad writes in his afterword to *The Agent:* the Agency "is clearly Meltzer's paradigm of society; a mindless machine of which we are all 'agents,' *including* those whom the machine supposedly serves. " . . . . The Agency is "a well-organised, self-sufficient, sexual underground. " In *The Agency* a young man is picked up by sexual agents and—like the woman in *Story of O*—spends the rest of the novel being forcibly indoctrinated with The Agency's tyrannical precepts. Brainwashed, he becomes an agent himself, ready to propagate the evil fantasies of his masters. In *The Agent* the satirical possibilities implied in *The Agency* are applied more broadly to various aspects of American society. Here Meltzer's deliberately ambiguous portrayal of two agents who may or may not be working for the same agency is often reminiscent of scenes from the movie *Dr. Strangelove*. The third volume in the trilogy, *How Many Blocks in the Pile?*, is constructed differently from the first two. In it, Meltzer creates an exaggerated portrait of the Agency's customers—a married couple who respond to sexual advertisements.

Meltzer's most ambitious erotic SF project is the Brain Plant Tetralogy. In classical Greek drama, a tetralogy is a group of four dramatic pieces, either four tragedies or three tragedies and a satire. Meltzer's Brain-Plant novels are not tragedies in the classical sense, and satire is a prominent feature of each of them; but his extrapolation of tendencies in American society of the late 1960's and their application in his prophetic fictions renders a tragic, scarifying vision. Meltzer's achievement in these four novels does not lie in the creation of characters, because they are either deliberate caricatures or disembodied voices, nor in the creation of a central fantasy. His projection of a future

American government ruled by "Military Industry" in which "Rads" (radicals) and "Rebs" (lower middle-class whites), "Snarks" (sexual anarchists) and black militants, are pacified by "Fun Zones" (ingenious Disneylands for the satisfaction of sexual fantasies) is simplistic—like R. Crumb cartoons, as Frank M. Robinson points out in his afterword to *Lovely*. Meltzer's achievement lies instead in the utterly convincing manner in which he argues his theme of exploitation through sex, power, and dreams. The Series, because of the extravagent, entertaining, violent, prophetic vision it conveys, is one of the high points of erotic SF literature.

—Michael Perkins

MELUCH, R(ebecca) M. American. Born in Ohio, 24 October 1956. Educated at the University of North Carolina, Greensboro, B. A. in theatre 1978; University of Pennsylvania, Philadelphia, M. A. in ancient history 1981. Since 1978, full-time writer. Since 1982, assistant instructor, Kim's Martial Arts School, Fairview Park, Ohio. Agent: Marie Rodell-Frances Collin Literary Agency, 110 West 40th Street, New York, New York 10018. Address: 29520 Schwartz Road, Westlake, Ohio 44145, U.S.A.

SCIENCE-FICTION PUBLICATIONS

Novels (series: Wind)

Sovereign. New York, New American Library, 1979; London, Arrow, 1980.
Wind Dancers. New York, New American Library, 1981.
Wind Child. New York, New American Library, 1982.
Jerusalem Fire. New York, New American Library, 1985.

*   *   *

R. M. Meluch is a relatively young writer (23 when her first novel was published) who paints her intergalactic adventure stories with a broad brush.

Sovereign, her first novel, is a self-contained saga of heroism thrust upon the person of a tormented young man. *Wind Child* and *Wind Dancer* combine to chronicle the return from virtual extermination of a race of shape-changers through the assistance of half-breed human/alien. In all of the novels, however, the characters rather than the plot grasp the reader's attention.

Sovereign is in fact a sort of character study predicated on a father-son conflict. The novel is divided into four parts, starting on the alien Arana, moving with the character, Teal, to earth, then to his own spacecraft, Sovereign, and then back to Arana. It follows Teal's heroic struggle for survival through a variety of interpersonal situations cast against an intergalactic war. As the 33rd and crucial generation of a long line of single, male children, Teal is dependent upon his father's tutoring for protection from side-effects of this breeding program. His birth causes the death of his mother and his father's rejection, starting a chain of events within which he must oppose ever larger aggregates of hostile beings. His father is his first enemy, while his second is the competing Brekk family, his third the invading "northern" tribes of the home planet, Arana, his fourth the alien Uelson race which threatens Arana as well as earth (Arana's social structure owes something to a Scottish model). Teal's long struggle to replace his father's missing affection takes him

first north to join a spacefaring race and then off-planet to battle the nefarious Uelsons in earth's behalf. These adventures, seemingly motivated by internal need rather than external compulsion, form the arena within which his heroic scope can be displayed. The focus of *Sovereign* is this character and all that flows from him, making the plot at times confusing but not without precedent in SF adventure tales.

Wind Dancer and *Wind Child*, while also based upon the existence of a race of genetically altered beings, is more reminiscent of H. Beam Piper than Doc Smith. A dying race of beings with 1sets of chromosomes is able to take three forms— human-like, animal, and wind. The wealthy terrans who have taken over their planet wish to deny and then to conceal their existence in order to hold their claim to a planet with no apparent indigenous population, a plot element borrowed from Piper's *Little Fuzzy*. *Wind Dancer* introduces the alien-human conflict and the characters, alien Niki, half-alien Laure, and human East, who will restore the race. *Wind Child* provides the human-alien savior, Daniel, who is similar in stature to Teal in *Sovereign*, to search out lost members of the race among the stars.

Alternations between the viewpoints of the wind-aliens and the humans provide this two-novel story with more controlled depth than found in her first novel, although all but a few central characters are embodiments of a single principle, mystery and aesthetic beauty in the alien dancer, Niki, evil in the rich Duchess Estelita and the military leader Admiral Czals, and unselfish but mischevious goodness in Daniel's close companion, Tavi.

All of Meluch's novels show a knowledge of SF as a genre and a genuine sensitivity to psychological development in the person of major characters. She has also obviously given a lot of thought to the cultures of her many worlds, although this comes through more strongly in *Wind Dancer* and *Wind Child*. If she devotes some serious attention to plot development, her evident stylistic strengths should bear out this early promise.

—Janice M. Bogstad

MEREDITH, Richard C(arlton). American. Born in Alderson, West Virginia, 21 October 1937. Educated at West Virginia State College, Institute, 1955-56; Pensacola Junior College, Florida, 1960-61; University of West Florida, Pensacola, B. A. 1972. Served in the United States Army, 1957-60, 1962. Married Joy Cecilia Gates in 1963; three children. Advertising Manager, Grice Electronics Inc., Pensacola, 1962-69; cartoonist and columnist ("Spinoffs"), Milton *Press-Gazette*, Florida, 1972-75; Editor, *Santa Rose Free Press*, Milton, 1975; copy editor, *National Enquirer*, Lantana, Florida, 1976-77; free-lance writer, illustrator, and graphic designer, 1977-79. Recipient: Phoenix Award, 1970. *Died in 1979.*

SCIENCE-FICTION PUBLICATIONS

Novels (series: Timeliner)

The Sky Is Filled with Ships. New York, Ballantine, 1969.
We All Died at Breakaway Station. New York, Ballantine, 1969.
At the Narrow Passage (Timeliner). New York, Putnam, 1973.
No Brother, No Friend (Timeliner). New York, Doubleday, 1976.
Run, Come See Jerusalem! New York, Ballantine, 1976.

Vestiges of Time (Timeliner). New York, Doubleday, 1978.
The Awakening. New York, St. Martin's Press, 1979.

Uncollected Short Stories

"Slugs," in *Knight* (Los Angeles), 1962.
"Choice of Weapons," in *Worlds of Tomorrow* (New York), March 1966.
"To the War Is Gone," in *Worlds of Tomorrow* (New York), November 1966.
"The Fifth Columbiad," in *Worlds of Tomorrow* (New York), February 1967.
"The Longest Voyage," in *Fantastic* (New York), September 1967.
"Earthcoming," in *The Future Is Now*, edited by William F. Nolan. Los Angeles, Sherbourne Press, 1970.
"Hired Man," in *If* (New York), February 1970.
"Time of the Sending," in *If* (New York), December 1971.
"Cold the Stars Are, Cold the Earth," in *Amazing* (New York), August 1978.

* * *

The protagonists of Richard C. Meredith's fiction generally are reluctant and/or disabled heroes who are forced by circumstances to attempt to solve the mysteries of the strange worlds in which they have previously been mere functionaries. As in traditional quest tales, they uncover even more mystery until a resolution, not always the solution they seek, is reached. They face frequent crises and perform heroically, if not always wisely, in response to external threats. They usually endure deep pain and are quite often physically injured—in fact, it seems that Meredith needs to put his protagonists through as much physical hell as possible before they are allowed the answers they seek or the revelations that there are some areas of human existence they will never fully understand. However, they are not the usual action-adventure sort of heroes. During their moments of flight or hiding, they reflect often upon their actions, regretting the emotional or physical pain they have caused and the violence, with its often questionable killings, that their need for self-preservation has precipitated. As pain is the recurring problem of the characters, violence is perhaps the aspect of Meredith's work that best sums up the science-fiction worlds he creates. Whether the story is about a contingent of handicapped warriors in outer space; a mercenary crossing alternate worlds, time, and space; or a time-traveller exploring facets of American history, the characters are frequently in a state of paranoiac apprehension, not knowing from where or when the next violent attack will come.

While Meredith's science fiction is thoroughly researched for its scientific and sociological aspects, he derives much of his inspiration from a finely honed sense of history. Science fiction is a field which attracts, in addition to hard-science promoters, social commentators, and literary aspirants, the history-influenced writer whose main impulse is to tamper with known history (time travel, alternate worlds) or to create complex future histories. Both of these impulses are found in Meredith's fiction and, in fact, he combines them skilfully in his timeliner trilogy and his time travel tour de force (*Run, Come See Jerusalem*). Many factors no doubt enter into an author's choice to write science fiction that has a strong historical bent, not the least of which is that it is definitely fun to play with history. Except for some dry leftover subjects, most of the exciting events and adventures of history have been adequately covered academically. On the other hand, the science-fiction writer can deal with history extensively in time travel and

alternate world stories. Additionally, such stories often necessitate speculation on historical subjects, an opportunity that Meredith takes full advantage of.

Run, Come See Jerusalem not only presents well-researched historical material but also gives full treatment to the what-if theme of the traveller effecting historical change by his actions in the past. Further, it juxtaposes two possible 21st-century futures against each other to make not only cautionary statements about contemporary trends but also detailed future histories rich in political and social implications. Meredith seems to have realized, along with a few other writers like Fritz Leiber, Jack Finney, and Robert Silverberg, that history can be very much a subject of science fiction, integrated comfortably with its fantastic plots and themes to create worlds just as imaginative as deep space colonies. Historically based science fiction helps to enlarge or at least vitalize our perception of historical matters. Perhaps as a result of this interest in history, Meredith's plots are extremely complicated and skilful. For example, events introduced early in his trilogy fit neatly into later portions of the story, and figure in a nearly apocalyptic finale that brings back into action most of the novels' surviving characters.

Meredith's best novel, *We All Died at Breakaway Station*, is an elegiac space opera which incorporates many elements similar to those in his time and alternate world sagas. It also features his most fully realized protagonist, the slightly embittered but resilient Absolom Bracer, a starship captain who has died in battle and been resurrected and put back together as more machine than man. Before he makes his valiant last stand as defender of Breakaway Station, he reviews his life as a warrior and ponders the more metaphysical questions regarding his place in a cold and alien universe. Like all Meredith heroes, he wonders if the effort and the pain are worth the result, that is, being the leader for a crew of the functioning wounded. He decides he does not regret his warrior life, especially since he has reached his life goal, being a starship captain. He is able to die courageously, also without regret. He may not have found satisfying answers, but he has asked the most important questions. In spite of Absolom's death, Meredith achieves in this novel a glorification of courage that is—oddly, in our times—quite inspiring. *We All Died at Breakaway Station* is a kind of Horatio-at-the-bridge epic that is given extra dimension by its main character's questing intelligence, by the way its heroism transcends the adventure story requirements of the genre, and because of the dramatic and poignant sacrifices of its disabled, tortured, but brave men and women. It is intriguing that similar bravery by the protagonist of a later novel, *Run, Come See Jerusalem*, results in a nearly opposite type of solution, the character's failure to create a better world where an already abominable one had existed.

Meredith's fiction is fast-paced, mysterious, and complex. He admirably blends philosophical reflection with high adventure to delineate the essential loneliness of his protagonists in an uncertain universe. A sympathetic observer of what is sometimes called the human condition, he infuses his novels and stories with intelligent compassion and a sense of what drives us to our sometimes disputable goals.

—Robert Thurston

MERRIL, Judith. Pseudonym for Josephine Juliet Grossman; also writes as Cyril Judd. Canadian. Born in New York City, 21 January 1923. Attended City College of New York, 1939-40.

Married 1) Daniel A. Zissman in 1940 (divorced, 1947), one daughter; 2) Frederik Pohl, *q. v.*, in 1949 (divorced, 1953), one daughter; 3) Daniel W. P. Sugrue in 1960 (divorced 1975). Research assistant and ghost writer, 1943-47; Editor, Bantam Books, New York, 1947-49. Since 1949, free-lance writer and lecturer: writing teacher, adult education program, Port Jervis, New York, 1963-64; director, Milford Science Fiction Writers Conference, 1956-61; book editor, *Fantasy and Science Fiction*, 1965-69; documentary scriptwriter, Canadian Broadcasting Corporation; commentator and performer, *Dr. Who*, TV Ontario. Lives in Toronto.

SCIENCE-FICTION PUBLICATIONS

Novels

Shadow on the Hearth. New York, Doubleday, 1950; London, Sidgwick and Jackson, 1953.
Gunner Cade (as Cyril Judd, with C. M. Kornbluth). New York, Simon and Schuster, 1952; London, Gollancz, 1964.
Outpost Mars (as Cyril Judd, with C. M. Kornbluth). New York, Abelard Press, 1952; London, New English Library, 1966; revised edition, as *Sin in Space*, New York, Galaxy, 1961.
The Tomorrow People. New York, Pyramid, 1960.

Short Stories

Out of Bounds. New York, Pyramid, 1960.
Daughters of Earth. London, Gollancz, 1968; New York, Doubleday, 1969.
Survival Ship and Other Stories. Toronto, Kakabeka, 1974.
The Best of Judith Merril. New York, Warner, 1976.

OTHER PUBLICATIONS

Other

"What Do You Mean: Science? Fiction?," in *SF: The Other Side of Realism*, edited by Thomas B. Clareson. Bowling Green, Ohio, Popular Press, 1971.

Editor, *Shot in the Dark*. New York, Bantam, 1950.
Editor, *Beyond Human Ken*. New York, Random House, 1952; London, Grayson, 1953.
Editor, *Beyond the Barriers of Space and Time*. New York, Random House, 1954; London, Sidgwick and Jackson, 1955.
Editor, *Human?* New york, Lion, 1954.
Editor, *Galaxy of Ghouls*. New York, Lion, 1955; as *Off the Beaten Orbit*, New York, Pyramid, 1959.
Editor, *S-F: The Year's Greatest Science-Fiction and Fantasy 1-4*, continued as *The Year's Best S-F, 5th* [to *11th*] *Annual*, and *SF12*. New York, Dell, 4 vols., 1956-59; New York, Simon and Schuster, 5 vols., 1960-64; New York, Delacorte Press, 3 vols., 1965-68; as *SF '57* [to *'59*], New York, Gnome Press, 3 vols., 1957-59; as *The Best of Sci-Fi*, London, Mayflower, 5 vols., 1963-70.
Editor, *SF: The Best of the Best*. New York, Delacorte Press, 1967; London, Hart Davis, 1968.
Editor, *England Swings SF*. New York, Doubleday, 1968; abridged edition, as *The Space-Time Journal*, London, Panther, 1972.

* * *

Judith Merril has been so prominent as a reviewer and an editor that her fiction has been somewhat eclipsed. Her most widely known story is her first, "That Only a Mother. " On one level this tale shows the power of love to blind the lover to the flaws of the beloved and to see only his or her best parts. On another, it is a horror story about the effects of atomic radiation. The two levels combine thematically: atomic energy is a beloved creation with great power to do good for mankind, but we delude ourselves if we refuse to see its potential dangers. Not only does this theme remain relevant to present-day problems; the story bears rereading for the pleasure of the word play, one of Merril's strengths throughout her work. Her finest novel, *Shadow on the Hearth*, also deals with the danger of atomic energy. It focuses on a Westchester woman with two daughters battling to survive the aftermath of a nuclear attack while her husband is trapped in Manhattan. Quietly rather than militantly feminist and ameliorative rather than separatist, Merril portrays the domestic reality of coping not only with the dangers of radiation but also with the unwelcome advances of a neighbor who has somehow managed to set himself up as an official of the emergency authorities who wishes to become her "protector. "

Working as one of the very few women in the SF field during an era when women were usually dumped with robots and aliens and treated as plot features rather than characters, Merril introduced a "woman's angle"—fiction unlikely to have been written by a man, usually with a female central character, yet still (against the so-called wisdom of the publishing trade) exciting to readers of both sexes. While "Project Nursemaid" (*Daughters of Earth*) does have a male viewpoint character, its main concern is the selection of candidates for foster-mothering babies born in space. "Daughters of Earth" is also quite unusual for its time, chronicling six generations of female space explorers. Merril vividly portrays the interactions and reactions between mother and daughter, who then becomes the mother against whom the next generation must react, and so on. Perhaps her most imaginative story is the novella "Homecalling" (*Daughters of Earth*). Again concerned with beauty in the eye of the beholder and the power of love, it is the story of a girl and her baby brother, shipwrecked on a planet with no other human life, who are adopted by a benevolent but repulsively alien mother.

Although it is always difficult to assess the contributions of each individual in collaborations, the two novels Merril wrote with C. M. Kornbluth as Cyril Judd (*Gunner Cade* and *Outpost Mars*) seem to have benefitted from the strengths of both writers, exhibiting Kornbluth's crisp prose, Merril's full-range view of human experience, and their mutual respect for irony.

—Elizabeth Anne Hull

———————

MERRITT, A(braham). American. Born in Beverly, New Jersey, 20 January 1884. Educated at Philadelphia High School. Married 1) Eleanor Ratcliffe (died); 2) Eleanor Humphrey; one daughter. Reporter, then night city editor, Philadelphia *Inquirer*, 1902-11; staff member from 1912, and Editor, 1937-43, *American Weekly. Died 30 August 1943.*

SCIENCE-FICTION PUBLICATIONS

Novels

The Moon Pool. New York and London, Putnam, 1919.

7 *Footprints to Satan*. New York, Boni and Liveright, and London, Richards, 1928.
Burn, Witch, Burn! New York, Liveright, 1933; London, Methuen, 1934.
Creep, Shadow! New York, Doubleday, 1934; as *Creep, Shadow, Creep!*, London, Methuen, 1935.
The Metal Monster. New York, Avon, 1946.
The Black Wheel, completed by Hannes Bok. New York, New Collectors' Group, 1947.

Short Stories

Thru the Dragon Glass. New York, ARRA, 1932.
Three Lines of Old French. Milheim, Pennyslvania, Bizarre Series, 1939.
The Fox Woman, and The Blue Pagoda, with Hannes Bok. New York, New Collectors' Group, 1946.
The Fox Woman and Other Stories, edited by Donald A. Wollheim. New York, Avon, 1949.

OTHER PUBLICATIONS

Novels

The Ship of Ishtar. New York and London, Putnam, 1926; original version, Los Angeles, Borden, 1949.
The Face in the Abyss. New York, Liveright, 1931; London, Futura, 1974.
Dwellers in the Mirage. New York, Liveright, 1932; London, Skeffington, 1933; original version, New York, Avon, 1944.

Other

The Story Behind the Story. Privately printed, 1942.
The Challenge of Beyond. Privately printed, 1954.

*

Bibliography: *A. Merritt: A Bibliography of Fantastic Writings* by Walter James Wentz, Los Angeles, Bibby, 1965.

* * *

A. Merritt was probably the most influential American science-fiction writer, after Edgar Rice Burroughs, though he is not nearly so well kown to the general public. A major reason for this is the paucity of his output (particularly as compared to Burroughs), though his relatively few novels have been almost continuously in print since World War II. He is generally regarded as a fantasist, but this is mainly a matter of changing standards in definition. A half century ago, many matters were regarded as open to "scientific" speculation that are not currently, particularly in the area of the occult. Three of Merritt's eight completed novels concern themselves with the occult (*Burn, Witch, Burn!, Creep, Shadow!*, and *Seven Footprints to Satan*, the last being a variation on the arch-criminal theme with occult and science-fiction overtones), and one (*The Ship of Ishtar*) is very definitely a fantasy set in an alternate world of Babylonian mythology.

The remaining four, however, are given enough of a pseudo-scientific rationale to qualify as science fiction in the romantic vein. There is a strong debt to H. Rider Haggard for the theme of "lost races" in what were then unknown corners of the world, as well as for the ever-popular idea of super-scientific knowledge from forgotten eras (certainly an idea back in vogue today). All this might be called anthropological speculation. *The Moon Pool* deals with a scientific party that penetrates the great caverns left beneath the Pacific when the Moon was ripped from the Earth. There they find the remnants of the ancient Lemurians, using the sophisticated technological instruments of their past. The conflict is with The Shining One, an entity created by the rulers of this land, three (implied) extra-terrestrials, and now turned against them. *The Face in the Abyss* takes place in an unknown part of the Andes. Again there are the remnants of a lost civilization, here ruled by the snake Mother, the last of a race of intelligent beings descended from reptilian antecedents. The lost culture of *Dwellers in the Mirage* is a curious mix of Amerindian, Mongol, and Norse. Its people inhabit a valley in Alaska, which due to volcanic activity and thermal layers gives the illusion of a wasteland; underneath the mirage is a "lost world" of unique life forms. *The Metal Monster* takes a slightly different theme; the title creature is an alien life form, sentient metallic beings with a sort of hive mentality reproducing themselves with astonishing vitality in the Himalayas.

Merritt wrote very much to pulp formula, that of rapidly paced adventure. There is inevitably conflict in these exotic locales, in which the protagonists from the outside world become involved, always on the "good" side. There are usually two women, one pure and beautiful to provide romantic interest for the hero, the other just the opposite; both are allied with the obvious sides of the conflict.

What Merritt brought to this formula that made his work so continuously popular was a remarkable writing style, called purple by his detractors, poetic by his followers. The super-scientific artifacts of the stories are given the barest minimum of scientific justification; their functions and activities are de-scribed in extremely visual, highly sensuous ways, as are the exotic flora, fauna, and natural phenomena. The result is far from the usual pulp writing of the time in its evocative imagery.

Because of their magazine origins and other factors, Merritt's works have often appeared in several variations and combin-ations. *The Moon Pool* is the combination of two shorter works ("The Moon Pool" and "The Conquest of the Moon Pool"), as is *The Face in the Abyss* ("The Face in the Abyss" and "The Snake Mother"). *Dwellers in the Mirage* has alternate endings. There is also a handful of short stories and fragments, two of which were completed by the artist Hannes Bok.

There can be no doubt that Merritt was of direct and considerable influence on what might be called the second generation of pulp science-fiction writers such as Kuttner, Moore, and Brackett, and through them on today's writers of the romantic school of SF.

—Baird Searles

MERWIN, Sam(uel Kimball), Jr. Also writes as Elizabeth Deare Bennett; Jacques Jean Ferrat; Matt Lee; Carter Sprague. American. Born in Plainfield, New Jersey, 28 April 1910. Educated at Phillips Academy, Andover, Massachusetts, graduated 1927; Princeon University, New Jersey, B. A. 1931; Boston Museum School of Fine Arts. Married 1) Lee Anna Vance in 1934 (died); 2) Marjory Kendal Davenport in 1959 (divorced); 3) Amanda Varela in 1972; two children. Reporter, Boston *Evening American*, 1932-33; New York Bureau Chief, Philadelphia *Inquirer*, 1936-37; Associate Editor, Dell pub-lishers, 1937-38; staff writer, *Country Home*, New York, 1938-39; sports and mystery editor, Standard Magazines, 1941-51, and King Size Publications, 1952-53: Editor, *Startling Stories*,

1945-51, *Fantastic Story Magazine*, 1950-51, *Wonder Stories Annual*, 1950-51, and *Thrilling Wonder Stories*, 1951-54; Editor, *Fantastic Universe*, 1953; Associate Editor, *Galaxy*, 1953-54; Editor, Renown Publications, 1955-56, 1975-79, and Brandon House, 1966-67. Agent: Foley Agency, 34 East 38th Street, New York, New York 10016, U.S.A.

SCIENCE-FICTION PUBLICATIONS

Novels

The House of Many Worlds. New York, Doubleday, 1951.
Killer to Come. New York, Abelard Press, 1953; London, Abelard Schuman, 1959.
The White Widows. New York, Doubleday, 1953; as *The Sex War*, New York, Galaxy, 1960.
Three Faces of Time. New York, Ace, 1955; London, Badger, 1960.
The Time Shifters. New York, Lancer, 1971.
Chauvinisto. Canoga Park, California, Major, 1976.

Uncollected Short Stories

"The Scourge Below," in *Thrilling Wonder Stories* (New York), October 1939.
" 'Dreaming' Down Axis Planes," in *Thrilling Wonder Stories* (New York), Summer 1944.
"No Greater Worlds," in *Thrilling Wonder Stories* (New York), Spring 1945.
"The Jimson Island Giant," in *Startling* (New York), Winter 1946.
"The Admiral's Walk," in *Thrilling Wonder Stories* (New York), December 1947.
"The Carriers," in *My Best Science Fiction Story*, edited by Leo Margulies and O. J. Friend. New York, Merlin, 1949.
"Forgotten Envoy," in *Startling* (New York), May 1949.
"The Tenth Degree," in *Thrilling Wonder Stories* (New York), October 1950.
"Exiled from Earth," in *Adventures in Tomorrow*, edited by Ken Crossen. New York, Greenberg, 1951; London, Lane, 1953.
"Exit Line," in *Possible Worlds of Science Fiction*, edited by Groff Conklin. New York, Greenberg, 1951.
"Short Order," in *Startling* (New York), March 1951.
"House of Many Worlds," in *Startling* (New York), September 1951.
"The Iron Deer," in *Thrilling Wonder Stories* (New York), December 1951.
"Judas Ram," in *Galaxy Reader*, edited by H. L. Gold. New York, Crown, 1952; London, Grayson, 1953.
"Star Tracks," in *Astounding* (New York), March 1952.
"Third Alternative," in *Fantastic Adventures* (New York), Spring 1952.
"Lambikin," in *Fantasy and Science Fiction* (New York), June 1952.
"Factor Unknown," in *Other Worlds* (Evanston, Indiana), June 1952.
"One Guitar," in *Fantastic Adventures* (New York), July 1952.
"Centaurus," in *Startling* (New York), March 1953.
"Distortion Pattern," in *Startling* (New York), April 1953.
"The Dark Side of the Moon," in *Space Stories* (New York), June 1953.
"There's Always Amanda," in *Fantastic Story* (New York), July 1953.
"Arbiter," in *Thrilling Wonder Stories* (New York), August 1953.

"Journey to Miseneum," in *Startling* (New York), August 1953.
"A Nice Thing to Know," in *Fantastic* (New York), February 1954.
"The Ambassador," in *If* (New York), March 1954.
"Wampum," in *Future* (New York), March 1954.
"The Wind Shines at Night," in *Thrilling Wonder Stories* (New York), Spring 1954.
"A World Apart," in *Fantastic Universe* (Chicago), May 1954.
"The Intimate Invasion," in *Future* (New York), June 1954.
"Summer Heat," in *Startling* (New York), Summer 1954.
"Process Shot," in *Thrilling Wonder Stories* (New York), Summer 1954.
"Poison Planet," in *Amazing* (New York), July 1954.
"It's Not the Heat," in *Beyond* (New York), September 1954.
"Sizzlesticks," in *Beyond 10* (New York), 1955.
"The Eye in the Window," in *Science Fiction Quarterly* (Holyoke, Massachusetts), May 1955.
"Pink Grass Planet," in *Fantastic Universe* (Chicago), May 1955.
"The Man from the Flying Saucer," in *Fantastic Universe* (Chicago), July 1955.
"Beyond the Door," in *Science Fiction Quarterly* (Holyoke, Massachusetts) August 1955.
"Day after Fear," in *Space Stories* (New York), September 1955.
"Star-Flight," in *Fantastic Universe* (Chicago), October 1955.
"Final Exam," in *Fantastic Universe* (Chicago), November 1955.
"Passage to Anywhere," in *Fantastic Universe* (Chicago), February 1956.
"The Vacationer," in *Original Science Fiction Stories* (Holyoke, Massachusetts), March 1956.
"It's All Yours," in *Fantastic Universe* (Chicago), November 1956.
"Service Elevator," in *Amazing* (New York), November 1956.
"The Stretcher," in *Original Science Fiction Stories* (Holyoke, Massachusetts), November 1956.
"Planet for Plunder," in *Satellite* (New York), February 1957.
"The Final Figure," in *Masters of Science Fiction*, edited by Ivan Howard. New York, Belmont, 1964.
"The Stretch," in *The Science Fiction Weight-Loss Book*, edited by Isaac Asimov, George R. R. Martin, and Martin H. Greenberg. New York, Crown, 1983.

Uncollected Short Stories as Carter Sprague

"The Rocket's Red Glare," in *Startling* (New York), June 1943.
"Climate—Disordered," in *Startling* (New York), March 1948.
"Journey for One," in *Startling* (New York), November 1949.
"The Star Slavers," in *Fantasy* (New York), Spring 1950.
"The Borghese Transparency," in *Thrilling Wonder Stories* (New York), April 1950.
"The Long Flight," in *Fantasy* (New York), Fall 1950.

Uncollected Short Stories as Matt Lee

"A Problem in Astrogation," in *Thrilling Wonder Stories* (New York), April 1948.
"Appointment in New Utrecht," in *Startling* (New York), March 1950.
"Final Haven," in *Thrilling Wonder Stories* (New York), February 1951.
"Deception," in *Thrilling Wonder Stories* (New York), April 1951.
"Letters of Fire," in *Startling* (New York), May 1951.

"I Do Not Like Thee," in *Fantastic Story* (New York), Summer 1951.

Uncollected Short Stories as Jacques Jean Ferrat

"Nightmare Tower," in *Fantastic Universe* (Chicago), July 1953.
"The Sane Men of Satan," in *Fantastic Universe* (Chicago), November 1953.
"Reel Life Films," in *Fantastic Universe* (Chicago), May 1954.
"The Sixth Season," in *Fantastic Universe* (Chicago), March 1955.
"The White Rain Came," in *Fantastic Universe* (Chicago), May 1955.
"Testing," in *Fantastic Universe* (Chicago), March 1956.
"Snowstorm on Mars," in *Fantastic Universe* (Chicago), June 1956.

OTHER PUBLICATIONS

Novels

Murder in Miniatures. New York, Doubleday, 1940.
Death in the Sunday Supplement. New York, Gateway, 1942.
The Big Frame. New York, Handi-Books, 1943.
The Flags Were Three, with Leo Margulies. New York, Curl, 1945; London, Hurst and Blackett, 1948.
Message from a Corpse. New York, Bouregy, 1945; London, Quality Press, 1947.
Knife in My Back. New York, Bouregy, 1945; London, Quality Press, 1947.
A Matter of Policy. New York, Bouregy, 1946; London, Quality Press, 1952.
Body and Soul (novelization of screenplay). Chicago, Century, 1947.
The Creeping Shadow. New York, Fawcett, 1952.
Regatta Summer (as Elizabeth Deare Bennett). New York, Dell, 1974.
Gower Court Manner (as Elizabeth Deare Bennett). New York, Dell, 1975.

Plays

Screenplay: *Manhunt in the Jungle*, with Owen Crump, 1958.

Television Plays: *The Star Slavers (Lights Out* series), 1951; *The Big Score (Alfred Hitchcock Presents* series), 1963.

Other

Confessions of a Scoundrel, with Guido Orlando. Philadelphia, Winston, 1954.

*

Sam Merwin, Jr. comments:

Although I have done more work in other fields, SF has been my favorite field since the mid-1950's. I have never sought to re- or in-form the world via such fiction, but have sought to entertain and, perhaps, to increase understanding through the introduction of speculative thought. I consider SF to be the other side of the IF.

*   *   *

Sam Merwin, Jr., is important because he is representative of a larger group of science-fiction writers. During his long career, he has written a number of intricately plotted formula novels. The principal characters and the bare bones of the story lines are remarkably similar; however, the locales and situational details are imaginatively conceived and extremely well executed.

Merwin's basic plot calls for an able but somewhat unlikely and relatively untried hero to be pitted against a group of one sex or the other who are scheming to overthrow the existing world order. The hero is usually assisted by a young and extra-ordinarily beautiful woman whose feats of strength and sexual prowess are matched only by his own. This remarkable couple is usually opposed by a fiendish mastermind who has somehow thwarted the aging process and lives undercover as a benign professor or in some similar disguise. Amazon-like women, superior mentally or physically or both, always figure promi-nently in Merwin's novels. They are not always on the side of evil; in *Chauvinisto* the Amazons control the world and have made it better, if somewhat homogenized, place to live. The denouement of each story occurs when the young hero almost single-handedly exposes the kingpin of the conspiracy and saves the world.

Merwin's short novels are composed of three major elements: the detective story, the conspiracy, and the spy novel. The first element, the detective story, is represented by at least one grisly murder which usually takes place in the opening chapter and the amateur sleuthing that the hero and his female friend do to solve the mystery of who runs the conspiracy. This conspiracy appears as a main thread of the plot in all of Merwin's novels. It is usually a pervasive and secret group that is plotting to control the world through ingenious schemes of disarming disguises and infiltration of the highest reaches of government. The spy element is represented by the exotic locales and the use of bugging devices and other sophisticated electronic espionage paraphernalia.

Some might be tempted to dismiss Merwin as a hack writer of formula science fiction. Such a quick dismissal would be entirely unjustified. While his novels do have many elements in common, they are set in vastly different locations, from the rarified atmosphere of a university think-tank to the female-dominated world of the 22nd century, and use a wide variety of secondary characters and subplots. In addition to being extremely readable these stories have dealt with some con-troversial issues such as the relationships between men and women; in the 1950's, for instance, Merwin was writing novels that portrayed women as the equal or dominant sex, as worthy adversaries and competent partners. All in all, Sam Merwin, Jr., has written a series of interesting and entertaining novels that have been enjoyed by readers of science fiction for 35 years.

—Alice Chambers Wygant

———————

MEYERS, Roy (Lethbridge). British. Born in Hounslow, Middlesex, 17 November 1910. Educated at University College, London; St. Bartholomew's Hospital Medical School, London, L. R. C. P. 1940, M. R. C. S. 1940. Married Mary Isobel Leasor in 1942; one son. Physician in general practice, Taunton, Somerset, 1944-74. Chairman of the Medical Board, Ministry for Social Security, 1945-74; Regional Medical Officer, Minis-try of Health, 1971-74. Former Director, Periwinkle Press. *Died 13 February 1974.*

SCIENCE-FICTION PUBLICATIONS

Novels (series: Dolphins in all books)

Dolphin Boy. New York, Ballantine, 1967; as *The Dolphin Rider*, London, Rapp and Whiting, 1968.
Daughters of the Dolphin. New York, Ballantine, 1968.
Destiny and the Dolphins. New York, Ballantine, 1969; London, Hale, 1971.

OTHER PUBLICATIONS

Novel

The Man They Couldn't Kill. Leicester, Blackfriars Press, 1944.

* * *

Long before it became fashionable, Roy Meyers was concerned about the quality of life in the sea and especially about the fate of humanity's underwater relatives, the dolphins and whales. Although Meyers may be considered a minor science fiction author, the questions and speculations he raised in the dolphin novels are important enough to transcend both the pedestrian writing style and the melodramatic plot. Luckily Meyers's education and interest enabled him to found the novels on a factual basis; otherwise they would have been rather ordinary romantic fantasies.

And the Dolphin Boy, born Sir John Averill, is quite a romantic figure. Exposed to radiation in an early fetal stage, John was born with slight physical abnormalities that would enable him to live for extended periods of time in the water. When his wealthy parents' Crab Island home and laboratory exploded, infant John, the sole survivor, was thrown into the ocean, where he was adopted by a school of dolphins. John was taught to swim and eat and live like a dolphin, but he was also taught that he was a human being, and that he would one day have to take his proper place among the "upper air creatures." Curiosity led John to teach himself to walk, and he began to follow ships around the Caribbean, in order to learn more about his own kind. When lovely Della Lord was swept overboard, John rescued her; this was his first encounter with another human. She taught him to speak English (his native tongue was Dolphinese) and instructed him in the rudiments of polite human behavior. Through several lucky coincidences, John, now a young man, made other human friends who helped him discover his identity and, incidentally, that he was very rich.

John's parents had been trying to develop a method of transmitting power through the air; with the resources at his command, John hired a staff to continue the experiments. One staff member, newly pregnant, was exposed to the same type of radiation that had affected John's mother. The woman died in childbirth, but her twin daughters were born with the same bodily abnormalities that John had, so he adopted them. He gave the infants to the dolphins to raise as he had been raised; as they grew older, he taught them to speak and walk and live on the land as humans. When Vinca and Synclaire were grown, John introduced them to society, and they were immediate successes. Some time later, John's Crab Island home was struck by a tidal wave, which opened a deep crack in the earth, from which escaping air promised to provide a perpetual power source. This was fortunate for them, because war broke out around the world; although nuclear weapons were not used, some nations resorted to biological warfare. Plagues and disease quickly wiped out all human life except for John, Syn, and Vinca. The rather vague conclusion (perhaps Meyers had

envisioned a fourth novel) leaves the reader to assume that the three protagonists may be entering a new underwater Garden of Eden with their friends the dolphins.

In these novels, Meyers presents strong contrasts between the serenity and simplicity of underwater life and our hectic, strident modern world. When the dolphin-raised humans are introduced to their own kind, they are truly alien, and they shock and surprise other people with their direct and honest dolphin-learned manners and morals. Meyers takes many opportunities for not-so-subtle commentary on the irrationality of some human customs, and, in fact, he cannot be accused of subtlety in any of his messages. As a writer, in fact, Meyers can most charitably be charactized as adequate. The flow of the narrative is uneven: long descriptive passages are interspersed with dramatic action, and occasional Serious Messages. He is most successful when he describes life under the sea; his feeling for the world of nature invests the writing with a touch of beauty. In handling the human characters, Meyers is often repetitious in description: every part of Syn and Vinca's bodies, for example, is called "pretty" at one time or another. The people are one-dimensional; the good characters have no vices, and the villians are all leering brutes, to be dispatched as expeditiously as possible.

Somehow, in spite of the awkward style and the episodic plotline the novels do impress upon the reader the beauty and the uniqueness of the ocean world. Meyers's dolphins are better friends to John, unacquainted as they are with avarice and cruelty, than many a human. And Meyers's arguments against whaling, illustrated with dignified and intelligent cetaceans, could scarcely be bettered by Greenpeace. Although his limitations as a writer are only too apparent, Meyers clearly showed himself to be a caring person with a creative imagination.

—Susan L. Nickerson

MILLER, Benj. See **LOOMIS, Noel M.**

MILLER, P(eter) Schuyler. American. Born 21 February 1912. Educated at Union College, Schenectady, New York, B. S. in chemistry 1932. Administrator in audio-visual education, Schenectady public schools; editor and technical writer, Fischer Scientific Company, Pittsburgh, 1949-74. Book reviewer ("The Reference Library"), *Astounding*, 1951-74; Editor, Pennsylvania Archaeologist ; Research Associate, Carnegie Museum. Recipient: Hugo Award, for non-fiction, 1963. *Died 12 October 1974.*

SCIENCE-FICTION PUBLICATIONS

Novel

Genus Homo, with L. Sprague de Camp. Reading, Pennsylvania, Fantasy Press, 1950.

Short Stories

The Titan. Reading, Pennsylvania, Fantasy Press, 1952; London, Weidenfeld and Nicolson, 1954.

Uncollected Short Stories

"The Red Plague," in *Wonder Stories* (New York), July 1930.
"Through the Vibrations," in *Amazing* (New York), May 1931.
"The Coils of Time," in *Astounding* (New York), May 1939.
"The Sands of Time," in *Adventures in Time and Space,* edited by Raymond J. Healy and J. Francis McComas. New York, Random House, 1946; London, Grayson, 1952.
"Over the River," in *The Sleeping and the Dead,* edited by August Derleth. Chicago, Pellegrini and Cudahy, 1947.
"The Chrysalis," in *Treasury of Science Fiction,* edited by Groff Conklin. New York, Crown, 1948.
"The Thing on Outer Shoal," in *Other Side of the Moon,* edited by August Derleth. New York, Pellegrini and Cudahy, 1949.
"The Man from Mars," in *From Off This World,* edited by Leo Margulies and Oscar J. Friend. New York, Merlin, 1949.
"Status Quondam," in *New Tales of Space and Time,* edited by Raymond J. Healy. New York, Holt, 1951.
"Trouble on Tantalus," in *Travelers in Space,* edited by Martin H. Greenberg. New York, Gnome Press, 1951.
"Daydream," in *Fantasy and Science Fiction* (New York), January 1956.
"Ship-in-a-Bottle," in *Davy Jones' Haunted Locker,* edited by Robert Arthur. New York, Random House, 1965.
"The Cave," in *Mars, We Love You,* edited by Jane Hipolito and Willis E. McNelly. New York, Doubleday, 1971.
"Tetrahedra of Space," in *Before the Golden Age,* edited by Isaac Asimov. New York, Doubleday, and London, Robson, 1974.
"Spawn," in *The Rivals of King Kong,* edited by Michel Parry. London, Coronet, 1978.
"Old Man Mulligan," in *The Great SF Stories 2 (1940),* edited by Isaac Asimov and Martin H. Greenberg. New York, DAW, 1979.
"As Never Was," in *The Arbor House Treasury of Science Fiction Masterpieces,* edited by Robert Silverberg and Martin H. Greenberg. New York, Arbor House, 1983.

OTHER PUBLICATIONS

Other

Alicia in Blunderland (parody), edited by Lloyd Arthur Eshbach. Philadelphia, Train, 1983.

*

Critical Study: *A Canticle for P. Schuyler Miller* by Sam Moskowitz, privately printed, 1975.

*   *   *

P. Schuyler Miller is best known for his reviews, covering most books worth mention over 23 years, a service of enormous value and influence. His approach was balanced optimism, looking for whatever values books had on any level. He kept history and context in mind, often interpolating short essays on ideas and trends. His criticism was neither bland nor shallow, but his more penetrating observations were briefly stated for the student to probe further. His own stories had made him a familiar name in the magazines from 1930, and his writing had developed somewhat as the general ambiance did.

In early years he was often compared to A. Merritt, though he is not very similar to modern eyes. Early Miller stories tend to be written in a florid style, though story and character are closer to real life than to heroic myth, and there is a down-to-earth

awareness of the natural world that gives a strongly visualised location. The impressions of landscape, forest and mountain, and living environment, contrast with many comtemporaries' romantically vague and perfunctory settings. His early story "The Red Plague" is "More of a well-written plot synopsis for a novel than a short story" as Sam Moskowitz remarks—true of innumerable early SF stories. There is a menace—a chain-reaction mineral blight of dust absorbing all surface water—and Martians, who have beaten the problem, provide the answer. But the voyage to Mars is vividly written and shows an original thinker's own vision of the remote prospect of space flight. "Through the Vibrations" and its sequel, "Cleon of Yzdral," has a world of abandoned automated cities, located on a different wavelength from Earth. "The Arrhenius Horror" is an exotic crystalline life form falling as particles from space. "If life is energy, why should it not rest where it will?" SF was opening new vistas of what other worlds might produce that was not Earth over again. Later Miller came back to the thought in "Spawn," a grim, powerful story of particles from beyond carrying elemental vitality that started new life in inanimate matter: a colloidal mass in the sea, a monster of gold, and a dead man revived as something else. "Tetrahedra of Space" deals with an invasion force of crystal beings from Mercury, not simply fought off but frightened off and diverted to more suitable Mars. "The Atom Smasher" predicts release of nuclear energy as an uncontrollable mountain-blasting discharge. "The Pool of Life" is an amorphous entity mentally controlling subhumans in a cave environment, treated as soberly as such a concept can be.

Many stories exploit the pre-war vision of the interplanetary future. "The Forgotten Man of Space" is about a man, marooned and adopted by primitive Martians, who dies protecting them from genocide by human exlpoiters. Several collaborations with Dennis and McDermott treat space piracy with amoral realism, the thoroughly evil pirate evading justice. "The Flame of Life" is an early Space Patrol episode, set on the rain-forest Venus of yore, as are others like "Old Man Mulligan," "Bird Walk," "Cuckoo," and "In the Good Old Summertime," introducing novel fauna. Others later move to the fanciful interstellar sphere. "Gleeps" lightly handles the intelligent alien mimicking people. "Trouble on Tantalus" goes back to the jungle adventure tradition on a world full of curiosities.

Miller's most distinctive work is the short novel "The Titan." Unfortunately it was revised into the idiom of the 1950's for its only complete publication (the original serialisation is incomplete). The change from first to third person lessens the impact of this story of crisis in an age-old, decadent Martian civilisation, told from a native leader's viewpoint, and the tighter style lacks the color and charm of the early version.

—Graham Stone

MILLER, Walter M(ichael), Jr. American. Born in New Smyrna Beach, Florida, 23 January 1922. Educated at the University of Tennessee, Knoxville, 1940-42; University of Texas, Austin, 1947-49. Served in the United States Army Air Force, 1942-45. Married Anna Louise Becker in 1945; three daughters and one son. Freelance writer. Recipient: Hugo Award, 1955, 1961. Address: c/o G. K. Hall, 70 Lincoln Street, Boston, Massachusetts 02111, U.S.A.

SCIENCE-FICTION PUBLICATIONS

Novel

A Canticle for Leibowitz. Philadelphia, Lippincott, and London, Weidenfeld and Nicolson, 1960.

Short Stories

Conditionally Human. New York, Ballantine, 1962; London Gollancz, 1963.
The View from the Stars . New York, Ballantine, and London, Gollancz, 1965.
The Best of Walter M. Miller, Jr. New York, Pocket Books, 1980.
The Darfstellar and Other Stories. London, Corgi, 1982.
The Science Fiction Stories of Walter M. Miller, Jr. Boston, Hall, 1984.

*   *   *

An engineer by profession, a Catholic by conversion, Walter M. Miller, Jr. brought both points of view to bear on the utilization of science and technology in some 41 stories and novellas of the 1950's, honing his writing skills to the peak achieved by his much-lauded novel, *A Canticle for Leibowitz*.

Amid his 1951 apprentice work, the novella "Dark Benediction" shows control of local color and romance psychology in a study of faith and prejudice. Gray and scaly "dermies," unable to control their urge to touch and transform others, are being exiled or killed. Sympathetic to one such mob victim in the early stages of her infection, Paul Oberlin takes her to priestly controlled Galveston Island, where he learns the truth. A meteor shower brought alien spores to Earth in an ironic invasion story that inverts the story of Pandora's Box. The benefits outweigh the disadvantages for those who are able to accept this gift of heaven's grace.

The next year, Miller published 15 pieces, eight of them good, three outstanding. A classic statement of wanderlust, "The Big Hunger" is a prose poem about waves of space travellers and homebodies over millennia of human change, if not development. An ironic commentary on conformity is "Command Performance." Resenting her suburban wifely role, Lisa resists her telepathic talent until it saves her from another telepath, intent on breeding supermen with her. With him eliminated, her loneliness sets in again, and she tries out her new communication channel, tentatively, as he too must once have done. "Conditionally Human" concerns playing God with life and death, as man elevates "lower" animals to substitute for babies in an overcrowded, overregulated world. Terry Norris, a veterinarian, must choose between killing a "neutroid" (a chimp-baby too smart and pretty and humanly viable, i. e., a deviant) or keeping his wife who wants children herself. Terry can't avoid playing God, but he plays it his way, killing his supervisor and taking a new job, helping to create more deviants. In making this choice, he opts for a race which "hasn't picked an apple yet," i. e., has no original sin.

Miller's best short story is "Crucifixus Etiam" (1953). Manue Nanti, a Peruvian laborer, works to help terraform Mars, and suffers acclimatization to the technology needed to keep him alive. Though he comes to realize he can never go home again to spend his earnings, he finds his sacrifice worthwhile, an act of faith in future generations.

In "The Ties that Bind" (1954), a novella pitting a far-future pacifist Earth society against the militarism of a fleet refueling at the old home world, the "innocent" pastoralists are the more

dangerous, their ancestry including the inner hell with which Earth once infected a whole galaxy. Ambitious formally, this tale of original sin interweaves viewpoints and themes with stanzas from the old ballad "Edward." "Death of a Spaceman" (1954; often reprinted as "Memento Homo") is a sentimental elegy to a man whose decrepit body lies in bed while his heart remains in space. A more ambitious variation on the theme of clipped wings is "The Hoofer" (1955), in which an itinerant entertainer comes home to Earth for the last time, his story combining slapstick with tragedy. "The Darfsteller" (1955) is a tale of technological displacement which also comments ironically on the paradox of free will and determinism. In telling the story of an aging matinee idol's near-tragic comeback, replacing a mannequin in an automated stage play, Miller adheres strictly to the actor's egotistical and stage-infatuated point of view. No mere entertainer, he is a genuine artist, for whom the "Maestro," the performance's mechanical producer-director, really has no tolerance. But though he is doomed to lose, the actor becomes more fully human by making this last stand. Miller's last published story, "The Lineman" (1957), portrays a day in the life of a lunar worker, when a travelling whorehouse put the crew off schedule. Mixing humor and pathos, Miller shows his main character learning to see that God created man and the universe on pretty equal footing.

These stories would be memorable enough, without his novel. But they pale by comparison with what may be the one universally acknowledged literary masterpiece to emerge from magazine SF. First published as three novellas, *A Canticle for Leibowitz* in book form is still a triptych. Each of its three "books" reaches six hundred years further into the future, viewing history from the vantage point of the Abbey of Leibowitz, somewhere in the American southwest. Each era is sharply etched, its characters clearly limned as plausible citizens of the City of God, simultaneously resisting and accommodating the City of Dys (Earthly life), as mankind struggles back from nuclear war to recycled Medieval, Renaissance, and Modern eras. Named for a Jewish engineer, a "booklegger" who memorized forbidden texts in the "Age of Simplicity" following the war, the Order of Leibowitz is committed to the preservation of knowledge, interpretation and use of which lie in secular hands.

In "Fiat Homo" (Let There Be Man), sheer survival is at issue, with marauding tribes threatening each other more than the Abbey. The story centers on Brother Francis's attempts to serve his order and mankind by finding, illuminating, and ultimately giving his life for a blueprint initialled by the Blessed Leibowitz and revealed to Francis by a wandering Jew. Church and State are in equilibrium in "Fiat Lux" (Let There Be Light). A secular scholar visits the Abbey to find his theories of electricity put into practice by Brother Kornhoer, providing artificial illumination over the objections of Brother Armbruster, the librarian, thus enabling the scholar to read—and misread—the Memorabilia. Between the Abbot and the scholar, a parasitic one-eyed Poet and the Wandering Jew, cross-dialogues reveal the misunderstandings that result from differing premises. The balance of power is secular again in "Fiat Voluntas Tua" (Thy Will Be Done), an allegory of contemporary history. As nuclear war erupts ("Lucifer is fallen"), the Abbot resists euthanasia clinics while Brother Joshua prepares to lead a remnant of clergy and children to Alpha Centauri, where another attempt will be made to temper technology with wisdom.

Moving enough in bare outline, the story is enriched in the telling. Olympian irony conveys "what fools these mortals be" even as warm humor makes us care about them. The comedy ranges from puns to slapstick to central symbols of misunderstanding. Elaborate jokes escape the confines of one book to echo in another (the blueprint of I, the dynamo and a fragment of *R. U. R.* in II, the Poet's satiric verse in III). Continuity is maintained by location and tradition; each era remembers its predecessors, sometimes mistakenly. Light imagery, the Wandering Jew and his eternal skepticism, an enigmatic statue of him and/or of Leibowitz carved in Book I all mock at pretenses to human wisdom. Names and events resound with symbolism, from the simple Francis to the equally simple old woman, Mrs. Grales, whose quest to have her second head, Rachel, blessed by the Abbot, is reversed at the end when Rachel awakes to bless the Abbot, pinned beneath rubble as the bombs fall, because she alone is untainted by original sin. A weighty but entertaining novel, science fiction's best exposure of the "human comedy," *A Canticle for Leibowitz* is a fitting capstone to Miller's writing career.

—David N. Samuelson

———————

MITCHELL, Clyde T. See **GARRETT, Randall.**

———————

MITCHISON, Naomi (Margaret, née Haldane). British. Born in Edinburgh, 1 November 1897; daughter of the scientist John Scott Haldane; sister of J. B. S. Haldane, *q. v.* Educated at Lynam's School, Oxford; St. Anne's College, Oxford. Served as a volunteer nurse, 1915. Married G. R. Mitchison (who became Lord Mitchison, 1964) in 1916 (died, 1970); three sons and two daughters. Labour Candidate for Parliament, Scottish Universities constituency, 1935; Member, Argyll County Council, 1945-66; Member, Highland Panel, 1947-64, and Highlands and Islands Development Council, 1966-76. Tribal Adviser, and Mmarona (Mother), to the Bakgatla of Botswana, 1963-73. D. Univ. : University of Stirling, Scotland, 1976; D. Litt. : University of Strathclyde, Glasgow, 1983. Honorary Fellow, St. Anne's College, 1980, and Wolfson College, 1983, Oxford. Officer, French Academy, 1924. C. B. E. (Commander, Order of the British Empire), 1985. Address: Carradale House, Carradale, Campbeltown, Scotland.

SCIENCE-FICTION PUBLICATIONS

Novels

Memoirs of a Spacewoman. London, Gollancz, 1962.
Solution Three. London, Dobson, and New York, Warner, 1975.
Not by Bread Alone. London, Boyars, 1983.

Uncollected Short Stories.

"After the Accident," in *The Year 2000*, edited by Harry Harrison. New York, Doubleday, 1970; London, Faber, 1971.
"Mary and Joe," in *Nova 1*, edited by Harry Harrison. New York, Delacorte Press, 1970; London, Sphere, 1975.
"Death of a Peculiar Boar," in *Worlds of Fantasy* (New York), Winter 1970.
"Miss Omega Raven" in *Nova 2*, edited by Harry Harrison.

New York, Walker, 1972; London, Sphere, 1975.
"The Factory," in *Nova 3*, edited by Harry Harrison. New York, Walker, 1973; London, Sphere, 1975.
"Out of the Waters," in *Nova 4*, edited by Harry Harrison. New York, Walker, 1974; London, Sphere, 1976.
"Valley of the Bushes," in *Andromeda 1*, edited by Peter Weston. London, Futura, 1976; New York, St. Martin's Press, 1979.
"The Finger," in *Best Science Fiction Stories of the Year 10*, edited by Gardner Dozois. New York, Dutton, 1981.
"Words," in *Despatches from the Frontiers of the Female Mind*, edited by Jen Green and Sarah Lefanu. London, Women's Press, 1985.

OTHER PUBLICATIONS

Novels

The Conquered. London, Cape, and New York, Harcourt Brace, 1923.
Cloud Cuckoo Land. London, Cape, 1925; New York, Harcourt Brace, 1926.
The Corn King and the Spring Queen. London, Cape, and New York, Harcourt Brace, 1931; as *The Barbarian*, New York, Cameron, 1961.
The Powers of Light. London, Cape, and New York, Peter Smith, 1932.
Beyond This Limit. London, Cape, 1935.
We Have Been Warned. London, Constable, 1935; New York, Vanguard Press, 1936.
The Blood of the Martyrs. London, Constable, 1939; New York, McGraw Hill, 1948.
The Bull Calves. London, Cape, 1947.
Lobsters on the Agenda. London, Gollancz, 1952.
Travel Light. London, Faber, 1952.
To the Chapel Perilous. London, Allen and Unwin, 1955.
Behold Your King. London, Muller, 1957.
When We Become Men. London, Collins, 1965.
Cleopatra's People. London, Heinemann, 1972.

Short Stories

When the Bough Breaks and Other Stories. London, Cape, and New York, Harcourt Brace, 1924.
Black Sparta: Greek Stories. London, Cape, and New York, Harcourt Brace, 1928.
Barbarian Stories. London, Cape, and New York, Harcourt Brace, 1929.
The Delicate Fire: Short Stories and Poems. London, Cape, and New York, Harcourt Brace, 1933.
The Fourth Pig: Stories and Verses. London, Constable, 1936.
Five Men and a Swan: Short Stories and Poems. London, Allen and Unwin, 1958.
Images of Africa. Edinburgh, Canongate, 1980.
What Do You Think Yourself? Scottish Short Stories. Edinburgh, Harris, 1982.

Plays

Nix-Nought-Nothing: Four Plays for Children (includes *My Ain Sel', Hobyah! Hobyah!, Elfen Hill*). London, Cape, 1928; New York, Harcourt Brace, 1929.
Kate Crackernuts: A Fairy Play. Oxford, Alden Press, 1931.
The Price of Freedom, with L. E. Gielgud (produced Cheltenham, 1949). London, Cape, 1931.
Full Fathom Five, with L. E. Gielgud (produced London, 1932).

An End and a Beginning and Other Plays (includes *The City and the Citizens, For This Man Is a Roman, In the Time of Constantine, Wild Men Invade the Roman Empire, Charlemagne and His Court, The Thing That is Plain, Cortez in Mexico, Akbar, But Still It Moves, The New Calendar, American Britons*). London, Constable, 1937; as *Historical Plays for Schools*, 2 vols., 1939.

As It Was in the Beginning, with L. E. Gielgud. London, Cape, 1939.

The Corn King, music by Brian Easdale, adaptation of the novel by Mitchison (produced London, 1950).

Spindrift, with Denis Macintosh (produced Glasgow, 1951). London, French, 1951.

Verse

The Laburnum Branch. London, Cape, 1926.
The Alban Goes Out. Harrow, Middlesex, Raven Press, 1939.
The Cleansing of the Knife and Other Poems. Edinburgh, Canongate, 1978.

Other (for children)

The Hostages and Other Stories for Boys and Girls. London, Cape, 1930; New York, Harcourt Brace, 1931.
Boys and Girls and Gods. London, Watts, 1931.
The Big House. London, Faber, 1950.
Graeme and the Dragon. London, Faber, 1954.
The Swan's Road. London, Naldrett Press, 1954.
The Land the Ravens Found. London, Collins, 1955.
Little Boxes. London, Faber, 1956.
The Far Harbour. London, Collins, 1957.
Judy and Lakshmi. London, Collins, 1959.
The Rib of the Green Umbrella. London, Collins, 1960.
The Young Alexander the Great. London, Parrish, 1960; New York, Roy, 1961.
Karensgaard: The Story of a Danish Farm. London, Collins, 1961.
The Young Alfred the Great. London, Parrish, 1962; New York, Roy, 1963.
The Fairy Who Couldn't Tell a Lie. London, Collins, 1963.
Alexander the Great. London, Longman, 1964.
Henny and Crispies. Wellington, New Zealand, Department of Education, 1964.
Ketse and the Chief. London, Nelson, 1965; New York, Nelson, 1967.
A Mochudi Family. Wellington, New Zealand, Department of Education, 1965.
Friends and Enemies. London, Collins, 1966; New York, Day, 1968.
The Big Surprise. London, Kaye and Ward, 1967.
Highland Holiday. Wellington, New Zealand, Department of Education, 1967.
African Heroes. London, Bodley Head, 1968; New York, Farrar Straus, 1969.
Don't Look Back. London, Kaye and Ward, 1969.
The Family at Ditlabeng. London, Collins, 1969; New York, Farrar Straus, 1970.
Sun and Moon. London, Bodley Head, 1970; Nashville, Nelson, 1973.
Sunrise Tomorrow. London, Collins, and New York, Farrar Straus, 1973.
The Danish Teapot. London, Kaye and Ward, 1973.
Snake! London, Collins, 1976.
The Little Sister, with works by Ian Kirby and Keetla Masogo. Cape Town, Oxford University Press, 1976.

The Wild Dogs, with works by Megan Biesele. Cape Town, Oxford University Press, 1977.
The Brave Nurse and Other Stories. Cape Town, Oxford University Press, 1977.
The Two Magicians, with Dick Mitchison. London, Dobson, 1978.
The Vegetable War. London, Hamish Hamilton, 1980.

Other

Anna Comnena. London, Howe, 1928.
Comments on Birth Control. London, Faber, 1930.
The Home and a Changing Civilisation. London, Lane, 1934.
Vienna Diary. London, Gollancz, and New York, Smith and Haas, 1934.
Socrates, with Richard Crossman. London, Hogarth Press, 1937; Harrisburg, Pennsylvania, Stackpole, 1938.
The Moral Basis of Politics. London, Constable, 1938; Port Washington, New York, Kennikat Press, 1971.
The Kingdom of Heaven. London, Heinemann, 1939.
Men and Herring: A Documentary, with Denis Macintosh. Edinburgh, Serif, 1949.
Other People's Worlds (travel). London, Secker and Warburg, 1958.
A Fishing Village on the Clyde, with G. W. L. Patterson. London, Oxford University Press, 1960.
Presenting Other People's Children. London, Hamlyn, 1961.
Return to the Fairy Hill (autobiography and sociology). London, Heinemann, and New York, Day, 1966.
The Africans: A History. London, Blond, 1970.
Small Talk: Memories of an Edwardian Childhood. London, Bodley Head, 1973.
A Life for Africa: The Story of Bram Fischer. London, Merlin Press, and Boston, Carrier Pigeon, 1973.
Oil for the Highlands? London, Fabian Society, 1974.
All Change Here: Girlhood and Marriage (autobiography). London, Bodley Head, 1975.
Sittlichkeit (lecture). London, Birkbeck College, 1975.
You May Well Ask: A Memoir 1920-1940. London, Gollancz, 1979.
Mucking Around: Five Continents over Fifty Years. London, Gollancz, 1981.
Among You, Taking Notes: The Wartime Diary of Naomi Mitchison 1939-45, edited by Dorothy Sheridan. London, Gollancz, 1985.

Editor, *An Outline for Boys and Girls and Their Parents*. London, Gollancz, 1932.
Editor, with Robert Britton and George Kilgour, *Re-Educating Scotland*. Glasgow, Scoop, 1944.
Editor, *What the Human Race Is Up To*. London, Gollancz, 1962.

*

Manuscript Collections: National Library of Scotland, Edinburgh; University of Texas, Austin.

Naomi Mitchison comments:

I like to present my characters—whether they are in the past or in the future—with interesting moral choices, and it seems to me that science-fiction writers are, or should be, the prophets and moralists of today. I am fairly well up in the biological sciences, but I am deeply uninterested in gadgets. A writer's job is to write about people with sympathy and insight.

* * *

In his 1946 introduction to *Brave New World*, Naomi Mitchison's friend and contemporary Aldous Huxley outlined a four-point plan for his own personal nightmare, a world in which foolproof techniques of conditioning had been perfected, social dissension obviated by keeping round pegs out of square holes, a harmless substitute for alcohol and narcotics introduced, and the human product standardised by eugenic techniques. What seemed to horrify Huxley most (coming as he did from a family of privileged, well-educated over-achievers) was the idea that the scientific state, instead of complicated random factors like inheritance, ambition, and opportunity, could determine a person's physical condition and social status. *Brave New World* is a piece of bitter and pessimistic polemic against science reducing noble, wild, and self-determining humanity to the status of laboratory mice.

The science fiction written by those scions of another family of privileged, well educated over-achievers, Naomi Mitchison and her brother J. B. S. Haldane, is mild and optimistic polemic promoting sundry brave new worlds in which all the elements that so unnerved Huxley have totally lost their power to disturb. In *Solution Three*, for instance, there are sleep-teaching, conditioning with hormones, a superior caste of cloned future leaders, blind obedience to a social code, cannabis, promiscuity, a constant struggle to improve the DNA, and as in Huxley's novel, a few round pegs chafing at the edges of their square holes. However, Mitchison's characters, controlled though they are, are by no means laboratory mice. After a certain amount of smoothing of curves and filling in of corners, the dissidents fit in, more or less; and while the author obviously views her future society as imperfect, its imperfections are no more sinister than those of the 20th century.

Naomi Mitchison's three science fiction novels are very different from each other, although *Memoirs of a Spacewoman* and *Solution Three* are to some extent bridged by her brother's unfinished *The Man with Two Memories*, in which the protagonist inherits the recollections of a subnormal citizen of a hugely advanced extra-terrestrial utopia of the remote past, complete with genetic and social engineering, drugs, free love, space travel, and talking animals. Free love, space travel, and talking animals are three of the four major preoccupations of the heroine of *Memoirs of a Spacewoman*, whose profession is to speed around the galaxy communicating with alien races; and her aliens are not the bug-eyed men of lesser writers' imaginations but genuinely strange beings such as the starfish-like individuals who, being radially rather than bilaterally symmetrical, cannot polarise choices into a right/left, right/wrong duality, and the caterpillars mercilessly tormented by their butterfly inheritors, who try to prevent them damaging their future bodies with too much infantile sex and creativity, all depicted with extraordinary sympathy and sensitivity. The spacewoman's other preoccupation is with motherhood, an emotion which she extends even to the leech-like parasitic embryos from another world which she experimentally nutures on her thighs, as well as to various children that she bears to sexually attractive and genetically compatible fathers and the haploid clone that she accidentally conceives while communicating with an over-excited Martian. There is no population problem in the spacewoman's world: even though almost every adventure is concluded by a conception, she spends so much time in relativistic time blackout in outer space that her family is well spaced-out.

Population is much more of a consideration in *Solution Three*. It is an obsession with the society which has conquered aggression and is ever struggling to keep the "popu-curve" dropping while cloning a master race from the two individuals who converted the world to homosexuality, thus stopping the explosion at a stroke (just as well, because the 20th-century pallative, the Green Revolution, is running into serious trouble). In her dedication, Mitchison refers to it as a "horrid idea", but as ever the book itself is sympathetic and optimistic, and one pauses to wonder whether a society where power is acquired by random heredity or aggression and where heterosexuality is enforced by social sanctions is really much more marvellous or much more free.

Mitchison returns to chronicle the doom of the Green Revolution in *Not by Bread Alone*, darkest and most realistic of her science fiction works, set in a near-future society dominated by the humanitarian face of a puppeteering multinational conglomerate, PAX. Advances in genetic engineering have made plentiful food for all a possibility, and PAX rushes ahead with implementing a global free-food programme (to liberate cash for more profitable forms of consumerism) without much regard for the possible pitfalls. The parallels with nuclear power are clear and frequently alluded to. Freefood fails tragically, but on a less disastrous scale than the average famine, and the book ends optimistically with some of PAX's former pocket scientists starting life and human cultural development on a fresh tack in a self-sufficient, nature-worshipping Australian Aboriginal homeland.

Naomi Mitchison views her Utopian creation with tolerant eye. Her societies are those in which emotion has its place, but in which reason is always the deciding factor. Greed, jealousy, nationalism, racism: all the possessive urges, and all the aggressive ones too, have been conquered. The scientific method is triumphant. The world has been inherited by progressive, liberal, thoroughly rational, scientifically inclined animal lovers, committed to natural childbirth, breastfeeding, pre-school education, free love, and vegetarianism. They are people not at all unlike the Haldane family (or the Huxley family for that matter). The rest of us round pegs will just have to fit in somehow.

—Lee Montgomerie

MONTELEONE, Thomas F. American. Born in Baltimore, Maryland, 14 April 1946. Educated at the University of Maryland, College Park, B. S. in psychology 1968, M. A. in English 1973. Married 1) Natalie Monteleone in 1969 (divorced, 1979), one son; 2) Linda Smith in 1981, one son. Psychotherapist, C. T. Perkins Hospital, Jessup, Maryland, 1969-78. Secretary, Science Fiction Writers of America, 1976-78. Recipient (for television play): Gabriel Award, 1984; International Television and Film Award, 1984. Agent: Howard Morhaim Literary Agency, 501 Fifth Avenue, New York, New York 10017. Address: 1366 Sudvale Road, Baltimore, Maryland 21208, U.S.A.

SCIENCE-FICTION PUBLICATIONS

Novels (series: Dragonstar)

Seeds of Change. Toronto, Laser, 1975.
The Time Connection. New York, Popular Library, 1976; London, Hale, 1979.
The-Time Swept City. New York, Popular Library, 1977.
The Secret Sea. New York, Popular Library, 1979; London, Hale, 1981.
Guardian. New York, Doubleday, 1980.

Night Things. New York, Fawcett, 1980.
Ozymandias. New York, Doubleday, 1981.
Day of the Dragonstar, with David F. Bischoff. New York, Berkley, 1983.
Night Train. New York, Pocket Books, 1984.
Night of the Dragonstar, with David F. Bischoff. New York, Berkley, 1985.

Short Stories

Dark Stars and Other Illuminations. New York, Doubleday, 1981.

Uncollected Short Stories

"Wendigo's Child," in *Monster Tales*, edited by Roger Elwood. Chicago, Rand McNally, 1973.
"The Imperfect Lover," in *Chrysalis 3*, edited by Roy Torgeson. New York, Zebra, 1978.
"Breath's a Ware That Will Not Keep," in *Nebula Winners 12*, edited by Gordon R. Dickson. New York, Harper, 1978.
"When Dark Descends," with Charles L. Grant, in *Chrysalis 4*, edited by Roy Torgeson. New York, Zebra, 1979.
"Sonate for Three Electrodes," in *Chrysalis 7*, edited by Roy Torgeson. New York, Zebra, 1980.
"Taking the Night Train," in *Night Voyages* (Freeburg, Illinois), Spring 1981.
"The Curandeiro," in *SF Story-Reader 15*. Munich, Heyne, 1981.
"Identity Crisis," in *Terrors*, edited by Charles L. Grant. New York, Pocket Books, 1982.
"Spare the Child," in *The Year's Best Horror Stories 11*, edited by Karl Edward Wagner. New York, DAW, 1983.
"The Mechanical Boy," in *Chrysalis 10*, edited by Roy Torgeson. New York, Doubleday, 1983.
"The Greatest Game," in *R-A-M: Random Access Messages of the Computer Age*, edited by Monteleone. Hasbrouck Heights, New Jersey, Hayden, 1984.
"The Cutty Black Sow," in *Sun Magazine*, October 1984.

OTHER PUBLICATIONS

Plays

U.F.O.!, with Grant Carrington (produced Ashton, Maryland, 1977).
Mister Magister (produced Silver Spring, Maryland, 1978). Included in *Dark Stars and Other Illuminations*, 1981.

Screenplays: *Sun-Treader*, 1983; *Three, Two, One: Countdown to Love*, 1984; *The Nowhere Man*, 1985.

Television Plays: *Mister Magister*, 1983; *Spare the Child*, 1983.

Other

"Fire and Ice," in *Algol* (New York), Summer 1975.
Introduction to *Isle of the Dead*, by Roger Zelazny. Boston, Gregg Press, 1976.
"Markets: Where and to Whom," in *Writing and Selling Science Fiction*. Cincinnati, Writer's Digest, 1976.
"Izat Knows the Way to Flushing," with Grant Carrington, in *Nickelodeon* (Kansas City), 1976.
"Science Fiction as Literature," in *Cerberus* (College Park, Maryland), Fall 1977.
Introduction to *Lords of the Starship*, by Mark Geston. Boston,

Gregg Press, 1978.
"The Gullibility Factor," in *Omni* (New York), 1979.

Editor, *The Arts and Beyond: Visions of Man's Aesthetic Future*. New York, Doubleday, 1977.
Editor, *R-A-M: Random Access Messages of the Computer Age*. Hasbrouck Heights, New Jersey, Hayden, 1984.

*

Manuscript Collection: University of Maryland, Baltimore.

Thomas F. Monteleone comments:
(1981) Although my early novels were little more than adventure fiction, I feel that the majority of my work intends to be more thought-provoking and imaginative. I think my short fiction reflects my desire to employ imagery, symbol, and ironic statement to create stories which make my readers think. I do not write "hard" SF; rather I find myself most comfortable in dealing with the softer sciences such as psychology, anthropology, and sociology. The main emphasis in my fiction seems to be *people*, and the way our technology and society influence them. Themes which are important to me are love, conscience, responsibility, creativity, and man's dual nature.
(1985) Since 1980, my writing has shifted away from SF *per se*, and explored the areas of horror, dark fantasy, and more speculative, "weird tales" kinds of fiction. I enjoy the greater freedom to explore character in the novel of suspense or horror. Although I am primarily a novelist now, I still write an occasional short story, and I believe the well-crafted short story is the most difficult form to master. Also, in recent years, I have become interested in writing for film and television, having had several pieces produced for both media. My intentions for the future are simple enough: keep writing.

* * *

One of the most promising new writers of science fiction adventure stories of the past several years has been Thomas F. Monteleone. His debut was a promotional novel for Laser Books, *Seeds of Change*, which used a well-worn theme to mediocre advantage. Denver Citiplex is a dehumanized, computer-governed city in which humans are mere cogs until a secret group causes a revolution. Fortunately, the novel was untypical of the kind of work Monteleone would shortly begin to produce.
The Time Connection is a time-spanning adventure story in the tradition of the best of Edmond Hamilton. A young man encounters a woman in the desert who tells him that she hears things silent to everyone else. Eventually they are transported to a barren future where alien war machines patrol the ruins of the planet, along with a few survivors of the alien invasion force that has caused the destruction, but no humans. They experience a number of adventures before encountering the hidden human civilization, adventures related in a clear, gripping style.
The Secret Sea was even better, this time emulating the tradition of Jules Verne. An adventurer travels to a parallel world and is taken aboard the Nautilus, subsequently discovering that it is this world that was the source of inspiration for many of Verne's adventure stories. The protagonist himself is caught up in the battle between Nemo and Robert Burton, Robur the Conqueror, in that alternate world.
A number of Monteleone's short stories were cobbled together into a future history of sorts in *The Time-Swept City*. In this case, the immortal city is Chicago, shown in a number of

brief glimpses as time passes. We see what happens when a cyborg falls in love, when a priest has to deal with the passing of the immunity of religion, and when people are bred in vats by genetically altered mothers, and what happens when that alteration gets out of control. In the latter portions of the book, Chicago has become an entity itself, the computers that govern it having progressed to the point where they constitute an Artificial Intelligence. People are reduced to implements, and interlopers are forbidden entry. There is a fascinating sequence where all humans are in coldsleep, and robots run the city, sometimes feuding among themselves. When a star traveller returns, he is unable to make the city recognize him as possessing any authority to act. It really isn't a novel, but many of the installments are fascinating, and the panoramic view of the future of the city works quite well.

Monteleone wrote two further novels about computers that have come to be more than they were intended. In *Guardian* and its sequel, *Ozymandias*, the sentient computer exists in a post-collapse world, existing in secret until discovered by a group of adventurers. Seeking to learn more about the world, it incarnates its intelligence in a human body and wanders around the world. Monteleone has also collaborated with David Bischoff on the novel *Day of the Dragonstar*, which relates the adventurers of a group of explorers sent to investigate a gigantic zoo in space, and those of the rescue team that must find them when they are routed by dinosaurs. A sequel, *Night of the Dragonstar*, has been announced for publication.

Monteleone's latest two novels have been in the horror genre. *Night Train* is set in the subways beneath Manhattan, and deals with a train that disappeared decades before and a series of psychopathic killings. More recently, *Night Things* is a more traditional monster story. An Indian burial mound is inadvertently disturbed, releasing a horde of small biting beasties that promptly begin dismembering and consuming all and sundry. They are both fairly good horror fiction, but not nearly as outstanding in their field as the earlier science-fiction novels are in that genre, and it is to be hoped that Monteleone has not completely left science fiction.

Most of his shorter fiction has been above average as well. Of particular note is "The Mechanical Boy," which deals with a young child who is diagnosed to have a mental disease because of his insistence that he is a machine and cannot function without electricity. The doctor handling his case believes that the problem is more complex than others realize, and soon learns that the boy can actually communicate with machines in some fashion and may indicate the next step in human evolution. The supernatural appears here as well, particularly in "When Dark Descends," written in collaboration with Charles L. Grant, and in "Spare the Child," a chilling story about what happens when you adopt a child by mail and then abandon her, if she happens to be related to a tribal priest.

—Don D'Ammassa

MOORCOCK, Michael. Has also written as Bill Barclay; Edward P. Bradbury; James Colvin; Desmond Reid. British. Born in Mitcham, Surrey, 18 December 1939. Served in the Air Training Corps. Married 1) Hilary Bailey in 1962, two daughters and one son; 2) Jill Riches in 1978; 3) Linda Steel in 1983. Editor, *Tarzan Adventures*, London, 1956-57, and Sexton Blake Library, Fleetway Publications, London, 1958-61; editor and writer for Liberal Party, 1962-63. Editor since 1964 and Publisher since 1967, *New Worlds*, London. Since 1955, songwriter and member of various rock bands including Hawkwind and Deep Fix. Recipient: British Science Fiction Association Award, 1966; Nebula Award 1967; Derleth Award, 1972, 1974, 1975, 1976; *Guardian* Fiction Prize, 1977; Campbell Memorial Award, 1979; World Fantasy Award, 1979. Guest of Honor, World Fantasy Convention, New York, 1976. Agent: Anthony Sheil Associates Ltd., 43 Doughty Street, London WC1N 2LF, England; or, Wallace and Sheil Inc., 177 East 70th Street, New York, New York 10021, U.S.A.

SCIENCE-FICTION PUBLICATIONS

Novels (series: Oswald Bastable; Jerry Cornelius; Jerry Cornell; Dancers at the End of Time; Karl Glogauer; Von Bek Family)

The Sundered Worlds. London, Compact, 1965; New York, Paperback Library, 1966; as *The Blood Red Game*, London, Sphere, 1970.

The Fireclown. London, Compact, 1965; New York, Paperback Library, 1967; as *The Winds of Limbo*, Paperback Library, 1969.

The Twilight Man. London, Compact, 1966; New York, Berkley, 1970; as *The Shores of Death*, London, Sphere, 1970.

Printer's Devil (as Bill Barclay). London, Compact, 1966.

Somewhere in the Night (as Bill Barclay). London, Compact, 1966; revised edition, as *The Chinese Agent* (Cornell), London, Hutchinson, and New York, Macmillan, 1970.

The Wrecks of Time. New York, Ace, 1967; revised edition, as *The Rituals of Infinity*, London, Arrow, 1971; New York, DAW, 1978.

The Final Programme (Cornelius). New York, Avon. 1968; London, Allison and Busby, 1969; revised edition, London, Fontana, 1979.

The Ice Schooner. London, Sphere, and New York, Berkley, 1969; revised edition, London, Harrap, 1985.

Behold the Man (Glogauer). London, Allison and Busby, 1969; New York, Avon, 1970.

The Black Corridor. London, Mayflower, and New York, Ace, 1969.

A Cure for Cancer (Cornelius). London, Allison and Busby, and New York, Holt Rinehart, 1971; revised edition, London, Fontana, 1979.

The Warlord of the Air (Bastable). London, New English Library, and New York, Ace, 1971.

An Alien Heat (Dancers), London, MacGibbon and Kee, and New York, Harper, 1972.

Breakfast in the Ruins (Glogauer). London, New English Library, 1972; New York, Random House, 1974.

The English Assassin (Cornelius). London, Allison and Busby, and New York, Harper, 1972; revised edition, London, Fontana, 1979.

The Land Leviathan (Bastable). London, Quartet, and New York, Doubleday, 1974.

The Hollow Lands (Dancers). New York, Harper, 1974; London, Hart Davis MacGibbon, 1975.

The Distant Suns, with Philip James. Llanfynydd, Dyfed, Unicorn Bookshop, 1975.

The Adventures of Una Persson and Catherine Cornelius in the Twentieth Century. London, Quartet, 1976.

The End of All Songs (Dancers). London, Hart Davis MacGibbon, and New York, Harper, 1976.

The Condition of Muzak (Cornelius). London, Allison and Busby, 1977; Boston, Gregg Press, 1978.

The Transformation of Miss Mavis Ming (Dancers). London, W. H. Allen, 1977; as *Messiah at the End of Time*, New York, DAW, 1978.

The Cornelius Chronicles (omnibus). New York, Avon, 1977.

Gloriana; or, The Unfulfill'd Queen. London, Allison and Busby, 1978; New York, Avon, 1979.

The Golden Barge. Manchester, Savoy, and New York, DAW, 1980.

The Russian Intelligence (Cornell). Manchester, Savoy, 1980.

The Entropy Tango (Cornelius). London, New English Library, 1981.

The Steel Tsar (Bastable). London, Mayflower, 1981; New York, DAW, 1982.

The War Hound and the World's Pain (Von Bek). New York, Pocket Books, 1981; London, New English Library, 1982.

Byzantium Endures. London, Secker and Warburg, 1981; New York, Random House, 1982.

The Brothel in Rösenstrasse (Von Bek). London, New English Library, 1982.

The Dancers at the End of Time (omnibus). London, Granada, 1983.

The Laughter of Carthage. London, Secker and Warburg, and New York, Random House, 1984.

Novels as Edward P. Bradbury (series: Michael Kane in all books)

Warrior of Mars. London, New English Library, 1981.

1. *Warriors of Mars*. London, Compact, 1965; New York, Lancer, 1966; as *The City of the Beast* (as Michael Moorcock), Lancer, 1980.
2. *Blades of Mars*. London, Compact, 1965; New York, Lancer, 1966; as *The Lord of the Spiders* (as Michael Moorcock), Lancer, 1970.
3. *The Barbarians of Mars*. London, Compact, 1965; New York, Lancer, 1966; as *The Masters of the Pit* (as Michael Moorcock), Lancer, 1970.

Short Stories

The Deep Fix (as James Colvin). London, Compact, 1966.

The Time Dweller. London, Hart Davis, 1969; New York, Berkley, 1971.

The Singing Citadel. London, Mayflower, and New York, Berkley, 1970.

The Jade Man's Eyes. Brighton, Unicorn Bookshop, 1973.

Moorcock's Book of Martyrs. London, Quartet, 1976.

The Lives and Times of Jerry Cornelius. London, Allison and Busby, 1976; New York, Dale, n. d.

Legends from the End of Time. London, W. H. Allen, and New York, Harper, 1976.

Dying for Tomorrow. New York, DAW, 1978.

My Experiences in the Third World War. Manchester, Savoy, 1980.

The Opium General and Other Stories. London, New English Library, 1984.

OTHER PUBLICATIONS

Novels

Caribbean Crisis (as Desmond Reid, with James Cawthorn). London, Fleetway, 1962.

Stormbringer. London, Jenkins, 1965; New York, Lancer, 1967; revised edition, New York, DAW, 1977.

The LSD Dossier (ghosted for Roger Harris). London, Compact, 1966.

The Jewel in the Skull. New York, Lancer, 1967; London, Mayflower, 1969; revised edition, New York, DAW, 1977.

Sorcerer's Amulet. New York, Lancer, 1968; as *The Mad God's Amulet*, London, Mayflower, 1969; revised edition, New York, DAW, 1977.

The Sword of the Dawn. New York, Lancer, 1968; London, Mayflower, 1969; revised edition, New York, DAW, 1977.

The Secret of the Runestaff. New York, Lancer, 1969; as *The Runestaff*, London, Mayflower, 1969; revised edition, New York, DAW, 1977.

The Eternal Champion. London, Mayflower, and New York, Dell, 1970; revised edition, New York, Harper, 1978.

Phoenix in Obsidian. London, Mayflower, 1970; as *The Silver Warriors*, New York, Dell, 1973.

The Swords Trilogy. New York, Berkley, 1977.

> *The Knight of the Swords*. London, Mayflower, and New York, Berkley, 1971.
>
> *The Queen of the Swords*. London, Mayflower, and New York, Berkley, 1971.
>
> *The King of the Swords*. London, Mayflower, and New York, Berkley, 1971.

The Sleeping Sorceress. London, New English Library, 1971; New York, Lancer, 1972; revised edition, as *The Vanishing Tower*, New York, DAW, 1977.

Elric of Melniboné. London, Hutchinson, 1972; as *The Dreaming City*, New York, Lancer, 1972.

The Bull and the Spear. London, Allison and Busby, and New York, Berkley, 1973.

Count Brass. London, Mayflower, 1973; New York, Dell, 1976

The Champion of Garathorm. London, Mayflower, 1973.

The Oak and the Ram. London, Allison and Busby, and New York, Berkley, 1973.

The Sword and the Stallion . London, Allison and Busby, and New York, Berkley, 1974.

The Quest for Tanelorn. London, Mayflower, 1975; New York, Dell, 1976.

The Sailor on the Seas of Fate. London, Quartet, and New York, DAW, 1976.

The Weird of the White Wolf. New York, DAW, 1977.

The Vanishing Tower. New York, DAW, 1977.

The Bane of the Black Sword. New York, DAW, 1977.

The History of the Runestaff (collection). London, Hart Davis MacGibbon, 1979.

The Great Rock 'n' Roll Swindle. London, Virgin, 1980.

Short Stories

The Stealer of Souls and Other Stories. London, Spearman, 1963; New York, Lancer, 1967.

Elric: The Return to Melniboné (cartoon), illustrated by Philippe Druillet. Brighton, Unicorn Bookshop, 1973.

Elric at the End of Time: Fantasy Stories. London, New English Library, 1984; New York, DAW, 1985.

Play

Screenplay: *The Land That Time Forgot*, with James Cawthorn, 1974.

Other

Preface to *The New SF*, edited by Langdon Jones, London, Hutchinson, 1969.

"Mal Dean," in *New Worlds 8*, edited by Hilary Bailey. London, Sphere, 1975.

Sojan (for children). Manchester, Savoy, 1977.

"New Worlds: A Personal History," in *Foundation 15* (London), January 1979.

"Wit and Humour in Fantasy," in *Foundation 16* (London), May 1979.

The Retreat from Liberty. London, Zomba, 1983.

Editor, *The Best of New Worlds*. London, Compact, 1965.

Editor, *Best SF Stories from New Worlds 1-8*. London, Panther, 8 vols., 1967-74; New York, Berkley, 6 vols., 1968-71.

Editor, *The Traps of Time*. London, Rapp and Whiting, 1968.

Editor (anonymously), *The Inner Landscape*. London, Allison and Busby, 1969.

Editor, *New Worlds Quarterly 1-5*. London, Sphere, 5 vols., 1971-73; New York, Berkley, 4 vols., 1971-73.

Editor, with Langdon Jones, *The Nature of the Catastrophe*. London, Hutchinson, 1971.

Editor, with Charles Platt, *New Worlds 6*. London, Sphere, 1973; as *New Worlds 5*, New York, Avon, 1974.

Editor, *Before Armageddon: An Anthology of Victorian and Edwardian Imaginative Fiction Published Before 1914*. London, W. H. Allen, 1975.

Editor, *England Invaded: A Collection of Fantasy Fiction*. London, W. H. Allen, and New York, Ultramarine, 1977.

Editor, *New Worlds: An Anthology*. London, Fontana, 1983.

*

Manuscript Collections: Bodleian Library, Oxford University; Sterling Library, Texas A and M University, College Station.

Critical Study: *The Entropy Exhibition: Michael Moorcock and the British "New Wave" in Science Fiction* by Colin Greenland, London, Routledge, 1983.

Michael Moorcock comments:

My work varies so widely that it attracts quite different readers. Most of it is not, in fact, generic SF—it's "fantasy," if anything—and much of it uses "genre borrowings" for specific ironic uses. Obsessions include imperialism, "trans-sexuality" (I don't believe in gender-roles as a survival trait—they're anti-survival now), racialism, how to live and grow in modern cities, etc. Modern pieties are another frequent target. I like change. I believe that people and things should be infinitely flexible. I am an anarchist in that I believe every individual should be self-governing and conscious of communal self-interest.

*   *   *

Michael Moorcock doesn't like SF: doubtless for that reason he has been one of the great impulses behind the New Wave, a notable editor of the genre, and its Proteus. Since his stories are "packed with personal symbols" one key to this paradoxical versatility lies in Moorcock's growing up during a crucial phase of British history. The only child of divorced parents, Moorcock was "brought up on an off-beat brand of Christian Mysticism." A professional writer and editor from an early age, and a Liberal party propagandist (now he supports the anarchist movement), he took over *New Worlds* and by publishing a range of the best authors, conservative as well as experimental, made it into one of the most challenging if misunderstood of SF magazines. Moorcock's dissatisfaction with SF was occasioned less by the inadequacies of the American pulps than by the complacency of an older generation of English writers. At a time when much SF was messianic and naive, he was influenced by the European mainstream, especially its *avant-garde*, believing the extension of the genre by such experimental techniques would produce work more ethically and psychologically relevant to the modern age. The exigencies as well as the opportunities of editing also shaped his own work. Because Moorcock was forced to finance *New Worlds* himself from hastily written stories, he wrote a copious amount of "swords and sorcery" fiction; so intertwined is his work in the two genres that the nature of his SF is moulded by the parodic experiments he began in the Elric stories and which culminate in *Gloriana*, that apotheosis of heroic burlesque—even if it does have a tinture of SF.

Remarkably little of his early SF lacks any merit, literary or intellectual. If the Michael Kane trilogy (a pastiche of Edgar Rice Burroughs) is a pot-boiler, the example of William Burroughs proved more encouraging; admittedly the ending of *The Rituals of Infinity* indicates the author is concerned less with the scientific than with the metaphysical validity of these stories.

The theme common to both Moorcock's fantasy and science fiction, the apocalypse, is first introduced in one of the Elric stories. Repeatedly his characters and their societies are faced with the question of how to react when confronted with racial extinction: thus in *The Twilight Man* the geodynamics memorably evoke the threat to human fertility posed by the possible unleashing of such cosmic forces by nuclear developments; in *The Black Corridor* Enoch Powell's anti-immigration policies, Celtic Nationalism, and sexism are powerfully satirized. *The Sundered Worlds* is notable for first presenting Moorcock's basic cosmology: one of the two "enlightened" protagonists sacrifices his life for the rest of mankind; the other preaches the gospel of the "multiverse" (the term probably derives from John Cowper Powys out of defiance of Chesterton), i. e., the occult existence of myriad universes in other dimensions which occasionally interact. The variant title (*The Blood Red Game*) underlines the message: there is a pattern to history, an existential gamble in which through self-knowledge humanity may survive. The appropriate eschatology, most fully stated in the ever more spell-binding fantasies, originates in Zoroastrianism which Moorcock admires (even if finally he demythologizes these beliefs): in the continual struggle between Chaos and Order, the balance is kept by the Cosmic Hand; the Zoroastrian historical perspective of time-cycles and millenary saviours inspired the mythos of the Eternal Champion who assumes different identities depending on which universe demands his reincarnation. The doubts often felt by and about the hero smack also of Brecht's epical theories.

Moorcock describes himself as "a faltering atheist with a deep irradicable religious sense"; in this ambivalence is rooted his fear of the dangers presented by the would-be saviour to his already threatened community; in *The Fireclown* one such target is amusingly L. Ron Hubbard. The risk run by the candidate himself is also the concern of the sensational *Behold the Man*. Moorcock now finds its iconoclasm hatefully deficient in humour, yet Glogauer's character is ambiguous enough for some to imterpret his actions as true *Imitatio Christi*, whereas in *The Black Corridor*, that sinister version of Harry Martinson's *Aniara*, the self-seeking head of the bourgeois family lost among Pascal's "infinite spaces" degenerates from appeasement to paranoia. More literary allusions are deployed in *The Ice Schooner* where Melville and Coleridge give symbolic as well as vivid circumstantial detail to a study of a new Ice Age hero who finally resists further social manipulation.

Moorcock has argued that while one of the major themes of 19th-century fiction concerned "the attempt of the individual to find personal freedom in a repressive society," today in the Western democracies (as heirs to the great radical and libertarian movements of the early years of this century) our problem is "how we should use this freedom." These themes are extensively explored in the markedly superior work Moorcock has done since the 1971 winding up of the original *New Worlds*. In the engagingly witty Oswald Bastable cycle, with its burlesque of the Edwardian utopias and wars-to-come of Verne, Kipling, E. Nesbit (and, hidden in the pseudonymic conundrums, Conrad and Lenin), Moorcock attacks the current nostalgia for Britain's imperial past; in *The War Lord of the Air*, *The Land Leviathan* and *The Steel Tsar* the lost time-traveller Bastable is educated into the realities of colonialism. Rather similar lessons are to be taken more to heart in the multiple "transincarnations" of Glogauer, whose "Second Coming" is the subject of that sardonic Brechtian experiment in alienation *Breakfast in the Ruins*. Armageddon is easier to depict than "a new heaven and a new earth"; and whereas in the exuberant Dancers at the End of Time series Moorcock can make hilarious use of Dickens, Shaw, Firbank, and of course Wells to ridicule both the wastefulness of the advanced countries and the "doomsters", ecological as well as religious, in *The Transformation of Miss Mavis Ming* he is over-indulgently whimsical.

The quintessence of Moorcock's achievement is the Jerry Cornelius series. At one time placed at the disposal of contributors to *New Worlds*, Cornelius has been progressively developed by Moorcock into a brilliant satirical device, a prism by means of which he does a spectrum analysis of 20th-century Western culture on the point of collapse. *The Final Programme* is a rewrite of some Elric stories in terms of *The Threepenny Novel*; starting with *A Cure for Cancer* the conventional narrative is decomposed into a series of apparently discrete images reflecting the non-linear mode in which, at least at a conscious level, modern life is increasingly conducted—a dazzling ironic synthesis of popular fictional formulae: detective, thriller, gothic horror, adventure, western, and not least science fiction. These are satirically related to 20th-century actualities in a manner often cinematic (though at other times the language is that of the computer or medicine or the theatre in and off the streets)—a montage of sensational headlines, authentic press stories, pop lyrics, fashion news, military and other advertisements, scientific reports, and subtly tampered-with extracts from scholarly authorities—yet the over-all effect of modernity is disturbed by a persistent sense of *déjà vu* that calls attention to a Jungian awareness of the spiritual heritage of archaic man surviving still in the depths of our unconscious, reinforced by the reappearance of situations or characters from Moorcock's other books. Through the burlesques of the different futures or pasts imagined by both society and the SF writer, Moorcock exposes the various illusions around which modern man has tried to build up a stable identity "against the tyranny of time and the human condition." Still, if Cornelius proves to be not "the Messiah of the age of science" but the *zeitgeist* itself, there is a punning kind of Messiah in the series: breaking through the muzak come the authentic voices of Bob Dylin, Jimi Hendrix, Schoenberg, Ives, and Messiaen whose collective presence helps to give structure and meaning to what might seem incoherence (particularly significant are the overarching allusions to Messiaen's *Turangalila Symphony*). Like the associated references to Vishnu and Shiva which open respectively the first and last books of the series, or the scientific evidence concerning "a hiss located in outer space [that] may be an echo of this explosive creation," these Messiaen references stress the importance of penetrating the illusion of *maya* to perceive the reality of the divine drama of *lila* enacted within the phenomena of the world. The two-part structure of the traditional harlequinade in which Cornelius finally appears obliquely suggests the unmasking desirable for his society. Paradoxically by departing from the strict conventions of the

genre, Moorcock as perhaps no other post-war British SF writer is able to tell home truths.

Eastern story-telling apparently suggested the principles by which he has continued to experiment with ways of distancing himself from SF: retrospectively Moorcock's homage to resourceful Scheherazade in *The Laughter of Carthage* illuminates his own art. With audiences the world over that range from the popular to the learned, arabesque narratives in the West have also stimulated just the sorts of literature, illustration, pantomine, movie, and opera as those which Moorcock delights to reshape; oriental collections of multitudinous tales within tales authenticated by chains of witnesses, their evidence tantalizingly discontinuous and imbricated, encyclopedias of genres combining the everyday and exotic, history and romance, facing tragicomically problems public, private, worldly, and spiritual, framed wisdom stories deploying space-time shifts, "the instrumental marvellous" (Todorov), inversions or replications of plot no less than protagonist, and all this in a manner—as Moorcock evidently has noted—that anticipates modernism's critique of the 19th-century aesthetic. Significantly, too, these Eastern structures admit of contraction as much as accretion, since compilations with the flexibility of *The Arabian Nights* help explain Moorcock's recent alternation between, on the one hand, multi-media *bricolage* as found elegantly minaturized in *The Entropy Tango* (where a snapshot of Major Nye shows him the double of Orwell), and, on the other hand, the vast, teeming canvases of the Pyat memoirs with their deceptive look of an old-style three-decker. Teasingly the alternative histories promised in titles like *Byzantium Endures* are but partially realized. The New Rome whose decline is chronicled here proves less Greek than Slav, Levantine, Cockney, and American, its citizens migrating from Kiev to Istanbul, Paris, London, Los Angeles: the industrial and commercial centres of the disintegrating 19th-century empires eclipsed by a west coast, where a like fall is on the cards. Ironically this geopolitical viewpoint imparts to seemingly traditional novels something of the estranged vision of SF as 20th-century history records events the equal of any bizarrerie imagined in *The Nomad of Time* cycle. Aspects of "The Russian Experiment" and the consequent East European exodus are metamorphosed into a perspective glass focused on the disparity between material and ethical progress in modern times. The powerful story "Crossing into Cambodia" (My Experiences in the Third World War) confronts Babel's cossacks with nuclear holocaust; a threat to Thatcher's England more light-heartedly treated in that coda to Corneliana, "The Alchemist's Question" (*The Opium General*). The novelist, though, requires conventions subtler and more panoramic. Wedding the extravagancies of a Münchhausen with the alibis of the picaro, conscripting the *dramatis personae* of Buchan to act *Greenmantle* -fashion alongside his existing troupes of maskers, Moorcock spins yarns about his anti-hero that are as enthralling as they are mordant. The parodies of Paustovsky, Piln'iak and Eisenstein in the first volume of the Pyat sequence, of D. W. Griffith, Nathanael West, Nabokov in the second, challenge oppression by Soviet and Fascist alike. With psychological acuteness Moorcock explores in practice as well as theory the paradox whereby, if the technological age is to be surveyed, even the mainstream novelist needs the expressiveness of SF, yet proportionately must he beware the crypto-authoritarian tendencies in such dangerous visions of the future or the past.

—Peter Caracciolo

MOORE, C(atherine) L(ucille). Also writes as Lewis Padgett. American. Born in Indianapolis, Indiana, 24 January 1911. Educated at the University of Southern California, Los Angeles, B. S. 1956 (Phi Beta Kappa), M. A. 1964. Married 1)Henry Kuttner, *q. v.*, in 1940 (died, 1958); 2) Thomas Reggie in 1963. Staff member, later President, Fletcher Trust Company, Indianapolis, 1930-40; Instructor in Writing and Literature, University of Southern California, 1958-61. Most of her work after 1940 was written in collaboration with Henry Kuttner, though not always acknowledged. Agent: Don Congdon Associates, 177 East 70th Street, New York, New York 10021. Address: c/o Boyd Correll, 1948 Hanscom Drive, South Pasadena, California 91030, U.S.A.

SCIENCE-FICTION PUBLICATIONS

Novels

Fury, with Henry Kuttner. New York, Grosset and Dunlap, 1950; London, Dobson, 1954; as *Destination Infinity*, New York, Avon, 1958.
Judgment Night (includes stories). New York, Gnome Press, 1952.
Doomsday Morning. New York, Doubleday, 1957; London, Consul, 1960.
Earth's Last Citadel, with Henry Kuttner. New York, Ace, 1964.
Valley of the Flame, with Henry Kuttner. New York, Ace, 1964.
The Time Axis, with Henry Kuttner. New York, Ace, 1965.
The Dark World, with Henry Kuttner. New York, Ace, 1965; London, Mayflower, 1966.
The Mask of Circe, with Henry Kuttner. New York, Ace, 1971.

Novels as Lewis Padgett, with Henry Kuttner

Tomorrow and Tomorrow, and The Fairy Chessmen. New York, Gnome Press, 1951; as *Tomorrow and Tomorrow* and *The Far Reality*, London, Consul, 2 vols., 1963; *The Fairy Chessmen* published as *Chessboard Planet*, New York, Galaxy, 1956.
Well of the Worlds. New York, Galaxy, 1953.
Beyond Earth's Gates. New York, Ace, 1954.

Short Stories

Shambleau and Others. New York, Gnome Press, 1953; abridged edition, London, Consul, 1961.
Northwest of Earth. New York, Gnome Press, 1954.
No Boundaries, with Henry Kuttner. New York, Ballantine, 1955; London, Consul, 1961.
Jirel of Joiry (collection). New York, Paperback Library, 1969; as *Black God's Shadow*, West Kingston, Rhode Island, Grant, 1977.
The Best of C. L. Moore, edited by Lester del Rey. New York, Doubleday, 1975.
Clash by Night and Other Stories, with Henry Kuttner, edited by Peter Pinto. London, Hamlyn, 1980.
Chessboard Planet and Other Stories, with Henry Kuttner. London, Hamlyn, 1983.

Short Stories as Lewis Padgett, with Henry Kuttner

A Gnome There Was. New York, Simon and Schuster, 1950.
Mutant. New York, Gnome Press, 1953; London, Weidenfeld and Nicolson, 1954.
Line to Tomorrow. New York, Bantam, 1954.

OTHER PUBLICATIONS

Novels with Henry Kuttner

The Brass Ring (as Lewis Padgett). New York, Duell, 1964; London, Sampson Low, 1947; as *Murder in Brass*, New York, Bantam, 1947.
The Day He Died (as Lewis Padgett). New York, Duell, 1947.

*

Manuscript Collection: Lovecraft Collection, Brown University Library, Providence, Rhode Island.

*   *   *

One of a handful of American women whose science-fiction and fantasy works were published during the 1930's, C. L. Moore has recently been rediscovered by enthusiastic readers and scholars. Her fiction is of significance not only for its own intrinsic merits but also for its influence on the evolution of this literary field. Alone and later in conjunction with Henry Kuttner, Moore introduced psychological analysis and sensuously evocative setting to a form which had been dominated by stereotyped characterization and technological gimmickry. Moore's works are also of interest in light of the 1970's explicitly feminist science fiction; some of her writing antedates this trend while other aspects of it reflect the beliefs and divided sensibility of a woman writer working without such published, politicized support.

"Shambleau" (1933), Moore's first story, innovatively, emphasized characterization, vivid imagery, and human sexuality in its depiction of an Earth adventurer, Northwest Smith, and his encounter with a Medusa-like alien. Through skillfully ambiguous imagery, Moore conveys the female attributes of this alien which, in themselves, simultaneously arouse and dismay her male protagonist. Smith, a conventionally hard-bitten but honorable hero whose illegal exploits are never immoral, figures in a series of stories which include "Black Thirst," "Scarlet Dream," and "Dust of God. " Moore began a chronologically parallel series of fantasy stories featuring Jirel of Joiry, an independent, resolute Warrior queen of the 15th century, in 1934. In "Black God's Kiss" Jirel braves the horrors of a supernatural, evil-ridden dimension in order to find a weapon she can use to overthrow her castle's conqueror. Avenging her warrior's honor and slain soldiers, Jirel discovers too late that she had really loved the briefly victorious Guillaume. In subsequent stories Jirel continues to triumph over the supernatural. "Quest of the Star Stone" (1937) (with Kuttner) is of special interest for both series: in it, Northwest Smith is magically transported back to the 15th century to confront Jirel.

After Moore's marriage in 1940, it is difficult to determine which stories are exclusively or predominantly hers and which Kuttner's because both writers—singly and in collaboration—used a total of 17 different pseudonyms. One story, however, written under her own name, stands clearly as Moore's work. "No Woman Born" (1944), the tale of a beautiful dancer caught in a theater fire whose severe burns force her rescuers to transfer her brain into a metal body, shines with Moore's glowing imagery and subtle questions about the nature of humanity. After the accident, Deidre's resilient physical grace stems from the ingenuity of futuristic engineering as much as from her own guiding memories of motion, but it is her will power, and her own values, that ultimately enable the sensation-deprived dancer to regard friendship and compassion more highly than her new, inhuman strength. "No Woman Born" is one of the first science-fiction treatments of cyborgs—creatures part human and part machine—to emphasize characterization rather than technological detail or innovation.

"Judgment Night" (1943), a novella also credited solely to Moore, illustrates not only her characteristic synaesthetic imagery but also her ambivalent stance towards independent womanhood. The psychological and ethical strengths Deidre manifests in "No Woman Born" are, in Moore's other works, either adulterated when the female protagonist *is* of woman born—mere flesh and blood—or else have disastrous consequences. Like Jirel of Joiry, Juille in "Judgment Night" is a warrior princess who must choose between adherence to an ethical code and the man she loves. Although circumstances conspire to remove this final decision from her grasp, Juille's cumulative hesitations and missteps seal both her lover's and her civilization's ultimate doom. While Moore presents Juille as a person who can admire her Amazon mentor's betrayal of her because this treachery stems from the woman's own sworn loyalties, the author undercuts this characterization by also presenting Juille as an incomplete woman seeking to capture "the despised femininity she had repudiated all her life." Within the galaxy-view Moore presents, it is impossible for a woman to be both psychologically strong and sexually or emotionally satisfied, to maintain her principles and still enjoy "a concert in color and motion." Juille is intially as unfamiliar with her body's needs and desires as she is with the extensive religiously taboo surfaces of her native planet. And the knowledge this character ultimately gains of both forbidden territories does little to forestall the "Judgment Night" that overtakes her. Moore leaves her protagonists together, "content" to "live each measured moment that remained to them with. . . vividness," but the reader knows that these moments are numbered.

Two of Moore and Kuttner's collaborations have been included in *The Science Fiction Hall of Fame*. "Mimsy Were the Borogroves" (1943) (as Lewis Padgett) plays with conventional notions of childhood and maturity: in it, two Earth children transport themselves into a different future dimension by deciphering the puzzles and games, scoffed at by their elders, that a time-travelling future scientist has lost. One of these puzzles is the *Through the Looking-Glass* quatrain beginning "Twas brillig. . . ." "Vintage Season" (1946) (as Lawrence O'Donnell) is a novella about time-travellers from the future whose vacations are spent witnessing crucial events in Earth's history. Its action centers upon the characters and personalities of these voyeurs and the reactions of their landlord, a contemporary young man who gradually comes to realize their origin and motivations. Although these dilettantes might avert disaster in his time, they selfishly choose not to. In addition to their numerous short stories, Moore and Kuttner also collaborated on one notable science-fiction novel, *Fury*, set on Venus and describing the aftermath of a failed utopia. Their later collaborative works are of less interest.

Moore's lasting contributions to science fiction and fantasy include not only her own classic works but also the models that she—and Kuttner—set for contemporary and future writers. Depth of characterization and setting, attention to the nuances of human motivation and interaction, recognition of the myths—and mythic quests—that shape human experience, and incorporation of sophisticated mainstream literary techniques—such as the use of a central intelligence in "No Woman Born": these are the innovations one may credit to Moore. Although feminist critics have recently begun to praise Moore for her strong heroine, Jirel of Joiry, at the same time they "excuse" or ignore her other works, such criticism does not recognize the full significance of her oeuvre. Technically

innovative, Moore's writing is also emblematic of women's authorial ambivalence in an explicitly patriarchal culture.

—Natalie M. Rosinsky

MOORE, Patrick (Caldwell-). British. Born in Pinner, Middlesex, 4 March 1923. Educated privately. Served in the Royal Air Force, 1940-45: Navigator, Bomber Command. Concerned in running a school, 1945-52; Director, Armagh Planetarium, Northern Ireland, 1965-68. Since 1957, Presenter, *The Sky at Night* television series, BBC, London. Since 1962, Editor, *Yearbook of Astronomy*. President, British Astronomical Association, since 1982. Also a composer. Recipient: Lorimer Gold Medal, 1962; Goodacre Gold Medal, 1968; Italian Astronomical Society Arturo Gold Medal, 1969; Jackson-Gwilt Medal, 1978; Astronomical Society of the Pacific Klumpke-Roberts Award, 1978. Fellow, Royal Astronomical Society. D. Sc. : University of Lancaster, 1974. O. B. E. (Officer, Order of the British Empire), 1968. Agent: Hilary Rubinstein, A. P. Watt Ltd., 26-28 Bedford Row, London WC1R 4HL. Address: Farthings, 39 West Street, Selsey, West Sussex, England.

SCIENCE-FICTION PUBLICATIONS

Novels (for children; series: Maurice Gray; Quest; Scott Saunders)

The Master of the Moon. London, Museum Press, 1952.
The Island of Fear. London, Museum Press, 1954.
The Frozen Planet. London, Museum Press, 1954.
Destination Luna. London, Lutterworth Press, 1955.
Quest of the Spaceways. London, Muller, 1955.
Mission to Mars (Gray). London, Burke, 1955.
World of Mists (Quest). London, Muller, 1956.
The Domes of Mars (Gray). London, Burke, 1956.
Wheel in Space. London, Lutterworth Press, 1956.
The Voices of Mars (Gray). London, Burke, 1957.
Peril on Mars (Gray). London, Burke, 1958; New York, Putnam, 1965.
Raiders on Mars (Gray). London, Burke, 1959.
Captives of the Moon. London, Burke, 1960.
Wanderer in Space. London, Burke, 1961.
Crater of Fear. London, Burke, and New York, Harvey House, 1962.
Invader from Space. London, Burke, 1963.
Caverns of the Moon. London, Burke, 1964.
Planet of Fire. Kingswood, Surrey, World's Work, 1969.
Spy in Space (Saunders). London, Armada, 1977.
Planet of Fear (Saunders). London, Armada, 1977.
The Moon Raiders (Saunders). London, Armada, 1978.
Killer Comet (Saunders). London, Armada, 1978.
The Terror Star (Saunders). London, Armada, 1979.
The Secret of the Black Hole (Saunders). London, Armada, 1980.

OTHER PUBLICATIONS

Plays

Perseus and Andromeda, music by Moore (produced Shoreham, Sussex, 1974).
Theseus, music by Moore (produced, 1982).

Other

Guide to the Moon. London, Eyre and Spottiswoode, and New York, Norton, 1953; revised edition, London, Colins, 1957; as *Survey of the Moon*, Eyre and Spottiswoode and Norton, 1963; revised edition, Guildford, Surrey, Lutterworth Press, 1976; as *New Guide to the Moon*, Norton, 1976.

Suns, Myths, and Men. London, Muller, 1954; revised edition, Muller, 1968; New York, Norton, 1969; as *The Story of the Man and the Stars*, New York, Norton, 1955.

Out into Space, with A. L. Helm. London, Museum Press, 1954.

The Boy's Book of Space. London, Burke, 1954; New York, Roy, 1956.

The True Book about Worlds Around Us. London, Muller, 1954; as *The Worlds Around Us*, New York, Abelard Schuman, 1956.

A Guide to the Planets. New York, Norton, 1954; London, Eyre and Spottiswoode, 1955; revised edition, London, Collins, 1957; Norton, 1960; Guildford, Surrey, Lutterworth Press, 1976; as *The New Guide to the Planets*, Norton, 1972.

The Moon, with Hugh Percival Wilkins. London, Faber, and New York, Macmillan, 1955.

Earth Satellite: The New Satellite Projects Explained. London, Eyre and Spottiswoode, 1955; as *Earth Satellites*, New York, Norton, 1956; revised edition, Norton, 1958.

The Planet Venus. London, Faber, 1956; New York, Macmillan, 1957; revised edition, 1959, 1961; with Garry Hunt, Faber, 1982.

Man-Made Moons. London, Newman Neame, 1956.

Making and Using a Telescope, with Hugh Percival Wilkins. London, Eyre and Spottiswoode, 1956; as *How to Make and Use a Telescope*, New York, Norton, 1956.

The True Book about the Earth. London, Muller, 1956.

Guide to Mars. London, Muller, 1956; New York, Macmillan, 1958; revised edition, Muller, 1965.

The True Book about Earthquakes and Volcanoes. London, Muller, 1957.

Isaac Newton (for children). London, Black, 1957; New York, Putnam, 1958.

Science and Fiction. London, Harrap, 1957; Folcroft, Pennsylvania, Folcroft Editions, 1970.

The Amateur Astronomer. London, Lutterworth Press, and New York, Norton, 1957; revised edition, Lutterworth Press, 1974; revised edition, as *Amateur Astronomy*, Norton, 1968.

The Earth, Our Home. New York, Abelard Schuman, 1957.

Your Book of Astronomy. London, Faber, 1958; revised edition, 1964, 1979.

The Solar System. London, Methuen, 1958; New York, Criterion, 1961.

The Boy's Book of Astronomy. London, Burke, and New York, Roy, 1958; revised edition, Burke, 1964.

The True Book about Man. London, Muller, 1959.

Man on the Moon. London, Newman Neame, 1959.

Rockets and Earth Satellites. London, Muller, 1959.

Astronautics. London, Methuen, 1960.

Star Spotter. London, Newman Neame, 1960.

Guide to the Stars. London, Eyre and Spottiswoode, and New York, Norton, 1960; revised edition, Guildford, Surrey, Lutterworth Press, 1974; as *The New Guide to the Stars*, New York, Norton, 1975.

Stars and Space. London, Black, 1960.

Conquest of the Air: The Story of the Wright Brothers. London, Lutterworth Press, 1961.

Navigation, with Henry Brinton. London, Methuen, 1961.

Astronomy. London, Oldbourne, 1961; as *The Picture History of Astronomy*, New York, Grosset and Dunlap, 1961; revised edition, 1972; revised edition, as *The Story of Astronomy*, London, Macdonald, 1972; revised edition, London, Macdonald and Jane's, 1977; revised edition, as *Patrick Moore's History of Astronomy*, London, Macdonald, 1983.

The Stars. London, Weidenfeld and Nicolson, 1962.

Exploring Maps, with Henry Brinton. London, Odhams Press, 1962; New York, Hawthorn, 1967.

Exploring Time, with Henry Brinton. London, Odhams Press, 1962.

The Astronomer's Telescope, with Paul Murdin. Leicester, Brockhampton Press, 1962.

Life in the Universe, with Francis J. Jackson. London, Routledge, and New York, Norton, 1962.

The Planets. London, Eyre and Spottiswoode, and New York, Norton, 1962.

The Observer's Book of Astronomy. London, Warne, 1962; 6th edition, 1978.

Telescopes and Observatories. London, Weidenfeld and Nicolson, and New York, Day, 1962.

Space in the Sixties. London, Penguin, 1963.

Exploring the Moon. London, Odhams Press, 1964.

The True Book about Roman Britain. London, Muller, 1964.

Exploring Weather, with Henry Brinton. London, Odhams Press, 1964.

The Sky at Night 1-7. London, Eyre and Spottiswoode, 2 vols., and London, BBC, 5 vols., 1964-80; vol. 1, New York, Norton, 1965.

Life on Mars, with Francis L. Jackson. London, Routledge, 1965; New York, Norton, 1966.

Exploring Other Planets, with Henry Brinton. London, Odhams Press, 1965; New York, Hawthorn, 1967.

Exploring the World. London, Oxford Unversity Press, 1966; New York, Watts, 1968.

The New Look of the Universe. London, Hodder and Stoughton, and New York, Norton, 1966.

Exploring the Planetarium. London, Odhams Press, 1966.

Legends of the Stars. London, Odhams Press, 1966.

Naked-Eye Astronomy. London, Lutterworth Press, and New York, Norton, 1966.

Basic Astronomy. Edinburgh, Oliver and Boyd, 1967.

Exploring Earth History, with Henry Brinton. London, Odhams Press, 1967.

The Craters of the Moon, with Peter J. Cattermole. New York, Norton, 1967.

The Amateur Astronomer's Glossary. London, Lutterworth Press, and New York, Norton, 1967; revised edition, as *The A-Z of Astronomy*, London, Fontana, and New York, Scribner, 1976.

Armagh Observatory: A History 1790-1967. Armagh, Armagh Observatory, 1967.

Exploring the Galaxies. London, Odhams Press, 1968.

Exploring the Stars. London, Odhams Press, 1968.

Space. London, Lutterworth Press, 1968; New York, Natural History Press, 1969.

The Sun and Its Influence, by Mervyn A. Ellison, revised edition. London, Routledge, and New York, Elsevier, 1968.

The Sun. London, Muller, and New York, Norton, 1968.

Moon Flight Atlas. London, Mitchell Beazley, and Chicago, Rand McNally, 1969; revised edition, Mitchell Beazley, 1970.

Astronomy and Space Research (bibliography). London, National Book League, 1969.

The Development of Astronomical Thought. Edinburgh, Oliver and Boyd, 1969.

The Atlas of the Universe. London, Mitchell Beazley, and Chicago, Rand Mcnally, 1970; revised edition, as *The Mitchell Beazley Concise Atlas of the Universe*, Mitchell

Beazley, 1974; as *The Concise Atlas of the Universe*, Rand McNally, 1974; revised edition, as *The New Atlas of the Universe*, New York, Crown, 1984.

Gunpowder, Treason: November 5, 1605, with Henry Brinton. London, Lutterworth Press, 1970.

Astronomy for O Level. London, Duckworth, 1970.

Seeing Stars. London, BBC, and Chicago, Rand McNally, 1971.

Mars, The Red World. Kingswood, Surrey, World's Work, 1971.

The Astronomy of Birr Castle. London, Mitchell Beazley, 1971.

Can You Speak Venusian: A Guide to Independent Thinkers. Newton Abbot, Devon, David and Charles, 1972; New York, Norton, 1973.

Challenge of the Stars, with David A. Hardy. London, Mitchell Beazley, and Chicago, Rand McNally, 1972; as *The New Challenge of the Stars*, London, Mitchell Beazley-Sidgwick and Jackson, 1977, Rand McNally, 1978.

How Britain Won the Space Race, with Desmond Leslie. London, Mitchell Beazley, 1972.

Stories of Science and Invention. London, Oxford University Press, 1972.

How to Recognise the Stars, with Lawrence Clarke. London, Corgi, 1972.

The Southern Stars. Cape Town, Timmins, 1972.

1001 Questions Answered about Astronomy, by James S. Pickering, revised edition. Guildford, Surrey, Lutterworth Press, 1972; New York, Dodd Mead, 1973.

Patrick Moore's Colour Star Atlas. Guildford, Surrey, Lutterworth Press, 1973; as *Color Star Atlas*, New York, Crown, 1973.

The Starlit Sky. Cape Town, Timmins, 1973.

Man the Astronomer. London, Priory Press, 1973.

Mars, with Charles A. Cross. London, Mitchell Beazley, and New York, Crown, 1973.

The Comets: Visitors from Space. Shaldon, Devon, Reid, 1973; revised edition, as *Comets*, New York, Scribner, 1976; as *Guide to Comets*, Guildford, Surrey, Lutterworth Press, 1977.

Watchers of the Stars: The Scientific Revolution. London, Joseph, and New York, Putnam, 1974.

Black Holes in Space, with Iain Nicolson. London, Ocean, 1974; New York, Norton, 1976.

The Astronomy Quiz Book. London, Carousel, 1974; revised edition, 1978.

The Young Astronomer and His Telescope. Shaldon, Devon, Reid, 1974.

Let's Look at the Sky: The Planets [*The Stars*]. London, Carousel, 2 vols., 1975.

Legends of the Planets. London, Luscombe, 1976.

The Next Fifty Years in Space. London, Luscombe, and New York, Taplinger, 1976.

The Stars Above. Norwich, Jarrold, 1976.

The Astronomy of Southern Africa, with Pete Collins. Cape Town, Timmins, and London, Hale, 1977.

The Atlas of Mercury, with Charles A. Cross. London, Mitchell Beazley, and New York, Crown, 1977.

Guide to Mars (not the same as 1956 book). Guildford, Surrey, Lutterworth Press, 1977; New York, Norton, 1978.

Wonder Why Book of Planets [*the Earth, Stars*]. London, Transworld, 3 vols., 1977-78; *Stars* published New York, Grosset and Dunlap, 1979.

Man's Future in Space. Hove, Sussex, Wayland, 1978.

The Guinness Book of Astronomy Facts and Feats. London, Guinness Superlatives, 1979.

Fun-to-Know-About Mysteries of Space (for children). London, Armada, 1979.

Out of Darkness: The Planet Pluto, with Clyde Tombaugh. Guildford, Surrey, Lutterworth Press, and Harrisburg, Pennsylvania, Stackpole, 1980.

The Pocket Guide to Astronomy. New York, Simon and Schuster, 1980; as *Patrick Moore's Pocket Guide to Astronomy*, London, Mitchell Beazley, 1982.

Everyman's Scientific Facts and Feats, with Magnus Pyke. London, Dent, 1981.

The Moon (atlas). London, Mitchell Beazley, and Chicago, Rand McNally, 1981.

Jupiter, with Garry Hunt. London, Mitchell Beazley, and Chicago, Rand McNally, 1981.

William Herschel, Astronomer and Musician. Sidcup, Kent, P. M. E. Erwood-Herschel Society, 1981.

The Unfolding Universe. London, Joseph-Rainbird, and New York, Crown, 1982.

Saturn, with Garry Hunt. London, Mitchell Beazley, and Chicago, Rand Mcnally, 1982.

What's New in Space? (for children). London, Carousel, 1982.

Countdown! or, How Nigh Is the End? London, Joseph-Rainbird, 1983.

Travellers in Space and Time. London, Park Lane, 1983; New York, Doubleday, 1984.

The Space Shuttle Action Book (for children). London, Aurum Press, and New York, Random House, 1983.

The Return of Halley's Comet, with John Mason. New York, Norton, 1984.

The Story of the Earth, with Peter Cattermole. London, Cambridge University Press, 1984; New York, Cambridge University Press, 1985.

Armchair Astronomy, Wellington, Northamptonshire, Stephens, 1984.

Stargazing: Astronomy Without a Telescope. London, Aurum Press, 1985.

Editor, *Space Exploration*. Cambridge, University Press, 1958.

Editor, *Practical Amateur Astronomy*. London, Lutterworth Press, 1963; as *A Handbook of Practical Amateur Astronomy*, New York, Norton, 1964.

Editor, *Against Hunting*. London, Gollancz, 1965.

Editor, *Some Mysteries of the Universe,* by William R. Corliss. London, Black, 1969.

Editor, *Astronomical Telescopes and Observatories*. Newton Abbot, Devon, David and Charles, and New York, Norton, 1973.

Editor, *Modern Astronomy: Selections from The Yearbook of Astronomy*. London, Sidgwick and Jackson, and New York, Norton, 1977.

Editor, *The Beginner's Book of Astronomy*. London, Sidgwick and Jackson, 1978.

Editor, with Garry Hunt, *The Atlas of the Solar System*. London, Mitchell Beazley, 1983.

Translator, *The Planet Mars*, by Gérard de Vaucouleurs. London, Faber, and New York, Macmillan, 1950; revised edition, Faber, 1951.

Translator, *The Structure of the Universe*, by Evry L. Schatzman. London, Weidenfeld and Nicolson, 1968.

Translator, *Quanta*, by J. Andrade e Silva and G. Lochak. London, Weidenfeld and Nicolson, 1969.

Translator, *Cosmology*, by Jean Émile Charon. London, Weidenfeld and Nicolson, 1970.

Translator, *The Planet Mercury* [*Mars*], by E. M. Antoniadi. Shaldon, Devon, Reid, 2 vols., 1974-75.

Recording: *The Ever Ready Band Plays Music by Patrick Moore*, Pye, 1979.

*

Patrick Moore comments:

My novels are written with the aim of entertaining; they are set in space and are for boys aged roughly 10 to 15. I try to keep a reasonably authentic background, though I am not above taking liberties (after all, Wells did!). I do, however, make a rule that any juvenile novels of mine avoid the sordid and unwholesome.

*   *   *

Patrick Moore's novels possess some special quality which is not shared by many of their contemporaries. Like the Biggles series, Moore's tales of interplanetary travel continue to be republished and find a steady readership. Unfortunately the quality which enables these novels to maintain their readership does not transmit itself to the adult reader. The children's books of a writer such as Ursula K. Le Guin can be identified as books of some merit even by adult standards. However, Moore's books tend to present a view of life and character that is narrow and unrealistic. The characters themselves are largely stock creations and are emotionally very limited. The story lines are repetitive and rely on a limited number of situations to maintain the excitement of the tale. (The main variations consist of altering the names of the chief characters, the settings, and the order of the incidents). Finally the stories themselves lack a human realism. Scientifically the stories are slightly behind the times but this is of little significance compared to the ease with which his juvenile heroes become incorporated into the adventure: this strains adult credulity, and probably that of many children as well. Despite this the books continue to attract readers at a time when many superior examples of the story-teller's craft fail to do so. Moore's books offer something beyond an adventure in space, something beyond the lack of literary polish. This something lies within the story.

A typical story line would go something like this: an honest courageous youth with a steady head on his shoulders by some means becomes associated with a research establishment engaged in the exploration of outer space. This establishment is staffed by a group of scientific internationalists who react strongly against national or political interests. A crisis occurs and the staff of the establishment are forced through circumstances to utilise the youth in a task of responsibility on a dangerous mission. The youth, despite the fact that he is not of outstanding intelligence or possessed of great knowledge, manages to win the respect of the scientists through a display of his basic qualities during the many dangers encountered throughout the mission, and, now accepted as an equal, has his future career as a respected member of an exploration team assured. In the series the youthful hero gradually occupies a more and more respected place among the ranks of the scientist/explorers. The appeal of this storyline is fairly obvious. It displays successful adolescent involvement in an adult world, though a greatly simplified and idealised one. A display of truth, integrity, and courage is sufficient to achieve one's desire, and there are no authority conflicts to establish problems between the adolescent and his elders, since the authority displayed by the scientists stems only from their great knowledge of a given situation, and the motivation for accepting their authority is made obvious: death in space if the mission fails. In this respect Moore's novels reflect an updating of traditional tales of this type, and in that context a fairly successful updating.

—Gary Coughlan

MOORE, Ward. American. Born in Madison, New Jersey, 10 August 1903. Self-educated. Married 1) Lorna Lenzi in 1942 (divorced); 2) Raylyn Crabbe in 1967; four daughters and three sons. Chicken farmer, bookshop clerk and manager, shipyard worker during World War II, house builder, gardener, ghost writer, copy editor, and book review editor; lived in California after 1929. *Died 29 January 1978.*

SCIENCE-FICTION PUBLICATIONS

Novels

Greener Than You Think. New York, Sloane, 1947; London, Gollancz, 1949.
Bring the Jubilee. New York, Farrar Straus, 1953; London, Heinemann, 1955.
Cloud by Day. London, Heinemann, 1956.
Joyleg, with Avram Davidson. New York, Pyramid, 1962.
Caduceus Wild, with R. Bradford. Los Angeles, Pinnacle, 1978.

Uncollected Short Stories

"Peacebringer" ("Sword of Peace"), in *The Big Book of Science Fiction,* edited by Groff Conklin. New York, Crown, 1950.
"Flying Dutchman," in *Adventures in Tomorrow,* edited by Ken Crossen. New York, Greenberg, 1951; London, Lane, 1953.
"We the People," in *Future Tense,* edited by Ken Crossen. New York, Greenberg, 1952; London, Lane, 1954.
"Measure of a Man," in *Fantasy and Science Fiction* (New York), August 1953.
"Lot," in *The Best from Fantasy and Science Fiction 3,* edited by Anthony Boucher and J. Francis McComas. New York, Doubleday, 1954.
"Rx Jupiter Save Us," in *Future* (New York), January 1954.
"Caution Advisable," in *Original Science Fiction Stories* (Holyoke, Massachusetts), March 1955.
"In Working Order," in *Original Science Fiction Stories* (Holyoke, Massachusetts), May 1955.
"Old Story," in *Fantasy and Science Fiction* (New York), September 1955.
"The Rewrite Man," in *Fantastic Universe* (Chicago), July 1956.
"No Man Pursueth," in *The Best from Fantasy and Science Fiction 6,* edited by Anthony Boucher. New York, Doubleday, 1957.
"Adjustment," in *The Best from Fantasy and Science Fiction 7,* edited by Anthony Boucher. New York, Doubleday, 1958.
"Lot's Daughter," in *A Decade of Fantasy and Science Fiction,* edited by Robert P. Mills. New York, Doubleday, 1960.
"Transient," in *Amazing* (New York), February 1960.
"The Fellow Who Married the Maxill Girl," in *The Best from Fantasy and Science Fiction 10,* edited by Robert P. Mills. New York, Doubleday, 1961.
"It Becomes Necessary" ("The Cold Peace"), in *The Year's Best S-F 7,* edited by Judith Merril. New York, Simon and Schuster, 1962.
"Rebel," in *Fantasy and Science Fiction* (New York), February 1962.
"The Second Trip to Mars" ("Dominions Beyond"), in *The Post Reader of Fantasy and Science Fiction.* New York, Doubleday, and London, Souvenir Press, 1964.
"The Mysterious Milkman of Bishop Street," in *Fantasy and Science Fiction* (New York), January 1965.
"Frank Merriwell in the White House," in *American Government Through Science Fiction,* edited by Joseph D. Olander and Martin H. Greenberg. New York, Random House, 1974.

"Durance," in *Epoch*, edited by Roger Elwood and Robert Silverberg. New York, Berkley, 1975.
"Wish Fiddle," in *Fantasy and Science Fiction* (New York), November 1975.
"A Class with Dr. Chang," in *Beyond Time*, edited by Sandra Ley. New York, Pocket Books, 1976.
"With Mingled Feelings. . .," in *Chrysalis 6*, edited by Roy Torgeson. New York, Kensington, 1979.
"Conversation Piece," in *Whispers 2*, edited by Stuart David Schiff. New York, Doubleday, 1979.

OTHER PUBLICATIONS

Novel

Breathe the Air Again. New York, Harper, 1942.

*   *   *

Ward Moore's science fiction began in 1947 with the publication of *Greener Than You Think*, a disaster novel in which a mysterious mutated "devilgrass" threatens the world. Moore also wrote a number of short stories, but no collected edition exists. This is a shame, since many of the stories are interesting and worthy of a larger audience. "Lot," for example, is a powerful story of a man obsessed with survival, who, with his family, is escaping the fallout of a nuclear attack, "Adjustment" shows Moore's humor in a tale of a man who can make his wishes come true. "The Mysterious Milkman of Bishop Street" shows still another dimension of Moore's ability, in a whimsical fantasy about a milkman too good to be endured.

Moore's reputation in science fiction, however, rests chiefly on a superlative work of alternate history, *Bring the Jubilee*. This fine novel, which ironically takes its title from the Civil War song "Marching Through Georgia," supposes that Lee's forces had taken the high ground before the Battle of Gettysburg, leading to victory there and eventually to victory in the "War of Southern Independence." Most of the novel shows the results of this turn of events on subsequent history: the Confederacy has become wealthy and powerful, expanding westward to California and southward into Central America, but the Northern States lead an impoverished, backward existence. The central character of the novel, Hodge Backmaker, is born into a poor farm family, and in 1938 goes to New York to expand his opportunities. The world of *Bring the Jubilee* is much more technologically backward than our historical one, and Hodge has trouble gaining the education he seeks. Events bring him to a center for study in Pennsylvania, established years before by Herbert Haggerwells, a major in the Confederate army who remained in the area. There Hodge finds his vocation, and begins to build himself a reputation in Civil War history, but his conclusions are challenged by an authority in the field. A descendant of the Major, Barbara Haggerwells, is a physicist; she has perfected a time machine, and she offers its use to Hodge to visit the Battle of Gettysburg and test his theories. Hodge is to learn painfully that even the fact of observation affects that which is studied. Arriving before dawn on the morning of the 1st of July, 1863, Hodge is spotted by advancing Confederate troops, and they halt to question him. A panic ensues in which the officer is killed, and when light breaks, Hodge recognizes the dead man as Herbert Haggerwells. With the advance interrupted, the Confederates never take the Round Tops, and the battle proceeds as our history knows it.

Born in 1921, Hodge dies in 1877, a broken man. He realizes his responsibility for the destruction of the world he knew. In addition to the adventure story and the imaginative construc-

tion of an alternative world, Moore has written a probing discussion of the controversy between free will and determinism, and the result is a work that is one of science fiction's best.

—Walter E. Meyers

———

MORGAN, Dan. British. Born in Holbeach, Lincolnshire, 24 December 1925. Educated at Spalding Grammar School. Served in the Royal Army Medical Corps, 1947-48. Married Georgina Congreve in 1973. Since 1958, Managing Director, Dan Morgan Ltd., men's clothing store, Spaulding. Professional Guitarist. Agent, Gerald Pollinger, Laurence Pollinger Ltd., 18 Maddox Street, London WIR OEU. Address: 1 Chapel Lane, Spalding, Lincolnshire PE11 1BP, England.

SCIENCE-FICTION PUBLICATIONS

Novels (series: Mind; Venturer 12)

Cee Tee Man. London, Panther, 1955.
The Uninhibited. London, Digit, 1961.
The Richest Corpse in Show Business. London, Compact, 1966.
The New Minds. London, Corgi, 1967; New York, Avon, 1969.
A Thunder of Stars (Venturer 12), with John Kippax. London, Macdonald, 1968; New York, Ballantine, 1970.
The Several Minds. London, Corgi, and New York, Avon, 1969.
The Mind Trap. London, Corgi, and New York, Avon, 1970.
Inside. London, Corgi, 1971; New York, Berkley, 1974.
Seed of Stars (Venturer 12), with John Kippax. New York, Ballantine, 1972; London, Pan, 1974.
The Neutral Stars (Venturer 12), with John Kippax. New York, Ballantine, 1973; London, Pan, 1975.
The High Destiny. New York, Berkley, 1973; London, Millington, 1975.
The Country of the Mind. London, Corgi, 1975.
The Concrete Horizon. London, Millington, 1976.

Uncollected Short Stories

"Alien Analysis," in *New Worlds* (London), January 1952.
"Home Is Tomorrow," in *Authentic* (London), July 1953.
"Amateur Talent," in *Authentic* (London), December 1953.
"Jerry Built," in *New Worlds* (London), June 1954.
"Psychic Twin," in *Authentic* (London), June 1954.
"Alcoholic Ambassador," in *Nebula* (Glasgow), August 1954.
"Forgive Them," in *Authentic* (London), September 1954.
"Trojan Hearse," with John Kippax, in *New Worlds* (London), December 1954.
"Cleansing Fires," in *Authentic* (London), December 1954.
"The Lesser Breed," in *Authentic* (London), February 1955.
"Kwakiutl," in *Authentic* (London), May 1955.
"Life Agency," in *New Worlds* (London), September 1955.
"The Earth Never Sets," in *Authentic* (London), March 1956.
"Wonkle," in *New Worlds* (London), April 1956.
"Controlled Flight," in *New Worlds* (London), May 1956.
"The Little Fleet," in *New Worlds* (London), August 1956.
"The Way I Am," in *Authentic* (London), August 1956.
"More Than Hormone," in *Nebula* (Glasgow), November 1956.
"The Whole Armour," in *New Worlds* (London), December 1956.
"The Humanitarian," in *New Worlds* (London), April 1957.

"The Unwanted," in *New Worlds* (London), February 1958.
"The Star Game," in *New Worlds* (London), June 1958.
"The Hard Way," in *Nebula* (Glasgow), November 1958.
"Insecurity Risk," in *New Worlds* (London), January 1959.
"Protected Planet," in *Future* (New York), April 1959.
"Drive Out of Mind," in *Fantastic* (New York), June 1960.
"Stopover Earth," in *New Worlds* (London), January 1961.
"Father," in *Amazing* (New York), July 1961.
"Emreth," in *New Writings in SF 3*, edited by John Carnell. London, Dobson, 1965; New York, Bantam, 1967.
"Parking Problem," in *New Writings in SF 4*, edited by John Carnell. London, Dobson, 1965; New York, Bantam, 1968.
"Third Party," in *New Worlds* (London), April 1965.
"Frozen Assets," in *Vision of Tomorrow* (Newcastle upon Tyne), December 1969.
"Flanagan's Law," in *Vision of Tomorrow* (Newcastle upon Tyne), February 1970.
"Scramble," in *Galaxy* (New York), February 1971.
"Canary," in *New Writings in SF 20*, edited by John Carnell. London, Dobson, 1972.
"Love in Limbo," in *Genesis* (New York), April 1974.
"The First Day of the Rest of Your Life," in *The Best of Science Fiction Monthly*, edited by Janet Sacks. London, New English Library, 1975.
"Young Tom," in *New Writings in SF 29*, edited by Kenneth Bulmer. London, Sidgwick and Jackson, 1976.

OTHER PUBLICATIONS

Other

Guitar. London, Corgi, 1965; revised edition, 1980; as *Playing the Guitar*, New York, Bantam, 1967.
Spanish Guitar. London, Corgi, 1982.
Beginning Windsurfing. London, Corgi, 1982.
You Can Play the Guitar, with Nick Penny. London, Carousel, 1983.

*

Dan Morgan comments:
A large number of my novels have been concerned with ESP—particularly the Mind series, of course. People have always interested me more than machines and continue to do so more than ever. The Venturer 12 series, written in collaboration with the late John Hynam (John Kippax), was likewise more concerned with character than hardware, and was labelled by one reviewer as "sophisticated Space Opera."
It may be of interest to note that the one book of mine which continues to stimulate the most comment and interest is *The Richest Corpse in Show Business*. Perhaps there is a clue in that this is the only avowedly humorous novel I have written—maybe I should have mined this vein further. At the moment my business commitments are so heavy that there just isn't time to write, but the bug is still there and I'll be back to it one of these days.

* * *

Although Dan Morgan is not the kind of author who attracts a devoted following, he is certainly underrated and generally overlooked. Most of his novels and short stories display sound storytelling ability, and all rely heavily on a fast-moving plot.
In collaboration with John Kippax, Morgan produced a space opera trilogy that enjoyed a brief popularity and was promptly forgotten. *A Thunder of Stars* introduced the Space

Corps, a professional military and exploratory organization. Against a muted background of alien encroachment, the protagonist must race against time to prevent disaster from a runaway reactor on a colony ship. In the sequel, *Seed of the Stars*, the governor of an established colony world is determined to wrest independence from the home world, even if it results in disaster for his charge. The Space Corps was pitted against another powerful but unscrupulous antagonist in *The Neutral Stars*, this time a private citizen investing his substantial wealth in highly secret research.
The idea of a single highly talented villain opposed by a well organized group is carried into Morgan's most effective series, the Mind series, which concentrates on a group of people with psi powers who band together for mutual support and enhancement of their powers. In each of these novels a different psionic menace appears, confronts the group in some fashion, and is ultimately vanquished. In one case, the problem is complicated by a schism within the organization itself, but the overall idea of the many banded together against the uncooperative opponent recurs throughout the series.
With one exception, the rest of Morgan's novels are fairly routine adventure stories. There is a struggle for power in reasonably familiar fashion on a far world in *The High Destiny*, interplanetary war and more telepathy in *The Uninhibited*, and contra-terrene matter in *Cee Tee Man*. An interesting novel that doesn't totally succeed is *Inside*, wherein an unconscionable experiment with human beings is conducted in a domed city on airless Mars. Totally untypical of Morgan is the satirical *The Richest Corpse in Show Business*. Although the barbed humor is generally directed at the television industry, there are good-natured swipes at nearly everything else along the way, including some satire of the genre itself.
Morgan's relative lack of popularity probably stems from his mining of conceptual veins already fairly well worked over. Competent but unoriginal stories of telepathy make little impression on readers after the surfeit of them provided during the Campbell years at *Analog*. Morgan is not really innovative, but does consistently maintain a degree of competence well above the average. His adventure novels are of the type that form the bulwark of the science-fiction genre.

—Don D'Ammassa

MORLEY, Wilfred Owen. See LOWNDES, Robert A. W.

MORRESSY, John. American. Born in Brooklyn, New York, 8 December 1930. Educated at St. John's University, New York, B. A. in English 1953; New York University, M. A. 1961. Served in the United States Army, 1953-55. Married Barbara Ann Turner in 1956. Writer and reviewer, Equitable Life, New York, 1957-59; Instructor, St. John's University, 1962-66; Assistant Professor, Monmouth College, West Long Branch, New Jersey, 1966-67. Since 1968, Associate Professor, Professor, and Writer-in-Residence, Franklin Pierce College, Rindge, New Hampshire. Writer-in-Residence, Worcester Consortium, Massachusetts, 1977; Visiting Writer and Elliott Professor of English, University of Maine, Orono, 1977-78. Recipient: Bread Loaf Writers Conference Fellowship, 1968; University of Colorado Writers Conference Fellowship, 1970; Balrog Award,

1984. Agent: Curtis Brown, 575 Madison Avenue, New York, New York 10022. Address: Apple Hill Road, East Sullivan, New Hampshire 03445, U.S.A.

SCIENCE-FICTION PUBLICATIONS

Novels (series: Ziax II)

Starbrat. New York, Walker, 1972; London, New English Library, 1979.
Nail Down the Stars. New York, Walker, 1973; London, New English Library, 1979; as *Stardrift*, New York, Popular Library, 1975.
The Humans of Ziax II (for children). New York, Walker, 1974.
Under a Calculating Star. New York, Doubleday, 1975; London, Sidgwick and Jackson, 1978.
The Windows of Forever (for children). New York, Walker, 1975.
A Law for the Stars. Toronto, Laser, 1976.
The Extraterritorial. Toronto, Laser, 1977.
Frostworld and Dreamfire. New York, Doubleday, 1977; London, Sidgwick and Jackson, 1979.
The Drought on Ziax II (for children). New York, Walker, 1978.
Ironbrand. Chicago, Playboy Press, 1980.
Graymantle. New York, Playboy Press, 1981.
Kingsbane. New York, Playboy Press, 1982.
The Mansions of Space. New York, Ace, 1983.

Uncollected Short Stories

"Accuracy," in *Fantasy and Science Fiction* (New York), December 1971.
"When the Stars Threw Down Their Spears," in *Fantasy and Science Fiction* (New York), January 1973.
"August Sunshine for Moe Joost," in *Isaac Asimov's Science Fiction Magazine* (New York), November 1979.
"No More Pencils, No More Books," in *The Best Science Fiction of the Year 9*, edited by Terry Carr. New York, Ballantine, 1980.
"A Hedge Against Alchemy," in *Fantasy and Science Fiction* (New York), April 1981.
"The Gifts of Conhoon," in *Fantasy and Science Fiction* (New York), September 1981.
"The Empath and the Savages," in *The Best of Omni Science Fiction 3*, edited by Ben Bova and Don Myrus. New York, Omni, 1982.
"The Last Jerry Fagin Show," in *The Best of Omni Science Fiction 4*, edited by Ben Bova and Don Myrus. New York, Omni, 1982.
"Final Version," in *Twilight Zone* (New York), January 1982.
"A Welcome Bit of Assistance," in *Fantasy and Science Fiction* (New York), March 1982.
"The Crystal of Caracodissa," in *Fantasy and Science Fiction* (New York), September 1982.
"The Hoppy Prince," in *Fantasy and Science Fiction* (New York), November 1982.
"A Rarebit of Magic," in *Fantasy and Science Fiction* (New York), January 1983.
"Short Timer," in *Isaac Asimov's Science Fiction Magazine* (New York), April 1983.
"Welcome to Wizcon," in *Fantasy and Science Fiction* (New York), May 1983.
"Wizard Goes A-Courtin'," in *Fantasy and Science Fiction* (New York), August 1983.
"Nothing to Lose, Nothing to Kick," in *Fantasy and Science Fiction* (New York), November 1983.
"Glory, Glory," in *Playboy* (Chicago), November 1983.
"Executives and Elevators," in *Fantasy and Science Fiction* (New York), January 1984.
"The Universal All-Purpose Fantasy Quiz," in *Twilight Zone* (New York), June 1984.
"Stoneskin," in *Fantasy and Science Fiction* (New York), June 1984.
"Hard Times in La Terre Jamais-Jamais," in *Fantasy Review* (Boca Raton, Florida), September 1984.
"Some Works of Noble Note," in *Fantasy and Science Fiction* (New York), March 1985.
"Two Fables," in *Fantasy and Science Fiction* (New York), June 1985.

OTHER PUBLICATIONS

Novels

The Blackboard Cavalier. New York, Doubleday, 1966; London, Gollancz, 1967.
The Addison Tradition. New York, Doubleday, 1968.
A Long Communion . New York, Walker, 1974; as *Displaced Persons*, New York, Popular Library, 1976.

Short Stories

Other Stories. Amherst, Massachusetts, Northern New England Review Press, 1983.

*

John Morressy comments:

I write science fiction because I find it to be the most interesting, enjoyable, and creative field open to a writer today and the one that may, in time, prove to be the most significant.

My books are founded on the assumption that the human race, in future ages, will behave much as it always has in the past. We are not yet civilized, and I find it hard to believe that we ever will be. After six or seven thousand years of recorded history and, according to some, progress, we still settle our ideological and economic conflicts by killing one another and laying waste to our planet. Piracy, slavery, and brigandage still thrive. In more countries than we can enumerate, torture is routinely inflicted on prisoners, trial and sentencing is a mockery of justice, and execution is quick and brutal. Under the circumstances, such cherished terms as "freedom" and "human dignity" are meaningless, almost silly. And all this is in the age of *Apollo, Voyager*, and *Explorer*, of organ transplants and laser surgery and micro-computers and an arm-long list of scientific and technological wonders.

My novels are set in a future spawned by this present. I envision the human race as surviving (though not without great suffering), eventually reaching the stars, encountering other worlds and other races, and making all the old mistakes over again, on a larger scale. I have tried to create a single future continuum and keep my novels within it. The novels are linked, not sequentially, but laterally. There is no one that must be read first, or last, in order to understand some grand design. A few characters, and places, and institutions, and events, appear in several of my novels; others are in one only. My novels are not attempts to predict the future, but glimpses of what might happen in one particular future. To me, that is the thing science fiction can do and no other genre can: it can give a reader a taste of the future without charging the full and non-refundable price of experiencing it in person.

* * *

Isaac Asimov has remarked that year in and year out his "juveniles"" are his steadiest sellers; and certainly Robert Heinlein's books for young readers have reached a wide audience. Similarly, several of John Morressy's works of science fiction, intended for children, will not be familiar even to avid readers of the genre. Yet they have received favorable reviews from library journals: *The Windows of Forever*, a time-travel story, was praised for the lesson of tolerance it conveys; likewise, the Ziax II novels, are noted for their ecological concerns.

Several of Morressy's science-fiction novels for adults are interesting for a plot technique reminiscent in some ways of Lawrence Durrell's *Alexandria Quartet*. The first of these, *Starbrat*, tells the story of Del Whitby, who, kidnapped as a child, later searches for information about his parentage. In the course of his adventures, he meets a man named Gariv, who has led a slaves'" revolt on the planet Xhanchos and is returning to his homeworld, Skorat, to be reunited with his queen, Nikkolope. Del gives the man a lift and says goodbye after putting him on Skorat. Some adventures ensue, and he later encounters a minstrel named Alladale. As the owner of a spaceship, Del accommodates Alladale in his need for transportation, parts with the minstrel, and heads for a planet named Mazat. There, in the company of six others, he saves the world from marauding pirates and is chosen king. In synopsis, the novel sounds like an episodic, run-of-the-mill space opera. But the story expands as we read more of Morressy's interwoven works.

In *Nail Down the Stars*, we meet Jolon Gallamor, the minstrel who had called himself Alladale when he met Del Whitby. Unknown to either of them at their meeting, Gallamor had also been on Xhanchos as one of the slaves when the revolt took place. He had ridden at the side of Gariv, the leader, and had later sung at the court of Queen Nikkolope; he left there suddenly when a murderous fight broke out at a banquet. Yet neither Del nor Jolon Gallamor, despite their travels, ever learns the whole story of the events they have been part of: *Under a Calculating Star* gives the reader a fuller picture. In that work we meet a confidence man named Kian Jorry. Jorry organizes an expedition for a raid on a long-abandoned but dangerous treasure trove, but the attempt is a failure. He winds up, disgruntled and weary, on Xhanchos shortly after the slave rebellion has succeeded. While there, he sees a picture of the beautiful Queen Nikkolope, and notices the close resemblance between himself and Gariv. He resolves to try one more audacious con-game: after killing Gariv in a fight the king has provoked, he decides to pose as Gariv, return to Skorat, and usurp the throne. It is in this assumed identity that he meets Del Whitby and is taken to the planet. Gallamor (Alladale) is playing at the banquet at which Jorry announces that King Gariv has returned; although Alladale is the only man there able to expose Jorry, the minstrel flees when the fight breaks out at Jorry's announcement. Each of the characters has only part of the truth; only the readers have the whole story of the sequence.

While *Frostworld and Dreamfire* introduces different characters, Morressy sets the work in the same milieu of the far future as the others. It is a time of lost knowledge and heroic action, a time that Morressy makes more familiar with each work.

—Walter E. Meyers

MORRIS, Janet E(llen). American. Born in Boston, Massa-

chusetts, 25 May 1946. Attended New York University, 1965-66. Married Christopher C. Morris in 1972 (divorced, 1975). Lighting designer, Chip Monck Enterprises, New York, 1963-64; night manager, 1970; bass player, Christopher Morris Band, 1975, 1977; songwriter and recording artist. Agent: Perry Knowlton, Curtis Brown, 575 Madison Avenue, New York, New York 10022. Address: Box 1073, Mashpee, Massachusetts 02649, U.S.A.

SCIENCE-FICTION PUBLICATIONS

Novels (series: Dream Dancer; Silistra)

High Couch on Silistra. New York, Bantam, 1977.
The Golden Sword (Silistra). New York, Bantam, 1977.
Wind from the Abyss (Silistra). New York, Bantam, 1978.
The Carnellian Throne (Silistra). New York, Bantam, 1979.
Dream Dancer. New York, Putnam, and London, Fontana, 1980.
Cruiser Dreams (Dancer). New York, Berkley, and London, Fontana, 1981.
Earth Dreams (Dancer). New York, Berkley, 1982.
The Forty-Minute War, with Chris Morris. New York, Baen, 1984.
Active Measures, with David A. Drake. New York, Baen, 1985.
Beyond Sanctuary. New York, Baen, 1985.

Uncollected Short Stories

"Raising the Green Lion," in *The Berkley Showcase 1*, edited by Victoria Schochet and John W. Silbersack. New York, Berkley, 1980.
"Vashanka's Minion," in *Tales from the Vulgar Unicorn*, edited by Robert Asprin. New York, Ace, 1980.
"A Man and His God," in *Shadows of Sanctuary*, edited by Robert Asprin. New York, Ace, 1981.
"Wizard Weather," in *Storm Season*, edited by Robert Asprin. New York, Ace, 1982.
"An End to Dreaming," in *Whispers* (Binghamton, New York), August 1982.
"High Moon," in *The Face of Chaos*, edited by Robert Asprin and Lynn Abbey. New York, Ace, 1983.
"What Women Do Best," with Chris Morris, in *Wings of Omen*, edited by Robert Asprin and Lynn Abbey. New York, Ace, 1984.

OTHER PUBLICATIONS

Novel

I, The Sun. New York, Bantam, 1980.

Other

Editor, *Afterwar*. New York, Baen, 1985.

*

Janet E. Morris comments:
(1981) The thrust of my work, over the long term and through a projected group of books, historical, contemporary, and speculative, is the evolution of consciousness, with an eye toward the genetic, societal, and philosophical influences thereon. Sophocles states that one law ever hold true: nothing vast enters into the world of mortals without a curse. I look for in

past history or create in my future histories moments of cataclysm in theaters both physical and mental. My intention is always to explore the thought that must precede any outward action, its struggle to reach a new, more tenable position from which to regard self and universe.

My work in history shall eventually include: Sargon of Agade's conquest of Ebla; Rammesseide Egypt in its position as the seat of Yawwhist tradition; the Seven Sages, those wonderful progenitors of pre-Socratic thought; as well as Suppiluliumas I of Hatti and his dealings with the short-lived Atenist rise in Egypt (*I, The Sun*). Another work samples alchemical thought at the time of the death of Paracelsus, father of chemotherapy.

My science-fictional excursions into the possible evolution of consiousness have all centered on man's apprehension of the physical world, and his sense of place in it. My areas of study are necessarily genetics, biology, sociobiology, philosophy, and physics, but the aim at all times is to *show* rather than *tell*. The more crystallized the tenets of my position in a particular book, the more I strive to present them in an experiental manner without technical discourse which might erect a barrier between myself and the reader.

My Silistra series openly treats sexual themes as well as the possible effect of mind on probability. My Dream Dancer books (in progress) treat the marriage of man and mechanical intelligence through the utilization of our mastery of the intelligence code, the decipherment of which is even now in progress, as well as man's attempt to emancipate himself from the prison of relativistic space. Both the above groups of books focus to some extent on women, but are in no sense "women's" books; rather, I feel that technology is the leveler of sexism and the liberator of those sexual types not included in the sub-set "hetrosexual male. "

Reading back over what I have written, I must add that I write primarily the book which I myself would like to read, the book I can imagine that you might like to read. My hope above all is to tender you, the reader, an excursion, a journey into another realm which, upon returning, you might find to some small degree has enriched your "present."

*   *   *

Rigorously intellectual, and ruthlessly demanding both of herself and of her readers, Janet E. Morris's first publication, *High Couch of Silistra,* established her as a writer to watch and a likely contender as the most controversial writer to emerge in the 1970's. Though the book did not contain graphic depictions of violence and sex, it immediately transcended the "barbarians and bondage" genre into which detractors tried to dump it. Morris's evocation of an old, elaborate culture literally bound by the metaphor of *chaldra,* chains symbolizing achievements and obligations, her complex literary style, and her concerns with cosmology and sociobiology (at a time when this issue was being hotly debated) demonstrated what have become hallmarks of Morris's work.

Her second series, the three Dream Dancer novels, shows the metamorphosis of Shebat from fey urchin to aristocrat when she is taken from a squalid future Earth and adopted into the noblest family in a culture that is actually a form of high-tech Helenism. In these three books Morris deals with Hellenistic concerns: politics and citizenship (to keep citizenship, voters must pass tests), study (by mental access to computer datapools), and even mythology and magic—all in an aureate style reminiscent of later Greek epic. The myth that she focuses on primarily is the story of Alexander the Great, the Persian Wars, and Alexander's bequeathing his Empire "to the

strongest. " But the most fascinating aspect of the series is Morris's creation of sentient cruisers, starships capable of traversing "sponge space" and bonding emotionally with their pilots. The cruisers are a metaphoric expression of Morris's interests in quantum mechanics and geochronometry, and are part of her ambition to "make the higher intellectual level more accessible" to readers.

Morris's fascination with ancient history dominates her one historical novel *I, The Sun,* a story of a Hittite God-King. Hellenism and the Persian Wars appear in the stories Morris has written for the Thieves' World anthologies about Tempus, prince, philospher, and immortal avatar to a war-god. These stories have now grown into a trilogy dealing with Tempus's wars: *Beyond Sanctuary, Beyond Wizardwall,* and *Beyond the Veil* (forthcoming). Both the enjoyment and intellectual challenge Morris has found in working with the other Thieves World writers are reflected in a series of collaborations: chiefly with Chris Morris, but works with C. J. Cherryh and David Drake are also planned, as is a collaborative anthology series, Heroes in Hell.

Some of her most recent work, *The Forty-Minute War* (written with Chris Morris) and *Active Measures* (written with David A. Drake), demonstrates remarkable expertise in a different kind of data-gathering—modern intelligence. These fast-paced novels are tales both of espionage and of ideas. *The Forty-Minute War* once again deals with geochronology and the effect of an observer upon the events observed; *Active Measures* involves the reader in the process of decoding. Additional books relating to modern intelligence techniques will no doubt be forthcoming.

Her most recent books show a trend away from her earlier lyricism to a kind of spare, tough prose. In addition, her collaborations show that this most intellectually independent of writers is a superb team player. And her development of the Heroes in Hell concept which she will edit indicates a willingness to share her stage with other writers capable of the originality and intensity she demands.

—Susan Shwartz

MORRISON, Richard. See **LOWNDES, Robert A. W.**

MORRISSEY, J. L. See **SAXON, Richard.**

MOULTON, Carl. See **TUBB, E. C.**

MULLER, John E. See **FANTHORPE, R. Lionel.**

MURDOCH, H. J. See McINTOSH, J. T.

MURNANE, Gerald. Australian. Born in Melbourne, Victoria, in 1939. Married; three sons. Lives in Macleod, Victoria. Address: c/o Norstrilia Press, P. O. Box 921, Carlton, Victoria 3053, Australia.

SCIENCE-FICTION PUBLICATIONS

Novels

Tamarisk Row. Melbourne, Heinemann, 1974.
A Lifetime on Clouds. Melbourne, Heinemann, 1976.
The Plains. Carlton, Victoria, Norstrilia Press, 1982; London, Penguin, 1984.
Landscape with Landscape. Carlton, Victoria, Norstrilia Press, 1985.

Uncollected Short Story

"Land Deal," in *Dreamworks*, edited by David King. Carlton, Victoria, Norstrilia Press, 1983.

*   *   *

Gerald Murnane may be dubbed a science-fiction writer by affinity with such speculative authors as J. G. Ballard, Brian Aldiss, and Christopher Priest. His first novel, *Tamarisk Row*, is a remarkable metafantasy, an obsessional study of the fantasies of a small boy in a country town in Victoria (and the pathetic attempts by his father to realize fantasies by gambling on horses), written in short mosaic chapters and, sometimes, extraordinarily long aspiring sentences. It is notable for its truthfulness, its sometimes embarrassing fidelity to the furtive or inexpressible dreams and crude realities of pre-pubescent life. *A Lifetime on Clouds* is about an adolescent boy's struggles with masturbation, and so, again, is a novel about the weaving of fantasies from the meagre facts and misleading suggestions offered by life, in this case, mainly those of Catholic secondary education in a Melbourne suburb. The ribald humour of the book fails to mask Murname's fierce satirical indictment of what was then (1953-54) a stultifying religious ethos.

The difference between fantasy and reality becomes blurred for 15-year-old Adrian Sherd; at one point he notes that his lustful fantasies about American film stars are not sanctioned by the behaviour of the few heroes he has seen on screen: "instead of courting them patiently . . . he had undressed them and defiled them only hours after their first meeting. It was all so absurd compared with what really happened in films." In *The Plains* the threshold has been crossed and we are presented with a mature man's fantasy of an Australia which is related to the real one only by inversion. All the wealth and values belong to the plainsmen of Inner Australia, who despise the busy city-dwellers of the coast. The narrator is an outsider, willing to spend his life making notes towards a film which will put on record the ever-elusive culture of the inner land, a land which is within Australia, because only Australia could have demanded its existence, yet a land which is beyond Australia, because it is too large and grand a vision to be comprehended by it. Murnane had adumbrated this vision in describing the yearnings of young Clement Killeaton in *Tamarisk Row* for what lies farther in,

farther north, beyond the farthest imaginable horizons of his wretchedly confined experience. Fantasies lie within fantasies in *The Plains,* a short memorable novel of considerable philosophical interest.

The Plains itself, slightly curtailed and adapted, might fit within the structure of Murnane's latest metafantasy, *Landscape with Landscape*, a kind of möbius box of six stories, each of which is written by the narrator of its predecessor (and the first story by the last narrator). The stories concern Melbourne men who are obsessed with the wish to see the landscape that is hidden by the landscape, or that is seen only by the figure in the landscape, and so on; people themselves are landscapes or owners of hidden landscapes, perhaps. In what may be the most interesting of these stories, "The Battle of Acosta Nu," Melbourne is located in Paraguay and the narrator, a descendant of Australian colonists, defines himself in relation to the Australian city which he has never seen.

Bruce Gillespie has remarked that both *The Plains* and *Tamarisk Row* "are guided by the proposition that, however one might perceive any object or idea in the universe, it is quite possible to perceive it in the *other* way as well." This insight seems particularly apt for the short story, "Land Deal," which presents a philosophically valid Aboriginal view of European colonists as having a possible existence only in dreams: their land deal is therefore a dream within a dream.

—Michael J. Tolley

MURRY, Colin Middleton. See COWPER, Richard.

NAHA, Ed. Also writes as D. B. Drumm. American. Born in Elizabeth, New Jersey, 10 June 1950. Educated at Newark State College, B. A. 1972. East Coast Publicity Manager, 1972-75, and Associate Producer of East Coast Artists and Repertory, 1975-77, CBS Records, New York; Co-Editor, *Future Life*, New York, 1977-80. Since 1980, columnist ("Screen Scoops"), New York *Post* ; since 1983, columnist ("Nahallywood"), *Heavy Metal*, New York; since 1983 columnist ("L. A. Offbeat"), *Starlog* , New York. Lives in Santa Monica, California. Agent: Frommer Price Literary Agency, 185 East 85th Street, New York, New York 10028, U.S.A.

SCIENCE-FICTION PUBLICATIONS

Novels (series: Harry Porter in both Naha books)

The Paradise Plot. New York, Bantam, 1980.
The Suicide Plague. New York, Bantam, 1982.
First, You Fight (as D. B. Drumm). New York, Dell, 1984.

Short Stories

Wanted. New York, Bantam, 1980.

OTHER PUBLICATIONS

Other

Horrors: From Screen to Scream. New York, Avon, 1975.

Science Fiction Aliens (for children). New York, Starlog, 1977.
Lillian Roxon's Rock Encyclopedia, revised edition. New York, Putnam, 1978.
The Rock Encyclopedia. New York, Grosset and Dunlap, 1978.
The Science Fictionary: An A-Z Guide to the World of SF Authors, Films, and TV Shows. New York, Putnam, 1980.
The Films of Roger Corman: Brilliance on a Budget. New York, Arco, 1982.
The Making of "Dune." New York, Berkley, and London, Target, 1984.

Plays

Screenplays: *Camp Bottomout*, 1984; *The Wizard Wars*, 1984.

* * *

Ed Naha is one of those rarities who have been able successfully to merge the science fiction and mystery genres. His first science-fiction novel, *The Paradise Plot*, introduced the character of Harry Porter, a newspaper reporter who always seems to be at the right spot at the right time, to get himself involved with world-shaking plots. In this first adventure, he is aboard Island One, an orbiting city established as part of mankind's movement toward the colonization of space. But not everything is peaceful in the colony, which has not cast off as many of the problems of the mother world as they might have thought.

Shortly after his arrival, Porter is thoroughly enmeshed in a complicated plot that involves a string of murders and a desperate political struggle both within the habitat and back on Earth. Although Porter is ultimately instrumental in solving the mystery, the revelations result in the closing down of Island One, although it is quite clear that this is probably a temporary measure. Naha's scientific background for the novel is convincing, and while Porter is essentially a stereotypical detective hero, he's a well-done stereotype involved in an engrossing mystery, livened up with excellent dialogue.

The sequel, *The Suicide Plague*, is even better. Porter, the last investigative reporter still working, is bewildered by a sudden rash of young suicides, uncovers a secret plot to assassinate the President of the United States, runs afoul of the Church of the Ancient Astronauts, a sinister and increasingly powerful new cult, searches for missing research scientists, solves the mystery of a murdered man who had telepathic powers, and helps to avert what might have resulted in a nuclear war. This obviously complex group of plots and subplots is woven skillfully together in a thoroughly satisfying fashion.

Naha also created "The Traveller," hero of an ongoing series of post-nuclear-holocaust novels published by Dell Books, although he may have written only the first in the series, *First, You Fight*. The series features a tough, well armed protagonist who is a professional soldier wandering through ruined America in his armored van, helping the weak, avoiding the mutants and power seekers among the survivors. It is a thoroughly violent action series, but displays none of the finesse of Naha's other work. He has also written extensively in the fields of science fiction, fantasy, and horror films, and in the history of popular music.

—Don D'Ammassa

NELSON, Ray (Radell Faraday Nelson). Also writes as R. N.

Elson; Jeffrey Lord. American. Born in Schenectady, New York, 3 October 1931. Educated at the Chicago Art Institute, 1954; Alliance Française, 1957-58; the Sorbonne, Paris, 1958; University of Chicago, B. A. 1960; Automation Institute, computer programmers certificate 1961; Peralta College, Berkeley, California, 1978. Married 1) Perdita Lilly in 1951 (divorced, 1955); 2) Lisa Mullikin in 1955 (divorced, 1958); 3) Kirsten Enge in 1958; one son. Worked for Inland Lakes Flying Service, Cadillac, Michigan, 1947-50, and Hudson Motor Company, Detroit, 1950-51; sign maker, Chicago, 1951-54; printer, Northside Poster Company, Chicago, 1954; artist, Artcraft Poster Company, Oakland, California, 1955-56; translator for Jean Linard, Vesoul, France, 1959; computer programmer, University of California Press, Berkeley, 1961-62. Since 1962, free-lance writer and artist: Co-Director, Berkeley Free University, 1967-68; Founder, Microcosm Fiction Workshop, later Ramona Street Regulars, 1967; since 1968, teaching assistant, Adams Junior High School, El Cerrito, California. President, California Writers Club, 1977-78. Recipient: Jack London Award, 1983. Address: 333 Ramona Avenue, El Cerrito, California 94530, U.S.A.

SCIENCE-FICTION PUBLICATIONS

Novels (series: Beggars)

The Ganymede Takeover, with Philip K. Dick. New York, Ace, 1967; London, Arrow, 1971.
Blake's Progress. Toronto, Laser, 1975.
Then Beggars Could Ride. Toronto, Laser, 1976.
The Ecolog. Toronto, Laser, 1977.
The Revolt of the Unemployables (Beggars). San Francisco, Anthelion, 1978.
Dimension of Horror (as Jeffrey Lord). Los Angeles, Pinnacle, 1979.
The Prometheus Man. Norfolk, Virginia, Donning, 1982.
Timequest. New York, Tor, 1985.

Uncollected Short Stories

"Turn Off the Sky," in *Fantasy and Science Fiction* (New York), August 1963.
"Eight O'Clock in the Morning," in *The Best from Fantasy and Science Fiction 13*, edited by Avram Davidson. New York, Doubleday, 1964.
"Losers Weepers," in *Nugget* (New York), 1964.
"Food," in *Gamma 4* (Los Angeles), 1965.
"The Great Cosmic Donut of Life," in *Fantasy and Science Fiction* (New York), September 1965.
"Time Travel for Pedestrians," in *Again, Dangerous Visions*, edited by Harlan Ellison. New York, Doubleday, 1972; London, Millington, 1976.
"Egyptian Christ," in *Orion* (Lakemont, Georgia), 1972.
"The City of the Crocodile," in *Fantastic* (New York), March 1974.
"A Song on the Rising Wind," in *Fantastic* (New York), November 1974.
"What Survives?," in *Uniquest* (Berkeley, California), 1976.
"Microcosm," in *Science Fiction Review* (Portland, Oregon), 1976.
"Who's the Red Queen?," in *Amazing* (New York), March 1976.
"Flesh Pearl," in *Amazing* (New York), December 1976.
"Two Futures," in *Uniquest* (Berkeley, California), 1977.
"Nightfall on the Dead Sea," in *Fantasy and Science Fiction*

(New York), September 1977.
"On the Edge of Futuria," in *Science-Fiction Review* (Portland, Oregon), 1978.
"Valse Triste," in *Weird Tales 2*, edited by Lin Carter. New York, Zebra, 1981.
"Story," in *Fifty Extremely SF Stories*, edited by Michael Bastraw. Center Harbor, New Hampshire, Niekas, 1982.

OTHER PUBLICATIONS

Novels

The Agony of Love. San Diego, Greenleaf, 1969.
Girl with the Hungry Eyes. San Diego, Greenleaf, 1969.

Novels as R. N. Elson

How to Do it. San Diego, Greenleaf, 1970.
Black Pussy. San Diego, Greenleaf, 1970.
Sex Happy Hippy. San Diego, Greenleaf, 1970.
The DA's Wife. San Diego, Greenleaf, 1970.

*

Ray Nelson comments:

(1981) For me, Jack London, not Hugo Gernsback, is the father of American Science Fiction, and my aim is to continue the tradition established at the beginning of this century by London and his friends. My three obsessive themes are radical utopianism, experimental occultism, and a love-fear romance with nature. In California these ideas are understood, particularly in the Bay Area (all but two of the living writers I admire live in California), but in New York, where there are no trees, my obsessions seem like nonsense. Most of my work has been published outside New York—places where there are trees and intuition and hope for a better life, and someday New York too will grudgingly lend me an ear, perhaps when I am safely dead.

(1985) In *Timequest* I have at last written the novel I always wanted to write, the book I hope posterity will remember me by, if it remembers me at all. Editors have helped me, from Roger Elwood who let me do the first version of a book no other editor would touch, through Hank Stein who encouraged me to put in everything previous length restrictions had forced me to leave out, to Terry Carr who suggested restoring even the parts I had left out for Hank Stein, but really *Timequest* represents my own basic attitudes and philosophy so well I am content to stand or fall on this one work, so well I may never write another book in this genre. Now I want to do something else: comedy, cartoons, songs. Maybe I'll steal a spraycan of paint and start drawing propellor beanies on subway walls.

*   *   *

Although Ray Nelson has never been one of the more prolific writers in the field, he has firmly established a reputation for himself on the basis of the generally high quality of his work. His first novel, *The Ganymede Takeover*, was written in collaboration with Philip K. Dick, and dealt with the domination of Earth by wormlike invaders from Ganymede, but it was written as a witty and satiric examination of individuals and societies, not the low grade movie plot it so resembles.

It would be almost a decade later that Nelson first appeared as sole author of a novel, in this case *Blake's Progress*, a serious contender for best novel of its year. Ostensibly, the central character was the poet, William Blake, a man capable of mentally travelling through time in company with his wife. It

soon becomes apparent, however, that it is she who dominates their relationship, has the more powerful intellect, and is in fact a far more interesting character than is her weak-willed husband.

Then Beggars Could Ride and *The Ecolog* appeared soon after. Each was entertaining in its own way, but both suffered in comparison to their predecessor. The former was a similar kaleidoscopic odyssey through time. The latter is a more conventional novel, pitting a determined, expert military man against a planet ruled by a ruthless matriarch. *Dimension of Horror*, an adventure in the "Richard Blade" series, was similarly competent but even less memorable.

The Prometheus Man, on the other hand, is one of the best dystopian novels of all time. Overpopulation, automation, and lethargy have weakened the fabric of society as the vast majority of the population is unemployable. In order to maintain order, most of these people are confined to camps where they are theoretically looked after, but the impersonal treatment leads predictably to unrest. The plot is complex and thoroughly worked out.

Nelson's short fiction is extremely good and equally infrequent. "Nightfall on the Dead Sea," for example, is a fine historical horror story putting a Roman soldier against a man cursed with immortality. "Time Travel for Pedestrians" aroused a degree of controversy because of its subject matter—time travel via masturbation—but its clear superiority of style and the maturity of its vision established it as a major accomplishment.

Nelson displays a fondness for the grotesque. A human is turned into an organic asteroid in "Flesh Pearl," and another becomes a rather unpleasant form of nourishment in "Food." Grotesquerie and the absurd are to be found in "The Great Cosmic Donut of Life" and "Turn Off the Sky" as well.

"Eight O'Clock in the Morning" takes a routine gimmick (aliens who can only be seen by a single human) but condenses what other writers would have extended to novel length into a few thousand words. Ancient history and the supernatural mix again in "The City of the Crocodile," and a man takes a spiritual journey to the land of the suicides in "Valse Triste." "A Song on the Rising Wind" examines the nature of violence and courage on a level rare in any field of writing, as a revolution brews among a society of sequestered unemployables in the obvious precursor to *The Prometheus Man*.

Although not a prolific writer, Nelson is a careful craftsman whose every story appears to reflect great concentration and commitment. He is not afraid to tackle controversial themes or ambitious goals, and maintains tight control of his work at all times. While his work is frequently idiosyncratic, this uniqueness of viewpoint is often what makes them stand out from the scores of similar works from lesser writers.

—Don D'Ammassa

NEVILLE, Kris (Ottman). American. Born in Carthage, Missouri, 9 May 1925. Educated at the University of California, Los Angeles, B. A. in English 1950. Served in the United States Army Signal Corps during World War II. Married Lil Johnson in 1957; five children. Worked in the plastics and chemistry industries: after 1965, staff member, Epoxylite Corporation, Anaheim, California. *Died 23 December 1980*.

SCIENCE-FICTION PUBLICATIONS

Novels

The Unearth People. New York, Belmont, 1964.
The Mutants. New York, Belmont, 1966.
Peril of the Starmen. New York, Belmont, 1967.
Special Delivery. New York, Belmont, 1967.
Bettyann. New York, Belmont, 1970.
Invaders on the Moon. New York, Belmont, 1970.

Short Stories

Mission: Manstop. North Hollywood, Nordon, 1971.
The Science Fiction of Kris Neville, edited by Barry N. Malzberg and Martin H. Greenberg. Carbondale, Southern Illinois University Press, 1984.

OTHER PUBLICATIONS

Novel

Run, The Spearmaker (in Japanese), with Lil Neville. Tokyo, Hayakawa Shobo, 1975.

Other

Epoxy Resins, with Henry Lee. New York, McGraw Hill, 1957.
Handbook of Epoxy Resins, with Henry Lee. New York, McGraw Hill, 1967.
New Linear Polymers, with Henry Lee. New York, McGraw Hill, 1967.
Handbook of Biomedical Plastics, with Henry Lee. Pasadena, California, Pasadena Technology Press, 1971.
Adhesive Restorative Dentistry, with Robert L. Ibsen. Philadelphia, Saunders, 1974.
Industrial Motor Users' Handbook of Insulation for Rewinds, with L. J. Regda. New York and Oxford, Elsevier, 1977.

Editor, with Henry Lee, *Handbook of Adhesive Bonding*, by Charles V. Cagle. New York, McGraw Hill, 1982.

*

Kris Neville commented:

(1980) I wrote the majority of my stories in the early 1950's. Having just graduated from UCLA with a degree in English literature, I was interested in introducing mainstream elements into science fiction (which I had been reading avidly since 1937)—shifting the emphasis to the impact of future technology on ordinary individuals. I also tried to seek out new perspectives—using female protagonists; playing with various viewpoints; seeing the future through the eyes of the old or young; portraying Earthmen in less than favorable lights; breaking taboos; making satirical comments (I was a socialist/humanist). In many of my shorts, I aimed for emotional effect. I was a trail blazer in my time.

By the mid-1950's, I'd run out of things to say. During the next decade, I kept my hand in with *The Unearth People* and an occasional short, and also revised earlier material into novels. I moved leftward philosophically to my present position: left wing anarchist. The shorts contained sharper social commentary ("Survival Problems"). I was particularly unhappy with the war in Vietnam ("The Price of Simeryl") and, later, Richard Nixon ("The Reality Machine"). During that decade, Lil and I wrote *Run, The Spearmaker*, a novel dealing with the evolution

of civilization at the beginning of human history. The translator called it a minor literary masterpiece. Pity it isn't available in English.

During the 1970's, in addition to half a dozen shorts that Lil and I collaborated on, we also did another novel, *Thorstein Macaulay*. It contains our best writing and most carefully considered political statements. It was about 10 years in the making. As of this writing (June 1979) we had not yet found a publisher for it.

*   *   *

Kris Neville's large output of stories seems to be equally divided among adventure SF, social SF, fantasy SF and fantasy. While he was known as a *Galaxy* school writer, his most characteristic work appears to be more melodramatic than ironic. Nevertheless, Neville will often subordinate adventure narrative to character interaction or to the character's response to those environmental or cultural forces that are by-products of future science and technology. Neville was a popular and critically respected author in the genre during the 1950's and 1960's, but his reputation as a craftsman seems to have been lost, perhaps as the result of the rather conventional plotting and characterization in his later work.

Neville's great theme is alienation, one which takes its most obvious form in stories that treat alien-human contact. He eschews the more sensational aspects of this theme in favor of the psychological dimensions implied in its use in the future world of SF. Novels like *Special Delivery, Earth Alert* (*If*, February 1953), and *The Mutants* deal with variations of the alien invasion theme or its analogues. *The Mutants*, a potentially timely treatment of the social implications of artificial insemination in a state utopia, fails to rise above the level of the melodramatic struggle of a few idealistic youths fighting to save the race from a progressively more repressive state control of human biology.

In the main, Neville was a writer typical of his time. He knew how to make good use of psychologically enriched characters and possessed more sensitivity toward character motivation and interaction than most of his colleagues. In many ways, he belongs in the Theodore Sturgeon camp of SF writers, although he does lapse into the action/adventure idiom more frequently than Sturgeon and his successors. Neville's style is also more direct, simple, and clear than Sturgeon's, better suited, perhaps, for the pot boilers he produced for Belmont. Neville was, it appears, in nearly every way a writer several cuts above the average who never quite made the success expected of him. Although he wrote SF, Neville gave little evidence of being deeply committed for or against science. It, like the future, is simply one of the unexamined, given elements of his stories. Whatever the cause, Neville produced a body of SF that refuses to move us deeply in any of the many ways in which less accomplished stylists have done by writing with more conviction, except in one notable case.

Neville may not deserve the obscurity into which his career has fallen if only for the sake of one superb story, "Bettyann" (1951; expanded into a novel, 1970; a sequel is "Bettyann's Children"). This story of a crippled orphan girl raised in a foster home whose sense of difference is confirmed when she discovers she is actually a member of an extra-terrestrial race is handled with the same kind of sensitivity and poignance as Daniel Keyes's "Flowers for Algernon," another story that grew successfully into a novel. In place of the overwriting of most SF melodrama, Neville has his subject and his characters fully under control. In "Bettyann" Neville manages understated effects brilliantly in a way that he approached in only a few other stories besides the sequel: "Old Man Henderson" and "Closing Time" are examples. "Bettyann" is one of those rare SF stories that could not be written in another genre but which deals profoundly with universal, human values. Bettyann's affirmation of a basic humanity which has become stronger in her nature than her lately discovered alien origins is an inspiring moment in literature. The two stories and the novel must be considered neglected masterpieces, which are only beginning to receive their due critical recognition.

—Donald L. Lawler

NICHOLS, Scott. See **SCORTIA, Thomas N.**

NIVEN, Larry (Laurence Van Cott Niven). American. Born in Los Angeles, California, 30 April 1938. Educated at California Institute of Technology, Pasadena, 1956-58; Washburn University, Topeka, Kansas, A. B. 1962; University of California, Los Angeles, 1962-63. Married Marylin Wosowati in 1969. Since 1964, free-lance writer. Recipient: Hugo Award, for story, 1967, 1972, 1975, 1976, for novel, 1971; Nebula Award, 1970; Ditmar Award, 1971. Address: 3961 Vanalden Avenue, Tarzana, California 91356, U.S.A.

SCIENCE-FICTION PUBLICATIONS

Novels (series: Known Space)

World of Ptavvs (Space). New York, Ballantine, 1966; London, Macdonald, 1968.
A Gift from Earth (Space). New York, Ballantine, 1968; London, Macdonald, 1969.
Ringworld (Space). New York, Ballantine, 1970; London, Gollancz, 1972.
The Flying Sorcerers, with David Gerrold. New York, Ballantine, 1971; London, Corgi, 1975.
Protector (Space). New York, Ballantine, 1973; Tisbury, Wiltshire, Compton Russell, 1976.
The Mote in God's Eye, with Jerry Pournelle. New York, Simon and Schuster, 1974; London, Weidenfeld and Nicolson, 1975.
Inferno, with Jerry Pournelle. New York, Pocket Books, 1976; London, Wingate, 1977.
A World Out of Time. New York, Holt Rinehart, 1976; London, Macdonald and Jane's 1977.
Lucifer's Hammer, with Jerry Pournelle. Chicago, Playboy Press, 1977.
The Magic Goes Away. New York, Ace, 1978; London, Futura, 1982.
The Ringworld Engineers (Space). New York, Holt Rinehart, and London, Gollancz, 1980.
The Patchwork Girl. New York, Ace, 1980; London, Macdonald, 1982.
Dream Park, with Steven Barnes. Huntington Woods, Michigan, Phantasia Press, 1981; London, Macdonald, 1983.
Oath of Fealty, with Jerry Pournelle. Huntington Woods, Michigan, Phantasia Press, 1981; London, Macdonald, 1982.
The Descent of Anansi, with Steven Barnes. New York, Tor, 1982.

The Integral Trees. New York, Ballantine, and London, Macdonald, 1984.
Footfall, with Jerry Pournelle. New York, Ballantine, and London, Gollancz, 1985.

Short Stories (series: Known Space)

Neutron Star (Space). New York, Ballantine, 1968; London, Macdonald, 1969.
The Shape of Space (Space). New York, Ballantine, 1969.
All the Myriad Ways. New York, Ballantine, 1971.
The Flight of the Horse. New York, Ballantine, 1973; London, Futura, 1975.
Inconstant Moon (omnibus). London, Gollancz, 1973.
A Hole in Space. New York, Ballantine, 1974; London, Futura, 1975.
Tales of Known Space. New York, Ballantine, 1975.
The Long Arm of Gil Hamilton (Space). New York, Ballantine, 1976; London, Futura, 1980.
Convergent Series. New York, Ballantine, 1979.
The Time of the Warlock, illustrated by Dennis Wolf. Minneapolis, SteelDragon Press, 1984.
Niven's Laws (includes articles). Philadelphia, Philcon, 1984.
Limits. New York, Ballantine, 1985.

OTHER PUBLICATIONS

Other

Editor, *The Magic May Return*. New York, Ace, 1981.
Editor, *More Magic*. New York, Berkley, 1984.

*

Manuscript Collection: George Arents Research Library, Syracuse University, New York.

* * *

Larry Niven learned his craft through his long familiarity with SF literature as a fan and through study of writers such as John W. Campbell, Jr., Heinlein, Asimov, and, later, Anderson, Clarke, and Clement. Niven sees himself rightly as carrying on and developing SF traditions and those of the related genre, popular fantasy. Everything Niven has written thus far has a strong genre identification, and his appeal as well as his fame has been until recently within the expanding universe of the SF and fantasy reader. Niven has tried his hand at nearly every major type of SF, including fantasy SF stories of time travel, parallel worlds, and sword and sorcery.

Niven's best and most characteristic work in SF has been done in series works. Among the lesser series are the delightful Hanville Svetz comic SF fantasies (*The Flight of the Horse*); the Leshy series, the best of which is "The Fourth Profession," culminating in *A World Out of Time;* the Draco's Tavern stories (*Convergent Series*); and the Jayberry Jensen teleportation stories, the best of which are "Flash Crowd" and "All the Bridges Rusting. "

The pre-eminent series, and possibly the best in SF history, has occupied Niven since the publication of his first story, "The Coldest Place" (1964). Known Space is the saga of the next 1200 years of human history, beginning in 1975 with the development of organbank technology on earth, chronicling the exploration of our galaxy and encounters with alien species, and culminating in the spread throughout the race of a mutant gene which incorporates the code for a psychic power that operates to protect the individual from harm and to promote and even guarantee maximum opportunities for happiness. The end result is a universe safe for future human development and for the generation of a species preferred by evolution through the cooperative union of genetics and psionics. In short, Niven's cosmology moves ultimately toward the realization of that universal hope of intelligent species expressed in the story "Convergent Series" (1967) that "There is a way to thwart entropy, to live forever." Many of Niven's critics have found in his ultimate triumphalism a weakness of vision, but it proceeds logically from Niven's traditionalism and from the philosophical assumptions underlying his fiction.

Between the present and dawn of the golden age in the Third Millennium, Niven chronicles the struggles of each generation to meet the challenges presented by the future development of modern technological advances that seem most revolutionary to Niven in biological and transportation engineering. The immediate impact of organ-transplant technology and the development of personal teleportation transfer stations is to polarize society into revolutionary and reactionary factions. Such new technologies "create new customs, new laws, new ethics, new crimes," as Niven observes. The potentiality for repressive and even ghoulish practices by both criminals and by society and its agents is dramatized powerfully in those stories set in the near future which strike the reader with the impact of social realism. Two of the Gil Hamilton stories, "Death by Ecstasy" and "The Defenseless Dead," present the official, police view of "organlegging," while stories like "Cloak of Anarchy," "The Jigsaw Man," and "Rammer" and the novel *A Gift from Earth* focus effectively on the kinds of abuse likely to grow from using criminals to supply body parts for organ banks. The teleportation stories like "Flash Crowd" extrapolate the technology and sociology of the displacement transfer booths. Typically, Niven's solution to the social and ethical problems of this chaotic world is technological. Unlike Huxley, Heinlein, and others who leave the technological base of their narrative in favor of moral speculations on human nature or social history, Niven follows through on his belief that moral values and ethical practice change with the alteration of basic social processes produced by technology.

The challenges of space exploration are even more dramatic because they allow Niven's imagination freer rein for invention. The smaller gravity of asteroids and planetary satellites affects all phases of the lives of the Belt inhabitants. Inevitably, the differences between Belters and Flatlanders (terrans) lead to separate and competing political and economic structures. The colonization of new worlds leads to the further specialization of the race and to the development of new characteristics peculiar to those from colony worlds of other star systems like Jinx and Wunderland. In his Known Space stories, Niven develops consequences implied in ecology-psychology interactions even more successfully than his mentors Asimov, Heinlein, and Herbert.

One of the great challenges of Known Space exploration comes from attempting to subdue alien environments of interstellar space and other worlds. Perhaps the most exotic of Niven's worlds is the Smoke Ring, a gaseous doughnut around a neutron star, a SF Noah's ark, carrying around in free fall all manner of flying life, especially the elegant flora of the title, *The Integral Trees*, so named because they are shaped as integral signs. Scattered among these trees are the descendants of the mutinous crew of the space craft *Discipline*, a future *Bounty*. After more than five centuries, while *Discipline* waits patiently outside the torus ring, the Quinn clan finds itself living on a dying tree. An expedition sets out to look for food, and encounters members of a rival clan from the other end of their

tree. Together, they explore their own Dalton-Quinn tree and subsequently the rarefied geography of the gas torus. Social life on the trees has devolved from the advanced scientific to a semi-feudal or in places tribal structure. Their quest leads the expedition into captivity and eventually to escape aboard one of *Discipline's* CARM (a module) where they encounter, electronically, Sharls Davis Kennedy, the legendary computer/cyborg policeman of the mother ship. The confrontation involving the conflicting loyalties of those aboard the CARM with the distant but electronically immanent Kendy is one of Niven's best pieces of writing. Despite Kendy's neofascist reflexes, he permits the survivors to live because, finally, his curiosity gets the better of his passion for order. Niven promises at least one sequel, provisionally called *The Smoke Ring*, in which we can expect to hear more from Kendy.

Critics who disparage Niven's writing do so on two counts. One is the critic's dislike of Niven's rather conventional optimism, even though there is a historical basis for Niven's positivism, and he is anything but naive about the abuse of technology. Niven's vision may be meliorative in the end, but humanity has to pay for its golden age with hard times to come. Critics have also objected to Niven's plotting difficulties in his novels, and there is no doubt that this is a weakness of his writing. At the same time, it must be said that Niven's use of cinematographic techniques of storytelling work well in his two most successful novels, *World of Ptavvs* and *Ringworld*. Few would deny Niven's extraordinary powers of invention and his ability to blend hard science extrapolation with soft science speculations and space opera adventure. To some degree the pleasure of reading Niven depends on the reader's growing awareness of the grand design of the series so that even the weaker novels and stories take on added dimensions.

At least brief mention should be made here of the appeal of Niven's plausible use of hard science speculations, especially in such glamor fields as biomedical engineering, space exploration, and exobiology. These are complemented brilliantly by Niven's extraordinary powers of naming. Niven's off-world inventions include an orismology of the colonized worlds of Known Space: Plateau, Home, Jinx, Wunderland, Down, and We Made It, with their inspired mixture of naive anthropocentricism, popular folk culture, and humor in a rather typically American combination. Niven is also especially good at suggesting ways in which the impact of these strange new worlds shapes the character and thinking of their inhabitants in the space of even a few generations.

Perhaps the two creations that give Niven's Known Space its distinctive richness and appeal are the alien creatures encountered by humanity in its exploration and expansion and the related discovery of universal history in the records, traditions, and artifacts of alien races, both living and dead. Niven's mythical history discloses three major eras in galactic history. The First is the ancient empire of the Thrint, known as Slavers, whose artifacts are occasionally to be found in stasis boxes, preserved from change, and prized by their finders for their technological importance. We actually meet a Thrint in *World of Ptavvs*, an encounter in which humanity barely escapes with life and freedom. The Thrint empire and its creatures were destroyed eventually during the suicidal revolution of the master technician slaves known as Tnuctipun. The second epoch was that of the Pak, remote ancestors in Niven's mythology of humans and other intelligent life forms, whose breeders had seeded the universe of Known Space and perhaps beyond. Although very ancient, Pak Protectors have survived to challenge the existence of their own unrecognized, mutated human descendants and to produce, accidentally, in what Niven intends to be an analogue of natural selection, a hybrid human protector, the Brennan monster, who ushers in a golden age of peace that lasts three centuries. The Third epoch begins with the Kzin-human wars and the acquisition of hyperdrive from the Outsiders, continues with Beowulf Shaeffer's discovery that the galactic core has exploded, and concludes with the discovery of the Great Pak artifact, Ringworld, and with the emergence of the Teela Brown gene. Niven's universal history is an ingenious and beautifully modulated bit of cosmic mythmaking.

A second distinctive creation is Niven's aliens. No SF writer has lavished as much energy in populating his fiction with such a variety of sentient beings: the ancient Thrint slavers; the enslaved master technician Tnuctipun; Pak Protectors; the bellicose, cat-like Kzinti; the cowardly, manipulative Puppeteers; the enigmatic space merchant Outsiders; and an oddity of other creatures including Grogs, Kdatlyno, and Bandersnatchi. Niven gives his readers far more than an alien bestiary, for he creates new species of intelligent beings who are both representative members of a type as well as distinctive individuals. Niven establishes the psychology, attitudes, and cultural identity of his aliens with rare economy and style. And yet we never feel that Niven has told us all he knows about his alien beings, their worlds, or their place in the cosmic history of Known Space.

Niven's collaborative work deserves brief mention here. His best collaborations have been with Jerry Pournelle, especially the cult favorite *Inferno* and the ponderous *Mote in God's Eye.* Niven has done a number of short stories and novels with Steven Barnes. Their best effort to date is *Dream Park* (1981), a science fantasy that entertains but fails to realize the potentials of its premise. So far, Niven's collaborations have been financial and social successes—writing is a solitary business—but indifferently rewarding to Niven admirers.

Niven also writes fantasy, and the chief modern influences on his writing in that genre have been Cabell, Dunsany, Howard, de Camp, and Fletcher Pratt. References, allusions, and analogues to the work of these writers are often deliberately worked into Niven's fantasy as echoes recalling the traditions he follows. So far, Niven has not attempted high or literary fantasy of the kind we associate with the tradition of Morris and Tolkien; rather, he writes in the fashion of popular adventure fantasies of Howard, Burroughs, and Brackett. Niven's best work in the Warlock series has been *The Magic Goes Away,* another novel that fails to live up to its original inspiration. The series also includes *The Magic May Return,* a collection of stories by other hands (Pournelle, Barnes, Ing, Saberhagen), edited by Niven who contributed one story to his own mythology, and *More Magic,* which is more of the same again.

Larry Niven deserves recognition as a major SF writer who has achieved excellence in individual stories and novels, but whose reputation will securely rest upon the foundation of his Known Space mythology. For readers unfamiliar with Niven's work, it is best to begin with the Gil Hamilton stories and *World of Ptavvs. Ringworld* should be saved for last since it comes virtually at the end of the Known Space saga. *Tales of Known Space* is invaluable for Niven's charts and editorial notes: and, although not up to the standard of the best novels, *Protector* forms an important link in the mythology no interested reader will want to overlook.

—Donald L. Lawler

NOBEL, Phil. See **FANTHORPE, R. Lionel.**

NOLAN, William F(rancis). American. Born in Kansas City, Missouri, 6 March 1928. Educated at Kansas City Art Institute, 1946-47; San Diego State College, California, 1947-48; Los Angeles City College, 1953. Married Marilyn Seal in 1970. Greeting card designer and cartoonist, Hall Brothers, Kansas City, 1945; mural painter, San Diego, 1949-50; aircraft inspector, Convair, San Diego, 1950-52; credit assistant, Blake Moffit and Towne Paper Company, Los Angeles, 1953-54; interviewer, California State Department of Employment, 1954-56. Since 1956, free-lance writer. Contributing Editor, *Chase,* Managing Editor, *GAMMA,* West Coast Editor, *Auto,* and Associate Editor, *Motor Sport Illustrated,* all Los Angeles, 1963-64; reviewer, Los Angeles *Times,* 1964-70. Recipient: American Library Association citation, 1960; Academy of Science Fiction and Fantasy award, for fiction and film, 1976; Maltese Falcon award, 1977. Honorary Doctorate: American River College, Sacramento, California, 1975. Lives in Agoura, California. Agent: Nat Sobel, 146 East 19th Street, New York, New York 10003, U.S.A.

SCIENCE-FICTION PUBLICATIONS

Novels (series: Logan; Sam Space)

Logan's Run, with G. C. Johnson. New York, Dial Press, 1967; London, Gollancz, 1968.
Space for Hire. New York, Lancer, 1971.
Logan's World. New York, Bantam, 1977; London, Corgi, 1978.
Logan's Search. New York, Bantam, 1980; London, Corgi, 1981.
Look Out for Space. New York, International Polygonics, 1985.

Short Stories

Impact-20. New York, Paperback Library, 1963; London, Corgi, 1966.
Alien Horizons. New York, Pocket Books, 1974.
Wonderworlds. London, Gollancz, 1977.
Things Beyond Midnight. Santa Cruz, California, Scream Press, 1984.

Uncollected Short Stories

"Sungrub," in *After the Fall,* edited by Robert Sheckley. New York, Ace, and London, Sphere, 1980.
"Trust Not the Man," in *Masques,* edited by J. N. Williamson. Baltimore, Maclay, 1984.
"Ceremony," in *Midnights,* edited by Charles L. Grant. New York, Tor, 1985.
"Of Time and Kathy Benedict," in *Whispers 5,* edited by Stuart David Schiff. New York, Doubleday, 1985.

OTHER PUBLICATIONS

Novels

Death Is for Losers. Los Angeles, Sherbourne Press, 1968.
The White Cad Cross-Up. Los Angeles, Sherbourne Press, 1969.

Plays

Visual Encounters (TV scripts). Baltimore, Maclay, 1986.

Screenplays: *The Legend of Machine-Gun Kelly,* 1975; *Logan's*

Run, 1976; *Burnt Offerings,* with Dan Curtis, 1976.

Television Plays: *The Joy of Living,* 1971; *The Norliss Tapes,* 1973; *Melvin Purvis, G-Man,* with John Milius, 1974; *The Turn of the Screw,* 1974; *The Kansas City Massacre,* with Bronson Howitzer, 1975; *Sky Heist,* with Rick Rosner, 1975; *Julie and Millicent and Therese* (in *Trilogy of Terror*), 1975; *Logan's Run* series, 1977; *First Loss,* 1981; *The Partnership,* 1981; *Terror at London Bridge,* 1985.

Verse

Twelve Poems. Northridge, California, Santa Susana Press, 1986.

Other

Adventure on Wheels: The Autobiography of a Road Racing Champion, with John Fitch. New York, Putnam, 1959.
Barney Oldfield. New York, Putnam, 1961.
Phil Hill: Yankee Champion. New York, Putnam, 1962.
Men of Thunder: Fabled Daredevils of Motor Sport. New York, Putnam, 1964.
Sinners and Supermen. North Hollywood, All Star, 1965.
John Huston: King Rebel. Los Angeles, Sherbourne Press, 1965.
Dashiell Hammett: A Casebook. Santa Barbara, California, McNally and Loftin, 1969.
Steve McQueen: Star on Wheels. New York, Putnam, 1972.
Carnival of Speed. New York, Putnam, 1973.
Hemingway: Last Days of the Lion. Santa Barbara, California, Capra Press, 1974.
The Ray Bradbury Companion. Detroit, Gale, 1975.
Hammett: A Life at the Edge (biography of Dashiell Hammett). New York, Congdon and Weed, 1983; London, Barker, 1984.
McQueen (biography of Steve McQueen). New York, Congdon and Weed, and London, Barker, 1984.
The Black Mask Boys. New York, Morrow, 1985.
The Work of Charles Beaumont (bibliography). San Bernardino, California, Borgo Press, 1985.

Editor, *Ray Bradbury Review.* San Diego, California, Nolan, 1952.
Editor, with Charles Beaumont, *Omnibus of Speed.* New York, Putnam, 1958; London, Paul, 1961.
Editor, with Charles Beaumont, *When Engines Roar.* New York, Bantam, 1964.
Editor, *Man Against Tomorrow.* New York, Avon, 1965.
Editor, *The Pseudo People: Androids in Science Fiction.* Los Angeles, Sherbourne Press, 1965; as *Almost Human,* London, Souvenir Press, 1966.
Editor, *3 to the Highest Power.* New York, Avon, 1968; London, Corgi, 1971.
Editor, *A Wilderness of Stars.* Los Angeles, Sherbourne Press, 1969; London, Gollancz, 1970.
Editor, *A Sea of Space.* New York, Bantam, 1970; London, Corgi, 1980.
Editor, *The Future Is Now.* Los Angeles, Sherbourne Press, 1970.
Editor, *The Human Equation.* Los Angeles, Sherbourne Press, 1971.
Editor, *The Edge of Forever,* by Chad Oliver. Los Angeles, Sherbourne Press, 1971.
Editor, with Martin H. Greenberg, *Science Fiction Origins.* New York, Fawcett-Popular Library, 1980.
Editor, *Max Brand's Best Western Stories.* New York, Dodd Mead, 1981; London, Hale, 1983; vol. 2, Dodd Mead, 1985.

Editor, *Max Brand: Western Giant.* Bowling Green, Ohio, Popular Press, 1986.

*

Bibliography: *William F. Nolan: A Checklist* by Charles E. Yenter, Tacoma, Washington, Charles E. Yenter, 1974; *The Work of William F. Nolan* by R. Reginald, San Bernardino, California, Borgo Press, 1986.

Manuscript Collection: Bowling Green State University, Bowling Green, Ohio.

Theatrical Activities:
Actor: **Films**—*The Intruder,* 1962; *The Legend of Machine-Gun Kelly,* 1975.

William F. Nolan comments:
As a writer I'm hard to pin down. Science fiction is just one of my many fields, and I take equal pride in my crime-suspense writing, auto-racing books, biographies, fantasy-terror fiction, thriller novels, and essays and book reviews. I keep fresh and excited as a writer by switching constantly from one genre to another. I enjoy doing SF, particularly the Logan novels, but I also enjoy all other types of writing. After 30 years as a professional, my work totals 895 items—and I figure my career has another 30 years to go.

* * *

William F. Nolan is best known for the creation of Logan who appeared in the novels *Logan's Run, Logan's World,* and *Logan's Search.* He has also written the mystery science-fiction novel *Space for Hire* and numerous short stories. His early influences included William Faulkner and Dashiell Hammett, but one of the greatest literary influences on his writing style and pacing technique is Ernest Hemingway, and in some respects it would be an accurate analysis to say Nolan is the contemporary, high-tech Hemingway of science fiction. Hints of this can be seen in *Space for Hire,* especially in the novel's central character, Samuel Space. During his early career, Nolan was influenced by Charles Beaumont (1929-67), and collaborated with Beaumont on some work; his literary friendship with such notable authors as Ray Bradbury, Robert Bloch, Ray Russell, and Richard Matheson is well known.

Nolan's ability to create and sustain a mood, construct characters with several levels of depth, and devise a tightly constructed plot is the hallmark of his fiction. With the Logan novels, Nolan created a fictional character whose interest and respect among science-fiction readers made him into a cult hero. Logan's appeal lies in his deterministic, moral approach to existence, and his strength to persevere against overwhelming odds and adversity.

Nolan is the author of over 700 works. Among his short fiction are the memorable stories "Jenny among the Zeebs," "Papa's Planet," "Lawbreaker," "The Underdweller," "The Day the Gorf Took Over," "Starblood," "Solution," and "The Joy of Living. " Each story concerns some aspect of survival, and the idea that struggle gives meaning to existence. Although the mood and plot are important in any Nolan story, the thrust is on character development—how the individual reacts to the situation and conflict; the character must make a logical decision as to what personal, moral, and social role is demanded and act accordingly. This is illustrated in three of Nolan's finest stories: "Starblood," "Jenny among the Zeebs," and "The Underdweller. " The existential side of Nolan, with its dark emphasis on the themes of conflict and struggle, is revealed in "The Underdweller," a morose and hauntingly strange story.

Noted as a writer gifted with the ability to create believable dialogue, Nolan has turned to screen and television writing in recent years, and the themes prevalent in his fiction are reflected there as well.

Nolan's contribution to science fiction is his keen insight into the sociological and psychological role of a character in any given situation, whether that situation involves confrontation with an alien entity, an alien environment, or with personal self. Nolan can translate a contemporary moral or social problem into any setting with ease, and his fiction can be compared favorably with other writers who show a similar concern: Ray Bradbury, Richard Matheson, and William Tenn. His character creations intrigue the reader with their sensitivity and empathic natures. The continued importance of William F. Nolan to scholars, sociologists, and readers of science fiction rests on his enduring creation of a universal culture hero: Logan. From a philosophical perspective, Nolan is Logan and Logan is Nolan.

—Harold Lee Prosser

NORMAN, John. Pseudonym for John (Frederick) Lange (Jr.). American. Born in Chicago, Illinois, 3 June 1931. Educated at the University of Nebraska, Lincoln, B. A. 1953; University of Southern California, Los Angeles, M. A. 1957; Princeton University, New Jersey, Ph. D. 1963. Served in the United States Army: Sergeant. Married Bernice L. Green in 1956; two sons and one daughter. Radio writer; story analyst, Warner Brothers; film writer, University of Nebraska; technical writer, Rocketdyne (North American Aviation); Instructor in Philosphy, Hamilton College, Clinton, New York, 1962-64. Since 1964, Member of the Department, and since 1967, Professor of Philosophy, Queens College, City University of New York. Address: Department of Philosophy, Queens College, Flushing, New York 11367, U.S.A.

SCIENCE-FICTION PUBLICATIONS

Novels (series: Gor)

Tarnsman of Gor. New York, Ballantine, 1966; London, Sidgwick and Jackson, 1969.
Outlaw of Gor. New York, Ballantine, 1967; London, Sidgwick and Jackson, 1970.
Priest-Kings of Gor. New York, Ballantine, 1968; London, Sidgwick and Jackson, 1971.
Nomads of Gor. New York, Ballantine, 1969; London, Sidgwick and Jackson, 1971.
Assassin of Gor. New York, Ballantine, 1970; London, Sidgwick and Jackson, 1971.
Ghost Dance. New York, Ballantine, 1970; London, Sphere, 1972.
Raiders of Gor. New York, Ballantine, 1971; London, Tandem, 1973.
Captive of Gor. New York, Ballantine, 1972; London, Tandem, 1973.
Hunters of Gor. New York, DAW, 1974; London, Tandem, 1975.
Marauders of Gor. New York, DAW, 1975; London, Universal, 1977.
Time Slave. New York, DAW, 1975.

Tribesmen of Gor. New York, DAW, 1976.
Slave Girl of Gor. New York, DAW, 1977; London, Universal, 1978.
Beasts of Gor. New York, DAW, 1978; London, Star, 1979.
Explorers of Gor. New York, DAW, 1979.
Fighting Slave of Gor. New York, DAW, 1980.
Guardsman of Gor. New York, DAW, 1981; London, Star, 1982.
Rogue of Gor. New York, DAW, 1981.
Blood Brothers of Gor. New York, DAW, 1982; London, Star, 1983.
Savages of Gor. New York, DAW, and London, Star, 1982.
Kajira of Gor. New York, DAW, and London, Star, 1983.
Players of Gor. New York, DAW, and London, Star, 1984.
Mercenaries of Gor. New York, DAW, 1985.

OTHER PUBLICATIONS as John Lange

Other

The Cognitivity Paradox: An Inquiry Concerning the Claims of Philosophy. Princeton, New Jersey, Princeton University Press, 1970.
Imaginative Sex. New York, DAW, 1975.

Editor, *Values and Imperatives: Studies in Ethics*, by Clarence I. Lewis. Stanford, California, Stanford University Press, 1969.

* * *

John Norman has written almost two dozen novels in the Gor series (the Chronicles of Counter-Earth), novels in the tradition of Edgar Rice Burroughs's Mars books or Andre Norton's Witch World stories. In these works, a character from contemporary Earth finds himself transported, often by inexplicable means, to an unfamiliar world where he is caught up in the events which are shaping the future of that world. And in such worlds, heroic action is almost always the means by which destiny is decided.

Norman's hero, Tarl Cabot, is transported to Gor, a planet on the opposite side of the sun from Earth and somehow shielded from any detection by Terran scientists. On Gor, Cabot is initiated into a way of life which the reader recognizes as medieval. All technological development, especially in weaponry, has been held in check by the Priest-Kings, and the men must fight with sword, spear, bow and arrow, and the like. For most of the known planet, the largest political unit is the city, and politics in and among cities is generally feudal. Gorean society is highly structured, and each person usually remains in the caste—warriors, bakers, scribes, etc.—into which he is born. But Gor and the Priest-Kings are in trouble and in need of heroics which only Tarl Cabot can provide.

As with any extended work of fantasy, the author's ability to detail convincingly a complex culture—or group of cultures—is important. Norman is quite good at this. In the first book, *Tarnsman of Gor*, such detail is necessary, and Norman provides a wealth of information on everything from the training of a warrior to the importance of a Home Stone. In what is possibly his best book to date, *Nomads of Gor*, he brings Cabot to the four tribes of the Wagon People, and the reader is treated to a fascinating descriptions of customs, habits, rituals, and all the other aspects of a complex cultural group. On Gor, the reader realizes, heroic action is not only possible, it is necessary; in other words, the culture is not just a backdrop for the action in Norman's books, it is an integral part of the action.

Heroic fantasies have always been considered male-escapist. The hero is muscular and skillful with weapons; he rescues the heroine who then succumbs to his over-powering maleness. Carries this aspect of heroic fantasy one step further than his predecessors. On Gor, most of the women are slaves, and those who are not are vaguely unhappy because a woman can be free only in total submission to a man. Some of the later books, *Slave Girl of Gor,* for example, focus less on Tarl Cabot than on the Earth woman brought to Gor. Such women are at first distressed by the culture in which they find themselves but soon realize the falseness of their previous (Terran) way of life. On Gor, Cabot says, women are free to be women; whereas, on Earth, they are forced to try to be men. This concept has lost Norman two groups of readers, the first violently opposed to his analysis of women, the second tired of hearing Cabot—or one of the women—explain and defend it book after book.

In literary terms it is the prolonged defense, not the attitude itself, which mars the novels, some of which mars the novels, some of which seem to have written solely to present examples of these ideas and attitudes of women. And Cabot's primary quest has suffered as well; to be sure, he still fights skirmishes against the enemies of the Priest-Kings, but what seemed to be the main plot-line of the series is barely progressing. This situation is unfortunate, for the Gor books are, in most other respects, good heroic fantasy.

—C. W. Sullivan III

NORTH, Andrew. See **NORTON, Andre.**

NORTON, Andre (Alice Mary Norton). Also writes as Andrew North; Allen Weston. American. Born in Cleveland, Ohio, in 1912. Educated at Western Reserve University, Cleveland, 1930-32. Children's Librarian, Cleveland Public Library, 1932-50; Special Librarian, Library of Congress, Washington, D. C., during World War II; editor, Gnome Press, New York, 1950-58. Recipient: Boys' Clubs of America Award, 1965; Grand Master of Fantasy Award, 1977; Gandalf Award, 1977; Grand Master Nebula Award 1983; Jules Verne Award 1984. Agent: Larry Sternig, 742 Robertson Street, Milwaukee, Wisconsin 53213. Address: 682 South Lakemont, Winter Park, Florida 32792, U.S.A.

SCIENCE-FICTION PUBLICATIONS

Novels (series: Astra; Beast Master; Forerunner; Janus; Shann Lantree; Moon Magic; Star Ka'at; Time Travel; Time War; Zero Stone)

Star Man's Son, 2250 A. D. New York, Harcourt Brace, 1952; London, Staples Press, 1953; as *Daybreak, 2250 A. D.,* New York, Ace, 1954.
Star Rangers. New York, Harcourt Brace, 1953; London, Gollancz, 1968; as *The Last Planet,* New York, Ace, 1955.
The Stars Are Ours! (Astra). Cleveland, World, 1954.
Star Guard. New York, Harcourt Brace, 1955; London, Gollancz, 1969.
The Crossroads of Time (Time Travel). New York, Ace, 1956; London, Gollancz, 1967.

Sea Siege. New York, Harcourt Brace, 1957.
Star Born (Astra). Cleveland, World, 1957; London, Gollancz, 1973.
Star Gate. New York, Harcourt Brace, 1958; London, Gollancz, 1970.
The Time Traders (Time War). Cleveland, World, 1958.
Secret of the Lost Race. New York, Ace, 1959; as *Wolfshead,* London, Hale, 1977.
The Beast Master. New York, Harcourt Brace, 1959; London, Gollancz, 1966.
Galactic Derelict (Time War) Cleveland, World, 1959.
Storm over Warlock (Lantree). Cleveland, World, 1960.
The Sioux Spaceman. New York, Ace, 1960; London, Hale, 1976.
Star Hunter. New York, Ace, 1961.
Catseye. New York, Harcourt Brace, 1961; London, Gollancz, 1962.
Eye of the Monster. New York, Ace, 1962.
The Defiant Agents (Time War). Cleveland, World, 1962.
Lord of Thunder (Beast Master). New York, Harcourt Brace, 1962; London, Gollancz, 1966.
Key Out of Time (Time War). Cleveland, World, 1963.
Judgment on Janus. New York, Harcourt Brace, 1963; London, Gollancz, 1964.
Ordeal in Otherwhere (Lantree). Cleveland, World, 1964.
Night of Masks. New York, Harcourt Brace, 1964; London, Gollancz, 1965.
The X Factor. New York, Harcourt Brace, 1965; London, Gollancz, 1967.
Quest Crosstime (Time Travel). New York, Viking Press, 1965; as *Crosstime Agent,* London, Gollancz, 1975.
Moon of Three Rings (Moon Magic). New York, Viking Press, 1966; London, Longman, 1969.
Victory on Janus. New York, Harcourt Brace, 1966; London, Gollancz, 1967.
Operation Time Search. New York, Harcourt Brace, 1967.
Dark Piper. New York, Harcourt Brace, 1968; London, Gollancz, 1969.
The Zero Stone. New York, Viking Press, 1968; London, Gollancz, 1974.
Postmarked the Stars. New York, Harcourt Brace, 1969; London, Gollancz, 1971.
Uncharted Stars (Zero Stone). New York, Viking Press, 1969; London, Gollancz, 1974.
Ice Crown. New York, Viking Press, 1970; London, Longman, 1971.
Android at Arms. New York, Harcourt Brace, 1971; London, Gollancz, 1972.
Exiles of the Stars (Moon Magic). New York, Viking Press, 1971; London, Longman, 1972.
Breed to Come. New York, Viking Press, 1972; London, Longman, 1973.
Here Abide Monsters. New York, Atheneum, 1973.
Iron Cage. New York, Viking Press, 1974; London, Kestrel, 1975.
Outside. New York, Walker, 1975; London, Blackie, 1976.
The Day of the Ness, with Michael Gilbert. New York, Walker, 1975.
Knave of Dreams. New York, Viking Press, 1975; London, Kestrel, 1976.
No Night Without Stars. New York, Atheneum, 1975; London, Gollancz, 1976.
Star Ka'at, with Dorothy Madlee. New York, Walker, 1976; London, Blackie, 1977.
Star Ka'at World, with Dorothy Madlee. New York, Walker, 1978.

Star Ka'ats and the Plant People, with Dorothy Madlee. New York, Walker, 1979.
Star Ka'ats and the Winged Warriors. New York, Walker, 1981.
Ten Mile Treasure. New York, Pocket Books, 1981.
Voorloper. New York, Ace, 1981.
Forerunner. New York, Pinnacle, 1981.
Moon Called. New York, Simon and Schuster, 1982.
Wheel of Stars. New York, Simon and Schuster, 1983.
Forerunner: The Second Venture. New York, Tor, 1985.

Novels as Andrew North (series: Solar Queen in all books)

Sargasso of Space. New York, Gnome Press, 1955; as Andre Norton, London, Gollancz, 1970.
Plague Ship. New York, Gnome Press, 1956; as Andre Norton, London, Gollancz, 1971.
Voodoo Planet. New York, Ace, 1959.

Short Stories

The Many Worlds of Andre Norton, edited by Roger Elwood. Radnor, Pennsylvania, Chilton, 1974; as *The Book of Andre Norton,* New York, DAW, 1975.
Perilous Dreams. New York, DAW, 1976.

OTHER PUBLICATIONS

Novels

The Prince Commands. New York, Appleton Century, 1934.
Ralestone Luck. New York, Appleton Century, 1938.
Follow the Drum. New York, Penn, 1942.
The Sword Is Drawn. Boston, Houghton Mifflin, 1944; London, Oxford University Press, 1946.
Scarface. New York, Harcourt Brace, 1948; London, Methuen, 1950.
Sword in Sheath. New York, Harcourt Brace, 1949; as *Island of the Lost,* London, Staples Press, 1953.
Murder for Sale (as Allen Weston, with Grace Hogarth). London, Hammond, 1954.
At Swords' Point. New York, Harcourt Brace, 1954.
Yankee Privateer. Cleveland, World, 1955.
Stand to Horse. New York, Harcourt Brace, 1956.
Shadow Hawk. New York, Harcourt Brace, 1960; London, Gollancz, 1971.
Ride Proud, Rebel! Cleveland, World, 1961.
Rebel Spurs. Cleveland, World, 1962.
Witch World. New York, Ace, 1963; London, Tandem, 1970.
Web of the Witch World. New York, Ace, 1964; London, Tandem, 1970.
Steel Magic. Cleveland, World, 1965; London, Hamish Hamilton, 1967; as *Gray Magic,* New York, Scholastic, 1967.
Three Against the Witch World. New York, Ace, 1965; London, Tandem, 1970.
Year of the Unicorn. New York, Ace, 1965; London, Tandem, 1970.
Octagon Magic. Cleveland, World, 1967; London, Hamish Hamilton, 1968.
Warlock of the Witch World. New York, Ace, 1967; London, Tandem, 1970.
Fur Magic. Cleveland, World, 1968; London, Hamish Hamilton, 1969.
Sorceress of the Witch World. New York, Ace, 1968; London, Tandem, 1970.
Dread Companion. New York, Harcourt Brace, 1970; London, Gollancz, 1972.

The Crystal Gryphon. New York, Atheneum, 1972; London, Gollancz, 1973.
Dragon Magic. New York, Crowell, 1972.
Forerunner Foray. New York, Viking Press, 1973; London, Longman, 1974.
The Jargoon Pard. New York, Atheneum, 1974; London, Gollancz, 1975.
Lavender-Green Magic. New York, Crowell, 1974.
Merlin's Mirror. New York, DAW, 1975; London, Sidgwick and Jackson, 1976.
The White Jade Fox. New York, Dutton, 1975; London, W. H. Allen. 1976
Red Hart Magic. New York, Crowell, 1976; London, Hamish Hamilton, 1977.
Wraiths of Time. New York, Atheneum, 1976; London, Gollancz, 1977.
The Opal-Eyed Fan. New York, Dutton, 1977.
Velvet Shadows. New York, Fawcett, 1977.
Quag Keep. New York, Atheneum, 1978.
Yurth Burden. New York, DAW, 1978.
Zarsthor's Bane. New York, Ace, 1978; London, Dobson, 1981.
Snow Shadow. New York, Fawcett, 1979.
Seven Spells to Sunday, with Phyllis Miller. New York, Atheneum, 1979.
Gryphon in Glory. New York, Atheneum, 1981.
Horn Crown. New York, DAW, 1981.
Caroline, with Enid Cushing. New York, Pinnacle, 1982.
'Ware Hawk. New York, Atheneum, 1983.
House of Shadows, with Phyllis Miller. New York, Atheneum, 1984.
Stand and Deliver. New York, Dell, 1984.

Short Stories

High Sorcery. New York, Ace, 1970.
Garan the Eternal. Alhambra, California, Fantasy, 1972.
Spell of the Witch World. New York, DAW, 1972; London, Prior, 1977.
Trey of Swords. New York, Grosset and Dunlap, 1977; London, Star, 1979.
Lore of the Witch World. New York, DAW, 1980.

Other

Rogue Reynard (for children). Boston, Houghton Mifflin, 1947.
Huon of the Horn (for children) New York, Harcourt Brace 1951.
"Living in 1980+," in *Library Journal* (New York), 15 September 1952.
Bertie and May (for children), with Bertha Stenn Norton. Cleveland, World, 1969; London, Hamish Hamilton, 1971.
"The Girl and the B. E. M.," in *Cassandra Rising,* edited by Alice Laurance. New York, Doubleday, 1978.

Editor, *Bullard of the Space Patrol,* by Malcolm Jameson. Cleveland, World, 1951.
Editor, *Space Service.* Cleveland, World, 1953.
Editor, *Space Pioneers.* Cleveland World, 1954.
Editor, *Space Police.* Cleveland, World, 1956.
Editor, with Ernestine Donaldy, *Gates to Tomorrow: An Introduction to Science Fiction.* New York, Atheneum, 1973.
Editor, *Small Shadows Creep: Ghost Children.* New York, Dutton, 1974; London, Chatto and Windus, 1976.
Editor, *Baleful Beasts and Eerie Creatures.* Chicago, Rand McNally, 1976.
Editor, with Robert Adams, *Magic in Ithkar.* New York, Tor, 1985.

*

Bibliography: *Andre Norton: A Primary and Secondary Bibliography* by Roger C. Schlobin, Boston, Hall, 1980.

Manuscript Collection: George Arents Research Library, Syracuse University, New York.

*   *   *

Andre Norton's early intention was to write fiction for boys, and she changed her name to enter this male-dominated market. Fortunately for the millions of readers who have made her one of the best selling of contemporary fantasy and science-fiction authors, she turned to these two forms in 1947 with her first published short story "People of the Crater" (later title: "Garin of Tav"). It is odd that Norton turned to science fiction at all. In fact, books like the *Beast Master* and its sequel, *Lord of Thunder*, weren't really science fiction at all. They were simply an experiment applying the form of a western to outer space and alien worlds. Actually, Norton has contempt for science and technology; they appear in her fiction only as vehicles and foils. In Ric Brooks's essay (in *The Many Worlds of Andre Norton*, 1974), she makes her stance quite clear: "Yes, I am anti-machine. The more research I do, the more I am convinced that when western civilizations turned to machines ..., they threw away parts of life ... [the lack of which] leads to much of our present frustration."

Even in Norton's science fiction, technology and science are incidental to plot and character. These major concerns reflect the influences of Edgar Rice Burroughs, H. Rider Haggard, A. Merritt, and Talbot Mundy, and Norton's respect for their fast-moving plots and memorable characters. For plot content, Norton's extensive research and affection for the mysterious and intriguing have led her to a number of specific motifs that occur throughout her fiction. Jewels frequently appear as powerful talismans, particularly in her fantasy novels. For example, as early as *At Swords' Point*, part of the Sword series that focuses on post-World-War-II espionage and the Netherlands during World War II, a set of jeweled miniature knights are central to a young man's search for his brother's murderer. Jewels are also important in *The Zero Stone*, the much heralded Witch World series, *Wraiths of Time*, and the gothic novels, particularly *The White Jade Fox* and *The Opal-Eyed Fan*. Frequently, these talismans are connected to an even more pervasive motif: the pseudo-science psychometry. This is formally defined as the detection of the residue of "memory" retained in an artifact by a sensitive. This plays a major role in the fantasy (with strong science-fiction elements) *Forerunner Foray*, in which Ziatha is drawn into a prehuman age through her reaction to a jewel; in *Wraiths of Time*, a crystal ankh and a staff contain the accumulated psychic power of a race.

Jewels and psychometry are two of the elements that give Norton's fiction its brooding depth, and together they provide a bridge between two other major Norton fascinations: history and speculative archaeology. Whether it be through references to prehistoric alien visits to Earth, as in *Merlin's Mirror*, or allusions to the prehistoric past, as in the Moon Magic series, Norton's fiction always has a resonance that goes beyond the immediate present to a more pervasive and often mysterious past. It is the characters' responsibility to discover the relevance of the past to themselves and their futures.

Yet none of these motifs or devices is the center of Andre Norton's fiction. Rather, the most important aspects are simply humanity and self-realization. Norton explains this in "On Writing Fantasy" (in *The Many Worlds of Andre Norton*): "But the first requirement for writing heroic . . . fantasy must be a deep interest in and a love for history itself. Not the history of dates, of sweeps and empires—but the kind of history which deals with daily life, the beliefs, and the aspirations of people long since dust. " Within the obvious cosmic scope, alien climes, antagonistic technology, vast quests, and fantastic forces of Norton's fiction, the characters are involved in crucial patterns of being, both for themselves and their fellows. While they are arrayed in mythic quests that grow from deep tradition, exist in a momentous present, and face a vital future, the characters remain pointedly human and humane. Most frequently, they move through what Northrop Frye calls "triumphant comedy." They struggle against an unlawful or unnatural order, undergo rites of passage to find realization, and establish new orders and freedoms. Kaththea (*Sorceress of the Witch World*) reflects this pattern as well as Norton's pioneering commitment to female characters. Shattered and disillusioned, Kaththea must find the faith to accept Hilarion, one of the enormously powerful "Old Ones" of the Witch World, if she is to save her family and regenerate her environment. Furtig, the mutated cat protagonist of *Breed to Come*, must overcome the mythology surrounding his long-departed human masters to unleash his own potentiality. Through the characters' agonizing trials, bondages and wastelands are destroyed, shape prejudice is eliminated, generative orders are established, and the protagonists and their fellows are ennobled. As Ric Brooks writes, "the chief value of Andre Norton's fiction may not lie in entertainment or social commentary, but in her 'reenchanting' us with her creations that renew our linkages to life."

Andre Norton's characters are always alone, alienated, fearful, and searching. They are admirable for their positive, if sometimes confused, values, and they are attractive in their frailty and their doubt. In spite of their varied shapes and alien abilities, they achieve the nobility and status of the healer as they cure themselves and others. Frequently, their solutions are androgynous—as for Simon Tregarth and Jaelithe in *Witch World*—and they do find the best of male and female. More significantly, their solutions to pain and loneliness are mythic and elemental and are a celebration of the bonds among man, animal, nature and cosmic order.

—Roger C. Schlobin

———————

NORVIL, Manning. See **BULMER, Kenneth.**

———————

NORWOOD, Warren. American. Born in Philadelphia, Pennsylvania, 21 August 1945. Educated at North Texas State University, Denton, B. A. 1972. Served in the United States Army, 1966-69: Bronze Star. Married 1) Mary Walker in 1965 (divorced, 1972); 2) Margot Biery in 1973; one daughter. Assistant Manager, University Bookstore, University of Texas, Arlington, 1973-76; Manager, Century Bookstore, Fort Worth, 1976-77; publisher's representative in Fort Worth, for Ballantine Books, 1978-79, and for Bantam Books, 1980-83; taught creative writing, Tarrant County Junior College, 1981-83. Agent: Richard Curtis Associates, 164 East 64th Street, New York, New York 10021. Address: 2428 Las Brisas, Fort Worth, Texas 76116, U.S.A.

SCIENCE-FICTION PUBLICATIONS

Novels (series: Double Spiral War; Windhover Tapes)

The Windhover Tapes:
    1. *An Image of Voices*. New York, Bantam, 1982.
    2. *Flexing the Warp*. New York, Bantam, 1983.
    3. *Fize of the Gabriel Ratchets*. New York, Bantam, 1983.
    4. *Planet of Flowers*. New York, Bantam, 1984.
The Seren Cenacles, with Ralph Mylius. New York, Bantam,
    1983.
Double Spiral War:
    1. *Midway Between*. New York, Bantam, 1984.
    2. *Polar Fleet*. New York, Bantam, 1985.

*   *   *

Warren Norwood's unusual first novel, *The Windhover Tapes: An Image of Voices,* received excellent reviews when it appeared in 1982, but earned its author the dubious honor of finishing last in the balloting for the John W. Campbell Award for best new writer of the year, behind "No Award." The book is a complex amalgam of 1930's-style space opera, obscure literary references to 17th-century poets like Michael Drayton and folklore characters like the Gabriel Ratchets, and a style which seems to fluctuate between Barry Malzberg-like monologue and the 18th-century epistolary novels of Samuel Richardson. The story takes place in the far future, when faster-than-light travel to other galaxies is routine and humanity has contacted and interbred with any number of alien races. Gerard Hopkins Manley is a contract diplomat and anthropological researcher, and the four "Windhover" novels relate his adventures with sentient flowers, pulp-style outer space empires, outspoken feminist ghosts, intelligent, wheeled avians, and other strange beings and situations. The first two books are made up entirely of Manley's first-person conversations with himself and his sentient space ship, Windhover. The later volumes are more conventional, third-person narratives. All four books contain numerous references to Manley's 19th-century English namesake, though Manley and those around him have apparently never heard of the poet.

The Windhover Tapes series is an enjoyable piece of work, but it has several flaws: the seeming irrelevance of most of the Hopkins material, Norwood's frequent inclusion of his own not very good poetry (including a travesty of Hopkins's "Windhover"), and the author's apparent fixation on human and humanoid mammary glands (Manley's beautiful alien wife has three). On the positive side, Norwood is doing some interesting stylistic experimentation, and his main character is a very unusual hero for science fiction—an emotional man who is not afraid to cry or dote upon his infant son and daughter, a man who is capable of space opera-style action, but who would really much rather talk things out sensibly.

That Norwood has considerable ability is clear; however, one cannot help but wish that he would take more time with his books. The Windhover series fluctuates markedly between startling originality and pulp cliché but maintains on the whole a fairly high level of excellence. The author's more recent novels, however, are generally less successful. *The Seren Cenacles*, co-authored with Ralph Mylius, is a well-written but poorly plotted tale of "alien terror" on a mining colony. The several political and industrial groups, military forces, and alien species contending for control of the situation are thrown at us willy nilly, without sufficient cultural context or satisfactory explanation. The book's basic premise, mining organic matter buried on distant worlds to ship to the galaxy's starving trillions, is not very believable, nor is the story's abrupt and

rather unlikely denouement. Likewise, *Midway Between*, the first volume of the Double Spiral War series, throws so many similar characters at the reader that it is virtually impossible to keep them straight. This space war novel, like all Norwood's books, is well written, but it is also talky, obscurely plotted, and considering its sub-genre, short on action.

In summary, Warren Norwood is a talented young writer with a knack for character development, fine prose, and experimentation, but he has considerable problems with plotting and background development. One can only hope that his prolific rate of publication will give him the financial stability he needs to ease his pace and refine his art.

—Michael M. Levy

NOURSE, Alan E(dward). American. Born in Des Moines, Iowa, 11 August 1928. Educated at Rutgers University, New Brunswick, New Jersey, B. A. 1951; University of Pennsylvania, Philadelphia, M. D. 1955. Served in the United States Navy, 1946-48: Hospitalman 3rd Class. Married Ann Jane Morton in 1952; three sons and one daughter. Intern, Virginia Mason Hospital, Seattle, Washington, 1955-56; free-lance writer, 1956-58; private medical practice, North Bend, Washington, 1958-64. Since 1964, free-lance writer. Owner, Chamberlain Press, 1953-55. Chairman of the Board, Tanner Electric Rural Electrification Co-op; President, Science Fiction Writers of America, 1968-69. Agent: Brandt and Brandt, 1501 Broadway, New York, New York 10036. Address: Rt. 1, Box 173, Thorp, Washington 98946, U.S.A.

SCIENCE-FICTION PUBLICATIONS

Novels

Trouble on Titan (for children). Philadelphia, Winston, 1954;
    London, Hutchinson, 1956.
A Man Obsessed. New York, Ace, 1955; revised edition, as *The
    Mercy Men*, New York, McKay, 1968; London, Faber, 1969.
Rocket to Limbo (for children). New York, McKay, 1957;
    London, Faber, 1964.
The Invaders Are Coming!, with J. A. Meyer. New York, Ace,
    1959.
Scavengers in Space (for children). New York, McKay, 1959;
    London, Faber, 1964.
Star Surgeon (for children). New York, McKay, 1960; London,
    Faber, 1962.
Raiders from the Rings (for children). New York, McKay, 1962;
    London, Faber, 1965.
The Universe Between. New York, McKay, 1965; London,
    Faber, 1966.
The Bladerunner. New York, McKay, 1974.
The Fourth Horseman. New York, Harper, 1983.

Short Stories

Tiger by the Tail. New York, McKay, 1961; London, Dobson,
    1962; as *Beyond Infinity,* London, Corgi, 1964.
The Counterfeit Man. New York, McKay, 1963; London,
    Dobson, 1964.
Psi High and Others. New York, McKay, 1967; London, Faber,
    1968.
Rx for Tomorrow. New York, McKay, 1971; London, Faber,
    1972.

OTHER PUBLICATIONS

Novels

Junior Intern. New York, Harper, 1955.
The Practice. New York, Harper, 1978; London, Futura, 1979.

Other

So You Want to Be a Doctor [*Lawyer, Scientist, Nurse* (with Eleanore Halliday), *Engineer* (with James C. Webbert), *Physicist, Chemist* (with James C. Webbert), *Surgeon, Architect* (with Carl Meinhardt)] (for children). New York, Harper, 9 vols., 1957-69.
Nine Planets. New York, Harper, 1960; revised edition, 1970.
The Management of a Medical Practice, with Geoffrey Marks. Philadelphia, Lippincott, 1963.
The Body. New York, Time, 1964; revised edition, New York, Time Life, 1980.
Universe, Earth, and Atom: The Story of Physics. New York, Harper, 1969.
Virginia Mason Medical Center: The First Fifty Years. Seattle, Virginia Mason Hospital Association, 1970.
Venus and Mercury (for children). New York, Watts, 1972.
Ladies' Home Journal Family Medical Guide. New York, Harper, 1973.
The Backyard Astronomer. New York, Watts, 1973.
The Giant Planets (for children). New York, Watts, 1974; revised edition, 1982.
The Outdoorsman's Medical Guide. New York, Harper, 1974.
The Asteroids (for children). New York, Watts, 1975.
Clear Skin, Healthy Skin (for children). New York, Watts, 1976.
Lumps, Bumps, and Rashes (for children). New York, Watts, 1976.
Viruses (for children). New York, Watts, 1976; revised edition, 1983.
The Tooth Book (for children). New York, McKay, 1977.
Vitamins (for children). New York, Watts, 1977.
Fractures, Dislocations, and Sprains (for children). New York, Watts, 1978.
Hormones (for children). New York, Watts, 1979.
Inside the Mayo Clinic. New York, McGraw Hill, 1979.
Menstruation: Just Plain Talk (for children). New York, Watts, 1980.
Your Immune System (for children). New York, Watts, 1980.

*

Manuscript Collection: Boston University.

*   *   *

Alan E. Nourse has several specialized interests which form a unifying theme in many of his short stories and novels. Most of them have a number of common stylistic characteristics linking him to the science-fiction writers of the 1950's. In his recent book, *The Bladerunner,* Nourse makes several frightening but logical extrapolations from current social problems.

A number of Nourse's novels, among them *Scavengers in Space, Trouble on Titan, Rocket to Limbo,* and *Raiders from the Rings,* are straightforward science fiction/adventure stories. Not surprisingly, however, since Nourse is a former practicing physician, his best stories deal with medicine. His most readable adventure story is *Star Surgeon* in which he develops an interesting concept, "Hospital Earth," where Earth utilizes its medical research and technology to serve as medical liaison for the galaxy. A number of stories revolve around Hoffman Center, a futuristic medical complex in Philadelphia, and Nourse develops a tantalizing concept, the "mercy men"—men who are recruited and paid for being guinea pigs. An additional theme Nourse frequently treats is the development, realization, and analysis of mental superpowers in individuals whom Nourse call "PSI high." In a number of his stories Nourse works with the concept of possible alternate universes that exist in other dimensions. Nourse frequently combines the medical and PSI themes, and in *The Universe Between* he adds to these the alternate dimension concept as well.

Like his contemporary Robert Heinlein, Nourse wrote "Juveniles" during the 1950's, and unlike Heinlein, continued to write them. These novels contain prototype characters, like the young male hero, and there are no overtly romantic scenes, but the prototype males may have female complements who are, for the 1950's and 1960's, surprisingly forceful. Because so many of Nourse's stories concern mental rather than scientific advancement, he seldom uses the "hard" science-fiction technique of describing in detail futuristic methods and machines; even in his medical-theme novels, where Nourse's familiarity with his subject clearly shows, he does not give his fiction much explicit scientific detail. In the Hoffman Center fiction Nourse does place some emphasis on the world-covering computer hook-up, but he generally expects his reader to take for granted the medical, scientific, and technological accomplishments of his future world. Nourse does not use the familiar 1950's social theme of nuclear disaster, although in his Hoffman Center fiction he postulates a social background which includes a devastating third world war. Like much of the science fiction of the 1950's, most of Nourse's relies for its primary interest on plot development and problem-solving rather than on character development, social philosophy, and other "new wave" techniques.

The Bladerunner is clearly aimed at a more mature audience. While it retains most stylistic characteristics of earlier Nourse novels, its theme is dystopian. Nourse based his novel on two premises: medical advancement would lead to increased longevity, survival of people with hereditary defects, and conquest of viral and bacterial diseases. In addition, the country would turn within 20 years entirely to socialized medicine. The consequences would be over-population and more virulent diseases requiring constant development of new medicines. Socialized medical care would have a price—sterilization—and to fulfill the needs of people unwilling to submit to sterilization, an army of underground doctors would work illegally, supplied and aided by "bladerunners." The plot of *The Bladerunner* centers on one doctor's fight to defeat the policies of socialized medicine and simultaneously to publicize a dangerous plague. While the plot and solution to the problem are entertaining, Nourse clearly wishes for *The Bladerunner* to serve as a warning against socialized medicine, and the diatribes against this evil are occasionally intrusive. Despite this flaw, *The Bladerunner* is the best of Nourse's science-fiction novels.

—Karren C. Edwards

———

NOWLAN, Philip Francis. Also wrote as Frank Phillips. American. Born in Philadelphia, Pennsylvania, in 1888. Educated at the University of Pennsylvania, Philadelphia, B. A. 1910. Married Teresa Marie Junker; four daughters and six sons. Worked for *Public Ledger, North American,* and *Retail Ledger;* collaborated with Dick Calkins on first science-fiction comic strip, *Buck Rogers,* 1929-40. *Died 1 February 1940.*

SCIENCE-FICTION PUBLICATIONS

Novel

Armageddon 2419 A. D. New York, Avalon, 1962; London,
Panther, 1976.

Uncollected Short Stories

"The Onslaught from Venus" (as Frank Phillips), in *Science
Wonder Stories* (New York), September 1929.
"The Time Jumpers," in *Amazing* (New York), February 1934.
"The Prince of Mars Returns," in *Fantastic Adventures*
(Chicago), February 1940.
"Space Guards," in *Astounding* (New York), May 1940.

OTHER PUBLICATIONS

Other

Buck Rogers on the Moons of Saturn. Racine, Wisconsin,
Whitman, 1934.
Buck Rogers in the Dangerous Mission. New York, Blue Ribbon
Press, 1934.
Buck Rogers and the Depth Men of Jupiter. Racine, Wisconsin,
Whitman, 1935.
*Buck Rogers, 25th Century, Featuring Buddy and Allura in
"Strange Adventures of the Spider Ship."* Chicago, Pleasure,
1935.
*Buck Rogers, 25th Century A. D., in the Interplanetay War with
Venus.* Racine, Wisconsin, Whitman, 1938.
Buck Rogers in the 25th Century 1-2, 7-8. Ann Arbor, Michigan,
Ed Aprill, 4 vols., 1964-68.
The Collected Works of Buck Rogers in the 25th Century, with
Dick Calkins and Rick Yager, edited by Robert C. Dille. New
York, Bonanza, 1969; revised edition, New York, A and W,
1977.

* * *

Although not as well known as Edgar Rice Burroughs or E. E.
Smith, Philip Francis Nowlan was probably their equal both as
a writer and as an influence on modern science fiction. In his first
story, "Armageddon 2419 A. D. " (*Amazing,* August 1928), he
introduced perhaps the most popular character in the history of
the genre, Anthony, or as he was later known, Buck Rogers.
Over the decades that followed Nowlan and others scripted
innumerable Buck Rogers comic strips. There were several
films, and a current successful television series is proof of Buck
Roger's continuing appeal.

In "Armageddon 2419 A. D. " Anthony Rogers, an engineer
exploring a Pennsylvania mine in 1929, is caught in a cave-in and
placed in suspended animation. Awakening in the 25th century,
he discovers that the United States is now ruled by Mongolians
and that Americans live in scattered communities, hiding from
the conquerers who consider them vermin. The Mongolians, or
Hans, a decadent, heartless race, rarely leave their cities and rely
on huge airships equipped with disintegrator rays to maintain
their dominance. Rogers has appeared at an opportune
moment, for the Americans, armed with newly developed anti-
gravity devices and rocket guns, are preparing to revolt.
Contributing a knowledge of 20th-century military tactics and a
certain primitive blood-thirstiness, Rogers soon becomes a
leader in the struggle. The American conquest is completed in
Nowlan's sequel, "The Airlords of Han. " (The two stories were
combined in the 1962 book *Armageddon 2419 A. D.*) Although

flawed by occasionally awkward language and handicapped by
the poorly considered choice of a first-person narrator, the
Anthony Rogers stories stand up quite well even today. The
action moves smoothly and the various military inventions and
tactics are intriguing. The stories are touched by the racism so
common in 1920's pulp fiction but, interestingly, are extremely
progressive in their treatment of women. Wilma Deering,
although occasionally given to the fainting spells and fits of
weeping which were *de riguer* for women in popular fiction, is in
general more competent and active than any female character in
science fiction prior to Joanna Russ's Alyx.

"The Onslaught from Venus" is a first-person account by a
member of the Airguard (the military arm of the Supernational
Commission of the Caucasioan League) who, captured by the
invading Venusians, first studies their civilization and then,
escaping, helps destroy it. Again the story is largely taken up
with inventive weaponry and tactics. The Venusians, who seem
quite human except for their skin color, are, like the Hans,
totally evil, totally decadent. They are incapable of even
considering coexistence and their complete extermination is
thus a necessity.

Nowlan published little science fiction in the years that
followed. His final story, and, after "Armageddon 2419 A. D.,"
probably his best, was "Space Guards. " In this tale the narrator
and his commanding officer, another of Nowlan's capable
women, are searching the jungles of Venus for the headquarters
of the criminal mastermind Tiger Madden. They're captured by
tribesmen who, again, are totally human except for their skin
color. Converting the natives to their side, the two Earth people
defeat Madden's troops in battle and then infiltrate his city.
Eventually they kidnap the villain and escape under fire. The
narrator saves his commander's life, disobeying her direct order
to abandon her. She at first considers court-martialing him but
then, as the story closes, decides to marry him instead. Despite
its silly ending and its somewhat old-fashioned plotting, "Space
Guards" is an interesting and exciting story.

Philip Nowlan was a talented writer, and, despite his small
output, he is one of the most influential science-fiction writers of
the Gernsback era.

—Michael M. Levy

NYE, Harold G. See **HARDING, Lee.**

O'BRIEN, Clancy. See **SMITH, George H.**

ODLE, E. V. British.

SCIENCE-FICTION PUBLICATIONS

Novel

The Clockwork Man. London, Heinemann, and New York,
Doubleday, 1923.

OTHER PUBLICATIONS

Novel

The History of Alfred Rudd. London, Collins, 1922.

Play

First Love (produced London, 1911).

Other

Editor, *Great Stories of Human Courage.* London, Lane, 1933.
Editor, *Quest and Conquest: An Anthology of Personal Adventures.* London, Macmillan, 1936.

* * *

There is little mystery about the title character of E. V. Odle's *The Clockwork Man,* for his origins become obvious right from the start. Through a malfunction of his clockwork mechanism he appears at a local village cricket match, having slipped back 8000 years from a future world established after a series of catastrophic wars. His bizarre behaviour and strange appearance throw the cricketers of 1920's England into confusion. Though at first glance human, he is internally a mass of cogs and wheels that are controlled by a "clock" set into the back of his head.

Most of the novel is concerned with the intellectual and moral challenges the Clockwork Man poses to his cricket-playing ancestors. His apparent ability to overcome the laws of time and space presents a prospect too bleak to contemplate to the middle-aged bachelor Dr. Allingham, primarily because he threatens, like the Doctor's free-thinking fiancée Lilian, a comfortable and complacent way of life. Gregg, a university graduate in his 20's, finds the existence of the Clockwork Man both believable and encouraging, the ideal outcome of man's quest for progress. Arthur Withers, a simple and contented bank clerk, sees only an unhappy soul, transported from a world devoid of emotion and trapped into one that can offer no acceptance.

Odle provides no clear answers to the questions he raises in this book. Is the Clockwork Man a manifestation of man's triumph over his physiological limitations, or merely a glorified puppet, a grim look into a future where, through his pursuit of happiness, man has become a slave to his own technology? The Clockwork Man forces the people he meets to re-examine their own lives. Are they superior to him, being free to act as they will? Or are they not as firmly fixed into their own mechanical patterns of behaviour and thought as he is into his loveless world of perpetual time and space change?

The Clockwork Man is undeniably a slow-moving and uneventful work of science fiction, and can hardly be considered an incisive allegory, but it is a thoughtful and well-constructed novel that shouldn't be *quite* so forgotten as it has apparently become.

—Judith Summers

O'DONNELL, K. M. See **MALZBERG, Barry N.**

O'DONNELL, Kevin, Jr. American. Born in Cleveland, Ohio, 29 November 1950. Educated at schools in Cleveland and Fairview Park; Seoul Foreign School, Korea, graduated 1968; Yale University, New Haven, Connecticut, 1968-72, B. A. in Chinese studies 1972. Married Lillian Tchang in 1974. Assistant Lecturer in English, Hong Kong Baptist College, 1972-73, and American English Language Institute, Taipei, Taiwan, 1973-74. Since 1976, free-lance writer. Managing Editor, 1979-81, and Publisher, 1981-83, *Empire*, New Haven, Connecticut. Agent: Howard Morhaim Literary Agency, 501 Fifth Avenue, New York, New York 10017, U.S.A.

SCIENCE-FICTION PUBLICATIONS

Novels (series: McGill Feighan)

Bander Snatch. New York, Bantam, 1979.
Mayflies. New York, Berkley, 1979.
Caverns (Feighan). New York, Berkley, 1981.
Reefs (Feighan). New York, Berkley, 1981.
War of Omission. New York, Bantam, 1982.
Lava (Feighan). New York, Berkley, 1982.
ORA: CLE. New York, Berkley, 1984.
Cliffs (Feighan). New York, Berkley, 1986.

Uncollected Short Stories

"The Hand *Is* Quicker," in *Analog* (New York), October 1973.
"The Tripper," in *Analog* (New York), October 1975.
"Shattered Hopes, Broken Dreams," in *Galaxy* (New York), January 1976.
"A Matter of Pride," in *Analog* (New York), February 1976.
"Hunger on the Homestretch," in *Galaxy* (New York), March 1976.
"Next Door Neighbor," in *Galileo 1* (New York), September 1976.
"In Xanadu," in *Galaxy* (New York), November 1976.
"Night Shift," in *Orbit 19*, edited by Damon Knight. New York, Harper, 1977.
"The Night Callers," in *Galileo* (New York), April 1977.
"A Meeting of Minds," in *Galaxy* (New York), June 1977.
"Information Station Sabbath," in *Analog* (New York), August 1977.
"Report to the Director," in *Empire* (New Haven, Connecticut), Fall 1977.
"Shadow Play," in *Swank* (New York), December 1977.
"Low Grade Ore," in *Isaac Asimov's Science Fiction Anthology 1*, edited by George H. Scithers. New York, Davis, 1978.
"The Gift of Prometheus," in *Analog* (New York), January 1978.
"Quinera 3," in *Analog* (New York), February 1978.
"Far from the Madding Crowd," in *Galileo* (New York), May 1978.
"Stalking the Timelines," in *Analog* (New York), September 1978.
"Tunnels of the Mind," in *Galileo* (New York), September 1978.
"Listen to the Rain," with Al Sirois, in *Tesseract*, Fall 1978.
"Do Not Go Gentle," in *Starry Messenger*, edited by Charles C. Ryan. New York, St. Martin's Press, 1979.
"The Dead of Winter," in *Isaac Asimov's Science Fiction Magazine* (New York), May 1979.
"Three Aliens," in *Destinies* (New York), October 1979.
"Old Friends," in *Analog* (New York), November 1979.
"The Raindrop's Role," in *Isaac Asimov's Science Fiction Magazine* (New York), November 1979.

"Temple Guardian," in *The Future at War 2*, edited by Reginald Bretnor. New York, Ace, 1980.

"Bloodsong," with Barry Longyear, in *Isaac Asimov's Science Fiction Magazine* (New York), December 1980.

"The Looking Glass of the Law," in *The Survival of Freedom*, edited by Jerry Pournelle and John F. Carr. New York, Fawcett, 1981.

"Younggold," in *The Berkley Showcase 4*, edited by Victoria Schochet and John W. Silbersack. New York, Berkley, 1981.

"Tears for Emily," in *Destinies* (New York), April 1981.

"Judo and the Art of Self-Government," in *Laughing Space*, edited by Isaac Asimov and J. O. Jeppson. Boston, Houghton Mifflin, and London, Robson, 1982.

"Marchianna," in *The Best of Omni Science Fiction 4*, edited by Ben Bova and Don Myrus. New York, Omni, 1982.

"Encroachment," in *The Berkley Showcase 5*, edited by Victoria Schochet and Melissa Singer. New York, Berkley, 1982.

"Oft in Offwana," with Al Sirois, in *Isaac Asimov's Science Fiction Magazine* (New York), February 1983.

"Linehan Alone," in *Amazing* (New York), July 1984.

"Thy Neighbor's Assets," in *Analog* (New York), April 1985.

OTHER PUBLICATIONS

Other

The Electronic Money Book, with the Haven Group. New York, Avon, 1984.

*

Kevin O'Donnell, Jr., comments:

When I write, I want the eventual readers to enjoy themselves; to think about themselves, others, and the future; and to feel at the end that they have experienced something worthwhile.

In one sense, science fiction is the opportunity to sample, vicariously and in advance, the consequences of choices human beings are making right now. I do not pretend to be a prophet, but I do attempt to depict potential futures, and those futures should ring as true to life as possible. Thus I stress verisimilitude in my writing, which poses a special challenge, since, by definition, what I write about has not happened yet, and probably never will. Before the words go on the paper, I have already spent a great deal of time trying to answer to my own satisfaction the question "What would it *really* be like if—?"

I give equal weight to characterization. Stereotypes are easy to work with—cardboard characters shuffle as easily as a deck of cards—but real people tangled in the webwork of their families, their friends, their pasts, and their present predicaments interest me much more than do mighty-thewed heroes or black-hearted villains. Don't get me wrong. I *like* heroes and villains. I also like shades of grey.

*   *   *

Possessed of one of the more entertaining new voices of science fiction, Kevin O'Donnell, Jr., infuses familiar SF themes and concepts with his own eager tone, the voice of the born story-teller. Among his shorter pieces, 6 have been recommended for Nebula Awards: "A Matter of Pride," a serious tale of epidemiology and prisoners of war, "Low Grade Ore" and "Temple Guardian," two stories of alien invaders, a time-travel short called "The Gift of Prometheus," a humorous story of censorship-via-computer, "Judo and the Art of Self-Government," and "Marchianna," of robots and asteroid mining. Emotional constants in O'Donnell's work are reliance upon individual strengths and the saving love of friends whether human or alien, and a suspicion of the corporate and bureaucratic. Humor is often achieved through a Chaplinesque stumbling over a plethora of detail.

His best-known work, *Mayflies*, utilizes two familiar themes: the hero interfaced with a computer and the generation starship. O'Donnell fuses these with energy and enthusiasm to create the memorable image of the immortal captain and controlling entity of a starship taking his human cargo across a thousand-year voyage, observing them with mingled compassion and disdain for their "mayfly" existence. Like a gardener, he cultivates, prunes, limits, and stimulates, and all the while we get an eerie sense of a human slowly developing into something *other* over the centuries. A similar tension between the hermetic and the oceanic pervades *ORA:CLE*, where the hero, Mr. Ale Elatey (AL L80) is liked by brain implant to a network of thousands of computer experts but never leaves the high-rise apartment where he and his wife live through their contacts on the network, and through other communication systems. As *Mayflies* may be said to reevaluate the experience of Heinlein's *Universe* and McCaffrey's *The Ship Who Sang*, *ORA:CLE* may be viewed as finding new possibilities in the closed environment of Silverberg's *The World Inside*.

O'Donnell's most ambitious project is the light-hearted Adventures of McGill Feighan, an open-ended series of picaresque travels among alien worlds by means of "flinging," a teleportation technique of which McGill is a rare possessor. The first four volumes in the series—*Caverns, Reefs, Lava,* and *Cliffs*—explore the intricacies of McGill's talent, human-alien encounter, the menace of a mob-like crime syndicate so powerfully parasitic it takes steps not to kill its host culture, and McGill's search for the Far Being, source of his flinging talent. Here O'Donnell's ability to compel sympathetic interest in his anomalous young hero helps him skirt the many improbabilities of the story line. Billed as "techno-fantasy," the inventive series shows a talent for humorous dialogue increasingly matched by pacing of incident and character development. A young writer still, O'Donnell shows great creative promise.

—Thomas P. Dunn

OFFUTT, Andrew J(efferson V.). Also writes as John Cleve. American. Born in Louisville, Kentucky, 16 August 1934 (?). Educated at the University of Louisville, B. A. in English 1955; M. A. in history; Ph. D. in psychology. Married Mary Joe McCarney McCabe in 1958; two daughters and two sons. Sales agent, Procter and Gamble, 1957-62; agency manager, Coastal States Life Insurance Company, Lexington, Kentucky, 1963-68; insurance agent, Andrew Offutt Associates, 1968-71. Since 1971, full-time writer: author of over 100 works under pseudonym John Cleve and others. Treasurer, 1973-76, and President, 1976-78, Science Fiction Writers of America. Recipient: *If* prize, 1954. Address: Funny Farm, Haldeman, Kentucky 40329, U.S.A.

SCIENCE-FICTION PUBLICATIONS

Novels

Evil Is Live Spelled Backwards. New York, Paperback Library, 1970.

The Castle Keeps. New York, Berkley, 1972; London, Magnum, 1978.

Messenger of Zhuvastou. New York, Berkley, 1973; London, Magnum, 1977.

Ardor on Aros. New York, Dell, 1973.

The Galactic Rejects (for children). New York, Lothrop, 1973.

The Genetic Bomb, with D. Bruce Berry. New York, Warner, 1975.

Chieftain of Andor. New York, Dell, 1976; as *Clansman of Andor*, London, Magnum, 1978.

My Lord Barbarian. New York, Ballantine, 1977; London, Magnum, 1979.

King Dragon. New York, Ace, 1980.

Novels as John Cleve (series: Spaceways in all books)

Of Alien Bondage. New York, Berkley, 1982.

Corundum's Woman. New York, Berkley, 1982.

Escape from Macho. New York, Berkley, 1982.

Satana Enslaved. New York, Berkley, 1982.

Master of Misfit. New York, Berkley, 1982.

Plunder. New York, Berkley, 1982.

The Manhuntress. New York, Berkley, 1982.

Under Twin Suns. New York, Berkley, 1982.

In Quest of Qalara. New York, Berkley, 1983.

The Yoke of Shen. New York, Berkley, 1983.

Star Slaver, with G. C. Edmondson. New York, Berkley, 1983.

The Iceworld Connection. New York, Berkley, 1983.

Jonuta Rising. New York, Berkley, 1983.

Assignment: Hellhole. New York, Berkley, 1983.

Starship Sapphire. New York, Berkley, 1984.

The Planet Murderer. New York, Berkley, 1984.

The Carnadyne Horde. New York, Berkley, 1984.

Race Across the Stars. New York, Berkley, 1984.

King of the Slavers. New York, Berkley, 1985.

Uncollected Short Stories

"And Gone Tomorrow," in *If* (New York), December 1954.

"Blacksword," in *Mind Partner,* edited by H. L. Gold. New York, Doubleday, 1961.

"Mandroid," with Robert Margroff and Piers Anthony, in *If* (New York), June 1966.

"The Forgotten Gods of Earth," in *If* (New York), December 1966.

"Swordsman of the Stars," with Robert Margroff, in *If* (New York), December 1967.

"Population Implosion," in *World's Best Science Fiction 1968,* edited by Donald A. Wollheim and Terry Carr. New York, Ace, 1968.

"The Defendant Earth," in *If* (New York), February 1969.

"The Book," with Robert Margroff, in *Orbit 8,* edited by Damon Knight. New York, Putman, 1970.

"Ask a Silly Question," in *Galaxy* (New York), July 1970.

"My Country, Right or Wrong," in *Protostars,* edited by David Gerrold and Stephen Goldin. New York, Ballantine, 1971.

"Sareva, In Memoriam," in *Fantasy and Science Fiction* (New York), March 1972.

"For Value Received," in *Again, Dangerous Visions,* edited by Harlan Ellison. New York, Doubleday, 1972; London, Millington, 1976.

"Meanwhile, We Eliminate," in *Future City,* edited by Roger Elwood. New York, Simon and Schuster, and London, Sphere, 1973.

"The Black Sorcerer of the Black Castle," in *Cosmic Laughter,* edited by Joe W. Haldeman. New York, Holt Rinehart, 1974.

"Tribute," with Robert Margroff, in *Eternity* (Sandy Springs, South Carolina), June 1974.

"Enchanté," in *Tomorrow,* edited by Roger Elwood. Philadelphia, Lippincott, 1976.

"Final Solution," in *Perry Rhodan 92-93*. New York, Ace, 1976.

"The Greenhouse Defect," in *Stellar Short Novels,* edited by Judy-Lynn del Rey. New York, Ballantine, 1976.

"Nekht Semerkeht," with Robert E. Howard, in *Swords Against Darkness,* edited by Andrew J. Offutt. New York, Zebra, 1977.

"Final Quest," in *Swords Against Darkness 2,* edited by Andrew J. Offutt. New York, Zebra, 1977.

"Shadowspawn," in *Thieves' World,* edited by Robert Asprin. New York, Ace, 1979; London, Penguin, 1984.

"Symbiote," in *New Terrors 2,* edited by Ramsey Campbell. New York, Pan, 1980.

"Little Boy Waiting at the Edge of the Darkwood," in *Elsewhere,* edited by Terri Windling and Mark Alan Arnold. New York, Ace, 1981.

"The Vivisectionist," in *Shadows of Sanctuary,* edited by Robert Asprin. New York, Ace, 1981.

"Godson," in *Storm Season,* edited by Robert Asprin. New York, Ace, 1982.

"Gone with the Gods," in *Analog's Lighter Side,* edited by Stanley Schmidt. New York, Davis, 1982.

"Rebels Aren't Born in Palaces," in *Wings of Omen,* edited by Robert Asprin and Lynn Abbey. New York, Ace, 1984.

"The Veiled Lady," in *Dead of Winter,* edited by Robert Asprin and Lynn Abbey. New York, Ace, 1985.

OTHER PUBLICATIONS

Novels

The Great 24-Hour Thing. Los Angeles, Orpheus Press, 1971.

Operation: Super Ms. New York, Berkley, 1974.

Sword of the Gael. New York, Zebra, 1975; London, Sphere, 1977.

The Undying Wizard. New York, Zebra, 1976.

Demon in the Mirror, with Richard K. Lyon. New York, Pocket Books, 1977.

Sign of the Moonbow. New York, Zebra, 1977.

The Mists of Doom. New York, Zebra, 1977.

Conan and the Sorcerer. New York, Grosset and Dunlap, 1978.

The Sword of Skelos. New York, Bantam, 1979.

The Iron Lords. New York, Harcourt Brace, 1979.

Shadows Out of Hell. New York, Berkley, 1980.

Conan the Mercenary (includes *Conan and the Sorcerer*). London, Sphere, 1980; *Conan the Mercenary* published New York, Ace, 1981.

When Death Birds Fly, with Keith Taylor. New York, Ace, 1980.

The Eyes of Sarsis, with Richard K. Lyon. New York, Pocket Books, 1980.

Web of the Spider, with Richard K. Lyon. New York, Pocket Books, 1981.

The Tower of Death, with Keith Taylor. New York, Ace, 1982.

The Lady of the Snowmist. New York, Ace, 1983.

Other

"How It Happened: One Bad Decision Leading to Another," in *Science-Fiction Studies* (Terre Haute, Indiana), July 1977.

"Stand Out," in *Writer's Digest* (Cincinnati), June 1978.

"VERYations on a Theme," in *Writer's Digest* (Cincinnati), 1979.

Editor, *Swords Against Darkness 1-5*. New York, Zebra, 5 vols., 1977-79.

* * *

Many science fiction and fantasy writers can be categorized according to the particular sub-genre in which they write. However, Andrew J. Offutt must be discussed in several sub-genres, from heroic fantasy to sociological science fiction.

Much of Offutt's early science fiction was obviously social criticism. *The Castle Keeps*, for example, is set in the same not-too-distant dystopian future as quite a bit of other science fiction; John Brunner's *Stand on Zanzibar* and *The Sheep Look Up* come immediately to mind. The world of *The Castle Keeps* is over-populated and poisonously polluted, and the society has devolved toward barbarism. The Andrews' home in the country is heavily fortified, and there is constant danger of being overrun by roving bands of looters and killers. In the city, the Caudills live inside a sealed-up apartment building from which they seldom emerge; outside, in spite of the official agencies, gangs are a threat by day and all-powerful by night. Throughout the novel, there are signs of how we, mid-20th-century Americans, got there.

Offutt can also write humorous science fiction and fantasy, often with a satiric bite. Short stories like "For Value Received" and "Population Implosion" satirize, among other things, one of Offutt's favorite targets, the medical profession. In "For Value Received," for example, he refers to the AMA as the American Magicians Association. In this story, Bob Barber is told that he cannot take his new baby daughter home before he pays the difference between what his insurance covers and the total bill. He refuses to do so, and Mary Ann Barber grows up in Saint Meinrad Medical Center. And *Ardor on Aros* is a humorous look at the heroic fantasy that Offutt himself seriously writes.

Offutt's heroic fantasy comes in two groups. The first group includes those stories which are essentially his own constructions, like *Messenger of Zhuvastou*. Scion Mark Keniston follows a beautiful woman, Elaine Dixon, supposedly his fiancée, to Helene, a planet which is the approximate cultural equivalent of early Imperial Rome. Because the planet is insulated from contact with more technologically advanced civilizations, Keniston must "go native" to follow Elaine onto the planet's surface. Disguised as an official messenger of the most powerful domain on the planet, Keniston sets out on his quest. The description of the planet and the portrayal of the heroic adventure are well-integrated so that the reader is able to envision quite clearly the world through which Keniston makes his way.

The second group of heroic fantasies, which seems to be occupying an increasing amount of Offutt's time, is based on characters created by Robert E. Howard. In fact, Offutt has selected one, Cormac mac Art, for extended consideration, and he admits, in the introduction to *Sword of the Gael*, that he is a Robert E. Howard fan and also "hopelessly in love with the Emerald Isle." This happy combination unites the heroic-age hero with a perfect historical setting, the Celtic/Viking period. Offutt skillfully mixes historical material from his own research with the literary history created by Howard to provide a cogent background for the adventures of Cormac mac Art and his Viking comrade, Wulfhere Skull-Splitter.

Heroic fantasy, socially critical science fiction, humor, and satire—Offutt writes them all and writes them well. His word output is tremendous, and not all of it is science fiction; many feel that not enough of it is science fiction.

—C. W. Sullivan III

OLIVER, (Symmes) Chad(wick). American. Born in Cincinnati, Ohio, 30 March 1928. Educated at the University of Texas, Austin, B. A. 1951; M. A. in English and anthropology 1952; University of California, Los Angeles, Ph. D. in anthropology 1961. Married Betty Jane Jenkins in 1952; two children. Instructor, 1955-59, Assistant Professor, 1959-62, Associate Professor, 1963-68, Department Chairman, 1967-71 and since 1980, and since 1968, Professor of Anthropology, University of Texas. Visiting Professor, University of California, Los Angeles, summer 1960; Research Anthropologist, National Science Foundation in East Africa, 1961-62. Recipient: Western Writers of America Spur Award, 1967. Agent: Scott Meredith Literary Agency, 845 Third Avenue, New York, New York 10022. Address: Department of Anthropology, University of Texas, Austin, Texas 78712-1086, U.S.A.

SCIENCE-FICTION PUBLICATIONS

Novels

Shadows in the Sun. New York, Ballantine, 1954; London, Reinhardt, 1955.
The Winds of Time. New York, Doubleday, 1957.
Unearthly Neighbors. New York, Ballantine, 1960; revised edition, New York, Crown, 1984.
The Shores of Another Sea. New York, New American Library, and London, Gollancz, 1971.
Giants in the Dust. New York, Pyramid, 1976.

Short Stories

Another Kind. New York, Ballantine, 1955.
The Edge of Forever, edited by William F. Nolan. Los Angeles, Sherbourne Press, 1971.

Uncollected Short Stories (series: Caravans Unlimited)

"King of the Hill," in *Again, Dangerous Visions*, edited by Harlan Ellison. New York, Doubleday, 1972; London, Millington, 1976.
"Second Nature," in *Future Quest*, edited by Roger Elwood. New York, Avon, 1973.
"Shaka" (Caravans), in *Continuum 1*, edited by Roger Elwood. New York, Putnam, 1974.
"Stability" (Caravans), in *Continuum 2*, edited by Roger Elwood. New York, Berkley, 1974.
"The Middle Man" (Caravans), in *Continuum 3*, edited by Roger Elwood. New York, Berkley, 1974.
"The Gift," in *Future Kin*, edited by Roger Elwood. New York, Doubleday, 1974.
"Monitor" (Caravans), in *Continuum 4*, edited by Roger Elwood. New York, Berkley, 1975.
"Community Study," in *Lone Star Universe*, edited by George W. Proctor and Steven Utley. Austin, Texas, Heidelberg, 1976.
"To Whom It May Concern," in *A Spadeful of Spacetime*, edited by Fred Saberhagen. New York, Ace, 1981.
"Meanwhile, Back on the Reservation," in *Analog* (New York), April 1981.
"Ghost Town," in *Analog* (New York), September 1983.

OTHER PUBLICATIONS

Novel

The Wolf Is My Brother. New York, New American Library, 1967; London, Jenkins, 1968.

Other

Mists of Dawn (for children). Philadelphia, Winston, 1952;
London, Hutchinson, 1954.
*Ecology and Cultural Continuity as Contributing Factors in the
Social Organization of the Plains Indians.* Berkeley, Univers-
ity of California Press, 1962.
The Discovery of Humanity: An Introduction to Anthropology.
New York, Harper, 1981.

*

Bibliography: by William F. Nolan, in *The Edge of Forever*,
1971.

Chad Oliver comments:

I wrote my first story when I was 14, and sold my first story (to
Anthony Boucher of *The Magazine of Fantasy and Science
Fiction*) when I was 22. I was a professional writer before I was
an anthropologist, and I suspect that I still am. I grew up with
science fiction and it has been an important part of my life.

I have written many kinds of stories and about all they have in
common is that I always tried to write as well as I could. I am not
interested in essays disguised as fiction; my stories are about
people and my opinion is that if they don't work on an emotional
level they don't work at all. I was strongly influenced by writers
outside the science-fiction field, notably Hemingway and
Steinbeck.

*   *   *

For a genre that deals freely in alien beings and cultures,
science fiction has often shown a marked tendency toward
simplistic anthropomorphism in handling such themes. Readers and editors who would demand the utmost verisimilitude
in fiction dealing with the natural sciences often allowed the
most naive applications of social science theory to pass
unnoticed in science-fiction stories, and it was not until well into
the 1950's that the social sciences began to take their place as
serious thematic material in popular science fiction. While
economics and sociology began to be treated with relative
sophistication by Frederik Pohl and other satirists of the *Galaxy*
-magazine school, the credit for introducing well-thoughtout
anthropological themes into popular American science fiction
of the 1950's rests almost solely with Chad Oliver. Himself a
professional anthropologist, Oliver dealt with alien cultures,
and the problems inherent in communicating with those
cultures, in a series of sympathetic and plausible stories and
novels that paved the way for later anthropological themes in
such writers as Ursula K. Le Guin.

Oliver's fiction tends heavily toward exposition and didacticism, but his pleasant, relaxed style and understated, non-heroic
characters work to make the lessons in cultural differentiation
and values easily palatable. When he treats a traditional theme,
such as the secret colonization of Earth by aliens in *Shadows in
the Sun,* he is apt to undercut the reader's expectations by
revealing early in the narrative the secret of the alien presence (in
this novel, they have completely taken over a small town in
Texas, without violence or murder), and focusing instead on the
more complex and interesting problem of what their motivations and values are. The equally familiar theme of the
generations-long space voyage, initially popularized by Robert
Heinlein in "Universe," in given a new twist in Oliver's
"Stardust" by the introduction of the problem of the culture
shock that the spaceship inhabitants might face if the
circumscribed environment that they have come to regard as the

universe is suddenly revealed to be only a machine. A "first
contact" story is also given a new twist, in "Scientific Method,"
by its simultaneous presentation from two opposing viewpoints. One of Oliver's favorite themes is the depiction of a
"primitive" alien culture that is really advanced, but in radically
different cultural terms from our own. This is the theme of "Rite
of Passage" and *Unearthly Neighbors;* the latter may be the most
carefully reasoned account of the problems of making contact
with an alien culture in all of science fiction.

Much of Oliver's fiction clearly draws on his own
experiences—his familiarity with small-town Texas culture in
Shadows in the Sun, his hobby of trout fishing in *The Winds of
Time,* his experiences in Kenya in *The Shores of Another Sea.* In
the last novel particularly the science-fiction theme seems to be
decidedly secondary to the portrayal of life on a baboonery in
the bush country of Kenya. Relatively few of his stories deal
with future societies, and his portrayals of technologically
advanced earth societies (as in *Unearthly Neighbors*) seem
somewhat stilted and uncomfortable. His real strengths lie in the
construction of hypothetical anthropological problems and his
graceful, understated style. Although he has produced relatively
little science fiction, what there is is valuable both for the specific
insights it offers and for the importance it holds in the
developing sophistication of the genre.

—Gary K. Wolfe

OLSEN, Bob (Alfred John Olsen, Jr.). American. Born in 1884.
Educated at Brown University, Providence, Rhode Island, A. B.
(Phi Beta Kappa). *Died 20 May 1956.*

SCIENCE-FICTION PUBLICATIONS

Short Stories

Rhythm Rides the Rocket. New York, Columbia, 1940.

Uncollected Short Stories (series: Four Dimensional; Justin
Pryor)

"Four Dimensional Surgery," in *Amazing* (New York),
February 1928.
"Four Dimensional Robberies," in *Amazing* (New York), May
1928.
"The Educated Pill," in *Amazing* (New York), July 1928.
"Four Dimensional Transit," in *Amazing Stories Quarterly*
(New York), Fall 1928.
"The Superperfect Bride," in *Amazing* (New York), July 1929.
"Flight in 1999," in *Air Wonder Stories* (New York), September
1929.
"The Phantom Teleview," in *Science Wonder Stories* (New
York), November 1929.
"Cosmic Trash," in *Science Wonder Stories* (New York), April
1930.
"The Man Who Annexed the Moon," in *Amazing* (New York),
February 1931.
"The Master of Mystery" (Pryor), in *Amazing* (New York),
October 1931.
"The Ant with a Human Soul," in *Amazing Stories Quarterly*
(New York), Spring-Summer 1932.
"Seven Sunstrokes" (Pryor), in *Amazing* (New York), April
1932.

"The Purple Monsters," in *Amazing* (New York), August 1932.
"Captain Brink of the Space Marines," in *Amazing* (New York), November 1932.
"The Pool of Death" (Pryor), in *Amazing* (New York), January 1933.
"The Crime Crusher," in *Amazing* (New York), June 1933.
"The Four Dimensional Escape," in *Amazing* (New York), December 1933.
"Peril among the Drivers," in *Amazing* (New York), March 1934.
"The Four Dimensional Auto-Parker," in *Amazing* (New York), July 1934.
"Noekken of Norway," in *Amazing* (New York), November 1934.
"Six-Legged Gangsters," in *Amazing* (New York), June 1935.
"The Isle of Juvenescence," in *Amazing* (New York), June 1936.
"The Space Marines and the Slavers," in *Amazing* (New York), December 1936.
"The Scourge of a Single Cell," in *Science Fiction* (Holyoke, Massachusetts), March 1940.
"Our Robot Maid," in *Future* (New York), November 1940.
"The Four Dimensional Roller-Press," in *Every Boy's Book of Science Fiction*, edited by Donald A. Wollheim. New York, Fell, 1951.
"The Drawbridge Horror," in *Phantom* (Bolton, Lancashire), July 1958.

OTHER PUBLICATIONS

Other

"Wanted: A Definition for SF," in *Future* (New York), Summer 1957.

* * *

Bob Olsen was among the earliest protégés of the editor Hugo Gernsback, who introduced him to *Amazing Stories* readers in 1927 and was soon pronouncing him "the possessor of a fertile mind with a turn for good writing." He begins with a series of ingenious treatments of the fourth dimension theme, to which he returned more than once in the course of earning a reputation over the next decade as a "distinguished" contributor, if only on account of his consistent popularity.

Some of his early offerings were more like popular lectures than stories, most of the dialogue emanating from his scientist hero, Professor Archimedes Banning, in "Four Dimension Transit" and "The Man Who Annexed the Moon"—a tale of the first lunar voyage, fairly typical of the period, which today seems uncannily predictive. Another stock character, Justin Pryor, a merchandising counsellor with a yen for criminal investigation, was featured in "The Master of Mystery" and "Seven Sunstrokes." An outstanding story was "The Ant with a Human Soul" in which the subject of a bizarre experiment in brain transference relates his experiences while "going native" among the ants. Two years later the author treated much the same idea to greater effect, with more human interest and less text-book detail, in "Peril Among the Drivers." And in "Six-Legged Gangsters" he told a simple story of formicary antics from the viewpoint of the insects themselves. He was also fascinated by the amoeba, a voracious specimen of which lurked in "The Pool of Death," another Justin Pryor mystery. It was to be found in its natural surroundings in "Noekken of Norway," which clearly betrayed the author's Scandinavian antecedents. And the amoeba-men of Titan were the villains "Captain Brink of the Space Marines" had to contend with.

In a mood close to satire, in "The Purple Monsters" he made light of an invasion of New York by nightmarish giants from Ganymede. "The Crime Crusher" brought criminals to book with a device which photographed their misdeeds in retrospect; and "The Four Dimensional Auto-Parker" offered a solution to a problem which, even in 1934, vexed Los Angeles motorists. By that time Olsen had also added jailbreaking to the list of possibilities—including surgery and bank robbery—presented by the exploitation of hyperspace.

—Walter Gillings

———————

O'NEILL, Joseph (James). Also wrote as Seosamh O'Neill. Irish. Born in Tuam, County Galway, 18 December 1878. Educated at St. Jarlath's College, Tuam, 1893-98; Queen's College, Galway, 1898-1901, B. A., M. A. in modern literature; Kuno Meyer's School of Irish Learning; Victoria College, Manchester; University of Freiburg, 1907. Married Mary Devenport in 1908. Taught at Queen's College, Galway, 1901-03; staff member, Department of Secondary Education: Inspector of Schools, from 1908, and Permanent Secretary, 1923-44; also civil service commissioner and local appointments commissioner, 1926-46. Recipient: Irish Academy of Letters Harmsworth Award, 1935. Member, Irish Academy of Letters. *Died 6 May 1952.*

SCIENCE-FICTION PUBLICATIONS

Novels

Wind from the North. London, Cape, 1934.
Land under England. London, Gollancz, and New York, Simon and Schuster, 1935.
Day of Wrath. London, Gollancz, 1936.

OTHER PUBLICATIONS

Novels

Philip. London, Gollancz, 1940.
Chosen by the Queen. London, Gollancz, 1947.

Play

The Kingdom-Maker (as Seosamh O'Neill), lyrics by Mary Devenport O'Neill. Dublin, Talbot Press, and London, Unwin, 1918.

* * *

Joseph O'Neill wrote five novels, a play, some criticism, some poetry and a few scholarly papers. Of his novels, three may be regarded as science fiction, though the connection is sometimes tenuous. *Wind from the North* is a well-written time-travel story of Norsemen in Dublin in the 11th century; the emphasis is on the conflict between the hero's 11th-century and 20th-century selves. *Day of Wrath* is a prophetic potboiler about an airwar involving "the Yellow Alliance" and Nazi aggressors against Russia, "the Latin Alliance," and, eventually, Great Britain and the United States; the aftermath of its poison gas and thermite bombs is a vivid picture of the breakdown of civilized behavior but it is not especially exciting either as science fiction or as novel.

Land under England is a work of power that was justly well received when first published and then almost forgotten until recently. It is doubtless worth noting that of all O'Neill's works only this one—despite the fact that *Wind from the North* received the Harmsworth Prize—was widely reviewed, and that only this one has been reprinted. Even so, except for passing references critical evaluation of the work is largely confined to reviews that appeared in 1935.

Part of the attraction of the novel is the development from an almost innocent beginning through an adventurous though fantastic journey into a world of horror that gradually becomes prophetic of doom not only for the protagonist but for the world at large. The story begins with devices like those of second-rate fantasy: the Julians are an old family tracing their origins back to Roman Britain; they live along the Roman Wall on property believed to possess the entrance to an underground world. There are half-believed stories of ancestors who have disappeared and returned with stories of a strange land beyond the mysterious entrance. Anthony Julian, the narrator, is the only child of two dramatically opposite types both of whom believe in the old legends, his father in the years following World War I, to the point of obsession; when he disappears, both wife and son are convinced that he has found the entrance. Tony, whose hero-worship of his father is the driving force of the book, is equally convinced that he will some day be found.

Tony's accidental discovery of the entrance in a dried-up pond and unhesitating plunge down the slope into the underworld are the obvious and expected result of what has gone before. What is not obvious or expected is what happens thereafter, and it is in this respect that the novel departs from the ordinary to become something of a minor masterpiece.

In this underground world are many curious, strange, and frequently alarming creatures, both plant and animal. But nothing is more curious, stranger, or more alarming than its human inhabitants. At first encounter they appear to be civilized and enough like the ancient Romans who had inhabited the land above that Tony speaks to them in Latin, but there is no reply and he realizes that all communication is through some kind of mind talk. When his early failure to understand this causes the master of the ship on which he first takes refuge to regard him as ill, and curable only by the Masters of Will and of Knowledge to whom he is sent, he soon learns that in this different and horrifying society control is through the minds of a few leaders who work their will on the rest of the populace. The remainder of the story deals with Tony's unceasing efforts to locate his father, to understand the ways of this fearful society, and eventually, his father obviously lost to him forever, to undertake the grueling flight back to the upper world.

If one pays attention only to the monstrous plants and animals and the even more monstrous leaders of the underworld society, *Land under England* remains only a good fantastic adventure. But if one remembers the time when it was written, it becomes a warning of the future that the totalitarian societies of the 1930's, especially that of Nazi Germany, might bring to England. When taken together with the search for self in *Wind from the North* and the polemical picture of brute mankind when the veneer of civilization is removed in *Day of Wrath*, it provides evidence of O'Neill's continuing effort to understand the hidden drives and motivations that still plague humanity. There are political and psychological aspects to this almost allegorical tale that move it to a higher level than most such works of the time, and O'Neill can justly be regarded as a minor but significant figure whose work prefigures the kind of social science fiction

and fantasy that became prominent in the immediate postwar years.

—Arthur O. Lewis

ORWELL, George. Pseudonym for Eric Arthur Blair. British. Born of English parents in Motihari, Bengal, India, 25 June 1903; brought to England, 1904. Educated at a convent school, Henley-on-Thames, Oxfordshire; St. Cyprian's, Eastbourne, Sussex, 1911-16; Wellington School, 1917; Eton College (King's Scholar), 1917-21. Served in the United Marxist Workers' Party militia in Catalonia, 1937: wounded in action; served in the Home Guard, 1940-43: Sergeant. Married 1) Eileen O'Shaughnessy in 1936 (died, 1945), one adopted son; 2) Sonia Mary Brownell in 1949. Served in the Imperial Indian Police in Burma: at Police Training School, Rangoon, 1922-23, Assistant Superintendent of Police at Myaungmya, 1923, Twante, 1924, Syriam, 1925, Insein, 1925-26, Moulmein, 1926, and Katha, 1927 (resigned 1927); lived in London, 1927, and Paris, 1928-29 (worked briefly as dishwasher, 1929); tutor, Southwold, Suffolk, 1930; lived in London, 1930-31; headmaster, The Hawthorns, Hayes, Middlesex, 1932-33, and teacher at Frays College, Uxbridge, 1933; worked at Booklovers' Corner bookshop, London, 1934-36; shopkeeper, Wallingford, Hertfordshire, 1936-40; talks producer in the Empire Department, BBC, London, 1941-43. Free-lance writer from 1935: reviewer, *New English Weekly*, 1935-36, *Time and Tide*, 1940-41, *Tribune*, 1940-47 (Literary Editor, 1943-45), and *Horizon*, 1940-49, all London; columnist ("London Letter"), *Partisan Review*, New York, 1941-46; Editor, with T. R. Fyvel, Searchlight Books series, Secker and Warburg, publishers, London, 1941-42; regular contributor, *Observer*, London, 1942-49 (war correspondent, 1945); columnist, Manchester *Evening News*, 1943-46. Lived on Jura, Hebrides Islands, Scotland, 1946-47. *Died 21 January 1950.*

SCIENCE-FICTION PUBLICATIONS

Novel

Nineteen Eighty-Four. London, Secker and Warburg, and New York, Harcourt Brace, 1949; edited by Bernard Crick, Oxford, Oxford University Press, 1984.

OTHER PUBLICATIONS

Novels

Burmese Days. New York, Harper, 1934; London, Gollancz, 1935.
A Clergyman's Daughter. London, Gollancz, and New York, Harper, 1935.
Keep the Aspidistra Flying. London, Gollancz, 1936; New York, Harcourt Brace, 1954.
Coming Up for Air. London, Gollancz, 1939; New York, Harcourt Brace, 1950.
Animal Farm: A Fairy Story. London, Secker and Warburg, 1945; New York, Harcourt Brace, 1946.

Plays

Radio Plays: *The Voyage of the Beagle,* from work by Darwin, 1946; *Animal Farm,* from his own novel, 1947.

Other

Down and Out in Paris and London. London, Gollancz, and New York, Harper, 1933.

The Road to Wigan Pier. London, Gollancz, 1937; New York, Harcourt Brace, 1958.

Homage to Catalonia. London, Secker and Warburg, 1938; New York, Harcourt Brace, 1952.

Inside the Whale and Other Essays. London, Gollancz, 1940.

The Lion and the Unicorn: Socialism and the English Genius. London, Secker and Warburg, 1941; New York, AMS Press, 1976.

Critical Essays. London, Secker and Warburg, 1946; as *Dickens, Dali and Others: Studies in Popular Culture*, New York, Reynal, 1946.

James Burnham and the Managerial Revolution. London, Socialist Book Centre, 1946.

The English People. London, Collins, 1947; New York, Haskell House, 1974.

Shooting an Elephant and Other Essays. London, Secker and Warburg, and New York, Harcourt Brace, 1950.

Such, Such Were the Joys. New York, Harcourt Brace, 1953; as *England, Your England and Other Essays*, London, Secker and Warburg, 1953.

A Collection of Essays. New York, Doubleday, 1954.

The Orwell Reader, edited by Richard H. Rovere. New York, Harcourt Brace, 1956.

Selected Essays. London, Penguin, 1957; as *Inside the Whale and Other Essays*, 1975.

Selected Writings, edited by George Bott. London, Heinemann, 1958.

Collected Essays. London, Secker and Warburg, 1961.

Decline of English Murder and Other Essays. London, Penguin, 1965.

The Collected Essays, Journalism, and Letters of George Orwell, edited by Sonia Orwell and Ian Angus. London, Secker and Warburg, 4 vols., 1968.

The Complete Works. New York, Harcourt Brace, 17 vols., 1984.

The War Broadcasts and *The War Commentaries*, edited by W. J. West. London, BBC Publications-Duckworth, 2 vols., 1985.

Editor, *Talking to India: A Selection of English Language Broadcasts to India.* London, Allen and Unwin, 1943.

Editor, with Reginald Reynolds, *British Pamphleteers 1: From the Sixteenth Century to the French Revolution.* London, Wingate, 1948.

*

Bibliography: "George Orwell: A Selected Bibliography" by Zoltan G. Zeke and William White, in *Bulletin of Bibliography 23* (Boston), May-August 1961; *George Orwell: An Annotated Bibliography of Criticism* by Jeffrey and Valerie Meyers, New York, Garland, 1977.

Manuscript Collection: University College, London.

Critical Studies (selection): *George Orwell* by Tom Hopkinson, London, Longman, 1953, revised edition, 1962; *George Orwell: A Literary Study* by John Atkins, London, Calder, 1954, New York, Ungar, 1955, revised edition, London, Calder and Boyars, 1971; *A Study of George Orwell, The Man and His Works* by Christopher Hollis, London, Hollis and Carter, and Chicago, Regnery, 1956; *The Crystal Spirit: A Study of George Orwell* by George Woodcock, Boston, Little Brown, 1966, London, Cape, 1967; *The Making of George Orwell: A Study in Literary History* by Keith Alldritt, London, Arnold, and New York, St. Martin's Press, 1969; *Orwell's Fiction* by Robert A. Lee, Notre Dame, Indiana, University of Notre Dame Press, 1969; *The World of George Orwell* edited by Miriam Gross, London, Weidenfeld and Nicolson, 1971, New York, Simon and Schuster, 1972; *Orwell* by Raymond Williams, London, Fontana, and New York, Viking Press, 1971, and *George Orwell: A Collection of Critical Essays* edited by Williams, Englewood Cliffs, New Jersey, Prentice Hall, 1974; *The Unknown Orwell* by Peter Stansky and William Abrahams, London, Constable, and New York, Knopf, 1972, *Orwell: The Transformation* by Stansky, London, Constable, 1979, New York, Knopf, 1980, and *On Nineteen Eighty-Four* edited by Stansky, New York, Freeman, 1984; *A Reader's Guide to George Orwell*, London, Thames and Hudson, 1975, Totowa, New Jersey, Rowman and Littlefield, 1977, and *George Orwell: The Critical Heritage*, London, Routledge, 1975, both edited by Jeffrey Meyers; *George Orwell and the Origins of 1984* by William Steinhoff, Ann Arbor, University of Michigan Press, 1975, as *The Road to 1984*, London, Weidenfeld and Nicolson, 1975; *The Road to Miniluv: George Orwell, The State and God* by Christopher Small, London, Gollancz, 1975, Pittsburgh, University of Pittsburgh Press, 1976; *Primal Dream and Primal Scream: Orwell's Development as a Psychological Novelist* by Richard I. Smyer, Columbia, University of Missouri Press, 1979; *George Orwell: A Life* by Bernard Crick, London, Secker and Warburg, 1980, Boston, Little Brown, 1981, revised edition, Secker and Warburg, 1981, and *Orwell Remembered* by Crick and Audrey Coppard, London, BBC, and New York, Facts on File, 1984; *Approaching 1984* by Donald McCormick, Newton Abbot, Devon, David and Charles, 1980; *George Orwell: The Road to 1984* by Peter Lewis, London, Heinemann, 1981; *George Orwell: A Personal Memoir* by T. R. Fyvel, London, Weidenfeld and Nicolson, 1982; *A George Orwell Companion* by J. R. Hammond, London, Macmillan, and New York, St. Martin's Press, 1982; *George Orwell's Guide Through Hell: A Psychological Study of 1984* by Robert Plank, San Bernardino, California, Borgo Press, 1984; *Orwell: The Road to Airstrip One* by Ian Slater, New York, Norton, 1985.

*   *   *

George Orwell's world-wide reputation as a writer of science fiction rests upon a single novel, *Nineteen Eighty-Four.* Such is the dynamic force of this work that the title of the book has become a universal symbol for the totalitarian nightmare. Although indisputably an SF novel, it differs from most other works in the genre by having an overt political purpose. In the author's own words he desired "to push the world in a certain direction, to alter other people's idea of the kind of society they should strive after. " His experiences while fighting alongside the Anarchists in the Spanish Civil War had opened his eyes to the "expedient inhumanities" which lay behind both international Communism and European Fascism. From now on in any conflict between the individual human being and the State Orwell was always to be found on the side of the underdog. Orwell's international stature was first established with *Animal Farm*, a classic Swiftian satire on the Soviet experiment. The runaway success of this work ensured that his next book would be given wide critical attention. When *Nineteen Eighty-Four* first appeared it was initially hailed in many quarters as a further trenchant indictment of Soviet Communism though, in fact, it is an indictment of absolutism of whatsoever political hue. Its conception owes a great deal to Eugene Zamyatin's *We* which Orwell had first read in a French translation some 20 years previously

The plot of *Nineteen Eighty-Four* is straightforward. The story follows the tragic fortues of Winston Smith, a minor civil servant, who lives and works in the London which has survived an atomic Third World War. This London is now the capital of Airstrip One, an off-shore province of Oceania, one of three constantly warring world-power blocs, Oceania, Eurasia, Eastasia. Under the absolute control of the Party and its Leader, Big Brother, the society of Oceania is stratified into the Inner Party (the rulers), the Party (the bureaucracy), and the rest (known collectively as the Proles). The complete ascendency of the Party is symbolized by the four Ministries which dominate Winston Smith's decaying urban metropolis. These are, in order of significance, the Ministry of Love, the Ministry of Truth, the Ministry of Peace, and the Ministry of Plenty:

> The Ministry of Love was the really frightening one. There were no windows in it at all. Winston had never been inside the Ministry of Love, nor within half a kilometre of it. The place was impossible to enter except on official business, and then only by penetrating through a maze of barbed-wire entanglements, steel doors and hidden machine-gun nests. Even the streets leading up to its outer barriers were roamed by gorilla-faced guards in black uniforms, armed with jointed truncheons.

Winston works in the Ministry of Truth whose slogans are "War is Peace. Freedom is Slavery. Ignorance is Strength." His job is to re-write items of recent history in Newspeak (the official Party language) in such a way that it accords with the official Party line. Watched over at all hours of the day and night by the ubiquitous telescreens of the dreaded Thought Police, Winston rebels against the system and commits the crime of falling in love with a fellow Party worker. For a brief spell he enjoys a precarious happiness only to learn, in what is surely one of the most horrendous passages in the whole of SF, that the Party has simply been toying with him all along. He is dragged into the Ministry of Love, and his total physical and spiritual degradation begins as the Party, in the person of the Torquemadian Senior Official O'Brien, sets about the task of extinguishing Winston's one precious spark of individual humanity—his moral conscience. The end is inevitable and horrifying. By a series of physical and psychological tortures Winston Smith as a person is totally erased and is then re-created in the Party's image until, in the end, "he loves Big Brother." Orwell's vision of a future in which the acquisition and tenure of absolute power is the only aspiration left to man is truly terrifying. "Power is not a means, it is an end," O'Brien tells Winston Smith. "If you want a picture of the future, imagine a boot stamping on a human face—for ever."

Nineteen Eighty-Four is a cautionary tale on a heroic scale; its initial impact on an immediately post-war world still groggy from the revelations of the Nazi extermination camps and the tales of Russian defectors to the West is not difficult to imagine. What still gives the story its tremendous emotional force is the intensity with which Orwell has expressed in fictional terms his passionately held belief in individual human freedom. All in all *Nineteen Eighty-Four* seems likely to retain its position as the most powerful as well as the most widely read science-fiction novel of the century.

—Richard Cowper

OSBORNE, David. See **SILVERBERG, Robert.**

PADGETT, Lewis. See **KUTTNER, Henry; MOORE, C. L.**

PALMER, Raymond A. Also wrote as Henry Gade; G. H. Irwin; Frank Patton; J. W. Pelkie; Wallace Quitman; A. R. Steber; Morris J. Steele. American. Born in Wisconsin, 1 August 1910. Crippled from childhood. Editor and publisher; Editor, *The Comet*, fan magazine, 1930; *Amazing Stories*, 1938-49; *Fantastic Adventures*, 1939-49; *Other Worlds* (later *Science Stories* and *Flying Saucers from Other Worlds*), 1950-57; *Imagination Science Fiction*, 1950; *Universe Science Fiction*, 1953-55; *Fate and Mystic* (later *Search*) in the 1950's; *The Hidden World* in the 1960's. *Died 15 August 1977.*

SCIENCE-FICTION PUBLICATIONS

Uncollected Short Stories

"The Time Ray of Jandra," in *Wonder Stories* (New York), June 1930.
"The Time Tragedy," in *Wonder Stories* (New York), December 1934.
"The Symphony of Death," in *Amazing* (New York), December 1935.
"Three from the Test Tube," in *Wonder Stories* (New York), November 1936.
"Matter Is Conserved," in *Astounding* (New York), April 1938.
"Catalyst Planet," in *Thrilling Wonder Stories* (New York), August 1938.
"Outlaw of Space" (as Wallace Quitman), in *Amazing* (New York), August 1938.
"The Vengeance of Martin Brand" (as G. H. Irwin), in *Amazing* (New York), August 1942; expanded edition, as "The Justice of Martin Brand," in *Other Worlds* (New York), July 1950.
"Red Coral," in *Other Worlds* (New York), May 1951.
"Tarzan Never Dies," in *Other Worlds* (New York), May 1955.

Uncollected Short Stories as A. R. Steber

"The Blinding Ray," in *Amazing* (New York), August 1938.
"Black World," in *Amazing* (New York), March 1940.
"When the Gods Make War," in *Amazing* (New York), July 1940.
"Moon of Double Trouble," in *Amazing* (New York), March 1945.

Uncollected Short Stories as Morris J. Steele

"Polar Prison," in *Amazing* (New York), December 1938.
"The Phantom Enemy," in *Amazing* (New York), February 1939.
"Weapon for a Wac," in *Amazing* (New York), September 1944.

Uncollected Short Stories as Henry Gade

"Pioneer—1957," in *Fantastic Adventures* (New York), November 1939.

"Liners of Space," in *Amazing* (New York), December 1939.
"The Invincible Crime Buster," in *Amazing* (New York), July 1941.

Uncollected Short Stories as Frank Patton

"The Test Tube Girl," in *Fantastic Adventures* (New York), January 1942.
"Doorway to Hell," in *Fantastic Adventures* (New York), February 1942.
"A Patriot Never Dies," in *Amazing* (New York), August 1943.
"War Worker," in *Amazing* (New York), September 1943.
"Jewels of the Toad," in *Fantastic Adventures* (New York), October 1943.
"Mahaffey's Mystery," in *Other Worlds* (New York), March 1950.
"The Identity of Sue Tenet," in *Other Worlds* (New York), December 1952.
"Question Please," in *Other Worlds* (New York), April 1953.
"Sure Thing," in *Science Stories* (Evanston, Illinois), February 1954.
"The Secret of Pierre Cotreau," in *Science Stories* (Evanston, Illinois), April 1954.

Uncollected Short Stories as J. W. Pelkie (series: Toka in all stories)

"King of the Dinosaurs," in *Fantastic Adventures* (New York), October 1945.
"Toka and the Man Bats," in *Fantastic Adventures* (New York), February 1946.
"Toka Fights the Big Cats," in *Fantastic Adventures* (New York), December 1947.
"In the Sphere of Time," *Planet* (New York), Summer 1948.

* * *

Raymond A. Palmer was one of the earliest science-fiction fans, his activities dating from the late 1920's, and his major influence was as an editor. His first important assignment was the editorship of *Amazing Stories*, taken over from the moribund Teck Publications in 1938 by Ziff-Davis. Palmer discarded the on-hand inventory, quickly filled the magazine with new, adventure-oriented stories, and (perhaps most important) refurbished its drab appearance to create a lively, colorful package. Simultaneously he worked to bring the contents of the magazine in line with its new appearance.

He was immediately successful, and the following year was able to add a companion magazine, *Fantastic Adventures*. In a number of ways, Palmer's career remarkably paralleled that of the legendary John W. Campbell, Jr. Each editor brought on a stable of new writers, in addition to retaining (or re-recruiting) the best writers of a previous administration. Each editor also ran afoul of reader resistance when he attempted to introduce a variety of pseudoscientific cult material in the 1940's and 1950's. For Campbell it was Dianetics, and other oddities; for Palmer, it was first the Shaver Mystery, and later an infatuation with Flying Saucers. Much given to hucksterism and juvenile promotional appeals, Palmer met strong resistance in science fiction and withdrew to concentrate on occult publishing after 1957. However, his real achievements as an editor have been sorely underrated, and an examination of files of the magazines he edited reveals an absolute treasure-trove of overlooked material, by many leading writers. He lured Edgar Rice Burroughs back to the science-fiction magazines after an absence of 12 years. Palmer was the first editor to publish stories by Isaac Asimov, for all that the latter prefers to emphasize his later association with Campbell in his reminiscences. It is to be hoped that as the lingering bad taste of "Shaverism," "Saucerism," and Palmer's other regretable antics fades away, his very significant editorial contribution to modern science fiction will be more appreciated.

Palmer's own fiction, upon review, indicates a considerable talent but one which was not applied sufficiently consistently to produce a coherent body of works. In Palmer's earliest work, for Gernsback's *Wonder Stories*, he shows strongly the influence of early writers in the field. "The Time Ray of Jandra" reads like a throwback to the early 19th century, with a first-person narrator explaining the circumstances of his birth and naming, and continuing through over-long paragraphs to detail a discovery tale in which he is purely an observer rather than a participant. Before long, Palmer had fallen into the pulp style. His stories of the 1930's and 1940's show a fully developed set of pulp characteristics: simplistic but highly colored characterization, heavy doses of violent action, a reliance on coincidence and a strongly romantic bent. An excellent example, further embellished with occasional pseudo-scientific asides, is "The Test Tube Girl" (as Frank Patton). In his few stories published in the 1950's, Palmer appears to have overcome the worse excesses of his pulp period, and to have moved toward a less heavy-handed and melodramatic approach.

—Richard A. Lupoff

PANGBORN, Edgar. Also wrote as Bruce Harrison. American. Born in New York City, 25 February 1909. Educated at Brooklyn Friends School, graduated 1924; Harvard University, Cambridge, Massachusetts, 1924-25; New England Conservatory of Music, 1927. Served in the United States Army Medical Corps, 1942-45. Farmer in Maine, 1939-42; writer from 1946. Lived in Voorheesville, New York. Recipient: International Fantasy Award, 1955. *Died 1 February 1976.*

SCIENCE-FICTION PUBLICATIONS

Novels

West of the Sun. New York, Doubleday, 1953; London, Hale, 1954.
A Mirror for Observers. New York, Doubleday, 1954; London, Muller, 1955.
Davy. New York, St. Martin's Press, 1964; London, Dobson, 1967.
The Judgment of Eve. New York, Simon and Schuster, 1966; London, Rapp and Whiting, 1968.
The Company of Glory. New York, Pyramid, 1975.
The Atlantean Nights Entertainment. San Francisco, Pennyfarthing Press, 1980.

Short Stories

Good Neighbors and Other Strangers. New York, Macmillan, 1972.
Still I Persist in Wondering. New York, Dell, 1978.

OTHER PUBLICATIONS

Novels

A-100 (as Bruce Harrison). New York, Dutton, 1930.

Wilderness of Spring. New York, Rinehart, 1958.
The Trial of Callista Blake. New York, St. Martin's Press, 1961;
London, Davies, 1962.

*

Manuscript Collection: Mugar Memorial Library, Boston
University.

*   *   *

Edgar Pangborn's work, according to Damon Knight,
reflects "the regreful, ironic, sorrowful, deeply joyous—and
purblind—love of the world and all in it. " Pangborn sees
wonder in the ordinary, removing the reader from mundane
perceptions. Some readers resent this heightening of the
conventional. Knight sees Pangborn's magic as a veil obscuring
the story. "The author will not get out of the way, but forces you
to look through his own misty substance at what he wants you to
see. " A moment of reflection reveals that this sort of reaction
indicates a matter of taste. Pangborn is an individual writer who
directs the reader's perceptions; he does not write to the reader's
order. Pangborn's view of life is tragic, comic, serious, and
speculatively imagainative; his range is wider than many critics
suspect. He is one of the few writers of SF and fantasy who was
also a major fiction writer. His ideas were not always original,
but he always managed to transform them.

"Angel's Egg," Pangborn's first story, is a powerful and very
moving alien-contact story which pleads for tolerance and
patience in regard to humankind's fate. Often reprinted, this
story would have been enough to make a name for any writer.
Pangborn's first SF novel, *West of the Sun,* is a deeply felt story
of interstellar castaways, notable for its vividly realized settings,
complex characters, and a painful knowledge of human failing.
The sense of being there with the characters is overwhelming. *A
Mirror for Observers,* a story of alien observers on earth who
struggle between being watchers and meddlers, reaches Stapledonian heights of thought and feeling about the fate of
humanity, but without the Stapledonian vistas. Pangborn's
focus is more personal and intimate. Pangborn regarded
Wilderness of Spring as a historical novel. Set in colonial New
England, there is much in the story's pioneer spirit to interest the
SF reader (one of the characters becomes a scientist). *The Trial
of Callista Blake* is a novel on the theme of capital punishment.

Davy is Pangborn's most famous novel. Set 300 years after a
nuclear holocaust, the book is a memoir written by the title
character who grows from a bondsman to an ambitious leader
concerned with the fate of humanity. Funny and tragic, bawdy
and adventurous in the manner of *Tom Jones, Davy* is one of the
lasting works of SF. A similar work, but one involving a female
counterpart to Davy, *The Judgment of Eve* is not as well known,
but, filled with the agony of choices, the book will please anyone
who has enjoyed Pangborn's work. It has been suggested that
the ambiguous ending might have been the result of editorial
pressure to avoid depicting a *ménage-à-quatre. The Company of
Glory* is set in the same world as *Davy* and *The Judgment of Eve*
(though the Pyramid edition was censored as being "too
faggoty") *Still I Persist in Wondering* contains most of the
shorter works set in the world of *Davy.*

Pangborn's body of work is of a consistent high quality. A
reader who responds to his work will want to read it all; but
Pangborn is clearly not for everyone who reads science fiction.
The narrow genre addict cannot enjoy Pangborn without
widening his reading horizons. His work addressed itself to the
great problems of life and death, the mystery of existence,
personal worth. Paradoxically, science fiction, though it claims

to be a literature of ideas and wide vision, rarely rises above the
entertainment formulas. Pangborn helped keep alive the
tradition of "high science fiction," even while the pejorative
genre association with SF dragged down serious receptions of
his work. Above everything else, Pangborn brought an
overpowering sense of beauty to science fiction. *West of the Sun*
glows with an unwearying light: "I give you birth and death and
the journey of our days and nights between them, the shining of
green fields, and patience of the forest, the little stars, the great
stars, the love and the thought, the labor and the laughter, the
good morning sky. " *A Mirror for Observers* breathes with an
unwaning love: "Never, beautiful Earth, never even at the
height of the human storms have I forgotten you, my planet
Earth, your forests and your fields, your oceans, the serenity of
your mountains; the meadows, the continuing rivers, the
incorruptible promise of returning spring. " In trying to make us
see, hear, and feel the important things that we so often forget,
Pangborn aspired to the utterance of music, his first love.

—George Zebrowski

———————

PANSHIN, Alexei. American. Born in Lansing, Michigan, 14
August 1940. Educated at the University of Michigan, Ann
Arbor, 1958-60; Michigan State University, East Lansing, B.A.
1965; University of Chicago, M. A. 1966. Served in the United
States Army, 1960-62. Married Cory Seidman in 1969; two sons.
Librarian, Brooklyn Public Library, 1966-67; Visiting Lecturer
in science fiction, Cornell University, Ithaca, New York,
summers 1971-72. Recipient: Hugo Award, for criticism, 1967;
Nebula Award, 1968. Address: R. D. 1, Box 168, Riegelsville,
Pennsylvania 18077, U.S.A.

SCIENCE-FICTION PUBLICATONS

Novels (series: Anthony Villiers)

Rite of Passage. New York, Ace, 1968; London, Sidgwick and
Jackson, 1969.
Star Well (Villiers). New York, Ace, 1968.
The Thurb Revolution (Villiers). New York, Ace, 1968.
Masque World (Villiers). New York, Ace, 1969.
Earth Magic, with Cory Panshin. New York, Ace, 1978;
London, Magnum, 1980.

Short Stories

Farewell to Yesterday's Tomorrow. New York, Putnam, 1975;
augmented edition, New York, Berkley, 1976.
Transmutations: A Book of Personal Alchemy. Elephant,
Pennsylvania, Elephant Books, 1982.

OTHER PUBLICATIONS

Other

Heinlein in Dimension: A Critical Analysis. Chicago, Advent,
1968.
"Short SF in 1968," in *Nebula Award Stories 5,* edited by James
Blish. New York, Doubleday, and London, Gollancz, 1970.
SF in Dimension: A Book of Explorations, with Cory Panshin.
Chicago, Advent, 1976.
Mondi Interiori (in Italian), with Cory Panshin. Milan, Editrice
Nord, 1978.

*

Manuscript Collection: Bowling Green University, Ohio.

Alexei Panshin comments:
My first aim as an Sf writer is to tell good stories. To me, that means the solidest, most complete, truest stories I can imagine. My second aim is to make every story new in some way: new characters, new settings, new style, new to myself. For me, each story has its own unique voice, its own autonomy, and I've got to find it and respect it and love it into being.
Most of the tme I write stories slowly, and I get published even more slowly. 20 years after I first began to write, I've published five novels and one book of stories. An editor wrote to my first agent: "I used to thing Panshin wrote this way because he was stubborn. Now I think he just doesn't have a very interesting imagination. " I don't know which it is. All that I know is that the SF that I want to write is still beyond me, but I haven't giving up trying.

* * *

Alexei Panshin began publishing science-fiction stories as an undergraduate. He had already conceived and begun writing the Nebula Award novel *Rite of Passage* while serving in the army. The novel, an acknowledged science-fiction classic, is an anthroipological novel of the maturation of Mia havero, the 19-year-old narrator recalling her one month "trial. " The time is 150 years after the earth has been destroyed. The trial is a survival test that all 14-year-olds living on the asteroid star "ships" must undergo on a colony planet in order to be adult citizens. The point of view of an adolescent girl and her maturation are well done, though she and her friend, Jimmy Dentremont, seem rather precocious, particularly at the conclusion of the novel. In its psychological realism and the careful delineation of the "ship" society and the colony planet culture, *Rite of Passage* is Panshin's major fiction achievement.
The three Villiers novels, *Star Well, The Thurb Revolution,* and *Masque World,* follow the adventures of the titled Anthony Villiers and his inscrutable, unpredictable alien companion, Torve, the frog-like Torg. Each novel takes place on a different planet near or in the weak Nashua Empire. Panshin incorporates many comic elements, parodying space operas, spy thrillers, novels of intrigue, and regency and picaresque novels. The narrator is a cynical observer of the human comedy who interrupts the narrative with epigrammatic comments and short essays on human folly and absurdity. While amusing, the literary parody is occasionally labored and the relativistic, amoral narrator can become wearing. However, the emphasis on style and manner is appropriate to the genres being parodied and to the character of a rebellious, wandering aristocrat whose adventures are precipitated by the failure of his father's remittance to arrive. Sometimes Panshin's learning is brought in rather obviously. The novels become increasingly pessimistic. *Masque World* has the weakest plot and ends the most grimly.
Farewell to Yesterday's Tomorrow includes stories written between 1966 and 1975 and shows how deeply affected Panshin was by the revolutionary 1960's and early 1970's in America. "The Sons of Prometheus," "A Sense of Direction," and "Arpad" employ the basis situation of the asteroid star "ships" from *Rite of Passage.* "Sky Blue" reflects a concern with the rapacious development of planets and, by extension, the exploitation of earth's ecology. "When the Vertical World Becomes Horizontal" preaches the need for freedom and spontaneity to replace rigid social assumptions and behaviour. Panshin's disillusionment with the failure of the counter culture

of the early 1970's is apparent in "How Can We Sink When We Can Fly?" "Lady Sunshine and the Beatus" (written with his wife Cory) is a quest story and a phantasmagoric version of the Beauty and the Beast fairy tale. It ends the collection optimisticaly and romantically.
Earth Magic, also in collaboration with his wife, is an intriguing heroic fantasy which follows the adventures of Haldane, the son of Black Morca, a barbaric warrior tyrant. It is an exploration of the themes of change, identity, and reality versus vision or magic.

—Diane Parkin-Speer

PASSANTE, Dom. See FEARN, John Russell.

PATTON, Frank. See PALMER, Raymond A. ; SHAVER, Richard S.

PEDLER, Kit (Christopher Magnus Howard Pedler). British. Born in London, 11 June 1927. Educated at Ipswich School; King's College, University of London; Westminster Medical School, London, M. B. B. S. 1953, Ph. D., Member, College of Pathologists. Married Una Freeston in 1949; two daughters and two sons. Physician and surgeon in London and Greenwich hospitals, 1953-57; in general practice briefly; Senior Lecturer, then Reader in Pathology, then founded and headed the Anatomy and Electron Microscopy Department, for 12 years, University of London: resigned in 1971 to become free-lance writer: author of many radio and television documentaries and features. Honorary Secretary, Royal Microscopy Society. *Died 27 May 1981.*

SCIENCE-FICTION PUBLICATIONS

Novels with Gerry Davis

Mutant 59, The Plastic Eater. London, Souvenir Press, 1971; New York, Viking Press, 1972.
Brainrack. London, Souvenir Press, 1974; New York, Pocket Books, 1975.
The Dynostar Menace. London, Souvenir Press, and New York, Scribner, 1975.

OTHER PUBLICATIONS

Plays

Radio Plays: *Sunday Lunch; Trial by Logic.*

Television Plays: *Doctor Who* series (8 plays, 3 with Gerry Davis); *The Robot* (documentary); *Doomwatch* series (39 plays with Gerry Davis); *Galenforce,* with Gerry Davis.

Other

The Quest for Gaia: A Book of Changes. London, Souvenir Press, 1979.

Mind Over Matter: A Scientist's View of the Paranormal. London, Thames-Methuen, 1981.

*

Kit Pedler commented:

(1981) My science fiction has always had to do with small logical extensions of current reality. I am currently engaged on "Document from the Year 3," for example, which deals (post hoc) with the evolution of homo sapiens, and "The Logon" which are the result of mating between a mould and a microchip!

* * *

Kit Pedler and Gerry Davis wrote three popular disaster novels following their collaboration on BBC-TV's Doomwatch series and their creation of the Cybermen for *Doctor Who.* Strong on the science background, these novels are sometimes markedly weak as fictions because of poor characterization and, particularly in *The Dynostar Menace*, a reliance on stylistic and suspense clichés. Nevertheless, the narratives are at times remarkably exciting and well-sustained, as in the well-executed main sequence in *Mutant 59, The Plastic Eater*, when a small group is trapped in the London Underground by fire and explosion. Further, the authors sometimes achieve nice ironic and satirical effects, for instance, by well-timed narrative switches of focus from one character to another in *Mutant 59.*

As prophets of doom, Pedler and Davis seem to be telling us that we are unwise to rely on over-complicated mechanisms that are vulnerable to simple accidents, caused by unforeseen weaknesses or dangers in materials, human error, or simply the over-complication itself. If we heeded their warnings, we would take immediate steps drastically to simplify our lives. At the end of their second and strongest novel, *Brainrack*, this solution is rendered highly appealing by an idyllic evocation of a London without motor vehicles. The solution, perhaps unfortunately, is more convincing than the threats, which are needlessly fantastic. It is not strictly necessary to postulate the existence of a mutant virus that feeds on plastic (and finds abundant food when a new sun-degradable plastic is marketed), in order to explain severe disasters to airliners, submarines, and London. That men brought up in cities are suffering irretrievable brain damage because of an unsuspected ingredient of petrol is a highly unconvincing explanation of the destruction of a new nuclear power plant. It does not seem very likely that a satellite reactor will disrupt the ozone layer of earth's atmosphere and burn large areas of the surface of our planet. (Human greed and negligence are sufficient explanations, as in a disaster novel that is not regarded as SF, John D. MacDonald's *Condominium*). However, these startling threats are piquant and intriguing, and, to be fair to the writers, they take ample account of familiar human nature as a contributory cause of the disasters. What they like to do, in fact, is to make their point by showing how easy it is for various weaknesses inherent in a system to compound each other: the "plastic eater" is simply the icing on the cake. Pedler and Davis are particularly convincing when, in the early part of *Brainrack*, they expose the "EMMY" (man-machine interface) dangers: most of us know how easy it is to hit the wrong keys on typewriters, or misread simple instructions, or confuse colour codes. There is a grand tour de force in *Brainrack*, a long sustained narrative account of the effects of meltdown on the workers in a nuclear reactor. This is vivid and horrific and, except that some people survive, for the sake of the story, highly convincing.

The Dynostar Menace stands apart from the other two novels in being set in a closed environment, a space lab, and having the form of a kind of hard SF version of Christie's *Ten Little Niggers*. In this sort of plot, versions of which can often be found in TV series (*Blake's Seven*) or films (*Alien*), the actual nature of the threat is almost bound to be subordinated to the excitement of detection (here, of a saboteur) in a race against time. Exceptional imaginative power and skill, particularly in characterization, are needed to lift such a hackneyed plot from cliché and perhaps it is here that we can see how a background in TV script-writing may have been a disadvantage, particularly to Davis. However, their three works together constitute a notable contribution to disaster fiction and they were perhaps a shade unlucky to have slightly anticipated the greatest market for this branch of the genre.

—Michael J. Tolley

PELKIE, J. W. See **PALMER, Raymond A.**

PERCY, Walker. American. Born in Birmingham, Alabama, 28 May 1916. Educated at the University of North Carolina, Chapel Hill, B. A. 1937; Columbia University, New York, M. D. 1941; intern at Bellevue Hospital, New York, 1942. Married Mary Bernice Townsend in 1946; two daughters. Contracted tuberculosis, gave up medicine, and became a full-time writer, 1943. Recipient: National Book Award, 1962; American Academy grant, 1967; National Catholic Book Award, 1972; Los Angeles *Times* award, for non-fiction, 1983. Address: P. O. Box 510, Covington, Louisiana 70433, U.S.A.

SCIENCE-FICTION PUBLICATIONS

Novel

Love in the Ruins: The Adventures of a Bad Catholic at a Time Near the End of the World. New York, Farrar Straus, and London, Eyre and Spottiswoode, 1971.

OTHER PUBLICATIONS

Novels

The Moviegoer. New York, Knopf, 1961; London, Eyre and Spottiswoode, 1963.
The Last Gentleman. New York, Farrar Straus, 1966; London, Eyre and Spottiswoode, 1967.
Lancelot. New York, Farrar Straus, and London, Secker and Warburg, 1977.
The Second Coming. New York, Farrar Straus, 1980; London, Secker and Warburg, 1981.

Other

The Message in the Bottle: How Queer Man Is, How Queer Language Is, and What One Has to Do with the Other. New York, Farrar Straus, 1975.
Lost in the Cosmos: The Last Self-Help Book. New York, Farrar Straus, 1983.
Novel-Writing in an Apocalyptic Time. New Orleans, Faust, 1984.

Conversations with Walker Percy, edited by Lewis A. Lawson and Victor A. Kramer. Jackson, University Press of Mississippi, 1985.

*

Manuscript Collection: University of North Carolina, Chapel Hill.

Critical Studies: *The Sovereign Wayfarer: Walker Percy's Diagnosis of the Malaise* by Martin Luschei, Baton Rouge, Louisiana State University Press, 1972; *Walker Percy: An American Search* by Robert Coles, Boston, Little Brown, 1978; *The Art of Walker Percy: Stratagems for Being* edited by Panthea Reid Broughton, Baton Rouge, Louisiana State University Press, 1979; *Walker Percy: Art and Ethics* edited by Jac Tharpe, Jackson, University Press of Mississippi, 1980; *Walker Percy and the Old Modern Age: Reflections on Language, Argument, and the Telling of Stories* by Patricia Lewis Poteat, Baton Rouge, Louisiana State University Press, 1985.

*   *   *

In *Love in the Ruins*, his only work of science fiction, Walker Percy uses a chaotic future to dramatize our present chaotic and amoral state. Dr. Thomas More observes the end of life-as-we-know-it, watching from his Louisiana vantage-point as America polarizes into abstraction and lust, the polarization cause by heavy sodium and chloride escaping into the atmosphere from underground. More has a machine which can measure and treat the disorders these heavy chemicals cause. The novel takes place in the future, and a new mechanical invention is crucial to the plot: it *is* science fiction. However, the science would pass no laboratory test—it is symbolically, not scientifically, logical. More is a great deal like his famous namesake; holding out against sin (he never stops believing in God and love) with humorous self-effacement, he beats the devil, here named Art Immelmann. Abstraction and lust are referred to by "technical" and rather medieval terms, angelism and bestialism. The heavy chemicals are sulfur and brimstone, welling up from hell, and More's invention is a lapsometer, which measures and treats nothing less than the disorders of the soul. America is going to hell because of its tendency to polarize into pure abstraction and pure lust, and because it has failed a simple moral test, by violating every right of the black people it transported from Africa.

In "Notes for a Novel about the End of the World" (in *The Message in the Bottle*), Percy makes it clear that we are not to take the strange signs and portents of *Love in the Ruins* as the ephemera of a disordered mind, though More is clearly disturbed. It is the world which is in disorder: "It may be useful to write a novel about the end of the world. Perhaps it is only through the conjuring up of catastrophe, the destruction of all Exxon signs, and the sprouting of vines in the church pews, that the novelist can make vicarious use of catastrophe in order that he and his reader may come to themselves. " By making vividly concrete America's spiritual ills, and by warning us through his description of a possible future, Percy hopes to make his readers aware of their present condition. The result of his concretion is a witty and humane novel written in the philosophical tradition of the American romantics and William Faulkner which makes meaningful and entertaining use of science-fiction devices.

Percy makes only passing reference to science fiction in later works. The eponymous anti-hero of *Lancelot* talks of a chivalric "Third Revolution" and Will Barrett of *Second Coming* expect's Jesus's reappearance, but neither future ever materializes and life-as-we-know-it continues. The curious *Lost in the Cosmos: The Last Self-Help Book*, a statement of philosophy and a satire of pop psychology, uses hypothetical aliens and space odysseys in hypothetical situations to illustrate hypothetical questions. While it does not use science fiction, it uses the tools of the genre to discuss ideas.

—Joan Gordon

———————

PEREGOY, Calvin. See McCLARY, Thomas.

———————

PETAJA, Emil (Theodore). American. Born in Milltown, Montana, 12 April 1915. Educated at Montana State University, Bozeman, 1936-38. Office worker, 1938-41; film technician, Technicolor Corporation, Hollywood, 1941-46; photographer, 1947-63. Since 1963, full-time writer: Chairman, Bokanalia Memorial Foundation; since 1972, owner, SISU Publishers, San Francisco. Agent: Forrest J. Ackerman, 2495 Glendower Avenue, Hollywood, California 90027. Address: P. O. Box 14126, San Francisco, California 94114, U.S.A.

SCIENCE-FICTION PUBLICATIONS

Novels (series: Green Planet; Kalevala)

Alpha Yes, Terra No! New York, Ace, 1965.
The Caves of Mars. New York, Ace, 1965.
Saga of Lost Earths (Kalevala). New York, Ace, 1965.
The Star Mill (Kalevala). New York, Ace, 1965.
Tramontane (Kalevala). New York, Ace, 1966.
The Stolen Sun (Kalevala). New York, Ace, 1967.
Lord of the Green Planet. New York, Ace, 1967.
The Prism. New York, Ace, 1968.
Doom of the Green Planet. New York, Ace, 1968.
The Time Twister (Kalevala). New York, Dell, 1968.
The Path Beyond the Stars. New York, Dell, 1969.
The Nets of Space. New York, Berkley, 1969.
Seed of the Dreamers. New York, Ace, 1970
Lost Earths (omnibus). New York, DAW, 1979.

Short Stories

Stardrift and Other Fantastic Flotsam. Los Angeles, Fantasy, 1971.

Uncollected Short Stories

"The Storm-King," in *Dark Things,* edited by August Derleth. Sauk City, Wisconsin, Arkham House, 1971.
"Terrible Quick Sword," in *Signs and Wonders,* edited by Roger Elwood. Old Tappan, New Jersey, Revell, 1972.
"Gola's Hell," in *Witchcraft and Sorcery 8* (Alhambra, California), 1972.
"The White Magician," in Witchcraft and Sorcery 10 (Alhambra, California), 1974.

OTHER PUBLICATIONS

Verse

As Dream and Shadow. San Francisco, SISU, 1972.

Other

And Flights of Angels: The Life and Legend of Hannes Bok. San Francisco, SISU, 1968.

Editor, *The Hannes Bok Memorial Showcase of Fantasy Art.* San Francisco, SISU, 1974.
Editor, *Photoplay Edition.* San Francisco, SISU, 1975.

*

Emil Petaja comments:

My writing endeavors have mainly been to entertain, except for the factual material concerning Hannes Bok and fantasy art in general, which serves to indicate my enthusiasm for these subjects. My novels about the Finnish legendry epic *Kalevala: The Land of Heroes* spring from a lifelong interest in this fine poetic work. I own six translations of the *Kalevala,* as well as the work in the original. Both my parents were Finnish.

*   *   *

Though Emil Petaja published short fiction sporadically during the 1940's and 1950's, his important works were written in the 1960's. Most of these novels were published by Ace Books, and even those that were not followed the Ace formula: heavy on action, with some superficial romance. Though Petaja never sought to go beyond this formula, his innovations within its structure are impressive. Petaja's choice of story-material is the source of his appeal, for into the traditional settings of science fiction he transferred mythic heroes and situations, devoting particular attention to his own Finnish myth-heritage, the Kalevala story-cycle. Petaja deftly contrasts the sterile safety of centralized civilization (into which the hero is born) with the barbaric but vital hardship of primitive culture (into which the hero is initiated), and though the author concedes the necessity for both milieus, he emphasizes the greater need for preserving humanity's potential. Unlike most Ace "common man" heroes, Petaja's protagonists are strong, romantic-minded men, slightly alienated in progressive society, but greatly attuned to the poetry of myths. Ultimately the hero's ability to empathize with mythic situations is the factor which saves all of humanity—whether directly by battling destructive forces or indirectly by mastering the situation with poetic insight (*Alpha Yes, Terra No!*)

In the Kalevala-based novels the hero's empathy is deep enough to propel his psyche upon astral journeys, becoming merged with a Finnish hero endowed with magic (psychic?) powers. These are probably the best of Petaja's works because of their belief in an actual existence of the Finnish mythos, even by means of rationalizations like psychic powers and alien entities. Thus the mythos provides the structural basis for evoking the poetry of Finnish culture. Earlier authors' works had also rationalized myths into science fiction (Henry Kuttner's *Mask of Circe*), but Petaja is virtually the first to maintain limited fidelity to the cultural content of the myths, rather than manipulating it to fit melodramatic purposes.

Less successful, but equally colorful, are the two books of a planteary culture modeled on Irish story-cycles, though no particular myths are emphasied by the plots of *Lord of the Green Planet* and *Doom of the Green Planet.* The supernatural creatures of Irish myth are robots and alien entities, while the "Irish" are merely transplanted humans from other planets, all brought together by a mad Fenian poet with super-scientific resources. Though entertaining these books do not have the poetry of the Kalevala books, for the Irish culture is merely a giant mock-up rather than a shamanistic culture like the Finns', seen as surviving into the future. Furthermore, though the mythos-structure is less articulated, Petaja displays more dislike for the "progressive" civilization beyond the Green Planet than in earlier novels, and greater cognizance of the conflict between the appeal of heroism and the necessities of humanism.

Of the non-related books, the best is *The Path Beyond the Stars* in which a man and woman traverse several time-periods attempting to acquire knowledge of the universe's destruction—which they ultimately cannot prevent, though they can become the Adam and Eve of another cosmos. The other novels have less imaginative scope, but, in a melodramatic way, they all work toward the same goal: regeneration of the heroes' mythopoetic faculties, and thus the redemption of the profane world.

Petaja's importance to science fiction is that of a precursor of the increased use of myth in late 1960's SF. At their best his works suggest an archaic heritage of man not unlike the findings of anthropologist Mircea Eliade—a heritage which most contemporary writers, SF and mainstream alike, have chosen to neglect.

—Gene Phillips

PHILLIFENT, John T. See **RACKHAM, John.**

PHILLIPS, Frank. See **NOWLAN, Philip Francis.**

PHILLIPS, Mark. See **GARRETT, Randall; JANIFER, Laurence M.**

PHILLIPS, Rog (Roger Phillips Graham). Also wrote as Clinton Ames; Robert Arnette; Franklin Bahl; Alexander Blade; Craig Browning; Gregg Conrad; P. F. Costello; Inez McGowan; Melva Rogers; Chester Ruppert; William Carter Sawtelle; A. R. Steber; Gerald Vance; John Wiley; Peter Worth. American. Born in Spokane, Washington, in 1909. Educated at Gonzaga University, Spokane, A. B. ; graduate study at the University of Washington, Seattle. Married 1) Mari Wolf; 2) Honey Wood in 1956. Power plant engineer; shipyard welder during World War II; free-lance writer after the war: Columnist ("The Club House"), *Amazing,* New York, 1948-53. *Died in 1965.*

SCIENCE-FICTION PUBLICATIONS

Novels

Time Trap. Chicago, Century, 1949.
Worlds Within. Chicago, Century, 1950.

World of If. Chicago, Century, 1951.
The Involuntary Immortals. New York, Avalon, 1959.

Uncollected Short Stories (series: Lefty Baker)

"Let Freedom Ring," in *Amazing* (New York), December 1945.
"Vacation in Shasta," in *Fantastic Adventures* (New York), February 1946.
"Atom War," in *Amazing* (New York), May 1946.
"The Mutants," in *Amazing* (New York), July 1946.
"Dual Personality," in *Fantastic Adventures* (New York), September 1946.
"The Space" (as Roger P. Graham), in *Amazing* (New York), September 1946.
"Battle of the Gods," in *Amazing* (New York), September 1946.
"The House," in *Amazing* (New York), February 1947.
"So Shall Ye Reap," in *Amazing* (New York), August 1947.
"The Uninvited Jest," in *Amazing* (New York), September 1947.
"The Despoilers," in *Amazing* (New York), October 1947.
"High Ears," in *Fantastic Adventures* (New York), October 1947.
"Squeeze Play" (Baker; as Craig Browning), in *Amazing* (New York), November 1947.
"And Eve Was," in *Amazing* (New York), November 1947.
"Hate," in *Amazing* (New York), January 1948.
"Twice to Die," in *Fantastic Adventures* (New York), February 1948.
"The Supernal Note," in *Amazing* (New York), July 1948.
"Starship from Sirius, in *Amazing* (New York), August 1948.
"The Cube Root of Conquest," in *Amazing* (New York), October 1948.
"The Unthinking Destroyer," in *Amazing* (New York), December 1948.
"Brainstorm" (as Alexander Blade), in *Fantastic Adventures* (New York), December 1948.
"The Can Opener," in *Fantastic Adventures* (New York), January 1949.
"The Immortal Menace" (Baker), and "M'Bong-Ah," in *Amazing* (New York), February 1949.
"Quite Logical," in *Thrilling Wonder Stories* (New York), April 1949.
"She," in *Fantastic Adventures* (New York), April 1949.
"Unthinkable," in *Amazing* (New York), April 1949.
"The Last Stronghold" (as Chester Ruppert), in *Amazing* (New York), May 1949.
"The Robot Men of Bubble City," in *Fantastic Adventures* (New York), July 1949.
"The Shortcut," in *Amazing* (New York), July 1949.
"The Awakening," in *Amazing* (New York), August 1949.
"The Tangential Semanticist," in *Fantastic Adventures* (New York), August 1949.
"Incompatible," in *Fantastic Adventures* (New York), September 1949.
"Matrix," in *Amazing* (New York), October 1949.
"Planet of the Dead," in *Fantastic Adventures* (New York), October 1949.
"The Insane Robot" (Baker), in *Fantastic Adventures* (New York), November 1949.
"Venus Trouble Shooter" (as John Wiley), in *Other Worlds* (Evanston, Indiana), November 1949.
"Beyond the Matrix of Time," in *Amazing* (New York), November 1949.
"The Miracle of Elmer Wilde," in *Other Worlds* (Evanston, Indiana), November 1949.
"To Give Them Welcome" (as Melva Rogers), in *Other Worlds* (Evanston, Indiana), January 1950.
"This Time," in *Other Worlds* (Evanston, Indiana), January 1950.
"The Pranksters," in *Amazing* (New York), February 1950.
"Detour from Tomorrow," in *Fantastic Adventures* (New York), March 1950.
"The Fatal Technicality," in *Other Worlds* (Evanston, Indiana), March 1950.
"The Mental Assassins" (as Greg Conrad), in *Fantastic Adventures* (New York), May 1950.
"Slaves of the Crystal Brain" (as William Carter Sawtelle), in *Amazing* (New York), May 1950.
"The Lost Bomb," in *Amazing* (New York), May 1950.
"If You Were Me . . .," in *Amazing* (New York), June 1950.
"Victims of the Vortex" (as Clinton Ames), in *Amazing* (New York), July 1950.
"Warrior Queen of Mars" (as Alexander Blade), in *Fantastic Adventures* (New York), September 1950.
"Holes in My Head," in *Other Worlds* (Evanston, Indiana), October 1950.
"One for the Robot—Two for the Same," in *Imagination* (Evanston, Illinois), October 1950.
"Weapon from the Stars," in *Amazing* (New York), October 1950.
"A Man Named Mars" (as A. R. Steber), in *Other Worlds* (Evanston, Indiana), October, 1950.
"Love My Robot," in *Startling* (New York), November 1950.
"Rescue Beacon" (as Craig Browning), in *Other Worlds* (Evanston, Indiana), November 1950.
"These Are My Children," in *Other Worlds* (Evanston, Indiana), January, March 1951.
"You'll Die Yesterday," in *Amazing* (New York), March 1951.
"Secret of the Flaming Ring" (as P. F. Costello), in *Fantastic Adventures* (New York), March 1951.
"In What Dark Mind," in *Fantastic Adventures* (New York), April 1951.
"Vampire of the Deep," in *Amazing* (New York), May 1951.
"The Lurker," in *Fantastic* (New York), May 1951.
"The Man from Mars," in *Other Worlds* (Evanston, Indiana), May 1951.
"Who Sows the Wind," in *Amazing* (New York), June 1951.
"The President Will See You," in *Fantastic Adventures* (New York), July 1951
"Step Out of Your Body, Please," in *Amazing* (New York), November 1951.
"Remember Not to Die!," in *Fantastic Adventures* (New York), November 1951.
"Checkmate for Aradjo," in *Amazing* (New York), December 1951.
"No Greater Wisdom," in *Amazing* (New York), January 1952.
"The Visitors," in *Amazing* (New York), February 1952.
"The Old Martians," in *If* (New York), March 1952.
"The Unfinished Equation" (as Robert Arnette), in *Fantastic Adventures* (New York), April 1952.
"A More Potent Weapon," in *Fantastic Adventures* (New York), April 1952.
"The World of Whispering Wings," in *Amazing* (New York), May 1952.
"Destiny Uncertain," in *Imagination* (Evanston, Illinois), May 1952.
"Black Angels Have No Wings," in *Amazing* (New York), August 1952.
"All the Answers," in *Science Fiction Quarterly* (Holyoke, Massachusetts), August 1952.
"The Man Who Lived Twice," in *Fantastic Adventures* (New York), August 1952.

"Adam's First Wife," in *Amazing* (New York), September 1952.

"I'll See You in My Dreams," in *Fantastic Adventures* (New York), September 1952.

"It's in the Cards," in *Fantastic Adventures* (New York), October 1952.

"It's Like This," in *Fantastic Story* (New York), November 1952.

"Visitors from Darkness," in *Amazing* (New York), December 1952.

"The Sorceress," in *Amazing* (New York), January 1953.

"Ye of Little Faith," in *If* (New York), January 1953.

"The Menace," in *Fantastic Adventures* (New York), February 1953.

"Your Funeral is Waiting," in *Amazing* (New York), March 1953.

"The Lost Ego," in *Imagination* (Evanston, Illinois), April 1953.

"The Cyberene," in *Imagination* (Evanston, Illinois), September 1953.

"The Phantom Truckdriver," in *Amazing* (New York), September 1953.

"Pariah," in *Science Stories* (Evanston, Illinois), October 1953.

"From This Dark Mind," in *Fantastic* (New York), December 1953.

"The Cosmic Junkman," in *Imagination* (Evanston, Illinois), December 1953.

"Repeat Performance," in *Imagination* (Evanston, Illinois), January 1954.

"Teach Me to Kill," in *Amazing* (New York), June 1957.

"A Handful of Sand," in *Amazing* (New York), April 1957.

"Homestead," in *Fantasy and Science Fiction* (New York), August 1957.

"Executioner No. 43," in *Venture* (Concord, New Hampshire), September 1957.

"The Cosmic Trap" (as Gerald Vance), in *Fantastic* (New York), November 1957.

"World of Traitors," in *Fantastic* (New York), November 1957.

"Truckstop," in *Imaginative Tales* (Evanston, Illinois), November 1957.

"Captain Peabody," in *If* (New York), December 1957.

"Game Preserve," in *SF '58*, edited by Judith Merril. New York, Dell, 1958.

"Lefty Baker's Nuthouse," in *Imaginative Tales* (Evanston, Illinois), January 1958.

"Love Me, Love My—," in *Fantasy and Science Fiction* (New York), February 1958.

"Venusian, Get Out!," in *Amazing* (New York), April 1958.

"It's Better Not to Know," in *Fantastic* (New York), April 1958.

"Refueling Station," in *Imaginative Tales* (Evanston, Illinois), May 1958.

"Ground Leave Incident," in *Venture* (Concord, New Hampshire), May 1958.

"Space Is for Suckers" (as P. F. Costello), and "Prophecy, Inc.," in *Amazing* (New York), June 1958.

"Services, Inc.," in *Fantasy and Science Fiction* (New York), June 1958.

"Jason's Secret," in *Fantastic* (New York), September 1958.

"In This Dark Mind" (as Inez McGowan), in *Fantastic* (New York), September 1958.

"Unto the Nth Generation," in *Amazing* (New York), December 1958.

"The Yellow Pill," in *SF '59*, edited by Judith Merril. New York, Dell, 1959.

"The Gallery," in *Amazing* (New York), January 1959.

"The Creeper in the Dream," in *Fantastic* (New York), February 1959.

"Keepers in Space," in *Fantastic* (New York), April 1959.

"The Only One Who Lived," in *Fantastic* (New York), May 1959.

"Camouflage," in *Amazing* (New York), June 1959.

"But Who Knows Huer or Huen?" (Baker), in *Fantastic* (New York), November 1961.

"Rat in the Skull," in *Introductory Psychology Through Science Fiction*, edited by Harvey A. Katz, Martin H. Greenberg, and Patricia S. Warrick. Chicago, Rand McNally, 1977.

Uncollected Short Stories as Peter Worth

"The Robot and the Pearly Gates," in *Amazing* (New York), January 1949.

"I Died Tomorrow," in *Fantastic Adventures* (New York), May 1949.

"Window to the Future," in *Amazing* (New York), May 1949.

"Lullaby," in *Amazing Annual* (New York), 1950.

"Null F," in *Fantastic Adventures* (New York), February 1950.

"The Master Ego," in *Fantastic Adventures* (New York), March 1951.

"The Imitators," in *Amazing* (New York), June 1951.

Uncollected Short Stories as Franklin Bahl

"Face Beyond the Veil," in *Fantastic Adventures* (New York), April 1950.

"The Justice of Tor," in *Fantastic Adventures* (New York), January 1951.

"Lady Killer," in *Amazing* (New York), February 1953.

*   *   *

Rog Phillips (the name by which Roger P. Graham was generally known to science-fiction readers) became a professional writer in his mid-thirties, after several years as a power plant engineer and shipyard welder, and quickly established himself as a prolific and reliable producer of pulp fiction. Phillips used many pseudonyms, including several house names.

Until 1950 Phillips wrote exclusively for the Ziff-Davis magazines; his SF and fantasy fiction appeared in *Amazing Stories* and *Fantastic Adventures*. Phillips wrote everything from featured novels to short stories and fillers. A large part of this output was routine work done to editorial order, but it was often a notch or two above the general level of quality in the magazines, and was very popular with the readers. The first work to attract wide attention was the novel, "So Shall Ye Reap." Starting with the premise that the five atomic bombs already exploded by 1947 had released enough radioactivity into the atmosphere to affect the genes of future generations, the novel offered a scenario of the next hundred and fifty years, in which mankind established an elaborate underground civilization and retreated from the Earth's surface. Although marred by polemical stretches and badly dated now, the story nevertheless has some effective scenes and an overall crude energy. A sequel, "Starship from Sirus," added human colonies on Mars and Venus and an insect-dominated Earth in the far future, and was quite different in tone from its predecessor.

Four memorable Phillips stories appeared in 1949. "M'Bong-Ah" was a novelette telling of the colonization of Venus and of the Earthman who became the natives' pawn in their resistance to the invasion. "Matrix" and "Beyond the Matrix of Time" together form a complex story of time paradox and alternate realities. *The Involuntary Immortals* is the story of a group of "accidental" immortals who band together to discover the source of their immortality and to protect themselves against the vengefulness of their own jealous relatives.

Starting in 1950 Rog Phillips's stories had begun to appear in a wider variety of magazines. "Rat in the Skull" is a memorable story of an experiment in rodent intelligence; "Ground Leave Incident" is a hard-boiled episode on a frontier planet; "Services, Inc. " is an offbeat deal-with-the-Devil story. By far the most successful story Phillips ever wrote is "The Yellow Pill," a brief tale of multiple subjective realities.

—R. E. Briney

PIERCY, Marge. American. Born in Detroit, Michigan, 31 March 1936. Educated at the University of Michigan, Ann Arbor (Hopwood Award, 1956, 1957), A. B. 1957; Northwestern University, Evanston, Illinois, M. A. 1958. Married Ira Wood (third marriage) in 1982. Instructor, Indiana University, Gary, 1960-62; Poet-in-Residence, University of Kansas, Lawrence, 1971; Visiting Lecturer, Thomas Jefferson College, Grand Valley State Colleges, Allendale, Michigan, 1975; staff member,Fine Arts Work Center, Provincetown, Massachusetts, 1976-77; Writer-in-Residence, College of the Holy Cross, Worcester, Massachusetts, 1976; held Butler Chair of Letters, State University of New York, Buffalo, 1977. Recipient: Borestone Mountain Award, 1968, 1974; National Endowment for the Arts grant, 1977. Agent: Lois Wallace, Wallace and Sheil Agency, 177 East 70th Street, New York, New York 10021. Address: Box 943, Wellfleet, Massachusetts 02667, U.S.A.

SCIENCE-FICTION PUBLICATIONS

Novels

Dance the Eagle to Sleep. New York, Doubleday, 1970; London, W. H. Allen, 1971.
Woman on the Edge of Time. New York, Knopf, 1976; London, Women's press, 1979.

OTHER PUBLICATIONS

Novels

Going Down Fast. New York, Simon and Schuster, 1969.
Small Changes. New York, Doubleday, 1973.
The High Cost of Living. New York, Harper, 1978; London, Women's Press, 1979.
Vida. New York, Summit, and London, Women's Press, 1980.
Braided Lives. New York, Summit, and London, Allen Lane, 1982.
Fly Away Home. New York, Summit, and London, Chatto and Windus, 1984.

Play

The Last White Class: A Play about Neighborhood Terror, with Ira Wood (produced Northampton, Massachusetts, 1978). Trumansburg, New York, Crossing Press, 1980.

Verse

Breaking Camp. Middletown, Connecticut, Wesleyan University Press, 1968.

Hard Loving. Middletown, Connecticut, Wesleyan University Press, 1969.
A Work of Artifice. Detroit, Red Hanrahan Press, 1970.
4-Telling, with others. Trumansburg,New York, Crossing Press, 1971.
When the Drought Broke. Santa Barbara, California, Unicorn Press, 1971.
To Be of Use. New York, Doubleday, 1973.
Living in the Open. New York, Knopf, 1976.
The Twelve-Spoked Wheel Flashing. New York, Knopf, 1978.
The Moon Is Always Female. New York, Knopf, 1980.
Circles on the Water: Selected Poems. New York, Knopf, 1982.
Stone, Paper, Knife. New York, Knopf, and London, Pandora Press, 1983.
My Mother's Body. New York, Knopf, 1985.

Recordings: *Laying Down the Tower,* Black Box, 1973; *Reading and Thoughts,* Everett Edwards, 1976; *At the Core,* Watershed, 1978.

Other

The Grand Coolie Damn. Boston, New England Free Press, 1970.
Parti-Colored Blocks for a Quilt. Ann Arbor, University of Michigan Press, 1982.

*   *   *

Marge Piercy is a fairly prolific author, with several books of poetry and fiction to her credit, but of these only two can be claimed for science fiction. *Dance the Eagle to Sleep* is only peripherally within the genre, a vivid though unsatisfying picture of an attempt by young people to break away from society and set up a tribal-based, loving, and supportive community. It does point forward, as do many of Piercy's other writings to her most successful work, *Woman on the Edge of Time,* a vision of future utopia.

In one sense *Woman on the Edge of Time* has had more attention than it deserves: science fiction, utopian, and, above all, feminist scholars have written about the book extensively. On the othe hand, this is the best written of the many feminist utopias that have appeared in recent years, and, unlike most utopian works, it is a novel with believable characters, an interesting plot, and potential for implementation. That it is also a careful, complete portrayal of the kind of society a reformer of the early 1970's would envisage as an ideal future only adds to its importance, in the field of utopian literature at least. There are, of course, many elements that are common to science fiction: travel through time, alternative futures, advanced technology— both physical and mental, new social and sexual groupings, and most important of all, extrapolation of current knowledge to plausible and far-reaching conclusions.

The heroine is Connie Ramos, Chicana, welfare-mother wrongly charged with abusing her daughter, patient against her will in a mental hospital, and victim of various experimental medical "treatments,"including implantations of electrodes in her brain. Beginning as scattered dream immpression, then in a real presence at first frightening to Connie, Luciente—"from a village in Massachusetts—Mattapoisset. Only I live there in 2137"—gets through to her as the first contact from a future into which she is soon able to journey more and more easily. The story of her horrible and inhuman experiences in the mental hospital is alternated with these visits to the pleasant new society of the 22nd century where many new friends teach her about their world. But always she is pulled back to the ugly world of doctors, ever-present nurses and attendants, and the ill-treated patients on whom they practice their cures and make their experiments, Connie's true 20th-century friends.

In Mattapoisset—utopian despite Piercy's claim that it is not but rather "the result of a full feminist revolution"—an ecologically responsible,loving, non-sexist (male and female pronouns have been replaced by "per") community has learned that its own existence is threatened by the possible outcome of the experiments being conducted at Rockover State Hospital. The contact with Connie is part of their attempt—there are four others, all also in mental hospitals or prisons—to prevent these undesirable consequences. Connie, it is apparent to Mattapoisset, can be a major factor in the conflict between technology wrongly used and the opposition and rebellion of those who want the kind of society that Mattapoisset represents. Bringing her to the right action, to fighting back against the system that has mistreated her, is a matter of showing her the beautiful future they represent as opposed to the dystopian society of her own day or the alternative future described in chapter 15 that would come as a result of her failure to act. Although the people of Mattapoisset are peaceful, they fight when necessary to defend their community—as Connie discovers on one of her visits, and they remind Connie that sometimes, especially in her time, the violence-prone must be resisted. Connie does take drastic action, but she is clearly doomed to end her days at Rockover.

Perhaps, as has been suggested by several critics, Connie's visits to the future are all hallucinations—certainly she has been sufficiently drugged to make such a suggestion reasonable. But hallucination or not, the story deals with a tormented victim of the evil in society, an almost-innocent, betrayed by those closest to her, who cannot understand why things work out for her as they do. The contrast with the beautiful world that might be is clearly the work of a reformer who feels deeply the injustices of this world and believes just as deeply in the things of which she writes. But, no matter what the motivating force behind its productions, this is an excellent novel, deserving of its warm critical reception. Piercy may never write another work that fits the science-fiction mold, but this work has earned her a permanent place in the utopian branch of the genre.

—Arthur O. Lewis

PIPER, H(enry) Beam. American. Born in Altoona, Pennsylvania, in 1904. Worked on the engineering staff of the Pennsylvania Railroad. *Died 11 November 1964.*

SCIENCE-FICTION PUBLICATIONS

Novels (series: Terran Federation)

Crisis in 2140, with John J. McGuire. New York, Ace, 1957.
A Planet for Texans, with John J. McGuire. New York, Ace, 1958.
Four-Day Planet (for children; Federation). New York, Putnam, 1961.
Little Fuzzy (Federation). New York, Avon, 1962.
Junkyard Planet (Federation). New York, Putnam, 1963; as *The Cosmic Computer*, New York, Ace, 1964.
Space Viking (Federation). New York, Ace, 1963; London, Sphere,1978.
The Other Human Race (Federation). New York, Avon, 1964;

as *Fuzzy Sapiens* New York, Ace, 1976.
Lord Kalvan of Otherwhen. New York, Ace, 1965; as *Gunpowder God*, London, Sphere, 1978.
The Fuzzy Papers (omnibus). New York, Doubleday, 1977.
Uller Uprising. New York, Ace, 1982.
Four-Day Planet, and Lone Star Planet. New York, Ace, 1984.
Fuzzies and Other People. New York, Ace, 1984.

Short Stories

Federation. New York, Ace, 1981.
Empire. New York, Ace, 1981.
Paratime. New York, Ace, 1981.
The Worlds of H. Beam Piper, edited by John F. Carr. New York, Ace, 1983.

OTHER PUBLICATIONS

Novel

Murder in the Gun Room. New York, Knopf, 1953.

Other

Editor, *A Catalogue of Early Pennsylvania and Other Firearms and Edged Weapons at "Restless Oaks," McElhattan, Pennsylvania.* Privately printed, 1927(?).

*   *   *

H. Beam Piper's science fiction is largely the stories of heroes (or heroines), with ideas apparently subordinate to the needs of plot and action. This is most evident in novels such as *A Planet for Texans, Four-Day Planet, Space Viking,* and *Lord Kalvan of Otherwhen.* The last two of these, especially, are fast-paced adventure yarns, with a well-developed central figure, but quite two-dimensional supporting charaters. In each case, the hero (Calvin Morrison in *Lord Kalvan of Otherwhen* Lucas Trask in *Space Viking*) is forced by circumstances totally beyond his control to enter a life radically different from the one that he had anticipated. A major difficulty each man must resolve is the ethical dilemma of the life which he perceives as central to his functioning. Thus, Morrison is caught in the field of an interdimension/time travel machine, while Trask on his wedding day has his bride-to-be killed by her rejected suitor. Morrison must agonize about the appropriateness of introducing more sophisticated weaponry into an essentially static culture, Trask the ethics of killing and looting even though the attached planets are decadent remnants of the "Old Federation." The ultimate results of the activities of each man are intrinsically the same as well: Morrison defeats Styphon's House (which opposed progress and sought to divide countries against one another) while Trask defeats the destructive forces both on Marduk and among the space vikings, establishing Tanith as a progressive planet which is destined to lead a new League of Civilized Worlds.

Perhaps his most famous works are *Little Fuzzy* and *The Other Human Race. Little Fuzzy* builds towards a dramatic courtroom scene in which good and evil clearly clash over the question of the sapience of the Fuzzies. Again there is a central heroic figure, Jack Holloway, discoverer of the Fuzzies. The ethical dilemma to be resolved is whether to recognize the Fuzzies as sentient, giving them *prima facie* right to their own planet and thereby displacing the human interests on the planet Zarathustra, or to allow them to be treated as charming and quick-to-learn animals, subjecting them to what is—for a sentient being—slavery. Holloway's determination and courage in the face of the bureaucratic opposition to the recognition of the Fuzzies as sentient has elements of the heroic physical challenges confronting Morrison and Trask, but it is primarily a moral courage in the face of social opposition. In *The Other Human Race* the same basic problem is repeated except that the ethical dilemma is whether or not to honor the governmental commitment to the Fuzzy Reservation in the face of economic pressures to open the Reservation for mining. There is the added problem of the radical increase in defective births among the Fuzzies. The apparently neutral position of doing nothing about Fuzzy rights is extensionally the same as the decision to exterminate the Fuzzy race, for the humans have it within their power to halt the flood of defective Fuzzy births. Again, in both books, the resolution of the ethical dilemma leaves the world rather significantly altered in the direction of progress-as-we-know-it.

A side light which may be of significant interest has to do with the name of the Fuzzies' planet—Zarathustra, the name of the central figure in the pre-Christian middle-Eastern religion Zoroastrianism (Zoroaster was also known as Zarathustra), similar to the Christian Manichean heresy, which argues the existence of two co-equal forces in the universe, Ahura Mazda (good) and Angra Mainyu (evil). An interesting speculation is that Piper was consciously trying to depict such a struggle in the Fuzzies novels. The planet's name might also have been an allusion to Friedrich Nietzsche's *Also Sprach Zarathustra*. This interpretation offers a potentially convoluted approach to the text because Nietzsche argued for the recognition of man *and superman*. Since the superman is exempt from the constraints of normal ethics, one might have expected a different conclusion.

Piper's other writings more or less follow the same pattern: the hero/heroine is struck by a major ethical problem— paternalism over proud people in *A Planet for Texans* ; revolution or economic slavery in *Four-Day Planet* ; human dependency upon its own machines in *Junkyard Planet* ; the dominance of scholarship by economics in 'Omnilingual. ' In each case the protagonist chooses honor and decency, but also, more significantly, the choice is made for progress. Those forces which support the status quo are doomed from the outset. In a Piper story one "knows" that the hero/heroine will prevail, but only after terrible difficulties. More impressive, however, is Piper's recognition that such successes must result in a significant alteration of the world on which they occur. Although Piper's works will never get him classed as a great writer, they certainly would get him listed as one whom the reader enjoys.

—Richard W. Miller

PISERCHIA, Doris (Elaine). Also writes as Curt Selby. American. Born in Fairmont, West Virginia, 11 October 1928. Educated at Fairmont State College, A. B. 1950; University of Utah, Salt Lake City, 1963-65. Served in the United States Navy, 1950-54: Lieutenant. Married Joseph John Piserchia in 1953; three daughters and two sons. Agent: Carnell Literary Agency, Rowneybury Bungalow, Sawbridgeworth, near Old Harlow, Essex CM20 2EX, England. Address: c/o DAW Books, 1633 Broadway, New York, New York 10019, U.S.A.

SCIENCE-FICTION PUBLICATIONS

Novels

Mister Justice. New York, Ace, 1973; London, Dobson, 1977.
Star Rider. New York, Bantam, 1974.
A Billion Days of Earth. New York, Bantam, 1976; London, Dobson, 1977.
Earthchild. New York, DAW, 1977; London, Dobson, 1979.
Spaceling. New York, Doubleday, 1978.
The Spinner. New York, DAW, 1980.
The Fluger. New York, DAW, 1980.
Earth in Twilight. New York, DAW, 1981.
Doomtime. New York, DAW, 1981.
Blood County (as Curt Selby). New York, DAW, 1981.
I, Zombie (as Curt Selby). New York, DAW, 1982.
The Dimensioneers. New York, DAW, 1982.
The Deadly Sky. New York, DAW, 1983.

Uncollected Short Stories

"Rocket to Gehenna," in *Fantastic* (New York), September 1966.
"Sheltering Dream," in *The Best Science Fiction for 1972*, edited by Frederik Pohl. New York, Ace, 1972.
"Last Train from Earth," in *If* (New York), August 1972.
"Empty Eden," in *If* (New York), December 1972.
"Half the Kingdom," in *Orbit 12*, edited by Damon Knight. New York, Putnam, 1973.
"Unbiased God," in *Galaxy* (New York), December 1973.
"1010," and "Naked and Afraid I Go," in *Orbit 13*, edited by Damon Knight. New York, Putnam, 1974.
"Limited Accommodations," in *Crisis*, edited by Roger Elwood. Nashville, Nelson, 1974.
"Quarantine," in *The Best from Galaxy 2*. New York, Award, 1974.
"Pale Hands," in *Orbit 15*, edited by Damon Knight. New York, Harper, 1974.
"Substance and Shadow," in *Galaxy* (New York), May 1974.
"Nature's Children," in *Galaxy* (New York), September 1974.
"A Typical Day," in *Best SF 1974*, edited by Harry Harrison and Brian Aldiss. Indianapolis, Bobbs Merrill, 1975.
"A Brilliant Curiosity," in *Orbit 16*, edited by Damon Knight. New York, Harper, 1975.
"Deathrights Deferred," in *Science Fiction Discoveries*, edited by Frederik and Carol Pohl. New York, Bantam, 1976.

*   *   *

Doris Piserchia's strongest asset in her novels has been the exotic and colorful settings she has created. *Star Rider*, for example, features a young girl who has a telepathic bond with a horse. The two of them can teleport themselves around the universe, encased by small pockets of environment. They are looking for a fabled world which turns out to be a ruined, deserted Earth tucked into another dimension. Her quest is complicated by a number of other parties involved not only in her quest, but interested as well in her mutant ability to transport herself across intergalactic as well as interstellar distances.

In *A Billion Days of Earth*, men have assumed godlike powers and many of the lower species of animal have acquired intelligence. A vigilante metes out his own brand of justice in *Mister Justice*. But the novels that followed these spent less time on characterization and more on setting and plot, with mixed results. *Earth Child* for instance is almost one constant chase-adventure-battle scene. Earth is being contested by Indigo, a plant that is becoming an ocean, and Emeroo, another plant that is much smaller in size but possibly more powerful in the long run. The last living human is a young girl named Ree, who spends much of her time flying giant insects and fighting the blueboys, plant growths that can move independently and who became increasingly human as the story progresses.

The plot of this novel shows up again in *Doomtime*, this time with gigantic trees battling for control of Earth, with the human race as pawns in their games. It shows up again in *Earth in Twilight*, except in this case the protagonist is a lone space explorer who returns to abandoned Earth to find it overgrown by a gigantic forest inhabited by newly sentient races and giant insects. The astronaut is a classic antihero, unable and perhaps unwilling to make any serious attempt to improve his situation, and the forest of Earth is itself really the strongest character in the novel.

Alien monsters figure even more centrally in two other novels, *The Fluger* and *The Spinner*. The first is rather minor: a gigantic alien wreaks havoc in a closed Earth city until eventually brought to its death by booby-trapped food. The second novel is considerably more interesting. An alien from another dimension spins a mysterious web over an entire city and begins to reproduce his kind in preparation for conquering the entire world.

Inter-dimensional adventures are another staple in Piserchia's novels. In *The Spaceling*, mutants can perceive different dimensions because of drifting rings that allow movement from one plane of existence to another. A young man is drafted into the effort to prevent an interdimensional invasion in *The Deadly Sky*. An extra-dimensional chase is the main plot of *The Dimensioneers*, which transports us from one weird environment to another so quickly that it is almost a comic book adventure without pictures.

Piserchia made more serious efforts at characterization in two recent novels published under the name "Curt Selby." *Blood County* is a supernatural adventure story involving a vampire who has set himself up as a virtual feudal lord. *I, Zombie*, despite the title, is straight science fiction. The recent dead are fitted with implants that allow them to be used as slave laborers with no will of their own, until one such body begins to reawaken its former personality and sets out to free others from their bondage.

Although an infrequent writer of short stories, Piserchia has had over a dozen published over the years, perhaps the most interesting of which are "Empty Eden," a variation of the "Dorian Gray" tale, "Deathrights Deferred," another story of reanimated corpses, and "Rocket to Gehenna," in which an asteroid cemetery is emptied by new tenants, a story marred by silly pseudoscience, but also featuring some of her best writing.

—Don D'Ammassa

PLATT, Charles. British. Born in Hertfordshire, 25 October 1944. Educated at Cambridge University, one year, and London College of Printing, two years. Worked for Clive Bingley, publishers, London, 1967; designer and production assistant, *New Worlds* magazine; free-lance photographer and book jacket designer. Recipient: *Locus* award, for non-fiction, 1985. Address: c/o Gollancz, 14 Henrietta Street, London WC2E 8QJ, England.

SCIENCE-FICTION PUBLICATIONS

Novels

The Garbage World. New York, Berkley, 1967; London, Panther, 1968.
The City Dwellers London, Sidgwick and Jackson, 1970; revised edition, as *Twilight of the City*, New York, Macmillan, 1977.
Planet of the Voles. New York, Putnam, 1971.
Sweet Evil. New York, Berkley, 1977.

Uncollected Short Stories

"One of Those Days," in *Science Fantasy* (Bournemouth), January 1965.
"Cultural Invasion," in *New Worlds* (London), November 1965.
"The Failures," in *New Worlds* (London), January 1966.
"A Taste of the Afterlife," in *New Worlds* (London), September 1966.
"The Total Experience Kick," in *The Best SF Stories from New Worlds 2*, edited by Michael Moorcock. London, Panther, and New York, Berkley, 1968.
"The Disaster Story," in *The Best SF Stories from New Worlds 3*, edited by Michael Moorcock. London, Panther, and New York, Berkley, 1968.
"Direction," in *The New SF*, edited by Langdon Jones. London, Hutchinson, 1969.
"The Rodent Laboratory," in *The Best SF Stories from New Worlds 5*, edited by Michael Moorcock. London, Panther, and New York, Berkley, 1969.
"Id," in *New Worlds* (London), March 1969.
"Lone Zone," in *The Best SF Stories from New Worlds 7*, edited by Michael Moorcock. London, Panther, 1971.
"Norman vs. America" (cartoon), in *Quark 4*, edited by Samuel R. Delany and Marilyn Hacker. New York, Paperback Library, 1971.
"A Cleansing of the System," in *New Worlds Quarterly 3*, edited by Michael Moorcock. London, Sphere, 1971; New York, Berkley, 1972.
"New York Times," in *Orbit 11*, edited by Damon Knight. New York, Putnam, 1973.
"Family Literature" and "The Motivation Chart," in *New Worlds Quarterly 5*, edited by Michael Moorcock. London, Sphere, 1973.
"The Coldness," in *New Worlds 6*, edited by Michael Moorcock and Charles Platt. London, Sphere, 1973; as *New Worlds 5*, New York, Avon, 1974.

OTHER PUBLICATIONS

Verse

Highway Sandwiches, with Thomas M. Disch and Marilyn Hacker. Privately printed, 1970.
The Gas. New York, Ophelia Press, 1970.

Other

"The Disaster Story," in *New Worlds* (London), March 1966.
"Expressing the Abstract," in *New Worlds* (London), July 1967.
"Fun Palace—Not a Freakout," in *New Worlds* (London), March 1968.
"The Responsive Environment," in *New Worlds* (London), May 1969.
Dream Makers: The Uncommon People Who Write Science

Fiction (interviews). New York, Berkley, 2 vols., 1980-82.
Graphics Guide to Commodore 64. Berkeley, California, Sybex, 1984.
Micromania: The Whole Truth about Home Computers, with David Langford. London, Gollancz, 1984; as *The Whole Truth Home Computer Handbook*, New York, Avon, 1984.

Editor, with Michael Moorcock, *New Worlds 6.* London, Sphere, 1973; as *New Worlds 5*, New York, Avon, 1974.
Editor, with Hilary Bailey, *New Worlds 7.* London, Sphere, 1974; as *New Worlds 6*, New York, Avon, 1975.

*   *   *

The science fiction written by the old *New Worlds* writers, of whom Charles Platt is a prolific and representative specimen, tends towards the antithesis of the scenario in which a macho hero saves (and preserves in an unchanged or improved state) the world from an alien threat before setting blasters for home, a beautiful but useless girl at his side. Theirs is the science fiction of despair looking to a future where things are inevitably worse. Their pet threats are those implicit in human or cosmic nature, and their totem motif is the inexorable unwinding of the universal mainspring. The entropy in Platt's fiction is the disorder created by the breakdown of the social mechanism rather than the heat death of the universe. His two major novels, *The Garbage World* and *The City Dwellers* (rewritten, with added love interest, as *Twilight of the City*), both concentrate on people coming to terms with the collapse, or loss of meaning, of the system which produced them.

In *The Garbage World* a two-man team arrive, ostensibly to repair a defective gravity generator but actually to blow up Kopra, the rubbish tip of the Asteroid Belt; its inhabitants, as befits the planet's name, pursue the anal pleasures of establishing pecking orders and hoarding trash in a landscape of shanty towns, stinking swamps, and gigantic mutated slugs, with a miserable climate exacerbated by a constant rain of space-going garbage packs. One of the new arrivals is converted to their insalubrious but unrepressed lifestyle, having fallen for the head man's dirty daughter; and after sundry erotic and other adventures in the sewerlike backwaters of the planet, both Kopra and the other official (clean-handed but dirty-dealing) are messily blown up, smothering the pleasures of the pleasure worlds of the Asteroid belt in a shower of excrement.

The City Dwellers has undergone several mutations between appearing as a series of disconnected short stories in *New Worlds* and being completely unified into *Twilight of the City.* This increase in order defies the second law of thermodynamics, but the story in all its forms goes along with it, forsaking the metaphor of *The Garbage World* in an attempt to depict with prophetic realism the degeneration of organised society. Trendy, hip characters from the pulsating, neon-lit heart of the city are forced, as the beat runs down, to abandon the twitching carcass and scrape an existence in the hostile countryside, finally returning to the rotting corpse to exterminate the last few worms which prey upon it.

There are no hairy-chested heroes in shiny suits and boots in Platt's novels. Even in *Planet of the Voles*, most space-operatic of his books, the protagonist struggles in hunger, rags, and filth through a hostile environment to confront a feared enemy and find it (although still an implacable enemy) jewelled, perfumed, and closer to him than he at first supposed. Platt's real heroes are small-time misfits: the coprotropic official of *The Garbage World*, the "socially inept" songwriter of *Twilight of the City*, the artist and the runt of the artificially reared crew of military men in *Planet of the Voles*. They survive where the perfect

specimens bite the dust, and in adjusting to the filth and pollution of the rubbish tip or the hardship of scraping a living on the land rapidly come to find, if not happiness, at least substance in the unsynthesised pleasures of life away from the glitter of the civilised artifice. The immaculate white gloves and the rhinestone-studded suit are well lost for such a reward. It is not optimism, but when the cake has been snatched away it is a crumb of consolation.

—Lee Montgomerie

POHL, Frederik. Also writes as James MacCreigh; Ernst Mason; Edson McCann; Jordan Park; Donald Stacy. American. Born in New York City, 26 November 1919. Served in the United States Air Force, in the United States and Italy, 1943-45: Sergeant. Married 1) Doris Baumgardt in 1940 (divorced, 1944); 2) Dorothy LesTina in 1945 (divorced, 1947); 3) Judith Merril, *q. v.*, in 1949 (divorced, 1953), one daughter; 4) Carol Metcalf Ulf in 1952 (divorced, 1981), two sons (one deceased) and one daughter; 5) Elizabeth Anne Hull in 1984. Editor, Popular Publications, New York, 1939-43; copywriter, Thwing and Altman, New York, 1946; Book Editor and Associate Circulation Manager, Popular Science Publication Company, New York, 1946-49; literary agent, New York, 1949-53; Features Editor, later Editor, *If*, New York, 1959-70; Editor, Galaxy Publishing Company, New York, 1961-69; Executive Editor, Ace Books, New York, 1971-72; Science Fiction Editor, Bantam Books, New York, 1973-79. Since 1976, Contributing Editor, *Algol*, New York. President, Science Fiction Writers of America, 1974-76; President, World SF, 1980-82 and current Vice-President (West); Mid-West Area Chair, Authors Guild of America. Recipient: Edward E. Smith Memorial Award, 1966; Hugo Award, for editing, 1966, 1967, 1968, for fiction, 1973, 1978; *Locus* award, 1973, 1978; Nebula Award, 1976, 1977; John W. Campbell Memorial Award, 1978; Prix Apollo (France), 1979; American Book Award, 1980. Guest of Honor, World Science Fiction Convention, 1972; Fellow, American Association for the Advancement of Science. Agent: Curtis Brown, 10 Astor Place, New York, New York 10003; or, Leslie Flood, Carnell Literary Agency, Rowneybury Bungalow, near Old Harlow, Essex CM20 2EX, England. Address: 855 South Harvard Drive, Palatine, Illinois 60067, U.S.A.

SCIENCE-FICTION PUBLICATIONS

Novels (series: Cuckoo's Saga; Jim Eden; Gateway; Starchild)

The Space Merchants, with C. M. Kornbluth. New York, Ballantine, 1953; London, Heinemann, 1955.
Search the Sky, with C. M. Kornbluth. New York, Ballantine, 1954; London, Digit, 1960.
Undersea Quest (for children; Eden), with Jack Williamson. New York, Gnome Press, 1954; London, Dobson, 1966.
Preferred Risk (as Edson McCann, with Lester del Rey). New York, Simon and Schuster, 1955; London, Methuen, 1983.
Gladiator-at-Law, with C. M. Kornbluth. New York, Ballantine, 1955; London, Digit, 1958.
Undersea Fleet (for children; Eden), with Jack Williamson. New York, Gnome Press, 1956; London, Dobson, 1968.
Slave Ship. New York, Ballantine, 1957; London, Dobson, 1961.
Undersea City (for children; Eden), with Jack Williamson. New

York, Gnome Press, 1958; London, Dobson, 1968.

Wolfbane, with C. M. Kornbluth. New York, Ballantine, 1959; London, Gollancz, 1960.

Drunkard's Walk. New York, Ballantine, 1960; revised edition, London, Gollancz, 1961.

The Starchild Trilogy, with Jack Williamson. New York, Doubleday, 1977; London, Penguin, 1980.

> *The Reefs of Space*. New York, Ballantine, 1964; London, Dobson, 1965.
>
> *Starchild*. New York, Ballantine, 1965; London, Dobson, 1966.
>
> *Rogue Star*. New York, Ballantine, 1969; London, Dobson, 1972.

A Plague of Pythons. New York, Ballantine, 1965; London, Gollancz, 1966; revised edition, as *Demon in the Skull*, New York, DAW, 1984.

The Age of the Pussyfoot. New York, Trident Press, 1969; London, Gollancz, 1970.

Farthest Star (Cuckoo's Saga), with Jack Williamson. New York, Ballantine, 1975; London, Pan, 1976.

Man Plus. New York, Random House, and London, Gollancz, 1976.

Gateway. New York, St. Martin's Press, and London, Gollancz, 1977.

Jem: The Making of a Utopia. New York, St. Martin's Press, and London, Gollancz, 1979.

Beyond the Blue Event Horizon (Gateway). New York, Ballantine, and London, Gollancz, 1980.

The Cool War. New York, Ballantine, and London, Gollancz, 1981.

Starburst. New York, Ballantine, and London, Gollancz, 1982.

Syzygy. New York, Bantam, 1982.

Wall Around a Star (Cuckoo's Saga), with Jack Williamson. New York, Ballantine, 1983.

Midas World. New York, St. Martin's Press, and London, Gollancz, 1983.

Heechee Rendezvous (Gateway). New York, Ballantine, and London, Gollancz, 1984.

The Years of the City. New York, Simon and Schuster, 1984; London, Gollancz, 1985.

The Merchants' War. New York, St. Martin's Press, 1984.

Black Star Rising. New York, Ballantine, 1985.

Short Stories

Danger Moon (as James MacCreigh). Sydney, American Science Fiction, 1953.

Alternating Currents. New York, Ballantine, 1956; London, Penguin, 1966.

The Case Against Tomorrow. New York, Ballantine, 1957.

Tomorrow Times Seven. New York, Ballantine, 1959.

The Man Who Ate the World. New York, Ballantine, 1960; London, Panther, 1979.

Turn Left at Thursday. New York, Ballantine, 1961.

The Wonder Effect, with C. M. Kornbluth. New York, Ballantine, 1962; London, Gollancz, 1967; revised edition, as *Critical Mass*, New York, Bantam, 1977.

The Abominable Earthman. New York, Ballantine, 1963.

The Frederik Pohl Omnibus. London, Gollancz, 1966; reprinted in part, as *Survival Kit*, London, Panther, 1979.

Digits and Dastards (includes essays). New York, Ballantine, 1966; London, Dobson, 1968.

Day Million. New York, Ballantine, 1970; London, Gollancz, 1971.

The Gold at Starbow's End. New York, Ballantine, 1972; London, Gollancz, 1973.

The Best of Frederik Pohl, edited by Lester del Rey. New York, Doubleday, 1975; London, Sidgwick and Jackson, 1977.

In the Problem Pit. New York, Bantam, and London, Corgi, 1976.

The Early Pohl. New York, Doubleday, 1976; London, Dobson, 1980.

Planets Three. New York, Berkley, 1982.

Pohlstars. New York, Ballantine, 1984.

Uncollected Short Stories

"The Kindly Isle," in *Isaac Asimov's Science Fiction Magazine* (New York), November 1984.

"Criticality," in *Analog* (New York), December 1984.

"The Saved," in *Playboy* (Chicago), February 1985.

OTHER PUBLICATIONS

Novels

A Town Is Drowning, with C. M. Kornbluth. New York, Ballantine, 1955; London, Digit, 1960.

Presidential Year, with C. M. Kornbluth. New York, Ballantine, 1956.

Sorority House (as Jordan Park, with C. M. Kornbluth). New York, Lion, 1956.

The God of Channel 1 (as Donald Stacy). New York, Ballantine, 1956.

Turn the Tigers Loose, with Walter Lasly. New York, Ballantine, 1956.

Edge of the City (novelization of screenplay). New York, Ballantine, 1957.

Other

"Long John Nebel and the Woodlouse," in *Library Journal* (New York), 1 November 1956.

Tiberius (biography; as Ernst Mason). New York, Ballantine, 1960.

Practical Politics 1972. New York, Ballantine, 1971.

"On Velocity Exercises," in *Those Who Can*, edited by Robin Scott Wilson. New York, New American Library, 1973.

"The Publishing of Science Fiction," in *Science Fiction, Today and Tomorrow*, edited by Reginald Bretnor. New York, Harper, 1974.

The Way the Future Was: A Memoir. New York, Ballantine, 1978; London, Gollancz, 1979.

Science Fiction: Studies in Film, with Frederik Pohl IV. New York, Ace, 1982.

Editor, *Beyond the End of Time*. New York, Permabooks, 1952.

Editor, *Shadow of Tomorrow*. New York, Permabooks, 1953.

Editor, *Star Science Fiction Stories 1-6*. New York, Ballantine, 6 vols., 1953-59; vols. 1 and 2, London, Boardman, 1954-55.

Editor, *Assignment in Tomorrow*. New York, Hanover House, 1954.

Editor, *Star Short Novels*. New York, Ballantine, 1954.

Editor, *Star of Stars*. New York, Doubleday, 1960; as *Star Fourteen*, London, Whiting and Wheaton, 1966.

Editor, *The Expert Dreamers*. New York, Doubleday, 1962; London, Gollancz, 1963.

Editor, *Time Waits for Winthrop and Four Other Short Novels from Galaxy*. New York, Doubleday, 1962.

Editor, *The Seventh* [through *Eleventh*] *Galaxy Reader*. New York, Doubleday, 5 vols., 1964-69; *Seventh* through *Tenth*, London, Gollancz, 4 vols., 1965-68; *Eighth*, as *Final*

Encounter, New York, Curtis, 1970; *Tenth*, as *Door to Anywhere*, New York, Curtis, 1970.

Editor, *The If Reader of Science Fiction*. New York, Doubleday, 1966; London, Whiting and Wheaton, 1967; second volume, New York, Doubleday, 1968.

Editor, *Nightmare Age*. New York, Ballantine, 1970.

Editor, *The Best Science Fiction for 1972*. New York, Ace, 1972.

Editor, with Carol Pohl, *Science Fiction: The Great Years*. New York, Ace, 1973; London, Gollancz, 1974; second volume, Ace, 1976.

Editor, with Carol Pohl, *Jupiter*. New York, Ballantine, 1973.

Editor, *The Science Fiction Roll of Honor*. New York, Random House, 1975.

Editor, with Carol Pohl, *Science Fiction Discoveries*. New York, Bantam, 1976.

Editor, *The Best of C. M. Kornbluth*. New York, Doubleday, 1976.

Editor, with Martin H. Greenberg and Joseph D. Olander, *Science Fiction of the 40's*. New York, Avon, 1978.

Editor, with Martin H. Greenberg and Joseph D. Olander, *Galaxy: Thirty Years of Innovative Science Fiction*. Chicago, Playboy Press, 1980; 2nd volume, New York, Ace, 1981.

Editor, *Nebula Winners 14*. New York, Harper, 1980; London, W. H. Allen, 1981.

Editor, with Martin H. Greenberg and Joseph D. Olander, *The Great Science Fiction Series*. New York, Harper, 1980.

Editor, *Yesterday's Tomorrows: Favorite Stories from Forty Years as a Science Fiction Editor*. New York, Berkley, 1982.

*

Manuscript Collection: Syracuse University Library, New York.

Frederik Pohl comments:

I write what interests me, in the hope that it will interest others. The things that particularly interest me are: The mismatch between what people say and what they do (U. S. presidents being only the most conspicuous example); The turbulence and elegance of science, particularly at its frontiers (science is my favorite spectator sport); The vulnerability and confusion inside the most plastic of human faces; The sound of language, and the amusing tricks that can be played with it; and Morality.

How thoroughly I communicate these concerns I can't easily tell, but when I stop trying I will stop writing.

*   *   *

A major figure in science fiction for more than four decades, Frederik Pohl in his best work combines technical extrapolation and penetrating social commentary with narrative complexity and a distinctive sardonic style. His 1950's short stories attracted attention with their satire of American consumer society, upending conventional expectations about economic planning ("Rafferty's Reasons"), social stratification ("My Lady Greensleeves"), and population stabilization ("The Census Takers"). The first of these "comic infernos" to gain major attention was "The Midas Plague,' in which increasing status in an overproducing economy accrues to people entitled to consume less. This tall tale multiplies complications for comic effect, satirizing the assumption that affluence is infinite. Best of the "consumer cycle," however, is "The Tunnel under the World," horror story based on penetrating insight into social manipulation by commercial interests. In it, Guy Burckhardt finds his mind imprisoned in a tiny automaton, at the mercy of a market research firm's controlled experiments. Derived partly from his advertising and sales experience, this motif of mind manipulation echoes throughout Pohl's work.

Collaborating since 1940, Pohl and C. M. Kornbluth gained fame with *The Space Merchants*. Its future dystopia run by advertising agencies is the setting for another tall tale, relating the fall from grace of ad executive Mitch Courtenay. Surviving addictive rations and a labor camp, he converts to the "Consies" (Conservationists) and subverts the admen's scheme to dump excess production and population on Venus. With sometimes manic humor, the novel moves swiftly to its climax, side-swiping venerable social institutions and incorporating a routine love-story plot. Other Pohl-Kornbluth collaborations were less impressive, especially where aliens are invoked to explain human failings (a Pohl weakness). *Gladiator-at-Law* took on the legal profession, *Search the Sky* attacked planetary isolationism, and *Wolfbane* was an occasionally chilling variation on the theme of aliens ruling human zombies. Another dystopian collaboration (with Lester del Rey), *Preferred Risk* is a lackluster exposé of dictatorship by worldwide insurance companies.

Another partnership, with Jack Williamson, began in the 1950's with formula-perfect adventure stories for children, *Undersea Quest, Undersea Fleet*, and *Undersea City*, overly reliant on coincidence, derring-do, and black-and-white characterizations. They also wrote *The Starchild Trilogy*, a straightforward if tedious entertainment lacking Pohl's verbal economy and social immediacy. Pohl's influence is more visible in Cuckoo's Saga (*Farthest Star* and *Wall Around a Star*) in which people are replicated on a multi-race starship bound for a distant artificial planet, but the plot wanders with multiple crises and undistinguished characterizations.

Pohl's own novels have generally grown from alien-fighting melodrama to fables of human folly. Exploring communication with animals in *Slave Ship*, he satirizes higher education in the dystopian *Drunkard's Walk*, and stresses the horrors of alien mind control in *A Plague of Pythons*. Just short of a comic masterpiece, *The Age of the Pussyfoot* tells how a man revived from cryogenic freezing finds a continually progressing world is not his oyster.

His chief advance in the 1960's he called "velocity exercises," minimal stories with little plot or dialogue. "The Martian Stargazers," for example, derives Martians' race suicide from their astrological lore. "Speed Trap" shows how the honors and trappings of a scientist's success thwart future creativity. Pohl perfected the form in "Day Million," a "love story" of the far future when "boy" and "girl" and "marriage" have been redefined.

His consistently best work emerged in the 1970's, however, and in longer forms. "The Merchants of Venus" is a tale of adventure with a happy ending, but its real interest lies in the setting, the hellish Venus of modern astronomy, and a socioeconomic situation little short of desperate. In "The Gold at the Starbow's End," a misfired experiment sends ten bright young people to explore a nonexistent planet orbiting Alpha Centaurus. Ten years of concentrated thinking turns them into supermen, creating their own world and returning to select colonists from a devastated Earth. A rare utopian story, "In the Problem Pit," shows ordinary people in a "think-tank" helping society surmount intractable obstacles. His finest treatment of mind control, "We Purchased People" is based on the "sale" of human criminals to alien remote control in a deal bringing trade to "backward" Earth from extraterrestrial civilizations.

Man Plus focuses on the transformation of Roger Torraway to help him survive on Mars; his self-control, his identity, even his sex are stripped away, making him more minus than plus.

The real "plus," man's computer network, narrates how it manipulated events to arrange its own survival on more worlds than one. Set in the future of "The Merchants of Venus," *Gateway* intertwines a lierally mechanical Freudian analysis with a story of chance-ridden space exploration via alien ships abondoned (by the "Heechee") on an asteroid. The throroughly dislikeable protagonist, Robinet Broadhead, stands in for human society depending for survival on a cosmic game of chance. Potentially heroic on the small scale, Broadhead's self-confrontation makes the book's emotional content as honest as its presentation is complex. In *Jem,* a tripartite division of Earth society (productive of food, energy, and people) is projected allegorically upon an alien planet, in conflict with three coexisting intelligent races of natives. The final amalgamation (ironically utopian) of all four races and all six life-styles is threatened by contact with a human colony near Alpha Centauri. Though lumbering and mechanical, the book has scenes and passages of undeniable power, and a dire message for mankind to cooperate or die.

After this spate of works confronting real problems and hard solutions in challenging narrative structures, most of Pohl's 1980s novels are disappointing sequels. *Beyond the Blue Event Horizon* and *Heechee Rendezvous* progressively increase the scope and the threat to human survival, losing the personal and temporal immediacy of *Gateway*. *Starburst* does something similar to its original, "The Gold at the Starbow's End. " *The Merchants' War* largely repeats *The Space Merchants,* and *Midas World* adds little to the "consumer cycle" of stories from which it is lamely constructed.

Of the non-sequels, *Syzygy* introduces a detached narrative voice, for a work of minimal science fiction concerning the difficulty of proving a negative. Though the "Jupiter Effect" precipitates no cataclysm, anxiety over it takes its toll on Los Angeles, less damaging than its own "routine" natural catastrophes. *The Cool War* suffers from a witless hero, all-powerful gangsters, and boring melodrama built on the conceit that East-West espionage is ruining Earth's "quality of life. " Only *The Years of the City* offers a ray of hope, in both outlook and technique. A set of linked stories, each a jump forward in the future of New York, it blends the technical and social inventiveness of *The Age of the Pussyfoot* with the optimism of "In the Problem Pit," the chronicle form mitigating its weak characterizations. A welcome reminder of Pohl's potential, it highlights by contrast the facile ideas and lame writing for which he is too often willing to settle.

—David N. Samuelson

PORGES, Arthur. Also writes as Peter Arthur; Pat Rogers. American. Born in Chicago, Illinois, 20 August 1915. Educated at Illinois Institute of Technology, Chicago, B. S. 1940. Taught mathematics at Illinois Institute of Technology, De Paul University, Chicago, and Western Military Academy: retired, 1975.

SCIENCE-FICTION PUBLICATIONS

Uncollected Short Stories (series: Ensign De Ruyter)

"The Rats," in *The Best Science-Fiction Stories 1952,* edited by E. F. Bleiler and T. E. Dikty. New York, Fell, 1952; London, Grayson, 1953.

'The Fly," in *The Best Science-Fiction Stories 1953,* edited by E. F. Bleiler and T. E. Dikty. New York, Fell, 1953; London, Grayson, 1955.

"Story Conference," in *Fantasy and Science Fiction* (New York), May 1953.

"Strange Birth," in *Fantasy and Science Fiction* (New York), June 1953.

"The Liberator," in *Fantasy and Science Fiction* (New York), December 1953.

"The Unwilling Professor," in *Dynamic* (New York), January 1954.

"The Grom," in *Fantasy and Science Fiction* (New York), November 1954.

"Guilty as Charged," in *The Best Science Fiction Stories and Novels 1955,* edited by T. E. Dikty. New York, Fell, 1955.

"The Ruum," in *Best SF,* edited by Edmund Crispin, London, Faber, 1955.

"Mop-Up," in *Galaxy of Ghouls,* edited by Judith Merril. New York, Lion, 1955.

"$1. 98," in *The Best from Fantasy and Science Fiction 4,* edited by Anthony Boucher. New York, Doubleday, 1955.

"The Tidings," in *Fantasy and Science Fiction* (New York), February 1955.

"The Box," in *Startling* (New York), Spring 1955.

"By a Fluke," in *Fantasy and Science Fiction* (New York), October 1955.

"The Logic of Rufus Weir," in *Fantasy and Science Fiction* (New York), November 1955.

"The Entity," in *Fantastic Universe* (Chicago), December 1955.

"Whirlpool," in *Fantastic Universe* (Chicago), March 1957.

"The Devil and Simon Flagg," in *Fantasia Mathematica,* edited by Clifton Fadiman. New York, Simon and Schuster, 1958.

"What Crouches in the Deep," in *Fantastic* (New York), March 1959.

"A Touch of Sun," in *Fantastic* (New York), April 1959.

"The Forerunner," in *Fantastic* (New York), July 1959.

"The Shakespeare Manuscript," in *Fantastic* (New York), August 1959.

"Security," in *Amazing* (New York), September 1959.

"Off His Rocker," in *Fantastic* (New York), February 1960.

"A Specimen for a Queen," in *Fantasy and Science Fiction* (New York), May 1960.

"Night Quake" (as Pat Rogers) and "Josephus," in *Fear* (Concord, New Hampshire), May 1960.

"The Fiftieth Year of April," in *Fantastic* (New York), June 1960.

"The Crime of Mr. Saver," in *Fantastic* (New York), August 1960.

"The Shadowsmith," in *Fantastic* (New York), September 1960.

"The Auto Hawks," in *Amazing* (New York), September 1960.

"Words and Music," in *If* (New York), September 1960.

"A Diversion for the Baron," in *Fantastic* (New York), November 1960.

"The Radio" (as Peter Arthur) and "The Melanas," in *Fantastic* (New York), December 1960.

"Degree Candidate" (as Peter Arthur) and "Dr. Blackadder's Clients," in *Fantastic* (New York), January 1961.

"The Other Side," in *Fantastic* (New York), February 1961.

"Revenge," in *Amazing* (New York), February 1961.

"Mulberry Moon," in *Fantastic* (New York), April 1961.

"The Arrogant Vampire," in *Fantastic* (New York), May 1961.

"One Bad Habit," in *Fantastic* (New York), June 1961.

"Report on the Magic Shop," in *Fantastic* (New York), August 1961.

"A Devil of a Day," in *Fantastic* (New York), August 1962.

"Mozart Annuity," in *Fantastic* (New York), November 1962.

"Emergency Operation," in *Great Science Fiction about Doctors*, edited by Groff Conklin and Noah D. Fabricant. New York, Macmillan, 1963.

"3rd Sister," in *Fantastic* (New York), January 1963.

"The Topper," in *Astounding* (New York), February 1963.

"Through Channels," in *Amazing* (New York), June 1963.

"The Formula," in *Amazing* (New York), July 1963.

"Controlled Experiment," in *Astounding* (New York), August 1963.

"The Rescuer," in *Yet More Penguin Science Fiction*, edited by Brian Aldiss. London, Penguin, 1964.

"Time-Bomb," in *Fantasy and Science Fiction* (New York), June 1964.

"Urned Reprieve" (De Ruyter), in *Amazing* (New York), October 1964.

"The Fanatic," in *Fantastic* (New York), December 1964.

"The Moths," in *Amazing* (New York), December 1964.

"Problem Child," in *The Year's Best S-F 10*, edited by Judith Merril. New York, Delacorte Press, 1965; London, Mayflower, 1967.

"Wheeler Dealer" (De Ruyter), in *Amazing* (New York), March 1965.

"Ensign De Ruyter, Dreamer," in *Amazing* (New York), April 1965.

"The Good Seed," in *Amazing* (New York), August 1965.

"Turning Point," in *Fantasy and Science Fiction* (New York), September 1965.

"A Civilized Community," in *Bizarre Mystery Magazine* (Concord, New Hampshire), October 1965.

"Dusty Answer" (De Ruyter), in *Amazing* (New York), October 1965.

"The Creep Brigade," in *Bizarre Mystery Magazine* (Concord, New Hampshire), November 1965.

"Pressure" (De Ruyter), in *Amazing* (New York), February 1966.

"Priceless Possession," in *Galaxy* (New York), June 1966.

"The Mirror," in *Fantasy and Science Fiction* (New York), October 1966.

"Solomon's Demon," in *Legends for the Dark*, edited by Peter Haining. London, New English Library, 1968.

"The Dragons of Tesla," in *Fantastic* (New York), October 1968.

*   *   *

Arthur Porges's fiction consists of some 70 short stories, often of 3,000 or fewer words. The corpus itself and many of the individual stories within it blend fantasy with science fiction. "Mop-Up," for instance, takes place in the realistic wreckage following a world war fought with atomic and biological weapons. Sharing what is left with the sole human survivor are a witch, a vampire, and a ghoul. Similarly, there appears to be no difference in feel or treatment between stories which are purely SF and other which are purely fantasy. Thus the djinn of "Solomon's Demon" and the robot speciman-gatherer of "The Ruum" are precisely equivalent in so far as the humans who come in contact with them are concerned: they are alien, enormously powerful, inexorable—and they must be stopped if the viewpoint characters are to survive.

The viewpoint character *doesn't* always survive a Porges story, a fact which contributes to the considerable tension of the best of them. The character does always struggle, however. The horror is not that caused by watching a man helpless in the face of the unknown; rather, it is aroused by seeing a strong and resourceful man overborne by a power or cunning still greater than his own. An excellent example of this is "The Rats," in which a lone man fights more-than-bestial rats against a backdrop of impending nuclear war. In his ultimate failure, the man turns over the world to antagonists who have proven themselves worthy at least to attempt to better Mankind's record.

Porges works against sharp, tersely drawn backgrounds; he has an enviable talent for choosing the right word or two which convinces a reader that the scene or character was written from life rather than merely studied. His work typically begins with a narrative hook which draws the reader into the body of the story. And even pedestrian stories are frequently enlivened by flashes of character which demonstrate a considerable depth of feeling. Regrettably, many of the stories *are* pedestrian. This is a result of their being based on gimmicks, often bits of scientific fact: parabolic reflectors concentrate light ("A Touch of Sun," "The Dragons of Tesla"); crickets chirp at a rate dependant on temperature ("The Formula"); a human body reduced to raw elements is a slight value ("$1.98"). While the development may be at least professional, only the gimmick itself is likely to stick in the reader's mind for any length of time. When the gimmick is integral to the story, however, the result can be extremely effective. "The Ruum" (humans can lose signigicant body weight by sweating) and "Solomon's Demon" (high voltage is harmless unless coupled with a path to ground) are striking examples of this synthesis; and "The Mirror," which turns on an analysis of multiple reflections, is a stunning horror story. If these are the exceptions, then in themselves they constitute a body which many writers must envy.

Despite his frequent use of factual gimmicks, Porges never neglects his characters. It is fitting that one of his last-published stories, "Priceless Possession," involves no gimmicks at all; only the question of what part of their souls three spacemen will pay to avoid losing a treasure which in money terms is priceless. This is not a sardonic story; and perhaps it is a story that is not without hope for humanity; but it is an indictment more damning than any shrill diatribe could have been. As if in summary of much of Porges's best work, men struggle but we cannot assume their victory; and our worst enemies may not be external to our hearts.

—David A. Drake

POURNELLE, Jerry (Eugene). Also writes as Wade Curtis. American. Born in Shreveport, Louisiana, 7 August 1933. Educated at the University of Iowa, Iowa City, 1953-54; University of Washington, Seattle, B. S. 1955, M. S. in statistics and systems engineering 1957, Ph. D. in psychology 1960, Ph. D. in political science 1964. Served in the United States Army 1950-52. Married Roberta Jane Isdell in 1959; four sons. Research Assistant, University of Washington Medical School, 1954-57; Aviation Psychologist and Systems Engineer, Boeing Corporation, Seattle, 1957-64; Manager of Special Studies, Aerospace Corporation, San Bernardino, California, 1964-65; Research Specialist and Proposal Manager, American Rockwell Corporation, 1965-66; Professor of Political Science, Pepperdine University, Los Angeles, 1966-69; Executive Assistant to the Mayor of Los Angeles, 1969-70. Since 1970, free-lance writer, lecturer, and consultant: regular contributor of non-fiction articles to *Galaxy*, 1974-78, and *Analog*. President, Science Fiction Writers of America, 1973-74. Recipient: John W. Campbell Award, 1973; Evans-Freehafer Award, 1977. Fellow, Operations Research Society of America, and American

Association for the Advancement of Science. Republic of Estonia Award of Honor, 1968; Officer, Military and Hospitaler Order of St. Lazarus of Jerusalem. Agent: Blassingame McCauley and Wood, 432 Park Avenue South, Suite 1205, New York, New York 10016. Address: 12051 Laurel Terrace, Studio City, California 91604, U.S.A.

SCIENCE-FICTION PUBLICATIONS

Novels (series: Falkenberg; Janissaries; Second Empire)

A Spaceship for the King (Empire). New York, DAW, 1973.
Escape from the Planet of the Apes (novelization of screenplay). New York, Award, 1974.
The Mote in God's Eye (Empire), with Larry Niven. New York, Simon and Schuster, 1974; London, Weidenfeld and Nicolson, 1975.
Birth of Fire. Toronto, Laser, 1976; New York, Pocket Books, 1978.
Inferno, with Larry Niven. New York, Pocket Books, 1976; London, Wingate, 1977.
West of Honor (Falkenberg). Toronto, Laser, 1976; New York, Pocket Books, 1978.
The Mercenary (Falkenberg). New York, Pocket Books, 1977.
Lucifer's Hammer, with Larry Niven. Chicago, Playboy Press, 1977.
Exiles to Glory. New York, Ace, 1978.
Janissaries. New York, Ace, 1979; London, Macdonald, 1981.
King David's Spaceship. New York, Pocket Books, 1980; London, Futura, 1981.
Oath of Fealty (Janissaries), with Larry Niven. Huntington Woods, Michigan, Phantasia Press, 1981; London, Macdonald, 1982.
Clan and Crown (Janissaries), with Roland Green. New York, Ace, 1982.
Footfall, with Larry Niven. New York, Ballantine, and London, Gollancz, 1985.

Short Stories

High Justice. New York, Pocket Books, 1977; London, Futura, 1980.

Uncollected Short Stories

"He Fell into a Dark Hole," in *Black Holes*, edited by Pournelle. New York, Fawcett, 1979.
"Spirals," with Larry Niven, and "Bind Your Sons to Exile," in *The Endless Frontier*, edited by Pournelle. New York, Ace, 1979.
"Reflex," with Larry Niven, and "His Truth Goes Marching On," in *There Will Be War*, edited by Pournelle and John F. Carr. New York, Tor, 1983.
"Manual of Operations," in *Men of War*, edited by Pournelle and John F. Carr. New York, Tor, 1984.

OTHER PUBLICATIONS

Novels as Wade Curtis

Red Heroin. New York, Berkley, 1969.
Red Dragon. New York, Berkley, 1971.

Other

The Strategy of Technology: Winning the Decisive War, with

Stefan T. Possony. New York, Dunellen, 1970.
"The Construction of Believable Societies," in *The Craft of Science Fiction*, edited by Reginald Bretnor. New York, Harper, 1976.
That Buck Rogers Stuff, edited by Gavin Claypool. Pasadena, California, Extequer, 1977.
The Mathematics of the Energy Crisis, with R. Gagliardi. Westmont, New Jersey, Intergalactic, 1978.
A Step Farther Out. London, W. H. Allen, 1980; New York, Ace, 1983.
Mutual Assured Survival: A Space-Age Solution to Nuclear Annihilation, with Dean Ing. New York, Baen, 1984.
The User's Guide to Small Computers. New York, Baen, 1985.

Editor, *20/20 Vision*. New York, Avon, 1974.
Editor, *Black Holes*. New York, Fawcett, 1979.
Editor, *The Endless Frontier*. New York, Ace, 1979.
Editor, with John F. Carr, *The Survival of Freedom*. New York, Fawcett, 1981.
Editor, with John F. Carr, *The Endless Frontier 2*. New York, Ace, 1982.
Editor, with John F. Carr, *Nebula Award Stories 16*. New York, Holt Rinehart, 1982; London, W. H. Allen, 1983.
Editor, with John F. Carr, *There Will Be War*. New York, Tor, 1983.
Editor, with John F. Carr, *Men of War*. New York, Tor, 1984.
Editor, with John F. Carr, *Blood and Iron*. New York, Tor, 1985.
Editor, with Jim Baen and John F. Carr, *Far Frontiers 1-4*. New York, Baen, 4 vols., 1985.
Editor, with John F. Carr, *Imperial Stars*. New York, Baen, 1985.
Editor, with John F. Carr, *Silicon Brains*. New York, Ballantine, 1985.
Editor, with John F. Carr, *Science Fiction Yearbook 1984*. New York, Baen, 1985.

*

Jerry Pournelle comments:
My work is intended to entertain. I may well have a serious message, but in my judgment fiction is best served if the characters in a story do not know they have a message to deliver. Science-fiction writers are bards of the sciences; we are not fundamentally different from the bards of Homeric times, who would travel about and, spying an encamped group, say, "If you'll fill my cup with wine and dish me a bowl of stew, I will tell you a story about a virgin and a bull that you just wouldn't believe. . . ."

*   *   *

Jerry Pournelle's science fiction has consistently portrayed technological advance as the most significant visible indication of mankind's progress. The most obvious form of benevolent innovation is the development of space travel, a theme which infuses much of his work. This theme is particularly evident in *A Spaceship for the King*, in which the salvation of an entire world rests upon its ability to develop rapidly a spacefaring technology. In *Exiles to Glory* humanity is jolted out of its introverted and short-sighted doldrums by a space effort financed by commercial organizations. The Martian colony in *Birth of Fire* is entirely dependent on advanced equipment from Earth for its very existence.

There is a well expressed admiration for the professional military man. Colonel Nathan MacKinnie, the protagonist of *A Spaceship for the King*, is a cashiered veteran unable to function properly within the organized military of his world. *Janissaries,* and its sequel *Clan and Clown,* co-authored with Roland Green, concerns a small group of professional soldiers kidnapped from Earth by aliens unwilling to fight their own battles. John Falkenberg, a recurring character in Pournelle's early fiction, is a highly skilled strategic and tactical planner who leads a successful career with a unit of mercenaries. Falkenberg and his companions are featured in the novel *West of Honor* and several shorter pieces, three of which were collected to form the book, *The Mercenary.* (one of the best stories in this series, "Silent Leges," was not included.)

The Falkenberg stories are set within the context of the CoDominium, a pragmatic alliance of the United States and the Soviet Union that eventually evolves in the world government and an interseller empire. Pournelle subscribes here to the concept of civilization as going through cycles of collapse and renewal, as decadence destroys the old order to make way for the vigorous new. One of the several novels Pournelle has written in collaboration with Larry Niven takes place several centuries after the fall of the CoDominium. This novel, *The Mote in God's Eye,* is possibly the best single work to have appeared under the Pournelle byline.

Mote was met with widely varied reader response. It is a much longer than average novel, and it concerns the first contact with an alien species that is biologically diversified in order to cope with the exigencies of survival within the confines of their own system. There is a well-paced and logically developed plot, a strong and sustained element of suspense, gradual revelation of the mystery of the alien culture, and several extremely effective scenes, particularly one in which a handful of aliens animate an empty human spacesuit. There was some adverse reaction to what some readers saw as stereotyped characterizations, particularly that of the single female character, a passive individual who demonstrates little initiative. There is little evidence of any sustained effort to fully develop characters, but *Mote* is nevertheless an enthralling novel of adventure and discovery, and the focus of the story is the unfolding mystery of the alien culture, not the reactions of the characters. To a degree, the traditional values of literature are subordinated in this type of novel.

The next collaborative novel, *Lucifer's Hammer,* features several strong female characters, possibly to counter the ealier criticism. *Lucifer's Hammer* is an end-of-the-world story on a panoramic scale. Following the collision of Earth with a comet, civilization collapses into barbarism and most of the physical features of the world are altered. Marketed as a mainstream disaster novel, it features an extremely large cast of characters, numerous plots and subplots and covers a span of decades. There is careful, plausible extrapolation of the slow decay of the few islands of comparatively advanced society that survive as the apparatus of civilization disappears. It is indicative of Pournelle's view of technology that the climactic battle is fought for control of a functional nuclear power plant.

Oath of Fealty, also written with Larry Niven, is set in an enormous self-contailned city-building that is theoretically a part of Los Angeles. Automatic defensive systems kill intruders, and interests unfriendly to the building administration use the incident in a political struggle that may determine the shape of future urban life throughout the world. Although less grandiose than the earlier collaborations, the novel is complexly plotted and the implications of each turn of events are explored in detail.

Pournelle makes use of traditional plots for the most part, such as interplanetary war and conquest, world disaster, war in space, first contact with aliens, commercial rivalries for political advantage, penal colonies on other worlds, etc. His themes are familiar as well, the importance of space travel as an outlet for

human endesvor, technological answers to problems confronting the human race, the value of individualism as opposed to collectivism, and the primacy of man over aliens because of our stronger competitive drive for survival.

But the familiarity of plot and theme should not be construed to mean a lack of ability. The de-emphasis of characterization does not imply a lack of depth in other areas. Pournelle develops his plots in a logical fashion, with a good sense of timing and judicious use of suspense and other devices. Most of his fiction is essentially adventure, with clear-out action and sympathetic, if not entirely realistic characters. Social issues, when they arise iln Pournelle's fiction, are dealt with consistently, as he makes no secret of his views. Shortsighted ecological protection and population control movements nearly destroy the space effort in *Exiles to Glory.* Government officials are almost invariably portrayed as corrupt or inept or both. Even at his most polemic, Pournelle carefully avoids disturbing the momentum of his stories with his discourses. But even while the implications of his work might infuriate, the inventiveness and smooth flow of his plotting will entertain.

—Don D'Ammassa

POWERS, L. C. See TUBB, E. C.

POWERS, Tim. American. Recipient: Philip K. Dick Memorial Award, 1984. Address: c/o Ace Books, 200 Madison Avenue, New York, New York 10016, U.S.A.

SCIENCE- FICTION PUBLICATIONS

Novels

The Skies Discrowned. Toronto, Laser, 1976.
The Drawing of the Dark. New York, Ballantine, 1979; London, Mayflower, 1981.
The Anubis Gates. New York, Ace, 1983; London, Chatto and Windus, 1985.
Dinner at Deviant's Palace. New York, Ace, 1985.

Uncollected Short Story

"The Way Down the Hill," in *Fantasy and Science Fiction* (New York), December 1982.

*   *   *

Tim Powers, along with James P. Blaylock and K. W. Jeter, is one of a group of science-fiction writers around San Francisco who are now gaining recognition; companions of the late Philip K. Dick, they are perhaps most known for the originality of their own voices. Powers's career, after an undistinguished beginning with science fiction for Laser books, produced two innovative and entertaining books unique in recent fantasy. One, *The Anubis Gates,* won the Philip K. Dick award for 1983. Now, with *Dinner at Deviant's Palace* and a forthcoming rewrite of his *The Skies Discrowned,* Powers is returning to science fiction with a voice in some ways more skillful than that he brought to fantasy.

The Drawing of the Dark— the title is a pun on the threatened decline of the West and the potent, magical Herzwesten beer that may be a key to saving it—concerns a 16th-century mercenary who is contacted by Merlin and finds he is the latest incarnation of King Arthur. Though pure fantasy, it shows a number of scientifical skills, including good presentation of Renaissance Europe, in some ways as foreign as an alien culture. Also, both *The Drawing of the Dark* and *The Anubis Gates* use a system of magic which, while not exactly a scientific technology, still clearly functions by stated rules: since a magician forsakes the natural earth, in the books, someone is safe if in touch with the earth, by direct contact or a grounding wire.

The Anubis Gates, however, is arguably science fiction, particularly in its major concern, time travel. In fact, magic and the science of Darrow Interdisciplinary Research Enterprises serve as equal, and equally plausible, vehicles for and explanations of travel into the past. Through various paradoxes and explanations, all of the mysteries of the novel—including the fate of the hero, Brendon Doyle; the mysterious life of the early 19th-century poet, William Ashbless; the Dancing Ape Madness; Lord Byron in two places at once—are shown to be perfectly logical effects of time travel or the actions of the magicians and others involved. (The theme of immortality through changing bodies, which is part of the explanation of events in the *The Anubis Gates*, also is treated in "The Way Down the Hill.") The handling of the historical settings is even stronger than in the earlier novel.

If *The Anubis Gates* is a fantasy novel with some of the strengths of science fiction, *Dinner at Deviant's Palace* is a science-fiction novel which at first seems to be fantasy. While the post-World War III setting—a Los Angeles where carefully preserved cars are towed on wagonbeds for their prestige value, and almost any vice can be purchased—is clearly science fiction, the setting holds a number of mysteries which seem inexplicable in scientific terms, including a cult that partakes of mass psychic communion, from whom the hero, Greg Rivas, is paid to liberate and de-program a woman he once loved. As the plot unfolds and connections appear, the reader discovers all the mysteries to be ingeniously linked, and explicable within the limits of science fiction.

Besides the facility with involved plots in which all is explained and shown to be related, and good description of societies in the past or future, careful depiction of his adventurer-hero in each book also marks Powers's works. These heroes, and other characters, seem constantly in pain due to their travails, in a way that is quite realistic but perhaps unpleasant. Powers also has a facination for the criminal underworld, which he presents with affection and energy but not sentimentality. Above all, Powers is an entertaining writer, humorous as well as able to present action. All of these qualities show, despite the less mature writing style, in *The Skies Discrowned;* probably, the rewrite will continue the trend of his increasingly able books.

—Bernadette Bosky

PRAGNELL, Festus. British. Born 16 January 1905. Worked as a policeman in London.

SCIENCE-FICTION PUBLICATIONS

Novels

The Green Man of Kilsona. London, Philip Allan, 1936; revised edition, as *The Green Man of Graypec*, New York, Greenberg, 1950.

Kastrove der Mächtige. Rastatt, Germany, Utopia-Zukunftsroman, 1966.

Uncollected Short Stories (series: Don Hargreaves)

"The Venus Germ," with R. F. Starzl, in *Wonder Stories* (New York), November 1932.

"Men of the Dark Comet," in *Wonder Stories* (New York), June 1933.

"The Isotope Man," in *Wonder Stories* (New York), August 1933.

"The Essence of Life," in *Amazing* (New York), August 1933.

"A Visit to Venus," in *Wonder Stories* (New York), August 1934.

"Ghost of Mars" (Hargreaves), in *Amazing* (New York), December 1938.

"War of the Human Cats," in *Fantastic Adventures* (New York), August 1940.

"Warlords" (Hargreaves), in *Amazing* (New York), October 1940.

"Kidnapped in Mars," in *Amazing* (New York), October 1941.

"Outlaw" (Hargreaves), in *Amazing* (New York), January 1942.

"Devil Birds of Deimos" (Hargreaves), in *Amazing* (New York), April 1942.

"Into the Caves of Mars" (Hargreaves), in *Amazing* (New York), August 1942.

"Twisted Giant of Mars" (Hargreaves), in *Amazing* (New York), May 1943.

"Conspirators of Phobos" (Hargreaves), in *Amazing* (New York), June 1943.

"Collision in Space," in *Amazing* (New York), July 1943.

"Madcap of Mars" (Hargreaves), in *Amazing* (New York), September 1943.

"The Machine God Laughs," in *The Machine God Laughs*, edited by William L. Crawford. Los Angeles, Griffin, 1949.

OTHER PUBLICATIONS

Novel

The Terror from Timorkal. London, Bear, 1946.

*   *   *

Festus Pragnell was among the small contingent of British writers who, lacking a suitable market at home, found a billet for their work in the American science-fiction magazines. Though he was far from being the most successful, he enjoyed the distinction of having his work approved by H. G. Wells.

Wells found that *The Green Man of Kilsona* contained a reference to "H. Geewells," a noted author on the electron world of Kilsona where Pragnell's hero finds himself in the body of an ape-man. Having read it, Wells wrote to Pragnell pronouncing it "a very good story indeed," but the resulting publicity was too late to help the sales of the novel. Pragnell's first story, "The Essence of Life," in which super-intelligent beings from Jupiter made a peaceful visit to Earth, appeared in *Amazing* 18 months after acceptance. "Men of the Dark Comet" is the tale of a wandering satellite inhabited by strange plant-creatures, and "The Isotope Men" deals with the destruction of a planet—now the Asteroid Belt—from which man's forebears came to Earth. The ideas were typical of the period, the writing no better or worse than editor Hugo

Gernsback was ready to accept at the rates which applied in those days of economic depression. And Pragnell, a spare-time scribbler, knew the pangs of unemployment.

In "A Visit to Venus" he painted a morbid picture of human bodies distorted by poisonous spores distributed by intending invaders. He was a man obsessed by the study of vitamins and other aspects of medicine which furnished him with plot-material while a daily pinch of baker's yeast supplied him with energy. He was fond of inventing bizarre forms of animal and vegetable life, and the effects of a strict religious upbringing against which he rebelled could be detected in his work. He protested, too, the rigid policies of editors who denied him the freedom of expression he craved. He had little success in his own country, but by the 1940's had found his metier in Ray Palmer's *Amazing Stories* where his lively tales of Don Hargreaves on Mars and its moons, replete with twisted giants and devil birds, suited its juvenile appeal.

—Walter Gillings

PRATCHETT, Terry. Address: c/o Smythe Ltd., P. O. Box 6, Gerrards Cross, Buckinghamshire SL9 8XA, England.

SCIENCE- FICTION PUBLICATIONS

Novels

Carpet People. Gerrards Cross, Buckinghamshire, Smythe, 1971.
The Dark Side of the Sun. Gerrards Cross, Buckinghamshire, Smythe, 1976.
Strata. Gerrards Cross, Buckinghamshire, Smythe, and New York, St. Martin's Press, 1981.
The Colour of Magic. Gerrards Cross, Buckinghamshire, Smythe, and New York, St. Martin's Press, 1983.

Uncollected Short Stories

"The Hades Business," in *The Unfriendly Future*, edited by Tom Boardman, Jr. London, FSB, 1965.
"Night Dweller," in *New Worlds* (London), November 1965.

*   *   *

Terry Pratchett's novel *Strata* was widely regarded as an amusing commentary on Larry Niven's award-winning novel Ringworld, which it resembles in many superficial ways. The protagonist is a human woman whose job is to oversee the construction of planets, the future homes of human and other races. She takes great pains to see that her subordinates do not plant anachronistic items in the strata of these planets, a diversion which appears to have an almost universal appeal. But from a mysterious visitor, she learns of the existence of a flat world lost in space, unknown to the rest of the universe, built in a fashion totally impossible to humanity, and inhabited by people totally indistinguishable from human beings.

Her curiosity is piqued, along with her sense of adventure, and she sets off with a number of companions, human and otherwise, in a quest to find the flat world. Unfortunately, a series of mishaps results in the loss of their guide, and the incapacitation of their spaceship in the atmosphere of their destination. After landing, they set off on an often hilarious romp among dragons, robots, aliens, and other creatures, as they explore this strange new environment. Pratchett is one of

the few genuinely funny writers practicing in the genre, and while it is hard to take much of what goes on in this novel (or his others) very seriously, it is consistantly amusing and entertaining.

The Dark Side of the Sun sounds like a much more serious novel. The protagonist is the rich heir to a powerful title who sets off on a quest to find the Jokers' World, home of a legendary alien species. The background of this novel is tied up with the manipulation of the laws of chance, another concept possibly borrowed from Niven's *Ringworld*. A series of assassination attempts are thwarted, generally through a strange combination of circumstances that seem to defy the laws of probability. As indeed they do. Once again, the delight of the book is in the richly creative backgrounds of alien species, religious and other philosophies, and bizarre settings. Pratchett's light-hearted approach succeeds in what would otherwise be just another adventure novel because of his wittiness and the density of material in a rather short novel.

Pratchett's most recent novel is *The Colour of Magic*, which is an iconoclastic view of fanasy adventures. The four related adventures are set in a flat world which really is held upon the backs of four gigantic elephants astride the shell of a gigantic tortoise swimming in space. The inhabitants of the world know this to be true because they have lowered observors over the edge to see for themselves.

Rincewind is certainly one of the least likely magicians ever to grace the pages of fiction. He agrees to provide his services as a guide to a visitor from another planet interested in exploring this strange world. Their travels bring them into encounters with malevolent animals, wizards, monsters, and other villains in an extremely funny spoof, which can only be compared to Jack Vance's "Dying Earth" stories at their very best. Pratchett seems particularly enamoured of anachronisms, which abound in this novel as well.

Pratchett seems to be neither a follower or a leader, more interested in exploring his own niche in the science fiction firmament. Humorous science fiction does not in general sell well and, as of this writing, only *Strata* has seen a mass market paperback edition in the United States. His style is certainly unique enough to attract a following, but it is unclear just how influential his work might ultimately be.

—Don D'Ammassa

PRATT, (Murray) Fletcher. Also wrote as George U. Fletcher. American. Born in Buffalo, New York, 25 April 1897. Attended Hobart College, Geneva, New York, 1915-16; University of Paris, 1931-33. Served in the War Library Service during World War I. Married Inga Marie Stephens. Librarian, 1918-20; staff member, Buffalo *Courier Express*, 1920-23; free-lance writer from 1923; regular contributor, American Mercury and *Saturday Review of Literature*; military advisor, *Time* and New York *Post* during World War II; staff member, Bread Loaf Writers Conference. President, Authors Club, 1941; Co-Founder, American Rocket Society. Recipient: United States Navy Award, 1957. *Died 10 June 1956.*

SCIENCE-FICTION PUBLICATIONS

Novels

Double in Space (*Project Excelsior, The Wanderer's Return*). New York, Doubleday, 1951.

Double Jeopardy. New York, Doubleday, 1952.
The Undying Fire. New York, Ballantine 1953; as *The Conditioned Captain,* in *Double in Space,* 1954.
Double in Space (Project Excelsior, The Conditioned Captain). London, Boardman, 1954.
Invaders from Rigel. New York, Avalon, 1960.
Alien Planet. New York, Avalon, 1962.
The Blue Star. New York, Ballantine, 1969.

OTHER PUBLICATIONS

Novels with L. Sprague de Camp

The Incomplete Enchanter. New York, Holt, 1941; London, Sphere, 1979.
Land of Unreason. New York, Holt, 1942.
The Carnelian Cube. New York, Gnome Press, 1948.
The Well of the Unicorn (by Pratt only, as George U. Fletcher). New York, Sloane, 1948.
The Castle of Iron. New York, Gnome Press, 1950.
Wall of Serpents. New York, Avalon, 1960.
The Compleat Enchanter: The Magical Adventures of Harold Shea (includes *The Incomplete Enchanter* and *The Castle of Iron*). New York, Doubleday, 1975; London, Sphere, 1979.

Short Stories

Tales from Gavagan's Bar, with L. Sprague de Camp. New York, Twayne, 1953; expanded edition, Philadelphia, Owlswick Press, 1978.

Other

The Heroic Years: Fourteen Years of the Republic 1801-1815. New York, Smith and Haas, 1934.
The Cunning Mulatto and Other Cases of Ellis Parker, American Detective. New York, Smith and Haas, 1935; as *Detective No. 1,* London, Methuen, 1936.
Ordeal by Fire: An Informal History of the Civil War. New York, Smith and Haas, 1935; revised edition, New York, Sloane, 1948; London, Lane, 1950; as *A Short History of the Civil War,* New York, Bantam, n. d.
Hail, Caesar! New York, Smith and Haas, 1936; London, Williams and Norgate, 1938.
The Navy: A History. New York, Doubleday, 1938.
Road to Empire: The Life and Times of Bonaparte the General. New York, Doubleday, 1939.
Sea Power and Today's War. New York, Harrison Hilton, 1939; London, Methuen, 1940.
Secret and Urgent: The Story of Codes and Ciphers. Indianapolis, Bobbs Merrill, and London, Hale, 1939.
Fletcher Pratt's Naval War Game. New York, Harrison Hilton, 1940.
Fighting Ships of the U. S. Navy. New York, Garden City Publishing Company, 1941.
America and Total War. New York, Smith and Durrell, 1941.
The U. S. Army. Racine, Wisconsin, Whitman, 1942.
What the Citizen Should Know about Modern War. New York, Norton, 1942.
The Navy Has Wings. New York, Harper, 1943.
My Life to the Destroyers, with Captain L. A. Abercrombie. New York, Holt, 1944.
The Navy's War. New York, Harper, 1944.
A Short History of the Army and Navy. Washington, D. C., Infantry Journal, 1944.
Fleet Against Japan. New York, Harper, 1946.

Empire of the Sea. New York, Holt, 1946.
Night Work: The Story of Task Force 39. New York, Holt, 1946.
A Man and His Meals, with Robeson Bailey. New York, Holt, 1947.
The Empire and Glory: Napoleon Bonaparte 1800-1806. New York, Sloane, 1948.
The Marines' War. New York, Sloane, 1948.
Eleven Generals: Studies in American Command. New York, Sloane, 1949.
The Third King. New York, Sloane, 1950.
War for the World: A Chronicle of Our Fighting Forces in World War II. New Haven, Connecticut, Yale University Press, 1950.
Prebble's Boys: Commodore Prebble and the Birth of American Sea Power. New York, Sloane, 1950.
Rockets, Jets, Guided Missiles, and Space Ships. New York, Random House, 1951; London, Sidgwick and Jackson, 1952.
The Monitor and the Merrimac. New York, Random House, 1951.
By Space Ship to the Moon (for children). New York, Random House, 1952; London, Publicity Products, 1953.
Stanton, Lincoln's Secretary of War. New York, Norton, 1953.
All about Rockets and Jets. New York, Random House, 1955.
The Civil War. New York, Garden City Books, 1955.
Famous Inventors and Their Inventions. New York, Random House, 1955.
The Battles that Changed History. New York, Doubleday, 1956.
Civil War on Western Waters. New York, Holt, 1956.
The Compact History of the United States Navy. New York, Hawthorn, 1957.

Editor, *World of Wonder.* New York, Twayne, 1951.
Editor, *Civil War in Pictures.* New York, Garden City Books, 1951.
Editor, *Petrified Planet.* New York, Twayne, 1952.
Editor, *Witches Three,* New York, Twayne, 1952.
Editor, *My Diary, North and South,* by Sir William Howard Russell. New York, Harper, 1954.

Translator, *The Great American Parade,* by H. J. Duteil. New York, Twayne, 1953.

* * *

Fletcher Pratt had an extremely varied writing career. While he is considered to be one of the pioneer science-fiction writers, he also wrote fantasy and produced an impressive list of historical nonfiction. In terms of science fiction, Pratt wrote mainly short fiction during his early years, with the exception of *Alien Planet.* The publisher's forword to the Ace edition of this novel accurately describes it as using "the traditional technique of the 'marvelous voyage' and the 'manuscript found in a bottle' . . . combined with a penetrating and satiric representation of human society through the method of exploring an alien culture. " It is a classic representation of the genre. Of course, much of the material is outdated but there remains some interesting philosophy, including the alien dissident's description of intelligent life as a disease infesting the planets which the divine spirit strives to destroy.

In 1939, Pratt met L. Sprague de Camp and his writing turned toward fantasy. Together they wrote a series of stories about a psychologist who finds himself projected into a number of parallel words which are based on our myths. Harold Shea, as he is called, makes his rounds of Norse mythology ("The Roaring Trumpet"), Spenser's *Faerie Queene* ("The Mathematics of

Logic"), Ariosto's *Orlando Furioso (The Castle of Iron)*, the Finnish *Kalevala (Wall of Serpents)* and the world of Irish myth ("The Green Magician"). The stories were unique in that they combined the then new field of sword-and-sorcery fantasy with a refreshing humor. The two writers wrote two additional fantasy novels, *Land of Unreason* and *The Carnelian Cube*, as well as a collection of short fantasy spoofs, *Tales from Gavagan's Bar*. The last, similar to Clarke's *Tales of the White Hart*, also showed the magical humor of Pratt and de Camp evident in the Harold Shea pieces. Pratt's solo novel *The Well of the Unicorn* is a fascinating creation by a master storyteller, one of the very best of fantasies.

Pratt's SF work *Double Jeopardy* details the adventures of George Helmfleet Jones, an agent with the Secret Service some time in the future. In his first adventure, Jones solves a case dealing with a matter transmitter; in the second, he is confronted by the theft of a large sum of money from a sealed, remote-controlled cargo rocket. *Double in Space* consists of two unrelated works. The first is born of the early Cold War with Russian and US space stations vying for superiority in space. The second is a take-off on the voyage of Ulysses set in the far distant future. In a similar vein, *The Undying Fire* follows the plot of Jason and the Golden Fleece. None of these works matches the caliber of Pratt's fantasy.

—Paul Swank

PREUSS, Paul. American. Born in Albany, Georgia, 7 March 1942. Educated at Yale University, New Haven, Connecticut, B. A. 1966. Served in the United States Air Force Reserve, 1960-66. Married 1) Marsha Pettit in 1963 (divorced, 1968), one daughter; 2) Karen Reiser in 1973. Marketing Planning Projects Director, Batten Barton Durstine & Osborn, New York, 1966-67; Floor Director, King-TV, 1967-68, and Unit Manager, 1968-69, Production Manager, 1969-70, and Creative Director, 1970-72, King Screen Productions, all in Seattle; Staff Consultant, Biological Science Curriculum Study, Boulder, Colorado, 1972-73; independent film producer, 1974-81, and associate producer, editor, and post-production supervisor, Lee Mendelson Film Productions and other companies, 1975-81. Since 1978, free-lance writer. Agent (literary): Diana Price, Frommer Price Literary Agency, 185 East 85th Street, New York, New York 10028, U.S.A.

SCIENCE-FICTION PUBLICATIONS

Novels

The Gates of Heaven. New York, Bantam, 1980.
Re-Entry. New York, Bantam, 1981.
Broken Symmetries. New York, Pocket Books, 1983; London, Penguin, 1984.
Human Error. New York, Tor, 1985.

Uncollected Short Story

"Small Bodies," in *The Planets*, edited by Byron Preiss. New York, Bantam, 1985.

*

Paul Preuss comments:

I am more interested in the social implications of the scientific endeavor than in gadgets, and I am even more interested in scientists than in science itself.

* * *

The novels that Paul Preuss has published since 1980, along with his competent popular science writing, demonstrate the continuing appropriateness of fiction and exposition for capturing the sense of both wonder and open-ended possibility that permeate modern science. The super science awe from the pulps and the precision of science itself combine in his work to suggest that hard science fiction is still a major mode of the genre. His first two fictions are the more fantastic as well as the less skillfully told; and it is not until *Broken Symmetries* that he achieves controlled storytelling, long passages of history of science exposition, and more plausible but nevertheless awesome recent science to create his best hard science fiction.

The determining theoretic notion for both The Gates of Heaven and *Re-Entry*, which may be the first two of a series of stories, is that paired black holes in orbit around one another provide a gateway to remote times and spaces. Not only does Preuss toy with this particular theoretic solution to the limitation of space/time but he also posits the usual plenitude of near-infinite alternate possibilities. Thus his hero in *Re-Entry* cleverly manages to journey backward in time to meet himself as his own tutor only to discover, both theoretically and fictionally, that there are an appalling number of variations possible to his lifeline. As Preuss speculates and marvels over this wonderful theoretic idea (though he does restore unity of character to his hero finally) he echoes Asimov, in particular, in *The End of Eternity*. But it is an old idea in the genre, and Preuss brings nothing startlingly new to it—except perhaps a rather more fanciful juxtaposition of epochs than some time-travel writers have used. In *Re-Entry* his key planet beyond the time-gate is one terraformed for biological engineering on Earth's Mesozoic and Cenozoic eras named Darwin.

If Preuss decided to abort this opening series of time-travel fictions in favor of what he has most recently accomplished in *Broken Symmetries*, it was a wise decision. Fanciful time travel and infinite possibilities for alternate universes are wonderful and stock themes in hard science fiction, but the sublime possibilities opened up by much actual scientific research and theory in our time can create similar effects in fiction—and more plausibly. Furthermore, his characterization and plotting in *Broken Symmetries* has matured and, also, paradoxically narrowed toward the more manageable range of mainstream fiction. He writes about real scientists and real scientific work in the manner of Gregory Benford in *Timescape* and infuses that realistic setting with the exciting sense of possibility that does exist at the pioneering edges of modern science. One does not need to travel to Darwin to create the sense of wonder in fiction or, for that matter, the sense of intellectual complexity that alternate universes suggest. The theory about sub-atomic particles and the technology of the gigantic particle accelerators offers "mad science" enough, and in this third novel Preuss combines those topics with fine sections of exposition about the history of particle theory and particle research in the 20th century as well as the impact of such research on potential nuclear holocaust. *Broken Symmetries* represents a movement on Preuss's part away from more pulpish writing and toward the more mainstream novel of modern science. What holds it closer to hard science fiction is the depth of the science and the pursuit of what is marvelous in the science and what is speculative.

Preuss developed those writing traits in his two earlier novels and, apparently, from a love of science fiction.

—Donald M. Hassler

PRIEST, Christopher. British. Born in Cheadle, Cheshire, in 1943. Educated at Warehouseman and Clerks' Orphan Schools, Manchester, 1951-59. Council Member, Science Fiction Foundation, and Editor, *Foundation,* for 2 years. Recipient: British Science Fiction Association Award, 1974, 1979; Ditmar Award (Australia) 1977, 1982. Agent: A. P. Watt Ltd., 26-28 Bedford Row, London WCIR 4HL, England; or, Ellen Levine Literary Agency, 432 Park Avenue South, New York, New York 10016, U.S.A.

SCIENCE-FICTION PUBLICATIONS

Novels

Indoctrinaire. London, Faber, and New York, Harper, 1970; revised edition, London, Pan, 1979.
Fugue for a Darkening Island. London, Faber, 1972; as *Darkening Island,* New York, Harper, 1972.
Inverted World. London, Faber, 1974; as *The Inverted World,* New York, Harper, 1974.
The Space Machine. London, Faber, and New York, Harper, 1976.
A Dream of Wessex. London, Faber, 1977; as *The Perfect Lover,* New York, Scribner, 1977.

Short Stories

Real Time World. London, New English Library, 1974.
An Infinite Summer. London, Faber, and New York, Scribner, 1979.

Uncollected Short Stories

"The Creation," in *Andromeda 3,* edited by Peter Weston. London, Futura, 1978.
"The Agent, " with David Redd, in *Aries 1,* edited by John Grant. Newton Abbot, Devon, David and Charles, 1979.
"The Miraculous Cairn," in *New Terrors 2,* edited by Ramsey Campbell. London, Pan, 1980.

OTHER PUBLICATIONS

Novels

The Affirmation. London, Faber, and New York, Scribner, 1981.
The Glamour. London, Cape, 1984; New York, Doubleday, 1985.

Other

Your Book of Film-Making (for children). London, Faber, 1974.

Editor, *Anticipations.* London, Faber, and New York, Scribner, 1978.
Editor, with Robert Holdstock, *Stars of Albion* (anthology of British science fiction). London, Pan, 1979.

*   *   *

Christopher Priest was one of the most promising new British science-fiction writers to become active in the 1970's. His fist novel *Indoctrinaire* (expanded from "The Interrogator"), reflected the type of story that dominated *New Worlds* at the time. Dr. Wentik is a researcher in investigating an experimental drug at a scientific installation in the Antarctic when he is shanghaied by the mysterious American government agent Astrourde. Shortly thereafter he is incarcerated in an enigmatic prison in the Brazilian highlands, in an area that somehow serves as a bridge between the present and the world two centuries from now. Wentik's attempts to escape his situation, or even to make some kind of sense of it, are reminiscent of Kafka. His efforts are largely ineffectual, although it does become increasingly clear to him that even his capters are without true freedom. Reality and fantasy merge at times, and the result is a kaleidoscopic novel that dilutes its effect by the lack of strong focus.

Fugue for a Darkening Island also features a weak and less than entirely admirable protagonist. Following a major war in Africa, the British Isles are rapidly inundated with refugees, an exodus that is met with indecisive hostility on the part of the British authorities. As the influx grows, order begins to disintegrate. Divergent opinions about the obligation to provide succor to the refugees lead to an increasingly violent factionalism. Government control over much of the country-side collapses; invidual neighborhoods wall themselves off from the outside world. Alan Whitman and his family are cast adrift in this world, and find that they are unable to control their own future. Frequently it is impossible even to distinguish those who uphold the law from those who break it. Priest makes no effort to plot his novel linearly. The viewpoint jumps back and forth through time, seemingly at random, so that the reader is almost simultaneously exposed to Whitman at all stages of his dissolution. But Priest holds his character at arm's length from us, and we can vaguely perceive his motivations; the nightmarish quality of his world remains that, for it never quite achieves reality.

Paradoxically, while the all too possible world shown in *Fugue for a Darkening Island* never acquires depth, the almost totally incredible setting of *Inverted World* is vividly realistic. It is a much more cohesive novel than anything Priest had written before. It features a strong sympathetic character, and some of the most innovative settings to appear in years. Helward Mann is a citizen of City Earth, an enormous construct that inches across the surface of its world by wincing itself across tracks picked up from beyond and laboriously replaced ahead. The city is in eternal pursuit of the Optimum, the place where environmental conditions are most like that of their home world. For this world, whatever it might be, is treacherous and changing. Behind them, physical features become broad and flat, time passes very rapidly in relation to the city itself, and a mysterious force increasingly attempts to pull laggers back to their destruction. Ahead, the distortions of time and space have exactly opposite attributes. As Mann is initiated into the guild responsible for scouting the future, he gradually matures and adjusts to the changing nature of his world. Idea is central here rather than character; nevertheless, Helward and his personal relationships with others from the city are well portrayed. Although less ambitious stylistically than Priest's earlier novels, *Inverted Worlds* is far more successful both as an adventure story and as a novel of ideas. Priest indulged in pastiche next, and *The Space Machine* is a witty and frequently funny examination of some of the situations first presented by H. G. Wells. This invocation of Martians invaders and time machines is carried a bit too far, unfortunately, and it is difficult to sustain interest through the end.

A Dream of Wessex is a far more successful novel in almost any terms, and is easy the high point of Priest's career. The Ridpath Project is a secret research installation where a group of people pool their subconscious minds to create a mutual dream world. Within this context, they can extrapolate the future possibilities of various aspects of the present. But there is trouble brewing. David Harkman, one of the dreamers, has lost his awareness of the real world and will not come out of trance. Julia Stretton, another participant, tries desperately to release him from the grip of the dream world, particularly when she learns of the imminent participation of a new dreamer, a man who considers the project to be nonsense. The dream world becomes more real to the reader than the project itself, and, despite the existence of Soviet domination over Britain, it is easy to see why Harkman is unconsciously reluctant to leave it for reality. Both of the central figures are fully realized personalities, and their awakening feelings for each other are convincing.

The Affirmation develops logically from the themes Priest has used in the past. Peter Sinclair is a young man who lives both in the London of our world and in Jethra of the Dream Archipelago, the setting for a number of Priest's short stories. In London, Sinclair is descending into madness following a series of personal disasters; in Jethra he has won the prize of immortality, but to secure it he must surrender all of his memories. Each man is writing a book set in the other universe, and each man has reached a point in his life where he must make significant decisions about his future. The intellectual nature of this struggle will not endear this novel to adventure-story readers, but Priest's skillful character development is at its best in this work.

Priest seems to be fusing reality and dreams increasingly in his fiction. It should be no surprise, therefore, to note that most of his better short stories also explore this interface. "Real Time World" describes the Observatory, supposedly an extra-dimensional establishment from which a small staff could observe the flora and fauna of other worlds, in actuality an experiment in itself on news deprivation with a staff throughly brainwashed about the nature of their situation. In "Palely Loitering" a man spends much of his life travelling back and forth across time bridges, always in pursuit of a young girl he does not have the courage to confront. His ultimate effort draws into question the immutability of the past and the reality of his own present. Two stories set within the context of the "Dream Archipelago" are also worth mentioning. "Whores" is an incident sliced out of time, wherein the protagonist encounters a series of inexplicable events, mutilations of a sort of people living in an area formerly occupied by enemy troops. Much of the story's impact is dissipated by the ambiguous ending, however, a problem that arises also with Priest's best short story, "The Watched. " Yvann Ordier is disturbed by his voyeuristic spying on a band of Qataari refugees. The Qataari have an obsessive need for privacy, and will literally starve to death rather than submit to being studied. At the same time, Ordier himself is compulsively wary of scintillas, tiny mechanical spy devices that are almost unavoidable. The result is a complex story of character, obsession, and personal decay.

The involuted, intellectualized nature of the conflict in Priest's recent fiction demonstrates a mature grasp of character and theme, but unfortunately is not as commercially successful as is fiction with more overt plots. The modest amount of fiction Priest has produced has enriched the field and quietly established him as one of the more innovative writers.

—Don D'Ammassa

PRIESTLEY, J(ohn) B(oynton). Also wrote as Peter Goldsmith. British. Born in Bradford, Yorkshire, 13 September 1894. Educated at Belle Vue School, Bradford; Trinity Hall, Cambridge, 1919-22, M. A. Served in the Duke of Wellington's and Devon regiments, 1914-1919. Married 1) Patricia Tempest (died, 1928), two daughters; 2) Mary Wyndham Lewis (divorced, 1952), two daughters and one son; 3) the writer Jacquetta Hawkes in 1953. Worked in a wool merchant's office after 1910; free-lance writer and publisher's reader in London after 1922; Director, Mask Theatre, London, 1938-39; radio lecturer on BBC programme "Postscripts" during World War II; regular contributor, *New Statesman*, London. President, P. E. N., London, 1936-37; United Kingdom Delegate, and Chairman, Unesco International Theatre Conference, Paris, 1947, and Prague, 1948; Chairman, British Theatre Conference, 1948; President, International Theatre Institute, 1949; Member, National Theatre Board, London, 1966-67. Recipient: Black Memorial Prize, 1930; Ellen Terry Award, 1948. LL. D. : University of St. Andrews; D. Litt. : University of Birmingham; University of Bradford, 1969. Honorary Freeman, City of Bradford, 1973; Honorary Student, Trinity Hall, Cambridge, 1978. Order of Merit, 1977. *Died 14 August 1984* .

SCIENCE-FICTION PUBLICATIONS

Novels

Adam in Moonshine. London, Heinemann, and New York, Harper, 1927.
The Doomsday Men. London, Heinemann, and New York, Harper, 1938.
The Magicians. London, Heinemann, and New York, Harper, 1954.
Low Notes on a High Level: A Frolic. London, Heinemann, and New York, Harper, 1954.
The Thirty-First of June. London, Heinemann, 1961; New York, Doubleday, 1962.
Snoggle (for children). London, Heinemann, 1971; New York, Harcourt Brace, 1972.

Short Stories

The Other Place and Other Stories of the Same Sort. London, Heinemann, and New York, Harper, 1953.

OTHER PUBLICATIONS

Novels

Benighted. London, Heinemann, 1927; as *The Old Dark House*, New York, Harper, 1928.
Farthing Hall, with Hugh Walpole. London, Macmillan, and New York, Doubleday, 1929.
The Good Companions. London, Heinemann, and New York, Harper, 1929.
Angel Pavement. London, Heinemann, and New York, Harper, 1930.
Faraway. London, Heinemann, and New York, Harper, 1932.
I'll Tell You Everything, with Gerald Bullett. New York, Macmillan, 1932; London, Heinemann, 1933.
Wonder Hero. London, Heinemann, and New York, Harper, 1933.
They Walk in the City: The Lovers in the Stone Forest. London, Heinemann, and New York, Harper, 1936.

Let the People Sing. London, Heinemann, 1939; New York, Harper, 1940.

Black-Out in Gretley: A Story of—and for—Wartime. London, Heinemann, and New York, Harper, 1942.

Daylight on Saturday: A Novel about an Aircraft Factory. London, Heinemann, and New York, Harper, 1943.

Three Men in New Suits. London, Heinemann, and New York, Harper, 1945.

Bright Day. London, Heinemann, and New York, Harper, 1946.

Jenny Villiers: A Story of the Theatre. London, Heinemann, and New York, Harper, 1947.

Festival at Farbridge. London, Heinemann, 1951; as *Festival*, New York, Harper, 1951.

Saturn over the Water. London, Heinemann, and New York, Doubleday, 1961.

The Shapes of Sleep: A Topical Tale. London, Heinemann, and New York, Doubleday, 1962.

Sir Michael and Sir George. London, Heinemann, 1964; Boston, Little Brown, 1965.

Lost Empires. London, Heinemann, and Boston, Little Brown, 1965.

Salt Is Leaving. London, Pan, 1966; New York, Harper, 1975.

It's an Old Country. London, Heinemann, and Boston, Little Brown, 1967.

The Image Men: Out of Town, and London End. London, Heinemann, 2 vols., 1968; Boston, Little Brown, 1 vol., 1969.

Found, Lost, Found; or The English Way of Life. London, Heinemann, 1976; New York, Stein and Day, 1977.

Short Stories

The Town Major of Miraucourt. London, Heinemann, 1930.

Albert Goes Through. London, Heinemann, and New York, Harper, 1933.

Going Up: Stories and Sketches. London, Pan, 1950.

The Carfitt Crisis and Two Other Stories. London, Heinemann, 1975.

Plays

The Good Companions (book only), with Edward Knoblock, lyrics by Harry Graham and Frank Eyton, music by Richard Addinsell, adaptation of the novel by Priestley (produced London and New York, 1931). London and New York, French, 1935.

Dangerous Corner (produced London and New York, 1932). London, Heinemann, and New York, French, 1932.

The Roundabout (produced Liverpool, London, and New York, 1932). London, Heinemann, and New York, French, 1933.

Laburnum Grove: An Immoral Comedy (produced London, 1933; New York, 1935). London, Heinemann, 1934; New York, French, 1935.

Eden End (produced London, 1934; New York, 1935). London, Heinemann, 1934; in *Three Plays and a Preface*, 1935.

Cornelius: A Business Affair in Three Transactions (produced Birmingham and London, 1935). London, Heinemann, 1935; New York, French, 1936.

Duet in Floodlight (produced Liverpool and London, 1935). London, Heinemann, 1935.

Three Plays and a Preface (includes *Dangerous Corner, Eden End, Cornelius*). New York, Harper, 1935.

Bees on the Boat Deck: A Farcical Tragedy (produced London, 1936). London, Heinemann, and Boston, Baker, 1936.

Spring Tide (as Peter Goldsmith), with George Billam (produced London, 1936). London, Heinemann, and New York, French, 1936.

The Bad Samaritan (produced Liverpool, 1937).

Time and the Conways (produced London, 1937; New York, 1938). London, Heinemann, 1937; New York, Harper, 1938.

I Have Been Here Before (produced London, 1937; New York, 1938). London, Heinemann 1937; New York, Harper, 1938.

Two Time Plays (includes *Time and the Conways* and *I Have Been Here Before*). London, Heinemann, 1937.

People at Sea (as *I Am a Stranger Here*, produced Bradford, 1937; as *People at Sea*, produced London, 1937). London, Heinemann, and New York, French, 1937.

Mystery of Greenfingers: A Comedy of Detection (produced London, 1938). London, French, 1937; New York, French, 1938.

The Rebels (produced Bradford, 1938).

When We Are Married: A Yorkshire Farcical Comedy (produced London, 1938; New York, 1939). London, Heinemann, 1938; New York, French, 1940.

Music at Night (produced Malvern, 1938; London, 1939). Included in *Three Plays*, 1943; in *Plays I*, 1948.

Johnson over Jordan (produced London, 1939). Published as *Johnson over Jordan: The Play, and All about It* (An Essay). London, Heinemann, and New York, Harper, 1939.

The Long Mirror (produced Oxford, 1940; London, 1945). Included in *Three Plays*, 1943; in *Four Plays*, 1944.

Good Night Children: A Comedy of Broadcasting (produced London, 1942). Included in *Three Comedies*, 1945; in *Plays II*, 1949.

Desert Highway (produced Bristol, 1943; London, 1944). London, Heinemann, 1944; in *Four Plays*, 1944.

They Came to a City (produced London, 1943). Included in *Three Plays*, 1943; in *Four Plays*, 1944.

Three Plays (includes *Music at Night, The Long Mirror, They Came to a City*). London, Heinemann, 1943.

How Are They at Home? A Topical Comedy (produced London, 1944). Included in *Three Comedies*, 1945; in *Plays II*, 1949.

The Golden Fleece (as *The Bull Market*, produced Bradford, 1944). Included in *Three Comedies*, 1945.

Four Plays (includes Music at Night, The Long Mirror, They Came to a City, Desert Highway). London, Heinemann, and New York, Harper, 1944.

Three Comedies (includes *Good Night Children, The Golden Fleece, How Are They at Home?*). London, Heinemann, 1945.

An Inspector Calls (produced Moscow, 1945; London, 1946; New York, 1947). London, Heinemann, 1947; New York, Dramatists Play Service, 1948(?).

Jenny Villiers (produced Bristol, 1946).

The Rose and Crown (televised, 1946). London, French, 1947.

Ever Since Paradise: An Entertainment, Chiefly Referring to Love and Marriage (also director: produced on tour, 1946; London, 1947). London and New York, French, 1949.

Three Time Plays (includes *Dangerous Corner, Time and the Conways, I Have Been Here Before*). London, Pan, 1947.

The Linden Tree (produced Sheffield and London, 1947; New York, 1948). London, Heinemann, and New York, French, 1948.

The Plays of J. B. Priestley:

1. *Dangerous Corner, I Have Been Here Before, Johnson over Jordan, Music at Night, The Linden Tree, Eden End, Time and the Conways*. London, Heinemann, 1948; as *Seven Plays*, New York, Harper, 1950.

2. *Laburnum Grove, Bees on the Boat Deck, When We Are Married, Good Night Children, The Good Companions, How Are They at Home?, Ever Since Paradise*. London, Heinemann, 1949; New York, Harper, 1951.

3. *Cornelius, People at Sea, They Came to a City, Desert*

Highway, An Inspector Calls, Home Is Tomorrow, Summer Day's Dream. London, Heinemann, 1950; New York, Harper, 1952.

Home Is Tomorrow (produced Bradford and London, 1948). London, Heinemann, 1949; in *Plays III*, 1950.

The High Toby: A Play for the Toy Theatre (produced London, 1954). London, Penguin-Pollock, 1948.

Summer Day's Dream (produced Bradford and London, 1949). Included in *Plays III*, 1950.

The Olympians, music by Arthur Bliss (produced London, 1949). London, Novello, 1949.

Bright Shadow: A Play of Detection (produced Oldham and London, 1950). London, French, 1950.

Treasure on Pelican (as *Treasure on Pelican Island*, televised, 1951; as *Treasure on Pelican*, produced Cardiff and London, 1952). London, Evans, 1953.

Dragon's Mouth: A Dramatic Quartet, with Jacquetta Hawkes (also director: produced Malvern and London, 1952; New York, 1955). London, Heinemann, and New York, Harper, 1952.

Private Rooms: A One-Act Comedy in the Viennese Style. London, French, 1953.

Mother's Day. London, French, 1953.

Try It Again (produced London, 1965). London, French, 1953.

A Glass of Bitter. London, French, 1954.

The White Countess, with Jacquetta Hawkes (produced Dublin and London, 1954).

The Scandalous Affair of Mr. Kettle and Mrs. Moon (produced Folkestone and London, 1955). London, French, 1956.

Take the Fool Away (produced Vienna, 1955; Nottingham, 1959).

These Our Actors (produced Glasgow, 1956).

The Glass Cage (produced Toronto and London, 1957). London, French, 1958.

The Thirty-First of June (produced Toronto and London, 1957).

A Pavilion of Masks (produced Germany, 1961; Bristol, 1963). London, French, 1958.

A Severed Head, with Iris Murdoch, adaptation of the novel by Murdoch (produced Bristol and London, 1963; New York, 1964). London, Chatto and Windus, 1964.

Screenplays: *Sing As We Go*, with Gordon Wellesley, 1934; *Look Up and Laugh*, with Gordon Wellesley, 1935; *We Live in Two Worlds*, 1937; *Jamaica Inn*, with Sidney Gilliat and Joan Harrison, 1939; *Britain at Bay*, 1940; *Our Russian Allies* 1941; *The Foreman Went to France* (*Somewhere in France*), with others, 1942; *Last Holiday*, 1950.

Radio Plays: *The Return of Jess Oakroyd*, 1941; *The Golden Entry*, 1955; *End Game at the Dolphin*, 1956; *An Arabian Night in Park Lane*, 1965.

Television Plays: *The Rose and Crown*, 1946; *Whitehall Wonders*, 1949; *Treasure on Pelican Island*, 1951; *You Know What People Are*, 1953; *The Stone Faces*, 1957; *Now Let Him Go*, 1957; *Lost City* (documentary), 1958; *The Rack*, 1958; *Doomsday for Dyson*, 1958; *The Fortrose Incident*, from his play *Home Is Tommorrow*, 1959; *Level Seven*, from the novel by Mordecai Roshwald, 1966; *The Lost Peace* series, 1966; *Anyone for Tennis*, 1968; *Linda at Pulteney's*, 1969.

Verse

The Chapman of Rhymes (juvenilia). London, Moring, 1918.

Other

Brief Diversions, Being Tales, Travesties, and Epigrams. Cambridge, Bowes and Bowes, 1922.

Papers from Lilliput. Cambridge, Bowes and Bowes, 1922.

I for One. London, Lane, 1923; New York, Dodd Mead, 1924.

Figures in Modern Literature. London, Lane, and New York, Dodd Mead, 1924.

The English Comic Characters. London, Lane, and New York, Dodd Mead, 1925.

George Meredith. London and New York, Macmillan, 1926.

Talking. London, Jarrolds, and New York, Harper, 1926.

(*Essays*). London, Harrap, 1926.

Open House: A Book of Essays. London, Heinemann, and New York, Harper, 1927.

Thomas Love Peacock. London and New York, Macmillan, 1927.

The English Novel. London, Benn, 1927; revised edition, London and New York, Nelson, 1935.

Apes and Angels: A Book of Essays. London, Methuen, 1928; as *Too Many People and Other Reflections*, New York, Harper, 1928.

The Balconinny and Other Essays. London, Methuen, 1929; as *The Balconinny*, New York, Harper, 1930.

English Humour. London and New York, Longman, 1929.

Self-Selected Essays. London, Heinemann, 1932; New York, Harper, 1933.

Four-in-Hand (miscellany). London, Heinemann, 1934.

English Journey, Being a Rambling But Truthful Account of What One Man Saw and Heard and Felt and Thought During a Journey Through England During the Autumn of the Year 1933. London, Heinemann-Gollancz, and New York, Harper, 1934.

Midnight on the Desert: A Chapter of Autobiography. London, Heinemann, 1937; as *Midnight on the Desert, Being an Excursion into Autobiography During a Winter in America, 1935-36*, New York, Harper, 1937.

Rain upon Godshill: A Further Chapter of Autobiography. London, Heinemann, and New York, Harper, 1939.

Britain Speaks (radio talks). New York, Harper, 1940.

Postcripts (radio talks). London, Heinemann, 1940; as *All England Listened*, New York, Chilmark Press, 1968.

Out of the People. London, Collins-Heinemann, and New York, Harper, 1941.

Britain at War. New York, Harper, 1942.

British Women Go to War. London, Collins, 1943.

Manpower: The Story of Britain's Mobilisation for War. London, His Majesty's Stationery Office, 1944.

Here Are Your Answers. London, Socialist Book Centre, 1944.

Letter to a Returning Serviceman. London, Home and Van Thal, 1945.

The Secret Dream: An Essay on Britain, America, and Russia. London, Turnstile Press, 1946.

Russian Journey. London, Writers Group of the Society for Cultural Relations with the USSR, 1946.

The New Citizen (address). London, Council for Education in World Citizenship, 1946.

Theatre Outlook. London, Nicholson and Watson, 1947.

The Arts under Socialism (lecture). London, Turnstile Press, 1947.

Delight. London, Heinemann, and New York, Harper, 1949.

The Priestley Companion: A Selection from the Writings of J. B. Priestley. London, Penguin-Heinemann, 1951.

Journey down a Rainbow (travel), with Jacquetta Hawkes. London, Cresset Press-Heinemann, and New York, Harper, 1955.

All about Ourselves and Other Essays, edited by Eric Gillett. London, Heinemann, 1956.

The Writer in a Changing Society (lecture). Aldington, Kent, Hand and Flower Press, 1956.

Thoughts in the Wilderness (essays). London, Heinemann, and New York, Harper, 1957.

The Art of the Dramatist: A Lecture Together with Appendices and Discursive Notes. London, Heinemann, 1957; Boston, The Writer, 1958.

Topside; or, The Future of England: A Dialogue. London, Heinemann, 1958.

The Story of Theatre (for children). London, Rathbone, 1959; as *The Wonderful World of the Theatre*, New York, Doubleday, 1959.

Literature and Western Man. London, Heinemann, and New York, Harper, 1960.

William Hazlitt. London, Longman, 1960.

Charles Dickens: A Pictorial Biography. London, Thames and Hudson, 1961; New York, Viking Press, 1962; as *Charles Dickens and His World*. Thames and Hudson, and Viking Press, 1969.

Margin Released: A Writer's Reminiscences and Reflections. London, Heinemann, and New York, Harper, 1962.

Man and Time. London, Aldus, and New York, Doubleday, 1964.

The Moments and Other Pieces. London, Heinemann, 1966.

The World of J. B. Priestley, edited by Donald G. MacRae. London, Heinemann, 1967.

Essays of Five Decades, edited by Susan Cooper. Boston, Little Brown, 1968; London, Heinemann, 1969.

Trumpets over the Sea, Being a Rambling and Egotistical Account of the London Symphony Orchestra's Engagement at Daytona Beach, Florida, in July-August 1967. London, Heinemann, 1968.

The Prince of Pleasure and His Regency 1811-1820. London, Heinemann, and New York, Harper, 1969.

The Edwardians. London, Heinemann, and New York, Harper, 1970.

Anton Chekhov. London, International Textbook, 1970.

Snoggle (for children). London, Heinemann, 1971; New York, Harcourt Brace, 1972.

Victoria's Heyday. London, Heinemann, and New York, Harcourt Brace, 1972.

Over the Long High Wall: Some Reflections and Speculations on Life, Death, and Time. London, Heinemann, 1972.

The English. London, Heinemann, and New York, Viking Press, 1973.

Outcries and Asides. London, Heinemann, 1974.

A Visit to New Zealand. London, Heinemann, 1974.

Particular Pleasures, Being a Personal Record of Some Varied Arts and Many Different Artists. London, Heinemann, 1975.

The Happy Dream: An Essay. Andoversford, Gloucestshire, Whittington Press, 1976.

English Humour (not the same as 1929 book). London, Heinemann, 1976.

Instead of the Trees: A Final Chapter of Autobiography. London, Heinemann, and New York, Stein and Day, 1977.

Seeing Stratford, illustrated by Arthur Keene. Stratford-on-Avon, Warwickshire, Celandine Press, 1982.

Editor, *Essayists Past and Present: A Selection of English Essays*. London, Jenkins, and New York, Dial Press, 1925.

Editor, *Fools and Philosophers: A Gallery of Comic Figures from English Literature*. London, Lane, and New York, Dodd Mead, 1925.

Editor, *Tom Moore's Diary: A Selection*. London, Cambridge University Press, 1925.

Editor, *The Book of Bodley Head Verse*. London, Lane, and New York, Dodd Mead, 1926.

Editor, *Our Nation's Heritage*. London, Dent, 1939.

Editor, *Scenes from London Life, from Sketches by Boz*, by Dickens. London, Pan, 1947.

Editor, *The Best of Leacock*. Toronto, McClelland and Stewart, 1957; as *The Bodley Head Leacock*, London, Bodley Head, 1957.

Editor, with Josephine Spear, *Adventures in English Literature*. New York, Harcourt Brace, 1963.

*

Bibliography: *J. B. Priestley: An Annotated Bibliography* by Alan Edwin Day, New York, Garland, and Stroud, Gloucestershire, Hodgkins, 1980.

Manuscript Collection: University of Texas, Austin.

Critical Studies: *J. B. Priestley* by Ivor Brown, London, Longman, 1957, revised edition, 1964; *J. B. Priestley: An Informal Study of His Work* by David Hughes, London, Hart Davis, 1958, Freeport, New York, Books for Libraries, 1970; *J. B. Priestley: Portrait of an Author* by Susan Cooper, London, Heinemann, 1970, New York, Harper, 1971; *J. B. Priestley* by Kenneth Young, London, Longman, 1977; *J. B. Priestley* by John Braine, London, Weidenfeld and Nicolson, 1978, New York, Barnes and Noble, 1979; *J. B. Priestley* by A. A. De Vitis and Albert E. Kalson, Boston, Twayne, 1980; *J. B. Priestley: The Last of the Sages* by John Atkins, London, Calder, and New York, Riverrun Press, 1981.

Theatrical Activities:
Director: **Plays**—*Ever Since Paradise*, tour, 1946, and London, 1947; *Dragon's Mouth*, London, 1952.

* * *

J. B. Priestley was possesed by a vision of life at its rare best—rich, vivid, eminently worth living. What makes him a science-fiction writer and not just another dreaming romantic is that he espouses theories of time that allow his characters (and conceivably his readers) actually to attain the rich life he envisions. Such theories—chronological simultaneity, serialism, multiple dimensions—are not easy to illustrate, but Priestley succeeds surprisingly well, in stories and novels and also in popular stage plays. As literary fashion moves on and Priestley's sedately conventional style falls from favor, it is his time stories, his personal ventures towards altered reality, that remain fresh and intriguing.

Priestley derived his theories from three souces: E. A. Abbott's idea that a fourth dimension would appear as time; J. W. Dunne's mathematical model of time as continuous, simultaneous, and serial; and P. D. Ouspensky's more philosophical view of time as a repeated circle which can be made to spiral morally up or down. What these concepts gave to Priestley was a non-religious hope. If there are other dimensions, then there might be somewhere to go after life's time ends. In the plays *Music at Night* and *Johnson over Jordan* characters withdraw after death into a higher observer-state similar to the Tibetan "Bardo. " Also, if all time is simultaneous then each minute is not murdered by the next, and the goodness of the past can be made accessible to those trapped in a bad present. Such comforting access is given to characters in the play *Time and the Conways* and in fiction such as "Night Sequence" and *The*

Magicians. And if precognition and time's recurrence are true, then the known future can be, paradoxically, changed, altered in a tiny moment to redirect the flow, as in the plays *Dangerous Corner* and *I Have Been Here Before.*

Priestley desires these comforts and powers because he sees the modern world as darkening fast. In a short grim tale called "The Grey Ones" he incarnates the powers of darkness into grey tentacled devils capable of human shape. Their weapons are boredom, blandness, and despair; they seek to dull the world down to a suburban hell. Priestley's fullest treatment of this theme, and of the time-conscious man's opposition to it, comes in *The Magicians.* The industrialist Ravenstreet leaves his company when it turns from exciting scientific quest to passionless bureaucracy. As he slides into despair he is tempted by a bitter elitist to help drug the masses into final lethargy. Ravenstreet almost agrees, but is saved by the intervention of three "magicians" whose mysterious abilities include precognition and hypnosis, and who seem to be involved in some larger struggle. They show Ravenstreet the difference between the "tick-tock time" he had been dying in, and "time alive" where his hopeful past still lives. They send him to re-experience crucial moments, and they also rearrange the present so that the drug's numbing secret is lost. At the end, Ravenstreet has reason to live, and the world is a little less grey. Priestley's time visions are not always cheering. In one of his most haunting stories, "The Statues," a tired man is granted exhilarating but temporary sight of huge glorious statues towering above a future London, and the contrast with the banal present saddens the rest of his life. In the well-crafted and widely anthologized "Mr. Strenberry's Tale" the title character is visited briefly by a time traveler from an advanced humanity's last black moment. The traveler vanishes, destroyed, but the terror stays.

Some of Priestley's stories have been classified as science fiction because they focus on some unusual bit of technology—the musical invention in *Low Notes on a High Level* or the earth-destroying transmitter in *The Doomsday Men.* But such devices usually turn out to be occasions for plot, not concepts in themselves, and plot for Priestley means romance, marriages, careers, and individual morale more than anything else. Even his children's book, *Snoggle,* which offers extra-terrestrial pets and invisible spaceships, spends most of its rather unsuccessful pages detailing the interactions of three ordinary children. Priestley began writing in 1910; he learned his craft in an earlier time than most science-fiction writers. His many romantic comedies now seem dated, his plots coercive and even clanking. But his parables of hope and despair remain compelling, and there are few science-fiction writers who can match him for the seriousness of his thinking about time.

—Karen G. Way

PROCTOR, George W. Also writes as Zach Wyatt. American. Address: c/o Pinnacle Books, 1430 Broadway, New York, New York 10018 U.S.A.

SCIENCE-FICTION PUBLICATIONS

Novels

The Esper Transfer. New York, Major, 1978.
Shadowman. New York, Fawcett, 1980.
Fire at the Center. New York, Fawcett, 1981.

Starwings. New York, Ace, 1984.
V: The Chicago Conversion (novelization of TV series). New York, Pinnacle, 1985.

Uncollected Short Stories

"Paperwork," in *Perry Rhodan 25* (Hollywood), June 1973.
"Gift Hearse," in *Perry Rhodan 35* (Hollywood), December 1974.
"The Migration," in *Lone Star Universe,* edited by Proctor and Steve Utley. Austin, Texas, Heidelberg, 1976.
"The Smile of Oisia," in *Swords Against Darkness 1,* edited by Andrew J. Offutt. New York, Zebra, 1977.
"A Kingdom Won," in *Swords Against Darkness 3,* edited by Andrew J. Offutt. New York, Zebra, 1978.
"Night of the Piasa," with J. C. Green, in *Nightmares,* edited by Charles L. Grant. New York, Doubleday, 1978.
"Death's Sweet Promise," in *Summermorn,* September 1979.
"The Good Is Oft Interred," in *Horrors,* edited by Charles L. Grant. New York, Berkley, 1981.
"The Gift of Life, The Debt of Death," in *Shadows of . . .* (Arlington, Texas), Spring 1982.
"The Nightbreeze on Watermelon Mountain," in *Softalk* (North Hollywood, California), August 1983.

OTHER PUBLICATIONS

Novels

Enemies. New York, Doubleday, 1983.
Death's Acolyte, with Robert E. Vardeman. New York, Ace, 1985.
A Yoke of Magic, with Robert E. Vardeman. New York, Ace, 1985.

Novels as Zach Wyatt

The Texians:
  The Texians. New York, Pinnacle, 1984.
  The Horse Marines. New York, Pinnacle, 1984.
  War Devils. New York, Pinnacle, 1984.
  Blood Moon. New York, Pinnacle, 1985.
  Death's Shadow. New York, Pinnacle, 1985.
  Comanche Ambush. New York, Pinnacle, 1985.

Other

Editor, with Steve Utley, *Lone Star Universe: Speculative Fiction from Texas.* Austin, Texas, Heidelberg, 1976.
Editor, with Arthur C. Clarke, *The Science-Fiction Hall of Fame 3: The Nebula Winners 1965-69.* New York, Avon, 1982.

*   *   *

In much of "hard science fiction," the technology overshadows characters and often becomes the protagonist. The science-fiction work of George W. Proctor shows a different and more human-oriented approach. Proctor relegates technology to the minor position of a plot device and concentrates on human and alien characters, showing little more than their reaction to technological gadgetry. In *Fire at the Center* the centerpiece isn't the technology of time travel or even what they hope to achieve by journeying into the past, but how the protagonists, Nils Kendler and Caltha Renenet, communicate psionically and the personal challenges and relationship this affords.

The central theme weaving throughout all Proctor's books is that of communication, no doubt a product of his training and work as a newspaper journalist. His first published novel, *The Esper Transfer,* is an uncomplicated, straightforward escape-chase plot, but the protagonist depends heavily on his telepathic talents and "oneness" with others of his race. The conflict comes more from within than from external forces. This is likewise true in *Shadowman.* Outwardly another escape-chase plot, the novel becomes more. Male and female join in telepathic contact and become lovers through this most intimate of contact.

Proctor carries this theme to its logical extension in *Starwings.* The protagonist, Radman Donalt, uses a collapsar as a time machine and becomes separated from his lover, Jenica, not only in space but in time. Fifteen years of time and the barriers of untold light years notwithstanding, Donalt enters Jenica's mind and they make love in the only way possible for them. "His mind merged with hers, Donalt led her to the bed. And there, her hands now hers, he made love to her."

This central theme of male-female, human-alien communication extends beyond Proctor's science fiction and into fantasy novels. While the structure and tone of his fantasy work is strongly influenced by Fritz Leiber's Fafhrd and the Gray Mouser stories, the basic themes are easily identifiable as belonging to Proctor.

The Nalcon and Hweir short stories transcend the usual genre offerings of sword-and-sorcery quest through the interplay between the main characters. Both are rogues and thieves, but their fierce friendship is obvious. They have discovered common ground, common affection, and fulfillment in one another in spite of divergent background as blond prince and black-skinned thief. This friendship and the strains placed upon it are more central to the stories than any quest.

In the *Swords of Raemllyn* heroic fantasy series, Proctor has created another way of examining male-female communication. While in *Death's Acolyte* there is Chal, a tongueless character who makes his wishes known to the heroine empathically, a more intriguing method of exploration lies with Goran One-Eye, an interdimensional being capable of massive shape changes. Goram, at first, lacks the control over this ability and is locked in a bulky male human body. By the second book, *A Yoke of Magic,* he shifts into female form and attempts to seduce his friend, Davin Anane, The byplay between the two, when Davin discovers the shape transformation, examines not only the limits of their friendship but also male-female roles and expectations.

Trying to sum up an author's works in a few words presents insurmountable problems, but the theme underlying virtually all of George W. Proctor's science fiction and fantasy works is both simple and beguiling: communication. How do men and women relate to one another, how would this be different if we were able to enter another's mind telepathically, how would our friendships and love alter if they were based on empathic rather than verbal considerations. Science fiction provides a suitable vehicle for Proctor's explorations for this enhanced communication.

—Robert E. Vardeman

PURDOM, Tom. (Thomas Edward Purdom). American. Born in New Haven, Connecticut, 19 April 1936. Educated at Lafayette College, Easton, Pennsylvania, 1952-54; Thomas Edison State College, Trenton, New Jersey, B. A. in social sciences 1977. Served in the United States Army Medical Corps,

1959-61. Married Sara Wescot in 1960; one son. Reservation agent, United Airlines, Philadelphia, 1957-58; science writer, University of Pennsylvania, Philadelphia, 1968-69; Visiting Professor of English, Temple University, Philadelphia, 1970-71; adjunct professor of English, Drexel University, Philadelphia, 1975; instructor in science fiction, Institute for Human Resources Development, Philadelphia, 1976-77. Vice-President, Science Fiction Writers of America, 1970-72. Agent: Scott Meredith Literary Agency, 845 Third Avenue, New York, New York 10022, U.S.A.

SCIENCE-FICTION PUBLICATIONS

Novels

I Want the Stars. New York, Ace, 1964.
The Tree Lord of Imeten. New York, Ace, 1966.
Five Against Arlane. New York, Ace, 1967.
Reduction in Arms. New York, Berkley, 1971.
The Barons of Behavior. New York, Ace, 1972; London, Dobson, 1977.

Uncollected Short Stories

"Grieve for a Man," in *Fantastic Universe* (Chicago), August 1957.
"A Matter of Privacy,' in *Science Fiction Quarterly* (Holyoke, Massachusetts), August 1957.
"The Man Who Wouldn't Sign Up," in *Infinity* (New York), October 1958.
"The Holy Grail," in *Star Science Fiction Stories 6,* edited by Frederik Pohl. New York, Ballantine, 1959.
"The Duel of the Insecure Man," in *Satellite* (New York), April 1959.
"Excellence," in *Amazing* (New York), October 1959.
"Soroman the Protector," in *Galaxy* (New York), August 1960.
"The Green Beret," in *Analog* (New York), January 1961.
"The Warriors," in *Amazing* (New York), June 1962.
"Greenplace," in *World's Best Science Fiction 1965,* edited by Donald A. Wollheim and Terry Carr. New York, Ace, 1965.
"Courting Time," in *Galaxy* (New York), February 1966.
"Toys," in *Crime Prevention in the Thirtieth Century,* edited by Hans S. Santesson. New York, Walker, 1969.
"A War of Passion," in *The Future Is Now,* edited by William F. Nolan. Los Angeles, Sherbourne Press, 1970.
"Moonchild," in *Future Quest,* edited by Roger Elwood. New York, Avon, 1973.
"The Chains of Freedom," in *Galaxy* (New York), May 1977.
"Reduction in Arms," in *International Relations Through Science Fiction,* edited by Martin H. Greenberg and Joseph D. Olander. New York, Watts, 1978.
"Moon Rocks," in *The Future at War 1,* edited by Reginald Bretnor. New York, Ace, 1979.

OTHER PUBLICATIONS

Other

"The Urban Hell," in *Worlds of Tomorrow* (New York), April 1964.
"The Alien Psyche," in *Worlds of Tomorrow* (New York), May 1965.
"SF's Creative Vigor," in *American Libraries* (Chicago), March 1974.
"Who's Going to Run Things in Twenty Three Hundred? And

How Are They Going to Do It?," in *Writing and Selling Science Fiction*. Cincinnati, Writer's Digest, 1976.

Editor, *Adventures in Discovery*. New York, Doubleday, 1969.

*

Tom Purdom comments:

My main aim as a fiction writer is to create the kind of stories I like to read—engrossing, well-plotted works that hold you from the first page to the end and really get you involved in the characters and the things that are happening to them. Once I jokingly said that the greatest living novelists were Alexander Solzhenitsyn, Ursula K. LeGuin, Richard Adams, and George Macdonald Fraser. I was poking a little fun at literary pomposity, but I would give a great deal to have written the better works of any of them.

The struggle that most interests me—and I think its mostly what I've written about and like to read about in SF—is the problem of adapting technology, especially the attempts to seize the opportunity it gives us without falling into all the traps it puts in front of us (some of which are not too obvious). I'm also fond of one of the things the man Santiago said about his fish: "It will feed many people and it will bring a good price on the market." I think science fiction has given a great many people a lot of things they needed, and it has even—especially recently—brought some of its practitioners a good price on the market.

* * *

Tom Purdom's career spans more than two decades. Though clearly distinguishable from one another, his early novels share the same narrative formula: the hero finds himself on an alien planet which is ruled by a dictator, either benign as in *Five Against Arlane* or malevolent as in *The Tree Lord of Imeten*. In either case, the hero struggles to overthrow tyranny and re-establish social equilibrium through bloodshed. In the aftermath of the battle against the tyrant, the hero emerges victorious from the rubble to announce that democratic liberties have been restored to the people. Great adulation of the Purdom hero follows the revolution, and the novel closes on a note of exhaustion as an infant republic comes uncertainly to life.

This well-worn plot serves as the basis for Purdom's most recent novels too, but in *The Barons of Behavior* he has achieved more interesting results. Here Purdom's subject is the potential threat which Skinnerian behaviorism poses to a free society. The novel opens in a world of the remote future in which the privileges and responsibilities of life in 20th-century America have been lost. Nurtured by democracy, the growth of lawlessness and violence has long ago become intolerable to society, and politicians, seeking a retardant, have turned to the behavioral sciences for help. And indeed they have found there willing social physicians. Thus a terrible triple alliance is formed of science, technology, and politics, whose aim it is to produce law and order, to provide security and comfort to the citizens of Windham County, Pennsylvania, but whose real accomplishment is to rob the human spirit of its civil liberties and to render the human will impotent. In *The Barons of Behavior* the orderly operation of society is insured by an arsenal of devices and techniques which can subvert individual free will. It can be numbed or stupified by insidious drugs; it can be forced to betray itself through the techniques of behaviour modification; or, most horribly, it can be bypassed altogether by devices surgically implanted in the brain. Opposed to the dehumanizing powers in control of society stands the Purdom hero, Ralph Nicholson, "psychotherapist to a psyched-out world," who manages to defeat the political machine of Martin Boyd despite the overwhelming odds against his doing so.

But this is familiar stuff to science-fiction readers. The science of control has inspired dozens of novels along the same line, the very best of which achieve truly chilling results. The atrocities committed against Alex in Burgess's *A Clockwork Orange,* for instance, evoke the archetypal fear humans have of being obliterated by forces beyond their comprehension, while his struggle to remain human and intact in the face of dehumanizing powers approaches Aristotle's definition of great tragedy, the purgation of fear and pity. Unfortunately, *The Barons of Behavior* never achieves such impact. Though Purdom's technological imagination is impressive, his ability to conceive and delineate character is not. Ralph Nicholson of *The Barons of Behavior* is as two-dimensional as Migel Lassamba of *Five Against Arlane*. Both are conventional super-heroes, men of endless resource and daring, but since they lack depth and delineation, their suffering appears rather more ludicrous than tragic, their lives more gratuitously violent than compelling, and their inevitable victory more contrived than earned.

Nevertheless, Purdom's interest in possibilities is genuine, and his grasp of the implications of behaviorism is very thorough. At his best, he is capable of constructing a shockingly plausible and horrifying vision of the future, a time when individual freedom is a suppressed, half-forgotten memory, abandoned centuries ago in pursuit of law and order. There is little anxiety in this world, even less disorder once chance factors have been all but eliminated. There are no dangers, except to the intellect and imagination. There is no physical suffering in the America of *The Barons of Behavior,* but there is no free thought either, no unapproved writing, no spontaneous creation of any kind. Men and women smile and go about their daily business, but their eyes appear vacant. They reflect no light. Birth and death are quiet, pre-arranged experiences.

—Marvin W. Hunt

———————

PYNCHON, Thomas. American. Born in Glen Cove, New York, 8 May 1937. Educated at Cornell University, Ithaca, New York, 1954-58, B. A. 1958. Served in the United States Navy. Former editorial writer, Boeing Aircraft, Seattle. Recipient: Faulkner Award, 1964; Rosenthal Memorial Award, 1967; National Book Award, 1974; American Academy Howells Medal, 1975. Agent: Candida Donadio and Associates, 11 West 57th Street, New York, New York 10019. Address: c/o Little Brown, 34 Beacon Street, Boston, Massachusetts 02106, U.S.A.

SCIENCE-FICTION PUBLICATIONS

Novel

Gravity's Rainbow. New York, Viking Press, and London, Cape, 1973.

OTHER PUBLICATIONS

Novels

V. Philadelphia, Lippincott, and London, Cape, 1963.
The Crying of Lot 49. Philadelphia, Lippincott, 1966; London, Cape, 1967.

Short Stories

Mortality and Mercy in Vienna. London, Aloes, 1976.
Low-lands. London, Aloes, 1978.
The Secret Integration. London, Aloes, 1980.
The Small Rain. London, Aloes, 1980(?).
Slow Learner: Early Stories. Boston, Little Brown, 1984;
London, Cape, 1985.

*

Bibliography: *Three Contemporary Novelists: An Annotated Bibliography* by Robert M. Scotto, New York, Garland, 1977; *John Barth, Jerzy Kosinski, and Thomas Pynchon: A Reference Guide* by Thomas P. Walsh and Cameron Northouse, Boston, Hall, 1977.

Critical Studies: *Thomas Pynchon* by Joseph V. Slade, New York, Warner, 1974; *Mindful Pleasures: Essays on Thomas Pynchon* edited by George Levine and David Leverenz, Boston, Little Brown, 1976; *The Grim Phoenix: Reconstructing Thomas Pynchon* by William M. Plater, Bloomington, Indiana University Press, 1978; *Pynchon: A Collection of Critical Essays* edited by Edward Mendelson Englewood Cliffs, New Jersey, Prentice Hall, 1978; *Pynchon: Creative Paranoia in Gravity's Rainbow* by Mark Richard Siegal, Port Washington, New York, Kennikat Press, 1978; *Thomas Pynchon: The Art of Allusion* by David Cowart, Carbondale, Southern Illinois University Press, 1980; *The Rainbow Quest of Thomas Pynchon* by Douglas A. Mackey, San Bernardino, Californa, Borgo Press, 1980; *Pynchon's Fictions: Thomas Pynchon and the Literature of Information* by John O. Stark, Athens, Ohio University Press, 1980; *A Reader's Guide to Gravity's Rainbow* by Douglas Fowler, Ann Arbor, Michigan, Ardis, 1980; *Thomas Pynchon* by Tony Tanner, London, Methuen, 1982; *Signs and Symptoms: Thomas Pynchon and the Contemporary World* by Peter L. Cooper, Berkeley, University of California Press, 1983.

*   *   *

Thomas Pynchon's novels are firmly entrenched in historic and technological realities, but question all orders and unities to suggest that, since man continually imposes patterns on his world, all patterns are suspect and potentially false, so much so that recorded "history" may be simply man imposing private interpretations on chaotic reality, just as man's mastery of bureaucratic and technological systems may well be his enslavement to his own creations. Pynchon's is a vision of a world in decline, one where personal choices are shaped by the necessities of science, language, history, and economics, where the victim in turn victimizes, where vast, shadowy conspiracies flourish, and where huge conglomerates seem to control events. His dominant themes include isolation, alienation, fragmentation, failure to communicate, degradation, entropy, the battle between men and machines and between established society and the preterites (the rebellious disinherited), the absurdities and ironies of modern existence, man's self-destructive potentials, the horrors of war, paranoia, and the question of multiple interpretations. Wastelands and undergrounds dominate his imagery.

His style, in tune with the complexity of his thematic concerns, is baroque, variegated, and multistructural, an intricate amalgam of Whitmanesque catalogs, Dickensian names, cryptic abbreviations, puns, analogical sequences, and historical and literary allusions. It runs the gamut of literary and cinematic modes, rapidly shifting, much like media events,

between comic-book fantasy and learned discourse on complex scientific and technological concerns: the organic chemistry, operant conditioning, rocket dynamics. It partakes of parody, farce, and black humor, jeremiad, apocalypse, and prophesy. Its geography is often allegorical, its conception mythic, its patterns analogical compounds—networks of interlocking images from personal to social to cosmic. Each novel focuses on some central mystery, a cryptogram in *The Crying of Lot 49,* an exlusive secret agent in *V,* a missing supersonic rocket in *Gravity's Rainbow,* which provides the supportive structure for diverse images encompassing a range of perspectives delineated by signs, codes, signals, patterns, and plots. Pynchon's last two works are like densely textured puzzles whose central images are visible only from a distance, while close up all seems chaos.

The Crying of Lot 49, the most accessible of Pynchon's novels, focuses on the quest of Oedipa Maas for the meaning of her ex-lover's will. Her synthesis of scattered clues, including a Jacobean tragedy, doodlings, acronyms, postage stamps, and graffiti, postulates the existence of a secret, 16th-century anti-postal service, the Tristero, perpetuated by W. A. S. T. E., an underground of the disenchanted. Ultimately she must question whether her discovery is a genuine conspiracy involving a parallel, secret America, a giant farcical hoax, or a paranoid projection of her own creation. In Pynchon it is a question of interpretation, one eye seeing chaos, another a system. This question of whether order, systems, patterns truly exist or are merely superimposed on chaotic reality is an essential concern of *V* and *Gravity's Rainbow* as well.

The central character of *V,* as his name suggests, "Stencil"'s his own pattern on an external blankness, but his various versions of himself, the elusive woman he pursues, and his world are all private dreams, products of his early conditioning and of his own paranoid inventiveness. He is played off against Benny Profane, an empiricist who becomes engulfed in incomprehensible details. Drawing on Henry Adams, Jorge Borges, thermodynamics, amd WWII film clips, Pynchon traces man's historic progression towards the moribund. The anarchistic V gradually replaces her flesh with cold machinery; an automaton named SHROUD walks the earth, and all the characters move towards annhilation near the rock of Malta. It is a nightmare world of genocide, dehumanization, dead landscapes, and man-machines.

Gravity's Rainbow continues the historic focus of *V,* tracing the end product of bureaucratic, technological system—a V-2 supersonic rocket that screams into view in the first lines of the novel (1945) and disintegrates the reader and his "theater," perhaps our civilisation, at its close. A satiric fantasy, an historic novel, a parody of various forms—part technological manual, part folk myth, part Kabbala, part pornography—it involves numerous plots and a cast of 400 characters and 1000 objects (including a talking light bulb, Richard Nixon, and King Kong), each with their own story. It begins with the quest of Lt. Slothrop, a New Englander of Puritan stock, whose sexuality is attuned to a mysterious, gravity-defying rocket for whom everybody is searching, but he ultimately dissolves over the Allied Zone, and the plot digresses in a myriad of directions, its only unity analogical. *Gravity's Rainbow,* with its labyrinthine complications, is a massive effort to seek through historic analysis the roots of man's mass death wish, his cultural programming for death, and to project a future/present when that wish might come true.

Pynchon suggests that modern man is paranoid, perhaps with good reason, compulsive, and self-destructive; his lethal technology is perhaps already beyond control, and he cannot be sure whether his perceptions of the world are valid or merely self-imposed. While breaking traditional patterns, he builds on our scientific and literary heritage. His works are eclectic and controversial, novels which verge on science fiction and partake of its techniques, while remaining difficult to categorize precisely.

—Gina Macdonald

QUITMAN, Wallace. See **PALMER, Raymond A.**

RACKHAM, John. Pseudonym for John Thomas Phillifent. British. Born in Durham, 10 November 1916. Served in the Royal Navy, 1935-47. Worked for the Central Electricity Generating Board in the early 1960's. *Died 16 December 1976.*

SCIENCE-FICTION PUBLICATIONS

Novels

Space Puppet. London, Pearson, 1954.
Jupiter Equilateral. London, Pearson, 1954.
The Master Weed. London, Pearson, 1954.
The Touch of Evil. London, Digit, 1963.
We, The Venusians. New York, Ace, 1965.
The Beasts of Kohl. New York, Ace, 1966.
Time to Live. New York, Ace, 1966; London, Dobson, 1969.
Danger from Vega. New York, Ace, 1966; London, Dobson, 1970.
The Double Invaders. New York, Ace, 1967.
Alien Sea. New York, Ace, 1968; London, Dobson, 1975.
The Proxima Project. New York, Ace, 1968.
The Treasure of Tau Ceti. New York, Ace, 1969.
Ipomoea. New York, Ace, 1969; London, Dobson, 1972.
The Flower of Doradil. New York, Ace, 1970.
The Anything Tree. New York, Ace, 1970; London, Dobson, 1977.
Beyond Capella. New York, Ace, 1971.
Dark Planet. New York, Ace, 1971.
Earthstrings. New York, Ace, 1972.
Beanstalk. New York, DAW, 1973.

Novels as John T. Phillifent

Genius Unlimited. New York, DAW, 1972.
Hierarchies. New York, Ace, 1973.
Life with Lancelot. New York, Ace, 1973.
King of Argent. New York, DAW, 1973.

Uncollected Short Stories

"Drog," in *Science Fantasy* (Bournemouth), February 1958.
"One-Eye," in *Astounding* (New York), May 1958.
"Nulook," in *Science Fantasy* (Bournemouth), April 1959.
"Curse Strings," in *Science Fantasy* (Bournemouth), November 1959.
"If You wish," in *If* (New York), November 1959.
"The Bright Ones," in *New Worlds* (London), May 1960.
"Idea Man," in *Galaxy* (New York), June 1960.
"Theory," in *New Worlds* (London), September 1960.

"The Science Fiction Ethic," in *New Worlds* (London), November 1960.
"The Black Cat's Paw," in *Science Fantasy* (Bournemouth), December 1960.
"Trial Run," in *New Worlds* (London), December 1960.
"Blink," in *New Worlds* (London), May 1961.
"The Veil of Isis," in Science Fantasy (Bournemouth), June 1961.
"The Trouble with Honey," in *New Worlds* (London), July 1961.
"The Stainless-Steel Knight," in *If* (New York), July 1961.
"Goodbye, Doctor Gabriel," in *New Worlds* (London), August 1961.
"Ankh," in *Science Fantasy* (Bournemouth), December 1961.
"The Dawson Diaries," in *New Worlds* (London), April, May 1962.
"Fire and Ice," in *Science Fantasy* (Bournemouth), December 1962.
"The Rainmaker," in *Science Fiction Adventures* (London), February 1963.
"Dossier," in *New Worlds* (London), April 1963.
"Confession," in *New Worlds* (London), May 1963.
"What You Don't Know," in *Science Fantasy* (Bournemouth), June 1963.
"With Clean Hands," in *Science Fantasy* (Bournemouth), August 1963.
"Dr. Jeckers and Mr. Hyde," in *Amazing* (New York), August 1963.
"Deep Freeze," in *New Worlds* (London), September 1963.
"Man-Hunt," in *New Worlds* (London), October 1963.
"Crux," in *New Worlds* (London), November 1963.
"The Last Salamander," in *Lambda 1 and Other Stories,* edited by John Carnell. New York, Berkley, 1964; London, Penguin, 1965.
"Hell-Planet," in *New Writings in SF 2,* edited by John Carnell, London, Dobson, 1964; New York, Bantam, 1966.
"Die and Grow Rich," in *New Worlds* (London), February 1964.
"God Killer," in *Science Fantasy* (Bournemouth), August 1964.
"Advantage," in *New Writings in SF 6* edited by John Carnell. London, Dobson, 1965; New York, Bantam, 1971.
"Room with a View," in *Science Fantasy* (Bournemouth), January 1965.
"Bring Back a Life," in *Science Fantasy* (Bournemouth), March 1965.
"A Way with Animals," in *Science Fantasy* (Bournemouth), August 1965.
"Computer's Mate," in *New Writings in SF 8,* edited by John Carnell. London, Dobson, 1966.
"Poseidon Project," in *New Writings in SF 9,* edited by John Carnell. London, Dobson, 1966; New York, Bantam, 1972.
"The God-Birds of Glentallach," in *Science Fantasy* (Bournemouth), January 1966.
"A Light Feint," in *Impulse* (London), April 1966.
"Catharsis," in *New Writings in SF 11,* edited by John Carnell. London, Dobson, 1968.
"The Divided House," in *New Writings in SF 13,* edited by John Carnell. London, Dobson, 1968.
"Stoop to Conquer," in *New Writings in SF 19,* edited by John Carnell. London, Dobson, 1971.
"Wise Child," in *New Writings in SF 22,* edited by Kenneth Bulmer. London, Sidgwick and Jackson, 1973.
"The Halted Village," in *New Writings in SF 25,* edited by Kenneth Bulmer. London, Sidgwick and Jackson, 1975.
"Heal Thyself," in *New Writings in SF 27,* edited by Kenneth Bulmer. London, Sidgwick and Jackson, 1976.

Uncollected Short Stories as John T. Phillifent

"Point," in *Fantastic* (New York), December 1961.
"Ethical Quotient," in *Analog* (New York), October 1962.
"Flying Fish," in *Analog* (New York), October 1964.
"Finnegan's Knack," in *Analog* (New York), January 1965.
"Aim for the Heel," in *Analog* (New York), July 1967.
"Incorrigible," in *Analog* (New York), April 1968.
"The Rites of Man," in *Analog* (New York), November 1968.
"All Fall Down," in *Analog* (New York), August 1969.
"The Fine Print," in *Analog* (New York), September 1971.
"Owe Me," in *Analog* (New York), May 1974.

OTHER PUBLICATIONS

Novels as John T. Phillifent

The Lonely Man. London, Boardman, 1965.
The Mad Scientist Affair. London, Souvenir Press, and New York, Ace, 1966.
The Corfu Affair. London, Sourvenir Press, 1967; New York, Ace, 1969.
The Power Cube Affair. London, Souvenir Press, and New York, Ace, 1968.

*   *   *

Under his own name and the pseudonym of John Rackham, John T. Phillifent produced a series of short adventure novels that made use of traditional science-fiction plots to present a fast-moving plot set against an exotic background. There is little doubt in the reader's mind that right will ultimately prevail, but the events along the way are the chief attraction.

To a great extent, Rackham repeated the situations he found most appealing. One of these is the Mowgli tale set in the future; one or more humans are returned to civilization after being raised among aliens, and the ensuing culture shock provides much of the basis of the story. This is the major plotline in *The Beasts of Kohl*, for example, where Earth has become considerably more benign but still unsettling to one not used to human ways. The same is true of the far better Phillifent novel, *Life with Lanceot*, in which the alien Shogleet rebuilds a damaged human with mechanical parts, and then tries to reintegrate him into human culture. Another recurring plot is the search for a fabulous treasure, be it gem, secret plans, or immortality drug. The protoganist of *The Treasure of Tau Ceti* is motivated by legends of priceless gems on that jungle world, but along the way he forces humans to recognize that the inhabitants of the planet are indeed intelligent. A secret agent searches for a rumored sentient plant in *The Anything Tree*. Another plant, this time one that will cure all humans diseases, is the target of another group of adventurers in *The Flowers of Doradil*. This time the major subplot is a crew of human smugglers determined to prevent the success of the hero's mission. Jewels are the quarry once again in the *Hierarchies* (Phillifent), this time purloined from their rightful owner. Another theme is that of secret alien or human manipulation of society. Secret aliens provoke a war between Earth and Venus in *Alien Sea* ; a new drug is revealed to be the tool of insidious would-be alien conquerors in *Ipomoea* ; human expansion into space is blocked by apparently invulnerable alien constructs in *Beyond Capella*. Secret human societies appear in *Earthstrings*, in which a human colony is wiped out as part of a plot by commercial magnates, and in *Genius Ulimited* (Phillifent), wherein a scientific colony is actually serving as a mask to conceal a plot for interstellar conquest.

Rackham did interject some commentary into his novels, and the earlier ones in particular seem to demonstrate his faith that mankind would grow out of its petty prejudices. In *We, The Venusians* Anthony Taylor passes as human because a pill changes his skin color and he cannot be identified as a native Greenie. Ultimately, the racial prejudice that forms the basis of the novel is reconciled as the two races eventually recognise each other's equality. In *The Beasts of Kohl* humanity has learned to accept the rights of whales on Earth and aliens in space. There is some evidence that Rackham became disillusioned in his last years. Nefarious plots are invariably human-instigated in the later novels, and the more enlightened humans cast themselves loose from the race, as in *King of Argent* (Phillifent), or even settle down among aliens, as does the hero of *Dark Planet*. Where the human refugees had favorable effects on a primitive alien race in *Danger from Vega*, they are presented as a danger to the interstellar community in *Genius Unlimited* (Phillifent) and, to a lesser extent, *Beyond Capella*. Other Standard plots appear here and there. There is rather dull interstellar war in *The Double Invaders*, and a rather amusing view of one in *Beanstalk*, which presents the familiar fairy tale as a distorted version of Earth's minor involvement in an interstellar war. Mankind's necessity to advance into the universe is central to *Beyond Capella* and *The Proxima Project*.

Rackham never produced what could fairly be termed an outstanding work. He made no attempt to tackle major social problems except in the most superficial way, and he broke no new ground in either style or plot. But he did produce a string of competently written light adventure novels that don't insult the intelligence of the reader. They are invariably unbeat, there is no confusion between heroes and villains, and any incompetence on the part of the central character is transitory. It is a simple universe in many ways that Rackham wrote about, and generally an entertaining one.

—Don D'Ammassa

RAND, Ayn. American. Born in St. Petersburg, now Leningrad, Russia, 2 February 1905; emigrated to the United States in 1926; naturalized, 1931. Educated at the University of Leningrad: graduated in history 1924. Married Frank O'Connor in 1929. Screenwriter, 1932-34, 1944-49. Editor, *The Objectivist*, New York, 1962-71, and *The Ayn Rand Letter*, New York, 1971-82. Visiting Lecturer at several universities, including Yale University, New Haven, Connecticut, Princeton University, New Jersey, Columbia University, New York, Harvard University and Massachusetts Institute of Technology, both Cambridge, and Johns Hopkins University, Baltimore. D. H. L. : Lewis and Clark College, Portland, Oregon, 1963. *Died 6 March 1982*.

SCIENCE-FICTION PUBLICATIONS

Novels

Anthem. London, Cassell, 1938; revised edition, Los Angeles, Pamphleteers, 1946.
Atlas Shrugged. New York, Random House, 1957.

OTHER PUBLICATIONS

Novels

We the Living. New York, Macmillan, and London, Cassell, 1936.

The Fountainhead. Indianapolis, Bobbs Merill, 1943; London, Cassell, 1947.

Short Stories

The Early Ayn Rand: A Selection from Her Unpublished Fiction, edited by Leonard Peikoff. New York, New American Library, 1984.

Plays

Night of January 16th (as *Woman on Trial,* produced Hollywood, 1934; New York, 1935; London, 1936; as *Penthouse Legend,* produced New York, 1973). New York, Longman, 1936.
The Unconquered, adaptation of her own novel *We the Living* (produced New York, 1940).

Screenplays: *You Came Along,* with Robert Smith, 1945; *Love Letters,* 1945; *The Fountainhead,* 1949.

Other

Textbook of Americanism. New York, Branden Institute, 1946.
Notes on the History of American Free Enterprise. New York, Platen Press, 1959.
Faith and Force: The Destroyers of the Modern World. New York, Branden Institute, 1961.
For the New Intellectual. New York, Random House, 1961.
The Objectivist Ethics. New York, Branden Institute, 1961.
America's Persecuted Minority: Big Business. New York, Branden Institute, 1962.
Conservatism: An Obituary (lecture). New York, Branden Institute, 1962.
The Fascist "New Frontier." New York, Branden Institute, 1963.
The Virtue of Selfishness: A New Concept of Egoism. New York, New American Library, 1965.
Capitalism: The Unknown Ideal, with others. New York, New American Library, 1966.
Introduction to Objectivist Epistemology. New York, The Objectivist, 1967.
The Romantic Manifesto: A Philosophy of Literature. Cleveland, World, 1970.
The New Left: The Anti-Industrial Revolution. New York, New American Library, 1971.
Philosophy: Who Needs It? Indianapolis, Bobbs Merrill, 1982.

*

Manuscript Collection: Library of Congress, Washington, D.C.

Critical Studies: *Who Is Ayn Rand? An Analysis of the Novels of Ayn Rand* by Nathaniel Branden, New York, Random House, 1962; *The Philosophic Thought of Ayn Rand* edited by Douglas J. Den Uyl and Douglas B. Rasmussen, Urbana, University of Illinois Press, 1984; *The Ayn Rand Companion* by Mimi Reisel Gladstein, Westport, Connecticut, Greenwood Press, 1984.

*   *   *

Considering her unvarying depictions of heroes and heroines as people adhering to unpopular views despite hostility and abuse, Ayn Rand must have been pleased at resembling them through the controversy she arouses by her novels. In spite of her claim to be an unswerving advocate of reason, her appeal is often violently emotional. She makes her readers long to identify themselves with her dynamic, creative, productive, intelligent, handsome, and ultimately victorious heroes (and thereby with the ideas associated with them). She also compels her readers to despise the cowardly, lazy, incompetent, vicious, ugly, and inevitably defeated spokesman for the ideas she abhors. Her two speculative novels, *Anthem* and *Atlas Shrugged,* stridently warn against shaping our future according to the ideas of Christianity, Marxism, liberalism, or any other viewpoint advocating self-sacrifice which, to her, means self-negation. In opposition to such ideals, they applaud man's ego as the source of all inventiveness, achievement, and happiness and capitalism as the system allowing the fullest expression of the ego. In spite of her stridency, Rand remains one of the most powerful—and thoughtful—defenders of conservative American values, portraying the businessman as the unacknowledged Atlas who carries the burden of civilization on his mighty shoulders.

Although *Anthem* and *Atlas Shrugged* are clearly intended as cautionary tracts expounding Rand's social and philosophical beliefs and fears, both present carefully detailed pictures of future societies. In creating these societies, Rand extrapolates the possible consequences of self-sacrificial goals on art, politics, economics, sex, and family and social relationships. *Anthem* is set in a new dark age which has come about after the collectivists have defeated all the individualists. In this world, technology has nearly ceased to exist since, for Rand, it is the product of individual curiosity, effort, and ability which have also nearly ceased to exist. At birth, all children are taken from their parents and placed in a communal home where they will be taught that they must devote their lives to working for the benefit of their brothers, act as all their brothers act, and think only what all their brothers think. No man is permitted to live as an individual and the word "I" is forbidden. However, one man known as Equality 7-2521 finds such a world uncomfortable, "transgresses," and through his "sinful" behavior rediscovers individualism, creativity, self-respect, and selective love and friendship—or, in short, Rand's own values. *Atlas Shrugged* is set in an America resembling that of the 1950's when the book was written. However, this America soon becomes transformed into a society trying to follow the Christian goal of loving one's brother like oneself and the Marxist principle "From each according to his ability, to each according to his need." The government assumes control over the economy, places all industries under a Unification Board, and attempts to redistribute the benefits earned by the most efficient companies to the least efficient ones on the assumption that the weaker companies have the greater need. The result of this policy of penalizing success and rewarding failure is that moochers rise to the highest levels of government (the head of the economic program is named Wesley Mouch) and the most productive businessmen have difficulty surviving. Having foreseen these developments, the superheroic protagonist, John Galt, leads the greatest producers and creators on strike, thus precipitating the collapse of the moochers' government and preparing the way for a new society founded on the Randian oath: "I swear—by my life and by my love of it—that I will never live for the sake of another man, nor ask another man to live for mine."

Both of Rand's speculative novels are major contributions to the field. Her passionate commitment to ideas about social structure is well suited to the speculative form, especially since it is coupled with an ability to give concrete embodiment to these ideas. Though the slim *Anthem* only sketches her ideas, it offers a good introduction to them. Longer than Samuel Delany's *Dhalgren* and talkier than Robert Heinlein's *I Will Fear No Evil,* the gigantic *Atlas Shrugged* spells them out fully in repetitious but often exciting, provocative, and even brilliant detail.

—Steven R. Carter

RANDALL, Marta. American. Born in Mexico City, 26 April 1948; moved to San Francisco at age 2. Educated at Berkeley High School, California; San Francisco State College, 1966-72. Married 1) Robert H. Bergstresser in 1966 (divorced, 1973), one son; 2) Christopher E. Conley in 1983. Since 1968, office manager, H. Zimmerman, Oakland, California. Taught at Clarion Writers workshop, East Lansing, Michigan, 1982, and at workshops at Portland State University, Cannon Beach, 1983, and University of California, Berkeley, 1984, 1985. Vice-President, 1981-82, and President, 1982-84, Science Fiction Writers of America. Agent: Richard Curtis, 164 East 64th Street, New York, New York 10021. Address: P. O. Box 13243, Station E, Oakland, California 94661, U.S.A.

SCIENCE-FICTION PUBLICATIONS

Novels (series: Kennerin Saga)

Islands. New York, Pyramid, 1976; revised edition, New York, Pocket Books, 1980.
A City in the North. New York, Warner, 1976.
Journey (Kennerin). New York, Pocket Books, 1978; London, Hamlyn, 1979.
Dangerous Games (Kennerin). New York, Pocket Books, 1980.
The Sword of Winter. New York, Pocket Books, 1983.
Those Who Favor Fire. New York, Pocket Books, 1984.

Uncollected Short Stories

"Smack Run" (as Marta Bergstresser), in *New Worlds 5*, edited by Michael Moorcock. London, Sphere, 1973.
"A Scarab in the City of Time," in *New Dimensions 5*, edited by Robert Silverberg. New York, Harper, 1975; London, Gollancz, 1976.
"Secret Rider," in *New Dimensions 6*, edited by Robert Silverberg. New York, Harper, and London, Gollancz, 1976.
"Megan's World," in *The Crystal Ship*, edited by Robert Silverberg. Nashville, Nelson, 1976; London, Millington, 1980.
"The State of the Art on Alyssum," in *New Dimensions 7*, edited by Robert Silverberg. New York, Harper, and London, Gollancz, 1977.
"The Captain and the Kid," in *Universe 9*, edited by Terry Carr. New York, Doubleday, 1979; London, Dobson, 1980.
"The View from Endless Scarp," in *Fantasy and Science Fiction* (New York), July 1979.
"Circus," in *New Dimensions 10*, edited by Robert Silverberg. New York, Harper, 1980.
"Singles," in *Shadows 5*, edited by Charles L. Grant. New York, Doubleday, 1981.
"On Cannon Beach," in *Isaac Asimov's Science Fiction Magazine* (New York), April 1984.
"Thank You, Mr. Halifax," in *Omni* (New York), November 1984.
"Undeniably Cute: A Cautionary Tale," in *Isaac Asimov's Science Fiction Magazine* (New York), February 1985.
"Sea Change," in *Isaac Asimov's Science Fiction Magazine* (New York), April 1985.

OTHER PUBLICATIONS

Other

Introduction to *Galaxies*, By Barry N. Malzberg. Boston, Gregg Press, 1980.

Editor, with Robert Silverberg, *New Dimensions 11-12*. New York, Pocket Books, 2 vols., 1980-81.
Editor, *The Nebula Awards 19*. New York, Arbor House, 1984.

*

Marta Randall comments:

I find it difficult to speak about my own fiction—primarily, I think, because of a conviction that stories must stand by themselves, and the hopes, opinion, or beliefs of their authors are ultimately irrelevant. I view science fiction as a tool, as a useful series of conventions with which to deal with a storyteller's basic task, that is, the exploration not of ideas, but of people. By using the devices of the genre the writer can pare away anything not relevant to the characters and their dilemmas, can, in effect, create a crucible in which to toss the characters and view their reactions. Last that sound pompous, I believe it equally important that science fiction remain, far more than general mainstream fiction, a genre in which one can tell stories, present adventures, write for the simple joy of creating wonderful things. My principal goal as a science-fiction writer is to meld these two approaches to the genre. It is a goal which I hope to be chasing for the rest of my professional life.

*   *   *

Marta Randall is a prolific and versatile writer. Her six novels span a variety of literary forms: science fiction, quasi-fantasy, and conventional novels. She has experimented with different literary modes as well: novels, short stories, novellas, and the editing of anthologies.

Her first two works, *Islands* and *A City in the North*, were published in 1976. *A City in the North* tells the story of an alien species, colonized and exploited by humans, who decide to tear asunder their social order in their revolt against their masters. The finale is ambiguous when the author posits that oppression does not lead to a higher morality on the part of the victim. *Journey* and *Dangerous Games* form a two-part saga of the Kennerin family who own the planet Aerie and attempt to create a society alternative to Earth.

In her last two novels Randall has increasingly moved away from science fiction. In *The Sword of Winter* she depicts a feudal society poised between change and stasis. The novel is neither science fiction nor fantasy; although it takes place on another planet, it is closer to a conventional historical novel. Her latest novel, *Those Who Favour Fire* is not science fiction at all, but rather a dystopian extrapolation of what could happen on the West Coast given urban crime, gang warfare, organized right-wing movements, and earthquakes.

Randall's works are representative of the feminist sub-genre in science fiction. This distinct sub-grouping emerged in the mid 1960's when women joined the ranks of science-fiction writers in substantial numbers for the first time. Almost to a woman, they wrote "soft" science fiction, concentrating on depicting alternative worlds which, when juxtaposed to their own, served to highlight the deleterious effects of sexism.

Many characteristics found in Randall's work are typical of traits found in feminist science fiction. First, her alternative worlds are not sexist. All her novels portray strong female characters who are decisive, independent, nurturing, and thoughtful. Second, Randall explores sexual taboos and alternative sexual modes openly and uninhibitedly, such as homosexuality, incest, and sensuality. Third, her imaginary worlds, although vivid, do not proffer an alternative view to the author's own social order. This shortcoming, shared with many feminist science-fiction writers, is most evident in *Journey* and *Dangerous Games* where Randall recreates monopoly capitalism and proffers it as a utopic social order to the reader.

Randall's strengths are many. Her novels are fast-paced and contain strong, well-developed characters. Her aliens in *Journey, Dangerous Games*, and especially *A City in the North* are believable and engaging. Her best science-fiction novel is her first, *Islands*. Here, she explores a society whose inhabitants have discovered the secret to immortality. Randall is brilliant in her speculations of the sciences, language, morality, psychology, phobias, and pathologies of immortal beings. The emotions of the heroine, who cannot achieve immortality and is an aging freak in a perpetually youthful society, are depicted masterfully. The finale is strongly reminiscent of Olaf Stapledon's *Star Maker*, where the heroine mutates to a higher level of consciousness, transcends the corporal, and merges with the world and cosmos.

—Hoda M. Zaki

RANDALL, Robert. See **GARRETT, Randall; SILVERBERG, Robert.**

RANKINE, John. Pseudonym for Douglas Rankine Mason; also writes as R. M. Douglas. British. Born in Hawarden, Flintshire, 26 September 1918. Educated at Heywood Grammar School, 1929-34; Chester Grammar School, 1934-37; Manchester University, 1937-39, 1946-48, B. A. Served in the Royal Signals, 1939-46: Lieutenant. Married Mary Cooper in 1945; two sons and two daughters. Headmaster, Somerville Junior School, 1954-67, and St. George's Primary School, 1967-78, both Wallasey, Cheshire. Agent: Leslie Flood, Carnell Literary Agency, Rowneybury Bungalow, Sawbridgeworth, near Old Harlow, Essex CM20 2EX. Address: Ghyll View, Hollens Farm, Grasmere, Cumbria, England.

SCIENCE-FICTION PUBLICATIONS

Novels

The Blockade of Sinitron (for children). London, Nelson, 1966.
Interstellar Two-Five. London, Dobson, 1966.
Never the Same Door. London, Dobson, 1967.
One Is One. London, Dobson, 1968.
Moons of Triopus. London, Dobson, 1968; New York, Paperback Library, 1969.
Binary Z. London, Dobson, 1969.
The Weisman Experiment. London, Dobson, 1969.
The Plantos Affair. London, Dobson, 1971.
The Ring of Garamas. London, Dobson, 1972.
Operation Umanaq. New York, Ace, 1973; London, Sidgwick and Jackson, 1974.

The Bromius Phenomenon. New York, Ace, 1973; London, Dobson, 1976.
The Fingalnan Conspiracy. London, Sidgwick and Jackson, 1973.
Moon Odyssey (novelization of TV series). London, Dobson, and New York, Pocket Books, 1975.
Lunar Attack (novelization of TV series). London, Dobson, 1975; New York, Pocket Books, 1976.
Astral Quest (novelization of TV series). London, Dobson, 1975; New York, Pocket Books, 1976.
Android Planet (novelization of TV series). London, Barker, and New York, Pocket Books, 1976.
Phoenix of Megaron (novelization of TV series). New York, Pocket Books, 1976.
The Thorburn Enterprise. London, Dobson, 1977.
The Vort Programme. London, Dobson, 1979.
The Star of Hesiock. London, Dobson, 1980.
Last Shuttle to Planet Earth. London, Dobson, 1980.

Novels as Douglas R. Mason

From Carthage Then I Came. New York, Doubleday, 1966; London, Hale, 1968; as *Eight Against Utopia*, New York, Paperback Library, 1967.
Ring of Violence. London, Hale, 1968; New York, Avon, 1969.
Landfall Is a State of Mind. London, Hale, 1968.
The Tower of Rizwan. London, Hale, 1968.
The Janus Syndrome. London, Hale, 1969.
Matrix. New York, Ballantine, 1970; London, Hale, 1971.
Satellite 54-Zero. New York, Ballantine, and London, Pan, 1971.
Horizon Alpha. New York, Ballantine, 1971; London, Hale, 1981.
Dilation Effect. New York, Ballantine, 1971; London, Hale, 1980.
The Resurrection of Roger Diment. New York, Ballantine, 1972.
The Phaeton Condition. New York, Putnam, 1973; London, Hale, 1974.
The End Bringers. New York, Ballantine, 1973; London, Hale, 1975.
Pitman's Progress. Morley, Yorkshire, Elmfield Press, 1976.
The Omega Worm. London, Hale, 1976.
Euphor Unfree. London, Hale, 1977.
Mission to Pactolus R. London, Hale, 1978.
The Typhon Intervention. London, Hale, 1981.

Uncollected Short Stories (series: Dag Fletcher)

"Two's Company" (Fletcher), in *New Writings in SF 1*, edited by John Carnell. London, Dobson, 1964; New York, Bantam, 1966.
"Maiden Voyage" (Fletcher), in *New Writings in SF 2*, edited by John Carnell. London, Dobson, 1964; London, Bantam, 1966.
"Six Cubed Plus 1," in *New Writings in SF 7*, edited by John Carnell. London, Dobson, 1966; New York, Bantam, 1971.
"Seventh Moon," in *Impulse* (London), May 1966.
"Pattern as Set," in *Impulse (London), July 1966.*
"Image of Destruction" (Fletcher), in *New Writings in SF 10*, edited by John Carnell. London, Dobson, 1967.
"Flight of the Plastic Bee," in *New Writings in SF 11*, edited by John Carnell. London, Dobson, 1968.
"Worm in the Bud" (Fletcher), in *New Writings in SF 12*, edited by John Carnell. London, Dobson, 1968.
"The Peacemakers," in *If* (New York), January 1968.

"Moonchip," in *Vision of Tomorrow* (Newcastle upon Tyne), December 1969.
"Second Run at the Data," in *Galaxy* (New York), February 1971.
"Link," in *Amazing* (New York), January 1973.

Uncollected Short Stories as Douglas R. Mason

"Traveller's Rest," in *New Worlds* (London), September 1965.
"Squared Out with Poplars," in *Worlds of Tomorrow* (New York), May 1967.
"Locust Years," in *Galaxy* (New York), November 1968.
"Dinner of Herbs," in *Vision of Tomorrow* (Newcastle upon Tyne), February 1970.
"Rejection Syndrome," in *Vision of Tomorrow* (Newcastle upon Tyne), April 1970.
"The Castoffs," in *If* (New York), February 1972.
"Algora One Six," in *New Writings in SF 21*, edited by John Carnell. London, Sidgwick and Jackson, 1973.

OTHER PUBLICATIONS

Novel as R. M. Douglas

The Darkling Plain. London, Hale, 1979.

*

John Rankine comments:
Science fiction is either escapist adventure—Hornblower in a star ship—or an allegory for our time—the dystopia, *Brave New World* bit. I tend to write the first as John Rankine and the second as Douglas R. Mason.
I hold the view that the biogrammar that determines the human make-up was laid down over such a long period that events like the technological revolution will not alter anything in the foreseeable future. Therefore my inhabitants of Wirral City in 4000 AD act in the same way as people of the present. Cain is still Cain and unable to change.

*   *   *

John Rankine, who also writes under his real name, Douglas R. Mason, envisions future battles waged by man against android, robot, computer, or physically recreated bionic man. Usually the machines' rigidity, their propensity toward predictable patterns, their lack of emotion, their machine nature is responsible for or aids in their ultimate defeat, while man's doubt, his emotion, his loyalty, his physical self, spurred by instinct, passion, and a need for action and for self-preservation, help him ultimately to conquer. Rankine continually deplores man's insidious tendency to sacrifice freedom and intellectual activity for the sake of comfort, stability, and pleasure, and asks if there can be true pleasure without conflict and pain. His heroes are constantly struck with the realization that they have never felt truly alive until they have tasted sweat, endured trauma, and shared danger. Rankine also wonders whether prolonging life through chemicals and mechanical replacements might not be ultimately self-destructive, immortality at the price of humanity and selfhood. Frequently his bionic characters are patronizing about real humans, and feel an intellectual sympathy with computers, attitudes that always doom them.
Rankine heroes are tough and manly but have sunk into the mindless apathy of modern regimentation only to be jarred into self-awareness and rebellion by a freak accident, a sudden intuition or insight, an irrepressible instinct. Occasionally they

articulate these attitudes in lines from Shakespeare or Keats. Often these men are attracted to cold, incredibly beautiful women who kepp them at a distance and intellectualize their relationship; ultimately, however, they learn that such women are either useless in a crisis or actively act against them, turning them over to robots for "readjustment." Usually the heroes are passionately aroused by a less perfect but more nubile woman who has worked with them unnoticed in the past, who fights in their cause, and who finally accepts a division of labor whereby the male is leader and warrior and the woman submits as helpmate, nurse, cook, and technician.
In *The End Bringers* androids rule, monitoring human emotions and repressing them with drugs, until a natural rebel uncovers a plot to eliminate all humanoids; rescuing hundreds before robots eviscerate them, he leads survivors to an air raid shelter from which revived humanity launches its attack on android tyrants. In *Matrix* city computers plan to eliminate all human life and use the free space to unify storage banks and achieve godhood, but a human administrator discovers the plan and fights back. In doing so he has to deal with conformists who not only disapprove of rebellion, but actively battle against it, blind to their own precarious predicament, or with doubters who understand his logic but question his motives, or with humanists who oppose the violence of his methods, violence that ultimately proves justified. In *From Carthage Then I Came* a computer, originally established to protect man from a cruel ice age, has monitored all life in the domed city for seven thousand years, but life is sterile, impersonal, and public. A few who have learned to evade mind probes unite in an escape plot, and, against difficult odds, outwit computers and robots, and start a new world in the wilderness, agrarian but free. These patterns with their Edenic themes are typical of much of Rankine's canon.
Basically Rankine writes about science's potential abuses, limiting man's potentiality, reducing originality, variety, and natural evolution, controlling his weather and his atmosphere, tampering with his mind. In *Satellite 54-Zero* a secret agent tries to penetrate a private scientific operation studying Jupiter, only to encounter the horror of mechanical failure in space, a scientific mind out of control, and a centaur transported from another dimension. In *Operation Umanaq* the Southern hemisphere plots to destroy the Northern by affecting weather conditions and producing another ice age, while a fast-acting Northern agent evades hitmen and suicide drugs to invade a Polar station and reset weather computers. *The Phaeton Condition* begins in a world so polluted by industrial waste that its oxygen supply is fast being depleted; an industrial giant who helped create this condition plans to exploit it further through a secret high-priced safe zone with its own underground oxygen reserves. Frequently Mason's scientists consider humans expendable and progress worth any danger. In *Moons of Triopus* the industrial advantages of exploiting a new planet are judged more important than slow, safe investigation, but politicians and businessmen learn too late that more rational beings may well view their selfish acts with contempt and act accordingly.
The "Dag Fletcher" series are all set in the same galaxy and involve lots of action, while his novelized episodes from TV *Space 1999*, are episodic, a progression of threats and dangers ranging from space brain anti-bodies to materialized nightmares to alien wars of annihilation. His short stories often focus on mathematics, "Six Cubed Plus 1" on the magical properties of special numbers and "Traveller's Rest" on topological oddities whereby time and language vary with the structure of space.

—Gina Macdonald

RAPHAEL, Rick. American. Born in New York City, 20 February 1919. Educated at Boise Junior College, Idaho; University of New Mexico Albuquerque, B. A. 1948; Colorado State University, Fort Collins. Served in the United States Army, 1936-45, and in the reserve service, 1945-65: retired as Captain: Bronze Star, Purple Heart, and service stars. Married 1) Dolores Raphael in 1941; 2) Elizabeth L. Van Schaick in 1958; one son and five daughters; 3) Donna E. Swenson in 1972. Newspaper reporter, writer, and editor, 1945-58; copy editor, *Idaho Daily Statesman,* Boise, 1958-59; assistant news editor and political editor, KBOI-TV and Radio, Boise, 1959-65; Press Secretary for Senator Frank Church, 1965-69; executive, J. C. Penney Company, 1969-79. Recipient: Radio-Television News Directors Award, for documentary, 1963. Agent: Scott Meredith Literary Agency, 845 Third Avenue, New York, New York 10022. Address: 5320 Thotland Road, Golden Valley, Minnesota 55422, U.S.A.

SCIENCE-FICTION PUBLICATIONS

Novel

Code Three. New York, Simon and Schuster, 1965; London, Gollancz, 1966.

Short Stories

The Thirst Quenchers. London, Gollancz, 1965.

OTHER PUBLICATIONS

Novels

The Defector. New York, Doubleday, 1980.
The President Must Die. New York, Norton, 1981.

*

Rick Raphael comments:
   Science fiction is the extrapolation of today's technology into tomorrow. But while science progresses, human nature and emotions remain unchanged. Tomorrow's man will merely have new tools to manifest his love, hate, fear, greed, and laughter.

*   *   *

In recent years Rick Raphael has turned to the suspense/thriller mode with such novels as *The President Must Die,* which, even though set for convenience in the 1990's (having been published in 1981) contains no science-fiction elements. Raphael's reputation as a pure science-fiction writer remains based upon the long stories which make up two books of classic SF: *The Thirst Quenchers* and *Code Three.* Most of the stories in question were originally published in *Analog* in the mid-1960's, and they exemplify that magazine's commitment to technological extrapolation and the rigorous if unobtrusive development of "lived-in" futures.
   Both the title story of *The Thirst Quenchers* and "Guttersnipe," collected in the same volume, deal with futures in which overpopulation has led to a scarcity of fresh water. Formidable managerial and technological resources are shown being used to maintain supplies. The different measures adopted in each story are threatened by disasters which generate the interest. Most notable in these stories is the patience and intelligence with which Raphael has worked out the operation of the agencies concerned with conserving the precious water; his technical descriptions are confidently and convincingly written.
   Code Three is really three novellas strung together in sequence; two of the three were originally published separately. Like much of Raphael's work, *Code Three* presents a dystopian future, in this case one dominated by five-mile-wide thruways providing routes for cars which travel at 400 miles per hour or more. The main characters of the book are officers who man a patrol car designed to cope with the dangers of driving on such roads—and the irresponsibilities of the civilian motorists, who often use their vehicles in a lunatic manner.
   Because of its episodic structure, *Code Three* lacks true cohesion as a novel. In the first two sections, the officers of the patrol car 56 deal efficiently with rampaging criminal vehicle (the cars, rather than the people, are the real charaters of this section), then with the reckless son of an important businessman. The son, like his father, thinks he is beyond law. He turns out to be likeable enough, and even shows signs of learning his lesson; however, the corrupt father is made to feel the full weight of the law when he tries to interfere criminally with the legal proceedings. In the last section, heroic romance suddenly changes to tragic irony: the main character, Ben Martin, is killed while testing a new type of patrol car, portentously known as "the bomb. ' His death is caused by an irresponsible young officer whose recklessness epitomizes what Martin had spent his life controlling. The sinister, ironic tone of this section meshes badly with the rest of the novel; yet the section itself is genuinely moving.
   Ultimately, Ben Martin is a futile scapegoat—slain by a guilty and irresponsible society, but without his death contributing a jot to society's redemption. While the society which Raphael has extrapolated no longer appears feasible—the development of more and more powerful motor vehicles having ceased to be the dominant trend that it was at this time of writing—*Code Three* is an effective and impressive technological parable, read in its proper context.
   As a science-fiction writer, Raphael is admirable when describing the more technical aspects of his projected societies' workings. He is less certain in handling his characters. his women are particularly stereotyped, while the male characters are seldom treated in psychological depth, and often engage in dialogue which is unbelievably sententious or downright corny (a criticism which applies to his recent mainstream work as well as to his science-fiction). Nonetheless, Raphael's admittedly minor contribution to the science-fiction genre has shown him to be a formidable and underrated talent whose hard-edged extrapolative ability is deserving of particular respect.

—Russell Blackford

RAYCRAFT, Stan. See **SHAVER, Richard S.**

RAYER, Francis G(eorge). Also wrote as George Longdon; Milward Scott; Roland Worcester. British. Born in Longdon, Worcestershire, 6 June 1921. Married Tessa Elizabeth Platt in 1957; two sons. Since 1945, self-employed technical designer and electronic engineer; also a technical journalist. *Died 11 July 1981.*

SCIENCE-FICTION PUBLICATIONS

Novels

Tomorrow Sometimes Comes. London, Home and Van Thal, 1951.
The Star Seekers. London, Pearson, 1954.
Cardinal of the Stars. London, Digit, 1964; as *Journey to the Stars*, New York, Arcadia House, 1964.
The Iron and the Anger. London, Digit, 1964; New York, Arcadia House, 1967.

Uncollected Short Stories (series: Mens Magna)

"Basic Fundamental," in *Fantasy* (London), August 1947.
"From Beyond the Dawn," in *New Worlds 3* (London), n. d.
"Necessity," in *New Worlds 5* (London), 1949.
"Fearful Barrier," in *Worlds at War*, edited by Francis G. Rayer. London, Temple, 1950.
"Adaptability," in *New Worlds* (London), Spring 1950.
"Quest," in *New Worlds* (London), Summer 1950.
"Deus ex Machina" (Mens Magna), in *New Worlds* (London), Winter 1950.
"Time Was," in *New Worlds* (London), Winter 1951.
"The Undying Enemy," in *Science Fantasy* (Bournemouth), Winter 1951.
"Coming of the Darakua," in *Authentic 17* (London), 1952.
"Earth Our New Eden," in *Authentic 20* (London), 1952.
"When Greed Steps In," in *Fantastic Adventures* (New York), January 1952.
"Plimsoll Line," in *Science Fantasy* (Bournemouth), Spring 1952.
"Man's Questing Ended," in *New Worlds* (London), July 1952.
"The Peacemaker" (Mens Magna), in *New Worlds* (London), September 1952.
"We Cast No Shadow," in *Authentic* (London), December 1952.
"Prison Trap," in *Laurie's Space Annual*. London, Laurie, 1953.
"Thou Pasture Us," in *Nebula* (Glasgow), Spring 1953.
"Traders' Planet," in *Science Fantasy* (Bournemouth), Spring 1953.
"Power Factor," in *New Worlds* (London), June 1953.
"Firstling," in *Nebula* (Glasgow), December 1953.
"Of Those Who Came" (as George Longdon), in *Gateway to Tomorrow*, edited by John Carnell. London, Museum Press, 1954.
"Seek Earthman No More," in *Science Fantasy 7* (Bournemouth), 1954.
"The Lava Seas Tunnel," in *Authentic* (London), March 1954.
"Space Prize," in *Science Fantasy* (Bournemouth), May 1954.
"Pipe Away Stranger," in *New Worlds* (London), June 1954.
"Come Away Home," in *New Worlds* (London), September 1954.
"Dark Summer," in *Science Fantasy* (Bournemouth), September 1954.
"Co-Efficiency Zero," in *Science Fantasy* (Bournemouth), December 1954.
"Kill Me This Man," in *New Worlds* (London), January 1955.
"Ephemeral This City" (Mens Magna), in *New Worlds* (London), March 1955.
"This Night No More," in *Nebula* (Glasgow), September 1955.
"Stormhead," in *New Worlds* (London), October 1955.
"The Jakandi Moduli," in *New Worlds* (London), December 1955.
"Hyperant," in *New Worlds* (London), March 1956.
"Consolidation Area," in *New Worlds* (London), April 1956.

"Culture Pattern," in *New Worlds* (London), May 1956.
"Period of Quarantine," in *New Worlds* (London), June 1956.
"Error Potential," in *New Worlds* (London), August 1956.
"Three-Day Tidal," in *New Worlds* (London), October 1956.
"Beacon Green," in *Nebula* (Glasgow), March 1957.
"Stress Complex," in *New Worlds* (London), June 1957.
"Painters of Narve," in *New Worlds* (London), March 1958.
"The Voices Beyond," in *New Worlds* (London), August 1958.
"Wishing Stone," in *Science Fantasy* (Bournemouth), August 1958.
"Searchpoint," in *New Worlds* (London), May 1959.
"Static Trouble," in *New Worlds* (London), February 1960.
"Alien," in *New Worlds* (New York), May 1960.
"Adjustment Period" (Mens Magna), in *Science Fiction Adventures* (London), September 1960.
"Sands Our Abode" (for children), in *Out of This World 3*, edited by Amabel Williams-Ellis and Mably Owen. London, Blackie, 1961.
"Spring Fair Moduli," in *New Worlds* (London), February 1961.
"Contact Pattern" (Mens Magna), in *Science Fiction Adventures* (London), March 1961.
"Sacrifice," in *New Worlds* (London), June 1962.
"Sixth Veil," in *New Worlds* (London), July 1962.
"Variant," in *New Worlds* (London), August 1962.
"Capsid," in *New Worlds* (London), December 1962.
"Aqueduct" in *New Worlds* (London), March 1963.

OTHER PUBLICATIONS

Novel

Lady in Danger. Dublin, Grafton, 1948.

Other

Modern Fiction-Writing Technique. London, Bond Street, 1960.
Repair of Domestic Electrical Appliances. London, Arco, 1961.
Electricity in the Home. London, Arco, 1962.
Amateur Radio. London, Arco, 1964.
Electricity in Your Home (as Millward Scott). London, Foyles, 1964.
Electrical Hobbies. London, Collins, 1964.
Transistor Receivers and Amplifiers. London, Focal Press, 1965.
The Pegasus Book of Radio Experiments (for children). London, Dobson, 1968.
The Pegasus Book of Electrical Experiments (for children). London, Dobson, 1968.
Popular Electronics and Computers. London, Arco, 1968; as *Electronics and Computers*, South Brunswick, New Jersey, A. S. Barnes, 1968.
The Pegasus Book of Electronic Experiments (for children). London, Dobson, 1969.
Electronics (as Roland Worcester). London, Hamlyn, 1969.
A Guide to Outdoor Building. London, Barker, 1970.
Handbook of IC Audio Preamplifier and Power Amplifier Construction. London, Babani Press, 1976.
Two Transistor Electronic Projects. London, Babani Press, 1976.
50 Projects Using Relays. London, Babani Press, 1977.
50 Field Effect Transistor Projects. London, Babani Press, 1977.
How to Make Walkie-Talkies. London, Babani Press, 1977.
Electronic Game Projects. London, Newnes, 1979.

Electronic Projects in Hobbies. London, Newnes, and Woburn, Massachusetts, Focal Press, 1979.
How to Build Your Own Solid State Oscilloscope. London, Babani Press, 1979.
Counter, Driver and Numerical Display Projects. London, Babani Press, 1979.
Radio Control for Beginners. London, Babani Press, 1980.
Electronic Test Equipment Construction. London, Babani Press, 1980.
Digital IC Projects. London, Babani Press, 1981.
Electronic Timer Projects. London, Babani Press, 1981.
Audio Projects. London, Babani Press, 1981.
Projects in Amateur Radio. London, Newnes, 1981.
Beginner's Guide to Amateur Radio. London, Newnes, 1982.
IC Projects for Beginners. London, Babani Press, 1982.

Editor, *Worlds at War.* London, Temple, 1950.

*

Francis G. Rayer commented:

(1981) My aim in writing science fiction was to show some aspects of the world as it could be within one or two generations. "Time Was," *Tomorrow Sometimes Comes*, and *The Star Seekers* were probably the best examples of this.

* * *

Much of the work produced by Francis G. Rayer is the routine potboiler that makes up the vast majority of published science fiction. In novels such as *The Iron and the Anger* he depicts the conflict between a typical unwillingly heroic human and some non-human menace, in this case homicidally inclined robots determined to wipe out the human race. At times, there is a more serious note to his fiction, but still only in a very limited sense. For example, *Cardinal of the Stars* points out what Rayer sees as the importance of humanity's progress into space, in this case in order to be able to defend itself from the encroachment of a hostile alien fleet. But the novel remains essentially a spy story set in the future, with the two-fisted hero determined to stop the series of sabataged space-ships and bombings from outer space that have begun to plague the world. Similarly, *Star Seekers* makes some tentative efforts toward philosophy, but remains essentially a potboiler about the dangers inherent in violating Einstein's laws and attempting to travel faster than light. Rayer's attempts here to avoid overt melodrama result in slow-paced scenes made even more ineffective by a turgid prose that is void of wit or clarity.

But there are times when Rayer is more than just a hack adventure writer. He was most successful with his series about an intelligent computer of unprecedented capacity that appears first as the administrator of a completely unemotional legal system in a short story, then progresses to taking complete control of humanity during a nuclear war in Rayer's best novel, *Tomorrow Sometimes Comes*. In a short story later in that same series, and possibly the best piece of short fiction Rayer wrote, the computer becomes "The Peacemaker," paradoxically by helping an alien race to invade Earth and conquer humanity for its own good. At the time Rayer wrote this story, this was certainly a far more novel and less acceptable conclusion than it would be now.

—Don D'Ammassa

REAMY, Tom. American. Born in Woodson, Texas, in 1935. Movie projectionist, technical illustrator, dispatcher for a concrete plant, assistant movie director and propman, photo-typositor, and house painter; Editor, *CriFanAc*, Dallas, in the 1950's and *Trumpet*, in the 1960's; Founder, with Ken Keller, Nickelodeon Graphics, Kansas City (worked on *Delap's SF & F Review* and *Chacol/Shayol*), and Editor, with Keller, *Nickelodeon*, 1975-77. Recipient: Nebula Award, 1975; John W. Campbell Award, 1976. *Died 5 November 1977.*

SCIENCE-FICTION PUBLICATIONS

Novel

Blind Voices. New York, Berkley, 1978; London, Sidgwick and Jackson, 1979.

Short Stories

San Diego Lightfoot Sue and Other Stories. Kansas City, Earthlight, 1980.

Uncollected Short Story

"M Is for the Million Things," in *New Voices 4*, edited by George R. R. Martin. New York, Berkley, 1981.

OTHER PUBLICATIONS

Play

Sting!, in *Six Science Fiction Plays* , edited by Roger Elwood. New York, Pocket Books, 1976.

* * *

From 1974, when his first stories appeared, Tom Reamy was considered a promising new writer and his progress watched with interest. His sudden death in 1977 meant that, instead of the long and prolific career and the steady increase in his already formidable powers his admirers expected, we have only one novel and a dozen short stories. But the novel, *Blind Voices*, and the best of the short stories need no special pleading as early experiments– they can stand on their own as successful and remarkable works. Tom Reamy's position is secure. Although he is often called a science-fiction writer, and won science-fiction awards, nearly all of Reamy's work would be better classified as fantasy. His stories skim along the edge of reality, firmly anchored in time and place, whether Depression-era, rural Kansas, or present-day Los Angeles, and the plots range between the subtlest of fantasies and the most visceral, outrageous horrors. His recurring themes are of human relationships, the frightening, dark side of sexuality, the triumph or destruction of the innocent, and monsters—from outer space, from Hollywood, from the id.

"Twilla," his first published story, shows the strong influence films—particularly low-budget horror films—had on Reamy, who worked in Hollywood and first tried his hand at script-writing. The plot of "Twilla" is straightforward and violent, full of vivid, visual descriptions with little time wasted on explanations. Like the films it emulates, the story seeks to entertain and shock, and it succeeds. There are some problems with plot construction and logic, but the story works as well as it does because of a solid grounding in reality, the accumulation of detail giving it a peculiar depth. In this, as in later stories, Reamy revealed his talent for selecting the perfect details to bring scenes and characters to life, from the utterly convincing names of even minor characters to precise descriptions of dress and furniture. "San Diego Lighfoot Sue," Reamy's own favorite and an award-winner, is the gentlest and most romantic of all his stories. The horror takes place off-stage and the emphasis is that of the so-called "mainstream," with the fantasy element almost superfluous. It is not the story, nor any sense of the fantastic, which remains to haunt the reader, but the characters—the vividly depicted Pearl and Daisy Mae; the extreme innocence and beauty of John Lee Peacock; the dying Grace Elizabeth; the hinted-at depths of the title character.

To my mind, Reamy's best and most powerful stories are "The Detweiler Boy" and "Under the Hollywood Sign," both set in a grittily real Los Angeles, both told in the first-person and using many of the conventions of the hard-boiled detective story, both probing the dark side of sexual desire and offering a complex vision of the conflict, on many levels, between innocence and evil. They are both disturbing stories which reveal love and need as the inseparable siamese twins of violence and destruction. In these stories people need each other and shy away from their need, knowing that sexual love will inevitable lead to death.

Blind Voices takes place in the American midwest during the Depression—a time and a place that Reamy makes convincingly his own. The story sets the fantastic creatures of a travelling wonder-show against the everyday lives of the people of Hawley, Kansas. It obviously owes much to works by Ray Bradbury, Charles Finney, and Theodore Sturgeon, but it shows Reamy's distinctive touch in the reworking of some familiar material, in the characterizations, the vivid style, and the dark undercurrent of sexuality which runs through all his writings. Although the material is that of fantasy, like *The Circus of Doctor Lao* or *Something Wicked This Way Comes*, an explanation near the end tips the book into science fiction.

—Lisa Tuttle

REAVES, J. Michael. American. Address: c/o Bantam Books, 666 Fifth Avenue, New York, New York 10019, U.S.A.

SCIENCE- FICTION PUBLICATIONS

Novels

Dragonworld, with Byron Preiss. New York, Bantam, 1979; London, Bantam, 1980; revised edition, New York, Bantam, 1983.
The Shattered World. New York, Pocket Books, n. d.
Sword of the Samurai, with Steve Perry. New York, Bantam, 1984.

Short Stories

Darkworld Detective. New York, Bantam, 1982.

Uncollected Short Stories

"The Breath of Dragons," in *Clarion 3*, edited by Robin Scott Wilson. New York, New American Library, 1973.
"The Century Feeling," in *Fantasy and Science Fiction* (New York), May 1974.

"Passion Play," in *Universe 5*, edited by Terry Carr. New York, Doubleday, 1975.
"The Sound of Someone Dying," in *Fantasy and Science Fiction* (New York), May 1976.
"Love among the Symbionts," in *Ascents of Wonder*, edited by David Gerrold and Stephen Goldin. New York, Popular Library, 1977.
"Shadetree," in *Horrors*, edited by Charles L. Grant. New York, Berkley, 1982.
"Werewind," in *Fantasy Annual 5*, edited by Terry Carr. New York, Pocket Books, 1982.
"The Tearing of Greymare House," in *Fantasy and Science Fiction* (New York), March 1983.

* * *

J. Michael Reaves is just now finding his own voice as a writer, making a true assessment of his work somewhat difficult and possibly premature. His 12 year career has seen eleven published short stories and six novels, two of them juvenile, three of them collaborative. Three other novels and a short story collection have been sold, and at least one collaborative novel remains unpublished. Reaves has supported himself through his apprenticeship by writing approximately 120 teleplays, treatments, bibles, and developments for the Saturday morning juvenile TV market, including both live-action and animated scripts. Not all of these programs have been produced, but the consistent level of work since 1975 has provided Reaves with the financial security to develop his craft slowly, and to be more selective with his books than he might have been otherwise. Further, many of these scripts were penned for science-fiction or fantasy programs, giving him a thorough grounding in a wide variety of plot elements common to both fields.

Reaves had been writing stories since his teen years, and had taken the usual round of creative writing courses in college. His first real break, however, was attending the Clarion Workshop for science fiction writers in 1972, where he had a chance to meet the professionals for the first time, and to have his stories torn apart by the experts. The result was his first professional sale, "The Breath of Dragons. " The choice of theme and setting in this story uncannily presages Reaves's later fiction. Perrin is a hunter on a planet where dragons are killed for their fire-producing bladders. The dragons look and fly like the creatures from children's fairy tales, but they're no match for man's superior future technology. Perrin also believes they're sentient beings, a theory no one else is willing to countenance. Perrin's attempts to prove the dragons' intelligence causes the accidental death of a crewmate; as he struggles to find a way out of his predicament, he is consumed (in an apparent act of kindness) by the very creatures he is striving to protect.

Reaves enjoys combining traditional science fiction and fantasy elements into one seemingly irreconcilable plot line, making the believability of one depend on the other. The images of dragons and similar creatures, of flying in general, of man and beast soaring above the grittiness of the everyday world, permeate his fiction. Even in *Hellstar* (forthcoming), where the world is a man-made, interstellar spaceship travelling slowly between the stars, we find constant pictures of man's attempts literally to rise above his environment. He imbues his key protagonists with a sense of responsibility for the worlds around them. The obvious caring demonstrated by Perrin in "The Breath of Dragons" is evident also in Amsel's dragonquest in *Dragonworld*, in Beorn's courage in *The Shattered World*, and even in the rather sardonic sense of justice evidenced by Kamus of Kadizar (*Darkworld Detective*).

In each of these stories the fantastic settings are counterbalanced by the reality of the people who must live in them. Those who evade their responsibilities must pay the price; correspondingly, those who act must suffer the consequences of their actions, consequences which are not always pleasant. Reaves sees the real drama in both life and literature in forcing recognizable individuals to make choices that will positively or negatively influence their lives—and even the universe—forever.

Thus, in Reaves's best novel to date, *The Shattered World*, the magicians must face the consequences of their ancient and irresponsible war that literally broke the world into fragments, Pandrogas and Amber cannot escape the harm caused by their affair, and Beorn, as attractive a thief as one will find in modern fantasy literature, still must pay a very high price indeed for his chosen profession. Yet they all persist in the face of severe adversity to keep on doing what each of them thinks is right and necessary and proper—for themselves, and even sometimes for others. For Reaves, the universe inevitable is a moral place where immorals fear to tread.

—R. Reginald

REED, Kit (née Craig). Also writes as Shelley Hyde. American. Born in San Diego, California. Educated at the College of Notre Dame of Maryland, Baltimore, B. A. 1954. Married Joseph Wayne Reed, Jr., in 1955; two sons and one daughter. Reporter, *St. Petersburg Times*, Florida, 1954-55; reporter, *Hamden Chronicle*, Connecticut, 1956, and *New Haven Register*, Connecticut, 1956-59; book reviewer, *New Haven Register* and *St. Petersburg Times*. Since 1974, Visiting Professor of English, Wesleyan University, Middletown, Connecticut. Recipient: New England Newspaperwoman of the Year award, 1958, 1959; Guggenheim Fellowship, 1964; Abraham Woursell Foundation five-year grant, 1965; Aspen Institute Rockefeller Fellowship, 1976. Agent: Carl Brandt, Brandt and Brandt, 1501 Broadway, New York, New York 10036. Address: 45 Lawn Avenue, Middletown, Connecticut 06457, U.S.A.

SCIENCE-FICTION PUBLICATIONS

Novels

Armed Camps. London, Faber, 1969; New York, Dutton, 1970.
Magic Time. New York, Berkley, 1979.

Short Stories

Mister da V. and Other Stories. London, Faber, 1967; New York, Berkley, 1973.
The Killer Mice. London, Gollancz, 1976.
Other Stories, and The Attack of the Giant Baby. New York, Berkley, 1981.

Uncollected Short Stories

"Tell Me Doctor—Please," in *Best Tales of Terror 2*, edited by Edmund Crispin. London, Faber, 1965.
"The Holdouts," in *Fantasy and Science Fiction* (New York), June 1977.
"Shan," in *Fantasy and Science Fiction* (New York), January 1978.
"Chicken Soup," in *New Terrors 1*, edited by Ramsey Campbell. London, Pan, 1980.

"Frontiers," in *Twilight Zone* (New York), May 1982.
"Sisohpromatem," in *Changes*, edited by Michael Bishop and Ian Watson. New York, Ace, 1982.
"The Bride of Bigfoot," in *Isaac Asimov's Science Fiction Magazine* (New York), July 1984.

OTHER PUBLICATIONS

Novels

Mother Isn't Dead, She's Only Sleeping. Boston, Houghton Mifflin, 1961.
At War as Children. New York, Farrar Straus, 1964.
The Better Part. New York, Farrar Straus, 1967; London, Hutchinson, 1968.
Cry of the Daughter. New York, Dutton, 1971.
Tiger Rag. New York, Dutton, 1973.
Captain Grownup. New York, Dutton, 1976.
The Ballad of T. Rantula. Boston, Little Brown, 1979.
Blood Fever (as Shelley Hyde). New York, Pocket Books, 1982.
Fort Privilege. New York, Doubleday, 1985.

Play

Radio Play: *The Bathyscaphe*, 1978.

Other

When We Dream (for children). New York, Hawthorn, 1967.
Story First: The Writer as Insider. Englewood Cliffs, New Jersey, Prentice Hall, 1982.

Editor, *Fat*. Indianapolis, Bobbs Merrill, 1974.

*

Manuscript Collection: Beinecke Library, Yale University, New Haven, Connecticut.

* * *

Kit Reed writes within several fiction genres. Her stories have been published in *Fiction* (Paris), *Town* (London), *Seventeen*, and a variety of science-fiction and fantasy magazines. Some of her stories are realistic, some impressionistic, some fantasy, some science fiction. And representatives of each of these types appear in the collection *Mister da V.* Reed does not write hard, or technologically oriented, science fiction; and although some of her stories do make use of traditional science-fiction devices or theories, those stories actually focus on the people in them and the ways in which those people are affected by their surroundings. While this is typical of science fiction in general, Reed seems to deal primarily with the people and to use the science-fiction elements as another writer might use a car or truck—as a detail necessary to the story.

In "Automatic Tiger" the full-sized mechanical tiger is not presented as an object of wonder. Edward Benedict accepts the tiger as no more than a special toy for his nephew. When he tries the tiger out, however, he decides to keep it. Having his own tiger gives Benedict confidence and changes his previously nondescript life. He becomes successful in business and in society—until he no longer has time for the tiger, which deteriorates. When he loses the tiger, his life collapses, and he is left much as he was when the story began. "Mister da V." is a story in which time travel is the traditional science-fiction device, but the story is really about the 20th-century family into which Leonardo da

Vinci is brought. The mother can see only the extra work that this "guest" necessitates. The twins like the strange toys he makes for them, but after he has gone and the toys are broken, they forget him. The father sees Leonardo as the source for a definitive biography. But the teen-aged girl sees a sweet, lonely, brilliant old man who seems to be sad because he will never get to do all the things he can envision.

This focus on people and the ways in which technology effects them is also at the heart of Reed's socially critical stories. One of her strongest pieces of social criticism is "Golden Acres," about a home for the elderly. In this future setting, an old person can use his negotiable assets to purchase a place in Golden Acres. Although these establishments look very attractive from the outside, they are extremely dehumanizing: all of the rooms are the same, the furniture is bolted down, and there is no place for personal effects or mementoes—what the management calls "clutter. " And when a person's funds run out—rent, medical care, etc. all add up—he is taken to the Tower of Sleep where his life is terminated.

"At Central," "Ordeal," and the novel *Armed Camps* are similar stories about societies in which technology has all but taken over. In "At Central" people watch television all the time (never going outside), pump their money into the appropriate slots when they see something they want, and have everything delivered. The people in "Ordeal" are all on "life fluid" and spend their time hooked up to the intravenous tubes which pump the purple liquid into their veins. In *Armed Camps* warfare is the one constant thing in the world; and although it seems that only champions fight and die, great numbers of people are killed each year. And instead of trying to end it, the top brass make sure that it will go on—forever, if possible.

In the final analysis, it is Reed's characters that carry her fiction—science fiction, fantasy, or mainstream. To be sure, the other aspects of her writing are not found wanting, but her characters—especially the women struggling to find themselves in an indifferent or hostile society, or struggling against various institutions—remain in the reader's mind.

—C. W. Sullivan III

REPP, Ed(ward) Earl. Also wrote as John Cody; Peter Field. American. Born in Pittsburgh, Pennyslvania, 22 May 1900. Married Margaret Louise Smith in 1925; one son. Newspaperman: reporter and feature writer for Hearst papers and others; screenwriter and publicity director for Warner Brothers, Columbia, and RKO; wrote westerns using the house name Peter Field. *Died 19 February 1979.*

SCIENCE-FICTION PUBLICATIONS

Short Stories

The Radium Pool. Los Angeles, Fantasy, 1949.
Stellar Missiles. Los Angeles, Fantasy, 1949.

Uncollected Short Stories (series: John Hale in all stories except "Rescue from Jupiter")

"The Scientific Ghost," in *Amazing* (New York), January 1939.
"The Curse of Montezuma," in *Amazing* (New York), May 1939.
"Brigade of the Dammed," in *Amazing* (New York 1939.

"John Hale Convicts a Killer," in *Amazing* (New York), July 1939.
"John Hale's Hollywood Mystery," in *Amazing* (New York), August 1939.
"Rescue from Jupiter," in *Science Fiction Qarterly* (Holyoke, Massachusetts), Spring 1941.
"The Light That Killed," in *Amazing* (New York), March 1943.
"The Black Pool," in *Amazing* (New York), November 1943.

OTHER PUBLICATIONS

Novels

Cyclone Jim. New York, Godwin, 1935; London, Wright and Brown, 1936.
Hell on the Pecos. New York, Godwin, 1935; London, Wright and Brown, 1936.
Gun Hawk. New York, Godwin, 1936; London Wright and Brown, 1937.
Hell in the Saddle. New York, Godwin, and London, Wright and Brown, 1936.
Suicide Ranch, New York, Godwin, 1936; London, Wright and Brown, 1937.
Empty Holsters (as John Cody). New York, Godwin, 1936. London, Wright and Brown, 1937
Canyon of the Forgotten. London, Wright and Brown, 1950.
Don Hurricane. London, Wright and Brown, 1950.
Hell's Hacienda. London, Wright and Brown, 1951.
Six-Gun Law. London, Wright and Brown, 1951.
Colt Carrier of the Rio. London, Ward Lock, 1952.
Desperado. London, Wright and Brown, 1954.
Blacksnake Trail (as Peter Field). New York, Pocket Books, 1959.

Plays

Screenplays: *The Cherokee Strip,* with Joseph K. Watson and Luci Ward, 1937; *The Old Wyoming Trail,* with J. Benton Cheney, 1937; *Prairie Thunder,* 1937; *Devil's Saddle Legion,* 1937; *Cattle Raiders,* with Joseph F. Poland and Folmer Blangsted, 1938; *Outlaws of the Prairie,* 1938; *Call of the Rockies,* 1938; *West of Cheyenne* 1938; *Rawhide Raiders,* 1941; *The Vigilantes Ride,* 1943; *Saddles and Sagebrush,* 1943; *The Last Horseman,* 1944; *Silver City Raiders,* 1944; *Six Gun Gospel,* with Jess Bowers, 1944; *Trigger Trial,* 1944; *Texas Panhandle,* 1945; *Galloping Thunder,* 1945; *Gunning for Vengeance,* with Louise Rosseau, 1946; *Heading West,* 1946; *Prairie Raiders,* 1946; *Terror Trail,* 1947; *The Lone Hand Texan,* 1947; *The Fighting Frontiersman* (serial), 1947; *The Stranger from Ponca City,* 1947; *Guns of Hate,* with Norman Houston, 1948; *Challenge of the Range,* 1948; *Storm over Wyoming,* 1950; *Rider from Tucson,* 1950; *Saddle Legion,* 1951; *Law of the Badlands,* 1951; *Gunplay,* 1951; *Cyclone Fury,* with Barry Shipman, 1952; *The Kid from Broken Gun,* with Barry Shipman, 1953; and short films.

Television Plays: for *The Lone Ranger, Arizona Rangers,* and *Broken Arrow* series.

*   *   *

For decades Ed Earl Repp was regarded in science-fiction circles as the ultimate example of the hack pulp writer, representing both the best and the worst elements of the pulp tradition. Never very interested in mingling, Repp had become a legendary figure, widely believed to have been dead for many years, when he was tracked down and interviewed shortly before his actual death in 1979. His statements indicated that his personal philosophy fit neatly into the pulp mold. He maintained that a commercial writer should produce 20 pages of manuscript a day. His formula for story construction was simple: place a sympathetic hero in dire peril and bring him through to triumph in the face of insurmountable odds. He has had little formal education (two years of high school), wandered from newspaper reporting into publicity work, and decided to try fiction when Edgar Rice Burroughs and Zane Grey independently recommended that he do so.

Repp produced scores of SF stories. Probably the best known is "The Radium Pool," wherein he uses a practical knowledge of geological exploration as background for an adventure tale typical of his work. The explorers—accompanied by a newpaper reporter who acts also as narrator—discover a mysterious glowing pool. There they discover evidence of alien intelligences with malign intentions toward the earth. In an atmosphere of isolation from the outside world, the explorers struggle against the alien forces, appear to be in hopeless straits, but ultimately triumph.

The characters in the story are typical of pulp science fiction: elderly professor, younger male companion, beautiful young woman who comes within the thrall of the villains and is ultimately rescued by the courageous newsman. The action is crude and physical, the pace a trifle less frenetic than in some pulp stories, the characterization vivid but simplistic.

Stellar Missiles (originally published as separate novelettes) is thematically similar to "The Radium Pool. " Ancient aliens existing in a state of suspended animation are discovered in two sites, one in Arizona and the other in Siberia. As a result of tampering with the aliens, the young son of the elderly scientist faces permanent suspended animation and in fact the entire earth is menaced. Other aspects aside, the story remarkably anticipates John W. Campbell's celebrated "Who Goes There?" (1938).

Repp's most successful shorter story is "The Red Dimension" (in *The Radium Pool*), a tale in which a scientist develops a technique for first observing, then physically entering, other vibrational planes of existence. In plot the story is unremarkable, concerning the usual pulp paraphernalia of hostile monstrosities, but in "The Red Dimension" Repp's prose, usually of a pedestrian flavor, achieves a number of descriptive moments little short of epiphanous.

Repp's science fiction is illuminated by an examination of samples of his western fiction. The latter appeared under such titles as *Suicide Ranch, Cyclone Jim*, and *Hell on the Pecos*. It is possible through the direct substitution of blasters for six-shooters, space-liners for stage-coaches, remote asteroids for isolated ranchos, and so on, to transform Repp's westerns into science fiction (or vice versa).

—Richard A. Lupoff

RESNICK, Mike (Michael Diamond Resnick). American. Born in Chicago, Illinois, 5 March 1942. Attended University of Chicago, 1959-62. Married Carol Cain in 1961; one daughter. File Clerk, Santa Fe Railroad, Chicago, 1962-65; Editor, *National Tattler*, 1965-66, and *National Insider*, 1966-69, for National Features Syndicate, Chicago; Editor and Publisher, Oligarch Publishing, Libertyville, Illinois, 1969-70. Since 1964, free-lace writer: has published over 200 novels (sex, gothic, romance) under pseudonyms. Breeder and exhibitor of collies, 1969-80, and columnist, *Collie Cues Magazine*, Hayward,

California, 1969-80; since 1976, owner of Briarwood Pet Motel, Cincinnati. Agent: Eleanor Wood, 432 Park Avenue South, Suite 1205, New York, New York 10016. Address: 11216 Gideon Lane, Cincinnati, Ohio 45249, U.S.A.

SCIENCE-FICTION PUBLICATIONS

Novels (series: Galactic Midway; Ganymede; Velvet Comet)

The Goddess of Ganymede. West Kingston, Rhode Island, Grant, 1967.
Pursuit on Ganymede. New York, Paperback Library, 1968.
Redbeard. New York, Lancer, 1969.
Battlestar Galactica 5: Galactica Discovers Earth, with Glen A. Larson. New York, Berkley, 1980.
The Soul Eater. New York, New American Library, 1981.
Birthright: The Book of Man. New York, New American Library, 1982.
Walpurgis III. New York, New American Library, 1982.
Tales of the Galactic Midway:
    1. *Sideshow*. New York, New American Library, 1982.
    2. *The Three-Legged Hootch Dancer*. New York, New American Library, 1983.
    3. *The Wild Alien Tamer*. New York, New American Library, 1983.
    4. *The Best Rootin' Tootin' Shootin' Gunslinger in the Whole Damned Galaxy*. New York, New American Library, 1983.
The Branch. New York, New American Library, 1984.
Tales of the Velvet Comet:
    1. *Eros Ascending*. Bloomfield Hills, Michigan, Phantasia Press, 1984.
    2. *Eros at Zenith*. Bloomfield Hills, Michigan, Phantasia Press, 1984.
    3. *Eros Descending*. New York, New American Library, 1985.
Adventures. New York, New American Library, 1985.

Short Stories

The Forgotten Sea of Mars. Baton Rouge, Louisiana, Camille E. Cazedessus, Jr., 1965.
Unauthorized Autobiographies. Detroit, Misfit Press, 1984.
The Inn of the Hairy Toad. New Orleans, Delta Con, 1985.

OTHER PUBLICATIONS

Other

Official Guide to the Fantastics. Florence, Alabama, House of Collectibles, 1976.
Official Guide to Comic Books and Big Little Books. Florence, Alabama, House of Collectibles, 1977.
Gymnastics and You: The Whole Story of the Sport. Chicago, Rand McNally, 1978.
Official Guide to Comic and Science Fiction Books. Orlando, Florida, House of Collectibles, 1979.

*

Mike Resnick comments:
I'm not at all sure that I write honest-to-God true-blue science fiction. What I write are morality plays, and if turning them into myths and fables of the future and setting them on alien worlds makes them more saleable, I have no objection to so doing. I have a hard time with fearless heroes and beautifuil princesses, so I tend to write about overmatched detectives and obsessed

ministers and frustrated stripteasers. I have a hard time with heroes who are all good and villains who are all bad, so my characters tend to be neither heroes nor villains, but fall into that in-between gray area that most of us inhabit. The future in which I set my stories is lived-in and a little bit shopworn around the edges; planets tend to look more like the outskirts of Indianapolis of Sioux City than those beautiful mechanized utopias that Frank Paul used to paint 40 and 50 years ago. I don't like puzzle or gimmick stories that leave the reader unmoved and untouched, and so I don't write them. I believe that every man and woman is ultimately responsible for his actions, and this is a theme that seems to recur through my novels.

I suppose if I had to sum up my work in a single sentence, it would be as follows: I am writing about adult characters who face adult problems in an adult universe, and I am writing these stories for an adult audience. This is, alas, rarer than you might think.

* * *

Mike Resnick wrote 250 pseudonymous novels before publishing under his own name, and he knows how to structure fiction to maintain the reader's interest. The characterization, however, is sometimes sacrificed in that major figures have vague backgrounds and hazy motivations: little is learned about Jericho in *Walpurgis III* except that he has assassinated a number of people; the Leather Madonna in *Eros Ascending* promises to explain how she became a madam but gives only fragments of information; and no real explanation is offered for Billybuck Dancer's compulsion to flirt with death. An original but sometimes disconcerting characteristic is Resnick's tendency near the end to kill off one or more major characters with whom the reader has thoroughly identified and then to conclude the work from the viewpoint of a minor character.

Resnick cites Olaf Stapledon as a writer who influenced him, and *Birthright: The Book of Man* presents his interpretation of a Stapledon subject, the rise and fall of the human race. Essentially a collection of short stories organized along a time line, the work presents a cynical view of man as he conquers and slaughters his way across the universe until other species unite to destroy him. This same cynicism and concern with slaughter are the focus of his novel *Walpurgis III*, in which the death-obsessed Conrad Bland systematically destroys cities while he sits in his church, like a contemporary Vlad Dracul, surrounded by tortured and dying victims on meat hooks. This "moral parable set in the future" (Resnick's term for his writings) contrasts the evil of Bland to that of his assassin. Like a gunfighter after the danger is over, Jericho must face a grateful but unsympathetic police force.

Although Resnick dislikes series novels, he has written one and is proceeding with a second; each, however, was planned as a limited series. Tales of the Galactic Midway, a four-volume work, follows the adventures of Thaddeus Flint and his sideshow acts through the carnival's five-year history. The characters, mostly carnival types, continue through the books; the aliens tend to have human emotions; and Flint's position at the end of the last novel exemplifies the cynical but fighting stance of many of Resnick's main characters. Although references are made in later volumes to events in the earlier ones, reading the books in order is not necessary. Tales of the Velvet Comet is another four-part work, but the volumes occur at fifty-year intervals, so only the setting—an elaborate house of prostitution—and its inherent problems remain the same. As in most of Resnick's works, the major characters have sublimated their humanity to their professions, whether it is murder,

espionage, prostitution, or corporate politics, and the positive characters tend to be minor or ineffectual, as is Rasputin in *Eros Ascending* or Sable in *Walpurgis III*, except for one action at the end.

A theme throughout his works is that people become obsessed with money, excitement, and evil if they have not found love; for example, Sable and Rasputin both resist temptation and both are family men whose pictures of wives and children are mentioned several times. When Bonhomme tries to bribe Rasputin by asking, "What are *you* looking for?" he glances at the pictures of his family and replies, "I found it a long time ago." Because of their themes, suspense, wide range of characters, and accessibility, most of his novels have been popular and have reached the Nebula preliminaries.

—Leonard G. Heldreth

REYNOLDS, Mack (Dallas McCord Reynolds). Also wrote as Todd Harding; Maxine Reynolds. American. Born in Corcoran, California, 12 November 1917. Attended public schools in Kingston, New York. Served in the United States Army Transportation Corps, during World War II; trained in the Marine Officers School, New Orleans: Navigator. Married Jeanette Wooley in 1947; two sons and one daughter. Editor, *Catskill Mountain Star*, Saugerties, New York, 1937-38, and *Oneonta News*, New York, 1939-40; IBM supervisor, San Pedro shipyards, California, 1940-43; National Organizer, Socialist Labor Party, 1946-52; foreign correspondent and travel editor, *Rogue*, 1953-63. *Died 29 January 1983.*

SCIENCE-FICTION PUBLICATIONS

Novels (series: Homer Crawford; Bat Hardin; Lagrangia; Joe Mauser; United Planets Organization; Julian West)

The Case of the Little Green Men. New York, Phoenix Press, 1951.
The Earth War (Mauser). New York, Pyramid, 1963; London, New English Library, 1965.
Planetary Agent X (United Planets). New York, Ace, 1965.
Time Gladiator (Mauser). London, New English Library, 1966; New York, Lancer, 1969.
Of Godlike Power. New York, Belmont, 1966; as *Earth Unaware*, 1968.
Dawnman Planet (United Planets). New York, Ace, 1966.
Space Pioneer. London, New English Library, 1966.
The Rival Rigellians. New York, Ace, 1967.
Computer War. New York, Ace, 1967.
After Some Tomorrow. New York, Belmont, 1967.
Mercenary from Tomorrow (Mauser). New York, Ace, 1968.
Code Duello (United Planets). New York, Ace, 1968.
Star Trek: Mission to Horatius. Racine, Wisconsin, Whitman, 1968.
The Space Barbarians. New York, Ace, 1969.
The Cosmic Eye. New York, Belmont, 1969.
Once Departed. New York, Curtis, 1970.
Computer World. New York, Curtis, 1970.
Blackman's Burden (Crawford). New York, Ace, 1972.
Border, Breed nor Birth (Crawford). New York, Ace, 1972.
Looking Backward, From the Year 2000 (West). New York, Ace, 1973; Morley, Yorkshire, Elmfield Press, 1976.

Commune 2000 A. D. (Hardin). New York, Bantam, 1974.
Depression or Bust. New York, Ace, 1974.
Ability Quotient. New York, Ace, 1975.
Amazon Planet (United Planets). New York, Ace, 1975.
The Five Way Secret Agent. New York, Ace, 1975.
Satellite City. New York, Ace, 1975.
Tomorrow Might Be Different. New York, Ace, 1975; London, Sphere, 1976.
The Towers of Utopia (Hardin). New York, Bantam, 1975.
Day after Tomorrow. New York, Ace, 1976.
Galactic Medal of Honor. New York, Ace, 1976.
Rolltown (Hardin). New York, Ace, 1976.
Section G: United Planets. New York, Ace, 1976.
After Utopia. New York, Ace, 1977.
Equality: In the Year 2000 (West). New York, Ace, 1977.
Perchance to Dream. New York, Ace, 1977.
Police Patrol 2000 A. D. New York, Ace, 1977.
Space Visitor. New York, Ace, 1977.
The Best Ye Breed (Crawford). New York, Ace, 1978.
Trample an Empire Down. New York, Nordon, 1978.
Brain World. New York, Nordon, 1978.
The Fracas Factor. New York, Nordon, 1978.
Lagrange Five. New York, Bantam, 1979.
Earth Unaware. New York, Nordon, 1979.
The Lagrangists, edited by Dean Ing. New York, Tor, 1983.
Chaos in Lagrangia. New York, Tor, 1984.
Space Search. New York, Dell, 1984.
Eternity , edited by Dean Ing. New York, Pocket Books, 1984.
Home Sweet Home 2010 A. D. , edited by Dean Ing. New York, Dell, 1984.
The Other Time, edited by Dean Ing. New York, Pocket Books, 1984.
Trojan Orbit, edited by Dean Ing. New York, Baen, 1985.

Short Stories

The Best of Mack Reynolds. New York, Pocket Books, 1976.
Compounded Interests. Cambridge, Massachusetts, NESFA Press, 1983.

Uncollected Short Stories

"Of Future Fears," in *Analog* (New York), October, November, December 1977.
"All Things to Us," in *Amazing* (New York), May 1978.
"A Halo for Horace," in *Amazing* (New York), February 1979.
"Toro," in *Amazing* (New York), May 1979.
"The Case of the Disposable Jalopy," in *Analog* (New York), October 1979.
"Golden Rule," in *Analog* (New York), March 1980.
"Hell's Fire," in *Fantasy and Science Fiction* (New York), June 1980.

OTHER PUBLICATIONS

Novels

Episode on the Riviera. Derby, Connecticut, Monarch, 1961.
A Kiss Before Loving. Derby, Connecticut, Monarch, 1961.
This Time We Love. Derby, Connecticut, Monarch, 1962.
The Kept Woman. Derby, Connecticut, Monarch, 1963.
The Jet Set. Derby, Connecticut, Monarch, 1964.
Sweet Dreams, Sweet Prince. London, New English Library, 1965.
Once Departed. New York, Curtis, 1970.
The House in the Kasbah (as Maxine Reynolds). New York, Beagle, 1972.
The Home of the Inquisitor (as Maxine Reynolds). New York, Beagle, 1972.
Four Letter World (as Todd Harding). San Diego, Greenleaf, 1972.

Other

Paradise for Males. New York, Plaza, 1957.
How to Retire Without Money. New York, Belmont, 1958.
The Expatriates. Evanston, Illinois, Regency, 1963.
Puerto Rican Patriot: The Life of Luis Muñoz Rivera. New York, Macmillan, 1969.
"What Do You Mean—Marxism?," in *Science-Fiction Studies* (Terre Haute, Indiana), Fall 1974.

Editor, with Fredric Brown, *Science-Fiction Carnival.* Chicago, Shasta, 1953.

*

Mack Reynolds commented:

(1981) Thirty years ago, when I first began writing science fiction, I soon arrived at the conclusion that a serious free-lancer in the field must be acquainted with the sciences he dealt with. The day of the space opera was rapidly disappearing, and the writer had best know what he was talking about. My background in the hard sciences was sketchy and I realized that I was out of my depth in them. However, I have had a lifelong interest in the social sciences and particularly in political economy. And, somewhat to my surprise, I discovered that few writers in our genre were so equipped. I decided to concentrate on stories with socio-economic backgrounds.

Many of us in our extrapolations do very well in portraying a future in which the sciences and technology have blossomed fantastically. We rejoice in faster-then-light travel, we colonize the galaxy, we have become immortal, we have matter transformers and transmitters. And what is our socio-economic system? Often it's feudalism, complete with galactic emperors, dukes, counts, and barons, sometimes swinging laser swords, whatever they are. We don't even have capitalism, not to speak of something in advance. What is the means of exchange? Often currency, silver and gold coins. What is the relationship between the sexes? What type of family prevails? The writers have returned to Victorian times.   Not one story in 25 in depicting the future ever considers that the private ownership of the means of production, the profit system, and class divided society, might one day end. American science fiction is myopic when it comes to forseeing an evolved social system. So is Soviet Science fiction. In the Soviets' case, they seem to have a fond belief that the millennium has been reached, that nothing lies beyond the state capitalism they have achieved, so there is no point in speculating on future socio-economics. The big difference is that even if a Soviet SF writer did attempt to look beyond their version of Utopia, it is unlikely that his story would ever see print. In the west we are still free to extrapolate in the field of political economy—we just don't. And, in my belief, science fiction is the poorer for it.

The world is going through an unprecedented period of revolutionary change, in science, in medicine, in technology, in the family relationship, in social systems, in the relationship between nations, between generations, between sexes. And if the future is to be a valid one we must buckle down to deciding just what we want. An end of war, an end of poverty, an end of the rape of our planet, a viable world government, are only a few of the goals we should keep ever in mind.

In my stories, I do not have any particular axe to grind. I have written stories (some humorous ones) both for and against every socio-economic system that I know of including socialism, in all its myriad forms, communism, syndicalism, anarchism, fascism, theocracy, technocracy, meritocracy, and industrial feudalism. It simply seems not to occur to the average person, even science fiction readers, that there is an alternative, or alternatives, to our present social system. I am attempting to bring home to them that there is, and possibly desirable alternatives at that.

*   *   *

A maverick socialist, Mack Reynolds is of that rare breed of American science-fiction writers specializing in socioeconomic speculation. Early in his writing career Reynolds switched from detective fiction to science fiction; but as the title of his first science-fiction novel (*The Case of the Little Green Men*) suggests, he never left the plots and characters of detective fiction entirely behind. Producing a strange amalgam of economics, politics, intrigue, action, and mystery, Reynolds became quite popular, and the readers of *Galaxy* and *If* once chose him as their favorite author.

Reynolds's popularity comes largely from his interplanetary fiction, such as his Section G: United Planets series. The premise is that a future confederation of diverse worlds pledges non-interference in each other's socioeconomic systems, but that anomalous worlds threaten this pledge. Crack agent Ronnie Bronston of the intelligence bureau Section G is, typically, the troubleshooter. A representative assignment, in *Dawnman Planet*, takes Ronnie to the super-capitalist world Phrygia, where the villanous Baron Wylie hides information about invading aliens who threaten the confederation. In *Code Duello* the troublesome world is Firenze, ruled by Florentine gentlemen preoccupied with dueling. The best in this series may be *The Rival Rigellians*, in which rival teams develop capitalism and socialism on their respective worlds until the natives rebel against both systems.

On the whole, though, Reynolds's short stories are both better written and better introductions to Reynolds ideas, for the irony of Reynolds's political thinking blends with the irony and reversal of the story form. In "Revolution" the U. S. tries to stop a democratic revolution within the U. S. S. R., since such a revolution would make a stronger Russia; in "Pacifist" a pacifist group uses terrorism to achieve its goals. "Compounded Interests," a time-loop story, suggests that anonymous financial interests control history. "Utopian" sets the premises for much of Reynolds's utopian fiction. Although one might expect a socialist's utopias to be pleasant places, Reynold's utopias are ambiguous; in this story the utopian leaders import a revolutionist from the past to keep them from going stale. The assumption behind these ironic stories is that change so dominates the late 20th century that what is revolutionary one day is reactionary the next.

The year 2000 series of near-future utopian novels is likewise ambiguous. Some worlds are rather pleasant places; others struggle with desperate boredom. Typically these worlds have put an end to the extremes of wealth and poverty (in fact, to social class). But the welfare state produces stagnation and decay. In *Computer World* Reynolds predicts, before computers were in vogue (1967), a world totally dependent on the computer. In *Commune 2000 A. D.* he gives us a world in which one can choose between many modes of dropping out. Reynolds's most ambitious works are his two updates of Bellamy, *Looking Backward, From the Year 2000* and *Equality: In the Year 2000*. Reynolds's 2000 resembles but also diverges from Bellamy's. Reynolds's Julian West is out of place in a world he cannot understand, a world which has transcended traditional ideologies and could be called socialism, collectivism, technocracy, archism, meritocracy, or, more accurately, none of these. Reynolds 2000—which he calls evolutionary rather than utopian—is more inevitable than it is attractive.

The Africa series (*Blackman's Burden; Border, Breed nor Birth; The Best Ye Breed*) likewise presents fixed ideologies in a changing world. Both the capitalist west and the socialist east struggle, often with strange results, to control African nationalism. In the Joe Mauser series (*Time Gladiator, The Earth War*, and others) Reynolds develops a world that has moved in a direction different from that of his utopias. The Earth contains a decadent class society in which one can advance only in the "fracases," a TV-age version of the Roman bread and circuses. Even protagonist Joe Mauser departs from the good-guy stereotypes in his disillusionment.

At his death Reynolds left several unfinished manuscripts which have been edited by Dean Ing. Some of these represent Reynolds at his best, particularly *The Other Time*, a time-paradox story containing a remarkably complete ethnology of 16th century Mexico. The Lagrangia series presents another ambiguous utopia, an orbiting colony which, because of its revolutionary production of power, is the source of fierce contention among rival forces on Earth.

Reynolds wrote too much, and his fiction contains grave flaws: sexism, macho-chauvinist heroes, super-slick dialogue, and melodramatic plots resolved often by pointless violence. Yet he takes seriously, as few writers do, the idea that the socioeconomic future will be stranger than we can imagine.

—Curtis C. Smith

RICHARDS, Edward. See **TUBB, E. C.**

RICHARDS, Henry. See **SAXON, Richard.**

RICHARDSON, Robert S. See **LATHAM, Philip.**

RICHMOND, Walt and Leigh. Americans. **RICHMOND, Walt(er F.):** Born in Memphis, Tennessee, 5 December 1922. Married Leigh Tucker; three children. Research physicist; President and Executive Director, Centric Foundation, Merritt Island, Florida. *Died 14 April 1977.* **RICHMOND, Leigh (née Tucker):** Educated at Louisiana State University, Baton Rouge; Tulane University, New Orleans. Married 1) Walt Richmond (died, 1977), three children; 2) Richard V. Donahue in 1979. Reporter, photographer, newspaper editor, and research anthropologist; President, Centric Foundation. Address: P.O. Box 908, Maggie Valley, North Carolina 28751, U.S.A.

SCIENCE-FICTION PUBLICATIONS

Novels

Shock Waves. New York, Ace, 1967.
The Lost Millennium. New York, Ace, 1967; as *SIVA!*, 1979.
Phoenix Ship. New York, Ace, 1969; expanded edition as *Phase Two*, 1980.
Gallagher's Glacier. New York, Ace, 1970; revised edition, 1979.
Challenge the Hellmaker. New York, Ace, 1976.
The Probability Corner. New York, Ace, 1977.

Short Stories

Positive Charge. New York, Ace, 1970.

Uncollected Short Story

"Antalogia," in *Analog* (New York), October 1973.

*

Leigh Richmond comments:

All of our books have been "hard core" or "hard science" science fiction, based on the results of research at the Centric Foundation. The next one, which should be published by the fall of 1986, is *How to Psi; or, Field Effect—The Pi-Phase of Physics*. This is not science fiction, but should be of interest to readers of the genre. It is a how-to book for using the psionic abilities consciously, as well as a detailed analysis of the electromagnetic structure which permeates and surrounds the body (seen as the aura) of which the psionic abilities are the sensory apparatus.

* * *

Walt and Leigh Richmond both grew up before the atomic bomb fell, when science seemed both simpler and more accessible. Understanding was not yet locked in moated research foundations—in those days (it seemed) a boy could invent anti-gravity with the right cardboard tubes and wires, and a few people thinking hard could uncover the secrets of the universe and Explain Everything. The Richmonds wanted to be among those few people, and in their eager stories the maverick amateurs always win. But because the Richmonds did not actually start writing until after the atomic bomb fell, their stories are also marked by a scorn for the current secrecy-bound scientific bureaucracy, and an appetite for apocalypse.

When the Richmonds' stories work, they successfully convey the excitement of individual discovery—the mind's reaction to its own new thinking, to its own awakening power. As a result, the Richmonds' most convincing characters tend to be children. An early story, "Poppa Needs Shorts," neatly details the way a four-year-old can combine pieces of information that an adult would keep rigidly separate. The same child, Oley, grows up in the novel *The Probability Corner* to learn how to read the mind of a computer and invent a matter transmitter in his cellar—all through his willingness to keep combining divergent types of knowledge. Such willingness, the Richmonds imply, is usually destroyed by modern education, and education is the most interesting topic in their novel *Phase Two*. The hero, S. T. A. R. Dustin, is injected with molecules of trained men's brains, whose knowledge is then activated in him through four years of computer testing. But the boy's real mental power develops from his efforts to recombine the facts on his own, preguessing the computer and eventually walking easily out of his political prison into new realms of science. The idea that the computer is an appropriate tool for the expanding mind is also pursued in *Challenge the Hellmaker*, where a group of friends on an orbital station accidentally invent a spacedrive while singlehandedly fighting off a world-wide military takeover. Though the heroes in the Richmonds' books are almost anachronistically individualistic, they are rarely isolated. Even little Oley feels secure in the center of his family, and the collaboration of friends (another means of combing divergent knowledge) is one of the more pleasant constants in the Richmonds' own collaboration.

When their stories do not work—or do not work consistently—they are flawed by unconvincing politics, hyperactive melodrama, and scientific explanations that are not only impossible but are also praised for their clarity by the other characters. The worst offender on all counts is *The Lost Millennium*, a novel that tries to explain all human and geologic history by proposing a prehistorical race of supermen who, through solar taps located in pyramids, possessed broadcast electrical power. The story covers so much so quickly—including all myths, many lectures on electricity, and an incomprehensible soap opera sub-plot—that the result is a fragmented scenario whose several apocalypses are the only relief.

Yet perhaps even *The Lost Millennium* is just part of the Richmonds' effort to scramble our brains into new connections. They were serious enough about the content of their work to form their own research group, the Centric Foundation, and before Walt Richmond's death in 1977 they planned to apply "relatively simple high school mathematics" to physics, and improve on the quantum theory. Few young science-fiction readers would fault their attack on education, and it is hard to resist the Richmonds' faith in the potentially supernatural power of individual thinking. Their eagerness and their determined amateur science ("'It's really quite easy,' he explained briskly") are part of an innocence science fiction has lost, and could never easily regain.

—Karen G. Way

———

ROBERT, Lionel. See **FANTHORPE, R. Lionel.**

———

ROBERTS, Keith (John Kingston). British. Born in Kettering, Northamptonshire, 20 September 1935. Educated at Northampton School of Art, National Diploma in Design 1956; Leicester College of Art, 1956-57. Has worked as a cartoon animator, and as an illustrator for advertising, magazines, and books. Editor, *SF Impulse*, London, 1966-67. Recipient: British Science Fiction Association award, 1982. Agent: Leslie Flood, Carnell Literary Agency, Rowneybury Bungalow, Sawbridgeworth, near Old Harlow, Essex CM20 2EX. Address: 23 New Street, Henley-on-Thames, Oxfordshire RG9 2BP, England.

SCIENCE-FICTION PUBLICATIONS

Novels

The Furies. London, Hart Davis, and New York, Berkley, 1966.
Pavane. London, Hart Davis, and New York, Doubleday, 1968.

The Inner Wheel. London, Hart Davis, and New York, Doubleday, 1970.
The Chalk Giants. London, Hutchinson, 1974; New York, Putnam, 1975.
Molly Zero. London, Gollancz, 1980.
Kiteworld. London, Gollancz, 1985.

Short Stories

Machines and Men. London, Hutchinson, 1973.
The Grain Kings. London, Hutchinson, 1976.
The Passing of the Dragons. New York, Berkley, 1977.
Ladies from Hell. London, Gollancz, 1979.

Uncollected Short Stories

"The Lordly Ones," in *Fantasy and Science Fiction* (New York), March 1980.
"The Comfort Station," in *Fantasy and Science Fiction* (New York), May 1980.
"Sphairistike," in *Fantasy and Science Fiction* (New York), February 1984.

OTHER PUBLICATIONS

Novels

The Boat of Fate. London, Hutchinson, 1971; Englewood Cliffs, New Jersey, Prentice Hall, 1974.
Anita. New York, Ace, 1970; London, Millington, 1976.

*

Keith Roberts comments:

I think if we survive our do-it-yourself Armageddon, the 20th century will be remembered as the Age of the pigeonhole. Everything has to have its tag; Stonehenge is a computer, etc. The particular label attached to me is science-fiction writer. I've nothing against it; but i really know very little science. I suppose I did write some technological fiction in the very early days. But I've simply tried to talk about characters who interested me, and events that moved or disturbed me. If that's science fiction, then so be it.

*   *   *

Keith Roberts is the Thomas Hardy of science fiction, a writer whose vision is deeply embedded in a particular place—the area of southwest England from Salisbury plain south to the Dorset downs and the Isle of Purbeck where Corfe Castle stands. That landscape is the spiritual centre of his work, from the alternate world of *Pavane*, the historical crumbling Roman Empire of *The Boat of Fate*, to the hallucinatory primitive 'future' of *The Chalk Giants*. This sense of place even affects the landscapes of the stories set on other worlds. Roberts's people live in a profoundly felt world, a phenomenal and perceived *lebenswelt* which actively influences their behaviour and beliefs. Roberts also shares with Hardy a desire to articulate the human struggle with passion, need, violence,and corruption of power; to explore humankind's tremendous will to survive in even the worst circumstances (ranging from the living death of survivors ot atomic attack to the machine-like behaviour demanded by the ruling class in the new Britain of *Molly Zero*); to incarnate the possibilities of love, and the kinds of penances people committed to others serve for the rest of guilty humanity. If his stories often seem extremely dark, thay are shot through with lightning strokes of passionate love and spiritual striving. They are full of powerful emotional currents, and the best of them are truly visionary.

Roberts began his career with a somewhat typically British disaster novel, *The Furies*. In it Britain is ravaged by giant wasps controlled by an alien intelligence. It's a good example of the sub-genre, and the descriptions, especially those of the wasps' underground nests, are strong; yet ironic self-destruction of the wasps and humanity's somewhat humble new beginning are quite conventional, as a quick look at *The Day of the Triffids* shows. *The Inner Wheel* is also an apprentice work, though a very good one. In this work Robert explores the theme of *homo gestalt* in a story that obviously owes a great deal to Theodore Sturgeon's *More Than Human*, yet especially in his handling of sexual love and the interactions of power and violence, he engages us with his singular emerging 'voice' Although his characterizations deepen in later works, in *The Inner Wheel* he is already using tone of voice and the small revealing gesture to present complex and humanly opaque individuals. Most important, his people *feel*, and because he renders their feelings with care and precision, we feel with and for them, as well.

In the stories in *Machines and Men* Roberts shows a wide-ranging imagination in his handling of SF themes, from ESP to flying saucers (revealing a capacity for comedy often ignored by his critics). Yet he sets tnem all in England, as if to say there's no need to go careening across the galaxy in order to explore either workings of the human heart or the awesome and awful possibilities of technological changes in society. "The Deeps" is especially interesting for its complex and subtle presentation of a new, underwater, society.

In the mosaic novel *Pavane*, which many critics agree is the finest of all alternate universe novels, Roberts comes into his own as a unique and major SF writer. Set in 20th-century England in an alternate universe where Elizabeth 1 was assassinated, the Spanish Armada won, and the Catholic Church has held power over most of the world until the present day, it is a superb complex chain of interlocked stories showing how, finally, the Church's attempt to hold civilization in stasis fail in the face of political and technological "progress. " We learn of the many social changes mostly by implications, however, for Roberts seeks to show us how particular people seek and find their destinies in such a world, a world after all not that different from our own in the sacrifices it demands of each person trying to live a "good" life. Roberts is a moral writer in that he insists that all persons face choices in life which will affect not only themselves but their families, friends, perhaps their whole societies. His people engage us because they face those moments of choice and bear the often terrible responsibilities they find there. Thus Brother John the artist, after he has seen and painted the Inquisition, finds he must turn heretic and preach against the Church, and the Lady Eleanor of Corfe Castle (which broods over so much of Roberts's fiction) is moved by compassion and political wit to do battle with the Pope, even at the cost of finally losing all. These people, and others, are troubling and passionate reflections of ourselves, and in their struggles we perforce recognize the possibilities our own lives offer. Yeats's line "In dreams begin responsibilities" could be taken as an epigraph to all Roberts's fiction, for his people break or make themselves in their struggles with precisely that recognition.

It certainly applies to the figures in that even darker novel of a future return to barbarism, *The Chalk Giants*. After an atomic war has literally torn Britain apart, Stan Potts, a lost little fatman, lies dreaming (or forseeing) passages in the story of humanity's return to an almost medieval culture in the centuries to come. Almost all the stories feature a character resembling

Martine, the woman he never dared to tell he adored. This fantasy lady is never in full control, though she is sometimes priestess, sometimes almost goddess, sometimes princess. The stories themselves are brooding meditations on the human capacity for love and violent hatred of others. Roberts's vision of humanity is not kindly; people will survive but they will often do so at any cost in pain and suffering, for themselves, yes, but especially for others. Yet sometimes suffering ia a kind of necessary penance, a recognition of human guilt. *The Chalk Giants* is a richly figured, awe-full book, yet like any good tragedy it is cathartic rather than simply depressing. The latter term could much better be applied to his later, and perhaps last, novel, *Molly Zero*, in which the vision of a blandly terroristic government controlling British youth in a dull bureaucratic future is barely transcended by a tour de force narration in the second person. But even here, as in *The Chalk Giants*, there are flashes of light in the darkness. These flashes, often the discovery of courage in love, even in love lost, occur in the best stories in *The Grain Kings* as well, such as the powerful 'Weih-nachtsabend' and the two stories set on the planet Xerxes, where humanity's technology has destroyed the natives' traditional way of life. 'Weihnachtsabend' is another example of Roberts's talent for alternative universes: this time it's a Britain conquered by the Third Reich, in which the most terrifying of the German gods hold power. But his vision has always had an apocalytic edge, like Blake's, as his brilliant collation of vampire legend and SF scenario of atomic war in "Kaeti's Nights" demostrates. Yet even this dark fable's power partly comes from Robert's expert invocation of village life in the British countryside. To know the land of Britain as Robert does is to know all its gods, the mythic inheritance which inheres in the very stuff of the language he uses with such visionary power. Balder, Tir-nan-Og, the spirits of place, the Old Ones, all live in Roberts's beloved landscape, as much a part of it as the trees and grass, the ruins of Corfe Castle, or the stones of the henge. Their special presence adds another element to the tapestries in which all the major threads of art and life—passion, compassion, love, courage, vision, humanity, and the human awareness of how easily these can be lost to their opposites, which are therefore also present in the warp and woof of his stories—are woven into rich and exciting patterns.

—Douglas Barbour

ROBESON, Kenneth. See **DENT, Lester; GOULART, Ron.**

ROBINETT, Stephen (Allen). American. Born in Long Beach, California, 13 July 1941. Educated at California State University, Long Beach, B. A. in history 1966; University of California Hastings College of the Law, San Francisco, J. D. 1971. Served in the United States Army: Sergeant. Married Louise Yeisley in 1969. Lawyer, 1971-73, then full-time writer. Agent: Hy Cohen, 111 West 57th Street, New York, New York 10019, U.S.A.

SCIENCE-FICTION PUBLICATIONS

Novels

Stargate. New York, St. Martin's Press, 1976; London Hale, 1978.

The Man Responsible. New York, Ace, 1978.

Short Stories

Projections. New York, Ace, 1979.

Uncollected Short Stories

"Guzman's Gardener," in *Analog Yearbook*, edited by Ben Bova. New York, Ace, 1978.
"Hell Creatures of the Third Planet,"in *The Best of Omni Science Fiction 3*, edited by Ben Bova and Don Myrus. New York, Omni, 1982.
"The President's Image," in *The Best of Omni Science Fiction 4*, edited by Ben Bova and Don Myrus. New York, Omni, 1982.

*   *   *

Stylist, theorist, storyteller, Stephen Robinett has written some of the funniest science fiction ever published. Whatever the "what if" situation, he is concerned with telling a story with grace and wit and style. True also of his non-SF and pseudonymous SF potboilers, this facet of his writing stands out in two novels and a clutch of short stories from "Mini-talent" to "The President's Image. " Once typed as an *Analog* writer, Robinett was first published by John W. Campbell, who liked his care with details, engaging style, and neutral attitude toward science and technology. Close extrapolation, narrow focus and a eye for the self-mocking detail mark even his early stories bylined Tak Hallus (Arabic for pen-name).

After two stories about matter transmitters, Robinett wrote a novel about big corporations and people on the make, in which two huge shipping concerns fight for their share, or more, of the 180-kilometer-wide tantalum ring through which drone freighters are transmitted to and from the stars. Set in near-future Orange County, California, and somewhere beyond the orbit of Mars, *Stargate* is also a detective story with a difference. The detective, who enters the story late, is a 75-year-old, cigar-smoking physical fitness buff, whose reconstruction of the crime is only part of the story. The narrator, an ambitious young project engineer, lives through consequent events and his success or failure hangs on their outcome. Revolutionary politics, utopian urban planning and a dead man's quest for immortality are involved in *The Man Responsible*, which cannibalizes earlier stories about a computer projection as corporation head and an almost-perfected method of transferring personality via synthesized RNA. A lawyer like Robinett, the hero has an essential interest only in recovering a client's $200 investment. Like a futuristic Philip Marlowe, he jousts with the forces of evil, ambition, and just plain flakiness in Southern California.

Collected in *Projections*, Robinett's best short fiction reveals in miniature his control of style, construction, local color, and humor. He plays it straight in "Tomus" and "Cynthia," ably exploiting the pathos of lost opportunities, but his zanier side dominates most of the others. In "Helbent 4" a self-conscious warship, having conquered the monstrous "Space Things," returns earlier in time to a parallel universe, where shocking us into taking the threat seriously costs it its "life. " "The Linguist" exploits his talent by selling engrams that strip away each language as soon as he has learned it. "The Satyr" is produced in real life by molecular engineering, but his "natural" proclivities cause distress to his maker and eventually to himself.

Excessive taxation is the enemy in "The Tax Man" where a trucker manages to beat the system. Birdlike aliens' threat to Earth is turned back by an Indian in full-feathered regalia in

"Powwow. " A "telesthesia projector" for subliminal comme-ricials gets an ad agency involved with politics and the law in the title story. A more recent story, "Hell Creatures of the Third Planet," finds a movie buff witnessing an insane attack by aliens on a movie studio parking lot and defending police and military forces. In each case, an appropriate narrator makes believable not only the everyday, but also the rididulous and the sublime. How they're told makes all the difference.

—David N. Samuelson

ROBINSON, Frank M(alcolm). American. Born in Chicago, Illinois, 9 August 1926. Educated at Beloit College, Wisconsin B. S. in physics in 1950 (Phi Beta Kappa); Northwestern University, Evanston, Illinois, M. S. in journalism 1955. Served as radar technician in the United States Navy, 1944-45, 1950-51. Office boy, Ziff-Davis Publishing Company, 1944; Assistant Editor, *Family Weekly*, 1955-56, and *Science Digest*, 1956-59; Editor, *Rogue*, 1959-65; Managing Editor, *Cavalier*, 1965-66; Editor, *Censorship Today*, 1967; staff writer, *Playboy*, 1969-73. Since 1973, free-lance writer. Agent: Curtis Brown, 575 Madison Avenue, New York, New York 10022, U.S.A.

SCIENCE-FICTION PUBLICATIONS

Novels

The Power. Philadelphia, Lippincott, 1956; London, Eyre and Spottiswoode, 1957.
The Glass Inferno, with Thomas N. Scortia. New York, Doubleday, 1974; London, Hodder and Stoughton, 1975.
The Prometheus Crisis, with Thomas N. Scortia. New York, Doubleday, 1975; London, Hodder and Stoughton, 1976.
The Nightmare Factor, with Thomas N. Scortia. New York, Doubleday, and London, Hodder and Stoughton, 1978.
The Gold Crew, with Thomas N. Scortia. New York, Warner, 1980; London, Panther, 1983.
The Great Divide, with John Levin. New York, Rawson Wade, 1982.

Short Stories

A Life in the Day of . . . and Other Short Stories. New York, Bantam, 1981.

Uncollected Short Stories

"The Girls from Earth," in *Out of This World 10*, edited by Amabel Williams-Ellis. London, Blackie, 1973.
"Situation Thirty," in *Combat SF*, edited by Gordon R. Dickson. New York, Ace 1981.
"The Oceans Are Wide," in *Starships*, edited by Isaac Asimov, Martin H. Greenberg, and Charles G. Waugh. New York, Fawcett, 1983.

OTHER PUBLICATIONS

Other

Editor, with Earl Kemp, *The Truth about Vietnam*. San Diego, Greenleaf, 1966.

Editor, with Nat Lehrman, *Sex, American Style*. Chicago, Playboy Press, 1971.

*

Frank M. Robinson comments:

I have no particular statement to make about my own variety of science fiction except that I like to read and write science fiction based upon extrapolations of current trends in the physical sciences, psychology, cultural anthropology, politics, etc. Conversely, I have little interest in the type of fantasy that has come to dominate the field in recent years.

*   *   *

Despite his background in physical science, Frank M. Robinson's stories are most often based on psychology or cultural anthropology. One such story, "The Fire and the Sword," is concerned with the reactions of Earthmen to a "perfect" alien society. Robinson chose this story to represent his work in the anthology *SF: Author's Choice 4* (edited by Harry Harrison, 1974). He worked entertaining variations on time travel in "Untitled Story," and produced a short novel of headlong action in "The Hunting Season. " "The Night Shift" is a clever short fantasy, and "The Oceans Are Wide" a short novel telling of a young boy's harsh passage to maturity in the warped society on board a generation-ship carrying colonists to a distant planetary system. Behind the editor's inappropriate title of "Dead End Kids of Space" was an entertaining story of the adventures of a survey team on a planet with a very confusing and unpredictable culture. Another light-hearted story with an anthropological basis was "The Santa Claus Planet" concern-ing a society in which the giving of gifts had been elevated into a ritual with decidedly sinister overtones. In another vein entirely, "Dream Street" was a deceptively simple story of a boy on the run from an orphanage, and of his longing to become a spaceman.

His first novel *The Power*, was published by Lippincott as part of a short-lived series of "novels of menace. " It lived up to its billing admirably. The story concerns a Navy-subsidized research team studying human endurance and survival charac-teristics. Results of an anonymous questionnaire suggest that one of the team members is a superman with an assortment of psychic powers, and the one team member who takes these results seriously promptly dies under mysterious circumstances. He leaves an uncompleted letter for team chairman William Tanner: "I want to tell you about Adam Hart. . . . " In his review of the book, Damon Knight characterized Robinson as "a gifted and sensitive writer" but found fault with his logic and with an anti-scientific tone to the book. Most readers and critics, on the other hand, found Tanner's nightmare battle against Adam Hart hair-raising and compulsively readable.

After the publication of *The Power*, Robinson temporarily gave up fiction writing and took a succession of editorial jobs. Occasionally another story would appear. "East Wind, West Wind" is a grim story of an inspector for Air Central, monitoring air quality in a smog-bound future Los Angeles in which all forms of air pollution, from cigarette smoking to internal combustion engines, are outlawed.

The collection, *A Life in the Day of . . . and Other Short Stories*, includes five of Robinson's stories from the 1950's and four later stories. The book is a reminder of just how good (and how underrated) Robinson's short fiction is, and is equally valuable for the extensive autobiographical commentary, which gives a vivid picture of the science fiction field in the 1950's and 1960's.

In 1973 Robinson began a very successful collaboration with Thomas N. Scortia. The team has produced a series of best-selling "disaster" novels, some of which are borderline science fiction. The first of these was *The Glass Inferno*, a story of a fire in a modern high-rise building. (Together with a similar book, *The Tower* by Richard Martin Stern, this was the basis for he popular film *The Towering Inferno*.) *The Prometheus Crisis* is about a reactor failure in a nuclear power plant, *The Nightmare Factor*, covert biological warfare. Even when not concerned with science-fiction ideas, these books exhibit the science-fiction writer's careful analysis of processes, both physical and mental. This attention to expository detail is not allowed to interfere with the pace of the story, and serves to enhance the realistic tone.

The Great Divide, a collaboration with John Levin, is a political thriller set in the late 1980's. The Second Constitutional Convention and a renewed oil crisis provide an unscrupulous California governor with the tools for a coup that would split the country into two warring camps. The efforts of a vice-presidential aide and a small group of friends to uncover and stop this scheme make a tense and uncomfortably convincing narrative.

—R. E. Briney

ROBINSON, Kim Stanley. American. Born in Waukegan, Illinois, 23 March 1952. Educated at the University of California, San Diego, B. A. in literature, 1974, Ph. D. 1982; Boston University, M. A. in English 1975. Married Lisa Howland Nowell in 1982. Visiting Lecturer, University of California, in Davis, 1982-84, 1985, and in San Diego, 1982, 1985. Recipient: World Fantasy Award, 1983; *Locus* Award, 1985. Agent: Patrick Delahunt, John Schaffner Associates, 114 East 28th Street, New York, New York 10016. Address: 17811 Romelle Avenue, Santa Ana, California 92705, U.S.A.

SCIENCE-FICTION PUBLICATIONS

Novels

The Wild Shore. New York, Ace, 1984; London, Futura, 1985.
Icehenge. New York, Ace, 1984; London, Futura, 1985.
The Memory of Whiteness. New York, Tor, and London, Futura, 1985.

Uncollected Short Stories

"Coming Back to Dixieland" and "In Pierson's Orchestra," in *Orbit 18*, edited by Damon Knight. New York, Harper, 1975.
"The Thing Itself," in *Clarion SF*, edited by Kate Wilhelm. New York, Berkley, 1977.
"The Disguise," in *Orbit 19*, edited by Damon Knight. New York, Harper, 1977.
"Venice Drowned," in *Universe 11*, edited by Terry Carr. New York, Doubleday, 1981.
"Exploring Fossil Canyon," in *Universe 12*, edited by Terry Carr. New York, Doubleday, 1982.
"Stone Eggs," in *Universe 13*, edited by Terry Carr. New York, Doubleday, 1983.
"Black Air," in *The Year's Best Science Fiction 1*, edited by Gardner Dozois and Jim Frenkel. New York, Bluejay, 1984.
"The Lucky Strike," in *Universe 14*, edited by Terry Carr. New York, Doubleday, 1984.

"Ridge Running," in *Fantasy and Science Fiction* (New York), January 1984.
"Mercurial," in *Universe 15*, edited by Terry Carr. New York, Doubleday, 1985.
"Green Mars," in *Isaac Asimov's Science Fiction Magazine* (New York), September 1985.

OTHER PUBLICATIONS

Other

The Novels of Philip K. Dick. Ann Arbor, Michigan, UMI Research Press, 1984.

* * *

Kim Stanley Robinson is one of the most promising new writers to burst onto the science fiction scene in the 1980's. Robinson gained instant respect with his short fiction, first published in *Orbit* . He gained a Nebula Award nomination for the haunting "Venice Drowned" in 1981; "To Leave a Mark" was nominated for a Hugo Award in 1982; "Black Air" won the World Fantasy Award and was also a Nebula and Hugo Award finalist.

But it was Robinson'S first novel, *The Wild Shore*, that gained him fame and a larger audience. It is a post-nuclear holocaust novel in which the U. N. has quarantined America. Henry, a 17-year-old version of Huck Finn, decides to explore his world and himself. Robinson displays his skills as a writer as he takes Henry through a series of adventures that culminate in an unforgettable rite of passage.

Robinson's next novel, *Icehenge*, is more difficult, and reveals a strong Philip K. Dick influence (this shouldn't be surprising because Robinson wrote his doctoral dissertation on Dick's work; a revised version was published as *The Novels of Philip K. Dick*). *In Icehenge* three narrators describe the same event in wildly different ways. This is a future in which individuals can live hundreds of years, but the government purges the data banks and controls information so that memories can last only 50 years. In an Orwellian sense, memory and history become fluid, relative. Yet a crisis occurs when the first expedition to Pluto finds a series of monoliths: the fact that Icehenge was constructed by humans is inescapable, but a total contradiction of established, official history. Robinson's brilliant realization of the characters of engineer Emma Weil and historian Hjalmar Nederland shows his growth as a writer.

—George Kelley

ROBINSON, Spider. American. Born in New York City, 24 November 1948. Educated at the State University of New York, Stony Brook, B. A. 1972; New York State University College. Plattsburgh. Married Jeanne Rubbicco in 1975; one daughter. Realty editor, *Long Island Commercial Review*, Syossett, New York, 1972-73. Since 1973, free-lance writer: reviewer, *Galaxy*, 1974-77, *Destinies*, 1977-79, and *Analog*, 1978-80. Chairman of the Executive Council, Writers Federation of Nova Scotia, 1981-83. Recipient: John W. Campbell Award, 1974; *Locus* award, for criticism, 1976, for fiction, 1977; Hugo Award, 1977, 1978, 1983; Nebula Award, 1977; Skylark award, 1977; Pat Terry Award (Australia), 1977; Canada Council grant, 1983, and Senior Arts Grant, 1984. Lives in Halifax, Nova Scotia, Canada. Agent: Eleanor Wood, Spectrum Literary Agency, 432

Park Avenue South, Suite 1205, New York, New York 10016, U.S.A.

SCIENCE-FICTION PUBLICATIONS

Novels

Telempath. New York, Berkley, 1976; London, Macdonald and Jane's, 1978.
Stardance, with Jeanne Robinson. New York, Dial Press, and London, Sidgwick and Jackson, 1979.
Mindkiller. New York, Holt Rinehart, 1982.
Night of Power. New York, Baen, 1985.

Short Stories

Callahan's Crosstime Saloon. New York, Ace, 1977.
Antinomy. New York, Dell, 1980.
Time Travelers Strictly Cash. New York, Ace, 1981.
Melancholy Elephants. Toronto, Penguin, 1984; New York, Tor, 1985.

Uncollected Short Story

"Stardance," with Jeanne Robinson, in *Nebula Winners 13*, edited by Samuel R. Delany. New York, Harper, 1980.

OTHER PUBLICATIONS

Other

Editor, *The Best of All Possible Worlds*. New York, Ace, 1980.

*

Manuscript Collection: Dalhousie University, Halifax, Nova Scotia.

*   *   *

In little more than a decade, Spider Robinson has established himself as an important writer and critic of contemporary SF. With three novels, two story collections, an anthology and two series of book reviews to his credit, Robinson has won a number of major awards; more important, he has shown himself able to combine successfully two themes that often seem incompatible in other SF writers: technological optimism and a critique of technological society.

Robinson's themes and style show a clear continuity from early stories and novellas such as those collected in *Callahan's Crosstime Saloon* through the apocalyptic novels *Telempath* and *Stardance* to the more recent SF mystery *Mindkiller*. The first, a collection of stories about the unusual clientele of a Long Island tavern, is a metaphorical *symposium* as well as a literal one: the gruff but kindly barkeep Callahan presides over a series of dialogues and encounters moving from a vision of social disintegration to one of restored community in the final story, which takes place on New Year's Eve. This comedic pattern appears in *Telempath* as well: here the remnant population of a post-catastrophe United States is threatened by powerful aliens as well as by conflict between technophiles and a naturalist cult, but the story ends in a love-feast marked by multiple marriages, restored filial relations, and administrative merger. In Mindkiller a professor whose life has disintegrated is restored by joining a conspiracy to change the world through a technique

known as mindwiping. And in *Stardance* the final vision is of a Dantesque redemption of humanity, flesh become incorruptible, and polymorphous sexual-spiritual communion among humanity's elect and plasmoid aliens who rather resemble angels.

The fitst-person narrator plays a similar role in the four fictions. Jake, frame-narrator of *Callahan's*, is nursing a spiritual wound—he was responsible for his wife's and daughter's deaths in an auto accident—but it is he who articulates the redemptive (*cross* -time) nature of Callahan's place. In *Telempath* Isham Stone has been nurtured on hatred, violence, and revenge, and early in the novel loses an arm and attempts to murer his father; yet it is Isham who evolves the ability to communicate with the aliens and who makes peace between the two factions of humanity. Charlie Armstead of *Stardance* is similarly wounded. An embittered dancer whose career was destroyed when his hip was damaged by a gunman's bullet, he works as a video specialist with the dancer Shara Drummond. This leads to communication with the alien entity that threatens Earth, and later to his dance company's transcendence of a corrupt and polluted planet, union with the aliens, and reunion with Shara. The importance of the disabled narrator redeemed through the shared experience of pain is underlined by the *Callahan* story "The Law of Conservation of Pain," in which a time traveler interferes with the early life of a blues singer. Rather than destroying her talent by obliterating the universe in which she suffered and was scarred, his interference creates a universe in which her songs of joy are as wrenching as her songs of pain ever were. The metaphor of the conservation laws makes joy and pain, like matter and energy, metonyms of the same reality. Curiously, the dual narrator of *Mindkiller* (English professor Norman/cat burglar Joe) comes to accept violence and a strong leader, beyond good and evil, as necessary to social progress, even though that individual has been directly responsible for much of Norman/Joe's personal misery.

It might seem paradoxical that Robinson, whose themes include the fragmentary and incomplete, as well as destructive, qualities of discursive thought and verbalized experience, should be so word-conscious a stylist. A hallmark of his writing is the pun, from the "Punday night" contests in *Callahan's* to the "abominable multi-level puns" swapped by Raoul and Charlie at the conclusion of *Stardance*. Especially in *Telempath*, the function of the pun is to deconstruct the reality asserted by the utterance in which it appears, suggesting that the universe of propositional language is created and provisional rather than given. Another feature making for dense verbal texture is a complex of allusions, especially to SF writers, situations, and language, but also to jazz and popular songs, and in *Stardance* to the traditions of modern dance and to the space colonization literature. Also notable is the high proportion of text devoted to dialogue and internal monologue (and in *Telempath* to documents), often reducing narration to mere stage directions. Such an "associative rhythm" (as Northrop Frye has termed it) is characteristic more of lyric poetry than of traditional prose fiction. Robinson's SF, which embodies a vision of *telempathy* (a secular version of the "communion of saints"), appropriately tends to be more lyric than narrative in style and structure.

The lyric quality of Robinson's SF suggests how he manages to fuse sharp critique with technological optimism. Such a collocation sits uneasily in the customary universe of hard SF, a universe governed by either/or, cause-and-effect logic. In *Telempath* and *Stardance* we view a world literally poisoned by the effects of modern technical society: pollution, overpopulation, war, crime, and madness. In *Callahan's*, redemption from this world is allotted only to those whose steps direct them to

Callahan's refuge and who are able to share in the bar's feast of love and empathy. In the two apocalyptic novels, redemption is communal: a remnant of humanity overcomes disintegration to move onto a new evolutionary plane of physical, intellectual and spiritual fusion. The fusion comes about partly through apparently fortuitous encounters with angels rationalized as plasmoids (alien entities embodied in the fourth phase of matter). But it occurs only when man makes benign use of his most advanced technologies to facilitate full communication. And it obliterates the oppositions which seem to structure the possibilities of human experience, including the one between technology and nature.

The lyric quality is nearly absent from *Mindkiller*, a more conventional SF mystery novel that seems to yield to the totalitarian temptations inherent in the "fusion" or "communion" motif of the earlier fictions. Like the others it portrays a society corrupt in all respects, but through a series of appearance/reality reversals, it tries to make us accept that its villain, a sinister practicioner of mind control, is really a benevolent scientist who wishes only to save the world. It is a novel promoting the theme that great ends justify any means, that urges the amorality of technology and of the visionary leader, and that naively reverses *1984*'s cynicism about the ends of power. The "associative rhythm" is muted, and even Robinson's wordplay seems strained and aimless. When Norman's identity is restored at the end, he speaks of the technology as "mindfill" as opposed to "mindkill," but we have the feeling that he and the other enthusiasts of mental surgery are little more than puppets mouthing a new party line.

Like all good SF writers, Robinson has created a myth of the future, one in which human initiative and technological advancement play an active part. In most versions of his myth, Robinson portrays humankind moving toward a quasi-mystical fusion in which individual consciousness retains its identity while merging into something greater than the self. Perhaps uncomfortable with the theological implications of those versions, Robinson has lately given us a version in which the individual consciousness remains atomistic and alone, to achieve union with others only through their common controller. It will be interesting to watch as the myth's two main variants contend for superiority in Robinson's future SF.

—John P. Brennan

ROCKLYNNE, Ross (Ross Louis Rocklin). American. Born in Cincinnati, Ohio, 21 February 1913. Educated at schools in Cincinnati. Married Frances Rosenthal in 1941 (divorced, 1947); two sons. Has worked as a story analyst for Warner Brothers and a literary agency, sewing machine salesman and repairman, cab driver, lumberjack, sales clerk, and building manager. Address: 2562 Military Avenue, Los Angeles, California 90064, U.S.A.

SCIENCE-FICTION PUBLICATIONS

Short Stories

The Men and the Mirror. New York, Ace, 1973.
The Sun Destroyers. New York, Ace, 1973.

Uncollected Short Stories

"The Doom That Came to Blagham," in *Witchcraft and Sorcery 10* (Alhambra, California), 1974.
"Emptying the Place," in *Fantastic* (New York), April 1975.

*   *   *

Ross Rocklynne was one of the important authors of magazine science fiction's middle years. He published his first story in *Astounding* in 1935, and for some 15 years was a regular contributor to a variety of science-fiction magazines. His works was of sufficiently high quality that L. Sprague de Camp wanted to include him as one of the 20 or so leading writers in the field for his *Science-Fiction Handbook* (1953). Both the key early anthologies of science fiction featured Ross Rocklynne stories: "Quietus" was in the Healy and McComas *Adventures in Time and Space* (1946) and "Jackdaw" was in the Groff Conklin *The Best of Science Fiction* (1946). Since 1950, Rocklynne's appearances have been sporadic.

Although he wrote some short novels, Rocklynne concentrated on shorter works. It is possible that his avoidance of the longer lengths has made his name less well known than it should be. Usually a careful craftsman, he wrote many types of science fiction: competent space operas, time-travel stories, effective mood pieces, scientific puzzle stories, detective stories, and yarns spun around the Big Idea. Typical of the latter was "The Moth" (*Astounding*, 1939). Here—in 14 pages—he presented what John Campbell called "a wholly new idea for a spaceship drive" and for good measure threw in a fairly sophisticated picture of competing corporations.

Rocklynne also wrote a series of stories about a character named Hallmeyer. They are unfortunately largely forgotten today. Dealing with a "Bureau of Transmitted Egos," they are early examples of reshaping human beings to live on alien worlds. More than that, Hallmeyer was a person who *cared*. The stories have an atmosphere of compassion, of questioning basic values, of sadness. (For example, see "Task to Lahri," *Planet*, Summer 1942.) Indeed, there is an elegiac quality that pervades many of Rocklynne's better stories. The experimental side of Rocklynne appears most notably in his *Darkness* stories (1940 to 1951). They are concerned with the fates of sentient stars, and the writing is far removed from the usual styles of pulp fiction. The series was reworked as *The Sun Destroyers*.

Ross Rocklynne was never less than a capable storyteller. However, he tried to be more than that: he pushed himself instead of always taking the easy way. He was a major creator of the science fiction of the past, but he was also one of those who pointed the way ahead.

—Chad Oliver

ROGERS, Pat. See **PORGES, Arthur.**

ROHMER, Richard. Canadian. Born in Hamilton, Ontario, 24 January 1924. Educated at Fort Erie High School, Ontario; Assumption College, University of Western Ontario, London, B. A. 1948; Osgoode Hall, Toronto; read law with Phelan O'Brien and Phelan: called to Ontario bar 1951, to Northwest

Territories bar 1970; Queen's Counsel, 1961. Served in the Royal Canadian Air Force, 1942-45: Distinguished Flying Cross, 1945; in the Royal Canadian Naval Reserve, 1946-48; Royal Canadian Air Force Auxiliary, 1950-53; Wing Commander; Honorary Colonel of 411 Air Reserve Squadron, 1971; Senior Air Reserve Adviser to the Chief of the Defence Staff and the Commander of Air Command: Brigadier-General, 1975; Commander, Air Reserve Group, 1976; Chief of Reserves of the Canadian Armed Forces, 1978-81: Major General. Married Mary Olivier Whiteside; two daughters. Since 1951, lawyer: Partner, Rohmer and Swayze; Counsel, Frost and Redway, Toronto; currently, Counsel, Macaulay Lipson and Joseph, Toronto, and Bellamy Besse Augaitis and Vandergust, Collingwood, Ontario. Chairman, Royal Commission on Book Publishing, 1971-72; Counsel, Royal Commission on Metropolitan Toronto, 1975-77. Since 1978, Chancellor, University of Windsor, Ontario. Recipient: Centennial Medal, 1967; Northwest Territories Commissioner's Award for Public Service, 1972; Jubilee Medal, 1977; Foundation for the Advancement of Canadian Letters award, 1984. LL. D. : University of Windsor. Commander, Order of St. John; Commander, Order of Military Merit, 1978. Address: 2180 Yonge Street, Toronto, Ontario M4S 2B9, Canada.

SCIENCE-FICTION PUBLICATIONS

Novels (series: Separation)

Ultimatum. Toronto, Clarke Irwin, and New York, Pocket Books, 1973.
Exxoneration. Toronto, McClelland and Stewart, 1974.
Exodus/UK. Toronto, McClelland and Stewart, 1975.
Separation. Toronto, McClelland and Stewart, 1976.
Balls! Don Mills, Ontario, General, 1979.
Periscope Red. Don Mills, Ontario, General, and New York, Beaufort, 1980.
Separation Two. Don Mills, Ontario, Paperjacks, 1981.
Triad. Don Mills, Ontario, General, 1981; New York, Beaufort, 1982.
Retaliation. Don Mills, Ontario, General, 1982.

OTHER PUBLICATIONS

Verse

Images. Don Mills, Ontario, General, 1981.

Other

The Green North: Mid-Canada. Toronto, Maclean Hunter, 1970.
The Arctic Imperative: An Overview of the Energy Crisis. Toronto, McClelland and Stewart, 1973.
E. P. Taylor (biography). Toronto, McClelland and Stewart, 1978.
Patton's Gap: An Account of the Battle of Normandy 1944. Don Mills, Ontario, General, New York, Beaufort, and London, Arms and Armour Press, 1981.
Massacre 747. Don Mills, Ontario, Paperjacks, 1984.
How to Write a Bestseller. Toronto, McClelland and Stewart, 1985.

*   *   *

Richard Rohmer's novels only qualify for the epithet "science fiction" by virtue of their settings, which are projections of the contemporary international political, economic, and military arena. As tales of the near future, they are ephemeral works, their fictional prognostications soon invalidated by historical reality (*Exodus/UK*, published in 1975, is set in the late 1970's, but the events narrated therein bear little resemblance to the actual political developments of the latter part of that decade). They perhaps fit more permanently, within the science-fiction framework, as alternative histories; nevertheless, their plots, characters, and narrative style have closer affinities with political thrillers than science fiction.

All the novels deal with various political and economic intrigues and are made convincing by Rohmer's personal knowledge of the worlds of the law, politics, and the military. His stories are particularly persuasive when they describe major global events, such as the bankruptcy of Britain, due to the withdrawal of Arab monies, in *Exodus/UK*; the events leading up to the annexation of Canada, in *Ultimatum*; the Canadian take-over of the two American banks, in *Retaliation*; the natural gas crisis, in *Balls*! But while the construction of such realistic scenarios is Rohmer's major strength, the presentation of his *dramstis peronae,* within these settings, is his major weakness. His characters are wooden and heavily stereotyped, given unrealistic dialogue (often for the sake of explication), and are frequently limited by a somewhat sexist representation. The male-female relationships are handled without subtlety—hard-drinking men seducing attractive and ambitious women—and conform to clichéd soap opera conventions (e. g., in *Retaliation* Samantha Scott, described as a handsome woman, unlikely to turn heads, is transformed when she removes her glasses).

All of the novels follow a consistent pattern of narrative technique, characterisation, and plot development. The chief part of each story is the description of an event (e. g., an energy crisis, take-over bid, military exercise) in which the characters are largely embodiments of certain prevailing elements within our society—what E. M. Forster would call "flat characters," built around a single idea or quality (the military man, the captain of industry, the superpower leader, etc). Inserted into general stream of the plot are some gratuitous digressions in a sensational vein (such as the Prime Minister's plane crash in *Exodus/UK* and the kidnapping of Dr. Huber's daughter in *Retaliation),* which do nothing to develop the characters or the plot and, I suspect, exist in order to make the rather impersonal central themes more immediately exciting. Another technique Rohmer uses, to this end, is the alternation of different streams, in an attempt to create an espisodic cliff-hanger effect. A number of the stories have sequels: *Ultimatum* is followed by *Exxoneration; Exodus/UK* is followed by *Separation* and *Separation Two; Periscope Red* is followed by *Triad.*

Rohmer's novels reflect some of the most powerful examples of social-Darwinism which occur in our society, particularly among the upper levels of international politics and multinational business, in which the balance of power shifts in vast, impersonal games of profit and loss. However, rather than questioning and analysing these games, Rohmer constructs his narratives in simple affirmation of his acute right-wing philosophies. At times his work reflects particularly Canadian concerns—such as the divisionalism in Canadian provinces and the threat of succession.

Rohmer is, on the one hand, a writer with an impressive imagination, has considerable experience in the areas about which he writes and presents imminently plausible projections of modern-day events, yet, on the other hand, he is very much limited by artificial and clumsy technique, awkward plots and bluntly stereotyped characterisations. Nevertheless, his books are popular with his audience, all of them best-sellers in his native Canada.

—Mark Warwick Leahy

ROSE, Lawrence W. See FEARN, John Russell.

ROSHWALD, Mordecai (Marceli). American. Born in Drohobycz, Poland, 26 May 1921. Educated at Hebrew University, Jerusalem, M. A. 1942, Ph. D. in philosophy 1947. Served in the Israeli Army, 1950-51. Married Miriam Wyszynski in 1945; one son. Lecturer, Israel Institute of Public Administration, Tel-Aviv, 1947-51, and Hebrew University, 1951-55. Since 1957, member of the Philosophy Department, now Professor, University of Minnesota, Minneapolis. Visiting Professor, Brooklyn College, Summer 1956, Israel Institute of Technology, Haifa, 1963-64, University of Bath, Spring 1966, and Simon Fraser University, Burnaby, British Columbia. Recipient: McKnight Foundation Humanities Award, 1962, 1963. Address: 314 Ford Hall, University of Minnesota, Minneapolis, Minnesota 55455; or, G-2 Glacier Drive, Nashua, New Hampshire 03062, U.S.A.

SCIENCE-FICTION PUBLICATIONS

Novels

Level Seven. London, Heinemann, 1959; New York, McGraw Hill, 1960.
A Small Armageddon. London, Heinemann, 1962; New York, New American Library, 1976.

Uncollected Short Stories

"The Politics of Ratology," in *The Nation* (New York), 17 September 1960.
"Awakening in Olympus," in *The Nation* (New York), 30 January 1967.

OTHER PUBLICATIONS

Other

Adam Ve'hinukno (Man and Education). Tel-Aviv, Dvir, 1954.
Humanism in Practice. London, Watts, 1955.
Moses, Leader, Prophet, Man, with Miriam Roshwald. New York, Yoseloff, 1969.

*

Mordecai Roshwald comments:
I became involved in fiction writing through concern about the menace to humanity from nuclear armament, as well as out of a sense of disenchantment with some aspects of modern life. However, an involvement in this kind of writing creates a momentum of its own, as it releases half-hidden emotions and sentiments in the writer's mind. Thus, in a way, I have become a

fiction writer, intent on not neglecting this kind of self-expression and public address, despite my regular academic commitments to teaching and scholarly research, as well as occasional journalistic writing. The diversity of my activity does not prevent me from looking for a common denominator, a philosophy common to these varied efforts. Indeed, I believe I have maintained a fairly consistent approach throughout the different modes of expression.

The science fiction I have written is very much coloured by social, political and cultural concern. Indeed, science fiction is for me a *form* of expression rather than an objective in its own right. In this sense I would classify it with such books as Swift's *Gulliver's Travels* or Huxley's *Brave New World,* rather than with some modern stories dealing with inter-stellar warfare, monsters from distant planets, and the like (unless such stories are used as parables). Though my main success as a fiction writer was due to the success of *Level Seven,* classified as science fiction, I do not feel restricted to this literary form.

*   *   *

Mordecai Roshwald's first book, *Level Seven,* is perhaps the most chilling of all warnings about the new and unlimited dangers of thermonuclear war—such as Nevil Shute's *On the Beach,* Eugene Burdick and Harvey Wheeler's *Fail Safe,* Peter George's *Red Alert,* and others. The story begins as the Push-button Officer X-127 is taken down the one-way escalator 4000 feet to Level 7, the deepest in his country's shelter system and the control centre for its offensive weapons. The personnel on this level have numbers and opinions, but not names and faces; they have an atomic reactor for power, synthetic food for 500 years, and taped music for amusement. Marriage is permitted and plans are made for raising children to carry on life as troglodytes after the inevitable war. Finally the order comes (set off, we learn, by an accidental rocket firing), X-127 and his colleagues push all their buttons and the surface of the planet is destroyed. Gradually, as the radiation penetrates deeper, the other Levels and those of the enemy and the neutrals falls silent. Level 7 itself is flooded with radiation from its faulty reactor, and X-127 dies with the others, huddled in his bunk and dreaming of the sun. The terrifying effect of *Level Seven* depends on the absolute inevitability of its outcome. The feeble protests of X-117, a button-pusher who refuses to do his duty, only underscore the iron determinism of the system. If the story were recast in more mundane and conventional form, using real characters instead of numbered abstractions, much of its unique capacity to convince and frighten would probably be lost.

We see the other side of the coin in Roshwald's second novel, *A Small Armageddon.* In this peculiar tale, a group of officers of the American nuclear submarine *Polar Lion* hold a clandestine drinking party while the ship is on patrol. When the captain finds them, a scuffle takes place in which the captain is killed. The submarine proceeds to cruise the world, exacting tribute under threat of its missiles. It is finally destroyed in an exchange of fire with a Minuteman base which has been taken over by religious fanatics. Meanwhile neo-Nazis have captured missile bases in Germany, and the African state of Qunta-Qunta announces its own demands, backed by three hydrogen bombs that it has managed to buy or steal.

Level Seven depends on the notion that heads of state are irresponsible maniacs. Its abstract nature enables the reader to believe this, at least enough to give the story a profound impact. *A Small Armageddon* requires us to believe that malcontents and fanatics can easily gain control of nuclear weapons. It fails because of Roshwald's failure to make either people or situations even remotely credible. Submarine officers are not sophomores who wait till the captain's asleep to hold booze parties. Armed Civilians cannot take over a functional missile base as bandits might a supermarket. *Level Seven* is an effective work produced by an author who cannot handle the demands of mainstream fiction; as such; the book is interesting as an SF boundary marker as well as for its own real and unique terror.

—E. R. Bishop

ROTSLER, William. Also writes as William Arrow; John Ryder Hall. American. Born in Los Angeles, California, 3 July 1926. Educated at Ventura Junior College, California, 1946; Los Angeles County Art Institute, 1947-50. Served in the United States Army, 1944-45. Married Marian Abney in 1953 (divorced, 1958); one daughter. Rancher in Camarillo, California, 1942-44, 1946; sculptor, 1950-59. Since 1959, photographer and film maker: writer, producer, and director of commercials, documentaries, and industrial and feature films. Recipient: *Locus* Award, for artwork, 1971, 1972, 1973; Hugo Award, for artwork, 1975, 1977, 1979. Guest of honor, 31st World Science Fiction Convention, 1973. Agent: Richard Curtis Associates, 164 East 64th Street, New York, New York 10021, U.S.A.

SCIENCE-FICTION PUBLICATIONS

Novels (series: Zandra)

Patron of the Arts. New York, Ballantine, 1974; Morley, Yorkshire, Elmfield Press, 1975.
Futureworld (novelization of screenplay; as John Ryder Hall). New York, Ballantine, 1976.
Man, The Hunted Animal (novelization of TV play; as William Arrow). New York, Ballantine, 1976.
To the Land of the Electric Angel. New York, Ballantine, 1976.
Visions of Nowhere (novelization of TV play; as William Arrow). New York, Ballantine, 1976.
Zandra. New York, Doubleday, 1978.
Iron Man: Call My Killer . . . Modok. New York, Pocket Books, 1979.
Dr. Strange. New York, Pocket Books, 1979.
The Far Frontier. Chicago, Playboy Press, 1980.
Shiva Descending, with Gregory Benford. New York, Avon, and London, Sphere, 1980.
The Hidden Worlds of Zandra. New York, Doubleday, 1983.

Short Stories

Star Trek II Short Stories. New York, Simon and Schuster, 1982.

Uncollected Short Stories

"Ship Me Tomorrow," in *Galaxy* (New York), June 1970.
"The Kong Papers," with Harlan Ellison, in *Partners in Wonder*, by Ellison. New York, Walker, 1971.
"After the End Before the Beginning," in *If* (New York), October 1971.
"Star Level," in *Amazing* (New York), March 1972.
"There's a Special Kind Needed Out There," in *Amazing* (New York), July 1972.
"Seed," in *Amazing* (New York), June 1973.
"Gerald Fitzgerald and the Time Machine," in *Vertex* (Los Angeles), October 1973.
"The Gods of Zar," in *Amazing* (New York), October 1973.
"War of the Magicians," in *Fantastic* (New York), November 1973.
"A la Mode Knights," in *Vertex* (Los Angeles), December 1973.
"The Immortality of Lazarus," in *Amazing* (New York), December 1973.
"Bohassian Learns," in *School and Society Through Science Fiction*, edited by Joseph D. Olander and Martin H. Greenberg. New York, Random House, 1974.
"A New Life," in *Fantastic* (New York), May 1974.
"The Raven and the Hawk," in *Analog* (New York), September 1974.
"Balance Point" and "The Conversation," in *Vertex* (Los Angeles), December 1974.
"Surprise Party," in *Vertex* (Los Angeles), April 1975.
"Landing Party," in *Vertex* (Los Angeles), August 1975.
"To Gain a Dream," in *Amazing* (New York), September 1975.
"Epic," in *Future Pastimes*, edited by Scott Edelstein. Nashville, Aurora, 1977.
"Parental Guidance Suggested," in *Fantasy and Science Fiction* (New York), January 1979.

OTHER PUBLICATIONS

Novels

Superstud. Los Angeles, Holloway, 1975.
Supermouth. Los Angeles, Holloway, 1975.
Supertongue and Other Turn Ons. Los Angeles, Holloway, 1975.
Sinbad and the Eye of the Tiger (novelization of screenplay; as John Ryder Hall). New York, Pocket Books, 1977.
Mr. Merlin 1-2 (novelizations of TV series). New York, Simon and Schuster, 2 vols., 1981; London, Beaver, 2 vols., 1982.
Grease 2 (novelization of screenplay). New York, Simon and Schuster, and London, Sphere, 1982.
Joanie Loves Chachi:
   1. *Secrets.* New York, Simon and Schuster, 1982.
   2. *A Test of Hearts.* New York, Simon and Schuster, 1982.
The Pirate Movie. New York, Simon and Schuster, 1982.
Distress Call. New York, Simon and Schuster, 1982.
Vice Squad. New York, Pinnacle, 1982.
The A-Team (novelizations of TV series):
   1. *Defense Against Terror.* New York, Simon and Schuster, 1983.
   2. *The Danger Maze.* New York, Simon and Schuster, 1983.
The Love Boat: Voyage of Love (novelization of TV series). New York, Simon and Schuster, 1983.
Magnum, P. I.: Maui Mystery (novelization of TV series). New York, Simon and Schuster, 1983.
The Vulcan Treasure. New York, Simon and Schuster, 1983.
Staying Alive. New York, Simon and Schuster, 1983.

Plays

Screenplays: *The Agony of Love,* 1966; *The Girl with Hungry Eyes,* 1966; *Four Kinds of Love,* 1967; *Suburban Pagans,* 1967; *Like It Is,* 1968; *Mantis in Lace (Lila),* 1968; *A Taste of Hot Lead,* 1969; *Shannon's Women,* 1969; *The Godson,* 1969; *She Did What He Wanted,* 1970; *Midnight,* 1970.

Other

Contemporary Erotic Cinema. New York, Ballantine, 1973.

*

Theatrical Activities:

Director: **Films**—all his screenplays.

Actor: **Films**—*The Notorious Daughter of Fanny Hill*, 1966; *The Agony of Love*, 1966; *Shannon's Women*, 1969; *The Secret Sex Life of Romeo and Juliet*, 1970.

* * *

William Rotsler is one of the few SF writers who has also achieved fame as a cartoonist. His distinctive style of cartooning has proven popular for over 30 years, and he writes frequently on the arts for such monthlies as *Adam*. It is little wonder, then, that Rotsler's first novel *Patron of the Arts*, is about the nature of the artistic process. Rotsler attempts in this novel to determine the social effects of a *Gesamstwerk*, an attempt at the total union of the arts through a synthesis of holography and electronic music. This novel succeeds to the extent that the ideas it contains are reflections of authentic experience, but Rotsler's extrapolative sense is not keen, and the novel can best be characterised as an interesting failure.

From his promising first novel, Rostler's work quickly declined. Rostler has tried a career as a commercial entertainer, but fails to provide that depth of charaterisation and intellection that the best popular writers, such as Paul Anderson and Gordon Dickson, provide. His later novels are mere repetition of formulas without any distinctive presence. His favourite formula is that of the Ship of Fools, a cast of various racial and sexual types gatherd together to face a perilous situation. Thus in *Zandra* the varied cast is drawn together after their cruiseship passes through the Bermuda Triangle into another dimension. In *Shiva Descending* (with Gregory Benford) the cast faces the familiar peril of a meteor about to destroy Earth. Rotsler and Benford mine this tired lode of apocalyptic fiction to little effect. Rostler's worst novel, however, is *The Far Frontier*. In this work, Rotsler fulfills the worst fantasies of those mundane critics who insist that science fiction is nothing more than Western formulas transported to a wider setting. Rostler has replied with a novel complete with interstellar Indians, space cows, and planet rustlers. Rarely does one read a novel where the writer rejoices in its trashy content; such, unfortunately, is the case with *The Far Frontier*.

Rotsler, then, after achieving promise as a first novelist, has reneged upon that promise with his later novels. He is less important for his writings than for his cartoons, which have the distinction and wit that his novels lack.

—Martin Morse Wooster

ROUSSEAU, Victor (Victor Rousseau Emanuel). Also wrote as H. M. Egbert. American. Born in London, in 1879. Lived in South Africa at the turn of the century; emigrated to the United States, and wrote for pulp magazines until 1941. *Died 5 April 1960*.

SCIENCE-FICTION PUBLICATIONS

Novels

The Messiah of the Cylinder. Chicago, McClurg, and London, Curtis Brown, 1917; as *The Apostle of the Cylinder*, London, Hodder and Stoughton, 1918.
Draught of Eternity (as H. M. Egbert). London, Long, 1924.

The Sea Demons (as H. M. Egbert). London, Long, 1924; as Victor Rousseau, Westport, Connecticut, Hyperion Press, 1976.

Uncollected Short Stories (series: Surgeon of Souls)

"Fruit of the Lamp," in *Argosy* (New York), 2 February 1918.
"The Eye of Balamok," in *All-Story Weekly* (New York), 17 January 1920.
"The Case of the Jailer's Daughter" (Surgeon), in *Weird Tales* (Indianapolis), September 1926.
"The Woman with the Crooked Nose" (Surgeon), in *Weird Tales* (Indianapolis), October 1926.
"The Tenth Commandment" (Surgeon), in *Weird Tales* (Indianapolis), November 1926.
"The Legacy of Hate" (Surgeon), in *Weird Tales* (Indianapolis), December 1926.
"The Mayor's Menagerie" (Surgeon), in *Weird Tales* (Indianapolis), January 1927.
"The Fetish of the Waxworks" (Surgeon), in *Weird Tales* (Indianapolis), February 1927.
"The Seventh Symphony" (Surgeon), in *Weird Tales* (Indianapolis), March 1927.
"The Chairs of Stuyvesant Baron" (Surgeon), in *Weird Tales* (Indianapolis), April 1927.
"The Man Who Lost His Luck" (Surgeon), in *Weird Tales* (Indianapolis), May 1927.
"The Dream That Came True" (Surgeon), in *Weird Tales* (Indianapolis), June 1927.
"The Ultimate Problem" (Surgeon), in *Weird Tales* (Indianapolis), July 1927.
"The Beetle Horde," in *Astounding* (New York), January 1930.
"The Atom Smasher," in *Astounding* (New York), May 1930.
"The Lord of Space," in *Astounding* (New York), August 1930.
"The Invisible Death," in *Astounding* (New York), October 1930.
"The Wall of Death," in *Astounding* (New York), November 1930.
"Outlaws of the Sun," in *Miracle* (New York), April-May 1931.
"Revolt on Inferno," in *Miracle* (New York), June-July 1931.
"The Curse of Amen-Ra," in *Strange Tales* (New York), October 1932.
"World's End," in *Argosy* (New York), 6 July 1933.
"The Stone Man of Ignota," in *Future* (New York), August 1941.
"Moon Patrol" in *Thrilling Wonder Stories* (New York), October 1941.
"The Seal Maiden," in *A. Merritt's Fantasy Magazine* (Kokomo, Indiana), February 1950.
"A Cry from Beyond," in *Fantastic Pulps*, edited by Peter Haining. New York, St. Martin's Press, 1975.

OTHER PUBLICATIONS

Novels

Derwent's Horse. London, Methuen, 1901.
Wooden Spoil. New York, Doran, 1919; London, Hodder and Stoughton, 1923.
The Big Muskeg. Cincinnati, Stewart Kidd, 1921; London, Hodder and Stoughton, 1923.
The Lion's Jaw. London, Hodder and Stoughton, 1923.
The Home Trail. London, Hodder and Stoughton, 1924.
The Big Man of Bonne Chance. London, Hodder and Stoughton, 1925.

The Golden Horde. London, Hodder and Stoughton, 1926.

Novels as H. M. Egbert

Jacqueline of Golden River. New York, Doubleday, 1920; London, Hodder and Stoughton, 1924.
My Lady of the Nile. London, Hodder and Stoughton, 1923.
The Big Malopo. London, Long, 1924.
Eric of the Strong Heart. London, Long, 1925.
Mrs. Aladdin. London, Long, 1925.
Salted Diamonds. London, Long, 1926.
Winding Trails. London, Long, 1927.

Novels as V. R. Emanuel

The Story of John Paul. London, Constable, 1923.
Middle Years. New York, Minton Balch, 1925.
The Selmans. New York, Dial Press, 1925.

Plays

Screenplays: *West of the Rainbow's End,* with Daisy Kent, 1926; *Wanderer of the West,* with Arthur Hoerl and W. Ray Johnston, 1927; *Prince of the Plains,* with Arthur Hoerl, 1927; *Lightnin' Shot,* with J. P. McGowan, 1928; *Trailin' Back,* with Arthur Hoerl and J. P. McGowan, 1928.

*   *   *

Victor Rousseau's stories spring out immediately and absorb the reader with global plots and bold valiance. Rousseau's rare talent is to combine medieval values and Louis L'Amour's style in the science-fiction context. The result provides sentimental satisfaction. The amusement in reading Rousseau is similar to the *Star Wars* experience in cinema. Both *The Messiah of the Cylinder* and *The Sea Demons* present strong heroes and execrable villains.

Even if the "daring sexual implications" that the promotion page of *The Sea Demons* promise are hard to find, there are enough imagination and activity in the macrocosmic plots to satisfy thrill-seeking readers. In *The Messiah of the Cylinder,* our hero (Arnold) and his foul antagonist are prep school mates. One of their school-mates, Herman Lagaroff, invents the 100-year time-lock cylinder that transports the two men (and the pristine maiden whom they both love) into the year 2017. The time forwarding is believably described, involving Arnold's tortuous arrival in the strange London of 2017: "I flung myself upon my face and prayed, with all my will, to die. " The story of these books is similar to Wells's *A Modern Utopia* and *When the Sleeper Wakes.* The time travelers in Rousseu's work are propelled into a barbarous authoritarian nightmare, however, where "the dull and the base" are categorized by size of cranium. "The Prophet Wells," as he is referred to by Rousseau, would be aghast at the cold brutality of the rational society as it is portrayed in *The Messiah.* The triumphant ending in *The Messiah* includes the destruction and overthrow of the (fascist) government, the outlawing of divorce, and a return to a "ruling class bound to its traditions of public service. " Where Wells asserts the final victory of reason, Rousseau longs for a futuristic theocracy. The priests would be happier than the scientists in Rousseau's future. Nonetheless, Rousseau exhibits a vivid technological imagination. He writes about solar power, plausible flying machines, and a communication network similar to the current and projected reality. The sinister government's effective propagandistic use of the media is a startling reminder of the current world situation.

The plot of *The Sea Demon* is of the canned-on-the-shelf variety, and the story is similar to *The Messiah.* The strange sea creatures who are struggling to take over the world are discovered by noble Captain Donald Paget. Gallantry overcoming the hideous threat is the main course: Donald "Raised the girl in his arms, and felt one of the blubbery flippers on his hand . . . the stinging flippers sucked the blood from his face and hands . . . But Donald could not lose with Ida's life at stake. " The battle to save the world intensifies to involve all governments and world resources. The story culminates in suicidal frenzy as the Queen Sea Beast dies of a broken heart and leaves the hordes without leadership, which we all know leads immediately to destruction.

The enduring impressions one gets of Rousseau are staunch traditionalism and faith in a well-ordered universe. Rousseau is good for a cheerful escape from heady ambiguity, and the pleasures of a frantic plot with the sugar-coated conclusion never in doubt.

—Peter Lynch

———

RUCKER, Rudy. American. Born in Louisville, Kentucky, 22 March 1946. Educated at Swarthmore College, Pennsylvania, B. A. in Mathematics 1967; Rutgers University, New Brunswick, New Jersey, M. A. 1969, Ph. D. 1973. Married Sylvia Bogsch in 1967; two daughters and one son. Assistant Professor, State University of New York, Geneseo, 1972-78; Alexander von Humboldt Foundation Research Grantee, University of Heidelberg, 1978-80; Associate Professor, Randolph-Macon Woman's College, Lynchburg, Virginia, 1980-82. Since 1982, free-lance writer. Recipient: Philip K. Dick Memorial Award, 1983. Agent: Susan Protter, 110 West 40th Street, New York, New York 10018. Address: 1324 Church Street, Lynchburg, Virginia 24504 U.S.A.

SCIENCE-FICTION PUBLICATIONS

Novels

White Light. London, Virgin, and New York, Ace, 1980.
Spacetime Donuts. New York, Ace, 1981.
Software. New York, Ace, 1982.
The Sex Sphere. New York, Ace, 1983.
Master of Space and Time. New York, Bluejay, 1984.
The Secret of Life. New York, Bluejay, 1985.

Short Stories

The Fifty-Seventh Franz Kafka. New York, Ace, 1983.

Uncollected Short Story

"Monument to the Third International," in *Fantasy and Science Fiction* (New York), December 1984.

OTHER PUBLICATIONS

Verse

Light Fuse and Get Away. Lynchburg, Virginia, Carp, 1983.

Other

Geometry, Relativity, and the Fourth Dimension . New York, Dover, and London, Constable, 1977.
Infinity and the Mind: The Science and Philosophy of the Infinite. Cambridge, Massachusetts, Birkhauser, and Brighton, Harvester, 1982.
The Fourth Dimension: Toward a Geometry of Higher Reality. Boston, Houghton Mifflin, 1984.
"Phil Dick Lives," in *PKDS Bulletin*, Fall 1984.
"What Do SF Writers Want?," in *SFWA Bulletin*, Winter 1984.

Editor, *Speculations on the Fourth Dimension: Selected Writings of Charles H. Hinton.* New York, Dover, and London, Constable, 1980.

*

Rudy Rucker comments:

An unusual thing about my work is that I write popular speculative mathematics books as well as fiction. To some degree the fiction serves as a laboratory for thought-experiments related to my scientific and philosophical investigations.

Another aspect of my fiction is that much of it is, on a higher level, autobiographical. I call the device of writing about one's life in SF terms *transrealism*. Taken in sequence, *Secret of Life*, *White Light*, and *Sex Sphere* make up a transrealist trilogy.

My non-fiction has largely been devoted to expanding the range of things that people are able to think and talk about. Infinity and higher dimensions are of particular interest to me.

*　　*　　*

In his works of science fiction and science fact, Rudy Rucker extrapolates new physical and psychological modes of existence from current possibilities. He pursues these extrapolations by exploring how the mind can manipulate the physical universe and hence distort our commonsense perceptions of the world. The results of these distortions are a renewed sense of wonder about the external world and an enhancement of the internal world through increased self awareness.

Rucker frequently takes his hero or heroes—and vicariously, of course, the reader—on a mental journey toward some higher plane of reality. Sometimes this journey involves altering our world by imagining a concept from theoretical physics into an everyday reality. In *Master of Space and Time*, Flectcher and Harry physically occupy Hilbert space and, in the process, allow an alternate version of Harry to escape into our world. This inversion of Harry's affable, disordered personality—Gerry Herber, a figment of Harry's imagination run wild—unleashes a reign of terror that preys upon the weakest elements of society. Herber threatens to eradicate the independent thought and action that made him a physical reality in the first place. Furthermore, Fletcher and Harry are themselves the product of Alwin Bitter's imagination. Bitter's preoccupation with Hilbert space willed them into existence and manipulated their experiment, and, like Gerry Herber, they threaten the balance of the physical world. Similarly, through the imagination, a young Alwin Bitter in *The Sex Sphere* achieves first the transformation of the city of Heidelberg into a degraded carnival of sexual activity and then a return to normalcy. A hypersphere trapped in three-dimensional space and the others it spawns have varacious sexual appetites and an intense aversion to human females. The emotional ties that bind Bitter to a normal life become increasingly precarious. When they reach a breaking point, he wills into existence a world in which sexual gratificiation becomes completely divorced from human involvement. There are no females, only sex spheres. Bitter's wife re-establishes ties with him, and he wills the sex spheres and his experiences in Germany away. In both of these novels, Rucker imagines for us a world transformed by an idea and infinite possibilities for the recursion of this transformation.

In addition to theoretical concepts, machines are also the catalysts for the journeys Rucker's heroes take. The possibilities opened up by computers form the basis for several of Rucker's novels, and like concepts, physical objects can alter everyday reality in unexpected ways. In *Infinity and the Mind*, Rucker suggests that computers may one day become self-replicating and through natural selection mimic the intuition and subtlety of human thought. Further, he speculates that because of more favorable environmental conditions on the moon, computers may eventually form their own separate society there. This speculation forms the basis of the novel *Software* in which an old man strives for immortality and a young man for his connection to the rest of the human race. In *Software* computers have achieved a rough parity with humans, and Rucker explores that delicate balance as humans fend off the computer's efforts to "eat their brains" and thus deprive them of their humanity. In *Spacetime Donuts*, the balance has shifted in favor of computers. They control most aspects of human activity, from dispensing food—a tasteless concoction called "dream food"—to plugging into the human consciousness every night and supplying mankind with dreams. Computers provide immediate gratification of all human needs, and men are little more than useless appendages of one large computer that rules the state. The novel explores one man's journey back to his own humanity with the help of theoretical physics and the revolution caused by that journey.

While the journeys prompted by ideas and technology threaten Rucker's heroes and their worlds, each journey ends in an affirmation of humanity. People become more aware and more open to their husbands, wives, lovers, children; people realize the best in themselves; people die because they are old and because death is the way the human race replenishes itself. This human affirmation brings a restoration of normalcy and with it an enhanced sense of wonder about the everyday world. This sense of wonder is what science fiction is all about.

—Terri Paul

RUPPERT, Chester. See **PHILLIPS, Rog.**

RUSS, Joanna. American. Born in New York City, 22 February 1937. Educated at Cornell University, Ithaca, New York, B. A. 1957; Yale University School of Drama, New Haven, Connecticut, M. F. A. 1960. Married Albert Amateau in 1963 (divorced, 1967). Lecturer in Speech, Queensborough Community College, New York, 1966-67; Instructor, 1967-70, and Assistant Professor of English, 1970-72, Cornell University; Assistant Professor of English, State University of New York, Binghamton, 1972-73, 1974-75, and University of Colorado, Boulder, 1975-77. Associate Professor, 1977-84, and since 1984, Professor of English, University of Washington, Seattle. Occasional book reviewer, *Fantasy and Science Fiction*, 1966-79. Recipient:

Nebula Award, 1972, 1983; National Endowment for the Humanities Fellowship, 1974; Hugo Award, 1983; *Locus* Award, 1983. Agent: Ellen Levine Literary Agency, 432 Park Avenue South, New York, New York 10016. Address: Department of English, University of Washington, Seattle, Washington 98195, U.S.A.

SCIENCE-FICTION PUBLICATIONS

Novels

Picnic on Paradise. New York, Ace, 1968; London, Macdonald, 1969.
And Chaos Died. New York, Ace, 1970.
The Female Man New York, Bantam, 1975; London, Star, 1977.
We Who Are About to . . . . New York, Dell, 1977.
Kittatinny: A Tale of Magic (for children). New York, Daughters, 1978.
The Two of Them. New York, Berkley, 1978.
On Strike Against God. New York, Out and Out, 1980.
Extra (Ordinary) People. New York, St. Martin's Press, 1984; London, Women's Press, 1985.

Short Stories

Alyx. Boston, Gregg Press, 1976.
The Adventures of Alyx. New York, Pocket Books, 1983.
The Zanzibar Cat. Sauk City, Wisconsin, Arkham House, 1983.

Uncollected Short Stories

"Nor Custom Stale," in *Fantasy and Science Fiction* (New York), September 1959.
"I Had Vacantly Crumpled It into My Pocket," in *Fantasy and Science Fiction* (New York), August 1964.
"Life in a Furniture Store, " in *Epoch* (Ithaca, New York), Fall 1965.
"Visiting, " in *Manhattan Review*, Fall 1966.
"Mr. Wilde's Second Chance," in *Fantasy and Science Fiction* (New York), September 1966.
"This Night at My Fire," in *Epoch* (Ithaca, New York), Winter 1966.
"Harry Longshanks," in *Fiction as Process*, edited by Carl Hartman and Hazard Adams. New York, Dodd Mead, 1968.
"Scenes from Domestic Life," in *Consumption* (Seattle), Fall 1968.
"This Afternoon," in *Cimarron Review* (Stillwater, Oklahoma), December 1968.
"Oh! She Has a Lover, " in *Kinesis 1* (Carbondale, Illinois), February 1969.
"The Throaways," in *Consumption* (Seattle), Spring 1969.
"What Really Happened," in *Just Friends 1*, October 1969.
"Window Dressing," in *New Worlds of Fantasy 2*, edited by Terry Carr. New York, Ace, 1970.
"The View from This Window," in *Quark 1*, edited by Samuel R. Delany and Marilyn Hacker. New York, Paperback Library, 1970.
"The Man Who Could Not See Devils," in *Alchemy and Academe*, edited by Anne McCaffrey. New York, Doubleday, 1970.
"Visiting Day," in *South* (Deland, Florida), Spring 1970.
"Cap and Bells," in *Discourse* (Moorhead, Minnesota), Summer 1970.
"Suffer a Sea-Change," in *William and Mary Review* (Williamsburg, Virginia), Fall 1970.

"Not for Love," in *Arlington Quarterly* (Arlington, Texas), Fall 1970.
"The Wise Man," in *Cimarron Review* (Stillwater, Oklahoma), October 1970.
"The Precious Object," in *Red Clay Reader 7* (Charlotte, North Carolina), November 1970.
"Foul Fowl," in *Little Magazine* (New York), Spring 1971.
"Dear Diary," in *Northwest Review* (Eugene, Oregon), Fall 1972.
"Laura, The Camp, and That Terrible Thing," in *Monmouth Review*, Spring 1973.
"Old Pictures," in *Little Magazine* (New York), Winter 1973.
"Reasonable People," in *Orbit 14*, edited by Damon Knight. New York, Harper, 1974.
"An Old Fashioned Girl," in *Final Stage*, edited by Edward L. Ferman and Barry N. Malzberg. New York, Charterhouse, 1974.
"Passages," in *Galaxy* (New York), January 1974.
"A Few Things I Know about Whileaway," in *The New Improved Sun*, edited by Thomas M. Disch. New York, Harper, 1975; London, Hutchinson, 1976.
"The Experimenter," in *Galaxy* (New York), October 1975.
"Dragons and Dimwits or . . . Lord of the Royalties," in *Fantasy and Science Fiction* (New York), December 1979.
"Little Tales from Nature," in *Woman Space*, edited by Claudia Laperti. Lebanon, New Hampshire, New Victoria, 1981.
"The Little Dirty Girl," in *Elsewhere 2*, edited by Terri Windling and Mark Alan Arnold. New York, Ace, 1982.
"Elf Hill," in *Fantasy and Science Fiction* (New York) November 1982.
"Sword Blades and Poppy Seed with Homage to (Who Else?) Amy Lowell,"in *Heroic Visions*, edited by Jessica Amanda Salmonson. New York, Ace, 1983.
"Main Street: 1953," in *Sinister Wisdom* (Lincoln, Nebraska), Fall 1983.

OTHER PUBLICATIONS

Play

Window Dressing, in *The New Woman's Theatre*, edited by Honor Moore. New York, Random House, 1977.

Other

"Daydream Literature and Science Fiction," in *Extrapolation* (Wooster, Ohio), December 1969.
"Genre," in *Clarion*, edited by Robin Scott Wilson. New York, New American Library, 1971.
"Communique from the Front: Teaching and the State of the Art," in *Colloquy*, May 1971.
"The Wearing Out of Genre Materials. " in *College English* (Urbana, Illinois), October 1971.
"The He-Man Ethos in Science Fiction," in *Clarion 2*, edited by Robin Scott Wilson. New York, New American Library, 1972.
"Images of Women in Science Fiction" and "What Can a Heroine Do? or, Why Women Can't Write," in *Images of Women in Fiction: Feminist Perspectives*, edited by Susan Cornillon. Bowling Green,Ohio, Popular Press, 1972.
"Setting," in *Those Who Can*, edited by Robin Scott Wilson. New York, New American Library, 1973.
"Speculations: The Subjectivity of Science Fiction," in *Extrapolation* (Wooster, Ohio), December 1973.
"'What If . . . ?' Literature," in *The Contemporary Literary Scene 1973*, edited By Frank N. Magill. Englewood, New

Jersey, Salem Press, 1974.

Introduction to *Tales and Stories*, by Mary Shelley. Boston, Hall, 1975.

"Towards an Aesthetic of Science Fiction," in *Science-Fiction Studies* (Terre Haute, Indiana), July 1975.

"Symposium: Women and Science Fiction," in *Khatru* (Baltimore), November 1975.

"Outta Space: Women Write Science Fiction," in *Ms* (New York), January 1976.

"Alien Monsters," in *Turning Points*, edited by Damon Knight. New York, Harper, 1977.

"S. F. and Technology as Mystifications," in *Science-Fiction Studies* (Terre Haute, Indiana), November 1978.

"Amor Vincit Foeminam: The Battle of the Sexes in S. F.," in *Science-Fiction Studies* (Terre Haute, Indiana), March 1980.

"Recent Feminist Utopias," in *Future Females*, edited by Marleen Barr. Bowling Green, Ohio, Popular Press, 1981.

How to Suppress Women's Writing. Austin, University of Texas Press, 1983; London, Women's Press, 1984.

Magic Mommas, Trembling Sisters, Puritans and Perverts: Feminist Essays. Trumansburg, New York, Crossing Press, 1985.

*   *   *

During the 1960's, Joanna Russ emerged as one of the most talented and provocative writers of science fiction's New Wave. While Russ identifies herself primarily as a feminist, she is equally well known for her experimental way of handling the conventional materials and narrative strategies of science fiction. Since Russ is opposed to all social fixities and intellectual givens, her major effort as a science-fiction writer has been to explore alternate realities and create new myths, especially ones which depict women as complex human subjects.

Russ's apprentice work is feminist only obliquely. Ostensibly she aims at an interesting mix of historic fantasy and the supernatural, a combination she continues to use in her later work. The initial run of stories exploits the theme of the after-life to fresh effect. "Nor Custom Stale," her first story, is untypically set in the future. It describes a bourgeois couple who live stubbornly immured in a future-tech "House" while catastrophic ages pass unnoticed outside; domestic monotony preserves them in a living death. Several of the stories are set in the 19th century, an era Russ understands but dislikes. "Mr. Wilde's Second Chance" is a wry account of the dead poet's renunciation of an opportunity to live a conventionally tasteful second life. In "There Is Another Shore . . .," a revenant young women, a kind of female Keats, returns to her deathplace in Rome to taste "the fullness of life" in romantic adventure. The ironic promise of this story—that if life for the 19th century woman was death, death was liberation—is also the germ for "My Dear Emily," whose sober young heroine is passionately emancipated when she becomes a vampire. Part of the wit of such stories is their literary allusiveness; "My Dear Emily" condenses the romantic plot of *Wuthering Heights*.

With her first Alyx stories, Russ introduces a character new to science fiction, an adventuress whose daring and cunning issue from her womanly strength. Set in ancient Phoenicia, these stories launch her on a career as a soldier of fortune. In her natural setting, Alyx is of necessity an outlaw sensibility—a rationalist in a world of superstitious mystique, an imaginist in a world of empty, brutal pragmatism: in short, Russ implies, the ancestor of the intelligent modern woman. *Picnic on Paradise*, also built around Alyx, casts her again as an outlaw, here a ruthlessly sensible, martially skilled Trans-Temp agent abstracted from Tyre to a future world wasted by advanced

capitalist war. Alyx is Russ's *agent provocateur* : neither Amazon nor androgyne, she foils both old and new notions of the feminine ideal. At the same time, her unromantic heroics are designed to satirize the "he-man ethos" of Sword and Sorcery. For all its modesty in plot and narrative strategy, *Picnic on Paradise* may be Russ's most inventive novel.

It was closely followed by another ground-breaking novel of the future and several increasingly accomplished shorter fantasies. *And Chaos Died* is at once a penetrating social critique and a lyrical celebration of a psionic near-utopia. Russ maroons her hero on a pastoral planet where he is drawn into an egalitarian community and taught psi-powers. What is really new in the novel is its style: the magic arbitrariness of the narrator's experience is rendered by a stream-of-expanding-consciousness technique that registers his initial nausea, then his growing joy, and finally his disgust when he is returned to a dystopic earth wholly given over to violence and mental imperialism. In the novelette "The Second Inquisition," Russ makes a poignantly funny story of one of her central concerns, a young girl's need for a worthy feminine model to counteract her social training in self-extinction. The tutelary genius in this case is a Trans-Temp agent from a non-sexist future world. The heroine of "The Zanzibar Cat" is yet another Alyx-like subversive ironist, a medieval miller's daughter who faces down a lord of Fantasyland. By the end of the tale, the humble milleress has grown into the mother of all meaning, the author. The archaic setting of "The Zanzibar Cat" and the Hellenistic background of "Poor Man, Beggar Man," a story that splits the historic Alexander into ego and ghostly alter ego, testify to Russ's continuing interest in unwritten history.

With "When It Changed" and "Nobody's Home," Russ reached a new level of achievement. These visions of an emancipated future for women on the wistfully named Whileaway are thorough reconstructions of the standard manless-world story. They are utopian, but only in a special sense: the particular virulence of male-dominated culture is no more, yet life remains unpredictably anguishing and rewarding.

The Female Man, a reconsideration of Whileawayan possibilities, has become an underground classic in both science-fiction and feminist circles. The book is built around the digressive journal of a present-day woman who encounters three other selves: the victim of an altered past even more oppressive of women than our own, an ambassador from a Whileawayan future, and an intermediary figure from a world split by gender war into Manland and Womanland. Each is, in her way, an Everywoman. Janet is Russ's ultimate heroine, "the Might-be of our dreams," the goal of feminine evolution. The way to Janet lies through Jael, or Alice Reasoner, the sex warrior based on Alyx; Jael knows that liberation must be won at hard cost. Joanna, the sometime narrator, and Jeanine are both confused products of a culture which invalidates their every aspiration. These four life histories are super-imposed on one another to create an anti-novel: narrative with dense novelistic details is interspersed with meditation, reverie, and fragments of the mythology and history of Whileaway. What holds all this together is impassioned articulation, a style as sensitive as ever to the bizarre complexities of women's lives, but here honed to laser precision by rage.

Russ distinguishes herself in *The Female Man* as radical intelligencer and stylist. Her next novel, *We Who Are About to . . .*, is a study of an hallucinating woman dying alone on an emptied planet. For all its eerie fascination, the book remains rather private and untransformed. In *The Two of Them*, Russ returns to the earlier mode of the politically and socially informed adventure. The Trans-Temp heroine of this novel has escaped from the stultifying world of America in the 1950's to become an agent in the future. Sent to a sexist society that owes something to the Arabian Nights and something to the Islamic world of today, she rescues a girl from a harem, discovering in the process the depth of her commitment to the child: " . . . it'll take longer than one woman's lifetime," she realizes, to free herself. Russ's own commitment to the liberation of the young has borne fruit in two recent short stories ("My Boat," "How Dorothy Kept Away the Spring") and *Kittatinny,* a fantasy written expressly for young girls.

Extra (Ordinary) People, Russ's latest work, evinces both a growing technical mastery and an increasingly subtle feminist consciousness in a series of tales about diverse female liberators. A wry, formally inventive book, *Extra (Ordinary) People* is comprised of five narratives, the first four centered on the extramundane adventures of these wise women and the last a romp of a parody—a plot outline for a lesbian historical romance. As a casual linking device, a fragment of a tutorial introduces each tale to a naive future "schoolkid." Repeating this structure, an ironic teaching and learning motif recurs in the stories proper: several of the heroine-mentors are isolated in dangerously ignorant, sexist societies of the past and future, and their often comic, always poignant reports are relayed as knowing letters home. Indeed, all of the stories present lessons in "the usual confusion and mess" of human sexuality. In the initial tale, the Hugo award-winning novella "Souls," for instance, a telepathic genius of a 12th-century abbess challenges the brutal sexual code of Viking invaders. In "The Mystery of the Young Gentleman" and "What Did You Do in the Revolution, Grandma?," lesbians in male disguise traverse sexual boundaries, demystifying their own "outlaw" sexuality and defamiliarizing orthodox sexual behavior as they go. Rendering from the inside the extraordinary sentience of her heroines as they struggle to endure or elude the meshes of simplistic alternate realities, Russ creates a fiction both immediate and ironically layered—a work of and about science fiction. *Extra (Ordinary) People* should keep Russ at the experimental forefront of the field.

—Carol L. Snyder

RUSSELL, Eric Frank. British. Born in Camberley, Surrey, 6 January 1905; grew up in Egypt. Served in the King's Regiment, 1922-26, and in the Royal Air Force, 1941-45. Married Ellen Russell in 1930; one daughter. Worked as a telephonist, quantity surveyor, and draughtsman. Founding Member, British Interplantary Society. Recipient: Hugo Award, 1955. *Died 28 February 1978.*

SCIENCE-FICTION PUBLICATIONS

Novels

Sinister Barrier. Kingswood, Surrey, World's Work, 1943; Reading, Pennsylvania, Fantasy Press, 1948.
Dreadful Sanctuary. Reading, Pennsylvania, Fantasy Press, 1951; London, Museum Press, 1953; revised edition, New York, Lancer, 1963; London, New English Library, 1967.
Sentinels from Space. New York, Bouregy, 1953; London, Museum Press, 1954.
Three to Conquer. New York, Avalon, 1956; London, Dobson, 1957.
Wasp. New York, Avalon, 1957; London, Dobson, 1958.

The Space Willies. New York Ace, 1958; revised edition, as *Next of Kin,* London, Dobson, 1959.
The Great Explosion. London, Dobson, and New York, Torquil, 1962.
With a Strange Device. London, Dobson, 1964; as *The Mind Warpers,* New York, Lancer, 1965.

Short Stories

Deep Space. Reading, Pennsylvania, Fantasy Press, 1954; London, Eyre and Spottiswoode, 1956.
Men, Martians, and Machines. London, Dobson, and New York, Roy, 1956.
Six Worlds Yonder. New York, Ace, 1958.
Far Stars. London, Dobson, 1961.
Dark Tides. London, Dobson, 1962.
Somewhere a Voice. London, Dobson, 1965; New York, Ace, 1966.
Like Nothing on Earth. London, Dobson, 1975.
The Best of Eric Frank Russell, edited by Alan Dean Foster. New York, Ballantine, 1978.

OTHER PUBLICATIONS

Other

Great World Mysteries. London, Dobson, and New York, Roy, 1957.
The Rabble Rousers. Evanston, Illinois, Regency, 1963.

* * *

Eric Frank Russell will always be remembered as the author of *Sinister Barrier,* the story which helped John W. Campbell launch the magazine *Unknown* in 1939. Boosted as "the greatest imaginative novel in two decades," it established the British writer at the centre of the international science-fiction scene where he remained a popular figure for more than 30 years. It also drew attention to the abundance of plot material in the much-maligned works of Charles Fort, whose philosophy of scepticism Russell upheld consistently on behalf of the Fortean Society.

The novel relies on the notion that the Earth belongs to an alien race which feeds on the human misery it causes. With consummate skill, goaded by Campbell, Russell presented it as a mystery story in the tradition of the detective pulps he had studied in preparing to write for the American market. His taut, racy style had first attracted attention in *Astounding Stories* in 1937, when "The Saga of Pelican West" showed the influence of Stanley G. Weinbaum which affected many writers at that time. His contributions to the British *Tales of Wonder* and *Fantasy* also revealed a refreshing touch of humor coupled with a vigorous approach that was rare in science fiction. Typical examples were "Vampire from the Void," set in his Liverpool habitat, and "I, Spy!" concerning a Martian visitant that could simulate any form of terrestrial life. His amusing tales of Jay Score, the robot space-pilot, and his crewmen were collected in *Men, Martians, and Machines.* War service curtailed his writing, but "Metamorphosite," a story about a galactic empire, and *Dreadful Sanctuary* returned him to front-rank status. A fast-moving tale about a secret society which sabotaged the first attempts at space-travel, *Dreadful Sanctuary* seriously considers mankind's irrational ways while posing the question "How do you know you're sane?"

All through the 1950's Russell's lucid narratives delighted

readers. He broke new ground with "First Person Singular" by adapting the Adam and Eve legend to an interstellar setting; in other stories he revealed an unsuspected flair for emotional themes and moral issues such as racial intolerance. "And There Were None" postulates the effect of passive resistance on planetary invaders, which later became the theme of his satirical novel *The Great Explosion. Three to Conquer* reflected the interest in *psionics* fostered by Campbell. "Allamagoosa" (Hugo) is a clever piece of nonsense. *Sentinels from Space*, in which a highly evolved species keeps a watch over lesser beings, derives something from Olaf Stapledon, with whom Russell maintained friendly contact after introducing him to American science fiction. *Wasp* is an action-thriller relating the escapades of a secret agent preparing the way for a Terran invasion of the Sirian Empire. Simplest of all Russell's novels is *With a Strange Device*, almost a straight mystery story about a conspiracy to sabotage a new defensive weapon. Almost as intriguing as any of his fiction, too, is his collection *Great World Mysteries* in which he delved into some of the enigmas which have baffled scientists over the past century or more.

—Walter Gillings

SABE, Quien. See **BATES, Harry.**

SABERHAGEN, Fred(erick Thomas) American. Born in Chicago, Illinois, 18 May 1930. Educated at Wright Junior College, Chicago, 1956-57. Served in the United States Air Force, 1951-55. Married Joan Dorothy Spicci in 1968; one daughter and two sons. Electronics technician, Motorola Inc., Chicago, 1956-62; assistant editor, *Encyclopaedia Britannica,* 1967-73. Freelance writer, 1962-67, and since 1973. Agent: Virginia Kidd, Box 278, Milford, Pennsylvania 18337, U.S.A.

SCIENCE-FICTION PUBLICATIONS

Novels (series: Berserker; Chup; Swords)

The Golden People. New York, Ace, 1964.
The Water of Thought. New York, Ace, 1965; complete edition, Los Angeles, Pinnacle, 1981.
The Empire of the East (Chup). New York, Ace, 1979; London, Macdonald, 1984.
The Broken Lands. New York, Ace, 1968.
The Black Mountains. New York, Ace, 1971.
Changeling Earth. New York, DAW, 1973.
Brother Assassin. New York, Ballantine, 1969; as *Brother Berserker,* London, Macdonald, 1969.
Berserker's Planet. New York, DAW, and London, Futura, 1975.
Specimens. New York, Popular Library, 1976
The Veils of Azlaroc. New York, Ace, 1978.
Love Conquers All. New York, Ace, 1979.
Mask of the Sun. New York, Ace, 1979.
Berserker Man. New York, Ace, 1979.
A Matter of Taste. New York, Ace, 1980.
Coils, with Roger Zelazny. New York, Tor, 1980.

The Berserker Wars. New York, Tor, 1981.
Octagon. New York, Ace, 1981; London, Sinclair Browne, 1984.
The First [Second, Third] Book of Swords. New York, Tor, 3 vols., 1983-84.
A Century of Progress. New York, Tor, 1983.
The Beserker Throne. New York, Simon and Schuster, 1985.

Short Stories

Berserker. New York, Ballantine, 1967.
The Book of Saberhagen. New York, DAW, 1975.
The Ultimate Enemy (Berserker). New York, Ace, 1979.
Earth Descended (Beserker). New York, Tor, 1982.

OTHER PUBLICATIONS

Novels

The Dracula Tape. New York, Warner, 1975.
The Holmes-Dracula File. New York, Ace, 1978.
An Old Friend of the Family. New York, Ace, 1979.
Thorn. New York, Ace, 1980.
Dominion. New York, Tor, 1982.

Other

Editor, *A Spadeful of Spacetime.* New York, Ace, 1981.
Editor, with Jean Saberhagen, *Pawn to Infinity.* New York, Ace, 1982.

*   *   *

Fred Saberhagen's gift is to dramatize familiar ideas with compelling thoroughness. For more than two decades his principal theme has been Life's war with Death across the evolutionary gradient. It is the very substance of his best-known work, the berserker stories. The berserkers are self-programming, self-replicating robotic spacecraft set by their "long-dead masters to destroy anything that lived." Fighting these ineradicable foes unites all life forms iln the galaxy and, ironically, stimulates progress that might not have otherwise come about without the machines' challenge. The berserkers are computerized demons, high-tech symbols of utter Evil.

This "divergent" series is a novelty in that it is organized around a common enemy instead of a continuing hero. However, its premise, which originally grew out of games theory, is not unique. (See Theodore Sturgeon's 1948 novella "There Is No Defence.") But Saberhagen has made it so completely his own, "his murderous mechanisms are the recognized standard in the field." (For the author's own account, see "The Berserker Story" in *Algol*, Summer, 1977.)

Initially, style was Saberhagen's weakest point, a fault most obvious in his Orpheus tale, "Starsong." But he has gradually come to make a virtue of plainness and subordinates the accidents of his prose to the substance of his story. Works like *Berserker Man* let the inherent mythic power of his subject matter operate unhindered.

A second weakness is that plot schematics occasionally hobble his natural flair for narration. Rigid one-to-one correspondences spoil *Love Conquers All* making it harshly polemical instead of effectively thematic. Arbitrariness also spoils the Swords trilogy which was created to serve as a computer game module—and reads like it.

On the positive side, Saberhagen's rendering technique is

usually strong and sure. For example, notice how economically he establishes the hideousness of the demons and their mortal minions in his excellent science fantasy trilogy *The Empire of the East*. This lively variation on the familiar "world where magic works" premise translates scientific laws into spells and back again, yielding such curiosities as a technologist djinn and valkyrie robots. Unlike the current wave of technophobic fantasies, science is the liberating force here, freeing Earth from "the Old Dark Mystery."

A sound scientific imagination is the cornerstone of Saberhagen's art. He can see a story in a Foucault pendulum ("Brother Berserker"), a black hole (*The Veils of Azarloc*), or even a squash seed ("Pressure"). He gives a biochemical basis to Paleolithic ritual in *The Water of Thought*.

But as the berserker stories demonstrate, he also draws inspiration from literature ("The Masque of the Red Shift"), the arts ("The Smile"), history ("Wings Out of Shadow"), and myth ("Some Events in the Templar Radiant"). He is especially deft at combining the factual and legendary aspects of a subject and then infusing the result with theological significance. "Stone Place" recreates Don John of Austria, Philip II of Spain, and the battle of Lepanto in a way G. K. Chesterton himself would have applauded. St. Francis of Assisi, Galileo, and the mystical theories of Pierre Teilhard de Chardin are brought together to beautiful effect in "Brother Berserker." (The mythic resonances of his work are explored in Sandra Miesel's afterwords to *Berserker Man* and *The First Book of Swords*.)

Furthermore, Saberhagen has edited anthologies about two of his personal enthusiasms, chess (*Pawn to Infinity*) and archeology (*A Spadeful of Spacetime*). His interests in gaming and history unite in alternate history tales such as *Mask of the Sun* and *A Century of Progress*.

Perhaps Saberhagen's greatest strength is the sheer conviction he brings to his work. Because he believes in his stories, he convinces his readers to do the same. His best characterizations are precisely those which ought to have been the most difficult: Brother Jovann, his St. Francis figure; Johann Karlsen, his Don John; and Draffut the Beast-Lord, a godlike dog. *Berserker Man's* child-hero Michel succeeds both as child and hero while at the same time carrying a heavy load of metaphysics on his shoulders.

Saberhagen can also make highly unpromising characters sympathetic: the second volume of *The Empire of the East* is told from the viewpoint of the first volume's villain. His excellent Dracula pastiches present the Count as entrancingly alien rather than monstrous and make him a force for rough justice. Placing this epitome of gothic horror in solidly realistic settings such as Renaissance Italy, Victorian London, and present-day Chicago intensifies his impact.

Saberhagen is unglamorous, ironic, and never sentimental. ("No world is safe for those who love," says the hero of "Young Girl at an Open Half-Door"). The unblinking eye he turns on evil records its horror with the utmost clarity. It allows no ambiguity: entities such as the berserkers and the demons are as totally depraved as any beings can be. They are to be fought without compromise or quarter.

Saberhagen's stated goal is "to impose different coordinates on the human condition," but the functions he plots are traditional Western Christian ones. Whatever the weaponry, his battles are wonder-wars between cosmic principles. Whatever the odds, he proclaims that Life will wear the final victor's crown.

—Sandra Miesel

ST. CLAIR, Margaret (née Neeley). American. Born in Hutchinson, Kansas, 17 February 1911. Educated at the University of California, Berkeley, M. A. 1933 (Phi Beta Kappa). Married Eric St. Clair in 1932. Horticulturist, St. Clair Rare Bulb Gardens, El Sobrante, California, 1938-41. Since 1945, full-time writer. Agent: Julie Fallowfield, McIntosh and Otis, 475 Fifth Avenue, New York, New York 10017. Address: Star Route, Manchester, California 95459, U.S.A.

SCIENCE-FICTION PUBLICATIONS

Novels

Agent of the Unknown. New York, Ace, 1956.
The Green Queen. New York, Ace, 1956.
The Games of Neith. New York, Ace, 1960.
Sign of the Labrys. New York, Bantam, and London, Corgi, 1963.
Message from the Eocene. New York, Ace, 1964.
The Dolphins of Altair. New York, Dell, 1967.
The Shadow People. New York, Dell, 1969.
The Dancers of Noyo. New York, Ace, 1973.

Short Stories

Three Worlds of Futurity. New York, Ace, 1964.
Change the Sky and Other Stories. New York, Ace, 1974.

Uncollected Short Stories

"The Sorrows of Witches," in *Amazons!* edited by Jessica Amanda Salmonson. New York, DAW, 1979.
"Wryneck, Draw Me," in *Chrysalis 8*, edited by Roy Torgeson. New York, Doubleday, 1980.
"The Hashed Brown Buggy," in *Chrysalis 9*, edited by Roy Torgeson. New York, Doubleday, 1981.

*

Margaret St. Clair comments:

It would take me days to write adequately about my work. So I shall only say that I think I am better at short fiction than at novels—the short story is more philosophical—and that I like my amusing stories better than the frightening ones, and prefer both classes to what I call "uplift."

I am not a natural writer. Writing is painful and difficult for me.

*   *   *

Margaret St. Clair is an example of a woman writer who did not have to disguise her sex in order to be succesful as a writer in a male-dominated field. She was able to write in a natural "female voice" at a time when some women writers of science fiction were outdoing the men in tough-flavored style, and, particularly in her fantasy short stories (generally written as by Idris Seabright), to introduce some sensitive characerization, including portrayals of housewives, single mothers, and young children, into a field which was highly technologically orientated. In common with others writing in the 1950's, St. Clair's fiction was oriented toward adventurous episodes, but she had a penchant for tackling controversial themes and for using gadgetry and environments symbolically.

Most of St. Clair's short fiction was published during the

1950's. Some of her astonishing output of approximately 130 stories may be found in *Three Worlds of Futurity* and *Change the Sky and Other Stories* ; both are representative of her work. Other individual stories are found in anthologies: "Short in the Chest" (in Greenberg and Olander's *Science Fiction of the 50's*, 1979), featuring Marine Major Sonya Briggs and a "philosophical robot" psychologist called a "huxley," is remarkable for its portrayal of women and its grappling with questions of sexuality. "New Ritual" (in Boucher's *The Best from Fantasy and Science Fiction*, 1954), also featuring a female protagonist, gives a futuristic twist to the plight of the dissatisfied housewife as a deep freeze turns everything from apricots to an inattentive husband into more desirable items. "Child of Void" (in Conklin's *Invaders of Earth*, 1952) shows a lonely boy grappling with the unknown in the form of a luminous egg which presents children with alluring visions of those things they most desire.

St. Clair's novels, not as consistently well-crafted as her shorter work, are usually adventures and may be relied upon to convey a message. *Agent of the Unknown* is set on the synthetic pleasure plantoid Fyon. An appealing non-comformist with a drinking problem finds purpose in life when he rescues from the edge of the sea a small but awe-inspiring "Weeping Doll," the creation of the master craftsman Vulcan. The protagonist muses "Sometimes I think everything in our world is synthetic, even happiness." While "Vulcan's Weeping Doll" passively changes in one world, *The Green Queen* and *The Games of Neith* both feature heroines as active characters who are chosen to inspire or lead their respective societies toward change. Histrionic talents, intelligence, and physical beauty are attributes possessed by the Green Queen, who lives in a post-holocaust society ripe for revolution, "a place where ten percent of the population monopolized eighty percent of the dwelling space and fifty percent of the unpolluted food, and where everybody, Uppers and Lowers alike, was always terribly afraid of damage from the omnipresent radioactive elements. . . ." In *The Games of Neith* Anassa, Priestess to the Goddess of Neith, possesses similar traits, and guides her seafaring society, which is threatening to return to the worship of primitave gods, to a new future. Anassa's relationship with Ehr'li Wan, a physics professor, is an excellent early example of a man and a woman in science fiction working in an equal part against evil forces.

The Shadow People is a striking work. Although the quality of the prose is uneven and the thrust of the narrative is excessively cheerless, an underworld of zombie-like people is memorably portrayed as scuttling through a rat-and-fungus-infested underworld in a hallucinatory, hopeless future. *Sign of the Labrys* portrays another dark underworld, this time inhabited by the survivors of a devastating plague who cower in damp caverns hacked out of rock until the hero, Sam Sewell, brings them awareness of an open, habitable world above ground. *Message from the Eocene* introduces Tharg, an ancient being of alien origin, who desperately attempts to overcome his condition of existing (for century upon century) as a disembodied sentient force so that he may convey a message to mankind. He eventually makes contact with a modern woman whose gift of mental sensitivity to unusual phenomena is sensitively portrayed.

St. Clair's best novel, *The Dolphins of Altair*, is a a moving work critical of man's disregard for the ecosystems of Earth. Members of a well-drawn, intelligent dolphin society conspire with a few enlightened humans to preserve the world for an unusual new future. *The Dancers of Noyo*, like *Agent of The Unknown*, relies upon a male protagonist to hold together a tale of the future. A quest for personal identity is set against a world dominated by powerful androids.

St. Clair's best work is tightly written shorter fiction which introduced unusual protagonists to the pages of science-fiction magazines. While some of her longer works suffer from over-ambitious exploration of diverse themes, the best of her novels are those most concerned with an individual's experience with the extraordinary, or a group's commitment to a visionary future.

—Rosemary Herbert

ST. JOHN, Philip. See **del REY, Lester.**

ST. PAUL, Sterner. See **MEEK, S. P.**

SALLIS, James. American. Born in Helena, Arkansas, 21 December 1944. Attended Tulane University, New Orleans, 1962-64. Married Jane Rose in 1964; one son. Worked as a college instructor and publisher's reader; Editor, *New Worlds*, London, 1969-70; now a full-time writer. Address: c/o William Morrow Inc., 105 Madison Avenue, New York, New York 10016, U.S.A.

SCIENCE-FICTION PUBLICATIONS

Short Stories

A Few Last Words. London, Hart Davis, 1969; New York, Macmillan, 1970.

Uncollected Short Stories

"This One," in *If* (New York), January 1970.
"Front and Centaur," in *New Worlds* (London), March 1970.
"Binaries" and "Only the Words Are Different," in *Orbit 9*, edited by Damon Knight. New York, Putnam, 1971.
"Mensuration," in *Quark 2*, edited by Samuel R. Delany and Marilyn Hacker. New York, Paperback Library, 1971.
"Field," in *Quark 3*, edited by Samuel R. Delaney and Marilyn Hacker. New York, Paperback Library, 1971.
"The Fly at Ciron," in *Fantasy and Science Fiction* (New York), December 1971.
"At the Fitting Shop" and "53rd American Dream," in *Again, Dangerous Visions*, edited by Harlan Ellison. New York, Doubleday, 1972; London, Millington, 1976.
"Doucement, S'Il Vous Plait," in *Orbit 11*, edited by Damon Knight. New York, Putnam, 1973.
"Echo," in *The Berserkers*, edited by Roger Elwood. New York, Simon and Schuster, 1973.
"Delta Flight 281" and "The First Few Kinds of Truth," in *Alternities*, edited by David Gerrold. New York, Dell, 1974.
"My Friend Zarathustra," in *Orbit 13*, edited by Damon Knight. New York, Putnam, 1974.
"The Invasion of Dallas," in *Lone Star Universe*, edited by

George W. Proctor and Steven Utley. Austin, Texas, Heidelberg, 1976.

"Miranda-Escobedo," in *Fantasy and Science Fiction* (New York), July 1976.

"One Road to Damascus," in *2076: The American Tricentennial*, edited by Edward Bryant. New York, Pyramid, 1977.

"La Fin d'une Monde (Intérieure)," in *Fantastic* (New York), June 1977.

"Jackson," in *Fantastic* (New York), December 1977.

"Changes," in *Fantastic* (New York), April 1978.

"Exigency and Martin Heidegger," in *Amazing* (New York), November 1978.

"They Will Not Hush," with David Lunde, in *Whispers 2*, edited by Stuart David Schiff. New York, Doubleday, 1979.

"Need," in *Isaac Asimov's Science Fiction Magazine* (New York), January 1985.

OTHER PUBLICATIONS

Other

Down Home: Country-Western. New York, Macmillan, 1971.

"The Writer as Teacher," in *Clarion 2*, edited by Robin Scott Wilson. New York, New American Library, 1972.

The Guitar Players: One Instrument and Its Masters in American Music. New York, Morrow, 1982.

Editor, *The War Book*. London, Hart Davis, 1969; New York, Dell, 1971.

Editor, *The Shores Beneath*. New York, Avon, 1970.

Editor, *Jazz Guitars: An Anthology*. New York, Morrow, 1984.

*   *   *

James Sallis's extraordinary fiction is distinguished by its honesty and meticulous artistry. With his highly imagistic stories, he has regularly displayed a finely honed mastery of sophisticated literary techniques and sharply etched psychological insights. Often the stories are clearly autobiographical, presenting painful indications of their author's personal difficulties, even his torments. They are not always easy to read, and it is sometimes hard to discern their intent or meaning, but they affect readers powerfully, at least those readers who demand more than thrill-seeking and fantastic adventures from the fiction they read. (It always sounds a bit pompous to score the escapist reader in such terms, but writers like Sallis, who employ quite subtle fictional devices, *do* demand more from their readers. In "My Friend Zarathustra" Sallis writes: "Yes— I mean what I say, and you must listen; must hear what's not said if you're to understand properly what is said.")

Many of his stories are moving portrayals of troubled or dazed individuals who are dissociated from their environments. In nearly every Sallis story the main character is helpless, or at least quite passive. Things are dreadfully confused in his private life or are being disrupted in the outside world. Sometimes nothing much is happening, but even then the character does not cope well. At the rare times when the character is able to act decisively, the action turns out to be futile or grotesque. (The disposal of the child in the brilliantly executed "Jim and Mary G." is a harrowing example of such futility and ugliness.) Usually the character is still helpless at the end of the story. In many stories, the protagonists are last seen merely waiting or going off into darkness or standing still as the world begins to disintegrate, literally or physically, around them. However Sallis dramatizes it, the main impression the reader receives

from most of the stories is of humankind trapped in environments upon which they can have no effect, and for which they no longer have any effective responses or reactions. In "Faces, Hands: The Kettle of Stars" a courier is halted from his message-carrying mission and stranded in an intergalactic waiting room, where he contemplates art in the form of an also-waiting alien singer whose destiny is repulsive servitude on another planet, an injustice the courier perceives but cannot affect. The protagonist of "The History Makers" occupies himself with letters or music or sitting at a window while whole time-accelerated civilizations grow, decline, and fall nearby. The only movement he makes is to move away from a city's encroaching border. Nevertheless, he is able to speculate on the exigencies of time, as manifested in the slow progress of a beetle across sand or in a review of his own life or in the odd inverted timescale of the cities. In "A Few Last Words" a man attempts to decide what to do as a doomed city more or less empties before his eyes.

In such stories the sense of dissociation is pronounced both in the relationship of character to setting and in the character's own "inner space," the phrase emphasized by interpreters of the new wave of science fiction as its primary subject matter. Sallis's characters, even at their most articulate, are often in danger of breaking up themselves in just about the same way the setting is crumbling around them. In one of his most effective and painful stories, "Binaries," the narrator-writer (who perceives his immediate environment as being regularly broken up and moved away) is in a state of dissociation with himself as a person and as a writer:

> Someone has written a collection of short stories and published them under my name; they have even put my photograph on the back cover. I received a copy in the morning post. Anonymous, no return address, postmarked Grnd Cntrl Stn. The stories reveal my deepest secrets. Only one person could have written them. Or had reason to. My attorney is investigating the possibility of a lawsuit against the publisher but, as the work was copyrighted in my own name, there seems little we can do. The publisher expressed to my attorney his desire to meet the author, his admiration for the book.

The passage's poignancy, its precise delineation of the character's troubled emotions, and—incidentally—its wrenching irony, are all hallmarks of the fiction of James Sallis.

Sallis also has an appealing knack for humorous, especially surrealistic, writing, which he uses in stories like "Kazoo," "The Creation of Bennie Good," and "Miranda-Escobedo." It is worth noting, however, that, even in these works, with their clever improvisations, sly allusions, and superb word-play, the sense of psychological and emotional dissociation generally remains, as dazed or momentarily baffled characters and even ghost-cops are disoriented by their absurd environments.

Sallis started publishing science fiction in the 1960's, a time when the field was being rattled by a number of literary experimenters who came to be dubbed, for better or for worse, the "new wave" of science fiction. He served some time as an editor of the British magazine *New Worlds*, the SF publication that became most associated with the new wave because it dared to publish the works of adventuresome writers during a period when many other SF markets were resisting anything that did not correspond with accepted approaches to the genre. Now that the new furore has somewhat subsided, upheld in print only by a few still petulant writers, it is clear that the contributions of the new wavers are legitimate literary extensions of established science-fiction traditions, and that Sallis's stories are among the best writings to emerge from the phenomenon. In recent years James Sallis, never prolific, has published few stories, but the ones that have been published exhibit the same care for literary details and intellectual concerns as the earlier stories. One recent story, "Changes," ranks with the best of his fiction.

—Robert Thurston

SARBAN. Pseudonym for John W. Wall. British.

SCIENCE-FICTION PUBLICATIONS

Novel

The Sound of His Horn. London, Davies, 1952; New York, Ballantine, 1960.

Short Stories

Ringstones and Other Curious Tales. London, Davies, and New York, Coward McCann, 1951.
The Doll Maker and Other Tales of the Uncanny. London, Davies, 1953; *The Doll Maker* published separately, New York, Ballantine, 1960.

*   *   *

The only true science-fiction novel to appear under the Sarban byline was *The Sound of His Horn*, a novel that evokes a mood of gloom and horror as well as anything that has ever been written. Kingsley Amis pointed out that it is one of the few novels ever to suggest a rural rather than urban dystopia, a future after Germany has won World War II and the other races of the world are viewed as little better than lower animals. Alan Querdilion wanders into an electrified fence while escaping from a German POW camp and finds himself somehow projected into a world where the Germans have already been victorious. After a brief period where he is the guest of a German landholder, he is set loose as prey for his host's periodic hunts.

Two other short novels appeared, both of which have been published as horror novels though the subject matter is such that they could as well be considered fantasies. In *The Doll Maker* a young girl is compelled to become a tutor at mysterious Brackenbine Hall, and soon falls under the influence of Niall Sterne, a peculiar reclusive man who roams the forests and exists only, it seems, for his collection of extremely lifelike dolls. In due course, the heroine learns of Sterne's connection with several past deaths, and comes to believe that he can transfer human souls into the dolls he creates. *The Doll Maker* also brilliantly creates a mood of despair and awakening horror. Sarban's skill at drawing the reader into his book is probably at its best, however, in *Ringstones*. A young woman is employed to tutor two young children at a remote estate, but soon becomes enmeshed in magic and the struggle to maintain her own personality and view of reality when faced with a form of existence that she had formerly considered only a dream. *Ringstones* is a haunting novel that is far more worthwhile than the hundreds of modern gothics which it in many ways resembles.

Although they are extremely hard to locate, Sarban also created several excellent shorter pieces. The most noteworthy of these are probably "Calmahain" and "Capra." In the former, two young children allow their fantasy world to become so real that it overflows into the real world and adults begin to experience elements of the fantasy. In the latter, a vicious lover's triangle at a costume party has unexpected results when the real God Pan makes an entry.

The most striking element in Sarban's fiction is obviously the evocation of a weird atmosphere, and the quiet construction of a world where things aren't quite as safe and logical as the characters have always believed. But the quality of the prose should not be overlooked either. Though couched in very formal style, Sarban's words flow and the current draws the reader along with it. There is never any hint that this is an amateur writing fiction as a hobby; the cool competent hand of the professional is obvious. Despite his small body of work, Sarban remains a unique and significant writer: the talent he displayed at creating a mood of slow despair has never been equalled.

—Don D'Ammassa

SARGENT, Pamela. American. Born in Ithaca, New York, 20 March 1948. Educated at the State University of New York, Binghamton, B. A. in philosophy 1968, M. A. 1970. Model and sales clerk, 1965-66; factory worker, Endicott Coil Company, 1966; sales clerk, Towne Distributors, 1966; typist, Harpur College, Binghamton, New York, 1966-67; office worker, Webster Paper Company, Albany, New York, 1969; teaching assistant in philosophy, State University of New York, Binghamton, 1969-71. Since 1971, free-lance writer and editor. Agent: Joseph Elder Agency, 150 West 87th Street, New York, New York 10024. Address: Box 486, Johnson City, New York 13790, U.S.A.

SCIENCE-FICTION PUBLICATIONS

Novels (series: Earthminds)

Cloned Lives. New York, Fawcett, 1976.
The Sudden Star. New York, Fawcett, 1979; as *The White Death*, London, Futura, 1980.
Watchstar (Earthminds). New York, Pocket Books, 1980.
The Golden Space. New York, Simon and Schuster, 1982.
The Alien Upstairs. New York, Doubleday, 1983.
Earthseed (for children). New York, Harper, 1983; London, Collins, 1984.
Eye of the Comet (for children; Earthminds). New York, Harper, 1984.
Homesmind (for children; Earthminds). New York, Harper, 1984.
Venus of Dreams. New York, Bantam, 1986.

Short Stories

Starshadows. New York, Ace, 1977.

Uncollected Short Stories

"Landed Minority," in *Fantasy and Science Fiction* (New York), September 1970.

"Matthew," in *Ten Tomorrows*, edited by Roger Elwood. New York, Fawcett, 1973.

"Darkness of Day," with George Zebrowski, in *Continuum 3*, edited by Roger Elwood. New York, Berkley, 1974.

"A Friend from the Stars" (for children), in *The Missing World and Other Stories*, edited by Roger Elwood. Minneapolis, Lerner, 1974.

"The Invisible Girl" (for children), in *The Killer Plants and Other Stories*, edited by Roger Elwood. Minneapolis, Lerner, 1974.

"Aunt Elvira's Zoo" (for children), in *Night of the Sphinx and Other Stories*, edited by Roger Elwood. Minneapolis, Lerner, 1974.

"Father," in *Amazing* (New York), February 1974.

"A Sense of Difference," in *And Walk Now Gently Through the Fire*, edited by Roger Elwood. Philadelphia, Chilton, 1975.

"Weapons," with George Zebrowski, in *Dystopian Visions*, edited by Roger Elwood. Englewood Cliffs, New Jersey, Prentice Hall, 1975.

"Exile," in *Fantasy and Science Fiction* (New York), December 1975.

"The Novella Race," in *Orbit 20*, edited by Damon Knight. New York, Harper, 1978.

"The Renewal," in *Immortal*, edited by Jack Dann. New York, Harper, 1978.

"The Summer's Dust," in *Fantasy and Science Fiction* (New York), July 1981.

"Out of Place," in *Twilight Zone* (New York), October 1981.

"The Broken Hoop," in *Twilight Zone* (New York), June 1982.

"The Shrine," in *Twilight Zone* (New York), December 1982.

"The Falling," with George Zebrowski, in *Isaac Asimov's Science Fiction Magazine* (New York), March 1983.

"Heavenly Flowers," in *Isaac Asimov's Space of Her Own*, edited by Shawna McCarthy. New York, Davis, 1983.

"The Old Darkness," in *Fantasy and Science Fiction* (New York), July 1983.

"Shrinker," in *Isaac Asimov's Science Fiction Magazine* (New York), November 1983.

"Fears," in *Light Years and Dark*, edited by Michael Bishop. New York, Berkley, 1984.

"Originals," in *Universe 15*, edited by Terry Carr. New York, Doubleday, 1985.

OTHER PUBLICATIONS

Other

"The Promise of Space: Transformations of a Dream," in *GCITRiverside Quarterly* (Regina, Saskatchewan), February 1972.

"Women in Science Fiction," in *Futures* (New York), October 1975.

Afterword to *The Fifth Head of Cerberus*, by Gene Wolfe. New York, Ace, 1976.

"On the Ouster of Stanislaw Lem from the SFWA: How It Happened," with George Zebrowski, in *Science-Fiction Studies* (Terre Haute, Indiana), July 1977.

"Aliens," with James E. Gunn, in *Contemporary Mythology*, edited by Patricia Warrick, Martin H. Greenberg, and Joseph D. Olander. New York, Harper, 1978.

"VIEWPOINT: In the Tradition of: An Immodest Proposal," in *Isaac Asimov's Science Fiction Magazine* (New York), May 1983.

Editor, *Women of Wonder: Science-Fiction Stories by Women about Women*. New York, Random House, 1975; London, Penguin, 1978.

Editor, *More Women of Wonder: Science-Fiction Novelettes by Women about Women*. New York, Random House, 1976; London, Penguin, 1979.

Editor, *Bio-Futures: Science Fiction Stories about Biological Metamorphosis*. New York, Random House, 1976.

Editor, *The New Women of Wonder: Science-Fiction Novelettes by Women about Women*. New York, Random House, 1978.

*

Manuscript Collection: David Paskow Science Fiction Collection, Temple University, Philadelphia.

* * *

A deft writer and editor, Pamela Sargent did not aspire to become a full-time writer. Moreover, once she turned to writing, she did not view herself as a *science-fiction* writer, even though that was what she wrote (and continues to write for the most part). For Sargent, who had only begun reading science fiction three years earlier, science fiction posed a special attraction. Indeed, she viewed science-fictional devices and literary inventions as useful metaphors for embellishing a story, and most of her earliest stories (i. e., "Landed Minority," "Oasis," "Gather Blue Rose," and "Julio 204" were about the near future and close to the present day.

Sargent soon concluded that science fictional ideas could be of interest for themselves, and endeavored to make her work both realistic and plausible. For the most part, this is her goal today. Sargent eschews prediction; she *does*, however, seek plausibility. The imaginary settings of her stories are typified by an underlying reality and possess a solid grounding in what we know of science (and people) today. In that sense, Sargent resembles several of the "hard" science-fiction writers who ground their work solidly in science, but, unlike many such writers, she also emphasizes characterization.

This is best illustrated by her first novel, *Cloned Lives*. At the time, she found little of what had been written about clones and the possibility of cloning human beings plausible. She asked herself several questions: Why did some writers think clones might have a telepathic connection? Would clones, in fact, be exceptionally close because of their identical genes, or might they become estranged, as some identical twins do? Why would anyone want to clone an individual in the first place? Her objective was to write a realistic story about clones who were believable people and whose problems, however heightened or altered by the fact that they were cloned, would mirror the struggle for identity that we all share. She also wished to underscore several of the real issues such as an attempt at biological engineering might present, rather than to concoct a myriad of bizarre adventures with strange cloned characters. *Cloned Lives* not only raised these issues, but did so with sensitivity and grace, artfulness and illumination. Ursula K. Le Guin called it "solidly realistic, humane, and well-proportioned," while *Bestsellers* termed it "an exceptional first novel."

In Sargent's first anthology, *Women of Wonder*, and the two which followed (*More Women of Wonder* and *The New Women of Wonder*), Sargent felt a special obligation to the scores of women writers who had made pioneering contributions to the science fiction field. She was buoyed when observing what other writers had done (and also observing some of the pitfalls some writers fell into when writing about female characters) to continue to develop well-rounded female characters in her own stories. Indeed, all of her works boast strong female characters in them, though, until recently (in "Fears" and in a novel that she is presently writing), she has not brought explicitly feminist concerns to the forefront. Each of the three anthologies include approximately ten science-fiction stories by women about women, as well as a cogently written introduction (and notes) by the editor. These essays, written in the classic scholarly manner, demonstrate Sargent's keen knowledge of the subject and her skillful research capabilities.

As for her goals, Sargent reflects: "I would like my work to be entertaining, believable (with some psychological resonance and truth about the human experience), emotionally involving, and maybe even, on occasion, intellectually stimulating." These goals have been amply realized in her work. For example, her anthology *Bio-Futures* features ten stories which explore biological metamorphosis, and which pose the question: Will we use these technological advances to transcend our biological destinies, or will we refuse to meddle with nature and reject them altogether? *Bio-Futures* represents an important first step in answering this weighty and often-debated question.

Sargent is a master of the short story, and *Star-shadows* includes some of her most well-crafted tales, among them "Shadows," "The Other Perceiver," and "Oasis." In addition to this work, Sargent has written several noteworthy novels, including *The Sudden Star* and *Watchstar*. The former, which raises a frightening vision of the future, suggests that the future rests not with mankind as we know it, but with a new mutant race. In the latter, Sargent chronicles the life of Daiya, a young girl from a telepathic society, who meets a boy whose people lack such mental powers. This novel, like Sargent's other works, combines the literary inventions of science fiction with the insights of psychology.

Sargent's characters are strikingly real people, characters who involve the reader, make the reader care what happens to them. As Sargent observes: 'Almost always, I have the experience of a character suddenly appearing in my mind, and have almost no notion of what this person's story is, then discovering the story by writing it; the characters always seem like real people to me, and often resist any attempt on my part to manipulate them for the sake of plot." Perhaps this is why *Publishers Weekly* has called Sargent "a sensitive writer of characterization rather than of cosmic gimmickry," and Michael Bishop has written, "Sargent, without fanfare and hoopla, has become a strikingly able and unusual story teller .... Her real forte is characterization, an ability to dissect and lay open the fears, passions, and yearnings of the intensely human people who invariably inhabit her books."

Lately, Sargent has written novels specifically for younger (teenage) readers: *Earthseed, Eye of the Comet,* and *Homesmind.* Artfully conceived, centrally developed, and well-plotted, these works constitute a natural progression of her literary talents. For example, part of *Cloned Lives* dealt with her characters, the Swensons, when they were young. *The Sudden Star* and *Watchstar* both include young characters, as does *The Golden Space,* which deals specifically with children and how they might act in a world of immortals, where only children would undergo growth and change. For Sargent, youthful experiences somehow seem more vivid, passionate, and exciting than what happens to many people later in life, when the decisions they made while young have overtaken them and set their lives along a certain path.

Modest by nature, Sargent seeks to cast a shadow on the field. Asked to assess her contribution, she opines: "I am reminded of the English writer, Jean Rhys, who said, 'All of writing is a huge lake. There are great rivers that feed the lake, like Tolstoy and Dostoevsky. And there are trickles, like Jean Rhys. All that matters is feeding the lake.' " Many writers strive to be remembered. Sargent is not particularly interested in that. She would much prefer to have some of her books or stories remembered, whether or not anyone recalled who wrote them. Sargent simply wishes to feed the lake.

—Jeffrey M. Elliot

SAWTRELLE, William Carter. See **PHILLIPS, Rog.**

SAXON, Richard. Pseudonym for Joseph Lawrence Morrissey; also writes as Henry Richards. American. Born in 1905.

SCIENCE-FICTION PUBLICATIONS

Novels

City of the Hidden Eyes (as J. L. Morrissey). London, Consul 1964.
Cosmic Crusade. London, Consul 1964; New York, Arcadia House, 1966.
Future for Sale. London, Consul 1964; New York, Arcadia House, 1965.
The Hour of the Phoenix. London, Consul 1964; as Henry Richards, New York, Arcadia House, 1965.
The Stars Came Down. London, Consul 1964; New York, Arcadia House, 1967.

*   *   *

Richard Saxon's career was begun and ended in a single year. Although none of his novels was exceptional enough to attract any particular interest, they are not as unprepossessing as their poor success might indicate.

For the most part, Saxon eschewed melodrama in a period when action and suspense were the main attractions for most genre devotees. The protagonists of *Future for Sale* invent a time machine with which they travel to both the past and the future, but with considerable less liveliness than in, for example, Wells's *The Time Machine.* In the past, one character relives a poignant moment in his own life; in the future, he discovers that a scientific dictatorship has been created which provides mankind with all of its material wants but which exacts in payment an irresistible drive for conformity. Far from leading a revolt, the hero returns to our own time, where a quarreling mob destroys the time machine utterly.

The Stars Came Down is also more reflective than active. Humanity's first trip to the stars is over, and the returnees discover that a new civilization has evolved on Earth during the relative five millennia that have passed since their departure. For the most part, the latter half of the novel consists of a quiet discourse on the nature of Utopian society.

The Hour of the Phoenix is Saxon's most lively novel. The drive into space is cut short as a new astronomical object appears, destined to destroy our world in the near future. The usual occurs, mobs riot, order breaks down into chaos, and through it all a small group attempts to make plans to allow humanity to carry on elsewhere in space. The waning chapters are a bit sentimental, and this is in balance no more than a very lightweight imitation of Wylie and Balmer's *When Worlds Collide*.

The Cosmic Crusade has another conventional plot, this time weighted with excessive ruminative discourses. An underground society slowly awakens to the reality of its existence and prepares to emerge onto the surface of its world. Once more, we are warned against the decay that inevitably accompanies conformity to the exclusion of individuality.

On balance, Saxon is a slightly above average writer whose talents might have developed had he remained active. The small body of essentially minor work which he produced are reasonable entertainments, but neither original enough or well-written enough to survive through the years.

—Don D'Ammassa

* * *

SAXTON, Josephine (née Howard). British. Born in Halifax, Yorkshire, 11 June 1935. Educated at Clare Hall County Secondary School, Halifax. Married 1) Geoffrey Banks in 1958, one son; 2) Colin Saxton in 1962 (divorced, 1983), one son and one daughter. Agent: Virginia Kidd, Box 278, Milford, Pennsylvania 18337, U. S. A. ; or, Maxine Jakubowski, 95 Finchley Lane, London N. W. 4. Address: 4 Albany Terrace, Flat 3, Leamington Spa, Warwickshire, CV32 5LP, England.

SCIENCE-FICTION PUBLICATIONS

Novels

The Hieros Gamos of Sam and An Smith. New York, Doubleday, 1969.
Vector for Seven; or, The Weltanshauung of Mrs. Amelia Mortimer and Friends. New York, Doubleday, 1971.
Group Feast. New York, Doubleday, 1971.
The Travails of Jane Saint. London, Virgin, 1981.

Uncollected Short Stories

"Nothing Much to Relate," in *Fantasy and Science Fiction* (New York), November 1967.
"Ne Deja Vu Pas," in *England Swings SF*, edited by Judith Merril. New York, Doubleday, 1968; as *The Space-Time Journal*, London, Panther, 1972.
"Light on Cader," in *Fantasy and Science Fiction* (New York), January 1968.
"The Consciousness Machine," in *Fantasy and Science Fiction* (New York), June 1968.
"Dormant Soul," in *Fantasy and Science Fiction* (New York), February 1969.
"The Triumphant Head," in *Alchemy and Academe*, edited by Anne McCaffrey. New York, Doubleday, 1970.
"Heads Africa, Tails America," in *Orbit 9*, edited by Damon Knight. New York, Putnam, 1971.
"Nature Boy," in *Quark 3*, edited by Samuel R. Delany and Marilyn Hacker. New York, Paperback Library, 1971.
"The Power of Time," in *New Dimensions 1*, edited by Robert

Silverberg. New York, Doubleday, 1971.
"The Wall," in *Best SF Stories from New Worlds 7*, edited by Michael Moorcock. London, Panther, 1971.
"Living Wild," in *Fantasy and Science Fiction* (New York), October 1971.
"Black Sabbatical," in *Fantasy and Science Fiction* (New York), December 1971.
"Elouise and the Doctors of the Planet Pergamon," in *Again, Dangerous Visions*, edited by Harlan Ellison. New York, Doubleday, 1972; London, Millington, 1976.
"In Memoriam, Jeannie," in *Stopwatch*, edited by George Hay. Nashville, Nelson, and London, New English Library, 1974.
"Lyserge of Anaglyptang," in *Science Fiction Monthly* (London), July 1975.
"Woe, Blight, and in Heaven, Laughs," in *Pulsar 1*, edited by George Hay. London, Penguin, 1978.
"Alien Sensation," in *Cassandra Rising*, edited by Alice Laurance. New York, Doubleday, 1978.
"The Snake Who Had Read Chomsky," in *Universe 11*, edited by Terry Carr. New York, Doubleday, 1981.
"To Market, To Market," in *Woman Space*, edited by Claudia Laperti. Lebanon, New Hampshire, New Victoria, 1981.
"No Coward Soul," in *Interzone* (Leeds), Autumn 1982.

*

Josephine Saxton comments:
I Have been called many kinds of writer: science-fiction editors say I am mainstream, mainstream editors say I am science fantasy, for example. I have written things with violent death in them, does this make me a writer of horror, detective, sadism, metaphysics? I refuse to be labelled, because metaphysical content embraces every possible experience and mode of existence which might be taken from real life, imaginary life. One theme seems to be emerging over the years which I was not aware of until I recently collected and revised my short stories, and that is a strong feminist theme. This does not make me a woman's writer, so forget it. I write about things which happen to people, for people to read; who needs more? I can say with authority that it takes just as much imagination to write well about something you do every day as it does to write about a trip to Aldebaran 62. People who only write and/or read SF are very narrow people and I don't wish to be identified with them, any more than if I set a story in the West of America I would want to be called a cowboy writer. Who started this ghetto of fiction, anyway? Publishers? Editors? It certainly couldn't have been thinking writers. However, if the only way I can get into print is by being labelled, then, I am a science-fiction writer. "Well, I bought this can of soup, but it tastes like nothing on earth to me. . . ?"

* * *

The flying saucer sighted twice in Josephine Saxton's *Vector for Seven* is definitely not an integral part of its plot. *Group Feast* and *The Hieros Gamos of Sam and An Smith* also do not stress science fiction's usual trappings. Instead of positing fantastic planets and alien creatures, Saxton focuses upon man confronting his absurd world. In contrast to a typical power fantasy, her novels emphasize aspects of human existence which are both finite and ridiculous. Her characters must come to terms with their material culture and their social relationships. The reader must also come to terms with Saxton's style. In addition to de-emphasizing the expected extrapolative characteristics of science fiction, she writes counter to the genre's allegorical clichés: the two "wild" children in *The Hieros Gamos* become a stereotypical married couple; Cora Caley, the rich self-obsessed heroine of *Group Feast*, does not suffer; the wanderings of the seven protagonists in *Vector for Seven* do not symbolize a death trip. Her technique causes one to question the validity of categorizing these novels as science fiction. An image of a barker standing outside of a circus tent shouting, "step right up folks and see the most terrible monster on Earth" helps to clarify this question. Those people whose curiosity is aroused venture within and view the promised exhibit: a mirror image of themselves. Similarly, marketing Saxton's work as science fiction attracts readers by establishing the expectation of fantastic characters. To continue the metaphor, like those who enter the tent, readers of Saxton's "science fiction" are directed toward an unexpected vision of man.

It is fair to call her work science fiction of the softest variety, a fiction of mundane existing technology—airplanes, buses, and an unusually long water pipe, for example—set against the background of a surreal vision of our world. Saxton's earthbound characters encounter such things as a department store which fulfills one's need without the necessity of remuneration (*The Hieros Gamos*) and a house with a seemingly limitless number of rooms (*Group Feast*). This is the way the world within that house ends: "there was a mushroom cloud containing caviar, shoes, bath mats, pot plants, priceless tapestries, parquet floors, starving cats, pickled peppers. . . telephones, crystal chandeliers and eight gallons of cooking oil full of sodden French-fried potatoes." Cora pedals off into the Australian sunset relieved to see the destruction of her innumerable possessions.

Journeys form the predominant image in Saxton's novels. But despite the character's incessant walking, driving, and pedaling, their travel through inner space is most important; they all complete a journey of inner mental change while confronting the juxtaposition between animalistic and civilized aspects of their existences. Cora contemplates an example of this juxtaposition while she eats: "this terrible animal content. . . the thrill of hot meat juices between the teeth, albeit that many of those teeth were the skilled products of orthodontists." Orthodontists artificially beautify meat-tearing teeth. We have many methods of masking or obliterating our natural characteristics. Saxton, on the other hand, will not allow us to forget nature. Description of all varieties of unpleasant bodily secretions are coupled with the novels' discussions of material good. *Vector for Seven*, for example, immediately presents us with the image of bird droppings spattering over a proper British lady's hat. And in *The Hieros Gamos*, after some years pass, the couple returns to a supermarket where they remove the excrement they previously left there. It comes as no surprise that Saxton's characters are obsessed with washing and with bathrooms.

These characters illustrate the absurdity of people's isolation and their mutual distrust. And Saxton's plots—as well as her titles—emphasize togetherness. In *Vector for Seven*, at the conclusion of their journey through a surreal landscape, individuals of differing age, gender, and class who were at first suspicious of each other form a trusting communal unit. Hence what Saxton views as the evil forces of society and materialism can no longer separate these people; members of this once disparate group can no longer feel, according to the initial opinion of one of their fellows, that "these days no one had any thoughtfulness for anyone. . . People did not like each other; it was the Labour government and the Commies, and the labour saving devices that had done all that. " While *Vector for Seven* fuses a group together, *Group Feast* breaks one apart. The

relationship between Cora and her servants is artificial and poisoned by the fact that money holds them together. Meaningful human interaction cannot take place in Cora's world; even an unrealistically freely flowing money supply does not stop one of the servants from setting out to murder Cora while she plays hostess at her fantastically sumptuous party. This party, which continues throughout the novel, is not the work's most thought-provoking group feast, however. We must not forget the cats who are locked in Cora's basement, wallowing in their own filth, having only each other to eat. Like these cats, Cora, who has clawed her way to the apex of the social pyramid, devours members of her own species: three people die during the course of her 24-hour party. Yet, as opposed to the hopeless situation of the imprisoned cats, there is hope for her. Despite her history of unfriendly friends and unloving lovers, when she abandones her property Cora has the potentiality to find a fulfilling relationship.

Unlike Cora and the characters in *Vector for Seven*, the lone male adolescent we meet at the beginning of *The Hieros Gamos* immediately assumes a significant place in the life of a fellow human being. He encounters a female baby attached to her dead mother and faces a dilemma: does he sacrifice his solitude or allow the baby to die? He decides in favor of life, and the two grow up in their own natural world which, at the same time, affords them free access to all the material they need. A description of them dressing in proper adult attire just before removing it to experience coitus is one example of the novel's preoccupation with man's civilized and animalistic behaviour. This text's most important *hieros gamos*, the Greek words for holy marriage, is the union between people's biological and man-made roles. Its protagonists are Everyman. And, like every man, they must be civilized. The two individuals who once called themselves "boy" and "baby" assume many roles and names until they become the suburban couple, Sam and An Smith. It is sad to see these surreal children develop into characters appropriate to an Erma Bombeck column. This is not to say, however, that Sam and An's relationship is devoid of positive aspects. An's life was saved and she in turn becomes the mother of a female child. In fact, life literally springs from death in all of Saxton's novels: in addition to the circumstances of An's birth, Cora is impregnated by someone who dies immediately after he ejaculates; and a gentleman in *Vector for Seven* expires while holding an infant who bears his name.

Like another of the travelers in *Vector for Seven*, members of the Smith family might think that "it was good having people in the house all together, living with one another instead of being alone and isolated, all of them in different homes, not even knowing each other or acknowledging the existence of other people. " *Group Feast*, then, best articulates the main idea of Saxton's work, an idea which Freud expressed in *Civilization and Its Discontents* : "Human life in common is only made possible when a majority comes together which is stronger than any separate individual and which remains united against all separate individuals. " Despite the novels' attention to the absurdity of the human condition, they celebrate human life, which, after all, depends upon the fulfillment of cultural as well as biological needs.

—Marleen S. Barr

SCHACHNER, Nat(han). Also wrote as Chan Corbett; Walter Glamis. American. Born in New York City, 16 January 1895.

Educated at the City College of New York, B. S. 1915; New York University, J. D. 1919. Served in the United States Army chemical warfare service, 1917-18. Married Helen Lichtenstein in 1919; one daughter. Chemist, New York City Department of Health, 1915-17; admitted to the New York Bar, 1919; practicing lawyer, New York, 1919-33; free-lance writer from 1933; Editorial Consultant, American Jewish Committee, 1945-51; Director of Public Relations, National Council of Jewish Women, 1954-55. President, American Rocket Society, 1933. *Died 2 October 1955.*

SCIENCE-FICTION PUBLICATIONS

Novel

Space Lawyer. New York, Gnome Press, 1953.

Uncollected Short Stories (series: Past, Present, and Future)

"The Tower of Evil," with Leo Zagat, in *Wonder Stories Quarterly* (New York), Summer 1930.
"In 20,000 A. D.," with Leo Zagat, in *Wonder Stories* (New York), September 1930.
"Back to 20,000 A. D.," with Leo Zagat, in *Wonder Stories* (New York), March 1931.
"The Emperor of the Stars," with Leo Zagat, in *Wonder Stories* (New York), April 1931.
"The Menace from Andromeda," with Leo Zagat, in *Amazing* (New York), April 1931.
"The Death-Cloud," with Leo Zagat, in *Astounding* (New York), May 1931.
"The Revolt of the Machines," with Leo Zagat, in *Astounding* (New York), July 1931.
"Venus Mines, Incorporated," with Leo Zagat, in *Wonder Stories* (New York), August 1931.
"Exiles of the Moon," with Leo Zagat, in *Wonder Stories* (New York), September 1931.
"Pirates of the Gorm," in *Astounding* (New York), May 1932.
"Slaves of Mercury," in *Astounding* (New York), September 1932.
"Emissaries of Space," in *Wonder Stories Quarterly* (New York), Fall 1932.
"The Time Express," in *Wonder Stories* (New York), December 1932.
"The Memory of the Atoms," with R. Lacher, in *Wonder Stories* (New York), January 1933.
"The Eternal Dictator," in *Wonder Stories* (New York), February 1933.
"The Robot Technocrat," in *Wonder Stories* (New York), March 1933.
"The Revolt of the Scientists," in *Wonder Stories* (New York), April, May, June 1933.
"The Orange God" (as Walter Glamis), and "Fire Imps of Vesuvius," in *Astounding* (New York), October 1933.
"Ancestral Voices," in *Astounding* (New York), December 1933.
"Redmask of the Outlands," in *Astounding* (New York), January 1934.
"The Time Imposter," in *Astounding* (New York), March 1934.
"He from Procyon," in *Astounding* (New York), April 1934.
"The 100th Generation," in *Astounding* (New York), May 1934.
"The Living Equation," in *Astounding* (New York), September 1934.

"The Great Thirst," in *Astounding* (New York), November 1934.
"Mind of the World," in *Astounding* (New York), March 1935.
"The Orb of Probability," in *Astounding* (New York), June 1935.
"The Son of Redmask," in *Astounding* (New York), August 1935.
"World Gone Mad," in *Amazing* (New York), October 1935.
"I Am Not God," in *Astounding* (New York), October, November 1935.
"The Isotope Men," in *Astounding* (New York), January 1936.
"Entropy," in *Astounding* (New York), March 1936.
"Reverse Universe," in *Astounding* (New York), June 1936.
"Pacifica," in *Astounding* (New York), July 1936.
"The Return of the Murians," in *Astounding* (New York), August 1936.
"The Saphrophyte Men of Venus," in *Astounding* (New York), October 1936.
"The Eternal Wanderer," in *Astounding* (New York), November 1936.
"Infra Universe," in *Astounding* (New York), December 1936, January 1937.
"Beyond Which Limits," in *Astounding* (New York), February 1937.
"Earthspin," in *Astounding* (New York), June 1937.
"Sterile Planet," in *Astounding* (New York), July 1937.
"Crystallized Thought," in *Astounding* (New York), August 1937.
"Lost in the Dimensions," in *Astounding* (New York), November 1937.
"City of the Rocket Horde," in *Astounding* (New York), December 1937.
"Negative Space," in *Astounding* (New York), April 1938.
"Island of the Individualists" (Past), in *Astounding* (New York), May 1938.
"The Sun World of Soldus," in *Astounding* (New York), October 1938.
"Simultaneous Worlds," in *Astounding* (New York), November 1938.
"Palooka from Jupiter," in *Astounding* (New York), February 1939.
"Worlds Don't Care," in *Astounding* (New York), April 1939.
"When the Future Dies," in *Astounding* (New York), June 1939.
"City under the Sea," in *Fantastic Adventures* (New York), September 1939.
"City of the Corporate Mind" (Past), in *Astounding* (New York), December 1939.
"Cold," in *Astounding* (New York), March 1940.
"Space Double," in *Astounding* (New York), May 1940.
"Master Gerald of Cambray," in *Unknown Worlds* (New York), June 1940.
"Runaway Cargo," in *Astounding* (New York), October 1940.
"The Return of Circe," in *Fantastic Adventures* (New York), August 1941.
"Beyond All Weapons," in *Astounding* (New York), November 1941.
"Eight Who Came Back," in *Fantastic Adventures* (New York), November 1941.
"The Ultimate Metal," in *The Best of Science Fiction*, edited by Groff Conklin. New York, Crown, 1946.
"Stratosphere Towers," in *Astounding* (New York), August 1954.
"Past, Present and Future," in *Before the Golden Age*, edited by Isaac Asimov. New York, Doubleday, and London, Robson, 1974.

"The Shining One," in *Visions of Tomorrow*, edited by Roger Elwood. New York, Pocket Books, 1976.

"City of the Cosmic Rays" (Past), in *Astounding Science Fiction July 1939*, by John W. Campbell, edited by Martin H. Greenberg. Carbondale, Southern Illinois University Press, 1981.

Uncollected Short Stories as Chan Corbett

"When the Sun Dies," in *Astounding* (New York), March 1935.
"Intra-Planetary," in *Astounding* (New York), October 1935.
"Ecce Homo," in *Astounding* (New York), June 1936.
"The Thought Web of Minipar," in *Astounding* (New York), November 1936.
"Beyond Infinity," in *Astounding* (New York), January 1937.
"Nova in Messier 33," in *Astounding* (New York), May 1937.
"When Time Stood Still," in *Astounding* (New York), June 1937.

OTHER PUBLICATIONS

Novels

By the Dim Lamps. New York, Stokes, 1941.
The King's Messenger. Philadelphia, Lippincott, 1942.
The Sun Shines West. New York, Appleton Century, 1943.
The Wanderer: A Novel of Dante and Beatrice. New York, Appleton Century, 1944; London, Melrose, 1948.

Other

Aaron Burr. New York, Stokes, 1937.
The Medieval Universities. New York, Stokes, and London, Allen and Unwin, 1938.
Alexander Hamilton. New York, Appleton Century, 1946.
The Price of Liberty: A History of the American Jewish Committee. New York, American Jewish Committee, 1948.
Thomas Jefferson. New York, Appleton Century Crofts, 1951.
Alexander Hamilton, Nation Builder. New York, McGraw Hill, 1952.
The Founding Fathers. New York, Putnam, 1954.

*   *   *

Nat Schachner was attracted for a time to the vigorous, young genre of pulp-magazine science fiction where he left an impression with his liberal ideas and earnest inventiveness. Schachner worked first as a chemist, spent a number of years in law practice, published hundreds of pieces of short fiction in the pulps (science, detective, mystery, western, and adventure stories), and wrote several scholarly books on history. During the Nazi threat before and during World War II he defended human liberties vigorously in all his writings—both pulp fiction and scholarly. Schachner's total commitment to the life of letters and to humanitarian values makes him a true 20th-century representative of the Romantics whom he said he loved as a child. He represents the writer as hero; and the heroic vigor of the science-fiction genre during the time that he was active in it corresponds well with his later American Revolutionary history. Schachner's hopeful ideas for progress through clever technology and rationality had their roots both in the 18th-century Enlightenment of Thomas Jefferson and in the pulp-fiction world of the early *Astounding*.

The first dozen or so of Schachner's science-fiction stories were written in collaboration with Arthur Leo Zagat, but it was with the "thought variant" stories of the F. Orlin Tremaine *Astounding* that the inventive lawyer began to hit his stride as a writer who would extrapolate into the future his liberal ideas about the present and eventually about the past. The first thought variant story was Schachner's "Ancestral Voices" (1933), and new idea stories followed rapidly for the rest of the decade. In his book on the science-fiction pulp magazines, Paul Carter calls Schachner the earliest of the "anti-Nazi Paul Reveres" whose speculative fictions increasingly explored the opportunities for sociological themes that could be related to current events. A rather stiff and primitive story called "The Eternal Wanderer" contains a crude courtroom scene about interplanetary law that anticipates Schachner's only science-fiction book *Space Lawyer* (made out of two later stories, "Old Fireball" and "Jurisdiction").

Schachner's best writing and most memorable contribution to letters is undoubtedly his historical work, and he properly gave up work for the pulps in order to pursue that research. But one cannot help thinking that his thought variant extrapolations were both inspired by his knowledge of the Enlightenment and contributed greatly to his understanding of it. One of his more carefully written and sophisticated fictions, "Past, Present, and Future" (1937), performs just that balancing between a nostalgia for the heroic and glorious lost past on the one hand and an awareness of the challenges in the present on the other that creates the ironic complexity of mind that is necessary for true liberal thinking. Schachner was a hero among writers not only for the vast amount of work that he got done but also for how he did it—less an artist than a propagandist for democracy.

—Donald M. Hassler

———

SCHENCK, Hilbert. American. Born in Boston, Massachusetts, 12 February 1926. Educated at Williams College, Williamstown, Massachusetts, B. A. in physics 1950; Stanford University, California, M. S. in mechanical engineering 1952. Served as an electronic technician in the United States Navy, 1944-46. Married 1) Mary Low Taylor in 1950; 2) Anne Thompson in 1983; six children. Test Engineer, Pratt & Whitney Aircraft, East Hartford, Connecticut, 1952-56; Assistant Professor to Professor, Clarkson College, Potsdam, New York, 1956-66; Professor, 1966-83, and Director, Scuba Safety Project, 1968-80, University of Rhode Island, Kingston. Agent: Virginia Kidd, Box 278, Milford, Pennsylvania 18337. Address: 92 Main Street, Box 816, Marion, Massachusetts 02738, U.S.A.

SCIENCE-FICTION PUBLICATIONS

Novels

At the Eye of the Ocean. New York, Pocket Books, 1980.
A Rose for Armageddon. New York, Pocket Books, 1982; London, Allison and Busby, 1984.

Short Stories

Wave Rider. New York, Pocket Books, 1980.

Uncollected Short Stories

"Tomorrow's Weather," in *Fantasy and Science Fiction* (New

York), April 1953.

"Me," in *The 5th Annual of the Year's Best S-F*, edited by Judith Merril. New York, Simon and Schuster, 1960.

"Memo at the Department of Agriculture," in *Fantasy and Science Fiction* (New York), April 1960.

"Ed Lear Wasn't So Crazy!," in *The 6th Annual of the Year's Best S-F*, edited by Judith Merril. New York, Simon and Schuster, 1961.

"Pun in Orbit," "Snip Snip," and "Wockyjabber," in *The Mathematical Magpie*, edited by Clifton Fadiman. New York, Simon and Schuster, 1962.

"The Theology of Water," in *Perpetual Light*, edited by Alan Ryan. New York, Warner, 1982.

"Hurricane Claude," in *Fantasy and Science Fiction* (New York), April 1983.

"The Geometry of Narrative," in *Analog* (New York), August 1983.

"Steam Bird," in *Fantasy and Science Fiction* (New York), April and May 1984.

"Silicon Muse," in *Analog* (New York), September 1984.

"Send Me a Kiss by Wire," in *Fantasy and Science Fiction* (New York), April 1985

OTHER PUBLICATIONS

Other

Shallow Water Diving for Pleasure and Profit, with Henry Kendall. Cambridge, Maryland, Cornell Maritime Press, 1950.

Underwater Photography, with Henry Kendall. Cambridge, Maryland, Cornell Maritime Press, 1954.

Shallow Water Diving and Spearfishing, with Henry Kendall. Cambridge, Maryland, Cornell Maritime Press, 1954.

Skin Diver's and Spearfisherman's Guide to American Waters. Cambridge, Maryland, Cornell Maritime Press, 1955.

Heat Transfer. Englewood Cliffs, New Jersey, Prentice Hall, 1959.

Thermodynamics, with R. Kenyon. New York, Ronald Press, 1961.

An Introduction to the Engineering Research Project. New York, McGraw Hill, 1962.

Fortran Methods in Heat Flow. New York, Ronald Press, 1963.

Theories of Engineering Experimentation. New York, McGraw Hill, 1963; 3rd edition, 1978.

Editor, *Introduction to Ocean Enginerering*. New York, McGraw Hill, 1975.

*

Hilbert Schenck comments:

My stories have been mainly concerned with the technology of ocean exploration, but also may contain fantasy elements. My first two novels are concerned both with the ocean and the area of Cape Cod, Mass. My novel *Steam Bird*, serialized last year in *F & SF* departs from these topics and is concerned with the flight of a nuclear-propelled aircraft, a project on which I worked in the 1950's at Pratt & Whitney Aircraft. Most recently, I have been fooling around with the idea of recursive fiction, that is, fiction that is concerned with its own creation. My two most recent fictions in *Analog* Are attempts to push the idea of recursion as far as it seems possible to go, although several other of my stories have recursive elements. My two Cape Cod novels represent attempts to introduce classic SF themes (the idea of

the superman and the idea of time travel) into a regional fiction setting. A third novel, not yet sold, adds a third basic SF theme, visitation from another world, into the Cape Cod geographic and historic situation.

*   *   *

Hilbert Schenck's connection with science fiction goes back to the 1950's, but his rise to prominence is relatively recent. While it is dangerous to draw conclusions about an author from his work, Schenck's writing has the ring of enthusiasm and sincerity about it. If this is as gen⁝⁚ ⁚e as it seems, then his fiction reflects his real beliefs and interests. Fortu⁚a⁚ely for his readers, he almost always avoids the trap of writing propaganda disguised as fiction.

The political position underlying his stories should be characterized as libertarian rather than conservative. "The Battle of Abaco Reef" is set in a communtiy, in the strong sense of the word, which wants no more than to be left alone to pursue goals which most Americans would probably accept by means which would also seem acceptable. Unforunately, the U. S. government does not find this acceptable. Fortunately, the community has the means to defend itself, the will to do so, and a moral stance which does not require them to be victims in the name of respect for life. At the same time, Schenck is vividly aware of the horrors of war, which tempers a belief in the possibility of just wars. The heroine of *A Rose for Armageddon* has all too realistic nightmares about a coming thermonuclear war.

Hope and optimism are characteristic of his stories, but not in the facile form seen in the problem-solving stories which were so common 30 years ago. When Schenck is writing about catastrophic events such as the imminent death of the ocean in "Three Days at the End of the World," it is clear that there is a real possibility of failure. Yet somehow, despite their weaknesses, his characters find in the depths of their souls the strength to rise to the occasion. That is the real subject of most of his stories, not how the doom that threatens is forestalled; and this is borne out by the fact that many of them end before the problem is solved.

Among Schenck's passions would seem to be the oceans and their dwellers, the local history of the islands off Cape Cod, and the technology of steam power. The members of the world of steam in " Steam Bird " are immersed in their subject and its history, about which they quarrel with the intensity of believing theologians. The descriptions of life in 19th-century Massachusetts in *At the Eye of the Ocean* are loving but not sentimental in their depictions both of riches and of grinding poverty, of enlightenment and of bigotry. And the oceans and their dwellers appear in so many places in such a wealth of detail that it is impossible to believe that the author simply worked up the subject for the stories.

A recurring theme in his work is spatio-temporal relations which define special places where the world changes for the right person at the right time. In *A Rose for Armageddon* two scientists find a place where it is possible to turn back the clock by analysing topography and the paths taken by people and animals on it. Abel Roon in *At the Eye of the Ocean* can sense the relations of sea floor, currents, and winds, which eventually lead him to a place at a time where he reaches a mystical enlightenment.

In passages such as these, Schenck's prose is almost lyrical; but when he turns to humor, as in "Steam Bird," his hand is heavy. Playing on the difference between the public image of right-thinking rectitude projected for political reasons and what the person behind the image really is, he exaggerates the contrast, an effective device which he carries too far. The result is that we cannot believe in the better side his characters must manifest to arrive at the happy ending.

Schenck writes well. His best work does not fit easily into established categories, and this may prevent his becoming widely popular. However, he is probably assured of a thoughtful and dedicated following, even if it be of relatively modest size.

—William M. Schuyler, Jr.

SCHMIDT, Stanley (Albert). American. Born in Cincinnati, Ohio, 7 March 1944. Educated at the University of Cincinnati, B. S. in physics 1966 (Phi Beta Kappa); Case Western Reserve University, Cleveland, M. A. 1968, Ph. D. 1969. Married Joyce Tokarz in 1979. Assistant Professor of Physics, Heidelberg College, Tiffin, Ohio, 1969-78. Since 1978, Editor, *Analog*, New York. Agent: Scott Meredith Literary Agency, 845 Third Avenue, New York, New York 10022. Address: c/o Analog, 380 Lexington Avenue, New York, New York 10017, U.S.A.

SCIENCE-FICTION PUBLICATIONS

Novels (series: Lifeboat Earth)

Newton and the Quasi-Apple. New York, Doubleday, 1975.
The Sins of the Fathers (Lifeboat Earth). New York, Berkley, 1976.
Lifeboat Earth. New York, Berkley, 1978.

Uncollected Short Stories

"A Flash of Darkness," in *Analog* (New York), September 1968.
"The Reluctant Ambassadors," in *Analog* (New York), December 1968.
"The Unreachable Stars," in *Analog* (New York), April 1971.
"May the Best Man Win," in *American Government Through Science Fiction*, edited by Joseph D. Olander and Martin H. Greenberg. New York, Random House, 1974.
"Lost Newton," in *Anthropology Through Science Fiction*, edited by Carol Mason, Martin H. Greenberg, and Patricia Warrick. New York, St. Martin's Press, 1974.
"A Thrust of Greatness," in *Analog* (New York), June 1976.
"His Loyal Opposition," in *Analog* (New York), July 1976.
"Caesar Clark," in *Analog* (New York), July 1977.
"Pinocchio," in *Analog* (New York), September 1977.
"Dark Age," in *Analog* (New York), December 1977.
"The Promised Land," in *Analog* (New York), January 1978.
"Panic," in *Isaac Asimov's Science Fiction Magazine* (New York), January-February 1978.
"A Midsummer Newt's Dream," in *Isaac Asimov's Science Fiction Magazine* (New York), June 1979.
"The Prophet," in *Analog's Golden Anniversary Anthology*, edited by Schmidt. New York, Davis, 1981.
"Camouflage," in *Twilight Zone* (New York), July 1981.
"Tweedlioop," in *Twilight Zone* (New York), November 1981.
"Mascots," in *Fantasy and Science Fiction* (New York), February 1982.
"War of Independence," in *Isaac Asimov's Science Fiction Magazine* (New York), August 1982.
". . . and Comfort to the Enemy," in *Aliens from Analog*, edited by Schmidt. New York, Davis, 1983.
"The Easy Way," in *Rigel* (Richmond, California), Summer 1983.
"The Folks Who Live on the Hill," in *Habitats*, edited by Susan Shwartz. New York, DAW, 1984.

OTHER PUBLICATIONS

Other

"Science Fiction Courses: An Example and Some Alternatives," in *American Journal of Physics* (New York), September 1973.
"Science Fiction and the Science Teacher," in *Extrapolation* (Wooster, Ohio), May 1976.
"Science in Science Fiction," in *Many Futures, Many Worlds*, edited by Thomas D. Clareson. Kent, Ohio, Kent State University Press, 1977.
"The Science of Science Fiction Writing," in *Writer's Digest* (Cincinnati), February 1983.
"Broccoli, Oranges, and Science Fiction," in *Twilight Zone* (New York), June 1985.

Editor, *Analog's Golden Anniversary Anthology*. New York, Davis, 1981.
Editor, *Analog: Reader's Choice*. New York, Davis, 1982.
Editor, *Analog's Children of the Future*. New York, Davis, 1982.
Editor, *Analog's Lighter Side*. New York, Davis, 1982.
Editor, *Analog: Writer's Choice*. New York, Davis, 1983.
Editor, *Analog's War and Peace*. New York, Davis, 1983.
Editor, *Aliens from Analog*. New York, Davis, 1983.
Editor, *From Mind to Mind*. New York, Davis, 1984.

*

Stanley Schmidt comments:
In all my fiction I try to tell entertaining stories about people in situations which are directly shaped by scientific or technological changes, with neither the human nor the technical parts of the foundation slighted in favor of the other. Probably the best examples to date of the type of thing I try to do are the Kyyra or Lifeboat Earth series, of which, to date, two books are complete: *The Sins of the Fathers* and *Lifeboat Earth*.

* * *

Stanley Schmidt seems to be one of the final products of the John Campbell influence on science fiction although it is probably too early in Schmidt's career to tell definitely. His three novels to date, however, as well as the short story versions of them that appeared in *Analog* all show the Campbell marks of hard science extrapolation, of positive-thinking problem-solving approaches to thorny human and social problems, and of two-dimensional human beings compared to a sense of rounded sublimity for whole planets and even galaxies. Schmidt's two later novels begin what will no doubt be a series in which galactic history unfolds much like Campbell taught the young Asimov to attempt sublime galactic history four decades ago. The first novel narrates a segment from the history of the planet Ymrek in which the natives seem more interesting than the human emissaries to the planet. Even if Schmidt had not told us that correspondence and ideas from Campbell influenced him, the effects of that influence are apparent in all three novels.

Schmidt is best when he begins to suggest the unresolved and, perhaps, unresolvable tensions that underlie the problems that must be resolutely solved by technology and engineering techniques; these interesting tensions lurking beneath the Campbell-like scenarios are almost exclusively associated with the alien species of the latter two novels. Although Ymrek is an interesting alien extrapolation, its natives are not nearly as symbolically (or scientifically) suggestive as the Kyyra who were originally from nearer the center of our galaxy and who literally set in motion all the action in *The Sins of the Fathers* and its sequel, *Lifeboat Earth*. The more suggestive passages appear in the first book of the series when the Kyyra seem to symbolize the dilemmas of maturation. We must destroy our pasts and even our gods to atone for our mistakes—almost Christian and yet more universal symbolism of the dying god.

The strength related to this symbolic suggestiveness is the detailed elaboration of the aliens themselves—his departure from Campbell. Without the concrete detail to make them credible, the Kyyra could suggest nothing. In fact, as Beldan conducts his human visitor on a tour of the immense Kyyra spaceship orbiting the earth, and explains to her the language and the customs of his people, the reader is reminded of the tours through Walden Two. These aliens are an advanced culture with a kind of social engineering that B. F. Skinner would admire. The Campbell positivism is not unlike Skinner's hopes for managing behaviour, and it is to Schmidt's credit that while the parallels are developed in his narrative, the dilemmas are lurking just beneath the surface that Campbell may not have noticed. We can anticipate, perhaps, more development of the Kyyra in future Schmidt stories; and we can wonder if their utopian, problem-solving traits will prevail or if the tragic implications in the death of their god will haunt Schmidt more.

—Donald M. Hassler

SCHMITZ, James H(enry). American. Born to American parents in Hamburg, Germany, 15 October 1911. Educated at Realgymnasium Obersekunda. Served in the United States Army Air Force during World War II. Married Betty Mae Chapman in 1957. Worked for International Harvester Company, in Germany, 1932-39; built automobile trailers in the United States after the war. Since 1961, full-time writer. Recipient: Invisible Little Man Award, 1973. Agent: Scott Meredith Literary Agency, 845 Third Avenue, New York, New York 10022, U.S.A.

SCIENCE-FICTION PUBLICATIONS

Novels (series: Telzey Amberdon)

A Tale of Two Clocks. New York, Torquil, 1962; as *Legacy*, New York, Ace, 1979.
The Universe Against Her (Telzey). New York, Ace, 1964.
The Witches of Karres. Philadelphia, Chilton, 1966.
The Demon Breed. New York, Ace, 1968; London, Futura, 1974.
The Eternal Frontiers. New York, Putnam, 1973; London, Sidgwick and Jackson, 1974.
The Lion Game (Telzey). New York, DAW, 1973; London, Sidgwick and Jackson, 1976.

Short Stories

Agent of Vega. New York, Gnome Press, 1960.
A Nice Day for Screaming and Other Tales of the Hub. Philadelphia, Chilton, 1965.
A Pride of Monsters. New York, Macmillan, 1970.
The Telzey Toy. New York, DAW, 1973; London, Sidgwick and Jackson, 1976.

Uncollected Short Stories

"One Step Ahead," in *If* (New York), April 1974.
"Aura of Immortality," in *If* (New York), June 1974.

*

Bibliography: *James H. Schmitz: A Bibliography* by Mark Owings, Baltimore, Croatan House, 1973.

* * *

James H. Schmitz is a craftsmanlike writer who has been a steady contributor to science-fiction magazines for over 20 years. The best of his shorter works are collected in *A Nice Day for Screaming* and *A Pride of Monsters*. In the first work the stories repeat a consistent theme that the universe is stranger than we can imagine, and that unexpected discoveries will meet us at every turn. Although the stories are set in the far future, humans (and others) continually encounter both creatures and behaviors they could not have foreseen, from the alien automated service-station for spaceships of the title story to an alien so intelligent it keeps humans for pets in "The Winds of Time." But aliens can be surprised too, as "The Other Likeness" shows: agents genetically engineered to resemble humans become so much like us that they begin to sympathize with humans against their masters. There are new machines, too, like the fear broadcaster of "The Tangled Web" or the half-men, half-machines of "The Machmen." And there are some things so strange yet so intelligent they can conceal their very existence from humans, like the forest-sized organism in "Balanced Ecology."

A Pride of Monsters collects stories that attempt to rejuvante the idea of "the monster" through tales of future encounters with alien life-forms. In "Lion Loose" Detective Bad-News Quillan, a favorite character of Schmitz's, meets a rug-sized creature with the ability to pass through solid matter, but it is not nearly so dangerous as the radiation creature of "The Searcher," which endangers a pair of private detectives working undercover against interstellar hijackers. "The Pork Chop Tree" is an alien plant whose very presence is addictive, a less forthright menace than the plant of "Greenface," a story which is unusual (for Schmitz) in being set in the present.

In his longer works, Schmitz has often shown a close cooperation between man and alien. The alien may be a machine, like the robot spaceships of the four thematically connected stories of *Agent of Vega*, or mutated animals, like the intelligent giant otters of *The Demon Breed*, who help to repel a threat to human civilization. The "aliens" may even be other humans, as in *The Eternal Frontiers*, in which the Swimmers have diverged so far from normal humanity as to be almost a different species. Rather than forming a close relationship, though, the two groups are keen competitors. And of course, there are aliens that, like those in *A Pride of Monsters*, are threats to humanity, ones such as the plasmoids in *A Tale of Two Clocks*.

A second theme that Schmitz has frequently used is that of supranormal mental powers: Telzey, a telepathic teen-aged girl, is the central character in a number of stories. Telepathy (and various other kinds of mental powers, chiefly psychokinesis) is central to Schmitz's most celebrated work, *The Witches of Karres*. The book is a fast-moving, episodic adventure story of an ordinary human, Captain Pausert, who becomes entangled with three psychically endowed girls. Its account of the wakening of telepowers in Pausert draws on familiar science-fiction recipes, mixing appropriately evil villains with nick-of-time escapes, and spicing the whole with an entertaining sense of humor.

—Walter E. Meyers

SCORTIA, Thomas N(icholas). Also writes as Scott Nichols. American. Born in Alton, Illinois, 29 August 1926. Educated at Washington University, St. Louis, A. B. 1949, graduate work 1950. Served in the United States Army Infantry, 1944-46, and chemical corps, 1951-53. Married Irene Baron in 1960 (divorced, 1968); one adopted son. Senior chemist, Union Starch and Refining Company, Granite City, Illinois, 1954-57; director of research, Chromalloy, Edwardsville, Illinois, 1957-60; group leader, Celanese Corporation, Asheville, North Carolina, 1960-61; section head, United Technology Corporation, Sunnyvale, California, 1961-70. Since 1970, full-time writer and lecturer: author of comics *Targos, Creepy* magazine, May 1972, and *Galactic Prime*, both illustrated by Jack Katz. Agent: William Morris Agency, 1350 Avenue of the Americas, New York, New York 10019. Address: 7177 Brydon Road, La Verne, California 91750, U.S.A.

SCIENCE-FICTION PUBLICATIONS

Novels

What Mad Oracle? Evanston, Illinois, Regency, 1961.
Artery of Fire. New York, Doubleday, 1972.
Earthwreck! New York, Fawcett, 1974; London, Coronet, 1975.
The Glass Inferno, with Frank M. Robinson. New York, Doubleday, 1974; London, Hodder and Stoughton, 1975.
The Prometheus Crisis, with Frank M. Robinson. New York, Doubleday, 1975; London, Hodder and Stoughton, 1976.
The Nightmare Factor, with Frank M. Robinson. New York, Doubleday, and London, Hodder and Stoughton, 1978.
The Gold Crew, with Frank M. Robinson. New York, Warner, 1980; London, Panther, 1983.

Short Stories

Caution! Inflammable! New York, Doubleday, 1975.
The Best of Thomas N. Scortia, edited by George Zebrowski. New York, Doubleday, 1981.

Uncollected Short Stories

"Fulfillment," in *Science Fiction Stories*, May 1957.
"Cat o' Nine Tales," in *Future* (New York), Summer 1957.
"Gag Rule," in *Science Fiction Stories*, July 1957.
"Genius Loci," in *Science Fiction Stories*, 1957.
"Cassandra" (as Scott Nichols), in *Science Fiction Quarterly*

(Holyoke, Massachusetts), August 1957.
"The Lonely Stars," in *Future* (New York), Fall 1957.
"Insane Planet," in *Fantastic Universe* (Chicago), February 1958.
"The Avengers," in *Science Fiction Stories*, September 1958.
"The Bomb in the Bathtub," in *Fourth Galaxy Reader*, edited by H. L. Gold. New York, Doubleday, 1959.
"The Renegade," in *Future* (New York), April 1959.
"Alien Night," in *Get Out of My Sky*. New York, Crest, 1960.
"Caliban," with Jim Harmon, in *Future* (New York), April 1960.
"The Destroyer," in *Fantastic* (New York), June 1965.
"Broken Image," in *Fantastic* (New York), November 1966.
"Wipeout," in *Swank*, February 1967.
"Superiority Complex," in *Analog* (New York), December 1968.
"Morality," in *Fantastic* (New York), December 1969.
"Judas Fish," in *The Year 2000*, edited by Harry Harrison. New York, Doubleday, 1970; London, Faber, 1971.
"The Good and Faithful," in *Two Views of Wonder*, edited by Scortia and Chelsea Quinn Yarbro. New York, Ballantine, 1973.
"Final Exam," in *The Other Side of Tomorrow*, edited by Roger Elwood. New York, Random House, 1973.
"The Tower," in *Children of Infinity*, edited by Roger Elwood. New York, Watts, 1973.
"Who Is Sylvia?," with Chelsea Quinn Yarbro, in *Vampires, Werewolves, and Other Monsters*, edited by Roger Elwood. Philadelphia, Curtis, 1974.
"Blood Brother," in *Future Kin*, edited by Roger Elwood. New York, Doubleday, 1974.
"The Armageddon Tapes 1-4," in *Continuum 1-4*, edited by Roger Elwood. New York, Putnam, 4 vols., 1974-75.
"The Worm," in *Beware More Beasts*. New York, Manor, 1975.
"Someday I'll Find You," in *Odyssey* (New York), April 1976.

OTHER PUBLICATIONS

Plays

Screenplays: *Endangered Species*, with Dalton Trumbo, 1976; *Darker Than You Think*, 1979.

Other

Editor, *Strange Bedfellows*. New York, Random House, 1972.
Editor, with Chelsea Quinn Yarbo, *Two View of Wonder*. New York, Ballantine, 1973.
Editor, with George Zebrowski, *Human-Machines: An Anthology of Stories about Cyborgs*. New York, Random House, 1975; London, Hale, 1977.

*   *   *

Thomas N. Scortia's first published story, "The Prodigy," immediately established him as an accomplished storyteller. Detailing a violent conflict with a paranormal child, the story reaches one of the few unguessable resolutions of the theme. "The Shores of Night" is a vision of a solar-system-wide civilization straining for the stars; here are the sounds and colors of change, as the human spirit readies itself with a new strength. Scortia writes with a virtuosity comparable to Bester's, with the high emotional content of a Lem in depicting "cruel miracles" at their most intense. This story belongs, to borrow the words of C. S. Lewis, "to those works of science fiction which are actual additions to life; they give, like certain rare dreams, sensations we naver had before, and enlarge our conception of the range of possible experience. " The work belongs to the period of Scortia's greatest attachment to the ideals of space travel. The story's success lies in its melding of personal loss with a haunting series of pictorial images.

His first novel, *What Mad Oracle?*, is based on Scortia's experience as a physico-chemist in the aerospace industry. It is a powerful story of engineers and corporations confronting the realities of American business and politics in the 1950's. SF in the sense that it shows the human impact of science and technology, the novel has a historical interest for SF readers.

As Scortia's involvement in aerospace increased, his SF production diminished; but stories continued to appear throughout the 1960's. One of the most notable is "Broken Image," depicting a future earth's attempts to have an ethical influence on an alien culture. Seldom has the theme of the saviour been given such a strong presentation. "The Destroyer" was an in-depth return to the theme of "The Prodigy," but this time the note was one of compassion. By 1970 Scortia was writing full time. The great success of this period is "The Weariest River," hailed by P. S. Miller and others as an instant classic on the theme of immortality, containing an original twist of great power; and *Artery of Fire*, a tense, taut novel of conflict over the building of an immense power system (the central image of the story is as strikingly original as that of Niven's *Ringworld*). John W. Campbell had turned down the novella version because he could not accept Scortia's prediction that fusion power would not be available by 1973 (appearing in 1960, the novella makes a striking contrast to "The Shores of Night" of four years before, prefiguring Scortia's critical approach to the products of technology).

Also appearing in the early 1970's was the novel *Earthwreck!* (the title was changed from *Endangered Species* without Scortia's consent), a strongly characterized story of human survival in space after an atomic war has devastated the earth. With the SF veteran Frank M. Robinson, Scortia wrote several disaster novels. These bestsellers earned the authors an international reputation, considerable monetary reward, and the often unfair scorn of the SF community. *The Prometheus Crisis* is of interest to SF readers because, in its depiction of a severe nuclear accident, the story is the legitimate descendant of such pioneering stories as Heinlein's "Blowups Happen" and del Rey's *Nerves*. There is a strong cautionary tone in all of Scortia's later work; it is the warning of the once idealistic, Campbell-influenced aerospace scientist who dreamed of space travel and found that human beings have a penchant for perverting any worthwhile project, from high-rise dwellings to atomic power plants.

Scortia's popular success outside the SF world is part of the continuing science fictionalization of our civilization, in the sense that many of the prophetic suggestions made by SF in the first half of this century, positive and negative, have become commonplace in the second half. That a veteran SF writer should take part in this infusion of what once would have been science-fiction themes and ideas into the body of popular fiction is not surprising. Scortia's special success lies in his genuine emotional and dramatic appeal to the average reader, and in showing how the real world has turned out to be more complex and full of human failure, darker than the idealistic SF on which he grew up had forseen. That human beings *can* do something is no longer enough; the problem is whether they will, or should.

Thomas N. Scortia's life might have been a science-fiction story, as written in some alternate dimension. He came to maturity in the 1950's, full of feeling and intellect, overflowing

with the wonder of human possibilities as pictured in Campbell's *Astounding*, only to learn that human beings don't always do their best for worthy dreams. One might say that Scortia's views were modified by the kind of satirical SF which Gold published in *Galaxy* (Gold himself was a Campbell writer who extended his master's approach to SF to include the "soft" social sciences). Scortia's stories of the 1950's and 1960's are powerful streams of thought and feeling, combined with rigorous speculation, flowing out of his critical but compassionate disappointment with the world. Though in his 50's, it is hard to think of Scortia as anything but a young man with his crowning work still to come. Some of it will be SF and some not. His work in aerospace enabled humanity to send probes into the outer solar system, while at the same time he was struggling in his fiction to understand the failing, often partly rational inner space of human nature.

—George Zebrowski

SCOT, Chesman. See **BULMER, Kenneth.**

SEABRIGHT, John. See **TUBB, E. C.**

SEARLS, Hank (Henry Hunt Searls, Jr.). American. Born in San Francisco, California, 10 August 1922. Educated at the University of California, Berkeley, 1940; United States Naval Academy, Annapolis, Maryland, B. S. 1944. Married Berna Ann Cooper;three children. Served in the United States Navy, 1941-54: Lieutenant Commander; writer for Hughes Aircraft, Culver City, California, 1955-56, Douglas Aircraft, Santa Monica, California, 1956-57, and Warner Brothers, Burbank, California, 1959. Since 1959, free-lance writer. Agent: Scott Meredith Literary Agency, 845 Third Avenue, New York, New York 10022, U.S.A.

SCIENCE-FICTION PUBLICATIONS

Novels

The Big X. New York, Harper, and London, Heinemann, 1959.
The Crowded Sky. New York, Harper, and London, Heinemann, 1960.
The Astronaut. London, Penguin, 1960; New York, Pocket Books, 1962.
The Pilgrim Project. New York, McGraw Hill, 1964; London, W. H. Allen, 1965.
The Hero Ship. Cleveland, World, and London, W. H. Allen, 1969.
Overboard. New York, Norton, and London, Raven, 1977.

Uncollected Short Story

" Martyr's Flight," in *Imagination* (Evanston, Ilinois), December 1955.

OTHER PUBLICATIONS

Novels

Pentagon. New York, Geis, 1971.
Never Kill a Cop. New York, Pocket Books, 1977.
Jaws 2 (novelization of screenplay). Universal City, Calfornia, MCA, and London, Pan, 1978.
Firewind. New York, Doubleday, 1981; London, Sphere, 1982.
Sounding. New York, Ballantine, 1982.
Blood Song. New York, Villard, 1984.

Other

"The Astronaut, The Novelist, and Cadwalder Goltz," in The Writer (Boston), September 1965.
The Lost Prince: Young Joe, The Forgotten Kennedy. Cleveland, World, 1969.

*   *   *

Hank Searls's stories revolve around the emerging space program, astronauts and their families, and whatever political machinations are most likely to create problems. His realistic contemporary fiction is built on timeliness, as each novel has foreshadowed a stage in man's actual venture into space.

The Big X explores some potential problems, both technical and human, of manned orbital space flight. Norco's X-F18, the experimental rocket-like ship of the title, must reach a speed of Mach 8 and prove maneuverable for Norco Aircraft to land the government contract for construction of the first manned spacecraft. Mitch Westerly, the test pilot for the Big X, knows he will probably be chosen as the first man in space if his testing is successful. But the test schedule grows tense as a psychopathic chief of operations orders more and more telemetering equipment mounted in the cockpit, despite Mitch's protests that the additional weight has made the ship unstable. The suspense of the impending Mach 8 test flight builds as Mitch must decide whether to push the plane beyond its limits, at the expense of the girl he wants to marry, and possibly his life, in order to provide telemetric data necessary to the space program. Besides an inside view of the politics of the aircraft industry, there is much authentic-sounding shop talk, as well as a love story with the turmoil surrounding the personal lives of men such as Mitch.

A story of our race for the moon, The Pilgrim Project begins as a routine orbital flight is mysteriously ordered to abort prematurely. Except for the commander, even the men aboard do not know that a top secret plan must be put in to effect immediately to land an American on the moon ahead of the Russians. The reader remains in a sustained sense of urgency and intrigue as NASA officials, Congressmen, the President, the media, and the astronauts themselves unravel clues about a plan so secret that even the man who originated it does not know it is about to be carried out. The tempo accelerates even more when it is discovered that the Russian moon shot carries a civilian cosmonaut, and the American astronauts are quickly switched to include the civilian Steve Lawrence in order to prove our equally peaceful intentions. When the Pilgrim Project is finally revealed, all concerned must re-evaluate their psychological and moral attitudes about what appears to be a heroic but suicidal one-way flight to the moon. Both Russians and Americans launch, and the race is neck and neck all the way. Several subplots weave throughout the story, providing continuous action.

It is clear that Hank Searl knows his way around both the thechnical and the human aspects of the space program, and if his stories have not retained their impact, it is only a matter of timing. The fictional Big X barely preceded North American's X-15, untested in free flight at the time, and The Pilgrim Project preceded the actual moon landing by less than five years. Still, Searls has incorporated enough human drama into his stories that these after-the-fact elements detract only negligibly for the modern reader.

—Myra Barnes

SELBY, Curt. See PISERCHIA, Doris.

SELLINGS, Arthur. Pseudonym for Robert Arthur Ley; also wrote as Martin Luther. British. Born in 1921. Worked in Customs and as an antiquarian book dealer. Died 24 September 1968.

SCIENCE-FICTION PUBLICATIONS

Novels

Telepath. New York, Ballantine, 1962; as The Silent Speakers, London, Dobson, 1963.
The Uncensored Man. London, Dobson, 1964; New York, Berkley, 1967.
The Quy Effect. London, Dobson, 1966; New York, Berkley, 1967.
Interminds (as Martin Luther). New York, Banner, 1967; London, Dobson, 1969.
The Power of X. London, Dobson, 1968; New York, Berkley, 1970.
Junk Day. London, Dobson, 1970.

Short Stories

Time Transfer and Other Stories. London, Joseph, 1956.
The Long Eureka. London, Dobson, 1968.

Uncollected Short Stories

"The Trial," in New Writings in SF 15, edited John Carnell. London, Dobson, 1969.
"The Legend and the Chemistry," in Fantasy and Science Fiction (New York), January 1969.
"The Dodgers," in Fantastic (New York), April 1969.
"The Last Time Around," in If (New York), November 1970.

*   *   *

Arthur Sellings was interested in how man reacts to the unknown, whether in outer space or on his own planet. He believed man is slowly evolving but that his essential self, with its present weaknesses and strengths, will endure—even if in unrecognizable forms. Thus his works explore man's inner space, his adaptability, his sense of responsibility, his psychological reactions (to holocaust, time travel, alien confrontation, genetic engineering), and his psychological potentialities (to control bodily shape, change reality, span dimensions, read thoughts). Notable among his short stories are "The Well-Trained Heroes," which deals with a special task force trained to predict and reduce urban tensions by becoming scapegoats, "Homecoming," wherein a disturbed space explorer discovers he has spent centuries in suspended animation and now resides amid aliens, "Verbal Agreement," about a cosmic salesman who learns, through poetry, to adapt a telepathic society to his needs, and "Start in Life," which records the robot training of five-year-old survivors of a starship plague.

Always Sellings's stories and novels focus on a well-developed central figure who must come to terms with the unexpected, while in the background large military complexes and political groups vie for power. In *The Power of X*, a conspiracy novel, an art dealer learns that other dimensions may be ones of time, not space, as he explores the dangers of "plying," a modern duplicating process which perfectly reproduces originals whether Old Masters or a living President. *The Quy Effect* depicts an aging inventor's struggle to perfect and publicize anti-gravity power, while *Intermind* focuses on a secret agent injected with a dead spy's memory. In *Telepath* young strangers, suddenly intimate due to unsuspected tele-pathic powers, combat the destiny of their life form until they gradually understand and communicate to others this mutant power which can transform man's future, opening up the potentiality for preserving racial memories through generations in space. The intriguing and suspenseful *Uncensored Man* focuses on a nuclear physicist's contact with another dimension, one where racial memories and the minds of earth's dead have accumulated and developed and now seek to reveal to man the power in his genes and in his physical and chemical heritage. The novel includes disappearing bodies, sympathetic, multi-personality beings warning of man's self-destructive blindless, and a hero who develops a full range of psi powers to protect the future of two dimensions. In Sellings's finest work, *Junk Day*, a cynical, gripping, post-holocaust tale of survival, a traumatized artist joins forces with a wary novitiate to tackle the junkman, a tough lower-class bully who, in a ruined world, is king of the London junkpile. The junkman's protection racket helps reunite dispersed humanity, while destroying the basic values that, from the artist's view, make life valuable. Ultimately his power is confirmed by overbearing scientists who set themselves up as gods of the new order, reconditioning and transforming those who fail to meet their interpretation of the ideal citizen.

Sellings's works have interesting themes, careful characteriz-ation, sensory detail, and satisfying suspense, all handled with discipline and restraint. Frequently a central character is an artist whose special power of perception, temperament, and intuitive insight raise him above the limitations of those around him. Sellings's typical pattern is for such a character, confronted with the unusual, first to doubt his sanity, but then rationally confirm his perceptions, and ultimately learn to deal with new powers or concepts, and understand and accept the responsi-bilities they entail.

—Gina Macdonald

SENARENS, Luis P(hilip). Also wrote as Captain Howard. American. Born in Brooklyn, New York, 24 April 1865. Educated at St. John's College, Brooklyn; law degree. Married in 1895; one son and one daughter. Free-lance writer from age 16: Editor, Frank Tousey publications, from 1904, and scenario writer from 1911; Editor, *Moving Picture Stories Weekly*, from 1913; retired in 1923. *Died in 1939.*

SCIENCE-FICTION PUBLICATIONS

Novels (series: Frank Reade, Jr.)

Frank Reade, Jr. and His Steam Wonder. New York, Tousey, 1884.
Frank Reade, Jr. and His Electric Boat. New York, Tousey, 1884.
Frank Reade, Jr. and His Adventures with His Latest Invention. New York, Tousey, 1884.
Frank Reade, Jr. and His Airship. New York, Tousey, 1884.
Frank Reade, Jr.'s Marvel; or, Above and Below Water. New York, Tousey, 1884.
Frank Reade, Jr. in the Clouds. New York, Tousey, 1885.
Frank Reade, Jr.'s Great Electric Tricycle and What He Did for Charity. New York, Tousey, 1885.
Frank Reade, Jr. and His Airship in Africa. New York, Tousey, 1885.
Across the Continent on Wings; or Frank Reade, Jr.'s Greatest Flight. New York, Tousey, 1886.
Frank Reade, Jr. Exploring Mexico in His New Airship. New York, Tousey, 1886.
The Electric Man; or Frank Reade, Jr. in Australia. New York, Tousey, 1887.
The Electric Horse; or, Frank Reade, Jr. and His Father in Search of the Lost Treasure of the Peruvians. New York, Tousey, 1888.
Frank Reade, Jr.'s Race Through the Clouds. New York, Tousey, 1888.
Frank Reade, Jr. and His Electric Team; or, In Search of a Missing Man. New York, Tousey, 1888.
Frank Reade, Jr.'s Search for a Sunken Ship; or, Working for the Government. New York, Tousey, 1889.
Frank Reade, Jr. in the Far West; or, The Search for a Lost Gold Mine. New York, Tousey, 1890.
Frank Reade, Jr. and His Queen Clipper of the Clouds. New York, Tousey, 1890.
Frank Reade, Jr. and His Monitor of the Deep; or, Helping a Friend in Need. New York, Tousey, 1890.
Frank Reade, Jr. Exploring a River of Mystery. New York, Tousey, 1890.
Frank Reade, Jr. and His Electric Air Yacht; or, The Great Inventor among the Aztecs. New York, Tousey, 1891.
Frank Reade, Jr. in a Sea of Sand and His Discovery of a Lost People. New York, Tousey, 1891.
Frank Reade, Jr. and His Greyhound of the Air; or, The Search for the Mountain of Gold. New York, Tousey, 1891.
From Pole to Pole; or, Frank Reade, Jr.'s Strange Submarine Voyage. New York, Tousey, 1891.
Frank Reade, Jr. and His Electric Coach; or, The Search for the Isle of Diamonds. New York, Tousey, 1891.
Frank Reade, Jr. and His Airship in Asia; or, A Flight Across the Steppes. New York, Tousey, 1892.
Frank Reade, Jr. and His Electric Ice Boat; or, Lost in the Land of Crimson Snow. New York, Tousey, 1892.
Frank Reade, Jr.'s Electric Cyclone; or, Thrilling Adventures in No Man's Land. New York, Tousey, 1892.
Frank Reade, Jr. and His New Steam Man; or, The Young Inventor's Trip to the Far West. New York, Tousey, 1892.

Frank Reade, Jr. with His New Steam Man in No Man's Land; or, On a Mysterious Trail. New York, Tousey, 1892.

Frank Reade, Jr. with His New Steam Man in Central America. New York, Tousey, 1892.

Frank Reade, Jr. with His New Steam Man in Texas; or, Chasing the Train Robbers. New York, Tousey, 1892.

Frank Reade, Jr. with His New Steam Man in Mexico; or, Hot Work among the Greasers. New York, Tousey, 1892.

Frank Reade, Jr. with His New Steam Man Chasing a Gang of "Rustlers," or, Wild Adventures in Montana. New York, Tousey, 1892.

Frank Reade, Jr. and His New Steam Horse; or, The Search for a Million Dollars. New York, Tousey, 1892.

Frank Reade, Jr. with His New Steam Horse among the Cowboys; or, The League of the Plains. New York, Tousey, 1892.

Frank Reade, Jr. with His New Steam Horse in the Great American Desert; or, The Sandy Trail of Death. New York, Tousey, 1892.

Frank Reade, Jr. with His New Steam Horse and the Mystery of the Underground Ranch. New York, Tousey, 1892.

Frank Reade, Jr. with His New Steam Horse in Search of an Ancient Mine. New York, Tousey, 1892.

Frank Reade, Jr. with His New Steam Horse in the North-West; or, Wild Adventures among the Blackfeet. New York, Tousey, 1892.

Frank Reade, Jr.'s Electric Air Canoe; or, The Search for the Valley of Diamonds. New York, Tousey, 1892.

Frank Reade, Jr.'s New Electric Submarine Boat "The Explorer"; or, To the North Pole under the Ice. New York, Tousey, 1893.

Frank Reade, Jr.'s New Electric Van; or, Hunting Wild Animals in the Jungles of India. New York, Tousey, 1893.

Frank Reade, Jr.'s "White Cruiser" of the Clouds; or, The Search for the Dog-Faced Men. New York, Tousey, 1893.

Frank Reade, Jr.'s Deep Sea Diver the "Tortoise"; or, The Search for a Sunken Island. New York, Tousey, 1893.

Frank Reade, Jr.'s New Electric Terror the "Thunderer"; or, The Search for the Tartar's Captive. New York, Tousey, 1893.

Frank Reade, Jr. and His Air-Ship. New York, Tousey, 1893.

Frank Reade, Jr.'s Latest Air Wonder the "Kite"; or, A Six Weeks' Flight Over the Andes. New York, Tousey, 1893.

Frank Reade, Jr.'s New Electric Invention the "Warrior"; or, Fighting the Apaches in Arizona. New York, Tousey, 1893.

Frank Reade, Jr.'s "Sea Serpent"; or, The Search for Sunken Gold. New York, Tousey, 1893.

Fighting the Slave Hunters; or, Frank Reade, Jr. in Central Africa. New York, Tousey, 1893.

Around the World Under Water; or, The Wonderful Cruise of a Submarine Boat. New York, Tousey, 1893.

Lost in the Land of Fire; or, Across the Pampas in the Electric Turret. New York, Tousey, 1893.

Six Weeks in the Great Whirlpool; or, Strange Adventures in a Submarine Boat. New York, Tousey, 1893.

Chased Across the Sahara; or, The Bedouins' Captive. New York, Tousey, 1893.

The Mystic Brand; or, Frank Reade, Jr. and His Overland Stage upon the Staked Plains. New York, Tousey, 1893.

Frank Reade, Jr. and His New Torpedo Boat; or, At War with the Brazilian Rebels. New York, Tousey, 1893.

Frank Reade, Jr. and His Magnetic Gun-Carriage; or, Working for the U. S. Mail. New York, Tousey, 1893.

Frank Reade, Jr. and His Engine of the Clouds; or, Chased Around the World in the Sky. New York, Tousey, 1893.

The Sunken Pirate; or, Frank Reade, Jr. in Search of Treasure at the Bottom of the Sea. New York, Tousey, 1893.

Frank Reade, Jr. and His Electric Air-Boat; or, Hunting Wild Beasts for a Circus. New York, Tousey, 1893.

The Black Range; or, Frank Reade, Jr. among the Cowboys with His New Electric Caravan. New York, Tousey, 1894.

From Zone to Zone; or, The Wonderful Trip of Frank Reade, Jr. with His Latest Air-Ship. New York, Tousey, 1894.

Frank Reade, Jr. and His Electric Prairie Schooner; or, Fighting the Mexican Horse Thieves. New York, Tousey, 1894.

Frank Reade, Jr. and His Electric Cruiser of the Lakes; or, A Journey Through Africa by Water. New York, Tousey, 1894.

Adrift in Africa; or, Frank Reade, Jr. among the Ivory Hunters with His New Electric Wagon. New York, Tousey, 1894.

Six Weeks in the Clouds; or, Frank Reade Jr.'s Air-Ship, The Thunderbolt of the Skies. New York, Tousey, 1894.

Frank Reade, Jr.'s Electric Air Racer; or, Around the Globe in Thirty Days. New York, Tousey, 1894.

Frank Reade, Jr. and His Flying Ice Ship; or, Driven Adrift in the Frozen Sky. New York, Tousey, 1894.

Frank Reade, Jr. and His Electric Sea Engine; or, Hunting for a Sunken Diamond Mine. New York, Tousey, 1894.

Frank Reade, Jr. Exploring a Submarine Mountain; or, Lost at the Bottom of the Sea. New York, Tousey, 1894.

Frank Reade, Jr.'s Electric Buckboard; or, Thrilling Adventures in North Australia. New York, Tousey, 1894.

Frank Reade, Jr.'s Search for the Sea Serpent; or, Six Thousand Miles under the Sea. New York, Tousey, 1894.

Frank Reade, Jr.'s Desert Explorer; or, The Underground City of the Sahara. New York, Tousey, 1894.

Frank Reade, Jr.'s New Electric Air-Ship the "Zephyr"; or, From North to South Around the Globe. New York, Tousey, 1894.

Across the Frozen Sea; or, Frank Reade, Jr.'s Electric Snow Cutter. New York, Tousey, 1894.

Lost in the Great Atlantic Valley; or, Frank Reade, Jr. and His Submarine Wonder the "Dart." New York, Tousey, 1894.

Frank Reade, Jr. and His New Electric Air-Ship the "Eclipse"; or, Fighting the Chinese Pirates. New York, Tousey, 1894.

Frank Reade, Jr.'s Clipper of the Prairie; or, Fighting the Apaches in the Far Southwest. New York, Tousey, 1894.

Under the Amazon for a Thousand Miles; or, Frank Reade, Jr.'s Wonderful Trip. New York, Tousey, 1894.

Frank Reade, Jr.'s Search for the Silver Whale; or, Under the Ocean in the Electric "Dolphin." New York, Tousey, 1894.

Frank Reade, Jr.'s Catamaran of the Air; or, Wild and Wonderful Adventures in North Australia. New York, Tousey, 1894.

Frank Reade, Jr.'s Search for a Lost Man in His Latest Air Wonder. New York, Tousey, 1894.

Frank Reade, Jr. in Central India; or, The Search for the Lost Savants. New York, Tousey, 1894.

The Missing Island; or, Frank Reade, Jr.'s Wonderful Trip under the Deep Sea. New York, Tousey, 1894.

Over the Andes with Frank Reade, Jr. in His New Air-Ship; or, Wild Adventures in Peru. New York, Tousey, 1894.

Frank Reade, Jr.'s Prairie Whirlwind; or, The Mystery of the Hidden Canyon. New York, Tousey, 1894.

Under the Yellow Sea; or, Frank Reade, Jr.'s Search for the Cave of Pearls with His New Submarine Cruiser. New York, Tousey, 1894.

Around the Horizon for Ten Thousand Miles; or, Frank Reade, Jr.'s Most Wonderful Trip with His Air-Ship. New York, Tousey, 1894.

Frank Reade, Jr.'s "Sky Scraper"; or, North and South Around the World. New York, Tousey, 1894.

Under the Equator from Ecuador to Borneo; or, Frank Reade, Jr.'s Greatest Submarine Voyage. New York, Tousey, 1894.

From Coast to Coast; or, Frank Reade, Jr.'s Trip Across Africa in

His Electric "Boomerang." New York, Tousey, 1894.

Frank Reade, Jr. and His Electric Car; or, Outwitting a Desperate Gang. New York, Tousey, 1894.

Lost in the Mountains of the Moon; or, Frank Reade, Jr.'s Great Trip with His New Air-Ship, the "Scud." New York, Tousey, 1894.

100 Miles Below the Surface of the Sea; or, The Marvelous Trip of Frank Reade, Jr.'s "Hardshell" Submarine Boat. New York, Tousey, 1894.

Abandoned in Alaska; or, Frank Reade, Jr.'s Thrilling Search for a Lost Gold Claim with His New Electric Wagon. New York, Tousey, 1894.

Around the Arctic Circle; or, Frank Reade, Jr.'s Most Famous Trip with His Air-Ship, The "Orbit." New York, Tousey, 1894.

Under Four Oceans; or, Frank Reade, Jr.'s Submarine Chase of a "Sea Devil." New York, Tousey, 1894.

From the Nile to the Niger; or, Frank Reade, Jr. Lost in the Soudan with His "Overland Omnibus." New York, Tousey, 1894.

The Chase of a Comet; or, Frank Reade, Jr.'s Most Wonderful Aerial Trip with His New Air-Ship, The "Flash." New York, Tousey, 1894.

Lost in the Great Undertow; or, Frank Reade, Jr.'s Submarine Cruise in the Gulf Stream. New York, Tousey, 1894.

From Tropic to Tropic; or, Frank Reade, Jr.'s Latest Tour with His Bicycle Car. New York, Tousey, 1894.

To the End of the Earth in an Air-Ship; or, Frank Reade, Jr.'s Great Mid-Air Flight. New York, Tousey, 1894.

The Underground Sea; or, Frank Reade, Jr.'s Subterranean Cruise in His Submarine Boat. New York, Tousey, 1894.

The Mysterious Mirage; or, Frank Reade, Jr.'s Desert Search for a Secret City with His New Overland Chaise. New York, Tousey, 1894.

The Electric Island; or, Frank Reade, Jr.'s Search for the Greatest Wonder on Earth with His Air-Ship, The "Flight." New York, Tousey, 1894.

For Six Weeks Buried in a Deep Sea Cave; or, Frank Reade, Jr.'s Great Submarine Search. New York, Tousey, 1894.

The Galleon's Gold; or, Frank Reade, Jr.'s Deep Sea Search. New York, Tousey, 1894.

Across Australia with Frank Reade, Jr. in His New Electric Car; or, Wonderful Adventures in the Antipodes. New York, Tousey, 1894.

Frank Reade, Jr.'s Greatest Flying Machine; or, Fighting the Terror of the Coast. New York, Tousey, 1894.

On the Great Meridian with Frank Reade, Jr. in His New Air-Ship; or, A Twenty-Five Thousand Mile Trip in Mid-Air. New York, Tousey, 1895.

Under the Indian Ocean with Frank Reade, Jr. ; or, A Cruise in a Submarine Boat. New York, Tousey, 1895.

Astray in the Selvas; or, The Wild Experiences of Frank Reade, Jr., Barney and Pomp, in South America with the Electric Car. New York, Tousey, 1895.

Lost in a Comet's Tail; or, Frank Reade, Jr.'s Strange Adventure with His New Air-Ship. New York, Tousey, 1895.

Six Sunken Pirates; or, Frank Reade, Jr.'s Marvelous Adventures in the Deep Sea. New York, Tousey, 1895.

Beyond the Gold Coast; or, Frank Reade, Jr.'s Overland Trip with His Electric Phaeton. New York, Tousey, 1895.

Latitude 90; or, Frank Reade, Jr.'s Most Wonderful Mid-Air Flight. New York, Tousey, 1895.

Afloat in a Sunken Forest; or, With Frank Reade, Jr. on a Submarine Cruise. New York, Tousey, 1895.

Across the Desert of Fire; or, Frank Reade, Jr.'s Marvelous Trip to a Strange Country. New York, Tousey, 1895.

Over Two Continents; or, Frank Reade, Jr.'s Long Distance Flight with His New Air-Ship. New York, Tousey, 1895.

The Coral Labyrinth; or, Lost with Frank Reade, Jr. in a Deep Sea Cave. New York, Tousey, 1895.

Along the Orinoco; or, With Frank Reade, Jr. in Venezuela. New York, Tousey, 1895.

Across the Earth; or, Frank Reade, Jr.'s Latest Trip with His New Air-Ship. New York, Tousey, 1895.

1,000 Fathoms Deep; or, With Frank Reade, Jr. in the Sea of Gold. New York, Tousey, 1895.

The Island in the Air; or, Frank Reade, Jr.'s Trip to the Tropics. New York, Tousey, 1895.

In the Wild Man's Land; or, With Frank Reade, Jr. in the Heart of Australia. New York, Tousey, 1895.

The Sunken Isthmus; or, With Frank Reade, Jr. in the Yucatan Channel, with His New Submarine Yacht, The "Sea Diver ." New York, Tousey, 1895.

The Lost Caravan; or, Frank Reade, Jr. on the Staked Plains with His "Electric Racer." New York, Tousey, 1895.

The Transient Lake; or, Frank Reade, Jr.'s Adventures in a Mysterious Country with His New Air-Ship, The "Spectre." New York, Tousey, 1895.

The Weird Island; or, Frank Reade, Jr.'s Strange Submarine Search for a Deep Sea Wonder. New York, Tousey, 1895.

The Abandoned Country; or, Frank Reade, Jr. Exploring a New Continent. New York, Tousey, 1895.

Over the Steppes; or, Adrift in Asia with Frank Reade, Jr. New York, Tousey, 1895.

The Unknown Sea; or, Frank Reade, Jr.'s Under-Water Cruise. New York, Tousey, 1895.

In the Black Zone; or, Frank Reade, Jr.'s Quest for the Mountain of Ivory. New York, Tousey, 1895.

The Lost Navigators; or, Frank Reade, Jr.'s Mid-Air Search with His New Air-Ship, The "Sky Flyer." New York, Tousey, 1895.

The Magic Island; or, Frank Reade, Jr.'s Deep Sea Trip of Mystery. New York, Tousey, 1895.

Through the Tropics; or, Frank Reade, Jr.'s Adventures in the Gran Chaco. New York, Tousey, 1895.

In White Latitudes; or, Frank Reade, Jr.'s Ten Thousand Mile Flight over the Frozen North. New York, Tousey, 1895.

Below the Sahara; or, Frank Reade, Jr. Exploring an Underground River, with His Submarine Boat. New York, Tousey, 1895.

The Black Mogul; or, Through India with Frank Reade, Jr. Abroad His "Electric Boomer." New York, Tousey, 1895.

The Missing Planet; or, Frank Reade, Jr.'s Quest for a Fallen Star with His New Air-Ship, "The Zenith." New York, Tousey, 1895.

The Black Squadron; or, Frank Reade, Jr. in the Indian Ocean with His Submarine Boat, The "Rocket." New York, Tousey, 1895.

The Prairie Pirates; or, Frank Reade, Jr.'s Trip to Texas with His Electric Vehicle, The "Detective." New York, Tousey, 1895.

Over the Orient; or, Frank Reade, Jr.'s Travels in Turkey with His New Air-Ship. New York, Tousey, 1895.

The Black Whirlpool; or, Frank Reade, Jr.'s Deep Sea Search for a Lost Ship. New York, Tousey, 1895.

The Silent City; or, Frank Reade, Jr.'s Visit to a Strange People with His New Electric "Flyer." New York, Tousey, 1895.

The White Desert; or, Frank Reade, Jr.'s Trip to the Land of Tombs. New York, Tousey, 1895.

Under the Gulf of Guinea; or, Frank Reade, Jr. Exploring the Sunken Reef of Gold with His New Submarine Boat. New

York, Tousey, 1895.

The Yellow Khan; or, Frank Reade, Jr. among the Thugs in Central India. New York, Tousey, 1895.

Frank Reade, Jr. in Japan, with His War Cruiser of the Clouds. New York, Tousey, 1895.

Frank Reade, Jr. in Cuba; or, Helping the Patriots with His Latest Air-Ship. New York, Tousey, 1895.

Chasing a Pirate; or, Frank Reade, Jr. on a Desperate Cruise. New York, Tousey, 1895.

In the Land of Fire; or, Frank Reade, Jr. among the Head Hunters. New York, Tousey, 1895.

7,000 Miles Underground; or, Frank Reade, Jr. Exploring a Volcano. New York, Tousey, 1895.

The Demon of the Clouds; or, Frank Reade, Jr. and the Ghosts of Phantom Island. New York, Tousey, 1895.

The Cloud City; or, Frank Reade, Jr.'s Most Wonderful Discovery. New York, Tousey, 1895.

The White Atoll; or, Frank Reade, Jr. in the South Pacific. New York, Tousey, 1895.

The Monarch of the Moon; or, Frank Reade, Jr.'s Exploits in Africa with His Electric "Thunderer." New York, Tousey, 1895.

37 Bags of Gold; or, Frank Reade, Jr. Hunting for a Lost Steamer. New York, Tousey, 1895.

The Lost Lake; or, Frank Reade, Jr.'s Trip to Alaska. New York, Tousey, 1895.

The Caribs' Cave; or, Frank Reade, Jr.'s Submarine Search for the Reef of Pearls. New York, Tousey, 1895.

The Desert of Death; or, Frank Reade, Jr. Exploring an Unknown Land. New York, Tousey, 1895.

A Trip to the Sea of the Sun; or, With Frank Reade, Jr. on a Perilous Cruise. New York, Tousey, 1895.

The Black Lagoon; or, Frank Reade, Jr.'s Submarine Search for a Sunken City in Russia. New York, Tousey, 1896.

The Mysterious Brand; or, Frank Reade, Jr. Solving a Mexican Mystery. New York, Tousey, 1896.

Across the Milky Way; or, Frank Reade, Jr.'s Great Astronomical Trip with His Air-Ship, "The Shooting Star." New York, Tousey, 1896.

Under the Great Lakes; or, Frank Reade, Jr.'s Latest Submarine Cruise. New York, Tousey, 1896.

The Magic Mine; or, Frank Reade, Jr.'s Trip up the Yukon with His Electric Combination Traveller. New York, Tousey, 1896.

Across Arabia; or, Frank Reade, Jr.'s Search for the Forty Thieves. New York, Tousey, 1896.

The Silver Sea; or, Frank Reade, Jr.'s Submarine Cruise in Unknown Waters. New York, Tousey, 1896.

In the Tundras; or, Frank Reade, Jr.'s Latest Trip Through Northern Asia. New York, Tousey, 1896.

The Circuit of Cancer; or, Frank Reade, Jr.'s Novel Trip Around the World with His New Air-Ship, The "Flight." New York, Tousey, 1896.

The Sacred Sea; or, Frank Reade, Jr.'s Submarine Exploits among the Dervishes of India. New York, Tousey, 1896.

The Land of Dunes; or, With Frank Reade, Jr. in the Desert of Gobi. New York, Tousey, 1896.

Six Days under Havana Harbor; or, Frank Reade, Jr.'s Secret Service Work for Uncle Sam. New York, Tousey, 1896.

The Sinking Star; or, Frank Reade, Jr.'s Trip into Space with His New Air-Ship "Saturn." New York, Tousey, 1896.

In the Gran Chaco; or, Frank Reade, Jr. in Search of a Missing Man. New York, Tousey, 1896.

The Lost Oasis; or, With Frank Reade, Jr. in the Australian Desert. New York, Tousey, 1896.

The Isle of Hearts; or, Frank Reade, Jr. in a Strange Sea with His

Submarine Boat. New York, Tousey, 1896.

Jack Wright and Frank Reade, Jr., The Two Young Inventors; or, Brains Against Brains. New York, Tousey, 1896.

Novels (series: Jack Wright)

Jack Wright, The Boy Inventor; or, Hunting for a Sunken Treasure. New York, Tousey, 1891.

Jack Wright and His Electric Turtle; or, Chasing the Pirates of the Spanish Main. New York, Tousey, 1891.

Jack Wright's Submarine Catamaran; or, The Phantom Ship of the Yellow Sea. New York, Tousey, 1891.

Jack Wright and His Ocean Racer; or, Around the World in Twenty Days. New York, Tousey, 1891.

Jack Wright and His Electric Canoe; or, Working the Revenue Service. New York, Tousey, 1891.

Jack Wright's Air and Water Cutter; or, Wonderful Adventures on the Wing and Afloat. New York, Tousey, 1891.

Jack Wright and His Magnetic Motor; or, The Golden City of the Sierras. New York, Tousey, 1891.

Jack Wright, The Boy Inventor, and His Under-Water Iron-clad; or, The Treasure of the Sandy Sea. New York, Tousey, 1892.

Jack Wright and His Electric Deer; or, Fighting the Bandits of the Black Hills. New York, Tousey, 1892.

Jack Wright and His Prairie Engine; or, Among the Bushmen of Australia. New York, Tousey, 1892.

Jack Wright and His Electric Air Schooner; or, The Mystery of a Magic Mine. New York, Tousey, 1892.

Jack Wright and His Electric Sea-Motor; or, The Search for a Drifting Wreck. New York, Tousey, 1892.

Jack Wright and His Ocean Sleuth-Hound; or, Tracking an Underwater Treasure. New York, Tousey, 1892.

Jack Wright and His Dandy of the Deep; or, Driven Afloat in the Sea of Fire. New York, Tousey, 1892.

Jack Wright and His Electric Torpedo Ram; or, The Sunken City of the Atlantic. New York, Tousey, 1892.

Jack Wright and His Deep Sea Monitor; or, Searching for a Ton of Gold. New York, Tousey, 1892.

Jack Wright, The Boy Inventor, Exploring Central Asia in His Magnetic Hurricane. New York, Tousey, 1892.

Jack Wright and His Ocean Plunger; or, The Harpoon Hunters of the Arctic. New York, Tousey, 1892.

Jack Wright and His Electric "Sea-Ghost"; or, A Strange Under-Water Journey. New York, Tousey, 1892.

Jack Wright, The Boy Inventor, and His Deep Sea Diving Bell; or, The Buccaneers of The Gold Coast. New York, Tousey, 1892.

Jack Wright, The Boy Inventor, and His Electric Tricycle-Boat; or, The Treasure of the Sun-Worshippers. New York, Tousey, 1892.

Jack Wright and His Undersea Wrecking Raft; or, The Mystery of a Scuttled Ship. New York, Tousey, 1892.

Jack Wright and His Terror of the Seas; or, Fighting for a Sunken Fortune. New York, Tousey, 1892.

Jack Wright and His Electric Diving Boat; or, Lost under the Ocean. New York, Tousey, 1892.

Jack Wright and His Submarine Yacht; or, The Fortune Hunters of The Red Sea. New York, Tousey, 1892.

Jack Wright and His Electric Gunboat; or, The Search for a Stolen Girl. New York, Tousey, 1893.

Jack Wright and His Electric Sea Launch; or, A Desperate Cruise for Life. New York, Tousey, 1893.

Jack Wright and His Electric Bicycle-Boat; or, Searching for Captain Kidd's Gold. New York, Tousey, 1893.

Jack Wright and His Electric Side-Wheel Boat; or, Fighting the Brigands of the Coral Isles. New York, Tousey, 1893.

Jack Wright's Wonder of the Waves; or, The Flying Dutchman of the Pacific. New York, Tousey, 1893.

Jack Wright and His Electric Exploring Ship; or, A Cruise Around Greenland. New York, Tousey, 1893.

Jack Wright and His Electric Man-of-War; or, Fighting the Sea Robbers of the Frozen Coast. new York, Tousey, 1893.

Jack Wright and His Submarine Torpedo-Tug; or, Winning a Government Reward. New York, Tousey, 1893.

Jack Wright and His Electric Sea-Demon; or, Daring Adventures under the Ocean. New York, Tousey, 1893.

Jack Wright and His Electric "Whale"; or, The Treasure Trove of the Polar Sea. New York, Tousey, 1893.

Jack Wright and His Electric Marine "Rover"; or, 50,000 Miles in Ocean Perils. New York, Tousey, 1893.

Jack Wright and His Electric Deep Sea Cutter; or, Searching for a Pirate's Treasure. New York, Tousey, 1893.

Jack Wright and His Electric Monarch of the Ocean; or, Cruising for a Million in Gold. New York, Tousey, 1893.

Jack Wright and His Electric Devil-Fish; or, Fighting the Smugglers of Alaska. New York, Tousey, 1893.

Jack Wright and His Electric Demon of the Plains; or, Wild Adventures among the Cowboys. New York, Tousey, 1893.

Jack Wright and His Electric Balloon Ship; or, 30,000 Leagues above the Earth. New York, Tousey, 1893.

Jack Wright and His Electric Locomotive; or, The Lost Mine of Death Valley. New York, Tousey, 1893.

Jack Wright and His Iron-Clad Air-Motor; or, Searching for a Lost Explorer. New York, Tousey, 1893.

Jack Wright and His Electric Tricycle; or, Fighting the Stranglers of the Crimson Desert. New York, Tousey, 1893.

Jack Wright and His Electric Dynamo Boat; or, The Mystery of a Buried Sea. New York, Tousey, 1893.

Jack Wright and His Flying Torpedo; or, the Black Demons of Dismal Swamp. New York, Tousey, 1893.

Jack Wright and His Prairie Privateer; or, Fighting the Western Road-Agents. New York, Tousey, 1893.

Jack Wright and His Naval Cruiser; or, Fighting the Pirates of the Pacific. New York, Tousey, 1893.

Jack Wright, The Boy Inventor, and His Whaleback Privateer; or, Cruising in the Behring Sea. New York, Tousey, 1893.

Jack Wright and His Electric Phantom Boat; or, Chasing the Outlaws of the Ocean. New York, Tousey, 1893.

Jack Wright and His Winged Gunboat; or, A Voyage to an Unknown Land. New York, Tousey, 1894.

Jack Wright and His Electric Flyer; or, Racing in the Clouds for a Boy's Life. New York, Tousey, 1894.

Jack Wright, The Boy Inventor's Electric Sledge Boat; or, Wild Adventures in Alaska. New York, Tousey, 1894.

Jack Wright and His Electric Express Wagon; or, Wiping Out the Outlaws of Deadwood. New York, Tousey, 1894.

Jack Wright and His Submarine Explorer; or, A Cruise at the Bottom of the Ocean. New York, Tousey, 1894.

Jack Wright and His Demon of the Air; or, A Perilous Trip in the Clouds. New York, Tousey, 1894.

Jack Wright and His Electric Ripper; or, Searching for a Treasure in the Jungle. New York, Tousey, 1894.

Jack Wright and His King of the Sea; or, Diving for Old Spanish Gold. New York, Tousey, 1894.

Jack Wright and His Electric Balloons; or, Cruising in the Clouds for a Mountain Treasure. New York, Tousey, 1894.

Jack Wright and His Imp of the Ocean; or, The Wreckers of Whirlpool Reef. New York, Tousey, 1894.

Jack Wright and His Electric Cab; or, Around the Globe on Wheels. New York, Tousey, 1894.

Jack Wright and His Flying Phantom; or, Searching for a Lost Balloonist. New York, Tousey, 1894.

Jack Wright and His Submarine Warship; or, Chasing the Demons of the Sea of Gold. New York, Tousey, 1894.

Jack Wright and His Prairie Yacht; or, Fighting the Indians of the Sea of Grass. New York, Tousey, 1894.

Jack Wright and His Electric Air Rocket; or, The Boy Exile of Siberia. New York, Tousey, 1894.

Jack Wright and His Submarine Destroyer; or, Warring Against the Japanese Pirates. New York, Tousey, 1894.

Jack Wright and His Electric Battery Diver; or, A Two Months' Cruise under Water. New York, Tousey, 1894.

Jack Wright and His Electric Stage; or, Leagued Against the James Boys. New York, Tousey, 1894.

Jack Wright and His Wheel of the Wind; or, The Jewels of the Volcano Dwellers. New York, Tousey, 1894.

Jack Wright and the Head-Hunters of the African Coast; or, The Electric Pirate Chaser. New York, Tousey, 1894.

3,000 Pounds of Gold; or, Jack Wright and His Electric Bat, Fighting the Cliff-Dwellers of the Sierras. New York, Tousey, 1894.

Jack Wright and the Wild Boy of the Woods; or, Exposing a Strange Mystery with the Electric Cart. New York, Tousey, 1894.

Jack Wright among the Demons of the Ocean with His Electric Sea-Fighter. New York, Tousey, 1894.

Jack Wright, The Wizard of Wrightstown and His Electric Dragon; or, A Wild Race to Save a Fortune. New York, Tousey, 1894.

Jack Wright's Electric Land-Clipper; or, Exploring the Mysterious Gobi Desert. New York, Tousey, 1894.

Skull and Cross-Bones; or, Jack Wright's Diving-Bell and the Pirates. New York, Tousey, 1895.

Jack Wright, The Boy Inventor, and His Phantom Frigate; or, Fighting the Coast Wreckers of the Gulf. New York, Tousey, 1895.

Jack Wright and His Air-Ship on Wheels; or, A Perilous Journey to Cape Farewell. New York, Tousey, 1895.

Jack Wright and His Electric Roadster in the Desert of Death; or, Chasing the Australian Brigand. New York, Tousey, 1895.

Jack Wright's Ocean Marvel; or, The Mystery of a Frozen Island. New York, Tousey, 1895.

Jack Wright and His Electric Soaring Machine; or, A Daring Flight Through Miles of Peril. New York, Tousey, 1895.

Jack Wright and His Electric Battery Car; or, Beating the Express Train Robbers. New York, Tousey, 1895.

Jack Wright and His Electric Sea Horse; or, Seven Weeks in Ocean Perils. New York, Tousey, 1895.

Jack Wright and His Electric Balloon Boat; or, A Dangerous Voyage above the Clouds. New York, Tousey, 1895.

In the Jungles of India; or, Jack Wright as a Wild Animal Hunter. New York, Tousey, 1895.

50,000 Leagues under the Sea; or, Jack Wright's Most Dangerous Voyage. New York, Tousey, 1895.

Jack Wright, The Boy Inventor, Working for the Union Pacific Railroad; or, Over the Continent on the "Electric." New York, Tousey, 1895.

Over the South Pole; or, Jack Wright's Search for a Lost Explorer with His Flying Boat. New York, Tousey, 1895.

Jack Wright and His Electric Air Monitor; or, The Scourge of the Pacific. New York, Tousey, 1895.

The Boy Lion Fighter; or, Jack Wright in the Swamps of Africa. New York, Tousey, 1895.

Jack Wright and His Electric Submarine Ranger; or, Afloat among the Cannibals of the Deep. New York, Tousey, 1895.

The Demon of the Sky; or, Jack Wright's $10,000 Wager. New

York, Tousey, 1895.

Adrift in the Land of Snow; or, Jack Wright and His Sledge-Boat on Wheels. New York, Tousey, 1896.

The Floating Terror; or, Jack Wright Fighting the Buccaneers of the Venezuelan Coast. New York, Tousey, 1896.

Lost in the Polar Circle; or, Jack Wright and His Aerial Explorer. New York, Tousey, 1896.

Jack Wright, The Boy Inventor, and the Smugglers of the Border Lakes; or, The Second Cruise of the Whaleback "Comet." New York, Tousey, 1896.

The Fatal Blue Diamond; or, Jack Wright among the Demon Worshippers with His Electric Motor. New York, Tousey, 1896.

Running the Blockade; or, Jack Wright Helping the Cuban Filibusters. New York, Tousey, 1896.

Jack Wright and Frank Reade, Jr., The Two Young Inventors; or, Brains Against Brains. New York, Tousey, 1896.

The Flying Avenger; or, Jack Wright Fighting for Cuba. New York, Tousey, 1896.

Jack Wright and His New Electric Horse; or, A Perilous Trip over Two Continents. New York, Tousey, 1896.

Over the Sahara Desert; or, Jack Wright Fighting the Slave Hunters. New York, Tousey, 1896.

Diving for a Million; or, Jack Wright and His Electric Ocean Liner. New York, Tousey, 1896.

Uncollected Serials (all published in *Happy Days*, New York)

"Young Frank Reade and His Electric Air Ship; or, a 10,000 Mile Search for a Missing Man," 14 October—2 December 1899; "Jack Wright, The Boy Inventor, and His Electric Flying Machine; or, A Record Trip Around the World," 29 March—19 April 1902; "Jack Wright and His Marvel of the Sea; or, Among the Demons of the Deep," 1 June—5 July 1902; "Jack Wright and His Ship of the Desert; or, Adventures in the Sea of Sand," 26 July—16 August 1902; "Jack Wright and His King of the Clouds; or, Around the World on Wings," 16 August—6 September 1902; "Jack Wright and His Submarine Boat; or, Working for the Navy," 20 September—11 October 1902; "Jack Wright and His Red Terror; or, Fighting the Bushmen of Australia," 1—22 November 1902; "Jack Wright and His Tandem Balloons; or, Hunting Wild Beasts in India," 29 November—27 December 1902; "Jack Wright and His Queen of the Deep; or, Exploring Submarine Caves," 10—31 January 1903; "Jack Wright and His Wonder of the Prairie; or, Perils among the Cowboys," 28 February—21 March 1903; "Jack Wright and His Flying Ice Boat; or, Adrift in the Polar Regions," 28 March—18 April 1903; "Jack Wright's Floating Terror; or, Fighting the Pirates," 25 April—16 May 1903; "Jack Wright's Electric Prairie Car; or, Hot Times with the Broncho Busters," 23 May—13 June 1903; "Jack Wright's Sky Scraper; or, After the Lost Balloonists," 20 June—11 July 1903; "Jack Wright's Sea Demon; or, Running the Blockade," 18 July—8 August 1903; "Jack Wright's Rapid Transit; or, Trailing the Cattle Punchers," 29 August—19 September 1903; "Jack Wright's Queen of the Air; or, After the Cliff Dwellers' Gold," 6—27 February 1904; "Jack Wright's King of the Plains; or, Calling Down the Cowboys," 3—24 December 1904.

Uncollected Short Story

"Frank Reade's Christmas in the Air," in *Muldoon's Christmas.* New York, Tousey, 1889.

OTHER PUBLICATIONS

Novels

Young Sleuths in Demijohn City; or, Waltzing William's Dancing School. New York, Tousey, 1894.

Young Sleuths on the Stage; or, An Act Not on the Bills. New York, Tousey, 1894.

Novels as Police Captain Howard

A. D. T.; or, The Messenger Boy Detective. New York, Champion, 1882.

The Girl Detective. New York, Champion, 1882.

The Mystery of One Night. New York, Champion, 1882.

Young Vidocq. New York, Champion, 1882.

Other

How to Become a Naval Cadet. New York, Tousey, 1891.

How to Become a West Point Military Cadet. New York, Tousey, 1891.

* * *

During his lifetime, Luis P. Senarens was referred to as "the American Jules Verne" and a comparison of the work of both writers indicates the similarity. Senarens was writing stories of airships suspended by helicopter blades ("helices") three years before the *Albatross* took off in *Robur le Conquérant (Clipper of the Clouds)* in 1886. His epic serial *Frank Reade, Jr. and His Queen Clipper of the Clouds* leaned heavily on Verne. Even the illustrations were identical, with three of those in Senarens's story also used in Verne's *Maitre du Monde (Master of the World)*. Senarens's story is basically a long air voyage hampered by the presence of several malcontents and a lunatic scientist intent on seizing Frank's vessel.

Frank Reade, boy inventor, was created by Harry Enton, who put himself through medical school writing dime novels and storypaper serials. The steam-driven robot in *The Steam Man of the Plains* (1876) is mainly a device for transporting Frank and his cousin, Charley Gorse, to the far West. The story is a tongue-in-cheek yarn of encounters with outlaws and Indians, named "Motzer-Ponum" and "Sholum Alarkum." Out west, Frank meets the comic Irishman, Barney Shea. Barney and the black man, Pomp (introduced in a later story), became regular members of the cast. The plot may be improbable, but the steam man (borrowed from Edward S. Ellis's 1865 *Steam Man of the Prairies*) is engaging and novel for its day. We are told just enough about how it works to make it plausible. Senarens seemed to take the stories more seriously then Enton when he stepped in with the fifth serial. He introduced Frank Reade, Jr., but kept Frank, Sr., and eventually gave Jr. a wife. No stylist, he often wrote in the choppy manner peculiar to writers paid by the line. Without the aid of a typewriter, he wrote fast, kept the plot moving, and the characters in hot water. In formula fiction the fascination is in the variation on the basic themes. A new airship, surpassing any effort of the imagination; a new type of submarine; electrified equipment to drive off enemies; aluminium bullet-proof armor; pneumatic revolvers; damsels in distress; gentlemen unjustly accused of murder; a race against time; evil men determined to steal the invention; the pranks of comic relief companions, forever quarrelling; the wonderfully strange foreign lands; the deadly beauty of an undersea cavern or ice-locked vessel. Along the way a bit of social comment: does the U. S. government protect citizens abroad? Do the workshops in Readestown provide enough jobs for the community?

Senarens himself claimed authorship of most of the Frank Reade stories and all of the companion series about Jack Wright, who lived in Wrightstown and whose specialty was inventing submarines. His adventures were novelettes cut from the same pattern as the Frank Reades. In 1894 the two raced each other around the world for $10,000. Jack's submarine won by 15 minutes because Frank set down his airship to save a girl on a runaway horse. The stories ended in 1904 when public sentiment decided the ideas were too bizarre and Senarens ran out of ideas, though they lived on in reprints.

Senarens's contribution to science fiction is in his early and imaginative use of so many scientific marvels harnessed for popular consumption to a mass market. Had it not been for the wonders of Senarens there might have been no Tom Swift.

—J. Randolph Cox

SERLING, (Edward) Rod(man). American. Born in Syracuse, New York, 25 December 1924. Educated at Antioch College, Yellow Springs, Ohio, B. A. 1950. Served as a paratrooper in the United States Army during World War II. Married Carolyn Kramer in 1948; two daughters. Writer, WLW-Radio, 1946-48, and WKRC-TV, 1948-53, both Cincinnati; free-lance writer from 1953; Producer of television series *The Twilight Zone*, 1959-64, and *Night Gallery*, from 1969; taught at Antioch College, 1950's, and Ithaca College, New York, 1970's. President, National Academy of Television Arts and Sciences, 1965-66; Member of the Council, Writers Guild of America West, 1965-67. Recipient: Emmy Award, for television plays, 1955, 1957, 1959; Sylvania Award, 1955, 1956; Christopher Award, 1956, 1971; Peabody Award, 1957; Hugo Award, for TV writing, 1960, 1961, 1962. D. H. L. : Emerson College, Boston, 1971; Alfred University, New York, 1972; Litt. D. : Ithaca College, 1972. *Died 28 June 1975*.

SCIENCE-FICTION PUBLICATIONS

Short Stories

Stories from the Twilight Zone. New York, Bantam, 1960.
More Stories from the Twilight Zone. New York, Bantam, 1961.
New Stories from the Twilight Zone. New York, Bantam, 1962.
From the Twilight Zone (selection). New York, Doubleday, 1962.
Night Gallery. New York, Bantam, 1971.
Night Gallery 2. New York, Bantam, 1972.

OTHER PUBLICATIONS

Novel

Requiem for a Heavyweight (novelization of screenplay). New York, Bantam, and London, Corgi, 1962.

Short Stories

The Season to Be Wary. Boston, Little Brown, 1967.

Plays

Requiem for a Heavyweight (televised, 1956). Included in *Patterns*, 1957; (revised version, produced New York, 1979).
Patterns: Four Television Plays (includes *Patterns, The Rack, Requiem for a Heavyweight, Old MacDonald Had a Curve*). New York, Simon and Schuster, 1957.
The Killing Season (produced New York, 1968).
The Lonely, in *Writing for Television*, edited by Max Wylie. New York, Cowles, 1970.
A Storm in Summer, in *Camera Two: Two Plays for Television*. Toronto, Holt Rinehart, 1972.

Screenplays: *Patterns*, 1956; *Saddle the Wind*, with Thomas Thompson, 1958; *Requiem for a Heavyweight*, 1962; *The Yellow Canary* , 1963; *Seven Days in May*, 1964; *Assault on a Queen*, 1966; *Planet of the Apes*, with Michael Wilson, 1968; *A Time for Predators*, 1971.

Television Plays: *Patterns*, 1955; *Requiem for a Heavyweight*, 1956; *Forbidden Area*, from the novel by Pat Frank, 1956; *The Comedian*, 1957; *The Doomsday Flight*, 1966; *The Movie Maker*, with Steve Bochko, 1967; *The Man*, 1971; *The Rack; Old MacDonald Had a Curve; Line of Duty; The Lonely; A Storm in Summer* ; and other plays for *U. S. Steel Hour, Playhouse 90, Hallmark Hall of Fame, Suspense, Twilight Zone, Night Gallery*, and *Danger* series.

*   *   *

One of the handful of scriptwriters who consistently produced quality drama during American television's "golden age" of the 1950's, Rod Serling demonstrated an interest in science-fiction themes as early as 1956, when he adapted Pat Frank's novels *Fobiden Area* for television. Later, as one of the few writers to be given relative artistic control over a TV series, he turned again to science fiction and fantasy with *The Twilight Zone*, an anthology series which began in 1959. *The Twilight Zone* is often cited as one of the first serious attempts to bring intelligent fantastic stories to television, and, in addition to the large number of scripts that Serling himself wrote for the series, he elicited scripts from major writers within the science fiction and fantasy field, including Richard Matheson, Charles Beaumont, and Ray Bradbury. A later TV series, *Night Gallery*, retained a few science-fiction stories but tended more toward fantasy and the supernatural. Serling also wrote the filmscripts for *Seven Days in May* and the hugely successful *Planet of the Apes*.

Serling adapted several of his *Twilight Zone* episodes as short stories. These often reveal the constraints of writing for television, and Serling for the most part made no effort to take advantage of the new form to develop or expand upon his initial scripts. The characters tend to be exaggerated stereotypes, easily recognizable in a half-hour TV format; the style is often precious or portentous, reflecting Serling's own opening and closing narrations for the original shows; and the fantastic elements are kept elementary and at times even simplistic. With their moralistic lessons and often sentimental tone, the tales work more as fables than as serious attempts at character or idea development.

Serling's attitude toward technology, for example, is decidedly ambiguous. When he writes of robots, he is unabashedly sentimental, as in "The Mighty Casey," which concerns a robot pitcher who nearly saves the Brooklyn Dodgers until he gets a mechanical heart which makes him too kind to strike out batters (the story is an odd combination of *Damn Yankees* and *The Wizard of Oz*), or "The Lonely," which concerns a prisoner sentenced to a lonely asteroid who finds companionship in a female robot brought by a kindly spaceship captain (a variation on a story by Ray Bradbury, who seems to be Serling's most consistent influence, even cropping up as a character name in a couple of Serling's stories). But in some stories mechanical contrivances become evil presences with minds of their own—a slot machine bent on destroying a compulsive gambler in "The Fever" or household appliances and a vengeful automobile in "A Thing about Machines. " The implicit technophobia of "A Thing about Machines," however, is undercut by the almost pathological hostility of the victim who is the central character. Other stories also reflect technophobia in their concern with escape into a simpler past life ("A Stop at Willoughby," "Walking Distance"). The relatively few that deal with the familiar science-fiction theme of alien presences, such as "Mr. Dingle, The Strong" or "The Monsters Are Due on Maple Street," treat them as little more than background for stories essentially concerned with character relations.

Not surprisingly, the major strength in Serling's writing is the convincing dialogue and his ability to sketch recognizable characters quickly—both skills well-suited to TV writing. His exposition is weak and at times even cloying, his themes and plots derivative. He is most likely to be remembered for his powerful non-science fiction dramas, such as *Patterns* or *Requiem for a Heavyweight*, and for his contribution in bringing serious, character-oriented fantastic tales—however familiar such tales may have been to veteran readers—to the television screen.

—Gary K. Wolfe

SERVISS, Garrett P(utnam). American. Born in Sharon Springs, New York, 24 March 1851. Educated at Cornell University, Ithaca, New York, B. S. 1872; Columbia University, New York, LL. B. 1874. Married Henrietta Gros le Blond in 1907. Editorial writer, New York *Sun*, to 1892; then lecturer on travel, history, and astronomy, and writer. *Died 25 May 1929.*

SCIENCE-FICTION PUBLICATIONS

Novels

The Moon Metal. New York, Harper, 1900.
A Columbus of Space. New York and London, Appleton, 1911.
The Second Deluge. New York, McBride Nast, and London, Richards, 1912.
Edison's Conquest of Mars. Los Angeles, Carcosa House, 1947; abridged edition, as *Invasion of Mars*, Reseda, California, Powell, 1969.

Uncollected Short Stories

"The Sky Pirate," in *Scrap Book* (New York), April 1909.
"The Moon Maiden," in *Argosy* (New York), May 1915.

OTHER PUBLICATIONS

Other

Astronomy with an Opera-Glass. New York, Appleton, 1888.

Wonders of the Lunar Worlds; or, A Trip to the Moon. New York, Urania, 1892.
Napoleon Bonaparte (lecture). Philadelphia, Morris, 1901.
Other Worlds: Their Nature, Possibilities, and Habitability in the Light of the Latest Discoveries. New York, Appleton, 1901.
Pleasures of the Telescope. New York, Appleton, 1901; London, Hirschfeld, 1902.
The Heavens Without a Telescope, with Leon Barritt. New York, Barritt, 1906.
Planet Tables, Moon Phases, and the Sun's Daily Position, with Leon Barritt. New York, Barritt, 1906.
The Barritt-Serviss Star and Planet Finder, Northern Hemisphere, with Leon Barritt, New York, Barritt, 1906.
The Moon. New York, Appleton, 1907; as *The Story of the Moon*, 1928.
Astronomy with the Naked Eye. New York, Harper, 1908.
Curiosities of the Sky. New York, Harper, 1909.
Round the Year with the Stars. New York, Harper, 1910.
Eloquence: Counsel on the Art of Public Speaking. New York, Harper, 1912.
Astronomy in a Nutshell. New York, Putnam, 1912.
The Einstein Theory of Relativity. New York, Fadman, 1923.
Riding Through Space: The Earth's Scenic Voyage. Springfield, Ohio, Corwell, 1923.

*   *   *

Most of the writings of Garrett P. Serviss were never read, or even suspected, by the generation which lauded his small but significant contribution to science fiction. As a staff writer for the New York *Sun*, and later or a newspaper syndicate, he produced many columns of popular science material, much of which was unsigned. Having made his name as the popular astronomer of his day, he wrote for several leading magazines on subjects ranging from "Facts and Fancies about Mars" to the Shakespeare-Bacon controversy. A series of articles (*Astronomy with an Opera-Glass*) in *Popular Science Monthly* was extended to become the first of a small library of works including such titles as *Other Worlds* and *Curiosities of the Sky*.

His first novel was serialised in 1898 in the New York *Evening Journal*, and was evidently designed to exploit the public interest engendered by H. G. Wells's *The War of the Worlds*. *Edison's Conquest of Mars* was in the nature of a sequel to the Wells classic, though it went far beyond the limits of imaginative conception that even the Master had essayed in a single story. The Martians, too, were rather more human than Wells's monstrous marauders; and they had no chance to launch a second invasion before the great American inventor had organised a counter-attack on Mars in a whole fleet of spaceships armed with deadly disintegrators. Though hurriedly written in a bombastic style, the story was remarkably inventive for its time, anticipating many of the devices which became the substance of later science fiction. No less remarkable is the fact that it was exhumed and published in hardcover only in 1947, having become legendary among fans who admired the author's subsequent stories.

One which attained classic status was *A Columbus of Space*, the tale of a voyage to Venus in an atomic-powered spaceship. Even more notable is *The Second Deluge*, in which a cosmic collision results in a universal flood. The story of how a latter-day Noah saved the human race from extinction proved so popular that it was twice reprinted by *Amazing*, where one reader found it so convincing that he wrote in asking for the plans of Cosmo Versál's ark so that he might save his family from the impending disaster. *The Moon Metal* concerned a mysterious metal originating in the lunar crater Tycho which replaced gold when this became as plentiful as iron. "The Sky Pirate" dared to predict air travel at 140 miles an hour in the year 1936; and "The Moon Maiden," the least of all his works, marked the last appearance of Serviss, in *Argosy*, the magazines which pioneered science fiction long before the advent of the specialist pulps.

—Walter Gillings

SEYMOUR, Alan. Australian. Born in Perth, Western Australia, 6 June 1927. Educated at Fremantle State School and Perth Modern School. Free-lance film and theatre critic and educational writer, Australian Broadcasting commission, late 1940's and 1950's; script editor and producer, BBC Television, London, 1974-1977. Theatre critic, *London Magazine*, 1963-65, and contributor to *Overland*, Melbourne, *Meanjin*, Melbourne and *Bulletin-Observer*, Sydney. Recipient: Sydney Journalists' Club Prize, 1960; Australian Council for the Arts grant, 1974. Address: 74 Upland Road, London SE22 0DB, England.

SCIENCE-FICTION PUBLICATIONS

Novel

The Coming Self-Destruction of the United States of America. London, Souvenir Press, 1969; New York, Grove Press, 1971.

OTHER PUBLICATIONS

Novel

The One Day of the Year. London, Souvenir Press, 1967.

Plays

Swamp Creatures (produced Canberra, 1958).
The One Day of the Year (produced Sydney and London, 1961). Sydney, Angus and Robertson, 1962; included in *Three Australian Plays*, London, Penguin, 1963.
The Gaiety of Nations (produced Glasgow, 1965; London, 1966).
A Break in the Music (produced Perth, 1966).
The Pope and the Pill (produced London, 1968).
Oh Grave, Thy Victory (produced Canberra, 1973).
Structures (produced Perth, 1974).
The Wind from the Plain, adaption of the novel by Yashar Kemal (produced Turku, Finland, 1974-75.
The Float (produced Adelaide, 1980).

Radio Plays: *Little Moron, 1956; A Winter Passion, 1960; Donny Johnson*, 1965 (Finland).

Television Plays: *The Runner*, 1962 (Australia); *Lean Liberty*, 1962; *And It Wasn't Just the Feathers*, 1964; *Auto-Stop*, 1965; *The Trial and Torture of Sir John Rampayne*, 1965; *Stockbrokers Are Smashing But Bankers Are Better*, 1965; *Fixation* , from work by Miles Tripp, 1973; *The Lotus, Tigers Are Better Looking, and Outside the Machine*, from stories by Jean Rhys, 1973-74; *Eustace and Hilda*, from the novels by L. P. Hartley,

1977; *Frost in May*, from the novel by Antonia White, 1982; *Sara Dene* series, 1982 (Australia).

*

Manuscript Collection: Mitchell Library, Sydney.

Theatrical Activities:
Director: **Plays**—*The One Day of the Year*, Australia tour, 1961. Operas for the Sydney Opera Group, 1953-57.

* * *

Alan Seymour produced his important science-fiction novel. *The Coming Self-Destruction of the United States of America*, when anxiety over Vietnam and racism were at fever pitch. Reviewers recognized its quality, but its plot and message, that racism will lead to guerilla civil war and the ruin of America, virtually guaranteed it would be no best seller. Such has been the fate of the host of works on these subjects, though Sam Greenlee's *The Spook Who Sat by the Door*, telling a similar tale, sold widely. In any case Seymour tells this story as well as it's been told. Its mysterious black revolutionary leader, "Hero," accurately recalls the authentic "Stagger Lee" of Black American folklore. Seymour keeps the focus on the experience of the individual human participants in the events with snippets of diaries, logs, tapes, and letters, and first-person narrating "editor. " The effect is a mosaic of awful concrete detail in place of sweeping abstraction that so often diminishes the impact of science-fiction. The sociology is excellent. That the political and economic theory that vaguely bolsters the novel is questionable matters not at all. America's racism is a fatal expression of its mono-cultural obsession and paranoia. In this context a black revolutionary effort will give no quarter, even to sympathetic whites. The result will be, therefore, ruinous as well for blacks.

Self-Destruction is a fine representative of the ruin-of-America and racial civil war stories that go back to Martin R. Deleny's *Blake; or, The Huts of America* (1859), W. E. B. Du Bois's *Dark Princess* (1928), Sinclair Lewis's *It Can't Happen Here* (1935),and Warren Miller's *The Siege of Harlem* (1964).

—John R. Pfeiffer

SHARKEY, Jack. (John Michael Sharkey). Also writes as Rick Abbot; Monk Ferris; Mike Johnson. American. Born in Chicago, Illinois, 6 May 1931. Educated at St. Mary's College, Winona, Minnesota, B. A. in English 1953. Served in the United States Army, 1955-56. Married Patricia Walsh in 1962; three daughters and one son. Since 1952, professional writer: Assistant Editor, *Playboy*, Chicago, 1963-64; Editor, *Aim*, later *Good Hands*, for Allstate Insurance, Northbrook, Illinois, 1964-75. Recipient: American Association of Industrial Editors prize, 1967; Inland Theatre League award, for play, 1984. Agent: (plays) Samuel French 45 West 25th Street, New York, New York 10010. Address: 24276 Ponchartrain Lane, El Toro, California 92630, U.S.A.

SCIENCE-FICTION PUBLICATIONS

Novels

The Secret Martians. New York, Ace, 1960.
Ultimatum in 2050 A. D. New York, Ace, 1965.

Uncollected Short Stories (series: Jerry Norcriss)

"The Captain of His Soul" and "The Obvious Solution," in *Fantastic* New York), March 1959.
"The Arm of Enmord," in *Fantastic* (New York), April 1959.
"Queen of the Green Sun," in *Fantastic* (New York), May 1959.
"Bedside Monster," in *Fantastic* (New York), June 1959.
"The Kink-Remover," in *Fantastic* (New York), July 1959.
"Let X = Alligators," in *Fantastic* (New York), August 1959.
"Dolce al Fine," in *Amazing* (New York), August 1959.
"The Blackbird," in *Fantastic* (New York), September 1959.
"Ship Ahoy!," in *Fantastic* (New York), October 1959.
"Minor Detail," in *Amazing* (New York), November 1959.
"The Man Who Was Pale," in *Fantastic* (New York), December 1959.
"Multum in Parvo," in *The Year's Best S-F 5*, edited by Judith Merril. New York, Simon and Schuster, 1960; London, Mayflower, 1966.
"Old Friends Are the Best" in *Amazing* (New York), March 1960.
"The Dope on Mars," in *Galaxy* (New York), August 1960.
"The Crispin Affair," in *Fantastic* (New York), July, August 1960.
"The Business, As Usual," in *Galaxy* (New York), August 1960.
"Squeeze," in *Fantastic* (New York), September 1960.
"Status Quaint," in *Fantastic* (New York), October 1960.
"According to the Plan," in *Fantastic* (New York), January 1961.
"The Contact Point," in *If* (New York), January 1961.
"A Thread in Time," in *Fantastic* (New York), February 1961.
"Night Caller," in *Fantastic* (New York), March 1961.
"The Flying Tuskers of Kiniik-Kinaak," in *If* (New York), May 1961.
"Are You Now or Have You Ever Been?," in *Fantastic* (New York), May 1961.
"One Small Drawback," in *Fantastic* (New York), August 1961.
"Arcturus Times Three" (Norcriss), in *Galaxy* (New York), October 1961.
"Robotum Delenda Est!," in *Fantastic* (New York), March 1962.
"Big Baby" (Norcriss), in *Galaxy* (New York), April 1962.
"Double or Nothing," in *Fantastic* (New York), May 1962.
"Behind the Door," in *Fantastic* (New York), August 1962.
"A Matter of Protocol" (Norcriss), in *Galaxy* (New York), August 1962.
"It's Magic, You Dope," in *Fantastic* (New York), November, December 1962.
"The Final Ingredient," in *Triple W*, edited by Rod Serling. New York, Bantam, 1963.
"The Leech," in *Fantastic* (New York), January 1963.
"The Smart Ones," in *Amazing* (New York), February 1963.
"The Trouble with Tweenity," in *Fantastic* (New York), July 1963.
"Collector's Item," in *Fantasy and Science Fiction* (New York), September 1963.
"The Aftertime," in *Fantastic* (New York), November 1963.
"The Creature Inside" (Norcriss), in *Worlds of Tomorrow* (New York), December 1963.
"The Awakening," in *Galaxy* (New York), February 1964.
"The Orginorg Way," in *Fantastic* (New York), February 1964.
"Survival of the Fittest," in *Fantasy and Science Fiction* (New York), March 1964.
"At the Feelies," in *Galaxy* (New York), April 1964.
"Illusion," in *Fantastic* (New York), June 1964.
"The Venus Charm," in *Fantastic* (New York), July 1964.

"Weetl," in *If* (New York), June 1964.
"Footnote to an Old Story," in *Fantastic* (New York), August 1964.
"The Colony That Failed" (Norcriss), in *Galaxy* (New York), August 1964.
"Hear and Obey," in *Fantastic* (New York), September 1964.
"The Grooves," in *Fantastic* (New York), October 1964.
"Breakthrough," in *Fantasy and Science Fiction* (New York), November 1964.
"The Seminarian," in *Amazing* (New York), November 1964.
"To Each His Own," in *The 6 Fingers of Time and 5 Other Science Fiction Novelets*. New York, Macfadden, 1965.
"The Twerlik," in *10th Annual Edition of the Year's Best SF*, edited by Judith Merril. New York, Delacorte Press, 1965; London, Mayflower, 1967.
"Trade-In," in *Best from Fantasy and Science Fiction 14*, edited by Avram Davidson. New York, Doubleday, 1965; London, Panther, 1967.
"Blue Boy," in *Amazing* (New York), January 1965.
"Look Out Below," in *Fantastic* (New York), March 1965.
"Essentials Only," in *Fantasy and Science Fiction* (New York), March 1965.
"The Trouble with Hyperspace," in *Fantastic* (New York), April 1965.
"The Glorious Fourth," in *Fantasy and Science Fiction* (New York), October 1965.
"Matrix Goose," in *Galaxy* (New York), August 1967.
"Life Cycle," in *If* (New York), September 1970.
"Conversation with a Bug" and "The Pool," in *From the "S" File*. Chicago, Playboy Press, 1971.
"Rate of Exchange," in *Galaxy* (New York), May 1971.
"Deadly Shade of Blue," in *Alfred Hitchcock's Tales to Fill You with Fear and Trembling*, edited by Eleanor Sullivan. New York, Dial Press, 1980.
"No Harm Done," in *Science Fiction from A to Z*, edited by Isaac Asimov, Martin H. Greenberg, and Charles G. Waugh. Boston, Houghton Mifflin, 1982.

OTHER PUBLICATIONS

Novels

Murder, Maestro, Please. New York and London, Abelard Schuman, 1960.
Death for Auld Lang Syne. New York, Holt Rinehart, 1962; London, Joseph, 1963.
The Addams Family. New York, Pyramid, 1965.

Plays

Here Lies Jeremy Troy (produced New York, 1965). New York, French, 1969.
M is for Million. New York, French, 1971.
How Green Was My Brownie. New York, French, 1972.
Kiss or Make Up. New York, French, 1972.
Meanwhile, Back on the Couch. . . . New York, French, 1973.
A Gentleman and a Scoundrel. New York, French, 1973.
Roomies. New York, French, 1974.
Spinoff. New York, French, 1974.
Who's on First? (produced Mount Prospect, Illinois, 1975). New York, French, 1975.
What a Spot!, with Dave Reiser. New York, French, 1975.
Saving Grace. New York, French, 1976.
Take a Number, Darling. New York, French, 1976.
The Creature Creeps! New York, French, 1977.

Dream Lover. New York, French, 1977.
Hope for the Best, with Dave Reiser. New York, French, 1977.
Rich Is Better. New York, French, 1977.
The Murder Room. New York, French, 1977.
Pushover, with Ken Easton. New York, French, 1977.
Once Is Enough. New York, French, 1977.
The Clone People (as Mike Johnson). New York, French, 1978.
Missing Link. New York, French, 1978.
Turnabout, with Ken Easton. New York, French, 1978.
Not the Count of Monte Cristo?, with Dave Reiser. New York, French, 1978.
Turkey in the Straw. New York, French, 1979.
Operetta!, with Dave Reiser. New York, French, 1979.
My Son the Astronaut. New York, French, 1980.
Par for the Corpse. New York, French, 1980.
Honestly Now! New York, French, 1981.
The Return of the Maniac (as Mike Johnson). New York, French, 1981.
Slow Down, Sweet Chariot, with Dave Reiser. New York, French, 1982.
Woman Overboard, with Dave Reiser. New York, French, 1982.
Your Flake or Mine? New York, French, 1982.
The Picture of Dorian Gray, with Dave Reiser, from the novel by Oscar Wilde. New York, French, 1982.
The Saloonkeeper's Daughter, with Dave Reiser. New York, French, 1982.
The Second Lady. New York, French, 1983.
And on the Sixth Day, with Dave Reiser. New York, French, 1984.

Other Plays: *How Green Was My Brownie; A Fine Monster You Are!; Double Exposure; And Then I Wrote*, with Mel Buttorff; *The Well Dressed Liar*, with George Abbott; *My Husband the Wife* (lyrics only, with Dave Reiser), book by Ira and Brady Rubin, music by Dave Reiser; as Rick Abbot—*Dracula: The Musical?*, *Beauty and the Beast. Really; June Groom; Play On!; But Why Bump Off Barnaby?; A Turn for the Nurse;* as Monk Ferris—*Don't Tell Mother!; This Must Be the Place!; Let's Murder Marsha!*—all published New York, French.

Other

Audition Pieces and Classroom Exercises. New York, French, n.d.

*

Jack Sharkey comments:

I enjoy writing imaginative fiction and stage plays because of the marvelous "elbow room" it allows me when plotting; unconfined by anything—even the force of gravity!—I can tell stories occurring in situations Polti never dreamed of, I can fly like a bird at the touch of the typewriter-key, and set my characters on any planet in the known or unknown universe without the bother of paying for rocket fuel!

*   *   *

Jack Sharkey started publishing science fiction in 1959, but produced little fiction of any kind after 1965. In that span of time, Sharkey sold about 50 stories and seven novels.

Sharkey's best-known series featured Jerry Norcriss, Space Zoologist. These stories were typical SF puzzle stories where Norcriss would "merge" minds with an alien organism in order to solve the enviromental puzzle and save a star colony. Two

novels which were serialized but never published in book form are "The Crispin Affair," a thrilling space opera, and "It's Magic, You Dope!," a wildly funny fantasy in the mode of Pratt and de Camp's *The Incomplete Enchanter*.

Sharkey's two SF novels published in book form are complete opposites. *The Secret Martians* is a first-person account of the mystery of the missing Space Scouts and the discovery of the ancient Martian civilization. The action is fast paced and laced with humor. *Ultimatum in 2050 A. D.* is the grim story, with overtones of *Logan's Run*, of revolt against an Earth Society where all its citizens are completely programmed. Sharkey's works are enjoyable, well written, and unfortunately completely out-of-print.

—George Kelley

———————

SHAVER, Richard S(harpe). Also wrote as Wes Amherst; Edwin Benson; Peter Dexter; Richard Dorset; Richard English; G. H. Irwin; Paul Lohrman; Frank Patton; Stan Raycraft. American. Born in 1907. Little is known of his life: probably a welder who lived in Pennsylvania. *Died 5 November 1975.*

SCIENCE-FICTION PUBLICATIONS

Short Stories

I Remember Lemuria, and The Return of Sathanas. Evanston Illinois, Venture, 1948.

Uncollected Short Stories (series: Red Dwarf)

"The Tale of the Red Dwarf," in *Fantastic Adventures* (New York), May 1947.
"Daughter of Night" (Dwarf), in *Amazing* (New York), December 1948.
"The Cyclops," in *Amazing* (New York), January 1949.
"The Cyclopeans," in *Fantastic Adventures* (New York), June 1949.
"Exiles of the Elfmounds," in *Amazing* (New York), July 1949.
"Erdis Cliff" (Dwarf), in *Amazing* (New York), September 1949.
"Where No Foot Walks" (as G. H. Irwin), and "The Fall of Lemuria," in *Other Worlds* (Evanston, Indiana), November 1949.
"Battle in Eternity," with Chester S. Geier, in *Amazing* (New York), November 1949.
"When the Moon Bounced" (as Frank Patton), and "Pillars of Delight" (as Stan Raycraft), in *Amazing* (New York), December 1949.
"Sons of the Serpent" (as Wes Amherst) in *Other Worlds* (Evanston, Indiana), January 1950.
"The Gamin" (as Peter Dexter), "Mahai's Wife" (as Edwin Benson), and "Lady," in *Other Worlds* (Evanston, Indiana), March 1950.
"The World of the Lost" (as Paul Lohrman), in *Fantastic Adventures* (New York), March 1950.
"We Dance for the Dom," in *Amazing* (New York), July 1950.
"The Palace of Darkness" (as Peter Dexter), in *Other Worlds* (Evanston, Indiana), September 1950.
"Glass Woman of Venus" (as G. H. Irwin) in *Other Worlds* (Evanston, Indiana), January 1951.
"Green Man's Grief," in *Future* (New York), January 1951.

"Yelisen," in *Other Worlds* (Evanston, Indiana), December 1951

"Of Stegner's Folly," in *If* (New York), March 1952.

"The Sun Smiths," in *Other Worlds* (Evanston, Indiana), July, August, October 1952.

"Beyond the Barrier," in *Other Worlds* (Evanston, Indiana), November, December 1952, January, February 1953.

"The Dark Goddess," in *Imagination* (Evanston, Illinois) February 1953.

"Paradise Planet," in *Imagination* (Evanston, Illinois) Spring 1953.

"She Was Sitting in the Dark" (as Richard Dorset), in *Science Stories* (Evanston, Illinois), December 1953.

"The Dream Makers," in *Fantastic* (New York), July 1958.

"The Heart of the Game" (as Richard English), in *Orbit 1,* edited by Damon Knight. New York, Putnam, and London, Whiting and Wheaton, 1966.

* * *

If Richard S. Shaver is discussed today, it is usually as a curiosity in the history of science fiction, or as an early example of that dim area where fiction shades into UFO's and ancient astronauts. This is to some extent justified but not altogether fair. Although "The Shaver Mystery" series was presented for the most part as fact, it is for more akin to the science fiction of its time, both in execution and in sources, than most realize; and, taken as fiction, the stories do have intrinsic interest and merit,

During his writing career, spanning three decades, Shaver's stories and "non-fiction" explications were published in a number of magazines, primarily under his longtime editor and advocate, Ray Palmer, at first in science-fiction magazines such as *Amazing Stories* and *Other Worlds,* and later lin "occult" publications such as *Hidden World.* A letter from Shaver (*Amazing,* December 1944) described the underground races called the "dero" and "tero" who had taught him the pre-catastrophe language of "Mantong. " Then, at Palmer's request, Shaver sent 10,000 word manuscript from which Palmer wrote a 31,000 word story, "I Remeber Lemuria!" Constructed for high drama and written in colorful and traditional pulp style, it told the story of "Mutan Mion of ancient Lemuria," and fully outlined the background and dogma of the Shaver Mystery. The Atlans and Titans, Shaver reports, had been immortal giants of advanced technology; then the sun began to age and give off "heavy metal radiation," causing aging and death. Most fled the earth for a planet with a younger sun, but others burrowed beneath the ground seeking protection from the poisonous rays. These are the dero and tero Shaver claimed to have met in the caves—struggling remnants of a once-great civilization. Of these two warring factions, the dero are by far the more interesting; Shaver has developed the quintessential conspiracy theory. Whenever anything goes wrong, the degenerate dero, crazed by the sun's rays and using the almost-magical machines left by the Elder Races, are responsible. Against this depravity the tero fight valiantly but often in vain, sometimes aided by sensitive surface men like Richard Shaver.

This is fairly basic stuff, at least in its psychological appeal both as archetype and as wish fulfillment, especially for *Amazing* with its younger and less demanding readership. What made it controversial was that, after the first story, the series was presented as fact. It is debatble whether Palmer believed this; it is probable that he saw it mainly as a way to increase circulation, at least at first. Shaver, however, apparently believed completely in his visit to the caves, in the voices that spoke to him from underground, and in what those voices told him. In the May 1978 *Science Fiction Review* Palmer announced that the eight years Shaver spent "in the caves" were actually spent in the Ypsilanti State Hospital as a paranoid schizophrenic. This sheds light on the style as well as the content of Shaver's writing:besides adventure-writing devices and techniques, Shaver's style is marked by "schizophrenese" characteristics such as disjointed sentences and, more importantly, word-dismantling and "clang associations. "

But it would be wrong to dismiss these writings as only psychotic ravings, or even as Shaver's ravings hammered into salable fiction by Palmer. For one thing, Shaver himself wrote for other magazines under a number of pseudonyms, including house names. Beyond that, the stories show an eclectic range of clearly literary influences. These include the lush fiction of A. Merritt, Wells's Morlocks and Eloi, and the fictional worldview of H. P. Lovecraft, from whose novel *At the Mountains of Madness* Shaver probably got the term "Elder Race. " Harry Warner, Jr. (in *All Our Yesterdays*) mentions a possible influence from E. R. Eddison, "Whom Shaver once identified as his literary idol" and *A Reader's Guide to Science Fiction* demonstrates patterning, perhaps conscious, after the planetary romances of Edgar Rice Burroughs. Possible sources in occult non-fiction include Charles Fort, the Theosophy of Mme. Blavatsky, and James Churchward's Mu series, which Shaver mentions in his first letter to Palmer. Shaver also mentions Edith Hamilton's writings on mythology—which his own works explain and correct. The Bible, especially the Edenic theme, is also an important source.

What results is an odd but fascinating blend of high adventure, outrageous "science," and elusive but striking systems of cosmic speculation. If the characters are sometimes flat, if the plots too often seem "boy meets girl, boy beats dero, boy wins girl"—and this is not always the case—the sheer wealth and strangeness of the concepts Shaver develops more than compensate for that. There is a kind of Stapledonian scope to Shaver, a sense of epic, and mythic, panoramas; the races, societies, and technologies with which he populates his universe are varied and often impressive. The appeal of Richard Shaver to the reader then and now is, as Palmer said, "One thing only, his unusual imagination. His strange sense of the unusual, his feeling for emotion, his sense of the beautiful and his sense of the outré." For that reason Shaver's writings, shrouded in controversy and now largely neglected, are worthy of new attention.

—Bernadette Bosky

SHAW, Bob (Robert Shaw). British. Born in Belfast, Northern Ireland, 31 December 1931. Educated at Technical High School, Belfast, 1944-46. Married Sarah Gourley in 1954; two daughters and one son. Prior to 1960 worked in the steel and aircraft industries and as a cab driver; Assistant Publicity Officer, 1960-66, and Press Officer, 1969-73, Short Bros. and Harland, aircraft manufacturers, Belfast; journalist, Belfast *Telegraph*, 1966-69; Publicity Officer, Vickers Shipbuilding Group, 1973-75. Recipient: British Science Fiction Association Award, 1975; Hugo Award, for criticism, 1979, 1980. Agent: A. P. Watt Ltd., 26-28 Bedford Row, London WC1R 4HL. Address: 66 Knutsford Road, Grappenhall, Warrington, Cheshire WA4 2PB, England.

SCIENCE-FICTION PUBLICATIONS

Novels (series: Orbitsville)

Night Walk. New York, Banner, 1967; London, New English Library, 1970.
The Two-Timers. New York, Ace, 1968; London, Gollancz, 1969.
Shadow of Heaven. New York, Avon, 1969; abridged edition, London, New English Library, 1970.
The Palace of Eternity. New York, Ace, 1969; London, Gollancz, 1970.
One Million Tomorrows. New York, Ace, 1970; London, Gollancz, 1971.
The Ground Zero Man. New York, Avon, 1971; London, Corgi, 1976; revised edition, as *The Peace Machine*, London, Gollancz, 1985.
Other Days, Other Eyes. New York, Ace, and London, Gollancz, 1972.
Orbitsville. London, Gollancz, and New York, Ace, 1975.
A Wreath of Stars. London, Gollancz, 1976; New York, Doubleday, 1977.
Medusa's Children. London, Gollancz, 1977; New York, Doubleday, 1979.
Who Goes Here? London, Gollancz, 1977; New York, Ace, 1978.
Ship of Strangers. London, Gollancz, 1978; New York, Ace, 1979.
Vertigo. London, Gollancz, 1978; New York, Ace, 1979.
Dagger of the Mind. London, Gollancz, 1979; New York, Ace, 1982.
Galactic Tours, illustrated by David Hardy. New York and London, Proteus, 1981.
The Ceres Solution. London, Gollancz, 1981; New York, DAW, 1984.
Orbitsville Departure. London, Gollancz, 1983; New York, DAW, 1985.
Fire Pattern. London, Gollancz, 1984.

Short Stories

The Enchanted Duplicator, with Walt Willis. Privately printed, 1954.
Tomorrow Lies in Ambush. London, Gollancz, and New York, Ace, 1973.
Cosmic Kaleidoscope. London, Gollancz, 1976; New York, Doubleday, 1977.
A Better Mantrap. London, Gollancz, 1982.

Uncollected Short Stories

"Aspect," in *Nebula* (Glasgow), August 1954.
"The Trespassers," in *Nebula* (Glasgow), December 1954.
"The Journey Alone," in *Nebula* (Glasgow), April 1955.
"Departure," in *Authentic* (London), October 1955.
"Sounds in the Dawn," in *Nebula* (Glasgow), January 1956.
"Barrier to Yesterday," in *Nebula* (Glasgow), March 1956.
"Dissolute Diplomat," with Walt Willis, in *If* (New York), January 1960.
"Hue and Cry," in *Amazing* (New York), July 1969.
"Cold Crucible," in *Vision of Tomorrow* (Sydney), August 1970.
"Altar Egoes," in *Beyond This Horizon*, edited by Christopher Carrell. Sunderland, Ceolfrith Press, 1973.
"A Glimpse of an Average Man's Working Day in the Year 2078," in *Shell-Times*, January 1978.

"The Edge of Time," with Malcolm Harris, in *Aries 1*, edited by John Grant. Newton Abbot, Devon, David and Charles, 1979.
"Well-Wisher," in *Fantasy and Science Fiction* (New York), November 1979.
"Love Me Tender," in *New Terrors 1*, edited by Ramsey Campbell. London, Pan, 1980.
"Go On, Pick a Universe," in *Fantasy and Science Fiction* (New York), June 1981.
"Aliens Aren't Human," in *Extro*, February 1982.
"Cutting Down," in *Isaac Asimov's Fiction Magazine* (New York), December 1982.
"Shadow of Wings," in *More Magic*, edited by Larry Niven. New York, Berkley, 1984.

OTHER PUBLICATIONS

Other

The Best of the Bushel. Epsom, Surrey, Paranoid-Inca Press, 1979.
The Eastercon Speeches. Epsom, Surrey, Paranoid-Inca Press, 1979.

*

Manuscript Collection: Science Fiction Foundation, North East London Polytechnic.

Critical Study: *Bob Shaw* by Brian M. Stableford (includes bibliography by Mike Ashley), n. p., British Science Fiction Association, 1981.

Bob Shaw comments:

It is very difficult, if not impossible, for an author to write objectively about his own work, but I sum up my output by saying that I write science fiction for people who don't read a great deal of science fiction. This doesn't mean that I curb my imagination. I'm quite prepared to deal with the most fantastic concepts, but I try to do it in such a way that the ideas can be appreciated by any reader. The technique involves a minimal use of in-group jargon and a very firm emphasis on relating every fictional event to real characters of a kind that the reader can immediately recognise and identify or empathise with. The universe is wonderful, but only when there is somebody there to wonder at it. Humour also plays an important role in my work, partly because I feel that science fiction shouldn't become too gloomy and portentous, mainly because one of the things we need most these days is a good laugh.

*   *   *

Bob Shaw stands in the forefront of those SF writers able to combine scientific concepts with humanistic concerns to the detriment of neither element. Most of his novels are centered upon the experiences of a protagonist who would become, in the hands of lesser writers, mere sterotypic "heroes"—whereas Shaw transforms such characters into figures of alternating strength and vulnerability, and thus consistent credibility. Shaw's protagonists perform heroic acts out of a pragmatic need for order and integrity rather than out of desires for escape or sensual indulgence.

The first "Slow Glass" story, "Light of Other Days," focuses on such a diaemna. "Slow glass," an idea that Shaw uses in various tales, is a special glass-substance that can slow down and "trap" light-images for years after their transmission. In "Light of Other Days" a federal judge must make a guilty ruling in a murder trial that will cost the defendant his life—in spite of the fact that a piece of "slow glass" may have trapped visual images proving or disproving the defendant's guilt. Rather than delaying the trial until the slow-glass image can develop, the judge makes his decision on the evidence at hand, a decision that signifies Shaw's commitment to the pre-eminence of humanity over technical constructs.

Several Shaw novels enable him to expand upon this confluence of human and scientific concerns, imparting to his novels a thematic texture enhanced by his rich, poetically evocative writing-style. *The Place of Eternity* is perhaps his best work, postulating what is termed a "panspermic" view of life— that is, the "concept of ubiquitous life. Justification for believing that every mind in existence was linked to every other mind. " With this philosophy in mind, Shaw constructs an interstellar conflict in which humanity is being gradually beaten down by an uncompromising race of aliens called the Pythsyccans (whose name Shaw certainly derives from the Greek "Python," monstrous enemy of the humanistic Apollo). Retreating from the unexplained alien attack, the human military takes refuge on Mnemosyne, a planet renowed for its natives' artistic accomplishments. The military's impositions on that culture lead ex-serviceman Mack Tavernor to side with the Mnemosyne natives, but ultimately he is killed in the conflict. However, on dying, his life-force finds verification of the panspermic theory when it encounters non-corporal beings called "Egons. " Through the Egons Tavernor learns how humanity's own technology and its contempt for the imagination-developing artistry symbolized by Mnenosyne are leading to its victimization by the Pythsyccans. In the tradition of archaic myth-saviors, Tavernor must be reborn in the body of his own unborn son before he can resolve the crisis.

The Two-Timers and *Vertigo* are two novels less cosmic in their scheme, but here as well Shaw's fine poetic diction and concern for the realistic concerns of humanity enhance concepts that could verge on melodrama, and make them into enthralling drama. In *The Two-Timers* John Breton loses his wife in a senseless street-killing, and becomes so traumatized by the event that he develops in himself psychic powers capable of transporting him to a parallel time-line, where he saves the life of another version of his wife. Thereafter he expects her to live the part of his deceased mate—much to the discomfort of both the women and the John Breton of that time-line. Interestingly enough, although the traumatized Breton eventually attempts to kill his rival in order to possess his "wife," Shaw maintains sympathy with all of the characters, and manages to resolve the dilemma without resorting to standard melodramatic clichés. In *Vertigo* Rob Hasson is an air-policeman who survives a devastating crash to earth which leaves him with a trauma regarding height, not unlike the protagonist of the Hitchcock movie of the same title. Similarly, Shaw's protagonist must overcome his trauma by forcing himself to endure it in the end, but, unlike the Hitchcock hero, who beats his vertigo through his monomaniacal obsession, Hasson's conquest of his fears is the outgrowth of a more gradual process of healing homeostasis. Shaw's heroes incarnate positive ideals, but he never loses sight of the intense efforts that must be put forth to live up to such ideals.

To be sure, some Shaw novels are of a more workmanlike nature, focusing more on a predictable world-endangering peril than on characters or concepts—for instance, *Medusa's Children*, about a colony life-form that dominates humans, and

A Wrath of Stars, about Earth's quasi-physical interaction with another world. Still, even when Shaw is less inspired, there are in his weaker novels moments of incisive character-study or intriguing conceptual elaboration that one never finds in the major works of other, more ballyhooed writers. At his weakest, Shaw is still stronger than most, and deserving of a more appreciative critical audience than he has thus far received.

—Gene Phillips

SHAW, Brian. See **TUBB, E. C.**

SHAW, Bryan. See **FEARN, John Russell.**

SHAWN, Frank S. See **GOULART, Ron.**

SHECKLEY, Robert. American. Born in New York City, 16 July 1928. Educated at New York University, B. A. 1951. Served in the United States Army, 1946-48. Married to Jay Rothbell. Agent: Marty Shapiro, Shapiro-Lichtman Talent, 8827 Beverly Boulevard, Los Angeles, California 90048, U.S.A.

SCIENCE-FICTION PUBLICATIONS

Novels

Immortality Delivered. New York, Avalon, 1958; revised edition, as *Immortality Inc.,* New York, Bantam, 1959; London, Gollancz, 1963.
The Status Civilization. New York, New American Library, 1960; London, New English Library, 1967.
Journey Beyond Tomorrow. New York, New American Library, 1962; London, Gollancz, 1964; as *Journey of Joenes,* London, Sphere, 1978.
The 10th Victim. New York, Ballantine, and London, Mayflower, 1966.
Mindswap. New York, Delacorte Press, and London, Gollancz, 1966.
Dimension of Miracles. New York, Dell, 1968; London, Gollancz, 1969.
Options. New York, Pyramid, 1975; London, Pan, 1977.
Crompton Divided. New York, Holt Rinehart, 1978; as *The Alchemical Marriage of Alistair Crompton,* London, Joseph, 1978.
Dramocles. New York, Holt Rinehart, 1983; London, New English Library, 1984.

Short Stories

Untouched by Human Hands. New York, Ballantine, 1954; London, Joseph, 1955.

Citizen in Space. New York, Ballantine, 1955; London, New English Library, 1969.
Pilgrimage to Earth. New York, Bantam, 1957; London, Corgi, 1959.
Store of Infinity. New York, Bantam, 1960.
Notions: Unlimited. New York, Bantam, 1960.
Shards of Space. New York, Bantam, and London, Corgi, 1962.
The People Trap. New York, Dell, 1968; London, Gollancz, 1969.
Can You Feel Anything When I Do This? New York, Doubleday, 1971; London, Gollancz, 1972; as *The Same to You Doubled and Other Stories, London, Pan, 1974*.
The Robert Sheckley Omnibus, edited by Robert Conquest. London, Gollancz, 1973.
The Robot Who Looked Like Me. London, Sphere, 1978.
The Wonderful World of Robert Sheckley. New York, Bantam, 1979; London, Sphere, 1980.
Is THAT What People Do? The Selected Short Stories of Robert Sheckley. New York, Holt Rinehart, 1984.

OTHER PUBLICATIONS

Novels

Calibre. 50. New York, Bantam, 1961.
Dead Run. New York, Bantam, 1961.
Live Gold. New York, Bantam, 1962.
The Man in the Water. Evanston, Illinois, Regency, 1962.
White Death. New York, Bantam, 1963.
The Game of X. New York, Delacorte Press, 1965; London, Cape, 1966.
Time Limit. New York, Bantam, and London, New English Library, 1967.

Play

Television Play: *Murder Club*, from his own story, 1961 (UK).

Other

Futuropolis: Impossible Cities in Science Fiction and Fantasy. New York, A and W, 1978; London, Big O, 1979.

Editor, *After the Fall: An Anthology*. New York, Ace, and London, Sphere, 1980.

*   *   *

Robert Sheckley is, if we must find a category for him, a metaphysical wit and satirist. His major theme, manifested in dozens of superb stories and novels, is that in an infinite universe "reality" is infinitely variegated, depending upon one's environmental or psychological framework. While some writers would regard this as a nihilistic nightmare, for Sheckley it offers an opportunity for unbounded imaginative romping—precisely the sort of freedom that SF so eagerly welcomes. "The quest for non-ordinary reality is something more than curiosity and wishful thinking," Sheckley once said in a rare public address ("The Search for the Marvellous," delivered at the Institute of Contemporary Arts, London, 1975); "We are too crowded in our everyday lives by replicas of ourselves and by the repetitious artifacts of our days and nights. But we do not quite believe in this prosaic world. Continually we are reminded of the strangeness of birth and death, the vastness of time and space, the unknowability of ourselves. " These somber thoughts

Sheckley clothes with highly imaginative and entertaining plots. For example, in *Dimension of Miracles* Carmody is brought to the galactic center for a prize he has won in the Intergalactic Sweepstakes. The prize is a sentient being in a gaily wrapped box which takes Carmody on a wild-goose chase through the universe in search of Earth (the Prize Committee does not know the co-ordinates for returning Carmody). Each episode makes it clear that the universe is such that one cannot go home again anyway, just as one cannot step into the same river twice. Carmondy's search for home is also a search for self, and on this matter he has quite a bit to learn—such as the fact that the shapes of objects and creatures are a function of environment. What is evil or ugly in one environment may well appear benevolent and lovely when transferred to another.

This idea of the universe as protean and magical serves as a satirical ploy for Sheckley. In "The Petrified World" (*Is THAT What People Do?*, original title, "Dreamworld," from *The People Trap*) Lanigan, whose real world is one in which objects are continually changing shape and color, suffers from a recurring nightmare: he keeps finding himself on a world where change is largely imperceptible. "The pavement never once yielded beneath his feet. Over there was the First National City Bank. It had been there yesterday . . . but, worse, it would be there without fail tomorrow, and the day after that . . . grotesquely devoid of possibilities. It would never become a tomb, an airplane . . . " Lanigan finally becomes trapped in his nightmare—the nightmare which, Sheckley is suggesting, is our nightmare.

No matter how absurb and wildly episodic Sheckley's plots sometimes become, the metaphysician is always lurking in the wings, cueing us with tidbits of cosmic wisdom which are themselves refreshing. For example, *Mindswap* introduces us to a universe in which people can change bodies like garments. Marvin Flynn gets swindled out of his body by the notorious body-pirate Ze Kraggash, whose ruling philosophy is "If a man cannot retain control of his own body, then he deserves to lose it. " During the galaxy-wide search Flynn begins to realize just how indeterminate bodies really are and how useless it is to attach any lasting importance to them. "The acceptance of indeterminacy was the beginning of wisdom," a hermit on some alien world tells him. And after he chases Ze Kraggash into the Twisted World, he attains ultimate wisdom: "Nothing is permanent except our illusions. "

Perhaps Sheckley's most dramatic rendering of the indeterminacy of selfhood is "Slaves of Time. " Like the solipsistic nightmare world of Robert Heinlen's "All You Zombies," this story (omitted, unfortunately, from *Is THAT What People Do?*) depicts some of the uncannily paradoxical things that can happen if one engages in some serious time traveling. Gleister builds a time machine and goes into the future. Because nature "can tolerate a paradox but abhors a vacuum," it instantaneously creates another Gleister to take the first Gleister's place. This new Gleister, identical to the other, but on a different reality-track, also builds a time machine and travels into the future. The inevitable, grim result: an endless stream of Gleisters, each following his own reality-track. "It is strange," Gleister/Mingus says at one point where all the Gleister manifestations convene, "that all of us are one person, yet we represent widely differing viewpoints. " And Gleister/Ergon replies, "It's not so strange . . . . One person is many people even under normal circumstances. "

Options offers yet another treatise on reality vs. illusion and mind-as-universe—embedded, but not too deeply, beneath a slapstick surface. Tom Mishkin, an intergalactic trader ("Frozen South African lobster tails, tennis shoes, air conditioners") finds himself stranded somewhere in the Lesser Megellanic Cloud, in need of a hard-to-get spare part for his ship. He is directed to Harmonia, a bizarre would where, as is almost always the case in Sheckley's cosmos, nothing is quite the way it seems. Mishkin and a mealy-mouthed robot set off on a mock-pilgrimage across Harmonia in search of the elusive spare part. To be sure, Harmonia is Tom Mishkin's disorderly mind strewn across an external milieu like an overstuffed closet that had burst open. Monsters pause in their deadly assaults to discuss metaphysical issues with him; carnival men entertain him; he meets poker players who think they are inside their hotel room in Manhatten (and very likely are). In one of the final episodes we get the sense that Mishkin is "really" just a little earth boy who has been engaged in a daydream that would make Walter Mitty's look dreary ("Tommy! Stop playing now!" "I'm not playing, Mom. This is real. " . . . "Put down that broom and come into the house at once. " "It's not a broom, it's a spaceship. Anyhow, my robot says . . . " "And bring that old radio in with you").

Many of Sheckley's works explore to some degree the nature of selfhood. The early, masterful tale, "Shape" (*Untouched by Human Hands* ; *Selected Stories*) is about a team of alien space explorers who possess the ability to change shape at will, but whose society has forbidden them to do so (shapes were assigned and had to be rigorously maintained). No wonder, then, that when they land on a strange planet called Earth, they are so awed by the multitude of shapes, that they cannot bring themselves to return home; instead they joyfully assume the shapes of trees, rocks, animals, humans. And in *Crompton Divided* Alistair Crompton, because of his multiple personality, is forced to undergo "Cleavage"—separation of the personalities, which are then placed in separate bodies and shipped, unknown to the main personality, to remote planets. Crompton, now mild-mannered but totally devoid of spunk, learns what has happened to him and, after raising sufficient funds by embezzling rare and exotic perfumes from his company, embarks on a galaxy-wide search for his lost selves. That this is yet another indictment of society for the pressures it exerts upon us to be consistent, predictable, content citizens is clear from the following passage:

> On all sides of him, the envious Crompton saw people with all their marvelous complexities and contradictions constantly bursting out of the stereotypes that society tried to force on them. He observed prostitutes who were not good-hearted, army sergeants who detested brutality, wealthy men who never gave a cent to charity. Irishmen who hated talking, Italians who could not carry a tune. . . . Most of the human race seemed to live lives of a wonderful and unpredictable richness, erupting into sudden passions and strange calms, saying one thing and meaning another.

For Sheckley, to be fully human means to house a repertoire of selves, willing and able to assume different roles, changing our minds when we want to. The only danger is that one can get carried away with the ability to manipulate reality and start trying to play God, conquering and subjugating with no regard for the well-being—the selfhood—of others. Such is the circumstance we encounter in Sheckley's latest novel, Dramocles. "Travelling between realities," the power-hungry Otho tells his son Dramocles, ruler of Glorm, is "the way to life everlasting. " Despite Otho's efforts to persuade him that the lives of mere mortals are irrelevant "when the rewards of godhood are within your grasp," Dramocles manages to resist.

Unlike the young man in Sheckley's "The Language of Love" who learned to express his deepest romantic feelings with such precision that his sweetheart quickly lost interest in him, Dramocles discovers that too much of a good thing can rob one of one's very humanity.

—Fred D. White

———

SHEFFIELD, Charles. Also writes as James Kirkwood. Born in England. Educated at St. John's College, Cambridge, B. A. and M. A. in mathematics, Ph. D. in theoretical physics. Formely President of the American Astronautical Society; currently Vice-President, Earth Satellite Corporation, and President, Science Fiction Writers of America. Address: 6812 Wilson Lane, Bethesda, Maryland 20817, U.S.A.

SCIENCE-FICTION PUBLICATIONS

Novels

Sight of Proteus. New York, Ace, 1978; London, Sidgwick and Jackson, 1980.
The Web Between the Worlds. New York, Ace, 1979; London, Sidgwick and Jackson, 1980.
My Brother's Keeper. New York, Ace, 1982.
Between the Strokes of Night. New York, Baen, 1985.

Short Stories

Vectors. New York, Ace, 1980.
Hidden Variables. New York, Ace, 1981.
Erasmus Magister. New York, Ace, 1982.
The McAndrew Chronicles. New York, Tor, 1983.

Uncollected Short Stories

"Murder in Triplicate," in *Amazing* (New York), 1978.
"The Grooves of Change," in *Amazing* (New York), 1979.
"That Strain Again," in *Microcosmic Tales,* edited by Isaac Asimov, Martin H. Greenberg, and Joseph D. Olander. New York, Taplinger, 1980.
"The Subtle Serpent, in *Stellar 5,* edited by Judy-Lynn del Rey. New York, Ballantine, 1980.
"Parasites Lost," in *Proteus,* edited by Richard S. McEnroe. New York, Ace, 1981.
"The Seventeen Year Locusts," in *Isaac Asimov's Science Fiction Magazine* (New York), 1982.
"The Mouths of Earth," in *Rigel* (Richmond, California), Winter 1982.
"Crocus Time," in *Weird Tales 4,* edited by Lin Carter. New York, Zebra, 1983.
"Accounting System" (as James Kirkwood), in *Analog* (New York), 1984.
"The Dominus Demonstration," in *Analog* (New York), April 1984.
"Nine Days' Wonder, in *Analog* (New York), October 1984.
"The Hostages of Zark," in *Analog* (New York), Mid-December 1984.
"Turnicate, Turnicate, Will Thou Be Mine," in *Isaac Asimov's Science Fiction Magazine* (New York), June 1985.

OTHER PUBLICATIONS

Novel

The Selkie, with David F. Bischoff. New York, Macmillan, 1982.

Other

Earthwatch: A Survey of the World from Space. London, Sidgwick and Jackson, and New York, Macmillan, 1981.
Man on Earth, London, Sidgwick and Jackson, and New York, Macmillan, 1983.
Space Careers, with Carol Rosin. New York, Morrow, 1984.

Editor, with John L. McLucas, *Commercial Operations in Space 1980-2000.* San Diego, American Astronautical Society, 1981.

Author of some 50 technical papers since 1965.

* * *

In a relatively short period Charles Sheffield has developed a substantial reputation as a writer of "hard" science fiction. His solid scientific background provides the technical basis for much of his work.

Sight of Proteus, his first novel, focuses on "form changing"—the machine-assisted ability to transmute the human body (look like anybody you please, or grow gills). Although form changing is outlawed in space and tightly controlled on Earth, illegal research eventually shows it to be the means of exploring space and of solving Earth's social problems. This novel is ultimately less concerned with the technology itself than with the impact of technology on society and the way that impact is handled.

Some of his other work is more concerned with technology. *The Web Between the Worlds,* for instance, deals with the construction of an elevator into space (a concept similar to Arthur C. Clarke's in *The Fountains of Paradise,* but devloped differently). Yet even here a secondary plot, dealing with genetic manipulation, emphasizes human values rather than mere technology. *The McAndrew Chronicles,* a series of 5 episodic "chronicles" dealing with the scientific adventures of a physicist and his pilot, have an almost completely technological emphasis. Most interesting is Sheffield's appendix which explains where a real science leaves off and science fiction begins.

His other two books are not so much science fiction as science fantasy. *Erasmus Magister* is a collection of three tales inspired by the life of Erasmus Darwin, gandfather of Charles. In each, Darwin investigates some apparently supernatural phenomenon and discovers a perfectly rational explanation for it. *The Selkie,* written with David Bischoff, is a strange mix of mystery, science, and horror. The Selkies are wereseals (explained as a mutation with an all-male population dependent upon certain genetic strains of human females to reproduce) living in northern Scotland. This is a more ambitious novel than the others, striving (not altogether successfully) to deal with a love motif and to characterize Mary Willis more fully.

Sheffield seems to be developing; as his control and depth of characterization rise to the level of his scientific understanding his fiction should become much more interesting.

—Robert Reilly

SHELDON, Roy. See **TUBB, E. C.**

———

SHEPARD, Lucius. Recipient: Clarion Award, 1984. Address: c/o Ace Books, 200 Madison Avenue, New York, New York 10016, U.S.A.

SCIENCE-FICTION PUBLICATIONS

Novel

Green Eyes. New York, Ace, 1984.

Uncollected Short Stories

"The Taylorsville Reconstruction," in *Universe 13,* edited by Terry Carr. New York, Doubleday, 1983.
"Solitario's Eyes," in *Fantasy and Science Fiction* (New York), September 1983.
"The Etheric Transmitter," in *The Clarion Awards,* edited by Damon Knight. New York, Doubleday, 1984.
"Black Coral," in *Universe 14,* edited by Terry Carr. New York, Doubleday, 1984.
"Salvador," in *Fantasy and Science Fiction* (New York), April 1984.
"A Traveler's Tale," in *Isaac Asimov's Science Fiction Magazine* (New York), July 1984.
"The Storming of Annie Kinsale," in *Isaac Asimov's Science Fiction Magazine* (New York), September 1984.
"The Night of White Bhairab," in *Fantasy and Science Fiction* (New York), October 1984.
"The Man Who Painted the Dragon Griaule," in *Fantasy and Science Fiction* (New York), December 1984.
"Reaper," in *Isaac Asimov's Science Fiction Magazine* (New York), December 1984.
"The End of Life as We Know It," in *Isaac Asimov's Science Fiction Magazine* (New York), January 1985.
"How the Wind Spoke at Madaket," in *Isaac Asimov's Science Fiction Magazine* (New York), April 1985.
"The Jaguar Hunter," in *Fantasy and Science Fiction* (New York), May 1985.

* * *

In the year and a half since 1983, Lucius Shepard has published one novel, *Green Eyes,* and about a dozen short stories. Other works are scheduled to appear in 1985. Shepard's superbly styled pieces have been nominated for several awards, and he has already won the Clarion Award. The work of William Gibson, Connie Willis, and David Palmer notwithstanding, Shepard has a solid claim to being the most auspicious new writer to enter the science fiction field in some time.

Shepard's work is remarkably of a piece. The majority of his stories take place in the present or near future and are set on or near the Caribbean or the Gulf of Mexico. Most walk the narrow border between fantasy and science fiction and many involve some form of possession. "Solitario's Eyes," for example, takes place somewhere on the Caribbean coast and details the strange relationship between an army officer of upper-class Castilian heritage, his beautiful Indian wife, and the native healer she seeks out during her pregnancy and then seduces. Her son, when born, appears to share some strange physical and psychic bond with the healer (since murdered by the army officer) and with his blind, possibly magical horse. In *Green Eyes* a scientific experiment in resurrecting the dead, set in the bayou country of Louisiana, goes awry, and leads its participants into a dark universe of perversion, murder, and voodoo. Both "Salvador" and "A Traveler's Tale" take place in the snake-infested swamps and forests of Central America and both involve spirit possession. In the former story an American soldier, stuck in an early 1990's Vietnam-like military campaign, is taken over by a native spirit seeking revenge against the gringoes. In the latter story an American is possessed by an alien who, half insane, has been haunting the swampy site of her spaceship's crash for centuries. Somewhat similar is "The Night of White Bhairab" in which an *Amityville Horror* -like demon, accidentally transported to Katmandu, gets its comeuppance at the hands of a rather novel Nepalese household spirit. Shepard's finest story may be "The Man Who Painted the Dragon Griaule. " With an ambience much like that of Le Guin's *Orsinian Tales*, "Griaule" is quite literally about a man who attempts to paint a 6000-foot long living but dormant dragon: not a picture of the dragon, it must be understood, but the body of the dragon itself.

Shepard's characters, like his settings, are remarkably consistent. His people are drifters, dreamers, and drug addicts, men and women with no real place to go and no real purpose, who end up on the edges of the civilized world. Many of them fall victim to strange events which they and we never fully understand. When they accomplish things—create works of art, make scientific discoveries, make babies—they usually do it almost in spite of themselves, and their creations are frequently two-edged swords. Shepard is a very talented writer, and to attempt a thumbnail analysis of his work is undoubtedly a disservice to him, but his clearly seems to be sensibility of a disenchanted member of the 1970's counter-culture. In the universe of Shepard's stories everything lies in disarray. Governments are corrupt, belief structures, those of the West at least, are dead, and, although good exists, it rarely prevails.

—Michael M. Levy

SHERMAN, Michael. See LOWNDES, Robert A. W.

SHERMAN, Peter Michael. See LOWNDES, Robert A. W.

SHERRED, T(homas) L. American. Born 27 August 1915. Attended Wayne State University, Detroit. Production line engineer; for many years worked in the Packard toolroom, Detroit; later worked in technical writing and advertising. *Died 16 April 1985.*

SCIENCE-FICTION PUBLICATIONS

Novels

Alien Island. New York, Ballantine, 1970.
Alien Main, with Lloyd Biggle, Jr. New York, Doubleday, 1985.

Short Stories

First Person, Peculiar. New York, Ballantine, 1972.

Uncollected Short Story

"Bounty," in *Again, Dangerous Visions,* edited by Harlan Ellison. New York, Doubleday, 1972.

*

Manuscript Collection: Spenser Research Library, University of Kansas, Lawrence.

* * *

T. L. Sherred's science fiction output was small but of excellent quality. The reason for this, as Sherred explained to Harlan Ellison in the introduction to "Bounty" in *Again, Dangerous Visions,* was " . . . I didn't write very much because I was too busy making a living; I only wrote when I got in a hole and needed cash. When I got the cash, of course, I had pulled out of the hole and didn't write any more . . . "

Sherred's most famous story is "E for Effort" published in *Astounding* (1947). Sherred takes ordinary people and elevates them to positions of great power. In "E for Effort" Ed Lefko is confronted by a television set that can look in on any scene in history. The implications, as developed by Sherred, are enormous. In "Eye for Iniquity" Sherred's main character can create ten-dollar bills out of thin air. "Cue for Quiet" presents us with a pipefitter who discovers that if he wishes hard enough, he can burst the noisy televisions, radios, and jukeboxes that annoy him. These stories are all included in Sherred's only short story collection, *First Person, Peculiar.*

Sherred's only solo novel, *Alien Island,* is a story of first contact. An alien commercial operation called the Regan Group opens relations with Earth by going through an ordinary laborer named Ken Jordan, a sometime alcoholic. By sharing minds with the Captain of the alien vessel, Jordan becomes changed, improved. The narrator of the novel is Dana Iverson, an American spy whose mission is to find out what Jordan and the aliens are planning. Jordan buys a Canadian island near Detroit and sets up a trading base: alien gold and other precious substances in return for Earth's luxury goods. Dana finds out what the Regan group is planning, yet finds their way of life attractive and joins them rather than reporting back to her superiors. The ending is bitter but appropriate.

—George Kelley

SHERRIFF, R(obert) C(harles). British. Born in Kingston upon Thames, Surrey, 6 June 1896. Educated at Kingston Grammar School; New College, Oxford, 1931-34. Served as a Captain in the East Surrey Regiment, 1917. Entered the Sun Insurance Company, 1914. Fellow, Society of Antiquaries; Fellow, Royal Society of Literature. *Died 13 November 1975.*

SCIENCE-FICTION PUBLICATIONS

Novel

The Hopkins Manuscript. London, Gollancz, and New York,

Macmillan, 1939; revised edition, as *The Cataclysm*, London, Pan, 1958, as *The Hopkins Manuscript*, Macmillan, 1963.

OTHER PUBLICATIONS

Novels

Journey's End, with Vernon Bartlett. London, Gollancz, and New York, Stokes, 1930.
The Fortnight in September. London, Gollancz, 1931; New York, Stokes, 1932.
Greengates. London, Gollancz, and New York, Stokes, 1936.
Chedworth. New York, Macmillan, 1944.
Another Year. London, Heinemann, and New York, Macmillan, 1948.
The Wells of St. Mary's. London, Heinemann, 1962.

Plays

Profit and Loss (produced Surbiton, Surrey, 1923).
Cornlow-in-the-Downs (produced Surbiton, Surrey, 1923).
Badger's Green (as *Mr. Birdie's Finger*, produced Surbiton, Surrey, 1926; revised version, as *Badger's Green*, produced London, 1930). London, Gollancz, 1930; New York, French, 1934; revised version (produced Wimbledon, 1961), London, French, 1962.
Journey's End (produced London, 1928; New York, 1929). London, Gollancz, and New York, Brentano's, 1929.
Windfall (produced London, 1934).
St. Helena, with Jeanne de Casalis (produced London and New York, 1936). London, Gollancz, 1934; New York, Stokes, 1935.
Two Hearts Doubled: A Playlet. London, French, 1935.
Goodbye Mr. Chips (screenplay), with Claudine West and Eric Maschwitz, in *The Best Pictures 1939-1940*, edited by Jerry Wald and Richard Macaulay. New York, Dodd Mead, 1940.
Mrs. Miniver (screenplay), with others, in *Twenty Best Film Plays*, edited by John Gassner and Dudley Nichols. New York, Crown, 1943.
Miss Mabel (produced London, 1948; Coonamesset, Massachusetts, 1950). London, Gollancz, 1949.
Quartet: Stories by W. Somerset Maugham, Screenplays by R. C. Sherriff. London, Heinemann, 1948; New York, Doubleday, 1949.
Trio: Stories and Screen Adaptations, with W. Somerset Maugham and Noel Langley. London, Heinemann, and New York, Doubleday, 1950.
Odd Man Out (screenplay), with F. L. Green, in *Three British Screen Plays*, edited by Roger Manvell. London, Methuen, 1950.
Home at Seven (produced London, 1950). London, Gollancz, 1950; New York, French, 1951.
The Kite, in *Action: Beacon Lights of Literature*, edited by Georgia G. Winn and others. Syracuse, New York, Iroquois, 1952.
The White Carnation (produced London, 1953). London, Heinemann, 1953.
The Long Sunset (broadcast, 1955; produced Manchester, 1955; London, 1961). London, Elek, 1956.
The Telescope (broadcast, 1956; produced London, 1957). Published in *Plays of the Year 15*, London, Elek, 1957.
A Shred of Evidence (produced London, 1960). London, French, 1961.

Screenplays: *The Old Dark House*, with Benn Levy, 1932; *The Invisible Man*, with Philip Wylie, 1933; *The Road Back*, with Chrles Kenyon, 1937; *Goodbye Mr. Chips*, with Claudine West and Eric Maschwitz, 1939; *The Four Feathers*, with Arthur Wimperis and Lajos Biro, 1936; *That Hamilton Woman (Lady Hamilton)*, with Walter Reisch, 1941; *Unholy Partners*, with others, 1941; *This Above All*, 1942; *Mrs. Miniver*, with others, 1942; *Stand By for Action*, with others, 1943; *Forever and a Day*, with others, 1944; *Odd Man Out*, with F. L. Green, 1947; *Quartet*, 1948; *Mr. Know-All* (in *Trio*), 1950; *No Highway (No Highway in the Sky)*, with Alec Coppel and Oscar Millard, 1951; *The Dam Busters*, 1955; *The Night My Number Came Up*, 1955; *Storm over the Nile*, with Lajos Biro and Arthur Wimperis, 1955.

Radio Plays: *The Long Sunset*, 1955; *The Night My Number Came Up*, 1956; *The Telescope*, 1956; *CArds with Uncle Tom*, 1958.

Television Play: *The Ogburn Story*, 1963.

Other

King John's Treasure (for children). London, Macmillan, 1954; New York, Macmillan, 1955.
No Leading Lady: An Autobiography. London, Gollancz, 1968.
The Siege of Swayne Castle (for children). London, Gollancz, 1973.

*   *   *

Although best known for his plays (the most recent of which include futuristic "visionary adapters"), R. C. Sherriff made two main contributions to science fiction, the 1933 screenplay of *The Invisible Man* and *The Hopkins Manuscript*, a story of planetary disaster. The screenplay focuses on the adverse psychological effects of physical transformation to depict the menace inherent in invisibility, while the novel contracts the menace of doomsday with the positive effects of crisis: growing loyalty, love, unity, and tolerance.

Though fanciful by scientific criteria, *The Hopkins Manuscript* is dramatic, imaginative, and mildly satiric. Its strength rests in its realistic psychological detail and its unusual point of view: an eccentric and rather Victorian Englishman, fussy, pompous, and endearing, a lunar scholar, breeder of prize poultry, upholder of rural values. He records his and his neighbors' reactions to the discovery that the moon, dislodged from its course and creating tornadoes and tidal waves as it nears earth, may well destroy all life; their preparation for survival, the actual catastrophe (the moon landing in mid-Atlantic), the attempt to rebuilt civilization are fascinating because of the mildly satiric and detailed characterization. Throughout Sherriff eulogizes the common rural Englishman as basically honest and hard-working, with a strong sense of responsibility, a love of the land and of the community; but laments the fact that he can be baffled, betrayed, and destroyed by greedy politicians who use patriotism as a weapon to forward private manias and to manipulate the simple commoner, who, left to himself, would life and let live. Ironically, after demonstrating man's capacity to overcome his vanity and selfishness in the common interest of survival against nature, he shows man's capacity for self-destruction in a meaningless and unnecessary war over the crashed moon's extensive wealth. Ultimately a Persian barbarian on a jihad so thoroughly destroys what remains of European civilization that years later an Abyssinian archeologist finds only traces of this lost civilization.

—Gina Macdonald

SHERWOOD, Nelson. See BULMER, Kenneth.

SHIEL, M(atthew) P(hipps). Also wrote as Gordon Holmes. British. Born on Montserrat Island, West Indies, 21 July 1865. Educated at Harrison College, Barbados; King's College, London; St. Bartholomew's Hospital Medical School, London. Married 1) Carolina García Gomez in 1898 (died), two daughters; 2) Mrs. Gerald Jewson c. 1918. Taught maths at a school in Derbyshire, two years. Granted Civil List pension, 1938. *Died 14 February 1947.*

SCIENCE-FICTION PUBLICATIONS

Novels

The Yellow Danger. London, Richards, 1898; New York, Fenno, 1899.
The Purple Cloud. London, Chatto and Windus, 1901; revised edition, London, Gollancz, 1929; New York, Vanguard Press, 1930.
The Lord of the Sea. London, Richards, and New York, Stokes, 1901; revised edition, New York, Knopf, 1924; London, Gollancz, 1929.
The Yellow Wave. London, Ward Lock, 1905.
The Isle of Lies. London, Laurie, 1909.
This Knot of Life. London, Everett, 1909.
The Dragon. London, Richards, 1913; New York, Clode, 1914; as *The Yellow Peril*, London, Gollancz, 1929.
This above All. New York, Vanguard Press, 1933; as *Above All Else*, London, Cole, 1943.
The Young Men Are Coming! London, Allen and Unwin, and New York, Vanguard Press, 1937.

Short Stories

Shapes in the Fire. London, Lane, and Boston, Roberts, 1896.
The Pale Ape and Other Pulses. London, Laurie, 1911.
The Invisible Voices, with John Gawsworth. London, Richards, 1935; New York, Vanguard Press, 1936.
The Best Short Stories of M. P. Shiel, edited by John Gawsworth. London, Gollancz, 1948.

OTHER PUBLICATIONS

Novels

The Rajah's Sapphire. London, Ward Lock, 1896.
Contraband of War. London, Richards, 1899; revised edition, London, Pearson, 1914; Ridgewood, New Jersey, Gregg Press, 1968.
Cold Steel. London, Richards, 1899; New York, Brentano's, 1900; revised edition, London, Gollancz, and New York, Vanguard Press, 1929.

The Man-Stealers. London, Hutchinson, and Philadelphia, Lippincott, 1900; revised edition, Hutchinson, 1927.
The Weird o' It. London, Richards, 1902.
Unto the Third Generation. London, Chatto and Windus, 1903.
The Evil That Men Do. London, Ward Lock, 1904.
The Lost Viol. New York, Clode, 1905; London, Ward Lock, 1908.
The Last Miracle. London, Laurie, 1907; revised edition, London, Gollancz, 1929.
The White Wedding. London, Laurie, 1908.
Children of the Wind. London, Laurie, 1923.
Dr. Krasinski's Secret. New York, Vanguard Press, 1929; London, Jarrolds, 1930.
The Black Box. New York, Vanguard Press, 1930; London, Richards, 1931.
Say Au R'Voir but Not Goodbye. London, Benn, 1933.

Novels as Gordon Holmes (with Louis Tracy)

An American Emperor. New York, Putnam, and London, Pearson, 1897.
The Late Tenant. New York, Clode, 1906; London, Cassell, 1907.
By Force of Circumstances. New York, Clode, 1909; London, Mills and Boon, 1910.
The House of Silence. New York, Clode, 1911; as *The Silent House,* London, Nash, 1911.

Short Stories

Prince Zaleski. London, Lane, and Boston, Roberts, 1895.
How the Old Woman Got Home. London, Richards, 1927; New York, Vanguard Press, 1928.
Here Comes the Lady. London, Richards, 1928.
Xélucha and Others. Sauk City, Wisconsin, Arkham House, 1975.
Prince Zaleski and Cummings King Monk. Sauk City, Wisconsin, Arkham House, 1977.

Verse

(*Poems*), edited by John Gawsworth. London, Richards, 1936.

Other

Science, Life, and Literature. London, Williams and Norgate, 1950.

Translator, *The Hungarian Revolution: An Eyewitness's Account,* by Charles Henry Schmitt. London, Worker's Socialist Federation, 1919.

*

Bibliography: *The Works of M. P. Shiel: A Study in Bibliography* by A. Reynolds Morse, Los Angeles, Fantasy, 1948.

*   *   *

Certainly one of the most idiosyncratic writers of fantastic fiction of the late 19th and early 20th centuries, M. P. Shiel is primarily remembered today for a single novel, *The Purple Cloud,* although during his own lifetime he was perhaps better known for his tales of imaginary warfare warning of Jewish conspiracies and invading hordes of Oriental devils. A capable stylist whose fine attention to detail can make the most unlikely fantasies persuasive, Shiel also aspired to philosophy, psychology, economics, and historical theory. Unfortunately, his intellectual theories are often no less bizarre than his imaginative situations, and tend to weaken most of his narratives.

Though Shiel produced more than 20 novels and a number of short stories, many of them are occult and historical romances, and relatively few are of interest to modern readers of science fiction. His first major work of science fiction followed in the tradition of future war narratives that became popular in England in the 1870's and 1880's. *The Yellow Danger* concerns the conquest by Japan and China of all Europe except for England, which successfully retaliates with torpedoes and biological warfare and finally comes to rule the world itself. The novel is as notable for its blatant racism as for its detailed and well-thought-out accounts of imaginary battle movements. In *The Lord of the Sea* Europe is again conquered, this time by Jews, and the retaliation comes from a kind of superman who constructs enormous floating fortresses to rule the seas, has the Jews banished to Palestine, and—in a decidedly strange denouement—reveals himself to be a Jew, and in fact the Second Coming! *This Knot of Life* combines themes from both novels in a tale of an Oriental invasion repelled by a European master race (literally called "Overmen") who invent a weapon that causes blindness. *The Young Men Are Coming!* concerns another favorite theme—the superiority of science to religion. A scientist is inspired (by aliens, who kidnap him to a moon of Jupiter) to set about a kind of reverse holy war to overthrow religion with science.

While few of these novels have retained readers, Shiel's masterpiece, *The Purple Cloud*, remains one of the most widely read end-of-the-world stories. Loosely modeled on Mary Shelley's *The Last Man* (1826), *The Purple Cloud* is essentially a study of conflicting creative and destructive impulses as characterized by a single man, Adam Jeffson, who conspires to be the first man to reach the north pole and returns to find the rest of humanity annihilated by a purple volcanic gas that has since dissipated. The "black" and "white" forces that struggled for Jeffson's personality even before he left for the pole create a strange and conflicting pattern of behavior in this last man. His only recreation becomes the burning of the huge cities that humanity left behind, and when he finds another survivor—a girl whose mind is a virtual *tabula rasa* from having lived alone in a dungeon her entire life (she was born just as the gas was dissipating)—he experiences a strange impulse to kill and eat her. But her companionship finally seems to restore a moral balance in Jeffson, and with her he sets out to start the race anew. Although the novel may not quite deserve the lavish praise heaped on it by H. G. Wells, Hugh Walpole, and Arthur Machen, it is an eerily fascinating and strangely powerful novel.

Shiel probably deserves greater attention than he has thus far received as an important figure in the history of science fiction. The intolerance and racial paranoia that characterize many of his works understandably put off many readers, but his works are not without substance, and at least one of them has become an acknowledged classic.

—Gary K. Wolfe

SHIRAS, Wilmar H(ouse). Also writes as Jane Howes. American. Born in Boston, Massachusetts, 23 September 1908.

Educated at Holy Names College, Oakland, California; University of California, Berkeley, M. A. 1956. Married Russell Shiras in 1927; three daughters and two sons. Address: 3720 Rhoda Avenue, Oakland, California 94602, U.S.A.

SCIENCE-FICTION PUBLICATIONS

Short Stories

Children of the Atom. New York, Gnome Press, 1953; London, Boardman, 1954.

Uncollected Short Stories

"Backward, Turn Backward," in *New Worlds of Fantasy 2*, edited by Terry Carr. New York, Ace, 1970.
"Shadow-Led," in *Fantastic* (New York), October 1971.
"Reality," in *Fantastic* (New York), February 1972.
"Bird-Song," in *Fantastic* (New York), April 1973.

OTHER PUBLICATIONS

Other

Slow Dawning (as June Howes). St. Louis, Herder, 1946.

*

Wilmar H. Shiras comments:
"In Hiding" grew out of my wondering whether very high-I. Q. children would have problems; the rest of the book deals with other such children and their problems.

*   *   *

Wilmar H. Shiras's total literary output has been far from copious, and even of the total number of works, not all have been science fiction. In fact, she is known almost entirely for a single volume, *Children of the Atom*. Though it reveals serious shortcomings and limitations, its virtues are even greater.

Children of the Atom originated in three stories published in *Astounding*; the author added two further stories, collecting the five into an episodic work which experienced a considerable vogue in the 1950's. ("In Hiding," the first story in the cycle, has been anthologized no fewer than a dozen times.) The basic premise of the stories, questionable even in 1948 and now recognized as an absurdity, is that an accident in a nuclear industrial plant will produce a uniform mutation in the offspring of all workers in the plant. Specifically, all children born to women pregnant at the time of the accident, or conceived by workers present at the accident, will be of genius-grade intelligence and of highly creative temperament. The author postulates, further, that all of the workers exposed to the accident will die within approximately two years, but that their children will be perfect. Shira's main concern is the problems of adjustment and development of these children in later years. Her major adult protagonists are a group of sympatheic educators and psychologists who discover the existence of these children (who are "in hiding"), and the existence of a network of communication among them. The author assumes that these mentally superior children will be automatically outcasts. The boys, with their inclination to study science, will not fit into a society which emphasizes athletics and violent competition; the girls, inclined toward art, will be similarly excluded from a society which emphasizes prettiness and socialization. Thus the children, in order to survive, hide their superiority beneath a veneer of assumed ordinariness.

Although the author's notions of mutation were quickly seen as absurd, her portrayal of the "superior" children—hyperintellectual adolescents, the boys frequently myopic and unathletic, the girls similarly not adept at the sex-role dictates of the day—struck a strong responsive chord in the typical science-fiction readers of the period. Both Marion Zimmer Bradley and Barry Malzberg, in notes published with a 1978 reissue of the book, comment upon the sense of identity felt by the original readers with the youngsters in the book. It is this uncanny identification of reader with character which gave the book its popularity in the 1950's. In later years the reading of science fiction gained a far greater acceptance in schools, *aficionados* ceased to be automatic outcasts, and this sense of identity became weakened although it did not cease altogether.

In its later segments the novel shows unfortunate tendencies to degenerate into piously one-sided theological argument-ation, and at the end the adult sponsors of the brilliant children are told by the children themselves that it will be best to terminate their experimental community and disperse them-selves among the general populace. This ending, too, has proved controversial among readers of the book, many of them indicating that they see in it a surrender to the very standards of mediocrity and conformism which the children had earlier sought to escape. Shiras has continued to produce short works of science fiction at long intervals. These have been uniformly pleasant, low-keyed, generally concerned with children, and have received little attention from readers.

—Richard A. Lupoff

SHIRLEY, John (Patrick). American. Born in Houston, Texas, 10 February 1953. High School education. Married Alexandra Allinne in 1982 (separated); twin sons. Has had various jobs including fruit picker, dancer, and office worker; regularly performs as lead singer with rock bands. Agent: Martha Millard, 357 West 19th Street, New York, New York 10019. Address: 624 North Beverly Drive, Beverly Hills, California 90210, U.S.A.

SCIENCE-FICTION PUBLICATIONS

Novels

Transmaniacon. New York, Zebra, 1979.
Dracula in Love. New York, Zebra, 1979.
Three-Ring Psychus. New York, Zebra, 1980.
City Come A-Walkin'. New York, Dell, 1981.
Cellars. New York, Avon, 1982; London, Sphere, 1983.
Eclipse. New York, Bluejay, 1985.

Uncollected Short Stories

"The Word 'Random,' Deliberately Repeated," in *Clarion 3*, edited by Robin Scott Wilson. New York, New American Library, 1973.
"Uneasy Chrysalids, Our Memories," in *Epoch*, edited by

Roger Elwood and Robert Silverberg. New York, Berkley, 1975.
"Silent Crickets," in *Fantastic* (New York), April 1975.
"What He Wanted," in *Amazing* (New York), November 1975.
"Under the Generator," in *Universe 6*, edited by Terry Carr. New York, Doubleday, 1976.
"The Almost Empty Rooms," in *New Dimensions 7*, edited by Robert Silverberg. New York, Harper, 1977.
"Will the Chill," in *Universe 9*, edited by Terry Carr. New York, Doubleday, 1979.
"The Gunshot," in *Oui* (New York), November 1980.
"The Belonging Kind," with William Gibson, in *Shadows 4*, edited by Charles L. Grant. New York, Doubleday, 1981.
"Quill Tripstickler Hits Bottom," in *Isaac Asimov's Science Fiction Magazine* (New York), Mid-December 1982.
"Triggering," in *The Second Omni Book of Science Fiction*, edited by Ellen Datlow. New York, Zebra, 1983.
". . . and the Angel with Television Eyes," in *Isaac Asimov's Science Fiction Magazine* (New York), May 1983.
"What Cindy Saw," in *Interzone: The First Anthology*, edited by John Clute, Colin Greenland, and David Pringle. London, Dent, 1985.
"The Unfolding," with Bruce Sterling, in *Interzone* (Leeds), Spring 1985.
"The Incorporated," in *Isaac Asimov's Science Fiction Magazine* (New York), July 1985.

OTHER PUBLICATIONS

Novel

The Brigade. New York, Avon, 1982; London, Sphere, 1983.

Plays

Screenplays: *Video Girl; The Other Side of Evil*.

*

John Shirley comments:

My early stories show that I was enamored of the surrealists; surrealist and expressionist painting influenced me more than writers. Although there was a political iconoclasm intrinsic to my writing, I've never sided with any particular political philosophy; I feel that the major political and economic theories have all been satirized even-handedly in my fiction. My newest novel, *Eclipse*—easily my most significant book—is essentially a political thriller set in the year 2020, when a non-nuclear world war has ravaged Europe, making it possible for an opportunisic cabal of genuine fascists to take over, through nationalistic puppets, one country after another. Essentially, Europe becomes a massive police state, and the heroes of *Eclipse* are the resistance. They're not Communists, particularly—that is, some are, some aren't. Nor are they radicals. They're simply the resistance to fascism. It happens I really and honestly believe that a resurgence of racism on a vast scale is about to transform Europe, due to the myopic and xenophobic reaction of European natives to the influx of third world immigrants, and also due to other sociological factors. *Eclipse* is a kind of warning novel about it, and an attempt to redefine the cultural backdrop of the near-future. The landscapes of bizarrities typical of much of my earlier writing, the attempt to realize abstractions in physical description—these are missing from *Eclipse*, at least in explicit manifestation. *Eclipse* is real life, contemporary life, seen through a science fiction lens. I've also given a much greater emphasis to characterization than ever before.

* * *

John Shirley probably is the most controversial younger sf writer. Some of his writing has acquired a cult following, but he has also been dismissed as a demented poseur. In fact, Shirley has worked hard to produce strong reactions. He would much rather offend readers than leave them unmoved. And his work generally does succeed because his ideas and images are too vivid to dismiss, pummeling readers in the pre-rational way Shirley intends.

In a recent letter, Shirley explains his purpose in his early sf and fantasy: "I was trying to make the impossible seem possible and palpably real, to make it seem so concrete and visualizable, so cinematically striking, that the reader would end by questioning his or her own sanity. I wanted people to question reality, their assumptions, political, social, existential, everything." In his early novels such as *Dracula in Love* and *City Come A-Walkin'*, Shirley's main character suffers because he is empty of purpose. He thus is attracted to an unchanging (but vicious) force trying to preserve itself; however he winds up on the side of an amoral but stability-shattering entity that plots to destroy that stifling "father" power. The novels' action is morally equivocal at best, with huge numbers of people being vividly mutilated and/or slaughtered. The central character never is sure he is doing the right thing, and Shirley offers the possibility that his thirst for freedom might actually be a craving for oblivion (in madness or death). *Transmaniacon* is probably the most successful of Shirley's early novels in demonstrating hatred of a status quo, thanks to its fierce images of bizarre obsessions; the novel's conclusion explicitly links escape from constraints with mortal danger, but Shirley's hero gladly makes that choice. Also memorable is *Three-Ring Psychus*, set *after* some people has been given psychic powers that let them transcend some physical limits; Shirley's characters discover that the change has given them new possibilities for growth but that some of the possibilities threaten the survival of human consciousness. The book ends with determined uncertainty.

Reading these novels is unsettling as much for the manner of their telling as for their content. The stories refuse to let a reader sink into them as comfortable escape fiction. The action lurches along. The characters let moral qualms interupt what the reader expects to be a smooth, exciting flow of action. On the other hand, what might be key personal decisions are summarized in an offhand manner. Shirley began experimenting with less obtrusively jarring narrative techniques when he turned away from science fiction briefly to write a mainstream suspense thriller (*The Brigade*), a horror fantasy in the vein of Stephen King (*Cellars*), and various pseudonymous action novels for paperback series (such as the "Traveler" series of post-WW III adventures, which are notable for Shirley's wholesale bloodletting and his bitter, witty contempt for the U. S. government responsible for launching the nucler missiles). Having returned to the science-fiction novel, he says that "Now, I'm trying to write with crystaline realism about *this* world, but I'm still trying to make my readers question their assumptions. I'm spending a great deal more time investigating character, and controlling tone, the overall quality of writing."

Shirley's early novels were paperbacks, now out of print and difficult to locate. It is even more difficult for a curious reader to seek out Shirley's short stories in the anthologies and magazines where they are scattered. The effort is worth it, however, for although Shirley's novels present his message more fully, some of his short stories are more successful at giving a burst of startling argument and stunning imagery that pry readers loose from their comfortable preconceptions. In particular, "The Almost Empty Rooms" plays with the idea of free will in a wry story of WW III seen as a frolic of event-animals whose cells are human beings. Another outstanding story, "What Cindy Saw," seems to begin as a study of mental illness, then becomes a surrealistic look at modern life, but ends by affirming the existence of a nightmarish world under the surface of normal "reality." In these and other short stories, Shirley demonstrates that he not only has an imagination that can take reality apart and put it together inside out; he also can seize a reader's attention and rivet it on *his* vision.

With that power and with a growing range of skills, Shirley is just entering his full maturity as a writer. He describes himself as "a performer," and his life as a writer may be compared to his other career as a rock musician. In a column for the semi-professional magazine *Thrust*, he describes himself being injured in a fight with an unappreciative member of the audience and considering quitting his band: "I got disgusted and thought 'What do I need this noise for?' But I'm singing tomorrow night, my lyrics my group and my risk." If this is a gutsy attitude for a young musician, it also is not a bad one for a beginning science-fiction writer. Shirley will keep writing because he cares so passionately about reaching more people in his audience, forcing them to listen for things they've been ignoring, showing them that they must give up the safety of their settled viewpoints to run the risks of freedom.

—Joe Sanders

SHUTE, Nevil (Nevil Shute Norway). British. Born in Ealing, London, 17 January 1899. Educated at Dragon School, Oxford; Shrewsbury School, Oxford; Royal Military Academy, Woolwich, London; Balliol College, Oxford, 1919-22, E. A. in engineering 1922. Served as a private in the Suffolk Regiment, British Army, 1918; commissioned in the Royal Naval Volunteer Reserve, 1940: Lieutenant Commander; retired 1945. Married Frances Mary Heaton in 1931; two daughters. Calculator, de Havilland Aircraft Company, 1923-24; Chief Calculator, 1924-28, and Deputy Chief Engineer, 1928-30, on the construction of Rigid Airship R. 100 for the Airship Guarantee Company: twice flew Atlantic in R. 100, 1930; Managing Director, Yorkshire Aeroplane Club Ltd., 1927-30; Founder and Joint Managing Director, Airspeed Ltd., airplane constructors, 1931-38. Lived in Australia after 1950. Fellow, Royal Aeronautical Society, 1934. *Died 12 January 1960.*

SCIENCE-FICTION PUBLICATIONS

Novels

What Happened to the Corbetts. London, Heinemann, 1939; as *Ordeal*, New York, Morrow, 1939.
An Old Captivity. London, Heinemann, and New York, Morrow, 1940.
No Highway. London, Heinemann, and New York, Morrow, 1948.
In the Wet. London, Heinemann, and New York, Morrow, 1953.
On the Beach. London, Heinemann, and New York, Morrow, 1957.

The Rainbow and the Rose. London, Heinemann, and New York, Morrow, 1958.

OTHER PUBLICATIONS

Novels

Marazan. London, Cassell, 1926.
So Disdained. London, Cassel, 1928; as *Mysterious Aviator*, Boston, Houghton Mifflin, 1928.
Lonely Road. London, Cassell, and New York, Morrow, 1932.
Ruined City. London, Cassell, 1938; as *Kindling,* New York, Morrow, 1938.
Landfall: A Channel Story. London, Heinemann, and New York, Morrow, 1940.
Pied Piper. New York, Morrow, 1941; London, Heinemann, 1942.
Pastoral. London, Heinemann, and New York, Morrow, 1944.
Most Secret. London, Heinemann, and New York, Morrow, 1945.
The Chequer Board. London, Heinemann, and New York, Morrow, 1947.
A Town Like Alice. London, Heinemann, 1950; as *The Legacy*, New York, Morrow, 1950.
Round the Bend. London, Heinemann, and New York, Morrow, 1951.
The Far Country. London, Heinemann, and New York, Morrow, 1952.
Requiem for a Wren. London, Heinemann, 1955; as *The Breaking Wave*, New York, Morrow, 1955.
Beyond the Black Stump. London, Heinemann, and New York, Morrow, 1956.
Trustee from the Toolroom. London, Heinemann, and New York, Morrow, 1960.
Stephen Morris. London, Heinemann, and New York, Morrow, 1961.

Play

Vinland the Good (screenplay). London, Heinemann, and New York, Morrow, 1946.

Other

Slide Rule: The Autobiography of an Engineer. London, Heinemann, and New York, Morrow, 1954.

*

Manuscript Collection: National Library of Australia, Canberra.

Critical Study: *Nevil Shute (Nevil Shute Norway)* by Julian Smith, Boston, Twayne, 1976.

*   *   *

Nevil Shute's science-fiction novels make up only a quarter of his output of 22 novels. Yet like all his work, the science fiction profits from Shute's ability to create strong, interesting characters. Although without exception ordinary middle-class people, living calm, almost prosaic lives, these characters are of interest because of their devotion to duty and their pursuit of some personal goal. These goals are as divergent as planting next year's garden in the face of death, finding a missing aircraft part, or providing proof for the Viking settlement in North America. But it is the people and their absorption in their goals in the face of gargantuan difficulties that draw the reader into the story. Shute's novels move at a very leisurely pace, full of details of country, city, and daily routine. Through the wealth of detail a verisimilitude develops so that the sufferings and triumphs of the characters are shared rather than observed. *On the Beach* is filled with characters who draw such interest. Peter and Mary Holmes calmly plant next spring's bulbs and buy a playpen for their daughter Jennifer, even though they know they will never see the bulbs bloom, nor see their daughter use the playpen. So slowly does the atomic fallout move that the Holmes's wait becomes the reader's wait as the worlds moves inexorably to its end.

No Highway, too, contains characters whose dedication to duty provides a way to live. Mr. Honey, a scientist studying metal fatigue, allows his daughter to locate the missing tail of a crashed plane through a clairvoyant hypnotic session. Unlike the characters who watch the proceedings, the reader is not shocked, for we are convinced, along with Honey, that the experiment is vital. *An Old Captivity, In the Wet, What Happened to the Corbetts*, and *The Rainbow and the Rose* are science-fiction works filled with ordinary people who face tremendous odds yet manage to survive.

—Walter E. Meyers

———

SILVA, Joseph. See **GOULART, Ron.**

———

SILVERBERG, Robert. Also writes as Walker Chapman; Ivar Jorgenson; Calvin M. Knox; David Osborne; Robert Randall; Lee Sebastian. American. Born in New York City, 15 January 1935. Educated at Columbia University, New York, A. B. 1956. Married Barbara H. Brown in 1956. Full-time writer: Associate Editor, *Amazing*, January 1969 issue, and Associate Editor, *Fantastic*, February-April 1969 issues. President, Science Fiction Writers of America, 1967-68. Recipient: Hugo Award, 1956, 1969; Nebula Award, for story, 1969, 1971, 1974, for novel, 1971; Jupiter award, 1973; Prix Apollo, 1976; *Locus* award, 1981. Guest of Honor, 28th World Science Fiction Convention, 1970. Agent: Scott Meredith Literary Agency, 845 Third Avenue, New York, New York 10022. Address: c/o Donald I. Fine Inc., 128 East 36th Street, New York, New York 10016, U.S.A.

SCIENCE-FICTION PUBLICATIONS

Novels (series: Majipoor; Nidor)

Revolt on Alpha C (for children). New York, Crowell, 1955.
The 13th Immortal. New York, Ace, 1957.
Master of Life and Death. New York, Ace, 1957; London, Sidgwick and Jackson, 1977.
The Shrouded Planet (Nidor; as Robert Randall, with Randall Garrett). New York, Gnome Press, 1957; London, Mayflower, 1964.

Invaders from Earth. New York, Ace, 1958; London, Sidgwick and Jackson, 1977.

Invincible Barriers (as David Osborne). New York, Avalon, 1958.

Stepsons of Terra. New York, Ace, 1958.

Aliens from Space (as David Osborne). New York, Avalon, 1958.

Starhaven (as Ivar Jorgenson). New York, Avalon, 1958.

Starman's Quest (for children). New York, Gnome Press, 1959.

The Dawning Light (Nidor; as Robert Randall, with Randall Garrett). New York, Gnome Press, 1959; London, Mayflower, 1964.

The Planet Killers. New York, Ace, 1959.

Lost Race of Mars (for children). Philadelphia, Winston, 1960.

Collision Course. New York, Avalon, 1961.

The Seed of Earth. New York, Ace, 1962; London, Hamlyn, 1978.

Recalled to Life. New York, Lancer, 1962; revised edition, New York, Doubleday, 1972; London Gollancz, 1974.

The Silent Invaders. New York, Ace, 1963; London, Dobson, 1975.

Regan's Planet. New York, Pyramid, 1964.

Time of the Great Freeze (for children). New York, Holt Rinehart, 1964.

A Pair from Space. New York, Belmont, 1965.

Conquerors from the Darkness (for children). New York, Holt Rinehart, 1965.

The Gate of Worlds (for children). New York, Holt Rinehart, 1967; London, Gollancz, 1978.

To Open the Sky. New York, Ballantine, 1967; London, Sphere, 1970.

Thorns. New York, Ballantine, 1967; London, Rapp and Whiting, 1969.

Those Who Watch. New York, New American Library, 1967; London, New English Library, 1977.

The Time-Hoppers. New York, Doubleday, 1967; London, Sidgwick and Jackson, 1968.

Planet of Death. New York, Holt Rinehart, 1967.

Hawksbill Station. New York, Doubleday, 1968; as *The Anvil of Time*, London, Sidgwick and Jackson, 1969.

The Masks of Time. New York, Ballantine, 1968; as *Vornan-19*, London, Sidgwick and Jackson, 1970.

Up the Line. New York, Ballantine, 1969.

Nightwings. New York, Avon, 1969; London, Sidgwick and Jackson, 1972.

Across a Billion Years (for children). New York, Dial Press, 1969; London, Gollancz, 1977.

The Man in the Maze (for children). New York, Avon, and London, Sidgwick and Jackson, 1969.

Three Survived (for children). New York, Holt Rinehart, 1969.

To Live Again. New York, Doubleday, 1969; London, Sidgwick and Jackson, 1975.

World's Fair 1992 (for children). Chicago, Follett, 1970.

Downward to the Earth. New York, Doubleday, 1970; London, Gollancz, 1977.

Tower of Glass. New York, Scribner, 1970; London, Panther, 1976.

A Robert Silverberg Omnibus. London, Sidgwick and Jackson, 1970.

The World Inside. New York, Doubleday, 1971; London, Millington, 1976.

A Time of Changes. New York, Doubleday, 1971; London, Gollancz, 1973.

Son of Man. New York, Ballantine, 1971; London, Panther, 1979.

The Book of Skulls. New York, Scribner, 1971; London, Gollancz, 1978.

Dying Inside. New York, Scribner, 1972; London, Sidgwick and Jackson, 1974.

The Second Trip. New York, Doubleday, 1972; London, Gollancz, 1979.

The Stochastic Man. New York, Harper, 1975; London, Gollancz, 1976.

Shadrach in the Furnace. Indianapolis, Bobbs Merrill, 1976; London, Gollancz, 1977.

Lord Valentine's Castle (Majipoor). New York, Harper, and London, Gollancz, 1980.

The Desert of Stolen Dreams. Columbia, Pennsylvania, Underwood Miller, 1981.

A Robert Silverberg Omnibus. New York, Harper, 1981.

Majipoor Chronicles. New York, Arbor House, and London, Gollancz, 1982.

Valentine Pontifex. New York, Arbor House, 1983; London, Gollancz, 1984.

Lord of Darkness. New York, Arbor House, and London, Gollancz, 1983.

The Conglomeroid Cocktail Party. New York, Arbor House, 1984; London, Gollancz, 1985.

Tom O'Bedlam. New York, Fine, 1985.

Sailing to Byzantium. Columbia, Pennsylvania, Underwood Miller, 1985.

Novels as Calvin M. Knox

Lest We Forget Thee, Earth. New York, Ace, 1958.
The Plot Against Earth. New York, Ace, 1959.
One of Our Asteroids Is Missing. New York, Ace, 1964.

Short Stories

Next Stop the Stars. New York, Ace, 1962; London, Dobson, 1979.

Godling, Go Home! New York, Belmont, 1964.

To Worlds Beyond. Philadelphia, Chilton, 1965; London, Sphere, 1969.

Needle in a Timestack. New York, Ballantine, 1966; London, Sphere, 1967; revised edition, Sphere, 1979.

To Open the Sky. New York, Ballantine, 1967.

The Calibrated Alligator (for children). New York, Holt Rinehart, 1969.

Dimension Thirteen. New York, Ballantine, 1969.

Parsecs and Parables. New York, Doubleday, 1970; London, Hale, 1973.

The Cube Root of Uncertainty. New York, Macmillan, 1970.

Moonferns and Starsongs. New York, Ballantine, 1971.

The Reality Trip and Other Implausibilities. New York, Ballantine, 1972.

Valley Beyond Time. New York, Dell, 1973.

Unfamiliar Territory. New York, Scribner, 1973; London, Gollancz, 1975.

Earth's Other Shadow. New York, New American Library, 1973; London, Millington, 1977.

Born with the Dead. New York, Random House, 1974; London, Gollancz, 1975.

Sundance and Other Science Fiction Stories. Nashville, Nelson, 1974; London, Abelard Schuman, 1975.

Sunrise on Mercury (for children). Nashville, Nelson, 1975; London, Gollancz, 1983.

The Feast of St. Dionysus. New York, Scribner, 1975; London, Gollancz, 1976.

The Shores of Tomorrow. Nashville, Nelson, 1976.
The Best of Robert Silverberg. New York, Pocket Books, 1976; London, Sidgwick and Jackson, 1977.
Capricorn Games. New York, Random House, 1976; London, Gollancz, 1978.
The Songs of Summer and Other Stories. London, Gollancz, 1979.
World of a Thousand Colors. New York, Arbor House, 1982.

OTHER PUBLICATIONS

Novel

Gilgamesh the King. New York, Arbor House, 1984; London, Gollancz, 1985.

Other

Treasures Beneath the Sea (for children). Racine, Wisconsin, Whitman, 1960.
First American into Space. Derby, Connecticut, Monarch, 1961.
Lost Cities and Vanished Civilizations (for children). Philadelphia, Chilton, 1962.
The Fabulous Rockefellers. Derby, Connecticut, Monarch, 1963.
Sunken History: The Story of Underwater Archaeology (for children). Philadelphia, Chilton, 1963.
15 Battles That Changed the World. New York, Putnam, 1963.
Home of the Red Man: Indian North America Before Columbus (for children). Greenwich, Connecticut, New York Graphic Society, 1963.
Empires in the Dust. Philadelphia, Chilton, 1963.
The Great Doctors (for children). New York, Putnam, 1964.
Akhnaten, The Rebel Pharaoh. Philadelphia, Chilton, 1964.
The Man Who Found Nineveh: The Story of Austen Henry Layard (for children). New York, Holt Rinehart, 1964; Kingswood, Surrey, World's Work, 1968.
Man Before Adam. Philadelphia, Macrae Smith, 1964.
The Loneliest Continent (as Walker Chapman). Greenwich, Connecticut, New York Graphic Society, 1965; London, Jarrolds, 1967.
Scientists and Scoundrels: A Book of Hoaxes. New York, Crowell, 1965.
The World of Coral (for children). New York, Duell, 1965.
The Mask of Akhnaten (for children). New York, Macmillan, 1965.
Socrates (for children). New York, Putnam, 1965.
The Old Ones: Indians of the American Southwest. Greenwich, Connecticut, New York Graphic Society, 1965.
Men Who Mastered the Atom. New York, Putnam, 1965.
The Great Wall of China. Philadelphia, Chilton, 1965.
Niels Bohr, The Man Who Mapped the Atom (for children). Philadelphia, Macrae Smith, 1965.
Forgotten by Time: A Book of Living Fossils (for children). New York, Crowell, 1966.
Frontiers of Archaeology. Philadelphia, Chilton, 1966.
Kublai Khan, Lord of Xanadu (for children; as Walker Chapman). Indianapolis, Bobbs Merrill, 1966.
The Long Rampart: The Story of the Great Wall of China. Philadelphia, Chilton, 1966.
Rivers (for children; as Lee Sebastian). New York, Holt Rinehart, 1966.
Bridges. Philadelphia, Macrae Smith, 1966.
To the Rock of Darius: The Story of Henry Rawlinson (for children). New York, Holt Rinehart, 1966.

The Dawn of Medicine. New York, Putnam, 1967.
The Adventures of Nat Palmer, Antarctic Explorer. New York, McGraw Hill, 1967.
The Auk, The Dodo, and the Oryx. New York, Crowell, 1967; Kingswood, Surrey, World's Work, 1969.
The Golden Dream: Seekers of El Dorado. Indianapolis, Bobbs Merrill, 1967.
Men Against Time: Salvage Archaeology in the United States. New York, Macmillan, 1967.
The Morning of Mankind. Greenwich, Connecticut, New York Graphic Society, 1967; Kingswood, Surrey, World's Work, 1970.
The World of the Rain Forest. New York, Meredith Press, 1967.
Light for the World: Edison and the Power Industry. Princeton, New Jersey, Van Nostrand, 1967.
Four Men Who Changed the Universe (for children). New York, Putnam, 1968.
Ghost Towns of the American West. New York, Crowell, 1968.
Mound Builders of Ancient America. Greenwich, Connecticut, New York Graphic Society, 1968.
The South Pole (for children; as Lee Sebastian). New York, Holt Rinehart, 1968.
Stormy Voyager: The Story of Charles Wilkes. Philadelphia, Lippincott, 1968.
The World of the Ocean Depths. New York, Meredith Press, 1968; Kingswood, Surrey, World's Work, 1970.
Bruce of the Blue Nile (for children). New York, Holt Rinehart, 1969.
The Challenge of Climate: Man and His Environment: New York, Meredith Press, 1969; Kingswood, Surrey, World's Work, 1971.
Vanishing Giants: The Story of the Sequoias. New York, Simon and Schuster, 1969.
Wonders of Ancient Chinese Science. New York, Hawthorn, 1969.
The World of Space. New York, Meredith Press, 1969.
If I Forget Thee, O Jerusalem: American Jews and the State of Israel. New York, Morrow, 1970.
Mammoths, Mastodons, and Man. New York, McGraw Hill, 1970; Kingswood, Surrey, World's Work, 1972.
The Pueblo Revolt. New York, Weybright and Talley, 1970.
The Seven Wonders of the Ancient World (for children). New York, Crowell Collier, 1970.
Before the Sphinx. New York, Nelson, 1971.
Clocks for the Ages: How Scientists Date the Past. New York, Macmillan, 1971.
To the Western Shore: Growth of the United States 1776-1853. New York, Doubleday, 1971.
Into Space, with Arthur C. Clarke. New York, Harper, 1971.
John Muir: Prophet among the Glaciers. New York, Putnam, 1972.
The Longest Voyage: Circumnavigation in the Age of Discovery. Indianapolis, Bobbs Merrill, 1972.
The Realm of Prester John. New York, Doubleday, 1972.
The World Within the Ocean Wave. New York, Weybright and Talley, 1972.
The World Within the Tide Pool. New York, Weybright and Talley, 1972.
"Introduction to *Sundance,*" in *Those Who Can,* edited by Robin Scott Wilson. New York, New American Library, 1973.
Drug Themes in Science Fiction. Rockville, Maryland, National Institute on Drug Abuse, 1974.
"The Profession of Science Fiction IX: Sounding Brass, Tinkling Cymbal," in *Foundation 7-8* (London), March 1975.

Editor, *Great Adventures in Archaeology*. New York, Dial Press, 1964; London, Hale, 1966.

Editor, *Earthmen and Strangers*. New York, Duell, 1966.

Editor (as Walker Chapman), *Antarctic Conquest*. Indianapolis, Bobbs Merrill, 1966.

Editor, *Voyagers in Time*. New York, Meredith Press, 1967.

Editor, *Men and Machines*. New York, Meredith Press, 1968.

Editor, *Mind to Mind*. New York, Meredith Press, 1968.

Editor, *Tomorrow's Worlds*. New York, Meredith Press, 1969.

Editor, *Dark Stars*. New York, Ballantine, 1969; London, Ballantine, 1971.

Editor, *Three for Tomorrow*. New York, Meredith Press, 1969; London, Gollancz, 1970.

Editor, *The Mirror of Infinity: A Critics' Anthology of Science Fiction*. New York, Harper, 1970; London, Sidgwick and Jackson, 1971.

Editor, *Science Fiction Hall of Fame 1*. New York, Doubleday, 1970; London, Gollancz, 1971.

Editor, *The Ends of Time*, New York, Hawthorn, 1970.

Editor, *Great Short Novels of Science Fiction*. New York, Ballantine, 1970; London, Pan, 1971.

Editor, *Worlds of Maybe*. New York, Nelson, 1970.

Editor, *Alpha 1-9*. New York, Ballantine, 5 vols., 1970-74; New York, Berkley, 4 vols., 1975-78.

Editor, *Four Futures*. New York, Hawthorn, 1971.

Editor, *The Science Fiction Bestiary*. New York, Nelson, 1971.

Editor, *To the Stars*. New York, Hawthorn, 1971.

Editor, *New Dimensions 1-12* (vols. 11 and 12 edited with Marta Randall). New York, Doubleday, 3 vols., 1971-73; New York, New American Library, 1 vol., 1974; New York, Harper, 6 vols., 1975-80; New York, Pocket Books, 2 vols., 1980-81; *5-7* published London, Gollancz, 3 vols., 1976-77.

Editor, *The Day the Sun Stood Still*. Nashville, Nelson, 1972.

Editor, *Invaders from Space*. New York, Hawthorn, 1972.

Editor, *Beyond Control*. Nashville, Nelson, 1972; London, Sidgwick and Jackson, 1973.

Editor, *Deep Space*. Nashville, Nelson, 1973; London, Abelard Schuman, 1976.

Editor, *Chains of the Sea*. Nashville, Nelson, 1973.

Editor, *No Mind of Man*. New York, Hawthorn, 1973.

Editor, *Other Dimensions*. New York, Hawthorn, 1973.

Editor, *Three Trips in Time and Space*. New York, Hawthorn, 1973.

Editor, *Mutants*. Nashville, Nelson, 1974; London, Abelard Schuman, 1976.

Editor, *Threads of Time*. Nashville, Nelson, 1974; London, Millington, 1975.

Editor, *Infinite Jests*. Radnor, Pennsylvania, Chilton, 1974.

Editor, *Windows into Tomorrow*. New York, Hawthorn, 1974.

Editor, with Roger Elwood, *Epoch*. New York, Berkley, 1975.

Editor, *Explorers of Space*. Nashville, Nelson, 1975.

Editor, *The New Atlantis*. New York, Hawthorn, 1975.

Editor, *Strange Gifts*. Nashville, Nelson, 1975.

Editor, *The Aliens*. Nashville, Nelson, 1976.

Editor, *The Crystal Ship*. Nashville, Nelson, 1976; London, Millington, 1980.

Editor, *Triax*. Los Angeles, Pinnacle, 1977; London, Fontana, 1979.

Editor, *Trips in Time*. Nashville, Nelson, 1977; London, Hale, 1979.

Editor, *Earth Is the Strangest Planet*. Nashville, Nelson, 1977.

Editor, *Galactic Dreamers*. New York, Random House, 1977.

Editor, *The Infinite Web*. New York, Dial Press, 1977.

Editor, *The Androids Are Coming*. New York, Elsevier Nelson, 1979.

Editor, *Lost Worlds, Unknown Horizons*. New York, Elsevier Nelson, 1979.

Editor, *The Edge of Space*. New York, Elsevier Nelson, 1979.

Editor, with Martin H. Greenberg and Joseph D. Olander, *Car Sinister*. New York, Avon, 1979.

Editor, with Martin H. Greenberg and Joseph D. Olander, *Dawn of Time: Prehistory Through Science Fiction*. New York, Elsevier Nelson, 1979.

Editor, *The Best of New Dimensions*. New York, Simon and Schuster, 1979.

Editor, with Martin H. Greenberg, *The Arbor House Treasury of Modern Science Fiction*. New York, Arbor House, 1980.

Editor, with Martin H. Greenberg, *The Arbor House Treasury of Great Science Fiction Short Novels*. New York, Arbor House, 1980.

Editor, with Martin H. Greenberg and Charles G. Waugh, *The Science Fictional Dinosaur*. New York, Avon, 1982.

Editor, *The Best of Randall Garrett*. New York, Pocket Books, 1982.

Editor, with Martin H. Greenberg, *The Arbor House Treasury of Science Fiction Masterpieces*. New York, Arbor House, 1983.

Editor, with Martin H. Greenberg, *Fantasy Hall of Fame*. New York, Arbor House, 1983.

Editor, *The Nabula Awards 18*. New York, Arbor House, 1983.

Editor, with Martin H. Greenberg, *The Time Travelers: A Science fiction Quartet*. New York, Fine, 1985.

*

Bibliography: in *Fantasy and Science Fiction* (New York), April 1974.

Manuscript Collection: Syracuse University, New York.

Critical Studies: "Robert Silverberg Issue" of *SF Commentary* (Melbourne), March 1977; *Robert Silverberg* by Thomas D. Clareson, Mercer Island, Washington, Starmont House, 1983.

*   *   *

Robert Silverberg's writing career spans four decades. A prolific writer, Silverberg's writing and themes have changed as the writer has matured and gained the skills of a master storyteller. In his revealing autobiographical essay, "Sounding Brass, Tinkling Cymbal" (*Hell's Cartographers*), Silverberg admits to producing over a million words per year of published material in his apprenticeship years 1955-59. Much of this was hackwork; stories like "Slaves of the Star Giants" and "Secret of the Green Invaders" and novels like *The Planet Killers* and *Stepsons of Terra*. Yet some of the stories were outstanding, like the dark "Road to Nightfall" and the clever "Translation Error," giving notice of the superb stories Silverberg was about to produce.

The late 1950's saw the decline and sudden contraction of the number of science-fiction magazines coupled with the declining market for science-fiction novels. Silverberg responded by shifting his main writing emphasis from SF to juvenile non-fiction where he achieved critical acclaim for excellent works like *Treasures Beneath the Sea*, *Empires in the Dust*, and *Lost Cities and Vanished Civilizations*. Silverberg also produced over a hundred soft-core pornopaperbacks most under the Don Elliot/Eliot pseudonym. Yet Silverberg did not entirely abandon the SF field during the years 1960-68. Frederik Pohl, then editor of *Galaxy*, *If* , and *Worlds of Tomorrow* SF magazines, invited Silverberg to write whatever he wanted. Silverberg, intrigued by the offer, submitted his now classic "To See the Invisible Man" (1962). Silverberg's narrator is punished by a future society for his crime of "coldness' by being completely ignored by everyone in that society for one year. Silverberg plays with the possibilities such a situation presents, showing the themes of the individual reacting against a society, even though the society is benign. "To See the Invisible Man" shows a shunned man in turn shunning a society: this is a sophisticated story light-years from Silverberg's earlier action adventure SF like "Battle for the Thousand Stars. "

The end of this transition period saw Silverberg begin to emerge as a powerful short-story witer. With "Flies," written for Harlan Ellison's *Dangerous Visions*, Silverberg breaks new ground. An alien race restores a dead starship pilot named Cassiday and enhances his powers. Sent back to Earth as a kind of transmitter for the aliens, Cassiday commits hideous acts of violence since his is incapable of emotion. The aliens, realizing their mistake, return Cassiday to their world and give him back his conscience, providing the means of self-torture. The story deals with major moral and religious themes, themes Silverberg will expand on in his major novels. Silverberg won his first Nebula Award for "Passengers," a horror story of humans dominated by parasitic aliens called Passengers who ride their host humans and utterly control them. "Passengers" explores the question of free will versus determinism, a major theme of later novels like *The Stochastic Man* and *Shadrach in the Furnace*.

Like the explosion of writing in Silverberg's early period, the years 1969-76 produce a similar flood of works; the difference was in the quality. *Nightwings* presents Silverberg's vision of the far future. Earth is a ruined planet, with the Americas sunk beneath the seas. Yet its super-science which produces genetically engineered Flyers coexists with a medieval political structure. Tomis the Watcher is a beautifully realized character who narrates this powerful story of hope, renewal, and redemption. In *Tower of Glass* Silverberg's dark vision returns. 23rd-century Earth is ruled by Simeon Krug, inventor of the android. His quest is to contact an alien race by building a mammoth tower of glass to send signals deep into space. At the same time, the androids are organizing to be granted person status instead of being consider property. The book abounds with racial and moral themes, yet the conclusion is very bitter. (About the time *Tower of Glass* was written, Silverberg suffered a fire to his house that destroyed part of his New York City home and left him depressed.)

A Time of Changes (Nebula Award) is a book misinterpreted as a vehicle for advocating the use of psychedelic drugs because of the dreamlike quality of many sections of book where the characters use a Sumaran drug which allows a person to link minds with another person. *Son of Man* is a strange blend of Olaf Stapledon and David Lindsay's *A Voyage to Arcturus* that results in a surreal plot that goes nowhere. But the characters Silverberg creates in Clay, Hanmer, and Ninameen remain unforgettable.

The World Inside presents some of Silverberg's more controversial solutions to overpopulation. Silverberg presents a world of gigantic living units, a thousand stories high, containing 800,000 people each. It is a unique future society that encourages sexual experimentation, encourages bearing children, encourages an anti-privacy culture. Contrast this to the situation Silverberg presents in *The Book of Skulls* where a student finds a manuscript in the rare books of a university library that promises immortality. This launches a quest that

results in what Barry N. Malzberg calls Silverberg's finest novel. Yet most critics consider *Dying Inside* Silverberg's best book. David Selig is a compelling character: he's forty years old and writes term papers for college students to make enough money to survive. He also has the power to listen to other people's thoughts. As a young man, he considered his power a curse, but now Selig finds he is gradually losing his power to receive the thoughts of others. Silverberg creates a complex, sympathic character whose plight—although strange and bizarre— becomes realistic and emotional through the exploration of the themes of loss, old age, racism, and change. In *Dying Inside*, Silverberg's powers as a novelist are most completely realized.

In 1976, *The Best of Robert Silverberg* appeared along with Silverberg's announcement that he was withdrawing from the SF field. Silverberg complained critics ignored his work and the science-fiction publishers failed to reward SF writers to the extent writers in other fields were rewarded. At the same time, other SF writers were announcing their flight from the science fiction ghetto: Harlan Ellison, Barry N. Malzberg, and Kurt Vonnegur. Ellison and Vonnegut fought to remove the SF label from their new works and reprinted ones. Yet Silverberg did not withdraw from the SF field completely: in the years 1976-79 he edited *New Directions* original SF anthology series as well as numerous SF theme anthologies—from 1966 to 1981 Silverberg edited over sixty SF anthologies.

As early as 1979 rumors abounded that Silverberg was working on a "big book. " Times had changed in publishing: science fiction and fantasy, often ignored and ill-funded lines, became much more popular with the success of *Star Wars* and the *Star Trek* movies. Silverberg received critical acclaim and a six-figure advance for *Lord Valentine's Castle*, in which he created a huge planet called Majipoor with twenty million human and alien beings. Valentine's quest is one of identity. He is a wandering juggler who is actually a king dethroned by treachery which robs him of his memory. The book lacks suspense: we know early on Valentine's quest will be successful, but Silverberg holds our interest for over 500 pages with adventures on Majipoor that are a delight. But the light fantasy of *Lord Valentine's Castle* gives way to the darker stories in *Majipoor Chronicles* where Silverberg explores in more detail his mammoth planet. "The Desert of Stolen Dreams" gives us a lesson in Majipoorean guilt when the main character faces the death of a companion. "The Soul-Painter and the Shapeshifter" shows us a love affair between Majipoor's humans and aliens. The other stories fill out Silverberg's marvellous creation with a detailed history and philosophy of Majipoor. This culminates in *Valentine Pontifex* where Valentine's promotion from Coronal to Pontifex bring him up against an awesome challenge: the Metamorphs, shape-shifting natives of Majipoor, have broken the thousand years of peace with an attempt to dominate the planet. The fate of the planet is in Valentine's hands and this seemingly concluding volume of the Majipoor saga generates the most suspense.

The Conglomeroid Cocktail Party, Silverberg's latest collection, contains some of his finest short stories. "The Pope of the Chimps" is a revealing study of religion as an experimental group of chimps begin to worship humans. "The Changeling" is a clever twist on alternate reality themes. "Gianni" is a marvelous time-travel story where scientists bring 18th-century musical prodigy Giovanni Pergolesi, who died at the age of 26, back to the future with deterministic results.

Silverberg's latest novel, the fantasy *Gilgamesh the King*, received excellent reviews in the *New York Times Book Review* and other literary journals. Silverberg takes us back to the ancient civilizations of 5000 years ago when the Sumerian god-king grew to maturity and reigned over an empire. With a blend of myth and magic, Silverberg makes Gilgamesh's narrative come alive despite the strangeness of the culture. *Gilgamesh the King* is Silverberg's best fantasy novel.

Robert Silverberg is certainly a giant in the field of science fiction, a writer whose long career has produced classic novels and short stories. The impressive fact that Silverberg continues to produce first-rate, sophisticated work only adds to his stature.

—George Kelley

SIMAK, Clifford D(onald). American. Born in Millville, Wisconsin, 3 August 1904. Attended the University of Wisconsin, Madison. Married Kay Kuchenberg in 1929; one son and one daughter. Reporter, 1924-76, News Editor, 1949-62, and Editor of Science Reading Series, 1962-76, Minneapolis *Star* and *Tribune*. Recipient: International Fantasy Award, 1953; Hugo Award, for story, 1959, 1981, for novel, 1964; First Fandom Hall of Fame Award, 1973; Grand Master Nebula Award, 1976, and Nebula Award, 1980; Jupiter Award, 1978; *Locus* award, 1981. Guest of Honor, 29th World Science Fiction Convention, 1971. Agent: Blassingame McCauley and Wood, 432 Park Avenue South, Suite 1205, New York, New York 10016, U.S.A.

SCIENCE-FICTION PUBLICATIONS

Novels

Cosmic Engineers. New York, Gnome Press, 1950; London, Magnum, 1982.
Time and Again. New York, Simon and Schuster, 1951; London, Heinemann, 1955; as *First He Died*, New York, Dell, 1953.
Empire. New York, Galaxy, 1951.
Ring Around the Sun. New York, Simon and Schuster, 1953; London, Consul, 1960.
Time Is the Simplest Thing. New York, Doubleday, 1961; London, Gollancz, 1962.
The Trouble with Tycho. New York, Ace, 1961.
They Walked Like Men. New York, Doubleday, 1962; London, Gollancz, 1963.
Way Station. New York, Doubleday, 1963; London, Gollancz, 1964.
All Flesh Is Grass. New York, Doubleday, 1965; London, Gollancz, 1966.
Why Call Them Back from Heaven? New York, Doubleday, and London, Gollancz, 1967.
The Werewolf Principle. New York, Putnam, 1967; London, Gollancz, 1968.
The Goblin Reservation. New York, Putnam, 1968; London, Rapp and Whiting, 1969.
Out of Their Minds. New York, Putnam, 1970; London, Sidgwick and Jackson, 1972.
Destiny Doll. New York, Putnam, 1971; London, Sidgwick and Jackson, 1972.
A Choice of Gods. New York, Putnam, 1972; London, Sidgwick and Jackson, 1973.
Cemetery World. New York, Putnam, 1973; London, Sidgwick and Jackson, 1975.

Our Children's Children. New York, Putnam, 1974; London, Sidgwick and Jackson, 1975.
Enchanted Pilgrimage. New York, Berkley, 1975; London, Sidgwick and Jackson, 1976.
Shakespeare's Planet. New York, Berkley, 1976; London, Sidgwick and Jackson, 1977.
A Heritage of Stars. New York, Berkley, 1977; London, Sidgwick and Jackson, 1978.
Mastodonia. New York, Ballantine, 1978; as *Catface*, London, Sidgwick and Jackson, 1978.
The Visitors. New York, Ballantine, 1980; London, Sidgwick and Jackson, 1981.
Project Pope. New York, Ballantine, and London, Sidgwick and Jackson, 1981.
Special Deliverance. New York, Ballantine, 1982; London, Severn House, 1983.
Where the Evil Dwells. New York, Ballantine, 1982; London, Severn House, 1984.

Short Stories

The Creator. Los Angeles, Crawford, 1946.
City. New York, Gnome Press, 1952; London, Weidenfeld and Nicolson, 1954.
Strangers in the Universe. New York, Simon and Schuster, 1956; abridged edition, London, Faber, 1958.
The Worlds of Clifford Simak. New York, Simon and Schuster, 1960; abridged edition, as *Aliens for Neighbours*, London, Faber, 1961; abridged edition, as *Other Worlds of Clifford Simak*, New York, Avon, 1962.
All the Traps of Earth. New York, Doubleday, 1962; as *All the Traps of Earth* and *The Night of the Puudly*, London, New English Library, 2 vols., 1964.
Worlds Without End. New York, Belmont, 1964; London, Jenkins, 1965.
Best Science Fiction Stories of Clifford Simak. London, Faber, 1967.
So Bright the Vision. New York, Ace, 1968.
The Best of Clifford D. Simak, edited by Angus Wells. London, Sidgwick and Jackson, 1975.
Skirmish: The Great Short Fiction of Clifford D. Simak. New York, Putnam, 1977.

Uncollected Short Stories

"Dusty Zebra," in *Alpha 9*, edited by Robert Silverberg. New York, Berkley, 1978.
"Brother," in *The 1978 Annual World's Best SF*, edited by Donald A. Wollheim. New York, DAW, 1978.
"Party Line," in *Destinies* (New York), November-December 1978.
"The Whistling Well," in *Dark Forces*, edited by Kirby McCauley. New York, Viking Press, 1980.
"Byte Your Tongue," in *Stellar 6*, edited by Judy-Lynn del Rey. New York, Ballantine, 1981.
"Grotto of the Dancing Deer," in *Nebula Award Stories 16*, edited by Jerry Pournelle. New York, Holt Rinehart, 1982; London, W. H. Allen, 1983.

OTHER PUBLICATIONS

Novel

The Fellowship of the Talisman. New York, Ballantine, 1978; London, Sidgwick and Jackson, 1980.

Other

"Faces of Science Fiction," in *Minnesota Libraries* (St. Paul),
September 1953.
The Solar System: Our New Front Yard (for children). New
York, St. Martin's Press, 1963.
Trilobite, Dinosaur, and Man: The Earth's Story. New York, St.
Martin's Press, and London, Macmillan, 1966.
Wonder and Glory: The Story of the Universe. New York, St.
Martin's Press, 1969.
Prehistoric Man . New York, St. Martin's Press, 1971.
"Room Enough for All of Us," in *Extrapolation* (Wooster,
Ohio), May 1972.

Editor, *From Atoms to Infinity: Readings in Modern Science.*
New York, Harper, 1965.
Editor, *The March of Science* (for children). New York, Harper,
1971.
Editor, *Nebula Award Stories 6.* New York, Doubleday, 1971.
Editor, *The Best of Astounding.* New York, Baronet, 1978.

*

Bibliography: *The Electric Bibliograph 1: Clifford D. Simak* by
Mark Owings, Baltimore, Alice and Jay Haldeman, 1971.

*   *   *

Who but Clifford D. Simak would expose invaders from
space by mobilizing skunks in a large midwestern city? Since
1931 he has retained popularity, writing about time machines
and mystic quests, a man in touch with his world. He is SF's
special ambassador to the stars, casually introducing robots,
goblins, sociable monstrosities, cyborg ships, and alien intelligences from shades to slugs. Perhaps his popularity is
explained by his engaging escapism: communication with other
beings is established; the war avoided; the talisman found; the
boy and girl (even werewolves) get together.

Much early and minor Simak is gadget SF. "The World of the
Red Sun" is a time-machine story with an uncharacteristically
unhappy ending, though his interest in time, man's destiny, and
illusion is obvious in this first publication. *The Trouble with
Tycho* is a treasure hunt on the moon. "The Answers," "The
Fence," "Beachhead," "Goodnight, Mr. James," "The Street
That Wasn't There," and "To Walk a City's Streets" are classic
stories. Although the message in "The Answer" is that life is an
insignificant accident, most disasters are avoided by courage
and determination. Such is the case in *They Walked Like Men,
Why Call Them Back from Heaven?, Out of Their Minds,* and
Our Children's Children up to *Where the Evil Dwells.* One man
who risks life and reputation to save mankind is joined by a
tough but feminine friend and at least one unique being. With
this mixed cast, what should be terrifying becomes humorous.
Another SF gadget is the robot. "How-2," "Earth for
Inspiration," "Installment Plan," "All the Traps of Earth,"
"Ogre," and "Lulu" feature strong-willed, people-loving
robots, stock characters in his works, companions, guides, and
occasionally scatter-brained troublemakers. Hezekiah of "Installment Plan" and *A Choice of Gods,* Richard Daniel of "All
the Traps of Earth," and Jenkins of *City* are interchangeable.
Although *Time and Again* is concerned with the plight of
human-looking androids, Simak's robots are usually obviously
machines in all but personality.

Simak frequently deals with time and parallel universes. His
ideal is a place outside time where things remain the same and a
body can rock peacefully on his front porch while auks and
dinosaurs frolic by the stream. He is unquestionably the leading
exponent of the pastoral mode in SF. "The Autumn Land,"
"Auk House," "New Folks' Home," "Kindergarten," "The
Sitters," "Retrograde Revolution," and "The Marathon
Photograph" offer simple, out-of-the-way retreats, often in the
Wisconsin countryside. "Neighbor" is perhaps the best
statement of Simak's ideal rural utopia where crops never fail,
machinery does not break down, and people are friends. A
house or a car waits to take someone to a higher existence. "The
Ghost of a Model-T" and "New Folks' Home" are particularly
appealing because they carry old men to new value. In
Mastodonia and *Cemetery World* the adventurers remain in
their isolated world, Adam, Eve, and machine. Simak's
characters share his love for home by returning to childhood
spots and fishing in *Ring Around the Sun, All Flesh Is Grass, Out
of Their Minds,* and *Cemetery World.* Small town distrust of
strangers often makes the plot move forward by sending the
heroes into hiding. In *Our Children's Children* ravening beasts
from time invade back yards, combining the everyday with the
fantastic.

Into the everyday, however, comes the world in which all
creatures are brothers and all time is linked. The most important
of Simak's works combine his themes into allegories of man's
need to establish peaceful, respectful communications with all
creation. As his world experienced the cold war, racism,
ecological deterioration, and loss of faith, Simak responded
with works that were at once good SF adventures and parables.
Cosmic Engineers is one of the earliest and most typical of the
works dealing with man's destiny. Two newspapermen, a
thousand-year-old lady mathematician, and a group of super-
robots save two universes. Their antagonists are the vicious
Hellhounds who reappear in *Enchanted Pilgrimage.* The
Cosmic Engineers summon every possible life form, including
nightmarish, misshapen creatures and goblins. Only man can
help—present and future. The one remaining man on Earth
explains that the others have migrated to the stars, pushing on to
their inheritance as masters of the universe; the Engineers were
their creation.

Interstellar cooperation also prevents total annihilation in
Way Station, Simak's masterpiece. A Civil War veteran, Enoch
Wallace, in spite of his 124 years, looks 30. Living alone with
only one friend, a mailman who delivers reading material and
supplies, he survives by selling precious jewels for less than their
worth. Enoch works for the Galaxy, running a way station for
interstellar travelers. When the CIA digs up the remains of an
extraterrestrial and he rescues a psychic deaf-mute, Lucy Fisher,
from a beating, Enoch is thrust into his troubled world. Just
when the world is on the brink of war and the Galaxy is torn by
strife because its talisman is lost, he is threatened by irate
townspeople and his station is to be closed by offended officials.
As Enoch packs his records and treasures, a ratlike saboteur
invades and he must kill him. Lucy is found to be a Guardian
when she reactivates the stolen talisman the rat had with him.
Because of Lucy, Earth is spared war and given Galactic status.

This improbably plotted book is significant for its messages of
universal brotherhood and the significance of life. It is also a
storehouse of Simak's materials. The talisman is a spiritual force
that unites planets. The ability of the Andromedans to adapt by
changing shape appears in *City* and *The Werewolf Principle.*
The picture cube, five-person sexual unit, companions created
by thought, affable aliens, lonely hero, old-fashioned romance,
bad government, powerful simple person, and narrator who
mulls over the meaning of his existence all are traits of Simak's
work. "The Big Front Yard" is a similar tale of the

establishment of a portal through which citizens of other worlds may pass peacefully. In *All Flesh Is Grass* a rural area is the entry point for a flower-like group-being that brings peace. "Mirage," "Contraption," "Limiting Factor," "Construction Shack," and *Time and Again* bring man into contact with far greater but non-threatening powers.

City is the most sweeping of his speculations about man's destiny among the stars. In eight stories written as myths passed on by the dogs and robots of the Webster family, Simak relates a history in which man takes to space, leaving his successors behind to doubt he ever existed. *City, The Creator, Time and Again*, and "Founding Father" suggest that man, as we know him, may not inherit the universe after all. In *Time Is the Simplest Thing* and *Ring Around the Sun* paranormals are resented and hunted.

Simak's recent works return to optimism and move into man-glorifying fantasy. All are quests for meaning in a vastly changed world. In *Cemetery World* Earth has become a glorified graveyard; in *A Choice of Gods* it has been left to robots, Indians, and a few conservatives. *Enchanted Pilgrimage, Destiny Doll, A Heritage of Stars, The Fellowship of the Talisman*, and *Where the Evil Dwells* have a medieval flavor, with ominous, degraded antagonists, magic, and waste lands, matching the interests of the times. They suggest a guiding cosmic principle.

Simak's work has great consistency. Names like Horton, Duncan, Hezekiah, Thorndyke, Bounce, and Bowser recur. Ideas like creating beings from thought, changing bodies for colonization, gateways to other world, and characters like long-winded, argumentative robots, friendly worms, mythical creatures like brownies, and strong-willed but malleable women are predictable. Above all, Simak insists on the dignity of all life and the irresponsibility of undervaluing any. Time stops while Simak spins his leisurely yarns.

—Mary S. Weinkauf

SINCLAIR, Upton. Also wrote as Frederick Garrison. American. Born in Baltimore, Maryland, 20 September 1878; moved with his family to New York City, 1888. Educated at the City College of New York, 1893-97, A. B. 1897; Columbia University, New York, 1897-1901. Married 1) Meta H. Fuller in 1900 (divorced, 1911); 2) Mary Craig Kimbrough in 1913 (died, 1961); 3) Mary Elizabeth Willis in 1961 (died, 1967). Writer from 1893; wrote Clif Faraday stories (as Ensign Clarke Fitch) and Mark Mallory stories (as Lieutenant Frederick Garrison) for various boys' weeklies, 1897-98; founded socialist community, Helicon Home Colony, Englewood, New Jersey, 1906-07; Socialist candidate for Congress, from New Jersey, 1906; settled in Pasadena, California, 1915; Socialist candidate for Congress, 1920, and for the United States Senate, 1922, and for Governor of California, 1926, 1930; moved to Buckeye, Arizona, 1953. Recipient: Pulitzer Prize, 1943; American Newspaper Guild Award, 1962. *Died 25 November 1968.*

SCIENCE-FICTION PUBLICATIONS

Novels

Prince Hagen. Boston, Page, and London, Chatto and Windus, 1903.

The Industrial Republic. New York, Doubleday, and London, Heinemann, 1907.
They Call Me Carpenter. New York, Boni and Liveright, and London, Laurie, 1922.
The Millennium: A Comedy of the Year 2000. Girard, Kansas, Haldeman Julius, 1924; London, Laurie, 1929.
Roman Holiday. New York, Farrar and Rinehart, and London, Laurie, 1931.
Our Lady. Emmaus, Pennsylvania, Rodale Press, and London, Laurie, 1938.

Uncollected Short Story

"Author's Adventure," in *The Fantastic Pulps*, edited by Peter Haining. New York, St. Martin's Press, 1975.

OTHER PUBLICATIONS

Novels

Springtime and Harvest: A Romance. New York, Sinclair Press, 1901; as *King Midas*, New York and London, Funk and Wagnalls, 1901.
The Journal of Arthur Stirling. New York, Appleton, and London, Heinemann, 1903.
Manassas. New York and London, Macmillan, 1904; as *Theirs Be the Guilt*, New York, Twayne, 1959.
The Jungle. New York, Doubleday, and London, Heinemann, 1906.
A Captain of Industry. Girard, Kansas, Appeal to Reason, and London, Heinemann, 1906.
The Metropolis. New York, Moffat Yard, and London, Laurie, 1908.
The Moneychangers. New York, Dodge, and London, Long, 1908.
Samuel the Seeker. New York, Dodge, and London, Long, 1910.
Love's Pilgrimage. New York, Kennerley, 1911; London, Heinemann, 1912.
Sylvia. Philadelphia, Winston, 1913; London, Long, 1914.
Damaged Goods. Philadelphia, Winston, and London, Hutchinson, 1913.
Sylvia's Marriage. Philadelphia, Winston, 1914; London, Laurie, 1915.
King Coal. New York, Macmillan, and London, Laurie, 1917.
Jimmie Higgins. London, Hutchinson, 1918; New York, Boni and Liveright, 1919.
The Spy. London, Laurie, 1919; as *100%: The Story of a Patriot*, privately printed, 1920; excerpt, as *Peter Gudge Becomes a Secret Agent*, Moscow, State Publishing House, 1930.
Oil! New York, Boni, and London, Laurie, 1927.
Boston. New York, Boni, 1928; London, Laurie, 1929; abridged edition, as *August 22nd*, New York, Universal, 1965; Bath, Chivers, 1971.
Mountain City. New York, Boni, 1929; London, Laurie, 1930.
The Wet Parade. New York, Farrar and Rinehart, and London, Laurie, 1931.
Co-op: A Novel of Living Together. New York, Farrar and Rinehart, and London, Laurie, 1936.
The Gnomobile. New York, Farrar and Rinehart, and London, Laurie, 1936.
Little Steel. New York, Farrar and Rinehart, and London, Laurie, 1938.
Marie Antoinette. New York, Vanguard Press, and London, Laurie, 1939; as *Marie and Her Lover*, Girard, Kansas,

Haldeman Julius, 1948.

World's End. New York, Viking Press, and London, Laurie, 1940.

Between Two Worlds. New York, Viking Press, and London, Laurie, 1941.

Dragon's Teeth. New York, Viking Press, and London, Laurie, 1942.

Wide Is the Gate. New York, Viking Press, and London, Laurie, 1943.

Presidential Agent . New York, Viking Press, 1944; London, Laurie, 1945.

Dragon Harvest. New York, Viking Press, and London, Laurie, 1945.

A World to Win. New York, Viking Press, 1946; London, Laurie, 1947.

Presidential Mission. New York, Viking Press, 1947; London, Laurie, 1948.

One Clear Call. New York, Viking Press, 1948; London, Laurie, 1949.

O Shepherd, Speak! New York, Viking Press, 1949; London, Laurie, 1950.

Another Pamela; or, Virtue Still Rewarded. New York, Viking Press, and London, Laurie, 1950.

The Return of Lanny Budd. New York, Viking Press, and London, Laurie, 1953.

What Didymus Did. London, Wingate, 1954; as *It Happened to Didymus*, New York, Sagamore Press, 1958.

The Cup of Fury. Great Neck, New York, Channel Press, 1956; London, Arco, 1957.

Affectionately Eve. New York, Twayne, 1961.

The Coal War: A Sequel to King Coal. Boulder, Colorado, Associated University Press, 1976.

Plays

Prince Hagen, adaptation of his own novel (produced San Francisco, 1909). Privately printed, 1909.

Plays of Protest (includes *Prince Hagen, The Naturewoman, The Machine, The Second-Story Man*). New York, Kennerley, 1912.

Hell: A Verse Drama and Photo-Play. Privately printed, 1923.

The Pot Boiler. Girard, Kansas, Haldeman Julius, 1924.

Singing Jailbirds (produced London, 1930). Privately printed, 1924.

Bill Porter. Privately printed, 1924.

Wally for Queen! The Private Life of Royalty. Privately printed, 1936.

A Giant's Strength. Girard, Kansas, Haldeman Julius, and London, Laurie, 1948.

The Enemy Had It Too. New York, Viking Press, 1950.

Three Plays (includes *The Second-Story Man, John D., The Indignant Subscriber*). Moscow, Progress, 1965.

Verse

Songs of Our Nation (as Frederick Garrison). New York, Marks Music, 1941.

Other

The Toy and the Man. Westwood, Massachusetts, Ariel Press, 1904.

Our Bourgeois Literature. Chicago, Kerr, 1905.

Colony Customs. Englewood, New Jersey, Sinclair, 1906.

The Helicon Home Colony. Englewood, New Jersey, Constitution, 1906.

A Home Colony: A Prospectus. New York, Jungle, 1906.

What Life Means to Me. Girard, Kansas, Appeal to Reason, 1906.

The Overman. New York, Doubleday, 1907.

Good Health and How We Won It, with Michael Williams. New York, Stokes, 1909; as *Strength and Health*, 1910; as *The Art of Health*, London, Health and Strength, 1909.

War: A Manifesto Against It. Girard, Kansas, Appeal to Reason, New York, Wilshire, and London, Clarion Press, 1909.

Four Letters About "Love's Pilgrimage. " Privately printed, 1911.

The Fasting Cure. New York, Kennerley, and London, Heinemann, 1911.

The Sinclair-Astor Letters: Famous Correspondence Between Socialist and Millionaire. Girard, Kansas, Appeal to Reason, 1914.

The Social Problem as Seen from the Viewpoint of Trade Unionism, Capital, and Socialism, with others. New York, Industrial Economics Department of the National Civic Federation, 1914.

Upton Sinclair: Biographical and Critical Opinions. Privately printed, 1917.

The Profits of Religion. Privately printed, 1918; London, Laurie, 1936.

Russia: A Challenge. Girard, Kansas, Appeal to Reason, 1919.

The High Cost of Living (address). Girard, Kansas, People's Press, 1919.

The Brass Check. London, Laurie, 1919; Pasadena, California, privately printed, 1920; excerpt, as *The Associated Press and Labor*, privately printed, 1920.

Press-titution. Girard, Kansas, Appeal to Reason, 1920.

The Crimes of the "Times": A Test of Newspaper Decency. Privately printed, 1921.

The Book of Life . Pasadena, California, Sinclair Paine, 1922; London, Laurie, 1934.

Mind and Body. New York, Macmillan, 1921; revised edition, Girard, Kansas, Haldeman Julius, 4 vols., 1950.

Love and Society. Pasasena, California, Sinclair Paine, 1922; revised edition, Girard, Kansas, Haldeman Julius, 4 vols., n.d.

The McNeal-Sinclair Debate on Socialism. Girard, Kansas, Haldeman Julius, 1921.

The Goose-Step: A Study of American Education. Privately printed, 1922; revised edition, n. d. ; London, Laurie, 1923.

Biographical Letter and Critical Opinions. Privately printed, 1922.

The Goslings. Privately printed, 1924; London, Laurie, 1930; excerpt, as *The Schools of Los Angeles, privately printed, 1924*.

Mammonart. Privately printed, 1925; London, Laurie, 1934.

Letters to Judd. Privately printed, 1926; revised edition, as *This World of 1949 and What to Do about It*, Girard, Kansas, Haldeman Julius, 1949.

The Spokesman's Secretary. Privately printed, 1926.

Money Writes! New York, Boni, 1927; London, Laurie, 1931.

The Pulitzer Prize and "Special Pleading. " Privately printed, 1929.

Mental Radio. New York, Boni, and London, Laurie, 1930; revised edition, Springfield, Illinois, Thomas, 1962.

Socialism and Culture. Girard, Kansas, Haldeman Julius, 1931.

Upton Sinclair on "Comrade" Kautsky. Moscow, Co-operative Publishing Society of Foreign Workers in the USSR, 1931.

American Outpost. New York, Farrar and Rinehart, 1932; as *Candid Reminiscences: My First Thirty Years*, London, Laurie, 1932.

I, Governor of California, and How I Ended Poverty. New York, Farrar and Rinehart, and London, Laurie, 1933.

Upton Sinclair Presents William Fox. Privately printed, 1933.

The Way Out—What Lies Ahead for America? New York, Farrar and Rinehart, and London, Laurie, 1933; revised edition, as *Limbo on the Loose: A Midsummer Night's Dream*, Girard, Kansas, Haldeman Julius, 1948.

EPIC Plan for California. New York, Farrar and Rinehart, 1934.

EPIC Answers: How to End Poverty in California. Los Angeles, End Poverty League, 1934.

Immediate EPIC. Los Angeles, End Poverty League, 1934.

The Lie Factory Starts. Los Angeles, End Poverty League, 1934.

An Upton Sinclair Anthology, edited by I. O. Evans. New York, Farrar and Rinehart, and London, Laurie, 1934; revised edition, Culver City, California, Murray and Gee, 1947.

Upton Sinclair's Last Will and Testament. Los Angeles, End Poverty League, 1934.

We, People of America, and How We Ended Poverty: A True Story of the Future. Pasadena, California, National EPIC League, 1934.

Depression Island. Pasadena, California, privately printed, and London, Laurie, 1935.

I, Candidate for Governor, and How I God Licked. New York, Farrar and Rinehart, 1935; as *How I Got Licked and Why*, London, Laurie, 1935.

What God Means to Me: An Attempt at a Working Religion. New York, Farrar and Rinehart, and London, Laurie, 1936.

The Flivver King. Girard, Kansas, Haldeman Julius, 1937; London, Laurie, 1938.

No Pasoran! (They Shall Not Pass). New York, Labor Press, and London, Laurie, 1937.

Terror in Russia: Two Views, with Eugene Lyons. New York, Richard R. Smith, 1938.

Upton Sinclair on the Soviet Union. New York, Weekly Masses, 1938.

Expect No Peace! Girard, Kansas, Haldeman Julius, 1939.

Telling the World. London, Laurie, 1939.

What Can Be Done about America's Economic Troubles? Girard, Kansas, Haldeman Julius, 1939.

Your Million Dollars. Privately printed, 1939; as *Letters to a Millionaire*, London, Laurie, 1939.

Is the American Form of Capitalism Essential to the American Form of Democracy? Girard, Kansas, Haldeman Julius, 1940.

Peace or War in America? Girard, Kansas, Haldeman Julius, 1940.

Index to the Lanny Budd Story, with others. New York, Viking Press, 1943.

To Solve the German Problem—A Free State? Privately printed, 1943.

A Personal Jesus: Portrait and Interpretation. New York, Evans, 1952; London, Allen and Unwin, 1954; as *Secret Life of Jesus*, Philadelphia, Mercury, 1962.

Radio Liberation Speech to the Peoples of the Soviet Union. New York, American Committee for Liberation from Bolshevism, 1955.

My Lifetime in Letters. Columbia, University of Missouri Press, 1960.

The Autobiography of Upton Sinclair. New York, Harcourt Brace, 1962; London, Allen and Unwin, 1963.

Editor, *The Cry for Justice: An Anthology of the Literature of Social Protest*. Philadelphia, Winston, 1915.

*

Bibliography: *Upton Sinclair: An Annotated Checklist* by Ronald Gottesman, Kent, Ohio, Kent State University Press, 1973.

Critical Studies: *This Is Upton Sinclair* by James Harte Lambert, Emmaus, Pennsylvania, Rodale Press, 1938; *The Literary Manuscripts of Upton Sinclair* by Ronald Gottesman and Charles L. P. Sinclair, Columbus, Ohio State University Press, 1972; *Upton Sinclair* by Jon A. Yoder, New York, Ungar, 1975; *Upton Sinclair, American Rebel* by Leon Harris, New York, Crowell, 1975; *Critics on Upton Sinclair* edited by Abraham Blinderman, Coral Gables, Florida, University of Miami Press, 1975; *Upton Sinclair* by William A. Bloodworth, Boston, Twayne, 1977.

*   *   *

Upton Sinclair is best known as a socialist muckraking novelist, and has a spectacular history as a much-admired and much-traduced political crusader. However, as an "Economic Scientist" he has experimented in both science fiction and fantasy, especially of the time-travel variety. Since his talents are journalistic and narrative rather than evocative of character and subtle human relations, his SF drama is less skilful than his novels are.

One group of novels takes America into a possible alternative world, consequent upon Sinclair being elected Governor of California and his EPIC programme being adopted by the USA. *I, Governor of California, and How I Ended Poverty* is fiction only in the sense that it projects a political campaign into the immediate future, emphasising the virtues and values of the co-operative movement that defeats the Depression. *We, People of America, and How We Ended Poverty* expands the canvas and the time-scale, but is still more argument than fiction. *Co-op* is a genuine fiction, but leaves the reader to debate whether President Roosevelt will or will not embrace the Co-operative Commonwealth ideal. That ideal is interesting in itself, uniting patriotism with socialist and collectivist principles, but the protagonists of the novel are more typical than individually memorable.

Genuinely science-fiction and fantasy novels are *The Millenium: A Comedy of the Year 2000*, a satirical parable on the need for socialism combined with social justice, and the rather stiffly Utopian *The Industrial Republic*. More striking juxtapositions of modern American assumptions with those of very different societies make *Prince Hagen* still interesting; the avaricious Nibelung ruler is impressed by the superior chicanery and greed of "Christian" American capitalism. In *Roman Holiday* a rich young American playboy, in the delirium following a motor-racing accident, finds himself back in patrician Rome, which tells him a great deal about his 20th-century life-style and society. *They Call Me Carpenter* also uses a rich and idle American as principal observer: laid out after a scuffle with "patriotic" demonstrators against the film *The Cabinet of Dr. Caligari*, he sees Christ step down from a cathedral window; inevitably "Carpenter" loves His fellow men, but is forced to denounce the press, the society's privileged, and especially the church that has deserted the revolutionary doctrines of its supposed Founder (the novel stops short of the crucifixion which its logic seems to entail). Sinclair's other major time-travel fantasy, *Our Lady*, is excellent in both research and the basic contrast between the mother of Jesus and the modern Californian Catholic world to which she is translated. Both her reaction to the ball-game where she first appears and her total alienation from any element of Roman Catholic faith which theoretically invokes her mingle comedy, pathos, and a genuine reverence for human spiritual exploration; even the exorcism climax has an obsessive power lacking in most of Sinclair's endings.

Most of Sinclair's immense number of novels were written too quickly, and stumble into structural faults as well as psychological shallowness. Yet the best of his writing carries immense compassion for human suffering and frustration, and the force and courage of his defence of human relations against capitalist priorities is worth the loss of many graces. Although genuinely convinced that all good art is primarily propaganda, Sinclair avoids portraying all capitalists or playboys as fools or or orges, and often relishes the sudden understanding that can spring up between characters socially alien to each other. In his drama there is genuine development between the versions of the "noble savage" girl in *The Naturewoman (Plays of Protest)* and *The Enemy Had It Too*, where the unspoiled maiden kills the sophisticated gangster by the use of flirtation and curare! Nonetheless, the exploration of Great Issues does not suit the stage, and mixing the world-disaster (or last-men) theme with the return-from-Mars, the noble savage, the satiric portrait, and the all-aboard-the-Ark themes makes even the latter too overloaded. It is for such novels as *Our Lady* that Sinclair most deserves the fantasy reader's attention.

—Norman Talbot

SIODMAK, Curt (Kurt Siodmak). American. Born in Dresden, Germany, 10 August 1902; brother of the film director Robert Siodmak. Educated at the University of Zurich, Ph. D. 1927. Married Henrietta De Perrot in 1931; one son. Railroad engineer and factory worker; film writer and director: worked for Gaumont British, 1931-37, and in the United States after 1937. Recipient: Bundespreis, for film, 1964. Lives in California. Agent: Paul R. Reynolds, 12 East 41st Street, New York, New York, 10017, U.S.A.

SCIENCE-FICTION PUBLICATIONS

Novels (series: Cory)

F. P. 1 Antwortet Nicht. Berlin, Keils, 1931; translated by H. W. Farrell as *F. P. 1 Does Not Reply*, Boston, Little Brown, 1933; as *F. P. 1 Fails to Reply*, London, Collins, 1933.
Donovan's Brain (Cory). New York, Knopf, 1943; London, Chapman and Hall, 1944.
Skyport. New York, Crown, 1959.
Hauser's Memory (Cory). New York, Putnam, 1968; London, Jenkins, 1969.
The Third Ear. New York, Putnam, 1971.
City in the Sky. New York, Putnam, 1974; London, Barrie and Jenkins, 1975.

Uncollected Short Stories

"Variations on a Theme," in *Fantasy and Science Fiction* (New York), June 1972.
"The P Factor," in *Fantasy and Science Fiction* (New York), September 1976.
"The Eggs from Lake Tanganyika," in *The Gernsback Awards 1, 1926*, edited by Forrest J. Ackerman. London, Turret, 1982.

OTHER PUBLICATIONS

Novels

Schluss in Tonfilmatelier. Berlin, Scherl, 1930.
Stadt Hinter Nebeln. Salzburg, Berglund, 1931.
Die Madonna aus der Markusstrasse. Leipzig, Goldmann, 1932.
Rache im Äther. Leipzig, Goldmann, 1932.
Bis ans Ende der Welt. Leipzig, Goldmann, 1933.
Die Macht im Dunkeln. Zurich, Morgarten, 1937.
Whomsoever I Shall Kiss. New York, Crown, 1952.
For Kings Only. New York, Crown, 1961.

Plays

Screenplays: *Menschen am Sonntag (People on Sunday)* (documentary), with Billy Wilder, 1929; *Le Bal*, 1931; *Der Mann der Seinen Mörder Sucht (Looking for His Murderer)*, 1931; *F. P. 1 Antwortet Nicht*, 1933; *Girls Will Be Boys*, with Clifford Grey and Roger Burford, 1934; *I Give My Heart*, with others, 1935; *The Tunnel (Transatlantic Tunnel)*, with L. DuGarde Peach and Clemence Dane, 1935; *It's a Bet*, with Frank Miller and L. DuGarde Peach, 1935; *Non-Stop New York*, with others, 1937; *Her Jungle Love*, with others, 1938; *The Invisible Man Returns*, with Lester Cole and Joe May, 1940; *The Ape*, with Richard Carroll, 1940; *Black Friday*, with Eric Taylor, 1940; *The Wolf Man*, with Gordon Kann, 1940; *The Invisible Woman*, with others, 1941; *Pacific Blackout*, with others, 1941; *Aloma of the South Seas*, with others, 1941 *Midnight Angel*, with others, 1941; *London Blackout Murders*, 1942; *The Invisible Agent*, 1942; *I Walked with a Zombie*, with Ardel Wray and Inez Wallace, 1943; *Frankenstein Meets the Wolf Man*, 1943; *The Mantrap*, 1943; *Son of Dracula*, with Eric Taylor, 1943; *False Faces*, 1943; *The Purple "V,"* with Bertram Millhauser, 1943; *House of Frankenstein*, with Edward T. Lowe, 1944; *The Climax*, with Lynn Starling, 1944; *Frisco Sal*, with Gerald Geraghty, 1945; *Shady Lady*, with others, 1945; *The Return of Monte Cristo*, with others 1946; *The Beast with Five Fingers*, with Harold Goldman, 1947; *Berlin Express*, with Harold Medford, 1948; *Tarzan's Magic Fountain*, with Harry Chandlee, 1949; *Four Days Leave*, with others, 1950; *Bride of the Gorilla*, 1951; *The Magnetic Monster*, with Ivan Tors, 1953; *Riders to the Stars*, 1954; *Creature with the Atom Brain*, 1955; *Earth vs. Flying Saucers*, with George Worthing Yates and Raymond Marcus, 1956; *Curucu, Beast of the Amazon*, 1956; *Love Slaves of the Amazon*, 1957; *The Devil's Messenger*, 1962; *Lightship*, 1963; *Ski Fever*, with Robert Joseph, 1967.

Television Plays: *13 Demon Street* series, 1959 (Sweden).

*

Theatrical Activities:
Director: **Films**—*Bride of the Gorilla*, 1951; *The Magnetic Monster*, 1953; *Curucu, Beast of the Amazon*, 1956; *Love Slaves of the Amazon*, 1957; *Ski Fever*, 1967.

*   *   *

As novelist, screenwriter, and film director, Curt Siodmak has had a long career, first in Germany and then in Hollywood, popularizing for the mass audience basic and extremely banal science-fiction motifs originated long before by other writers: an airfield floating in mid-ocean, the building of a trans-Atlantic tunnel or a spaceport, experiments with artificially induced telepathy or genetic manipulation all provide formulaic grist for some very melodramatic mills. Siodmak's protagonists in his novels and films are either Frankensteinian mad scientists in the grand pulp tradition or strong-willed and far-sighted entrepreneurial over-reachers in the Faustian/Ayn Rand mold. Indeed, perhaps the only redeeming feature of Siodmak's early German science-fiction work of the 1930's is that the films based on his novels (three versions of *F. P. 1 Does Not Reply* and two versions of *Transatlantic Tunnel*) utilized some impressive special effect. Not even that much can be said for most of the movies based on his Hollywood screenplays in the 1940's, which were invariably low-budget programmers, that attempted to milk tried-and-true monster-movie formulas that had long been dried out.

Siodmak is best known, however, within both the science-fiction field and the mainstream of literary and cinematic popular culture, as the creator of *Donovan's Brain,* which has itself been adapted three time for the movies, with varying degrees of success: *The Lady and the Monster* (1947, with Erich von Stroheim), *Donovan's Brain* (1953, with Lew Ayres), and *The Brain* (1963, with Peter Van Eyck). In all of its manifestations, the story has held up durably and has retained to a certain extent its queasy fascination. The reclusive scientist-physician Patrick Cory extracts the still-living brain of the powerful industrialist Warren Horace Donovan after an airplane crash had mangled the tycoon's elderly body. Despite the stereotypical warnings of his devoted wife and an alcoholic colleague, Cory establishes telepathic contact with the disembodied brain, which, nurtured by chemicals, is growing daily in size and telepathic power. The brain quickly takes control of Cory's body, forcing it to wreak vengeance on Donovan's enemies. What gives Siodmak's novel its inherent power is not only its central theme of physical possession caused by unchecked and thus finally destructive scientific research, but also the first-person narration from Cory's panicky point of view. Unfortunately, the story eventually degenerates into unduly complicated histrionics detailing Donovan's desire to pay off an old debt by intruding on a murder investigation involving the heir of one of Donovan's early business partners. By plunging Donovan and his hapless, progressively will-less surrogate into such a desultory and pointless subplot so late in the proceedings, Siodmak conveniently sidesteps the more somber medical, legal, and metaphysical implications of his initially intriguing concept.

Siodmak's later novels continued his career-long tendency to graft mainstream genres onto science-fiction settings. Thus, *City in the Sky* is a kind of *Grand Hotel* in orbit, mixed in with political intrigue and prison-escape heroics, while *Skyport* is like a space-age *Fountainhead*. A bit more interesting to the genuine science-fiction enthusiast are *The Third Ear,* which concerns the chemically created cultivation of ESP abilities, and *Hauser's Memory,* Siodmak's belated sequel to *Donovan's Brain,* with the intrepid Cory again blazing new scientific trails, transplanting a German chemist's overactive, revenge-minded RNA onto another ill-fated human guinea pig. Despite the pseudo-scientific trappings, both books are relatively straightforward espionage thrillers, demonstrating again that Siodmak's talents lie in welding worn-out science-fiction themes with other conventional, pop-cultural formulas.

—Kenneth Jurkiewicz

SKALDASPILLIR, Sigfridur. See BROXON, Mildred Downey.

SKY, Kathleen. American. Born in Alhambra, California, 5 August 1943. Married Stephen Goldin, *q. v.,* in 1972 (divorced, 1982). Children's barber, Bullock's Department Store, Pasadena, California, 1964-71; volunteer worker for the Humane Society, Pasadena, 1972; film extra. Since 1968, free-lance writer. Agent: Joseph Elder Agency, 150 West 87th Street, Apartment 6-D New York, New York 10024, U.S.A.

SCIENCE-FICTION PUBLICATIONS

Novels

Birthright. Toronto, Laser, 1975.
Ice Prison. Toronto, Laser, 1976.
Vulcan! New York, Bantam, 1978.
Death's Angel. New York, Bantam, 1980.
Witchdame. New York, Berkley, 1985.

Uncollected Short Stories

"One Ordinary Day, with Box," in *Generation,* edited by David Gerrold and Stephen Goldin. New York, Dell, 1972.
"Lament of the Keeku Bird," in *The Alien Condition,* edited by Stephen Goldin. New York, Ballantine, 1973.
"Door to Malequar," in *Vertex* (Los Angeles), June 1975.
"A Daisychain for Pav," in *Odyssey* (New York), Summer 1976.
"Motherbreast," in *Cassandra Rising,* edited by Alice Laurance. New York, Doubleday, 1978.
"Painting the Roses Red," with Stephen Goldin, in *Science Fiction Times,* May 1980.
"The Devil Behind the Leaves," with Stephen Goldin, in *Fantasy Book* (Pasadena, California), October 1981.

OTHER PUBLICATIONS

Other

The Business of Being a Writer, with Stephen Goldin. New York, Harper, 1982.

*

Kathleen Sky comments:

It's difficult to analyze my fiction on the basis of past output because I know that my best work still lies ahead of me. Nevertheless, I recognize some themes in my books that will continue to appear. Just as blacks and Chicanos need strong positive images in their literature, I feel that the increasing number of women who read science fiction will require strong female characters to give them a postive self-image. It's easy to write a strong woman as a bitch, but much harder to write her as a loving, caring person (the "mother" aspect). Nevertheless, I try. In my forthcoming fantasy series, *The Witchdame Trilogy,* I have a strong character, Princess Elizabeth, who eventually becomes the queen of her realm and consequently a strong mother figure. In my novel *Shalom,* there are several strong women, most notably Judith, who eventually becomes a mother figure to her entire planet.

In writing about strong women, I find I need strong male characters to match them. It's no use liberating only one gender; men and women need to share their strengths equally. I fell that everyone is psychologically bisexual—that is, each human being has both masculine and feminine components to his personality. Only by bringing out *all* the strengths, masculine and feminine, can people truly become liberated from the stereotypes of the past. Because of this, I reject the role of the traditional feminist. Too many of the radical women writers tend to view men as an enemy to be overcome. In doing so, they are doing more harm to themselves than to their supposed enemies. I view men and women as but two halves of a single race. If one side loses, we all do; only by having both sides succeed can humanity be the victor.

* * *

Kathleen Sky is good at understanding a special variety of emotion: the grief of a creature coerced by its own nature into a task both valuable to others and costly to itself. One could say it is a woman's grief—Sky makes it into the grief of a tired little man, or a green alien, or a Vulcan. Sky has the visibly struggling competence of a new writer, but also a depth of emotional perception which is already formed. The plight of her characters is both cleverly illustrated and deeply felt.

"One Ordinary Day, with Box," her first story, functions with the simplicity of a parable. A little old man travels from place to place with a big black box. To those who reach inside, the box gives what they need, but not what they want. The disparity between imagined want and true need runs like a moral lesson through this quick, effective tale, but the emotional focus is finally on the old man himself. Scorned by the people that the box has frustrated and insulted, he goes off alone, and at last reaches into the box himself. He is given another box. His need, the box implies, is to continue his thankless task, his unappreciated giving.

Sometimes the task is change itself. In the somewhat overwritten but surprisingly moving "Lament of the Keeku Bird" Sky details the painful process of an alien initiation ritual, a menopause by violence in which a female creature makes a ceremonial journey that wears off her sexuality. The writing task is difficult—Sky narrates in the first person present from the alien's point of view and thus must develop landscape, species, and personality all indirectly. The development is coherent and interesting; Sky manages not only to establish a believable extraterrestrial world but also to show the beginnings of personal change, the openings of thought in what was at first a thoughtless breeding animal. The mingling of grief and triumph at the end is consistent with Sky's awareness of the inner price to be paid for anything of value.

This awareness is carried into Sky's Star Trek novel, *Vulcan!* Enough young science-fiction writers have written Star Trek continuations that it may become a set exercise for entering the craft. As such it provides a useful device of classification: *Trek to Madworld* by Sky's husband, Stephen Goldin, is whimsical and extravagant; Sky's version has a deeper concentration on personality, and is in effect a serious consideration of what it means to be a Vulcan or to love one. The fan's potential delight in this can be easily imagined, and Sky does well in capturing Spock's angular appeal, his passionless speech, his promise of intensities withheld. Her portrayal of Katalya Tremain, the scientist who tries to hate Vulcans in order to avoid loving them, is less consistent, but the book as a whole works. Sky transmits both Spock's calm appreciation of the powers he has and his regret at his limitations. He helps Tremain to change but cannot change himself. His last request to the women is that she help him to rediscover his childhood imagination and thus find a way out of his box of logical competence.

Sky's style is as yet unremarkable; she chooses the nearest words to communicate what she envisions—the view from inside a sensitive mind looking at a landscape both alien and alienating, where endurance is a value and change expensive. This view is one that lends itself to science fiction, to making new landscapes and locating characters in them emotionally as well as sensually. Sky's work is not an investigation into science or ideas, but into experience, and she succeeds, even in her career's outset, in making the experiences both strange and believable.

—Karen G. Way

SLADEK, John (Thomas). Also writes as Thom Demijohn; Cassandra Knye; Richard A. Tilms; James Vogh. American. Born in Waverly, Iowa, 15 December 1937. Educated at College of St. Thomas, St. Paul, Minnesota, 1955-56; University of Minnesota, Minneapolis, 1956-59. Married in 1970, one child. Engineering assistant, University of Minnesota, 1959-61; technical writer, Technical Publications Inc., St. Louis Park, Minnesota, 1961-62; switchman, Great Northern Railway, Minneapolis, 1962-63; draftsman, New York, 1964-65. Editor, with Pamela A. Zoline, *Ronald Reagan: The Magazine of Poetry*, London, 1968. Recipient: British Science Fiction Association Award, 1984. Agent: Richard Curtis Associates, 164 East 64th Street, New York, New York 10021, U. S. A. ; or, A. P. Watt Ltd., 26-28 Bedford Row, London WC1R 4HL, England.

SCIENCE-FICTION PUBLICATIONS

Novels (series: Roderick)

The Reproductive System. London, Gollancz, 1968; New York, Avon, 1974; as *Mechasm*, New York, Ace, 1969.
The Müller-Fokker Effect. London, Hutchinson, 1970; New York, Morrow, 1971.
Roderick; or, The Education of a Young Machine. London, Granada, 1980; abridged edition, New York, Pocket Books, 1982.
Roderick at Random. London, Granada, 1983.
Tik-Tok. London, Gollancz, 1983.

Short Stories

The Steam-Driven Boy and Other Strangers. London, Panther, 1973.
Keep the Giraffe Burning. London, Panther, 1977.
The Best of John Sladek. New York, Pocket Books, 1981.
Alien Accounts. London, Panther, 1982.
The Lunatics of Terra. London, Gollancz, 1984.

OTHER PUBLICATIONS

Novels

The House That Fear Built (as Cassandra Knye, with Thomas M. Disch). New York, Paperback Library, 1966.
The Castle and the Key (as Cassandra Knye). New York, Paperback Library, 1967.

Black Alice (as Thom Demijohn, with Thomas M. Disch). New York, Doubleday, 1968; London, W. H. Allen, 1969.
Black Aura . London, Cape, 1974; New York, Walker, 1979.
Invisible Green. London, Gollancz, 1977; New York, Walker, 1979.

Other

The New Apocrypha: A Guide to Strange Science and Occult Beliefs. London, Hart Davis MacGibbon, 1973; New York, Stein and Day, 1974
Arachne Rising: The Thirteenth Sign of the Zodiac (as James Vogh). London, Hart Davis MacGibbon, 1977.
The Cosmic Factor (as James Vogh). London, Hart Davis MacGibbon, 1978.
Judgement of Jupiter (as Richard A. Tilms). London, New English Library, 1980.

*

John Sladek comments:

Most of my novels and short stories are set in the near future, in a recognizable America in which technology has either solved all of our problems or failed to solve any of them, or something else entirely has happened. Something else entirely is always happening in science fiction, I understand. My work is usually called satire or black humor, but it also reflects my preoccupation with certain thems.

I am endlessly fascinated by machines which can mimic or displace human beings. So a number of my characters are robots (such as "The Steam-Driven Boy") or computers or cyborgs, or selfreplicating machines (as in *Mechasm*). This theme informs *Roderick; or The Education of a Young Machine*, first of a two-part novel which attempts to cover the entire "life" history of a robot learning machine, and efforts to assimilate him into human society.

A parallel concern is with dehumanizing processes—ways in which governments and other institutions, mistakenly modelled on machines, attempt to reduce their citizens or members to mechanical components. This is the argument of three novellas, "Masterson and the Clerks," "The Communicants," and "The Great Wall of Mexico," and of at least a dozen short stories, and it creeps into the novels, too. It seems almost as though machines, evolving rapidly towards a kind of mimetic humanity, are meeting humans on the way down.

People do of course escape the process of robotization, and one escape route is madness, another recurring theme. Most of the stories in *Keep the Giraffe Burning* seem to deal with mad people (as well as bad, sad, and silly people) and how they succeed at their madness. As the title indicates, these stories are steeped in Surrealism; they are meant to blur the border between dream and reality.

That border is blurred by science fiction all the time. Science fiction, it seems to me, constitutes the right brain hemisphere of contemporary fiction (the dreaming part). My work, if it isn't buried in the hypothalamus or the hippocampus or something, is probably somewhere near the lobotomy scars.

*   *   *

John Sladek's literary accomplishment since his start as an expatriate American with the British New Wave in the late 1960's has been steady, significant, and generally not adequately appreciated in the genre though his conventions and effects are firmly in the science fiction tradition. But since he experiments with a variety of narrative modes (usually within the same fiction) and often dazzles his reader with complexity of tone and allusion, he is often set aside as a rather non-science-fictional satirist and a writer who is most brilliant in his short pieces. He does pun continuously and wonderfully; writes the one-liner of bitter disgust as well as any black humorist; and creates the short, surreal image with the energy of Robert Coover or Richard Brautigan or his fellow Iowa expatriate Thomas M. Disch, whom he often names in his fictions and with whom he has colloborated. Sladek should not be categorized as a black humorist, however, or simply as a mainstream writer of experimental fiction.

His most ambitious novel to date, *The Müller-Fokker Effect*, with the defiant pun in the title is an early example of deconstruction, satiric disgust, and yet wonderfully modern intricacy in which sympathy for disembodied intelligence, artificial intelligence run wild, replaces usual characterization. The financial tycoon who eventually reassembles the technical writer and later author of *The American Book of the Dead* who has been deconstructed on four "M-F tapes" is named Mac Hines, or "machines. " What Sladek's punning supports is a sustained program of speculation about the interfaces between mind and machine. This theme was also introduced in his first novel and most recently has reached another full expression in his robot novels, the two volume "education" of Roderick Wood (the little robot who is a Tin Woodman with a heart) and the story of Tik-Tok, who is the violent obverse of Roderick.

In other words, Sladek's treatment of the mind/machine theme may be not only stylistically too experimental for the American SF market but also too divergent from Asimov's. Actually from his early parody of "Iclick as-i-move" that first appeared in *The Steam-Driven Boy* through incisive analysis in the Roderick texts to the ultimate violation of the Three Laws in *Tik-Tok*, Sladek has carried on a running debate with Asimov and with over-simplifications in thinking about machine intelligence. One might conclude that for Sladek Asimov is the Whig progressive, the hopeful journalist of the new science and of our new inflationary universe whereas Sladek sees himself as the Tory Swift for whom the human animal and progressive technology (the media are a main target for his satire) have become disgusting Yahoo thoughts. He does show continually real sympathy for "other" intelligence. The sympathy, then, brings him back to hard science fiction so that his readers learn and do not just experience Tory disgust. Realizing with Shakespeare in *The Winter's Tale* that no art changes nature unless "the art itself is nature," Sladek at his science fiction best speculates about the nature of things and the position of man and machines in nature—closer, in fact, to Asimov than to black humor.

—Donald M. Hassler

SLESAR, Henry. Also writes O. H. Leslie. American. Born in Brooklyn, New York, 12 June 1927. Educated in public schools. Served in the United States Air Force, 1946-47. Married 1) Oenone Scott in 1953; 2) Jan Maakestad in 1970; 3) Manuela Jone in 1974; one daughter and one son. Advertising Executive: Vice-President and Creative Director, Robert W. Orr Inc., New York, 1949-57; Fuller and Smith and Ross, New York, 1957-60; West Wir and Bartel, New York, 1960-64. President and Creative Director, Slesar and Kanzer, New York, 1964-69, and since 1974, Slesar and Manuela. Recipient: Mystery Writers of

America Edgar Allan Poe Award, for novel, 1960, for television serial, 1977; Emmy Award, 1974. Agent: Jerome S. Siegel Associates, 8733 Sunset Boulevard, Hollywood, California 90069. Address: 125 East 72nd Street, New York, New York 10021, U.S.A.

SCIENCE-FICTION PUBLICATIONS

Uncollected Short Stories

"The Brat," in *Imaginative Tales* (Evanston, Illinois), September 1955.
"The Bloodless Laws," in *Fantastic Universe* (Chicago), May 1956. "The Monument," in *Amazing* (New York), July 1956.
"A Message from Our Sponsor," in *Infinity* (New York), October 1956.
"Sleep It Off," in *Amazing* (New York), November 1956.
"The Chimp," in *Fantastic* (New York), December 1956.
"Repeat Broadcast," in *Amazing* (New York), December 1956.
"Who Am I," in *Super Science Fiction* (New York), December 1956.
"Thought for Today," in *if* (New York), December 1956.
"20 Million Miles to Earth," from screenplay, in *Amazing Stories Science Fiction Novel 1* (New York), 1957.
"Dream Town," in *Fantastic Universe* (Chicago), January 1957.
"Heart," in *Amazing* (New York), January 1957.
"Beauty Contest," in *Fantastic* (New York), February 1957.
"Mr. Loneliness," in *Super Science Fiction* (New York), February 1957.
"The Goddess of World 21," in *Fantastic* (New York), March 1957.
"25 Words or Less," in *Fantastic Universe* (Chicago), April 1957.
"Brainchild," in *if* (New York), April 1957.
"Bottle Baby," in *Fantastic* (New York), April 1957.
"The Metal Martyr," in *Fantastic* (New York), May 1957.
"The Babbit from Bzlfsk," in *Amazing* (New York), June 1957.
"Ben's Idea," in *Satellite* (New York), June 1957.
"Desire Women," in *Super Science Fiction* (New York), June 1957.
"The Show Must Go On," in *Infinity* (New York), July 1957.
"The Secret of Marracott Deep," in *Fantastic* (New York), July 1957.
"A God Named Smith," in *Amazing* (New York), July 1957.
"Monster on Stage 4," in *Amazing* (New York), August 1957.
"Traveling Man," in *Fantastic* (New York), August 1957.
"Saucer/Saucer," in *Fantastic* (New York), September 1957.
"The Success Machine," in *Amazing* (New York), September 1957.
"Jewel of Ecstasy," in *Fantastic* (New York), February 1958.
"The Night We Died," in *Amazing* (New York), February 1958.
"The Moon Chute," in *Amazing* (New York), March 1958.
"The Genie Takes a Wife," in *Fantastic* (New York), March 1958.
"Brother Robot," in *Amazing* (New York), May 1958.
"The Man Who Took It with Him," in *Fantastic* (New York), June 1958.
"No Place to Go. " in *Amazing* (New York), July 1958.
"Garden of Evil," in *Amazing* (New York), August 1958.
"The Delegate from Venus," in *Amazing* (New York), October 1958.
"Deadly Satellite," in *Amazing* (New York), December 1958.
"The Eleventh Plague," in *Fantastic* (New York), December 1958.

"The Blonde from Space," in *Amazing* (New York), January 1959.
"Like Father—Like Son," in *Fantastic* (New York), February 1959.
"Job Offer," in *Satellite* (New York), April 1959.
"The Worth of a Man," in *Fantastic* (New York), June 1959.
"The Trigger," in *Amazing* (New York), June 1959.
"The Traveling Couch," in *Amazing* (New York), August 1959.
"The Toy," in *Fantastic* (New York), September 1959.
"The Invisible Man Murder Case," in *Invisible Men*, edited by Basil Davenport. New York, Ballantine, 1960.
"My Father the Cat," in *The Fantastic Universe Omnibus*, edited by Hans S. Santesson. Englewood Cliffs, New Jersey, Prentice Hall, 1960; London, Panther, 1962.
"Who Is Mrs. Myob," in *Fantastic* (New York), September 1960.
"Long Shot," in *Fantastic* (New York), November 1960.
"Very Small, Very Fine," in *Amazing* (New York), November 1960.
"Chief," in *The Year's Best S-F 6*, edited by Judith Merril. New York, Simon and Schuster, 1961; London, Mayflower, 1963.
"Discoverers," in *Fantastic* (New York), April 1961.
"The Self-Improvement of Salvatore Ross," in *Fantasy and Science Fiction* (New York), May 1961.
"Policeman's Lot," in *Fantastic* (New York), August 1961.
"The Stuff," in *Galaxy* (New York), August 1961.
"The Living End," in *Fantastic* (New York), November 1961.
"The Candidate," in *The Fiend in You*, edited by Charles Beaumont. New York, Ballantine, 1962.
"Way-Station," in *Fantasy and Science Fiction* (New York), January 1963.
"Jobo," in *Amazing* (New York), May 1963.
"Before the Talent Dies," in *No Limits*, edited by Joseph W. Ferman. New York, Ballantine, 1964.
"Beside the Golden Door," in *Amazing* (New York), February 1964.
"Prisoner in Orbit," in *Amazing* (New York), April 1964.
"The Knocking in the Castle," in *Fantastic* (New York), November 1964.
"The Rats of Dr. Picard," in *Bizarre Mystery* (Concord, New Hampshire), October 1965.
"After," in *The Playboy Book of Science Fiction and Fantasy*, edited by Ray Russell. Chicago, Playboy Press, 1966; London, Souvenir Press, 1967.
"I Remember Oblivion," in *Fantasy and Science Fiction* (New York), March 1966.
"The Jam," in *The Playboy Book of Horror and the Supernatural*, edited by Ray Russell. Chicago, Playboy Press, 1967; London, Souvenir Press, 1968.
"The Moving Finger Types," in *Fantasy and Science Fiction* (New York), September 1968.
"Ball of the Centuries," in *Fantastic* (New York), December 1968.
"Cry, Baby, Cry," in *Startling Mystery* (New York), Spring 1970.
"Examination Day," "Melodramine," and "Victory Parade," in *From the "S" File*. Chicago, Playboy Press, 1971.
"I Do Not Like Thee, Dr. Feldman," in *Weird Show*. Chicago, Playboy Press, 1971.
"Survivor No. 1 (The Man with the Green Nose)," with Harlan Ellison, in *Partners in Wonder*, by Ellison. New York, Walker, 1971.
"Legacy of Terror," in *Satan's Pets*, edited by Vic Ghidalia. New York, Manor, 1972.
"The Rise and Fall of the Fourth Reich," in *Fantasy and Science*

Fiction (New York), August 1975.

"My Mother the Ghost," in *Tricks and Treats*, edited by Joe Gores and Bill Pronzini. New York, Doubleday, 1976.

"Melodramine," in *Spaced Out*, edited by Michel Parry. London, Panther, 1978.

"A Woman's Help," in *Alfred Hitchcock Presents: The Master's Choice*. New York, Random House, 1979.

"Light Fingers," in *Alfred Hitchcock's Tales to Fill You with Fear and Trembling*, edited by Eleanor Sullivan. New York, Dial Press, 1980.

"The Slave," in *Alfred Hitchcock's Tales to Make Your Teeth Chatter*, edited by Eleanor Sullivan. New York, Dial Press, 1980.

"Good Morning! This Is the Future," "Speak," and "The Penalty," in *Microcosmic Tales*, edited by Isaac Asimov, Martin H. Greenberg, and Joseph D. Olander. New York, Taplinger, 1980.

"Prez," in *Terrors*, edited by Charles L. Grant. New York, Pocket Books, 1982.

"The Movie Makers," in *Hollywood Unreel*, edited by Martin H. Greenberg and Charles G. Waugh. New York, Taplinger, 1982.

"The Girl Who Found Things," in *Alfred Hitchcock's Fatal Attractions*, edited by Elana Lore. New York, Davis, 1983.

Uncollected Short Stories as O. H. Leslie

"Death Rattle," in *Fantastic* (New York), December 1956.

"Marriages Are Made in Detroit," in *Amazing* (New York), December 1956.

"Reluctant Genius," in *Amazing* (New York), January 1957.

"My Robot," in *Fantastic* (New York), February 1957.

"Abe Lincoln—Android," in *Fantastic* (New York), April 1957.

"The Dope," in *Super Science Fiction* (New York), June 1957.

"No Room in Heaven," in *Amazing* (New York), June 1957.

"The Marriage Machine," in *Fantastic* (New York), July 1957.

"Inheritance," in *Fantastic* (New York), August 1957.

"Space Boat," in *Fantastic* (New York), January 1958.

"Danger Red," in *Fantastic* (New York), February 1958.

"The Mind Merchants," in *Amazing* (New York), February 1958.

"The Creators," in *Amazing* (New York), March 1958.

"The Search for Murphy's Bride," in *Fantastic* (New York), March 1958.

"Mission Murder," in *Amazing* (New York), November 1958.

"The Seven Eyes of Captain Dark," in *Amazing* (New York), January 1959.

"The Chair," in *Amazing* (New York), April 1964.

OTHER PUBLICATIONS

Novels

The Gray Flannel Shroud. New York, Random House, 1959; London, Deutsch, 1960.

Enter Murderers. New York, Random House, 1960; London, Gollancz, 1961.

The Bridge of Lions. New York, Macmillan, 1963; London, Gollancz, 1964.

The Seventh Mask (novelization of TV play). New York, Ace, 1969.

The Thing at the Door. New York, Random House, 1974; London, Hamish Hamilton, 1975.

Short Stories

A Bouquet of Clean Crimes and Neat Murders. New York, Avon, 1960.

A Crime for Mothers and Others. New York, Avon, 1962.

Plays

Screenplays: *The Eyes of Annie Jones*, with Louis Vittes, 1963; *Two on a Guillotine*, with John Kneubuhl, 1965; *Murders in Rue Morgue*, with Christopher Wicking, 1970.

Radio Plays: *CBS Radio Mystery Theatre* (39 plays).

Television Plays: *Forty Detectives Later, Insomnia, Coming Home, The Hat Box, Keep Me Company, The Honey, The Man with Two Faces, The Last Escape, The Horseplayer, A Crime for Mothers, Incident in a Small Jail, A Woman's Help, The Throwback, Servant Problem, The Matched Pearl, First Class Honeymoon, The Right Kind of Medicine, Most Likely to Succeed, The Test, Burglar Proof, The Case of M. J. H., and The Kerry Blue (in Alfred Hitchcock Presents* series), 1955-61; *The Self-Improvement of Salvatore Ross*, with Jerry McNeeley (in *Twilight Zone* series), 1963; *The Edge of Night* series, 1968-79; *Honeymoon with a Stranger*, with David Harmon, from a novel by Robert Thomas, 1969; 100 scripts for other series.

*   *   *

The magazine *TV Guide* once called Henry Slesar "the writer with the largest audience in America." This accolade, whether true or not, was due primarily to the fact that Slesar spent nine years as head writer for the daytime TV serial *The Edge of Night*, and also wrote 100 teleplays for *Alfred hitchcock Presents* and other dramatic TV series, as well as plays for CBS Radio Mystery Theater. Most of Slesar's work in science fiction has been in the short story form. (His only SF novel is a version of the film *Twenty Million Miles to Earth*, not published in hardcover, although the suspense novel *The Bridge of Lions* may be considered borderline science fiction.) About 20 of his stories have been anthologized, most notably such excellent and provocative short-shorts as "Examination Day," "The Jam," "After" (four post-apocalyptic vignettes), and "Victory Parade." The best of Slesar's work is not only entertaining but offers quite horrifying statements on human folly and cruelty ("Examination Day"). Clever O. Henry-type surprise endings are also used to good advantage, as they are in his mystery short stories.

—Bill Pronzini

SLOANE, William M(illigan, III). Also wrote as William Milligan. American. Born in Plymouth, Massachusetts, 15 August 1906. Educated at Hill School, graduated, 1925; Princeton University, New Jersey, A. B. 1929 (Phi Beta Kappa). Married Julie Hawkins in 1930; one son and two daughters. Publisher: in Play Department, 1929-31, and Editorial Department, 1931, Longmans Green and Company; Manager, Fitzgerald Publishing Company, 1932-37; Associate Editor, Farrar and Rinehart, 1937-38; Manager of the Trade Department, 1939-46, and Vice-President, 1944-46, Henry Holt and Company; President, William Sloane Associates, 1946-52;

Editorial Director, Funk and Wagnalls Company and Wilfred Funk Inc., 1952-55; Director, Rutgers University Press, 1955-74. Director, Council on Books in Wartime; Chairman of the Editorial Committee, Armed Services Editions, 1943-44; staff member, Bread Loaf Writers Conference, 1946-72. President, Association of American University Presses, 1969-70. *Died 25 September 1974.*

SCIENCE-FICTION PUBLICATIONS

Novels

To Walk the Night. New York, Farrar and Rinehart, 1937; London, Barker, 1938; revised edition, New York, Dodd Mead, 1954.
The Edge of Running Water. New York, Farrar and Rinehart, 1939; London, Methuen, 1940; as *The Unquiet Corpse,* New York, Dell, 1946.
The Rim of Morning (omnibus). New York, Dodd Mead, 1964.

Uncollected Short Story

"Let Nothing You Dismay," in *Stories for Tomorrow*, edited by William M. Sloane. New York, Funk and Wagnalls, 1954; London, Eyre and Spottiswoode, 1955.

OTHER PUBLICATIONS

Plays

Back Home: A Ghost Play. New York, Longman, 1931.
Runner in the Snow: A Play of the Supernatural , adaptation of the story "I Saw a Woman Turn Into a Wolf" by W. B. Seabrook. Boston, Baker, 1931.
Digging Up the Dirt, adaptation of a play by Bert J. Norton. New York, Longman, 1931.
Crystal Clear. New York, Longman, 1932.
Ballots for Bill: A Light-Hearted Comedy of Politics, with William Ellis Jones. New York, Fitzgerald, 1933.
The Silence of God: A Play for Christmas. Boston, Baker, 1933.
Art for Art's Sake. Boston, Baker, 1934.
The Invisible Clue (as William Milligan). New York, Fitzgerald, 1934.
Gold Stars for Glory. Boston, Baker, 1935.

Other

Editor, *Space, Space, Space.* New York, Watts, 1953.
Editor, *Stories for Tomorrow.* New York, Funk and Wagnalls, 1954; London, Eyre and Spottiswoode, 1955.

* * *

William M. Sloane had an extremely brief career as a science-fiction writer, completing two novels and a single short story, but those two novels have probably won him a permanent place in the history of the genre. He blended science and horror with consummate skill, and his calm, smooth-paced novels are more successful at developing suspense and tension than most of the lurid thrillers that reach the bestseller lists.

To Walk the Night utilizes a plot device so standard, so familiar, that is has long since become a cliché avoided even by the less inventive film makers, but in the hands of a writer with Sloane's talent it is transformed into an entirely new vehicle.

Two young men make a surprise visit to an old friend, and arrive just in time to see his body mysteriously incinerated as if from within. Although they are unable to explain the peculiar nature of his death, they are freed by the authorities. But one of them has become infatuated with the unexpected widow of his late friend. The perceptive reader will realize fairly soon that the mysterious death resulted from the scientist's researches into the nature of reality. Sloane leaves myriad hints of other oddities as well, the widow's awkwardness in familiar human situations, the disappearance of a young girl with virtually no intelligence, the mystery of yet another death, this time clearly suicide. Despite the fact that the reader has a clear idea what comprises the general nature of the mystery, the details provide the true suspense, and the climactic confrontation is one of the most effective scenes in the genre.

The Edge of Running Water broke no new ground either, and moves even further toward the supernatural, while still retaining the scientific rationale of its mystery. Although the characters are not as well drawn in this story of a man convinced he can develop a machine that will enable him to communicate with the dead, the element of suspense is just as expertly handled. There is little overt action, even though one character is eventually killed and another destroyed, propelled into another universe, but the reader's attention is unlikely to waver despite this fact.

Both novels have been published as mysteries, which they are, as horror stories, which they are, and science fiction, which they also are. Sloane's sole foray into more conventional science fiction, "Let Nothing You Dismay," is singularly unremarkable, a pedestrian examination of human refugees adjusting to a new world after the death of Earth. He was at his best at greater length, using a familiar setting and coloring it with a series of hints of something totally unfamiliar. His style was highly advanced for his time, and both novels are free of archaic anomalies and outdated prose. It seems clear that had Sloane chosen to pursue his career as a genre writer, he would have become one of the dominant forces within it.

—Don D'Ammassa

* * *

SMITH, Clark Ashton. American. Born 13 January 1893. Left school at 14. Married in 1954. Writer and artist: regular contributor to *Weird Tales* in the early 1930's; ceased writing in 1936. *Died 14 August 1961.*

SCIENCE-FICTION PUBLICATIONS

Short Stories

The Immortals of Mercury. New York, Stellar, 1932.
Tales of Science and Sorcery. Sauk City, Wisconsin, Arkham House, 1964; London, Panther, 1976.
Other Dimensions. Sauk City, Wisconsin, Arkham House, 1970; London, Panther, 2 vols., 1977.

OTHER PUBLICATIONS

Short Stories

The Double Shadow and Other Fantasies. Privately printed, 1933.
The White Sybil. Everett, Pennsylvania, Fantasy, 1935 (?).

Out of Space and Time (includes verse). Sauk City, Wisconsin, Arkham House, 1942; London, Spearman, 1971.

Lost Worlds. Sauk City, Wisconsin, Arkham House, 1944; London, Spearman, 1971.

Genius Loci. Sauk City, Wisconsin, Arkham House, 1948; London, Spearman, 1972.

The Abominations of Yondo. Sauk City, Wisconsin, Arkham House, 1960; London, Spearman, 1972.

Zothique, Hyperborea, Xiccarph, Poseidonis (selections), edited by Lin Carter. New York, Ballantine, 4 vols., 1970-73.

The Mortuary. Glendale, California, Squires, 1971.

Prince Alcouz and the Magician. Glendale, California, Squires, 1977.

The City of the Singing Flame, edited by Donald Sidney-Fryer. New York, Pocket Books, 1981.

The Monster of the Prophecy , edited by Donald Sidney-Fryer. New York, Pocket Books, 1983.

Verse

The Star-Treader and Other Poems. San Francisco, Robertson, 1912.

Odes and Sonnets. San Francisco, Book Club of California, 1918.

Ebony and Crystal: Poems in Verse and Prose. Privately printed 1923.

Sandalwood. Privately printed, 1925.

Nero and Other Poems. Lakeport, California, Futile Press, 1937.

The Dark Chateau and Other Poems. Sauk City, Wisconsin, Arkham House, 1951.

Spells and Philtres. Sauk City, Wisconsin, Arkham House, 1958.

Poems in Prose. Sauk City, Wisconsin, Arkham House, 1964.

Grotesques and Fantastiques. Saddle River, New Jersey, Gerry de la Ree, 1973.

Klarkash-ton and Monstro Lieriv, with Virgil Finlay. Saddle River, New Jersey, Gerry de la Ree, 1974.

Fugitive Poems. Privately printed, 4 vols., 1974-75.

Other

Planets and Dimensions: Collected Essays., edited by Charles K. Wolfe. Baltimore, Mirage Press 1973.

The Black Book of Clark Ashton Smith. Sauk City, Wisconsin, Arkham House, 1979.

*

Bibliography: *The Tales of Clark Ashton Smith: A Bibliography* by G. L. Cockcroft, Melling, New Zealand, Cockcroft, 1952; *Emperor of Dreams: A Clark Ashton Smith Bibliography* by Donald Sidney-Fryer and others, West Kingston, Rhode Island, Grant, 1978.

Critical Studies: *In Memoriam Clark Ashton Smith* edited by Jack L. Chalker, Baltimore, Anthem, 1963; *The Last of the Great Romantic Poets* by Donald Sidney-Fryer, Albuquerque, Silver Scarab Press, 1973; *The Fantastic Art of Clark Ashton Smith* by Dennis Rickard, Baltimore, Mirage Press, 1973.

*   *   *

Clark Ashton Smith was a contributor to the early science-fiction and fantasy pulp magazines whose output, despite its unevenness, became a seminal influence on modern science fiction. Jack Vance, Harlan Ellison, Theodore Sturgeon, Fritz Leiber, H. P. Lovecraft, Robert E. Howard, and Ray Bradbury, among others, were influenced by his work.

Smith's earliest short stories—he wrote no novels—are the primitive interplanetary narratives common in the pulp magazines. Of these, "Marooned in Andromeda" and "The Amazing Planet" Are typical. They recount the adventures of the crew of the space ship *Alcoyne* on distant worlds, and are odysseys of perilous adventure distinguished only by Smith's exotic language and bizarre imagination.

Smith, also a poet, was concerned mainly with the poetry of death and the alien. His protagonists are decidely unheroic, being either misfits or rogues who seek other worlds because they do not fit into their own. In "The Monster of the Prophecy" the suicidal poet Theophilus Alvor agreeably becomes the instrument through which the Antarean wizard Vizaphmal assumes control of his world. This lack of virtue does not prevent Alvor from finding true love in the arms of an Antarean woman. Similarly, the renegade and thief Datu Buang lives out his life in peace after assass- inating an evil ruler with the aid of his consort in "As It Is Written. "

The search for a better reality is the predominant theme in Smith. In his haunting classic, "The City of the Singing Flame," the author Giles Angarth discovers the gateway to another dimension where the Singing Flame lures the unwary into its fires. Angarth finds himself finally drawn to the flame and discovers it is the entrance to still another, better, reality beyond.

Those stories set wholly on other worlds, in which he gives his poetic vision free rein, are considered Smith's best. Among these are the sardonic tales of the world of Xiccarpth and those set on the continent of Zothique in the last days of Earth. In "The Maze of Maal Dweb" the hunter Tiglari seeks his kidnapped lover in the stronghold of Xiccarph's tyrant, Maal Dweb, but falls victim to the tyrant's powers. Maal Dweb, on the other hand, is the protagonist of "The Flower-Women. " It is a peculiarity of Smith's fiction that the amoral flourish and the good become the victims of ironic fates. Like Tiglari, the hero of "The Demon of the Flower" ultimately fails to rescue the woman he loves from the plant ruler of his world. The tales of Zothique, although set in Earth's distant future, are closer to fantasy. In these Smith's macabre poetic vision is at its highest. "Xeethra" is a poignant story of a goat- herd who partakes of strange fruit and imagines himself the ruler of a distant land. He goes in search of that land, only to find it in ruins. "The Last Hieroglyph" is an ironic tale of an astrologer, Nushain, who reads in the stars that he must go on a journey which will fulfill his destiny. At the voyage's end, he meets his end. "The Weaver in the Vault" relates the weird doom of two individuals who desecrate a tomb. Hope and futility are expertly balanced in "The Isle of the Torturers. "

Despite the weird trappings of his stories, Smith's work cannot be rightfully labeled as horror stories. He was a fatalist who delighted in spinning phantasms, not terror. With rare exceptions ("Master of the Asteroid" and "The Dweller in the Gulf"), his work is too remote from reality to evoke a convincing mood of horror and his imaginings thus fascinate instead of terrify. The power of Smith's writing, and the reason for its widespread influence, lay in the fact that Smith shared with many of his protagonists a yearning for a reality *truer* than the one he knew, and he discovered a language which enabled him to express his unique vision.

—Will Murray

SMITH, Cordwainer. Pseudonym for Paul Myron Anthony Linebarger; also wrote as Felix C. Forrest; Carmichael Smith. American. Born in Milwaukee, Winsconsin, 11 July 1913. Educated at schools in Honolulu, Shanghai, and Baden Baden; University of Nanking, 1930; North China Union Language School, 1931; George Washington University, Washington, D. C., A. B. 1933 (Phi Beta Kappa); Oxford University, 1933; American University, Washington, D. C., 1934; University of Chicago, 1935; John Hopkins University, Baltimore, M. A. 1935; Ph. D. 1936; University of Michigan, Ann Arbor, 1937, 1939; Washington School of Psychiatry, certificate in psychiatry 1955; Universidad Interamericana, 1959-60. Served in the United States Army Intelligence Service, 1942-66: helped found Office of War Information, served in Chungking, 1942-46, and as consultant to British Forces in Malaya, 1950, and to 8th Army, Korea, 1950-52: Lieutenant Colonel. Married 1) Margaret Snow in 1936 (divorced, 1949), two daughters; 2) Genevieve Cecilia Collins in 1950. Instructor, Harvard University, Cambridge, Massachusetts, 1936-37; Instructor, then Associate Professor, Duke University, Durham, North Carolina, 1937-46; Professor of Asiatic Politics, Johns Hopkins University School of Advanced International Studies, Washington, D. C., 1946-66. Visiting Professor, University of Pennsylvania, Philadelphia, 1955-56, and Australian National University, Canberra, 1957. President, American Peace Society. *Died 6 August 1966.*

SCIENCE-FICTION PUBLICATIONS

Novels (series: Instrumentality in all books)

The Planet Buyer. New York, Pyramid, 1964.
The Underpeople. New York, Pyramid, 1968.
Norstrilia (omnibus). New York, Ballantine, 1975.

Short Stories (series: Instrumentality)

You Will Never Be the Same. Evanston, Illinois, Regency, 1963.
Space Lords (Instrumentality). New York, Pyramid, 1965; London, Sidgwick and Jackson, 1969.
Quest of the Three Worlds. New York, Ace, 1966.
Under Old Earth and Other Explorations. London, Panther, 1970.
Stardreamer. New York, Beagle, 1971.
The Best of Cordwainer Smith, edited by J. J. Pierce. New York, Doubleday, 1975.
The Instrumentality of Mankind. New York, Ballantine, 1979.

OTHER PUBLICATIONS

Novels

Ria (as Felix C. Forrest). New York, Duell, 1947.
Carola (as Felix C. Forrest). New York, Duell, 1948.
Atomsk (as Carmichael Smith). New York, Duell, 1949.

Other as P. M. A. Linebarger

The Political Doctrines of Sun Yat-Sen. Baltimore, Johns Hopkins University Press, 1937.
Government in Republican China. New York, McGraw Hill, 1938.
The China of Chiang Kai-shek. Boston, World Peace Foundation, 1941.

Psychological Warfare. Washington, D. C., Infantry Journal Press, 1948; revised edition, Washington, D. C., Combat Forces Press, 1954.
Far Eastern Governments and Politics, with Djang Chu and Ardath W. Burks. New York, Van Nostrand, 1952.

Editor, *The Gospel of Chung Shan,* by Paul Linebarger. Privately printed, 1932.
Editor, *The Ocean Men,* by Paul Linebarger. Washington D. C., Mid-Nation, 1937.

*

Critical Studies: *Exploring Cordwainer Smith* (includes bibliography) edited by Andrew Porter, New York, Algol Press, 1975; *Concordance to Cordwainer Smith* by Anthony Lewis, Jr., Cambridge, Mussachusetts, NESFA Press, 1984.

*   *   *

Paul Linebarger, who wrote science fiction under the name Cordwainer Smith, certainly stands as one of the most unusual and imaginative writers of fantastic literature of this century. Though his total output of fiction is relatively small, Smith's reputation and influence have grown consistently since his death in 1966. Virtually his entire science fiction output was in print in book form by early 1979, and the theme that ties most of these stories together—a future galactic civilization called the Instrumentality of Mankind—has emerged as one of the most striking and detailed future history constructs in all of science fiction. His non-science-fiction novels *Ria* and *Carola* also reveal the strength of imagination, idiosyncratic style, and sensitivity to character that make his better-known work stand out.

Smith was a Christian, a romantic, and a shrewd political theorist who had written under his own name an internationally influential text on psychological warfare. All of these strains come together in his fiction, giving it a complexity and depth of meaning that are sometimes confusing to readers encountering one of his stories for the first time. The first of his mature stories to be published (his first science-fiction story, "War No. 81-Q," had appeared when he was only 15), "Scanners Live in Vain," appeared in 1950, and clearly implied a more detailed imaginary universe than the story itself explained. Set early in the history of the Instrumentality, the tale concerns a threat posed to the guild of "scanners"—humans mechanically restructured to survive in space—by the discovery of a new and safer means of space travel. In a characteristically bizarre Smith touch, the new method depends on lining the spaceships with oysters to insulate the passengers from harm. Clearly, this odd version of a technological breakthrough represented an event of historical important to this future world, but the nature of that world itself remained unclear.

During the next decade and a half, Smith gradually filled in some of the gaps. Following a series of disastrous wars that nearly reduced Earth to barbarism, humanity gradually recovers its vitality, aided by a powerful family called the Vomacts, descended from the daughters of a Nazi scientist who were placed in suspended animation in orbit and who returned following the wars ("Mark Elf" and "The Queen of the Afternoon"). The Vomacts help give rise to the universal government called the Instrumentality, which initially explores space with the aid of scanners, briefly replaces these with the oyster-shell ships, and in turn replaces these with ships powered by massive photonic sails ("The Lady Who Sailed *The Soul,*"

"Think Blue, Count Two"). Finally, a near-instantaneous form of space travel, called planoforming, is discovered ("The Colonel Came Back from the Nothing-at-All," "The Burning of the Brain"), but planoforming ships are subject to attacks by hideous, incorporeal outer-space "dragons" and must be protected by telepathic technicians called pinlighters, sometimes assisted by telepathic cats ("The Game of Rat and Dragon"). As the Instrumentality grows increasingly powerful and decadent—offering humans near-immortality through a life-extending drug called stroon—its economy comes to depend on a slave class of converted animals called underpeople. Aided by a few heroic underpeople and the sympathetic Jestocost family, the underpeople finally attain civil rights ("The Dead Lady of Clown Town," "Under Old Earth," "The Ballad of Lost C'Mell"), and a renaissance of humanism, the Rediscovery of Man, set in ("Alpha Ralpha Boulevard," *Norstrilia*). In the far distant future, civilization finally seems to be achieving some kind of stability (*Quest of the Three Worlds*), but the actual conclusion of the history of the Instrumentality, if planned by Smith, was not completed during his lifetime.

Although there is an abundance of political and social satire in Smith's work—the Instrumentality is clearly not a simple utopia—what stands out most are the memorable characters of near-mythic proportions, the romantic legends he weaves, and the oddly nostalgic style, reminiscent of oral history or folktales, in which he writes. Smith has a unique ability to make a romance between a man and a cat convincing ("The Game of Rat and Dragon") or to make an unconsummated romance between a servant girl and a lord as powerful as a medieval legend ("The Ballad of Lost C'Mell"). Occasionally, he turns to actual legends for his source material; "The Dead Lady of Clown Town" is a retelling of the Joan of Arc legend, with Joan made into an underperson converted from a dog. In other cases, he turns to literary culture for his sources; "Drunkboat" is essentially a tour de force on themes from Arthur Rimbaud. "Golden the Ship Was—Oh! Oh! Oh!" is at once a satire on the bureaucracy of war and a retelling of the Trojan horse story—with the horse becoming a 90-million-mile-long decoy spaceship used to frighten an enemy while the second-level bureaucrats drop poisonous bombs. Other of his stories are supposedly based on Chinese narrative techniques, and occasionally he deliberately plays games with the reader, such as working anagrammatic references to the Kennedy-Oswald assassinations into *Quest of the Three Worlds*.

One wonders, at times, whether Smith's curious style and unusual way of structuring stories is due to his great sophistication or to his ingenuousness as a writer. *Norstrilia* does not stand up as well as do many of the short stories, partly because the narrative tends to ramble, partly because the style seems to grow self-conscious over such an extended narrative. But Smith's short fiction includes some of science fiction's finest stories, but demonstrates that an author need not abandon sensitive insights into love and ethics in order to create imaginary universes of great imagination.

—Gary K. Wolfe

―――――

SMITH, Doc. See **SMITH, E. E.**

―――――

SMITH, E(dward) E(lmer). American. Born in Sheboygan,

Wisconsin, 1 May 1890. Educated at the University of Idaho, Moscow; George Washington University, Washington, D. C., Ph. D. in food chemistry 1919. Served in an explosives arsenal during World War II. Married Jeanne Craig MacDougall; one daughter and one son. Worked as ranch hand, lumberjack, silver miner, and surveyor, before coming chemist, specializing in food mixes: Manager of General Mix Division of J. W. Allen and Company, 1945-57. Recipient: First Fandom Hall of Fame Award (as "Doc" Smith), 1964. Guest of Honor, 2nd World Science Fiction Convention, 1940. *Died 31 August 1965.*

SCIENCE-FICTION PUBLICATIONS

Novels (series: Lensman; Lord Tedric; Skylark)

The Skylark of Space, with Mrs. Lee Hawkins Garby. Proovidence, Rhode Island, Buffalo, 1946; revised edition, New York, Pyramid, 1958; London, Digit, 1959.
Spacehounds of IPC. Reading, Pennsylvania, Fantasy Press, 1947; London, Panther, 1974.
Skylark Three. Reading, Pennsylvanis, Fantasy Press, 1948; London, Panther, 1974.
The History of Civilization (Lensman):
  Triplanetary. Reading, Pennsylvania, Fantasy Press, 1948; London, Boardman, 1954.
  First Lensman. Reading, Pennsylvania, Fantasy Press, 1950; London, Boardman, 1955.
  Galactic Patrol. Reading, Pennsylvania, Fantasy Press, 1950; London, W. H. Allen, 1971.
  Gray Lensman. Reading, Pennsylvania, Fantasy Press, 1951; London, W. H. Allen, 1971.
  Second Stage Lensman. Reading, Pennsylvania, Fantasy Press, 1953; London, W. H. Allen, 1972.
  Children of the Lens. Reading, Pennsylvania, Fantasy Press, 1954; London, W. H. Allen, 1972.
Skylark of Valeron. Reading, Pennyslvania, Fantasy Press, 1949.
The Vortex Blaster (Lensman). New York, Gnome Press, 1960; as *Masters of the Vortex*, New York, Pyramid, 1968; London, W. H. Allen, 1972.
The Galaxy Primes. New York, Ace, 1965; London, Panther, 1975.
Subspace Explorers. New York, Canaveral Press, 1965; London, Panther, 1975.
Skylark DuQuesne. New York, Pyramid, 1966; London, Panther, 1974.
Masters of Space. London, Futura, 1976.
Lord Tedric, with Gordon Eklund. New York, Baronet, 1978.
Lord Tedric: Alien Worlds. London, Wright, 1978.
Space Pirates, with Gordon Eklund. New York, Baronet, 1979; as *Lord Tedric: The Space Pirates*, London, Wingate, 1979.
Lord Tedric: The Black Knight of the Iron Sphere. London, Star, 1979.
Lord Tedric: Alien Realms. London, Star, 1980.
Subspace Encounter, edited by Lloyd Arthur Eshbach. New York, Berkley, 1983.

Short Stories

The Best of E. E. ("Doc") Smith. London, Futura, 1975.

OTHER PUBLICATIONS

Other

What Does This Convention Mean? A Speech Delivered at the

Chicago 1940 World's Science Fiction Convention. Privately printed, 1941.

"The Epic of Space," in *Of Worlds Beyond*, edited by Lloyd Arthur Eshbach. Chicago, Advent, 1964.

Galactic Roamer (interview with Thomas Sheridan). West Warwick, Rhode Island, Necronomicon Press, 1977.

*

Critical Study: *The Universes of E. E. Smith* by Ron Ellik and Bill Evans, Chicago, Advent, 1966.

*   *   *

It is difficult if not impossible to overestimate the impact of E. E. "Doc" Smith on 20th-century science fiction. He developed and perfected the space opera, a form which had existed only in a rudimentary state prior to his work. As one of the two major forms of "pulp" science fiction, space opera should be distinguished from interplanetary romance. The latter, with strong roots in 19th-century works, was perfected about 1912 by Edgar Rice Burroughs, and continued in later years by innumerable others of whom the greatest was probably Leigh Brackett. In interplanetary romance an adventurer is transported rapidly by any convenient means to an alien planet. This planet is generally primitive, inhabited by non-technological societies, and in these societies the adventurer rises by means of derring-do not very different from those described in the works of Rafael Sabatini. The space opera, in contrast, involves the clash of two or more technologically advanced societies. The protagonist society is normally human; the antagonist may be human or otherwise. Major segments of the action take place in outer space, usually in spaceships or fleets of spaceships quite comparable to 20th-century navies. A frequent sub-theme of space opera is the interplantary or interstellar alliance of wildly differing intelligent species.

Precursors of space opera may be found in works of the late 19th and early 20th centuries. Smith's contemorary Edmond Hamilton actually preceded Smith into print with relevant works, starting with *Across Space*, serialized in *Weird Tales* from September 1926. However, with the appearance of Smith's *The Skylark of Space* in *Amazing Stories* in 1928, Smith achieved pre-eminence in the field and never was surpassed. (Smith actually began the novel in 1915 and completed it in 1919.) A secondary point concerns the role of Mrs. Lee Hawkins Garby in the writing of the book. It is widely known that Smith asked Mrs. Garby to assist him with "the love interest." The usually perceptive critic Paul A. Carter infers from this that "so incidental was the heroine to the plot that the author himself need pay no attention to her!" Carter quite misinterprets Smith's motive: Smith was concerned that he might delineate his heroine and "the love interest" inadequately, and sought assistance in doing a proper job. (The result was still thoroughly stilted and unsatisfying, and in later works Smith omitted the collaboration. With passing years, Smith's delineation of character—regardless of gender—improved substantially, but neither characterization nor dialogue nor "the love interest" was ever his strongest suit.)

Once Smith was established, numerous others wrote within the arena he had created. The two who did so most effectively were Hamilton and Jack Williamson. Clifford Simak, in *Cosmic Engineers*, produced a single, brilliant space opera. John W. Campbell, Jr., before switching his energies from authorship to editing, also wrote a number of such works. More recently the film *Star Wars* has been classed by many viewers as the "purest" space opera yet produced in dramatic form. The bulk of Smith's works falls into two series. The Skylark series runs to four volumes. It opens with a thoroughly familiar love triangle, the rival suitors being the noble, brilliant Richard Seaton and the villainous, brilliant "Blacky" DuQuesne. When Seaton invents an atomic-powered spaceship, he and DuQuesne proceed to battle on an ever-growing canvas for the favor of the lovely and accomplished Dorothy Vaneman. Upon this rudimentary framework, Smith built the most audacious and energetic series of super-scientific adventures—often harking back to the geographic wonder-tales of Verne—written up to that time.

But Smith's Lensman cycle exceeded even the Skylark series in scope, audacity, and power. They represent space opera at its very peak of development; the two central volumes of the series, *Galactic Patrol* and *Gray Lensman*, certainly embody both the greatest virtues and the greatest faults of the space-opera form. These novels are based on the premise that a cosmic struggle is taking place, between the Arisians, godlike protectors of the galaxy, and the Eddorians, satanic invaders and destroyers from another galaxy. The epic spans eons of time and inconceivable volumes of space, in the tradition of the works of Olaf Stapledon. Its central phase involves a family saga, the most notable character being Kimball Kinnison, Smith's supreme hero. In sequence after sequence, seemingly cosmic struggles between the two great forces are seen to be merely local incidents in the titanic war which only Smith fully knows. The Lensman are a cosmic "elite corps" of the forces of Arisia; as such they are carefully selected individuals of the highest intellectual, physical, and moral perfection. Each receives, as badge of membership in this corps, a lens which not only identifies its owner but amplifies that owner's outstanding abilities into the superhuman range. Smith's advocates have suggested that the struggle between Arisia and Eddore, if it is to be read as more than a grand but literal-minded adventure, may be considered a sort of Juedo-Christian allegory, with the Arisians representing the forces of Heaven and the Eddorians the Adversary. In this regard, congruences are obvious between the series and Tolkien's *Lord of the Rings*. Both cycles, in this aspect, are further comparable to Wagner's great operatic cylce. On the other hand, Smith's critics have pointed out that the elitism, the (at least implicit) racism, the ruthlessness, and the authoritarianism involved in Lens philosophy make the works more Nazi-like than Biblical in theme.

In addition to his two major series, Smith wrote a number of other works. *Spacehounds of IPC* is a charming retelling of the babes-in-the-woods story, with boy and girl castaway on an alien planet. *The Galaxy Primes* is an unsuccessful attempt to write a more modern novel with psionic themes. *Subspace Explorers* is a very readable volume intended as the first of three in a final series. The other two volumes never appeared but it is believed that Smith had completed at least a draft of the second before his death.

Smith was the very paradigm of the great "primitive" novelist, perhaps comparable to Grandma Moses in painting. Where the formal or academic novelist may be judged on the basis of subtlety of characterization, polish of style, complexity of plot, ambiguity of theme—and, in the case of the science-fiction writer, detail, plausibility, and accuracy of scientific background—the primitive novelist is subject to a quite different set of criteria—*vividness* rather than subtlety of characterization, *dynamism* rather than polish of style, *power* rather than complexity of plot, and *directness* rather than ambiguity of theme. In the case of the science-fiction writer in particular, the primitive may be judged by the audacity, emotional and structural effect of any scientific postulate not obviously absurd. By these criteria, Smith was the absolute champion of his realm.

—Richard A. Lupoff

———

SMITH, Evelyn E. Also writes as Delphine C. Lyons. American. Born in 1927. Writer and crossword puzzle compiler. Lives in New York.

SCIENCE-FICTION PUBLICATIONS

Novels

The Perfect Planet. New York, Avalon, 1962.
Valley of Shadows (as Delphine C. Lyons). New York, Lancer, 1968.
Unpopular Planet. New York, Dell, 1975.

Uncollected Short Stories

"Nightmare on the Nose," in *Fantastic Universe* (Chicago), November 1953.
"Baxbr Daxbr," in *Time to Come* edited by August Derleth. New York, Farrar Straus, 1954.
"Not Fit for Children" and "Tea Tray in the Sky," in *Second Galaxy Reader of Science Fiction,* edited by H. L. Gold. New York, Crown, 1954; London, Grayson, 1955.
"Call Me Wizard," in *Beyond* (New York), January 1954.
"The Agony of the Leaves," in *Beyond* (New York), July 1954.
"At Last I've Found You," in *Fantasy and Science Fiction* (New York), October 1954.
"Collector's Item," in *Galaxy* (New York), December 1954.
"The Laminated Woman," in *Fantastic Universe* (Chicago), December 1954.
"Helpfully Yours," in *Galaxy* (New York), February 1955.
"The Big Jump, " in *Fantastic Universe* (Chicago), March 1955.
"Man's Best Friend," in *Galaxy* (New York), April 1955.
"The Princess and the Physicist," in *Galaxy* (New York), June 1955.
"The Faithful Friend," in *Fantasy and Science Fiction* (New York), June 1955.
"Teregram," in *Fantastic Universe* (Chicago), June 1955.
"Dragon Lady," in *Beyond* (New York), June 1955.
"The Good Husband," in *Fantastic Universe* (Chicago), August 1955.
"The Doorway," in *Fantastic Universe* (Chicago), September 1955.
"Weather Prediction," in *Fantastic Universe* (Chicago), October 1955.
"Jack of No Trades," in *Galaxy* (New York), October 1955.
"Floyd and the Eumenides," in *Fantastic Universe* (Chicago), December 1955.
"The Captains's Mate," in *Fantasy and Science Fiction* (New York), March 1956.
"The Venus Trap," in *Galaxy* (New York), June 1956.
"Mr. Replogle's Dream," in *Fantastic Universe* (Chicago), December 1956.
"Woman's Touch," in *Super Science Fiction* (New York), February 1957.
"The Ignoble Savages," in *Galaxy* (New York), March 1957.
"The Lady from Aldebaran," in *Fantastic Universe* (Chicago), March 1957.

"The 4D Bargain," in *Saturn* (Holyoke, Massachusetts), May 1957.
"Outcast of Mars," in *Fantasy and Science Fiction* (New York), May 1957.
"The Man Outside," in *Galaxy* (New York), August 1957.
"The Weegil," in *Super Science Fiction* (New York), December 1957.
"The Vilbar Party," in *The Third Galaxy Reader*, edited by H. L. Gold. New York, Doubleday, 1958.
"The Blue Tower," in *Galaxy* (New York), February 1958.
"My Fair Planet," in *Galaxy* (New York), March 1958.
"Two Suns of Morcali," in *Fantastic Universe* (Chicago), July 1958.
"Once a Greech," in *Worlds That Couldn't Be and 8 Other SF Novelets,* edited by H. L. Gold. New York, Doubleday, 1959.
"The People Upstairs," in *Fantastic Universe* (Chicago), March 1959.
"The Alternate Host," in *Fantastic Universe* (Chicago), September 1959.
"Send Her Victorious," in *Fantasy and Science Fiction* (New York), February 1960.
"The Hardest Bargain," in *Mind Partner and 8 Other Novelets from Galaxy,* edited by H. L. Gold. New York, Doubleday, 1961.
"Sentry of the Sky," in *Galaxy* (New York), February 1961.
"Robert E. Lee at Moscow," in *Fantasy and Science Fiction* (New York), October 1961.
"Softly While You're Sleeping," in *The Best from Fantasy and Science Fiction 11,* edited by Robert P. Mills. New York, Doubleday, 1962.
"They Also Serve," in *Fantasy and Science Fiction* (New York), September 1962.
"The Last of the Spode," in *17 x Infinity,* edited by Groff Conklin. New York, Dell, 1963.
"The Martian and the Magician," in *Fifty Short Science Fiction Tales,* edited by Isaac Asimov and Groff Conklin. New York, Macmillan, 1963.
"Little Gregory," in *Fantasy and Science Fiction* (New York), February 1964.
"Calliope and Gherkin and the Yankee Doodle Thing," in *The Best from Fantasy and Science Fiction 19,* edited by Edward L. Ferman. New York, Doubleday, 1971.
"A Day in the Suburbs," in *Sociology Through Science Fiction,* edited by John W. Milstead and others. New York, St. Martin's Press, 1974.
"Gerda," in *Dragon Tales,* edited by Isaac Asimov, Martin H. Greenberg, and Charles G. Waugh. New York, Fawcett, 1982.
"The Most Sentimental Man," in *Last Man on Earth,* edited by Isaac Asimov, Martin H. Greenberg, and Charles G. Waugh. New York, Fawcett, 1982.

OTHER PUBLICATIONS

Other

The Building Book (for children). New York, Howell Soskin, 1947.

*   *   *

Although Evelyn E. Smith's individual works of SF vary greatly in style, mood, and focus, it is possible to characterize her work as making a wry statement about human nature. Here is an author who is optimistic in spite of herself; even in those works which focus on post-nuclear holocaust worlds, humanity has survived and—whether or not its representatives are honorable or otherwise admirable—they do possess the ability to meet wild challenges and to survive their own foibles.

Smith's comments on human nature range from sharp and ironical to light and ludicrous. Her first story, "The Last of thw Spode," is a terse portrayal of three Britishers who, by a twist of fate, seem to be the sole survivors of nuclear holocaust. A "correct" professor and a young chap join a figure of British womanhood in an afternoon tea at the end of the world. As the Spode teapot is poured out, they reveal their chief concern as to whether or not their tea supply will last them to the end of their days. "No point in anything, really," the young chap remarks. "We must face the facts, lad," the professor says and then adds, in a gem of understatement, "pity about the Bodleian, though." "The Hardest Bargain" envisions another post-holocaust future, in which the American populace is weakened with hunger and racial debility. Presidential advisor Dr. Livingston, who believes that "the thinking man is the despairing man," urges President Buchbinder to accept extraterrestrial aid in decontaminating the lands, but when the earthlings fail to keep their bargain to pay the extraterrestrial Foma in famous works of art, the Foma reveals his true identity as a pied piper to the robots which are so desperately needed by human society. "Not Fit for Children" is representative of Smith's more lighthearted stories. Here a group of alien children pose as war-dancing "natives" on an asteroid-like space chip which is visited regularly by human tourists. In payment for their antics, the children receive coins which are melted down by their disbelieving elders into metal which is needed to repair their space ship.

Most of Smith's short stories appeared during the 1950's; just as they varied in seriousness of theme as well as sophistication of writing technique, her novels represent the extremes of the author's abilities. *The Perfect Planet* shares the wry ironic tone of so many of her shorter works, as the author tells an amusing but insubstantial tale of two astronauts, one male and one female, who land on a planet populated by vain health enthusiasts who foist their obsession with slim, perfect physiques upon the slightly pudgy, space-weary duo. While the book does have some impact as a critique of mindless conformity, sadly the astronauts, who start out as rebelious to the ways of this world, come to have a fondness for the pampered inhabitants of "the perfumed planet." The initially gutsy female astronaut Moodie comes to value herself as an alluring female using charm, artifice, and cosmetics to enhance her self-worth while the captain learns to be protective of his changed space partner. *Unpopular Planet* is also preoccupied with questions of sexual identity. While it, too, features some portrayals of women which would not please feminists—the hero's partner is a female who is fully mature sexually although mentally and chronologically she is but three years old—such characterization is used with more sophisticated satirical purpose. An aspiring musician, Nicholas Piggot, careens perplexedly yet enthusiastically through a series of picaresque adventures observed by blue dragons. They turn out not to be the result of drunken fancy but to be "real" beings from another dimension who have a particular genetic purpose in store for the hero, who rises from life as an unknown in subterranean Manhattan to become father of a new future.

—Rosemary Herbert

SMITH, George H(enry). Also writes as M. J. Deer; Jan Hudson; Jerry Jason; Clancy O'Brien; Diana Summers. American. Born in Vicksburg, Mississippi, 27 October 1922. Educated at the University of Southern California, Los Angeles, B. A. 1950. Served in the United States Navy, 1942-45. Married M. Jane Deer in 1950. Since 1950, free-lance writer. Address: 4113 West 180th Street, Torrance, California 90504, U.S.A.

SCIENCE-FICTION PUBLICATIONS

Novels (series: Annwn)

Satan's Daughter. New York, Epic, 1961.
1976: Year of Terror. New York, Epic, 1961.
Scourge of the Blood Cult. New York, Epic, 1961.
The Coming of the Rats. New York, Pike, 1961; London, Digit, 1964.
Doomsday Wing. Derby, Connecticut, Monarch, 1963.
The Unending Night. Derby, Connecticut, Monarch, 1964.
The Forgotten Planet. New York, Avalon, 1965.
The Psycho Makers (as Jerry Jason). New York, Tempo, 1965.
The Four Day Weekend. New York, Belmont, 1966.
Druids' World (Annwn). New York, Avalon, 1967.
Kar Kaballa (Annwn). New York, Ace, 1969.
Witch Queen of Lochlann (Annwn). New York, New American Library, 1969; London, Hale, 1981.
The Second War of the Worlds (Annwn). New York, DAW, 1976.
The Island Snatchers (Annwn). New York, DAW, 1978.

Uncollected Short Stories

"The Last Spring," in *Startling* (New York), August 1953.
"The Savages," in *Universe* (Evanston, Illinois), December 1953.
"The Ordeal of Colonel Johns," in *If* (New York), June 1954.
"The Last Crusade," in *If* (New York), February 1955.
"The Unwanted," in *Spaceway* (Alhambra, California), February 1955.
"Witness," in *If* (New York), May 1955.
"At the Bridge," in *Other Worlds* (Evanston, Indiana), July 1955.
"Bridge to Limbo," in *Pacific Stars and Stripes* (Tokyo), 3 October 1955.
"Shrine of Hate," in *Original Science Fiction Stories* (Holyoke, Massachusetts), January 1956.
"Elected," in *Science Fiction Quarterly* (Holyoke, Massachusetts), February 1956.
"The Other Army," in *Original Science Fiction Stories* (Holyoke, Massachusetts), September 1956.
"The Ships in the Sky," in *Fantastic Universe* (Chicago), February 1957.
"The Barbarian," in *Jem* (Union City, New Jersey), August 1957.
"In the Beginning," in *Good Humour*, March 1958.
"The Night the TV Went Out," in *Future* (New York), April 1958.
"Hello, Terra Central!," in *Original Science Fiction Stories* (Holyoke, Massachusetts), July 1958.
"Benefactor," in *Fantastic Universe* (Chicago), August 1958.
"Perfect Marriage," in *Original Science Fiction Stories* (Holyoke, Massachusetts), January 1959.
"Ego-Transfer Machine," in *Super Science Fiction* (New York), February 1959.

"The Last Days of L. A.," in *If* (New York), February 1959.
"Paradox Lost," in *Original Science Fiction Stories* (Holyoke, Massachusetts), February 1959.
"Conquerors Return," in *Gallant*, May 1959.
"The Bare Facts," in *Original Science Fiction Stories* (Holyoke, Massachusetts), July 1959.
"Specimens," in *Super Science Fiction* (New York), August 1959.
"Too Robot to Marry," in *Fantastic Universe* (Chicago), October 1959.
"The Outcasts," in *Now and Beyond*, edited by Ivan Howard. New York, Belmont, 1965.
"The Night Before," in *Galaxy* (New York), April 1966.
"The Look," in *Galaxy* (New York), August 1966.
"The Plague," in *Famous Science Fiction* (New York), Winter 1966.
"In the Imagicon," in *Nebula Award Stories 2*, edited by Brian Aldiss and Harry Harrison. New York, Doubleday, and London, Gollancz, 1967.
"In the Land of Love," in *Worlds of Tomorrow 24* (New York), 1970.
"A Matter of Freedoms" (as Clancy O'Brien) and "Flame Tree Planet," in *Flame Tree Planet*, edited by Roger Elwood. St. Louis, Concordia, 1973.
"Take Me To Your Leader," in *Microcosmic Tales*, edited by Isaac Asimov, Martin H. Greenberg, and Joseph D. Olander. New York, Taplinger, 1980.
"The Great Secret," in *Science Fiction from A to Z*, edited by Isaac Asimov, Martin H. Greenberg, and Charles G. Waugh. Boston, Houghton Mifflin, 1982.

OTHER PUBLICATIONS

Novels

A Place Called Hell (as M. J. Deer, with M. Jane Deer Smith). New York, France, 1963.
Flames of Desire (as M. J. Deer, with M. Jane Deer Smith). New York, France, 1963.
The Devil's Breed. Chicago, Playboy Press, 1979.
The Rogues. Chicago, Playboy Press, 1980.
The Firebrands. Chicago, Playboy Press, 1980.

Novels as Diana Summers

Wild Is the Heart. Chicago, Playboy Press, 1978.
Love's Wicked Ways. Chicago, Playboy Press, 1978.
Fallen Angel. Chicago, Playboy Press, 1981.
Louisiana. New York, Dell, 1984.
The Emperor's Lady. New York, Charter, 1984.

Other

Who Is Ronald Reagan? New York, Pyramid, 1968.
Martin Luther King, Jr. New York, Lancer, 1971.

Other as Jan Hudson

Hell's Angels. San Diego, Greenleaf, 1965; London, New English Library, 1967; as *The New Barbarians*, New English Library, 1973.
The People in the Saucers. San Diego, Greenleaf, 1967.
Bikers at War. London, New English Library, 1976.

*

George H. Smith comments:

(1981) Science fiction was my first love in writing, and I've done it off and on for the last 25 years. Five of my novels are set in the imaginery Celtic other world called Annwn. I am currently committed to a series of historical novels so it will be some time before I get back to science fiction, but when I do I hope to continue the Annwn series.

* * *

The career of George H. Smith as a writer of science fiction is a peculiar one. Since most of his early novels were written for small paperback houses specializing in lurid action and violent sex, there is a certain crudity about them that masks his positive values as a writer. It was not until the 1970's that Smith began to sell novels to the more prestigious paperback houses, and the quality of his novels seems to have improved proportionally.

The early novels made use of a standard set of characters. The typical male protagonist was an indecisive man who had some insight into the future and realized that a significant change was coming to the world, but who was unable to communicate this to those around him. Typically, he spends the first half of each novel infatuated with a woman obviously unsuited for him, gradually awakening to the fact that some third character is actually the person with whom he wishes to spend his life. This is the pattern of *The Coming of the Rats*, for example; the hero finally convinces his totally impractical girlfriend to accompany him to a remote cave as nuclear war hovers just over the horizon. In the aftermath, the rats of the title challenge man for supremacy with predictable results. The pattern repeats itself in *Doomsday Wing*, also about a nuclear war, this time threatening to extinguish all life on Earth, and *The Unending Night*, wherein runaway nuclear reactors knock Mars out of its orbit, and threaten to pull our own planet away from the warmth of the sun. In the former the dedicated military man cannot convince his ambitious wife of the importance of serving his country, and in the latter a hyper-liberated woman is convinced that the best thing that can happen to the human race is for it to descend to a primitive culture. The scientist hero of the latter is thoroughly enamored of her until she proves insane. This basic arrangement of characters also appears in *The Four Day Weekend*, involving a plot by secret aliens to take over the world by reprogramming the computers that direct our motor vehicles. Although there is some amusing satire here, it is rather silly most of the time, possibly the worst of Smith's novels.

Suprisingly enough, one of his better novels was published by a softcore pornography publisher. *1976: Year of Terror* is set in a future America in which the Libertarian Party has seized power by assassination and clever plotting by the head of the Federal Security Police. Opposed to him is a secret agent intent on finding the missing Vice-President and restoring democratic rule to the country. This anticipates a number of thrillers along similar lines, and is fairly well written.

Somewhere along the line, Smith became interested in mythology and druidism. It crops up first in *Druid's World*, a fairly dull novel, then to much better effect in *Witch Queen of Lochlann*, written in the mode of the stories made famous by *Unknown* magazine. Duffus January is a magician of sorts who undertakes to restore the rightful queen to the throne of Lochlann, a Welsh alternate world where magic works. A low-key sword and sorcery tale, this seems to have set the stage for a major series of novels. *Kar Kaballa* is named for the king of the Gogs, a barbaric nation of nomads whose existence is barely noted by their neighbors, the civilized inhabitants of Avalon, a nation comparable to 19th-century England in our universe.

Dylan MacBride, a young adventurer, is convinced that the imminent freezing of the channel between Avalon and the northern regions will result in a massive invasion, but he is unable to convince anyone in authority of the seriousness of the threat. Despondent, he seems doomed to failure when he encounters a man from our own universe who plans to sell Gatling guns to the alternate world. Smith went on to chronicle the Martian invasion of his alternate world in *The Second War of the Worlds*, an entertaining novel throughout, and a magical plot to destroy civilization in *The Island Snatchers*, the weakest in the series. These latter books are far better than his earlier efforts, with more complex characters, a quieter and more careful style, and more significant care taken in establishing settings, mood, and suspense.

Although he has written shorter pieces, Smith's only interesting story is "In the Imagicon," an enigmatic piece about a machine that allows its user to create the mental world of his choosing. It seems unlikely that Smith will add to his reputation with short stories, but it is quite possible that his novels will continue to improve.

—Don D'Ammassa

SMITH, George O(liver). American. Born in Chicago, Illinois, 9 April 1911. Attended the University of Chicago, 1929-30. Served as an editorial engineer, National Defense Research Council, 1944-45. Married 1) Helen Kunzler in 1936 (divorced, 1948), one daughter and one son; 2) Dona Louise Stebbins in 1949 (died, 1974), one son. Radio Serviceman, Chicago, 1932-35; radio engineer: General Household, 1935-38, Wells-Gardiner, 1938-40, Philco, 1940-42, 1946-51, Crosley, 1942-44; Manager, Emerson Radio components engineering, 1951-57; Analyst, ITT Defense Communications, 1959-74. Reviewer, *Space Science Fiction. Died.*

SCIENCE-FICTION PUBLICATIONS

Novels

Pattern for Conquest: An Interplanetary Adventure. New York, Gnome Press, 1949; London, Clerke and Cockeran, 1951.
Nomad. Philadelphia, Prime Press, 1950.
Operation Interstellar. Chicago, Century, 1950.
Hellflower. New York, Abelard Press, 1953; London, Lane, 1955.
Highways in Hiding. New York, Gnome Press, 1956; abridged edition, as *The Space Plague*, New York, Avon, 1957.
Troubled Star. New York, Avalon, 1957.
Fire in the Heavens. New York, Avalon, 1958.
The Path of Unreason. New York, Gnome Press, 1958.
Lost in Space. New York, Avalon, 1959.
The Fourth "R." New York, Ballantine, 1959; as *The Brain Machine*, New York, Lancer, 1968.

Short Stories

Venus Equilateral. Philadelphia, Prime Press, 1947; enlarged edition, London, Futura, 2 vols., 1975; and as *The Complete Venus Equilateral*, New York, Ballantine, 1976.
Worlds of George O. New York, Bantam, 1982.

OTHER PUBLICATIONS

Other

Mathematics, The Language of Science (for children). New York, Putnam, 1961.
Scientists' Nightmares. New York, Putnam, 1972.

*   *   *

When one mentions "the golden age of science fiction," several stereotypes come to mind, including bug-eyed aliens who act like humans, humans who act like supermen, mysterious gadgets and even more mysteriouse ray guns. Fortunately, much of the science fiction written during this period did not employ such stereotypes. A few became classics. Many more, while certainly not classics, have to be considered as good, solid science fiction.

One such work is George O. Smith's *Highways in Hiding*. Although it might be classified as a science-fiction mystery, it moves fast enough and has enough action to keep your attention. In fact, it is difficult to put down. The characterizations are only adequate, but the plot is well thought out, involving psychic phenomena, a mysterious disease, and a baffling disappearance. There is a political message here, too, which is common in Smith's works: the fruits of science should be for all and not just the elite. *The Fourth "R"* is another Smith work which makes use of this underlying idea. This time it is the Holden Electromechanical Educator which promises to be mankind's salvation. However, Jimmy Holden's parents, who developed the device, are murdered by an unscrupulous business associate who wishes the device to further his own aims. Because Jimmy's parents had used the device on him, he is no ordinary five-year-old, but practically an adult trapped in a child's body, and his adventures protecting the device make a very clever work.

Fire in the Heavens, Nomad, Hellflower, and *Troubled Star* are less interesting. The first has a lot of science but not much plot: the sun is about to go nova and a young scientist who doesn't believe in the Law of Conservation of Energy or in neutrinos must save the day. The plot of *Hellflower* is a little worn, though suspenseful. Space pilot Farradyne crashes his ship, killing 33 people. He is banished to the Venusian fungus field until a federal agent gives him a chance to prove himself anew by becoming an undercover agent and helping to break the hellflower smuggling ring. *Troubled Star* may not have been intended as a tongue-in-cheek stab at 1950's science fiction, but I take it as such. Dusty Britton of the space patrol has so many TV followers that, when a group of aliens plan to make Sol into a three-day variable beacon, they approach Dusty to be their spokesman. In *Nomad* humans are made out to be monsters who use sub-science life forms for vivisections and who annihilate the "10th" planet of the solar system with little provocation. It is a particularly frightening projection of the future of mankind.

No discussion of Smith's works would be complete without mentioning *Venus Equilateral*. Venus Equilateral Relay Station is a manned satellite circling the sun at the orbit of Venus, but 60 degrees ahead of that planet. It's purpose is to relay radio transmissions among the inhabited planets whenever the sun interferes with direct transmission. The stories mostly concern technical problems and their solution by the station's scientists. Most of the problems are archaic by today's standards, but the stories are of interest, at least from a historical perspective. Many of the stereotypes of golden age science fiction are found here.

—Paul Swank

SMITH, L. Neil. Address: c/o Ballantine Books, 201 East 50th Street, New York, New York 10020, U.S.A.

SCIENCE-FICTION PUBLICATIONS

Novels (series: Lando Calrissian)

Their Majesties' Buccaneers. New York, Ballantine, 1981.
The Venus Belt. New York, Ballantine, 1981.
The Nagasaki Vector . New York, Ballantine, 1983.
Lando Calrissian and the Flamewind of Oseon. New York, Ballantine, 1983.
Lando Calrissian and the Mindharp of Sharu. New York, Ballantyne, 1983.
Lando Calrissian and the Starcave of ThonBoka. New York, Ballantine, 1983.
Tom Paine Maru. New York, Ballantine, 1984; London, Futura, 1985.

Uncollected Short Stories

"Grimm's Law," in *Stellar 5*, edited by Judy-Lynn del Rey. New York, Ballantine, 1980.
"Grandfather Clause," in *Stellar 6*, edited by Judy-Lynn del Rey. New York, Ballantine, 1981.
"Folger's Factor," in *Stellar 7*, edited by Judy-Lynn del Rey. New York, Ballantine, 1981.

*   *   *

The stories of the North American Confederation are a product of the Libertarian movement which in recent years has sprung up to question the idea that increased government power is the answer to anything. It was once summed up as "How to hate your government on principle." L. Neil Smith's stories are, like those of F. Paul Wilson and J. Neil Schulmann, openly propandising for this movement which claims a great deal of support from the more individualilst wing of science-fiction. In calling them propaganda I imply no necessary criticism although as I indicate below I feel their political viewpoint may make for one major flaw in the series.

All the stories follow much the same pattern: a naive but basically decent individual is gradually introduced to the world view of Libertarianism, the idea that aggression is wrong no matter for what cause and that the State is organized aggression. (This gives the stories a built-in excuse for explaining to the newcomer What Is Going On And Why.) The Confederacy is a world in which Government has been gradually abolished over the past 200 years, starting with the execution of George Washington during the Whiskey Rebellion, and the stories find their villans (who tend to be smooth sophists with sado-masochistic tendencies) from the Hamiltonians, who are trying to reestablish Death and Taxes. As the central character sees a stateless world in action he comes to question the values of his own world and eventually comes round to identify with the forces of Anarchy (wearing the white hats).

Much of the fun comes, as with all parallel-world stories, from the distorting mirror it holds up to our own world. Most vivid in my memory are John Wayne (who in the confederacy never abandoned his real name) going off to shoot a space opera in the Asteroids ("Only thing th' people wanna see, these . . . days. Feels downright silly 'thout a . . . horse under me") and Senator Proxmire as a science-fiction writer. In fact Smith takes a great delight in placing politicians in the shady or menial roles he feels they would occupy in an ideal world, like Dante assigning his enemies a precise place in hell.

Another strength lies in the creation of eccentric minor characters to contrast with the more staid heroes. For some reason his non-humans (although he never tries to make them truly alien in their thinking) are the most entertaining; I think especially of Mr. Meep, the chimpanzee restauranteur ("Our Food Untouched By Human Hands") and "Georgie" the computer/ship/mistress of the hero in *The Nagasaki Victor* ("The Ship Who What?"). One thing you can count on with Smith, he will never resist the temptation to make a silly joke or wisecrack.

The major faults of the series are two: firstly a love of "in jokes" and obscure references, either to the lore of science fiction or to Libertarian political writings. A certain amount of this is tolerable, even fun but by *Tom Paine Maru* it has turned into a incestuous reference back to the earlier novels which must be irritating to those coming to the later work first. The second fault is the determinedly upbeat nature of the stories which prevents them from achieving any emotional depth. Libertarianism is an optimistic philosophy, rejecting as sickness the idea that suffering is necessary to the human condition. But Smith seems to be prevented by this from showing suffering by his major characters who though they have to make choices never have to pay prices. At the end of *Tom Paine Maru* he dangles before us the possibility of the heroine's death only to say a moment later "Yah, fooled you! I didn't really mean it. " That such childishness is not a necessary characteristic of Libertarian writers may be seen by contrasting Smith with J. Neil Schulmann's *The Rainbow Cadenza*.

—Michael Cule

SOHL, Jerry (Gerald Allan Sohl). Also writes as Nathan Butler; Roberta Jean Mountjoy; Sean Mei Sullivan. American. Born in Los Angeles, California, 2 December 1913. Attended Central College, Chicago, 1933-34. Served in the United States Army Air Force, 1942-45: Sergeant. Married Jean Gordon in 1942; one son and two daughters. Reporter, telegraph editor, photographer, and feature writer, Bloomington *Daily Pantagraph*, Illinois, 1945-58. Since 1958, free-lance writer: staff writer for *Star Trek, Alfred Hitchcock Presents*, and *The New Breed*; also concert pianist. Agent: Joseph Elder Agency, 150 West 87th Street, New York, New York 10024. Address: P.O. Box 1336, Thousand Oaks, California 91360, U.S.A.

SCIENCE-FICTION PUBLICATIONS

Novels

The Haploids. New York, Rinehart, 1952.
Costigan's Needle. New York, Rinehart, 1953; London, Grayson, 1955.
The Transcendent Man. New York, Rinehart, 1953.
The Altered Ego. New York, Rinehart, 1954.
Point Ultimate. New York, Rinehart, 1955.
The Mars Monopoly. New York, Ace, 1956; London, Satellite, 1958.
The Time Dissolver. New York, Avon, 1957; London, Sphere, 1967.
The Odious Ones. New York, Rinehart, 1959; London, Consul, 1961.

One Against Herculum. New York, Ace, 1959.
Night Slaves. New York, Fawcett, 1965.
The Anomaly. New York, Curtis, 1971.
I, Aleppo. Toronto, Laser, 1976.
Death Sleep. New York, Fawcett, 1983.

Uncollected Short Stories

"The Seventh Order," in *Galaxy* (New York), March 1952.
"The Ultroom Error," in *Space* (New York), May 1952.
"Brink's Bounty," in *Galaxy* (New York), January 1955.
"The Hand," in *Imagination* (Evanston, Illinois), January 1955.
"The Elroom," in *If* (New York), March 1955.
"The Invisible Enemy," in *Imaginative Tales* (Evanston, Illinois), September 1955.
"Death in Transit," in *Infinity* (New York), June 1956.
"Counterweight," in *If* (New York), November 1959.
"The Little Red Bag," in *If* (New York), January 1960.
"Jelna," in *Fantasy and Science Fiction* (New York), August 1972.
"Mr. Moyachki," in *Playboy* (Chicago), May 1974.
"Before a Live Audience," in *Future Corruption*, edited by Roger Elwood. New York, Warner, 1975.
"The Service," in *The Year's Best Horror Stories 5*, edited by Gerald W. Page. New York, DAW, 1977.

OTHER PUBLICATIONS

Novels

Prelude to Peril, New York, Rinehart, 1957.
The Lemon Eaters. New York, Simon and Schuster, and London, Cassell, 1967.
The Spun Sugar Hole. New York, Simon and Schuster, 1971.
The Resurrection of Frank Borchard. New York, Simon and Schuster, 1973.
Supermanchu, Master of Kung Fu (as Sean Mei Sullivan). New York, Ballantine, 1974.
Night Wind (as Roberta Jean Mountjoy). New York, Coward McCann, 1981.
Black Thunder (as Roberta Jean Mountjoy). New York, Berkley, 1983.

Novels as Nathan Butler

Dr. Josh. New York, Fawcett, 1973.
Mamelle. New York, Fawcett, 1974.
Blow-Dry. New York, Fawcett, 1976.
Mamelle, The Goddess. New York, Fawcett, 1977.
Kaheesh. New York, Fawcett, 1983.

Plays

Screenplays: *Twelve Hours to Kill*, 1960; Monster of Terror (*Die Monster, Die!*), 1965; *Frankenstein Conquers the World*, with Kaoru Mabuchi and Reuben Bercovitch, 1966.

Television Plays: *The Corbomite Maneuver* (*Star Trek* series), 1966; *Night Slaves*, from his own novel, 1970; and episodes for *Naked City, Route 66, M-Squad, G.E. Theater, Markham, Border Patrol, Twilight Zone, The Invaders, The Outer Limits, Target: The Corrupters, Man from Atlantis*, and *The Next Step Beyond* series.

Other

Underhanded Chess. New York, Hawthorn, 1973.
Underhanded Bridge. New York, Hawthorn, 1975.

Manuscript Collection: University of Wyoming, Laramie.

*

Jerry Sohl comments:
The corpus of my science-fiction work reflects, I believe, rather accurately what was fashionable in the genre from 1950 to 1970, moving from gimmick as story to people as story. Although superior to what it was prior to 1970, today's science fiction is often too abstruse to be understood.

While I continue to write science fiction now and then, my interest has shifted to mainstream and I am at the moment at work on a super-suspense novel entitled *The Pacem Complex* as well as novels I can only describe as *avant-garde*, one entitled *Mortal Coils* and the other *The Gold Triskelion*.

*   *   *

Like many fans-turned-writers, Jerry Sohl reveals an appreciative understanding of the surface structures of science-fiction narratives but often fails at deeper levels of conceptualization and extrapolation. Although Sohl has contributed little of originality to the genre, he is in many ways a representative popular writer of the 1950's, skilled in generating an initial sense of mystery and wonder, but often confusing or even absurd in his resolutions.

Most of his novels and stories deal with familiar science-fiction themes. *The Transcendent Man*, for example, borrows a premise from Charles Fort via earier treatments by Eric Frank Russel, L. Ron Hubbard, and others: the idea that humanity's intelligence and civilization are the creations of a vastly superior race of invisible aliens who feed off the emotional energy generated by catastrophes such as war and plagues. Although these aliens, called the Capellans in this novel, might serve as an interesting metaphor for the paradoxical quality in human nature that somehow accounts for both creative and destructive impulses, Sohl develops the story into little more than an adventure narrative concerning one supernormal human who discovers the alien secret and, in the end, singlehandedly takes on the task of maintaining civilization. *Point Ultimate*, Sohl's contribution to the literature of dystopia, concerns a world conquered by communists who seem to come right out of the nightmares of Joe McCarthy, and quickly descends into a welter of germ warfare, gypsies, underground railways, and secret Martian colonies. *The Altered Ego* involves the somewhat more intriguing notion of a society which has learned how to resurrect important citizens after death, but soon becomes a familiar tale of chases and conspiracies.

Sohl's more successful novels are those in which the science-fiction element is kept fairly simple or relegated to the background. *The Time Dissolver* is an intriguing amnesia mystery for most of its length, with the protagonist and his wife awaking one morning to find that their memories from 1946 to 1957 have disappeared—and that, consequently, they do not even know each other. The carefully wrought details of the investigation into the missing years of their lives provide a suspenseful narrative, and the rather weak explanation concerning a memory-dissolving machine does not interfere greatly with the overall impact of the novel. *Costigan's Needle*, an exploration of the parallel-universe theme, is perhaps Sohl's best novel: an account of a group of people who pass into a parallel world through a needle-shaped machine invented by a Chicago scientist, only to find themselves trapped in the other world and forced to spend years redesigning the technology that will enable them to build another machine (which, it turns out, will only enable them to enter another of an apparently infinite series of parallel worlds). Understandably, the people choose not to abandon this new world that they have created with their own hands. Although the characters in the novel are a familiar assortment of popular fiction stereotypes, the exploration of the problems inherent in trying to recreate a sophisticated technology from raw materials is well-handled.

Sohl has had relatively little influence on the genre, although one of his novels, *Night Slaves*—concerning a community dominated by alien visitors—provided the basis for a television movie. A writer with undeniable skill in constructing suspenseful situations, and one who enjoyed some popularity during the 1950's, his works in retrospect seem weakened by inadequate conceptualization of the scientific and social ideas he dealt with.

—Gary K. Wolfe

SOMERS, Bart. See **FOX, Gardner F.**

SPENCER, Leonard G. See **GARRETT, Randall.**

SPINRAD, Norman (Richard). American. Born in New York City, 15 September 1940. Educated at the City College of the City University of New York, B. S. 1961. Since 1963, full-time writer. President, Science Fiction Writers of America, 1980-81. Recepient: Prix Apollo, 1974; Jupiter Award, 1975. Address: c/o Bantam Books, 666 Fifth Avenue, New York, New York 10019, U.S.A.

SCIENCE-FICTION PUBLICATIONS

Novels

The Solarians. New York, Paperback Library, 1966; London, Sphere, 1979.
Agent of Chaos. New York, Belmont, 1967; London; Corgi, 1981.
The Men in the Jungle. New York, Doubleday, 1967; London, Sphere, 1972.
Bug Jack Barron. New York, Walker, 1969; London, Macdonald, 1970.
The Iron Dream. New York, Avon, 1972; London, Panther, 1974.
Riding the Torch. New York, Dell, 1978.
A World Between. New York, Pocket Books, 1979; London, Arrow, 1980.
Songs from the Stars. New York, Simon and Schuster, 1980; London, Sidgwick and Jackson, 1981.

The Void Captain's Tale. New York, Pocket Books, 1983.
Child of Fortune. New York, Bantam, 1985.

Short Stories

The Last Hurrah of the Golden Horde. New York, Doubleday, 1970; London, Macdonald, 1971.
No Direction Home. New York, Pocket Books, 1975; London, Millington, 1976.
The Star-Spangled Future. New York, Ace, 1979.

Uncollected Short Stories

"Prime Time" in *The 1981 Annual World's Best SF*, edited by Donald A. Wollheim. New York, DAW, 1981.
"Perchance to Dream," in *Isaac Asimov's Science Fiction Magazine* (New York), June 1983.
"Street Meat," in *Isaac Asimov's Science Fiction Magazine* (New York), Mid-December 1983.

OTHER PUBLICATIONS

Novel

Passing Through the Flame. New York, Putnam, 1975.

Plays

Television Plays: for *Star Trek* series.

Other

Fragments of America. North Hollywood, Now Library Press, 1970.
" *Stand on Zanzibar* : The Novel as Film," in *SF: The Other Side of Realism*, edited by Thomas D. Clareson. Bowling Green, Ohio, Popular Press, 1971.
Experiment Perilous: Three Essays on Science Fiction, edited by Andrew Porter. New York, Algol Press, 1976.
Staying Alive: A Writer's Guide. Norfolk, Virginia, Donning, 1983.

Editor, *The New Tomorrows*. New York, Belmont, 1971.
Editor, *Modern Science Fiction*. New York, Doubleday, 1974.

*

Bibliography: *Le Livre d'Or de Norman Spinrad* by Patrice Duvic, Paris, Presses Pocket, n. d.

*   *   *

Norman Spinrad's most original and insightful fiction emerges from his remarkable grasp of the potential impacts of the communication revolution on American ways of living, loving, and dying. He can create for us the archetypes and myths we need to understand the new electronic milieu which he sees overloading our senses and sensitivities, creating a "multivalued, post Age-of-Reason reality. " Spinrad helps us to imagine what we are becoming in the hands of the "media pros" and even what might happen if the "pros" had a case of conscience and a commitment to something more than improving the ratings.

In what remains his best novel, *Bug Jack Barron*, Spinrad creates the ultimate American TV hero, who, in the style of Joe

Pine, electronically extends his brand of kick-em-in-the-ass confrontation of the power structure into the tube minds and hearts of all the "losers" and "suckers" sitting in front of the glass teat. Barron is a latter day cousin of Robin Hood and Billy the Kid – the bad guy turned good cowboy; hating authority, power and civilization; riding to danger with his tube blazing; shooting it out verbally at OK TV studio; and walking into the fade out with his sexetary, after Sweet Sara, his good-hearted whore and first love has laid down her life for him and changed him from hired gun (or mouth) to public hero number one and president of the United States. It may be familiar, but it's the stuff of which democracy is made. Americans have to believe the good guy could save the damned town. Spinrad, in fact, accurately predicts Ronald Reagan's two terms as town savior, invents the format that has made Ted Koppel's *Nightline* a success, and prepares us for the recent poll that indicates a substantial percentage of the electorate think that Phil Donahue would make a fine president. His sense of the relationships between politics and the media is as accurate as it is frightening.

Similarly, in *A World Between* Spinrad's strongest writing and most effective imagining occur as he describes the media campaigns used to influence public opinion in a totally participatory electronic democracy. In *Riding the Torch,* a novella that is in the main a typical science-fiction confrontation between man and the uncaring universe, Spinrad's protagonist is an artist producing sensos, total recreations of experience. His task is to help mankind face the truth about having to live forever in space. Despite his own fears and doubts the artist achieves affirmation and hope. At least Spinrad himself is seeking to make such an affirmation.

Spinrad's hope that the electronic media can serve the common good, is not, however, mindless optimism, and four of his best short stories explore the manipulation that the media message can produce. "National Pastime" finds a TV producer inventing a modern gladiatorial version of football that capitalizes on race hatred, sexual intolerance and the national love of violence to win the ratings "wars. " "Blackout" details the sheep-like response to an alien take-over created by stopping the flow of network news. "The Conspiracy," an interesting experiment in style, uses news-flash diction and headline typography to reveal and/or parody the growing sense of paranoia that leads many to a conspiratorial view of modern life. "The Big Flash" explores the possibilities of using a media-hyped rock group to sell the populace on the ultimate death trip, a thermo-nuclear flash. In each of these stories Spinrad is raising serious questions about the ethical vacuum that produces the wasteland we call the entertainment industry.

All of this is not to say that Spinrad has not written or imagined well in a multiplicity of other areas. In fact, with the exception of Burgess in *A Clockwork Orange*, no one writing speculative fiction has explored 20th-century manifestations of violence and sadism more thoroughly. *The Men in the Jungle* is an account of the crimes men and women commit in running revolutions to "free" or "save" one another and comes too close to the truths of living in Northern Ireland, Afghanistan, Lebanon, and Central America. In *The Iron Dream* Spinrad imagines an alternative past in which Adolf Hitler as a science-fiction writers gives us a novel bad enough to be pulp science-fiction, and which, unbelievably, in the real world was sold to Nazi Germany. His earlier novels, *The Solarians* and *Agent of Chaos*, reveal the same concern with the problems of government, power, individual freedom, and social responsibility found in the later work. A more recent novel, *The Void Captain's Tale*, returns to these themes turning them around a search for self and transcendence. The captain telling the tale

plays Ishmael to his female pilot's Ahab. Her quest for ultimate experience serves as the literal force driving their ship through space and time toward an unutterable union with the universe which is achieved through a kind of perpetual platform orgasm. A Moby-Dick indeed. Only a writer with Spinrad's talent can make all this even marginally believable, and his continuing experimentation with style, language, and point of view produces some fine moments in an interesting failure.

Spinrad's short stories are among the best of the past 20 years. *The Last Hurrah of the Golden Horde* contains stories published between 1963 and 1969. The works are tightly stuctured and contain flashes of brilliant characterization. As might be expected, several of the stories tend to be formulaic, but "Carcinoma Angels," "The Last of the Romany," "The Ersatz Ego," "It's a Bird! It's a Plane!," "The Entropic Gang Bang Caper," and the title story reveal a command of the form, an active sense of humor, an a whimsical imagination. In *No Direction Home* there is little that could be called conventional science fiction. In terms of topics, themes, and approaches we are in a universe that is Spinradian. The stories are highly crafted and the characters are well drawn; to use Spinrad's own distinction, the stories are "speculative fiction," a modern form that seeks to explore the "could-be-but-isn't. " They cross whatever boundaries there are that define what Spinrad calls "science fiction as a commercial genre-cum-subculture. " In *The Star-Spangled Future* Spinrad reprints several stories from his other collections with a series of annotations and essays that make clear the way in which he sees speculative fiction-science fiction as the literature of the American present. What the collection makes clear is that Norman Spinrad is a sensitive observer of his culture, a skilled craftsman of the short story, and one of the best writers of his generation. Let us hope that the failings of his last two novels are not signs the he is no longer able to avoid the problems of the "genre-cum-subculture" so clearly delineated in his essays and notes in *Modern Science Fiction. The Void Captain's Tale* ought to have been a better book than it is. It does not provide the intellegent criticisms and affirmations that characterize Spinrad's earlier work; unlike his best work it does little to help us understand and shape ourselves and our world.

—Thomas D. Bacig

SPRAGUE, Carter. See **MERWIN, Sam, Jr.**

SPRUILL, Steven. American. Born in Battle Creek, Michigan, 20 April 1946. Educated at Andrews University, Berrien Springs, Michigan, B. A. in biology 1968; Catholic University of America, Washington, D. C., M. A. in psychology 1979, Ph. D. in clinical psychology 1981. Married Nancy Lyon in 1969. Biological technician, Hazleton Laboratories, Falls Church, Virginia, 1969-73; psychology intern, Veterans Administration Hospital, Washington, D. C., 1978-79, and Mt. Vernon Community Health Center, Alexandria, Virginia, 1979-80. Since 1981, full-time writer. Agent: Al Zuckerman, 21 West 26th Street, New York, New York 10010. Address: 123 North Park Drive, Arlington, Virginia 22203, U.S.A.

SCIENCE-FICTION PUBLICATIONS

Novels (series: Elias Kane)

Keepers of the Gate. New York, Doubleday, and London, Hale, 1977.
The Psychopath Plague (Kane). New York, Doubleday, and London, Hale, 1978.
Hellstone, New York, Playboy, 1980.
The Imperator Plot (Kane). New York, Doubleday, 1983.
The Genesis Shield. New York, Pinnacle, 1985.

Uncollected Short Stories

"Prime Culture," in *Aries 1*, edited by John Grant. Newton Abbot, Devon, David and Charles, 1979.
"The Janus Equation," in *Binary Star 4*. New York, Dell, 1980.

*

Steven Spruill comments:

My purpose in writing is primarily to entertain the reader and produce an emotional experience in the process. I believe people read in order to feel. Consequently, I consider it extremely important to write in the technical sense in such a way that the reader feels him or herself to *be* the viewpoint character, wanting what that character wants, fearing what he or she fears, and sensing along with the character. In the process or writing this way I feel it is quite important for the author to remain as nearly invisible as possible.

In addition, I prefer the extraordinay to the ordinary (which is all too readily available to us in real life) when I structure the plots of my novels. Consequently, most of my novels are concerned with the bizarre, the complicated, the strange, and the psychological, hopefully made clear through "simple" writing, and engaging through the hopes, needs, fears, and, in general, the emotional journey of the characters through their rather baroque plots and landscapes. I might sum up my position as a writer by naming the two other authors I most admire—Bob Shaw and Ken Follett.

* * *

Reviewers have not been especially kind to Steven Spruill. His non-science-fiction novels were given bad reviews, and a pre-publication reviewer accurately suggested that his first science-fiction nove, *Keepers of the Gate*, was not only uninspired and routine but one that the reader could skip and not miss anything of significance. On the other hand, despite several less than enthusiastic reviews, his Elias Kane novels, *The Psychopath Plague* and *The Imperator Plot*, which bear a superficial resemblance to Asimov's Elijah Baley series, are well plotted, well written, and entertaining. Elias, a former Navy lieutenant, is highly intelligent, possessed of eidetic memory, and has spent years in various educational institutions studying, among other things, psychology, criminology, physics, and biology. A superman he is not, for he makes the kind of errors caused by human fallibility and emotion, a touch that obviously draws heavily on Spruill's background as clinical psychologist.

In *The Psychopath Plague* for some unknown reason people are being seized by a compulsion to maim or even kill anyone who happens to be nearby. The computers predict a rate of increase in outbreaks that will soon alter Earth society beyond reclamation. Despite the usual false clues and attempts to stop him that are common to such works, Elias, aided by the

Cephantine Pendrake, locates the source of the contamination, pinpoints the criminals, and wins his true love Elizabeth, the million-credit reward, and the gratitude of the Imperator, who rules Earth and the nine, sometimes rebellious, colonies.

In *The Imperator Plot* three years of happiness with Elizabeth end when Elias is summoned by the Imperator to head the investigation of an assassination plot. Unfortunately the assassin strikes first, Elizabeth dies saving Elias, and the Imperator, his body destroyed, is saved only because his personal physician, Martha Reik, quickly attaches his uninjured head to an advanced life support system. The extent of the real plot is uncovered only after a long series of harrowing experiences and sidetracks, during which Elias learns much about himself and humanity.

What lifts these novels from the ordinary is often at first reading almost unnoticeable. Thus, in *The Psychopath Plague* only further reflection shows parallels between a seemingly insignificant conversation about the difference between perception and reality, between the human being's belief that his or her thoughts can control behaviour and the view of all other intelligent creatures in the galaxy that this belief is irrational and that it is really environment, physical, mental, and emotional, that controls all behavior, including that of humanity. Since the attack on Earth is alien, partly physical and partly through the tremendous mental powers of the innocent-appearing invaders, it is a nice touch that this discussion is conducted with a friendly alien not yet identified as part of the problem.

In *The Imperator Plot* the significance of the demands of the bodiless head for a new body, for a way to experience the pleasure of eating, even the desire for a human touch on its forehead, is not at first obvious. Only later do certain questions arise: How would the Imperator deprived of all sensation accept the situation? What would be the effect on his behaviour? How does it affect his Ornyl bodyguard? An integral part of the solution is Elias's own experience of a temporary total sensory deprivation and his subsequent understanding of both self and the Ornyl.

Spruill's human characters are well developed and believable, their actions made plausible by the motivations established early on. He also has an inventive turn of mind where aliens are concerned, and some of his creations are most interesting: Pendrake, the Cephantine, is an orange-skinned giant of enormous strength from a species known for its inability to permit violence or death, empathetic with all plant and animal life, and respected as incapable of uttering a falsehood; his absolute loyalty to Elias who has gambled him out of slavery is a major ingredient in the successful investigations. The musal trees have overrun their planet with their roots and eliminated the fauna except for two species; they use one of these, the humanoid Krythians, to create technical devices and serve as bodyguards to the illusory, comical, penguin-like traders, the Chirpones, who actually carry out their plot. The Moitans, "fish-people," are an advanced technological civilization. The Ornyls, humanoid giant insects, are fierce warriors; their binding to their chosen masters in irrevocable and complete. In every case the behavior of these aliens is consistent with the internal psychology established for them when they first appear on the scene.

Spruill writes well, invents interesting plots, and uses his own technical knowledge effectively. He is a comparative newcomer to science fiction, but he appears to have a major career in the field awaiting him.

—Arthur O. Lewis

STABLEFORD, Brian M(ichael). Also writes as Brian Craig. British. Born in Shipley, Yorkshire, 25 July 1948. Educated at Manchester Grammar School; University of York, B. A. (honours) in biology 1969, D. Phil, in sociology 1979. Married Vivien Owen in 1973; one son and one daughter. Lecturer in Sociology, University of Reading, Berkshire, 1976 and since 1977. Address: 113 St. Peter's Road, Reading, Berkshire RG6 1PG, England.

SCIENCE-FICTION PUBLICATIONS

Novels (series: Daedalus; Dies Irae; Hooded Swan)

Cradle of the Sun. New York, Ace, and London, Sidgwick and Jackson, 1969.
The Blind Worm. New York, Ace, and London, Sidgwick and Jackson, 1970.
The Days of Glory (Dies Irae). New York, Ace, and Manchester, Five Star, 1971.
In the Kingdom of the Beasts (Dies Irae). New York, Ace, 1971; London, Quartet, 1974.
Day of Wrath (Dies Irae). New York, Ace, 1971; London, Quartet, 1974.
To Challenge Chaos. New York, DAW, 1972.
Halcyon Drift (Swan). New York, DAW, 1972; London, Dent, 1974.
Rhapsody in Black (Swan). New York, DAW, 1973; London, Dent, 1975.
Promised Land (Swan). New York, DAW, 1974; London, Dent, 1975.
The Paradise Game (Swan). New York, DAW, 1974; London, Dent, 1976.
The Fenris Device (Swan). New York, DAW, 1974; London, Pan, 1978.
Swan Song. New York, DAW, 1975; London, Pan, 1978.
Man in a Cage. New York, Day, 1975.
The Face of Heaven. London, Quartet, 1976.
The Mind-Riders. New York, DAW, 1976; London, Fontana, 1977.
The Florians (Daedalus). New York, DAW, 1976; London, Hamlyn, 1978.
Critical Threshold (Daedalus). New York, DAW, 1977; London, Hamlyn, 1979.
The Realms of Tartarus. New York, DAW, 1977.
Wildeblood's Empire (Daedalus). New York, DAW, 1977; London, Hamlyn, 1979.
The City of the Sun (Daedalus). New York, DAW, 1978; London, Hamlyn, 1980.
The Last Days of the Edge of the World (for children). London, Hutchinson, 1978; New York, Berkley, 1985.
Balance of Power (Daedalus). New York, DAW, 1979; London, Hamlyn, 1984.
The Walking Shadow. London, Fontana, 1979.
The Paradox of Sets (Daedalus). New York, DAW, 1979.
Optiman. New York, DAW, 1980; as *War Games*, London, Pan, 1981.
The Castaways of Tanagar. New York, DAW, 1981.
Journey to the Center. New York, DAW, 1982.
The Gates of Eden. New York, DAW, 1983.

Uncollected Short Stories

"Beyond Time's Aegis" (as Brian Craig, with Craig Mackintosh), in *Science Fantasy* (Bournemouth), November 1965.

"The Man Who Came Back," in *SF Impulse* (London), October 1966.
"Inconstancy," in *SF Impulse* (London), February 1967.
"Prisoner in the Ice," in *Vision of Tomorrow* (Newcastle upon Tyne), November 1969.
"Story with a Happy Ending," in *Science Fiction Monthly* (London), June 1974.
"Sad Story," in *Science Fiction Monthly* (London), August 1974.
"An Offer of Oblivion," in *Amazing* (New York), December 1974.
"The Sun's Tears," in *The 1975 Annual World's Best SF*, edited by Donald A. Wollheim. New York, DAW, 1975.
"Judas Story," in *The Year's Best Horror Stories 3*, edited by Richard Davis. New York, DAW, 1975.
"The Conqueror," in *Science Fiction Monthly* (London), April 1975.
"The Engineer and the Executioner," in *The 1976 Annual World's Best SF*, edited by Donald A. Wollheim. New York, DAW, 1976.
"Captain Fagan Died Alone," in *The DAW Science Fiction Reader*, edited by Donald A. Wollheim. New York, DAW, 1976.
"Skinned Alive," in *Weekend Fiction Extra* (London), September 1978.
"Mortification of the Flesh," in *Ad Astra* (London), vol. 1, no. 5, 1979.
"Security," in *Western Mail* (Cardiff), 24 November 1979.
"Second Chance," in *Pictures at an Exhibition*, edited by Ian Watson. Cardiff, Greystoke Mobray, 1981.
"Verstehen," in *Pilger durch Raum und Zeit*, edited by P. Wilfert. Munich, Goldmann, 1982.

OTHER PUBLICATIONS

Other

"The Evolution of Science Fiction," in Beyond This Horizon, edited by Christopher Carrell. Sunderland, Ceolfrith Press, 1973.
"The Robot in Science Fiction," in *Vector* (Reading), July-August 1973.
"Machines and Inventions," in *Vector* (Reading), Spring 1974.
"SF: A Sociological Perspective," in *Fantastic* (New York), March 1974.
"SF: The Nature of the Medium," in *Amazing* (New York), August 1974.
"The Social Role of Science Fiction," in *Algol* (New York), Summer 1975.
"The Metamorphosis of Robert Silverberg," in *Science Fiction Monthly 3* (London), 1976.
"William Watson's Prospectus for Science Fiction," in Foundation 10 (London), June 1976.
"Opening Minds," in *Vector* (Reading), August-September 1976.
"Edgar Fawcett," in *Vector* (Reading), November-December 1976.
The Mysteries of Modern Science. London, Routledge, 1977; Totowa, New Jersey, Littlefield Adams, 1980.
"Insoluble Problems: Barry Malzberg's Career in Science Fiction," in Foundation 11-12 (London), March 1977.
"Icaromenippus; or, The Future of Science Fiction," in *Vector* (Reading), May-June 1977.
"The Needs and Demands of the Science Fiction Reader," in *Vector* (Reading), September-October 1977.

"The Marriage of Science Fiction," in *Encyclopedia of Science Fiction*, edited by Robert Holdstock. London, Octopus, and Baltimore, Hoen, 1978.

"Science Fiction and the Image of the Future," in *Foundation 14* (London), September 1978.

"Scientific Imagination in Literature 1-4," in *Social Biology and Human Affairs* (London), vol. 43, no. 1, 1978; vol. 45, no. 1, 1980; vol. 48, no. 1, 1983; vol. 48, no. 2, 1983.

"Locked in the Slaughterhouse: The Novels of Kurt Vonnegut," in *Arena* (Canterbury), September 1978.

"The Best of Hamilton and Brackett," in *Vector* (Reading), November-December 1978.

A Clash of Symbols: The Triumph of James Blish. San Bernardino, California, Borgo Press, 1979.

"Notes Toward a Sociology of Science Fiction," in *Foundation 15* (London), January 1979.

"Social Design in Science Fiction," in *Amazing* (New York), February 1979.

"The Utopian Dream Revisited: Socioeconomic Speculation in the SF of Mack Reynolds," in *Foundation 16* (London), May 1979.

"The Future Between the Wars: The Speculative Fiction of John Gloag," in *Foundation 20* (London), October 1980.

Masters of Science-Fiction: Essays on Science-Fiction Authors. San Bernardino, California, Borgo Press, 1981.

Bob Shaw. N. p., British Science Fiction Association, 1981.

The Science in Science Fiction, with Peter Nicholls and David Langford. London, Joseph, 1982; New York, Knopf, 1983.

"The Realistic Romances of Edgar Fawcett," in *Foundation 24* (London), February 1982.

"Man-Made Catastrophe in SF," in *The End of the World*, edited by Eric S. Rabkin, Martin H. Greenberg, and Joseph D. Olander. Carbondale, Southern Illinois University Press, 1983.

"The Politics of Evolution: Philosophical Themes in the Speculative Fiction of M. P. Shiel," in *Foundation 27* (London), February 1983.

"Against the New Gods: The Speculative Fiction of S. Fowler Wright," in *Foundation 29* (London), November 1983.

Future Man: Brave New World or Genetic Nightmare? London, Granada, and New York, Crown, 1984.

"Future Wars 1890-1950," in *Metaphones*, no. 9-10, 1984.

"Marxism, SF and the Poverty of Prophecy," in *Foundation 32* (London), November 1984.

The Sociology of Science Fiction. San Bernardino, California, Borgo Press, 1985.

The Third Millennium: A History of the World AD 2000-3000, with David Langford. London, Sidgwick and Jackson, and New York, Knopf, 1985.

Scientific Romance in Britain. London, Fourth Estate, 1985.

Articles in *The Science Fiction Encyclopedia* edited by Peter Nicholls, New York, Doubleday, and London, Granada, 1979; *Survey of Science Fiction Literature*, 5 vols., 1979, *Critical Survey of Short Fiction*, 1981, *Survey of Modern Fantasy Literature*, 1983, *Critical Survey of Long Fiction*, 1983, and *Critical Survey of Long Fiction (Foreign-Language Writers)*, 1984, all edited by Frank N. Magill, Englewood Cliffs, New Jersey, Salem Press; *Anatomy of Wonder* edited by Neil Barron, New York, Bowker, 2nd edition, 1981; *Science Fiction Writers*, 1983, and *Supernatural Fiction Writers*, 1985, both edited by E. F. Bleiler, New York, Scribner; *The Science Fiction Source Book* edited by David Wingrove, New York, Van Nostrand Reinhold, 1984.

*   *   *

Prolific in his reviews and criticism of science fiction, Brian M. Stableford is likely to be better remembered for them than for most of his fiction.

He writes genuine science-fiction novels, whole-heartedly adopting the conventions, devices, motifs, and themes that characterize space opera or galactic adventure. He adopts these elements with gusto, interweaving among them elements of modern detective, western, and mystery stories. What he does, he does well; a Stableford novel is always an interesting read, entertaining and engaging if not intellectually profound or thought-provoking. A biologist and sociologist by training, he uses his learning well to provide background material for his tales, but he does not seem to want to explore the ramifications of the social, biological, or ecological systems he is good at creating. Critics and reviewers generally agree that Stableford will raise important questions: he will query, for instance, the nature of Mankind and its place in the Universe, only to have his cynical central character utter a wise-acre crack that sidetracks the thought. It is true the sarcasm and cynicism ordinarily reflect his hero's hard-boiled nature, but the promise of a realistically drawn person considering significant relations of important human concerns never materializes, and the character remains a prop. Nonetheless, Stableford by impulse and by training seems to have more in him than he lets out in his fiction; this impression may very well indicate that he has an idea that the purpose of fiction is more to entertain than to philosophize. And this thesis seems to be borne out simply by the content, the volume, and the general excellence of his reviewing and criticism.

The general assertions made above are supported by a quick look at Stableford's major efforts in the novel. The earliest important novel was *Halcyon Drift*. One of the six "Swan" novels, it is formula science fiction. The main character, the cynical Grainger—a kind of hard-boiled space pilot—crashes or an out-of-the-way planet and before being rescued becomes symbiotic host to a benevolent parasite. The Earth he returns to is as morally empty as the social life of one of those detectives on whom Stableford seems to have modelled Grainger. Accepting a job to find a lost spaceship, Grainger experiences various adventures, finds the ship, and destroys its cargo in fidelity to a promise made to an old alien colleague who helped in the quest but who did not survive. Grainger thus satisfies a need to vent his anger at the injustice and stupidity of the human race. He escapes easily from various dangers and relaxes until another commission comes along. The story contains rich thematic possibilities for exploration: the degeneration of Earth-side institutions is hinted at, and the ship Grainger uses in his quest, the "Hooded Swan," is imaginatively conceived, as is the reaction of the jungle on the planet Hallsthammer to the presence of forms of life alien to it. But none of these and other interesting possibilities is developed or explored.

The same phenomenon occurs in the other five novels of this series and in the more recent works. For instance, the recent novel *Journey to the Center* features a hard-boiled hero of the Grainger type, and *The Gates of Eden* is a mystery story; both are ultimately judged unsuccessful by most critics. Although the premises are interesting and the backgrounds are well worked out, the stories seem finally too formulaic and appear to be hurried toward conclusion so that the deeper significance of the people and situations are left unexplored. As one reviewer pointed out, Stableford does not seem to want to take his art seriously. He is, consequently, among the best of the light adventure science fiction writers, and he brings to the genre an ease with the conventions of other popular literary genres such as the mystery and the western.

But his copious criticism and his reviews are not to be faulted.

To his criticism he brings a strong craftman's awareness, and he bolsters this awareness with the sense of place and time he derives from his professional training as a sociologist.

—Alexander J. Butrym

STALLMAN, Robert. American. Born in 1930. *Died in August 1980.*

SCIENCE-FICTION PUBLICATIONS

Novels (series: The Beast)

The Book of the Beast:
1. *The Orphan.* New York, Pocket Books, 1980; London, Granada, 1981.
2. *The Captive.* New York, Pocket Books, 1981; London, Granada, 1982.
3. *The Beast.* New York, Pocket Books, 1982; as *The Book of the Beast*, London, Granada, 1982.

* * *

Robert Stallman's exquisite fantasy novel *The Orphan* was published in March 1980. By August 1980 he was dead of cancer at fifty. He had completed two more volumes of the series, published posthumously, *The Captive* and *The Beast.* The vangard novel, *The Orphan*, would have been enough: it was so good that it was nominated for a Hugo Award in 1981—a great honor because it was the only work of fiction that Stallman wrote.

Summarized very superficially, the three volumes of the Book of the Beast narrate the four-year maturation process of an other-worldly creature and the mate who will finally join him in love. *The Orphan* begins in mid-1930's south-western Michigan at the farm of Catherine and Martin Nordmeyer, where the "Beast" appears for the first time and "shifts" into the person of Robert Lee Burney, a boy of about five. Robert is adopted by the kindly Nordmeyers. So begins the kinship of the Beast and the matriarchal line of Aunt "Cat" as the six major episodes of the three volumes unfold. With Aunt Cat and her husband Martin, Robert/Beast begin to mature. But the idyllic summer months end in tragedy when drifters terrorize the Nordmeyers and Martin is killed by an errant shotgun blast, even as the Beast, shifting from Robert's five-year-old person to its physically and mentally superhuman self, intervenes to save the family. Witnessing the connection between the Beast and Robert, Aunt Cat, driven insane with grief at the loss of Martin, hounds it until it flees and arrives in Illinois as early teen-aged Charles Cahill to live with Grandmother Stumway, Aunt Cat's mother. Charles goes to school for the year, at the end of which the Beast, in a fit of springtime lust, is discovered coupling, as Charles, with a cow. He shifts to Beast and flees to Chicago. *Orphan* is a stunning work.

In *The Captive* the beast joined with the person of Barry Golden, falls in love with Rene, daughter of Aunt Cat. Rene's alcoholic husband, William Hegel, nearly succeeds in killing Barry in a car/train wreck. Shifted into Beast, however, Barry/Beast survive, only to be held in captivity in an open cage by a farmer. Escaped and reunited with Rene (divorced from William), Barry, Rene and her daughter Mina move to Arizona.

All is not finally well until Barry/Beast rescue kidnapped Rene and Mina from William and his American-Nazi training cell mustered in the mountains. In *The Beast* the Beast's female partner-to-be saves the life of George (Bo) Beaumont from cancer. Bo is the father of Charles Cahill of *The Orphan.* Bo believes Charles is dead in his early teens. Charles is dead, provisionally. But the Beast can make Charles live if Bo wishes, though Bo must relinquish the life of a woman he loves in exchange. Bo chooses Charles's life. The two beasts finally get together in a mystical marriage, leaving Bo reunited with his resurrected son, and Barry, also permanently resurrected, with Rene and Mina.

The adventure of the Beast in *The Orphan* is a pristine metaphor. The successor volumes, *The Captive* and *The Beast*, provide ethers, metaphysics, transcendence, and substantial explanation. Ironically, they are lesser in quality than *The Orphan* just because their purpose is to finish its story and to explain its vision. Aesthetic considerations aside, the three volumes together are in initiation story, a tale of a Beast's quest that tells us, thereby, about human quests. It is full of lovely natural-state settings and objects plucked from contexts by the super senses of the Beast to convey a feeling of seeing the essence of the landscapes, the flora, the animals—indeed the very furniture and trinkets in the Nordmeyer farm house. It evokes many wonderful traditional motifs. Principally there is the shape-shifter tale such as that about the bear-man in the ancient Icelandic Grettissaga, and reused by Tolkien in the Beorn character of *The Hobbit.* We may also remember R. L. Stevenson's *The Strange Case of Dr. Jekyll and Mr. Hyde*, or think of Robert Silverberg's sinister tale "Passengers." It recalls "beauty and the beast" stories. It erects an occult universe and, in the relationship of the Beast to its "persons," reinterprets notions of the golem and zombie. The basic narrative gives the reader humor, cleverness, and, best of all and mostly, unposturing clarity.

In a telephone interview Mrs. Stallman has spoken of her husband's interest in the Jungian notion of a collective unconscious. The suggestion is helpful in an attempt to explain what a meaning of the story might be. Surely the elegance of the tale is rooted in the daring simple obviousness of its theme. The theme is a progress that beings, "there is a Beast in all of us . . . ." It feels and tastes things more sensually. It is physically stronger. It is smarter. Its appetites are keener—for food, for sex, for beauty. It loves music. It is the foundation of our emotions. It is the source of our creative drive. In the story the Beast might be the novelist himself—is, in fact, when he is personed with writer Barry Golden. The Beast is always trying to fit itself into the human world. It participates in virtually all of our meaningful existence. But it is not us. It is not human. It can be a guiltless maverick to our human ideas of order and morality. It is amoral, yet innocent. It is heedlessly curious, willing to learn what may be fatally dangerous for humans to know. Therefore, it is a mistake to imagine that humanity and Beast are an identity—or even a unity. People are always human. Beasts are only Beasts.

—John R. Pfeiffer

STAPLEDON, (William) Olaf. British. Born near Wallasey, Cheshire, 10 May 1886. Educated at Abbotsholme School; Balliol College, Oxford, M. A. 1909; University of Liverpool, Ph. D. 1925. Served in the Friends' Ambulance Unit in France,

1916-19. Married Agnes Zena Miller in 1919; one son and one daughter. Assistant Headmaster, Manchester Grammar School, 1910; worked for Alfred Holt and Company, shippers, Liverpool and Port Said, 1911; Lecturer in History and English, Workers' Educational Association, University of Liverpool, 1912-15; after World War I, Lecturer in Philosophy and Psychology, University of Liverpool. *Died 6 September 1950.*

SCIENCE-FICTION PUBLICATIONS

Novels

Last and First Men: A Story of the Near and Far Future. London, Methuen, 1930; New York, Cape and Smith, 1931.
Last Men in London. London, Methuen, 1932; Boston, Gregg Press, 1976.
Odd John. London, Methuen, 1935; New York, Dutton, 1936.
Starmaker. London, Methuen, 1937; New York, Berkley, 1961.
Darkness and the Light. London, Methuen, 1942; Westport, Connecticut, Hyperion Press, 1974.
Sirius. London, Secker and Warburg, 1944; included in *To the End of Time*, 1953.
Death into Life. London, Methuen, 1946.
The Flames. London, Secker and Warburg, 1947.
Worlds of Wonder (includes *The Flames; Death into Life; Old Man in New World*). Los Angeles, Fantasy, 1949.
A Man Divided. London, Methuen, 1950.
To the End of Time: The Best of Olaf Stapledon, edited by Basil Davenport. New York, Funk and Wagnalls, 1953.
Nebula Maker. Hayes, Middlesex, Bran's Head, 1976; New York, Dodd Mead, 1982.
Nebula Maker and Four Encounters. New York, Dodd Mead, 1983.

Short Stories

Old Man in New World. London, Allen and Unwin, 1944.
Four Encounters. Hayes, Middlesex, Bran's Head, 1976.
Far Future Calling: Uncollected Science Fiction and Fantasies, edited by Sam Moskowitz. Philadelphia, Trainer, 1980.

OTHER PUBLICATIONS

Verse

Latter-Day Psalms. Liverpool, Young, 1914.

Other

A Modern Theory of Ethics: A Study of the Relations of Ethics and Psychology. London, Methuen, and New York, Dutton, 1929.
Waking World. London, Methuen, 1934.
New Hope for Britain. London, Methuen, 1939.
Saints and Revolutionaries. London, Heinemann, 1939.
Philosophy and Living. London, Penguin, 2 vols., 1939.
Beyond the "Isms." London, Secker and Warburg, 1942.
The Seven Pillars of Peace. London, Common Wealth, 1944.
Youth and Tomorrow. London, St. Botolph, 1946.
The Opening of the Eyes, edited by Agnes Z. Stapledon. London, Methuen, 1954.

*

Bibliography: *Olaf Stapledon: A Bibliography* by Harvey J. Satty and Curtis C. Smith, Westport, Connecticut, Greenwood Press, 1984.

Critical Studies: *Olaf Stapledon* by Patrick A. McCarthy, Boston, Hall, 1982; *Olaf Stapledon, A Man Divided* by Leslie A. Fiedler, New York and Oxford, Oxford University Press, 1983.

*   *   *

Between the age of Verne and Wells and the Golden Age of American science fiction in the 1940's, the greatest achievement in the genre belongs, without much question, to Olaf Stapledon. Future history, galactic wars and empires, sympathetic presentation of alien psychologies and cultures, science and technology conceived critically in their reaction upon society (and even upon sexuality), man's mind itself seen as radically mutating, evolving toward a trans-earthly destiny either tragic or superhuman (or both), and in that evolution exploring the depths of time and space in the quest to find some ultimate meaning in the Universe—these themes and motifs enter the genre, or receive for the first time ample and serious treatment, in Stapledon's work.

Last and First Men, the most ambitious and systematic of future histories, is also memorable as the first attempt in science fiction to create a full-scale apocalyptic "myth" (Stapledon's own term in his Preface). Man's future is projected here through unprecedented magnitudes of time and change, not because of some compulsive need in Stapledon to write a "titanic" book, but because only a vast, flexibly protean counter-myth could challenge effectively the dominant patterns of belief—orthodoxies both of right-wing religion and left-wing politics—that he saw usurping the sense of the future in his time. Not from any irrepressible pessimism in himself but to demolish—or shock awake—such complacencies among his readers, Stapledon has his First Men perish after a few more millennia of steadily degenerating civilization. World-unity of a sort, the First World State, is achieved, but only through a tyrannous, super-technologized culture. After several million years, the Second Men emerge, gifted with larger bodies and more acute senses, but these amiable semi-Utopian giants fail to reconcile their will to universal human communion with their cosmic awareness, especially after that awareness is fatally darkened by a long and hopeless conflict with invading, biologically alien, intelligent "clouds" from Mars. Not until the Last Men, sixteen species later—that is, almost two billennia and several interplanetary migrations later—do we learn in retrospect what the controlling model of transcendence, the ideal relationship of human will to cosmic reality, is in Stapledon's myth.

The Last (Eighteenth) Men are, in one sense, the First of Men—the first to attain full humanity, to "awaken" thoroughly from animal "sleep," to develop latent powers of both body and mind beyond man's evolutionary childhood to something like "maturity. " The great civilization that flowers on Neptune succeeds in remaking man's nature by correcting the tragic imbalance of powers, and especially the will to overtranscendence, of the earlier species (e. g., the abstract intellectuality of the Fourth Men, the love of tragic "ecstasy" that lures the Flying Men on Venus to racial suicide). Although their bodies are made superstrong by artificial atoms, man's mammalian sexuality has not now been left behind but enlarged and enhanced in sensibility, so as to become the sympathetic basis of world-community. The "racial mind" achieved on Neptune is thus both—and equally—human and "astronomical" in its modes of consciousness; it has both psychic and electromagnetic dimension, capable of reaching telepathically far out into galactic space and far back through historical time (hence the virtual omniscience, where the past is concerned, of the narrator, one of the Last Men). The supreme test of this transcendent "spirit" comes when radiation from a supernova dooms the Neptunian race to extinction: they plan to "seed" the galaxy with artificial life-spores but they themselves—and with them the entire human past—cannot escape obliteration. What enables the Neptunians to meet, and even "salute," this fate without despair is not only their tragic wisdom about the cosmos but a renewed influx of animal courage and "loyalty to life," gained from telepathic interaction with the primitive minds of the First Men. It is really therefore the indomitable will of all humanity in time that speaks through the well-known words of the young prophet, last-born of the Last Men, which close Stapledon's epic "symphony":

> Man himself, at the very least, is music, a brave theme that makes music also of its vast accompaniment, its matrix of storms and stars. . . . It is very good to have been mad. And so we may go forward together with laughter in our hearts, and peace, thankful for the past, and for our own courage. For we shall make after all a fair conclusion to this brief music that is man.

Starmaker takes the mythic history of "spirit" beyond the solar system into all space and time. This may not be, as Stapledon himself thought, his best book but it is certainly his most marvellously inventive. The first-person narrator (we may think of him as Stapledon) finds himself magically transported from a suburban hillside at night on a disembodied journey to the stars, where he is soon joined by like-minded spirits from other worlds. At first the telepathic abilities of the travellers are limited to their own level of experience—to their sympathetic awareness of "the human crisis" that results whenever a planet's civilization develops transcendent consciousness and struggles toward world-community. Very few of these worlds achieve Utopia; most succumb to war or cataclysm; and even many of those that emerge triumphantly from the crisis lapse into a "mad" imperialism of galactic conquest. A true community of "minded worlds" is at last realized, but its survival is not assured until the traumatic discovery that stars, too, are "living minds." Only after this breakthrough does the ever-enlarging communion of spiritual travellers become the multi-galactic "cosmical mind"—and only then does the narrator, now the "I" of this supremely human spirit, attain the long-sought vision of the Star Maker. Himself evolving, this neo-Bergsonian yet teleology-minded Deity, experimenting with one cosmos after another (our own, a middling success, occurs about halfway through His education) may be Stapledon's boldest and most brilliant but not therefore his best invention in the book. The Creator-God of this cosmos seems to me surpassed, even in sublimity, by many of its psychozoic creatures (the Nautiloids, the Plant Men, the symbiotic Arachnids and Ichthyoids). More indifferent Star than man-inspiring God, the Star Maker remains, almost by definition, a loveless Deity, despite Stapledon's insistence that He is worthy of "adoration." And at the end this ambiguity of attitude seems to have become intentional. For when the traveler returns to his suburban hill, he finds that he needs "two lights for guidance," the human and the astral, living radiances linked in a symbiosis of "spirit." The human warmth of "our little glowing atom of community" is defined and valued by its dialectical contrast with "the cold light of the stars," in whose "crystal ecstasy . . . even the dearest love is frostily assessed."

Stapledon's later drift toward mysticism, which takes increasingly religious (though always agnostic) form after *Starmaker*, was first strongly evident in *Odd John*. Between his two myth-histories Stapledon wrote two novels—the first of which, *Last Men in London*, generally fails to wed philosophical fantasy (his Last Man narrator reappears here as a time-explorer trying to "influence" a young First Man's mind) with autobiographical realism (the novel faithfully reproduces Stapledon's experiences before and during World War I). The second novel, *Old John*, has become, however, a justly popular classic of the genre because it dramatizes both the good and evil latent in the post-Nietzschean myth of the Superman. The intrepid, ultra-intelligent John (he too acquires telepathic powers) is in many ways a hero, even a martyr, of Stapledonian "spirit," and the island-colony in the Pacific that he establishes with other "super-normals" is, in its organization and way of life, a model of Stapledon's philosophical ideal of "Personality-in-Community." But in the effort to make his colony secure and viable John commits a series of tactical murders, with little or no remorse; and such acts would have been for Stapledon (not in this book to be confused with his narrator, a rather servile hero-worshipper) violations of the only surely real vehicale of spirit, namely, "human personality," without reverence for which no society can long endure. And such is the fate awaiting John's colony, which rapidly perishes—or vanishes. Hopelessly threatened by all the world's powers, the colonists blow themselves up, confident that the "music" of their minds, their immortal being, is destined for new and greater realms of Spirit.

What is tragically wrong with John is clear by contrast with Stapledon's protagonist in the last of his four major works of fiction. The eponymous hero of *Sirius* is a hero without hands—and therefore free of the supple-handed John's delusions of power through manipulations of men and their world. Sirius is a huge Alsatian sheepdog, with an artificially mutated brain capable of reaching all but the very highest levels of human intelligence. Like John, Sirius rebels against his human conditioning, but this time the will to transcendence is informed by a passional commitment to love (love of Plaxy, the girl with whom he has been raised as an "equal") and by profounder intuitions of "spirit," gained through this love and the life-sympathies of his animal being. Yet, again not unlike John, Sirius never reconciles the two halves of his being; he continually succumbs to a violent "wolf-madness" seemingly rooted in his nature. And at the end, as Plaxy stands in the moorland dawn over the dead body of her lover—he has been hunted down by a rifle-armed pack of human wolves—we are left looking more to the skies than to earth for hope.

The theme of divided consciousness, of an insuperable, darkly ambiguous contradiction in man's nature, haunts most of Stapledon's fiction in his last decade. It appears throughout *Darkness and the Light*, where man's future prospects for good and evil are divided into alternate time-streams, and even the Utopian triumph of the Light scenario is threatened by inscrutable forces of cosmic Darkness. It is much less apparent in the exceptional *Death into Life*, neither a novel nor a myth-narrative so much as a work of visionary rhetoric designed to promote the belief that death is a passage to higher forms of cosmically immortal Spirit. It returns with a vengeance in *The Flames*, a novella of ambiguous fantasy, where the protagonist, a mental patient, may be hallucinating or actually encountering (at the end he dies mysteriously in a fire) a race of flame-like beings—self-declared aborigines of the Sun, in some ways spokesman of Stapledonian "spirit" yet also lethally dangerous to man and his planet. The theme finds consummation in the semi-autobiographical novel *A Man Divided,* a Psychic Double story, where the philosophically awakened Victor struggles unsuccessfully with his "doltish" other self, who in turn rebels against the former's "beatitude," until both perish together in an act of suicide, despite the efforts of the loving Maggie to save both her husbands.

Offsetting the decline of Stapledon's prophetic confidence in his last years was a generally finer command of the art and craftsmanship of fiction. First strikingly apparent in *Sirius,* which is perhaps his most aesthetically satisfying fiction, the greater range and variety of his literary skills are most observable in several fantastic short stories written in this period (or slightly earlier)—three of which, "A Modern Magician," "Arms Out of Hand," and "The Man Who Became a Tree," show Stapledon succeeding impressively in a form that he had hitherto avoided. Not that Stapledon in the 1930's was ever a stylistically incompetent writer, as he is sometimes said to be. The theme of the myth-histories necessarily demanded prose of a certain rarefied abstraction and austerity of feeling. And if his purely narrative talents were then sometimes weak, his poetic and dramatic powers—the powers, in a word, of a gifted myth-maker's imagination—were always demonstrably present. Certainly if his literary abilities had not been in large measure commensurate with his intellectural originality, Stapledon would never have exercised so great an influence on, or have won the continued admiration of, so many science-fiction writers in our time, most notably Clifford D. Simak, Cordwainer Smith, Arthur C. Clarke, Brian W. Aldiss, Ursula K. Le Guin, and Stanislaw Lem.

—John Kinnaird

STASHEFF, Christopher. American. Born in Mt. Vernon, New York, in January 1944. Educated at the University of Michigan, Ann Arbor, B. A. 1965, M. A. 1966; University of Nebraska, Lincoln, Ph. D. in theater 1972. Married Mary Miller in 1973; three daughters and one son. Instructor, 1972-77, and since 1977, Assistant Professor of Speech and Theater, Montclair State College, New Jersey. Agent: Spectrum Literary Agency, 432 Park Avenue South, New York, New York 10016. Address: Department of Speech and Theater, Montclair State College, Upper Montclair, New Jersey 07043, U.S.A.

SCIENCE-FICTION PUBLICATIONS

Novels (series: Rod Gallowglass)

The Warlock in Spite of Himself (Gallowglass). New York, Ace, 1969.
King Kobold (Gallowglass). New York, Ace, 1971; revised edition, as *King Kobold Revived*, 1984.
A Wizard in Bedlam. New York, Doubleday, 1979; London, Mayflower, 1982
The Warlock Unlocked (Gallowglass). New York, Ace, 1982.
Escape Velocity (Gallowglass). New York, Ace, 1983.
The Warlock Enraged (Gallowglass). New York, Ace, 1985.

OTHER PUBLICATIONS

Plays

The Three-Legged Man (produced Lincoln, Nebraska, 1970).

Cotton-Eye Joe (produced Lincoln, Nebraska, 1970).
Joey Win (produced Lincoln, Nebraska, 1971).

*

Christopher Stasheff comments:

I'm not concerned with the novel as an end in itself, but as a means towards the end of trying to awaken the audience to an awareness of the issues I consider important, and to convey some vital facts and a few opinions. I'm also trying to reverse some trends I discern in popular literature, which I believe to be detrimental to us as people and as society. But none of this will do any good if no one reads it; so, first and foremost, I try to entertain.

* * *

Christopher Stasheff wrote a wild and ribald mixture of science fiction and fantasy with his first novel, the fabulous *The Warlock in Spite of Himself.* Rodney d'Armond, who renames himself Rod Gallowglass, and his goofy robot, Fess, arrive on Gramarye, a planet where magic works. Their mission is to bring democracy to this feudal society. They find themselves kidnapped by elves, encounter ghosts and goblins, and meet other legendary creatures. Gallowglass falls in love with a lovely witch and saves Gramayre from a force from the future who are intent on preserving Gramarye's feudalism. All of this is told in a bold, swashbuckling style with great humor. *The Warlock in Spite of Himself* is more than a successful blending of science fiction and sword and sorcery; it is wonderful entertainment.

The original sequel to *The Warlock in Spite of Himself, King Kobold,* received negative reviews, chiefly from Lester del Rey who was reviewer for *Worlds of If.* When Stasheff's publishers wanted to re-release the book, Stasheff insisted on rewriting the book to take into account del Rey's criticisms. The rewritten book, *King Kobold Revived,* is better than the original 1971 edition. Rod Gallowglass has to save Gramarye from an evil band of time-travelling Neanderthals who are the latest weapon in the transtemporal wars. To defeat them, Gallowglass needs the assistance of a power witch and a clever wizard; however, the plot revolves around their reluctance to get involved and Gallowglass's attempts to recruit them.

The Warlock Unlocked carries the story farther: Gramarye is still threatened by sinister time-travelers, and Rod Gallowglass is its main defender. The plot centers around the attempt to cause a rift between the Church and the State. Rod Gallowglass is cunningly trapped and sent with his family to an alternate world. There he must defeat wicked elves and monsters before he can return to Gramarye to save it from ruin.

Escape Velocity is a "prequel" to the Warlock series and answers some of the questions about Gramayre's origin. But too much of the action takes place on decadent Earth, and the lead characters, Dar and Samantha, tend to deliver speeches on sociopolitics rather than engage in the glib dialog Stasheff is famous for.

The Warlock in Spite of Himself remains Stasheff's best book with each sequel or prequel diminished from the original vision. Stasheff's lone non-series book, *A Wizard in Bedlam,* reworks Stasheff's themes about bringing democracy to a feudal planet and lacks the charm of the Warlock books.

—George Kelley

STATTEN, Vargo. See **FEARN, John Russell.**

———————

STEBER, A. R. See **PALMER, Raymond A.; PHILLIPS, Rog.**

———————

STEELE, Morris J. See **PALMER, Raymond A.**

———————

STEFFANSON, Con. See **GOULART, Ron.**

———————

STEPHENSON, Andrew M(ichael). British. Born in Maracaibo, Venezuela, 8 October 1946. Educated at Rottingdean Pre-Preparatory School, Sussex, 1956-60; Stowe School, Buckinghamshire, 1960-65; City University, London, B. Sc. (honours) in electrical and electronic engineering 1969. Design engineer, Plessey Telecommunications Research, Taplow, Buckinghamshire, 1969-76. European Representative, Science Fiction Writers of America, 1976-78. Lives in High Wycombe, Buckinghamshire. Agent: Frances Collin, Marie Rodell-Frances Collin Literary Agency, 110 West 40th Street, New York, New York 10018, U.S.A.

SCIENCE-FICTION PUBLICATIONS

Novels

Nightwatch. London, Futura, 1977; New York, Dell, 1979.
The Wall of Years. London, Futura, 1979; New York, Dell, 1980.

Uncollected Short Stories

"Holding Action," in *Analog* (New York), 1971.
"The Giant Killers," in *Andromeda 1*, edited by Peter Weston. London, Futura, 1976; New York, St. Martin's Press, 1979.

*

Andrew M. Stephenson comments:
The notion of making any sort of introductory statement on my work repels me: it feels as though I am being required to define what I wrote about, whereas the work itself is sufficient definition. All I will say is that I am content to be described (where relevant) as a writer of science fiction, provided my works are judged on their *individual* merits, not as samples of "science fiction," whatever that may be.

*   *   *

Andrew M. Stephenson began his career in SF as an illustrator. "The Giant Killers," like *Nightwatch*, is highly technophilic but at the same time possesses a deep concern and sensitivity for human and animal suffering. Whereas in the short story man is seen at war against himself, in the novel he is seen pitted against an alien intruder. It is a competent if unoriginal novel about semi-sentient machines and their creator, set mainly on the moon.

A much lengthier and far more successful novel is *The Wall of Years*, moulding together two traditional SF themes—time travel and parallel worlds—into a story which is both convincing and compelling. Experiments into parallel worlds reveal that there are nearby worlds of possibility and that the majority of these are engaged in warfare. The bonds that separate the worlds break and they begin to intermingle. As the world falls into chaos some humans escape into the future of the 26th century where they set about trying to stabilise their own history (in this alternate world). The protagonist, Jerlan Nilssen, goes back to the time of Alfred the Great to ensure that history is not changed by an outside agency which might wish to see the future city destroyed. Stephenson ties the plot threads tightly together and manages to portray accurately the clash between modern and 9th-century worldviews. There is, again, a marked sensitivity, but with a much more defined skill in the writing. The crudity of the dark ages is well drawn, and the nobility is subdued as Stephenson leads us through the laws of necessity that govern behaviour in those times. By comparison, the world of the 21st century (the time of the break-up of reality as the parallel worlds impose upon one another) is not so well focused, and seems to hint that Stephenson's future direction may be toward historical fiction, or like Keith Roberts, toward charting parallel worlds based on the past.

With a quite clear command over the intricacies of plot and a constantly improving style, Andrew M. Stephenson appears one of the most promising of the young British SF writers, although his reputation at present rests upon a single book.

—David Wingrove

———————

STERLING, Brett. See **HAMILTON, Edmond.**

———————

STERLING, Bruce. American. Born in Brownsville, Texas, 14 April 1954. Educated at the University of Texas, Austin, 1972-76, B. A. in Journalism 1976. Married Nancy Baxter in 1979. Agent: Merrilee Heifetz, Writers House, 21 West 26th Street, New York, New York 10010. Address: 809-C West 12th Street, Austin, Texas 78701, U.S.A.

SCIENCE-FICTION PUBLICATIONS

Novels

Involution Ocean. New York, Jove, 1977; London, New English Library, 1980.
The Artificial Kid. New York, Harper, 1980; London, Penguin, 1985.
Schismatrix. New York, Arbor House, 1985.

Uncollected Short Stories

"Man-Made Self," in *Lone Star Universe*, edited by George W.

Proctor and Steve Utley. Austin, Texas, Heidelberg, 1976.
"Spider Rose," in *Fantasy and Science Fiction* (New York), August 1982.
"Cicada Queen," in *Universe 13*, edited by Terry Carr. New York, Doubleday, 1983.
"Swarm," in *The Nebula Awards 18*, edited by Robert Silverbert. New York, Arbor House, 1983.
"Spook," in *Fantasy and Science Fiction* (New York), April 1983.
"Red Star, Winter Orbit," with William Gibson, in *Omni* (New York), July 1983.
"Twenty Evocations: Life in the Mechanist/Shaper Era," in *Interzone* (Leeds) Spring 1984.
"Sunken Gardens," in *Omni* (New York), June 1984.
"Telliamed," in *Fantasy and Science Fiction* (New York), September 1984.
"The Unfolding," with John Shirley, in *Interzone* (Leeds), Spring 1985.
"Dinner in Audoghast," in *Isaac Asimov's Science Fiction Magazine* (New York), May 1985.

*   *   *

Although not prolific, Bruce Sterling is one of the most respected younger sf writers. Part of this reputation is due to Sterling's apparent self-assurance; even his early writing is deft in structure and cooly precise in style. He seems to believe in himself. Actually, even in his first publications (*Involution Ocean* and *The Artificial Kid*), Sterling began exploring the very nature of self-control as his protagonists gain experience and self-knowledge in bizarre future secieties. Each character must adjust to so many unsettling situations that it would be comforting if he could find someone else who has found a way to interpret experience and act effectively. Instead, the young narrators see that older people generally drift toward death because they have tried different beliefs and roles until no faith is convincing enough to hold their attention. The few old men who do manage to cling to one purpose do so with a foolish fanaticism that also leads to death. At first, Sterling's protagonists escape confusion by using drugs (*Involution Ocean*) or edited versions of experience (*The Artificial Kid*) to give themselves an illusion of controlled action pursuing significant goals. When events strip them of their illusions, they must begin to explore the notion of commitment. They come to realize how much any belief depends on lies or contrivance, but they also recognize that humans cannot long exist without belief.

From the beginning of his career, then, Sterling was grappling with a major human concern: believing in a set of values gives consciousness a center but narrows it; how can one gain the focus that faith makes possible without the accompanying destructiveness? Sterling considers this repeatedly in his series of short stories describing the struggle between the Shapers (who have restructured people through biosciences) and the Mechs (who augment human powers through mechanical means). Each of these movements, the factions they spawn, and the subfactions *they* produce, attempts to dominate the race after most of "humanity" has abandoned Earth and begun to spread through space. In form, the stories give glimpses of events that readers must strain to intrepret and connect. In substance, the stories focus on characters who attempt to find something that they can confidently assert in their confusing milieu. Conclusions tend to be somewhat equivocal, as in "Swarm," which challenges readers' comfortable assumption that humanity equals exploring, intelligence equals mastery. With wit and ironic ambiguity, Sterling describes the multiplicity of beliefs that develop as human consciousness is fragmented.

The Shaper series concludes with *Schismatrix*, in which Sterling shows one man's trying out many identities and beliefs. Even though the book does explain the future history into which the Shaper stories fit, this remains so complex that the reader (like Sterling's hero) is challenged to grasp nuances and adapt to them rapidly, avoiding both confusion and staleness. No one faith finally satisfies Sterling's protagonist. The important thing is that his wide sympathy and flexibility eventually make him a fit companion for a Presence that has observed humanity's development but disdains the idea of taking part in its unrestricted evolution even if that might lead to godlike consciousness and power: "I want what I already have! Eternal wonder, eternally fulfilled . . . . Not the eternal even, just the Indefinite, that's where all the beauty is . . . . I'll wait out the heat-death of the Universe to see what happens next! And in the meantime, isn't it something, all of it?"

That statement may or may not be Sterling's own final position, but it certainly does reflect his central subject: the wonder of the "human" response to experience, the fascinating ways people liberate or limit themselves. In his latest short fiction, such as "Dinner in Audoghast," he continues to examine a debate between different human certainties, showing how small "certainties" lead to cruelty because they are determinedly ignorant of others.

Thanks to his ability to center on a key human concern with intelligence and skill, Bruce Sterling already has created an impressively mature body of work. He is not satisfied. He considers himself just past the "apprentice" stage of his career. Almost certainly, his future work will disturb readers' complacency with even greater impact. As the protagonist of *The Artificial Kid* concludes, "Just wait till the Kid grows up."

—Joe Sanders

STEVENS, Francis. Pseudonym for Gertrude Barrows Bennett. American. Born in Minneapolis, Minnesota, 18 September 1884. Widow; one daughter. Disappeared in September 1939.

SCIENCE-FICTION PUBLICATIONS

Novels

The Heads of Cerberus. Reading, Pennsylvania, Polaris Press, 1952.
Claimed! New York, Avalon, 1966.
The Citadel of Fear. New York, Paperback Library, 1970.

Uncollected Short Stories

"The Nightmare," in *All-Story* (New York), 14 April 1917.
"Behind the Curtain," in *All-Story* (New York), 7 September 1918.
"The Elf Trap," in *Argosy* (New York), 5 July 1919.
"Serapion," in *Argosy* (New York), 19 June—10 July 1920.
"Sunfire," in *Weird Tales* (Chicago), July-August, September 1923.
"Friend Island," in *Under the Moons of Mars*, edited by Sam Moskowitz. New York, Harper, 1970.

"Unseen—Unfeared," in *Horrors Unknown*, edited by Sam Moskowitz. New York, Walker, 1971.

*   *   *

The body of writing for which the name Francis Stevens is remembered was published during a span of little more than six years (1917-23), and was probably written in an even shorter period. Gertrude Barrows Bennett, the woman who used the pseudonym Francis Stevens, wrote under pressure of economic necessity, and stopped when the immediate need for extra income was removed. Through the years those readers who have fallen under the spell of her remarkable fantasies have had cause to regret not only the premature cessation of her fiction-writing, but also the fact that some already-completed work remained unpublished (and is now presumed to be lost).

Francis Stevens wrote mainly for *All-Story* and *Argosy* magazines during the same period in which the first of A. Merritt's fantasies were published. It has been said that some readers thought Francis Stevens was a pen-name of Merritt's. The conjecture could just as easily have gone the other way, for when Steven's first major novel, *The Citadel of Fear*, appeared, Merritt had published only a few short works. Merritt was, in fact, a great admirer of Stevens's work, and was instrumental in having several of her stories reprinted during the 1940's. Although the first part of *The Citadel of Fear*, which takes place in the lost city of Tlapallan in an uncharted corner of Mexico, is superficially similar to Merritt's work, Stevens replaced Merritt's romantic/tragic outlook with a much more down-to-earth viewpoint. The story, while forfeiting none of its appeal as an exotic lost-race adventure, is told with liveliness and humor, to which the hints of darker things form an effective counterpoint. In the latter two-thirds of the novel, the very real and concrete evil of Tlapallan reappears in the quiet American countryside, and a succession of mysterious events builds up to a climactic confrontation between supernatural forces.

The second of Francis Stevens's three major works, *The Heads of Cerberus*, was serialized in *The Thrill Book* in 1919. Like *The Citadel of Fear* the novel opens with an episode of Merrittesque fantasy, involving a substance called the Dust of Purgatory which transports people into the strange alternate world of Ulithia. But once the main characters have passed through Ulithia and find themselves in a future Philadelphia in the year 2118, the novel becomes political and social satire of a high order. The two parts of the novel fit somewhat oddly together, but each is so good in itself that one is willing to accept the discontinuity between them. In the introduction to the Polaris Press edition, P. Schuyler Miller is quoted as saying that the novel "can be read as perhaps the first work of fantasy to envisage the parallel-time-track concept, with an added variation that so far as I know has not been reused since"—the idea that times moves at different rates in the alternate tracks.

The third of Stevens's important works is *Claimed!* Here the focus of attention is a carved oblong box found on a volcanic island in the Atlantic. The box comes into the possession of millionare Jesse Robinson, whose creed is, "What I want, I get—and what I get, I keep. " The novel tells, in a straightforward narrative without any of the subplots or side-trips evident in earlier works, of the attempts at recovery of the box by the supernatural being who had created it many thousands of years in the past.

Three novels by Francis Stevens have so far appeared only in magazine form. Her first work was the short novel "The Nightmare," of which Stevens herself said that its only merit was "a rather grotesque originality. " "Serapion" is a grim and powerful story of psychic possession which stands up well in comparison to more recent works on the same theme. "Sunfire" was a return to both the lost-race fantasy and the light-hearted narrative style of earlier works.

Of Stevens's short works, "Friend Island" is notable for its background of a future world when women are the dominant gender, but the story itself is little more than an extended joke. (It is probably nothing more than coincidence that the byline "Francis Stevens" appeared on a story called "The Curious Experience of Thomas Dunbar" in the March 1904 issue of *Argosy*.)

—R. E. Briney

STEWART, George R(ippey). American. Born in Sewickley, Pennsylvania, 31 May 1895. Educated at Pasadena High School, California; Princeton University, New Jersey, A. B. 1917 (Phi Beta Kappa); University of California, Berkeley, M. A. 1920; Columbia University, New York, Ph. D. 1922. Served in the United States Army Ambulance Service, 1917-19; civilian technician, United States Navy, 1944. Married Theodosia Burton in 1924; one daughter and one son. Instructor, University of Michigan, Ann Arbor, 1922-23. Member of the English Department from 1923, Professor of English, 1942-62, then Emeritus, University of California. Taught at the University of Michigan, summer 1926, Duke University, Durham, North Carolina, summer 1939; Fellow in Creative Writing, Princeton University, 1942-43; Fulbright Professor, University of Athens, 1952-53. Recipient: International Fantasy Award, 1951; American Association for State and Local History Award, 1963; Hillman Award, 1969. L. H. D. : University of California, 1963. *Died 22 August 1980.*

SCIENCE-FICTION PUBLICATIONS

Novel

Earth Abides. New York, Random House, 1949; London, Gollancz, 1950.

OTHER PUBLICATIONS

Novels

East of the Giants. New York, Holt, 1938; London, Harrap, 1939.
Doctor's Oral. New York, Random House, 1939.
Storm. New York, Random House, 1941; London, Hutchinson, 1942.
Fire. New York, Random House, 1948; London, Gollancz, 1951.
Sheep Rock. New York, Random House, 1951.
The Years of the City. New York, Random House, 1955.

Other

The Technique of English Verse. New York, Holt, 1930.
Bret Harte, Argonaut and Exile. Boston, Houghton Mifflin, 1931.
A Bibliography of the Writings of Bret Harte in the Magazines and Newspapers of Calilfornia 1857-1871. Berkeley, University of California Press, 1933.

Ordeal by Hunger: The Story of the Donner Party. New York, Holt, and London, Cape, 1936; revised edition, Boston, Houghton Mifflin, 1960.

English Composition. New York, Holt, 2 vols., 1936.

John Phoenix, Esq. New York, Holt, 1937.

Take your Bible in One Hand: The Life of William Henry Thomes. San Francisco, Colt Press, 1939.

Names on the Land. New York, Random House, 1945; revised edition, Boston, Houghton Mifflin, 1958, 1967.

Man: An Autobiography. New York, Random House, 1946; London, Cassell, 1948.

The Year of the Oath: The Fight for Academic Freedom at the University of California, with others. New York, Doubleday. 1950.

U. S. 40. Boston, Houghton Mifflin, 1953.

American Ways of Life. New York, Doubleday, 1954.

To California by Covered Wagon (for children). New York, Random House, 1954.

N. A. 1: The North-South Continental Highway. Boston, Houghton Mifflin, 1957.

Pickett's Charge. Boston, Houghton Mifflin, 1959.

Donner Pass and Those Who Crossed It. San Franciso, California Historical Society, 1960.

The California Trail. New York, McGraw Hill, 1962; London, Eyre and Spottiswoode, 1964.

Committee of Vigilance: Revolution in San Francisco 1851. Boston, Houghton Mifflin, 1964.

This California, photographs by Michael Bry. Berkeley, California, Diablo Press, 1965.

Good Lives. Boston, Houghton Mifflin, 1967.

The Department of English of the University of California on the Berkeley Campus. Berkeley, University of California, 1968.

Not So Rich as You Think. Boston, Houghton Mifflin, 1968.

American Place-Names. New York, Oxford University Press, 1970.

Names on the Globe. New York, Oxford University Press, 1975.

American Given Names: Their Origin and History in the Context of the English Language. New York, Oxford University Press, 1979.

Editor, *The Luck of Roaring Camp and Selected Stories and Poems*. by Bret Harte. New York, Macmillan, 1928.

Editor, *Map of the Emigrant Road from Independence, Missouri, to St. Francisco*, by T. H. Jefferson. San Francisco, California Historical Society, 1945.

Editor, *The Opening of the California Trail*, by Moses Shallenberger. Berkeley, University of California Press, 1953.

*

Manuscript Collection: Bancroft Library, University of California, Berkeley.

Critical Study: *George R. Stewart* by John Caldwell, Boise, Idaho, Boise State University, 1981.

*   *   *

In 1951, George R. Stewart received the first of the International Fantasy Awards for *Earth Abides*, the only one of his novels to fall into the SF genre. He is also the author of non-fiction works which, like his novels, all touch on some aspect of American history or culture.

Earth Abides inverts the famous story of Ishi, the last wild Indian in North America, a story recently retold by Theodora

Kroeber in *Ishi in Two Worlds* (1962). Ishi, the last member of the Yahi, a tribe of California Indians long thought to be extinct, emerged from his Stone Age world to live in the early 20th-century world of trolley cars and electric lights. He was rescued by an anthropologist at the University of California, and taken to live in its Museum of Anthropology, then located in San Francisco, where he passed his remaining years. He showed the anthropologists the native Yahi way of making and hunting with a bow and arrow, and of making fire. With these lessons Ishi paid his way and enjoyed the fruits of civilization, which for him were mainly glue (for the easier feathering of arrows) and matches. His name in Yahi means "man. "

The hero of *Earth Abides* is named Ish, which in Hewbrew also means "man. " Ish is one of a very few to survive a pandemic disease to see civilization collapse and his descendants return to the life of Stone Age hunters like that of Ishi. Ish is the last of the civilised Americans as Ishi is the last of the aboriginal Americans. Naked, hungry, and weakened by snake bite, the real Ishi stumbled into industrial America on 29 August 1911. The last of the Yahi, he wandered down from his native hills into the corral of a slaughter-house near Oroville, California. There he fell exhausted, was jailed as a "wild man," was finally recognised for what he was, and taken to the museum in San Francisco. Weakened by snake bite, the fictional Ish stumbles out of the same hills into a dead civilization, its populace almost wiped out by some deadly virus. He had been studying the ecology of the Sacramento Valley, Ishi's tribal home, for a master's degree at the University of California. Throughout the novel, Ish watches with ecological detachment the transformation of a world emptied of men.

He returns to his home in a suburb of San Francisco, overlooking the Golden Gate bridge. The few survivors he gathers around him facetiously call themselves the "Tribe. " Everybody forages in stores for food and other goods, trying to maintain the old way of life under new conditions. One couple brings home a bridge lamp and a fancy radio set, even though no electricity is available. Even Ish, the only one to think about the future, teaches spelling and arithmatic, although the world is so depopulated it cannot sustain occupational specialities based on literacy. At last Ish realises the futility of his classroom lessons and school is dismissed. He then teaches the children a game, which he knows will have to become a way of life once there are no more store goods to scavenge: he teaches them how to make and use the bow and arrow, and how to make fire without matches, the same technology he knew from his study of anthropology to have been the basis for sucessful living by our pre-civilized ancestors.

In time, the tribe departs the crumbling ruins of San Francisco. By then Ish is an old man and the tribe, now skilled hunters, sets out to cross the bridge to new lands. Crossing the bridge, Ish slows to a stop. Before he dies, he reflects on the course of human history and the fate of his grandchildren and others of their generation, who squat in a half circle around him. "They were very young in age, at least by comparison with him, and in the cycle of mankind they were many thousands of years younger than he. He was the last of the old; they were the first of the new. But whether the new would follow the course which the old had followed, that he did not know. " But the moral of the novel is certain. Inverting the story of Ishi, Stewart dramatises the humanistic fact that man is man, be he civilised or tribal; that a Stone Age culture is just as valid a setting for being human as is an industrial culture.

—Leon Stover

STEWART, Will. See **WILLIAMSON, Jack.**

STINE, G. Harry. See **CORREY, Lee.**

STINE, Hank (Henry Eugene Stine). American. Born in Sikeston, Missouri, 13 April 1945. Married Christine Annette Kindred in 1966 (divorced, 1968); one child. Film director; Editor, *Galaxy*, 1978-79. Editor, Starblaze Books, Norfolk, Virginia. Agent: Jeremy P. Tarcher Inc., 9110 Sunset Boulevard, Suite 250, Los Angeles, California 90069, U.S.A.

SCIENCE-FICTION PUBLICATIONS

Novel

Season of the Witch. New York, Essex House, 1968.

Uncollected Short Story

"No Exit," in *Fantastic* (New York), June 1971.

OTHER PUBLICATIONS

Novels

Thrill City. New York, Essex House, 1969.
The Prisoner: A Day in the Life (novelization of TV series). New York, Ace, 1970; London, Dobson, 1979.
The Prisoner 2: A Day in the Life (novelization of TV series). London, Dobson, 1979.

* * *

Hank Stine's *Season of the Witch* included a moodpiece "Postscript" by Harlan Ellison, was given a warm welcome by the few critics who found it, and then allowed to drift into obscurity. It is notable as a special combination of science fiction and pornagraphic detail and rhetoric. The quality of the novel artistically justifies this radical strategy and invites association with other well-known peices of science fiction that have employed it. In *Season of the Witch* Andre Fuller rapemurders Josette Kovacs under the influence of a hallucinogen. He is punished in a low-population civilization by having his brain put into his victim's body. His own body is given to someone else. He/she, as Celeste Fuller, begins an odyssey in which, after confusion and pain, Celeste makes a new and happy life as a woman and a wife. Plot and setting are minimal. The story combines dramatic narrative and stream-of-consciousness in a tight control of point-of-view that vividly exposes the painful psychological transformation of Fuller from male to female. The shock to the male psyche directly experiencing the vulnerability of the female body is stunningly revealed. The pornographic elements of the novel can titillate only briefly before the reader is plunged into the agony of the ordeal. Where science fiction as well as pornography are often male chauvinist, the novel might raise male consciousness.

Explicit sexual descriptions as well as sex-changing effects are not rare in important science fiction works. They appear in such novels as Theodore Sturgeon's *Venus Plus X*, Norman Spinrad's *Bug Jack Barron*, Robert Heinlein's *I Shall Fear No Evil*, ike Dolinsky's *Mind One*, David Gerrold's *The Man Who Folded Himself*, and Sam Delany's *Dhalgren*.

—John R. Pfeiffer

STOCKTON, Frank R. (Francis Richard Stockton). American. Born in Philadelphia, Pennsylvania, 5 April 1834. Educated at Zane Street School, 1840-48, and Central High School, 1848-52, both in Philadelphia. Married Marian Edwards Tuttle in 1860. Apprenticed as a wood-engraver in 1852, and worked as an engraver until 1870. Assistant Editor, *Hearth and Home*, 1868-73, and *St. Nicholas* magazine, 1873-78, both New York. Regular contributor to *Scribner's Magazine.* Died 20 April 1902.

SCIENCE-FICTION PUBLICATIONS

Novels

The Great War Syndicate. New York, Collier, and London, Longman, 1889.
The Great Stone of Sardis. New York and London, Harper, 1898.

Short Stories

The Science Fiction of Frank R. Stockton, edited by Richard Gid Powers. Boston, Gregg Press, 1976.

OTHER PUBLICATIONS

Novels

The Late Mrs. Null. New York, Scribner, and London, Sampson Low, 1886.
The Hundredth Man. New York, Century, and London, Sampson Low, 1887.
The Stories of the Three Burglars. New York, Dodd Mead, and London, Sampson Low, 1890.
The Merry Chanter. New York, Century, and London, Sampson Low, 1890.
Ardis Claverden. New York, Dodd Mead, and London, Sampson Low, 1890.
The House of Martha. Boston, Houghton Mifflin, and London, Osgood, 1891.
The Squirrel Inn. New York, Century, and London, Sampson Low, 1891.
Pomona's Travels. New York, Scribner, and London, Cassell, 1894.
The Adventures of Captain Horn. New York, Scribner, and London, Cassell, 1895.
Mrs. Cliff's Yacht. New York, Scribner, and London, Cassell, 1896.
The Girl at Cobhurst. New York, Scribner, and London, Cassell, 1898.
The Novels and Stories. New York, Scribner, 23 vols., 1899-1904.

A Bicycle in Cathay. New York, Harper, 1900.
The Captain's Toll Gate, edited by Marian E. Stockton. New York, Appleton, and London, Cassell, 1903.

Short Stories

Rudder Grange. New York, Scribner, 1879; Edinburgh, Douglas, 1883.
The Lady or the Tiger? and Other Stories. New York, Scribner, and Edinburgh, Douglas, 1884.
The Transferred Ghost. New York, Scribner, 1884.
The Casting Away of Mrs. Lecks and Mrs. Aleshine. New York, Century, and London, Sampson Low, 1886.
The Christmas Wreck and Other Stories. New York, Scribner, 1886; as *A Borrowed Month and Other Stories,* Edinburgh, Douglas, 1887.
The Dusantes. New York, Century, and London, Sampson Low, 1888.
Amos Kilbright, His Adscititious Experiences, with Other Stories. New York, Scribner, and London, Unwin, 1888.
The Rudder Grangers Abroad. New York, Scribner, and London, Sampson Low, 1891.
The Watchmaker's Wife and Other Stories. New York, Scribner, 1893; as *The Shadrach and Other Stories,* London, W. H. Allen, 1893.
A Chosen Few. New York, Scribner, 1895.
A Story-Teller's Pack. New York, Scribner, and London, Cassell, 1897.
The Associate Hermits. New York and London, Harper, 1898.
The Vizier of the Two-Horned Alexander. New York, Century, and London, Cassell, 1899.
Afield and Afloat. New York, Scribner, and London, Cassell, 1901.
John Gayther's Garden. New York, Scribner, and London, Cassell, 1903.
The Magic Egg and Other Stories. New York, Scribner, 1907.
Stories of New Jersey. New Brunswick, New Jersey, Rutgers University Press, 1984.

Other (for children)

Ting-a-Ling. Boston, Hurd and Stoughton, 1870; London, Ward and Downey, 1889.
Roundabout Rambles in Lands of Fact and Fancy. New York, Scribner, 1872.
What Might Have Been Expected. New York, Dodd Mead, 1874; London, Routledge, 1875.
Tales Out of School. New York, Scribner, 1875.
A Jolly Friendship. New York, Scribner, and London, Kegan Paul, 1880.
The Floating Prince and Other Fairy Tales. New York, Scribner, and London, Ward and Downey, 1881.
Ting-a-Ling Tales. New York, Scribner, 1882.
The Story of Viteau. New York, Scribner, and London, Sampson Low, 1884.
The Bee-Man of Orn and Other Fanciful Tales. New York, Scribner, 1887; London, Sampson Low, 1888.
The Queen's Museum. New York, Scribner, 1887.
Personally Conducted. New York, Scribner, and London, Sampson Low, 1889.
The Clocks of Rondaine and Other Stories. New York, Scribner, and London, Sampson Low, 1892.
Fanciful Tales, edited by Julia E. Langworthy. New York, Scribner, 1894.
Captain Chap; or, The Rolling Stones. Philadelphia, Lippincott,

and London, Nimmo, 1896; as *The Young Master of Hyson Hall,* Lippincott, 1899.
New Jersey, from the Discovery of the Scheyichbi to Recent Times. New York, Appleton, 1896; as *Stories of New Jersey,* New York, American Book Company, 1896.
The Buccaneers and Pirates of Our Coasts. New York, Macmillan, 1898.
Kate Bonnet. New York, Appleton, and London, Cassell, 1902.
Stories of the Spanish Main. New York, Macmillan, 1913.
The Poor Count's Christmas. New York, Stokes, 1927.

*

Critical Study: *Frank R. Stockton* by Martin I. J. Griffin, Philadelphia, University of Pennsylvania Press, 1939 (includes bibliography).

* * *

Frank R. Stockton's science fiction has been neglected in histories of the field, perhaps because his literary reputation has suffered such eclipse in this century (he was highly praised during his life-time), and because science fiction was only a small part of his literary output. Except in his two important novels, *The Great War Syndicate* and *The Great Stone of Sardis,* his science fiction was light and humorous popular magazine fiction. A recent collection, *The Science Fiction of Frank R. Stockton,* assembles all his SF stories (and *The Great Stone of Sardis*), and the introduction by Richard Gid Powers is notable for its disdain for his lack of "seriousness."

Most of Stockton's SF stories have a similar plot: a gentleman amateur wins fame and fortune and gets the girl by means of an invention. This is true in "My Terminal Moraine," *The Great Stone of Sardis,* "My Translatophone," and, to a certain extent, "A Tale of Negative Gravity." The remainder are fantasies laced with contemporary science: "The Water Devil" concerns the trans-Atlantic cable and a ship whose cargo is electricity; "Amos Kilbright" is a ghost story: "The Knife That Killed Po Hancy" is a Jekyll and Hyde story concerning blood transfusions. Powers points out that *The Great Stone of Sardis* (the stone is a great diamond at the earth's core) combines Jules Verne's books *Journey to the Center of the Earth* and *The Adventures of Captain Hatteras* in a novel of polar exploration (Clewes, the amateur scientist/hero is first to reach the North Pole) and geological theory (Clewes invents an "Artesian Ray" to explore the interior of the earth). Clewes's adventures (set in 1947) are a significant contribution to the development of the "wonders of science" novel.

Stockton's major novel, however, is *The Great War Syndicate.* Although not mentioned in I. F. Clarke's *Voices Prophesying War,* Stockton's novel of a war between the US and England, fought using such new technology as an ultimate weapon (a disintegrator), is perhaps the most important SF novel in the "future war" tradition between *The Battle of Dorking* (1871) and *The War of the Worlds* (1898). World peace, capitalism, and the English language are enforced by an Anglo-American syndicate using the threat of ultimate destruction. The novel surpasses its many contemporaries, which characteristically dealt with politics, military tactics, and unimaginative technology (with minor innovations such as a new gun which would cause tactics to change) and were warnings clothed in fictional attributes. *The Great War Syndicate* is a true science-fiction vision of a new world created by a war to end war and a weapon to end war, the archetype of that naive hope which led to the building and use of the first atomic bombs and the "pax Americana."

That Stockton's immediate followers in this mode were for the most part popular hacks (e. g., George Griffith) has not enhanced his reputation as progenitor. However, despite its failings as a novel (principally a lack of adequate characterization), *The Great War Syndicate* repays serious examination.

—David G. Hartwell

STORM, Eric. See **TUBB, E. C.**

STRATFORD, H. Philip. See **BULMER, Kenneth.**

STRATTON, Thomas. See **COULSON, Robert; DE WEESE, Gene.**

STRETE, Craig (Kee). American. Born in Fort Wayne, Indiana, 6 May 1950; son of a Cherokee Indian father. Educated at Wright State University, Dayton, Ohio, B. A. in theatre arts 1974; University of California, Irvine, M. F. A. 1978. Married to Countess Irmgard Margaretha Christina Von Dam. Since 1980, foreign rights and international acquisitions editor, De Knipscheer, Amsterdam, and Rogner & Bernhard, Munich. Editor, *Red Planet Earth*, 1974-75; Managing Editor, *East West Players Newsletter*, 1984-85. Co-Founder and Director, Society of Ethnic Literature in Translation. Agent: (novels) Kirby McCauley Ltd., 432 Park Avenue South, Suite 1509, New York, New York 10016; (juveniles) Curtis Brown Ltd., 10 Astor Place, New York, New York 10003. Address: P.O. Box 9487, North Hollywood, California 91609, U.S.A.

SCIENCE-FICTION PUBLICATIONS

Short Stories

Als Al het Andere Faalt. Amersterdam, Knipscheer, 1976; expanded edition, as *If All Else Fails*, New York, Doubleday, 1980.
The Bleeding Man and Other Science Fiction Stories (for children). New York, Greenwillow, 1977.
Dreams That Burn in the Night. New York, Doubleday, 1982.

OTHER PUBLICATIONS

Novel

Burn Down the Night. New York, Warner, 1982.

Plays

Paint Your Face on a Drowning in the River (produced Los Angeles, 1984).
A Sunday Visit with Great Grandfather, and The Arrow That Kills with Love (produced New York, 1984).

Screenplays: *Killing Moves*, 1975; *Honor Code*, 1976; *Blodets Röst*, 1978; *Sous les toits de nuit*, 1978.

Television Plays (under pseudonyms): for *Streets of San Francisco*, *Baretta*, and *McCloud* series.

Verse

In Geronimo's Doodkist. Amsterdam, Knipscheer, 1978.
Dark Journey. Amsterdam, Knipscheer, 1979.

Other (for children)

Paint Your Face on a Drowning in the River. New York, Greenwillow, 1978.
Oom Coyote en de Bisonpizza. Amsterdam, Knipscheer, 1978.
When Grandfather Journeys into Winter. New York, Greenwillow, 1979.
Spiegel je gezicht. Amsterdam, Knipscheer, 1979.
Twee Spionnen in het Huis van de Liefde. Amsterdam, Knipscheer, 1981.
Met de Pijn die het Liefheeft en Haat. Amsterdam, Knipscheer, 1983.

*   *   *

Craig Strete has the flamboyance of R. A. Lafferty and Norman Spinrad, combining flights of fantasy with intense social criticism. He capitalizes on his Indian heritage in theme, motif, humor, plot, story-telling technique, and subjects of social criticism, leaning heavily on the mythic to generate a felling of universality. His works are relatively short and indicate fascination with the sound and rhythm of sentences, giving the poetic effect of the native American oral tradition. Exaggeration, word play, and comic, low-key dialogue are characteristic. Because he often omits transitions, becomes pyrotechnical, and demands close attention, Strete is not to be read rapidly.

Strete's recurrent theme is society's attempt to mold human beings into productive working parts of the white man's big world machine. What does not work is thrown out (the old man of "Time Deer"), or put to better use, providing blood for transfusions ("Bleeding Man") or adding color to movies ("A Horse of a Different Technicolor"). "Bleeding Man," his most conventionally narrated work, is most illustrative of the clash that occurs when emotionless bureaucracy meets the supernatural. On one level, it is a parable of the policy of first making war with Indians and then studying them. "Time Deer" similarly contrasts values. "A Horse of a Different Technicolor," a horror story of mind control, and "Why Has the Virgin Mary Never Entered the Wigwam of Standing Bear?" attack materialism and forced conformity, using television as a metaphor for the regimented spectator/consumer life. In fact, the stories published in *The Bleeding Man* frequently refer to cultural conflict and genocide.

Strete's novels for children, published under the name Craig Kee Strete, though not science fiction, should be taken into account as contributing to understanding the more complex stories. In "Paint Your Face on a Drowning River" Old Cat tells his grandson, who is about to leave the reservation, about his early life. The story is part of "Time Deer" and prophetic of the young man's life in the white world.

—Mary S. Weinkauf

STURGEON, Theodore (Hamilton). Also wrote as Frederick R. Ewing; Ellery Queen. American. Born Edward Hamilton Waldo in Staten Island, New York, 26 February 1918; name changed on adoption, 1929. Attended Overbrook High School, Philadelphia. Married 1) Dorothy Fillingame in 1940, two daughters; 2) Mary Mair in 1949; 3) Marion Sturgeon in 1951, four children; 4) Wina Golden in 1969, one son. Salesman in early 1930's; seaman, 1935-38; hotel manager, West Indies, 1940-41; assistant chief steward for U. S. Army, 1941; bulldozer operator, Puerto Rico, 1942-43; advertising copy editor, 1944; literary agent, 1946-47; circulation staff member, *Fortune* and *Time,* New York, 1948-49; story editor, *Tales of Tomorrow,* 1950; feature editor, 1961-64, and contributing editor, 1972-74, *If,* New York; television writer, 1966-75. Book reviewer, *Venture,* 1957-58, *Galaxy,* 1972-74, and New York *Times,* 1974-75; columnist, *National Review,* New York, 1961-73. Recipient: *Argosy* prize, 1947; International Fantasy award, 1954; Nebula Award, 1970; Hugo Award, 1971. Guest of Honor, 20th World Science Fiction Convention, 1962. *Died 8 May 1985.*

SCIENCE-FICTION PUBLICATIONS

Novels

The Dreaming Jewels. New York, Greenberg, 1950; London, Nova, 1955; as *The Synthetic Man,* New York, Pyramid, 1957.
More Than Human. New York, Farrar Straus, 1953; London, Gollancz, 1954.
The Cosmic Rape. New York, Dell, 1958.
Venus Plus X. New York, Pyramid, 1960; London, Gollancz, 1969.
Voyage to the Bottom of the Sea (novelization of screenplay). New York, Pyramid, 1961.
. . . and My Fear Is Great; Baby Is Three. New York, Universal, 1965.

Short Stories

"It." Philadelphia, Prime Press, 1948.
Without Sorcery. Philadelphia, Prime Press, 1948.
E Pluribus Unicorn. New York, Abelard Press, 1953; London, Abelard Schuman, 1960.
Caviar. New York, Ballantine, 1955; London, Sidgwick and Jackson, 1968.
A Way Home. New York, Funk and Wagnalls, and London, Mayflower, 1955.
Thunder and Roses. London, Joseph, 1957.
A Touch of Strange. New York, Doubleday, 1958; London, Hamlyn, 1978.
Aliens 4. New York, Avon, 1959.
Beyond. New York, Avon, 1960.
Not Without Sorcery. New York, Ballantine, 1961.
Sturgeon in Orbit. New York, Pyramid, 1964; London, Gollancz, 1970.
The Joyous Invasions. London, Gollancz, 1965.

Starshine. New York, Pyramid, 1966; London, Gollancz, 1968.
Sturgeon Is Alive and Well. New York, Putnam, 1971.
The Worlds of Theodore Sturgeon. New York, Ace, 1972.
To Here and the Easel. London, Gollancz, 1973.
Case and the Dreamer. New York, New American Library, 1973; London, Pan, 1974.
Visions and Venturers. New York, Dell, 1978; London, Gollancz, 1979.
Maturity. Minneapolis, Science Fiction Society, 1979.
The Golden Helix. New York, Doubleday, 1979.
The Stars Are the Styx. New York, Dell, 1979.
Slow Sculpture. New York, Pocket Books, 1982.
Alien Cargo. New York, Bluejay, 1984.

OTHER PUBLICATIONS

Novels

I, Libertine (as Frederick R. Ewing). New York, Ballantine, 1956.
The King and Four Queens. New York, Dell, 1956.
Some of Your Blood. New York, Ballantine, 1961; London, Sphere, 1967.
The Player on the Other Side (as Ellery Queen). New York, Random House, 1963.
The Rare Breed. New York, Fawcett, 1966.

Short Stories

Sturgeon's West. New York, Doubleday, 1973.

Plays

It Should Be Beautiful (produced Woodstock, New York, 1963?).
Psychosis: Unclassified, adaptation of his novel *Some of Your Blood* (produced 1977).

Radio Plays: *Incident at Switchpath,* 1950; *The Stars Are the Styx,* 1953; *Mr. Costello Here,* 1956; *Saucer of Loneliness,* 1957; *The Girl Had Guts, The Skills of Xanadu,* and *Affair with a Green Monkey,* all in the 1960's; *More Than Human,* 1967.

Television Plays: *Mewhu's Jet* and *The Adoptive Ultimate,* from fiction by Stanley Weinbaum (*Beyond Tomorrow* series), *They Came to Bagdad,* from the novel by Agatha Christie (*Playhouse 90* series), *Ordeal in Space,* from story by Robert Heinlein, and *The Sound Machine,* from story by Roald Dahl (both *CBS Stage 14* series)—all 1950's; *Dead Dames Don't Dial* (*Schlitz Playhouse* series), 1959; *Shore Leave,* 1966, and *Amok Time,* 1967 (both *Star Trek* series); *Killdozer!,* with Ed MacKillop, from the story by Sturgeon, 1974; *The Pylon Express* (*Land of the Lost* series), 1975-76.

Other

"Why I Selected Thunder and Roses," in *My Best Science Fiction Story,* edited by Leo Margulies and O. J. Friend. New York, Merlin Press, 1949.
"The Mover, the Shaker," in *I Have No Mouth, And I Must Scream,* by Harlan Ellison. New York, Pyramid, 1967.
"The Wonder-Full Age," in *Science Fiction Tales,* edited by Roger Elwood. New York, Random House, 1973.
"Why?," in *Clarion 3,* edited by Robin Scott Wilson. New York, New American Library, 1973.

"All the Effingers at Once," in *Mixed Feelings*, by Geo. Alec Effinger. New York, Harper, 1974.
"Science Fiction, Morals, and Religion," in *Science Fiction, Today and Tomorrow*, edited by Reginald Bretnor. New York, Harper, 1974.

Comic Books: wrote *Iron Munro* (2 issues), 1940; *How to Build Boats*, 1940; *It*, 1972; *Killdozer!*, 1974; *Microcosmic God*, 1976.

Editor, *New Soviet Science Fiction*. London, Collier Macmillan, 1980.

*

Bibliography: *Theodore Sturgeon: A Primary and Secondary Bibliography* by Lahna F. Diskin, Boston, Hall, 1980.

Critical Studies: *Theodore Sturgeon* by Lucy Menger, New York, Ungar, 1981; *Theodore Sturgeon* by Lahna F. Diskin, Mercer Island, Washington, Starmont House, 1981.

*   *   *

In Kurt Vonnegut's fictional universe, Kilgore Trout writes SF stories pregnant with emotion and philopsophy, but relegated to the unread pages of pornographic magazines, while he ekes out a living with odd jobs. Trout's most likely model is Theodore Sturgeon, whose much-anthologized stories have made him probably the best *loved* of all SF writers. Inclined toward magic and fantasy, unashamedly romantic and psychologically penetrating, Sturgeon commonly writes about the yearning for wholeness that characterizes love in a disjointed, repressive society. This emotional edge and his mastery of styles, using a classically restrained vocabulary, make him second only to Heinlein as a contemporary model for other SF writers. Bradbury and Delany acknowledge their debt openly; others, like Vonnegut, are more indirect. Beside extensive writing outside SF, Sturgeon's fantasies fill over a dozen volumes of stories and several novels, plus the novelization of the movie, *Voyage to the Bottom of the Sea*.

Of his earliest work, *It* and "Killdozer" concern menaces whose life and terrestrial origins are in question. The latter is a compelling metaphor of machine malevolence. Another horror story, extraordinarily sensuous, is "Bianca's Hands" which tells of an idiot with beautiful hands that work without conscious direction, eventually strangling her lover. Other early stories include "Shottle Bop," about a mysterious shop selling talents pople inevitably misuse, and "Microcosmic God" in which a misanthropic scientist drives the evolution of a race of tiny creatures who propitiate him with remarkable inventions. "Maturity" concerns a charming self-educated polymath whose perpetual youthful irresponsibility stems from a glandular defect; when it is corrected medically, he ripens and dies. The maturing of a society is the subject of "Thunder and Roses" in which a beautiful entertainer, dying from radiation sickness, persuades the men at a key military base in an America crippled by nuclear attack to spare their enemy and the human race.

Sturgeon's first novel, *The Dreaming Jewels*, is a mad melodrama of circus freaks and humanoid products of living crystals. Its few poetic moments cannot overcome simplistic conflicts among telepathic cardboard characters, but elements in it look forward to *More Than Human*, which won the International Fantasy Award. In "Baby Is Three" a boy finds out in a marathon psychiatric session why he tried to kill his foster mother. With the analyst's vocabulary and his own repressed memories, he discovers his role as the central ganglion of a multi-person form, or gestalt, whose other members are also children with parapsychological powers complementing his own. Actually killing off the governess in the middle section of the novel, Sturgeon begins it with the youthful outcasts and an older "idiot" coalescing into the gestalt's "first draft," and ends it with the addition of a moral component who binds the entity to homo sapiens while he opens the door to the superior race, homo gestalt. Written in a vivid, impressionistic style, this parable of social organization and psychological integration became for many readers the one SF classic. Completing this parapsychological trilogy, *The Cosmic Rape* finds another outcast repelling a group-mind invasion by uniting Earth's mental forces over the galaxy-spanning alien being. In the process, he breaks through his isolation and finds himself, while healing the fragmentation of the individualistic human race.

Featuring magic and wish-fulfillment, aliens and esp, Sturgeon's stories exploit the most peripheral of science-fiction content. In "Saucer of Loneliness" a girl learns from a miniature flying saucer that someone is lonelier than she is. Though it brings tribulations, it sustains her through them, finally bringing the love of the narrator, who saves her from suicide. "The World Well Lost" appears to concern a pair of aliens, "loverbirds" fron Dirnadu, a planet closed to mankind. It is really about the love between two human space crewmen, which literally "cannot speak its name," and which taints the entire human race from the perpective of the aliens, whose gender differences are more pronounced. Apparent homosexuality also surfaces in "Affair with a Green Monkey" in which a slightly built young man is rescued from thugs by a pompously "well-adjusted" psychologist. Overbearingly tolerant, the host throws his wife and his guest together, and a platonic affair develops. Its consummation is prevented not by the guest's being gay but by his being an alien, far too well-endowed sexually for interspecies sex. But what may seem merely a dirty joke is in fact a sensitive plea for understanding, tolerance, and tenderness.

Closer to hard science fiction, "Bulkhead" (originally "Who?") tells of an astronaut kept company by the childish half of his artificially split personality, supposedly beyond a bulkhead which actually separates him from the vacuum of space. More utopian is the far-future pastoral world of "The Skills of Xanadu" where people are integrated by means of "belts" that virtually transcend technology, freeing them to realize their (and our) potential. Three other tales show the variety of Sturgeon's production in the 1950's. In "The Girl Had Guts" a symbiotic alien saves human lives by becoming a false digestive system, vomited out in times of peril. Marooned on Mars, a man disguises from himself, with lyrical impressions and memories, his impending death as the first human to take this next evolutionary step into an alien environment ("The Man Who Lost the Sea"). The comic elegy "Like Young" suggests that fun-loving otters have already inherited the Earth from a doomed human race.

Never avoiding controversy, Sturgeon anticipated by a decade Le Guin's Gethenians in *Venux Plus X*. In alternating chapters, suburbanites talk about sexual variety and stereotypes, and a downed aviator with macho hangups fails to be integrated into a utopian society of surgically created bisexuals. Flirting with another taboo, *Some of Your Blood* takes the vampire theme seriously, probing its causes in a fictional case history of a man's bizarre need. Like these novels, Sturgeon's later stories tend to be talky, as well as controversial. "When You Care, When You Love" extends love to one's own creation, a cloned replica of a lost beloved. "If All Men Were Brothers,

Would You Want One to Marry Your Sister?" posits a world in which keeping sex in the family is the "healthy" rule, not a frequently broken proscription. In perhaps his best story about healing, "Slow Sculpture" compares it to raising bonsai plants (Hugo and Nebula awards). His more recent work is less successful. A case in point is "Case and the Dreamer"; ambitious but diffuse, it is about an astronaut and his lover, resurrected by an indrawn human race to explore the universe for it, in the company of a clownish "god" (the dreamer) with whom their ship's computer has fallen in love.

A *science-fiction* writer largely by courtesy, Sturgeon equates "science" with "wisdom," not with hardware and limitations. Moving even when they are talky, his fantasies are wrought from emotional experiences his readers recognize as theirs, but which his skill with words can distance artistically. As unselfishly giving and fiscally "irresponsible" as the protagonist of "Maturity," Sturgeon never profited much financially from his writing. But he turned his suffering into beauty, encapsulating in fiction the longing for alternatives which characterizes many people's fascination with science fiction and fantasy.

—David N. Samuelson

SUCHARITKUL, Somtow. Also writes as S.P. Somtow. Born in Bangkok, Thailand, in 1952; grew up in Europe. Educated at Eton College; Cambridge University, B.A., M.A. Conductor and composer: Director, Bangkok Opera Society, 1977-78, and Asian Composer's Conference-Festival, Bangkok, 1978; compositions include *Gongula 3* and *Star Maker—An Anthology of Universes.* Recipient: John W. Campbell Award, 1981; *Locus* award, 1982. Address: 3621 Greenway Place, Alexandria, Virginia 22302-2005, U.S.A.

SCIENCE-FICTION PUBLICATIONS

Novels (series: Inquestor)

Inquestor:
  1. *Light on the Sound.* New York, Pocket Books, 1982.
  2. *The Throne of Madness.* New York, Pocket Books, 1983.
  3. *Utopia Hunters.* New York, Pocket Books, 1984.
Starship and Haiku. New York, Pocket Books, 1984.
The Darkling Wind. New York, Bantam, 1985.

Short Stories

Mallworld. Norfolk, Virginia, Donning, 1981.
Fire from the Wine-Dark Sea. Norfolk, Virginia, Donning, 1983.
The Aquiliad. New York, Pocket Books, 1983.

Uncollected Short Stories

"The Fallen Country," in *Elsewhere 2,* edited by Terri Windling and Mark Alan Arnold. New York, Ace, 1982.
"Remembrances," in *Isaac Asimov's Science Fiction Magazine* (New York), 15 March 1982.
"Scarlet Snow," in *Isaac Asimov's Science Fiction Magazine* (New York), May 1982.
"The Shattered Horse," in *Amazing* (New York), May 1984.
"The Comet That Cried for Its Mother," in *Amazing* (New York), September 1984.

OTHER PUBLICATIONS

Novel

Vampire Junction (as S.P. Somtow). Norfolk, Virginia, Donning, 1984.

*   *   *

Often described as "droll," "cosmic," "symbolic," "myth-opoetic," "startlingly original," and "inventive," but also as "cryptic," "unrestrained," "ponderous," and "convoluted," the works of Somtow Sucharitkul echo the familiar, either historical (Romans, Olmecs, lost tribes of Israel), or present (the threat of nuclear holocaust, lab-born plagues, and the slaughter of whales), or pseudo-mythic (Bigfoot, flying saucers, and vampires), but also partake of the alien and the bizarre (sentient suns, cities in the heads of monstrous snakes, a Throne of Madness, a Utopia of the dead, a dust sculptures, a web dancer, and a rainbow king). Sucharitkul is at his best exploring sentient cultures grudgingly forced to face the common bonds that link them despite appearance, tradition, and culture, whether they be earthlings and lizards (*The Alien Swordmaster*), Windbringers and Inquestors (*Light on the Sound*), Selespridons and humans (*Mallworld*), Romans and American Indians (*The Aquiliad*) or whales and Japanese (*Starship and Haiku*). His works, whether set eons in the future or in an alternate antiquity, show benevolence and compassion devolving into a mass blood lust until salvation comes from some unexpected quarter, some unknown hero who spearheads a resistance, engages in a strategic game of life and death with thousands of lives or thousands of planets at stake, and proves his/her mettle defending old-fashioned values, goodness, justice, and family. Often it is the very young or the very old in Sucharitkul's works who are the most perceptive and the most attuned to the pain and the tragedy of other sentient beings.

In *The Alien Swordmaster,* one of the *V* series, a ninjitsu expert and a Japanese-American anthropologist shelter an orphan and aid an alien Martial Arts Master to counter a saurian plot to retake the earth through a well-trained cadre of soulless Martial Arts killers; in doing so they find love and family and self-respect.

Light on the Sounds, the first of the Inquestor series, introduces those vigilant guardians of the Dispersal of Man, the anti-Utopian, omnipotent, immortal, absentminded, despotic Inquestors. Because they need the disembodied brains of a whale-like sentient race (Windbringers) to power their faster than light vehicles, they have developed a race of deaf and dumb humans genetically designed to be impervious to the beauty of light and sound, the Windbringers' only defense. Ultimately a sympathetic Inquestor heretic leads the fight to save both races. In *The Throne of Madness* (second in the series) Inquestor despotism, cruelty, and madness sends more rebels across the galaxy seeking the means to destroy the Inquest and in so doing experiencing numerous wonders. *Utopia Hunters* provides the history of the Inquest through a series of ornate, and moving, linked tales told a young "lightweaver," Jenjen, by an ancient. They reveal the sadness, the guilt, the madness that afflict beings who must destroy worlds in order to preserve them. Chosen to fashion a great lightsculpture celebrating the Inquest's crusade against utopias, Jenjen gradually learns to overcome her fear of darkness and to see in her own conflicts and creations the dark that is a texture in every light and that threatens and Inquest and yet could save it. She finally learns to understand the need to destroy false utopias that blind man to truth and make him a slave to false hopes. The final tale of the destruction of flaming phoenixes that will rise no more sums up the paradoxes of dark and light.

Fire from the Wine-Dark Sea, a short story collection, includes two early Inquestor stories and a precursor of *Starship and Haiku,* entitled "The Last Line of the Haiku," a compact, intriguing piece. *Starship and Haiku* juxtaposes the modern and the ancient, the technological and the artistic in a story of a dying earth, its land and seas polluted, its inhabitants diseased and mutated. Therein the Japanese prove to be the offspring of whales, and, led by a madman, commit mass *seppuku* for having slaughtered their ancestors. But a hybrid race, whale and human, will survive in space.

The Aquiliad delineates an alternative world wherein the Roman Empire extends to America and an Indian Chief aids the Romans in their search for China. An evil time-traveller, pre-columbian genetic engineering, flying saucers and cops helping Olmecs are only a few of the unusual twists of this sprawling plot. The narrator, a dim-witted general favored by Nero, continually clashes with the aged Indian, whose Latin wordplay is the wittiest part of the novel.

Mallworld is a delightful series of bizarre glimpses of the inhabitants of a futuristic shopping mall world being investigated by a superior alien race, the Selespridons, who are fascinated by the strength of the human spirit and appalled by human barbarism and bad taste. It depicts a world of the unexpectedly familiar transformed: St. Betty Crocker, St. Martin Luther King Kong, a nude female Pope, babies custom designed at Storkways, Inc., suicide parlors featuring death by vampire, a megacredit card system that permits the shopping spree of the century, and the Bible belt, a mixture of Amish, Buddhist, and Hare Krishna, and the center of that ancient art, reading. Yet amid this modern insanity, man struggles to create, to free his body and soul, to achieve human dignity, love and understanding, and so touches the heart of jaded aliens that they cannot escape man's pull.

In sum, Sucharitkul creates worlds and languages, customs and cultures in narratives that are gripping, moving, well-crafted set pieces, with dense prose and metaphorical overtones, though at times his attempts at complex poetic diction and epic scope distract and obscure. Always he is a wildly imaginative mythmaker, projecting topsy turvy worlds that somehow remain human, entertaining, and compelling. He offers an Eastern perspective on art and nature, and a humanistic concern for man and his world.

—Gina Macdonald

SUTTON, Andrew. See **TUBB, E. C.**

SUTTON, Jeff and Jean. American. **SUTTON, Jeff(erson Howard):** Born in Los Angeles, California, 25 July 1913. Educated at San Diego State College, B. A. 1954, M. A. 1956. Served in the United States Marine Corps, 1941-45: Technical Sergeant. Married Eugenia Geneva Hansen in 1941; one son and one daughter. Photographer, International News Photos, Los Angeles, 1937-40; reporter, photographer, public relations writer for General Dynamics Astronautics; free-lance writer

and editorial consultant to aerospace industries from 1960. *Died 31 January 1979.* **SUTTON, Jean** (Eugenia Geneva Sutton, née Hansen): Born in Denmark, Wisconsin, 5 July 1916. Educated at the University of Wisconsin, Madison, 1934-37; University of California, Los Angeles, B. A. in economics 1940; San Diego State University, M. A. in education 1959. Personnel worker, U.S. Steel, Los Angeles, 1940-41; construction company timekeeper, San Diego, 1942-45; lathe operator, Douglas Aircraft, Santa Monica, California, and social worker in Los Angeles; Executive Secretary, San Diego City Council, 1949-52; Administrative Assistant, San Diego State College, 1953-55; social studies teacher, San Diego county high schools, 1958-71. Since 1971, consultant assistant. Agent: Scott Meredith Literary Agency, 845 Third Avenue, New York, New York 10022. Address: 4325 Beverly Drive, La Mesa, California 92041, U.S.A.

SCIENCE-FICTION PUBLICATIONS

Novels by Jeff Sutton

First on the Moon. New York, Ace, 1958.
Bombs in Orbit. New York, Ace, 1959.
Spacehive. New York, Ace, 1960.
The Atom Conspiracy. New York, Avalon, 1963.
Apollo at Go (for children). New York, Putnam, 1963; London, Mayflower, 1964.
The Missile Lords. New York, Putnam, 1963; London, Sidgwick and Jackson, 1964.
Beyond Apollo (for children). New York, Putnam, 1966; London, Gollancz, 1967.
H-Bomb over America. New York, Ace, 1967.
The Man Who Saw Tomorrow. New York, Ace, 1968.
Whisper from the Stars. New York, Dell, 1970.
Alton's Unguessable. New York, Ace, 1970.
The Mindlocked Man. New York, DAW, 1972.
Cassady. New York, St. Martin's Press, 1979; London, Hale, 1981.

Novels by Jeff and Jean Sutton (for children)

The River. New York, Belmont, 1966.
The Beyond. New York, Putnam, 1968.
The Programmed Man. New York, Putnam, 1968.
Lord of the Stars. New York, Putnam, 1969.
Alien from the Stars. New York, Putnam, 1970.
The Boy Who Had the Power. New York, Putnam, 1971.

Uncollected Short Stories by Jeff Sutton

"The Third Empire," in *Spaceway* (Alhambra, California), February 1955.
"The Man Who Had No Brains," in *Amazing* (New York), September 1961.
"Forerunner," in *Androids, Time Machines, and Blue Giraffes,* edited by Roger Elwood and Vic Ghidalia. Chicago, Follett, 1973.
"After Ixmal," in *Space Opera,* edited by Brian Aldiss. London, Weidenfeld and Nicolson, 1974; New York, Doubleday, 1975.

*

Manuscript Collection: San Diego State University.

* * *

Jeff Sutton's career as a writer of SF has been checkered. In spite of the fact that its melodramatic plot of conflict between the United States and Russia is a reflection in miniature of the then Cold War, *First on the Moon*, his first novel, was considered promising because its technological detailing seemed authentic, perhaps owing to the author's engineering background. His second novel, *Bombs in Orbit*, again elicited some praise for its handling of technological details and for what appeared to be an increased skill in manipulating plot and creating suspense. However, the next two novels, *Spacehive* and *The Atom Conspiracy*, aroused substantial critical misgivings. No one doubted Sutton's ability to describe technological processes, current and extrapolated, and to suggest thereby verisimilitude. But plotting and characterization seemed more and more throwbacks to 1930's space opera; further, Sutton's style increasingly manifested an embarrassing fondness for cliché.

The Atom Conspiracy aptly illustrates Sutton's limitations. Its portrait of the Empire of Earth in 2449 when research in the atom is outlawed because of previous nuclear catastrophes, and a World Government is directed by an elite Council of Six who possess the highest IQ, is neither original nor convincing. The world looks and society functions very much the way they do today, and the Council of Six appear no better or worse than anyone with normal IQ. For reasons not entirely clear the Empire also looks with disdain upon anyone with ESP powers. The novel's hero, Max Krull, a government agent and a secret ESPer, is sent to investigate the circumstances behind the death by nuclear burning of a long-missing man. Most of the action, consisting of conventional intrigue, flight and chase, confrontations with supposedly all-powerful figures, and a gingerly touch of sex, is designed to keep Max from being where it was foretold he would be regardless of anything done to prevent it. Finally, Sutton's use of ESP owes more to a need for narrative gimmicks than a desire to investigate seriously an important topic.

Perhaps believing that his ability for describing technological processes and penchant for conventional plotting and characterization might be better utilized in children's SF, Sutton pointed his next novel, *Apollo at Go*, at the juvenile market. Buoyed by the novel's positive acceptance, Sutton turned out seven additional children's SF novels, most of which were written in collaboration with his wife Jean. (Several more Jeff Sutton adult SF novels have been published but none has made any stir.) Unfortunately, after initial acceptance and subsequent tinkering to find other effective ways of attracting young readers, the Suttons have been unable to come up with the one unqualified success that would establish them as significant authors of SF. Still their children's SF is as good as the representative Nourse or Lightner juvenile, and superior to a typical Hugh Walters story. *The Programmed Man, Lord of the Stars*, and *Alien from the Stars*, in particular, are all action-packed, quick-moving novels. Considered as a whole, then, Jeff Sutton's SF, whether intended for adults or children, has fallen short of the first rank. Although always solid in its depiction of technological process and procedures and usually adequately grounded in its scientific speculation, his fiction has yet to move beyond the merely competent and predictable and to achieve originality and literary distinction.

—Francis J. Molson

SZILARD, Leo. American. Born in Budapest, Hungary, 11 February 1898; emigrated to the United States, 1937; naturalized, 1943. Educated at the Budapest Institute of Technology; University of Berlin, D. Phil. 1922. Married Gertrud Weiss in 1951. Staff member, University of Berlin, 1925-32; research worker in nuclear physics, St. Bartholomew's Hospital, London, and Clarendon Laboratory, Oxford, 1934-38; staff member at Columbia University, New York, 1939-42, and, with Enrico Fermi, University of Chicago, 1942-46: devised chain reaction system with Fermi; resident fellow, Salk Institute of Biological Studies, La Jolla, California, 1964. Recipient: Atoms for Peace Prize, 1959. *Died 30 May 1964.*

SCIENCE-FICTION PUBLICATIONS

Short Stories

The Voice of the Dolphins and Other Stories. New York, Simon and Schuster, and London, Gollancz, 1961.

OTHER PUBLICATIONS

Other

The Collected Works of Leo Szilard, edited by Bernard T. Feld and Gertrud Weiss Szilard. Cambridge, Massachusetts Institute of Technology, 1972.
Leo Szilard: His Version of the Facts: Selected Recollections and Correspondence, edited by Spencer R. Weart and Gertrud Weiss Szilard. Cambridge, Massachusetts Institute of Technology Press, 1978.

* * *

Leo Szilard will always be remembered more for his involvement with the atomic bomb than for his literary achievements. His sole work of science fiction, *The Voice of the Dolphins and Other Stories*, is of interest more because it is written by a famous physicist than for any particular merit. All the stories are told in dry, lecture-tour manner, rather like the crudest efforts of the Gernsback era. Szilard was a vigorous thinker but he showed no interest in character development or plot. Instead, he merely presented ideas. The title story concerns efforts by dolphins to control the human race, using scientific organizations as fronts. They do fairly well for a while. All this is told in straight exposition, as a "non-fact" history. Some of the political predictions have turned out to be uncannily on the mark, others way off. "My Trial as a War Criminal" concerns the possible guilt of the early atomic bomb scientists. The others are less important. "Report on 'Grand Central Terminal'" has future extraterrestrial archeologists puzzling over pay toilets.

—Darrell Schweitzer

TAINE, John. Pseudonym for Eric Temple Bell. American. Born in Aberdeen, Scotland, 7 February 1883. Educated at the University of London, 1902; Stanford University, California, A. B. 1904 (Phi Beta Kappa); University of Washington, Seattle, A. M. 1908; Columbia University, New York, Ph. D. 1912. Married Jessie Lillian Brown in 1910; one child. Professor of Mathematics, University of Washington, 1912-26, and California Institute of Technology, Pasadena, 1927-53. Vice President, American Mathematical Society, 1926; President, Mathematical Association of America, 1931-33. Recipient: Bocher Prize, for academic work, 1920-24. Vice-President, American Academy of Arts and Sciences, 1930; Member, National Academy of Sciences. *Died 21 December 1960.*

SCIENCE-FICTION PUBLICATIONS

Novels

The Purple Sapphire. New York, Dutton, 1924.
Quayle's Invention. New York, Dutton, 1927.
The Gold Tooth. New York, Dutton, 1927.
Green Fire. New York, Dutton, 1928.
The Greatest Adventure. New York, Dutton, 1929.
The Iron Star. New York, Dutton, 1930.
Before the Dawn. Baltimore, Williams and Wilkins, 1934.
The Time Stream. Providence, Rhode Island, Buffalo, 1946.
The Forbidden Garden. Reading, Pennsylvania, Fantasy Press, 1947.
The Cosmic Geoids, and One Other. Los Angeles, Fantasy, 1949.
Seeds of Life. Reading, Pennsylvania, Fantasy Press, 1951; London, Rich and Cowan, 1955.
The Crystal Horde. Reading, Pennsylvania, Fantasy Press, 1952; as *White Lily,* in *Seeds of Life, and White Lily,* New York, Dover, 1966.
G. O. G. 666. Reading, Pennsylvania, Fantasy Press, 1954; London, Rich and Cowan, 1955.

Uncollected Short Stories

"Twelve Eighty-Seven," in *Astounding* (New York), May 1935.
"Tomorrow," in *Marvel* (New York), April-May 1939.
"The Ultimate Catalyst," in *My Best Science Fiction Story,* edited by Leo Margulies and O. J. Friend. New York, Merlin Press, 1949.

OTHER PUBLICATIONS

Verse

Recreations (as J. T.). Boston, Gorham Press, 1915.
The Singer (as J. T.). Boston, Gorham Press, 1916.

Other as Eric Temple Bell

The Cyclotomic Quinary Quintic. New York, Columbia University, 1912.
An Arithmetic Theory of Certain Numerical Functions. Seattle, University of Washington, 1915.
Algebraic Arithmetic. New York, American Mathematical Society, 1927.
Debunking Science. Seattle, University of Washington Book Store, 1930.
The Queen of the Sciences . Baltimore, Williams and Wilkins, 1931.
Numerology. Baltimore, Williams and Wilkins, 1933.
The Handmaiden of the Sciences. Baltimore, Williams and Wilkins, and London, Baillière, 1937.
Men of Mathematics. New York, Simon and Schuster, and London, Gollancz, 1937.
Man and His Lifebelts. Baltimore, Williams and Wilkins, 1938.

"Why Science Fiction?" (as John Taine) in *Startling* (New York), March 1939.
The Development of Mathematics. New York, McGraw Hill, 1940; revised edition, 1945.
The Magic of Numbers. New York, McGraw Hill, 1946.
Mathematics, Queen and Servant of Science. New York, McGraw Hill, 1951; London, Bell, 1952.
The Last Problem . New York. Simon and Schuster, 1961; London, Gollancz, 1962.

* * *

John Taine was the pseudonym used by the prominent research mathematician Eric Temple Bell in his science-fiction novels. Taine was a respected science-fiction novelist during the 1920's who turned to the pulp SF magazines with the depression. His best work blended theoretical inquiry into the unknown with high adventure in the H. Rider Haggard tradition, and he combined sound science with a rare story-telling ability.

The major preoccupation in Taine's handful of novels is that of technological disaster. In almost all his work, scientific inquiry into the unknown precipitates an impending catalcysm. These disasters can be man-made, as in *Seeds of Life,* natural, as in *The Iron Star,* or accidental, as the monsters created in *White Lily.* In *The Greatest Adventure* and *The Purple Sapphire* unknown cataclysms in remote antiquity have their effect on the modern world. *The Time Stream* links the destruction of a future world with the great San Francisco earthquake.

Taine's novels invariably focus on individuals who band together to quest into the unknown. Often, he teams a scientist with an adventurer. On one level his narratives function as scientific mystery stories in which inexplicable phenomena screen a hidden truth. Taine slowly—in *White Lily,* ponderously—reveals the solution through his close-mouthed scientist characters. At times complete and final answers are withheld in order to maintain a sense of wonder and mystery. This is particularly true in *The Greatest Adventure* and *The Purple Sapphire,* both of which concern survivals of ancient super-civilizations of Earth's past. In *The Greatest Adventure* an Antarctic expedition uncovers the remnants of such a civilization. Under the ice is a city which had entombed itself alive rather than allow the possibility of escape to the mutated creatures spawned when they discovered the secret of life. The expedition inadvertently activates the menace. Taine concentrates on the biological nightmares, and neither explores nor identifies the ancient civilization, but this enhances the power of the novel. On the other hand, this reserve limits the otherwise excellent *Purple Sapphire.* Three seekers of fortune discover a fantastic city in the heart of Central Asia where a degraded theocracy guards its technological marvels against the day its true inhabitants return. They do not return, and the three successfully rescue the kidnapped daughter of a British General but lose the secret of transmuting matter.

Genetic mutation is a theme Taine finds fascinating. Two novels, *Seeds of Life* and *G. O. G. 666,* deal with the consequences of human genetic tampering. *Seeds of Life* chronicles the brief career of a dissolute research scientist, Neils Bork, who becomes a superman when exposed to radiation. Bork, who considers human life beneath contempt, masterminds a fiendish plan to eradicate all humans, but is stymied when he regresses and falls in love with the women he has chosen as the instrument of annihilation. A similar figure is Gog, the hulking travesty of a man whom plant geneticist Dr. Clive Chase encounters in his investigation of a Soviet plan to liberate its workers from drudgery in *G. O. G. 666*. Gog is the keystone of the plan, and he hides a secret darker than that of Neils Bork. *G. O. G. 666* is somewhat marred by its Cold War preoccupations. *White Lily* also depicts Russia in an uncomplimentary light. In China, two despicable Russian agents foment revolution. Against this bloody backdrop, a US soldier has unwittingly introduced silicon-based lifeforms on Earth, which run unchecked.

Considered to be his greatest work, *The Time Stream* is a complex excursion into the dynamics of time travel and cyclical universes. The Time Stream is the medium by which ten individuals from the future send their minds back to 20th-century San Francisco. There they live new lives in an attempt to determine if a scientifically forbidden marriage will result in the destruction of their world. Although somewhat confusing in its narrative structure, *The Time Stream* is nevertheless a compelling example of imaginative writing. Of his other works, *The Iron Star*, a novel of a destructive asteroid, and "The Ultimate Catalyst" are noteworthy.

—Will Murray

TALL, Stephen. Pseudonym for Compton Newby Crook. American. Born in Rossville, Tennessee, 14 June 1908. Educated at George Peabody College (now Vanderbilt University), Nashville, B. S. 1932, M. A. 1933; Johns Hopkins University, Baltimore; Arizona State University, Tempe. Served as an intelligence officer in the Office of Strategic Services, 1943-45: Captain. Married Lucy Beverly Courtney; three children. Science teacher, Appalachian State University, Boone, North Carolina, Middle Tennessee State University, Murfreesboro, Tennessee Polytechnic Institute, Western Reserve University, Cleveland, College of William and Mary, Williamsburg, Virginia, and Episcopal Academy, Philadelphia, 1933-39. Instructor, then Professor of Biology and Department Chairman, 1939-73, and from 1973, Professor Emeritus, Towson State University, Baltimore. Ranger and naturalist with the National Park Service, eight summers. Recipient: National Science Foundation grants for ecological study. *Died 15 June 1981.*

SCIENCE-FICTION PUBLICATIONS

Novels

The Ramsgate Paradox. New York, Berkley, 1976.
The People Beyond the Wall. New York, DAW, 1980.

Short Stories

The Stardust Voyages. New York, Berkley, 1975.

Uncollected Short Stories

"Lights on Precipice Peak," in *Galaxy* (New York), October 1955.
"Allison, Carmichael, and Tattersall," in *Galaxy* (New York), April 1970.
"The Angry Mountain," in *Fantasy and Science Fiction* (New York), June 1970.

"Talk with the Animals," in *Analog* (New York), September 1970.
"The Mad Scientist and the FBI," in *Galaxy* (New York), December 1970.
"This Is My Country," in *Galaxy* (New York), February 1971.
"Space Bounce," in *If* (New York), October 1973.
"Chlorophyll," in *Fantasy and Science Fiction* (New York), June 1976.
"The Rock and the Pool," in *Galaxy* (New York), December 1976.
"The Man Who Saved the Sun," in *Fantasy and Science Fiction* (New York), January 1977.
"The King Is Dead, Long Live the Queen!," in *Amazing* (New York), January 1978.
"Home Is the Hunter," in *Analog* (New York), August 1979.
"The Merry Men of Methane," in *Fantasy and Science Fiction* (New York), May 1980.
"The Hot and Cold Running Waterfall," in *Fantasy Annual 4*, edited by Terry Carr. New York, Pocket Books, 1981.

*

Stephen Tall commented:

(1981) I was born in Tennessee near the Big River, the Mississippi, the son of a country doctor and a cultured, sensitive mother. The levees, the cotton fields, the cypress swamps, and the cane breaks were my first playgrounds. And in our home books and good reading always had status. Respect for knowledge and how it is acquired was instilled early.

I have always been a biologist writing fiction, not the other way around. I write because I like to tell a good story, and because the mechanics of good writing are pleasing to me. My stories are about what I know, and about what I have concern for. They have always reflected my awareness of and interest in the living world other than man. I wrote stories based on ecology before the word was generally familiar. I regard science fiction as almost the ideal medium for expressing ecological concerns: any species, any race, anywhere.

*   *   *

Approximately half of Stephen Tall's science fiction concerns the crew of the interstellar explorer ship *Stardust* : six short stories collected as *The Stardust Voyages* and one of the two published novels, *The Ramsgate Paradox*. They are in many ways from the same mold as the television program *Star Trek*. A crew of 400 staffs the ship as it makes its way from one star system to another, but for all practical purposes, there are only three characters. Roscoe Kissinger is the obligatory hero, not too long on brains, but courageous to a fault. Equally necessary is Lindy Peterson, the attractive female scientist whose major significance seems to be to require rescue by Roscoe. The last is Pegleg Williams, the tried and true best friend, comic relief, and jack of all trades. There is also an elderly woman whose psychic abilities manifest themselves in her cryptic paintings.

There is no doubt that the entire series is built around pure stereotypes. Nevertheless, some of the adventures have been very well received. Perhaps the best known is "The Bear with a Knot on His Tail", in which the star Mizar is about to explode and the *Stardust* arrives to carry off significant records and frozen germ plasma of the local intelligent species. Perhaps the most interesting, however, is the first, "Seventy Light-Years from Sol" (retitled "A Star Called Cyrene"). This time our protagonists land on a planet inhabited by two very distinct races. The first consists of featureless vari-colored cubes who can teleport themselves about from one location to another, and do so frequently in order to escape the predations of a species of carnivorous wheel. But now the cubes face a new threat, invasion from a nearby island of formless blobs, against which they have no defense. Human policy is to avoid taking sides in local squabbles, but the crew decides that offering advice is not tantamount to interference. This strange twist of logic seems not to present any problems to the characters or the author, and the story is well written enough for us to ignore the chauvinism. These two stories set the pattern for the rest of the series, in which the three central characters meet and overcome a variety of menaces ranging from a manifestation of ancient Greek gods to mutated giant crabs. The latter appear in "The Invaders," another above-average story that suffers from problems of internal logic.

A non-series story of note is "Allison, Carmichael, and Tattersall" which seems to have been molded at least in part by recollection of the Arcot, Morey, and Wade stories of John W. Campbell Jr. Indeed, much of Tall's fiction would not have been out of place in the 1930's, although the level of literary achievement is substantially higher. This was also the beginning of a truncated series, and is a satisfying light adventure story marred by over-reliance on coincidence, a flaw which appears in many of the other stories as well.

The Ramsgate Paradox is distinguished from the shorter *Stardust* pieces only by length, making no serious effort to add substantial depth to the characters. The second novel, *The People Beyond the Wall*, is also a return to a tradition largely abandoned in the genre, the Utopian novel. A pair of adventurers set off to explore an area of glacier in the Antarctic and find themselves in a hidden land where people have returned to a pastoral existence unmarred by organized strife. Although this is probably the most ambitious work Tall produced, it falls prey eventually to an internal problem of most such novels; the plot begins to slow to a crawl as the varied aspects of the totally sane but rather dull society are revealed. Tall loses control totally in the final chapters, jumping forward years in time, introducing new characters, and confusing the reader. Nevertheless, the early chapters are quite well done, and the move away from the repetitiveness of the *Stardust* stories is promising.

—Don D'Ammassa

* * *

TATE, Peter. British. Journalist. Agent: Virginia Kidd, Box 278, Milford, Pennsylvania 18837, U. S. A. Address: 3 Seaway Avenue, Friars Cliff, Christchurch, Hampshire, England.

SCIENCE-FICTION PUBLICATIONS

Novels

The Thinking Seat. New York, Doubleday, 1969; London, Faber, 1970.
Gardens One to Five. New York, Doubleday, 1971; as *Gardens, 1,2,3,4,5,* London, Faber, 1971.
Country Love and Poison Rain. New York, Doubleday, 1973.
Moon on an Iron Meadow. New York, Doubleday, 1974.
Faces in the Flames. New York, Doubleday, 1976.
Greencomber. New York, Doubleday, 1979.

Short Stories

Seagulls under Glass. New York, Doubleday, 1975.

Although Peter Tate can be a futurist, an allegorist, and a fantasist, in his major work he is a realist who utilizes current trends in natural and social science as well as technology for conveying his values. His concept of science fiction is a "work styled in protest at a particular facet of . . . technology and using research to qualify that protest" (introduction to "The Post-Mortem People" in *Seagulls Under Glass*). Unlike futurists who project their characters onto other planets, eons removed from the present, Tate remains on a familiar earth only a few years distanced from the copyright date. He chooses recognizable settings (Waukegan, Zimbabwe, New Forest) and with them creates an illusion that his scientific and technological projections have already left the laboratory and are threatening the balance in man and nature. Likewise, he interweaves imagined crises with references to current headlines (Che Guevara, Vorster, Kent State, Mozambique), thus enabling the reader to fuse fabrication with newspaper fact. Sobering is his recognition that heroes sometimes die. Tate further asserts the realness of his fictions by overlapping characters and plots. Simeon and Tomorrow Julie star in *The Thinking Seat, Moon on an Iron Meadow,* and *Faces in the Flames* ; Scarlatti and Prinz counter each other in *Gardens one to Five* and *Faces in the Flames.* Famous Gogan slips in and out of *The Thinking Seat, Gardens One to Five* and *Faces in the Flames* ; and Shem of *Gardens One to Five* is a memory in *Faces in the Flames.* Even more interesting than overlapping is Tate's technique of using fiction to authenticate fiction, as in *Moon on an Iron Meadow* where he returns to the buildings, people, and atmosphere created 50 years before by his mentor Ray Bradbury (*Something Wicked This Way Comes*).

Many of Tate's plots are compelling in their fast-paced intrigue ("Skyhammer"); their allegorical assessment of social and political foces (*Gardens One to Five*); or their subtle ambivalence between realism and fantasy (*Greencomber*). A few are bizarre. In "Mars Pastorale" a defenseless poppy seed invades a defenseless human's throat; in "Post-Mortem People" licensed ghouls stalk dying men for healthy body parts; in "The Gloom Pattern"—whose science, says Tate, is "bunkum"—a youngster is sucked up from his earthly existence on an "ecstasy beam" when he craves a sad man's happiness. Tate's humor surfaces in the provocative "Same Autumn in a Different Park. " In this parody of the Adam-Eve story, Addison springs from the side of Tina who with the help of "molecular rejig" turns into an apple which is eaten by the new Adam.

Tate sees the world as essentially good; but it has been contaminated by ignorance, indifference, misguided heroics, self-serving, and malice. As in Bradbury's *Something Wicked This Way Comes,* the spirit of evil is pervasive and its confrontation inevitable. It periodically erupts in such "bodies" as the United Nations, desalination plants, canisters of biological weapons, defoliants, contaminated rabbits, atom bombs, church "Prinzes," and Hitlerian megalomaniacs. Once this force is loose, balance between good and evil can be restored only by a figure who embodies the spirit of pristine Christianity: "the time of authenticity on the lake shores of Nazareth before two thousand years of controversy and schism and compromise and commerce had muddied the waters beyond perception" (*Faces in the Flames*). Simeon, along with Shem, Nelso Ojukwe (*Faces in the Flames*), Greencomber, and Adams ("Mainchance"), insists on rational, willed self-involvement—even to the point of death—against any sort of manipulation of humans. Like the Galilean, all of these hereos provoke action in the quiescent; by the force of their integrity, they transform

Judases and self-deceivers into disciples. A developing theme from *The Thinking Seat* to *Greencomber* is individual and social transformation effected by altruistic love.

Tate enjoys language. He puns, makes memorable metaphors, and sometimes achieves a mesmerizing lyricism. His use of myth is haunting: blood is the price for exaltation; life consciously saved counterbalances that which is wantonly taken; love dispels enslaving myths created by malevolent scientists. At times he mistakes clichés for original expression, or reaches too far for an apt comparison. But Tate is a stimulating writer who structures complex materials into convincing fictions.

—Rosemary Coleman

TEMPLE, William F(rederick). British. Born in London, 9 March 1914. Educated at Gordon School, London, 1919-27; Woolwich Polytechnic, London, 1928-30. Served in the Royal Artillery, 1940-46. Married Joan Streeton in 1939; one daughter and one son. Head Clerk, Stock Exchange, London, 1930-50. Editor, British Interplanetary Society *Bulletin. Died.*

SCIENCE-FICTION PUBLICATIONS

Novels (series: Martin Magnus)

Four-Sided Triangle. London, Long, 1949; New York, Fell, 1951.
Martin Magnus, Planet Rover (for children). London, Muller, 1955.
Martin Magnus on Venus (for children). London, Muller, 1955.
Martin Magnus on Mars (for children). London, Muller, 1956.
The Automated Goliath, The Three Suns of Amara. New York, Ace, 1962.
Battle on Venus. New York, Ace, 1963.
Shoot at the Moon. New York, Simon and Schuster, and London, Whiting and Wheaton, 1966.
The Fleshpots of Sansato. London, Macdonald, 1968.

Uncollected Short Stories

"The Kosso," in *Thrills.* London, Philip Allan, 1935.
"Lunar Lilliput," in *Tales of Wonder 2* (Kingswood, Surrey), 1938.
"Mr. Craddock's Amazing Experience," in *Amazing* (New York), February 1939.
"Experiment in Genius," in *Tales of Wonder* (Kingswood, Surrey), Summer 1940.
"The Monster on the Border," in *Super Science* (Kokomo, Indiana), November 1940.
"The Three Pylons," in *New Worlds 1* (London), 1946.
"Miracle Town," in *Thrilling Wonder Stories* (New York), October 1948.
"The Brain Beast," in *Super Science* (Kokomo, Indiana), July 1949.
"For Each Man Kills," in *Amazing* (New York), March 1950.
"Martian's Fancy," in *New Worlds* (London), Summer 1950.
"Wisher Take All," in *Other Worlds* (Evanston, Indiana), July 1950.
"The Bone of Contention," in *Thrilling Wonder Stories* (New York), October 1950.

"Forget-Me-Not," in *The Best Science Fiction Stories 1951*, edited by E. F. Bleiler and T. E. Dikty. New York, Fell, 1951.
"Conditioned Reflex," in *Other Worlds* (Evanston, Indiana), January 1951.
"You Can't See Me," in *Fantastic Adventures* (New York), June 1951.
"Double Trouble," in *Science Fantasy* (Bournemouth), Winter 1951.
"A Date to Remember," in *Invaders of Earth*, edited by Groff Conklin. New York, Vanguard Press, 1952; London, Weidenfeld and Nicolson, 1953.
"The Two Shadows," in *The Best Science-Fiction Stories 1952*, edited by E. F. Bleiler and T. E. Dikty. New York, Fell, 1952; London, Grayson, 1953.
"Counter-Transference," in *The Best Science-Fiction Stories 1953*, edited by E. F. Bleiler and T. E. Dikty. New York, Fell, 1953; London, Grayson, 1955.
"Way of Escape," in *Science Fiction Adventures in Dimension*, edited by Groff Conklin. New York, Vanguard Press, 1953; London, Grayson, 1955.
"Immortal's Playthings," in *Authentic* (London), January 1953.
"Field of Battle," in *Other Worlds* (Evanston, Indiana), February 1953.
"Mind Within Mind," in *Authentic* (London), May 1953.
"Limbo," in *Nebula* (Glasgow), Summer 1953.
"Pawn in Revolt," in *Nebula* (Glasgow), Autumn 1953.
"Destiny Is My Enemy," in *Nebula* (Glasgow), September 1953.
"Moon Wreck," in *Boy's Own Paper* (London), November 1953.
"Explorers of Mars," in *Authentic Book of Space*, edited by Herbert J. Campbell. London, Panther, 1954.
"Pilot's Hands," in *Nebula* (Glasgow), February 1954.
"Errand of Mercy," in *Authentic* (London), March 1954.
"Space Saboteur," in *Boy's Own Paper* (London), March 1954.
"Eternity," in *Science Fantasy* (Bournemouth), February 1955.
"Man in a Maze," in *Authentic* (London), February 1955.
"The Lonely," in *Imagination* (Evanston, Illinois), July 1955.
"Better Than We Know," in *Science Fiction Quarterly* (Holyoke, Massachusetts), August 1955.
"Mansion of Love," in *Nebula* (Glasgow), September 1955.
"Uncle Buno," in *Science Fantasy* (Bournemouth), November 1955.
32 stories, in *Rocket* (London), April to November 1956.
"The Girl from Mars," in *Heiress* (London), September 1956.
"Outside Position," in *Nebula* (Glasgow), November 1956.
"A Date to Remember," in *Nebula* (Glasgow), July 1957.
"Against Goliath," in *Nebula* (Glasgow), August 1957.
"Brief Encounter," in *Nebula* (Glasgow), October 1957.
"War Against Darkness," in *Nebula* (Glasgow), June 1958.
"The Different Complexion," in *New Worlds* (London), October 1958.
"Imbalance," in *Nebula* (Glasgow), May 1959.
"Magic Ingredient," in *Science Fantasy* (Bournemouth), December 1959.
"The Whispering Gallery," in *Zacherley's Midnight Snacks*, edited by Zacherley. New York, Ballantine, 1960.
"'L' Is for Lash," in *Amazing* (New York), July 1960.
"Sitting Duck," in *New Worlds* (London), November 1960.
"The Unknown," in *Amazing* (New York), March 1961.
"A Trek to Na-Abiza," in *Science Fiction Adventures* (London), July 1961.
"Beyond the Line," in *Fantastic* (New York), September 1964.
"A Niche in Time," in *World's Best Science Fiction 1965*, edited by Donald A. Wollheim and Terry Carr. New York, Ace, 1965.

"The Legend of Ernie Deacon," in *Analog* (New York), March 1965.

"Coco-Talk," in *New Writings in SF 7*, edited by John Carnell. London, Dobson, 1966; New York, Bantam, 1971.

"Echo," in *Famous Science Fiction* (New York), Winter 1967.

"The Year Dot," in *If* (New York), January 1969.

"When in Doubt—Destroy!," in *Vision of Tomorrow* (Newcastle upon Tyne), August 1969.

"The Undiscovered Country," in *A Sea of Space*, edited by William F. Nolan. New York, Bantam, 1970.

"Life of the Party," in *Vision of Tomorrow* (Newcastle upon Tyne), February 1970.

"The Impatient Dreamers," in *Vision of Tomorrow* (Newcastle upon Tyne), June 1970.

"The Unpicker," in *Androids, Time Machines, and Blue Giraffes*, edited by Roger Elwood and Vic Ghidalia. Chicago, Follett, 1973.

"The Man Who Wasn't There," in *Amazing* (New York), November 1978.

"The Smile of the Sphinx," in *The Best Animal Stories of Science Fiction and Fantasy*, edited by Donald J. Sobol. New York, Warne, 1979.

"The Green Car," in *The Thirteen Crimes of Science Fiction*, edited by Isaac Asimov, Martin H. Greenberg, and Charles G. Waugh. New York, Doubleday, 1979.

OTHER PUBLICATIONS

Novel

The Dangerous Edge. London, Long, 1951.

Other

The True Book about Space Travel. London, Muller, 1954; as *The Prentice-Hall Book about Space Travel*, New York, Prentice Hall, 1955.

*

William F. Temple commented:

(1981) I've read SF since childhood. At first, uncritically: I didn't notice it was only two-dimensional, i. e., lacked depth, especially in characterization. Then critically: I decided to try to add that third dimension in my writing. Then despairingly: Nobody noticed that I had. Then cynically: Nobody wanted it, anyway. They preferred their robots. Then uncaringly: I don't bother to write it any more.

* * *

Most critics would agree that the golden age of modern science fiction occurred in the 1930's. Then were found the pulp magazines with such visionary editors as John Campbell to encourage and develop the writers who were to become almost legendary figures in the field. While Asimov, van Vogt, and others were honing their skills in the United States, William F. Temple was drawn to science fiction in England. Temple's interest, like that of his counterparts across the sea, was fostered by his companionship with Arthur C. Clarke, John Wyndham, and John Christopher. In the early days of science fiction there seemed to work among such individuals a kind of cross current which stimulated and sustained them in the creation of materials at which conventional critics of the day looked askance. Only the hardy survived those pioneering times to bring forth such books as *Childhood's End* and *No Blade of Grass*. That Temple was of durable stuff was demonstrated by what he went through to turn out what was perhaps his most notable work, *Four-Sided Triangle*. While serving in Africa with the Eighth Army in World War II, Temple converted what had been a short story into novel length. Despite the novel's publication delay, its survival qualities could not be extinguished. In a fascinating variation of the trite, a woman selects one of the two suitors who vie for her. The man who loses uses a matter-copying device to create an "exact" duplicate of her—which loads the novel's plot structure engrossingly.

Some readers may find Temple's work a bit stuffy at times, but his plots employ interesting contrasts and conflicts: a group of explorers investigates the alien topography of the Moon, but the real territory to be mapped is the unknown personality of warring party members. His story ideas are usually quite interesting, as in a short story like "A Date to Remember." This yarn seems almost banal in some ways—a wife about to bring forth a child, rainy night, success/failure conflict of two old school chums. Then we discover the central idea, that Martians have long "passed" as Earthlings, struggling to civilize the inhabitants of Earth while disguised as Byron, Pasteur, Haydn, and others throughout the centuries.

—Robert H. Wilcox

———

TENN, William. Pseudonym for Philip Klass. American. Born in Des Moines, Iowa, 8 November 1919. Educated at Iowa State University, Ames, B.S. 1941. Served in the United States Army during World War II. Consulting Editor, *Fantasy and Science Fiction*, New York, 1958. Since 1966, Member of the Department of English, Pennsylvania State University, University Park. Address: Department of English, Pennsylvania State University, University Park, Pennsylvania 16802, U.S.A.

SCIENCE-FICTION PUBLICATIONS

Novel

Of Men and Monsters. New York, Ballantine, 1968; London, Pan, 1971.

Short Stories

Of All Possible Worlds. New York, Ballantine, 1955; enlarged edition, London, Joseph, 1956.

The Human Angle. New York, Ballantine, 1956.

Time in Advance. New York, Bantam, 1958; London, Gollancz, 1963.

The Seven Sexes. New York, Ballantine, 1968.

The Square Root of Man. New York, Ballantine, 1968; London, Pan, 1971.

The Wooden Star. New York, Ballantine, 1968; London, Pan, 1971.

Uncollected Short Stories

"On Venus, Have We Got a Rabbi," in *The Best Science Fiction of the Year 4*, edited by Terry Carr. New York, Ballantine, and London, Gollancz, 1975.

"Bernie the Faust," in *Dark Sins, Dark Dreams*, edited by Barry N. Malzberg and Bill Pronzini. New York, Doubleday, 1978.

"There Were People on Bikini," in *The Best of Omni Science Fiction 5*, edited by Don Myrus. New York, Omni, 1983.

OTHER PUBLICATIONS

Novel

A Lamp for Medusa. New York, Belmont, 1968.

Other

"The Fiction in Science Fiction," in *Science Fiction Adventures* (New York), March 1954.
"Jazz Then, Musicology Now," in *Fantasy and Science Fiction* (New York), May 1972.

Editor, *Children of Wonder*. New York, Simon and Schuster, 1953; as *Outsiders*, New York, Permabooks, 1954.
Editor, with Donald E. Westlake, *Once Against the Law*. New York, Macmillan, 1968.

*   *   *

"The incredible William Tenn," as he has been dubbed by Brian Aldiss, started a whole school of comic and satiric science fiction in the 1940's. Tenn quickly perfected a way of looking at things, at once funny, bitter, and serious, that made him the natural heir to the nearly silent tradition of Swift and Voltaire. Sheckley, Pohl, Ellison, Russell, Goulart, Knight, Kagan, Eisenberg, Brown, Lafferty, and Malzberg have all echoed Tenn's work at one time or another. A serious humorist, Tenn has had a double problem. The science-fiction genre has always made if difficult to tell serious writers from entertainers, through the manner of publications and because the entertainers often claim to be serious, or have it claimed for them; also, satirists and funny men have rarely risen high in the genre (in terms of awards and sales). Tenn was a pioneer whose example was imitated by writers who developed in different ways, but who also became known for the angle opened up by Tenn, thus diffusing the effect he might have had if his plumage had not been confused with that of imitators. Tenn imitations might have been more acceptable to some editors of the 1950's because they were watered-down versions of Tenn-like material—less serious and not so critical of the world and human nature. Tenn's stories are always a bit disturbing at some level, even when they are breathlessly readable, amusing, or cute.

An outgoing but sensitive man, Tenn fell silent by the end of the 1960's, even as his work was gathered into an impressive, though editorially flawed, six-volume set from Ballantine. One suspects that neglect made him feel that perhaps his work was not worthy. He went on to become an excellent college teacher, leaving behind a body of work sufficient to secure the reputation of any major writer in this field, and a name often confused with another Klass in various reference works. He published one story in the 1970's, "On Venus, Have We Got a Rabbi," which Damon Knight called "the great story he was talking about in the fifties." It was well received, garnering award nominations and appearing in a best of the year collection. There have been recent signs that he will soon have several works, including a new novel, to offer his readers. Tenn was also the editor of *Children of Wonder*, a pioneering theme anthology which was notable for its variety of stories and non-parochial choice of authors. Two incisive essays, "The Fiction in Science Fiction" and "Jazz Then, Musicology Now," are both required reading

for anyone who cares about the ideals of literate science fiction, if not its practice.

Notable stories from Tenn's first two decades include "Brooklyn Project," which Fritz Leiber has called a "Marvelously cynical" time-travel story, and "Firewater!," one of the most sophisticated stories ever published by John W. Campbell, with its unforgettable lament by Larry for the loss of what he was and what he cannot be as humanity struggles to keep its sanity before the seemingly superior aliens who have taken up residence on earth. The story should have taken all the awards. "Generation of Noah" is one of the finest atomic threat stories ever written. "Of All Possible Worlds," "Wednesday's Child" (a fascinating sequel to the much reprinted classic "Child's Play"), "Time Waits for Winthrop," "Eastward Ho!," and "The Malted Milk Monster" all drew honorable mentions in Judith Merril's best of the year collections, while "Bernie the Faust" took pride of place as the first story in the 1964 collection. "Time Waits for Winthrop" shows a remarkable use of exotic ideas, among them fairly advanced biological concepts, another feature of Tenn's stories that makes them unusual for the 1950's. "The Discovery of Morniel Mathaway" shows an understanding of the creative process that is usually beyond most SF writers. Jacques Sadoul has called it "the most beautiful example of a temporal paradox offered by science fiction." "The Custodian," with its plea for the blending of art and utility, and "Down among the Dead Men," with its clever use of offstage space opera to heighten a pathetic predicament, both manage to do what few SF stories can do—move us emotionally and intellectually on a mature level.

Tenn is always a master of situations, which at first prod and intrigue, then provoke curiosity, make us laugh a bit, then explode into some thoughtful irony or observation. Once you catch on to a Tenn situation, you can't stop reading. The satirical tones of irony, mockery, slapstick, and occasional bitterness do wonders for genre materials, precisely because Tenn joins these materials to human experience outside the insular worlds of SF wish-fulfillment and power fantasy. The science-fiction materials are all there, strong and clear, but just as you're about to accept the story at its face value Tenn hits you with something real and painful. He's a very sly writer, inserting polished, precise narratives into our minds through unexpected channels. Many of his stories have the effect of blossoming into a single line of great beauty and illumination; but always the aesthetic fires are banked by irony and, above all, eloquent wit, behind which sits the ultimate authority of an author who has something to say, who sometimes seems to believe with Oscar Wilde that eloquence and wit alone can make the scales fall from human eyes. One senses an author laughing and crying at the same time, writing, exhibiting intellect and dramatic talent within the confines of a narrow genre.

Tenn's two long works are the novel *Of Men and Monsters* and the short novel *A Lamp for Medusa*. The second work is easily worthy of having appeared in *Unknown Worlds*. Funny, atmospheric, and wonderfully paced, this neglected work has seen only a shabby book appearance. It is not surprising, given Tenn's tendencies, that is recalls the poise of the *Unknown Worlds* tradition, since that magazine was the only sizable market for humorous work of the early 1940's, and Tenn's only antecedent within the SF genre.

Of Men and Monsters, a story of humanity living in the walls of the houses of giant aliens who have occupied the earth, is a vivid, energetically paced story which best embodies one of Tenn's main points: that humanity is not what it thinks itself to be, that implicit in our biological history is a nature not of our making; we may glimpse it, even understand it at time, but it may be a while before we can remake ourselves, if ever. In his awareness of biological and anthropological complexities, Tenn has at the center of his work the most thoroughgoing of science-fiction methods: the collision of the possible with the actual, with the actual displaying fantastic holding power. Eric the Eye, the Lilliputian viewpoint character of the novel, learns that his society is not what he thought it was, that its rites of passage are a sham, and finally that human beings are not what he thought they were either; since change seems unlikely on a radical scale, he accepts this human nature and joins the plan to make of it something pervasive and influential. Eric becomes part of the reverse invasion of human vermin as they begin the infestation of the great alien starships. The story is very vivid, the characters charming (Eric meets Rachel Esthersdaughter, one of the nicest nice Jewish girls in all science fiction). The death of Eric's uncle is shatteringly presented. There are great wonder and awesome confrontation, sharply realized. Most importantly, there is an anthropological sophistication in the depiction of social systems; the aliens are properly terrifying, puzzling, and *other*. Tenn's tendency to romance, compassion, and brief, hard-bitten sentimentality shows through his bitterness just enough to be believable. The novel may be compared to Daniel Galouye's *Dark Universe* and Thomas M. Disch's *The Genocides*.

It is regrettable that Tenn stopped his development in the 1960's, when it was clear that the continuous practice of his craft, coupled with his acute and constant rethinking of the nature of fiction and science fiction, would certainly have produced a mighty progress over his very worthy body of work. Now that he seems poised at the start of his most mature period, it remains to be seen whether he will continue the main line suggested by his previous work, or whether his silence is a sign that he has been developing a new direction. He can do anything he wants, except hack work ("I have no talent for it," he has said). Few writers have ever suggested so much promise at the start of their sixth decade. Tenn belongs to the great generation of Asimov, Heinlein and Clarke. He is the most perfect example of the failure of the awards system within the science-fiction community, and an obvious candidate for the Grand Master Nebula Award. His work is a clear example that SF can be literature, that it can provoke us to see, fell, and think. Tenn belongs to that unbroken chain of sayers who expose our delusions and foibles, our willful blindness and stupidity, and who ultimately stand against death and the amnesia of generations. "Tenn is another artist," Damon Knight has written, "who won't stop till he's had the last word."

—George Zebrowski

TENNANT, Emma (Christina). Also writes as Catherine Aydy. British. Born in London, 20 October 1937. Educated at St. Paul's Girls' School, London. Has one son and two daughters. Travel correspondent, *Queen*, London, 1963; features editor, *Vogue*, London, 1966; Editor, *Bananas*, London, 1975-78. Agent: Gill Coleridge, Anthony Sheil Associates, 43 Doughty Street, London WC1N 2LF. Address: 78 Elgin Crescent, London W. 11, England.

SCIENCE-FICTION PUBLICATIONS

Novels

The Time of the Crack. London, Cape, 1973; as *The Crack*, London, Penguin, 1978.
The Last of the Country House Murders. London, Cape, 1974; New York, Nelson, 1976.
Hotel de Dream. London, Gollancz, 1976.
Queen of Stones. London, Cape, 1982.

OTHER PUBLICATIONS

Novels

The Colour of Rain (as Catherine Aydy). London, Weidenfeld and Nicolson, 1964.
The Bad Sister. London, Gollancz, and New York, Coward McCann, 1978.
Wild Nights. London, Cape, 1979; New York, Harcourt Brace, 1980.
Alice Fell. London, Cape, 1980.
Woman Beware Woman. London, Cape, 1983; as *The Half-Mother*, Boston, Little Brown, 1985.
Black Marina. London, Faber, 1985.

Other (for children)

The Boggart. London, Granada, 1980.
The Search for Treasure Island. London, Penguin, 1981.
The Ghost Child. London, Heinemann, 1984.

Other

Editor, *Bananas*. London, Quartet-Blond and Briggs, 1977.
Editor, *Saturday Night Reader*. London, W. H. Allen, 1979.

*   *   *

Emma Tennant's fiction explores realms of satirical, psychological, and apocalyptic fantasy, worlds where past and present, reality and illusion, mingle freely, if often uneasily. Although a sophisticated humor marks much of her work, a sense of futility and loss ultimately prevails, and Tennant's novels generally conclude on despondent if inconclusive notes.

The threat of apocalypse which frequently underscores this sense of failure is emphasized most fully in Tennant's first novel, *The Time of the Crack*. In this tale a cataclysmic earthquake levels London and splits the Thames, creating a startling image for what one character refers to as a "schizophrenic society" and providing a visual metaphor for Tennant's contrast between a collapsed city and "the other side," an idyllic world where life will be perfect. The characters in the novel strive to reach this promised land—particularly the women, banded together and led by a charismatic liberated leader named Medea Smith. Of course, as in all of Tennant's stories, the striving is usually in vain and the paradise does not measure up to its illusion.

The apocalyptic shadow is less ominous in *Hotel de Dream*, but the lure of an alternate reality is even stronger. The occupants of a seedy boarding house in Kensington, *The Westringham*, escape the fetid and oppressive atmosphere of the hotel and of their failed lives by sleeping, dreaming their various versions of a British paradise—royalty, position, exotic adventure, wealth; but gradually, they begin to wander in and out of one another's dreams, and soon the force of the collective dream overtakes and controls them, and the outside world as well. The ultimate failure of the dream world to transcend reality suggest not only the futility of fantasizing but also the failure of a past England of aristocratic grandeur and glory to connect with the modern world. As Mrs. Routledge, the hotel's despairing owner, feels, the future "only seemed capable of presenting itself as a revamped and frequently misty version of the past. "

This sense of collapsed time also permeates Tennant's other two novels, *The Last of the Country House Murders* and *Woman Beware Woman*, both of which are rooted in the murder and gothic mystery genre but are reshaped by Tennant's peculiar vision and clever plotting. The first one, set in an overpopulated future after an unspecified Revolution, centers around the government's plan to arrange the murder of the last great country-estate occupant—with his knowledge—as a means of bolstering the vital tourist trade. Again, reality and fantasy intertwine: long-dead relatives of the estate owner casually appear, and an intriguing character named Cedric suspects that the entire usiverse is an optical illusion. This novel, satirizing such groups as tourists, decadent aristocrats, and bumbling government authorities, is probably Tennant's most entertaining, though it does broach some thin political commentary.

The outcome is more grim in *Woman Beware Woman*, the most sophisticated of these novels. The setting shifts from England to southern Ireland, where a prominent writer is found dead near his seaside estate; the narrator, Minnie, who practically grew up with this family, returns to the estate after a ten-year absence, only to become entangled in an increasingly bizarre psychological web of circumstance. This is a tale of love and passion, jealousy and obsession, but is lifted above mere melodrama by Tennant's skillful and imaginative plot structure, by the supernatural allusions (the widow's mother is said to have possessed "the eye"), and by the disturbed narrator, whose chilling unreliability gradually becomes apparent.

Tennant's obvious concern with women—their desires and needs, their roles, obligations, and subjugation—receives its darkest, most sinister treatment in this novel, which ends in betrayal: woman against woman, a contrast to the bond of sisterhood suggested in *The Time of the Crack* and *Hotel de Dream*.

Tennant is an imaginative author whose clever plots unfold in futuristic and fantastic settings juxtaposed with the ordinary: a run-down hotel filled with dream, a crowd of regressing psychoanalysis patients at a funfair, a cracked river in London, a British manor house where a reddish-haired dandy is trying to decide on his murderer. Against these backgrounds, Tennant sets characters who often serve simply as allegorical roles; they are, for the most part, thin, cardboard-like, easily disposed of, and usually recognizable types.

Nor are Tennant's themes especially new: the end of the world, dreams as reality, utopian promise, social and political satire, the gothic mystery or murder of manners—most of these have long traditions. Rather, it is her particular blending of these elements, along with her peculiarly beguiling style, humor, and imagination, that distinguishes Tennant's works.

However, Tennant offers no solutions, no alternatives, in the quirky worlds she creates, where characters are caught between a failed past and a bleak future. She merely implies that we cannot return to a treasured past and that illusions of an idyllic future are false. Perhaps these stories are warnings, perhaps only nihilistic views disguised as satire, or perhaps merely reflections of the human condition and its absurdity.

—Karen Charmaine Blansfield

TENNESHAW, S. M. See **GARRETT, Randall; SILVERBERG, Robert.**

TEVIS, Walter (Stone). American. Born in San Francisco, California, 28 February 1928. Educated at the University of Kentucky, Lexington, M. A. 1956; University of Iowa, Iowa City, M. F. A. 1961. Served in the United States Navy. Divorced; one son and one daughter. Worked for Kentucky highway department in 1950's and early 1960's; after 1965, Professor of English, Ohio University, Athens. *Died 9 August 1984.*

SCIENCE-FICTION PUBLICATIONS

Novels

The Man Who Fell to Earth. New York, Fawcett, and London, Muller, 1963.
Mockingbird. New York, Doubleday, and London, Hodder and Stoughton, 1980.
The Steps of the Sun. New York, Doubleday, 1983; London, Gollancz, 1984.

Short Stories

Far from Home. New York, Doubleday, 1981; London, Gollancz, 1983.

OTHER PUBLICATIONS

Novel

The Hustler. New York, Harper, 1959; London, Joseph, 1960.
The Queen's Gambit. New York, Random House, and London, Heinemann, 1983.
The Color of Money. New York, Warner, 1984; London, Severn House, 1985.

*

Walter Tevis commented:

(1981) I suppose I write disguised autobiographies. The idea, as far as I know, is to move other people. I feel alienated from other people sometimes; when I was younger the feeling was stronger than it is now. My major characters are alienated, by virtue of being pool players, from Mars, robots, the only people alive who can read, or alcoholics. I like to write about people under psychological stress, and when I write I am very serious about it.

*   *   *

Thomas Jerome Newton, in *The Man Who Fell to Earth*, is an emissary from the dying planet of Anthea, sent to prepare a refuge and transportation for its last few survivors. We never learn his real name. By introducing advanced Anthean technology Newton amasses the necessary millions of dollars, but attracts the attentions of the FBI who imprison and interrogate him, blinding him in the process. Eventually released, he abandons his project and dwindles into perpetual alcoholic exile. Earth, though they colonised it in the first place, is no place for Antheans. Walter Tevis's novel is the classic refutation of the alien invasion theme in SF. He reduces the interplanetary war to a case of depression, the story of the loneliest man in the world. Newton could save mankind, but represents a threat to the American economy. He is disabled not by military might or scientific ingenuity, but by smothering bureaucracy. Seeing Newton decrepit and drunk in a bar, Nathan Bryce, his only human confidant, reflects that he "certainly would not have been the first means of possible salvation to get the official treatment. " Christ, it seems, was an Anthean too. The failure of Newton's mission is a slow, pathetic crucifixion. Bryce remembers Thoreau's dictum: "quiet desperation" is the mood of the novel, an unobstrusive tragedy in an unostentatious style that conceals irony, bitterness, and ultimately cold fury. "I worked very hard to become an imitation human being. . . . " Newton says. "And of course I succeeded. "

Mockingbird is altogether less original and distinctive. In a future America run and serviced by robots human faculties, emotions, and even social urges have been eroded. The senior robot, Bob Spofforth (Mark Nine), is an interesting figure of moral ambivalence, sexless and immortal, but plagued by human dreams that slipped in under his mental programming. As in Bradbury's *Fahrenheit 451*, literacy is suppressed but the hero learns to read, and is emboldened to further rebellion when he meets a woman less obedient to convention than he is. The book is efficiently plotted and written, but suffers from too much formula and too little variation.

Tevis's only collection, *Far from Home*, divides neatly into six competent but routine novelty stories, mostly from *Galaxy* at the end of the 1960's, and seven more searching pieces from 1979-80, including four previously unpublished highly Freudian self-examinations. These latter fictions demand to be read with a sympathy for their author which they do not altogether repay, but it seems that in its primary therapeutic purpose Tevis's writing finally, if precariously, succeeded. *The Steps of the Sun* tells how a big, rich, glum, impotent American restores himself and his impoverished nation by an illegal venture into space. In Tevis's quaintly benevolent cosmos, Ben Belson swiftly finds not only "safe" uranium but also a perfect analgesic and a sentient planet that hauls him through his self-induced psychological crisis. What is hard is bringing these gifts back to Earth, whose authorities treat the returning explorer with all the suspicion and hostility they showed to the extra-terrestrial benefactor in *The Man Who Fell to Earth*. Whereas Thomas Jerome Newton is last seen drunk and defeated, Ben Belson's life on the run culminates in a period of stringent purification in a bleak, utopian China before a final symbolic tableau in which he and his wife switch on all the lights of a New York dark for 30 years and more. *The Steps of the Sun* annoys those who insist on reading science fiction literally, but as a fantasy quest through a damaged psyche it is effective and affecting. It ended Tevis's melancholy career on a hopeful note.

—Colin Greenland

————

THANET, Neil. See FANTHORPE, R. Lionel.

————

THOMAS, Cogswell. See COGSWELL, Theodore R. ; THOMAS, Ted.

————

THOMAS, D(onald) M(ichael). British. Born in Redruth, Cornwall, 27 January 1935. Educated at Redruth Grammar School; University High School, Melbourne; New College, Oxford, B. A. (honours) in English, 1958, M. A. Served in the British Army (national service), 1953-54. Has two sons and one daughter. Teacher, Teignmouth Grammar School, Devon, 1959-63; Senior Lecturer in English, Hereford College of Education, 1964-78. Visiting Lecturer in English, Hamline University, St. Paul, Minnesota, 1967; Creative Writing Teacher, American University, Washington, D. C., 1982. Recipient: Richard Hillary Memorial Prize, 1960; Cholmondeley Award, 1978; *Guardian* -Gollancz Fantasy Novel prize, 1979; Los Angeles *Times* prize, 1981; Silver Pen Award, 1982. Address: 10 Greyfriars Avenue, Hereford HR4 0BE, England.

SCIENCE-FICTION PUBLICATIONS

Novels

The Flute-Player. London, Gollancz, and New York, Dutton, 1979.
Birthstone. London, Gollancz, 1980.
The White Hotel. London, Gollancz, and New York, Viking Press, 1981.
Ararat. London, Gollancz, and New York, Viking Press, 1983.
Swallow. London, Gollancz, and New York, Viking Press, 1984.

Uncollected Short Stories

"Seeking a Suitable Donor," in *The New SF*, edited by Langdon Jones. London, Hutchinson, 1969.
"Labyrinth," in *New Worlds* (London), April 1969.

Plays

Radio Plays: *You Will Hear Thunder*, 1981; *Boris Godunov*, from play by Pushkin, 1984.

Verse

Personal and Possessive. London, Outposts, 1964.
Penguin Modern Poets 11, with D. M. Black and Peter Redgrove. London, Penguin, 1968.
Two Voices. London, Cape Goliard Press, and New York, Grossman, 1968.
The Lover's Horoscope: Kinetic Poem. Laramie, Wyoming, Purple Sage, 1970.
Logan Stone. London, Cape Goliard Press, and New York, Grossman, 1971.
The Shaft. Gillingham, Kent, Arc, 1973.
Lilith-Prints. Cardiff, Second Aeon, 1974.
Symphony in Moscow. Richmond, Surrey, Keepsake Press, 1974.
Love and Other Deaths. London, Elek, 1975.
The Rock. Knotting, Bedfordshire, Sceptre Press, 1975.
Orpheus in Hell. Knotting, Bedfordshire, Sceptre Press, 1977.

The Honeymoon Voyage. London, Secker and Warburg, 1978.
Dreaming in Bronze. London, Secker and Warburg, 1981.
Selected Poems. London, Secker and Warburg, and New York, Viking Press, 1983.
News from the Front, with Sylvia Kantaris. Todmorden, Lancashire, Arc, 1983.

Other

The Devil and the Floral Dance (for children). London, Robson, 1978.

Editor, *The Granite Kingdom: Poems of Cornwall.* Truro, Cornwall, Barton, 1970.
Editor, *Poetry in Crosslight.* London, Longman, 1975.
Editor, *Songs from the Earth: Selected Poems of John Harris, Cornish Miner, 1820-84.* Padstow, Cornwall, Lodenek Press, 1977.

Translator, *Requiem, and Poem Without a Hero*, by Anna Akhmatova. London, Elek, and Athens, Ohio University Press, 1976.
Translator, *Way of All the Earth*, by Anna Akhmatova. London, Secker and Warburg, and Athens, Ohio University Press, 1979.
Translator, *Invisible Threads*, by Evtushenko. New York, Macmillan, 1981.
Translator, *The Bronze Horseman and Other Poems*, by Pushkin. London, Secker and Warburg, and New York, Viking Press, 1982.
Translator, *A Dove in Santiago*, by Evtushenko. London, Secker and Warburg, 1982; New York, Viking Press, 1983.
Translator, *You Will Hear Thunder*, by Anna Akhmatova. London, Secker and Warburg, and Athens, Ohio University Press-Swallow Press, 1985.

*

D. M. Thomas comments:
Most of my science-fiction poetry is collected in one publication, *Penguin Modern Poets 11* (1968). Since then I have remained interested in the mythic aspect of SF, but have moved away from "pure" SF into other areas of myth.

*   *   *

D. M. Thomas's SF writing is largely restricted to his earlier poetry, published from the mid-1960's through the 1970's. Since that time he has turned increasingly to fiction, and he has gained considerable attention, especially for *The White Hotel*, *Ararat*, and its recent sequel, *Swallow*. Thomas's work in these forms is unified by common themes, particularly by the emotional and psychological structures that link sex, love, death, and artistic creation.

Thomas's SF poetry is often narrative, relying on SF settings and tropes to explore the emotional tangles that might arise in these placements with effective imagery, striking metaphors, and evocative language and tone. Poems like "Missionary," "A Dead Planet," and "The Strait" tell the stories we identify with science fiction—alien contacts and troubles with androids. Other poems show Thomas moving confidently across a variety of forms: from the evocative lyrics of "Fire Victims" and "Elegy for an Android" to striking dramatic monologues reminiscent of Browning like "Tithonus" and "Hera's Spring." The poet

can produce both the traditional dialogue "A Conversation upon the Shadow" and visually stimulating concrete poems like "Symbiosis" and "Mercury." In most of these, Thomas demonstrates his skill at reworking the mythic inspirations supplied by science-fiction stories. The most striking examples of this latter strategy are "The Strait," based on Bradbury's *Marionettes Inc.*, and "Hera's Spring," arising in response to Clarke's *The City and the Stars*. The former work poignantly captures the painful emotions aroused when a living woman must be replaced by an android duplicate. In "Hera's Spring" the motherly speaker tries to allay the sudden sense of loss and sorrow that a newly reminded Jeserac faces when he realizes the hundreds of lives he has lived before his present existence.

Thomas often relies on the myths of SF to emphasize isolation and alienation, love, sex, and violence, concerns especially apparent in his formally innovative, tabular poem "Hospital of Transplanted Hearts." In its multiple possibilities for reading and interpretation, this work seems to anticipate Calvino's *Castle of the Crossed Destinies*. In "The Head-Rape" Thomas explores the need for personal mental seclusion, especially in the complex and powerfully charged atmosphere of sexual violence—here as brutalization, but in "A Conversation upon the Shadow" as part of intimacy and love.

These themes continued to fascinate Thomas, and his later work often returns to them, often published in *New Worlds*. Indeed, pieces appearing in this periodical reveal Thomas's progression from poetry within the genre to work belonging more in the mainstream. Long and extremely complex poems like *Two Voices* and "Computer 70: Dreams and Love Poems" still rely on technology and estranged settings to examine love and sorrow; and the former is particularly evocative of a post-holocaust survivor's experience balanced by the reflections of a woman who is both the unwilling human and the mythic earth mother. "Mr. Black's Poems of Innocence" marks the first of Thomas's incursions into the social sciences for his estranging material, and the poem is a masterpiece of parody mixed with serious, if fictionalized, psychotherapy. A mute schizophrenic suffers operant conditioning therapy, but between his outward, verbal answers we read his inner figurative musings. These center on a fantasy of his own entrapment and isolation, first associated with being a trapped sweep in a labyrinthine chimney, and then with passages from Rider Haggard's *King Solomon's Mines*. This latter material is especially important because it returns in yet another guise in Thomas's latest novel, *Swallow*, where once again the writer feels compelled to rework the figures of desire, greed, and death.

Although Thomas published several more pieces in *New Worlds*, these were increasingly removed from the usual settings and tropes marking SF. With the series that appeared in September 1979 ("Primitive Behavior," "A Letter From Marina," "Fathers, Sons and Lovers," and "The Woman to Freud"), he seemed to have given up the technological side of SF altogether. Here, we find material anticipating that in *The White Hotel*—for example, in the next to last, a historical fictionalization of the letters preceding the suicide of one of Freud's disciples, and in the last the sexual fantasy about a hysteria victim and Freud's son, which becomes the first section of the "Don Giovanni" section in the novel.

Throughout his work, Thomas shows the potentiality of science fiction's myths for poetic expression. We can only hope that he will again turn his prodigious skills in this direction.

—Len Hatfield

THOMAS, K. See **FEARN, John Russell.**

THOMAS, Ted (Theodore L. Thomas). Also writes as Leonard Lockhard; Cogswell Thomas. American. Born in New York City, 13 April 1920. Educated at Massachusetts Institute of Technology, S. B. 1947; Georgetown University, Washington, D. C., J. D. 1953. Served in the United States Army, 1943-46: 1st Lieutenant. Married Virginia Kent Paton in 1947; two daughters and one son. Chemical engineer, American Cyanamid Company, Stamford, Connecticut, 1947-50. Patent lawyer, in Washington, D. C., 1950-55, and since 1955, for Armstrong Cork Company, Lancaster, Pennsylvania. Columnist ("Science for Everybody"), Stamford *Advocate*, 1949-79, and columnist ("The Science Springboard"), *Fantasy and Science Fiction*, New York, 1964-67. Chairman, Lancaster Zoning Board of Adjustments, 1966-70, and Lancaster Narcotics and Dangerous Drugs Committee, 1970-71. Address: 1284 Wheatland Avenue, Lancaster, Pennsylvania 17603, U. S. A.

SCIENCE-FICTION PUBLICATIONS

Novels

The Clone, with Kate Wilhelm. New York, Berkley, 1965; London, Hale, 1968.
Year of the Cloud, with Kate Wilhelm. New York, Doubleday, 1970.

Uncollected Short Stories

"The Revisitor," in *Space Science Fiction* (New York), September 1952.
"The Fatal Third," in *Planet* (New York), November 1953.
"The Penultimate Weapon," in *Future* (New York), January 1954.
"The Disciplinarian," in *Blue Book* (Chicago), October 1954.
"Trial Without Combat," in *Future 28* (New York), 1955.
"The Far Look," in *SF: 57*, edited by Judith Merril. Philadelphia, Gnome Press, 1957.
"The Disappearing Man," in *Science Fiction Stories*, July 1957.
"Mars Trial," in *Future* (New York), Summer 1957.
"Twice-Told Tales," in *Super Science Fiction* (New York), August 1957.
"The Attractive Nuisance," in *Science Fiction Quarterly* (Holyoke, Massachusetts), August 1957.
"Just Rub a Lamp," in *Science Fiction Stories*, September 1957.
"The Sound of the Wind," in *Science Fiction Stories*, June 1958.
"The Law School," in *Analog* (New York), June 1958.
"The Back of a Hand," in *Future* (New York), June 1958.
"The Destroyer," in *Science Fiction Stories*, September 1958.
"Satellite Passage," in *SF: 59*, edited by Judith Merril. Philadelphia, Gnome Press, 1959.
"The Good Work," in *If* (New York), February 1959.
"Broken Tool," in *Analog* (New York), July 1959.
"New Model Spaceman," in *Future* (New York), August 1959.
"The Sound of Screaming," in *Amazing* (New York), October 1960.
"The Crackpot," in *Analog* (New York), November 1960.
"The Flames of Life," in *Amazing* (New York), December 1960.
"The Moon v. Nansen," in *New Worlds* (London), February 1961.

"Passage to Malish," in *Fantastic* (New York), August 1961.
"Day of Succession," in *A Century of Science Fiction*, edited by Damon Knight. New York, Simon and Schuster, 1962; London, Gollancz, 1963.
"The Spy," in *If* (New York), May 1962.
"Test," in *Best from Fantasy and Science Fiction 12*, edited by Avram Davidson. New York, Doubleday, 1963.
"The Weather Man," in *Analog 2*, edited by John W. Campbell, Jr. New York, Doubleday, 1964.
"The Soft Woman," in *Fantastic* (New York), February 1964.
"The Lonely Man," in *The Eighth Galaxy Reader*, edited by Frederik Pohl. New York, Doubleday, 1965.
"Manfire," in *Worlds of Tomorrow* (New York), January 1965.
"Lunar Landing," in *Fantasy and Science Fiction* (New York), September 1965.
"December 28th," in *The Playboy Book of Science Fiction and Fantasy*. New York, Paperback Library, 1966.
"The Doctor," in *Orbit 2*, edited by Damon Knight. New York, Putnam, 1967.
"The Being in the Tank," in *Galaxy* (New York), August 1967.
"The Other Culture," in *Analog* (New York), January 1969.
"Welcome, Centaurians," in *Galaxy* (New York), January 1969.
"The Weather on the Sun," in *Orbit 8*, edited by Damon Knight. New York, Putnam, 1970.
"The Intruder," in *A Pocketful of Stars*, edited by Damon Knight. New York, Doubleday, 1971; London, Gollancz, 1972.
"The Tour," in *Fantasy and Science Fiction* (New York), March 1971.
"The Swan Song of Dame Horse," in *Analog* (New York), June 1971.
"Motion Day at the Courthouse," in *Analog* (New York), October 1971.
"Paradise Regained" (as Cogswell Thomas, with Theodore R. Cogswell), in *Saving Worlds*, edited by Roger Elwood and Virginia Kidd. New York, Doubleday, 1973.
"Early Bird," with Theodore R. Cogswell, in *Astounding*, edited by Harry Harrison. New York, Random House, 1973; London, Sidgwick and Jackson, 1974.
"The Rescuers," in *Fantasy and Science Fiction* (New York), September 1974.
"Players at Null-G," with Theodore R. Cogswell and Algis Budrys, in *Fantasy and Science Fiction* (New York), July 1975.
"The Family Man," in *Fantasy and Science Fiction* (New York), March 1978.
"Ceramic Incident," in *The Analog Anthology 1*, edited by Stanley Schmidt. New York, Davis, 1980.
"The Innocents' Refuge," in *Travels Through Time*, edited by Isaac Asimov, Martin H. Greenberg, and Charles G. Waugh. Milwaukee, Raintree, 1981.

Uncollected Short Stories as Leonard Lockhard (series: Patent Attorney in all stories)

"Improbable Profession" (with Charles L. Harness), September 1952, "That Professional Look" (with Charles L. Harness), January 1954, "The Curious Profession," April 1956, "The Professional Touch," February 1959, "The Lagging Profession," January 1961, "The Professional Approach," September 1962, and "Professional Dilemma," October 1964, all in *Astounding* (New York). "The Magnificent Profession," in *Fantastic Universe* (Chicago), November 1955.

*   *   *

Over a period of more then two decades, Ted Thomas has produced a small but steady stream of short stories of unusually high calibre. Although he has yet to produce a novel that is solely his own work, he has collaborated with Kate Wilhelm twice at novel length, and in each case the end product has been of superior quality. *The Clone*, for example, based on a short story of the same name by Thomas alone, is one of the most frightening and plausible tales of biochemistry gone wild. An amorphous creature is spawned in the sewers of a major city, able to absorb virtually any other organic structure—including people—upon contact.

The Year of the Cloud deals with the theme of world disaster. The Earth passes through a strange interstellar cloud that has catastrophic effects on the planet. Tidal waves and volcanic activity are only short-term problems. The oceans turn into a gelatin-like substance and water is in short supply everywhere. The disaster is seen through the eyes of a number of characters, some of whom are working to reverse the effects of the cloud. But the cloud eventually proves to be a mixed blessing in this story, which combines scientific investigation with straightforward adventure.

Thomas himself is best known for his short stories, including those set against a background where the Weather Control Board controls the Earth because of its ability to affect the lifestyles and commercial undertakings of everyone on Earth. In "The Weather Man" a section of Australia refuses to abide by their authority and is threatened with a drought as a consequence. In "The Weather on the Sun" the efficacy of the government is endangered when the nature of the sun begins to alter, with unpredictable effects on the weather of our own planet.

"Satellite Passage" is a poignant tale of the near passage of two manned satellites, one from the United States and one from the Soviet Union. As the time of passage nears, there is considerable worry by the Americans that the Russians will commit some overt act of violence, but ultimately there is an accident in space and a Soviet cosmonaut is rescued by the Americans. Thomas also portrays the effects of a prolonged stay by a team of two men on the moon in "The Far Look." After experiencing a number of near disasters, the returning men possess a difference in demeanor that is quite noticeable.

Thomas assumed that H. G. Wells was correct about the Martians in "Day of Succession." When a ruthless general begins destroying the inhabitants of landing space vessels without warning, the authorities remove him from authority. The next capsule unleashes a technological onslaught against which human armies cannot stand, and the general assassinates the President in order to resume his program of eradication. A criminal is sentenced to be hanged each year in "December 28th," then brought back to life and allowed to recover in time for his next execution.

Thomas's use of irony is perhaps best illustrated in "The Doctor." A physician is stranded in prehistoric times when an accident destroys his time machine. He attempts to help the local residents by using his medical skills, but his attempts to extract teeth, set bones, etc. are viewed as hostile acts, as his intentions are totally misunderstood. Similarly, in "The Tour" a scientist realizes that visiting politicians do not understand his policy of using drugs to treat incurable murderers, and he subsequently commits murder himself in order to protect his program.

Thomas has several times collaborated with Theodore Cogswell, most notably with "Early Bird", a humorous tale of a human space pilot whose ship becomes transformed when it arrives on a most peculiar planet, evolving in a strange merge of mechanical and organic development, and in "Paradise Regained," in which political exiles decide to terraform the planet upon which they have been confined. "The Players at Null-G", written with Cogswell and Algis Budrys, is a humorous spoof of the time-travel story.

—Don D'Ammassa

THOMSON, Edward. See **TUBB, E. C.**

THORPE, Trebor. See **FANTHORPE, R. Lionel.**

THURSTON, Robert (Donald). American. Born in Lockport, New York, 28 October 1936. Educated at the University of Buffalo, now State University of New York, B. A. in English 1959, M. A. 1967. Served in the United States Army Air Defense Command, 1960-62. Married 1) Joan K. Sullivan in 1964 (died, 1980), one son; 2)Rosemary E. Fox in 1982. Reporter, *Union-Sun and Journal,* Lockport, 1959-60; Assistant Professor, Alliance College, Cambridge Springs, Pennsylvania, 1967-68; Manager, Glen Art Book Store, Williamsville, New York, 1968-71. Recipient: Clarion Workshop Award, 1970. Agent: Sharon Jarvis, Jarvis Braff Ltd., 260 Willard Avenue, Staten Island, New York 10314. Address: 200 Cabrini Boulevard, No. 19, New York, New York 10033, U. S. A.

SCIENCE-FICTION PUBLICATIONS

Novels (series: Battlestar Galactica)

Alicia II. New York, Berkley, 1978.
Battlestar Galactica, with Glen A. Larson. New York, Berkley, and London, Futura, 1978.
Battlestar Galactica 2: The Cylon Death Machine, with Glen A. Larson. New York, Berkley, 1979.
Battlestar Galactica 3: The Tombs of Kobol, with Glen A. Larson. New York, Berkley, 1979.
Battlestar Galactica 4: The Young Warriors, with Glen A. Larson. New York, Berkley, 1980.
A Set of Wheels. New York, Berkley, 1983.
Q Colony. New York, Berkley, 1985.

Uncollected Short Stories

"Stop Me Before I Tell More," in *Orbit 9,* edited by Damon Knight. New York, Putnam, 1971.
"Wheels," "Anaconda," and "The Last Desperate Hour," in *Clarion,* edited by Robin Scott Wilson. New York, New American Library, 1971.
"Get FDR!," "Punchline," and "The Good Life," in *Clarion 2,* edited by Robin Scott Wilson. New York, New American Library, 1972.

"Goodbye Shelley, Shirley, Charlotte, Charlene," in *Orbit 11*, edited by Damon Knight. New York, Putnam, 1972.

"Carolyn's Laughter," in *Fantasy and Science Fiction* (New York), January 1972.

"She/Her," in *Infinity 5*, edited by Robert Hoskins. New York, Lancer, 1973.

"Up Against the Wall," in *School and Society Through Science Fiction*, edited by Martin H. Greenberg and Joseph D. Olander. New York, Random House, 1974.

"Soundtrack: The Making of a Thoroughbred," in *Fantastic* (New York), May 1974.

"Under Siege," in *Fantasy and Science Fiction* (New York), July 1974.

"Searching the Ruins," in *Amazing* (New York), August 1974.

"The Hippie-Dip File," in *Social Problems Through Science Fiction*, edited by Martin H. Greenberg and others. New York, St. Martin's Press, 1975.

"Theodora and Theodora," in *New Dimensions 5*, edited by Robert Silverberg. New York, Harper, 1975.

"Jack and Betty," in *Orbit 16*, edited by Damon Knight. New York, Harper, 1975.

"Dream by Number," in *Fantasy and Science Fiction* (New York), September 1975.

"The Haunted Writing-Manual," in *Fantastic* (New York), October 1975.

"Groups," in *Fantastic* (New York), February 1976.

"If That's Paradise, Toss Me an Apple," in *Amazing* (New York), March 1976.

"One Magic Ring, Used," in *Fantastic* (New York), May 1976.

"Parker Frightened on a Tightrope," in *Fantastic* (New York), November 1976.

"Aliens," in *Fantasy and Science Fiction* (New York), December 1976.

"The Kingmakers," in *New Voices in Science Fiction*, edited by George R. R. Martin. New York, Macmillan, 1977.

"The Mars Ship," in *Fantasy and Science Fiction* (New York), June 1977.

"Wheels Westward," in *Cosmos* (New York), November 1977.

"What Johnny Did on His Summer Vacation," with Joe Haldeman, in *Rod Serling's Other Worlds*. New York, Bantam, 1978.

"The Bulldog Nutcracker," in *Chrysalis 2*, edited by Roy Torgeson. New York, Kensington, 1978.

"Seedplanter," in *Chrysalis 3*, edited by Roy Torgeson. New York, Kensington, 1978.

"Vibrations," in *Chrysalis 4*, edited by Roy Torgeson. New York, Kensington, 1979.

"The Oonaa Woman," in *The Berkley Showcase 3*, edited by Victoria Schochet and John W. Silbersack. New York, Berkley, 1981.

"Alternate 51: Bliss," in *The Berkley Showcase 4*, edited by Victoria Schochet and John W. Silbersack. New York, Berkley, 1981.

"The Wanda Lake Number," in *Light Years and Dark*, edited by Michael Bishop. New York, Berkley, 1984.

"The Fire at Sarah Siddons," in *Isaac Asimov's Science Fiction Magazine* (New York), August 1984.

OTHER PUBLICATIONS

Novels

Rugger 1: For the Silverfish. New York, Avon, 1985.
Rugger 2: In Justice's Prison. New York, Avon, 1985.

Other

Introduction to *Early Science Fiction Stories of Thomas M. Disch, The Big Time* by Fritz Leiber, *Dark Universe* by Daniel F. Galouye, *Driftglass* by Samuel R. Delany, *Today We Choose Faces* by Roger Zelazny, and *The Game Players of Titan* by Philip K. Dick. Boston, Gregg Press, 6 vols., 1972-79.

*   *   *

Robert Thurston established himself as a significant new writer in the science-fiction genre on the basis of his short fiction and has only recently turned to original novels, some of which develop themes presented earlier in short form.

One of Thurston's earliest short stories, "Carolyn's Laughter," hovered around the border between science fiction and the supernatural. A young man is troubled by memories of his first wife, now deceased, and eventually resorts to a computer medium in a half-hearted effort to contact her spirit. Carolyn had agreed to have her organs used in transplants, and there is some evidence that she may have reached across the borderline between life and death in an effort to reclaim the parts of her body that survived. This theme recurs in a very recent story, "The Fire at Sarah Siddons," in which a man's life is completely dominated by a message he receives from his dead wife.

Both stories are well plotted, but the outstanding quality of these and most of Thurston's short fiction is the detailed and convincing development of characters. "Under Siege," for example, works only because of its fine characterization. Within the context of a racist police state, a white liberal with a black wife is plagued by the constant silent presence of a black man. The growing tensions among the three are superbly handled, and the story might well have attracted much serious attention if it had been published in mainstream markets.

Time travel is ostensibly the subject of "Kingmakers," in which a man travels through the past to write a biography of a pivotal figure, but the four visits he makes, spaced widely apart in the lifespan of both men, cause tensions and contrasts that are the main focus of the story. Thurston's short stories run the gamut from comic to surreal, occasionally strongly plot oriented but more frequently concerned with character and theme. Doppelgangers show up frequently, with inexplicable duplicate women in "Goodbye Shelley, Shirley, Charlotte, Charlene," a host of people with no apparent pasts in "Searching the Ruins," and two virtually identical wives in "Theodore and Theodore. " Some of his stories deal with controversial themes, such as "Aliens," wherein a human male is used as a sex object by non-humanoid aliens, and "The Oonaa Woman," also quite explicitly sexual in subject matter.

Thurston's first novel, *Alicia II*, was uneven. As might be expected, Thurston did a remarkable job of developing his characters as human beings. Voss Geraghty callously accepts the society he lives in, one which classifies people early in their lives, designating some as "rejects" whose bodies will be confiscated in young adulthood to become the home of non-rejects. But Geraghty's new body was sabotaged by its former owner, and cannot function sexually. Following this blow to his view of the world, he must then re-examine much of what he believes about his own society. Unfortunately, the setting of the novel is unconvincing, and the long delay before the advent of organized resistance to its system is not particularly credible.

A Set of Wheels was a bit of a disappointment after the promise of Thurston's first novel. In the not too distant future, a young man becomes involved in a love affair with an illegal automobile. The setting is brutal and dirty, a world of clandestine repair shops, police nearly as corrupt as the people they hunt, love tainted by mistrust and self-interest. Thurston uses unconventional dialogue, perhaps to emphasize the depersonalization of his future, but it also serves to flatten his characters as well.

Q Colony, his most recent novel, uses "The Oonaa Woman" as its opening and proceeds from there to provide a history of a failed human research colony on an alien world. It is easily Thurston's most successful full-length effort. The characters are not particularly admirable or heroic, but they are certainly original and convincing. The Oonaa and humans can interbreed, which might not make much sense scientifically, but it is an effective device by which to launch the tale of two colliding cultures and their different sets of values. As Thurston continues to develop as a writer, his themes have become more mature and complex, and the consequent rewards to be derived from his work become greater as well.

—Don D'Ammassa

TILLEY, Patrick. British. Born in Southend, Essex, 4 July 1928. Educated at Royal Grammar School, Newcastle upon Tyne; King's College of Art, University of Durham. Married in 1951; two sons and one daughter. Graphic designer and illustrator, 1954-68, then free-lance writer. Production illustrator, *Oh, What a Lovely War!,* 1969, and technical adviser, A Bridge Too Far, 1977. Agent: A. D. Peters, 10 Buckingham Street, London WC2N 6BU, England; or, Peter Matson, 32 West 40th Street, New York, New York 10018, U. S. A. Address: Pen-yr-Allt, Llanrhychwyn, Trefriw, Gwynedd LL27 0YX, North Wales.

SCIENCE-FICTION PUBLICATIONS

Novels

Fade-Out. London, Hodder and Stoughton, and New York, Morrow, 1975.
The Amtrak Wars:
  1. *Cloud Warrior.* London, Sphere, 1983; New York, Macmillan, 1984.
  2. *First Family.* London, Sphere, 1985.

OTHER PUBLICATIONS

Novels

Whatever Happened to the Likely Lads? (novelization of TV series). London, BBC, 1973.
Mission. London, Joseph, and Boston, Little Brown, 1981.

Plays

Screenplays: *Wuthering Heights,* 1970; *People That Time Forgot,* 1977; *The Legacy,* 1977.

Television Plays: *Crane* series (3 episodes), 1959.

*

Patrick Tilley comments:

The books I write are designed primarily as entertainment but they are, essentially, about the human condition. For me, the elements of a story should go together like a Swiss watch. The plot has to have a logical basis; the story should not insult the reader's intelligence. A writer's job is to communicate with his readers as simply and effectively as possible. He should not make them reach for a dictionary, or try to impress other writers with the quality of his prose.

*   *   *

One of the hallmarks of writers of stature is that they can take a standard plot and do something novel with it, something that makes it stand out among a crowd of similar stories. Perhaps one of the oldest, most overdone situations in science fiction is the invasion of Earth by aliens in flying saucers, and almost as hoary a plot is the first contact story. So it is particularly interesting that Patrick Tilley's debut novel, *Fade-Out,* is in fact a melding of both of these into a novel that should have been derivative and uninspired. The result was quite the contrary.

Borrowing from the film *The Day the Earth Stood Still,* Tilley has his aliens cut off all power to human machinery during their landing. Soon the government of the United States must cope with a mysterious vehicle and its inhabitants who either cannot or will not communicate, but who possess abilities far beyond those of the human race. The novel covers several months of tentative and then increasingly strident attempts by the government to regain control of the situation. Tilley has done in this novel much the same thing that Michael Crichton did for the space plague in *The Andromeda Strain,* that is, examine the situation in incredible detail, and portray the unfolding events in such convincing fashion that the reader is convinced that this really is the way things would happen.

Tilley's second novel, *Mission,* on the other hand, was further from the mainstream of science fiction, although it also is pervaded by a sense of absolute conviction about the sequence of events, the details of official reaction, and the manner in which the characters react to the situation. A dead body is discovered bearing the same wounds as those of Jesus when he died on the cross. But shortly after the body is declared officially dead, there are signs of life. The medical staff is understandably amazed, but their investigation is cut short when their patient mysteriously disappears from the hospital. The protagonist finds his life disrupted even further when his missing patient reappears, apparently quite healthy, and identifies himself as being Jesus himself. At this point, readers might dismiss the novel as an allegorical religious fantasy, but Tilley has more surprises in store. "Jesus" is actually an alien from another universe, using a human body from our far past, travelling through time because, to his/its perceptions, all times are simultaneous and it is an act of will to move from one to the other. In fact, the protagonist ends up travelling back through time himself in what is a very strange adventure novel, more ambitious than *Fade-Out,* and in some ways more interesting, but less successful as entertainment.

The most recent Tilley novel as of this writing is *The Cloud Warrior,* as different from its predecessors as they were from each other. Once again Tilley uses a standard science-fiction theme as the background for his story, in this case a post-nuclear-collapse civilization. The comparatively primitive culture that survives is essentially tribal, and the hero, one of the Wingmen, is captured by his enemies, the Mutes. His sojourn as a prisoner exposes him to the culture of the rival tribe and, rather than continuing to view them as an opposing force, he begins to accept them as individual human beings. Peace begins to occur to him as more desirable than conflict or even triumph. But how can the gulf between the tribes be overcome?

The Cloud Warrior appears to be the beginning of a series, so presumably Tilley will have room to develop his future society even further. It is in this kind of detailed construction of setting that he excels, and it is likely that he will attract an increasing readership as his reputation grows.

— Don D'Ammassa

TIPTREE, James, Jr. Pseudonym for Alice Sheldon, née Bradley. American. Born in Chicago, Illinois, in 1916. Educated at Sarah Lawrence College, Bronxville, New York; University of California, Berkeley; George Washington University, Washington, D. C., Ph. D. in psychology 1967. Served in the United States Army Air Force, 1942-46. Married 1) William Davey in 1934 (divorced, 1938); 2) Huntington Denton Sheldon in 1945. Worked as an art critic, for the Central Intelligence Agency, in personal business, and as college teacher and experimental psychologist. Recipient: Nebula Award, 1973, 1976, 1977; Hugo Award, 1974, 1977; *Locus* award, 1984. Agent: Virginia Kidd, Box 278, Milford, Pennsylvania 18337. Address: 6037 Ramshorn Place, McLean, Virginia 22101, U.S.A.

SCIENCE-FICTION PUBLICATIONS

Novels

Up the Walls of the World. New York, Berkley, and London, Gollancz, 1978.
Brightness Falls from the Air. New York, Tor, 1985.

Short Stories

Ten Thousand Light-Years from Home. New York, Ace, 1973; London, Eyre Methuen, 1975.
Warm Worlds and Otherwise. New York, Ballantine, 1975.
Star Songs of an Old Primate. New York, Ballantine, 1978.
Out of the Everywhere and Other Extraordinary Visions. New York, Ballantine, 1981.

Uncollected Short Stories

"Excursion Fare," in *Stellar 7*, edited by Judy-Lynn del Rey. New York, Ballantine, 1981.
"Liros: A Tale of Quintana Roo," in *Isaac Asimov's Wonders of the World*, edited by Kathleen Moloney. New York, Davis, 1982.
"The Boy Who Waterskied to Forever," in *Fantasy and Science Fiction* (New York), October 1982.
"Beyond the Dead Reef," in *Fantasy and Science Fiction* (New York), January 1983.

*

Critical Study: *The Fiction of James Tiptree, Jr.* by Gardner Dozois, New York, Algol Press, 1977.

*   *   *

With the revelation that James Tiptree, Jr., is Alice ("Raccoona") Sheldon, the SF community that had praised Tiptree for treating feminist themes in a "masculine" style had to rethink its categories. In fact, Tiptree is simply a gifted writer who brings to her feminist concerns a critical knowledge of traditionally male domains—"all the huge authoritarian organizations," as one of her heroines puts it, "for doing unreal things."

Tiptree's early work is marked by a certain manic inventiveness and a preoccupation with far-future sex and science. Some of the best of these tightly written short stories are pure farce: "Birth of a Salesman," for instance, turns on the proposition that commercial packaging meant for distant client planets may trigger bizarre sexual and religious reactions among alien dockworkers. With powerfully dark stories like "The Last Flight of Dr. Ain," however, it became clear that Tiptree is more than a comic artist. Indeed, the twists of her fiction suggest a deeply skeptical turn of mind, wary of all absolutes, suspicious of all power.

These stories often have errant sexuality in the foreground. Human types encounter aliens whose sexual morphology is unstable or haploid ("All the Kinds of Yes," "Your Haploid Heart"), animal orgiasts who form delicious Lovepiles ("Painwise"), primitive mud-beings who offer "gentle glubbering" satisfaction ("The Milk of Paradise"). Tiptree exploits such situations to satirize our own sexual parochialism and, occasionally, to make a further points: even on alternate worlds or among weirdly equipped life forms, sexual existence is pain for the powerless.

In two overtly feminist stories, Tiptree's work revealed a new clarity and firmness of purpose. "The Girl Who Was Plugged In" translates social truths into grotesque literal images; it describes a near-future society that secretly uses devastatingly attractive waldos to sell goods and preserve the commercial status quo. The girl of the title is a monstrous socio-sexual reject who finds momentary happiness wired into an empty android playgirl. "The Women Men Don't See" is a vivid story of the invisible real women in our own world, surviving, as the protagonist tells the Hemingwayesque narrator, "by ones and twos in the chinks of your world-machine."

By one means or another, every recent Tiptree story condemns that world-machine as a tyrannical yet ultimately doomed system. Typically, her protagonists live anxiously on its margins. In "The Psychologist Who Wouldn't Do Awful Things to Rats" the system is the present scientific establishment, and the hero, himself a ratman of sorts, a "failed" researcher, "failed" because humanely dedicated. "Houston, Houston, Do You Read?" is Tiptree's most powerful anti-system work and a landmark in the recent feminist revival of the manless world story. In it, Tiptree identifies the male ethos of aggression and domination with life-plague. An epidemic in the past has left only women, their clones, and androgenic creations to refashion human existence. This history, patchily revealed to the crew of a NASA ship plunged 300 years into the future, is intercut with the scientist narrator's memories of their rescue and his efforts to comprehend a stunningly different reality.

An extension of this concern with sexual politics often surfaces in the short works and wholly informs the novella "A Momentary Taste of Being": the ambivalent force of the biologic urge itself, mercilessly driving toward the completion or transformation of species. The title of one of these stories, "Love Is the Plan, The Plan Is Death," could serve for them all. In "A Momentary Taste of Being" humanity is forced to the stars to fertilize like spermatozoa alien ova. Surrender to the female half of a zygote is seen by most as an estatic taste of being, but the narrator, a quasi-objective male doctor, sees it as doom—"Sex equals death." The death literally occurs; the worth of the sacrifice remains a matter of faith.

For *Up the Walls of the World*, her first novel, Tiptree creates an epic transformational journey through space and time for a group of painfully human telepaths. In alternating chapters that shift from our own botched world to a dying parallel world and into the center of a vast star-destroying being, a drama of destruction versus creation unfolds. Philosophically rich and formally ambitious, the novel is evidence of Tiptree's powers.

In sharp contrast to her expansive first novel, Tiptree's second, *Brightness Falls from the Air*, is a tightly constructed thriller. In cast and situation, the novel recalls the film noir, *Key Largo*: during a tense day and night, an outpost planet in the far future is taken over by thugs while a nova front, the auroral detritus of an exploded star, approaches. As the conflict develops between three planet administrators, their tourist allies, and the gangster types, Tiptree exploits the thriller form to consider the recurrence of evil and the permanence of the past. The planet is the site of an old crime against its native race of flying creatures, now threatened anew; the female administrator has been responsible for the murder of the star whose husks, as they pass, bring momentary "time-flurries," allowing instant revision of the immediate past. Intriguing as these possibilities are, the mix of thriller action and philosophical speculation never quite jells, and the novel lacks the trenchant wit, psychological clarity, and sexual percipience of the earlier stories. *Brightness Falls from the Air* is, however, clearly the work of an accomplished artist still reaching for new forms.

—Carol L. Snyder

———————

TORRO, Pel. See **FANTHORPE, R. Lionel.**

———————

TRAIN, Arthur (Cheney). American. Born in Boston, Massachusetts, 6 September 1875. Educated at Prince School, Boston; Boston Latin School; St. Paul's School, Concord, New Hampshire; Harvard University, Cambridge, Massachusetts, A. B. 1896, LL. B. 1899; admitted to the Massachusetts bar 1899. Married 1) Ethel Kissam in 1897 (died, 1923), three daughters and one son; 2) Helen C. Gerard in 1926, one son. Lawyer: worked in firm of Robinson Biddle and Ward, 1900; Assistant District Attorney for New York, 1901-08; in private practice (Train and Olney, later Perkins and Train) after 1908; Attorney General, Commonwealth of Massachusetts. Prolific story writer from 1904. President, National Institute of Arts and Letters, 1941-45. *Died 22 December 1945.*

SCIENCE-FICTION PUBLICATIONS

Novels (with Robert William Wood)

The Man Who Rocked the Earth. New York, Doubleday, 1915.
The Moon Maker. Hamburg, New York, Krueger, 1958.

Short Stories

Mortmain. New York, Appleton, 1907.

OTHER PUBLICATIONS

Novels

The Butler's Story. New York, Scribner, and London, Laurie, 1909.
The Confessions of Artemas Quibble. New York, Scribner, 1911.
"C. Q. "; or, In the Wireless House. New York, Century, 1912.
The World and Thomas Kelly. New York, Scribner, 1917.
As It Was in the Beginning. New York, Macmillan, 1921.
The Hermit of Turkey Hollow. New York, Scribner, 1921.
His Children's Children. New York, Scribner, and London, Nash, 1923.
The Needle's Eye. New York, Scribner, 1924.
The Lost Gospel. New York, Scribner, 1925.
The Blind Goddess. New York, Scribner, 1926.
High Winds. New York, Scribner, and London, Nash, 1927.
Ambition. New York, Scribner, and London, Nash, 1928.
The Horns of Ramadan. New York, Scribner, 1928; London, Nash, 1929.
Illusion. New York, Scribner, and London, Nash, 1929.
Paper Profits. New York, Liveright, and London, Mathews and Marrot, 1930.
The Adventures of Ephraim Tutt. New York, Scribner, 1930.
Princess Pro Tem. New York, Scribner, 1932.
No Matter Where. New York, Scribner, 1933.
Jacob's Ladder. New York, Scribner, 1935.
Manhattan Murder. New York, Scribner, 1936; as *Murderers' Medicine*, London, Constable, 1937.
Tassels on Her Boots . New York, Scribner, and London, Hutchinson, 1940.
Yankee Lawyer—Autobiography of Ephraim Tutt. New York, Scribner, 1943.

Short Stories

McAllister and His Double. New York, Scribner, and London, Newnes, 1905.
Tutt and Mr. Tutt. New York, Scribner, 1920.
By Advice of Counsel. New York, Scribner, 1921.
Tut, Tut! Mr. Tutt. New York, Scribner, 1923; London, Nash, 1924.
Page Mr. Tutt. New York, Scribner, 1926.
When Tutt Meets Tutt. New York, Scribner, 1927.
Tutt for Tutt. New York, Scribner, 1934.
Mr. Tutt Takes the Stand . New York, Scribner, 1936.
Mr. Tutt's Case Book (omnibus). New York, Scribner, 1936.
Old Man Tutt. New York, Scribner, 1938.
Mr. Tutt Comes Home. New York, Scribner, 1941.
Mr. Tutt Finds a Way. New York, Scribner, 1945.
Mr. Tutt at His Best, edited by Harold R. Medina. New York, Scribner, 1961.

Other

The Prisoner at the Bar. New York, Scribner, 1906; London, Laurie, 1907; revised edition, 1908; revised edition, as *From the District Attorney's Office*, 1939.
True Stories of Crime from the District Attorney's Office. New York, Scribner, and London, Laurie, 1908.
Courts, Criminals, and the Camorra. New York, Scribner, and London, Chapman and Hall, 1912.
The Earthquake. New York, Scribner, 1918.
Courts and Criminals (selection). New York, Scribner, 1921.
On the Trail of the Bad Men. New York, Scribner, 1925.

Puritan's Progress. New York, Scribner, 1931.
The Strange Attacks on Herbert Hoover. New York, Day, 1932.
My Day in Court (autobiography). New York, Scribner, 1939.

Editor, *The Goldfish, Being the Confessions of a Successful Man.* New York, Century, 1914.

*   *   *

While serving as Assistant District Attorney for New York County, Arthur Train began to write stories about the procession of human comedy and tragedy that passed through the criminal court building. Train wrote fewer than 100 short stories and only one short novel about Mr. Ephraim Tutt, Counsellor and Attorney at Law, but it is for Mr. Tutt that he will always be remembered. The Lincolnesque lawyer with his frock coat, stove pipe hat, and fondness for stogies is a vivid part of American folklore. Most of his books deal with human nature and not with crime or the law, but his few attempts at fantasy suggest he had abilities in that direction which ought to have been exercised further. Unfortunately, he often allowed the literary conventions of the day to undercut his imagination. The wonderfully weird theme of the dead man's hand grafted onto the wrist of Sir Richard Mortmain (*Mortmain*), which thus gives him the fingerprints of a murderer, is marred by the revelation that it has all been a dream.

The Man Who Rocked the Earth, written with the scientist Robert Williams Wood, was planned to demonstrate Wood's theories that the man who exploded the atom would be master of the world, able to dictate peace and banish war forever. The story features the mysterious commander Pax of the atomic-powered *Flying Ring*, and has echoes of Jules Verne's *Clipper of the Clouds* and *Master of the World.* The "lavender ray" which can tilt the earth's axis and level the Atlas Mountains to force the world powers to stop the war is never completely explained scientifically, yet it has a plausibility that only a creative writer can give. Train claimed never to have understood Wood's scientific data, but found it didn't matter in telling the story. Some parts of it turned out to be strangely prophetic. The description of the German bombardment of Paris from a distance of 60 miles came true several years later. The story is told in a lively style which overcomes the obvious propaganda of its theme.

The ending makes the publication of a sequel, *The Moon Maker*, inevitable (it was serialized in 1916-17, but not published in book form for 40 years). The physicist Professor Benjamin Hooker, having captured the *Flying Ring* from Pax (who has disappeared), takes it into outer space to deflect or destroy an asteroid which may destroy the earth. There is more scientific detail in the story as well as the added presence of a mathematician and romantic interest, Rhoda Gibbs, who accompanies Hooker on the mission. Forced to land on the moon to replace a uranium cylinder for the trip home, the party demonstrates some of the real problems in space survival when Rhoda loses sight of the ship. Absent-minded scientist and would-be feminist, Hooker and Rhoda are near caricatures, but very appealing. Their marriage at the end of the story seems a proper romantic outcome to their adventure, while Train's imaginative and humorous use of traditional themes in science fiction make his work of more than historical interest.

—J. Randolph Cox

TRENT, Olaf. See **FANTHORPE, R. Lionel.**

TRIMBLE, Louis (Preston). Also wrote as Stuart Brock; Gerry Travis. American. Born in Seattle, Washington, 2 March 1917. Educated at Eastern Washington State College, Cheney, B. A. 1950, Ed. M. 1953; University of Washington, Seattle, 1952-53, 1955, 1956-57; University of Pennsylvania, Philadelphia, 1955-56. Served as an editor in the United States Army Corps of Engineers Architects Divison. Married 1) Renee Eddy in 1938 (died, 1951), one daughter; 2)Jacquelyn Whitney in 1952; 3) Mary Todd in 1974. English teacher, Bonners Ferry High School, Idaho, 1946-47; instructor in Spanish and English, Eastern Washington State College, 1950-54; Instructor, 1956-59, Assistant Professor, 1959-65, Associate Professor, 1965-76, and Professor of Humanities and Social Studies, 1976-80, now Emeritus, University of Washington. Participated in English as a Second Language Seminars in Yugoslavia, 1972-74, 1976. Member of the Executive Board, Western Writers of America, 1963-64. Agent: Scott Meredith Literary Agency, 845 Third Avenue, New York, New York 10022, U. S. A. Address: 2 Radnor Terrace, Totnes, Devon TQ9 5JW England.

SCIENCE-FICTION PUBLICATIONS

Novels

Anthropol. New York, Ace, 1968.
The Noblest Experiment in the Galaxy. New York, Ace, 1970.
Guardians of the Gate, with Jacqueline Trimble. New York, Ace, 1972.
The City Machine. New York, DAW, 1972.
The Wandering Variables. New York, DAW, 1972.
The Bodelan Way. New York, DAW, 1974.

Uncollected Short Story

"Probability," in *If* (New York), April 1954.

OTHER PUBLICATIONS

Novels

Fit to Kill. New York, Phoenix Press, 1941.
Date for Murder. New York, Phoenix Press, 1942.
Tragedy in Turquoise. New York, Phoenix Press, 1942.
Design for Dying. New York, Phoenix Press, 1945.
Murder Trouble. New York, Phoenix Press, 1945 London, Wells Gardner, 1949.
Give Up the Body. Seattle, Superior, 1946.
You Can't Kill a Corpse. New York, Phoenix Press, 1946.
Valley of Violence. Philadelphia, Macrae Smith, 1948; London, Corgi, 1951.
The Case of the Blank Cartridge. New York, Phoenix Press, 1949.
The Tide Can't Wait. New York, Bouregy, 1949; London, Wright and Brown, 1959.
Gunsmoke Justice. Philadelphia, Macrae Smith, 1950; London, Corgi, 1951.
Blonds Are Skin Deep. New York, Lion, 1950.
Gaptown Law. Philadelphia, Macrae Smith, 1950.

Fighting Cowman. New York, Popular, 1952; Manchester, World Distributors, 1956.

Crossfire. New York, Avalon, 1953.

Bullets on Bunchgrass. New York, Avalon, 1954.

Stab in the Dark. New York, Ace, 1956.

The Virgin Victim. New York, Mercury, 1956.

Nothing to Lose But My Life. New York, Ace, 1957.

Mountain Ambush. New York, Avalon, 1958.

The Smell of Trouble. New York, Ace, 1958.

Cargo for the Styx. New York, Ace, 1959.

The Corpse Without a Country. new York, Ace, 1959.

Obit Deferred. New York, Ace, 1959.

Til Death Do Us Part. New York, Ace, 1959.

The Duchess of Skid Row. New York, Ace, 1960.

Girl on a Slay Ride. New York, Avon, 1960.

Love Me and Die. New York, Ace, 1960.

Deadman and Canyon. New York, Ace, 1961.

Montana Gun. New York, Hillman, 1961; London, White Lion, 1972.

The Surfside Caper. New York, Ace, 1961.

Siege at High Meadow. New York, Ace, 1962.

The Dead and the Deadly. New York, Ace, 1963.

The Man from Colorado. New York, Ace, 1963.

Wild Horse Range. New York, Ace, 1963.

Trouble at Gunsight. New York, Ace, 1964.

The Desperate Deputy of Cougar Hill. New York, Ace, 1965; London, Severn House, 1979.

The Holdout in the Diablos. New York, Ace, 1965.

Showdown in the Cayuse. New York, Ace, 1966.

Standoff at Massacre Buttes. New York, Ace, 1967.

Marshal of Sangaree. New York, Ace, 1968.

West to the Pecos. New York, Ace, 1968.

The Hostile Peaks. New York, Ace, 1969; London, Severn House, 1979.

Trouble Valley. New York, Ace, 1970; London, Severn House, 1979.

The Lonesome Mountains. New York, Ace, 1970.

The Ragbag Army. New York, Ace, 1971.

Novels as Gerry Travis

Tarnished Love. New York, Phoenix Press, 1942.

A Lovely Mask for Murder. New York, Avalon, 1956.

The Big Bite. New York, Avalon, 1957.

Novels as Stuart Brock

Death Is My Lover. New York, Mill, 1948.

Just Around the Coroner. New York, Mill, 1948.

Railtown Sheriff. New York, Bouregy, 1949; London, Barker, 1959.

Bring Back Her Body. New York, Ace, 1953.

Double-Cross Ranch. New York, Avalon, 1954; London, Barker, 1957.

Action at Boundary Peak. New York, Avalon, 1955.

Whispering Canyon. New York, Avalon, 1955.

Forbidden Range. New York, Avalon, 1956.

Killer's Choice. New York, Graphic, 1956.

Other

Sports of the World. Los Angeles, Golden West, 1938.

Working Papers in English for Science and Technology, with Robert Bley-Vroman and Larry Selinker. Seattle, University of Washington, 1972.

New Horizons: A Reader in Scientific and Technical English, (and *Teachers' Guide*), with others. Zagreb, Skolska Knjiga, 2 vols., 1975.

Course Materials for Non-Native Speakers Planning to Enter U.S. Universities to Study Science or Technology, with Mary Todd Trimble. San Francisco, Pacific American Institute, 1977.

English for Multinational Business, with Mary Todd Trimble. Washington, D. C., International Communication Agency, 1978.

Editor, *Criteria for Highway Benefit Analysis.* Seattle, University of Washington-National Academy of Sciences, 3 vols., 1964-65;revised edition, with Robert G. Hennes, Washington, D. C., National Highway Research Board, 1966-67.

Editor, *Incorporation of Shelter into Apartments and Office Buildings.* Washington, D. C., Office of Civil Defense, 1965.

Editor, with Karl Drobnic and Mary Todd Trimble, *English for Specific Purposes: Scientific and Technical English.* Corvallis, Oregon State University Press, 1978.

*

Bibliography: in *English for Academic and Technical Purposes: Studies in Honor of Louis Trimble* edited by Larry Selinker and others, Rowley, Massachusetts, Newbury House, 1981.

Manuscript Collections: University of Oregon Library,Eugene; University of Wyoming, Laramie.

*

Louis Trimble comments:

The basic purpose of my science fiction is to entertain while at the same time commenting on some of the unchanging characteristics of humans. I have chosen one of the least complicated ways of showing this—by setting my books several thousand years in the future, when "earth-originated" people have spread throughout the galaxy, colonizing. In some cases they conquered and at times displaced native peoples; in others living harmoniously with them or mixing (when possible). By using this galaxy and this time period in all of my books. I hope to show that in several thousand years there has been little change in political attitudes, social attitudes, and—in fact—the way people act and think.

*   *   *

Louis Trimble made his debut as a science-fiction novelist in 1968 with the publications of *Anthropol.* Trimble has mastered one form of the futuristic novel, the lyrical fantasy, quite handily. Especially entertaining are *The Wandering Variables, The City Machine,* and *The Bodelan Way,* books which share a motif of whimsical fantasy underpinning the rather standard fare of futuristic gadgetry and intergalactic conflict. In each the setting reminds one of the more familiar works of C. S. Lewis and Jules Verne; there are botanical wildernesses, shimmering islands, stark winter steppes, deep pools, and medieval valleys.

The lyrical tone is a result of the presence of fantastic goddesses, women of divine birth or superior knowledge, who accompany kind-hearted and competent, if somewhat insecure, males on their adventures. Because Trimble's novels transpire under this divine feminine sanction, the gratuitous violence typical of so much popular science fiction is diminished, and in its place has come the spirit of romance. His books move from loss to reacquisition, from discord to harmony, from problem to solution.

However, Trimble often achieves the effect of romance at the expense of sound narrative construction. There is frequently too much fortuitous coincidence in his books, too many miraculous rescues of the protagonists, too little real threat of failure or death. We are too rarely awe-struck by what happens and too often left incredulous. Neither are his romances of the heart or of the head: his problems tend to be created and resolved by machines rather than by human experience. The problem for Trimble's characters is always to escape physical threat or to build a new city or to return to a familiar planet. Thus only rarely, as in the final scenes of *The Bodelan Way* and *Guardians of the Gate,* does the solution involve the emotional or intellectual growth we demand of first-rate fiction. There is altogether too little development of Trimble's characters and too little engagement of our deeper human sympathies in his situations. Another difficulty arises from the fact that Trimble's novels sometimes cannot sustain their futurism through an entire narrative. In particular, *The Wandering Variables* and *The City Machine* retain their futurism only through the initial phase of exposition before finding their true subject in earth's Middle Ages. At the center of these books are dirt floors, oxdrawn carts, and bellicose medieval clans. Consequently, one feels that in these books science fiction is more peripheral than central, more a vehicle to Trimble's real interest, which is in the past rather than the future.

Nevertheless, after more than 50 books Trimble has developed a prose style which is elaborate yet efficient, and vividly descriptive yet never excessive. Like so many others, his narratives are fastpaced and full of action, yet one does not have the sensation that their pace and action are purely an exploitation of commercial appeal. More often, one feels that though Trimble's novels may fall short of the very best, his concern with the remote future is sincere and his imagination sufficient to include the human condition in that future. For young readers initiating themselves into the worlds of futuristic literature, Trimble's works are fine preparation for the more distant and rewarding vision of Lewis and others like him.

—Marvin W. Hunt

TROUT, Kilgore. See **FARMER, Philip José.**

TUBB, E(dwin) C(harles). British. Also writes as Chuck Adams; Stuart Allen; Anthony Armstrong; Ted Bain; Alice Beecham; Anthony Blake; L. T. Bronson; Raymond L. Burton; Morley Carpenter; Julian Carey; Jud Cary; Julian Cary; J. F. Clarkson; Norman Dale; Robert D. Ennis; James Evans; James S. Farrow; James R. Fenner; R. H. Godfrey; Charles S. Graham; Charles Grey; Volsted Gridban; Alan Guthrie; D. W. R. Hill; George Holt; Gill Hunt; Alan (or Allan) Innes; E. F. Jackson; Gordon Kent; Gregory Kern; King Lang; Mike Lantry; P. Lawrence; Chet Lawson; Nigel Lloyd; Robert Lloyd; Frank T. Lomas; Ron Lowam; Arthur Maclean; Carl Maddox; Phillip Martyn; John Mason; Carl Moulton; L. C. Powers; M. L. Powers;

Edward Richards; Paul Schofield; John Seabright; Brian Shaw; Roy Sheldon; John Stevens; Eric Storm; Andrew Sutton; Edward Thomson; Ken Wainwright; Frank Weight; Douglas West; Eric Wilding; Frank Winnard. British. Born in London, 15 October 1919. Married Iris Kathleen Smith in 1944; two daughters. Has worked as a welfare officer, catering manager, and printing machine salesman. Editor, *Authentic Science Fiction*, London, 1956-57, and *Eye and Vector*, 1958-60. Recipient: Cytricon Award, 1955; Eurocon Award, 1972. Guest of Honor, World Science Fiction Convention, Heidelberg, 1970. Agent: Carnell Literary Agency, Rowneybury Bungalow, Sawbridgeworth, near Old Harlow, Essex CM20 2EX. Address: 67 Houston Road, London SE23 2RL, England.

SCIENCE-FICTION PUBLICATIONS

Novels (series: Dumarest; Space 1999)

Saturn Patrol (as King Lang). London, Curtis, 1951.
Planetfall (as Gill Hunt). London, Curtis, 1951.
Argentis (as Brian Shaw). London, Curtis, 1952.
Alien Impact. London, Hamilton, 1952.
Atom War on Mars. London, Panther, 1952.
The Mutants Rebel. London, Panther, 1953.
Venusian Adventure. London, Comyns, 1953.
Alien Life. London, Paladin, 1954.
The Living World (as Carl Maddox). London, Pearson, 1954.
World at Bay. London, Panther, 1954.
The Metal Eater (as Roy Sheldon). London, Panther, 1954.
Journey to Mars. London, Scion, 1954.
Menace from the Past (as Carl Maddox). London, Pearson, 1954.
City of No Return. London, Scion, 1954.
The Stellar Legion. London, Scion, 1954.
The Hell Planet. London, Scion, 1954.
The Resurrected Man. London, Scion, 1954.
Alien Dust. London, Boardman, 1955; New York, Avalon, 1957.
The Space-Born. New York, Ace, 1956; London, Digit, 1961.
Touch of Evil (as Arthur Maclean). London, Fleetway, 1959.
Moon Base. London, Jenkins, and New York, Ace, 1964.
Death Is a Dream. London, Hart Davis, and New York, Ace, 1967.
The Winds of Gath (Dumarest). New York, Ace, 1967; as *Gath*, London, Hart Davis, 1968.
C. O. D. Mars. New York, Ace, 1968.
Derai (Dumarest). New York, Ace, 1968; London, Arrow, 1973.
S. T. A. R. Flight. New York, Paperback Library, 1969; London, Hale, 1980.
Toyman (Dumarest). New York, Ace, 1969; London, Arrow, 1973.
Escape into Space. London, Sidgwick and Jackson, 1969.
Kalin (Dumarest). New York, Ace, 1969; London, Arrow, 1973.
The Jester at Scar (Dumarest). New York, Ace, 1970; London, Arrow, 1977.
Lallia (Dumarest). New York, Ace, 1971; London, Arrow, 1977.
Technos (Dumarest). New York, Ace, 1972; London, Arrow, 1977.
Century of the Manikin. New York, DAW, 1972; London, Millington, 1975.
Mayenne (Dumarest). New York, DAW, 1973; London, Arrow, 1977.

Veruchia (Dumarest). New York, Ace, 1973; London, Arrow, 1977.
Jondelle (Dumarest). New York, DAW, 1973; London, Arrow, 1977.
Zenya (Dumarest). New York, DAW, 1974; London, Arrow, 1978.
Breakaway (Space 1999; novelization of TV series). London, Futura, and New York, Pocket Books, 1975.
Eloise (Dumarest). New York, DAW, 1975; London, Arrow, 1978.
Eye of the Zodiac (Dumarest). New York, DAW, 1975; London, Arrow, 1978.
Collision Course (Space 1999; novelization of TV series). London, Futura, 1975; New York, Pocket Books, 1976.
Jack of Swords (Dumarest). New York, DAW, 1976; London, Arrow, 1979.
Alien Seed (Space 1999; novelization of TV series). New York, Pocket Books, and London, Barker, 1976.
Spectrum of a Forgotten Sun (Dumarest). New York, DAW, 1976; London, Arrow, 1980.
Rogue Planet (Space 1999; novelization of TV series). New York, Pocket Books, and London, Futura, 1976.
Earthfall (Space 1999; novelization of TV series). London, Futura, 1977.
Haven of Darkness (Dumarest). New York, DAW, 1977; London, Arrow, 1980.
Prison of Night (Dumarest). New York, DAW, 1977; London, Arrow, 1980.
The Primitive. London, Futura, 1977.
Incident on Ath (Dumarest). New York, DAW, 1978.
The Quillian Sector (Dumarest). New York, DAW, 1978; London, Arrow, 1982.
Stellar Assignment. London, Hale, 1979.
Web of Sand (Dumarest). New York, DAW, 1979; London, Arrow, 1983.
Death Wears a White Face. London, Hale, 1979.
Iduna's Universe (Dumarest). New York, DAW, 1979; London, Arrow, 1985.
The Luck Machine. London, Dobson, 1980.
The Terra Data (Dumarest). New York, DAW, 1980; London, Arrow, 1985.
Pawn of the Omphalos. New York, Fawcett, 1980.
Earth Is Heaven (Dumarest). New York, DAW, 1982.
The Coming Event. New York, DAW, 1982.
Stardeath. New York, Ballantine, 1983.
Melome (Dumarest). New York, DAW, 1983.
Angado (Dumarest). New York, DAW, 1984.
Symbol of Terra. New York, New American Library, 1984.

Novels as Volsted Gridban

Alien Universe. London, Scion, 1952.
Reverse Universe. London, Scion, 1952.
Planetoid Disposals Ltd. London, Milestone, 1953.
De Bracy's Drug. London, Scion, 1953.
Fugitive of Time. London, Milestone, 1953.

Novels as Charles Grey

The Wall. London, Milestone, 1953.
Dynasty of Doom. London, Milestone, 1953.
Tormented City. London, Milestone, 1953.
Space Hunger. London, Milestone, 1953.
I Fight for Mars. London, Milestone, 1953.
The Extra Man. London, Milestone, 1954.

The Hand of Havoc. London, Merit, 1954.
Enterprise 2115. London, Merit, 1954; as *The Mechanical Monarch* (as E. C. Tubb), New York, Ace, 1958.

Novels as Gregory Kern (series: Cap Kennedy in all books)

Galaxy of the Lost. New York, DAW, 1973; London, Mews, 1976.
Slave Ship from Sergan. New York, DAW, 1973; London, Mews, 1976.
Monster of Metelaze. New York, DAW, 1973.
Enemy Within the Skull. New York, DAW, 1974.
Jewel of Jarhen. New York, DAW, 1974; London, Mews, 1976.
Seetee Alert! New York, DAW, 1974; London, Mews, 1976.
The Gholan Gate. New York, DAW, 1974.
The Eater of Worlds. New York, DAW, 1974.
Earth Enslaved. New York, DAW, 1974.
Planet of Dread. New York, DAW, 1974.
Spawn of Laban. New York, DAW, 1974.
The Genetic Buccaneer. New York, DAW, 1974.
A World Aflame. New York, DAW, 1974.
The Ghosts of Epidoris. New York, DAW, 1975.
Mimics of Dephene. New York, DAW, 1975.
Beyond the Galactic Lens. New York, DAW, 1975.
Das Kosmiche Duelle. Bergisch Gladbach, Germany, Bastei, 1976.
Galactiad. New York, DAW, 1983.

Novels as Edward Thomson (series: Atilus in all books)

Atilus the Slave. London, Futura, 1975.
Atilus the Gladiator. London, Futura, 1975.
Gladiator. London, Futura, 1978.

Short Stories

Ten from Tomorrow. London, Hart Davis, 1966.
A Scatter of Stardust. New York, Ace, 1972; London, Dobson, 1976.

Uncollected Short Stories

"No Short Cuts," in *New Worlds 10* (London), Summer 1951.
"Greek Gift," in *New Worlds 11* (London), Autumn 1951.
"Grounded," in *Science Fantasy* (Bournemouth), Winter 1951.
"Third Party," in *New Worlds 14* (London), March 1952.
"Alien Impact," in *Authentic* (London), May 1952.
"First Effort" (as L. T. Bronson), in *Worlds of Fantasy* (London), September 1952.
"Heroes Don't Cry" (as Gordon Kent), in *New Worlds 19* (London), January 1953.
"Dark Solution," in *Nebula* (Glasgow), Spring 1953.
"Confessional," in *Science Fantasy* (Bournemouth), Spring 1953.
"Freight," in *Nebula* (Glasgow), Summer 1953.
"Lone Wolf" (as Eric Storm), in *Authentic* (London), August 1953.
"The Pilot," in *Nebula* (Glasgow), Autumn 1953.
"The Troublemaker," in *Nebula* (Glasgow), September 1953.
"Conversation Piece," in *Authentic* (London), October 1953.
"Subtle Victory," in *Authentic* (London), November 1953.
"Tea Party," in *Nebula* (Glasgow), December 1953.
"The Inevitable Conflict," in *Vargo Statten's Science Fiction Magazine* (Luton, Bedfordshire), January 1954.

"Test Piece" (as Morley Carpenter), in *Vargo Statten's Science Fiction Magazine* (Luton, Bedfordshire), February 1954.

"Emancipation," in *Nebula* (Glasgow), February 1954.

"Sword of Tormain" (as Eric Storm), in *Planet* (New York), March 1954.

"Episode," in *Nebula* (Glasgow), April 1954.

"Death Deferred," in *Authentic* (London), May 1954.

"Tomorrow," in *Science Fantasy* (Bournemouth), May 1954.

"Illusion" (as Anthony Armstrong) and "Forbidden Fruit," in *Vargo Statten's Science Fiction Magazine* (Luton, Bedfordshire), May 1954.

"Occupational Hazard," in *Science Fantasy* (Bournemouth), July 1954.

"Project One," in *Nebula* (Glasgow), August 1954.

"Logic," in *Authentic* (London), September 1954.

"Homeward Bound" (as Anthony Armstrong), in *British Science Fiction Magazine* (Luton, Bedfordshire), September 1954.

"Hidden Treasure of Kalin," in *Authentic* (London), October 1954.

"Closing Time," in *Nebula* (Glasgow), October 1954.

"Into Thy Hands," in *New Worlds 29* (London), November 1954.

"Star Haven," in *Authentic* (London), December 1954.

"The Robbers," in *New Worlds 30* (London), December 1954.

"The Enemy Within Us," in *Science Fantasy* (Bournemouth), December 1954.

"Death-Wish" (as Eric Wilding) and "Nonentity," in *Authentic* (London), February 1955.

"School for Beginners," in *New Worlds 32* (London), February 1955.

"Lover, Where Art Thou?" (as Alice Beecham) and "Murder Most Innocent," in *Authentic* (London), March 1955.

"Snowflake," in *Flying Review*, March 1955.

"The Veterans" (as Norman Dale), in *New Worlds 33* (London), March 1955.

"Poor Henry," in *Science Fantasy* (Bournemouth), April 1955.

"Forgetfulness" (as Phillip Martyn) and "No Place for Tears" (as R. H. Godfrey), in *New Worlds 34* (London), April 1955.

"Agent," in *Science Fantasy* (Bournemouth), June 1955.

"Ethical Assassin," in *Authentic* (London), June 1955.

"Perac," in *New Worlds 37* (London), July 1955.

"Decision," in *Authentic* (London), August 1955.

"See No Evil," in *New Worlds 38* (London), August 1955.

"One Every Minute," in *Authentic* (London), September 1955.

"Planetbound," in *Nebula* (Glasgow), September 1955.

"The Predators," in *Science Fantasy* (Bournemouth), September 1955.

"That Zamboni," in *Authentic* (London), October 1955.

"Unwanted Eden" (as Eric Wilding) and "The Shell Game," in *Authentic* (London), November 1955.

"Quis Custodiet," in *Nebula* (Glasgow), November 1955.

"Venus for Never," in *Authentic* (London), December 1955.

"Prime Essential" (as Frank Weight) and "Lawyer at Large," in *New Worlds 42* (London), December 1955.

"Mistake on Mars," in *Authentic* (London), January 1956.

"Investment," in *Nebula* (Glasgow), January 1956.

"When He Died" (as Anthony Blake), in *Authentic* (London), February 1956.

"Asteroids," in *Authentic* (London), February 1956.

"The Moron" (as John Seabright) and "Dying to Live," in *Nebula* (Glasgow), March 1956.

"Man in Between" (as Carl Moulton) and "A Woman's Work," in *Authentic* (London), March 1956.

"Tailor Made" (as Anthony Blake), in *Authentic* (London), March 1956.

"Time to Kill," in *Galaxy* (New York), April 1956.

"The Letter" (as Alice Beecham) and "Secret Weapon" (as Frank T. Lomas), in *Authentic* (London), April 1956.

"Like a Diamond" (as Alice Beecham), in *Authentic* (London), June 1956.

"Into the Empty Dark," in *Nebula* (Glasgow), July 1956.

"Wishful Thinking" (as Carl Moulton), in *Authentic* (London), July 1956.

"Reluctant Farmer," in *Nebula* (Glasgow), November 1956.

"Mistaken Identity" (as D. W. R. Hill), in *Science Fantasy* (Bournemouth), December 1956.

"YOU Go," in *Galaxy* (New York), December 1956.

"Special Pleading" (as Phillip Martyn) and "A Fine Day for Dying," in *Science Fantasy* (Bournemouth), February 1957.

"Man of Imagination," in *Nebula* (Glasgow), March 1957.

"The Devil's Dictionary" (as Edward Richards), "The Ancient Alchemist" (as John Mason), "The Artists' Model" (as Robert D. Ennis), "The Witch of Peronia" (as L. C. Powers), "The Dolmen" (as Raymond L. Burton), and "Snake Vengeance" (as Andrew Sutton), all in *Supernatural Stories*, April 1957.

"Ad Infinitum," in *Science Fantasy* (Bournemouth), June 1957.

"Sentimental Journey," in *Nebula* (Glasgow), August 1957.

"Food for Friendship," in *Authentic* (London), August 1957.

"Second from the Sun" (as Ron Lowam) and "Linda" (as James Evans), in *Authentic* (London), September 1957.

"Pride of Possession" (as Ron Lowam), in *Authentic* (London), October 1957.

"Training Aid," in *Nebula* (Glasgow), January 1958.

"Requiem for a Harvey," in *New Worlds 68* (London), February 1958.

"The Touch of Reality," in *Nebula* (Glasgow), March 1958.

"The Wanton Jade," in *Nebula* (Glasgow), May 1958.

"The Beatific Smile," in *Nebula* (Glasgow), June 1958.

"Way Out" (as Robert Lloyd), "Conflagration" (as Stuart Allen), and "Talk Not at All," in *Nebula* (Glasgow), August 1958.

"Sell Me a Dream" (as Stuart Allen) and "Wallpaper War," in *Nebula* (Glasgow), November 1958.

"Beware?," in *Science Fantasy* (Bournemouth), December 1958.

"Somebody Wants You," in *Science Fantasy* (Bournemouth), August 1959.

"Galactic Destiny," in *Science Fiction Adventures* (London), October 1959.

"The Window," in *Science Fantasy* (Bournemouth), November 1959.

"Good-By, Gloria" (as Ted Bain) and "Orange," in *If* (New York), November 1959.

"Man of War," in *New Worlds 93* (London), April 1960.

"Too Bad!," in *Science Fantasy* (Bournemouth), April 1960.

"Grit," in *Science Fiction Adventures* (London), May 1960.

"Iron Head," in *Science Fiction Adventures* (London), September 1960.

"Memories Are Important," in *New Worlds 99* (London), October 1960.

"Umbrella in the Sky," in *Science Fiction Adventures* (London), January 1961.

"Gigolo," in *New Worlds 104* (London), March 1961.

"Jackpot," in *New Worlds 107* (London), June 1961.

"The Seekers," in *New Writings in SF 6*, edited by E. H. Carnell. London, Dobson, 1965; New York, Bantam, 1971.

"The Life Buyer," in *New Worlds 149* (London), April 1965.

"An Answer for Augustus," in *Tangent*, September 1965.

"Boomerang," in *Science Fantasy* (Bournemouth), September 1965.

"State of Mind," in *Science Fantasy* (Bournemouth), October 1965.

"As Others See Us," in *Science Fantasy* (Bournemouth), December 1965.

"In Vino Veritas," in *Science Fantasy* (Bournemouth), January 1966.

"Sing Me No Sorrows," in *Science Fantasy* (Bournemouth), February 1966.

"Secret Weapon," in *New Worlds 162* (London), May 1966.

"Quarry," in *Vision of Tomorrow* (Sydney), December 1969.

"Trojan Horse," in *Vision of Tomorrow* (Sydney), January 1970.

"Full-Five," in *Vision of Tomorrow* (Sydney), March 1970.

"A Matter of Survival," in *Vision of Tomorrow* (Sydney), June 1970.

"Spawn of Jupiter," in *Vision of Tomorrow* (Sydney), August 1970.

"The Winner," in *New Writing in Horror and the Supernatural 1*, edited by David Sutton. London, Sphere, 1971.

"Mistaken Identity," in *Space 1*, edited by Richard Davis. London, Abelard Schuman, 1973.

"Death God's Doom," in *Witchcraft and Sorcery* (Alhambra, California), Winter 1973.

"Lazarus," in *Beyond This Horizon*, edited by Christopher Carrell. Sunderland, Ceolfrith Press, 1974.

"Made to Be Broken," in *New Writings in SF 23*, edited by Kenneth Bulmer. London, Sidgwick and Jackson, 1974.

"Face to Infinity," in *New Writings in SF 28*, edited by Kenneth Bulmer. London, Dobson, 1976.

"Random Sample," in *New Writings in SF 29*, edited by Kenneth Bulmer. London, Sidgwick and Jackson, 1976.

"Block-Buster," in *Diversifier* (Oroville, California), July 1976.

"Read Me This Riddle," in *New Writings in SF 30*, edited by Kenneth Bulmer. London, Corgi, 1978.

"The Captain's Dog," in *The Androids Are Coming*, edited by Robert Silverberg. New York, Elsevier Nelson, 1979.

"Blood in the Mist," in *Heroic Fantasy*, edited by Gerald W. Page and Hank Reinhardt. New York, DAW, 1979.

Uncollected Short Stories as Charles Grey

"Intrigue on Io," in *Tales of Tomorrow* (London), September 1952.

"There's No Tomorrow," in *Worlds of Fantasy* (London), September 1952.

"Helping Hand," in *Wonders of the Spaceways* (London), December 1952.

"Honour Bright," in *Futuristic* (London), August 1953.

"Visiting Celebrity," in *Futuristic* (London), November 1953.

"Museum Piece," in *Futuristic* (London), Spring 1954.

"Accolade," in *New Writings in SF 23*, edited by Kenneth Bulmer. London, Sidgwick and Jackson, 1974.

Uncollected Short Stories as George Holt

"Emergency Exit," in *British Science Fiction Magazine* (Luton, Bedfordshire), September 1954.

"Skin Deep," in *British Science Fiction Magazine* (Luton, Bedfordshire), December 1954.

"Oversight," in *British Science Fiction Magazine* (Luton, Bedfordshire), March 1955.

"Brutus," in *Authentic* (London), April 1955.

"Kalgan the Golden," in *British Space Fiction Magazine* (Luton, Bedfordshire), August 1955.

"Lost Property," in British Space Fiction Magazine (Luton, Bedfordshire), December 1955.

"The Answer," in *British Space Fiction Magazine* (Luton, Bedfordshire), February 1956.

Uncollected Short Stories as Julian Carey or Julian Cary

"Repair Job," May 1955, "Blow the Man Down," October 1955, "Cure for Dreamers," April 1956, "The Give-Away Worlds," August 1956, and "Combination Calamitous," January 1957, all in *Authentic* (London).

Uncollected Short Stories as Alan Guthrie

"Samson," in *New Worlds 35* (London), May 1955.

"No Space for Me," in *New Worlds 37* (London), July 1955.

"Dear Ghost," in *Science Fantasy* (Bournemouth), September 1955.

"The Pensioners," in *New Worlds 43* (London), January 1956.

"Emergency Call," in *New Worlds 45* (London), March 1956.

"Breathing Space," in *Science Fantasy* (Bournemouth), August 1956.

"Thirty-Seven Times," in *New Worlds 55* (London), January 1957.

"The Greater Ideal," in *New Worlds 56* (London), February 1957.

Uncollected Short Stories as Douglas West

"The Dogs of Hanooie," in *Science Fantasy* (Bournemouth), September 1955.

"Number Thirteen," in *Authentic* (London), May 1956.

"Point of View," in *Authentic* (London), July 1956.

"Reward for a Hero," in *Authentic* (London), September 1956.

"Legal Eagle," in *Authentic* (London), December 1956.

"Dead Weight," in *Authentic* (London), March 1957.

Uncollected Short Stories as Ken Wainwright

"Sleeve of Care," February 1956, "The Big Secret," June 1956, "Enemy of the State," November 1956, and "Grzdle," June 1957, all in *Authentic* (London).

Uncollected Short Stories as Frank Winnard

"First Impression," February 1956, 'Misplaced Person," July 1956, and "Melly and the Martian," January 1957, all in *Authentic* (London).

Uncollected Short Stories as Alan (or Allan) Innes

"The Long Journey," March 1956, "The Dilettantes," April 1956, "The Spice of Danger," May 1956, "We, The Brave," January 1957, all in *Authentic* (London).

Uncollected Short Stories as Nigel Lloyd

"Upstairs," March 1957, "The Honest Philosopher," April 1957, "Eve No Adam," May 1957, "There's Only One Winner," June 1957, "Patient of Promise," July 1957, all in *Authentic* (London).

OTHER PUBLICATIONS

Novels

The Fighting Fury (as Paul Schofield). London, Spencer, 1955.
Assignment New York (as Mike Lantry). London, Spencer, 1955.
Comanche Capture (as E. F. Jackson). London, Spencer, 1955.
Sands of Destiny (as Jud Cary). London, Spencer, 1955.
Men of the Long Rifle (as J. F. Clarkson). London, Spencer, 1955.
Scourge of the South (as M. L. Powers). London, Spencer, 1956.
Vengeance Trail (as James S. Farrow). London, Spencer, 1956.
Quest for Quantrell (as John Stevens). London, Spencer, 1956.
Trail Blazers (as Chuck Adams). London, Spencer, 1956.
Drums of the Prairie (as P. Lawrence). London, Spencer, 1956.
Men of the West (as Chet Lawson). London, Spencer, 1956.
Wagon Trail (as Charles S. Graham). London, Spencer, 1957.
Colt Vengeance (as James R. Fenner). London, Spencer, 1957.
Target Death. London, Micron, 1961.
Lucky Strike. London, Fleetway, 1961.
Calculated Risk. London, Fleetway, 1961.
Too Tough to Handle. London, Fleetway, 1962.
The Dead Keep Faith. London, Fleetway, 1962.
The Spark of Anger. London, Fleetway, 1962.
Full Impact. London, Fleetway, 1962.
I Vow Vengeance. London, Fleetway, 1962.
Gunflash. London, Fleetway, 1962.
Hit Back. London, Fleetway, 1962.
One Must Die. London, Fleetway, 1962.
Suicide Squad. London, Fleetway, 1962.
Airbourne Commando. London, Fleetway, 1963.
No Higher Stakes. London, Fleetway, 1963.
Penalty of Fear. London, Fleetway, 1963.

*

Bibliography: in *Science Fiction Collector* 7, February 1980.

*   *   *

The quantity of E. C. Tubb's output can be gauged by the fact that he has used nearly 60 pseudonyms. Since 1951 he has been turning out novels and stories on a monthly basis, occasionally editing on the side; Michael Ashley in *The History of the Science Fiction Magazine* calls Tubb "an inspired fiction machine." His popularity, well established in England, is now sizable in America as well. He is quick to turn ideas into stories set out in hard, clear prose, and many of his plots have been repeated by younger writers, not always with as much success.

Tubb writes of a hostile universe where men seek to dominate each other, and nowhere is it as hostile or extensive as in the Dumarest saga. Stretching now to a score of novels, the long quest of Earl Dumarest for his lost Earth is an effective device for creating science-fiction adventure. Reticent, grim, dressed in grey, and quick with a knife, Dumarest travels from planet to planet pursued by the Cyclan, cold zealots whose emotions have been surgically removed and who are psychically linked to an organic computer of a million embalmed brains. They want Dumarest because he has the secret to another kind of psychic linking, and Dumarest wants his mythical Earth because it is his own home. In effect the books form a 20-novel chase sequence. Some aspects become repetitive—for example, the description of Low and High travelling (frozen vs. time-accelerated) is transferred almost verbatim from book to book. And in each

story Dumarest is injured in ghastly detail, which he stoically endures until advanced medicine repairs him. But the planets are different—vivid landscapes and weathers similar only in their exoticism and their evironmental exacerbation of the baser emotions. There is also range in the interpersonal plots. Sometimes Dumarest finds friends, sometimes only enemies; sometimes the lush women (all of whom desire him) have to be taught a lesson, and sometimes they do not; and in *Jondelle*, with creditable devotion, Dumarest defends a child. All this escapes being ludicrous through the stolid understatement in Tubb's competent style, and through the character of Dumarest himself, who is so determined and so quiet that he remains something of an enigma even after repeated adventures. That he has no sense of humor can be attributed to the desperate situations his author devises for him, situations in which genuine heroism can only consist of bleak courage and violent action.

Violence is important to Tubb; his interest in it is conscious and explicitly defended, not only in the Dumarest series but in novels like *Century of the Manikin* as well. The "manikins" are people who have been conditioned to believe violence is wrong. They live on a decadent, drug-controlled Earth where sex is so free that the only secret pleasure is violent. It takes a 20th-century woman, thawed out from cryogenic sleep, to tell them that men need weapons and honest fighting in order to be truly masculine and alive. Like almost every woman in Tubb's books, she finds male combat sexually exciting. But violence is not Tubb's only theme, however much it motivates his characters. His plots cover the full range of traditional science fiction, from first-contact riddles like "Random Sample," to sad tales of awakening computers like "J Is for Jeanne," and even to mood pieces like "The Last Day of Summer," where a man waits for the Bureau of Euthanasia. Tubb can also play with concepts of time and space; in *S. T. A. R. Flight* the instantaneous transport Gates of the dictatorial Kaltich are a puzzle to be solved, rather bloodily, by Earth's resistance organization.

E. C. Tubb is a good candidate for the theory that science fiction is essentially conservative. Against varying backgrounds of unexplained technology, Tubb talks about the most basic human passions. And however many suns are in the sky, the framework for ethical decision remains the same. For Tubb, the old values matter in the new places—matter more, since the strangeness isolates the grasping nature of men in plainer sight. Dumarest appears as a appropriate alter-ego for a man whose prose is lean and unsentimental. Tubb works in a highly colored imaginative landscape, but like Dumarest he does his job quickly and then moves on, convictions unchanged, to the next world.

—Karen G. Way

TUCKER, (Arthur) Wilson ("Bob"). American. Born in Deer Creek, Illinois, 23 November 1914. Educated at Normal High School, Illinois. Married 1) Mary Jan Joestine in 1937 (divorced, 1942); 2) Fern Delores Brookes in 1953; one daughter and four sons. Motion picture projectionist, 1933-72, and electrician for 20th Century Fox and the University of Illinois at Urbana and at Normal. Publisher of many fan magazines: *The Planetoid*, 1932, *Science Fiction News Letter, D'Journal, Le Zombie*, 1938-75, *Fantasy and Weird Fiction*, 1938-39, *Yearbook of Science, Fanewscard Weekly, Fanzine Yearbook*, 1941-45, *Fapa Variety*. President, National Fantasy Fan Federation,

1942-43. Recipient: Hugo Award, for criticism, 1970; John W. Campbell Memorial Award, 1976. Guest of Honor, 25th World Science Fiction Convention, 1967. Agent: Curtis Brown, 10 Astor Place, New York, New York 10003, U.S.A.

SCIENCE-FICTION PUBLICATIONS

Novels

The City in the Sea. New York, Rinehart, 1951; London, Nova, 1955.
The Long Loud Silence. New York, Rinehart, 1952; London, Lane, 1953; revised edition, New York, Lancer, 1970.
The Time Masters. New York, Rinehart, 1953; revised edition, New York, Doubleday, 1971; London, Gollancz, 1973.
Wild Talent. New York, Rinehart, 1954; London, Joseph, 1955; as *Man from Tomorrow*, New York, Bantam, 1955.
Time Bomb. New York, Rinehart, 1955; as *Tomorrow Plus X*, New York, Avon, 1957.
The Lincoln Hunters. New York, Rinehart, 1958; London, Phoenix House, 1961.
To the Tombaugh Station. New York, Ace, 1960.
The Year of the Quiet Sun. New York, Ace, 1970; London, Hale, 1971.
Ice and Iron. New York, Doubleday, 1974; revised edition, New York, Ballantine, and London, Gollancz, 1975.
Resurrection Days. New York, Pocket Books, 1981.

Short Stories

The Science-Fiction Subtreasury. New York, Rinehart, 1954; as *Time: X*, New York, Bantam, 1955.
The Best of Wilson Tucker. New York, Pocket Books, 1982.

OTHER PUBLICATIONS

Novels

The Chinese Doll. New York, Rinehart, 1946; London, Cassell, 1948.
To Keep or Kill. New York, Rinehart, 1947; London, Cassell, 1950.
The Dove. New York, Rinehart, 1948; London, Cassell, 1950.
The Stalking Man. New York, Rinehart, 1949; London, Cassell, 1950.
Red Herring. New York, Rinehart, 1951; London, Cassell, 1953.
The Man in My Grave. New York, Rinehart, 1956; London, Macdonald, 1958.
The Hired Target. New York, Ace, 1957.
Last Stop. New York, Doubleday, 1963; London, Hale, 1965.
A Procession of the Damned. New York, Doubleday, 1965; London, Hale, 1967.
The Warlock. New York, Doubleday, 1967; London, Hale, 1968.
This Witch. New York, Doubleday, 1971; London, Gollancz, 1972.

Other

"How to Write an Sf Story," in *Fantasy Fan*, November 1933.
The Neo-Fan's Guide to Science Fiction Fandom. Privately printed, 1955.
"The Bamboo Mite Gap" (introduction), in *Charles Fort Never Mentioned Wombats*, by Gene DeWeese and Robert Coulson. New York, Doubleday, 1977.

*

Wilson Tucker comments:
I write to entertain an editor, his readers, and myself, in that order. If I fail to entertain the editor, there will be no readers; if I fail to entertain the readers my own livelihood will be reduced accordingly. Some critics have said that my books may paint a bleak picture for humanity but that I always offer hope and sunshine for the future. That's news to me. I had always believed that I was writing adventure and offering entertainment, nothing more.

*   *   *

Wilson Tucker's stories have the modesty of realistic black and white films. His casts are small, his scale intimate, and his settings familiar. He develops his plots and characters using human actions and reactions. He prefers concrete imagery to abstract verbiage: he tells by showing. In *The Years of the Quiet Sun*, for example, shots of the same swimming pool in four different years give instant summaries of intervening events at the site. Indeed, the cinematic flow of Tucker's narratives may reflect his 40 years' experience as a motion picture projectionist.

Tucker's style is economical and unadorned. He understates so much that careless readers sometimes miss the full implications of his text, such as clues to the hero's race in *The Year of the Quiet Sun* or the practice of cannibalism in *The Long Loud Silence*. He actually had to revise the ending of *Ice and Iron* after its initial publication to supply additional explanations. Characterization is his strongest gift. His heroes are marked by a certain ornery ordinariness and a stubborn integrity that the critic Bruce Gillespie calls "the ability neither to give in to the world nor to push it around" (*SF Commentary 43*, 1976). These heroes crave simplicity and distrust institutions. They wield their talents—anything from telepathy to acting to survival skills—without bravado. They establish prickly, often unsatisfactory relationships with heroines as stubborn as themselves. Tucker sensibly combines appreciation of feminine charms with respect for feminine strength.

Historical, not physical, sciences have been Tucker's major inspiration. His personal enthusiasm for history and archeology fuels the well-researched vitality of *The Lincoln Hunters* and *The Year of the Quiet Sun*. The human dimensions of time travel have seldom been better portrayed in SF, for instance in the chief Lincoln-hunter's joy at meeting people from past eras: "They were living *now* and he was among them." Although he does plot with time paradoxes, Tucker always makes time travel a means rather than an end in itself. In *The Lincoln Hunters* it enables the author to place his hero in two radically different environments—a sterile, repressive future and a burgeoning, liberal past—and then generates a eucatastrophe to leave him in the happier world. Tucker keeps restating the proposition that life itself is a kind of time machine operating at the maximum rate of one second per second.

A poignant version of temporal translation is achieved through extreme longevity in *The Time Masters*. A marooned extraterrestrial who had been Gilgamesh in ancient Sumer waits thousands of years while the mayfly lives of ordinary humans flicker out around him before he finds an alternative to both loneliness and escape. The hero of *The Time Masters* reappears in a minor role in *Time Bomb*, a novel in which mechanical time travel changes history by eliminating a McCarthy-like villain in his larval stage. This premise is inverted in Tucker's finest work,

The Year of the Quiet Sun, when data gleaned from temporal research preserve a villain and trigger a catastrophic world race war. Every element in this honest, solidly built book meshes securely and unobtrusively to present a close-up of Armageddon.

Tucker thriftily incorporated the same research on Biblical archeology and the Dead Sea Scrolls used for *The Year of the Quiet Sun* into his mystery novel This Witch. He prefers doing mysteries because he finds them easier and more fun to write than SF, but his dual careers cross-fertilize each other. He often uses SF elements (even facts about SF fandom) in his mysteries and employs mystery/thriller conventions in his SF. (Compare the espionage apparatus and psychic elements in *Wild Talent* and *The Warlock*.) The clearest instance of Tucker's debt to the hard-boiled mystery styles of the 1940's is *The Long Loud Silence*. Its protagonist is a mono-maniac scrambling for survival in a plague-devasted eastern United States. Although the unrelenting brutality of his novel cost it popular acceptance on its initial publication, it remains a chilling reflection of Cold War attitudes.

Yet despite the grimness that underlies much of his professional work, Tucker has been one of SF fandom's favorite humorists—in person and in print—for half a century. His close friend Robert Bloch calls him "a legend in his own time." Tucker's chief handicap as a writer is an excess of humility— even after a score of novels he still refuses to think of himself as a professional writer. But the author of *The Year of the Quiet Sun* need stand in awe of no one.

—Sandra Miesel

TUREK, Ian Francis. See **BINDER, Eando.**

TUREK, Ione Frances. See **BINDER, Eando.**

TURNER, George (Reginald). Australian. Born in Melbourne, Victoria, 8 October 1916. Educated in Victoria state schools; at University High School, Melbourne. Served in the Australian Imperial Forces, 1939-45. Employment officer, Commonwealth Employment Service, Melbourne, 1945-49, and Wangaratta, Victoria, 1949-50; textile technician, Bruck Mills, Wangaratta, 1951-64; senior employment officer, Volkswagen Ltd., Melbourne, 1964-67; beer transferrer, Carlton and United Breweries, Melbourne, 1970-77. Since 1970, science fiction reviewer, Melbourne *Age*. Recipient: Miles Franklin Award, 1963; Commonwealth Literary Fund award, 1968; Ditmar award, 1984. Agent: Carl Routledge, 22 Knoll House, Carlton Hill, London N. W. 8, England. Address: 87 Westbury Street, Balaclava, Victoria 3183, Australia.

SCIENCE-FICTION PUBLICATIONS

Novels (series: Ethical Culture in all books)

Beloved Son. London, Faber, 1978; New York, Pocket Books, 1979.

Vaneglory. London, Faber, 1981.
Yesterday's Men. London, Faber, 1983.

Uncollected Short Stories

"In a Petri Dish Upstairs," in *Rooms of Paradise*, edited by Lee Harding. Melbourne, Quartet, 1978; New York, St. Martin's Press, 1979.
"A Pursuit of Miracles," in *Universe 12*, edited by Terry Carr. New York, Doubleday, 1982.
"Feedback," in *Dreamworks*, edited by David King. Melbourne, Norstrilia Press, 1984.
"The Fittest," in *Urban Fantasies*, edited by David King and Russell Blackford. Melbourne, Ebony Press, 1985.
"On the Nursery Floor," in *Strange Attractors*, edited by Damien Broderick. Sydney, Hale and Iremonger, 1985.

OTHER PUBLICATIONS

Novels

Young Man of Talent. London, Cassell, 1959; as *Scobie*, New York, Simon and Schuster, 1959.
A Stranger and Afraid. London, Cassell, 1961.
The Cupboard under the Stairs. London, Cassell, 1962.
A Waste of Shame. Melbourne and London, Cassell, 1965.
The Lame Dog Man. Melbourne, Cassell, 1967; London, Cassell, 1968.
Transit of Cassidy. Melbourne, Nelson, 1978; London, Hamish Hamilton, 1979.

Other

"Science Fiction as Literature," in *The Visual Encyclopedia of Science Fiction*, edited by Brian Ash. London, Pan, 1977.
"Frederik Pohl as a Creator of Future Societies," in *The Stellar Gauge*, edited by Michael J. Tolley and Kirpal Singh. Melbourne, Norstrilia Press, 1980.
"Australian Science Fiction 1950-1980," in *Science Fiction: A Review of Speculative Literature* (Perth, Western Australia), 1983.
In the Heart or in the Head (autobiography). Melbourne, Norstrilia Press, 1984.

Editor, *The View from the Edge*. Melbourne, Norstrilia Press, 1977.

*

George Turner comments:

Since it is my personal view (admittedly shared by few contemporary SF writers) that SF long ago lost its way among erotica, exotica, wishdreams, metaphysical guesswork, "mind-blowing" conceptions, and plain bad writing, I prefer to maintain a low key in my own work. To this end I have concentrated on simple, staple SF ideas, mostly those which have become conventions in the genre, injected without background or discussion into stories on the understanding that readers know all they need about such things. So in *Beloved Son* I used only the everyday ingredients of the genre—genetic manipulation, telepathy, the nature of World War III, the politics of renaissance—in order to rethink them and point out that all is not as obvious as conventional SF usage would have the readers believe.

My work will always be concerned with how human beings

behave—as all fiction ultimately must be. Super-heroes, super-intelligences, and unlikely worlds created for melodrama or the spelling out of doubtful metaphors for the future of man do not interest me. My SF method remains the same as for my mainstream novels—set characters in motion in a speculative situation and let them work out their destinies with a minimum of auctorial interference.

* * *

A well-known and prize-winning mainstream novelist of the 1960's, George Turner has earned a reputation as Australia's most rigorous and astute science-fiction critic and reviewer. (He claims, with justification, that his "thirty-year apprenticeship" in the writer's craft has given him "the critical confidence to stand in awe of no-one but Shakespeare and Tolstoy. ") His autobiography, *In the Heart or in the Head*, shows his lifelong commitment to literature, expounds his view of the history and shortcomings of the SF genre, and acts as a model for literary criticism in its engrossing blend of the personal and the critical, the subjective and the objective.

Turner's reputation as an SF writer rests upon the three novels of his Ethical Culture series: *Beloved Son, Vaneglory*, and *Yesterday's Men* (which, though linked, do not form a trilogy). Each book is set in the post-holocaust reconstructed world of the 21st century. The Collapse of 1992 (caused by genetic interference with food-crops, worsened by the spread of mutated-disease epidemics, and climaxed by hysterical nuclear bombing) has left the world's population greatly reduced, but within half a century a new world has emerged. Built on the Ethic of Non-Interference, the new culture relies upon an imprinted fear of the greed, obscenity, and cruelty of the past, and many of these old-world ills have genuinely been overcome – but only through fear and ignorance, not intellectual resolve.

Old social problems soon emerge, for dissent against the new order grows. But new problems also arise; experiments in cloning lead to attempts to tinker with human genetic stock (in *Beloved Son*), and further manipulations take place after the discovery of mutant humans with a lifespan of centuries (*Vaneglory*). (*Yesterday's Men* draws the series to an intellectually satisfying close when the new society finally seeks to learn the truth about the "barbarians" of the 20th century . . . and discovers that human nature has not (and possibly cannot) change.

Ostensibly, the three novels are about the abuses and consequences of supposed "progress" in the biological sciences, but they are more centrally concerned with the pitfalls of romantic idealism and utopian thinking. The emblem of this sad, depleted future is the Security Headquarters building: "Plain, ugly, efficient and temporary, it was uncompromisingly an administrative block. Like this entire civilization, it was there only to serve a passing purpose and be torn down. It symbolized with repellent neatness a world with an immutable past and a hopefully solid future but only a ramshackle, disposable present. "

The compelling wisdom of Turner's novels lies in his ability to see with this kind of clarity: to perceive the shabby present amid the rosy dreams of the future. Such qualities have attracted charges of dourness, cynicism, and pessimism, but these accusations miss the point of the novels' achievement. The books may be forthright and uncompromising in their judgements of man and society, but they are also honest – bluntly, harshly honest. To use a phrase from *Beloved Son*, they deal with "the unholy competence of man," demonstrating that man's wisdom is less than his ability, and that the human talent

for self-delusion and naive dreaming can be disastrous in its consequences. Just as *Brave New World* and *Nineteen Eighty-Four* brought home to an earlier generation the general socio-political dangers posed by the unevaluated advancement of science, so Turner's work brings home to our age the dangers lurking in the test tubes of the biologists and the fatal weaknesses inherent in man's slothful complacency. The Ethical Culture novels can fitly be mentioned side by side with Huxley's and Orwell's classics; they are a major work of science-fiction.

—Van Ikin

TUTTLE, Lisa. American. Born in Houston, Texas, 16 September 1952. Educated at Syracuse University, New York, B. A. in English 1973. Editor of the fan magazine *Mathom*, 1968-70; television columnist, Austin American Statesman, Texas, 1976-79. Recipient: John W. Campbell Award, 1974; Nebula Award, 1982. Agent: Howard Morhaim, 501 Fifth Avenue, New York, New York 10017, U. S. A.; or, A. P. Watt Ltd., 26-28 Bedford Row, London WC1R 4HP, England.

SCIENCE-FICTION PUBLICATIONS

Novels

Windhaven, with George R. R. Martin. New York, Pocket Books, 1981; London, New English Library, 1982.
Familiar Spirit. New York, Berkley, and London, New English Library, 1983.

Uncollected Short Stories

"Stranger in the House," in *Clarion 2*, edited by Robin Scott Wilson. New York, New American Library, 1972.
"Till Human Voices Wake Us . . . ," in *Clarion 3*, edited by Robin Scott Wilson. New York, New American Library, 1973.
"I Have Heard the Mermaids," in *Survival from Infinity*, edited by Roger Elwood. New York, Watts, 1974.
"Changelings," in *Best SF 75*, edited by Harry Harrison and Brian Aldiss. Indianapolis, Bobbs Merrill, and London, Weidenfeld and Nicolson, 1976.
"Woman Waiting," in *Lone Star Universe*, edited by George W. Proctor and Steven Utley. Austin, Texas, Heidelberg, 1976.
"Stone Circle," in *Amazing* (New York), March 1976.
"Mrs. T," in *Amazing* (New York), September 1976.
"Tom Sawyer's Sub-Orbital Escapade," with Steven Utley, in *Ascents of Wonder*, edited by David Gerrold and Stephen Goldin. New York, Popular Library, 1977.
"The Family Monkey," in *New Voices in Science Fiction*, edited by George R. R. Martin. New York, Macmillan, 1977.
"Flies by Night," with Steven Utley, in *SF Choice 77*, edited by Mike Ashley. London, Quartet, 1977.
"Kin to Kaspar Hauser," in *Galaxy* (New York), April 1977.
"Sangre," in *Fantastic* (New York), June 1977.
"The Horse Lord," in *The Year's Best Horror Stories 6*, edited by Gerald W. Page. New York, DAW, 1978.
"A Mother's Heart: A True Bear Story," in *Isaac Asimov's Science Fiction Magazine* (New York), January-February 1978.

"Uncoiling," with Steven Utley, in *Fantastic* (New York), April 1978.

"The Hollow Man," in *New Voices 2*, edited by George R. R. Martin. New York, Harcourt Brace, 1979.

"In the Arcade," in *The Year's Best Horror Stories 7*, edited by Gerald W. Page. New York, DAW, 1979.

"The Birds of the Moon," in *Fantastic* (New York), January 1979.

"Sun City," in *New Terrors 1*, edited by Ramsey Campbell. London, Pan, 1980.

"Where the Stones Grow," in *Dark Forces*, edited by Kirby McCauley. New York, Viking Press, 1980.

"Bug House," in *Fantasy and Science Fiction* (New York), June 1980.

"The Other Mother," in *Fantasy and Science Fiction* (New York), December 1980.

"A Spaceship Built of Stone," in *The 1981 Annual World's Best SF*, edited by Donald A. Wollheim. New York, DAW, 1981.

"Need," in *Shadows 4*, edited by Charles L. Grant. New York, Doubleday, 1981.

"Dollburger," in *Horrors*, edited by Charles L. Grant. New York, Berkley, 1981.

"The Bone Flute," in *Fantasy and Science Fiction* (New York), May 1981.

"Treading the Maze," in *Fantasy and Science Fiction* (New York), November 1981.

"A Friend in Need," in *The Year's Best Fantasy Stories 8*, edited by Arthur W. Saha. New York, DAW, 1982.

"Wives," in *The Best from Fantasy and Science Fiction 24*, edited by Edward L. Ferman. New York, Doubleday, 1982.

"The Memory of Wood," in *Fantasy and Science Fiction* (New York), September 1982.

"The Nest," in *Fantasy and Science Fiction* (New York), April 1983.

"The Cure," in *Light Years and Dark*, edited by Michael Bishop. New York, Berkley, 1984.

"Redcap," in *Fantasy and Science Fiction* (New York), September 1984.

"Children of the Centaur," in *Amazing* (New York), September 1984.

"The Other King," in *Isaac Asimov's Science Fiction Magazine* (New York), December 1984.

"No Regrets," in *Fantasy and Science Fiction* (New York), May 1985.

"Flying to Byzantium," in *Twilight Zone* (New York), May 1985.

OTHER PUBLICATIONS

Novel

Angela's Rainbow. Limpsfield, Surrey, Dragon's World, 1983.

Other

Catwitch (for children). Limpsfield, Surrey, Dragon's World, and New York, Doubleday, 1983.
Children's Literary Houses, with Rosalind Ashe. Limpsfield, Surrey, Dragon's World, 1984.

*   *   *

George R. R. Martin has called Lisa Tuttle's writing "distinctive, delightful," and Ted White attributed to her "a reputation for strong stories which deal with human responses to the unusual."

Tuttle has called her first story, "Stranger in the House," a "going home story." A young woman returns home and attempts to regain her childhood. This is a theme writers such as Bradbury and Ellison have used to produce stories of ineffable sadness, but Tuttle goes a step further to produce a work of genuine horror, catching an aspect of our desire to relive the past that few writers seem to understand. It was a fitting start. Tuttle quickly revealed herself as a writer of interesting variety and skill.

It's just as important that she's revealed herself as a writer of highly original horror fiction. "Changelings," for example, is a nicely extrapolated sociological vignette about a society that employs surgery to cure anti-social behavior; in it, a father is betrayed by his pre-school-age child. "Flies by Night," written with Steven Utley, is a psychological study of a woman who longs to turn into a fly. "Stone Circle" is a complex character study set in a near-future welfare state. "In the Arcade" depicts a future where racism is offered as a sideshow attraction. "Sangre" and "The Horse Lord" are almost, but not quite, conventional, the first juxtaposing the story of a woman's affair with her stepfather with a tale of vampirism, the other telling of a family that encounters Indian superstition that turns out to be justified—again, parents are betrayed by their children.

In "The Family Monkey" a rural Texas couple saves an alien from a crashed spaceship and adopts it as a servant. The story is simple and straightforward: the alien is saved, becomes a sort of family retainer, is discovered years later by its own people, and leaves. The story acquires a remarkable depth, however, because Tuttle's interest lies not with the plot, or even the alien, but with character relationships. Relationship provides the focus of most of her work, in fact. "The Hollow Man," set in the near future, concerns a woman whose husband commits suicide. She has him brought back to life through new medical techniques only to discover the flesh has been revived, but nothing else. Cold and indifferent, the husband lacks even the interest necessary to kill himself. The tragedy of the ending is classically inevitable, and quite powerful.

Little of Tuttle's fiction takes place away from the Earth. In "Wives," one of the few set on another planet, aliens are permitted by their Earthman conquerers to exist only so long as they pretend to be the human's wives. "The Birds of the Moon" is set on Earth, but tells about a woman whose astronaut husband has been to the moon. The voyage has changed him, and his wife hallucinates about beings—strange, ugly birds—which live on the moon. As with many of Tuttle's stories, the line between hallucination and reality is impossible to discern, particularly in man-woman relationships. In "Flies by Night" the women who longs to be a fly is captured by men who have become spiders—or so she believes.

As striking as such images are in a writer of Tuttle's talent, they never dominate her stories; neither, for that matter, does her interest in relationships. If anything, they seem to provide a focus for what appears to be a still-emerging concern for the nature of her characters' humanity. In "Bug House" a young woman, visiting an aunt who lives in a lonely isolated house, finds her aunt sick and the house overrun by insects. When the aunt dies, it is apparently as the victim of a strange young man whose connection with her, the house, the insects, becomes apparent only when it's too late. As in "Stone Circle" sex is treated as a numbing, enslaving element.

"Flying to Byzantium," another "going home" story, is about a writer elevated from a drab, lonely life by the modest success of a fantasy novel. At a science-fiction convention, she finds herself forced, through a confrontation with her readers, back into her hated, previous existence. The story permits some cogent observations on the problems of being a writer in the 1980's, and its last paragraph is a powerful as the idea itself. But the story fails to satisfy, possibly because the matter-of-fact style in which most of it is written fails to deliver the emotional impact it demands. "Need" is a far more successful story in which a young woman's fears and insecurities lead her into a situation that neatly brings a twist to the conventional ghost story plot— but in a way that is emotional and satisfying: few writers other than Tuttle could have pulled it off.

Windhaven, written with George R. R. Martin, is not typical Tuttle fiction, but it would be wrong to call it typical Martin, either. It's a superb collaborative effort set on a planet whose inhabitants, descendants of the survivors of a spaceship wreck, are dependent on the skills of messengers who travel on artificial wings, similar to hang gliders. It's good, solid science fiction, carefully crafted. It makes the most of Martin's eye for the exotic and ability to plot, and Tuttle's graceful style and sensitivity to people.

Tuttle's first solo novel, *Familiar Spirit*, is more in line with her short fiction. A commercial horror novel, it is well written, carefully plotted, and marked with Tuttle's customary vivid characterization. Its weakness lies in an unsatisfying formula ending. Even so, it's head and shoulders above all but a handful of the horror novels of its decade.

In the mid-1980's, it's difficult to appraise Lisa Tuttle's career, in part because she is at that period of transition, apparently, from the short story to the novel. While *Familiar Spirit* makes fewer demands on her talent than such shorter works as "The Family Monkey" or "The Hollow Man," her skills and the several themes she has been developing, seem to demand the longer form.

—Gerald W. Page

TWAIN, Mark. Pseudonym for Samuel Langhorne Clemens. American. Born in Florida, Missouri, 30 November 1835; grew up in Hannibal, Missouri. Married Olivia Langdon in 1870 (died, 1904); one son and three daughters. Printer's apprentice from age 12; helped brother with Hannibal newspapers, 1850-52; worked in St. Louis, New York, Philadelphia, Keokuk, Iowa, and Cincinnati, 1853-57; river pilot's apprentice, on the Mississippi, 1857: licensed as a pilot, 1859; went to Nevada as secretary to his brother, then in the service of the governor, and also worked as a goldminer, 1861; staff member, *Territorial Enterprise*, Virginia City, Nevada, 1862-64; moved to San Francisco, 1864; writer from 1867, lecturer from 1868; Editor, *Buffalo Express*, New York, 1868-71; moved to Hartford, Connecticut, and became associated with the Charles L. Webster Publishing Company, 1884: went bankrupt, 1894 (last debts paid, 1898). M. A. : Yale University, New Haven, Connecticut, 1888; Litt. D. : Yale University, 1901; Oxford University, 1907; LL. D. : University of Missouri, Columbia, 1902. *Died 21 April 1910.*

SCIENCE-FICTION PUBLICATIONS

Novel

A Connecticut Yankee in King Arthur's Court. New York, Webster, and London, Chatto and Windus, 1889.

Short Stories

The Science Fiction of Mark Twain, edited by David Ketterer. Hamden, Connecticut, Shoe String Press, 1984.

OTHER PUBLICATIONS

Novels

The Innocents Abroad; or, The New Pilgrims' Progress. Hartford, Connecticut, American Publishing Company, 1869; London, Routledge, 2 vols., 1872.
The Innocents at Home. London, Routledge, 1872.
The Gilded Age: A Tale of Today, with Charles Dudley Warner. Hartford, Connecticut, American Publishing Company, 1873; London, Routledge, 3 vols., 1874; *The Adventures of Colonel Sellers, Being Twain's Share of "The Gilded Age,"* edited by Charles Neider, New York, Doubleday, 1965; London, Chatto and Windus, 1966.
The Adventures of Tom Sawyer. London, Chatto and Windus, and Hartford, Connecticut, American Publishing Company, 1876.
A Tramp Abroad. Hartford, Connecticut, American Publishing Company, and London, Chatto and Windus, 1880.
The Prince and the Pauper. London, Chatto and Windus, and Boston, Osgood, 1881.
The Adventures of Huckleberry Finn (Tom Sawyer's Companion). London, Chatto and Windus, 1884; New York, Webster, 1885.
The American Claimant. New York, Webster, and London, Chatto and Windus, 1892.
Pudd'nhead Wilson: A Tale. London, Chatto and Windus, 1894; as *The Tragedy of Pudd'nhead Wilson*, Hartford, Connecticut, American Publishing Company, 1894.
Personal Recollections of Joan of Arc . . . . New York, Harper, and London, Chatto and Windus, 1896.
A Double Barrelled Detective Story. New York, Harper, and London, Chatto and Windus, 1902.
Extracts from Adam's Diary. New York, and London, Harper, 1904.
Eve's Diary. New York and London, Harper, 1906.
A Horse's Tale. New York and London, Harper, 1907.
Simon Wheeler, Detective, edited by Franklin R. Rogers. New York, New York Public Library, 1963.
The Complete Novels, edited by Charles Neider. New York, Doubleday, 2 vols., 1964.
Mississippi Writings (Library of America). New York, Literary Classics of the United States, and London, Cambridge University Press, 1982.

Short Stories

The Celebrated Jumping Frog of Calaveras County and Other Sketches, edited by John Paul. New York, Webb, 1867.
A True Story and the Recent Carnival of Crime. Boston, Osgood, 1877.
Date 1601: Conversation as It Was by the Social Fireside in the Time of the Tudors. Privately printed, 1880; as *1601 . . . ,* edited by Franklin J. Meine, Chicago, privately printed, 1939.
The Stolen White Elephant Etc. London, Chatto and Windus, and Boston, Osgood, 1882.
Merry Tales. New York, Webster, 1892.
The £1,000,000 Bank-Note and Other New Stories. New York, Webster, and London, Chatto and Windus, 1893.
Tom Sawyer Abroad. New York, Webster, and London, Chatto and Windus, 1894.

Tom Sawyer Abroad, Tom Sawyer, Detective, and Other Stories.
New York, Harper, 1896; as *Tom Sawyer, Detective, as Told by Huck Finn, and Other Tales.* London, Chatto and Windus, 1897.

The Man That Corrupted Hadleyburg and Other Stories and Essays. New York, Harper, and London, Chatto and Windus, 1900.

A Dog's Tale. London, National Anti-Vivisection Society, and New York, Harper, 1904.

The $30,000 Bequest and Other Stories. New York, Harper, 1906; London, Harper, 1907.

Extract from Captain Stormfield's Visit to Heaven. New York and London, Harper, 1909; revised edition, as *Report from Paradise*, edited by Dixon Wecter, New York, Harper, 1952.

The Mysterious Stranger: A Romance. New York, Harper, 1916; London, Harper, 1917.

The Curious Republic of Gondour and Other Whimsical Sketches. New York, Boni and Liveright, 1919.

The Mysterious Stranger and Other Stories. New York and London, Harper, 1922.

The Adventures of Thomas Jefferson Snodgrass, edited by Charles Honce. Chicago, Covici, 1928.

A Boy's Adventure. Privately printed, 1928.

Jim Smiley and His Jumping Frog, edited by Albert Bigelow Paine. Chicago, Pocahontas Press, 1940.

A Murder, A Mystery, and a Marriage. Privately printed, 1945.

The Complete Short Stories, edited by Charles Neider. New York, Hanover House, 1957.

The Complete Humorous Sketches and Tales, edited by Charles Neider. New York, Doubleday, 1961.

Mark Twain's Satires and Burlesques, edited by Franklin R. Rogers. Berkeley, University of California Press, 1967.

Mark Twain's Mysterious Stranger Manuscripts , edited by William M. Gibson. Berkeley, University of California Press, 1969.

Mark Twain's Hannibal, Huck, and Tom, edited by Walter Blair. Berkeley, University of California Press, 1969.

Early Tales and Sketches, edited by Edgar M. Branch and Robert H. Hirst. Berkeley, University of California Press, 2 vols., 1979-81.

Wapping Alice. Berkeley, California, Friends of the Bancroft Library, 1981.

Plays

Colonel Sellers as a Scientist, with William Dean Howells, adaptation of the novel *The Gilded Age* by Twain and Charles Dudley Warner (produced New Brunswick, New Jersey, and New York, 1887). Published in *The Complete Plays of William Dean Howells*, edited by Walter J. Meserve, New York, New York University Press, 1960.

Ah Sin, with Bret Harte, edited by Frederick Anderson (produced Washington, D. C., 1877). San Francisco, Book Club of California, 1961.

The Quaker City Holy Land Excursion: An Unfinished Play. Privately printed, 1927.

Verse

On the Poetry of Mark Twain, with Selections from His Verse, edited by Arthur L. Scott. Urbana, University of Illinois Press, 1966.

Other

Mark Twain's (Burlesque) Autobiography and First Romance.
New York, Sheldon, 1871.

Memoranda: From the Galaxy. Toronto, Canadian News and Publishing Company, 1871.

Roughing It. London, Routledge, and Hartford, Connecticut, American Publishing Company, 1872.

A Curious Dream and Other Sketches. London, Routledge, 1872.

Screamers: A Gathering of Scraps of Humour, Delicious Bits, and Short Stories. London, Hotten, 1872.

Sketches. New York, American News Company, 1874.

Sketches, New and Old. Hartford, Connecticut, American Publishing Company, 1875.

Old Times on the Mississippi. Toronto, Belford, 1876.

Punch, Brothers, Punch! and Other Sketches. New York, Slote Woodman, 1878.

An Idle Excursion. Toronto, Belford, 1878.

A Curious Experience. Toronto, Gibson, 1881.

LIfe on the Mississippi. London, Chatto and Windus, and Boston, Osgood, 1883.

Facts for Mark Twain's Memory Builder. New York, Webster, 1891.

How to Tell a Story and Other Essays. New York, Harper, 1897; revised edition, 1900.

Following the Equator: A Journey Around the World. Hartford, Connecticut, American Publishing Company, 1897; as *More Tramps Abroad*, London, Chatto and Windus, 1897.

The Writings of Mark Twain. Hartford, Connecticut, American Publishing Company, and London, Chatto and Windus, 25 vols., 1899-1907.

The Pains of Lowly Life. London, London Anti-Vivisection Society, 1900.

English as She Is Taught. Boston, Mutual, 1900; revised edition, New York, Century, 1901.

To the Person Sitting in Darkness. New York, Anti-Imperialist League, 1901.

Edmund Burke on Croker, and Tammany (lecture). New York, Economist Press, 1901.

My Dé but as a Literary Person, with Other Essays and Stories. Hartford, Conecticut, American Publishing Company, 1903.

Mark Twain on Vivisection. New York, New York Anti-Vivisection Society, 1905(?).

King Leopold's Soliloquy: A Defense of His Congo Rule. Boston, Warren, 1905; revised edition, 1906; London, Unwin, 1907.

Editorial Wild Oats. New York, Harper, 1905.

What Is Man? (published anonymously). New York, DeVinne Press, 1906; as Mark Twain, London, Watts, 1910.

Mark Twain on Spelling (lecture). New York, Simplified Spelling Board, 1906.

The Writings of Mark Twain (Hillcrest Edition). New York and London, Harper, 25 vols., 1906-07.

Christian Science, with Notes Containing Corrections to Date. New York and London, Harper, 1907.

Is Shakespeare Dead? From My Autobiography. New York and London, Harper, 1909.

Mark Twain's Speeches, edited by F. A. Nast. New York and London, Harper, 1910; revised edition, 1923.

Queen Victoria's Jubilee. Privately printed, 1910.

Letter to the California Pioneers. Oakland, California, Dewitt and Snelling, 1911.

What Is Man? and Other Essays. New York, Harper, 1917; London, Chatto and Windus, 1919.

Mark Twain's Letters, Arranged with Comment, edited by Albert Bigelow Paine. New York, Harper, 2 vols., 1917; shortened version, as *Letters*, London, Chatto and Windus, 1920.

Moments with Mark Twain, edited by Albert Bigelow Paine. New York, Harper, 1920.

The Writings of Mark Twin (Definitive Edition), edited by Albert Bigelow Paine. New York, Gabriel Wells, 37 vols., 1922-25.

Europe and Elsewhere. New York and London, Harper, 1923.

Mark Twain's Autobiography, edited by Albert Bigelow Paine. New York and London, Harper, 2 vols., 1924.

Sketches of the Sixties by Bret Harte and Mark Twain . . . from "The Californian," 1864-67. San Francisco, John Howell, 1926.

The Suppressed Chapter of "Following the Equator. Privately printed, 1928.

A Letter from Mark Twain to His Publisher, Chatto and Windus. San Francisco, Penguin Press, 1929.

Mark Twain the Letter Writer, edited by Cyril Clemens. Boston, Meador, 1932.

Mark Twain's Works. New York, Harper, 23 vols., 1933.

The Family Mark Twain. New York, Harper, 1935.

The Mark Twain Omnibus , edited by Max J. Herzberg. New York, Harper, 1935.

Representative Selections, edited by Fred L. Patee. New York, American Book Company, 1935.

Mark Twain's Notebook, edited by Albert Bigelow Paine. New York, Harper, 1935.

Letters from the Sandwich Islands, Written for the "Sacramento Union," edited by G. Ezra Dane. San Francisco, Grabhorn Press, 1937; London, Oxford University Press, 1938.

The Washoe Giant in San Francisco, Being Heretofore Uncollected Sketches . . . , edited by Franklin Walker. San Francisco, George Fields, 1938.

Mark Twain's Western Years, Together with Hitherto Unreprinted Clemens Western Items, by Ivan Benson. Stanford, California, Stanford University, 1938.

Letters from Honolulu Written for the "Sacramento Union," edited by Thomas Nickerson. Honolulu, Thomas Nickerson, 1939.

Mark Twain in Eruption: Hitherto Unpublished Pages about Men and Events, edited by Bernard De Voto. New York, Harper, 1940.

Travels with Mr. Brown, Being Heretofore Uncollected Sketches Written for the San Francisco "Alta California" in 1866 and 1867, edited by Franklin Walker and G. Ezra Dane. New York, Knopf, 1940.

Republican Letters, edited by Cyril Clemens. Webster Groves, Missouri, International Mark Twain Society, 1941.

Letters to Will Brown . . . , edited by Theodore Hornberger. Austin, University of Texas, 1941.

Letters in the "Muscatine Journal," edited by Edgar M. Branch. Chicago, Mark Twain Association of America, 1942.

Washington in 1868, edited by Cyril Clemens. Webster Groves, Missouri, International Mark Twain Society, and London, Laurie, 1943.

Mark Twain, Business Man, edited by Samuel Charles Webster. Boston, Little Brown, 1946.

The Letters of Quintus Curtius Snodgrass, edited by Ernest E. Leisy. Dallas, Southern Methodist University Press, 1946.

The Portable Mark Twain, edited by Bernard De Voto. New York, Viking Press, 1946; London, Penguin, 1977.

Mark Twain in Three Moods: Three New Items of Twainiana, edited by Dixon Wecter. San Marino, California, Friends of the Huntington Library, 1948.

The Love Letters of Mark Twain, edited by Dixon Wecter. New York, Harper, 1949.

Mark Twain to Mrs. Fairbanks, edited by Dixon Wecter. San Marino, California, Huntington Library, 1949.

Mark Twain to Uncle Remus 1881-1885, edited by Thomas H. English. Atlanta, Emory University Library, 1953.

Twins of Genius (letters to George Washington Cable), edited by Guy A. Cardwell. East Lansing, Michigan State College Press, 1953.

Mark Twain of the "Enterprise" . . . , edited by Henry Nash Smith and Frederick Anderson. Berkeley, University of California Press, 1957.

Traveling with Innocents Abroad: Mark Twain's Original Reports from Europe and the Holy Land, edited by Daniel Morley McKeithan. Norman, University of Oklahoma Press, 1958.

The Autobiography of Mark Twain, edited by Charles Neider. New York, Doubleday, 1959.

The Art, Humor, and Humanity of Mark Twain, edited by Minnie M. Brashear and Robert M. Rodney. Norman, University of Oklahoma Press, 1959.

Mark Twain and the Government, edited by Svend Petersen. Caldwell, Idaho, Caxton Printers, 1960.

Mark Twain-Howells Letters: The Correspondence of Samuel L. Clemens and William Dean Howells 1872-1910, edited by Henry Nash Smith and William M. Gibson. Cambridge, Massachusetts, Harvard University Press, 2 vols., 1960; abridged edtion, as *Selected Mark Twain-Howells Letters*, 1967.

Your Personal Mark Twain . . . . New York, International Publishers, 1960.

Life as I Find It: Essays, Sketches, Tales, and Other Material, edited by Charles Neider. New York, Doubleday, 1961.

The Travels of Mark Twain, edited by Charles Neider. New York, Doubleday, 1961.

Contributions to "The Galaxy," 1868-1871, edited by Bruce R. McElderry. Gainesville, Florida, Scholars Facsimiles and Reprints, 1961.

Mark Twain on the Art of Writing, edited by Martin B. Fried. Buffalo, Salisbury Club, 1961.

Letters to Mary, edited by Lewis Leary. New York, Columbia University Press, 1961.

The Pattern for Mark Twain's "Roughing It": Letters from Nevada by Samuel and Orion Clemens, 1861-1862, edited by Franklin R. Rogers. Berkeley, University of California Press, 1961.

Letters from the Earth, edited by Bernard De Voto. New York, Harper, 1962.

Mark Twain on the Damned Human Race, edited by Janet Smith. New York, Hill and Wang, 1962.

Selected Shorter Writings, edited by Walter Blair. Boston, Houghton Mifflin, 1962.

The Complete Essays, edited by Charles Neider. New York, Doubleday, 1963.

Mark Twain's San Francisco, edited by Bernard Taper. New York, McGraw Hill, 1963.

The Forgotten Writings of Mark Twain, edited by Henry Duskus. New York, Citadel Press, 1963.

General Grant by Matthew Arnold, with a Rejoinder by Mark Twain (lecture), edited by John Y. Simon. Carbondale, Southern Illinois University Press, 1966.

Letters from Hawaii, edited by A. Grove Day. New York, Appleton Century Crofts, 1966; London, Chatto and Windus, 1967.

Which Was the Dream? and Other Symbolic Writings of the Later Years, edited by John S. Tuckey. Berkeley, University of California Press, 1967.

The Complete Travel Books, edited by Charles Neider. New

York, Doubleday, 1967.

Letters to His Publishers, 1867-1894, edited by Hamlin Hill. Berkeley, University of California Press, 1967.

Clemens of the "Call": Mark Twain in California, edited by Edgar M. Branch. Berkeley, University of California Press, 1969.

Correspondence with Henry Huttleston Rogers, 1893-1909, edited by Lewis Leary. Berkeley, University of California Press, 1969.

Man Is the Only Animal That Blushes—or Needs to: The Wisdom of Mark Twain, edited by Michael Joseph. Los Angeles, Stanyan Books, 1970.

Mark Twain's Quarrel with Heaven: Captain Stormfield's Visit to Heaven and Other Sketches, edited by Roy B. Browne. New Haven, Connecticut, College and University Press, 1970.

Everybody's Mark Twain, edited by Caroline Thomas Harnsberger. South Brunswick, New Jersey, A. S. Barnes, and London, Yoseloff, 1972.

Fables of Man, edited by John S. Tuckey. Berkeley, University of California Press, 1972.

A Pen Warmed Up In Hell: Mark Twain in Protest, edited by Frederick Anderson. New York, Harper, 1972.

The Choice Humorous Works of Mark Twain. London, Chatto and Windus, 1973.

Mark Twain's Notebooks and Journals, edited by Frederick Anderson and others. Berkeley, University of California Press, 1975 (and later volumes).

Letters from the Sandwich Islands, edited by Joan Abramson. Norfolk Island, Australia, Island Heritage, 1975.

Mark Twain Speaking, edited by Paul Fatout. Iowa City, University of Iowa Press, 1976.

The Mammoth Cod, and Address to the Stomach Club. Milwaukee, Maledicta, 1976.

The Comic Mark Twain Reader, edited by Charles Neider. New York, Doubleday, 1977.

Mark Twain Speaks for Himself, edited by Paul Fatout. West Lafayette, Indiana, Purdue University Press, 1978.

The Devil's Race-Track: Mark Twain's Great Dark Writings: The Best from "Which Was the Dream" and "Fables of Man," edited by John S. Tuckey. Berkeley, University of California Press, 1980.

The Selected Letters of Mark Twain, edited by Charles Neider. New York, Harper, 1982.

Translator, *Slovenly Peter (Der Struwwelpeter).* New York, Limited Editions Club, 1935.

*

Bibliography: *A Bibliography of the Works of Mark Twain, Samuel Langhorne Clemens* by Merle Johnson, New York, Harper, revised edition, 1935; in *Bibliography of American Literature 2* by Jacob Blanck, New Haven, Connecticut, Yale University Press, 1957; *Mark Twain: A Reference Guide* by Thomas Asa Tenney, Boston, Hall, 1977; *Mark Twain International: A Bibliography and Interpretation of His Worldwide Popularity* edited by Robert H. Rodney, Westport, Connecticut, Greenwood Press, 1982.

Critical Studies (selection): *Mark Twain: A Biography* by Albert Bigelow Paine, New York, Harper, 3 vols., 1912, abridged edition, as *A Short Life of Mark Twain,* 1920; *Mark Twain: The Man and His Work* by Edward Wagenknecht, New Haven, Connecticut, Yale University Press, 1935, revised edition, Norman, University of Oklahoma Press, 1961, 1967;

Mark Twain: Man and Legend by De Lancey Ferguson, Indianapolis, Bobbs Merrill, 1943; *A Casebook on Mark Twain's Wound* edited by Lewis Leary, New York, Crowell, 1962; *Discussions of Mark Twain* edited by Guy A. Cardwell, Boston, Heath, 1963; *Mr Clemens and Mark Twain: A Biography* by Justin Kaplan, New York, Simon and Schuster, 1966, London, Cape, 1967; *Mark Twain: The Fate of Humor* by James M. Cox, Princeton, New Jersey, Princeton University Press, 1966; *The Art of Mark Twain* by William M. Gibson, New York, Oxford University Press, 1976; *Mark Twain: A Collection of Criticism* edited by Dean Morgan Schmitter, New York, McGraw Hill, 1976; *Mark Twain* by Robert Keith Miller, New York, Ungar, 1983; *The Authentic Mark Twain: A Literary Biography of Samuel L. Clemens* by Everett Emerson, Philadelphia, University of Pennsylvania Press, 1984.

*   *   *

Frequently Twain's science-fiction works are labeled as mimetic fiction (ultimately what occurs can be explained as dreams rather than actual time travel resulting from scientific extrapolation), still his dystopic creations and employment of the ideology of science within or preceding the dream structures qualifies some of his works as science fiction. In other works his use of alternate settings and actual scientific extrapolation outside of the dream/reality contexts appears, particularly in his shorter and sometimes incomplete stories.

Report from Paradise, The Mysterious Stranger, and *Letters from the Earth* are fantasy rather than science fiction: satires on man's place in the universe in which science is neither used as a tool to create the condition of the stories nor as a thematic consideration within them. Twain's fascination with comets, particularly Halley's comet, is evidenced in "Captain Stormfield's Visit to Heaven," "A Letter from a Comet," and "A Curious Pleasure Excursion." The interstellar travel included in each is either in or on a comet rather than in any kind of man-made space vessel and relegates these writings as fantasy.

Several of Twain's shorter works, "Mental Telegraphy," "Mental Telegraphy Again," and "My Platonic Sweetheart" focus on parapsychology in which Twain professed a firm belief, thus excluding them from his science-fiction works. Two other stories which have been classified as science fiction by some are "Earthquake Almanac" and "Petrified Man." However, both depend on natural phenomenon rather than on extrapolated science, social or physical.

Twain does extrapolate on technology of his time, predicting long distance telephone service in "The Loves of Alonzo Fitz Clarence and Rosannah Ethelton," and long distance balloon flight in *Tom Sawyer Abroad* and in the incomplete manuscripts of "A Murder, A Mystery, and a Marriage," and "The Mysterious Balloonist." However, *The Comedy of Those Extraordinary Twins* is neither extrapolative nor predictive, it being based on the Tocci Twins. Physical science extrapolation is used in "Sold to Satan" where Satan is made of radium, and Twain predicts the isolation of various elements by Madame Curie, and in the incomplete "Shackleford's Ghost" where a man becomes invisible after taking a potion created after numerous experiments by the local scientist.

Two works containing alternate settings, "The Curious Republic of Gondour" and "History 1,000 Years from Now," are seeming utopias. In "Curious Republic" weighted universal suffrage has developed; education, common sense, and, to a lesser extent, money earn the citizens extra votes. In the incomplete manuscript "History" society has evolved from a democracy to a monarchy. Three incomplete works by Twain employ alternate settings: "The Generation Iceberg," "The Secret History of Eddypus, The World-Empire," and "3000 Years among the Microbes." In "3000" Twain satirizes the human condition. By having a wizard accidently turn a man into a cholera microbe instead of a bird, Twain creates a setting which affords a distancing from reality which has been a science-fiction technique used by many writers to allow social criticism without immediately alienating the reader. The setting is the diseased body of a tramp within which millions of microbes live where nations have their own languages, customs, and governments, all patterned after nations existing during the early 20th century. The microbes are not described as aliens; instead they look, act, talk, and think precisely as man does. This setting allows Twain to comment on his favorite themes: the stupidity of government officials, the hypocrisy of organized religions, the prejudices evident in class systems, the problem of the lie – here related to the tall tale. The microbe tells his friends about the real world and they compliment him on his poetic inspiration—with one exception he is flatly not believed.

Unlike Hank of *Connecticut Yankee in King Arthur's Court*, the microbe does not introduce new technology to the society. Instead the society is ahead of his time, having a device which records thoughts and images and condenses them to perfectly understandable encapsulations of facts and meanings. Notably, a religious scientist reveals to the microbe a world view akin to Twain's by expounding on the absurdity of man's false sense of superiority. Technology is celebrated when a microscope is used to discover that on every level of organism the cycle of life is the same; thereby enforcing the moral treatise of the absurdity of man's presumptious superiority.

In "The Secret History of Eddypus, the World-Empire," Twain presents a 29th-century dystopia ruled by the Christian Science church which is comparable to the late 18th-century lifestyle, dominated by religious persecution, arrogance, and misinformation. He presents no new technology, scientific inquiry having been effectively stopped by the church. He shows the absurdities of organized religion which perpetuates the status quo, encourages a distinct disrespect for truth, and consistently and with a vengence destroys knowledge for fear that it would abrogate the power of the church. The narrator has begun to write a history of the world, all such references having been destroyed by the church and replaced by the church's version. The history is a humorous mish-mash of erroneous facts until the 19th-century section which contains an accurate delineation of scientific discoveries and their effects, focusing on evolution, both biological and societal, in which he identifies circumstances and environment as those factors which chart the course of the world.

In "The Generation Iceberg" Twain speculates on the type of society which would evolve in a group totally isolated. This fascination with isolated groups and the effect of their exposure to technology is also evident in "A Murder, A Mystery, and A Marriage" as well as *A Connecticut Yankee in King Arthur's Court*.

"From the 'London Times' of 1904," "The Great Dark," and *A Connecticut Yankee in King Arthur's Court* all reflect the increasing cynicism of Twain's later years. In the confusion of dream and reality accompanied by alteration of time and space, Twain creates different worlds for his protagonists to struggle in. These dystopias present Twain's perception of the unchanging human condition; man as a petty being, always willing to prey on his fellowman.

The comic relief in *Connecticut Yankee* (a literary burlesque of Malory's *Morte d'Arthur*) erupts through Twain's satire of the age of chivalry whose precepts had been adopted by the Old South, a frequent target of Twain's social criticism in his mainstream works. But primarily Twain investigates the effects of industrialization on a pre-industrial society which was a matter of public concern both in relation to the United States and to our foreign policy at the time. In this view, Twain attacked Social Darwinism: the establishment of an industrialized, capitalistic society where the common man was once again suppressed by the financial power of a few individuals who had gained their power through that technological revolution.

Hank, the protagonist of *Connecticut Yankee*, a 19th-century common working man, rises to power in King Arthur's Court through creative use of his technical skills and scientific knowledge. By introducing industrialization, Hank attempts to change the economic, political, and intellectual structures of a nation of oppressed people, but his failure results not so much through the powers of the church and state as through his own failure. He succumbs to one of the primary evils of capitalism (according to Twain): once Hank gains power, he becomes self-absorbed. The megalomanic Hank instigates a civil war (purportedly in the name of creating a viable civilization for the common man) which results in the ultimate destruction of all that he has established. What makes *Connecticut Yankee* science fiction is not just the question of whether Hank actually experiences time travel and suspended animation or whether he dreams it. Instead it is Twain's questioning of the effects of technology, his concentration on the idea of technology in another time and space.

The problem of dream versus reality occurs again in "The Great Dark." Whereas in *Connecticut Yankee* the protagonist goes back in time to a setting already familiar to the reader, in "The Great Dark" Twain concentrates on establishing a setting in which circumstance, not time, is important. Presenting a tiny world as seen through a microscope, Twain creates a whole watery universe filled with monsters, destruction, and suffering for his protagonist to attempt to survive in. Like Hank, Mr. Edwards returns to the present no longer accepting it as real, finding his other existence to have all the qualities of reality and his present that of the dream. This exploration of dream versus reality is closely linked with temporal/spatial relationships so that time and setting become an integral part of what makes these works science fiction. In *Connecticut Yankee*, science, or at least technology, is a thematic consideration, whereas in "The Great Dark" technology is used only as a tool to create the setting in which the characters must question temporal/spatial relationships. Twain embarks on another approach to science in "From the 'London Times' of 1904." Instead of employing a thematic consideration of technology as in *Connecticut Yankee* or using an already existing scientific instrument to create the circumstances of the story as in "The Great Dark," Twain invents the telectroscope (television) to use in conjunction with his usual exploration of thought and visual transference in temporal/spatial relationships.

In these works, Twain, as an early writer of science fiction, presents three different approaches still frequently used in the genre. Additionally, through his social criticism, Twain is one of the first mainstream writers to present dystopias rather than utopias to show by comparison rather than by contrast the inequities of the social institutions he questions: religion, government, taxes, prejudice, slavery, censorship, and politics. Yet his dark view of man is made bearable through his caustic humor. He invokes our laughter even as we accept with humility his accusations of our greed, jealousy, lack of common sense, thirst for power, cruelty, and ultimately the smallness of mind of the human beast.

—Jane B. Weedman

UTLEY, Steven. American. Born in 1948. Address: c/o Heidelberg Publishers, 1003 Brown Building, Austin, Texas 78701, U.S.A.

SCIENCE-FICTION PUBLICATIONS

Uncollected Short Stories

"The Unkindest Cut of All," in *Perry Rhodan 20*. New York, Ace, 1972.

"Parrot Phrase," in *Perry Rhodan 24*. New York, Ace, 1973.

"The Queen and I," in *Perry Rhodan 31*. New York, Ace, 1973.

"Crash Cameron and the Slime Beast," in *Vertex* (Los Angeles), June 1973.

"The Reason Why," in *Vertex* (Los Angeles), December 1973.

"Hung Like an Elephant," with Joe Pumilia, and "Womb, with a View," in *Alternities*, edited by David Gerrold. New York, Dell, 1974.

"Sport," in *Best SF 1973*, edited by Harry Harrison and Brian Aldiss. New York, Putnam, and London, Sphere, 1974.

"Deeper Than Death," in *Vertex* (Los Angeles), April 1974.

"Act of Mercy," in *Galaxy* (New York), July 1974.

"Big Black Whole" and "Time and Variance," in *Galaxy* (New York), August 1974.

"Amber Eyes," in *Galaxy* (New York), December 1974.

"The Great Red Spot," with Joe Pumilia, and "Dear Mom, I Don't Like It Here," in *Vertex* (Los Angeles), February 1975.

"Caring for Your Edaphosaurus," in *Vertex* (Los Angeles), August 1975.

"The Other Half," in *Galaxy* (New York), September 1975.

"Custer's Last Jump," with Howard Waldrop, in *Universe 6*, edited by Terry Carr. New York, Doubleday, 1976; London, Dobson, 1978.

"Predators," in *The Ides of Tomorrow*, edited by Terry Carr. Boston, Little Brown, 1976.

"Ghost Seas," in *Lone Star Universe*, edited by George W. Proctor and Steven Utley. Austin, Texas, Heidelberg, 1976.

"Sic Transit . . . ?," with Howard Waldrop, in *Stellar 2*, edited by Judy-Lynn del Rey. New York, Ballantine, 1976.

"Getting Away," in *Galaxy* (New York), January 1976.

"Larval Stage," in *Galaxy* (New York), July 1976.

"Ocean," in *Fantastic* (New York), August 1976.

"The Man at the Bottom of the Sea," in *Galaxy* (New York), October 1976.

"The Thirteenth Labor," in *Stellar 3*, edited by Judy-Lynn del Rey. New York, Ballantine, 1977.

"Black as the Pit, from Pole to Pole" with Howard Waldrop, in *New Dimensions 7*, edited by Robert Silverberg. New York, Harper, and London, Gollancz, 1977.

"Sidhe," in *More Devil's Kisses*, edited by Linda Lovecraft. London, Corgi, 1977.

"In Brightest Day, In Darkest Night," in *Fantastic* (New York), February 1977.

"Passport for a Phoenix," in *Galaxy* (New York), April 1977.

"Spectator Sport," in *Amazing* (New York), July 1977.

"The Maw," in *Fantasy and Science Fiction* (New York), July 1977.

"Flies by Night," with Lisa Tuttle, in *SF Choice 77*, edited by Mike Ashley. London, Quartet, 1977.

"Tom Sawyer's Sub-Orbital Escapade," with Lisa Tuttle, in *Ascents of Wonder*, edited by David Gerrold and Stephen Goldin. New York, Popular Library, 1977.

"Losing Streak," in *Fantasy and Science Fiction* (New York), January 1977.

"Our Vanishing Triceratops," with Joe Pumilia, in *Amazing* (New York), March 1977.

"Time and Hagakure," in *Asimov's Choice: Black Holes and Bug-Eyed Monsters* , edited by George H. Scithers. New York, Dale, 1978.

"Deviation from a Theme," in *The Rivals of King Kong*, edited by Michel Parry. London, Corgi, 1978.

"Uncoiling," with Lisa Tuttle, in *Fantastic* (New York), April 1978.

"Personal Column," in *Sex in the 21st Century*, edited by Michel Parry and Milton Subotsky. London, Panther, 1979.

"The Man Who Ran Up the Clock," in *Fantastic* (New York), January 1979.

"Leaves," in *Amazing* (New York), February 1979.

"Genocide Man," in *Fantasy and Science Fiction* (New York), April 1979.

"Upstart," in *The Best from Fantasy and Science Fiction 23*, edited by Edward L. Ferman. New York, Doubleday, 1980.

OTHER PUBLICATIONS

Other

Editor, with George W. Proctor, *Lone Star Universe: Speculative Fiction from Texas*. Austin, Texas, Heidelberg, 1976.

*

Steven Utley comments:

I don't have much to say, meaningful or otherwise, about my stories. I did, of course, think rather highly of some of my own work when I wrote it. I was possessed of considerable enthusiasm for what I was about. Disenchantment with the SF field, when it set in, set in hard, and now time has made all the difference. Anymore, I view my having been a writer as just a phase, like puberty, into which I entered at one point in my life and from which I emerged, not exactly unscathed, at a subsequent point. I've done some writing since the, ah, divorce, but I no longer *think* of myself as a writer, only as someone who every now and then misses the actual grueling work of sitting in front of the typewriter for hours on end. Most of my energy goes into other pursuits which are quite unrelated to SF and, more to the point, quite satisfying.

*   *   *

Between 1972 and 1979, Steven Utley established a reputation as a prolific author of short stories and novelettes, either alone or in collaboration with a number of other Texas-based writers, almost notably Howard Waldrop and Lisa Tuttle. With George W. Proctor he edited a volume of SF and fantasy by Texans, *Lone Star Universe*, whose appearance Harlan Ellison hailed as a "watershed event." Working exclusively at less-than-novel length, Utley has produced fiction either competent but undistinguished or astonishing for its inventive mordancy. At his best, his pervasive angst leavened with humor, angry wit, or local color, he has written chilling horror stories ("Ghost Seas"), scathingly funny satires ("Upstart"), outrageous pastiches ("Black as the Pit, from Pole to Pole," with Waldrop), and evocative, melancholy science fiction ("The Man at the Bottom of the Sea"). The strongest contemporary influences on Utley's development appear to be the October landscapes of Ray Bradbury, the ironic pessimism of the later Robert Silverberg, the pop-culture eclecticism of Philip José Farmer, and the manic-depressive black humor of Barry N. Malzberg, whose style and subject matter Utley affectionately parodies in "Losing Streak. " In one conspicuous but hardly damning sense, then, he is a writer still in the process of discovering his own voice and métier.

"Custer's Last Jump," with Waldrop, first secured wide recognition of Utley's talents. It postulates a frontier America in which the Oglala Sioux, equipped with Krupp monoplanes, defeat the 7th Cavalry of George Armstrong Custer and its airborne auxiliary, the 505th Balloon Infantry. Told in earnest text-book prose, this off-the-wall tour de force concludes with a "Suggested Reading" list as whacky and authentic-seeming as the "historical" matter preceding it. This final bibliographic fillip may owe something to Farmer's convolute appendices in the mock-biography *Tarzan Alive*.

A second Utley-Waldrop collaboration, "Black as the Pit, from Pole to Pole," pays homage to Farmer (again), Mary Shelley, Poe, Verne, Burroughs, and others. Its protagonist is that quintessential symbol of alienation, the Frankenstein monster, and its setting is the perilous hollow interior of the earth. Although the disparate elements of this tale do not always mesh convincingly, sheer narrative *chutzpah* often effectively disguises the fact. Like "Custer's Last Jump," it has been much discussed and anthologized.

Among Utley's solo efforts "Upstart" is a pointed, and hilarious, satire of the spacefarer-as-superman ethos in science fiction, perhaps the last word on this indefatigable idiocy. "Ghost Seas," meanwhile, invokes the desolate West Texas landscape in the service of a terrifying tale of avarice and revenge. "The Man at the Bottom of the Sea" demonstrates Utley's ability to dramatize, poignantly, a private sense of loss; it is notable for a calm descriptive overlay at odds with the emotional intensity of its characters.

Another effective story, set against the historical backdrop of World War II, is "Time and Hagakure," wherein the son of a Japanese kamikaze pilot attempts to preserve his own sanity by mediating, through time, the salvation of his doomed father. In "Getting Away" Utley makes effective use of his deep-seated interest in dinosaurs—creatures which frequently raise their huge, anomalous heads in his fiction—to give his protagonist a means of psychological escape from a polluted and regimented future.

In many ways Utley has been an undervalued writer, perhaps because he shows little interest in writing a novel. The fact that even his best short stories and novelettes remain uncollected has also obscured his accomplishment.

—Michael Bishop

VANCE, Gerald. See **GARRETT, Randall; PHILLIPS, Rog.**

VANCE, Jack (John Holbrook Vance). Also writes as Peter Held; Ellery Queen; Alan Wade. American. Born in San Francisco, California, 28 August 1916. Educated at the University of California, Berkeley, B. A. 1942. Married Norma Ingold in 1946; one son. Self-employed writer. Recipient: Mystery Writers of America Edgar Allan Poe Award, 1960; Hugo Award, 1963, 1967; Nebula Award, 1966; Jupiter Award, 1974; World Fantasy Life Achievement award, 1984. Agent: Kirby McCauley Ltd., 425 Park Avenue South, New York, New York, 10016. Address: 6383 Valley View Road, Oakland, California 94611, U.S.A.

SCIENCE-FICTION PUBLICATIONS

Novels (series: Alastor; Big Planet; Dying Earth; Durdane; Keith Gersen; Lyonesse; Tschai)

The Space Pirate. New York, Toby Press, 1953; abridged edition, as *The Five Gold Bands*, New York, Ace, 1963; London, Granada, 1980.
Vandals of the Void (for children). Philadelphia, Winston, 1953.
To Live Forever. New York, Ballantine, 1956; London, Sphere, 1976.
Big Planet. New York, Avalon, 1957; London, Coronet, 1977.
The Languages of Pao. New York, Avalon, 1958.
Slaves of the Klau. New York, Ace, 1958.
The Dragon Masters. New York, Ace, 1963; London, Dobson, 1965.
The Houses of Iszm, Son of the Tree. New York, Ace, 1964; *Son of the Tree* published separately, London, Mayflower, 1974.
The Star King (Gersen). New York, Berkley, 1964; London, Dobson, 1966.
The Killing Machine (Gersen). New York, Berkley, 1964; London, Dobson, 1967.
Monsters in Orbit. New York, Ace, 1965; London, Dobson, 1977.
Space Opera. New York, Pyramid, 1965; London, Coronet, 1982.
The Blue World. New York, Ballantine, 1966; London, Mayflower, 1976.
The Brains of Earth. New York, Ace, 1966; London, Dobson, 1975; as *Nopalgarth*, New York, DAW, 1980.
The Palace of Love (Gersen). New York, Berkley, 1967; London, Dobson, 1968.
City of the Chasch (Tschai). New York, Ace, 1968; London, Dobson, 1975.
Emphyrio. New York, Doubleday, 1969.
Servants of the Wankh (Tschai). New York, Ace, 1969; London, Dobson, 1975.
The Dirdir (Tschai). New York, Ace, 1969; London, Dobson, 1975.
The Pnume (Tschai). New York, Ace, 1970; London, Dobson, 1975.
The Anome (Durdane). New York, Dell, 1973; London, Hodder and Stoughton, 1975; as *The Faceless Man*, New York, Ace, 1978.
The Brave Free Men (Durdane). New York, Dell, 1973; London, Hodder and Stoughton, 1975.
Trullion: Alastor 2262. New York, Ballantine, 1973; London, Mayflower, 1979.
The Asutra (Durdane). New York, Dell, 1974; London, Hodder and Stoughton, 1975.
The Gray Prince. Indianapolis, Bobbs Merrill, 1974; London, Coronet, 1976.
Marune: Alastor 933. New York, Ballantine, 1975; London, Coronet, 1978.

Showboat World (Big Planet). New York, Pyramid, 1975; London, Coronet, 1977.
Maske: Thaery. New York, Berkley, 1976; London, Fontana, 1978.
Wyst: Alastor 1716. New York, DAW, 1978.
The Face (Gersen). New York, DAW, 1979; London, Dobson, 1980.
The Book of Dreams (Gersen). New York, DAW, 1981.
Lyonesse. New York, Berkley, 1983; London, Panther, 1984.
Cugel's Saga (Dying Earth). New York, Pocket Books, 1983.
Rhialto the Marvellous (Dying Earth). New York, Baen, 1984.
Lyonesse 2: The Green Pearl. New York, Berkley, 1985.

Short Stories (series: Dying Earth)

The Dying Earth. New York, Curl, 1950; London, Mayflower, 1972.
Future Tense. New York, Ballantine, 1964; as *Dust of Far Suns,* New York, DAW, 1981.
The World Between and Other Stories. New York, Ace, 1965; as *The Moon Moth and Other Stories,* London, Dobson, 1976.
The Eyes of the Overworld (Dying Earth). New York, Ace, 1966; London, Mayflower, 1972.
The Many Worlds of Magnus Ridolph. New York, Ace, 1966; London, Dobson, 1977.
The Last Castle. New York, Ace, 1967.
Eight Fantasms and Magics. New York, Macmillan, 1969; as *Fantasms and Magics,* London, Mayflower, 1978.
The Worlds of Jack Vance. New York, Ace, 1973.
The Best of Jack Vance. New York, Pocket Books, 1976.
Green Magic. San Francisco, Underwood Miller, 1979.
The Bagful of Dreams. San Francisco, Underwood Miller, 1979.
The Seventeen Virgins. San Francisco, Underwood Miller, 1979.
Galactic Effectuator. Columbia, Pennsylvania, Underwood Miller, 1980.
The Narrow Land. New York, DAW, 1982; London, Coronet, 1984.
Lost Moons. Columbia, Pennsylvania, Underwood Miller, 1982.

OTHER PUBLICATIONS

Novels as John Holbrook Vance

Isle of Peril (as Alan Wade). New York, Curl, 1957.
Take My Face (as Peter Held). New York, Curl, 1957.
The Man in the Cage. New York, Random House, 1960; London, Boardman, 1961.
The Fox Valley Murders. Indianapolis, Bobbs Merrill, 1966; London, Hale, 1967.
The Pleasant Grove Murders. Indianapolis, Bobbs Merrill, 1967; London, Hale, 1968.
The Deadly Isles. Indianapolis, Bobbs Merrill, 1969; London, Hale, 1970.
Bad Ronald. New York, Ballantine, 1973.
The House on Lily Street. San Francisco, Underwood Miller, 1979.
The View from Chickweed's Window. San Francisco, Underwood Miller, 1979.

Novels as Ellery Queen

The Four Johns. New York, Pocket Books, 1964; as *Four Men Called John,* London, Gollancz, 1976.

A Room to Die In. New York, Pocket Books, 1965.
The Madman Theory. New York, Pocket Books, 1966.

Plays

Television Plays: *Captain Video* (6 episodes), 1952-53.

*

Bibliography: *Fantasms: A Bibliography of the Literature of Jack Vance* by Daniel J. H. Levack and Tim Underwood, San Francisco, Underwood Miller, 1978.

Manuscript Collection: Mugar Memorial Library, Boston University.

Critical Studies: *Jack Vance, Science Fiction Stylist* by Richard Tiedman, Wabash, Indiana, Coulson, 1965; *Jack Vance* edited by Tim Underwood and Chuck Miller, New York, Taplinger, 1980.

* * *

Jack Vance's works will never fit any definition of science fiction or fantasy. In fact what makes his stories distinctive is the fact that he writes science fiction that feels like fantasy and fantasy that feels like science fiction. In over the 30 years he has been writing, Vance has distinguished himself for his ability to create fictional worlds with a richness of detail and inner logic rarely encountered in either science fiction or fantasy. If, for example, a future Earth is described as in *The Dying Earth* and *The Eyes of the Overworld,* the reader's attention is soon focused on the remarkable creatures that share this world with humanity rather than on a particularly original plot or a strongly stated theme. His plots are usually based on classical and Germanic mythology, medieval romance, and earlier space operas. What prevents such yarns as *The Eyes of the Overworld, Slaves of the Klau,* and most of his novel series from becoming repetitive is the setting, newly invented for each work. A Vance story teases the reader; there is always something new added to top what he has already done.

The six interconnected stories that make up *The Dying Earth* illustrate well Vance's use of fantasy in science fiction. Using a popular science-fiction devise, a future in which magic has replaced science, Vance leads his characters on a series of adventures reminiscent of the quest in fantasy. Though the stories are populated with magicians, half-humans, tree creatures, and deamons, the air cars, antigravity devices, and the great machines of science fiction are equally present. Vance combines a folklore atmosphere with a science-fiction future and theme (humans can overcome any hardship they have the will to overcome). The stories read like fantasy, but they mean like science fiction.

It is this balance between fantasy and science fiction that Vance returns to so often in his works. *Big Planet, Son of the Tree, The Houses of Iszm,* the Tschai, Durdane, and Gersen series all show Vance's lavish care in settings. And their human characters are just as lovingly presented. Each is identifiably human despite the strangeness of the world he or she inhabits. Vance has occassionally been accused of spending too much time on his settings. Recent works such as *Wyst: Alastor 1716* sometimes appear to sacrifice plot to the details of their worlds. But if there are times when attention to imaginative details upsets the balance between story and setting, there are also times when that balance is magnificently maintained.

The *Languages of Pao* is such an achievement, a classic science-fiction story. Using a simple plot of palace intrigue, Vance explores the complicated issue of the interconnection of man's perception of himself and his world with his universal use of language. Does language so filter a speaker's sense of his world through providing names for each object and experience that human perception is limited to what is contained within the language? Can these limits be expanded? What is the cost of such expansion? Vance raises each of these questions, and he finds satisfying answers for each. What allows for the successful resolution of the novel is the care with which Vance first presents the worlds of Pao and Breakness. Pao is a passive world in which a massive population is favored by a planet with a geology that sees to all its needs. The planet Breakness, however, is rugged, harsh, indifferent to the needs of its inhabitants. On Pao, "The typical Paonese saw himself as a cork on a sea of a million waves, lofted, lowered, thrust aside by incomprehensible forces—if he thought of himself as a discrete personality at all." The people of Breakness, on the other hand, can only see themselves as individuals. On a world in which the individual is in constant danger, concern for individual identity remains uppermost. Given these two worlds, and the care with which Vance develops their contrasting natures, the exploration of the languages of each world and their implications for mankind as the race confronts a future that increasingly demands flexibility is both believable and happily clever. *The Languages of Pao* deals with a complex concept with significant implications for humanity's future, but does so in a straightforward story that dramatizes the issue without trivializing it. The balance between setting and theme is largely responsible for this success.

Perhaps the most endearing characteristic in Vance's work is the way in which he turns the unusual into the familiar. What starts out as a totally alien world ends up as comfortably recognizable. This process usually results from Vance's interest in the social customs and cultural institutions of his fictional worlds. *Big Planet*, for example, contains many such descriptions, and *Space Opera* has the same in a more humorous vein. "Moon Moth" combines the detective story with science fiction and, at the same time, presents a credible picture of a society in which all people wear masks and use music as an important aid in communication. In each of these works what becomes significant is not the strangeness of the societies but the fact that they are all human societies. No matter how alien the environment or the customs, humanity remains identifiably human.

The Dragon Master is perhaps Vance's finest and most poetic example of his ability to translate the strange into the familiar. Using a rather evocative vocabulary, Vance describes the world of Aerlith as a place of wind and stone with a few beautiful, fertile valleys. Genetic engineering has become commonplace on Aerlith and appears to be tinged with a bit of magic, and this allows Vance plenty of room for introducing some of his most exotic creatures. Yet, by the end of the novel Aerlith is not an alien world. Because Vance carefully shows how his human characters (particularly Joaz Banbeck) have learned to live with its strangeness and not lose their human traits, the world and its society are believable. The reader is convinced that given such circumstances human beings would create just such a society on such a world. While *The Dragon Masters* is Vance's most successful attempt at the union of the bizarre and the common, *The Last Castle, The Blue World, Emphyrio,* and *The Anome* all illustrate his love for this technique.

Finally, there is the range of styles Vance writes with. In 1983 two novels were published that illustrate just how broad that range is. *Lyonesse* is based on Celtic folklore and is written in a lush and intricate language worthy of these elaborate tales. Its plot is equal to its language. *Cugel's Saga* (part of the Dying Earth series) is the opposite. Based on Norse mythology, its language is sparse and understated. In both novels, Vance exhibits his talent in using words to evoke the atmosphere most fitting to the world he creates. Readers who are familiar with the traditions of Celtic and Norse literature will appreciate what he has achieved. Those who are not will still respond to the radically different voices with which each work resonates.

Jack Vance creates by taking extremes that initially threaten to tear a story apart. But these forces finally come together in worlds in which every element appears exactly as it should. Vance creates neither science-fiction nor fantasy worlds. They are Jack Vance worlds.

—Stephen H. Goldman

VAN LHIN, Eric. See **del REY, Lester.**

VAN SCYOC, Sydney J(oyce). American. Born in Mt. Vernon, Indiana, 27 July 1939. Educated at Florida State University, Tallahassee; University of Hawaii, Honolulu; Chabot College, Hayward, California; California State University, Hayward. Married Jim R. Van Scyoc in 1957; one daughter and one son. Since 1962, free-lance writer. Secretary, 1975-77, and President, 1977-79, Starr King Unitarian Church, Hayward. Agent: Howard Morhaim Literary Agency, 501 Fifth Avenue, New York, New York 10017. Address: 2636 East Avenue, Hayward, California 94541, U.S.A.

SCIENCE-FICTION PUBLICATIONS

Novels (series: Darkchild)

Saltflower. New York, Avon, 1971.
Assignment: Nor'Dyren. New York, Avon, 1973.
Starmother. New York, Berkley, 1976.
Cloudcry. New York, Berkley, 1977.
Sunwaifs. New York, Berkley, 1981.
Darkchild. New York, Berkley, 1982; London, Penguin, 1984.
Bluesong (Darkchild). New York, Berkley, 1983; London, Penguin, 1984.
Starsilk (Darkchild). New York, Berkley, 1984.

Uncollected Short Stories

"Shatter the Wall," in *Galaxy* (New York), February 1962.
"Bimmie Says," in *Galaxy* (New York), October 1962.
"Pollony Undiverted," in *Galaxy* (New York), February 1963.
"Zack with His Scar," in *Fantasy and Science Fiction* (New York), March 1963.
"Cornie on the Walls," in *Fantastic* (New York), August 1963.
"Soft and Soupy Whispers," in *Galaxy* (New York), April 1964.
"One Man's Dream," in *Fantasy and Science Fiction* (New York), November 1964.
"The Dead Ones," in *Worlds of Tomorrow* (New York), January 1965.
"A Visit to Cleveland General," in *World's Best Science Fiction*

1969, edited by Donald A. Wollheim and Terry Carr. New York, Ace, and London, Gollancz, 1969.
"Unidentified Fallen Object," in *Fantasy and Science Fiction* (New York), January 1969.
"Little Blue Hawk," in *Galaxy* (New York), May 1969.
"Summons to the Medicmat," in *Worlds of Tomorrow* (New York), Spring 1971.
"Noepti-Noe," in *Galaxy* (New York), November 1972.
"When Petals Fall," in *Two Views of Wonder,* edited by Thomas M. Scortia and Chelsea Quinn Yarbro. New York, Ballantine, 1973.
"Mnarra Mobilis," in *The Best from If 2.* New York, Award, 1974.
"Skyveil," in *Galaxy* (New York), April 1974.
"Aberrant," in *Analog* (New York), June 1974.
"Sweet Sister, Green Brother," in *The Best from Galaxy 3,* edited by James Baen. New York, Award, 1975.
"Deathsong," in *The 1975 Annual World's Best SF,* edited by Donald A. Wollheim and Arthur W. Saha. New York, DAW, 1975; Morley, Yorkshire, Elmfield Press, 1976.
"Nightfire," in *Cassandra Rising,* edited by Alice Laurance. New York, Doubleday, 1978.
"Mountain Wings," in *Isaac Asimov's Science Fiction Magazine* (New York), November 1979.
"Darkmorning," in *Isaac Asimov's Science Fiction Magazine* (New York), March 1980.
"Stonefoal," in *Isaac Asimov's Science Fiction Magazine* (New York), August 1980.
"Laughing Man," in *Isaac Asimov's Science Fiction Magazine* (New York), November 1980.
"Bluewater Dreams," in *Isaac Asimov's Science Fiction Magazine* (New York), March 1981.
"The Teaching," in *Isaac Asimov's Science Fiction Magazine* (New York), April 1982.
"Fire-Caller," in *Isaac Asimov's Space of Her Own,* edited by Shawna McCarthy. New York, Davis, 1983.

*

Manuscript Collection: California State University, Fullerton.

Sydney J. Van Scyoc comments:

My earlier short fiction was set on Earth in the non-too-distant future and dealt primarily with individuals struggling against an increasingly dehumanizing technological society. I took several years off from writing in the mid 1960's, while my children were very young. Soon after I began writing again, I found my focus had shifted to short fiction set on other planets and dealt primarily with communities struggling against inexplicable alien environments. I am increasingly intrigued now by the genetic and social changes which I believe will overtake the human race once we begin to colonize other planets. I prefer not to deal in much detail with the inevitable technological changes we will see. Instead I like to set my fiction on isolated worlds inhabited by a relatively small human population. My personal orientation is increasingly pantheistic, and in my longer fiction I am attempting to deal with the spiritual relationship of human to environment.

*   *   *

Sydney J. Van Scyoc's early stories are set on earth not very far in the future and show the dehumanization of persons in an advanced technological society. The dehumanization is primarily apparent in the characters' lack of personal freedom and conscious choice in such stories as "Pollony Undiverted," "Soft and Soupy Whispers," and the chilling "Visit to Cleveland General. " The recent "Nightfire" is an unusual story in which a stalemated war in North America has confined 12 million non-combatants as virtual hostages in orbit above the earth for 41 years. The protagonist, Corneil Rothler, in a carefully planned coup d'etat ruthlessly engineers a truce alone.

A major shift in her work becomes apparent in the long short story "Little Blue Hawk," set in the 21st century; this story focuses on the personal and social costs of human genetic engineering. Van Scyoc's interest in the relationship of human with alien species and an alien ecology appears in "Noepti-Noe," "Sweet Sister, Green Brother," and "Aberrant. " These stories emphasize the interdependence and unity of all life forms.

Van Scyoc's impressive first novel, *Saltflower,* takes the basic premise of a dying race seeding earth to generate a transpecies who will be able to reproduce and be viable. The novel is set on earth in the year 2024, and follows the adventures of one of the "transracial" children, Hadley Greer, who is under surveillance by the US government agency SIBling. Most of the action takes place at the Purification Colony's headquarters near Salt Lake City. The Purification Colony is a cult headed by a psychotic leader, Dr. Braith. The novel deftly blends government intrigue, and burgling, religious fanaticism, mysterious murders, and credible alien consciousness, reactions, and biology.

Assignment: Nor'Dyren is an anti-utopian novel with strong satiric elements. It begins on earth in the not-too-distant future with a maintenance sub-engineer, Tollan Bailey, attempting to get a job in the huge company CalMega. Only a few people are employed; the rest live comfortable, futile lives without realizing the social controls that narrow their existence. Bailey wins a trip to the planet Nor'Dyren inhabited by three humanoid species whose rigid social roles and asexual inter-species marriage are leading to a breakdown of the moneyless economy and culture. The Gonnegon are the thinkers and administrators, the Allegon serve, and the Berregon manufacture. The novel follows Bailey's attempts to understand the culture and his maturation. He is an appealing character, particularly in his enchantment with trying to repair machines on Nor'Dyren and help the aliens. The anthropologist Laarica Johns, sent to aid him in his legal battle, discovers the reason for the de-evolution on Nor'Dyren with the help of Patt, a rebellious Berregon. The satire of earth bureaucracy, rigid social and sexual roles, and crippling cultural assumptions both on earth and Nor'Dyren is effective. The novel is an impassioned plea for a humane culture in which persons can be free to develop their capacities and make ethical choices.

Starmother presents the pathos of ostracized human mutants on a colony world, a race of aliens, the dirads, and the testing of the young protagonist, Jahna Swiss, a cadet of the Service Corps from the planet Peace. The novel alternates the points of view of Jahna, Zuniin, an alienated social outcast, and a young mother, Piety, who is a victim of the superstition and fanaticism of the puritanical human colonists, known as The First Fathers, on the planet Nelding. The alien planet, the various social groups, and species are vividly realized. Suspense is generated by the attempt of Zuniin to kill Jahna out of insane jealousy and xenophobia. Jahna's ethical dilemma and her final commitment to the mutant children enrich the novel. Van Scyoc contrasts the civilization of Peace, Jahna's planet, with Nelding, showing the deficiencies of rigid social roles, fanatic religion, and superstition which make life unbearable on the unlovely Nelding.

Cloudcry is an expansion and development of the short story

"Deathsong. " Around the core of the earlier story of an encounter with still-powerul alien artifacts resembling flutes by members of two humanoid races on an alien planet, Van Scyoc has added the framestory of the human space adventurer Verron's search for the man-leopards of the planet Rumar and the complication of a deadly space disease called bloodblossom. Verrons is exiled on the quarantine plant, Selmarii, along with another human, Sadler Wells, and a sentient bird-man alien because they have the disease. Aleida, one of the descendants of the ancient race, has psionic powers and heightens them with a crystal which focuses solar energy. The radiation from the light dancer's flute cures the bloodblossom disease. Verrons leaves the abandoned isolation planet haunted by the prospect of Aleida and a new race of powerful light dancers who do not share humane values, *Cloudcry*, like Van Scyoc's other novels, is distinguished by vivid imagery and sensuous detail, particularly when she portrays non-human perceptions and consciousness.

Sunwaifs continues the author's focus on humans struggling to adapt on uncongenial planets. The sunwaifs are six children born with paranormal mutant abilities, resulting from unusual solar activity during their conception on the harsh planet Destiny. In two alternating points of view over 14 years, the reader follows their development and deepening relationship with the planet. The adaptation of the other humans is aided by the mutant teenagers' increasing understanding of the planet ecology. The climax and resolution of personal and social difficulties comes from an ecological pantheism based on cooperation with natural forces. This hopeful ending promises further enrichment of all intelligent life on the planet Destiny.

Two short stories, "Mountain Wings" and "Darkmorning," set on the harsh planet Brakrath, show the promising direction of Van Scyoc's imagination. This promise is brilliantly fulfilled in the following three novels, set primarily on the same planet. The trilogy, *Darkchild, Bluesong*, and *Starsilk*, forms a major achievement demonstrating her strengths as a science-fiction writer: invention of believable alien environments and psychologies which are truly strange, powerful new myths, and striking relationships of humans and aliens with action plots and memorable characters. Perhaps the finest invention is the sentient starsilk which appears in each novel. The starsilk can form a symbiotic relationship with various sentient beings, providing the occasion for effective poetic description; various types of consciousness are presented which have been a strength of Van Scyoc's style for some years. Also notable is the sun goddess myth which functions to explain the harnessing of solar energy and is the basis for the testing of characters in all three novels. The individual works fit together in a satisfying whole with an epic sweep encompassing several planets, but each novel can be enjoyed independently as good adventure science fiction.

—Diane Parkin-Speer

---

van VOGT, A(lfred) E(lton). American. Born near Winnipeg, Manitoba, Canada, 26 April 1912. Educated in schools in Manitoba, graduated 1928; University of Ottawa; University of California, Los Angeles. Served in the Department of National Defense, Ottawa, 1939-41. Married Lydia I. Brayman (second marriage) in 1979. Census clerk, Ottawa, 1931-32; western representative, Maclean Trade Papers, Winnipeg, 1936-39. Managing Director, Hubbard Dianetic Research Foundation of California, Los Angeles, 1950-53; co-owner, Hubbard Dianetic Center, Los Angeles, 1953-61, and President, Califor-

nia Association of Dianetic Auditors, 1958-81. Recipient: Manuscripters Literature Award, 1948; Count Dracula Society Ann Radcliffe Award, 1968; Academy of Science Fiction, Fantasy, and Horror Films Award, 1979. B. A. : Golden Gate College, Los Angeles. Guest of Honor, 4th World Science Fiction Convention, 1946, European Science Fiction Convention, 1978 and Metz Festival, France, 1985. Agent: Leslie Flood, Carnell Literary Agency, Rowneybury Bungalow, Sawbridgeworth, near Old Harlow, Essex CM20 2EX, England. Address: P. O. Box 3065, Hollywood, California 90078, U.S.A.

SCIENCE-FICTION PUBLICATIONS

Novels (series: Clane; Gilbert Gosseyn; Weapon Shop)

Slan. Sauk City, Wisconsin, Arkham House, 1946; revised edition, New York, Simon and Schuster, 1951; London, Weidenfeld and Nicholson, 1953.
The Weapon Makers (Weapon Shop). Providence, Rhode Island, Hadley, 1947; revised edition, New York, Greenberg, 1952; London, Weidenfeld and Nicolson, 1954; as *One Against Eternity*, New York, Ace, 1955.
The Book of Ptath. Reading, Pennsylvania, Fantasy Press, 1947; as *Two Hundred Million A. D. *, New York, Paperback Library, 1964.
The World of A (Gosseyn). New York, Simon and Schuster, 1948; revised edition, as *The World of Null-A*, London, Dobson, 1969; New York, Berkley, 1970.
The Voyage of the Space Beagle. New York, Simon and Schuster, 1950; London, Grayson, 1951; *as Mission: Interplanetary*, New York, New American Library, 1952.
The House That Stood Still. New York, Greenberg, 1950; London, Weidenfeld and Nicolson, 1953; revised edition, as *The Mating Cry*, New York, Galaxy, 1960; as *Undercover Aliens*, London, Panther, 1976.
The Weapon Shops of Isher. New York, Greenberg, 1951; London, Weidenfeld and Nicolson, 1952.
The Mixed Men. New York, Gnome Press, 1952; as *Mission to the Stars*, New York, Berkley, 1955; London, Digit, 1960.
The Universe Maker. New York, Ace, 1953; in *The Universe Maker, and The Proxy Intelligence*, London, Sidgwick and Jackson, 1976.
Planets for Sale, with E. Mayne Hull. New York, Fell, 1954; London, Panther, 1978.
The Pawns of Null-A (Gosseyn). New York, Ace, 1956; London, Digit, 1960; as *The Players of Null-A*, New York, Berkley, 1966.
Empire of the Atom (Clane). Chicago, Shasta, 1957; London, New English Library, 1975.
The Mind Cage. New York, Simon and Schuster, 1957; London, Panther, 1960.
Triad (omnibus). New York, Simon and Schuster, 1959.
The War Against the Rull. New York, Simon and Schuster, 1959; London, Panther, 1961.
Siege of the Unseen. New York, Ace, 1959; as *The Three Eyes of Evil*, with *Earth's Last Fortress*, London, Sidgwick and Jackson, 1973.
The Wizard of Linn (Clane). New York, Ace, 1962; London, New English Library, 1976.
The Beast. New York, Doubleday, 1963; as *Moonbeast*, London, Panther, 1969.
Rogue Ship. New York, Doubleday, 1965; London, Dobson, 1967.

The Winged Man, with E. Mayne Hull. New York, Doubleday, 1966; London, Sidgwick and Jackson, 1967.
A Van Vogt Omnibus 1-2. London, Sidgwick and Jackson, 2 vols., 1967-71.
The Silkie . New York, Ace, 1969; London, New English Library, 1973.
Quest for the Future. New York, Ace, 1970; London, Sidgwick and Jackson, 1971.
Children of Tomorrow. New York, Ace, 1970; London, Sidgwick and Jackson, 1972.
The Battle of Forever. New York, Ace, 1971; London, Sidgwick and Jackson, 1972.
The Darkness on Diamondia. New York, Ace, 1972; London, Sidgwick and Jackson, 1974.
Future Glitter. New York, Ace, 1973; London, Sidgwick and Jackson, 1976; as *Tyranopolis*, London, Sphere, 1977.
The Secret Galactics. Englewood Cliffs, New Jersey, Prentice Hall, 1974; London, Sidgwick and Jackson, 1975; as *Earth Factor X*, New York, DAW, 1976.
The Man with a Thousand Names. New York, DAW, 1974; London, Sidgwick and Jackson, 1975.
The Anarchistic Colossus. New York, Ace, 1977; London, Sidgwick and Jackson, 1978.
Supermind. New York, DAW, 1977; London, Sidgwick and Jackson, 1978.
Renaissance. New York, Pocket Books, 1979.
Cosmic Encounter. New York, Doubleday, 1980; London, New English Library, 1981.
Computerworld. New York, DAW, 1983; as *Computer Eye*, Beverly Hills, California, Morrison Raven Hill, 1985.
Null-A Three (Gosseyn). New York, DAW, and London, Sphere, 1985.

Short Stories

Out of the Unknown, with E. Mayne Hull. Los Angeles, Fantasy, 1948; London, New English Library, 1970; expanded edition, Reseda, California, Powell, 1969; as *The Sea Thing and Other Stories*, London, Sidgwick and Jackson, 1970.
Masters of Time. Reading, Pennsylvania, Fantasy Press, 1950; as *Earth's Last Fortress*, New York, Ace, 1960; *The Changeling* published separately, New York, Macfadden Bartell, 1967; in *The Three Eyes of Evil, and Earth's Last Fortress* , London, Sidgwick and Jackson, 1973.
Away and Beyond. New York, Pellegrini and Cudahy, 1952; London, Panther, 1963.
Destination: Universe! New York, Pellegrini and Cudahy, 1952; London, Weidenfeld and Nicolson, 1953.
The Twisted Men. New York, Ace, 1964.
Monsters. New York, Paperback Library, 1965; London, Corgi, 1970; as *The Blal*, New York, Zebra, 1976.
The Far-Out Worlds of A. E. van Vogt. New York, Ace, 1968; London, Sidgwick and Jackson, 1973; expanded edition, as *The Worlds of A. E. van Vogt*, Ace, 1974.
More Than Superhuman. New York, Dell, 1971; London, New English Library, 1975.
The Proxy Intelligence and Other Mind Benders. New York, Paperback Library, 1971.
M33 in Andromeda. New York, Paperback Library, 1971.
The Book of van Vogt. New York, DAW, 1972; as *Lost: Fifty Suns*, DAW, 1979; London, New English Library, 1980.
The Best of A. E. van Vogt. London, Sphere, 1974.
The Best of A. E. van Vogt. New York, Pocket Books, 1976.
The Gryb. New York, Zebra, 1976; London, New English Library, 1980.

Pendulum. New York, DAW, 1978; London, New English Library, 1982.

OTHER PUBLICATIONS

Novel

The Violent Man. New York, Farrar Straus, 1962.

Other

"Complication in the Science Fiction Story," in *Of Worlds Beyond*, edited by Lloyd Arthur Esbach. Reading, Pennsylvania, Fantasy Press, 1947; London, Dobson, 1965.
The Hypnotism Handbook, with Charles Edward Cooke. Los Angeles, Griffin, 1956.
"Introduction" to *The Pseudo-People*, edited by William F. Nolan. Los Angeles, Sherbourne Press, 1965; as *Almost Human*, London, Souvenir Press, 1966.
The Money Personality. West Nyack, New York, Parker, 1972; Wellingborough, Northamptonshire, Thorsons, 1975; as *Unlock Your Money Personality*, Beverly Hills, California, Morrison Raven Hill, 1983.
"The Development of a Science Fiction Writer," in *Foundation 3* (London), March 1973.
Reflections of A. E. van Vogt. Lakemont, Georgia, Fictioneer, 1975.

*   *   *

In the stories of A. E. van Vogt all things are possible, for saying makes them so. It seems of little moment that any event logically follow the preceding one or that one character dominate the action. For readers expecting tightly structured plots, careful characterization, polished prose style, and a logical extrapolation van Vogt affords a field day for criticism. (For a classic lambasting on such matters see Damon Knight's "Cosmic Jerrybuilder: A. E. van Vogt" in *In Search of Wonder.*) But for the reader willing to submit his reason to another's wide-ranging imagination van Vogt is a "good read. '

Van Vogt's canon offers a melange of intriguing situations spiced with telepathy, teleportation, shape control, inner and outer space, mass consciousness, time shifts, technological wonders beyond count. Humans, super-creatures, androids, and aliens perform an intricate dance of adventure on a cosmic stage, existing in past, present, and future time, out-of-time and space as we know them, and often out-of-phase with each other. Incidents bombard us, with little transition to ease the pace. Disconcerting as this can be, it does have the trade-off value of keeping one in continual suspense. In "Complication in the Science Fiction Story" van Vogt explained his method of writing scenes in 800-word blocks, the first one to introduce both scene and story purpose. As the main plot develops logically in succeeding scenes, van Vogt adds a secondary plot and minor plot threads deriving from "theme science and atmosphere." While one may question the success of the logical development, there is no argument about van Vogt's ability to handle the minor threads skillfully to induce a sense of mystery, wonder, and suspense.

Since van Vogt writes both short stories and novels, often combining the former to create the latter, a mixed sampling of these modes makes a valid introduction to his characters, situations, and techniques. One especially notices van Vogt's emphasis on superior beings, well exemplified in *The Mixed Men*, a novel combining three short stories. In the earliest story of this group, "The Storm," we meet three super-creatures: the Dellian robots, physically and mentally advanced over man; the non-Dellian robots, higher in creativity; and the Mixed Men of human form but with double brains. Another superhuman, Gilbert Gosseyn of *The World of Null-A*, also has the extra brain, in addition possessing the ability to evade death, thus becoming a more godlike entity than Captain Maltby of the Mixed Men.

Van Vogt's catalog of aliens ranges from BEM's to intelligent forms fearsome in appearance but cooperative in action, once accepted by men. In *The Voyage of the Space Beagle* four aliens appear; the catlike Coeurl, the Ixtl, the Riim folk (a colony-psyche), and the anabis. All four pose grave problems to the expedition whose aim is "to explore limits of deep space and contact alien life forms." By contrast, two sympathetic aliens aid men in *The War Against the Rull*. For mutual survival they contribute their telepathetic ability and energy-conducting bodies respectively. The inimical Rull in turn infiltrates human society, using its capability to assume human form. This minor theme of replication appears in many van Vogt tales, starting with "Vault of the Beast" (1940), with the ultimate example being the title character of *The Silkie* which can shift from fish to bullet-like spaceship to human form to innumerable other shapes for its own purposes and protection.

These aliens often educate man about his own nature. In *The Replicators* a harmless alien assumes the form of its first human contact, an ex-Marine full of anger and aggressiveness. The resultant trouble is predictable. A more gentle lesson comes from the super-intelligent, catlike creature in "The Cataaaaa." On assignment to study man on earth the Cat does so from the stage of a carnival freak show. The title, linking the Cat with the spontaneous awed exclamation of the carnival crowd, spotlights the human response. The Cat's response comes in the final act of his study when he communicates to one man the conclusion that the basic human characteristic is self-dramatisation. This may well be the most agreeable comment van Vogt can offer about humans. All too often the enemy turns out to be one of our own. In the power struggle which runs as a major theme throughout van Vogt's stories, the specific enemy is often the trusted man-in-charge. Morlake of "The Earth Killers" tracks down the destroyers of civilization, only to find them racists headed by a power-driven ex-senator pretending to be the altruistic guardian of the people.

Critics note in van Vogt a predilection for the power of monarchy, such as held by the Isher empire in *The Weapon Shops of Isher* and the House of Linn in *Empire of the Atom*. More notable is van Vogt's sense of the drama inherent in all authoritarian systems. Finding authority operating all around us, he exploits the emotional possibilities in such situations as the struggle of the "dynasties" in *Rogue Ship*, the parent-child confrontations in *Children of Tomorrow*, and the professional friction aboard the *Space Beagle*. However, van Vogt always supplies an antithesis to authoritarianism. Most intriguing are those single characters who perform this duty, those superior beings motivated by a sense of mission and possessing a gift or a powerful idea to be manipulated for benefit of all. The combination is varied: Lesley Craig and "toti-potency" in *Masters of Time* ; Elliot Grosvenor and "Nexialism" on the *Space Beagle* ; Robert Hedrock and the Weapon Shops opposing Isher power; Gilbert Gosseyn with Null-A training (here van Vogt gives a nod to Alfred Korzybski's *Theory of General Semantics*); and others. A natural extension of this balance is a recognition of the cyclic nature of human society in the character of Morton Cargill of *The Universe Maker*. The most famous "saviour" of human values and idealism is Johnny

Cross of *Slan*, the novel usually considered van Vogt's most outstanding. A member of a mutant group hated and persecuted by the majority, the slan Johnny Cross is a telepath, superior both in intelligence and physique to ordinary men. From childhood his training points toward the end of bringing slans and normal men closer together in harmony. He must contend not only with John Petty, the human chief of the secret police, but alos with Kier Gray, the head of the government and a slan passing as a normal human.

Slan epitomizes van Vogt's major thematic issues: the tenacity of the life force whatever its form, the need of cooperative effort for mutual survival, and an overwhelming optimism that a consciousness shared with all life forms can work only to a mutual benefit. For the new reader approaching van Vogt, *Slan* provides a satisfactory entry into van Vogt's provocative and imaginative worlds.

For the seasoned reader of van Vogt, *Computerworld* over 35 years later addresses these major issues in the context of a very contemporary concern: computerized control. In the near-future of 2094 the omnipresent, multiform computer has relieved humans of all onerous labor but has sapped them of moral energy. Through Eye-O ports it tracks human activity, registering data for identification and correcting aberrant behaviour with weapons of graduated power. Questions arise. Who will control this force? How can the spiritual sense necessary for humanness exist in the strictly logical environment of the machine? The protagonist-computer asks the key question: "How does a human differ from a machine?" Only when it develops a "sense of self" comes the recognition that uniqueness requires cooperative understanding for co-existence, that recognition being a basic van Vogtian theme.

—Hazel Pierce

VARDRE, Leslie. See **DAVIES, L. P.**

VARLEY, John. American. Born in Austin, Texas, in 1947. Attended Michigan State University, East Lansing, 1966. Married Anet Mconel; three sons. Since 1973, free-lance writer. Recipient: *Locus* award, 1977, 1979 (twice), 1981, 1982 (twice); Jupiter Award, 1978; Nebula Award, 1978, 1985; Hugo Award, 1979, 1982; Prix Apollo, 1979. Lives in Eugene, Oregon. Agent: Kirby McCauley Ltd., 425 Park Avenue South, New York, New York 10016, U.S.A.

SCIENCE-FICTION PUBLICATIONS

Novels (series: Cirocco Jones)

The Ophiuchi Hotline. New York, Dial Press, 1977; London, Sidgwick and Jackson, 1978.
Titan (Jones). New York, Berkley, and London, Sidgwick and Jackson, 1979.
Wizard (Jones). New York, Berkley, 1980; London, Futura, 1981.
Millennium. New York, Berkley, 1983; London, Sphere, 1985.
Demon (Jones). New York, Putnam, 1984.

Short Stories

The Persistence of Vision. New York, Dial Press, 1978; as *In the Hall of the Martian Kings*, London, Sidgwick and Jackson, 1978.
The Barbie Murders and Other Stories. New York, Berkley, 1980; London, Futura, 1983.

Uncollected Short Stories

"Options," in *Universe 9*, edited by Terry Carr. New York, Doubleday, 1979.
"Blue Champagne," in *New Voices 4*, edited by George R. R. Martin. New York, Berkley, 1981.
"The Pusher," in *The Best Science Fiction of the Year 11*, edited by Terry Carr. New York, Pocket Books, and London, Gollancz, 1982.
"PRESS ENTER," in *Isaac Asimov's Science Fiction Magazine* (New York), May 1984.

OTHER PUBLICATIONS

Plays

Screenplays: *Galaxy*, 1978; *Millennium*, 1983.

*

Manuscript Collection: Special Collections, Temple University, Philadelphia.

*   *   *

Although John Varley has produced relatively few novels, he merits consideration for his inventiveness. His first novel, *The Ophiuchi Hotline*, takes place in a time in the future after mysterious invaders have come to our solar system and done away with human technology. This novel exhibits an environmentalist's bias in that the Invaders have abolished Earth's industrial-technical system to save whales and dolphins who, as some have long suspected, outclass humans in their intellectual potentiality. Yet someone out there wants human-kind to survive, for, over the decades, a "hotline" to a mysterious presence in another part of the universe continues to feed the remaining people information vital to their survival. Part of the story revolves around the attempt to discover who these "good Samaritans" are. For a short novel, *The Ophiuchi Hotline* certainly does not lack action; in fact, so much goes on that the plot at times becomes confusing.

Varley exhibits better control over his enthusiasm for inventing new worlds and improbable beings in his series consisting of *Wizard, Titan*, and *Demon* which chronicle the adventures of a displaced earth women, Cirocco Jones, sometimes-NASA-spaceship-pilot and adventurer. Not content simply to send her to another planet—in this case Saturn—to struggle against aliens, Varley turns the planet itself into a sentient being, the quasi-goddess Gaea. The trilogy follows Jones's transformation from friendly adventurer learning about Gaea's whimsical personality, to an alcoholic "wizard" in Gaea's employ, and finally to the only adversary who can vanquish the "goddess"-gone-mad and save the many lifeforms that populate this fascinating ring world. In this series we are asked to consider space opera from a moderately feminist point of view. At least that seems to be the perspective Varley wants his readers to take, for most of his major characters are either completely female or oddly bisexual. In some ways his focus on lesbian relationships is gratuitous; ultimately, the romantic couplings and jealousies add little to the trilogy's sense of entertainment which, in fact, is derived from the familiar quest-adventure motif found so frequently in science fiction.

Millennium considers an equally odd topic, human catastrophes. It seems that for as long as people have been mass-murdering each other or having accidents involving large numbers of people, a group of time travelers have been snagging the victims and whisking them through a time port to the far-future. These time travelers stand close to the end of life on earth; these kidnapping efforts represent their attempt to perpetuate life at a time millions of years beyond their immediate destruction. Varley combines and makes interesting twists on catastrophe/Bermuda Triangle themes, theories concerning the nature of time, and an old-fashioned love story between future alien and 20th-century deadbeat. The results entertain because *Millennium* resists the standard clichés of time travel and end-of-the-world tales.

Varley's short stories concern themselves with the same topics that he raises in his novels: speculations of the quality of life in the future, cloning, the nature of the alien "personality," to name a few. Like his novels, these stories are entertaining, and, like his novels, they also demand a certain degree of patient toleration on the part of their reader. Varley likes to pack his writing with action, gadgets, and many characters. Frequently the reader must untangle some of the snarls this type of writing inevitably creates. Although such roughness can irritate, Varley is a writer worth reading: he entertains because he isn't afraid to take risks with his plots, characters, or inventive view of the future. Furthermore, he takes fresh and timely perspectives on old chestnuts: love, war, the environment, and a human's place in the universe.

—Melissa E. Barth

———

VERRILL, A(lpheus) Hyatt. Also wrote as Ray Ainsbury. American. Born in New Haven, Connecticut, 23 July 1871. Educated at Yale University School of Fine Arts, New Haven; studied zoology with his father. Married 1)Kathryn L. McCarthy in 1892, four children; 2) Lida Ruth Shaw in 1944. Natural history illustrator for *Webster's International Dictionary*, 1896, and for *Clarendon Dictionary;* invented the autochrome process of photography, 1920; explorer and archaeologist: lived in Domenica, 1903-06, British Guiana, 1913-17, and Panama, 1917-21, and made expeditions to Central and South America, the West Indies, and Mexico, to 1950; did undersea excavation in the West Indies, 1933-34; established the Anhlarka experimental gardens and natural science museum, Florida, 1940; eastablished shell business, Lake Worth, Florida, 1944. *Died 14 November 1954.*

SCIENCE-FICTION PUBLICATIONS

Novels

Uncle Abner's Legacy. New York, Holt, 1915.
The Golden City (for children). New York, Duffield, 1916.
The Trial of the Cloven Foot (for children). New York, Dutton, 1918.
The Trail of the White Indians (for children). New York, Dutton, 1920.

The Boy Adventurers in the Land of the Monkey Men (for children). New York, Putnam, 1923.

The Bridge of Light. Reading, Pennsylvania, Fantasy Press, 1950.

When the Moon Ran Wild (as Ray Ainsbury). London. Consul, 1962.

Uncollected Short Stories

"Through the Crater's Rim," in *Amazing* (New York), December 1926.

"The Man Who Could Vanish," in *Amazing* (New York), January 1927.

"The Plague of the Living Dead,"in *Amazing* (New York), April 1927.

"The Voice from the Inner World," in *Amazing* (New York), July 1927.

"The Ultra-Elixir of Youth," in *Amazing* (New York), August 1927.

"The Astounding Discoveries of Doctor Mentiroso," in *Amazing* (New York), November 1927.

"The Psychological Solution," in *Amazing* (New York), January 1928.

"The King of the Monkey Men," in *Amazing Stories Quarterly* (New York), Spring 1928.

"The World of the Giant Ants," in *Amazing Stories Quarterly* (New York), Fall 1928.

"Into the Green Prism," in *Amazing* (New York), March 1929.

"Death From the Skies," in *Amazing* (New York), October 1929.

"Vampires of the Desert," in *Amazing* (New York), December 1929.

"Beyond the Green Prism," in *Amazing* (New York), January 1930.

"The Feathered Detective," in *Amazing* (New York), April 1930.

"The Non-Gravitational Vortex," in *Amazing* (New York), June 1930.

"Monsters of the Ray," in *Amazing Stories Quarterly* (New York), Summer 1930.

"A Visit to Suari," in *Amazing* (New York), July 1930.

"The Dirigibles of Death," in *Amazing Stories Quarterly* (New York), Winter 1930.

"The Treasures of the Golden God," in *Amazing* (New York), January 1933.

"The Death Drum," in *Amazing* (new York), May 1933.

"Through the Andes," in *Amazing* (New York), September 1934.

"The Inner World," in *Amazing* (New York), June 1935.

"The Mummy of Ret-Seh," in *Fantastic Adventures* (New York), May 1939.

"Beyond the Pole," in *The Gernsback Awards 1, 1926,* edited by Forrest J Ackerman. London, Turret, 1982.

"The Exterminator," in *Caught in the Organ Draft,* edited by Isaac Asimov, Martin H. Greenberg, and Charles G. Waugh, New York, Farrar Straus, 1983.

OTHER PUBLICATIONS

Novels (for children)

The American Crusoe. New York, Dodd Mead, 1914.
The Cruise of the Cormorant. New York, Holt, 1915.
In Morgan's Wake. New York, Holt, 1915.
Marooned in the Forest. New York, Harper, 1916.

Jungle Chums. New York, Holt. 1916.

The Boy Adventurers in the Forbidden Land [*in the Land of El Dorando, in the Unknown Land*]. New York, Putman, 3 vols., 1922-24.

The Deep Sea Hunters [*in the Frozen Sea, in the South Seas*]. New York, Appleton, 3 vols., 1922-24.

The Radio Detectives [*in the Jungle, Southward Bound, under the Sea*]. New York, Appleton, 4 vols, 1922.

Bartons Mills: A Saga of the Pioneers. New York, Appleton, 1932.

The Incas' Treasure House. Boston, Page, 1932; London, Harrap, 1936.

Before the Conquerors. New York, Dood Mead, 1935.

The Treasure of the Bloody Gut. New York, Putman, 1937.

Other

Gasolene Engines: Their Operation, Use and Care. New York, Henley, 1912.

Knots, Splices, and Rope Work. New York, Henley, 1912; revised edition, 1917, 1922.

Harper's Book for Young Naturalists [*Gardeners*]. New York, Harper, 2 vols, 1913-14.

Harper's Wireless [*Aircraft, Gasoline Engine*] *Book.* New York, Harper, 3 vols, 1913-14.

Cuba Past and Present. New York, Dodd Mead, 1914; revised edition, 1920.

South and Central American Trade Conditions of Today. New York, Dodd Mead, 1914; revised edition, 1919.

Porto Rico Past and Present. New York, Dodd Mead, 1914.

Pets for Pleasure and Profit. New York, Scribner, 1915.

The Boys' Outdoor Vacation Book. New York, Dodd Mead, 1915.

The Amateur Carpenter. New York, Dodd Mead, 1915.

The Boy Collector's Handbook. New York, McBride, 1915.

Isles of Spice and Palm. New York Appleton, 1915.

A-B-C of Automobile Driving. New York, Harper, 1916.

TThe Real Story of the Whaler. New York, Appleton, 1916.

The Ocean and Its Mysteries. New York, Duffield, 1916.

The Book of the Motor Boat [*Sailboat*]. New York, Appleton, 2 vols, 1916.

The Book of the West Indies. New York, Dutton, 1917.

The Book of Camping. New York, Knopf, 1917.

How to Operate a Motor Car. Philadelphia, McKay, 1918.

Getting Together with Latin America. New York, Dutton, 1918.

Islands and Their Mysteries. New York, Duffield, 1920; London, Melrose, 1922.

Panama, Past and Present. New York, Dodd Mead, 1921.

The Boys' Book of Whalers [*Carpentry, Buccaneers*]. New York, Dodd Mead, 3 vols., 1922-23.

Radio for Amateurs. New York, Dodd Mead, and London, Heinemann, 1922.

Rivers and Their Mysteries. New York, Duffield, 1922.

The Home Radio. New York, Harper, 1922; revised edition, 1924; revised edition, as *The Home Radio Up to Date*, with E. E. Verrill, 1927.

In the Wake of the Buccaneers. New York, Century, and London, Parsons, 1923.

The Real Story of the Pirate. New York, Appleton, 1923.

Smugglers and Smuggling. New York, Duffield, and London, Allen and Unwin, 1924.

Love Stories of Some Famous Pirates. London, Collins, 1924.

Panama [*Cuba, Jamaica, West Indies*] *of Today.* New York, Dodd Mead, 4 vols., 1927-31.

The American Indian. New York, Appleton, 1927.

Old Civilization of the New World. Indianapolis, Bobbs Merrill, and London, Williams and Norgate, 1929.

Thirty Years in the Jungle. London, Lane, 1929.

Great Conquerors of South and Central America. New York, Appleton, 1929.

Lost Treasure. New York, Appleton, 1930.

Gasoline-Engine Book for Boys. New York, Harper, 1930.

Under Peruvian Skies. London, Hurst and Blackett, 1930.

Secret Treasure. New York, Appleton, 1931.

The Inquisition. New York, Appleton, 1931.

Romantic and Historic Maine [Florida, Virginia]. New York, Dodd Mead, 3 vols., 1933-35.

Our Indians. New York, Putnam, 1935.

They Found Gold. New York and London, Putnam, 1936; as *Carib Gold*, London, Collins, 1939.

The Heart of Old New England. New York, Dodd Mead, 1936.

Along New England Shores. New York, Putnam, 1936.

Sea Shells [Insects, Reptiles, Birds, Fish, Animals] and Their Stories. Boston, Page, and London, Harrap, 6 vols., 1936-39.

My Jungle Trails. Boston, Page, and London, Harrap, 1937.

Foods America Gave the World. Boston, Page, 1937.

Minerals, Metals and Gems. Boston, Page, 1939.

Wonder Plants and Plant Wonders. New York, Appleton Century, 1939.

Perfumes and Spices. Boston, Page, 1940.

Wonder Creatures of the Sea. New York, Appleton Century, 1940.

Strange Prehistoric Animals and Their Stories. Boston, Page, 1948.

The Strange Story of Our Earth. Boston, Page, 1952.

America's Ancient Civilization, with R. Verrill. New York and London, Putnam, 1954.

* * *

A. Hyatt Verrill was one of the more distinguished writers who helped in the development of *Amazing Stories* during its early years, and who continued to contribute to it until the mid-1930's. Many of his stories were set in the South American jungles with which he was so familiar, or dealt with ancient civilisations whose cultures he studied for more than half a century. But he did not limit himself to such themes, drawing on astronomy, biology, optics, atomic physics, and fourth-dimension theory for ideas which he developed with equal facility.

The magazine was only six months old when his first offering, "Beyond the Pole," dealing with a race of intelligent crustaceans discovered in the Antarctic, appeared late in 1926. It compared favourably with the stories of Wells and Verne which almost monopolised those early issues, while the editor, Hugo Gernsback, contrived to nurture new writers to displace them. Some of Verrill's longer stories went to fill out the inch-thick *Amazing Stories Quarterly*; "The World of the Giant Ants" was remarkable for its engrossing narrative combined with an enlightening insight into its subject. Even more fascinating was "Into the Green Prism," with its sequel, "Beyond the Green Prism," which sought to dispel the storm of controversy over the scientific fallacies it raised. "The Astounding Discoveries of Doctor Mentiroso" began the endless argument in the readers' columns over the time-travel theme. "Death from the Skies" was about a bombardment of Earth by the Martians, and "The Bridge of Light" took readers to a hidden city where the Mayas still thrived. Verrill's flights of imagination reached their peak in 1931 with "Monsters of the Ray" and "When the Moon Ran Wild"; but his later contributions, such as "The Death Drum"

and "Through the Andes," were pure adventure tales which reflected the gradual decline of *Amazing*.

—Walter Gillings

———

VIDAL, Gore (Eugene Luther Vidal, Jr.). Has also written as Edgar Box. American. Born in West Point. New York, 3 October 1925. Educated at Los Alamos School, New Mexico, 1939-40; Phillips Exeter Academy, New Hampshire, 1940-43. Served in the United States Army, 1943-46: Warrant Officer. Editor, E. P. Dutton, publishers, New York, 1946. Member, Advisory Board, *Partisan Review*, New Brunswick, New Jersey, 1960-71; Democratic-Liberal candidate for Congress, New York, 1960; Member, President's Advisory Committee on the Arts, 1961-63; Co-Chairman, New Party, 1968-71. Recipient: Mystery Writers of America award, for television play, 1954; National Book Critics Circle award, for criticism, 1983. Address: Ravello, Salerno, Italy; or c/o Random House Inc., 201 East 50th Street, New York, New York 10022, U.S.A.

SCIENCE-FICTION PUBLICATIONS

Novels

Messiah. New York, Dutton, 1954; London, Heinemann, 1955; revised edition, Boston, Little Brown, 1965; Heinemann, 1968.

Myra Breckinridge. Boston, Little Brown, and London, Blond, 1968.

Myron. New York, Random House, 1974; London, Heinemann, 1975.

Kalki. New York, Random House, and London, Heinemann, 1978.

Duluth. New York, Random House, and London, Heinemann, 1983.

OTHER PUBLICATIONS

Novels

Williwaw. New York, Dutton, 1946; London, Panther, 1965.

In a Yellow Wood. New York, Dutton, 1947; London, New English Library, 1967.

The City and the Pillar. New York, Dutton, 1948; London, Lehmann, 1949; revised edition, Dutton, and London, Heinemann, 1965.

The Season of Comfort. New York, Dutton, 1949.

Dark Green, Bright Red. New York, Dutton, and London, Lehmann, 1950.

A Search for the King: A Twelfth Century Legend. New York, Dutton, 1950; London, New English Library, 1967.

The Judgment of Paris. New York, Dutton, 1952; London, Heinemann, 1953; revised edition, Boston, Little Brown, 1965; Heinemann, 1966.

Three: Williwaw, A Thirsty Evil, Julian the Apostate. New York, New American Library, 1962.

Julian. Boston, Little Brown, and London, Heinemann, 1964.

Washington, D. C. Boston, Little Brown, and London, Heinemann, 1967.

Two Sisters: A Memoir in the Form of a Novel. Boston, Little Brown, and London, Heinemann, 1970.

Burr. New York, Random House, 1973; London, Heinemann, 1974.

1876. New York, Random House, and London, Heinemann, 1976.

Creation. New York, Random House, and London, Heinemann, 1981.

Lincoln. New York, Random House, and London, Heinemann, 1984.

Novels as Edgar Box

Death in the Fifth Position. New York, Dutton, 1952; London, Heinemann, 1954.

Death Before Bedtime. New York, Dutton, 1953; London, Heinemann, 1954.

Death Likes It Hot. New York, Dutton, 1954; London, Heinemann, 1955.

Short Stories

A Thirsty Evil: Seven Short Stories. New York, Zero Press, 1956; London, Heinemann, 1958.

Plays

Visit to a Small Planet (televised, 1955). Included in *Visit to a Small Planet and Other Television Plays*, 1956; revised version (produced New York, 1957; London, 1960), Boston, Little Brown, 1957; in *Three Plays*, 1962.

Honor (televised, 1956). Published in *Television Plays for Writers: Eight Television Plays*, edited by A. S. Burack, Boston, The Writer, 1957; revised version, as *On the March to the Sea: A Southron Comedy* (produced Bonn, Germany, 1961), in *Three Plays*, 1962.

Visit to a Small Planet and Other Television Plays (includes *Barn Burning, Dark Possessions, The Death of Billy the Kid, A Sense of Justice, Smoke, Summer Pavilion, The Turn of the Screw*). Boston, Little Brown, 1956.

The Best Man: A Play about Politics (produced New York, 1960). Boston, Little Brown, 1960; in *Three Plays*, 1962.

Three Plays (includes *Visit to a Small Planet, The Best Man, On the March to the Sea*). London, Heinemann, 1962.

Romulus: A New Comedy, adaptation of a play by Friedrich Dürrenmatt (produced New York, 1962). New York, Dramatists Play Service, 1962.

Weekend (produced New York, 1968). New York, Dramatists Play Service, 1968.

An Evening with Richard Nixon and . . . (produced New York, 1972). New York, Random House, 1972.

Screenplays: *The Catered Affair*, 1956; *I Accuse*, 1958; *The Scapegoat*, with Robert Hamer, 1959; *Suddenly Last Summer*, with Tennessee Williams, 1960; *The Best Man*, 1964; *Is Paris Burning?*, with Francis Ford Coppola, 1966; *Last of the Mobile Hot-Shots*, 1970.

Television Plays: *Barn Burning*, from the story by Faulkner, 1954; *Dark Possession*, 1954; *Smoke*, from the story by Faulkner, 1954; *Visit to a Small Planet*, 1955; *The Death of Billy the Kid*, 1955; *A Sense of Justice*, 1955; *Summer Pavilion*, 1955; *The Turn of the Screw*, from the story by Henry James, 1955; *Honor*, 1956; *The Indestructible Mr. Gore*, 1960.

Other

Rocking the Boat (essays). Boston, Little Brown, 1962; London, Heinemann, 1963.

Sex, Death, and Money (essays). New York, Bantam, 1968.

Reflections upon a Sinking Ship (essays). Boston, Little Brown, and London, Heinemann, 1969.

Homage to Daniel Shays: Collected Essays 1952-1972. New York, Random House, 1972; as *Collected Essays 1952-1972*, London, Heinemann, 1974.

Matters of Fact and of Fiction: Essays 1973-1976. New York, Random House, and London, Heinemann, 1977.

Great American Families, with others. New York, Norton, and London, Times Books, 1977.

Sex Is Politics and Vice Versa. Los Angeles, Sylvester and Orphanos, 1979.

Views from a Window: Conversations with Gore Vidal, with Robert J. Stanton. Secaucus, New Jersey, Lyle Stuart, 1980.

The Second American Revolution and Other Essays 1976-1982. New York, Random House, 1982; as *Pink Triangle and Yellow Star and Other Essays*, London, Heinemann, 1982.

Editor, *Best Television Plays*. New York, Ballantine, 1956.

*

Bibliography: *Gore Vidal: A Primary and Secondary Bibliography* by Robert J. Stanton, Boston, Hall, and London, Prior, 1978.

Manuscript Collection: University of Wisconsin, Madison.

Critical Studies: *Gore Vidal* by Ray Lewis White, New York, Twayne, 1968; *The Apostate Angel: A Critical Study of Gore Vidal* by Bernard F. Dick, New York, Random House, 1974; *Gore Vidal* by Robert F. Kiernan, New York, Ungar, 1982.

*   *   *

Only a part of Gore Vidal's varied literary production strongly relates to science fiction and fantasy: two plays, *An Evening with Richard Nixon* and *Visit to a Small Planet*, and five novels, *Messiah, Myra Breckenridge, Myron, Kalki,* and *Duluth*. Vidal's "Edgar Box" detective novels are similar to science-fiction formula writing, while his many historical novels, *Julian, Creation, Washington, D. C., Burr, 1876,* and *Lincoln*, have some Utopian elements. In *Julian* and *Creation* Vidal speculates about an alternative development of the West out of the grip of Christianity and Greek thought. Julian and Persian thought, Persian religions, which ponder the origin and purpose of man and the world, provide alternatives to the dominant patterns of Western thought, religions, and social institutions. The Washington tetralogy is mostly realistic historical fiction. Some of the characters reappear in *Burr, Lincoln,* and *1876*, the latter resembling a Henry James novel with Europeanized Americans, Charles and the Princess, socially evaluating the politics and manners of the United States while pursuing marriage for the Princess and a writing career for Charles. *Lincoln*, while not debunking the great man in the manner of Charles Beard, focuses on Lincoln's shrewd political savvy and strength, although, as in the rest of the tetralogy, all the major political figures of the period are examined such as Seward and Chase.

An *Evening with Richard Nixon*, dramatically showing the high points of Nixon's career, does so by framing Nixon's own words and some fictional dialogue and action with a chorus and narrative commentary by former Presidents George Washington, John Kennedy, and Dwight Eisenhower. These fantastic characters are used for satiric purposes, not only by their views of Nixon but by their views of one another. Only Washington seems genuinely decent; the others are mocked. The play *Visit to a Small Planet* uses a typical science-fiction action, alien invasion, for satiric purposes. What is devalued by Kreton, unintentionally because he loves it, is man's hostility. By performing a miracle of telekinesis, Kreton nearly starts a war between Russia and the United States, prevented only by Delton 4, who as deus ex machina, hauls Kreton (cretin) away, bending time prior to Kreton's visit. Of course, Kreton's plan depends on destructive human passion, which projects hostility from a visit, glories in hate, and is secretive about love, as the Conrad-Ellen plot illustrates.

Messiah, a memoir by Eugene Luther, is a futuristic retelling of the Christ story and the development of Christianity, except the Good News by John Cave, the Christ figure, is that death is good. Luther, writing about the year 2000 in Luxor, Egypt about his involvement with Cave, recounts his relationships with Clarissa, a witch-like woman supposedly over 2000 years old, Iris, who becomes a new Virgin Mary, and Paul Himmel, a PR version of St. Paul. In an opening similar to H. G. Wells's *War of the Worlds*, Marx, Freud, and modern science have failed to organize the world well, so a new mystic, John Cave, argues that death is a friend to be embraced. Luther likes the message, but sees it as the existentialists would, that life's value increases because of death. As Cave is forced to practice what he preaches and is killed, Eugene is forced to flee the Cavites, realizing later that he should have been the Messiah.

Myra Breckinridge, also a memoir, is a comic, Frankenstein-like sex-change story. Though treated as soft pornography, Vidal's satiric targets are frequently sophisticated, such as Robbe-Grillet's theories of anthropomorphic projection in *For a New Novel*. When Myra says "Nothing is *like* anything else. Things are themselves entirely and do not need interpretation, only a minimal respect for their precise integrity," Robbe-Grillet is being reduced. Though the novel's action climaxes with Myra's sodomizing of Rusty and winning her inheritance from Buck Loner, as Myra goes through two sex changes, the satire caused by her alien encounter with the world is subtly clever. *Myron*, the sequel to *Myra Breckinridge*, uses a staple of fantasy, the alternate universe, as Myron is pushed into his television set while watching *Siren of Babylon* by the suppressed personality of Myra. As Myron seeks to return to his wife, Mary Ann, by finding the exit to the film in production, Myra seeks to change cinematic history, thereby changing cultural history—even Watergate and the election of Richard Nixon. Myra, as many science-fiction authors have fabulated, is trying to manipulate the present by changing the past.

Kalki is a dystopian novel in which a former GI poses as the Hindu god Kalki and poisons the world population except for four chosen followers. Though a mystery plot dominates the novel with its two catastrophes, the poisoning and the doublecross of Kelly by Giles, Vidal's social concerns are still present. The memoir and additional narrative voices, common in *Two Sisters, Julian, Messiah*, and other Vidal novels, combine with science-fiction and Utopian strategies so that Vidal's satire, his social criticism and liberal social message, appears with the ease of Petronius and the power of Juvenal.

Duluth, a satire on middle America, is not as biting as *Kalki* because it has too many targets. Vidal's Duluth features a good deal of changed geography—New Orleans and Tulsa are surprisingly close, which is possibly a slap at geology's plate techtonics. Narrative action has many strands; however, a mayoral election ending in assassination, a pull-out from the race by the present mayor, and the successful candidacy of a former black crime figure is prominent. Through the figures of

Rosemary Kantor Klein and Chloris Craig, romance novels and melodramatic serials such as *Dynasty* and *Dallas* are mocked along with Derridean notions of erasure, as parts of Duluth are temporarily wiped out by Kantor Klein's word processor. All human action is erased permanently, though, when the alien centipedes from outer space who have crashed their space ship in a Duluth swamp eradicate human life in disgust at their stock market losses.

If satire is the ridiculing of a specific person, practice, or object, Vidal has thousands of satiric targets in *Duluth*. Though he is primarily a realistic novelist, one can expect Vidal to continue to experiment with science-fiction, Utopian fiction, and fantasy, for they are all strategies of him primary aim, satire.

—Craig Wallace Barrow

VINCENT, Harl. Pseudonym for Harold Vincent Schoepflin. American. Born in Buffalo, New York, in 1893. Married; one daughter. Engineer and free-lance writer. *Died 5 May 1968.*

SCIENCE- FICTION PUBLICATIONS

Novel

The Doomsday Planet. New York, Belmont, 1966.

Uncollected Short Stories

"The Golden Girl of Munan," in *Amazing* (New York), June 1928.
"The Ambassador from Mars," in *Amazing* (New York), September 1928.
"The War of the Planets," in *Amazing* (New York), January 1929.
"Venus Liberated," in *Amazing Stories Quarterly* (New York), Summer 1929.
"The Menace from Below," in *Science Wonder Stories* (New York), July 1929.
"Barton's Island," in *Amazing* (New York), August 1929.
"Yellow Air Peril," in *Air Wonder Stories* (New York), September 1929.
"Through the Air Tunnel," in *Air Wonder Stories* (New York), October 1929.
"The Microcosmic Buccaneers," in *Amazing* (New York), November 1929.
"The Colloidal Nemesis," in *Amazing* (New York), December 1929.
"The Seventh Generation," in *Amazing Stories Quarterly* (New York), Winter 1929.
"Old Crompton's Secret," in *Astounding* (New York), February 1930.
"Callisto at War," in *Amazing* (New York), March 1930.
"Before the Asteroids," in *Science Wonder Stories* (New York), March 1930.
"The Return to Subterrania," in *Science Wonder Stories* (New York), April 1930.
"The Terror of Air-Level Six," in *Astounding* (New York), July 1930.
"Silver Dome," in *Astounding* (New York), August 1930.
"Free Energy," in *Amazing* (New York), September 1930.
"Vagabonds of Space," in *Astounding* (New York), November 1930.

"Gray Denim," in *Astounding* (New York), December 1930.

"Tanks under the Seas," in *Amazing* (New York), January 1931.

"Terrors Unseen," in *Astounding* (New York), March 1931.

"Invisible Ships," in *Amazing Stories Quarterly* (New York), April 1931.

"Too Many Boards," in *Amazing* (New York), April 1931.

"Beyond the Dark Nebula," in *Argosy* (New York), 4 April 1931.

"The Moon Weed," in *Astounding* (New York), August 1931.

"The Copper-Clad World," in *Astounding* (New York), September 1931.

"Red Twilight," in *Argosy* (New York), 12 September 1931.

"A Matter of Ethics," in *Amazing* (New York), October 1931.

"Sky Corps," with Charles Roy Cox, in *Amazing* (New York), December 1931.

"Power," in *Amazing* (New York), January 1932.

"Creatures of Vibration," in *Astounding* (New York), January 1932.

"Water-Bound World," in *Amazing Stories Quarterly* (New York), Spring-Summer 1932.

"Vulcan's Workshop," in *Astounding* (New York), June 1932.

"Thia of the Drylands," in *Amazing* (New York), July 1932.

"Faster than Light," in *Amazing Stories Quarterly* (New York), Fall-Winter 1932.

"Roadways of Mars," in *Amazing* (New York), December 1932.

"Once in a Blue Moon," in *Amazing Stories Quarterly* (New York), Winter 1932.

"When the Comet Returned," in *Amazing* (New York), April 1933.

"Cavern of Thunders," in *Amazing* (New York), July 1933.

"Whisper of Death," in *Amazing* (New York), November 1933.

"Telegraph Plateau," in *Astounding* (New York), November 1933.

"Master of Dreams," in *Amazing* (New York), January 1934.

"Lost City of Mars," in *Astounding* (New York), February 1934.

"Cat's Eye," in *Amazing* (New York), April 1934.

"The Barrier," in *Amazing* (New York), September 1934.

"Cosmic Rhythm," in *Astounding* (New York), October 1934.

"The Explorers of Callisto," in *Amazing* (New York), January 1935.

"Energy," in *Astounding* (New York), January 1935.

"Valley of the Rukh," in *Amazing* (New York), February 1935.

"The Plane Compass," in *Astounding* (New York), June 1935.

"Parasite," in *Amazing* (New York), July 1935.

"Return of the Prowler," in *Astounding* (New York), November 1938.

"Prince Deru Returns," in *Amazing* (New York), December 1938.

"Newscast," in *Marvel* (New York), April-May 1939.

"The Devil Flower," in *Fantastic Adventures* (New York), May 1939.

"The Morons," in *Astounding* (New York), June 1939.

"The Mystery of the Collapsing Skyscrapers," in *Amazing* (New York), August 1939.

"Lighting Strikes Once," in *Marvel* (New York), August 1939.

"Power Plant," in *Astounding* (New York), November 1939.

"Neutral Vessel," in *Astounding* (New York), January 1940.

"High Frequency War," in *Astounding* (New York), February 1940.

"Undersea Prisoner," in *Amazing* (New York), February 1940.

"Gravity Island," in *Super Science* (Kokomo, Indiana), March 1940.

"Master Control," in *Astonishing* (Chicago), April 1940.

"Deputy Correspondent," in *Astounding* (New York), June 1940.

"Trouble Shooter," in *Super Science* (Kokomo, Indiana), July 1940.

"Other World," in *Astonishing* (Chicago), October 1940.

"Lunar Station," in *Comet* (Springfield, Massachusetts), January 1941.

"Grave of the Achilles," in *Captain Future* (New York), Winter 1941.

"Voice from the Void," in *Amazing* (New York), June 1942.

"Life Inside a Wall," in *The Moon Conquerors*. London, Swan, 1943.

"Rex," in *The Coming of the Robots*, edited by Sam Moskowitz. New York, Macmillan, 1963.

"Prowler of the Wastelands," in *Strange Signposts*, edited by Roger Elwood and Sam Moskowitz. New York, Holt Rinehard, 1966.

"Invader," in *If* (New York), September 1967.

"Lethal Planetoid," in *Spaceway* (Alhambra, California), January 1969.

"Space Storm," in *Famous Science Fiction* (New York), Spring 1969.

"Wanderer of Infinity," in *The Pulps*, edited by Tony Goodstone. New York, Chelsea House, 1970.

*   *   *

Of Harl Vincent's stories, few are familiar to the present generation of readers. With the possible exception of "Barton's Island," none of his tales has been granted "classic" status, and most of his output was of an order consistent with the pulps of the 1930's. Yet he will be remembered by a few as a writer who, even when conforming to strict editorial policies (which he did with remarkable facility), never failed to evoke the sense of wonder which is vital to science fiction.

Following his initial appearance in 1928 with "The Golden Girl of Munan," he soon became a favourite with *Amazing Stories* readers. His full-length novel, "Venus Liberated," was typical: a tale of interplanetary adventure, full of incident, yet told with restraint and with equal regard for both scientific and romantic interest. "Barton's Island," the story of an inventive genius at odds with a future dictator, revealed a penchant for novel variations on more realistic themes. In "The Colloidal Nemesis" the War of Extermination ended abruptly in 1953 when the Western Alliance let loose on the Asiatics a monstrous mass of devouring protoplasm. He was not so original that he could ignore the note of menace which resounded through science fiction's pages in those days. As well as arriving from Callisto, the threat lurked among the super-apes of Subterrania, or loomed up from the microcosmos. But his ideas were so diverse and his hand so adroit that, having catered equally to *Science Wonder* and *Air Wonder Stories*, he was able to produce a string of lusty tales for the new *Astounding* which further enlarged the field in 1930. "Vagabonds of Space" and "The Copper-Clad World" were typical of the formalised space opera on which the magazine relied for much of its appeal.

Meanwhile, *Amazing* continued to feature Vincent's work in more reflective mood, as "Power," a significant tale of conflicting forces in 23rd-century New York which hinted at nuclear fission as a new source of energy. Several of his stories at this period were set in the "drylands" of Mars, among the superstitious savages of the parched plains between the canals ("Red Twilight" and "Beyond the Dark Nebula"), "Faster Than Light" brought back the heroes who had liberated Venus for another adventure in remoter realms.

When *Astounding* reappeared under new management towards the end of 1933, Vincent was among those who found their way back into its pages. But, except for "Cosmic Rhythm," he was not particularly successful in meeting its "thought-variant" demands; and some of his more interesting concepts, such as "Parasite," were still to be found in *Amazing*. By 1942 he seemed to have given up writing; but in 1966 he made a brief comeback with *The Doomsday Planet*, an interplanetary adventure.

—Walter Gillings

VINGE, Joan (Carol) D(ennison). American. Born in Baltimore, Maryland, 2 April 1948. Educated at San Diego State University, California, B. A. in anthropology 1971. Married 1) Vernor Vinge, *q. v.*, in 1972 (divorced, 1979); 2) the publisher James R. Frenkel in 1980. Salvage archaeologist, San Diego County, 1971. Recipient: Hugo Award, 1978, 1981; *Locus* awar, 1981. Agent: Merrilee Heifetz, Writers House Inc., 21 West 26th Street, New York, New York 10010. Address: 26 Douglas Road, Chappaqua, New York 10514, U.S.A.

SCIENCE-FICTION PUBLICATIONS

Novels

The Outcasts of Heaven Belt. New York, New American Library, 1978; London, Futura, 1981.
The Snow Queen. New York, Dial Press, and London, Sidgwick and Jackson, 1980.
Psion (for children). New York, Delacorte Press, 1982; London, Futura, 1983.
Return of the Jedi Storybook (novelization of screenplay; for children). New York, Random House, and London, Futura, 1983.
The Dune Storybook (novelization of screenplay). New York, Putnam, 1984.
World's End. New York, Bluejay, 1984.
Ladyhawke (novelization of screenplay). New York, New American Library, 1985.

Short Stories

Fireship. New York, Dell, 1978; as *Fireship, and Mother and Child,* London, Sidgwick and Jackson, 1981.
Eyes of Amber and Other Stories. New York, New American Library, 1979; London, Futura, 1981.
Phoenix in the Ashes. New York, Bluejay, 1985.

Uncollected Short Stories

"Exorcycle," in *Issac Asimov's Science Fiction Magazine* (New York), January 1980.
"Tam Lin," in *Imaginary Lands,* edited by Robin McKinley. New York, Berkley, 1982.

OTHER PUBLICATIONS

Novels (novelizations of sceenplays)

Mad Max: Beyond the Thunderdome. New York, Warner, 1985.

Return to Oz. New York, Ballantine, 1985.
Santa Claus. New York, Putman, 1985.

Other

Tarzan, King of Apes (for children). New York, Random House, 1983.

*

Manuscript Collection: Elizabeth Charter Science Fiction Collection, San Diego University.

Joan D. Vinge comments:

(1981) Because I have a degree in anthropology, I tend to write anthropological science fiction, with an emphasis on the interaction of different cultures (human and alien) and of individual people to their surroundings. The importance of communication across barriers of alienness often becomes a theme in my stories. Mythology and music also influence my work; my novel *The Snow Queen* was in large part inspired by Robert Graves's *The White Goddess*. I have written several stories with a "hard" science background, thanks to the borrowed expertise of my husband, who is a mathematician and also a science-fiction writer; however, I've written other stories which I hope cover a wide range of moods and styles, I feel as if I'm just beginning to explore the infinite possibilities of the future.

* * *

Joan D. Vinge has produced a wide variety of fiction within the genre, from popular stories for children and young people (for example, the *Return of the Jedi Storybook, Ladyhawke,* and an excellend young adult novel, *Psion*), to adult works that have twice won the Hugo Award (*Eyes of Amber* and *The Snow Queen*). Vinge writes within the milieu established by New Wave SF writers like Le Guin, Russ, and McIntyre; and Vinge uses the freedom won by these writers to explore characters' emotional and psychological responses to the new worlds she envisions. Her emphasis on feelings will sometimes render her work too sentimental for some readers, but her skill at depicting the inner states of her characters—human or alien—makes her stories often insightful and compelling.

In her best work, Vinge balances the evocation of personal struggle with her considerable understanding of physical and social science, as in shorter works such as "Phoenix in the Ashes," "Mother and Child," and most of the tales in her important collection *Eyes of Amber,* especially the title novella, "To Bell the Cat," and "Crystal Ship. " In all of these, once a firm scientific base is established, Vinge goes on to explore the ways characters deal with common human emotions. Variously focusing on human/alien contacts, exploitation, and the failures of communication, these stories keep our attention and enlarge our sensibilities. A compulsive explainer (as evidenced by the afterwords following every story in her two collections), Vinge is also a deft one. Her stories are subtle and pithy.

But beyond her excellence in stories of novella length, Vinge is also effective in the novel. In the longer works, Vinge has often demonstrated her skill at capturing the mental life of the protagonists, espcially on their telepathic jaunts through space and time. Her depiction of Cat's mentalistic journey and discoveries in *Psion,* and of the mindlink experiences of Moon in *The Snow Queen,* and the frighteningly evocative near-madness suffered by BZ Gundhalinu in the sequel come to mind. But in addition to these personalistic qualities in her stories, Vinge also consistently displays a powerful social conscience, and much of her writing either directly or tangentially addresses major social issues. A central motivation in all these novels is the need to resist the institutionalized abuse of beings and resources, and the author pays particular attention to the various forms of prejudice that oppress the gifted (the telepathic in *Psion*). She also gives special attention to the sufferings of the lower social classes and of women: beyond his special gift, Cat's troubles also stem from his being poor; issues of class pervade the fabric of the Snow Queen novels, especially in references to the Kharemoughi social structure, and the struggles of women in a male-dominate culture are epitomized in the sufferings of Jerusha PalaThion in *The Snow Queen* (these concerns also dominate stories like "Mother and Child" and "Phoenix in the Ashes"). BZ's near breakdown in *World's End* powerfully suggests the ways that rigid social structures oppress even those they privilege.

Vinge's interests also extend to reworkings of powerful mythic materials, and her understanding and application of Robert Graves's *The White Goddess* help to make *The Snow Queen* even more resonant. In effect, the novel argues for an ecologically conserservative, heart-oriented, yet technologically aware culture through its major figures: the Winter Queen's association with exploitive technolgy and her Summer counterpart's beginnings in a naive but profoundly correct mother religion form the basic opposition in the tale, which is ultimately overcome when the Summer Queen comes to power having learned the values of technology. The opposing mythic forces are united in the new queen, promising a new social order. The revisionary unification of opposing social systems is also a crucial part of Vinge's earlier *The Outcasts of Heaven's Belt*, though there the opposing figures are female and male.

When readers recollect a Joan Vinge story, it won't be ideas separated from their personal and social ramifications that come to mind. Instead, we remember the characters and their feelings—Moon Dawntreader Summer, Arienhrod, Jerusha, BZ, T'uupieh, Etaa, Tarawassie and Moon Shadow, Amanda and Cristavoa. These are characters working through the trouble and delight generated by the friction between the individual and culture. We can look forward to much writing from Joan D. Vinge that will be culturally and personally satisfying.

—Len Hatfield

VINGE, Vernor (Steffen). American. Born in Waukesha, Wisconsin, 2 October 1944. Educated at Michigan State University, East Lansing, M. S. 1966; University of California, San Diego, M. A. 1968, Ph. D. 1971. Married Joan Carol Dennison (i. e., Joan D. Vinge, *q. v.*), in 1972 (divorced, 1979). Assistant Professor, 1972-78, and since 1978, Associate Professor of Mathematics, San Diego State University. Address: Department of Mathematics, San Diego State University, San Diego, California 92182, U.S.A.

SCIENCE-FICTION PUBLICATIONS

Novels

Grimm's World. New York, Berkley, 1969; London, Hamlyn, 1978.

The Witling. New York, DAW, and London, Dobson, 1976.
True Names, in *Binary Star 5*. New York, Dell, 1981.
The Peace War. New York, Bluejay, 1984.

Uncollected Short Stories

"Apartness," in *World's Best Science Fiction 1966*, edited by Donald A. Wollheim and Terry Carr. New York, Ace, 1966.
"The Accomplice," in *If* (New York), April 1967.
"Bookworm, Run!," in *Analog 6*, edited by John W. Campbell, Jr. New York, Doubleday, 1968.
"The Science Fair," in *Orbit 9*, edited by Damon Knight. New York, Putnam, 1971.
"Just Peace," in *Analog* (New York), December 1971.
"Original Sin," in *Analog* (New York), December 1972.
"Long Shot," in *Best Science Fiction Stories of the Year 1972*, edited by Lester del Rey. New York, Dutton, 1973.
"Bomb Scare," in *Tomorrow, and Tomorrow, and Tomorrow* . . ., edited by B. Heintz and others. New York, Holt Rinehart, 1974.
"The Whirligig of Time," in *Stellar 1*, edited by Judy-Lynn del Rey. New York, Ballantine, 1974.
"The Peddler's Apprentice," in *Best Science Fiction Stories of the Year 1975*, edited by Lester del Rey. New York, Dutton, 1976.
"Conquest by Default," in *Analog's War and Peace*, edited by Stanley Schmidt. New York, Davis, 1983.
"Gemstone," in *Analog* (New York), October 1983.

* * *

Vernor Vinge is not a prolific writer but his significance is considerably greater than the size of his output because of the high quality of much of his work. Especially in his best stories, Vinge deals with extreme social situations, with crises within a society or with intercultural conflict. Much of his work is permeated with a melancholy awareness of the evanescence of all human institutions. Typically, Vinge's characters are faced with some personal problem arising out of social change. The furnish the best possible solution given the initial conditions, but it is never more than a half-solution, and they must live with their failure as well as with their success.

Vinge's first two novels, both set on other planets, move in the characteristic Vinge pattern. *Grimm's World*, set on a retrogressed colony planet now climbing back to high technology, centers on the intrigues and struggles of a native-born superwoman whose only intellectual equals are two visitors from a higher interstellar culture. The novel focuses our greatest sympathy not on the superhumans but on the ordinary people caught up in their machinations. The various cultures of this largely archipelagic, metal-poor world, and especially its alternative technologies, are described in fascinating elaboration. *The Witling* has many of the same story elements (covert interplanetary visitors, an emotionally crippled woman genius, a person of ordinary capacity caught up in all this, a pet with psionic powers), but the combination is less successful. For one thing, much of the exposition is taken up with a brilliantly logical but never quite believable development of a world where practically everyone has an inborn ability to teleport. The title (which Vinge uses to mean approximately "half-wit") is a pun: at first it is applied in scorn to Pelio, the native hero who lacks his race's usual teleportational ability, but by the end it applies with more justification to the genius heroine. In a typical Vinge twist-of-the-knife ending, she suffers brain damage which both impairs her intellect and renders her a more balanced, happier person, a suitable partner for the love-stricken Pelio.

In his next two novels, Vinges returns to Earth. The widely acclaimed *True Names* features a computer net perceived by its users as a magical realm, and centers on a struggle by hobbyist "wizards" against a bloated Federal bureaucracy on the one hand, and against the mysterious malevolent Mailman on the other. The same loving elaboration applied to teleportation in *The Witling* is here put to a more plausible initial premise (the "magic" computer net), with brilliant results. As in previous novels, *True Names* features superhumans, but this time they attain that status largely by computer interface, rather than solely on the basis of their inborn talents. The love affair, within the "magical" realm where youth can be eternal, between the young hero and the old heroine (so ancient she had actually worked as a keypunch operator!) recalls, probably intentionally, a similar relationship in Heinlein's "Magic Incorporated." The technological innovation put to scrutiny in *The Peace War* is the stasis field, described in a few throw-away lines in Heinlein's *Beyond This Horizon* and perhaps best used before *The Peace War* in Niven's Known Space series. Vinge finds a variety of new applications for the idea, using it as an offensive weapon, a shield, a prison, and a time machine. In a combination of previous superman notions *The Peace War's* main viewpoint character is a genius even unassisted, and something unprecedented when interfaced with computers. Like *Grimm's World*, *The Peace War* depicts an elaborate sociological situation growing out of its basic assumptions (chiefly use of the stasis field, progress in genetic engineering and electronics, and the deliberate suppression of high-powered machinery). As in *True Names*, there is a romance blighted by age disparity—this time between a woman Air Force captain, newly emerged from stasis, and her onetime lover, who has aged throughout the fifty years since she was entrapped.

Both *True Names* and *The Peace War* show a considerable mellowing in tone over Vinge's previous work, which had been powerful and effective, but generally so bleak in outlook that it was made bearable only by the sparsity of the author's production. True, most of the human race is wiped out offstage in *The Peace War*, and the threat of bureaucracy is not entirely gone by the end of *True Names*, but life does now seem to be dealing Vinge viewpoint characters somewhat better cards. At the very least, the author is demonstrating his control of a wider range of approaches. Vernor Vinge has one of the most enviable "batting averages" in SF; any work under his name must be assumed to be a serious award contender, not so much because of name recognition (lessened by his slow rate of production) as by its consistent quality. It would be pleasant if Vinge could learn to write just as well more quickly, but even failing this, the steady accumulation of solid work will indeed earn him a major reputation with the passing of years.

—Patrick L. McGuire

VONNEGUT, Kurt, Jr. American. Born in Indianapolis, Indiana, 11 November 1922. Educated at Cornell University, Ithaca, New York, 1940-42; Carnegie Institute, Pittsburgh, 1943; University of Chicago, 1945-47. Served in the United States Army Infantry, 1942-45; Purple Heart. Married 1) Jane Marie Cox in 1945 (divorced 1979), one son and two daughters; 2) Jill Krementz in 1979. Police Reporter, Chicago City News Bureau, 1946; worked in public relations for the General Electric Company, Schenectady, New York, 1947-50. Since 1950, free-lance writer. Since 1965, teacher, Hopefield School, Sandwich, Massachusetts. Visiting Lecturer, Writers Workshop, University of Iowa, Iowa City, 1965-67, and Harvard University, Cambridge, Massachusetts, 1970-71; Visiting Professor, City University of New York, 1973-74. Recipient: Guggenheim Fellowship, 1967; American Academy grant, 1970. M. A.: University of Chicago, 1971; Litt. D.: Hobart and William Smith Colleges, Geneva, New York, 1974. Member, American Academy, 1973. Agent: Donald C. Farber, 600 Madison Avenue, New York, New York, 10022, U.S.A.

SCIENCE-FICTION PUBLICATIONS

Novels

Player Piano. New York, Scribner, 1952; London, Macmillan, 1953; as *Utopia 14*, New York, Bantam, 1954.
The Sirens of Titan. New York, Dell, 1959; London, Gollancz, 1962.
Cat's Cradle. New York, Holt Rinehart, and London, Gollancz, 1963.
Slaughterhouse-Five; or, The Children's Crusade. New York, Delacorte Press, 1969; London, Cape, 1970.

Short Stories

Canary in a Cat House. New York, Fawcett, 1961.
Welcome to the Monkey House: A Collection of Short Works. New York, Delacorte Press, 1968; London, Cape, 1969.

Uncollected Short Stories

"2BRO2B," in *If* (New York), January 1962.
"The Big Space Fuck," in *Again, Dangerous Visions,* edited by Harlan Ellison. New York, Doubleday, 1972; London, Millington, 1976.

OTHER PUBLICATIONS

Novels

Mother Night. New York, Fawcett, 1962; London, Cape, 1968.
God Bless You, Mr. Rosewater; or, Pearls Before Swine. New York, Holt Rinehart, and London, Cape, 1965.
Breakfast of Champions; or, Goodbye, Blue Monday. New York, Delacorte Press, and London, Cape, 1973.
Slapstick; or, Lonesome No More! New York, Delacorte Press, and London, Cape, 1976.
Jailbird. New York, Delacorte Press, and London, Cape, 1979.
Deadeye Dick. New York, Delacorte Press, 1982; London, Cape, 1983.

Plays

Happy Birthday, Wanda June (as *Penelope*, produced Cape Cod, Massachusetts, 1960; revised version, as *Happy Birthday, Wanda June*, produced New York, 1970; London, 1977). New York, Delacorte Press, 1970; London, Cape, 1973.
The Very First Christmas Morning, IN *Better Homes and Gardens* (Des Moines, Iowa), December 1962.
Between Time and Timbuktu; or, Prometheus-5: A Space Fantasy (televised, 1972; produced New York, 1976). New York, Delacorte Press, 1972; London, Panther, 1975.
Fortitude, in *Wampeters, Foma, and Granfalloons*, 1974.

Timesteps (produced Edinburgh, 1979).
God Bless You, Mr. Rosewater, adaptation of his own novel (produced New York, 1979).

Television Play: *Between Time and Timbuktu*, 1972.

Other

"Science Fiction," in *Page 2: The Best of "Speaking of Books" from the New York Times Book Review*, edited by Francis Brown. New York, Holt Rinehart, 1970.
Wampeters, Foma, and Granfalloons: Opinions. New York, Delacorte Press, 1974; London, Cape, 1975.
Sun Moon Star. New York, Harper, and London, Hutchinson, 1980.
Palm Sunday: An Autobiographical Collage. New York, Delacorte Press, and London, Cape, 1981.
Fates Worse Than Death. Nottingham, Spokesman, 1980(?).

*

Bibliography: *Kurt Vonnegut, Jr.: A Descriptive Bibliography and Annotated Secondary Checklist* by Asa B. Pieratt, Jr., and Jerome Klinkowitz, Hamden, Connecticut, Shoe String Press, 1974.

Critical Studies: *Kurt Vonnegut, Jr.* by Peter J. Reed, New York, Warner, 1972; *Kurt Vonnegut: Fantasist of Fire and Ice* by David H. Goldsmith, Bowling Green, Ohio, Popular Press, 1972; *The Vonnegut Statement* edited by Jerome Klinkowitz and John Somer, New York, Delacorte Press, 1973, London, Panther, 1975, *Vonnegut in America: An Introduction to the Life and Work of Kurt Vonnegut* edited by Klinkowitz and Donald L. Lawler, New York, Delacorte Press, 1977, and *Kurt Vonnegut* by Klinkowitz, London, Methuen, 1982; *Kurt Vonnegut, Jr.* by Stanley Schatt, Boston, Twayne, 1976; *Kurt Vonnegut* by James Lundquist, New York, Ungar, 1977; *Vonnegut: A Preface to His Novels* by Richard Giannone, Port Washington, New York, Kennikat Press, 1977; *Kurt Vonnegut: The Gospel from Outer Space* by Clark Mayo, San Bernardino, California, Borgo Press, 1977; *Vonnegut's Duty-Dance with Death: Theme and Structure in Slaughterhouse-Five* by Monica Loeb, Umeå, Sweden, Umeå Studies in the Humanities, 1979.

* * *

What is Kurt Vonnegut's relationship of SF? It would not only be too simple to say that he began as a SF writer and later drifted away from the "lodge"—it would also be misleading. For one thing, Vonnegut never identified with the "lodge"; for another, he has continued to use SF as a mine of metaphors for his sad, zany fictions chronicling the decline and dissolution of Middle American culture. The bizarre holocaustal scenario of *Cat's Cradle* has shrunk in *Deadeye Dick* to the depopulation of Midland City by a neutron bomb, but the weirdness that every reader perceives as the dominant mode of Vonnegut's fiction (whether it be diagnosed as black humor or absurdist fantasy) is nothing more or less than that of SF.

There are at least two ways to go wrong. One is to take straight Eliot Rosewater's much-quoted drunken speech to a SF writers' convention ("I love you sons of bitches. . . . You're all I read any more. . . . Your're the only ones with guts enough to *really* care about the future. . . .") which appears in *God Bless You, Mr. Rosewater*. Eliot is a compassionate and humane drunken lunatic, to be sure, but all the same he is a drunken lunatic. Even

so he admits that SF writers "can't write for sour apples," while claiming that Kilgore Trout, the dean of hacks, is "the greatest writer alive today."

Another is to focus on Vonnegu's remark (in a *New York Times Book Review* essay on "Science Fiction") that since writing *Player Piano* he has "been a soreheaded occupant of a file drawer labeled 'science fiction,'" and that he wants out, "particularly since so many serious critics regularly mistake the drawer for a urinal." The urinal mistake is not Vonnegut's: he attributes it to critics who didn't study enough science in college, and he goes on to provide a clear-headed and sympathetic account of the SF writer's "lodge" and the SF branch of the publishing industry.

So unravelling Vonnegut's SF connection is not easy, nor should it be. Perhaps the best approach is to consider Donald L. Lawler's analysis of *The Sirens of Titan*. Lawler claims that the "narrative shell" of *Sirens* is "space opera," and that it serves Vonnegut as "an enabling form of satire." Lawler is right to see the satirical punch of the novel as arising from its SF form and content; he errs only in identifying the relevant SF type as space opera, for the SF form that is the opposite of the "shaggy dog story" Lawler finds in the novel is the apocalypse, the kind of SF story that portrays a catastrophic transformation of the human scene in order to reveal the purpose of human history. One of the most ambitious of SF's apocalyptic fictions is Arthur C. Clarke's *Childhood's End*, published five years before *The Sirens of Titan*. In 1978 Vonnegut called Clarke's novel one of SF's few masterpieces ("All of the others were written by me"). *Childhood's End* portrays the end of human evolution on earth, revealing that the latent destiny of humankind is to transform its last generation into a collective immaterial entity that will soar away from its planetary home and join the Overmind, a godlike union of similar "racial" consciousnesses which is gradually taking over the universe. The apocalyptic revelation of *Sirens* is a shaggy dog indeed, for its plot discloses that fifty thousand years of human history have had one trivial purpose: to ensure the delivery of a repair part for the spacecraft of an alien courier stranded on Titan. Not only that, the courier discovers that the message he has spent his being to carry from one end of the galaxy to the other is the merest ejaculation: *Greetings.*

The foregoing ilustrates one way in which Vonnegut utilizes SF conventions—by writing against them, even to the point of parody. SF stories, whether they end well or badly for their protagonists, generally embody a romantic concept of human purpose: whether immanent or extrinsic, whether foreordained or created by human striving against nature, the destiny of humankind is noble and important. It is a struggle to dominate and to make sense of the universe. *The Sirens of Titan* uses its SF motifs to counter this tradition. Its "hero," Malachi Constant ("the eternal pilgrim") learns, along with Winston Niles Rumfoord and the rest of mankind, that the "outward push" is pointless, that there is no meaning to the universe, and there is no god but "God the Utterly Indifferent."

Another indicator of Vonnegut's relationship to SF is of course the feckless SF writer Kilgore Trout, who appears regularly in much of Vonnegut's fiction. He was promised his freedom in *Breakfast of Champions* (which was also supposed to be Vonnegut's final novel), but was pressed into service again for *Jailbird*. Trout knows and cares little about science, writes terribly, and has earned neither critical nor popular acclaim: his books can be found, remaindered and misleadingly titled, only in pornographic bookstores. His fate as a SF writer is far worse than that of the late Theodore Sturgeon, but his name is almost certainly a wicked parody of Sturgeon's. Kilgore Trout, however, is clearly also an *alter ego* of Vonnegut. His novel

2BR02B, so admired by Eliot Rosewater, appears to involve the situation of *Player Piano*, Vonnegut's first novel, with the addition of Ethical Suicide Parlors for population control, themselves an appurtenance of the *Playboy* story "Welcome to the Monkey House" (written about the same time as *God Bless You, Mr. Rosewater*). Trout may be partly an execrable old hack who smells bad, but he is also a loveabe fellow whose fictions are based on big, imaginative concepts like that of Sturgeon's *The Cosmic Rape*, the title of which is parodied and the plot of which is inverted in Vonnegut's notorious "The Big Space Fuck," published in *Again, Dangerous Visions*.

Kilgore Trout represents Vonnegut's interface with SF; he is no more a portrait of Sturgeon than he is of Vonnegut. He is perhaps Vonnegut's chief SF metaphor—the writer whose vision outstrips his knowledge and his craft. In that his condition is Sturgeon's—but also Vonnegut's, and any writer's. Perhaps he also represents any writer's (and any reader's) fear of becoming an old, derelict failure—or of actually being one already. Perhaps, more specifically, he embodies some nagging fear of his author that what he has created might just possibly be a bunch of worthless, second-rate SF.

Vonnegut's SF (many of the early stories, *Player Piano, The Sirens of Titan, Cat's Cradle*, and *Slaughterhouse-Five*), is not second-rate. *Player Piano*, perhaps, has suffered unfair competition from the major dystopian novels of its time: *Nineteen Eighty-Four, Farenheit 451*, and *The Space Merchants*, all of which have similar plots involving the rebellion of an insider against an oppressive social order. But like the others the story of Paul Proteus has a unique target—in its case automated production—and like the others it presents a plausible vision of one of our possible futures. In fact, in the details of its extrapolation it misses on only a couple of points: the virtual elimination of vacuum tubes by solid state devices and the failure of US government and industry to merge fully in management of the economy. *The Sirens of Titan* is not only the parody of apocalyptic SF discussed above: published at the beginning of the age of space, it is a satirical critique of a society obsessed with technological accomplishments that lead to litle more than "empty heroics, low comedy, and pointless death. " *Cat's Cradle*, with its story that couhterpoints the careless disposal of a doomsday weapon with the history of a harmless cult religion, is perhaps even stronger in its denunciation of the follies of technological society. The discoverer of Ice-Nine, the substance that destroys the planet by freezing all its water, irresponsibly leaves the fatal chunk to his three less than normal offspring. Dr. Felix Hoenikker was already the "father of the A-Bomb," a scientist who would play with any dangerous research idea suggested by the military sources of his funding. Contrasted with him is the playful Bokonon, creator of a religion he realized was lies and illusions (a fiction), but knew would relieve the miserable lives of the inhabitants of his poor Caribbean island. Bokonon is a holy fool who has created a warm extended family; Hoenikker is a man of reason who has neglected his children. The dreams of reason prove more fatal than the illusions of religion.

Slaughterhouse-Five is the perfect marriage of Vonnegut's SF with his more "mundane" themes. "Billy Pilgrim has come unstuck in time"; but unlike the purposeful time travelers of SF convention (but much like the Winston Niles Rumfoord of *The Sirens of Titan*, jerked around by the chrono-synclastic infundibulum), this unlikely hero lives all the moments of his life simultaneously, including his POW captivity in Dresden during the firebombing and his captivity in an exhibit on the planet Tralfamadore. From this perspective, optometrist Billy sees that the universe is mechanically preordained, and that the soution is to try living only the happy moments. Billy, of course,

is regarded as a harmless lunatic (especially since he is a devoted fan of SF writer Kilgore Trout). Again, however, it is not the holy fools and lunatic dreamers who run the death camps and firebomb Dresden—it is a different kind of madman, who has polluted the stream of reason that trickles so weakly in a Billy, a Bokonon, and an Eliot Rosewater.

With *Slaughterhouse-Five* Vonnegut's fiction becomes more personal, and the line begins to blur between fictional narrative and autobiographical essay. The auctorial voice becomes more direct, and hard to distinguish from those of first-person narrators who are clearly, like Trout, avatars of Kurt Vonnegut, Jr. In the much-maligned *Breakfast of Champions*, the author-narrator actually appears in a coctail lounge occupied by several of the novel's characters, and at its conclusion he confronts a pathetic Kilgore Trout. But though he tries to dismiss Trout, Vonnegut's SF roots will not disappear so easily. In *Slapstick* he employs a Troutian conceit (telepathic intelligence-boosting between twins) and a vague post-holocaust setting to articulate the idea of artificial extended families as an antidote for the rootlessness and minimal selfhood of contemporary Americans. In *Deadeye Dick* a freak neutron bomb accident (the stuff of a low-budget 1950's SF film, one would think) is a metaphor for the demolition of the rich cultural matrix of a place like the Indianapolis of Vonnegut's forebears.

Looking back, we can see that Vonnegut has been writing about two things since the beginning—the loss of Indianapolis Union Station and the way of life it stood for (noble despite its racism, its pretentiousness, and its abuse and neglect of the poor), and what we seem to be replacing it with (a racist, pretentious, exploitative vulgarity). Kurt Vonnegut, Jr. may not be a bonafide SF writer—by his own admission he is not a member of the "lodge" and did not read SF pulps as a kid. If he is not, he remains an ornament to SF, for without the SF devices that give shape to his fiction, he would have been unable to say most of what he wanted to say. If his chronicle of the never-ending Great Depression—of contemporary American life—has any enduring value, that is due in large measure to the fact that Vonnegut cut his literary teeth on SF.

—John P. Brennan

WAINWRIGHT, Ken. See **TUBB, E. C.**

WALDROP, Howard. American. Born in Houston, Mississippi, 15 September 1946. Educated at Arlington High School, Texas, 1962-65; University of Texas, Arlington, 1965-70, 1972-74. Served as an information specialist in the United States Army, 1970-72. Linotype operator, Arlington *Daily News*, 1965-68; advertising copywriter, Lindell-Keyes, Dallas, 1972; auditory research subject, Dynastat Inc., Austin, 1975-80. Recipient: Nebula Award, 1980; World Fantasy Award, 1981. Agent: Joseph Elder Agency, 150 West 87th Street, No. 6-D, New York, New York 10024. Address: P. O. Box 49335, Austin, Texas 78765, U.S.A.

SCIENCE-FICTION PUBLICATIONS

Novels

The Texas-Israeli War: 1999, with Jake Saunders. New York,
Ballantine, 1974.
Them Bones. New York, Ace, 1984.

Uncollected Short Stories

"Lunchbox," in *Analog* (New York), May 1972.
"Mono no Aware," in *Haunt of Horror* (New York), August
1973.
"A Voice and Bitter Weeping," with Jake Saunders, in *The Best
from Galaxy 2*. New York, Award, 1974.
"My Sweet Lady Jo," in *Universe 4*, edited by Terry Carr. New
York, Random House, 1974.
"Time and Variance," in *Vertex* (Los Angeles), August 1974.
"Sic Transit. . .?" with Steve Utley, in *Stellar 2*, edited by Judy-
Lynn del Rey. New York, Ballantine, 1976.
"Mary Margaret Road-Grader," in *Orbit 18*, edited by Damon
Knight. New York, Harper, 1976.
"Sun Up!," with Al Jackson, in *Faster Than Light*, edited by
Jack Dann and George Zebrowski. New York, Harper, 1976.
"Custer's Last Jump," with Steve Utley, in *Universe 6*, edited by
Terry Carr. New York, Doubleday, 1976; London, Dobson,
1978.
"Unsleeping Beauty and the Beast," in *Lone Star Universe*,
edited George W. Proctor and Steve Utley. Austin, Texas,
Heidelberg, 1976.
"Save a Place in the Lifeboat for Me," in *Nickelodeon 2* (Kansas
City), 1976.
"Der Untergang des Abendlandesmenschen," in *Chacal 1*
(Overland Park, Kansas), 1976.
"Men of Greywater Station," with George R. R. Martin, in
Songs of Stars and Shadows, by Martin. New York, Pocket
Books, 1977.
"Adventures of the Grinder's Whistle," in *Chacal 2* (Overland
Park, Kansas), 1977.
"Black as the Pit, From Pole to Pole," with Steve Utley, in *New
Dimensions 7*, edited by Robert Silverberg. New York,
Harper, and London, Gollancz, 1977.
"Dr. Hudson's Secret Gorilla," in *The Rivals of King Kong*,
edited by Michel Parry. London, Corgi, 1978.
"Horror, We Got," in *Shayol 3* (Overland Park, Kansas), 1979.
"All about Strange Monsters of the Recent Past," in *Shayol 4*
(Overland Park, Kansas), 1980.
"Billy Big-Eyes," in *Berkley Showcase 1*, edited by Victoria
Schochet and John W. Silbersack. New York, Berkley, 1980.
"The Ugly Chickens," in *Universe 10*, edited by Terry Carr. New
York, Doubleday, 1980.
"Green Brother," in *Shayol 5* (Overland Park, Kansas), 1982.
"God's Hooks," in *Universe 12*, edited by Terry Carr. New
York, Doubleday, 1982.
". . . the World, As We Know't," in *Shayol 6* (Overland Park,
Kansas), 1982.
"Ike at the Mike," in *The First Omni Book of Science Fiction*,
edited by Ellen Datlow, New York, Zebra, 1983.
"Man-Mountain Gentian," in *The Year's Best Science Fiction
1*, edited by Gardner Dozois and Jim Frenkel. New York,
Bluejay, 1984.
"Helpless, Helpless," in *Light Years and Dark*, edited by
Michael Bishop. New York, Berkley, 1984.
"Flying Saucer Rock and Roll," in *Omni* (New York), January
1985.
"Heirs of the Perisphere," in *Playboy* (Chicago), July 1985.

*   *   *

It is necessary to know something about Howard Waldrop
the person in order to understand something vital about
Howard Waldrop the writer. Waldrop the person loves to
reenact bits, pieces, and whole chunks of everything from Three
Stooges comedies to *Casablanca*. It is his best party trick. He sets
the scene with a few words and a gesture, he makes the faces, he
does the voices. The result is neither impersonation nor
interpretation, but something in between. Approximation.
Pastiche. Onlooking film purists have been known to complain
that he misses the letter of his model. But the spirit is always
there, and often it is enhanced. The Waldrop version can be
better than the original.

Everything that goes into the warehouse of information that
is Waldrop's memory does not simply come back out but comes
out skewed. He claims Thomas Wolfe, R. A. Lafferty, and
Philip José Farmer as seminal literary influences and credits a
Lin Carter novel with his deciding to become a writer. ("If *The
Wizard of Lemuria* could be published, I knew anything *I* wrote
could be published. ") What seems to have given Waldrop's
fiction its particular bent, however, was a remark made by
Farmer at a long-ago science-fiction convention: "Mine your
Childhood. " Childhood for Waldrop is the 1950's, and, like his
favorite moments in old films, that decade has been warped out
of true by immersion in his brain chemicals.

So every bad brain-transplant and worse ape-on-the-loose
movie he ever saw re-emerges, complete with Mad Scientist, Evil
Assistant, and Beautiful Woman, in "Dr. Hudson's Secret
Gorilla"; the title itself is a twisted homage to an old soap opera
called *Dr. Hudson's Secret Journal*. Every comedian who ever
made him laugh returns in "Save a Place in the Lifeboat for
Me," on a mission to save the lives of three rock 'n' roll stars who
bear more than passing resemblance to Buddy Holly, Richie
Valens, and the Big Bopper—all killed in the same airplane
crash in 1959, all as beloved of Waldrop as Buster Keaton,
Abbott and Costello, and the Marx Brothers. Waldrop
especially loves the science-fiction films of the 1950's; inevitably,
in "All About Strange Monsters of the Recent Past" (another
title that pays tribute, this time to Roy Chapman Andrews,
whose *All About Strange Beasts of the Past* enriched many a
1950's childhood besides Waldrop's), those films' giant
arthropods, marauding Martian invaders, and revivified
prehistoric animals enter our reality. Civilization As We Know
It is destroyed. "God," muses the story's hero. "Japan must
have gone first. " And in "Ike at the Mike" Waldrop offers his
most skewed vision of the decade: a promising young politician
named E. Aaron Presley attends a farewell performance by jazz-
great Dwight Eisenhower, on clarinet. George S. Patton sits in
on drums.

Sometimes, of course, these whacko conceptions founder in
faulty execution. Sometimes, the ideas themselves simply are
not strong enough to support much wordage. The notion of
importing Israeli mercenaries to a Lone Star State defending its
oil against the other forty-nine is clever enough to sustain
Waldrop and Jake Saunders's "A Voice and Bitter Weeping"
but bogs down in a dreary and interminable combat yarn in their
subsequent novel-length expansion, plokingly titled *The Texas-
Israeli War: 1999*, almost as soon as the original material is left
behind.

Still, Waldrop's level of competence has risen sharply in
recent years. He hit his stride with "The Ugly Chickens," which
won the Nebula Awardd in 1980. This tragicomic journal of a
young ornithologist's search for the last surviving dodoes in, of
all places, Mississippi contains a perfectly charming episode in

which the narrator daydreams of those hapless fowl dancing to Pachelbel's *Canon in D* before the King and Queen of Holland.

In Waldrop's first solo novel, *Them Bones*, an archeological team working in Louisiana in the late 1920's digs into a pre-Columbian burial mound and discovers first the remains of horses and then other, even more disturbing anachronisms. "Meanwhile," in the past but not far from the future site of the mound, Madison Yazoo Leake, a time-traveler from the 21st century, finds Greek-speaking Amerindians and meets traders from the Old World—an Islamic empire, heir to mighty Carthage, which crushed Rome in the Punic Wars. Oddity piles upon oddity and the very structure of time seems to fray as the novel cuts back and forth from the bewildered archeologists to Leake. *Them Bones* is a thoroughly engaging work, part mystery story, part action-adventure romp, and, like "The Ugly Chickens," amply demonstrates that Waldrop's technical skills have at last caught up with his non-stop imagination.

Waldrop's strengths as a writer are considerable. He is a tireless, meticulous researcher. He writes fine, pared-down prose and has a knack for the startling turn of phrase. He possesses humor, compassion, and a vast curiosity, and he loves to tinker with reality. Buster Keaton may have evoked guffaws in quite the way that Waldrop says he did, Rome may not have defeated Carthage and gone on to conquer most of the known world, Eisenhower may have become not a general and a president but the world's greatest jazz clarinetist instead. Waldrop can tell you that a thing was so or was not so, and while he is telling you, you are absolutely convinced.

—Steven Utley

WALLACE, (Richard Horatio) Edgar. British. Born in Greenwich, London, 1 April 1875. Educated at St. Peter's School, London; Board School, Camberwell, London, to age 12. Served in the Royal West Kent Regiment in England, 1893-96, and in the Medical Staff Corps in South Africa, 1896-99; bought his discharge, 1899; served in the Lincoln's Inn branch of the Special Constabulary, and as a special interrogator for the War Office, during World War I. Married 1) Ivy Caldecott in 1901 (divorced, 1919), two daughters and two sons; 2) Violet King in 1921, one daughter. Worked in a printing firm, shoe shop, rubber factory, and as a merchant seaman, plasterer, and milk delivery boy, in London, 1886-91; South African Correspondent for Reuter's 1899-1902, and the London *Daily Mail*, 1900-02; Editor, *Rand Daily News*, Johannesburg, 1902-03; returned to London: Reporter, *Daily Mail*, 1903-07, and *Standard*, 1910; Racing Editor, and later Editor, *The Week-End*, later *The Week-End Racing Supplement*, 1910-12; Racing Editor and Special Writer, *Evening News*, 1910-12; founded *Bilbury's Weekly* and *R. E. Walton's Weekly*, both racing papers; Editor, *Ideas* and *The Story Journal*, 1913; Writer, and later Editor, *Town Topics*, 1913-16; regular contributor to the *Birmingham Post*, and *Thomson's Weekly News*, Dundee; Racing Columnist, *The Star*, 1927-32, and *Daily Mail*, 1930-32; Drama Critic, *Morning Post*, 1928; Founder, *The Bucks Mail*, 1930; Editor, *Sunday News*, 1931. Chairman of the Board of Directors, and film writer/director, British Lion Film Corporation. President, Press Club, London, 1923-24. *Died 10 February 1932.*

SCIENCE-FICTION PUBLICATIONS

Novels

1925: The Story of a Fatal Peace. London, Newnes, 1915.
The Green Rust. London, Ward Lock, 1919; Boston, Small Maynard, 1920.
Captains of Souls. Boston, Small Maynard, 1922; London, Long, 1923.
The Day of Uniting. London, Hodder and Stoughton, 1926; New York, Mystery League, 1930.
Planetoid 127 (includes *The Sweizer Pump*). London, Readers Library, 1929.

OTHER PUBLICATIONS

Novels

The Four Just Men. London, Tallis Press, 1906; revised edition, 1906; revised edition, Sheffield, Weekly Telegraph, 1908; Boston, Small Maynard, 1920.
Angel Esquire. Bristol, Arrowsmith, 1908; Boston, Small Maynard, 1920.
The Council of Justice. London, Ward Lock, 1908.
The Duke in the Suburbs. London, Ward Lock, 1909.
Captain Tatham of Tatham Island. London, Gale and Polden, 1909; revised edition, as *The Island of Galloping Gold*, London, Newnes, 1916; as *Eve's Island*, Newnes, 1926.
The Nine Bears. London, Ward Lock, 1910; as *The Other Man*, New York, Dodd Mead, 1911; as *Silinski, Master Criminal*, Cleveland, World, 1930; as *The Cheaters*, London, Digit, 1964.
Private Selby. London, Ward Lock, 1912.
The Fourth Plague. London, Ward Lock, 1913; New York, Doubleday, 1930.
Grey Timothy. London, Ward Lock, 1913, as *Pallard the Punter*, 1914.
The River of Stars. London, Ward Lock, 1913.
The Man Who Bought London. London, Ward Lock, 1915.
The Melody of Death. Bristol, Arrowsmith, 1915; New York, Dial Press, 1927.
The Clue of the Twisted Candle. Boston, Small Maynard, 1916; London, Newnes, 1917.
A Debt Discharged. London, Ward Lock, 1916.
The Tomb of Ts'in. London, Ward Lock, 1916.
The Just Men of Cordova. London, Ward Lock, 1917.
Kate Plus Ten. London, Ward Lock, and Boston, Small Maynard, 1917.
The Secret House. London, Ward Lock, 1917; Boston, Small Maynard, 1919.
Down under Donovan. London, Ward Lock, 1918.
The Man Who Knew. Boston, Small Maynard, 1918; London, Newnes, 1919.
Those Folk of Bulboro. London, Ward Lock, 1918.
The Daffodil Mystery. London, Ward Lock, 1920; as *The Daffodil Murder*, Boston, Small Maynard, 1921.
Jack o' Judgment. London, Ward Lock, 1920; Boston, Small Maynard, 1921.
The Book of All Power. London, Ward Lock, 1921.
The Angel of Terror. Boston, Small Maynard, and London, Hodder and Stoughton, 1922; as *The Destroying Angel*, London, Pan, 1959.
Number Six. London, Newnes, 1922.
The Crimson Circle. London, Hodder and Stoughton, 1922; New York, Doubleday, 1929.

The Flying Fifty-Five. London, Hutchinson, 1922.

Mr. Justice Maxell. London, Ward Lock, 1922.

The Valley of Ghosts. London, Odhams Press, 1922; Boston, Small Maynard, 1923.

The Books of Bart. London, Ward Lock, 1923.

The Clue of the New Pin. Boston, Small Maynard, and London, Hodder and Stoughton, 1923.

The Green Archer. London, Hodder and Stoughton, 1923; Boston, Small Maynard, 1924.

The Missing Million. London, Long, 1923; as *The Missing Millions*, Boston, Small Maynard, 1925.

The Dark Eyes of London. London, Ward Lock, 1924; New York, Doubleday, 1929.

Double Dan. London, Hodder and Stoughton, 1924; as Diana of Kara-Kara, Boston, Small Maynard, 1924.

The Face in the Night. London, Long, 1924; New York, Doubleday, 1929.

Room 13. London, Long, 1924.

Flat 2. New York, Garden City Publishing Company, 1924; revised edition, London, Long, 1927.

The Sinister Man. London, Hodder and Stoughton, 1924; Boston, Small Maynard, 1925.

The Three Oaks Mystery. London, Ward Lock, 1924.

Blue Hand. London, Ward Lock, 1925; Boston, Small Maynard, 1926.

The Black Avons. London, Gill, 1925; as *How They Fared in the Times of the Tudors, Roundhead and Cavalier, From Waterloo to the Mutiny*, and *Europe in the Melting Pot*, 4 vols., 1925.

The Daughters of the Night. London, Newnes, 1925.

The Fellowship of the Frog. London, Ward Lock, 1925; New York, Doubleday, 1928.

The Gaunt Stranger. London, Hodder and Stoughton, 1925; as *The Ringer*, New York, Doubleday, 1926.

The Hairy Arm. Boston, Small Maynard, 1925; as *The Avenger*, London, Long, 1926.

A King by Night. London, Long, 1925; New York, Doubleday, 1926.

The Strange Countess. London, Hodder and Stoughton, 1925; Boston, Small Maynard, 1926.

The Three Just Men. London, Hodder and Stoughton, 1925; New York, Doubleday, 1930.

Barbara on Her Own. London, Newnes, 1926.

The Black Abbot. London, Hodder and Stoughton, 1926; New York, Doubleday, 1927.

The Door with Seven Locks. London, Hodder and Stoughton, and New York, Doubleday, 1926.

The Joker. London, Hodder and Stoughton, 1926; as *The Colossus*, New York, Doubleday, 1932.

The Man from Morocco. London, Long, 1926; as *The Black*, New York, Doubleday, 1930.

The Million Dollar Story. London, Newnes, 1926.

The Northing Tramp. London, Hodder and Stoughton, 1926; New York, Doubleday, 1929; as *The Tramp*, London, Pan, 1965.

Penelope of the Polyantha. London, Hodder and Stoughton, 1926.

The Square Emerald. London, Hodder and Stoughton, 1926; as *The Girl from Scotland Yard*, New York, Doubleday, 1927.

The Terrible People. London, Hodder and Stoughton, and New York, Doubleday, 1926.

We Shall See! London, Hodder and Stoughton, 1926; as *The Gaol Breaker*, New York, Doubleday, 1931.

The Yellow Snake. London, Hodder and Stoughton, 1926.

Big Foot. London, Long, 1927.

The Feathered Serpent. London, Hodder and Stoughton, 1927;

New York, Doubleday, 1928.

The Forger. London, Hodder and Stoughton, 1927; as *The Clever One*, New York, Doubleday, 1928.

The Hand of Power. London, Long, 1927; New York, Mystery League, 1930.

The Man Who Was Nobody. London, Ward Lock, 1927.

The Ringer (novelization of stage play). London, Hodder and Stoughton, 1927.

The Squeaker. London, Hodder and Stoughton, 1927; as *The Squealer*, New York, Doubleday, 1928.

Terror Keep. London, Hodder and Stoughton, and New York, Doubleday, 1927.

The Traitor's Gate. London, Hodder and Stoughton, and New York, Doubleday, 1927.

The Double. London, Hodder and Stoughton, and New York Doubleday, 1928.

The Thief in the Night. London, Readers Library, 1928.

The Flying Squad. London, Hodder and Stoughton, 1928; New York, Doubleday, 1929.

The Gunner. London, Long, 1928; as *Gunman's Bluff*, New York, Doubleday, 1929.

The Twister. London, Long, 1928; New York, Doubleday, 1929.

The Golden Hades. London, Collins, 1929.

The Green Ribbon. London, Hutchinson, 1929; New York, Doubleday, 1930.

The India-Rubber Men. London, Hodder and Stoughton, 1929; New York, Doubleday, 1930.

The Terror. London, Detective Story Club, 1929.

The Calendar. London, Collins, 1930; New York, Doubleday, 1931.

The Clue of the Silver Key. London, Hodder and Stoughton, 1930; as *The Silver Key*, New York, Doubleday, 1930.

The Lady of Ascot. London, Hutchinson, 1930.

White Face. London, Hodder and Stoughton, 1930; New York, Doubleday, 1931.

On the Spot. London, Long, and New York, Doubleday, 1931.

The Coat of Arms. London, Hutchinson, 1931; as *The Arranways Mystery*, New York, Doubleday, 1932.

The Devil Man. London, Collins, and New York, Doubleday, 1931; as *The Life and Death of Charles Peace, 1932*.

The Man at the Carlton. London, Hodder and Stoughton, 1931; New York, Doubleday, 1932.

The Frightened Lady. London, Hodder and Stoughton, 1932; New York, Doubleday, 1933.

When the Gangs Came to London. London, Long, and New York, Doubleday, 1932.

Short Stories

Smithy. London, Tallis Press, 1905; revised edition, as *Smithy, Not to Mention Nobby Clark and Spud Murphy*, London, Newnes, 1914.

Smithy Abroad: Barrack Room Sketches. London, Hulton, 1909.

Sanders of the River. London, Ward Lock, 1911; New York, Doubleday, 1930.

The People of the River. London, Ward Lock, 1912.

Smithy's Friend Nobby. London, Town Topics, 1914; as *Nobby*, London, Newnes, 1916.

The Admirable Carfew. London, Ward Lock, 1914.

Bosambo of the River. London, Ward Lock, 1914.

Bones, Being Further Adventures in Mr. Commissioner Sanders' Country. London, Ward Lock, 1915.

Smithy and the Hun. London, Pearson, 1915.

The Keepers of the King's Peace. London, Ward Lock, 1917.
Lieutenant Bones. London, Ward Lock, 1918.
Tam o' the Scouts. London, Newnes, 1918; as *Tam of the Scoots, Boston*, Boston, Small Maynard, 1919; as *Tam*, Newnes, 1919.
The Fighting Scouts. London, Pearson, 1919.
The Adventures of Heine. London, Ward Lock, 1919.
Bones in London. London, Ward Lock, 1921.
The Law of the Four Just Men. London, Hodder and Stoughton, 1921; as *Again the Three Just Men*, New York, Doubleday, 1933.
Sandi, The King-Maker. London, Ward Lock, 1922.
Bones of the River. London, Newnes, 1923.
Chick. London, Ward Lock, 1923.
Educated Evans. London, Webster, 1924.
The Mind of Mr. J. G. Reeder. London, Hodder and Stoughton, 1925; as *The Murder Book of Mr. J. G. Reeder*, New York, Doubleday, 1929.
More Educated Evans. London, Webster, 1926.
Mrs. William Jones and Bill. London, Newnes, 1926.
Sanders. London, Hodder and Stoughton, 1926; as *Mr. Commissioner Sanders*, New York, Doubleday, 1930.
The Brigand. London, Hodder and Stoughton, 1927.
Good Evans! London, Webster, 1927; as *The Educated Man— Good Evans!*, London, Collins, 1929.
The Mixer. London, Long, 1927.
Again Sanders. London, Hodder and Stoughton, 1928; New York, Doubleday, 1929.
Again the Three Just Men. London, Hodder and Stoughton, 1928; as *The Law of the Three Just Men*, New York, Doubleday, 1931; as *Again the Three*, London, Pan, 1968.
Elegant Edward. London, Readers Library, 1928.
The Orator. London, Hutchinson, 1928.
Again the Ringer. London, Hodder and Stoughton, 1929; as *The Ringer Returns*, New York, Doubleday, 1931.
Four Square Jane. London, Readers Library, 1929.
The Big Four. London, Readers Library, 1929.
The Black. London, Readers Library, 1929; augmented edition, London, Digit, 1962.
The Ghost of Down Hill (includes *The Queen of Sheba's Belt*). London, Readers Library, 1929.
The Cat Burglar. London, Newnes, 1929.
Circumstantial Evidence. London, Newnes, 1929; Cleveland, World, 1934.
Fighting Snub Reilly. London, Newnes, 1929; Cleveland, World, 1934.
The Governor of Chi-Foo. London, Newnes, 1929; Cleveland, World, 1934.
The Little Green Man. London, Collins, 1929.
The Prison-Breakers. London, Newnes, 1929.
Forty-Eight Short Stories. London, Newnes, 1929.
For Information Received. London, Newnes, 1929.
The Lady of Little Hell. London, Newnes, 1929.
The Lone House Mystery. London, Collins, 1929.
Red Aces. London, Hodder and Stoughton, 1929; New York, Doubleday, 1930.
The Reporter. London, Readers Library, 1929.
The Iron Grip. London, Readers Library, 1930.
Killer Kay. London, Newnes, 1930.
The Stretelli Case and Other Mystery Stories (omnibus). Cleveland, World, 1930.
The Lady Called Nita. London, Newnes, 1930.
The Guv'nor and Other Stories. London, Collins, 1932; as *Mr. Reeder Returns*, New York, Doubleday, 1932; as *The Guv'nor and Mr. J. G. Reeder Returns*, Collins, 2 vols., 1933-34.

Sergeant Sir Peter. London, Chapman and Hall, 1932; as *Sergeant Dunn C. I. D.*, London, Digit, 1962.
The Steward. London, Collins, 1932.
The Last Adventure. London, Hutchinson, 1934.
The Woman from the East and Other Stories. London, Hutchinson, 1934.
Nig-Nog (omnibus). Cleveland, World, 1934.
The Undisclosed Client. London, Digit, 1962.
The Man Who Married His Cook and Other Stories. London, White Lion, 1976.
Unexpected Endings. Oxford, Edgar Wallace Society, 1979.
Two Stories, and The Seventh Man. Oxford, Edgar Wallace Society, 1981.
The Sooper and Others, edited by Jack Adrian. London, Dent, 1984.

Plays

An African Millionaire (produced South Africa, 1904). London, Davis Poynter, 1972.
The Forest of Happy Dreams (produced London, 1910; New York, 1914). Published in *One-act Play Parade*, London, Hodder and Stoughton, 1935.
Dolly Cutting Herself (produced London, 1911).
Sketches, in *Hullo, Ragtime* (produced Lodon, 1912).
Sketches, in *Hullo, Tango!* (produced London, 1912).
Hello, Exchange! (sketch; produced London, 1913; as *The Switchboard*, produced New York, 1915).
The Manager's Dream (sketch; produced London, 1913).
Sketches, in *Business as Usual* (produced London, 1914).
The Whirligig (revue), with Wal Pink and Albert de Courville, music by Frederick Chappelle (produced London, 1919; as *Pins and Needles*, produced New York, 1922).
M'Lady (produced London, 1921).
The Whirl of the World (revue), with Albert de Courville and William K. Wells, music by Frederick Chappelle (produced London, 1924).
The Looking Glass (revue), with Albert de Courville, music by Frederick Chappelle (produced London, 1924).
The Ringer, adaptation of his own novel *The Gaunt Stranger* (produced London, 1926). London, Hodder and Stoughton, and New York, French, 1929.
The Mystery of Room 45 (produced London, 1926).
The Terror, adaptation of his own novel *Terror Keep* (produced Brighton and London, 1927). London, Hodder and Stoughton, 1929.
Double Dan, adaptation of his own novel (produced Blackpool and London, 1926).
A Perfect Gentlman (produced London, 1927).
The Yellow Mask, music by Vernon Duke, lyrics by Desmond Carter (produced Birmingham, 1927; London, 1928).
The Flying Squad, adaptation of his own novel (produced Oxford and London, 1928). London, Hodder and Stoughton, 1929.
The Man Who Changed His Name (produced London, 1928; New York, 1932). London, Hodder and Stoughton, 1929.
The Squeaker, adaptation of his own novel (produced London, 1928; as *Sign of the Leopard*, produced New York, 1928). London, Hodder and Stoughton, 1929.
The Lad (produced Wimbledon, 1928; London, 1929).
Persons Unknown (produced London, 1929).
The Calendar (also director: produced Manchester and London, 1929). London, French 1932.
On the Spot (produced London and New York, 1930).
The Mouthpiece (produced London, 1930).

Smoky Cell (produced London, 1930).

Charles III, adaption of a play by Curt Götz (produced London, 1931.)

The Old Man (produced London, 1931).

The Case of the Frightened Lady (produced London, 1931). London, French, 1932; as *Criminal at Large* (produced New York, 1932), New York, French, 1934.

The Green Pack (produced London, 1932). London, French, 1933.

Screenplays: *Nurse and Martyr, 1915; The Ringer,* 1928; *Valley of the Ghosts,* 1928; *The Forger,* 1928; *Red Aces,* 1929, *The Squeaker,* 1930; *Should a Doctor Tell?,* 1930; *The Hound of the Baskervilles,* with V. Gareth Gundrey, 1931; *The Old Man,* 1931; *King Kong,* with others, 1933.

Verse

The Mission That Failed! A Tale of the Raid and Other Poems. Cape Town, Maskew Miller, 1898.

Nicholson's Nek. Cape Town, Eastern Press, 1900.

War! and Other Poems. Cape Town, Eastern Press, 1900.

Writ in Barracks. London, Methuen, 1900.

Other

Unofficial Despatches. London, Hutchinson, 1901.

Famous Scottish Regiments. London, Newnes, 1914.

Fieldmarshall Sir John French and His Campaigns. London, Newnes, 1914.

Heroes All: Gallant Deeds of War. London, Newnes. 1914.

The Standard History of the War. London, Newnes, 4 vols. 1914-16.

War of the Nations, vols 2-11. London. Newnes. 1914-19.

Kitchener's Army and the Territorial Forces: The Full Story of a Great Achievement. London, Newnes, 6 vols., 1915.

People: A Short Autobiography. London, Hodder and Stoughton, 1926; New York, Doubleday, 1929.

This England. London, Hodder and Stoughton, 1927.

My Hollywood Diary. London, Hutchinson, 1932.

A Fragment of Medieval Life. St. Peter Port, Guernsey, Toucan Press, 1977(?).

Ghostwriter: *My Life,* by Evelyn Thaw, London, Long, 1914.

*

Bibliography: *A Guide to the First Editions of Edgar Wallace* by Charles Kiddle, Motcombe, Dorset, Ivory Head Press, 1981.

Critical Studies: *Edgar Wallace—Each Way* by Robert G. Curtis, London, Long, 1932; *Edgar Wallace* by Ethel V. Wallace, London, Hutchinson, 1932; *Edgar Wallace: The Biography of a Phenomenon* by Margaret Lane, London, Heinemann, 1938, New York, Doubleday, 1939, revised edition London, Hamish Hamilton, 1964.

Theatrical Activities:
Director: **Plays**—*The Calendar,* Manchester and London, 1929; *Brothers* by Herbert Ashton, Jr., London, 1929. **Films**—*Red Aces,* 1929 *The Squeaker,* 1930.

*   *   *

Edgar Wallace is not a name which comes to mind as a writer

of science fiction. Were it not for the integral part which the fantastic plays in some of his plots they might be classed among his other thrillers. Even his stories of high adventure about Sanders of the River have skirmishes with the fantastic if witch doctors can be so classified. The difficulty in discussing Wallace's science fiction arises from its dual nature. The mystery critic's convention of not revealing the ending of the story has to be discarded in discussing Wallace. To explain what makes the science fiction is to give away the solutions to their mysteries.

Apart from the Sanders stories, Wallace's earliest use of a science-fiction theme is *1925: The Story of a Fatal Peace* which deals with the consequences for Britain if Germany is not totally beaten in World War I. During the Festival of Schleswig-Holstein in 1925 the Germans attempt to invade Britain in the very transport which had brought British veterans to the German Festival. An interesting device in the story is the submarine detector activated by the sound of propellers, invented by Sir John Venniman. The preface frankly proclaims the story's propangandistic purpose. *The Green Rust* involves a scheme by a German scientist to infest the rest of the world's grain crops with a bacteria, thus putting Germany in a position of power. A layman's view of science and of scientists dominated both *Planetoid 127* and *The Day of Uniting.* The second work recalls a traditional theme in early science fiction, the impending destruction of the world and the effect the knowledge of this has on the characters. The humorous view of science by the non-scientist is combined with the moral dilemma over whether to protect the population from panic by keeping the disaster a secret against the objective view of their need to know. The impending disaster itself is the explanation for the mysterious incidents in the first half of the story, but the conclusion may still come as a surprise to all but the most alert reader. The title refers to the officially proclaimed day for families to be reunited before the end of the world. Professor Colson's "sound strainer" in *Planetoid 127* by which he talks to his alter ego on the planet Vulcan is a thing of "instruments, of wires that spun across the room like the web of a spider, of strange machines which seemed to be endowed with perpetual motion. " Events on the other world often being in advance of those on earth, Colson is able to predict the future. This knowledge enables him to manipulate the stock market to his advantage until an unscrupulous gentleman kills him for his secret. The planet Vulcan is on the opposite side of the Sun from the Earth and thus the story has been called the earliest example of the "twin world" theme. It is obvious that the dominant theme in the story itself is the mis-use of scientific knowledge. *Captains of Souls* is a tour de force for Wallace. The transfer of the souls of the two men, Ambrose Sault and Robert Morelle, is an intriguing device which allows the author to explore his characters in depth and also results in a happy ending with retribution for all.

—J. Randolph Cox

WALLACE, F(loyd) L. American. Lives in California.

SCIENCE-FICTION PUBLICATIONS

Novel

Address: Centauri. New York, Gnome Press, 1955.

Uncollected Short Stories

"Hideaway," in *Astounding* (New York), February 1951.
"Student Body," in *Crossroads in Time*, edited by Groff Conklin. New York, Permabooks, 1953.
"Worlds in Balance," in *Science Fiction Plus* (Philadelphia), May 1953.
"The Music Master," in *Imagination* (Evanston, Illinois), November 1953.
"The Seasoned Traveler," in *Universe* (Evanston, Illinois), December 1953.
"Forget Me Nearly," in *Galaxy* (New York), June 1954.
"The Man Who Was Six," in *Galaxy* (New York), September 1954.
"Simple Psiman," in *Startlin* (New York), Fall 1954.
"The Impossible Voyage Home," in *Science Fiction Adventures in Mutation*, edited by Groff Conklin. New York, Vanguard Press, 1955.
"The Assistant Self," in *Fantastic Universe* (Chicago), March 1956.
"Little Thing for the House," in *Astounding* (New York), July 1956.
"The Nevada Virus," in *Venture* (Concord, New Hampshire), September 1957.
"End as a World," in *The Third Galaxy Reader*, edited by H. L. Gold. New York, Doubleday, 1958.
"Tangle Hold," in *5 Galaxy Short Novels*, edited by H. L. Gold. New York, Doubleday, 1958.
"Mezzerow Loves Company," in *World That Couldn't Be and 8 Other SF Novelets*, edited by H. L. Gold. New York, Doubleday, 1959.
"Delay in Transit," in *Bodyguard and 4 Other Short SF Novels from Galaxy*, edited by H. L. Gold. New York, Doubleday, 1960.
"Second Landing," in *Amazing* (New York), January 1960.
"Privates All," in *Fatasy and Science Fiction* (New York), September 1961.
"Accidental Flight," in *Time Waits for Winthrop and Four Other Short Novels*, edited by Frederick Pohl. New York, Doubleday, 1962.
"Bolden's Pets," in *Great Science Fiction about Doctors*, edited by Groff Conklin and Noah D. Fabricant. New York, Macmillan, 1963.
"Big Ancestor," in *Five-Odd*, edited by Groff Conklin. New York, Pyramid, 1964.
"Growing Season," in *Frozen Planet and 4 Other SF Novellas*. New York, Macfadden, 1966.
"The Deadly Ones," in *Flying Saucers*, edited by Isaac Asimov, Martin H. Greenberg, and Charles G. Waugh. New York, Fawcett, 1982.

OTHER PUBLICATIONS

Novels

Three Times a Victim. New York, Ace, 1957.
Wired for Scandal. New York, Ace, 1959.

*   *   *

Still a hazy figure in the history of science fiction, F. L. Wallace was one of the field's most outstanding and least appreciated writers during the 1950's. His only SF novel, *Address: Centauri*, is a minor work that was an expansion of his very good story "Accidental Flight" (*Galaxy*, 1952). Wallace's other SF stories are of high quality, characterized by a depth and a thoroughness uncommon to the field in the 1950's. Among his most noteworthy stories are "Delay in Transit"; "Big Ancestor," a powerful commentary on the human race and its future direction; "Student Body," which features one of the very best descriptions and development of an alien life form in all of science fiction; "Bolden's Pets," wherein Wallace brilliantly employs the unique concept of *positive* parasitism; "Mezzerow Loves Company"; "Tangle Hold"; and "The Impossible Voyage Home. "

—Martin H. Greenberg

———

WALLACE, Ian. Pseudonym for John Wallace Pritchard. American. Born in Chicago, Illinois, 4 December 1912. Educated at the University of Michigan, Ann Arbor, B. A. in English 1934, M. A. in educational psychology 1939, graduate study 1949-51; Wayne University, now Wayne State University, Detroit, education certificate 1936, Ed. D. 1957. Served as a clinical psychologist in the United States Army during World War II: Captain. Married Elizabeth Paul in 1938; two sons. Psychology Technician, Clinical Psychologist, Department Head, Administrative Assistant, Director, and Divisional Director, Board of Education, Detroit, 1934-74; now retired. Part-time lecturer in education, Wayne State University, 1955-74. Lives near Asheville, North Carolina. Address: c/o DAW Books, 1633 Broadway, New York, New York 10019, U.S.A.

SCIENCE-FICTION PUBLICATIONS

Novels (series: Croyd; St. Cyr and U. Tuli)

Croyd. New York, Putnam, 1967.
Dr. Orpheus (Croyd). New York, Putnam, 1968.
Deathstar Voyage (St. Cyr). New York, Putnam, 1969; London, Dobson, 1972.
The Purloined Prince (St. Cyr). New York, McCall, 1971.
Pan Sagittarius. New York, Putnam, 1973.
A Voyage to Dari (Croyd). New York, DAW, 1974.
The World Asunder. New York, DAW, 1976; London, Dobson, 1978.
The Sign of the Mute Medusa (St. Cyr). New York, Popular Library, 1977.
Z-Sting (Croyd). New York, DAW, 1978.
Heller's Leap. New York, DAW, 1979.
The Lucifer Comet. New York, DAW, 1980.
The Rape of the Sun. New York, DAW, 1982.

OTHER PUBLICATIONS as John Wallace Pritchard

Novel

Every Crazy Wind. New York, Dodd Mead, 1952.

Other

Frank Cody, A Realist in Education, with others. New York, Macmillan, 1943.
Off to Work, with Paul H. Voelker. Pittsburgh, Stanwix House, 1962.

Author-editor-publisher of numerous Detroit Board of Education textbooks and teaching guides, 1942-74.

*

Ian Wallace comments:

I aim my books at well-educated or self-educated minds. For them, I try to write pleasurable, frequently startling, coherently designed stories, taking advantage of fantasy to enlarge their scope, but disciplining the tales with logic and with scientific and philosophic theory. I try to portray humans living at the highest levels of their humanity, entailing many-sided intelligence, emotion intelligently guided and expressed, and human fellow-feeling for all the different kinds of humans (including some weird-bodied instances on other planets); that, for me, is both a moral issue and a taste preference.

* * *

Ian Wallace is a modern SF writer who, like many authors who developed during the 1960's, shows more concern for the "soft sciences" of psychology and history than for the "hard sciences" of physics and biology that preoccupied the SF milieu from the 1930's through the 1950's. Wallace's novels tend toward great complexity, a factor which proves an advantage in some works, and a detriment in others.

Wallace's most famous novels are his earliest—*Croyd* and *Dr. Orpheus*. These deal with the adventures of Croyd, a humanoid being possessed of great psychic powers, with special emphasis on the ability to move himself through time. The complexity of the subject matter is well balanced, especially in *Dr. Orpheus*, in which a madman attempts to subjugate humanity with a drug called Anagonon, which robs a subject of the inclination to question orders. Behind him, however, stands the additional threat of a race of arthropodal aliens, whose motive for disseminating the drug involves rendering humanity into a docile herd of mammalian food-sources in which to implant their eggs. Croyd must combat this threat by travelling through time to research the problem's beginnings, which necessitates a journey to ancient Greece at the time of Heraclitus, whose philosophy figures into the novel in a significant manner. Despite the apparent irrelevance of some plot-threads, Wallace draws them together in an engaging tour de force.

In later novels, however, the complexities come too thick and fast for the reader to catch his breath. *A Voyage to Dari* is an exceptionally diffuse novel in which a wide variety of plot complexities fail to gell, including:(1) a political situation between two planets roughly parallel to India and colonial Britain, (2) an alien marriage rite that requires three genetic donors to spawn a child, (3) Croyd losing his powers, and (4) a space-dwelling, brainlike organism that reproduces Earth-medieval imagery as its mental "universe" and favors feudalism over democracy. Another Croyd novel, *Z-Sting*, is little more than *Fail-Safe* with SF trappings, but this simpler structure is undermined by another Wallace weakness, a penchant for unrealistic, mechanically detached dialogue. When in *Z-Sting* a female character suggests to Croyd the possibility of their having a liaison, he responds that it is "not long-range probable." A non-Croyd novel, *The World Asunder*, also strains credulity in that its protagonists, who must grapple with a madman called Kali out either to control or to destroy Earth (the motives are never clear), are all incredibly well-versed in the psychology necessary to analyze the madman—so well-versed that they often seem to speaking in the same voice. Yet here and there Wallace voices some interesting, if didactic insights, as

when one character says, "I suppose you know that you must never totally reject your dark side; it is where you get your depth".

In some ways, Wallace is more successful dealing with less involved plots. More readable than the save-the-world opuses are the St. Cyr SF-detective genre-pieces, which include the novels *The Purloined Prince*, *The Sign of the Mute Medusa*, and *Deathstar Voyage*. *Deathstar Voyage*, with its colorful settings and rigorously pursued logic-problems, is probably the best of these, in which the policeman Claudine St. Cyr must identify a madman aboard a space-vessel by analyzing his psychic powers and psychological proclivities.

In recent years, Wallace's novels continue to show the same fluctuations of quality. *The Rape of the Sun*, all about aliens who steal Earth's solar system to make of it a present to their princess, is, like *The World Asunder*, heavy on talk and slim in motivations (at the end, when the alien leader is shamed by circumstances that prompt him to desert his mission, he curiously decides that he wants to go back to Earth in the body of one of the protagonists—an action which makes no sense in light of the alien's character, but certainly makes for an emotional finish.) However, *The Lucifer Comet*, also a late work, may well be his second-best work, after *Dr. Orpheus*. Taking his cue from the popular myth of the struggle of angels and devils for the soul of man, Wallace posits two superhuman aliens who both desire to bring into being a planetary race of humans who follow their respective philosophies. However, rather than "good" and "evil," Wallace's "Quarfar" and "Narfar" symbolize something closer to "progress" and "antiprogress." Quarfar is the Prometheus of the real world, who brought it into scientific development; Narfar is a nature-loving, Neanderthal-like savage who prefers the simple life. In addition to giving the reader an interesting view of what life on Earth might have become under the sway of Narfar, Wallace succeeds in making the character of the "devil" quite likeable—which proves tragically affecting when he is unintentionally betrayed by the Earth-woman he loves. There are still some questionable plot-devices in *Lucifer Comet*, but overall, it shows that Wallace's innate creativity is high, and that he only requires a substantial idea in which to develop that propensity.

—Gene Phillips

WALLIS, B. See **WALLIS, G. C.**

WALLIS, B. and G. C. See **WALLIS, G. C.**

WALLIS, G(eorge) C. Also wrote as B. Wallis; B. and G. C. Wallis. British. Partner in a printing firm, Sheffield, prior to World War II; after the war worked in cinema management; wrote comics as John Stanton.

SCIENCE-FICTION PUBLICATIONS

Novels

The Children of the Sphinx. London, Simpkin Marshall, 1924.
The Call of Peter Gaskell. Kingswood, Surrey, World's Work, 1948.

Uncollected Short Stories

"The Last King of Atlantis," in *Short Stories* (London), 1896-97.
"World Wreckers," in *Scraps*, 1908
'Wireless War," with A. J. Andrews, in *Comic Life*, 1909
"The Terror from the South," in *Comic Life*, 1909.
"The World at Bay" (as B. and G. C. Wallis), in *Amazing* (New York), November 1928.
"The Mother World" (as B. and G. C. Wallis), in *Amazing Stories Quarterly* (New York), Summer 1933.
"The Voyage of the Neutralia," in *Weird Tales* (Indianapolis), 1937.
"The Orbit Jumper," in *Tales of Wonder* (Kingswood, Surrey), Winter 1938
"Invaders from the Void," in *Fantasy 3* (London), 1939.
"Voyage of Sacrifice," in *Tales of Wonder* (Kingswood, Surrey), Spring 1939.
"Across the Abyss," in *Tales of Wonder* (Kingswood, Surrey), Summer 1939.
"The Crystal Menace," in *Tales of Wonder* (Kingswood, Surrey), Autumn 1939.
"Under the Dying Sun," in *Tales of Wonder* (Kingswood, Surrey), Summer 1940.
"The Red Spheres," in *Tales of Wonder* (Kingswood, Surrey), Spring 1941.
"The Cosmic Cloud," in *Tales of Wonder* (Kingswood, Surrey), Autumn 1941.
"The Power Supreme," in *Tales of Wonder* (Kingswood, Surrey), Winter 1941.
"From Time's Dawn" (as B. Wallis), in *Fantastic Novel* (New York), May 1950.
"The Great Sacrifice," in *Worlds Apart*, edited by George Locke. London, Cornmarket Reprints 1972.
"The Last Days of Earth," in *Science Fiction by the Rivals of H. G. Wells*, edited by Alan K. Russell. Secaucus, New Jersey, Castle 1979.

OTHER PUBLICATIONS

Novel

Taquita the Pearl. London, Stockwell, 1924.

*   *   *

The writing career of G. C. Wallis started at the turn of the last century, when the stories of Wells, Shiel, and Griffith were delighting the readers of the *Strand* and *Pearson's*. A list of his published tales, delicately printed by the Sheffield firm in which he was a partner, con- tains almost a hundred titles, including *The Children of the Sphinx*, a novel which the *Literary World* found "full of swing and interest." By then he had published half a dozen magazine serials, such as "The Last King of Atlantis" and "World Wreckers," and 40-odd short stories which appeared in a variety of publications from the *Penny Magazine* to *Tit-Bits*.

Only some of these tales were science fiction, which was often to be found in juvenile papers like the *Boy's Friend, Union Jack*, and *Lot-o'-Fun*. To such as these he contributed another 40-odd stories and serials, some under the name of John Stanton and a few in collaboration with a certain A. Anthony. Though most of his heroes were "Fighting the Spaniards," "In Peril in Persia," or "In the Grip of the Mafia," there were others who ventured to the "City at the South Pole," who voyaged "In Trackless Space," or joined in the "Wireless War."

Like several of his contemporaries who were the real pioneers of science fiction, Wallis played with ideas of cosmic proportions long before they became the stock-in-trade of the pulp magazines of a more advanced period. In "The Great Sacrifice" he anticipated writers like John Russell Fearn by destroying the outer planets (excepting Pluto, yet undiscovered) with the aid of the Martians, who finally exploded their own world so that Earth might escape the meteor stream invading the solar system. The notion that the Martians might not be the monsters that Wells made them was fairly well established among the writers who followed in the wake of Flammarion. Another early Wallis story, "The Last Days of Earth," shows all too obviously the influence of the French astronomer's *Omega: The Last Days of the World*.

In acknowledgment of a Canadian cousin's help in placing his manuscripts in America, many of Wallis's stories were by-lined B. & Geo. C. Wallis, Bruce & G. C. Wallis, or simply B. Wallis. He made several appearances in *Weird Tales*, where a four-part serial, "The Star Shell," typified the kind of science-fantasy with which the editor Farnsworth Wright sought to offset the competition of *Amazing Stories* when it appeared in 1926. Within two years the writer had made his bow in Hugo Gernsback's magazine with "The World at Bay," dealing with an invasion of the surface world by a subterranean race (a tale simple and exciting enough to be serialised also in London *Daily Herald*). Though just as simply told, with his usual touches of romantic interest, "The Mother World" contained some of Wallis's most thoughtful speculations upon the origin and destiny of the human species. An unlikely party of space-travellers is lured to a distant world whose godlike inhabit- ants have the power to expunge all life on other planets where they have planted their seed, should it fail to reach maturity—and man's fate is in the balance.

A pedestrian thriller, "The Voyage of the Neutralia," depicting lesser forms of life on Mars and Venus, marked his last appearance in *Weird Tales* in 1937. His sole contribution to the British *Fantasy*, "Invaders from the Void," was equally conventional; and when *Tales of Wonder* became established it featured several stories which, though fresh from his still brisk pen, mostly stemmed from ideas he had developed years earlier. His last novel, *The Call of Peter Gaskell*, concerned a mysterious Inca queen in a lost city in the Amazon jungle, and proved so close to Rider Haggard, yet so difficult to read, that a devastating critique in *Fantasy Review* was headed "She-Who-Must-Be-Avoided."

—Walter Gillings

———————

WALTERS, Hugh Pseudonym for Walter Llewellyn Hughes. British. Born in Bilston, Staffordshire, 15 June 1910. Educated at St. Martin's School; Bilston Central School; Dudley Grammar School, 1923-26; Wednesbury College, 1939-41; Wolverhampton Polytechnic, 1941-43. Married 1) Doris

Higgins in 1933, one son and one daughter; 2) Susan Hughes in 1977. Since 1954, Managing Director, Bransteds Ltd., engineers, and Chairman, Walter Hughes Ltd., furnishings. Justice of the Peace, 1947-74. Agent: John Farquharson Ltd., 8 Bell Yard, London WC2A 2JU. Address: 16 Elm Avenue, Bilston, West Midlands WV14 6AS, England.

SCIENCE-FICTION PUBLICATIONS

Novels (for children; series: Chris Godfrey in all books)

Blast off at Woomera. London, Faber, 1957; as *Blast-Off at 0300*, New York, Criterion, 1958.
The Domes of Pico. London, Faber, 1958; as *Menace from the Moon*, New York, Criterion, 1959.
Operation Columbus. London, Faber, 1960; as *First on the Moon*, New York, Criterion, 1961.
Moon Base One. London, Faber, 1961; as *Outpost on the Moon*, New York, Criterion, 1962.
Expedition Venus. London, Faber, 1962; New York, Criterion, 1963.
Destination Mars. London, Faber, 1963; New York, Criterion, 1964.
Terror by Satellite. London, Faber, and New York, Criterion, 1964.
Mission to Mercury. London, Faber, and New York, Criterion, 1965.
Journey to Jupiter. London, Faber, 1965; New York, Criterion, 1966.
Spaceship to Saturn. London, Faber, and New York, Criterion, 1967.
The Mohole Mystery. London, Faber, 1968; as *The Mohole Menace*, New York, Criterion, 1969.
Nearly Neptune. London, Faber, 1969; as *Neptune One Is Missing*, New York, Washburn, 1969.
First Contact? London, Faber, 1971; Nashville, Nelson, 1973.
Passage to Pluto. London, Faber, and Nashville, Nelson, 1973.
Tony Hale, Space Detective. London, Faber, 1973.
Murder on Mars. London, Faber, 1975.
Boy Astronaut. London, Abelard Schuman, 1977.
The Caves of Drach. London, Faber, 1977.
The Last Disaster. London, Faber, 1978.
The Blue Aura. London, Faber, 1979.
First Family on the Moon. London, Abelard Schuman, 1979.
The Dark Triangle. London, Faber, 1981.
School of the Moon. London, Abelard Schuman, 1981.

*

Hugh Walters comments:

All my books are for young people in the 9-11 and 11-16 age groups. I believe that books for this readership should 1) entertain, which is the primary object; 2) educate painlessly (astronomy, mathematics, geology, etc.); 3) inspire the young people of today to become the scientists and technicians of tomorrow.

*   *   *

Hugh Walters has devoted his entire writing career to children's SF, and the results have been mixed. At first, his novels were welcomed as filling a void in SF publishing, being praised as the way SF should be written for children. Gradually critical opinion shifted as Walter's fiction came to be seen as repetitive, formula-bound, and even carelessly written; and the attention it received from the review media in both SF and children's literature virtually ceased. In the face of critical neglect and sometimes even open scorn, the wonder is, then, that Walter's novels continue to be published and have retained popularity for as long as they have. Obviously, his publishers are satisfied that the young audience Walters writes for does read and enjoy his novels and, ignoring adult disapproval, even puts pressure upon librarians to keep his books in circulation and order new titles as they appear. This phenomeneon is readily understood once it is perceived that Walter's fiction is the result of his attempt to wed the formulas and expectations of boy's series books and SF. In other words, Walter's SF manifests both the strengths and weaknesses of children's series fiction writing.

On one hand, Walters's SF celebrates the exploits of youthful, dashing, and resourceful protagonists that boys chaffing under the dullness of their routine-filled lives enthusiastically identify with. In *Operation Columbus* Chris Godfrey, hero of Walters's SF, is the first person on the moon and he also magnanimously saves the life of his young Russian rival, Serge Smyslov, who had previously disabled Chris's space craft. Chris then pilots the Russian space ship safely to earth in spite of not being familiar with the controls. In *Terror by Satellite* Tony Hale, who appears in some of the Godfrey books, is the remaining link between earth and the Observatory, the space satellite taken over by its crazed commander, Hendriks, who threatens to destroy earth; through his skill in electronics Tony proves indispensable as Chris successfully retakes control of the Observatory. Of more than passing interest is that Walters is clearly a knowledgeable author of children's books, and is careful to balance Chris, the public-school boy born to privilege and noblesse oblige, with Tony, the son of lower-class shop-keeping parents. In this way, many different kinds of young readers may be able to identify with Walter's protagonists. Further, although he does emphasize action and the various dangers of space exploration— emphases obviously intended to capture the attention of young readers—Walters does not neglect space technology and weaponry. Described in detail, these are usually up-to-date or plausibly extrapolated so that youngsters looking for "nuts and bolts SF" are readily satisfied.

On the other hand, Walters's SF exhibits the weaknesses characteristic of most series fiction: conventional, two-dimensional characterization, repetitive and predictable plotting, and dull, pedestrian writing. As a result of these weaknesses, Walters has rightfully been denied major status. At the same time, however, it would be unfair to dismiss Walters as just another author of series SF, another Victor Appleton II or John Blaine. For, in view of his strenths it is clear that Walter's work is definitely a cut or two above typical series SF.

—Francis J. Molson

WANDREI, Donald. American. Born in 1908. Founding Editor, with August Derleth, Arkham House, 1939-42. Recipient: World Fantasy Life Achievement Award, 1984. Address: 1152 Portland Avenue, St. Paul, Minnesota 55104, U.S.A.

SCIENCE- FICTION PUBLICATIONS

Novel

The Web of Easter Island. Sauk City, Wisconsin, Arkham House, 1948; London, Consul, 1961.

Short Stories

The Eye and the Finger. Sauk City, Wisconsin, Arkham House, 1944.
Strange Harvest. Sauk City, Wisconsin, Arkham House, 1965.

OTHER PUBLICATIONS

Verse

Ecstasy and Other Poems. Athol, Massachusetts, Cook, 1928.
Dark Odyssey. St. Paul, Webb, 1931.
Poems for Midnight. Sauk City, Wisconsin, Arkham House, 1964.

Other

Editor, with August Derleth, *The Outsider and Others*, by H. P. Lovecraft. Sauk City, Wisconsin, Arkham House, 1939.
Editor, with August Derleth, *Beyond the Wall of Sleep*, by H. P. Lovecraft. Sauk City, Wisconsin, Arkham House, 1943.
Editor, with August Derleth, *Marginalia*, by H. P. Lovecraft. Sauk City, Wisconsin, Arkham House, 1944.
Editor, with August Derleth, *Selected Letters 1911-1924, 1925-1929, 1929-1931*, by H. P. Lovecraft. Sauk City, Wisconsin, Arkham House, 3 vols., 1965-71.

*   *   *

Donald Wandrei's short SF appeared in a variety of pulp, slick, and academic outlets from 1926 to 1953. Wandrei was a frequent contributor to *Weird Tales*, but most of his appearances there were SF, not fantasy; his novel, *The Web of Easter Island*, is SF despite its close connection to H. P. Lovecraft's Cthulhu Mythos. Throughout the body of Wandrei's work runs a fascination with science, scientists, and the scientific attitude. Despite their scientific form, however, the stories are almost invariably horror stories. Considered as such, many of them work very well indeed. An ill-conceived experiment may bloodily destroy the experimenter in front of his wife—or may release atomic bonds, allowing the Earth to slump into a formless mass. Aliens invade across space or dimensional boundaries, doing enormous, graphically described damage. Human warfare sets into motion events which destroy the universe, the Earth, or simply civilization. Natural processes bring the universe to a quiet end or sterilize all life on Earth.

The unity of the stories is deeper than the horrifying nature of the events alone: there is also the coldness with which the events are perpetrated. A well-written illustration of this tendency is "The Witch-Makers." An adventurer trying to escape with the jeweled idol he stole from an African tribe stumbles into the camp of a pair of scientists. They have chosen to camp in an uncivilized area so that no one will interfere with their experiments in mind-transfer among animals. They experiment on the unwilling adventurer until they kill him, feeling neither compassion nor dislike for their human guinea pig. The effect is chilling.

Regrettably, Wandrei had little scientific background, a factor which severely weakens some of his best-known stories and most of the minor ones. "Colossus" and "Colossus Eternal," in effect the two halves of a novella, have a truly cosmic conclusion, but they are riddled with—and indeed built upon—repeated misunderstandings of basic concepts such as the periodic table and the difference between mass and volume.

Likewise, the universe of "The Red Brain" is being choked with dust which glues all the stars to blackness, a notion, whatever its validity in 1927, which has not aged well but which is crucial to the plot.

However, when Wandrei wrote of characters and settings with which he was personally familiar, he consistently created stories of great reality and impact. The Upper Minnesota Farmer and his wife in "The Crystal Bullet" are tersely and ably described. They are bewildered by the object which falls in their woodlot; and while they react to the object, they do not halt the story to explain the event as Wandrei's scientists would have felt compelled to do. Similarly, the overworked reporter of "Infinity Zero" is wholly real. He is so wrapped up in the everyday horrors of war-time news-gathering that it is some time before he realizes that he has witnessed the beginning of the process which will end the world in a few weeks.

The Web of Easter Island adds a level of compassion and, perhaps, hope to the horror it shares with the shorter fiction. A statuette turns up in a British cemetary amid buried structures built in the prehuman past. The statuette proceeds westward from one doomed carrier to another. It is studied and finally pursued by an archeologist who realizes that it is only a portion of a living being which will open our dimension to its own and the creatures thereof—unless stopped. The confrontation on Easter Island is not a final confrontation: there can be no final victory over such an opponent. But Mankind has found a champion, and at whatever cost to that individual there will be someone to protect the Earth beyond the foreseeable future.

The bulk of Wandrei's work is flawed, but there is some merit in the worst of it. At his best, Wandrei wrote fiction that was the equal of anything of its type.

—David A. Drake

WATER, Silas. See LOOMIS, Noel M.

WATERLOO, Stanley. American. Born in St. Clair County, Michigan, 21 May 1846. Educated at the University of Michigan, Ann Arbor, A. B. 1869. Married Anna C. Kitten in 1874. Journalist and editor: reporter in Chicago, 1870-71; co-owner, St. Louis *Journal*, 1872; editor, St. Louis *Republic Chronicle* and *Globe-Democrat* ; founded St. Paul *Day* ; writer, Chicago *Tribune* ; editor in chief, Chicago *Mail* ; editor, Washington *Critic and Capitol*. A. M. : University of Michigan, 1898. *Died 11 October 1913.*

SCIENCE- FICTION PUBLICATIONS

Novels

The Story of Ab: A Tale in the Time of the Cave Men. Chicago, Way and Williams, 1897.
Armageddon. Chicago, Rand McNally, 1898.
A Son of the Ages. New York, Doubleday, and London, Curtis Brown, 1914.

Short Stories

The Wolf's Long Howl. Chicago, Stone, 1899.

OTHER PUBLICATIONS

Novels

A Man and a Woman. Chicago, Schulte, 1892; London, Redway, 1896.
An Odd Situation. Chicago, Morrill Higgins, 1893; London, Black, 1896.
The Launching of a Man. Chicago, Rand McNally, 1899.
The Seekers. Chicago, Stone, 1900.
The Cassowary. Chicago, Monarch, 1906.

Other

How It Looks. New York, Brenmtano's 1888.
Honest Money. Chicago, Equitable, 1895.
These Are My Jewels (for children). Chicago, Coolidge and Waterloo, 1902.

Editor, with John Wesley Hanson Jr., *Famous American Men and Women.* Chicago, Wabash, 1896; as *Eminent Sons and Daughters of Columbia*, Chicago, International, 1896; as *Our Living Leaders*, Chicago, Monarch, 1896.
Editor, *The Parties and the Men; or, Political Issues of 1896.* Chicago, Conkey, 1896.
Editor, *The Story of a Strange Career.* New York, Appleton, 1902.

* * *

In discussing Stanley Waterloo's novels it is necessary to differentiate between the conception and the execution of the works. *The Story of Ab* is an early realistic novel of prehistoric man. Jack London admitted plagiarizing it for his *Before Adam*, and Waterloo's novel predated even H. G. Wells's spendid "A Story of the Stone Age" by some months. (Lang's still earlier "The Romance of the First Radical" differs from both works in being based in anthropology, not archeology, and being primarily a vehicle for social comment.) Similarly, *Armageddon* was probably the first of the fictional attempts to presage World War I with its weaponry and fabric of alliances. Writers as fine as Wells and Shiel (and many of lesser note) again followed in Waterloo's footsteps. On the other hand, Waterloo's execution (with a few brief exceptions) ranged from poor to worse. Both these novels as well as mainstream novels by Waterloo show signs of hasty construction and a basic lack of writing talent.

The Story of Ab is a serious attempt at the biography of a Stone Age (perhaps Neanderthal) man, told through significant incidents. Ab does many of the things that prehistoric heroes have done in more recent fiction: he hunts mammoths, domesticates dogs, slays a sabre-toothed tiger, invents the bow, and wages the first war. He does *not* tame fire. Waterloo claims to have based his novel on the best contemporary scientific opinion. Fire had been used by men long before the rise of Ab's subspecies, and Waterloo refused to take artistic license with scientific fact. While our knowledge of prehistory has greatly increased in the years since the book was published, Waterloo's obvious care keeps the novel from being badly dated. Indeed, Waterloo's picture of the Clam People combing tide flats for food and scuttling deeper in the water when danger threatens anticipates that drawn by Elaine Morgan in her 1972 treatise

The Descent of Woman. However, the incidents of Ab's life are only incidents. Some of them are spun into short skeins, but there is no connected purpose controlling the action of the novel. In general, chapters stand or fall on their own merits. There is little preparation for later events and almost no character development.

Armageddon is also rich in exciting material: the creation of the first airship, the building of a sea-level canal through Nicaragua, the greatest sea battle of all time, and, for that matter, a romance between parties of widely differing social positions. Waterloo's failure to make any of this material interesting results from a combination of flaws. First, there are not realized characters. Second, matters of large moment are trivialized by their handling. For instance, the novel's description of the international political situation descends beneath the level of national stereotype to the anthropomorphization of nations *as* national steretypes. Third, the gritty details which could create the illusion of reality in a fictional world are absent. From the evidence of the novel, Waterloo simply did not know enough about the gadgetry of the present to be able to describe realistically the gadgetry of his future.

In sum, Waterloo was imaginative and was capable of good research. His writing, however, was generally pedestrian and invariably hasty. *The Story of Ab* remains readable, especially for younger people; *Armageddon* is at most of historical interest.

—David A. Drake

———

WATKINS, William Jon. American. Born in Coaldale, Pennsylvania, 19 July 1942. Educated at Neshaminy High School, Langehorne, Pennsylvania; Rutgers University, New Brunswick, New Jersey, B. S. 1964, M. Ed. 1965. Married Sandra Lee Preno in 1961; three children. Instructor, Delaware Valley College, Doyleston, Pennsylvania, 1965-68; high school teacher, Asbury Park, New Jersey, 1968-69. Instructor, 1969-70, Assistant Professor, 1970-71, and since 1971, Associate Professor of Humanities, Brookdale Community College, Lincroft, New Jersey. Recipient: Per Se Award, for play, 1970. Agent: Collier Associates, 875 Avenue of the Americas, New York, New York 10001. Address: 1406 Garven Avenue, Ocean, New Jersey 07712, U.S.A.

SCIENCE-FICTION PUBLICATIONS

Novels

Ecodeath, with Gene Snyder. New York, Doubleday, 1972.
Clickwhistle. New York, Doubleday, 1973.
The God Machine. New York, Doubleday, and London, Angus and Robertson, 1973.
The Litany of Sh'reev, with Gene Snyder. New York, Doubleday, 1976.
What Rough Beast. Chicago, Playboy Press, 1980.
Centrifugal Rickshaw Dancer. New York, Warner, 1985.

Uncollected Short Stories

"Ten Micro Novels," in *Vertex* (Los Angeles), December 1974.
"The Last Ten Micro Novels," in *Vertex* (Los Angeles), August 1975.
"Like Sno-Humped Fields Afraid of Rain," in *2076: The*

American Tricentennial, edited by Edward Bryant. New York, Pyramid, 1977.
"Untitled," in *New Worlds 10*, edited by Hilary Bailey. London, Corgi, 1977.
"Coming of Age in Henson's Tube," in *Asimov's Choice: Black Holes and Bug-Eyed Monsters*, edited by George H. Scithers. New York, Davis, 1977.
"Butcher's Thumb," in *Shadows*, edited by Charles L. Grant. New York, Doubleday, 1978.
"The People's Choice," in *Space Mail 2*, edited by Isaac Asimov, Martin H. Greenberg, and Charles G. Waugh. New York, Fawcett, 1982.
"Bear Smacking," in *Landmarks*. Chicago, Scott Foresman, 1983.
"Rites of Passage," in *Pulpsmith* (New York), August 1984.
"The Recent Unpleasantness with the Post Awful," in *Twilight Zone* (New York), 1985.

OTHER PUBLICATIONS

Plays

The Judas Wheel (produced Warrensburg, Missouri, 1970). New York, Smith, 1969.
A Kind of a Hole. Elgin, Illinois, Performance, 1974.

Verse

Five Poems. Chula Vista, California, Word Press, 1968.

Other

A Fair Advantage (for children). Englewood Cliffs, New Jersey, Prentice Hall, 1975.
Tracker, with Tom Brown, Jr. Englewood Cliffs, New Jersey, Prentice Hall, 1978.
The Psychic Experiment Book. Englewood Cliffs, New Jersey, Prentice Hall, 1980.
The Psychic Diet Book. Asbury Park, New Jersey, Grappling Press, 1980.
Suburban Wilderness. New York, Putnam, 1981.
Who's Who in New Jersey Wrestling. Asbury Park, New Jersey, Grappling Press, 1981.

*   *   *

William Jon Watkins's novels, two of which were written with Gene Snyder, show man as a corrupt evil-doer who creates his own doomsday crises in which he barely avoids the total extinction of human life on Earth.

In *Ecodeath* Earth is about to die from water pollution. Two characters, Watkins and Snyder, start out as opponents but soon pool forces in order to rescue mankind. They use teleportation and finally link their mindpower to transport a small group of survivors to a pollution-free parallel earth of the future by telekinesis. Mankind survives because Watkins realizes that time implies parallel worlds existing simultaneously in infinity.

In *Clickwhistle* extraterrestrial beings take possession of the minds of killer whales to send computerized commands to atomic missiles stored in submarines. Dr. Pearson, a dolphin authority, defeats the aliens with the help of dolphins but other human beings are either evil-doers or slaves of dark political powers. Intrigue and betrayal run rampant while Orcas and dolphins battle. Earth is saved when dolphins triumph but men will forever live in fear of political bosses.

The God Machine shows perpetual and total warfare between a totalitarian worldwide state machine of Orwell's *Nineteen Eighty-Four* type and a highly technological underground opponent. Sophisticated weapons and tactics improve with the need to accelerate extermination. A reduction machine, the "micronizer," is central to several plot twists. Ecological negligence is the trademark of the status quo. An unbreathable atmosphere makes the use of masks and air filters universal. Neither side is a definite winner in the end.

In *The Litany of Sh'reev* Sh'reev uses mental powers to heal and save lives while a chronic state of revolutionary wars wrecks civilization. Empire is run by the will of an absolute and totalitarian ruler who destroys extant royal families to seize their wealth. The revolutionaries are ESPers who reject the increase of oppression. Sh'reev gets his spiritual power from Tao techniques. His mind fuses with those of the sick and dying in a state called Sh'aela. Eternal Return in its Eastern version provides further existences for Sh'reev.

The central action of *What Rough Beast* is the hunt for one huge, extraterrestrial, telekinetic, furry humanoid female who lands on Earth in order to help humans acquire her talents. Corporation mentality as the villainous hunter is aided by an almost sentient computer, Slic 1000, and his offspring Tad. There is an ironical twist when corporational man, dominated by a rigid mentality, becomes a dehumanized animal backbiting other corporate members in the struggle for power and rewards while the computers become humanized. The hero and savior is Lth, the alien furry female whose telepathic abilities merge with Tad in order to confer superhuman status upon man. Mankind is saved when sentient microcomputers become an implanted standard stabilizing device in human brains.

Although Watkins's novels are simply constructed and appropriate for juvenile audiences they deal with the vital issue of man's chances of survival. In each instance, man brings a catastrophic end upon himself and an environment he can neither preserve nor duplicate, and avoids self-annihilation by the slightest margin. Watkins implies that mankind, part angel but mostly beast, is on a cyclical course and will probably repeat its past mistakes. In *What Rough Beast*, Watkins introduces two new solutions to the "scorpion syndrome," man against himself. One is Lth's Superwoman mentality; the other is brain microcomputer implantation. In both cases, Watkins suggests that man can not be his own master.

—Eric A. Fontaine

WATSON, Ian. British. Born in North Shields, Northumberland, 20 April 1943. Educated at Tynemouth School, 1948-59; Balliol College, Oxford, 1960-65, B. A. (honours) in English 1963, B. Litt. 1965, M. A. 1966. Married Judith Jackson in 1962; one daughter. Lecturer, University College, Dar es Salaam, Tanzania, 1965-67, and Tokyo University of Education, 1967-70; Lecturer, 1970-75, and Senior Lecturer in Complementary Studies, 1975-76, Birmingham Polytechnic Art and Design Centre; Writer-in-Residence, Nene College, Northampton, 1984. Since 1975, features editor and regular contributor, *Foundation*, London; since 1983, European Editor, *Science Fiction Writers of America Bulletin*. Recipient: Prix Apollo (France), 1975; Orbit Award, 1976; British Science Fiction Association Award, 1978; Southern Arts Association bursary, 1978. Address: Bay House, Banbury Road, Moreton Pinkney, near Daventry, Northamptonshire, England.

SCIENCE-FICTION PUBLICATIONS

Novels

The Embedding. London, Gollancz, 1973; New York, Scribner, 1975.
The Jonah Kit. London, Gollancz, 1975; New York, Scribner, 1976.
The Martian Inca. London, Gollancz, and New York, Scribner, 1977.
Alien Embassy. London, Gollancz, 1977; New York, Ace, 1978.
Miracle Visitors. London, Gollancz, and New York, Ace, 1978.
The Gardens of Delight. London, Gollancz, 1980; New York, Pocket Books, 1982.
Under Heaven's Bridge, with Michael Bishop. London, Gollancz, 1981; New York, Ace, 1982.
Deathhunter. London, Gollancz, 1981.
Chekhov's Journey. London, Gollancz, 1983.
Converts. London, Granada, 1984; New York, St. Martin's Press, 1985.
Trilogy (Yaleen):
  The Book of the River. London, Gollancz, 1984.
  The Book of the Stars. London, Gollancz, 1985.
  The Book of Being. London, Gollancz, 1985.

Short Stories

God's World. London, Gollancz, 1979.
The Very Slow Time Machine. London, Gollancz, and New York, Ace, 1979.
Sunstroke and Other Stories. London, Gollancz, 1982.
Slow Birds and Other Stories. London, Gollancz, 1985.

Uncollected Short Stories

"Roof Garden under Saturn," in *New Worlds 195* (London), 1969.
"The Sex Machine," in *New Worlds 199* (London), 1970.
"The Tarot Pack Megadeath," in *New Worlds 200* (London), 1970.
"EA 5000: Report on the Effects of a Riot Gas," in *Stopwatch*, edited by George Hay. London, New English Library, 1974.
"The Ghosts of Luna," in *New Worlds 7*, edited by Charles Platt and Hilary Bailey. London, Sphere, 1974; as *New Worlds 6*, New York, Avon, 1975.
"The False Braille Catalogue," in *Ad Astra 4*, 1979.
"The Big Buy," in *Ad Astra 12*, 1980.
"A Cage for Death," in *The Best of Omni Science Fiction 6*, edited by Don Myrus. New York, Omni, 1981.
"The Ultimate One-Word First Contact Story," in *Alien Encounters*, edited by Jan Howard Finder. New York, Taplinger, 1982.
"Of Ground, and Ocean, and Sky," in *Science Fiction Review 47*, 1983.
"Showdown on Showdown," in *Isaac Asimov's Science Fiction Magazine* (New York), September 1983.
"The Dome of Whispers," in *Imagine*, Setpember 1983.
"We Remember Babylon," in *Habitats*, edited by Susan Shwartz. New York, Ace, 1984.
"Letters from the Monkey Alphabet," in *Last Wave 2*, (New York), Winter 1984.
"Samathiel's Summons," in *Fantasy Book* (Pasadena, California), December 1984.
"On the Dream Channel Panel," in *Amazing* (New York), March 1985.

OTHER PUBLICATIONS

Other

Japan: A Cat's Eye View (for children). Osaka, Bunken, 1969.
"SF Idea Capsules for Art Students," in *Foundation 5* (London), January 1974.
"Le Guin's *Lathe of Heaven* and the Role of Dick: The False Reality as Mediator," in *Science-Fiction Studies* (Terre Haute, Indiana), March 1975.
"The Forest as Metaphor for Mind," in *Science-Fiction Studies* (Terre Haute, Indiana), November 1975.
"Towards an Alien Linguistics," in *Vector 71* (Reading), 1975.
"The Greening of Ballard," in *J. G. Ballard: The First Twenty Years*, edited by James Goddard and David Pringle. Hayes, Middlesex, Bran's Head, 1976.
"Science Fiction: Form Versus Content" and "Fancy Going to the Vats?," in *Foundation 10* (London), June 1976.
"W(h)ither Science Fiction?," in *Vector 78* (Reading), 1976.
Japan Tomorrow (for children). Osaka, Bunken, 1977.
"The Crudities of Science Fiction," in *Arena* (Canterbury), March 1978.
"Some Sufist Insights into the Nature of Inexplicable Events," in *SFWA Bulletin* (Sea Cliff, New York), 1979.
"A Rhetoric of Recognition: The Science Fiction of Michael Bishop," in *Foundation 19* (London), 1980.
"UFOs, Science, and the Inexplicable," in *Arena 11* (Canterbury), 1980.

Editor, *Pictures at an Exhibition: A Science Fiction Anthology*. Cardiff, Greystoke Mobray, 1981.
Editor, with Michael Bishop, *Changes*. New York, Ace, 1982.

*

Manuscript Collection: Science Fiction Foundation, North-East London Polytechnic.

Ian Watson comments:
My books are all primarily about the relationship between reality and consciousness (testing out this theme variously by way of linguistics, speculation about cetacean intelligence, evolution, novel life forms, the UFO mythos, etc.) and whether any kind of ultimate understanding of the nature of reality and the reason for life and the universe may or may not be arrived at. Intersecting this is frequently—particularly in my earlier books—a strong socio-political underpinning to events. A dialectic of history and transcendence is at work. I regard my fiction as a research programme, in fictional form, into the nature of existence and the nature of knowledge.

* * *

"SF is founded upon the exploration of ideas, rather than stylistics. It is a community of ideas; in its sum, it composes what one might call an 'idea-myth,' the idea-myth of man in the universe," Ian Watson wrote in "The Crudities of Science Fiction." That Watson should define science fiction in terms of its speculative content, with particular emphasis on myth and ontology, provides a telling gloss on both the form and the substance of his novels and stories. A former academic whose work displays not only a serious metaphysical bent but also an engaging internationalism in his choice of settings and characters, Ian Watson vaulted to prominence with the publication of *The Embedding*. Few novel-length debuts are so dazzling, either for their structural brilliance or for the multifaceted complexity of their intellectual speculations, and reviewers responded with laudatory comparisons to the works of Arthur C. Clarke and Stanislaw Lem. Later J. G. Ballard emphatically styled Ian Watson "the most interesting British SF writer of ideas—or, more accurately, the *only* British SF writer of ideas" (*New Statesman*). Christopher Priest, likewise commenting on Watson's talent for launching cerebral flights of fancy within the expansive parameters of science fiction, has described his novels as having "a Wagnerian quality to them, with immense clashings of intellectual bravura and cosmic event" (Introduction to *Anticipations*, 1978).

One idea exploited in different guises or subtle variations from novel to novel is Watson's strategically held "belief" that consensus reality, or the world of everyday experience, is ripe for transcendence. The means of transcending our human limitations or the prison of the physical universe may differ from one fictional foray to the next, but the fact that there does exist a transcendent mental set or cosmic continuum to which we may or should aspire remains a conspicuous constant. Although Watson usually embeds this idea in a scrupulously rational context (often it is a research project or a scientific mission), a strong element of the primordial or the mystical (from meta-linguitics to Sufism) lends his several restatements of the concept a rich and endlessly ramifying ambiguity. Indeed, Watson is especially adept at legitimizing the paranormal with the argot of technological discourse. Good examples of this technique include not only the recent stories "The Very Slow Time Machine" and "The Rooms of Paradise," but the mind-bogglingly open-ended novel *Miracle Visitors*, whose concluding sentence, rendered almost after the fashion of a haiku or a koan, points directly to the metaphysical beyond with which Watson is so obsessed: "Somewhere else,/Khidr smiled."

The structural complexity of Watson's work, as a matter of fact, almost certainly stems from his preoccupation with ideas. In *The Embedding*, for instance, the agency for arriving at the freedom and omnipotence of "Other-Reality" is a language, a distilled grammar of perception permitting its speakers to encompass "This-Reality" physco-biologically and so to transcend it. Language, then, is the unifying element of the complicated, threefold plot. First, in an English hospital a group of Pakistani orphans are learning artificial languages as "probes at the frontiers of mind. " Second, a French anthropologist in the Amazon is studying a tribe of Indians whose use of a local drug enables them to alter their day-to-day language into an otherwise incomprehensible embedded language of transcedent perception and control. Finally, an alien race called the Sp'thra, whose name means "Signal Traders," arrive on Earth and as part of their ongoing "Language inventory" of the galaxy ask for six living human brains programmed with six different terrestrial grammars. By this inventory the Sp'thra hope to excape "This-Reality" for the ineffable "Other-Reality" now inhabited by a transcendent alien species called the "Change Speakers. " Watson's ending, however, is both apocalyptic and enigmatic.

His next two novels follow a somewhat similar pattern. In *The Jonah Kit* escape from this illusory universe lies within the grasp only of the world's whales. By forming a "Thought Star"—a cetacean computer whose living components reach out with their minds to an alternate continuum—and by later committing mass suicide, these self-aware sea breasts abstract themselves from the homocentric madnesses of man. In *The Martian Inca*, on the other hand, transcendence derives from a viral activator in the soil of Mars. This mysterious catalyst triggers a

dormant genetic program in our DNA for releasing the superhuman in every adult representative of the species—but humanity, in the person of a bourgeois American astronaut, resists the transformation and the novel ends on a decidedly downbeat note. Although as complex and inventive as *The Embedding*, these books cast a dark and somewhat fatalistic spell. (*The Martian Inca*, incidentally, contains the seminal idea for Watson's story "The Very Slow Time Machine. ")

Between *The Martian Inca* and *Alien Embassy* an interesting change apparently took place in Watson's thinking. His fourth novel—besides boasting his most appealing protagonist, Lila Makindi, who also narrates her own story—is noteworthy for framing the moral dilemma of a young African woman who sees the conscious formulation of humanity's next evolutionary step as a betrayal of the species *as it exists at present*. Watson cannily dramatizes the poignancy of Lila's dilemma even as he establishes forceful arguments for the necessity of society's taking the step that so appalls her. Although beyond is better, getting there may entail fearful hardships and the cruelty of institutionalized deceit. A departure from as well as a recognizable sequel to his previous work, *Alien Embassy* shows Watson opting for a hard-nosed humanistic compassion for his characters. For just that reason, it may be his most moving novel to date

Miracle Visitors, perhaps an even more structurally complex novel than *The Embedding*, partakes of this same auctorial generosity and openmindedness. Here Watson's presiding metaphor for transcendence is the phenomenon of the UFO experience, which, because it manifests itself to different characters in different ways, establishes at least three separate subjective "realities" within the novel's conceptual framework. Imagine a Philip K. Dick novel sustained by undiluted intellectual rigor, and you have some idea of the tone and the narrative effects of *Miracle Visitors*. Its most striking bravura passage details a trip to the moon in a Ford Thunderbird. Although an intrinsically wacky, if not downright duncish, concept, Watson handles it with admirable pokerfaced dexterity—just as he does the psychological portraiture of his principal characters, even if the major part of his own sympathy seems to lie with the consciousness research, John Deacon. The book's final lines, "Somewhere else, / Khidr smiled," are therefore a kind of password phrase hinting at both the reality and the benevolence of Watson's hoped-for beyond. They also provide a clue to his own aesthetic orientation to the problem of demonstrable human limitations; the desire to know what some have labeled unknowable, Watson implies, is precisely what makes us human.

The Very Slow Time Machine, although lacking the eerily brilliant story "The Rooms of Paradise," contains a full-course feast of Watson's short fiction—from the title story to the early and nightmarish "Thy Blood Like Milk" to the playful and admonitory "Programmed Love Story" to the concluding complex mini-novel "The Event Horizon. " In addition, Watson has written *God's World*, which he describes as "a kind of companion novel to *Miracle Visitors*," although neither a sequel nor a blatant parallel, and *The Gardens of Delight*, in which Watson creates a world based on the famous triptych by Hieronymus Bosch.

A fascinating *intermezzo* in Watson's career is *Under Heaven's Bridge*, co-authored with Michael Bishop without the two writers ever having met. That Watson is hardly a typical British SF writer—an "odd duck" according to Cy Chauvin in *Foundation*, "the most madcap, daring major figure" writes Gregory Benford in the same journal—is pointed up by this transatlantic co-creation which seamlessly fuses preoccupations (numinous, human, and exotic) common to both Bishop and Watson. British authors typically also write at least one disaster novel; but Watson has not done so.

His next novel *Deathhunter* took as theme a peaceful, apparently utopian near-future society founded upon euthanasia and the denial of an afterlife; but all is not quite as it seems. *Locus* hailed *Deathhunter* as "a watershed, bringing a new lightness to his metaphsical concerns"—humor, irony, sprightliness of touch. These new elements—broadening Watson's scope and writerly repertoire—were even more evident in his next novel, *Chekhov's Journey*, concerning a scheme hatched up by a Soviet film unit to improve the performance of their lead actor (an Anton Chekhov look-alike) by means of "reincarnation by hypnosis," a scheme which goes awry in a delightful counterpointing of time present, timeship future, and the past where Chekhov's genuine historic journey across Siberia mutates into an investigation by him of the Tunguska explosion. As well as being a loving, convincing reconstruction of 19th-century Russia, the novel combines "comedy and thought-provoking inventiveness with a sophistication rare in SF" (*Locus*). American readers, alas, were to be deprived of their own editions of these two richly rewarding breakthrough novels due to the lack of perspicacity of U.S. editors.

The comic tendency climaxed in Watson's next novel, *Converts*, a fantastic slapstick tale about the pitfalls and pratfalls of taking evolution into one's own hands with a viral DNA drug which enables people to become the creatures of their own secret dreams. A witty homage to Ovid's Metamorphoses, Converts is also deeply satirical of the new fndamentalist "born-again" Christianity, showing how Watson remains an astute political and social commentator even while at his most outrageously, and hilariously, fantastic.

In the meantime Watson's second story collection, *Sunstroke*, appeared, confirming his position as one of the more prolific of short-fiction writers—as well as one with the most varied of tone, from the dark irony of "Nightmares," through the politically committed satire of "Returning Home," to the parodic comedy of "The Call of the Wild: The Dog-Flea Version" and the haunting, adventurous metaphysical domain of "The Milk of Knowledge."

Next, to the surprise of some readers, but to the pleasure of others who had seen the signposts of the new "light touch," Watson wrote an exotic adventure trilogy set on a distant world: *The Book of the River, The Book of the Stars*, and *The Book of Being*. Metaphysical concerns are still present, but even more noteworthy are the exuberance and informality of style, the vivid characterizatio and the memorable inventiveness of Watson's world divided by a great river, on one side of which a repressive male-dominated society rules, while on the other side is a female-led river-faring civilization—and in the midst, preventing intercourse between the two, a giant enigmatic alien creature, whose nature is gradually revealed. The first-person heroine of all three volumes is riverwoman Yaleen; and it's worth remarking how many of Watson's books have had heroines rather than heroes: *Alien Embassy, God's World*, and now the Yaleen cycle of novels told in her own lively irreverent voice. Few male SF authors have so frequently, so successfully, or so naturally developed female characters as their principals.

In the time since his *Sunstroke* collection Watson has already published enough short fiction, mainly in American magazines and anthologies, to fill at least two more collections. A whole range of voices is present in these: the playful ("Ghost Lecturer," a tale about the world-view of Roman philosopher Lucretius), the comic ("On the Dream Channel Panel"), the

parodic ("The Bloomsday Revolution"), the political ("Cruising": Watson is a convinced nuclear disarmer), the horrific ("The Flesh of Her Hair" and "White Socks"), the wittily fantastic as in "In the Mirror of the Earth," the emotionally moving (the Nebula- and Hugo-nominated "Slow Birds"), the satiric, and the experimental.

Just over forty, Watson has already produced a formidable *oeuvre*. The breadth of his intellectual interests, along with the nimbleness of his imagination and his wholehearted commitment to the possibilities of the field, ensures that no attempt to assess either the direction or the quality of 20th-Century science fiction can ignore his remarkable contribution.

—Jeffrey M. Elliot and Michael Bishop

WEBB, Sharon. American. Born in Tampa, Florida, 29 February 1936. Attended Tampa public schools; Florida Southern College, Lakeland, 1953-56; Miami-Dade College School of Nursing, 1970-72. Married Bryan Webb in 1956; three children. Free-lance writer, 1959-65; Registered Nurse, Baptist Hospital, Miami, 1972-73, and in Blairsville, Georgia, 1973-81. Since 1979, free-lance writer. Agent: Adele Leone Agency, 26 Nantucket Place, Scarsdale, New York 10583. Address: Route 2, Box 2600, Blairsville, Georgia 30512, U.S.A.

SCIENCE-FICTION PUBLICATIONS

Novels (series: Kurt Kraus in all books except *The Adventures of Terra Tarkington*)

Earthchild. New York, Atheneum, 1982.
Earth Song. New York, Atheneum, 1983.
Ram Song. New York, Atheneum, 1984.
The Adventures of Terra Tarkington. New York, Bantam, 1985.

Uncollected Short Stories

"Hitch on the Bull Run," in *Isaac Asimov's Science Fiction Magazine* (New York), June 1979.
"Sharing Time in the Gallery," in *Isaac Asimov's Science Fiction Magazine* (New York), November 1979.
"Miss Nottworthy and the Aliens," in *Other Worlds*, edited by Roy Torgeson. New York, Zebra, 1979.
"Itch on the Bull Run," in *Space Mail 1*, edited by Isaac Asimov, Martin H. Greenberg, and Joseph D. Olander. New York, Fawcett, 1980.
"The Cathedral in Dying Time," in *Chrysalis 8*, edited by Roy Torgeson. New York, Doubleday, 1980.
"Transference," in *Isaac Asimov's Science Fiction Magazine* (New York), July 1980.
"Rare Bird," in *Isaac Asimov's Science Fiction Magazine* (New York), September 1980.
"Variation on a Theme from Beethoven," in *1981 Annual World's Best SF*, edited by Donald A. Wollheim. New York, DAW, 1981.
"The Dust of Creeds Outworn," in *Isaac Asimov's Science Fiction Magazine* (New York), February 1981.
"Sand," in *Isaac Asimov's Science Fiction Magazine* (New York), March 1981.
"Twitch on the Bull Run," in *Isaac Asimov's Science Fiction Magazine* (New York), April 1981.

"Bridges," in *Isaac Asimov's Science Fiction Magazine* (New York), May 1981.

"Bitch on the Bull Run," in *Isaac Asimov's Science Fiction Magazine* (New York), June 1981.

"Reliquary for an Old Soul," in *Isaac Asimov's Science Fiction Magazine* (New York), September 1981.

"Our Man in Vulnerable," in *Isaac Asimov's Science Fiction Magazine* (New York), October 1981.

"Niche on the Bull Run," and "Switch on the Bull Run," in *Space Mail 2*, edited by Isaac Asimov, Martin H. Greenberg, and Charles G. Waugh. New York, Fawcett, 1982.

"Slow Virus," in *Parsec* (Russellville, Alabama), June 1982.

"Threshold," in *Amazing* (New York), November 1982.

"The Syncopated Man," in *Amazing* (New York), March 1983.

"Shadows from a Small Template," in *Isaac Asimov's Space of Her Own*, edited by Shawna McCarthy. New York, Davis, 1983; London, Hale, 1984.

"With Gl-oon'sha, Dreams Come," in *Amazing* (New York), January 1984.

"Misplaced Friends," in *Softalk* (North Hollywood, California), February and March 1984.

"A Demon in Rosewood," in *Shadows 8*, edited by Charles L. Grant. New York, Doubleday, 1985.

OTHER PUBLICATIONS

Other

R. N. New York, Zebra, 1982.

*

Manuscript Collection: University of Georgia, Athens.

Sharon Webb comments:

The sciences I studied in nursing school gave me the confidence to write something that I had loved since childhood: science fiction. Thirty stories and three sf books later, I can look back and see that this "tool" of science, while useful to the genre, is not essential to the writing of it. The real tool of sf is the use of metaphor to describe the human condition, and it is this, I believe, that explains the seductiveness of science fiction for the reader.

*   *   *

Sharon Webb has only been writing for the last few years, but she has been impressive. Following a non-fiction book about nursing school and the humorous Terra Tarkington, R. N., stories in *Asimov's Science Fiction Magazine*, Webb began work on the novelette "Variation on a Theme from Beethoven," an early version of part of *Earth Song*, the second volume of the *Earth Song Triad*, her most significant work so far. The trilogy explores how human beings respond to immortality either thrust unwillingly upon them, denied them, chosen by them, or denied by them. The Mouat-Gari immortality process, given to the children of earth at first without their consent, only works for children whose growth has not been completed. It tends to freeze people in a youthful maturity, allowing them to live forever. While the triad moves to events a few hundred years beyond our times and includes some of the usual science-fiction hardware, such as the Ram, a space ship similar to Clarke's Rama, and Utopian thinking similar to Asimov's in the Foundation series, there is an even greater conservatism in Webb—she stays close to what she knows: medicine, music,

writing, and locations in the southeast such as Tampa, Atlanta, Chattanooga, and the Blue Ridge Mountains. In many respects, particularly in her concern for people's motivations and reactions, Webb is a realistic social novelist doing "What if?" experiments with her characters much like Ursula K. Le Guin. Although immortality for human beings may seem an undeniable good, Webb sees a trade-off much as we might see in Homer or the Greek tragedians: her thesis is that creativity is dependent upon mortality which immortals consequently do not share—creative work thus becomes for mortals a substitute for immortality, a way to live on after death.

Earthchild traces the beginning of the effects of immortality on human beings and moves to the establishment of an immortal solar government with headquarters on earth, WorldCo. The initial effect of immortality on the children of earth is hatred, as the immortal children are hunted and killed by groups of mortals, sometimes their own relatives. So much butchery occurs that the children have to be taken from their parents and raised in a fortified, protected environment where they are forced into training for government work in a plan similar to Plato's. Two immortals have special significance, Kurt Kraus, a man who loses his art, music, to the Mouat-Gari immortality process, as well as his family, and Silvio Tarantino, a cherubic looking immortal whose lust for power and manipulation of people is as sinister as Hitler's or Asimov's Mule. After a generation, it becomes clear that immortality and creativity are at odds; consequently, Kurt Kraus, who has become the Minister of Culture, designs a planned environment, Renascence, where gifted children may study their art or science and then choose to live through their work and die or to live eternally.

Earth Song continues the cultural developments of Renascence nearly 200 years after Mouat-Gari. Two children of Renascence must choose between mortality and art, Liss McNabb and David Defour, while Silvio Tarantino, through control of the propaganda apparatus in WorldCo. Communication, plots a revolution of earth's solar colonies. The villain is foiled through David's art, Kurt's courage, and the skills of a child with Down's Syndrome. This plot, though skillful, only provides the suspense of the novel. The book's real fascination, just as in *Earthchild*, is in human motivation. What does it feel like to be alienated from a father dying of cancer who wishes to kill his immortal son? To know that one will outlive his parents and brothers and know that they know this will happen? To choose between immortality and the prospects of immortality through one's own creativity?

Sharon Webb's writing is extremely sensitive. Though she uses symbolic narrative, her chief ploy aids narrative compression and characterization, situational irony. Kurt Kraus, for instance, who tells his dying father, "I'm going to watch you die," soon finds that he institutes death to save earth's creativity at Renascence; he triumphs but grieves. David Defour and Liss are caught in equally powerful ironic situations through their choices involving immortality and their love. The *Earth Song Triad* is a powerful beginning by a writer with great potential.

—Craig Wallace Barrow

WEIGHT, Frank. See **TUBB, E. C.**

WEINBAUM, Stanley G(rauman). American. Born in Louisville, Kentucky, in 1902. Educated at public schools in Milwaukee; University of Wisconsin, Madison, B. Chem. Engr. 1923. Married Margaret Weinbaum. Worked as movie theatre manager. *Died 14 December 1935.*

SCIENCE-FICTION PUBLICATIONS

Novels

The New Adam. Chicago, Ziff Davis, 1939; London, Sphere, 1974.
The Black Flame. Reading, Pennsylvania, Fantasy Press, 1948.
The Dark Other. Los Angeles, Fantasy, 1950.

Short Stories

Dawn of Flame. New York, Ruppert, 1936.
A Martian Odyssey and Others. Reading, Pennsylvania, Fantasy Press, 1949.
The Red Peri. Reading, Pennsylvania, Fantasy Press, 1952.
The Best of Stanley G. Weinbaum. New York, Ballantine, 1974; London, Sphere, 1977.

*

Critical Studies: *After Ten Years: A Tribute to Stanley G. Weinbaum* edited by Gerry de la Ree and Sam Moskowitz, Westwood, New Jersey, de la Ree, 1945.

*   *   *

It is now formulaic to include the term "tragic death" with each mention of the name Stanley G. Weinbaum. His total career as a writer lasted from the publication of "A Martian Odyssey" in the July 1934 issue of *Wonder Stories* to his death in December 1935. Almost every critic who discusses the early years of pulp science fiction singles out Weinbaum as a unique voice who never had the chance to develop fully his powers as a writer. While one can never know just how far these powers would have in fact developed, a number of conclusions can be drawn, based on the short stories published during Weinbaum's career and a number of stories published after his death.

With his very first story Weinbaum managed to break a number of standard formulae in pulp fiction. "A Martian Odyssey" not only attempted to portray aliens as creatures unlike man but went so far as to present one such creature in a highly sympathetic light. Weinbaum seems to have been one of the first, if not the first, to realize that aliens may differ from humans in not only their outer appearance but their inner thought processes as well. His invention of the bib-bird-like creature Tweel in "A Martian Odyssey" stands as a major step in the genre because it undertakes the difficult task of describing the actions of a creature that clearly thinks differently. Given its non-human nature, Weinbaum uses a human character's interaction with Tweel to bring out the alien's basic nature. While both the human character and the reader begin the story amused at the weird actions of Tweel, this amusement is changed to admiration and respect by the end of the story. Tweel first grasps the possibility of communication between alien and human, and is able to make use of the human language while the human character gives up any chance of comprehending Tweel's. Tweel shows the greater understanding of the other aliens on Mars, and looks more at home on Mars, even though he too is an explorer from another planet. In other words, with Tweel readers were given an alternative to the murderous aliens of H. G. Wells, and many writers were soon imitating Weinbaum.

But Weinbaum's stories were not successful simply because he had invented a new attitude toward aliens. In the stories that followed (all in *Wonder Stories*) Weinbaum continued to emphasize the fact that his aliens lived by systems of logic that were different from man's, and it is the fact that these different systems were both strange *and* internally consistent that won him a wide audience. The care with which Weinbaum created new aliens and described their alienness was unique to the pulp fiction of its time. Thus, even in a story such as "Paradise Planet" in which alien forms on Venus do menace humans, the threat originates in the nature of life on Venus and not in some anthropomorphic desire to rape and pillage humanity.

As *Wonder Stories* continued to publish stories by Weinbaum almost monthly, a second reason for his popularity became apparent: his stories contained a good deal of humor. This humor was often achieved at the expense of human character and human science. Thus in a series of stories based on a delightfully "mad" scientist named Professor Haskel van Manderpootz ("The Worlds of If," "The Ideal," and "The Point of View"), inventions constantly appear that seem to have no other reason for existence than the fact that they constantly complicate the life of Dixon Wells, a young and somewhat lovesick romantic.

Weinbaum's treatment of aliens and his use of humor, however, did not free him from all of the pulp formulas. In "Pygmalion's Spectacles," for example, Weinbaum refuses to bring the story to its logical, tragic conclusion. A young man, while wearing spectacles that allow the wearer to take full part in an illusion, falls in love with a dream woman. When the dream ends and he must take off the glasses, he remains in love with the woman. Weinbaum, however, begs the whole issue of illusion and reality when at the end of the story a living counterpart of the dream woman is produced. Given the strength with which Weinbaum evokes the dream world and the sadness that the hero undergoes with its loss, one feels that "Pygmalion's Spectacles" could have been a better story. Weinbaum's ties to pulp fiction can also be seen in *The Black Flame*, which contains two versions of the same story. The first version, "Dawn of Flame" is a competent but uninspired story of the innocent young man who meets the exotic and erotic immortal woman. Reminiscent of H. Rider Haggard's *She*, the story contains some powerfully sexual scenes but basically remains a formula story. In the second version, "The Black Flame," however, Weinbaum rewrites the story and adds the paraphernalia of a pulp story complete with happy ending. The mixture of these two separate traditions was less than successful, and "The Black Flame" seems to be constantly struggling to make up its mind as to exactly what it wants to be.

On those occasions when Weinbaum does completely overcome his pulp environment, however, the fiction he produces is both sensitive and moving. In "The Adoptive Ultimate" he refuses to opt for the happy ending, and in the *The New Adam* Weinbaum takes the stock superman character and turns him into a sympathetic character who is alone in a world of mere humans. Because of the first-person narration the reader is able to see a side of such a character that rarely was portrayed before Weinbaum's treatment, and never so carefully or intimately. Lester del Rey calls the hero of *The New Adam* "a rather helpless failure," but such a characterization refuses to take into account what caused that failure, what it was in the nature of being a superman that led to it. And it is Weinbaum's investigation of exactly these questions in a sympathetic and painstaking manner that makes the novel so readable.

Works like *The New Adam* are rare in science fiction. Too often they are ignored when they do appear, and such was particularly true during the great age of the pulps. Weinbaum is remembered best for his aliens and the strange worlds he created for his stories in *Wonder Stories*. Thus, "A Martian Odyssey" remains Stanley Weinbaum's best known work. While such stories have had a significant effect on the direction science fiction was to take in the 1940's, *The New Adam* deserves far more notice than it has received to date.

—Stephen H. Goldman

WELLMAN, Manly Wade. Also writes as Gans T. Field. American. Born in Kamundongo, Angola, 21 May 1903; brother of the writer Paul I. Wellman. Educated at Wichita State University, Kansas, A. B. 1926; Columbia University, New York, B. Lit. 1927. Married Frances Obrist in 1930; one son. Reporter and feature writer, Wichita *Beacon*, 1927-30, and *Eagle*, 1930-34; assistant project supervisor, WPA Writers Project, New York, 1936-38; Instructor of Creative Writing, Elon College, North Carolina, 1962-70, and University of North Carolina evening college, Chapel Hill, 1963-73. Recipient: Ellery Queen Award, 1946; American Association for State and Local History certificate, 1973; H. P. Lovecraft Award, 1975. Agent: Kirby McCauley Ltd., 425 Park Avenue South, New York, New York 10016, U.S.A.

SCIENCE-FICTION PUBLICATIONS

Novels

The Invading Asteroid. New York, Stellar, 1932.
Sojarr of Titan. New York, Crestwood, 1949.
The Beasts from Beyond. Manchester, World, 1950.
The Devil's Planet. Manchester, World, 1951.
Twice in Time. New York, Avalon, 1957.
Giants from Eternity. New York, Avalon, 1959.
The Dark Destroyers. New York, Avalon, 1959.
Island in the Sky. New York, Avalon, 1961.
The Solar Invasion. New York, Popular Library, 1968.
Sherlock Holmes's War of the Worlds, with Wade Wellman. New York, Warner, 1975.
The Beyonders. New York, Warner, 1977.

Short Stories

Worse Things Waiting. Chapel Hill, North Carolina, Carcosa, 1973.
Lonely Vigils. Chapel Hill, North Carolina, Carcosa, 1981.

Uncollected Short Stories

"Goodman's Place," in *Night Chills*, edited by Kirby McCauley. New York, Avon, 1975.
"The Beasts That Perish," in *Whispers 3*, 1975.
"The Petey Car," in *Superhorror*, edited by Ramsey Campbell. London, W. H. Allen, 1976; New York, St. Martin's Press, 1977.
"Straggler from Atlantis," in *Swords Against Darkness 1*, edited

by Andrew J. Offutt. New York, Zebra, 1977.
"Where the Woodbine Twineth," in *The Year's Best Horror Stories 5*, edited by Gerald W. Page, New York, DAW, 1977.
"The Dakwa," in *Whispers*, edited by Stuart David Schiff. New York, Doubleday, 1977.
"The Dweller in the Temple," in *Swords Against Darkness 2*, edited by Andrew J. Offutt. New York, Zebra, 1977.
"The Vampire in America," in *First World Fantasy Awards*, edited by Gahan Wilson. New York, Doubleday, 1977.
"Caretaker," in *Fantasy and Science Fiction* (New York), October 1977.
"The Guest of Dzinganji," in *Swords Against Darkness 3*, edited by Andrew J. Offutt. New York, Zebra, 1978.
"Ever the Faith Endures," in *The Year's Best Horror Stories 6*, edited by Gerald W. Page. New York, DAW, 1978.
"Hundred Years Gone," in *Fantasy and Science Fiction* (New York), March 1978.
"The Spring," in *Shadows 2*, edited by Charles L. Grant. New York, Doubleday, 1979.
"Chastel," in *The Year's Best Horror Stories 7*, edited by Gerald W. Page. New York, DAW, 1979.
"Trill Coster's Burden," in *Whispers 2*, edited by Stuart David Schiff. New York, Doubleday, 1979.
"The Edge of the World," in *Swords Against Darkness 4*, edited by Andrew J. Offutt. New York, Zebra, 1979.
"The Seeker in the Fortress," in *Heroic Fantasy*, edited by Gerald W. Page and Hank Reinhardt. New York, DAW, 1979.
"Toad's Foot," in *Fantasy and Science Fiction* (New York), April 1979.
"The Ghastly Priest Doth Reign," in *The World Fantasy Awards 2*, edited by Stuart David Schiff and Fritz Leiber. New York, Doubleday, 1980.
"Owls Hoot in the Daytime," in *Dark Forces*, edited by Kirby McCauley. New York, Viking Press, 1980.
"Yare," in *New Terrors 1*, edited by Ramsey Campbell. London, Pan, 1980.
"What of the Night," in *Fantasy and Science Fiction* (New York), March 1980.
"Nobody Ever Goes There," in *Weird Tales 3*, edited by Lin Carter. New York, Zebra, 1981.
"Rouse Him Not," in *The Year's Best Horror Stories 11*, edited by Karl Edward Wagner. New York, DAW, 1983.
"Along about Sundown," in *Whispers* (Binghamton, New York), October 1983.

OTHER PUBLICATIONS

Novels

Romance in Black (as Gans T. Field). London, Utopian, 1946.
A Double Life (novelization of screenplay). Chicago, Century, 1947.
Find My Killer. New York, Farrar Straus, 1947; London, Sampson Low, 1948.
Fort Sun Dance. New York, Dell, and London, Corgi, 1955.
Candle of the Wicked. New York, Putnam, 1960.
Not at These Hands. New York, Putnam, 1962.
The Old Gods Waken. New York, Doubleday, 1979.
After Dark. New York, Doubleday, 1980.
The Lost and the Lurking. New York, Doubleday, 1981.
The Hanging Stones. New York, Doubleday, 1982.
What Dreams May Come. New York, Doubleday, 1983.
The Voice from the Mountain. New York, Doubleday, 1984.
The School of Darkness. New York, Doubleday, 1985.

Novels (for children)

The Sleuth Patrol. New York, Nelson, 1947.
The Mystery of Lost Valley. New York, Nelson, 1948.
The Raiders of Beaver Lake. New York, Nelson, 1950.
The Haunts of Drowning Creek. New York, Holiday House, 1951.
Wild Dogs of Drowning Creek. New York, Holiday House, 1952.
The Last Mammoth. New York, Holiday House, 1953.
Gray Riders: Jeb Stuart and His Men. New York, Aladdin, 1954.
Rebel Mail Runner. New York, Holiday House, 1954.
Flag on the Levee. New York, Washburn, 1955.
To Unknown Lands. New York, Holiday House, 1956.
Young Squire Morgan. New York, Washburn, 1956.
Lights over Skeleton Ridge. New York, Washburn, 1957.
The Ghost Battalion. New York, Washburn, 1958.
Ride, Rebels! New York, Washburn, 1959.
Appomattox Road. New York, Washburn, 1960.
Third String Center. New York, Washburn, 1960.
Rifles at Ramsour's Mill. New York, Washburn, 1961.
Battle for King's Mountain. New York, Washburn, 1962.
Clash on the Catawba. New York, Washburn, 1962.
The River Pirates. New York, Washburn, 1963.
Settlement on Shocco. Winston-Salem, North Carolina, Blair, 1963.
The South Fork Rangers. New York, Washburn, 1963.
The Master of Scare Hollow. New York, Washburn, 1964.
A True Story of the Revolting and Bloody Crimes of Sergeant Stanlas, U. S. A. Wichita, Kansas, Four Ducks Press, 1964.
The Great Riverboat Race. New York, Washburn, 1965.
Mystery at Bear Paw Gap. New York, Washburn, 1965.
Battle at Bear Paw Gap. New York, Washburn, 1966.
The Specter of Bear Paw Gap. New York, Washburn, 1966.
Jamestown Adventure. New York, Washburn, 1967.
Brave Horse: The Story of Janus. Williamsburg, Virginia, Colonial Williamsburg, 1968.
Carolina Pirate. New York, Washburn, 1968.
Frontier Reporter. New York, Washburn, 1969.
Mountain Feud. New York, Washburn, 1969.
Napoleon of the West: A Story of the Aaron Burr Conspiracy. New York, Washburn, 1970.
Fast Break Five. New York, Washburn, 1971.

Short Stories

Who Fears the Devil? Sauk City, Wisconsin, Arkham House, 1963.

Play

Many Are the Hearts. Raleigh, North Carolina Confederate Centennial Commission, 1961.

Other

Giant in Gray: A Biography of Wade Hampton of South Carolina. New York, Scribner, 1949.
Dead and Gone: Classic Crimes of North Carolina. Chapel Hill, University of North Carolina Press, 1954.
Rebel Boast: First at Bethel—Last at Appomattox. New York, Holt, 1956.
Fastest on the River. New York, Holt, 1957.
The Life and Times of Sir Archie, with Elizabeth Amis Blanchard. Chapel Hill, University of North Carolina Press, 1958.
The County of Warren, North Carolina, 1586-1917. Chapel Hill, University of North Carolina Press, 1959.
They Took Their Stand: The Founders of the Confederacy. New York, Putnam, 1959.
The Rebel Songster, with Frances Wellman. New York, Heritage House, 1959.
Harpers Ferry, Prize of War. Charlotte, North Carolina, McNally and Loftin, 1960.
The County of Gaston, with Robert F. Cope. Gastonia, North Carolina, Gaston County Historical Society, 1961.
The County of Moore 1847-1947. Southern Pines, North Carolina, Moore County Historical Association, 1962.
Winston-Salem in History: The Founders. Winston-Salem, North Carolina, Blair, 1966.
The Kingdom of Madison: A Southern Mountain Fastness and Its People. Chapel Hill, University of North Carolina Press, 1973.
The Story of Moore County. Southern Pines, North Carolina, Moore County Historical Association, 1974.

*

Manly Wade Wellman comments:

I came to America from an African wilderness, but with strong family heritage and association in the American west and south. I began by wanting to write of the fantastic, the imaginative. I wrote in other fields, too, but now I've returned to that first love. A writer must find himself out all alone, must understand himself, use himself in all he writes. More than by years or ability or reputation, your life is measured by the work you do. You pave your road by your writing, and travel it always into new wonders and perils and joys and sorrows. You find and use things out of sight and sound of all others. It's part of you, like the blood in your veins, the breath in your nostrils.

I look back on more than half a century of writing, and hope to keep on until they say the last words over me.

*   *   *

The bulk of Manly Wade Wellman's writing has been outside the science-fiction field. A popular writer during the heyday of the SF pulps, he is best known today as a fantasy author and for his fiction and nonfiction work in the field of Southern regionalism.

Wellman began selling SF as early as 1927 with "Back to the Beast" in *Weird Tales*. In 1930 he turned to writing as a full-time profession, and in 1934 moved to New York in order to be closer to his markets. After "Outlaws on Callisto" made the cover of the April 1936 *Astounding Stories*, Wellman became a client of the noted agent, Julius Schwartz, under whose direction he became part of the Better Publications stable. There Wellman became a regular contributor to *Thrilling Wonder Stories* and *Startling Stories*. These popular pulps, aimed at an adolescent readership, were well suited to Wellman's brisk, simple narrative style, and the bulk of his SF appeared in these and similar pulps. Most of his SF books are reprints of his earlier work, although recently he has begun to write fantasy.

Wellman's first book publication was *The Invading Asteroid*. It set the tone for the sort of space opera Wellman was to become known for. He created a consistent futuristic setting of the 30th century, and utilized this for some 16 of his stories. Wellman's 30th century was pretty much the same as the 20th, with the addition of interplanetary travel and extraterrestrials. Nonetheless, so well-liked was Wellman's future world that fans cried "plagiarism" when Nelson Bond utilized certain of these elements for a story of his own, and Wellman had to explain that Bond had done so with his permission.

Sojarr of Titan is a "Tarzan of outer space" pastiche written at editor Leo Margulies's request. *The Beasts from Beyond* made use of the idea of invasion at the intersection point of bubble universes that Wellman returned to in *The Beyonders*. *The Devil's Planet*, part of his 30th-century series, is a murder mystery set on Mars that teams a human and an android as detectives, and appears to be the archetype of Asimov's *Caves of Steel*. *Twice in Time* is a novel of a man who travels through time to become Leonardo da Vinci. It is Wellman's most important SF work and remains a superior time-travel novel. *The Dark Destroyers* has Earthmen throwing off the yoke of extraterrestrial conquest. In *Giants from Eternity*, Pasteur, Darwin, Newton, Edison, and Curie are brought back to life to combat an alien growth that threatens to engulf the Earth. In *Island in the Sky* a future gladiator rebels against a technological dictatorship that holds Earth in thrall. A final reprint from the pulp days, *The Solar Invasion* is Wellman's one fling at writing a Captain Future episode.

During the 1960's Wellman collaborated with his son, Wade Wellman, for a series of droll pastiches that placed Doyle's Sherlock Holmes and Watson alongside Professor Challenger in the London of Wells's *War of the Worlds*. These were expanded and collected as *Sherlock Holmes's War of the Worlds*, a book which ranks among the best of the Holmes pastiches. *The Beyonders* is a routine novel of invasion by creatures from another dimension, with the saving charm of its Southern mountain setting.

While even the best of Wellman's SF seems naive and badly dated to modern readers, the same is not true for his fantasy writing, which remains some of the finest in this genre. The best of his short fantasy fiction has been collected in *Who Fears the Devil?*, *Worse Things Waiting*, and *Lonely Vigils*. *Lonely Vigils* collects the cases of three occult investigators, Judge Pursuivant, Professor Enderby, and John Thunstone, whose separate series originally appeared in *Weird Tales* and *Strange Stories*. *Who Fears the Devil?* collects the adventures of a wandering balladeer, named simply "John," who confronts supernatural evil in the southern Appalachians. The stories originally appeared in *The Magazine of Fantasy and Science Fiction* during the 1950's.

Recently Wellman has revived these characters for a series of novels, that, although marketed as SF, definitely belong to the category of fantasy. *The Old Gods Waken*, *After Dark*, *The Lost and the Lurking*, *The Hanging Stones*, and *The Voice of the Mountain* all feature John. Judge Pursuivant makes a guest appearance in *The Hanging Stones*, while John Thunstone returns as the hero of *What Dreams May Come* and *The School of Darkness*.

—Karl Edward Wagner

WELLS, H(erbert) G(eorge). Also wrote as Reginald Bliss. British. Born in Bromley, Kent, 21 September 1866. Educated at Mr. Morley's Bromley Academy until age 13: certificate in book-keeping; apprentice draper, Rodgers and Denyer, Windsor, 1880; pupil-teacher at a school in Wookey, Somerset, 1880; apprentice chemist in Midhurst, Sussex, 1880-81; apprentice draper, Hyde's Southsea Drapery Emporium, Hampshire,

1881-83; student/assistant, Midhurst Grammar School, 1883-84; studied at Normal School (now Imperial College) of Science, London (Editor, *Science School Journal*), 1884-87; taught at Holt Academy, Wrexham, Wales, 1887-88, and at Henley House School, Kilburn, London, 1889; B. Sc. (honours) in zoology 1890, and D. Sc. 1943, University of London. Married 1) his cousin Isabel Mary Wells in 1891 (separated, 1894; divorced, 1895); 2) Amy Catherine Robbins in 1895 (died, 1927), two sons; had one daughter by Amber Reeves, and one son by the writer Rebecca West, the writer Anthony West. Tutor, University Tutorial College, London, 1890-93. Full-time writer from 1893: theatre critic, *Pall Mall Gazette*, London, 1895. Member of the Fabian Society, 1903-08; Labour Candidate for Parliament, for the University of London, 1922, 1923; lived mainly in France, 1924-33. D. Lit. : University of London, 1936. Honorary Fellow, Imperial College of Science and Technology, London. *Died 13 August 1946.*

SCIENCE-FICTION PUBLICATIONS

Novels

The Time Machine: An Invention. London, Heinemann, and New York, Holt, 1895.
The Island of Doctor Moreau. London, Heinemann, and New York, Stone and Kimball, 1896.
The Invisible Man: A Grotesque Romance. London, Pearson, and New York, Arnold, 1897.
The War of the Worlds. London, Heinemann, and New York, Harper, 1898.
When the Sleeper Wakes. London and New York, Harper, 1899; revised edition, as *The Sleeper Wakes*, London, Nelson, 1910.
The First Men in the Moon. London, Newnes, and Indianapolis, Bowen Merrill, 1901.
The Food of the Gods, and How It Came to Earth. London, Macmillan, and New York, Scribner, 1904.
A Modern Utopia. London, Chapman and Hall, and New York, Scribner, 1905.
In the Days of the Comet. London, Macmillan, and New York, Century, 1906.
The War in the Air, and Particularly How Mr. Bert Smallways Fared While It Lasted. London, Bell, and New York, Macmillan, 1908.
The World Set Free: A Story of Mankind. London, Macmillan, and New York, Dutton, 1914.
Men Like Gods. London, Cassell, and New York, Macmillan, 1923.
The Shape of Things to Come: The Ultimate Resolution. London, Hutchinson, and New York, Macmillan, 1933; revised edition, as *Things to Come* (film story), London, Cresset Press, and New York, Macmillan, 1935.
The Croquet Player. London, Chatto and Windus, 1936; New York, Viking Press, 1937.
Star Begotten: A Biological Fantasia. London, Chatto and Windus, and New York, Viking Press, 1937.
The Holy Terror. London, Joseph, and New York, Simon and Schuster, 1939.

Short Stories

The Stolen Bacillus and Other Incidents. London, Methuen, 1895.
The Plattner Story and Others. London, Methuen, 1897.
Thirty Strange Stories. New York, Arnold, 1897.

Tales of Space and Time. London, Harper, and New York, Doubleday, 1899.

Twelve Stories and a Dream. London, Macmillan, 1903; New York, Scribner, 1905.

The Country of the Blind and Other Stories. London, Nelson, 1911; revised edition of *The Country of the Blind*, London, Golden Cockerel Press, 1939.

The Door in the Wall and Other Stories. New York, Kennerley, 1911; London, Richards, 1915.

The Short Stories of H. G. Wells. London, Benn, 1927; New York, Doubleday, 1929.

28 Science Fiction Stories. New York, Dover, 1952.

Selected Short Stories. London, Penguin, 1958.

Best Science Fiction Stories of H. G. Wells. New York, Dover, 1966.

OTHER PUBLICATIONS

Novels

The Wonderful Visit. London, Dent, and New York, Macmillan, 1895.

The Wheels of Chance . London, Dent, and New York, Macmillan, 1896.

Love and Mr. Lewisham. London, Harper, and New York, Stokes, 1900.

The Sea Lady: A Tissue of Moonshine. London, Metheun, and New York, Appleton, 1902.

Kipps. London, Macmillan, and New York, Scribner, 1905.

Tono-Bungay. New York, Duffield, 1908; London, Macmillan, 1909.

Ann Veronica. London, Unwin, and New York, Harper, 1909.

The History of Mr. Polly. London, Nelson, and New York, Duffield, 1910.

The New Machiavelli. London, Lane, and New York, Duffield, 1911.

Marriage. London, Macmillan, and New York, Duffield, 1912.

The Passionate Friends. London, Macmillan, and New York, Harper, 1913.

The Wife of Sir Isaac Harman. London and New York, Macmillan, 1914.

Boon (as Reginald Bliss). London, Unwin, and New York, Doran, 1915.

Bealby. London, Methuen, and New York, Macmillan, 1915.

The Research Magnificent. London and New York, Macmillan, 1915.

Mr. Britling Sees It Through. London, Cassell, and New York, Macmillan, 1916.

The Soul of a Bishop. London, Cassell, and New York, Macmillan, 1917.

Joan and Peter. London, Cassell and New York, Macmillan, 1918.

The Undying Fire. London, Cassell, and New York, Macmillan, 1919.

The Secret Places of the Heart. London, Cassell, and New York, Macmillan, 1922.

The Dream. London, Cape, and New York, Macmillan, 1924.

Christina Alberta's Father. London, Cape, and New York, Macmillan, 1925.

The World of William Clissold. London, Benn, 3 vols., and New York, Doran, 2 vols., 1926.

Meanwhile: The Picture of a Lady. London, Benn, and New York, Doran, 1927.

Mr. Blettsworthy on Rampole Island. London, Benn, and New York, Doubleday, 1928.

The King Who Was a King: The Book of a Film. London, Benn, and New York, Doubleday, 1929.

The Autocracy of Mr. Parham. London, Heinemann, and New York, Doubleday, 1930.

The Bulpington of Blup. London, Hutchinson, 1932; New York, Macmillan, 1933.

Man Who Could Work Miracles (film story). London, Cresset Press, and New York, Macmillan, 1936.

Brynhild. London, Methuen, and New York, Scribner, 1937.

The Camford Vistitation. London, Methuen, 1937.

Apropos of Dolores. London, Cape, and New York, Scribner, 1938.

The Brothers. London, Chatto and Windus, and New York, Viking Press, 1938.

The Holy Terror. London, Joseph, and New York, Simon and Schuster, 1939.

Babes in the Darkling Wood. London, Secker and Warburg, and New York, Alliance, 1940.

All Aboard for Ararat. London, Secker and Warburg, 1940; New York, Alliance, 1941.

You Can't Be Too Careful: A Sample of Life 1901-1951. London, Secker and Warburg, 1941; New York, Putnam, 1942.

The Wealth of Mr. Waddy, edited by Harris Wilson. Carbondale, Southern Illinois University Press, 1969.

Short Stories

Select Conversations with an Uncle (Now Extinct) and Two Other Reminiscences. London, Lane, and New York, Merriman, 1895.

A Cure for Love. New York, Scott, 1899.

The Vacant Country. New York, Kent, 1899.

Tales of the Unexpected [of Life and Adventure, of Wonder], edited by J. D. Beresford. London, Collins, 3 vols., 1922-23.

The Valley of Spiders. London, Collins, 1964.

The Cone. London, Collins, 1965.

The Man with the Nose and Other Uncollected Short Stories, edited by J. R. Hammond, London, Athlone Press, 1984.

Plays

Kipps, with Rudolf Besier, adaptation of the novel by Wells (produced London, 1912).

The Wonderful Visit, with St. John Ervine, adaptation of the novel by Wells (produced London, 1921).

Hoopdriver's Holiday, adaptation of his novel *The Wheels of Chance*, edited by Michael Timko. Lafayette, Indiana, Purdue University English Department, 1964.

Screenplays: *H. G. Wells Comedies* (*Bluebottles, The Tonic, Daydreams*), with Frank Wells, 1928; *Things to Come*, 1936; *The Man Who Could Work Miracles*, 1936.

Other

Text-Book of Biology. London, Clive, 2 vols., 1893.

Honours Physiography, with R. A. Gregory. London, Hughes, 1893.

Certain Personal Matters: A Collection of Material, Mainly Autobiographical. London, Lawrence and Bullen, 1897.

Anticipations of the Reaction of Mechanical and Scientific Progress upon Human Life and Thought. London, Chapman and Hall, 1901; New York, Harper, 1902.

The Discovery of the Future (lecture). London, Unwin, 1902;

New York, Huebsch, 1913; revised edition, London, Cape, 1925.

Mankind in the Making. London, Chapman and Hall, 1903; New York, Scribner, 1904.

The Future in America: A Search after Realities. London, Chapman and Hall, and New York, Harper, 1906.

Faults of the Fabian (lecture). Privately printed, 1906.

Socialism and the Family. London, Fifield, 1906; Boston, Ball, 1908.

Reconstruction of the Fabian Society. Privately printed, 1906.

This Misery of Boots. London, Fabian Society, 1907; Boston, Ball, 1908.

Will Socialism Destroy the Home? London, Independent Labour Party, 1907.

New Worlds for Old. London, Constable, and New York, Macmillan, 1908; revised edition, London, Constable, 1914.

First and Last Things: A Confession of Faith and Rule of Life. London, Constable, and New York, Putnam, 1908; revised edition, London, Cassell, 1917; London, Watts, 1929.

Floor Games (for children). London, Palmer, 1911; Boston, Small Maynard, 1912.

The Labour Unrest. London, Associated Newspapers, 1912.

War and Common Sense. London, Associated Newspapers, 1913.

Liberalism and Its Party. London, Good, 1913.

Little Wars (children's games). London, Palmer, and Boston, Small Maynard, 1913.

An Englishman Looks at the World, Being a Series of Unrestrained Remarks upon Contemporary Matters. London, Cassell, 1914; as *Social Forces in England and America*, New York, Harper, 1914.

The War That Will End War. London, Palmer, and New York, Duffield, 1914; reprinted in part as *The War and Socialism*, London, Clarion Press, 1915.

The Peace of the World. London, Daily Chronicle, 1915.

What Is Coming? A Forecast of Things after the War. London, Cassell, and New York, Macmillan, 1916.

The Elements of Reconstruction. London, Nisbet, 1916.

War and the Future. London, Cassell, 1917; as *Italy, France, and Britain at War*, New York, Macmillan, 1917.

God the Invisible King. London, Cassell, and New York, Macmillan, 1917.

A Reasonable Man's Peace. London, Daily News, 1917.

In the Fourth Year: Anticipations of a World Peace. London, Chatto and Windus, and New York, Macmillan, 1918; abridged edition, as *Anticipations of a World Peace*, Chatto and Windus, 1918.

British Nationalism and the League of Nations. London, League of Nations Union, 1918.

History Is One. Boston, Ginn, 1919.

The Outline of History, Being a Plain History of Life and Mankind. London, Newnes, 2 vols., and New York, Macmillan, 2 vols., 1920 (and later revisions).

Russia in the Shadows. London, Hodder and Stoughton, 1920; New York, Doran, 1921.

The Salvaging of Civilisation. London, Cassell, and New York, Macmillan, 1921.

The New Teaching of History, with a Reply to Some Recent Criticisms of "The Outline of History." London, Cassell, 1921.

Washington and Hope of Peace. London, Collins, 1922; as *Washington and the Riddle of Peace*, New York, Macmillan, 1922.

The World, Its Debts, and the Rich Men. London, Finer, 1922.

A Short History of the World. London, Cassell, and New York,

Macmillan, 1922; revised edition, London, Penguin, 1946.

Socialism and the Scientific Motive (lecture). Privately printed, 1923.

The Story of a Great Schoolmaster, Being a Plain Account of the Life and Ideas of Sanderson of Oundle. London, Chatto and Windus, and New York, Macmillan, 1924.

The P. R. Parliament. London, Proportional Representation Society, 1924.

A Year of Prophesying. London, Unwin, 1924; New York, Macmillan, 1925.

Works (Atlantic Edition). London, Unwin, and New York, Scribner, 28 vols., 1924.

A Forecast of the World's Affairs. New York, Encyclopaedia Britannica, 1925.

Works (Essex Edition). London, Benn, 24 vols., 1926-27.

Mr. Belloc Objects to "The Outline of History." London, Watts, 1926.

Democracy under Revision (lecture). London, Hogarth Press, and New York, Doran, 1927.

Wells' Social Anticipations, edited by H. W. Laidler. New York, Vanguard Press, 1927.

In Memory of Amy Catherine Wells. Privately printed, 1927.

The Way the World Is Going: Guesses and Forecasts of the Years Ahead. London, Benn 1928; New York, Doubleday, 1929.

The Open Conspiracy: Blue Prints for a World Revolution. London, Gollancz, and New York, Doubleday, 1928; revised edition, London, Hogarth Press, 1930; revised edition, as *What Are We to Do with Our Lives?*, London, Heinemann, and New York, Doubleday, 1931.

The Common Sense of World Peace (lecture). London, Hogarth Press, 1929.

Imperialism and the Open Conspiracy. London, Faber, 1929.

The Adventures of Tommy (for children). London, Harrap, and New York, Stokes, 1929.

The Science of Life: A Summary of Contemporary Knowledge about Life and Its Possibilities, with Julian Huxley and G. P. Wells. London, Amalgamated Press, 3 vols., 1930; New York, Doubleday, 4 vols., 1931; revised edition, as *Science of Life Series,* London, Cassell, 9 vols., 1934-37.

The Problem of the Troublesome Collaborator. Privately printed, 1930.

Settlement of the Trouble Between Mr. Thring and Mr. Wells: A Footnote to The Problem of the Troublesome Collaborator. Privately printed, 1930.

The Way to World Peace. London, Benn, 1930.

The Work, Wealth, and Happiness of Mankind. New York, Doubleday, 2 vols., 1931; London, Heinemann, 1 vol., 1932; revised edition, Heinemann, 1934; as *The Outline of Man's Work and Wealth,* Doubleday, 1936.

After Democracy: Addresses and Papers on the Present World Situation. London, Watts, 1932.

What Should Be Done Now? New York, Day, 1932.

Experiment in Autobiography: Discoveries and Conclusions of a Very Ordinary Brain (since 1866), London, Gollancz-Cresset Press, 2 vols., and New York, Macmillan, 1 vol., 1934.

Stalin-Wells Talk: The Verbatim Record, and A Discussion, with others. London, New Statesman and Nation, 1934.

The New America: The New World. London, Cresset Press, and New York, Macmillan, 1935.

The Anatomy of Frustration: A Modern Synthesis. London, Cresset Press, and New York, Macmillan, 1936.

The Idea of a World Encylopaedia. London, Hogarth Press, 1936.

World Brain. London, Methuen, and New York, Doubleday, 1938.

Travels of a Republican Radical in Search of Hot Water. London, Penguin, 1939.

The Fate of Homo Sapiens: An Unemotianal Statement of the Things That Are Hapening to Him Now and of the Immediate Possibilities Confronting Him. London, Secker and Warburg, 1939; as *The Fate of Man,* New York, Alliance, 1939.

The New World Order, Whether It Is Obtainable, How It Can Be Obtained, and What Sort of World a World at Peace Will Have to Be. London, Secker and Warburg, and New York, Knopf, 1940.

The Rights of Man; or, What Are We Fighting For? London, Penguin, 1940.

The Common Sense of War and Peace: World Revolution or War Unending? London, Penguin, 1940.

The Pocket History of the World. New York, Pocket Books, 1941.

Guide to the New World: A Handbook of Constructive World Revolution. London, Gollancz, 1941.

The Outlook for Homo Sapiens (revised versions of *The Fate of Homo Sapiens* and *The New World Order).* London, Secker and Warburg, 1942.

Science and the World-Mind. London, New Europe, 1942.

Phoenix: A Summary of the Inescapable Conditions of World Reorganization. London, Secker and Warburg, 1942; Girard, Kansas, Haldeman Julius, n. d.

A Thesis on the Quality of Illusion in the Continuity of Individual Life of the Higher Metazoa, with Particular Reference to the Species Homo Sapiens. Privately printed, 1942.

The Conquest of Time. London, Watts, 1942.

The New Rights of Man. Girard, Kansas, Haldeman Julius, 1942.

Crux Ansata: An Indictment of the Roman Catholic Church. London, Penguin, 1943; New York, Agora, 1944.

The Mosley Outrage. London, Daily Worker, 1943.

'42 to '44: A Contemporary Memoir upon Human Behaviour During the Crisis of the World Revolution. London, Secker and Warburg, 1944.

Marxism vs. Liberalism (interview with Stalin). New York, Century, 1945.

The Happy Turning: A Dream of Life. London, Heinemann, 1945.

Mind at the End of Its Tether. London, Heinemann, 1945.

Mind at the End of Its Tether, and The Happy Turning. New York, Didier, 1945.

The Desert Daisy (for children), edited by Gordon N. Ray. Urbana, University of Illinois Press, 1957.

Henry James and H. G. Wells: A Record of Their Friendship, Their Debate on the Art of Fiction, and Their Quarrel, edited by Leon Edel and Gordon N. Ray. Urbana, University of Illinois Press, and London, Hart Davis, 1958.

Arnold Bennett and H. G. Wells: A Record of a Personal and Literary Friendship, edited by Harris Wilson. London, Hart Davis, 1960.

George Gissing and H. G. Wells: Their Friendship and Correspondence, edited by Royal A. Gettman. London, Hart Davis, 1961.

Journalism and Prophecy 1893-1946, edited by W. Warren Wagar. Boston, Houghton Mifflin, 1964; abridge edition, London, Bodley Head, 1965.

Early Writings in Science and Science Fiction, edited by Robert M. Philmus and David Y. Hughes. Berkeley, University of California Press, 1975.

H. G. Wells's Literary Criticism, edited by Patrick Parrinder and Robert M. Philmus. Brighton, Harvester Press, 1980.

H. G. Wells in Love, edited by G. P. Wells. London, Faber, 1984.

Editor, with G. R. S. Taylor and Frances Evelyn Warwick, *The Great State: Essays in Construction.* London, Harper, 1912; as *Socialism and the Great State,* New York, Harper, 1914.

*

Bibliography: *H. G. Wells: A Comprehensive Bibliography* , London, H. G. Wells Society, 1966, revised edition, 1968; *Herbert George Wells: An Annotated Bibliography of His Works* by J. R. Hammond, New York, Garland, 1977.

Manuscript Collection: University of Illinois, Urbana.

Critical Studies (selection): *The World of H. G. Wells* by Van Wyck Brooks, New York, Mitchell Kennerley, and London, T. Fisher Unwin, 1915; *H. G. Wells: A Biography,* London, Longman, 1951; *The Early H. G. Wells: A Study of the Scientific Romances* by Bernard Bergonzi, Manchester, Manchester University Press, 1961, and *H. G. Wells: A Collection of Critical Essays* edited by Bergonzi, Englewood Cliffs, New Jersey, Prentice Hall, 1976; *H. G. Wells: An Outline* by F. K. Chaplin, London, P. R. Macmillan, 1961; *H. G. Wells and the World State* by W. Warren Wagar, New Haven, Connecticut, Yale University Press, 1961; *The Life and Thought of H. G. Wells* by Julius Kagarlitsky (translated by Moura Budberg), London, Sidgwick and Jackson, 1966; *H. G. Wells* by Richard Hauer Costa, New York, Twayne, 1967; *H. G. Wells: His Turbulent Life and Times* by Lovat Dickson, London, Macmillan, 1969; essay in *A Soviet Heretic* by Yevgeny Zamyatin (translated by Mirra Ginsburg), Chicago, University of Chicago Press, 1970; *H. G. Wells* by Patrick Parrinder, Edinburgh, Oliver and Boyd, 1970, New York, Capricorn, 1977, and *H. G. Wells: The Critical Heritage* edited by Parrinder, London, Routledge, 1972; *The Time Traveller: The Life of H. G. Wells* by Norman and Jeanne Mackenzie, London, Weidenfeld and Nicolson, 1973, as *H. G. Wells: A Biography,* New York, Simon and Schuster, 1973; *H. G. Wells: Critic of Progress* by Jack Williamson, Baltimore, Mirage Press, 1973; *H. G. Wells and Rebecca West* by Gordon N. Ray, New Haven, Connecticut, Yale University Press, and London, Macmillan, 1974; *The Scientific Romances of H. G. Wells* by Stephen Gill, Cornwall, Ontario, Vesta, 1975; *Anatomies of Egotism: A Reading of the Last Novels of H. G. Wells* by Robert Bloom, Lincoln, University of Nebraska Press, 1977; *H. G. Wells and Modern Science Fiction* edited by Darko Suvin and Robert M. Philmus, Lewisburg, Pennsylvania, Buckness University Press, 1977; *H. G. Wells: A Pictorial Biography* by Frank Wells, London, Jupiter, 1977; *The H. G. Wells Scrapbook* edited by Peter Haining, London, New English Library, 1978; *Who's Who in H. G. Wells* by Brian Ash, London, Elm Tree, 1979; *H. G. Wells, Discoverer of the Future: The Influence of Science on His Thought* by Roslynn D. Haynes, New York, New York University Press, and London, Macmillan, 1980; *H. G. Wells: Interviews and Recollections* edited by J. R. Hammond, London, Macmillan, 1980; *The Science Fiction of H. G. Wells: A Concise Guide* by P. H. Niles, Clifton Park, New York, Auriga, 1980; *The Science Fiction of H. G. Wells* by Frank McConnell, New York, Oxford University Press, 1981; *H. G. Wells and the Culminating Ape: Biological Themes and Imaginative Obsessions* by Peter Kemp, London, Macmillan, and New York, St. Martin's Press, 1982; *The Logic of Fantasy: H. G. Wells and Science Fiction* by John Huntington, New York, Columbia University Press, 1982; *H. G. Wells* by Robert Crossley, Mercer Island, Washington, Starmont House, 1984; *H. G. Wells: Aspects of a Life* by Anthony West, London,

Hutchinson, and New York, Random House, 1984; *H. G. Wells* by John Batchelor, London, Cambridge University Press, 1985.

* * *

Bernard Bergonzi, in his monograph *The Early H. G. Wells*, notes somewhat caustically that if Wells had died in 1900, like his young American friend Stephen Crane, "he would be remembered primarily as a literary artist. " The 45 years of ardent "pamphleteering" that followed would not have occurred, and Well's place in the firmament of high culture would have been more secure, unshadowed by the embarrassment of his crusades for public enlightenment, or even by his sometimes awkward attempts after 1900 to write mainstream fiction. From the perspective of literary criticism as it is practiced in the second half of the 20th century, Bergonzi's judgment is hard to fault. What Wells produced between 1894 and 1901, from the earliest short stories in *The Pall Mall Budget* to *The First Men in the Moon*, was not only the most imaginative and artistically satisfying science fiction of any novelist of his generation, but also the best writing of his long career. None of the mainstream novels, sociological tracts, prophetic manifestos, collections of journalism, or encyclopedic surveys of science and history that Wells published after 1900 bears comparison, as art, with his early science fiction. Most of his later science fiction also suffers when measured against the standards he set for himself between 1894 and 1901.

Fortunately for his literary soul, Wells did more than enough in his salad days to win admission to the ranks of the immortals. From 1894 to 1901 his output of fantasy and science fiction (chiefly the latter) came to six novels and more than 30 short stories; most of these captured immediate public and critical acclaim. *The Time Machine*, the first of the novels, is a profound dystopian parable and the archetype of all time-travel stories in 20th-century science fiction. *The Island of Dr. Moreau* retells the Frankenstein tale, with dark satirical touches reminiscent of Swift. *The Invisible Man* furnishes the model for every later warning in science fiction of the Faustian potentiality for human self-destruction in the powers of science. *The War of the Worlds* is the first great story of interplanetary conflict, and *When the Sleeper Wakes* inspired Zamyatin's *We* and Huxley's *Brave New World*. In *The First Men in the Moon* Wells produced a masterful fantasia on the theme of biological engineering and one of the first credible accounts of space travel.

Several of the short stories have the same archetypal quality as the early novels. The deadliness of nature disclosed by modern science, which has supplied the raw material for a huge literature of disaster in our century, was a subject thoroughly exploited by Wells in his early stories, and in a few others written just after 1901. Apart from *The War of the Worlds*, which can also be read as a Darwinian fairy-tale, there were stories of man-eating orchids and cephalopods, giant birds and spiders, world-conquering ant hordes, and, in "The Star," an astrophysical disaster story of classical discipline, which seems almost to have been carved in ice. In "A Story of the Stone Age" Wells was among the first writers to make imaginative use of modern anthropology. "The New Accelerator" and "A Dream of Armageddon" carry further the admonitions in *The Invisible Man* on the perils of science and technology. "You know the silly way of the ingenious sort of men who make these things," the dreamer tells the narrator in "A Dream of Armageddon," recalling the weapons research in his nightmare of future life. "They turn 'em out as beavers build dams, and with no more sense of the rivers they're going to divert and the lands they're going to flood!"

The flow of science fiction from Well's pen did not stop in 1901, but time sapped his creative powers and eroded his craftsmanship. He grew careless. Between 1902 and 1914 he wrote six fantasy and science-fiction novels and a dozen stories. From 1914 until his death another five science-fiction novels made their appearance, three filmscripts, and several works located in a literary no-man's-land halfway between speculative and mainstream fiction. In his later work some of the warnings and anxieties of the first novels emerge again, and new ground is broken as well. What chiefly distinguishes Wells's science fiction after 1901 is its heightened political consciousness. Scenarios of global war fought with diabolical weapons alternate with visions of a technocratic worldwide utopia. Wells foresaw tank warfare in 1903 ("The Land Ironclads"), massive bombardment of cities by aircraft in 1908 (*The War in the Air*), and atomic bombs in 1914 (*The World Set Free*). He satirized fascism in *The Autocracy of Mr. Parham* and turned it to his advantage in *The Holy Terror*. His three major utopian novels, *A Modern Utopia, Men Like Gods*, and *The Shape of Things to Come*, are landmarks in that extraordinarily difficult genre.

Writing in 1934, Wells took stock of the "incurable habit with literary critics to lament some lost artistry and innocence in my early work and to accuse me of having become polemical in my later years. " In his defense, he observed—quite correctly—that his work had always been concerned with contemporary issues and with "life in the mass. " So far, so true. But Wells could not bring himself to admit the decline of imagination and technique that overtook his later fiction. The success of such eminently polemical writers of science fiction as George Orwell and Walter M. Miller, Jr., who has as many axes to grind as Wells at his worst, suffices to show that Wells did not go wrong by abandoning "pure" literature for "pamphleteering. " He merely let impatience and irritability diminish the effectiveness of his art. But the size of his achievement remains formidable. Well's best work is superb, and grandly paradigmatic. No other early writer of science fiction opened so many pathways. He is also a singularly universal figure. One may wonder if even one significant writer in the genre anywhere in the world in this century has missed reading H. G. Wells. Quite simply, he is to science fiction what Albert Einstein is to modern physics, or Pablo Picasso to modern art.

—W. Warren Wagar

WELLS, John J. See **BRADLEY, Marion Zimmer; COULSON, Juanita.**

WERNHEIM, John. See **FEARN, John Russell.**

WEST, Douglas. See **TUBB, E. C.**

WEST, Wallace (George). American. Born in Walnut Hills, Kentucky, 22 May 1900. Educated at Butler University, Indianapolis, A. B. 1924 (Phi Beta Kappa); Indiana University Law School, Bloomington, LL. B. 1925. Assistant to the Director of Radio Censorship during World War II. Married Claudia M. Weyant in 1928. Farmer, barber, and telegrapher; lawyer, Calvin and West, in the 1920's; journalist, United Press; publicity officer, Paramount Pictures; editor, *ROTO, Voice of Experience, Song Hits*, and *Movie Mirror* ; publicity writer for CBS Radio, and news writer and commentator for ABC, NBC, and Mutual radio; polution control expert, American Petroleum Institute, 1947-58; consultant, Air Pollution Control Administration; now retired.

SCIENCE-FICTION PUBLICATIONS

Novels

The Bird of Time. New York, Gnome Press, 1959.
Lords of Atlantis. New York, Avalon, 1960.
The Memory Bank. New York, Avalon, 1961.
River of Time. New York, Avalon, 1963.
The Time-Lockers. New York, Avalon, 1964.
The Everlasting Exiles. New York, Avalon, 1967.

Short Stories

Outposts in Space. New York, Avalon, 1962.

Uncollected Short Stories

"A Thing of Beauty," in *Magazine of Horror* (New York), August 1963.
"Glimpses of the Moon," in *Great Science Fiction about the Moon*, edited by T. E. Dikty. New York, Fell, 1967.
"The Last Filibuster," in *Galaxy* (New York), February 1967.
"Dust," in *Famous Science Fiction* (New York), Spring 1967.
"Steamer Time?," in *Analog* (New York), September 1968.
"A Thing of Beauty," in *The Unspeakable People*, edited by Peter Haining. London, Frewin, 1969.
"The 'Last Man' Mess," in *WT50: A Tribute to Weird Tales*. Chicago, Advent, 1974.

OTHER PUBLICATIONS

Novels

Jimmy Allen in The Sky Parade (novelization of screenplay). New York, Lynn, 1936.
Thirteen Hours by Air (novelization of screenplay). New York, Lynn, 1936.

Other

Betty Boop in Snow-White (adaptation of screenplay; for children). Racine, Wisconsin, Whitman, 1934.
Alice in Wonderland (novelization of screenplay; for children). Racine, Wisconsin, Whitman, 1934.
Paramount Newsreel Men with Admiral Byrd in Little America. Racine, Wisconsin, Whitman, 1934.
Our Good Neighbors in Latin America. New York, Noble, 1942.
Our Good Neighbors in Soviet Russia, with James P. Mitchell. New York, Noble, 1945.
Down to the Sea in Ships. New York, Noble, 1947.

Find a Career in Electronics. New York, Putnam, 1959.
Clearing the Air. New York, American Petroleum Institute, 1961.
Conserving Our Waters. New York, American Petroleum Institute, 1964(?).
The Amazing Inventor from Laurel Creek (for children). New York, Putnam, 1967.

*   *   *

Shortly after the end of World War II, a number of science-fiction enthusiasts became small-time book publishers, dealing exclusively in fantasy and science fiction. Many of the oldtime favorite magazine authors found that they could rework their earlier short stories or novelettes into full-length novels for an appreciate audience. Wallace West was one of the "names" thus uncovered to the book-buying world, and his novels are such expansions and conflations. *Lords of Atlantis*, though, was originally published as a series of novelettes; it retells the Greek myths as the memories of an invasion from Mars in a combination of the author's ingenuity and ironic humor.

Wallace West was never a full-time writer. He wrote stories because he enjoyed reading science fiction and enjoyed writing it. He could tailor his plots to any magazine's requirements, and some of his stories are wildly melodramatic in the old "pulp" manner; but even those examples offer humor and speculation beyond the level of pulp entertainment. A number of the early stories were the first to present themes that are very familiar. The Feminist movement foreshadowed today's Women's Liberation, and there were those Feminists who felt that a truly decent society could exist only if males were completely subjugated to females—if not dispensed with altogether. In "The Last Man" (*Amazing*, February 1929) West draws an amusing yet grim portrait of a world where that "final solution" has been achieved. The last man is a museum exhibit; there are no more wars and sex conflict is a thing of the past. But is the world a utopia? The picture is not enticing.

West was concerned with air and water pollution decades before it became a public issue. In 1935, West wrote a short story, "Dust," which shows what happens when several elements of runaway pollution peak simultaneously. The story was rejected in 1935; he effectively rewrote and updated the tale for publication in 1967. "The Phantom Dictator," his best-remembered story, showed the possibilities of subliminal propagandizing some 20 years before Vance Packard's *The Hidden Persuaders*. (That story was subsumed, with other themes, in his novel *The Time-Lockers*.)

Wallace West was well-educated and widely read in many fields—literature, history, and the theater—as well as science. He used the entire range of his learning, in addition to his wry sense of humor, to write stories that stimulated thought as well as provided entertainment; that is why so many of them are still a pleasure to read and have not grown stale with time. He cared too much for the joys of science fiction to preach to or condescend to his readers, however seriously he himself might consider some of the themes, and would be the first to snort if some academic found his work "significant. "

—Robert A. W. Lowndes

_____

WHEATLEY, Dennis (Yates). British. Born in London, 8 January 1897. Educated at Dulwich College, London, 1908; H.

M. S. Worcester, 1909-13; privately in Germany, 1913. Married 1) Nancy Robinson in 1923, one son; 2) Joan Gwendoline Johnstone in 1931. Served in the Royal Field Artillery, City of London Brigade, 1914-17; 36th Ulster Division, 1917-19 (invalided out); recommissioned in Royal Air Force Volunteer Reserve, 1939; Member, National Recruiting Panel, 1940-41; Member, Joint Planning Staff of War Cabinet, 1941-44; Wing Commander, 1944-45: United States Army Bronze Star. Joined his father's wine business, Wheatley and Son, London, 1914; worked in the business, 1919-26; sole owner, 1926-31. Editor, Dennis Wheatley's Library of the Occult, Sphere Books, London, from 1973 (over 40 volumes). Received Livery of Vintners' Company, 1918, and Distillers' Company, 1922. Fellow, Royal Society of Arts, and Royal Society of Literature. *Died 11 November 1977.*

SCIENCE-FICTION PUBLICATIONS

Novels

Such Power Is Dangerous. London, Hutchinson, 1933.
Black August. London, Hutchinson, and New York, Dutton, 1934.
The Fabulous Valley. London, Hutchinson, 1934.
They Found Atlantis. London, Hutchinson, and Philadelphia, Lippincott, 1936.
The Secret War. London, Hutchinson, 1937.
Uncharted Seas. London, Hutchinson, 1938.
Sixty Days to Live. London, Hutchinson, 1939.
The Man Who Missed the War. London, Hutchinson, 1945.
Star of Ill-Omen. London, Hutchinson, 1952.

OTHER PUBLICATIONS

Novels

The Forbidden Territory. London, Hutchinson, and New York, Dutton, 1933.
The Devil Rides Out. London, Hutchinson, 1935; New York, Bantam, 1967.
The Eunuch of Stamboul. London, Hutchinson, and Boston, Little Brown, 1935.
Murder Off Miami. London, Hutchinson, 1936; as *File on Bolitho Blane*, New York, Morrow, 1936.
Contraband. London, Hutchinson, 1936.
Who Killed Robert Prentice? London, Hutchinson, 1937; as *File on Robert Prentice*, New York, Greenberg, 1937.
The Malinsay Massacre. London, Hutchinson, 1938; New York, Rutledge Press, 1981.
The Golden Spaniard. London, Hutchinson, 1938.
The Quest of Julian Day. London, Hutchinson, 1939.
Herewith the Clues! London, Hutchinson, 1939.
The Scarlet Imposter. London, Hutchinson, 1940; New York, Macmillan, 1942.
Three Inquisitive People. London, Hutchinson, 1940.
Faked Passports. London, Hutchinson, 1940; New York, Macmillan, 1943.
The Black Baroness. London, Hutchinson, 1940; New York, Macmillan, 1942.
Strange Conflict. London, Hutchinson, 1941.
The Sword of Fate. London, Hutchinson, 1941; New York, Macmillan, 1944.
"V" for Vengeance. London, Hutchinson, and New York, Macmillan, 1942.

Codeword—Golden Fleece. London, Hutchinson, 1946.
Come into My Parlour. London, Hutchinson, 1946.
The Launching of Roger Brook. London, Hutchinson, 1947; New York, Ballantine, 1973.
The Shadow of Tyburn Tree. London, Hutchinson, 1948; New York, Ballantine, 1973.
The Haunting of Toby Jugg. London, Hutchinson, 1948; New York, Ballantine, 1974.
The Rising Storm. London, Hutchinson, 1949.
The Second Seal. London, Hutchinson, 1950.
The Man Who Killed the King. London, Hutchinson, 1951; New York, Putnam, 1965.
To the Devil—A Daughter. London, Hutchinson, 1953; New York, Bantam, 1968.
Curtain of Fear. London, Hutchinson, 1953.
The Island Where Time Stands Still. London, Hutchinson, 1954.
The Dark Secret of Josephine. London, Hutchinson, 1955.
The Ka of Gifford Hillary. London, Hutchinson, 1956; New York, Ballantine, 1973.
The Prisoner in the Mask. London, Hutchinson, 1957.
Traitors' Gate. London, Hutchinson, 1958.
The Rape of Venice. London, Hutchinson, 1959.
The Satanist. London, Hutchinson, 1960; New York, Bantam, 1967.
Vendetta in Spain. London, Hutchinson, 1961.
Mayhem in Greece. London, Hutchinson, 1962.
The Sultan's Daughter. London, Hutchinson, 1963.
Bill for the Use of a Body. London, Hutchinson, 1964.
They Used Dark Forces. London, Hutchinson, 1964.
Dangerous Inheritance. London, Hutchinson, 1965.
The Wanton Princess. London, Hutchinson, 1966.
Unholy Crusade. London, Hutchinson, 1967.
The White Witch of the South Seas. London, Hutchinson, 1968.
Evil in a Mask. London, Hutchinson, 1969.
Gateway to Hell. London, Hutchinson, 1970; New York, Ballantine, 1973.
The Ravishing of Lady Mary Ware. London, Hutchinson, 1971.
The Strange Story of Linda Lee. London, Hutchinson, 1972.
The Irish Witch. London, Hutchinson, 1973.
Desperate Measures. London, Hutchinson, 1974.

Short Stories

Mediterranean Nights. London, Hutchinson, 1942; revised edition, London, Arrow, 1963.
Gunmen, Gallants, and Ghosts. London, Hutchinson, 1943; revised edition, London, Arrow, 1963.

Play

Screenplay: *An Englishman's Home* (*Madmen of Europe*), with others, 1939.

Other

Old Rowley: A Private Life of Charles II. London, Hutchinson, 1933; as *A Private Life of Charles II,* 1938.
Red Eagle: A Life of Marshal Voroshilov. London, Hutchinson, 1937.
Invasion (war game). London, Hutchinson, 1938.
Blockade (war game). London, Hutchinson, 1939.
Total War. London, Hutchinson, 1941.
The Seven Ages of Justerini's. London, Riddle Books, 1949; revised edition, as *1749-1965: The Eight Ages if Justerini's,* Aylesbury, Buckinghamshire, Dolphin, 1965.

Alibi (war game). London, Geographia, 1951.

Stranger Than Fiction. London, Hutchinson, 1959.

Saturdays with Bricks and Other Days under Shell-Fire. London, Hutchinson, 1961.

The Devil and All His Works. London, Hutchinson, and New York, American Heritage Press, 1971.

The Time Has Come: The Memoirs of Dennis Wheatley. London, Arrow, 1981.

The Young Man Said 1897-1914. London, Hutchinson, 1977.

Officer and Temporary Gentleman 1914-1919. London, Hutchinson, 1978.

Drink and Ink 1919-1977, edited by Anthony Lejeune. London, Hutchinson, 1979.

The Deception Planners: My Secret War, edited by Anthony Lejeune. London, Hutchinson, 1980.

Editor, *A Century of Horror Stories*. London, Hutchinson, 1935; Freeport, New York, Books for Libraries, 1971; selection as *Quiver of Horror* and *Shafts of Fear*, London, Arrow, 2 vols., 1965; as *Tales of Strange Doings* and *Tales of Strange Happenings*, Hutchinson, 2 vols., 1968.

Editor, *A Century of Spy Stories*. London, Hutchinson, 1938.

Editor, *Uncanny Tales*. London, Sphere, 2 vols., 1974.

*

Bibliography: *Fyra Decennier med Dennis Wheatley: En Biografi & Bibliografi* by Iwan Hedman and Jan Alexandersson, privately printed, 1963; revised edition, Strägnäs, Sweden, DAST, 1973.

*   *   *

In 40 years, Dennis Wheatley published some 60 books of detection, adventure, fantasy, and romance. While his plots may seem fantastic, his is not a name which comes to mind when science-fiction writers are mentioned. Many of those which may be classed in the genre are only marginally science fiction in theme. The fantasy is often only a framework for a story of romance and adventure. His stories of black magic may give him one claim to belong to the field.

The heroes of two of his major series of thrillers, the Duke de Richleau and Gregory Sallust, become involved with the occult in some of their adventures. *The Devil Rides Out*, which concerns a classic confrontation between the forces of good and evil (Richleau and a group of Satanists in contemporary London) is considered his best novel in the genre. In the sequel, *Strange Conflict*, the success of the Nazis in World War II is traced to their use of the supernatural. This fancy is also the theme of a later work, *They Used Dark Forces,* in which the occult is turned upon Hitler himself. Richleau's third black magic adventure is *Gateway to Hell*. Other black magic novels which do not involve recurring characters from the major series are *The Haunting of Toby Jugg, To the Devil a Daughter, The Ka of Gifford Hillary*, and *The Satanist*. While there is a definite attempt to make the reader believe in the occult in these novels (one is uncertain of the extent to which the author is being creative or reporting his own belief) it must be admitted that the supernatural is described in such detail that the reader is never really frightened. Actual malevolence is never as convincing as the suggestion of the possibility that ghosts exist. The diabolists could just as well have been gangsters. The ghost hunter stories in *Gunmen, Gallants, and Ghosts* and the lurking fears in *The Haunting of Toby Jugg* more successfully evoke the true shudder.

More traditional science-fiction motifs occur in some of his other novels. *Black August* is a Wellsian story of England in the future during a Communist revolution. In *The Fabulous Valley* the heirs to a diamond field in Africa have only a knobkerrie, a necklace of monkey skulls, and a leopard skin to tell them where to find the treasure, in a story of high adventure in the Haggard vein. A somewhat incongruously diverse group of adventurers find a lost race in *They Found Atlantis* ; while the plot may not appear original to us there is a sound foundation of archeology and anthropology behind the telling of the story. *Uncharted Seas* is another lost-race story in which the shipwrecked protagonists are cast adrift on the open sea and discover a continent made of seaweed. A more conventional thriller, *The Secret War*, is a speculative fantasy about an anti-war league called the "Millers of God" who assassinate war profiteers. Also in the Wellsian vein is *Sixty Days to Live*, the story of the comet scheduled to strike the earth. The bulk of the novel concerns three men in love with the same woman and a world gone mad. A third lost-race story is *The Man Who Missed the War:* Philip Vaudell tries to float a raft across the Atlantic, is diverted to the Antarctic, and discovers a warm climate and a people cut off from the world. In *Star of Ill Omen* a British secret agent discovers the secret behind flying saucers and travels from Argentina to Mars. One of the novels often found on lists of Wheatley's fantasy, *Such Power is Dangerous*, has little to recommend it apart from a fascinating idea of motion picture studios combining to shape public opinion through the films they produce. It is more satiric than fantastic.

Even in fantasy, Wheatley's strength lies in his having discovered that what the readers wanted was what he enjoyed writing for them. His adventure stories are far better than the elements of fantasy with which he filled them. A study of Wheatley is a study of public taste.

—J. Randolph Cox

———

WHITE, James. British. Born in Belfast, Northern Ireland, 7 April 1928. Educated at St. John's Primary School, 1935-41, and St. Joseph's Secondary Technical School, 1942-43, both Belfast. Married Margaret Sarah Martin in 1955; one daughter and two sons. Salesman and manager in several tailoring stores, Belfast, 1943-65. Technical clerk, 1965-66, publicity assistant, 1966-68, and publicity officer, 1968-84, Shorts Aircraft, Belfast. Patron, Irish Science Fiction Association, 1974; Council Member, British Science Fiction Association, 1975. Recipient: Europa Award, 1972. Agent: Leslie Flood, Carnell Literary Agency, Rowneybury Bungalow, Sawbridgeworth, near Old Harlow, Essex CM20 2EX, England. Address: 2 West Drive, Portstewart BT55 7ND, Northern Ireland.

SCIENCE-FICTION PUBLICATIONS

Novels (series: Sector General)

The Secret Visitors. New York, Ace, 1957; London, Digit, 1961.

Second Ending. New York, Ace, 1962.

Star Surgeon (Sector). New York, Ballantine, 1963; London, Corgi, 1967.

Escape Orbit. New York, Ace, 1965; as *Open Prison*, London, New English Library, 1965.

The Watch Below. New York, Ballantine, and London, Whiting and Wheaton, 1966.

All Judgment Fled. London, Rapp and Whiting, 1968; New York, Walker, 1969.
Tomorrow Is Too Far. New York, Ballantine, and London, Joseph, 1971.
Dark Inferno. London, Joseph, 1972; as *Lifeboat*, New York, Ballantine, 1972.
The Dream Millennium. London, Joseph, and New York, Ballantine, 1974.
Underkill. London, Corgi, 1979.
Ambulance Ship (Sector). New York, Ballantine, 1979; London, Corgi, 1980.
Star Healer (Sector). New York, Ballantine, 1985.

Short Stories (series: Sector General)

Hospital Station (Sector). New York, Ballantine, 1962; London, Corgi, 1967.
Deadly Litter. New York, Ballantine, 1964; London, Corgi, 1968.
The Aliens Among Us. New York, Ballantine, 1969; London, Corgi, 1970.
Major Operation (Sector). New York, Ballantine, 1971.
Monsters and Medics. London, Corgi, and New York, Ballantine, 1977.
Future Past. New York, Ballantine, 1982.
Sector General. New York, Ballantine, 1983.

Uncollected Short Stories

"Federation World," in *Analog* (New York), August 1980.
"The Scourge," in *The 1983 Annual World's Best SF*, edited by Donald A. Wollheim and Arthur W. Saha. New York, DAW, 1983.
"Something of Value," in *Analog* (New York), February 1985.

*

James White comments:
I have always felt that the best stories are those in which ordinary people are faced with extraordinary situations, and my early attraction to science fiction, both as a very young reader and later as a writer, was that it was the only genre which allowed ordinary people to be faced with truly extraordinary situations. My favourite of these is the one in which Earth-human characters make first contact with an extraterrestrial species. The attempts to understand the behaviour and thought processes of the aliens frequently illuminate the human condition as well, and the problem of learning to understand and adapt to a totally alien viewpoint places in proper perspective the very minor differences of skin pigmentation and politics which bedevil our own culture.

*   *   *

One of the most memorable of James White's many intriguing settings is to be found in *The Watch Below*: a colony survives for several generations trapped inside the hull of a tanker torpedoed during World War II. In their effort to keep themselves sane, one of the things the first generation does is to attempt to recall every story any of them has ever read. One survivor has read a few works in the relatively new genre of science fiction. He particularly remembers a Doc Smith novel with a character "who was a winged dragon with scales, claws, four extensible eyes, and a lot of other visually horrifying features and who was more human than some of the human characters." Now, since

The Watch Below is a "first contact" story, there are reasons of plot for this introduction of this tribute to the idea of interspecific brotherhood. But beyond this, the tradition of the fraternity of all intelligent life which first took firm hold in magazine SF in the mid-1930's is one which has had a marked impact on White himself as an author.

Most of White's stories involve extraterrestrials, and these beings are a varied lot indeed, including creatures indistinguishable from terrestrials in *The Secret Visitors*, aquatic lifeforms in *The Watch Below*, chlorine-breathers in *Open Prison*, and giant caterpillar-like tree-dwellers in *All Judgment Fled*. All these varieties together, and others besides, can be found at once in *Hospital Station* and the other books in White's series about Sector Twelve General Hospital, a multi-environmental hospital in deep space with staff and patients from a diverse galactic culture. Indeed, as an author White is quite fond of the field of medicine, perhaps seeing in it a paradigm of the cooperation and fellowship which should embrace all intelligent beings. Even outside the Sector General series, physicians are important characters in *The Secret Visitors, The Watch Below, All Judgment Fled*, and *Underkill*.

But soldiers figure almost as prominently as doctors in White's work. One section of *Hospital Station* is given over to the hero's realization that the Monitor Corps performs a necessary police function. White is not happy about this fact of life. Indeed, in at least three different books characters are relieved to have it turn out that the lifeforms they were forced to kill are only animals, and not intelligent beings after all. And beyond such justified violence, White's work also depicts some conflicts based on honest misunderstanding, and others stemming from deliberate selfishness and greed. But with one exception, the accent in White's work is not on the existence of such abominations but on the possibility of doing something about them. White's stories almost always close with harmony restored, or at least with such a restoration anticipated. This stubborn optimism has been one of White's trademarks.

A second trademark, already alluded to, is his inventiveness regarding environments. If his most brilliant achievement in this area is the sunken tanker in *The Watch Below*, other instances are almost equally imaginative—the prison planet of *Open Prison*, the alien starship overrun with laboratory animals in *All Judgment Fled*, the energy-poor world of the "powerdown" in *Underkill*, and others.

White's work does have its defects. His human characters are too much alike, and sometimes their actions are inadequately motivated. Often White's extra-terrestrials have incongruously human—indeed, Western—psychologies, whatever their external forms. White's fascinating environments are also sometimes a little too visibly contrived. Until fairly recently, the single most serious accusation that could be brought against White was his utopianism, his seeming belief that no group of intelligent beings could willfully persist in wrongdoing once they had had the right path pointed out to them. White, however, effectively countered any such accusation with *Underkill*, a novel presumably growing out of White's experience of the civil unrest in his home of Northern Ireland. In this novel, extra-terrestrials—playing as it were the part of an Old-Testament Yahweh—find mankind so depraved (particularly by the ethnic and sectarian hatreds that lead to terrorism) that they see no solution but to destroy all the Earth's population save for a chosen remnant of ten million, and to start over with those. Unlike other White books, *Underkill* is charged with a bitterness and forcefulness reminiscent of Jonathan Swift. However, after this aberration, White's next several books went back with no obvious difficulty to the seeming utopianism of the Sector General series. This return to a familiar path could have been based on commercial considerations, since *Underkill* failed to find an American publisher. (Presumably its bitterness was judged to be unviable in an American market that was beginning to emerge from the gloom of much Vietnam-era sf.) In any case, *Underkill* makes it clear that in his other books, White is presenting a view of human relations as they ought to be, not as he actually takes them to be. White is not naive—merely hopeful.

—Patrick L. McGuire

WHITE, Ted (Theodore Edward White). Also writes as Ron Archer; Norman Edwards. American. Born in Washington, D.C., 4 February 1938. Educated in public schools in Falls Church, Virginia. Married 1)Sylvia Dees in 1958; 2) Robin Postal in 1966;one child. Head of foreign department, Scott Meredith Literary Agency, 1963; Assistant Editor, 1963-67, and Associate Editor, 1967-68, *Fantasy and Science Fiction;* Associate Editor, Lancer Books, 1966; Managing Editor, 1969, and Editor, 1970-78, *Amazing* and *Fantastic* ; Co-Editor, *Void* fan magazine, 1959-68; Editor, *Heavy Metal,* New York, 1979-81. Recipient: Hugo Award, for criticism, 1968. Agent: Henry Morrison Inc., 320 McLain Street, Bedford Hills, New York 10705, U.S.A.

SCIENCE-FICTION PUBLICATIONS

Novels

Invasion from 2500 (as Norman Edwards, with Terry Carr). Derby, Connecticut, Monarch, 1964.
Android Avenger. New York, Ace, 1965.
Phoenix Prime. New York, Lancer, 1966.
The Sorceress of Qar. New York, Lancer, 1966.
The Jewels of Elsewhen. New York, Belmont, 1967.
Lost in Space (novelization of TV play; as Ron Archer, with Dave Van Arnam). New York, Pyramid, 1967.
Secret of the Marauder Satellite. Philadelphia, Westminster Press, 1967.
Sideslip, with Dave Van Arnam, New York, Pyramid, 1968.
Captain America: The Great Gold Steal. New York, Bantam, 1968.
The Spawn of the Death Machine. New York, Paperback Library, 1968.
No Time Like Tomorrow (for children). New York, Crown, 1969.
By Furies Possessed. New York, New American Library, 1970.
Star Wolf! New York, Lancer, 1971.
Trouble on Project Ceres (for children). Philadelphia, Westminster Press, 1971.
Forbidden World, with David F. Bischoff. New York, Popular Library, 1978.

Uncollected Short Stories

"I, Executioner," in *If* (New York), March 1963.
"Policy Conference," in *Gamma* (North Hollywood), September 1965.
"The Peacock King," in *Fantasy and Science Fiction* (New York), November 1965.

"The Secret of the City," in *Startling* (New York), Fall 1966.
"Wednesday Noon," in *Fantasy and Science Fiction* (New York), February 1968.
"Saboteur," in *If* (New York), March 1969.
"Only Yesterday," in *Amazing* (New York), July 1969.
"It Could Be Anywhere," in *Fantastic* (New York), October 1969.
"A Girl Like You," in *Amazing* (New York), March 1971.
"Wolf Quest," in *Fantastic* (New York), April 1971.
"Growing Up Fast in the City," in *Amazing* (New York), May 1971.
"Junk Patrol," in *Amazing* (New York), September 1971.
"Things Are Tough All Over," in *Fantastic* (New York), December 1971.
"Stella," in *And Walk Now Gently Through the Fire* . . ., edited by Roger Elwood. Philadelphia, Chilton, 1972.
"4148 PM, October 6, 197-, Late Afternoon, on Christopher Street," in *Amazing* (New York), January 1972.
"Dandy," in *Demon Kind,* edited by Roger Elwood. New York, Avon, 1973.
"Phoenix," with Marion Zimmer Bradley, in *The Best from Amazing Stories,* edited by Ted White. New York, Manor, 1973; London, Hale, 1976.
" . . . and Another World Above," in *Fantasy* (New York), January 1974.
"Sixteen and Vanilla," in *Vertex* (Los Angeles), June 1974.
"Manhattan Square Dance," in Amazing (New York), August 1974.
"Doc Phoenix (The Man Who Enters the Wind)," in *Weird Heroes 2,* edited by Byron Preiss. New York, Pyramid, 1975.
"Under the Mad Sun," in *Amazing* (New York), May 1975.
"What Is Happening to Sarah Anne Lawrence?," in *Amazing* (New York), September 1975.
"Welcome to the Machine," in *Amazing* (New York), June 1976.
"Vengeance Is Mine," in *Fantastic* (New York), June 1977.

OTHER PUBLICATIONS

Other

Editor, *The Best from Amazing Stories.* New York, Manor, 1973; London, Hale, 1976.
Editor, *The Best from Fantastic.* New York, Manor,1973; London, Hale, 1976.

* * *

Ted White, like many writers of his generation, first achieved prominence as a fan. He was responsible for what was recognised as the first fanzine devoted exclusively to comics in 1953; his fanzine *Void* helped advance both his career and that of Gregory Benford.

White's career as a novelist was relatively short. His novels tend to be all of a type, in that they usually deal with supermen with neuroses. Thus *The Spawn of the Death Machine,* a novel much better than its title suggests, concerns an android in a post-apocalyptic future who wanders about determining the limits of his powers. In *Phoenix Prime* the cab-driver Maximillan Quest learns that he is an incomplete superman and is rushed to another dimension to fight a cosmic war. White's novels are essentially imitative, at times reminding one of Heinlein, at other times of Van Vogt; while his work is competent, he has not achieved any writing of the first rank, save for certain sections of the fascinating failure, *The Jewels of Elsewhen*, White's favorite among his own works.

White's distinction is as an editor, more than as a writer. White was editor of *Amazing Stories* and *Fantastic Science Fiction* for some ten years; he returned the magazines to a policy of publishing orginal fiction, and developed some of the talented young writers of the 1970's

—Martin Morse Wooster

WIBBERLEY, Leonard (Patrick O'Connor). Also wrote as Leonard Holton; Patrick O'Connor; Christopher Webb. Irish. Born in Dublin, 9 April 1915. Educated at Ring College, Ireland; Abbey House, Romsey, Hampshire; Cardinal Vaughan's School, London, 1925-30; El Camino College, Torrance, California. Served in the Trinidad Artillery Volunteers, 1938-40: Lance Bombardier. Married Katherine Hazel Holton in 1948; two daughters and four sons. Reporter, *Sunday Dispatch*, 1931-32, *Sunday Express*, 1932-34, and *Daily Mirror*, 1935-36, all London; editor, Trinidad *Evening News*, 1936; oilfield worker, Trinidad, 1936-43; cable editor, Associated Press, New York, 1943-44; New York correspondent and bureau chief, London *Evening News*, 1944-46; editor, Independent Journal, San Rafael, California, 1947-49; reporter and copy editor, Los Angeles *Times*, 1950-54; columnist, San Francisco *Chronicle*. Died 22 November 1983.

SCIENCE-FICTION PUBLICATIONS

Novels (series: Mouse)

The Mouse That Roared. Boston, Little Brown, 1955; London, Corgi, 1959; as *The Wrath of Grapes*, London, Hale, 1955.
The Mouse on the Moon. New York, Morrow, 1962; London, Muller, 1964.
Encounter Near Venus (for children). New York, Farrar Straus, 1967; London, Macdonald, 1968.
Journey to Untor (for children). New York, Farrar Straus, 1970; London, Macdonald, 1971.

OTHER PUBLICATIONS

Novels

Mrs. Searwood's Secret Weapon. Boston, Little Brown, 1954; London, Hale, 1955.
McGillicuddy McGotham. Boston, Little Brown, 1956; London, Hale, 1958.
Take Me to Your President. New York, Putnam, 1957.
Beware of the Mouse. New York, Putnam, 1958.
The Quest for Excalibur. New York, Putnam, 1959.
The Hands of Cormac Joyce. New York, Putnam, 1960; London, Muller, 1962.
Stranger at Killknock. New York, Putnam, 1961; London, Muller, 1963.
A Feast of Freedom. New York, Morrow, 1964.
The Island of the Angels. New York, Morrow, 1965.
The Centurion. New York, Morrow, 1966.
The Road from Toomi. New York, Morrow, 1967.
Adventures of an Elephant Boy. New York, Morrow, 1968.
The Mouse on Wall Street. New York, Morrow, 1969.

Meeting with a Great Beast. New York, Morrow, 1971; London, Chatto and Windus, 1972.
The Testament of Theophilus. New York, Morrow, 1973; as *Merchant of Rome*, London, Cassell, 1974.
The Last Stand of Father Felix. New York, Morrow, 1974.
1776—and All That. New York, Morrow, 1975.
One in Four. New York, Morrow, 1976.
Homeward to Ithaka. New York, Morrow, 1978.
The Mouse That Saved the West. New York, Morrow, 1981.

Novels as Leonard Holton

The Saint Maker. New York, Dodd Mead, 1959; London, Hale, 1960.
A Pact with Satan. New York, Dodd Mead, 1960; London, Hale, 1961.
Secret of the Doubting Saint. New York, Dodd Mead, 1961.
Deliver Us from Wolves. New York, Dodd Mead, 1963.
Flowers by Request. New York, Dodd Mead, 1964.
Out of the Depths. New York, Dodd Mead, 1966; London, Hammond, 1967.
A Touch of Jonah. New York, Dodd Mead, 1968.
A Problem in Angels. New York, Dodd Mead, 1970.
The Mirror of Hell. New York, Dodd Mead, 1972.
The Devil to Play. New York, Dodd Mead, 1974.
A Corner of Paradise. New York, St. Martin's Press, 1977.

Fiction (for children)

The King's Beard. New York, Farrar Straus, 1952; London, Faber, 1954.
The Secret of the Hawk. New York, Farrar Straus, 1953; London, Faber, 1956.
Deadmen's Cave. New York, Farrar Straus, and London, Faber, 1954.
The Wound of Peter Wayne. New York, Farrar Straus, 1955; London, Faber, 1957.
Kevin O'Connor and the Light Brigade. New York, Farrar Straus, 1957; London, Harrap, 1959.
John Treegate's Musket. New York, Farrar Straus, 1959.
Peter Treegate's War. New York, Farrar Straus, 1960.
Sea Captain from Salem. New York, Farrar Straus, 1961.
The Time of the Lamb. New York, Washburn, 1961.
Treegate's Raiders. New York, Farrar Straus, 1962.
Attar of the Ice Valley. New York, Farrar Straus, 1968; London, Macdonald, 1969.
Leopard's Prey. New York, Farrar Straus, 1971.
Flint's Island. New York, Farrar Straus, 1972; London, Macdonald, 1973.
Red Pawns. New York, Farrar Straus, 1973.
The Last Battle. New York, Farrar Straus, 1976.
Perilous Gold. New York, Farrar Straus, 1978.
Little League Family. New York, Doubleday, 1978.
The Crime of Martin Coverly. New York, Farrar Straus, 1980.

Fiction (for children) as Patrick O'Connor

The Lost Harpooner. New York, Washburn, 1947; London, Harrap, 1959.
Flight of the Peacock. New York, Washburn, 1954.
The Society of Foxes. New York, Washburn, 1954.
The Watermelon Mystery. New York, Washburn, 1955.
Gunpowder for Washington. New York, Washburn, 1956.
The Black Tiger. New York, Washburn, 1956.
Mexican Road Race. New York, Washburn, 1957.

Black Tiger at Le Mans. New York, Washburn, 1958.
The Five-Dollar Watch Mystery. New York, Washburn, 1959.
Black Tiger at Bonneville. New York, Washburn, 1960.
Treasure at Twenty Fathoms. New York, Washburn, 1961.
Black Tiger at Indianapolis. New York, Washburn, 1962.
The Raising of the Dubhe. New York, Washburn, 1964.
Seawind from Hawaii. New York, Washburn, 1965.
South Swell. New York, Washburn, 1967; London, Macdonald, 1968.
Beyond Hawaii. New York, Washburn, 1969; as Leonard Wibberley, London, Macdonald, 1970.
A Car Called Camellia. New York, Washburn, 1970.

Fiction (for children) as Christopher Webb

Matt Tyler's Chronicle. New York, Funk and Wagnalls, 1958; London, Macdonald, 1966.
Mark Toyman's Inheritance. New York, Funk and Wagnalls, 1960.
The River of Pee Dee Jack. New York, Funk and Wagnalls, 1962.
The Quest of the Otter. New York, Funk and Wagnalls, 1963; London, Macdonald, 1965.
The "Ann and Hope" Mutiny. New York, Funk and Wagnalls, 1966; London, Macdonald, 1967.
Eusebius, The Phoenician. New York, Funk and Wagnalls, 1969; London, Macdonald, 1970.

Plays

The Heavenly Quarterback. Chicago, Dramatic Publishing Company, 1968.
Gift of a Star. Chicago, Dramatic Publishing Company, 1969.
The Vicar of Wakefield, adaptation of the novel by Oliver Goldsmith. Chicago, Dramatic Publishing Company, n. d.
Black Jack Rides Again. Chicago, Dramatic Publishing Company, 1971.
1776—and All That. Chicago, Dramatic Publishing Company, 1973.
Once, In a Garden. Chicago, Dramatic Publishing Company, 1975.

Ballet Scenario: *Encounter near Venus*, 1978.

Verse (for children)

The Ballad of the Pilgrim Cat. New York, Washburn, 1962.
The Shepherd's Reward. New York, Washburn, 1963.

Other

The Trouble with the Irish (or the English, Depending on Your Point of View). New York, Holt, 1956; London, Muller, 1958.
The Coming of the Green. New York, Holt, 1958.
No Garlic in the Soup (on Portugal). New York, Washburn, 1959; London, Faber, 1960.
The Land That Isn't There: An Irish Adventure. New York, Washburn, 1960.
Yesterday's Land: A Baja California Adventure. New York, Washburn, 1961.
Ventures into the Deep: The Thrill of Scuba Diving. New York, Washburn, 1962.
Ah Julian! A Memoir of Julian Brodetsky. New York, Washburn, 1963.

Fiji: Islands of the Dawn. New York, Washburn, 1964.
Toward a Distant Island: A Sailor's Odyssey. New York, Washburn, 1966.
Something to Read. New York, Washburn, 1967.
Hound of the Sea. New York, Washburn, 1969.
Voyage by Bus. New York, Morrow, 1971.
The Shannon Sailors: A Voyage to the Heart of Ireland. New York, Morrow, 1972.
The Good-Natured Man: A Portrait of Oliver Goldsmith. New York, Morrow, 1979.

Other (for children)

The Coronation Book: The Dramatic Story in History and Legend. New York, Farrar Straus, 1953.
The Epics of Everest. New York, Farrar Straus, 1954; London, Faber, 1955.
The Life of Winston Churchhill. New York, Farrar Straus, 1956; revised edition, 1965.
John Barry, Father of the Navy. New York, Farrar Straus, 1957.
Wes Powell, Conqueror of the Grand Canyon. New York, Farrar Straus, 1958.
Zebulon Pike, Soldier and Explorer. New York, Funk and Wagnalls, 1961.
Man of Liberty: A Life of Thomas Jefferson. New York, Farrar Straus, 1968.
1. *Young Man from the Piedmont: The Youth of Thomas Jefferson*. New York, Farrar Straus, 1963.
2. *A Dawn in the Trees: Thomas Jefferson, The Years 1776 to 1789*. New York, Farrar Straus, 1964.
3. *The Gales of Spring: Thomas Jefferson, The Years 1789 to 1801*. New York, Farrar Straus, 1965.
4. *Time of the Harvest: Thomas Jefferson, The Years 1801 to 1826*. New York, Farrar Straus, 1966.
Guarneri: Story of a Genius. New York, Farrar Straus, 1974; London, Macdonald and Jane's, 1976.

*

Manuscript Collection: University of Southern California, Los Angeles.

* * *

Leonard Wibberley's science fiction for adults is limited to two books of a series on the Duchy of Grand Fenwick, *The Mouse That Roared* and *The Mouse on the Moon*. The scientific element in them, and the others in the series, is quite thin, bordering upon the fantastic. The only element of *The Mouse That Roared* that seems at all science-fictional is Dr. Kokintz's "Quadium Bomb." It is supposedly based upon quadium, the unstable isotope of hydrogen that follows deuterium and tritium. The bomb itself is built in a lead shoebox and uses a hairpin as a triggering device (which ultimately doesn't work). The essence of the story, however, is the extolling of the presumed virtues of smallness. Wibberley seems to assume that there is some sort of Rousseau-like principle at work in nations, that size and density of population virtually force immoral behavior upon the inhabitants of large countries. This is apparent when the rulers of Grand Fenwick realize that large nations cannot be trusted to handle a "doomsday device" but a coalition of little nations can. *The Mouse on the Moon* is a virtual repeat of *The Mouse That Roared*. The now-famous Dr. Kokintz discovers that an extract of the Duchy's wine, Pinot

Grand Fenwick, is the basis for the world's most powerful rocket fuel. The Prime Minister has obtained a $50,000,000 grant from the US (under the guise of starting a space program, but really to improve the castle's plumbing), so the Duchy enters the space race. As in *The Mouse That Roared* Grand Fenwick succeeds in besting the world's "Great Powers. " When the Russian and American spacemen arrive on the moon, they find Grand Fenwickians already in possession of it. Of course, again, the little countries accept their responsibilities, where the big ones hadn't, and agree to keep the moon free for all humanity.

Wibberley's science fiction for children seems only slightly more juvenile in plot and thesis. *Encounter Near Venus* tells of four children who, almost despite the aid of their child-hating uncle, save an Edenic Venusian moon from the deadly clutches of Ka the Smiler. On a simplified basis it is quite reminiscent of C. S. Lewis's Narnia chronicles. In *Journey to Untor* the message is again that the big and/or mature lack flexibility and sensitivity to the world around them, while the small and/or immature, when given the opportunity, have those properties and the will to use them in the most responsible manner possible.

In general, Wibberley's supposed science-fiction writings are so categorized only as a recognition that they employ gimmicks which nominally belong to that realm. In actuality they are fairly simple-minded morality stories written in a clever and entertaining fashion.

—Richard W. Miller

WILDER, Cherry. Pseudonym for Cherry Barbara Grimm, née Lockett. New Zealander. Born in Auckland, 3 September 1930. Educated at Canterbury University College, Christchurch, B. A. 1952. Married 1) A. J. Anderson in 1952; 2) H. K. F. Grimm in 1963, two daughters. Lived in Australia, 1954-76: high school teacher, editorial assistant, theatre director; regular reviewer from Sydney *Morning Herald* and *The Australian*, 1964-74. Recipient: Australia Council grant, 1973, 1975. Agent: Virginia Kidd, Box 278, Milford, Pensylvania 18337, U. S. A. Address: 19 Egelsbacher Strasse, 6070 Langen/Hessen, West Germany.

SCIENCE-FICTION PUBLICATIONS

Novels (series: Torin)

The Luck of Brin's Five (for children; Torin). New York, Atheneum, 1977; London, Angus and Robertson, 1979.
The Nearest Fire (for children; Torin). New York, Atheneum, 1980.
Second Nature. New York, Pocket Books, 1982.
The Tapestry Warriors (for children; Torin). New York, Atheneum, 1983.

Uncollected Short Stories

"The Ark of James Carlyle," in *New Writings in SF 24*, edited by Kenneth Bulmer. London, Sidgwick and Jackson, 1974.
"The Phobos Transcripts," in *New Writings in SF 26*, edited by Kenneth Bulmer. London, Sidgwick and Jackson, 1975.
"Way Out West," in *Science Fiction Monthly* (London), August 1975.
"The Remittance Man," in *The Ides of Tomorrow*, edited by

Terry Carr. Boston, Little Brown, 1976.
"Double Summer Time," in *New Writings in SF 29*, edited by Kenneth Bulmer. London, Sidgwick and Jackson, 1976.
"Point of Departure," in *The Zeitgeist Machine*, edited by Damien Broderick. London, Angus and Robertson, 1977.
"The Recollectors," in *New Writings in SF 30*, edited by Kenneth Bulmer. London, Corgi, 1977.
"The Lodestar," in *Cosmos* (New York), May 1977.
"Mab Gallen Recalled," in *Millennial Women*, edited by Virginia Kidd. New York, Dell, 1978.
"The Falldown of Man," in *Rooms of Paradise*, edited by Lee Harding. New York, St. Martin's Press, 1979.
"Dealers in Light and Darkness," in *20 Houses of the Zodiac*, edited by Maxim Jakubowski. London, New English Library, 1979.
"Odd Man Search," in *Alien Worlds*, edited by Paul Collins. St. Kilda, Victoria, Void, 1979.
"A Long Bright Day by the Sea of Utner," in *Chrysalis 5*, edited by Roy Torgeson. New York, Zebra, 1979.
"The Gingerbread House," in *New Terrors 1*, edited by Ramsey Campbell. London, Pan, 1980.
"The Dreamers of Deliverance," in *Distant Worlds*, edited by Paul Collins. St. Kilda, Victoria, Cory and Collins, 1981.
"Cabin Fever," in *Frontier Worlds*, edited by Paul Collins. St. Kilda, Victoria, Cory and Collins, 1983.
"Kaleidoscope," in *Omni* (New York), July 1983.
"Something Coming Through," in *Interzone* (Brighton), Winter 1983.

OTHER PUBLICATIONS

Novels (series: Hylor in all books)

A Princess of the Chameln. New York, Atheneum, 1984.
Yorath the Wolf. New York, Atheneum, 1984.
The Summer's King. New York, Atheneum, 1985.

*

Manuscript Collection: de Grummond Collection, University of Southern Mississippi, Hattiesburg.

*   *   *

Cherry Wilder's first published SF short story, "The Ark of James Carlyle," launched a bountiful career in the field. The story displays her considerable narrative skill and the gently evocative style charactertistic of her work. Wilder creates highly original landscapes, people with unique aliens—far removed from the classic little green men and bug-eyed monsters of pulp SF. She attributes this inventiveness to the influence of the Australian bush, in which she lived for a number of years. Human contact with aliens, a theme common to the rest of her work, is the subject of "The Ark of James Carlyle. " Carlyle is serving at a weather station, on an island of a newly explored planet which is inhabited by baboon-like mammals called Quogs, child-like aliens who are described with affectionate humour. Carlyle's relationship with the Quogs is revolutionised when the island is flooded by torrential seasonal rains. The humans have recklessly chopped down the single tree of the island, a giant mee-haw tree, which the Quogs used as a refuge from the rapidly rising waters. Carlyle saves them, by improvising the raft and it is on this that his relationship with the Quogs undergoes a delicate transformation, with the Quogs using telepathic dreams to communicate with Carlyle and help him contact the rest of the explorative team. A subtly ecological message is mixed with the idea of empathising with alien species.

In "The Phobos Transcripts" Wilder uses alternating narrative styles to describe three different perspectives of the same event: a vast transcendental alien's possession of an astronaut's body. One of the themes of this story is the effect of loneliness—in particular the loneliness of isolation, which results in the alien breaking its covenant and the madness of one of the crew of a survey ship. The three crew members are changed by the contact with the alien – the madness healed and transformed into religious zeal.

First contact is dealt with in a unique way in "Double Summer Time." A basic SF theme—an invasion of aliens who can mimic other lifeforms—is transformed into a charming, unusual, and complex story in Wilder's hands. Human characters include a radical "greenie," her scientist uncle, and a security robot, indistinguishable from human beings. Various perspectives are explored: the cynical contempt of the professor, the patronising amusement of the secret service man, the passionate involvement of the environmentalist, who falls in love with a "tree" which later becomes a man. The aliens can tamper with the flow of time, and the last part of the story is an intricately woven pattern of different time streams. Andrew Marvell's "The Garden" and "To His Coy Mistress" act as a kind of referential symbolism throughout the story. It is a complex story which demands re-reading.

"Point of Departure" begins an alien-human contact saga, continued in *The Luck of Brin's Five* and *The Nearest Fire*. In these works Wilder details the world of a marsupial race, called Moruians, who live in a society whose strength is in its tradition of tightly knit families, known as "Fives." The old ways are seen threatened by new ideas, and new technologies such as electricity (fire-metal-magic) and photography (silk-beam copy) are looked on with fear and suspicion. Into this world comes Scott Gale, a member of a survey team, when his small ship crashes near some bush-weavers. He is adopted by Brin's Five as their "Luck" – an abnormal or disabled person who brings good luck to a family, acting as a kind of living talisman or familiar. The story is told through the young eyes of Dorn Brinroyan. One sees the growth of Dorn, from the naive member of a family, to a wise individualistic character (from Dorn Brinroyan, to Dorn-U-Dorn). Ideas of turning misfortune into luck, of encompassing the disabled within society without the need for patronising charity, of aliens learning and changing and growing from intimate contact are developed in this story. Technology, as opposed the craft, is discussed at length.

The story is continued in *The Nearest Fire*, this time told from the perspective of Yolo Harn, a female miner sent to a prison settlement for assault. It details the story of the other members of the bio-survey team and their reunion with Scott Gale. Although immensely pleased to be reunited with his fellow humans, he has developed attachments to his new family (a transition from Scott Gale to Escott Garl Brinroyan). The great strength of these stories is Wilder's ability to create a convincing and engrossing alien culture, encompassing conventional SF themes (such as telepathy) and injecting them with a refreshing original approach. *The Nearest Fire* ends with a promise of new adventures, told from yet another perspective. (A minor problem is reading these stories recalls James Carlyle's difficulty in recognising the gender of the cryptorchidian Quogs – it is very difficult keeping track of the character's names and sex. The list of character's names at the front is very useful but a glossary of Moruian terms might also prove worthwhile.)

Wilder's work is optimistic and hopeful. She presents contact with aliens, so often a violent and ugly event is SF, as a gradual learning process, in which all concerned grow and change. This can perhaps be best summed up with a quote from "The Ark of James Carlyle" describing the effects of his contact with the Quogs: "The distance between Carlyle and the landing party could not be taken up in a few small steps. They saw tomorrow's man, who by some chance operation of good-will, some accident of understanding, reached forward into new modes of being." Wilder's effortless prose, her charming characters, her moving plots and beautiful descriptions make her books a joy to read, and they are a positive and exciting contribution to the genre.

—Mark Warwick Leahy

WILDING, Eric. See **TUBB, E. C.**

WILEY, John. See **PHILLIPS, Rog.**

WILHELM, Kate (Gertrude, née Meredith). American. Born in Toledo, Ohio, 8 June 1928. Married 1) Joseph B. Wilhelm in 1947 (divorced, 1962), two sons; 2) Damon Knight, *q. v.*, in 1963, one son. Co-Director, Milford Science Fiction Writers Conference, 1963-72; Lecturer, Clarion Science Fiction Writers Conference, since 1968, and Tulane University, New Orleans, 1971. Recipient: Nebula Award, 1968; Hugo Award, 1977; Jupiter Award, 1977; *Locus* Award, 1977. Agent: Brandt and Brandt, 1501 Broadway, New York, New York 10036. Address: 1645 Horn Lane, Eugene, Oregon 97404, U.S.A.

SCIENCE-FICTION PUBLICATIONS

Novels

The Clone, with Ted Thomas. New York, Berkley, 1965; London, Hale, 1968.
The Nevermore Affair. New York, Doubleday, 1966.
The Killer Thing. New York, Doubleday, 1967; as *The Killing Thing*, London, Jenkins, 1967.
Let the Fire Fall. New York, Doubleday, 1969; London, Panther, 1972.
Year of the Cloud, with Ted Thomas. New York, Doubleday, 1970.
Abyss. New York, Doubleday, 1971.
Margaret and I. Boston, Little Brown, 1971.
The Clewiston Test. New York, Farrar Straus, 1976; London, Hutchinson, 1977.
Where Late the Sweet Birds Sang. New York, Harper, 1976; London, Arrow, 1977.
Juniper Time. New York, Harper, 1979; London, Hutchinson, 1980.
A Sense of Shadow. Boston, Houghton Mifflin, 1981.
Oh, Susannah! Boston, Houghton Mifflin, 1982.
Welcome, Chaos. Boston, Houghton Mifflin, 1983.

Short Stories

The Mile-Long Spaceship. New York, Berkley, 1963; as *Andover
    and the Android,* London, Dobson, 1966.
The Downstairs Room. New York, Doubleday, 1968.
The Infinity Box. New York, Harper, 1975; London, Arrow,
    1979.
Somerset Dreams and Other Fictions. New York, Harper, 1978;
    London, Hutchinson, 1979.
Listen, Listen. Boston, Houghton Mifflin, 1981.

Uncollected Short Stories

"Strangeness, Charm, and Spin," in *Light Years and Dark,*
    edited by Michael Bishop. New York, Berkley, 1984.
"O Femina," in *Omni* (New York), May 1985.

OTHER PUBLICATIONS

Novels

More Bitter Than Death. New York, Simon and Schuster, 1963;
    London, Hale, 1965.
City of Cain. Boston, Little Brown, 1974; London, Gollancz,
    1975.
Fault Lines. New York, Harper, 1977; London, Hutchinson,
    1978.

Other

"Something Happens," in *Clarion,* edited by Robin Scott
    Wilson. New York, New American Library, 1971.
"The Source," in *Clarion 3,* edited by Robin Scott Wilson. New
    York, New American Library, 1973.
Better Than One, with Damon Knight. Cambridge, Massa-
    chusetts, NESFA Press, 1980.

Editor, *Nebula Award Stories 9.* London, Gollancz, 1974; New
    York, Harper, 1975.
Editor, *Clarion SF.* New York, Berkley, 1977.

*

Manuscript Collection: Syracuse University, New York.

*   *   *

Kate Wilhelm has said that about half of her published work
is science fiction, though much of the rest contains elements of
fantasy. Her first novel was a mystery; later works such as
Margaret and I and *Fault Lines* are novels of contemporary life,
though *Margaret and I* makes use of a speculative element by
portraying the protagonist's subconscious as a separate
character. Wilhelm is primarily a writer who skillfully uses genre
elements—suspenseful plots, scientific or technological notions, and slick prose—to produce fiction as satisfying and as
well-rounded as any being written today.

Wilhelm's technique, in most of her work, is to introduce a
character or set of characters in a commonplace setting, then to
reveal the unusual or uncommon elements of the story through
the thoughts and actions of the people in it. Her characters are
some of the most fully realized people to be found in science
fiction. Her style is the smooth, almost slick manner of so much
"women's magazine" fiction, complete with the details of
domestic and everyday life; this manner of telling her stories
makes the contrast and tension between the usual and the
unusual even more striking. This technique can be seen in
Wilhelm's first novel, *More Bitter Than Death.* A young couple,
Eve and Grant, return to Grant's home, where the body of
Grant's murdered mother has been found. Eve must come to
terms with her husband, who is one of those suspected of the
murder, and Grant must deal with long-suppressed feelings
about his home and family. The problems raised here are
resolved by the book's conclusion, though in her later work
Wilhelm's characters find answers more difficult to come by, life
more complex, and reconcillations more problematic. The
problem Eve and Grant face, that of having to understand the
past and to reconcile it with their future hopes in the midst of
unusual events, is present in Wilhelm's later work, and is
especially prominent in her science fiction. These same
problems are depicted movingly in the novella "Somerset
Dreams," ostensibly a story about dream research in a dying
town.

In two early science-fiction novels, Wilhelm writes about
standard science-fiction themes. In *The Killer Thing* a computerized robot which is trying to kill all life must be destroyed;
in *Let the Fire Fall* an alien landing on Earth and the rise of a new
religion are shown. *The Killer Thing* shows Wilhelm's mastery of
the technique of suspense. Though it is set in the familiar future
of colonized planets so common in SF, the book shows the
author's concern with the moral issues raised by space travel and
human greed. *Let the Fire Fall* begins in the familiar, almost
cozy, environs of a small American city. This novel is written in
an uncharacteristically breezy style; the author's strong
opinions about organized religion and cults are not concealed,
and the new religion is much like some rather disturbing present-
day cults. These books, and early pieces such as "The Mile-Long
Spaceship" and "Stranger in the House," are better than
average stories, but it is in later works that Wilhelm shows her
real strengths.

Wilhelm, unlike many writers, is a master of both the novel
and shorter forms of fiction. Her short story "Baby, You Were
Great" shows a world where it is possible, through brain-
implanted electrodes, to live a celebrity's life vicariously and to
feel all her emotions as well. Her Nebula Award-winning "The
Planners" concerns biological research, and "The Funeral"
depicts a rigid future society. But these stories are not simply
intellectual adventures comfortably removed from us in time.
"The Planners" shows a scientist who does not fully comprehend the moral and ethical implications of his research, "The
Funeral" reveals the crippling constraints in which adults often
place children, and "Baby, You Were Great" takes place in a
world uncomfortably like our own.

Wilhelm's work gains much of its strength by showing us life
as it is lived, as so many works of science fiction do not. Her
stories are easily accessible, but they are not ecapist entertainments which one can read and then put aside; the issues she
raises are present in our lives. She is a concerned writer, but she
does not moralize and she does not lapse into despair. Many of
her works, notably *City of Cain,* a novel about a plot to build an
underground city where experiments will be conducted on
survivors of atomic and environmental disasters, show the
dangers of excessive power thoughtlessly used. One especially
strong novella, "The Infinity Box," shows the corrupting
influence of power from the inside; the story is made more
disturbing by the fact that the protagonist is a likeable,
intelligent, and sympathetic man who is altered and changed
simply by having the power to enter another person's mind.
Where Late the Sweet Birds Sang (Hugo Award) has been called
the best treatment of cloning in science fiction by many critics.

But the novel is also about the often destructive strategies human beings can employ in order to survive, and it shows the author's concern with the damage we have done to the earth, a common theme in her work.

Wilhelm's abilities are at their height in *The Clewiston Test* and *Juniper Time*. *The Clewiston Test* is both a feminist novel and a psychological thriller which presents issues in the context of a suspenseful story. The isolation of the protagonist, Anne Clewiston, who is recovering from a serious accident, is symbolic of the isolation felt by so many women; the scientific project in the novel is used as a plot device to illuminate the personal conflicts of the characters, as well as to present issues about human experimentation. *Juniper Time* tells the story of two people, Jean Brighton and Arthur Cluny, who are the children of astronauts. The two grow up in a drought-plagued world in which the dream of space exploration, the goal to which their fathers had devoted themselves, has died. The conflicts in the book reflect our own predicament; we must live with our technology, however uneasily, and cannot turn back, but we must conserve what is valuable of the past, and keep future hopes from being perverted to unworthy and short-sighted ends.

A recent novel, *Welcome, Chaos*, also unites many of Wilhelm's concerns and techniques, and deals with the dilemmas that immortality might raise. In an earlier novella, "April Fool's Day Forever,'h the author also dealt with immortality; there, the price of endless life turned out to be the loss of the bond with the collective unconscious and all creative forces. In *Welcome, Chaos* Wilhelm, in the context of a thriller, asks difficult questions: What if the serum that makes immortality possible kills half of those people who are exposed to it? Should such a serum be limited to only a few? How will its protection against the effects of radiation affect the nuclear balance of terror? It is to Wilhelm's credit that she attempts to give answers, however tentative, to these questions.

In her science fiction, Kate Wilhelm holds a mirror to our world, and in her work we can see the dilemmas present in our uneasy, late-20th-century lives.

—Pamela Sargent

WILLIAMS, John A(lfred). Also writes as J. Dennis Gregory. American. Born in Jackson, Mississippi, 5 December 1925. Educated at Central High School, Syracuse, New York; Syracus University, A. B. 1950. Served in the United States Navy, 1943-46. Married 1) Carolyn Clopton in 1947 (divorced), two sons; 2) Lorrain Isaac in 1965, one son. Member of the public relations department, Doug Johnson Associates, Syracuse, 1952-54, and Arthur P. Jacobs Company; staff member, CBS, Hollywood and New York, 1954-55; publicity director, Comet Press Books, New York, 1955-56; publisher and editor, *Negro Market Newsletter*, New York, 1956-57; staff member, Abelard-Schuman, publishers, New York, 1957-58; director of information, American Committee on Africa, New York, 1958; European correspondent, *Ebony* and *Jet* magazines, 1958-59; announcer, WOV Radio, New York, 1959; Africa correspondent, *Newsweek*, New York, 1964-65. Regents Lecturer, University of California, Santa Barbara, 1972; Distinguished Professor of English, LaGuardia Community College, City University of New York, 1973-75; Visiting Professor, University of Hawaii, Summer 1974, and Boston University, 1978-79. Since 1979, Professor of English, Rutgers University, New Brunswick, New Jersey. Member of the Editorial Board, *Audience*, Boston, 1970-72; Contributing Editor, *American Journal*, New York, 1972. Recipient: American Academy grant, 1962; Syracuse University Outstanding Achievement Award, 1970; National Endowment for the Arts grant, 1977; Before Columbus Foundation award, 1983. Litt. D. : Southeastern Massachusetts University, North Dartmouth, 1978. Address: 693 Forest Avenue, Teaneck, New Jersey 07666, U.S.A.

SCIENCE-FICTION PUBLICATIONS

Novels

Sons of Darkness, Sons of Light. Boston, Little Brown, 1969; London, Eyre and Spottiswoode, 1970.
Captain Blackman. New York, Doubleday, 1972.

OTHER PUBLICATIONS

Novels

The Angry Ones. New York, Ace, 1960; as *One for New York*, Chatham, New Jersey, Chatham Bookseller, 1975.
Night Song. New York, Farrar Straus, 1961; London, Collins, 1962.
Sissie. New York, Farrar Straus, 1963; as *Journey Out of Anger*, London, Eyre and Spottiswoode, 1968.
The Man Who Cried I Am. Boston, Little Brown, 1967; London, Eyre and Spottiswoode, 1968.
Mothersill and the Foxes. New York, Doubleday, 1975.
The Junior Bachelor Society. New York, Doubleday, 1976.
! Click Song. Boston, Houghton Mifflin, 1982.
The Bahama Account. New York, New Horizon Press, 1985.

Other

Africa: Her History, Lands, and People. New York, Cooper Square, 1962.
The Protectors (on narcotics agents; as J. Dennis Gregory), with Harry J. Anslinger. New York, Farrar Straus, 1964.
This Is My Country, Too. New York, New American Library, 1964; London, New English Library, 1966.
The Most Native of Sons: A Bibliography of Richard Wright. New York, Doubleday, 1970.
The King God Didn't Save: Reflections on the Life and Death of Martin Luther King, Jr. New York, Coward McCann, 1970; London, Eyre and Spottiswoode, 1971.
Flashbacks: A Twenty-Year Diary of Article Writing. New York, Doubleday, 1973.
Minorities in the City. New York, Harper, 1975.

Editor, *The Angry Black*. New York, Lancer, 1962.
Editor, *Beyond the Angry Black*. New York, Cooper Square, 1967.
Editor, with Charles F. Harris, *Amistad I* and *II*. New York, Knopf, 2 vols., 1970-71.

*

Manuscript Collection: Syracuse University, New York.

Critical Study: *The Evolution of a Black Writer: John A. Williams* by Earl Cash, New York, Third Press, 1974.

* * *

As a sensitive black writer, John A. Williams is alert to discriminatory literary restrictions and chafes against them. His article "The Literary Ghetto" contends that the critical practice of comparing black writers only to black writers denies them the rights to compete with whites and to be taken seriously when they examine issues and emotions common to all men. Although his fiction concentrates on the manifold ways in which blacks have been oppressed and have reacted to that oppression, he also depicts similar maltreatment accorded to Jews and others, the need for man to transcend his progenitor, the killer ape, the differences between casual affairs and emotional commitments. Moreover, he welcomes—and merits—comparison with such contemoraries as Mailer and Styron.

Williams's novels *The Man Who Cried I Am*, *Sons of Darkness, Sons of Light*, and *Captain Blackman* demonstrate that he also rejects the critical practice of placing future-oriented fiction in a literary ghetto. These novels blend mainstream, experimental, thriller, and speculative fiction techniques into artistic wholes that confound many critics. Like Doris Lessing's Martha Quest series, *The Man Who Cried I Am* starts with a realistic delineation of social and political forces at work in the modern era as experienced by a protagonist and ends with a vision of the future those forces have shaped. The protagonist, Max Reddick, is a black man whose advances from job-seeker to journalist to presidential speechwriter reveal increasingly subtle refusals by whites to share power. Thus, he is not surprised to confront the King Alfred plan, the American government's proposal to put all blacks into concentration camps and gas them if some blacks move from rioting to rebellion over unfilled promises. The more extensively speculative *Sons of Darkness, Sons of Light* show how a racial war could develop in the United States from one black man's decision to initiate the assassin-ation of whites who kill blacks as an alternative to the random violence of riots. Both blacks and whites readily comprehend the "eye for an eye" philosophy behind such assassinations and both escalate the number of eyes to be exchanged. However, Williams never repudiates retaliatory violence by blacks but raises unresolved moral and practical questions about it. *Captain Blackman* also combines realism and extrapolation but examines the distant past before considering the future. Like Twain's Connecticut Yankee, Capatain Blackman receives a wound that jolts him back in time while leaving his present knowledge intact. Blackman then experiences life as a typical black soldier from the Revolutionary War to Vietnam. Since he has thus encountered two hundred years of white callousness, his decision not to accept intergration into a white army that countenances My Lai massacres and contemplates nuclear holocausts gains added meaning. His achieved goal of infiltrating light-skinned blacks into key positions to take over the nuclear strike and dismantle it is not only a blow for black power but also an attempt to substitute decency for destructive-ness. All three novels reflect Williams's belief that man must comprehend his personal, racial, national, and evolutionary history to alter himself and his society. He also feels that in an oppressive society manhood depends on the willingness to strive for change. It is his longing for change that leads him to link mainstream and speculative fiction.

Williams also refuses to segregate fiction from fact and the personal from political. His background as journalist and poet makes him aware of the fictive in much so-called fact and the reality behind fantasy. Both *The Man Who Cried I Am* and *Captain Blackman* intermingle historical persons with fictional characters and actual occurrences with invented ones to illuminate his view of history. Both works also analyze the interrelationships between the social and the individual. In *The Man Who Cried I Am*, for example, the social impinges on the personal when Max's white-imposed joblessness prompts his girlfriend to undergo an abortion. And the personal impinges on the social when Max's "friend" Harry Ames risks leaving the King Alfred plan unexposed by giving it to Max because he is jealous of Max and expects him to die for possessing it. Such insightful juxtapositions, plus that of the realistic with the speculative, place Williams among the best contemporary writers.

—Steven R. Carter

WILLIAMS, Paul O(sborne). American. Born in Chatham, New Jersey, 17 January 1935. Educated at Principia College, Elsah, Illinois, B. A. 1956; University of Pennsylvania, Philadelphia, M. A. 1958, Ph. D. 1962. Married 1) Nancy Ellis in 1961 (divorced, 1984), one daughter and one son; 2) Kerry Lynn Blau in 1985. Instructor, 1961-62, and Assistant Professor of English, 1962-64, Duke University, Durham, North Carolina. Assistant Professor, 1964-68, Associate Professor, 1968-77, Professor of English, 1977-81, and since 1981, Cornelius and Muriel Wood Professor of Humanities, Principia College. Member, Board of Trustees, Village of Elsah, 1969-75; President, Greater St. Louis Historical Association, 1975, and Thoreau Society, 1977; Director, Elsah Museum, 1981-84. Recipient: John W. Campbell Award, 1983. Address: Human-ities Division, Principia College, Elsah, Illinois 62028, U.S.A.

SCIENCE-FICTION PUBLICATIONS

Novels (series: Pelbar in all books)

The Breaking of Northwall. New York, Ballantine, 1981.
The Ends of the Circle. New York, Ballantine, 1981.
The Dome in the Forest. New York, Ballantine, 1981.
The Fall of the Shell. New York, Ballantine, 1982.
An Ambush of Shadows. New York, Ballantine, 1983.
The Song of the Axe. New York, Ballantine, 1984.

OTHER PUBLICATIONS

Other

Elsah: A Historic Guidebook, with Charles B. Hosmer. Elsah, Illinois, Historic Elsah Foundation, 1967.
The McNair Family of Elsah, Illinois: Uncommon Common Men. Elsah, Illinois, Historic Elsah Foundation, 1982.

* * *

The Pelbar cycles consists of six novels based on the hypothesis that a nuclear war occurred in the late 20th/early 21st century. Focusing on the land area of Urstadge (the United States and southwestern Canada), Paul O. Williams surmises that despite the devastation, isolated groups of people survived. His series, set about 1000 years after the devastation, explores these groups of people when they are large and stable enough to be expanding beyond their borders.

The cycle is rich in detail about political systems, languages, games, architecture, dress, food, weaponry, technology, music, art, education. William's societies are influenced by his knowledge of Native Americans, especially in the Mississippi River valley; his scholarship in 19th-century American romanticism, especially Thoreau; his Christian Science religion which offers strong female models; his reading of western expeditions, particularly that of Lewis and Clark; and his clear love for the immensity of the land, the endurance of nature and its patterns, and the symbolism and power of the Mississippi River, a feature he has watched from the limestone cliffs just north of St. Louis where he has lived for many years.

The cycle depicts humankind moving toward unity as the individual societies realize the advantages of open trade, exchange of knowledge and skills, and their common historical and religious foundations. The impetus for the move toward unification comes from the Pelbar, people living in three elaborately designed stone cities along the Heart River (Mississippi). Individual novels echo the cycle's movement from fragmentation to federation by depicting journeys by psychological and physical discovery by young protagonists. Each protagonist's search culminates not only in a return home and a new or renewed marriage but also in a treaty or agreement with other societies.

The cyclic nature of these novels is evident in a number of ways but most clearly in its open-endedness; although certain individuals or social groups reach agreements about the sharing of responsibilities, land, or resources, there is always the potential for separation and renewed isolation. Underneath the movement toward unity is the potential for injustice, tyranny, and destruction. How these conflicting desires for unity and for power are handled by individuals is the real focus of the series. The solutions affect the married couple (William's ideal for human fulfillment and social unity) and the nature of individual societies. Unification in the cycle requires the combined skills of different heroes—the visionary, the inventor/technician, the diplomat, the social leader, the rebel, the explorer, the military strategist, the warrior.

The Breaking of Northwall, besides providing background, recounts the influences that lead the people of Northwall, the northernmost Pelbar city, to share knowledge and to intermarry with the other two valley tribes of the valley, the Sentani and the Shumai. The external tribes are hunters and nomads; the Pelbar offer these intelligent, honorable peoples a high level of culture and a settled existence. The Ends of the Circle tells of the personal quest of Ahroe, a young Pelbar wife, for Stel, her husband who has fled West to escape the severe domination of Ahroe's family. In Pelbar society, women are the administrators and men are laborers. The adventures of both Ahroe and Stel lead them to an increased understanding of human love and hate, men and women, social order and change. The Dome in the Forest is an account of the emergence of a small group of "the ancients" from a sealed dome where they have perpetuated themselves through several generations for over 1000 years. Even more isolated than the Pelbar, they bring with them advanced technology and reason but lack the social skills, emotions, and intuitions of their rescue party composed of Pelbar, Sentani, and Shumai.

The Fall of the Shell turns to the third and most conservative Pelbar city where twin adolescent boys defy the harsh rule and are punished severely. One twin is imprisoned in the city and contemplates the architectural and social structure of his society; the other escapes to journey south on the river and return with great knowledge of new societies. By different routes, the twins learn the basic human virtues of love, forbearance, kindness, and goodwill. An Ambush of Shadows depicts the strained marriage of Ahroe and Stel as she goes to the Heart River Federation Convention as a diplomat and he travels north to seek contact with new societies. The Song of the Axe, the only novel to use non-Pelbars as protagonists, recounts a journey that began at the end of The Dome in the Forest. Tor, a Shumai axeman, and his nephew, Tristal, travel far into the northwest. Although Tor, a man of intuition and vision, chooses not to return to the Heart, he helps shape his nephew so that he does returns with the combined skill of the diplomat and the explorer.

The Fall of the Shell best exemplifies the themes and structure of the cycle. The concept that each society is in artifact and that its design determines its strengths and weaknesses is universal in the cycle. Williams uses the nautilus shell and the Mississippi River as symbols of the beauty, limitations, and potentiality of human society. The river/highway gives access to a variety of human societies and greater knowledge of the single religion that underlies all of the Urstadge societies. The shell is rich in ambiguity for a shell can house mature life as a society shelters its citizens, but it may also inhibit life and have to be cracked open.

—Elizabeth Cummins Cogell

WILLIAMS, Robert Moore. American. Born in Farmington, Missouri, 19 June 1907. Educated at the University of Missouri Columbia, B. A. in journalism. Married Margaret Jelley in 1938 (divorced, 1952); one daughter. Full-time wrilter, 1937-72. Died in 1977

SCIENCE-FICTION PUBLICATIONS

Novels (series:Jongor; Zanthar)

The Chaos Fighters New York, Ace, 1955.
Conquest of the Space Sea. New York, Ace, 1955.
Doomsday Eve New York, Ace, 1957.
The Blue Atom. New York, Ace, 1958.
World of the Masterminds. New York, Ace, 1960.
The Day They H-Bombed Los Angeles. New York, Ace, 1961.
The Darkness Before Tomorrow. New York, Ace, 1962.
King of the Fourth Planet. New York, Ace, 1962.
Walk Up the Sky. New York, Avalon, 1962.
The Star Wasps. New York, Ace, 1963.
Flight From Yesterday. New York, Ace, 1963.
The Lunar Eye. New York, Ace, 1964.
The Second Atlantis. New York, Ace, 1965.
Vigilante—21st Century. New York, Lancer, 1967.
Zanthar of the Many Worlds. New York, Lancer, 1967.
Zanthar of the Edge of Never. New York, Lancer, 1968.
The Bell from Infinity. New York, Lancer, 1968.
Zanthar at Moon's Madness. New York, Lancer, 1968.
Zanthar at Trip's End. New York, Lancer, 1968.
Beachhead Planet. New York, Dell, and London, Sidgwick and Jackson, 1970.
Jongor of Lost Land. New York, Popular Library, 1970.
Return of Jongor. New York, Popular Library, 1970.
Jongor Fights Back New York, Popular Library, 1970.
Now Comes Tomorrow. New York, Curtis, and London, Sidgwick and Jackson, 1971.

Short Stories

The Void Beyond and Other Stories. New York, Ace, 1958.
To the End of Time. New York, Ace, 1960.
When Two Worlds Meet. New York, Curtis, 1970.

Uncollected Short Story

"Now Comes Tomorrow," in *Science Fiction Special 6.*
London, Sidgwick and Jackson, 1973.

OTHER PUBLICATIONS

Other

Love Is Forever, We Are for Tonight (atuobiography). New
York, Curtis, 1970.

*   *   *

During the editorship of Ray Palmer in the 1940's, *Amazing
Stories* and *Fantastic Adventures* were juvenile action pulps
principally written by a stable of writers under their own bylines and an assortment of house names. Robert Moore
Williams was part of this stable, producing scores of stories
including a few under the name Russell Storm. (It is not clear
which stories he wrote under house names, but it's probable that
most of the stories published prior to 1951 under the name E. K.
Jarvis are his.) Even today, Williams is largely associated with
these magazines and their juvenile policy, but the truth is he was
one of only a handful of writers of those years who were able to
cut across policy boundaries and sell stories to almost all the
existing science-fiction magazines. He appeared often, for
example, in both *Thrilling Wonder* and *Startling,* and also in
John Campbell's *Astounding* (Campbell thought enough of his
talents to mention him in his essay for Lloyd Eshbach's *Of
Worlds Beyond*). In fact, of these writers, Williams is unique in
sustaining a continuous career as an SF writer through to the
1970's

Although Williams wrote almost 200 stories, it is possible
from one of his collections to get a good feel for his approaches
and talent. The stories in *When Two Worlds Meet* are linked
through a common background of Earthman conflict although
the background details of Mars and the Martians are
inconsistent. The title story tells of an Earthman who tries to
learn the secret behind a "god weapon" that allows one race to
subjugate another. "Aurochs Came Walking" concerns a
shaman's crystal ball that turns out to be a control device for a
machine built by ancient Martians. In "The Sound of Bugles"
Martians show an Earthman the secret of creating such
resources as food and housing from pure thought. The weakest
story in the book is probably "When the Spoilers Came,"
marred by an unconvincing and rather sentimental resolution,
something not especially common in the fiction of Williams
whose romantic streak more often manifested itself as a mildly
ironic cynicism. "The Final Frontier," in which a dying Marian
wields strange powers to thwart exploitative Earthman, is only
technically better. The best story in the book is "On Pain of
Death," a suspense story about a group of Earthman trapped in
a strange prison that may be either a particularly efficient
machine or a test of their worthiness to live.

Again and again, Williams's fiction deals with machines that
bestow godlike powers, or ordinary humans who possess a
special rapport with machines or elemental energies. In "The
Night the General Left Us" a mathematician's love of machines
is returned by a model rocket that attacks a general who orders
the man arrested. "The Smallness Beyond Thought" deals with
an eccentric hermit whose ability to grow food without water is
related to his ability to sense the flow of electromagnetic and less
familiar forms of energy.

It should not be assumed that William is playing with the
traditional science-fiction theme of the superman. Rather, his
work expresses a basically mystical view of the world. This is
borne out by "The Grove of God" (*Other Worlds,* 1956), whose
editor described it as too taboo-breaking for other magazines.
An expedition of space explorers from Earth lands on a planet
where they discover god-like humans living in a primitive
paradise. They discover that the planet is actually Earth, to
which they have returned through some sort of application of
Lorenz-Fitzgerald principle that none of the scientists seem to
have been aware of. The narrative is as awkward and downright
clumsy as the idea, something surprising in the work of a
professional as experienced as Williams. Ironically, another
stroy by him in that issue ("The Steogar" as by Russell Storm)
deals more effectively with similar material: a research scientist
at a government installation acquires godlike abilities through
the agency of a miraculous invention.

Williams turned to novels for the growing paperback markets
in 1955 with *The Chaos Fighter.* During the next decade and a
half Williams produced almost 30 books. By and Large they
were not too different from the mass of his magazine fiction and
they abound with such concepts as aliens trying to control
human detiny, Earthman exploiting alien planets, and humans
with miraculous powers. Williams did manage, in *The Day They
H-Bombed Los Angeles* and *The Second Atlantis,* to find
interesting ways to destroy Southern California. The Jongor
series consist of Burroughs-like lost-land stories, and the
Zanthar series are about a super scientist who seems as
interested in the occult as in physics. The last, appropriately
called *Zanthar at Trip's End,* has him coping with a machine
that blows the souls out of people's bodies.

The strangest of Williams's books, however, is a slim volume
titled *Love Is Forever, We Are for Tonight.* Although its called
science fiction on one cover and a "strange and fantastic novel of
a man trapped in an inner world of fear and evil" on the other,
the book is autobiography with no pretense of being fiction. It
begins with some fairly evocative description of his childhood
and youth but soon focuses on Williams's interest in and
experiences with such things as dianetics, hallucinogenic gases,
and communes (in the 1950's). The style reminds one of Ray
Palmer's in his editorials for *Other Worlds,* but Palmer's
delightful flamboyance and self-directed humor are missing and
missed. The book is often vague and evasive, but some facts
about the man crop up and the portions dealing with dianetics,
while not particularly revealing, might hold interest for anyone
curious about the impact of that cult on the SF field.

Williams doesn't seem to have very often probed deeply into
any of his ideas or themes, and this makes some of his work,
while perfectly readable on the surface, seem disturbingly
incomplete. His best work tends to be stories of adventure and
suspense, such as "On Pain of Death," and stories about
determined human beings trying to survive, such as "Last Ship
Out" where two disfigured survivors of atmomic war try to
battle their way on board a spaceship bound for Mars. The story
is slight but compact and straightforward and very readable. It
satisfies more than the ponderous "Grove of God," reminding
us that Williams is more likely to be at his best writing about
people and situations than about ideas.

—Gerald W. Page

WILLIAMSON, Jack (John Stewart Williamson). Also wrote as Will Stewart. American. Born in Bisbee, Arizona, 29 April 1908. Educated at Richland High School, New Mexico; West Texas State University, Canyon, 1928-30; University of New Mexico, Albuquerque, 1931-32; Eastern New Mexico University, Portales, B. A. (summa cum laude), M. A. 1957; University of Colorado, Boulder, Ph. D. 1964. Weather forecaster in the United States Army, 1942-45: Staff Sargeant. Married Blanche Slaten Harp in 1947; two step-children. Writer from 1928; wire editor, Portales *News Tribune,* 1947; created comic strip *Beyond Mars* New York *Sunday News,* 1952-55; Instructor in English, New Mexico Military Institute, Roswell, 1958-60, and University of Colorado, 1960; Professor of English, Eastern New Mexico University, 1960-77, now retired. President, Science Fiction Writers of America, 1978-80. Recipient: Pilgrim Award, 1973; Grand Master Nebula Award, 1975. Guest of Honor, 35th World Science Fiction Convention, 1977. Agent: Scott Meredith Literary Agency, 845 Third Avenue, New York, New York 10022. Address: Box 761, Portales, New Mexico 88130, U.S.A.

SCIENCE-FICTION PUBLICATIONS

Novels (series: Cuckoo's Saga; Jim Eden; Legion of Space; Seetee; Starchild)

The Girl from Mars, with Miles J. Breuer. New York, Stellar, 1929.
The Legion of Space. Reading, Pennsylvania, Fantasy Press, 1947; London, Sphere, 1977.
The Humanoids. New York, Simon and Schuster, 1949; London, Museum Press, 1953.
The Green Girl. New York, Avon, 1950.
The Cometeers (Legion). Reading, Pennsylvania, Fantasy Press, 1950; London, Sphere, 1977; expanded section published as *One Against the Legion,* New York, Pyramid, 1967; London, Sphere, 1977.
Seetee Shock (as Will Stewart). New York, Simon and Schuster, 1950; Kingswood, Surrey, World's Work, 1954.
Seetee Ship (as Will Stewart). New York, Gnome Press, 1951.
Dragon's Island. New York, Simon and Schuster, 1951; London, Museum Press, 1954; as *The Not-Men,* New York, Belmont, 1968.
The Legend of Time. Reading, Pennsylvania, Fantasy Press, 1952; as *The Legion of Time* and *After World's End,* London, Digit, 2 vols., 1961.
Undersea Quest (Eden), with Frederik Pohl. New York, Gnome Press, 1954; London, Dobson, 1966.
Dome Around America. New York, Ace, 1955; London, Faber, 1964.
Star Bridge, with James E. Gunn. New York Gnome Press, 1955; London, Sidgwick and Jackson, 1978.
Undersea Fleet (Eden), with Frederik Pohl. New York, Gnome Press, 1956; London, Dobson, 1968.
Undersea City (Eden), with Frederik Pohl. Hicksville, New York, Gnome Press, 1958; London, Dobson, 1968.
The Trial of Terra. New York, Ace, 1962.
The Starchild Trilogy, with Frederik Pohl. New York, Doubleday, 1977; London, Penguin, 1980.
  The Reefs of Space. New York, Ballantine, 1964; London, Dobson, 1965.
  Starchild. New York, Ballantine, 1965; London, Dobson, 1966.
  Rogue Star. New York, Ballantine, 1969; London, Dobson, 1972.

Bright New Universe. New York, Ace, 1967; London, Sidgwick and Jackson, 1969.
Trapped in Space (for children). New York, Doubleday, 1968.
The Moon Children. New York, Putnam, 1972; Morley, Yorkshire, Elmfield Press, 1975.
Farthest Star (Cuckoo's Saga), with Frederik Pohl. New York, Ballantine, 1975; London, Pan, 1976.
The Power of Blackness. New York, Berkley, 1976; London, Sphere, 1978.
Brother to Demons, Brother to God. Indianapolis, Bobbs Merrill, 1979; London, Sphere, 1981.
The Humanoid Touch. New York, Holt Rinehart, 1980; London, Sphere, 1982.
The Birth of a New Republic, with Miles J. Breuer. New Orleans, P. D. A., 1981.
Manseed. New York, Ballantine, 1982.
The Queen of the Legion. New York, Pocket Books, 1983; London, Sphere, 1984.
Wall Around a Star (Cuckoo's Saga), with Frederik Pohl. New York, Ballantine, 1983.
Lifeburst. New York, Ballantine, 1984.

Short Stories

Lady in Danger. London, Utopian, 1945(?).
The Pandora Effect. New York, Ace, 1969.
People Machines. New York, Ace, 1971.
The Early Williamson. New York, Doubleday, 1975; London, Sphere, 1978.
Dreadful Sleep. Chicago, Weinberg, 1977.
The Best of Jack Williamson. New York, Ballantine, 1978.
The Alien Intelligence. New Orleans, P. D. A., 1980.

OTHER PUBLICATIONS

Novels

Darker Than You Think. Reading, Pennsylvania, Fantasy Press, 1948; London, Sphere, 1976.
Golden Blood. New York, Lancer, 1964.
The Reign of Wizardry. New York, Lancer, 1964.

Other

"The Logic of Fantasy," in *Of Worlds Beyond,* edited by Lloyd Arthur Eshbach. Reading, Pennsylvania, Fantasy Press, 1947; London, Dobson, 1965.
"Why I Selected Star Bright," in *My Best Science Fiction Story,* edited by Leo Margulies and O. J. Friend. New York, Merlin Press, 1949.
"As I Knew Hugo," in *Extrapolation* (Wooster, Ohio), May 1970.
"Science Fiction Comes to College," in *Extrapolation* (Wooster, Ohio), May 1971.
"Science Fiction: Emerging from Its Exile in Limbo," in *Publishers Weekly* (New York), 5 July 1971.
Teaching Science Fiction. Privately printed, 1972.
H. G. Wells, Critic of Progress. Batimore, Mirage Press, 1973.
"The Years of Wonder," in *Voices for the Future,* edited by Thomas D. Clareson. Bowling Green, Ohio, Popular Press, 1976.
"The Next Century of Science Fiction," in *Analog* (New York), February 1978.
"The Case Against the Critics," in *Analog* (New York), April 1980.

Wonder's Child: My Life In Science Fiction. New York, Bluejay, 1984.

Editor, *Teaching Science Fiction for Tomorrow.* Philadelphia, Owlswick Press, 1980.

*

Bibliography: *Jack Williamson: A Primary and Secondary Bibliography* by Robert E. Myers, Boston, Hall, 1980.

Manuscript Collection: Special Collections, Eastern New Mexico University Library, Portales.

Jack Williamson comments:

I began writing at 20, hardly half-educated but dazzled with visions of science and intoxicated with science-fiction as a device for exploring the possible. In the 50 years since, the known unverse has vastly expanded and science filction has grown as fast. Now at 70 I'm still held by the unfolding of science and still excited about science fiction. As a career, it has been rewarding. Though in the first few decades the pay in money was meager, there were always rich compensations in the satisfactions of creating, in the fine friendships, in the opportunities to observe the explosions of scientific knowledge and the human impacts of science and technology. The writers and readers of science fiction form a special community, still tiny when I first discovered it, inhabited by the most able and interesting people I have known. Belonging to it has been a privilege.

*   *   *

Jack Williamson occupies the same place in the history of science fiction that Richard Strauss occupies in the history of music. Both men were artistic prodigies who first achieved recognition in their early twenties; both represented, as they grew older, a dynamic conservative branch of their art that used the techniques of their heirs to refine their own skills. Thus Strauss tended, as he aged, towards a neo-classic style that was late Romanticism freed of ostentation; thus Williamson, in the past decade, has returned to the characters of his early novels, echoing Strauss's return to the forms of his youth.

Williamson's early life was spent in a covered wagon on one of the last frontiers, that of rural New Mexico. His first story resulted from reading one of the first numbers of *Amazing Stories;* it was "The Metal Man" (1928). In a crude but enthusiastic way, it established one of Williamson's *leitmotifs* : the interface between man and machine, as the hero becomes a technological object, a "person-machine. " After several early novels that have never been published in book form (e. g. "The Stone from the Green Star") Williamson first earned a reputation as a master of space opera with *The Legion of Space* (1934). This novel put Williamson in the same rank with such galaxy-conquerors as John W. Campbell and E. E. "Doc" Smith; but the novel resembles those of his contemporaries only in its exuberance. Unlike Campbell and Smith, Williamson was not espousing either technocracy, as Campbell did, or the joys of physics unchecked by any intellectual bound, as Smith did. Williamson is neither pro- nor anti-technology; while there is a great deal of gimcrack physics scattered throughout the text, the central device that allows the heros to conquer their foes, AKKA, can be activated only by a few scraps and an act of will; its operation is never explained. *The Legion of Space* is important because it is the first sign that SF was moving away from the epic of technocracy; although it is what Alexei Panshin

would call a lost-race novel of space (much of the action is standard lost-race adventure transported to the jungle-covered moon of Jupiter, Titan), it is still an advance over other, duller works of the time and can still be read with pleasure. Its sequels are better written but less entertaining. Williamson was one of the few writers of the 1930's who could write with equal facility for the *Astounding* of F. Orlin Tremaine and the *Astounding* of John Campbell. It is generally forgotten that *One Against the Legion* was published in Campbell's *Astounding.* Campbell prodded Williamson to excellence in much the same way as he prodded other writers; Williamson's best work dates from this period, and the only novel that Williamson produced after 1948 that achieves excellence is a result of a Campbell-inspired fragment of 1941.

Williamson's three great works deal with the same theme: the eternal tension of society. Man, Aristotle teaches, is a social animal; it is the degree to which an individual must participate in society without abandoning free will that Williamson seeks to find in *Darker Than You Think, The Humanoids,* and *Star Bridge.*

Darker Than You Think is a result of the two years Williamson spent in psychoanalysis in the late 1930's. Ostensibly it concerns a war between lycanthropy and humanity for dominance; but the werewolves are seen as agents of freedom, creatures that put the lie to scientific and psychoanalytic explanations with mystical truth that transcends attempts at rationalization. But freedom, in this novel, requires a price, a sum of dependence, of eternal vigilance. It is as if the werewolves were organised anarchists, determined to preserve absolute liberty with a new order. Added to this, Williamson has produced what is the best explanation of lycanthropy extent (it depends on probablistic physics, a theme deepened in *The Humanoids*). *Darker Than You Think* is an excellent thriller as well, being the finest novel of the occult produced by a science-fiction writer.

Williamson continued his search for controlling agents in his best work, *The Humanoids.* In two ancillary works designed to match each other as thesis and antithesis, "With Folded Hands" and "The Equalizer," Williamson ruminated on the use and abuse of technology. The former introduces a classic dystopian theme, that of robots following a categorical imperative to its logical limit; the latter shows that technology can preserve as well as destroy free will. But these two novellas are two halves of a larger whole; they can not be read apart, and consequently they lose some of their artistic impact. Only in *The Humanoids* does Williamson attempt a synthesis; and he does this by relying on the old Campbellian warhorse, that of psionic power, as Williamson combines metaphysics with particle physics and the laws of probability to produce a new unified field theory. It is hard for the modern reader to accept psionics with the willingness of those in the late 1940's; but Williamson transcends mere reciting of psionic power to examine the epistemological foundations behind that power. Williamson also examines the fate of those who have accepted the humanoid categorical imperative, producing an examination of the middle ground between the two cultures of pure technocracy and pure mysticism that still retains its impact. *The Humanoids* is Williamson's best novel, a classic dystopia and the single best work on robot instrumentalities outside the work of Isaac Asimov.

Williamson began a rapid decline after *The Humanoids* ; for the next dozen years, he produced works only in collaboration. These collaborations with Frederik Pohl are minor entertainments, the earlier novels such as *Undersea City* being competent juveniles, but rapidly declining to reach a nadir with *Starchild,* the worst novel of either author. Williamson's other "collaboration" is not that at all, but is instead the completion of a Williamson fragment by James Gunn. This novel, *Star Bridge*, is Williamson's last important work, an examination of the processes of political change no less searching than his examination of psychoanalysis in *Darker Than You Think* and of technology in *The Humanoids*. The dialectic between individual and society here is less distinct; the chief representative of individualism is an assassin who does not know what he stands for, the society a corporate state whose internal dynamic has been spent.

After *Star Bridge*, Williamson began a creative drought which lasted 27 years. During this period Williamson's only important work was non-fiction; he began an academic career in the late 1950's, his dissertation forming part of *H. G. Wells, Critic of Progress*. Williamson's novels during this period returned to stories that would have achieved minor billing in *Planet Stories* ; such a work as *The Power of Blackness* suffers from a black hero so characterless that Williamson can find no other descriptive qualities for him than the color of his skin. By the 1980's, Williamson was reduced to writing unneeded sequels to his major works; *The Humanoid Touch* is a minor, darker pastiche of *The Humanoids*, while *The Queen of the Legion* is a frothy conceit lacking in the force of its predecessors.

Manseed marked a new phase in Williamson's career. This tale of a latent superman struggling to discover the limits of his powers, while seriously flawed, marked a new seriousness in Williamson's career. Williamson followed *Manseed* with a collaboration with Frederik Pohl, *Wall Around a Star*, one of the few novels to use linguistics as the scientific base for its intricate plot.

Williamson's most recent novel, *Lifeburst*, is his most important since *The Humanoids*. In *Lifeburst* Williamson returns to his eternal theme—in relations between man and the world. *Lifeburst* is a surprisingly dark exploration of galactic power politics, with the power struggles between clans used as a metaphor for sexual and social tension. Gritty and imaginative, *Lifeburst* is to Williamson what *Capriccio* was to Richard Strauss: an autumnal masterpiece that ensures that Williamson, unlike most writers of his generation, remains a major force in science fiction in his fifth decade as a professional writer.

—Martin Morse Wooster

WILLIS, Connie (Constance E. Willis). American. Born in Denver, Colorado, 31 December 1945. Educated at the University of Northern Colorado, Greeley, B. A. in English and elementary education 1967. Married Courtney W. Willis in 1967; one daughter. Teacher in elementary and junior high schools, Branford, Connecticut, 1967-69; substitute teacher, Woodland Park, Colorado, 1974-81. Since 1982, full-time writer. Recipient: National Endowment for the Arts grant, 1982; Nebula Award (twice), 1982; Hugo Award, 1983. Agent: Patrick Delahunt, John Schaffner Associates, 114 East 28th Street, New York, New York 10016. Address: 1716 13th Avenue, Greeley, Colorado 80631, U.S.A.

SCIENCE-FICTION PUBLICATIONS

Novel

Water Witch, with Cynthia Felice. New York, Ace, 1982.

Short Stories

Fire Watch. New York, Bluejay, 1985.

*

Connie Willis comments:

I love the short story. People are constantly telling me how the short story is dying and how it is economically impossible to make a career out of writing short stories, but I still love the short story, and I've been writing them for 20 years. I think I like the variety of moods, styles, and themes I can explore in the short story, which I have always felt was the most successful form of science fiction. It is necessary to work with only a few characters, to create worlds with only a few words and hints of background, and to make everything in the story do double duty. It's an exciting challenge. I have written everything from screwball comedies to mysteries to fairy tales and have found to my delight that science fiction welcomes them all.

I have always been fascinated by the problem of time and our place in it, and science fiction has allowed me to explore that theme in a variety of ways. I have written stories that involve the impact of the past on the present and on the future and on the far-reaching and sometimes devastating effects time travel would have on us. My story "Fire Watch" concerns a history department at Oxford that has time travel at its disposal. It can make a wonderful teaching tool, but the lessons to be learned are not always the simple ones of discovering the past. I plan to do several stories using the Oxford history department and a novel in which a young woman living in Washington, D. C., begins to dream Robert E. Lee's dreams. The theme of time is one of endless possibilities and I find the stories unfolding one after the other as if I hadn't even begun.

*　　*　　*

Connie Willis has very quietly become one of the most interesting writers of short fiction of recent years, despite a relatively small body of work, and despite the fact that it is spread among science fiction, fantasy, and supernatural fiction. It is in science fiction, however, that she particularly stands out, as recent Hugo and Nebula awards attest. Her sole novel to date, *Water Witch*, written with Cynthia Felice, was an interesting but not outstanding story of a shrewd and not particularly honest con artist on a planet where water is in short supply. It was entertaining, but nothing upon which to base a reputation. The recent publication of *Fire Watch*, her first short-story collection, should go a long way toward correcting that situation.

The title story of the collection concerns a man who travels back through time to the London Blitz as part of his training in the study of history. He becomes involved with the efforts to save an historic cathedral from destruction, waiting on the roof during each air raid to extinguish incendiary bombs before they can do any great damage. He becomes involved emotionally with his fellow defenders and ultimately learns more about himself than he does about the Blitz. In "A Letter from the Clearys" Willis illustrates the strongest point of her fiction, her ability to create entirely convincing characters, in this case, a young woman struggling for mental equilibrium in the paranoid, near-primitive aftermath of a nuclear war.

"All My Darling Daughters" is set in an orbiting finishing school for rich, but probably not particularly loved adolescents. The protagonist is a feisty, opinionated young woman who uses unorthodox methods to combat a new vice among the male students, an alien pet that completely sublimates their sexual drives. Willis maturely and deftly handles a very controversial theme.

"The Sidon in the Mirror" is an even more complex story. The setting this time is a small mining colony on the surface of a burnt-out star. The main characters are the staff and clientele of a bordello catering to the miners, and the story centers on the sado-masochistic relationships among them. Once again, Willis avoids sensationalism and grotesquerie and concentrates on the personalities of her characters and the destructive and self-destructive forces that impinge upon them. This is perhaps her most successful single work.

Another outstanding story, this time with a more conventional plot, is "The Curse of Kings. " An archaeological expedition on a primitive world uncovers a fabulous treasure, but most of their complement are immediately struck down by a bizarre and fatal ailment. Is it in fact a curse of some sort, a virus held in the burial chamber perhaps? Or is it a plot by a native chieftain jealous of the treasure and equally concerned to conceal the sordid facts of his race's earlier exploits? A reporter finds himself a bit too intimately involved in the unravelling of events as he learns that the planet's past history was not quite what he had expected.

A number of other short stories bear mention. "Daisy, in the Sun" is another of those stories where the finely developed character of the protagonist is the main focus and the plot, which involves survival of consciousness following the death of our sun. "Blued Moon" is typical of her work, a quite funny tale of what happens when the disposal of industrial wastes works to affect the laws of probability. It is genuinely humorous, a rarity in the science-fiction genre.

"Samaritan" is another of her best stories, set in a future where most of the organized churches have combined into one ecumenical body to resist a host of new beliefs. A minister and his assistant differ when their orangutan servant apparently requests that he be baptized into the faith. Predictably, some church members are aghast at the possibility of their church accepting an "animal" as a member, and the minister himself is torn between two conflicting urges. The resolution is inevitable, given the context and tone of the story, but nonetheless satisfying for all that.

Willis has also written some unusually good ghost stories, notably "The Service for the Burial of the Dead", "Distress Call", and "Substitution Trick. " Her writing in general shows great versatility and a real talent for fine characterization that should make her one of the leaders in the field for the forseeable future.

—Don D'Ammassa

WILSON, Colin (Henry). British. Born in Leicester, 26 June 1931. Educated at Gateway Secondary Technical School, Leicester, 1942-47. Served in the Royal Air Force, 1949-50. Married 1) Dorothy Betty Troop in 1951 (marriage dissolved), one son; 2) Pamela Joy Stewart in 1960, two sons and one daughter. Laboratory Assistant, Gateway School, 1948-49; tax collector, Leicester and Rugby, 1949-50; labourer and hospital porter in London, 1951-53; salesman for the magazines *Paris Review* and *Merlin*, Paris, 1953. Since 1954, full-time writer. British Council Lecturer in Germany, 1957; Writer-in-Residence, Hollins College, Virginia, 1966-67; Visiting Profes-

sor, University of Washington, Seattle, 1968; Professor, Institute of the Mediterranean (Dowling College, New York), Mallorca, 1969; Visiting Professor, Rutgers University, New Brunswick, New Jersey, 1974. Agent: David Bolt Associates, Cedar House, High Street, Ripley, Surrey GU23 6AE. Address: Tetherdown, Trewallock Lane, Gorran Haven, Cornwall, England.

SCIENCE-FICTION PUBLICATIONS

Novels

The Mind Parasites. London, Barker, and Sauk City, Wisconsin, Arkham House, 1967.
The Philosopher's Stone. London, Barker, 1969; New York, Crown, 1971.
The Space Vampires. London, Hart Davis MacGibbon, and New York, Random House, 1976.

Short Story

The Return of the Lloigor. London, Village Press, 1974.

Uncollected Short Story

"Timeslip," in *Aries 1*, edited by John Grant. Newton Abbot, Devon, David and Charles, 1979.

OTHER PUBLICATIONS

Novels

Ritual in the Dark. London, Gollancz, and Boston, Houghton Mifflin, 1960.
Adrift in Soho. London, Gollancz, and Boston, Houghton Mifflin, 1961.
The World of Violence. London, Gollancz, 1963; as *The Violent World of Hugh Greene*, Boston, Houghton Mifflin, 1963.
Man Without a Shadow: The Diary of an Existentialist. London, Barker, 1963; as *The Sex Diary of Gerard Sorme*, New York, Dial Press, 1963.
Necessary Doubt. London, Barker, and New York, Simon and Schuster, 1964.
The Glass Cage: An Unconventional Detective Story. London, Barker, 1966; New York, Random House, 1967.
The Killer. London, New English Library, 1970; as *Lingard*, New York, Crown, 1970.
The God of the Labyrinth. London, Hart Davis, 1970; as *The Hedonists*, New York, New American Library, 1971.
The Black Room. London, Weidenfeld and Nicholson, 1971; New York, Pyramid, 1975.
The Schoolgirl Murder Case. London, Hart Davis MacGibbon, and New York, Crown, 1974.
The Janus Murder Case. London, Granada, 1984.

Plays

Viennese Interlude (produced Scarborough, Yorkshire, and London, 1960).
Strindberg (as *Pictures in a Bath of Acid*, produced Leeds, Yorkshire, 1971; as *Strindberg: A Fool's Decision*, produced London, 1975). London, Calder and Boyars, 1970; New York, Random House, 1971.
Mysteries (produced Cardiff, 1979).

Other

The Outsider. London, Gollancz, and Boston, Houghton Mifflin, 1956.

Religion and the Rebel. London, Gollancz, and Boston, Houghton Mifflin, 1957.

The Age of Defeat. London, Gollancz, 1959; as *The Stature of Man*, Boston, Houghton Mifflin, 1959.

Encylopaedia of Murder, with Patricia Pitman. London, Barker, 1961; New York, Putnam, 1962.

The Strength to Dream: Literature and the Imagination. London, Gollancz, and Boston, Houghton Mifflin, 1962.

Origins of the Sexual Impulse. London, Barker, and New York, Putnam, 1963.

Rasputin and the Fall of the Romanovs. London, Barker, and New York, Farrar Straus, 1964.

Brandy of the Damned: Discoveries of a Musical Eclectic. London, Baker, 1964; as *Chords and Discords: Purely Personal Opinions on Music*, New York, Crown, 1966; augmented edition, as *Colin Wilson on Music*, London, Pan, 1967.

Beyond the Outsider: The Philosophy of the Future. London, Barker, and Boston, Houghton Mifflin, 1965.

Eagle and Earwig (essays). London, Baker, 1965.

Introduction to the New Existentialism. London, Hutchinson, 1966; Boston, Houghton Mifflin, 1967; as *The New Existentialism*, London, Wildwood House, 1980.

Sex and the Intelligent Teenager. London, Arrow, 1966; New York, Pyramid, 1968.

Voyage to a Beginning (autobiography). London, Cecil and Amelia Woolf, 1966; New York, Crown, 1969.

Bernard Shaw: A Reassessment. London, Hutchinson, and New York, Atheneum, 1969.

A Casebook of Murder. London, Frewin, 1969; New York, Cowles, 1970.

Poetry and Mysticism. San Francisco, City Lights, 1969; London, Hutchinson, 1970.

The Strange Genius of David Lindsay, with E. H. Visiak and J. B. Pick. London, Baker, 1970; as *The Haunted Man*, San Bernardino, California, Borgo Press, 1979.

The Occult. New York, Random House, and London, Hodder and Stoughton, 1971.

New Pathways in Psychology: Maslow and the Post-Freudian Revolution. New York, Taplinger, and London, Gollancz, 1972.

Order of Assassins: The Psychology of Murder. London, Hart Davis, 1972.

L'Amour: The Ways of Love, photographs by Piero Rimaldi. New York, Crown, 1972.

Strange Powers. London, Latimer New Dimensions, 1973; New York, Random House, 1975.

Tree by Tolkien. London, Covent Garden Press-Inca, 1973; Santa Barbara, California, Capra Press, 1974.

Hermann Hesse. London, Village Press, and Philadelphia, Leaves of Grass Press, 1974.

Wilhelm Reich. London, Village Press, and Philadelphia, Leaves of Grass Press, 1974.

Jorge Luis Borges. London, Village Press, and Philadelphia, Leaves of Grass Press, 1974.

A Book of Booze. London, Gollancz, 1974.

The Unexplained. Lake Oswego, Oregon, Lost Pleiade Press, 1975.

Mysterious Powers. London, Aldus, and Danbury, Connecticut, Danbury Press, 1975; as *They Had Strange Powers*, New York, Doubleday, 1975; revised edition, as *Mysteries of the Mind*, with Stuart Holroyd, Aldus, 1978.

The Craft of the Novel. London, Gollancz, 1975.

Enigmas and Mysteries. Danbury, Connecticut, Danbury Press, and London, Aldus, 1976.

The Geller Phenomenon. London, Aldus, 1976.

Mysteries: An Investigation into the Occult, The Paranormal, and the Supernatural. London, Hodder and Stoughton, 1978; New York, Putnam, 1980.

Science Fiction as Existentialism. Hayes, Middlesex, Bran's Head, 1978.

The Search for the Real Arthur, with *King Arthur Country in Cornwall*, by Brenda Duxbury and Michael Williams. Bodmin, Cornwall, Bossiney, 1979.

Starseekers. London, Hodder and Stoughton, 1980; New York, Doubleday, 1981.

The War Against Sleep: The Philosophy of Gurdjieff. Wellingborough, Northamptonshire, Aquarian Press, and York Beach, Maine, Weiser, 1980.

Frankenstein's Castle. Sevenoaks, Kent, Ashgrove Press, 1980; Salem, New Hampshire, Salem House, 1982.

Anti-Sartre, with an Essay on Camus. San Bernardino, California, Borgo Press, 1981.

The Quest for Wilhelm Reich. London, Granada, and New York, Doubleday, 1981.

Witches. Limpsfield, Surrey, Dragon's World, 1981; New York, A and W, 1982.

Poltergeist! A Study in Destructive Haunting. London, New English Library, 1981; New York, Putnam, 1982.

Access to Inner Worlds: The Story of Brad Absetz. London, Rider, 1983.

Encyclopaedia of Modern Murder 1962-1982, with Donald Seaman. London, Barker, 1983; New York, Putnam, 1985.

Psychic Detectives; The Story of Psychometry and the Paranormal in Crime Detection. London, Pan, 1984.

A Criminal History of Mankind. London, Granada, and New York, Putnam, 1984.

Lord of the Underworld: Jung and the Twentieth Century. Wellingborough, Northamptonshire, Aquarian Press, 1984.

The Essential Colin Wilson. London, Harrap, 1985.

Existential Essays, edited by Howard F. Dossor. Bath, Ashgrove Press, 1985.

Editor, *Colin Wilson's Men of Mystery*. London, W. H. Allen, 1977.

Editor, *Dark Dimensions: A Celebration of the Occult*. New York, Everest House, 1978.

Editor, with John Grant, *The Book of Time*. Newton Abbot, Devon, David and Charles, 1980.

Editor, with John Grant, *The Directory of Possibilities*. Exeter, Webb and Bower, and New York, Rutledge Press, 1981.

*

Manuscript Collection: University of Texas, Austin.

Critical Studies: *The Angry Decade* by Kenneth Allsop, London, Owen, 1958; *The World of Colin Wilson* by Sidney Campion, London, Muller, 1963; "The Novels of Colin Wilson" by R. H. W. Dillard, in *Hollins Critic* (Hollins College, Virginia), October 1967; *Colin Wilson* by John A. Weigel, New York, Twayne, 1975; *Colin Wilson: The Outsider and Beyond* by Clifford P. Bendau, San Bernardino, California, Borgo Press, 1979; *The Novels of Colin Wilson* by Nicolas Tredell, London, Vision Press, 1982; *An Odyssey of Freedom: Four*

Themes in Colin Wilson's Novels by K. Gunnar Bergstrom, Uppsala, Sweden, University of Uppsala, 1983.

* * *

Colin Wilson is an enormously energetic and eclectic writer whose works include non-fiction and fiction of many classes. For his world view he acknowledges a seminal and continuing influence of Bernard Shaw, whose long science-fantasy play *Back to Methuselah* is a sort of mainspring for Wilson's science-fiction novels.

In the Preface to *The Mind Parasites* Wilson remarks that the work is his first attempt at fantasy and likely his last. It was not. At least two more have followed. In *The Mind Parasites* Professor Gilbert Austin discovers a counter-life entity competing with humanity for life energy from the wellspring of creation. Throughout history the parasites have masked from men mankind's own true powers—which are enormous, even godlike. Austin and his cohorts turn the tide of battle in favor of man, after themselves becoming considerably advanced in this "natural" power. Similarly, in *The Philosopher's Stone* Howard Lester seeks and finds the answer to the problem of death. The power of the will to live has been blocked by the "Old Ones," a superspecies millions of years old that caused and then intercepted the evolution of man. Long asleep, the Old Ones may soon awaken. Lester hopes to lead men to confront them as "Masters" where they once served the Old Ones as slaves. *The Space Vampires* streamlines in style and strategy a similar tale. Spaceship Commander Carlsen discovers a gigantic interstellar craft to perverted aliens from the star-system Rigel. These creatures cheat death by absorbing life energy from host species such as humanity. Fortunately for mankind, sane Rigelians catch up with the vampire Rigelians just in time. Carlsen acts as the medium of the saviours, and in the process learns wholesome means by which mankind can be "immortal".

There are an enthusiam and bright-eyed bombast about these tales that make it not unrewarding to read them as parodies of science fiction. This may account for a number of the elements common in the three works, though one need not forego taking them seriously as well. Each is furnished with a preface acknowledging a debt to H. P. Lovecraft or August Derleth. Each manifests considerable erudition exhibiting Wilson's encyclopaedic knowledge of the occult as well as the arts and history: ancient mythologies are found to have considerable basis in fact. Each story presents an intellectual power fantasy. The hero, in whom a panoply of parapsychological abilities is emerging, seems torn between visions of mankind as mean, gullible, and cowardly and man with a destiny of vaulting grandeur. These heroes, after lifting the yoke of mental slavery from humanity, win a form of personal transcendence, a step in the direction of joining the advanced intelligent life that lives throughout the universe.

Of the three *The Space Vampires* is the shortest and slickest. *The Philosopher's Stone* bogs us down and seems precisely repetitive of *The Mind Parasites* whose patient narrative, nicely deployed scenic hyperboles, and wonderful message were Wilson's first, best attempt after all.

—John R. Pfeiffer

WILSON, F(rancis) Paul. American. Born in Jersey City, New Jersey, 17 May 1946. Married Mary Murphy in 1969; two daughters. Since 1974, physician, Cedar Bridge Medical Group, Bricktown, New Jersey. Recipient: Prometheus Award, 1979. Agent: Albert Zuckerman, Writers House, 21 West 26th Street, New York, New York 10010, U.S.A.

SCIENCE-FICTION PUBLICATIONS

Novels (series: LaNague Federation)

Healer (LaNague). New York, Doubleday, 1976; London, Sidgwick and Jackson, 1977.
Wheels Within Wheels (LaNague). New York, Doubleday, 1979; London, Sidgwick and Jackson, 1980.
An Enemy of the State (LaNague). New York, Doubleday, 1980.
The Keep. New York, Morrow, 1981; London, New English Library, 1982.
The Tomb. Binghamton, New York, Whispers Press, 1984.

Uncollected Short Stories

"The Cleaning Machine," in *Startling Mystery Stories* (New York), March 1971.
"Higher Centers," in *Analog* (New York), April 1971.
"The Man with the Anteater," in *Analog* (New York), July 1971.
"The Sound of Wings," in *Eerie* (New York), July 1971.
"Ratman," in *Analog* (New York), August 1971.
"With Silver Bells and Cockle Shells . . . ," in *Creepy* (New York), March 1972.
"Pard," in *Analog* (New York), December 1972.
"He Shall Be John," in *Fiction 4* (Boston), 1973; expanded version, as "The Tery," in *Binary Star 2,* New York, Dell, 1979.
"Lipidleggin'," in *Asimov's Choice: Dark Stars and Dragons,* edited by George H. Scithers. New York, Davis, 1978.
"To Fill the Sea and Air," in *Isaac Asimov's Science Fiction Anthology 2,* edited by George H. Scithers. New York, Davis, 1979.
"Demonsong," in *Heroic Fantasy,* edited by Gerald W. Page and Hank Reinhardt. New York, DAW, 1979.
"Green Winter," in *Analog* (New York), 5 January 1981.
"Be Fruitful and Multiply," in *Perpetual Light,* edited by Alan Ryan. New York, Warner, 1982.
"Soft," in *Masques,* edited by J. N. Williamson. Baltimore, Maclay, 1984.
"The Last 'One Mo' Once Golden Oldies Revival,' " in *Shadows 8,* edited by Charles L. Grant. New York, Doubleday, 1985.

*

F. Paul Wilson comments:
Frankly, I'm hesitant about making a statement about my work. I have no long-range goals, no grand theme I'm pursuing (at least not consciously). My prime personal interests are achieving personal autonomy and living an honorable life while remaining a participant in modern civilization (oxymoronic as that may sound). Surely my work reflects that, but to what degree I don't know. In my writing, I'm most interested in telling a good story, in writing the kind of book *I* would wish to plunk down money for. Anything beyond that is gravy.

* * *

F. Paul Wilson is undoubtedly one of the most interesting of the younger science-fiction authors. He is a praticing physician, plays musical instruments and composes music, a physical-fitness advocate, the father of two daughters, recipient of the first annual Prometheus Award (for *Wheels Within Wheels*), and was encouraged and developed by editor-writer John Campbell. Wilson's erudite background in literature, science, and medicine slip unobtrusively into his writings in a manner that fascinates and intrigues the reader.

To understand some of the major themes in Wilson's work, it is important to look at one of the major early influences on his writing, Albert Camus. If struggle gives meaning to life, then that struggle must of necessity have a valid cause worth fighting and dying for. This is evident in Wilson's novel *An Enemy of the State,* which is concerned with the LaNague Federation. The central character, Peter LaNague, is a true existential hero, and in some philosophical aspects is beyond good and evil as Friedrich Nietzsche might envision.

All Wilson characters are involved to one degree or another in conflict and struggle to establish a meaningful existence. (Generally speaking, this is true of all fiction writing since World War One.) Through commitment to struggle, the Wilson characters have made the choice to have the courage to be, and by so doing, establish meaning in a void of nothingness. Courage to be means to struggle for essence, among other things, and in Wilson's fiction, the characters make this choice no matter what the outcome may be. Each character seeks to be realized in his or her existence; otherwise, reality rapidly gives way to illusion and illusion gives way to nothingness.

Another major theme that runs through Wilson's writing like a gossamer spider web is the conflict between good and evil at every level of existence and action. To seek either means the character must have the courage to be one or the other; yet, there is no such thing as pure good or pure evil, for each contains mirror fragments of the other to function rationally in an existential universe. To defend either requires that the situational ethics through which each exists and functions must be examined in depth before definition of the situation can become known. Consequently, justification of each character's definition must be analyzed in those terms. In whatever genre Wilson works in, the conflict between good and evil is an intricate part of the structure. Other themes in Wilson's writing include equality, individuality, fear, loneliness, and sexuality.

Wilson's fiction clearly reveals his careful attention to plot construction for character development. Character development is interwoven into the plot in a subtle manner so that every character action reflects attributes necessary for the character's existence and moral code. Every Wilson character has a moral code, and Wilson's prose style is reminiscent at times of William Faulkner.

The continued importance of Wilson to scholars, sociologists, and readers of science fiction rests on his unique skill at presenting complex philosophical themes in a clear, direct manner that instructs as it entertains. F. Paul Wilson's contribution to science fiction is his philosophical insights into social themes and social trends, and his concern over the struggle between good and evil for superiority.

—Harold Lee Prosser

WILSON, Gabriel. See **CUMMINGS, Ray.**

WILSON, Richard. American. Born in Huntington Station, New York, 23 September 1920. Educated at Brooklyn College, 1935-36; University of Chicago, 1947-48. Served in the United States Army Signal Corps and Air Force, 1942-46. Married 1) Jessica Gould in 1941 (divorced, 1944); 2) Doris Owens in 1950 (divorced, 1967); 3) Frances Daniels in 1967 (divorced, 1982); one son and one step-daughter. Reporter, Copyreader, and assistant drama critic, Fairchild Publications, New York, 1941-42; Chief of Bureau, Transradio Press, Chicago, Washington, D. C., and New York, 1946-51; reporter, and deputy to the North American editor, Reuters, New York, 1951-64; Director, Syracuse University News Bureau, New York, 1964-80, and University Editor, 1980-82. Recipient: Nebula Award, 1968. Agent: Leslie Flood, Carnell Literary Agency, Rowneybury Bungalow, Sawbridgeworth, near Old Harlow, Essex CM20 2EX, England. Address: 1711-A Boston Avenue, Fort Pierce, Florida 33450, U.S.A.

SCIENCE-FICTION PUBLICATIONS

Novels

The Girls from Planet 5. New York, Ballantine, 1955; London, Hale, 1968.
And Then the Town Took Off. New York, Ace, 1960.
30-Day Wonder. New York, Ballantine, 1960; London, Icon, 1963.

Short Stories

Those Idiots from Earth. New York, Ballantine, 1957.
Time Out for Tomorrow. New York, Ballantine, 1962; London, Mayflower, 1967.

Uncollected Short Stories (series: Harry Protagonist)

"Friend of the Family," in *Star 2* (Derby, Connecticut), 1953.
"The Enemy," in *Infinity* (New York), October 1957.
"Man Working," in *Star* (Derby, Connecticut), November 1958.
"Frostbite," in *Future* (New York), February 1959.
"The Carson Effect," in *The Year's Best S-F 10,* edited by Judith Merril. New York, Delacorte Press, 1965.
"Box," in *New Worlds* (London), February 1965.
"The Eight Billion," in *Fantasy and Science Fiction* (New York), July 1965.
"Watchers in the Glade," in *The Ninth Galaxy Reader,* edited by Frederik Pohl. New York, Doubleday, and London, Gollancz, 1966.
"Deserter," in *Impulse* (Bournemouth), March 1966.
"Inside Out," in *Impulse* (Bournemouth), December 1966.
"Green Eyes," in *Impulse* (Bournemouth), January 1967.
"The Evil Ones," in *If* (New York), February 1967.
"9-9-99," in *Galaxy* (New York), August 1967.
"The South Waterford Rumble Club," in *Galaxy* (New York), December 1967.
"Mother to the World," in *Orbit 3,* edited by Damon Knight. New York, Putnam, 1968.
"See Me Not," in *World's Best Science Fiction 1968,* edited by Donald A. Wollheim and Terry Carr. New York, Ace, and London, Gollancz, 1968.
"Harry Protagonist, Undersec for Overpop," in *Magazine of Horror* (New York), December 1969.
"A Man Spekith," in *World's Best Science Fiction 1970,* edited

by Donald A. Wollheim and Terry Carr. New York, Ace, and London, Gollancz, 1970.

"If a Man Answers," in *If* (New York), January 1970.

"Have It Your Own Way," in *The Most Thrilling Science Fiction Ever Told* (New York), Winter 1970.

"The Day They Had the War," in *Fantasy and Science Fiction* (New York), June 1971.

"The Far King," in *Asimov's Choice: Comets and Computers*, edited by George H. Scithers. New York, Davis, 1978.

"Harry Protagonist, Brain-Drainer," in *100 Great Science Fiction Short-Short Stories*, edited by Isaac Asimov, Martin H. Greenberg, and Joseph D. Olander. New York, Doubleday, and London, Robson, 1978.

"The Story Writer," in *The 1980 Annual World's Best SF*, edited by Donald A. Wollheim. New York, DAW, 1980.

"Gone Past," in *Destinies* (New York), Fall 1980.

"The Nineteenth Century Spaceship," in *Last Wave* (New York), August 1984.

"Lark Thou Never Wert," in *Pandora* (Tampa, Florida), December 1984.

OTHER PUBLICATIONS

Plays

Jack and Jill (produced Syracuse, New York, 1965).
Another Time, in *Modern Radio Production*. Belmont, California, Wadsworth, 1985.

Radio Play: *Inside Story* (*X Minus One* series), 1955.

Other

"Syracuse University Science-Fiction Collections," in *Worlds of Tomorrow* (New York), May 1967.
Syracuse University: The Critical Years (vol. 3 of university history). Syracuse, New York, Syracuse University, 1984.

*

Manuscript Collection: Bird Library, Syracuse University, New York.

*   *   *

Richard Wilson's career as a writer breaks quite nicely into two stages. In his early years, Wilson was a satirical humorist in the mode of Henry Kuttner and Robert Sheckley, whose stories were frequently infused with a grim humor and a sharp eye for humanity's foibles. The three novels written at this time are cases in point. *The Girls from Planet 5* takes a pair of old standby plots and fuses them, with delighted results. America has become a matriarchy, where only one state still upholds the macho ideal—Texas, naturally. Into this strife-ridden world come invaders from another world, but invaders who are actually beautiful women. Frustrated by their loss of pre-eminence, the Texan patriarchs are not willing to become a minor backwater in an increasingly female universe. Aliens appear again in *And Then the Town Took Off*, a shorter novel that details the effect upon the citizens of Superior, Ohio, when their city uproots itself from Earth and rises into space to become a separate planet. This rollicking escapade pokes amusing if unconscious fun at James Blish's famous "Cities in Flight" series. The third and best of the novels is *30-Day Wonder* which takes what should be an ideal situation and turns it

completely around. The Monolithians are alien visitors who express their determination to obey scrupulously all human laws and regulations, and ensure that all humans in their vicinity will do the same. The effect on rush-hour traffic of several automobiles sedately travelling well within the speed limit is just the beginning of an increasingly taxing month of the human race.

Although most of Wilson's early short stories such as "Those Idiots from Earth," were satirical or actively funny, his most well-known story of that period was very serious. The heroine of "Love" is a blind human girl living on Mars, who is in love with one of the despised Martian natives. When her father forbids her to have anything futher to do with him, she runs off for one last meeting, and together they discover an ancient artifact that may well cure her sight. It is a touching tale told somewhat awkwardly, but effective.

The awkwardness left during the years that followed, and several of Wilson's more recent works are outstanding. "Mother to the World" won a Nebula award for its tender, effective portrayal of the last man on Earth and the last woman, a gentle but retarded individual whose tolerance and flexibility overcome the horrors of their situation. Wilson returned to the last man theme in "A Man Spekith" in which a disc jockey and a computer remain in orbit, looking down over the corpse of the Earth. "See Me Not" is one of the few recent treatments of invisibility that contains any novelty. "The Carson Effect" portrays a wave of philanthropy on the eve of the last day of the world, an ending that is miscalculated and never happens, much to the consternation of those who have given away their fortunes. "The Story Writer" is a complex, engrossing story that contains enough complexity for a brace of novels. An aging successful pulp writer sits in flea markets, writing stories for people as a whim, until he finds himself a character in one of his own stories, the tale of the meeting of our own race and another that has reached us through another plane of existence in their flight from a ravaged homeworld. In this as in the other later stories, Wilson employs a rich, witty style that is a delight in itself; the expertly handled plots and characters are almost superfluous.

—Don D'Ammassa

WILSON, Robert Anton. American. Born in Brooklyn, New York, 18 January 1932. Educated at Brooklyn Polytechnic Institute; New York University, Paideia University, B. S., M.A. 1978, Ph. D. 1981. Married Arlen Riley in 1959; four children. Engineering aide, Ebasco Inc., New York, 1950-56; salesman, Doubleday, publishers, 1957; copywriter, Popular Club, Passaic, New Jersey, 1959-62; Sales Manager, Antioch Bookplate, Yellow Springs, Ohio, 1962-65; astrology columnist, *National Mirror*, and Editor, *Jaguar*, 1965; Associate Editor, *Playboy,* Chicago, 1965-71. Agent: Al Zuckerman, Writers House, 21 West 26th Street, New York, New York 10001, U.S.A.

SCIENCE-FICTION PUBLICATIONS

Novels (series: Illuminatus; Schrödinger's Cat)

Illuminatus! The Eye in the Pyramid, The Golden Apple, Leviathan, with Robert Shea. New York, Dell, 3 vols., 1975; London, Sphere, 3 vols., 1976; one vol. edition, Dell, 1984.

Schrödinger's Cat:
   The Universe Next Door. New York, Pocket Books, 1979; London, Sphere, 1980.
   The Trick Top Hat. New York, Pocket Books, 1980; London, Sphere, 1981.
   Homing Pigeons. New York, Pocket Books, 1981; London, Sphere, 1982.
Masks of the Illuminati. New York, Pocket Books, and London, Sphere, 1981.
The Earth Will Shake. Los Angeles, Tarcher, 1982.
The Widow's Son. New York, Bluejay, 1985.

OTHER PUBLICATIONS

Novel

The Sex Magicians. Los Angeles, Jaundice Press, 1974.

Play

Illuminatus! (produced Liverpool, 1976; London, 1977; Seattle, 1978).

Other

Playboy's Book of Forbidden Words. Chicago, Playboy Press, 1972.
Sex and Drugs. Chicago, Playboy Press, 1973; London, Mayflower, 1975.
The Book of the Breast. Chicago, Playboy Press, 1974.
Cosmic Trigger: Final Secret of the Illuminati. Berkeley, California, And/Or Press, 1977; London, Abacus, 1979.
Neuropolitics, with Timothy Leary. Culver City, California, Peace Press, 1977.
The Illuminati Papers. Berkeley, California, And/Or Press, 1980; London, Sphere, 1982.
Right Where You Are Sitting Now: Further Tales of the Illuminati. Berkeley, California, And/Or Press, 1982.
Prometheus Rising. Santa Monica, California, Prometheus Press, 1983.

*

Robert Anton Wilson comments:

I define my writing as guerilla ontology—that is, a literary expression of the discoveries of physical relativity (Einstein), cultural relativity (anthropology), neurological relativity (Korzybski, Leary) and the new head-spaces opened to us by psychedelics, bio-feedback, scientific study of yoga, etc. Each of my books presents not one map of reality, but several; the humor, the suspense, and the philosophical meaning (if any) derive from the search for the one reality, never quite found, which will synthesize or include all the alternative reality-tunnels presented. As in quantum physics, the isolated observer or omniscient narrator does not exist in my world; it is a participatory universe in which each entity projects/creates its own surrounding experential continuum.

*   *   *

George, you're too serious.
Don't you known how to play?
Did you ever think that life is
maybe a game? There is no
difference between life and a
game, you know.

Games of all sorts and at all levels abound throughout Robert Anton Wilson's books. Those most typical in this respect are perhaps *Masks of the Illuminati*, whose overall structure is that of a detective story (the most formal sort of literary game, and here played with strict attention to the rules) and whose subject is the mind-game played on an innocent seeking occult knowledge. And Wilson would solemnly assure us that the book is part of the mind-game he is playing with his readers, Operation Mindfuck, to lead them to some level of further awareness.

Some readers will find that last level, Wilson's philosophical pretensions, spoils the books for them. But insofar as he's serious about anything, Wilson is serious about bringing home to people the limits that their own viewpoints impose on them and the possibility of transcending those limits. To this end Wilson makes a mockery of all political viewpoints (including the anarchism he himself espouses) and in *Prometheus Rising* tries to give some structure to a course of self-liberation. Perhaps the "Trancendental Agnosticism" that has come to Wilson from drinking too deep of too many springs of ultimate wisdom, from hearing too many Ultimate Truths, contradict each other; perhaps it's too much a product of the late 1960's to appeal to the True Believers who infest more recent decades. But happily Wilson doesn't seem to have noticed and continues to pillory our "normal primate behaviour."

And if you want to just sit back, forget the message and look at the scenery, Wilson will keep you happily entertained, stealing from any source that pleases him, Joyce, Lovecraft, Tolkien, or "Elephant Doody Comix" and throwing up the lunatic touches of characterisation that make the patchwork structures of his novels shine.

Drake let out a small fart, an incredible thing, it seemed to George, for the leader of all organised crime in America to do.
Wildeblood was by no means a simple or uncomplicated WoMan. The sex-change operation had only been stage one in a plan to totally transform himself. After that she intended to become a nun.
   George decided . . . to grow his hair long, smoke dope and become a musician. He succeeded in two of these ambitions.

Wilson's viewpoint is determinedly optimistic, as his essays on Buckminster Fuller and on the conquest of stupidity show. Yet there is in his novels alongside the jugglers and buffoons a sense of pain and tragedy that isn't diminished by its futility. To quote Wilson's own motto: "It isn't true unless it makes you laugh, but you don't understand it until it makes you cry."

The author solemnly warrants and guarantees that there are no flat lies and only one hidden joke in the above . . . paragraphs.

—Michael Cule

WINGRAVE, Anthony. See **WRIGHT, S. Fowler.**

WINIKI, Ephraim. See **FEARN, John Russell.**

WINNARD, Frank. See TUBB, E. C.

WINTER, H. G. See BATES, Harry.

WODHAMS, Jack. Australian. Born in Dagenham, Essex, England, 3 September 1931; emigrated to Australia in 1955. Has worked as a weighing-machine mechanic, brush salesman, a porter in mental hospital, taxi and truck driver, bartender, welder, and magician's assistant. Currently mailvan driver, Brisbane. Guest of Honor, Melbourne Science Fiction Convention, 1968. Address: P. O. Box 48, Caboolture, Queensland 4510, Australia.

SCIENCE-FICTION PUBLICATIONS

Novels

The Authentic Touch. New York, Curtis, 1971.
Looking for Blücher. St. Kilda, Victoria, Void, 1980.
Ryn. St. Kilda, Victoria, Cory and Collins, 1982.

Short Stories

Future War. St. Kilda, Victoria, Cory and Collins, 1982.

Uncollected Short Stories

"The Pearly Gates of Hell," in *Analog* (New York), September 1967.
"The Cure-All Merchant," in *Analog* (New York), November 1967.
"The Helmet of Hades," in *New Writtings in SF 11,* edited by John Carnell. London, Corgi, 1968.
"The God Pedlars," in *Analog* (New York), February 1968.
"Handyman," in *Analog* (New York), April 1968.
"The Fuglemen of Recall," in *Analog* (New York), August 1968.
"Homespinner," in *Galaxy* (New York), October 1968.
"Try Again," in *Amazing* (New York), November 1968.
"Split Personality," in *Analog* (New York), November 1968.
"The Form Master," in *Analog* (New York), December 1968.
"Hey but No Presto," in *Analog* (New York), April 1969.
"A Run of Deuces," in *Fantasy and Science Fiction* (New York), June 1969.
"The Empty Balloon," in *Analog* (New York), July 1969.
"Androtomy and the Scion," in *Analog* (New York), August 1969.
"Anchor Man," in *Vision of Tomorrow* (Newcastle upon Tyne), August 1969.
"Star Hunger," in *Galaxy* (New York), August 1969.
"The Visitors," in *Analog* (New York), September 1969.
"Undercover Weapon," in *Vision of Tomorrow* (Newcastle upon Tyne), December 1969.
"There Is a Crooked Man," in *Analog 7,* edited by John W. Campbell, Jr. New York, Doubleday, 1970.
"The Ill Wind" in *Vision of Tomorrow* (Newcastle upon Tyne), January 1970.

"On Greatgrandfather's Knee," in *Vision of Tomorrow* (Newcastle upon Tyne), February 1970.
"Dali, For Instance," in *Analog* (New York), February 1970.
"Wrong Rabbit," in *Analog* (New York), March 1970.
"Zwoppover," in *Vision of Tomorrow* (Newcastle upon Tyne), April 1970.
"Beau Farscon Regrets," in *Analog* (New York), July 1970.
"Top Billing," in *Analog* (New York), September 1970.
"Enemy by Proxy," in *Amazing* (New York), November 1970.
"Big Time Operator," in *Analog* (New York), December 1970.
"Sprog," in *Analog* (New York), January 1971.
"The Pickle Barrel," in *Analog* (New York), February 1971.
"Knight Arrant," in *Analog* (New York), September 1971.
"Foundling's Father," in *Analog* (New York), December 1971.
"Stormy Bellwether," in *Analog* (New York), January 1972.
"Budnip," in *Analog* (New York), August 1972.
"Lien Low," in *Void 1* (St. Kilda, Victoria), 1975.
"The 200-1 Asset," in *Void 2* (St. Kilda, Victoria), 1975.
"Squawman," in *Void 3* (St. Kilda, Victoria), 1976.
"The Masque Behind the Face," in *Void 4* (St. Kilda, Victoria), 1976.
"The Giveaway," in *Void 5* (St. Kilda, Victoria), 1977.
"The Butterfly Must Die," in *Envisaged Worlds,* edited by Paul Collins. St. Kilda, Victoria, Void 1978.
"Jade Elm," in *Other Worlds,* edited by Paul Collins. St. Kilda, Victoria, Void, 1978.
"One Clay Foot," in *Alien Worlds,* edited by Paul Collins. St. Kilda, Victoria, Void, 1979.
"Whosa Whatsa?," in *The Seven Deadly Sins of Science Fiction,* edited by Isaac Asimov, Martin H. Greenberg, and Charles G. Waugh. New York, Fawcett, 1980.
"Armstrong," in *Distant Worlds,* edited by Paul Collins. St. Kilda Victoria, Cory and Collins, 1981.
"Mostly Meantime," in *Analog* (New York), February 1981.
"Freeway," in *Amazing* (New York), November 1981.
"The Making of a Gaffa," in *Rigel* (Richmond, California), Spring 1982.
"Telepathetique," in *Fantasy Book* (Pasadena, California), May 1982.
"Premonition," in *Twilight Zone* (New York), September 1982.
"The Hide," in *Future Worlds,* edited by Paul Collins. St. Kilda, Victoria, Cory and Collins, 1983.
"Gauntlet's World," in *Rigel* (Richmond, California), Summer 1983.
"The Maroon Is Rue," in *Fantasy Book* (Pasadena, California), August 1983.

*   *   *

It is well known that science fiction tends to emphasis content at the expense of style, but the positive influence this has had on narrative techniques is not always appreciated. Writers have been encouraged to create methods better adapted to its needs than traditional story-telling procedures. Jack Wodhams is one such writer. The way his stories are constructed could have been evolved in tradition short story writing. Smooth, effortless, controlled, a typical Wodhams story moves irresistibly ahead, mostly carried by dialog with a minimum of description and explanation. Indeed, when the author intrudes to fill in background or discuss principles, the pace slows or falters. There may be a firm single viewpoint, or a focus of action on a continuing situation if it is required. Often there are frequent scene changes as the action unfolds through related events. Characters tend to be no more than voices whose conversation shows what is happening, details of motivation unknown and irrelevant. The effect at its best is of the story happening, not being reported. It has much in common with modern film scripts, but it emerged naturally in science fiction as the field matured and a sophisticated readership developed.

Wodham's stories usually grow out of an original scientific premise, often a revaluation of a familiar speculation. They may bring out new objects or snags or turn a familiar argument around, often for a surprise ending. Some are in the venerable "dangerous invention" tradition. Thus "Stormy Bellwether" devastatingly sets out the bad news about person-to-person television. "The Fuglemen of Recall" has criminal exploitation of a memory recording and transfer process. "The Empty Balloon" looks at a "mind-reading" device working on sub-vocalised verbal thinking, an uncomfortable possibility, with a spy plot. In "Androtomy and the Scion" a cloned duplicate brain, in rapport with the original, gives the forces of evil new powers for coercion. "Split Personality" has an even more macabre atrocity, a felon physically dissected into living left and right halves for use as a better form of radio for an interstellar expedition.

The author's awareness of the social implications of radical new techniques, their value for oppression by ever-ready authority or for private anti-social acts, shows in many other stories. Thus "Whosa Whatsa" explores the utter ruin of traditional legal assumptions and conventions implicit in human sex reversal, and its impact on adultery, divorce, custody, and inheritance. "The Form Master" brings out the weakness of the coming world data bank, including its use for fraud by selective use of false input. In "Sprog" the inventor of a system of predicting future events cannot get a hearing and ends up exploiting the gullible as an ordinary fortune-teller. In "The Cure-All Merchant" behavior modification drugs have been refined into effective specifics for all problems, but a practitioner treats patients just as well by suggestion. One group of stories deals with the hazards and misuses of matter-transmission systems. "There Is a Crooked Man" shows future crime and detection in action. In "Wrong Rabbit" communication is accidentally opened with another world. "Top Billing" looks at duplication of people transmitted. "Hey but No Presto" shows a future form of hijacking. Among the stories of the interstellar future, "Star Hunger" is an excellent look at the need to reach the stars, the drive for habitable new worlds, and the danger of failure.

Wodhams's first two novels are similar, though episodic and with more complexity of detail. *The Authentic Touch* uses the setting of a planet settled with re-creations of past epochs for jaded tourists of an opulent future, which tends to get out of control through too much realism. *Looking for Blücher* has a thin framing device to link up a series of shared hallucinatory adventures—easy stuff to write no doubt but not very satisfactory reading. It is really a disappointing waste of effort. *Ryn* does not seem to qualify as science fiction despite a vague gesture at rationalising its theme of reincarnation of metempsychosis. But it is a strongly unified work, strictly following the logic of its premises, and a compelling study of a victim of circumstances trying to cope with his narrowly restricted situation: as an infant with full consciousness and memory of a previous adult life in another milieu.

An interesting recent group of stories looks with loathing at some ideas about the possibilities of war in the distant future which are commonly found and accepted in science fiction, bringing out their absurdity as well as obscenity. In "Pet" the dehumanised military caste isolated from its sponsoring society is seen: the fighter accidentally acquiring a civilian captive insists on keeping the creature as a pet. One innovation in

"Butcher Mackerson" is the custom of drafting the handicapped to carry on a permanent ritual conflict, clearly an inverted form of eugenics. All the characters in these stories have a total ethical vacuity and no sense of any meaning underlying the fighting, but we may draw our own conclusions.

Perhaps Wodham's writing is so typical of *Analog*, where most of his stories have been published, that he does not seem distinctive, despite his considerable originality and individuality.

—Graham Stone

WOLF, Gary K. American. Born in Berwyn, Illinois, 24 January 1941. Educated at the University of Illinois, Urbana, B.S. 1963, M.S. 1969. Served in the United States Air Force, in Vietnam, 1963-69: Major. Vice-President and Creative Director, Crosson Austin Wolf, advertising and public relations, Amherst, New Hampshire. Agent: Bill Reiss, Paul R. Reynolds Inc., 71 West 23rd Street, New York, New York 10010, U.S.A.

SCIENCE-FICTION PUBLICATIONS

Novels

Killerbowl. New York, Doubleday, 1975; London, Sphere, 1976.
A Generation Removed. New York, Doubleday, 1977.
The Resurrectionist. New York, Doubleday, 1979.
Who Censored Roger Rabbit? New York, St. Martin's Press, 1981.

Uncollected Short Stories

"Love Story," in *Worlds of Tomorrow* (New York), Winter 1970.
"Dissolve," in *Orbit 11*, edited by Damon Knight. New York, Putnam, 1973.
"Therapy," in *Orbit 13*, edited by Damon Knight. New York, Putnam, 1974.
"The Bridge Builder," in *Orbit 14*, edited by Damon Knight. New York, Harper, 1974.
"Slammer," in *Fantasy and Science Fiction* (New York), March 1974.
"Dr. Rivet and Supercon Sal," in *Fantasy and Science Fiction* (New York), January 1976.

*   *   *

Gary K. Wolf's "Love Story" opens with a marriage ceremony during which the couple involved are required to relive briefly their pasts. Their civilization at first seems typically dystopian—conception occurs artificially, each fetus is properly programmed, children are raised in state facilities—yet Wolf cleverly reverses the situation, making it clear that the children are both well cared for and happy. We briefly tour a culture where there is no excess population, where everyone is content and virtually immortal. Our protagonists grow to adulthood, fall in love, and live together. Eventually they decide to have children and, their twin babies born artificially, they prepare for marriage. "Love Story" ends with a jolt. The priest at the ceremony hands them each a wafer. Eucharist-like, symbolic of their love, poisoned. They give up immortality to provide space for their babies.

"Dissolve" argues that television, because of its documentary-like quality and its oversimplification of moral problems, is drastically distorting our view of reality. The story jumps montage-like between a TV talk-show discussion of this problem, a number of typical television programs, and a young couple living in a bombed out TV studio after an atomic war. The girl is dying from radiation sickness but the boy, immersed in the simplistic television mind set, seems to think that he can save her by making a video-tape in which she is cured. A grim story, it is very effective.

"Therapy" is a slight, funny piece about a computer marriage counselor, one of its less successful cases, and a robot elevator which thinks it's the computer's mother. "The Bridge Builder" is a gripping story set in a world where the main transportation system is the Bridge, a matter transmitter. The protagonist builds bridges, repairs them, and is, in fact, fatally addicted to their use. "Slammer" and "Dr. Rivet and Supercon Sal" are both wildly comic tales reminiscent of Ron Goulart. The first concerns a prissy momma's boy who, mistakenly arrested for breaking into his own car and interred in a city reserved entirely for criminals, decides to stay there and become one. The second details the adventures of two shysters out to make a fast buck. He's a failure with people, but can do anything with machines. She's just the reverse. Their partner in crime is a rogue robot kitchenette. The story ends with one of the most hilarious chase scenes in recent fiction.

Wolf's novels, as a rule, are not of the same quality as his short fiction. *Killerbowl*, the best of them, is set in the world of street football, a cross between our current sport and guerilla warfare. The playing field covers several square city blocks, knives, clubs, and rifles are routinely issued, and the millions of fans keep statistics not only on touchdowns but on kills. T. R. Mann, a veteran quarterback, has been marked for assassination because he isn't bloody enough. The novel is very effective, but seems derivative of William Harrison's well-known story "Roller Ball Murder" (1973). Less successful are *A Generation Removed*, which involves a near-future America where only those under 20 can hold political office and where those over 55 are "euthed," and *The Resurrectionist*, which details the adventures of a Bridge (see "The Bridge Builder") who must rescue a defector lost in the lines during transmission. Both novels suffer from weaknesses of plot, characterization, and style. All three books involve basically the same character motivation; a competent middle-aged protagonist, while working for the System, discovers it to be corrupt, and, finding himself in jeopardy, sets out vigilante-style to destroy it.

In summary, Wolf is a talented but uneven writer who seems most at home with short fiction. His best work is found in such slightly avant-garde stories as "Dissolve" and "The Bridge Builder," and in the broad comedy of "Slammer" and "Dr. Rivet."

—Michael M. Levy

WOLFE, Bernard. American. Born in New Haven, Connecticut, 28 September 1915. Educated at Yale University, New Haven, 1931-36, B.A. 1935 (Phi Beta Kappa). Married Dolores Michaels in 1964. Taught at Bryn Mawr College, Pennsylvania, 1936; Trotsky's secretary, Mexico, 1937; served in the United States Merchant Marine, 1937-39; Editor, *Mechanix* *Illustrated*, New York, 1944-45; ghostwriter for Billy Rose's syndicated column, "Pitching Horseshoes," 1947-50; taught creative writing, University of California, Los Angeles, 1966-68. Screenwriter, Universal-International Productions, and Tony Curtis Productions, Hollywood. *Died 27 October 1985.*

SCIENCE-FICTION PUBLICATIONS

Novel

Limbo. New York, Random House, 1952; abridged edition, as *Limbo 90*, London, Secker and Warburg, 1953.

Uncollected Short Stories

"Self Portrait," in *The Robot and the Man*, edited by Martin H. Greenberg. New York, Gnome Press, 1953.
"The Never Ending Penny," in *The Year's Best S-F 6*, edited by Judith Merril. New York, Simon and Schuster, 1961; London, Mayflower, 1963.
"The Dot and Dash Bird," in *The Playboy Book of Science Fiction and Fantasy*, edited by Ray Russell. Chicago, Playboy Press, 1966; London, Souvenir Press, 1967.
"The Biscuit Position" and "The Girl with the Rapid Eye Movements," in *Again, Dangerous Visions*, edited by Harlan Ellison. New York, Doubleday, 1972; London, Millington, 1976.

OTHER PUBLICATIONS

Novels

Really the Blues, with Mezz Mezzrow. New York, Random House, 1946; London, Musicians Press, 1947.
The Late Risers: Their Masquerade. New York, Random House, 1954; London, Consul, 1962; as *Everything Happens at Night*, New York, New American Library, 1963.
In Deep. New York, Knopf, 1957; London, Secker and Warburg, 1958.
The Great Prince Died. New York, Scribner, and London, Cape, 1959; as *Trotsky Dead*, Los Angeles, Wollstonecraft, 1975.
The Magic of Their Singing. New York, Scribner, 1961.
Come On Out, Daddy. New York, Scribner, 1963.
Memoirs of a Not Altogether Shy Pornographer. New York, Doubleday, 1972.
Logan's Gone. Los Angeles, Nash, 1974.
Lies. Los Angeles, Wollstonecraft, 1975.

Short Stories

Move Up, Dress Up, Drink Up, Burn Up. New York, Doubleday, 1968.

Plays

Television Plays: *Assassin!*, 1955; *The Ghost Writer*, 1955; *The Five Who Shook the Mighty*, 1956.

Other

Full Disclosure, edited by Annette Welles. Los Angeles, Wollstonecraft, 1975.
Julie: The Life and Times of John Garfield. Los Angeles, Wollstonecraft, 1976.

Translator, with Alice Backer, *The Plot*, by Egon Hostovsky. London, Cassell, 1961.

*

Critical Study: *Bernard Wolfe* by Carolyn Geduld, New York, Twayne, 1972.

*   *   *

A lifelong enemy of science fiction, to judge from his comments in Harlan Ellison's *Again, Dangerous Visions*, Bernard Wolfe has written a few science fiction stories and a celebrated dystopian novel. The stories are tightly written, but *Limbo* is a masterpiece.

Zany, action-packed, Joycean in style, *Limbo* is formally and conceptually complex and unremittingly analytical, both politically and psychologically. Most effectively of Wolfe's novels, it argues Dr. Edmund Bergler's acceptance of ambivalence opposition to "pseudo-aggression." Alongside Korzybskian semantics, cybernetics, and various technological fantasies (van Vogt is cited by name in the Afterword), Bergler's neo-Freudian theories are entertained in an entertaining manner. Besides its Dantesque associations, the novel's title signifies voluntary amputation, the absurdist idea for literal "disarmament" Dr. Martine left behind in a journal when he deserted World War III's automated carnage. Self-exiled among the relatively primitive Mandunji for 18 years, he has perfected their traditional cure for evil spirits, lobotomy. When civilization invades his island in 1990, Martine feels compelled to return to the mainland, where he finds the postwar "Inland Strip" and its great power rival, the "East Union," have taken his gallows humor seriously.

As in Plato's *Republic*, the state is the individual writ large; only Martine, as its unwitting begetter, can end this travesty, after he comes to know himself. Others are little more than extensions of him, for or against the prosthetic limbs that are more dangerous than their originals. Tom, son of his loins, is the ultimate pacifist, a basket case, and a spokesman for the Anti-Pros. Children of Martine's thought are his former colleague, now President Helder (hero) and the charismatic Theo (god) whose wartime amputation by Martine started the whole chain of ideas. performing a social lobotomy, Martine removes both party "heads," returning with Theo to his tropical island. There, his healthy native son, Rambo (for Arthur Rimbaud), is leading a similar revolution against single-minded solutions.

Not a prediction of 1990, *Limbo* is a metaphorical extension of a literal malaise, most dangerous among the technologically sophisticated whose dependence on their tools blinds them to their own responsibility. Self-amputation is no answer to the human dilemma, rather a symptom of it. This central absurdity is the most important of many estranging devices integrated into a thoroughly modernist novel; its vision of wholeness and balance is both its form and its substance. Wolfe does not simply arouse anxiety about the uncontrollable, or appease it with an appeal to contemplate the artwork. *Limbo* locates the trouble's source in the individual, whose recognition of the problem is the necessary first step toward its solution.

This therapy may not have worked for Wolfe, whose subsequent novels belabored Berglerian analysis without winning much of an audience. Nor has post-1952 American society been self-evidently more able to laugh at and accept its ambivalence. The book's acceptance in SF circles is marginal; reviewed at arm's length, it has often been ignored in historical studies of the genre. Though its direct influence is questionable,

Limbo is still a harbinger of more stylish, sexy, complex novels to come. On its literary merits, *Limbo* is the "great American dystopia."

—David N. Samuelson

WOLFE, Gene (Rodman). American. Born in Brooklyn, New York, 7 May 1931. Educated at Texas A and M University, College Station, 1949, 1952; University of Houston, B.S. 1956; Miami University. Served in the United States Army, 1952-54. Married Rosemary Frances Dietsch in 1956; two sons and two daughters. Project engineer, Procter and Gamble, 1956-72; Senior Editor, *Plant Engineering*, Barrington, Illinois, 1972-84. Recipient: Nebula Award, 1973, 1982; Rhysling Award, for verse, 1978; *Locus* Award, 1982; World Fantasy Award, 1982; British Science Fiction Association Award, 1982; British Fantasy Award, 1983; John W. Campbell Memorial Award, 1984. Agent: Virginia Kidd, Box 278, Milford, Pennsylvania 18337. Address: P. O. Box 69, Barrington, Illinois 60010, U.S.A.

SCIENCE-FICTION PUBLICATIONS

Novels (series: Book of the New Sun)

Operation ARES. New York, Berkley, 1970; London, Dobson, 1977.
The Shadow of the Torturer (New Sun). New York, Simon and Schuster, 1980.
The Claw of the Conciliator (New Sun), New York, Simon and Schuster, 1981.
The Sword of Lictor (New Sun). New York, Simon and Schuster, and London, Sidgwick and Jackson, 1982.
The Citadel of the Autarch (New Sun). New York, Simon and Schuster, and London, Sidgwick and Jackson, 1983.

Short Stories

The Fifth Head of Cerberus. New York, Scribner, 1972.
The Island of Doctor Death and Other Stories and Other Stories. New York, Pocket Books, 1980.
Gene Wolfe's Book of Days. New York, Doubleday, 1981.

Uncollected Short Stories

"Tarzan of the Grapes," in *Mother Was a Lovely Beast*, edited by Philip José Farmer. Radnor, Pennsylvania, Chilton, 1974.
"To the Dark Tower Came," in *Orbit 19*, edited by Damon Knight. New York, Harper, 1977.
"Our Neighbour by David Copperfield," in *Rooms of Paradise*, edited by Lee Harding. Melbourne, Quartet, 1978; New York, St. Martin's Press, 1979.
"The Woman Who Loved the Centaur Pholus," in *Isaac Asimov's Science Fiction Anthology 4*, edited by George H. Scithers. New York, Davis, 1980.
"Suzanne Delage," in *Edges*, edited by Ursula K. Le Guin and Virginia Kidd. New York, Pocket Books, 1980.
"A Criminal Proceeding," in *Interfaces*, edited by Ursula K. Le Guin and Virginia Kidd. New York, Ace, 1980.
"The Detective of Dreams," in *Dark Forces*, edited by Kirby McCauley. New York, Viking Press, 1980.
"Kevin Malone," in *New Terrors 1*, edited by Ramsey Campbell. London, Pan, 1980.

"In Looking-Glass Castle," in *TriQuarterly* (Evanston, Illinois), Fall 1980.

"The Horars of War," in *Combat SF*, edited by Gordon R. Dickson. New York, Ace, 1981.

"The Marvelous Brass Chessplaying Automaton," in *Pawn to Infinity*, edited by Fred and Joan Saberhagen. New York, Ace, 1982.

"Last Day," in *Speculations*, edited by Isaac Asimov and Alice Laurance. Boston, Houghton Mifflin, 1982.

"The Woman the Unicorn Loved," in *The Best Science Fiction of the Year 11*, edited by Terry Carr. New York, Pocket Books, 1982.

"The Dark of the June," in *Changes*, edited by Michael Bishop and Ian Watson. New York, Ace, 1982.

"Cherry Jubilee," in *Isaac's Science Fiction Magazine* (New York), 18 January 1982.

"The Last Thrilling Wonder Story," in *Isaac Asimov's Science Fiction Magazine* (New York), June 1982.

"A Solar Labyrinth," in *Fantasy and Science Fiction* (New York), April 1983.

"Four Wolves," in *Amazing* (New York), May 1983.

"From the Desk of Gilmer C. Merton," in *Fantasy and Science Fiction* (New York), June 1983.

"Creation," in *Omni* (New York), November 1983.

"The Map," in *Light Years and Dark*, edited by Michael Bishop. New York, Berkley, 1984.

"Redbeard," in *Masques*, edited by J. N. Williamson. Baltimore, Maclay, 1984.

"A Cabin on the Coast," in *Fantasy and Science Fiction* (New York), February 1984.

"The Traveller," in *Amazing* (New York), January 1985.

"The Woman Who Went Out," in *Fantasy and Science Fiction* (New York), June 1985.

OTHER PUBLICATIONS

Novels

Peace. New York, Harper, 1975.
The Devil in a Forest (for children). Chicago, Follett, 1976.
The Castle of the Otter. Willimantic, Connecticut, Ziesing, 1982.
The Wolfe Archipelago. WIllimantic, Connecticut, Ziesing, 1983.
Plant Engineering. Cambridge, Massachusetts, NESFA Press, 1984.

*

Bibliography: in *The Castle of the Otter*, 1982.

Gene Wolfe comments

I am frequentley called an *Orbit* writer, by which the callers appear to mean an obscurantist. I do not feel the term is justified. I try to bring pleasure to my readers on more than one level; but that, I think, is a characteristic of virtually all good fiction. I avoid private symbolism, and usually provide more than enough clues for such small puzzles as I set. If I show a man lying when it is to his advantage to lie, I assume that my reader is intelligent enough to see that the man in question is a liar—and so on.

My heroes are often boys or young men trying to find a place in the world (Tacky Babcock in "The Island of Doctor Death and Other Stories," Mark in *The Devil in a Forest*, Number Five in *The Fifth Head of Cerberus* and so on); perhaps despite a conscious conviction to the contrary, I feel that the most adventurous years are between 10 and 30. But I have written about old women too, and young ones, aliens, and middle-aged men. Recently I wrote a story—"The War Beneath the Tree"—in which the chief character was an automated teddy bear.

I think I am still at least as much a reader as a writer. I like Proust, Chesterton, Dickens (I've done a Dickens story: "Our Neighbor by David Copperfield"), Washington Irving, Lewis Carroll (not just *Alice*), Kipling, Maugham, Wells, John Fowles, R. A. Lafferty, Ursula K. Le Guin, Kate Wilhelm, Jorge Luis Borges, Tolkein, and C. S. Lewis. If you like half or more of those writers (for example, Maugham as far as the 'h') you should probably try me. Trembling, I throw myself on the mercy of the court.

*   *   *

With the publication of his tetralogy *The Book of the New Sun*, Gene Wolfe has entered the ranks of the major contemporary writers of science fiction. The far-future world of Urth through which Wolfe's characters move is a world of beauty and horror, one in which humanity's great accomplishments are not only past, but also nearly forgotten, and in which the lack of resources makes the knowledge that remains nearly useless.

In this work's first volume, *The Shadow of the Torturer*, we follow Wolfe's hero, Severian, through his apprenticeship among the Seekers for Truth and Penitence, a guild of torturers who administer the punishments meted out by the authorities of the Commonwealth Severian serves. When Severian helps the prisoner Thecla, whom he has grown to love, commit suicide, he is expelled from the Citadel where his guild resides, and must leave the great walled city of Nessus to become an executioner in distant Thrax. During his journey out of Nessus, he joins a troupe of players, meets the mysterious young woman Dorcas, who cannot recall her past, and accidentally acquires a gem, the Claw of the Conciliator, which has the power to heal. In *The Claw of the Conciliator*, Severian continues on his journey as he is pursued by the woman Agia, who seeks revenge for the death of her brother, whom Severian has executed. Severian participates in a bizarre feast with the rebel leader Vodalus and rejoins Dr. Talos's troupe, who are to perform at the House Absolute, a residence of the Autarch who rules the Commonwealth. In *The Sword of the Lictor*, Severian reaches Thrax, spares a woman he was supposed to execute, learns that the Claw may have raised Dorcas from the dead, and then flees Thrax, still pursued by the vengeful Agia; he eventually loses his sword, *Terminus Est*, in a battle with the giant Baldanders. In *The Citadel of the Autarch*, Severian comes to the battlefield where his commonwealth is waging war against the Ascians, once again meets Agia, the rebel Voladus, and the Autarch, and discovers his own destiny.

This all-too-brief summary might make *The Book of the New Sun* seem yet another series of novels about a fantastic quest in a fantasy world, but Wolfe's work is much more than that. Wolfe is mindful of Arthur C. Clarke's dictum that a sufficiently advanced technology would be indistinguishable from magic (through it would not *be* magic), and the fantastic elements in this work are solidly grounded in science-fictional traditions and in the carefully developed technology of this future society. The tower in which the torturers live is clearly an old spaceship. The Claw's healing powers may be the result of its ability to twist time, to return an ailing or dead person to a time when he was healthy or alive. The Hall of Mirrors in the House Absolute, where Severian loses his friend Jonas, is actually a room of portals leading to other worlds, while Jonas is himself a cyborg and spacefarer from the past. The house where the anchorite Ash resides has windows that reveal both the past and future possibilities. Various unusual creatures populate the wilder areas of Urth; some are the products of past genetic alterations, but others are alien in origin. One of the most terrifying of these is the alzabo, which can lure its victims by speaking to them in the voice of someone it has already killed.

Even those elements in these books which might otherwise seem merely throwbacks to a past society are not simply the past grafted onto the future, but are logical developments. The cavalry used by the Commonwealth in its war makes use of genetically altered beasts and various sophisticated weapons. Severian's own guild of torturers and executioners might be a distant offshoot of those who once manipulated and altered the human body. All of the developments we look toward in our own future—space travel, the settling of other worlds, advances in biology—are in Urth's distant past, and its people live out their lives on a depleted planet under a dying sun. *The Book of the New Sun* can be grouped with such far-future narratives as William Hope Hodgson's *The Nightland*, Arthur C. Clarke's *The City and the Stars*, and some of the novels of Jack Vance, but Wolfe's skillful use of obscure and unusual words lends much to his atmospheric depiction of a world quite unlike our own.

Most of Wolfe's earlier work is extremely atsmospheric. Though many of its props are familiar to science fiction readers, the author's oblique manner forces us to see these devices with fresh eyes. An early Wolfe story, "Trip, Trap," has a standard plot, that of a man landing on an alien world and trying to communicate with its inhabitants. The author, however, tells the story through a message sent by the man to his superior and a letter dictated by one of the aliens, alternating between the two points of view so that we see how differently the two perceive the same events.

Wolfe's first science-fiction novel, *Operation Ares*, is ostensibly about a Martian attempt to invade the earth, but the author plays with this old theme. The "Martians' are Earthpeople who were sent to Mars by NASA, only to be abandoned by a United States that has given up science and technology. The novel's plot has apparently been modeled on a game of chess, and *Operation Ares* is not up to the standards of the author's later work. Its pace is too rapid topward the end, since the original manuscript was cut before publication; the protagonist, John Castle, is one of the few characters who stand out clearly. But in several scenes, particularly those at the beginning of the novel and those in which we see John pressed into service as a welfare worker in New York, Wolfe's ability to write suspenseful and frightening narratives is displayed.

Wolfe's short fiction is especially noteworthy, and he is a prolific master of this form. Three stories deserve special attention, since they are related and are among Wolfe's best work. "The Island of Doctor Death and Other Stories," written in the second person, tells of a young boy who begins to see the people and events around him mirror those in a pulp magazine he is reading. "The Death of Doctor Island" is, according to the author, the first story reversed, a mirror image of it; Doctor Island is an artificial world in which disturbed people needing treatment dwell, and again a boy is the central character. "The Doctor of Death Island" is the same story turned inside out; a prisoner is serving a life sentence, but the catch here is that he, and everyone else, is immortal. Each story shows a character imprisoned or confined in some way, each ends in violence and the character's understanding of what has happened to him. Two protagonists are boys, one is an older man; two female characters are threatened by death in the first two stories, while the man in the third is himself threatened by a woman. The stories conclude when the main characters are, in different ways, freed from the circumstances around them. A fourth story,

"Death of the Island Doctor," in which a young couple takes a seminar with a professor named Dr. Insula, is a coda to this series and follows the pattern of the first three stories.

The Devil in a Forest, a fantasy novel published for younger readers, demonstrates Wolfe's concern in much of his work for the young boy finding his place in the world. This book tells the story of a medieval peasant boy whose village is involved with a highwayman. The boy, trying to sort out good from evil, finds that the world is a good deal more ambiguous than it once seemed. Another novel, *Peace*, was published as a "serious" novel, but this remarkable work deserves mention here. *Peace* reveals the inner life of a man who is apparently reflecting on his life after his own death; we are shown the man's memories and associations so vividly and subtly that, by the novel's end, we feel we know this other mind as well as our own. The book's manner is at times reminiscent of Marcel Proust, at other times of Thomas Wolfe, but it is Gene Wolfe's style that prevails. *Peace* is, in its own way, a novel of "speculative" fiction and a major American novel that has been neglected.

One of Wolfe's most important works is *The Fifth Head of Cerberus*, a group of three novellas that forms a novel. The second novella, " 'A Story' by John V. Marsch," is supposedly a tale written by a character who appears briefly in the first novella and is the main character of the third; it is an imaginative depiction of an alien culture. The first novella, "The Fifth Head of Cerberus," is considered to be one of the most intriguing treatments of cloning in science fiction. The background of the book includes many traditional science-fictional elements; an alien culture, the settling of other planets, biological experimentation, and space travel are among them. Yet *The Fifth Head of Cerberus* raises a great many questions about its characters and its world that it never fully answers; it reflects the ambiguity of life rather than the clarity of a dramatic paradigm. It is a quality this book shares with that rich and varied work, *The Book of the New Sun*.

The last volume of *The Book of the New Sun* ends with Severian, now the Autarch and the representative of Urth, embarking on another quest as he travels into space, where, if he passes a certain test, his race may be judged ready to enter space once again, and a new sun may be created in the embers of the old. Much could be written about the symbols, particularly those of the rose and the sun, that Wolfe uses in his tetralogy, but the spiritual nature of Severian's quest should also be mentioned. He begins as a torturer, one who inflicts pain, and ends as one who wants to reform his old guild, not because of what it has inflicted on its victims, but because, as Severian puts it, "it is intolerable that good men should spend a lifetime dispensing pain."

In an essay about how he came to write his tetralogy, "Helioscape' (in *The Castle of the Otter*), Wolfe has said that the existence of pain, contrary to what some might argue, might tend to prove God's reality, for through pain it is possible to learn compassion. Wolfe writes:

> It has been remarked thousands of times that Christ died under torture. . . . But no one ever seems to notice that the instruments of torture were wood, nails, and a hammer; that the man who built the cross was undoubtedly a carpenter too; that the man who hammered in the nails was as much a carpenter as a soldier. . . . Very few seem even to have noticed that although Christ was a "humble carpenter," the only object we are specifically told he made was not a table or a chair, but a whip.
>
> And if Christ knew not only the pain of torture but the pain of being a torturer (as it seems certain to me that he

did), then the dark figure is also capable of being a heroic and even holy figure. . . .

Severian, who has acquired the memories of the previous Autarchs and now carries them inside himself, may bring the rebirth of the dying Urth.

Gene Wolfe is a writer for the thinking reader; he will reward anyone searching for intelligence, crafted prose, involving stories, and atmospheric detail. He is the heir of many literary traditions—pulp stories, fantasy, adventurer stories of all kinds, and serious literature—and he makes use of all of them. His work can be read with pleasure many times; new discoveries are made with each reading, and the stories linger in one's mind.

—Pamela Sargent

WOLLHEIM, Donald A(llen). Also writes as David Grinnell. American. Born in New York City, 1 October 1914. Educated at New York University, B. A. Married Elsie Balter in 1943; one daughter. Editor, *Stirring Science Stories*, 1941-42, *Cosmic Stories*, 1941, *Out of This World Adventures*, 1950, *10 Story Fantasy*, 1951; Editor, Avon Books, 1947-52, and Ace Books, 1952-67; editorial consultant, *Saturn*, 1957-58. Since 1971, publisher and editor, DAW Books. Recipient: Hugo Award, for editing, 1964, and Special Award, 1975; 33rd World Science Fiction Covention Award, 1975; World Fantasy Award, 1981; British Fantasy Award, 1984. Address: 66-17 Clyde Street, Rego Park, New York 11374, U.S.A.

SCIENCE-FICTION PUBLICATIONS

Novels (for children; series: Mike Mars)

The Secret of Saturn's Rings [*the Martian Moons, the Ninth Planet*]. Philadelphia, Winston, 3 vols., 1954-59.
One Against the Moon. Cleveland, World, 1956.
Mike Mars, Astronaut [*at Cape Canaveral (at Cape Kennedy), Flies the X-15, in Orbit, Flies the Dyna-Soar, South Pole Spaceman, and the Mystery Satellite, Around the Moon*]. New York, Doubleday, 8 vols., 1961-64.

Novels as David Grinnell (series: Ajax Calkins)

Across Time. New York, Avalon, 1957.
The Edge of Time. New York, Avalon, 1958.
The Martian Missile. New York, Avalon, 1959.
Destiny's Orbit (Calkins). New York, Avalon, 1961.
Destination: Saturn (Calkins), with Lin Carter. New York, Avalon, 1967.
To Venus! To Venus! New York, Ace, 1970.

Short Stories

Two Dozen Dragon Eggs. Reseda, California, Powell, 1969; London, Dobson, 1977.
The Men from Ariel. Cambridge, Massachusetts, NESFA Press, 1982.

OTHER PUBLICATIONS

Other

Lee de Forest: Advancing the Electronic Age (for children). Chicago, Encyclopaedia Britannica Press, 1962.

The Universe Makers: Science Fiction Today. New York, Harper, 1971; London, Gollancz, 1972.

Editor, *The Pocket Book of Science Fiction*. New York, Pocket Books, 1943.
Editor, *Portable Novels of Science*. New York, Viking Press, 1945.
Editor, *Avon Bedside Companion: A Treasury of Tales for the Sophisticated*. New York, Avon, 1947.
Editor, *Avon Detective Mysteries 3*. New York, Avon, 1947.
Editor, *Avon Fantasy Reader 1-18*. New York, Avon, 18 vols., 1947-51.
Editor, *Avon Western Reader 3-4*. New York, Avon, 2 vols., 1947.
Editor, *Where the Girls Were Different and Other Stories*, by Erskine Caldwell. New York, Avon, 1948.
Editor, *Yesterday's Love and Eleven Other Stories*, by James T. Farrell. New York, Avon, 1948.
Editor, *Yvedtte and Other Stories*, by Maupassant. New York, Avon, 1949.
Editor, *Avon Book of New Stories of the Great Wild West*. New York, Avon, 1949.
Editor, *The Fox Woman and Other Stories*, by A. Merritt. New York, Avon, 1949.
Editor, *The Girl with the Hungry Eyes and Other Stories*. New York, Avon, 1949.
Editor, *A Hell of a Good Time and Other Stories*, by James T. Farrell. New York, Avon, 1950.
Editor, *The Avon All-American Fiction Reader*. New York, Avon, 1951.
Editor, *Avon Science-Fiction Reader 1-3*. New York, Avon, 3 vols., 1951-52.
Editor, *Flight into Space*. New York, Fell, 1950; London, Cherry Tree, 1951.
Editor, *Every Boy's Book of Science-Fiction*. New York, Fell, 1951.
Editor, *Giant Mystery Reader*. New York, Avon, 1951.
Editor, *Hollywood Bedside Reader*. New York, Avon, 1951.
Editor, *Let's Go Naked*. New York, Pyramid, 1952.
Editor, *Prize Science Fiction*. New York, McBride, 1953; as *Prize Stories of Space and Time*, London, Weidenfeld and Nicolson, 1953.
Editor, *Adventures in the Far Future*. New York, Ace, 1954.
Editor, *Tales of Outer Space*. New York, Ace, 1954.
Editor, *The Ultimate Invader and Other Science-Fiction*. New York Ace, 1954.
Editor, *Adventures on Other Planets*. New York, Ace, 1955.
Editor, *Terror in the Modern Vein*. New York, Hanover House, 1955; abridged edition, as *Terror [and More Terror] in the Modern Vein*, London, Digit, 2 vols., 1961.
Editor, *The End of the World*. New York, Ace, 1956.
Editor, *The Earth in Peril*. New York, Ace, 1957.
Editor, *Men on the Moon*. New York, Ace, 1958.
Editor, *The Hidden Planet*. New York, Ace, 1959.
Editor, *The Macabre Reader*. New York, Ace, 1959; London, Digit, 1960.
Editor, *More Macabre*. New York, Ace, 1961.
Editor, *More Adventures on Other Planets*. New York, Ace, 1963.
Editor, *Swordsmen in the Sky*. New York, Ace, 1964.
Editor, with Terry Carr, *World's Best Science Fiction 1965* [to *1971*]. New York, Ace, 1965-71; *1968* to *1971* vols. published London, Gollancz, 4 vols., 1969-71; first 4 vols. published as *World's Best Science Fiction: First* [to *Fourth*] *Series*, Ace, 1970.

Editor, *Operation Phantasy: The Best from the Phantagraph.* Rego Park, New York, Phantagraph Press, 1967.

Editor, with George Ernsberger, *The Avon Fantasy Reader* [and *2nd Reader*]. New York, Avon, 2 vols., 1969.

Editor, *A Quintet of Sixes.* New York, Ace, 1969.

Editor, *Ace Science Fiction Reader.* New York, Ace, 1971; as *A Trilogy of the Future,* London, Sidgwick and Jackson, 1972.

Editor, *The 1972* [to *1985*] *Annual World's Best SF* (first 4 and last 4 vols. edited with Arthur W. Saha). New York, DAW, 14 vols., 1972-1985; first 8 vols. published as *Wollheim's World's Best SF 1-8,* 8 vols., 1977-85; 1974-1975 vols. published as *The World's Best Short Stories* 1-2, Morley, Yorkshire, Elmfield Press, 1975-76; *World's Best SF 4-6,* London, Dobson, 3 vols., 1979-81.

Editor, *The Best from the Rest of the World: European Science Fiction.* New York, Doubleday, 1976.

Editor, *The DAW Science Fiction Reader.* New York, DAW, 1976.

*

Manuscript Collections: Syracuse University, New York; University of Wyoming, Laramie (includes correspondence).

*   *   *

Although Donald A. Wollheim made his first sale while still in his teens ("The Man from Ariel," *Wonder Stories,* January 1934) and has written about 20 volumes of a science fiction, his greatest impact on science fiction has been in capacities other than that of author. Wollheim was one of the pioneering fan publishers in the 1930's, founded the influential Fantasy Amateur Press Association (which still exists), and was a founding member of the original Futurian Society. The Futurians, founded in New York in 1938, were an odd combination of science-fiction club, radical political movement, communal residential society, and literary mutual aid association. At one point Futurians controlled no fewer than seven science-fiction pulp magazines—*Stirring Science Stories* and *Cosmic Stories* edited by Wollheim, *Super Science Stories* and *Astonishing* edited by Frederik Pohl, and *Future, Science Fiction,* and *Science Fiction Quarterly* edited by Robert A. W. Lowndes.

Since the Futurians numbered among their membership such young talents as James Blish, Damon Knight, Isaac Asimov, Judith Merril, and Richard Wilson, in addition to the three editors, there was a constant flow of material into the magazines. Wollheim's *Stirring* was the most interesting of the seven, divided into science-fiction and fantasy sections. Wollheim later edited *The Pocket Book of Science Fiction* (1943), generally regarded as the first significant science-fiction anthology, and helped A. A. Wyn in the creation of Ace Books in 1952. At Ace, Wollheim was known for his keen choices and successful mixture of commercially popular and artistically valid works. Besides publishing many important new SF writers, he was responsible for publication of the first mass-market editions of Tolkien's *The Lord of the Rings* and of many of the science-fiction works of Edgar Rice Burroughs. In 1972 Wollheim left Ace to create DAW Books, the first mass publisher devoted entirely to science fiction. At DAW, Wollheim has continued his formula of mixing pulp-style adventure series with significant works.

Notwithstanding the greater importance of Wollheim's work as editor and publisher, his own production of fiction has been substantial. In the 1950's he wrote three juvenile novels in the

"Secret of. . . . " series; all are set in the intermediate-near future and deal with the exploration of the solar system. In the 1960's Wollheim produced eight novels featuring the juvenile hero Mike Mars; these are set even closer in the future than the previous series. Among Wollheim's other novels, many readers have found amusement in *Destiny's Orbit* and its sequel *Destination: Saturn.* These amusing space opera-comedies feature Ajax Calkins, introduced in a series of short stories written by Wollheim under the pseudonym Martin Pearson. Also of interest is the novel *Edge of Time,* regarded by many as the definitive (although far from the first) treatment of the macro/micro-universe theme.

A good collection of Wollheim's shorter fiction is *Two Dozen Dragon Eggs.* The short stories tend toward extreme simplicity of plot and minimal characterization, concentrating on a mix of atmosphere and "idea. " "The Rag Thing" and "Mimic," probably Wollheim's two best stories, are both included in this collection. Wollheim's short critical volume, *The Universe Makers,* is one of the most cohesive and convincing statements of philosophy to date in the context of science fiction.

—Richard A. Lupoff

WOODCOTT, Keith. See **BRUNNER, John.**

WOODS, Lawrence. See **LOWNDES, Robert A. W.**

WORTH, Peter. See **PHILLIPS, Rog.**

WRIGHT, Austin Tappan. American. Born in Hanover, New Hampshire, 20 August 1883. Educated at Harvard University, Cambridge, Massachusetts, A. B. 1905, LL. B. 1908. Corporation and admiralty lawyer: practiced with firm of Brandeis Dunbar and Nutter, Boston, 1908-16; Professor of Law, University of California, Berkeley, 1916-24, and University of Pennsylvania, Philadelphia, 1924-31. *Died 18 September 1931.*

SCIENCE-FICTION PUBLICATIONS

Novel

Islandia. New York, Farrar and Rinehart, 1942.

*

Critical Studies: *An Introduction to Islandia* by Basil Davenport, New York Farrar and Rinehart, 1942; *The Islandian World of Austin Wright* by Lawrence Clark Powell, privately printed, 1957.

*   *   *

The reputation of Austin Tappan Wright rests on only one work, but it is safe to say there is nothing quite like *Islandia* in all of literature. If one can make a fine semantic distinction between science fiction and speculative fiction, Wright's novel is more the latter than the former. His "speculation" is in the area of geography and, spinning off that, sociology and cultural anthropology.

Islandia is a nation located on the southern half of the Karain subcontinent in the southern hemisphere. It is civilized but isolationist, and for it Wright has created the most detailed and in-depth of all fictional cultures. There are discernible elements of Japan, Madagascar, Indonesia, and India, but the sum total is curiously more Western than Eastern, more homely than exotic. Islandia is revealed to the reader in all its richness by the action of the novel, which takes place in the early part of this century. The country has decided to end its isolation from the rest of the world, and a few representatives of other governments are allowed in. One of these is a young American diplomat, John Lang; we learn about Islandia through his eyes as he travels the country and becomes acquainted and involved with her people.

The novel is peripherally a remarkable portrait of the nationalistic power plays that were occurring at the turn of the century, and a fine character sketch of an intelligent, moral young American confronted with values different from his own. But it is Islandia and the wonderful cast of characters with which it is peopled that is Wright's most notable achievement.

—Baird Searles

───────────

WRIGHT, Kenneth. See **del REY, Lester.**

───────────

WRIGHT, S(ydney) Fowler. Also wrote as Sydney Fowler; Alan Seymour; Anthony Wingrave. British. Born 6 January 1874. Educated at King Edward's School, Birmingham. Married 1) Nellie Ashbarry in 1895 (died, 1918), three sons and three daughters; 2) Truda Hancock in 1920, one son and three daughters. Accountant in Birmingham from 1895. Editor, *Poetry* (later *Poetry and the Play*) magazine, Birmingham, 1920-32. *Died 25 February 1965.*

SCIENCE-FICTION PUBLICATIONS

Novels

The Amphibians: A Romance of 500,000 Years Hence. London, Merton Press 1925.
Deluge. London, Fowler Wright, 1927; New York, Cosmopolitan, 1928.
The Island of Captain Sparrow. London, Gollancz, and New York, Cosmopolitan, 1928.
The World Below (includes *The Amphibians*). London, Collins, 1929; New York, Longman, 1930; *The World Below* published as *The Dwellers,* London, Panther, 1954.
Dawn. New York, Cosmopolitan, 1929; London, Harrap, 1930.
Dream; or, The Simian Maid. London, Harrap, 1931.

Beyond the Rim. London, Jarrolds, 1932.
Prelude in Prague: A Story of the War of 1938. London, Newnes, 1935; as *The War of 1938,* New York, Putnam, 1936.
The Vengeance of Gwa (as Anthony Wingrave). London, Butterworth, 1935.
Four Days War. London, Hale, 1936.
Megiddo's Ridge. London, Hale, 1937
The Hidden Tribe. London, Hale, 1938.
The Adventure of Wyndham Smith. London, Jenkins, 1938.
The Screaming Lake. London, Hale, 1939.
The Adventure in the Blue Room (as Sydney Fowler). London, Rich and Cowan, 1945.
Spiders' War. New York, Abelard Press, 1954.

Short Stories

The New Gods Lead (as Sydney Fowler). London, Jarrolds, 1932.
The Witchfinder. London, Books of Today, 1945.
Justice, and The Rat. London, Books of Today, 1945 (?).
The Throne of Saturn. Sauk City, Wisconsin, Arkham House, 1949; London, Heinemann, 1951.

OTHER PUBLICATIONS

Novels

Elfin. London, Harrap, and New York, Longman, 1930
Seven Thousand in Israel. London, Jarrolds, 1931.
Red Ike, with J. M. Denwood. London, Hutchinson, 1931; as *Under the Brutchstone.* New York, Coward McCann, 1931.
Lord's Right in Languedoc. London, Jarrolds, 1933.
Power. London, Jarrolds, 1933
David. London, Butterworth, 1934.
Ordeal of Barata. London, Jenkins, 1939.
The Siege of Malta: Founded on an Unfinished Romance by Sir Walter Scott. London, Muller, 1942.

Novels as Sydney Fowler

The King Against Anne Bickerton. London, Harrap, 1930; as *The Case of Anne Bickerton,* New York, Boni, 1930; as *Rex V. Anne Bickerton,* London, Penguin, 1947.
The Bell Street Murders. London, Harrap, and New York, Macaulay, 1931.
By Saturday. London, Lane, 1931.
The Hanging of Constance Hillier. London, Jarrolds, 1931; New York, Macaulay, 1932.
Crime & Co. New York, Macaulay, 1931; as *The Hand- Print Mystery,* London, Jarrolds, 1932.
Arresting Delia. London, Jarrolds, and New York, Macaulay, 1933.
The Secret of the Screen. London, Jarrolds, 1933.
Who Else But She? London, Jarrolds, 1934.
Three Witnesses. London, Butterworth, 1935.
The Attic Murder. London, Butterworth, 1936.
Was Murder Done? London, Butterworth, 1936.
Post-Mortem Evidence. London, Butterworth, 1936.
Four Callers in Razor Street. London, Jenkins, 1937.
The Jordans Murder. London, Jenkins, 1938; New York, Curl, 1939.
The Murder in Bethnal Square. London, Jenkins, 1938.
The Wills of Jane Kanwhistle. London, Jenkins, 1939.
The Rissole Mystery. London, Rich and Cowan, 1941.

A Bout with the Mildew Gang. London, Eyre and Spottiswoode, 1941.

Second Bout with the Mildew Gang. London, Eyre and Spottiswoode, 1942.

Dinner in New York. London, Eyre and Spottiswoode, 1943.

The End of the Mildew Gang. London, Eyre and Spottiswoode, 1944.

Too Much for Mr. Jellipot. London, Eyre and Spottiswoode, 1945.

Who Murdered Reynard? London, Rich and Cowan, 1947.

With Cause Enough? London, Harvill Press, 1954.

Verse

Scenes from the Morte d'arthur (as Alan Seymour). London, Erskine MacDonald, 1919.

Some Songs of Bilitis. Birmingham, Poetry, 1921.

The Song of Songs and Other Poems. London, Merton Press, 1925; New York, Cosmopolitan, 1929.

The Ballad of Elaine . London, Merton Press 1926.

The Riding of Lancelot: A Narrative Poem. London, Fowler Wright, 1929.

Other

Police and Public: A Political Pamphlet. London, Fowler Wright, 1929.

The Life of Walter Scott: A Biography. London, Poetry League, 1932; New York, Haskell House, 1971.

Should We Surrender Colonies? London, Readers' Library, 1939.

Editor, *Voices on the Wind: An Anthology of Contemporary Verse*. London, Merton Press, 3 vols., 1922-24.

Editor, *Poets of Merseyside: An Anthology of Present-Day Liverpool Poetry*. London, Merton Press 1923.

Editor, with R. Crompton Rhodes, *Poems: Chosen by Boys and Girls*. Oxford, Blackwell, 4 vols., 1923-24.

Editor, *Birmingham Poetry 1923-24*. London, Merton Press, 1924.

Editor, *From Overseas: An Anthology of Contemporary Dominion and Colonial Verse*. London, Merton Press, 1924.

Editor, *Some Yorkshire Poets*. London, Merton Press, 1924.

Editor, *A Somerset Anthology of Modern Verse 1924*. London, Merton Press 1924.

Editor, *The County Series* (verse anthologies). London, Fowler Wright, 13 vols., 1927-30.

Editor, *The Last Days of Pompeii: A Redaction*, by Edward Bulwer-Lytton. London, Vision Press, 1948.

Translator, *The Inferno*, by Dante. London, Fowler Wright, 1928.

Translator, *Marguerite de Valois*, by Dumas Père. London, Temple, 1947.

Translator, *The Purgatorio*, by Dante. Edinburgh, Oliver and Boyd, 1954.

* * *

S. Fowler Wright escaped being an accountant and poetry magazine editor with tales of fantasy, adventure, detection, and disaster. This prolific and versatile author began writing fantasy at 50.

His early novels reflect the influence of H. G. Wells. Wright, however, had such a pessimistic view of man's devolution that most human beings and their social customs vanish with dramatic flourishes. *The World Below* features a time- machine trip 500,000 years ahead to encounter Amphibians, delicate, web-footed, and cerebral, and Dwellers, gigantic seekers of knowledge through scientific investigation. The hero is most like the lizard-like Killers, who boil and eat victims. Much of the conversation between him and his amphibian companion reveals man's mistreatment of other living things, while many of the adventures show how close he is to bestiality when he throws reason aside in panic.

In *Beyond the Rim* descendants of British Puritans live in an Antarctic theocracy, raided occasionally by the Anabaptist horde from the volcanic hell nearby. The explorers include two strong women, one of whom remains while the other and her lover return home, but never to tell the real story. Similarly, in *The Island of Captain Sparrow* Charlton Fogle is shipwrecked where a pirate established a kingdom for his men and their women. Already present were a race of satyrs, providing meat, and a tribe of handsome natives decimated by disease brought by the outsiders. Charlton and Marcelle, intended for Sparrow's ugly, vicious heir, fall in love. At the book's spectacular climax the giant rokas, birds used for agricultural work, turn on the pirates, leaving the young lovers and the last native child to start over.

Deluge narrates a cataclysmic flood in which a hero and two heroines survive the barbarity to which most civilized people descend and found a new order. Martin Webster and Claire Arlington are among the few who adapt to living with nature. Because she is the kind of woman men put on a pedestal, Helen Webster also survives with her children. Some men—a murderer among them—become humane while others degenerate into ravaging, rapacious beasts who must be exterminated. At the end of this engrossing novel, Wright surprises his readers by allow- ing Martin to have both women. What's more—with noble psychological struggles—the women love each other. In *Dawn*, its sequel, Wright goes back in time to introduce new characters and repeat the flood's horrors. Defeat of the threatening gang and escape from another flood promise a future.

In *Dream* and its sequel, *Spiders' War*, Marguerite Leinster enjoys dangerous adventures with the help of a psychologist-magician. In the first she dreams of an ape-girl fighting off the river rats that challenge human supremacy. In *Spiders' War* she goes into a future where the threat to divided humanity stalks in the form of giant spiders. Her man, a scholar of 20th-century history, is also a warrior-leader. Together they organize three hostile groups against the intelligent monsters. *The Vengeance of Gwa* contrasts similar groups, ranging from starving barbarism to bored perfection, in a tale of an evil queen and her well-deserved end.

Prelude in Prague, Four Days War, and *Megiddo's Ridge* form a trilogy dealing with an ugly near-future in which Germany conquers Europe, by the use of a freezing gas, air raids, and political terrorism. In this apocalyptic disaster culminating in the destruction of the powerful forces of Von Teufel, Wright creates and kills a large cast of interesting characters, including a double agent and a woman pilot. He also vents anger at British underestimation of Germany, lack of preparation for war, and callousness about highway moralities. As in *Deluge* he warns readers that, while they vegetate, their neighbors hover a step from savagery.

In addition, Wright produced numerous short stories—light fantasy, medieval romance, mystery, and satire. Among the best are "Justice" and "Original Sin," a short version of *The Adventure of Wyndham Smith*. Society can be so perfect that only mass suicide can abolish boredom. So often does Wright annihilate mankind that it is not surprising that the heroine of his last story, "The Better Choice," prefers to remain a cat.

—Mary S. Weinkauf

WYLIE, Philip (Gordon). Also wrote as Leatrice Homesley. American. Born in Beverly, Massachusetts, 12 May 1902. Educated at Montclair High School, New Jersey; Princeton University, New Jersey, 1920-23. Member of the Board, Office of Facts and Figures, 1942; with Bureau of Personnel, United States Army Air Force, 1945. Married 1) Sally Ondeck in 1928 (divorced, 1937), one daughter; 2) Frederica Ballard in 1938. Staff member, *The New Yorker*, 1925-27; Advertising Manager, Cosmopolitan Book Corporation, 1927-28; Screenwriter, Paramount Pictures, 1931-33, and MGM, 1936-37; Editor, Farrar and Rinehart, publishers, New York, 1944. Member of the Council, Authors Guild, 1945. Consultant to the Federal Civil Defense Administration, 1949-71. Recipient: Freedom Foundation Gold Medal, 1953; Hyman Memorial Trophy, 1959. D. Litt. : University of Miami; Florida State University, Tallahassee. *Died 26 October 1971.*

SCIENCE-FICTION PUBLICATIONS

Novels

Gladiator. New York, Knopf, 1930.
The Murderer Invisible. New York, Farrar and Rinehart, 1931.
The Savage Gentleman. New York, Farrar and Rinehart, 1932.
When Worlds Collide, with Edwin Balmer. New York, Stokes, and London, Paul, 1933.
After Worlds Collide, with Edwin Balmer. New York, Stokes, and London, Paul, 1934.
Finnley Wrenn: A Novel in a New Manner. New York, Farrar and Rinehart, 1934.
The Disappearance. New York, Rinehart, and London, Gollancz, 1951.
Tomorrow! New York, Rinehart, 1954.
Triumph. New York, Doubleday, 1963.
Los Angeles: A. D. 2017 (novelization of TV play). New York, Popular Library, 1971.
The End of the Dream. New York, Doubleday, 1972; Morley, Yorkshire, Elmfield Press, 1975.

Short Stories

Night unto Night. New York, Farrar and Rinehart, 1944.
Three to Be Read. New York, Rinehart, 1952; *Experiment in Crime* and *The Smuggled Atom Bomb* published separately, New York, Avon, 2 vols., 1956.
The Answer. New York, Rinehart, and London, Muller, 1956.

Uncollected Short Story

"Jungle Journey (The Paradise Crater)," in *Masterpieces of Science Fiction*, edited by Sam Maskowitz. Cleveland, World, 1967.

OTHER PUBLICATIONS

Novels

Heavy Laden. New York, Knopf, 1928.

Babes and Sucklings. New York, Knopf, 1929; as *The Party*, New York, Popular Library, 1966(?).
Blondy's Boy Friend (as Leatrice Homesley). New York, Chelsea House, 1930.
Footprint of Cinderella. New York, Farrar and Rinehart, 1931; as *9 Rittenhouse Square*, New York, Popular Library, 1959.
Five Fatal Words, with Edwin Balmer. New York, Long and Smith, 1932; London, Paul, 1933.
The Golden Hoard, with Edwin Balmer. New York, Stokes, 1934.
As They Reveled. New York, Farrar and Rinehart, 1936.
Too Much of Everything. New York, Farrar and Rinehart, and London, Chapman and Hall, 1936.
The Shield of Silence, with Edwin Balmer. New York, Stokes, 1936; London, Collins, 1937.
An April Afternoon. New York, Farrar and Rinehart, 1938.
Danger Mansion. Los Angeles, Bantam, 1941.
The Other Horseman. New York, Farrar and Rinehart, 1942.
Corpses at Indian Stones. New York, Farrar and Rinehart, 1943.
Opus 21. New York, Rinehart, 1949; London, Consul, 1962.
They Were Both Naked. New York, Doubleday, 1965.
Autumn Romance. New York, Lancer, 1965.
A Resourceful Lady. New York, Popular Library, 1966.
The Spy Who Spoke Porpoise. New York, Doubleday, 1969.

Short Stories

The Big Ones Get Away!. New York, Farrar and Rinehart, 1940.
Salt Water Daffy. New York, Farrar and Rinehart, 1941.
Fish and Tin Fish: Crunch and Des Strike Back. New York, Farrar and Rinehart, 1944.
Fifth Mystery Book, with others. New York, Farrar and Rinehart, 1944.
Selected Short Stories. New York, Editions for the Armed Services, 1946.
Crunch and Des: Stories of Florida Fishing. New York, Rinehart, 1948.
The Best of Crunch and Des. New York, Rinehart, 1954.
Treasure Cruise and Other Crunch and Des Stories. New York, Rinehart, 1956.

Plays

Screenplays: *Island of Lost Souls*, with Waldemar Young, 1932; *The Invisible Man*, with R. C. Sherriff, 1933; *Murders in the Zoo*, 1933; *The King of the Jungle*, with Fred Niblo, Jr., 1933; *Death in Paradise Canyon*, with Saul Elkins and Norman Foster, 1936.

Other

The Army Way: A Thousand Pointers for New Soldiers, with William W. Muir. New York, Farrar and Rinehart, 1940.
Generation of Vipers. New York, Farrar and Rinehart, 1942; revised edition, Rinehart, and London, Muller, 1955.
An Essay on Morals. New York, Rinehart, 1947.
Denizens of the Deep: True Tales of Deep-Sea Fishing. New York, Rinehart, 1953.
The Innocent Ambassadors. New York, Rinehart, 1957; London, Muller, 1958.
The Lerner Marine Laboratory at Bimini, Bahamas. New York, American Museum of Natural History, 1960.
The Magic Animal. New York, Doubleday, 1968.
Sons and Daughters of Mom. New York, Doubleday, 1971.

*

Manuscript Collection: Princeton University, New Jersey.

Critical Study: *Philip Wylie* by Truman Frederick Keefer, Boston, Twayne, 1977.

* * *

Philip Wylie's science fiction represents only a small portion of his profile output of magazine stories, novels, polemics, and screenplays. Wylie consciously and carefully placed himself in the "popular" market where his strongly moralistic and iconoclastic eye could not only observe and criticise but where his work would be read by large numbers. For, unlike the satirist, Wylie passionately believed that his pen could contribute to the sweeping away of cant and the creation of a modern and sane society.

Gladiator was accepted for publication in 1928 but Wylie's publishers held it for two years until he had produced two non-science fictions works. In it and in *The Murderer Invisible* he set the pattern for his ventures in the science-fiction idiom. In both novels the scientific projections (a genetically produced superman and an invisible man) are put in place quickly and without fuss as in H. G. Wells's novels, and the real stress lies on what the innovation can reveal about human nature and human society. Hugo Danner, the superman in *Gladiator*, observes the futility of human greed and of things like fraternity parties, football games, and the stock market. Through Hugo Wylie poses the problem of what could be done to improve the lot of man even by a superman if the masses would not change themselves. In *The Murderer Invisible* moral issues emerge because a scientist, William Carpenter, seriously wronged in a previous career on the commodities market, develops invisibility with intentions of a fair revenge and further use for the good of mankind. But he becomes a megalomaniac and attempts to take over the world for its own good. In these novels Wylie keeps calling his characters back to reckonings of conscience and analyses of the society which they are trying to change. These real and central concerns of his work were continued in *The Savage Gentleman*, a novel about a child educated away from mankind which offers a Tarzan-like variation on the single-man-against-society theme of the earlier novels.

Wylie's most optimistic venture into SF comes in two novels written in collaberatin with Edwin Balmer, *When Worlds Collide* and *After Worlds Collide*. In these cosmic disaster stories two planets, a gas giant with an Earthlike planet in orbit about it, enter the solar system and destroy the Earth when the gas giant brushes against it. *When Worlds Collide* chronicles the discovery of the threat and the desperate efforts of a group of scientists to build rockets to get them onto Bronson Beta, the smaller of the invaders. Several parties succeed and the second novel deals with their survival on Bronson Beta, their discovery of a high civilisation there, and the conflicts between the American party and a Japanese-Chinese-Soviet party which has also survived. These novels contain a good deal of Wylie's most careful scientific prognostication in astronomy, earth physics, and in the prediction of human behaviour in times of extreme crisis, although the extrapolations about rocketry and inter-planetary travel are considerably flawed.

Time spent in Hollywood, war work, and the pursuit of other kinds of writing leave a gap in Wylie's SF output until the publication of *The Disappearance*. The simple but very elegant premise of this novel is a world in which all of the women disappear in an instant from the world of the men and all of the men disappear from the world of the women. Although no real explanation is offered for this split in the stream of reality, the device is a perfect instrument for some very carefully considered opinions on the roles of the sexes, particularly in modern America. Wylie cleverly sets a great deal of the novel in a family unit very much like his own which lives in Miami and has all the domestic complications that society tends to produce. On one level the novel is fascinating because chapters taking place in exactly the same surroundings trace the varied collapse of the two worlds, the men having an all-out atomic war and a return to savagery while the women struggle with technological collapse. But in addition to the outward struggle there runs through the book some very serious contemplation of the double standard and the fragility of male-female relationships.

Wylie's next three SF works deal in various ways with his deep concern for the dangers of nuclear war, a phenomenon about which he was particularly well informed because of his activities in civil defence organisation. *Tomorrow!* is a detailed portrait of a nuclear attack on an American city and the civil defence response. He is heavily critical of the failure of face and prepare for this inevitability, and his realistically detailed picture of the carnage is both blunt and sobering. *The Answer* is a brief allegory in which both the Americans and the Russians bring down an angel in their bomb tests. The angel was carrying the message "Love one another" to mankind. *Triumph* paints the most horrible picture of holocaust, in which virtually the only survivors in the northern hemisphere are 14 people in a supershelter prepared by a farsighted millionaire.

Wylie's posthumous legacy to mankind, *The End of the Dream*, is his prediction of the pollution death of the world. Like John Brunner's novel of the same year, *The Sheep Look Up*, *The End of the Dream* ties together projections of man's mistreatment of the environment to foresee mass deaths from air pollution in the cities, a rice blight which leaves most of the world starving, and a particularly horrible mutation of an ocean leech which sucks the life from millions. *The End of the Dream* is a fitting culmination of Wylie's career, for it combines his anger against human foolishness with his obvious desire to warn and thus influence the future positively. From *Gladiator* to *The End of the Dream* Philip Wylie has used the science-fiction mode and the style of the popular writer to reach and caution the widest possible audience in his life-long crusade to save man from his own foolishness and blinkered views.

—Peter A. Brigg

WYNDHAM, John. Pseudonym for John Wyndham Parkes Lucas Beynon Harris; also wrote as John Beynon; Johnson Harris. British. Born in Knowle, Warwickshire, 10 July 1903. Educated at Bedales School, Petersfield, Hampshire; also read for the Bar. Served in the Royal Signals during World War II. Married Grace Wilson in 1963. *Died 11 March 1969.*

SCIENCE-FICTION PUBLICATIONS

Novels

The Secret People (as John Beynon). London, Newnes, 1935; as John Wyndham, New York, Fawcett, 1973.
Planet Plane (as John Beynon). London, Newnes, 1936; revised edition, as *Stowaway to Mars*, London, Nova, 1953.
The Day of the Triffids. New York, Doubleday, and London,

Joseph, 1951; as *Revolt of the Triffids*, New York, Popular Library, 1952.

The Kraken Wakes. London, Joseph, 1953; as *Out of the Deeps*, New York, Ballantine, 1953.

Re-Birth. New York, Ballantine, 1955; as *The Chrysalids*, London, Jospeh, 1955.

The Midwich Cuckoos. London, Joseph, 1957; New York, Ballantine, 1958; as *Village of the Damned,*, Ballantine, 1960.

The Outward Urge (as John Wyndham and Lucas Parkes). London, Jospeh, and New York, Ballantine, 1959.

Trouble with Lichen. London, Joseph, and New York, Ballantine, 1960.

Chocky. New York, Ballantine, and London, Joseph, 1968.

Web. London, Joseph, 1979.

Short Stories

Jizzle. London, Dobson, 1954.

The Seeds of Time. London, Joseph, 1956.

Tales of Gooseflesh and Laughter. New York, Ballantine, 1956.

Consider Her Ways and Others. London, Joseph, 1961.

The Infinite Moment. New York, Ballantine, 1961.

The Best of John Wyndham. London, Sphere, 1973; as *The Man from Beyond and Other Stories*. London, Joseph, 1975.

Short Stories as John Beynon

Sleepers of Mars. London, Coronet, 1973.

Wanderers of Time. London, Coronet, 1973.

Exiles on Asperus. London, Severn House, 1979.

OTHER PUBLICATIONS

Novels

Foul Play Suspected (as John Beynon). London, Newnes, 1935.

Love in Time (as Johnson Harris). London, Utopian, 1946.

Verse

'Melia Ann: A Fantasy of the W. I. Taunton, Somerset, Wessex Press, 1953.

* * *

J. B. Harris had been writing long before the reading public first heard of John Wyndham. Beginning in 1930, he published—primarily in the US and under several pseudonyms—a great many short stories and several novels. Eventually it was the novel *The Day of the Triffids* which in 1951 brought Harris wide public recognition and permanently affixed to him the pseudonym under which he had published it: John Wyndham. Wyndham is justifiably considered to be the truest disciple of H. G. Wells in English literature. He himself said that of all science fiction he was most influenced by two of Wells's novels, *The Time Machine* and *War of the Worlds*. Indeed, Wyndham more than once dealt with themes raised in those novels, such as displacement in time and invasion from outerspace, though Wells's influence on Wyndham was not restricted to thematic borrowing.

Wyndham loves to write about perfectly familiar things, some everyday occurence, and let the fantastic element help him uncover unprecedented and unforeseen possibilities in that daily routine. Only one of his novels, *The Outward Urge*, deals with other worlds. In his other novels and stories the action is set on Earth and in time frames not all that distant from ours. Nor does he burden us with technical minutiae. Being a firm opponent of the Jules Verne school of science fiction, resurrected and modernized in the US by Hugo Gernsback, Wyndham uses technical—and other—detail only insofar as he or any other writer needs it: for the sake of credibility, realism, authenticity. In addition Wyndham has the ability—decidedly not within any other writer's reach—to compel us to suspend disbelief by being true to human character. Damon Knight correctly observed that Wyndham achieved his objective with down-to-earth means, that is, making us believe the most unbelievable things simply because they happened to people whom we all knew well. Wyndham's imagination is very tactile, sequential, logical. He follows the Wellsian method of the "single premise. " In each of his books there is, then, one fantastic assumption; something in the world has changed and all subsequent changes follow as a consequence. Wyndham has the inventiveness to illustrate with many examples the impact of an event on all realms of life. All this causes Wyndham's fantasy novels to be part of the basic current of literature. He has no use for space opera; instead he practices a special kind of "realism in fantasy. " One of his tasks has been the exploration of possibilities created by application of science-fiction motifs to various types of short stories. That is the guiding principle behind the collection *Seeds of Time*. Here again there can be no doubt about the influence of H. G. Wells.

The influence of Wells also determined the basic theme of Wyndham's writings. He is usually concerned with some catastrophe, cosmic or social, which results in the discovery of hitherto hidden dangers in daily life, in the revelation of character under novel circumstances, in the disclosure of defects in the society. In searching for his "single fantastic premise" Wyndham displays a degree of imagination which belies his ostensibly traditional manner. In *The Day of the Triffids*, which remains Wyndham's best-known novel, he showed his greatest originality. The novel deals with the disintegration of the social order under the impact of two events—a rain of meteors which has blinded most of the human race, and the appearance of mobile carnivorous plants. In two other novels Wyndham writes about the invasion of Earth by beings from other planets. In the first of these, *The Kraken Wakes*, invaders from space who can exist only under conditions of enormous pressure, establish a bridgehead deep under the ocean. In an attempt to wipe out the human race, they melt down the polar ice caps; the resulting flooding of the continents almost brings about the desired end. All this occurs under Cold War conditions, with mutual suspicion between the great powers preventing them from joining forces against the invaders. In the final analysis the catastrophe is caused by human divisiveness. In *The Midwich Cuckoos* the subject matter is not so much invasion as a kind of "penetration" from space. Here the non-earthlings isolate the village of Midwich and a few other places on Earth from their surroundings and put their inhabitants to sleep. Nine months later there appear in those localities children of non-earthly origin who are evidently destined to become the rulers of all mankind. Their intellectual and spiritual superiority is such that the earthlings submit without protest, even to the point of taking actions clearly detrimental to themselves. What makes these children from outer space so superior is their capacity to communicate constantly with each other by telepathy. Thus, while remaining individual beings, they form at the same time a formidable collective force. Anything learned by one becomes immediately part of everyone's knowledge. And the group also has the abllility to channel everyone's will in one direction.

Eventually the extra-planetary colony becomes so dangerous to Earth that it must be destroyed.

Telepathy is a rather common theme in Wyndham's fiction. It serves as a means of demonstrating its relationship to various forms of collectivism. The collectivism of the non-earthlings in *The Midwich Cuckoos*, for instance, reminds one of a fascist order. *The Chrysalids* provides an example of another sort of collectivist order. *The Chrysalids* takes place many centuries after a devastating nuclear war. Enclaves of life are cut off from one another by vast areas of radioactive contamination. Random mutations are occurring. As a result people, animals, and plants become so grotesquely disfigured that their hideousness exceeds even that which Wells anticipated in *The Island of Doctor Moreau*. These circumstances have given rise to puritanical communities seeking salvation by suppressing anything "different." Should anything new turn out to be superior to the old, these puritans are all the more eager to suppress it. They are convinced that they themselves represent the only kind of perfection possible, and at the very thought that elsewhere there might live people of a different color they fly into a rage. Nevertheless, life, movement, progress win out even here. These horrible, monstrous families produce children similar to those who tried to control Midwich. They differ in one respect, though: they hate cruelty. According to Wyndham these children who feel themselves to be members of one single family will not merely rebuild the old world: they will build a new and better one. *Trouble with Lichen* is the least interesting of Wyndham's novels. Taking the theme of Shaw's *Back to Methuselah*, he discusses the possibilities a vastly extended life expectancy could open for mankind.

—Julius Kagarlitsky

YARBRO, Chelsea Quinn. Also writes as Terry Nelson Bonner; Vanessa Pryor. American. Born in Berkeley, California, 15 September 1942. Attended San Francisco State College, 1960-63. Married Donald P. Simpson in 1969 (divorced, 1982). Theatre manager and playwright, Mirthmakers Children's Theatre, San Francisco, 1961-64; children's counsellor, 1963; cartographer, C. E. Erickson and Associates, Oakland, California, 1963-70; composer; card and palm reader, 1974-78. Secretary, Science Fiction Writers of America, 1970-72. Agent: Ellen Levine Literary Agency, 432 Park Avenue South, Suite 1205, New York, New York 10016. Address: 1921 El Dorado Avenue, Berkeley, California 94707, U.S.A.

SCIENCE-FICTION PUBLICATIONS

Novels

Time of the Fourth Horseman. New York, Doubleday, 1976; London, Sidgwick and Jackson, 1980.
False Dawn. New York, Doubleday, 1978; London, Sidgwick and Jackson, 1979.
Hyacinths. New York, Doubleday, 1983.
Nomads (novelization of screenplay). New York, Bantam, 1984.

Short Stories

Cautionary Tales. New York, Doubleday, 1978; expanded edition, New York, Warner, and London, Sidgwick and Jackson, 1980.
On Saint Hubert's Thing. New Castle, Virginia, Cheap Street, 1982.
Signs and Portents. Santa Cruz, California, Dream Press, 1984.
The Saint-Germain Chronicles. New York, Pocket Books, 1983.

Uncollected Short Stories

"Postures of Prophesy," in *If* (New York), September 1969.
"False Dawn," in *Strange Bedfellows*, edited by Thomas N. Scortia. New York, Random House, 1972.
"A Time of the Fourth Horseman," in *Infinity 3*, edited by Robert Hoskins. New York, Lancer, 1972.
"Who Is Sylvia?," with Thomas N. Scortia, in *Vampires, Werewolves, and Other Monsters*, edited by Roger Elwood. Philadelphia, Curtis, 1974.
"Training Twofoots," in *If* (New York), March-April 1974.
"Do I Dare to Eat a Peach?," in *Shadows 8*, edited by Charles L. Grant. New York, Doubleday, 1985.

OTHER PUBLICATIONS

Novels

Ogilvie, Tallant, and Moon. New York, Putnam, 1976.
Hôtel Transylvania: A Novel of Forbidden Love. New York, St. Martin's Press, 1978; London, New English Library, 1981.
Music When Sweet Voices Die. New York, Putnam, 1979.
The Palace. New York, St. Martin's Press, 1979; London, New English Library, 1981.
Blood Games. New York, St. Martin's Press, 1980.
Ariosto. New York, Pocket Books, 1980.
Dead and Buried (novelization of screenplay). New York, Warner, and London, Star, 1980.
Sins of Omission. New York, New American Library, 1980.
Path of the Eclipse. New York, St. Martin's Press, 1981.
Tempting Fate. New York, St. Martin's Press, 1982.
A Taste of Wine (as Vanessa Pryor). New York, Pocket Books, 1982.
The Godforsaken. New York, Warner, 1983.
The Making of Australia 5: The Outback (as Terry Nelson Bonner). New York, Dell, 1983.
The Mortal Glamour. New York, Bantam, 1985.
To the High Redoubt. New York, Warner, 1985.

Play

The Little-Girl Dragon of Alabaster-on-Fenwick (produced San Francisco, 1973).

Other

Messages from Michael on the Nature of the Evolution of the Human Soul. Chicago, Playboy Press, 1979.
"Cinderella's Revenge: Twists on Fairy Tales and Mythic Themes in the Work of Stephen King," in *Fear Itself*, edited by Tim Underwood and Chuck Miller. Columbia, Pennsylvania, Underwood Miller, 1982.
Locadio's Apprentice (for children). New York, Harper, 1984.
Four Horses for Tishtry (for children). New York, Harper, 1985.

Editor, with Thomas N. Scortia, *Two Views of Wonder*. New York, Ballantine, 1973.

*

Chelsea Quinn Yarbro comments:

My work, for the most part, has to do with some aspect of love and survival, though that should be interpreted in its broadest sense. Music has very much influenced me, not only as subject matter, but structurally as well. Since I make my living as a writer, I do, in a pragmatic sense, write for money. However, I regard writing as an art, and feel that within certain realistic limitations a part of my responsibility is to maintain and protect the integrity of my work.

*   *   *

Chelsea Quinn Yarbro's first collection of short fiction is appropriately called *Cautionary Tales*, a title which fits a lot of work in the genre of SF. Although she loves opera and has based at least three stories on operas, and although she creates strong characters and likes to put them in moments of confrontation which feel like grand opera duets (as James Tiptree, Jr., points out in the introduction to *Cautionary Tales*), Yarbro is most easily characterized as a dystopian SF writer whose horrible speculations on the future are meant as dire warnings, predictions she hopes will *not* come true. But all categories, even useful ones, tend to be too narrow and simplistic. Yarbro is not simply a prophet of hard times to come; it just happens that a lot of her stories occur in rather harsh and unfriendly worlds. This makes for very stark conflict, and lots of passion, pain, romance, violence, terror, adventure, and love, all of them marshalled into evocative form by a strong and vivid talent.

What is most obvious once you read the stories is that Yarbro finds the very starkness of ultimate situations aesthetically exciting. In *Time of the Fourth Horseman, False Dawn*, "Allies," "The Generalissimo's Butterfly," "Dead in Irons," and *Hyacinths* (as well as in the cycle of historical fantasies about le Compte de Saint-Germain), her protagonists must continually battle for physical, psychological, *and* moral balance against the final enemy in whatever form: plague, ecological breakdown and the descent to barbarism, an alien death-force, the corruption of political power, slavery in the hold of a giant FTL cargo ship, the degeneration of art in the service of greed, or the various dogmas enlightened people have fought throughout history. Their heroism is not the easy kind found in escapist adventures; it is, rather, hard won and often of little value to anyone except the protagonist, and then only as a psychological talisman with which to face oncoming destruction. But Yarbro's morality is fiercely held to, in both her characters and her style of presenting them. As well (remember the opera), love can light up portions of a grim life if like Thea, of *False Dawn*, you're especially lucky. But if, like Jehanne Bliss, of *Hyacinths*, you throw away love for power, you may lose both power and the power to love. Moreover, love will not solve any problems, really, though its presence helps a person carry on. Certainly the act of loving, even when that love may not be returned, is presented as a positive virtue, something to hold on to in the midst of destructive chaos.

If many of the stories and the three novels are extremely dark, there are some lighter moments, especially in the short stories. "Frog Pond," whose protagonist later becomes Thea of *False Dawn*, is, despite its post-apocalyptic setting, a social comedy. "Disturb Not My Slumbering Fair" is a kind of Hitchcockian black comedy thriller about the trials and tribulations of a young ghoul, while "Lammas Night" is a historical sketch revealing the kind of wit Yarbro brings to the series of five novels and five stories concerning the ageless, charming, and essentially good vampire, le Comte de Saint-Germain. Interestingly, these tales are full of the operatic colour and larger-than-life

romance which Yarbro tends to eschew in the bleak spaces of her pure SF works. Nevertheless, these narratives, too, point to the inherent cruelty and power hunger of so much of humanity throughout the ages, and, in every one of the novels, Saint-Germain, and the readers, must face the dark side of the human heart.

But there are ways to introduce such colour into SF worlds. "Un Bel Di" is a story of a confrontation between two alien races that is also a variation on the structure of *Madame Butterfly*. "The Fellini Beggar," surely one of Yarbro's finest stories, gathers together a number of significant motifs in her work: her ability to suggest through telling details the lineaments of a whole world, in this case another post-apocalyptic Earth; her delight in the beauty to be found even in the midst of rubble; and her recognition that emotion and the absolute need to satisfy it are continually changing with personal circumstances—this beggar allowed Fellini to "use" him brutally in his final film because it was a worthy exchange for his personal grail, the manuscript which allowed him to *know* exactly how Puccini had planned to finish *Turandot*. This, like all Yarbro's fiction, is 160 proof, and meant to satisfy a discriminating palate.

—Douglas Barbour

YEP, Laurence (Michael). American. Born in San Francisco, California, 14 June 1948. Educated at Marquette University, Milwaukee (Dretzka Award, 1968), 1966-68; University of California, Santa Cruz, B. A. in English 1970; State University of New York, Buffalo, Ph. D. in English 1975. Part-time English teacher, Foothill College, Mountain View, California, 1975, and San Jose City College, California, 1975-76. Recipient: Book-of-the-Month-Club Fellowship, 1970; International Reading Association award, for children's book, 1976; National Council for the Social Studies Woodson Award, 1976; Boston *Globe-Horn Book* award, for children's book, 1977; Women's International League for Peace and Freedom Jane Addams Award, 1978. Agent: Pat Berens, Sterling Lord Agency, 660 Madison Avenue, New York, New York 10021. Address: 921 Populus Place, Sunnyvale, California 94086, U.S.A.

SCIENCE-FICTION PUBLICATIONS

Novels

Sweetwater (for children). New York, Harper, 1973; London, Faber, 1976.
Seademons. New York, Harper, 1977.
Shadow Lord. New York, Pocket Books, 1985.

Uncollected Short Stories

"The Selchey Kids," in *World's Best Science Fiction 1969*, edited by Donald A. Wollheim and Terry Carr. New York, Ace, and London, Gollancz, 1969.
"The Electric Neon Mermaid," in *Quark 2*, edited by Samuel R. Delany and Marilyn Hacker. New York, Paperback Library, 1971.
"In a Sky of Daemons," in *Protostars*, edited by David Gerrold and Stephen Goldin. New York, Ballantine, 1971.
"The Looking-Glass Sea," in *Strange Bedfellows*, edited by Thomas N. Scortia. New York, Random House, 1972.

"My Friend Klatu," in *Signs and Woders*, edited by Roger Elwood. Old Tappen, New Jersey, Revell, 1972.

"The Eddystone Light," in *Demon Kind*, edited by Roger Elwood. New York, Avon, 1973.

OTHER PUBLICATIONS

Novels (for children)

Dragonwings. New York, Harper, 1975.
Child of the Owl. New York, Harper, 1977.
Sea Glass. New York, Harper, 1979.
The Mark Twain Murders. New York, Four Winds Press, 1982.
Kind Hearts and Gentle Monsters. New York, Harper, 1982.
Dragon of the Lost Sea. . New York, Harper, 1982.
Liar, Liar. New York, Morrow, 1983.
The Serpent's Children. New York, Harper, 1984.
The Tom Sawyer Fires. New York, Morrow, 1984.

*

Laurence Yep comments:

Growing up as a Chinese in America, I felt much like Ralph Ellison's "invisible man": without form and without shape. In my studies and in my teaching, I pursued the psychological figure of the Stranger, both in the American classics and in the works of popular culture. In writing science-fiction stories about aliens and alienated heroes, I was also unconsciously seeking my own identity. I've used the results to good effect in my children's books on Chinese-Americans. When I'm having problems with a historical novel, I still find it useful to do a science-fiction story on a similar theme.

* * *

Laurence Yep is making his mark as a writer of realism as well as SF fantasy for adults and children. In his children's novels depicting Chinese-American experience in San Francisco, *Dragonwings, Child of the Owl*, and *Sea Glass* , Yep, himself Chinese-American, has deliberately and effectively sought to combat racial stereotyping, and these novels have been praised because they have repaired some of the harm inflicted by racist persistence in describing Chinese or Chinese-Americans as characters resembling Charlie Chan or Fu Manchu, or playing the seemingly omnipresent houseboy, gardener, or launderer. The impact of these novels largely derives from the author's frank, sympathetic rendering of the painful clash between an old generation of Chinese in America who, while mindful of the opportunities their new home provides, still cherish the folkways of their mother country, and a young generation, convinced of the importance of change and the necessity of becoming American, who are tempted to deny the value of their ancestral past. It is surely not coincidental that a similar clash is the thematic center of *Sweetwater*, a most distinguished children's SF novel.

Set on Harmony some centuries in the future, *Sweetwater* describes the efforts of the Silkies, descendants of the Anglic starship crew who had brought the first colonists and then been forced to remain, to maintain their own distinctive society—one lived in harmony with the sea which dominates their lives—and resist the blandishments of the descendants of the first colonists, who are enamored of the latest technology. The Sikies are led by Captain Inigo Priest whose son, Tyree, is both the narrator and moral center of the novel. His several ethical choices, making up a great part of the plot, encapsulate the novel's focus upon the conflict between tradition and the necessity of change and growth. The most prominent element is the setting created for Harmony, in particular, its ecology. Not knowing that the planet is subject to cyclic flooding, the settlers, aided by the Argans, an indigenous race resembling spiders, built on the flood plain. When the waters rise, the settlement, Old Sion, is abandoned by all except the Silkies who struggle to wrest a livelihood from the sea. *Sweetwater* also concerns the development of an artist, a relatively rare topic in children's fiction of any kind, as Tyree senses within himself a gift for music which his parents disdain. Secretly abetted by Amadeus, an old Argan (the many references to music and the Old Testament contribute to the allusive richness of the novel), Tyree gradually internalizes the expressive nature of music and its centrality in any life that aspires for wholeness. Both thematic complexity and verbal richness, then, make *Sweetwater* superior SF.

A subsequent SF novel, *Seademons*, describes Fancyfree, a world colonized by the Folk, other descendants of the Anglics. Unlike the Silkies, the Folk do not live in harmony with the Sea-demons, intelligent life forms native to Fancyfree, until catastrophe forces them to. Like *Sweetwater*, *Seademons* dramatizes a clash between tradition and change, and its most prominent element too is the sea-dominant setting. Also *Seademons*, a densely written and poetically evocative novel like *Sweetwater*, effectively incorporates Celtic lore into its plot. Recently Yep seems to be aiming for versatility. He has written *Shadow Lord*, a volume in the Star Trek series; two young adult novels; and *Dragon of the Lost Sea*, a retelling of a Chinese legend. The merit of the last, in particular its witty interplay between a young boy and the ancient dragon, suggests that Yep, in spite of his desire for versatility, writes most distinctively whenever he focuses on the clash between generations and their conflicting values and draws upon his Chinese-American heritage.

—Francis J. Molson

YERMAKOV, Nicholas. Also writes as Simon Hawke. American. Born in New York City, 30 September 1951. Educated at Valley Forge Military Academy, Pennsylvania; American University, Washington, D. C. ; Hofstra University, Hempstead, New York, B. A. in English and communications 1974. Has worked as musician, broadcaster, journalist, salesman, bartender, and factory worker. Agent: Adele Leone Agency, 26 Nantucket Place, Scarsdale, New York 10583. Address: P. O. Box 18111, Denver, Colorado 80218, U.S.A.

SCIENCE-FICTION PUBLICATIONS

Novels (series: Battlestar Galactica; Boomerang)

Journey from Flesh. New York, Berkley, 1981.
Last Communion (Boomerang). New York, New American Library, 1981.
Fall into Darkness. New York, Berkley, 1982.
Clique. New York, Berkley, 1982.
Epiphany (Boomerang). New York, New American Library, 1982.
Battlestar Galactica 6: The Living Legend, with Glen A. Larson. New York, Berkley, 1982.
Battlestar Galactica 7: War of the Gods, with Glen A. Larson. New York, Berkley, 1982.
Jehad (Boomerang). New York, New American Library, 1984.

Uncollected Short Stories

"Writer's Block," in *Galaxy* (New York), February 1978.
"The Surrogate Mouth," in *Galaxy* (New York), November-December 1978.
"Ecch, The Young Gnome," in *Heavy Metal* (New York), July 1979.
"The Whisper of Banshees," in *Fantasy and Science Fiction* (New York), August 1979.
"Melpomene, Calliope. . . and Fred," in *The Year's Best Fantasy Stories 7*, edited by Arthur W. Saha. New York, DAW, 1981.
"Tomorrow Mourning," in *Chrysalis 9*, edited by Roy Torgeson. New York, Doubleday, 1981.
"Crash Course for the Ravers," in *The Berkley Showcase 3*, edited by Victoria Schochet and John W. Silbersack. New York, Berkley, 1981.
"Drift Away," in *Proteus*, edited by Richard S. McEnroe. New York, Ace, 1981.
"Far Removed from the Scene of the Crime," in *Horrors*, edited by Charlie L. Grant. New York, Berkley, 1981.
"The Orpheus Implant," in *Fantasy and Science Fiction* (New York), February 1981.
"The ECM War," in *Fantasy and Science Fiction* (New York), April 1981.
"Hamburger Heaven," in *Perpetual Light*, edited by Alan Ryan. New York, Warner, 1982.
"Fortunes of a Fool," in *Dragon* (Lake Geneva, Wisconsin), February 1985.

OTHER PUBLICATIONS

Novels as Simon Hawke

The Ivanhoe Gambit. New York, Ace, 1984.
The Timekeeper Conspiracy New York, Ace, 1984.
The Pimpernel Plot. New York, Ace, 1984.
The Zenda Vendetta. New York, Ace, 1985.
The Nautilus Sanction. New York, Ace, 1985.

*

Nicholas Yermakov comments:

I approach my writing with a musician's sensibilities, which is to say that I enjoy "playing different kinds of music." I practice hard, I play often, and I continually seek to improve, but the driving force is the sheer joy of playing and the appreciation of the listener, or in this case, the reader. Writing is not so much a profession or an art as it is a lifestyle. Writers are fringe people. We deal in dreams. We shape them, hone them, polish them, nurture them lovingly, then share them. It's a craft, perhaps more ethereal than most, but no less demanding. Its special attraction is that it can never be truly mastered. But I'll keep on trying, just the same.

*   *   *

A member of what might be called the post-New Wave generation in American science fiction, Nicholas Yermakov is nothing if not eclectic. An admirer of literary radicals in the genre like Harlan Ellison, Norman Spinrad, and Samuel R. Delany, he is nevertheless quite traditional in plotting and style—as Simon Hawke, he is even responsible for the Time Wars series, and he has also written a couple of Battlestar Galactica novelizations.

Yermakov's serious works are full of allusions to both literary classics (Oscar Wilde and Samuel Taylor Coleridge are among his heroes) and such modern authors and gurus as Tom Wolfe, Marshall McLuhan, and Robert Anton Wilson. From all of them, he takes a sense of personal moral responsibility and a distrust of false values and manipulation of whatever kind.

His philosophy perhaps emerges most explicitly in *Clique*, where Ross Cleary, one of those most responsible for the fashion in holographic "auras" behind which people hide their true selves, breaks with the System to lead a movement against their use. But the movement's ideal of being true to one's self, of becoming "clean" of all deception and hypocrisy, later degenerates into an ideology—with Cleary turning into a guru as domineering as his earlier advertising-executive persona.

Yermakov sympathizes with the libertarian movement, but doesn't seem to have enough faith in it to write utopian works. The Boomerang trilogy (*Last Communion, Epiphany, Jehad*) is set in an authoritarian future in which a few decent people try to defend the native culture of a newly discovered world against the ruthlessly amoral designs of the Directorate.

The Shades, as the natives of Boomerang are called, are a unique species. They can absorb the minds and memories of dying members of their kind, so that all their "dead" live on as entities which form gestalts like Jungian archetypes. For the Directorate, after the failure of a drug that promised immortality, the Shades are a godsend. Unknown to present-day explorers, colonists are sent into the *past*—in what turns out to be a successful experiment to acquire the Shades' form of "immortality" for humanity through calculated genocide.

Although full of plot complications involving time travel and conspiracy, the real tension of the series is a *moral* one. The colonists are as much victims as the Shades, all knowledge of their true origin and purpose having been suppressed—and, ironically, they do create a viable hybrid culture by absorbing the Shades (who had never had a *society*, nor the need for one). And the heroes like Paul Tabarde, who had hoped to save the Shades, end up as the defenders of the colonists against the Directorate's obscene plan to "harvest" them like a crop.

Yermakov became known for taking strange turns even in his first novel, *Journey from Flesh*, expanded from a short story: the same alien reptile that at first seems to be a parasite, draining the life from the host that is addicted to it, turns out also to hold out the hope of immortality—at the cost of turning the seeming parasites into the victims themselves.

Having held almost every kind of job imaginable (rock musician, security guard, factory worker, book store clerk, motorcycle salesman), Yermakov can write authoritatively from many viewpoints. But for all that, and the moral-philosophical issues in his SF, he insists that "the primary aim of my work is to be a good storyteller."

—John J. Pierce

YOUNG, Michael (Dunlop) ; Baron Young of Dartington. British. Born in Manchester, 9 August 1915. Educated at Dartington Hall School, Devon; University of London, B. Sc., M: A., Ph. D. ; Gray's Inn, London: called to the Bar. Married 1) Joan Lawson in 1945, two sons and daughter 2) Sasha Moorsom in 1960, one son and one daughter. Director of Political and Economic Planning, 1941-45; Secretary, Research Department, Labour Party, 1945-51. Since 1953, Director, Institute of Community Studies, London. Chairman, Social Science Research Council, 1965-68; Visiting Professor, Ahmadu Bello University, Nigeria, 1972; Chairman, National Consumer Council, 1975-77. Chairman, 1956-65, and since 1965 President, Consumer's Association; Chairman, 1962-71, and since 1971 President, National Extension College. Fellow, Churchill College, Cambridge, 1961-66. Since 1942, Trustee, Dartington Hll. Litt. D. : University of Sheffield, 1965; Hon. Dr. : Open University, 1973; D. Litt. : Universe of Adelaide, 1974. Created Baron Young of Dartington, 1978. Address: Institute of Community Studies, 18 Victoria Park Square, London E2 9PF, England.

SCIENCE-FICTION PUBLICATIONS

Novel

The Rise of the Meritocracy 1870-2033: An Essay on Education and Equality. London, Thames and Hudson, 1958; New York, Random House, 1959.

OTHER PUBLICATIONS

Other

Will the War Make Us Poorer?, with Henry Bunbury. London, Oxford University Press, 1943.
Civil Aviation. London, Pilot Press, 1944.
There's Work for All, with Theodore Prager. London, Nicholson and Watson, 1945.
Labour's Plan for Plenty. London, Gollancz, 1947.
What Is Socialised Industry?. London, Fabian Publications, 1947.
Small Man, Big World: A Discussion of Socialist Democracy. London, Labour Publications, 1949.
Fifty Million Unemployed (on India). London, Labour Party, 1952.
Family and Kinship in East London, with Peter Willmott. London, Routledge, and Glencoe, Illinois, Free Press, 1957; revised edition, London, Penguin, 1962.
Family and Class in a London Suburb, with Peter Willmott. London, Routledge, 1960; New York, Humanities Press, 1961.
New Look at Comprehensive Schools, with Michael Armstrong. London, Fabian Society, 1964.
Innovation and Research in Education. London, Routledge, 1965.
Learning Begins at Home, with Patrick McGeeney. London, Routledge, 1968.
Is Equality a Dream? (lecture). London, Hinden Memorial Fund, 1972.
The Symmetrical Family: A Study of Work and Leisure in the London Region with Peter Willmott. London, Routledge, 1973; New York, Pantheon, 1974.
Mutual Aid in a Selfish Society, with Marianne Rigge. London, Mutual Aid Press, 1979.
Distance Teaching for the Third World, with others. London, Routledge, 1980.
Building Societies and the Consumer: A Report, with Marianne Rigge. London, National Consumer Council, 1981.
The Elmhirsts of Dartington: The Creation of an Utopian Community. London, Routledge, 1982.
Revolution from Within: Co-operatives and Co-operation in British Industry, with Marianne Rigge. London, Weidenfeld and Nicolson, 1983.

Editor, *Forecasting and the Social Sciences*. London, Heinemann, 1968.
Editor, *Poverty Report 1974* [and *1975*]. London, Temple Smith, 2 vols., 1974-75.

*   *   *

With doctorates in sociology and economics, Michael Young is dominantly an academic. It is difficult, in fact, to tell if *The Rise of the Meritocracy* is literature or sociology. Young uses the handy and familiar future perspective in order to persuade the reader that the world has evolved into a complete meritocracy by the year 2034.

The form of the book is a historical-sociological analysis of the present (2034 AD) social situation in Great Britiain. Young takes us step by step up the rungs of educational reform that rendered a system of happy justice on the basis of education to fit the intelligence of the individual. This transformation from "an aristocracy of wealth to an aristocracy of merit" produces a smooth and durable social order. It becomes evident through the book that Young may be more infatuated with the aristocracy than the merit. The villians of this fantasy are the socialists who stupidly support equal and uniform education for all, therefore enslaving the gifted to mediocrity. In fact, some of the more cogent points in the book are made on the subject of education as "social leveling" on one hand, and the potentiality wasted by a system that excludes talented lower-class children from educational opportunity on the other. Part of the scenario Young builds is Britain surging ahead in productivity "thanks mainly to the scientific management of talent. " In the meritorious future students do not have to wash dishes, and in fact are paid a 60% higher wage than industrial workers.

The Rise of the Meritocracy is surely unique in form, as it has no characters and no plot, and is footnoted as an academic work would be. In fact Young may be accused of dressing up his bizarre political notions in literary garb and selling it on the basis of its being a bi-genre novelty. But this would be too harsh; Young deserves credit for his inventiveness and believable scenario construction.

—Peter Lynch

***

YOUNG, Robert F(ranklin). American. Born in Silver Creek, New York, 8 June 1915. Served in the United States Army during World War II. Married Regina M. Sadusky in 1941; one daughter. Inspector in a non-ferrous foundry, now retired. Agent: Scott Meredith Literary Agency, 845 Third Avenue, New York, New York 10022, U.S.A.

SCIENCE-FICTION PUBLICATIONS

Novels

La Quête de la Sainte Grille. Paris, Opta, 1975.
Starfinder. New York, Pocket Books, 1980.
The Last Yggdrasill. New York, Ballantine, 1982.
Eridahn. New York, Ballantine, 1983.
The Vizier's Second Daughter. New York, DAW, 1985.

Short Stories

The Worlds of Robert F. Young. New York, Simon and

Schuster, 1965; London, Gollancz, 1966.
A Glass of Stars. Jacksonville, Illinois, Harris Wolfe, 1968.
Le Pays d'esprit. Paris, Oswald, 1982.

Uncollected Short Stories

"Pithecanthropus Astralis," in *Venture* (Concord, New Hampshire), August 1969.
"The Ogress," in *The Future Is Now*, edited by William F. Nolan. Los Angeles, Sherbourne Press, 1970,
"Reflections," in *Galaxy* (New York), March 1970.
"To Touch a Star," in *If* (New York), April 1970.
"A Ship Will Come," in *Worlds of Fantasy* (New York), Winter 1970.
"Genesis 500," in *Analog* (New York), February 1972.
"The Hand," in *Galaxy* (New York), March 1972.
"Whom The Gods Love," in *If* (New York), December 1972.
"The Years," in *Best SF 1972*, edited by Harry Harrison and Brian Aldiss. New York, Putnam, 1973; as *The Year's Best Science Fiction 6*, London, Sphere, 1973.
"Remnants of Things Past," in *Fantasy and Science Fiction* (New York), April 1973.
"Girl Saturday," in *Galaxy* (New York), May 1973.
"The Adventures of the Last Earthman in Search of Love," in *Amazing* (New York), June 1973.
"The Giantess," in *Fantasy and Science Fiction* (New York), July 1973.
"Ghosts," in *Best Science Fiction Stories of the Year*, edited by Lester del Rey. New York, Dutton, 1974.
"No Deposit, No Refill," in *Amazing* (New York), February 1974.
"The Star of Stars," in *Fantasy and Science Fiction* (New York), March 1974.
"Tinkerboy," in *Galaxy* (New York), May 1974.
"New Route to the Indies," in *Amazing* (New York), August 1974.
"Spacetrack," in *Fantasy and Science Fiction* (New York), September 1974.
"Hex Factor," in *Fantasy and Science Fiction* (New York), November 1974.
"The Decayed Leg Bone," in *Amazing* (New York), December 1974.
"Perchance to Dream," in *Fantastic* (New York), February 1975.
"Techmech," in *Fantastic* (New York), June 1975.
"Lord of Rays," in *Amazing* (New York), July 1975.
"The Curious Case of Henry Dickens," in *Fantasy and Science Fiction* (New York), August 1975.
"Shakespeare of the Apes," in *Fantasy and Science Fiction* (New York), December, 1975.
"Clay Suburb," in *The Best Science Fiction of the Year 5*, edited by Terry Carr. New York, Ballantine, and London, Gollancz, 1976.
"Above This Race of Men," in *Amazing* (New York), January 1976.
"Ghur R'Hut Urr," in *Amazing* (New York), June 1976.
"PRNDLL," in *Fantasy and Science Fiction* (New York), June 1976.
"Milton Inglorious," in *Fantasy and Science Fiction* (New York), September 1976.
"The Day the Limited Was Late," in *Fantasy and Science Fiction* (New York), March 1977.
"Fleuve Red," in *Fantastic* (New York), September 1977.
"The Space Roc," in *Amazing* (New York), January 1978.

"The Journal of Nathaniel Worth," in *Fantastic* (New York), July 1978.
"The Winning of Gloria Grandonwheels," in *Amazing* (New York), August 1978.
"Hologirl," in *Fantasy and Science Fiction* (New York) August 1978.
"Crutch," in *Amazing* (New York), November 1978.
"The First Mars Mission," in *Fantasy and Science Fiction* (New York), May 1979.
"Project Hi-Rise," in *The Best from Fantasy and Science Fiction 23*, edited by Edward L. Ferman. New York, Doubleday, 1980.
"The Tents of Kedar," in *Fantasy and Science Fiction* (New York), December 1980.
"Yours,—Guy," in *Shadows 4*, edited by Charles L. Grant. New York, Doubleday, 1981.
"The Summer of the Fallen Star," in *Fantasy and Science Fiction* (New York), April 1981.
"Invitation to the Waltz," in *Fantasy and Science Fiction* (New York), March 1982.
"Dark Space," *in Isaac Asimov's Science Fiction Magazine* (New York), March 1982.
"Earthscape," *in Isaac Asimov's Science Fiction Magazine* (New York), May 1982.
"Universes," in *Isaac Asimov's Science Fiction Magazine* (New York), August 1982.
"The Moon of Advanced Learing," in *Isaac Asimov's Science Fiction Magazine* (New York), October 1982.
"Glimpses," in *Isaac Asimov's Science Fiction Magazine* (New York), February 1983.
"The Lost Earthman," in *Fantasy and Science Fiction* (New York), November 1983.
"The Princess of Akkir," in *Isaac Asimov's Science Fiction Magazine* (New York), March 1984.
"Divine Wind," in *Fantasy and Science Fiction* (New York), April 1984.
"Glass Houses," in *Fantasy and Science Fiction* (New York), November 1984.
"Findokin's Way," in *Isaac Asimov's Science Fiction Magazine* (New York), November 1984.
"Mars Child," in *Amazing* (New York), January 1985.

*

Robert F. Young comments:
My books and stories deal with a variety of subjects. My motive in writing most of them stems in part from a fascination for science fiction dating from the long-ago years when I discovered Edgar Rice Burroughs and H. G. Wells, and in part from the genre's capability of providing a writer with the opportunity to make the impossible seem possible.

*   *   *

In an introductory essay to Robert F. Young's *A Glass of Stars*, Fritz Leiber remarks: "And I say that the field to which Robert F. Young has many times proven his claim is that of romantic love. The magic potion of which he is master creator is the love philter. " It could be further noted that the potion is not meant merely for the characters in his stories, but to captivate the audience that reads them. Robert F. Young's realm is the realm of boy meets girl, not in some bygone era but on other worlds or in a future mired in the sins of our own time, crass commercialism and the violation of the environment. Almost always Young surveys his domain with the force of his sense of humor, inserting it at the proper junctures so as not to allow "boy meets girl" to become soap opera. Young skillfully weaves his plots in such a manner that the reader can only smile at the fact that the man and woman are together, living happily ever after, in the end.

An especially fine example of Young's plot-twisting talent is the story "L'Arc de Jeanne," which takes place on the planet Ceil Bleu, near the key city of Fleur du Sud. This is a planet committed to the Psycho-Phenomenalist Church. We find it under attack by the forces of the evil tyrant O'Riordan. All that stands in the way of conquest is a young maiden who rides a "magnificent black stallion" and is armed with what appears to be a magic bow and arrow. O'Riordan wants the maiden captured, and sends a computer-selected young man guaranteed to be irresistible to the maiden, to win her affection. The story evolves in such a manner that Young's Joan of Arc must burn at the stake, yet Young manages the plot so that the story ends happily.

Young's conservations concerns show forth in "To Fell a Tree." A young treeman has the task of felling a glorious 1000-foot tree, a job his company has been hired to do by a rather greedy village. The tree is so enormous that he must live in the tree for a number of days in order to bring it down. While in the tree he meets a dryad, the spirit of the tree, who is seen slowly dying as the tree is cut down, a tree the sap of which looks just like blood. Young's talent as a weaver of words is revealed in this story, along with his passionate concern for nature's living forms.

Young, a shrewd commentator on the crassness of commercialism, has a special fondness for the crudities of the automotive world. In "Romance in a Twenty-First-Century Used-Car-Lot" the auto industry has managed to miniaturize cars sufficiently so that they can be worn as clothing, and then convinced the public that not wearing them is obscene. Those who don't wear cars are called nudists and consigned to a nudist colony. "It wasn't hard to do," Howard Highways tells Arabella Grille, "because people had been wearing their cars unconsciously all along. " Then there is Emily ("Emily and the Bards Sublime"), an assistant curator of a museum. She is extremely fond of the android poets, especially Lord Tennyson. One day she is told that the poets must go to make room for a display of 20th-century art, cars, that is. Mr. Brandon tells her she will be taking over the new exhibit; "Mr. Brandon handed her the big book he was carrying. ' An Analysis of the Chrome Motif in Twentieth Century Art. Read it religiously, Miss Meredith. It's the most important book of our century.' "

However, Young's first love is romance, and he is willing to go to, or to manipulate, the ends of time to bring his loved ones together. "The Dandelion Girl," "The Girl Who Made Time Stop," and "Mine Eyes Have Seen The Glory" are all examples of first-rate stories that entail clever use of the intricacies of time as the fourth dimension. Robert Young's gift as a story teller is brought out in these tales, for by the end of each story the reader has been moved to believe in the possibility of romantic love even when it entails bending the known laws of physics.

In a recent novel, *Starfinder,* Young also makes much use of the intricacies of time travel. The book deals with giant creatures—space whales—who can dive into the past, spaceships constructed from the carcases of these creatures, and one man's relationship to both the spacecraft and one of the creatures. Young takes full advantage of the paradoxes of time travel as he spins yet another story of romance across the eons. The reader should be forewarned, however, that Young's romanticism takes something of a rather sexist turn in its portrayal of one of the most important female characters and

the planet she helps rule. The reader might also wish to know that several segments of *Starfinder* were first published in short story versions over a number of years.

—Mitchell Aboulafia

ZACHARY, Hugh. See **HUGHES, Zach.**

ZAGAT, Arthur Leo. American. Born in New York City, in 1895. Educated at City College of New York, B. A. ; Bordeaux University; Fordham University Law School, New York, LL. D. Served in the United States Army during World War I, and with the Office of War Information during World War II. Married Ruth Zagat; one daughter. Founded Writers Workshop at New York University. Member of the Council, Authors League of America. *Died 3 April 1949.*

SCIENCE-FICTION PUBLICATIONS

Novel

Seven Out of Time. Reading, Pennsylvania, Fantasy Press, 1949.

Uncollected Short Stories

"The Tower of Evil," with Nat Schachner, in *Wonder Stories Quarterly* (New York), Summer 1930.
"In 20,000 A. D.," with Nat Schachner, in *Wonder Stories* (New York), September 1930.
"Back to 20,000 A. D.," with Nat Schachner, in *Wonder Stories* (New York), March 1931.
"The Emperor of the Stars," with Nat Schachner, in *Wonder Stories* (New York), April 1931.
"The Menace from Andromeda," with Nat Schachner, in *Amazing* (New York), April 1931.
"The Death-Cloud," with Nat Schachner, in *Astounding* (New York), May 1931.
"The Revolt of the Machines," with Nat Schachner, in *Astounding* (New York), July 1931.
"Venus Mines Incorporated," with Nat Schachner, in *Wonder Stories* (New York), August 1931.
"Exiles of the Moon," with Nat Schachner, in *Wonder Stories* (New York), September 1931.
"The Great Dome on Mercury," in *Astounding* (New York), April 1932.
"When the Sleepers Woke," in *Astounding* (New York), November 1932.
"The Living Flame," in *Astounding* (New York), February 1934.
"Spoor of the Bat," in *Astounding* (New York), July 1934.
"Beyond the Spectrum," in *Astounding* (New York), August 1934.
"The Land Where Time Stood Still," in *Thrilling Wonder Stories* (New York), August 1936.
"Flight of the Silver Eagle," in *Thrilling Wonder Stories* (New York), April 1937.

"Lost in Time," in *Thrilling Wonder Stories* (New York), June 1937.

"Drink We Deep," in *Argosy* (New York), 31 July-4 September 1937.

"The Cavern of the Shining Pool," in *Thrilling Wonder Stories* (New York), October 1937.

"Island in the Sky," in *Argosy* (New York), 17 December 1937.

"The Green Ray," in *Thrilling Wonder Stories* (New York), August 1938.

"Tomorrow," in *Argosy* (New York), 27 May 1939.

"Children of Tomorrow," in *Argosy* (New York), 17 June 1939.

"Bright Flag of Tomorrow," in *Argosy* (New York), 9 September 1939.

"Thunder Tomorrow," in *Argosy* (New York), 16 March 1940.

"Sunrise Tomorrow," in *Argosy* (New York), 8-15 June 1940.

"The Long Road to Tomorrow," in *Argosy* (New York), 1-22 March 1941.

"The Two Moons of Tranquillia," in *Weird Tales* (New York), January 1943.

"Jungle Interlude," in *Argosy* (New York), February 1943.

"Sunward Flight," in *Super Science* (Kokomo, Indiana), February 1943.

"Venus Station," in *Science Fiction Stories* (New York), April 1943.

"The Lanson Screen," in *Best of Science Fiction*, edited by Groff Conklin. New York, Crown, 1946.

"Slaves of the Lamp," in *Astounding* (New York), August, September 1946.

"Grim Rendezvous," in *Thrilling Wonder Stories* (New York), December 1946.

"The Faceless Men," in *Thrilling Wonder Stories* (New York), April 1948.

"No Escape from Destiny," in *Startling* (New York), May 1948.

*   *   *

Arthur Leo Zagat is essentially an early 1930's figure, to be seen in the context of science fiction broadening, diversifying, and acquiring a definite character as more magazines emerged.

His relatively small science-fiction output reflected a personal interest in futuristic ideas; as with many others of the time whose overall output was trivial hack work, he showed originality and vision in science fiction. Every cliché began as an inspiration. Though his stories ranged over a variety of themes, his main contribution was to space flight. This was then something predicted for the indefinite future, but it was a vision that excited that generation as no other. The spectacluar progress of aviation had made a profound impression, clearly made obvious the pace of technological change, and raised imagination from the ground.

Interplanetary travel had a long literary tradition, but, aside from its use as a springboard to introduce a Utopia or a reflection on man's follies, its emphasis had always been on the initial problems to be solved. By the time SF was firmly established, readers had gone over that ground many times and were ready to go beyond it. Early 1930's science fiction tried to imagine regular traffic between worlds, and settled into a picture analogous to ocean shipping as it had been in earlier times when it was more hazardous and maritime countries more remote and diverse. Zagat helped build up the image of a dangerous yet established trade, of interplanetary shipping lines and business rivalries, of a rough spaceport district analogous to the traditional waterfront, of a rough frontier class of spacemen, with occasional piracy and clashes with natives, or a well-disciplined space service to keep order.

Inevitably this led to the repetitive action stories Tucker aptly tagged space opera. It tended to trivialise space flight by glossing over the problems, though it popularised the concept. Its rather optimistic view had a strong appeal in its time. Zagat's stories such as "The Great Dome on Mercury," "Spoor of the Bat," and "The Cavern of the Shining Pool" were good entertainment, and added to the movement's repertory of expectations. World-scale conflict of East and West, another standard theme, was exploited in "The Death-Cloud," "The Green Ray," and "Flight of the Silver Eagle," dated, but showing what then seemed good probabilities: a world shrunk by better communications, conflict mainly airborn, death-rays and other devices.

And there are many other themes, all fairly new and treated originally—unearthlike life, the amorphous "Menace from Andromeda," logically evolved; a nonhuman inteligent race in "The Emperor of the Stars" sympathetically treated without humanising it; invisible subterranean beings in "Beyond the Spectrum"; machine intelligence in "The Revolt of the Machines"; the world depopulated and left to a few chance survivors in "When the Sleepers Woke"; big business replacing traditional state power in "Exiles of the Moon" and "Lost in Time"; glimpses of future custom and folklore, even sport, in "Sunward Flight"; dangerous inventions in "The Lanson Screen," the defensive shield that became a deadly prison.

Zagat's only book, *Seven Out of Time*, drew on elements he had used before and clearly suffers from spinning out the suspense in a six-part serial. The early chapters with their missing-person plot and eery touches contrast with the strange remote world of millions of years hence, where the group of dehumanised monsters evolved from us try to recover the insights and motivations they have lost by studying their kidnapped people of our own and earlier times. Dated and plausable only as symbolic fantasy even in 1939, it has merit for the message it presents even today.

The volume of science fiction still appearing in the general fiction magazines through the 1930's is generally overlooked, but it was considerable and, though mostly less original, it has interest. *Seven Out of Time* first ran in *Argosy* which had a long history of including science fiction on its merits. Perhaps a better novel serialised there, never made a book, is "Drink We Deep," though hampered by its use of the primitive diary-letter form. This mystery with seemingly supernatural elements developed into a wild extravaganza of early science-fiction fancies, with size-change to bring the leading characters from everyday America into a minature people's realm under a lake, with scientific marvels and a possible menace to the human world, plot elements reminiscent of Burroughs or Merritt, and some memorable scenes. The 1939-41 series of six tales beginning with "Tomorrow" was discontinued without resolution, perhaps because its background of a future America enslaved by the Yellow Peril came to be less a stock theme than an uncomfortable possibility. But its treatment with a group of children growing into Noble Savages in a wilderness retreat to lead revolt was an unusual concept.

Zagat's first works were written with Nat Schachner, whose role cannot be distinguished. The writing is conventional, the human interest elementary, with characterisation going little beyond stock figures. But it is competent, good of its kind in its time, and it has conviction.

—Graham Stone

ZAHN, Timothy. American. Born in Chicago, Illinois, 1

September 1951. Educated at Michigan State University, East Lansing, 1969-73, B. A. in physics 1973; University of Illinois, Urbana, 1973-79, M. S. in physics 1975. Married Anna L. Zahn in 1979; one son. Since 1980, full-time writer. Recipient: Hugo Award, 1984. Agent: Russell Galen, Scott Meredith Literary Agency, 845 Third Avenue, New York, New York 10022. Address: 2014 Vawter Street, Apt. 2, Urbana, Illinois 61801, U.S.A.

SCIENCE-FICTION PUBLICATIONS

Novels

The Blackcollar. New York, DAW, 1983.
A Coming of Age. New York, Bluejay, 1985.
Cobra. New York, Baen, 1985.
Spinneret. New York, Bluejay, 1985.

Uncollected Short Stories

"Ernie," in *Analog* (New York), July 1979.
"The Dreamsender," in *Analog* (New York), July 1980.
"A Lingering Death," in *Analog* (New York), December 1980.
"The Challenge," in *The Space Gamer* (Austin, Texas), December 1980.
"The Energy Crisis of 2215," in *Amazing* (New York), March 1981.
"Hollow Victory," in *Analog* (New York), 30 March 1981.
"Red Thoughts at Morning," in *Analog* (New York), 27 April 1981.
"Fantasy World," in *The Space Gamer* (Austin, Texas), May 1981.
"The Price of Survival," in *Analog* (New York), 22 June 1981.
"The Giftie Gie Us," in *Analog* (New York), 20 July 1981.
"Sword's Man," in *The Space Gamer* (Austin, Texas), September 1981.
"Loophole," in *Analog* (New York), 14 September 1981.
"Raison d'Etre," in *Analog* (New York), 12 October 1981.
"Job Inaction," in *Analog* (New York), 9 November 1981.
"Houseguest," in *Fantasy and Science Fiction* (New York), January 1982.
"When Johnny Comes Marching Home," in *Analog* (New York), 4 January 1982.
"Symmkyn's Edge," in *The Space Gamer* (Austin, Texas), February 1982.
"Origin," in *Isaac Asimov's Science Fiction Magazine* (New York), 15 February 1982.
"Final Solution," in *Analog* (New York), 1 March 1982.
"Unitive Factor," in *Analog* (New York), May 1982.
"Between a Rock and a High Place," in *Analog* (New York), July 1982.
"The Peaceful Man," in *Fantasy and Science Fiction* (New York), September 1982.
"Dragon Pax," in *Rigel* (Richmond, California), Fall 1982.
"Dark Thoughts at Noon," in *Analog* (New York), December 1982.
"Pawn's Gambit," in *The 1983 Annual World's Best SF*, edited by Donald A. Wollheim. New York, DAW, 1983.
"The Shadows of Evening," in *Fantasy and Science Fiction* (New York), March 1983.
"The Final Report on the Lifeline Experiment," in *Analog* (New York), May 1983.
"Warlord," in *Analog* (New York), July 1983.
"Curtain Call," in *Rigel* (Richmond, California), Summer 1983.

"Expanded Charter," in *Analog* (New York), Mid-September 1983.
"The Cassandra," in *Analog* (New York), November 1983.
"The Damocles Mission," in *Ares* (Lake Geneva, Wisconsin), Winter 1983.
"Cascade Point," in *Analog* (New York), December 1983.
"Vampire Trap," in *The Fantasy Gamer* (Austin, Texas), February-March 1984.
"Bête Noire," in *Analog* (New York), March 1984.
"Teamwork," in *Analog* (New York), April 1984.
"Return to the Fold," in *Analog* (New York), September 1984.
"Cordon Sanitaire," in *Alien Stars*. New York, Baen, 1985.
"Music Hath Charms," in *Analog* (New York), April 1985.

*

Timothy Zahn comments

There are as many definitions of "science fiction" as there are writers, readers, and critics; but to me the important word here is "fiction," and fiction means telling a story. I enjoy speculating in my stories—playing the "if-then" game—and when I can make a point about humanity or society as well I feel I am helping, in a small way, to fulfill the promise of depth and richness that science fiction has always offered its readers. But the basic story *must* be worth reading; must hold the readers' attention and firmly draw them into the world the writer has created. Otherwise any message is likely to be lost, or never read at all.

The number-one goal in my writing, therefore, is to entertain my audience—to entertain with high adventure, as in *The Blackcollar*; to entertain with details of an unusual society, as in *A Coming of Age*; to entertain with scientific-puzzle stories, as in many of my shorter stories. But the entertainment must be there. Always. It's part of the job.

*   *   *

Timothy Zahn is one of the newest holders of the reputation of "an *Astounding/Analog* writer". During the five years of his career to date, most of his work has appeared as novelettes in that magazine. His stories emphasize an intellectual challenge in a context of the growth of mankind, astronomically and metaphysically. His characters are intelligent and likeable, although due to the brevitiy of the stories they are seldom more than stereotypes of technicians: stick figures to present and solve the problem. This has begun to change with the recent publication of two novels which have given Zahn more room for character development.

A common theme is the expansion of humanity into space, often involving conflict with an alien civilization. In "Hollow Victory" two biomedics must deduce the cause of the critical illness of an alien ambassador, using clues about the Thrulmodi physiology and the nature of the planet on which the first human-Thrulmodi conference is taking place. "Unitive Factor" is set on an exploratory ship manned by a team of humans and aliens who find each other sociologically dislikeable. The story, involving a space rescue utilizing an incomprehensible deep-space life form, emphasizes the need of the two cultures to work together. A sequel, "Bête Noire," goes deeper into the ecology of the fascinating space life forms. "Cascade Point" (Hugo winner) is the point in space at which a ship makes its transition to another stellar system. An unexplained phenomenon is the appearance surrounding each person aboard ship of multiple images of himself, from alternate time-lines. The story relates how an experiment to use this phenomenon for psychotherapeutic purposes ends up revealing more about the phenomenon itself, and how the embittered narrator comes to prefer his actual career to that shown by his more glamorous cascade-point images. *The Blackcollar*, Zahn's first novel, is a military-combat thriller in which a commando unit with chemically-augmented physical abilities fights the alien conquerers of Earth. Zahn sets up the question, if the entire human space civilization was unable to defeat the aliens thirty years earlier, what chance does a single Resistance unit have today? He answers it in a melodramatic yet plausible manner.

Another common theme is the elevation of society to a higher mental plane, and the psychological stresses that this creates. In "Dark Thoughts at Noon" two telepaths are kidnapped by a technician who wants mechanically to duplicate their talents for his own benefit. The methods that the unscrupulous Green uses to stymie Ted's and Colleen's natural powers, and the manner by which Green is finally thwarted, are cleverly worked out. "The Final Report on the Lifeline Experiment" tells how an intellectual experiment to find out by telepathy at what point a human fetus becomes a "real person" is converted into a political crisis by pro- and anti-abortion activists. "The Cassandra" starts with a mutation that enables the humans of a colony planet to foretell death, and ends with a speculation that the death of any sentient being may affect the structure of the universe.

Zahn's second novel, *A Coming of Age*, is set on a planet where a mutation two hundred years earlier resulted in all children developing telekinetic powers at the age of five, which they lose at puberty. Several strong characters are developed, notably a 13-year-old girl who fears the coming loss of her ability, an adult detective and his preteen assistant who are investigating a kidnapping, a scientist doing research on the biology of the telekinetic phenomenon, and a criminal plotting to take advantage of it. Zahn slowly reveals one facet at a time of this unique society, and ties each one in as an important element of his mystery. *A Coming of Age* is Zahn's most ambitious and his best-developed work, and indicates that he will become an increasingly important SF author during the next few years.

—Frederick Patten

ZEBROWSKI, George. American. Born in Villach, Austria, 28 December 1945. Attended the State University of New York, Binghamton, 1964-69. Copy editor, Binghamton *Evening Press*, 1967; filtration plant operator, New York, 1969-70; lecturer in science fiction, State University of New York, Binghamton, Spring 1971; Editor, *SFWA Bulletin*, 1970-75, and since 1983; since 1983, General Editor and Consultant, Crown, publishers, New York. Free-lance writer and lecturer. Agent: Joseph Elder Agency, 150 West 87th Street, New York, New York 10024. Address: Box 486, Johnson City, New York 13790, U.S.A.

SCIENCE-FICTION PUBLICATIONS

Novels (series: Omega Point)

The Omega Point. New York, Ace, 1972; London, New English Library, 1974.
The Star Web. Toronto, Laser, 1975.
Ashes and Stars. New York, Ace, 1977; London, New English Library, 1978.
Macrolife.New York, Harper, 1979; London, Futura, 1980.

The Omega Point Trilogy (includes *The Omega Point* and *Ashes and Stars*, both revised, and *Mirror of Minds*). New York, Ace, 1983.
Sunspacer (for children). New York, Harper, 1984.
The Stars Will Speak (for children). New York, Harper, 1985.

Short Stories

The Monadic Universe and Other Stories New York, Ace, 1977; augmented edition, 1985.
A Silent Shout. Tulsa, Educational Development Corporation, 1979.
The Firebird. Tulsa, Educational Development Corporation, 1979.

Uncollected Short Stories

"Dark, Dark, the Dead Star," with Jack Dann, in *If* (New York), July-August 1970.
"Listen, Love," with Jack Dann, in *New Worlds Quarterly 2*, edited by Michael Moorcock. London, Sphere, and New York, Berkley, 1971.
"Trap," with Jack Dann, in *Coming Through*, edited by Nina C. Woessner and William D. Sheldon. Boston, Allyn and Bacon, 1972.
"Fountain of Force," with Grant Carrington, in *Inifinity 4*, edited by Robert Hoskins. New York, Lancer, 1972.
"OD," with Jack Dann, in *Omega*, edited by Roger Elwood. New York, Walker 1974.
"Adrift in Space" (for children), in *Adrift in Space and Other Stories*, edited by Roger Elwood. Minneapolis, Lerner, 1974.
"Darkness of Day," with Pamela Sargent, in *Continuum 3*, edited by Roger Elwood. New York, Berkley, 1974.
"Thirty-Three and One Third," with Jack Dann, in *Long Night of Waiting and Other Stories*, edited by Roger Elwood. Nashville, Aurora, 1974.
"The Flower That Missed the Morning" (for children), with Jack Dann, in *The Killer Plants and Other Stories*, edited by Roger Elwood. Minneapolis, Lerner, 1974.
"Journey to Another Star" (for children), in *Journey to Another Star and Other Stories*, edited by Roger Elwood. Nashville, Aurora, 1974.
"The Iron Butterfly" (for children), in *Current Science*, 20 February 1974.
"Faces Forward," with Jack Dann, and "Weapons,"with Pamela Sargent, in *Dystopian Visions*, edited by Roger Elwood. Englewood Cliffs, Prentice Hall, 1975.
"Yellowhead," with Jack Dann, in *New Constellations*, edited by Thomas M. Disch and Charles Naylor. New York, Harper, 1976.
"Transfigured Night," in *Immortal*, edited by Jack Dann. New York, Harper, 1978.
"Fire of Spring," in *Chillers*, July 1981.
"Earth Around His Bones," in *Chillers*, September 1981.
"The Alternate," in *Chillers*, November 1981.
"The Falling," with Pamela Sargent, in *Isaac Asimov's Science Fiction Magazine* (New York), March 1983.
"The Sea of Evening," in *Isaac Asimov's Science Fiction Magazine* (New York), July 1983.
"The Eichmann Variations," in *Light Years and Dark*, edited by Michael Bishop. New York, Berkley, 1984.
"The City of Thought and Steel," in *Isaac Asimov's Scienced Fiction Magazine* (New York), March 1984.
"Gödel's Doom," in *Popular Computing* (London), February 1985.

OTHER PUBLICATIONS

Other

Introduction to *Horror Tales*, edited by Roger Elwood. Chicago, Rand McNally, 1974.

"Whatever Gods There Be: Space-Time and Deity in Science Fiction," in *Strange Gods*, edited by Roger Elwood. New York, Simon and Schuster, 1974.

"Science Fiction and the Visual Media," in *Science Fiction: Today and Tomorrow*, edited by Reginald Bretnor. New York, Harper, 1974.

Introduction to *Things to Come*, by H. G. Wells. Boston, Gregg Press, 1975.

"Afterword" to *The Space Beyond and Other Short Novels*, by John W. Campbell, Jr. New York, Pyramid, 1976.

"On the Ouster of Stanislaw Lem from the SFWA: How It Happened," with Pamela Sargent, and "Why It Happened," in *Science-Fiction Studies* (Terre Haute, Indiana), July 1977.

"More Than Human? Androids, Cyborgs, and Others," with Patricia S. Warrick, in *Contemporary Mythology*, edited by Warrick, Martin H. Greenberg, and Joseph D. Olander. New York, Harper, 1978.

"Herding Words: A Journal," with Jeffrey M. Elliot, in *Foundation* (London), July 1983.

Introduction to *The Forgotten Planet* by Murray Leinster; *The Joy Makers* by James E. Gunn; *Men, Martians, and Machines* by Eric Frank Russell; *The Paradox Men* by Charles L. Harness; *The Shores of Another Sea, Unearthly Neighbors*, and *Shadows in the Sun* by Chad Oliver; and *Greater Than You Think* by Ward Moore, New York, Crown, 8 vols., 1984-85.

Editor. *Tomorrow Today*. Santa Cruz, California, Unity Press, 1975.

Editor, with Thomas N. Scortia, *Human-Machines: An Anthology of Stories about Cyborgs*. New York, Ramdom House, 1975; London, Hale, 1977.

Editor, with Jack Dann, *Faster Than Light: An Anthology of Stories about Interstellar Travel*. New York, Harper, 1976.

Editor, *The Best of Thomas N. Scortia*. New York, Doubleday, 1981.

Editor, with Isaac Asimov and Martin H. Greenberg, Creations: The Quest for Origins in Story and Science. New York, Crown, 1983; London, Harrap, 1984.

Editor, *Nebula Awards 20*. San Diego, Harcourt Brace, 1985.

*

Bibliography: *The Work of George Zebrowski: An Annotated Bibliography and Guide* by Jeffrey M. Elliot, San Bernardino, California, Borgo Press, 1985.

Manuscript Collection: Paskow Science Fiction Collection, Temple University, Philadelphia.

*   *   *

There is, contends George Zebrowski, an aspect to writing that is akin to prayer, to pleading with the nameless fact of existence, on behalf of one's characters. Superficially, a fiction writer tells lies, fabricating events and characters; but on a deeper level, a writer tells the truth about his characters and events, finding what is meaningful about these things for the reader and himself. Some writers never get past the point of telling lies, of fabricating events and characters in a facile simulation of what literature, at its best, is about. However technically skilled such work is, it has one feature which betrays it: the inauthentic work fades in the reader's mind, however dazzling the initial reading might have seemed. This is not true of George Zebrowski.

Macrolife, Zebrowski's most ambitious work, depicts with Stapledonian scope the evolution of artificial space colonies (or macrolife). Jack Bulero, a 21st-century businessman in charge of the world's largest corporation, inadvertently precipitates a disaster that threatens to destroy earth. Blamed for the catastrophe, his family is forced to seek asylum in a space colony where Richard Bulero, the visionary younger son, realizes that macrolife has the potentiality to become the next logical step in man's evolutionary development. Freed from the drawbacks of natural planets, with their scarcity of resources and other limitations, macroworlds offer man the opportunity for almost limitless expansion and social experimentation. This dream is tested in the second section of the novel when a descendant of the Bulero clan becomes sentimentally attracted to the savage inhabitants of a decayed natural world, only to find that his primitivistic yearnings are not only impossible but deadly. The novel concludes on an apocalyptic note: as the last remnants of macrolife huddle around a few dying dwarf stars, a reconstructed descendant of the Buleros is called on to aid in an apparent miracle: the rebirth of the cosmos.

Imaginative rebirth, with its philosophic and religious implications, is the dominant motif of *The Monadic Universe*, a collection of stories. "Monadic Universe" charts the nightmarish voyage of the last survivors of earth's destruction. Hurtling through deep space, they must confront the terrible truth that they cannot return to their normal space-time continuum without unleashing forces that would destroy the entire cosmos. Their only hope lies in a leap of faith so unimaginable that it drives the rigidly rationalistic captain to his death. Self-enclosed space systems as a metaphor for human isolation and regeneration also appear in the Christian Praeger series. A struggling city youth in "Assassins of Air," Praeger decides to quit the "recycling gangs" roaming the polluted city and trafficking in bootleg automobile parts. Sensitive and idealistic, he seeks to obtain an education that will help him to combat pollution, but his former cohorts drive him from the city with murderous fury. In "Parks of Rest and Culture" he becomes so disillusioned with the seemingly insoluble problems of earth that he enlists as a space colonist, dreaming of an idyllic new life "filled with elegant people, full-leafed trees casting broad shadows." Several years later Praeger, now a seasoned space colonist, encounters his old friend Julian, "The Water Sculptor," a reclusive artist in an orbiting studio. When Julian commits suicide rather than return to the crass and corrupt earth, Praeger not only learns a poignant lesson about the human condition but also has a deeper insight into the transformative power of art and the imagination.

Other stories in this collection, such as "Starcrossed" and "First Love, First Fear," explore the paradoxes of eroticism in an utterly alien context. In "Heathen God" a priest of a proudly "enlightened" interstellar empire is shocked to discover that a gnome-like alien is actually the worship-starved "father" of the human race. The religious implications of an "alien god" are also taken up in "Interpose," a story whose account of the Jesus-as-alien theme is as subtle as its punning title.

Major stories of the late 1970's and early 1980's include "The Word Sweep," "The Eichmann Variations" (a Nebula Award finalist), and "Gödel's Doom." This last work is overtly based on the philosophy of mathematics, and is one of the few science fiction stories in which mathematics is treated accurately. The story was reprinted in the Bertrand Russell Society quarterly, the only story to be so honored by that journal.

Zebrowski's science fiction is a way of grasping and communicating human experience, past, present, and future; it is a form of phenomenological description in areas too complex for quantification. This is the grist with which serious writers deal, witnessing their times, refining language, transmitting feelings, thoughts, and a sense of beauty. The critical possibilities of Zebrowski's work suggest that the creation of genuine future alternatives may, when it is combined with the tools of literary expression, become a supremely affecting art form.

Writers, argues Zebrowski, must be prepared to risk being demolished, psychologically, by the "facts" of their careers, by how they are perceived. "Artistic failure" is a curious process; there is no way to prove it is happening, since some of the best writers often receive the most vehement condemnation (and no money), and the worst the highest praise (while the money teems). Beware the voices of *both* praise and condemnation; both speak from shifting positions, and can be very damaging in how they affect a writer's new work.

Arriving in the United States as a displaced person while still a child (his parents were captured by the Nazis), Zebrowski is preoccupied with exile, loss, and the need to find meaning and identity in a strange environment. Thomas N. Scortia has compared Zebrowski's style and background to that of another deracinated Polish writer, Joseph Conrad, whose "prose . . . is alternatively complex and leanly descriptive" and whose "themes reflect the intellectual heritage of Middle Europe. " Michael Bishop has written: "Together with his metaphysical imagination, his hard-earned understanding of science and technology, and his maturing skills as a delineator of character, his mastery of a distinctive prose style makes it impossible to regard Zebrowski as just another journeyman yarnspinner. . . . The strides he has made on a stylistic level— the increases in metaphorical aptness, in the beauty and simplicity of his images—cry out for applause. " Serious and original as well as stimulating and entertaining, Zebrowski has proven a promising new voice whose work deserves a wider readership.

—Jeffrey M. Elliot and Anthony Manousos

ZEIGFRIED, Karl. See **FANTHORPE, R. Lionel.**

ZELAZNY, Roger (Joseph). Also writes as Harrison Denmark. American. Born in Cleveland, Ohio, 13 May 1937.Educated at Noble School, 1943-49, Shore Junior High School, 1949-52, and Euclid Senior High School, 1952-55, all Euclid, Ohio; Western Reserve University, Cleveland (Foster Poetry Award, 1957, 1959), 1955-59, B. A. in English 1959; Columbia University, New York, 1959-60, M. A. 1962. Served in the Ohio National Guard, 1960-63, and the United States Army Reserve, 1963-66. Married 1) Sharon Steberl in 1964 (divorced, 1966); 2) Judith Callahan in 1966, two sons and one daughter. Claims representative, Cleveland, 1963-65, and claims specialist, Baltimore, 1965-69, Social Security Administration. Since 1969, freelance writer and lecturer. Secretary-Treasurer,

Science Fiction Writers of America, 1967-68. Recipient: Nebula Award, 1965 (2 awards), 1975; Hugo Award, for novel, 1966, 1968, for story, 1976, 1982; Prix Apollo, 1972; American Library Association award, 1976; *Locus* award, 1984. Guest of Honor, 32nd World Science Fiction Convention, 1974, and Australian National Science Fiction Convention, 1978. Agent: Kirby McCauley Ltd., 425 Park Avenue South, New York, New York 10016. Address: 1045 Stagecoach Road, Santa Fe, New Mexico 87501, U.S.A.

SCIENCE-FICTION PUBLICATIONS

Novels (series: Amber)

This Immortal. New York, Ace, 1966; London, Hart Davis, 1967.
The Dream Master. New York, Ace, 1966; London, Hart Davis, 1968.
Lord of Light. New York, Doubleday, 1967; London, Faber, 1968.
Isle of the Dead. New York, Ace, 1969; London, Rapp and Whiting, 1970.
Creatures of Light and Darkness. New York, Doubleday, 1969; London, Faber, 1970.
Damnation Alley. New York, Putnam, 1969; London, Faber, 1971.
Nine Princes in Amber. New York, Doubleday, 1970; London, Faber, 1972.
Jack of Shadows. New York, Walker, 1971; London, Faber, 1973.
The Guns of Avalon (Amber). New York, Doubleday, 1972; London, Faber, 1974.
Today We Choose Faces. New York, New American Library, 1973; London, Millington, 1974.
To Die in Italbar. New York, Doubleday, 1973; London, Faber, 1975.
Sign of the Unicorn (Amber). New York, Doubleday, 1975; London, Faber, 1977.
Doorways in the Sand. New York, Harper, 1976; London, W. H. Allen, 1977.
The Hand of Oberon. New York, Doubleday, 1976; London, Faber, 1978.
Bridge of Ashes. New York, New American Library, 1976.
Deus Irae, with Philip K. Dick. New York, Doubleday, 1976; London, Gollancz, 1977.
The Courts of Chaos (Amber). New York, Doubleday, 1978; London, Faber, 1980.
The Chronicles of Amber (omnibus). New York, Doubleday, 2 vols., 1979.
Roadmarks. New York, Ballantine, 1979; London, Futura, 1981.
Coils, with Fred Saberhagen. New York, Tor, 1980.
The Changing Land. New York, Ballantine, 1981.
Eye of the Cat. New York, Pocket Books, 1982.
Dilvish, The Damned. New York, Ballantine, 1982.
Trumps of Doom (Amber). New York, Arbor House, 1985.

Short Stories

Four for Tomorrow. New York, Ace, 1967; as *A Rose for Ecclesiastes*, London, Hart Davis, 1969.
The Doors of His Face, The Lamps of His Mouth, and Other Stories. New York, Doubleday, 1971; London, Faber, 1973.

My Name Is Legion. New York, Ballantine, 1976; London, Faber, 1979.
The Last Defender of Camelot. New York, Pocket Books, 1980.
Unicorn Variations. New York, Pocket Books, 1983.

Uncollected Short Stories

"Conditional Benefits," in *Thurban I*, August-September 1953.
"Mr. Fuller's Revolt," in *Literary Cavalcade* (New York), October 1954.
"The Teachers Rode a Wheel of Fire," in *Fantastic* (New York), October 1962.
"Moonless in Byzantium," in *Amazing* (New York), December 1962.
"On the Road to Splenoba," in *Fantastic* (New York), January 1963.
"Final Dining," in *Fantastic* (New York), February 1963.
"The Borgia Hand," in *Amazing* (New York), March 1963.
"Nine Starships Waiting," in *Fantastic* (New York), March 1963.
"Circe Has Her Problems," in *Amazing* (New York), April 1963.
"Monologue for Two" (as Harrison Denmark) and "Threshold of the Prophet," in *Fantastic* (New York), May 1963.
"Mine Is the Kingdom" (as Harrison Denmark), in *Amazing* (New York), August 1963.
"The New Pleasure," in *Double: Bill*, August 1964.
"Passage to Dilfar," in *Fantastic* (New York), February 1965.
"Of Time and Yan," in *Fantasy and Science Fiction* (New York), June 1965.
"The Drawing," in *Algol* (New York), September 1965.
"The Injured," in *Kronos 2*, 1965.
"The House of the Hanged Man," in *Double: Bill*, September 1966.
"A Knight for Merytha," in *Kallikanzaros*, September 1967.
"He That Moves," in *If* (New York), January 1968.
"Stowaway," in *Odd*, Summer 1968.
"Song of the Blue Baboon," in *If* (New York), August 1968.
"The Last Inn on the Road," with Dannie Plachta, in *Rest SF Stories from New Worlds 5*, edited by Michael Moorcock. London, Panther, and New York, Berkley, 1969.
"The Year of the Good Seed," with Dannie Plachta, in *Galaxy* (New York), December 1969.
"Heritage," in *Cetacean 6* (Baltimore), 1969.
"King Solomon's Ring," in *On Our Way to the Future*, edited by Terry Carr. New York, Ace, 1970.
"The Man in the Corner of Now and Forever," in *Exile 7*, 1970.
"Come to Me Not in Winter's White," with Harlan Ellison, in *Partners in Wonder* by Ellison, New York, Walker, 1971.
"The Malatesta Collection," in *The Best from Fantastic*, edited by Ted White. New York, Manor, 1973; London, Hale, 1976.
"The Misfit," in *The Best from Amazing Stories*, edited by Ted White. New York, Manor, 1973; London, Hale, 1976.
"The Salvation of Faust," in *The Black Magic Omnibus*, edited by Peter Haining. New York, Taplinger, 1976.
"Thelinde's Song," in *Realms of Wizardry*, edited by Lin Carter. New York, Doubleday, 1976.
"Garden of Blood," in *Sorcerer's Apprentice* (New York), Summer 1979.
"The White Beast," in *Whispers* (Binghamton, New York), October 1979.
"The Devil and the Dancer," in *Chrysalis 10*, edited by Roy Torgeson. New York, Doubleday, 1983.
"Dayblood," in *Twilight Zone* (New York), June 1985.

OTHER PUBLICATIONS

Novels

The Bells of Shoredan. Columbia, Pennsylvania, Underwood Miller, 1979.
Changeling. New York, Ace, 1980.
Madwand. Huntingon Woods, Michigan, Phantasia Press, 1981.

Verse

Poems. N. p., Discon, 1974.
To Spin Is Miracle Cat. Columbia, Pennsylvania, Underwood Miller, 1982.

Other

"In Praise of His Spirits Noble and Otherwise," in *From the Land of Fear*, by Harlan Ellison. New York, Belmont, 1967.
The Authorized Illustrated Book of Roger Zelazny, illustrated by Gray Morrow. New York, Baronet, 1978.

Editor, *Nebula Award Stories 3*. New York, Doubleday, and London, Gollancz, 1968.

*

Bibliography: *Roger Zelazny: A Primary and Secondary Bibliography* by Joseph L. Sanders, Boston, Hall, 1980; *Amber Dreams: A Roger Zelazny Bibliography* by Daniel J. H. Levack, Columbia, Pennsylvania, Underwood Miller, 1983.

Manuscript Collections: George Arents Research Library, Syracuse University, New York; Special Collections, University of Maryland, Baltimore.

Critical Study: *A Reader's Guide to Roger Zelazny* by Carl B. Yoke, West Linn, Oregon, Starmont House, 1979.

Roger Zelazny comments:

My earlier writing involved considerable use of mythological materials. I have, however, attempted to diversify over the years. I write both fantasy and science fiction, as well as mixtures of the two. My objectives vary from book to book, but in general I begin with character in mind rather than plot. Among my personal favorites are the *Lord of Light* and *Doorways in the Sand*.

*   *   *

A writer who constantly challenges himself, Roger Zelazny is difficult to categorize. He has successfully written both fantasy and "hardcore" science fiction, his work has been both light and serious in tone, he is adept at all lengths, he has tackled most of the standard science-fiction themes. Even his style has changed since he published his first short story in 1962—from one that was highly mythic and richly poetic to one that is more controlled, economical, and precise. Yet despite the wide variation in tone, content, and style of his work, there are definite and consistent characteristics in his writing. Certain themes recur; certain kinds of character reappear. Perhaps it is in his characterization that the threads which link his works are most easily seen.

Zelazny's ability to create believable characters is probably his single most important contribution to science fiction. Even though his protagonists usually possess some ability or talent which makes them "larger-than-life," they remain entirely credible. They prize their self-reliance, personal integrity, and individualism. They must develop their own unique abilities and talents. And, since growth is a result of experience, the psychological growth of the characters is directly linked to their adventures. Frequently, Zelazny's stories begin with his protagonist disillusioned, alienated, or geographically isolated, and, whatever the circumstances, the specific conditions of his situation set him off on some kind of quest. In addition to attaining some physical objective, however, Zelazny's heroes are also set off unconsciously on a psychological quest—which is to achieve a metamorphosis of a personality, to raise their level of consciousness. If successful, this new maturity brings the disparate elements of their personalities into harmony, gives them a broader and deeper knowledge of themselves and the worlds in which they live, and creates the possibility for love. Of Zelazny's best works, the Amber novels, "A Rose for Ecclesiastes," and "The Doors of His Face, The Lamps of His Mouth" use protagonists who achieve metamorphosis in the course of the story, while *Lord of Light* and *This Immortal* tells stories which could not happen until after their protagonists have achieved this growth.

Zelazny's recurrent themes are integrally related to the psychological quests of his heroes. Vanity, greed, power, guilt, and revenge block metamorphosis and must be overcome before it can occur. Immortality permits a character to achieve a fuller realization of his capabilities. Zelazny recognizes that as long as a healthy person lives, psychological growth will continue. Love and fertility, in all their possible forms, are the positive benefits of metamorphosis. Self-reliance, personal integrity, and indivdualism are the keys to achieving it. Renewal, or restoration, which appears so frequently in Zelazny's stories, is an encompassing theme which signals both physical and psychological success.

Zelazny's most important works are the stories "A Rose for Ecclesiastes," "The Doors of His Face, The Lamps of His Mouth," and "Home Is the Hangman" and the novels *This Immortal, The Dream Master, Lord of Light,* and the five Amber books. "A Rose for Ecclesiastes" and "The Doors of His Face, The Lamps of His Mouth" are renewal stories, and both Gallinger, the conceited Earth poet, and Carlton Davits, the bankrupt baitman, must overcome their vanity in order to achieve personality metamorphosis. Each does, and in the process Gallinger saves the Martians from racial suicide and restores fertility to the planet, whilst Davits brings both his and his ex-wife's personalities into harmony and creates a healthy relationship. "Home Is the Hangman," one of Zelazny's "no-name detective" stories, presents a unique twist on the metamorphosis motif. In it, the Hangman, a combination telefactor and computer, returns to Earth after many years in space to show its teachers that it has overcome the neurosis they created for it. The anthropomorphic machine has successfully integrated the elements of its personality, while, ironically, one of its teachers, Jessie Brockden, is so overpowered by guilt that he believes that the machine has returned to kill him.

This immortal presents a protagonist, Conrad Nomikos, who has already achieved maturity by the time the story begins, so the focus of the story shifts from achieving metamorphosis to the role of the hero in restoring the irradiated Earth. A revolutionary group believes that the Vegans, a superior alien culture, are about to begin a wholesale exploitation of the planet, when in truth they are testing Conrad's worth to inherit and subsequently restore it.

The Dream Master presents the only instance in Zelazny's writing where a protagonist fails to achieve metamorphosis. Because his particular personality fault, once again pride, continues to dominate, Dr. Charles Render, a neuroparticipation therapist, is ultimately drawn into the madness of one of his patients. His vanity has prevented him from seeing the limits of his abilities. In one of Zelazny's more interesting attempts to expand a novel through the use of myth, he links Render to the Scandinavian *ragnarok* and Eileen, his patient, to Arthurian legend. The *ragnarok* represents Render's view of the world and signifies the psychologically deterministic course of his life. The Arthurian material characterizes Eileen's chivalric and highly idealized view of the world. Though the concept is ingenious, the use of symbolic mythic sequences tends to confuse meaning for the perceptive reader rather than clarify it. In addition to illustrating the dangers inherent in allusion, it also illustrates the danger of assuming that Zelazny is attempting to translate whole bodies of myth into science fiction.

Lord of Light, undoubtedly Zelazny's best novel, also treats renewal—in this case the renewal of a society. By the time the story begins, Sam, the Protagonist, has long since passed on to a higher state of consciousness. The world of Urath is ruled by colonists who have virtually become gods. They patterned the new after the Hindu culture that they left behind on Earth, and they have achieved virtual immortality because they have the technology for body transfer. Unfortunately, their power has corrupted them. They exploit the masses, their own descendants, and refuse to let them share their technological benefits. Society is repressive and stagnant, and Sam sets out to change it. Of course, he accomplishes his reform mission.

The Amber novels treat both the physical and psychological sides of renewal—the restoration of the land and the metamorphosis of personality. Corwin, the protagonist, journeys from youthful and romantic idealism to pragmatism in the course of his adventures to keep his universe from being absorbed back into chaos. In the process, he learns that the most important reason for living is psychologically healthy human relationships. A dramatization of Zelazny's form and chaos philosophy, the Amber novels also show how man should relate to the basic forces of the universe.

The Amber novels are not only a major fantasy work, they are also an excellent window on Zelazny's capabilities. Criticized by some who feel that he has not achieved the stature projected for him when he broke into science fiction more than 15 years ago, Zelazny has perhaps more than any other writer brought the techniques, style, and language of serious literature to the field. There can be no question of his stature, for he has written several major works, but his greatest contribution may in the end prove to be that he has brought characters who are psychologically credible, who are sympathetic, who have depth and scope, to a literature famous for its cardboard figures.

Zelazny's most recent stories display two interesting lines of development. First, in *Changeling, Madwand,* and *Eye of Cat,* he consciously uses Jungian images and concepts to shape his stories, much as he did in "The Doors of His Face, The Lamps of His Mouth. " Such usage reinforces the renewal theme, which pervades his work and which is evident in these stories, especially in terms of the personality growth of his characters. This technique is very similar to what he did in his early writing with mythology.

Second, his most recent work clearly leans toward fantasy, but it is fantasy that has been hedged. By that I mean that he takes great care to treat the worlds of these new stories as if they were simply governed by physical laws different from our own. Magic, supernatural events, and other motifs and devices usually unexplained in fantasy are handled as if they were a normal part of some other reality in these worlds. In *Changeling* and *Madwand,* for instance, magic is a skill. There are different forms of it, there are rules to govern its use, and there are various degrees of adeptness in its practice. In short, Zelazny provides means for his characters to tap into and use the basic forces that govern their story worlds. Though these forces are different from our own, he implies that lying beneath both sets is something common. In this work, Zelazny is probing the question of reality and offering up different scenarios as possibilities. I suspect that his concern for verisimilitude is prompted by his reading about the chaotic, illogical, and irrational world of sub-atomic physics and his longtime interst in the Quabalah.

The questions of different realities is one with which he has flirted in the past. The Amber novels end, for example, with Corwin inscribing a new universe, one which may incorporate entirely new physical laws. *The Changing Land,* too, ends with a castle passing through the end of time to a new creation. And while *Trumps of Doom,* which re-opens the Amber series with a new story line focusing on Merlin, is too busy charting a course to map out how this second set of novels will probe the question of reality, it does provide a perfect opportunity to deal with it by raising the issue of Corwin's whereabouts.

While Zelazny's ultimate intention may be nothing more than providing us with a series of imagined alternatives, evidence indicates that he will continue to probe the question of reality in his future work.

—Carl B. Yoke

ZETFORD, Tully. See BULMER, Kenneth.

FOREIGN-LANGUAGE
WRITERS

ABE, Kobo (1924—). Japanese. *Inter Ice Age 4*, 1970.

* * *

Science fiction is but a small part of Kobo Abe's work, though his creations in other genres have tinges of science-fiction character. He is, however, regarded in Japan as a major literary figure mainly because of his plays.

As a medical school graduate, Abe has the technical knowledge for outstanding work in science fiction. Also relevant is his creation of psychological novels in the 1960's, as well as his propensity for experimental literary work, combining his familiarity with European 20th-century trends with the characteristic Japanese mindfulness of indigenous cultural tradition. One important example of this is the mask, for centuries a major resource of Japanese drama. His novel *Tanin no kao* (The Face of Another) is scarcely science fiction, but has technological content, the methods by which a realistic mask is substituted for a horribly disfigured face. Here the hero compares himself to the monsters of television, and the film is replete with the organ-filled laboratories of the Frankenstein tradition.

The greatest science-fiction work of Abe is *Inter Ice Age 4* in which the forthcoming inundation of the Earth by melting polar ice caps is to be dealt with by modifying human embryos to produce gill-breathers. Very important in predicting the disaster here is computer technology, and we are told that the computers have also discerned Communism as the shape of things to come. However, says a leading character, Communism *would* fit the predictions of a machine; it neglects free will. The computers are also described as scanning a human mind completely, then engaging in dialogue with the "individual" stored in their data banks. When this dialogue with the "data bank ghost" is extended even to the mind of a newly dead person, one sees an old Japanese concept in action (the 11th-century novel *Tale of Genji*, as well as the modern film *Rashomon*). Abe's philosophy of present-future relationships is especially significant. *Inter Ice Age 4* comments that "The future is not to be judged by us," but rather it "sits in judgment on the present." It gives a verdict of guilty, says Abe, and the people of the present, confident in the continuity of their microcosm, are to be scorned. This author's vision may have been enhanced by a sense of alienation from his immediate present. Also monumental in his work is an eager confrontation with the great borderlines between life and death, between illusion and reality, and between the inner and outer worlds of human beings.

—Frank H. Tucker

ANDREVON, Jean-Pierre (1937—). French. "Observation of Quadragnes," in *View from Another Shore*, edited by Franz Rottensteiner, 1973; "The Time of the Big Sleep," in *A Shocking Thing*, edited by Damon Knight, 1974.

* * *

Jean-Pierre Andrevon is perhaps the best-known French SF writer, though he became a professional fairly late (31). He quickly became the most prolific contributor to the main Parisian SF monthly, *Fiction*, both as a critic and short-story writer, introducing political views in both fields, to the delight of progressive readers and the (very vocal) fury of the more conventional ones. He was one of the first to explode the taboos of sex ("Observation of Quadragnes") as well as death (*Le*

Reflux de la Nuit), to strip the glamour from war on the earth ("Retour à Broux") as well as in space (*La Guerre des Gruulls*), and to denounce the excesses of technology. In his anthologies —the 3 volumes of *Retour à la Terre* (whose title clearly express the intention of re-focussing SF on the problems of our world), the 2 volumes of *Compagnons en Terre Etrangère* — he rallied round him a whole school of young writers who shared his preoccupation with imminent perils (pollution, overpopulation, the misuse of nuclear energy, social and international conflicts).

Andrevon should not, however, be considered as a pure son of the protest movement of 1968: contrary to many of his followers who tended to reduce their SF to ideological tracts, and whose readership consequently dwindled very fast, he never forgot that he was expected to tell stories, and to tell them well. In his first novel, *Les Hommes-Machines contre Gandahar*— a sort of *Great Dictator* of the future, with a strange time-controlling creature thrown in as game-master — the libertarian message and the appeal of mystery and adventure were already cleverly blended. Putting to use both his sense of everyday dialogue (to the inclusion of slang and vulgarisms) and the eye of the painter that he also is, he unites truly poetic visions with the most implacable realism, which he sometimes tempers with fantasy and humour, as in *L'Immeuble d'en face* and *Hôpital Nord* (both recently published in collaboration with Philippe Cousin, a disciple with a strong personality of his own).

Though he has kept exploring his main obsessions (death and sex in *Il Faudra Bien Se Résoudre à Mourir Seul*) and concerns (the follies of mankind and the endangered future of the planet in *Paysages de Mort* and *Dans les Décors Truqués*; more particularly the nuclear peril in *Neutron*), Andrevon has achieved a great diversity of themes and approaches: his latest anthology, *L'Oreille contre les Murs*, is an attempt to launch a modern fantastic school; *Le Travail du Furet à l'Intérieur du Poulailler*, though about overpopulation, is in the form a thriller; *Le Désert du Monde* and *Cauchemar . . . Cauchemars* have something of Philip K. Dick's interplay of reality and Illusion; *La Fée et le Géomètre* shows that writing for young people does not entail self-censorship of one's convictions.

The latter book is indeed one of Andrevon's finest expressions of his ideology, which has shifted from Trotskyist marxism to ecology — harmony between various social groups being now subject in his opinion to saner relationships between man and his environment. The main short-coming that he has been reproached with is that, because of the huge gap between his views of the ideal future and the present evils he denounces, he has failed to imagine any acceptable transition: in his novel *Le Temps des Grandes Chasses* an idyllic society emerges only after world-wide disaster; and in *Le Monde Enfin* our planet finds beauty and balance again at the cost of . . . the disappearance of humanity!

Yet, by the abundance and variety of his production, his rich characterization, and the wide resources of his style as well as by the warning function he often gives his fiction, Andrevon's stature in French SF can be compared to John Brunner's in Britain.

—George W. Barlow

BARJAVEL, René (1911—). French. *Ashes, Ashes*, 1967; *Future Times Three*, 1970; *The Ice People*, 1970; *The Immortals*, 1974.

* * *

René Barjavel's science-fiction work contrasts pastoral utopias full of love with war-torn dystopias full of distrust. Although *Le Diable l'Emporte, Colomb de la Lune*, and *L'Homme Forte* have not been translated, *Ashes, Ashes, Future Times Three, The Ice People*, and *The Immortals*, available in English, are passionately anti-war, erotic, and satiric, relating vividly penned horrors and sentimental romance.

Although Barjavel is a screenwriter, journalist, and writer of romantic novels, *Future Times Three* is typical science fiction, dealing with the paradoxes and dangers of time travel. Playful escapades in the near future and malicious forays into the 19th century echo Wells's *Invisible Man*, and the specialized races of 100,000 A.D. follow Stapledon. Exploring the future, mathematician and physicist brood over questions of God and causality. This episodic novel declares — like Faust — that man cannot safely extend beyond God.

In traveling to 2052, St. Menoux learns the fate of the survivors of *Ashes, Ashes*, in which some inexplicable sunspot phenomenon cuts off electricity and the world goes mad. Fire and bloodshed purge a decadent technological society on the verge of all-out war. As in the earlier novel, the pure love of two young people provides hope. The heroes, however, are ruthless killers who fight their way into the country to found a pastoral society where books and inventions are forbidden.

One of the numerous Swiftian sallies of *Ashes, Ashes* explains the system of freezing ancestors. In *The Ice People* South Pole explorers find two gorgeous bodies from 900,000 years earlier, obviously remnants of a vastly advanced society destroyed by atomic holocaust. Unfrozen, Elea transmits her memories of her perfect love with Paikan and her selection as the mate to be preserved for the mastermind, Coban. This Romeo and Juliet tale is set against political turmoil of past and present. Only a coalition of scientists and students might save the world, though Elea and Paikan are destroyed.

Using the actual backdrop and leaders of his own time, *The Immortals* examines the frightening long-range political effects of a drug that defeat death and disease. Since immortality is contagious, all those involved in research have been isolated on an Aleutian paradise. They are, however, human time bombs doomed to annihilation by world powers when scientists learn there is nowhere for man in space. Although pessimistic, Barjavel didactically asserts the values of love and peace.

—Mary S. Weinkauf

BELYAEV, Aleksandr (1884-1942). Russian. *The Amphibian*, n.d.; *The Struggle in Space*, 1965; *Professor Dowell's Head*, 1980.

* * *

Aleksandr Belyaev's first SF stories were published in adventure journals in 1925 and his first book in 1926. He wrote about 30 SF stories, about 20 novels, and a dozen articles or prefaces (e.g., to Jack London's novels) which make of him the first penetrating Russian SF critic. He used the breathtaking Vernean adventure plot or the current detective-thriller-SF (from Wells, London, Renard, Burroughs or A. Tolstoy) with an isolated and romantically alienated hero, either a scientist with humanistic ideals, a biologically modified man who is a naive child of nature (Ichthyander in his most popular novel, *The Amphibian Man*, or Ariel in the novel of the same title), or quite openly an artist (such as Presto in the two variant novels *The Man Who Lost His Face* and *The Man Who Found His Face*). This bearer of the novum and of the desire for freedom is opposed to and hounded by the cruel power of wicked scientists and financiers; most interestingly, he is at the center of an extreme situation or novum validated by a bold scientific technique. This is usually biological adaptation, including the changing use of the senses, and, most prominently, a sundering of brain from body as in *Professor Dowell's Head* (much superior to Renard's *New Bodies for Old*) or various, often humorous and folktale-like, scientific inventions in the "Professor Wagner" cycle. Such works are imbued with an aching lyricism and a vibrant humanistic vehemence. But often Belyaev's hero triumphs thanks to an essentially fairytale metamorphosis that allows him to vanquish physical gravity and social injustice. The black-and-white opposition of his threatened hero to a grotesque capitalist environment becomes then a form of escapism into a wicked Ruritania.

In the late 1920's and early 1930's Belyaev's SF was interrupted by a campaign against the genre. From 1934 he largely shifted his focus to short-range technological anticipation and (more interestingly) to interplanetary work and struggles, domesticating the notions of Tsiolkovsky and early Soviet rocket experimenters. For all his shortcomings, Belyaev's basic concern with human metamorphosis striving for freedom and the external resistance and inner anxieties it provokes have not only made of him at least the equal of any interwar German, French, or US SF writer, and a lasting influence in Russia, but also an author who remains of interest today.

—Darko Suvin

BORGES, Jorge Luis (1899—). Argentine. *Ficciones*, 1962; *Labyrinths*, 1962; *The Aleph and Other Stories 1933-1969*, 1970; *The Book of Sand*, 1977.

* * *

Jorge Luis Borges has been called "the greatest living writer in the Spanish language today." His literary achievements secured him a post as director of the Argentine National Library in 1955, though blindness obliged him to retire in 1973.

Primarily a miniaturist and poet, Borges has been attracted throughout his long career by themes which transcend our normal reality, and many of his short stories are frankly science-fictional. In "Tlön, Uqbar, Orbis Tertius" he describes how our Earth is gradually being taken over by another, invented version of the world. His pitiable title character in "Funes the Memorious" is endowed with a memory which will not permit him to forget anything, yet this talent cripples him as a person. "Dr. Brodie's Report" gives an account of a visit to an imaginary African tribe halfway between apes and humans, who possess a religion, the concept of poetry, and a rudimentary ability to foretell the future. "The Aleph" is a point within which the whole world, past and future, can be seen. "The Zahir" is a satirical variation on a similar motif: an object which obsesses its beholder, sometimes a man or a tiger, but at present a common coin. Paradoxes connected with infinity abound in Borges's work, for instance, in *The Library of Babel*, which is an endless store of incomprehensible books, and *The Book of Sand*, which appears to be a sort of scripture, but contains literally countless leaves. He has also long been fascinated by fabulous animals, and indeed devoted an entire volume to the subject, a sort of bestiary of the nonexistent: *The Book of Imaginary Beings* (with Margarita Guerrero).

It is known that Borges has occasionally been influenced by authors of SF or near-SF, including Poe and Lovecraft; in turn his elegant economy of style and his ability to compress long complex arguments into a few pages have earned him the admiration of many younger SF writers, who not infrequently imitate him, though with scant success.

—John Brunner

BOULLE, Pierre (1912—). French. *Planet of the Apes*, 1963 (as *The Monkey Planet*, 1964); *Garden on the Moon*, 1964; *Time Out of Mind and Other Stories*, 1966; *Because It Is Absurd* (stories), 1971; *Desperate Games*, 1973; *The Marvellous Palace and Other Stories*, 1977; *The Good Leviathan*, 1979; *The Whale of the Victoria Cross*, 1983.

* * *

Like the venerable minister-priest of the Religion of Doubt who is the narrator of the six "*histoires perides*" that make up *The Marvelous Palace and Other Stories*, Pierre Boulle has viewed his main function throughout his prolific and varied career as his duty "to arouse curiosity by the prospect of an enigma." In Boulle's wryly laconic fables, the enigmatic takes many forms: in *The Good Leviathan*, an oil supertanker capable of miraculous cures; in *The Whale of the Victoria Cross*, another kind of good leviathan, one that sacrifices itself to save its friends on the British fleet during the Falklands conflict; in "The Heart of the Galaxy" (*Because It Is Absurd*), a message from the stars, engendered by an immense expenditure of energy, which— much to the consternation of the scientists on earth who decipher it— turns out to be an advertising slogan; in *Desperate Games* a world government of Nobel Prize-winning scientists who cure all of mankind's social ills but must devise destructive war games to prevent the universal ennui that sets in when man is left with nothing to struggle against. Boulle's style is too arch and his stance too knowing for his science-fiction tales to be called cautionary, just as his espionage stories set in the Far East are too coolly ironic to be labeled merely escapist thrillers: even a casual reader must have anticipated that the astronaut escaping from *Planet of the Apes*— undoubtedly Boulle's best-known SF work and the basis for the popular film series— was returning to an Earth in which a similar evolutionary movement had taken its inevitable course.

Most recently, Boulle's double-edged, deadpan observance of man's social and political foibles has even taken him to the Throne of Heaven itself. When Boulle, in *Trouble in Paradise*, has the Virgin Mary coming back to Earth to help patch up a quarrel between the bickering members of the Holy Trinity, only to become a media celebrity and prime minister of France, her eventual triumphant ascension back to Paradise as Supreme Goddess could be construed as either a pro- or anti-feminist statement. In all of Boulle's work, however, the tone may be cynical or obscure but it is rarely morose, since Boulle remains detached from the delusions, vanities, and follies of technocratic man confronting the remorselessness of an implacable Nature and the unchangingness of his own proud and enigmatic heart.

—Kenneth Jurkiewicz

BOYE, Karin (1900-41). Swedish. *Kallocain*, 1966.

* * *

Karin Boye was a distinguished Swedish poet and a disciple of the radical French pacifist Henri Barbusse. She committed suicide a year after the publication of *Kallocain* in 1940. She was one of those intellectuals horrified by the rise of Nazism, and she returned disappointed from a journey to the Soviet Union, a country she had considered a hope for the future. Her anxieties and her experiences with Nazism and Stalinism are clearly reflected in her novel, one of the few dystopias written by a woman. Her work uncannily anticipates many of the black features that Orwell made known in *Nineteen Eighty-Four*, in particular the total surveillance of citizens by spy-lenses in their private homes, the concept of a thought police and thought crime, and the thoroughgoing division of the world into (two) big states which are so antagonistic to each other that they deny their enemy the common human ancestry. Leo Kall, a chemist and inventor of the epynomous truth serum Kallocain, is a citizen of the "world state" in the 21st century— a "fellow soldier," for the country's organization is thoroughly militaristic. The police are omnipresent, and citizens are urged to denounce their friends and relatives and to join in communal "hate sessions." The fear of spies is so great that even simple geographical data are treated as secrets of state. Leo Kall is deeply distrustful of his immediate superior Edo Rissen, one of the few human beings who have kept their individualism, and he suspects that his wife is unfaithful to him. Knowing very well that under the influence of his new drug all are equally guilty, Kall decides to attack and to denounce Rissen, who is promptly sentenced. In the end the "world state" is invaded by the "universal state," which is, we may assume, different only by name, and Kall serves his new masters with equal zeal. The psychological conflicts of the hero are depicted powerfully, and the novel reflects a deep fear of the rise of totalitarianism and an all-powerful state that inexorably crushes the individual.

—Franz Rottensteiner

BRAUN, Johanna (1929—), and **Günter** (1928—). East German. *The Great Magician's Error*, 1972; *Uncanny Phenomena on Omega 11*, 1974; *The Mistake Factor* (stories), 1975; *Conviva Ludibundus*, 1978; *The Utofant: A Periodical from the Third Millennium Found in the Future*, 1981; *The Spherico-Transcendental Design*, 1983; *The Inaudible Sounds*, 1984.

* * *

Johanna and Günter Braun, a married couple, were newspaper reporters and editors before they turned free-lance writers. They published 9 juvenile adventures, historical novels, TV plays, and experimental prose such as *Eve and the New Adam* touching on equal rights for women and sparking off much public discussion. At the beginning of the 1960's they entered into full possession of their narrative voice— ironical, lyrically oriented toward characterization rather than plot, and strongly concerned with the integrity of people enmeshed into politics and economics. *An Objective Angel*, for instance, deals with the societal and personal implications of modern technology in contemporary East Germany. In the 1970's they published four SF books.

The Great Magician's Error, a juvenile novel, is a folktale-like parable on a country ruled by a Magician whose power is founded on the soporific effects of a special pear, in its natural state both inebriating and stimulating. Helped by a snake-like girl, the young hero, drawn to pranks and interesting knowledge rather than obedience, manages to defeat the despotic rule, in an analogy to Stalinism's rule and fall. In their collection of stories, *The Mistake Factor*, the central conflict is between critical socialist humanism and technocratic self-satisfaction. The collection contains at least three small masterpieces. In "Choosing Astronauts" the earthy and quirky independence of Merkur and Elektra (heroes of the second novel) amounts to an *exemplum* not only for the fitness of astronauts but of people in general to cohabit. "The Jingling of Caesar's Cowbells," told by an involved narrator changing her opinion, is a tour de force of economy and clarity, successfully blending the East European "production tale" with understated sexiness and graceful wit. Best of all is the title story: in a utopian future the narrator is sent to investigate the malfunctioning of the central computer. The setting is an inertia-inducing centre near the Bertolt Brecht Lake with rejuvenating qualities, and the story opposes the rejuvenation associated with a critical and anti-bureaucratic marxism to the huge but tired technocracy which concealed the malfunctioning because the machine had become a soothing idol.

In the second novel, *Uncanny Phenomena on Omega 11*, the erotic and cognitive interplay between the playful Merkur and the serious Elektra, from grudging mutual acceptance through connubial bliss and the ups and downs of team-work to final growing apart, possesses a gentle power. The adventure-puzzle on a foreign planet with a treacherous exploiting race, whom our heroes circumvent by brain not brawn, suggests the uses of playfulness fused with work as antidote to class isolation and specialization. *Conviva Ludibundus* is named after a marine bio-electronic life-form which is the indispensable link in the production of a mussel containing all the nutrients necessary for a future humanity. Instead of the gardener-like encouragement by the narrator, the Conviva is subjected to rationalization and enclosures by his successor, a typical hardworking, unimaginative, upwardly mobile, pompous scientist. His hunt for the Conviva in a super-technological Vernean vehicle manages, by misusing scraps of knowledge, to turn it for a time into the producer of uneatable giant mussels and of unnecessary data from the seabed. A global catastrophe is only averted by the narrator's girlfriend who unwittingly deprograms the Conviva (a one-celled being which can come together in many shapes) by leading it into mobile self-constructs and aquatic ballet. This key scene of the novel is not unworthy of comparison with some of Lem's *Solaris*. The upshot is that art is the only antidote to elitist power and technocratic breakdown: a darker and weightier conclusion in a text with a more powerful antagonist, putting up stronger obstacles to utopian ethics. But the satire remains accompanied by comedy and wit, by the constant disrespectful and funny inversion of received authority.

In the 1980's, the Brauns have, keeping to their constant horizons, become more embattled, faced with what they perceive as a stronger bureaucratic or "cold current" in the GDR (East Germany). Among other things, they have left the official GDR Union of Writers. This attitude, and the attendant pragmatic pressures on them as free-lance writers, has resulted in a genre diversification of their writings. Outside of SF this has led to some brilliant works of travelog, Hoffmannesque fantasy, essays, a fictional biography of Socrates as parable on the difficulties of an independent and disrespectful thinker, and even a book of witty culinary recipes crossbred with erotics. In SF, the result has been a number of short stories published in various East and West German anthologies, and the books *The Utofant: A Periodical from the Third Millennium Found in the Future* (1981), *The Spherico-Transcendental Design* (1983), and *The Inaudible Sounds* (1984)— the two latter, just as the Socrates book, published only in West Germany. These are more fragmentary and as a rule briefer than their earlier writings, but just as elegant and ironical. Thus, increasingly dark and forlorn, the Brauns' playful cognizing is part of the "warm current" in socialism, colliding with the cold one. Their artful manipulation of narrative voices, their commitment to the feminine principle amusingly associated with sexual emotions, productive self-management, and critical intelligence place them at the pivot of East German SF, and on the map of the best world SF.

—Darko Suvin

BRYUSOV, Valery (1873-1924). Russian. *The Republic of the Southern Cross and Other Stories*, 1918.

* * *

Valery Bryusov, from a rich merchant family, became a leader of Russian Symbolist poetry, publishing a dozen books of formidably erudite and polished verse, as well as stories, plays, brilliant verse translations from many languages (including the complete poetry of Poe), and interesting criticism of poetry. His esoteric disdain for the multitude changed after the 1904-05 revolution into a growing acceptance of social responsibility and sympathy for the revolutionary destruction of the "ugly and shameful" capitalist order. He thus became one of the few prominent non-Marxists to take an active part in Soviet cultural life, and in 1920 even joined the communist party.

Bryusov had a long-standing interest in a "scientific poetry" akin to SF. Two of his major preoccupations were more obviously SF. From the 1890's he was haunted by the fall of world civilization, envisioned as a giant symbolic city. In his play *Youth* (1904) a revolt of youth shatters the glass dome that bars the city from sunshine and open space; the revolt both seeks liberation and exposes the city to the risk of death (see also his story "The Last Martyrs"). Written after the defeat of the 1905 revolution, his Poesque story "The Republic of the Southern Cross" is frankly dystopian: an enclosed industrial city on the South Pole falls prey to an epidemic leading the afflicted to do the opposite from what they wish to do; a resolute bourgeois minority fighting for order is overwhelmed by the brutalized inhabitants. Raskolnikov's dream at the end of *Crime and Punishment* blends here with a parable on the great social convulsions of our century. Bryusov's second SF theme is one of cosmic contacts, treated both in his poetry and in a number of unfinished stories and plays, and influenced by the utopian philosopher Fyodorov and his disciple Tsiolkovsky, by Poe, Wells, and most of all Flammarion; as in this last writer such contacts often involved a cometary world. His old theme of catastrophe and a distant presentiment of a possible new world lent themselves well to the widespread post-1917 equation of the social revolution with man's leap into interplanetary space. Bryusov thus became the link between, on the one hand, the tradition of Russian utopianism, 19th-century European SF, and philosophic speculation leading from Leibniz to Spengler, and, on the other, early Soviet "Cosmist" poetry and SF. Bryusov's peculiar double horizon, embracing both dystopia and utopia is his greatest strength: he clearly managed to influence both Zamyatin and Mayakovsky, and, through them as well as directly, most prewar Russian SF.

—Darko Suvin

BULGAKOV, Mikhail (1891-1940). Russian. *Heart of a Dog*, 1968; *Diaboliad and Other Stories*, 1972.

* * *

"The stars will remain when the shadows of our presence and our deeds have vanished from the eath. There is no man who does not know that. Why, then, will we not turn our eyes towards the stars?" This is the leitmotiv of Mikhail Bulgakov's science fiction: the nature of a true relationship between a Kantian universe and a human existence of thought and action.

Bulgakov's early science-fiction stories established an allegoric parallel between scientific discovery and social revolution, using every technique from slapstick comedy to black humor and horror, to show the absurdity and danger of trying to impose human purposes on reality. In "The Fatal Eggs" (*Diaboliad*), based on H.G. Wells's *The Food of the Gods*, mammoth artificially hatched serpents almost devour Moscow. In "The Crimson Island"— "Jules Verne translated into Aesopian"— an involuted rebellion results in nothing but a drunken revel and a telegram to the West: "Go (indecipherable) your (indecipherable) mother."

The novella *Heart of a Dog* exhibits Bulgakov's characteristic literary method: a fantastic realism that is a combination of grotesque action and a naturalistic background, with a satiric intent, serving a philosophical idea. It concerns a Moscow professor who transforms a dog into a man in a rejuvenation experiment. The identification of professor and Lenin, rejuvenation and revolution is implicit. Within a week, the new creation has a vocabulary of "every known Russian swearword"; he can't button his fly, eats toothpaste, and has fleas: he is immediately made a Commissar. His mature virtues include greed, viciousness, and "cosmic stupidity." Disgusted, the professor curses the attempt to substitute the artificial for the authentic, whether dog for man or dogma for life, and reverses the experiment.

Bulgakov's science-fiction plays range from burlesque to near-tragedy, but all deal with the ontological theme. In *Bliss* a wondrous future utopia is revealed to be inadequate and boring compared to the mystery of reality and the adventure of living. In *Ivan Vasilievich* Ivan the Terrible's farcical misadventures in modern Moscow revolve around a confusion of definitions and roles with actualities. The best of the type, however, both in character development and seriousness of thought, is the tragicomedy *Adam and Eve*. In a war-devastated Leningrad, a few surviving men and one woman must choose between reality and ideology, represented by the pacifist Yefrosimov, whose anti-gas invention saved them, and Adam Krasovsky, who wants to risk annihilation for the sake of Communism. In the end, Eve chooses Yefrosimov for her mate because, as she tells Adam, "the forest and the singing of the birds, and the rainbow, this is real, but you with your frenzied cries are unreal."

The Master and Margarita is Bulgakov's masterpiece of indefinable genre and indeterminate meaning, wherein Satan visits Moscow, punishing evil, driving rationalists insane, and "putting the fear of God" into atheists. In it, the science-fiction theme converges with all of Bulgakov's other themes, styles, and techniques, and is fully realized. In *The Master and Margarita* reality is infinite, eternal, and transcendent; time and space are relative; man is immortal. Living according to the demands of universal truth is a moral duty for which man is held accountable. "Cowardice is the worst sin of all" for a character like Pontius Pilate whose "mind is too closed" and whose life is too cramped." Yet man's denial and betrayal of reality cannot alter it. "All will be as it should," the devil promises; "that is how the world is made."

By his science-fiction model of a surreal method to present a multi-dimensional universe, and by the example of his artistic courage, Bulgakov obliged Russian writers to contemplate "the shadows of man's presence" from the perspective of the stars and therefore "to a complete truth of thought and word."

—Jana I. Tuzar

BUZZATI, Dino (1906-72). Italian. *Larger Than Life*, 1962; *Catastrophe* (stories), 1965.

* * *

Although Dino Buzzati became first widely known with his novel *The Tartar Steppe* (1940), his real strength is in his short stories, concise, absurd, wonderful fables and parables of modern existence, often fantasies. Buzzati has frequently been compared to Kafka, and although there is a certain similarity in the mysteries both writers touch upon, their differences are quite marked, both in style and rhythm and their manner of story-telling.

Actually, Buzzati is much more a fantasist than Kafka, showing the influences of E.T.A. Hoffmann and Gogol, as well as of fairy and folk tales. Often his stories are allegorical. This is marked in his brief novel *The Secret of the Old Forest* which revolves around the conflict between nature and civilization; the spirits of an old forest, untouched by human hands for centuries, wage a war against the greedy owner who starts exploiting the old trees. The absurdity of existence and the vanity of human ambitions is the subject of Buzzati's best novel, *The Tartar Steppe*. Isolated in a lonely fortress at the border of a big desert, engaging in senseless military drill, the commander of the small forces garrisoned in the fort spends his whole life waiting for an invasion that never comes, and when rumors seem to indicate that the dreaded onslaught of the Tartars may come, he is already an old man, falls ill and dies. An obsessive concern with military duties and a senseless waiting for an event that may never come, is turned into parable of the futility of human existence when all aspirations for transcendent meaning are destroyed by accidental death. Compared to this puzzling and disturbing novel, Buzzati's only SF novel proper, *Larger Than Life*, is an uninspired computer story; a big computer is programmed with the personality of a woman, and this mawkish story is not better than countless other SF novels of big computers.

Generally, Buzzati's few genuine SF stories tend to be weak and unoriginal, lacking the power of his fantastic stories. There are a few tales of time travel, the atomic bomb, the end of the world, and flying saucers. Much more impressive are his stories that blend the everyday and the fantastic in an intricate, inseparable manner, and are told with the economy and eye for factual details of the journalist that Buzzati was. Buzzati declared: " . . .fantasy should be as close as possible to journalism. The right word is not 'banalising,' although in fact a little of this is involved. Rather, I mean that the effectiveness of a fantastic story will depend on its being told in the most simple and practical terms." Something that would have been applauded by Edmund Wilson. By quite simple means, in elegantly turned stories, Buzzati manages to convey alternatively a sense of wonder, horror, the absurdity of existence, the bewildering complexity of modern society, and the inexplicable workings of fate. Strive as they might, his characters have a particular destiny waiting for them from which they cannot escape. Often their whole efforts prove to be in vain, and a long wait or a long search turns out ultimately to be a waste of their lives, as in "The Colomber" or "The Walls of Anagoor." Buzzati's most impressive story is probably "The Slaying of the Dragon"— the story of a hunt for a murderous monster, turned upside down. There the human hunters show only base motives, vanity and greed, while the dragon alone exhibits courage, compassion, and dignity. "Seven Floors" is another parable of modern existence, the story of a hospital, which the patients enter in perfectly good health at the seventh floor, and are gradually moved down to the basement where they arrive terminally ill.

Buzzati's stories are characterized by a search for meaning; they express the existential fears of modern man and interpret the anxieties of modern civilization, explore the labyrinthic existence of cities and the threats of machinery. Their dreamlike mood is often underpinned by an ironical sense of humor and they exhibit a deep feeling for their fellow-sufferers. They show the absurdity of existence, but the hope for salvation is nevertheless a redeeming feature in them; for all their sometimes ferocious criticism of human beings they do not condemn but leave open an avenue of hope.

—Franz Rottensteiner

CALVINO, Italo (1923-1985). Italian. *Cosmicomics* (stories), 1968; *T Zero*, 1969 (as *Time and the Hunter*, 1970); *The Watchers and Other Stories*, 1971; *Invisible Cities*, 1974; *The Castle of Crossed Destinies*, 1977.

*   *   *

Italo Calvino is perhaps better known as a writer of fantasy/surreal/experimental fiction than as the creator of science fiction. Yet at some points these two branches of fiction intersect with interesting results. His first science-fiction work, *Cosmicomics*, considers the origin of the universe, the development of life, and the advance of human consciousness and technology— all from the perspective of the "cell/narrator," Qfwfq, who has been present as an observer in one form or another from the beginning of time. This collection of vignettes pre-dates Douglas Adams's *Hitchhiker's Guide to the Galaxy* by many years and takes the same wry perspective on the struggle to survive on the planet Earth and in the universe. Calvino uses the science-fiction format as his vehicle for observing human foibles, in much the same way that any writer of science fiction places "human" protagonists in alternate universes and times to explore how any creature, human or otherwise, handles challenges.

T Zero considers the meaning of time, space, motion, and values. In this episodic series Calvino investigates such

polarities as unity and multiplicity, past and present, chaos and order, probability and certainty. As in most of his work, Calvino experiments as much with narrative form as an expression of observed "reality" as he does with creating entertaining characters and plots.

Calvino also makes use of arcane subjects in order to explore the nature of the universe. For example, he patterns the events in *The Castle of Crossed Destinies* on the array of cards in the Tarot pack. The cards and the things they stand for shift meaning as he sets them in different time frames: one grouping shows us such figures as Faust, Parsifal, and Oedipus from the perspective of a medieval castle; another examines them as they would manifest themselves in a more modern setting.

Stylistically similar is *Invisible Cities* in which an imaginary Marco Polo meets with an improbable Kublai Khan to describe the cities of his empire. Each chapter explores a different city in this imaginary world and provides accompanying dialogues between Polo and the Khan.

Calvino is rewarding to read, for his work not only challenges our assumptions about time, ethics, and perception but also forces us to re-examine the comfortable methods we generally employ to avoid dealing with paradox. He explores these topics thematically at the same time that he makes conscious efforts to extend and distort the boundaries of conventional fiction. His fiction has as much to do with the structure and nature of fiction itself as it does with characters and plot. For this reason, Calvino can be grouped with such writers of fantasy as Jorge Luis Borges, Umberto Eco, Donald Barthelme, and Robert Coover, all of whom want their readers to be aware of what it means to be a *reader*, a participant in their fictions.

—Melissa E. Barth

CAPEK, Karel (1890-1938). Czech. Fiction— *Krakatit*, 1925 (as *An Atomic Fantasy*, 1948); *The Absolute at Large*, 1927; *War with the Newts*, 1937. Plays— *R.U.R. (Rossum's Universal Robots)*, 1923; *And So Ad Infinitivum (The Life of the Insects)*, 1923 (as *The Insect Play*, 1923; as *The World We Live In*, 1933); *The Macropulos Secret*, 1925; *Adam the Creator*, 1929; *Power and Glory*, 1937.

*   *   *

Karel Capek was a prolific author of stories, essays, novels, travelogues, plays, and newspaper articles. The word "robot" was coined by his brother Josef (his collaborator in some works), but its blend of psycho-physiology and politics expresses precisely Karel's preoccupation with contemporary inhumanity, opposing Natural Man to Unnatural Pseudo-Man, a manlike, reasoning, but unfeeling being associated with capitalist technology and the social extremes of upper-class tycoon and working-class multitude. Capek's heroes range from small employees and craftsmen to doctors and deviant scientists, and his most stubborn values arise from peasant confidence in traditional things and relationships. In the plays, this is openly expressed by his small people and ideological arbiters, such as Nana in *R.U.R.* or Kristina in *The Makropoulos Secret*, while in the novels it is implied by key actions such as the final return to normality in *Krakatit* and *The Absolute at Large*. Yet Capek was also spellbound and terrified by the workers' world of factories and the power of capitalists (e.g., Bondy from both the latter novel and *War with the Newts*).

In Capek's first SF phase, after World War I, the tension between the little people (the audience he was writing for) and the catastrophic forces of technology and violence is largely vitiated by the ambiguity between a menace to man and to the middle class: does it arise from aliens created by the large industry, its capitalists and engineers, or from the workers? The robots of *R.U.R.*, synthetic androids outwardly like men, are mass-produced to be "workers with the minimum amount of requirements," i.e. without the non-exploitable emotions. In their first story, "System" (1908), the Capeks had shown a workers' revolt in such circumstances; the machine-men of *R.U.R.* are technological stand-ins for workers (and for Wells's Morlocks) but also, simultaneously, inhuman aliens "without history." Their creation doesn't lead to Domin's engineering utopia with Nietzschean supermen but to genocidal revolt. Yet during the play they grow more like a new human order than like inhuman aliens, more workers than machines; reacquiring feelings, they usher in a new cycle of creation. This oscillation, parallel to one between psychological and collective drama, has dated *R.U.R.* This holds even more strongly for *Adam the Creator* and *The Makropoulos Secret* (about the elixir of longevity). In *And So Ad Infinitivum* the flighty erotics of upper-class "golden youth," the acquisitive sentimentalities of the petty bourgeoisie, and the militarism and deathlust racism of incipient fascism are personified as insects in a bitter satire, Capek's best stage play.

Capek's SF strength lies in his novels. *The Absolute at Large* presents another supposedly utopian but destructive invention: the Absolute or God, mass-produced as a by-product of atomic fission in "karburators" that supply cheap energy. The novel passes in sarcastic review its abuses by church and state, corporations and individuals, academics and journalists: both the economy and personal relations collapse. Absolutized sectarian and national fanaticism leads to the "Greatest War," which peters out only when all "atomotors" have been destroyed along with most people. Yet it isn't clear why the Absolute, a "mystical Communism," must bend itself to capitalist economy and competitive psychology, or work disparately in things (overpopulation of industrial goods only) and in people (destructiveness matching the overpopulation). The power unleashed is simply a chaotic magnification of acquisitive economics and psychology. This makes for brilliant if spotty social satire, in which the little people outlast the highminded idea, but hardly for consistent SF.

In *Krakatit* the naive genius who pierces the secret of atomic fission finds a parallel "destructive chemistry" in Dostoevskian fevered nightmares, dissociations of memory, and explosive human encounters, and develops from "value-free" science to painful recognition of the primacy and dangers of human relationships. Capek integrated here popular literature— detection mystery and epic adventure from Homer through the folktale to pulp thrillers— into poetic and committed modern SF. The love and heroism of sensational melodrama and the counter-creation of the mad-scientist tradition are balanced by a sympathetic, suffering, and relatively complex hero, who rejects a series of erotic-cum-political temptations— not only the established class and new personal power but also the idyllic retreat. He is left with a resolve to achieve useful warmth instead of destructive explosions, and emerges from the fog of yearning into the clarity of moderation. Though the novel doesn't quite fuse realism and allegory, ethical moderation and folktale certainties, it largely succeeds in transcending the opposition between scientific progress and human happiness. For the first and last time in Capek's SF, a believable hero fights back successfully at destructive forces within himself and society.

Capek's second phase comprises some minor, marginally SF stories, *War with the Newts*, and one play. The rise of Nazism dispelled his illusions of the little man's instinctual rightness and the relativity of truth. Instead of satirizing the intellect, he wrote sharply against irrationalism, "be it the cult of will, of the soil, of the subconscious, of the mass instincts, or of the violence of the powerful." The pseudo-human becomes clearly evil when the Salamanders become analogous to the Nazi aggressors. Their rise is interwoven with a satire on the illusion industries which screen biological and social reality from mankind— the exotic and juvenile adventure romance, sensational tabloid news-paper, Hollywood movies, pseudo-scientific polls and inter-views in newspapers. Scientists and academics are as timid and ideologically limited as the public at large, but the real villains are the capitalists who finance the menace through the Salamander Syndicate— an industrial utopianism satirized in the minutes of its meeting. The Salamanders, who began as exotic pets, become an "extremely cheap labor force" parallel to the transformation of competitive merchant-buccaneering into a global exploitative corporation aiming at a new Atlantis— which will end as Atlantis did. An appendix on the Salamander's sexual life shows that their "Collective Male" horde is capable of politics and technics but not of real sociability: the Syndicate is the greatest illusion of them all. Progressing to a powerful alternate society, learning well mankind's combination of slavery and stock-market, aggression and ideological propa-ganda, they begin their assault. Capek's satire is here most bitter, topical, and precise. Startlingly, even his beloved small people are found guilty of complacency as continents crumble around them.

The satire of literary, journalistic, and essayistic forms in this novel is also a critique of SF. The history of the Salamanders echoes Wells's *Island of Dr. Moreau*, Conan Doyle's *Lost World*, and the animal fable; the global overview latches onto Wells's later SF and France's *Penguin Island*; it ends with Wellsian havoc-wreaking aliens— but also with an open question, much superior to ordinary SF: "No cosmic catastrophes, nothing but state, official, economic, and other causes . . . ." The menace could have been stopped— if people had organized to fight it, if "All the industries. All the banks. All the different states" had not financed "this End of the World." Such writing makes of Capek not only the pioneer of all anti-fascist and anti-militarist SF but also (together with Zamyatin) the most significant SF writer between the World Wars. True, *War with the Newts* didn't quite manage to overcome this ambiguity: the Salamanders are at the beginning a wronged inferior race and yet grow into an embodiment of both the Nazis and robotized masses. Russia, moreover, is presented as a Tsarist state: Capek couldn't deal with socialism or any positive radical novelty. He dealt in catastrophes, and concentrated his fire almost entirely on bourgeois society. Conversely, such a love-hate relationship led the communist bureaucracy in Czechoslovakia to neglect him in the early 1950's, though he has since been rehabilitated.

Capek's evolution is not simple. One of his best works, *Krakatit*, is early, and his final SF play, *Power and Glory*— a critique of fascism, militarism, and subservient medicine— is second rate. But in a few works he left a precious heritage. He— rather than Burroughs or Gernsback— is the missing link between Wells and a literature which will be both entertaining (which means popular) and cognitively (which means also formally) avant garde. He infused the legacy of the adventure novel and melodramatic thriller, French and British SF, and German fantasy with the prospects of modern poetry, painting, and movies as well as with an eager and constant interest in societal relationships, in natural and physical sciences, and above all in the richly humorous and idiomatic language of the street and the little people. In that way, he is the most "American" of the often elitist European SF writers. And yet he is also not only intensely Czech, but a "European local patriot" for whom Europe meant culture and humanism; when they were betrayed, the Salamanders— read fascists— had arrived.

—Darko Suvin

FRANKE, Herbert W. (1927—). Austrian. *The Orchid Cage*, 1973; *Zone Null*, 1974.

* * *

Writer, scientist, spelunker, computer expert, and academic, Herbert W. Franke writes novels, short stories, and works on science for laymen which revolve around computers, information science, and the potentialities of psychological manipulation through electronic sensory stimulation. His earlier novels emphasized dominant military-industrial systems allied to conformist drug cultures, radioactive desolations, the decadent games of satiated mass cultures, entrapment in plastic environments, and the definition of enforced "superiority" as conformity to one man's monomaniacal obsessions. Some of the novels of the late 1970's and early 1980's portray superman-obsessed leaders who use electronic simulations to test and delude their trainees (*Schule für Übermenschen*). From *Glasfalle* to *Kälte des Weltraums* tyrants are a continuing thread, but the later novels allow their heroes more freedom. Although Franke's portrayal of enforced "superiority" remains harsh, a hero may submit voluntarily to the training school rigors in the beginning and survive the tyrant in the end (*Schule für Übermenschen*). Franke continues his analysis of scientists' responsibility for the state of affairs in *Keine Spur vom Leben* and *Tod eines Unsterblichen*. Most striking is the development of the entertainment theme from *The Orchid Cage* through *Zone Null* and *Sirius Transit* (1979) with its ultimate amusement parks. There the dominant personality is a "Star" who manipulates the masses by faking the conquest of a distant planet. Though some of his characters show a modest development, the novels are ironic in outline and analytical in the disclosure of unifying social, political, and psychological systems. With the enduring themes of heroes who question and survive, critical encounters with "superiority," and analyses of the psychological potentialities of advanced technology, Franke continues to plumb the long-term problems of survival for the individual and the species.

—Alice Carol Gaar

GAIL, Otto (1896-1956). German. "The Stone from the Moon," in *Science Wonder Quarterly*, Spring 1930; *By Rocket to the Moon* (for children), 1931; *The Shot into Infinity*, 1975.

* * *

Otto Gail, the German popular science and science-fiction writer, was closely associated with rocketry pioneers such as Hermann Oberth, and influential in development of realistic

depiction of space travel in Anglo-American and even Soviet SF. All three of Gail's science fiction novels were translated into English.

Until the appearance of *The Shot into Infinity* in *Wonder Stories Quarterly* in 1929 there was little technical realism in Anglo-American SF devoted to the conquest of space. Victorian devices like anti-gravity were still common, and even when rockets were used they tended to be built by precocious inventors right in their back yards. Gail, also the author of a 1928 non-fiction work of popularization, *With Rocket Ships into Space*, was familiar with the work of Oberth and other theorists. And if he did not *fully* realize the logistical problems of the Space Age, he was certainly aware space travel would be a massive undertaking. *The Shot into Infinity* mixes Vernean SF with romantic melodrama. August Korf, the hero, has been working on a multi-stage liquid-fuel rocket — a project that has languished for lack of funding (partly due to his own stubbornness: he is too proud to appeal to the world for help). A rival has stolen his earlier plans for a solid-fuel craft, and sent an astronaut to the Moon. Alas, solid fuel proves inadequate, and the luckless pilot is trapped in lunar orbit. So naturally Korf speeds completion of his *Geryon* to attempt a rescue, and of course the dying pilot turns out to be his former true love, who was impatient with his caution and wanted to *go* herself. Amid the melodrama, there remain realistic scenes of acceleration, stage separation, space walks, and the like. Too, there is the sense that reality is unforgiving, as in Tom Godwin's later "The Cold Equations," and, above all, a sense of *mission*: space travel as a *cause*. *The Shot into Infinity* is ancestor to such later works as Robert A. Heinlein's "The Man Who Sold the Moon" and Arthur C. Clarke's *Prelude to Space*.

"The Stone from the Moon" is less interesting; although it features a space station, the plot centers on an occult Lost Atlantis theme. *By Rocket to the Moon* is strictly juvenile. Despite the earlier influence of Konstantin Tsiolkovsky, Gail's work seems to have had some impact on Soviet SF through translations. Aleksandr Belyaev tries to go *The Shot into Infinity* one better with *A Leap into Nothingness* (1933), with even more attention to logistics and outdoes "The Stone from the Moon" with the space station in *KETStar* (1936).

—John J. Pierce

JESCHKE, Wolfgang (1936—). German. "A Little More Than Twelve Minutes," in *New Writings in SF*, edited by Kenneth Bulmer, 1975; "The King and the Dollmaker," in *The Best from the Rest of the World: European Science Fiction*, edited by Donald A. Wollheim, 1976; *The Last Day of Creation*, 1982; "The Land of Osiris," in *Isaac Asimov's Science Fiction Magazine*, March 1985.

* * *

Although Wolfgang Jeschke's output is small— so far one novel, 13 short stories, several poems, and a number of radio dramas— he ranks among Germany's most important writers. Yet he is much better known as editor (since 1972) of Wilhelm Heyne's successful SF line— the largest in Europe.

As a writer, he is almost the exact opposite of somebody like H.W. Franke (generally considered to be the most important SF writer in Germany), who is more interested in content than in the manner of expressing it, and who has turned a style severe and austere into a virtue. Jeschke is a more natural writer, interested in a tale well told, rich in background, narrative turns, and incident. Mood and stylistic qualities are often more important than plot, subject matter, or theme. Consequently, many of his stories are variations on well-known SF themes or build upon previous SF. His first professionally published story, "Der Türmer," is typical of this: a sentient and telepathic plant on a far planet comes into contact with a lonely human being, striving like the humans to conquer space and to spread its seeds on other planets. One of Jeschke's favorite topics is time-travel and its paradoxes, as in one of his earliest stories, "Supernova," later revised as "The Gap in the Mountain"— an earthman is caught in a time-loop. Similarly in "A Little More Than Twelve Minutes" time travelers from the future wait for the building of the first time machine so that they can return home. Sometimes Jeschke's stories contain mythical allusions or provide SF versions of classical tales, as in "Sirens on the Shore." His imminent death is made bearable for a dying spaceman by aliens that project his inmost longings into his mind. This character of wish-fulfillment is also evident in "The Gate of Night," in which the after-effects of an atomic war are undone by mutants who create another reality track, thus giving mankind another chance. Other early stories feature a horrible new disease, the transplantation of human memories into robot bodies or the long voyage to the stars by human beings who have forgotten their origins and purpose. These are well-written but not terribly original, old-fashioned and slight stories. Of quite a different order is the long story "The King and the Dollmaker," another time-travel tale, but this time a virtuoso performance, so complex and well-constructed a story that it can stand besides the best time-travel stories, a tour de force that turns artifice into a high art, although this was recognized (upon its appearance in Donald A. Wollheim's *The Best from the Rest of World*) only by perceptive critics like Michael Bishop.

Jeschke's newer stories are both more substantial in content, and more experimental in form. "Heike the Heretic's Writings" is a skilful arrangement of real and fictitious newspaper reports, essays, speeches of politicians, news, and quotations from books, all relating to the current political state of the world, while "The Land of Osiris" offers a journey through a post-atomic Africa, and a contact with an alien visitor.

Jeschke's first novel, *The Last Day of Creation*, again turns back to time-travel. The book starts with the discovery of a series of mysterious artifacts that are both a spoof on Erich von Däniken's ancient astronauts theories and the saintly traditions of the Roman Catholic Church. The discoveries are taken by the American authorities to mean that their project is viable: to travel back into the past in order to change the present, to steal the Arab oil from under the noses of the sheikhs. But from the beginning, everything goes wrong, the time troops arrive in little groups, spaced years apart, and are already awaited by superior and better-equipped enemy forces. They are not even all from the same future but from alternate futures, and they are soon stranded in the past, for no return is possible, and all that is left to them is fighting for their bare survival in the jungles of the Mediterranean (then not yet a sea), with only dim prospects of a golden Atlantis in the Bermudas ahead. Jeschke's novel is both an engaging fast-paced adventure story, and a narrative with deeper meanings, satiric both of the current situation of the world and other SF stories depicting attempts to improve history by time-travel.

—Franz Rottensteiner

JEURY, Michel (1934—). French. *Chronolysis*, 1980.

* * * *

When *Le Temps Incertain* (*Chronolysis*) appeared in 1973, a new author arrived in French science fiction and established himself immediately at his peak. Michel Jeury was neither a young writer nor a newcomer. Born in 1934, he had already published in 1960 (under the pseudonym of Albert Higon) *Aux Etoiles du Destin* and *La Machine du Pouvoir*, which attempted a synthesis between the French tradition of the *roman d'anticipation* and recent American science fiction. Then for more than ten years Jeury was silent. Of humble, peasant background, which had already placed him apart in the social universe of science fiction, he spent many difficult years and had nearly ceased writing entirely. This origin, these difficulties, these uncertainties on the order of the world, are essential to the understanding of his work.

In *Chronolysis* two futures, the one dominated by a multinational fascist HKH, the other more human and asserted by intelligent computers, the Phords, dispute our present, which will decide their existence. Both futures have use of the weapon *chronolyse*, which permits sending agents into the past, or rather projecting their personality there. But the chronolitic drug is not as certain as a machine, because it acts upon the mind. Robert Holzach thus enters into a universe of uncertainty where the past, the present, the future, and the possible encounter each other and are superimposed, alternatively. He's a man hunted to the depths of his own psyche. So well is this done that the novel has the characteristics of a realistic nightmare, without becoming hallucinatory.

Jeury is so remarkable for creating the social fabric of a period that he specializes both in economic problems and the hesitations of the real, as well as an anguish that is sometimes precise, other times diffuse. Therefore, certain commentators relate Jeury to Philip K. Dick. But one can also discern in the *principe d'incertitude* the influence of Robbe-Grillet. If this is the case, Jeury brings to the *nouveau roman* a simplicity of writing and an almost prophetic content which it ordinarily lacks. In reality, Jeury invents— and does not cease to explore in his major works— a personal world that is somber, even pessimistic, controlled by vast social machines, by informational networks, by the omnipresence of tyranny, by the image, the falsification of the real for the benefit of the dominant groups.

In this universe where nothing is ever exactly as it seems, the central character, a little man, flees, tries to survive and even bring about a better world, a utopia like that in *La Fête du changement*, perhaps Jeury's most brilliant novel but a utopia without rules.

The result defies all analytic description. If *Chronolysis* and its successors have known an instant success, it is in the dissolution of the framework of the real and in joining the philosophic themes then developed by Lyotard, Deleuze, and Guttari, whom Jeury probably hadn't yet read.

The little man hunted is evidently Jeury himself, perceiving the crushing of his social group by the great forces fighting among themselves for absolute supremacy.

One finds again these preoccupations, this obsession, in his later works, notably in *Soleil chaud, poisson des profondeurs* and in *Les Animaux de Justice*. But with *Les Yeux Geants* the writer was to go further yet, describing the encounter between a society in crisis in the beginning of the 21st century and an absolute strangeness, an extra-terrestrial who manifests himself always in an elusive manner. The novel is a long progression towards the discovery of the other as indicated by the last sentence: "the ending of this story can never be written with human words." In this terrain, Jeury has surpassed, in my judgment, Stapledon, Clarke, and Lem. He borders on the frontier of mysticism without ever letting himself be taken into its pitfalls, and shows that it is a question at the same time of a mediated perception and a social phenomenon. He has thus profoundly renewed science fiction; too much perhaps for its habitual public.

The other side of the coin is that the narrowness of the French quest for science fiction works of high quality limits Jeury to producing more commercial work, where he is less comfortable. His skill even in describing problematic unknown universes in dissolution prevents him from producing simple and manichaean works which please the larger public. And that is precisely because his characters, without being anti-heroes, cannot and will not dominate the conflicts that confront them. If science fiction is a literature obsessed by theory, Jeury introduces to it, exaggerated by the taste of the majority, doubt.

The drama, and I weigh my words, is that Jeury, as with so many other writers of breadth, might find himself prevented from writing what he is and obliged to turn away from and devalue his talent. This would be an immense loss for French literature and for world-wide science fiction. The reader will profit from consulting my preface to the *Livre d'or de Michel Jeury* (Presses-Pocket, 1982) where I develop the ideas briefly sketched here on the sense, the importance, and the genesis of Jeury's work.

—Gérard Klein (translated by Ann K. Smith)

KELLERMANN, Bernhard (1879-1951). German. *The Tunnel*, 1915.

* * *

Bernhard Kellermann's only science fiction novel, *The Tunnel*, was influential in development of a school of SF better known in the Soviet Union than in the West. "Industrial science fiction," as it was later christened by Soviet critics, goes beyond the strict invention-adventure format of Jules Verne as represented in both the *voyages extraordinaires* and the juvenile SF (dime novels, Tom Swift, etc.) which imitated them: vast engineering projects change both the face of the world and ordinary people's lives. But no more than in straight Vernean SF is there any *fundamental* change in society. Early examples include André Laurie's *New York to Brest in Seven Hours* (1888, France), involving construction of a transatlantic oil pipeline, and Luigi Motta's *The Submarine Tunnel* (1912, Italy), which anticipates the project in Kellermann's novel.

The Tunnel was undoubtedly the most popular of these; it was translated into English within a year, and was still remembered fondly enough two decades later to inspire three movie versions, *The Tunnel* (1933, in simultaneous French and German versions) and *Transatlantic Tunnel* (1935, Britain). Even the novel reads like a cross between Verne and Cecil B. DeMille. Mac Allan, the hero, is an idealistic engineering genius typical of invention SF. But realization of his dream requires billions of dollars and entire armies of workers— and costs thousands of lives. Kellermann realizes the scale of logistics for such a project, from an artificial Niagara to provide electric power to a new city to house workers. Although gigantic boring machines do the basic tunneling work, the toll on human life is great— and the

project is nearly doomed by an explosion that kills nearly 3,000 and leads to strikes and riots. Despite being made a scapegoat for the disaster and being sent to jail (his wife and child already having been killed by rioters), Allan eventually redeems himself and completes the tunnel. Through it all, there are no basic moral or social questions: Western civilization is united by the ideals of science and engineering; there are no wars or serious international disputes. Even the scientific imagination is shortsighted: the possibility of *air* travel across the Atlantic is curtly dismissed.

Kellermann's collected works were translated in 1930 in the Soviet Union, where his sympathy for the Bolshevik Revolution struck a responsive chord. *The Tunnel* undoubtedly helped inspire Aleksandr Kazantsev's *Arctic Bridge* (1946), involving a similar project across the Arctic Ocean, as well as such industrial sf novels as Aleksandr Belyaev's *Under the Arctic Sky* (1938), Grigori Adamov's *The Banishment of the Lord* (1946), Vladimir Nemtsov's *Golden Bottom* (1948) and Kazantsev's *Northern Jetty* (1952), devoted to Siberian development and similar projects.

—John J. Pierce

KLEIN, Gérard (1937—). French. *The Day Before Tomorrow*, 1972; *Star Masters' Gambit*, 1973; *The Overlords of War*, 1973.

* * *

Gérard Klein has been a prolific writer of science fiction as well as an important editor, publisher, and critic. He has produced considerable critical writing about American science fiction, and the influence of such writers as Silverberg, Dick, and Brunner can be seen frequently in his work. His first novel, *Star Masters' Gambit*, falls into the pulp tradition of adventure action narrative and space opera. One French critic argues that Klein wished to revive the Romantic tradition of the bildungsroman; and a later novel, *The Overlords of War*, is drawn from Klein's own personal experience with the French Algerian crisis. His more than 60 science-fiction short stories show a wide literary influence as well as a preciousness and polish in style at times that seems peculiarly French. The reader can move from space opera set on Uranus and told straight to first-person monologues suggestive of Malzberg's *Beyond Apollo* to Swiftian irony set like an 18th-century *conte philosophique* to fantastic aliens such as Snarks in his most widely known story, "Jonah." Without doubt Klein is important and influential in the current science-fiction scene in Europe.

—Donald M. Hassler

KOMATSU, Sakyo (1931—). Japanese. *Japan Sinks*, 1976 (*The Death of the Dragon*, 1978).

* * *

Sakyo Komatsu has written widely in science fiction, other types of fiction, and non-fiction. He was characterized in the early 1970's, when a number of his major works were published and his fame spread, as one of the "Big Five" of Japanese science fiction writers, the others being Tsutsui Yasutaka, Hoshi Shin'ichi, Mitsuse Ryū, and Mayumura Taku. That grouping left aside Abe Kobo, who may have exceeded the "Big Five" in fame, but is by no means an SF specialist, having produced much mainstream literature.

Komatsu himself is not at all a tightly specialized SF writer. He is sometimes called the Robert Heinlein of Japan, while Hoshi is contrastingly referred to as Japan's Ray Bradbury. Like Heinlein, Komatsu gives much thought to political and international problems, and both writers have had a diversified cultural, technical, and occupational background. For Komatsu, this diversified experience contributes to his ability to present natural and realistic narratives, and contributed particularly to his great success with *Japan Sinks*.

One may also say that Komatsu resembles Isaac Asimov in his continuing output of non-fiction and fiction other than SF. His non-fiction often gets into futurology, as in *Mirai Gijutsu to Ningen Shakai* (Future Technology and Human Society, co-authored with Kato Hidetoshi, 1983), which explores the way in which our dreams of today may be realized in the future. His *Nihon Bunka no Shikaku* (The Dead Space of Japanese Civilization, 1977) is a critical examination of Japanese culture. Komatsu's critical writings include a piece of SF criticism in English, "H. G. Wells and Japanese Science Fiction," found in a book he wrote with Judith Merril, Tetsu Yano, and Robert Philmus, *H. G. Wells and Modern Science Fiction* (1977). Komatsu has also written mysteries, detective stories, and travel books— these last help to account for his impressive physical descriptions.

His story "Fukurokoji" (Blind Alley) is a summary of his futurology, and is included in his book, *Hoshi Koroshi* (Star Killer)— a title drawn from another very original story in that volume. In the same book are his skilled narratives of the birth and death of our moon, "Kaigo" (Conjunction) and "Wareta Kagami" (The Broken Mirror). The title story of another collection, *Chi ni wa Heiwa* (Peace on Earth) was nominated for the Naoki Prize, while a short-short-story therein, "Koppu Ippai no Senso" (A Full Cup of War) deals with the development and hazards of nuclear war. The story "Hokusai no Sekai" (The World of Hokusai) was one of the first Japanese SF stories to appear in Russian for Soviet readers.

Japan Sinks enlarged his status greatly, selling over four million copies in Japan, appearing in translation in the United States and other countries, and leading to a motion picture which has been widely exhibited in Japan and abroad. By the 1980's he was referred to in publications as "Mr. Chimbotsu" (Mr. Submersion) and as "the man who sank Japan." In this novel he makes plausible, with abundant data from geology and physics, what would otherwise be regarded as highly fantastic, the submergence of virtually the entire Japanese archipelago as the result of sliding plates, earthquakes, and terrific volcanic action. The loss of Japan in a mere year or so of time is the fantastic element here. The same process extending over millions of years would not be so questionable— nor might it make much of a narrative.

Komatsu has called this novel a fable, and it surely can be read as a caution against insularity in Japan or any nation. On the question of the surviving Japanese people and their culture after their land disappears, Komatsu says that beyond ethnocentric and insular nationalism is a better, enriched identity, that one's own language and customs can be kept, while enhanced by a global blending. He also considers the often problematic question of how peoples in distress may interact with the nations to which they call for help.

Japan Sinks and its forthcoming sequel are to be rated against a number of other SF stories of cataclysms— and inevitably to be compared even with those novels which treat the end of the Mother Earth or of the entire human race. Such themes, of course, offer the SF writer a fine chance to deal with the essence of humanity and human destiny. Komatsu's variegated preparation enables him to deal superbly with this challenge.

—Frank H. Tucker

LASSWITZ, Kurd (1848-1910). German. *Two Planets*, 1971.

* * *

In the literature of space travel Kurd Lasswitz's *Two Planets* merits notice, particularly for its acknowledged impact upon a generation of German scientist-engineers. After the initial 1897 publication translations fostered audiences throughout Europe. Lasswitz's thousand-page novel (abridged in the English translation) focuses on the conflict of values when intellectually and ethically superior but physically similar Martians ("Nume") invade Earth ("Ba").

Three explorers accidentally discover the Martian land station at Earth's North Pole. Their balloon runs afoul of the "abaric" or anti-gravity field used to propel craft to a solar-powered, ring-shaped satellite. Despite this peaceful contact a subsequent misunderstanding between Martians and the crew of an English warship precipitates military reactions from Earth, soon nullified by superior Martian weapons utilizing repulsion rather than destruction. Ensuing events admit no victory for Earth. The Martians reduce Earth to protectorate status and institute a stringent system of education. Ironically they in turn suffer a re-awakening of the corrupting urge to power. Only through such efforts as those of La, a Nume, and the explorer Saltner does compromise occur. Offering a microcosmic solution for the macrocosmic problem, these two fulfill destiny, or "reason within timeless will," by becoming one with love: "To follow destiny is freedom; to satisfy it is dignity."

Even as the novel gains philosophical complexity, it suffers weak plotting and characterization. Its great strength lies in description and exposition. In detail Lasswitz describes the Martian utopia as a society accommodating freedom of the individual moral will. His scientific and technological exposition of establishment of space stations, utilization of solar energy, synthetic food, and the healthy balance of scientific and humanitarian concerns prophetically foreshadows contemporary interests.

—Hazel Pierce

LEM, Stanislaw (1921—). Polish. *Solaris*, 1971; *Memoirs Found in a Bathtub*, 1973; *The Invincible*, 1973; *The Investigation*, 1974; *The Cyberiad*, 1974; *The Futurological Congress*, 1974; *The Star Diaries*, 1976 (as *Memoirs of a Space Traveller*, 1982); *Mortal Engines*, 1977; *The Chain of Chance*, 1978; *Tales of Pirx the Pilot*, 1979 (*More Tales*, 1982); *A Perfect Vacuum*, 1979; *Return from the Stars*, 1980; *The Cosmic Carnival*, 1981; *Imaginary Magnitude*, 1984; *His Master's Voice*, 1984.

* * *

One of the most respected and innovative of modern science fiction writers, Stanislaw Lem can pride himself on the linguistic versatility, the humanism, the scientific accuracy, and the intellectual virtuosity of his creations. He takes the genre seriously, and has used it to explore man's limits and man's potentials, to satirize his governments, his pretensions, his militancy, his delusions, his failure of imagination. His attack encompasses East and West, man the tourist and man the bureaucrat, man the technician and man the theoretician. In *Microworlds: Writings on Science Fiction and Fantasy* (1985) Lem criticizes writers for squandering the potential of science fiction, resorting to clichéd patterns and devices and rehashing old tales instead of initiating experiments and evolving processes of discovery to heighten human awareness and to challenge the intellect. These last mentioned goals he has made his own. He has been compared to both Swift and Voltaire for the wit and seriousness of his vision, and the controversy of his ideas. His cynicism, his sense of man's alienation and Sisyphean dilemma, his understanding of the limits of theories and interpretations, his willingness to face the human condition, explore and criticize it, his unique geopolitical vantage point lend his works significance and distinction.

Lem's treatment of the alien is intriguing and intelligent, for, unlike those writers whose anthropomorphism he attacks as banal and absurd, he focuses on the truly unknown and unknowable, with man limited by nature and experience and the alien beyond human reason and human understanding. In *Solaris* scientists, confronted with a possibly sentient, collodial ocean capable of materializing their deepest obsessions, collect reams of data and even develop an anti-field to exorcize their psychic mirrors, but are "dumbfounded" by alien phenomena whose essence remains forever mysterious. Their observations, theories, and methodology ultimately serve only to reveal themselves and their needs; yet they deny even these (as in Kelvin's rejection of Rheya, an innocent ocean creation, an exact duplicate of his lost love). In *The Invincible* man measures his limits against the alien, whose nature remains elusive. The probing and measuring of a new planet reveals "undefinable formations," an inexplicable black cloud, and puzzling signs of the mayhem that eventually force the human observers to recognize their vincibility; their specialists can study and their destructive machines attack, but man remains stymied, more in tune with a befuddled robot than with the dark, inscrutable configuration that defies interpretation. The main character, Rohan, stands in "numbed awe," and concludes that "not everywhere has everything been intended for us." In *Return from the Stars* the central figure, Hal Bregg, tells his girlfriend about an inexplicable incident on a dusty planetoid, one "like nothing. We have no referents. No analogies," while Doctor Digóras in *Memoirs of a Space Traveller* finds himself the subject of an experiment he thought he was conducting, and stands helpless, "without a chance of understanding" before two amorphous fungoids. "Eden" and the stories of Ijon Tichy and Pilot Pirx continue this theme. Man stands alone, alienated from his universe, misunderstanding his fellow creatures, redeemed only when he shows respect for other life forms and gains insights into his own nature.

Related to Lem's image of man projecting the familiar onto the alien is his focus on man's obsession with theorizing and hypothesizing, seeking a pattern amid the random chance of myriad realities. *Philosophy of Chand* and *Summa technologiae* (philosophical essays which provide keys to his views) establish his absurdist attitudes toward man's search for meaning amid meaninglessness. In both *The Investigation* and *The Chain of Chance* private investigators try to unravel bizarre mysteries, in the former resurrection of corpses, in the latter a series of deaths and disappearances at an Italian seaside resort. A chain of coincidences is countered with deductive reasoning, causal arguments, and the laws of probability seemingly to explain the inexplicable. *His Master's Voice* delineates man's attempts to interpret a pulsating stream of neutrino radiation as some sort of stellar code. 25,000 specialists advance divergent hypotheses to decode the so-called message, with explanations ranging from a technological gift from a dying civilization to a formula for the ultimate weapon; all are convincingly detailed, but reveal more about the theorists than the reality. The penetrating description of the formulation of scientific theories and their social impact, the controversy and the conspiracies are the heart of the novel, but the role of chance and the problem of communication (between worlds, societies, and individuals) are also central.

Memoirs Found in a Bathtub continues the focus on militarism and global destruction first introduced in Lem's early "social realism," *Astronauts, The Magellan Nebula*, and "Sesame." The record of what happened in the "Third Pentagon" after an American revolution, the memoirs expose a bureaucratic hell in which intelligence gathering and surveillance are turned inward as the Pentagon invents functions, and nameless characters are caught in a senseless maze filled with double agents, secret codes, loyalty tests, polygraph mittens, and "Seminars on Applied Agony." The reminiscences of Ijon Tichy, tourist of the universe and protagonist of *The Star Diaries, The Futurological Congress*, and *Memoirs of a Space Traveller*, point up the ridiculousness of human institutions and doctrines in a more comic vein. Tichy is average and mundane, yet his outrageous adventures, recorded in a free-wheeling, episodic diary, tilts at scientists and scientific laws, concepts of progress and nature, repression, jargon, and even "unaccommodated man" with delightful informality and gusto. In the 7th Voyage Tichy gets caught in a time warp and splits into multiple selves, while in the 4th he finds his cultural assumptions about personal identity challenged. In *The Futurological Congress* he encounters revolution and chemical warfare, drug therapy and psychemization, and a "pitifully empty" world which changes grass to cheese without the cow. In *Space Traveller* "Phools" consent to their own destruction, a scientist discovers that the mechanical beings he has created are as real as he, and Tichy realizes that eternal life without body or social contact is eternal hell.

Mortal Engines and *The Cyberiad* are fables, robot legends, at times comic, at times nearly tragic, satiric parodies of human avarice, cruelty, and stupidity. They include stories of a pirate drowned in a paper sea of trivial information, soldiers plugged together for greater efficiency, and a tyrant ironically saved by his greed and suspicion, but ultimately trapped in a dream about dreaming. Despite the fairy tale quality of many of these stories, "Dragons of Probability" is scientifically sound, and "The Mask," the powerful story of a robot programmed to kill the man she has come to love, verge on pathos. Here and elsewhere Lem tackles the question of artificial intelligence, suggesting that consciousness brings pain, but deserves respect.

Tales of Pirx the Pilot also deals with man vs. machines. Pirx is tough and courageous in his own way, prosaic and bumbling but irresistible. His training mission teaches him the inadequacy of textbook knowledge and the importance of sheer guts, and his first mission the limits of technology and the need for close observation; his last adventure involves deciphering the final acts of a long dead crew from the encoded memories of a psychically wounded robot. In contrast, Hal Bregg of *Return from the Stars* is a worn-out astronaut, returning home after harrowing adventures only to find himself overpowered by changes on earth which make it alien and intimidating. He finds aggressions medically neutralized, sophisticated robots in charge, social customs incomprehensible, and risk and challenge lost concepts; yet he learns to assert his humanity and to find love and meaning and a new life.

Clearly Lem enjoys variety and experimentation. His *Imaginary Magnitude* consists of introductions to nonexistent books, while *A Perfect Vacuum* has clever reviews of nonexistent books, including a review of Lem's reviews. His science fiction ranges from realism to fantasy, from comedy to tragedy, from the technological to the poetic. Lem is fond of situations that lend themselves to multiple interpretations and that leave the final reality ambiguous. Mirrors, masks, and multiple levels add to the confusion and to the depth of his message. Double and triple puns, intentional ambiguities, codes, neologisms, cybernetic and futuristic jargon, and carefully selected proper names add to the fun and the potential possible interpretations. *The Cosmic Carnival* provides a good panoramic selection of Lem's best.

—Gina Macdonald

MAUROIS, André (1885-1967). French. *The Next Chapter: The War Against the Moon*, 1927; *Voyage to the Island of the Articoles*, 1928; *A Private Universe* (stories), 1932; *The Thought-Reading Machine*, 1938; *The Weigher of Souls, and The Earth Dwellers*, 1963.

* * *

The scores of diverse books published by André Maurois show the varied experience and interests of the man. His family business of cloth manufacturing claimed his attention in early life and the first World War also delayed his full-time devotion to writing, thus helping to carry out the advice of his mentor, Emile Chartier, that he should experience the real world amply before turning to a life of literary creativity. Certainly his novels and short stories evince a mastery of human nature and profound understanding of the French and English character. His careful analysis and biographies of Percy and Mary Shelley, Charles Dickens, Honoré de Balzac, and other authors contributed further to this, as did his many works of history and commentary on modern affairs.

Maurois gave only a fraction of his literary attention to science fiction, and his typical works in this genre are novellas. In these, as always with Maurois, we see reflections of the universal curiosity to which he himself gives major credit for his successes. Always also there is the readiness to interpret discerningly. In *The Thought-Reading Machine* a professor makes a machine to detect the passing thoughts of the targeted persons, but Maurois discerns that transient thoughts are of quite limited value. In *Voyage to the Island of the Articoles* the author imagines a South Sea island society, but he is also satirizing the purblindness of his European contemporaries. Maurois's close acquaintance with H.G. Wells and with even more innovation-minded Frenchmen of his time did not prevent him from warning against rapid changes in society. He also warned of the destructiveness of then undeveloped "ray" and atomic weapons. *The Next Chapter* contemplates wars of genocidal scope— with 30 million deaths in 1947 alone. Equally imaginative, for 1927, is his description of the marshalling of the media to shape and control public opinion on a grand scale. The author's historical works show that he knew how this opinion-moulding had worked in the propaganda for the wars before 1927. The ambitious re-casting of national opinion is shown as the benevolent but arbitrary project of the powerful magnates who control the media of the world, and Maurois envisions unforeseen, even catastrophic, effects from this tampering with the outlook of the masses.

In quality, the science fiction of Maurois can be ranked among the early classics, with impressive insights into human affairs.

—Frank H. Tucker

MAYAKOVSKY, Vladimir (1893-1930). Russian. *The Bedbug* (play), 1960; *The Bathhouse*, in *Complete Plays*, 1968.

* * *

Vladimir Mayakovsky, the Futurist poet and playwright, is one of the brightest stars in the great constellation of modern Russian literature. His paradoxical fusion of lyrical tenderness and oratorical violence marks a decisive change and renewal in it. Some of his works— even though, or perhaps because, only partly SF— are most representative of the embattled utopianism of the Soviet structure of feeling 1917-30. In poems such as "About It," "150,000,000," and "The Fifth International," in short propagandist pieces such as *Before and Now*, in film scenarios, and most clearly in his three post-revolutionary plays, the mainspring of Mayakovsky's creation was the tension between anticipatory utopianism and recalcitrant reality. An admirer of Wells and London, Mayakovsky wrote his witty masterpiece *Mystery Buffo* to celebrate the first anniversary of the October revolution, envisaging it as a second cleansing Flood in which the working classes, inspired by a poetic vision from the future, get successively rid of their masters, devils, heaven, and (in the 1921 version) economic chaos, and finally achieve a Terrestrial Paradise of reconciliation with Things around them. The revolution is thus both political and cosmic, it is an irreversible and eschatological, irreverent and mysterious, earthy and tender return to direct relationships of men with a no longer alien universe. No wonder that Mayakovsky's two later plays become satirical protests against the threatening separation of the classless heavens from the Earth. The future heavens of the sun-lit Commune remain the constant horizon of Mayakovsky's imaginative experiments, and it is by its values that the grotesque tendencies of petty-bourgeois restoration in *The Bedbug* or of bureaucratic degeneration in *The Bathhouse* are savaged. Indeed, in the second part of both plays, the future— though too vaguely imagined from scenic purposes— irrupts into the play. In *The Bedbug* it absorbs and quarantines the petty "bedbugus normalis" in its bestiary. In *The Bathhouse* the newly proclaimed Soviet Five-Year-Plan slogan of "Time forward!" materializes into the invention of a time machine that communicates with and leaps into the future, sweeping along the productive and the downtrodden characters but spewing out the bureaucrats. The victory over time was for Mayakovsky a matter of central political, cosmic, and personal importance: intrigued by Fyodorov and by Einstein's theory of relativity, he firmly expected it to make immortality possible for men. His suicide in 1930 cut him off in the middle of a fierce fight against the bureaucrats whom he envisaged as holding time back and who engineered the failure of Meyerhold's production of *The Bathhouse*.

—Darko Suvin

NESVADBA, Josef (1926—). Czech. "The Last Secret Weapon of the Third Reich," in *The Year's Best S-F 10*, edited by Judith Merril, 1965; "Mordair," in *Czech and Slovak Short Stories*, 1967; "The Planet Circè," in *New Writing from Czechoslovakia*, edited by George Theiner, 1969; "Vampire Ltd.," in *Other Worlds, Other Seas*, edited by Darko Suvin, 1970; *In the Footsteps of the Abominable Snowman* (stories), 1970 (as *The Lost Face*, 1971); "Captain Nemo's Last Adventure," in *View from Another Shore*, edited by Franz Rottensteiner, 1973.

* * *

Josef Nesvadba is a practicing psychiatrist. Almost all of his stories are introverted, brooding, and hauntingly effective probings of humanist morality and the "small people" that inhabit the real world of modern, Soviet-dominated Czechoslovakia. Those stories which have appeared in English show his penchant for intellectual and psychological questions; Nesvadba's tales are rarely "upbeat" as they dig beneath appearances, peel away affectations, and discover a universality in man that transcends the hated memories of the Nazis, the heavy presence of Soviet power, and the occasionally wistful reflections about Britons and somewhat distant Americans.

One major collection has appeared in translation, *In the Footsteps of the Abominable Snowman*. The best in this assortment is "The Death of an Apeman," a wry retelling of the Tarzan story with a typical twist: the nobleman (German, not English) must commit suicide once he has learned what "civilized" men are like. "Expedition in the Opposite Direction" tells of time travel gone afoul, especially when one's sense of *déjà vu* cannot prevent the inevitable; "The Trial Nobody Ever Heard Of" focuses on petty scientists and their academic wars extrapolated by analogy into the Nazi murderers and their callous inhumanity; "The Lost Face" suggests that even plastic surgery cannot change essentials; "The Chemical Formula of Destiny" examines the uniqueness of genius; "Inventor of His Own Undoing" asks what would happen if everyone worked for fun; "Doctor Moreau's Other Island" grumpily predicts man's inevitable degeneracy; and the title story is a moving tale of wanderlust, perhaps indicative of Nesvadba's sense of isolation.

Other stories which have appeared in English include "Mordair," that suggests a cheap and inhumane solution to fuel costs; "Vampire Ltd.," a beautifully crafted tale of the soul-sucking qualities of the modern automobile; "Captain Nemo's Last Adventure," one of Nesvadba's best, showing the wanderlust and the eternal search for "The Fundamental Question of Life" and its "Final Answer"; "The Planet Circè" which examines the dangers of total indolence and complete satisfaction of childhood desires; and "The Last Secret Weapon of the Third Reich" which recalls the nightmare of the Nazi ability to pit Czech against Czech.

Nesvadba writes with great dexterity, and his stories deserve wider attention in the West. He represents a brand of science fiction quite distinct from either the Russian variety, which sometimes smothers good writing in the cocoon of socialistic theorizing, or from the American-British science fiction, which tends to focus on disasters (man-made or natural) or how heroes with mechanical know-how can undo cosmic evils. Nesvadba is a clear descendent in Czech literature of Hasek and perhaps Polacek, but not Capek. The zest of Capek's furious and ironic humor does not appear in Nesvadba's writing. The vision is narrowed, and Capek's wide-ranging internationalism has been replaced by a poignant sadness, an inner reflection of the fate of the Czech nation.

—John Scarborough

RENARD, Maurice (1875-1939). French. *New Bodies for Old*, 1923; *Blind Circle*, with Albert Jean, 1928; *The Hands of Orlac*, 1929; *The Flight of the Aerofix*, 1932.

* * *

Maurice Renard is considered a pioneer of French SF and one of the most important SF writers of the period 1910-30. His first novel, a wildly impressionist fantasy akin to Wells's *The Island of Dr. Moreau*, albeit with more overt sexuality that sometimes rises to strange ecstasies, was *New Bodies for Old*, in which the brain of the hero is transplanted into a bull by one of the proverbial mad scientists of science fiction; the novel ends with an even more fantastic identity change that brings to mind demoniac possession. A similar grafting experiment on a more modest scale (a pianist is given the hands of a criminal), but with hardly less gruesome consequences, appears in the more glib and weaker *The Hands of Orlac*, which is probably better known since it was filmed twice. In *L'Homme Truqué*, finally, a giant is given a pair of electric eyes which turns the world into a nightmarish vision. *Un Homme Chez les Microbes* is an elegant and sophisticated treatment of the journey into a microscopic world, a theme often mishandled in American SF by Ray Cummings. Renard's most ambitious novel, however, is *Le Pé ril Bleu*, an almost surrealist work with strong Fortean overtones. It introduces a strange civilization of etheric lifeforms, the Oniweig, living on top of our atmosphere and fishing for objects in the air as we might fish the deep seas. They abduct humans and experiment with them, returning them to the surface of Earth only as a rain of picked bones and skeletons. Another SF novel is *Le Maître de la Lumière*, a fantastic mystery novel about duplicated bodies. His short stories tend towards the mystical and fantastic; a common theme is the relativity of perception, and their favorite device a distortion of perspective: time and space, other dimensions, mirrors, and changed sense organs figure prominently in them, and he is fond of joining together opposites, cold reason as well as feverish dreams.

—Franz Rottensteiner

STRUGATSKY, Boris (1933—), and **Arkady** (1925—). Soviet. *Far Rainbow*, 1967; *Hard to Be a God*, 1973; *The Final Circle of Paradise*, 1976; *Monday Begins on Saturday*, 1977; *Roadside Picnic*, 1977; *Prisoners of Power*, 1977; *Tale of the Troika*, 1977; *Definitely Maybe*, 1978; *Noon: 22nd Century* (stories), 1978; *The Ugly Swans*, 1978; *Far Rainbow and The Second Invasion from Mars*, 1979; *The Snail on the Slope*, 1980; *Beetle in the Anthill*, 1980; *Space Apprentice*, 1981; *Escape Attempt*, 1982; *Aliens, Travelers and Other Strangers*, 1984.

* * *

Boris and Arkady Strugatsky's early cycle— the trilogy *The Country of Crimson Clouds*, *A Voyage to Amaltheia*, *The Space Apprentice*, and the short stories in *Six Matches* and *Noon: 22nd Century*— is an optimistic "future history" on or near Earth, a not quite systematic series with interlocking characters progressing through the next two centuries. The young explorers and scientists, and their vivid and variegated surroundings, are shown in adventure-packed action leading to ethical choice. In this first idyllic cycle, except for some surviving egotism and capitalism, conflicts take place "between the good and the better," basically between man and nature. The societies depicted, based on friendship, community, equality, shared property, and shared values, have overcome modern worries about overpopulation, pollution, and mechanical dehumanization, but still face human problems of man's limitations and failures, torments of conscience, boredom, and unhappiness. Some of these early tales, only recently published in English, focus on human frailty: the short stories of *Aliens, Travelers and Other Strangers* which spoof the complications caused by a greedy time-travelling art collector or make wry comments on the space hero cult, and *Space Apprentice* which focuses on the adventures of a galactic hitch-hiker who sees greed, ambition, and jealousy dividing workers and threatening the security of communities, and who finally sacrifices his life for knowledge. It is such failures that darken the somewhat aseptically bright horizons.

The dialectics of innocence and experience, of utopian ethics and historical destructiveness provide the Strugatskys' main tension in their second phase (1962-65). In *Escape Attempt* a holiday jaunt leads to a brutal planet where barbaric masters force enslaved masses, made subhuman by cruel abuse, to test out alien weaponry that moves endlessly across a frozen wateland. Communication and assistance prove impossible due to divergent *a priori* premises, and even attack proves futile. This interest in utopian ethics tested by inhuman and apparently irresistible destruction continues in the Strugatskys' first masterpieces, *Far Rainbow* and *Hard to Be a God*. All three books involve a theme the Strugatskys explore throughout their canon, that of interference in the history of an alien planet, and of the moral, logical, and social problems arising therefrom. On the small planet Far Rainbow a physical Black Wave, unintentionally produced by a joyous community of experimenting creators, destroys them in a clear historical parable. The novel focuses on the decisions involved in the final 24 hours before destruction: whether to rely on logic and preserve the knowledge stored on the planet or to act humanely and save the children, the biological future. Almost all remaining heroes of the first cycle die here; only the children, and the mysterious deathless man-robot Kamill (a lonely and powerless Reason), survive. In *Hard to Be a God*, a very successful domestication of a historical novel, the conflict of militant philistinism, stupidity, and social entropy with utopia is faced without natural science disguises— and therefore the richer and subtler consequences. The hero is an emissary from classless Earth to a feudal planet, instructed to observe without interfering. However, the Earth historians' projection of progress turns out to be wrong; organized obscurantism is killing off intellectuals and destroying all human values. The planet triggers readers' memories of human history as the worst excesses of the medieval and the fascistic merge (ignorance, superstitious hatred of intelligence, violence, and oppression), and revolt simply leads to more calamity. Outside interference would introduce a new benevolent dictatorship, but the Earthling "gods" are trapped in a dilemma— their humanism and ethical sense compel them to reduce suffering, to save those they love and respect, yet in so doing they will introduce weapons that will be misused, and will push the planet's progress forward so rapidly that its inhabitants will be deprived of their own history, a history that would humanize them and that would form the dark base for their brighter future. *The Final Circle of Paradise* (originally *Predatory Things of Our Age*!) returns to the anticipatory universe of the first cycle. An apparent utopia, democratic,

peaceful, unified, and abundantly wealthy, proves spiritually regressive, endangered by too much ease and a new hedonism, summed up in "slug," a mysterious addictive substance that provides instant pleasures, but that destroys thought and binds man in a dehumanizing cycle of self-gratification. The protagonist, a Soviet cosmonaut turned UN agent, flushes out the demoralizing pleasure centers and seeks to overcome them through education and conflict. The ending is left open, the outcome uncertain, the warning clear.

Running into increasing pressures, the Strugatskys opted in their third phase (1965-68) for parables with increasingly satirical overtones, joining formal mastery to sociological bewilderment. The protagonists provide the privileged point of view, often a naive glance at a disharmonious world with monopolized information channels. In *The Second Invasion from Mars* the philistine protagonist, keeping a diary of the Martian invasion, happily conforms to the new bosses, who use local traitors, economic corruption, misinformation, and modern business practices, instead of heat rays and gases, to enslave and conquer. Renewable body fluids become big business, and only the active opposition of the strongly independent can possibly keep the human race from becoming the Martians' dumb, complacent sheep. The work is infused with details that relate the action directly to Soviet society: farmers celebrated for productivity, long shopping lines, ill-will towards POWs, alcoholism, persecution of the press, incomprehensible news reports of new wheat deals.

In the two interlocked stories of *The Snail on the Slope* a fantastic and symbolic forecast is seen indistinctly from inside and outside by protagonists painfully struggling to understand. The "Kandid" narrator juxtaposes his stream of consciousness with rural idioms, infuriatingly repetitive and monotonous as the life whose flavor they convey: the dearth of information and this impossibility of generalizing, the "vegetable way of life" bereft of history and subject to unknown destructive forces. The "Pepper" narrator views the forest from the bureaucracy supposedly managing it. The two protagonists come to stand for the alternatives of modern intellectuals faced with power: accommodation versus refusal. Though a culmination of the Strugatskys' escape from politics into ethics, the novel is among their most interesting creations, and the Kandid part a gem of contemporary Russian literature. The work has not been published as a single volume in Russian. The English edition, following the authors' guidelines, alternates between chapters belonging to the two parts.

The Ugly Swans was published abroad in an edition repudiated by the authors. In a Shchedrinian satiric city, persistent rainfall signifies the end of a morally corrupt society; the children evolve to higher intelligence and justice with the help of mutant "Wetters," midwives of the New. Boundaries between past and future blur, the fantastic (multiplying "rainmen," sudden metamorphoses) and the realistic (quarreling police factions, paramilitary Fascists) merge. The setting is the West, but the capital is Moscow, and unrelenting fog inundates all. Lepers, harbingers of the future, are pied-pipers, leading children from the past. Contradictions and metamorphoses are the essence of this novel, whose title is a counterproject to H.C. Andersen's optimistic fairy tale. As in the former novel, the puzzles are left unsolved: all we can infer from the final exodus of the children, through the ambiguous protagonist— a politically suspect writer— and the hardboiled, polemical vernacular, is that our species is doomed.

The novels *Monday Begins on Saturday* and *Tale of the Troika* are linked by the main character. The updating of folktale to embody the "magic" of modern alienated sciences and society results in a loose picaresque work ranging from fun to the Goyaesque horrors of charlatanism and bureaucratic power. *Monday* deals primarily with the use and abuse of science. The director of the Scientific Institute for Magic, studying human happiness, has split into scientist and administrator who lives backward; the demagogic charlatan Vybegallo plans a happy Universal Consumer and his homunculus is destroyed just short of consuming the universe. *Troika* shows a bureaucratic triumvirate "rationalizing" a country of unexplained phenomena. The Troika's semiliterate jargon and fossilized pseudo-democratic slogans, its incompetent quid pro quos and malapropisms, make for wildly hilarious black humour. Somewhat uneven, this is perhaps the Strugatskys' weightiest experiment.

The post-1968 novels can be thought of as their fourth phase, somber and uneven, often of juvenile heroics amid increasing alienation and desperation. *Prisoners of Power* is a very good adventure wherein the uptopian protagonist, a Terran explorer marooned on a planet wasted by nuclear holocaust, fights a military dictatorship and its new persuasion technologies. But to change this world he too must change, experience its cruelties and ignorance, unravel its mysteries. The masterly depiction of various social strata bereft of history, the insights into both oligarchy and underground politics, contrast with the super-hero and the happy ending. In *Beetle in the Anthill* the choice is again between ethics and survival; a space explorer is suspected of being programmed by aliens to destroy the human race. The racy mystery, told by a confused Terran security officer, ends with the security chief, ex-space hero, murdering the suspect—just in case. *Hotel "To the Lost Climber", Kid from Hell*, and *Space Mowgli* are entertaining lightweights. The first is a mystery with a SF twist. In the second, humane interference in a grotesque war between equally violent societies produces a limited peace, but failure to truly change a trained killer from one of the societies, after prolonged intellectual and emotional contact, suggests conflict is inevitable, people cannot be changed, peace is doomed. In the third, a "wolfchild" tale, contact with a humanoid— modified for survival and raised to manhood by an incomprehensible alien life form— raises false hopes of bridging the gulf between human and alien. The weightiest work is *Roadside Picnic*, simultaneously a folktale, utopian quest, and straight psychological novel, with a rich array of standpoints and vernaculars. In it Earthlings seek meaning amid the strange and dangerous discarded leavings of unknown cosmic travelers. The story centers around one of the blackmarketeers who penetrates the alien Zones to steal artifacts and to perhaps find knowledge/salvation. The alien influence is catalytic, showing up man as greedy and ignorant, ingenious and courageous. In *Definitely Maybe*, a chilling tale verging on the supernatural and a very dark parable, an unknown force disrupts the lives, work, and happiness of the world's leading scientists, whose groping hypotheses include a supercivilization threatening Earth's progress and the universal laws of nature asserting themselves to control destiny. The somber prevails, but the tough-minded clarity of relationships and a glimmer of utopian brightness persist.

The Strugatskys' work is at the heart of Soviet SF; its polemic acted as an aesthetic and ideological icebreaker. From static utopian brightness in a near future they have moved through a return to the complex dynamics of history to an unresolvable tension between the necessity of utopian ethics and the inhuman inscrutable powers of anti-utopian stasis. There are deficiencies in their vision: the junction of ethics with either politics and philosophy has remained unclear, the localization of events has oscillated somewhat erratically; the socio-philosophic criticism

has sometimes fitted only loosely into the SF framework. Their writing is at times obscure, at times consciously illogical. Nonetheless, half a dozen of their works approach major literature. Their later phases are a legitimate continuation of the Gogol vein and of the great Soviet tradition of Ilf and Petrov or Olesha, at the borders of SF and satirical fantasy, as in Mayakovsky's late plays, Lem, Kafka, or Carroll. The predatory bestiary into which people without cognitive ethics are transmuted, the strange countries and monsters becoming increasingly horrible suggest that *Gulliver's Travels* is their final source. The Strugatskys' work has some of Swift's fascination with language— a mimicry of bureaucratic and fanatic jargon, irony and parody, colloquialisms and neologisms. Their satire of official language, though alien to Westerners, is masterful, as is their control of conversational idiom. They are polemical at the deepest level of wordcraft and vision, making untenable what they termed the "fiery banalities" of the genre.

The Strugatskys' works are full of humor, irony, exciting action, and a clear sense of historical inevitability. They infuse scientific and technological elements with typically Russian ones, from dachas to central committees. They mix historical realities and future settings (and often seem careless about the precise motivation of their story's framework). In *Escape Attempt*, for example, a central character turns out to be an escapee from a Nazi concentration camp flung into a better future by sheer will power. The Strugatskys introduce characters *in medias res* and leave readers gradually to work out relationships. The main characters are complex— at times contradictory— in nature; they are changed by events, and grow and evolve with experience.

Within the Russian tradition, the best of the later Strugatskys reads like an updating of Shchedrin's fables and chronicle of Foolsville. However, the hero and ideal reader is no longer Shchedrin's *muzhik*, but the contemporary scientific and cultural intellectual, the reader of Voznesensky and Voltaire, Wiener and Wells. Many Strugatsky passages read as a hymn to young scientists who are also citizen-activists, inner-directed by and toward "constant cognition of the unknown." The central source of the Strugatskys is an ethics of cognition, sprung from a confluence of utopianism and modern philosophy of science. With all its oscillations from bright to somber horizons, such a confluence transcends Russian borders and marks their rightful place in world SF and literature.

—Darko Suvin and Gina Macdonald

TENDRYAKOV, Vladimir (1923—). Soviet. *Three, Seven, Ace, and Other Stories*, 1973; *A Topsy-Turvy Spring* (stories), 1978.

*   *   *

"A Lifelong Journey" is a departure from Vladimir Tendryakov's usual realistic stories of rural life and moral decision into a "scientific-fantastic" metaphor of human existence. Told in a matter-of-fact linear style, it is the story of the scientist Bartenyev whose disembodied mind is sent on an interstellar voyage while the rest of him works, loves, and dies on earth. The central conflict is Cartesian. The rational mind may hold all of time and space in itself and "be greater than all the universe," yet, isolated in space, it is inhumanly unhappy and "the most meaningless thing" in creation. Similarly, "it is necessary simply to live," but the body alone is purposeless, and "there is no more terrible unhappiness than the happiness of comfort."

Aside from the unifying potentiality of artistic experience and of natural beauty, Tendryakov offers no solution for the contradictions in humanity. His world is constructed to move always in a dual pattern, exclusive and complementary, of good-evil, life-death, thought-being. He warns that any attempt at one-sided reduction leads to falsification of reality and loss of movement; and "to crave motionlessness is just as unnatural as for a healthy individual to think of the grave." "The future disturbs me," Tendryakov writes, because the "tormenting puzzles" of the human situation will not only obtain in the future, but will become more urgent with increasing knowledge and power. "To describe the future as a rosy Eden populated with the blessed, means to deceive oneself." His hope is that as science once discovered the laws governing matter and the processes of life, so now it will uncover the essential nature and laws of "thinking life," that mankind may learn to cope with the perennial problems of its existence. "Our future is real," Tendryakov says; "we have to take it seriously."

—Jana I. Tuzar

TERTZ, Abram. Pseudonym for Andrey Sinyavsky (1925—). Soviet. *The Icicle and Other Stories*, 1963 (as *Fantastic Stories*, 1963); *The Makepeace Experiment*, 1965; "Pkhentz," in *Soviet Short Stories 2*, 1968.

* * *

Abram Tertz, a literary critic who, after six years in Soviet prison camps, now lives in Paris, can be only marginally claimed for SF, though he has written on the subject. *The Makepeace Experiment* has strong SF aspects, both in its use of thought-reading and thought-control powers by means of which the hero Makepeace becomes for a while ruler of the town of Lyubimov, and as a satirical parable in the vein of Gogol, Shchedrin, and Dostoevsky on Russian messianic utopianism. However, the psi powers are ultimately shown to be a gift from a historical ghost who is exorcised at the same time as the robot tanks break through, and the whole narrative system of the story leads one to call it a fantastic parable. Similarly inconclusive is the clairvoyance in "The Icicle," which the government tries to use but which is lost with the death of the hero's beloved. But the short story "Pkhentz" is brilliant SF, a simultaneously sad, grotesque, and terrible parable on an individual Alien isolated in a claustrophobic, menacing, and repugnant everyday life. Though grounded in the banalities and pettinesses of Soviet reality, it has implications for all situations where stifling social pressures pervade the most intimate strivings of alienated exceptions, who see it with a foreign and estranging eye yet slowly lose their original insight.

—Darko Suvin

TOLSTOY, Alexey (1882-1945). Russian. *The Deathbox*, 1934 (as *The Garin Death Ray*, 1955); *Aelita*, 1957.

* * *

Alexey Tolstoy published two collections of poetry before he turned away from both verse and Symbolism to stories and novels in the tradition of 19th-century realism. He emigrated to Germany after the Bolshevik revolution, but returned to Russia in 1923 and became a leading and privileged exponent of the official Socialist Realism, especially in a number of historical novels.

Tolstoy became the first classic writer of Russian SF by giving the fast-developing genre the accolade of literary quality and respectability, much as his model Wells did. In *Aelita* this blend is enriched with a lyrical component, the love of Los, the inventor of the rocketship, for the Martian princess Aelita. Los, the creative intellectual, with his vacillations and individualist concerns, is contrasted to but also allied with Gusev, a shrewd man of the people and fearless fighter who leads the revolt of Martian workers (the Martians are descendants of the Atlantans) against the decadent dictatorship of the Engineers' Council. If the standard adventure and romance were taken over from Wells and pulp SF (e.g., Benoit's *Atlantis* and Burroughs's *A Princess of the Moon*) or indeed from theosophy, the politics are diametrically opposed to Lasswitz's and Bogdanov's idea of a Martian benevolent technocracy. Yet if the workers' uprising led by a Red Army man was a clear parable for the times, such as could have been shared by all Soviet SF from Mayakovsky to Zamyatin, the dejected and somewhat hasty return which has Los listening at the end to the desperate wireless calls of his beloved is clearly of a Wellsian gloom (*The First Men in the Moon*). But this ambiguity, which sometimes strains the plot mechanics, makes also for an encompassing of differing attitudes and levels that follows Bogdanov by envisaging the price as well as the necessity of an activist happiness. This is achieved by plastic characterization, differentiated language, and consistent verisimilitude. Tolstoy's second novel, *The Deathbox* (four versions from 1926 to 1937), is a retreat to the "catastrophe" novel: Vernean adventures and Chestertonian detections and conspiracies center around a well-drawn amoral scientist who beats the capitalist industry kings at their own game but comes to grief when faced with popular revolt. It moves fast if jerkily; as Tolstoy had training in engineering, its science is believable (atomic disintegration of a transuranium element is posited as well as something resembling lasers), and it remains a prototype of the anti-imperialist and antifascist satire-thriller melodrama, always a vigorous strand in Russian SF. The two novels, as well as the stories "Blue Cities" and "The League of the Five" and several plays (including an adaptation of Capek's *R.U.R.*), blended SF adventures (interplanetary flight, the revolt of machines, or global struggle for a new scientific invention) with a utopian pathos arising from revolutionary social perspectives in a way calculated to please almost all segments of the reading public. This blend was to remain the basic Soviet SF tradition till Yefremov, and indeed to the end of the 1960's.

—Darko Suvin

TSIOLKOVSKY, Konstantin (1857-1935). Russian. *Beyond the Planet Earth*, 1960; *The Call of the Cosmos* (miscellany), 1963.

* * *

Konstantin Tsiolkovsky lost most of his hearing as a boy, and grew up a lonely eccentric. He became a provincial teacher, writing scientific papers all the while— particularly on aeronautics (from balloons to jet aircraft) and interplanetary travel. A self-made mathematician, he often rediscovered already known hypotheses; yet he also created the theory of rocket flight for interplanetary space (formula for attaining cosmic velocities). Disregarded before the revolution, he was elected to the Socialist Academy in 1918 and given a pension in 1921, when he devoted himself entirely to writing. His SF tales *On the Moon* and *Beyond the Planet Earth* and his anticipatory fictionalized essays bordering on SF, *Dreams of Earth and Heaven: The Effects of Universal Gravitation*, as well as some other anticipatory essays, are collected in *The Call of the Cosmos*, while other essays are collected in *Life in Interstellar Environment*; a number of utopian visions, notably *Sorrow and Genius*, have been relatively slighted.

The deep-seated obsession in all of Tsiolkovsky's writings is liberation from earthly and indeed universal gravity. The cosmic alternative— on rocket spaceships, satellite stations, asteroids, or space colonies— is accompanied by diverse aspects of bliss: perpetual Spring, physical ease and health, utopian-socialist democracy, unheard-of technological achievements, "heavenly life without sorrow," and finally immortality— possibly for individuals and certainly for the human species moving from sun to sun through billions of years. When touching on such a cluster of beatific desires Tsiolkovsky's clear but very pedestrian style rises to passages of a naive poetry, e.g., in descriptions of life-forms on the low-gravity Moon. This is also what makes for the peculiar hybrid genre of these writings, oscillating between fantastic idea and scientific (or populariz-ing) prose, with the stories just on this and the essays just on that side of an imaginary halfway house. Visionary essays seem the primary form of his expression, while the tales are primarily an attempt at reaching a wider readership. Thus even their clumsy plots and non-existent characterization are an interesting testimonial to the genesis of one kind of SF, the "literature of ideas" (in Tsiolkovsky this embraces also speculations on "etheric" beings, on a photonic phase of mankind and universe, on reversing entropy).

The main literary influences on Tsiolkovsky seem to have been the eccentric Russian philosopher of cosmic utopianism and this-worldly resurrection N.F. Fyodorov, Verne, and Flammarion. In his turn, he stands behind all Soviet writings on cosmic travel, in fiction from Tolstoy and Belyaev to Yefremov and Altov, and in science from Oberth and others down to the Sputnik and Yostok constructors. He remains one of the great pioneers of modern SF, particularly important for his refusal to discriminate between utopia and science.

—Darko Suvin

VARSHAVSKY, Ilya (1909—). Russian. "In Man's Own Image," in *Russian Science Fiction 1968*, edited by Robert Magidoff, 1968; "Out in Space," in *Last Door to Aiya*, edited by Mirra Ginsburg, 1968; "A Raid Takes Place at Midnight," in *Russian Science Fiction 1969*, edited by Robert Magidoff, 1969; "Preliminary Research," in *The Ultimate Threshold*, edited by Mirra Ginsburg, 1970; "Biocurrents, Biocurrents," "Lectures on Parapsychology," "The Noneaters," and "Somp," in *Others Worlds, Other Seas*, edited by Darko Suvin, 1970; "Robby," in *Path into the Unknown*, 1973; "Escape," in *Best SF 1973*, edited by Harry Harrison and Brian Aldiss, 1974.

* * *

Ilya Varshavsky's main interests are thinking machines, space travel, and advanced medical and mechanical technology. His attitude toward science is generally humorous or ironic, but at times bitingly satiric or questioning. He expresses nostalgia for the beauty and spirit of the 20th century.

Varshavsky's machines are subject not only to the laws of mathematical logic but to those of self-organization which demand that robots eventually develop the impulses and drives of humans. For example, when confronted with "death," they are impelled to reproduce themselves ("Homunculus"); rather than harm their robot children, they choose a life of frustration ("Conflict"); thoughts of soccer and redheads can subvert them ("The Duel"); like any vocabulary-gifted human, they can develop into pompous, abusive, tricky, intellectually perverse beings ("Robby"). Of interest to Varshavsky is the relationship between language and humanness, as well as the obstacles to a robot's thinking processes posed by connotation, non-objective reality, and accidental characteristics.

Varshavsky uses space travel to examine his ideas on closed-circuit systems (animal organisms in "The Noneaters"; time in "The Trap"); the effects of man on other life forms ("Lilac Planet"; "The Noneaters"); the continuity of human qualities, from petty to heroic ("The Return"). He twits simpleton-scientists ("Somp"; "Lectures on Parapsychology"; "A Raid Takes Place at Midnight"); castigates those who sell their minds to blind projects ("Preliminary Research"); and satirizes science-fiction writers who do anything for a plot. He questions both means and ends of psycho-scientists ("Escape") and ponders the human complications of organ transplants ("Plot for a Novel").

—Rosemary Coleman

VERCORS. Pseudonym for Jean Bruller (1902—). French. *You Shall Know Them*, 1953 (as *Borderline*, 1954; as *The Murder of the Missing Link*, 1955); *The Insurgents*, 1956; *Sylva*, 1962.

* * *

Although never really considered a genre writer, Vercors contributed two interesting and well-crafted novels to the field. *Sylva* is a poetic fantasy about a fox that changes magically into a human woman before the eyes of a hunter. The man falls in love with this wereperson, but the peculiarities of her origin provide rather unusual stresses in their married life. *Sylva* bears more than a passing resemblance to David Garnett's Fantasy *Lady into Fox*, though with a more coherent plot. There are traces of satire as well, much in the tradition of John Collier's *His Monkey Wife* or Mikhail Bulgakov's *Heart of a Dog*. But Vercors is less a humorist than a novelist, and his novel portrays a touching love story that transcends the gimmick that might otherwise seem central to the story.

At the same time, *Sylva* reflects the concerns mentioned in his more significant novel, *You Shall Know Them*. We are told in the latter that "all man's troubles arise from the fact that we do not know what we are and do not agree on what we want to be." The relevance to the lady into fox theme is obvious, but the statement has equal validity when applied to the latter novel. A thoughtful man becomes aware of the existence of a sub-human race on Earth, the legendary missing link in our own evolutionary climb. Concerned about their exploitation by the rest of humanity, he embarks on a bizarre course to determine their legal humanity. He sires a child which he then kills, confessing himself a murderer and surrendering to the authorities. The stage is hereby set for a precedent-setting murder trial, for if the protagonist is indeed guilty of murder, then the sub-humans must be considered our equals and be protected by the law. If they are not to be considered as human, then he has not in fact committed anything worse than cruelty to animals. In conception, this is one of the finest novels in the genre, establishing and examining a genuine ethical question with ruthless realism. At the same time, it is a well-balanced, craftily written tale that should appeal to all readers. Indeed, the novel has been marketed as a mystery, which in at least one sense it is. But it is also that most rare of creations, a novel of science fiction that tells us something about ourselves and our society.

Only one other of Vercors's novels can truly be said to be science fiction. *The Insurgents* chronicles one man's search for physical immortality, and the perils and prices inherent in both the search and the attainment. Thematically it is remarkably similar to Aldous Huxley's *After Many a Summer*, and in some ways is more effectively handled.

—Don D'Ammassa

VERNE, Jules (1828-1905). French. *Five Weeks in a Balloon*, 1869; *From the Earth to the Moon*, 1869, complete version, 1873 (as *The American Gun Club*, 1874; as *The Baltimore Gun Club*, 1874) (sequels: *All Around the Moon*, 1876; *The Purchase of the North Pole*, 1890); *A Journey to the Centre of the Earth*, 1871; *Twenty Thousand Leagues under the Sea*, 1872; *Doctor Ox and Other Stories*, 1874; *A Floating City, and The Blockade Runners*, 1874; *From the Clouds to the Mountains*, 1874 (as *Dr. Ox's Experiment*, n.d.); *The Mysterious Island: Shipwrecked in the Air* (as *Dropped from the Clouds*), *Abandoned*, *The Secret of the Island*, 3 vols., 1874-75; *The Voyages and Adventures of Captain Hatteras: The English at the North Pole, The Field of Ice*, 2 vols., 1874-76; *Hector Servadoc*, 1877 (as *To the Sun*, 1878; as *Off on a Comet*, 1957; as *Homeward Bound*, 1965; as *Anomalous Phenomena*, 1965); *The Begum's Fortune*, 1879 (as *500 Millions of the Begum*, 1879); *The Steam House: The Demon of Cawnpore, Tigers and Traitors*, 2 vols., 1881; *The Clipper of the Clouds*, 1887 (as *Robur the Conqueror*, 1887; as *A Trip Around the World in a Flying Machine*, 1887) (sequel: *Master of the World*, n.d.); *Adventures of a Chinaman in China*, 1889; *The Winter amid the Ice and Other Stories*, 1890; *The Castle of the Carpathians*, 1893; *The Floating Island*, 1896 (as *Propeller Island*, 1961); *For the Flag*, 1897 (as *Facing the Flag*, 1897); *An Antarctic Mystery*, 1898 (as *The Mystery of Arthur Gordon Pym*, 1960); *The Chase of the Golden Meteor*, 1909 (as *Hunt for the Meteor*, 1965); *The Master of the World*, 1914; *The Lottery Ticket, and The Begum's Fortune*, 1919; *The Barsac Mission: The City in the Sahara, Into the Niger Bend*, 2 vols., 1960; *Village in the Treetops*, 1964.

* * *

The key biographical fact in Jules Verne's life, for the understanding of his *voyages extraordinaires*, is his induction, at the height of his fame, into the French Legion of Honor by none other than Ferdinand de Lesseps, builder of the Suez Canal and a disciple of Henri Saint-Simon. Saint-Simon is the pre-Marxist patriarch of socialism, whose disciples coined the very word for "socialism," and who meant by it what we mean by the word

"technocracy." They worshipped industrial production as a world-wide process, not merely the international proletarian worker as in later Marxism, and their slogan was "The whole world belongs to mankind." Their romantic globalism is captured in Verne's most famous novel, *Around the World in Eighty Days*. The Saint-Simonians were apostles of world transport and a world-industrial civilization, to which the Suez Canal was a programmatic contribution.

Their view was that the industrial revolution would make for the socialist revolution, replacing the feudalistic love of war with peaceful production, and Catholic theology with science; thereby uniting mankind in universal association for the exploitation of nature, instead of being divided for the exploitation of man by man. Verne's great novelization of this doctrinal thesis is *From the Earth to the Moon*.

Verne wrote this novel during the fourth year of the American Civil War. As a Saint-Simonian socialist, he pondered on American wartime technology, wondering how it might be converted to peacetime industry. How redirect these destructive energies into a creative project? His answer, as the war concluded, was symbolically to melt down its entire arsenal of cannons in the casting of the *Columbiad* for the peaceful colonization of space and the development of interplanetary travel. But the moonshot is not America's project alone.

While a civilian spinoff of her military technology, the Baltimore Gun Club that initiated the project raises funds for it from a world-wide subscription. All humanity is drawn into it with a collective enthusiasm. The Gun Club itself is internationalized on the model of the Council of Newton— the name Saint-Simon gave the brain center of his technocratic council of world direction— as it calls upon scientific talent wherever it is to be found, including the world's astronomers to track the moon capsule in flight. Moreover, the Gun Club's council of directors wins to its purpose the happy collaboration of the American work force, organized on a gigantic scale as one national workshop of united interests. This is a harbinger of Saint-Simon's prophecy: "All men shall work; they will regard themselves as laborers attached to one workshop and whose efforts will be directed by the supreme Council of Newton."

In its exalted atmosphere of class collaboration between captains of industry and the proletarian workers, all this in the service of man's harmonious conquest of nature, the novel is a technocratic hymn to the partnership of knowledge and work, science and labor. The arts of war are again translated into peaceful production in Verne's model mining community, Coal City, in *Black Diamonds*. Coal City is a veritable military colony, where its miners live and work together inside the mine itself, a huge underground cavern lit by the promethian light of electricity. Here they live with and for their work, under the direction of their chief engineer, a former army engineer, together constituting "a peaceful army of labor" that toils in harmony and collective joy. With their division of labor modeled after that of the armed forces, they are able to realize the ideals of fraternity and equality. All are united in "one big family with the same interests."

So, too, in *The Mysterious Island*. The scientifically versatile army engineer, Capt. Cyrus Harding, leads the survivors of a balloon crash to salvation through endurance and their zeal for hard work, epitomizing the Saint-Simonian motto, "Down with idlers." The island is a microcosm of the socialist utopia, the well-regulated and fraternal cooperation of humanity in the exploitation of the globe in the light of scientific knowledge. At the end of the novel, Capt. Nemo appears, and gives them his blessing after they have proved themselves by their readiness for labor. "You love this island," he says on his deathbed in his submarine. "You have changed it by your efforts and it is truly yours."

Capt. Nemo's all-electric submarine is itself a miniature Saint-Simonian world, with its crew of international sailors who speak a universal synthetic language. Observing their grim and robotlike round of tireless work under Capt. Nemo's direction, Ned Land in *Twenty Thousand Leagues Under the Sea* suspects that they, too, are "run by electricity." Their work, however, is not peaceful production; it is making war for peace, the business of sinking British ships, punishing them for their nation's world-dividing colonial wars. In this Capt. Nemo is like the hero of *Robur the Conqueror* and *The Master of the World*. He does his vengeance by smiting the world's warships from out of the sky in his airplane, *The Terror*, by way of enforcing the union of nations and a cooperative oneness in the "economic and political ways of the world." For the whole world belongs to mankind.

—Leon Stover

WERFEL, Franz (1890-1945). Austrian. *Star of the Unborn*, 1946.

* * *

Franz Werfel fled from Nazi Germany, finding refuge in California, the setting of his single contribution to utopian science fiction, *Star of the Unborn*. His expressionism, poetic skill, love for the lush music and grand passions of the opera, religious mysticism, and experience in a society as surreal as fiction combine in a novel much like Olaf Stapledon's vast future panoramas, Dante's *Inferno*, and *Gulliver's Travels*.

Star of the Unborn envisions a huge underground city full of decadent, beautiful, ethereal souls who live over 200 years and avoid physical contact. Summoned from the past to be a wedding guest, F.W. is guided by his old friend, B.H. Unfortunately, since his glasses were left behind, F.W. never sees the world with complete sharpness. The novel tours a world 100,000 years in the future, vividly reporting social customs and chronicling long philosophical conversations. What little plot there is revolves around the atavistic bridegroom, Io-Do, and the lovely bride, Io-La, who develops a crush on F.W. More like a long poetic satire than a blueprint for an ideal world, it is full of brilliant scenes and paradoxes. "I am doing my utmost to avoid any invention in this narrative," Werfel insists.

Star of the Unborn is organized around the three days of F.W.'s visit. In "Irongray Turf" he encounters Mental Man and his society, which uses a "travel puzzle" to move destinations to individuals and prints its news in the stars. In "Djebel and Jungle" he meets the Jew, Idiot, and Worker of the Era, travels in space with an elementary chronosopher class, has three questions answered by the High Floater, and witnesses the first shot of a revolution. In "Flight from the Wintergarden" he visits the Jungle where people drink beer and remain earthy and the Wintergarden where Mental Man goes for Antiception, a sometimes horror-producing form of euthanasia. Finally, the Grand Bishop of the powerful Catholic Church returns him to April 1943.

—Mary S. Weinkauf

WITKIEWICZ, Stanislaw (1885-1939). Wrote as Witkacy. Polish. *Insatiability*, 1977; plays—*The Madman and the Nun and Other Plays*, 1968; *The Cuttlefish*, in *Treasury of the Theatre 2*, edited by Bernard F. Dukore and John Gassner, 1969; *Tropical Madness: Four Plays*, 1972.

* * *

Labelled old-fashioned by his peers but *avant-garde* and prophetic by modern critics, a precursor of the Theater of the Absurd, a forewarner of Hitler-like aberrations and Red Chinese power, Stanislaw Witkiewicz defies categorization. At times parodying Shakespeare, Ibsen, Chekhov, Stendhal, or Strindberg, Witkacy combines the wit and urbanity of an Oscar Wilde with the dramatic sensitivity and the sense of the absurd of a Samuel Beckett, the artistic perception of unity in fragmentation of a Picasso with the Renaissance conception of individual discord, disintegration, lunacy, and crisis as microcosmic reflections of the world at large. In both novels and plays he paints horrifying images of anti-utopias, characterized by exploding violence, the destruction of the individual, and the emergence of a totalitarian state of insect-like automatons. These mechanized men in mass are summed up most graphically in "the mobile yellow wall," a solid block of completely depersonalized Chinese soldiers who encircle Poland in *Insatiability*. The way "THEY" destroy art, language, creativity, and individuality, and harness man's sexual energies to produce a neutral social machine, bland, boring, and bogged down in mindless bureaucratic red tape and senseless cruelty, is Orwellian in conception. So too is his emphasis on fear tactics and collective madness. He envisions the destruction of contemporary civilization by mechanization and egalitarian levelling, with clone-like technocrats the wave of the future, a "dusk of mechanized grayness," not physical dissolution only but psychological too. The title of one of his plays destroyed during World War II sums up his final vision: *The End of the World*.

In a childhood play, *Cockroaches*, a preview of his adult concerns, an army of identical gray insects from America invades a city, while in *The Cuttlefish* a Renaissance pope, a modern artist, and a potential dictator debate ethical, political, and artistic relativity. In *The Mother* the individuals are bloodsuckers, ultimately trapped in a room with no exits, dominated by a giant tube used by the mechanized workers of the State to suck out life. In *The Crazy Locomotive*, set against a hurtling cinematic backdrop, the machine that will supposedly carry man to higher knowledge ends up in a headlong collision, death and a pile of human and mechanical debris with "no help possible." *They* suggests a vast conspiracy, a dread and secret menace that bans art and crushes artists. In *The Madman and the Nun* the authorities, represented by a Freudian psychologist, imprison the artist, imposing physical and psychological restraints on his humanity, but at the end are forced to question their own sanity and the sanity of all systems which limit the individual. *The Water Hen* ends in revolution, with grenades exploding, heaps of corpses in the street, advocates of community property "banging away in fine style," and thinking man resigned to his fate, playing out a card hand amid chaos, the final call a "Pass." *The Shoemakers* envisions revolution after revolution— capitalism overturned by a fascist coup followed by a worker's rebellion in turn overthrown by nameless, identical technocrats who annihilate freedom and uniqueness and make boredom the ultimate reality.

Like his plays, Witkacy's novels are a kaleidoscopic mixture of the erotic, the philosophical, and the apocalyptic. They follow the adventures and musings of an artist who struggles against domination, but who ultimately fails, partly due to his own weakness, partly due to the disintegration of society around him, partly due to historical inevitability. *Farewell to Autumn* (1927), set in an unspecified future world, concentrates on a period of change, with metaphorical winter coming, an old regime failing, and "the amorphous anthill" dominating. As a bourgeois democratic revolution is followed by the reign of "Levellers," the artist hero seeks escape in cocaine and sex and faraway places, but finally succumbs to the horror of the new system: petty regimentation, a drab daily routine, and futile, fatal boredom. In a number of his works, Witkacy focuses on the debilitating power of drugs that paralyze those individuals who might have stood against the State. In "Sluts and Butterflies" he portrays whites, in the face of the vitality of primitives; resorting to pills as substitutes for real feelings; "Mother" includes a cocaine party, a sign of social decadence and a refusal to face facts; *Insatiability* predicts the Chinese use of a very special pill (and accompanying mystic pseudo-philosophy) to pacify and lull the European enemy populace, and thereby to effect the takeover of Russia and then Poland. The latter, Witkacy's most famous novel, is a black comedy of chaos and loss, with the hero seeking personal identity in a world where identity is slowly but definitely being annihilated. Therein government has become a sport, news reporting false, women dominant, sexuality absurd, madness the norm. The Chinese, "flawless, fearless machines," threaten Poland and all of Western culture, first with painless palliatives, then with the possibility of crossbreeding to produce an Oriental-Occidental hybrid that is totally deindividualized. In this work, as is true throughout Witkacy's canon, sexual perversions, emasculated males and destructive, insatiable females are harbingers of totalitarian sterility, and images of the insect world sum up collective society. At their victory banquet the Chinese serve rat's tails in a bedbug sauce; Witkacy's childhood nightmare is realized; the world is in chains, and lunacy prevails. The fate of the individual and of society follow parallel courses; decapitation of victors and victims occurs after the human mind has already become extinct.

Witkacy's tone is mocking, irreverent, ironic. He depicts man baffled by an inexplicable universe, waging a hopeless battle for identity and control. Images of imprisonment, restraint, confinement are played off against those of stifled creativity. His characters are oversexed misfits, the lunatic fringe (the bastions of sanity in a world gone mad)— neurotic artists, criminals, demonic women, and mathematical geniuses, indulging in self-gratification, seeking thrills and oblivion, but sometimes making a last frenzied stand before being engulfed by historical inevitability. His works are full of fake deaths and resurrected corpses, as fantasy and psychological realism meet in a symbolic, metaphorical world of the grotesque. His style is an incredibly varied hodge-podge of forms: a new language of insults and obscenities, allusions, puns, jokes in mock Russian, parody, polemic, digression, political and philosophical argument, buffoonery, free-for-alls, cabaret routines, accelerated and decelerated tempos, anti-climaxes, sight gags, masks, and disclosures and exposures; although the triple puns, multiple connotations, and amazing manipulation of sound and meaning are lost in translation, his style remains impressively versatile. His future includes a Ministry of the Mechanization of Culture, a Department of Metaphysical Absurdity, a Commissariat of Sexual Nonsense, a Council for the Production of Handmade Crap, and an organization of Vigilant Youth. Characters split in two, corpses prove dummies or return unscathed, the aging process is eliminated, and time and space are confused.

His works are not science fiction as we generally envision it; but they are science fiction in the sense of fantastic creations that project political worlds that could well (and in some cases did) evolve in the very near future.

—Gina Macdonald

YEFREMOV, Ivan (1907-72). Russian. *A Meeting over Tuscarora* (stories), 1946; *Stories*, 1954; *Andromeda*, 1959.

* * *

Ivan Yefremov, with degrees in geology and biology, was Professor of Paleontology at the Paleontological Institute in Moscow. His first book of stories was *A Meeting over Tuscarora*, hovering between folk legends, sea and historical romance, scientific popularization, and SF. His first "cosmic" novella was "Stellar Ships" (*Stories*), but it is *Andromeda* which is his breakthrough, the bearer of the post-Stalinist "thaw" in SF, and the supreme achievement of its first phase (1957-63). *Andromeda* achieved this position after a long and acrimonious public debate, unheard of in the USSR since the enthronement of dogmatic literary policy and the Stalinist purges of the 1930's. Against violent ideological opposition, this debate resulted in 1957-58 in the victory of the new wave, which wanted to build upon the pristine Soviet tradition, in abeyance since the Leninist 1920's. The opinion of "warm stream" critics, and of the thousands of readers who wrote to the author, newspapers, and periodicals, that this was a liberating turning-point in Soviet SF, finally prevailed.

Andromeda creatively revived the classical utopian and socialist vision, which looks forward to a unified, affluent, humanist, classless, and stateless world. The novel is situated in year 408 of the Era of the Great Ring, when mankind has established communicational contact with inhabitants of distant constellations who pass information to each other through a ring of inhabited systems. The Earth itself is administered— by analogy with the associative centers of the human brain— by an Astronautic Council and an Economic Council which tallies all plans with existing possibilities; their specialized research academies correspond to man's sensory centers. Within this framework of the body politic, Yefremov concentrates on new ethical relationships of disalienated men. For all the theatrical loftiness of his characters, whose emotions are rarely less than sublime, they can learn through painful mistakes and failures, as distinct from the desperado and superman clichés of "socialist realism" or much American SF after Gernsback.

The novel's strong narrative sweep full of action, from fistfights to encounters with electrical predators and a robotspaceship from the Andromeda nebula, is imbued with the joy and romance of cognition. Yefremov's strong anthropocentric bent places the highest value on creativity, a simultaneous adventure of deed, thought, and feeling, resulting in physical and ethical beauty. Even his title indicates not only a constellation but also the chained Greek beauty rescued from a monster (here, class egotism and violence, personified in the novel as a bull, and often bearing hallmarks of Stalinism) by a flying hero endowed with superior science. Astronautics thus don't evolve into a new uncritical cult, but are claimed as a humanist discipline, in one of the most significant fusions of physical sciences, social sciences, ethics, and art established as the norm for Yefremov's new people. Such a connection is embodied even in the compositional oscillation between cosmic and terrestrial chapters, where the "astronautic" Erg-Nisa subplot is finally integrated with the "earthly" Darr-Veda subplot by means of the creative beauty of science united to art (Mven-Chara and Renn-Evda). Furthermore, this future is not the arrested, pseudo-perfect end of history— that weak point of optimistic utopianism. Freed from economic and power worries, people must still redeem time through a dialectics of personal creativity and societal teamwork mediated by functional beauty, shown in Dar's listening to the "Cosmic Symphony in F-minor, Color Tone 4.75 u." Creativity is always countered by entropy, and self-realization paid for in effort and suffering. In fact, several very interesting approaches to a Marxist "optimistic tragedy" can be found in Andromeda, e.g., in Mven's "happy Fall": the failed and destructive "null-space" experiment finally leads to great advances. Significantly, the accent on beauty and responsible freedom places at the center of the novel female heroines, interacting with the heroes and contributing to the emotional motivation of new utopian ethics— in contrast to the US SF of those times.

True, Andromeda has somewhat dated. In a number of places its dialog, motivation, and rhythm flag, and it falls back on melodrama and preaching. Yefremov's characters tend to be plaster-of-Paris statuesque, and his incidents often exploit the quantitatively grandiose: Mven blows up a satellite and half a mountain, Veda loses the greatest anthropological find ever; Erg is manly, Nisa is pure. One feels in Andromeda the presence of an unsophisticated reader, who is, as Yefremov wrote, "still attracted to the externals, decorations, and theatrical effects of the genre," and the presence of the erotic, philosophic, and literary taboos of the cultural context. Yefremov's epistemology is a naive anthropocentrism: the 19th-century view of man as subject and the universe as object of a cognition that is ever expanding, if necessary through a basic social change yet without major existential consequences. Doubt and the menace of entropy are only external enemies— e.g., the electric predators of a far-off planet; if any epistemological opaqueness ever becomes internalized in a man, then he is a melodramatic villain, such as Pour Hyss.

Yefremov's ideology is thus receptive only to a certain romantically codified range of creativity. His limitations are more clearly manifested in his later works. In The Heart of the Serpent Terrans meeting a fluorine-based mankind put an end to its loneliness by promising to transmute fluorine into oxygen. This story— an avowed counterblast to Leinster's "First Contact" with its aggressive and acquisitive presuppositions— might be a legitimate pacifist-socialist allegory for changing US capitalist meritocrats into Russian socialist ones, yet it is curiously ethnocentric. Yefremov's last SF novel, The Hour of the Bull, demonstrates this even more clearly. Though he took from Lem and the Strugatskys the device of showing heroes (and heroines) facing anti-utopia, his old preachiness reaches monumental proportions; and the fascist regime of Tormans seems nearer to US pulp SF of the 1930's and 1940's, or indeed to the weirdnesses of Lindsay (from whom the planet's name is taken), than to either the reactionary capitalism or Maoism which Yefremov declared he wanted to hit in one fell swoop. Such parochial views preclude a full development of imaginative SF vistas.

Yet any discussion of such vistas in Soviet SF was made possible by Yefremov's pioneering effort. Andromeda has polyphonic scope and a large number of protagonists; it is Tolstoian rather than Flaubertian. Not limited to the consciousness of one central hero, it is one of the first utopias in world literature which successfully shows new characters creating, and being created by, a new society, i.e., the personal working out of a collective utopia (analogous to what Scott did for the historical novel). Yefremov's unfolding the narration as if the anticipated future were already a normative present unites the classic "looking backward" of utopian anticipations with the modern Einsteinian conception of different coordinate systems with autonomous norms: 20th-century science and the age-old Russian folk dreams of a just and happy society meet in his novel. This meeting made it a nodal point of the Russian and socialist SF tradition, and enabled it to usher in the second Golden Age of Soviet SF— an age which closed with the 1960's.

—Darko Suvin

ZAMYATIN, Yevgeny (1884-1937). Russian. We, 1924.

* * *

Yevgeny Zamyatin wrote some 40 books of fiction, fables, plays, and essays. After the October Revolution he became a prominent figure in key literary groups, but from 1921 he incurred much critical disfavor, eventually culminating in a campaign of vilification, especially after We was published in an émigré journal. He died in Paris shunned both by Soviet officialdom and right-wing émigrés.

As all post-revolutionary Russian SF, We (written in 1920) deals with the relation of the new Heavens and the old Earth. It incorporates significant features of Zamyatin's novella satrizing life-crushing bourgeois respectability and clerical philistinism written in England during World War I (sex coupons, Taylorite "table of compulsory salvation" through minutely regulated daily occupations). In We the Revolution, sunlike principle of life and movement, is opposed to Entropy, principle of dogmatic evil and death. Zamyatin thought of himself as a utopian, more revolutionary than the latter-day Bolsheviks. He is thus not primarily anti-Soviet— even though the increasingly dogmatic high priests of Soviet letters thought so. Extrapolating the repressive possibilities of every strong state and technocratic set-up, including the socialist ones, Zamyatin describes a Unique State 12 centuries hence having for its leader "the Benefactor" (a prototype for Orwell), where art is a public utilitarian service, and science a guide for linear, undeviating happiness. Zamyatin's sarcasm against abstract utopian prescriptions takes on Dostoevskian and Shchedrinian overtones against the totally rationalized city. The only irrational element left is people, like the narrator, the mathematician and rocketship builder D-503, and the temptress from the undergound movement who for a moment makes of him a deviant. But man has a built-in instinct for slavery, the rebellion fails, and all the citizen "Numbers" are subjected to brain surgery removing the possibility of harmful imagination.

A practicing scientist, committed to the scientific method, Zamyatin could not seriously blame it for the deformation of life. How was it then that a certain rationalism, claiming to be scientific, became harmful? Zamyatin could answer this only in mythical terms: the victory of any lofty ideal causes it to turn repressive. To the extent that We equates Leninist Communism with institutionalized Christianity and models its fable on an inevitable Fall from Eden ending in ironical crucifixion, it has a strong anti-utopian streak. Instead of motivations, it advances through powerful recurring images, unable to reconcile rationalism and irrationalism, science and art (including the art of love). Zamyatin's political ideology conflicts here with his experimental approach: a meaningful exploration would have to be conducted in terms of the least alienating utopia imaginable— one in which there is no misuse of natural sciences by a dogmatic science of man.

Yet the basic values of *We* imply a stubborn vision of a classless new moral world free from all social alienations, a vision common to Anarchism and libertarian Marxism. Zamyatin confronts absolutistic control— extrapolated from both tsarist-bourgeois and early socialist state practices— with a utopian-socialist norm. As he wrote: "We do not turn to those who reject the present in the name of a return to the past, nor to those hopelessly stupefied by the present, but to those who can see the far-off tomorrow— and in the name of tomorrow, in the name of man, we judge the present." His novel brought to SF the realization that the new world cannot be a static changeless paradise of a new religion— albeit of steel, mathematics, and interplanetary flights. The materialist utopia must subject itself to a constant scrutiny; its values are for Zamyatin centered in an ever-developing human personality and expressed in irreducible and subversive erotic passion. For all its resolute one-sidedness, the uses of Zamyatin's bitter and paradoxical warning in a dialectical utopianism seem obvious.

The expressionistic language of *We*, manipulated for speed and economy ("a high voltage of every word"), helps to subsume the protagonist's defeat under the novel's concern for the integrity of man's knowledge (science) and practice (love and art). By sensitively subjecting the deformities it describes to the experimental examination and hyperbolic magnification of SF, Zamyatin's method makes it possible to identify and cope with them. In his own vocabulary, the protagonist's defeat is of the day but not necessarily of the epoch. The defeat in the novel *We* is not the defeat of the novel itself, but an exasperated shocking of the reader into thought and action. Zamyatin's encyclopedic knowledge embraced the SF tradition before and after Wells, from the utopias through the planetary and underground novels to the anticipations of Odoevsky, About, Bellamy, Morris, Lasswitz, Willbrandt, Jack London, and most notably Anatole France. *We* is thus a document of an acute clash between the "cold" and the "warm" utopia: it probably fails to attain full consistency because of the one-sided assumptions, but Zamyatin remains a heretic socialist.

Zamyatin also wrote the SF story "A Story about the Most Important Thing," interleaving developments on three levels— an episode of the Russian civil war, the death of a caterpillar, and four people on a dying "star" (planet, asteroid?) rushing toward destruction on Earth. Its lyrical investigation of the kinds of love and death that are "the most important thing" doesn't quite come off, but presents an interesting literary experiment.

—Darko Suvin

MAJOR FANTASY WRITERS

DUNSANY, Lord; Edward John Moreton Drax Plunkett, 18th Baron Dunsany (1878-1957). Irish. *The Gods of Pegana* (stories), 1905; *Time and the Gods* (stories), 1906; *The Sword of Wellaran and Other Stories,* 1908; *A Dreamer's Tales,* 1910; *The Book of Wonder: A Chronicle of Little Adventures at the Edge of the World,* 1912; *Fifty-One Tales,* 1919 (as *The Food of Death,* 1974); *Tales of Wonder,* 1916 (as *The Last Book of Wonder,* 1916); *Tales of Three Hemispheres,* 1919; *The Chronicles of Rodriguez,* 1922 (as *Don Rodriguez: Chronicles of Shadow Valley,* 1922); *The King of Elfland's Daughter,* 1924; *The Charwoman's Shadow,* 1926; *The Blessing of Pan,* 1927; *The Travel Tales of Mr. Joseph Jorkens,* 1931; *The Curse of the Wise Woman,* 1933; *Mr. Jorkens Remembers Africa* (stories), 1934; *Jorkens Has a Large Whisky* (stories), 1940; *The Fourth Book of Jorkens* (stories), 1948; *The Man Who Ate the Phoenix* (stories), 1949; *The Strange Journeys of Colonel Polders,* 1950; *Jorkens Borrows Another Whisky* (stories), 1954; *At the Edge of the World* (selection), 1970; *Beyond the Fields We Know* (selection), 1972; *God, Men, and Ghosts* (selection), 1972.

* * *

While Lord Dunsany may have been a minor figure in Irish literature, the extent of his role in the development of modern fantasy is major. He was a critical influence on H.P. Lovecraft, L. Sprague de Camp, and Fritz Leiber, and his play *King Argimenes and the Unknown Warrior* is one of the sources for Fletcher Pratt's *The Well of the Unicorn.* From his first book, *The Gods of Pegana,* in which he creates an entire pantheon, to his Jorkens series of adventure stories based on his travels in Algeria and the Sudan, to his masterpiece *The King of Elfland's Daughter,* Dunsany belongs with William Morris and George MacDonald as the generating forces of modern fantasy.

Dunsany's fantasy is characterized by his exotic settings; difficult, if creative and frequently numinous, prose; and stalwart protagonists and alluring, exquisite heroines. His ability to create vivid setting is partially explained by his relationship with Sidney H. Sime; Sime's drawings inspired "The Distressing Tale of Thangobrind the Jeweller, and of the Doom that Befell Him" (in *The Book of Wonder*). Dunsany's visual settings are evident in the country village and the activities of love in *The Blessing of Pan* and in the fictional Spanish Golden Age in *The Chronicles of Don Rodriguez* and *The Charwoman's Shadow.* However, his greatest stylistic triumph is the much-heralded *The King of Elfland's Daughter,* and in this novel all the qualities of his fantastic fictions are epitomized. Drawing on the themes of alienation and identity and the structure of the quest, which characterize much of his canon, Dunsany creates an interplay between the world of faery and everyday with his innovative proper names, coined phrases, and characterizations. In the novel Alveric falls in love with an elfin princess, but after she bears him a son she can no longer endure the crude society of mankind and returns to faery. Alveric's quest for his wife provides ample opportunity for Dunsany's ability to create numinous wonder, and the quest is resolved through love and harmony.

The on-going reprinting of Dunsany's tales—especially "The Sword of Welleran" and "The Fortress Unvanquishable Save for Sacnoth"— demonstrates Dunsany's continuing influence on the literature of fantasy, the lasting appeal of his fantastic settings, and his role as a progenitor of modern fantasy literature in all its varieties and techniques.

—Roger C. Schlobin

EDDISON, E(ric) R(ucker) (1882-1945). British. *The Worm Ouroboros,* 1922; *Styrbiorn the Strong,* 1926; *Mistress of Mistresses: A Vision of Zimiamvia,* 1935; *A Fish Dinner in Memison,* 1941; *The Menzentian Gate,* 1958.

* * *

William Morris was an important influence on many later writers, including E.R. Eddison. Eddison's *Styrbiorn the Strong,* a historical romance, is based on materials found in the Norse and Icelandic sagas, and is often considered, with Haggard's *Eric Brighteyes,* one of the best modern depictions of the Viking Age. Four years later, Eddison published *Egil's Saga,* a prose translation of an Icelandic saga. In both works, Eddison mentions Morris's romances and translations.

Eddison's fame, however, rests largely on a work which has much in common with saga and historical romance but is actually pure fantasy, *The Worm Ouroboros.* It is both romantic and epic, filled with the lavish description and heroic adventure that delight fantasy readers. And at the end of the novel, just as the reader and the characters are wishing that it could go on forever, their wish is granted, the action begins all over again, and the plot of the novel, like the worm of the title, becomes circular and eats its own tail. Eddison's Zimiamvian trilogy— *Mistress of Mistresses, A Fish Dinner in Memison,* and *The Menzentian Gate*— which follows *The Worm Ouroboros* and is set in the heaven of the world depicted in that novel, is less successful. Most critics agree that the philosophy Eddison propounds in the Zimiamvian trilogy makes the novels difficult to read, and most readers find them harder going than *The Worm Ouroboros.* *The Menzentian Gate* is especially difficult because it was finished and published after Eddison's death.

—C.W. Sullivan III

MORRIS, William (1834-96). British. *The Earthly Paradise* (verse), 3 vols., 1868-70, revised edition, 1890; *The Story of Sigurd the Volsung and the Fall of the Niblungs* (verse), 1876; *A Dream of John Ball, and A King's Lesson,* 1888; *A Tale of the House of the Wolfings,* 1889; *The Roots of the Mountains Wherein Is Told Somewhat of the Lives of the Men of Burgdale . . .,* 1889; *News from Nowhere,* 1890; *The Story of the Glittering Plain Which Has Been Also Called the Land of Living Men, or the Acre of the Undying,* 1891; *The Wood Beyond the World,* 1894; *Child Christopher and Goldilind the Fair,* 1895; *The Well at the World's End,* 1896; *The Hollow Land,* 1897; *The Water of the Wondrous Isles,* 1897; *The Sundering Flood,* 1897; *Golden Wings,* 1900; *The Hollow Land and Other Contributions to the Oxford and Cambridge Magazine,* 1903.

* * *

It is impossible to summarise the contribution of William Morris to his age, which he abominated, and to our own, which would not much have impressed him. As social thinker, as designer and influence upon both arts and crafts (and especially those of everyday life), as poet (though his biggest works are not much to our contemporary taste) and as the first great Englishman to declare himself a communist, he is unique and irreplacable. Yet it may be that the ten great prose fictions of the last ten years of his life offer his most lasting influence and his finest work. In these romances he invented the modern fantasy novel, set in an imagined, glamorous and self-consistent world, a "secondary creation," as Tolkien was later to call it.

Morris was directly influenced by saga, epic, and medieval romance: he in fact translated many sagas, as well as *The Odyssey*, *The Aeneid*, *Beowulf*, and some romances— the most important of which, *Havelock the Dane*, became the prose romance *Child Christopher*. The list of influencing genres would not be complete, however, without the wealth of folktales that he knew and used (mostly in verse) which give a pervasive colouring to the prose romances proper. Two of the ten books are time-travel stories, two evoke "barbaric" pre-history, and the other six are more or less radical redesignings of the patterns of quest-romance.

A Dream of John Ball takes a modern protagonist back into the time of the Peasants' Revolt, a period whose arts, crafts, and architecture delighted Morris, and with whose social turmoil he strongly identified. The time-traveller learns the impotence of "knowing the future": he cannot help John Ball and the other rebels, and the nightlong climactic discussion with Ball in the church is more enlightening to "modern man" than to the radical priest. The book's initial and lasting charm lies in the eager clarity with which the medieval setting is evoked.

News from Nowhere is a much larger companion work, a journey into and within a future world that is described in the same energetic, clear-edged style. This future world is the Commonwealth of "Nowhere," into which the protagonist dreams England has been transformed by revolution. It is the finest Utopia in English, the only one thoroughly worth living and working in, and Morris wrote it for a small radical audience, the readership of his leftwing magazine *Commonwealth*, who would find it worth living and working for.

News from Nowhere at times seems to divide between too much "history" of how this post-governmental England came into being and too easy a celebration of its early-summer idyllic aspects, but the time-traveller joins and justifies these contraries. The wise and subtle treatment of his responses to— and his salutary effect on— the people of Nowhere carries the narrative and powers its journey into the heart of England and of community. Contemporary readers knew the open secret that "William Guest" was Morris, and recognised every stage in his journey as part of Morris's life. His strength of longing also creates the intrepid soul-mate Ellen, who will safeguard and reshape Nowhere in its future, because she has met and loved the man that dreamed it.

A Tale of the House of the Wolfings and *The Roots of the Mountains*, between the two time-travel stories, explore two forms of the high barbaric society that Morris (like Marx and Engels) much preferred to high-capitalist civilisation. In *A Tale of the House of the Wolfings* the Gothic tribe's heroic resistance to Roman imperialism focusses upon the indomitable war-leader Thiodolf, but his love-affair with the nature-goddess and part-time Valkyrie Wood-Sun almost prevents the completion of his necessary selfless death. In *The Roots of the Mountains* another warrior-hero finds that the destiny of his people depends on both battle and his personal leadership, but the Gothic tribes are united and the Huns driven from that side of the mountains without his having to pay the final price. Goldmane is a more complex and contemporary hero than Thiodolf; both wildwood magic and personal luck and beauty protect him instead of destroying him.

The Story of the Glittering Plain evokes a later, Teutonic tribal world, and the hero, Hallblithe, has to pursue a Viking group that has kidnapped his betrothed. The quest takes him beyond this conflict, however, to an earthly paradise in which youth is permanently renewed and sensuous delight is not only guaranteed but insisted upon. Hallblithe detests the Glittering Plain; he eventually escapes from paradise and is reunited with his love. In a similar short romance, Golden Walter flees a miserable failed marriage, following mysterious visions that take him to the Wood Beyond the World. There his sexual helplessness teaches him to grow, both by his being forced to lie with the Lady of that Wood and by his being forbidden even to touch the Maid he loves. Eventually, the Maid is responsible for the Lady's death, and the two survivors find a new life as welcome rulers of a strange city through the mountains.

In these short romances and their great successors, *The Well at the World's End* and *The Water of the Wondrous Isles*, Morris creates a world akin to an unchurched version of medieval north-western Europe. There is active magic in these worlds, both for good and for ill, and usually associated with a wise and beautiful woman (or two or more contrasting power-women). Natural and life-enhancing magic is available to the very rare adventurer who reaches the Well at the World's End, but the book focusses on Ralph's adventures travelling there and back, especially his contact with the two loves of his life: one is a Power-Lady, the other a beautiful and courageous "ordinary" girl who becomes far more astonishing than the Lady.

The Water of the Wondrous Isles has an even more revolutionary effect upon our expectations of the quest: the protagonist or "hero" is a girl. A witch has stolen Birdalone and reared her to be a trap for lustful males, but she escapes, naked and resolute, into the wide world. She travels among literally wondrous isles and is caught up in a typical male quest, whose heroes leave her in a safe, smug castle while they sail off to rescue their ladies. Since she has never been taught that ladies are supposed to be passive, she escapes this protection too, and causes a much more perilous and passionate story. Three kinds of power-women influence her life, but her own developing integrity brings a qualified happy ending to her story.

The last, and incomplete, romance, *The Sundering Flood*, returns to a male hero, aided by chthonic magic and doing great deeds even as a boy. Osberne's female counterpart, Elfhild, was never properly filled out, and the book has accepted the limitations of an Icelandic saga, whereas the major romances explore their own psychological and magical structuring forces in a more demanding way.

The enactment of archetypal events, the rich evocation of psychological fears and needs, and the unhurried delight in both adventure and environment, make Morris's best romances a valuable experience— Yeats described them as books he always read very slowly, so as not to come too soon to the end. Their radical political stance and keen celebration of female personality are also remarkable, when so many fantasies are (rightly or wrongly) associated with high-church conservatism. Like Ellen in *News from Nowhere*, the Maid, Ursula, and Birdalone are courageous and enterprising people, not baits or rewards for more "real" male protagonists.

Morris created his own language, with something of the texture of 14th-century English, but as unlike it as Spenser's is unlike Malory's. The resultant style is an unique experience, shapely and pleasurable, emphasising physical rather than abstract aspects of experience, while retaining a tapestried sense of distance. The romances are designed for a future society's audience, freed from the frantic busyness of his own age just as the folk of his Nowhere are. This audience loves a good story with both circumstantiality and wonders whether in an old folktale, a Dickens fiction, or a "reactionary novel." It delights in so active and sensuous a world, so radical and lucid a use of traditional conventions. Morris invented the fantasy set in an invented and magical pseudo-medieval land, but he also invented a fantastic future audience that could appreciate it.

—Norman Talbot

—————

PEAKE, Mervyn (1911-68). British. The Gormenghast books: *Titus Groan*, 1946, *Gormenghast*, 1950, and *Titus Alone*, 1959; *Mr. Pye*, 1953.

* * *

Peake's major fictional works are the three books which relate the heritage, childhood, and adolescence of Titus, 77th Earl of Gormenghast. They are often inaccurately called the Gormenghast Trilogy, but the third volume is not set in Gormenghast, nor were they designed as a trilogy. Peake certainly intended a fourth book, and would probably have written more.

Gormenghast is an immense, ancient castle of crumbling stone and suffocating ritual, set in a wild and dreary land. Its inhabitants, from Count Sepulchrave, suffused in laudanum and antiquarian gloom, down to Swelter, the mountainous chef, make up one of the greatest gallery of grotesques in English literature. Every aspect of their existence is dictated by the Master of Ritual from the Books of the Law, though the observances and ceremonies are so old that no one can even remember their significance. Seizing on his shadowy castle and its atmosphere of doom, many critics have called Peake a gothic writer, but the label is misleading. He makes almost no use of the supernatural, which is essential to Gothic, and his descriptive writing has a visual and tactile solidity foreign to the genre. His characters, with their extraordinary forms and names— Flay, Muzzlehatch, Prunesquallor— are caricatures whose robust and energetic presence recalls Dickens or Rabelais, not Walpole or Radcliffe. Again, Peake is farcical as well as horrific; he writes out of a relish for life and colour that is hostile to Gothic morbidity, sunlight to its vampires.

Titus Groan is the story of Titus's birth and the ripples of disturbance that spread inexorably from it. He is a natural rebel, impulsive, moody, idealistic; his arrival coincides with the rise of Steerpike, a more sinister figure, who works his way up from kitchen the highest place of power by insinuation, flattery, violence, and murder. The prose is deep, dense, eloquent, and richly detailed. Peake was a painter, and when he used purple he knew exactly what shade and texture he needed.

Gormenghast, which tells of Titus's truant childhood, the growing horror and inhumanity of Steerpike, and their eventual, inevitable confrontation, moves more quickly. Once set going, "change, that most unforgivable of all heresies," spreads like contagion. The rituals are disrupted. Love shows itself in strange distortions, ungainly, absurd, or corrupt. Steerpike is exposed and hunted. Peake loses none of his control as his plot gains momentum. He portrays the adolescent tumult in all its quicksilver ambiguity. Titus's experience of life and death both in and outside the castle brutally confirm his individuality, the impossibility that he will stay there. Disobeying his mother by going in to fight the cornered villain, he is attacking the Master of Ritual and manipulator of lives, powers of Gormenghast that he hates; but he is also ridding the castle of the man who would crush it to dominate it.

Titus Alone is entirely different again, which has put off readers who (unlike Peake) are more interested in Gormenghast than in Titus and the rest of the world. It is, though rarely acknowledged as such, science fiction, from a class somewhere between Huxley's *Brave New World* and Harness's *The Rose*. Titus wanders, exiled and imperilled, in a strange land, a meticulous parody of modern Europe with furnishings and fittings that place it in an imminent, unpleasant future. He is arrested in a city of crystal towers and rockets; he is pursued by machine-like police and a robot flying eye, and hides in the refugee camp of the Under-River with all the malcontents and victims of a damaged civilisation; he falls into the hands of Cheeta, the corrupt daughter of the master of the death factory. Wherever he goes, no one has heard of Gormenghast, and few will believe it exists. Where *Titus Groan* was ponderous and slow, *Titus Alone* is fast and elusive. We barely glimpse the scenes as they whirr by. The effect is intentional, frightening in a way that Peake's other horror fiction never is; but the mysteries and frustrations of the book are, unavoidably, too many. Peake's last illness was well upon him when he began it, and his ability to express his ideas deteriorated as he wrote. The moral vision, at once urgent and subtle, emerges in flashes, or dimly; the novel is a characteristic document of the 20th century, damaged, hallucinatory, but intensely purposeful. (Langdon Jones's 1970 edition is the best possible version of what Peake had in mind.)

"Boy in Darkness" tells an extra story of Titus Groan, though without naming him. After the rituals of his 14th birthday he slips away from the castle into the wilderness, where he meets two old creatures called Goat and Hyena. They take him to the Blind Lamb, a malevolent deity who lives deep in an abandoned mine where once, like Comus, he commanded a rout of beasts transformed from human originals. The Goat and the Hyena are the last of this crew. He begins the metamorphosis of Titus, who fights back at the last minute for his humanity and that of the two pathetic courtiers. More sombre than almost any episode in the novels, "Boy in Darkness" has been read by some as spiritual, perhaps blasphemous, allegory, though interpretation was never the purpose of Peake's imaginings. Certainly the story is his most chilling and sensuous exercise in the macabre, far superior to the merely gruesome "Same Time, Same Place" and the ghoulish "Danse Macabre." *Mr. Pye*, Peake's only other novel, was unsuccessful when it was published because of expectations aroused by the Titus books. It is comic fantasy of a very different kind: a remarkable mixture of farce and fable, lighter in tone than the Titus books, but more exclusively adult in appeal. Set on Sark, it records the misadventures of a charming, irritating, self-appointed missionary whose work of disseminating love among the close, suspicious islanders is upset when God, "the Great Pal," rewards him rather too literally.

It can be said that Mervyn Peake lived before his time, and died too soon. Best known during his life for his dense, vigorous illustration of works by authors from Carroll to Coleridge, he also produced poetry, paintings, plays for radio and stage, and theatrical designs, as well as the prose fantasy for which he is now most famous. An eccentric to his own generation, he has been rightly honoured as a master by the next— unfortunately too late to know or benefit by it.

—Colin Greenland

—————

TOLKIEN, J.R.R. (1892-1973). British. *The Hobbit, or, There and Back Again*, 1937; *Farmer Giles of Ham*, 1949; *The Lord of the Rings: The Fellowship of the Ring*, 1954, *The Two Towers*, 1955, *The Return of the King*, 1956, revised edition, 1966; *The Adventures of Tom Bombadil and Other Verses from the Red*

Book, 1962; *Tree and Leaf*, 1964; *Smith of Wootton Major*, 1967; *The Road Goes Ever On* (verse), 1968; *Bilbo's Last Song*, 1974; *The Father Christmas Letters* (juvenile), 1976; *The Silmarillion*, edited by Christopher Tolkien, 1977; *Unfinished Tales of Numenór and Middle-Earth*, edited by Christopher Tolkien, 1980; *The History of Middle-Earth* (*The Book of Lost Tales*, parts 1 and 2, *The Lays of Beleriand*), edited by Christopher Tolkien, 1983-85.

* * *

In 1937, J.R.R. Tolkien published *The Hobbit*. The story, now a classic of the genre, introduces the reader to hobbits and their culture in Middle-Earth. As the tale develops, we are to meet characters that step into Bilbo's adventure out of folk legend and fairy story: a wizard, dwarfs bent upon revenge and the recovery of a fabulous treasure, trolls, goblins, elves both magical and dangerous, a bear-man changeling, and above all the great dragon Smaug. Much of the story's success depends upon the way in which Tolkien introduces us to the character of Bilbo Baggins, the hobbit whose uneventful life as a comfortable bachelor at Bag End is forever upset by the intervention of Gandalf the wizard who leads Thorin Oakenshield and his company of dwarfs to Bilbo's door with the promise that Bilbo will prove to be a daring and resourceful burglar, and just the person needed to win back the treasure of the dwarfs from Smaug. Bilbo is an unwilling adventurer who loves his comfortable hobbit hole and his reputation as a respectable member of a community of innocent, good-natured burghers. Tolkien manages successfully the difficult task of keeping the comic dimensions of Bilbo's character pleasantly in focus while at the same time developing the equally endearing qualities of good humor, humility, moral courage, and a temperate mind.

In the course of the action, two things are happening. The first is the discovery of the shape, constitution, and nature of Middle-Earth and its wondrous if sometimes menacing inhabitants. Tolkien opens a prospect of unexplored territory in fairyland, and rarely misses an opportunity to enrich the reader's imagination with new and permanent boundary markers. The second is that, in the course of the action, Bilbo comes to discover his limitations but also his own powers and his place in the wide world. Tolkien has shaped the action of Bilbo's quest as correlative to the experience of growing up. His adventures remind us with the solicitude of a wise parent: be yourself, trust your instincts for good, overcome your belittling fears, be generous and brave always, be courteous, especially in strange company or in foreign lands, be resourceful, and the world will discover your worth and praise your accomplishments, and you will be numbered with the mighty and powerful.

Since Bilbo's initiation into life is one of the substructures shaping this narrative, part of his learning experience comes from rubbing elbows with creatures of other kinds and species. He learns about the special virtues, powers, and shortcomings of dwarfs, elves, orcs, goblins, wizards, and men. He learns a bit of the history and lore of Middle-Earth and of the polite conventions that make common action possible between variant races and species. In learning these things, Bilbo comes to understand himself better as a hobbit and to see his place and that of his kind in the great scheme of things, although the full revelation of that awaits *The Lord of the Rings*. Bilbo learns to his surprise, discomfort, and eventual satisfaction that he has a role to play in life and in the great adventures of the wide world—even of the wild world.

Tolkien made a revision of *The Hobbit* after he had completed the trilogy *The Lord of the Rings*. The revision was a major one,

raising the tone and characterization considerably above the original child's story level to the threshold of the legendary, making it more consistent with the great sequel to which, in a way, it gave birth. Also Tolkien made some adjustments in the details of the original story so as to bring them into line with the more serious mythology of the trilogy.

In the end, the greatness of the trilogy has to be assessed on the basis of what Tolkien attempted. The trilogy is, of course, fantasy, an extension of the fairy-story elements of *The Hobbit* into the heroic tradition. Some critics have called it "high fantasy," others myth, still others saga, legend, even science fiction and "super science fiction." Tolkien himself described the trilogy as "feigned history," and as such it is best understood. Feigned history is imagined history, which is not at all the same thing as imaginary history.

The appearance of *Unfinished Tales* and *The History of Middle-Earth* throws new light on Christopher Tolkien's extraordinary contributions as editor of *The Silmarillion* and offers sufficient background evidence that *The Silmarillion* continued to mature in Tolkien's mind as much after the writing of *The Lord of the Rings* as before. Although the published *The Silmarillion* is unfinished and not the work the author hoped to produce, what we have is incomparable. *The Silmarillion* is best read as the scripture and legendary history of the elves. Nor is it presumed that the history was all given in the same voice, style, or at the same moment. All three of the major branches of the elves (Vanyar, Noldor, Teleri) seem to have their temperaments represented in the various books: the Vanyar in "Ainulindale," the Teleri in "Valaquenta," and the Noldor in "Quenta Silmarillion." As such, *The Silmarillion* is Tolkien's elvish scripture, a feigned sacred writing: the revelation, lore, and practice from which we are to surmise those myths and legends grew that gave birth eventually to the hobbit records of the last war against Sauron in *The Lord of the Rings*. The feigned history of *The Lord of the Rings* which includes its own epic-heroic-legendary transformations now ultimately rests upon the elvish revelations of *The Silmarillion*. If the gods be absent from *The Lord of the Rings*, as many critics once complained (even though gods are very much felt), they are present and immanent in *The Silmarillion*.

Clearly, *The Salmarillion* is the foundation of Tolkien's Middle-Earth and everything in it. He began writing parts of the Silmaril mythos before he went off to World War I, declaring to his future wife and to friends that his intention was to create a mythology for England. *The Silmarillion* was to be an English epic fit to rival Homer and Virgil, the stated ambition of every major English poet since Spenser. As the other poets, Tolkien rests his epic claims on language, but in his case it is not merely the narrative language but the languages of the subtexts of Middle-Earth. In the case of *The Silmarillion*, especially elvish. More than any work of its type, *The Silmarillion* grew out of language, both received and invented.

Tolkien's genius for naming grew directly out of his interest in developing imaginary languages spoken by beings all the more imaginary for dwelling in the world of faerie. Tolkien's world is the backward extension of the one we know from romance, legend, folklore, and fairy tale. Thus the revelation at the beginning of "Ainulindale" that the elvish name for Eru, the creator, was Iluvatar is revelation indeed, but perhaps more of elvishness than divinity. Tolkien is at his best when working at the roots of words and at the heart of languages wherein the inquiring mind discovers itself reflected in its most basic operations. Thus, the Tolkien power of name-giving is reflexive, revealing both the thing named and the namer— here the elves—but it stirs hidden responses in the receptive reader to the universal sense of the power of names, when they are the right names. And Tolkien is almost infallibly right in his naming, perhaps because his inspirations come from an understanding of the nature and practice of language similar to that which a scientist might develop after long study of the secrets of nature. Inventing names is Tolkien's chief (but not only) method of activating the power of language structures to both quicken the imagination and convey the assurance that existence follows upon the name, as indeed in Tolkien's world it truly does.

We cannot separate Tolkien's interest in and experiments with languages both real and imagined from his vision of faerie, a vision that grew with his exploration of its imaginative potential. Tolkien revealed that the vision was in his words "a gift," and it remained for him all his life a hobby and a pastime, bound up with both his scholarship as an Oxford don and his parenting of his own children. Many of the key episodes that anchored *The Silmarillion* in Tolkien's imagination were visions, visual images, which Tolkien felt he was obliged to find the explanation of. He always held that Middle-Earth was a world discovered rather than dreamed up. It was to be found in the logic of cause and effect: an imagined language extended itself necessarily to ethology, and thence to geology, geography, botany, zoology and so on, producing the coherent infrastructures of a realized secondary world suited to the imagination.

No critical estimate of Tolkien and *The Silmarillion* would be worth producing without a word on style. Thanks to the publication of some of the earlier drafts of Silmarillion materials, we can assess the process by which Tolkien's mature style developed. How fortunate literature has been that Tolkien's elvish mythology did not enjoy an early success. The early drafts are discovered to be stylistically mannered, artificial in the bad sense, and feebly imitative of 19th-century aesthetic models. As Tolkien's imagination expanded so did the range of his style. Finally, he found the proper voices for his elves in *The Silmarillion*, which contains elements of the most lyrical prose ever written in English. *The Silmarillion* is, moreover, rich in sustained, inspired story-telling, in mythic and epic elements that range from the literature of revelation to the tragic beauty of elvin history in Middle-Earth, an accounting of a species exiled by fate and by choice from felicity. In addition to numerous instances in the published version of *The Silmarillion*, readers should not overlook two jewels of heroic and tragic narrative reaching that rarest of all literary achievements, the sublime, in the stories of Tuor and Turin, both found in *Unfinished Tales*.

The Lord of the Rings and *The Silmarillion* are not merely great fantasy; they are great literature. Tolkien will continue to interest scholars and students who have already begun the exhaustive study of his work, its sources, inspirations, and its elements. There is little doubt that Tolkien will eventually take his place somewhere in the neo-romantic movement which followed the aestheticism and decadence of the late 19th century. He has already been placed in the tradition of writers like Rider Haggard and William Morris, and the influences of the Eddas, the Kalevala, Anglo-Saxon, and Middle English romance have already been noted and will doubtless yield more secrets in the future. Nor should we ignore the influence of the Inklings and their interest in Tolkien's work during the long, difficult years before recognition came. Other students will consider the relation or at least the parallels to contemporary writers of fantasy like Mervyn Peake and Austin Tappan Wright. In the end, it may be that Tolkien will be understood best when linked and compared to James Joyce, an unlikely pairing, perhaps, but one that is full of telling comparisons and contrasts.

—Donald L. Lawler

TITLE
INDEX

The following list of titles includes all novels and short story collections (designated "s") listed in the Science-Fiction Publications section of the entries in the book. The name(s) in parenthesis after the title is meant to direct the reader to the appropriate entry where full publication information is given. Series characters or locales (noted in the fiction lists) are listed here, even if their names do not appear in specific titles of works. The abbreviations "for" and "fan" indicate entrants in the Foreign-Language Writers and Major Fantasy Writers appendices.

A for Andromeda (F. Hoyle), 1962
A for Anything (D. Knight), 1961
Abandon Galaxy (Fox, as Somers), 1967
Abandoned (Verne, for), 1874
Abbs (Hyne), 1929
Ability Quotient (Reynolds), 1975
Abode of Life (Correy), 1982
Abominable Earthman (s Pohl),1963
Above All Else (Shiel), 1943
Absolute at Large (Capek, for), 1927
Absolutely Perfect House (Mayhar), 1983
Abyss (Keller), 1948
Abyss (Wilhelm), 1971
Accidental Earth (Kelley), 1968
Across a Billion Years (Silverberg), 1969
Across the Ages (Fearn, as Statten), 1952
Across the Sea of Stars (Benford),1984
Across the Sea of Stars (Clarke), 1959
Across Time (Wollheim, as Grinnell), 1957
Actions and Reactions (s Kipling), 1909
Active Measures (Drake, J. Morris), 1985
Adam in Moonshine (Priestley), 1927
Adam Link series (s Binder)
Adam the Creator (Capek, for), 1929
Address: Centauri (F. Wallace), 1955
Adventure in the Blue Room (S. Wright, as Fowler), 1945
Adventure of the Peerless Peer (Farmer), 1974
Adventure of Wyndham Smith (S. Wright), 1938
Adventures (Resnick), 1985
Adventures of a Chinaman in China (Verne, for), 1889
Adventures of a Solicitor (s Hyne, as Chesney), 1898
Adventures of a Two–Minute Werewolf (DeWeese), 1983
Adventures of Alyx (s Russ), 1983
Adventures of Terra Tarkington (Webb), 1985
Adventures of Tom Bombadil (Tolkien, fan), 1962
Adventures of Una Persson and Catherine Cornelius in the Twentieth Century (Moorcock), 1976
Adversary (May), 1984
Aelita (Tolstoy, for), 1957
Affair with Genius (s Green), 1969
After Doomsday (P. Anderson), 1962
After Many a Summer (Huxley), 1939
After Many a Summer Dies the Swan (Huxley), 1939
After Some Tomorrow (Reynolds), 1967
After Things Fell Apart (Goulart), 1970
After 12,000 Years (Coblentz), 1950
After Utopia (Reynolds), 1977
After Worlds Collide (Wylie), 1934
After World's End (Williamson), 1961
Afterglow (England), 1965
Against Infinity (Benford), 1983
Against the Fall of Night (Clarke), 1953
Age (Aldiss), 1967
Age of Miracles (Brunner), 1973
Age of the Pussyfoot (Pohl), 1969
Agency series (Meltzer)
Agent (Meltzer),1968
Agent of Chaos (Spinrad), 1967

Agent of the Terran Empire (s P. Anderson), 1965
Agent of the Unknown (St. Clair), 1956
Agent of Vega (P. Anderson), 1983
Agent of Vega (s Schmitz), 1960
Ahead of Time (s Kuttner), 1953
Airs of Earth (s Aldiss), 1963
Airtrust (England), 1915
Alas, Babylon (Frank), 1959
Alastor series (Vance)
Alchemical Marriage of Alistair Crompton (Sheckley), 1978
Aldair series (Barrett)
Aleph (Borges, for), 1970
Algorithm (Gawron), 1978
Alice's World (Lundwall), 1971
Alicia II (Thurston), 1978
Alien (Davies),1968
Alien (A. Foster), 1979
Alien (R.Jones), 1951
Alien Accounts (s Sladek),1982
AlienArt (Dickson), 1973
Alien Cargo (s Sturgeon), 1984
Alien Debt (Busby), 1984
Alien Dust (Tubb), 1955
Alien Embassy (Watson), 1977
Alien from Arcturus (Dickson), 1956
Alien from the Stars (Fanthorpe), 1959
Alien from the Stars (Sutton), 1970
Alien Heat (Moorcock), 1972
Alien Horizons (s Nolan), 1974
Alien Impact (Tubb), 1952
Alien Intelligence (s Williamson), 1980
Alien Island (Sherred), 1970
Alien Life (Tubb), 1954
Alien Main (Biggle, Sherred), 1985
Alien Minds (E. Evans), 1955
Alien Ones (Fanthorpe, as Brett), 1963
Alien Planet (Pratt), 1962
Alien Realms (E.E. Smith), 1980
Alien Sea (Rackham), 1968
Alien Seed (Tubb), 1976
Alien Universe (Tubb, as Gridban), 1952
Alien Upstairs (Sargent), 1983
Alien Way Dickson), 1965
Alien Worlds (E.E. Smith), 1978
Aliens (s Leinster), 1960
Aliens Among US (s J. White), 1969
Aliens for Neighbours (s Simak),1961
Aliens 4 (s Sturgeon), 1959
Aliens from Space (Silverberg, as Osborne), 1958
Aliens, Travellers and Other Strangers (Strugatsky, for), 1984
All Around the Moon (Verne, for), 1876
All Darkness Met (Cook), 1980
All Flesh is Grass (Simak), 1965
All Fools' Day (Cooper), 1966
All for His Country (Giesy), 1915
All Judgment Fled (J. White), 1968
All My Sins Remembered (Joe Haldeman), 1977
All the Colors of Darkness (Biggle), 1963

All the Myriad Ways (s Niven), 1971
All the Sounds of Fear (s Ellison), 1973
All the Traps of Earth (s Simak), 1962
All These Earths (Busby), 1978
All Times Possible (Eklund), 1974
Alley God (s Farmer), 1962
Allies of Antares (Bulmer, as Akers), 1981
Alnians series (Hoskins)
Alone Against Tomorrow (s Ellison), 1971
Alph (Maine), 1972
Alpha Centauri—or Die! (Brackett), 1963
Alpha Yes, Terra No! (Petaja), 1965
Als Al het Andere Faalt (s Strete), 1976
Altar on Asconal (Brunner), 1965
Alteration (Amis), 1976
Altered Ego (Sohl), 1954
Alternate Martians (Chandler), 1965
Alternate Orbits (s Chandler), 1971
Alternating Currents (s Pohl), 1956
Alton's Unguessable (Sutton), 1970
Aluminum Man (Edmondson), 1975
Always the Blackknight (Hoffman), 1970
Alyx (s Russ), 1976
Amazon Planet (Reynolds), 1975
Amazon Strikes Again (Fearn), 1954
Amazon's Diamond Quest (Fearn), 1953
Amber series (Zelazny)
Amberdon, Telzey series (Schmitz)
Ambulance Ship (J. White), 1979
Ambush of Shadows (P. Williams), 1983
American Gun Club (Verne, for), 1874
Among the Dead and Other Events Leading Up to the Apocalypse (s Bryant), 1973
Amphibian (Belyaev, for), n.d.
Amphibians (S. Wright), 1925
Amsirs and the Iron Thorn (Budrys), 1967
Amtrak War series (Tilley)
Anackire (Lee), 1983
Analogue Men (D. Knight), 1962
Anarchistic Colossus (van Vogt), 1977
Anasazi (s Ing), 1980
Ancient, My Enemy (s Dickson), 1974
Ancient of Days (Bishop), 1985
And All the Stars a Stage (Blish), 1971
And Chaos Died (Russ), 1970
...and My Fear Is Great (Sturgeon), 1965
And Not Make Dreams Your Master (Goldin), 1981
...and Others Shall Be Born (F. Lond), 1968
And So Ad Infinitivum (The Life of the Insects) (Capek, for), 1923
...and Some Were Human (s del Rey), 1948
And Strange at Ecbatan the Trees (Bishop), 1976
And the Stars Remain (Berry), 1952
And Then the Town Took Off (Richard Wilson), 1960
And Then There'll Be Fireworks (Elgin), 1981
Andover and the Android (s Wilhelm), 1966
Android (Fanthorpe, as Zeigfried), 1962
Android at Arms (Norton), 1971
Android Avenger (T. White), 1965
Android Planet (Rankine), 1976
Androids (F.Long), 1969
Andromeda (Yefremov, for), 1959
Andromeda Breakthrough (F. Hoyle), 1964
Andromeda Gun (Boyd), 1974
Andromeda Strain (Crichton),1969
Angado (Tubb), 1984
Angel of the Revolution (Griffith), 1893

Angel with a Sword (Cherryh), 1985
Angels and Spaceships (s F. Brown),1954
Angry Espers (Biggle), 1961
Angry Ghost (Dent, as Robeson), 1977
Angry Planet (Cross), 1945
Animal People (Coblentz), 1970
Annals of Klepsis (Lafferty), 1983
Annihilation (Fearn, as Statten) 1950
Annihilation Factor (Bayley), 1972
Annihilist (Dent, as Robeson), 1968
Annwn series (George H. Smith)
Anomalous Phenomena (Verne, for), 1965
Anomaly (Sohl), 1971
Anome (Vance), 1973
Another End (King), 1971
Another Fine Myth (Asprin), 1978
Another Heaven, Another Earth (Hoover),1981
Another Kind (s Oliver), 1955
Another Tree in Eden (Duncan), 1956
Answer (s Wylie), 1956
Antarctic Mystery (Verne, for), 1898
Anthem (Rand), 1938
Anthonology (s Anthony), 1985
Anthropol (Trimble), 1968
Antic Earth (Charbonneau), 1967
Anti-Death League (Amis), 1966
Antigeos series (Capon)
Antigrav (Fisk), 1978
Anti-Man (Koontz), 1970
Antinomy (s S. Robinson), 1980
Anton York, Immortal (s Binder), 1965
Anubis Gates (Powers), 1983
Anvil of Time (Silverberg), 1969
Anything Box (s Henderson),1965
Anything Tree (Rackham), 1970
Anything You Can Do...(Garrett, as Langart), 1963
Anywhen (s Blish), 1970
Ape and Essence (Huxley), 1948
Apocalypse Brigade (Coppel), 1981
Apocalypses (Lafferty), 1977
Apollo at Go (Sutton), 1963
Apology for Rain (Gawron), 1974
Apostle of the Cylinder (Rousseau),1918
Appointment at Bloodstar (Goldin), 1978
Apprentice Adept series (Anthony)
Approaching Oblivion (s Ellison), 1974
Aquarius Mission (Caidin), 1968
Aquiliad (s Sucharitkul), 1983
Archipelago (Lafferty), 1979
Arcot, Morey, and Wade series (Campbell)
Arctic Bridge (s Meek), 1944
Arcturus Landing (Dickson), 1978
Ardor on Aros (Offutt), 1973
Arena of Antares (Bulmer, as Akers), 1974
Argentis (Tubb, as Shaw), 1952
Argos series (Lessing)
Ark, Simon series (s Hoch)
Arm of the Starfish (L'Engle), 1965
Armada of Antares (Bulmer, as Akers), 1976
Armageddon (Waterloo), 1898
Amageddon Rag (Martin), 1983
Armageddon 2419 A.D. (Nowlan), 1962
Armed Camps (Reed), 1969
Arrive at Easterwine (Lafferty), 1971
Arsenal of Miracles (Fox), 1964
Artery of Fire (Scortia), 1972

Artifact (Benford), 1985
Artificial Kid (Sterling), 1980
Artificial Man (Davies), 1965
As on a Darkling Plain (Bova), 1972
As the Curtain Falls (Chilson), 1974
As the Green Star Rises (L. Carter), 1975
As You Were (s Kuttner), 1955
Ascendancies (Compton), 1980
Ascension (Grant), 1977
Ashes and Stars (Zebrowski), 1977
Ashes, Ashes (Barjavel, for), 1967
Asleep in the Afternoon (Large), 1938
Assassin of Gor (Norman), 1970
Assault on the Gods (Goldin), 1977
Assignment: Hellhole (Offutt, as Cleve), 1983
Assignment in Eternity (s Heinlein), 1953
Assignment in Nowhere (Laumer), 1968
Assignment: Nor'Dyren (Van Scyoc), 1973
Asteroid Man (Fanthorpe), 1960
Astra series (Norton)
Astral Quest (Rankine), 1975
Astronaut (Searls), 1960
Astronauts Must Not Land (Brunner), 1963
Asutra (Vance), 1974
Asylum Piece (s Kavan), 1940
Asylum World (Jakes), 1969
At the Earth's Core (E. Burroughs), 1922
At the Edge of the World (Dunsany, fan), 1970
At the Eye of the Ocean (Schenck), 1980
At the Mountains of Madness (s Lovecraft), 1964
At the Narrow Passage (Meredith), 1973
At the Seventh Level (Elgin), 1972
Atilus series (Tubb, as Thomson)
Atlantean Nights Entertainment (Pangborn), 1980
Atlantic Abomination (Brunner), 1960
Atlas Shrugged (Rand), 1957
Atom Conspiracy (Sutton), 1963
Atom War on Mars (Tubb), 1952
Atomic Fantasy (Capek, for), 1948
Atomic Nemesis (Fanthorpe, as Zeigfried), 1962
Atoms and Evil (s Bloch), 1962
Atoms of Empire (s Hyne), 1904
Aton series (Anthony)
Atrocity Exhibition (s Ballard), 1970
Attack from Atlantis (del Rey), 1953
Attack on the Giant Baby (s Reed), 1981
Attar series (Joe Haldeman, as Graham)
Aurelia (Lafferty), 1982
Austin, Steve series (Caidin)
Authentic Touch (Wodhams), 1971
Automated Goliath (Temple), 1962
Autumn Angels (Cover), 1975
Autumn People (s Bradbury), 1965
Avatar (P.Anderson), 1978
Avenger series (Goulart, as Robeson)
Avenger of Antares (Bulmer,as Akers), 1975
Avengers Battle the Earth-Wrecker (Binder), 1967
Avengers of Carrig (Brunner), 1969
Avenging Goddess (s Fanthorpe), 1964
Avenging Martian (Fearn, as Statten), 1951
Aventine (s Killough), 1982
Awakening (Meredith), 1979
Away and Beyond (s van Vogt), 1952
Awful Egg (Dent, as Robeson), 1978
Ayesha (Haggard), 1905

B.E.A.S.T. (Maine), 1966
Babel-17 (Delany), 1966
Baby is Three (Sturgeon), 1965
Back to the Stone Age (E. Burroughs), 1937
Backward in Time (Kelley), 1979
Badge of Infamy (del Rey), 1963
Bagful of Dreams (s Vance), 1979
Balance of Power (Stableford), 1979
Baley, Elijah series (Asimov)
Ballad of Beta-2 (Delany), 1965
Ballroom of the Skies (MacDonald), 1952
Balls! (Rohmer), 1979
Baltimore Gun Club (Verne, for), 1874
Bander Snatch (O'Donnell), 1979
Barbarian of World's End (L. Carter), 1977
Barbarians of Mars (Moorcock, as Bradbury), 1965
Barbie Murders (s Varley), 1980
Barefoot in the Head (Aldiss), 1969
Barnard's Planet (Boyd), 1975
Barnstormer in Oz (Farmer), 1982
Barons of Behavior (Purdom), 1972
Barrier 346 (Fanthorpe, as Zeigfried), 1965
Barrier World (Charbonneau), 1970
Barsac Mission (Verne, for), 1960
Barton series (Busby)
Bastable, Oswald series (Moorcock)
Bathhouse (Mayakovsky, for), 1968
Battle Circle series (Anthony)
Battle for the Planet of the Apes (Gerrold), 1973
Battle for the Stars (Hamilton), 1961
Battle of Forever (van Vogt), 1971
Battle of Wizards (Hubbard), 1949
Battle on Mercury (del Rey, as Van Lhin), 1953
Battle on Venus (Temple), 1963
Battlefield Earth: A Saga of the Year 3000 (Hubbard), 1983
Battlestar Galactica series (Goulart, Resnick, Thurston, Yermakov)
Beachhead Planet (R. Williams), 1970
Beanstalk (Rackham), 1973
Bearing an Hourglass (Anthony), 1984
Beast (J. Fast), 1981
Beast series (Stallman)
Beast (van Vogt), 1963
Beast Master series (Norton)
Beast That Shouted Love at the Heart of the World (s Ellison), 1969
Beastchild (Koontz), 1970
Beasts (Crowley), 1976
Beasts from Beyond (Wellman), 1950
Beasts of Antares (Bulmer, as Akers), 1980
Beasts of Gor (Norman),1978
Beasts of Kohl (Rackham), 1966
Beautiful Biting Machine (s Lee), 1984
Because It Is Absurd (Boulle, for), 1971
Beckoning Hand (s Allen), 1887
Beckoning Lights (M. Hughes), 1982
Bedbug (Mayakovsky, for), 1960
Bedlam Planet (Brunner), 1968
Beetle in the Anthill (Strugatsky, for), 1980
Before Adam (London), 1907
Before the Dawn (Taine), 1934
Beggars series (Nelson)
Begum's Fortune (Verne, for), 1879
Behind the Walls of Terra (Farmer), 1970
Behold the Man (Moorcock), 1969
Behold the Stars (Bulmer), 1965
Believers' World (Lowndes), 1961
Bell from Infinity (R. Williams), 1968

Bell Tree (Hoover), 1982
Beloved Son (Turner), 1978
Beneath the Shattered Moons (Bishop), 1977
Beneath Your Very Boots (Hyne), 1889
Benefits (Fairbairns), 1979
Benita (Haggard), 1906
Ben's Bed (Mann), 1985
Bernards magiska sommar (Lundwall), 1975
Bernhard the Conqueror (Lundwall), 1973
Berserker series (Saberhagen)
Best Laid Schemes (s Eisenberg), 1971
Best Rootin' Tooton' Gunslinger in the Whole Damned Galaxy
    (Resnick), 1983
Best Ye Breed (Reynolds), 1978
Better Mantrap (s Shaw), 1982
Bettyann (Neville), 1970
Between Planets (Heinlein), 1951
Between the Strokes of Night (Sheffield), 1985
Beyond (s Sturgeon),1960
Beyond (Sutton), 1968
Beyond Another Sun (Godwin), 1971
Beyond Apollo (Malzberg), 1972
Beyond Apollo (Sutton), 1966
Beyond Bedlam (s Guin), 1973
Beyond Capella (Rackham), 1971
Beyond Earth's Gates (Kuttner and C.Moore, as Padgett), 1954
Beyond Eden (Duncan), 1955
Beyond Heaven's River (Bear), 1980
Beyond Infinity (s Nourse), 1964
Beyond Santuary (J. Morris), 1985
Beyond the Barrier (D. Knight), 1964
Beyond the Barrier of Space (Fanthorpe, as Torro), 1969
Beyond the Beyond (s P.Anderson), 1969
Beyond the Black Enigma (Fox, as Somers), 1965
Beyond the Blue Event Horizon (Pohl), 1980
Beyond the Burning Lands (Christopher), 1971
Beyond the Dark River (M. Hughes), 1979
Beyond the Eleventh Hour (R. Gordon, as Hough), 1961
Beyond the Farthest Star (E. Burroughs), 1964
Beyond the Fields we Know (Dunsany, fan), 1972
Beyond the Galactic Lens (Tubb, as Kern), 1975
Beyond the Galactic Rim (Chandler), 1963
Beyond the Gates of Dream (s L. Carter), 1969
Beyond the Great Oblivion (England), 1965
Beyond the Moon (Hamilton), 1950
Beyond the Planet Earth (Tsiolkovsky, for), 1960
Beyond the Resurrection (Eklund), 1973
Beyond the Rim (S. Wright), 1932
Beyond the Silver Sky (Bulmer), 1961
Beyond the Stars (Cummings), 1963
Beyond the Tomorrow Mountains (Engdahl), 1973
Beyond the Vanishing Point (Cummings), 1958
Beyond the Veil (Fanthorpe, as Thanet), 1964
Beyond the Void (Fanthorpe, as Muller), 1965
Beyond Thirty (s E. Burroughs), 1955
Beyond This Horizon (Heinlein), 1948
Beyond Time (Fanthorpe, as Muller), 1962
Beyonders (Wellman), 1977
Bicentennial Man (s Asimov), 1976
Big Ball of Wax (Mead), 1954
Big Bang (Goulart), 1982
Big Black Mark (Chandler), 1975
Big Death (Maine), 1978
Big Eye (Ehrlich), 1949
Big Jump (Brackett), 1955
Big Planet series (Vance)

Big Show (s Laumer), 1972
Big Sun of Mercury (Asimov, as French), 1974
Big Time (Leiber), 1961
Big X (Searls), 1959
Biggles—Charter Pilot (Johns), 1943
Bilbo's Last Song (Tolkien, fan), 1974
Bill, The Galactic Hero (H. Harrison), 1965
Billenium (s Ballard), 1962
Billion Days of Earth (Piserchia), 1976
Binary (Crichton, as Lange), 1972
Binary Z (Rankine), 1969
Bioblast! (Gallun), 1985
Bird of Time (Effinger), 1985
Bird of Time (West), 1959
Birds of Prey (Drake), 1984
Birth of a New Republic (Breuer, Williamson), 1981
Birth of Fire (Pournelle), 1976
Birth of the People's Republic of Antarctica (Batchelor), 1983
Birthgrave series (Lee)
Birthright (Resnick), 1982
Birthright (Sky), 1975
Bitter Pill (Chandler), 1974
Bitter Reflection (s Fanthorpe), 1964
Black August (Wheatley), 1934
Black Avengers (Fearn, as Statten), 1953
Black Bargain (Fearn, as Statten), 1953
Black, Black Witch (Dent, as Robeson), 1981
Black Chariots (Goulart, as Robeson), 1974
Black Cloud (F. Hoyle), 1957
Black Company series (Cook)
Black Corridor (Moorcock), 1969
Black Druid (s F. Long), 1975
Black Easter (Blish), 1968
Black Flame (Weinbaum), 1948
Black Fox (Heard), 1950
Black Galaxy (Leinster), 1954
Black God's Shadow (s C. Moore), 1977
Black Grail (Broderick), 1985
Black Hole (A. Foster), 1979
Black in Time (Jakes), 1970
Black Infinity (Fanthorpe, as Brett), 1961
Black Knight of the Iron Sphere (E.E. Smith), 1979
Black Legion of Callisto (L. Carter), 1972
Black Lion (Fanthorpe), 1979
Black Mountains (Saberhagen), 1971
Black Opal (Ash), 1915
Black Roads (Hensley), 1976
Black Star (L. Carter), 1973
Black Star Passes (s Campbell), 1953
Black Star Rising (Pohl), 1985
Black Venus's Tale (s A. Carter), 1980
Black Wheel (Merritt), 1947
Black Yacht (Baxter), 1982
Blackcollar (Zahn), 1983
Blackman's Burden (Reynolds), 1972
Black-Wing of Mars (Fearn, as Stratten), 1953
Bladerunner (Nourse), 1974
Blades of Mars (Moorcock, as Bradbury), 1965
Bladesman of Antares (Bulmer, as Akers), 1975
Blake's Progress (Nelson), 1975
Blake's Seven series (T. Hoyle)
Blal (s van Vogt), 1976
Blast off at Woomera (Walters), 1957
Blast-Off at 0300 (Walters), 1958
Blazon (Bulmer), 1970
Bleeding Man (s Strete), 1977

Blessing of Pan (Dunsany, fan), 1927
Blessing Papers (Barnwell), 1980
Blind Circle (Renard, for), 1928
Blind Man and the Elephant (Griffin), 1982
Blind Spot (Flint, Hall), 1951
Blind Voices (Reamy), 1978
Blind Worm (Stableford), 1970
Blindfold from the Stars (High), 1979
Blindman's World (s Bellamy), 1898
Blockade of Sinitron (Rankine), 1966
Blockade Runners (Verne, for), 1874
Blood and Burning (s Budrys), 1978
Blood Brothers of Gor (Norman), 1982
Blood Countess (Goulart, as Robeson), 1975
Blood County (Piserchia, as Selby), 1981
Blood Music (Bear), 1985
Blood Red Game (Moorcock), 1970
Blooded on Arachne (s Bishop), 1982
Bloodhype (A. Foster), 1973
Bloodstar Conspiracy (Goldin), 1978
Bloodworld (Janifer), 1968
Bloody Chamber (s A. Carter), 1979
Bloody Sun (Bradley), 1964
Blown (Farmer), 1969
Blue Adept (Anthony), 1981
Blue Atom (R. Williams), 1958
Blue Aura (Walters), 1979
Blue Barbarians (Coblentz), 1958
Blue Face (Edmondson), 1972
Blue Hawk (Dickinson), 1976
Blue Juggernaut (Fanthorpe, as Fane), 1965
Blue Pagoda (s Merritt), 1946
Blue Star (Pratt), 1969
Blue World (Vance), 1966
Bluesong (Van Scyoc), 1983
Boats of the "Glen Carrig" (Hodgson), 1907
Bodelan Way (Trimble), 1974
Body Snatchers (Finney), 1955
Bolo series (Laumer)
Bolts: A Robot Dog (Key), 1966
Bombs in Orbit (Sutton), 1959
Bond (Ehrlich), 1980
Bones of Zora (de Camp), 1983
Book of Being (Watson), 1985
Book of Days (s G. Wolfe), 1981
Book of Dreams (Vance), 1981
Book of Lost Tales (Tolkien, fan), 1983
Book of Martyrs (s Moorcock), 1976
Book of Ptath (van Vogt), 1947
Book of Rack the Healer (Z. Hughes), 1973
Book of Sand (Borges, for), 1977
Book of Skulls (Silverberg), 1971
Book of the Beast (Stallman), 1982
Book of the New Sun (G. Wolfe)
Book of the River (Watson), 1984
Book of the Stars (Watson), 1985
Book of Wonder (Dunsany, fan), 1912
Boomerang series (Yermakov)
Boosted Man (Bulmer, as Zetford), 1974
Border, Breed nor Birth (Reynolds), 1972
Borderline (Vercors, for), 1954
Born in Captivity (Berry), 1952
Born Leader (McIntosh), 1954
Born of Luna (Fearn, as Statten), 1951
Born of Man and Woman (s Matheson), 1954
Born to Exile (Eisenstein), 1978

Born Under Mars (Brunner), 1967
Born with the Dead (s Silverberg), 1974
Boss of Terror (Dent, as Robeson), 1976
Bow Down to Nul (Aldiss), 1960
Box of Nothing (Dickinson), 1985
Boy Adventurers in the Land of the Monkey Men (Verrill), 1923
Boy Astronaut (Walters), 1977
Boy Who Had the Power (Sutton), 1971
Boys from Brazil (Levin), 1976
Brain Machine (George O. Smith), 1968
Brain Plant series (Meltzer)
Brain Twister (Garrett as Phillips, Janifer), 1962
Brain Wave (P. Anderson), 1954
Brain World (Reynolds), 1978
Brainrack (G. Davis, Pedler), 1974
Brains of Earth (Vance), 1966
Brain-Stealers (Leinster), 1954
Branch (Resnick), 1984
Brand New World (Cummings), 1964
Brand of the Werewolf (Dent, as Robeson), 1965
Brass Dragon (Bradley), 1969
Brave Free Men (Vance), 1973
Brave New World (Huxley), 1932
Breakaway (Tubb), 1975
Breakfast in the Ruins (Moorcock), 1972
Breaking Earth (s Laumer), 1981
Breaking of Northwall (P. Williams), 1981
Breaking Point (s Gunn), 1972
Breakthrough (Cowper), 1967
Breed to Come (Norton), 1972
Bride from the Desert (s Allen), 1896
Bridge of Ashes (Zelazny), 1976
Bridge of Light (Verrill), 1950
Bridgehead (Drake), 1985
Briefing for a Descent into Hell (Lessing), 1971
Brigands of the Moon (Cummings), 1931
Bright Companion (E. Llewellyn), 1980
Bright New Universe (Williamson), 1967
Brightness Falls from the Air (Tiptree), 1985
Bring Back Yesterday (Chandler), 1961
Bring the Jubilee (W. Moore), 1953
Brinkman (Goulart), 1981
British Barbarians (Allen), 1895
Briton or Boer? (Griffith), 1897
Broke Down Engine (s Goulart), 1971
Broken Cycle (Chandler), 1975
Broken Lands (Saberhagen), 1968
Broken Sword (P. Anderson), 1954
Broken Symmetries (Preuss), 1983
Bromius Phenomenon (Rankine), 1973
Brontomek! (Coney), 1976
Bronze King (Charnas), 1985
Bronze of Eddarta (Garrett), 1983
Brooks, Clifford series (Fearn, as Gridban)
Brothel in Rösenstrasse (Moorcock), 1982
Brother Assassin (Saberhagen), 1969
Brother Berserker (Saberhagen), 1969
Brother Jonathan (Kilian), 1985
Brother to Demons, Brother to God (Williamson), 1979
Brothers of Earth (Cherryh), 1976
Bug Jack Barron (Spinrad), 1969
Bug Wars (Asprin), 1979
Bumsider (MacApp), 1972
Burn, Witch, Burn! (Merritt), 1933
Burning (Gunn), 1972
Burning Mountain (Coppel), 1983

Burning World (Ballard), 1964
Businessman (Disch), 1984
But What of Earth? (Anthony, R. Coulson), 1976
Butterfly Kid (C. Anderson), 1967
Butterfly Planet (High), 1971
Buy Jupiter (s Asimov), 1975
By Airship to Ophir (Ash), 1911
By Furies Possessed (T. White), 1970
By Rocket to the Moon (Gail, for), 1913
By the Light of the Green Star (L. Carter), 1974
Bypass to Otherness (s Kuttner), 1961
Byworlder (P. Anderson), 1971
Byzantium Endures (Moorcock), 1981

C.O.D. Mars (Tubb), 1968
Cabrito (s Lafferty), 1976
Cachalot (A. Foster), 1980
Cache from Outer Space (Farmer), 1962
Caduceus Wild (W. Moore), 1978
Cage a Man (Busby), 1973
Cageworld series (Kapp)
Cal, Veg, and Aquilon series (Anthony)
Calculated Risk (Maine), 1960
Calibrated Alligator (s Silverberg), 1969
Calkins, Ajax series (Wollheim)
Call of Peter Gaskell (Wallis), 1948
Call of the Cosmos (Tsiolkovsky, for), 1963
Call of the Savage (Kline), 1937
Call of the Werewolf (s Fanthorpe), 1958
Call of the Wild (s Fanthorpe), 1965
Callahan's Crosstime Saloon (s S. Robinson), 1977
Caller from Overspace (Lymington), 1979
Calling Dr. Patchwork (Goulart), 1978
Callisto series (L. Carter)
Calrissian, Lando series (L. Smith)
Caltraps of Time (s Masson), 1968
Camberwell Miracle (Beresford), 1933
Camp Concentration (Disch), 1968
Can You Feel Anything When I Do This? (s Sheckley), 1971
Canary in a Cat House (s Vonnegut), 1961
Candy Man (King), 1971
Canopus in Argos: Archives series (Lessing)
Canopy of Time (s Aldiss), 1959
Canticle for Leibowitz (W. Miller), 1960
Cape (Caidin), 1971
Capella's Golden Eye (C. Evans), 1980
Capitol (s Card), 1978
Capricorn Games (s Silverberg), 1976
Captain America: The Great Gold Steal (T. White), 1968
Captain Blackman (J. Williams), 1972
Captain Future series (Hamilton)
Captain Ishmael (Griffith), 1901
Captains of Souls (E. Wallace), 1922
Captive (Stallman), 1981
Captive of Gor (Norman) 1972
Captive Scorpio (Bulmer, as Akers), 1978
Captive Universe (H. Harrison), 1969
Captives of the Flame (Delany), 1963
Captives of the Moon (P. Moore), 1960
Caravan (Goldin), 1975
Cardinal of the Stars (Rayer), 1964
Carefully Considered Rape of the World (Mead), 1966
Cargo Unknown (Dent, as Robeson), 1980
Carlisle, Gerry series (s A. Barnes)
Carnadyne Horde (Offutt, as Cleve), 1984
Carnellian Throne (J. Morris), 1979

Carpet People (Pratchett), 1971
Carson of Venus (E. Burroughs), 1939
Cartoon Crimes (Goulart, as Robeson), 1974
Carty (Fox), 1977
Case Against Tomorrow (S Pohl), 1957
Case and the Dreamer (s Sturgeon), 1973
Case of Conscience (Blish), 1958
Case of the Little Green Man (Reynolds), 1951
Casey Agonistes (s McKenna), 1973
Cassady (Sutton), 1979
Castaways of Tanagar (Stableford), 1981
Castaways' World (Brunner), 1963
Castle Keeps (Offutt), 1972
Castle of Crossed Destinies (Calvino, for), 1977
Castle of the Carpathians (Verne, for), 1893
Castle Roogna (Anthony), 1979
Cat Karina (Coney), 1982
Cataclysm (Fearn, as Statten), 1951
Cataclysm (Sherriff), 1958
Catacomb Years (Bishop), 1979
Catalyst (Fearn, as Statten), 1951
Catalyst (Harness), 1980
Catastrophe (Buzzati, for), 1965
Catastrophe Planet (Laumer), 1966
Catch a Falling Star (Brunner), 1968
Catch the Star Winds (Chandler), 1969
Catface (Simak), 1978
Catfang (Fisk), 1980
Cat's Cradle (Vonnegut), 1963
Catseye (Norton), 1961
Caution! Inflammable! (s Scortia), 1975
Cautionary Tales (s Yarbo), 1978
Cave Girl (s E. Burroughs), 1925
Caverns (O'Donnell), 1981
Caverns of the Moon (P. Moore), 1964
Caves of Drach (Walters), 1977
Caves of Karst (Hoffman), 1969
Caves of Mars (Petaja), 1965
Caves of Steel (Asimov), 1954
Caviar (s Sturgeon), 1955
Cee Tee Man (Morgan), 1955
Celestial Blueprint (s Farmer), 1962
Celestial Steam Locomotive (Coney), 1983
Cellars (Shirley), 1982
Cemetery World (Simak), 1973
Centaur Aisle (Anthony), 1982
Centauri Device (M. Harrison), 1974
Centrifugal Rickshaw Dancer (Watkins), 1985
Centurion's Vengeance (s Fanthorpe), 1961
Century of Progress (Saberhagen), 1983
Century of the Manikin (Tubb), 1972
Century's End (Griffin), 1981
Cerberus (Chalker), 1982
Ceres Solution (Shaw), 1981
Chain of Chance (Lem, for), 1978
Chain Reaction (Hodder-Williams), 1959
Chaining the Lady (Anthony), 1978
Chalk Giants (Roberts), 1974
Challenge (Bulmer), 1954
Challenge the Hellmaker (Richmond), 1976
Challenger, Professor series (Doyle)
Chameleon Corps (s Goulart), 1972
Change Song (Hoffman), 1972
Change the Sky (s St. Clair), 1974
Change War (s Leiber), 1978
Changeling (s van Vogt), 1967

Changeling Earth (Saberhagen), 1973
Changeling Worlds (Bulmer), 1959
Changes series (Dickinson)
Changing Land (Zelazny), 1981
Channel's Destiny (Lichtenberg), 1982
Chanur series (Cherryh)
Chaos (Fanthorpe, as Bell), 1964
Chaos Fighters (R. Williams), 1955
Chaos in Lagrangia (Reynolds), 1984
Chaos Weapon (Kapp), 1977
Chapayeca (Edmondson), 1971
Chariot of Apollo (s Fanthorpe), 1962
Chariots of Ra (Bulmer), 1972
Charisma (Coney), 1975
Charles Fort Never Mentioned Wombats (R. Coulson, DeWeese),
    1977
Charon (Chalker), 1982
Charwoman's Shadow (Dunsany, fan), 1926
Chase of the Golden Meteor (Verne, for), 1909
Chauvinisto (Merwin), 1976
Checkpoint Lambda (Leinster),1966
Cheetah–Girl (s Blayre), 1923
Chekhov's Journey (Watson), 1983
Chessboard Planet (Kuttner and C. Moore, as Padgett), 1956
Chessmen of Mars (E. Burroughs), 1922
Chicago Conversion (Proctor), 1985
Chieftain of Andor (Offutt), 1976
Child Buyer (Hersey), 1960
Child Christopher and Goldilind the Fair (W. Morris, fan), 1895
Child of Fortune (Spinrad), 1985
Childhood's End (Clarke), 1953
Children of Atlantis (Harding), 1976
Children of Morrow (Hoover), 1973
Children of the Atom (s Shiras), 1953
Children of the Lens (E.E. Smith), 1954
Children of the Sphinx (Wallis), 1924
Children of the Stars series (J. Coulson)
Children of Tomorrow (van Vogt), 1970
Chinese Agent (Moorcock), 1970
Chocky (Wyndham), 1968
Choice of Gods (Simak), 1972
Chorale (Malzberg), 1978
Chrestomathy (s Laumer), 1984
Christmas Eve (Kornbluth), 1956
Chromosome Game (Hodder–Williams), 1984
Chronicles of Amber (Zelazny), 1979
Chronicles of Rodriguez (Dunsany, fan), 1922
Chronocules (Compton), 1970
Chronolysis (Jeury), 1980
Chronopolis (s Ballard), 1971
Chrysalids (Wyndham), 1955
Chthon (Anthony), 1967
Chtorr series (Gerrold)
Chup series (Saberhagen)
Cinnabar (Bryant), 1976
Circuit-Breaker (MacLeod), 1978
Circumpolar! (Lupoff), 1984
Circus of Hells (P. Anderson), 1970
Circus World (s Longyear), 1980
Cirque (T. Carr), 1977
Citadel of Fear (Stevens), 1970
Citadel of the Autarch (G. Wolfe), 1983
Cities in Flight series (Blish)
Cities of the Red Night (W. Burroughs), 1981
Citizen in Space (s Sheckley), 1955
Citizen of the Galaxy (Heinlein), 1957

City (s Simak), 1952
City and the Stars (Clarke), 1956
City at World's End (Hamilton), 1951
City Come A-Walkin' (Shirley), 1981
City Dwellers (Platt), 1970
City in the North (Randall), 1976
City in the Sahara (Verne, for), 1960
City in the Sea (Tucker), 1951
City in the Sky (Siodmak), 1974
City Machine (Trimble), 1972
City of a Million Legends (Lichtenberg), 1985
City of a Thousand Suns (Delany), 1965
City of Baraboo (Longyear), 1980
City of Brass (s Hoch), 1971
City of Darkness (Bova) 1976
City of Glass (Loomis), 1955
City of Gold and Lead (Christopher), 1967
City of Illusions (Le Guin), 1967
City of No Return (Tubb), 1954
City of Sorcery (Bradley), 1984
City of the Beast (Moorcock), 1980
City of the Chasch (Vance), 1968
City of the Hidden Eyes (Saxon, as Morrissey), 1964
City of the Moon (Leinster), 1957
City of the Sun (Stableford), 1978
City on the Edge of Forever (Ellison), 1977
City Outside the World (L. Carter), 1977
City under the Sea (Bulmer), 1957
City under the Sea (Fairman), 1963
Claimed! (Stevens), 1966
Clan and Crown (Pournelle), 1982
Clane series (van Vogt)
Clans of the Alphane Moon (Dick), 1964
Clansman of Andor (Offutt), 1978
Clash by Night (s Kuttner, C. Moore), 1980
Clash of Cymbals (Blish), 1959
Clash of Star-Kings (Davidson), 1966
Clash of the Titans (A. Foster), 1981
Claw of the Conciliator (G. Wolfe), 1981
Clay's Ark (O. Butler), 1984
Clewiston Test (Wilhelm), 1976
Clickwhistle (Watkins), 1973
Cliffs (O'Donnell), 1986
Climate Incorporated (Fearn), 1985
Clinton, Rex series (Johns)
Clipper of the Clouds (Verne, for), 1887
Clique (Yermakov), 1982
Cloak of Aesir (s Campbell), 1952
Clock of Time (s Finney), 1958
Clockwork Man (Odle), 1923
Clockwork Orange (Burgess), 1962
Clockwork Traitor (Goldin), 1976
Clockwork's Pirates (s Goulart), 1971
Clone (Cowper), 1972
Clone (T.Thomas, Wilhelm), 1965
Cloned Lives (Sargent), 1976
Close to Critical (Clement), 1964
Closed Worlds (Hamilton), 1968
Cloud by Day (W. Moore), 1956
Cloud on Silver (Christopher), 1964
Cloud Walker (Cooper), 1973
Cloud Warrior (Tilley), 1983
Cloudcry (Van Scyoc), 1977
Cluster series (Anthony)
Cobra (Zahn), 1985
Code Duello (Reynolds), 1968

Code of the Lifemaker (Hogan), 1983
Code Three (Raphael), 1965
Coelura (McCaffrey), 1983
Coils (Saberhagen, Zelazny), 1980
Coils of Time (Chandler), 1964
Coins of Murph (Kelley), 1971
Cold Cash War (Asprin), 1977
Cold Victory (s P. Anderson), 1982
Cold War in a Country Garden (Gutteridge), 1971
Collapsing Cosmoses (s Lovecraft), 1977
Collision Course (Bayley), 1973
Collision Course (Silverberg), 1961
Collision Course (Tubb), 1975
Collision with Chronos (Bayley), 1977
Colonial Survey (Leinster), 1957
Colony (Bova), 1978
Colors of Space (Bradley), 1963
Colossus series (D. Jones)
Colour of Magic (Pratchett), 1983
Colour Out of Space (s Lovecraft), 1964
Columbus of Space (Serviss), 1911
Come, Hunt an Earthman (High), 1973
Comet Halley (F. Hoyle), 1985
Comet Kings (Hamilton), 1969
Cometeers (Williamson), 1950
Comic Inferno (s Aldiss), 1973
Coming Event (Tubb), 1982
Coming of Age (Zahn), 1985
Coming of the Rats (George H. Smith), 1961
Coming of the Strangers (Lymington), 1961
Coming of the Terrans (s Brackett), 1967
Coming Self-Destruction of the United States of America (Seymour),
    1969
Commander–1 (George), 1965
Committed Men (M. Harrison), 1971
Commodore at Sea (s Chandler), 1979
Common Enemy (Beresford), 1942
Commune 2000 A.D. (Reynolds), 1974
Communipath series (Elgin)
Company of Glory (Pangborn), 1975
Compass Rose (s Le Guin), 1982
Compleat Feghoot (s Bretnor, as Briarton), 1975
Compleat Werewolf (s Boucher), 1969
Complete Robot (s Asimov), 1982
Compounded Interests (s Reynolds), 1983
Computer Connection (Bester), 1975
Computer Eye (van Vogt), 1985
Computer War (Reynolds), 1967
Computer World (Reynolds), 1970
Computerworld (van Vogt), 1983
Concrete Horizon (Morgan), 1976
Concrete Island (Ballard), 1974
Conditon of Muzak (Moorcock), 1977
Conditionally Human (s W. Miller), 1962
Conditoned Captain (Pratt), 1954
Conehead (Fox), 1973
Confederation Matador (Bone), 1978
Conflict (s P. Anderson), 1983
Conglomeroid Cocktail Party (Silverberg), 1984
Connecticut Yankee in King Arthur's Court (Twain), 1889
Conquerors from the Darkness (Silverberg), 1965
Conquest of the Amazon (Fearn), 1976
Conquest of the Planet of the Apes (Jakes), 1972
Conquest of the Space Sea (R. Williams), 1955
Conquests (s P. Anderson), 1981
Conscience Interplanetary (Green), 1972

Consider Her Ways (Grove), 1947
Consider Her Ways (s Wyndham), 1961
Continent Makers (s de Camp), 1953
Continuous Katherine Mortenhoe (Compton), 1974
Contraband from Otherspace (Chandler), 1967
Contraband Rocket (Correy), 1955
Convergent series (s Niven), 1979
Conversations (Malzberg), 1975
Converts (Watson), 1984
Conviva Ludibundus (Braun, for), 1978
Cool War (Pohl), 1981
Coramonde series (Daley)
Corlay series (Cowper)
Cornelius, Jerry series (Moorcock)
Cornell, Jerry series (Moorcock)
Corona (Bear), 1984
Corpus Earthling (Charbonneau), 1960
Corridors of Time (P. Anderson), 1965
Corundum's Woman (Offutt, as Cleve), 1982
Cory series (Siodmak)
Cosmic Carnival (Lem, for), 1981
Cosmic Checkmate (MacLean), 1962
Cosmic Computer (Piper), 1964
Cosmic Crusade (Saxon), 1966
Cosmic Encounter (van Vogt), 1980
Cosmic Engineers (Simak), 1950
Cosmic Exodus (Fearn, as Holt), 1953
Cosmic Eye (Reynolds), 1969
Cosmic Flame (Fearn, as Statten), 1950
Cosmic Geoids (Taine), 1949
Cosmic Kaleidoscope (s Shaw), 1976
Cosmic Manhunt (de Camp), 1954
Cosmic Puppets (Dick), 1957
Cosmic Rape (Sturgeon), 1958
Cosmic Spies (McIntosh), 1972
Cosmicomics (Calvino, for), 1968
Costigan's Needle (Sohl), 1953
Count Zero (Gibson), 1985
Count-Down (Maine), 1959
Counter-Clock World (Dick), 1967
Counterfeit Man (s Nourse), 1963
Counterfeit World (Galouye), 1964
Counterfeits (Kelley), 1967
Country Love and Poison Rain (Tate), 1973
Country of the Blind (s Wells), 1911
Country of the Mind (Morgan), 1975
Courts of Chaos (Zelazny), 1978
Courtship Rite (Kingsbury), 1982
Cowboy Heaven (Goulart), 1979
Crack (Tennant), 1978
Crack in Space (Dick), 1966
Crack in the Sky (Lupoff), 1976
Crack of Doom (Cromie), 1895
Crackpot (Goulart), 1977
Crader, Carl, and Earl Jazine series (Hoch)
Cradle of the Sun (Stableford), 1969
Craig, Commander series (Fox)
Crash (Ballard), 1973
Crash (Lundwall), 1982
Crashing Suns (s Hamilton), 1965
Crater of Fear (P. Moore), 1962
Crawford, Homer series (Reynolds)
Crawling Fiend (s Fanthorpe, as Fane), 1960
Creator (s Simak), 1946
Creature from Beyond Infinity (Kuttner), 1968
Creature from the Black Lagoon (Fearn, as Statten), 1954

Creatures of Light and Darkness (Zelazny), 1969
Creatures of the Abyss (Leinster), 1961
Creep, Shadow! (Merritt), 1934
Creep, Shadow, Creep! (Merritt), 1935
Crewel Lye (Anthony), 1985
Criminal Croesus (Griffith), 1904
Crimson Capsule (Coblentz), 1967
Crimson Planet (Fanthorpe, as Muller), 1961
Crimson Serpent (Dent, as Robeson), 1974
Crisis in 2140 (Piper), 1957
Crisis on Cheiron (J. Coulson), 1967
Crisis on Conshelf Ten (M. Hughes), 1975
Crisis 2000 (Maine), 1956
Critical Mass (s Kornbluth and Pohl), 1977
Critical Threshold (Stableford), 1977
Crompton Divided (Sheckley), 1978
Croquet Player (Wells), 1936
Cross of Fire (Malzberg), 1982
Cross the Stars (Drake), 1984
Crossroads of Time (Norton), 1956
Crosstime Agent (Norton), 1975
Crowded Sky (Searls), 1960
Crown of the Sword God (Bulmer, as Norvil), 1980
Croyd series (I. Wallace)
Crucible of Evil (F. Long, as L. Long), 1974
Crucible of Time (Brunner), 1983
Cruiser Dreams (J. Morris), 1981
Cryptozoic! (Aldiss), 1968
Crystal Horde (Taine), 1952
Crystal Singer (McCaffrey), 1982
Crystal World (Ballard), 1966
Cube Root of Uncertainty (s Silverberg), 1970
Cuckoo's Egg (Cherryh), 1985
Cuckoo's Saga series (Pohl, Williamson)
Cugel's Saga (Vance), 1983
Cult (Ehrlich), 1978
Cultural Survey series (Biggle)
Cure for Cancer (Moorcock), 1971
Curious Fragments (s London), 1975
Currents of Space (Asimov), 1952
Curse of the Khan (s Fanthorpe), 1966
Curse of the Totem (s Fanthorpe), 1962
Curse of the Wise Woman (Dunsany, fan), 1933
Cursed (England), 1919
Custodians (s Cowper), 1976
Cuttlefish (Witkiewicz, for), 1969
Cyberiad (Lem, for), 1974
Cybernetic Brains (R. Jones), 1962
Cybernetic Controller (Bulmer), 1952
Cyborg series (Caidin)
Cyborg King (Goulart), 1981
Cycle of Fire (Clement), 1957
Cycle of Nemesis (Bulmer), 1967
Cyclops in the Sky (Fanthorpe, as Roberts), 1960
Cyclon Death Machine (Thurston), 1979
Cyrion (s Lee), 1982
Czar of Fear (Dent, as Robeson), 1968

D-99 (Fyfe), 1962
Daedalus series (Stableford)
Dagger in the Sky (Dent, as Robeson), 1969
Dagger of the Mind (Shaw), 1979
d'Alembert Family series (Goldin)
Daleth Effect (H. Harrison), 1970
Damnation Alley (Zelazny), 1969
Dance of the Apocalypse (Eklund), 1976

Dance of the Hag (Leigh), 1983
Dance the Eagle to Sleep (Piercy), 1970
Dancer from Atlantis (P. Anderson), 1971
Dancers at the End of Time series (Moorcock)
Dancers in the Afterglow (Chalker), 1978
Dancers of Noyo (St. Clair), 1973
Dancing Gods series (Chalker)
Danger! (s Doyle), 1918
Danger: Dinosaurs! (Hunter, as Marsten), 1953
Danger from Vega (Rackham), 1966
Danger—Human (s Dickson), 1970
Danger Moon (s Pohl, as MacCreigh), 1953
Danger Planet (Hamilton, as Sterling), 1968
Dangerous Games (Randall), 1980
Darcy, Lord series (Garrett)
Dare (Farmer), 1965
Darfstellar (s W. Miller), 1982
Dark (J. Herbert), 1980
Dark Beasts (s F. Long), 1963
Dark Between the Stars (s P. Anderson), 1981
Dark Boundaries (Fearn, as Lorraine), 1953
Dark Carnival (s Bradbury), 1947
Dark Continuum (Fanthorpe, as Muller), 1964
Dark December (Coppel), 1960
Dark Design (Farmer), 1977
Dark Destroyers (Wellman), 1959
Dark Dimensions (s Chandler), 1971
Dark Dominion (Duncan), 1954
Dark Enemy (Holly), 1965
Dark Inferno (J. White), 1972
Dark Intruder (s Bradley), 1964
Dark is the Sun (Farmer), 1979
Dark Light Years (Aldiss), 1964
Dark Mind (Kapp), 1965
Dark of the Woods (Koontz), 1970
Dark Other (Weinbaum), 1950
Dark Piper (Norton), 1968
Dark Planet (Holly), 1962
Dark Planet (Rackham), 1971
Dark Side of Earth (s Bester), 1964
Dark Side of the Sun (Pratchett), 1976
Dark Star (A. Foster), 1979
Dark Stars and Other Illuminations (Monteleone), 1981
Dark Symphony (Koontz), 1970
Dark Tides (s Russell), 1962
Dark Triangle (Walters), 1981
Dark Universe (Galouye), 1961
Dark Wing (MacLean), 1979
Dark World (Kuttner, C. Moore),1965
Darkchild series (Van Scyoc)
Darkening Island (Priest), 1972
Darker Drink (s Fanthorpe), 1962
Darkest of Nights (Maine), 1962
Darkling Wind (Sucharitkul), 1985
Darkness and Dawn (England), 1914
Darkness and the Light (Stapledon), 1942
Darkness Before Tomorrow (R. Williams), 1962
Darkness in My Soul (Koontz), 1972
Darkness on Diamondia (van Vogt), 1972
Darkness upon the Ice (Forstchen), 1985
Darkover series (Bradley)
Darkworld Detective (s Reaves), 1982
Darzek, Jan series (Bester)
Daughters of Earth (s Merril), 1968
Daughters of the Dolphin (Meyers), 1968
Davy (Pangborn), 1964

Dawn (S. Wright), 1929
Dawn in Andromeda (Large), 1956
Dawn of Flame (s Weinbaum), 1936
Dawn of Mutants (Fanthorpe, as Roberts), 1959
Dawning Light (Garrett and Silverberg, as Randall), 1959
Dawnman Planet (Reynolds), 1966
Day after Judgement (Blish), 1971
Day after Tomorrow (Heinlein), 1951
Day after Tomorrow (Reynolds), 1976
Day Before Forever (Laumer), 1968
Day Before Tomorrow (Klein, for), 1972
Day by Night (Lee), 1980
Day for Damnation (Gerrold), 1984
Day It Rained Forever (s Bradbury), 1959
Day Million (s Pohl), 1970
Day of Forever (s Ballard), 1967
Day of the Burning (Malzberg), 1974
Day of the Dissonance (A. Foster), 1984
Day of the Dragonstar (Bischoff, Monteleone), 1983
Day of the Drones (Lightner), 1969
Day of the Giants (del Rey), 1959
Day of the Klesh (M. Foster), 1979
Day of the Ness (Norton), 1975
Day of the Star Cities (Brunner), 1965
Day of the Triffids (Wyndham), 1951
Day of Their Return (P. Anderson), 1974
Day of Timestop (Farmer), 1968
Day of Uniting (E. Wallace), 1926
Day of Wrath (O'Neill), 1936
Day of Wrath (Stableford), 1971
Day Star (Geston), 1972
Day the Machines Stopped (Anvil), 1964
Day the Oceans Overflowed (Fontenay), 1964
Day the World Died (Fanthorpe, as Muller), 1962
Day the World Stopped (Coblentz), 1968
Day They H–Bombed Los Angeles (R. Williams), 1961
Daybreak, 2250 A.D. (Norton), 1954
Daymares (s F. Brown), 1968
Days of Glory (Stableford), 1971
Days of Grass (Lee), 1985
Dayworld (Farmer), 1985
De Bracy's Drug (Tubb, as Gridban), 1953
Dead is the Blue (Ehrlich), 1964
Dead Letter (Ehrlich), 1958
Dead Moon (Kelley), 1979
Deadfall (Laumer), 1971
Deadliest Show in Town (McQuay), 1982
Deadline to Pluto (Fearn, as Statten), 1951
Deadly Dwarf (Dent, as Robeson), 1968
Deadly Image (Cooper), 1958
Deadly Litter (s J. White), 1964
Deadly Silents (Killough), 1981
Deadly Sky (Fairman, as Jorgensen), 1970
Deadly Sky (Piserchia), 1983
Dealing in Futures (s Joe Haldeman), 1985
Death by Gaslight (Kurland), 1982
Death Cell (Goulart), 1971
Death Dolls of Lyra (Holly), 1977
Death Had Yellow Eyes (Dent, as Robeson), 1982
Death Has Two Faces (s. Fanthorpe), 1964
Death in Florence (Effinger), 1978
Death in Silver (Dent, as Robeson), 1968
Death into Life (Stapledon), 1946
Death is a Dream (Tubb), 1967
Death Machine (Goulart, as Robeson), 1975
Death Note (s Fanthorpe), 1958

Death of Grass (Christopher), 1956
Death of the Dragon Komatsu, for), 1978
Death Rays of Ardilla (Johns), 1959
Death Sentence (Kelley), 1979
Death Sleep (Sohl), 1983
Death Watch (Compton), 1981
Death Wears a White Face (Tubb), 1979
Deathbeast (Gerrold), 1978
Deathbird Stories (s Ellison), 1975
Deathbox (Tolstoy, for), 1934
Deathhunter (Watson), 1981
Deathless Amazon (Fearn), 1955
Death's Angel (Sky), 1980
Death's Deputy (Hubbard), 1948
Death's Master (Lee), 1979
Deathstar Voyage (I. Wallace), 1969
Deathworld series (H. Harrison)
Deathworms of Kratos (Cooper, as Avery), 1975
Deceivers (Bester), 1981
Decision at Doona (McCaffrey), 1969
Decreation (Fearn, as Statten), 1952
Deep (Crowley), 1975
Deep Fix (s Moorcock, as Colvin), 1966
Deep Range (Clarke), 1957
Deep Reaches of Space (Chandler), 1964
Deep Space (s Russell), 1954
Deep Waters (s Hodgson), 1967
Deeper Than the Darkness (Benford), 1970
Defiance (Bulmer), 1963
Defiant Agents (Norton), 1962
Definitely Maybe (Strugatsky, for), 1978
Delaney, Mike series (Maine)
Delia of Vallia (Bulmer, as Akers), 1982
Delikon (Hoover), 1977
Deluge (S. Wright), 1927
Delusion World (Dickson), 1961
Delusion's Master (Lee), 1981
Demolished Man (Bester), 1953
Demon (Varley), 1984
Demon Breed (Schmitz), 1968
Demon in the Skull (Pohl), 1984
Demon Island (Goulart, as Robeson), 1975
Demon of Cawnpore (Verne, for), 1881
Demon of Scattery (P. Anderson, Broxon), 1979
Demon Seed (Koontz), 1973
Demons (Bulmer), 1965
Demons of the Upper Air (s F. Long), 1969
Demons' World (Bulmer), 1964
Demu Trilogy (Busby), 1980
Denver is Missing (D.Jones), 1971
Denver's Double (Griffith), 1901
Depression or Bust (Reynolds), 1974
Derai (Tubb), 1968
Derrick Devil (Dent, as Robeson), 1973
Descent of Anansi (S. Barnes, Niven), 1982
Desert of Stolen Dreams (Silverberg), 1981
Desire of the Eyes (s Allen), 1895
Desperate Games (Boulle, for), 1973
Destination Infinity (Kuttner, C. Moore), 1958
Destination Luna (P. Moore), 1955
Destination Mars (Walters), 1963
Destination Moon (s Heinlein), 1979
Destination: Saturn (L. Carter, Wollheim as Grinnell), 1967
Destination: Universe! (s van Vogt), 1952
Destination: Void (F. Herbert), 1966
Destined Maid (Griffith), 1898

Destiny and the Dolphins (Meyers), 1969
Destiny Doll (Simak), 1971
Destiny Times Three (Leiber), 1957
Destiny's Orbit (Wollheim, as Grinnell), 1961
Destroy the U.S.A. (Leinster), 1946
Destruction of the Temple (Malzberg), 1974
Deus Irae (Dick, Zelazny), 1976
Deviates (R. Jones), 1959
Devil and the Doctor (Keller), 1940
Devil from the Depths (s Fanthorpe), 1961
Devil Genghis (Dent, as Robeson), 1974
Devil Is Dead (Lafferty), 1971
Devil on My Back (M. Hughes), 1984
Devil on the Moon (Dent, as Robeson), 1970
Devil World (Eklund), 1979
Devil's Children (Dickinson), 1970
Devil's Game (P. Anderson), 1980
Devil's Peak (Ball), 1972
Devil's Planet (Wellman), 1951
Devil's Scrapbook (s Bixby), 1964
Devil's Tor (Lindsay), 1932
Devil–Tree of El Dorado (Ash, as Aubrey), 1896
Devolutionist (Flint), 1965
Devouring Fire (Fearn, as Statten), 1951
Dextra series (Lake)
Dhalgren (Delany), 1975
di Stefano, Angelo series (Janifer)
Diaboliad (Bulgakov, for), 1972
Diabolist (Fairman, as Jorgensen), 1973
Diabols (Mackelworth),1969
Diamond Contessa (Bulmer), 1983
Dies Irae series (Stableford)
Different Light (Lynn), 1978
Digital Wristwatch of Philip K. Dick (s Lupoff), 1985
Digits and Dastards (s Pohl), 1966
Dilation Effect (Rankine, as Mason), 1971
Dilke, Matthew series (Gutteridge)
Dilvish, The Damned (Zelazny), 1982
Dimension A (Davies), 1969
Dimension of Horror (Nelson, as Lord), 1979
Dimension of Miracles (Sheckley), 1968
Dimension Thirteen (s Silverberg), 1969
Dimensioneers (Piserchia), 1982
Dinner at Deviant's Palace (Powers), 1985
Dinosaur Beach (Laumer), 1971
Dinosaur Planet series (McCaffrey)
Dinosaur Tales (s Bradbury), 1983
Diploids and Other Flights of Fancy (s MacLean), 1962
Dirdir (Vance), 1969
Direct Descent (F. Herbert), 1980
Dirty Tricks (s Effinger), 1978
Disappearance (Wylie), 1951
Disaster Area (s Ballard), 1967
Displaced Person (Harding), 1979
Dispossessed (Le Guin), 1974
Distant Stars (Delany), 1981
Distant Suns (Moorcock), 1975
Diversity of Creatures (s Kipling), 1917
Divide and Rule (de Camp), 1948
Divine Invasion (Dick), 1981
Do Androids Dream of Electric Sheep? (Dick), 1968
Doc Savage series (Dent, as Robeson)
Dr. Adder (Jeter), 1984
Dr. Bloodmoney (Dick), 1965
Dr. Cyclops (Kuttner), 1967
Dr. Futurity (Dick), 1960

Dr. Heidenhoff's Progress (Bellamy), 1880
Dr. Orpheus (I. Wallace), 1968
Doctor Ox series (Verne, for)
Doctor Rat (Kotzwinkle), 1976
Dr. Scofflaw (Goulart), 1979
Dr. Strange (Rotsler), 1979
Dr. Strangelove (George), 1963
Dr. Time (Goulart, as Robeson), 1974
Doctor to the Galaxy (Lightner), 1965
Doctor to the Stars (s Leinster), 1964
Doctor Who series (G. Davis)
Does Anyone Else Have Something Further to Add? (s Lafferty), 1974
Doings of Raffles Haw (Doyle), 1892
Doll Maker (s Sarban), 1953
Dolphin Boy (Meyers), 1967
Dolphin Island (Clarke), 1963
Dolphin Rider (Meyers), 1968
Dolphins series (Meyers)
Dolphins of Altair (St. Clair), 1967
Dom and Va (Christopher), 1973
Domain (J. Herbert), 1984
Dome Around America (Williamson), 1955
Dome in the Forest (P. Williams), 1981
Dome World (McLaughlin), 1962
Domes of Mars (P. Moore), 1956
Domes of Pico (Walters), 1958
Domino (Cowper), 1971
Don Rodriguez (Dunsany, fan), 1922
Donovan's Brain (Siodmak), 1943
Don't Bite the Sun (Lee), 1976
Don't Pick the Flowers (D. Jones), 1971
Doom of the Green Planet (Petaja), 1968
Doomed World (Fanthorpe), 1960
Doomfarers of Coramonde (Daley), 1977
Doomsday Eve (R. Williams), 1957
Doomsday Exhibit (s Fairman), 1971
Doomsday Gene (Boyd), 1973
Doomsday Men (Bulmer), 1968
Doomsday Men (Priestley), 1938
Doomsday Morning (C. Moore), 1957
Doomsday on Ajiat (s N. Jones), 1968
Doomsday Planet (Vincent), 1966
Doomsday Wing (George H. Smith), 1963
Doomsman (Ellison), 1967
Doomstar (Hamilton), 1966
Doomtime (Piserchia), 1981
Door in the Wall (s Wells), 1911
Door into Fire (Duane), 1979
Door into Shadow (Duane), 1984
Door into Summer (Heinlein), 1957
Door Through Space (Bradley), 1961
Doors of His Face, The Lamps of His Mouth (s Zelazny), 1971
Doors of the Universe (Engdahl), 1981
Doorways in the Sand (Zelazny), 1976
Doppelganger Gambit (Killough), 1979
Doppelgangers (Heard), 1947
Dorsai series (Dickson)
Dosadi Experiment (F. Herbert), 1977
Double, Double (Brunner), 1969
Double Illusion (High), 1970
Double Invaders (Rackham), 1967
Double Jeopardy (Pratt), 1952
Double Man (Binder), 1971
Double Meaning (D. Knight), 1974
Double Phoenix, The Firebird (Cooper), 1971
Double Spiral War series (Norwood)

Double Star (Heinlein), 1956
Douglas Convolution (E. Llewellyn), 1979
Down Here in the Dream Quarter (s Malzberg), 1976
Down in the Black Gang (s Farmer), 1971
Down to Earth (Capon), 1954
Down to Earth (Charbonneau), 1967
Downbelow Station (Cherryh), 1981
Downstairs Room (s Wilhelm), 1968
Downtime (Felice), 1985
Downtiming the Night Side (Chalker), 1985
Downward to the Earth (Silverberg), 1970
Dracula in Love (Shirley), 1979
Dragon (Coppel), 1977
Dragon (Shiel), 1913
Dragon and the George (Dickson), 1976
Dragon Hoard (Lee), 1984
Dragon in the Sea (F. Herbert), 1956
Dragon Masters (Vance), 1963
Dragon on a Pedastal (Anthony), 1983
Dragonard series (Jakes)
Dragondrums (McCaffrey), 1979
Dragonflight (McCaffrey), 1968
Dragonquest (McCaffrey), 1971
Dragonrider series (McCaffrey)
Dragon's Egg (Forward), 1980
Dragon's Island (Williamson), 1951
Dragonsinger (McCaffrey), 1977
Dragonsong (McCaffrey), 1976
Dragonstar series (Bischoff, Monteleone)
Dragonworld (Reaves), 1979
Dramaturges of Yan (Brunner), 1972
Dramocles (Sheckley), 1983
Draught of Eternity (Rousseau, as Egbert), 1924
Drawing of the Dark (Powers), 1979
Dread Empire series (Cook)
Dread Visitor (Berry), 1952
Dreadful Sanctuary (Russell), 1951
Dreadful Sleep (s Williamson), 1977
Dream (S. Wright), 1931
Dream, Benjamin's Dream, Benjamin's Bicentennial Blast (s
　Asimov), 1976
Dream Chariots (Bulmer, as Norvil), 1977
Dream Dancer series (J. Morris)
Dream Master (Zelazny), 1966
Dream Millennium (J. White), 1974
Dream of Debs (s London), 1912 (?)
Dream of John Ball (W. Morris, fan), 1888
Dream of Kinship (Cowper), 1981
Dream of Wessex (Priest), 1977
Dream of X (Hodgson), 1912
Dream Park (S. Barnes, Niven), 1981
Dreamers (Gunn), 1980
Dreamer's Tales (Dunsany, fan), 1910
Dreamfields (Jeter), 1976
Dreaming Dragons (Broderick), 1980
Dreaming Earth (Brunner), 1963
Dreaming Jewels (Sturgeon), 1950
Dreams That Burn in the Night (s Strete), 1982
Dreamsnake (McIntyre), 1978
Dreamstone (Cherryh), 1983
Drew, Clayton series (Fearn)
Driftglass (s Delany), 1971
Drinking Sapphire Wine (Lee), 1977
Dropped from the Clouds (Verne, for), 1874
Drought (Ballard), 1965
Drought on Ziax II (Morressy), 1978

Drowned World (Ballard), 1962
Drug of Choice (Crichton, as Lange), 1970
Druid (s Fanthorpe, as Brett), 1959
Druid Stones (Fox, as Majors), 1965
Druids' World (George H. Smith), 1967
Drums of Tapajos (Meek), 1961
Drunkard's Walk (Pohl), 1960
Dueling Machine (Bova), 1969
Duluth (Vidal), 1983
Dumarest series (Tubb)
Dune series (F. Herbert)
Dune Storybook (J. Vinge), 1984
Dunjer series (Haiblum)
Duplicated Man (Blish, Lowndes), 1959
Duplicators (Leinster), 1964
Durdane series (Vance)
Dushau series (Lichtenberg)
Dust Destroyer (Fearn, as Stratten), 1953
Dust of Death (Dent, as Robeson), 1969
Dust of Far Suns (s Vance), 1981
Dwellers (S. Wright), 1954
Dwellers of the Deep (Malzberg, as O'Donnell), 1970
Dying Earth series (Vance)
Dying for Tomorrow (s Moorcock), 1978
Dying Inside (Silverberg), 1972
Dying Man (D. Knight), 1967
Dying of the Light (Martin), 1977
Dynasty of Doom (Tubb, as Grey), 1953
Dyno-Depressant (Fearn, as Gridban), 1953
Dynostar Menace (G. Davis, Pedler), 1975

E Pluribus Unicorn (s Sturgeon), 1953
E.S.P. Worm (Anthony), 1970
E.T.: The Book of the Green Planet (Kotzwinkle), 1985
E.T., The Extra-Terrestrial (Kotzwinkle), 1982
Earth Abides (Stewart), 1949
Earth Book of Stormgate (s P. Anderson), 1978
Earth Cult (T. Hoyle), 1979
Earth Descended (s Saberhagen), 1982
Earth Dreams (J. Morris), 1982
Earth Dwellers (Maurois, for), 1963
Earth Enslaved (Tubb, as Kern), 1974
Earth Factor X (van Vogt), 1976
Earth Gods Are Coming (Bulmer), 1960
Earth Has Been Found (D. Jones), 1979
Earth in Twilight (Piserchia), 1981
Earth Invader (Garrett), 1983
Earth Is Heaven (Tubb), 1982
Earth Is Room Enough (s Asimov), 1957
Earth Magic (Panshin), 1978
Earth Quarter (D. Knight), 1970
Earth Song (Webb), 1983
Earth Tripper (Kelley), 1973
Earth 2 (Fearn, as Statten), 1955
Earth Two (Kelley), 1979
Earth Unaware (Reynolds), 1968
Earth War (Reynolds), 1963
Earth Will Shake (Robert Anton Wilson), 1982
Earthblood (R. Brown, Laumer), 1966
Earthbound (Lesser), 1952
Earthchild (Piserchia), 1977
Earthchild (Webb), 1982
Earthdark (M. Hughes), 1977
Earthfall (Tubb), 1977
Earthlight (Clarke), 1955
Earthly Paradise (W. Morris, fan), 1868

Earthman, Come Home (Blish), 1955
Earthman, Go Home! (P. Anderson), 1960
Earthman, Go Home (s Ellison), 1964
Earthman on Venus (Farley), 1950
Earthman's Burden (s P. Anderson, Dickson), 1957
Earthminds series (Sargent)
Earth's Last Citadel (Kuttner, C. Moore), 1964
Earth's Last Fortress (s van Vogt), 1960
Earth's Long Shadow (Bulmer), 1961
Earth's Other Shadow (s Silverberg), 1973
Earthseed (Sargent), 1983
Earthstrings (Rackham), 1972
Earthwind (Holdstock), 1977
Earthworks (Aldiss), 1965
Earthwreck! (Scortia), 1974
East Wind Coming (Cover), 1979
Eater of Worlds (Tubb, as Kern), 1974
Echo in the Skull (Brunner), 1959
Echo round His Bones (Disch), 1967
Eclipse (Felice), 1982
Eclipse (Shirley), 1985
Eclipse Express (Fearn, as Statten), 1952
Eclipse of Dawn (Eklund), 1971
Eclipsing Binaries (Goldin), 1983
Ecodeath (Watkins), 1972
Ecolog (Nelson), 1977
Ecotopia series (Callenbach)
Eden, Jim series (Pohl, Williamson)
Eden Cycle (Gallun), 1974
Edge (s Beaumont), 1966
Edge in My Voice (s Ellison), 1984
Edge of Beyond (Johns), 1958
Edge of Forever (s Oliver), 1971
Edge of Running Water (Sloane), 1939
Edge of Time (Wollheim, as Grinnell), 1958
Edge of Tomorrow (s H. Fast), 1961
Edict (Ehrlich), 1971
Edison's Conquest of Mars (Serviss), 1947
Egg-Shaped Thing (Hodder-Williams), 1967
Eight Against Utopia (Rankine, as Mason), 1967
Eight Fantasms and Magics (s Vance), 1969
Eight Keys to Eden (Clifton), 1960
Eighty-Minute Hour (Aldiss), 1974
Einstein Intersection (Delany), 1967
Elak of Atlantis (s Kuttner), 1985
Elana series (Engdahl)
Electric Crocodile (Compton), 1970
Electric Forest (Lee), 1979
Electric Sword Swallowers (Bulmer), 1971
Element (s F. Hoyle), 1967
Elephant Song (Longyear), 1981
Eleventh Commandment (del Rey), 1962
Elixir of Hate (England), 1976
Eloise (Tubb), 1975
Elsewhere, Elsewhen, Elsehow (s deFord), 1971
Emancipatrix (Flint), 1965
Embedding (Watson), 1973
Embryo (Charbonneau), 1976
Emerald Forest (Holdstock), 1985
Emperor of Mars (Fearn), 1950
Emperor of the Last Days (Goulart), 1977
Emperor of the World (Hyne), 1915
Emperor, Swords, Pentacles (Gotlieb), 1982
Emphyrio (Vance), 1969
Empire series (Asimov)
Empire (s Piper), 1981

Empire (Simak), 1951
Empire: A Visual Novel (Delany), 1978
Empire 99 (Goulart), 1980
Empire of Chaos (Bulmer), 1953
Empire of the Atom (van Vogt), 1957
Empire of the East (Saberhagen), 1979
Empire of the World (Hyne), 1910
Empire of Time (Kilian), 1978
Empire of Two Worlds (Bayley), 1972
Empire Star (Delany), 1966
Empires of Flux and Anchor (Chalker), 1984
Empress Irene series (Chandler)
Empress of Outer Space (Chandler), 1965
Empty People (Malzberg, as O'Donnell), 1969
Empty World (Christopher), 1977
Enchanted Duplicator (s Shaw), 1954
Enchanted Pilgrimage (Simak), 1975
Enchantress from the Stars (Engdahl), 1970
Enchantress of World's End (L. Carter), 1975
Encounter (Holly), 1959
Encounter Near Venus (Wibberley), 1967
Encounter Three (Caidin), 1978
Encounter with Space (Bulmer), 1952
End Bringers (Rankine, as Mason), 1973
End of All Songs (Moorcock), 1976
End of Eternity (Asimov), 1955
End of Exile (Bova), 1975
End of the Dream (Wylie), 1972
End of the Dreams (s Gunn), 1975
End of the Empire (Gilliland), 1983
End of the Matter (A. Foster), 1977
End of the World News (Burgess), 1982
Ender's Game (Card), 1985
Endless Shadow (Brunner), 1964
Endless Universe (Bradley), 1979
Endless Voyage (Bradley), 1975
Ends of the Circle (P. Williams), 1981
Enemies from Beyond (Laumer), 1967
Enemies of the System (Aldiss), 1978
Enemy of My Enemy (Davidson), 1966
Enemy of the State (F. Wilson), 1980
Enemy Stars (P. Anderson), 1959
Enemy Within the Skull (Tubb, as Kern), 1974
Energy Pirate (F. and G. Hoyle), 1982
Engine Summer (Crowley), 1979
England's Peril (Le Queux), 1899
English Assassin (Moorcock), 1972
English at the North Pole (Verne, for), 1874
Enigma from Tantalus (Brunner), 1965
Enormous Hourglass (Goulart), 1976
Enquiries of Dr. Eszterhazy (s Davidson), 1975
Enslaved Brains (Binder), 1965
Enterprise 2115 (Tubb, as Grey), 1954
Entropy Effect (McIntyre), 1981
Entropy Tango (Moorcock), 1981
Entry to Elsewhen (s Brunner), 1972
Envoy to New Worlds (s Laumer), 1963
Eon (Bear), 1985
Epiphany (Yermakov), 1982
Equality (Bellamy), 1897
Equality (Reynolds), 1977
Equator (Aldiss), 1961
Erasmus Magister (s Sheffield), 1982
Erewhon (S. Butler), 1872
Erewhon Revisisted (S. Butler), 1901
Eric Brighteyes (Broxon, as Skaldaspillir), 1979

Eric John Stark, Outlaw of Mars (Brackett), 1982
Eric of Zanthodon (L. Carter), 1982
Eridahn (R. Young), 1983
Eros Ascending (Resnick), 1984
Eros at Zenith (Resnick), 1984
Eros Descending (Resnick), 1985
Escape! (Bova), 1970
Escape Across the Cosmos (Fox), 1964
Escape Attempt (Strugatsky, for), 1982
Escape from Macho (Offutt, as Cleve), 1982
Escape from New York (McQuay), 1981
Escape from Splatterbang (Fisk), 1978
Escape from the Planet of the Apes (Pournelle), 1974
Escape into Space (Tubb), 1969
Escape on Venus (E. Burroughs), 1946
Escape Orbit (J. White), 1965
Escape Plus Ten (s Bova), 1984
Escape to Infinity (Fanthorpe, as Zeigfried), 1963
Escape to Nowhere (Karp), 1955
Escape to Tomorrow (Effinger), 1975
Escape to Witch Mountain (Key), 1968
Escape Velocity (Stasheff), 1983
Escapement (Maine), 1956
Esper (Blish), 1958
Esper Transfer (Proctor), 1978
Eternal Conflict (Keller), 1949
Eternal Frontiers (Schmitz), 1973
Eternal Lover (s E. Burroughs), 1925
Eternal Man (C. Long), 1964
Eternal Savage (s E. Burroughs), 1963
Eternity (Reynolds), 1984
Eternity Brigade (Goldin), 1980
Ethical Culture series (Turner)
Ethical Engineer (H. Harrison), 1964
Euphor Unfree (Rankine, as Mason), 1977
(Even) More Compleat Feghoot (s Bretnor, as Briarton), 1980
Everlasting Exiles (West), 1967
Evil Earths (Kuttner), 1976
Evil Eye (Fisk), 1980
Evil Gnome (Dent, as Robeson), 1976
Evil in the Family (Hoskins, as Corren), 1972
Evil Is Live Spelled Backwards (Offutt), 1970
Evil That Men Do (Brunner), 1969
Excommunication (s Aldiss), 1975
Exile of Time (Cummings), 1964
Exile on Vlahil (Mayhur), 1984
Exile Waiting (McIntyre), 1975
Exiled From Earth (Bova), 1971
Exiled in Space (Fanthorpe, as Torro), 1968
Exiles series (Bova)
Exiles at the Well of Souls (Chalker), 1978
Exiles of the Stars (Norton), 1971
Exiles of Time (Bond), 1949
Exiles on Asperus (s Wyndham, as Beynon), 1979
Exiles to Glory (Pournelle), 1978
Exit Humanity (Fanthorpe, as Brett), 1960
Exit Life (Fearn, as Gridban), 1953
Exodus/UK (Rohmer), 1975
Exorcists (Fanthorpe, as Muller), 1965
Expanded Universe (s Heinlein), 1980
Expedition to Earth (s Clarke), 1953
Expedition Venus (Walters), 1962
Expendables series (Cooper, as Avery)
Experiment in Crime (s Wylie), 1956
Experiment in Terra (Goulart), 1984
Explorations (s P. Anderson), 1981

Explorers (s Kornbluth), 1954
Explorers into Infinity (Cummings), 1965
Explorers of Gor (Norman), 1979
Exterminator! (W. Burroughs), 1973
Extinction Bomber (R. Gordon, as Hough), 1956
Extra Man (Tubb, as Grey), 1954
Extra (Ordinary) People (Russ), 1984
Extraterritorial (Morressy), 1977
Extro (Bester), 1975
Exxoneration (Rohmer), 1974
Eyas (Kilian), 1982
Eye among the Blind (Holdstock), 1976
Eye and the Finger (s Wandrei), 1944
Eye in the Pyramid (Robert Anton Wilson), 1975
Eye in the Sky (Dick), 1957
Eye of Istar (Le Queux), 1897
Eye of Karnak (Fanthorpe, as Muller), 1962
Eye of the Cat (Zelazny), 1982
Eye of the Comet (Sargent), 1984
Eye of the Heron (Le Guin), 1982
Eye of the Lens (s L. Jones), 1972
Eye of the Monster (Norton), 1962
Eye of the Queen (Mann), 1982
Eye of the Vulture (Goulart), 1977
Eye of the Zodiac (Tubb), 1975
Eyes series (S. Gordon)
Eyes of Amber (s J. Vinge), 1979
Eyes of Fire (Bishop), 1980
Eyes of Heisenberg (F. Herbert), 1966
Eyes of the Overworld (s Vance), 1966

F.P. 1 Antwortet Nicht (Siodmak), 1931
F.P. 1 Does Not Reply (Siodmak), 1933
F.P. 1 Fails to Reply (Siodmak), 1933
Fabulous Riverboat (Farmer), 1971
Fabulous Valley (Wheatley), 1934
Face (Vance), 1979
Face in the Dark (s Fanthorpe), 1961
Face in the Night (Fanthorpe, as Brett), 1962
Face of Fear (Fanthorpe, as Torro), 1963
Face of Heaven (Stableford), 1976
Face of X (Fanthorpe, as Roberts), 1960
Faceless Man (Vance), 1978
Faceless Planet (Fanthorpe, as Brett), 1960
Faces in the Flames (Tate), 1976
Faces Outside (s McAllister), 1985
Facial Justice (Hartley), 1960
Facing the Flag (Verne, for), 1897
Faded Sun series (Cherryh)
Fade–Out (Tilley), 1975
Fahrenheit 451 (Bradbury), 1953
Fairy Chessman (Kuttner and C. Moore, as Padgett), 1951
Faith of Tarot (Anthony), 1980
Falcons of Narabedla (Bradley), 1964
Falkenberg series (Pournelle)
Fall into Darkness (Yermakov), 1982
Fall of Chronopolis (Bayley), 1974
Fall of Colossus (D. Jones), 1974
Fall of Moondust (Clarke), 1961
Fall of the Dream Machine (Koontz), 1969
Fall of the Shell (P. Williams), 1982
Fall of the Towers series (Delany)
Fallen Spaceman (Harding), 1973
Falling Astronauts (Malzberg), 1971
Falling Torch (Budrys), 1959
Falling Toward Forever (Eklund), 1975

False Dawn (Yarbro), 1978
False Fatherhood (Chandler), 1968
False Night (Budrys), 1954
Familiar Spirit (Tuttle),1983
Fängelsestaden (Lundwall), 1978
Fantasms and Magics (s Vance), 1978
Fantastic Island (Dent, as Robeson), 1966
Fantastic Stories (Tertz, for), 1963
Fantastic Voyage (Asimov), 1966
Fantastic Voyage II (Farmer), 1985
Fantasy (s P. Anderson), 1981
Far and Away (s Boucher), 1955
Far Call (Dickson), 1978
Far Ends of Time and Earth (Asimov), 1979
Far from Home (s Tevis), 1981
Far Frontier (Rotsler), 1980
Far Future Calling (s Stapledon), 1980
Far Out (s D. Knight), 1961
Far Rainbow (Strugatsky, for), 1967
Far Reality (Kuttner and C. Moore, as Padgett), 1963
Far Side of Evil (Engdahl), 1971
Far Stars (s Russell), 1961
Far Sunset (Cooper), 1967
Far Traveller (Chandler), 1977
Farewell, Earth's Bliss (Compton), 1966
Farewell to Yesterday's Tomorrow (s Panshin), 1975
Farfetch (Lichtenberg), 1985
Farmer Giles of Ham (Tolkien, fan), 1949
Farmer in the Sky (Heinlein), 1950
Farnham's Freehold (Heinlein), 1964
Farthest Star (Pohl, Williamson), 1975
Fat Chance (Laumer), 1975
Fatal Fire (Bulmer), 1962
Father Christmas Letters (Tolkien, fan), 1976
Father of Lies (Brunner), 1968
Father to the Stars (s Farmer), 1981
Faustus Pentacle series (Broderick)
Fear (Hubbard), 1951
Fear Cay (Dent, as Robeson), 1966
Fear That Man (Koontz), 1969
Fear Today, Gone Tomorrow (s Bloch), 1971
Feast of St. Dionysus (s Silverberg), 1975
Feast Unknown (Farmer), 1969
Feathered Octopus (Dent, as Robeson), 1970
Federation (s Piper), 1981
Feelies (Farren), 1978
Feighan, McGill series (O'Donnell)
Fellowship of the Hand (Hoch), 1973
Fellowship of the Ring (Tolkien, fan), 1954
Female Man (Russ), 1975
Fenris Device (Stableford), 1974
Fever Dreams and Other Fantasies (s Bloch, Bradbury), 1970
Fevre Dream (Martin), 1982
Few Last Words (Sallis), 1969
Ficciones (Borges, for), 1962
Field of Ice (Verne, for), 1874
Fiends (Fanthorpe), 1959
Fifth Head of Cerberus (s G. Wolfe), 1972
Fifth Planet (F. and G. Hoyle), 1963
Fifty-seventh Franz Kafka (s Rucker), 1983
Fight for Life (Leinster), n.d.
Fighting Man of Mars (E. Burroughs), 1931
Fighting Slave of Gor (Norman), 1980
Figment of a Dream (s Keller), 1962
Final Blackout (Hubbard), 1948
Final Circle of Paradise (Strugatsky, for), 1976

Final Doors (s Hensley), 1981
Final Encyclopedia (Dickson), 1984
Final Programme (Moorcock), 1968
Final War (Keller), 1949
Final War (s Malzberg, as O'Donnell), 1969
Find the Changeling (Benford, Eklund), 1980
Find the Feathered Serpent (Hunter), 1952
Fingalnan Conspiracy (Rankine), 1973
Fingers of Darkness (s Fanthorpe), 1961
Finish Line (Goldin), 1976
Finnley Wren (Wylie), 1934
Fire at the Center (Proctor), 1981
Fire from the Wine-Dark Sea (s Sucharitkul), 1983
Fire in His Hands (Cook), 1984
Fire in the Abyss (S. Gordon), 1983
Fire in the Heavens (George O. Smith), 1958
Fire of the Witches (F. Long, as L. Long), 1971
Fire Past the Future (Maine), 1960
Fire Pattern (Shaw), 1984
Fire Time (P. Anderson), 1974
Fire Watch (s Willis), 1985
Fireball (Christopher), 1981
Firebird (Harness), 1981
Firebird (s Zebrowski), 1979
Fireclown (Moorcock), 1965
Fire-Eater (Goulart), 1970
Fireflood (s McIntyre), 1979
Firemantle (Mackelworth), 1968
Fires of Azeroth (Cherryh), 1979
Fires of Scorpio (Bulmer, as Akers), 1983
Fireship (s J. Vinge), 1978
Fireworks (s A. Carter), 1974
First Channel (Lichtenberg), 1980
First Contact? (Walters), 1971
First Family (Tilley), 1985
First Family on the Moon (Walters), 1979
First He Died (Simak), 1953
First Lensman (E.E. Smith), 1950
First Men in the Moon (Wells), 1901
First on Mars (R. Gordon), 1957
First on the Moon (Sutton), 1958
First on the Moon (Walters), 1961
First One and Twenty (s Gloag), 1946
First Person, Peculiar (s Sherred), 1972
First Through Time (R. Gordon), 1962
First to the Stars (R. Gordon), 1959
First Train to Babylon (Ehrlich), 1955
First, You Fight (Naha, as Drumm), 1984
Fish Dinner in Memison (Eddison, fan), 1941
Fistful of Digits (Hodder–Williams), 1968
Fittest (McIntosh), 1955
Five Against Arlane (Purdom), 1967
Five Against Venus (Latham), 1952
Five Faces of Fear (Fanthorpe, as Thorpe), 1960
Five Gold Bands (Vance), 1963
500 Millions of the Begum (Verne, for), 1879
Five Steps to Tomorrow (Binder), 1970
Five to Twelve (Cooper), 1968
Five Way Secret Agent (Reynolds), 1975
Five Weeks in a Balloon (Fox), 1962
Five Weeks in a Balloon (Verne, for), 1869
Fize of the Gabriel Ratchets (Norwood), 1983
Flame Goddess (Fanthorpe, as Roberts), 1961
Flame Mass (Fanthorpe), 1961
Flame of Iridar (L. Carter), 1967
Flame Upon the Ice (Forstchen), 1984

Flamers (Fisk), 1979
Flames (Stapledon), 1947
Flaming Falcons (Dent, as Robeson), 1968
Flandry, Dominic series (P. Anderson)
Flash Gordon (Cover), 1980
Flash Gordon series (Goulart, as Steffanson)
Flesh (Farmer), 1960
Flesh in the Furnace (Koontz), 1972
Fleshpots of Sansato (Temple), 1968
Flexing the Warp (Norwood), 1983
Flicka i fönster vid världens kant (Lundwall), 1980
Fliers of Antares (Bulmer, as Akers), 1975
Flight from Neveryon (Delany), 1985
Flight from Rebirth (McIntosh), 1971
Flight from Yesterday (R. Willliams), 1963
Flight into Yesterday (Harness), 1953
Flight of Dragons (Dickinson), 1979
Flight of Exiles (Bova), 1972
Flight of the Aerofix (Renard, for), 1932
Flight of the Dragonfly (Forward), 1984
Flight of the Horse (s Niven), 1973
Flight of the Valkyries (s Fanthorpe), 1958
Flight of Time (Capon), 1960
Flight to Opar (Farmer), 1976
Flight to the Lonesome Place (Key), 1969
Flinx series (A.Foster)
Floating City (Verne, for), 1874
Floating Continent (de Camp), 1966
Floating Gods (M. Harrison), 1983
Floating Island (Verne, for), 1896
Floating Worlds (Holland), 1976
Floating Zombie (D. Jones), 1975
Florians (Stableford), 1976
Flow My Tears, The Policeman Said (Dick), 1974
Flower of Doradil (Rackham), 1970
Flowers for Algernon (Keyes), 1966
Fluger (Piserchia), 1980
Fluke (J. Herbert), 1977
Flux (Goulart), 1974
Flying Eyes (Holly), 1962
Flying Fortunes in an Encounter with Rubberface (Cross), 1952
Flying Goblin (Dent, as Robeson), 1977
Flying Legion (England), 1920
Flying Sorcerers (Gerrold, Niven), 1971
Fog (J. Herbert), 1975
Folsom Flint (s Keller), 1969
Food for Demons (s E. Evans), 1958
Food of Death (Dunsany, fan), 1974
Food of the Gods (Wells), 1904
Fools' Harvest (Cox), 1939
Fool's Hill (Lupoff), 1978
Footfall (Niven, Pournelle), 1985
For England's Sake (Cromie), 1889
For Love of Mother-Not (A. Foster), 1983
For Texas and Zed (Z. Hughes), 1976
For the Flag (Verne, for), 1897
Forbidden (Fanthorpe, as Brett), 19o3
Forbidden Area (Frank), 1956
Forbidden Garden (Taine), 1947
Forbidden Planet (Fanthorpe, as Muller), 1961
Forbidden Tower (Bradley), 1977
Forbidden World (Bischoff, T. White), 1978
Force 97X (Fanthorpe, as Torro), 1965
Foreign Constellations (s Brunner), 1980
Forerunner series (Norton)
Forever Machine (Clifton), 1967

Forever War (Joe Haldeman), 1974
Forgetful Robot (Fairman), 1968
Forgotten Colony (Binder), 1972
Forgotten Door (Key), 1965
Forgotten News (s Finney), 1983
Forgotten Planet (Leinster), 1954
Forgotten Planet (George H. Smith), 1965
Forgotten Sea of Mars (s Resnick), 1965
Forlorn Hope (Drake), 1984
Fomula 29X (Fanthorpe, as Torro), 1963
Forschungskreuzer Saumarez (Bulmer), 1960
Fortress of Solitude (Dent, as Robeson), 1968
Fortune for Kregen (Bulmer, as Akers), 1979
Fortunes of Brak (s Jakes), 1980
Forty-Minute War (J. Morris), 1984
40000 in Gehenna (Cherryh), 1983
Forward in Time (s Bova), 1973
Foundation series (Asimov)
Foundations of Paradise (Clarke), 1979
Four Came Back (Caidin), 1968
Four Day Weekend (George H. Smith), 1966
Four Days War (S. Wright), 1936
Four Encounters (s Stapledon), 1976
Four for Tomorrow (s Zelazny), 1967
Four from Planet 5 (Leinster), 1959
Four Lords of the Diamond series (Chalker)
Fourth Hemisphere (Lake), 1980
Fourth Mansions (Lafferty), 1969
Four-Day Planet (Piper), 1961
Four-Dimensional Nightmare (s Ballard), 1963
Four-Sided Triangle (Temple), 1949
Fourth Horseman (Nourse), 1983
Fourth "R" (George O. Smith), 1959
Fox, The Dog and the Griffin (P. Anderson), 1966
Fox Woman (s Merritt), 1946
Fracas Factor (Reynolds), 1978
Frames series (Ball)
Frankenstein Factory (Hoch), 1975
Frankenstein Unbound (Aldiss), 1973
Fratricide Is a Gas (Gutteridge), 1975
Freckled Shark (Dent, as Robeson), 1972
Friday (Heinlein), 1982
Friends Come in Boxes (Coney), 1973
From Carthage Then I Came (Rankine, as Mason), 1966
From Death to the Stars (Hubbard), 1953
From Outer Space (Clement), 1957
From Realms Beyond (Fanthorpe, as Brett), 1963
From the Clouds to the Mountain (Verne, for), 1874
From the Earth to the Moon (Verne, for), 1869
From the Heart of Darkness (s Drake), 1983
From the Land of Fear (s Ellison), 1967
From the Oceans, From the Stars (Clarke), 1962
From This Day Forward (s Brunner), 1972
From What Far Star? (Berry), 1953
Frontier of the Dark (Chandler), 1984
Frontier's Secret (Binder, as Turek), 1973
Froomb! (Lymington), 1964
Frostworld and Dreamfire (Morressy), 1977
Frozen Limit (Fearn, as Gridban), 1954
Frozen Planet (Fanthorpe, as Torro), 1960
Frozen Planet (P. Moore), 1954
Frozen Planet of Azuron (F. and G. Hoyle), 1982
Frozen Sky (Harding), 1976
Frozen Tomb (s Fanthorpe, as Brett), 1962
Fugitive from Time (High), 1978
Fugitive in Transit (E. Llewellyn), 1985

Fugitive of the Stars (Hamilton), 1965
Fugitive of Time (Tubb, as Gridban), 1953
Fugue for a Darkening Island (Priest), 1972
Fun with Your New Head (s Disch), 1971
Funeral for the Eyes of Fire (Bishop), 1975
Funnyfingers (s Lafferty), 1976
Furies (Roberts), 1966
Furious Future (s Budrys), 1964
Further Adventures of Halley's Comet (Batchelor), 1981
Furthest (Elgin), 1971
Fury (Kuttner, C. Moore), 1950
Fury from Earth (McLaughlin), 1963
Fury Out of Time (Biggle), 1965
Future, Captain series (Hamilton)
Future for Sale (Saxon), 1964
Future Glitter (van Vogt), 1973
Future History series (Heinlein)
Future Imperfect (s Gunn), 1964
Future Past (s J. White), 1982
Future Sanctuary (Harding), 1976
Future Tense (s Vance), 1964
Future Times Three (Barjavel, for), 1970
Future War (s Wodhams), 1982
Futureworld (Rotsler, as Hall), 1976
Futurological Congress (Lem, for), 1974
Fuzzies and Other People (Piper), 1984
Fuzzy Papers (Piper), 1977
Fuzzy Sapiens (Piper), 1976

G–Bomb (Fearn, as Statten), 1952
G.O.G. 666 (Taine), 1954
Gadget Man (Goulart), 1971
Galactiad (Tubb, as Kern), 1983
Galactic Breed (Brackett), 1955
Galactic Cluster (s Blish), 1959
Galactic Derelict (Norton), 1959
Galactic Diplomat (s Laumer), 1965
Galactic Effectuator (s Vance), 1980
Galactic Empire series (Brunner)
Galactic Intrigue (Bulmer), 1953
Galactic Medal of Honor (Reynolds), 1976
Galactic Midway series (Resnick)
Galactic Odyssey (Laumer), 1967
Galactic Patrol (E.E. Smith), 1950
Galactic Pot-Healer (Dick), 1969
Galactic Rejects (Offutt), 1973
Galactic Sibyl Sue Blue (R. Brown), 1963
Galactic Takeover Bid (McIntosh), 1973
Galactic Tours (Shaw), 1981
Galactic Troubadours (Lightner), 1965
Galactic Whirlpool (Gerrold), 1980
Galactica Discovers Earth (Resnick), 1980
Galaxies (Malzberg), 1975
Galaxies Like Grains of Sand (s Aldiss), 1960
Galaxy Builder (s Laumer), 1984
Galaxy Mission (Hamilton), 1969
Galaxy of Strangers (s Biggle), 1976
Galaxy of the Lost (Tubb, as Kern), 1973
Galaxy Primes (E.E. Smith), 1965
Galaxy 666 (Fanthorpe, as Torro), 1963
Gallagher's Glacier (Richmond), 1970
Gallowglass, Rod series (Stasheff)
Gambles with Destiny (s Griffith), 1898
Game of Empire (P. Anderson), 1985
Game-Players of Titan (Dick), 1963
Gameplayers of Zan (M. Foster), 1977

Games of Neith (St. Clair), 1960
Gamesman (Malzberg), 1975
Gandalara series (Garrett)
Ganymean series (Hogan)
Ganymede series (Resnick)
Ganymede Takeover (Dick, Nelson), 1967
Garbage World (Platt), 1967
Garden of Winter (Eklund), 1980
Garden on the Moon (Boulle, for), 1964
Gardens of Delight (Watson), 1980
Gardens One to Five (Tate), 1971
Gardens, 1,2,3,4,5, (Tate), 1971
Garin Death Ray (Tolstoy, for), 1955
Garments of Caean (Bayley), 1976
Gäst i Frankensteins hus (Lundwall), 1976
Gate of Ivrel (Cherryh), 1976
Gate of Time (Farmer), 1966
Gate of Worlds (Silverberg), 1967
Gates of Creation (Farmer), 1966
Gates of Eden (Stableford), 1983
Gates of Heaven (Preuss), 1980
Gates of the Universe (R. Coulson, DeWeese), 1975
Gates of Time (Barrett), 1970
Gateway series (Pohl)
Gateway to Elsewhere (Leinster), 1954
Gateway to Never (Chandler), 1972
Gath (Tubb), 1968
Gather, Darkness! (Leiber), 1950
Gather in the Hall of the Planets (Malzberg, as O'Donnell), 1971
Gemini God (Kilworth), 1981
Gender Genocide (Cooper), 1972
General Zapped an Angel (s H. Fast), 1970
Generation Removed (Wolf), 1977
Genesis Machine (Hogan), 1978
Genesis Shield (Spruill), 1985
Genesis Two (Davies), 1969
Genetic Bomb (Offutt), 1975
Genetic Buccaneer (Tubb, as Kern), 1974
Genetic General (Dickson), 1960
Genial Dinosaur (Fearn, as Gridban), 1954
Genius Unlimited (Rackham, as Phillifent), 1972
Genocides (Disch), 1965
Gentle Giants of Ganymede (Hogan), 1978
Genus Homo (de Camp, P. Miller), 1950
Gerald Knave: Survivor series (Janifer)
Gersen, Keith series (Vance)
Get Off My World (Binder), 1971
Get Off My World! (s Leinster), 1966
Get Off the Unicorn (s McCaffrey), 1977
Geta (Kingsbury), 1984
Getaway World (Goldin), 1977
Getting into Death (s Disch). 1973
Gholan Gate (Tubb, as Kern), 1974
Ghost Breaker (s Goulart), 1971
Ghost Dance (Norman), 1970
Ghost Light (s Leiber), 1984
Ghost Pirates (Hodgson), 1909
Ghost Rider (s Fanthorpe), 1959
Ghosts of Epidoris (Tubb, as Kern), 1975
Giant Stumbles (Lymington), 1960
Giants from Eternity (Wellman), 1959
Giants in the Dust (Oliver), 1976
Giants of Universal Park (F. and G. Hoyle), 1982
Giants' Star (Hogan), 1981
Gift (Dickinson), 1973
Gift from Earth (Niven), 1968

Gift of the Manti (Bone), 1977
Giggling Ghosts (Dent, as Robeson), 1971
Ginger Star (Brackett), 1974
Girl from Mars (Breuer, Williamson), 1929
Girl from Tomorrow (Fanthorpe, as Zeigfried), 1966
Girl in the Golden Atom (Cummings), 1922
Girl, The Gold Watch, and Everything (MacDonald), 1962
Girl with the Jade Green Eyes (Boyd), 1978
Girl with the Symphony in Her Fingers (Coney), 1975
Girls from Planet 5 (Richard Wilson), 1955
Give Daddy the Knife, Darling (Lymington), 1969
Give Warning to the World (Brunner), 1974
Gladiator (Tubb, as Thomson), 1978
Gladiator (Wylie), 1930
Gladiator-at-Law (Kornbluth, Pohl), 1955
Glass Hammer (Jeter), 1985
Glass Inferno (F.Robinson, Scortia), 1974
Glass Man (Goulart, as Robeson),1975
Glass of Dyskornis (Garrett), 1982
Glass of Stars (s R. Young), 1968
Glogauer, Karl series (Moorcock)
Gloriana (Moorcock), 1978
Glory Game (Laumer), 1973
Glory Planet (Chandler), 1964
Glory Road (Heinlein), 1963
Glory That Was (de Camp), 1960
Glow of Candles (s Grant),1981
Glue Factory (Meltzer), 1969
Gnome There Was (s Kuttner and C. Moore, as Padgett), 1950
Goblin Reservation (Simak), 1968
God Killers (Baxter), 1966
God Machine (Caidin), 1969
God Machine (Watkins), 1973
God Makers (F. Herbert), 1972
God, Men, and Ghosts (Dunsany, fan), 1972
God of Tarot (Anthony), 1979
Goddess of Ganymede (Resnick), 1967
Goddess of Mars (Fearn), 1950
Goddess of the Night (s Fanthorpe), 1963
Godfrey, Chris series (Walters)
Godling, Go Home! (s Silverberg), 1964
Gods and Golems (s del Rey), 1973
Gods Laughed (s P.Anderson), 1982
Gods Look Down (T. Hoyle), 1978
Gods of Darkness (Fanthorpe, as Zeigfried), 1962
Gods of Mars (E. Burroughs), 1918
Gods of Pegana (Dunsany, fan), 1905
Gods of Riverworld (Farmer), 1983
Gods of the Greataway (Coney), 1984
Gods of Xuma (Lake), 1978
Gods, or Demons? (Lightner), 1973
Gods Themselves (Asimov), 1972
God's World (s Watson), 1979
Godsfire (Felice), 1978
Godwhale (Bass), 1974
Goggle-Eyed Pirates (Goulart, as Shawn), 1974
Gold at Starbow's End (s Pohl), 1972
Gold Crew (F. Robinson, Scortia), 1980
Gold Ogre (Dent, as Robeson), 1969
Gold Star (Z. Hughes), 1983
Gold the Man (Green), 1971
Gold Tooth (Taine), 1927
Golden Age (FitzGibbon), 1975
Golden Amazon series (Fearn)
Golden Ape (Fairman, as Chase; Lesser), 1959
Golden Apple (Robert Anton Wilson), 1975

Golden Apples of the Sun (s Bradbury), 1953
Golden Barge (Moorcock), 1980
Golden Blight (England), 1916
Golden Chalice (Fanthorpe), 1961
Golden Circle (Goulart, as Shawn), 1973
Golden City (Verrill), 1916
Golden Dream (Mayhur), 1983
Golden Enemy (Key), 1969
Golden Gate (s Lafferty), 1983
Golden Helix (s Sturgeon), 1979
Golden Man (Dent, as Robeson), 1984
Golden Man (s Dick), 1980
Golden People (Saberhagen), 1964
Golden Peril (Dent, as Robeson), 1970
Golden Scorpio (Bulmer, as Akers), 1978
Golden Space (Sargent), 1982
Golden Sword (J. Morris), 1977
Golden Torc (May), 1981
Golden Warrior (s Fanthorpe, as Roberts), 1958
Golden Wings (W. Morris, fan), 1900
Golden Witchbreed (Gentle), 1983
Gold-Finder (Griffith), 1898
Golem (Bester), 1980
Goliah: A Utopian Essay (s London), 1973
Good Leviathan (Boulle, for), 1979
Good Neighbors and Other Strangers (s Pangborn), 1972
Good Taste (s Asimov), 1977
Good-bye to Earth (Kelley), 1979
Gor series (Norman)
Gordon, Flash series (Goulart, as Steffanson)
Gordon, John series (Hamilton)
Gorgon (s Lee), 1985
Gorgon Festival (Boyd), 1972
Gormenghast (Peake, fan), 1950
Goslings (Beresford), 1913
Gosseyn, Gilbert series (van Vogt)
Grain Kings (s Roberts), 1976
Grand Adventure (s Farmer), 1984
Grand Illusion (Fearn, as Statten), 1953
Grand Jubilee (Elgin), 1981
Grand Wheel (Bayley), 1977
Grandon, Robert series (Kline)
Graveyard of the Damned (s Fanthorpe), 1962
Gravity's Rainbow (Pynchon), 1973
Gray, Maurice series (P. Moore)
Gray Aliens (Holly), 1963
Gray Lensman (E.E. Smith), 1951
Gray Prince (Vance), 1974
Graymantle (Morressy), 1981
Grayspace Beast (Eklund), 1976
Great Divide (F. Robinson), 1982
Great Explosion (Russell), 1962
Great Fetish (de Camp), 1978
Great Fog (s Heard), 1944
Great Imperium series (L. Carter)
Great Magician's Error (Braun, for), 1972
Great Pirate Syndicate (Griffith), 1899
Great Stone of Sardis (Stockton), 1898
Great Taboo (Allen), 1890
Great Time Machine Hoax (Laumer), 1964
Great War in England in 1897 (Le Queux), 1894
Great War Syndicate (Stockton), 1889
Great Weather Syndicate (Griffith), 1906
Great White Queen (Le Queux), 1898
Greatest Adventure (Taine), 1929
Greatheart Silver (s farmer), 1982

Green Brain (F. Herbert), 1966
Green Death (Dent, as Robeson), 1971
Green Drift (Lymington), 1965
Green Eagle (Dent, as Robeson), 1968
Green Eyes (Shepard), 1984
Green Fire (Taine), 1928
Green Gene (Dickinson), 1973
Green Girl (Williamson), 1950
Green Hills of Earth (s Heinlein), 1951
Green Magic (s Vance), 1979
Green Man of Graypec (Pragnell), 1950
Green Man of Kilsona (Pragnell), 1936
Green Millennium (Leiber), 1953
Green Odyssey (Farmer), 1957
Green Planet (Holly), 1960
Green Planet series (Petaja)
Green Queen (St. Clair), 1956
Green Ray (Le Queux), 1944
Green Rust (E. Wallace), 1919
Green Star series (L. Carter)
Greencomber (Tate), 1979
Greener Thank You Think (W. Moore), 1947
Greetings from Earth (Goulart), 1983
Greks Bring Gifts (Leinster), 1964
Gremlins, Go Home! (Bová, Dickson), 1974
Grey Ones (Lymington), 1960
Greybeard (Aldiss), 1964
Greylorn (s Laumer), 1968
Grimes, John series (Chandler)
Grimm's World (V. Vinge), 1969
Grinny (Fisk), 1973
Grip of Fear (s Fanthorpe), 1961
Ground Zero Man (Shaw), 1971
Groundstar Conspiracy (Davies), 1972
Group Feast (Saxton), 1971
Growing Up in Tier 3000 (Gotschalk), 1975
Gryb (s van Vogt), 1976
Guardian (Monteleone), 1980
Guardian of Isis (M. Hughes), 1981
Guardians (Christopher), 1970
Guardians of the Gate (Trimble), 1972
Guardians of the Tomb (s Fanthorpe, as Roberts), 1958
Guardians of Time (s P. Anderson), 1961
Guardsman of Gor (Norman), 1981
Guernica Night (Malzberg), 1974
Gulliver of Mars (Arnold), 1964
Gun for Dinosaur (s de Camp), 1963
Gunner Cade (Kornbluth and Merril, as Judd), 1952
Gunpowder God (Piper), 1978
Guns of Avalon (Zelazny), 1972
Gwen, In Green (Z. Hughes, as Zachary), 1974
Gypsy series (Goulart)

H-Bomb over America (Sutton), 1967
Hadon of Ancient Opar (Farmer), 1974
Hail Hibbler (Goulart), 1980
Hain series (Le Guin)
Halcyon Drift (Stableford), 1972
Half Past Human (Bass), 1971
Halflings (s Brackett), 1973
Haljan series (Cummings)
Hamelin Plague (Chandler), 1963
Hammer's Slammers (s Drake), 1979
Hampdenshire Wonder (Beresford), 1911
Han Solo series (Daley)
Hand from Gehenna (s Fanthorpe, as Nobel), 1964

Hand of Doom (Fanthorpe), 1960
Hand of Ganz (Haiblum), 1985
Hand of Havoc (Tubb, as Grey), 1954
Hand of the Oberon (Zelazny), 1976
Hand of Zei (de Camp), 1963
Handful of Darkness (s Dick), 1955
Handful of Time (s R. Brown), 1963
Hands of Orlac (Renard, for), 1929
Haploids (Sohl), 1952
Happy New Year, Herbie (s Hunter), 1963
Hard to Be a God (Strugatsky, for), 1973
Hard Way Up (s Chandler), 1972
Hardin, Bat series (Reynolds)
Harper Hall series (McCaffrey)
Harper of Titan (Hamilton), 1967
Harrigan's File (s Derleth), 1975
Hart's Hope (Card), 1983
Hastings Conspiracy (Coppell), 1980
Hate Genius (Dent, as Robeson), 1979
Haunted Earth (Koontz), 1973
Haunted Pool (s Fanthorpe, as Thorpe), 1958
Haunted Stars (Hamilton), 1960
Haunted Woman (Lindsay), 1922
Hauser's Memeory (Siodmak), 1968
Have Space Suit—Will Travel (Heinlein), 1958
Have You Seen These? (s Asimov), 1974
Haven of Darkness (Tubb), 1977
Hawk among the Sparrows (s McLaughlin), 1976
Hawk in Silver (Gentle), 1977
Hawkmistress (Bradley), 1982
Hawksbill Station (Silverberg), 1968
Hawkshaw (Goulart), 1972
He Could Stop the World (Dent, as Robeson), 1970
He Owned the World (Maine), 1960
Heads of Cerberus (Stevens), 1952
Healer (Dickinson), 1983
Healer (Meltzer), 1969
Healer (F. Wilson), 1976
Heart of a Dog (Bulgakov, for), 1968
Heart of Stone Dear (s Lafferty), 1983
Heart of the World (Haggard), 1895
Heartsease (Dickinson), 1969
Heaven Makers (F. Herbert), 1968
Heavenly Host (s Asimov), 1975
Hector Servadac (Verne, for), 1877
Heechee Rendezvous (Pohl), 1984
Hegira (Bear), 1979
Heirs of Babylon (Cook), 1972
Hell Below (Dent, as Robeson), 1980
Hell Fruit (Fearn, as Rose), 1953
Hell Has Wings (s Fanthorpe), 1962
Hell Planet (Tubb), 1954
Heller's Leap (I. Wallace), 1979
Hellflower (George O. Smith), 1953
Hellhound Project (Goulart), 1975
Helliconia series (Aldiss)
Hello America (Ballard), 1981
Hello, Lemuria (Goulart), 1979
Hello Summer, Goodbye (Coney), 1975
Hellquad (Goulart), 1984
Hell's Gate (Koontz), 1970
Hell's Pavement (D. Knight), 1955
Hellstone (Spruill), 1980
Hellstrom's Hive (F. Herbert), 1973
Herds (Goldin), 1975
Here Abide Monsters (Norton), 1973

Heritage of Hastur (Bradley), 1975
Heritage of Stars (Simak), 1977
Heritage of the Star (Engdahl), 1973
Hermes Fall (Baxter), 1978
Hermes 3000 (Kotzwinkle), 1972
Hero of Downways (Coney), 1973
Hero Ship (Searls), 1969
Heroes and Villains (A. Carter), 1969
Heroics (Effinger), 1979
Herovit's World (Malzberg), 1973
Hestia (Cherryh), 1979
Heu-Heu (Haggard), 1924
Hex (Dent, as Robeson), 1968
Hidden Tribe (S. Wright), 1938
Hidden Universe (Farley), 1950
Hidden Variables (s Sheffield), 1981
Hidden World (Coblentz), 1957
Hidden Worlds of Zandra (Rotsler), 1983
Hierarchies (Rackham, as Phillifent), 1973
Hieros Gamos of Sam and An Smith (Saxton), 1969
Hiero's Journey (Lanier), 1973
High Couch on Silistra (J. Morris), 1977
High Crusade (P. Anderson), 1960
High Crystal (Caidin), 1974
High Destiny (Morgan), 1973
High Hex (Janifer), 1969
High Justice (s Pournelle), 1977
High Side (Ehrlich), 1969
High Tension (s Ing), 1982
High Vacuum (Maine), 1957
High Way Home (Fisk), 1973
High-Rise (Ballard), 1975
Highways in Hiding (George O. Smith), 1956
Highwood (Barrett), 1972
His Master's Voice (Lem, for), 1984
History of Civilization (E.E.Smith), from 1948
History of Middle-Earth (Tolkien, fan), 1983
Hit or Myth (Asprin), 1983
Hitch-Hiker series (Adams)
Hobbit (Tolkien, fan), 1937
Hoenig, Robby series (Dickson)
Hoka! (s P. Anderson, Dickson), 1983
Holding Wonder (s Henderson), 1971
Hole in Space (s Niven), 1974
Hole in the World (Lymington), 1974
Hole in the Zero (Joseph), 1967
Hollow Land (W. Morris, fan), 1897
Hollow Lands (Moorcock), 1974
Holy Terror (Wells), 1939
Home from the Shore (Dickson), 1978
Home is the Martian (Bulmer, as Kent), 1954
Home Sweet Home 2010 A.D. (Reynolds), 1984
Homebrew (s P. Anderson), 1976
Homesmind (Sargent), 1984
Homeward and Beyond (s P. Anderson), 1975
Homeward Bound (Verne, for), 1965
Homeworld (H. Harrison), 1980
Homing Pigeons (Robert Anton Wilson), 1981
Homunculus (Keller), 1949
Honeymoon in Hell (s F. Brown), 1958
Honeymoon in Space (Griffith), 1901
Hooded Swan series (Stableford)
Hook, Ryder series (Bulmer, as Zetford)
Hopkins Manuscript (Sherriff), 1939
Horde (Green), 1976
Horizon Alpha (Rankine, as Mason), 1971

Horn of Time (s. P. Anderson), 1968
Horns on Their Heads (s Lafferty), 1976
Horror Expert (F. Long), 1961
Horror from the Hills (F. Long), 1963
Horror on the Asteroid (s Hamilton), 1936
Hospital Horror (Binder), 1973
Hospital Station (s J. White), 1962
Hostage for Hinterland (Darney), 1976
Hostage of Zir (de Camp), 1977
Hot Sleep (Card), 1978
Hot Spot (Leinster), 1969
Hot Time in Old Town (McQuay), 1981
Hot Wireless Sets, Aspirin Tablets, The Sandpaper Sides Of Used
   Matchboxes, and Something that Might Have Been Castor Oil
   (Compton), 1971
Hotel de Dream (Tennant), 1976
Hothouse (Aldiss), 1962
Hounds of Tindalos (s F. Long), 1946
Hour at the Gate (A. Foster), 1984
Hour of the Horde (Dickson), 1970
Hour of the Phoenix (Saxon), 1964
House Between the Worlds (Bradley), 1980
House in November (Laumer), 1970
House of Many Worlds (Merwin), 1951
House of Sleep (Kavan), 1947
House of the Deadly Nightshade (F. Long, as L. Long), 1972
House of the Wolfings (W. Morris, fan), 1889
House of Zeor (Lichtenberg), 1974
House on the Borderland (Hodgson), 1908
House That Stood Still (van Vogt), 1950
Houses of Iszm (Vance), 1964
How Many Blocks in the Pile? (Meltzer), 1968
How the Gods Wove in Kyrannon (Mayhar), 1979
Hrolf Kraki's Saga (P. Anderson), 1973
Human Angle (s Tenn), 1956
Human Error (Preuss), 1985
Humanity Prime (McAllister), 1971
Humanoid Touch (Williamson), 1980
Humanoids (Williamson), 1949
Humans of Ziax II (Morressy), 1974
Hundredth Millennium (Brunner), 1959
Hunger (s Beaumont), 1957
Hunt for the Meteor (Verne, for), 1965
Hunter and the Trap (H. Fast), 1967
Hunter of the Worlds (Cherryh), 1976
Hunter Out of Time (Fox), 1965
Hunters of Gor (Norman), 1974
Hunters of Jundagai (Bulmer), 1971
Hunters of the Red Moon (Bradley), 1973
Hyancinths (Yarbro), 1983
Hybrid (Jakes), 1969
Hydra Monster (Goulart, as Shawn), 1973
Hyperspace (Fanthorpe), 1959

I, Aleppo (Sohl), 1976
I Am Lazarus (s Kavan), 1945
I Am Legend (Matheson), 1954
I Came, I Saw, I Wondered (Fearn, as Gridban), 1954
I Fight for Mars (Tubb, as Grey), 1953
I Have No Mouth, and I Must Scream (s Ellison), 1967
I Hope I Shall Soon Arrive (s Dick), 1985
I Inside (A. Foster), 1984
I Love Galesburg in the Springtime (s Finney), 1963
I.Q. Merchant (Boyd), 1972
I Remember Lemuria (s Shaver), 1948
I, Robot (a Asimov), 1950

I Sing the Body Electric! (s Bradbury), 1969
I Spy… (Fearn, as Statten)
I, The Machine (Fairman), 1968
I Want the Stars (Purdom), 1964
I Will Fear No Evil (Heinlein), 1970
I, Zombie (Piserchia, as Selby), 1982
Ice (Kavan), 1967
Ice and Iron (Tucker), 1974
Ice Crown (Norton), 1970
Ice Monkey (s M. Harrison), 1983
Ice People (Barjavel, for), 1970
Ice Prison (Sky), 1976
Ice Prophet (Forstchen), 1983
Ice Schooner (Moorcock), 1969
Icehenge (K. Robinson), 1984
Icequake (Kilian), 1979
Icerigger (A. Foster), 1974
Iceworld (Clement), 1953
Iceworld Connection (Offutt, as Cleve), 1983
Icicle (Tertz, for), 1963
Identity Plunderers (Haiblum), 1984
Idle Pleasures (s Effinger), 1983
Iduna's Universe (Tubb), 1979
If All Else Fails (s Strete), 1980
If the Stars Are Gods (Benford, Eklund), 1977
Illuminatus series (Robert Anton Wilson)
Illustrated Man (s Bradbury), 1951
Image of the Beast (Farmer), 1968
Image of Voices (Norwood), 1982
Imaginary Magnitude (Lem, for), 1984
Immortal (Gunn), 1970
Immortal of World's End (L. Carter), 1976
Immortality Delivered (Sheckley) 1958
Immortality Inc. (Sheckley), 1959
Immortals (Barjavel, for), 1974
Immortals (Berry, as Garner), 1953
Immortals (Fanthorpe, as Brett), 1962
Immortals (s Farley), 1946
Immortals (Gunn), 1962
Immortals of Mercury (s Clark Ashton Smith), 1932
Impact-20 (s Nolan), 1963
Imperator Plot (Spruill), 1983
Imperial Earth (Clarke), 1975
Imperial Stars (Goldin), 1976
Imperium series (Laumer)
Implosion (D. Jones), 1967
Impossible? (s Janifer), 1968
Impossible Man (s Ballard), 1966
Impossible World (Binder), 1970
Impossibles (Garrett as Phillips, Janifer), 1963
Imram (Barnwell), 1981
In and Out of the Quandary (s Hoffman), 1982
In Caverns Below (Coblentz), 1975
In Deep (s D. Knight), 1963
In Iron Years (s Dickson), 1980
In Our Hands, The Stars (H. Harrison), 1970
In Quest of Qalara (Offutt, as Cleve), 1983
In Solitary (Kilworth), 1977
In the Beginning (Christopher), 1972
In the Days of the Comet (Wells), 1906
In the Enclosure (Malzberg), 1973
In the Footsteps of the Abominable Snowman (Nesvadba, for), 1970
In the Green Star's Glow (L. Carter), 1976
In the Hall of the Martian Kings (s Varley), 1978
In the Hands of Glory (Eisenstein), 1981
In the Kingdom of the Beasts (Stableford), 1971

In the Ocean of Night (Benford), 1977
In the Pocket (s Malzberg), 1971
In the Problem Pit (s Pohl), 1976
In the Valley of the Statues (s Holdstock), 1982
In the Wet (Shute), 1953
In Vericonium (M. Harrison), 1982
Inaudible Sounds (Braun, for), 1984
Incandescent Ones (F. and G. Hoyle), 1977
Incarnations of Immortality series (Anthony)
Incident on Ath (Tubb), 1978
Inconstant Moon (s Niven), 1973
Incredible Planet (Campbell), 1949
Incredible Tide (Key), 1970
Incredulist (s Fanthorpe, as Roberts), 1954
Indestructible (Berry, as Garner), 1954
Indian Mystery (Allen), 1902
Indiana Jones and the Temple of Doom (Kahn), 1984
Indoctrinaire (Priest), 1970
Industrial Republic (Sinclair), 1907
Infernal Desire Machines of Dr. Hoffman (A. Carter), 1972
Inferno (Fearn, as Statten), 1950
Inferno (F. and G. Hoyle), 1973
Inferno (Niven, Pournelle), 1976
Infinite Brain (C. Long), 1957
Infinite Cage (Laumer), 1972
Infinite Dreams (s Joe Haldeman), 1978
Infinite Man (Galouye), 1973
Infinite Moment (s Wyndham), 1961
Infinite Summer (s Priest), 1979
Infinite Worlds of Maybe (del Rey), 1966
Infinitive of Go (Brunner), 1980
Infinity Box (s Wilhelm), 1975
Infinity Concerto (Bear), 1984
Infinity Machine (Fanthorpe, as Muller), 1962
Inherit the Stars (Hogan), 1977
Inheritor (Bradley), 1984
Inheritors (Chandler), 1972
Inheritors (Golding), 1955
Inheritors of Earth (P. Anderson, Eklund), 1974
Inn of the Hairy Toad (s Resnick), 1985
Inner Circle (J. Fast), 1979
Inner Cosmos (Fearn, as Statten), 1952
Inner Wheel (Roberts), 1970
Inquestor series (Sucharitkul)
Insane City (Bulmer), 1971
Insatiability (Witkiewicz, for), 1977
Insect Invasion (Cummings), 1967
Insect Play, 1923 (Capek, for), 1933
Inside (Morgan), 1971
Inside Outside (Farmer), 1964
Insider (C. Evans), 1981
Instrumentality series (Cordwainer Smith)
Insurgents (Vercors, for), 1956
Intangibles Inc. (s Aldiss), 1969
Integral Trees (Niven), 1984
Intelligence Gigantic (Fearn), 1943
Inter Ice Age 4 (Abe, for), 1970
Interface (Adlard), 1971
Interloper (Fearn, as Statten), 1953
Interminds (Sellings, as Luther), 1967
Interplanetary Hunter (A. Barnes), 1956
Interpreter (Aldiss), 1961
Interstellar Empire (Brunner), 1976
Interstellar Two-Five (Rankine), 1966
Interworld (Haiblum), 1977
Into Deepest Space (F. and G. Hoyle), 1974

Into Plutonian Depths (Coblentz), 1950
Into the Aether (Lupoff), 1974
Into the Alternative Universe (Chandler), 1964
Into the Niger Bend (Verne, for), 1960
Into the Slave Nebula (Brunner), 1968
Into the Tenth Millennium (Capon), 1956
Intruders (Fanthorpe, as Fane), 1963
Invader from Space (P. Moore), 1963
Invader on My Back (High), 1968
Invaders series (Laumer)
Invaders are Coming! (Nourse), 1959
Invaders from Earth (Silverberg), 1958
Invaders from Rigel (Pratt), 1960
Invaders from the Infinite (Campbell), 1961
Invaders of Space (Leinster), 1964
Invaders on the Moon (Neville), 1970
Invading Asteroid (Wellman), 1932
Invasion: Earth (H. Harrison), 1982
Invasion from 2500 (T. Carr and T. White, as Edwards) 1964
Invasion of Mars (Serviss), 1969
Invasion of 1910 (Le Queux), 1906
Invasion of the Body Snatchers (Finney), 1961
Inverted World (Priest), 1974
Investigation (Lem, for), 1974
Invincible (Lem, for), 1973
Invincible Barriers (Silverberg, as Osborne), 1958
Invisible Cities (Calvino, for), 1974
Invisible Death (L. Carter), 1975
Invisible Man (Wells), 1897
Invisible Voices (s Shiel), 1935
Invisibility Affair (R. Coulson and DeWeese, as Stratton), 1967
Involuntary Immortals (Phillips), 1959
Involution Ocean (Sterling), 1977
In-World (Fanthorpe, as Roberts), 1960
Ion War (Kapp), 1978
Ipomoea (Rackham), 1969
Iron and the Anger (Rayer), 1964
Iron Cage (Norton), 1974
Iron Dream (Spinrad), 1972
Iron Heel (London), 1908
Iron Hoop (FitzGibbon), 1949
Iron Man: Call My Killer...Modok (Rotsler), 1979
Iron Skull (Goulart, as Robeson), 1975
Iron Star (Taine), 1930
Iron Thorn (Budrys), 1968
Ironbrand (Morressy), 1980
Irrational Numbers (s Effinger), 1976
Is THAT What People Do? (s Sheckley), 1984
Isis series (M. Hughes)
Island (Huxley), 1962
Island Called Moreau (Aldiss), 1981
Island in the Sky (Wellman), 1961
Island of Captain Sparrow (S. Wright), 1928
Island of Doctor Death (s G. Wolfe), 1980
Island of Dr. Moreau (Goulart, as Silva), 1977
Island of Doctor Moreau (Wells), 1896
Island of Fear (P. Moore), 1954
Island People (Coblentz), 1971
Island Snatchers (George H. Smith), 1978
Islandia (A. Wright), 1942
Islands (Randall), 1976
Islands in the Sky (Clarke), 1952
Islands of Space (Campbell), 1957
Isle of Lies (Shiel), 1909
Isle of the Dead (Zelazny), 1969
Isotope Man (Maine), 1957

It (s Sturgeon), 1948
It Came from Schenectady (Longyear), 1984
It Can't Happen Here (S. Lewis), 1935
It Was the Day of the Robot (F. Long), 1963
It's a Mad, Mad, Mad Galaxy (s Laumer), 1968
Ivan Greet's Masterpiece (s Allen), 1893

Jack of Eagles (Blish), 1952
Jack of Shadows (Zelazny), 1971
Jack of Swords (Tubb), 1976
Jacket (London), 1915
Jack-in-the-Box Planet (Hoskins), 1978
Jade Man's Eyes (s Moorcock), 1973
Jagged Orbit (Brunner), 1969
Jagger, The Dog from Elsewhere (Key), 1976
Jameson, Professor series (s N. Jones)
Jamie the Red (Dickson), 1984
Jan series (Kline)
Jandar of Callisto (L.Carter), 1972
Janissaries series (Pournelle)
Janus series (Norton)
Janus Syndrome (Rankine, as Mason), 1969
Japan Sinks (Komatsu, for), 1976
Jason, Son of Jason (Giesy), 1966
Jaws of Death (Allen), 1889
Jaws That Bite, The Claws That Catch (Coney), 1975
Jehad (Yermakov), 1984
Jem (Pohl), 1979
Jeremy Case (DeWeese), 1976
Jerusalem Fire (Meluch), 1985
Jester at Scar (Tubb), 1970
Jesus Incident (F. Herbert), 1979
Jesus on Mars (Farmer), 1979
Jewel of Arwen (s Bradley), 1974
Jewel of Jarhen (Tubb, as Kern), 1974
Jewels of Aptor (Delany), 1962
Jewels of Elsewhen (T. White), 1967
Jirel of Joiry (s C. Moore), 1969
Jitterbug (McQuay), 1984
Jiu San (Dent, as Robeson), 1981
Jizzle (s Wyndham), 1954
Job: A Comedy of Justice (Heinlein), 1984
John Carstairs, Space Detective (s F. Long), 1949
John Carter of Mars (s E. Burroughs), 1964
Jonah (J. Herbert), 1981
Jonah Kit (Watson), 1975
Jondelle (Tubb), 1973
Jones, Cirocco series (Varley)
Jongor series (R. Williams)
Jonuta Rising (Offutt, as Cleve), 1983
Jorkens, Joseph series (Dunsany, fan)
Joshua Son of None (Freedman), 1973
Journey (Randall), 1978
Journey Between Worlds (Engdahl), 1970
Journey Beyond Tomorrow (Sheckley), 1962
Journey from Flesh (Yermakov), 1981
Journey into Darkness (F. Long), 1967
Journey into Space (Chilton), 1954
Journey into Terror (Effinger), 1975
Journey of Joenes (Sheckley), 1978
Journey to Jupiter (Walters), 1965
Journey to Mars (Tubb), 1954
Journey to the Center (Stableford), 1982
Journey to the Centre of the Earth (Verne, for), 1871
Journey to the Stars (Rayer), 1964
Journey to the Underground World (L. Carter), 1979

Journey to Untor (Wibberley), 1970
Joy in Our Cause (s Emshwiller), 1974
Joy Makers (Gunn), 1961
Joyleg (Davidson, W. Moore), 1962
Joyous Invasions (s Sturgeon), 1965
Judas Mandala (Broderick), 1982
Judges of Hades (s Hoch), 1971
Judgment Night (C. Moore), 1952
Judgment of Dragons (Gotlieb), 1980
Judgment of Eve (Pangborn), 1966
Judgment on Janus (Norton), 1963
Juggernaut (Fanthorpe, as Fane), 1960
Julia and the Bazooka (s Kavan), 1970
Junction (Dann), 1981
Jungle Girl (E. Burroughs), 1932
Jungle Kids (s Hunter), 1956
Jungle of Stars (Chalker), 1976
Juniper Time (Wilhelm), 1979
Junk Day (Sellings), 1970
Junkyard Planet (Piper), 1963
Jupiter Equilateral (Rackham), 1954
Jupiter Laughs (s Cooper), 1979
Jupiter Legacy (H. Harison), 1970
Jupiter Project (Benford), 1975
Justice (s S. Wright), 1945 (?)
Justice of Revenge (Griffith), 1900
Juxtaposition (Anthony), 1982

Kajira of Gor (Norman), 1983
Kalee's Shrine (Allen), 1886
Kalevala series (Petaja)
Kalin (Tubb), 1969
Kalki (Vidal), 1978
Kallocain (Boyle, for), 1966
Kampus (Gunn), 1977
Kandar (Bulmer), 1969
Kane, Elias series (Spruill)
Kane, Michael series (Moorcock, as Bradbury)
Kar Kaballa (George H. Smith), 1969
Kar-Chee Reign (Davidson), 1966
Karma (Darney), 1980
Karma Affair (Darney), 1978
Karma Corps (Barrett), 1984
Karns, Joe series (R. Coulson, DeWeese)
Kastrove der Mächtige (Pragnell), 1966
Keegan series (Ball)
Keep (F. Wilson), 1981
Keep the Giraffe Burning (s Sladek), 1977
Keeper (Holly), 1976
Keeper of the Isis Light (M. Hughes), 1980
Keepers of the Gate (Spruill), 1977
Keepers of the Secrets (Farmer), 1983
Kellory the Warlock (L. Carter), 1984
Kelly Country (Chandler), 1983
Kelwin (Barrett), 1970
Kenmore, Joe series (Leinster)
Kennedy, Cap series (Tubb, as Kern)
Kennerin series (Randall)
Key out of Time (Norton), 1963
Key to Irunium (Bulmer), 1967
Key to Venudine (Bulmer), 1968
Keys to Dimensions series (Bulmer)
Khi to Freedom (Mayhar), 1982
Kif Strikes Back (Cherryh), 1985
Kill the Dead (Lee), 1980
Killbird (Z. Hughes), 1980

Killer (Drake), 1984
Killer Comet (P. Moore), 1978
Killer Mice (s Reed), 1976
Killer Pine (Gutteridge), 1973
Killer Thing (Wilhelm), 1967
Killer to Come (Merwin), 1953
Killerbowl (Wolf), 1975
Killing Machine (Vance), 1964
Killing Thing (Wilhelm), 1967
Kindred (O.Butler), 1979
King and Joker (Dickinson), 1976
King David's Spaceship (Pournelle), 1980
King Dragon (Offutt), 1980
King Kobold series (Stasheff)
King Kull (s L. Carter), 1967
King Maker (Dent, as Robeson), 1975
King of Argent (Rackham, as Phillifent), 1973
King of Elfland's Daughter (Dunsany, fan), 1924
King of Eolim (R. Jones), 1975
King of Terror (Dent, as Robeson), 1984
King of the Dead (Ash, as Aubrey), 1903
King of the Fourth Planet (R. Williams), 1962
King of the Slavers (Offutt, as Cleve), 1985
King of the Stars (Kelley), 1979
King Solomon's Mines (Haggard), 1885
Kingdom of the Cats (Gotlieb), 1985
King's Lesson (Morris, fan), 1888
King's Oak (s Cromie), 1897
Kings of Space (Johns), 1954
Kingsbane (Morressy), 1982
Kingslayer (Hubbard), 1949
Kinsman (Bova), 1979
Kirlian Quest (Anthony), 1978
Kiteworld (Roberts), 1985
Kittatinny (Russ), 1978
Klekton series (Jakes)
Knave, Gerald series (Janifer)
Knave in the Hand (Janifer), 1979
Knave of Dreams (Norton), 1975
Knight of Ghosts and Shadows (P. Anderson), 1974
Knights of the Limits (s Bayley), 1978
Known Space series (Niven)
Kosmiche Duelle (Tubb, as Kern), 1976
Krakatit (Capek, for), 1925
Kraken Wakes (Wyndham), 1953
Kraus, Kurt series (Webb)
Kren series (Lichtenberg)
Kronk (Cooper), 1971
Krozair of Kregen (Bulmer, as Akers), 1977
Krull (A. Foster), 1983
Kuldasak (Cowper), 1972

Labyrinths (Borges, for), 1962
Ladder in the Sky (Brunner, as Woodcott), 1962
Ladies' Day (Bloch), 1968
Ladies from Hell (s Roberts), 1979
Lady Decides (Keller), 1950
Lady in Danger (s Williamson), 1945 (?)
Ladyhawke (J. Vinge), 1985
Lagrange Five (Reynolds), 1979
Lagrangia series (Reynolds),
Lagrangists (Reynolds), 1983
Lair (J. Herbert), 1979
Lake of Gold (Griffith), 1903
Lallia (Tubb), 1971
Lampton Dreamers (Davies), 1966

LaNague Federation series (F. Wilson)
Land Beyond the Gate (s Eshbach), 1984
Land Beyond the Map (Bulmer), 1965
Land Leviathan (Moorcock), 1974
Land of Always-Night (Dent, as Robeson), 1966
Land of Fear (Dent, as Robeson), 1973
Land of Hidden Men (E. Burroughs), 1963
Land of Mist (Doyle), 1925
Land of Terror (E. Burroughs), 1944
Land of Terror (Dent, as Robeson), 1935
Land of the Giants (Leinster), 1968
Land That Time Forgot (s E. Burroughs), 1924
Land Under England (O'Neill), 1935
Landfall Is a State of Mind (Rankine, as Mason), 1968
Lando Calrissian series (L. Smith)
Landscape with Landscape (Murnane), 1985
Languages of Pao (Vance), 1958
Lani People (Bone), 1962
Lankar of Callisto (L. Carter), 1975
Lantree, Shann series (Norton)
Larger Than Life (Buzzati, for), 1962
Last Amazon (Chandler), 1984
Last and First Men (Stapledon), 1930
Last Astronaut (Fanthorpe, as Torro), 1963
Last Castle (s Vance), 1967
Last Communion (Yermakov), 1981
Last Continent (Cooper), 1969
Last Day of Creation (Jeschke, for), 1982
Last Days of the Edge of the World (Stableford), 1978
Last Defender of Camelot (s Zelazny), 1980
Last Disaster (Walters), 1978
Last Fathom (Caidin), 1967
Last Gasp (T. Hoyle), 1983
Last Hurrah of the Golden Horde (s Spinrad), 1970
Last Leap (s Galouye), 1964
Last Man on Earth (Fanthorpe, as Fane), 1960
Last Martian (Fearn, as Statten), 1952
Last Master (Dickson), 1984
Last Men in London (Stapledon), 1932
Last of the Country House Murders (Tennant), 1974
Last of the Great Race (Coblentz), 1964
Last Orders (s Aldiss), 1977
Last Planet (Norton), 1955
Last President (Kurland), 1980
Last Shuttle to Planet Earth (Rankine), 1980
Last Space Ship (Leinster), 1949
Last Spin (s Hunter), 1960
Last Starfighter (A. Foster), 1984
Last Starship from Earth (Boyd), 1968
Last Transaction (Malzberg), 1977
Last Valkyrie (Fanthorpe, as Roberts), 1961
Last Yggdrasill (R. Young), 1982
Lathe of Heaven (Le Guin), 1971
Laugh of Death (Dent, as Robeson), 1984
Laughter in Space (Fearn, as Statten), 1952
Laughter of Carthage (Moorcock), 1984
Lava (O'Donnell), 1982
Lavalite World (Farmer), 1977
Law for the Stars (Morressy), 1976
Laxham Haunting (Lymington), 1976
Lays of Beleriand (Tolkien, fan), 1983
Lazarus Effect (F. Herbert), 1983
Leaky Establishment (Langford), 1984
Leaves of Time (Barrett), 1971
Left Hand of Darkness (Le Guin), 1969
Legacy (Bone), 1976

Legacy (Schmitz), 1979
Legacy of Evil (F. Long, as L. Long), 1973
Legacy of the Stars (Hoskins, as Gregory), 1979
Legend of Miaree (Z. Hughes), 1974
Legend of Time (Williamson), 1952
Legends from the End of Time (s Moorcock), 1976
Legion (Grant), 1979
Legion of Space series (Williamson)
Legion of Time (Williamson), 1961
Legion of the Lost (Fanthorpe, as Torro), 1962
Legions of Antares (Bulmer, as Akers), 1981
Lensman series (E.E. Smith)
Lepidus the Centurion (Arnold), 1901
Ler series (M. Foster)
Lesson for the Damned (Ball), 1971
Lest Darkness Fall (de Camp), 1941
Lest Earth Be Conquered (F. Long), 1966
Lest We Forget Thee, Earth (Silverberg, as Knox), 1958
Let the Fire Fall, (Wilhelm), 1969
Let the Spaceman Beware! (P. Anderson), 1963
Letters of the Altrurian Traveller (1893-1894) (Howells), 1961
Level Seven (Roshwald), 1959
Leviathan (Robert Anton Wilson), 1975
Leviathan's Deep (J. Carr), 1979
Liberty's World (Killough), 1985
Lie Destroyer (Fearn, as Statten), 1953
Lies, Inc (Dick), 1984
Lieut. Gullivar Jones: His Vacation (Arnold), 1905
Life Everlasting (s Keller), 1947
Life for Kregen (Bulmer, as Akers), 1979
Life for the Stars (Blish), 1962
Life in the Day of...(s F. Robinson), 1981
Life, the Universe, and Everything (Adams), 1982
Life with Lancelot (Rackham, as Phillifent), 1973
Lifeboat (H. Harrison), 1977
Lifeboat (J. White), 1972
Lifeboat Earth series (Schmidt)
Lifeburst (Williamson), 1984
Lifekeeper (McQuay), 1980
Lifeship (Dickson, H. Harrison), 1976
Lifetime on Clouds (Murnane), 1976
Light a Last Candle (King), 1969
Light at the End of the Universe (s T. Carr), 1976
Light Fantastic (s Bester), 1976
Light on the Sound (Sucharitkul), 1982
Light That Never Was (Biggle), 1972
Lightning World (Fanthorpe, as Thorpe), 1960
Lights in the Sky Are Stars (F. Brown), 1953
Like Nothing on Earth (s Russell), 1975
Lilith (Chalker), 1981
Limbo (B. Wolfe), 1952
Limbo 90 (B. Wolfe), 1953
Limits (s Niven), 1985
Lincoln Hunters (Tucker), 1958
Line to Tomorrow (s Kuttner and C. Moore, as Padgett), 1954
Liners of Time (Fearn), 1947
Lion Game (Schmitz), 1973
Lion Men of Mongo (Goulart, as Steffanson), 1974
Lion of Comarre (Clarke), 1968
Lisa Kane (Lupoff), 1976
Listen, Listen (s Wilhelm), 1981
Listen! The Stars! (Brunner), 1963
Listeners (Gunn), 1972
Listeners (Leinster), 1969
Litany of Sh'reev (Watkins), 1976
Little, Big (Crowley), 1981

Little Fuzzy (Piper), 1962
Little Green Spaceman (Fisk), 1974
Little Knowledge (Bishop), 1977
Little People (Christopher), 1967
Lives and Times of Jerry Cornelius (s Moorcock), 1976
Lives You Wished to Lead But Never Dared (s Hubbard), 1978
Living Fire Menace (Dent, as Robeson), 1971
Living Legend (Yermakov), 1982
Living Way Out (s Guin), 1967
Living World (Tubb, as Maddox), 1954
Lizard Lords (Coblentz), 1964
Llana of Gathol (s E. Burroughs), 1948
Loafers of Refuge (Green), 1965
Logan series (Nolan)
Lone Star Planet (Piper), 1984
Lonely Astronomer (Fearn, as Gridban), 1954
Lonely Vigils (s Wellman), 1981
Long After Midnight (s Bradbury), 1976
Long Afternoon of Earth (Aldiss), 1962
Long Arm of Gil Hamilton (s Niven), 1976
Long Eureka (s Sellings), 1968
Long Loud Silence (Tucker), 1952
Long Night (s P. Anderson), 1983
Long Night (Caidin), 1956
Long Patrol (Goulart), 1984
Long Result (Brunner), 1965
Long Shot for Rosinante (Gilliland), 1981
Long Sleep (Koontz, as Hill), 1975
Long Tomorrow (Brackett),1955
Long Twilight (Laumer), 1969
Long View (Busby), 1976
Long Way Home (P. Anderson), 1975
Long Winter (Christopher), 1962
Look Out for Space (Nolan), 1985
Looking Backward, From the Year 2000 (Reynolds), 1973
Looking Backward 2000-1887 (Bellamy), 1888
Looking for Blücher (Wodhams), 1980
Lord Kalvan of Otherwhen (Piper), 1965
Lord of Darkness (Silverberg), 1983
Lord of Death (Flint), 1965
Lord of Labour (Griffith), 1911
Lord of Light (Zelazny), 1967
Lord of the Apes (Effinger), 1976
Lord of the Flies (Golding), 1954
Lord of the Green Planet (Petaja), 1967
Lord of the Rings (Tolkien, fan), 1954
Lord of the Sea (Shiel), 1901
Lord of the Spiders (Moorcock), 1970
Lord of the Stars (Sutton), 1969
Lord of the Trees (Farmer), 1970
Lord of Thunder (Norton), 1962
Lord of Tranerica (Coblentz), 1966
Lord Tedric series (Eklund, E.E. Smith)
Lord Tyger (Farmer), 1970
Lord Valentine's Castle (Silverberg), 1980
Lords of Atlantis (West), 1960
Lords of Creation (Binder), 1949
Lords of the Psychon (Galouye), 1963
Lords of the Starship (Geston), 1967
Lords of the Triple Moons (Mayhar), 1983
Los Angeles: A.D. 2017 (Wylie), 1971
Lost–A Moon (Capon), 1956
Lost Cavern (s Heard), 1948
Lost Comet (Coblentz), 1964
Lost Continent (s E. Burroughs), 1963
Lost Continent (Hyne), 1900

Lost Earths (Petaja), 1979
Lost Face (Nesvadba, for), 1971
Lost: Fifty Suns (s van Vogt), 1980
Lost Giant (Dent, as Robeson), 1980
Lost in Space (George O. Smith), 1959
Lost in Space (T. White, as Archer), 1967
Lost Legacy (s Heinlein), 1960
Lost Millennium (Richmond), 1967
Lost Moons (s Vance), 1982
Lost Oasis (Dent, as Robeson), 1965
Lost on Venus (E. Burroughs), 1935
Lost Perception (Galouye), 1966
Lost Race of Mars (Silverberg), 1960
Lost Star (Hoover), 1979
Lost World (Doyle), 1912
Lost World of Cronus (Kapp), 1982
Lost World of Time (L. Carter), 1969
Lost Worlds (L. Carter), 1980
Lottery Ticket (Verne, for), 1919
Lotus Caves (Christopher), 1969
Love Ain't Nothing But Sex Misspelled (s Ellison), 1968
Love and Napalm (s Ballard), 1972
Love Conquers All (Saberhagen), 1979
Love Eternal (Haggard), 1918
Love in the Ruins (Percy), 1971
Love Not Human (Dickson), 1981
Lovecraft's Book (Lupoff), 1985
Lovely (Meltzer), 1969
Lovers (Farmer), 1961
Low Notes on a High Level (Priestley), 1954
Low-Flying Aircraft (s Ballard), 1976
Luana (A. Foster), 1974
Lucifer Comet (I. Wallace), 1980
Lucifer's Hammer (Niven, Pournelle), 1977
Luck of Brin's Five (Wilder), 1977
Lunar Attack (Rankine), 1975
Lunar Eye (R. Williams), 1964
Lunatics of Terra (s Sladek), 1984
Luck Machine (Tubb), 1980
Lyonesse series (Vance)

M33 in Andromeda (s van Vogt), 1971
Macabre Ones! (Fanthorpe, as Fane), 1964
Machine in Shaft Ten (s M. Harrison), 1975
Machine That Thought (s Gallun, as Callahan), 1940
Machineries of Joy (s Bradbury), 1964
Machines and Men (s Roberts), 1973
Macrolife (Zebrowski), 1979
Macropulos Secret (Capek, for), 1925
Macroscope (Anthony), 1969
Mad Empress of Callisto (L. Carter), 1975
Mad Eyes (Dent, as Robeson), 1969
Mad Goblin (Farmer), 1970
Mad Mesa (Dent, as Robeson), 1972
Mad Metropolis (High), 1966
Madman and the Nun (Witkiewicz, for), 1968
Madonna of the Music Halls (Le Queux), 1897
Madrone Tree (Duncan), 1949
Magic Goes Away (Niven), 1978
Magic Inc. (Heinlein), 1950
Magic Island (Dent, as Robeson), 1977
Magic Labyrinth (Farmer), 1980
Magic Man (s Beaumont), 1965
Magic Meadow (Key), 1975
Magic Time (Reed), 1979
Magician of Mars (Hamilton), 1959

Magicians (Gunn), 1976
Magicians (Priestley), 1954
Magnetic Brain (Fearn, as Gridban), 1953
Magnificent MacInnes (Mead), 1949
Magnus, Martin series (Temple)
Mahatma and the Hare (Haggard), 1911
Mahogany Trinrose (Lichtenberg), 1981
Main Experiment (Hodder-Williams), 1964
Majii (Dent, as Robeson), 1971
Majipoor series (Silverberg)
Major Corby and the Unidentified Flapping Object (DeWeese), 1979
Major Operation (s J. White), 1971
Make Room! Make Room! (H. Harrison), 1966
Makepeace Experiment (Tertz, for), 1965
Maker of the Universes (Farmer), 1965
Makeshift God (Griffin), 1979
Makeshift Rocket (P. Anderson), 1962
Making of the Representative for Planet 8 (Lessing), 1982
Male Response (Aldiss), 1961
Malicia Tapestry (Aldiss), 1976
Mallworld (s Sucharitkul), 1981
Malone, Kenneth J. series (Garrett as Phillips, Janifer)
Man Divided (Stapledon), 1950
Man from Atlantis (Goulart, as Robeson), 1974
Man from Beyond (Fanthorpe, as Muller), 1965
Man from Beyond (s Wyndham), 1975
Man from Maybe (Kelley), 1974
Man from Tomorrow (Fearn, as Statten), 1952
Man from Tomorrow (Tucker), 1955
Man in a Cage (Stableford), 1975
Man in Duplicate (Fearn, as Statten), 1953
Man in the Bird Cage (MacLean), 1971
Man in the High Castle (Dick), 1962
Man in the Maze (Silverberg), 1969
Man in the Tree (D. Knight), 1984
Man Obsessed (Nourse), 1955
Man of Bronze (Dent, as Robeson), 1935
Man of Earth (Budrys), 1958
Man of Many Minds (E. Evans), 1953
Man of Metal (Fanthorpe, as Torro), 1970
Man of Two Worlds (Fearn, as Statten), 1953
Man of Two Worlds (R. Jones), 1963
Man on the Meteor (Cummings), 1952
Man out of Nowhere (Davies), 1965
Man Plus (Pohl), 1976
Man Responsible (Robinett), 1978
Man Returned (s Broderick), 1965
Man the Fugitive (Effinger), 1974
Man, The Hunted Animal (Rotsler, as Arrow), 1976
Man Who Ate the Phoenix (Dunsany, fan), 1949
Man Who Ate the World (s Pohl), 1960
Man Who Awoke (Manning), 1975
Man Who Came Back (Fanthorpe, as Thanet), 1964
Man Who Conquered Time (Fanthorpe, as Muller), 1962
Man Who Corrupted the Earth (Edmondson), 1980
Man Who Couldn't Die (s Fanthorpe), 1960
Man Who Couldn't Sleep (Maine), 1958
Man Who Counts (P. Anderson), 1978
Man Who Fell to Earth (Tevis), 1963
Man Who Fell Up (Dent, as Robeson), 1982
Man Who Folded Himself (Gerrold), 1973
Man Who Had No Idea (s Disch), 1982
Man Who Japed (Dick), 1956
Man Who Limped (s Kline), 1946
Man Who Loved Mars (L. Carter), 1973
Man Who Loved Morlocks (Lake), 1981

Man Who Loved the Midnight Lady (s Malzberg), 1980
Man Who Made Models (s Lafferty), 1984
Man Who Mastered Time (Cummings), 1929
Man Who Melted (Dann), 1984
Man Who Missed the War (Wheatley), 1945
Man Who Owned the World (Maine), 1961
Man Who Rocked the Earth (Train), 1915
Man Who Saw Tomorrow (Sutton). 1968
Man Who Shook the Earth (Dent, as Robeson), 1969
Man Who Sold the Moon (s Heinlein), 1950
Man Who Upset the Universe (Asimov), 1955
Man Who Used the Universe (A. Foster), 1983
Man Who Vanished into Space (Johns), 1963
Man Who Wanted Stars (McLaughlin), 1965
Man Who Was Scared (Dent, as Robeson) 1981
Man with a Thousand Names (van Vogt), 1974
Man with Absolute Motion (Loomis, as Water), 1955
Man with Nine Lives (Ellison), 1960
Man with Three Eyes (Griffith), n.d.
Man with Two Memories (Haldane), 1976
Man Without a Planet (L. Carter), 1966
Man Without a Planet (del Rey, Fairman), 1969
Manalone (Kapp), 1977
Mandala (Bischoff), 1983
Man-Eater (s E. Burroughs), 1955
Manhounds of Antares (Bulmer, as Akers), 1974
Manhuntress (Offutt, as Cleve), 1982
Manifest Destiny (s Longyear), 1980
Mankind on the Run (Dickson), 1956
Mankind under the Leash (Disch), 1966
Manna (Correy), 1984
Manna (Gloag), 1940
Man's Understanding (s Hyne), 1933
Manseed (Williamson), 1982
Mansions of Space (Morressy), 1983
Many Worlds of Magnus Ridolph (s Vance), 1966
Many-Colored Land (May), 1981
Maracot Deep (s Doyle), 1929
Marauders of Gor (Norman), 1975
March of the Robots (Fanthorpe, as Brett), 1961
Marching Morons (s Kornbluth), 1959
Mardrömmen (Lundwall), 1976
Margaret and I (Wilhelm), 1971
Marion's Wall (Finney), 1973
Mark of the Beast (Fanthorpe, as Muller), 1964
Marooned (Caidin), 1964
Marooned on Mars (del Rey), 1952
Marriages Between Zones Three, Four, and Five (Lessing), 1980
Mars series (E. Burroughs)
Mars series (Kline)
Mars, Mike series (Wollheim)
Mars Is My Destination (F. Long), 1962
Mars Monopoly (Sohl), 1956
Martian Chronicles (s Bradbury), 1950
Martian Inca (Watson), 1977
Martian Martyrs (s Binder, as Coleridge), 1940
Martian Missile (Wollheim, as Grinnell), 1959
Martian Odyssey (s Weinbaum), 1949
Martian Sphinx (Brunner, as Woodcott), 1965
Martian Time-Slip (Dick), 1964
Martian Visitors (F. Long), 1964
Martian Way (s Asimov), 1955
Martians, Go Home (F. Brown), 1955
Marune: Alastor 933 (Vance), 1975
Marvellous Palace (Boulle, for). 1977
Mask of Chaos (Jakes), 1970

Mask of Circe (Kuttner, C. Moore), 1971
Mask of the Sun (Saberhagen), 1979
Maske: Thaery (Vance), 1976
Masks of Scorpio (Bulmer, as Akers), 1984
Masks of the Illuminati (Robert Anton Wilson), 1981
Masks of Time (Silverberg), 1968
Masque World (Panshin), 1969
Master Caliban! (Gotlieb), 1976
Master Mind of Mars (E. Burroughs), 1928
Master Must Die (Fearn, as Gridban), 1953
Master of Life and Death (Silverberg), 1957
Master of Misfit (Offutt, as Cleve), 1982
Master of Space (Clarke), 1961
Master of Space and Time (Rucker), 1984
Master of the Dark Gate (Jakes), 1970
Master of the Moon (P. Moore), 1952
Master of the Stars (Hoskins), 1976
Master of the World (Verne, for), 1914
Master Weed (Rackham), 1954
Masters of Everon (Dickson), 1980
Masters of Evolution (D. Knight), 1959
Masters of Flux and Anchor (Chalker), 1985
Masters of Space (E.E. Smith), 1976
Masters of the Maze (Davidson), 1965
Masters of the Pit (Moorcock), 1970
Masters of the Vortex (E.E. Smith), 1968
Masters of Time (s van Vogt), 1950
Mastodonia (Simak), 1978
Matilda's Stepchildren (Chandler), 1979
Mating Center (F. Long), 1961
Mating Cry (van Vogt), 1960
Matrix (Rankine, as Mason), 1970
Matter for Men (Gerrold), 1983
Matter of Taste (Saberhagen), 1980
Matter of Time (Cook), 1985
Matter, Space, and Time series (Cummings)
Maturity (s Sturgeon), 1979
Mauri and Kith (s P. Anderson), 1982
Mauser, Joe series (Reynolds)
Maxwell's Demons (s Bova), 1979
Mayday Orbit (P. Anderson), 1961
Mayenne (Tubb), 1973
Mayfair Magician (Griffith), 1905
Mayflies (O'Donnell), 1979
Maza of the Moon (Kline), 1930
Maze of Death (Dick), 1970
Mazes of Scorpio (Bulmer, as Akers), 1982
McAndrew Chronicles (s Sheffield), 1983
McKie, Jorj X. series (F. Herbert)
Mechanical Monarch (Tubb), 1958
Mechasm (Sladek), 1969
Med Service series (Leinster)
Meddlers (Bone), 1976
Medicine for Melancholy (s Bradbury), 1959
Medusa (Chalker), 1983
Medusa's Children (Shaw), 1977
Meeting at Infinity (Brunner), 1961
Meeting over Tuscarora (Yefremov, for), 1946
Meeting Place (s Beresford), 1929
Megiddo's Ridge (S. Wright), 1937
Melancholy Elephants (s S. Robinson), 1984
Melome (Tubb), 1983
Memoirs Found in a Bathtub (Lem, for), 1973
Memoirs of a Space Traveller (Lem, for), 1982
Memoirs of a Spacewoman (Mitchison), 1962
Memoirs of a Survivor (Lessing), 1974

Memory Bank (West), 1961
Memory of Whiteness (K. Robinson), 1985
Men and the Mirror (s Rocklynne), 1973
Men from Ariel (s Wollheim), 1982
Men in the Jungle (Spinrad), 1967
Men Inside (Malzberg), 1973
Men into Space (s Leinster), 1960
Men Like Gods (Wells), 1923
Men, Martians, and Machines (s Russell), 1956
Men of Avalon (s Keller), 1935 (?)
Menace from Earth (s Heinlein), 1959
Menace from Mercury (Fanthorpe, as La Salle), 1954
Menace from the Moon (Walters), 1959
Menace from the Past (Tubb, as Maddox), 1954
Menace of the Saucers (Binder), 1969
Menace under Marwood (Lanier), 1983
Mendelov Conspiracy (Caidin), 1969
Mental Monster (Dent, as Robeson), 1973
Mental Wizard (Dent, as Robeson), 1970
Mention My Name in Atlantis (Jakes), 1972
Menzentian Gate (Eddison, fan), 1958
Mercenaries of Gor (Norman), 1985
Mercenary (Anthony), 1984
Mercenary (Pournelle), 1977
Mercenary from Tomorrow (Reynolds), 1968
Merchanter's Luck (Cherryh), 1982
Merchants of Disaster (Dent, as Robeson), 1969
Merchants' War (Pohl), 1984
Mercy Men (Nourse), 1968
Mermaid Reef (s Fanthorpe), 1959
Merman's Children (P. Anderson), 1979
Merry Christmas, Ms. Minerva (Cooper), 1978
Mesklin series (Clement)
Message from the Eocene (St. Clair), 1964
Messenger of Zhuvastou (Offutt), 1973
Messiah (Vidal), 1954
Messiah at the End of Time (Moorcock), 1978
Messiah Choice (Chalker), 1985
Messiah of the Cylinder (Rousseau), 1917
Metal Eater (Tubb, as Sheldon), 1954
Metal Giants (s Hamilton), 1932 (?)
Metal Monster (Merritt), 1946
Metallic Muse (s Biggle), 1972
Meteor Man (Laumer, as Le Baron), 1968
Meteor Menace (Dent, as Robeson), 1964
Methuselah's Children (Heinlein), 1958
Michaelmas (Budrys), 1977
Micro Infinity (Fanthorpe, as Muller), 1962
Micro Men (Fearn, as Statten), 1950
Microscopic Ones (Fanthorpe, as Brett), 1960
Midas Man (Dent, as Robeson), 1970
Midas World (Pohl), 1983
Midnight at the Well of Souls (Chalker), 1977
Midsummer Century (Blish), 1972
Midsummer Tempest (P. Anderson), 1974
Midway Between (Norwood), 1984
Midwich Cuckoos (Wyndham), 1957
Midworld (A. Foster), 1975
Mightiest Machine (Campbell), 1947
Mike Mars series (Wollheim)
Mile Beyond the Moon (s Kornbluth), 1958
Mile-Long Spaceship (s Wilhelm), 1963
Millennium (Bova), 1976
Millennium (Sinclair), 1924
Millennium (Varley), 1983
Million Cities (McIntosh), 1963

Million Year Hunt (Bulmer), 1964
Mimics of Dephene (Tubb, as Kern), 1975
Mind series (Morgan)
Mind Behind the Eye (Green), 1972
Mind Cage (van Vogt), 1957
Mind Force (Fanthorpe, as Brett), 1961
Mind from Outer Space (Binder), 1972
Mind Master (Gunn), 1982
Mind of Mr. Soames (Maine), 1961
Mind of My Mind (O. Butler), 1977
Mind Parasites (C. Wilson), 1967
Mind Spider (s Leiber), 1961
Mind Switch (D. Knight), 1965
Mind Thing (F. Brown), 1961
Mind Traders (Holly), 1966
Mind Trap (Morgan), 1970
Mind Warpers (Russell), 1965
Mind Wizards of Callisto (L. Carter), 1975
Mindbridge (Joe Haldeman), 1976
Mindflight (Goldin), 1978
Mindkiller (S. Robinson), 1982
Mindlocked Man (Sutton), 1972
Mindmix (Kelley), 1972
Mind-Riders (Stableford), 1976
Mindswap (Sheckley), 1966
Mind-Twisters Affair (R. Coulson and DeWeese, as Stratton), 1967
Mindworm (s Kornbluth), 1955
Miners in the Sky (Leinster), 1967
Minerva Experiment (Hogan), 1981
Miracle Visitors (Watson), 1978
Mirkheim (P. Anderson), 1977
Mirror for Observers (Pangborn), 1954
Mirror Friend, Mirror Foe (Asprin), 1979
Mirror Image (Coney), 1972
Mirror of Minds (Zebrowski), 1983
Misplaced Persons (Harding), 1979
Missile Lords (Sutton), 1963
Missing Angel (Cox), 1947
Missing Man (MacLean), 1975
Missing Men of Saturn (Latham), 1953
Mission: Interplanetary (van Vogt), 1952
Mission: Manstop (s Neville), 1971
Mission of Gravity (Clement), 1954
Mission to a Star (F. Long), 1964
Mission to Horatius (Reynolds), 1968
Mission to Mars (P. Moore), 1955
Mission to Mercury (Walters), 1965
Mission to Moulokin (A. Foster), 1979
Mission to Pactolus (Rankine, as Mason), 1978
Mission to the Heart Stars (Blish), 1965
Mission to the Moon (del Rey), 1956
Mission to the Stars (Bulmer, as Kent), 1953
Mission to the Stars (van Vogt), 1955
Mission to Universe (Dickson), 1965
Missionaries (Compton), 1972
Mistake Factor (Braun, for), 1975
Mr. Adam (Frank), 1946
Mister da V. (s. Reed), 1967
Mr. Jorkens Remembers Africa (Dunsany, fan), 1934
Mister Justice (Piserchia), 1973
Mr. Mergenthwirker's Lobblies (s Bond), 1946
Mr. Pye (Peake, fan), 1953
Mistress of Mistresses (Eddison, fan), 1935
Mists of Avalon (Bradley), 1983
Mixed Feelings (s Effinger), 1974
Mixed Men (van Vogt), 1952

Mockingbird (Tevis), 1980
Moderan (Bunch), 1971
Modern Utopia (Wells), 1905
Mohole Menace (Walters), 1969
Mohole Mystery (Walters), 1968
Molecule Men (F. and G. Hoyle), 1971
Molly Zero (Roberts), 1980
Molt Brother (Lichtenberg), 1982
Moment of Eclipse (s Aldiss), 1970
Moment of the Magician (A. Foster), 1984
Monadic Universe (s Zebrowski), 1977
Monday Begins on Saturday (Strugatsky, for), 1977
Monella series (Ash, as Aubrey)
Monitor Found in Orbit (s Coney), 1974
Monitor, The Miners and the Shree (Killough), 1980
Monitors (Laumer), 1966
Monkey Planet (Boulle, for), 1964
Monkeys Have No Tails in Zamboanga (s Meek), 1935
Monster from Earth's End (Leinster), 1959
Monster from Out of Time (F. Long), 1970
Monster Maker (Fisk), 1979
Monster Men (E. Burroughs), 1929
Monster of Loch Ness (F. Hoyle), 1971
Monster of Metelaze (Tubb, as Kern), 1973
Monsters (Dent, as Robeson), 1965
Monsters (s van Vogt), 1965
Monsters and Medics (s J. White), 1977
Monsters and Such (s Leinster), 1959
Monsters in Orbit (Vance), 1965
Monsters of Juntonheim (Hamilton), 1950
Monte Cristo 99 (Jakes), 1970
Monument (Biggle), 1974
Moon (J. Herbert), 1985
Moon Base (Tubb), 1964
Moon Base One (Walters), 1961
Moon Called (Norton), 1982
Moon Children (Williamson), 1972
Moon Is a Harsh Mistress (Heinlein), 1966
Moon is Hell! (Campbell), 1951
Moon Magic series (Norton)
Moon Maid (s E. Burroughs), 1926
Moon Maker (Train), 1958
Moon Men (s E. Burroughs), 1962
Moon Metal (Serviss), 1900
Moon Moth (s Vance), 1976
Moon Odyssey (Rankine), 1975
Moon of Mutiny (del Rey), 1961
Moon of Three Rings (Norton), 1966
Moon on an Iron Meadow (Tate), 1974
Moon People (Coblentz), 1964
Moon Pool (Merritt), 1919
Moon Raiders (P. Moore), 1978
Moon Wolf (s Fanthorpe), 1964
Moonbase One (R. Jones), 1971
Moonbeast (van Vogt), 1969
Moonferns and Starsongs (s Silverberg), 1971
Moons for Sale (Fearn, as Gridban), 1953
Moons of Jupiter (Asimov, as French), 1974
Moons of Triopus (Rankine), 1968
Moonstar Odyssey (Gerrold), 1977
More Than Human (Sturgeon), 1953
More Than Superhuman (s van Vogt), 1971
More Things in Heaven (Brunner), 1973
Moreau's Other Island (Aldiss), 1980
Moreta, Dragonlady of Pern (McCaffrey), 1983
Morgaine series (Cherryh)

Morgan, Jet series (Chilton)
Mörkrets furste (Lundwall), 1975
Morlock Night (Jeter), 1979
Morphodite series (M. Foster)
Morrow series (Hoover)
Mortal Engines (Lem, for), 1977
Mortal Gods (J. Fast), 1978
Mortals and Monsters (s del Rey), 1965
Mortmain (s Train), 1907
Mote in God's Eye (Niven, Pournelle), 1974
Mother and Child (s J. Vinge), 1981
Motherearth (McQuay), 1985
Motherlines (Charnas), 1979
Motion Menace (Dent, as Robeson), 1971
Mountain Monster (Dent, as Robeson), 1976
Mouse series (Wibberley)
Mouse on the Moon (Wibberley), 1962
Mouse That Roared (Wibberley), 1955
Mouthpiece of Zitu (Giesy), 1965
Müller-Fokker Effect (Sladek), 1970
Multiface (Adlard), 1975
Multi-Man (Fearn, as Statten), 1954
Multiple Man (Bova), 1976
Mummy and Miss Nitocris (Griffith), 1906
Mummy and the Girl (Griffith), n.d.
Munitions Master (Dent, as Robeson), 1971
Murchison, Jake series (Cartmill)
Murder and Magic (s Garrett), 1979
Murder in Millennium VI (Gray), 1951
Murder in the Clinic (s Hamilton), 1946
Murder Madness (Leinster), 1931
Murder of the Missing Link (Vercors, for), 1955
Murder of the U.S.A. (Leinster, as Jenkins), 1946
Murder on Mars (Walters), 1975
Murderer Invisible (Wylie), 1931
Mutant (s Kuttner and C. Moore, as Padgett), 1953
Mutant 59, The Plastic Eater (G. Davis, Pedler), 1971
Mutant Weapon (Leinster), 1959
Mutants (s Dickson), 1970
Mutants (Neville), 1966
Mutants are Coming (Haiblum), 1984
Mutants Rebel (Tubb), 1953
Mute (Anthony), 1981
Mutiny in Space (Davidson), 1964
My Brother's Keeper (Sheffield), 1982
My Enemy, My Ally (Duane), 1984
My Experiences in the Third World (s Moorcock), 1980
My Lord Barbarian (Offutt), 1977
My Name is Legion (s Zelazny), 1976
My Petition for More Space (Hersey), 1974
My Science Project (McQuay), 1985
Myra Breckinridge (Vidal), 1968
Myron (Vidal), 1974
Mysterious Island (Verne, for), 1874
Mysterious Planet (del Rey, as Wright), 1953
Mystery of Arthur Gordon Pym (Verne, for), 1960
Mystery of the Green Ray (Le Queux), 1915
Mystery of the Sea Horse (Goulart, as Shawn), 1973
Mystery of the Third Mine (Lowndes), 1953
Mystery on Happy Bones (Dent, as Robeson), 1979
Mystery on the Snow (Dent, as Robeson), 1972
Mystery under the Sea (Dent, as Robeson), 1968
Mystic Mullah (Dent, as Robeson), 1965
Mythago Wood (Holdstock), 1984
Myth-ing Person (Asprin), 1984
Mythmaster (Kelley), 1973

Myths of the Near Future (s Ballard), 1982

Nagasaki Vector (L. Smith), 1983
Nail Down the Stars (Morressy), 1973
Naked Beach (Ehrlich), 1979
Naked Edge (Ehrlich), 1961
Naked Lunch (W. Burroughs), 1959
Naked Sun (Asimov), 1957
Naked to the Stars (Dickson), 1961
Narrow Land (s Vance), 1982
Native Tongue (Elgin), 1984
Natives of Space (s Clement), 1965
Natural State (D. Knight), 1967
Navigator of Rhada (Coppel, as Gilman), 1968
Navigator's Sindrome (J. Carr), 1983
Neanderthal Planet (s Aldiss), 1970
Nearest Fire (Wilder), 1980
Nearly Neptune (Walters), 1969
Nebogipfel at the End of Time (s Lupoff), 1979
Nebula Alert (Chandler), 1967
Nebula Maker (Stapledon), 1976
Nebula X (Fearn, as Statten), 1950
Necromancer (Dickson), 1962
Needle (Clement), 1950
Needle in a Timestack (s Silverberg), 1966
Negative Minus (Fanthorpe), 1963
Negative Ones (Fanthorpe, as Muller), 1965
Nemesis (Fanthorpe, as Fane), 1964
Nemesis from Terra (Brackett), 1961
Nemesis of Evil (L. Carter), 1975
Nemo (Goulart), 1977
Neptune One Is Missing (Walters), 1969
Neptune's Cauldron (Coney), 1981
Neq the Sword (Anthony), 1975
Nerves (del Rey), 1956
Nets of Space (Petaja), 1969
Neural Atrocity (Farren), 1977
Neuron World (Fanthorpe), 1965
Neutral Stars (Kippax, Morgan), 1973
Neuromancer (Gibson), 1984
Neutron Star (s Niven), 1968
Never Let Up (Maine), 1964
Never the Same Door (Rankine), 1967
Nevermore Affair (Wilhelm), 1966
Neveryó (s Delany), 1983
New Adam (Weinbaum), 1939
New America (s P. Anderson), 1982
New Arrivals, Old Encounters (s Aldiss), 1979
New Bodies for Old (Renard for), 1923
New Eden (Hyne), 1892
New Found Land (Christopher), 1983
New Gods Lead (s S. Wright, as Fowler), 1932
New Life (s Binder, as Coleridge), 1940
New Messiah (Cromie), 1902
New Minds (Morgan), 1967
New Pleasure (Gloag), 1933
New Satellite (Fearn, as Statten), 1951
New Sun series (G. Wolfe)
New World series (Kahn)
Neweden series (Leigh)
News From Elsewhere (s Cooper), 1968
News From Nowhere (W. Morris, fan), 1890
Newton and the Quasi-Apple (Schmidt), 1975
Next Chapter: War Against the Moon (Maurois, for), 1927
Next Crusade (Cromie), 1896
Next Door to the Sun (Coblentz), 1960

Next of Kin (Russell), 1959
Next Stop the Stars (s Silverberg), 1962
Nice Day for Screaming (s Schmitz), 1965
Nidor series (Silverberg)
Night Creature (Ball), 1974
Night Face (s P. Anderson) 1979
Night Fear (s F. Long), 1979
Night Gallery series (s Sterling)
Night Land (Hodgson), 1912
Night Mare (Anthony), 1983
Night of Delusions (Laumer), 1972
Night of Fire and Blood (Kelley), 1979
Night of Kadar (Kilworth), 1978
Night of Light (Farmer), 1966
Night of Masks (Norton), 1964
Night of Power (S. Robinson), 1985
Night of the Big Heat (Lymington), 1959
Night of the Dragonstar (Bischoff, Monteleone), 1985
Night of the Puudly (s Simak), 1964
Night of the Robots (Ball), 1972
Night of the Saucers (Binder), 1971
Night of the Wolf (s Leiber), 1966
Night of the Wolf (F. Long), 1972
Night Ride and Other Journeys (s Beaumont), 1960
Night Slaves (Sohl), 1965
Night Songs (Grant), 1984
Night Spiders (s Lymington), 1964
Night Things (Monteleone), 1980
Night Train (Monteleone), 1984
Night unto Night (s Wylie), 1944
Night Walk (Shaw), 1967
Nightfall (s Asimov), 1969
Nightflyers (s Martin), 1985
Nightmare (Fanthorpe, as Brett), 1962
Nightmare Blue (Dozois, Effinger), 1975
Nightmare Express (Haiblum), 1979
Nightmare Factor (F. Robinson, Scortia), 1978
Nightmare Journey (Koontz), 1975
Nightmare Seasons (Grant), 1982
Nightmares and Daydreams (s Bond), 1968
Nightmares and Geezenstacks (s F. Brown), 1961
Nightmares from Space (DeWeese), 1981
Night's Daughter (Bradley), 1985
Night's Master (Lee), 1978
Nightwatch (Stephenson), 1977
Nightwings (Silverberg), 1969
Nightwitch Devil (Goulart, as Robeson), 1974
Nightworld series (Bischoff)
Nine Billion Names of God (s Clarke), 1967
Nine Hundred Grandmothers (s Lafferty), 1970
Nine Princes in Amber (Zelazny), 1970
Nine Tomorrows (s Asimov), 1959
1985 (Burgess), 1978
Nineteen Eighty-Four (Orwell), 1949
Nineteen Impressions (s Beresford), 1918
1976: Year of Terror (George H. Smith), 1961
1925: The Story of a Fatal Peace (E. Wallace), 1915
98.4 (Hodder-Williams), 1969
99% (Gloag), 1944
Nitrogen Fix (Clement), 1980
No Blade of Grass (Christopher), 1957
No Boundaries (s Kuttner, C. Moore), 1955
No Brother, No Friend (Meredith), 1976
No Direction Home (s Spinrad), 1975
No Doors, No Windows (s Ellison), 1975
No Enemy But Time (Bishop), 1982

No Future in It (s Brunner), 1962
No Grave Need I (Fearn), 1984
No Highway (Shute), 1948
No Man Friday (R. Gordon), 1956
No Man's World (Bulmer), 1961
No Man's World (Caidin), 1967
No Night Without Stars (Norton), 1975
No Other Gods but Me (s Brunner), 1966
No Place on Earth (Charbonneau), 1958
No Room for Man (Dickson), 1963
No Time for Heroes (Lundwall), 1971
No Time Like the Future (s Bond), 1954
No Time Like Tomorrow (s Aldiss), 1959
No Time Like Tomorrow (T. White), 1969
No Truce wirh Terra (High), 1964
No Way Back (Fanthorpe, as Zeigfried), 1964
No Witchcraft for Sale (s Lessing), 1956
No World of Their Own (P. Anderson), 1955
Noblest Experiment in the Galaxy (Trimble), 1970
Nomad (George O. Smith), 1950
Nomads (Yarbro), 1984
Nomads of Gor (Norman), 1969
Noman Way (McIntosh), 1964
Nonborn King (May), 1983
None But Man (Dickson), 1969
Non-Statistical Man (s R. Jones), 1964
Non-Stop (Aldiss), 1958
Noon: 22nd Century (Strugatsky, for), 1978
Nopalgarth (Vance), 1980
Nor Crystal Tears (A. Foster), 1982
Norby series (Asimov)
Noren series (Engdahl)
Norman Conquest 2066 (McIntosh), 1977
Norstrilia (Cordwainer Smith), 1975
Northwest of Earth (s C. Moore), 1954
Not Before Time (s Brunner), 1968
Not By Bread Alone (Mitchison), 1983
Not This August (Kornbluth), 1955
Not to Mention Camels (Lafferty), 1976
Not Without Sorcery (s Sturgeon), 1961
Notions: Unlimited (s Sheckley), 1960
Not-Men (Williamson), 1968
Nova (Delany), 1968
Nova Express (W. Burroughs), 1964
Now Comes Tomorrow (R. Williams), 1971
Now Then (s Brunner), 1965
Now to the Stars (Johns), 1956
Now Wait for Last Year (Dick), 1966
Now You See It/Him/Them (R. Coulson, DeWeese), 1975
Nowhere Place (Lymington), 1969
Null–A Three (van Vogt), 1985
Number of the Beast (Heinlein), 1980
Numquam (Durrell), 1970
Nutzenbolts (s Goulart), 1975

Oath of Fealty (Niven, Pournelle), 1981
Occam's Razor (Duncan), 1957
Ocean on Top (Clement), 1973
Oceans of Venus (Asimov, as French), 1973
Octagon (Saberhagen), 1981
October Country (s Bradbury), 1955
October the First Is Too Late (F. Hoyle), 1966
October's Baby (Cook), 1980
Odan series (Bulmer, as Norvil)
Odd Job No. 101 (s Goulart), 1975
Odd John (Stapledon), 1935

Odd Science Fiction (F. Long), 1964
Odds Are Murder (McQuay), 1983
Odious Ones (Sohl), 1959
Odyssey of Nine (Fearn, as Statten), 1953
Odyssey to Earthdeath (Kelley), 1968
Of Alien Bondage (Offutt, as Cleve), 1982
Of All Possible Worlds (s Tenn), 1955
Of Earth Foretold (Bulmer), 1961
Of Godlike Power (Reynolds), 1966
Of Men and Monsters (Tenn), 1968
Of Other Worlds (s C. Lewis), 1966
Of Time and Stars (s Clarke), 1972
Off Center (s D. Knight), 1965
Off on a Comet (Verne, for), 1957
Off-Worlders (Baxter), 1966
Ogre, Ogre (Anthony), 1982
Oh, Susannah! (Wilhelm), 1982
Old Captivity (Shute), 1940
Old Die Rich (s Gold), 1955
Old Man in New World (s Stapledon), 1944
Ole Doc Methuselah (s Hubbard), 1970
O'Leary series (Laumer)
Olga Romanoff (Griffith), 1894
Omega Man (Matheson), 1971
Omega Point series (Zebrowski)
Omega Worm (Rankine, as Mason), 1976
Omha Abides (MacApp), 1968
Omicron Invasion (Goldin), 1984
Omnibus of Time (s Farley), 1950
Omnivore (Anthony), 1968
On a Pale Horse (Anthony), 1984
On a Planet Alien (Malzberg), 1974
On Saint Hubert's Thing (s Yarbro), 1982
On Strike Against God (Russ), 1980
On the Beach (Shute), 1957
On the Flip Side (Fisk), 1983
On the Red World (Kelley), 1979
On the Run (Dickson), 1979
On the Symb-Socket Circuit (Bulmer), 1972
On Wheels (Jakes), 1973
On Wings of Song (Disch), 1979
Once Departed (Reynolds), 1970
Once There Was a Giant (s Laumer), 1971
One (Karp), 1953
One Against Eternity (van Vogt), 1955
One Against Herculum (Sohl), 1959
One Against the Legion (Williamson), 1967
One Against the Moon (Wollheim), 1956
One Hundred and Two H-Bombs (s Disch), 1966
One in Three Hundred (McIntosh), 1954
One Is One (Rankine), 1968
One Million Centuries (Lupoff), 1967
One Million Tomorrows (Shaw), 1970
One of Our Asteroids Is Missing (Silverberg, as Knox), 1964
One Step from Earth (s H. Harrison), 1970
One Winter in Eden (s Bishop), 1984
One-Eye (S. Gordon), 1973
One-Eyed Mystic (Dent, as Robeson), 1982
Open Prison (J. White), 1965
Operation ARES (G. Wolfe), 1970
Operation Chaos (P. Anderson), 1971
Operation Columbus (Walters), 1960
Operation Interstellar (George O. Smith), 1950
Operation Nuke (Caidin), 1973
Operation: Outer Space (Leinster), 1954
Operation Terror (Leinster), 1962

Operation Time Search (Norton), 1967
Operation Umanaq (Rankine), 1973
Operation Venus (Fearn), 1950
Ophiuchi Hotline (Varley), 1977
Opium General (s Moorcock), 1984
Optiman (Stableford), 1980
Options (Sheckley), 1975
Or All the Seas with Oysters (s Davidson), 1962
ORA: CLE (O'Donnell), 1984
Oracle of the Thousand Hands (Malzberg), 1968
Orbit One (Fanthorpe, as Muller), 1962
Orbit Unlimited (P. Anderson), 1961
Orbitsville series (Shaw)
Orchid Cage (Franke, for), 1973
Ordeal (Shute), 1939
Ordeal in Otherwhere (Norton), 1964
Organ Bank Farm (Boyd), 1970
Orion (Bova), 1984
Orion Shall Rise (P. Anderson), 1984
Orn (Anthony), 1971
Orphan (Stallman). 1980
Orphan Star (A. Foster), 1977
Orphans of the Sky (s Heinlein), 1963
Ossian's Ride (F. Hoyle), 1959
Other Days, Other Eyes (Shaw), 1972
Other Dimensions (s Clarke Ashton Smith), 1970
Other Eyes Watching (Fearn, as Cross), 1946
Other Foot (D. Knight), 1966
Other Half of the Planet (Capon), 1952
Other Half of the Sun (Capon), 1950
Other Human Race (Piper), 1964
Other Log of Phileas Fogg (Farmer), 1973
Other Passenger (s Cross), 1944
Other Place (s Priestley), 1953
Other Side of Green Hills (Cross), 1947
Other Side of Here (Leinster), 1955
Other Side of Nowhere (Leinster), 1964
Other Side of the Sky (s Clarke), 1961
Other Side of Time (Laumer), 1965
Other Sky (s Laumer), 1968
Other Stories and The Attack of the Giant Baby (s Reed), 1981
Other Time (Reynolds), 1984
Other Times, Other Worlds (s MacDonald), 1978
Other World (Dent, as Robeson), 1968
Our Children's Children (Simak), 1974
Our Friends from Frolix 8 (Dick), 1970
Our Lady (Sinclair), 1938
Out (Meltzer), 1969
Out from Ganymede (s Malzberg), 1974
Out of Bounds (s Merril), 1960
Out of Chaos (McIntosh), 1965
Out of Darkness (Fanthorpe), 1960
Out of My Mind (s Brunner), 1967
Out of the Abyss (England), 1965
Out of the Dead City (Delany), 1968
Out of the Deeps (Wyndham), 1953
Out of the Everywhere (s Tiptree), 1981
Out of the Mouth of the Dragon (Geston), 1969
Out of the Night (Fanthorpe, as Muller), 1965
Out of the Silence (Cox), 1925
Out of the Silent Planet (C. Lewis), 1938
Out of the Silent Sky (s Biggle), 1977
Out of the Storm (s Hodgson), 1975
Out of the Sun (Bova), 1968
Out of the Unknown (s Hull, van Vogt), 1948
Out of Their Minds (Simak), 1970

Out of This World (s Leinster), 1958
Out There Where the Big Ships Go (s Cowper), 1980
Outcasts of Heaven Belt (J. Vinge), 1978
Outerworld (Haiblum), 1979
Outland (A. Foster), 1981
Outlaw of Gor (Norman), 1967
Outlaw World (Hamilton), 1969
Outlaws of Mars (Kline), 1961
Outlaws of the Air (Griffith), 1895
Outlaws of the Moon (Hamilton), 1969
Outpost Mars (Kornbluth and Merril, as Judd), 1952
Outpost of Jupiter (del Rey), 1963
Outpost on the Moon (Walters), 1962
Outposter (Dickson), 1972
Outposts in Space (s West), 1962
Outside (Norton), 1975
Outside the Universe (Hamilton), 1964
Outward Bound (J. Coulson), 1982
Outward Urge (Wyndham), 1959
Outworlder (L. Carter), 1971
Ova Hamlet Papers (s Lupoff), 1979
Over the Edge (s Ellison), 1970
Overboard (Searls), 1977
Overkill (Crichton, as Lange), 1972
Overlay (Malzberg), 1972
Overloaded Man (s Ballard), 1967
Overlords of War (Klein, for), 1973
Overman Culture (Cooper), 1971
Owl and the Pussycat (Cross), 1946
Owl Time (s M. Foster), 1985
Ox (Anthony), 1975
Ozark series (Elgin)
Ozymandias (Monteleone), 1981

Pail of Air (s Leiber), 1964
Paingod and Other Delusions (s Ellison), 1965
Pair from Space (Silverberg), 1965
Palace of Eternity (Shaw), 1969
Palace of Love (Vance), 1967
Pale Ape and Other Pulses (s Shiel), 1911
Pale Rider (A. Foster), 1985
Palos series (Giesy)
Pan Sagittarius (I. Wallace), 1973
Panchronicon Plot (Goulart), 1977
Pandora Effect (s Williamson), 1969
Pandora Stone (Grenleaf), 1984
Pandora's Planet (Anvil), 1972
Panic O'Clock (Hodder-Williams), 1973
Paper Dolls (Davies), 1964
Paradise Game (Stableford), 1974
Paradise Plot (Naha), 1980
Paradox Lost (s F. Brown), 1973
Paradox Men (Harness), 1955
Paradox of Sets (Stableford), 1979
Paratime (s Piper), 1981
Parric family series (Grant)
Parsecs and Parables (s Silverberg), 1970
Particle Theory (s Bryant), 1980
Parting of Arwen (s Bradley), 1974
Partners in Wonder (s Ellison), 1971
Passage of Arms (Cook), 1985
Passage to Pluto (Walters), 1973
Passing of the Dragons (s Roberts), 1977
Passion of New Eve (A. Carter), 1977
Passport to Eternity (s Ballard), 1963
Past Master (Lafferty), 1968

Past Through Tomorrow: Future History Stories (s Heinlein), 1967
Past Times (s P. Anderson), 1984
Pastel City (M. Harrison), 1971
Patchwork Girl (Niven), 1980
Path Beyond the Stars (Petaja), 1969
Path of Unreason (George O. Smith), 1958
Patient Dark (Bulmer), 1969
Patron of the Arts (Rotsler), 1974
Pattern for Conquest (George O. Smith), 1949
Patternists series (O. Butler)
Patternmaster (O. Butler), 1976
Pattern of Chaos (Kapp), 1972
Pavane (Roberts), 1968
Paw of God (R. Gordon), 1967
Pawn of the Omphalos (Tubb), 1980
Pawns of Null-A (van Vogt), 1956
Pays d'esprit (s R. Young), 1982
Peace Machine (Shaw), 1985
Peace War (V. Vinge), 1984
Pebble in the Sky (Asimov), 1950
Peculiar Exploits of Brigadier Ffellowes (s Lanier), 1977
Pelbar series (P. Williams)
Pellucidar series (E. Burroughs)
Pendulum (Christopher), 1968
Pendulum (s van Vogt), 1978
Penultimate Truth (Dick), 1964
People Beyond the Wall (Tall), 1980
People Machines (s Williamson), 1971
People Maker (D. Knight), 1959
People Minus X (Gallun), 1957
People: No Different Flesh (Henderson), 1966
People of the Abyss (England), 1965
People of the Comet (Hall), 1948
People of the Mist (Haggard), 1894
People of the Talisman (Brackett), 1964
People of the Wind (P. Anderson), 1973
People Trap (s Sheckley), 1968
Perchance to Dream (Reynolds), 1977
Peregrine (P. Anderson), 1978
Perelandra (C. Lewis), 1943
Perfect Lover (Priest), 1977
Perfect Planet (Evelyn E. Smith), 1962
Perfect Vacuum (Lem, for), 1979
Peril from Space (Bulmer, as Maras), 1955
Peril in the North (Dent, as Robeson), 1984
Peril of the Starmen (Neville), 1967
Peril on Mars (P. Moore), 1958
Perilous Dreams (s Norton), 1976
Perilous Galaxy (Fanthorpe, as Muller), 1962
Periscope Red (Rohmer), 1980
Perry's Planet (Jack C. Haldeman), 1980
Persistence of Vision (s Varley), 1978
Petrified Planet (Fearn, as Statten), 1951
Phaeton Condition (Rankine, as Mason), 1973
Phantom series (Goulart, as Shawn)
Phantom City (Dent, as Robeson), 1966
Phantom Crusader (s Fanthorpe, as Brett), 1963
Phantom Ones (Fanthorpe, as Torro), 1961
Pharaoh's Ghost (Dent, as Robeson), 1981
Phase IV (Malzberg), 1973
Phase Two (Richmond), 1980
Phenomena X (Fanthorpe, as Muller), 1966
Philosopher's Stone (C. Wilson), 1969
Phobos, The Robot Planet (Capon), 1955
Phoenix (Cowper), 1968
Phoenix in the Ashes (s J. Vinge), 1985

Phoenix of Megaron (Rankine), 1976
Phoenix Prime (T. White), 1966
Phoenix Ship (Richmond), 1969
Phoenix Without Ashes (Bryant, Ellison), 1975
Phthor (Anthony), 1975
Phu Nham (P. Anderson, Dickson), 1984
Picnic on Paradise (Russ), 1968
Piece of Martin Cann (Janifer), 1968
Pilgrim Project (Searls), 1964
Pilgrimage (Henderson), 1961
Pilgrimage to Earth (s Sheckley), 1957
Pillars of Eternity (Bayley), 1982
Pioneer 1990 (Fearn, as Statten), 1953
Pirate Isle (Dent, as Robeson), 1983
Pirate of the Pacific (Dent, as Robeson), 1967
Pirate of World's End (L. Carter), 1978
Pirate's Ghost (Dent, as Robeson), 1971
Pirates of Rosinante (Gilliland), 1982
Pirates of Venus (E. Burroughs), 1934
Pirates of Zan (Leinster), 1959
Pirx the Pilot series (Lem, for)
Pitman's Progress (Rankine, as Mason), 1976
Plague from Space (H. Harrison), 1965
Plague of Demons (Laumer), 1965
Plague of Pythons (Pohl), 1965
Plague of Sound (Goulart, as Steffanson), 1974
Plague Ship (Norton, as North), 1956
Plains (Murnane), 1982
Planet Buyer (Cordwainer Smith), 1964
Planet Called Krishna (de Camp), 1966
Planet Called Treason (Card), 1979
Planet Called Utopia (McIntosh), 1979
Planet Explorer (Leinster), 1957
Planet for Texans (Piper), 1958
Planet in Peril (Christopher), 1959
Planet Killers (Silverberg), 1959
Planet Mappers (E. Evans), 1955
Planet Murderer (Offutt, as Cleve), 1984
Planet of Death (F. and G. Hoyle), 1982
Planet of Death (Silverberg), 1967
Planet of Dread (Tubb, as Kern), 1974
Planet of Exile (Le Guin), 1966
Planet of Fear (P. Moore), 1977
Planet of Fire (P. Moore), 1969
Planet of Flowers (Norwood), 1984
Planet of Judgment (Joe Haldeman), 1977
Planet of Light (R. Jones), 1953
Planet of No Return (P. Anderson), 1957
Planet of No Return (H. Harrison), 1981
Planet of Peril (Kline), 1929
Planet of the Apes (Boulle, for), 1963
Planet of the Apes series (Effinger)
Planet of the Damned (H. Harrison), 1962
Planet of the Double Sun (s N. Jones), 1967
Planet of the Dreamers (MacDonald), 1953
Planet of the Voles (Platt), 1971
Planet of Treachery (Goldin), 1982
Planet of Your Own (Brunner), 1966
Planet of Youth (Coblentz), 1952
Planet Patrol (Dorman), 1978
Planet Plane (Wyndham, as Beynon), 1936
Planet Poachers (Lightner), 1965
Planet Probability (Ball), 1973
Planet Run (Dickson, Laumer), 1967
Planet Savers (Bradley), 1979
Planet Seekers (Fanthorpe, as Barton), 1964

Planet Story (H. Harrison), 1979
Planet Strappers (Gallun), 1961
Planet Wizard (Jakes), 1969
Planetary Agent X (Reynolds), 1965
Planeteers (s Campbell), 1966
Planetfall (Tubb, as Hunt), 1951
Planetoid Disposals Ltd. (Tubb, as Gridban), 1953
Planetoid 127 (E. Wallace), 1929
Planets for Sale (Hull, van Vogt), 1954
Planets in Peril (Hamilton), 1969
Planets Three (s Pohl), 1982
Plantos Affair (Rankine), 1971
Plattner Story (s Wells), 1897
Platypus of Doom and Other Nihilists (s Cover), 1976
Player Piano (Vonnegut), 1952
Players at the Game of People (Brunner), 1980
Players of Gor (Norman), 1984
Players of Null-A (van Vogt), 1966
Pliocene Exile series (May)
Plot Against The Earth (Silverberg, as Knox), 1959
Plunder (Goulart), 1972
Plunder (Offutt, as Cleve), 1982
Plunge into Space (Cromie), 1890
Pluribus (Kurland), 1975
Pnume (Vance), 1970
Podkayne of Mars (Heinlein), 1963
Pohlstars (s Pohl), 1984
Point Ultimate (Sohl), 1955
Poison Belt (Doyle), 1913
Poison Island (Dent, as Robeson), 1971
Poison Oracle (Dickinson), 1974
Polar Fleet (Norwood), 1985
Polar Treasure (Dent, as Robeson), 1965
Police Patrol 2000 A.D. (Reynolds), 1977
Police Your Planet (del Rey, as Van Lhin), 1956
Politician (Anthony), 1985
Pollinators of Eden (Boyd), 1969
Poltergeist (Kahn), 1982
Polymath (Brunner), 1974
Pool of Fire (Christopher), 1968
Port Eternity (Cherryh), 1982
Port of Peril (Kline), 1949
Porter, Harry series (Naha)
Positive Charge (s Richmond), 1970
Possessors (Christopher), 1965
Postman (Brin), 1985
Postmarked the Stars (Norton), 1969
Power (Janifer), 1974
Power (F. Robinson), 1956
Power and Glory (Capek, for), 1937
Power Ball (Lymington), 1981
Power of Blackness (Williamson), 1976
Power of X (Sellings), 1968
Power Sphere (Fanthorpe, as Brett), 1963
Practice Effect (Brin), 1984
Prayer Machine (Hodder-Williams), 1976
Preferred Risk (del Rey and Pohl, as McCann), 1955
Prelude in Prague (S. Wright), 1935
Prelude to Chaos (E. Llewellyn), 1983
Prelude to Mars (Clarke), 1965
Prelude to Space (Clarke), 1951
Prescot, Dray series (Bulmer, as Akers)
Preserver (M. Foster), 1985
Preserving Machine (s Dick), 1969
Pretender (Anthony), 1979
Pride of Chanur (Cherryh), 1982

Pride of Monsters (s Schmitz), 1970
Priest-Kings of Gor (Norman), 1968
Priests of Psi (s F. Herbert), 1980
Primal Urge (Aldiss), 1961
Prime Number (s H. Harrison), 1970
Primitive (Tubb), 1977
Prince Hagen (Sinclair), 1903
Prince in Waiting (Christopher), 1970
Prince of Peril (Kline), 1930
Prince of Scorpio (Bulmer, as Akers), 1974
Princes of Earth (Kurland), 1978
Princess of Mars (E. Burroughs), 1917
Princess of the Atom (Cummings), 1950
Printer's Devil (Moorcock, as Barclay), 1966
Prism (Petaja), 1968
Prison of Night (Tubb), 1977
Prison Satellite (Kelley), 1979
Prisoner (Disch), 1969
Prisoner of Blackwood Castle (Goulart), 1984
Prisoner of Fire (Cooper), 1974
Prisoner of the Planets (J. Fast), 1980
Prisoner of Zhamanak (de Camp), 1982
Prisoners of Power (Strugatsky, for), 1977
Prisoners of Space (del Rey, Fairman), 1968
Prisoners of the Sky (MacApp), 1969
Prisoners of the Stars (Asimov), 1979
Pritcher Mass (Dickson), 1972
Private Cosmos (Farmer), 1968
Private Universe (Maurois, for), 1932
Pro (Dickson), 1978
Probability Corner (Richmond), 1977
Probability Man (Ball), 1972
Prodigal Sun (High), 1964
Productions of Time (Brunner), 1967
Professor Dowell's Head (Belyaev, for), 1980
Profundis (Cowper), 1979
Programmed Man (Sutton), 1968
Project Avalon (T. Hoyle), 1979
Project Barrier (s Galouye), 1968
Project Excelsior (Pratt), 1951
Project 40 (F. Herbert), 1973
Project Jupiter (F. Brown), 1954
Project Pope (Simak), 1981
Projection Barrier (Fanthorpe, as Zeigfried), 1964
Projections (s Robinett), 1979
Prometheus Crisis (F. Robinson, Scortia), 1975
Prometheus Man (Nelson), 1982
Promised Land (Stableford), 1974
Propeller Island (Verne, for), 1961
Prostho Plus (Anthony), 1971
Protector (Niven), 1973
Protectorate (Farren), 1984
Proteus Operation (Hogan), 1985
Proud Enemy (Busby), 1975
Proud Robot: The Complete Galloway Gallegher Stories (s Kuttner), 1983
Proxima Project (Rackham), 1968
Proxy Intelligence and Other Mind Benders (s van Vogt), 1971
Pry, Charles series (Large)
Psi High (s Nourse), 1967
Psi Hunt (Kurland), 1980
Psion (J. Vinge), 1982
Psionic Menace (Brunner, as Woodcott), 1963
Pstalemate (del Rey), 1971
Psychedelic-40 (Charbonneau), 1965
Psychlone (Bear), 1979

Psycho Makers (George H. Smith, as Jason), 1965
Psychogeist (Davies), 1966
Psychopath Plague (Spruill), 1978
Psychotechnic League (s P. Anderson), 1981
Pulling Through (Ing), 1983
Puppet Masters (Heinlein), 1951
Puppies of Terra (Disch), 1978
Purchase of the North Pole (Verne, for), 1890
Pure Blood (McQuay), 1985
Purity Plot (Goldin), 1978
Purloined Planet (L. Carter), 1969
Purloined Prince (I. Wallace), 1971
Purple Book (Farmer), 1982
Purple Cloud (Shiel), 1901
Purple Dragon (Dent, as Robeson), 1978
Purple Sapphire (s Blayre), 1921
Purple Sapphire (Taine), 1924
Purple Wizard (Fearn, as Gridban), 1953
Purple Zombie (Goulart, as Robeson), 1974
Pursuit on Ganymede (Resnick), 1968
Puzzle of the Space Pyramids (Binder), 1971
Puzzle Planet (Lowndes), 1961

Q series (T. Hoyle)
Q Colony (Thurston), 1985
Quality of Mercy (Compton), 1965
Quantrill series (Ing)
Quatermain, Allan series (Haggard)
Quatermass (Kneale), 1979
Quayle's Invention (Taine), 1927
Queen of Air and Darkness (s P. Anderson), 1973
Queen of Atlantis (Ash, as Aubrey), 1899
Queen of Life (Flint), 1965
Queen of Stones (Tennant), 1982
Queen of the Legion (Williamson), 1983
Queen of Zamba (de Camp), 1977
Queen Sheba's Ring (Haggard), 1910
Quench the Burning Stars (Bulmer), 1970
Quest series (P. Moore)
Quest Beyond the Stars (Hamilton), 1969
Quest Crosstime (Norton), 1965
Quest for the Future (van Vogt), 1970
Quest for the Perfect Planet (Johns), 1961
Quest for the Well of Souls (Chalker), 1978
Quest for the White Witch (Lee), 1978
Quest of Qui (Dent, as Robeson), 1965
Quest of the DNA Cowboys (Farren), 1976
Quest of the Gypsy (Goulart), 1976
Quest of the Spaceways (P. Moore), 1955
Quest of the Spider (Dent, as Robeson), 1935
Quest of the Three Worlds (s Cordwainer Smith), 1966
Question and Answer (P. Anderson), 1978
Quests of Simon Ark (s Hoch), 1984
Quête de la Sainte Grille (R. Young), 1975
Quicksand (Brunner), 1967
Quiet of Stone (Leigh), 1984
Quillian Sector (Tubb), 1978
Quincunx of Time (Blish), 1973
Quirke, Adam series (Fearn, as Gridban)
Quy Effect (Sellings), 1966

R.U.R. (Rossum's Universal Robots (Capek, for), 1923
R-Master (Dickson), 1973
Race Across the Stars (Offutt, as Cleve), 1984
Race Against Time (Anthony), 1973
Radar Alert (Fanthorpe, as Zeigfried), 1963

Radio Beasts (Farley), 1964
Radio Man series (Farley)
Radio Planet (Farley), 1964
Radium Pool (s Repp), 1949
Radium Seekers (Ash), 1905
Rag, A Bone, and a Hank of Hair (Fisk), 1980
Ragged Edge (Christopher), 1966
Raid of "Le Vengeur" (s Griffith), 1974
Raiders from the Rings (Nourse), 1962
Raiders of Gor (Norman), 1971
Raiders on Mars (P. Moore), 1959
Rainbow and the Rose (Shute), 1958
Rains of Eridan (Hoover), 1977
Rakehells of Heaven (Boyd), 1969
Ralph 124C41+ (Gernsback), 1925
Ram Song (Webb), 1984
Ramsgate Paradox (Tall), 1976
Random Factor (Maine), 1971
Ranger Boys in Space (Clement), 1956
Ransom, Dr. Elwin series (C. Lewis)
Rape of the Sun (I. Wallace), 1982
Rat (s S. Wright), 1945 (?)
Rat Race (Bester), 1984
Rat Report (FitzGibbon), 1980
Rats (J. Herbert), 1974
Ravens of the Moon (Grant), 1978
Rax (Coney), 1975
Reach for Tomorrow (s Clarke), 1956
Reactor XK9 (Fanthorpe, as Muller), 1963
Reade, Frank, Jr., series (Senarens)
Real People (Beresford), 1929
Real Time World (s Priest), 1974
Reality Forbidden (High), 1967
Reality Trip and Other Implausibilities (s Silverberg), 1972
Realms of Tartarus (Stableford), 1977
Rebel in Time (H. Harrison), 1983
Rebel of Antares (Bulmer, as Akers), 1980
Rebel of Rhada (Coppel, as Gilman), 1968
Rebel Worlds (P. Anderson), 1969
Rebellious Stars (Asimov), 1954
Rebels of the Red Planet (Fontenay), 1961
Rebel's Quest (Busby), 1985
Rebirth (McClary), 1944
Re-Birth (Wyndham), 1955
Recall Not Earth (MacApp), 1970
Recalled to Life (Silverberg). 1962
Recipe for Diamonds (Hyne), 1893
Recruit for Andromeda (Lesser), 1959
Red Alert (George, as Bryant), 1959
Red as Blood (s Lee), 1983
Red Hawk (Lynn), 1983
Red Insects (Fearn, as Statten), 1951
Red Journey Back (Cross), 1954
Red Men of Mars (Fearn), 1950
Red Moon (Goulart, as Robeson), 1974
Red One (s London), 1918
Red Peri (Weinbaum), 1952
Red Planet (Chilton), 1956
Red Planet (Heinlein), 1949
Red Skull (Dent, as Robeson), 1967
Red Snow (Dent, as Robeson), 1969
Red Spider (Dent, as Robeson), 1979
Red Terrors (Dent, as Robeson), 1976
Redbeard (Resnick), 1969
Reduction in Arms (Purdom), 1971
Redward Edward Papers (s Davidson), 1978

Reefs (O'Donnell), 1981
Reefs of Earth (Lafferty), 1968
Reefs of Space (Pohl, Williamson), 1964
Reel (Janifer), 1983
Re-Entry (Preuss), 1981
Refugee (Anthony), 1983
Regan's Planet (Silverberg), 1964
Regiments of Night (Ball), 1972
Rehearsal Night (F. Long), 1981
Reincarnation in Venice (Ehrlich), 1979
Reincarnation of Peter Proud (Ehrlich), 1974
Relatives (Effinger), 1973
Remaking of Sigmund Freud (Malzberg), 1985
Remarkable Exploits of Lancelot Biggs, Spaceman (s Bond), 1950
Remember Tomorrow (s Kuttner), 1954
Renaissance (R. Jones), 1951
Renaissance (van Vogt), 1979
Rendezvous on a Lost World (Chandler), 1961
Rendezvous with Rama (Clarke), 1973
Renegade of Callisto (L. Carter), 1978
Renegade of Kregan (Bulmer, as Akers), 1976
Renegade Star (Fearn, as Statten), 1951
Renegades of Time (R. Jones), 1975
RenSime (Lichtenberg), 1984
Repairmen of Cyclops (Brunner), 1965
Report on Probability A (Aldiss), 1968
Reproductive System (Sladek), 1968
Republic of the Southern Cross (Bryusov, for) 1918
Requiem for a Ruler of Worlds (Daley), 1985
Rest in Agony (Fairman, as Jorgensen), 1963
Rest of the Robots (s Asimov), 1964
Restaurant at the End of the Universe (Adams), 1980
Restoree (McCaffrey), 1967
Resurgam (s Fanthorpe), 1957
Resurgent Dust (Berry, as Garner), 1953
Resurrected Man (Tubb), 1954
Resurrection Day (Dent, as Robeson), 1969
Resurrection Days (Tucker), 1981
Resurrection of Roger Diment (Rankine, as Mason), 1972
Resurrectionist (Wolf), 1979
Retaliation (Rohmer), 1982
Retief series (Laumer)
Return (s Fanthorpe, as Brett), 1959
Return (Fanthorpe, as Torro), 1964
Return (Haiblum), 1973
Return from the Stars (Lem, for), 1980
Return from Witch Mountain (Key), 1978
Return of Jongor (R. Williams), 1970
Return of Nathan Brazil (Chalker), n.d.
Return of Retief (Laumer), 1985
Return of Sathanas (s Shaver), 1948
Return of Skull-Face (Lupoff), 1977
Return of the Jedi (Kahn), 1983
Return of the Jedi Storybook (J. Vinge), 1983
Return of the King (Tolkien, fan), 1956
Return of the Lloigor (s C. Wilson), 1974
Return of Zeus (Fanthorpe, as Muller), 1962
Return to Earth (Berry), n.d.
Return to Earth (Hoover), 1980
Return to Mars (Johns), 1955
Return to Otherness (s Kuttner), 1962
Return to the Stars (Hamilton), 1970
Return to Tomorrow (Harding), 1976
Return to Tomorrow (Hubbard), 1954
Reunion with Tomorrow (Bloch), 1978
Revelations (Malzberg), 1972

Reverse Universe (Tubb, as Gridban), 1952
Revolt in 2100 (s Heinlein), 1953
Revolt of Aphrodite (Durrell), 1974
Revolt of the Galaxy (Goldin), 1985
Revolt of the Triffids (Wyndham), 1952
Revolt of the Unemployables (Nelson), 1978
Revolt on Alpha C (Silverberg), 1955
Revolution (Beresford), 1921
Revolution from Rosinante (Gilliland), 1981
Revolving Boy (Friedberg), 1966
Rhada series (Coppel, as Gilman)
Rhapsody in Black (Stableford), 1973
Rhialto (Vance), 1984
Rhythm Rides the Rocket (s Olsen), 1940
Richest Corpse in Show Business (Morgan), 1966
Riddle of the Tower (Beresford), 1944
Riddley Walker (Hoban), 1980
Riding the Torch (Spinrad), 1978
Right Hand of Dextra (Lake), 1977
Rim Gods (s Chandler), 1968
Rim of Morning (Sloane), 1964
Rim of Space (Chandler), 1961
Rim of the Unknown (s F. Long), 1972
Rim Worlds series (Chandler)
Ring (Anthony), 1968
Ring Around the Sun (Simak), 1953
Ring of Endless Light (L'Engle), 1980
Ring of Garamas (Rankine), 1972
Ring of Ritornel (Harness), 1968
Ring of Truth (Lake), 1983
Ring of Violence (Rankine, as Mason), 1968
Ringing Changes (s Lafferty), 1984
Ring-Rise, Ring-Set (M. Hughes), 1982
Rings of Ice (Anthony), 1974
Rings of Saturn (Asimov, as French), 1974
Rings of Tantalus (Cooper, as Avery), 1975
Ringstones (s Sarban), 1951
Ringtime (s Disch), 1983
Ringworld series (Niven)
Rise of the Meritocracy 1870-2033 (M. Young), 1958
Rissa series (Busby)
Rite of Passage (Panshin), 1968
Rites of Ohe (Brunner), 1963
Rithian Terror (D. Knight), 1965
Rituals of Infinity (Moorcock), 1971
Rival Rigellians (Reynolds), 1967
River (Sutton), 1966
River and the Dream (R. Jones), 1977
River of Eternity (Farmer), 1983
River of Time (West), 1963
Riverworld series (Farmer)
Rivets and Sprockets (Key), 1964
Road Goes Ever On (Tolkien, fan), 1968
Road to Corlay (Cowper), 1978
Road to the Rim (Chandler), 1967
Roadmarks (Zelazny), 1979
Roadside Picnic (Strugatsky, for), 1977
Roar Devil (Dent, as Robeson), 1977
Robot Novels (Asimov), 1971
Robot Revolt (Fisk), 1981
Robot Who Looked Like Me (s Sheckley), 1978
Robots and Changelings (s del Rey), 1958
Robots and Empire (Asimov), 1985
Robots, Androids, and Mechanical Oddities (s Dick), 1985
Robots Have No Tails (s Kuttner, as Padgett), 1952
Robots of Dawn (Asimov), 1983

Robur the Conqueror (Verne, for), 1887
Rocannon's World (Le Guin), 1966
Rock of Three Planets (Lightner), 1963
Rocket from Infinity (del Rey), 1966
Rocket Journey (del Rey, as St.John), 1952
Rocket Man (Correy), 1955
Rocket Pilot (del Rey, as St. John), 1955
Rocket Ship Galileo (Heinlein), 1947
Rocket to Limbo (Nourse), 1957
Rocket to Luna (Hunter, as Marsten), 1952
Rocket to the Morgue (Boucher, as Holmes), 1942
Rockets in Ursa Major (F. and G. Hoyle), 1969
Rockets to Nowhere (del Rey, as St. John), 1954
Rodent Mutation (Fanthorpe, as Fane), 1961
Roderick series (Sladek)
Rogue Bolo (Laumer), 1985
Rogue Dragon (Davidson), 1965
Rogue in Space (F. Brown), 1957
Rogue Moon (Budrys), 1960
Rogue of Gor (Norman), 1981
Rogue Planet (Tubb), 1976
Rogue Queen (de Camp), 1951
Rogue Ship (van Vogt), 1965
Rogue Star (Pohl, Williamson), 1969
Roller Coaster World (Bulmer), 1972
Rolling Stones (Heinlein), 1952
Rolltown (Reynolds), 1976
Roman Holiday (Sinclair), 1931
Roman Twilight (s Fanthorpe, as Trent), 1963
Romance of the Golden Star (Griffith), 1897
Roots of the Mountains (W. Morris, fan), 1889
Rork! (Davidson), 1965
Rose (s Harness), 1966
Rose for Armageddon (Schenck), 1982
Rose for Ecclesiastes (s Zelazny), 1969
Rosinante series (Gilliland)
Ruins of Isis (Bradley), 1978
Rule Golden (D. Knight), 1967
Rule of the Door and Other Fanciful Regulations (s Biggle), 1967
Rule of the Pagbeasts (McIntosh), 1956
Ruler of the World (McIntosh), 1976
Run, Come See Jerusalem! (Meredith), 1976
Runaway Robot (del Rey, Fairman), 1965
Runaway World (Coblentz), 1961
Runes of the Lyre (Mayhar), 1982
Running Man (Holly), 1963
Russian Hide-and-Seek (Amis), 1980
Russian Intelligence (Moorcock), 1980
Rx for Tomorrow (s Nourse), 1971
Ryn (Wodhams), 1982

SOS from Mars (Cross), 1954
S.O.S. from Three Worlds (s Leinster), 1966
S.T.A.R. Flight (Tubb), 1969
Sabella (Lee), 1980
Sacred Locomotive Flies (Lupoff), 1971
Sacred Skull (Griffith), 1908
Saga of Grittel Sundotha (Mayhar), 1985
Saga of Lost Earths (Petaja), 1965
Sailing to Byzantium (Silverberg), 1985
St. Cyr and U. Tuli series (I. Wallace)
St. Francis Effect (Z. Hughes), 1976
Saint–Germain Chronicles (s Yarbro), 1983
Saliva Tree and Other Strange Growths (s Aldiss), 1966
Saltflower (Van Scyoc), 1971
Salvage and Destroy (E. Llewellyn), 1984

Sam Space series (Nolan)
Same to You Doubled (s Sheckley), 1974
San Diego Lightfoot Sue (s Reamy), 1980
Sanctuary in the Sky (Brunner), 1960
Sandkings (s Martin), 1981
Sands of Eternity (s Fanthorpe), 1963
Sands of Mars (Clarke), 1951
Sandworld (Lupoff), 1976
Sandwriter (M. Hughes), 1985
Santaroga Barrier (F. Herbert), 1968
Sardonyx Net (Lynn), 1981
Sargasso of Space (Norton, as North), 1955
Sargasso Ogre (Dent, as Robeson), 1967
Satan Black (Dent, as Robeson), 1980
Satana Enslaved (Offutt, as Cleve), 1982
Satan's Daughter (George H. Smith), 1961
Satan's World (P. Anderson), 1969
Satellite (Fanthorpe), 1960
Satellite City (Reynolds), 1975
Satellite 54-Zero (Rankine, as Mason), 1971
Saturn Patrol (Tubb, as Lang), 1951
Saunders, Scott series (P. Moore)
Savage Gentleman (Wylie), 1932
Savage Is Loose (Ehrlich), 1974
Savage Pellucidar (s E. Burroughs), 1963
Savage Scorpio (Bulmer, as Akers), 1978
Savages of Gor (Norman), 1982
Scanner Darkly (Dick), 1977
Scarlet Plague (London), 1915
Scatter of Stardust (s Tubb), 1972
Scavenger Hunt (Goldin), 1975
Scavengers in Space (Nourse), 1959
Scheme of Things (del Rey, Fairman), 1966
Schimmelhorn File (s Bretnor), 1979
Schismatrix (Sterling), 1985
School of the Moon (Walters), 1981
Schrödinger's Cat series (Robert Anton Wilson)
Science Metropolis (Fearn, as Statten), 1952
Science-Fiction Subtreasury (s Tucker), 1954
Scop (Malzberg), 1976
Scorpio Attack (T. Hoyle), 1981
Scorpion God (s Golding), 1971
Scourge of Screamers (Galouye), 1968
Scourge of the Atom (Fearn, as Gridban), 1953
Scourge of the Blood Cult (George H. Smith), 1961
Screaming Face (Lymington), 1963
Screaming Lake (S. Wright), 1939
Screaming Man (Dent, as Robeson), 1981
Scudder's Game (Compton), 1985
Sea Angel (Dent, as Robeson), 1970
Sea Beasts (Chandler), 1971
Sea Demons (Rousseau, as Egbert), 1924
Sea Girl (Cummings), 1930
Sea Magician (Dent, as Robeson), 1970
Sea Siege (Norton), 1957
Sea Thing (s Hull, van Vogt), 1970
Seademons (Yep), 1977
Seagulls under Glass (s Tate), 1975
Sea-Horse in the Sky (Cooper), 1969
Sealed Sarcophagus (s Fanthorpe), 1965
Search for Ka (Garrett), 1984
Search for Spock (McIntyre), 1984
Search for the Sun (Kapp), 1981
Search for Zei (de Camp), 1962
Search the Sky (Kornbluth, Pohl), 1954
Season of the Witch (Stinc), 1968

Seasons in Flight (s Aldiss), 1984
Second Atlantis (R. Williams), 1965
Second Deluge (Serviss), 1912
Second Empire series (Pournelle)
Second Ending (J. White), 1962
Second Invasion from Mars (Strugatsky, for), 1979
Second Nature (Wilder), 1982
Second Satellite (Latham, as Richardson), 1956
Second Stage Lensman (E.E.Smith), 1953
Second Trip (Silverberg), 1972
Second War of the Worlds (George H. Smith), 1976
Secret Agent of Terra (Brunner), 1962
Secret Galactics (van Vogt), 1974
Secret Martians (Sharkey), 1960
Secret of Life (Rucker), 1985
Secret of Saturn's Rings (Wollheim), 1954
Secret of Sinharat (Brackett), 1964
Secret of the Black Hole (P. Moore), 1980
Secret of the Black Planet (s Lesser), 1965
Secret of the Island (Verne, for), 1874
Secret of the Lost Race (Norton), 1959
Secret of the Marauder Satellite (T. White), 1967
Secret of the Martian Moons (Wollheim), 1954
Secret of the Ninth Planet (Wollheim), 1954
Secret of the Red Spot (Binder), 1971
Secret of the Sky (Dent, as Robeson), 1967
Secret of the Snows (s Fanthorpe), 1957
Secret of the Sunless World (MacApp), 1969
Secret of ZI (Bulmer), 1958
Secret People (R.Jones), 1956
Secret People (Wyndham, as Beynon), 1935
Secret Scorpio (Bulmer, as Akers), 1977
Secret Sea (Moteleone), 1979
Secret Sin (Le Queux), 1913
Secret Songs (s Leiber), 1968
Secret under Antarctica (Dickson), 1963
Secret under the Caribbean (Dickson), 1964
Secret under the Sea (Dickson), 1960
Secret Visitors (J. White), 1957
Secret War (Wheatley), 1937
Secrets of Stardeep (Jakes), 1969
Secrets of Synchronicity (J. Fast), 1977
Section G: United Planets (Reynolds), 1976
Sector General series (J. White)
Seed of Earth (Silverberg), 1962
Seed of Evil (s Bayley), 1979
Seed of Light (Cooper), 1959
Seed of Stars (Kippax, Morgan), 1972
Seed of the Dreamers (Petaja), 1970
Seed of the Gods (Z. Hughes), 1974
Seedling Stars (s Blish), 1957
Seeds of Change (Monteleone), 1975
Seeds of Life (Taine), 1951
Seeds of Time (s Wyndham), 1956
Seeker (Bischoff), 1976
Seekers of Shar Nuhn (Mayhar), 1980
Seeking the Mythical Future (T. Hoyle), 1977
Seeklight (Jeter), 1975
Seetee series (Williamson, as Stewart)
Seetee Alert! (Tubb, as Kern), 1974
Seg the Bowman (Bulmer, as Akers), 1984
Sense of Obligation (H. Harrison), 1967
Sense of Shadow (Wilhelm), 1981
Sensitives (Charbonneau), 1968
Sentenced to Prism (A. Foster), 1985
Sentimental Agents (Lessing), 1983

Sentinel (s Clarke), 1983
Sentinel Stars (Charbonneau), 1964
Sentinels from Space (Russell), 1953
Separation (Rohmer)
September, Skua series (A. Foster)
Seren Cenacles (Norwood), 1983
Serpent's Reach (Cherryh), 1980
Servants of the Wankh (Vance), 1969
Serving in Time (Eklund), 1975
Set of Wheels (Thurston), 1983
Seven Agate Devils (Dent, as Robeson), 1973
Seven Conquests (s P. Anderson), 1967
Seven Days to Never (Frank), 1957
7 Footprints to Satan (Merritt), 1928
Seven from the Stars (Bradley), 1962
Seven Out of Time (Zagat), 1949
Seven Sexes (s Tenn), 1968
Seven Steps to the Arbiter (Hubbard), 1975
Seven Steps to the Sun (F. and G. Hoyle), 1970
Seventeen Virgins (s Vance), 1979
Several Minds (Morgan), 1969
Sex and the High Command (Boyd), 1970
Sex Machine (Mead), 1949
Sex Sphere (Rucker), 1983
Sex War (Merwin), 1960
Shade of Time (Duncan), 1946
Shadow Girl (Cummings), 1946
Shadow Lord (Yep), 1985
Shadow Man (Fanthorpe, as Barton), 1966
Shadow of All Night Falling (Cook), 1979
Shadow of Alpha (Grant), 1976
Shadow of Earth (Eisenstein), 1979
Shadow of Heaven (Shaw), 1969
Shadow of the Torturer (G. Wolfe), 1980
Shadow on the Hearth (Merril), 1950
Shadow Over Mars (Brackett), 1951
Shadow People (St. Clair), 1969
Shadow Play (s Beaumont), 1964
Shadowfire (Lee), 1979
Shadowkeep (A. Foster), 1984
Shadowline (Cook), 1982
Shadowman (Proctor), 1980
Shadows in the Sun (Oliver), 1954
Shadows Linger (Cook), 1984
Shadrach in the Furnace (Silverberg), 1976
Shaggy Planet (Goulart), 1973
Shakehole (Mackelworth), 1981
Shakespeare's Planet (Simak), 1976
Shambleau (s C. Moore), 1953
Shann Lantree series (Norton)
Shape Changer (Laumer), 1972
Shape of Fear (F. Long, as L. Long), 1971
Shape of Space (s Niven), 1969
Shape of Terror (Dent, as Robeson), 1982
Shape of Things to Come (Wells), 1933
Shapes in the Fire (s Shiel), 1896
Shards of Space (s Sheckley), 1962
Sharra's Exile (Bradley), 1981
Shattered People (Hoskins), 1975
Shattered World (Reaves), n.d.
She series (Haggard)
Sheep Look Up (Brunner), 1972
Shepherd (Holly), 1977
Shepherd Moon (Hoover), 1984
Sherlock Holmes's War of the Worlds (Wellman), 1975
Shield (P. Anderson), 1963

Shikasta (Lessing), 1979
Shining Strangers (Bova), 1973
Ship from Outside (Chandler), 1963
Ship of Shadows (s Leiber), 1979
Ship of Strangers (Shaw), 1978
Ship That Sailed the Time Stream (Edmondson), 1965
Ship Who Sang (McCaffrey), 1969
Ships of Durostorum (Bulmer), 1970
Ships to the Stars (s Leiber), 1964
Shipwrecked in the Air (Verne, for), 1874
Shiva Descending (Banford, Rotsler), 1980
Shock series (s Matheson)
Shock Waves (s Matheson), 1970
Shock Waves (Richmond), 1967
Shockwave Rider (Brunner), 1975
Shoot at the Moon (Temple), 1966
Shores of Another Sea (Oliver), 1971
Shores of Death (Moorcock), 1970
Shores of Kansas (Chilson), 1976
Shores of Space (s Matheson), 1957
Shores of Tomorrow (s Silverberg), 1976
Shot into Infinity (Gail, for), 1975
Showboat World (Vance), 1975
Shrine (J. Herbert), 1983
Shrinking Man (Matheson), 1956
Shrouded Abbot (s Fanthorpe), 1964
Shrouded Planet (Garrett and Silverberg, as Randall), 1957
Shuttle Down (Correy), 1981
Sibyl Sue Blue (R. Brown), 1966
Sideshow (Resnick), 1982
Sideslip (T. White), 1968
Sidewise in Time (s Leinster), 1950
Siege of Faltara (Darney), 1978
Siege of the Unseen (van Vogt), 1959
Siege of Wonder (Geston), 1976
Siege Perilous (del Rey, Fairman), 1966
Sight of Proteus (Sheffield), 1978
Sign of the Burning Hart (Keller), 1938
Sign of the Labrys (St. Clair), 1963
Sign of the Mute Medusa (I. Wallace), 1977
Sign of the Unicorn (Zelazny), 1975
Signs and Portents (s Yarbro), 1984
Signs and Wonders (s Beresford), 1921
Silence Is Deadly (Biggle), 1977
Silent Invaders (Silverberg), 1963
Silent Multitude (Compton), 1966
Silent Shout (s Zebrowski), 1979
Silent Sky (s Biggle), 1979
Silent Speakers (Sellings), 1963
Silent Voice (Hodder-Williams), 1977
Silistra series (J. Morris)
Silkie (van Vogt), 1969
Silmarillion (Tolkien, fan), 1977
Silver Eggheads (Leiber), 1962
Silver Horse (Lynn), 1984
Silver Locusts (s Bradbury), 1951
Silver Metal Lover (Lee), 1982
Sime/Gen series (Lichtenberg)
Simulacra (Dick), 1964
Simulacron-3 (Galouye), 1964
Sin in Space (Kornbluth and Merril, as Judd), 1961
Sinful Ones (s Leiber), 1953
Singing Citadel (s Moorcock), 1970
Singing Stones (J. Coulson), 1968
Single Combat (Ing), 1983
Singularity Station (Ball), 1973

Sinister Barrier (Russell), 1943
Sins of the Fathers (Schmidt), 1976
Sioux Spaceman (Norton), 1960
Sirens of Titan (Vonnegut), 1959
Sirian Experiments (Lessing), 1981
Sirius (Stapledon), 1944
Siscoe, Nick and Ross Block series (Haiblum)
SIVA! (Richmond), 1979
Six Gates from Limbo (McIntosh), 1968
Six Worlds Yonder (s Russell), 1958
Six-Gun Planet (Jakes), 1970
Sixth Column (Heinlein), 1949
Sixty Days to Live (Wheatley), 1939
Skaith series (Brackett)
Skeeve and Aahz series (Asprin)
Skies Discrowned (Powers), 1976
Skirmish (s Simak), 1977
Skua September series (A. Foster)
Sky Is Falling (del Rey), 1963
Sky Is Filled With Ships (Meredith), 1969
Sky Pirates of Callisto (L. Carter), 1973
Sky Ripper (Drake), 1983
Skyfall (H. Harrison), 1977
Skylark series (E.E.Smith)
Skynappers (Brunner), 1960
Skyport (Siodmak), 1959
Skyrocket Steele (Goulart), 1980
Slan (van Vogt), 1946
Slaughterhouse-Five (Vonnegut), 1969
Slave Girl of Gor (Norman), 1977
Slave Planet (Janifer), 1963
Slave Ship (Pohl), 1957
Slave Ship from Sergan (Tubb, as Kern), 1973
Slavers of Space (Brunner), 1960
Slaves of Heaven (Cooper), 1974
Slaves of Ijax (Fearn), 1948
Slaves of the Klau (Vance), 1958
Slaves of the Spectrum (Bulmer, as Kent), 1954
Sleep Eaters (Lymington), 1973
Sleep Has His House (Kavan), 1948
Sleeper Wakes (Wells), 1910
Sleepers of Mars (s Wyndham, as Beynon), 1973
Sleepwalker's World (Dickson), 1971
Slippery (s Lafferty), 1985
Slipt (A. Foster), 1984
Slitherers (Fearn), 1984
Slow Birds (s Watson), 1985
Slow Fall to Dawn (Leigh), 1981
Slow Sculpture (s Sturgeon), 1982
Small Armageddon (Roshwald), 1962
Small Assassin (s Bradbury), 1962
Small Changes (s Clement), 1969
Smile on the Void (S. Gordon), 1981
Smith of Wootton Major (Tolkien, fan), 1967
Smuggled Atom Bomb (s Wylie), 1956
Snail on the Slope (Strugatsky, for), 1980
Snake in His Bosom (s Lafferty), 1983
Sneak Preview (Bloch), 1971
Snoggle (Priestley), 1971
Snow Queen (J. Vinge), 1980
Snow White and the Giants (McIntosh), 1968
Snows of Ganymede (P. Anderson), 1958
Snow-White Soliloquies (MacLeod), 1970
So Bright the Vision (s Simak), 1968
So Close to Home (s Blish), 1961
So Dark a Heritage (F. Long), 1966

So Long, and Thanks for All the Fish (Adams), 1984
Sodom and Gomorrah Business (Malzberg), 1974
Soft Come the Dragons (s Koontz), 1970
Soft Machine (W. Burroughs), 1961
Soft Targets (Ing), 1979
Softly By Moonlight (Fanthorpe, as Fane), 1963
Software (Rucker), 1982
Sojarr of Titan (Wellman), 1949
Solar Invasion (Wellman), 1968
Solar Lottery (Dick), 1955
Solar Queen series (Norton, as North)
Solarians (Spinrad), 1966
Solaris (Lem, for), 1971
Sold—For a Space Ship (High), 1973
Soldier, Ask Not (Dickson), 1967
Solipsism Samba (s Broderick), 1985
Solitary Hunters (Keller), 1948
Solution Three (Mitchison), 1975
Some Dreams are Nightmares (s Gunn), 1974
Some Notes on Xi Bootis (Clement), 1959
Some Will Not Die (Budrys), 1961
Some Women of the University (s Blayre), 1934
Somerset Dreams (s Wilhelm), 1978
Something Answered (DeWeese), 1983
Something Wicked This Way Comes (Bradbury), 1962
Somewhere a Voice (s Russell), 1965
Somewhere in the Night (Moorcock, as Barclay), 1966
Somewhere Out There (Fanthorpe, as Fane), 1963
Son of Kronk (Cooper), 1970
Son of Man (Silverberg), 1971
Son of the Ages (Waterloo), 1914
Son of the Morning (s Gotlieb), 1983
Son of the Stars (R. Jones), 1952
Son of the Tree (Vance), 1964
Song for Lya (s Martin), 1976
Song of Earth series (Coney)
Song of Phaid the Gambler (Farren), 1981
Song of the Axe (P. Williams), 1984
Songbirds of Pain (s Kilworth), 1984
Songmaster (Card), 1980
Songs from the Stars (Spinrad), 1980
Songs of Stars and Shadows (s Martin), 1977
Songs of Summer (Silverberg), 1979
Songs the Dead Men Sing (s Martin), 1983
Sons of Darkness, Sons of Light (J. Williams), 1969
Sorcerer's Son (Eisenstein), 1979
Sorcerer's World (Broderick), 1970
Sorceress of Qar (T.White), 1966
Sos the Rope (Anthony), 1968
Soul Eater (Resnick), 1981
Soul of the Robot (Bayley), 1974
Soul Rider series (Chalker)
Soul-Singer of Tyrnos (Mayhar), 1981
Sound of His Horn (Sarban), 1952
Sound of Winter (Cover),1976
Source of Magic (Anthony), 1979
South Pole (Dent, as Robeson), 1974
Sovereign (Meluch), 1979
Soylent Green (H. Harrison), 1973
Space Apprentice (Strugatsky, for), 1981
Space Ark (Lightner), 1968
Space Barbarians (Godwin), 1964
Space Barbarians (Reynolds), 1969
Space Beyond (s Campbell), 1976
Space by the Tale (s Bixby), 1964
Space Cadet (Heinlein), 1948

Space Captain (Leinster), 1966
Space Chantey (Lafferty), 1968
Space Circus (Goulart, as Steffanson), 1974
Space Doctor (Correy), 1981
Space Dreamers (Clarke), 1969
Space Eater (Langford), 1982
Space Family Stone (Heinlein), 1969
Space for Hire (Nolan), 1971
Space Fury (Fanthorpe), 1962
Space Guardians (Ball), 1975
Space Gypsies (Leinster), 1967
Space Gypsies (Lightner), 1974
Space Hawk (Bates, as Gilmore), 1952
Space Hostages (Fisk), 1967
Space Hunger (Tubb, as Grey), 1953
Space Lash (s Clement), 1969
Space Lawyer (Schachner), 1953
Space Lords (s Cordwainer Smith), 1965
Space Machine (Priest), 1976
Space Mercenaries (Chandler), 1965
Space Merchants (Kornbluth, Pohl), 1953
Space 1999 series (Tubb)
Space No Barrier (Fanthorpe, as Torro), 1964
Space Olympics (Lightner), 1967
Space on My Hands (s F. Brown), 1951
Space Opera (Vance), 1965
Space Pioneer (Reynolds), 1966
Space Pirate (Vance) 1953
Space Pirates (Eklund, E.E. Smith), 1979
Space Plague (Lightner), 1966
Space Plague (George O. Smith), 1957
Space Platform (Leinster), 1953
Space Prison (Godwin), 1960
Space Puppet (Rackham), 1954
Space Salvage (Bulmer), 1953
Space, Sam series (Nolan)
Space Scavengers (s Cartmill), 1975
Space Search (Reynolds), 1984
Space Skimmer (Gerrold), 1972
Space Sorcerers (McIntosh), 1972
Space Station No. 1 (F. Long), 1957
Space Swimmers (Dickson), 1967
Space, Time, and Nathaniel (s Aldiss), 1957
Space Trap (J. Coulson), 1976
Space Trap (Fanthorpe, as Bell), 1964
Space Trap (M. Hughes), 1983
Space Treason (Bulmer), 1952
Space Tug (Leinster), 1953
Space Tyrant series (Anthony)
Space Vampires (C. Wilson), 1976
Space Viking (Piper), 1963
Space Visitor (Reynolds), 1977
Space War (s N. Jones), 1967
Space War Blues (Lupoff), 1978
Space Warp (Fearn, as Statten), 1952
Space Willies (Russell), 1958
Space Winners (Dickson), 1965
Space-Born (Tubb), 1956
Space-Borne (Fanthorpe), 1959
Spacehawk, Inc. (Goulart), 1974
Spacehive (Sutton), 1960
Spacehounds of IPC (E.E. Smith), 1947
Spaceling (Piserchia), 1978
Spacemen, Go Home (Lesser), 1962
Spacepaw (Dickson), 1969
Spaceship for the King (Pournelle), 1973

Spaceship to Saturn (Walters), 1967
Spacetime Donuts (Rucker), 1981
Space-Time Juggler (Brunner), 1963
Spaceways (Maine), 1953
Spaceways series (Offutt, as Cleve)
Spaceways Satellite (Maine), 1958
Spacial Delivery (Dickson), 1961
Spartan Planet (Chandler), 1969
Spawn of Laban (Tubb, as Kern), 1974
Spawn of the Death Machine (T. White), 1968
Speak for Earth (Brunner, as Woodcott) 1961
Speaking of Dinosaurs (High), 1974
Speaking Stone (Dent, as Robeson), 1983
Spear (J. Herbert), 1978
Special Deliverance (Simak), 1982
Special Delivery (Neville), 1967
Special Mission (Fanthorpe, as Muller), 1963
Specials (Charbonneau), 1967
Specimens (Saberhagen), 1976
Specter Is Haunting Texas (Leiber), 1969
Spectre of Darkness (Fanthorpe, as Muller), 1965
Spectrum of a Forgotten Sun (Tubb), 1976
Spell for Chameleon (Anthony), 1977
Spell Sword (Bradley), 1974
Spellsinger series (A. Foster)
Spherico-Transcedental Design (Braun, for), 1983
Sphinx (Lindsay), 1923
Spider in the Bath (Lymington), 1975
Spiders' War (S. Wright), 1954
Spin the Glass Web (Ehrlich), 1952
Spinner (Piserchia), 1980
Spinneret (Zahn), 1985
Spirit of the Bambatse (Haggard), 1906
Spirits of Flux and Anchor (Chalker), 1984
Splendid Freedom (s Darney), 1980
Splendor and Misery of Bodies, of Cities (Delany), 1985
Splinter of the Mind's Eye (A. Foster), 1978
Split Infinity (Anthony), 1980
Split Second (Kilworth), 1979
Spock, Messiah! (Cogswell), 1976
Spock Must Die! (Blish), 1970
Spook Hole (Dent, as Robeson), 1972
Spook Legion (Dent, as Robeson), 1967
Spot of Life (Hall), 1965
Spotted Men (Dent, as Robeson), 1977
Sprockets: A Little Robot (Key), 1963
Spy in Space (P. Moore), 1977
Square Root of Man (s Tenn), 1968
Square Root of Tomorrow (s Cooper), 1970
Squares of the City (Brunner), 1965
Squeaking Goblin (Dent, as Robeson), 1969
Stadium Beyond the Stars (Lesser), 1960
Stained-Glass World (Bulmer), 1976
Stainless Steel Rat series (H. Harrison)
Stalking the Nightmare (s Ellison), 1982
Stand on Zanzibar (Brunner), 1968
Standing Joy (Guin), 1969
Star Beast (Heinlein), 1954
Star Begotten (Wells), 1937
Star Born (Norton), 1957
Star Bridge (Gunn, Williamson), 1955
Star Circus (Lightner), 1977
Star City (Bulmer, as Zetford), 1974
Star Colony (Laumer), 1981
Star Conquerors (Bova), 1959
Star Courier (Chandler), 1977

Star Diaries (Lem, for), 1976
Star Dog (Lightner), 1973
Star Driver (Correy), 1980
Star Dwellers (Blish), 1961
Star Fall (Bischoff), 1980
Star Fox (P. Anderson), 1965
Star Gate (Norton), 1958
Star Gold (Kelley), 1979
Star Guard (Norton), 1955
Star Hawks series (Goulart)
Star Healer (J. White), 1985
Star Hunter (Norton), 1961
Star Ka'at series (Norton)
Star King (Vance), 1964
Star Kings (Hamilton), 1949
Star Light (Clement), 1971
Star Light, Star Bright (s Bester), 1976
Star Loot (Chandler), 1980
Star Magicians (L. Carter), 1966
Star Man's Son, 2250 A.D. (Norton), 1952
Star Masters' Gambit (Klein, for), 1973
Star Mill (Petaja), 1965
Star of Danger (Bradley), 1965
Star of Hesiock (Rankine), 1980
Star of Ill-Omen (Wheatley), 1952
Star of Life (Hamilton), 1959
Star of the Unborn (Werfel, for), 1946
Star Prince Charlie (P. Anderson, Dickson), 1975
Star Probe (Green), 1976
Star Quest (Koontz), 1968
Star Rangers (Norton), 1953
Star Rebel (Busby), 1984
Star Rider (Piserchia), 1974
Star Road (s Dickson), 1973
Star Rogue (L. Carter), 1970
Star Rover (London), 1915
Star Seekers (Lesser), 1953
Star Seekers (Rayer), 1954
Star Shall Abide (Engdahl), 1972
Star Shine (s F. Brown), 1956
Star Slaver (Edmondson and Offutt, as Cleve), 1983
Star Smashers of the Galaxy Rangers (H. Harrison), 1973
Star Songs of an Old Primate (s Tiptree), 1978
Star Spring (Bischoff), 1982
Star Surgeon (Nourse), 1960
Star Surgeon (J. White), 1963
Star Treasure (Laumer), 1971
Star Trek series (s Blish; A. Foster; Joe Haldeman; McIntyre; Reynolds; s Rotsler)
Star Trek: The Day of the Dove (Bixby), 1978
Star Trove (Bulmer), 1970
Star Venturers (Bulmer), 1969
Star Virus (Bayley), 1970
Star Wars (A. Foster, as Lucas) 1976
Star Wasps (R. Williams), 1963
Star Watchman (Bova), 1964
Star Ways (P. Anderson), 1956
Star Web (Zebrowski), 1975
Star Well (Panshin), 1968
Star Winds (Bayley), 1978
Star Witches (Lymington), 1965
Star Wolf! (T. White), 1971
Star-Anchored, Star-Angered (Elgin), 1979
Starblood (Koontz), 1972
Starbrat (Morressy), 1972
Starburst (s Bester), 1958

Starburst (Pohl), 1982
Starchild series (Pohl, s Williamson)
Starcrossed (Bova), 1975
Star-Crowned Kings (Chilson), 1975
Stardance (S. Robinson), 1979
Stardeath (Tubb), 1983
Stardreamer (s Cordwainer Smith), 1971
Stardrift (Morressy), 1975
Stardrift (s Petaja), 1971
Stardroppers (Brunner), 1972
Stardust Voyages (s Tall), 1975
Starfinder (R. Young), 1980
Starfishers series (Cook)
Starflight 3000 (Mackelworth), 1972
Starfollowers of Coramonde (Daley), 1979
Stargate (Robinett), 1976
Starhaven (Silverberg, as Jorgenson), 1958
Starhiker (Dann), 1977
Starkahn of Rhada (Coppel, as Gilman), 1970
Starless World (Eklund), 1978
Starlight (s Bester), 1976
Starmaker (Stapledon), 1937
Starman (A. Foster), 1984
Starman Jones (Heinlein), 1953
Starman's Quest (Silverberg), 1959
Starmen (Brackett), 1952
Starmen of Llyrdis (Brackett), 1976
Starmother (Van Scyoc), 1976
Starquake! (Forward), 1985
Starr, David series (Asimov, as French)
Starr, Lucky series (Asimov, as French)
Stars Are Ours (Bulmer), 1953
Stars Are Ours! (Norton), 1954
Stars Are the Styx (s Sturgeon), 1979
Stars Came Down (Saxon), 1964
Stars' End (Cook), 1982
Stars in My Pocket Like Grains of Sand (Delany), 1984
Stars in Shroud (Benford), 1978
Stars, Like Dust (Asimov), 1951
Stars My Destination (Bester), 1957
Stars Will Speak (Zebrowski), 1985
Starseed on Gye Moor (Lymington), 1977
Starshadows (s Sargent), 1977
Starshine (s Sturgeon), 1966
Starship (Aldiss), 1959
Starship (s P. Anderson), 1982
Starship and Haiku (Sucharitkul), 1984
Starship Death (Garrett), 1982
Starship Sapphire (Offutt, as Cleve), 1984
Starship Through Space (Correy), 1954
Starship Troopers (Heinlein), 1959
Starsilk (Van Scyoc), 1984
Star-Spangled Future (s Spinrad), 1979
Starstormers series (Fisk)
Starswarm (s Aldiss), 1964
Startide Rising (Brin), 1983
Starwings (Proctor), 1984
Starwolf series (Hamilton)
Starworld (H. Harrison), 1981
Station in Space (s Gunn), 1958
Stations of Nightmare (s Farmer), 1982
Status Civilisation (Sheckley), 1960
Steam House (Verne, for), 1881
Steam-Driven Boy and Other Strangers (s Sladek), 1973
Steel Crocodile (Compton), 1970
Steel of Raithskar (Garrett), 1981

Steel, The Mist and the Blazing Sun (Anvil), 1983
Steel Tsar (Moorcock), 1981
Stella Fregelius (Haggard), 1904
Stellar Assignment (Tubb), 1979
Stellar Legion (Tubb), 1954
Stellar Missiles (s Repp), 1949
Step to the Stars (del Rey), 1954
Stepford Wives (Levin), 1972
Steppe (Anthony), 1976
Steps of the Sun (Tevis), 1983
Stepsons of Terra (Silverberg), 1958
Still I Persist in Wondering (s Pangborn), 1978
Still Small Voice of Trumpets (Biggle), 1968
Stitch in Snow (McCaffrey), 1984
Stochastic Man (Silverberg), 1975
Stolen Bacillus (s Wells), 1895
Stolen Faces (Bishop), 1977
Stolen Souls (s Le Queux), 1895
Stolen Sphere (Cross), 1953
Stolen Submarine (Griffith), 1904
Stolen Sun (Petaja), 1967
Stone God Awakens (Farmer), 1970
Stone in Heaven (P Anderson), 1979
Stone Man (Dent, as Robeson), 1976
Stone That Never Came Down (Brunner), 1973
Stonehenge (H. Harrison), 1972
Store of Infinity (s Sheckley), 1960
Stork Factor (Z. Hughes), 1975
Storm God's Fury (s Fanthorpe, as Fane), 1962
Storm Lord (Lee), 1976
Storm of Wings (M. Harrison), 1980
Storm over Warlock (Norton), 1960
Stormqueen (Bradley), 1978
Story of Ab (Waterloo), 1897
Story of Sigurd the Volsung and the Fall of the Niblungs (Morris, fan), 1876
Story of the Glittering Plain (W. Morris, fan), 1891
Story of Ulla (s Arnold), 1895
Stowaway to Mars (Wyndham), 1953
Strange Doings (s Lafferty), 1971
Strange Harvest (s Wandrei), 1965
Strange Invaders (A. Llewellyn), 1934
Strange Journeys of Colonel Polders (Dunsany, fan), 1950
Strange Ones (Fanthorpe, as Torro), 1963
Strange Papers of Dr. Blayre (s Blayre), 1932
Strange Relations (s Farmer), 1960
Strange Seas and Shores (s Davidson), 1971
Strange Stories (s Allen), 1884
Strange Stories of Hospitals (s Ash, as Aubrey), 1898
Strange Wine (s Ellison), 1978
Strange Worlds (Farley), 1952
Stranger in a Strange Land (Heinlein), 1961
Stranger in the Shadow (s Fanthorpe), 1966
Stranger Than You Think (s Edmondson), 1965
Strangers (Dozois, Effinger), 1978
Strangers in Paradise (Anvil), 1969
Strangers in the Universe (s Simak), 1956
Strangler's Moon (Goldin), 1976
Strata (Pratchett), 1981
Street of Queer Houses (s Keller), 1976
Streetlethal (S. Barnes), 1983
Strength of Stones (Bear), 1981
Strength of the Strong (s London), 1911
Stress Pattern (Barrett), 1974
Stroka Prospekt (s Lupoff), 1982
Struggle in Space (Belyaev, for), 1965

Styrbiorn the Strong (Eddison, fan), 1926
Suaine and the Crow-God (S. Gordon), 1975
Subb (MacApp), 1971
Submarine Mystery (Dent, as Robeson), 1971
Subspace Encounter (E.E. Smith), 1983
Subspace Explorers (E.E. Smith), 1965
Subterfuge (Maine), 1959
Such Power Is Dangerous (Wheatley), 1933
Sudden Star (Sargent), 1979
Sugar in the Air (Large), 1937
Suicide Plague (Naha), 1982
Suiciders (McIntosh), 1973
Sun Destroyers (s Rocklynne), 1973
Sun Makers (Fearn, as Statten), 1950
Sun Saboteurs (D. Knight), 1961
Sun Smasher (Hamilton), 1959
Sunbound (Felice), 1981
Sunburst (Fisk), 1980
Sunburst (Gotlieb), 1964
Sundance (s Silverberg), 1974
Sundered Worlds (Moorcock), 1965
Sundering Flood (W. Morris, fan), 1897
Sundiver (Brin), 1980
Sundog (Ball), 1965
Sung in Shadow (Lee), 1983
Sunken World (Coblentz), 1948
Sunless World (s N. Jones), 1967
Sunrise on Mercury (s Silverberg), 1975
Sun's End (Lupoff), 1984
Suns of Scorpio (Bulmer, as Akers), 1973
Sunspacer (Zebrowski), 1984
Sunstroke (s Watson), 1982
Sunwaifs (Van Scyoc), 1981
Sunworld (Kelley), 1979
Super Barbarians (Brunner), 1962
Superluminal (McIntyre), 1983
Superman III (Kotzwinkle), 1983
Supermind (Garrett as Phillips, Janifer), 1963
Supermind (van Vogt), 1977
Survey Ship (Bradley), 1980
Survival! (Dickson), 1984
Survival Game (Kapp), 1976
Survival Kit (s Pohl), 1979
Survival Margin (Maine), 1968
Survival Project (Fanthorpe, as Muller), 1966
Survival Ship (s Merril), 1974
Survival World (F. Long), 1971
Survivor (O. Butler), 1978
Survivor (J. Herbert), 1976
Survivor (Janifer), 1977
Survivors (Bradley), 1979
Survivors (Godwin), 1958
Suspension (Fanthorpe, as Fane), 1964
Swain, Mathew series (McQuay)
Swamp Rats (Goulart, as Shawn), 1974
Swan Song (Stableford), 1975
Sweeney's Island (Christopher), 1964
Sweet Dreams (Frayn), 1973
Sweet Evil (Platt), 1977
Sweets from a Stranger (s Fisk), 1982
Sweetwater (Yep), 1973
Sweizer Pump (E. Wallace), 1929
Swiftly Tilting Planet (L'Engle), 1978
Sword above the Night (Lymington), 1962
Sword for Kregen (Bulmer, as Akers), 1979
Sword of Aldones (Bradley), 1962

Sword of Aradel (Key), 1977
Sword of Lictor (G. Wolfe), 1982
Sword of Rhiannon (Brackett), 1953
Sword of the Samurai (Reaves), 1984
Sword of the Spirits series (Christopher)
Sword of Tomorrow (s Kuttner), 1955
Sword of Wellaran (Dunsany, fan), 1908
Sword of Winter (Randall), 1983
Sword Swallower (Goulart), 1968
Swordbearer (Cook), 1982
Swords series (Bulmer)
Swords series (Saberhagen)
Swords of Chaos (s Bradley), 1982
Swords of Mars (E. Buroughs), 1936
Swords of the Barbarians (Bulmer), 1970
Swordships of Scorpio (Bulmer, as Akers), 1973
Swordsman of Mars (Kline), 1960
Sylva (Vercors, for), 1962
Symbol of Terra (Tubb), 1984
Syn (R. Jones), 1969
Synaptic Manhunt (Farren), 1976
Syndic (Kornbluth), 1953
Synthajoy (Compton), 1968
Synthetic Man (Sturgeon), 1957
Synthetic Men of Mars (E. Burroughs), 1940
Synthetic Ones (Fanthorpe, as Roberts), 1961
Systemic Shock (Ing), 1981
Syzygy (Coney), 1973
Syzygy (Pohl), 1982

T Zero (Calvino, for), 1969
T.H.E.M. (Edmondson), 1974
THX 1138 (Bova), 1971
Tactics of Conquest (Malzberg), 1974
Tactics of Mistake (Dickson), 1971
Takeoff (s Garrett), 1979
Takeoff (Kornbluth), 1952
Takeover (Edmondson), 1984
Takers (Ehrlich), 1961
Tale of the House of the Wolfings (W. Morris, fan), 1889
Tale of the Troika (Strugatsky, for), 1977
Tale of Two Clocks (Schmitz), 1962
Talent for the Invisible (Goulart), 1973
Talents, Incorporated (Leinster), 1962
Tales from the Nightside (s Grant), 1981
Tales from the White Hart (s Clarke), 1957
Tales from Underwood (s Keller), 1952
Tales of Gooseflesh and Laughter (s Wyndham), 1956
Tales of Known Space (s Niven), 1975
Tales of Nevèryön (s Delany), 1979
Tales of Science and Sorcery (s Clark Ashton Smith), 1964
Tales of Space and Time (s Wells), 1899
Tales of Ten Worlds (s Clarke), 1962
Tales of the Flying Mountains (s P. Anderson), 1970
Tales of Three Hemispheres (Dunsany, fan), 1919
Tales of Three Planets (s E. Burroughs), 1964
Tales of Wonder (Dunsany, fan), 1916
Talking Devil (Dent, as Robeson), 1982
Tallons of Scorpio (Bulmer, as Akers), 1983
Tam, Son of the Tiger (Kline), 1962
Tama series (Cummings)
Tamarisk Row (Murnane), 1974
Tamastara (s Lee), 1984
Tambu (Asprin), 1979
Tanar of Pellucidar (E. Burroughs), 1930
Tapestry of Magics (Daley), 1983

Tapestry of Time (Cowper), 1982
Tapestry Warriors (Wilder), 1983
Tara of the Twilight (L. Carter), 1979
Tar-Aiym Krang (A. Foster), 1972
Target: Terra (Janifer), 1968
Tarnsman of Gor (Norman), 1966
Tarot series (Anthony)
Tarrano the Conqueror (Cummings), 1930
Tartarus Incident (Greenleaf), 1983
Tarzan at the Earth's Core (E. Burroughs), 1930
Tau Zero (P. Anderson), 1970
Tcity series (Adlard)
Technicolor Time Machine (H. Harrison), 1967
Technos (Tubb), 1972
Tedric, Lord series (Eklund, E.E. Smith)
Telempath (S. Robinson), 1976
Telepath (Sellings), 1962
Telepathist (Brunner), 1965
Telepower (Hoffman), 1967
Television Detective (Keller), 1938
Telzey Amberdon series (Schmitz)
Temple of Fire (Ash, as Ashley) 1905
Ten Deadly Men (Fairman, as Jorgensen), 1975
Ten from Infinity (Fariman, as Jorgensen), 1963
Ten from Tomorrow (s Tubb), 1966
Ten Mile Treasure (Norton), 1981
Ten Million Years to Friday (Lymington), 1967
Ten Thousand Light-Years from Home (s Tiptree), 1973
Ten Ton Snake (Dent, as Robeson), 1982
Ten Years to Doomsday (C. Anderson, Kurland), 1964
Tenth Planet (Cooper), 1973
10th Victim (Sheckley), 1966
Terminal Beach (s Ballard), 1964
Terminal Man (Crichton), 1972
Terra Data (Tubb), 1980
Terran Federation series (Piper)
Terror by Satellite (Walters), 1964
Terror in the Bay (Binder, as Turek), 1971
Terror in the Navy (Dent, as Robeson), 1969
Terror of the Air (Le Queux), 1920
Terror Star (P. Moore), 1979
Terror Version (Lymington), 1982
Test of Fire (Bova), 1982
Testament of Andros (s Blish), 1977
Texas-Israeli War: 1999 (Waldrop), 1974
Texts of Festival (Farren), 1973
Tharkol, Lord of the Unknown (Hamilton), 1950
That Hideous Strength (C. Lewis), 1945
Theatre of Timesmiths (Kilworth), 1984
Their Majesties' Buccaneers (L.Smith), 1981
Them Bones (Waldrop), 1984
Then Beggars Could Ride (Nelson), 1976
Thendara House (Bradley), 1983
There is No Darkness (Jack C. Haldeman, Joe Haldeman), 1983
There Will be Time (P. Anderson), 1972
These Savage Futurians (High), 1967
They Call Me Carpenter (Sinclair), 1922
They Died Twice (Dent, as Robeson), 1981
They Found Atlantis (Wheatley), 1936
They Never Came Back (Fanthorpe, as Brett), 1962
They Shall Have Stars (Blish), 1956
They Walked Like Men (Simak), 1962
They'd Rather Be Right (Clifton), 1957
Thief of Llarn (Fox), 1966
Thief of Thoth (L. Carter), 1968
Thing (s Campbell), 1952

Thing (A. Foster), 1982
Thing from Sheol (s Fanthorpe, as Fane), 1963
Thing in the Cellar (s Keller), 1940
Thing of the Past (Fearn, as Gridban), 1953
Things Beyond Midnight (s Nolan), 1984
Things to Come (Wells), 1935
Thinking Seat (Tate), 1969
Thinktank That Leaked (Hodder-Williams), 1979
Third Ear (Siodmak), 1971
Third Eye (s Cogswell), 1968
Third from the Sun (s Matheson), 1955
Third Level (s Finney), 1957
Thirst! (Maine), 1977
Thirst Quenchers (s Raphael), 1965
Thirteen O'Clock (s Kornbluth), 1970
13th Immortal (Silverberg), 1957
30-Day Wonder (Richard Wilson), 1960
Thirty-First of February (s Bond), 1949
Thirty-First of June (Priestley), 1961
Thirty-Four East (Coppel), 1974
This above All (Shiel), 1933
This Crowded Earth (Bloch), 1968
This Darkening Universe (Biggle), 1975
This Fortress World (Gunn), 1955
This Immortal (Zelazny), 1966
This Is the Way the World Begins (McIntosh), 1977
This Island Earth (R. Jones), 1952
This Knot of Life (Shiel), 1909
This Perfect Day (Levin), 1970
This Sentient Earth (T. Hoyle), 1979
This Strange Tomorrow (F. Long), 1966
This Time of Darkness (Hoover), 1980
This World Is Taboo (Leinster), 1961
Thorburn Enterprise (Rankine), 1977
Thorns (Silverberg), 1967
Those Gentle Voices (Effinger), 1976
Those Idiots from Earth (s Richard Wilson), 1957
Those Who Favor Fire (Randall), 1984
Those Who Watch (Silverberg), 1967
Thought Projector (s Keller), 1930
Thought-Reading Machine (Maurois, for), 1938
Thousand-Headed Man (Dent, as Robeson), 1964
Thousandstar (Anthony), 1980
Thousand-Year Plan (Asimov), 1955
1,000-Year Voyage (Fearn, as Statten), 1954
Three Eternals (s Binder), 1949
Three Eyes of Evil (s van Vogt), 1973
Three Faces of Time (F. Long), 1969
Three Faces of Time (Merwin), 1955
Three Hearts and Three Lions (P. Anderson), 1961
334 (Disch), 1972
Three Lines of Old French (s Merritt), 1939
Three, Seven, Ace (Tendryakov), 1973
Three Steps Spaceward (F. Long), 1963
Three Stigmata of Palmer Eldritch (Dick), 1965
Three Suns of Amara (Temple), 1962
Three Survived (Silverberg), 1969
Three Thousand Years (McClary), 1954
Three to Be Read (s Wylie), 1952
Three to Conquer (Russell), 1956
Three Worlds of Furturity (s St. Clair), 1964
Three Worlds to Conquer (P. Anderson), 1964
Three-Eyes (S. Gordon), 1975
Three-Legged Hootch Dancer (Resnick), 1983
Three-Ring Psychus (Shirley), 1980
Threshold of Eternity (Brunner), 1959

Thrice upon a Time (Hogan), 1980
Throne of Madness (Sucharitkul), 1983
Throne of Saturn (s S. Wright), 1949
Through a Glass, Clearly (s Asimov), 1967
Through Elegant Eyes (s Lafferty), 1983
Through Space and Time with Ferdinand Feghoot (s Bretnor, as Briarton), 1962
Through the Barrier (Fanthorpe, as Torro), 1963
Through the Eye of a Needle (Clement), 1978
Through the Eye of a Needle (Howells), 1907
Through the Eye of Time (T. Hoyle), 1977
Thru the Dragon Glass (s Merritt), 1932
Thunder and Roses (s Sturgeon), 1957
Thunder of Stars (Kippax, Morgan), 1968
Thunderhead (Laumer), 1968
Thunderworld (Z. Hughes), 1982
Thurb Revolution (Panshin), 1968
Thursday Toads (Lightner), 1971
Thuvia, Maid of Mars (E. Burroughs), 1920
Ticket That Exploded (W. Burroughs), 1962
Tide (Z. Hughes), 1974
Tide Went Out (Maine), 1958
Tides of Kregen (Bulmer, as Akers), 1976
Tides of Time (Brunner), 1984
Tiers series (Farmer)
Tiger by the Tail (s Nourse), 1961
Tiger Girl (s Hamilton), 1945 (?)
Tiger in the Stars (Z. Hughes), 1976
Tiger! Tiger! (Bester), 1956
Tiger! Tiger! (s Gunn), 1983
Tigers and Traitors (Verne, for), 1881
Tik–Tok (Sladek), 1983
Tiltangle (Mackelworth), 1970
Time series (L'Engle)
Time and Again (Finney), 1970
Time and Again (Simak), 1951
Time and Stars (s P. Anderson), 1964
Time and the Gods (Dunsany, fan), 1906
Time and the Hunter (Calvino, for), 1970
Time and the Riddle (s H. Fast), 1975
Time Appointed (Fearn, as Statten), 1954
Time Axis (Kuttner, C. Moore), 1965
Time Bender (Laumer), 1966
Time Bomb (Tucker), 1955
Time Bridge (Fearn, as Statten), 1952
Time Connection (Monteleone), 1976
Time Dissolver (Sohl), 1957
Time Dweller (s Moorcock), 1969
Time Enough for Love: The Lives of Lazarus Long (Heinlein), 1973
Time Factor (R. Gordon), 1964
Time for a Change (McIntosh), 1967
Time for the Stars (Heinlein), 1956
Time Gate (Jakes), 1972
Time Gladiator (Reynolds), 1966
Time in Advance (s Tenn), 1958
Time Is the Simplest Thing (Simak), 1961
Time Jumper (Greenleaf), 1981
Time Machine (Wells), 1895
Time Masters (Tucker), 1953
Time Mercenaries (High), 1968
Time Must Have a Stop (Huxley), 1944
Time of Changes (Silverberg), 1971
Time of the Crack (Tennant), 1973
Time of the Eye (s Ellison), 1974
Time of the Fourth Horseman (Yarbro), 1976
Time of the Great Freeze (Silverberg), 1964

Time of the Warlock (s Niven), 1984
Time: 110100 (Kelley), 1972
Time Out for Tomorrow (s Richard Wilson), 1962
Time Out of Joint (Dick), 1959
Time Out of Mind (Boulle, for), 1966
Time Out of Mind (Cowper), 1973
Time Patrolman (P. Anderson), 1983
Time Rogue (Kelley), 1970
Time Safari (s Drake), 1982
Time Shifters (Merwin), 1971
Time Slave (Norman), 1975
Time Snake and Superclown (King), 1976
Time Storm (Dickson), 1977
Time Story (S. Gordon), 1972
Time Stream (Taine), 1946
Time Terror (Dent, as Robeson), 1981
Time Thieves (Koontz), 1972
Time to Live (Rackham), 1966
Time to Teleport (Dickson), 1960
Time Traders (Norton), 1958
Time Transfer (s Sellings), 1956
Time Trap (Fearn, as Statten), 1952
Time Trap (Fisk), 1976
Time Trap (Kelley), 1977 (?)
Time Trap (Kuttner), 1976
Time Trap (Laumer), 1970
Time Trap (Phillips), 1949
Time Travel series (Norton)
Time Travelers Strictly Cash (s S. Robinson), 1981
Time Tunnel (Leinster), 1964
Time Twister (Petaja), 1968
Time Twisters (Holly), 1964
Time War (L. Carter), 1974
Time War series (Norton)
Time When (s McCaffrey), 1975
Time: X (s Tucker), 1955
Time-Echo (Fanthorpe, as Roberts), 1959
Time-Hoppers (Silverberg), 1967
Time-Jump (s Brunner), 1973
Timeless Ones (Fanthorpe, as Torro), 1963
Timeliner (Maine), 1955
Timeliner series (Meredith)
Time-Lockers (West), 1964
Timepiece (Ball), 1968
Timepit (Ball), 1971
Timepivot (Ball), 1970
Timequest (Nelson), 1985
Time's Dark Laughter (Kahn), 1982
Time's Last Gift (Farmer), 1972
Times Without Number (Brunner), 1962
Timescape (Benford), 1980
Timescoop (Brunner), 1969
Timeservers (Griffin), 1985
Timeslip! (Leinster), 1967
Timestop! (Farmer), 1970
Time-Swept City (Monteleone), 1977
Timetipping (s Dann), 1980
Timetracks (s Laumer), 1972
Timewinders (Kapp), 1980
Tin Angel (Goulart), 1973
Tin Men (Frayn), 1965
Tin Woodman (Bischoff), 1979
Tio sanger och Alltid Lady Macbeth (Lundwall), 1975
Titan (s P. Miller), 1952
Titan (Varley), 1979
Titan's Daughter (Blish), 1961

Tithonian Factor (s Cowper), 1984
Titus Alone (Peake, fan), 1959
Titus Groan (Peake, fan), 1946
To Challenge Chaos (Stableford), 1972
To Conquer Chaos (Brunner), 1964
To Control the Stars (Hoskins), 1977
To Die in Italbar (Zelazny), 1973
To Escape the Stars (Hoskins), 1978
To Here and the Easel (s Sturgeon), 1973
To Keep the Ship (Chandler), 1978
To Live Again (Silverberg), 1969
To Live Forever (Vance), 1956
To Open the Sky (s Silverberg), 1967
To Outer Space (Johns), 1957
To Outrun Doomsday (Bulmer), 1967
To Prime the Pump (Chandler), 1971
To Renew the Ages (R. Coulson), 1976
To Ride Pegasus (McCaffrey), 1973
To Sail the Century Sea (Edmondson), 1981
To Sing Strange Songs (s Bradbury), 1979
To the Dark Tower (F. Long, as L. Long), 1969
To the End of Time (Stapledon), 1953
To the End of Time (s R. Williams), 1960
To the Land of the Electric Angel (Rotsler), 1976
To the Stars series (H. Harrison)
To the Sun (Verne, for), 1878
To the Tombaugh Station (Tucker), 1960
To the Ultimate (Fearn, as Statten), 1952
To Venus! To Venus! (Wollheim, as Grinnell), 1970
To Walk the Night (Sloane), 1937
To Worlds Beyond (s Silverberg), 1965
To Worlds Unknown (Johns), 1960
To Your Scattered Bodies Go (Farmer), 1971
Today We Choose Faces (Zelazny), 1973
Tom O'Bedlam (Silverberg), 1985
Tom Paine Maru (L. Smith), 1984
Tomato Cain (s Kneale), 1949
Tomb (F. Wilson), 1984
Tombs of Kobol (Thurston), 1979
Tomorrow! (Wylie), 1954
Tomorrow and Tomorrow (Eldershaw), 1947
Tomorrow and Tomorrow (Hunter, as Collins), 1979
Tomorrow and Tomorrow (Kuttner and C. Moore, as Padgett), 1951
Tomorrow and Tomorrow and Tomorrow (Eldershaw), 1983
Tomorrow Came (s Cooper), 1963
Tomorrow City (M. Hughes), 1978
Tomorrow Is Too Far (J. White), 1971
Tomorrow Knight (Kurland), 1976
Tomorrow Lies in Ambush (s Shaw), 1973
Tomorrow Midnight (s Bradbury), 1966
Tomorrow Might Be Different (Reynolds), 1976
Tomorrow People (Merril), 1960
Tomorrow Plus X (Tucker), 1957
Tomorrow Revealed (Atkins), 1955
Tomorrow Sometimes Comes (Rayer), 1951
Tomorrow Testament (Longyear), 1983
Tomorrow Times Seven (s Pohl), 1959
Tomorrow's Gift (s Cooper), 1958
Tomorrow's Heritage (J. Coulson), 1981
Tomorrow's Son (Hoskins), 1977
Tomorrow's World (Hunter, as Collins), 1956
To-morrow's Yesterday (Gloag), 1932
Tongues of the Moon (Farmer), 1964
Tonight We Steal The Stars (Jakes), 1969
Tony Hale, Space Detective (Walters), 1973
Too Long a Sacrifice (Broxon), 1981

Too Many Magicians (Garrett), 1967
Topsy-Turvy Spring (Tendryakov, for), 1978
Torin series (Wilder)
Tormented City (Tubb, as Grey), 1953
Torrent of Faces (Blish, N. Knight), 1967
Tortured Planet (C. Lewis), 1958
Torturing Mr. Amberwell (s Disch), 1985
Total Eclipse (Brunner), 1974
Touch of Evil (Rackham), 1963
Touch of Evil (Tubb, as Maclean), 1959
Touch of Infinity (s Ellison), 1960
Touch of Infinity (s H. Fast), 1973
Touch of Strange (s Sturgeon), 1958
Tower of Glass (Silverberg), 1970
Tower of Rizwan (Rankine, as Mason), 1968
Tower of the Edge of Time (L. Carter), 1968
Tower of the Medusa (L. Carter), 1969
Tower of Zanid (de Camp), 1958
Towers of Toron (Delany), 1964
Towers of Utopia (Reynolds), 1975
Toymaker (s R. Jones), 1951
Toyman (Tubb), 1969
Trace of Dreams (Eklund), 1972
Trace of Memory (Laumer), 1963
Trader to the Stars (s P. Anderson), 1964
Trail of the White Indians (Verrill), 1920
Traitor to the Living (Farmer), 1973
Tramontane (Petaja), 1966
Trample an Empire Down (Reynolds), 1978
Transatlantic Tunnel, Hurrah! (H. Harrison), 1972
Transcendent Man (Sohl), 1953
Transfer to Yesterday (Haiblum), 1973
Transfigurations (Bishop), 1979
Transfinite Man (Kapp), 1964
Transformation of Miss Mavis Ming (Moorcock), 1977
Transformer (M. Foster), 1983
Transit (Cooper), 1964
Transit to Scorpio (Bulmer, as Akers), 1972
Transmaniacon (Shirley), 1979
Transmigration (McIntosh), 1970
Transmigration of Timothy Archer (Dick), 1982
Transmission Error (Kurland), 1970
Transmitters (Broderick), 1984
Transmutations (s Panshin), 1982
Transvection Machine (Hoch), 1971
Trantorian Empire series (Asimov)
Trapped in Space (Williamson), 1968
Travails of Jane Saint (Saxton), 1981
Travel Tales of Mr. Joseph Jorkens (Dunsany, fan), 1931
Traveler from Altruria (Howells), 1894
Traveler in Black (Brunner), 1971
Treasure in the Heart of the Maze (J. Carr), 1985
Treasure of Tau Ceti (Rackham), 1969
Treasures of Morrow (Hoover), 1976
Tree and Leaf (Tolkien, fan), 1964
Tree Lord of Imeten (Purdom), 1966
Tree of Swords and Jewels (Cherryh), 1983
Trek to Madworld (Goldin), 1979
Trembling World (Fearn, as Del Martia), 1949
Triad (Rohmer), 1981
Triad (van Vogt), 1959
Trial of Terra (Williamson), 1962
Trial of the Cloven Foot (Verrill), 1918
Triangle (Asimov), 1961
Tribesmen of Gor (Norman), 1976
Trick Top Hat (Robert Anton Wilson), 1980

Trillions (Fisk), 1971
Trip Around the World in a Flying Machine (Verne, for), 1887
Trip to Mars (Ash), 1909
Triplanetary (E.E. Smith), 1948
Triple Détente (Anthony), 1974
Triple World (Fanthorpe), 1965
Triplicity (Disch), 1980
Tripods series (Christopher)
Triton (Delany), 1976
Triton (Hubbard), 1949
Triumph (Wylie), 1963
Triumph of Time (Blish), 1958
Triune Man (Lupoff), 1976
Trojan Orbit (Reynolds), 1985
Tron (Daley), 1982
Tropical Madness (Witkiewicz, for), 1972
Trouble on Project Ceres (T. White), 1971
Trouble on Titan (Nourse), 1954
Trouble Twisters (s P. Anderson), 1966
Trouble with Lichen (Wyndham), 1960
Trouble with Treaties (s MacLean), 1975
Trouble with Tycho (Simak), 1961
Trouble with You Earth People (s MacLean), 1980
Troubled Star (George O. Smith), 1957
Troyana (Meek), 1962
True Names (V. Vinge), 1981
Trullion: Alastor 2262 (Vance), 1973
Trumps of Doom (Zelazny), 1985
Tsaddik of the Seven Wonders (Haiblum), 1971
Tschai series (Vance)
Tsunami (Kilian), 1983
Tunc (Durrell), 1968
Tunnel (Kellermann, for), 1915
Tunnel in the Sky (Heinlein), 1955
Tunnel Terror (Dent, as Robeson), 1979
Tunnel Through the Deeps (H. Harrison), 1972
Tunnel Through Time (del Rey, Fairman), 1966
Tunnel Through Time (Leinster), 1966
Turn Left at Thursday (s Pohl), 1961
Turning On (s D. Knight), 1966
Turning Wheel (s Dick), 1977
Twelve Fair Kingdoms (Elgin), 1981
Twelve Stories and a Dream (s Wells), 1903
21st Century Sub (F. Herbert), 1956
Twenty-Second Century (s Christopher), 1954
Twenty Thousand Leagues Under the Sea (Verne, for), 1872
Twice in Time (Wellman), 1957
Twice Twenty Two (s Bradbury), 1966
Twice upon a Time (Fontenay), 1958
Twilight Ancestor (s Fanthorpe), 1963
Twilight at the Well of Souls (Chalker), 1980
Twilight Journey (Davies), 1967
Twilght Man (Moorcock), 1966
Twilight of Briareus (Cowper), 1974
Twilight of the City (Platt), 1977
Twilight River (Eklund), 1979
Twilight World (P. Anderson), 1961
Twilight Zone series (s Serling)
Twin of the Amazon (Fearn), 1954
Twin Planets (High), 1967
Twin Worlds (s N. Jones), 1967
Twisted Men (s van Vogt), 1964
Twists in Time (s Leinster), 1960
Two Dozen Dragon Eggs (s Wollheim), 1969
Two Faces of Tomorrow (Hogan), 1979
Two Hawks from Earth (Farmer), 1979

Two Hours to Doom (George, as Bryant), 1958
Two Hundred Million A.D. (van Vogt), 1964
200 Years to Christmas (McIntosh), 1961
Two of Them (Russ), 1978
Two Planets (Lasswitz, for), 1971
Two Tales and Eight Tomorrows (s H. Harrison), 1965
2018 (Lundwall), 1975
2001: A Space Odyssey (Clarke), 1968
2010: Odyssey Two (Clarke), 1982
2000 Years On (Fearn, as Statten), 1950
Two to Conquer (Bradley), 1980
Two Towers (Tolkien, fan), 1955
Two Worlds (P. Anderson), 1978
Two-Eyes (S. Gordon), 1974
Two-Timers (Shaw), 1968
Typewriter in the Sky (Hubbard), 1951
Typhon Intervention (Rankine, as Mason), 1981
Tyranopolis (van Vogt), 1977
Tyrant of Hades (Kapp), 1982
Tyrant of Time (s Eshbach), 1955

U.F.O. 517 (Fanthorpe, as Fane), 1966
Ubik (Dick), 1969
Ugly Swans (Strugatsky, for), 1978
Ulcer Culture (Bulmer), 1969
Uller Uprising (Piper), 1982
Ultimate Adventure (Hubbard), 1970
Ultimate Enemy (s Saberhagen), 1979
Ultimate Jungle (Coney), 1979
Ultimate Man (Fanthorpe, as Muller), 1961
Ultimate Weapon (Campbell), 1966
Ultimate World (Gernsback), 1971
Ultimatum (Rohmer), 1973
Ultimatum in 2050 A.D. (Sharkey), 1965
Ultimax Man (Laumer), 1978
Ultra Spectrum (Fearn, as Statten), 1953
Unaccompanied Sonata (s Card), 1981
Unauthorized Autobiographies (s Resnick), 1984
Unborn Tomorrow (s Cooper), 1971
Uncanny Phenomena on Omega 11 (Braun, for), 1974
Uncensored Man (Sellings), 1964
Uncertain Midnight (Cooper), 1958
Uncharted Seas (Wheatley), 1938
Uncharted Stars (Norton), 1969
Uncle Abner's Legacy (Verrill), 1915
Unconfined (Fanthorpe), 1965
Undefeated (s Laumer), 1974
Under a Calculating Star (Morressy), 1975
Under Compulsion (s Disch), 1968
Under Heaven's Bridge (Bishop, Watson), 1981
Under Old Earth and Other Explorations (s Cordwainer Smith), 1970
Under Pressure (F. Herbert), 1974
Under the Green Star (L. Carter)
Under the Triple Suns (Coblentz), 1955
Under Twin Suns (Offutt, as Cleve), 1982
Undercover Aliens (van Vogt), 1976
Underkill (J. White), 1979
Underlay (Malzberg), 1974
Underpeople (Cordwainer Smith), 1968
Undersea City (Pohl, Williamson), 1958
Undersea Fleet (Pohl, Williamson), 1956
Undersea Quest (Pohl, Williamson), 1954
Undying Fire (Pratt), 1953
Unearth People (Neville), 1964
Unearthly Neighbors (Oliver), 1960
Unending Night (George H. Smith), 1964

Unexpected Dimension (s Budrys), 1960
Unfamiliar Territory (s Silverberg), 1973
Unfinished Tales of Númenór and Middle-Earth (Tolkien, fan), 1980
Unforsaken Hiero (Lanier), 1983
Unicorn Girl (Kurland), 1969
Unicorn Variations (s Zelazny), 1983
Uninhibited (Morgan), 1961
Uninvited (Fanthorpe, as Muller), 1961
United Planets Organization series (Reynolds)
Universe (s Heinlein), 1951
Universe Against Her (Schmitz), 1964
Universe Between (Nourse), 1965
Universe Day (Malzberg, as O'Donnell), 1971
Universe Maker (van Vogt), 1953
Universe Next Door (Robert Anton Wilson), 1979
Unknown Danger (Leinster), 1969
Unknown Destiny (Fanthorpe, as Fane), 1964
Unknown Tomorrow (Le Queux), 1910
Unlimited Dream Company (Ballard), 1979
Un-Man (s P. Anderson), 1962
Unorthodox Engineers (Kapp), 1979
Unpleasant Profession of Jonathan Hoag (s Heinlein), 1959
Unpopular Planet (Evelyn E. Smtih), 1975
Unquiet Corpse (Sloane), 1946
Unreasoning Mask (Farmer), 1981
Unseen (Fanthorpe, as Barton), 1964
Unsleeping Eye (Compton), 1974
Unteleported Man (Dick), 1966
Unto the Last Generation (J. Coulson),1975
Unto Zeor, Forever (Lichtenberg), 1978
Untouched by Human Hands (s Sheckley), 1954
Unwise Child (Garrett), 1962
Up the Line (Silverberg), 1969
Up the Walls of the World (Tiptree), 1978
Up to the Sky in Ships (s Chandler), 1982
Uplift series (Brin)
Upside Downsidc (Goulart), 1982
Uranium 235 (Fanthorpe, as Muller), 1962
Ursus of Ultima Thule (Davidson), 1973
Usual Lunacy (Compton), 1978
Utofant (Braun, for), 1981
Utopia 14 (Vonnegut), 1954
Utopia Hunters (Sucharitkul), 1984
Utopia minus X (R. Gordon), 1966
Utopia 3 (Effinger), 1980
Utopia 239 (R. Gordon), 1955

Vacation in Space (Kelley), 1979
Valdar the Oft-Born (Griffith), 1895
Vale of the Sad Banana (Lymington), 1984
Valencies (Broderick), 1983
Valentina (Delaney), 1984
Valentine Pontifex (Silverberg), 1983
Valis series (Dick)
Valley Beyond Time (s Silverberg), 1973
Valley of Creation (Hamilton), 1964
Valley of Pretenders (Fearn, as Clive), 1942
Valley of Shadows (Evelyn E. Smith, as Lyons), 1968
Valley of the Flame (Kuttner, C. Moore), 1964
Valley Where Time Stood Still (L. Carter), 1974
Vampire Tapestry (Charnas), 1980
Van Rijn, Trader series (P. Anderson)
Vandals of the Void (Vance), 1953
Vaneglory (Turner), 1981
Vanguard from Alpha (Aldiss), 1959
Vanished Jet (Blish), 1968

Vanisher (Dent, as Robeson), 1970
Var the Stick (Anthony), 1972
Variable Man (s Dick), 1957
Vassals of Venus (Bulmer, as Kent), 1954
Vault of the Ages (P. Anderson), 1952
Vazkor, Son of Vazkor (Lee), 1978
Vector Analysis (Jack C. Haldeman), 1978
Vector for Seven (Saxton), 1971
Vectors (s Sheffield), 1980
Veiled Lady (Goulart, as Shawn), 1973
Veils of Azlaroc (Saberhagen), 1978
Velvet Comet series (Resnick)
Venetian Court (Harness), 1984
Vengeance of Gwa (S. Wright, as Wingrave), 1935
Vengeance of Siva (Fanthorpe, as Muller), 1962
Vengeance of the Dancing Gods (Chalker), 1985
Venom of Argus (Cooper, as Avery), 1976
Venom Seekers (Berry), 1953
Venomous Serpent (Ball), 1974
Venturer 12 series (Kippax, Morgan)
Venus series (E. Burroughs)
Venus Belt (L. Smith), 1981
Venus Equilateral (s George O. Smith), 1947
Venus Hunters (s Ballard), 1980
Venus of Dreams (Sargent), 1986
Venus on the Half-Shell (Farmer, as Trout), 1975
Venus Plus X (Sturgeon), 1960
Venus Venture (Fanthorpe, as Muller), 1961
Venusian Adventure (Tubb), 1953
Vermilion Sands (s Ballard), 1971
Vertigo (Shaw), 1978
Veruchia (Tubb), 1973
Very Private Life (Frayn), 1968
Very Slow Time Machine (s Watson), 1979
Vestiges of Time (Meredith), 1978
Viagens Interplanetarias series (de Camp)
Vicinity Cluster (Anthony), 1979
Victory for Kregen (Bulmer, as Akers), 1980
Victory on Janus (Norton), 1966
View from the Stars (s W. Miller), 1965
Vigilante—21st Century (R. Williams), 1967
Village in the Treetops (Verne, for), 1964
Village of the Damned (Wyndham), 1960
Villiers, Anthony series (Panshin)
Violet Apple (Lindsay), 1976
Virgin Planet (P. Anderson), 1959
Viriconium series (M. Harrison)
Virility Gene (Bulmer, as Zetford), 1975
Viscous Circle (Anthony), 1982
Visible Man (s Dozois), 1977
Vision of Tarot (Anthony), 1980
Vision of the Damned (s Fanthorpe), 1965
Visions and Venturers (s Sturgeon), 1978
Visions of Nowhere (Rotsler, as Arrow), 1976
Visitors (Simak), 1980
Vizier's Second Daughter (R. Young), 1985
Voice Commands (Fearn, as Clive), 1942
Voice of the Dolphins (s Szilard), 1961
Voice Out of Ramah (Killough), 1979
Voices in the Dark (s Cooper), 1960
Voices of Mars (P. Moore), 1957
Voices of Time (s Ballard), 1962
Void Beyond (s R. Williams), 1958
Void Captain's Tale (Spinrad), 1983
Volcano (Fisk), 1980
Volcano Ogre (L. Carter), 1976

Volkhavaar (Lee), 1977
Volteface (Adlard), 1972
Von Bek Family series (Moorcock)
Voodoo Hell Drums (s Fanthorpe, as Thorpe), 1961
Voodoo Planet (Norton, as North), 1959
Voorloper (Norton), 1981
VOR (Blish), 1958
Vornan-19 (Silverberg), 1970
Vort Programme (Rankine), 1979
Vortex Blaster (E.E. Smith), 1960
Voyage from Yesteryear (Hogan), 1982
Voyage of the Eighth Mind (Lymington), 1980
Voyage of the Space Beagle (van Vogt), 1950
Voyage to Arcturus (Lindsay), 1920
Voyage to Dari (I. Wallace), 1974
Voyage to the Bottom of the Sea (R. Jones), 1965
Voyage to the Bottom of the Sea (Sturgeon), 1961
Voyage to the City of the Dead (A. Foster), 1984
Voyage to the Island of the Articoles (Maurois, for), 1928
Voyage to Venus (C. Lewis), 1953
Voyager in Night (Cherryh), 1984
Voyagers (Bova), 1981
Voyages and Adventures of Captain Hatteras (Verne, for), 1974
Vulcan! (Sky), 1978
Vulcan's Hammer (Dick), 1960

Wagered World (Janifer), 1969
Wailing Asteroid (Leinster), 1960
Waiting for the End of the World (Harding), 1983
Waiting World (Fanthorpe), 1958
Waking of the Stone (Lymington), 1978
Waldo (Heinlein), 1950
Waldo, Genius in Orbit (Heinlein), 1958
Walk Through To-morrow (Fanthorpe, as Zeigfried), 1962
Walk to the End of the World (Charnas), 1974
Walk Up the Sky (R. Williams), 1962
Walkers on the Sky (Lake), 1976
Walking Shadow (s Fanthorpe, as Fane), 1964
Walking Shadow (Stableford), 1979
Wall (Tubb, as Grey), 1953
Wall Around a Star (Pohl, Williamson), 1983
Wall Around the World (s Cogswell), 1962
Wall of Years (Stephenson), 1979
Walpurgis III (Resnick), 1982
Wanderer (Leiber), 1964
Wanderer in Space (P. Moore), 1961
Wanderer of Space (Fearn, as Statten), 1950
Wanderers of Time (s Wyndham, as Beynon), 1973
Wandering Variables (Trimble), 1972
Wandl the Invader (Cummings), 1961
Wanted (s Naha), 1980
Wanting Factor (DeWeese), 1980
Wanting Seed (Burgess), 1962
War Against the Rull (van Vogt), 1959
War for the Lot (Lanier), 1969
War Games (Stableford), 1981
War Games of Zelos (Cooper, as Avery), 1975
War Hound and the World's Pain (Moorcock), 1981
War in the Air (Wells), 1908
War of Dreams (A. Carter), 1974
War of 1938 (S. Wright), 1936
War of Omission (O'Donnell), 1982
War of Shadows (Chalker), 1979
War of the Gods (Yermakov), 1982
War of the Wing-Men (P. Anderson), 1958
War of the Worlds (Wells), 1898

War of Two Worlds (P. Anderson), 1959
War with the Gizmos (Leinster), 1958
War with the Newts (Capek, for), 1937
War with the Robots (s H. Harrison), 1962
Wargames (Bischoff), 1983
Warlock (Koontz), 1972
Warlock Enraged (Stasheff), 1985
Warlock in Spite of Himself (Stasheff), 1969
Warlock of Rhada (Coppel, as Gilman), 1985
Warlock Unlocked (Stasheff), 1982
Warlock's Gift (Mayhar), 1982
Warlord of Kor (T. Carr), 1963
Warlord of the Air (Moorcock), 1971
Warlords of Mars (E. Burroughs), 1919
Warlords of Xuma (Lake), 1983
Warlord's World (Anvil), 1975
Warm Worlds and Otherwise (s Tiptree), 1975
Warrior of Llarn (Fox), 1964
Warrior of Mars (Fearn), 1950
Warrior of Mars (Moorcock, as Bradbury), 1981
Warrior of Scorpio (Bulmer, as Akers), 1973
Warrior of World's End (L. Carter), 1974
Warriors of Dawn (M. Foster), 1975
Warriors of Day (Blish), 1953
Warriors of Mars (Moorcock, as Bradbury), 1965
Wasp (Russell), 1957
Watch Below (J. White), 1966
Watchers (Calvino, for), 1971
Watchers of the Dark (Biggle), 1966
Watchers of the Forest (s Fanthorpe), 1958
Watching World (Fanthorpe), 1966
Watchstar (Sargent), 1980
Water of the Wondrous Isles (W. Morris, fan), 1897
Water of Thought (Saberhagen), 1965
Water Witch (Felice, Willis), 1982
Waters of Centaurus (R. Brown), 1970
Waters of Lethe (Keller), 1937
Wave Rider (s Schenck), 1980
Wave Without a Shore (Cherryh), 1981
Waves (M. Foster), 1980
Way Back (Chandler), 1976
Way Home (s Sturgeon), 1955
Way of the Gods (s Kuttner), 1954
Way Station (Simak), 1963
We (Zamyatin, for), 1924
We All Died at Breakaway Station (Meredith), 1969
We Can Build You (Dick), 1972
We Claim These Stars (P. Anderson), 1959
We, The Venusians (Rackham), 1965
We Who Are About to... (Russ), 1977
Wealth of the Void (Fearn, as Statten), 1954
Weapon from Beyond (Hamilton), 1967
Weapon Makers (van Vogt), 1947
Weapon Shop series (van Vogt)
Weathermakers (Bova), 1967
Weathermonger (Dickinson), 1968
Web (Wyndham), 1979
Web Between the Worlds (Sheffield), 1979
Web of Darkness (Bradley), 1984
Web of Easter Island (Wandrei), 1948
Web of Everywhere (Brunner), 1974
Web of Light (Bradley), 1982
Web of Sand (Tubb), 1979
Web of the Chozen (Chalker), 1978
Web of the Magi (s Cowper), 1980
Web of Time (Harding), 1979

Weeping May Tarry (del Rey, R. Jones), 1978
Weeping Sky (Harding), 1977
Weigher of Souls (Maurois, for), 1963
Weird Tales of Terror and Detection (s Heard), 1946
Weisman Experiment (Rankine), 1969
Welcome, Chaos (Wilhelm), 1983
Welcome to Mars (Blish), 1967
Welcome to the Monkey House (s Vonnegut), 1968
Well at the World's End (W. Morris, fan), 1896
Well of Darkness (Garrett), 1983
Well of Shiuan (Cherryh), 1978
Well of the Worlds (Kuttner and C. Moore as Padgett), 1953
Well World series (Chalker)
Werewolf among Us (Koontz), 1973
Werewolf at Large (s Fanthorpe), 1960
Werewolf Principle (Simak), 1967
Werewolves of Kregen (Bulmer, as Akers), 1985
West, Julian series (Reynolds)
West of Eden (H. Harrison), 1984
West of Honor (Pournelle), 1976
West of the Sun (Pangborn), 1953
Westminster Disaster (F. and G. Hoyle), 1978
Whale of the Victoria Cross (Boulle, for), 1983
What Did I Do Tomorrow? (Davies), 1972
What Dreams May Come (Beresford), 1941
What Entropy Means to Me (Effinger), 1972
What Happened to the Corbetts (Shute), 1939
What Mad Oracle? (Scortia), 1961
What Mad Universe (F. Brown), 1949
What Rough Beast (Watkins), 1980
What Strange Stars and Skies (s Davidson), 1965
What's Become of Screwloose? (s Goulart), 1971
What's It Like Out There (s Hamilton), 1974
Wheel in Space (P. Moore), 1956
Wheel of Stars (Norton), 1983
Wheelie in the Stars (Fisk), 1976
Wheels of If (s de Camp), 1948
Wheels Within Wheels (F. Wilson), 1979
Wheelworld (H. Harrison), 1981
When Chaugnar Walks (s F. Long), 1978
When Harlie Was One (Gerrold), 1972
When Smuts Goes (Keppel-Jones), 1947
When the Birds Fly South (Coblentz), 1945
When the Dream Dies (Chandler), 1981
When the Green Star Calls (L. Carter), 1973
When the Kissing Had to Stop (FitzGibbon), 1960
When the Moon Ran Wild (Verrill, as Ainsbury), 1962
When the Sky Burned (Bova), 1973
When the Sleeper Wakes (Wells), 1899
When the Star Kings Die (Jakes), 1967
When the Waker Sleeps (Goulart), 1975
When the World Shook (Haggard), 1919
When They Come from Space (Clifton), 1962
When Trouble Beckons (McQuay), 1981
When Two Worlds Meet (s R. Williams), 1970
When Worlds Collide (Wylie), 1933
Whenabouts of Burr (Kurland), 1975
Where Eternity Ends (s Binder), 1950
Where No Stars Guide (Kippax), 1975
Where No Sun Shines (Kelley), 1979
Where the Evil Dwells (Simak), 1982
Where the Sweet Birds Sang (Wilhelm), 1976
Where Time Winds Blow (Holdstock), 1982
Whetted Bronze (Bulmer, as Norvil), 1978
Whiff of Madness (Goulart), 1976
Whipping Star (F. Herbert), 1970

Whirligig of Time (Biggle), 1979
Whirlpool of Stars (Bulmer, as Zetford), 1974
Whirlwind of Death (s Fanthorpe), 1960
Whisker of Hercules (Dent, as Robeson), 1981
Whisper from the Stars (Sutton), 1970
White Death (Sargent), 1980
White Dragon (McCaffrey), 1978
White Fang Goes Dingo (s Disch), 1971
White Light (Rucker), 1980
White Lily (Taine), 1966
White Lotus (Hersey), 1965
White Mountains (Christopher), 1967
White Plague (F. Herbert), 1982
White Rose (Cook), 1985
White Widows (Merwin), 1953
Who? (Budrys), 1958
Who Can Replace a Man? (s Aldiss), 1966
Who Censored Roger Rabbit? (Wolf), 1981
Who Goes Here? (Shaw), 1977
Who Goes There? (s Campbell), 1948
Who Is Lewis Pindar? (Davies), 1966
Who Made Stevie Crye? (Bishop), 1984
...Who Needs Enemies? (s A. Foster), 1984
Who Needs Men? (Cooper), 1972
Whole Man (Brunner), 1964
Why Call Them Back From Heaven? (Simak), 1967
Why I Want to Fuck Ronald Reagan (s Ballard), 1968
Wicked Cyborg (Goulart), 1978
Widow's Son (Robert Anton Wilson), 1985
Wild Alien Tamer (Resnick), 1983
Wild Boys (W. Burroughs), 1971
Wild Country (Ing), 1985
Wild Jack (Christopher), 1974
Wild Seed (O. Butler), 1980
Wild Shore (K. Robinson), 1984
Wild Talent (Tucker), 1954
Wildeblood's Empire (Stableford), 1977
Wildings of Westron (Lake), 1977
Wildsmith (Goulart), 1972
Wilk are among Us (Haiblum), 1975
Wind series (Meluch)
Wind Child (Meluch), 1982
Wind Dancers (Meluch), 1981
Wind from a Burning Woman (s Bear), 1983
Wind from Nowhere (Ballard), 1962
Wind from the Abyss (J. Morris), 1978
Wind from the North (O'Neill), 1934
Wind from the Sun (s Clarke), 1972
Wind in the Door (L'Engle), 1973
Wind of Liberty (Bulmer), 1962
Wind Whales of Ishmael (Farmer), 1971
Windhaven (Martin, Tuttle), 1981
Windhover Tapes series (Norwood)
Windows (Compton), 1979
Windows of Forever (Morressy), 1975
Winds of Altair (Bova), 1973
Winds of Change (s Asimov), 1983
Winds of Gath (Tubb), 1967
Winds of Limbo (Moorcock), 1969
Winds of Time (Oliver), 1957
Wind's Twelve Quarters (s Le Guin), 1975
Wine of the Dreamers (MacDonald), 1951
Winged Man (Hull, van Vogt), 1966
Winners (s P. Anderson), 1981
Winter amid the Ice (Verne, for), 1890
Winter of the World (P. Anderson), 1975

Winter's Children (Coney), 1974
Winter's Tale (Helprin), 1983
Winter's Youth (Gloag), 1934
Wisdom's Daughter (Haggard), 1923
Witch (Lindsay), 1976
Witch of Kregen (Bulmer, as Akers), 1985
Witch of the Dark Gate (Jakes), 1972
Witch Queen of Lochlann (George H. Smith), 1969
Witch Tree (F. Long, as L. Long), 1971
Witchdame (Sky), 1985
Witches of Karres (Schmitz), 1966
Witchfinder series (Ball)
Witchfinder (s S. Wright), 1945
Witching Hour (s Gunn), 1970
With a Finger in My I (s Gerrold), 1972
With a Strange Device (Russell), 1964
With a Tangled Skein (Anthony), 1985
With Friends Like These (s A. Foster), 1977
With Mercy Toward None (Cook), 1985
Without Sorcery (s Sturgeon), 1948
Witling (V. Vinge), 1976
Wizard (Varley), 1980
Wizard in Bedlam (Stasheff), 1979
Wizard of Anharitte (Kapp), 1975
Wizard of Linn (van Vogt), 1962
Wizard of Starship Poseidon (Bulmer), 1963
Wizard of Venus (s E. Burroughs), 1970
Wizards of Senchuria (Bulmer), 1969
Wolf Hollow Bubbles (s Keller), 1934 (?)
Wolfbane (Kornbluth, Pohl), 1959
Wolfhead (Harness), 1978
Wolfling (Dickson), 1969
Wolf's Long Howl (s Waterloo), 1899
Wolfshead (Norton), 1977
Wolves of Memory (Effinger), 1981
Woman a Day (Farmer), 1960
Woman from Another Planet (F. Long), 1960
Woman on the Edge of Time (Piercy), 1976
Woman Who Loved the Moon (s Lynn), 1981
Wonder (Beresford), 1917
Wonder Effect (s Kornbluth and Pohl), 1962
Wonder Stick (Coblentz), 1929
Wonder War (Janifer), 1964
Wonderbolt (Capon), 1955
Wonderful Adventures of Phra the Phoenician (Arnold), 1890
Wonderworlds (s Nolan), 1977
Wood Beyond the World (W. Morris, fan), 1894
Wooden Star (s Tenn), 1968
Woodrow Wilson Dime (Finney), 1968
Word for World Is Forest (Le Guin), 1976
World Aflame (Bulmer), 1954
World Aflame (Tubb, as Kern), 1974
World and Thorinn (D. Knight), 1981
World Asunder (I. Wallace), 1976
World at Bay (Capon), 1953
World at Bay (Tubb), 1954
World Below (S. Wright), 1929
World Between (Spinrad), 1979
World Between (s Vance), 1965
World Called Solitude (Goldin), 1981
World Ends in Hickory Hollow (Mayhar), 1985
World Enough and Time (Kahn), 1980
World Grabbers (Fairman), 1964
World in Peril (Chilton), 1960
World in Winter (Christopher), 1962
World Inside (Silverberg), 1971

World Jones Made (Dick), 1956
World Masters (Griffith), 1903
World Menders (Biggle), 1971
World of A (van Vogt), 1948
World of a Thousand Colors (s Silverberg), 1982
World of Chance (Dick), 1956
World of Difference (Cooper), 1980
World of If (Phillips), 1951
World of Mists (P. Moore), 1956
World of Null-A (van Vogt), 1969
World of Ptavvs (Niven), 1966
World of Shadows (Harding), 1975
World of the Future (Fanthorpe, as Zeigfried), 1964
World of the Gods (Fanthorpe, as Torro), 1960
World of the Masterminds (R. Williams), 1960
World of the Starwolves (Hamilton), 1968
World of Tiers series (Farmer)
World of Tomorrow (Fanthorpe, as Zeigfreid), 1963
World of Women (Beresford), 1913
World Out of Mind (McIntosh), 1953
World Out of Time (Niven), 1976
World Peril of 1910 (Griffith), 1907
World Set Free (Wells), 1914
World Shuffler (Laumer), 1970
World Swappers (Brunner), 1959
World That Never Was (Fanthorpe, as Zeigfried), 1963
World We Live In (Capek, for), 1933
World Without Children (D. Knight), 1970
World Without End (Joe Haldeman), 1979
World Without Men (Maine), 1958
World Without Stars (P. Anderson), 1966
World Wreckers (Bradley), 1971
Worlds series (Joe Haldeman)
Worlds Apart (Cowper), 1974
Worlds Apart (Joe Haldeman), 1983
Worlds Apart (Kelley), 1979
Worlds Apart (McIntosh), 1958
World's End series (L. Carter)
World's End (J. Vinge), 1984
World's Fair Goblin (Dent, as Robeson), 1969
World's Fair 1992 (Silverberg), 1970
Worlds for the Taking (Bulmer), 1966
Worlds of Eclos (R. Gordon), 1961
Worlds of George O. (s George O. Smith), 1982
Worlds of the Imperium (Laumer), 1962
Worlds of the Wall (MacApp), 1969
Worlds of Wonder (s Johns), 1962
Worlds of Wonder (Stapledon), 1949
Worlds to Conquer (Fearn, as Statten), 1952
Worlds Within (Phillips), 1950
Worlds Without End (s Simak), 1964
Worm Ouroboros (Eddison, fan), 1922
Worse Than Murder (Duncan), 1954
Worse Things Waiting (s Wellman), 1973
Worthing Chronicle (Card), 1983
Wounded Sky (Duane), 1983
Wrath of Grapes (Wibberley), 1955
Wrath of Khan (McIntyre), 1982
Wreath of Stars (Shaw), 1976
Wrecks of Time (Moorcock), 1967
Wright, Jack series (Senarens)
Wrinkle in the Skin (Christopher), 1965
Wrinkle in Time (L'Engle), 1962
Wrong End of Time (Brunner), 1971
Wyoming Sun (s Bryant), 1980
Wyst: Alastor 1716 (Vance), 1978

X Factor (Norton), 1965
X-Machine (Fanthorpe, as Muller), 1962
Xanth series (Anthony)
Xanthe and the Robots (MacLeod), 1977
Xeno (D. Jones), 1979
Xenogenesis (s deFord), 1969
Xuma series (Lake)

Yaleen series (Watson)
Yank at Valhalla (Hamilton), 1973
Year Dot (Lymington), 1972
Year of the Cloud (T. Thomas, Wilhelm), 1970
Year of the Comet (Christopher), 1955
Year of the Painted World (Mackelworth), 1975
Year of the Quiet Sun (Tucker), 1970
Year 2018! (Blish), 1957
Year When Stardust Fell (R. Jones), 1958
Years of the City (Pohl), 1984
Yellow Cloud (Dent, as Robeson), 1971
Yellow Danger (Shiel), 1898
Yellow Fraction (R. Gordon), 1969
Yellow God (Haggard), 1908
Yellow Peril (Shiel), 1929
Yellow Wave (Shiel), 1905
Yesterday's Children (Gerrold), 1972
Yesterday's Men (Turner), 1983
Ylana of Callisto (L. Carter), 1977
Yoke of Shen (Offutt, as Cleve), 1983
Yonder (s Beaumont), 1958
You Remember Me! (Fisk), 1984
You Sane Men (Janifer), 1965
You Shall Know Them (Vercors, for), 1953
You Will Never Be The Same (s Cordwainer Smith), 1963
Young Men Are Coming! (Shiel), 1937
Young Warriors (Thurston), 1980
You're All Alone (s Leiber), 1972
Youth Madness (Coblentz), 1944 (?)

Z Formations (Fearn, as Shaw), 1953
Z-Sting (I. Wallace), 1978
Zandra series (Rotsler)
Zanthar series (R. Williams)
Zanzibar Cat (s Russ), 1983
Zap Gun (Dick), 1967
Zarathustra Refugee Planet series (Brunner)
Zarkon series (L. Carter)
Zelde M'Tana (Busby), 1980
Zen Gun (Bayley), 1983
Zenya (Tubb), 1974
Zero Hour (Fearn, as Statten), 1953
Zero Minus X (Fanthorpe, as Zeigfried), 1962
Zero Stone series (Norton)
Zhorani (Bulmer, as Maras), 1953
Ziax II series (Morressy)
Zone Null (Franke, for), 1974

NOTES
ON
ADVISERS
AND
CONTRIBUTORS

ABOULAFIA, Mitchell. Associate Professor of Philosophy and the Humanities, University of Houston, Clear Lake City. Author of *The Self-Winding Circle: A Study of Hegel's System*, 1982, and *The Mediating Self*, forthcoming. **Essay:** Robert F. Young.

ALDISS, Brian. See his own entry.

ARBUR, Rosemarie. Associate Professor of English, Lehigh University, Bethlehem, Pennsylvania. Author of *Leigh Brackett, Marion Zimmer Bradley, Anne McCaffrey: A Primary and Secondary Bibliography*, 1982, *Computer-Assisted Preparation of Texts*, 1982, *Marion Zimmer Bradley: A Reader's Guide*, 1985, and of articles in journals and collections. **Essays:** Leigh Brackett; Marion Zimmer Bradley.

BACIG, Thomas D. Professor of English, University of Minnesota, Duluth; Editor of *Minnesota English Newsletter*. Author of articles in *Arizona English Bulletin, Minnesota English Journal*, and *Choice*. Editor of *Newman Annual*, 1961. **Essay:** Norman Spinrad.

BARBOUR, Douglas. Professor of English, University of Alberta, Edmonton; Poetry Editor, *Canadian Forum*. Author of several books of poetry–the most recent being *Visible Visions: The Selected Poems*, 1984–and *Worlds Out of Words: The SF Novels of Samuel R. Delany*, 1979, and articles on Delany, Tolkien, and Zelazny. **Essays:** Brian Aldiss; Edward Bryant; Samuel R. Delany; Carol Emshwiller; Phyllis Gotlieb; Barry N. Malzberg; Keith Roberts; Chelsea Quinn Yarbro.

BARLOW, George W. Teacher of English in Grenoble, France. Author of short stories and essays in French science-fiction magazines; editor and translator of *Le Livre d'Or de John Brunner*, 1979, *Le Livre d'Or d'Arthur Clarke*, 1981, and *Le Livre d'Or de Harry Harrison*, 1985. **Essays:** Jean-Pierre Andrevon (foreign-language); J.G. Ballard; Thomas M. Disch; Aldous Huxley.

BARNES, Myra. Teacher. Author of *Linguistics and Language in Science Fiction-Fantasy*, 1975. **Essay:** Hank Searls.

BARR, Marleen S. Assistant Professor of English, Virginia Polytechnic Institute and State University, Blacksburg. Author of *Alien to Femininity: Women and Contemporary Science Fiction*, forthcoming. Editor of *Future Females: A Critical Anthology*, 1981, *Women and Utopia: Critical Interpretations* (with Nicholas Smith), 1983, and the feminist SF issue of *Women's Studies International Forum*, June 1984. **Essays:** Suzy McKee Charnas; Zoë Fairbairns; Josephine Saxton.

BARROW, Craig Wallace. Professor of English, University of Tennessee, Chattanooga. Author of *Montage in James Joyce's Ulysses*, 1980, and of essays on science fiction, contemporary fiction, and Irish literature. Editor, with Reed Sanderlin, *Politics, Society, and the Humanities*, 1984. **Essays:** Piers Anthony (with Diana Barrow); Jack L. Chalker; William Kotzwinkle; Gore Vidal; Sharon Webb.

BARROW, Diana. Head of the English Department, Notre Dame High School, Chattanooga, and graduate student in English, University of Tennessee, Chattanooga. Editor of the literary magazine of the Tennessee Philological Association. **Essay:** Piers Anthony (with Craig Wallace Barrow).

BARTH, Melissa E. Assistant Professor of English, Appalachian State University, Boone, North Carolina. Author of *A Reader's Guide to Stephen R. Donaldson* (forthcoming), essays on Donald Barthelme, Thomas Tryon, and Evelyn Waugh, and book reviews in *Modern Fiction Studies* and *Washington Book Review*. **Essays:** Italo Calvino (foreign-language); John Varley.

BERMAN, Ruth. Free-lance writer. Author of *Patterns of Unification in Lewis Carroll's Sylvie and Bruno*, 1974, SF and fantasy stories in magazines, and reviews for *F and SF Review*. Poetry editor of *Mythlore*. **Essay:** Isidore Haiblum.

BISHOP, E.R. Associate Professor of Mathematics, Acadia University, Wolfville, Nova Scotia. **Essay:** Mordecai Roshwald.

BISHOP, Michael. See his own entry. **Essays:** Steven Utley; Ian Watson (with Jeffrey M. Elliot).

BLACKFORD, Russell. Partner in Ebony Books, Melbourne, Australia. Author of *The Tempting of the Witch King* (a fantasy novel), 1983, SF and fantasy stories, and regular articles in *Science Fiction: A Review of Speculative Literature*. Co-editor of *Urban Fantasies* (forthcoming). **Essays:** John Calvin Batchelor; Damien Broderick; William S. Burroughs; Rick Raphael.

BLANSFIELD, Karen Charmaine. Free-lance writer. Author of reviews in *Mid-American Review* and *San Francisco Chronicle*. Has taught at East Carolina University, Greenville, North Carolina, and University of Delaware, Newark; former assistant editor of the journal *Teaching English in the Two-Year College*. **Essays:** E.C. Large; Emma Tennant.

BOGSTAD, Janice M. Library Assistant, University of Wisconsin, Madison; Ph.D. candidate in comparative literature, University of Wisconsin. Author of *An Introduction to Fantasy and Science Fiction* (with F.J. Lemoine), 1985, and of articles in journals. Former editor of the magazines *Janus* and *New Moon: Journal of SF and Critical Feminism*. **Essays:** M.A. Foster; Ardath Mayhar; R.M. Meluch.

BOSKY, Bernadette. Teaching Assistant in English, Duke University, Durham, North Carolina. Author of articles on Le Guin, Peter Straub, and Stephen King. **Essays:** David A. Drake; Suzette Haden Elgin; Tim Powers; Richard S. Shaver.

BRENNAN, John P. Assistant Professor of English, Indiana University-Purdue University, Fort Wayne. Author of articles on Le Guin, Kornbluth, and Pohl. **Essays:** John Brunner; James P. Hogan; L. Ron Hubbard; Spider Robinson; Kurt Vonnegut, Jr.

BRIGG, Peter A. Associate Professor of English, University of Guelph, Ontario. Author of articles in *Arthur C. Clarke*, 1977, *Ursula K. Le Guin*, 1979, *Survey of Science Fiction Literature*, 1979, and in several periodicals including *Mosaic* and *Science-Fiction Studies*. **Essays:** Jerome Bixby; Lester del Rey; Philip Wylie.

BRINEY, R.E. Professor of Computer Science and Chairman of the Computer Science Department, Salem State College, Massachusetts; editor, *Rohmer Review*; a founder, Advent publishers. Author of *SF Bibliographies* (with Edward Wood), 1972, essays in *The Mystery Writer's Art*, 1971, *The Conan Grimoire*, 1971, and *The Mystery Story*, 1976, and of articles and bibliographies in journals. Editor of *Master of Villainy: A Biography of Sax Rohmer*, 1972; co-editor of *Multiplying Villainies: Selected Mystery Criticism* by Anthony Boucher, 1973; contributing editor of *Encyclopedia of Mystery and Detection*, 1976, and *Encyclopedia of Frontier and Western Fiction*, 1983. Contributing editor of the journal *Views and Reviews*, 1972-75; member of the editorial board, Mystery Library, 1975-80, and Collection of Mystery Classics (Bantam Books), 1985. **Essays:** Juanita Coulson; Robert Coulson; August Derleth; Gene DeWeese; Curme Gray; Henry Kuttner; Rog Phillips; Frank M. Robinson; Francis Stevens.

BRIZZI, Mary T. Associate Professor of English, Kent State University, Kent, Ohio; associate editor, *Extrapolation.* Author of *Philip José Farmer: A Reader's Guide,* 1980, and *Anne McCaffrey: A Reader's Guide,* forthcoming. **Essays:** Philip José Farmer; H.F. Heard; Anne McCaffrey.

BRUNNER, John. See his own entry. **Essays:** Jorge Luis Borges (foreign-language); Rudyard Kipling.

BUTRYM, Alexander J. Associate Professor of English, Seton Hall University, South Orange, New Jersey; Director of the program to train teachers of technical writing, Fund for the Improvement of Post-Secondary Education. Author of "For Suffering Humanity: Ethics of Scientists in S-F," in *The Transcendent Adventure,* edited by Robert Reilly, 1984. **Essays:** Sam J. Lundwall; Brian M. Stableford.

CARACCIOLO, Peter. Lecturer in English, Royal Holloway and Bedford New College, London University. Author of articles on Dryden, Defoe, Emily Brontë, Wilkie Collins, Le Fanu, Doyle, Chesterton, Lady Gregory, Wyndham Lewis, Doris Lessing, Keith Roberts, and the landscape garden. SF reviewer, *The Tablet,* 1977-82. **Essay:** Michael Moorcock.

CARTER, Gay E. Reference Librarian, University of Houston, Clear Lake City. **Essay:** Phyllis Eisenstein.

CARTER, Steven R. Teacher in San Juan, Puerto Rico. Author of articles on mystery fiction, black literature, and science fiction in *Dimensions of Detective Fiction, Popular Culture Association Newsletter,* and *Armchair Detective.* **Essays:** Ayn Rand; John A. Williams.

CHAPMAN, Edgar L. Associate Professor of English and Foreign Languages, Bradley University, Peoria, Illinois. Author of articles on Patrick White, Suzette Haden Elgin, Thomas Berger, Talbot Mundy, Philip José Farmer, Hope Mirrlees, Clifford D. Simak, Philip K. Dick, and Frank Herbert, and forthcoming books on Farmer and Robert Silverberg. **Essays:** Arthur Byron Cover; John Crowley; Mike McQuay.

COGELL, Elizabeth Cummins. Assistant Professor of English, University of Missouri, Rolla; member of the editorial board, *Extrapolation.* Author of *Ursula K. Le Guin: A Primary and Secondary Bibliography,* 1983, and an article on Darko Suvin in *Essays in Arts and Sciences,* August 1980. **Essay:** Paul O. Williams.

COLBERT, Robert E. Associate Professor of English, Louisiana State University, Shreveport. Author of articles on Brian Aldiss's criticism, James Blish's criticism, Stanley Elkin, Saul Bellow, F.R. Leavis, and Ford Madox Ford, and of conference papers on Doris Lessing's SF and on C.M. Kornbluth's satire. **Essay:** Russell M. Griffin.

COLEMAN, Rosemary. Associate Professor of Literature, Illinois Benedictine College, Lisle. **Essays:** Peter Tate; Ilya Varshavsky (foreign-language).

COUGHLAN, Gary. Teacher. **Essay:** Patrick Moore.

COWPER, Richard. See his own entry. **Essay:** George Orwell.

COX, J. Randolph. Reference and Documents Librarian, and Associate Professor, St. Olaf College, Northfield, Minnesota; reviewer of popular culture for *Choice.* Author of bibliographies and studies of John Buchan, M.R. James, the Nick Carter authors, George Harmon Coxe, and others for *Dime Novel Roundup, Baker Street Journal, Edgar Wallace Newsletter, English Literature in Transition, Armchair Detective,* and other journals; contributor of the dime novel sections to *Mystery, Detective, and Espionage Magazines,* 1983, and *Detective and Mystery Fiction: An International Bibliography of Secondary Sources,* 1985. **Essays:** Ron Goulart; Luis P. Senarens; Arthur Train; Edgar Wallace; Dennis Wheatley.

CULE, Michael. Actor. Has worked with Ken Campbell's Science Fiction Theatre of Liverpool; appeared in the stage and TV versions of *The Hitch-Hiker's Guide to the Galaxy.* **Essays:** Randall Garrett; David Langford; L. Neil Smith; Robert Anton Wilson.

CUSHING, Charles. Adult Services Librarian, Hamilton Public Library, Ontario. **Essays:** Robert Abernathy; Charles L. Harness.

D'AMMASSA, Don. Materials and Advertising Manager, Taunton Silversmiths; editor of *Mythologies* amateur magazine. SF critic for *Science Fiction Chronicle,* and reviewer for *Delap's F & SF Review, WSFA Journal, SF Booklog,* and other periodicals. **Essays:** William Barnwell; Neal Barrett, Jr.; Barrington John Bayley; David F. Bischoff; J.F. Bone; Mildred Downey Broxon; David R. Bunch; Paul Capon; D.G. Compton; Alfred Coppel; Lee Correy; Arsen Darnay; Joseph H. Delaney; Peter Dickinson; Larry Eisenberg; E. Everett Evans; William R. Forstchen; H.B. Fyfe; Stephen Goldin; Jack C. Haldeman; Philip E. High; Christopher Hodder-Williams; Robert Holdstock; J. Hunter Holly; Laurence Manning; Dean McLaughlin; Thomas F. Monteleone; Dan Morgan; Ed Naha; Ray Nelson; Doris Piserchia; Jerry Pournelle; Terry Pratchett; Christopher Priest; John Rackham; Francis G. Rayer; Sarban; Richard Saxon; William M. Sloane; George H. Smith; Stephen Tall; Ted Thomas; Robert Thurston; Patrick Tilley; Vercors (foreign-language); Connie Willis; Richard Wilson.

DRAKE, David A. See his own entry. **Essays:** Arthur Porges; Donald Wandrei; Stanley Waterloo.

DUNN, Thomas P. Associate Professor of English, Miami University, Oxford, Ohio; member of the editorial board, *Extrapolation.* Editor, with Richard D. Erlich, *The Mechanical God: Machines in Science Fiction,* 1982, and *Clockwork Worlds: Mechanized Environments in SF,* 1983. Associate editor of *The Year's Scholarship in Science Fiction, Fantasy, and Horror Literature,* 1980-84. **Essays:** H.M. Hoover; Kevin O'Donnell, Jr.

EDWARDS, Karren C. Teacher. **Essays:** Fenton Ash; Alan E. Nourse.

EDWARDS, Malcolm. Administrator, Science Fiction Foundation, London, and editor, *Foundation,* London. Editor of *Vector,* 1972-74; SF editor for Gollancz publishers, 1976-77.

EGGELING, John. SF bibliographer.

EISENSTEIN, Alex. Author of several SF short stories with Phyllis Eisenstein. **Essay:** C.M. Kornbluth.

ELKINS, Charles. Associate Professor of English, Director of the Humanities Program, and Associate Dean for College Programs, Florida International University, Miami; co-editor, *Science-Fiction Studies.* Author of a chapter in *Isaac Asimov,* 1977, and of essays in *Survey of Science Fiction Literature,* 1979, and periodicals.

ELLIOT, Jeffrey M. Associate Professor of Political Science, North Carolina Central University, Durham. Author of 41 books and 450 articles and reviews; some of his books on SF and fantasy include *Science Fiction Voices, Fantasy Voices, Pulp Voices,* and *Science*

Fiction Masters; co-author of autobiographies of Raymond Z. Gallun (*Skyclimber*, 1981), and Stanton A. Coblentz (*Adventures of a Free-lancer*, 1984). Editor of the SF-fantasy anthology *Kindred Spirits*, 1984. **Essays:** Pamela Sargent; Ian Watson (with Michael Bishop); George Zebrowski (with Anthony Manousos).

FEELEY, Gregory. Free-lance writer and critic. Author of a forthcoming biography of James Blish, *Alchemy under Pressure*. **Essays:** Glen Cook; Jack Dann; Felix C. Gotschalk; Donald Kingsbury.

FONTAINE, Eric A. Free-lance writer; author of articles on French and Latin American literature. **Essay:** William Jon Watkins.

FRANE, Jeff. Free-lance writer. Author of *Fritz Leiber*, 1980. Co-editor of *A Fantasy Reader*, 1981. **Essays:** Charles L. Grant; Elizabeth A. Lynn.

FROESE, Robert. Assistant Professor of English, University of Maine, Machias. **Essay:** Alfred Bester.

GAAR, Alice Carol. Assistant University Librarian, Florida State University Library, Tallahassee. Co-author of *Deutsche Stunden*, 1964, and author of articles in *Robert A. Heinlein*, 1978, *Quarber Merkur, Science Fiction Studies*, and *SForum*. **Essay:** Herbert W. Franke (foreign-language).

GARNER, John V. High school language director. **Essay:** Mark S. Geston.

GILLINGS, Walter. Editor and publisher of British science fiction from the 1930's; editor of *Tales of Wonder, Scientifiction, Fantasy Review, Science Fantasy,* and *Cosmos Science-Fantasy Review;* associate editor of Utopian Publications, and founding director of Nova Publications. Died 1979. **Essays:** Miles J. Breuer; S.P. Meek; Bob Olsen; Festus Pragnell; Eric Frank Russell; Garrett P. Serviss; A. Hyatt Verrill; Harl Vincent; G.C. Wallis.

GOLDMAN, Stephen H. Associate Professor of English, University of Kansas, Lawrence. Author of articles in *Survey of Science Fiction*, 1979 and *Science-Fiction Studies*. **Essays:** Tom Godwin; James E. Gunn; Daniel Keyes; Jack Vance; Stanley G. Weinbaum.

GORDON, Joan. Graduate student, University of Iowa, Iowa City. Author of a two-volume correspondence course on SF and of a forthcoming book on Joe Haldeman. **Essays:** Joe Haldeman; Walker Percy.

GREENBERG, Martin H. Professor of Regional Analysis, University of Wisconsin, Green Bay; series co-editor of Alternatives (Southern Illinois University Press) and Writers of the Twenty-First Century (Taplinger). Co-author of *Index to Stories in Thematic Anthologies of Science Fiction*, 1978. Editor of more than 100 anthologies and single-author collections. **Essays:** Christopher Anvil; Chan Davis; F.L. Wallace.

GREENLAND, Colin. Free-lance writer. Author of *The Entropy Exhibition: Michael Moorcock and the British "New Wave" in Science Fiction*, 1983, and *Daybreak on a Different Mountain* (novel), 1984. Co-editor of *Interzone* magazine, 1982-85, and *Interzone: The First Anthology*, 1985. **Essays:** Mick Farren; Langdon Jones; Mervyn Peake (fantasy); Walter Tevis.

HALL, Hal W. Head, Special Formats Division, Texas A and M University, College Station. Compiler of *Science Fiction Book Review Index 1923-73, 1974-79,* and annual volumes since 1980, and

of the annual Science Fiction and Fantasy Research Index. Guest editor of *Science Fiction Collections*, 1983.

HARBOTTLE, Philip J. Local government officer. Author of *The Multi-Man* (on John Russell Fearn), 1968, and a forthcoming biography of Fearn, *The Blackpool Wonder*, and *Vultures of the Void: A Bibliographic Survey of British Science Fiction 1946-1956* (with Stephen Holland), forthcoming. Research consultant and contributor, *The Visual Encyclopaedia of Science Fiction*, 1977. **Essay:** John Russell Fearn.

HARDING, Lee. See his own entry.

HARRIS, Rose Flores. Instructor in English, Galveston College, Texas. **Essays:** H.H. Hollis; George R.R. Martin.

HARTWELL, David G. Consulting editor, Tor Books and Arbor House, New York; SF editor, Gregg Press, Boston. Author of *Age of Wonders: Exploring the World of Science Fiction*, 1985. Former SF editor for Signet-New American Library, Berkley-Putnam, and Timescape-Pocket Books. **Essays:** Peter George; Frank R. Stockton.

HASSLER, Donald M. Professor of English, Kent State University, Kent, Ohio; President, Science Fiction Research Association, 1985-86. Author of *The Comedian as the Letter D: Erasmus Darwin's Comic Materialism*, 1973, *Erasmus Darwin*, 1974, *Comic Tones in Science Fiction: The Art of Compromise with Nature*, 1982, and *Hal Clement*, 1982. Editor of *Patterns of the Fantastic*, 2 vols., 1983-84, and co-editor, *Death and the Serpent: Immortality in Science Fiction and Fantasy*, 1985. **Essays:** Harry Bates; James Blish; Hal Clement; Raymond Z. Gallun; David H. Keller; Gérard Klein (foreign-language); Norman L. Knight; Murray Leinster; Paul Preuss; Nat Schachner; Stanley Schmidt; John Sladek.

HATFIELD, Len. Instructor in English, Indiana University, Bloomington; book review editor, *Victorian Studies.* Author of articles on Yeats and May Sinclair, and reviews for *Fantasy Review.* Assistant editor, *College English*, 1982-84. **Essays:** Greg Bear; D.M. Thomas; Joan D. Vinge.

HECHT, Sharon-Ilona. Technical editor for a NASA contractor. **Essay:** M.K. Joseph.

HELDRETH, Leonard G. Professor of English, Northern Michigan University, Marquette. Author of articles on the SF film, E.B. White, and Wordsworth, and forthcoming studies of vampires in literature and Fred Saberhagen. **Essay:** Mike Resnick.

HERBERT, Rosemary. Reference Librarian, Harvard University, Cambridge, Massachusetts; University Press columnist, *Christian Science Monitor.* Free-lance writer on the world of books: frequent contributor to *Publishers Weekly, Boston Review, Armchair Detective,* and other publications. **Essays:** Arthur Conan Doyle; Ursula K. Le Guin; Margaret St. Clair; Evelyn E. Smith.

HILLS, Norman L. Director of Data Processing, Servi Share, Inc. Author of articles on Harness and Leiber. **Essays:** Lawrence Durrell; Jean Mark Gawron; Fritz Leiber.

HOLM, Janis Butler. Assistant Professor of English, Ohio University, Athens. Author of articles on literary theory, textual bibliography, Tudor cultural history, and women's studies. **Essay:** Sheila MacLeod.

HUGHES, Terry. Free-lance writer. **Essay:** Lee Hoffman.

HULL, Elizabeth Anne. Associate Professor of English, William

Rainey Harper College, Palatine, Illinois; North American Secretary of World SF, and editor of *World SF Newsletter*. Author of essays in *Clockwork Worlds, Extrapolation, Essays in Arts and Sciences, Destinies,* and *Starlog Science Fiction Yearbook*; contributor to *Locus, Science Fiction Chronicle,* and *Fantasy Review*. **Essays:** Lloyd Biggle, Jr.; Robert A. Heinlein; Judith Merril.

HUNT, Marvin W. Graduate student in English, University of North Carolina, Chapel Hill. Author of a travel narrative, "The Road to Key West," in the Winston-Salem *Journal,* December 1984. **Essays:** Paul W. Fairman; Tom Purdom; Louis Trimble.

IKIN, Van. Senior Tutor in English, University of Western Australia, Nedlands; Editor of *Science Fiction: A Review of Speculative Literature*; SF columnist for the Sydney *Morning Herald*. Editor of *Australian Science Fiction,* 1982. **Essays:** John Baxter; Frank Bryning; Lee Harding; George Turner.

JONES, Anne Hudson. Associate Professor of Literature and Medicine, Institute for the Medical Humanities, University of Texas Medical Branch, Galveston; Editor-in-Chief of the journal *Literature and Medicine,* and member of the editorial board, *Medical Heritage*. Author of several articles on feminist science fiction and on literature and medical ethics. Editor of *Literature and Medicine: Images of Healers,* 1983. **Essay:** Katherine MacLean.

JONES, Robert L. Scientific Programmer, Lunar and Planetary Institute, Universities Space Research Association. Former Professor of English and Department Chairman, Radford University, Virginia. **Essay:** Damon Knight.

JURKIEWICZ, Kenneth. Assistant Professor of English, Central Michigan University, Mount Pleasant. Author of articles on space movies, Ramsey Campbell, and Saki. **Essays:** Pierre Boulle (foreign-language); Mark Helprin; Curt Siodmak.

KAGARLITSKY, Julius. Free-lance critic; member of the editorial board, Library of Modern SF. Author of *The Life and Thought of H.G. Wells,* 1966; *What Does It Mean, SF?,* 1974; *Western Theatre of the 18th Century in the Eyes of Russian Critics,* 1976; *Shakespeare and Voltaire,* 1980; *Theatre for All Ages,* 1986. Editor of a 15-volume edition of works by Wells, 1964. Former Professor at the State Theatrical Institute, Moscow. **Essay:** John Wyndham.

KELLEY, George. Professor of Business Administration, Erie Community College-City Campus, Buffalo. Contributor to *Twentieth-Century Crime and Mystery Writers, Twentieth-Century Western Writers, Mass Market Publishing in America, Poison Pen, Mystery and Detective Monthly, DAPA-EM,* and *Academy of Management Review.* **Essays:** Michael Bishop; Mark Clifton; Miriam Allen deFord; Gardner Dozois; Cynthia Felice; M. John Harrison; Joe L. Hensley; Trevor Hoyle; Zach Hughes; Dean Ing; K.W. Jeter; Leo P. Kelley; Crawford Kilian; Milton Lesser; Edward Llewellyn; Kim Stanley Robinson; Jack Sharkey; T.L. Sherred; Robert Silverberg; Christopher Stasheff.

KETTERER, David. Professor of English, Concordia University, Montreal. Author of *New Worlds for Old: The Apocalyptic Imagination, Science Fiction, and American Literature,* 1974, *The Rationale of Deception in Poe,* 1979, *Frankenstein's Creation: The Book, The Monster, and Human Reality,* 1979, and *Imprisoned in a Tesseract: The Life and Work of James Blish,* forthcoming. Editor of *The Science Fiction of Mark Twain,* 1984.

KINNAIRD, John. Late Member of the English Department, University of Maryland, College Park. Died 1980. **Essays:** J.B.S. Haldane; Olaf Stapledon.

KLEIN, Gérard. See his entry in the foreign-language appendix. Editor, Editions Robert Laffont, Paris, and consultant economist. Author of novels (*Le Gambit des Etoiles,* 1958, *Les Seigneurs de la Guerre,* 1971), short stories (*Les Perles du Temps,* 1958, *La Loi du Talion,* 1973, *Histoires comme si...,* 1985), and the critical book *Malaise dans la science-fiction américaine,* 1979. **Essay:** Michel Jeury (foreign-language).

KOHLER, Vince. Staff writer and SF reviewer, *The Oregonian,* Portland. **Essay:** John Kippax.

LAKE, David. See his own entry. **Essays:** Russell Hoban; C.S. Lewis.

LAWLER, Donald L. Professor of English, East Carolina University, Greenville, North Carolina; Editor of *Victorians Institute Journal.* Co-author of *Vonnegut in America,* 1977, and author of *Approaches to Science Fiction,* 1978, and articles on 19th- and 20th-century British and American writers. Contributing editor of *Survey of Science Fiction Literature,* 1979, consulting editor of *Survey of Modern Fantasy Literature,* 5 vols., 1983, and editor of a forthcoming edition of Wilde's *The Picture of Dorian Gray.* **Essays:** Anthony Boucher; David Brin; Avram Davidson; David Gerrold; Fred and Geoffrey Hoyle; Otis Adelbert Kline; Richard Matheson; Kris Neville; Larry Niven; J.R.R. Tolkien (fantasy).

LEAHY, Mark Warwick. Graduate student, University of Adelaide, South Australia. **Essays:** Sylvia Engdahl; Richard Rohmer; Cherry Wilder.

LEVY, Michael M. Assistant Professor of English, University of Wisconsin, Menomonie; assistant editor of *Menomonie Review.* Author of articles on *Paradise Lost* and *Doctor Who,* and of reviews for *Fantasy Review.* **Essays:** Warren Norwood; Philip Francis Nowlan; Lucius Shepard; Gary K. Wolf.

LEWIS, Arthur O. Professor of English Emeritus, Pennsylvania State University, University Park; member of the advisory board, *Alternative Futures.* Author of many books; those on SF-related topics include *Of Men and Machines,* 1963, *American Utopias: Selected Short Fiction,* 1971, *Utopian Literature in the Pennsylvania State University Libraries: A Selected Bibliography,* 1984. Editor of *Utopian Literature,* 41 vols., 1971, and the SF issue, 1976, and Utopian Studies issue, 1981, of *Journal of General Education.* **Essays:** Ernest Callenbach; Joseph O'Neill; Marge Piercy; Steven Spruill.

LOWENKOPF, Shelly. Adjunct Professor, Professional Writing Program, University of Southern California, Los Angeles. Author of more than 40 books (fiction and non-fiction), and of numerous essays and reviews. Former director, Dell Publishing California Office, and former editor-in-chief, American Bibliographical Center-Clio Press and Ross-Erikson Inc. **Essays:** Lin Carter; A. Bertram Chandler; Madeleine L'Engle.

LOWNDES, Robert A.W. See his own entry. **Essay:** Wallace West.

LUNAN, Duncan. Free-lance writer; SF critic for the Glasgow *Herald.* Author of *Men and the Stars,* 1974 (in USA: *Interstellar Contact*), *New Worlds for Old,* 1979, and *Man and the Planets,* 1983 (all non-fiction), many articles and papers, and 16 short stories (including "The Comet, The Cairn, and the Capsule," 1972). **Essay:** Charles Chilton.

LUPOFF, Richard A. See his own entry. **Essays:** Edwin L.

Arnold; Robert Asprin; Eando Binder; Robert Bloch; Edgar Rice Burroughs; Orson Scott Card; Stanton A. Coblentz; George Allan England; Hugo Gernsback; H.L. Gold; Michael Kurland; Frank Belknap Long; Raymond A. Palmer; Ed Earl Repp; Wilmar H. Shiras; E.E. Smith; Donald A. Wollheim.

LYNCH, Peter. Free-lance writer, Houston. **Essays:** Gordon Eklund; Victor Rousseau; Michael Young.

MACDONALD, Andrew. Director of Freshman English and English as a Second Language, Loyola University, New Orleans. Author of articles on Jonson, Shakespeare, English as a second language, SF, and popular culture. **Essays:** Martin Caidin (with Gina Macdonald); Arthur Keppel-Jones; Doris Lessing.

MACDONALD, Gina. Assistant Professor of English, Loyola University, New Orleans. Author of articles on Shakespeare, Robert Greene, English as a second language, popular culture, and SF. **Essays:** Kingsley Amis; Brian N. Ball; Martin Caidin (with Andrew Macdonald); William Golding; Frank Herbert; Robert Hoskins; Stanislaw Lem (foreign-language); Charles R. Long; Thomas McClary; Thomas Pynchon; John Rankine; Arthur Sellings; R.C. Sherriff; Somtow Sucharitkul; Boris and Arkady Strugatsky (foreign-language; with Darko Suvin); Stanislaw Witkiewicz (foreign-language).

MANOUSOS, Anthony. Member of the Department of English, Carleton College, Northfield, Minnesota. Author of articles in *Dictionary of American Science Fiction Writers*, and on D.H. Lawrence and Swift. **Essays:** L.P. Davies; George Zebrowski (with Jeffrey M. Elliot).

McGUIRE, Patrick L. Civil servant, U.S. Federal government. Author of *Red Stars: Political Aspects of Soviet Science Fiction*, 1985, and articles on Joe Haldeman, the Strugatskys, C.J. Cherryh, and Poul Anderson. Consulting editor, *Survey of Science Fiction Literature*, 1979; translator of works of Soviet SF. **Essays:** C.J. Cherryh; Keith Laumer; Vernor Vinge; James White.

MEAD, David G. Associate Professor of English, Corpus Christi State University, Texas. Author of articles an Amis, Cummings, and Eliot. **Essay:** William Gibson.

MEYERS, Walter E. Professor of English, North Carolina State University, Raleigh; member of the editorial board, *Science Fiction Studies*. Author of *Aliens and Linguists*, 1980. Consulting editor, *Survey of Science Fiction Literature*, 1979. **Essays:** T.J. Bass; Rosel George Brown; Rex Gordon; H. Rider Haggard; Neil R. Jones; David Karp; Ward Moore; John Morressy; James H. Schmitz; Nevil Shute.

MIESEL, Sandra. Free-lance writer. Author of *Myth, Symbol, and Religion in Lord of the Rings*, 1973, *Against Time's Arrow: The High Crusade of Poul Anderson*, 1978, *Dreamrider*, 1982, and of articles in *Amazing, SF Monthly, Isaac Asimov's Science Fiction Magazine*, and other periodicals; also writes introductions and afterwords for Gregg Press and Ace Books. Editor of story collections for Tor Books and Baen Books. **Essays:** Poul Anderson; Steven Barnes; Gordon R. Dickson; Alexis A. Gilliland; Zenna Henderson; R.A. Lafferty; Fred Saberhagen; Wilson Tucker.

MILLER, Richard W. Associate Professor of Philosophy, University of Missouri, Rolla. **Essays:** H. Beam Piper; Leonard Wibberley.

MOLSON, Francis J. Professor of English, Central Michigan University, Mount Pleasant. Author of chapters on SF for children in *Anatomy of Wonder, The Art and Aesthetics of Fantasy*, and *The Science Fiction Reference Book*, and of articles on Le Guin, Emily Dickinson, Frances Hodgson Burnett, and other writers. **Essays:** Monica Hughes; Alexander Key; Alice Lightner; Jeff and Jean Sutton; Hugh Walters; Laurence Yep.

MONTGOMERIE, Lee. Free-lance writer. Past contributor to *Foundation*. **Essays:** W.E. Johns; Naomi Mitchison; Charles Platt.

MORRISON, Michael A. Associate Professor, University of Oklahoma, Norman. Author of an article on Clive Barker, and of numerous reviews in *Fantasy Review, Washington Post Book World*, and other periodicals. **Essay:** James Herbert.

MURRAY, Will. Editorial Director of Odyssey Publications and free-lance writer. Author or co-author of *The Man Behind Doc Savage*, 1974, *The Duende History of The Shadow Magazine*, 1979, and *The Assassin's Handbook*; articles in *Starlog, Lovecraft Studies, Crypt of Cthulhu, Xenophile, Etchings and Odysseys*, and fiction in *Ellery Queen's Mystery Magazine, Eldritch Tales*, and other magazines. Past editor of the magazines *Duende* and *Skullduggery*. **Essays:** Lester Dent; Clark Ashton Smith; John Taine.

NELLIS, Marilyn K. Assistant Professor, Liberal Studies Center, Clarkson University, Potsdam, New York. **Essays:** Brian C. Daley; James Kahn.

NICKERSON, Susan L. Director, Roseville Public Library, California. Reviewer for *Fantasy Review* and *Science-Fiction Studies*. **Essay:** Roy Meyers.

OLIVER, Chad. See his own entry. **Essays:** Edmond Hamilton; Ross Rocklynne.

ORODENKER, Richard. Associate Professor of English, Peirce Junior College, Philadelphia. Author of criticism and fiction in *North American Review, Benzene, Studies in Short Fiction*, and other publications. **Essay:** F.M.Busby.

PAGE, Gerald W. Writer and editor. Author of many SF and fantasy stories since 1963. Editor of the anthologies *Year's Best Horror Stories 4-7, Nameless Places*, and *Heroic Fantasy* (with Hank Reinhardt); former editor of *Witchcraft and Sorcery Magazine* and consultant editor of *Amazing*. **Essays:** Bryan Berry; Nelson S. Bond; Charles L. Fontenay; Gardner F. Fox; Raymond F. Jones; Lisa Tuttle; Robert Moore Williams.

PARKIN-SPEER, Diane. Associate Professor of English, Southwest Texas State University, San Marcos. Author of articles on Heinlein, John Lilburne, and alien ethics and religion, and of reviews in *Fantasy Review*. **Essays:** Alexei Panshin; Sydney J. Van Scyoc.

PATTEN, Frederick. Catalog librarian in an aerospace technical library. Author of the guide to comic books in *Magazines for Libraries*, and of reviews of SF in *Library Journal, Science Fiction Review, Locus*, and other publications. Publisher and co-editor of *Delap's F & SF Review*, 1975-77. **Essays:** C.C. MacApp; Timothy Zahn.

PAUL, Terri. Senior Scientific Programmer, McDonnell Douglas Technical Services Company, Houston. Author of articles on Pohl, women in SF, time travel, and technical writing. **Essay:** Rudy Rucker.

PERKINS, Michael. Free-lance writer. Author of *Evil Compan-*

ions (novel), 1968, *Down Here* (stories), 1969, *The Secret Record* (criticism), 1976, and *The Persistence of Desire* (poetry), 1977. Editor of *Ulster Arts* magazine, 1977-79, and former editor for Tompkins Square Press and Croton Press. **Essay:** David Meltzer.

PFEIFFER, John R. Professor of English, Central Michigan University, Mount Pleasant; bibliographer, *Shaw Annual.* Author of *Fantasy and Science Fiction: A Critical Guide*, 1971, and essays on Brunner, Le Guin, Huxley, Morris, and Carroll; co-author of a chapter on the modern period in *Anatomy of Wonder*, 1976 (revised 1981). Special editor of "GBS and Science Fiction" issue of *Shaw Review.* **Essays:** John Christopher; Alan Seymour; Robert Stallman; Hank Stine; Colin Wilson.

PHILLIPS, Gene. Librarian. Author of fantasy stories. **Essays:** Kenneth Bulmer; Robert Chilson; Alan Dean Foster; Colin Kapp; Emil Petaja; Bob Shaw; Ian Wallace.

PHILMUS, Robert M. Professor of English, Concordia University, Montreal. Author of *Into the Unknown: The Evolution of Science Fiction from Francis Godwin to H.G. Wells.* 1970 (2nd edition 1983), and a chapter on early SF in *Anatomy of Wonder*, 1976 (revised 1981). Co-editor of *H.G. Wells: Early Writings in Science and Science Fiction*, 1975, *H.G. Wells and Modern Science Fiction*, 1977, and *H.G. Wells's Literary Criticism*, 1980.

PIERCE, Hazel. Professor of English, Kearney State College, Kearney, Nebraska; member of the editorial board, *Platte Valley Review.* Author of *Philip K. Dick*, 1982, *A Literary Symbiosis: Science Fiction / Fantasy / Mystery*, 1983, and essays on Asimov, Bradbury, and Dick in *Writers of the 21st Century* volumes, and on Blake and Byron. **Essays:** George Alec Effinger; Kurd Lasswitz (foreign-language); Phillip Mann; A.E. van Vogt.

PIERCE, John J. Associate editor, Private Label magazine. Author of essays on Cordwainer Smith. Editor of *The Best of Cordwainer Smith*, 1975, *Norstrilia*, 1975, *The Best of Murray Leinster*, 1978, and *The Best of Raymond Z. Gallun*, 1978. Former editor of *Galaxy*, and of the fanzines *Renaissance* and *Tension, Apprehension, and Dissension.* **Essays:** Otto Gail (foreign-language); Bernhard Kellermann (foreign-language); Nicholas Yermakov.

PRATT, Nick. Free-lance photographer; also book reviewer. **Essay:** R.W. Mackelworth.

PRIEST, Christopher. See his own entry.

PRONZINI, Bill. Author of 35 novels and several hundred stories, articles, and essays. Editor of numerous thematic anthologies. **Essays:** Arthur K. Barnes; Charles Beaumont; Cleve Cartmill; Edward D. Hoch; Evan Hunter; Henry Slesar.

PROSSER, Harold Lee. Sociologist and writer; instructor at Drury College, Springfield, Missouri. Author of *Dandelion Seeds* (stories), 1974, *Goodbye, Lon Chaney, Jr., Goodbye* (novelette), 1978, and *Summer Wine* 1979, stories in *Cold Sweat*, 1985, and *Missouri Short Fiction*, 1985, and forthcoming books on Charles Beaumont and Robert Bloch. **Essays:** William Greenleaf; Stephen Leigh; William F. Nolan; F. Paul Wilson.

QUINN, Joseph A. Associate Professor of English, University of Windsor, Ontario. Author of articles and reviews in *Chesterton Review, University of Windsor Review, Christianity and Literature,* and *Alternative Futures.* **Essays:** John Atkins; Constantine FitzGibbon; L.P. Hartley; Alun Llewellyn; Noel M. Loomis.

RABKIN, Eric S. Professor of English, University of Michigan, Ann Arbor. Author of *The Fantastic in Literature*, 1976, *Science Fiction: History, Science, Vision* (with Robert Scholes), 1977, and *Arthur C. Clarke*, 1979. Co-editor of *The End of the World*, 1983. **Essay:** Arthur C. Clarke.

REGINALD, R. Full Librarian (Chief Cataloger), California State University, San Bernardino; publisher, Borgo Press. Author of 30 books, including *Cumulative Paperback Index 1939-1959, Contemporary Science Fiction Authors, Science Fiction and Fantasy Literature: A Checklist, Paperback Price Guide, Things to Come, Visions of Tomorrow, Lords Temporal and Lords Spiritual, Analytical Congressional Directory,* and *Tempest in a Teapot,* and of 100 articles. Editor of six SF reprint series. **Essays:** R. Lionel Fanthorpe; Bruce McAllister; J. Michael Reaves.

REILLY, Robert. Professor of English, Rider College, Lawrenceville, New Jersey. Author of *The Transcendent Adventure: Studies of Religion in Science Fiction/Fantasy*, 1984, and articles on Ray Bradbury. **Essays:** Douglas Adams; D.F. Jones; Vincent King; Charles Sheffield.

RIES, Lawrence R. Assistant Director of the University Without Walls, Skidmore College, Saratoga Springs, New York. Author of *Wolf Masks: Violence in Contemporary Poetry*, 1977. **Essay:** Sterling E. Lanier.

ROSINSKY, Natalie M. Instructional designer and technical trainer for industry. Author of *Feminist Futures: Contemporary Women's Speculative Fiction*, 1984, an essay on C.L. Moore, and an article in *The Lost Tradition: A History of Mothers and Daughters in Literature*, 1979. **Essays:** Vonda N. McIntyre; C.L. Moore.

ROTTENSTEINER, Franz. Editor of Suhrkamp's Fantastic Library series (24 annual vols.). Author of *The Science Fiction Book*, 1975, and *The Fantasy Book*, 1978. Editor of *The Slaying of the Dragon: Modern Tales of the Playful Imagination*, 1984, and *Microworlds*, by Lem, 1985. **Essays:** Karin Boye (foreign-language); Dino Buzzati (foreign-language); Wyman Guin; E.M. Hull; Wolfgang Jeschke (foreign-language); Maurice Renard (foreign-language).

RUSS, Joanna. See her own entry. **Essay:** H.P. Lovecraft.

SAMUELSON, David N. Professor of English, California State University, Long Beach; member of the editorial board, *Science Fiction Studies* and *Survey of Science Fiction Literature.* Author of *Visions of Tomorrow: Six Voyages from Outer to Inner Space*, 1975, *Arthur C. Clarke: A Primary and Secondary Bibliography*, 1984, and essays on Aldiss, Benford, Brunner, Clarke, Delany, Heinlein, Miller, Pohl, and Bernard Wolfe. **Essays:** Isaac Asimov; Gregory Benford; John Boyd; Anthony Burgess; Max Ehrlich; Howard Fast; Walter M. Miller, Jr.; Frederik Pohl; Stephen Robinett; Theodore Sturgeon; Bernard Wolfe.

SANDERS, Joe. Professor of English, Lakeland Community College, Mentor, Ohio; Associate Editor of *The Year's Scholarship in Science Fiction, Fantasy, and Horror Literature* since 1980. Author of *Roger Zelazny: A Primary and Secondary Bibliography*, nine essays in *Survey of Fantasy Literature*, 1983, and an article on Richard Condon in *Extrapolation*, 1984. **Essays:** John Shirley; Bruce Sterling.

SARGENT, Pamela. See her own entry. **Essays:** Cecelia Holland; Kate Wilhelm; Gene Wolfe.

SATTY, Harvey J. President of the Olaf Stapledon Society. Author of *Olaf Stapledon: A Bibliography* (with Curtis C. Smith), 1984. **Essays:** Chester Anderson; Robert L. Forward; John Gloag.

SCARBOROUGH, John. Professor of Ancient History and the History of Medicine, University of Kentucky, Lexington. Author of *Roman Medicine*, 1969, *Facets of Hellenic Life*, 1976, "Medicine in Science Fiction," in *The Science Fiction Encyclopedia*, 1979, and articles on Rider Haggard, Wyndham, Lem, Anthony, and von Däniken. Editor of *Byzantine Medicine*, 1984. **Essay:** Josef Nesvadba (foreign-language).

SCHLOBIN, Roger C. Associate Professor of English and Special Assistant to the Chancellor, Purdue University North Central Campus, Westville, Indiana; editor for Garland and Starmont publishers. Author of *A Research Guide to Science Fiction Studies* (with Marshall B. Tymn and L.W. Currey), 1977, *The Year's Scholarship in Science Fiction and Fantasy* (with Tymn), 1979, *The Literature of Fantasy* (bibliography), 1979, *Andre Norton: A Primary and Secondary Bibliography*, 1980, and *Urania's Daughters: A Checklist of Women Science Fiction Writers 1697-1982*, 1983. **Essays:** Lord Dunsany (fantasy); Andre Norton.

SCHOLES, Robert. Professor of English, Brown University, Providence, Rhode Island; general editor, Masters of Science Fiction series. Author of *The Fabulators*, 1969, *Structural Fabulation*, 1975, and *Science Fiction: History, Science, Vision* (with Eric S. Rabkin), 1977.

SCHUYLER, William M., Jr. Professor of Philosophy, University of Louisville, Kentucky. Author of articles and chapters on philosophy and SF. **Essays:** Diane Duane; Hilbert Schenck.

SCHWEITZER, Darrell. Free-lance writer; assistant editor, *Amazing*; SF critic, Philadelphia *Inquirer*. Author of *The Dream Quest of H.P. Lovecraft*, 1978, *We Are All Legends* (stories), 1981, *The Shattered Goddess* (novel), 1982, *Tom O'Bedlam's Night Out* (stories), 1985, and a forthcoming study of Lord Dunsany. Editor of *Essays Lovecraftian*, 1976, *Science Fiction Voices 1*, 1979, *Discovering Modern Horror Fiction*, 1985, and *Exploring Fantasy Worlds*, 1985. **Essays:** L. Sprague de Camp; Barry Longyear; Leo Szilard.

SEARLES, Baird. Owner and manager, The Science Fiction Shop, New York; film columnist, *Amazing*, and book columnist, *Isaac Asimov's Science Fiction Magazine*. Author or co-author of a study of Heinlein, *The Science Fiction Quiz Book*, 1974, *A Reader's Guide to Science Fiction [Fantasy]*, 2 vols., 1979-82, and many reviews. **Essays:** A. Merritt; Austin Tappan Wright.

SEIDEL, Kathryn Lee. Assistant Professor of English, University of Maryland, College Park. Author of *The Southern Belle in American Fiction: Her Rise and Fall*, 1985, and articles on Russ, Piercy, Le Guin, Faulkner's women, Ellen Glasgow's satire, and writing anxiety. **Essay:** Dean R. Koontz.

SHWARTZ, Susan. Information Coordinator, BEA Associates, and free-lance writer and editor. Author of a forthcoming novel, short fiction in *Analog*, *Fantasy Book*, and other periodicals, and of articles and reviews. Editor of the anthologies *Hecate's Cauldron*, 1982, *Habitats*, 1984, and *Moonsinger's Friends*, 1985. **Essays:** Jayge Carr; Jacqueline Lichtenberg; Janet E. Morris.

SMITH, Curtis C. Professor of Literature, University of Houston, Clear Lake City. Author of *Olaf Stapledon: A Bibliography* (with Harvey J. Satty), 1984. Editor of *Twentieth-Century Science-Fiction Writers*, 1981 (2nd edition 1986). **Essays:** Laurence M. Janifer; Philip Latham; Jack London; Robert A.W. Lowndes; Mack Reynolds.

SNYDER, Carol L. Associate Professor of Humanities, University of Houston, Clear Lake City. **Essays:** Joanna Russ; James Tiptree, Jr.

SNYDER, Judith. Teacher and free-lance writer. **Essays:** Gertrude Friedberg; Lee Killough.

STABLEFORD, Brian M. See his own entry.

STAPLES, Katherine. Translator of works by Henri Rousseau and of *Les Illuminations* by Rimbaud. **Essay:** J.T. McIntosh.

STEPHENSEN-PAYNE, Philippa. Free-lance writer. **Essay:** Nicholas Fisk.

STONE, Graham. Author of *Australian Science Fiction Index 1925-1967*, 1968 (supplement 1976), *Index to British Science Fiction Magazines 1934-1954*, 1980, and *Notes on Australian Science Fiction*, 1985. **Essays:** Christopher Blayre; Erle Cox; Ray Cummings; Lloyd Arthur Eshbach; P. Schuyler Miller; Jack Wodhams; Arthur Leo Zagat.

STOVER, Leon. Professor of Anthropology, Illinois Institute of Technology, Chicago. Author of the novels *Stonehenge*, with Harry Harrison, 1972 (revised as *Stonehenge: Where Atlantis Died*, 1983) and *The Shaving of Karl Marx*, 1982, and several works of nonfiction, including *La Science-Fiction Américaine*, 1972, *The Cultural Ecology of Chinese Civilization*, 1973, *Stonehenge: The Indo-European Heritage* with Bruce Kraig, 1978 (British edition: *Stonehenge and the Origins of Europe*), and *The Prophetic Soul: A Reading of H.G. Wells's "Things to Come"*, forthcoming. **Essays:** John W. Campbell, Jr.; Harry Harrison; George R. Stewart; Jules Verne (foreign-language).

SULLIVAN, C.W., III. Associate Professor of English, East Carolina University, Greenville, North Carolina; editor of *Children's Folklore Newsletter*. Author of articles in *Survey of Science Fiction Literature*, 1979, and reviews in *Fantasy Review*. Editor of *As Tomorrow Becomes Today*, 1974. **Essays:** E.R. Eddison (fantasy); Harlan Ellison; Pat Frank; John Hersey; John Norman; Andrew J. Offutt; Kit Reed.

SUMMERS, Judith. Free-lance writer. Author of the novel *Dear Sister*, 1985. **Essay:** E.V. Odle.

SUVIN, Darko. Professor of English and Comparative Literature, McGill University, Montreal. Author of *Russian Science Fiction 1956-1974: A Bibliography*, 1976, *Pour Une Poétique de la Science-Fiction*, 1977, *Metamorphoses of Science Fiction*, 1979, *Victorian Science Fiction in the UK: The Discourses of Knowledge and of Power*, 1983, and *To Brecht and Beyond*, 1984. Editor of *Other Worlds, Other Seas*, 1970, *Science Fiction Studies* (with R.D. Mullen), 2 vols., 1976-78, and *H.G. Wells and Modern Science Fiction* (with Robert M. Philmus), 1977. **Essays:** Grant Allen; Edward Bellamy; Aleksandr Belyaev (foreign-language); Johanna and Günter Braun (foreign-language); Valery Bryusov (foreign-language); Samuel Butler; Karel Capek (foreign-language); Robert Cromie; George Griffith; C.J. Cutcliffe Hyne; William Le Queux; Vladimir Mayakovsky (foreign-language); Boris and Arkady Strugatsky (foreign-language; with Gina Macdonald); Abram Tertz (foreign-language); Alexey Tolstoy (foreign-language); Konstantin Tsiolkovsky (foreign-language); Ivan Yefremov (foreign-language); Yevgeny Zamyatin (foreign-language).

SWANK, Paul. Assistant Professor of Educational Psychology, University of Houston, University Park. **Essays:** Fletcher Pratt; George O. Smith.

TALBOT, Norman. Professor of English, University of Newcastle, New South Wales; managing editor, Nimrod Publications. Author of several books of poetry, the most recent being *Find the Lady* and *Overhill Faraway*, and works of literary criticism. Editor of anthologies of poetry and prose. **Essays:** William Morris (fantasy); Upton Sinclair.

THURSTON, Robert. See his own entry. **Essays:** Richard M. McKenna; Richard C. Meredith; James Sallis.

TOLLEY, Michael J. Reader in English, University of Adelaide, South Australia; editorial adviser, *Blake Studies.* Author of 20 essays on Blake and reviews for *SF and F Book Review* and *Fantasy Review*, mainly on Australasian writing. Co-editor of *William Blake's Designs for Edward Young's Night Thoughts*, 2 vols., 1980, and *The Stellar Gauge: Essays on Science Fiction Writers*, 1980. **Essays:** Mark Adlard; Angela Carter; Michael G. Coney; Michael Frayn; Joseph Green; Lindsay Gutteridge; David Lake; John D. MacDonald; Gerald Murnane; Kit Pedler and Gerry Davis.

TUCK, Donald H. Bibliographer and industrial manager. Author of *A Handbook of Science Fiction and Fantasy*, 1954 (revised edition, 2 vols., 1959), and *The Encyclopedia of Science Fiction and Fantasy*, 3 vols., 1974-83.

TUCKER, Frank H. Professor of History, Colorado College, Colorado Springs. Author of *The White Conscience*, 1969, a chapter in *Robert A. Heinlein*, 1978, *The Frontier Spirit and Progress*, 1980, and articles in *Russian Affairs, Japanese Affairs, Intellect*, and *Extrapolation.* **Essays:** Kobo Abe (foreign-language); Sakyo Komatsu (foreign-language); André Maurois (foreign-language).

TURNER, George. See his own entry. **Essays:** J.D. Beresford; M. Barnard Eldershaw; Pip Maddern.

TUTTLE, Lisa. See her own entry. **Essay:** Tom Reamy.

TUZAR, Jana I. Doctoral student, University of Chicago. **Essays:** Mikhail Bulgakov (foreign-language); Vladimir Tendryakov (foreign-language).

TYMN, Marshall B. Professor of English, Eastern Michigan University, Ypsilanti; director of the National Workshop on Teaching Science Fiction; Editor of the Contributions to the Study of Science Fiction and Fantasy series. Author of *Thomas Cole's Poetry*, 1972, *A Research Guide to Science Fiction Studies* (with Roger C. Schlobin and L.W. Currey), 1977, *Index to Stories in Thematic Anthologies of Science Fiction*, 1978, *American Fantasy and Science Fiction* (bibliography), 1979, *Fantasy [Horror] Literature: A Core Collection and Reference Guide*, and numerous articles, essays, and bibliographies. Editor of the annual bibliography *The Year's Scholarship in Science Fiction, Fantasy, and Horror Literature*, and of *Thomas Cole: Collected Essays and Prose Sketches*, 1980.

UNDERWOOD, Marylyn J. Member of the Department of English, Victoria College, Texas. Author of *First Principles* (with Gary M. Underwood), 2 vols., 1978-83, and articles on SF, James Thurber, and Chipita Rodriguez. **Essay:** Ben Bova.

UTLEY, Steven. See his own entry. **Essays:** Ralph Milne Farley; Howard Waldrop.

VARDEMAN, Robert E. Free-lance writer; president of the Cenotaph Corporation. Author of *Sandcats of Rhyl*, 1978, *The Klingon Gambit*, 1981, *Mutiny on the Enterprise*, 1983, *The Cenotaph Road*, 1983 (and 5 other books in the series), *The Quaking Lands*, 1985

(and 3 other books in the Jade Demons series), and *To Demons Bound* (with George W. Proctor), 1985 (and 5 other books in the Swords of Raemllyn series). Editor, *SFWA Forum*, 1978-79, and Vice-President, SFWA, 1979-80. **Essay:** George W. Proctor.

WAGAR, W. Warren. Professor of History, State University of New York, Binghamton; member of the editorial board, *Futures Research Quarterly.* Author of *H.G. Wells and the World State*, 1961, *The City of Man*, 1963, *Building the City of Man*, 1971, *Good Tidings: The Belief in Progress from Darwin to Marcuse*, 1972, *Books in World History*, 1973, *World Views: A Study in Comparative History*, 1977, and *Terminal Visions: The Literature of Last Things*, 1982. Editor of *H.G. Wells: Journalism and Prophecy*, 1964, *European Intellectual History since Darwin and Marx*, 1967, *Science, Faith, and Man*, 1968, *The Idea of Progress since the Renaissance*, 1969, *History and the Idea of Mankind*, 1971, and *The Secular Mind: Transformations of Faith in Modern Europe*, 1982. **Essay:** H.G. Wells.

WAGNER, Karl Edward. Free-lance writer; editor of *Carcosa.* Author of *Darkness Weaves*, 1970, *Death Angel's Shadow*, 1973, *Bloodstone*, 1975, *Dark Crusade*, 1976, *Legion from the Shadows*, 1976, *Night Winds*, 1978, *The Road of Kings*, 1978, *In a Lonely Place*, 1983, *Killer* (with David A. Drake), 1985, and *The Book of Kane*, 1985. Editor of *The Year's Best Horror Stories 8-14*, the authorized Conan series, and *Echoes of Valor*, forthcoming. **Essay:** Manly Wade Wellman.

WATSON, Ian. See his own entry. **Essay:** David I. Masson.

WAY, Douglas E. Retired businessman. **Essays:** J.U. Giesy; Austin Hall and Homer Eon Flint.

WAY, Karen G. Teaching Assistant, Department of English, Rutgers University, New Brunswick, New Jersey. Past editor of *Lovejoy's Guidance Digest.* **Essays:** Jonathan Fast; Nancy Freedman; J.B. Priestley; Walt and Leigh Richmond; Kathleen Sky; E.C. Tubb.

WEEDMAN, Jane B. Assistant Professor of English, Texas Tech University, Lubbock. Author of *Samuel R. Delany*, 1982, and articles on Delany, James White, and E.E. Smith. Editor of *Women Worldwalkers: New Dimensions of Science Fiction and Fantasy*, forthcoming. **Essays:** Anna Kavan; Mark Twain.

WEINKAUF, Mary S. Professor of English and Head of the Department, Dakota Wesleyan University, Mitchell, South Dakota. Author of *Early Poems by a Late Beginner*, 1976, *Lew Archer, Humanist Priest*, 1985, forthcoming studies of S. Fowler Wright and Ngaio Marsh, and of articles and reviews in *Fantasy and Science Fiction Book Review, SFRA Newsletter, Extrapolation, Studies in English Literature, Texas Quarterly*, and other periodicals. **Essays:** René Barjavel (foreign-language); Octavia E. Butler; William Dean Howells; Tanith Lee; Sinclair Lewis; Julian May; Clifford D. Simak; Craig Strete; Franz Werfel (foreign-language); S. Fowler Wright.

WELCH, Dennis M. Associate Professor of English and Humanities, Virginia Polytechnic and State University, Blacksburg. Author of articles on Tennyson, science and literature, Sturgeon, Blake, and Shelley. **Essay:** Theodore R. Cogswell.

WHITE, Fred D. Assistant Professor of English, University of Santa Clara, California. Author of *Composition: Art and Craft* (forthcoming), and articles in *San Jose Studies, Arizona Quarterly, Journal of English Teaching Techniques, The Writing Instructor*, and other publications. **Essay:** Robert Sheckley.

WILCOX, Robert H. Professor Emeritus, Glendale College,

Arizona. Former consulting editor, *Amazing*, and editor-in-chief, Industrial Publications, New York. **Essays:** Fredric Brown; Louis Charbonneau; J. Francis McComas; William F. Temple.

WILDER, Cherry. See her own entry. **Essay:** Ira Levin.

WINGROVE, David. Free-lance writer. Author of *Apertures: A Study of the Writings of Brian Aldiss* (with Brian Griffin), 1984. Editor of *The Science Fiction Source Book*, 1984, and *The Science Fiction Film Source Book*, 1985. **Essays:** Richard Cowper; Christopher Evans; Mary Gentle; Garry Kilworth; Andrew M. Stephenson.

WOLFE, Gary K. Dean, Evelyn T. Stone College, Roosevelt University, Chicago. Author of *The Known and the Unknown: The Iconography of Science Fiction*, 1979, *Elements of Research*, 1979, *David Lindsay*, 1982, and articles in *Dictionary of Literary Biography, Survey of Science Fiction Literature*, and periodicals. **Essays:** Ray Bradbury; Edmund Cooper; John Keir Cross; Jack Finney; William Hope Hodgson; Nigel Kneale; David Lindsay; John Lymington; Chad Oliver; Rod Serling; M.P. Shiel; Cordwainer Smith; Jerry Sohl.

WOLFE, Gene. See his own entry. **Essay:** Algis Budrys.

WOLK, Anthony. Professor of English, Portland State University, Oregon. Author of articles on Philip K. Dick and on language philosophy and language testing. **Essays:** Philip K. Dick; Shepherd Mead.

WOOD, Susan. Assistant Professor of English, University of British Columbia, Vancouver. Author of essays on fantasy, SF, and Canadian literature. Editor of *The Language of the Night* by Le Guin, 1979, and of the science-fiction and fantasy issue of *Room of One's Own*. Died 1980. **Essays:** Terry Carr; Frederick Philip Grove.

WOOSTER, Martin Morse. Washington Editor, *Harper's Magazine*. Author of articles in *Esquire, Wall Street Journal, Chicago Tribune, Fantasy Review,* Toronto *Star*, Boston *Globe*, and other publications. **Essays:** Reginald Bretnor; Richard A. Lupoff; William Rotsler; Ted White; Jack Williamson.

WYGANT, Alice Chambers. Reference Librarian, Moody Medical Library, Galveston, Texas. **Essays:** Sonya Dorman; G.C. Edmondson; Stuart Gordon; Sam Merwin, Jr.

YOKE, Carl B. Assistant to the Associate Vice-President for the Extended University, and Associate Professor of English, Kent State University, Kent, Ohio; associate editor of *Extrapolation*. Author of *A Reader's Guide to Roger Zelazny*, 1979, *Roger Zelazny and Andre Norton: Proponents of Individualism* (forthcoming), and articles on Jakes, Galouye, Crichton, Joan Vinge, Maine, Kuttner, C.L. Moore, Merritt, Moorcock, and other SF and fantasy writers. Co-editor of *Death and the Serpent: Immortality in Science Fiction and Fantasy*, 1985. **Essays:** Michael Crichton; Daniel F. Galouye; John Jakes; Charles Eric Maine; Roger Zelazny.

ZAKI, Hoda M. Assistant Professor of Political Science, Hampton University, Virginia. Reviewer for *Hypatia: A Journal of Feminist Philosophy*, Hampton and Newport News *Daily Press*, and the National Women's Studies Association's *Newsletter*. **Essay:** Marta Randall.

ZEBROWSKI, George. See his own entry. **Essays:** David Duncan; Edgar Pangborn; Thomas N. Scortia; William Tenn.